RAND McNALLY

Volume 1: Guide
136th Edition

Commercial
Atlas & Marketing Guide
The First Place to Look for Up-to-Date Business Planning Data!
2005

Population, Economic, and Geographic Data for more than 120,000 U.S. places—complete with large-scale, detailed maps.

How to Order the Commercial Atlas & Marketing Guide

To order the Rand McNally 2005 Commercial Atlas & Marketing Guide, please contact Rand McNally at 1-800-678-7263.

The information in this Atlas was collected directly from the sources cited or from other sources considered reliable. The Atlas is published for general reference and not as a substitute for independent verification by users of this information when circumstances warrant. While care and diligence have been used in its preparation, the Publisher does not guarantee the accuracy of the information.

Contents | Volume 1

Volume 2 Contents on next page

Contents | Volume 2

Preface

Through the *Commercial Atlas & Marketing Guide*, Rand McNally brings together the most current economic and geographic information. With maps, tables and charts, this *Atlas* combines maximum demographic coverage of the United States with an authoritative interpretation of business data.

The *Commercial Atlas & Marketing Guide* is organized into two volumes. Volume 1 includes an Introduction to the Atlas, Economic Data section, Population Data section and Map section. Volume 2 includes Statistics by State and a State Index that includes references to the state maps in Volume 1.

The Introduction to the Atlas includes a Table of Contents and a Glossary of Terms that provides definitions of terms and concepts used throughout the atlas.

The Economic section describes business activity for states, counties, cities, Trading Areas, Metropolitan Statistical Areas (MSAs), and the latest Core Based Statistical Areas (CBSAs) announced by the Office of Management and Budget (OMB) in 2003.

The Population section provides 2000 Census figures and current population estimates for states, counties, Metropolitan Statistical Areas, Core Based Statistical Areas, and Ranally Metro Areas (RMAs). In addition, projected population figures for Metropolitan Statistical Areas, Core Based Statistical Areas, and counties are presented.

The Maps section includes maps of Minor Civil Divisions, and maps of the fifty states and the District of Columbia. The state map pages also include detailed inset maps for important cities.

The State Statistics section includes a list of Principal Places ranked by population, and a Business Data table that includes all the counties in each state. The State Index is arranged alphabetically by state. This section provides location information and statistics for virtually all inhabited places in the United States. In fact, over 120,000 places (including townships and counties) are described in the State Index. Of these, more than 41,000 have populations that are not available through the U.S. Census Bureau and are provided exclusively by Rand McNally.

Once again, Rand McNally is proud to present the *Commercial Atlas and Marketing Guide,* the oldest annually published reference atlas in existence. This edition of the *Commercial Atlas & Marketing Guide* continues to represent Rand McNally's unique background in research, mapmaking, and publishing.

Glossary of Terms

Annexation Population: Population of a place following annexation (expansion of boundary) since the 2000 Census. In the State Index, this population figure is preceded by the symbol Ⓐ.

Apparel Store Sales*: Sales for establishments engaged primarily in selling new clothing and related articles. It includes men's and women's clothing stores, family and children's clothing stores, shoe stores and other clothing and clothing accessories stores. Not included are apparel and accessories sales made in department or general merchandise stores, or custom tailoring.

Bank: In the State Index, places with one or more full-service banks are indicated with a Ⓢ symbol. The source of this information is Thomson Financial Publishing.

Basic Trading Area: An area surrounding at least one Basic Trading Center. Each Basic Trading Area is named after one or more cities which are its Basic Trading Centers. All Basic Trading Area boundaries follow county lines and are drawn to include the county or counties whose residents make the bulk of their shopping goods purchases in the area's Basic Trading Center or its suburbs. Some Basic Trading Areas have two or more Basic Trading Centers, generally because residents may conveniently shop at either one.

Basic Trading Center: A city which serves as a center for shopping goods purchases for the surrounding area. Shopping goods are those retail items a shopper ordinarily travels some distance to purchase and for which he or she compares qualities, styles and prices before buying. Most sales of shopping goods are made through general merchandise or apparel stores. Basic Trading Centers also serve their surroundings with various specialized services, such as medical care, entertainment, higher education and a daily newspaper.

Census Designated Place (CDP): A geographic entity defined by the U.S. Census Bureau that serves as the statistical counterpart of an incorporated place for the purpose of presenting census data. CDPs are defined for areas with concentrations of population, housing and commercial structures that are identifiable by name, but are not located within incorporated places. A CDP may contain one or more unincorporated places within its established boundaries. Census designated places are specifically identified in the State Indexes. CDPs with the designation "Census Area Only" are those that Rand McNally has determined to be not locally recognized.

Census Population: Official U.S. Census Bureau population resulting from the 2000 Population and Housing Census of the United States. *See also: Final Census Population, Revised Census Population, and Special Census Population.*

Combined Statistical Area (CSA): A geographic area consisting of two or more adjacent Core Based Statistical Areas (CBSAs) with a high degree of employment interchange. *See also: Core Based Statistical Area.*

Consolidated Metropolitan Statistical Area (CMSA): Contains two or more Primary Metropolitan Statistical Areas (PMSAs) that are considered as a single unit for statistical purposes due to their economic and social integration. To qualify as a CMSA, the metropolitan area as a whole must have a population of at least one million.

Core Based Statistical Area (CBSA): A metropolitan area consisting of the county or counties associated with an urban core having a population of at least 10,000, plus adjacent counties having a high degree of social and economic integration with the core as measured through commuting ties. Counties or county equivalents form the building blocks for CBSAs for the entire U.S. Current CBSA definitions were announced by the Office of Management and Budget (OMB) effective June 6, 2003. CBSAs are more current definitions of metropolitan areas than the older Metropolitan Statistical Areas (MSAs) as defined and revised by the OMB through June 30, 1999. The *Commercial Atlas and Marketing Guide* provides data on both CBSAs and MSAs. *See also: Metropolitan Core Based Statistical Area; Micropolitan Core Based Statistical Area; Combined Statistical Area; Metropolitan Statistical Area.*

County: The primary political subdivision of every state except Alaska. The total number of counties in each state is specified in the Counties: Population/Income/Sales table on pages 52-73, and also in the State Statistics section for each state in Volume 2.

Most places in the U.S. are included within a county. Areas not included in any county are Alaska, the District of Columbia and certain independent cities.

A number of counties do not function as political entities (in Connecticut and Rhode Island, for example). Although there are no county officials or functions, the name and boundaries of each county are well known locally.

In Louisiana, county-level subdivisions are called parishes. In Alaska, the *Commercial Atlas & Marketing Guide* recognizes Alaska's census areas and boroughs as county equivalents.

County Subdivision: This term is used by the U.S. Census Bureau as a generic name for primary divisions of counties and statistically equivalent areas. There are two main categories of County Subdivisions:

- Those that are delineated by the Census Bureau in cooperation with state and local governments for data presentation purposes. The census-only divisions are called "Census County Divisions" (CCDs) or "Census Subareas" in Alaska.

- Those that have an intrinsic governmental or administrative function. These are referred to as "Minor Civil Divisions" (MCDs). They include an impressive and diverse mixture of legal entities with different governmental and administrative functions, the most important of which are townships.

There is enormous variability in terms of the importance, function and local recognition of townships. In some states, mostly located in New England, townships are of such importance that they essentially function as incorporated places. At the other extreme, there are states in which the townships have virtually no governmental significance and may be almost unknown to local residents.

Many MCD states include MCDs other than townships, including boroughs, gores and precincts. In addition, MCD states may contain incorporated places that are independent of any MCD and "unorganized territories" that are not part of an MCD or an independent incorporated place.

The *Commercial Atlas* contains township data for a subset of MCD states that can be broadly grouped into two main categories.

Northeastern Group (9 states: CT, ME, MA, NH, NJ, NY, PA, RI, VT). In these states, counties are divided into townships or "towns". Other types of MCDs, as well as unorganized territories, may also occur. In these states, townships are important administratively and are well known locally. In the six New England states (CT, ME, MA, NH, RI, VT) the "towns" are much more important in local life than the counties themselves. Moreover, these "towns" and townships possess most or all of the powers exercised by incorporated places.

In most states outside of the Northeast, a "town" is a built-up community, usually smaller than a city but larger than a village. In many Northeastern states, however, a "town" is a fairly large area (15 square miles or even larger), containing a central village having the same name as the "town" and possibly other villages, smaller localities and farms. Only rarely do the villages within the "town" have a separate corporate status. Such "towns" come closer to the townships found in the Midwest than the incorporated places known as "towns" in other states.

Because of this, the Census Bureau does not consider these "towns" to be incorporated places. The *Commercial Atlas* follows this practice. "Towns" in New England and New York are listed in the State Indexes but are not identified as incorporated places.

In Pennsylvania and New Jersey, townships have much the same character as "towns" in New England and New York. Both these states also have incorporated cities and numerous incorporated boroughs that are similar to villages in other states.

The State Indexes for the Northeastern states include entries for the "towns" and townships with active governments as recognized by the U.S. Census of Governments. The indexes also indicate the "town" or township in which each indexed place is located. Each of these indexes has a head note describing the Minor Civil Divisions in the state.

Great Lakes Group (5 states: IL, IN, MI, OH, WI). In these states, as in most of the Midwest, most counties are divided into townships. However, these divisions are considerably

---

* Estimates for economic activity in this edition of the *Atlas* are based on data from the U.S. Census Bureau's 1997 Economic Census and utilize the North American Industry Classification System (NAICS); estimates from editions of the *Atlas* before 2001 are based on census data using the 1987 Standard Industrial Classification (SIC) system. Trade statistics are not directly comparable between systems. Consult U.S. Census Bureau documentation for further information.

less significant administratively and are less well known than in the Northeast. Though they may possess legal status, they are usually not thought of locally as "incorporated". One exception is Wisconsin, where townships do retain much local importance and are officially called "towns" just as in New England.

The relationship between townships and incorporated places is variable among and even within these states. Larger places are generally independent of any township, while smaller places often remain within the township for governmental purposes.

For the five Great Lake states, the State Indexes list the townships with active governments as recognized by the U.S. Census of Governments. For Michigan, Ohio and Wisconsin, location by township is provided for each place. Each of these indexes has a head note describing the Minor Civil Divisions in the state.

The remaining states represent a mixture of conditions. Some are CCD-only states where townships and other MCDs do not exist. These include many of the Western, Southwestern and Southeastern states. In other cases MCDs may exist but have little local significance governmentally or do not figure prominently in local knowledge. The *Commercial Atlas* does not include township data for such states.

Cross-References and Alternate Names: Cities and towns that are known by more than one name (e.g. places whose post office name differs from their corporate name, or the name used by a railroad serving them) are shown in the State Indexes under all such names.

Disincorporated Place: A place that has lost its corporate status and no longer functions as a legal municipality.

Disposable Income (DI): Represents an estimate of a household's purchasing power or after-tax income. The proportion of household income left after taxes is estimated from special studies conducted by the Census Bureau to simulate household taxes. Four types of taxes are deducted: Federal individual income taxes, State individual income taxes, FICA (Social Security) and Federal retirement payroll taxes, and property taxes for owner-occupied housing.

Duplicated Name: A place name representing two or more places located in the same state. All such places are distinguished in the State Indexes by indicating the county in which each place is located.

Estimated Population: Population estimates as of 7/1/04 are available for all counties, all populated places with a population of more than 20,000 people and selected places with fewer than 20,000 people. The source of these population estimates is Devonshire Associates Ltd. and Scan/US, Inc. In the State Index, these population figures are preceded by the symbol ◆. *See also: Rand McNally Population Estimates for Unincorporated Places.*

Final Census Population: 2000 Census population of a place. In the State Indexes, this population figure is preceded by the symbol ©.

FIPS (Federal Information Processing Standards) Place Code: County and state codes established by the federal government for the purpose of standardizing the coding of statistical information made available through various reference sources.

Food Store Sales*: Sales for establishments selling food and beverages primarily for home consumption. Not included are sales for establishments primarily selling items prepared on premises, such as bakeries.

Furniture, Home Furnishings and Appliance Store Sales*: Sales for establishments selling furniture and home furnishings, plus electronics and appliances. Not included are sales from custom manufacturing.

General Merchandise Store Sales*: Sales from department stores, general merchandise stores, warehouse clubs, and superstores.

Health, Drug and Personal Care Sales*: Total sales for establishments primarily engaged in the sale of prescription and nonprescription drugs, cosmetics and toiletries, optical goods, food (health) supplements, and other health and personal care products.

Household: A household consists of all persons occupying a single housing unit (a house, apartment, room or group of rooms) whether related or not. Persons residing in institutions, college dormitories or military barracks are living in group quarters rather than within households and are not included in household counts.

Incorporated Place: A place which has met the various legal requirements for its respective state for incorporation as a municipality. The rules for incorporation vary widely from state to state; some states have only a few incorporated places, while others have a great many. The *Commercial Atlas and Marketing Guide* follows the same standards in determining which places are incorporated as are used by the U.S. Census Bureau. Incorporated places are specifically identified in the State Indexes.

Generally speaking, incorporated places are the only localities that have official legal boundaries.

Places incorporated since 2000 have the year of incorporation specified by a date after the incorporation symbol.

Census populations are available for all incorporated places. For places incorporated since the 2000 Census, population figures are estimates, usually for the date of incorporation. Though the Census was taken as of April 1, 2000, usually it did not report separately any place incorporated after January 1, 2000.

See also: Unincorporated Place.

Independent City: These cities are administered independently of any adjoining county, and have the status of separate counties. The term is commonly used to refer to Baltimore, MD; St. Louis, MO; Carson City, NV; and 39 cities in Virginia. In the cases of Baltimore and St. Louis, there is also a Baltimore County, MD and a St. Louis County, MO (each separate from the city).

All of the larger cities in Virginia are independent cities. Users of statistics may find it difficult to treat cities as separate units in this one state, preferring to combine the cities with an adjoining county. A list of such combinations is given in a footnote to the County Business Data table for Virginia, which is located in Volume 2 of the *Commercial Atlas & Marketing Guide.*

In the State Index, the name of each independent city is followed by "Independent City".

Major Trading Area: An area consisting of two or more Basic Trading Areas. A Major Trading Area's boundaries follow the boundaries of its Basic Trading Areas. Each Major Trading Area is named after one or more cities which are its Major Trading Centers.

Major Trading Center: A city within a Major Trading Area that serves as one of the trading area's primary centers of wholesaling, distribution, banking, and specialized services such as advertising.

Map Key: Index to the location of a place on the appropriate state map.

Market Ability Index (MAI): A measure of a market's potential, expressed as a percentage of the U.S. total. It is calculated by multiplying .5 times the percent of the total Disposable Income, .3 times the percent of Total Retail Sales, and .2

times the percent of Total Population. The sum of these weighted percents is the Market Ability Index.

Median Household Income: This figure divides the Disposable Income distribution into two equal parts with one-half of the households above it, the other half below it.

Metropolitan Area: A large urban center that includes the central city, its suburbs, and the satellite communities whose economic and social life is tied to the city.

Metropolitan Core Based Statistical Area: A Core Based Statistical Area (CBSA) associated with at least one urban core having a population of at least 50,000. The Metropolitan Core Based Statistical Area comprises the central county or counties containing the core, plus adjacent counties having a high degree of social and economic integration with the core as measured through commuting ties. *See also: Core Based Statistical Area; Micropolitan Core Based Statistical Area.*

Metropolitan Statistical Area (MSA): A metropolitan area as defined and revised by the Office of Management and Budget (OMB) through June 30, 1999. An area qualifies for recognition as a Metropolitan Statistical Area in one of two ways: the area has (1) a city of at least 50,000 population, or (2) an urbanized area of at least 50,000 with a total metropolitan population of at least 100,000. MSAs are defined in terms of entire counties, except in the six New England states (Connecticut, Maine, Massachusetts, New Hampshire, Rhode Island and Vermont), where they are defined in terms of cities and towns. In addition to the county containing the main city, an MSA may include counties having strong economic and social ties to the central county. *See also: Core Based Statistical Area.*

Micropolitan Core Based Statistical Area: A Core Based Statistical Area (CBSA) associated with at least one urban core having a population of at least 10,000 but less than 50,000. The Micropolitan Core Based Statistical Area comprises the central county or counties containing the core, plus adjacent counties having a high degree of social and economic integration with the core as measured through commuting ties. *See also: Core Based Statistical Area; Metropolitan Core Based Statistical Area.*

Military Installation: All important Army, Navy, Marine Corps, and Air Force bases and other establishments are shown on the Major Military Installations map on pages 34-35. The map also includes Coast Guard stations, but excludes recruiting stations.

Minor Civil Division: *See County Subdivision.*

New England City and Town Area (NECTA): A metropolitan area in New England conceptually similar to a Core Based Statistical Area but based on cities and towns rather than counties. NECTAs are defined using the same criteria as Metropolitan and Micropolitan Core Based Statistical Areas. *See also: Core Based Statistical Area; Metropolitan Core Based Statistical Area; Micropolitan Core Based Statistical Area.*

New England County Metropolitan Area (NECMA): A NECMA provides county-based data for metropolitan areas in Connecticut, Maine, Massachusetts, New Hampshire, Rhode Island and Vermont. Because MSAs for these states are defined in terms of cities and towns rather than by

---

* Estimates for economic activity in this edition of the *Atlas* are based on data from the U.S. Census Bureau's 1997 Economic Census and utilize the North American Industry Classification System (NAICS); estimates from editions of the *Atlas* before 2001 are based on census data using the 1987 Standard Industrial Classification (SIC) system. Trade statistics are not directly comparable between systems. Consult U.S. Census Bureau documentation for further information.

county, the NECMA offers data consistent with those for MSAs throughout the rest of the country.

Passenger Car Registrations: The total number of non-commercial automobiles registered.

Per Capita Income: Average income per person; arrived at by dividing the Disposable Income by the total population.

Place incorporated in recent years: A place that has been incorporated in recent years is shown in the State Index with the year of incorporation noted.

Place indicated as "pop included with" another place: Any place listed in the State Index with the "pop included with" designation is within the generally accepted limits of another place, and the population is included in the figure for that place.

Place listed as "rural": Any place listed in the State Index with the "rural" designation is an open-country locality with a locally recognized name, although no concentrated area of settlement exists and the population is scattered over a wide area. Populations are not available for these places.

Population: The total number of people living in an area. Populations for all counties, townships, and many places are provided by the U.S. Census Bureau. Annual population estimates for important places are provided by Devonshire Associates Ltd. and Scan/US, Inc. Populations are estimated by Rand McNally for unincorporated places that are not provided by the U.S. Census Bureau. Population includes people living in group quarters such as colleges, plus permanently assigned armed forces, but generally excludes tourists and transients unless otherwise stated. *See also: Final Census Population, Estimated Population, Rand McNally Population Estimates for Unincorporated Places, Revised Census Population, and Special Census Population.*

Population Change: The increase or decrease in population, determined by comparing the population of a place at one point in time to the population of the place at a second point in time. The amount of change is expressed as a percentage (gain or loss) from the earlier population.

Population Projection: The projected total number of people that will be living in an area at the beginning of the stated year.

Post Office: A facility maintained by the U.S. Postal Service for the purpose of processing and distributing mail. In the State Index, all places that have a Post Office, Branch Post Office, Community Post Office, or Postal Station are identified with a special symbol **P**. If a place does not have its own post office, it may or may not be recognized as a place (an acceptable "last line") according to the Postal Service. If a place is not an acceptable last line, then the index entry indicates the name of the post office to which its mail should be addressed. For example, the index entry for Tinyplace, AL shows "mail Someplace **Z**12345". In this example, Someplace is an acceptable last line on an envelope, while Tinyplace is not. For places indicated as "pop included with" another place, if no mailing point is stated, the mailing point is the same as that for the incorporated place in which it is included.

Previous Census Population: 1990 Census population of a place. In the State Indexes, this population figure is preceded by the symbol Ⓟ.

Primary Metropolitan Statistical Area (PMSA): Any metropolitan area which is a component of a Consolidated Metropolitan Statistical Area.

Principal Business Center: A city of significant economic importance within its region or state based on a number of criteria, including population, total retail sales volume, shopping goods volume, volume of wholesaling, the number of headquarters of major corporations, banking activity and hospital facilities. Another important factor is circulation statistics for locally published daily newspapers, the extent of the area in which they circulate and the degree to which they undergo competition locally with newspapers from other cities. Principal Business Centers include, but are not limited to, Basic Trading Centers and Major Trading Centers. *See also: Ranally City Ratings.*

Projected Population Change: The increase or decrease in population, determined by comparing the Projected Population to the Estimated Population. The amount of change is expressed as a percentage (gain or loss) from the Estimated Population.

Processing and Distribution Center: A large U.S. Postal Service facility for processing and distributing mail to/from all of the smaller post offices in one or more ZIP Code Service Areas. Processing and Distribution Centers are usually located in "hub" cities that serve as the natural centers of local transportation.

Ranally City Ratings: The Ranally City Ratings classify Principal Business Centers by assigning each a rating which reflects the city's relative business and economic importance. Special thanks to Editorial Consultant, Richard L. Forstall, for his major contributions in the development of the Ranally City Rating System.

The Ranally City Rating utilizes a number of criteria, including population, total retail sales volume, shopping goods volume, volume of wholesaling, the number of headquarters of major corporations, banking activity and hospital facilities. Another important factor is circulation statistics for locally published daily newspapers, the extent of the area in which they circulate and the degree to which they undergo competition locally with newspapers from other cities. All of these variables are used to determine the extent to which the city is a shopping focus for the surrounding area and the degree of business competition from neighboring cities.

Because the Ranally City Rating employs a much more comprehensive set of criteria than systems based solely on population, it provides a more reliable and broad-based indicator of a city's relative economic importance. Used alone, population may give a misleading impression of a city's actual importance. For example, many smaller cities within metropolitan areas are important business centers for surrounding suburbs, despite having relatively modest populations. Likewise, urban centers in different parts of the country may have nearly the same population totals but still vary greatly in their relative importance.

The meaning of the city ratings are as follows:

Each city rating includes a number and one or more letters. The **number** indicates the city's general level of importance and is the most significant item in the rating. Within each general level, the **number of capital letters** used distinguishes the more important cities (for which two or more letters are used) from the less important cities, which have only one capital letter. Finally, a **lower-case letter** is used to identify certain special groups of suburbs.

The specific letter, **A, B, C,** or **S,** indicates the city's status as a trading center for its immediate area. A city rated **A** is a **primary** Basic Trading Center—the most important center of shopping for a wide surrounding area.

A **B** city is a **secondary** Basic Trading Center—the second (or third) most important center for its area. Both **A** and **B** cities are mentioned in the titles of Basic Trading Areas. For example, in the Minneapolis-St. Paul Basic Trading Area, Minneapolis is a primary center and is rated **A**, and St. Paul is a secondary center and is rated **B**.

Cities designated **C** do not qualify as Basic Trading Centers, but are within the trading area of a larger city. Cities designated **S** are actually within the Ranally Metro Area of a larger city—they are suburbs or satellite cities.

The specific city ratings are described below. All of the Principal Business Centers appear in a table on pages 74-87.

Rating 1—National Business Centers. Each of these cities is an independent center of large-scale financial and wholesaling activity, as well as a very large retailing center. Each has a large tributary territory in which its dominant importance is overwhelming. Firms with nationwide distribution are almost certain to have important branches or outlets in every one of these cities. Each city rated **1** has at least $850 million annual sales of general merchandise and apparel stores in its urban area (including immediate suburbs) and has daily newspapers whose total circulation is over 300,000.

1-AAAA. New York City is the only city with this rating, in recognition of its unique business importance and nationwide economic influence.

1-AAA. Los Angeles and Chicago have been recognized with this special rating, as the only cities besides New York whose economic importance and influence operate over a large part of the U.S.

1-AA—Major national business centers. These cities are distinguished from the **1-A**s, the next lower category, by a greater volume of retailing, financial activity, newspaper circulation, etc. They account for most of the headquarters of firms that do a nationwide range of business. Their annual urban area shopping goods volume ranges from $1.5 to $4.5 billion, and their Sunday newspaper circulation ranges upward from 500,000. In over-all business importance these cities are comparable with the leading cities of many foreign countries.

1-A—Other national business centers. These cities are only slightly less important than the **1-AA**s. They include many of the cities most often selected as branch headquarters by major firms, but they are less likely to be headquarters for national firms.

Rating 2—Regional Business Centers. The business importance of these cities operates on a regional rather than a national scale. A regional center is likely to be the largest city within a radius of 100 to 150 miles. It is an important wholesaling center and the headquarters of many businesses of regional scope; it has branch offices or assembly plants of some of the larger national concerns, but only rarely has headquarters of such firms. The **2**s are divided into two general groups: **2-AA** and **2-A**. The smallest **2-AA** cities have annual general merchandise and apparel stores sales volume in their urban area of at least $280 million, and dailies with a total circulation of at least 100,000. Most **2-AA** cities have morning dailies. The **2-A** cities generally have at least $185 million general merchandise and apparel store sales volume and 50,000 daily newspaper circulation.

2-AA—Major regional business centers. The largest of these cities are only slightly less important than the **1-A** centers. It is worth noting that major regional centers in the North and on the West Coast are rated **1**, while many of those in the South are rated **2**. Though they are of great importance for their immediate area, the overall importance of most Southern cities is still not comparable to that of major cities in the North and West with their large concentrations of manufacturing and other activities of long standing. Many of the **2-AA** cities are growing rapidly and some of them will probably qualify for a **1** rating before long.

2-BB, 2-CC. Fort Worth, St. Paul, Oakland, San Jose and similar cities, within the metropolitan areas of larger cities, are rated **2-BB**. Newark, NJ is the only **2-CC** city.

2-A, 2-B, 2-C—Other regional business centers. The **2-A** cities are regional centers of somewhat lesser importance than the **2-AA**s. Several are major industrial centers of a size great enough to qualify for this rating, in spite of the lack of a large tributary area.

The **2-B** cities are mainly secondary central cities of large metropolitan areas. Like Newark, St. Paul, and Oakland mentioned above, their close relationship to a large metropolis should not obscure their major importance in many respects.

2-S These cities are key business centers in major metropolitan areas, though not large enough to be recognized as central cities. Typically, their retailing volume is very high but serves only a limited section of the metropolitan area. Such activities as wholesaling may also be important. These centers represent the choice of many businesses as the best locations for supplying consumer products to the suburban sections of the chief metropolitan areas.

Rating 3—Significant Local Business Centers. The cities rated **3** are those whose business importance is significant, but is typically local rather than regional. They are usually the largest place within a radius of fifty miles or so, but a larger center rated **2** or **1** is usually not far away, and a **3** city will have close connections with this larger center, especially for wholesaling, finance, and similar activities that do not directly involve the consumer. Cities rated **3** serve their immediate areas as the main source for shopping goods, are important as general retailing centers, but are usually not important for wholesaling. The **3** cities have daily newspapers, but their circulation is limited to the immediate area.

3-AA, 3-BB, 3-CC—Major local business centers. Approximately the upper quarter of the **3**s are of sufficient importance to be rated as a separate group. They show some tendency to move up into **2** status, but so far have not developed a large enough tributary area to do so, often because of proximity to a larger center. Generally the **3-AA** centers have at least $100 million annual urban-area general merchandise

* Estimates for economic activity in this edition of the *Atlas* are based on data from the U.S. Census Bureau's 1997 Economic Census and utilize the North American Industry Classification System (NAICS); estimates from editions of the *Atlas* before 2001 are based on census data using the 1987 Standard Industrial Classification (SIC) system. Trade statistics are not directly comparable between systems. Consult U.S. Census Bureau documentation for further information.

and apparel stores and a daily of at least 25,000 circulation. Most of these cities are Basic Trading Centers, but there are also some **3-BB**s (secondary Basic Trading Centers) and **3-CC**s.

3-SS. This is an additional group of suburban shopping centers of significance comparable to that of the **3-AA** cities.

3-A, 3-B, 3-C—Other significant local business centers. These cities usually have a well-defined but limited tributary area, outside of which they have relatively little influence. Nearly all have $35 to $100 million annual volume in general merchandise and apparel store sales, a daily with 10,000 circulation and at least one general hospital.

3-S. These are suburban shopping centers of importance comparable to those of the **3-A** cities outside of metropolitan areas. Typically they supply shopping goods to their own population and to a few adjoining suburbs. Many have a daily newspaper and most have a general hospital. However, most suburbs with over $100 million in shopping goods sales are rated **3** even if they lack these other characteristics.

Rating 4—Other Local Business Centers. The cities rated **4** are local business centers which are of some importance, but do not qualify for a **3** rating in one respect or another. Some are isolated centers in hilly or mountainous areas in the West or South, whose local importance is unquestioned, but whose tributary area is simply too small to support a larger business center. Some are established centers for declining mining or agricultural districts. Others are centers of small tributary areas in prosperous farming or industrial regions, in each case with larger centers (rated **3** or even **2**) close by. Most **4**s have a daily newspaper with 7,000 or more circulation, as well as at least $14 million in annual general merchandise and apparel stores, and a general hospital.

4-A. These are small Basic Trading Centers. Most of them are in relatively isolated areas, especially in the West, and a few have very small populations. But in each case they are clearly the chief local shopping focus for their area.

4-B, 4-C. These cities (not suburbs) are within the Basic Trading Areas of larger cities. Many are found in well-developed agricultural or industrial areas, which are able to support local trading centers spaced quite close together.

4-S. These suburban centers are of moderate retailing importance, though some have sizable populations.

Special Groups of Suburbs. A lower-case letter at the end of the Ranally City Rating is used to identify two special categories of suburban business centers. The letter **m** concluding the rating identifies suburbs where a major portion of total retail volume and shopping-goods sales are accounted for by a large mall or planned shopping center (or, in a few cases, two or more such centers). Such suburbs may have only a small "downtown" in the traditional sense; although their sales volume may be larger than that of some Basic Trading Centers, they generally lack a daily newspaper or a hospital and do not have a wide range of other professional and business services. The letter **r** concluding the rating identifies suburbs which are of modest importance as shopping-goods centers, but which have substantial non-shopping-goods retailing (for example, automobile dealers). Many of these suburbs are also important employment centers, with numerous workers commuting in from other suburbs or from the area's main city.

Collectively the rated cities include about 45 percent of the nation's population, but about 60 percent of the total retail sales and about 70 percent of shopping-goods sales. Counting activity in immediate suburban areas, the rated cities account for almost 90 percent of all shopping-goods sales. Over 90 percent of U.S. daily newspaper circulation originates in the rated cities.

Business centers below the level of the rated cities are mostly small in size and very local in importance—such as numerous county-seat towns of the Midwest and South. One group of exceptions are business and shopping centers located in unincorporated suburban communities. Details of the business activity for these places appear only in limited form in the Economic Census and it is not possible to rate them on a comparable basis with that of other business centers.

See also: Principal Business Center.

Ranally Manufacturing Unit (RMU): Each Ranally Manufacturing Unit represents one millionth of the U.S. total value added by manufacture, according to the 1997 Census of Manufactures.

Ranally Metro Area (RMA): Rand McNally's definition of a metropolitan area. Like Metropolitan Statistical Areas (MSAs) and Core Based Statistical Areas (CBSAs), RMAs include one or more central cities, satellite communities and suburbs. Unlike MSAs and CBSAs, RMAs are not restricted to following county boundaries. For this reason, RMAs provide a better portrayal of the extent of urban and suburban development than MSAs or CBSAs. While MSAs and CBSAs are useful for making general comparisons between major urban centers or for summarizing the importance of a given area for business purposes the RMA offers a more precise look at areas of concentrated population.

There are two basic criteria that determine inclusion within an RMA. In general, an area must have 1) at least 70 people per square mile and 2) at least 20% of the labor force must commute to the central urban area of the RMA. These requirements provide general guidelines for drawing consistent boundaries for RMAs across the nation.

A comparison of the MSA and RMA for a single city clearly demonstrates the difference between the two methods of definition and their subsequent uses. For example, the MSA of Charleston, SC includes the entire counties of Berkeley, Charleston, and Dorchester. Relatively large in size, this MSA covers a total of 2,592 square miles. 87% of its population, however, is concentrated in the 635-square-mile RMA for Charleston. Thus, the MSA exaggerates the actual extent of Charleston's concentrated marketable area, while the RMA defines with more accuracy the area of Charleston's development and economic influence.

In general the population threshold for RMAs is 50,000. Selected areas of less than 50,000 are also defined as RMAs because they either have populations close to 50,000, include a central city of an official MSA, or are of special significance to the state. *See also: Metropolitan Statistical Area.*

Ranally Population Unit (RPU): Each Ranally Population Unit represents one millionth of the U.S. total population.

Ranally Sales Units (RSU): Each Ranally Sales Unit represents one millionth of the U.S. total volume for a sales category. RSUs are presented for Total Retail Sales, General Merchandise Store Sales and Apparel Store Sales. The value appearing in the RSU column is computed by dividing the area's dollar sales value by the U.S. total dollar sales value and multiplying the result by one million.

Rand McNally & Co. Designated Place (RMC Place): A place that has not met the legal requirements of its state for incorporation as a municipality, and is not defined as a Census Designated Place. These are unincorporated places not reported by the U.S. Census Bureau. These places are identified by Rand McNally by consulting a variety of map and statistical sources. Populations for these places are Rand McNally estimates that refer to the central or built-up sections of these places. *See also: Incorporated Place; Census Designated Place; Rand McNally Population Estimates for Unincorporated Places.*

Rand McNally Population Estimates for Unincorporated Places: Population estimates for unincorporated places that are not reported separately by the U.S. Census Bureau. Rand McNally secures these estimates by contacting local authorities and consulting a variety of map and statistical sources. In the State Index these population figures are preceded by the symbol ●.

Retail Trade Sales*: Net sales for establishments engaged in retail trade. Receipts from repairs and other services are included, but retail sales by non-retailers such as service establishments and wholesalers are not. Sales and other taxes collected from customers and credit charges are not included. Total retail sales are all-encompassing, including (among others) general merchandise and apparel store sales.

Revised Census Population: Revision of final 2000 Census figures. In the State Indexes, this population figure is preceded by the symbol Ⓡ.

Shopping Goods Sales*: Retail items that the shopper ordinarily travels some distance to purchase, and for which he or she compares qualities, styles and prices from store to store before buying. Shopping goods represent the best category of distinguishing the towns to which the buying public travels. Such towns are natural centers for other activities such as entertainment, education and medical care. Most sales of shopping goods are made through general merchandise or apparel stores.

Special Census Population: Census population figure taken at a time other than the normal Census. In the State Indexes, this population figure is preceded by the symbol Ⓢ.

Township and "Town": Commonly used generic term for minor civil divisions (MCDs) in the U.S. Townships and "towns" are indexed in the State Index for Connecticut, Illinois, Indiana, Maine, Massachusetts, Michigan, New Hampshire, New Jersey, New York, Ohio, Pennsylvania, Rhode Island, Vermont, and Wisconsin. Maps displaying townships (and other selected MCDs) for these states appear on pages 255-271 of the *Commercial Atlas*. The information on the township or "town" is given in a separate entry in the State Index. These entries are specifically identified as MCDs in the index. *See also: County Subdivision.*

Unincorporated Place: *See Rand McNally Designated Place.*

Value Added By Manufacture: The value added to raw materials during the manufacturing process.

ZIP Code: Numerical codes assigned by the U.S. Postal Service to speed the distribution of mail. The *Commercial Atlas & Marketing Guide* specifies the correct ZIP Code for cities, towns and rural areas where there are residents to receive mail; all ZIP Codes shown in the Index are preceded by a "**Z**" symbol.

For places where the name of the town is not recognized by the U.S. Postal Service as an acceptable "last line" on an envelope, the place name that should instead be shown is given immediately before the ZIP code. For example, an index entry for Tinyplace, AL shows "mail Someplace **Z** 12345". In this example, Someplace is an acceptable last line on an envelope, while Tinyplace is not.

Some ZIP Codes are assigned to individual companies or entities (Unique ZIP Codes) while others are used exclusively for mail box deliveries. In the *Commercial Atlas & Marketing Guide*, no distinction is made between delivery, unique or post office box ZIP Codes. All are reported in the same manner.

Many large cities have each been assigned multiple ZIP Code areas. Index entries for these major multi-zoned cities specify ZIP information as one or more ranges. Megaburg, CA, for example, might show ZIP Codes of **Z** 55055-99, **Z** 55150-99, and **Z** 55250.

USPS definitions of city boundaries do not necessarily correspond to legal corporate boundaries. The ZIP Codes listed in this atlas for a given city include ZIPs for which the USPS considers that city name to be an acceptable last line.

The mail delivery area of numerous other communities is also subdivided by ZIP Code, usually into just a few zones. ZIP information for these minor multi-zoned cities is also presented in the index as

---

* Estimates for economic activity in this edition of the *Atlas* are based on data from the U.S. Census Bureau's 1997 Economic Census and utilize the North American Industry Classification System (NAICS); estimates from editions of the *Atlas* before 2001 are based on census data using the 1987 Standard Industrial Classification (SIC) system. Trade statistics are not directly comparable between systems. Consult U.S. Census Bureau documentation for further information.

a range, although generally singular and shorter than those of major multi-zoned cities. For more information on ZIP codes, consult the U.S. Postal Service web site at http://www.usps.com/zip4/zipfaq.htm.

ZIP Code Service Area: An area surrounding an U.S. Postal Service Processing and Distribution Center. These areas are defined by the first three digits, or prefix, of the five-digit ZIP Code. As the ZIP Code system has evolved, ZIP Code Service Areas have become widely recognized as a useful and practical means for delineating marketing units. The three-digit Zip Code prefixes that define the Service Areas are conveniently available as part of mailing addresses, and no further coding or allocation to county or sales area is required.

Each ZIP Code Service Area surrounds a large post office, many of which operate as Processing and Distribution Centers serving between 40 and 75 other post offices in the area. The Processing and Distribution Center is usually located at the natural center of local transportation patterns. As a result, Service Areas generally represent economically homogeneous units of value to the marketer in defining prospective customers, establishing market potential, measuring market penetration and maximizing corporate resources. Service Areas are shown on the ZIP Code Service Areas map (pages 18-19) and are listed in the table called ZIP Code Service Areas: Population/Sales on pages 20-21.

The ZIP Code system assigns over 40,000 different five-digit codes to individual post offices, individual branch offices (in medium-sized cities) and individual postal delivery areas (in large cities). Because many Processing and Distribution Centers require more than one three-digit prefix, the number of prefixes exceeds the number of Service Areas. The extra prefixes are necessary either to handle individually zoned cities within a Service Area or because the area has a large number of separate post offices. In most cases, however, within any given Service Area, the prefixes are consecutive. Thus, in northern Illinois, ZIP Code prefixes 600 and 602 are used for post offices in the northern portion of the Chicago metropolitan area, 601, 603, and 605 for Chicago's western suburbs, and 604 for the southern suburbs. Consequently, Chicago's three-digit ZIP Code Service Area comprises prefixes 606-608 inclusive. The prefix 606 is used for Chicago proper and several bordering suburbs; 607 and 608 for several other adjacent suburbs. Some further subdivision of the Chicago metropolitan area by ZIP Codes is theoretically possible, but there is no advantage in doing so. The areas served by the north and west suburban prefixes could be distinguished from one another, but the current boundaries separating them simply reflect postal convenience and have little or no marketing significance.

Likewise, it would be possible to distinguish Chicago and suburbs such as Evanston and Oak Park from their surroundings, but the areas served by these post offices do not necessarily correspond to the corporate limits of these cities. For example, the Evanston Post Office (ZIP Code delivery areas 60201-04 and 60208-09) serves a sizable portion of the neighboring village of Skokie, so the Skokie residents of that area have ZIP Codes beginning with 602 instead of the Skokie Post Office's 600. The area served by the Chicago Post Office includes Norridge and several other suburban communities that have codes beginning 606.

Besides the combinations reflected in the Postal Service's official list, a few additional combinations of three-digit areas have been made for purposes of the ZIP Code Service Areas table. For example, the Brockton MA Service Area (023-024) has been treated along with Boston (017-024), because by itself it comprises neither a coherent independent area nor a useful subdivision of the greater Boston metropolitan area. There are also a few areas listed in the table under a name that differs from the one used by the Postal Service. For example, 208-209 appears as Rockville, MD, not Suburban Maryland.

This classification has been made primarily from the point of view of the business user interested in retail distribution through existing trading centers. Of course, there are other important marketing considerations relative to smaller areas. One example is the setting up of sales territories or territories for branch offices, where a center is chosen not so much because local people shop there as because it is a convenient place from which to cover the surrounding district.

ZIP Code Service Areas in principal do not cross state lines. With minor exceptions, if a Processing and Distribution Center services territory in another state, that portion of its area is given its own three-digit prefix. Many users will want to ignore state lines and combine these separate areas. *See also: ZIP Code, ZIP Code Service Area Classification Codes.*

ZIP Code Service Area Classification Codes: Codes developed by Rand McNally to indicate the degree to which ZIP Code Service Areas conform to city trading areas as defined on the Rand McNally Trading Areas Map *(see pages 22-23)*. Because ZIP Code Service Areas were developed to provide postal service, they usually include with each city the territory conveniently served from it by rail and other ground transportation. In many cases, these areas conform very closely to those of the city's trading area as defined by Rand McNally. However, there are also many ZIP Code Service Areas that differ significantly from what would generally be considered the trading area of the city. To aid users of ZIP Code Service Areas, Rand McNally has classified the Service Areas according to the degree to which they represent realistic trading areas.

Service Areas are classified by a letter (**A, B, C, D, M, W,** or **X**) followed in some cases by a number to indicate a subcategory of the main group. The classifications are as follows:

A—Accurate as a trading area. All of the Service Area is essentially served for retailing from one trading center, and its boundaries match quite closely the boundaries of the center's trading area. Some Service Areas encompass two or even three cities so close to one another that most shoppers can readily visit any one of them. Such Areas are classified as **A**, provided the Processing and Distribution Center city is also the most important of the multiple trading centers.
Service Areas classed as **A** sometimes have a trading area extending across a state line. The designation is still **A** if essentially all of the center's trading territory within the home state is within the Service Area.

A2—Cross-line area. The Service Area is served from a Processing and Distribution Center outside the state, but it conforms fairly closely to the portion of the corresponding trading area that is within the state. Most users will want to combine such areas with the portion across the state line. To aid in making these combinations, the ZIP prefix for the parent Service Area is given in parentheses after the **A2** classification.

B—Fairly accurate as a trading area. These in turn divide into:

B1—Fairly accurate, but larger than the actual trading area. The Processing and Distribution Center city is the most important trading center in the Area, but the Service Area is somewhat larger than the trading territory, and includes counties or districts whose residents would rarely if ever visit the Processing and Distribution Center city for shopping. For most marketing purposes, however, the Area is a fairly accurate approximation of the trading area.

B2—Fairly accurate, but smaller than the actual trading area. Many of these Areas center on large cities, whose actual trading areas are significantly more extensive than the Postal Service arrangements recognize. The outlying portions of their trading areas are often separate Service Areas for postal purposes and are classified as **W1** or **W2** (see below).

C—Multicentered Service Area. These Service Areas have two or more trading centers, too far apart to be treated as adjacent centers of a single trading area. Thus, they are not single units for shopping.
The **C** Service Areas are good examples of situations which may provide quite satisfactory units for sales territories and related purposes, so long as it is recognized that they do not represent the trading area for any single city. In several cases a **C** Area is closely related to a city across a state line and has that city's ZIP prefix specified.

C1. The Service Area has two trading centers, and the Processing and Distribution Center city is the most important.

C2. The Service Area has two trading centers, but the Processing and Distribution Center city is *not* the most important. It would be misleading to treat these Service Areas as comprising the shopping area of the city named, when in fact there is a more important shopping focus elsewhere in the Service Area.

C3. The Service Area has three or more trading centers, which are relatively independent of one another. The Processing and Distribution Center city may or may not be the most important of these trading centers.

D—Fairly accurate as a trading area, but the Processing and Distribution Center is not the trading center. The Processing and Distribution Center city is a fairly important trading center, but is not the most important in the Area, as comparison with the Rand McNally Trading Areas Map will show. These Areas form satisfactory units if the presence of the more important trading center is recognized. In some cases the ZIP prefix of a nearby city across a state line is specified.

M—Metropolitan Service Area. The Service Area is a well-defined central or outlying portion of a major metropolitan area. Because sections of all metropolitan areas are not readily distinguishable in ZIP Code terms, some *Atlas* users will want to combine these into one Area with their main city (whose ZIP prefix is specified following the classification).

W—Weak Service Area. The Service Area represents a somewhat accurate trading area, but is centered on a relatively small town that does not qualify as a Rand McNally Basic Trading Center. Many of these centers are in fairly remote regions in the Appalachians or the West. For mail distribution purposes they may still be the convenient centers for serving their surroundings. However, residents of these areas would often not be satisfied with the limited range of goods available in the stores of such small communities, and they would go further afield for their shopping to larger cities. For marketing purposes, most of the **W** Areas could logically be combined with the neighboring Service Area with whose trading center they are most closely associated. The ZIP Codes for these stronger areas are specified following the **W** classifications.

W1. The Service Area, usually with a rather small population, does represent fairly closely the trading area of the designated Processing and Distribution Center city.

W2. The Service Area is considerably larger than the territory served for trading purposes by the designated center. An example is Jasper, AL (355). This small city northwest of Birmingham is a significant shopping center for Walker County, its immediate vicinity, but not for the several additional counties or portions of counties to the west which are also included in 355. Residents of these counties would probably travel past Jasper to Birmingham more often than to any other city. Thus, Area 355 decidedly exaggerates the area realistically served for shopping by Jasper. However, such an area could be served by a salesman from Jasper quite readily, if it were desired to recognize it separately from a larger Birmingham area.

X—Unsatisfactory as a Trading Area. This small group of Areas defies treatment as marketing units. Sometimes this is because the Processing and Distribution Center city selected is very limited in importance. Or it is because the shape of the area does not conform at all closely to actual trading patterns.

See also: ZIP Code Service Area, Basic Trading Area.

* Estimates for economic activity in this edition of the *Atlas* are based on data from the U.S. Census Bureau's 1997 Economic Census and utilize the North American Industry Classification System (NAICS); estimates from editions of the *Atlas* before 2001 are based on census data using the 1987 Standard Industrial Classification (SIC) system. Trade statistics are not directly comparable between systems. Consult U.S. Census Bureau documentation for further information.

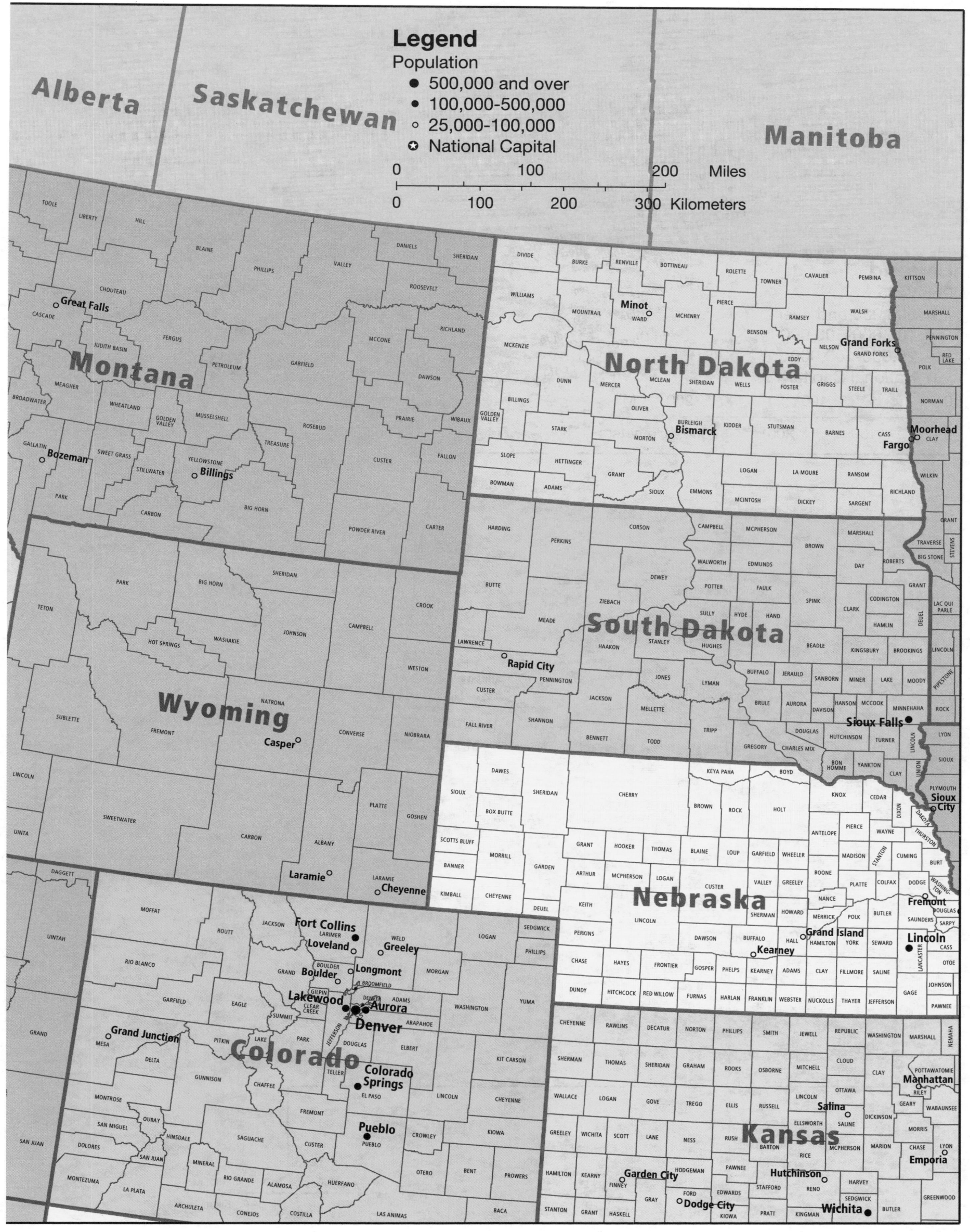

Legend
Population
- ● 500,000 and over
- ● 100,000-500,000
- ○ 25,000-100,000
- ✪ National Capital

0   100   200   Miles

0   100   200   300 Kilometers

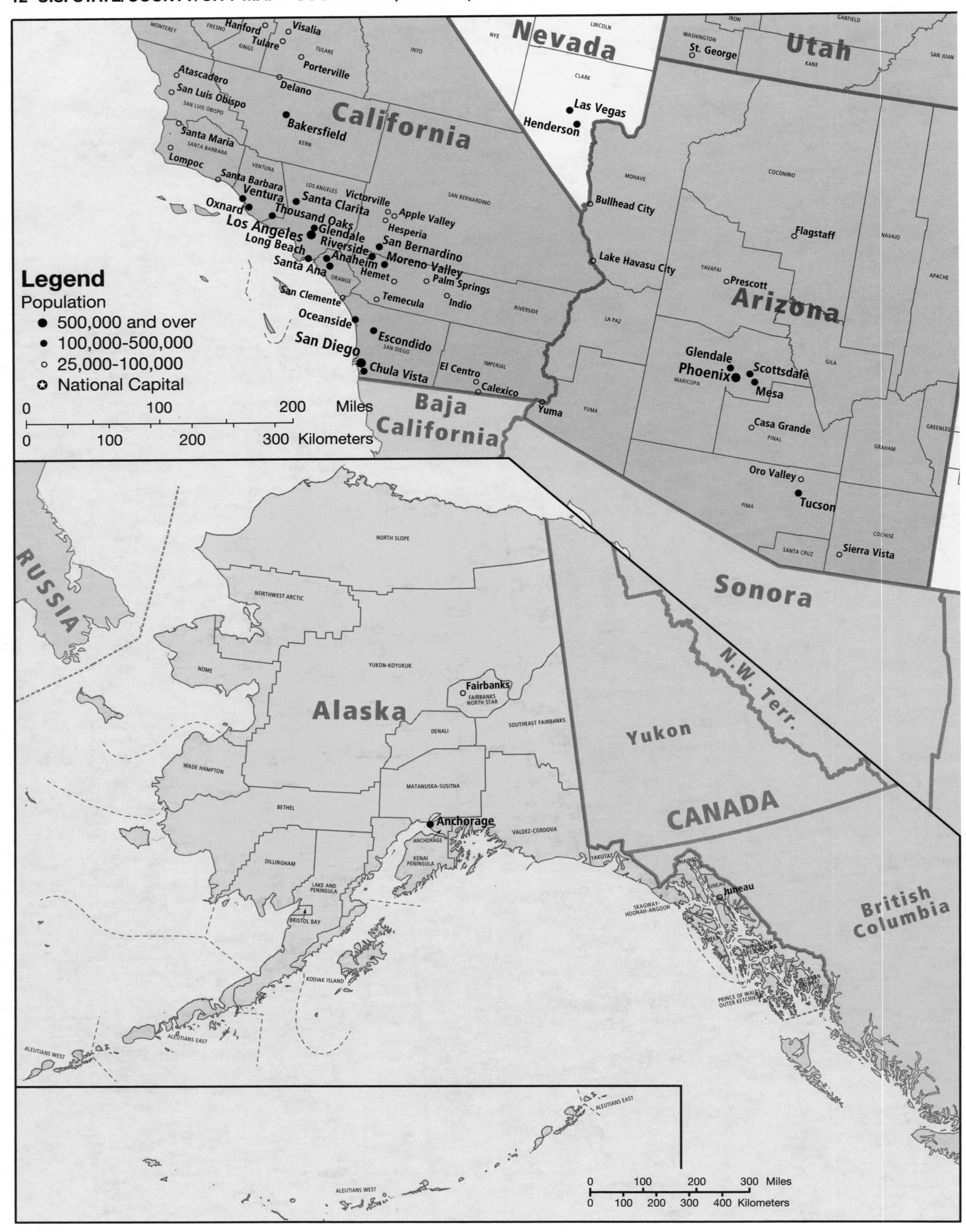

Legend
Population
- ● 500,000 and over
- ● 100,000-500,000
- ○ 25,000-100,000
- ✪ National Capital

0   100   200   Miles

0   100   200   300   Kilometers

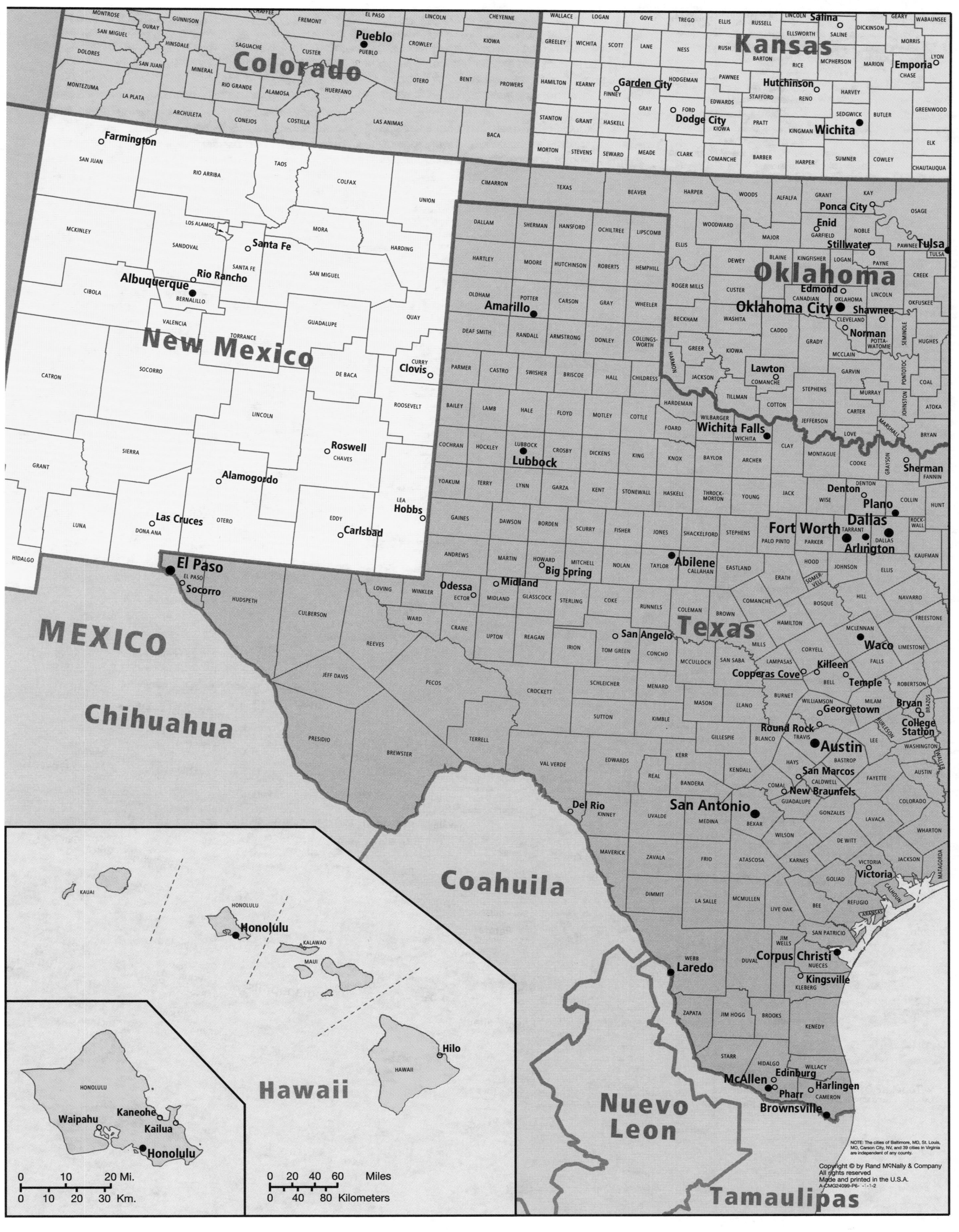

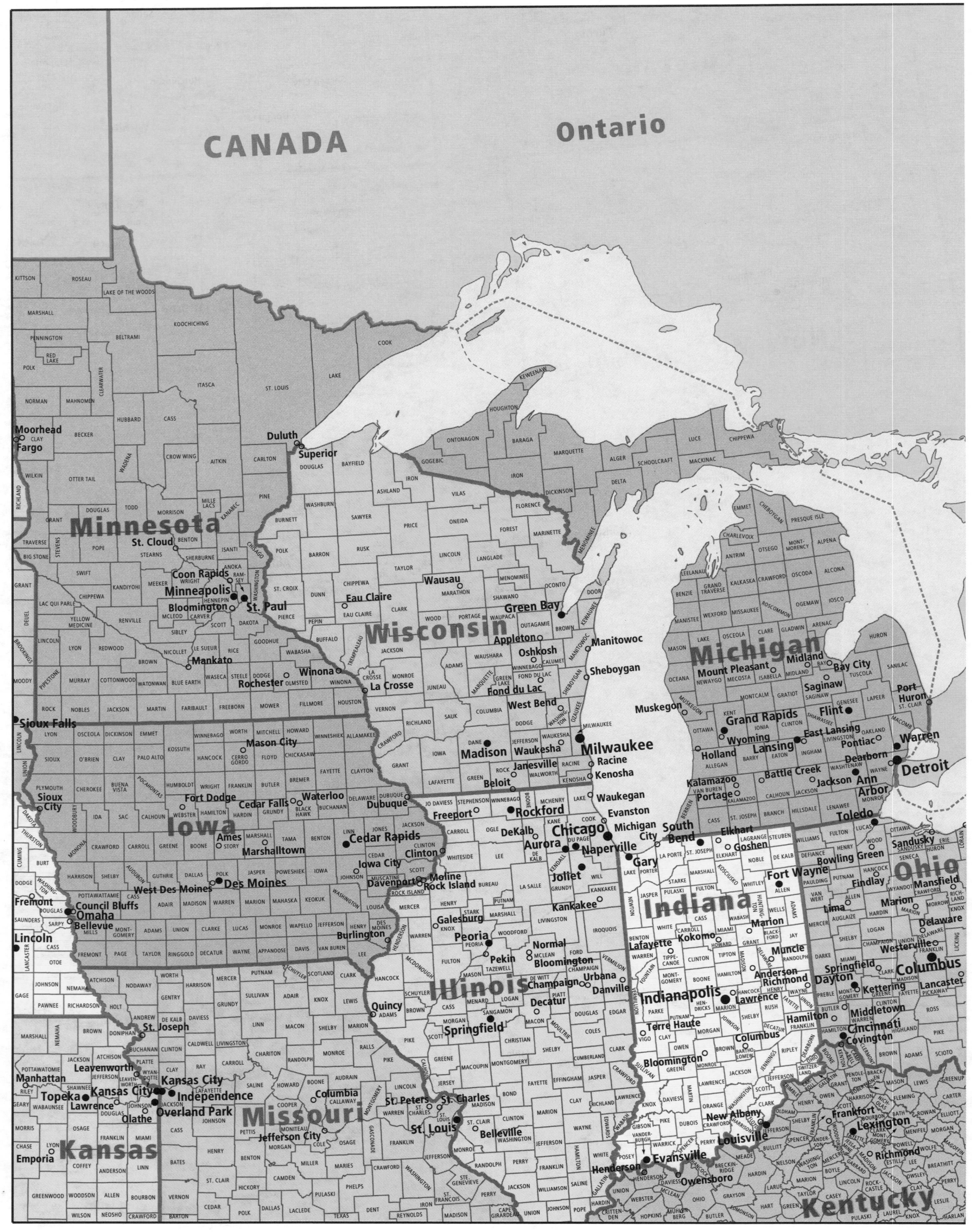

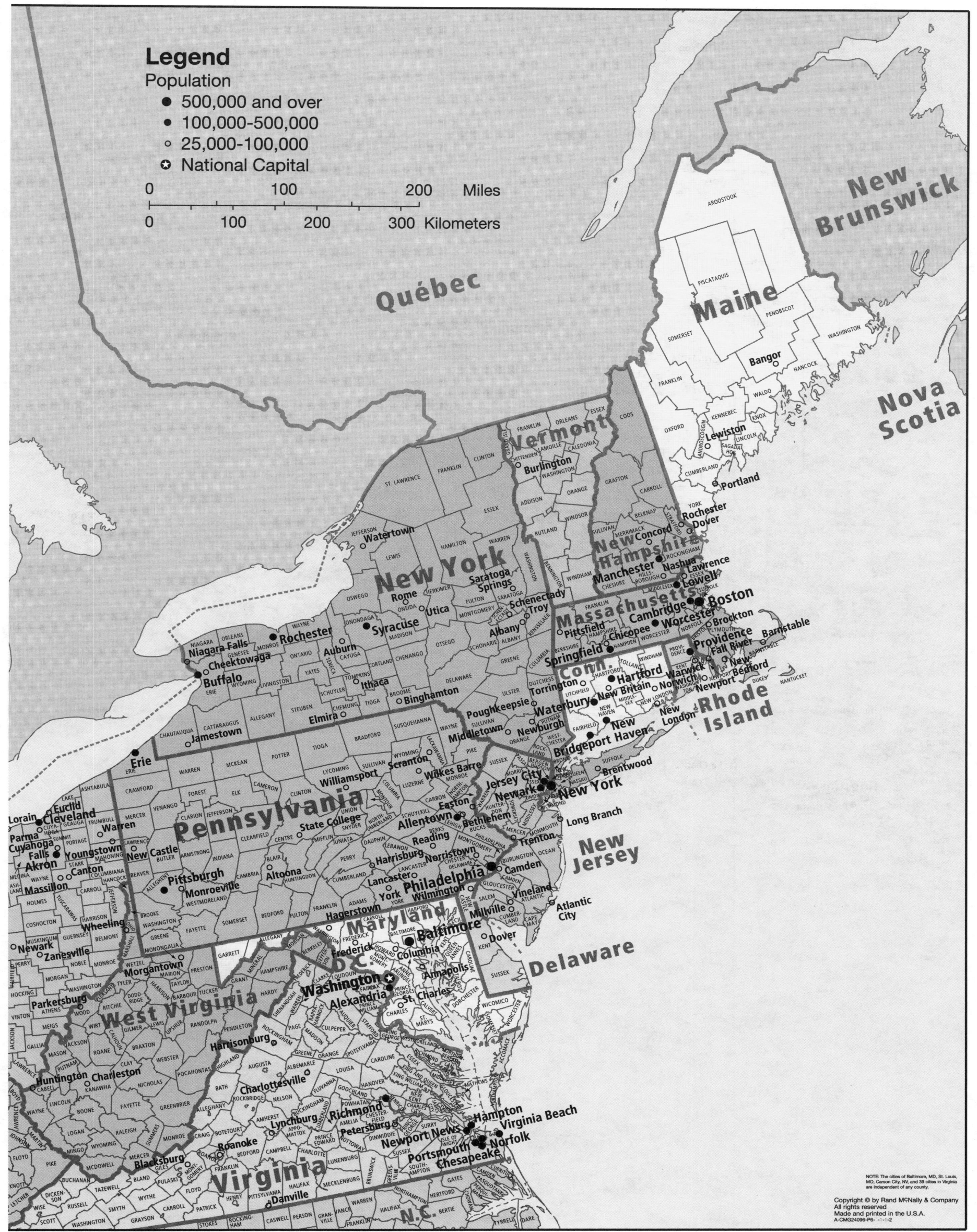

Legend

Population

- ● 500,000 and over
- ● 100,000-500,000
- ○ 25,000-100,000
- ⊛ National Capital

```
0          100          200     Miles
0     100     200     300 Kilometers
```

New Brunswick

Québec

Nova Scotia

Maine

AROOSTOOK

PISCATAQUIS

SOMERSET

FRANKLIN

OXFORD

PENOBSCOT

WASHINGTON

Bangor

HANCOCK

WALDO

KNOX

LINCOLN

SAGADAHOC

CUMBERLAND

YORK

Portland

Vermont

New Hampshire

Lewiston

Rochester
Dover

Concord

Manchester

Nashua
Lawrence
Lowell

Burlington

New York

Watertown

Saratoga
Springs

Rome

Utica

Syracuse

Schenectady
Troy

Albany

Rochester

Niagara Falls
Cheektowaga

Buffalo

Auburn

Ithaca

Binghamton

Elmira

Jamestown

Erie

Massachusetts

Boston
Cambridge Worcester
Brockton

Pittsfield
Springfield Chicopee

Providence
Fall River   Barnstable
New Bedford
Newport

Conn.

Hartford
New Britain
Waterbury
Torrington
New London
Norwich

Rhode Island

Poughkeepsie

Middletown
Newburgh

Bridgeport New Haven

Brentwood

Scranton
Wilkes Barre

Williamsport

Pennsylvania

State College

Jersey City
Newark   New York

Easton
Allentown Bethlehem

Reading

Long Branch

New Jersey

Lorain
Cleveland
Euclid
Parma
Cuyahoga
Falls
Akron
Youngstown
New Castle

Warren

Pittsburgh
Monroeville

Canton
Massillon

Wheeling

Newark
Zanesville

Parkersburg

Morgantown

Harrisburg

Lancaster
York

Norristown

Philadelphia

Trenton

Camden

Vineland

Atlantic City

Millville

Altoona

Hagerstown

Maryland

Frederick

Baltimore

Columbia

Annapolis

Dover

Delaware

West Virginia

Washington

Alexandria

St. Charles

Huntington Charleston

Harrisonburg

Charlottesville

Lynchburg

Roanoke

Blacksburg

Virginia

Richmond

Petersburg

Newport News
Portsmouth
Chesapeake

Hampton
Virginia Beach
Norfolk

Danville

N.C.

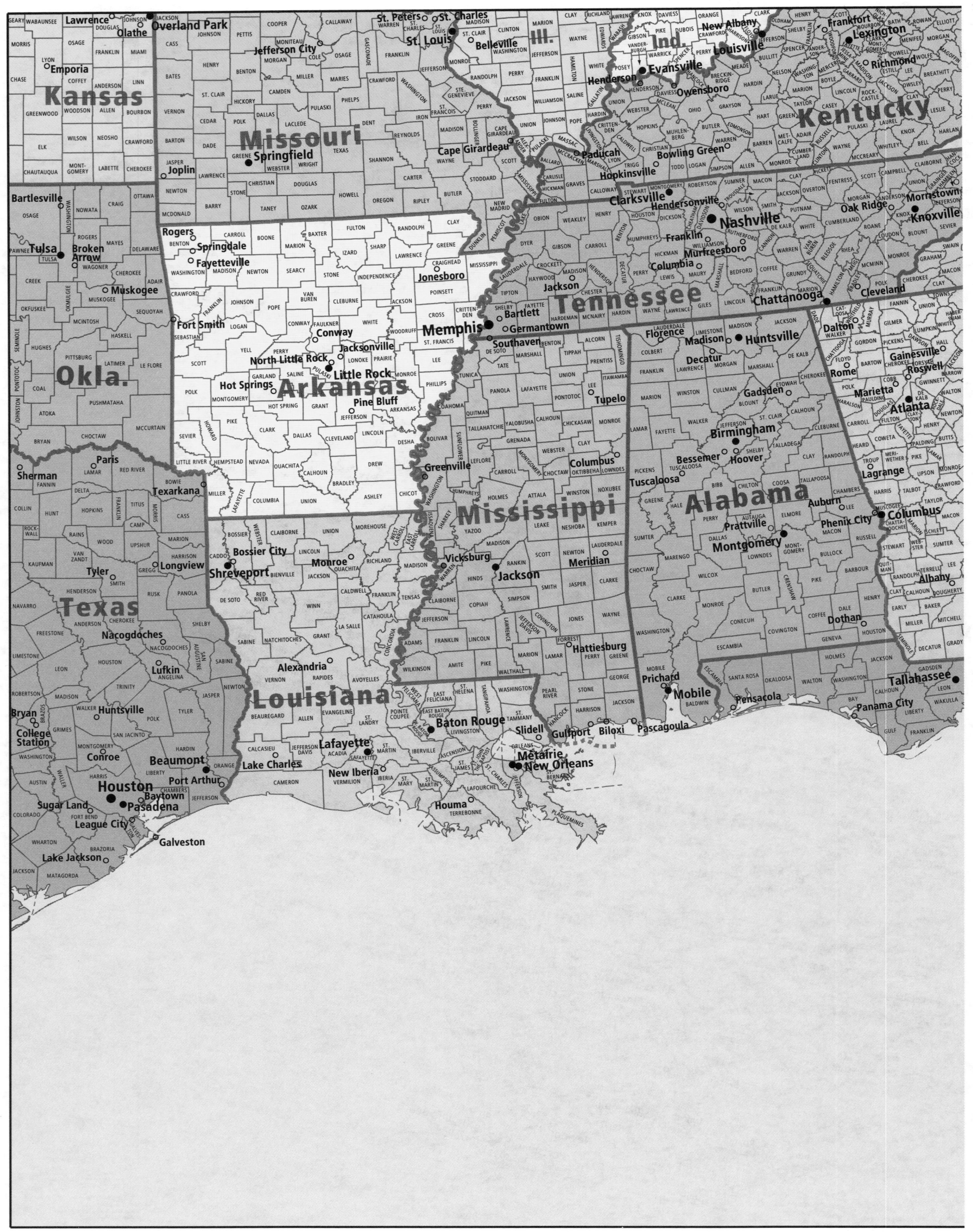

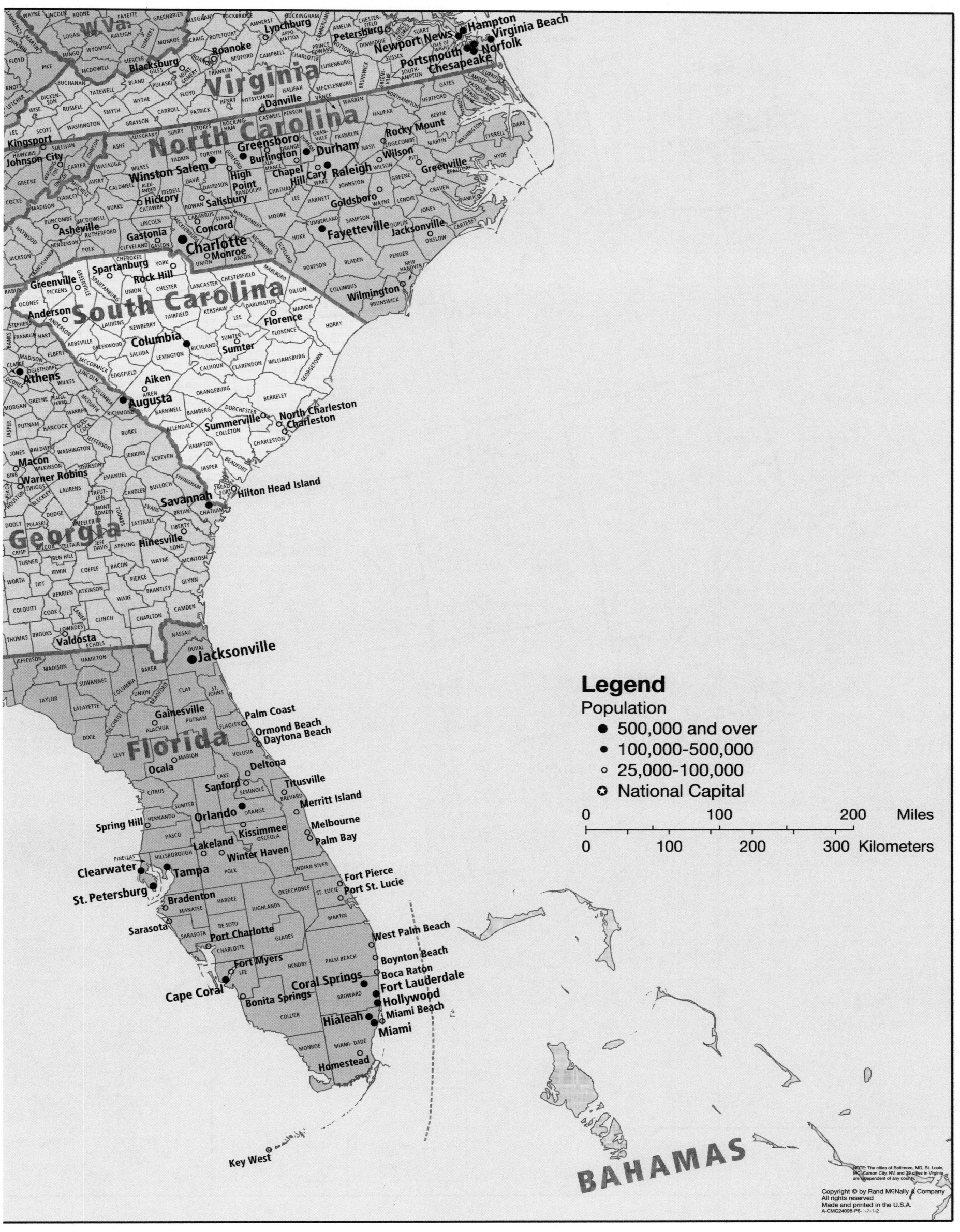

Legend
Population
- ● 500,000 and over
- ● 100,000-500,000
- ○ 25,000-100,000
- ⊚ National Capital

0   100   200   Miles

0   100   200   300   Kilometers

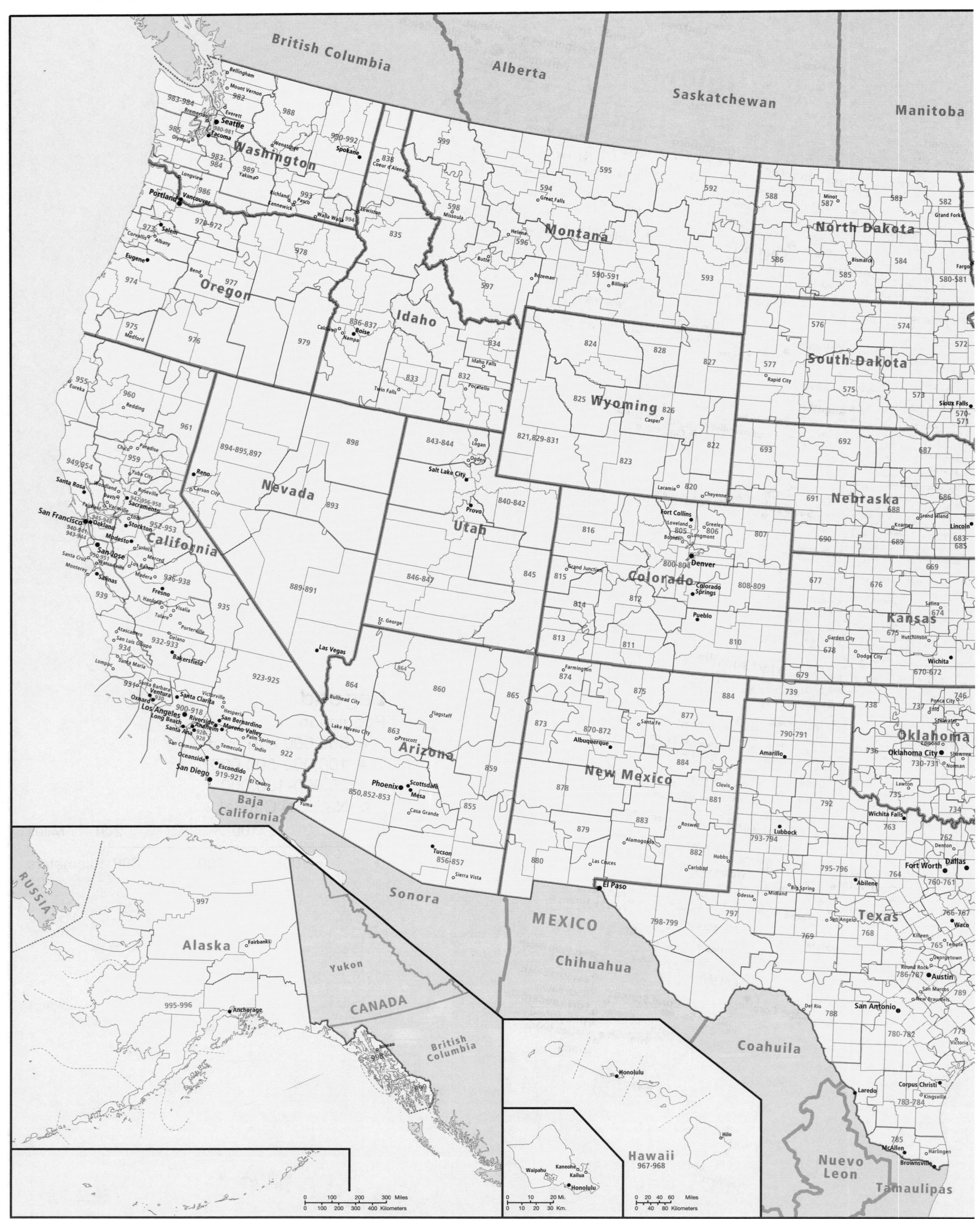

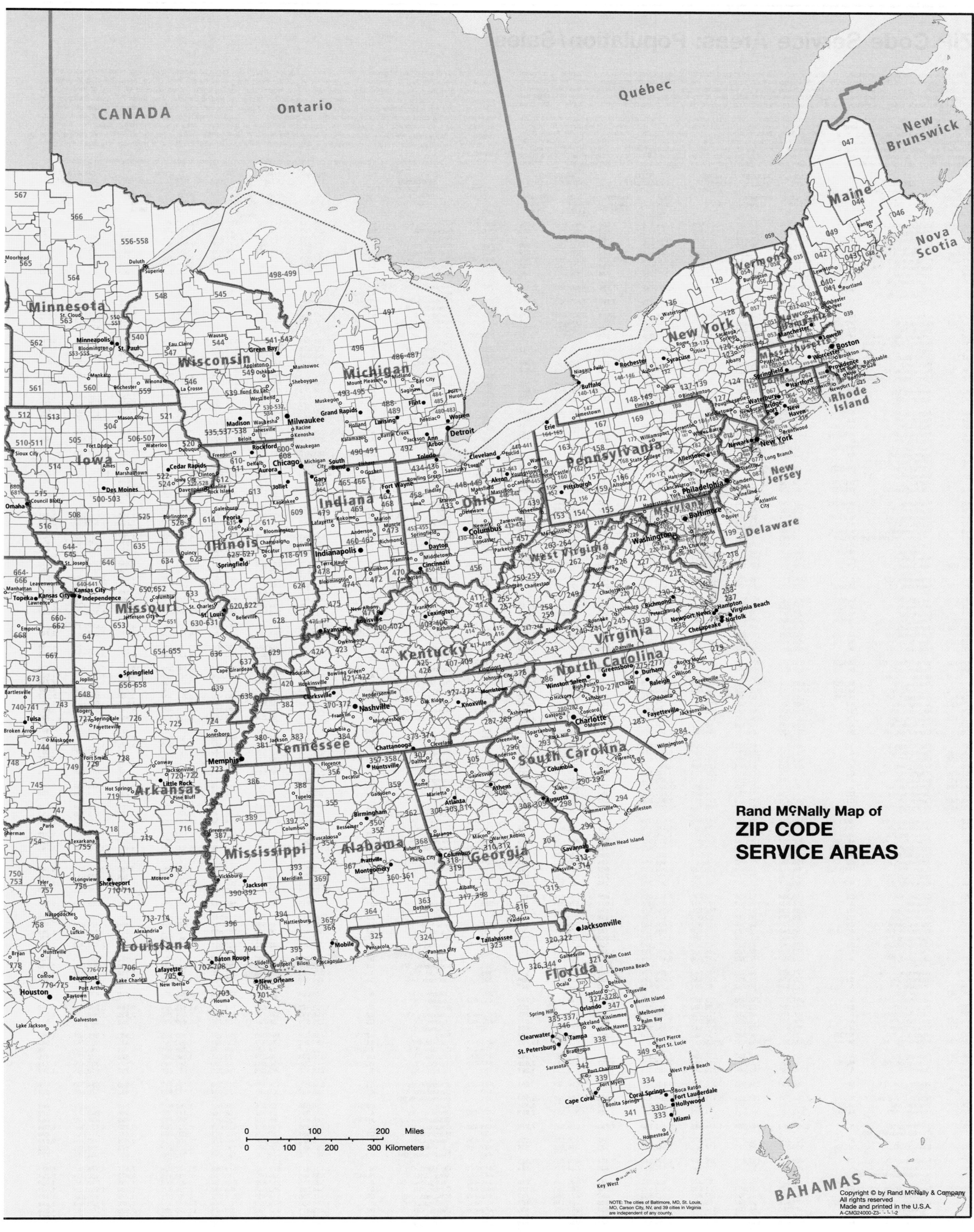

Rand M&Nally Map of
ZIP CODE
SERVICE AREAS

NOTE: The cities of Baltimore, MD, St. Louis,
MO, Carson City, NV, and 39 cities in Virginia
are independent of any county.

ZIP Code Service Areas: Population/Sales

This table provides current marketing information for areas identified by 3-digit ZIP Codes. Each Service Area is served by a Postal Service Processing and Distribution Center usually located in its principal city or the principal city of an adjacent area. The Processing and Distribution Centers and the area served by each one appear on the map on pages 18–19. ZIP Code Service Areas have received increasing attention as marketing units because of the great convenience they afford in allotting sales prospects, inquiries, etc., since the ZIP Codes for these areas are already available as part of the mailing address and no further coding or allocation to county or sales area is required.

Since the ZIP Areas were set up originally to provide postal service, they usually include with each city the territory conveniently served from it by rail and other ground transportation. In many cases the boundaries of the ZIP Area conform very closely to those of the city's trading area as defined on the Rand McNally Trading Area Map (see pages 22–23). However, many ZIP Areas differ significantly from what would generally be considered the trading area of the city. To aid users of ZIP Areas, Rand McNally has classified the Service Areas according to the degree to which they represent realistic trading areas for the principal cities named.

Areas classified **A** conform closely to the actual trading areas of the cities. Those classified **B** are reasonably similar, but are either somewhat larger (**B1**) or somewhat smaller (**B2**) than the city's actual trading area. Areas denoted **C** contain more than one distinct center and do not constitute single areas for retail sales purposes, though they might be satisfactory units for sales territories or branch offices. In Areas denoted **D**, the main trading center is not the town designated by the Post Office. Areas denoted **M** constitute convenient portions of large metropolitan areas rather than independent trading areas. Areas denoted **W**, many of them in thinly populated regions, center on towns which have only a weak status as regional trading centers; often, these ZIP Areas are larger than the trading area served from their center. Finally, the Areas classified **X** either have very small towns as centers or consist of essentially unrelated territory, and cannot be considered meaningful marketing units. Rand McNally recommends combining the **X** Areas with the adjoining Area with which each is most closely related; the ZIP Code of this related Area is stated in parentheses following the **X** classification. Many users will also want to combine some of the **M** and **W** areas with adjoining areas, to treat whole metropolitan areas as units or to eliminate disproportionately small areas. Suggested combinations for all of the **M** and **W** areas are specified following the classification.

A further discussion of the classification and a detailed explanation of the categories appear in the Introduction on pages 5–9.

ZIP CODE	SECTIONAL CENTER OR PRINCIPAL CITY	CLASSIFICATION	POPULATION Estimated 7/1/04	HOUSEHOLDS Estimated 7/1/04	AUTO REGISTRATIONS 2003	TOTAL RETAIL SALES 2003 Sales ($1,000)	TOTAL RETAIL SALES Ranally Sales Units	SHOPPING GOODS SALES** 2003 Sales ($1,000)	SHOPPING GOODS SALES** Ranally Sales Units
010-011	Springfield, MA	B2	632,935	244,897	379,663	6,454,316	**1,899**	964,808	**1,486**
012	Pittsfield, MA	A	132,083	56,261	87,137	1,557,685	**458**	262,885	**405**
013	Greenfield, MA	W1(010)	84,252	35,097	57,916	642,819	**189**	59,952	**92**
014	Fitchburg, MA	W1(015)	211,006	79,589	138,913	2,583,037	**760**	324,465	**500**
015-016	Worcester, MA	B2	550,556	211,297	347,586	6,247,445	**1,837**	895,857	**1,379**
017-024	Boston, MA	B2	4,036,731	1,563,111	2,405,095	52,597,842	**15,473**	8,356,317	**12,866**
025	Buzzards Bay, MA	X(026)	118,919	48,797	85,672	1,807,970	**532**	172,260	**265**
026	Hyannis, MA	B2	160,716	71,146	119,579	2,528,034	**744**	356,040	**548**
027	Providence, RI (MA Part)	C3(028)	530,793	209,504	336,162	6,446,742	**1,896**	1,496,489	**2,304**
028-029	Providence, RI (RI Part)	A	1,084,804	429,611	701,246	10,761,398	**3,166**	1,635,363	**2,518**
030-031	Manchester, NH	B2	522,662	196,549	369,766	10,384,819	**3,054**	2,321,946	**3,575**
032-033	Concord, NH	W2(030)	246,940	97,268	179,385	3,583,201	**1,054**	508,244	**783**
034	Keene, NH	B2	83,882	32,684	60,521	1,521,327	**448**	188,967	**291**
035	Littleton, NH (NH Part)	W2(042)	45,808	19,852	33,189	886,086	**261**	46,818	**72**
036	Bellows Falls, VT (NH Part)	W1(034)	13,087	5,422	10,224	121,918	**36**	11,132	**17**
037	White River Jct., VT (NH Part)	D	76,203	30,521	53,402	1,450,567	**427**	233,094	**359**
038	Portsmouth, NH	B1	315,049	126,510	235,570	5,968,981	**1,756**	1,024,762	**1,578**
039	Portsmouth, NH (ME Part)	A2(038)	50,904	20,721	38,715	420,644	**124**	100,904	**155**
040-041	Portland, ME	B2	440,557	181,968	313,545	7,121,886	**2,095**	1,067,357	**1,643**
042	Auburn, ME	D	175,961	73,165	125,297	2,274,834	**669**	296,363	**456**
043	Augusta, ME	A	80,306	34,019	59,237	1,237,994	**364**	163,469	**252**
044	Bangor, ME	B2	169,730	70,537	120,968	2,286,726	**673**	333,991	**514**
045	Bath, ME	W2(040)	49,962	21,835	38,808	643,143	**189**	26,941	**41**
046	Ellsworth, ME	W2(044)	72,578	31,777	54,598	939,493	**276**	117,729	**181**
047	Houlton, ME	D	73,624	31,618	53,268	702,163	**207**	113,466	**175**
048	Rockland, ME	W1(044)	41,449	17,945	30,591	561,941	**165**	63,127	**97**
049	Waterville, ME	B1	158,622	65,862	113,093	1,909,501	**562**	230,567	**355**
050	White River Junction, VT (VT Part)	D1(037)	62,454	25,927	47,009	522,765	**154**	16,329	**25**
051	Bellows Falls, VT (VT Part)	W1(034)	29,838	12,878	22,541	288,794	**85**	26,260	**40**
052	Bennington, VT	W1(057)	33,529	13,747	23,396	709,792	**209**	133,185	**205**
053	Brattleboro, VT	W1(034)	37,480	15,964	28,019	464,358	**137**	25,878	**40**
054	Burlington, VT	B2	228,193	89,774	162,556	3,507,314	**1,032**	467,913	**720**
056	Montpelier, VT	W1(054)	84,891	35,111	60,342	979,820	**288**	77,054	**119**
057	Rutland, VT	B2	84,015	33,985	58,431	1,157,508	**340**	138,680	**214**
058	St. Johnsbury, VT	W1(054)	58,049	23,673	40,837	591,081	**174**	61,376	**95**
059	Littleton, NH (VT Part)	X(054)	3,644	1,489	2,621	2,000	**1**	0	**0**
060-061	Hartford, CT	M	953,161	378,620	630,939	11,984,818	**3,526**	1,988,292	**3,062**
062	Willimantic, CT	M(060)	159,506	58,002	108,424	1,049,892	**309**	111,785	**172**
063	New London, CT	A	260,321	102,953	180,854	3,271,469	**962**	601,144	**926**
064-066	New Haven, CT	C1	1,223,822	471,169	791,865	15,601,798	**4,589**	2,260,891	**3,481**
067	Waterbury, CT	A	330,271	129,766	220,795	4,050,847	**1,192**	557,055	**858**
068-069	Stamford, CT	M(100)	580,816	216,904	402,626	13,903,865	**4,090**	1,491,772	**2,296**
070-076,079	Newark, NJ	M(100)	3,890,241	1,407,375	2,104,781	46,752,125	**13,752**	7,296,460	**11,235**
077	Monmouth, NJ	M(100)	613,614	232,285	410,748	8,527,144	**2,508**	1,481,135	**2,280**
078	Dover, NJ	M(100)	365,747	132,982	257,266	5,299,852	**1,559**	911,993	**1,404**
080-084	South Jersey, NJ	M(189)	1,843,990	693,140	1,143,487	22,633,415	**6,659**	3,634,231	**5,596**
085-086	Trenton, NJ	A	558,485	200,725	347,245	5,891,188	**1,733**	824,493	**1,269**
087	Lakewood, NJ	M(100)	448,531	180,810	289,470	5,499,454	**1,618**	732,548	**1,128**
088-089	New Brunswick, NJ	M(100)	985,216	351,531	629,324	14,189,861	**4,174**	2,154,214	**3,316**
100-104	New York, NY	M	3,408,941	1,395,657	748,403	36,787,414	**10,822**	12,502,754	**19,248**
105-108	White Plains, NY	M(100)	1,036,376	375,423	592,937	12,914,526	**3,799**	2,370,864	**3,650**
109	Suffern, NY	M(100)	516,910	168,188	300,411	5,698,730	**1,676**	1,366,832	**2,104**
110-116	Brooklyn-Queens-Nassau, NY	M(100)	5,630,286	1,958,358	1,760,097	37,290,971	**10,968**	6,786,064	**10,448**
117-118	Hicksville, NY	M(100)	1,642,813	539,328	1,062,689	21,822,726	**6,419**	3,624,757	**5,581**
119	Riverhead, NY	M(100)	240,923	90,440	162,638	3,269,518	**962**	629,303	**969**
120-123	Albany, NY	B2	902,926	368,549	586,145	9,401,191	**2,766**	1,458,862	**2,246**
124	Kingston, NY	B1	156,600	63,864	105,460	1,608,698	**473**	223,626	**344**
125-126	Poughkeepsie, NY	C1	529,150	190,499	339,271	4,893,589	**1,440**	813,778	**1,253**
127	Monticello, NY	X(100)	98,155	37,438	60,172	708,077	**208**	42,926	**66**
128	Glens Falls, NY	B1	221,423	88,471	149,222	2,449,388	**721**	474,103	**730**
129	Plattsburgh, NY	B1	161,925	61,231	101,869	1,514,414	**445**	216,725	**334**
130-132	Syracuse, NY	A	793,710	314,671	500,527	8,074,331	**2,376**	1,282,314	**1,975**
133-135	Utica, NY	A	401,528	157,457	250,762	3,507,411	**1,031**	571,290	**879**
136	Watertown, NY	B2	236,333	87,024	138,696	2,303,371	**678**	362,061	**557**
137-139	Binghamton, NY	C1	356,786	143,612	232,103	3,472,150	**1,021**	612,074	**943**
140-143	Buffalo, NY	A	1,296,495	523,695	788,811	12,505,951	**3,679**	2,039,218	**3,140**
144-146	Rochester, NY	A	1,092,601	432,793	714,977	11,492,079	**3,381**	1,829,427	**2,817**
147	Jamestown, NY	C3	184,498	72,671	114,945	1,567,996	**461**	314,565	**484**
148-149	Elmira, NY	C1	337,425	132,274	212,644	2,962,800	**872**	487,477	**750**
150-152	Pittsburgh, PA	M	1,546,464	666,847	973,119	18,905,624	**5,562**	3,032,154	**4,668**
153	Washington, PA	W2(150)	180,258	71,311	123,662	1,821,699	**536**	212,604	**327**
154	Uniontown, PA	W1(150)	152,107	62,495	103,091	1,416,370	**417**	291,813	**449**
155	Somerset, PA	W2(159)	90,013	35,672	65,174	1,140,397	**335**	116,516	**179**
156	Greensburg, PA	M(150)	308,037	126,144	220,091	3,298,949	**970**	464,094	**715**
157	Indiana, PA	A	115,432	45,629	79,718	1,064,976	**313**	189,533	**292**
158	Du Bois, PA	B1	93,472	38,445	65,511	995,289	**293**	136,529	**210**
159	Johnstown, PA	B2	150,424	61,452	98,954	1,446,568	**426**	230,012	**354**
160	Butler, PA	W1(150)	194,178	74,864	138,733	2,062,630	**607**	321,729	**495**
161	New Castle, PA	C1	230,395	91,111	154,491	2,700,416	**794**	528,420	**814**
162	Kittanning, PA	W2(150)	89,675	35,743	61,807	973,278	**286**	123,390	**190**
163	Oil City, PA	C3	153,334	62,468	103,220	2,173,930	**639**	296,814	**457**
164-165	Erie, PA	A	314,634	123,807	199,607	3,437,385	**1,012**	576,791	**888**
166	Altoona, PA	B2	208,224	82,618	142,350	2,244,576	**660**	397,624	**612**
167	Bradford, PA	B2	50,558	20,114	32,069	401,572	**118**	22,131	**34**
168	State College, PA	C1	184,714	69,574	122,367	2,001,189	**589**	388,305	**598**
169	Wellsboro, PA	A2(148)	66,550	25,924	46,678	504,428	**148**	58,506	**90**
170-171	Harrisburg, PA	A	738,982	300,354	520,120	9,731,736	**2,863**	1,328,639	**2,046**
172	Chambersburg, PA	B1	188,442	73,739	142,592	1,897,328	**558**	225,514	**347**
173-174	York, PA	A	473,529	184,748	346,037	4,467,313	**1,314**	773,500	**1,191**
175-176	Lancaster, PA	A	458,799	170,378	295,606	6,401,444	**1,883**	916,828	**1,412**
177	Williamsport, PA	A	171,690	68,923	115,583	1,908,771	**561**	338,468	**521**
178	Sunbury, PA	C1	229,608	88,432	153,436	2,229,325	**656**	329,677	**508**
179	Pottsville, PA	A	125,430	50,782	83,691	1,360,882	**400**	160,497	**247**
180-181	Lehigh Valley (Bethlehem), PA	A	657,827	258,403	452,892	7,857,056	**2,311**	1,145,111	**1,763**
182	Hazleton, PA	B1	126,095	53,391	88,680	1,215,868	**358**	200,262	**308**
183	East Stroudsburg, PA	A	168,476	60,812	117,239	1,900,831	**559**	490,515	**755**
184-185	Scranton, PA	A	308,841	126,221	206,312	3,224,196	**948**	527,904	**813**
186-187	Wilkes-Barre, PA	A	306,615	129,251	209,547	3,558,327	**1,047**	575,500	**886**
188	Montrose, PA	X(137)	75,745	30,590	53,862	766,160	**225**	95,521	**147**
189-194	Philadelphia, PA	M	3,833,202	1,495,454	2,139,757	47,724,228	**14,037**	7,009,645	**10,792**
195-196	Reading, PA	A	401,478	152,263	265,536	4,419,517	**1,300**	873,532	**1,345**
197-198	Wilmington, DE	M(189)	514,926	200,603	342,048	7,808,729	**2,297**	1,314,911	**2,025**
199	Dover, DE	A	312,397	122,490	219,278	3,963,064	**1,166**	842,235	**1,297**
200,202-205	Washington, D.C.	M	560,780	256,593	235,775	3,435,653	**1,010**	618,263	**951**
201,220-223	Northern Virginia, VA	M(200)	2,034,681	791,551	1,471,810	26,607,656	**7,828**	5,588,492	**8,604**
206-207	Waldorf, MD	M(200)	1,260,423	453,229	816,283	11,817,835	**3,476**	2,033,757	**3,131**
208-209	Rockville, MD	M(200)	942,221	351,891	614,514	11,303,099	**3,325**	1,878,957	**2,893**
210-212,214	Baltimore, MD	A	2,401,803	944,684	1,494,642	26,461,760	**7,784**	5,009,131	**7,713**
215	Cumberland, MD (MD Part)	A	102,701	40,677	70,376	1,061,687	**312**	200,576	**309**
216	Easton, MD	X(210)	160,355	64,275	118,082	1,947,779	**573**	349,165	**538**
217	Frederick, MD	C2	446,725	162,615	325,298	4,954,846	**1,458**	879,769	**1,355**
218	Salisbury, MD	A	165,887	65,048	112,781	2,141,400	**630**	534,915	**824**
219	Northeastern Maryland, MD	X(189)	94,834	34,976	67,370	822,422	**242**	140,578	**216**
224-225	Fredericksburg, VA	B1	362,175	131,993	271,959	3,563,498	**1,048**	763,165	**1,175**
226	Winchester, VA	A	162,300	64,395	127,831	2,217,556	**652**	473,388	**729**
227	Culpeper, VA	W2(200)	71,975	26,547	55,723	700,362	**206**	67,110	**103**
228	Harrisonburg, VA	A	149,150	56,101	114,572	1,812,750	**533**	282,455	**435**
229	Charlottesville, VA	B2	230,269	93,340	177,052	2,054,376	**604**	399,603	**615**
230-232	Richmond, VA	M	1,025,312	422,294	774,209	12,033,928	**3,540**	2,495,653	**3,843**
233-237	Norfolk, VA	B2	1,552,804	591,397	1,028,500	16,183,349	**4,760**	3,538,037	**5,448**
238	Petersburg, VA	M(230)	316,572	121,668	227,854	2,548,835	**750**	591,829	**911**
239	Farmville, VA	W2(230)	101,581	38,540	68,720	682,638	**201**	67,750	**104**
240-241	Roanoke, VA	C1	559,857	236,412	449,700	6,088,366	**1,791**	1,270,279	**1,956**
242	Bristol, VA	A	191,983	81,987	142,155	2,163,459	**636**	409,092	**630**
243	Pulaski, VA	W2(240)	153,502	65,285	119,271	1,407,586	**414**	204,646	**315**
244	Staunton, VA	B1	137,270	55,807	108,424	1,312,827	**386**	124,859	**192**
245	Lynchburg, VA	C1	361,050	148,914	274,088	3,857,525	**1,135**	728,329	**1,121**
246	Bluefield, WV (VA Part)	A2(247)	70,549	29,522	52,540	759,426	**223**	172,008	**265**
247-248	Bluefield, WV (WV Part)	B1	102,751	44,499	67,327	977,398	**287**	232,326	**358**
249	Lewisburg, WV	X(258)	52,595	22,534	39,847	412,513	**121**	96,667	**149**
250-253	Charleston, WV	B2	325,168	138,955	218,482	3,901,525	**1,147**	737,210	**1,135**
254	Martinsburg, WV	A	153,599	61,009	113,272	1,114,629	**328**	208,565	**321**
255-257	Huntington, WV	B1	265,744	112,987	175,587	2,692,608	**793**	511,266	**788**
258-259	Beckley, WV	B2	135,693	56,376	89,062	1,485,374	**437**	343,496	**529**
260	Wheeling, WV	C1	137,158	59,890	96,038	1,017,432	**299**	169,216	**261**
261	Parkersburg, WV	A	131,841	55,693	92,349	1,687,305	**496**	456,695	**703**
262	Buckhannon, WV	W2(263)	82,906	33,723	56,006	691,396	**203**	120,518	**186**
263-264	Clarksburg, WV	B2	142,635	58,513	96,658	1,401,046	**412**	310,343	**478**
265	Morgantown, WV	C1	163,277	68,306	112,534	1,574,642	**463**	398,792	**614**
266	Gassaway, WV	X(250)	32,715	13,408	22,325	350,319	**103**	66,748	**103**
267	Cumberland, MD (WV Part)	A2(215)	51,963	21,228	38,570	344,469	**101**	86,606	**133**
268	Petersburg, WV	W2(228)	33,840	14,123	26,423	187,141	**55**	19,638	**30**
270-274	Greensboro, NC	C1	1,676,359	686,331	1,277,186	20,463,519	**6,020**	3,405,552	**5,243**
275-277	Raleigh, NC	C1	1,525,808	619,600	1,136,380	20,677,621	**6,082**	3,678,619	**5,663**
278	Rocky Mount, NC	C1	516,092	206,535	353,039	5,732,692	**1,686**	986,325	**1,519**
279	Elizabeth City, NC	W1(233)	184,728	74,427	130,681	2,221,786	**654**	398,973	**614**
280-282	Charlotte, NC (NC Part)	A	1,764,145	714,946	1,305,531	22,331,929	**6,569**	4,035,705	**6,214**
283	Fayetteville, NC	A	777,878	297,885	521,628	7,535,372	**2,217**	1,601,069	**2,465**
284	Wilmington, NC	A	395,091	173,687	302,802	5,355,971	**1,576**	899,879	**1,385**
285	Kinston, NC	C3	435,110	171,727	303,536	4,613,859	**1,357**	852,305	**1,312**
286	Hickory, NC	C1	606,152	246,770	477,808	7,530,257	**2,215**	1,390,437	**2,141**
287-289	Asheville, NC	A	636,693	270,513	490,299	7,960,351	**2,341**	1,466,837	**2,258**
290-292	Columbia, SC	C3	1,034,762	407,478	712,394	10,863,911	**3,196**	2,322,585	**3,576**
293	Spartanburg, SC	A	372,030	146,773	260,487	4,251,504	**1,251**	849,868	**1,308**
294	Charleston, SC	A	647,673	258,699	429,636	7,116,625	**2,093**	1,678,318	**2,584**
295	Florence, SC	C3	569,152	230,696	381,026	7,426,332	**2,185**	1,710,668	**2,634**
296	Greenville, SC	C1	882,067	354,066	639,670	10,363,673	**3,049**	1,967,035	**3,028**
297	Charlotte, NC (SC Part)	A2(280)	294,173	117,091	215,842	2,810,096	**827**	449,076	**691**
298	Augusta, GA (SC Part)	A2(308)	207,636	80,833	143,603	1,476,422	**434**	304,442	**469**
299	Savannah, GA (SC Part)	A2(313)	181,473	67,632	114,221	2,310,704	**680**	489,160	**753**
300-303,311	Atlanta, GA	B1	4,767,670	1,830,498	3,357,991	62,297,113	**18,324**	11,285,824	**17,376**
304	Swainsboro, GA	X(313)	209,304	76,798	132,472	1,784,431	**525**	346,354	**533**
305	Gainesville, GA	B1	533,184	203,281	402,137	6,194,237	**1,822**	1,380,971	**2,126**
306	Athens, GA	B1	341,925	134,172	255,734	3,401,798	**1,001**	657,137	**1,012**
307	Chattanooga, TN (GA Part)	C1(373)	338,061	129,039	242,525	3,420,656	**1,006**	653,705	**1,006**
308-309	Augusta, GA (GA Part)	B2	360,456	137,036	236,199	4,064,332	**1,195**	884,209	**1,361**
310,312	Macon, GA	A	663,360	251,167	444,363	6,561,927	**1,930**	1,328,030	**2,045**
313-314	Savannah, GA (GA Part)	B2	391,631	151,048	256,276	4,305,168	**1,267**	1,061,022	**1,633**
315	Waycross, GA	C2	304,818	117,905	204,479	3,125,412	**919**	620,899	**956**
316	Valdosta, GA	A	171,254	65,202	114,189	1,733,980	**510**	312,825	**482**
317, 398	Albany, GA	A	484,852	181,429	299,501	4,941,047	**1,454**	934,853	**1,439**
318-319	Columbus, GA	A	270,629	103,486	174,100	2,715,505	**799**	561,208	**864**
320,322	Jacksonville, FL	A	1,368,587	546,175	929,385	16,629,255	**4,891**	2,971,439	**4,575**
321	Daytona Beach, FL	B1	496,898	227,436	358,546	5,082,940	**1,495**	876,408	**1,349**
323	Tallahassee, FL	B2	384,717	156,690	268,862	3,973,892	**1,169**	802,250	**1,235**
324	Panama City, FL	B1	313,782	123,253	210,239	3,279,315	**965**	736,435	**1,134**
325	Pensacola, FL	C1	622,541	261,688	457,762	7,148,104	**2,103**	1,601,421	**2,466**
326,344	Gainesville, FL	C1	701,614	298,670	494,831	7,301,445	**2,148**	1,348,953	**2,077**
327-328,347	Orlando, FL	C3	2,104,676	841,403	1,451,708	27,485,211	**8,085**	5,539,110	**8,528**
329	Melbourne, FL	C1	573,205	261,128	430,105	6,706,108	**1,973**	1,394,737	**2,147**
330-333	Miami, FL	A	4,149,648	1,598,888	2,465,690	49,760,123	**14,638**	9,412,429	**14,492**
334	West Palm Beach, FL	A	1,357,496	630,670	962,735	18,122,148	**5,331**	3,827,119	**5,892**
335-337, 346	Tampa, FL	A	2,601,119	1,167,620	1,815,307	34,493,339	**10,147**	5,636,605	**8,678**
338	Lakeland, FL	A	632,120	263,012	421,534	6,685,077	**1,966**	1,225,510	**1,887**
339	Fort Myers, FL	A	623,945	268,847	424,022	8,126,692	**2,391**	1,782,780	**2,745**
341	Naples, FL	A	340,148	141,477	232,066	4,757,204	**1,399**	907,650	**1,397**
342	Sarasota, FL	A	700,824	310,731	480,929	8,705,309	**2,561**	1,530,799	**2,357**
349	Fort Pierce, FL	A	372,566	158,649	252,901	4,125,594	**1,214**	667,689	**1,028**
350-352	Birmingham, AL	B2	1,204,752	484,545	884,159	14,171,622	**4,169**	3,041,326	**4,683**
354	Tuscaloosa, AL	B2	200,278	83,234	146,568	2,232,464	**657**	473,977	**730**
355	Jasper, AL	W2(350)	160,004	66,240	124,562	1,403,038	**413**	254,119	**391**
356	Decatur, AL	C2	354,820	145,947	282,988	3,966,598	**1,167**	922,387	**1,420**
357-358	Huntsville, AL	B2	367,630	151,019	292,427	4,316,220	**1,270**	1,070,074	**1,648**
359	Gadsden, AL	A	271,804	109,576	207,582	2,727,256	**802**	637,995	**982**
360-361	Montgomery, AL	A	484,570	189,710	332,206	5,173,554	**1,521**	1,186,104	**1,826**
362	Anniston, AL	A	176,718	73,338	139,844	1,526,894	**449**	351,128	**541**
363	Dothan, AL	A	221,360	90,520	163,373	2,683,356	**789**	613,366	**944**
364	Evergreen, AL	X(365)	105,682	44,025	78,265	946,703	**278**	170,582	**263**
365-366	Mobile, AL	B2	603,502	233,344	410,434	6,043,929	**1,778**	1,518,105	**2,337**
367	Selma, AL	B1	123,043	48,361	77,334	866,450	**255**	199,754	**308**
368	Opelika, AL	C1	222,034	93,678	169,477	1,725,293	**508**	436,538	**672**
369	Meridian, MS (AL Part)	A2(393)	21,486	8,789	15,083	125,696	**37**	8,563	**13**
370-372	Nashville, TN	B2	1,691,612	683,880	1,264,351	22,801,181	**6,707**	5,107,532	**7,864**
373-374	Chattanooga, TN (TN Part)	C1	716,564	293,930	547,982	7,931,172	**2,333**	1,779,286	**2,739**
376	Johnson City, TN	C2	396,894	171,383	321,261	4,159,389	**1,224**	992,975	**1,529**
377-379	Knoxville, TN	A	1,167,246	489,847	911,299	15,639,894	**4,600**	3,338,643	**5,141**
375, 380-381	Memphis, TN (TN Part)	A	1,126,858	435,223	711,239	13,096,795	**3,852**	3,014,283	**4,641**
382	McKenzie, TN	X(380)	114,963	47,747	85,922	1,034,415	**304**	289,617	**446**
383	Jackson, TN	A	279,572	113,962	204,992	2,928,561	**861**	714,767	**1,100**
384	Columbia, TN	W2(370)	174,504	68,355	130,817	1,476,835	**434**	317,861	**489**
385	Cookeville, TN	B1	214,216	89,505	169,072	1,988,482	**585**	483,990	**745**
386	Memphis, TN (MS Part)	A2(380)	366,441	136,797	244,792	3,312,870	**975**	791,412	**1,218**
387	Greenville, MS	B2	136,335	45,691	67,136	1,378,586	**406**	324,006	**499**
388	Tupelo, MS	B2	252,948	100,402	183,513	2,745,162	**808**	908,156	**1,398**
389	Grenada, MS	W2(387)	116,030	44,718	70,361	961,532	**283**	240,521	**370**
390-392	Jackson, MS	B1	780,380	292,513	502,611	8,683,161	**2,554**	2,116,902	**3,259**
393	Meridian, MS (MS Part)	B1	208,263	80,540	137,337	1,910,156	**562**	480,818	**740**
394	Hattiesburg, MS	C1	352,417	133,999	239,853	3,429,734	**1,009**	1,006,862	**1,550**
395	Gulfport, MS	A	379,455	151,193	271,483	4,126,247	**1,214**	1,136,025	**1,749**
396	McComb, MS	B1	129,800	50,401	86,965	1,186,222	**349**	303,120	**467**
397	Columbus, MS	A	170,654	67,092	116,918	1,629,385	**479**	408,922	**630**
400-402	Louisville, KY (KY Part)	B2	1,055,472	441,637	751,787	11,175,784	**3,288**	2,259,736	**3,480**
403-406	Lexington, KY	B2	806,197	337,119	592,492	8,891,250	**2,615**	1,868,173	**2,876**
407-409	London, KY	C3	216,574	86,721	137,767	1,892,295	**556**	536,607	**826**
410	Cincinnati, OH (KY Part)	A2(450)	459,038	184,049	329,287	5,302,255	**1,560**	1,051,567	**1,619**
411-412	Ashland, KY	B1	189,382	76,879	132,001	1,603,195	**472**	352,783	**543**
413-414	Campton, KY	X(403)	63,065	24,437	39,323	336,401	**98**	44,254	**68**
415-416	Pikeville, KY	B2	110,008	46,214	73,775	1,099,322	**323**	270,777	**416**
417-418	Hazard, KY	W2(403)	75,305	30,893	49,590	582,443	**171**	137,476	**211**
420	Paducah, KY	A	219,568	93,228	165,220	2,557,881	**752**	710,285	**1,094**
421-422	Bowling Green, KY	C1	344,250	136,387	243,039	3,194,929	**940**	634,700	**978**
423	Owensboro, KY	A	166,480	66,951	122,404	1,512,663	**445**	370,985	**571**
424	Evansville, IN (KY Part)	C2(476)	136,035	55,506	98,550	1,262,673	**371**	261,371	**402**
425-426	Somerset, KY	A	136,896	56,937	98,146	1,177,757	**346**	242,017	**372**
427	Elizabethtown, KY	X(400)	168,967	68,729	125,011	1,695,882	**499**	431,590	**664**
430-432	Columbus, OH	A	1,809,159	756,511	1,353,011	25,334,284	**7,452**	4,437,990	**6,834**
433	Marion, OH	C1	181,051	69,888	132,611	1,601,769	**471**	311,844	**480**
434-436	Toledo, OH	A	816,823	332,686	585,770	10,109,216	**2,974**	1,933,316	**2,976**
437-438	Zanesville, OH	B1	258,423	100,685	190,464	2,306,612	**678**	364,531	**562**
439	Steubenville, OH	C3	183,159	76,126	133,242	1,996,183	**587**	504,514	**777**
440-441	Cleveland, OH	M	2,131,912	878,828	1,432,393	26,572,334	**7,817**	4,176,661	**6,431**
442-443	Akron, OH	M(440)	833,140	334,002	613,719	10,104,418	**2,972**	1,452,964	**2,237**
444-445	Youngstown, OH	A	532,515	217,828	385,354	5,901,486	**1,735**	948,155	**1,459**
446-447	Canton, OH	B1	644,392	250,648	458,498	7,356,601	**2,164**	1,251,663	**1,927**
448-449	Mansfield, OH	C3	441,756	174,435	324,522	4,350,071	**1,279**	896,526	**1,381**
450-452	Cincinnati, OH	A	1,674,595	679,529	1,201,184	20,143,397	**5,926**	3,820,854	**5,883**
453-455	Dayton, OH	B2	1,083,911	452,762	808,075	12,570,285	**3,698**	2,606,564	**4,014**
456	Chillicothe, OH	C3	342,961	135,596	249,493	2,910,990	**856**	658,234	**1,013**
457	Athens, OH	C2	157,307	61,323	115,679	1,271,775	**374**	178,738	**275**
458	Lima, OH	C1	370,101	143,150	274,759	4,380,848	**1,289**	877,064	**1,350**
460-462	Indianapolis, IN	A	1,811,347	730,529	1,322,565	24,613,442	**7,240**	5,036,634	**7,754**
463-464	Gary, IN	M(600)	779,632	296,955	518,919	8,661,905	**2,548**	1,682,692	**2,591**
465-466	South Bend, IN	C1	610,042	230,126	411,170	7,713,389	**2,269**	1,526,443	**2,350**
467-468	Fort Wayne, IN	A	619,764	241,358	445,152	7,419,350	**2,183**	1,547,061	**2,382**
469	Kokomo, IN	C3	317,189	126,812	232,986	3,417,765	**1,005**	650,778	**1,002**
470	Cincinnati, OH (IN Part)	A2(450)	113,466	44,141	92,754	909,206	**267**	78,477	**121**
471	Louisville, KY (IN Part)	A2(400)	273,870	112,327	215,895	2,828,399	**832**	543,379	**837**
472	Columbus, IN	C1	200,948	78,887	152,800	2,246,440	**661**	530,830	**817**
473	Muncie, IN	C3	323,579	131,268	243,472	3,441,383	**1,012**	747,526	**1,151**
474	Bloomington, IN	A	251,759	104,351	197,237	2,366,563	**696**	523,960	**807**
475	Washington, IN	X(476)	158,739	61,996	117,729	1,974,475	**581**	298,992	**460**
476-477	Evansville, IN (IN Part)	B2	299,405	123,928	224,997	4,212,028	**1,239**	940,100	**1,447**
478	Terre Haute, IN	A	183,859	72,714	131,846	3,324,041	**978**	621,101	**956**

Source: Devonshire Associates Ltd. and Scan/US, Inc. 2004.

** Estimates for Retail Sales, including Shopping Goods Sales, are based on data from the U.S. Census Bureau's 1997 Economic Census and utilize the North American Industry Classification System (NAICS). Shopping Goods include sales data for general merchandise and apparel stores.

ZIP Code Service Areas: Population / Sales, *Continued*

ZIP CODE	SECTIONAL CENTER OR PRINCIPAL CITY	CLASS-IFICA-TION	POPULA-TION Estimated 7/1/04	HOUSE-HOLDS Estimated 7/1/04	AUTO REGISTRA-TIONS 2003	TOTAL RETAIL SALES 2003 Sales ($1,000)	TOTAL RETAIL SALES Ranally Sales Units	SHOPPING GOODS SALES** 2003 Sales ($1,000)	SHOPPING GOODS SALES** Ranally Sales Units
479	Lafayette, IN	B1	288,389	110,579	205,435	3,195,775	940	700,531	1,079
480-483	Detroit, MI	A	4,776,167	1,891,297	3,248,532	65,776,551	19,348	13,433,038	20,682
484-485	Flint, MI	B1	678,311	267,889	494,138	7,913,156	2,327	1,710,177	2,633
486-487	Saginaw, MI	A	638,413	259,164	465,081	8,027,271	2,361	1,693,126	2,607
488-489	Lansing, MI	B1	773,770	297,160	556,002	8,941,652	2,630	2,472,967	3,807
490-491	Kalamazoo, MI	C3	861,097	342,340	625,475	8,789,340	2,586	2,262,100	3,482
492	Jackson, MI	C1	357,225	133,783	252,244	3,713,984	1,092	871,630	1,342
493-495	Grand Rapids, MI	C3	1,269,186	478,176	885,584	15,895,943	4,676	3,777,709	5,816
496	Traverse City, MI	A	265,236	107,958	200,677	3,613,697	1,063	777,795	1,198
497	Gaylord, MI	C3	235,122	95,644	170,257	3,095,664	911	569,479	877
498-499	Iron Mountain, MI	C3	267,047	110,759	193,722	2,706,550	796	524,208	807
500-503	Des Moines, IA	A	837,088	331,756	629,843	9,590,749	2,822	1,615,205	2,487
504	Mason City, IA	A	108,550	45,441	87,812	1,228,010	361	219,865	339
505	Fort Dodge, IA	A	127,964	51,627	98,523	1,387,314	408	226,221	348
506-507	Waterloo, IA	B2	242,827	96,799	187,779	2,772,777	816	464,314	715
508	Creston, IA	W2(500)	33,995	14,283	28,746	290,754	86	35,293	54
510-511	Sioux City, IA	B2	174,845	66,939	126,220	2,154,331	634	334,654	515
512	Sheldon, IA	W2(510)	43,333	15,967	32,296	522,028	154	40,185	62
513	Spencer, IA	W2(510)	47,848	20,264	38,384	679,012	200	110,555	170
514	Carroll, IA	W2(500)	48,036	19,231	37,249	543,868	160	83,515	129
515	Omaha, NE (IA Part)	A2(680)	145,871	57,067	109,556	1,898,165	558	205,106	316
516	Shenandoah, IA	W2(680)	24,900	9,991	19,210	202,493	60	31,939	49
520	Dubuque, IA	B2	138,772	54,265	102,266	1,776,951	523	282,972	436
521	Decorah, IA	W1(506)	60,170	23,456	46,211	562,622	166	60,057	92
522-524	Cedar Rapids, IA	C1	430,274	172,730	330,410	5,313,935	1,563	954,080	1,468
525	Ottumwa, IA	A	112,582	46,115	87,509	1,271,425	374	260,516	401
526	Burlington, IA	A	107,794	43,314	82,185	1,336,422	393	253,064	390
527-528	Rock Island, IL (IA Part)	A2(612)	264,767	105,304	195,618	3,541,710	1,042	635,080	977
530-532,534	Milwaukee, WI	B1	2,204,646	891,795	1,495,859	24,076,038	7,082	4,263,248	6,564
535,537-538	Madison, WI	C1	832,182	341,147	614,750	12,648,030	3,720	1,926,194	2,966
539	Portage, WI	W2(535)	189,898	75,030	140,886	2,172,833	639	406,498	626
540	St. Paul, MN (WI Part)	A2(553)	133,195	50,346	105,482	1,286,790	379	270,709	417
541-543	Green Bay, WI	C3	544,561	219,161	405,124	6,172,830	1,817	1,414,975	2,179
544	Wausau, WI	C3	383,409	152,266	287,951	4,894,794	1,440	1,020,412	1,571
545	Rhinelander, WI	W1(544)	94,180	40,433	73,190	1,192,025	351	193,303	298
546	La Crosse, WI	A	234,767	93,022	172,380	2,651,963	780	504,664	777
547	Eau Claire, WI	B1	247,943	97,904	191,297	3,480,011	1,024	761,099	1,172
548	Spooner, WI	X(556)	182,543	75,939	140,781	1,982,963	583	377,098	581
549	Oshkosh, WI	C2	458,286	186,134	342,213	6,231,816	1,833	1,156,208	1,780
550-551	St. Paul, MN	M(553)	1,350,777	520,835	954,269	17,558,057	5,165	2,920,700	4,497
553-555	Minneapolis, MN	M	1,884,981	764,020	1,356,370	32,930,076	9,687	5,729,077	8,821
556-558	Duluth, MN	A	297,908	124,721	221,438	3,259,794	959	639,825	985
559	Rochester, MN	C1	315,488	124,937	233,090	3,403,873	1,001	689,198	1,061
560	Mankato, MN	A	253,648	99,712	189,485	2,615,563	769	455,214	701
561	Windom, MN	D	93,520	37,915	71,629	823,112	242	59,021	91
562	Willmar, MN	B1	147,582	58,388	109,210	1,611,621	474	228,044	351
563	St. Cloud, MN	B1	292,275	111,559	214,275	3,847,614	1,132	739,546	1,139
564	Brainerd, MN	A	139,777	57,250	106,463	1,575,251	463	252,168	388
565	Detroit Lakes, MN	X(580)	165,620	65,265	123,078	1,751,915	515	265,823	409
566	Bemidji, MN	B1	90,567	35,550	65,251	988,315	291	173,860	268
567	Thief River Falls, MN	W2(582)	69,524	27,865	51,757	615,344	181	55,411	85
570-571	Sioux Falls, SD	B1	300,770	118,760	234,574	11,383,726	3,349	898,609	1,383
572	Watertown, SD	A	71,299	28,585	57,832	1,033,922	304	93,572	144
573	Mitchell, SD	C2	81,071	32,307	63,885	1,241,760	365	128,143	197
574	Aberdeen, SD	B2	58,422	24,215	46,291	1,219,250	359	83,515	129
575	Pierre, SD	W2(573)	54,494	20,286	39,519	598,567	176	85,996	132
576	Mobridge, SD	W2(574)	22,313	7,953	15,373	157,691	46	16,438	25
577	Rapid City, SD	A	178,939	69,142	137,741	2,842,338	836	586,778	903
580-581	Fargo, ND	B2	168,348	71,733	135,390	2,881,210	847	448,757	691
582	Grand Forks, ND	B2	96,223	38,413	72,046	1,687,935	497	342,898	528
583	Devils Lake, ND	W2(582)	50,810	19,805	37,382	466,377	137	50,407	78
584	Jamestown, ND	W2(580)	48,300	20,365	41,291	528,988	156	64,295	99
585	Bismarck, ND	A	124,224	50,754	101,991	1,653,716	486	282,493	435
586	Dickinson, ND	A	39,191	16,200	32,972	525,870	155	63,118	97
587	Minot, ND	A	80,728	32,700	66,653	1,098,231	323	166,410	256
588	Williston, ND	A	23,756	10,022	19,697	303,755	89	58,776	91
590-591	Billings, MT	B2	197,785	79,883	152,089	2,523,699	742	473,395	729
592	Wolf Point, MT	W2(590)	34,351	13,647	27,655	296,089	87	17,106	26
593	Miles City, MT	W1(590)	34,449	14,154	29,860	336,541	99	44,333	68
594	Great Falls, MT	B1	128,773	51,201	97,717	1,375,477	405	274,726	423
595	Havre, MT	W1(594)	30,493	11,696	22,925	246,310	72	32,679	50
596	Helena, MT	A	70,374	28,917	57,743	786,531	231	139,947	215
597	Butte, MT	C1	142,181	58,426	115,953	1,792,558	527	264,862	408
598	Missoula, MT	A	179,936	72,691	143,779	2,107,202	620	436,917	673
599	Kalispell, MT	B1	103,979	42,496	84,377	1,144,461	337	237,328	365
600-608	Chicago, IL	M	8,583,584	3,090,211	4,860,647	99,891,439	29,383	16,813,574	25,886
609	Kankakee, IL	A	163,181	61,970	109,449	1,678,413	494	340,168	524
610-611	Rockford, IL	C1	534,676	209,626	378,214	5,939,784	1,747	1,090,787	1,679
612	Rock Island, IL (IL Part)	A	215,612	87,084	155,397	2,424,562	713	366,521	564
613	La Salle, IL	A	151,602	61,325	109,313	2,079,841	612	389,007	599
614	Galesburg, IL	C1	150,311	59,949	107,222	1,444,646	425	311,539	480
615-616	Peoria, IL	B2	365,966	146,655	257,802	4,558,870	1,341	788,588	1,214
617	Bloomington, IL	A	224,962	85,625	157,333	2,871,664	845	489,673	754
618-619	Champaign, IL	C1	387,345	154,937	264,524	4,369,643	1,285	1,034,096	1,592
620,622	St. Louis, MO (IL Part)	M(630)	752,852	294,518	522,500	7,729,326	2,274	1,477,899	2,276
623	Quincy, IL	B1	113,009	44,511	81,066	1,177,508	346	224,078	345
624	Effingham, IL	W2(625)	149,148	58,898	110,333	1,697,242	499	233,644	360
625-627	Springfield, IL	C1	488,052	199,280	348,151	5,777,695	1,700	1,119,055	1,723
628	Centralia, IL	D	217,024	87,962	155,731	2,164,858	637	408,553	629
629	Carbondale, IL	B1	226,574	93,299	156,478	2,020,893	594	466,945	719
630-631	St. Louis, MO (MO Part)	M	1,653,095	687,785	1,132,038	20,917,316	6,153	3,781,934	5,822
633	St. Charles, MO	M(630)	428,712	158,126	316,012	3,839,399	1,129	743,591	1,145
634	Hannibal, MO	A	67,941	27,159	50,133	557,298	164	79,669	123
635	Kirksville, MO	A	61,703	25,180	46,093	510,521	150	83,540	129
636	Flat River, MO	X(630)	127,496	49,038	88,527	972,855	286	215,808	332
637	Cape Girardeau, MO	B2	120,553	47,568	85,988	1,635,097	481	376,520	580
638	Sikeston, MO	W2(637)	126,360	50,769	79,041	1,378,472	405	201,799	311
639	Poplar Bluff, MO	A	81,654	33,911	57,340	736,770	217	148,010	228
640-641	Kansas City, MO	B2	1,097,982	449,913	771,540	14,155,965	4,164	2,415,065	3,718
644-645	St. Joseph, MO	A	184,172	73,327	131,562	1,983,294	584	413,452	636
646	Chillicothe, MO	W2(640)	74,222	30,668	56,559	505,737	149	82,999	128
647	Harrisonville, MO	X(640)	118,113	46,904	89,319	1,002,622	295	175,847	271
648	Joplin, MO	B2	182,353	70,877	126,522	1,927,777	567	469,079	722
650,652	Columbia, MO	A	391,540	155,633	286,305	4,267,995	1,255	773,344	1,191
651	Jefferson City, MO	A	65,116	26,498	47,269	1,260,235	371	295,007	454
653	Sedalia, MO	A	101,150	40,760	72,745	824,995	243	171,526	264
654-655	Rolla, MO	B1	201,893	77,166	140,352	1,802,291	530	317,931	489
656-658	Springfield, MO	B1	653,939	267,960	484,249	7,475,551	2,199	1,380,179	2,125
660-662	Kansas City, KS	A2(640)	941,822	367,187	697,576	11,886,087	3,497	2,452,314	3,776
664-666	Topeka, KS	C1	350,280	141,994	267,620	3,826,945	1,126	843,466	1,299
667	Fort Scott, KS	D	119,016	48,002	92,451	1,055,267	310	260,970	402
668	Emporia, KS	B2	63,338	25,040	48,686	534,479	157	93,173	143
669	Concordia, KS	W2(674)	26,672	11,324	22,871	192,468	57	19,515	30
670-672	Wichita, KS	A	670,535	261,866	486,705	7,010,123	2,062	1,543,029	2,375
673	Independence, KS	D	62,920	25,925	48,428	551,052	162	108,973	168
674	Salina, KS	B2	135,125	54,568	108,038	1,696,820	499	340,123	524
675	Hutchinson, KS	C1	122,647	49,030	93,162	1,223,184	360	216,733	334
676	Hays, KS	A	58,497	24,480	48,108	688,407	203	119,576	184
677	Colby, KS	W2(676)	32,169	13,402	28,054	375,763	111	59,296	91
678	Dodge City, KS	C2	121,282	41,352	79,672	1,302,671	383	239,384	369
679	Liberal, KS (KS Part)	B1	29,768	9,966	17,788	372,523	110	91,258	141
680-681	Omaha, NE (NE Part)	B2	721,952	286,502	518,233	10,221,871	3,006	1,701,098	2,619
683-685	Lincoln, NE	B1	401,129	161,714	304,926	4,448,740	1,309	804,929	1,239
686	Columbus, NE	W1(680)	72,888	28,056	57,534	733,944	216	70,592	109
687	Norfolk, NE	A	133,862	50,968	101,473	1,406,998	414	209,624	323
688	Grand Island, NE	A	158,326	60,276	122,039	2,008,927	591	494,264	761
689	Hastings, NE	A	74,679	29,969	61,064	718,587	211	80,883	125
690	McCook, NE	A	26,364	10,921	22,884	348,355	102	62,375	96
691	North Platte, NE	B1	78,737	32,792	66,790	1,722,802	507	157,666	243
692	Valentine, NE	W1(691)	9,288	3,976	8,082	117,485	35	11,901	18
693	Alliance, NE	D	71,037	28,798	56,745	829,486	244	170,877	263
700-701	New Orleans, LA	B2	1,119,904	460,842	651,968	12,299,064	3,617	2,895,424	4,457
703	Thibodaux, LA	C2	266,418	96,778	156,031	2,866,149	843	646,325	995
704	Hammond, LA	B1	383,431	144,213	252,320	3,953,733	1,163	772,883	1,190
705	Lafayette, LA	A	598,726	226,590	359,134	6,783,867	1,996	1,584,043	2,439
706	Lake Charles, LA	A	251,302	98,896	164,815	2,630,047	774	737,642	1,136
707-708	Baton Rouge, LA	A	700,745	269,431	462,502	8,238,218	2,423	1,808,587	2,784
710-711	Shreveport, LA	B2	462,875	183,139	294,546	5,010,160	1,474	1,106,390	1,704
712	Monroe, LA	B2	330,027	128,456	202,360	3,387,952	997	947,770	1,459
713-714	Alexandria, LA	B1	390,690	146,480	234,517	3,384,153	996	780,478	1,202
716	Pine Bluff, AR	A	178,694	67,461	108,512	1,735,151	510	442,081	681
717	Camden, AR	D	115,116	46,315	75,939	1,070,178	315	305,769	471
718	Texarkana, TX (AR Part)	A2(755)	127,629	49,822	84,234	884,384	260	229,468	353
719	Hot Springs National Park, AR	B1	163,643	70,587	119,249	1,753,465	516	486,200	749
720-722	Little Rock, AR	B2	839,438	342,964	588,037	10,842,390	3,190	2,649,445	4,079
723	Memphis, TN (AR Part)	A2(380)	182,615	67,677	99,798	1,790,684	527	430,171	662
724	Jonesboro, AR	B1	206,274	83,311	143,689	2,128,385	626	645,790	994
725	Batesville, AR	W1(720)	101,912	42,408	75,419	930,061	274	292,148	450
726	Harrison, AR	A	134,387	57,120	101,951	1,303,526	383	378,261	582
727	Fayetteville, AR	A	362,368	138,381	251,567	4,115,275	1,211	1,420,528	2,187
728	Russellville, AR	A	116,594	44,611	81,135	1,101,669	324	260,521	401
729	Fort Smith, AR (AR Part)	B2	213,891	82,984	144,523	2,457,309	723	753,958	1,161
730-731	Oklahoma City, OK	B2	1,202,051	487,401	855,021	13,740,021	4,041	2,785,386	4,288
734	Ardmore, OK	A	86,583	34,597	61,374	794,890	234	192,205	296
735	Lawton, OK	B1	204,371	76,206	133,737	1,613,619	475	491,724	757
736	Clinton, OK	W2(730)	54,740	21,437	39,553	581,803	171	125,379	193
737	Enid, OK	A	103,149	40,806	76,151	964,519	284	228,417	352
738	Woodward, OK	W1(730)	30,054	12,324	24,303	322,449	95	96,085	148
739	Liberal, KS (OK Part)	A2(679)	28,006	10,025	19,480	190,845	56	38,308	59
740-741	Tulsa, OK	B2	946,271	388,381	685,720	11,024,601	3,243	2,599,137	4,001
743	Vinita, OK	X(740)	126,182	49,806	92,136	789,210	232	190,031	293
744	Muskogee, OK	B1	217,479	84,755	147,519	1,728,576	508	487,782	751
745	McAlester, OK	B1	89,205	34,706	59,863	676,172	199	198,829	306
746	Ponca City, OK	A	57,754	24,015	42,833	511,360	150	149,668	230
747	Durant, OK	X(750)	83,966	33,288	56,791	564,782	166	138,277	213
748	Shawnee, OK	C1	190,614	72,870	132,873	1,251,210	368	368,647	568
749	Fort Smith, AR (OK part)	A2(729)	110,367	41,321	73,746	698,567	205	164,731	254
750-753	Dallas, TX	M	3,738,264	1,408,147	2,477,175	49,303,420	14,504	9,847,488	15,161
754	Greenville, TX	X(750)	314,874	118,404	214,087	2,940,430	865	586,735	903
755	Texarkana, TX (TX Part)	A	124,511	47,941	81,553	1,447,277	426	342,904	528
756	Longview, TX	A	318,163	122,977	214,402	3,456,001	1,017	675,547	1,040
757	Tyler, TX	A	317,673	121,618	214,481	3,950,495	1,162	952,485	1,466
758	Palestine, TX	W2(757)	119,286	39,985	67,863	845,979	249	133,085	205
759	Lufkin, TX	B1	247,231	93,377	158,001	2,423,104	713	494,364	761
760-761	Fort Worth, TX	M(750)	1,884,584	698,101	1,257,967	23,943,707	7,044	3,760,520	5,790
762	Denton, TX	X(760)	317,400	117,515	223,653	3,719,127	1,094	749,842	1,154
763	Wichita Falls, TX	B2	172,877	67,422	117,109	1,819,066	535	378,117	582
764	Stephenville, TX	W2(760)	133,875	51,535	92,962	1,096,564	323	178,077	274
765	Temple, TX	A	416,197	149,224	267,141	3,291,633	968	563,646	868
766-767	Waco, TX	A	321,813	120,183	207,740	3,255,491	958	681,483	1,049
768	Brownwood, TX	B1	87,607	33,993	59,859	862,300	254	155,687	240
769	San Angelo, TX	B2	123,246	48,873	82,571	1,343,003	395	292,661	451
770-775	Houston, TX	B2	5,369,276	1,960,022	3,373,985	61,670,814	18,140	12,979,032	19,983
776-777	Beaumont, TX	B1	409,815	158,934	261,565	4,763,134	1,401	946,919	1,458
778	Bryan, TX	B1	260,863	98,774	174,385	2,847,099	837	602,303	927
779	Victoria, TX	A	163,399	60,043	103,972	1,685,755	496	352,318	542
780-782	San Antonio, TX	C1	2,193,299	775,951	1,314,326	24,626,167	7,244	5,068,386	7,803
783-784	Corpus Christi, TX	A	520,245	188,440	305,759	5,119,555	1,506	1,049,471	1,615
785	McAllen, TX	C3	1,107,116	313,327	494,068	8,620,776	2,536	2,399,776	3,695
733, 786-787	Austin, TX	A	1,483,594	590,616	1,062,179	29,452,287	8,660	3,500,924	5,390
788	Uvalde, TX	C3	170,802	53,946	87,591	1,288,772	379	313,166	482
789	La Grange, TX	W2(770)	67,860	26,068	47,244	642,950	189	78,841	121
790-791	Amarillo, TX	B1	422,227	155,651	277,416	4,481,665	1,318	770,088	1,186
792	Childress, TX	W2(793)	36,133	13,683	24,005	217,898	64	24,291	37
793-794	Lubbock, TX	B2	368,044	138,183	236,406	4,296,810	1,263	794,672	1,223
795-796	Abilene, TX	A	215,255	81,431	141,561	2,289,477	673	467,606	720
797	Midland, TX	C3	347,636	128,025	217,840	3,852,873	1,133	861,250	1,326
798-799	El Paso, TX	A	736,573	235,041	398,419	6,646,163	1,955	1,804,307	2,778
800-804	Denver, CO	B2	2,564,140	1,016,567	1,879,882	33,653,358	9,901	6,119,796	9,423
805	Longmont, CO	X(800)	419,293	162,248	333,020	5,234,399	1,540	951,565	1,465
806	Brighton, CO	X(800)	209,061	71,547	146,331	2,034,217	598	350,699	540
807	Fort Morgan, CO	X(800)	67,868	25,064	49,523	621,102	183	84,655	130
808-809	Colorado Springs, CO	B1	584,118	218,688	416,031	7,415,712	2,181	1,346,957	2,074
810	Pueblo, CO	B2	224,922	86,816	158,146	2,259,247	665	528,123	813
811	Alamosa, CO	W2(810)	70,523	27,530	53,608	570,455	168	72,098	111
812	Salida, CO	W2(800)	83,323	30,697	60,414	671,353	197	91,457	141
813	Durango, CO	A	61,907	25,144	49,119	836,065	246	106,962	165
814	Montrose, CO	W2(815)	78,728	31,953	63,315	758,805	223	97,495	150
815	Grand Junction, CO	B2	123,533	49,238	95,957	1,536,601	452	379,286	584
816	Glenwood Springs, CO	W2(815)	136,769	51,659	104,031	2,062,038	607	357,052	550
820	Cheyenne, WY	A	116,864	47,864	93,536	1,725,006	507	345,095	531
821,829-831	Rock Springs, WY	B1	97,093	37,788	80,238	1,409,700	415	245,592	379
822	Wheatland, WY	W2(826)	23,028	9,625	20,129	204,115	60	20,660	32
823	Rawlins, WY	W1(826)	15,729	6,493	13,311	193,771	57	14,297	22
824	Worland, WY	W2(590)	49,584	20,131	40,925	517,999	152	87,774	135
825	Riverton, WY	B1	34,695	13,444	26,598	419,379	123	76,940	118
826	Casper, WY	B2	83,005	34,005	66,774	1,019,001	300	221,636	341
827	Gillette, WY	W1(826)	49,591	18,945	43,267	451,394	133	95,741	147
828	Sheridan, WY	W1(590)	34,110	14,685	28,081	407,265	120	70,132	108
832	Pocatello, ID	B1	163,254	57,211	119,246	1,527,343	449	211,643	326
833	Twin Falls, ID	A	169,026	61,518	124,210	1,944,789	572	383,420	590
834	Idaho Falls, ID	B2	167,201	56,186	117,737	1,768,497	520	392,244	604
835	Lewiston, ID (ID Part)	B2	66,508	26,988	54,151	694,931	204	114,910	177
836-837	Boise, ID (ID Part)	A	596,796	218,338	428,797	7,308,766	2,150	1,415,394	2,179
838	Spokane, WA (ID Part)	A2(990)	225,876	87,420	175,952	3,088,851	909	405,305	624
840-842	Salt Lake City, UT	B2	1,581,307	513,866	1,050,327	20,923,993	6,154	4,037,848	6,217
843-844	Ogden, UT	C1	319,628	103,629	213,356	3,723,084	1,095	896,299	1,380
845	Price, UT	X(840)	52,744	18,574	37,362	470,295	138	89,668	138
846-847	Provo, UT	C2	434,207	134,129	284,031	4,344,467	1,278	759,071	1,169
850,852-853	Phoenix, AZ	B1	3,887,395	1,456,844	2,474,499	44,926,722	13,216	7,777,744	11,975
855	Globe, AZ	X(850)	89,435	32,680	58,450	556,385	164	125,590	193
856-857	Tucson, AZ	B1	1,086,954	431,326	715,933	9,636,819	2,834	1,959,344	3,016
859	Show Low, AZ	X(850)	66,234	23,532	43,230	538,811	159	98,051	151
860	Flagstaff, AZ	A	167,156	54,952	95,870	1,469,715	432	370,888	571
863	Prescott, AZ	B1	187,462	79,101	143,974	1,759,638	518	358,262	552
864	Kingman, AZ	A2(889)	171,359	71,103	124,723	1,750,119	515	292,728	451
865	Gallup, NM (AZ Part)	A2(873)	63,330	17,869	23,652	131,801	39	11,661	18
870-872	Albuquerque, NM	B2	820,532	323,559	580,866	9,464,737	2,785	2,015,015	3,102
873	Gallup, NM (NM Part)	A	69,946	20,554	32,117	715,390	210	183,124	282
874	Farmington, NM	A	124,976	42,468	80,312	1,361,676	401	387,865	597
875	Santa Fe, NM	A	224,003	93,104	175,116	2,446,269	720	602,666	928
877	Las Vegas, NM	W2(870)	41,706	16,626	29,950	347,208	102	58,834	91
878	Socorro, NM	X(870)	18,577	7,326	12,777	71,487	21	5,003	8
879	Truth or Consequences, NM	W1(880)	18,310	7,543	12,990	110,258	32	8,480	13
880	Las Cruces, NM	B1	244,890	87,383	160,007	1,858,275	547	396,193	610
881	Clovis, NM	A	66,113	25,307	45,226	564,372	166	146,938	226
882	Roswell, NM	C3	167,379	62,217	109,986	1,380,303	406	329,087	507
883	Carrizozo, NM	X(798)	79,129	31,438	58,150	603,901	178	145,805	224
884	Tucumcari, NM	W2(790)	16,995	6,981	12,519	165,645	49	15,373	24
889-891	Las Vegas, NV	A	1,679,019	637,439	1,043,295	19,263,099	5,666	3,834,574	5,904
893	Ely, NV	W1(894)	9,685	3,582	6,971	45,426	13	2,536	4
894-895,897	Reno, NV (NV Part)	B2	578,312	222,780	416,622	6,848,870	2,015	1,020,596	1,571
898	Elko, NV	W2(894)	48,656	16,761	32,876	446,389	131	56,324	87
900-918	Los Angeles, CA	M	10,715,586	3,484,793	5,862,908	101,194,745	29,771	19,961,076	30,733
919-921	San Diego, CA	A	2,953,554	1,058,486	1,893,279	32,967,866	9,698	6,224,688	9,583
922	Palm Springs, CA	C1	697,625	237,087	385,401	6,823,823	2,007	1,419,031	2,185
923-925	San Bernardino, CA	M(900)	2,371,645	748,249	1,354,362	18,505,604	5,443	3,368,928	5,186
926-928	Santa Ana, CA	M(900)	2,937,828	958,700	1,838,011	38,493,346	11,322	7,514,223	11,569
930	Oxnard, CA	M(900)	670,506	212,009	417,827	6,800,596	2,000	958,249	1,475
931	Santa Barbara, CA	B2	184,560	67,657	126,822	2,588,636	761	394,731	608
932-933	Bakersfield, CA	C1	1,146,625	339,245	577,291	8,614,710	2,534	1,586,273	2,442
934	San Luis Obispo, CA	C2	458,168	163,118	310,868	4,705,120	1,384	780,811	1,202
935	Mojave, CA	X(900)	463,032	150,936	280,054	3,797,642	1,117	700,975	1,079
936-938	Fresno, CA	A	1,064,648	328,222	557,260	8,218,015	2,417	1,405,603	2,164
939	Salinas, CA	A	387,296	115,228	212,703	4,171,438	1,227	754,225	1,161
940-941,943-944	San Francisco, CA	M	1,754,658	721,940	1,127,116	29,804,542	8,766	7,186,776	11,065
942,956-958	Sacramento, CA	B2	2,149,670	785,664	1,410,384	22,565,441	6,638	3,918,057	6,032
945-948	Oakland, CA	M(940)	2,911,791	1,061,096	1,926,173	31,979,779	9,407	5,349,789	8,236
949,954	North Bay, CA	M(940)	867,004	335,290	619,782	11,282,308	3,319	1,743,866	2,685
950-951	San Jose, CA	M(940)	1,694,639	568,425	1,162,835	24,013,923	7,064	4,509,677	6,943
952-953	Stockton, CA	C3	1,473,142	477,713	860,377	11,849,669	3,486	2,079,258	3,201
955	Eureka, CA	A	159,818	63,779	108,413	1,432,690	421	207,991	320
959	Marysville, CA	C2	491,543	183,898	338,918	4,289,508	1,262	714,979	1,101
960	Redding, CA	A	297,117	117,862	213,932	2,651,517	780	425,918	656
961	Reno, NV (CA Part)	A2(894)	127,633	47,341	89,315	1,014,126	298	132,526	204
967-968	Honolulu, HI	B1	1,272,786	429,751	718,842	13,859,392	4,077	4,278,443	6,587
970-972	Portland, OR (OR Part)	A	1,811,828	715,295	1,258,397	25,812,222	7,593	6,062,945	9,334
973	Salem, OR	A	559,972	210,904	388,406	5,614,321	1,651	1,425,607	2,195
974	Eugene, OR	C3	531,356	218,850	401,245	6,044,573	1,778	1,339,447	2,062
975	Medford, OR	A	271,403	108,932	206,085	4,070,997	1,198	836,496	1,288
976	Klamath Falls, OR	A	69,440	27,841	52,142	744,526	219	162,258	250
977	Bend, OR	A	185,218	72,720	147,310	2,432,999	716	569,222	876
978	Pendleton, OR	B1	141,453	53,171	105,151	1,740,745	512	258,066	397
979	Boise, ID (OR Part)	A2(836)	32,050	10,369	19,723	402,570	118	117,639	181
980-981	Seattle, WA	B2	2,017,033	844,210	1,484,990	30,401,616	8,943	6,319,725	9,730
982	Everett, WA	C1	806,924	305,567	604,592	8,790,442	2,586	1,615,444	2,487
983-984	Tacoma, WA	C1	1,067,749	405,420	770,852	10,625,656	3,125	2,339,846	3,602
985	Olympia, WA	C1	434,380	170,093	329,497	4,616,166	1,358	1,118,833	1,723
986	Portland, OR (WA Part)	A2(970)	529,968	198,393	384,362	4,517,761	1,329	1,004,365	1,546
988	Wenatchee, WA	A	200,671	72,060	139,535	2,080,161	612	405,883	625
989	Yakima, WA	A	264,364	88,561	170,177	2,289,581	674	522,635	805
990-992	Spokane, WA (WA Part)	A	558,161	218,580	403,399	5,772,808	1,698	1,239,719	1,909
993	Pasco, WA	C2	305,541	105,422	209,468	3,102,279	913	696,925	1,073
994	Lewiston, ID (WA Part)	A2(835)	20,713	8,511	16,329	196,962	58	82,712	127
995-996	Anchorage, AK	A	461,136	163,669	289,160	6,161,091	1,812	1,542,411	2,375
997	Fairbanks, AK	B1	121,075	42,315	68,930	1,367,968	402	383,646	591
998	Juneau, AK	B2	49,453	19,085	30,544	503,737	148	155,581	240
999	Ketchikan, AK	W1(998)	21,057	8,216	12,138	262,596	77	34,911	54
	U.S. Totals		293,687,162	112,708,735	193,017,681	3,399,544,000	1,000,000	649,513,000	1,000,000

Source: Devonshire Associates Ltd. and Scan/US, Inc. 2004.

** Estimates for Retail Sales, including Shopping Goods Sales, are based on data from the U.S. Census Bureau's 1997 Economic Census and utilize the North American Industry Classification System (NAICS). Shopping Goods include sales data for general merchandise and apparel stores.

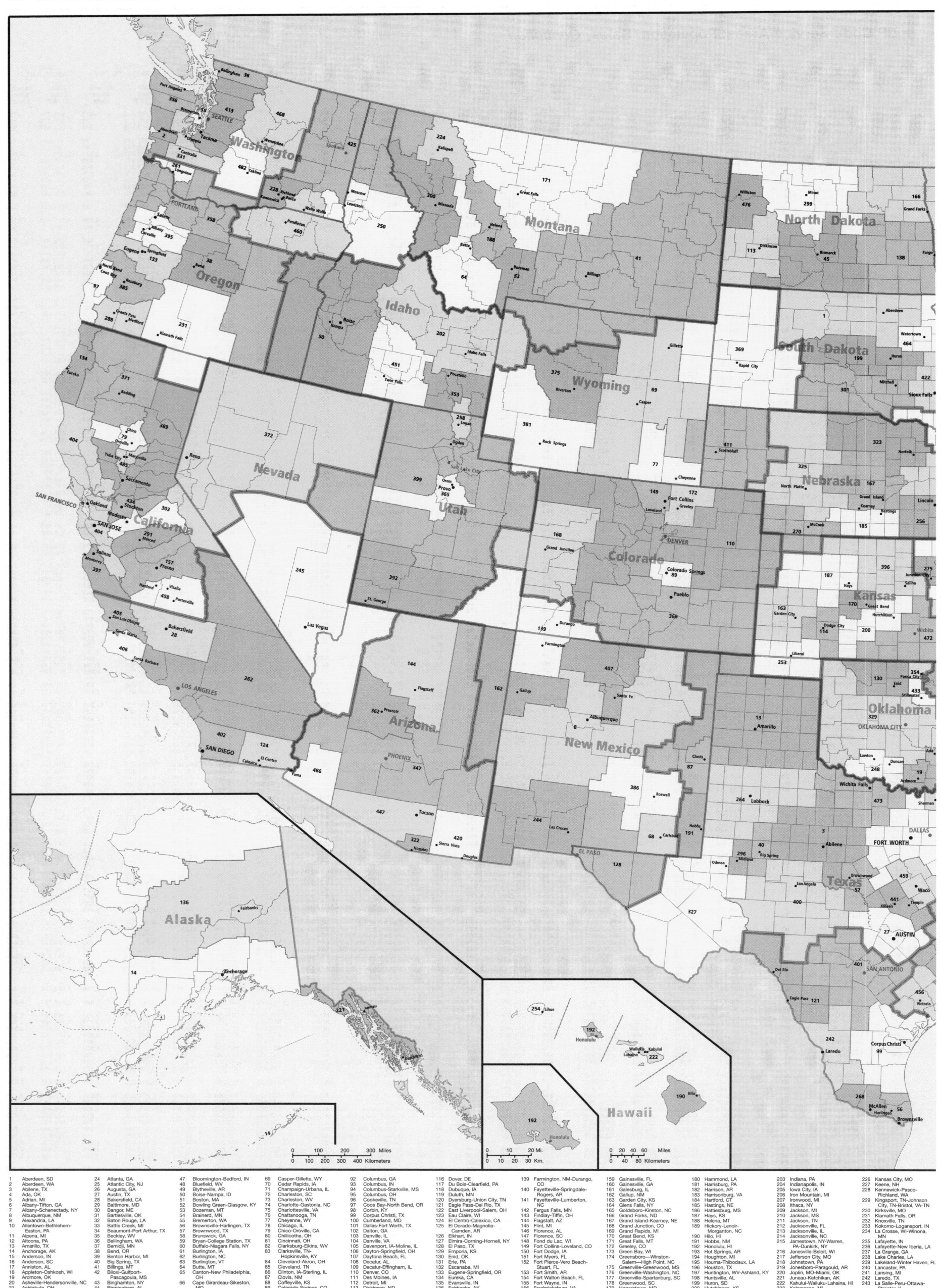

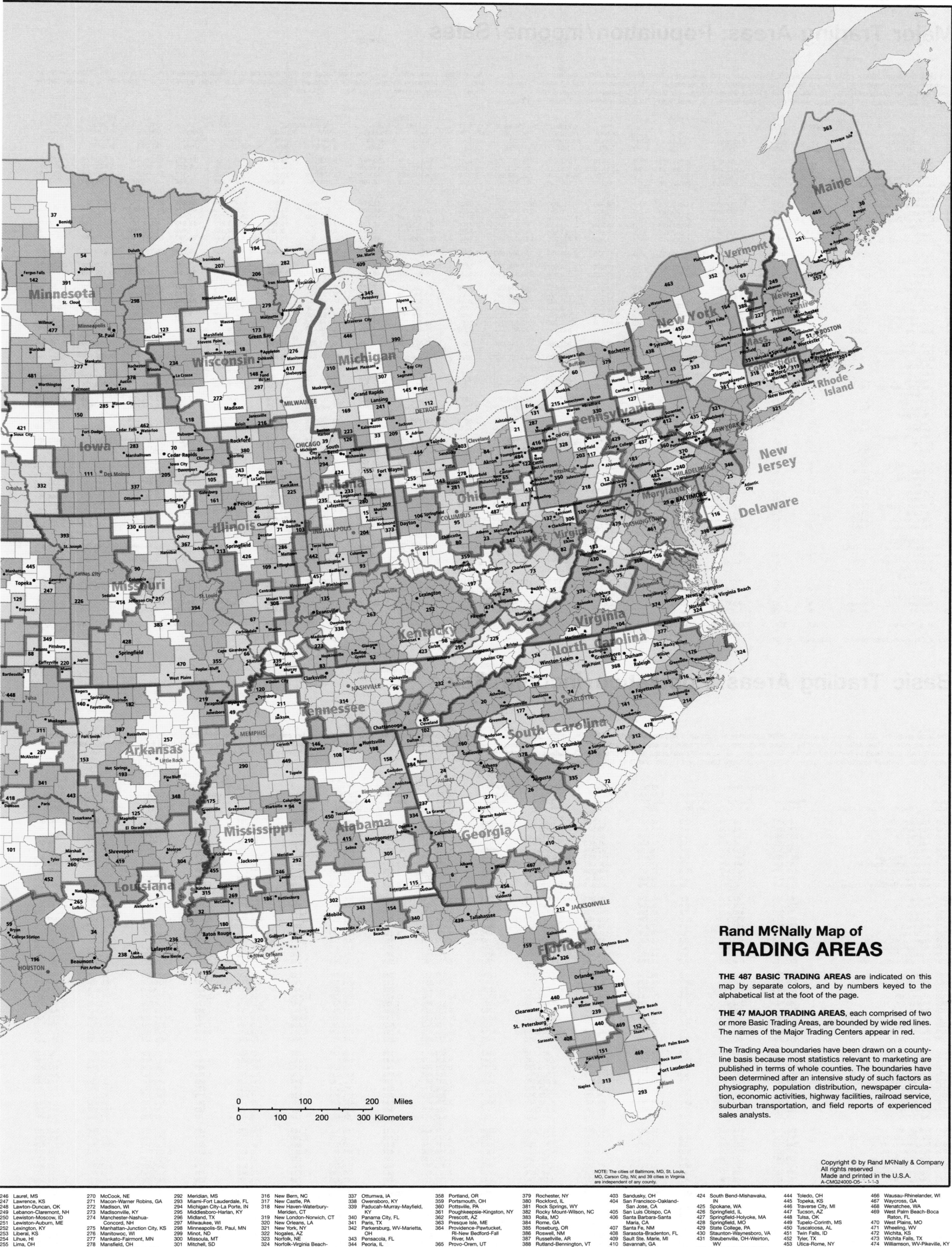

Rand McNally Map of
TRADING AREAS

THE 487 BASIC TRADING AREAS are indicated on this map by separate colors, and by numbers keyed to the alphabetical list at the foot of the page.

THE 47 MAJOR TRADING AREAS, each comprised of two or more Basic Trading Areas, are bounded by wide red lines. The names of the Major Trading Centers appear in red.

The Trading Area boundaries have been drawn on a county-line basis because most statistics relevant to marketing are published in terms of whole counties. The boundaries have been determined after an intensive study of such factors as physiography, population distribution, newspaper circulation, economic activities, highway facilities, railroad service, suburban transportation, and field reports of experienced sales analysts.

NOTE: The cities of Baltimore, MD, St. Louis, MO, Carson City, NV, and 39 cities in Virginia are independent of any county.

Major Trading Areas: Population / Income / Sales

This table gives the 2000 Census population, 2004 estimates of population and households, and 2003 estimates of income, purchasing power, retail sales (total and by various store groups) and passenger car registrations for the 47 Major Trading Areas as defined by Rand McNally. The Major Trading Areas are combinations of Basic Trading Areas as shown on the map on pages 22-23. Statistics for Total Retail Sales, General Merchandise, Apparel Store, Food Store Sales, and Health and Drug Store Sales in this edition are estimates based on data from the U.S. Census Bureau, and utilize the 1997 North American Industry Classification System (NAICS). A detailed explanation of Retail Trade, and Major and Basic Trading Areas, can be found in the Introduction on pages 5-9.

NO.	MAJOR TRADING AREA	MTA ABBREV.	NUMBER OF BASIC AREAS	NUMBER OF COUN-TIES	POPULATION Estimate 7/1/04	POPULATION Census 4/1/00	% Change 4/1/90-4/1/00	PER CAPITA INCOME 2003	HOUSE-HOLDS Estimate 7/1/04	DISPOSABLE INCOME 2003 ($1,000)	MARKET ABILITY INDEX 2003	TOTAL RETAIL SALES 2003 Sales ($1,000)	TOTAL RETAIL SALES Ranally Sales Units	GENERAL MERCHANDISE 2003 Sales ($1,000)	GENERAL MERCHANDISE Ranally Sales Units	APPAREL STORE 2003 Sales ($1,000)	APPAREL STORE Ranally Sales Units	FOOD STORE SALES 2003 ($1,000)	HEALTH & DRUG STORE 2003 ($1,000)	PASSEN-GER CAR REGIS-TRATIONS 2003
01	Atlanta	ATL	14	156	9,395,891	8,731,699	25.8	19,479	3,614,510	183,023,170	3.1941	110,143,278	32,397	15,843,836	33,634	5,573,600	31,235	16,118,466	4,880,778	6,550,399
03	Birmingham	BIR	10	55	3,612,736	3,555,114	9.6	17,447	1,463,687	63,030,690	1.1387	39,357,956	11,578	7,019,591	14,901	1,755,239	9,833	5,332,553	1,961,311	2,694,647
05	Boston-Providence	BOS-	14	47	10,262,975	10,009,759	5.9	22,228	4,051,746	228,120,540	3.8590	134,583,586	39,587	13,478,169	28,611	7,935,802	44,472	24,404,288	8,718,019	6,627,057
07	Buffalo-Rochester	BUF-	4	19	2,778,092	2,792,296	0.5	19,777	1,109,996	54,943,440	.9089	27,730,449	8,158	3,104,097	6,589	1,371,268	7,686	5,148,736	1,804,006	1,753,022
09	Charlotte-Greensboro-Greenville-Raleigh	C-G-G-R	23	134	12,227,231	11,613,265	19.1	18,643	4,941,030	227,952,630	4.0904	145,779,520	42,874	20,574,806	43,677	6,826,314	38,260	20,749,062	7,889,024	8,875,955
11	Chicago	CHI	18	84	13,575,288	13,220,193	9.5	20,431	5,038,491	277,358,760	4.7082	157,057,328	46,200	20,317,681	43,128	7,577,929	42,474	21,382,157	11,908,213	8,337,383
13	Cincinnati-Dayton	CIN-	9	71	4,921,632	4,888,525	3.6	18,667	2,022,886	91,872,950	1.6121	54,691,157	16,087	8,677,380	18,421	2,132,158	11,949	7,703,489	3,428,475	3,527,416
15	Cleveland	CLEV	10	25	5,072,714	5,084,468	2.8	18,996	2,049,931	96,359,640	1.7104	60,263,306	17,727	7,207,233	15,299	2,679,383	15,018	8,788,167	5,250,053	3,527,699
17	Columbus	COL	6	29	2,484,063	2,392,826	11.5	19,873	1,021,265	49,366,930	.8765	31,787,503	9,351	4,424,224	9,393	1,392,353	7,802	4,112,089	1,412,549	1,842,024
19	Dallas-Fort Worth	DAL-	22	210	12,504,258	11,688,918	20.6	18,961	4,739,236	237,088,360	4.2935	157,819,682	46,422	21,744,482	46,164	6,850,947	38,393	20,648,730	6,582,440	8,330,589
21	Denver	DEN	12	105	5,237,698	4,907,635	26.5	20,752	2,041,407	108,691,550	1.8849	66,684,265	19,617	9,650,932	20,485	2,461,438	13,792	9,185,709	2,245,470	3,902,902
23	Des Moines-Quad Cities	DES-	13	102	3,176,773	3,157,069	5.0	17,992	1,264,631	57,155,750	1.0877	42,748,044	12,572	5,127,279	10,882	1,136,359	6,370	5,162,256	1,778,229	2,395,490
25	Detroit	DET	18	84	10,844,299	10,658,459	6.6	20,225	4,270,562	219,325,590	3.8532	138,096,828	40,625	24,525,917	52,069	5,448,811	30,534	16,412,704	8,322,185	7,613,931
27	El Paso-Albuquerque	ELP-	8	37	2,643,993	2,533,752	19.9	14,984	960,957	39,618,250	.7496	25,720,441	7,569	4,790,943	10,171	1,152,238	6,457	3,169,575	1,254,750	1,713,142
29	Honolulu	HON	4	5	1,272,696	1,211,537	9.3	19,407	429,724	24,699,580	.4224	13,845,580	4,073	2,707,801	5,748	1,566,698	8,779	2,440,661	1,114,719	718,816
31	Houston	HOU	6	46	6,799,743	6,307,777	21.5	18,572	2,506,442	126,283,840	2.2336	76,906,321	22,623	12,248,468	26,001	4,006,461	22,453	11,691,046	3,548,209	4,298,127
33	Indianapolis	IND	11	54	3,424,165	3,333,121	10.5	18,935	1,374,354	64,837,700	1.1730	42,954,895	12,632	7,344,138	15,589	1,520,590	8,520	4,449,800	2,601,562	2,517,382
35	Jacksonville	JAX	7	49	2,908,443	2,740,381	20.5	18,298	1,156,040	53,218,920	.9424	32,216,851	9,474	4,762,900	10,110	1,432,590	8,030	4,842,984	1,649,368	1,977,160
37	Kansas City	K.C.	9	71	3,299,848	3,202,863	9.9	19,034	1,321,033	62,808,020	1.1062	38,341,753	11,281	6,174,619	13,108	1,310,752	7,346	5,018,706	1,928,622	2,402,913
39	Knoxville	KNOX	3	38	2,001,418	1,944,407	12.9	16,418	845,575	32,859,810	.6332	24,129,352	7,098	4,216,492	8,947	1,096,714	6,147	3,243,903	1,357,579	1,552,986
41	Little Rock	L.R.	9	61	2,465,816	2,385,905	16.3	16,116	987,369	39,740,030	.7559	27,674,494	8,144	6,811,739	14,457	894,238	5,012	2,846,380	1,110,010	1,712,665
43	Los Angeles-San Diego	L.A.-	7	16	23,918,509	22,223,875	16.1	18,420	7,975,043	440,567,560	7.5728	241,896,522	71,157	28,515,646	60,533	17,810,396	99,815	40,110,850	12,899,107	13,949,097
45	Louisville-Lexington-Evansville	L-L-E	9	117	4,003,379	3,905,399	9.8	17,546	1,653,478	70,243,950	1.2534	42,307,104	12,443	7,267,772	15,427	1,684,485	9,443	4,979,692	2,604,763	2,917,065
47	Memphis-Jackson	MEM-	11	94	3,798,729	3,761,294	8.5	15,605	1,456,577	59,281,000	1.1227	39,818,421	11,716	7,872,301	16,715	1,820,362	10,206	4,544,478	2,324,225	2,459,221
49	Miami-Fort Lauderdale	MIA-	5	13	6,984,713	6,436,114	25.3	20,681	2,868,718	144,450,370	2.4891	86,635,086	25,485	10,318,111	21,904	6,698,470	37,539	12,562,622	6,115,838	4,448,124
51	Milwaukee	MILW	16	66	5,049,618	4,941,046	8.8	19,726	2,047,027	99,607,670	1.7456	61,272,015	18,023	9,408,582	19,971	1,661,431	9,311	8,252,010	2,760,631	3,618,908
53	Minneapolis-St. Paul	MPLS-	23	211	6,821,456	6,621,619	10.6	20,112	2,723,383	137,194,630	2.5014	96,398,616	28,355	13,506,276	28,672	2,823,962	15,822	12,131,894	4,008,775	5,055,493
55	Nashville	NASH	3	43	2,269,776	2,165,007	22.5	19,365	914,540	43,955,200	.7815	27,993,031	8,233	4,995,540	10,603	1,261,501	7,069	3,612,905	1,460,800	1,695,780
57	New Orleans-Baton Rouge	N.O.-	13	67	5,509,210	5,399,308	9.6	16,735	2,163,905	92,198,840	1.6948	59,177,699	17,407	11,263,817	23,911	2,734,099	15,325	8,017,300	3,581,456	3,573,490
59	New York	N.Y.	20	94	28,857,708	28,198,690	6.8	22,491	10,781,246	649,050,060	10.3665	316,067,584	92,977	29,787,333	63,234	27,665,969	155,049	53,104,215	24,158,213	14,974,463
61	Oklahoma City	O.C.	8	50	2,074,171	2,029,571	8.1	16,305	825,888	33,818,530	.6194	21,055,594	6,195	4,163,167	8,835	675,945	3,785	2,493,955	1,134,643	1,464,985
63	Omaha	OMA	7	90	1,831,213	1,794,352	8.1	18,071	727,156	33,091,940	.6128	22,895,749	6,729	3,110,202	6,603	703,674	3,945	3,071,783	1,270,628	1,381,797
65	Philadelphia	PHIL	11	37	9,753,181	9,510,948	6.5	21,091	3,760,807	205,700,090	3.4958	119,327,918	35,104	11,818,406	25,087	6,730,293	37,719	20,037,833	8,122,498	6,032,424
67	Phoenix	PHOE	7	13	5,474,965	4,906,177	39.8	18,711	2,075,101	102,441,930	1.7770	58,741,648	17,279	8,488,374	18,017	2,169,711	12,159	8,537,563	2,842,740	3,523,306
69	Pittsburgh	PGH	12	42	4,003,675	4,048,998	-1.3	17,229	1,663,660	68,979,020	1.2542	43,636,996	12,834	5,455,479	11,581	1,761,480	9,871	6,999,593	3,197,688	2,681,880
71	Portland	POR	9	35	3,966,888	3,738,321	22.2	19,130	1,555,553	75,888,190	1.3610	49,245,180	14,491	9,279,168	19,700	2,103,472	11,788	7,144,876	1,601,178	2,844,052
73	Richmond-Norfolk	RICH-	7	97	4,391,599	4,242,383	10.5	18,468	1,755,224	81,103,350	1.4242	48,061,627	14,142	7,574,702	16,083	2,219,477	12,438	7,030,007	2,555,990	3,185,747
75	St. Louis	ST.L.	12	103	5,118,975	5,018,297	7.6	18,259	2,058,863	93,468,540	1.6602	57,044,851	16,782	9,051,481	19,213	1,767,328	9,904	7,860,174	3,269,140	3,608,033
77	Salt Lake City	S.L.C.	8	65	3,554,489	3,319,967	29.0	16,496	1,190,137	58,634,320	1.1295	43,143,666	12,694	6,921,937	14,695	1,513,573	8,482	6,496,783	1,050,040	2,429,682
79	San Antonio	SANT	6	40	4,031,386	3,716,676	24.4	13,754	1,346,838	55,446,810	1.1065	39,957,554	11,751	6,463,278	13,722	2,416,505	13,545	6,737,769	1,541,420	2,229,311
81	San Francisco-Oakland-San Jose	SF-O-SJ	13	58	14,534,980	13,782,432	15.9	22,195	5,197,769	322,597,790	5.2249	163,797,628	48,181	19,502,336	41,398	10,658,616	59,737	30,467,461	8,940,209	9,340,429
83	Seattle	SEAT	11	48	5,477,507	5,231,647	19.5	21,170	2,131,312	115,957,780	1.9687	67,218,508	19,775	11,116,477	23,599	3,332,298	18,675	10,490,686	2,509,427	3,922,249
85	Spokane-Billings	SPOK-	11	87	2,260,530	2,178,445	16.9	16,278	883,646	36,797,380	.6985	25,643,456	7,544	4,092,430	8,687	752,882	4,217	4,154,253	907,560	1,718,231
87	Tampa-St. Petersburg-Orlando	T-SP-O	7	20	7,281,281	6,660,705	22.9	20,705	3,143,870	150,760,460	2.6018	90,933,388	26,746	12,007,124	25,490	4,404,768	24,684	13,307,409	5,573,350	5,074,675
89	Tulsa	TUL	4	20	1,256,254	1,224,694	11.7	17,345	509,517	21,789,790	.3894	13,053,921	3,839	2,731,054	5,796	381,662	2,139	1,562,498	700,872	901,915
91	Washington-Baltimore	WASH-	9	67	9,347,921	8,799,742	13.1	24,703	3,620,861	230,924,160	3.5417	102,908,075	30,270	13,438,506	28,525	6,108,485	34,237	17,479,759	5,768,456	6,228,704
93	Wichita	WICH	8	66	1,205,277	1,206,230	7.3	17,074	467,744	20,579,360	.3727	12,779,572	3,759	2,175,774	4,615	452,277	2,534	1,893,169	545,783	886,915
	U. S. Totals		487	3141	293,687,162	281,421,906	13.2	19,691	112,708,735	5,782,884,870	100.0000	3,399,544,000	1,000,000	471,078,000	1,000,000	178,435,000	1,000,000	505,933,000	192,191,000	193,017,681

Source: Devonshire Associates Ltd. and Scan/US, Inc. 2004.

Basic Trading Areas: Population / Income / Sales

This table gives the 2000 Census population, 2004 estimates of population and households, and 2003 estimates of income, purchasing power, retail sales (total and by various store groups) and passenger car registrations for the 487 Basic Trading Areas (BTAs) as defined by Rand McNally. The Basic Trading Areas are shown on the map on pages 22-23. Statistics for Total Retail Sales, General Merchandise, Apparel Store, Food Store Sales, and Health and Drug Store Sales in this edition are estimates based on data from the U. S. Census Bureau, and utilize the 1997 North American Industry Classification System (NAICS). A detailed explanation of Retail Trade, and Major and Basic Trading Areas, can be found in the Introduction on pages 5-9.

BTA NO.	BASIC TRADING AREA	POPULATION Estimate 7/1/04	POPULATION Census 4/1/00	% Change 4/1/90-4/1/00	PER CAPITA INCOME 2003	HOUSE-HOLDS Estimate 7/1/04	DISPOSABLE INCOME 2003 ($1,000)	MARKET ABILITY INDEX 2003	TOTAL RETAIL SALES 2003 Sales ($1,000)	TOTAL RETAIL SALES Ranally Sales Units	GENERAL MERCHANDISE 2003 Sales ($1,000)	GENERAL MERCHANDISE Ranally Sales Units	APPAREL STORE 2003 Sales ($1,000)	APPAREL STORE Ranally Sales Units	FOOD STORE SALES 2003 ($1,000)	HEALTH & DRUG STORE 2003 ($1,000)	PASSEN-GER CAR REGIS-TRATIONS 2003
001	Aberdeen, SD	83,077	86,789	-2.4	14,531	33,100	1,207,190	.0288	1,433,961	421	88,105	189	11,394	65	78,772	12,396	62,943
002	Aberdeen, WA	91,301	88,178	6.2	15,555	36,524	1,420,190	.0244	677,968	200	112,619	239	9,625	54	174,472	55,872	65,285
003	Abilene, TX	255,040	261,706	3.4	14,665	97,401	3,740,180	.0740	2,754,517	811	458,797	976	72,110	404	331,216	112,806	169,048
004	Ada, OK	55,350	55,053	4.5	12,654	21,550	700,400	.0140	465,241	137	133,542	283	14,632	82	57,700	24,137	38,014
005	Adrian, MI	101,344	98,890	8.1	19,258	37,894	1,951,730	.0346	1,228,128	361	242,181	514	16,434	92	138,341	72,763	73,111
006	Albany-Tifton, GA	361,850	355,474	9.4	13,681	134,665	4,950,530	.0996	3,618,498	1,066	524,487	1,112	135,513	758	588,219	166,025	222,508
007	Albany-Schenectady, NY	1,067,671	1,047,324	1.8	21,277	434,661	22,716,960	.3677	11,176,542	3,288	1,244,372	2,642	543,341	3,046	1,692,608	740,348	697,309
008	Albuquerque, NM	878,243	831,850	20.8	17,876	346,982	15,699,540	.2831	9,920,813	2,919	1,748,555	3,713	332,713	1,864	980,171	533,316	621,151
009	Alexandria, LA	269,006	270,223	-3.5	13,489	100,540	3,628,570	.0710	2,398,805	705	519,657	1,103	76,148	427	297,519	149,816	162,771
010	Allentown-Bethlehem-Easton, PA	776,747	740,395	7.8	20,869	305,639	16,210,200	.2761	9,403,351	2,767	979,519	2,079	367,959	2,063	1,723,108	631,887	533,539
011	Alpena, MI	66,929	67,759	6.8	16,356	29,048	1,094,680	.0203	715,563	210	106,481	226	21,219	118	108,795	46,293	52,249
012	Altoona, PA	222,418	224,714	0.9	15,740	89,461	3,500,750	.0701	2,788,430	820	386,278	819	66,077	371	413,888	171,427	157,093
013	Amarillo, TX	411,930	410,323	7.9	15,765	154,439	6,493,900	.1233	4,457,900	1,313	573,458	1,216	159,648	894	481,853	185,083	275,576
014	Anchorage, AK	483,813	456,392	17.3	20,536	170,104	9,935,470	.1744	6,314,171	1,857	1,342,257	2,850	245,298	1,375	1,031,413	83,108	293,383
015	Anderson, IN	177,855	181,866	1.7	17,857	72,139	3,175,950	.0556	1,820,969	535	280,009	594	38,833	218	217,792	128,990	132,238
016	Anderson, SC	359,767	347,350	13.8	16,908	146,021	6,082,960	.1076	3,456,356	1,016	522,579	1,109	114,490	642	596,026	215,426	273,055
017	Anniston, AL	163,455	163,006	0.7	15,882	68,078	2,595,950	.0467	1,482,690	436	308,726	656	39,647	222	233,541	66,356	128,784
018	Appleton-Oshkosh, WI	468,337	452,355	13.3	20,143	188,786	9,433,930	.1668	6,052,381	1,780	819,618	1,739	205,956	1,155	779,177	235,415	352,499
019	Ardmore, OK	92,684	90,772	8.1	14,005	36,878	1,298,060	.0253	895,015	264	188,727	400	27,753	155	119,696	57,366	65,398
020	Asheville-Hendersonville, NC	632,075	608,250	19.3	17,388	268,110	10,990,240	.2091	8,052,565	2,366	1,186,551	2,519	320,983	1,798	1,145,321	433,167	486,060
021	Ashtabula, OH	103,234	102,728	2.9	16,316	40,105	1,684,410	.0290	837,567	246	121,774	259	24,400	137	142,532	71,498	73,630
022	Athens, GA	222,745	207,668	25.1	16,433	88,304	3,660,370	.0683	2,424,651	712	354,724	753	167,142	937	336,056	108,464	170,443
023	Athens, OH	134,943	130,742	5.6	12,977	52,021	1,751,130	.0325	913,411	269	113,276	240	25,011	140	213,609	68,981	97,383
024	Atlanta, GA	4,892,700	4,407,446	37.9	22,454	1,878,535	109,860,030	1.8492	64,164,487	18,874	8,365,720	17,759	3,335,362	18,692	9,272,544	2,575,751	3,462,500
025	Atlantic City, NJ	368,557	354,878	11.1	21,221	142,561	7,821,170	.1325	4,515,980	1,329	469,557	997	317,234	1,778	1,056,306	285,181	213,356
026	Augusta, GA	605,032	590,218	13.1	16,620	232,388	10,055,690	.1787	5,735,373	1,686	961,644	2,041	246,734	1,383	859,725	295,641	404,543
027	Austin, TX	1,499,582	1,325,029	47.3	22,656	595,395	33,975,100	.6555	29,430,626	8,659	2,401,133	5,098	1,098,605	6,157	3,277,523	1,409,754	1,071,406
028	Bakersfield, CA	729,553	661,645	21.7	13,779	226,881	10,052,420	.1858	5,580,342	1,642	732,780	1,556	216,564	1,214	895,681	350,750	390,843
029	Baltimore, MD	2,690,679	2,606,003	7.2	22,799	1,048,378	61,344,350	.9715	29,224,813	8,597	3,770,428	8,003	1,669,615	9,358	5,202,186	1,843,845	1,705,024
030	Bangor, ME	331,036	323,784	2.2	16,735	140,161	5,539,810	.1082	4,272,884	1,257	464,407	986	91,466	513	988,424	173,302	241,501
031	Bartlesville, OK	49,164	48,996	1.9	18,003	20,493	885,110	.0145	401,693	118	135,138	287	13,880	78	34,488	20,620	36,732
032	Baton Rouge, LA	727,706	705,760	13.2	17,770	279,440	12,931,440	.2349	8,323,377	2,447	1,490,811	3,165	346,887	1,944	1,097,510	395,026	477,866
033	Battle Creek, MI	245,095	240,527	5.7	18,416	96,952	4,513,750	.0781	2,531,754	744	558,659	1,186	57,295	321	326,436	142,956	177,222
034	Beaumont-Port Arthur, TX	463,147	467,106	8.1	16,346	179,429	7,570,500	.1426	5,164,466	1,519	833,934	1,770	203,048	1,139	733,467	276,852	295,781
035	Beckley, WV	165,997	166,963	-0.1	14,117	69,690	2,343,360	.0458	1,617,667	476	336,247	714	30,374	169	182,913	120,050	113,840
036	Bellingham, WA	179,561	166,814	30.5	18,388	71,394	3,301,690	.0602	2,206,779	649	395,974	841	93,233	523	482,145	104,046	135,400
037	Bemidji, MN	69,605	66,449	15.3	14,687	26,702	1,022,260	.0214	888,675	262	131,901	280	37,643	211	169,070	32,624	49,591
038	Bend, OR	174,663	153,558	49.5	18,381	68,392	3,210,480	.0603	2,342,284	690	497,679	1,057	69,344	388	364,135	68,882	138,660
039	Benton Harbor, MI	162,816	162,453	0.7	17,983	66,098	2,927,880	.0504	1,585,823	466	298,008	633	29,166	163	230,436	105,137	115,292
040	Big Spring, TX	34,657	35,762	3.4	12,907	11,916	447,310	.0089	307,444	91	51,763	110	8,420	47	41,703	13,259	19,461
041	Billings, MT	315,239	312,138	7.5	16,263	127,263	5,126,820	.0989	3,774,804	1,111	558,652	1,186	106,273	596	498,277	117,700	249,297
042	Biloxi-Gulfport-Pascagoula, MS	405,152	396,754	16.8	17,628	160,456	7,142,130	.1269	4,245,104	1,249	1,036,132	2,200	137,635	771	491,985	185,494	289,597
043	Binghamton, NY	344,202	345,959	-3.0	17,931	139,171	6,171,730	.1043	3,117,155	917	403,577	858	96,909	543	532,518	248,801	227,429
044	Birmingham, AL	1,343,594	1,319,776	10.0	18,279	541,598	24,559,630	.4378	15,150,905	4,457	2,495,407	5,297	729,535	4,087	2,127,079	751,754	991,351
045	Bismarck, ND	130,047	129,398	4.6	17,842	53,393	2,320,280	.0441	1,721,193	506	250,427	532	33,787	190	190,520	100,657	107,451
046	Bloomington, IL	245,152	238,092	10.3	19,544	92,717	4,791,370	.0853	3,083,981	908	399,770	848	137,996	774	357,323	188,686	167,992
047	Bloomington-Bedford, IN	246,030	240,734	10.5	16,249	101,921	3,997,820	.0719	2,325,444	684	439,966	934	78,640	441	339,593	133,274	191,833
048	Bluefield, WV	163,139	168,756	-8.3	13,000	69,337	2,120,740	.0443	1,677,271	493	347,435	738	41,392	232	242,935	155,134	114,009
049	Blytheville, AR	67,768	72,026	-9.3	12,163	26,053	824,260	.0169	577,226	170	103,999	221	13,668	77	85,842	34,208	39,218
050	Boise-Nampa, ID	644,161	584,008	40.2	17,090	235,067	11,008,870	.2084	7,869,346	2,315	1,313,050	2,787	226,329	1,269	1,115,229	250,455	460,546
051	Boston, MA	4,452,771	4,391,344	6.2	24,996	1,723,822	111,299,830	1.8013	60,701,542	17,855	5,700,756	12,102	4,396,572	24,640	10,266,378	4,205,252	2,714,924
052	Bowling Green-Glasgow, KY	262,056	254,561	14.3	15,857	107,376	4,155,470	.0766	2,577,287	759	412,863	875	89,599	502	324,155	158,431	193,596
053	Bozeman, MT	90,763	83,525	28.5	17,596	36,569	1,597,040	.0310	1,238,402	364	129,620	275	37,136	208	192,291	33,249	74,336
054	Brainerd, MN	103,900	97,550	24.3	16,899	43,112	1,755,830	.0335	1,271,337	374	218,321	463	9,875	55	165,879	38,485	79,540
055	Bremerton, WA	243,450	231,969	22.3	19,816	90,966	4,824,290	.0783	2,263,687	666	520,165	1,104	67,059	376	338,124	110,073	177,217
056	Brownsville-Harlingen, TX	391,958	355,309	27.9	9,480	114,664	3,715,660	.0840	2,851,056	838	649,080	1,377	196,477	1,101	540,429	115,231	177,531
057	Brownwood, TX	62,633	63,037	9.3	14,160	24,001	886,860	.0177	648,669	191	100,597	212	19,743	111	72,087	33,463	42,467
058	Brunswick, GA	81,832	78,415	10.2	19,756	36,269	1,616,660	.0285	1,011,043	298	151,307	321	85,764	481	155,186	49,603	61,666
059	Bryan-College Station, TX	195,011	184,885	22.4	13,878	74,689	2,706,380	.0546	2,032,602	598	368,615	783	93,680	524	290,674	49,105	132,704
060	Buffalo-Niagara Falls, NY	1,199,068	1,213,535	-1.5	19,522	485,681	23,408,220	.3875	11,724,898	3,449	1,250,510	2,654	662,473	3,713	2,112,315	916,383	726,617
061	Burlington, IA	131,770	136,489	-0.8	17,086	53,312	2,251,470	.0416	1,505,861	443	222,689	473	36,053	202	238,661	68,874	101,009
062	Burlington, NC	138,548	130,800	20.9	18,658	56,281	2,585,040	.0472	1,747,387	514	210,583	447	106,370	596	236,792	102,793	105,187
063	Burlington, VT	418,921	406,799	10.2	19,218	167,030	8,050,830	.1469	5,525,766	1,627	422,366	897	212,077	1,191	1,011,734	323,702	297,711
064	Butte, MT	64,362	67,256	3.1	15,343	27,827	987,490	.0190	682,049	201	74,206	158	32,241	181	130,841	31,542	52,432

Source: Devonshire Associates Ltd. and Scan/US, Inc. 2004.
. . . Represents a change of less than 0.1%

Basic Trading Areas: Population / Income / Sales, *Continued*

BTA NO.	BASIC TRADING AREA	POPULATION Estimate 7/1/04	POPULATION Census 4/1/00	% Change 4/1/90-4/1/00	PER CAPITA INCOME 2003	HOUSE-HOLDS Estimate 7/1/04	DISPOSABLE INCOME 2003 ($1,000)	MARKET ABILITY INDEX 2003	TOTAL RETAIL SALES 2003 Sales ($1,000)	TOTAL RETAIL SALES Ranally Sales Units	GENERAL MERCHANDISE 2003 Sales ($1,000)	GENERAL MERCHANDISE Ranally Sales Units	APPAREL STORE 2003 Sales ($1,000)	APPAREL STORE Ranally Sales Units	FOOD STORE SALES 2003 ($1,000)	HEALTH & DRUG STORE 2003 ($1,000)	PASSEN-GER CAR REGIS-TRATIONS 2003
065	Canton-New Philadelphia, OH	536,362	534,503	4.1	17,960	214,691	9,633,290	.1746	6,202,224	**1,824**	864,777	**1,836**	285,844	**1,602**	957,845	533,816	395,864
066	Cape Girardeau-Sikeston, MO	191,798	189,401	4.2	15,066	75,627	2,889,680	.0586	2,332,684	**687**	416,362	**884**	51,928	**290**	237,138	107,599	129,242
067	Carbondale-Marion, IL	214,433	214,191	2.2	14,454	87,775	3,099,380	.0595	2,056,517	**604**	437,769	**930**	67,361	**378**	278,001	104,282	148,377
068	Carlsbad, NM	51,476	51,658	6.3	14,681	19,673	755,700	.0137	409,266	**120**	76,011	**161**	13,585	**76**	73,217	23,461	35,248
069	Casper-Gillette, WY	151,827	146,211	8.2	18,229	61,174	2,767,730	.0496	1,747,830	**515**	304,547	**646**	32,668	**183**	239,105	38,524	125,650
070	Cedar Rapids, IA	296,712	289,492	11.1	19,803	118,593	5,875,670	.1034	3,676,965	**1,082**	513,965	**1,091**	171,324	**959**	472,582	174,680	231,149
071	Champaign-Urbana, IL	239,495	230,197	3.5	18,059	95,187	4,325,070	.0782	2,768,387	**815**	503,565	**1,070**	132,636	**744**	362,182	193,903	161,968
072	Charleston, SC	713,665	680,311	9.0	18,018	285,566	12,858,880	.2275	7,677,563	**2,257**	1,296,098	**2,752**	484,579	**2,716**	1,299,115	362,883	473,952
073	Charleston, WV	482,610	486,731	1.1	16,236	203,791	7,835,610	.1470	5,275,752	**1,552**	805,364	**1,709**	174,145	**977**	688,641	389,067	326,046
074	Charlotte-Gastonia, NC	2,246,673	2,078,083	24.4	20,352	904,949	45,725,410	.7863	26,964,020	**7,931**	3,610,335	**7,663**	1,161,561	**6,508**	3,727,615	1,469,333	1,650,081
075	Charlottesville, VA	241,699	228,045	19.9	19,083	96,433	4,612,440	.0797	2,656,442	**781**	322,632	**686**	129,885	**729**	458,161	150,825	185,180
076	Chattanooga, TN	583,689	568,186	11.2	17,649	237,496	10,301,790	.1827	6,108,421	**1,797**	1,006,464	**2,137**	306,257	**1,716**	876,408	381,150	437,957
077	Cheyenne, WY	116,770	113,621	9.3	17,264	47,829	2,015,940	.0406	1,723,287	**507**	315,243	**669**	29,533	**165**	198,007	30,647	93,456
078	Chicago, IL	9,405,026	9,098,316	11.2	21,277	3,404,592	200,106,090	3.3284	108,533,325	**31,926**	12,448,491	**26,424**	5,997,775	**33,613**	14,973,121	8,989,067	5,408,248
079	Chico-Oroville, CA	240,946	229,624	11.0	15,468	92,944	3,726,950	.0680	2,195,977	**646**	324,500	**689**	77,736	**436**	451,891	152,965	168,845
080	Chillicothe, OH	103,093	101,040	8.0	16,091	39,855	1,658,820	.0297	939,622	**277**	218,718	**465**	22,901	**129**	171,829	60,084	75,655
081	Cincinnati, OH	2,224,929	2,170,768	9.1	20,668	898,706	45,983,740	.7792	26,066,909	**7,667**	3,814,372	**8,097**	1,121,541	**6,286**	3,745,190	1,426,347	1,607,792
082	Clarksburg-Elkins, WV	190,554	190,767	0.1	14,271	77,539	2,719,460	.0534	1,916,057	**564**	354,081	**752**	59,709	**333**	252,831	116,371	127,937
083	Clarksville, TN-Hopkinsville, KY	270,944	265,119	20.3	16,059	102,704	4,351,070	.0783	2,524,554	**743**	569,442	**1,208**	98,129	**549**	251,950	97,176	187,035
084	Cleveland-Akron, OH	2,995,077	2,993,610	3.4	20,083	1,219,085	60,151,460	1.0513	37,092,442	**10,912**	3,918,082	**8,318**	1,694,454	**9,497**	5,372,314	3,587,217	2,055,867
085	Cleveland, TN	107,156	104,015	19.1	16,849	43,530	1,805,440	.0321	1,037,640	**305**	189,521	**403**	34,377	**192**	122,296	69,439	83,384
086	Clinton, IA-Sterling, IL	145,655	147,772	-0.1	17,848	58,792	2,599,630	.0461	1,550,728	**455**	235,130	**499**	21,383	**120**	237,402	87,869	108,861
087	Clovis, NM	75,654	75,318	6.0	13,187	28,461	997,680	.0192	619,193	**183**	121,551	**258**	26,486	**148**	78,791	29,405	51,087
088	Coffeyville, KS	59,574	61,512	-3.1	14,338	24,313	854,190	.0150	397,189	**116**	74,216	**157**	10,095	**57**	70,026	28,966	45,317
089	Colorado Springs, CO	582,962	537,484	31.3	19,915	217,598	11,609,510	.2043	7,281,101	**2,142**	1,150,804	**2,443**	191,586	**1,074**	801,447	279,729	414,826
090	Columbia, MO	223,936	216,756	13.8	16,998	89,768	3,806,500	.0710	2,590,548	**762**	407,239	**864**	66,315	**372**	323,887	119,036	160,446
091	Columbia, SC	700,532	668,081	17.5	19,170	280,116	13,429,050	.2376	8,351,037	**2,456**	1,509,496	**3,205**	398,449	**2,234**	1,143,451	423,265	497,135
092	Columbus, GA	370,856	364,510	6.5	15,342	143,489	5,689,770	.1058	3,545,730	**1,042**	601,279	**1,276**	196,688	**1,101**	530,156	207,191	241,096
093	Columbus, IN	157,936	155,281	11.6	18,515	61,989	2,924,140	.0503	1,621,245	**476**	288,837	**613**	100,968	**566**	200,018	101,248	122,097
094	Columbus-Starkville, MS	171,202	174,971	5.1	13,844	67,817	2,370,080	.0467	1,655,721	**487**	335,169	**712**	69,924	**391**	234,590	86,675	118,150
095	Columbus, OH	1,773,443	1,692,240	14.5	21,609	742,396	38,322,070	.6732	25,051,562	**7,369**	3,232,799	**6,863**	1,171,093	**6,563**	3,033,710	997,326	1,326,287
096	Cookeville, TN	143,007	138,089	17.4	14,489	59,123	2,071,970	.0397	1,376,877	**406**	240,112	**509**	52,082	**293**	209,021	65,311	111,777
097	Coos Bay-North Bend, OR	85,175	83,916	5.4	16,022	37,068	1,364,640	.0248	816,047	**240**	181,621	**385**	16,466	**92**	147,073	39,617	65,822
098	Corbin, KY	149,993	144,931	13.1	11,029	58,967	1,654,230	.0366	1,370,326	**402**	316,489	**672**	46,152	**259**	141,767	76,637	96,570
099	Corpus Christi, TX	552,441	548,161	9.6	14,713	197,552	8,127,960	.1552	5,361,961	**1,577**	843,560	**1,791**	235,326	**1,319**	955,161	204,225	321,030
100	Cumberland, MD	163,633	163,356	4.2	15,128	65,590	2,475,480	.0453	1,439,207	**423**	246,535	**523**	46,019	**258**	234,968	119,321	116,062
101	Dallas-Fort Worth, TX	6,156,363	5,571,828	28.7	21,123	2,302,252	130,038,990	2.2360	78,450,987	**23,076**	10,614,640	**22,534**	3,914,905	**21,941**	10,605,174	3,148,201	4,104,452
102	Dalton, GA	129,405	120,031	21.7	17,187	48,839	2,224,020	.0435	1,755,183	**516**	226,995	**482**	61,298	**343**	254,638	64,871	90,835
103	Danville, IL	108,946	110,292	-3.5	16,574	43,686	1,805,690	.0322	1,044,499	**307**	171,921	**365**	23,885	**134**	172,413	68,392	75,948
104	Danville, VA	168,234	171,012	7.9	15,298	70,137	2,573,630	.0472	1,511,488	**445**	267,153	**567**	42,273	**237**	284,660	84,608	128,050
105	Davenport, IA-Moline, IL	429,075	429,924	2.4	18,738	171,815	8,040,010	.1468	5,438,870	**1,599**	755,561	**1,604**	200,725	**1,125**	690,276	337,315	310,141
106	Dayton-Springfield, OH	1,217,191	1,219,933	1.0	20,062	504,176	24,419,660	.4152	13,717,269	**4,035**	2,229,050	**4,732**	509,455	**2,855**	1,932,969	736,825	908,664
107	Daytona Beach, FL	542,645	493,175	23.5	20,372	245,026	11,054,840	.1836	5,769,501	**1,698**	770,128	**1,635**	219,433	**1,230**	968,057	386,603	398,756
108	Decatur, AL	147,582	145,867	10.9	18,193	60,090	2,684,900	.0479	1,655,638	**487**	238,893	**507**	65,839	**369**	168,352	86,024	116,816
109	Decatur-Effingham, IL	243,058	248,778	0.5	17,357	97,750	4,218,820	.0807	3,138,799	**924**	453,238	**962**	89,945	**506**	405,631	170,900	175,882
110	Denver, CO	2,892,052	2,712,488	30.8	23,125	1,140,561	66,878,970	1.1100	37,930,413	**11,158**	4,982,800	**10,577**	1,800,381	**10,091**	5,609,241	1,341,639	2,128,039
111	Des Moines, IA	834,716	804,543	10.4	19,144	331,872	15,979,980	.2801	9,659,723	**2,840**	1,289,857	**2,738**	301,009	**1,687**	1,376,367	456,004	630,459
112	Detroit, MI	5,032,403	4,965,944	5.5	22,177	1,984,462	111,604,370	1.9122	68,527,198	**20,159**	10,862,822	**23,060**	3,066,495	**17,184**	8,147,450	4,650,610	3,444,756
113	Dickinson, ND	34,379	35,772	-5.9	15,042	14,093	517,140	.0110	476,414	**141**	52,537	**112**	10,293	**58**	56,739	24,629	28,486
114	Dodge City, KS	43,754	42,837	14.4	14,402	14,602	630,140	.0130	514,681	**151**	83,404	**177**	12,817	**71**	55,052	12,131	27,841
115	Dothan-Enterprise, AL	228,431	223,605	6.4	16,412	93,528	3,749,100	.0719	2,707,659	**797**	512,640	**1,088**	101,868	**570**	268,691	109,450	169,185
116	Dover, DE	339,569	313,107	24.6	18,138	133,285	6,159,110	.1138	4,236,754	**1,247**	588,365	**1,249**	265,768	**1,489**	560,865	212,490	239,269
117	Du Bois-Clearfield, PA	128,651	129,314	4.1	15,059	51,879	1,937,380	.0368	1,280,788	**377**	161,393	**343**	37,330	**209**	202,664	71,038	89,625
118	Dubuque, IA	180,625	179,707	1.8	17,097	70,986	3,088,170	.0575	2,101,266	**617**	282,543	**600**	48,136	**269**	277,952	99,688	132,801
119	Duluth, MN	414,689	413,956	3.3	17,151	173,718	7,112,290	.1292	4,478,209	**1,317**	731,910	**1,553**	96,754	**541**	671,136	205,159	309,514
120	Dyersburg-Union City, TN	118,887	120,330	5.6	15,144	47,629	1,800,430	.0342	1,188,824	**350**	287,889	**611**	62,813	**353**	138,217	59,782	82,481
121	Eagle Pass-Del Rio, TX	123,461	117,380	16.4	9,238	37,821	1,140,510	.0262	899,141	**265**	176,248	**374**	80,825	**453**	223,584	19,107	60,068
122	East Liverpool-Salem, OH	111,328	112,075	3.5	15,685	43,451	1,746,210	.0314	992,742	**292**	98,533	**209**	20,824	**117**	173,190	73,404	80,842
123	Eau Claire, WI	200,687	195,408	8.2	17,284	79,379	3,468,690	.0721	3,231,128	**951**	639,348	**1,357**	106,712	**597**	347,818	147,416	154,484
124	El Centro-Calexico, CA	151,466	142,361	30.2	10,979	41,707	1,662,980	.0370	1,392,918	**410**	261,116	**554**	82,208	**461**	254,019	62,708	71,483
125	El Dorado-Magnolia-Camden, AR	102,399	105,766	-2.8	14,305	41,293	1,464,860	.0282	971,538	**287**	242,209	**514**	45,521	**254**	124,018	50,365	68,006
126	Elkhart, IN	278,381	268,804	14.3	17,786	101,336	4,951,240	.0895	3,141,973	**925**	450,160	**955**	40,666	**229**	356,524	153,574	183,697
127	Elmira-Corning-Hornell, NY	313,021	313,154	-0.6	17,230	124,648	5,393,280	.0947	3,031,401	**891**	408,686	**869**	96,952	**543**	538,954	175,214	208,609
128	El Paso, TX	781,579	748,239	15.1	12,188	251,738	9,525,770	.1965	6,901,539	**2,030**	1,423,356	**3,021**	443,103	**2,483**	890,856	326,354	430,825
129	Emporia, KS	47,674	47,830	3.6	15,267	18,690	727,830	.0135	448,305	**133**	70,839	**151**	19,920	**112**	68,738	18,460	35,788
130	Enid, OK	83,622	85,696	-0.4	15,737	33,930	1,315,930	.0244	816,032	**241**	186,274	**395**	18,777	**105**	124,202	37,360	62,536
131	Erie, PA	279,718	280,843	1.9	17,187	111,157	4,807,540	.0901	3,333,544	**981**	445,349	**945**	129,279	**725**	546,498	194,903	176,959
132	Escanaba, MI	46,959	47,423	2.9	16,868	19,799	792,120	.0140	450,857	**133**	53,637	**114**	16,216	**91**	70,260	25,263	35,261
133	Eugene-Springfield, OR	332,896	322,959	14.2	17,777	136,131	5,917,890	.1118	4,302,190	**1,266**	807,668	**1,715**	128,392	**720**	679,603	134,140	246,882
134	Eureka, CA	156,509	154,025	8.0	15,456	62,322	2,419,030	.0442	1,427,490	**419**	158,416	**336**	48,961	**275**	323,699	113,782	105,712
135	Evansville, IN	525,981	523,510	3.7	17,759	215,342	9,341,080	.1746	6,581,736	**1,937**	1,034,540	**2,194**	245,985	**1,378**	782,288	329,257	394,526
136	Fairbanks, AK	100,893	97,458	5.8	19,356	36,802	1,952,890	.0344	1,219,624	**358**	305,039	**648**	34,701	**194**	110,354	13,470	65,702
137	Fairmont, WV	56,470	56,598	-1.1	15,391	24,156	869,130	.0158	505,817	**149**	111,506	**237**	8,265	**46**	80,110	34,573	39,369
138	Fargo, ND	319,223	316,537	6.2	17,250	131,329	5,506,470	.1093	4,513,206	**1,328**	572,521	**1,214**	122,194	**685**	467,618	216,229	250,222
139	Farmington, NM-Durango, CO	224,237	208,285	28.0	15,127	81,202	3,391,950	.0656	2,387,239	**704**	431,918	**917**	65,978	**369**	329,671	68,611	155,943
140	Fayetteville-Springdale-Rogers, AR	365,442	325,364	46.2	16,998	139,557	6,211,650	.1149	4,113,058	**1,211**	1,301,371	**2,762**	117,847	**660**	354,245	121,114	253,916
141	Fayetteville-Lumberton, NC	681,569	663,154	16.1	15,844	261,501	10,798,520	.1992	6,733,933	**1,982**	1,128,656	**2,397**	302,595	**1,696**	943,411	372,126	461,339
142	Fergus Falls, MN	134,799	131,271	9.2	16,361	54,515	2,205,400	.0411	1,465,370	**432**	233,881	**497**	24,518	**138**	211,575	57,623	103,197
143	Findlay-Tiffin, OH	153,971	152,886	3.6	18,728	60,838	2,883,620	.0511	1,777,870	**524**	299,534	**636**	45,635	**255**	204,231	88,786	115,501
144	Flagstaff, AZ	122,854	116,320	20.4	16,664	44,020	2,047,190	.0374	1,282,069	**377**	284,754	**604**	31,842	**178**	226,079	29,172	80,390
145	Flint, MI	516,834	507,828	1.5	19,398	209,029	10,025,790	.1759	6,115,058	**1,799**	1,215,355	**2,580**	192,285	**1,078**	698,374	403,337	370,662
146	Florence, AL	188,646	191,015	10.4	16,002	77,572	3,018,660	.0554	1,878,223	**553**	413,560	**878**	75,236	**422**	233,468	91,199	148,598
147	Florence, SC	263,425	259,343	8.4	14,891	102,154	3,922,580	.0769	2,848,491	**838**	430,532	**915**	126,230	**708**	433,776	180,523	168,160
148	Fond du Lac, WI	97,983	97,296	8.0	19,536	38,650	1,914,180	.0329	1,099,443	**323**	211,554	**449**	23,267	**130**	159,938	50,532	71,829
149	Fort Collins-Loveland, CO	271,165	251,494	35.1	21,864	107,740	5,928,820	.1012	3,560,752	**1,047**	603,249	**1,281**	139,359	**781**	480,045	104,785	220,754
150	Fort Dodge, IA	123,676	128,475	-2.5	16,551	50,503	2,046,950	.0369	1,214,561	**357**	168,522	**358**	20,178	**113**	183,851	53,113	97,560
151	Fort Myers, FL	714,104	629,301	31.3	20,995	306,971	14,992,860	.2572	8,946,143	**2,632**	1,403,676	**2,981**	530,961	**2,976**	1,316,658	547,351	484,634
152	Fort Pierce-Vero Beach-Stuart, FL	480,733	432,373	26.7	22,090	216,618	10,619,410	.1748	5,695,561	**1,676**	752,563	**1,597**	295,497	**1,655**	914,661	444,274	345,548
153	Fort Smith, AR	335,801	326,881	15.8	14,487	129,877	4,864,720	.0946	3,350,894	**985**	923,271	**1,961**	80,302	**450**	415,379	143,388	228,631
154	Fort Walton Beach, FL	228,712	211,099	23.1	21,930	101,254	5,015,660	.0858	3,046,205	**896**	529,447	**1,124**	208,421	**1,168**	381,635	147,129	182,590
155	Fort Wayne, IN	730,858	715,480	10.6	18,871	284,558	13,792,170	.2455	8,689,194	**2,556**	1,455,977	**3,090**	307,692	**1,723**	1,034,614	434,501	530,535
156	Fredericksburg, VA	192,972	165,316	32.6	20,419	71,749	3,940,200	.0694	2,507,640	**738**	510,244	**1,083**	78,847	**442**	301,003	107,905	146,845
157	Fresno, CA	1,003,162	922,516	22.1	13,501	309,778	13,543,840	.2538	7,751,818	**2,280**	1,028,372	**2,183**	312,576	**1,752**	1,425,308	478,421	522,409
158	Gadsden, AL	194,570	191,899	10.3	15,370	78,835	2,990,510	.0537	1,647,168	**484**	348,251	**740**	58,442	**328**	294,948	98,945	149,965
159	Gainesville, FL	333,586	320,199	22.9	15,310	130,226	5,107,190	.0954	3,225,709	**948**	478,546	**1,017**	140,952	**791**	594,270	143,069	225,911
160	Gainesville, GA	283,099	246,560	44.7	18,244	105,503	5,164,900	.0897	2,917,063	**858**	484,093	**1,028**	166,136	**931**	340,285	139,808	210,636
161	Galesburg, IL	72,176	74,571	-1.3	16,724	28,609	1,207,080	.0220	749,939	**220**	154,544	**328**	14,195	**80**	110,713	41,051	49,920
162	Gallup, NM	139,571	144,221	17.9	8,912	41,432	1,243,850	.0282	897,122	**264**	152,517	**323**	51,892	**291**	152,016	23,106	63,531
163	Garden City, KS	70,712	73,686	13.3	15,008	24,382	1,061,260	.0206	759,097	**223**	114,341	**242**	29,520	**165**	113,414	19,597	46,981
164	Glens Falls, NY	127,334	124,345	4.9	19,244	50,896	2,450,470	.0416	1,332,449	**392**	120,576	**256**	99,993	**560**	213,546	82,321	85,248
165	Goldsboro-Kinston, NC	243,413	241,014	10.9	15,144	95,835	3,686,180	.0700	2,440,486	**717**	374,885	**796**	97,176	**544**	372,061	132,367	169,232
166	Grand Forks, ND	196,882	203,087	-5.1	16,100	78,867	3,169,890	.0632	2,548,246	**750**	369,795	**783**	61,831	**347**	304,462	103,187	147,076
167	Grand Island-Kearney, NE	150,796	149,977	6.0	15,737	58,459	2,373,130	.0476	1,920,449	**566**	399,120	**848**	65,394	**367**	169,236	73,909	118,611
168	Grand Junction, CO	268,700	246,119	31.6	17,382	106,190	4,670,490	.0874	3,253,184	**957**	534,540	**1,134**	66,526	**372**	506,947	98,452	208,974
169	Grand Rapids, MI	1,126,690	1,079,340	17.8	19,249	421,404	21,687,850	.3879	14,013,475	**4,122**	2,786,720	**5,915**	477,916	**2,678**	1,372,839	612,334	782,153
170	Great Bend, KS	37,288	38,989	-4.4	15,016	15,124	559,920	.0109	401,425	**119**	63,093	**134**	8,648	**49**	71,675	22,287	28,758
171	Great Falls, MT	160,724	164,305	2.0	14,727	63,507	2,367,040	.0460	1,633,161	**480**	266,787	**567**	40,444	**227**	242,060	63,356	121,921
172	Greeley, CO	220,667	180,936	37.3	16,913	76,443	3,732,100	.0638	1,875,716	**552**	261,111	**554**	24,309	**136**	242,183	53,013	157,962
173	Green Bay, WI	368,215	355,786	14.6	19,375	148,055	7,134,030	.1269	4,540,813	**1,335**	950,926	**2,019**	115,054	**644**	549,514	133,413	273,206
174	Greensboro--Winston-Salem--High Point, NC	1,509,499	1,454,066	17.1	19,026	621,408	28,719,830	.5205	19,190,058	**5,643**	2,477,105	**5,260**	854,771	**4,792**	2,496,824	1,151,380	1,154,018
175	Greenville-Greenwood, MS	199,191	209,666	-2.0	10,545	68,681	2,100,480	.0483	1,869,542	**551**	343,880	**730**	78,588	**440**	235,216	93,473	100,625
176	Greenville-Washington, NC	253,130	247,820	13.2	15,192	102,928	3,845,630	.0773	3,026,250	**890**	343,576	**728**	146,350	**821**	457,363	158,960	173,862
177	Greenville-Spartanburg, SC	949,306	914,473	16.0	18,133	377,675	17,213,430	.3136	11,349,191	**3,338**	1,557,403	**3,306**	554,671	**3,109**	1,534,130	663,225	675,654
178	Greenwood, SC	78,208	76,229	11.4	16,209	31,003	1,267,680	.0230	767,845	**226**	145,737	**309**	40,233	**226**	125,461	43,444	52,641
179	Hagerstown, MD-Chambersburg, PA-Martinsburg, WV	391,227	366,345	11.8	18,664	153,926	7,302,050	.1250	3,988,431	**1,174**	571,080	**1,212**	136,769	**767**	639,514	221,737	282,751
180	Hammond, LA	114,752	111,113	16.2	13,478	42,709	1,546,610	.0315	1,171,370	**344**	206,181	**438**	34,201	**192**	147,681	57,391	68,914
181	Harrisburg, PA	712,963	698,708	6.7	19,949	289,380	14,222,830	.2556	9,523,790	**2,802**	981,077	**2,083**	325,648	**1,825**	1,380,790	503,993	501,321
182	Harrison, AR	94,344	92,314	24.0	14,053	39,168	1,325,830	.0257	881,506	**260**	245,102	**521**	20,785	**117**	99,365	32,315	71,266
183	Harrisonburg, VA	155,935	152,235	18.1	15,598	59,158	2,432,200	.0472	1,758,999	**517**	250,658	**531**	49,042	**275**	265,741	97,180	118,909
184	Hartford, CT	1,186,956	1,148,618	2.2	26,395	467,168	31,330,290	.4795	14,476,166	**4,258**	1,272,994	**2,702**	1,069,247	**5,993**	2,502,419	1,079,752	799,511
185	Hastings, NE	71,790	73,440	0.8	16,165	28,706	1,160,470	.0210	682,379	**200**	69,896	**148**	10,974	**62**	134,768	38,093	58,713
186	Hattiesburg, MS	188,539	182,113	12.5	13,818	71,307	2,605,270	.0536	2,058,459	**606**	557,996	**1,185**	73,076	**410**	187,139	135,983	125,875
187	Hays, KS	57,485	60,018	-1.5	15,851	23,993	911,190	.0185	777,850	**229**	101,614	**216**	32,985	**185**	124,135	27,302	48,077
188	Helena, MT	72,640	70,150	19.4	18,289	29,801	1,328,480	.0234	792,674	**233**	128,824	**273**	11,674	**65**	139,793	22,472	59,799
189	Hickory-Lenoir-Morganton, NC	352,521	341,851	16.9	18,165	142,926	6,403,660	.1160	4,138,266	**1,217**	589,803	**1,251**	146,720	**822**	530,183	248,052	277,715
190	Hilo, HI	161,480	148,677	23.6	17,181	58,557	2,774,430	.0493	1,616,503	**476**	330,370	**701**	95,334	**534**	384,822	103,208	101,893
191	Hobbs, NM	55,610	55,511	-0.5	13,200	20,136	734,040	.0144	481,606	**142**	87,874	**187**	16,851	**94**	63,323	23,656	35,788
192	Honolulu, HI	911,719	876,156	4.8	19,820	301,773	18,070,470	.3029	9,586,291	**2,820**	1,932,186	**4,102**	1,213,597	**6,801**	1,460,075	815,873	491,636
193	Hot Springs, AR	143,011	138,969	18.3	16,394	62,420	2,344,520	.0439	1,560,736	**460**	370,710	**787**	42,865	**240**	173,665	73,781	105,285
194	Houghton, MI	47,327	47,063	4.4	13,573	18,462	642,350	.0127	444,833	**130**	75,535	**160**	16,681	**93**	87,025	17,445	31,507
195	Houma-Thibodaux, LA	273,625	271,365	2.9	15,004	99,220	4,105,600	.0806	3,003,018	**884**	629,510	**1,337**	92,224	**518**	510,851	167,558	159,825
196	Houston, TX	5,527,291	5,045,022	24.4	19,254	2,018,784	106,424,210	1.8549	63,270,120	**18,612**	9,717,042	**20,627**	3,469,339	**19,443**	9,702,626	2,939,697	3,476,024
197	Huntington, WV-Ashland, KY	367,619	368,924	1.4	14,906	154,137	5,479,750	.1043	3,618,951	**1,064**	666,202	**1,414**	164,722	**923**	472,203	350,671	257,156
198	Huntsville, AL	532,485	509,873	15.9	19,746	218,183	10,514,400	.1843	6,472,653	**1,904**	1,231,197	**2,613**	327,283	**1,833**	841,017	263,926	422,400
199	Huron, SD	51,559	53,386	0.4	16,506	21,235	851,010	.0182	829,137	**244**	72,671	**155**	24,770	**138**	39,813	21,937	41,219
200	Hutchinson, KS	125,265	128,235	2.5	16,288	49,481	2,040,310	.0368	1,208,292	**355**	182,852	**388**	30,347	**171**	158,687	44,836	94,680
201	Hyannis, MA	258,516	246,737	20.8	23,797	111,295	6,151,920	.1059	3,971,395	**1,168**	182,662	**388**	285,994	**1,603**	952,661	265,812	190,613
202	Idaho Falls, ID	236,647	223,017	17.2	15,725	81,280	3,721,200	.0711	2,576,012	**758**	439,631	**934**	78,903	**443**	398,161	78,981	171,234
203	Indiana, PA	88,892	89,605	-0.4	14,140	34,895	1,256,920	.0250	918,658	**270**	153,968	**327**	25,096	**141**	145,092	47,127	60,915
204	Indianapolis, IN	1,644,237	1,552,963	17.5	21,113	664,013	34,714,280	.6160	23,108,093	**6,797**	3,909,709	**8,300**	878,000	**4,920**	2,231,839	1,479,415	1,201,167
205	Iowa City, IA	138,449	131,676	13.8	18,369	55,900	2,543,120	.0469	1,756,834	**517**	239,718	**509**	59,232	**332**	301,270	83,903	103,332
206	Iron Mountain, MI	44,844	45,698	2.5	16,396	19,301	735,280	.0137	494,588	**145**	78,127	**166**	13,474	**76**	83,516	27,944	33,530
207	Ironwood, MI	31,511	32,049	-3.1	14,457	13,792	455,570	.0089	314,381	**92**	39,900	**84**	9,663	**54**	55,282	11,352	22,658
208	Ithaca, NY	102,983	96,501	2.6	18,179	39,852	1,872,090	.0299	758,836	**223**	72,786	**155**	32,607	**183**	186,312	57,099	62,802
209	Jackson, MI	210,926	204,949	6.1	18,166	79,204	3,831,580	.0664	2,146,069	**631**	545,151	**1,158**	51,820	**290**	235,772	102,763	145,477
210	Jackson, MS	693,182	677,489	10.1	15,767	258,242	10,929,470	.2103	7,767,033	**2,284**	1,526,805	**3,240**	302,032	**1,692**	872,873	457,198	446,839
211	Jackson, TN	290,683	287,020	12.4	16,079	118,057	4,673,890	.0864	2,985,019	**878**	583,166	**1,238**	127,250	**715**	336,393	171,780	212,113
212	Jacksonville, FL	1,477,907	1,358,825	21.9	20,360	590,003	30,090,350	.5150	17,462,760	**5,135**	2,352,598	**4,993**	773,905	**4,336**	2,483,786	878,308	1,004,433
213	Jacksonville, IL	69,868	70,609	-0.3	16,386	27,334	1,144,870	.0198	578,877	**170**	84,869	**180**	16,727	**94**	96,888	39,325	49,463
214	Jacksonville, NC	146,634	150,355	0.3	14,600	53,106	2,140,860	.0420	1,534,013	**451**	261,489	**555**	47,943	**269**	197,933	55,794	95,880
215	Jamestown, NY-Warren, PA-Dunkirk, NY	179,504	183,613	-1.8	16,822	71,799	3,019,650	.0561	2,010,497	**591**	259,608	**551**	51,435	**288**	299,394	102,372	114,134

Continued on next page

Source: Devonshire Associates Ltd. and Scan/US, Inc. 2004.
. . . Represents a change of less than 0.1%

Basic Trading Areas: Population / Income / Sales, *Continued*

BTA NO.	BASIC TRADING AREA	POPULATION Estimate 7/1/04	POPULATION Census 4/1/00	% Change 4/1/90-4/1/00	PER CAPITA INCOME 2003	HOUSE-HOLDS Estimate 7/1/04	DISPOSABLE INCOME 2003 ($1,000)	MARKET ABILITY INDEX 2003	TOTAL RETAIL SALES 2003 Sales ($1,000)	TOTAL RETAIL SALES Ranally Sales Units	GENERAL MERCHANDISE 2003 Sales ($1,000)	GENERAL MERCHANDISE Ranally Sales Units	APPAREL STORE 2003 Sales ($1,000)	APPAREL STORE Ranally Sales Units	FOOD STORE SALES 2003 ($1,000)	HEALTH & DRUG STORE 2003 ($1,000)	PASSENGER CAR REGIS-TRATIONS 2003
216	Janesville-Beloit, WI	253,823	246,066	14.7	19,539	99,347	4,959,420	.0860	2,933,824	863	502,139	1,066	49,123	275	422,882	141,347	185,684
217	Jefferson City, MO	168,058	163,616	15.7	17,903	65,095	3,008,750	.0557	2,053,421	604	324,748	689	29,209	163	265,727	80,390	122,874
218	Johnstown, PA	227,679	232,621	-3.6	14,546	91,625	3,311,910	.0627	2,109,312	620	236,822	503	58,434	327	346,047	152,151	151,798
219	Jonesboro-Paragould, AR	184,989	181,062	13.6	14,844	74,284	2,746,010	.0539	1,985,279	584	535,336	1,136	90,785	510	190,526	84,237	127,911
220	Joplin, MO-Miami, OK	253,010	247,343	15.0	14,418	98,747	3,647,880	.0699	2,394,194	704	490,651	1,041	50,983	285	286,682	108,432	178,647
221	Juneau-Ketchikan, AK	71,193	73,082	5.9	23,173	27,527	1,649,760	.0261	780,293	231	140,984	299	55,025	307	200,360	21,587	42,995
222	Kahului-Wailuku-Lahaina, HI	138,013	128,241	27.6	19,522	47,444	2,694,250	.0492	1,874,641	551	302,956	643	202,723	1,136	403,376	141,222	85,229
223	Kalamazoo, MI	384,987	377,288	7.1	18,746	152,916	7,216,920	.1276	4,423,495	1,301	1,145,091	2,431	141,253	791	489,109	215,438	281,114
224	Kalispell, MT	81,063	74,471	25.8	16,408	32,674	1,330,090	.0258	998,648	294	208,225	442	19,172	107	142,619	23,731	65,277
225	Kankakee, IL	136,680	135,167	6.4	17,897	51,369	2,446,150	.0431	1,433,670	422	275,012	584	44,420	249	158,211	102,364	90,587
226	Kansas City, MO	2,139,575	2,049,447	11.4	20,728	857,635	44,349,750	.7643	26,644,105	7,838	4,013,128	8,520	984,551	5,519	3,314,780	1,379,502	1,542,694
227	Keene, NH	121,070	118,041	5.7	18,957	48,852	2,295,150	.0458	2,002,384	589	168,705	358	46,028	258	332,935	83,601	88,429
228	Kennewick-Pasco-Richland, WA	215,499	191,822	27.9	17,905	75,145	3,858,460	.0698	2,458,913	723	502,225	1,066	66,090	370	431,707	99,354	152,681
229	Kingsport, TN-Johnson City, TN-Bristol, VA-TN	716,844	707,899	8.5	15,657	307,808	11,223,430	.2131	7,616,705	2,240	1,356,328	2,878	282,585	1,584	1,102,098	480,687	565,499
230	Kirksville, MO	56,626	57,351	3.2	13,671	23,270	774,140	.0145	467,265	138	68,704	147	12,015	67	73,702	29,243	42,518
231	Klamath Falls, OR	81,917	80,646	8.2	14,770	32,964	1,209,900	.0230	791,497	234	149,134	316	13,959	79	154,871	28,118	61,977
232	Knoxville, TN	1,167,564	1,118,107	17.9	17,429	489,264	20,349,790	.3939	15,706,092	4,621	2,630,959	5,583	784,823	4,399	1,947,312	807,640	909,179
233	Kokomo-Logansport, IN	191,496	192,308	4.0	19,061	77,772	3,650,140	.0637	2,168,506	638	397,947	844	57,250	321	235,775	158,720	143,056
234	La Crosse, WI-Winona, MN	324,481	320,367	8.3	16,779	127,944	5,444,420	.0995	3,438,749	1,012	542,700	1,153	62,294	348	465,734	99,907	237,532
235	Lafayette, IN	283,089	275,303	11.2	17,163	107,957	4,858,630	.0886	3,085,120	907	606,198	1,288	95,113	532	321,762	160,881	199,824
236	Lafayette-New Iberia, LA	558,492	548,154	10.4	14,464	212,248	8,077,810	.1632	6,281,626	1,848	1,156,358	2,454	245,933	1,379	827,463	409,212	337,014
237	La Grange, GA	71,816	69,791	8.8	16,189	27,981	1,162,640	.0220	799,746	235	108,781	231	38,708	217	135,911	33,028	48,328
238	Lake Charles, LA	283,526	283,429	9.3	16,180	110,177	4,587,470	.0856	3,018,062	887	732,494	1,554	106,662	597	378,397	151,468	181,933
239	Lakeland-Winter Haven, FL	518,809	483,924	19.4	19,073	217,966	9,895,440	.1713	5,716,090	1,681	873,686	1,855	196,846	1,103	977,731	287,481	353,833
240	Lancaster, PA	486,469	470,658	11.3	19,463	180,573	9,468,350	.1739	6,676,478	1,964	579,937	1,231	367,776	2,061	1,109,981	332,301	314,284
241	Lansing, MI	522,508	509,246	4.0	19,589	204,523	10,235,420	.1782	6,133,994	1,804	1,375,708	2,920	209,162	1,172	751,123	322,061	376,098
242	Laredo, TX	243,808	216,446	41.6	9,376	66,646	2,285,920	.0584	2,492,899	733	477,060	1,014	297,757	1,669	395,744	99,204	107,329
243	La Salle-Peru-Ottawa-Streator, IL	153,473	153,098	3.2	18,749	60,781	2,877,480	.0536	2,074,094	610	330,799	703	59,558	334	288,091	112,541	109,416
244	Las Cruces, NM	258,140	249,902	26.7	12,517	93,440	3,231,230	.0629	1,967,819	579	352,930	750	51,199	287	277,189	83,278	170,241
245	Las Vegas, NV	1,855,794	1,568,418	82.8	19,143	709,420	35,525,460	.6190	21,026,297	6,185	2,863,733	6,079	1,271,752	7,127	3,309,723	899,216	1,169,992
246	Laurel, MS	83,562	83,107	5.0	13,217	31,657	1,104,480	.0213	685,204	202	144,254	306	23,708	132	78,027	44,967	56,128
247	Lawrence, KS	103,909	99,962	22.2	16,965	40,944	1,762,840	.0319	1,084,623	319	155,726	331	56,394	316	198,476	47,982	76,691
248	Lawton-Duncan, OK	177,652	180,897	1.7	14,505	66,335	2,576,790	.0463	1,348,167	397	352,994	750	36,731	205	161,370	67,717	117,657
249	Lebanon-Claremont, NH	185,340	179,619	7.2	19,466	76,287	3,607,900	.0666	2,582,276	760	249,462	529	63,454	355	563,265	102,855	135,224
250	Lewiston-Moscow, ID	123,353	123,481	12.2	15,667	49,173	1,932,580	.0359	1,228,196	362	248,250	527	24,020	134	269,267	58,503	96,967
251	Lewiston-Auburn, ME	226,290	221,126	-0.3	16,888	94,965	3,821,650	.0755	3,062,685	901	307,281	652	37,345	208	574,873	141,180	161,470
252	Lexington, KY	960,178	927,633	13.7	17,333	398,348	16,642,300	.2971	9,962,139	2,930	1,594,773	3,384	452,414	2,538	1,241,949	652,134	693,520
253	Liberal, KS	61,937	62,064	15.0	14,792	21,311	916,200	.0172	569,069	168	100,967	213	28,500	160	90,668	20,554	40,197
254	Lihue, HI	61,484	58,463	14.2	18,874	21,950	1,160,430	.0210	768,146	226	142,289	302	55,045	308	192,388	54,416	40,058
255	Lima, OH	250,324	251,414	0.7	17,731	96,788	4,438,560	.0796	2,752,813	810	504,007	1,070	77,256	434	319,615	185,784	183,613
256	Lincoln, NE	360,221	346,818	12.1	18,443	145,390	6,643,610	.1183	4,121,746	1,211	655,080	1,391	125,352	702	616,415	264,956	271,246
257	Little Rock, AR	988,281	963,155	13.0	17,548	406,536	17,341,900	.3258	12,326,012	3,625	2,660,376	5,645	407,840	2,286	1,189,148	444,150	697,935
258	Logan, UT	109,025	102,720	29.3	13,470	32,976	1,468,530	.0293	1,047,968	308	191,711	407	30,325	170	166,101	28,536	72,690
259	Logan, WV	36,468	37,710	-12.4	12,892	15,041	470,150	.0106	464,256	137	67,777	144	13,229	74	73,592	50,827	22,638
260	Longview-Marshall, TX	321,071	314,446	7.4	15,763	124,297	5,060,890	.0961	3,459,644	1,016	567,687	1,205	109,326	612	506,929	164,690	216,480
261	Longview, WA	99,569	96,772	13.3	17,823	38,545	1,774,600	.0310	1,010,378	298	215,269	457	17,384	97	192,428	39,572	75,201
262	Los Angeles, CA	17,556,372	16,391,590	12.7	18,227	5,700,623	319,999,850	5.4914	173,252,845	50,964	20,131,165	42,734	13,331,957	74,717	28,922,480	9,378,090	9,971,564
263	Louisville, KY	1,530,990	1,486,048	9.8	19,305	635,402	29,556,060	.5023	16,136,864	4,746	2,717,724	5,770	617,052	3,458	1,839,740	997,459	1,116,008
264	Lubbock, TX	415,551	409,227	4.2	14,240	154,375	5,917,550	.1210	4,695,841	1,381	676,053	1,433	195,305	1,094	711,279	149,219	264,552
265	Lufkin-Nacogdoches, TX	164,026	162,058	12.5	14,284	61,998	2,342,890	.0466	1,719,168	506	304,476	647	72,251	405	298,395	60,361	105,459
266	Lynchburg, VA	162,053	161,946	4.8	16,533	65,908	2,679,190	.0533	2,165,704	636	321,085	682	67,603	378	289,960	154,919	118,901
267	McAlester, OK	54,776	54,645	7.3	13,186	21,337	722,300	.0142	481,324	142	141,333	300	14,895	83	38,120	18,521	36,529
268	McAllen, TX	715,030	623,060	46.9	8,416	198,627	6,017,530	.1516	5,759,701	1,694	1,119,781	2,378	433,102	2,427	918,124	238,691	316,493
269	McComb-Brookhaven, MS	115,003	114,119	6.4	12,676	44,857	1,457,770	.0304	1,128,770	333	249,254	528	48,209	271	112,072	60,410	78,377
270	McCook, NE	32,755	33,749	-7.8	15,104	13,844	494,720	.0100	408,845	119	55,968	119	7,351	42	54,282	17,995	28,440
271	Macon-Warner Robins, GA	685,839	662,942	12.5	15,570	259,470	10,678,400	.1985	6,767,227	1,992	1,075,470	2,284	283,909	1,593	1,084,097	344,698	456,650
272	Madison, WI	717,335	682,098	15.0	20,701	296,780	14,849,890	.2767	11,268,073	3,315	1,357,728	2,881	294,782	1,652	1,216,541	426,400	534,603
273	Madisonville, KY	46,961	46,519	0.9	15,478	19,422	726,850	.0136	461,681	136	99,767	212	27,544	154	57,417	38,572	33,612
274	Manchester-Nashua-Concord, NH	653,188	617,057	14.1	21,879	254,597	14,291,390	.2719	11,771,266	3,462	1,590,126	3,376	493,884	2,768	1,799,143	411,077	466,596
275	Manhattan-Junction City, KS	115,275	117,821	-4.1	15,042	45,517	1,734,000	.0327	1,114,109	328	193,217	409	42,055	236	177,682	31,441	88,178
276	Manitowoc, WI	81,775	82,887	3.1	19,213	33,021	1,571,170	.0255	714,591	210	146,084	310	11,334	64	125,916	17,862	60,246
277	Mankato-Fairmont, MN	251,997	250,632	2.2	17,729	99,299	4,467,670	.0782	2,533,020	744	357,535	759	62,389	350	432,165	114,512	189,345
278	Mansfield, OH	228,057	228,341	3.1	17,388	90,046	3,965,520	.0713	2,437,932	717	463,365	983	67,537	378	305,164	159,577	167,231
279	Marinette, WI-Menominee, MI	68,182	68,710	5.0	16,372	28,676	1,116,270	.0194	579,277	171	129,601	275	15,006	84	97,384	27,718	51,911
280	Marion, IN	105,142	108,363	-0.8	16,618	41,062	1,747,290	.0315	1,050,723	309	135,134	287	38,593	216	123,029	68,684	74,965
281	Marion, OH	100,636	97,845	6.3	17,181	37,767	1,729,070	.0295	878,941	259	188,046	399	22,112	124	131,844	48,410	71,465
282	Marquette, MI	74,359	74,496	-6.7	17,004	30,647	1,264,400	.0229	779,214	229	156,994	333	23,600	133	109,368	43,665	55,541
283	Marshalltown, IA	56,833	57,414	3.1	16,918	22,144	961,510	.0169	527,776	156	81,224	173	22,996	129	88,649	31,039	43,209
284	Martinsville, VA	90,957	92,753	2.4	15,081	38,809	1,371,730	.0253	823,281	242	171,959	366	34,496	193	130,802	55,582	71,516
285	Mason City, IA	113,873	116,657	-1.8	17,298	47,676	1,969,730	.0365	1,317,242	388	217,333	462	23,368	130	189,783	37,669	92,091
286	Mattoon, IL	62,494	64,449	3.4	15,904	25,364	993,910	.0197	778,082	229	201,720	428	9,506	53	73,869	47,136	44,912
287	Meadville, PA	89,668	90,366	4.9	15,527	34,875	1,392,310	.0252	799,528	235	81,499	173	20,749	116	133,921	49,372	58,613
288	Medford-Grants Pass, OR	272,902	256,995	22.9	16,502	109,551	4,503,330	.0935	4,071,661	1,198	736,441	1,564	99,284	556	468,137	116,965	207,254
289	Melbourne-Titusville, FL	515,004	476,230	19.4	22,229	228,764	11,447,810	.1835	5,603,865	1,648	916,795	1,946	235,423	1,319	919,936	384,085	382,238
290	Memphis, TN	1,592,565	1,553,276	11.2	16,966	608,065	27,019,230	.4953	17,363,186	5,109	3,083,744	6,549	922,087	5,169	1,890,339	1,082,429	1,001,500
291	Merced, CA	256,241	227,684	18.2	13,496	78,086	3,458,170	.0616	1,614,601	475	271,148	576	43,168	242	317,810	90,700	139,900
292	Meridian, MS	207,296	209,027	4.5	13,436	81,019	2,785,230	.0547	1,866,188	550	406,699	864	48,617	274	254,724	112,606	137,905
293	Miami-Fort Lauderdale, FL	4,211,224	3,955,969	21.0	18,781	1,630,601	79,092,790	1.4174	50,631,779	14,893	5,584,256	11,854	3,918,738	21,961	7,110,389	3,772,053	2,506,762
294	Michigan City-La Porte, IN	109,775	110,106	2.8	17,742	41,606	1,947,620	.0356	1,280,452	377	223,881	475	120,176	674	134,138	82,101	74,565
295	Middlesboro-Harlan, KY	117,010	118,401	-2.3	10,996	48,503	1,286,590	.0262	806,556	237	229,205	486	29,307	164	194,493	69,252	78,308
296	Midland, TX	124,215	120,755	8.2	18,126	47,651	2,251,530	.0424	1,644,940	484	285,960	607	75,888	425	187,045	55,674	83,264
297	Milwaukee, WI	1,877,172	1,849,490	5.6	20,829	764,702	39,099,540	.6543	21,347,068	6,279	3,062,927	6,501	681,086	3,817	3,184,592	1,357,590	1,263,093
298	Minneapolis-St. Paul, MN	3,447,778	3,293,598	15.9	22,983	1,370,888	79,241,640	1.3806	52,225,246	15,360	7,235,527	15,362	1,856,738	10,405	6,808,694	2,262,258	2,478,388
299	Minot, ND	113,197	118,459	-3.4	14,663	45,620	1,659,850	.0344	1,416,530	418	155,759	330	27,414	154	170,132	65,734	92,254
300	Missoula, MT	183,588	175,320	25.9	15,685	74,316	2,879,600	.0563	2,138,543	629	391,062	830	46,013	257	333,963	61,367	147,269
301	Mitchell, SD	82,903	84,187	0.1	12,976	31,390	1,075,740	.0252	1,146,939	336	101,410	215	14,201	79	107,038	22,855	62,494
302	Mobile, AL	675,391	663,075	11.6	16,343	262,734	11,037,700	.2007	6,723,070	1,976	1,306,496	2,772	365,433	2,049	948,527	381,232	462,129
303	Modesto, CA	563,828	501,498	19.7	16,171	184,638	9,117,780	.1630	5,178,871	1,523	732,586	1,555	183,349	1,027	1,027,398	348,603	333,036
304	Monroe, LA	327,564	331,088	2.1	14,001	127,795	4,586,290	.0905	3,245,128	953	760,969	1,617	110,238	618	413,876	151,144	201,043
305	Montgomery, AL	488,775	484,647	10.0	16,448	193,208	8,039,270	.1496	5,301,149	1,560	961,543	2,041	226,804	1,270	729,814	311,444	338,579
306	Morgantown, WV	115,017	111,200	6.4	14,763	47,439	1,698,040	.0322	1,099,015	323	215,260	457	63,393	355	125,813	74,893	79,194
307	Mount Pleasant, MI	139,316	136,888	15.5	14,853	52,547	2,069,200	.0388	1,289,964	380	323,655	688	33,340	187	151,072	59,903	97,650
308	Mount Vernon-Centralia, IL	121,174	122,656	2.8	16,183	48,337	1,960,950	.0383	1,472,043	434	239,931	510	35,694	200	146,386	75,223	86,967
309	Muncie, IN	179,280	182,024	-0.2	16,030	72,283	2,873,870	.0531	1,812,105	533	376,426	799	59,118	331	207,936	102,213	134,217
310	Muskegon, MI	231,188	225,347	8.9	16,843	90,297	3,893,980	.0718	2,540,032	748	620,742	1,318	64,427	362	304,652	163,721	165,445
311	Muskogee, OK	168,412	164,258	10.8	12,794	65,059	2,154,600	.0421	1,356,499	398	321,601	682	31,860	178	230,692	65,903	111,990
312	Myrtle Beach, SC	214,999	196,629	36.5	18,682	91,843	4,016,570	.0819	3,690,442	1,086	611,740	1,299	391,423	2,194	536,626	149,542	154,459
313	Naples, FL	297,488	251,377	65.3	24,228	122,501	7,207,470	.1199	4,228,159	1,244	421,375	895	411,527	2,306	713,495	233,244	201,527
314	Nashville, TN	1,855,825	1,761,799	23.3	20,224	752,713	37,532,160	.6635	24,091,600	7,084	4,185,986	8,886	1,111,290	6,227	3,151,934	1,298,312	1,396,968
315	Natchez, MS	70,243	72,775	-0.6	11,863	27,667	833,290	.0176	628,962	185	178,369	379	20,917	117	81,300	28,863	44,221
316	New Bern, NC	176,015	174,134	12.4	18,045	73,678	3,176,240	.0573	2,028,845	598	316,927	673	68,086	382	308,841	87,912	129,107
317	New Castle, PA	93,007	94,643	-1.7	15,756	37,010	1,465,450	.0267	873,282	257	103,569	220	12,674	71	145,503	57,560	62,926
318	New Haven-Waterbury-Meriden, CT	1,037,023	1,006,201	2.9	25,118	406,820	26,048,350	.4121	13,179,211	3,877	1,211,367	2,571	663,622	3,719	2,144,077	959,492	673,484
319	New London-Norwich, CT	379,266	368,179	3.0	24,438	148,251	9,268,520	.1432	4,225,437	1,243	524,673	1,113	179,175	1,004	721,424	290,580	264,044
320	New Orleans, LA	1,434,883	1,430,273	4.6	17,606	580,490	25,262,910	.4538	15,593,332	4,587	2,681,517	5,694	902,258	5,056	2,270,496	1,151,497	868,802
321	New York, NY	20,084,590	19,620,902	8.7	23,099	7,313,968	463,935,600	7.3080	218,537,459	64,286	19,429,157	41,242	22,783,712	127,684	36,087,889	17,382,810	9,172,337
322	Nogales, AZ	40,833	38,381	29.3	11,327	12,760	462,500	.0106	436,479	128	104,751	222	47,253	265	88,596	12,094	22,791
323	Norfolk, NE	109,932	112,342	-0.2	14,584	42,834	1,603,280	.0326	1,266,181	372	160,957	342	27,701	156	156,591	58,096	86,210
324	Norfolk-Virginia Beach-Newport News-Hampton, VA	1,872,308	1,784,356	9.1	18,147	718,110	33,977,620	.5950	19,697,962	5,798	3,098,462	6,578	1,081,303	6,058	2,883,175	928,937	1,262,646
325	North Platte, NE	85,288	86,263	7.5	15,935	33,888	1,359,050	.0258	922,615	269	145,832	310	17,150	96	131,351	47,359	69,806
326	Ocala, FL	286,954	258,916	32.9	17,412	123,754	4,996,440	.0912	3,225,186	949	498,732	1,059	83,149	466	433,921	186,643	199,083
327	Odessa, TX	208,106	209,080	-2.0	13,506	76,026	2,810,670	.0563	2,030,992	598	405,010	859	54,477	305	284,057	89,556	127,345
328	Oil City-Franklin, PA	102,349	104,276	-1.5	15,019	40,901	1,537,170	.0298	1,075,900	316	122,950	261	31,866	178	200,584	66,541	69,441
329	Oklahoma City, OK	1,479,853	1,434,827	9.9	17,080	593,070	25,275,700	.4586	15,798,374	4,646	2,825,180	5,996	523,774	2,935	1,863,903	860,247	1,049,507
330	Olean, NY-Bradford, PA	236,929	238,984	-0.1	16,077	92,490	3,808,990	.0651	1,816,257	535	200,515	426	40,283	226	370,254	167,437	151,255
331	Olympia-Centralia, WA	350,453	325,360	25.7	19,535	137,959	6,846,060	.1183	3,993,208	1,175	879,131	1,866	118,653	666	738,719	148,269	270,604
332	Omaha, NE	1,020,431	991,763	9.5	19,068	404,035	19,457,680	.3575	13,573,535	3,992	1,623,349	3,445	449,751	2,520	1,809,140	770,220	748,771
333	Oneonta, NY	109,358	109,731	1.8	16,562	43,419	1,811,180	.0320	1,014,403	298	109,960	233	18,079	101	147,873	55,271	72,435
334	Opelika-Auburn, AL	156,405	151,675	22.3	15,695	65,111	2,454,740	.0438	1,345,810	396	270,129	573	55,084	309	255,216	47,231	120,063
335	Orangeburg, SC	122,131	123,425	7.8	13,743	47,400	1,678,410	.0324	1,075,183	316	130,573	277	41,791	234	194,703	79,382	79,065
336	Orlando, FL	1,912,510	1,697,906	35.1	20,582	761,426	39,362,490	.6969	25,645,422	7,543	3,518,099	7,468	1,661,920	9,313	3,428,365	1,401,293	1,306,327
337	Ottumwa, IA	123,055	124,054	0.9	15,517	50,232	1,909,460	.0362	1,292,494	379	231,041	489	29,690	167	206,943	52,434	96,544
338	Owensboro, KY	166,023	164,630	4.8	16,437	66,791	2,728,980	.0482	1,511,155	444	327,291	695	43,351	243	183,628	113,515	122,078
339	Paducah-Murray-Mayfield, KY	232,198	232,585	7.1	16,593	98,386	3,852,960	.0720	2,583,778	759	562,616	1,196	125,233	703	249,605	150,086	175,073
340	Panama City, FL	213,913	201,086	17.5	17,269	85,305	3,694,040	.0667	2,298,612	676	487,971	1,037	84,452	473	355,728	126,004	145,723
341	Paris, TX	96,130	95,149	6.4	14,054	38,728	1,350,990	.0260	880,814	258	168,719	359	33,846	189	111,013	50,759	65,960
342	Parkersburg, WV-Marietta, OH	180,488	182,549	1.4	16,664	75,272	3,007,680	.0574	2,166,524	637	444,768	945	63,402	355	251,510	121,409	130,642
343	Pensacola, FL	434,387	412,153	19.7	19,068	176,993	8,282,890	.1411	4,519,358	1,330	756,204	1,605	179,965	1,008	666,395	295,741	303,602
344	Peoria, IL	458,895	461,289	1.2	19,036	183,173	8,735,670	.1539	5,345,557	1,571	755,467	1,604	139,661	782	819,947	369,240	327,726
345	Petoskey, MI	112,271	107,276	24.9	18,076	45,963	2,029,440	.0408	1,776,871	523	268,639	570	65,697	368	260,394	75,424	83,401
346	Philadelphia, PA-Wilmington, DE-Trenton, NJ	6,315,353	6,184,346	4.8	22,195	2,421,449	140,171,240	2.3368	78,701,322	23,151	7,244,367	15,379	4,717,011	26,435	13,239,729	5,782,826	3,716,768
347	Phoenix, AZ	3,916,048	3,462,432	44.0	19,453	1,466,525	76,176,930	1.3206	44,784,226	13,174	6,017,552	12,774	1,658,694	9,296	6,219,533	2,138,714	2,492,448
348	Pine Bluff, AR	150,723	154,005	0.7	13,396	55,923	2,019,010	.0408	1,474,532	434	316,245	671	65,738	368	185,267	123,482	90,157
349	Pittsburg-Parsons, KS	90,762	92,459	1.7	14,150	36,620	1,284,270	.0258	958,295	282	216,607	461	23,883	134	160,204	47,274	69,921
350	Pittsburgh, PA	2,444,329	2,471,759	-1.4	18,557	1,027,006	45,358,220	.8060	28,020,931	8,242	3,092,639	6,566	1,291,432	7,238	4,541,722	2,146,002	1,603,579
351	Pittsfield, MA	132,813	134,953	-3.2	20,327	56,564	2,699,630	.0461	1,559,390	459	144,111	306	120,070	673	319,913	115,743	87,675
352	Plattsburgh, NY	120,870	118,745	-3.6	17,519	46,710	2,117,580	.0378	1,283,210	377	155,512	331	57,864	325	224,771	73,549	78,735
353	Pocatello, ID	100,470	100,943	12.6	15,323	36,392	1,539,510	.0298	1,095,186	323	157,301	333	19,433	109	175,025	49,059	73,699
354	Ponca City, OK	47,032	48,080	0.0	15,683	19,785	737,600	.0140	498,805	147	136,583	290	12,712	71	50,706	30,538	34,386
355	Poplar Bluff, MO	152,568	154,045	3.9	12,938	63,319	1,973,930	.0403	1,452,105	429	240,066	509	25,446	142	213,035	92,011	105,502
356	Port Angeles, WA	95,889	90,478	18.1	18,824	41,910	1,805,050	.0293	807,332	238	154,647	329	23,198	130	210,784	36,252	76,534
357	Portland-Brunswick, ME	545,846	521,184	10.5	20,682	225,934	11,289,000	.2071	8,192,371	2,409	677,940	1,439	517,826	2,902	1,642,291	316,332	394,479
358	Portland, OR	2,262,025	2,114,640	25.1	20,629	886,942	46,664,390	.8176	29,451,600	8,665	5,351,455	11,361	1,541,478	8,639	4,100,756	937,492	1,587,276
359	Portsmouth, OH	90,604	93,287	-0.1	12,972	35,986	1,175,270	.0223	679,932	200	111,926	238	24,327	136	119,570	52,908	63,281
360	Pottsville, PA	147,221	150,336	-1.5	15,903	60,111	2,341,200	.0435	1,496,557	440	131,524	279	31,556	177	277,785	213,434	99,248
361	Poughkeepsie-Kingston, NY	476,417	457,899	7.8	22,016	176,503	10,488,660	.1631	4,520,609	1,330	504,801	1,072	256,131	1,435	886,630	276,299	313,075
362	Prescott, AZ	189,588	167,517	55.5	17,740	79,896	3,363,380	.0565	1,644,997	484	297,003	630	44,109	247	338,416	63,090	145,395
363	Presque Isle, ME	73,272	73,938	-15.0	14,719	31,453	1,078,520	.0204	695,130	204	99,864	212	13,418	75	162,373	41,627	53,034
364	Providence-Pawtucket, RI-New Bedford-Fall River, MA	1,635,332	1,582,997	4.8	19,915	645,096	32,567,900	.5469	17,438,480	5,130	2,043,845	4,338	1,093,558	6,128	3,321,275	1,620,497	1,048,874
365	Provo-Orem, UT	416,085	376,774	39.9	14,326	117,341	5,961,030	.1174	4,250,508	1,250	810,841	1,721	141,362	792	710,129	74,681	261,529
366	Pueblo, CO	323,662	312,828	17.6	14,035	122,478	4,542,610	.0876	2,997,090	883	611,872	1,297	37,516	209	471,995	118,640	227,027
367	Quincy, IL-Hannibal, MO	182,945	184,825	4.3	15,154	71,223	2,772,380	.0522	1,785,226	523	285,620	606	32,732	184	283,591	99,543	129,517

Source: Devonshire Associates Ltd. and Scan/US, Inc. 2004.
. . . Represents a change of less than 0.1%

Basic Trading Areas: Population / Income / Sales, *Continued*

BTA NO.	BASIC TRADING AREA	POPULATION Estimate 7/1/04	POPULATION Census 4/1/00	% Change 4/1/90-4/1/00	PER CAPITA INCOME 2003	HOUSE-HOLDS Estimate 7/1/04	DISPOSABLE INCOME 2003 ($1,000)	MARKET ABILITY INDEX 2003	TOTAL RETAIL SALES 2003 Sales ($1,000)	TOTAL RETAIL SALES Ranally Sales Units	GENERAL MERCHANDISE 2003 Sales ($1,000)	GENERAL MERCHANDISE Ranally Sales Units	APPAREL STORE 2003 Sales ($1,000)	APPAREL STORE Ranally Sales Units	FOOD STORE SALES 2003 ($1,000)	HEALTH & DRUG STORE 2003 ($1,000)	PASSEN-GER CAR REGIS-TRATIONS 2003
368	Raleigh-Durham, NC	1,633,027	1,475,053	35.4	21,894	663,226	35,753,580	.6077	21,224,074	**6,244**	2,655,503	**5,637**	1,008,408	**5,651**	3,109,756	1,028,264	1,223,698
369	Rapid City, SD	202,629	196,855	8.6	15,526	78,489	3,145,930	.0682	3,080,109	**905**	505,349	**1,073**	93,879	**525**	253,568	98,124	158,557
370	Reading, PA	388,909	373,638	11.0	19,644	147,702	7,639,890	.1301	4,256,088	**1,252**	525,747	**1,116**	342,408	**1,919**	683,206	249,524	256,404
371	Redding, CA	297,360	276,618	9.2	16,207	118,032	4,819,270	.0851	2,614,128	**769**	370,611	**787**	53,717	**301**	543,460	136,959	214,145
372	Reno, NV	642,040	589,751	34.3	20,064	245,651	12,881,640	.2206	7,422,331	**2,183**	898,616	**1,906**	190,574	**1,070**	1,267,091	383,911	461,086
373	Richmond, IN	101,988	104,034	-0.9	16,821	41,710	1,715,590	.0325	1,206,842	**355**	223,181	**473**	29,099	**162**	177,308	74,523	75,474
374	Richmond-Petersburg, VA	1,311,798	1,256,479	15.2	20,358	532,940	26,705,830	.4510	14,853,628	**4,370**	2,403,690	**5,103**	681,957	**3,823**	2,190,869	879,392	974,116
375	Riverton, WY	48,297	48,975	4.5	15,105	19,122	729,530	.0144	546,270	**161**	90,800	**193**	7,194	**40**	75,573	10,911	37,949
376	Roanoke, VA	671,281	664,313	9.0	17,501	282,831	11,747,930	.2154	7,721,897	**2,272**	1,115,767	**2,370**	271,876	**1,525**	1,030,478	371,748	538,668
377	Roanoke Rapids, NC	77,908	79,456	4.1	12,730	30,994	991,730	.0200	684,354	**201**	97,423	**207**	28,925	**162**	114,966	45,412	50,462
378	Rochester-Austin-Albert Lea, MN	267,147	255,927	9.8	20,201	107,404	5,396,520	.0928	3,159,552	**929**	582,415	**1,237**	82,518	**462**	394,041	122,036	199,423
379	Rochester, NY	1,162,591	1,156,164	3.3	21,251	460,026	24,706,580	.4002	12,178,797	**3,583**	1,393,465	**2,958**	617,076	**3,459**	2,366,773	617,814	761,016
380	Rockford, IL	470,732	456,277	10.7	19,887	183,092	9,361,240	.1584	5,150,307	**1,515**	760,405	**1,614**	165,444	**929**	830,203	314,072	331,233
381	Rock Springs, WY	59,643	59,027	3.6	19,335	23,082	1,153,190	.0205	721,235	**212**	96,663	**205**	14,945	**83**	113,829	13,663	49,347
382	Rocky Mount-Wilson, NC	220,962	216,840	8.8	16,132	87,383	3,564,640	.0671	2,402,890	**706**	287,299	**610**	124,660	**698**	297,095	142,528	152,045
383	Rolla, MO	112,377	104,820	6.7	13,621	41,313	1,530,670	.0285	866,245	**255**	157,188	**334**	14,075	**79**	105,945	26,671	74,648
384	Rome, GA	134,540	128,692	11.8	15,372	50,432	2,068,100	.0380	1,246,196	**367**	260,109	**552**	53,402	**299**	170,773	86,467	91,008
385	Roseburg, OR	102,953	100,399	6.1	15,988	41,645	1,646,060	.0291	891,484	**262**	180,243	**383**	23,823	**134**	176,421	47,329	80,480
386	Roswell, NM	80,930	80,793	15.3	14,231	31,349	1,151,730	.0217	712,546	**210**	166,795	**354**	28,938	**163**	106,823	41,482	55,844
387	Russellville, AR	100,826	98,389	20.2	14,099	38,311	1,421,530	.0281	1,010,939	**298**	217,120	**460**	22,557	**127**	114,767	37,178	69,558
388	Rutland-Bennington, VT	100,773	100,394	2.5	18,090	41,625	1,823,020	.0369	1,618,249	**476**	123,586	**262**	128,760	**722**	278,935	90,067	70,931
389	Sacramento, CA	2,244,255	2,001,001	20.8	20,662	829,065	46,370,760	.7595	23,318,228	**6,859**	2,652,095	**5,630**	1,226,819	**6,875**	4,266,322	1,007,559	1,489,661
390	Saginaw-Bay City, MI	640,668	638,851	3.8	17,517	258,910	11,222,680	.2142	8,318,274	**2,448**	1,461,669	**3,103**	424,640	**2,380**	951,432	434,569	467,083
391	St. Cloud, MN	310,984	287,947	18.1	18,307	114,690	5,693,060	.1056	3,988,799	**1,174**	582,914	**1,238**	67,769	**379**	571,821	113,063	228,398
392	St. George, UT	161,402	140,919	69.2	13,985	54,252	2,257,240	.0483	2,022,489	**596**	283,283	**602**	60,944	**340**	289,402	39,500	107,128
393	St. Joseph, MO	195,052	196,619	2.7	15,788	78,102	3,079,410	.0571	1,958,514	**577**	352,130	**747**	30,423	**170**	288,945	70,926	139,922
394	St. Louis, MO	2,925,094	2,873,395	4.8	20,430	1,176,784	59,760,100	1.0088	33,198,507	**9,766**	5,069,666	**10,761**	1,127,918	**6,321**	4,898,914	2,176,291	2,035,831
395	Salem-Albany-Corvallis, OR	554,788	528,436	20.1	17,298	204,315	9,596,900	.1699	5,568,039	**1,638**	1,159,658	**2,462**	193,343	**1,083**	861,453	189,062	380,500
396	Salina, KS	140,008	144,345	0.7	16,297	57,714	2,281,780	.0437	1,632,404	**479**	275,199	**584**	51,549	**288**	231,943	67,473	114,183
397	Salinas-Monterey, CA	418,251	401,762	13.0	17,064	123,111	7,137,110	.1276	4,236,459	**1,246**	473,268	**1,005**	285,175	**1,598**	741,345	267,217	230,362
398	Salisbury, MD	195,055	186,608	14.5	17,817	77,304	3,475,260	.0657	2,530,480	**745**	497,367	**1,055**	168,738	**945**	410,948	155,444	132,830
399	Salt Lake City-Ogden, UT	1,717,659	1,629,189	24.6	17,525	571,311	30,101,670	.5742	22,336,081	**6,571**	3,411,466	**7,243**	887,251	**4,973**	3,358,396	455,120	1,158,645
400	San Angelo, TX	158,858	161,869	3.9	15,398	62,767	2,446,130	.0463	1,634,760	**478**	277,498	**590**	51,817	**291**	229,804	45,156	107,354
401	San Antonio, TX	2,004,688	1,856,320	21.3	17,040	731,528	34,159,230	.6311	22,592,795	**6,644**	3,197,549	**6,788**	1,173,017	**6,576**	3,704,727	864,962	1,246,860
402	San Diego, CA	2,966,135	2,813,833	12.6	20,344	1,059,703	60,342,670	1.0169	33,222,905	**9,773**	3,825,198	**8,120**	2,426,068	**13,596**	5,326,312	1,680,462	1,896,665
403	Sandusky, OH	138,855	139,038	4.5	19,252	55,258	2,673,270	.0458	1,498,159	**441**	258,927	**549**	58,500	**328**	216,834	109,630	101,639
404	San Francisco-Oakland-San Jose, CA	7,321,723	7,237,170	12.7	27,119	2,719,573	198,560,840	3.0815	98,134,912	**28,867**	11,157,032	**23,683**	7,847,273	**43,978**	18,164,645	5,340,008	4,900,144
405	San Luis Obispo, CA	254,929	246,681	13.6	20,201	98,521	5,149,890	.0859	2,720,316	**800**	246,788	**524**	150,585	**844**	543,527	192,222	190,418
406	Santa Barbara-Santa Maria, CA	404,260	399,347	8.0	19,379	138,188	7,834,290	.1368	4,700,898	**1,383**	454,866	**966**	331,262	**1,856**	859,109	335,658	258,132
407	Santa Fe, NM	229,817	218,804	25.4	20,096	95,141	4,618,480	.0779	2,524,096	**743**	438,861	**932**	164,831	**924**	359,632	155,142	180,359
408	Sarasota-Bradenton, FL	681,633	622,168	21.2	22,167	301,100	15,109,710	.2528	8,594,700	**2,527**	1,000,790	**2,125**	498,737	**2,795**	1,331,929	555,481	466,498
409	Sault Ste. Marie, MI	57,119	57,510	12.7	14,681	21,419	838,570	.0159	536,042	**158**	70,643	**150**	22,970	**128**	94,738	22,655	35,839
410	Savannah, GA	790,759	754,491	19.7	16,373	298,767	12,946,750	.2422	8,677,254	**2,551**	1,414,419	**3,003**	492,991	**2,764**	1,292,141	361,013	510,448
411	Scottsbluff, NE	99,324	101,597	-0.4	15,271	40,701	1,516,730	.0373	1,967,279	**578**	193,954	**413**	23,541	**133**	193,768	57,343	80,361
412	Scranton--Wilkes-Barre--Hazleton, PA	663,945	672,498	-0.9	16,919	277,256	11,233,030	.2103	7,712,718	**2,269**	991,581	**2,105**	335,558	**1,881**	1,407,977	536,995	450,366
413	Seattle-Tacoma, WA	3,375,700	3,232,492	19.3	22,930	1,351,295	77,405,190	1.2918	44,488,534	**13,086**	6,441,709	**13,674**	2,581,033	**14,464**	6,375,471	1,789,378	2,473,305
414	Sedalia, MO	94,972	92,562	16.1	15,043	38,561	1,428,660	.0269	908,470	**267**	154,404	**327**	18,701	**104**	132,936	40,685	69,998
415	Selma, AL	69,266	71,409	-4.1	10,922	27,432	756,540	.0155	485,056	**142**	92,074	**195**	21,572	**120**	86,317	36,734	42,418
416	Sharon, PA	119,795	120,293	-0.6	16,241	47,178	1,945,620	.0405	1,759,998	**518**	245,942	**522**	163,746	**918**	228,125	107,358	79,080
417	Sheboygan, WI	113,582	112,646	8.4	20,355	45,994	2,311,980	.0379	1,149,763	**338**	226,999	**482**	16,678	**93**	182,279	51,099	81,145
418	Sherman-Denison, TX	186,640	178,371	17.4	16,437	71,622	3,067,790	.0573	2,046,523	**602**	470,367	**999**	38,243	**215**	239,026	78,646	128,801
419	Shreveport, LA	607,540	605,690	3.8	15,107	238,552	9,177,820	.1760	6,249,714	**1,839**	1,149,358	**2,440**	242,159	**1,358**	835,967	280,682	384,432
420	Sierra Vista-Douglas, AZ	123,522	117,755	20.6	15,016	47,093	1,854,760	.0322	881,412	**259**	165,558	**351**	26,535	**149**	187,070	22,214	82,354
421	Sioux City, IA	340,158	344,417	4.7	16,083	129,065	5,470,840	.1563	9,714,760	**2,858**	477,354	**1,011**	124,538	**700**	532,523	156,073	246,314
422	Sioux Falls, SD	259,193	244,947	17.9	18,827	102,895	4,879,780	.1051	5,121,068	**1,506**	714,680	**1,517**	84,863	**475**	398,340	204,838	204,751
423	Somerset, KY	128,999	124,982	12.1	12,295	53,444	1,586,020	.0324	1,122,138	**330**	201,709	**429**	37,154	**208**	159,142	88,672	92,082
424	South Bend-Mishawaka, IN	356,725	354,754	7.2	17,780	139,341	6,342,560	.1182	4,438,481	**1,306**	799,491	**1,697**	157,556	**883**	537,514	297,569	247,451
425	Spokane, WA	774,358	741,519	21.0	16,356	302,069	12,665,370	.2390	8,703,750	**2,561**	1,290,752	**2,739**	309,838	**1,735**	1,394,766	325,733	571,306
426	Springfield, IL	270,738	267,461	5.0	19,886	111,898	5,383,850	.0937	3,241,889	**953**	550,362	**1,168**	90,925	**510**	440,339	198,654	192,548
427	Springfield-Holyoke, MA	691,167	680,014	1.0	19,479	269,913	13,463,310	.2241	6,876,412	**2,023**	689,313	**1,463**	327,408	**1,835**	1,412,300	508,321	420,831
428	Springfield, MO	692,694	660,151	23.9	15,738	283,485	10,901,680	.2133	8,130,059	**2,391**	1,249,657	**2,651**	288,931	**1,620**	946,845	323,284	512,173
429	State College, PA	143,518	135,758	9.7	15,772	52,665	2,263,590	.0432	1,572,637	**463**	206,017	**437**	90,830	**509**	222,749	82,855	92,657
430	Staunton-Waynesboro, VA	114,968	111,524	11.2	17,809	46,489	2,047,420	.0370	1,287,668	**379**	196,585	**417**	39,969	**224**	220,064	80,806	91,850
431	Steubenville, OH-Weirton, WV	127,547	132,008	-7.4	16,455	54,147	2,098,810	.0357	1,010,343	**297**	175,748	**373**	32,493	**182**	203,887	107,682	91,989
432	Stevens Point-Marshfield-Wisconsin Rapids, WI	217,093	214,617	6.6	17,668	86,153	3,835,640	.0701	2,512,539	**740**	485,498	**1,031**	41,627	**234**	293,385	29,138	163,130
433	Stillwater, OK	83,202	79,601	9.7	14,324	33,003	1,191,750	.0226	752,637	**221**	198,534	**421**	26,669	**149**	78,258	38,757	60,958
434	Stockton, CA	700,091	604,152	17.9	16,685	228,896	11,681,090	.1955	5,302,059	**1,560**	680,125	**1,444**	222,175	**1,246**	964,199	364,671	413,230
435	Stroudsburg, PA	159,381	138,687	44.9	18,883	56,652	3,009,580	.0523	1,746,834	**514**	263,869	**560**	167,624	**939**	350,528	113,936	109,779
436	Sumter, SC	159,736	157,267	5.2	14,319	60,198	2,287,240	.0420	1,284,950	**377**	168,411	**357**	59,362	**333**	205,266	65,345	100,809
437	Sunbury-Shamokin, PA	191,986	191,962	2.5	15,771	74,164	3,027,720	.0550	1,786,024	**525**	213,316	**452**	34,816	**196**	293,363	100,862	126,272
438	Syracuse, NY	785,833	780,716	-1.3	19,403	310,764	15,247,800	.2556	7,961,451	**2,342**	857,005	**1,820**	368,342	**2,064**	1,561,691	558,112	493,199
439	Tallahassee, FL	513,524	502,539	19.9	17,097	204,810	8,779,500	.1575	5,294,897	**1,557**	829,716	**1,761**	221,799	**1,243**	858,638	336,130	349,342
440	Tampa-St. Petersburg-Clearwater, FL	2,823,726	2,628,386	16.8	20,857	1,265,834	58,893,730	1.0225	36,378,624	**10,700**	4,428,895	**9,402**	1,509,261	**8,458**	5,247,471	2,371,765	1,967,940
441	Temple-Killeen, TX	372,441	354,952	21.7	15,892	133,087	5,918,800	.1033	3,032,416	**892**	444,217	**943**	84,221	**472**	445,300	63,823	237,095
442	Terre Haute, IN	242,800	245,348	3.5	15,602	96,375	3,788,260	.0829	3,804,560	**1,118**	552,883	**1,173**	113,455	**636**	291,466	136,819	175,989
443	Texarkana, TX-AR	271,242	270,420	5.6	14,173	105,184	3,844,340	.0738	2,514,954	**739**	531,789	**1,129**	98,334	**550**	332,155	91,354	177,896
444	Toledo, OH	791,153	789,378	0.9	19,020	322,586	15,047,950	.2688	9,606,395	**2,826**	1,491,248	**3,167**	346,127	**1,939**	1,366,723	547,856	565,542
445	Topeka, KS	259,619	258,820	5.3	18,463	106,217	4,793,380	.0841	2,831,138	**833**	527,918	**1,121**	83,842	**470**	390,264	183,919	201,074
446	Traverse City, MI	260,573	247,138	20.8	18,189	105,782	4,739,500	.0910	3,663,834	**1,077**	647,612	**1,377**	134,840	**757**	491,608	174,931	197,015
447	Tucson, AZ	907,511	843,746	26.5	17,888	365,815	16,233,410	.2752	8,272,791	**2,434**	1,284,384	**2,726**	326,802	**1,831**	1,268,524	505,873	600,419
448	Tulsa, OK	979,104	949,928	13.6	18,278	399,652	17,895,890	.3178	10,898,540	**3,207**	2,200,099	**4,670**	325,827	**1,826**	1,227,292	585,384	707,876
449	Tupelo-Corinth, MS	327,519	323,239	10.8	15,228	129,810	4,987,410	.0942	3,273,306	**963**	899,660	**1,910**	142,748	**800**	328,860	171,295	237,022
450	Tuscaloosa, AL	255,932	254,017	6.8	16,105	105,163	4,121,730	.0759	2,576,815	**758**	417,301	**886**	109,013	**612**	349,326	145,480	186,551
451	Twin Falls, ID	169,040	162,397	18.7	15,241	61,518	2,576,270	.0510	1,946,077	**573**	314,653	**668**	69,027	**386**	284,340	73,707	124,211
452	Tyler, TX	329,524	313,226	16.1	15,666	121,574	5,162,440	.1013	3,876,245	**1,140**	716,877	**1,523**	213,060	**1,194**	497,293	172,012	212,703
453	Utica-Rome, NY	297,571	299,896	-5.3	17,516	117,786	5,212,330	.0891	2,695,644	**793**	385,726	**819**	101,736	**570**	444,071	253,056	183,229
454	Valdosta, GA	170,549	166,053	19.3	13,879	64,943	2,366,980	.0474	1,734,995	**510**	218,554	**463**	96,089	**540**	236,066	61,087	114,085
455	Vicksburg, MS	60,193	61,475	3.8	15,903	23,537	957,230	.0181	643,413	**189**	122,921	**261**	31,717	**178**	86,124	25,917	39,147
456	Victoria, TX	166,742	165,277	10.2	15,907	61,365	2,652,390	.0493	1,701,903	**501**	291,908	**620**	61,482	**345**	287,487	70,726	106,226
457	Vincennes-Washington, IN	94,312	94,897	1.2	14,757	37,133	1,391,730	.0269	951,289	**280**	133,849	**284**	31,522	**177**	103,283	56,795	66,522
458	Visalia-Porterville-Hanford, CA	539,564	497,482	20.3	12,331	154,576	6,653,400	.1250	3,480,656	**1,024**	536,701	**1,139**	138,264	**775**	730,501	180,245	269,021
459	Waco, TX	315,094	303,669	12.4	14,983	117,978	4,720,930	.0909	3,235,000	**952**	508,485	**1,080**	171,554	**962**	563,063	122,888	203,930
460	Walla Walla, WA-Pendleton, OR	178,941	174,458	15.1	15,225	65,302	2,724,410	.0534	1,994,316	**586**	293,828	**624**	59,981	**337**	378,667	70,554	126,946
461	Washington, DC	5,139,785	4,769,729	15.8	27,616	1,977,811	141,938,430	2.0754	56,418,895	**16,594**	6,868,670	**14,581**	3,757,128	**21,057**	9,644,156	2,937,631	3,400,546
462	Waterloo-Cedar Falls, IA	262,176	266,449	2.1	16,856	103,741	4,419,210	.0825	2,990,966	**881**	412,341	**875**	77,727	**437**	365,996	139,568	202,020
463	Watertown, NY	304,846	301,747	1.9	15,282	112,427	4,658,560	.0854	2,750,695	**809**	305,219	**648**	86,282	**483**	447,149	228,923	180,691
464	Watertown, SD	74,716	75,962	1.9	15,465	30,097	1,155,460	.0240	1,009,995	**296**	71,200	**151**	27,844	**156**	102,934	22,781	59,518
465	Waterville-Augusta, ME	171,739	168,002	1.4	17,046	71,940	2,927,390	.0581	2,397,398	**705**	277,413	**589**	42,951	**240**	441,342	104,280	122,663
466	Wausau-Rhinelander, WI	248,151	244,048	10.9	18,146	100,710	4,503,050	.0863	3,466,001	**1,020**	608,513	**1,292**	75,252	**422**	424,500	75,893	188,191
467	Waycross, GA	117,132	113,264	14.4	13,354	44,484	1,564,200	.0319	1,188,836	**350**	244,210	**518**	29,630	**166**	159,310	55,165	76,000
468	Wenatchee, WA	221,409	213,481	28.2	14,613	78,418	3,235,360	.0623	2,175,994	**641**	365,569	**776**	40,704	**228**	428,209	85,418	151,997
469	West Palm Beach-Boca Raton, FL	1,281,164	1,167,094	30.7	25,397	592,027	32,537,840	.5198	17,133,442	**5,040**	2,156,242	**4,577**	1,541,747	**8,641**	2,507,419	1,118,916	909,653
470	West Plains, MO	77,272	77,090	14.8	12,817	32,867	990,380	.0195	640,231	**189**	154,529	**328**	15,702	**88**	87,003	35,567	59,938
471	Wheeling, WV	206,762	211,493	-3.8	15,601	87,602	3,225,780	.0600	2,038,462	**599**	341,267	**723**	74,710	**420**	341,453	152,323	148,014
472	Wichita, KS	668,828	656,056	9.8	18,209	261,137	12,178,560	.2120	6,916,753	**2,035**	1,254,303	**2,661**	257,910	**1,445**	1,047,595	331,603	486,198
473	Wichita Falls, TX	218,813	222,462	6.3	15,804	85,599	3,458,130	.0633	2,121,768	**624**	371,680	**789**	55,712	**312**	340,250	111,210	150,449
474	Williamson, WV-Pikeville, KY	173,075	175,453	-5.5	11,814	72,022	2,044,670	.0434	1,573,151	**463**	299,006	**635**	52,973	**297**	245,476	146,645	113,990
475	Williamsport, PA	161,596	164,514	1.6	15,847	65,007	2,560,770	.0500	1,919,021	**565**	259,856	**551**	79,410	**445**	324,619	129,639	108,372
476	Williston, ND	24,780	25,498	-7.3	14,811	10,259	367,010	.0076	304,589	**90**	51,078	**108**	7,643	**43**	41,324	16,715	19,908
477	Willmar-Marshall, MN	123,441	126,335	2.1	16,899	48,842	2,086,080	.0381	1,317,395	**388**	171,764	**364**	21,627	**120**	190,402	47,706	91,467
478	Wilmington, NC	353,488	329,281	31.9	19,277	156,729	6,814,270	.1282	5,111,321	**1,504**	662,103	**1,405**	200,538	**1,125**	742,347	277,901	272,339
479	Winchester, VA	176,936	162,105	17.9	19,237	70,512	3,403,750	.0625	2,383,168	**701**	400,892	**851**	72,441	**406**	323,082	134,569	140,557
480	Worcester-Fitchburg-Leominster, MA	784,595	750,963	5.8	21,778	300,867	17,087,140	.2811	9,059,973	**2,665**	882,285	**1,873**	405,829	**2,274**	1,627,115	628,138	500,744
481	Worthington, MN	94,962	96,475	-0.1	16,636	38,764	1,579,800	.0290	1,004,226	**296**	80,677	**172**	21,520	**120**	156,321	44,582	73,166
482	Yakima, WA	263,845	255,943	18.7	13,576	88,413	3,581,830	.0692	2,290,919	**674**	458,384	**973**	63,769	**358**	400,635	61,952	169,827
483	York-Hanover, PA	497,040	473,043	13.2	20,168	193,910	10,024,220	.1614	4,643,266	**1,366**	618,645	**1,313**	157,835	**885**	888,442	229,394	364,473
484	Youngstown-Warren, OH	470,620	482,671	-2.0	17,764	194,085	8,360,010	.1512	5,309,170	**1,561**	708,986	**1,505**	214,048	**1,200**	711,746	363,279	337,974
485	Yuba City-Marysville, CA	151,010	139,149	13.5	14,753	51,097	2,227,910	.0395	1,120,098	**330**	218,867	**465**	28,829	**162**	243,792	75,167	92,878
486	Yuma, AZ	174,609	160,026	49.7	13,194	58,992	2,303,760	.0445	1,439,675	**423**	334,372	**710**	34,477	**193**	209,344	71,584	99,509
487	Zanesville-Cambridge, OH	191,460	188,410	5.7	15,137	73,954	2,898,160	.0542	1,837,443	**540**	226,617	**481**	87,835	**491**	309,588	116,340	140,592
	U. S. Totals	293,687,162	281,421,906	13.2	19,691	112,708,735	5,782,884,870	100.0000	3,399,544,000	**1,000,000**	471,078,000	**1,000,000**	178,435,000	**1,000,000**	505,933,000	192,191,000	193,017,681

Source: Devonshire Associates Ltd. and Scan/US, Inc. 2004.
. . . Represents a change of less than 0.1%

150 Largest Basic Trading Areas: Population / Income / Sales

This table lists the 150 largest Basic Trading Areas (BTAs), as defined by Rand McNally, ranked by July 1, 2004 estimated population. The data shown are consistent with the data in the BTA table which appears on pages 24-27. The Basic Trading Areas are shown on the map which appears on pages 22-23. Statistics for Total Retail Sales, General Merchandise, Apparel Store, Food Store Sales and Health and Drug Store Sales in this edition are estimates based on data from the U.S. Census Bureau, and utilize the 1997 North American Industry Classification System (NAICS). A detailed explanation of Retail Trade and Trading Areas can be found in the Introduction on pages 5-9.

RANK	BASIC TRADING AREA	POPULATION Estimate 7/1/04	POPULATION Census 4/1/00	% Change 4/1/90-4/1/00	PER CAPITA INCOME 2003	HOUSE-HOLDS Estimate 7/1/04	DISPOSABLE INCOME 2003 ($1,000)	MARKET ABILITY INDEX 2003	TOTAL RETAIL SALES 2003 Sales ($1,000)	TOTAL RETAIL SALES Ranally Sales Units	GENERAL MERCHANDISE 2003 Sales ($1,000)	GENERAL MERCHANDISE Ranally Sales Units	APPAREL STORE 2003 Sales ($1,000)	APPAREL STORE Ranally Sales Units	FOOD STORE SALES 2003 ($1,000)	HEALTH & DRUG STORE 2003 ($1,000)	PASSEN-GER CAR REGIS-TRATIONS 2003
1	New York, NY	20,084,590	19,620,902	8.7	23,099	7,313,968	463,935,600	7.3080	218,537,459	**64,286**	19,429,157	**41,242**	22,783,712	**127,684**	36,087,889	17,382,810	9,172,337
2	Los Angeles, CA	17,556,372	16,391,590	12.7	18,227	5,700,623	319,999,850	5.4914	173,252,845	**50,964**	20,131,165	**42,734**	13,331,957	**74,717**	28,922,480	9,378,090	9,971,564
3	Chicago, IL	9,405,026	9,098,316	11.2	21,277	3,404,592	200,106,090	3.3284	108,533,325	**31,926**	12,448,491	**26,424**	5,997,775	**33,613**	14,973,121	8,989,067	5,408,248
4	San Francisco-Oakland-San Jose, CA	7,321,723	7,237,170	12.7	27,119	2,719,573	198,560,840	3.0815	98,134,912	**28,867**	11,157,032	**23,683**	7,847,273	**43,978**	18,164,645	5,340,008	4,900,144
5	Philadelphia, PA-Wilmington, DE-Trenton, NJ	6,315,353	6,184,346	4.8	22,195	2,421,449	140,171,240	2.3368	78,701,322	**23,151**	7,244,367	**15,379**	4,717,011	**26,435**	13,239,729	5,782,826	3,716,768
6	Dallas-Fort Worth, TX	6,156,363	5,571,828	28.7	21,123	2,302,252	130,038,990	2.2360	78,450,987	**23,076**	10,614,640	**22,534**	3,914,905	**21,941**	10,605,174	3,148,201	4,104,452
7	Houston, TX	5,527,291	5,045,022	24.4	19,254	2,018,784	106,424,210	1.8549	63,270,120	**18,612**	9,717,042	**20,627**	3,469,339	**19,443**	9,702,626	2,939,697	3,476,024
8	Washington, DC	5,139,785	4,769,729	15.8	27,616	1,977,811	141,938,430	2.0754	56,418,895	**16,594**	6,868,670	**14,581**	3,757,128	**21,057**	9,644,156	2,937,631	3,400,546
9	Detroit, MI	5,032,403	4,965,944	5.5	22,177	1,984,462	111,604,370	1.9122	68,527,198	**20,159**	10,862,822	**23,060**	3,066,495	**17,184**	8,147,450	4,650,610	3,444,756
10	Atlanta, GA	4,892,700	4,407,446	37.9	22,454	1,878,535	109,860,030	1.8492	64,164,487	**18,874**	8,365,720	**17,759**	3,335,362	**18,692**	9,272,544	2,575,751	3,462,500
11	Boston, MA	4,452,771	4,391,344	6.2	24,996	1,723,822	111,299,830	1.8013	60,701,542	**17,855**	5,700,756	**12,102**	4,396,572	**24,640**	10,266,378	4,205,252	2,714,924
12	Miami-Fort Lauderdale, FL	4,211,224	3,955,969	21.0	18,781	1,630,601	79,092,790	1.4174	50,631,779	**14,893**	5,584,256	**11,854**	3,918,738	**21,961**	7,110,389	3,772,053	2,506,762
13	Phoenix, AZ	3,916,048	3,462,432	44.0	19,453	1,466,525	76,176,930	1.3206	44,784,226	**13,174**	6,017,552	**12,774**	1,658,694	**9,296**	6,219,533	2,138,714	2,492,448
14	Minneapolis-St. Paul, MN	3,447,778	3,293,598	15.9	22,983	1,370,888	79,241,640	1.3806	52,225,246	**15,360**	7,235,527	**15,362**	1,856,738	**10,405**	6,808,694	2,262,258	2,478,388
15	Seattle-Tacoma, WA	3,375,700	3,232,492	19.3	22,930	1,351,295	77,405,190	1.2918	44,488,534	**13,086**	6,441,709	**13,674**	2,581,033	**14,464**	6,375,471	1,789,378	2,473,305
16	Cleveland-Akron, OH	2,995,077	2,993,610	3.4	20,083	1,219,085	60,151,460	1.0513	37,092,442	**10,912**	3,918,082	**8,318**	1,694,454	**9,497**	5,372,314	3,587,217	2,055,867
17	San Diego, CA	2,966,135	2,813,833	12.6	20,344	1,059,703	60,342,670	1.0169	33,222,905	**9,773**	3,825,198	**8,120**	2,426,068	**13,596**	5,326,312	1,680,462	1,896,665
18	St. Louis, MO	2,925,094	2,873,395	4.8	20,430	1,176,784	59,760,100	1.0088	33,198,507	**9,766**	5,069,666	**10,761**	1,127,918	**6,321**	4,898,914	2,176,291	2,035,831
19	Denver, CO	2,892,052	2,712,488	30.8	23,125	1,140,561	66,878,970	1.1100	37,930,413	**11,158**	4,982,800	**10,577**	1,800,381	**10,091**	5,609,241	1,341,639	2,128,039
20	Tampa-St. Petersburg-Clearwater, FL	2,823,726	2,628,386	16.8	20,857	1,265,834	58,893,730	1.0225	36,378,624	**10,700**	4,428,895	**9,402**	1,509,261	**8,458**	5,247,471	2,371,765	1,967,940
21	Baltimore, MD	2,690,679	2,606,003	7.2	22,799	1,048,378	61,344,350	.9715	29,224,813	**8,597**	3,770,428	**8,003**	1,669,615	**9,358**	5,202,186	1,843,845	1,705,024
22	Pittsburgh, PA	2,444,329	2,471,759	-1.4	18,557	1,027,006	45,358,220	.8060	28,020,931	**8,242**	3,092,639	**6,566**	1,291,432	**7,238**	4,541,722	2,146,002	1,603,579
23	Portland, OR	2,262,025	2,114,640	25.1	20,629	886,942	46,664,390	.8176	29,451,600	**8,665**	5,351,455	**11,361**	1,541,478	**8,639**	4,100,756	937,492	1,587,276
24	Charlotte-Gastonia, NC	2,246,673	2,078,083	24.4	20,352	904,949	45,725,410	.7863	26,964,020	**7,931**	3,610,335	**7,663**	1,161,561	**6,508**	3,727,615	1,469,333	1,650,081
25	Sacramento, CA	2,244,255	2,001,001	20.8	20,662	829,065	46,370,760	.7595	23,318,228	**6,859**	2,652,095	**5,630**	1,226,819	**6,875**	4,266,322	1,007,559	1,489,661
26	Cincinnati, OH	2,224,929	2,170,768	9.1	20,668	898,706	45,983,740	.7792	26,066,909	**7,667**	3,814,372	**8,097**	1,121,541	**6,286**	3,745,190	1,426,347	1,607,792
27	Kansas City, MO	2,139,575	2,049,447	11.4	20,728	857,635	44,349,750	.7643	26,644,105	**7,838**	4,013,128	**8,520**	984,551	**5,519**	3,314,780	1,379,502	1,542,694
28	San Antonio, TX	2,004,688	1,856,320	21.3	17,040	731,528	34,159,230	.6311	22,592,795	**6,644**	3,197,549	**6,788**	1,173,017	**6,576**	3,704,727	864,962	1,246,860
29	Orlando, FL	1,912,510	1,697,906	35.1	20,582	761,426	39,362,490	.6969	25,645,422	**7,543**	3,518,099	**7,468**	1,661,920	**9,313**	3,428,365	1,401,293	1,306,327
30	Milwaukee, WI	1,877,172	1,849,490	5.6	20,829	764,702	39,099,540	.6543	21,347,068	**6,279**	3,062,927	**6,501**	681,086	**3,817**	3,184,592	1,357,590	1,263,093
31	Norfolk-Virginia Beach-Newport News-Hampton, VA	1,872,308	1,784,356	9.1	18,147	718,110	33,977,620	.5950	19,697,962	**5,798**	3,098,462	**6,578**	1,081,303	**6,058**	2,883,175	928,937	1,262,646
32	Nashville, TN	1,855,825	1,761,799	23.3	20,224	752,713	37,532,160	.6635	24,091,600	**7,084**	4,185,986	**8,886**	1,111,290	**6,227**	3,151,934	1,298,312	1,396,968
33	Las Vegas, NV	1,855,794	1,568,418	82.8	19,143	709,420	35,525,460	.6190	21,026,297	**6,185**	2,863,733	**6,079**	1,271,752	**7,127**	3,309,723	899,216	1,169,992
34	Columbus, OH	1,773,443	1,692,240	14.5	21,609	742,396	38,322,070	.6732	25,051,562	**7,369**	3,232,799	**6,863**	1,171,093	**6,563**	3,033,710	997,326	1,326,287
35	Salt Lake City-Ogden, UT	1,717,659	1,629,189	24.6	17,525	571,311	30,101,670	.5742	22,336,081	**6,571**	3,411,466	**7,243**	887,251	**4,973**	3,358,396	455,120	1,158,645
36	Indianapolis, IN	1,644,237	1,552,963	17.5	21,113	664,013	34,714,280	.6160	23,108,093	**6,797**	3,909,709	**8,300**	878,000	**4,920**	2,231,839	1,479,415	1,201,167
37	Providence-Pawtucket, RI-New Bedford-Fall River, MA	1,635,332	1,582,997	4.8	19,915	645,096	32,567,900	.5469	17,438,480	**5,130**	2,043,845	**4,338**	1,093,558	**6,128**	3,321,275	1,620,497	1,048,874
38	Raleigh-Durham, NC	1,633,027	1,475,053	35.4	21,894	663,226	35,753,580	.6077	21,224,074	**6,244**	2,655,503	**5,637**	1,008,408	**5,651**	3,109,756	1,028,264	1,223,698
39	Memphis, TN	1,592,565	1,553,276	11.2	16,966	608,065	27,019,230	.4953	17,363,186	**5,109**	3,083,744	**6,549**	922,087	**5,169**	1,890,339	1,082,429	1,001,500
40	Louisville, KY	1,530,990	1,486,048	9.8	19,305	635,402	29,556,060	.5023	16,136,864	**4,746**	2,717,724	**5,770**	617,052	**3,458**	1,839,740	997,459	1,116,008
41	Greensboro--Winston-Salem--High Point, NC	1,509,499	1,454,066	17.1	19,026	621,408	28,719,830	.5205	19,190,058	**5,643**	2,477,105	**5,260**	854,771	**4,792**	2,496,824	1,151,380	1,154,018
42	Austin, TX	1,499,582	1,325,029	47.3	22,656	595,395	33,975,100	.6555	29,430,626	**8,659**	2,401,133	**5,098**	1,098,605	**6,157**	3,277,523	1,409,754	1,071,406
43	Oklahoma City, OK	1,479,853	1,434,827	9.9	17,080	593,070	25,275,700	.4586	15,798,374	**4,646**	2,825,180	**5,996**	523,774	**2,935**	1,863,903	860,247	1,049,507
44	Jacksonville, FL	1,477,907	1,358,825	21.9	20,360	590,003	30,090,350	.5150	17,462,760	**5,135**	2,352,598	**4,993**	773,905	**4,336**	2,483,786	878,308	1,004,433
45	New Orleans, LA	1,434,883	1,430,273	4.6	17,606	580,490	25,262,910	.4538	15,593,332	**4,587**	2,681,517	**5,694**	902,258	**5,056**	2,270,496	1,151,497	868,802
46	Birmingham, AL	1,343,594	1,319,776	10.0	18,279	541,598	24,559,630	.4378	15,150,905	**4,457**	2,495,407	**5,297**	729,535	**4,087**	2,127,079	751,754	991,351
47	Richmond-Petersburg, VA	1,311,798	1,256,479	15.2	20,358	532,940	26,705,830	.4510	14,853,628	**4,370**	2,403,690	**5,103**	681,957	**3,823**	2,190,869	879,392	974,116
48	West Palm Beach-Boca Raton, FL	1,281,164	1,167,094	30.7	25,397	592,027	32,537,840	.5198	17,133,442	**5,040**	2,156,242	**4,577**	1,541,747	**8,641**	2,507,419	1,118,916	909,653
49	Dayton-Springfield, OH	1,217,191	1,219,933	1.0	20,062	504,176	24,419,660	.4152	13,717,269	**4,035**	2,229,050	**4,732**	509,455	**2,855**	1,932,969	736,825	908,664
50	Buffalo-Niagara Falls, NY	1,199,068	1,213,535	-1.5	19,522	485,681	23,408,220	.3875	11,724,898	**3,449**	1,250,510	**2,654**	662,473	**3,713**	2,112,315	916,383	726,617
51	Hartford, CT	1,186,956	1,148,618	2.2	26,395	467,168	31,330,290	.4795	14,476,166	**4,258**	1,272,994	**2,702**	1,069,247	**5,993**	2,502,419	1,079,752	799,511
52	Knoxville, TN	1,167,564	1,118,107	17.9	17,429	489,264	20,349,790	.3939	15,706,092	**4,621**	2,630,959	**5,583**	784,823	**4,399**	1,947,312	807,640	909,179
53	Rochester, NY	1,162,591	1,156,164	3.3	21,251	460,026	24,706,580	.4002	12,178,797	**3,583**	1,393,465	**2,958**	617,076	**3,459**	2,366,773	617,814	761,016
54	Grand Rapids, MI	1,126,690	1,079,340	17.8	19,249	421,404	21,687,850	.3879	14,013,475	**4,122**	2,786,720	**5,915**	477,916	**2,678**	1,372,839	612,334	782,153
55	Albany-Schenectady, NY	1,067,671	1,047,324	1.8	21,277	434,661	22,716,960	.3677	11,176,542	**3,288**	1,244,372	**2,642**	543,341	**3,046**	1,692,608	740,348	697,309
56	New Haven-Waterbury-Meriden, CT	1,037,023	1,006,201	2.9	25,118	406,820	26,048,350	.4121	13,179,211	**3,877**	1,211,367	**2,571**	663,622	**3,719**	2,144,077	959,492	673,484
57	Omaha, NE	1,020,431	991,763	9.5	19,068	404,035	19,457,680	.3575	13,573,535	**3,992**	1,623,349	**3,445**	449,751	**2,520**	1,809,140	770,220	748,771
58	Fresno, CA	1,003,162	922,516	22.1	13,501	309,778	13,543,840	.2538	7,751,818	**2,280**	1,028,372	**2,183**	312,576	**1,752**	1,425,308	478,421	522,409
59	Little Rock, AR	988,281	963,155	13.0	17,548	406,536	17,341,900	.3258	12,326,012	**3,625**	2,660,376	**5,645**	407,840	**2,286**	1,189,148	444,150	697,935
60	Tulsa, OK	979,104	949,928	13.6	18,278	399,652	17,895,890	.3178	10,898,540	**3,207**	2,200,099	**4,670**	325,827	**1,826**	1,227,292	585,384	707,876
61	Lexington, KY	960,178	927,633	13.7	17,333	398,348	16,642,300	.2971	9,962,139	**2,930**	1,594,773	**3,384**	452,414	**2,538**	1,241,949	652,134	693,520
62	Greenville-Spartanburg, SC	949,306	914,473	16.0	18,133	377,675	17,213,430	.3136	11,349,191	**3,338**	1,557,403	**3,306**	554,671	**3,109**	1,534,130	663,225	675,654
63	Honolulu, HI	911,719	876,156	4.8	19,820	301,773	18,070,470	.3029	9,586,291	**2,820**	1,932,186	**4,102**	1,213,597	**6,801**	1,460,075	815,873	491,636
64	Tucson, AZ	907,511	843,746	26.5	17,888	365,815	16,233,410	.2752	8,272,791	**2,434**	1,284,384	**2,726**	326,802	**1,831**	1,268,524	505,873	600,419
65	Albuquerque, NM	878,243	831,850	20.8	17,876	346,982	15,699,540	.2831	9,920,813	**2,919**	1,748,555	**3,713**	332,713	**1,864**	980,171	533,316	621,151
66	Des Moines, IA	834,716	804,543	10.4	19,144	331,872	15,979,980	.2801	9,659,723	**2,840**	1,289,857	**2,738**	301,009	**1,687**	1,376,367	456,004	630,459
67	Toledo, OH	791,153	789,378	0.9	19,020	322,586	15,047,950	.2688	9,606,395	**2,826**	1,491,248	**3,167**	346,127	**1,939**	1,366,723	547,856	565,542
68	Savannah, GA	790,759	754,491	19.7	16,373	298,767	12,946,750	.2422	8,677,254	**2,551**	1,414,419	**3,003**	492,991	**2,764**	1,292,141	361,013	510,448
69	Syracuse, NY	785,833	780,716	-1.3	19,403	310,764	15,247,800	.2556	7,961,451	**2,342**	857,005	**1,820**	368,342	**2,064**	1,561,691	558,112	493,199
70	Worcester-Fitchburg-Leominster, MA	784,595	750,963	5.8	21,778	300,867	17,087,140	.2811	9,059,973	**2,665**	882,285	**1,873**	405,829	**2,274**	1,627,115	628,138	500,744
71	El Paso, TX	781,579	748,239	15.1	12,188	251,738	9,525,770	.1965	6,901,539	**2,030**	1,423,356	**3,021**	443,103	**2,483**	890,856	326,354	430,825
72	Allentown-Bethlehem-Easton, PA	776,747	740,395	7.8	20,869	305,639	16,210,200	.2761	9,403,351	**2,767**	979,519	**2,079**	367,959	**2,063**	1,723,108	631,887	533,539
73	Spokane, WA	774,358	741,519	21.0	16,356	302,069	12,665,370	.2390	8,703,750	**2,561**	1,290,752	**2,739**	309,838	**1,735**	1,394,766	325,733	571,306
74	Fort Wayne, IN	730,858	715,480	10.6	18,871	284,558	13,792,170	.2455	8,689,194	**2,556**	1,455,977	**3,090**	307,692	**1,723**	1,034,614	434,501	530,535
75	Bakersfield, CA	729,553	661,645	21.7	13,779	226,881	10,052,420	.1858	5,580,342	**1,642**	732,780	**1,556**	216,564	**1,214**	895,681	350,750	390,843
76	Baton Rouge, LA	727,706	705,760	13.2	17,770	279,440	12,931,440	.2349	8,323,377	**2,447**	1,490,811	**3,165**	346,887	**1,944**	1,097,510	395,026	477,866
77	Madison, WI	717,335	682,098	15.0	20,701	296,780	14,849,890	.2767	11,268,073	**3,315**	1,357,728	**2,881**	294,782	**1,652**	1,216,541	426,400	534,603
78	Kingsport, TN-Johnson City, TN-Bristol, VA-TN	716,844	707,899	8.5	15,657	307,808	11,223,430	.2131	7,616,705	**2,240**	1,356,328	**2,878**	282,585	**1,584**	1,102,098	480,687	565,499
79	McAllen, TX	715,030	623,060	46.9	8,416	198,627	6,017,530	.1516	5,759,701	**1,694**	1,119,781	**2,378**	433,102	**2,427**	918,124	238,691	316,493
80	Fort Myers, FL	714,104	629,301	31.3	20,995	306,971	14,992,860	.2572	8,946,143	**2,632**	1,403,676	**2,981**	530,961	**2,976**	1,316,658	547,351	484,634
81	Charleston, SC	713,665	680,311	9.0	18,018	285,566	12,858,880	.2275	7,677,563	**2,257**	1,296,098	**2,752**	484,579	**2,716**	1,299,115	362,883	473,952
82	Harrisburg, PA	712,963	698,708	6.7	19,949	289,380	14,222,830	.2556	9,523,790	**2,802**	981,077	**2,083**	325,648	**1,825**	1,380,790	503,993	501,321
83	Columbia, SC	700,532	668,081	17.5	19,170	280,116	13,429,050	.2376	8,351,037	**2,456**	1,509,496	**3,205**	398,449	**2,234**	1,143,451	423,265	497,135
84	Stockton, CA	700,091	604,152	17.9	16,685	228,896	11,681,090	.1955	5,302,059	**1,560**	680,125	**1,444**	222,175	**1,246**	964,199	364,671	413,230
85	Jackson, MS	693,182	677,489	10.1	15,767	258,242	10,929,470	.2103	7,767,033	**2,284**	1,526,805	**3,240**	302,032	**1,692**	872,873	457,198	446,839
86	Springfield, MO	692,694	660,151	23.9	15,738	283,485	10,901,680	.2133	8,130,059	**2,391**	1,249,657	**2,651**	288,931	**1,620**	946,845	323,284	512,173
87	Springfield-Holyoke, MA	691,167	680,014	1.0	19,479	269,913	13,463,310	.2241	6,876,412	**2,023**	689,313	**1,463**	327,408	**1,835**	1,412,300	508,321	420,831
88	Macon-Warner Robins, GA	685,839	662,942	12.5	15,570	259,470	10,678,400	.1985	6,767,227	**1,992**	1,075,470	**2,284**	283,909	**1,593**	1,084,097	344,698	456,650
89	Sarasota-Bradenton, FL	681,633	622,168	21.2	22,167	301,100	15,109,710	.2528	8,594,700	**2,527**	1,000,790	**2,125**	498,737	**2,795**	1,331,929	555,481	466,498
90	Fayetteville-Lumberton, NC	681,569	663,154	16.1	15,844	261,501	10,798,520	.1992	6,733,933	**1,982**	1,128,656	**2,397**	302,595	**1,696**	943,411	372,126	461,339
91	Mobile, AL	675,391	663,075	11.6	16,343	262,734	11,037,700	.2007	6,723,070	**1,976**	1,306,496	**2,772**	365,433	**2,049**	948,527	381,232	462,129
92	Roanoke, VA	671,281	664,313	9.0	17,501	282,831	11,747,930	.2154	7,721,897	**2,272**	1,115,767	**2,370**	271,876	**1,525**	1,030,478	371,748	538,668
93	Wichita, KS	668,828	656,056	9.8	18,209	261,137	12,178,560	.2120	6,916,753	**2,035**	1,254,303	**2,661**	257,910	**1,445**	1,047,595	331,603	486,198
94	Scranton--Wilkes-Barre--Hazleton, PA	663,945	672,498	-0.9	16,919	277,256	11,233,030	.2103	7,712,718	**2,269**	991,581	**2,105**	335,558	**1,881**	1,407,977	536,995	450,366
95	Manchester-Nashua-Concord, NH	653,188	617,057	14.1	21,879	254,597	14,291,390	.2719	11,771,266	**3,462**	1,590,126	**3,376**	493,884	**2,768**	1,799,143	411,077	466,596
96	Boise-Nampa, ID	644,161	584,008	40.2	17,090	235,067	11,008,870	.2084	7,869,346	**2,315**	1,313,050	**2,787**	226,329	**1,269**	1,115,229	250,455	460,546
97	Reno, NV	642,040	589,751	34.3	20,064	245,651	12,881,640	.2206	7,422,331	**2,183**	898,616	**1,906**	190,574	**1,070**	1,267,091	383,911	461,086
98	Saginaw-Bay City, MI	640,668	638,851	3.8	17,517	258,910	11,222,680	.2142	8,318,274	**2,448**	1,461,669	**3,103**	424,640	**2,380**	951,432	434,569	467,083
99	Asheville-Hendersonville, NC	632,075	608,250	19.3	17,388	268,110	10,990,240	.2091	8,052,565	**2,366**	1,186,551	**2,519**	320,983	**1,798**	1,145,321	433,167	486,060
100	Shreveport, LA	607,540	605,690	3.8	15,107	238,552	9,177,820	.1760	6,249,714	**1,839**	1,149,358	**2,440**	242,159	**1,358**	835,967	280,682	384,432
101	Augusta, GA	605,032	590,218	13.1	16,620	232,388	10,055,690	.1787	5,735,373	**1,686**	961,644	**2,041**	246,734	**1,383**	859,725	295,641	404,543
102	Chattanooga, TN	583,689	568,186	11.2	17,649	237,496	10,301,790	.1827	6,108,421	**1,797**	1,006,464	**2,137**	306,257	**1,716**	876,408	381,150	437,957
103	Colorado Springs, CO	582,962	537,484	31.3	19,915	217,598	11,609,510	.2043	7,281,101	**2,142**	1,150,804	**2,443**	191,586	**1,074**	801,447	279,729	414,826
104	Modesto, CA	563,828	501,498	19.7	16,171	184,638	9,117,780	.1630	5,178,871	**1,523**	732,586	**1,555**	183,349	**1,027**	1,027,398	348,603	333,036
105	Lafayette-New Iberia, LA	558,492	548,154	10.4	14,464	212,248	8,077,810	.1632	6,281,626	**1,848**	1,156,358	**2,454**	245,933	**1,379**	827,463	409,212	337,014
106	Salem-Albany-Corvallis, OR	554,788	528,436	20.1	17,298	204,315	9,596,900	.1699	5,568,039	**1,638**	1,159,658	**2,462**	193,343	**1,083**	861,453	189,062	380,500
107	Corpus Christi, TX	552,441	548,161	9.6	14,713	197,552	8,127,960	.1552	5,361,961	**1,577**	843,560	**1,791**	235,326	**1,319**	955,161	204,225	321,030
108	Portland-Brunswick, ME	545,846	521,184	10.5	20,682	225,934	11,289,000	.2071	8,192,371	**2,409**	677,940	**1,439**	517,826	**2,902**	1,642,291	316,332	394,479
109	Daytona Beach, FL	542,645	493,175	23.5	20,372	245,026	11,054,840	.1836	5,769,501	**1,698**	770,128	**1,635**	219,433	**1,230**	968,057	386,603	398,756
110	Visalia-Porterville-Hanford, CA	539,564	497,482	20.3	12,331	154,576	6,653,400	.1250	3,480,656	**1,024**	536,701	**1,139**	138,264	**775**	730,501	180,245	269,021
111	Canton-New Philadelphia, OH	536,362	534,503	4.1	17,960	214,691	9,633,290	.1746	6,202,224	**1,824**	864,777	**1,836**	285,844	**1,602**	957,845	533,816	395,864
112	Huntsville, AL	532,485	509,873	15.9	19,746	218,183	10,514,400	.1843	6,472,653	**1,904**	1,231,197	**2,613**	327,283	**1,833**	841,017	263,926	422,400
113	Evansville, IN	525,981	523,510	3.7	17,759	215,342	9,341,080	.1746	6,581,736	**1,937**	1,034,540	**2,194**	245,985	**1,378**	782,288	329,257	394,526
114	Lansing, MI	522,508	509,246	4.0	19,589	204,523	10,235,420	.1782	6,133,994	**1,804**	1,375,708	**2,920**	209,162	**1,172**	751,123	322,061	376,098
115	Lakeland-Winter Haven, FL	518,809	483,924	19.4	19,073	217,966	9,895,440	.1713	5,716,090	**1,681**	873,686	**1,855**	196,846	**1,103**	977,731	287,481	353,833
116	Flint, MI	516,834	507,828	1.5	19,398	209,029	10,025,790	.1759	6,115,058	**1,799**	1,215,355	**2,580**	192,285	**1,078**	698,374	403,337	370,662
117	Melbourne-Titusville, FL	515,004	476,230	19.4	22,229	228,764	11,447,810	.1835	5,603,865	**1,648**	916,795	**1,946**	235,423	**1,319**	919,936	384,085	382,238
118	Tallahassee, FL	513,524	502,539	19.9	17,097	204,810	8,779,500	.1575	5,294,897	**1,557**	829,716	**1,761**	221,799	**1,243**	858,638	336,130	349,342
119	York-Hanover, PA	497,040	473,043	13.2	20,168	193,910	10,024,220	.1614	4,643,266	**1,366**	618,645	**1,313**	157,835	**885**	888,442	229,394	364,473
120	Montgomery, AL	488,775	484,647	10.0	16,448	193,208	8,039,270	.1496	5,301,149	**1,560**	961,543	**2,041**	226,804	**1,270**	729,814	311,444	338,579
121	Lancaster, PA	486,469	470,658	11.3	19,463	180,573	9,468,350	.1739	6,676,478	**1,964**	579,937	**1,231**	367,776	**2,061**	1,109,981	332,301	314,284
122	Anchorage, AK	483,813	456,392	17.3	20,536	170,104	9,935,470	.1744	6,314,171	**1,857**	1,342,257	**2,850**	245,298	**1,375**	1,031,413	83,108	293,383
123	Charleston, WV	482,610	486,731	1.1	16,236	203,791	7,835,610	.1470	5,275,752	**1,552**	805,364	**1,709**	174,145	**977**	688,641	389,067	326,046
124	Fort Pierce-Vero Beach-Stuart, FL	480,733	432,373	26.7	22,090	216,618	10,619,410	.1748	5,695,561	**1,676**	752,563	**1,597**	295,497	**1,655**	914,661	444,274	345,548
125	Poughkeepsie-Kingston, NY	476,417	457,899	7.8	22,016	176,503	10,488,660	.1631	4,520,609	**1,330**	504,801	**1,072**	256,131	**1,435**	886,630	276,299	313,075
126	Rockford, IL	470,732	456,277	10.7	19,887	183,092	9,361,240	.1584	5,150,307	**1,515**	760,405	**1,614**	165,444	**929**	830,203	314,072	331,233
127	Youngstown-Warren, OH	470,620	482,671	-2.0	17,764	194,085	8,360,010	.1512	5,309,170	**1,561**	708,986	**1,505**	214,048	**1,200**	711,746	363,279	337,974
128	Appleton-Oshkosh, WI	468,337	452,355	13.3	20,143	188,786	9,433,930	.1668	6,052,381	**1,780**	819,618	**1,739**	205,956	**1,155**	779,177	235,415	352,499
129	Beaumont-Port Arthur, TX	463,147	467,106	8.1	16,346	179,429	7,570,500	.1426	5,164,466	**1,519**	833,934	**1,770**	203,048	**1,139**	733,467	276,852	295,781
130	Peoria, IL	458,895	461,289	1.2	19,036	183,173	8,735,670	.1539	5,345,557	**1,571**	755,467	**1,604**	139,661	**782**	819,947	369,240	327,726
131	Pensacola, FL	434,387	412,153	19.7	19,068	176,993	8,282,890	.1411	4,519,358	**1,330**	756,204	**1,605**	179,965	**1,008**	666,395	295,741	303,602
132	Davenport, IA-Moline, IL	429,075	429,924	2.4	18,738	171,815	8,040,010	.1468	5,438,870	**1,599**	755,561	**1,604**	200,725	**1,125**	690,276	337,315	310,141
133	Burlington, VT	418,921	406,799	10.2	19,218	167,030	8,050,830	.1469	5,525,766	**1,627**	422,366	**897**	212,077	**1,191**	1,011,734	323,702	297,711
134	Salinas-Monterey, CA	418,251	401,762	13.0	17,064	123,111	7,137,110	.1276	4,236,459	**1,246**	473,268	**1,005**	285,175	**1,598**	741,345	267,217	230,362
135	Provo-Orem, UT	416,085	376,774	39.9	14,326	117,341	5,961,030	.1174	4,250,508	**1,250**	810,841	**1,721**	141,362	**792**	710,129	74,681	261,529
136	Lubbock, TX	415,551	409,227	4.2	14,240	154,375	5,917,550	.1210	4,695,841	**1,381**	676,053	**1,433**	195,305	**1,094**	711,279	149,219	264,552
137	Duluth, MN	414,689	413,956	3.3	17,151	173,718	7,112,290	.1292	4,478,209	**1,317**	731,910	**1,553**	96,754	**541**	671,136	205,159	309,514
138	Amarillo, TX	411,930	410,323	7.9	15,765	154,439	6,493,900	.1233	4,457,900	**1,313**	573,458	**1,216**	159,648	**894**	481,853	185,083	275,576
139	Biloxi-Gulfport-Pascagoula, MS	405,152	396,754	16.8	17,628	160,456	7,142,130	.1269	4,245,104	**1,249**	1,036,132	**2,200**	137,635	**771**	491,985	185,494	289,597
140	Santa Barbara-Santa Maria, CA	404,260	399,347	8.0	19,379	138,188	7,834,290	.1368	4,700,898	**1,383**	454,866	**966**	331,262	**1,856**	859,109	335,658	258,132
141	Brownsville-Harlingen, TX	391,958	355,309	27.9	9,480	114,664	3,715,660	.0840	2,851,056	**838**	649,080	**1,377**	196,477	**1,101**	540,429	115,231	177,531
142	Hagerstown, MD-Chambersburg, PA-Martinsburg, WV	391,227	366,345	11.8	18,664	153,926	7,302,050	.1250	3,988,431	**1,174**	571,080	**1,212**	136,769	**767**	639,514	221,737	282,751
143	Reading, PA	388,909	373,638	11.0	19,644	147,702	7,639,890	.1301	4,256,088	**1,252**	525,747	**1,116**	342,408	**1,919**	683,206	249,524	256,404
144	Kalamazoo, MI	384,987	377,288	7.1	18,746	152,916	7,216,920	.1276	4,423,495	**1,301**	1,145,091	**2,431**	141,253	**791**	489,109	215,438	281,114
145	New London-Norwich, CT	379,266	368,179	3.0	24,438	148,251	9,268,520	.1432	4,225,437	**1,243**	524,673	**1,113**	179,175	**1,004**	721,424	290,580	264,044
146	Temple-Killeen, TX	372,441	354,952	21.7	15,892	133,087	5,918,800	.1033	3,032,416	**892**	444,217	**943**	84,221	**472**	445,300	63,823	237,095
147	Columbus, GA	370,856	364,510	6.5	15,342	143,489	5,689,770	.1058	3,545,730	**1,042**	601,279	**1,276**	196,688	**1,101**	530,156	207,191	241,096
148	Atlantic City, NJ	368,557	354,878	11.1	21,221	142,561	7,821,170	.1325	4,515,980	**1,329**	469,557	**997**	317,234	**1,778**	1,056,306	285,181	213,356
149	Green Bay, WI	368,215	355,786	14.6	19,375	148,055	7,134,030	.1269	4,540,813	**1,335**	950,926	**2,019**	115,054	**644**	549,514	133,413	273,206
150	Huntington, WV-Ashland, KY	367,619	368,924	1.4	14,906	154,137	5,479,750	.1043	3,618,951	**1,064**	666,202	**1,414**	164,722	**923**	472,203	350,671	257,156

Source: Devonshire Associates Ltd. and Scan/US, Inc. 2004.

Business/Manufactures, by State

STATE	STATE ABBRE-VIATION†	FIPS STATE CODE‡	BANK DEPOSITS, 12/31/03‡‡ Number of Banks	BANK DEPOSITS, 12/31/03‡‡ Total Deposits ($1,000)	TOTAL WHOLESALE TRADE, 1997* Estab-lishments	TOTAL WHOLESALE TRADE, 1997* Sales ($1,000)	MANUFACTURES, 1997* Number of Establishments	MANUFACTURES, 1997* Establishments With 20 or More Employees	MANUFACTURES, 1997* Total Employees	MANUFACTURES, 1997* Value Added by Manufacture Total ($1,000)	MANUFACTURES, 1997* Value Added by Manufacture Ranally Mfg. Units	AUTOMOBILE REGISTRATIONS Automobiles Registered 2003††	AUTOMOBILE REGISTRATIONS Automobiles Registered 2000**
Alabama	AL	01	162	60,300,000	6,315	40,986,328	5,444	2,089	352,618	29,221,522	**15,998**	3,324,005	3,114,091
Alaska	AK	02	7	5,700,000	784	2,989,820	488	102	10,770	1,159,253	**635**	402,080	370,973
Arizona	AZ	04	50	56,000,000	6,689	45,899,068	4,917	1,370	193,616	26,898,948	**14,726**	3,680,325	3,272,230
Arkansas	AR	05	170	37,700,000	3,619	27,515,382	3,316	1,248	230,153	19,346,813	**10,592**	1,873,302	1,785,861
California	CA	06	318	614,700,000	57,841	548,864,451	49,418	15,266	1,809,667	195,872,810	**107,234**	21,676,396	20,372,623
Colorado	CO	08	180	61,100,000	7,383	60,310,393	5,480	1,264	173,069	20,673,048	**11,318**	3,410,192	3,137,147
Connecticut	CT	09	63	69,600,000	5,283	76,167,938	5,844	1,926	252,330	27,295,212	**14,943**	2,335,064	2,267,536
Delaware	DE	10	34	96,800,000	906	12,585,529	675	232	41,084	5,389,453	**2,951**	561,796	533,235
District of Columbia	DC	11	5	15,600,000	348	3,918,622	200	35	2,858	170,849	**94**	235,770	217,821
Florida	FL	12	304	268,200,000	31,214	187,079,940	15,992	3,628	433,149	40,213,354	**22,016**	11,656,363	10,229,301
Georgia	GA	13	345	124,900,000	13,978	163,782,649	9,083	3,301	533,830	55,550,096	**30,412**	6,119,599	5,481,753
Hawaii	HI	15	8	21,200,000	1,872	7,147,462	921	159	15,109	1,262,448	**691**	718,816	684,415
Idaho	ID	16	18	12,600,000	1,980	10,127,777	1,647	419	66,184	6,393,062	**3,500**	1,020,031	944,739
Illinois	IL	17	769	281,800,000	21,951	275,968,383	17,953	6,572	887,350	95,287,251	**52,167**	7,775,171	7,260,999
Indiana	IN	18	206	80,300,000	8,896	66,350,132	9,303	3,946	625,692	67,210,944	**36,796**	4,512,006	4,173,377
Iowa	IA	19	422	52,100,000	5,399	35,453,705	3,749	1,413	235,880	28,673,277	**15,698**	2,239,502	2,099,301
Kansas	KS	20	380	44,900,000	5,085	42,209,864	3,309	1,151	193,742	17,650,640	**9,663**	2,038,938	1,915,734
Kentucky	KY	21	243	56,100,000	5,051	37,242,872	4,218	1,712	288,405	38,337,622	**20,989**	2,956,274	2,705,637
Louisiana	LA	22	170	52,600,000	6,390	46,972,265	3,545	1,170	165,777	29,066,923	**15,913**	2,779,013	2,559,794
Maine	ME	23	40	16,100,000	1,726	7,305,592	1,812	513	82,288	6,530,588	**3,575**	949,427	880,559
Maryland	MD	24	122	77,900,000	6,283	54,906,650	3,996	1,213	163,992	18,721,618	**10,249**	3,619,286	3,426,815
Massachusetts	MA	25	209	172,400,000	9,993	112,792,386	9,554	3,313	417,135	44,337,768	**24,274**	3,957,361	3,760,685
Michigan	MI	26	178	137,100,000	13,936	159,432,288	16,045	5,753	833,429	93,809,468	**51,358**	7,091,799	6,525,706
Minnesota	MN	27	486	97,400,000	9,348	99,444,542	8,091	2,728	382,530	36,629,931	**20,054**	3,696,214	3,395,174
Mississippi	MS	28	103	32,900,000	3,173	18,445,224	3,008	1,282	227,800	17,088,506	**9,355**	1,920,660	1,757,459
Missouri	MO	29	377	91,600,000	9,522	91,411,852	7,497	2,498	371,448	43,186,072	**23,643**	4,061,108	3,814,641
Montana	MT	30	80	11,300,000	1,574	7,596,802	1,160	179	19,611	1,732,158	**948**	732,175	688,762
Nebraska	NE	31	270	31,500,000	3,157	38,015,440	1,960	612	106,690	10,822,657	**5,925**	1,319,548	1,237,634
Nevada	NV	32	37	31,900,000	2,253	12,806,893	1,615	408	37,849	3,298,077	**1,806**	1,499,732	1,353,743
New Hampshire	NH	33	31	29,700,000	2,033	11,371,112	2,328	757	98,934	11,320,082	**6,197**	941,925	856,901
New Jersey	NJ	34	146	196,300,000	17,812	227,309,002	11,812	3,828	409,788	50,101,691	**27,429**	5,183,488	4,944,083
New Mexico	NM	35	60	16,700,000	2,182	7,397,572	1,593	293	39,664	13,440,222	**7,358**	1,309,844	1,236,492
New York	NY	36	206	580,700,000	37,499	319,697,562	23,908	6,689	785,891	76,999,763	**42,155**	8,924,727	8,615,553
North Carolina	NC	37	104	147,000,000	12,284	98,080,086	11,306	4,621	773,548	78,638,044	**43,052**	6,298,393	5,674,382
North Dakota	ND	38	104	11,000,000	1,604	8,618,382	704	188	21,956	1,802,403	**987**	507,265	477,318
Ohio	OH	39	304	211,000,000	17,322	160,415,587	17,974	6,897	984,201	112,491,355	**61,585**	8,258,075	7,651,217
Oklahoma	OK	40	278	44,300,000	5,191	32,132,263	4,087	1,191	164,060	17,233,699	**9,435**	2,500,715	2,360,076
Oregon	OR	41	38	37,300,000	5,943	53,679,098	5,768	1,675	213,111	25,077,180	**13,729**	2,578,438	2,411,395
Pennsylvania	PA	42	270	208,000,000	17,138	159,354,185	17,128	6,357	826,521	86,212,087	**47,198**	7,920,514	7,364,754
Rhode Island	RI	44	15	17,800,000	1,590	7,602,702	2,535	704	75,599	5,484,173	**3,002**	701,181	682,914
South Carolina	SC	45	97	44,900,000	5,035	34,179,799	4,450	1,873	346,142	33,657,787	**18,427**	2,896,655	2,671,612
South Dakota	SD	46	94	15,700,000	1,402	7,874,169	888	292	46,539	3,880,867	**2,125**	595,047	555,129
Tennessee	TN	47	208	86,700,000	8,234	82,626,370	7,407	2,906	483,823	44,355,170	**24,283**	4,348,750	3,978,403
Texas	TX	48	698	297,300,000	33,346	323,111,661	21,808	6,788	959,665	129,390,041	**70,837**	14,256,695	12,791,932
Utah	UT	49	64	85,000,000	3,277	21,271,857	2,860	861	119,140	11,343,518	**6,210**	1,584,885	1,393,778
Vermont	VT	50	19	8,800,000	941	4,731,383	1,226	340	42,533	4,044,564	**2,214**	445,805	413,235
Virginia	VA	51	141	129,700,000	7,868	61,046,705	5,986	2,042	370,595	43,563,006	**23,849**	5,463,924	4,902,369
Washington	WA	53	100	81,500,000	10,039	75,397,750	7,801	2,159	328,511	30,434,838	**16,662**	4,512,912	4,261,854
West Virginia	WV	54	74	22,300,000	1,956	10,290,356	1,505	517	72,813	9,310,976	**5,097**	1,244,035	1,139,393
Wisconsin	WI	55	311	95,900,000	8,025	57,192,863	9,936	3,905	562,479	54,947,083	**30,082**	3,969,663	3,629,972
Wyoming	WY	56	46	7,800,000	800	2,547,065	503	90	8,448	1,031,057	**564**	412,792	385,272
United States			9,164	5,087,900,000	453,470	4,059,657,778	363,753	120,475	16,888,016	1,826,589,974	**1,000,000**	193,017,681	178,365,779

† U.S. Postal Service standard abbreviation for state names.
‡ Federal Information Processing Standards (FIPS) codes for states, as published by the National Bureau of Standards, U.S. Department of Commerce.
‡‡ Source: Statistical Abstract of the United States: 2004-2005.
* Source: U.S. Bureau of the Census.
†† Source: Devonshire Associates Ltd. and Scan/US, Inc. 2004.
** Data compiled by Devonshire Associates Ltd. and Scan/US, Inc. 2001.

Retail Sales, by State

STATE	FIPS STATE CODE†	RETAIL SALES TOTAL, 2003‡* Sales ($1,000)	RETAIL SALES TOTAL, 2003‡* Ranally Sales Units	RETAIL SALES TOTAL, 1997* Sales ($1,000)	RETAIL SALES TOTAL, 1997* Ranally Sales Units	RETAIL SALES TOTAL, 1992** Sales ($1,000)	RETAIL SALES TOTAL, 1992** Ranally Sales Units	SHOPPING GOODS†† TOTAL, 2003‡* Sales ($1,000)	SHOPPING GOODS†† TOTAL, 2003‡* Ranally Sales Units	SHOPPING GOODS†† TOTAL, 1997* Sales ($1,000)	SHOPPING GOODS†† TOTAL, 1997* Ranally Sales Units	GENERAL MERCHANDISE STORES 2003‡* Sales ($1,000)	APPAREL & ACCESSORIES STORES 2003‡* Sales ($1,000)	HEALTH & DRUG STORES 2003‡* Sales ($1,000)	FOOD STORES 2003‡* Sales ($1,000)	FURNITURE, HOME FURNISHING & APPLIANCE STORES 2003‡* Sales ($1,000)	AUTOMOTIVE DEALERS 2003‡* Sales ($1,000)
Alabama	01	47,869,124	**14,080**	36,623,327	**14,882**	27,733,562	**14,636**	10,874,252	**16,742**	7,605,392	**16,291**	8,692,589	2,181,663	2,416,340	6,673,254	1,878,353	12,583,091
Alaska	02	8,314,088	**2,446**	6,251,372	**2,540**	4,981,919	**2,629**	2,123,303	**3,269**	1,533,403	**3,285**	1,788,280	335,023	118,165	1,342,127	295,606	1,753,782
Arizona	04	60,709,448	**17,857**	43,960,933	**17,864**	29,365,954	**15,498**	10,984,133	**16,911**	7,574,645	**16,225**	8,776,765	2,207,368	2,926,679	8,921,980	2,993,609	16,870,288
Arkansas	05	30,093,872	**8,855**	21,643,695	**8,795**	15,925,313	**8,404**	8,291,609	**12,766**	4,819,230	**10,323**	7,331,064	960,545	1,230,502	3,171,092	1,109,929	8,262,275
California	06	377,404,791	**111,017**	263,118,346	**106,921**	224,593,152	**118,524**	71,275,561	**109,737**	51,304,332	**109,895**	44,262,037	27,013,524	20,565,700	66,055,029	28,206,126	97,527,667
Colorado	08	57,617,687	**16,951**	40,536,034	**16,472**	28,532,646	**15,058**	10,479,951	**16,135**	7,056,296	**15,115**	8,201,622	2,278,329	2,010,478	8,231,077	3,948,238	15,591,001
Connecticut	09	49,806,992	**14,651**	34,938,893	**14,198**	27,753,739	**14,647**	7,004,477	**10,784**	5,655,183	**12,114**	3,943,062	3,061,415	3,147,093	7,764,901	2,698,764	12,312,685
Delaware	10	11,760,062	**3,460**	8,236,970	**3,347**	6,491,936	**3,426**	2,155,158	**3,318**	1,569,710	**3,362**	1,540,177	614,981	656,918	1,780,576	954,219	3,120,525
District of Columbia	11	3,408,245	**1,003**	2,788,831	**1,133**	3,586,625	**1,893**	614,298	**946**	558,663	**1,197**	145,053	469,245	481,206	940,510	258,447	117,468
Florida	12	212,175,371	**62,409**	151,191,241	**61,438**	118,741,770	**62,665**	40,224,246	**61,930**	28,992,896	**62,104**	27,544,533	12,679,713	13,555,446	31,050,963	12,837,674	63,281,209
Georgia	13	104,473,500	**30,730**	72,212,484	**29,344**	49,940,017	**26,355**	20,011,656	**30,810**	13,464,419	**28,841**	14,825,265	5,186,391	4,528,319	15,093,586	5,608,496	28,440,150
Hawaii	15	13,845,580	**4,073**	11,317,752	**4,599**	11,250,217	**5,937**	4,274,499	**6,581**	4,025,448	**8,623**	2,707,801	1,566,698	1,114,719	2,440,661	504,012	2,529,214
Idaho	16	16,352,387	**4,814**	11,649,609	**4,734**	7,726,843	**4,078**	2,924,297	**4,502**	1,892,114	**4,053**	2,495,026	429,271	555,695	2,489,674	819,954	4,435,812
Illinois	17	145,710,068	**42,860**	108,002,177	**43,888**	85,765,697	**45,262**	25,539,168	**39,321**	20,204,186	**43,278**	18,490,509	7,048,659	11,192,197	20,333,294	9,193,554	38,708,959
Indiana	18	76,264,128	**22,432**	57,241,650	**23,261**	42,373,476	**22,362**	15,415,310	**23,734**	10,998,165	**23,559**	12,742,454	2,672,856	4,554,552	8,378,432	3,312,935	20,247,419
Iowa	19	35,056,752	**10,310**	26,723,822	**10,859**	19,959,786	**10,534**	5,809,458	**8,944**	4,539,020	**9,723**	4,745,603	1,063,855	1,640,777	4,879,104	1,733,888	9,833,915
Kansas	20	30,716,045	**9,035**	22,571,918	**9,172**	17,566,800	**9,271**	6,387,764	**9,835**	4,390,088	**9,404**	5,120,974	1,266,790	1,456,353	4,438,950	1,767,447	8,143,080
Kentucky	21	42,260,060	**12,428**	33,332,675	**13,545**	25,267,776	**13,335**	9,164,732	**14,110**	6,735,095	**14,427**	7,415,661	1,749,071	2,780,005	5,305,305	1,704,730	10,983,826
Louisiana	22	48,523,208	**14,270**	35,807,894	**14,551**	27,806,373	**14,674**	11,269,897	**17,351**	7,519,239	**16,107**	9,139,874	2,130,023	2,866,560	6,668,639	2,048,638	12,368,437
Maine	23	18,080,289	**5,317**	12,737,087	**5,176**	10,286,757	**5,429**	2,511,596	**3,867**	2,093,023	**4,483**	1,813,632	697,964	749,012	3,723,597	549,323	4,317,718
Maryland	24	60,450,524	**17,783**	46,428,206	**18,866**	37,624,742	**19,856**	11,016,684	**16,961**	8,597,434	**18,416**	7,652,465	3,364,219	3,402,675	10,830,571	3,598,074	17,237,300
Massachusetts	25	80,785,302	**23,763**	58,578,048	**23,804**	47,663,248	**25,154**	12,877,192	**19,826**	10,206,959	**21,864**	7,255,897	5,621,295	5,913,933	14,396,539	4,870,893	19,495,157
Michigan	26	128,365,324	**37,760**	93,706,078	**38,078**	71,523,046	**37,745**	28,071,642	**43,220**	19,499,555	**41,769**	22,978,581	5,093,061	7,748,758	15,214,693	6,859,968	37,259,224
Minnesota	27	70,948,964	**20,871**	48,097,982	**19,545**	35,622,218	**18,799**	12,227,995	**18,826**	8,264,490	**17,703**	9,955,951	2,272,044	3,013,581	9,560,017	4,389,277	18,397,491
Mississippi	28	29,353,211	**8,639**	20,774,508	**8,442**	14,780,984	**7,800**	7,710,400	**11,871**	4,492,439	**9,623**	6,629,705	1,080,695	1,601,382	3,312,054	1,084,800	7,439,262
Missouri	29	65,707,730	**19,332**	51,269,881	**20,834**	37,918,234	**20,011**	12,118,411	**18,658**	9,888,877	**21,182**	10,192,466	1,925,945	3,620,047	8,623,093	2,660,547	17,681,283
Montana	30	10,614,488	**3,122**	7,779,112	**3,161**	6,246,712	**3,297**	1,920,328	**2,957**	1,390,384	**2,978**	1,640,523	279,805	344,921	1,604,676	403,331	2,933,013
Nebraska	31	22,569,932	**6,633**	16,529,333	**6,717**	11,521,818	**6,080**	3,763,801	**5,795**	2,819,227	**6,039**	3,089,792	674,009	1,198,067	2,972,244	1,323,587	5,485,910
Nevada	32	26,588,237	**7,822**	18,220,790	**7,404**	11,546,436	**6,093**	4,910,505	**7,560**	3,512,726	**7,524**	3,484,703	1,425,802	1,204,678	4,208,328	1,307,676	6,565,463
New Hampshire	33	23,893,063	**7,028**	15,812,027	**6,425**	11,099,193	**5,857**	4,330,967	**6,668**	2,875,100	**6,159**	3,419,023	911,944	861,928	3,988,780	1,362,781	6,435,126
New Jersey	34	108,684,617	**31,972**	79,914,892	**32,474**	63,109,174	**33,305**	17,019,371	**26,203**	13,967,808	**29,920**	9,663,099	7,356,272	7,157,799	19,829,135	7,924,210	28,725,623
New Mexico	35	19,163,663	**5,640**	14,984,454	**6,089**	11,279,262	**5,952**	4,295,839	**6,614**	2,788,711	**5,974**	3,554,349	741,490	969,660	2,256,342	875,563	4,987,297
New York	36	184,067,719	**54,145**	139,303,944	**56,607**	118,885,698	**62,740**	37,973,982	**58,465**	29,089,261	**62,311**	19,080,822	18,893,160	15,727,930	30,431,174	11,708,474	38,610,981
North Carolina	37	104,325,590	**30,685**	72,356,763	**29,403**	49,564,327	**26,157**	18,700,332	**28,791**	12,198,301	**26,129**	14,082,382	4,617,950	5,639,210	14,536,034	5,481,612	29,233,912
North Dakota	38	9,158,577	**2,697**	6,702,134	**2,723**	4,696,871	**2,479**	1,479,521	**2,278**	1,148,405	**2,460**	1,243,759	235,762	457,880	958,312	424,766	2,404,105
Ohio	39	136,773,683	**40,233**	102,938,830	**41,830**	79,030,973	**41,708**	24,397,758	**37,563**	19,350,352	**41,449**	18,668,355	5,729,403	9,170,449	19,270,480	7,252,073	36,687,758
Oklahoma	40	35,434,102	**10,424**	27,065,555	**10,998**	21,212,771	**11,195**	8,249,306	**12,701**	5,629,926	**12,060**	7,177,620	1,071,686	1,887,068	4,285,633	1,683,536	10,083,468
Oregon	41	46,822,313	**13,777**	33,396,849	**13,571**	24,170,222	**12,756**	10,762,494	**16,570**	7,128,228	**15,269**	8,720,416	2,042,078	1,426,266	6,704,837	2,623,838	11,893,832
Pennsylvania	42	145,109,009	**42,687**	109,948,462	**44,678**	87,787,842	**46,329**	22,358,361	**34,423**	18,566,576	**39,771**	15,030,581	7,327,780	10,075,015	24,179,500	6,582,394	37,358,522
Rhode Island	44	10,750,673	**3,163**	7,505,754	**3,050**	6,734,282	**3,554**	1,633,856	**2,516**	1,209,085	**2,590**	957,954	675,902	1,143,477	2,105,585	505,230	2,632,708
South Carolina	45	46,577,029	**13,696**	33,634,264	**13,668**	24,743,214	**13,058**	9,762,145	**15,030**	6,332,483	**13,565**	7,208,418	2,553,727	2,483,253	7,159,615	2,064,163	12,013,597
South Dakota	46	18,643,300	**5,481**	11,707,133	**4,757**	5,108,398	**2,696**	1,899,026	**2,924**	1,210,935	**2,594**	1,622,620	276,406	385,056	989,470	339,645	2,788,731
Tennessee	47	71,056,732	**20,902**	50,813,221	**20,648**	37,508,350	**19,795**	16,027,205	**24,676**	10,389,135	**22,254**	12,470,271	3,556,934	3,983,306	8,856,237	3,077,154	19,884,778
Texas	48	266,234,582	**78,314**	182,516,112	**74,167**	130,686,364	**68,968**	51,798,606	**79,750**	35,237,668	**75,481**	38,630,480	13,168,126	11,288,000	37,916,175	15,839,763	75,559,552
Utah	49	29,437,510	**8,661**	19,964,601	**8,113**	12,373,482	**6,530**	5,777,637	**8,895**	3,435,212	**7,358**	4,659,955	1,117,682	592,029	4,494,871	1,883,809	7,794,166
Vermont	50	8,218,275	**2,419**	5,898,646	**2,397**	4,734,763	**2,499**	947,151	**1,458**	726,043	**1,555**	577,615	369,536	463,438	1,480,456	311,294	2,108,027
Virginia	51	86,111,217	**25,331**	62,569,924	**25,426**	48,048,593	**25,357**	17,588,465	**27,080**	12,311,328	**26,372**	13,177,237	4,411,228	4,398,343	12,503,309	5,654,306	21,910,597
Washington	53	72,333,303	**21,279**	52,472,866	**21,323**	40,909,824	**21,590**	15,334,354	**23,609**	9,966,496	**21,349**	11,890,507	3,443,847	3,006,491	11,452,141	3,973,669	17,638,435
West Virginia	54	17,843,892	**5,248**	14,057,933	**5,713**	11,194,130	**5,908**	3,760,411	**5,790**	2,773,789	**5,942**	3,140,755	619,656	1,398,368	2,325,919	556,151	4,731,358
Wisconsin	55	66,732,238	**19,627**	50,520,463	**20,529**	38,350,527	**20,239**	12,283,076	**18,911**	8,489,600	**18,185**	10,457,690	1,825,386	2,954,461	8,922,128	3,255,444	16,720,158
Wyoming	56	6,347,503	**1,868**	4,530,537	**1,841**	3,554,153	**1,876**	1,180,815	**1,818**	815,025	**1,746**	1,042,029	138,786	126,808	881,902	236,027	1,577,640
United States		3,399,544,000	**1,000,000**	2,460,886,012	**1,000,000**	1,894,880,209	**1,000,000**	649,513,000	**1,000,000**	466,842,105	**1,000,000**	471,078,000	178,435,000	192,191,000	505,933,000	192,538,000	895,703,000

† Federal Information Processing Standards (FIPS) codes for states, as published by the National Bureau of Standards, U.S. Department of Commerce.
‡ Source: Devonshire Associates Ltd. and Scan/US, Inc. 2004.
* Data based on 1997 NAICS classification system; not directly comparable with 1987 SIC system data.
** Data based on 1992 SIC classification system; not directly comparable with NAICS data.
†† Shopping Goods figures are the combination of Apparel and General Merchandise sales.

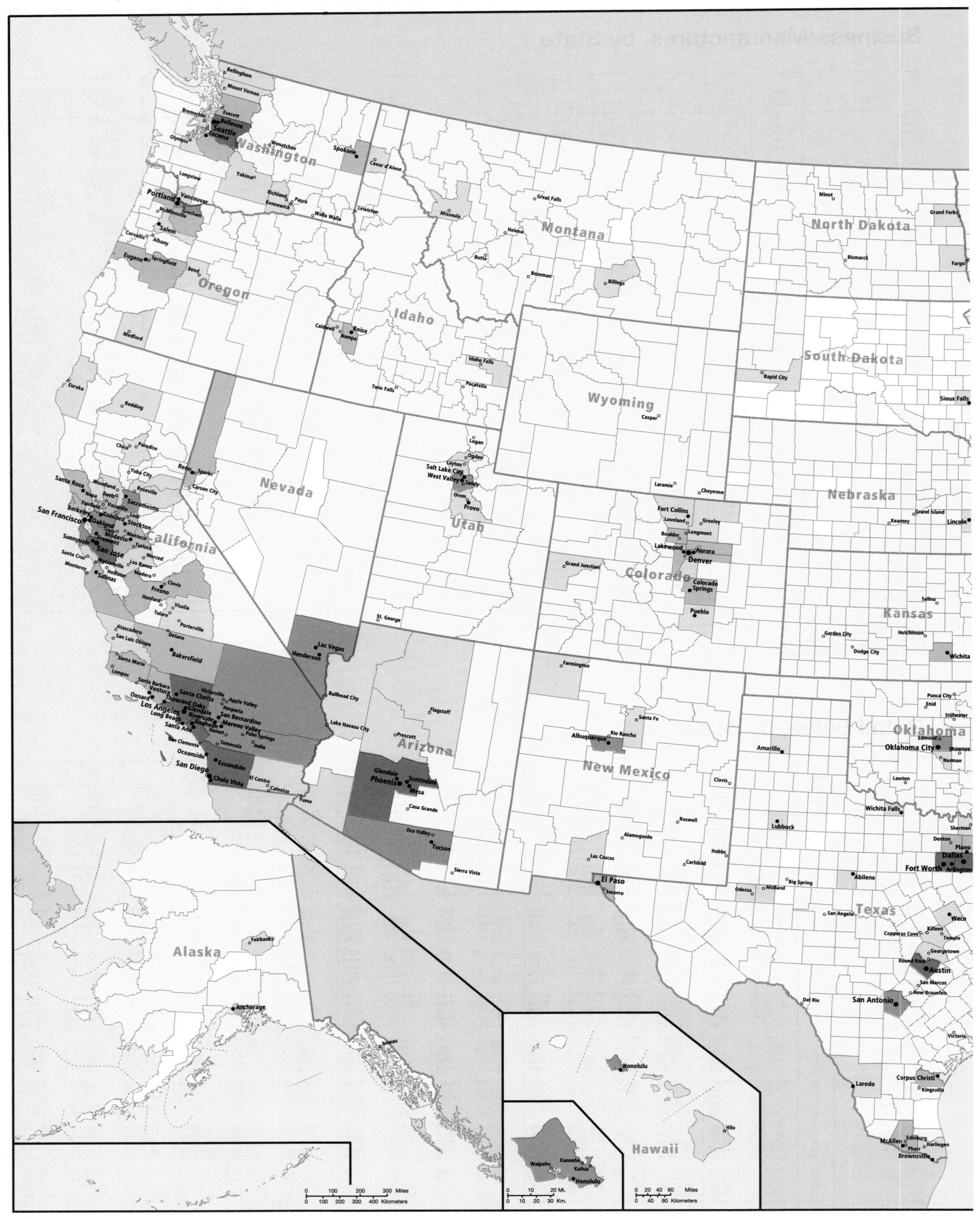

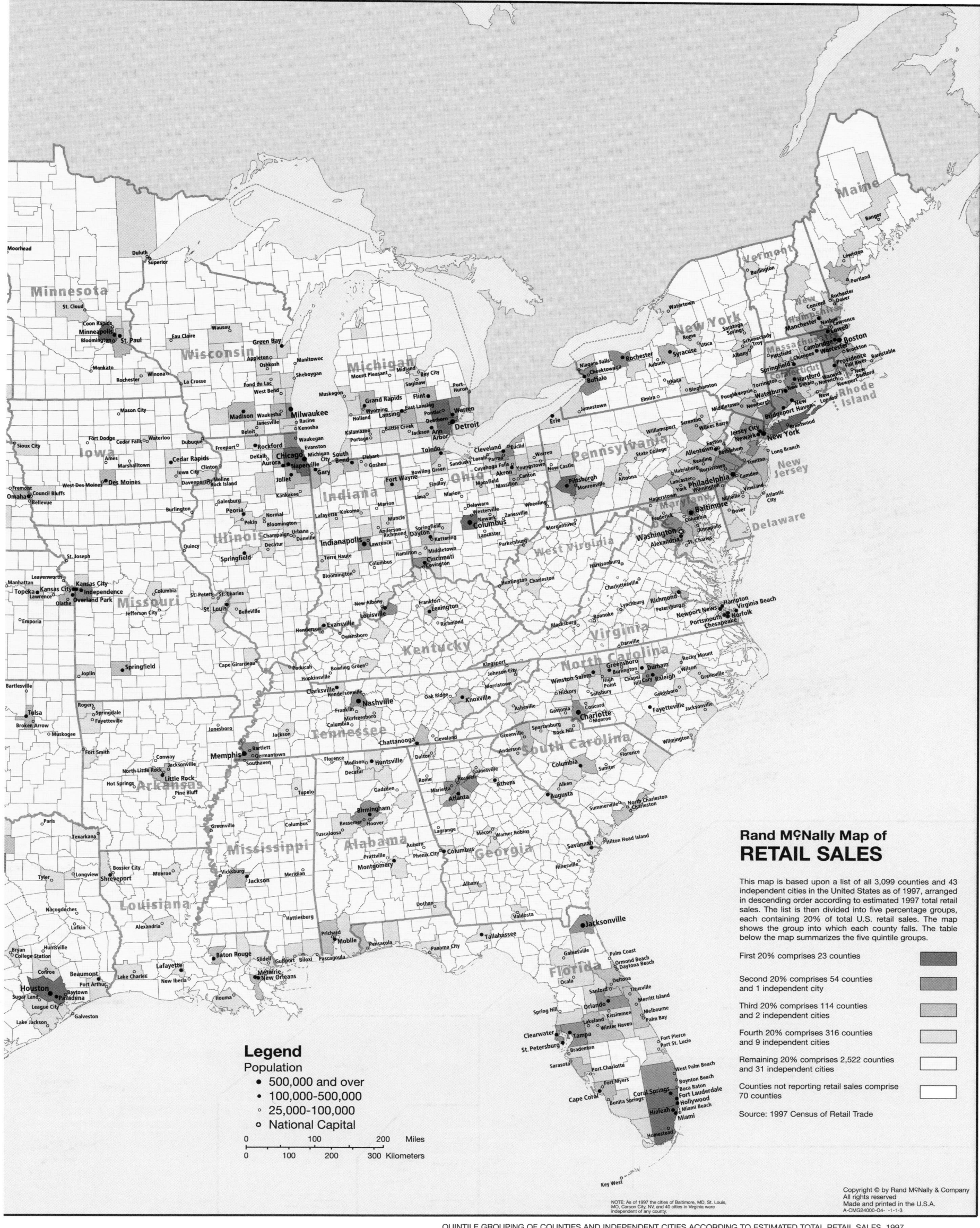

Rand McNally Map of
RETAIL SALES

This map is based upon a list of all 3,099 counties and 43 independent cities in the United States as of 1997, arranged in descending order according to estimated 1997 total retail sales. The list is then divided into five percentage groups, each containing 20% of total U.S. retail sales. The map shows the group into which each county falls. The table below the map summarizes the five quintile groups.

First 20% comprises 23 counties

Second 20% comprises 54 counties and 1 independent city

Third 20% comprises 114 counties and 2 independent cities

Fourth 20% comprises 316 counties and 9 independent cities

Remaining 20% comprises 2,522 counties and 31 independent cities

Counties not reporting retail sales comprise 70 counties

Source: 1997 Census of Retail Trade

Legend
Population
- ● 500,000 and over
- • 100,000-500,000
- ○ 25,000-100,000
- ⊙ National Capital

| 0 | 100 | 200 Miles |
| 0 | 100 | 200 | 300 Kilometers |

NOTE: As of 1997 the cities of Baltimore, MD, St. Louis, MO, Carson City, NV, and 40 cities in Virginia were independent of any county.

QUINTILE GROUPING OF COUNTIES AND INDEPENDENT CITIES ACCORDING TO ESTIMATED TOTAL RETAIL SALES, 1997

Group	Range in retail sales of counties and independent cities in each group — Largest	Smallest	Total retail sales of each group	Retail sales of each group plus all preceding groups	% of total U.S. value added contained in each group	% of total U.S. retail sales contained in each group plus all preceding groups	Number of counties & indep. cities in each group	% of the total number of counties & indep. cities in each group	Numbers of counties & indep. cities in each group plus all preceding groups	% of the total number of counties & indep. cities in each group plus all preceding groups
1	$69,534,164 to	12,825,281	500,716,144	500,716,144	20.4	20.4	23	0.7	23	0.7
2	12,662,922 to	6,497,655	487,653,772	988,369,916	19.9	40.3	55	1.8	78	2.5
3	6,491,770 to	2,759,547	485,382,377	1,473,752,293	19.8	60.1	116	3.7	194	6.2
4	2,754,452 to	891,209	490,501,062	1,964,253,355	19.9	80.0	325	10.3	519	16.5
5	890,734 to	332	490,866,097	2,455,119,452	20.0	100.0	2,553	81.3	3,072	97.8
*Counties reporting no retail sales			Dollar figures are in thousands				70	2.2	3,142	100.0

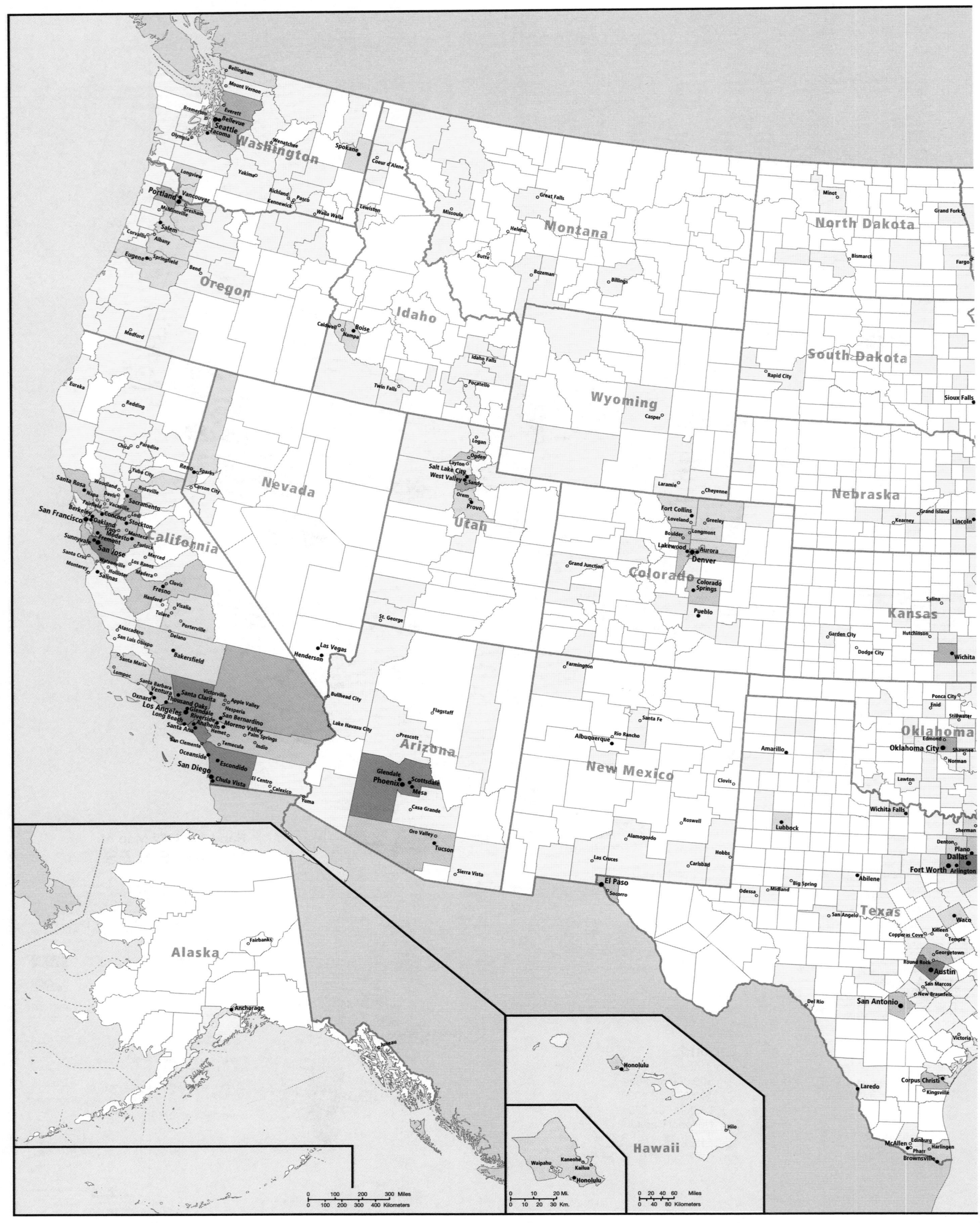

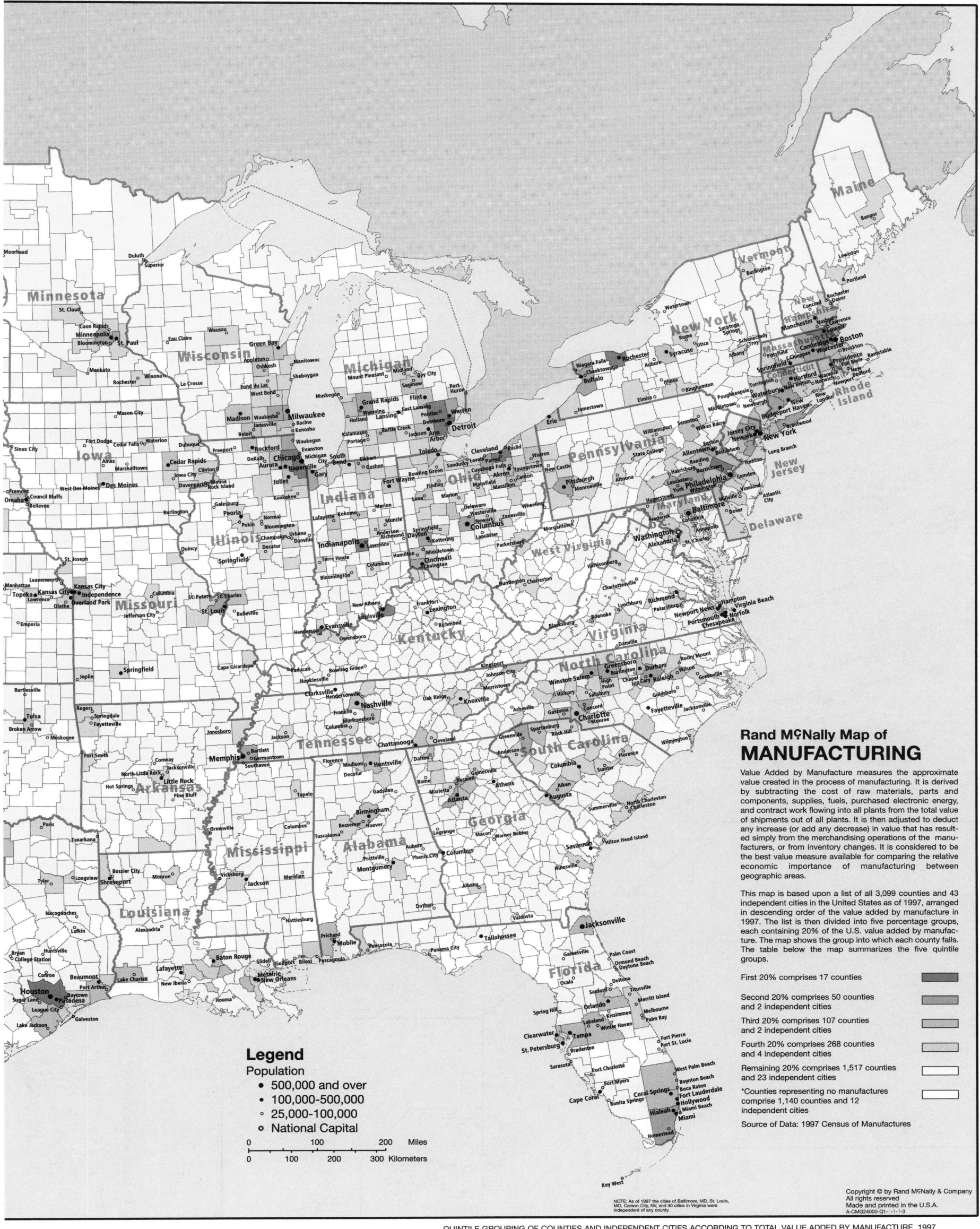

Rand McNally Map of
MANUFACTURING

Value Added by Manufacture measures the approximate value created in the process of manufacturing. It is derived by subtracting the cost of raw materials, parts and components, supplies, fuels, purchased electronic energy, and contract work flowing into all plants from the total value of shipments out of all plants. It is then adjusted to deduct any increase (or add any decrease) in value that has resulted simply from the merchandising operations of the manufacturers, or from inventory changes. It is considered to be the best value measure available for comparing the relative economic importance of manufacturing between geographic areas.

This map is based upon a list of all 3,099 counties and 43 independent cities in the United States as of 1997, arranged in descending order of the value added by manufacture in 1997. The list is then divided into five percentage groups, each containing 20% of the U.S. value added by manufacture. The map shows the group into which each county falls. The table below the map summarizes the five quintile groups.

First 20% comprises 17 counties

Second 20% comprises 50 counties and 2 independent cities

Third 20% comprises 107 counties and 2 independent cities

Fourth 20% comprises 268 counties and 4 independent cities

Remaining 20% comprises 1,517 counties and 23 independent cities

*Counties representing no manufactures comprise 1,140 counties and 12 independent cities

Source of Data: 1997 Census of Manufactures

Legend
Population
- ● 500,000 and over
- ● 100,000-500,000
- ◦ 25,000-100,000
- ⊙ National Capital

```
0        100        200   Miles
0    100    200    300  Kilometers
```

NOTE: As of 1997 the cities of Baltimore, MD, St. Louis, MO, Carson City, NV, and 40 cities in Virginia were independent of any county.

QUINTILE GROUPING OF COUNTIES AND INDEPENDENT CITIES ACCORDING TO TOTAL VALUE ADDED BY MANUFACTURE, 1997

Group	Range in value added of counties and independent cities in each group — Largest	Smallest	Total value added of each group	Value added of each group plus all preceding groups	% of total U.S. value added contained in each group	% of total U.S. value added contained in each group plus all preceding groups	Number of counties & indep. cities in each group	% of the total number of counties & indep. cities in each group	Numbers of counties & indep. cities in each group plus all preceding groups	% of the total number of counties & indep. cities in each group plus all preceding groups
1	$53,692,011 to	10,999,196	359,926,496	359,926,496	20.5	20.5	17	0.5	17	0.5
2	10,459,875 to	4,578,744	343,781,647	703,708,143	19.6	40.1	52	1.7	69	2.2
3	4,452,897 to	2,319,323	350,580,035	1,054,288,178	19.9	60.0	109	3.5	178	5.7
4	2,317,378 to	765,725	351,313,142	1,405,601,320	20.0	80.0	272	8.7	450	14.3
5	765,645 to	5,372	350,723,151	1,756,324,471	20.0	100.0	1,540	49.0	1,990	63.4
*Counties reporting no manufactures							1,152	36.6	3,142	100.0

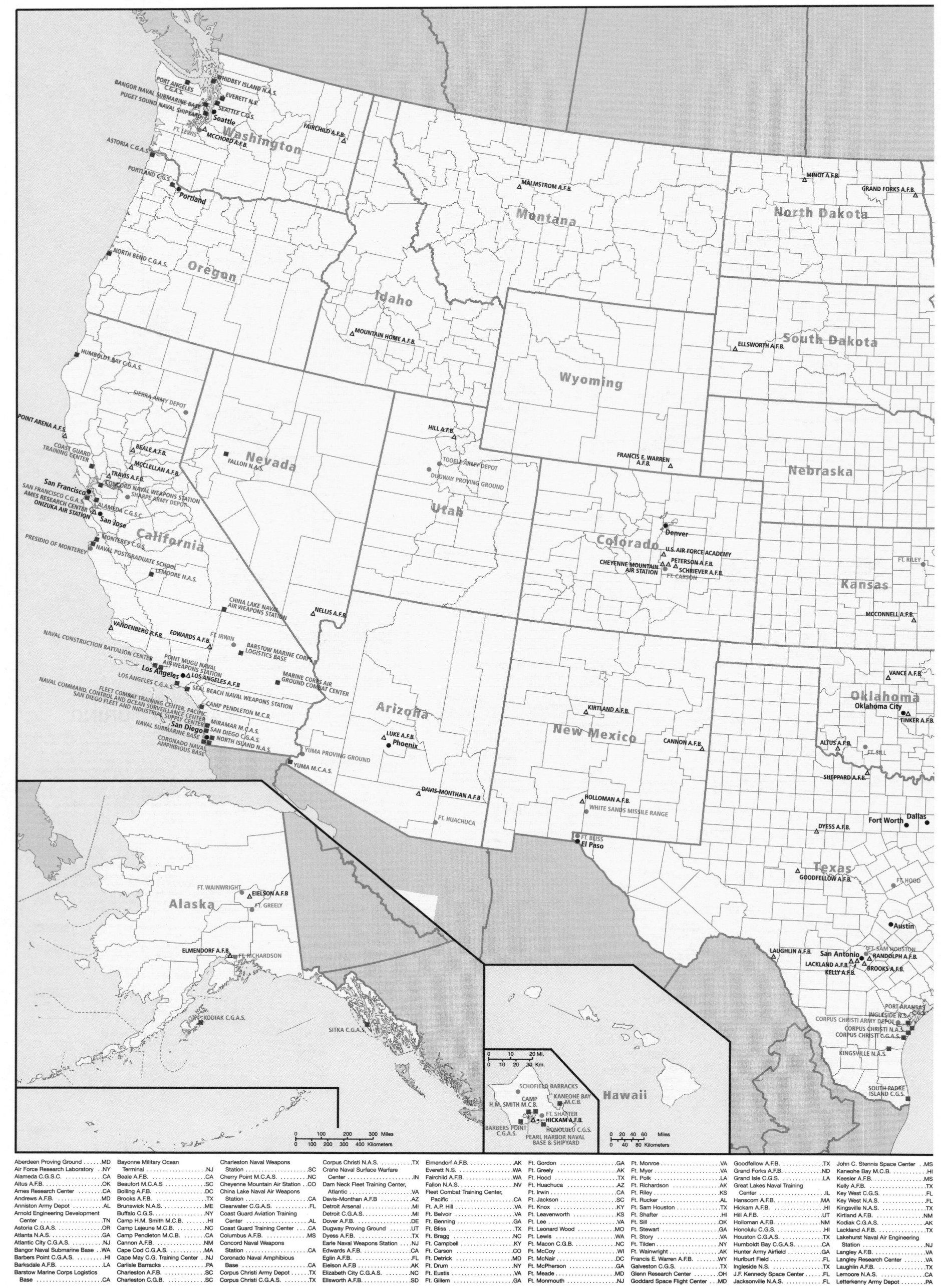

This map, in a state/county outline format, shows major military installations in the U.S. All branches of the U.S. military are included: Army, Navy, Air Force, Marine Corps, Coast Guard, and the National Aeronautics and Space Administration (NASA). The legend in the lower right portion of the map indicates the symbol used for each type of military installation.

The table below the map lists the official name of each installation and the state in which it is located.

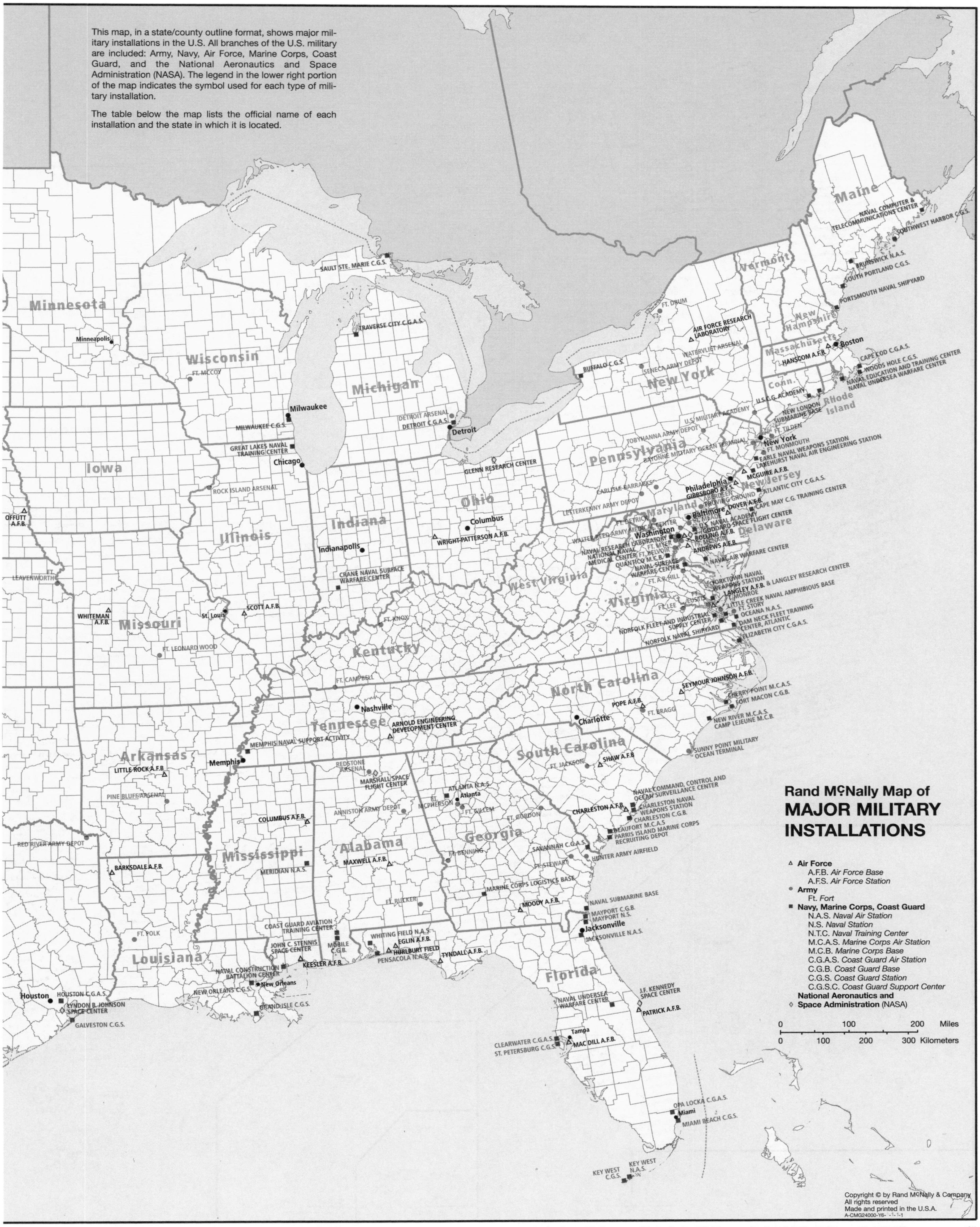

**Rand McNally Map of
MAJOR MILITARY
INSTALLATIONS**

△ **Air Force**
A.F.B. *Air Force Base*
A.F.S. *Air Force Station*
● **Army**
Ft. *Fort*
■ **Navy, Marine Corps, Coast Guard**
N.A.S. *Naval Air Station*
N.S. *Naval Station*
N.T.C. *Naval Training Center*
M.C.A.S. *Marine Corps Air Station*
M.C.B. *Marine Corps Base*
C.G.A.S. *Coast Guard Air Station*
C.G.B. *Coast Guard Base*
C.G.S. *Coast Guard Station*
C.G.S.C. *Coast Guard Support Center*
National Aeronautics and
◇ **Space Administration (NASA)**

| 0 | 100 | 200 Miles |
| 0 | 100 200 | 300 Kilometers |

Little Creek Naval Amphibious Base	VA
Little Rock A.F.B.	AR
Los Angeles A.F.B	CA
Los Angeles C.G.A.S.	CA
Luke A.F.B.	AZ
Lyndon B. Johnson Space Center	TX
MacDill A.F.B.	FL
Malmstrom A.F.B.	MT
Marine Corps Air Ground Combat Center	CA
Marine Corps Logistics Base	GA
Marshall Space Flight Center	AL
Maxwell A.F.B.	AL
Mayport C.G.B.	FL
Mayport N.S.	FL
McChord A.F.B.	WA
McClellan A.F.B.	CA
McConnell A.F.B.	KS
McGuire A.F.B.	NJ
Memphis Naval Support Activity	TN
Meridian N.A.S.	MS
Miami Beach C.G.S.	FL
Milwaukee C.G.S.	WI
Minot A.F.B.	ND
Miramar M.C.A.S.	CA
Mobile C.G.B.	AL
Monterey C.G.S.	CA
Moody A.F.B.	GA
Mountain Home A.F.B.	ID
National Naval Medical Center	MD
Naval Air Warfare Center	MD
Naval Command, Control and Ocean Surveillance Center	CA
Naval Command, Control and Ocean Surveillance Center	MS
Naval Construction Battalion Center	CA
Naval Construction Battalion Center	MS
Naval Education and Training Center	RI
Naval Postgraduate School	CA
Naval Research Laboratory	DC
Naval Submarine Base	CA
Naval Submarine Base	GA
Naval Surface Warfare Center	VA
Naval Undersea Warfare Center	FL
Naval Undersea Warfare Center	CA
Nellis A.F.B.	NV
New London Submarine Base	CT
New Orleans C.G.S.	LA
New River M.C.A.S.	NC
Norfolk Fleet and Industrial Supply Center	VA
Norfolk Naval Shipyard	VA
North Bend C.G.A.S.	OR
North Island N.A.S.	CA
Oceana N.A.S.	VA
Offutt A.F.B.	NE
Onizuka Air Station	CA
Opa Locka C.G.A.S.	FL
Parris Island Marine Corps Recruiting Depot	SC
Patrick A.F.B.	FL
Pearl Harbor Naval Base & Shipyard	HI
Pensacola N.A.S.	FL
Peterson A.F.B.	CO
Pine Bluff Arsenal	AR
Point Arena A.F.S.	CA
Point Mugu Naval Air Weapons Station	CA
Pope A.F.B.	NC
Port Angeles C.G.A.S.	WA
Port Aransas C.G.S.	TX
Portland C.G.S.	OR
Portsmouth Naval Shipyard	NH
Presidio of Monterey	CA
Puget Sound Naval Shipyard	WA
Quantico M.C.B.	VA
Randolph A.F.B.	TX
Red River Army Depot	TX
Redstone Arsenal	AL
Robins A.F.B.	GA
Rock Island Arsenal	IL
San Diego C.G.A.S.	CA
San Diego Fleet and Industrial Supply Center	CA
San Francisco C.G.A.S.	CA
Sault Ste. Marie C.G.S.	MI
Savannah C.G.A.S.	GA
Schofield Barracks	HI
Schriever A.F.B.	CO
Scott A.F.B.	IL
Seal Beach Naval Weapons Station	CA
Seattle C.G.S.	WA
Seneca Army Depot	NY
Seymour Johnson A.F.B.	NC
Sharpe Army Depot	CA
Shaw A.F.B.	SC
Sheppard A.F.B.	TX
Sierra Army Depot	CA
Sitka C.G.A.S.	AK
South Padre Island C.G.S.	TX
South Portland C.G.S.	ME
Southwest Harbor C.G.S.	ME
St. Petersburg C.G.S.	FL
Sunny Point Military Ocean Terminal	NC
Tobyhanna Army Depot	PA
Tooele Army Depot	UT
Travis A.F.B.	CA
Tyndall A.F.B.	FL
U.S. Air Force Academy	CO
U.S. Coast Guard Academy	CT
U.S. Military Academy	NY
U.S. Naval Academy	MD
Vance A.F.B.	OK
Vandenberg A.F.B.	CA
Walter Reed Army Medical Center	DC
Watervliet Arsenal	NY
Whidbey Island N.A.S.	WA
White Sands Missile Range	NM
Whiteman A.F.B.	MO
Whiting Field N.A.S.	FL
Woods Hole C.G.S.	MA
Wright-Patterson A.F.B.	OH
Yorktown Naval Weapons Station	VA
Yuma M.C.A.S.	AZ
Yuma Proving Ground	AZ

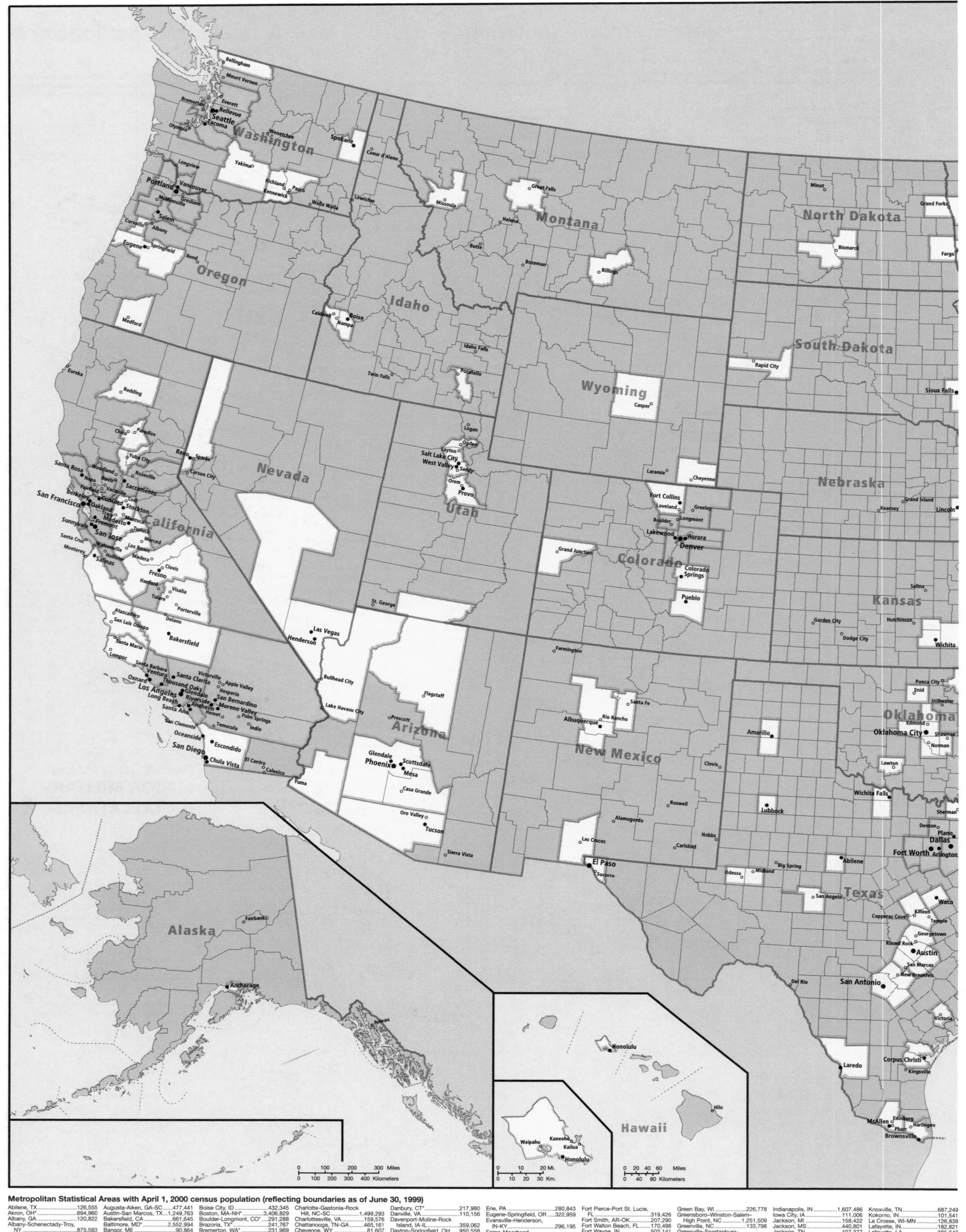

Metropolitan Statistical Areas with April 1, 2000 census population (reflecting boundaries as of June 30, 1999)

Abilene, TX..........126,555
Akron, OH*..........694,960
Albany, GA..........120,822
Albany-Schenectady-Troy, NY..........875,583
Albuquerque, NM..........712,738
Alexandria, LA..........126,337
Allentown-Bethlehem-Easton, PA..........637,958
Altoona, PA..........129,144
Amarillo, TX..........217,858
Anchorage, AK..........260,283
Ann Arbor, MI*..........578,736
Anniston, AL..........112,249
Appleton-Oshkosh-Neenah, WI..........358,365
Asheville, NC..........225,965
Athens, GA..........153,444
Atlanta, GA..........4,112,198
Atlantic-Cape May, NJ*..........354,878
Auburn-Opelika, AL..........115,092

Augusta-Aiken, GA-SC..........477,441
Austin-San Marcos, TX..........1,249,763
Bakersfield, CA..........661,645
Baltimore, MD*..........2,552,994
Bangor, ME..........90,864
Barnstable-Yarmouth, MA..........162,582
Baton Rouge, LA..........602,894
Beaumont-Port Arthur, TX..........385,090
Bellingham, WA..........166,814
Benton Harbor, MI..........162,453
Bergen-Passaic, NJ*..........1,373,167
Billings, MT..........129,352
Biloxi-Gulfport-Pascagoula, MS..........363,988
Binghamton, NY..........252,320
Birmingham, AL..........921,106
Bismarck, ND..........94,719
Bloomington, IN..........120,563
Bloomington-Normal, IL..........150,433

Boise City, ID..........432,345
Boston, MA-NH*..........3,406,829
Boulder-Longmont, CO*..........291,288
Brazoria, TX*..........241,767
Bremerton, WA*..........231,969
Bridgeport, CT*..........459,479
Brockton, MA*..........255,459
Brownsville-Harlingen-San Benito, TX..........335,227
Bryan-College Station, TX..........152,415
Buffalo-Niagara Falls, NY..........1,170,111
Burlington, VT..........169,391
Canton-Massillon, OH..........406,934
Casper, WY..........66,533
Cedar Rapids, IA..........191,701
Champaign-Urbana, IL..........179,669
Charleston, WV..........251,662
Charleston-North Charleston, SC..........549,033

Charlotte-Gastonia-Rock Hill, NC-SC..........1,499,293
Charlottesville, VA..........159,576
Chattanooga, TN-GA..........465,161
Davenport-Moline-Rock Island, IL-IA..........359,062
Cheyenne, WY..........81,607
Chicago, IL*..........8,272,768
Chico-Paradise, CA..........203,171
Cincinnati, OH-KY-IN*..........1,646,395
Clarksville-Hopkinsville, TN-KY..........207,033
Cleveland-Lorain-Elyria, OH*..........2,250,871
Colorado Springs, CO..........516,929
Columbia, MO..........135,454
Columbia, SC..........536,691
Columbus, GA-AL..........274,624
Columbus, OH*..........1,540,157
Corpus Christi, TX..........380,783
Corvallis, OR..........78,153
Cumberland, MD-WV..........102,008
Dallas, TX*..........3,519,176

Danbury, CT*..........217,980
Danville, VA..........110,156
Dayton-Springfield, OH..........950,558
Daytona Beach, FL..........493,175
Decatur, AL..........145,867
Decatur, IL..........114,706
Denver, CO*..........2,109,282
Des Moines, IA..........456,022
Detroit, MI*..........4,441,551
Dothan, AL..........137,916
Dover, DE..........126,697
Dubuque, IA..........89,143
Duluth-Superior, MN-WI..........243,815
Dutchess County, NY*..........280,150
Eau Claire, WI..........148,337
El Paso, TX..........679,622
Elkhart-Goshen, IN..........182,791
Elmira, NY..........91,070
Enid, OK..........57,813

Erie, PA..........280,843
Eugene-Springfield, OR..........322,959
Evansville-Henderson, IN-KY..........296,195
Fargo-Moorhead, ND-MN..........174,367
Fayetteville, NC..........302,963
Fayetteville-Springdale-Rogers, AR..........311,121
Fitchburg-Leominster, MA*..........142,284
Flagstaff, AZ-UT..........122,366
Flint, MI*..........436,141
Florence, AL..........142,950
Florence, SC..........125,761
Fort Collins-Loveland, CO..........251,494
Fort Lauderdale, FL*..........1,623,018
Fort Myers-Cape Coral, FL..........440,888

Fort Pierce-Port St. Lucie, FL..........319,426
Fort Smith, AR-OK..........207,290
Fort Walton Beach, FL..........170,498
Fort Wayne, IN..........502,141
Fort Worth-Arlington, TX*..........1,702,625
Fresno, CA..........922,516
Gadsden, AL..........103,459
Gainesville, FL..........217,955
Galveston-Texas City, TX*..........250,158
Gary, IN*..........631,362
Glens Falls, NY..........124,345
Goldsboro, NC..........113,329
Grand Forks, ND-MN..........97,478
Grand Junction, CO..........116,255
Grand Rapids-Muskegon-Holland, MI..........1,088,514
Great Falls, MT..........80,357
Greeley, CO*..........180,936

Green Bay, WI..........226,778
Greensboro-Winston-Salem-High Point, NC..........1,251,509
Greenville, NC..........133,798
Greenville-Spartanburg-Anderson, SC..........962,441
Hagerstown, MD*..........131,923
Hamilton-Middletown, OH*..........332,807
Harrisburg-Lebanon-Carlisle, PA..........629,401
Hartford, CT..........1,183,110
Hattiesburg, MS..........111,674
Hickory-Morganton-Lenoir, NC..........341,851
Honolulu, HI..........876,156
Houma, LA..........194,477
Houston, TX*..........4,177,646
Huntington-Ashland, WV-KY-OH..........315,538
Huntsville, AL..........342,376

Indianapolis, IN..........1,607,486
Iowa City, IA..........111,006
Jackson, MI..........158,422
Jackson, MS..........440,801
Jackson, TN..........107,377
Jacksonville, FL..........1,100,491
Jacksonville, NC..........150,355
Jamestown, NY..........139,750
Janesville-Beloit, WI..........152,307
Jersey City, NJ*..........608,975
Johnson City-Kingsport-Bristol, TN-VA..........480,091
Johnstown, PA..........232,621
Jonesboro, AR..........82,148
Joplin, MO..........157,322
Kalamazoo-Battle Creek, MI..........452,851
Kankakee, IL*..........103,833
Kansas City, MO-KS..........1,776,062
Kenosha, WI*..........149,577
Killeen-Temple, TX..........312,952

Knoxville, TN..........687,249
Kokomo, IN..........101,541
La Crosse, WI-MN..........126,838
Lafayette, IN..........182,821
Lafayette, LA..........385,647
Lake Charles, LA..........183,577
Lakeland-Winter Haven, FL..........483,924
Lancaster, PA..........470,658
Lansing-East Lansing, MI..........447,728
Laredo, TX..........193,117
Las Cruces, NM..........174,682
Las Vegas, NV-AZ..........1,563,282
Lawrence, KS..........99,962
Lawrence, MA-NH*..........396,230
Lawton, OK..........114,996
Lewiston-Auburn, ME..........90,830
Lexington, KY..........479,198
Lima, OH..........155,084
Lincoln, NE..........250,291

* Primary Metropolitan Statistical Area

This map shows the official **Metropolitan Statistical Areas** (MSAs) as defined and published by the Office of Management and Budget (OMB) on December 31, 1992, and as revised through June 30, 1999. The general "metropolitan area" concept is that of a geographic area consisting of a large population nucleus together with adjacent communities and areas having a high degree of economic and social integration with that nucleus. The major purpose of defining these areas is to enable all Federal statistical agencies to use common definitions when studying metropolitan characteristics. The Federal government makes available various types of data for each of these MSAs; they are also used by many state and local agencies.

OMB follows specific rules in determining MSA status. An area qualifies for recognition as a Metropolitan Statistical Area in one of two ways: the area has **(1)** a city of at least 50,000 population, or **(2)** an urbanized area of at least 50,000 with a total metropolian population of at least 100,000. (Urbanized areas are defined by the Census Bureau and include the continuously built-up territory in and around each large city.) MSAs are defined in terms of entire counties, except in the six New England states where they are defined in terms of cities and towns (townships). In addition to including the county containing the main city, an MSA may also include additional counties having strong economic and social ties to the central county. If a metropolitan area has more than one million population and meets certain other requirements, it is designated a **Consolidated Metropolitan Statistical Area** (CMSA) and consists of several component areas which are termed **Primary Metropolitan Statistical Areas** (PMSAs). Federal statistics are issued both for the CMSAs and their constituent PMSAs.

New England County Metropolitan Areas (NECMAs) have also been defined in order to provide a uniform set of county-based metropolitan areas, as a convenience for users whose data are not available on a subcounty basis. Generally, each NECMA includes those counties that have more than half of their populations included in the corresponding MSA or CMSA; however, some NECMAs include more than one MSA located in the same county. Names of NECMAs are based on those of the associated MSAs and PMSAs. NECMAs are not shown on this map.

All metropolitan area boundaries are outlined on this map in red. MSAs are untinted while CMSAs and their component PMSAs are identified by the presence of a red tint. The alphabetical list below the map includes all MSAs and PMSAs with their 2000 census population. The table at the right margin of the map lists each CMSA and its component PMSAs, along with their 2000 census populations.

Metropolitan Statistical Areas as defined by OMB differ from **Ranally Metro Areas** in that MSA boundaries, except for the six New England states, are based solely upon county boundaries. Although RMAs offer the most precise look at areas of concentrated population, the use of MSAs is sometimes more convenient for the compilation of detailed statistics or for making general comparisons. Statistical information on MSAs, PMSAs and CMSAs is presented in the Population, Income and Sales Data tables for Metropolitan Statistical Areas found on pages 40-44.

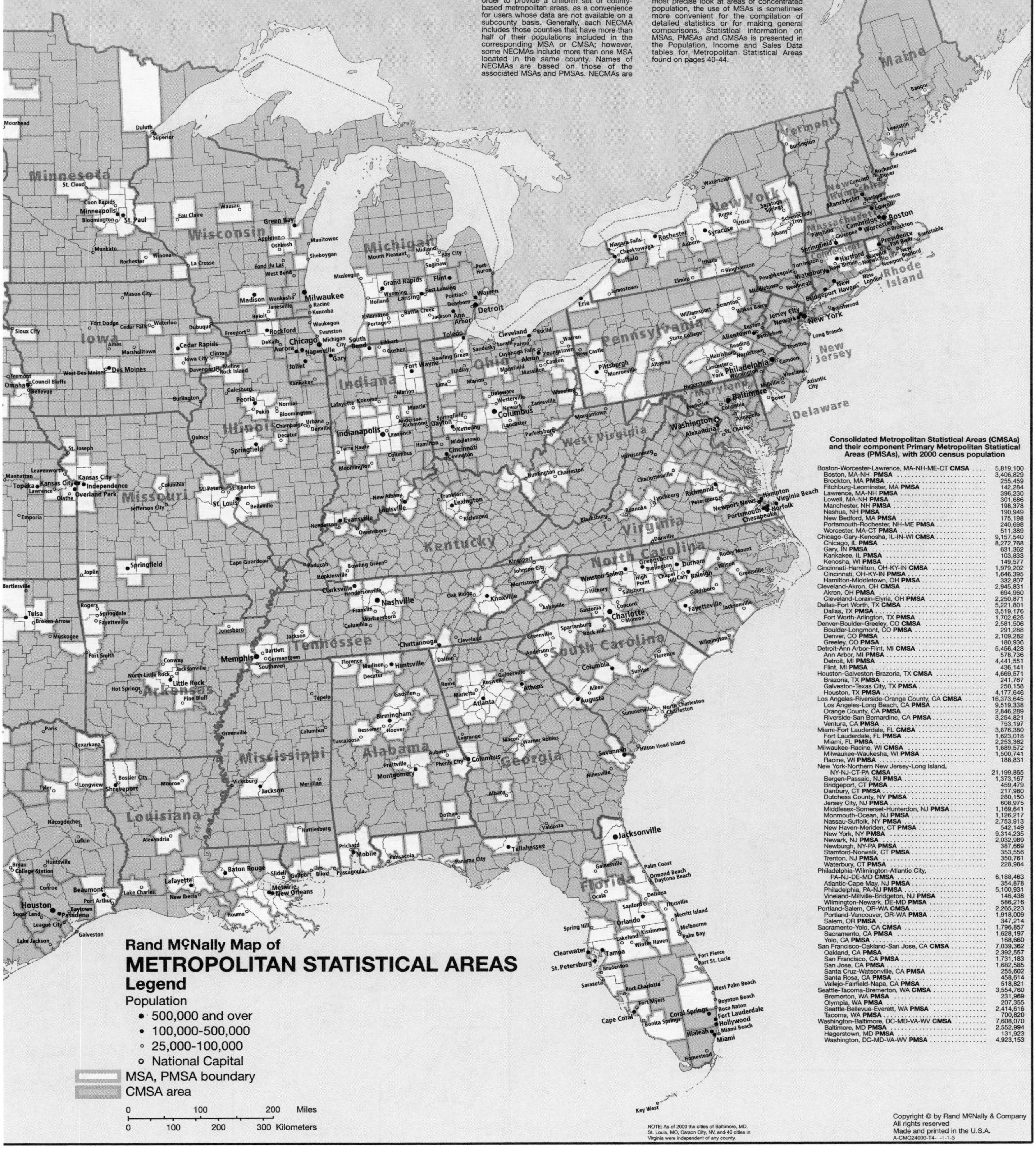

Rand McNally Map of
METROPOLITAN STATISTICAL AREAS
Legend

Population
- 500,000 and over
- 100,000-500,000
- 25,000-100,000
- National Capital

MSA, PMSA boundary
CMSA area

0 100 200 Miles
0 100 200 300 Kilometers

NOTE: As of 2000 the cities of Baltimore, MD, St. Louis, MO, Carson City, NV, and 40 cities in Virginia were independent of any county.

Consolidated Metropolitan Statistical Areas (CMSAs) and their component Primary Metropolitan Statistical Areas (PMSAs), with 2000 census population

Boston-Worcester-Lawrence, MA-NH-ME-CT **CMSA**	5,819,100
Boston, MA-NH **PMSA**	3,406,829
Brockton, MA **PMSA**	255,459
Fitchburg-Leominster, MA **PMSA**	142,284
Lawrence, MA-NH **PMSA**	396,230
Lowell, MA-NH **PMSA**	301,686
Manchester, NH **PMSA**	198,378
Nashua, NH **PMSA**	190,949
New Bedford, MA **PMSA**	175,198
Portsmouth-Rochester, NH-ME **PMSA**	240,698
Worcester, MA-CT **PMSA**	511,389
Chicago-Gary-Kenosha, IL-IN-WI **CMSA**	9,157,540
Chicago, IL **PMSA**	8,272,768
Gary, IN **PMSA**	631,362
Kankakee, IL **PMSA**	103,833
Kenosha, WI **PMSA**	149,577
Cincinnati-Hamilton, OH-KY-IN **CMSA**	1,979,202
Cincinnati, OH-KY-IN **PMSA**	1,646,395
Hamilton-Middletown, OH **PMSA**	332,807
Cleveland-Akron, OH **CMSA**	2,945,831
Akron, OH **PMSA**	694,960
Cleveland-Lorain-Elyria, OH **PMSA**	2,250,871
Dallas-Fort Worth, TX **CMSA**	5,221,801
Dallas, TX **PMSA**	3,519,176
Fort Worth-Arlington, TX **PMSA**	1,702,625
Denver-Boulder-Greeley, CO **CMSA**	2,581,506
Boulder-Longmont, CO **PMSA**	291,288
Denver, CO **PMSA**	2,109,282
Greeley, CO **PMSA**	180,936
Detroit-Ann Arbor-Flint, MI **CMSA**	5,456,428
Ann Arbor, MI **PMSA**	578,736
Detroit, MI **PMSA**	4,441,551
Flint, MI **PMSA**	436,141
Houston-Galveston-Brazoria, TX **CMSA**	4,669,571
Brazoria, TX **PMSA**	241,767
Galveston-Texas City, TX **PMSA**	250,158
Houston, TX **PMSA**	4,177,646
Los Angeles-Riverside-Orange County, CA **CMSA**	16,373,645
Los Angeles-Long Beach, CA **PMSA**	9,519,338
Orange County, CA **PMSA**	2,846,289
Riverside-San Bernardino, CA **PMSA**	3,254,821
Ventura, CA **PMSA**	753,197
Miami-Fort Lauderdale, FL **CMSA**	3,876,380
Fort Lauderdale, FL **PMSA**	1,623,018
Miami, FL **PMSA**	2,253,362
Milwaukee-Racine, WI **CMSA**	1,689,572
Milwaukee-Waukesha, WI **PMSA**	1,500,741
Racine, WI **PMSA**	188,831
New York-Northern New Jersey-Long Island, NY-NJ-CT-PA **CMSA**	21,199,865
Bergen-Passaic, NJ **PMSA**	1,373,167
Bridgeport, CT **PMSA**	459,479
Danbury, CT **PMSA**	217,980
Dutchess County, NY **PMSA**	280,150
Jersey City, NJ **PMSA**	608,975
Middlesex-Somerset-Hunterdon, NJ **PMSA**	1,169,641
Monmouth-Ocean, NJ **PMSA**	1,126,217
Nassau-Suffolk, NY **PMSA**	2,753,913
New Haven-Meriden, CT **PMSA**	542,149
New York, NY **PMSA**	9,314,235
Newark, NJ **PMSA**	2,032,989
Newburgh, NY-PA **PMSA**	387,669
Stamford-Norwalk, CT **PMSA**	353,556
Trenton, NJ **PMSA**	350,761
Waterbury, CT **PMSA**	228,984
Philadelphia-Wilmington-Atlantic City, PA-NJ-DE-MD **CMSA**	6,188,463
Atlantic-Cape May, NJ **PMSA**	354,878
Philadelphia, PA-NJ **PMSA**	5,100,931
Vineland-Millville-Bridgeton, NJ **PMSA**	146,438
Wilmington-Newark, DE-MD **PMSA**	586,216
Portland-Salem, OR-WA **CMSA**	2,265,223
Portland-Vancouver, OR-WA **PMSA**	1,918,009
Salem, OR **PMSA**	347,214
Sacramento-Yolo, CA **CMSA**	1,796,857
Sacramento, CA **PMSA**	1,628,197
Yolo, CA **PMSA**	168,660
San Francisco-Oakland-San Jose, CA **CMSA**	7,039,362
Oakland, CA **PMSA**	2,392,557
San Francisco, CA **PMSA**	1,731,183
San Jose, CA **PMSA**	1,682,585
Santa Cruz-Watsonville, CA **PMSA**	255,602
Santa Rosa, CA **PMSA**	458,614
Vallejo-Fairfield-Napa, CA **PMSA**	518,821
Seattle-Tacoma-Bremerton, WA **CMSA**	3,554,760
Bremerton, WA **PMSA**	231,969
Olympia, WA **PMSA**	207,355
Seattle-Bellevue-Everett, WA **PMSA**	2,414,616
Tacoma, WA **PMSA**	700,820
Washington-Baltimore, DC-MD-VA-WV **CMSA**	7,608,070
Baltimore, MD **PMSA**	2,552,994
Hagerstown, MD **PMSA**	131,923
Washington, DC-MD-VA-WV **PMSA**	4,923,153

Little Rock-North Little Rock, AR	583,845
Longview-Marshall, TX	208,780
Los Angeles-Long Beach, CA*	9,519,338
Louisville, KY-IN	1,025,598
Lowell, MA-NH*	301,686
Lubbock, TX	242,628
Lynchburg, VA	214,911
Macon, GA	322,549
Madison, WI	426,526
Manchester, NH*	198,378
Mansfield, OH	175,818
McAllen-Edinburg-Mission, TX	569,463
Medford-Ashland, OR	181,269
Melbourne-Titusville-Palm Bay, FL	476,230
Memphis, TN-AR-MS	1,135,614
Merced, CA	210,554
Miami, FL*	2,253,362
Middlesex-Somerset-Hunterdon, NJ*	1,169,641
Milwaukee-Waukesha, WI*	1,500,741
Minneapolis-St. Paul, MN-WI	2,968,806
Missoula, MT	95,802
Mobile, AL	540,258
Modesto, CA	446,997
Monmouth-Ocean, NJ*	1,126,217
Monroe, LA	147,250
Montgomery, AL	333,055
Muncie, IN	118,769
Myrtle Beach, SC	196,629
Naples, FL	251,377
Nashua, NH*	190,949
Nashville, TN	1,231,311
Nassau-Suffolk, NY*	2,753,913
Newark, NJ*	2,032,989
New Bedford, MA*	175,198
Newburgh, NY-PA*	387,669
New Haven-Meriden, CT*	542,149
New London-Norwich, CT-RI	293,566
New Orleans, LA	1,337,726
New York, NY*	9,314,235
Norfolk-Virginia Beach-Newport News, VA-NC	1,569,541
Oakland, CA*	2,392,557
Ocala, FL	258,916
Odessa-Midland, TX	237,132
Oklahoma City, OK	1,083,346
Olympia, WA*	207,355
Omaha, NE-IA	716,998
Orange County, CA*	2,846,289
Orlando, FL	1,644,561
Owensboro, KY	91,545
Panama City, FL	148,217
Parkersburg-Marietta, WV-OH	151,237
Pensacola, FL	412,153
Peoria-Pekin, IL	347,387
Philadelphia, PA-NJ*	5,100,931
Phoenix-Mesa, AZ	3,251,876
Pine Bluff, AR	84,278
Pittsburgh, PA	2,358,695
Pittsfield, MA	84,699
Pocatello, ID	75,565
Portland, ME	243,537
Portland-Vancouver, OR-WA*	1,918,009
Portsmouth-Rochester, NH-ME*	240,698
Providence-Fall River-Warwick, RI-MA	1,188,613
Provo-Orem, UT	368,536
Pueblo, CO	141,472
Punta Gorda, FL	141,627
Racine, WI*	188,831
Raleigh-Durham-Chapel Hill, NC	1,187,941
Rapid City, SD	88,565
Reading, PA	373,638
Redding, CA	163,256
Reno, NV	339,486
Richland-Kennewick-Pasco, WA	191,822
Richmond-Petersburg, VA	996,512
Riverside-San Bernardino, CA*	3,254,821
Roanoke, VA	235,932
Rochester, MN	124,277
Rochester, NY	1,098,201
Rockford, IL	371,236
Rocky Mount, NC	143,026
Sacramento, CA*	1,628,197
Saginaw-Bay City-Midland, MI	403,070
St. Cloud, MN	167,392
St. Joseph, MO	102,490
St. Louis, MO-IL	2,603,607
Salem, OR*	347,214
Salinas, CA	401,762
Salt Lake City-Ogden, UT	1,333,914
San Angelo, TX	104,010
San Antonio, TX	1,592,383
San Diego, CA	2,813,833
San Francisco, CA*	1,731,183
San Jose, CA*	1,682,585
San Luis Obispo-Atascadero-Paso Robles, CA	246,681
Santa Barbara-Santa Maria-Lompoc, CA	399,347
Santa Cruz-Watsonville, CA*	255,602
Santa Fe, NM	147,635
Santa Rosa, CA*	458,614
Sarasota-Bradenton, FL	589,959
Savannah, GA	293,000
Scranton–Wilkes-Barre–Hazleton, PA	624,776
Seattle-Bellevue-Everett, WA*	2,414,616
Sharon, PA	120,293
Sheboygan, WI	112,646
Sherman-Denison,TX	110,595
Shreveport-Bossier City, LA	392,302
Sioux City, IA-NE	124,130
Sioux Falls, SD	172,412
South Bend, IN	265,559
Spokane, WA	417,939
Springfield, IL	201,437
Springfield, MA	591,932
Springfield, MO	325,721
Stamford-Norwalk, CT*	353,556
State College, PA	135,758
Steubenville-Weirton, OH-WV	132,008
Stockton-Lodi, CA	563,598
Sumter, SC	104,646
Syracuse, NY	732,117
Tacoma, WA*	700,820
Tallahassee, FL	284,539
Tampa-St. Petersburg-Clearwater, FL	2,395,997
Terre Haute, IN	149,192
Texarkana,TX-AR	129,749
Toledo, OH	618,203
Topeka, KS	169,871
Trenton, NJ*	350,761
Tucson, AZ	843,746
Tulsa, OK	803,235
Tuscaloosa, AL	164,875
Tyler, TX	174,706
Utica-Rome, NY	299,896
Vallejo-Fairfield-Napa, CA*	518,821
Ventura, CA*	753,197
Victoria, TX	84,088
Vineland-Millville-Bridgeton, NJ*	146,438
Visalia-Tulare-Porterville, CA	368,021
Waco, TX	213,517
Washington, DC-MD-VA-WV*	4,923,153
Waterbury, CT*	228,984
Waterloo-Cedar Falls, IA	128,012
Wausau, WI	125,834
West Palm Beach-Boca Raton, FL	1,131,184
Wheeling, WV-OH	153,172
Wichita Falls, TX	140,518
Wichita, KS	545,220
Williamsport, PA	120,044
Wilmington, NC	233,450
Wilmington-Newark, DE-MD*	586,216
Worcester, MA-CT*	511,389
Yakima, WA	222,581
Yolo, CA*	168,660
York, PA	381,751
Youngstown-Warren, OH	594,746
Yuba City, CA	139,149
Yuma, AZ	160,026

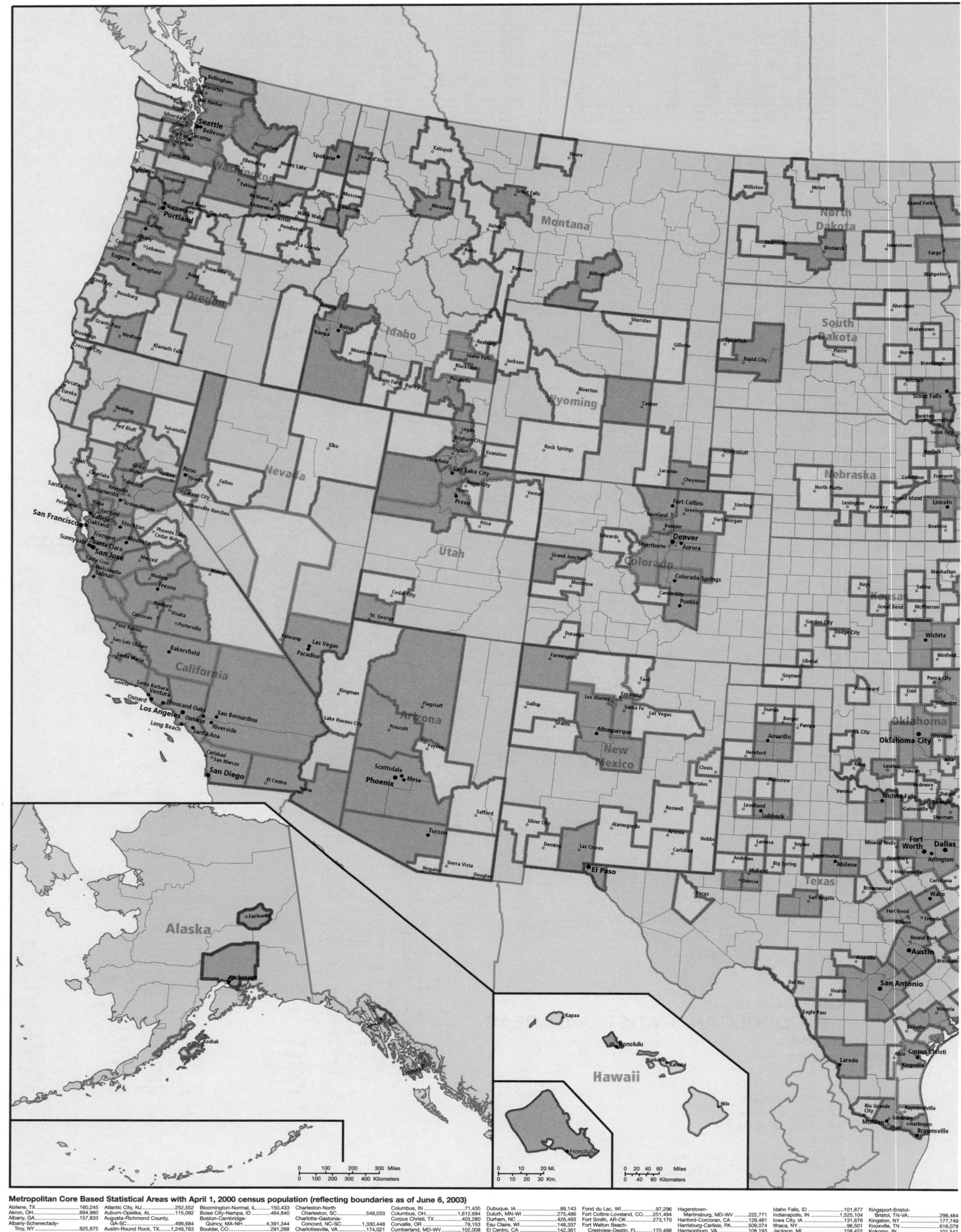

Metropolitan Core Based Statistical Areas with April 1, 2000 census population (reflecting boundaries as of June 6, 2003)

Abilene, TX	160,245	
Akron, OH	694,960	
Albany, GA	157,833	
Albany-Schenectady-Troy, NY	825,875	
Albuquerque, NM	729,649	
Alexandria, LA	145,035	
Allentown-Bethlehem-Easton, PA-NJ	740,395	
Altoona, PA	129,144	
Amarillo, TX	226,522	
Ames, IA	79,981	
Anchorage, AK	319,605	
Anderson, IN	133,358	
Anderson, SC	165,740	
Ann Arbor, MI	322,895	
Anniston-Oxford, AL	112,249	
Appleton, WI	201,602	
Asheville, NC	369,171	
Athens-Clarke County, GA	166,079	
Atlanta-Sandy Springs-Marietta, GA	4,247,981	
Atlantic City, NJ	252,552	
Auburn-Opelika, AL	115,092	
Augusta-Richmond County, GA-SC	499,684	
Austin-Round Rock, TX	1,249,763	
Bakersfield, CA	661,645	
Baltimore-Towson, MD	2,552,994	
Bangor, ME	144,919	
Barnstable Town, MA	222,230	
Baton Rouge, LA	705,973	
Battle Creek, MI	137,985	
Bay City, MI	110,157	
Beaumont-Port Arthur, TX	385,090	
Bellingham, WA	166,814	
Bend, OR	115,367	
Billings, MT	138,904	
Binghamton, NY	252,320	
Birmingham-Hoover, AL	1,052,238	
Bismarck, ND	94,719	
Blacksburg-Christiansburg-Radford, VA	151,272	
Bloomington, IN	175,506	
Bloomington-Normal, IL	150,433	
Boise City-Nampa, ID	464,840	
Boston-Cambridge-Quincy, MA-NH	4,391,344	
Boulder, CO	291,288	
Bowling Green, KY	104,166	
Bremerton-Silverdale, WA	231,969	
Bridgeport-Stamford-Norwalk, CT	882,567	
Brownsville-Harlingen, TX	335,227	
Brunswick, GA	93,044	
Buffalo-Niagara Falls, NY	1,170,111	
Burlington, NC	130,800	
Burlington-South Burlington, VT	198,889	
Canton-Massillon, OH	406,934	
Cape Coral-Fort Myers, FL	440,888	
Carson City, NV	52,457	
Cedar Rapids, IA	237,230	
Champaign-Urbana, IL	210,275	
Charleston, WV	309,635	
Charleston-North Charleston, SC	549,033	
Charlotte-Gastonia-Concord, NC-SC	1,330,448	
Charlottesville, VA	174,021	
Chattanooga, TN-GA	476,531	
Cheyenne, WY	81,607	
Chicago-Naperville-Joliet, IL-IN-WI	9,098,316	
Chico, CA	203,171	
Cincinnati-Middletown, OH-KY-IN	2,009,632	
Clarksville, TN-KY	232,000	
Cleveland, TN	104,015	
Cleveland-Elyria-Mentor, OH	2,148,143	
Coeur d'Alene, ID	108,685	
College Station-Bryan, TX	184,885	
Colorado Springs, CO	537,484	
Columbia, MO	145,666	
Columbia, SC	647,158	
Columbus, GA-AL	281,768	
Columbus, IN	71,435	
Columbus, OH	1,612,694	
Corpus Christi, TX	403,280	
Corvallis, OR	78,153	
Cumberland, MD-WV	102,008	
Dallas-Fort Worth-Arlington, TX	5,161,544	
Dalton, GA	120,031	
Danville, IL	83,919	
Danville, VA	110,156	
Davenport-Moline-Rock Island, IA-IL	376,019	
Dayton, OH	848,153	
Decatur, AL	145,867	
Decatur, IL	114,706	
Deltona-Daytona Beach-Ormond Beach, FL	443,343	
Denver-Aurora, CO	2,157,756	
Des Moines, IA	481,394	
Detroit-Warren-Livonia, MI	4,452,557	
Dothan, AL	130,861	
Dover, DE	126,697	
Dubuque, IA	89,143	
Duluth, MN-WI	275,486	
Durham, NC	426,493	
Eau Claire, WI	148,337	
El Centro, CA	142,361	
Elizabethtown, KY	107,547	
Elkhart-Goshen, IN	182,791	
Elmira, NY	91,070	
El Paso, TX	679,622	
Erie, PA	280,843	
Eugene-Springfield, OR	322,959	
Evansville, IN-KY	342,815	
Fairbanks, AK	82,840	
Fargo, ND-MN	174,367	
Farmington, NM	113,801	
Fayetteville, NC	336,609	
Fayetteville-Springdale-Rogers, AR-MO	347,045	
Flagstaff, AZ	116,320	
Flint, MI	436,141	
Florence, SC	193,155	
Florence-Muscle Shoals, AL	142,950	
Fond du Lac, WI	97,296	
Fort Collins-Loveland, CO	251,494	
Fort Smith, AR-OK	273,170	
Fort Walton Beach-Crestview-Destin, FL	170,498	
Fort Wayne, IN	390,156	
Fresno, CA	799,407	
Gadsden, AL	103,459	
Gainesville, FL	232,392	
Gainesville, GA	139,277	
Glens Falls, NY	124,345	
Goldsboro, NC	113,329	
Grand Forks, ND-MN	97,478	
Grand Junction, CO	116,255	
Grand Rapids-Wyoming, MI	740,482	
Great Falls, MT	80,357	
Greeley, CO	180,936	
Green Bay, WI	282,599	
Greensboro-High Point, NC	643,430	
Greenville, NC	152,772	
Greenville, SC	559,940	
Gulfport-Biloxi, MS	246,190	
Hagerstown-Martinsburg, MD-WV	222,771	
Hanford-Corcoran, CA	129,461	
Harrisburg-Carlisle, PA	509,074	
Harrisonburg, VA	108,193	
Hartford-West Hartford-East Hartford, CT	1,148,618	
Hattiesburg, MS	123,812	
Hickory-Lenoir-Morganton, NC	341,851	
Hinesville-Fort Stewart, GA	71,914	
Holland-Grand Haven, MI	238,314	
Honolulu, HI	876,156	
Hot Springs, AR	88,068	
Houma-Bayou Cane-Thibodaux, LA	194,477	
Houston-Baytown-Sugar Land, TX	4,715,407	
Huntington-Ashland, WV-KY-OH	288,649	
Huntsville, AL	342,376	
Idaho Falls, ID	101,677	
Indianapolis, IN	1,525,104	
Iowa City, IA	131,676	
Ithaca, NY	96,501	
Jackson, MI	158,422	
Jackson, MS	497,197	
Jackson, TN	107,377	
Jacksonville, FL	1,122,750	
Jacksonville, NC	150,355	
Janesville, WI	152,307	
Jefferson City, MO	140,052	
Johnson City, TN	181,607	
Johnstown, PA	152,598	
Jonesboro, AR	107,762	
Joplin, MO	157,322	
Kalamazoo-Portage, MI	314,866	
Kankakee-Bradley, IL	103,833	
Kansas City, MO-KS	1,836,038	
Kennewick-Richland-Pasco, WA	191,822	
Killeen-Temple-Fort Hood, TX	330,714	
Kingsport-Bristol-Bristol, TN-VA	298,484	
Kingston, NY	177,749	
Knoxville, TN	616,079	
Kokomo, IN	101,541	
La Crosse, WI-MN	126,838	
Lafayette, IN	178,541	
Lafayette, LA	239,086	
Lake Charles, LA	193,568	
Lakeland, FL	483,924	
Lancaster, PA	470,658	
Lansing-East Lansing, MI	447,728	
Laredo, TX	193,117	
Las Cruces, NM	174,682	
Las Vegas-Paradise, NV	1,375,765	
Lawrence, KS	99,962	
Lawton, OK	114,996	
Lebanon, PA	120,327	
Lewiston, ID-WA	57,961	
Lewiston-Auburn, ME	103,793	
Lexington-Fayette, KY	408,326	

This map shows Core Based Statistical Areas (CBSAs) as announced by the Office of Management and Budget (OMB) effective June 6, 2003. A CBSA is a metropolitan area consisting of the county or counties associated with an urban core having a population of at least 10,000, plus adjacent counties having a high degree of social and economic integration with the core as measured through commuting ties. CBSAs are more current definitions of metropolitan areas than the older Metropolitan Statistical Areas (MSAs) as defined and revised by the OMB through June 30, 1999.

The term CBSA refers collectively to Metropolitan CBSAs and Micropolitan CBSAs. Metropolitan CBSAs are associated with at least one urban core having a population of at least 50,000, while Micropolitan CBSAs are associated with at least one urban core having a population of at least 10,000 but less than 50,000.

Combined Statistical Areas (CSAs) consist of two or more adjacent CBSAs with a high degree of employment interchange.

Counties or county equivalents form the building blocks for CBSAs for the entire U.S. The largest city in each CBSA is designated the principal city. Other cities may also be principal cities if specific population and employment criteria are met. The title of each CBSA consists of the names of up to three of its principal cities, plus the name of each state into which the CBSA extends.

This map shows both Micropolitan and Metropolitan CBSAs in different colors. CSA boundaries are also shown.

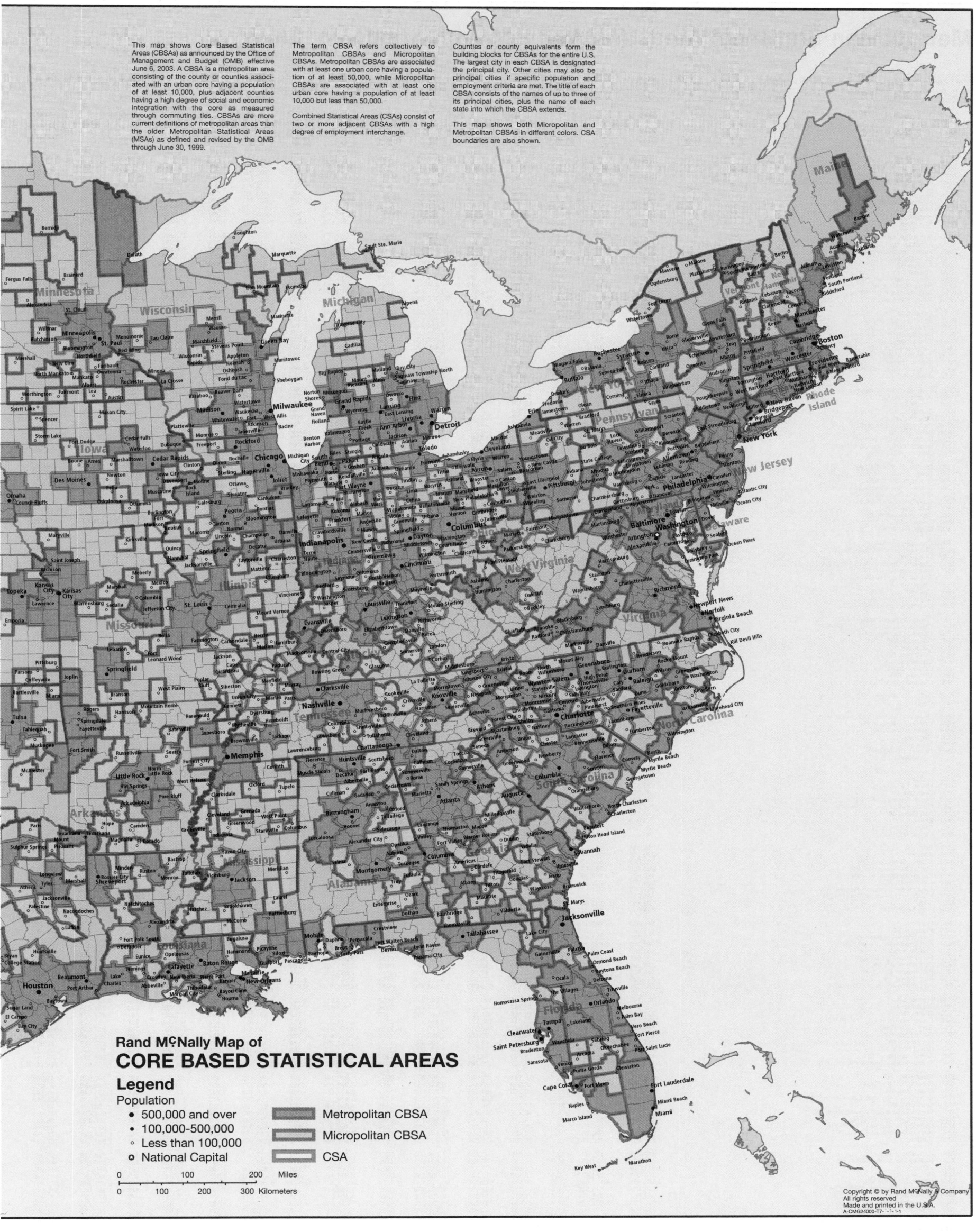

Rand McNally Map of
CORE BASED STATISTICAL AREAS

Legend
Population
- ● 500,000 and over
- • 100,000-500,000
- ○ Less than 100,000
- ⊙ National Capital

▨ Metropolitan CBSA
☐ Micropolitan CBSA
☐ CSA

| 0 | 100 | 200 Miles |
| 0 | 100 | 200 | 300 Kilometers |

Metropolitan Statistical Areas (MSAs): Population / Income / Sales#

This table provides population and marketing information for each of the 331 MSAs and PMSAs. Included are all of the data items given for Basic Trading Areas in the table starting on page 24. Data are from Devonshire Associates Ltd. and Scan/US, Inc. 2004. Also included are codes for MSAs published in the FIPS series of the National Bureau of Standards. A map showing the MSAs, with a detailed explanation of how they are determined, appears on pages 36-37. For information on the Ranally Metro Areas (RMAs), whose boundaries differ from those of the MSAs, see the table on pages 126-127.

CODE	METROPOLITAN STATISTICAL AREA	POPULATION Estimate 7/1/04	POPULATION Census 4/1/00	POPULATION % Change 4/1/90-4/1/00	PER CAPITA INCOME 2003	HOUSEHOLDS Estimate 7/1/04	DISPOSABLE INCOME 2003 ($1,000)	MARKET ABILITY INDEX 2003	TOTAL RETAIL SALES 2003 Sales ($1,000)	TOTAL RETAIL SALES Ranally Sales Units	GENERAL MERCHANDISE 2003 Sales ($1,000)	GENERAL MERCHANDISE Ranally Sales Units	APPAREL STORE SALES 2003 Sales ($1,000)	APPAREL STORE SALES Ranally Sales Units	FOOD STORE SALES 2003 ($1,000)	HEALTH & DRUG STORE SALES 2003 ($1,000)
0040	Abilene, TX	124,966	126,555	5.8	16,319	48,929	2,039,260	.0409	1,676,253	493	364,443	774	57,487	322	193,312	67,243
0080	Akron, OH (PMSA)	703,530	694,960	5.7	20,270	288,070	14,260,790	.2526	9,231,659	2,716	949,148	2,015	365,016	2,046	1,289,167	791,147
0120	Albany, GA	125,195	120,822	7.3	15,319	46,770	1,917,800	.0391	1,585,537	467	303,991	646	72,454	406	250,576	58,890
0160	Albany-Schenectady-Troy, NY	894,569	875,583	1.6	21,784	365,332	19,487,310	.3157	9,776,471	2,876	1,112,250	2,361	535,299	3,001	1,372,276	647,465
0200	Albuquerque, NM	759,193	712,738	21.0	18,702	302,189	14,198,270	.2551	9,136,804	2,688	1,679,936	3,566	321,107	1,799	844,165	503,142
0220	Alexandria, LA	127,716	126,337	-4.0	14,314	48,977	1,828,070	.0384	1,572,058	462	373,937	794	65,982	370	180,477	98,802
0240	Allentown-Bethlehem-Easton, PA	665,446	637,958	7.2	19,938	263,264	13,267,640	.2312	8,062,162	2,372	851,652	1,808	323,584	1,814	1,435,608	561,692
0280	Altoona, PA	126,555	129,144	-1.1	16,075	52,018	2,034,420	.0417	1,752,849	516	316,759	672	58,130	326	267,824	121,301
0320	Amarillo, TX	226,760	217,858	16.2	16,610	85,720	3,766,460	.0746	3,011,460	886	419,156	890	124,225	696	251,546	129,332
0380	Anchorage, AK	274,398	260,283	15.0	22,488	100,252	6,170,610	.1105	4,355,756	1,281	1,057,357	2,245	209,835	1,176	511,166	47,012
0440	Ann Arbor, MI (PMSA)	622,300	578,736	18.1	23,364	237,874	14,539,490	.2437	8,574,571	2,522	1,470,152	3,121	287,239	1,609	935,302	401,861
0450	Anniston, AL	112,234	112,249	-3.3	16,515	47,412	1,853,520	.0344	1,213,266	357	270,566	574	36,994	207	176,829	51,711
0460	Appleton-Oshkosh-Neenah, WI	372,541	358,365	13.7	20,783	150,343	7,742,360	.1368	5,045,676	1,484	701,353	1,488	196,624	1,102	592,168	204,798
0480	Asheville, NC	234,482	225,965	17.8	18,158	99,466	4,257,810	.0812	3,212,650	945	497,034	1,055	175,631	984	384,718	191,736
0500	Athens, GA	160,455	153,444	21.5	16,222	65,228	2,602,980	.0497	1,841,677	541	301,540	640	82,934	465	252,908	78,416
0520	Atlanta, GA	4,570,501	4,112,198	38.9	22,906	1,754,099	104,691,600	1.7622	61,850,085	18,194	8,043,762	17,075	3,264,121	18,295	8,869,200	2,408,217
0560	Atlantic-Cape May, NJ (PMSA)	368,557	354,878	11.1	21,221	142,561	7,821,170	.1325	4,515,980	1,329	469,557	997	317,234	1,778	1,056,306	285,181
0580	Auburn-Opelika, AL	120,927	115,092	32.1	15,916	50,646	1,924,700	.0344	1,074,311	316	212,560	451	52,646	295	208,266	33,042
0600	Augusta-Aiken, GA-SC	492,040	477,441	15.0	17,539	188,840	8,629,940	.1530	5,079,956	1,494	898,436	1,907	233,736	1,310	721,888	237,488
0640	Austin-San Marcos, TX	1,415,292	1,249,763	47.7	22,947	561,961	32,477,300	.6303	28,689,214	8,440	2,281,526	4,844	1,085,483	6,083	3,148,162	1,386,529
0680	Bakersfield, CA	729,553	661,645	21.7	13,779	226,881	10,052,420	.1858	5,580,342	1,642	732,780	1,556	216,564	1,214	895,681	350,750
0720	Baltimore, MD (PMSA)	2,635,941	2,552,994	7.2	22,837	1,025,342	60,196,130	.9507	28,414,112	8,358	3,697,296	7,848	1,633,456	9,155	5,055,123	1,789,340
0730	Bangor, ME	92,098	90,864	-0.8	17,745	38,360	1,634,293	.0351	1,667,355	490	219,113	467	47,698	267	285,136	71,143
0740	Barnstable-Yarmouth, MA	170,164	162,582	20.5	23,730	73,655	4,038,024	.0684	2,469,226	727	154,462	328	157,960	886	600,710	175,506
0760	Baton Rouge, LA	626,070	602,894	14.1	18,636	245,812	11,667,190	.2106	7,606,623	2,237	1,420,953	3,017	341,266	1,913	952,775	359,783
0840	Beaumont-Port Arthur, TX	381,930	385,090	6.6	16,834	147,921	6,429,600	.1227	4,650,610	1,368	746,358	1,584	194,534	1,090	630,665	250,353
0860	Bellingham, WA	179,561	166,814	30.5	18,388	71,394	3,301,690	.0602	2,206,779	649	395,974	841	93,233	523	482,145	104,046
0870	Benton Harbor, MI	162,816	162,453	0.7	17,983	66,098	2,927,880	.0504	1,585,823	466	298,008	633	29,166	163	230,436	105,137
0875	Bergen-Passaic, NJ (PMSA)	1,402,356	1,373,167	7.4	26,344	503,348	36,944,300	.5904	19,883,736	5,849	1,837,976	3,901	1,618,652	9,071	3,466,180	1,266,914
0880	Billings, MT	134,394	129,352	14.0	17,704	54,783	2,379,280	.0484	2,120,345	624	389,726	827	70,846	397	212,932	63,204
0920	Biloxi-Gulfport-Pascagoula, MS	369,960	363,988	16.5	17,932	147,932	6,634,010	.1182	4,034,839	1,187	991,452	2,105	136,388	764	455,361	167,207
0960	Binghamton, NY	250,793	252,320	-4.6	18,483	101,911	4,635,420	.0790	2,475,857	728	356,641	758	95,881	537	435,767	196,783
1000	Birmingham, AL	946,208	921,106	9.6	19,491	380,583	18,442,620	.3273	11,707,936	3,444	1,820,107	3,864	636,585	3,567	1,594,497	553,431
1010	Bismarck, ND	97,478	94,719	13.0	18,994	40,230	1,851,510	.0354	1,438,682	423	246,014	522	32,045	179	148,249	83,697
1020	Bloomington, IN	123,639	120,563	10.6	16,262	52,250	2,010,580	.0381	1,394,254	410	291,567	619	59,345	333	194,840	66,862
1040	Bloomington-Normal, IL	158,878	150,433	16.5	20,577	60,568	3,269,280	.0581	2,158,777	635	294,644	625	128,048	718	227,004	144,519
1080	Boise City, ID	490,178	432,345	46.1	18,184	180,322	8,913,570	.1687	6,609,386	1,944	1,139,141	2,418	207,788	1,165	867,259	207,440
1120	Boston, MA-NH (PMSA)	3,452,130	3,406,829	5.5	25,889	1,357,201	89,371,074	1.4146	46,096,733	13,561	4,115,948	8,732	3,944,707	22,103	7,775,391	3,449,624
1125	Boulder-Longmont, CO (PMSA)[1]	280,533	291,288	29.3	24,908	112,423	6,987,540	.1145	3,962,671	1,166	385,734	819	126,037	706	729,202	128,964
1145	Brazoria, TX (PMSA)	269,789	241,767	26.1	19,523	92,394	5,267,100	.0842	2,299,176	676	524,335	1,113	58,745	329	344,993	82,707
1150	Bremerton, WA (PMSA)	243,450	231,969	22.3	19,816	90,966	4,824,290	.0783	2,263,687	666	520,165	1,104	67,059	376	338,124	110,073
1160	Bridgeport, CT (PMSA)	466,775	459,479	3.6	22,365	175,027	10,439,547	.1906	7,764,125	2,286	564,391	1,198	445,735	2,497	990,406	413,229
1200	Brockton, MA (PMSA)	266,153	255,459	8.1	20,608	93,889	5,484,961	.1028	4,229,009	1,245	327,081	693	81,161	454	611,250	213,163
1240	Brownsville-Harlingen-San Benito, TX	371,857	335,227	28.9	9,563	109,025	3,556,070	.0806	2,774,996	816	641,360	1,361	195,601	1,096	531,733	106,356
1260	Bryan-College Station, TX	162,171	152,415	25.1	13,684	61,901	2,219,150	.0464	1,835,194	540	347,968	739	92,157	516	241,085	42,860
1280	Buffalo-Niagara Falls, NY	1,156,288	1,170,111	-1.6	19,600	470,582	22,662,690	.3756	11,435,256	3,364	1,227,487	2,605	661,291	3,706	2,043,522	900,419
1305	Burlington, VT	173,586	169,391	11.8	21,114	68,986	3,665,111	.0708	3,057,260	899	311,463	662	128,387	720	494,440	170,202
1320	Canton-Massillon, OH	407,161	406,934	3.3	18,397	162,941	7,490,370	.1367	5,012,905	1,474	691,501	1,468	239,306	1,341	727,029	449,795
1350	Casper, WY	68,763	66,533	8.7	17,576	28,287	1,208,590	.0232	917,121	270	190,011	403	22,242	125	108,499	19,530
1360	Cedar Rapids, IA	197,521	191,701	13.6	20,875	80,191	4,123,340	.0744	2,872,078	845	447,566	950	120,082	673	374,981	149,724
1400	Champaign-Urbana, IL	189,076	179,669	3.8	17,848	75,340	3,374,700	.0620	2,245,429	661	485,103	1,030	92,343	518	297,615	167,268
1440	Charleston-North Charleston, SC	578,716	549,033	8.3	18,762	232,024	10,857,930	.1907	6,506,338	1,913	1,101,200	2,338	413,126	2,315	1,082,356	277,047
1480	Charleston, WV	247,465	251,662	0.5	18,856	106,886	4,666,210	.0880	3,481,537	1,024	563,098	1,195	143,355	804	391,157	252,899
1520	Charlotte-Gastonia-Rock Hill, NC-SC	1,648,241	1,499,293	29.0	21,888	671,061	36,076,240	.6125	21,335,074	6,276	2,848,716	6,047	980,987	5,497	2,779,355	1,108,325
1540	Charlottesville, VA	168,816	159,576	21.7	19,884	67,746	3,356,720	.0600	2,214,226	652	309,345	657	126,650	710	371,432	117,009
1560	Chattanooga, TN-GA	476,717	465,161	9.6	18,494	195,528	8,816,560	.1579	5,276,920	1,640	921,343	1,955	298,417	1,673	763,793	338,324
1580	Cheyenne, WY	84,872	81,607	11.6	18,223	33,925	1,546,640	.0303	1,264,795	372	198,396	421	22,697	127	146,267	25,711
1600	Chicago, IL (PMSA)	8,558,311	8,272,768	11.6	21,500	3,081,858	183,999,930	3.0531	99,647,029	29,312	11,133,626	23,633	5,660,774	31,725	13,745,635	8,327,600
1620	Chico-Paradise, CA	213,422	203,171	11.6	15,710	83,496	3,352,780	.0619	2,084,387	613	302,336	642	76,186	427	422,545	147,515
1640	Cincinnati, OH-KY-IN (PMSA)	1,680,493	1,646,395	7.9	20,967	684,327	35,234,210	.6050	21,061,796	6,196	3,115,573	6,613	1,025,827	5,749	2,912,642	1,160,037
1660	Clarksville-Hopkinsville, TN-KY	212,112	207,033	22.2	16,230	78,603	3,442,530	.0631	2,146,371	631	525,541	1,116	94,533	529	173,464	70,547
1680	Cleveland-Lorain-Elyria, OH (PMSA)	2,239,967	2,250,871	2.2	20,112	917,281	45,050,120	.7827	27,265,297	8,020	2,958,359	6,281	1,321,633	7,407	3,989,913	2,796,478
1720	Colorado Springs, CO	560,804	516,929	30.2	19,819	208,812	11,114,350	.1975	7,166,545	2,108	1,150,622	2,443	190,170	1,066	768,575	274,941
1740	Columbia, MO	142,884	135,454	20.5	18,274	58,480	2,611,020	.0487	1,863,303	548	297,344	631	54,706	307	214,028	75,677
1760	Columbia, SC	565,436	536,691	18.4	19,810	227,194	11,201,340	.2011	7,451,868	2,192	1,368,576	2,906	376,713	2,112	969,619	364,404
1800	Columbus, GA-AL	281,559	274,624	5.3	16,158	109,891	4,549,520	.0837	2,852,718	839	470,540	999	178,751	1,001	422,354	170,137
1840	Columbus, OH	1,614,311	1,540,157	14.5	21,957	681,950	35,445,620	.6237	23,486,517	6,909	3,057,216	6,490	1,019,604	5,714	2,767,089	914,804
1880	Corpus Christi, TX	384,106	380,783	8.8	15,859	139,636	6,091,530	.1152	4,131,445	1,215	668,101	1,418	193,675	1,085	715,029	158,981
1890	Corvallis, OR	79,726	78,153	10.4	19,582	32,175	1,561,160	.0243	609,433	179	82,549	175	24,628	138	136,155	28,413
1900	Cumberland, MD-WV	100,473	102,008	0.4	14,953	40,132	1,502,400	.0285	982,642	289	232,915	494	42,687	239	153,863	82,351
1920	Dallas, TX (PMSA)	3,900,657	3,519,176	31.5	22,107	1,465,557	86,231,560	1.4545	50,211,022	14,770	7,211,634	15,310	2,700,602	15,136	6,895,737	2,030,127
1930	Danbury, CT (PMSA)	228,211	217,980	12.6	27,035	82,483	6,169,601	.1047	4,050,832	1,192	371,178	788	282,948	1,586	688,261	222,662
1950	Danville, VA	108,169	110,156	1.3	15,496	46,142	1,676,150	.0316	1,097,461	323	198,693	421	33,492	188	192,389	56,712
1960	Davenport-Moline-Rock Island, IA-IL	357,656	359,062	2.3	18,891	144,362	6,756,410	.1252	4,808,297	1,414	667,384	1,417	189,352	1,061	598,628	308,995
2000	Dayton-Springfield, OH	945,928	950,558	-0.1	20,424	399,525	19,319,570	.3313	11,312,803	3,327	1,975,612	4,194	458,726	2,570	1,529,222	606,476
2020	Daytona Beach, FL	542,645	493,175	23.5	20,372	245,026	11,054,840	.1836	5,769,501	1,698	770,128	1,635	219,433	1,230	968,057	386,603
2030	Decatur, AL	147,582	145,867	10.9	18,193	60,090	2,684,900	.0479	1,655,638	487	238,893	507	65,839	369	168,352	86,024
2040	Decatur, IL	110,093	114,706	-2.1	18,388	45,406	2,024,380	.0388	1,560,720	459	284,280	603	50,446	283	216,372	109,137
2080	Denver, CO (PMSA)[1]	2,239,478	2,109,282	30.0	23,174	884,070	51,896,650	.8662	30,024,921	8,832	4,308,975	9,147	1,345,192	7,539	4,158,108	1,009,491
2120	Des Moines, IA	483,114	456,022	16.1	20,764	193,718	10,031,420	.1750	6,195,047	1,822	853,756	1,813	228,718	1,281	819,287	303,591
2160	Detroit, MI (PMSA)	4,466,850	4,441,551	4.1	22,004	1,767,309	98,289,920	1.6904	60,800,681	17,886	9,618,308	20,401	2,792,305	15,648	7,291,963	4,286,316
2180	Dothan, AL	141,592	137,916	5.3	16,888	57,789	2,391,160	.0474	1,932,561	569	379,415	806	83,263	466	180,075	73,824
2190	Dover, DE	136,821	126,697	14.1	17,831	51,808	2,439,640	.0448	1,634,075	481	336,656	715	44,077	247	195,425	69,449
2200	Dubuque, IA	90,309	89,143	3.2	17,549	35,087	1,584,810	.0308	1,245,748	366	204,332	434	31,824	178	148,726	70,539
2240	Duluth-Superior, MN-WI	242,578	243,815	1.6	17,336	102,207	4,205,370	.0777	2,819,194	829	518,427	1,100	72,173	404	379,604	140,921
2281	Dutchess County, NY (PMSA)	294,234	280,150	8.0	23,067	105,960	6,787,060	.1043	2,893,122	851	352,228	748	190,468	1,067	564,313	160,219
2290	Eau Claire, WI	151,741	148,337	7.8	17,719	61,246	2,688,700	.0568	2,634,523	775	545,765	1,158	100,713	564	287,391	94,843
2320	El Paso, TX	713,340	679,622	14.9	12,037	226,278	8,586,800	.1799	6,462,611	1,901	1,356,263	2,879	425,599	2,385	831,659	312,642
2330	Elkhart-Goshen, IN	190,535	182,791	17.0	18,034	69,272	3,436,030	.0660	2,636,787	776	432,046	917	35,241	198	276,343	119,557
2335	Elmira, NY	90,205	91,070	-4.3	17,997	35,627	1,623,380	.0298	1,092,065	321	190,558	405	53,956	302	157,479	68,541
2340	Enid, OK	56,916	57,813	1.9	16,295	23,194	927,440	.0174	620,785	183	145,515	309	17,180	96	98,379	26,289
2360	Erie, PA	279,718	280,843	1.9	17,187	111,157	4,807,540	.0901	3,333,544	981	445,349	945	129,279	725	546,498	194,903
2400	Eugene-Springfield, OR	332,896	322,959	14.2	17,777	136,131	5,917,890	.1108	4,302,190	1,266	807,668	1,715	128,392	720	679,603	134,140
2440	Evansville-Henderson, IN-KY	299,416	296,195	6.2	18,873	124,639	5,650,850	.1065	4,287,765	1,262	762,265	1,618	202,620	1,135	443,994	221,295
2520	Fargo-Moorhead, ND-MN	180,577	174,367	13.7	18,232	74,906	3,292,320	.0680	3,077,853	906	451,918	959	91,991	516	271,043	146,309
2560	Fayetteville, NC	304,324	302,963	10.3	17,357	118,570	5,282,290	.0972	3,493,381	1,028	695,105	1,476	168,128	942	434,080	148,723
2580	Fayetteville-Springdale-Rogers, AR	351,068	311,121	47.5	17,154	134,011	6,022,250	.1117	4,042,942	1,190	1,284,182	2,726	117,622	659	350,219	117,229
2600	Fitchburg-Leominster, MA (PMSA)	145,019	142,284	3.0	19,495	56,349	2,827,084	.0508	1,868,415	547	173,219	369	93,666	525	348,571	99,961
2620	Flagstaff, AZ-UT	128,880	122,366	20.2	16,592	46,355	2,138,420	.0389	1,315,804	387	285,037	605	32,242	180	237,900	30,869
2640	Flint, MI (PMSA)	444,011	436,141	1.3	19,539	181,093	8,675,620	.1515	5,238,928	1,541	1,038,212	2,204	183,929	1,031	608,615	347,323
2650	Florence, AL	141,000	142,950	8.9	17,078	59,396	2,407,980	.0445	1,604,167	472	378,407	803	72,513	406	171,876	65,218
2655	Florence, SC	129,181	125,761	10.0	16,191	49,954	2,091,520	.0429	1,820,488	536	303,217	644	86,872	487	225,269	102,383
2670	Fort Collins-Loveland, CO	271,165	251,494	35.1	21,864	107,740	5,928,820	.1012	3,560,752	1,047	603,249	1,281	139,359	781	480,045	104,785
2680	Fort Lauderdale, FL (PMSA)	1,764,315	1,623,018	29.3	21,989	747,072	38,796,200	.6810	25,541,193	7,513	2,758,291	5,855	1,486,450	8,330	3,491,409	1,626,468
2700	Fort Myers-Cape Coral, FL	508,350	440,888	31.6	21,735	219,630	11,049,150	.1922	7,029,399	2,068	988,622	2,099	443,513	2,486	986,313	442,891
2710	Fort Pierce-Port St. Lucie, FL	357,906	319,426	27.2	21,236	155,543	7,594,610	.1252	3,987,293	1,173	507,921	1,078	135,595	759	652,399	314,490
2720	Fort Smith, AR-OK	214,506	207,290	17.8	15,270	83,057	3,275,540	.0652	2,515,007	739	667,518	1,418	67,905	381	288,631	105,115
2750	Fort Walton Beach, FL	180,485	170,498	18.6	23,214	81,167	4,189,840	.0711	2,557,865	752	468,067	994	183,928	1,031	285,709	117,808
2760	Fort Wayne, IN	515,722	502,141	10.1	18,986	202,993	9,791,550	.1754	6,307,857	1,856	1,127,630	2,394	217,304	1,218	697,635	338,146
2800	Fort Worth-Arlington, TX (PMSA)	1,883,211	1,702,625	25.1	20,175	698,010	37,994,410	.6688	24,036,467	7,070	2,687,262	5,705	1,053,332	5,903	3,254,314	956,554
2840	Fresno, CA	1,003,162	922,516	22.1	13,501	309,778	13,543,840	.2538	7,751,818	2,280	1,028,372	2,183	312,576	1,752	1,425,308	478,421
2880	Gadsden, AL	102,945	103,459	3.6	15,783	42,212	1,624,740	.0296	962,832	283	197,166	419	41,883	235	187,328	55,255
2900	Gainesville, FL	225,339	217,955	20.0	16,166	91,355	3,642,780	.0696	2,576,067	758	374,123	794	132,681	744	467,971	106,898
2920	Galveston-Texas City, TX (PMSA)	272,122	250,158	15.1	20,011	106,277	5,445,530	.0870	2,419,704	712	413,687	878	149,310	837	487,505	149,368
2960	Gary, IN (PMSA)	642,735	631,362	4.4	18,997	245,511	12,210,110	.2125	7,158,945	2,106	1,080,330	2,293	240,561	1,348	977,665	543,114
2975	Glens Falls, NY	127,394	124,345	4.9	19,244	50,898	2,450,470	.0416	1,332,449	392	120,576	256	99,993	560	213,546	82,321
2980	Goldsboro, NC	113,028	113,329	8.3	15,911	44,258	1,798,380	.0346	1,286,204	378	226,878	482	56,081	314	170,727	62,907
2985	Grand Forks, ND-MN	95,100	97,478	-5.5	16,004	37,219	1,522,000	.0303	1,545,462	455	294,376	625	46,105	258	150,561	57,640
2995	Grand Junction, CO	127,075	116,255	24.8	16,763	50,551	2,130,220	.0407	1,540,898	453	347,773	738	31,679	178	205,091	40,014
3000	Grand Rapids-Muskegon-Holland, MI	1,133,518	1,088,514	16.1	19,507	426,766	22,111,920	.3972	14,593,889	4,293	3,031,710	6,435	501,970	2,813	1,366,619	668,285
3040	Great Falls, MT	79,349	80,357	3.4	16,141	32,601	1,280,800	.0252	989,385	291	223,772	475	22,782	128	109,989	41,908
3060	Greeley, CO (PMSA)[1]	220,667	180,936	37.3	16,913	76,443	3,732,100	.0638	1,875,716	552	261,111	554	24,309	136	242,183	53,013
3080	Green Bay, WI	236,097	226,778	16.5	20,278	94,899	4,787,460	.0877	3,417,482	1,005	818,139	1,737	88,904	498	354,646	101,190
3120	Greensboro--Winston-Salem--High Point, NC	1,308,675	1,251,509	19.2	19,765	539,415	25,866,150	.4621	16,919,287	4,976	2,106,360	4,473	801,850	4,494	2,148,538	1,006,356
3150	Greenville, NC	140,223	133,798	24.0	16,079	56,933	2,254,600	.0463	1,950,066	574	211,126	448	117,144	657	258,694	92,355
3160	Greenville-Spartanburg-Anderson, SC	1,004,256	962,441	15.9	18,279	399,967	18,357,290	.3384	12,611,430	3,709	1,764,790	3,746	624,010	3,497	1,691,626	731,466
3180	Hagerstown, MD (PMSA)	138,354	131,923	8.7	18,511	52,912	2,561,100	.0458	1,617,258	476	276,893	588	42,981	241	256,199	86,461
3200	Hamilton-Middletown, OH (PMSA)	346,371	332,807	14.2	21,345	135,917	7,393,210	.1154	3,165,589	931	461,306	979	61,907	347	531,475	168,698
3240	Harrisburg-Lebanon-Carlisle, PA	643,547	629,401	7.0	20,421	261,966	13,141,920	.2363	8,927,130	2,626	910,112	1,932	306,222	1,716	1,284,021	475,386
3280	Hartford, CT	1,223,067	1,183,110	2.2	26,005	479,099	31,805,651	.4816	13,959,486	4,109	1,296,053	2,751	944,013	5,290	2,385,089	1,107,334
3285	Hattiesburg, MS	117,751	111,674	13.1	14,815	45,008	1,744,500	.0371	1,579,853	465	477,565	1,014	64,444	361	114,189	106,062
3290	Hickory-Morganton-Lenoir, NC	352,521	341,851	16.9	18,165	142,926	6,403,660	.1160	4,138,266	1,217	589,803	1,251	146,720	822	530,183	248,052
3320	Honolulu, HI	911,719	876,156	4.8	19,820	301,773	18,070,470	.3029	9,586,291	2,820	1,932,186	4,102	1,213,597	6,801	1,460,075	815,873
3350	Houma, LA	198,351	194,477	6.4	15,568	71,352	3,087,850	.0610	2,360,449	695	477,923	1,015	76,947	432	388,063	105,806
3360	Houston, TX (PMSA)	4,595,351	4,177,646	25.8	19,614	1,679,706	90,131,170	1.5774	54,978,827	16,172	8,289,468	17,597	3,155,929	17,686	8,231,298	2,575,461
3400	Huntington-Ashland, WV-KY-OH	313,136	315,538	1.0	15,306	132,481	4,792,860	.0904	3,131,978	921	608,693	1,292	155,764	873	381,044	315,542
3440	Huntsville, AL	355,704	342,376	16.8	21,319	148,388	7,732,470	.1305	4,408,012	1,296	884,283	1,877	227,112	1,272	579,797	171,413
3480	Indianapolis, IN	1,695,006	1,607,486	16.4	21,083	687,260	35,735,210	.6333	23,681,000	6,965	4,019,032	8,532	901,457	5,052	2,289,703	1,536,109
3500	Iowa City, IA	116,938	111,006	15.5	18,537	47,437	2,167,730	.0404	1,554,147	457	220,859	469	55,000	308	270,763	77,087
3520	Jackson, MI	163,516	158,422	5.8	18,372	61,219	3,004,140	.0530	1,801,553	530	486,032	1,032	45,211	253	190,509	85,531
3560	Jackson, MS	457,428	440,801	11.5	17,908	172,842	8,191,450	.1559	6,105,362	1,796	1,218,256	2,586	265,516	1,488	608,387	330,138
3580	Jackson, TN	110,436	107,377	18.3	17,750	44,215	1,960,220	.0396	1,722,683	507	382,036	811	110,247	618	151,297	90,390
3600	Jacksonville, FL	1,204,735	1,100,491	21.4	21,668	489,865	26,104,270	.4408	15,075,439	4,434	1,952,141	4,144	713,757	4,000	2,134,586	757,997
3605	Jacksonville, NC	146,634	150,355	0.3	14,600	53,106	2,140,860	.0420	1,534,013	451	261,489	555	47,943	269	197,933	55,794
3610	Jamestown, NY	137,003	139,750	-1.5	16,599	54,280	2,274,060	.0391	1,147,289	337	182,331	387	28,227	158	227,354	80,263
3620	Janesville-Beloit, WI	155,545	152,307	9.2	19,859	62,205	3,088,910	.0555	2,063,534	607	359,494	763	32,652	183	282,095	98,760
3640	Jersey City, NJ (PMSA)	606,768	608,975	10.1	19,564	230,298	11,870,940	.1835	4,478,993	1,318	376,234	799	508,737	2,851	872,848	396,886
3660	Johnson City-Kingsport-Bristol, TN-VA	487,711	480,091	10.1	16,614	211,669	8,102,670	.1520	5,525,720	1,625	1,048,519	2,225	228,312	1,281	700,585	314,504
3680	Johnstown, PA	227,679	232,621	-3.6	14,546	91,625	3,311,910	.0627	2,109,312	620	236,822	503	58,434	327	346,047	152,151
3700	Jonesboro, AR	85,334	82,148	19.1	15,727	34,061	1,342,040	.0281	1,210,679	356	330,305	701	77,711	436	91,604	43,446
3710	Joplin, MO	163,621	157,322	16.6	15,072	64,006	2,466,140	.0484	1,804,711	531	419,953	892	46,048	258	163,155	79,283
3720	Kalamazoo-Battle Creek, MI	461,120	452,851	5.4	18,885	186,779	8,708,460	.1540	5,363,685	1,578	1,450,904	3,080	167,064	936	515,255	283,508
3740	Kankakee, IL (PMSA)	106,207	103,833	7.9	17,954	39,387	1,906,840	.0346	1,230,032	362	251,524	534	43,569	244	124,754	53,925
3760	Kansas City, MO-KS	1,863,851	1,776,062	12.2	21,564	748,899	40,192,810	.6912	24,548,449	7,221	3,611,899	7,667	950,889	5,331	2,975,922	1,254,630
3800	Kenosha, WI (PMSA)	158,255	149,577	16.7	19,561	60,514	3,092,510	.0487	1,265,061	372	201,089	427	94,119	527	200,957	76,540
3810	Killeen-Temple, TX	327,158	312,952	22.6	15,912	116,082	5,205,700	.0914	2,737,070	805	410,838	872	81,203	455	393,524	48,250
3840	Knoxville, TN	720,109	687,249	17.3	18,922	304,926	13,626,120	.2712	11,827,267	3,480	1,854,356	3,936	667,996	3,743	1,326,691	574,926
3850	Kokomo, IN	101,227	101,541	4.7	20,974	42,915	2,123,170	.0375	1,385,222	407	327,176	694	34,854	195	134,753	98,680

Metropolitan Statistical Areas (MSAs): Population / Income / Sales#, *Continued*

CODE	METROPOLITAN STATISTICAL AREA	POPULATION Estimate 7/1/04	POPULATION Census 4/1/00	% Change 4/1/90-4/1/00	PER CAPITA INCOME 2003	HOUSE-HOLDS Estimate 7/1/04	DISPOSABLE INCOME 2003 ($1,000)	MARKET ABILITY INDEX 2003	TOTAL RETAIL SALES 2003 Sales ($1,000)	TOTAL RETAIL SALES Ranally Sales Units	GENERAL MERCHANDISE 2003 Sales ($1,000)	GENERAL MERCHANDISE Ranally Sales Units	APPAREL STORE SALES 2003 Sales ($1,000)	APPAREL STORE SALES Ranally Sales Units	FOOD STORE SALES 2003 ($1,000)	HEALTH & DRUG STORE 2003 ($1,000)
3870	La Crosse, WI-MN	129,119	126,838	9.0	17,711	51,815	2,286,770	.0439	1,739,488	**512**	328,342	**697**	36,142	**202**	227,580	47,403
3880	Lafayette, LA	394,628	385,647	11.8	15,125	152,433	5,968,610	.1211	4,827,890	**1,421**	964,233	**2,046**	198,484	**1,113**	578,079	317,888
3920	Lafayette, IN	190,622	182,821	13.2	16,749	72,212	3,192,740	.0599	2,182,187	**642**	509,669	**1,082**	85,285	**478**	203,378	117,736
3960	Lake Charles, LA	184,005	183,577	9.2	17,572	74,088	3,233,420	.0603	2,249,684	**662**	538,185	**1,142**	91,221	**511**	274,045	119,468
3980	Lakeland-Winter Haven, FL	518,809	483,924	19.4	19,073	217,966	9,895,440	.1713	5,716,090	**1,681**	873,686	**1,855**	196,846	**1,103**	977,731	287,481
4000	Lancaster, PA	486,469	470,658	11.3	19,463	180,573	9,468,350	.1739	6,676,478	**1,964**	579,937	**1,231**	367,776	**2,061**	1,109,981	332,301
4040	Lansing-East Lansing, MI	458,301	447,728	3.5	20,004	182,777	9,167,820	.1606	5,685,892	**1,672**	1,278,910	**2,715**	207,150	**1,161**	673,930	297,591
4080	Laredo, TX	219,931	193,117	44.9	9,311	58,756	2,047,880	.0538	2,387,548	**702**	472,368	**1,003**	296,511	**1,662**	370,036	96,388
4100	Las Cruces, NM	184,554	174,682	28.9	12,499	63,683	2,306,790	.0444	1,344,907	**396**	259,830	**552**	39,961	**224**	154,238	70,219
4120	Las Vegas, NV-AZ	1,850,678	1,563,282	83.3	19,153	707,390	35,446,380	.6178	21,009,850	**6,180**	2,863,514	**6,079**	1,271,752	**7,127**	3,307,295	894,880
4150	Lawrence, KS	103,909	99,962	22.2	16,965	40,944	1,762,840	.0319	1,084,623	**319**	155,726	**331**	56,394	**316**	198,476	47,982
4160	Lawrence, MA-NH (PMSA)	413,761	396,230	12.2	22,667	150,856	9,378,641	.1509	4,733,394	**1,393**	800,913	**1,699**	245,364	**1,374**	875,457	288,251
4200	Lawton, OK	113,664	114,996	3.1	14,565	40,239	1,655,550	.0289	779,898	**229**	245,081	**520**	21,843	**122**	72,711	30,150
4240	Lewiston-Auburn, ME	93,140	90,830	-3.0	17,574	39,075	1,636,881	.0349	1,649,816	**485**	211,141	**449**	22,358	**125**	239,385	60,675
4280	Lexington, KY	502,488	479,198	18.0	20,112	213,434	10,106,000	.1795	6,566,002	**1,931**	1,009,857	**2,143**	352,317	**1,975**	716,761	379,822
4320	Lima, OH	154,917	155,084	0.5	17,786	60,607	2,755,340	.0522	2,019,631	**594**	414,268	**879**	63,657	**357**	189,660	120,518
4360	Lincoln, NE	264,249	250,291	17.2	19,213	107,177	5,076,970	.0902	3,206,420	**943**	559,295	**1,187**	111,717	**626**	493,547	221,103
4400	Little Rock-North Little Rock, AR	606,101	583,845	13.8	19,424	251,553	11,772,820	.2206	8,786,253	**2,584**	1,742,933	**3,699**	318,576	**1,785**	743,404	277,719
4420	Longview-Marshall, TX	215,225	208,780	7.7	16,251	83,189	3,497,720	.0691	2,751,508	**809**	493,769	**1,048**	91,774	**514**	360,853	112,989
4480	Los Angeles-Long Beach, CA (PMSA)	9,980,271	9,519,338	7.4	17,007	3,253,579	169,739,220	2.9601	92,102,910	**27,093**	10,418,455	**22,116**	7,736,176	**43,356**	15,567,979	5,237,037
4520	Louisville, KY-IN	1,049,861	1,025,598	8.1	20,632	447,993	21,660,610	.3669	12,238,548	**3,600**	2,074,920	**4,404**	502,346	**2,815**	1,388,270	772,146
4560	Lowell, MA-NH (PMSA)	303,591	301,686	7.5	21,345	108,107	6,480,147	.1009	2,736,638	**805**	200,617	**425**	89,458	**503**	533,349	201,986
4600	Lubbock, TX	252,962	242,628	9.0	15,382	98,160	3,891,160	.0818	3,504,726	**1,031**	536,684	**1,139**	164,044	**919**	496,093	106,005
4640	Lynchburg, VA	218,030	214,911	10.8	17,436	88,786	3,801,670	.0684	2,344,758	**689**	344,595	**732**	70,070	**392**	304,261	170,489
4680	Macon, GA	338,900	322,549	10.9	17,606	132,213	5,966,570	.1111	4,134,860	**1,216**	665,955	**1,414**	204,694	**1,147**	581,825	176,689
4720	Madison, WI	456,369	426,526	16.2	22,239	191,747	10,149,360	.1798	6,914,106	**2,034**	889,619	**1,888**	241,263	**1,352**	833,571	318,717
4760	Manchester, NH (PMSA)	210,181	198,378	14.2	21,971	80,597	4,617,810	.0830	3,268,354	**960**	512,415	**1,087**	127,797	**715**	483,131	135,007
4800	Mansfield, OH	173,916	175,818	1.0	17,451	69,649	3,034,990	.0558	2,008,228	**591**	415,086	**881**	58,513	**327**	232,377	129,596
4880	McAllen-Edinburg-Mission, TX	656,072	569,463	48.5	8,644	182,386	5,671,110	.1419	5,457,211	**1,605**	1,064,900	**2,261**	420,429	**2,356**	833,469	231,799
4890	Medford-Ashland, OR	192,822	181,269	23.8	17,054	76,466	3,288,420	.0707	3,296,101	**970**	569,323	**1,209**	84,470	**473**	347,160	87,002
4900	Melbourne-Titusville-Palm Bay, FL	515,004	476,230	19.4	22,229	228,764	11,447,810	.1835	5,603,865	**1,648**	916,795	**1,946**	235,423	**1,319**	919,936	384,085
4920	Memphis, TN-AR-MS	1,178,084	1,135,614	12.7	18,588	454,941	21,897,800	.3928	13,968,165	**4,109**	2,381,739	**5,056**	819,485	**4,593**	1,453,839	894,457
4940	Merced, CA	238,219	210,554	18.0	13,234	71,028	3,152,650	.0571	1,544,511	**454**	256,600	**545**	38,860	**218**	298,155	86,520
5000	Miami, FL (PMSA)	2,368,141	2,253,362	16.3	16,237	848,751	38,452,660	.7039	23,817,798	**7,006**	2,737,682	**5,812**	2,321,232	**13,009**	3,289,971	2,034,323
5015	Middlesex-Somerset-Hunterdon, NJ (PMSA)	1,236,285	1,169,641	14.7	29,098	441,732	35,973,700	.5487	17,388,807	**5,115**	1,543,590	**3,276**	1,092,322	**6,122**	2,887,475	912,783
5080	Milwaukee-Waukesha, WI (PMSA)	1,518,392	1,500,741	4.8	21,091	626,347	32,024,760	.5377	17,828,356	**5,244**	2,468,920	**5,241**	607,112	**3,403**	2,663,965	1,200,135
5120	Minneapolis-St. Paul, MN-WI	3,117,850	2,968,806	16.9	23,599	1,239,180	73,576,940	1.2830	49,271,803	**14,494**	6,752,377	**14,336**	1,762,104	**9,874**	6,271,900	2,151,420
5140	Missoula, MT	99,453	95,802	21.8	16,676	40,452	1,658,450	.0346	1,528,262	**450**	329,816	**700**	38,925	**218**	173,741	41,515
5160	Mobile, AL	554,939	540,258	13.3	16,905	215,349	9,381,040	.1693	5,716,074	**1,681**	1,129,778	**2,398**	334,609	**1,876**	769,574	320,389
5170	Modesto, CA	506,378	446,997	20.6	15,862	162,035	8,032,070	.1459	4,753,556	**1,398**	669,983	**1,422**	178,855	**1,002**	913,403	315,443
5190	Monmouth-Ocean, NJ (PMSA)	1,194,230	1,126,217	14.2	26,646	461,891	31,821,320	.4890	15,014,622	**4,417**	1,469,156	**3,119**	899,817	**5,042**	3,027,352	925,760
5200	Monroe, LA	148,118	147,250	3.6	16,229	60,235	2,403,800	.0467	1,793,330	**528**	499,482	**1,060**	92,642	**519**	175,892	80,637
5240	Montgomery, AL	341,047	333,055	13.9	18,107	133,223	6,175,490	.1136	4,186,480	**1,232**	792,318	**1,682**	200,979	**1,126**	516,664	244,283
5280	Muncie, IN	117,094	118,769	-0.7	16,012	47,338	1,874,870	.0364	1,381,187	**406**	331,237	**703**	55,373	**310**	137,963	69,463
5330	Myrtle Beach, SC	214,999	196,629	36.5	18,682	91,843	4,016,570	.0819	3,690,442	**1,086**	611,740	**1,299**	391,423	**2,194**	536,626	149,542
5345	Naples, FL	297,488	251,377	65.3	24,228	122,501	7,207,470	.1199	4,228,159	**1,244**	421,375	**895**	411,527	**2,306**	713,495	233,244
5350	Nashua, NH (PMSA)	199,522	190,949	13.5	23,975	74,978	4,783,616	.0953	4,557,046	**1,340**	715,002	**1,520**	177,753	**995**	616,349	136,025
5360	Nashville, TN	1,305,357	1,231,311	25.0	21,839	533,849	28,507,770	.5070	19,443,915	**5,718**	3,233,566	**6,865**	988,463	**5,539**	2,369,919	1,046,125
5380	Nassau-Suffolk, NY (PMSA)	2,823,190	2,753,913	5.5	26,883	944,853	75,895,570	1.2057	40,475,642	**11,906**	3,927,759	**8,337**	3,362,636	**18,845**	5,969,684	2,859,514
5400	New Bedford, MA (PMSA)	175,615	175,198	-0.3	19,472	69,573	3,419,540	.0553	1,558,967	**459**	243,872	**516**	71,688	**402**	320,894	113,923
5480	New Haven-Meriden, CT (PMSA)	558,806	542,149	2.3	25,384	217,158	14,184,918	.2228	7,046,455	**2,074**	569,423	**1,208**	440,585	**2,468**	1,165,560	520,528
5520	New London-Norwich, CT-RI	300,479	293,566	1.0	24,891	119,236	7,479,164	.1214	4,117,840	**1,210**	515,570	**1,094**	203,424	**1,140**	672,007	269,477
5560	New Orleans, LA	1,339,327	1,337,726	4.1	17,870	542,216	23,933,970	.4286	14,779,516	**4,348**	2,493,129	**5,294**	876,417	**4,912**	2,170,408	1,105,888
5600	New York, NY (PMSA)	9,449,241	9,314,235	9.0	19,496	3,516,152	184,222,140	2.8951	74,637,532	**21,956**	7,093,249	**15,057**	12,074,493	**67,668**	12,194,376	8,200,113
5640	Newark, NJ (PMSA)	2,080,714	2,032,989	6.1	25,266	748,659	52,571,660	.8198	25,323,919	**7,450**	1,660,994	**3,525**	1,738,863	**9,746**	4,824,662	1,780,829
5660	Newburgh, NY-PA (PMSA)	423,860	387,669	15.5	21,069	145,809	8,930,310	.1428	4,158,453	**1,223**	684,571	**1,453**	376,001	**2,107**	612,899	246,159
5720	Norfolk-Virginia Beach-Newport News, VA-NC	1,649,035	1,569,541	8.8	18,502	628,301	30,510,690	.5288	17,309,532	**5,094**	2,782,538	**5,907**	968,063	**5,423**	2,404,178	788,060
5775	Oakland, CA (PMSA)	2,481,548	2,392,557	14.9	25,854	910,856	64,158,440	.9689	27,783,114	**8,172**	2,998,426	**6,365**	1,513,360	**8,481**	5,542,436	1,375,606
5790	Ocala, FL	286,954	258,916	32.9	17,412	123,754	4,996,440	.0912	3,225,186	**949**	498,732	**1,059**	83,149	**466**	433,921	186,643
5800	Odessa-Midland, TX	243,009	237,132	5.1	16,218	91,901	3,941,070	.0780	3,102,129	**913**	618,214	**1,312**	121,450	**680**	383,961	117,885
5880	Oklahoma City, OK	1,131,827	1,083,346	13.0	18,082	459,286	20,465,960	.3693	13,076,515	**3,846**	2,285,527	**4,851**	448,620	**2,515**	1,463,530	713,738
5910	Olympia, WA (PMSA)	226,479	207,355	28.6	21,081	90,097	4,774,330	.0817	2,831,219	**833**	658,091	**1,397**	78,248	**439**	496,829	97,280
5920	Omaha, NE-IA	750,455	716,998	12.1	19,980	297,793	14,994,260	.2754	10,729,850	**3,157**	1,351,732	**2,870**	393,241	**2,203**	1,385,436	600,049
5945	Orange County, CA (PMSA)	2,991,519	2,846,289	18.1	23,134	989,208	69,206,970	1.1471	39,088,814	**11,498**	4,547,424	**9,653**	3,141,259	**17,605**	6,027,801	2,162,963
5960	Orlando, FL	1,851,873	1,644,561	34.3	20,739	737,616	38,405,230	.6825	25,416,119	**7,476**	3,495,555	**7,420**	1,661,395	**9,310**	3,372,844	1,393,435
5990	Owensboro, KY	92,851	91,545	5.0	17,937	37,583	1,665,490	.0297	1,020,908	**300**	225,267	**478**	38,656	**217**	109,897	72,292
6015	Panama City, FL	157,510	148,217	16.7	18,652	64,529	2,937,810	.0539	2,015,801	**593**	435,643	**925**	81,428	**456**	299,060	98,266
6020	Parkersburg-Marietta, WV-OH	149,426	151,237	1.4	17,179	62,705	2,566,950	.0503	2,025,162	**596**	429,487	**912**	62,642	**351**	221,717	109,673
6080	Pensacola, FL	434,387	412,153	19.7	19,068	176,993	8,282,890	.1411	4,519,358	**1,330**	756,204	**1,605**	179,965	**1,008**	666,395	295,741
6120	Peoria-Pekin, IL	346,613	347,387	2.4	19,918	138,610	6,903,930	.1223	4,421,329	**1,300**	616,300	**1,308**	117,726	**659**	664,142	297,071
6160	Philadelphia, PA-NJ (PMSA)	5,185,302	5,100,931	3.6	22,050	2,000,270	114,335,950	1.9085	64,223,991	**18,892**	5,638,401	**11,970**	3,946,842	**22,119**	10,757,555	4,748,610
6200	Phoenix-Mesa, AZ	3,698,598	3,251,876	45.3	19,860	1,390,757	73,453,060	1.2676	43,123,015	**12,685**	5,754,543	**12,215**	1,636,357	**9,171**	5,887,002	2,114,223
6240	Pine Bluff, AR	82,445	84,278	-1.4	13,976	30,359	1,152,220	.0238	933,401	**275**	187,094	**397**	55,965	**314**	129,323	102,357
6280	Pittsburgh, PA	2,332,585	2,358,695	-1.5	18,741	982,599	43,715,910	.7760	27,098,464	**7,971**	3,023,500	**6,419**	1,282,646	**7,188**	4,387,682	2,025,969
6320	Pittsfield, MA	82,558	84,699	-4.5	20,156	35,977	1,664,023	.0286	960,909	**284**	80,799	**172**	80,835	**454**	212,567	71,067
6340	Pocatello, ID	75,644	75,565	14.4	15,671	27,584	1,185,420	.0234	903,112	**266**	153,687	**326**	18,959	**106**	145,567	41,229
6400	Portland, ME	251,488	243,537	10.1	21,304	105,022	5,357,693	.1053	4,760,267	**1,402**	415,344	**880**	250,874	**1,406**	899,238	196,292
6440	Portland-Vancouver, OR-WA (PMSA)	2,064,660	1,918,009	26.6	20,989	805,998	43,334,910	.7577	27,462,972	**8,079**	4,981,840	**10,575**	1,438,297	**8,061**	3,670,572	842,358
6450	Portsmouth-Rochester, NH-ME (PMSA)	256,051	240,698	7.8	23,252	103,309	5,953,801	.1103	4,675,075	**1,378**	496,161	**1,054**	245,229	**1,373**	720,470	186,732
6480	Providence-Fall River-Warwick, RI-MA	1,229,484	1,188,613	4.8	19,449	484,930	23,912,381	.4038	12,839,618	**3,778**	1,445,281	**3,068**	845,850	**4,738**	2,359,453	1,279,986
6520	Provo-Orem, UT	407,123	368,536	39.8	14,363	114,713	5,847,380	.1153	4,189,283	**1,232**	806,151	**1,711**	141,362	**792**	704,861	73,449
6560	Pueblo, CO	151,054	141,472	15.0	15,098	58,747	2,280,620	.0447	1,659,496	**488**	395,824	**840**	30,025	**168**	218,342	61,578
6580	Punta Gorda, FL	157,100	141,627	27.6	20,982	71,830	3,296,280	.0530	1,568,354	**461**	366,846	**779**	83,926	**470**	252,565	99,775
6600	Racine, WI (PMSA)	193,383	188,831	7.9	20,192	75,070	3,904,770	.0646	2,000,747	**589**	328,944	**698**	47,858	**268**	321,126	122,733
6640	Raleigh-Durham-Chapel Hill, NC	1,328,146	1,187,941	38.9	23,223	546,749	30,842,920	.5192	18,376,719	**5,406**	2,283,168	**4,847**	930,779	**5,215**	2,594,121	864,240
6660	Rapid City, SD	92,908	88,565	8.9	17,302	37,133	1,607,490	.0379	2,003,457	**589**	417,197	**886**	84,303	**472**	173,874	75,403
6680	Reading, PA	388,909	373,638	11.0	19,644	147,702	7,639,890	.1301	4,256,088	**1,252**	525,747	**1,116**	342,408	**1,919**	683,206	249,524
6690	Redding, CA	179,590	163,256	11.0	16,828	70,586	3,022,140	.0528	1,632,661	**480**	274,967	**584**	44,756	**251**	319,925	87,215
6720	Reno, NV	380,688	339,486	33.3	20,389	147,051	7,761,940	.1365	4,927,460	**1,449**	767,107	**1,628**	165,864	**930**	743,396	194,817
6740	Richland-Kennewick-Pasco, WA	215,499	191,822	27.9	17,905	75,145	3,858,460	.0698	2,458,913	**723**	502,225	**1,066**	66,090	**370**	431,707	99,354
6760	Richmond-Petersburg, VA	1,044,758	996,512	15.1	21,627	428,842	22,595,390	.3794	12,797,495	**3,766**	2,174,738	**4,617**	633,173	**3,549**	1,828,511	759,973
6780	Riverside-San Bernardino, CA (PMSA)	3,763,495	3,254,821	25.7	16,568	1,190,886	62,352,000	1.0820	32,473,181	**9,552**	4,207,194	**8,931**	1,932,948	**10,833**	5,780,775	1,423,456
6800	Roanoke, VA	236,385	235,932	5.1	19,712	104,040	4,659,640	.0892	3,712,447	**1,092**	576,209	**1,223**	157,320	**882**	452,741	167,994
6820	Rochester, MN	133,562	124,277	16.7	22,785	54,231	3,043,170	.0530	1,995,060	**587**	455,521	**967**	66,575	**373**	199,272	72,562
6840	Rochester, NY	1,102,049	1,098,201	3.4	21,495	437,550	23,688,360	.3826	11,651,582	**3,428**	1,355,331	**2,877**	534,997	**2,999**	2,284,893	586,878
6880	Rockford, IL	387,465	371,236	12.6	20,145	150,219	7,805,440	.1321	4,338,742	**1,277**	639,669	**1,358**	147,039	**825**	704,827	249,267
6895	Rocky Mount, NC	145,152	143,026	7.3	15,821	55,470	2,296,510	.0420	1,389,971	**408**	165,999	**352**	80,735	**452**	168,128	86,148
6920	Sacramento, CA (PMSA)	1,842,845	1,628,197	21.5	21,137	683,523	38,952,280	.6367	19,765,983	**5,814**	2,439,432	**5,179**	1,126,460	**6,313**	3,478,390	818,945
6960	Saginaw-Bay City-Midland, MI	403,326	403,070	0.9	18,338	161,152	7,396,110	.1426	5,788,836	**1,703**	1,152,722	**2,448**	363,828	**2,039**	543,711	300,521
6980	St. Cloud, MN	176,070	167,392	12.4	17,788	65,598	3,131,890	.0619	2,585,072	**761**	485,538	**1,031**	60,761	**340**	324,406	77,711
7000	St. Joseph, MO	101,433	102,490	4.9	17,467	42,139	1,771,690	.0328	1,198,486	**353**	287,997	**611**	21,835	**122**	150,321	45,353
7040	St. Louis, MO-IL	2,651,207	2,603,607	4.5	20,979	1,071,356	55,619,040	.9341	30,901,201	**9,090**	4,750,381	**10,083**	1,098,666	**6,157**	4,567,369	2,050,522
7080	Salem, OR (PMSA)	367,908	347,214	24.9	16,849	130,863	6,199,000	.1128	3,871,527	**1,139**	789,346	**1,676**	136,871	**767**	556,517	124,085
7120	Salinas, CA	418,251	401,762	13.0	17,064	123,111	7,137,110	.1276	4,236,459	**1,246**	473,268	**1,005**	285,175	**1,598**	741,345	267,217
7160	Salt Lake City-Ogden, UT	1,401,430	1,333,914	24.4	17,906	467,808	25,094,290	.4842	19,473,859	**5,728**	3,094,313	**6,569**	775,845	**4,348**	2,750,678	392,394
7200	San Angelo, TX	103,389	104,010	5.6	16,149	41,302	1,669,670	.0320	1,193,948	**351**	241,597	**513**	46,860	**263**	165,713	36,321
7240	San Antonio, TX	1,722,612	1,592,383	20.2	17,341	629,687	29,872,110	.5505	19,817,186	**5,829**	2,885,576	**6,126**	1,106,928	**6,204**	3,039,566	787,336
7320	San Diego, CA	2,966,135	2,813,833	12.6	20,344	1,059,703	60,342,670	1.0169	33,222,905	**9,773**	3,825,198	**8,120**	2,426,068	**13,596**	5,326,312	1,680,462
7360	San Francisco, CA (PMSA)	1,682,970	1,731,183	8.0	30,593	688,594	51,487,220	.8009	27,316,734	**8,036**	3,136,463	**6,658**	3,295,298	**18,468**	4,882,998	1,660,518
7400	San Jose, CA (PMSA)	1,675,734	1,682,585	12.4	29,915	586,292	50,130,310	.7861	27,026,688	**7,950**	3,149,778	**6,686**	2,287,248	**12,818**	4,358,160	1,341,238
7460	San Luis Obispo-Atascadero-Paso Robles, CA	254,929	246,681	13.6	20,201	98,521	5,149,890	.0859	2,720,316	**800**	246,788	**524**	150,585	**844**	543,527	192,222
7480	Santa Barbara-Santa Maria-Lompoc, CA	404,260	399,347	8.0	19,379	138,188	7,834,290	.1368	4,700,898	**1,383**	454,866	**966**	331,262	**1,856**	859,109	335,658
7485	Santa Cruz-Watsonville, CA (PMSA)	250,198	255,602	11.3	23,542	91,446	5,890,220	.0942	2,967,816	**873**	302,380	**642**	153,966	**863**	615,612	266,818
7490	Santa Fe, NM	157,592	147,635	26.1	22,817	65,653	3,595,830	.0591	1,957,741	**576**	393,771	**836**	144,840	**812**	241,466	112,968
7500	Santa Rosa, CA (PMSA)	468,851	458,614	18.1	23,674	174,821	11,099,560	.1798	5,877,135	**1,729**	619,805	**1,316**	256,127	**1,435**	1,187,270	345,374
7510	Sarasota-Bradenton, FL	647,224	589,959	20.5	22,658	289,616	14,664,530	.2443	8,331,292	**2,450**	976,820	**2,074**	496,718	**2,784**	1,292,386	548,115
7520	Savannah, GA	307,995	293,000	13.5	18,342	121,256	5,649,240	.1028	3,741,300	**1,100**	694,530	**1,474**	206,990	**1,160**	521,531	132,810
7560	Scranton--Wilkes-Barre--Hazleton, PA	614,462	624,776	-2.1	16,989	257,645	10,439,140	.1952	7,157,244	**2,106**	938,315	**1,992**	326,966	**1,833**	1,285,643	497,082
7600	Seattle-Bellevue-Everett, WA (PMSA)	2,496,295	2,414,616	18.8	24,252	1,021,038	60,539,450	1.0042	35,212,324	**10,358**	4,844,127	**10,283**	2,242,194	**12,566**	4,991,139	1,410,945
7610	Sharon, PA	119,795	120,293	-0.6	16,241	47,178	1,945,620	.0405	1,759,998	**518**	245,942	**522**	163,746	**918**	228,125	107,358
7620	Sheboygan, WI	113,582	112,646	8.4	20,355	45,994	2,311,980	.0379	1,149,763	**338**	226,999	**482**	16,678	**93**	182,279	51,099
7640	Sherman-Denison, TX	116,532	110,595	16.4	17,785	45,226	2,072,480	.0389	1,481,541	**436**	372,920	**792**	32,470	**182**	172,110	55,084
7680	Shreveport-Bossier City, LA	394,221	392,302	4.2	16,302	156,808	6,426,760	.1234	4,634,290	**1,363**	847,236	**1,799**	192,491	**1,079**	586,687	199,816
7720	Sioux City, IA-NE	123,569	124,130	7.9	16,375	45,942	2,023,440	.0398	1,580,770	**465**	233,422	**495**	60,740	**341**	235,568	62,804
7760	Sioux Falls, SD	187,360	172,412	23.8	19,915	75,158	3,731,200	.0836	4,368,137	**1,285**	643,959	**1,367**	65,830	**369**	351,776	182,304
7800	South Bend, IN	266,508	265,559	7.5	17,775	104,015	4,737,260	.0911	3,620,979	**1,065**	700,006	**1,486**	140,246	**786**	399,407	257,464
7840	Spokane, WA	435,145	417,939	15.7	17,174	170,747	7,473,250	.1385	5,018,057	**1,476**	886,324	**1,881**	231,274	**1,296**	770,118	205,222
7880	Springfield, IL	205,434	201,437	6.3	21,081	86,436	4,330,730	.0739	2,539,671	**747**	448,852	**953**	80,482	**451**	334,831	160,456
7920	Springfield, MO	344,995	325,721	23.2	17,168	143,829	5,922,880	.1170	4,791,863	**1,409**	720,493	**1,529**	105,176	**590**	461,796	207,558
8000	Springfield, MA	603,755	591,932	0.7	19,208	233,886	11,596,686	.1955	6,129,987	**1,803**	542,859	**1,151**	308,028	**1,726**	1,271,520	480,477
8040	Stamford-Norwalk, CT (PMSA)	363,586	353,556	7.2	40,815	138,441	14,839,624	.2223	7,852,816	**2,310**	263,468	**559**	557,332	**3,123**	923,042	331,430
8050	State College, PA	143,518	135,758	9.7	15,772	52,665	2,263,590	.0432	1,572,637	**463**	206,017	**437**	90,830	**509**	222,749	82,855
8080	Steubenville-Weirton, OH-WV	127,547	132,008	-7.4	16,455	54,147	2,098,810	.0357	1,010,343	**297**	175,748	**373**	32,493	**182**	203,887	107,682
8120	Stockton-Lodi, CA	654,288	563,598	17.3	16,392	210,061	10,725,080	.1822	5,087,457	**1,497**	677,193	**1,438**	219,393	**1,230**	911,463	340,141
8140	Sumter, SC	106,361	104,646	2.0	15,246	40,297	1,621,630	.0297	959,454	**282**	136,905	**291**	50,276	**282**	128,249	45,197
8160	Syracuse, NY	737,104	732,117	-1.4	19,587	292,002	14,437,390	.2404	7,411,093	**2,180**	799,327	**1,698**	360,769	**2,022**	1,428,189	527,700
8200	Tacoma, WA (PMSA)	753,288	700,820	19.6	19,217	281,633	14,476,220	.2441	7,660,414	**2,253**	1,311,305	**2,784**	277,368	**1,554**	1,116,419	309,143
8240	Tallahassee, FL	288,589	284,539	21.8	19,406	120,962	5,600,290	.0987	3,477,596	**1,022**	602,949	**1,280**	167,210	**937**	552,299	220,739
8280	Tampa-St. Petersburg-Clearwater, FL	2,574,498	2,395,997	15.9	21,239	1,157,320	54,679,370	.9513	34,351,447	**10,104**	4,164,175	**8,840**	1,446,023	**8,104**	4,811,738	2,259,763
8320	Terre Haute, IN	147,496	149,192	1.1	15,676	59,461	2,312,180	.0582	3,179,528	**935**	495,330	**1,051**	106,130	**595**	200,142	94,896
8360	Texarkana, TX-AR	132,208	129,749	8.0	15,062	50,531	1,991,340	.0402	1,584,069	**466**	306,315	**650**	79,403	**445**	170,818	41,392
8400	Toledo, OH	620,144	618,203	0.7	18,942	254,495	11,746,760	.2139	7,949,520	**2,338**	1,292,148	**2,744**	318,923	**1,787**	1,104,698	447,550
8440	Topeka, KS	171,175	169,871	5.5	19,419	71,974	3,324,050	.0605	2,278,937	**670**	477,160	**1,013**	75,794	**425**	295,682	164,466
8480	Trenton, NJ (PMSA)	365,448	350,761	7.7	25,680	133,605	9,384,820	.1447	4,366,020	**1,284**	398,348	**846**	330,116	**1,850**	753,962	416,720
8520	Tucson, AZ	907,511	843,746	26.5	17,888	365,815	16,233,410	.2752	8,272,791	**2,434**	1,284,384	**2,726**	326,802	**1,831**	1,268,524	505,873
8560	Tulsa, OK	829,509	803,235	13.3	19,040	341,229	15,793,530	.2811	9,974,562	**2,935**	1,954,354	**4,148**	313,548	**1,757**	1,079,190	542,665
8600	Tuscaloosa, AL	166,903	164,875	9.5	17,741	69,787	2,960,990	.0545	1,988,420	**585**	344,218	**731**	96,127	**539**	243,985	106,668
8640	Tyler, TX	186,882	174,706	15.5	17,504	72,108	3,271,110	.0660	2,829,077	**832**	474,715	**1,008**	187,114	**1,049**	337,370	129,863
8680	Utica-Rome, NY	297,571	299,896	-5.3	17,516	117,786	5,212,330	.0891	2,695,644	**793**	385,726	**819**	101,736	**570**	444,071	253,056
8720	Vallejo-Fairfield-Napa, CA (PMSA)	551,336	518,821	15.0	21,927	189,566	12,089,340	.1895	5,375,799	**1,581**	750,931	**1,594**	318,173	**1,783**	1,122,819	238,833
8735	Ventura, CA (PMSA)	802,627	753,197	12.6	22,864	258,964	18,351,220	.2961	9,381,128	**2,760**	941,078	**1,998**	513,106	**2,876**	1,505,559	540,323
8750	Victoria, TX	85,853	84,088	13.1	16,969	30,982	1,456,800	.0287	1,163,146	**342**	236,603	**502**	51,763	**290**	156,770	50,391
8760	Vineland-Millville-Bridgeton, NJ (PMSA)	150,283	146,438	6.1	17,007	50,856	2,555,870	.0455	1,488,762	**438**	144,840	**307**	48,684	**273**	322,667	121,082
8780	Visalia-Tulare-Porterville, CA	398,103	368,021	18.0	12,544	117,213	4,993,740	.0943	2,716,977	**799**	427,942	**908**	106,651	**598**	549,480	145,301
8800	Waco, TX	221,739	213,517	12.9	15,426	83,405	3,420,440	.0655	2,358,225	**694**	434,782	**923**	83,366	**467**	383,400	91,734
8840	Washington, DC-MD-VA-WV (PMSA)	5,326,575	4,923,153	16.6	27,313	2,049,946	145,486,130	2.1408	58,917,498	**17,330**	7,392,681	**15,693**	3,879,721	**21,743**	9,890,576	3,047,385
8880	Waterbury, CT (PMSA)	234,728	228,984	3.3	23,056	91,614	5,412,003	.0862	2,658,124	**783**	320,523	**680**	111,020	**622**	529,230	204,370
8920	Waterloo-Cedar Falls, IA	125,922	128,012	3.4	16,904	50,103	2,128,580	.0428	1,787,507	**526**	297,139	**631**	58,515	**328**	206,762	93,056
8940	Wausau, WI	127,589	125,834	9.0	19,297	50,040	2,462,120	.0466	1,887,978	**555**	362,120	**769**	42,550	**238**	218,595	38,765
8960	West Palm Beach-Boca Raton, FL	1,243,157	1,131,184	31.0	25,735	577,999	31,992,820	.5094	16,783,738	**4,937**	2,107,777	**4,474**	1,528,403	**8,566**	2,438,488	1,097,284
9000	Wheeling, WV-OH	149,538	153,172	-3.8	15,785	64,006	2,360,440	.0455	1,691,503	**497**	300,727	**638**	70,216	**394**	264,938	117,677
9040	Wichita, KS[2]	527,608	512,351	12.8	18,757	205,477	9,896,290	.1732	5,857,946	**1,723**	1,120,026	**2,377**	233,233	**1,307**	841,766	268,947
9080	Wichita Falls, TX	137,823	140,518	7.8	16,180	53,232	2,229,960	.0424	1,558,576	**459**	308,977	**656**	45,828	**257**	230,937	74,403

Metropolitan Statistical Areas (MSAs): Population / Income / Sales#, *Continued*

CODE	METROPOLITAN STATISTICAL AREA	POPULATION Estimate 7/1/04	POPULATION Census 4/1/00	% Change 4/1/90-4/1/00	PER CAPITA INCOME 2003	HOUSE-HOLDS Estimate 7/1/04	DISPOSABLE INCOME 2003 ($1,000)	MARKET ABILITY INDEX 2003	TOTAL RETAIL SALES 2003 Sales ($1,000)	Ranally Sales Units	GENERAL MERCHANDISE 2003 Sales ($1,000)	Ranally Sales Units	APPAREL STORE SALES 2003 Sales ($1,000)	Ranally Sales Units	FOOD STORE SALES 2003 ($1,000)	HEALTH & DRUG STORE 2003 ($1,000)
9140	Williamsport, PA	117,940	120,044	1.1	16,296	47,574	1,921,940	.0378	1,491,653	439	223,336	474	62,585	351	255,638	108,531
9160	Wilmington-Newark, DE-MD (PMSA)	614,320	586,216	14.2	22,618	236,718	13,894,600	.2381	8,622,549	2,537	1,062,778	2,256	391,369	2,193	1,405,545	496,413
9200	Wilmington, NC	254,768	233,450	36.3	21,066	117,472	5,366,910	.1022	4,351,845	1,280	583,827	1,239	178,499	1,001	589,821	223,099
9240	Worcester, MA-CT (PMSA)	536,389	511,389	6.9	21,870	206,638	11,730,876	.1938	6,347,171	1,870	674,455	1,431	289,385	1,620	1,085,081	453,513
9260	Yakima, WA	228,066	222,581	17.9	13,316	74,206	3,037,030	.0593	1,979,472	582	431,605	916	60,404	339	329,183	54,696
9270	Yolo, CA (PMSA)	187,466	168,660	19.5	17,468	65,200	3,274,600	.0537	1,434,376	422	92,016	195	28,130	158	338,545	70,836
9280	York, PA	398,969	381,751	12.4	20,544	157,278	8,196,390	.1339	4,069,282	1,197	563,866	1,197	146,775	823	757,223	207,738
9320	Youngstown-Warren, OH	581,948	594,746	-1.0	17,366	237,536	10,106,220	.1826	6,301,912	1,853	807,519	1,714	234,872	1,317	884,937	436,683
9340	Yuba City, CA	151,010	139,149	13.5	14,753	51,097	2,227,910	.0395	1,120,098	330	218,867	465	28,829	162	243,792	75,167
9360	Yuma, AZ	174,609	160,026	49.7	13,194	58,992	2,303,760	.0445	1,439,675	423	334,372	710	34,477	193	209,344	71,584
	U. S. Totals	237,101,488	225,948,810	13.9	20,621	90,651,200	4,889,177,980	83.5634	2,849,115,645	838,102	389,887,053	827,647	161,556,998	905,389	418,018,756	164,400,182

Source: Devonshire Associates Ltd. and Scan/US, Inc. 2004.

Estimates for Total Retail Sales, General Merchandise, Apparel Store Sales, Food Store Sales, and Health and Drug Store Sales are based on data from the U.S. Census Bureau's 1997 Economic Census and utilize the North American Industry Classification System (NAICS).

[1] Census population includes a portion of Broomfield county.

[2] Data exclude Harvey County, Kansas (7/1/04 estimated population 33,707) which fails to meet published standards for MSA inclusion, but has been included with the Wichita MSA as the result of Congressional action.

Consolidated Metropolitan Statistical Areas (CMSAs): Population / Income / Sales#

CMSAs are MSAs of one million or more population that meet certain requirements officially established by the Office of Management and Budget (OMB). Each CMSA constitutes a comprehensive definition of one of the nation's large metropolitan complexes. Within each CMSA, the Bureau defines component portions termed PMSAs. Data for PMSAs are included in the table on page 37. Both CMSAs and PMSAs appear on the map on pages 36-37.

CODE	CONSOLIDATED METROPOLITAN STATISTICAL AREAS	POPULATION Estimate 7/1/04	POPULATION Census 4/1/00	POPULATION % Change 4/1/90-4/1/00	PER CAPITA INCOME 2003	HOUSEHOLDS Estimate 7/1/04	DISPOSABLE INCOME 2003 ($1,000)	MARKET ABILITY INDEX 2003	TOTAL RETAIL SALES 2003 Sales ($1,000)	TOTAL RETAIL SALES **Ranally Sales Units**	GENERAL MERCHANDISE 2003 Sales ($1,000)	GENERAL MERCHANDISE **Ranally Sales Units**	APPAREL STORE SALES 2003 Sales ($1,000)	APPAREL STORE SALES **Ranally Sales Units**	FOOD STORE SALES 2003 ($1,000)	HEALTH & DRUG STORE 2003 ($1,000)
07	Boston-Worcester-Lawrence, MA-NH-ME-CT	5,958,412	5,819,100	6.7	24,175	2,301,497	144,047,550	2.3577	80,070,802	**23,558**	8,259,682	**17,526**	5,366,209	**30,064**	13,369,943	5,278,184
14	Chicago-Gary-Kenosha, IL-IN-WI	9,465,508	9,157,540	11.1	21,257	3,427,270	201,209,390	3.3489	109,301,067	**32,152**	12,666,569	**26,887**	6,039,023	**33,844**	15,049,011	9,040,779
21	Cincinnati-Hamilton, OH-KY-IN	2,026,864	1,979,202	8.9	21,031	820,244	42,627,420	.7204	24,227,386	**7,127**	3,576,879	**7,592**	1,087,734	**6,096**	3,444,117	1,328,735
28	Cleveland-Akron, OH	2,943,497	2,945,831	3.0	20,150	1,205,351	59,310,910	1.0353	36,496,956	**10,736**	3,907,507	**8,296**	1,686,648	**9,453**	5,279,080	3,587,625
31	Dallas-Fort Worth, TX	5,783,868	5,221,801	29.3	21,478	2,163,567	124,225,970	2.1233	74,247,488	**21,840**	9,898,896	**21,015**	3,753,934	**21,039**	10,150,051	2,986,682
34	Denver-Boulder-Greeley, CO[1]	2,740,678	2,581,506	30.4	22,847	1,072,936	62,616,290	1.0445	35,863,308	**10,550**	4,955,820	**10,520**	1,495,538	**8,381**	5,129,493	1,251,468
35	Detroit-Ann Arbor-Flint, MI	5,533,161	5,456,428	5.2	21,959	2,186,276	121,505,030	2.0856	74,614,180	**21,949**	12,118,671	**25,726**	3,263,473	**18,288**	8,835,879	5,035,500
42	Houston-Galveston-Brazoria, TX	5,137,262	4,669,571	25.2	19,630	1,878,377	100,843,800	1.7486	59,697,707	**17,560**	9,227,490	**19,588**	3,363,984	**18,852**	9,063,795	2,807,536
49	Los Angeles-Riverside-Orange County, CA	17,537,912	16,373,645	12.7	18,226	5,692,637	319,649,410	5.4853	173,046,034	**50,903**	20,114,151	**42,698**	13,323,489	**74,670**	28,882,115	9,363,779
56	Miami-Fort Lauderdale, FL	4,132,456	3,876,380	21.4	18,693	1,595,823	77,248,860	1.3849	49,358,990	**14,519**	5,495,973	**11,667**	3,807,683	**21,339**	6,781,380	3,660,791
63	Milwaukee-Racine, WI	1,711,775	1,689,572	5.1	20,990	701,417	35,929,530	.6023	19,829,104	**5,833**	2,797,864	**5,939**	654,970	**3,671**	2,985,091	1,322,868
70	New York-Northern NJ-Long Island, NY-NJ-CT-PA	21,728,432	21,199,865	8.4	23,262	7,937,030	505,447,512	7.9506	237,993,197	**70,014**	21,433,085	**45,494**	24,029,725	**134,665**	39,470,252	18,858,115
77	Philadelphia-Wilmington-Atlantic City, PA-NJ-DE-MD	6,318,462	6,188,463	5.0	21,937	2,430,405	138,607,590	2.3246	78,851,282	**23,196**	7,315,576	**15,530**	4,704,129	**26,363**	13,542,072	5,651,287
79	Portland-Salem, OR-WA	2,432,568	2,265,223	26.3	20,363	936,861	49,533,910	.8705	31,334,498	**9,218**	5,771,186	**12,251**	1,575,168	**8,828**	4,227,089	966,442
82	Sacramento-Yolo, CA	2,030,311	1,796,857	21.3	20,798	748,723	42,226,880	.6904	21,200,359	**6,236**	2,531,448	**5,374**	1,154,590	**6,471**	3,816,935	889,781
84	San Francisco-Oakland-San Jose, CA	7,110,637	7,039,362	12.6	27,403	2,641,575	194,855,090	3.0194	96,347,286	**28,341**	10,957,783	**23,261**	7,824,172	**43,848**	17,709,295	5,228,387
91	Seattle-Tacoma-Bremerton, WA	3,719,512	3,554,760	19.7	22,749	1,483,734	84,614,290	1.4083	47,967,645	**14,110**	7,333,689	**15,568**	2,664,869	**14,935**	6,942,511	1,927,443
97	Washington-Baltimore, DC-MD-VA-WV	8,100,870	7,608,070	13.1	25,706	3,128,200	208,243,360	3.1373	88,948,868	**26,164**	11,366,869	**24,129**	5,556,158	**31,139**	15,201,898	4,923,186
	Totals	114,412,185	109,423,176	12.5	21,962	42,351,923	2,512,742,792	41.3379	1,339,396,159	**394,006**	159,729,138	**339,061**	91,351,495	**511,946**	209,880,008	84,108,589

Source: Devonshire Associates Ltd. and Scan/US, Inc. 2004.

[1] Census population includes a portion of Broomfield county.

New England County Metropolitan Areas (NECMAs): Population / Income / Sales#

CODE	NEW ENGLAND COUNTY METROPOLITAN AREAS	POPULATION Estimate 7/1/04	POPULATION Census 4/1/00	POPULATION % Change 4/1/90-4/1/00	PER CAPITA INCOME 2003	HOUSEHOLDS Estimate 7/1/04	DISPOSABLE INCOME 2003 ($1,000)	MARKET ABILITY INDEX 2003	TOTAL RETAIL SALES 2003 Sales ($1,000)	TOTAL RETAIL SALES **Ranally Sales Units**	GENERAL MERCHANDISE 2003 Sales ($1,000)	GENERAL MERCHANDISE **Ranally Sales Units**	APPAREL STORE SALES 2003 Sales ($1,000)	APPAREL STORE SALES **Ranally Sales Units**	FOOD STORE SALES 2003 ($1,000)	HEALTH & DRUG STORE 2003 ($1,000)
0733	Bangor, ME	147,681	144,919	-1.1	16,681	61,206	2,463,420	.0509	2,209,724	**650**	278,391	**591**	50,449	**283**	427,296	83,225
0743	Barnstable-Yarmouth, MA	231,645	222,230	19.1	23,742	100,221	5,499,830	.0935	3,415,754	**1,005**	174,648	**371**	229,079	**1,284**	801,769	241,440
1123	Boston-Worcester-Lawrence-Lowell-Brockton, MA-NH	6,186,809	6,057,826	6.5	24,042	2,393,059	148,744,620	2.4502	84,167,045	**24,757**	8,824,317	**18,733**	5,525,052	**30,964**	14,173,302	5,570,242
1303	Burlington, VT	204,838	198,889	12.3	20,637	80,861	4,227,310	.0795	3,282,264	**966**	310,507	**660**	156,077	**875**	563,362	179,025
3283	Hartford, CT	1,186,956	1,148,618	2.2	26,395	467,168	31,330,290	.4795	14,476,166	**4,258**	1,272,994	**2,702**	1,069,247	**5,993**	2,502,419	1,079,752
4243	Lewiston-Auburn, ME	106,865	103,793	-1.4	17,501	44,561	1,870,230	.0390	1,762,740	**519**	215,665	**458**	23,086	**129**	262,314	67,601
5483	New Haven-Bridgeport-Stamford-Danbury-Waterbury, CT	1,751,503	1,706,575	4.6	27,405	666,309	48,000,640	.7865	28,568,613	**8,404**	2,012,429	**4,272**	1,757,149	**9,847**	4,103,659	1,614,566
5523	New London-Norwich, CT	265,499	259,088	1.6	25,332	104,602	6,725,490	.1054	3,310,747	**974**	430,241	**913**	173,428	**972**	509,295	214,890
6323	Pittsfield, MA	132,813	134,953	-3.2	20,327	56,564	2,699,630	.0461	1,559,390	**459**	144,111	**306**	120,070	**673**	319,913	115,743
6403	Portland, ME	272,577	265,612	9.2	21,003	113,068	5,724,970	.1170	5,541,891	**1,630**	521,839	**1,108**	379,457	**2,127**	989,094	216,268
6483	Providence-Warwick-Pawtucket, RI	998,644	962,886	5.1	19,167	392,386	19,140,620	.3202	9,819,616	**2,889**	929,747	**1,973**	612,680	**3,433**	1,938,523	1,048,417
8003	Springfield, MA	618,736	608,479	0.9	19,319	239,516	11,953,370	.2015	6,351,419	**1,869**	645,916	**1,371**	315,869	**1,770**	1,298,551	477,431
	Totals	12,104,566	11,813,868	5.4	23,824	4,719,521	288,380,420	4.7693	164,465,370	**48,380**	15,760,803	**33,458**	10,411,643	**58,350**	27,889,496	10,908,602

Source: Devonshire Associates Ltd. and Scan/US, Inc. 2004.

Metropolitan Statistical Areas (MSAs): State Totals for Population / Income / Sales#

	POPULATION Estimate 7/1/04	POPULATION Census 4/1/00	% Change 4/1/90-4/1/00	PER CAPITA INCOME 2003	HOUSEHOLDS Estimate 7/1/04	DISPOSABLE INCOME 2003 ($1,000)	MARKET ABILITY INDEX 2003	TOTAL RETAIL SALES 2003 Sales ($1,000)	TOTAL RETAIL SALES **Ranally Sales Units**	GENERAL MERCHANDISE 2003 Sales ($1,000)	GENERAL MERCHANDISE **Ranally Sales Units**	APPAREL STORE SALES 2003 Sales ($1,000)	APPAREL STORE SALES **Ranally Sales Units**	FOOD STORE SALES 2003 ($1,000)	HEALTH & DRUG STORE 2003 ($1,000)
Alabama	3,186,831	3,108,959	11.2	18,300	1,286,233	58,319,770	1.0459	36,766,501	**10,815**	6,749,231	**14,328**	1,854,851	**10,393**	4,887,557	1,779,156
Alaska	274,398	260,283	15.0	22,488	100,252	6,170,610	.1105	4,355,756	**1,281**	1,057,357	**2,245**	209,835	**1,176**	511,166	47,012
Arizona	5,079,978	4,527,000	41.4	19,051	1,931,405	96,780,620	1.6761	55,897,054	**16,442**	7,929,785	**16,832**	2,062,191	**11,556**	7,925,719	2,798,553
Arkansas	1,392,748	1,321,019	19.1	17,495	553,356	24,365,720	.4656	18,134,557	**5,334**	4,367,909	**9,271**	657,284	**3,684**	1,650,910	672,301
California	34,796,160	32,750,394	13.7	20,011	11,804,633	696,297,970	11.6356	367,746,066	**108,175**	43,192,542	**91,691**	26,718,009	**149,737**	63,858,392	19,983,980
Colorado	3,850,776	3,607,656	29.8	21,832	1,498,851	84,070,300	1.4286	49,790,999	**14,646**	7,453,289	**15,822**	1,886,771	**10,574**	6,801,547	1,732,787
Connecticut	3,353,288	3,256,900	3.5	26,784	1,293,789	89,813,547	1.4195	46,981,256	**13,827**	3,843,492	**8,156**	2,972,957	**16,658**	7,239,506	3,035,240
Delaware	656,304	626,962	13.4	21,804	253,550	14,310,140	.2517	9,435,022	**2,776**	1,299,355	**2,759**	395,076	**2,214**	1,453,393	529,776
District of Columbia	560,725	572,059	-5.7	26,337	256,560	14,767,850	.1959	3,408,245	**1,003**	145,053	**308**	469,245	**2,630**	940,510	481,206
Florida	16,124,509	14,837,497	23.4	20,732	6,768,259	334,290,730	5.7675	201,591,559	**59,297**	26,173,533	**55,563**	12,208,605	**68,418**	29,007,271	12,892,047
Georgia	6,193,884	5,666,664	30.2	21,397	2,383,469	132,531,970	2.2783	80,525,458	**23,687**	11,236,098	**23,851**	4,202,035	**23,552**	11,422,648	3,238,353
Hawaii	911,719	876,156	4.8	19,820	301,773	18,070,470	.3029	9,586,291	**2,820**	1,932,186	**4,102**	1,213,597	**6,801**	1,460,075	815,873
Idaho	565,822	507,910	40.4	17,848	207,906	10,098,590	.1921	7,512,498	**2,210**	1,292,828	**2,744**	226,747	**1,271**	1,012,825	248,669
Illinois	10,871,095	10,541,708	10.1	21,057	3,999,092	228,908,720	3.8401	126,970,339	**37,349**	15,609,718	**33,134**	6,614,277	**37,070**	17,674,400	10,136,240
Indiana	4,530,319	4,389,903	10.8	19,367	1,805,852	87,737,290	1.5952	59,815,687	**17,595**	10,545,760	**22,385**	2,125,834	**11,913**	6,231,979	3,603,997
Iowa	1,365,087	1,326,133	10.5	19,331	543,660	26,388,970	.4879	18,906,384	**5,561**	2,732,810	**5,803**	695,909	**3,899**	2,445,733	949,629
Kansas[1]	1,558,507	1,488,194	14.3	20,872	613,080	32,529,810	.5588	19,413,563	**5,710**	3,291,916	**6,988**	934,575	**5,238**	2,674,333	985,976
Kentucky	2,030,455	1,973,102	10.9	20,118	849,740	40,848,490	.7032	24,006,492	**7,061**	3,951,397	**8,387**	1,113,351	**6,241**	2,836,679	1,497,786
Louisiana	3,412,436	3,370,210	6.7	17,158	1,351,921	58,549,670	1.0901	39,823,840	**11,716**	7,615,079	**16,167**	1,935,448	**10,849**	5,306,426	2,388,089
Maine	482,071	466,606	5.3	20,165	200,870	9,721,011	.1912	8,462,436	**2,491**	850,691	**1,807**	425,258	**2,382**	1,450,036	344,521
Maryland	5,168,760	4,911,040	10.6	24,098	1,958,837	124,554,880	1.9203	55,686,687	**16,380**	6,923,400	**14,696**	3,129,141	**17,537**	9,977,569	3,108,966
Massachusetts	6,217,954	6,101,425	5.4	23,626	2,419,375	146,907,019	2.3751	77,224,233	**22,721**	7,021,945	**14,897**	5,432,741	**30,443**	13,586,096	5,690,222
Michigan	8,315,758	8,169,466	6.1	21,023	3,271,067	174,821,360	3.0434	109,433,858	**32,191**	19,816,957	**42,069**	4,577,864	**25,653**	12,356,339	6,776,074
Minnesota	3,616,897	3,463,360	15.0	22,814	1,440,221	82,517,260	1.4544	56,082,170	**16,499**	8,046,366	**17,083**	1,957,812	**10,970**	7,104,867	2,444,917
Mississippi	1,074,771	1,023,662	17.1	18,010	414,731	19,356,820	.3561	13,079,165	**3,848**	2,986,362	**6,340**	481,440	**2,698**	1,332,924	681,004
Missouri	3,901,177	3,794,801	8.7	20,359	1,593,389	79,425,840	1.3802	48,475,092	**14,260**	7,405,712	**15,719**	1,501,582	**8,417**	6,159,282	2,805,179
Montana	313,196	305,511	13.2	16,981	127,836	5,318,530	.1082	4,637,992	**1,365**	943,314	**2,002**	132,553	**743**	496,662	146,627
Nebraska	946,627	899,838	14.3	19,876	377,517	18,815,610	.3390	12,685,736	**3,732**	1,790,308	**3,800**	466,014	**2,611**	1,763,647	753,187
Nevada	2,054,960	1,747,736	72.4	19,691	782,620	40,465,120	.7029	24,157,806	**7,106**	3,358,888	**7,130**	1,404,903	**7,874**	3,715,921	1,011,995
New Hampshire	781,892	739,699	12.3	23,108	299,599	18,067,807	.3459	15,434,638	**4,540**	2,613,469	**5,549**	624,748	**3,497**	2,369,885	546,827
New Jersey	8,707,156	8,414,350	8.9	25,358	3,199,381	220,796,870	3.4614	108,684,617	**31,972**	9,663,099	**20,512**	7,356,272	**41,227**	19,829,135	7,157,799
New Mexico	1,101,339	1,035,055	23.0	18,251	431,525	20,100,890	.3586	12,439,452	**3,660**	2,333,536	**4,954**	505,908	**2,835**	1,239,868	686,329
New York	17,729,441	17,473,058	5.8	20,940	6,618,418	371,257,770	5.9259	170,937,298	**50,283**	17,729,246	**37,636**	18,470,372	**103,512**	27,906,789	14,800,029
North Carolina	5,815,666	5,437,056	24.3	20,494	2,380,787	119,185,310	2.0999	76,278,973	**22,437**	10,237,168	**21,732**	3,623,053	**20,302**	9,976,833	3,992,675
North Dakota	290,202	283,966	10.3	18,424	120,867	5,346,550	.1126	5,271,204	**1,551**	871,482	**1,849**	162,825	**912**	452,845	254,335
Ohio	9,291,714	9,213,776	4.4	20,066	3,825,379	186,448,620	3.2733	116,557,419	**34,284**	15,888,381	**33,729**	5,080,518	**28,472**	15,940,666	7,946,110
Oklahoma	2,172,200	2,098,362	12.2	18,123	879,453	39,367,010	.7065	24,735,520	**7,276**	4,666,071	**9,904**	802,914	**4,500**	2,777,529	1,327,140
Oregon	2,647,740	2,502,366	21.7	19,832	1,038,310	52,510,630	.9537	36,184,700	**10,645**	6,579,187	**13,967**	1,711,263	**9,591**	4,800,896	1,010,797
Pennsylvania	10,482,379	10,391,529	3.1	19,622	4,187,405	205,685,840	3.6087	126,512,211	**37,217**	13,002,135	**27,601**	6,809,752	**38,165**	20,991,696	8,823,159
Rhode Island	1,021,546	986,351	5.1	19,293	401,827	19,708,655	.3272	9,895,094	**2,912**	899,689	**1,910**	609,164	**3,412**	1,946,026	1,065,550
South Carolina	2,953,934	2,806,962	15.9	18,611	1,181,741	54,975,310	.9957	36,194,568	**10,645**	5,738,532	**12,183**	2,061,646	**11,555**	5,196,675	1,833,946
South Dakota	280,268	260,977	18.3	19,049	112,291	5,338,690	.1215	6,371,594	**1,874**	1,061,156	**2,253**	150,133	**841**	525,650	257,707
Tennessee	4,010,190	3,862,144	16.7	19,497	1,636,055	78,187,030	1.4377	55,378,122	**16,289**	9,429,715	**20,017**	3,100,873	**17,377**	6,374,350	3,058,695
Texas	19,280,576	17,691,880	24.9	18,664	7,043,518	359,849,290	6.5317	238,796,156	**70,243**	34,738,999	**73,747**	12,286,288	**68,854**	33,186,986	10,219,486
Utah	1,814,579	1,708,496	27.4	17,102	584,856	31,032,900	.6010	23,696,878	**6,970**	3,900,747	**8,281**	917,606	**5,142**	3,467,360	467,540
Vermont	173,586	169,391	11.8	21,114	68,986	3,665,111	.0708	3,057,260	**899**	311,463	**662**	128,387	**720**	494,440	170,202
Virginia	5,898,831	5,528,068	15.8	23,220	2,318,750	136,970,270	2.2122	70,940,388	**20,870**	11,011,185	**23,376**	3,994,644	**22,386**	10,073,577	3,475,012
Washington	5,168,055	4,899,154	21.4	21,299	2,018,549	110,075,470	1.8597	62,988,388	**18,528**	10,201,355	**21,655**	3,217,265	**18,031**	9,544,775	2,595,961
West Virginia	770,618	765,568	2.3	17,906	328,744	13,798,950	.2483	8,660,045	**2,547**	1,541,640	**3,271**	376,792	**2,112**	1,031,898	700,287
Wisconsin	3,748,729	3,640,308	9.3	20,620	1,522,703	77,299,090	1.3413	47,326,464	**13,920**	7,517,109	**15,956**	1,515,730	**8,492**	6,351,695	2,385,989
Wyoming	153,635	148,140	10.2	17,934	62,212	2,755,230	.0535	2,181,915	**642**	388,407	**824**	44,939	**252**	254,766	45,241
U. S. Totals	237,101,488	225,948,810	13.9	20,621	90,651,200	4,889,177,980	83.5634	2,849,115,645	**838,102**	389,887,053	**827,647**	161,556,998	**905,389**	418,018,756	164,400,182

Source: Devonshire Associates Ltd. and Scan/US, Inc. 2004.

Estimates for Total Retail Sales, General Merchandise, Apparel Store Sales, Food Store Sales, and Health and Drug Store Sales are based on data from the U.S. Census Bureau's 1997 Economic Census and utilize the North American Industry Classification System (NAICS).

[1] Data for Kansas excludes Harvey Co. See footnote 2 on page 42.

150 Largest Metropolitan Statistical Areas (MSAs): Population / Income / Sales#

The table lists the 150 largest Metropolitan Statistical Areas (MSAs) and Primary Metropolitan Statistical Areas (PMSAs), ranked by July 1, 2004 estimated population. The data shown are consistent with the data on the MSA Table which appears on pages 40-42. A map showing the MSAs, with a detailed explanation of how they are determined, appears on pages 36-37. An explanation of MSAs may also be found in the Introduction on pages 5-9.

RANK	METROPOLITAN STATISTICAL AREA	POPULATION Estimate 7/1/04	POPULATION Census 4/1/00	POPULATION % Change 4/1/90-4/1/00	PER CAPITA INCOME 2003	HOUSEHOLDS Estimate 7/1/04	DISPOSABLE INCOME 2003 ($1,000)	MARKET ABILITY INDEX 2003	TOTAL RETAIL SALES 2003 Sales ($1,000)	TOTAL RETAIL SALES Ranally Sales Units	GENERAL MERCHANDISE 2003 Sales ($1,000)	GENERAL MERCHANDISE Ranally Sales Units	APPAREL STORE SALES 2003 Sales ($1,000)	APPAREL STORE SALES Ranally Sales Units	FOOD STORE SALES 2003 ($1,000)	HEALTH & DRUG STORE 2003 ($1,000)
1	Los Angeles-Long Beach, CA (PMSA)	9,980,271	9,519,338	7.4	17,007	3,253,579	169,739,220	2.9601	92,102,910	27,093	10,418,455	22,116	7,736,176	43,356	15,567,979	5,237,037
2	New York, NY (PMSA)	9,449,241	9,314,235	9.0	19,496	3,516,152	184,222,140	2.8951	74,637,532	21,956	7,093,249	15,057	12,074,493	67,668	12,194,376	8,200,113
3	Chicago, IL (PMSA)	8,558,311	8,272,768	11.6	21,500	3,081,858	183,999,930	3.0531	99,647,029	29,312	11,133,626	23,633	5,660,774	31,725	13,745,635	8,327,600
4	Washington, DC-MD-VA-WV (PMSA)	5,326,575	4,923,153	16.6	27,313	2,049,946	145,486,130	2.1408	58,917,498	17,330	7,392,681	15,693	3,879,721	21,743	9,890,576	3,047,385
5	Philadelphia, PA-NJ (PMSA)	5,185,302	5,100,931	3.6	22,050	2,000,270	114,335,950	1.9085	64,223,991	18,892	5,638,401	11,970	3,946,842	22,119	10,757,555	4,748,610
6	Houston, TX (PMSA)	4,595,351	4,177,646	25.8	19,614	1,679,706	90,131,170	1.5774	54,978,827	16,172	8,289,468	17,597	3,155,929	17,686	8,231,298	2,575,461
7	Atlanta, GA	4,570,501	4,112,198	38.9	22,906	1,754,099	104,691,600	1.7622	61,850,085	18,194	8,043,762	17,075	3,264,121	18,295	8,869,200	2,408,217
8	Detroit, MI (PMSA)	4,466,850	4,441,551	4.1	22,004	1,767,309	98,289,920	1.6904	60,800,681	17,886	9,610,308	20,401	2,792,305	15,648	7,291,963	4,286,316
9	Dallas, TX (PMSA)	3,900,657	3,519,176	31.5	22,107	1,465,557	86,231,560	1.4545	50,211,022	14,770	7,211,634	15,310	2,700,602	15,136	6,895,737	2,030,127
10	Riverside-San Bernardino, CA (PMSA)	3,763,495	3,254,821	25.7	16,568	1,190,886	62,352,000	1.0820	32,473,181	9,552	4,207,194	8,931	1,932,948	10,833	5,780,775	1,423,456
11	Phoenix-Mesa, AZ	3,698,598	3,251,876	45.3	19,860	1,390,757	73,453,060	1.2676	43,123,015	12,685	5,754,543	12,215	1,636,357	9,171	5,887,002	2,114,223
12	Boston, MA-NH (PMSA)	3,452,130	3,406,829	5.5	25,889	1,357,201	89,371,074	1.4146	46,096,733	13,561	4,115,948	8,732	3,944,707	22,103	7,775,391	3,449,624
13	Minneapolis-St. Paul, MN-WI	3,117,850	2,968,806	16.9	23,599	1,239,180	73,576,940	1.2830	49,271,803	14,494	6,752,377	14,336	1,762,104	9,874	6,271,900	2,151,420
14	Orange County, CA (PMSA)	2,991,519	2,846,289	18.1	23,134	989,208	69,206,970	1.1471	39,088,814	11,498	4,547,424	9,653	3,141,259	17,605	6,027,801	2,162,963
15	San Diego, CA	2,966,135	2,813,833	12.6	20,344	1,059,703	60,342,670	1.0169	33,222,905	9,773	3,825,198	8,120	2,426,068	13,596	5,326,312	1,680,462
16	Nassau-Suffolk, NY (PMSA)	2,823,190	2,753,913	5.5	26,883	944,853	75,895,570	1.2057	40,475,642	11,906	3,927,759	8,337	3,362,636	18,845	5,969,684	2,859,514
17	St. Louis, MO-IL	2,651,207	2,603,607	4.5	20,979	1,071,356	55,619,040	.9341	30,901,201	9,090	4,750,381	10,083	1,098,666	6,157	4,567,369	2,050,522
18	Baltimore, MD (PMSA)	2,635,941	2,552,994	7.2	22,837	1,025,342	60,196,130	.9507	28,414,112	8,358	3,697,296	7,848	1,633,456	9,155	5,055,123	1,789,340
19	Tampa-St. Petersburg-Clearwater, FL	2,574,498	2,395,997	15.9	21,239	1,157,320	54,679,370	.9513	34,351,447	10,104	4,164,175	8,840	1,446,023	8,104	4,811,738	2,259,763
20	Seattle-Bellevue-Everett, WA (PMSA)	2,496,295	2,414,616	18.8	24,252	1,021,038	60,539,450	1.0042	35,212,324	10,358	4,844,127	10,283	2,242,194	12,566	4,991,139	1,410,945
21	Oakland, CA (PMSA)	2,481,548	2,392,557	14.9	25,854	910,856	64,158,440	.9689	27,783,114	8,172	2,998,426	6,365	1,513,360	8,481	5,542,436	1,375,606
22	Miami, FL (PMSA)	2,368,141	2,253,362	16.3	16,237	848,751	38,452,660	.7039	23,817,798	7,006	2,737,682	5,812	2,321,232	13,009	3,289,971	2,034,323
23	Pittsburgh, PA	2,332,585	2,358,695	-1.5	18,741	982,599	43,715,910	.7760	27,098,464	7,971	3,023,500	6,419	1,282,646	7,188	4,387,682	2,025,969
24	Cleveland-Lorain-Elyria, OH (PMSA)	2,239,967	2,250,871	2.2	20,112	917,281	45,050,120	.7827	27,265,297	8,020	2,958,359	6,281	1,321,633	7,407	3,989,913	2,796,478
25	Denver, CO (PMSA)[1]	2,239,478	2,109,282	30.0	23,174	884,070	51,896,650	.8662	30,024,921	8,832	4,308,975	9,147	1,345,192	7,539	4,158,108	1,069,491
26	Newark, NJ (PMSA)	2,080,714	2,032,989	6.1	25,266	748,659	52,571,660	.8198	25,323,919	7,450	1,660,994	3,525	1,738,863	9,746	4,824,662	1,780,829
27	Portland-Vancouver, OR-WA (PMSA)	2,064,660	1,918,009	26.6	20,989	805,998	43,334,910	.7577	27,462,972	8,079	4,981,840	10,575	1,438,297	8,061	3,670,572	842,358
28	Fort Worth-Arlington, TX (PMSA)	1,883,211	1,702,625	25.1	20,175	698,010	37,994,410	.6688	24,036,467	7,070	2,687,262	5,705	1,053,332	5,903	3,254,314	956,554
29	Kansas City, MO-KS	1,863,851	1,776,062	12.2	21,564	748,899	40,192,810	.6912	24,548,449	7,221	3,611,899	7,667	950,889	5,331	2,975,922	1,254,630
30	Orlando, FL	1,851,873	1,644,561	34.3	20,739	737,616	38,405,230	.6825	25,416,119	7,476	3,495,555	7,420	1,661,395	9,310	3,372,844	1,393,435
31	Las Vegas, NV-AZ	1,850,678	1,563,282	83.3	19,153	707,390	35,446,380	.6178	21,009,850	6,180	2,863,514	6,079	1,271,752	7,127	3,307,295	894,880
32	Sacramento, CA (PMSA)	1,842,845	1,628,197	21.5	21,137	683,523	38,952,280	.6367	19,765,983	5,814	2,439,432	5,179	1,126,460	6,313	3,478,390	818,945
33	Fort Lauderdale, FL (PMSA)	1,764,315	1,623,018	29.3	21,989	747,072	38,796,200	.6810	25,541,193	7,513	2,758,291	5,855	1,486,450	8,330	3,491,409	1,626,468
34	San Antonio, TX	1,722,612	1,592,383	20.2	17,341	629,687	29,872,110	.5505	19,817,186	5,829	2,885,576	6,126	1,106,928	6,204	3,039,566	787,336
35	Indianapolis, IN	1,695,006	1,607,486	16.4	21,083	687,260	35,735,210	.6333	23,681,000	6,965	4,019,032	8,532	901,457	5,052	2,289,703	1,536,109
36	San Francisco, CA (PMSA)	1,682,970	1,731,183	8.0	30,593	688,594	51,487,220	.8009	27,316,734	8,036	3,136,463	6,658	3,295,298	18,468	4,882,998	1,660,518
37	Cincinnati, OH-KY-IN (PMSA)	1,680,493	1,646,395	7.9	20,967	684,327	35,234,210	.6050	21,061,796	6,196	3,115,573	6,613	1,025,827	5,749	2,912,642	1,160,037
38	San Jose, CA (PMSA)	1,675,734	1,682,585	12.4	29,915	586,292	50,130,310	.7861	27,026,688	7,950	3,149,778	6,686	2,287,248	12,818	4,358,160	1,341,238
39	Norfolk-Virginia Beach-Newport News, VA-NC	1,649,035	1,569,541	8.8	18,502	628,301	30,510,690	.5288	17,309,532	5,094	2,782,538	5,907	968,063	5,423	2,404,178	788,060
40	Charlotte-Gastonia-Rock Hill, NC-SC	1,648,241	1,499,293	29.0	21,888	671,061	36,076,240	.6125	21,335,074	6,276	2,848,716	6,047	980,987	5,497	2,779,355	1,108,325
41	Columbus, OH	1,614,311	1,540,157	14.5	21,957	681,950	35,445,620	.6237	23,486,517	6,909	3,057,216	6,490	1,019,604	5,714	2,767,089	914,804
42	Milwaukee-Waukesha, WI (PMSA)	1,518,392	1,500,741	4.8	21,091	626,347	32,024,760	.5377	17,828,356	5,244	2,468,920	5,241	607,112	3,403	2,663,965	1,200,135
43	Austin-San Marcos, TX	1,415,292	1,249,763	47.7	22,947	561,961	32,477,300	.6303	28,689,214	8,440	2,281,526	4,844	1,085,483	6,083	3,148,162	1,386,529
44	Bergen-Passaic, NJ (PMSA)	1,402,356	1,373,167	7.4	26,344	503,348	36,944,300	.5904	19,883,736	5,849	1,837,976	3,901	1,618,652	9,071	3,466,180	1,266,914
45	Salt Lake City-Ogden, UT	1,401,430	1,333,914	24.4	17,906	467,808	25,094,290	.4842	19,473,859	5,728	3,094,313	6,569	775,845	4,348	2,750,678	392,394
46	New Orleans, LA	1,339,327	1,337,726	4.1	17,870	542,216	23,933,970	.4286	14,779,516	4,348	2,493,129	5,294	876,417	4,912	2,170,408	1,105,888
47	Raleigh-Durham-Chapel Hill, NC	1,328,146	1,187,941	38.9	23,223	546,749	30,842,920	.5192	18,376,719	5,406	2,283,168	4,847	930,779	5,215	2,594,121	864,240
48	Greensboro--Winston-Salem--High Point, NC	1,308,675	1,251,509	19.2	19,765	539,415	25,866,150	.4621	16,919,287	4,976	2,106,360	4,473	801,850	4,494	2,148,538	1,006,356
49	Nashville, TN	1,305,357	1,231,311	25.0	21,839	533,849	28,507,770	.5070	19,443,915	5,718	3,233,566	6,865	988,463	5,539	2,369,919	1,046,125
50	West Palm Beach-Boca Raton, FL	1,243,157	1,131,184	31.0	25,735	577,999	31,992,820	.5094	16,783,738	4,937	2,107,777	4,474	1,528,403	8,566	2,438,488	1,097,284
51	Middlesex-Somerset-Hunterdon, NJ (PMSA)	1,236,285	1,169,641	14.7	29,098	441,732	35,973,700	.5487	17,388,807	5,115	1,543,590	3,276	1,092,322	6,122	2,887,475	912,783
52	Providence-Fall River-Warwick, RI-MA	1,229,484	1,188,613	4.8	19,449	484,930	23,912,381	.4038	12,839,618	3,778	1,445,281	3,068	845,850	4,738	2,359,453	1,279,986
53	Hartford, CT	1,223,067	1,183,110	2.2	26,005	479,099	31,805,651	.4816	13,959,486	4,109	1,296,053	2,751	944,013	5,290	2,385,089	1,107,334
54	Jacksonville, FL	1,204,735	1,100,491	21.4	21,668	489,865	26,104,270	.4408	15,075,439	4,434	1,952,141	4,144	713,757	4,000	2,134,586	757,997
55	Monmouth-Ocean, NJ (PMSA)	1,194,230	1,126,217	14.2	26,646	461,891	31,821,320	.4890	15,014,622	4,417	1,469,156	3,119	899,817	5,042	3,027,352	925,760
56	Memphis, TN-AR-MS	1,178,084	1,135,614	12.7	18,588	454,941	21,897,800	.3928	13,968,165	4,109	2,381,739	5,056	819,485	4,593	1,453,839	894,457
57	Buffalo-Niagara Falls, NY	1,156,288	1,170,111	-1.6	19,600	470,582	22,662,690	.3756	11,435,256	3,364	1,227,487	2,605	661,291	3,706	2,043,522	900,419
58	Grand Rapids-Muskegon-Holland, MI	1,133,518	1,088,514	16.1	19,507	426,766	22,111,920	.3972	14,593,889	4,293	3,031,710	6,435	501,970	2,813	1,366,619	668,285
59	Oklahoma City, OK	1,131,827	1,083,346	13.0	18,082	459,286	20,465,960	.3693	13,076,515	3,846	2,285,527	4,851	448,620	2,515	1,463,530	713,738
60	Rochester, NY	1,102,049	1,098,201	3.4	21,495	437,550	23,688,360	.3826	11,651,582	3,428	1,355,331	2,877	534,997	2,999	2,284,893	586,878
61	Louisville, KY-IN	1,049,861	1,025,598	8.1	20,632	447,993	21,660,610	.3669	12,238,548	3,600	2,074,920	4,404	502,346	2,815	1,388,270	772,146
62	Richmond-Petersburg, VA	1,044,758	996,512	15.1	21,627	428,842	22,595,390	.3794	12,797,495	3,766	2,174,738	4,617	633,173	3,549	1,828,511	759,973
63	Greenville-Spartanburg-Anderson, SC	1,004,256	962,441	15.9	18,279	399,967	18,357,290	.3384	12,611,430	3,709	1,764,790	3,746	624,010	3,497	1,691,626	731,466
64	Fresno, CA	1,003,162	922,516	22.1	13,501	309,778	13,543,840	.2538	7,751,818	2,280	1,028,372	2,183	312,576	1,752	1,425,308	478,421
65	Birmingham, AL	946,208	921,106	9.6	19,491	380,583	18,442,620	.3273	11,707,936	3,444	1,820,107	3,864	636,585	3,567	1,594,497	553,431
66	Dayton-Springfield, OH	945,928	950,558	-0.1	20,424	399,525	19,319,570	.3313	11,312,803	3,327	1,975,612	4,194	458,726	2,570	1,526,222	606,476
67	Honolulu, HI	911,719	876,156	4.8	19,820	301,773	18,070,470	.3029	9,586,291	2,820	1,932,186	4,102	1,213,597	6,801	1,460,075	815,873
68	Tucson, AZ	907,511	843,746	26.5	17,888	365,815	16,233,410	.2752	8,272,791	2,434	1,284,384	2,726	326,802	1,831	1,268,524	505,873
69	Albany-Schenectady-Troy, NY	894,569	875,583	1.6	21,784	365,332	19,487,310	.3157	9,776,471	2,876	1,112,250	2,361	535,299	3,001	1,372,276	647,465
70	Tulsa, OK	829,509	803,235	13.3	19,040	341,229	15,793,530	.2811	9,974,562	2,935	1,954,354	4,148	313,548	1,757	1,079,190	542,665
71	Ventura, CA (PMSA)	802,627	753,197	12.6	22,864	258,964	18,351,220	.2961	9,381,128	2,760	941,078	1,998	513,106	2,876	1,505,559	540,323
72	Albuquerque, NM	759,193	712,738	21.0	18,702	302,189	14,198,270	.2551	9,136,804	2,688	1,679,936	3,566	321,107	1,799	844,165	503,142
73	Tacoma, WA (PMSA)	753,288	700,820	19.6	19,217	281,633	14,476,220	.2441	7,660,414	2,253	1,311,305	2,784	277,368	1,554	1,116,419	309,143
74	Omaha, NE-IA	750,455	716,998	12.1	19,980	297,793	14,994,260	.2754	10,729,850	3,157	1,351,732	2,870	393,241	2,203	1,385,436	600,049
75	Syracuse, NY	737,104	732,117	-1.4	19,587	292,002	14,437,390	.2404	7,411,093	2,180	799,327	1,698	360,769	2,022	1,428,189	527,700
76	Bakersfield, CA	729,553	661,645	21.7	13,779	226,881	10,052,420	.1858	5,580,342	1,642	732,780	1,556	216,564	1,214	895,681	350,750
77	Knoxville, TN	720,109	687,249	17.3	18,922	304,926	13,626,120	.2712	11,827,267	3,480	1,854,356	3,936	667,996	3,743	1,326,691	574,926
78	El Paso, TX	713,340	679,622	14.9	12,037	226,278	8,586,800	.1799	6,462,611	1,901	1,356,263	2,879	425,599	2,385	831,659	312,642
79	Akron, OH (PMSA)	703,530	694,960	5.7	20,270	288,070	14,260,790	.2526	9,231,659	2,716	949,148	2,015	365,016	2,046	1,289,167	791,147
80	Allentown-Bethlehem-Easton, PA	665,446	637,958	7.2	19,938	263,264	13,267,640	.2312	8,062,162	2,372	851,652	1,808	323,584	1,814	1,435,608	561,692
81	McAllen-Edinburg-Mission, TX	656,072	569,463	48.5	8,644	182,386	5,671,110	.1419	5,457,211	1,605	1,064,900	2,261	420,429	2,356	833,469	231,799
82	Stockton-Lodi, CA	654,288	563,598	17.3	16,392	210,061	10,725,080	.1822	5,087,457	1,497	677,193	1,438	219,393	1,230	911,463	340,141
83	Sarasota-Bradenton, FL	647,224	589,959	20.5	22,658	289,616	14,664,530	.2443	8,331,292	2,450	976,820	2,074	496,718	2,784	1,292,386	548,115
84	Harrisburg-Lebanon-Carlisle, PA	643,547	629,401	7.0	20,421	261,966	13,141,920	.2363	8,927,130	2,626	910,112	1,932	306,222	1,716	1,284,021	475,386
85	Gary, IN (PMSA)	642,735	631,362	4.4	18,997	245,511	12,210,110	.2125	7,158,945	2,106	1,080,330	2,293	240,561	1,348	977,665	543,114
86	Baton Rouge, LA	626,070	602,894	14.1	18,636	245,812	11,667,190	.2106	7,606,623	2,237	1,420,953	3,017	341,266	1,913	952,775	359,783
87	Ann Arbor, MI (PMSA)	622,300	578,736	18.1	23,364	237,874	14,539,490	.2437	8,574,571	2,522	1,470,152	3,121	287,239	1,609	935,302	401,861
88	Toledo, OH	620,144	618,203	0.7	18,942	254,495	11,746,760	.2139	7,949,520	2,338	1,292,148	2,744	318,923	1,787	1,104,698	447,550
89	Scranton--Wilkes-Barre--Hazleton, PA	614,462	624,776	-2.1	16,989	257,645	10,439,140	.1952	7,157,244	2,106	938,315	1,992	326,966	1,833	1,285,643	497,082
90	Wilmington-Newark, DE-MD (PMSA)	614,320	586,216	14.2	22,618	236,718	13,894,600	.2381	8,622,549	2,537	1,062,778	2,256	391,369	2,193	1,405,545	496,413
91	Jersey City, NJ (PMSA)	606,768	608,975	10.1	19,564	230,298	11,870,940	.1835	4,478,993	1,318	376,234	799	508,737	2,851	872,848	396,886
92	Little Rock-North Little Rock, AR	606,101	583,845	13.8	19,424	251,553	11,772,820	.2206	8,786,253	2,584	1,742,933	3,699	318,576	1,785	743,404	277,719
93	Springfield, MA	603,755	591,932	0.7	19,208	233,886	11,596,686	.1955	6,129,987	1,803	542,859	1,151	308,028	1,726	1,271,520	480,477
94	Youngstown-Warren, OH	581,948	594,746	-1.0	17,366	237,536	10,106,220	.1826	6,301,912	1,853	807,519	1,714	234,872	1,317	884,937	436,683
95	Charleston-North Charleston, SC	578,716	549,033	8.3	18,762	232,024	10,857,930	.1907	6,506,338	1,913	1,101,200	2,338	413,126	2,315	1,082,356	277,047
96	Columbia, SC	565,436	536,691	18.4	19,810	227,194	11,201,340	.2011	7,451,868	2,192	1,368,576	2,906	376,713	2,112	969,619	364,404
97	Colorado Springs, CO	560,804	516,929	30.2	19,819	208,877	11,114,350	.1975	7,166,545	2,108	1,150,622	2,443	190,170	1,066	768,575	274,941
98	New Haven-Meriden, CT (PMSA)	558,806	542,149	2.3	25,384	217,158	14,184,918	.2228	7,046,455	2,074	569,423	1,208	440,585	2,468	1,165,560	520,528
99	Mobile, AL	554,939	540,258	13.3	16,905	215,349	9,381,040	.1693	5,716,074	1,681	1,129,778	2,398	334,609	1,876	769,574	320,389
100	Vallejo-Fairfield-Napa, CA (PMSA)	551,336	518,821	15.0	21,927	189,566	12,089,340	.1895	5,375,799	1,581	750,931	1,594	318,173	1,783	1,122,819	238,833
101	Daytona Beach, FL	542,645	493,175	23.5	20,372	245,026	11,054,840	.1836	5,769,501	1,698	770,128	1,635	219,433	1,230	968,057	386,603
102	Worcester, MA-CT (PMSA)	536,389	511,389	6.9	21,870	206,638	11,730,876	.1938	6,347,171	1,870	674,455	1,431	289,385	1,620	1,085,081	453,513
103	Wichita, KS[2]	527,608	512,351	12.8	18,757	205,477	9,896,290	.1732	5,857,946	1,723	1,120,026	2,377	233,233	1,307	841,766	268,947
104	Lakeland-Winter Haven, FL	518,809	483,924	19.4	19,073	217,966	9,895,440	.1713	5,716,090	1,681	873,686	1,855	196,846	1,103	977,731	287,481
105	Fort Wayne, IN	515,722	502,141	10.1	18,986	202,993	9,791,550	.1754	6,307,857	1,856	1,127,630	2,394	217,304	1,218	697,635	338,146
106	Melbourne-Titusville-Palm Bay, FL	515,004	476,230	19.4	22,229	228,764	11,447,810	.1835	5,603,865	1,648	916,795	1,946	235,423	1,319	919,936	384,085
107	Fort Myers-Cape Coral, FL	508,350	440,888	31.6	21,735	219,630	11,049,150	.1922	7,029,399	2,068	988,622	2,099	443,513	2,486	986,313	442,891
108	Modesto, CA	506,378	446,997	20.6	15,862	162,035	8,032,070	.1459	4,753,556	1,398	669,983	1,422	178,855	1,002	913,403	315,443
109	Lexington, KY	502,488	479,198	18.0	20,112	213,434	10,106,000	.1795	6,566,002	1,931	1,009,857	2,143	352,317	1,975	716,761	379,822
110	Augusta-Aiken, GA-SC	492,040	477,441	15.0	17,539	188,840	8,629,940	.1530	5,079,956	1,494	898,436	1,907	233,736	1,310	721,888	237,488
111	Boise City, ID	490,178	432,345	46.1	18,184	180,322	8,913,170	.1687	6,609,386	1,944	1,139,141	2,418	207,788	1,165	867,259	207,440
112	Johnson City-Kingsport-Bristol, TN-VA	487,711	480,091	10.1	16,614	211,669	8,102,670	.1520	5,525,720	1,625	1,048,519	2,225	228,312	1,281	700,585	314,504
113	Lancaster, PA	486,469	470,658	11.3	19,463	180,573	9,468,350	.1739	6,676,478	1,964	579,937	1,231	367,776	2,061	1,109,981	332,301
114	Des Moines, IA	483,114	456,022	16.1	20,764	193,718	10,031,420	.1743	6,195,047	1,822	853,756	1,813	228,718	1,281	819,287	303,591
115	Chattanooga, TN-GA	476,717	465,161	9.6	18,494	195,528	8,816,560	.1579	5,576,920	1,640	921,343	1,955	298,417	1,673	763,793	338,324
116	Santa Rosa, CA (PMSA)	468,851	458,614	18.1	23,674	174,821	11,099,560	.1798	5,877,135	1,729	619,805	1,316	256,127	1,435	1,187,270	345,374
117	Bridgeport, CT (PMSA)	466,775	459,479	3.6	22,365	175,027	10,439,547	.1906	7,764,125	2,286	564,391	1,198	445,735	2,497	990,406	413,229
118	Kalamazoo-Battle Creek, MI	461,120	452,851	5.4	18,885	186,779	8,708,460	.1540	5,363,685	1,578	1,450,904	3,080	167,064	936	515,255	283,508
119	Lansing-East Lansing, MI	458,301	447,728	3.5	20,004	182,777	9,167,820	.1606	5,685,892	1,672	1,278,910	2,715	207,150	1,161	673,930	297,591
120	Jackson, MS	457,428	440,801	11.5	17,908	172,842	8,191,450	.1559	6,105,362	1,796	1,218,256	2,586	265,516	1,488	608,387	330,138
121	Madison, WI	456,369	426,526	16.2	22,239	191,747	10,149,360	.1798	6,914,106	2,034	889,619	1,888	241,263	1,352	833,571	318,717
122	Flint, MI (PMSA)	444,011	436,141	1.3	19,539	181,093	8,675,620	.1515	5,238,928	1,541	1,038,212	2,204	183,929	1,031	608,615	347,323
123	Spokane, WA	435,145	417,939	15.7	17,174	170,747	7,473,250	.1385	5,018,057	1,476	886,324	1,881	231,274	1,296	770,118	205,222
124	Pensacola, FL	434,387	412,153	19.7	19,068	176,993	8,282,890	.1411	4,519,358	1,330	756,204	1,605	179,965	1,008	666,395	295,741
125	Newburgh, NY-PA (PMSA)	423,860	387,669	15.5	21,069	145,809	8,930,310	.1428	4,158,453	1,223	684,571	1,453	376,001	2,107	612,899	246,159
126	Salinas, CA	418,251	401,762	13.0	17,064	123,111	7,137,110	.1276	4,236,459	1,246	473,268	1,005	285,175	1,598	741,345	267,217
127	Lawrence, MA-NH (PMSA)	413,761	396,230	12.2	22,667	150,856	9,378,641	.1509	4,733,394	1,393	800,913	1,699	245,364	1,374	875,457	288,251
128	Canton-Massillon, OH	407,161	406,934	3.3	18,397	162,941	7,490,370	.1367	5,012,905	1,474	691,501	1,468	239,306	1,341	727,029	449,795
129	Provo-Orem, UT	407,123	368,536	39.8	14,363	114,713	5,847,380	.1153	4,189,283	1,232	806,151	1,711	141,362	792	704,861	73,449
130	Santa Barbara-Santa Maria-Lompoc, CA	404,260	399,347	8.0	19,379	138,188	7,834,290	.1368	4,700,898	1,383	454,866	966	331,262	1,856	859,109	335,658
131	Saginaw-Bay City-Midland, MI	403,326	403,070	0.9	18,338	161,152	7,396,110	.1426	5,788,836	1,703	1,152,722	2,448	363,828	2,039	543,711	300,521
132	York, PA	398,969	381,751	12.4	20,544	157,278	8,196,390	.1339	4,069,282	1,197	563,866	1,197	146,775	823	757,223	207,738
133	Visalia-Tulare-Porterville, CA	398,103	368,021	18.0	12,544	117,213	4,993,740	.0943	2,716,977	799	427,942	908	106,651	598	549,480	145,301
134	Lafayette, LA	394,628	385,647	11.8	15,125	152,433	5,968,610	.1211	4,827,890	1,421	964,233	2,046	198,484	1,113	578,079	317,888
135	Shreveport-Bossier City, LA	394,221	392,302	4.2	16,302	156,808	6,426,760	.1234	4,634,290	1,363	847,236	1,799	192,491	1,079	586,687	199,816
136	Reading, PA	388,909	373,638	11.0	19,644	147,702	7,639,890	.1301	4,256,088	1,252	525,747	1,116	342,408	1,919	683,206	249,524
137	Rockford, IL	387,465	371,236	12.6	20,145	150,219	7,805,440	.1321	4,338,742	1,277	639,669	1,358	147,039	825	704,827	249,267
138	Corpus Christi, TX	384,106	380,783	8.8	15,859	139,636	6,091,530	.1152	4,131,445	1,215	668,101	1,418	193,675	1,085	715,029	158,981
139	Beaumont-Port Arthur, TX	381,930	385,090	6.6	16,834	147,921	6,429,600	.1227	4,650,610	1,368	746,358	1,584	194,534	1,090	630,665	250,353
140	Reno, NV	380,688	339,486	33.3	20,389	147,051	7,761,940	.1365	4,927,460	1,449	767,107	1,628	165,864	930	743,396	194,817
141	Appleton-Oshkosh-Neenah, WI	372,541	358,365	13.7	20,783	150,343	7,742,360	.1368	5,045,676	1,484	701,353	1,488	196,624	1,102	592,168	204,798
142	Brownsville-Harlingen-San Benito, TX	371,857	335,227	28.9	9,563	109,025	3,556,070	.0806	2,774,996	816	641,360	1,361	195,601	1,096	531,733	106,356
143	Biloxi-Gulfport-Pascagoula, MS	369,960	363,988	16.5	17,932	147,932	6,634,010	.1182	4,034,839	1,187	991,452	2,105	136,388	764	455,361	167,207
144	Atlantic-Cape May, NJ (PMSA)	368,557	354,878	11.1	21,221	142,561	7,821,170	.1325	4,515,980	1,329	469,557	997	317,234	1,778	1,056,306	285,181
145	Salem, OR (PMSA)	367,908	347,214	24.9	16,849	130,863	6,199,000	.1128	3,871,527	1,139	789,346	1,676	136,871	767	556,517	124,085
146	Trenton, NJ (PMSA)	365,448	350,761	7.7	25,680	133,605	9,384,820	.1447	4,366,020	1,284	398,348	846	330,116	1,850	753,962	416,720
147	Stamford-Norwalk, CT (PMSA)	363,586	353,556	7.2	40,815	138,441	14,839,624	.2223	7,852,816	2,310	263,468	559	557,332	3,123	923,042	331,430
148	Huntsville, AL	362,704	342,376	16.8	21,319	148,388	7,732,470	.1305	4,408,012	1,296	884,283	1,877	227,112	1,272	579,797	171,413
149	Fort Pierce-Port St. Lucie, FL	357,906	319,426	27.2	21,220	155,543	7,594,610	.1252	3,987,293	1,173	507,921	1,078	135,595	759	652,399	314,490
150	Davenport-Moline-Rock Island, IA-IL	357,656	359,062	2.3	18,891	144,362	6,756,410	.1252	4,808,297	1,414	667,384	1,417	189,352	1,061	598,628	308,995

Estimates for Total Retail Sales, General Merchandise, Apparel Store Sales, Food Store Sales, and Health and Drug Store Sales are based on data from the U.S. Census Bureau's 1997 Economic Census and utilize the North American Industry Classification System (NAICS).

[1] Census population includes a portion of Broomfield county.

[2] Data exclude Harvey County, Kansas (7/1/04 estimated population 33,707) which fails to meet published standards for MSA inclusion, but has been included with the Wichita MSA as the result of Congressional action.

Source: Devonshire Associates Ltd. and Scan/US, Inc. 2004.

Core Based Statistical Areas (CBSAs): Population / Income / Sales#†

This table provides population and marketing information for each Metropolitan CBSA and for all Micropolitan CBSAs as a group. Included are all of the data items given for Basic Trading Areas in the table starting on page 24. Data are from Devonshire Associates Ltd. and Scan/US, Inc. 2004. Also included are CBSA FIPS codes. A map showing the CBSAs, with a detailed explanation of how they are determined, appears on pages 38-39. For information on the Ranally Metro Areas (RMAs), whose boundaries differ from those of the CBSAs, see the table on pages 126-127.

CODE	CORE BASED STATISTICAL AREA	POPULATION Estimate 7/1/04	POPULATION Census 4/1/00	% Change 4/1/90-4/1/00	PER CAPITA INCOME 2003	HOUSE-HOLDS Estimate 7/1/04	DISPOSABLE INCOME 2003 ($1,000)	MARKET ABILITY INDEX 2003	TOTAL RETAIL SALES 2003 Sales ($1,000)	TOTAL RETAIL SALES Ranally Sales Units	GENERAL MERCHANDISE 2003 Sales ($1,000)	GENERAL MERCHANDISE Ranally Sales Units	APPAREL STORE SALES 2003 Sales ($1,000)	APPAREL STORE SALES Ranally Sales Units	FOOD STORE SALES 2003 ($1,000)	HEALTH & DRUG STORE 2003 ($1,000)
10180	Abilene, TX	157,948	160,245	8.3	15,552	59,940	2,456,420	.0492	1,951,980	574	381,098	809	58,645	329	210,145	71,916
10420	Akron, OH	703,530	694,960	5.7	20,270	288,070	14,260,790	.2526	9,231,659	2,716	949,148	2,015	365,016	2,046	1,289,167	791,147
10500	Albany, GA	162,223	157,833	7.7	14,936	60,692	2,422,990	.0477	1,773,466	522	311,984	662	75,573	423	290,389	69,900
10580	Albany-Schenectady-Troy, NY	845,300	825,875	2.0	22,081	345,122	18,665,030	.3014	9,338,794	2,747	1,066,101	2,263	520,678	2,919	1,296,966	616,121
10740	Albuquerque, NM	775,936	729,649	21.7	18,586	308,223	14,421,760	.2591	9,239,198	2,718	1,680,359	3,567	321,444	1,801	858,890	506,985
10780	Alexandria, LA	146,661	145,035	-2.7	14,299	56,317	2,097,130	.0425	1,632,174	480	376,715	800	65,982	370	184,423	101,230
10900	Allentown-Bethlehem-Easton, PA-NJ	776,747	740,395	7.8	20,869	305,639	16,210,200	.2761	9,403,351	2,767	979,519	2,079	367,959	2,063	1,723,108	631,887
11020	Altoona, PA	126,555	129,144	-1.1	16,075	52,018	2,034,420	.0417	1,752,849	516	316,759	672	58,130	326	267,824	121,301
11100	Amarillo, TX	235,287	226,522	15.5	16,670	88,973	3,922,290	.0769	3,045,743	896	419,318	890	124,351	697	252,918	129,662
11180	Ames, IA	83,964	79,981	7.7	16,929	30,985	1,421,410	.0258	880,205	259	164,956	350	36,753	206	145,918	35,233
11260	Anchorage, AK	345,540	319,605	20.1	21,960	125,280	7,587,970	.1340	5,082,299	1,495	1,142,505	2,426	225,729	1,265	643,803	61,438
11300	Anderson, IN	130,409	133,358	2.1	17,867	52,787	2,330,070	.0408	1,337,055	393	226,170	480	32,209	181	168,264	98,737
11340	Anderson, SC	173,238	165,740	14.1	17,671	69,852	3,061,330	.0557	1,976,565	581	309,476	657	87,099	488	315,932	122,398
11460	Ann Arbor, MI	343,273	322,895	14.1	22,856	135,907	7,845,780	.1371	5,202,501	1,530	846,525	1,797	217,383	1,218	569,099	240,364
11500	Anniston-Oxford, AL	112,234	112,249	-3.3	16,515	47,412	1,853,520	.0344	1,213,266	357	270,566	574	36,994	207	176,829	51,711
11540	Appleton, WI	213,551	201,602	15.3	21,044	83,554	4,493,880	.0802	3,040,001	894	453,810	963	126,309	708	374,728	85,008
11700	Asheville, NC	385,591	369,171	19.9	18,343	164,470	7,072,740	.1350	5,386,669	1,584	728,627	1,546	246,536	1,381	661,500	302,324
12020	Athens-Clarke County, GA	174,053	166,079	22.1	16,238	70,544	2,826,220	.0530	1,887,176	554	302,118	641	82,934	465	256,162	82,238
12060	Atlanta-Sandy Springs-Marietta, GA	4,719,358	4,247,981	38.4	22,702	1,809,292	107,137,870	1.8008	62,669,946	18,435	8,088,545	17,171	3,346,251	18,754	9,016,906	2,471,415
12100	Atlantic City, NJ	266,864	252,552	12.6	20,882	100,111	5,572,680	.0947	3,215,273	946	412,580	876	217,853	1,221	682,910	190,310
12220	Auburn-Opelika, AL	120,927	115,092	32.1	15,916	50,646	1,924,700	.0344	1,074,311	316	212,560	451	52,646	295	208,266	33,042
12260	Augusta-Richmond County, GA-SC	515,207	499,684	14.7	17,290	197,259	8,907,760	.1584	5,243,476	1,542	906,628	1,924	235,924	1,322	754,220	247,507
12420	Austin-Round Rock, TX	1,415,292	1,249,763	47.7	22,947	561,961	32,477,300	.6303	28,689,214	8,440	2,281,526	4,844	1,085,483	6,083	3,148,162	1,386,529
12540	Bakersfield, CA	729,553	661,645	21.7	13,779	226,881	10,052,420	.1858	5,580,342	1,642	732,780	1,556	216,564	1,214	895,681	350,750
12580	Baltimore-Towson, MD	2,635,941	2,552,994	7.2	22,837	1,025,342	60,196,130	.9507	28,414,112	8,358	3,697,296	7,848	1,633,456	9,155	5,055,123	1,789,340
12620	Bangor, ME	147,681	144,919	-1.1	16,681	61,206	2,463,420	.0509	2,209,724	650	278,391	591	50,449	283	427,296	83,225
12700	Barnstable Town, MA	231,645	222,230	19.1	23,742	100,221	5,499,830	.0935	3,415,754	1,005	174,648	371	229,079	1,284	801,769	241,440
12940	Baton Rouge, LA	727,723	705,973	13.2	17,814	279,668	12,963,740	.2350	8,307,961	2,442	1,491,216	3,166	347,124	1,946	1,093,197	391,446
12980	Battle Creek, MI	139,106	137,985	1.5	18,718	57,969	2,603,740	.0454	1,519,459	447	407,580	865	38,743	217	160,456	95,039
13020	Bay City, MI	109,229	110,157	-1.4	18,379	45,170	2,007,490	.0384	1,531,992	451	331,992	705	47,788	268	152,433	75,791
13140	Beaumont-Port Arthur, TX	381,930	385,090	6.6	16,834	147,921	6,429,600	.1227	4,650,610	1,368	746,358	1,584	194,534	1,090	630,665	250,353
13380	Bellingham, WA	179,561	166,814	30.5	18,388	71,394	3,301,690	.0602	2,206,779	649	395,974	841	93,233	523	482,145	104,046
13460	Bend, OR	133,790	115,367	53.9	19,248	53,268	2,575,130	.0496	2,062,744	607	494,038	1,049	64,588	362	296,027	49,603
13740	Billings, MT	144,234	138,904	14.3	17,643	59,061	2,544,750	.0509	2,165,803	637	389,726	827	71,793	402	220,538	65,032
13780	Binghamton, NY	250,793	252,320	-4.6	18,483	101,911	4,635,420	.0790	2,475,857	728	356,641	758	95,881	537	435,767	196,783
13820	Birmingham-Hoover, AL	1,079,089	1,052,238	10.0	18,944	433,567	20,442,380	.3654	13,037,366	3,835	2,092,263	4,441	676,907	3,793	1,773,260	634,458
13900	Bismarck, ND	97,478	94,719	13.0	18,994	40,230	1,851,510	.0354	1,438,682	423	246,014	522	32,045	179	148,249	83,697
13980	Blacksburg-Christiansburg-Radford, VA	153,009	151,272	7.5	14,936	60,927	2,285,270	.0442	1,597,885	470	297,975	633	43,002	241	213,683	80,502
14020	Bloomington, IN	180,031	175,506	12.0	16,151	74,771	2,907,610	.0526	1,719,124	506	355,396	754	60,141	337	245,974	91,415
14060	Bloomington-Normal, IL	158,878	150,433	16.5	20,577	60,568	3,269,280	.0581	2,158,777	635	294,644	625	128,048	718	227,004	144,519
14260	Boise City-Nampa, ID	524,915	464,840	45.4	17,931	192,987	9,412,420	.1764	6,725,318	1,978	1,140,423	2,421	208,330	1,168	905,562	211,288
14460	Boston-Cambridge-Quincy, MA-NH	4,452,771	4,391,344	6.2	24,996	1,723,822	111,299,830	1.8013	60,701,542	17,855	5,700,756	12,102	4,396,572	24,640	10,266,378	4,205,252
14500	Boulder, CO	280,533	269,814	29.1	24,908	112,423	6,987,540	.1145	3,962,671	1,166	385,734	819	126,037	706	729,202	128,964
14540	Bowling Green, KY	108,712	104,166	19.7	17,438	44,572	1,895,690	.0354	1,311,956	386	236,899	503	73,389	411	131,919	53,100
14740	Bremerton-Silverdale, WA	243,450	231,969	22.3	19,816	90,966	4,824,290	.0783	2,263,687	666	520,165	1,104	67,059	376	338,124	110,073
14860	Bridgeport-Stamford-Norwalk, CT	904,001	882,567	6.6	30,224	334,894	27,322,330	.4561	17,926,178	5,273	934,028	1,983	1,149,371	6,441	2,396,980	817,269
15180	Brownsville-Harlingen, TX	371,857	335,227	28.9	9,563	109,025	3,556,070	.0806	2,774,996	816	641,360	1,361	195,601	1,096	531,733	106,356
15260	Brunswick, GA	97,306	93,044	13.2	18,840	42,224	1,833,290	.0318	1,053,072	310	152,601	324	86,080	483	166,184	51,654
15380	Buffalo-Niagara Falls, NY	1,156,288	1,170,111	-1.6	19,600	470,582	22,662,690	.3756	11,435,256	3,364	1,227,487	2,605	661,291	3,706	2,043,522	900,419
15500	Burlington, NC	138,548	130,800	20.9	18,658	56,281	2,585,040	.0472	1,747,387	514	210,583	447	106,370	596	236,792	102,793
15540	Burlington-South Burlington, VT	204,838	198,889	12.3	20,637	80,861	4,227,310	.0795	3,282,264	966	310,507	660	156,077	875	563,362	179,025
15940	Canton-Massillon, OH	407,161	406,934	3.3	18,397	162,941	7,490,370	.1367	5,012,905	1,474	691,501	1,468	239,306	1,341	727,029	449,795
15980	Cape Coral-Fort Myers, FL	508,350	440,888	31.6	21,735	219,630	11,049,150	.1922	7,029,399	2,068	988,622	2,099	443,513	2,486	986,313	442,891
16180	Carson City, NV	56,233	52,457	29.7	18,970	21,701	1,066,760	.0212	927,961	273	53,850	114	1,745	10	156,266	105,836
16220	Casper, WY	68,763	66,533	8.7	17,576	28,287	1,208,590	.0232	917,121	270	190,011	403	22,242	125	108,499	19,530
16300	Cedar Rapids, IA	244,390	237,230	12.6	20,244	98,206	4,947,520	.0879	3,237,789	953	477,117	1,013	122,834	688	414,700	159,248
16580	Champaign-Urbana, IL	219,572	210,275	3.7	18,083	87,529	3,970,450	.0716	2,519,943	742	498,563	1,059	95,668	537	335,333	183,208
16620	Charleston, WV	305,986	309,635	0.6	17,654	130,915	5,401,750	.1008	3,763,965	1,107	582,070	1,235	144,059	808	470,411	278,964
16700	Charleston-North Charleston, SC	578,716	549,033	8.3	18,762	232,024	10,857,930	.1907	6,506,338	1,913	1,101,200	2,338	413,126	2,315	1,082,356	277,047
16740	Charlotte-Gastonia-Concord, NC-SC	1,470,003	1,330,448	29.8	22,345	602,683	32,847,930	.5571	19,602,323	5,766	2,646,389	5,617	926,940	5,194	2,486,119	978,597
16820	Charlottesville, VA	183,913	174,021	20.9	19,723	74,122	3,627,400	.0638	2,265,895	667	309,921	658	127,458	715	389,541	119,413
16860	Chattanooga, TN-GA	488,857	476,531	10.0	18,410	200,415	8,999,930	.1610	5,656,736	1,663	931,010	1,976	299,207	1,677	771,836	342,749
16940	Cheyenne, WY	84,872	81,607	11.6	18,223	33,925	1,546,640	.0303	1,264,795	372	198,396	421	22,697	127	146,267	25,711
16980	Chicago-Naperville-Joliet, IL-IN-WI	9,405,026	9,098,316	11.2	21,277	3,404,592	200,106,090	3.3284	108,533,325	31,926	12,448,491	26,424	5,997,775	33,613	14,973,121	8,989,067
17020	Chico, CA	213,422	203,171	11.6	15,710	83,496	3,352,780	.0619	2,084,387	613	302,336	642	76,186	427	422,545	147,515
17140	Cincinnati-Middletown, OH-KY-IN	2,058,374	2,009,632	8.9	21,001	833,063	43,228,550	.7288	24,347,704	7,162	3,578,925	7,597	1,088,721	6,102	3,474,232	1,334,996
17300	Clarksville, TN-KY	238,045	232,000	22.6	16,291	89,400	3,878,000	.0698	2,277,439	670	538,331	1,143	95,193	532	199,023	76,366
17420	Cleveland, TN	107,156	104,015	19.1	16,849	43,530	1,805,440	.0321	1,037,640	305	189,521	403	34,377	192	122,296	69,439
17460	Cleveland-Elyria-Mentor, OH	2,136,733	2,148,143	2.2	20,295	877,176	43,365,710	.7537	26,427,730	7,774	2,836,585	6,022	1,297,232	7,270	3,847,381	2,724,980
17660	Coeur d'Alene, ID	120,129	108,685	55.7	16,722	45,406	2,008,850	.0384	1,461,817	430	200,422	425	48,677	273	245,170	51,863
17780	College Station-Bryan, TX	195,011	184,885	22.4	13,878	74,689	2,706,380	.0546	2,032,602	598	368,615	783	93,680	524	290,674	49,105
17820	Colorado Springs, CO	582,962	537,484	31.3	19,915	217,598	11,609,510	.2043	7,281,101	2,142	1,150,804	2,443	191,586	1,074	801,447	279,729
17860	Columbia, MO	152,833	145,666	19.4	18,012	62,254	2,752,790	.0509	1,895,365	557	298,360	633	55,200	310	224,344	77,519
17900	Columbia, SC	678,866	647,158	18.0	19,288	271,665	13,094,270	.2312	8,121,937	2,388	1,461,358	3,102	391,616	2,196	1,104,551	415,843
17980	Columbus, GA-AL	288,724	281,768	5.7	16,090	112,635	4,645,610	.0854	2,892,433	851	474,625	1,008	179,515	1,005	427,765	173,256
18020	Columbus, IN	72,553	71,435	12.2	19,548	28,769	1,418,280	.0243	799,523	235	148,891	316	53,440	300	105,411	57,214
18140	Columbus, OH	1,693,064	1,612,694	14.8	21,863	711,298	37,016,120	.6479	24,084,728	7,085	3,114,519	6,612	1,026,104	5,750	2,879,390	943,488
18580	Corpus Christi, TX	408,027	403,280	9.7	15,844	149,535	6,464,610	.1214	4,287,745	1,261	695,672	1,477	198,700	1,113	763,556	160,495
18700	Corvallis, OR	79,726	78,153	10.4	19,582	32,175	1,561,160	.0243	609,433	179	82,549	175	24,628	138	136,155	28,413
19060	Cumberland, MD-WV	100,473	102,008	0.4	14,953	40,132	1,502,400	.0285	982,642	289	232,915	494	42,687	239	153,863	82,351
19100	Dallas-Fort Worth-Arlington, TX	5,720,764	5,161,544	29.4	21,519	2,136,210	123,103,990	2.1099	74,314,243	21,860	9,970,829	21,167	3,745,975	20,995	9,998,227	2,946,274
19140	Dalton, GA	129,405	120,031	21.7	17,187	48,839	2,224,020	.0435	1,755,183	516	226,995	482	61,298	343	254,638	64,871
19180	Danville, IL	82,467	83,919	-4.9	16,270	33,283	1,341,740	.0248	858,593	253	169,014	359	22,640	127	137,428	58,020
19260	Danville, VA	108,169	110,156	1.3	15,496	46,142	1,676,150	.0316	1,097,461	323	198,693	422	33,492	188	192,389	56,712
19340	Davenport-Moline-Rock Island, IA-IL	374,674	376,019	2.1	18,885	151,084	7,075,850	.1301	4,913,588	1,445	679,541	1,443	190,384	1,067	610,777	312,800
19380	Dayton, OH	845,439	848,153	0.5	20,594	357,985	17,411,280	.2977	10,158,179	2,988	1,735,989	3,686	431,765	2,419	1,342,338	491,936
19460	Decatur, AL	147,582	145,867	10.9	18,193	60,090	2,684,900	.0479	1,655,638	487	238,893	507	65,839	369	168,352	86,024
19500	Decatur, IL	110,093	114,706	-2.1	18,388	45,406	2,024,380	.0388	1,560,720	459	284,280	603	50,446	283	216,372	109,137
19660	Deltona-Daytona Beach-Ormond Beach, FL	476,562	443,343	19.6	20,089	215,582	9,573,780	.1631	5,410,480	1,592	719,210	1,527	211,817	1,187	893,089	358,640
19740	Denver-Aurora, CO	2,337,049	2,179,240	30.7	23,285	921,916	54,418,490	.8985	30,460,849	8,960	4,356,686	9,248	1,347,655	7,553	4,236,864	1,085,958
19780	Des Moines, IA	509,323	481,394	15.6	20,607	204,097	10,495,510	.1817	6,384,753	1,877	861,094	1,829	229,830	1,288	846,810	314,243
19820	Detroit-Warren-Livonia, MI	4,492,464	4,452,557	4.8	22,202	1,773,948	99,740,930	1.7090	61,289,437	18,030	9,672,534	20,533	2,789,100	15,630	7,328,480	4,281,485
20020	Dothan, AL	134,089	130,861	8.7	16,546	55,584	2,218,610	.0452	1,909,878	562	363,431	771	82,265	461	179,309	74,264
20100	Dover, DE	136,821	126,697	14.1	17,831	51,808	2,439,640	.0448	1,634,075	481	336,656	715	44,077	247	195,425	69,449
20220	Dubuque, IA	90,309	89,143	3.2	17,549	35,087	1,584,810	.0308	1,245,748	366	204,332	434	31,824	178	148,726	70,539
20260	Duluth, MN-WI	276,062	275,486	2.3	17,366	115,215	4,793,970	.0875	3,090,259	909	553,870	1,175	72,947	408	425,059	154,679
20500	Durham, NC	454,080	426,493	23.8	20,825	189,975	9,456,370	.1584	5,184,875	1,526	512,260	1,088	270,260	1,514	920,987	312,899
20740	Eau Claire, WI	151,741	148,337	7.8	17,719	61,246	2,688,700	.0568	2,634,523	775	545,765	1,158	100,713	564	287,391	94,843
20940	El Centro, CA	151,466	142,361	30.2	10,979	41,707	1,662,980	.0370	1,392,918	410	261,116	554	82,208	461	254,019	62,708
21060	Elizabethtown, KY	110,057	107,547	6.6	17,318	42,431	1,905,950	.0343	1,170,936	344	250,726	533	58,498	328	99,084	56,788
21140	Elkhart-Goshen, IN	190,535	182,791	17.0	18,034	69,272	3,436,030	.0660	2,636,787	776	432,046	917	35,241	198	276,343	119,557
21300	Elmira, NY	90,205	91,070	-4.3	17,997	35,627	1,623,380	.0298	1,092,065	321	190,558	405	53,956	302	157,479	68,541
21340	El Paso, TX	713,340	679,622	14.9	12,037	226,278	8,586,800	.1799	6,462,611	1,901	1,356,263	2,879	425,599	2,385	831,659	312,642
21500	Erie, PA	279,718	280,843	1.9	17,187	111,157	4,807,540	.0901	3,333,544	981	445,349	945	129,279	725	546,498	194,903
21660	Eugene-Springfield, OR	332,896	322,959	14.2	17,777	136,131	5,917,890	.1118	4,302,190	1,266	807,668	1,715	128,392	720	679,603	134,140
21780	Evansville, IN-KY	346,581	342,815	5.5	18,394	143,502	6,374,920	.1198	4,662,329	1,372	814,297	1,728	208,187	1,166	505,130	238,148
21820	Fairbanks, AK	87,045	82,840	6.6	19,956	31,711	1,737,030	.0312	1,166,641	343	299,064	635	34,508	193	97,107	13,360
22020	Fargo, ND-MN	180,577	174,367	13.7	18,232	74,906	3,292,320	.0680	3,077,853	906	451,918	959	91,991	516	271,043	146,309
22140	Farmington, NM	124,961	113,801	24.2	13,937	42,462	1,741,540	.0356	1,362,112	401	346,139	735	41,368	232	147,324	41,633
22180	Fayetteville, NC	343,212	336,609	13.2	16,906	131,814	5,802,500	.1052	3,586,986	1,056	702,675	1,492	168,678	945	468,641	155,360
22220	Fayetteville-Springdale-Rogers, AR-MO	387,515	347,045	44.9	16,721	147,765	6,479,530	.1198	4,236,529	1,247	1,303,952	2,767	118,052	661	408,743	125,206
22380	Flagstaff, AZ	122,854	116,320	20.4	16,664	44,020	2,047,190	.0374	1,282,069	377	284,754	604	31,842	178	226,079	29,172
22420	Flint, MI	444,011	436,141	1.3	19,539	181,093	8,675,620	.1515	5,238,928	1,541	1,038,212	2,204	183,929	1,031	608,615	347,323
22500	Florence, SC	197,296	193,155	9.6	15,715	76,867	3,100,520	.0608	2,337,905	688	361,572	768	108,121	606	334,795	138,955
22520	Florence-Muscle Shoals, AL	141,000	142,950	8.9	17,078	59,396	2,407,980	.0445	1,604,167	472	378,407	803	72,513	406	171,876	65,218
22540	Fond du Lac, WI	97,983	97,296	8.0	19,536	38,650	1,914,180	.0329	1,099,443	323	211,554	449	23,267	130	159,938	50,532
22660	Fort Collins-Loveland, CO	271,165	251,494	35.1	21,864	107,740	5,928,820	.1012	3,560,752	1,047	603,249	1,281	139,359	781	480,045	104,785
22900	Fort Smith, AR-OK	281,742	273,170	16.7	14,765	108,522	4,160,000	.0816	2,987,004	878	800,726	1,701	71,529	401	374,247	123,340
23020	Fort Walton Beach-Crestview-Destin, FL	180,485	170,498	18.6	23,214	81,167	4,189,840	.0711	2,557,865	752	468,067	994	183,928	1,031	285,709	117,808
23060	Fort Wayne, IN	402,608	390,156	10.1	19,308	160,633	7,773,560	.1393	5,065,354	1,490	978,547	2,078	200,064	1,121	533,792	288,823
23420	Fresno, CA	866,423	799,407	19.8	13,541	269,842	11,732,460	.2231	7,104,904	2,090	970,831	2,061	301,911	1,692	1,214,541	433,499
23460	Gadsden, AL	102,945	103,459	3.6	15,783	42,212	1,624,740	.0296	962,832	283	197,166	419	41,883	235	187,328	55,255
23540	Gainesville, FL	241,335	232,392	21.5	15,995	97,017	3,860,190	.0730	2,620,298	771	375,339	797	132,681	744	479,702	110,562
23580	Gainesville, GA	161,175	139,277	45.9	18,827	58,724	3,034,450	.0521	1,689,280	497	323,483	687	47,462	266	181,864	83,409
24020	Glens Falls, NY	127,334	124,345	4.9	19,244	50,896	2,450,470	.0416	1,332,449	392	120,576	256	99,993	560	213,546	82,321
24140	Goldsboro, NC	113,028	113,329	8.3	15,911	44,258	1,798,380	.0346	1,286,204	378	226,878	482	56,081	314	170,727	62,907
24220	Grand Forks, ND-MN	95,100	97,478	-5.5	16,004	37,219	1,522,000	.0333	1,545,462	455	294,376	625	46,105	258	150,561	57,640
24300	Grand Junction, CO	127,075	116,255	24.8	16,763	50,551	2,130,220	.0407	1,540,898	453	347,773	738	31,679	178	205,091	40,014
24340	Grand Rapids-Wyoming, MI	768,430	740,482	14.6	19,201	289,500	14,755,000	.2671	9,880,515	2,906	1,851,881	3,931	352,570	1,976	891,877	446,099
24500	Great Falls, MT	79,349	80,357	3.4	16,141	32,601	1,280,800	.0252	989,385	291	223,772	475	22,782	128	109,989	41,908
24540	Greeley, CO	220,667	180,926	37.3	16,913	76,443	3,732,100	.0638	1,875,716	552	261,111	554	24,309	136	242,183	53,013
24580	Green Bay, WI	293,914	282,599	16.0	19,900	117,838	5,848,850	.1043	3,810,393	1,120	833,279	1,769	90,186	505	427,594	112,138
24660	Greensboro-High Point, NC	666,943	643,430	19.1	19,789	276,895	13,198,200	.2387	8,968,096	2,638	1,092,366	2,319	404,136	2,265	1,135,820	551,736
24780	Greenville, NC	160,525	152,772	23.9	15,737	64,178	2,526,170	.0506	2,011,580	592	213,809	454	117,144	657	275,729	94,795
24860	Greenville, SC	584,065	559,940	18.6	18,610	232,657	10,869,420	.1983	7,315,362	2,152	987,107	2,096	339,854	1,905	952,644	389,823
25060	Gulfport-Biloxi, MS	249,739	246,190	18.4	17,496	101,273	4,369,410	.0800	2,851,077	839	698,746	1,483	107,647	603	301,374	129,687
25180	Hagerstown-Martinsburg, MD-WV	242,248	222,771	15.6	18,620	94,376	4,510,690	.0767	2,403,099	707	396,664	842	104,382	585	372,552	139,425
25260	Hanford-Corcoran, CA	141,461	129,461	27.6	11,732	37,363	1,659,660	.0307	763,680	225	108,758	231	31,613	177	181,021	34,944
25420	Harrisburg-Carlisle, PA	520,152	509,074	7.3	20,822	213,483	10,830,400	.1940	7,355,835	2,164	722,807	1,534	278,217	1,559	1,057,504	405,259
25500	Harrisonburg, VA	111,322	108,193	22.7	15,376	40,521	1,711,720	.0355	1,488,950	438	224,896	477	40,293	226	202,960	74,334
25540	Hartford-West Hartford-East Hartford, CT	1,186,956	1,148,618	2.2	26,395	467,168	31,330,290	.4795	14,476,166	4,258	1,272,994	2,702	1,069,247	5,993	2,502,419	1,079,752
25620	Hattiesburg, MS	130,073	123,812	13.0	14,615	49,578	1,901,080	.0396	1,620,094	477	484,113	1,028	64,930	364	122,720	110,415
25860	Hickory-Lenoir-Morganton, NC	352,521	341,851	16.9	18,165	142,926	6,403,660	.1160	4,138,266	1,217	589,803	1,251	146,720	822	530,183	248,052
25980	Hinesville-Fort Stewart, GA	69,055	71,914	22.0	13,735	24,099	948,470	.0165	408,149	120	90,356	192	17,953	101	56,363	11,007
26100	Holland-Grand Haven, MI	252,694	238,314	26.9	20,891	90,801	5,278,990	.0893	2,991,989	880	749,974	1,592	94,721	531	278,265	106,669
26180	Honolulu, HI	911,719	876,156	4.8	19,820	301,773	18,070,470	.3029	9,586,291	2,820	1,932,186	4,102	1,213,597	6,801	1,460,075	815,873
26300	Hot Springs, AR	92,118	88,068	20.0	17,312	41,928	1,594,770	.0311	1,248,087	367	312,850	664	38,691	217	120,441	58,699
26380	Houma-Bayou Cane-Thibodaux, LA	198,351	194,477	6.4	15,568	71,352	3,087,850	.0610	2,360,449	695	477,923	1,015	76,947	432	388,063	105,806
26420	Houston-Baytown-Sugar Land, TX	5,187,158	4,715,407	25.2	19,599	1,897,350	101,663,440	1.7618	60,014,131	17,654	9,252,065	19,640	3,382,371	18,955	9,117,678	2,819,147
26580	Huntington-Ashland, WV-KY-OH	285,902	288,649	0.2	15,520	121,645	4,437,150	.0833	2,888,944	850	581,437	1,234	147,444	826	341,163	297,563
26620	Huntsville, AL	362,704	342,376	16.8	21,319	148,388	7,732,470	.1305	4,408,012	1,296	884,283	1,877	227,112	1,272	579,797	171,413
26820	Idaho Falls, ID	108,893	101,677	14.6	16,533	37,776	1,800,370	.0351	1,363,845	401	306,515	651	31,851	178	192,802	47,637
26900	Indianapolis, IN	1,616,900	1,525,104	17.8	21,197	653,495	34,273,110	.6066	22,689,052	6,673	3,846,247	8,165	876,562	4,912	2,181,248	1,455,903
26980	Iowa City, IA	138,449	131,676	13.8	18,369	55,900	2,543,120	.0469	1,756,834	517	239,718	509	59,232	332	301,270	83,903
27060	Ithaca, NY	102,983	96,501	2.6	18,179	39,852	1,872,090	.0299	758,836	223	72,786	155	32,607	183	186,312	57,099
27100	Jackson, MI	163,516	158,422	5.8	18,372	61,219	3,004,140	.0530	1,801,553	530	486,032	1,032	45,211	253	190,509	85,531
27140	Jackson, MS	513,973	497,197	11.2	17,308	193,505	8,895,610	.1691	6,473,402	1,905	1,301,508	2,763	270,673	1,517	666,464	365,773
27180	Jackson, TN	110,436	107,377	18.3	17,750	44,215	1,960,220	.0396	1,722,683	507	382,036	811	110,247	618	151,297	90,390

Core Based Statistical Areas (CBSAs): Population / Income / Sales#†, Continued

CODE	CORE BASED STATISTICAL AREA	POPULATION Estimate 7/1/04	POPULATION Census 4/1/00	% Change 4/1/90-4/1/00	PER CAPITA INCOME 2003	HOUSE-HOLDS Estimate 7/1/04	DISPOSABLE INCOME 2003 ($1,000)	MARKET ABILITY INDEX 2003	TOTAL RETAIL SALES 2003 Sales ($1,000)	TOTAL RETAIL SALES Ranally Sales Units	GENERAL MERCHANDISE 2003 Sales ($1,000)	GENERAL MERCHANDISE Ranally Sales Units	APPAREL STORE SALES 2003 Sales ($1,000)	APPAREL STORE SALES Ranally Sales Units	FOOD STORE SALES 2003 ($1,000)	HEALTH & DRUG STORE 2003 ($1,000)
27260	Jacksonville, FL	1,228,504	1,122,750	21.4	21,558	497,528	26,483,630	.4471	15,231,569	**4,480**	1,973,993	**4,190**	715,024	**4,007**	2,176,928	768,741
27340	Jacksonville, NC	146,634	150,355	0.3	14,600	53,106	2,140,860	.0420	1,534,013	**451**	261,489	**555**	47,943	**269**	197,933	55,794
27500	Janesville, WI	155,545	152,307	9.2	19,859	62,205	3,088,910	.0555	2,063,534	**607**	359,494	**763**	32,652	**183**	282,095	98,760
27620	Jefferson City, MO	143,594	140,052	16.0	18,458	55,338	2,650,460	.0486	1,793,299	**527**	310,703	**659**	26,946	**150**	219,820	72,646
27740	Johnson City, TN	187,591	181,607	13.2	16,275	80,682	3,052,950	.0573	2,054,674	**605**	385,911	**819**	125,442	**704**	245,098	121,051
27780	Johnstown, PA	148,535	152,598	-6.4	14,525	60,133	2,157,510	.0416	1,455,184	**428**	194,854	**414**	35,359	**198**	276,792	104,805
27860	Jonesboro, AR	110,679	107,762	15.1	15,098	44,126	1,671,070	.0338	1,344,174	**395**	353,812	**751**	78,162	**439**	119,678	54,725
27900	Joplin, MO	163,621	157,322	16.6	15,072	64,006	2,466,140	.0484	1,804,711	**531**	419,953	**892**	46,048	**258**	163,155	79,283
28020	Kalamazoo-Portage, MI	322,014	314,866	7.3	18,958	128,810	6,104,720	.1086	3,844,226	**1,131**	1,043,323	**2,215**	128,321	**719**	354,799	188,470
28100	Kankakee-Bradley, IL	106,207	103,833	7.9	17,954	39,387	1,906,840	.0346	1,230,032	**362**	251,524	**534**	43,569	**244**	124,754	93,525
28140	Kansas City, MO-KS	1,925,595	1,836,038	12.2	21,378	772,932	41,166,020	.7074	24,965,001	**7,342**	3,716,868	**7,890**	953,702	**5,346**	3,040,182	1,272,430
28420	Kennewick-Richland-Pasco, WA	215,499	191,822	27.9	17,905	75,145	3,858,460	.0698	2,458,913	**723**	502,225	**1,066**	66,090	**370**	431,707	99,354
28660	Killeen-Temple-Fort Hood, TX	347,063	330,714	23.0	15,926	123,423	5,527,190	.0969	2,888,916	**850**	420,155	**892**	82,598	**463**	411,687	56,125
28700	Kingsport-Bristol-Bristol, TN-VA	300,120	298,484	8.3	16,826	130,987	5,049,720	.0947	3,471,046	**1,020**	662,608	**1,406**	102,870	**577**	455,487	193,453
28740	Kingston, NY	182,183	177,749	7.5	20,318	70,543	3,701,600	.0588	1,627,487	**479**	152,573	**324**	65,662	**368**	322,318	116,080
28940	Knoxville, TN	643,341	616,079	15.2	19,141	273,658	12,314,110	.2435	10,569,943	**3,110**	1,711,283	**3,632**	420,316	**2,355**	1,167,051	538,607
29020	Kokomo, IN	101,227	101,541	4.7	20,974	42,915	2,123,170	.0375	1,385,222	**407**	327,176	**694**	34,854	**195**	134,753	98,680
29100	La Crosse, WI-MN	129,119	126,838	9.0	17,711	51,815	2,286,770	.0439	1,739,488	**512**	328,342	**697**	36,142	**202**	227,580	47,403
29140	Lafayette, IN	186,417	178,541	12.4	16,928	71,027	3,155,600	.0592	2,170,179	**639**	487,339	**1,035**	83,611	**468**	191,893	109,428
29180	Lafayette, LA	245,778	239,086	14.5	17,232	96,621	4,235,140	.0860	3,699,976	**1,089**	721,764	**1,532**	161,851	**907**	368,972	234,047
29340	Lake Charles, LA	193,633	193,568	9.1	17,475	77,630	3,383,820	.0626	2,288,569	**673**	543,814	**1,154**	91,221	**511**	289,364	119,952
29460	Lakeland, FL	518,809	483,924	19.4	19,073	217,966	9,895,440	.1713	5,716,090	**1,681**	873,686	**1,855**	196,846	**1,103**	977,731	287,481
29540	Lancaster, PA	486,469	470,658	11.3	19,463	180,573	9,468,350	.1739	6,676,478	**1,964**	579,937	**1,231**	367,776	**2,061**	1,109,981	332,301
29620	Lansing-East Lansing, MI	458,301	447,728	3.5	20,004	182,777	9,167,820	.1606	5,685,892	**1,672**	1,278,910	**2,715**	207,150	**1,161**	673,930	297,591
29700	Laredo, TX	219,931	193,117	44.9	9,311	58,756	2,047,880	.0538	2,387,548	**702**	472,368	**1,003**	296,511	**1,662**	370,036	96,388
29740	Las Cruces, NM	184,554	174,682	28.9	12,499	63,683	2,306,790	.0444	1,344,907	**396**	259,830	**552**	39,961	**224**	154,238	70,219
29820	Las Vegas-Paradise, NV	1,637,622	1,375,765	85.5	19,574	620,349	32,054,670	.5564	19,011,943	**5,593**	2,590,700	**5,500**	1,238,316	**6,940**	2,927,642	777,477
29940	Lawrence, KS	103,909	99,962	22.2	16,965	40,944	1,762,840	.0319	1,084,623	**319**	155,726	**331**	56,394	**316**	198,476	47,982
30020	Lawton, OK	113,664	114,996	3.1	14,565	40,239	1,655,550	.0289	779,898	**229**	245,081	**520**	21,843	**122**	72,711	30,150
30140	Lebanon, PA	123,395	120,327	5.8	18,733	48,483	2,311,520	.0423	1,571,295	**462**	187,305	**398**	28,005	**157**	226,517	70,127
30300	Lewiston, ID-WA	58,451	57,961	12.9	16,990	24,012	993,080	.0188	708,657	**209**	184,274	**391**	10,800	**61**	123,558	27,291
30340	Lewiston-Auburn, ME	106,865	103,793	-1.4	17,501	44,561	1,870,230	.0390	1,762,740	**519**	215,665	**458**	23,086	**129**	262,314	67,601
30460	Lexington-Fayette, KY	426,494	408,326	17.2	20,850	182,897	8,892,490	.1577	5,875,286	**1,728**	841,380	**1,785**	317,551	**1,780**	630,731	340,223
30620	Lima, OH	108,137	108,473	-1.2	17,241	42,785	1,864,400	.0376	1,597,704	**470**	367,555	**780**	46,191	**259**	132,113	97,404
30700	Lincoln, NE	280,966	266,787	16.5	19,123	113,321	5,372,960	.0949	3,316,866	**975**	577,161	**1,225**	112,143	**628**	498,726	227,264
30780	Little Rock-North Little Rock, AR	633,708	610,518	14.1	19,291	262,285	12,224,550	.2274	8,899,092	**2,617**	1,776,498	**3,770**	318,812	**1,786**	766,679	282,051
30860	Logan, UT-ID	109,025	102,720	29.3	13,470	32,976	1,468,530	.0293	1,047,968	**308**	191,711	**407**	30,325	**170**	166,101	28,536
30980	Longview, TX	199,528	194,042	7.8	16,182	77,142	3,228,820	.0634	2,489,363	**732**	464,619	**986**	78,959	**442**	347,241	105,916
31020	Longview, WA	95,850	92,948	13.2	17,792	37,022	1,705,340	.0301	1,001,310	**295**	212,859	**452**	17,384	**97**	191,898	39,276
31100	Los Angeles-Long Beach-Santa Ana, CA	12,971,790	12,365,627	9.7	18,420	4,242,787	238,946,190	4.1072	131,191,725	**38,591**	14,965,879	**31,769**	10,877,435	**60,961**	21,595,780	7,400,000
31140	Louisville, KY-IN	1,198,515	1,161,975	10.0	20,338	503,792	24,375,560	.4092	13,227,081	**3,890**	2,142,103	**4,548**	518,818	**2,908**	1,495,463	819,693
31180	Lubbock, TX	259,602	249,700	8.6	15,282	100,546	3,967,170	.0834	3,562,461	**1,048**	537,545	**1,141**	164,717	**923**	515,522	108,227
31340	Lynchburg, VA	231,742	228,616	10.9	17,383	94,225	4,028,470	.0722	2,447,064	**719**	348,738	**741**	71,712	**401**	332,802	179,459
31420	Macon, GA	227,227	222,368	7.6	16,840	88,709	3,826,400	.0721	2,681,481	**788**	485,203	**1,030**	131,680	**738**	388,324	139,294
31460	Madera, CA	136,739	123,109	39.8	13,247	39,936	1,811,380	.0307	646,914	**190**	57,541	**122**	10,665	**60**	210,767	44,922
31540	Madison, WI	534,379	501,774	16.1	21,802	222,637	11,650,780	.2146	8,783,205	**2,584**	1,026,224	**2,178**	252,590	**1,416**	929,642	346,073
31700	Manchester-Nashua, NH	398,775	380,841	13.3	22,726	152,823	9,062,560	.1736	7,717,723	**2,270**	1,155,385	**2,453**	304,995	**1,709**	1,064,120	259,831
31900	Mansfield, OH	128,091	128,852	2.2	17,420	50,750	2,231,330	.0429	1,684,909	**496**	397,813	**844**	53,078	**297**	174,139	81,338
32580	McAllen-Edinburg-Pharr, TX	656,072	569,463	48.5	8,644	182,386	5,671,110	.1419	5,457,211	**1,605**	1,064,900	**2,261**	420,429	**2,356**	833,469	231,799
32780	Medford, OR	192,822	181,269	23.8	17,054	76,466	3,288,420	.0707	3,296,101	**970**	569,323	**1,209**	84,470	**473**	347,160	87,002
32820	Memphis, TN-MS-AR	1,249,702	1,205,204	12.9	18,305	480,832	22,875,320	.4105	14,456,493	**4,253**	2,489,377	**5,285**	825,463	**4,627**	1,493,064	919,941
32900	Merced, CA	238,219	210,554	18.0	13,234	71,028	3,152,650	.0571	1,544,511	**454**	256,600	**545**	38,860	**218**	298,155	86,520
33100	Miami-Fort Lauderdale-Miami Beach, FL	5,375,613	5,007,564	23.5	20,322	2,173,822	109,241,680	1.8943	66,142,729	**19,456**	7,603,750	**16,141**	5,336,086	**29,905**	9,219,868	4,758,075
33140	Michigan City-La Porte, IN	109,775	110,106	2.8	17,742	41,606	1,947,620	.0356	1,280,452	**377**	223,881	**475**	120,176	**674**	134,138	82,101
33260	Midland, TX	119,655	116,009	8.8	18,305	46,067	2,190,260	.0412	1,600,790	**471**	285,960	**607**	75,888	**425**	182,330	53,538
33340	Milwaukee-Waukesha-West Allis, WI	1,518,392	1,500,741	4.8	21,091	626,347	32,024,760	.5377	17,828,356	**5,244**	2,468,920	**5,241**	607,112	**3,403**	2,663,965	1,200,135
33460	Minneapolis-St. Paul-Bloomington, MN-WI	3,117,850	2,968,806	16.9	23,599	1,239,180	73,576,940	1.2830	49,271,803	**14,494**	6,752,377	**14,336**	1,762,104	**9,874**	6,271,900	2,151,420
33540	Missoula, MT	99,453	95,802	21.8	16,676	40,452	1,658,450	.0346	1,528,262	**450**	329,816	**700**	38,925	**218**	173,741	41,515
33660	Mobile, AL	399,635	399,843	5.6	15,819	152,735	6,321,850	.1148	3,735,954	**1,099**	796,502	**1,691**	159,638	**895**	512,300	206,288
33700	Modesto, CA	506,378	446,997	20.6	15,862	162,035	8,032,070	.1459	4,753,556	**1,398**	669,983	**1,422**	178,855	**1,002**	913,403	315,443
33740	Monroe, LA	171,146	170,053	4.4	16,017	69,452	2,741,170	.0524	1,930,984	**568**	519,897	**1,103**	92,974	**521**	212,160	85,628
33780	Monroe, MI	152,069	145,945	9.2	21,641	57,434	3,290,970	.0534	1,655,186	**487**	319,220	**678**	56,627	**317**	191,344	93,565
33860	Montgomery, AL	354,386	346,528	13.6	17,853	138,358	6,327,020	.1162	4,233,247	**1,246**	800,152	**1,699**	200,979	**1,126**	523,663	246,613
34060	Morgantown, WV	115,017	111,200	6.4	14,763	47,439	1,698,040	.0322	1,099,015	**323**	215,260	**457**	63,393	**355**	125,813	74,893
34100	Morristown, TN	128,445	123,081	22.4	15,740	52,132	2,021,680	.0385	1,395,601	**411**	264,342	**561**	41,049	**230**	172,052	75,366
34580	Mount Vernon-Anacortes, WA	111,156	102,979	29.4	18,370	41,628	2,041,940	.0384	1,490,007	**438**	281,875	**598**	60,566	**339**	212,366	60,042
34620	Muncie, IN	117,094	118,769	-0.7	16,012	47,338	1,874,870	.0364	1,381,187	**406**	331,237	**703**	55,373	**310**	137,963	69,463
34740	Muskegon-Norton Shores, MI	173,945	170,200	7.1	17,223	68,024	2,995,780	.0552	1,977,190	**582**	527,223	**1,119**	54,416	**305**	204,944	128,039
34820	Myrtle Beach-Conway-North Myrtle Beach, SC	214,999	196,629	36.5	18,682	91,843	4,016,570	.0819	3,690,442	**1,086**	611,740	**1,299**	391,423	**2,194**	536,626	149,542
34900	Napa, CA	133,946	124,279	12.2	22,584	48,804	3,024,970	.0481	1,452,122	**427**	87,608	**186**	125,152	**701**	369,317	82,039
34940	Naples-Marco Island, FL	297,488	251,377	65.3	24,228	122,501	7,207,470	.1199	4,228,159	**1,244**	421,375	**895**	411,527	**2,306**	713,495	233,244
34980	Nashville-Davidson--Murfreesboro, TN	1,389,376	1,311,789	25.1	21,436	566,503	29,783,080	.5276	19,889,768	**5,849**	3,310,027	**7,027**	996,971	**5,587**	2,462,695	1,078,959
35300	New Haven-Milford, CT	847,502	824,008	2.5	24,399	331,415	20,678,310	.3304	10,642,435	**3,131**	1,078,401	**2,289**	607,778	**3,406**	1,706,678	797,297
35380	New Orleans-Metairie-Kenner, LA	1,318,235	1,316,510	4.1	17,916	535,050	23,617,510	.4235	14,673,543	**4,317**	2,489,535	**5,286**	876,417	**4,912**	2,131,086	1,101,031
35620	New York-Northern New Jersey-Long Island, NY-NJ-PA	18,735,483	18,323,002	8.8	22,813	6,824,880	427,405,790	6.7022	196,107,217	**57,688**	17,839,877	**37,868**	21,256,522	**119,126**	32,996,658	16,282,004
35660	Niles-Benton Harbor, MI	162,816	162,453	0.7	17,983	66,098	2,927,880	.0504	1,585,823	**466**	298,008	**633**	29,166	**163**	230,436	105,137
35980	Norwich-New London, CT	265,499	259,088	1.6	25,332	104,602	6,725,490	.1054	3,310,747	**974**	430,241	**913**	173,428	**972**	509,295	214,890
36100	Ocala, FL	286,954	258,916	32.9	17,412	123,754	4,996,440	.0912	3,225,186	**949**	498,732	**1,059**	83,149	**466**	433,921	186,643
36140	Ocean City, NJ	101,693	102,326	7.6	22,111	42,450	2,248,490	.0378	1,300,707	**383**	56,977	**121**	99,381	**557**	373,396	94,871
36220	Odessa, TX	123,354	121,123	1.8	14,193	45,834	1,750,810	.0368	1,501,339	**442**	332,254	**705**	45,562	**255**	201,630	64,347
36260	Ogden-Clearfield, UT	476,951	442,656	25.8	17,543	154,038	8,367,310	.1517	5,317,040	**1,564**	947,833	**2,012**	146,125	**819**	848,133	109,399
36420	Oklahoma City, OK	1,144,287	1,095,421	12.8	18,079	464,505	20,687,690	.3717	13,035,439	**3,834**	2,207,799	**4,686**	447,625	**2,509**	1,473,089	692,412
36500	Olympia, WA	226,479	207,355	28.6	21,081	90,097	4,774,330	.0817	2,831,219	**833**	658,091	**1,397**	78,248	**439**	496,829	97,280
36540	Omaha-Council Bluffs, NE-IA	801,189	767,041	11.8	19,834	317,131	15,890,860	.2901	11,130,228	**3,275**	1,359,230	**2,886**	395,984	**2,218**	1,441,414	616,912
36740	Orlando, FL	1,851,873	1,644,561	34.3	20,739	737,616	38,405,230	.6825	25,416,119	**7,476**	3,495,555	**7,420**	1,661,395	**9,310**	3,372,844	1,393,435
36780	Oshkosh-Neenah, WI	158,990	156,763	11.7	20,432	66,789	3,248,480	.0566	2,005,674	**590**	247,543	**525**	70,315	**394**	217,440	119,790
36980	Owensboro, KY	111,124	109,875	5.0	17,642	44,942	1,960,490	.0343	1,116,526	**328**	229,538	**487**	38,656	**217**	126,717	79,823
37100	Oxnard-Thousand Oaks-Ventura, CA	802,627	753,197	12.6	22,864	258,964	18,351,220	.2961	9,381,128	**2,760**	941,078	**1,998**	513,106	**2,876**	1,505,559	540,323
37340	Palm Bay-Melbourne-Titusville, FL	515,004	476,230	19.4	22,229	228,764	11,447,810	.1835	5,603,865	**1,648**	916,795	**1,946**	235,423	**1,319**	919,936	384,085
37460	Panama City-Lynn Haven, FL	157,510	148,217	16.7	18,652	64,529	2,937,810	.0539	2,015,801	**593**	435,643	**925**	81,428	**456**	299,060	98,266
37620	Parkersburg-Marietta, WV-OH	162,712	164,624	1.7	17,030	67,899	2,770,950	.0536	2,095,461	**617**	438,360	**931**	63,402	**355**	234,021	111,888
37700	Pascagoula, MS	155,413	150,564	14.1	17,841	59,183	2,772,720	.0469	1,394,027	**410**	337,386	**717**	29,989	**168**	190,611	55,807
37860	Pensacola-Ferry Pass-Brent, FL	434,387	412,153	19.7	19,068	176,993	8,282,890	.1411	4,519,358	**1,330**	756,204	**1,605**	179,965	**1,008**	666,395	295,741
37900	Peoria, IL	365,775	366,899	2.3	19,857	146,334	7,263,210	.1276	4,523,862	**1,330**	617,644	**1,311**	118,036	**661**	677,785	305,743
37980	Philadelphia-Camden-Wilmington, PA-NJ-DE-MD	5,799,622	5,687,147	4.6	22,110	2,236,988	128,230,550	2.1466	72,846,541	**21,429**	6,701,179	**14,226**	4,338,211	**24,312**	12,163,100	5,245,024
38060	Phoenix-Mesa-Scottsdale, AZ	3,698,598	3,251,876	45.3	19,860	1,390,757	73,453,060	1.2676	43,123,015	**12,685**	5,754,543	**12,215**	1,636,357	**9,171**	5,887,002	2,114,223
38220	Pine Bluff, AR	105,584	107,341	0.4	13,595	37,911	1,435,430	.0284	995,884	**293**	194,128	**412**	56,210	**315**	139,996	108,425
38300	Pittsburgh, PA	2,404,027	2,431,087	-1.5	18,638	1,011,774	44,806,500	.7956	27,697,371	**8,147**	3,082,330	**6,544**	1,291,132	**7,236**	4,492,970	2,114,185
38340	Pittsfield, MA	132,813	134,953	-3.2	20,327	56,564	2,699,630	.0461	1,559,390	**459**	144,111	**306**	120,070	**673**	319,913	115,743
38540	Pocatello, ID	82,971	83,103	13.7	15,442	30,090	1,281,210	.0251	947,787	**279**	154,338	**327**	19,433	**109**	153,211	42,688
38860	Portland-South Portland-Biddeford, ME	510,775	487,568	10.5	20,763	210,713	10,605,030	.1948	7,739,008	**2,276**	666,059	**1,414**	510,079	**2,859**	1,535,545	296,960
38900	Portland-Vancouver-Beaverton, OR-WA	2,075,083	1,927,881	26.5	20,972	810,015	43,519,560	.7602	27,483,047	**8,085**	4,981,840	**10,575**	1,438,297	**8,061**	3,677,838	843,089
38940	Port St. Lucie-Fort Pierce, FL	357,906	319,426	27.2	21,220	155,543	7,594,610	.1252	3,987,293	**1,173**	507,921	**1,078**	135,595	**759**	652,399	314,490
39100	Poughkeepsie-Newburgh-Middletown, NY	664,094	621,517	9.6	22,088	231,447	14,668,650	.2322	6,806,419	**2,002**	978,011	**2,076**	561,093	**3,144**	1,135,631	396,977
39140	Prescott, AZ	189,588	167,517	55.5	17,740	79,896	3,363,380	.0565	1,644,997	**484**	297,003	**630**	44,109	**247**	338,416	63,090
39300	Providence-New Bedford-Fall River, RI-MA	1,635,332	1,582,997	4.8	19,915	645,096	32,567,900	.5469	17,438,480	**5,130**	2,043,845	**4,338**	1,093,558	**6,128**	3,321,275	1,620,497
39340	Provo-Orem, UT	416,085	376,774	39.9	14,326	117,341	5,961,030	.1174	4,250,508	**1,250**	810,841	**1,721**	141,362	**792**	710,129	74,681
39380	Pueblo, CO	151,054	141,472	15.0	15,098	58,747	2,280,620	.0447	1,659,496	**488**	395,824	**840**	30,025	**168**	218,342	61,578
39460	Punta Gorda, FL	157,100	141,627	27.6	20,982	71,830	3,296,280	.0530	1,568,354	**461**	366,846	**779**	83,926	**470**	252,565	99,775
39540	Racine, WI	193,383	188,831	7.9	20,192	75,070	3,904,770	.0646	2,000,747	**589**	328,944	**698**	47,858	**268**	321,126	122,733
39580	Raleigh-Cary, NC	911,301	797,071	47.3	24,193	371,773	22,047,240	.3722	13,547,177	**3,985**	1,817,305	**3,858**	670,995	**3,760**	1,750,243	571,253
39660	Rapid City, SD	117,781	112,818	9.3	17,033	46,496	2,006,140	.0448	2,201,788	**647**	424,036	**901**	86,319	**483**	187,308	78,381
39740	Reading, PA	388,909	373,638	11.0	19,644	147,702	7,639,890	.1301	4,256,088	**1,252**	525,747	**1,116**	342,408	**1,919**	683,206	249,524
39820	Redding, CA	179,590	163,256	11.0	16,828	70,586	3,022,140	.0528	1,632,661	**480**	274,967	**584**	44,756	**251**	319,925	87,215
39900	Reno-Sparks, NV	384,239	342,885	33.3	20,419	148,610	7,845,900	.1375	4,936,356	**1,452**	767,107	**1,628**	166,226	**932**	744,305	194,817
40060	Richmond, VA	1,150,973	1,096,957	15.6	21,215	469,750	24,417,590	.4073	13,361,603	**3,931**	2,185,048	**4,639**	638,822	**3,581**	1,922,958	786,818
40140	Riverside-San Bernardino-Ontario, CA	3,763,495	3,254,821	25.7	16,568	1,190,886	62,352,000	1.0820	32,473,181	**9,552**	4,207,194	**8,931**	1,932,948	**10,833**	5,780,775	1,423,456
40220	Roanoke, VA	291,205	288,309	7.4	19,372	126,620	5,641,260	.1052	4,134,402	**1,216**	627,184	**1,331**	165,974	**931**	513,895	178,057
40340	Rochester, MN	175,153	163,618	15.3	21,854	69,997	3,827,730	.0649	2,254,139	**663**	462,361	**982**	67,785	**380**	253,624	85,057
40380	Rochester, NY	1,042,130	1,037,831	3.5	21,618	414,464	22,528,540	.3645	11,200,585	**3,295**	1,291,364	**2,741**	517,944	**2,903**	2,214,017	566,798
40420	Rockford, IL	334,044	320,204	12.9	20,196	129,921	6,746,450	.1163	3,993,279	**1,175**	607,860	**1,290**	144,964	**813**	669,329	238,494
40580	Rocky Mount, NC	145,152	143,026	7.3	15,821	55,470	2,296,510	.0420	1,389,971	**408**	165,999	**352**	80,735	**452**	168,128	86,148
40660	Rome, GA	94,225	90,565	11.5	15,797	35,418	1,488,480	.0280	991,673	**292**	214,757	**456**	49,258	**276**	103,109	65,750
40900	Sacramento--Arden-Arcade--Roseville, CA	2,030,311	1,796,857	21.3	20,798	748,723	42,226,880	.6904	21,200,359	**6,236**	2,531,448	**5,374**	1,154,590	**6,471**	3,816,935	889,781
40980	Saginaw-Saginaw Township North, MI	209,117	210,039	-0.9	17,419	81,984	3,642,550	.0737	3,169,109	**932**	578,286	**1,228**	275,821	**1,546**	294,087	145,571
41060	St. Cloud, MN	176,070	167,392	12.4	17,788	65,598	3,131,890	.0619	2,585,072	**761**	485,538	**1,031**	60,761	**340**	324,406	77,711
41100	St. George, UT	108,436	90,354	86.1	14,542	36,802	1,576,890	.0343	1,509,158	**444**	206,294	**438**	52,171	**292**	198,002	27,281
41140	St. Joseph, MO-KS	122,599	122,336	5.6	16,489	48,811	2,021,480	.0374	1,318,431	**388**	289,384	**614**	21,868	**122**	168,958	48,580
41180	St. Louis, MO-IL	2,747,415	2,698,687	4.6	20,789	1,108,215	57,115,590	.9597	31,592,542	**9,293**	4,808,411	**10,207**	1,105,126	**6,193**	4,681,186	2,086,819
41420	Salem, OR	367,908	347,214	24.9	16,849	130,863	6,199,000	.1128	3,871,527	**1,139**	789,346	**1,676**	136,871	**767**	556,517	124,085
41500	Salinas, CA	418,251	401,762	13.0	17,064	123,111	7,137,110	.1276	4,236,459	**1,246**	473,268	**1,005**	285,175	**1,598**	741,345	267,217
41540	Salisbury, MD	113,889	109,391	11.9	16,639	42,577	1,895,040	.0364	1,384,753	**408**	290,801	**617**	57,951	**325**	181,347	85,298
41620	Salt Lake City, UT	1,016,207	968,858	26.1	18,190	343,458	18,484,430	.3608	14,942,479	**4,395**	2,202,106	**4,675**	702,153	**3,935**	2,115,978	302,204
41660	San Angelo, TX	105,120	105,781	5.7	16,180	41,997	1,700,880	.0324	1,195,311	**351**	241,597	**513**	46,860	**263**	165,713	36,321
41700	San Antonio, TX	1,854,472	1,711,703	21.6	17,270	676,131	32,027,530	.5891	21,068,159	**6,196**	2,980,108	**6,327**	1,116,149	**6,257**	3,285,955	808,729
41740	San Diego-Carlsbad-San Marcos, CA	2,966,135	2,813,833	12.6	20,344	1,059,703	60,342,670	1.0169	33,222,905	**9,773**	3,825,198	**8,120**	2,426,068	**13,596**	5,326,312	1,680,462
41780	Sandusky, OH	78,417	79,551	3.6	20,237	32,184	1,586,900	.0274	941,112	**277**	206,509	**438**	50,006	**280**	117,156	69,561
41860	San Francisco-Oakland-Fremont, CA	4,164,518	4,123,740	11.9	27,769	1,599,450	115,645,660	1.7698	55,099,848	**16,208**	6,134,889	**13,023**	4,808,658	**26,949**	10,425,434	3,036,124
41940	San Jose-Sunnyvale-Santa Clara, CA	1,732,851	1,735,819	13.1	29,594	602,990	51,282,100	.8039	27,476,573	**8,082**	3,204,551	**6,802**	2,295,067	**12,862**	4,468,811	1,364,979
42020	San Luis Obispo-Paso Robles, CA	254,929	246,681	13.6	20,201	98,521	5,149,890	.0859	2,720,316	**800**	246,788	**524**	150,585	**844**	543,527	192,222
42060	Santa Barbara-Santa Maria-Goleta, CA	404,260	399,347	8.0	19,379	138,188	7,834,290	.1368	4,700,898	**1,383**	454,866	**966**	331,262	**1,856**	859,109	335,658
42100	Santa Cruz-Watsonville, CA	250,198	255,602	11.3	23,542	91,446	5,890,220	.0942	2,967,816	**873**	302,380	**642**	153,966	**863**	615,612	266,818
42140	Santa Fe, NM	138,622	129,292	30.7	20,935	57,574	2,902,080	.0510	1,871,483	**551**	391,438	**831**	142,197	**797**	198,157	110,379
42220	Santa Rosa-Petaluma, CA	468,851	458,614	18.1	23,674	174,821	11,099,560	.1798	5,877,135	**1,729**	619,805	**1,316**	256,127	**1,435**	1,187,270	345,374
42260	Sarasota-Bradenton-Venice, FL	647,224	589,959	20.5	22,658	289,616	14,664,530	.2443	8,331,292	**2,450**	976,820	**2,074**	496,718	**2,784**	1,292,386	548,115
42340	Savannah, GA	307,995	293,000	13.5	18,342	121,256	5,649,240	.1028	3,741,300	**1,100**	694,530	**1,474**	206,990	**1,160**	521,531	132,810
42540	Scranton--Wilkes-Barre, PA	549,692	560,625	-2.5	17,114	232,147	9,407,410	.1763	6,528,589	**1,921**	861,310	**1,829**	306,501	**1,718**	1,190,018	453,584
42660	Seattle-Tacoma-Bellevue, WA	3,171,685	3,043,878	18.9	23,150	1,271,838	73,423,950	1.2254	42,438,914	**12,483**	6,116,628	**12,985**	2,512,922	**14,083**	5,998,962	1,694,877
43100	Sheboygan, WI	113,582	112,646	8.4	20,355	45,994	2,311,980	.0379	1,149,763	**338**	226,999	**482**	16,678	**93**	182,279	51,099
43300	Sherman-Denison, TX	116,532	110,595	16.4	17,785	45,226	2,072,480	.0389	1,481,541	**436**	372,920	**792**	32,470	**182**	172,110	55,084
43340	Shreveport-Bossier City, LA	379,073	375,965	4.5	16,335	150,373	6,192,250	.1182	4,392,052	**1,292**	805,798	**1,711**	183,191	**1,027**	541,120	191,964
43580	Sioux City, IA-NE-SD	142,792	143,053	8.9	16,664	53,469	2,379,540	.0947	7,301,511	**2,148**	233,422	**495**	60,740	**341**	264,906	66,493
43620	Sioux Falls, SD	201,734	187,093	21.9	19,655	80,771	3,965,010	.0877	4,494,856	**1,322**	643,959	**1,367**	66,160	**371**	354,750	187,221
43780	South Bend-Mishawaka, IN-MI	317,967	316,663	6.8	17,891	124,276	5,688,590	.1047	3,837,330	**1,129**	708,062	**1,503**	142,891	**801**	441,894	270,890
43900	Spartanburg, SC	263,575	253,791	11.9	17,658	103,158	4,654,080	.0862	3,173,259	**933**	462,662	**982**	129,536	**726**	417,776	215,655
44060	Spokane, WA	435,145	417,939	15.7	17,174	170,747	7,473,250	.1385	5,018,057	**1,476**	886,324	**1,881**	231,274	**1,296**	770,118	205,222
44100	Springfield, IL	205,434	201,437	6.3	21,081	86,436	4,330,730	.0739	2,539,671	**747**	448,852	**953**	80,482	**451**	334,831	160,456
44140	Springfield, MA	691,167	680,014	1.0	19,479	269,913	13,463,310	.2241	6,876,412	**2,023**	689,313	**1,463**	327,408	**1,835**	1,412,300	508,321
44180	Springfield, MO	389,665	368,374	23.3	16,682	160,518	6,500,430	.1280	5,132,095	**1,509**	778,420	**1,652**	108,006	**606**	536,260	223,210
44220	Springfield, OH	142,925	144,742	-1.9	18,956	57,971	2,709,270	.0460	1,449,668	**426**	256,832	**545**	30,877	**173**	231,995	132,395
44300	State College, PA	143,518	135,758	9.7	15,772	52,665	2,263,590	.0432	1,572,637	**463**	206,017	**437**	90,830	**509**	222,749	82,855
44700	Stockton, CA	654,288	563,598	17.3	16,392	210,061	10,725,080	.1822	5,087,457	**1,497**	677,193	**1,438**	219,393	**1,230**	911,463	340,141
44940	Sumter, SC	106,361	104,646	2.0	15,246	40,297	1,621,630	.0297	959,454	**282**	136,905	**291**	50,276	**282**	128,249	45,197

Core Based Statistical Areas (CBSAs): Population / Income / Sales#†, Continued

CODE	CORE BASED STATISTICAL AREA	POPULATION Estimate 7/1/04	Census 4/1/00	% Change 4/1/90-4/1/00	PER CAPITA INCOME 2003 ($1,000)	HOUSEHOLDS Estimate 7/1/04	DISPOSABLE INCOME 2003 ($1,000)	MARKET ABILITY INDEX 2003	TOTAL RETAIL SALES 2003 Sales ($1,000)	Ranally Sales Units	GENERAL MERCHANDISE 2003 Sales ($1,000)	Ranally Sales Units	APPAREL STORE SALES 2003 Sales ($1,000)	Ranally Sales Units	FOOD STORE SALES 2003 ($1,000)	HEALTH & DRUG STORE 2003 ($1,000)
45060	Syracuse, NY	655,449	650,154	-1.5	19,766	260,632	12,955,600	.2165	6,781,841	1,995	712,363	1,513	343,366	1,924	1,314,851	467,463
45220	Tallahassee, FL	330,177	320,304	23.6	19,051	136,318	6,290,160	.1088	3,627,111	1,066	608,524	1,291	168,444	944	601,027	232,307
45300	Tampa-St. Petersburg-Clearwater, FL	2,574,498	2,395,997	15.9	21,239	1,157,320	54,679,370	.9513	34,351,447	10,104	4,164,175	8,840	1,446,023	8,104	4,811,738	2,259,763
45460	Terre Haute, IN	169,396	170,943	2.6	15,424	67,411	2,612,830	.0634	3,305,316	972	512,318	1,087	108,064	606	216,215	100,212
45500	Texarkana, TX-Texarkana, AR	132,208	129,749	8.0	15,062	50,531	1,991,340	.0402	1,584,069	466	306,315	650	79,403	445	170,818	41,392
45780	Toledo, OH	661,399	659,188	0.8	19,068	271,511	12,611,450	.2286	8,447,768	2,485	1,321,643	2,807	324,354	1,817	1,182,481	472,292
45820	Topeka, KS	226,731	224,551	6.8	18,991	93,085	4,305,870	.0752	2,554,211	751	496,988	1,055	79,377	445	342,060	172,768
45940	Trenton-Ewing, NJ	365,448	350,761	7.7	25,680	133,605	9,384,820	.1447	4,366,020	1,284	398,348	846	330,116	1,850	753,962	416,720
46060	Tucson, AZ	907,511	843,746	26.5	17,888	365,815	16,233,410	.2752	8,272,791	2,434	1,284,384	2,726	326,802	1,831	1,268,524	505,873
46140	Tulsa, OK	886,021	859,532	12.9	18,696	363,016	16,564,680	.2949	10,343,623	3,044	2,059,466	4,371	319,925	1,793	1,142,592	558,925
46220	Tuscaloosa, AL	195,077	192,034	9.0	16,808	80,512	3,278,800	.0602	2,097,720	617	358,142	761	97,052	545	275,502	114,994
46340	Tyler, TX	186,882	174,706	15.5	17,504	72,108	3,271,110	.0660	2,829,077	832	474,715	1,008	187,114	1,049	337,370	129,863
46540	Utica-Rome, NY	297,571	299,896	-5.3	17,516	117,786	5,212,330	.0891	2,695,644	793	385,726	819	101,736	570	444,071	253,056
46660	Valdosta, GA	123,021	119,560	20.5	14,284	46,884	1,757,200	.0364	1,456,291	428	201,815	428	88,759	498	183,373	43,188
46700	Vallejo-Fairfield, CA	417,390	394,542	15.9	21,717	140,762	9,064,370	.1414	3,923,677	1,154	663,323	1,408	193,021	1,082	753,501	156,794
46940	Vero Beach, FL	122,827	112,947	25.2	24,627	61,075	3,024,800	.0496	1,708,268	503	244,642	519	159,902	896	262,262	129,783
47020	Victoria, TX	113,403	111,663	12.3	16,652	41,144	1,888,420	.0359	1,340,823	395	257,232	546	57,088	320	209,401	52,919
47220	Vineland-Millville-Bridgeton, NJ	150,283	146,438	6.1	17,007	50,856	2,555,870	.0455	1,488,762	438	144,840	307	48,684	273	322,667	121,082
47260	Virginia Beach-Norfolk-Newport News, VA-NC	1,656,100	1,576,370	8.8	18,493	631,044	30,626,410	.5304	17,321,808	5,098	2,782,538	5,908	968,399	5,426	2,405,325	788,584
47300	Visalia-Porterville, CA	398,103	368,021	18.0	12,544	117,213	4,993,740	.0943	2,716,977	799	427,942	908	106,651	598	549,480	145,301
47380	Waco, TX	221,739	213,517	12.9	15,426	83,405	3,420,440	.0655	2,358,225	694	434,782	923	83,366	467	383,400	91,734
47580	Warner Robins, GA	123,475	110,765	24.2	19,588	47,679	2,418,660	.0411	1,338,286	394	191,144	406	58,498	328	182,002	37,920
47900	Washington-Arlington-Alexandria, DC-VA-MD-WV	5,179,798	4,796,183	16.3	27,551	1,993,702	142,708,760	2.0960	57,695,266	16,970	7,221,135	15,329	3,808,065	21,343	9,724,167	2,981,653
47940	Waterloo-Cedar Falls, IA	161,643	163,706	3.2	17,148	64,107	2,771,910	.0532	2,055,123	605	316,488	672	61,868	347	246,323	107,125
48140	Wausau, WI	127,589	125,834	9.0	19,297	50,040	2,462,120	.0466	1,887,978	555	362,120	769	42,550	238	218,595	38,765
48260	Weirton-Steubenville, WV-OH	127,547	132,008	-7.4	16,455	54,147	2,098,810	.0357	1,010,343	297	175,748	373	32,493	182	203,887	107,682
48300	Wenatchee, WA	102,502	99,219	26.5	16,039	37,283	1,644,060	.0320	1,219,738	359	233,690	496	27,525	154	229,375	42,448
48540	Wheeling, WV-OH	149,538	153,172	-3.8	15,785	64,006	2,360,440	.0455	1,691,503	497	300,727	638	70,216	394	264,938	117,677
48620	Wichita, KS	586,332	571,166	11.7	18,629	228,064	10,922,760	.1897	6,269,005	1,844	1,192,543	2,531	248,202	1,391	932,851	282,840
48660	Wichita Falls, TX	149,063	151,524	7.9	16,266	57,706	2,424,590	.0455	1,637,748	482	310,345	659	46,467	261	238,255	75,558
48700	Williamsport, PA	117,940	120,044	1.1	16,296	47,574	1,921,940	.0378	1,491,653	439	223,336	474	62,585	351	255,638	108,531
48900	Wilmington, NC	299,048	274,532	37.2	20,437	135,026	6,111,590	.1138	4,591,501	1,351	591,267	1,255	185,424	1,040	656,474	236,236
49020	Winchester, VA-WV	112,471	102,997	22.4	18,576	44,686	2,089,240	.0399	1,605,681	472	355,190	754	57,248	321	179,262	104,659
49180	Winston-Salem, NC	442,297	421,961	16.7	19,940	182,853	8,819,330	.1580	5,846,125	1,719	774,596	1,645	280,777	1,574	717,320	323,855
49340	Worcester, MA	784,595	750,963	5.8	21,778	300,867	17,087,140	.2811	9,059,973	2,665	882,285	1,873	405,829	2,274	1,627,115	628,138
49420	Yakima, WA	228,066	222,581	17.9	13,316	74,206	3,037,030	.0593	1,979,472	582	431,605	916	60,404	339	329,183	54,696
49620	York-Hanover, PA	398,969	381,751	12.4	20,544	157,278	8,196,390	.1339	4,069,282	1,197	563,866	1,197	146,775	823	757,223	207,738
49660	Youngstown-Warren-Boardman, OH-PA	590,415	602,964	-1.7	17,455	241,263	10,305,630	.1917	7,069,168	2,079	954,927	2,027	377,795	2,118	939,871	470,637
49700	Yuba City, CA	151,010	139,149	13.5	14,753	51,097	2,227,910	.0395	1,120,098	330	218,867	465	28,829	162	243,792	75,167
49740	Yuma, AZ	174,609	160,026	49.7	13,194	58,992	2,303,760	.0445	1,439,675	423	334,372	710	34,477	193	209,344	71,584
	Micropolitan Statistical Area Totals	30,034,218	29,412,298	10.0	16,228	11,702,873	487,405,540	9.0556	316,905,065	93,225	52,706,414	111,879	11,579,749	64,892	48,966,496	16,130,159
	U.S. Totals	274,129,922	261,992,238	13.6	20,038	104,998,830	5,493,122,910	94.7450	3,238,790,398	952,715	452,554,531	960,683	175,155,745	981,614	477,511,871	183,330,633

Source: Devonshire Associates Ltd. and Scan/US, Inc. 2004.

Estimates for Total Retail Sales, General Merchandise, Apparel Store Sales, Food Store Sales, and Health and Drug Store Sales are based on data from the U.S. Census Bureau's 1997 Economic Census and utilize the North American Industry Classification System (NAICS).

† CBSA totals are for Metropolitan Core Based Statistical Areas. A U.S. total for Micropolitan Core Based Statistical Areas is also provided.

Combined Statistical Areas (CSAs): Population/Income/Sales#

CSAs are groups of two or more adjacent CBSAs with a high degree of employment interchange.

CODE	COMBINED STATISTICAL AREAS	POPULATION Estimate 7/1/04	POPULATION Census 4/1/00	POPULATION % Change 4/1/90-4/1/00	PER CAPITA INCOME 2003	HOUSE-HOLDS Estimate 7/1/04	DISPOSABLE INCOME 2003 ($1,000)	MARKET ABILITY INDEX 2003	TOTAL RETAIL SALES 2003 Sales ($1,000)	TOTAL RETAIL SALES Ranally Sales Units	GENERAL MERCHANDISE 2003 Sales ($1,000)	GENERAL MERCHANDISE Ranally Sales Units	APPAREL STORE SALES 2003 Sales ($1,000)	APPAREL STORE SALES Ranally Sales Units	FOOD STORE SALES 2003 ($1,000)	HEALTH & DRUG STORE 2003 ($1,000)
102	Albany-Corvallis-Lebanon, OR	186,880	181,222	11.8	18,182	73,452	3,397,900	.0571	1,696,513	499	370,312	786	56,472	316	304,936	64,978
104	Albany-Schenectady-Amsterdam, NY	1,140,691	1,118,095	1.9	21,217	464,215	24,202,580	.3938	12,108,949	3,562	1,335,999	2,836	636,616	3,568	1,814,133	792,377
112	Ames-Boone, IA	110,209	106,205	6.8	17,265	41,422	1,902,800	.0338	1,111,534	327	203,738	432	39,639	222	177,911	47,024
118	Appleton-Oshkosh-Neenah, WI	372,541	358,365	13.7	20,783	150,343	7,742,360	.1368	5,045,676	1,484	701,353	1,488	196,624	1,102	592,168	204,798
120	Asheville-Brevard, NC	415,007	398,505	19.5	18,437	177,198	7,651,560	.1441	5,622,738	1,653	784,191	1,664	254,973	1,428	712,866	311,602
122	Atlanta-Sandy Springs-Gainesville, GA-AL	5,045,068	4,548,344	37.1	22,336	1,932,397	112,687,980	1.8988	65,832,561	19,365	8,655,778	18,375	3,445,944	19,313	9,478,534	2,628,997
132	Baton Rouge-Pierre Part, LA	750,952	729,361	12.8	17,700	288,140	13,292,140	.2403	8,406,550	2,471	1,515,026	3,217	347,124	1,946	1,113,993	395,918
138	Beckley-Oak Hill, WV	126,492	126,799	1.6	13,970	52,093	1,767,050	.0363	1,405,186	414	301,221	640	29,447	165	153,749	96,675
140	Bend-Prineville, OR	154,810	134,549	51.1	18,821	61,321	2,913,620	.0551	2,193,671	646	494,844	1,051	66,085	370	325,238	65,222
142	Birmingham-Hoover-Cullman, AL	1,157,590	1,129,721	10.3	18,763	465,487	21,719,750	.3890	13,851,720	4,075	2,219,039	4,710	696,240	3,901	1,903,078	673,179
148	Boston-Worcester-Manchester, MA-NH	5,843,682	5,715,698	6.9	24,258	2,259,196	141,756,350	2.3372	80,858,202	23,784	8,143,311	17,288	5,225,057	29,283	13,545,467	5,221,961
154	Brownsville-Harlingen-Raymondville, TX	391,958	355,309	27.9	9,480	114,664	3,715,660	.0840	2,851,056	838	649,080	1,377	196,477	1,101	540,429	115,231
160	Buffalo-Niagara-Cattaraugus, NY	1,239,456	1,254,066	-1.5	19,378	502,976	24,018,120	.3999	12,223,245	3,596	1,352,853	2,871	688,701	3,860	2,176,362	964,973
164	Cape Girardeau-Sikeston-Jackson, MO-IL	132,796	130,734	6.9	15,745	52,494	2,090,930	.0425	1,748,357	515	357,925	760	48,680	272	184,291	90,044
172	Charlotte-Gastonia-Salisbury, NC-SC	2,064,635	1,897,034	26.3	20,916	833,007	43,183,680	.7377	25,352,119	7,457	3,405,134	7,228	1,114,849	6,246	3,430,036	1,359,560
174	Chattanooga-Cleveland-Athens, TN-GA	647,130	629,561	11.8	17,939	264,876	11,608,700	.2076	7,160,003	2,105	1,203,978	2,556	343,129	1,923	964,767	438,583
176	Chicago-Naperville-Michigan City, IL-IN-WI	9,621,008	9,312,255	11.1	21,199	3,485,585	203,960,550	3.3986	111,043,809	32,665	12,923,896	27,433	6,161,520	34,531	15,232,013	9,164,692
178	Cincinnati-Middletown-Wilmington, OH-KY-IN	2,100,487	2,050,175	9.0	20,957	849,874	44,019,420	.7437	24,933,402	7,334	3,644,964	7,737	1,094,936	6,137	3,562,237	1,352,975
180	Claremont-Lebanon, NH-VT	214,679	207,845	7.3	19,308	87,975	4,145,000	.0750	2,781,640	819	254,814	540	63,817	357	599,814	113,826
184	Cleveland-Akron-Elyria, OH	2,943,497	2,945,831	3.0	20,150	1,205,351	59,310,910	1.0353	36,496,956	10,736	3,907,507	8,296	1,686,648	9,453	5,279,080	3,587,625
188	Clovis-Portales, NM	63,743	63,062	7.0	13,300	24,320	847,780	.0165	551,956	163	121,015	257	25,787	144	69,361	27,247
192	Columbia-Newberry, SC	715,942	683,266	17.5	19,104	286,393	13,677,230	.2412	8,392,908	2,468	1,510,662	3,207	399,532	2,240	1,152,718	430,088
194	Columbus-Auburn-Opelika, GA-AL	432,893	420,965	11.2	15,749	172,159	6,817,810	.1242	4,045,242	1,190	696,641	1,479	232,374	1,301	653,004	211,231
198	Columbus-Marion-Chillicothe, OH	1,920,053	1,835,189	13.7	21,264	797,242	40,828,560	.7170	26,434,408	7,777	3,577,947	7,596	1,210,819	6,786	3,243,392	1,067,715
200	Columbus-West Point, MS	81,884	83,565	3.9	14,410	30,941	1,179,920	.0248	1,024,407	301	222,686	473	46,077	258	129,409	56,533
202	Corbin-London, KY	94,038	88,580	15.4	12,441	37,305	1,169,970	.0252	980,344	288	239,286	508	20,536	115	73,765	44,953
204	Corpus Christi-Kingsville, TX	439,671	435,243	9.2	15,607	160,668	6,861,760	.1297	4,586,811	1,349	763,098	1,620	211,857	1,187	809,775	172,056
206	Dallas-Fort Worth, TX	5,918,901	5,346,119	29.2	21,374	2,213,521	126,510,800	2.1693	76,179,757	22,408	10,268,487	21,799	3,826,710	21,446	10,310,320	3,033,487
212	Dayton-Springfield-Greenville, OH	1,080,951	1,085,094	0.4	20,211	452,234	21,847,070	.3721	12,415,836	3,652	2,096,922	4,452	480,463	2,692	1,717,322	657,350
214	Deltona-Daytona Beach-Palm Coast, FL	542,645	493,175	23.5	20,372	245,026	11,054,840	.1836	5,769,501	1,698	770,128	1,635	219,433	1,230	968,057	386,603
216	Denver-Aurora-Boulder, CO	2,617,582	2,449,054	30.6	23,459	1,034,339	61,406,030	1.0130	34,423,520	10,126	4,742,420	10,067	1,473,691	8,259	4,966,066	1,214,922
218	Des Moines-Newton-Pella, IA	579,709	550,659	14.4	20,345	231,506	11,794,270	.2044	7,141,264	2,099	933,267	1,982	241,597	1,354	962,683	357,177
220	Detroit-Warren-Flint, MI	5,431,817	5,357,538	5.1	22,010	2,148,382	119,553,300	2.0510	73,386,052	21,588	11,876,491	25,212	3,247,040	18,196	8,697,538	4,962,736
222	Dothan-Enterprise-Ozark, AL	228,431	223,605	6.4	16,412	93,528	3,749,100	.0719	2,707,659	797	512,640	1,088	101,868	570	268,691	109,450
232	Eau Claire-Menomonie, WI	193,240	188,195	8.5	17,323	76,490	3,347,440	.0695	3,113,463	916	628,743	1,334	105,387	590	341,964	145,398
242	Fairmont-Clarksburg, WV	147,965	148,742	-0.0	15,219	61,646	2,251,810	.0437	1,605,380	473	312,672	664	55,884	312	202,882	103,935
244	Fargo-Wahpeton, ND-MN	204,940	199,503	11.5	18,027	84,417	3,694,470	.0748	3,271,597	963	456,830	969	95,370	535	303,925	156,526
248	Findlay-Tiffin, OH	131,174	129,978	3.8	18,868	51,794	2,474,960	.0447	1,629,506	480	292,593	621	44,346	248	179,769	71,278
252	Fond du Lac-Beaver Dam, WI	185,465	183,193	9.9	19,045	71,444	3,532,170	.0596	1,868,688	549	359,642	763	39,156	219	239,921	65,137
256	Fort Polk South-De Ridder, LA	83,720	85,517	-7.1	14,343	30,473	1,200,780	.0212	573,353	168	130,142	276	15,999	90	55,200	18,417
258	Fort Wayne-Huntington-Auburn, IN	562,961	548,416	11.0	18,853	220,158	10,613,510	.1887	6,644,146	1,955	1,173,470	2,491	222,202	1,245	747,210	352,868
260	Fresno-Madera, CA	1,003,162	922,516	22.1	13,501	309,778	13,543,840	.2538	7,751,818	2,280	1,028,372	2,183	312,576	1,752	1,425,308	478,421
266	Grand Rapids-Muskegon-Holland, MI	1,306,806	1,254,661	15.8	19,238	489,299	25,140,220	.4458	15,794,441	4,646	3,214,549	6,823	513,660	2,879	1,554,421	743,088
268	Greensboro--Winston-Salem--High Point, NC	1,474,109	1,414,656	18.1	19,374	606,611	28,559,100	.5129	18,760,139	5,517	2,401,759	5,100	864,605	4,846	2,443,232	1,130,735
273	Greenville-Spartanburg-Anderson, SC	1,172,803	1,128,104	15.5	18,071	468,544	21,193,860	.3850	13,820,857	4,065	1,969,209	4,180	656,444	3,679	1,922,045	813,882
274	Gulfport-Biloxi-Pascagoula, MS	405,152	396,754	16.8	17,628	160,456	7,142,130	.1269	4,245,104	1,249	1,036,132	2,200	137,635	771	491,985	185,494
276	Harrisburg-Carlisle-Lebanon, PA	643,547	629,401	7.0	20,421	261,966	13,141,920	.2363	8,927,130	2,626	910,112	1,932	306,222	1,716	1,284,021	475,386
278	Hartford-West Hartford-Willimantic, CT	1,300,723	1,257,709	2.6	26,042	510,817	33,873,320	.5173	15,390,856	4,527	1,367,425	2,902	1,074,994	6,025	2,714,548	1,155,441
288	Houston-Baytown-Huntsville, TX	5,287,717	4,815,122	24.9	19,471	1,930,332	102,956,350	1.7874	60,875,567	17,907	9,398,782	19,952	3,419,039	19,161	9,258,704	2,856,646
290	Huntsville-Decatur, AL	510,286	488,243	15.0	20,415	208,478	10,417,370	.1784	6,063,650	1,783	1,123,176	2,384	292,951	1,641	748,149	257,436
292	Idaho Falls-Blackfoot, ID	152,191	143,412	13.5	15,757	51,831	2,398,030	.0458	1,661,447	489	336,106	714	32,401	181	249,961	55,791
294	Indianapolis-Anderson-Columbus, IN	1,933,566	1,843,588	15.6	20,699	779,712	40,022,440	.7060	25,880,888	7,611	4,369,895	9,277	973,965	5,458	2,585,159	1,673,842
296	Ithaca-Cortland, NY	151,712	145,100	1.4	17,682	58,614	2,682,500	.0451	1,309,193	385	130,463	277	40,180	225	319,814	87,510
297	Jackson-Humboldt, TN	158,277	155,529	13.4	17,058	63,839	2,699,930	.0521	2,049,317	603	438,999	932	115,610	648	195,690	105,842
298	Jackson-Yazoo City, MS	542,282	525,346	11.2	16,933	202,766	9,182,490	.1757	6,721,488	1,978	1,333,457	2,831	275,194	1,542	696,249	375,598
304	Johnson City-Kingsport-Bristol (Tri-Cities), TN-VA	487,711	480,091	10.1	16,614	211,669	8,102,670	.1520	5,525,720	1,625	1,048,519	2,225	228,312	1,281	700,585	314,504
312	Kansas City-Overland Park-Kansas City, MO-KS	1,993,187	1,901,070	12.1	21,165	797,686	42,185,240	.7249	25,424,527	7,478	3,832,874	8,137	960,833	5,386	3,098,968	1,291,745
314	Knoxville-Sevierville-La Follette, TN	812,881	779,013	16.6	18,517	343,990	15,052,320	.2958	12,506,614	3,680	1,967,734	4,176	675,894	3,787	1,464,469	627,026
316	Kokomo-Peru, IN	137,405	137,623	2.8	19,996	57,018	2,747,610	.0478	1,664,270	489	333,751	708	38,611	216	177,398	124,889
318	Lafayette-Acadiana, LA	523,429	512,720	10.7	14,780	199,389	7,736,290	.1562	6,088,267	1,791	1,132,164	2,403	243,019	1,363	784,602	384,109
320	Lafayette-Frankfort, IN	220,356	212,407	11.9	16,946	83,634	3,734,240	.0687	2,416,314	711	514,155	1,092	86,202	483	225,734	128,991
324	Lake Charles-Jennings, LA	224,648	225,003	8.1	16,856	89,201	3,786,760	.0710	2,601,430	765	620,807	1,317	95,386	534	320,699	136,759
330	Lansing-East Lansing-Owosso, MI	531,124	519,415	3.4	19,803	210,713	10,517,990	.1850	6,562,022	1,930	1,456,052	3,091	215,506	1,208	763,689	353,606
332	Las Vegas-Paradise-Pahrump, NV	1,674,272	1,408,250	85.5	19,533	635,569	32,703,180	.5664	19,230,345	5,657	2,591,782	5,502	1,239,038	6,944	2,972,525	817,179
336	Lexington-Fayette--Frankfort--Richmond, KY	629,233	602,773	17.4	19,628	266,610	12,350,650	.2179	7,736,153	2,275	1,235,396	2,621	390,274	2,188	865,253	459,582
338	Lima-Van Wert-Wapakoneta, OH	184,075	184,743	-0.0	17,873	72,270	3,289,950	.0612	2,296,246	675	455,257	966	68,957	387	234,063	135,684
340	Little Rock-North Little Rock-Pine Bluff, AR	810,124	785,024	12.7	18,166	327,056	14,716,540	.2761	10,612,920	3,121	2,183,614	4,634	408,301	2,288	967,107	423,816
346	Longview-Marshall, TX	262,444	256,152	7.8	16,001	100,704	4,199,390	.0808	3,028,038	890	543,382	1,153	98,785	553	416,230	129,084
348	Los Angeles-Long Beach-Riverside, CA	17,537,912	16,373,645	12.7	18,226	5,692,637	319,649,410	5.4853	173,046,034	50,903	20,114,151	42,698	13,323,489	74,670	28,882,115	9,363,779
350	Louisville-Elizabethtown-Scottsburg, KY-IN	1,332,297	1,292,482	9.7	20,012	555,869	26,662,550	.4503	14,610,835	4,297	2,442,025	5,185	578,033	3,240	1,616,836	892,916
352	Lubbock-Levelland, TX	282,456	272,416	7.2	15,159	108,821	4,281,640	.0895	3,764,093	1,107	564,489	1,198	169,032	947	545,684	115,264
354	Lumberton-Laurinburg, NC	162,220	159,337	14.7	12,652	59,394	2,052,450	.0422	1,520,452	447	209,191	444	67,768	380	225,795	75,796
356	Macon-Warner Robins-Fort Valley, GA	375,193	356,801	12.6	17,606	145,309	6,605,730	.1200	4,244,041	1,248	686,565	1,458	205,054	1,149	609,525	185,380
358	Madison-Baraboo, WI	591,173	556,999	16.2	21,537	245,931	12,731,990	.2357	9,680,378	2,848	1,161,992	2,466	270,988	1,519	1,051,667	377,534
360	Mansfield-Bucyrus, OH	173,916	175,818	1.0	17,451	69,649	3,034,990	.0558	2,008,228	591	415,086	881	58,513	327	232,377	129,596
372	Midland-Odessa, TX	243,009	237,132	5.1	16,218	91,901	3,941,070	.0780	3,102,129	913	618,214	1,312	121,450	680	383,961	117,885
376	Milwaukee-Racine-Waukesha, WI	1,711,775	1,689,572	5.1	20,990	701,417	35,929,530	.6023	19,829,104	5,833	2,797,864	5,939	654,970	3,671	2,985,091	1,322,868
378	Minneapolis-St. Paul-St. Cloud, MN-WI	3,436,228	3,271,888	16.4	23,128	1,357,818	79,473,720	1.3901	53,175,698	15,642	7,408,052	15,728	1,864,380	10,447	6,849,698	2,288,437
380	Mobile-Daphne-Fairhope, AL	554,939	540,258	13.3	16,905	215,349	9,381,040	.1693	5,716,074	1,681	1,129,778	2,398	334,609	1,876	769,574	320,389
384	Monroe-Bastrop, LA	201,714	201,074	3.2	15,430	81,027	3,112,400	.0601	2,200,568	647	568,649	1,207	97,994	549	250,937	99,798
388	Montgomery-Alexander City, AL	406,218	400,205	12.7	17,607	160,214	7,152,140	.1298	4,564,119	1,343	871,976	1,852	212,103	1,188	581,099	266,269
392	Morristown-Newport, TN	163,011	156,646	20.7	15,210	66,712	2,479,390	.0468	1,621,067	477	333,113	707	48,713	273	214,748	88,862
396	Myrtle Beach-Conway-Georgetown, SC	274,864	252,426	32.6	18,375	116,162	5,050,660	.1008	4,356,974	1,282	746,611	1,585	446,770	2,504	644,802	200,962
400	Nashville-Davidson--Murfreesboro--Columbia, TN	1,463,732	1,381,287	25.2	21,333	595,646	31,225,800	.5512	20,577,712	6,051	3,427,826	7,277	1,026,971	5,755	2,576,983	1,110,984
406	New Orleans-Metairie-Bogalusa, LA	1,362,195	1,360,436	4.0	17,742	552,861	24,168,080	.4339	14,970,158	4,404	2,534,685	5,382	885,240	4,961	2,184,381	1,122,474
408	New York-Newark-Bridgeport, NY-NJ-CT-PA	21,888,232	21,361,797	8.4	23,233	8,002,189	508,531,540	8.0061	240,012,532	70,603	21,514,205	45,668	24,026,387	134,648	39,749,627	18,988,543
416	Oklahoma City-Shawnee, OK	1,212,183	1,160,942	12.7	17,878	490,201	21,671,330	.3894	13,552,871	3,986	2,344,548	4,976	473,093	2,652	1,536,145	735,180
420	Omaha-Council Bluffs-Fremont, NE-IA	837,058	803,201	11.5	19,715	331,583	16,502,180	.3042	11,854,234	3,488	1,471,367	3,124	411,223	2,303	1,511,004	662,088
422	Orlando-The Villages, FL	1,912,510	1,697,906	35.1	20,582	761,426	39,362,490	.6969	25,645,422	7,543	3,518,099	7,468	1,661,920	9,313	3,428,365	1,401,293
424	Paducah-Mayfield, KY-IL	134,855	135,793	6.0	16,909	57,778	2,280,240	.0446	1,770,380	520	438,483	931	94,857	532	157,168	102,666
426	Peoria-Canton, IL	403,241	405,149	2.1	19,479	161,027	7,854,810	.1379	4,819,303	1,417	665,551	1,413	125,395	702	734,969	329,186
428	Philadelphia-Camden-Vineland, PA-NJ-DE-MD	5,949,905	5,833,585	4.7	21,981	2,287,844	130,786,420	2.1921	74,335,302	21,867	6,846,019	14,533	4,386,895	24,585	12,485,766	5,366,106
430	Pittsburgh-New Castle, PA	2,497,034	2,525,730	-1.5	18,531	1,048,784	46,271,950	.8223	28,570,653	8,404	3,185,899	6,764	1,303,807	7,307	4,638,473	2,171,745
438	Portland-Lewiston-South Portland, ME	617,640	591,361	8.2	20,198	255,274	12,475,260	.2338	9,501,748	2,795	881,724	1,872	533,165	2,988	1,797,859	364,561
450	Raleigh-Durham-Cary, NC	1,467,394	1,314,589	37.9	22,536	599,600	33,068,980	.5570	19,400,996	5,708	2,436,512	5,173	952,146	5,335	2,792,180	928,748
464	Rochester-Batavia-Seneca Falls, NY	1,137,836	1,131,543	3.2	21,362	450,876	24,306,590	.3937	12,023,399	3,537	1,384,174	2,938	615,921	3,453	2,327,081	606,271
466	Rockford-Freeport-Rochelle, IL	435,367	420,215	11.2	20,043	169,794	8,726,250	.1479	4,860,441	1,430	727,201	1,544	162,672	913	796,753	290,201
472	Sacramento--Arden-Arcade--Truckee, CA-NV	2,172,596	1,930,149	21.6	20,937	806,184	45,488,550	.7394	22,453,535	6,605	2,567,694	5,451	1,208,099	6,771	4,161,254	986,711
474	Saginaw-Bay City-Saginaw Township North, MI	318,346	320,196	-1.1	17,748	127,154	5,650,040	.1121	4,701,101	1,383	910,278	1,933	323,609	1,814	446,520	221,362
476	St. Louis-St. Charles-Farmington, MO-IL	2,806,063	2,754,328	4.7	20,651	1,130,605	57,948,300	.9760	32,168,780	9,463	4,964,678	10,539	1,123,959	6,299	4,760,642	2,134,608
480	Salisbury-Ocean Pines, MD	164,439	155,934	17.4	17,923	64,423	2,947,230	.0556	2,136,598	629	378,078	802	156,345	876	329,800	130,384
482	Salt Lake City-Ogden-Clearfield, UT	1,556,404	1,469,474	26.0	17,904	517,253	27,865,890	.5301	20,769,918	6,109	3,199,464	6,793	858,281	4,810	3,063,744	419,409
488	San Jose-San Francisco-Oakland, CA	7,167,754	7,092,596	12.8	27,346	2,658,273	196,006,880	3.0372	96,797,171	28,473	11,012,556	23,377	7,831,991	43,892	17,819,946	5,252,128
492	Santa Fe-Espanola, NM	179,180	170,482	27.9	19,293	72,969	3,456,960	.0613	2,180,922	642	401,794	853	144,518	810	260,995	142,177
496	Savannah-Hinesville-Fort Stewart, GA	377,050	364,914	15.1	17,498	145,355	6,597,710	.1193	4,149,450	1,220	784,886	1,666	224,943	1,261	577,894	143,818
500	Seattle-Tacoma-Olympia, WA	3,772,492	3,604,165	19.8	22,677	1,504,222	85,549,830	1.4229	48,295,707	14,207	7,388,809	15,685	2,669,246	14,960	7,029,248	1,939,996
508	Shreveport-Bossier City-Minden, LA	420,366	417,796	4.0	16,139	166,993	6,784,350	.1296	4,783,573	1,407	871,560	1,851	195,079	1,094	606,540	207,474
512	Sioux City-Vermillion, IA-NE-SD	155,884	156,590	8.3	16,278	58,350	2,537,450	.0981	7,432,978	2,187	240,216	509	61,092	343	284,120	69,632
526	Sunbury-Lewisburg-Selinsgrove, PA	173,959	173,726	2.4	15,511	66,883	2,698,280	.0494	1,615,391	475	208,986	443	32,710	184	253,427	97,576
532	Syracuse-Auburn, NY	737,104	732,117	-1.4	19,587	292,002	14,437,390	.2404	7,411,093	2,180	799,327	1,698	360,769	2,022	1,428,189	527,700
534	Toledo-Fremont, OH	723,132	720,980	0.7	19,050	296,116	13,776,000	.2483	9,058,026	2,665	1,423,436	3,023	337,056	1,888	1,280,690	505,485
538	Tulsa-Bartlesville, OK	935,185	908,528	12.3	18,659	383,509	17,449,790	.3094	10,745,316	3,162	2,194,604	4,658	333,805	1,871	1,177,080	579,545
540	Tyler-Jacksonville, TX	234,746	221,365	15.1	16,577	89,227	3,891,350	.0779	3,198,277	941	549,472	1,167	194,845	1,092	404,228	142,619
542	Union City-Martin, TN-KY	73,797	75,097	4.4	15,334	30,143	1,131,610	.0207	665,553	196	165,704	351	31,622	178	70,942	33,073
548	Washington-Baltimore-Northern Virginia, DC-MD-VA-WV	8,023,042	7,538,385	13.1	25,821	3,098,265	207,166,280	3.1192	88,544,164	26,044	11,412,223	24,225	5,524,689	30,964	15,156,735	4,921,658
554	Wausau-Merrill, WI	157,785	155,475	9.2	18,964	62,272	2,992,180	.0558	2,183,654	642	405,060	860	46,936	263	256,798	52,046
556	Wichita-Winfield, KS	622,050	607,457	10.8	18,445	242,062	11,473,530	.1998	6,595,168	1,940	1,234,955	2,621	256,467	1,437	996,108	308,812
558	Williamsport-Lock Haven, PA	155,213	157,958	1.3	15,882	62,360	2,465,030	.0485	1,888,818	556	257,768	547	79,410	445	318,479	127,178
564	York-Hanover-Gettysburg, PA	497,040	473,043	13.2	20,168	193,910	10,024,220	.1614	4,643,266	1,366	618,645	1,313	157,835	885	888,442	229,394
566	Youngstown-Warren-East Liverpool, OH-PA	701,743	715,039	-1.0	17,174	284,714	12,051,840	.2231	8,061,910	2,371	1,053,460	2,236	398,618	2,235	1,113,061	544,041
	Totals	181,741,992	174,028,784	12.7	21,089	69,170,941	3,832,738,290	64.6675	2,170,229,759	638,381	285,572,372	606,212	126,139,184	706,914	322,310,228	126,800,042

Source: Devonshire Associates Ltd. and Scan/US, Inc. 2004.

Core Based Statistical Areas (CBSAs): State Totals for Population/Income/Sales#†

	POPULATION Estimate 7/1/04	POPULATION Census 4/1/00	POPULATION % Change 4/1/90-4/1/00	PER CAPITA INCOME 2003	HOUSE-HOLDS Estimate 7/1/04	DISPOSABLE INCOME 2003 ($1,000)	MARKET ABILITY INDEX 2003	TOTAL RETAIL SALES 2003 Sales ($1,000)	TOTAL RETAIL SALES Ranally Sales Units	GENERAL MERCHANDISE 2003 Sales ($1,000)	GENERAL MERCHANDISE Ranally Sales Units	APPAREL STORE SALES 2003 Sales ($1,000)	APPAREL STORE SALES Ranally Sales Units	FOOD STORE SALES 2003 ($1,000)	HEALTH & DRUG STORE 2003 ($1,000)
Alabama	3,198,418	3,133,253	10.2	17,995	1,290,258	57,557,130	1.0356	36,249,194	10,663	6,693,886	14,210	1,720,130	9,639	4,846,797	1,757,177
Alaska	432,585	402,445	17.1	21,556	156,991	9,325,000	.1652	6,248,940	1,838	1,441,570	3,061	260,237	1,458	740,910	74,798
Arizona	5,093,160	4,539,485	41.1	19,124	1,939,480	97,400,800	1.6812	55,762,547	16,403	7,955,056	16,885	2,073,587	11,620	7,929,365	2,783,941
Arkansas	1,593,424	1,516,451	18.8	17,245	636,274	27,478,220	.5215	19,871,158	5,844	4,784,291	10,154	697,534	3,909	1,859,544	764,512
California	35,146,204	33,075,450	13.9	19,939	11,900,401	700,772,400	11.7211	370,352,548	108,942	43,617,190	92,592	26,839,650	150,419	64,404,082	20,105,373
Colorado	3,970,505	3,676,685	30.4	21,934	1,545,418	87,087,300	1.4677	50,341,482	14,808	7,501,181	15,923	1,890,650	10,596	6,913,174	1,754,042
Connecticut	3,203,958	3,114,281	3.4	26,859	1,238,079	86,056,420	1.3714	46,355,527	13,636	3,715,663	7,887	2,999,824	16,812	7,115,373	2,909,209
Delaware	656,304	626,962	13.4	21,804	253,550	14,310,140	.2517	9,435,022	2,776	1,299,355	2,759	395,076	2,214	1,453,393	529,776
District of Columbia	560,725	572,059	-5.7	26,337	256,560	14,767,850	.1959	3,408,245	1,003	145,053	308	469,245	2,630	940,510	481,206
Florida	16,262,606	14,973,073	23.4	20,730	6,828,571	337,121,110	5.8164	203,290,682	59,797	26,395,900	56,034	12,363,393	69,285	29,297,366	13,019,843
Georgia	7,109,688	6,526,455	29.2	20,767	2,729,426	147,644,980	2.5463	89,020,537	26,185	12,522,126	26,581	4,626,531	25,930	12,585,198	3,649,926
Hawaii	911,719	876,156	4.8	19,820	301,773	18,070,470	.3029	9,586,291	2,820	1,932,186	4,102	1,213,597	6,801	1,460,075	815,873
Idaho	886,755	807,044	35.8	17,276	325,490	15,319,250	.2906	11,084,858	3,261	1,907,015	4,048	317,991	1,783	1,600,570	371,735
Illinois	11,038,991	10,713,406	9.9	20,987	4,066,669	231,673,210	3.8892	128,521,813	37,805	15,813,762	33,568	6,645,549	37,246	17,924,760	10,247,053
Indiana	4,831,753	4,686,372	10.7	19,251	1,922,768	93,017,960	1.6834	62,308,559	18,328	10,920,408	23,180	2,299,638	12,887	6,543,641	3,787,609
Iowa	1,610,036	1,563,592	10.0	19,037	637,210	30,650,780	.5606	21,087,133	6,203	2,975,961	6,320	745,618	4,178	2,757,238	1,038,808
Kansas	1,716,425	1,644,292	13.7	20,539	673,713	35,253,150	.6022	20,450,086	6,014	3,477,841	7,383	955,386	5,354	2,859,435	1,022,272
Kentucky	2,344,447	2,272,494	11.4	19,875	971,778	46,595,440	.7988	26,796,832	7,881	4,367,871	9,273	1,218,487	6,830	3,100,885	1,620,285
Louisiana	3,380,600	3,340,667	6.8	17,251	1,336,463	58,318,610	1.0812	39,285,709	11,556	7,426,661	15,767	1,895,706	10,626	5,208,385	2,331,103
Maine	765,321	736,280	6.2	19,519	316,480	14,938,680	.2847	11,711,472	3,445	1,160,115	2,463	583,614	3,271	2,225,155	447,786

Core Based Statistical Areas (CBSAs): State Totals for Population / Income / Sales[#][†], Continued

	POPULATION Estimate 7/1/04	POPULATION Census 4/1/00	% Change 4/1/90-4/1/00	PER CAPITA INCOME 2003	HOUSE-HOLDS Estimate 7/1/04	DISPOSABLE INCOME 2003 ($1,000)	MARKET ABILITY INDEX 2003	TOTAL RETAIL SALES 2003 Sales ($1,000)	TOTAL RETAIL SALES Ranally Sales Units	GENERAL MERCHANDISE 2003 Sales ($1,000)	GENERAL MERCHANDISE Ranally Sales Units	APPAREL STORE SALES 2003 Sales ($1,000)	APPAREL STORE SALES Ranally Sales Units	FOOD STORE SALES 2003 ($1,000)	HEALTH & DRUG STORE 2003 ($1,000)
Maryland	5,282,649	5,020,431	10.7	23,937	2,001,414	126,449,920	1.9567	57,071,440	16,788	7,214,202	15,313	3,187,092	17,862	10,158,916	3,194,264
Massachusetts	6,430,333	6,324,590	5.4	23,600	2,508,314	151,758,960	2.4580	80,229,661	23,600	7,247,883	15,386	5,564,380	31,185	14,245,647	5,889,561
Michigan	8,242,444	8,099,288	6.1	20,988	3,240,995	172,992,740	3.0063	107,590,152	31,649	19,437,756	41,264	4,523,592	25,350	12,171,761	6,650,100
Minnesota	3,691,972	3,534,372	14.9	22,722	1,468,995	83,890,420	1.4761	56,612,314	16,655	8,088,649	17,173	1,959,796	10,981	7,204,676	2,471,171
Mississippi	1,250,448	1,194,552	16.6	17,356	478,379	21,703,200	.3982	14,186,040	4,175	3,228,479	6,855	494,307	2,771	1,475,382	764,763
Missouri	4,184,769	4,069,962	9.2	20,040	1,700,070	83,860,730	1.4608	51,085,796	15,026	7,808,866	16,574	1,533,063	8,592	6,582,533	2,907,486
Montana	323,036	315,063	13.4	16,976	132,114	5,484,000	.1107	4,683,450	1,378	943,314	2,002	133,500	748	504,268	148,456
Nebraska	989,460	942,503	13.9	19,774	393,597	19,566,000	.3507	12,945,489	3,808	1,812,573	3,847	467,675	2,620	1,801,581	764,581
Nevada	2,078,094	1,771,107	70.4	19,714	790,660	40,967,330	.7151	24,876,261	7,318	3,411,657	7,242	1,406,288	7,882	3,828,213	1,078,130
New Hampshire	812,101	770,433	12.3	22,963	311,443	18,648,430	.3559	15,788,939	4,644	2,584,506	5,487	637,229	3,571	2,461,638	546,185
New Jersey	8,707,156	8,414,350	8.9	25,358	3,199,381	220,796,870	3.4614	108,684,617	31,972	9,663,099	20,512	7,356,272	41,227	19,829,135	7,157,799
New Mexico	1,224,073	1,147,424	24.0	17,460	471,942	21,372,170	.3901	13,817,700	4,066	2,677,765	5,685	544,970	3,054	1,358,608	729,216
New York	17,686,761	17,415,517	5.9	20,981	6,599,867	371,093,510	5.9192	170,658,407	50,201	17,575,194	37,309	18,491,337	103,629	27,928,540	14,781,284
North Carolina	5,868,355	5,485,424	24.3	20,398	2,407,069	119,705,500	2.1154	77,112,670	22,683	10,301,707	21,868	3,647,295	20,438	10,097,133	3,987,689
North Dakota	290,202	283,966	10.3	18,424	120,867	5,346,550	.1126	5,271,204	1,551	871,482	1,849	162,825	912	452,845	254,335
Ohio	9,225,408	9,140,806	4.6	20,178	3,800,081	186,146,470	3.2641	116,314,480	34,214	15,914,603	33,785	5,078,246	28,458	15,864,509	7,870,678
Oklahoma	2,233,399	2,157,030	12.3	17,933	901,635	40,052,550	.7172	24,805,135	7,297	4,658,913	9,889	794,339	4,452	2,815,581	1,306,064
Oregon	2,781,530	2,617,733	22.9	19,804	1,091,578	55,085,760	1.0033	38,247,443	11,252	7,073,225	15,016	1,775,851	9,953	5,096,923	1,060,400
Pennsylvania	10,409,907	10,319,747	3.0	19,653	4,159,590	204,590,300	3.5883	125,828,335	37,016	12,941,993	27,474	6,774,698	37,969	20,932,105	8,820,531
Rhode Island	1,084,664	1,048,319	4.5	19,612	429,549	21,272,810	.3527	10,750,673	3,163	957,954	2,033	675,902	3,787	2,105,585	1,143,477
South Carolina	3,152,101	3,001,853	15.8	18,434	1,258,825	58,104,780	1.0455	37,235,810	10,950	5,884,123	12,492	2,030,276	11,380	5,435,859	1,918,367
South Dakota	332,681	312,495	17.1	18,745	132,492	6,236,040	.1860	12,393,631	3,645	1,067,995	2,268	152,479	854	566,341	268,034
Tennessee	4,278,161	4,122,288	16.8	19,255	1,743,335	82,376,200	1.5076	57,139,257	16,807	9,834,730	20,877	2,938,528	16,466	6,620,023	3,206,544
Texas	19,548,867	17,944,548	24.9	18,616	7,137,540	363,921,730	6.6072	241,299,673	70,980	34,998,097	74,297	12,308,985	68,984	33,535,684	10,231,553
Utah	2,114,661	1,970,033	30.6	16,882	680,910	35,700,710	.6907	26,992,952	7,939	4,356,500	9,248	1,071,841	6,006	4,019,898	538,577
Vermont	204,838	198,889	12.3	20,637	80,861	4,227,310	.0795	3,282,264	966	310,507	660	156,077	875	563,362	179,025
Virginia	6,392,423	6,007,063	15.8	22,686	2,512,863	145,019,510	2.3615	76,184,130	22,411	11,896,606	25,257	4,141,463	23,213	10,793,569	3,752,806
Washington	5,430,735	5,153,165	21.5	21,064	2,116,152	114,393,900	1.9458	66,482,459	19,556	10,972,218	23,291	3,317,493	18,592	10,115,262	2,725,804
West Virginia	994,678	983,274	3.4	17,154	420,693	17,062,760	.3061	10,276,484	3,022	1,791,615	3,802	442,207	2,478	1,278,526	821,198
Wisconsin	3,982,539	3,868,673	9.4	20,534	1,615,182	81,776,080	1.4256	50,687,918	14,908	7,880,408	16,727	1,551,607	8,693	6,680,653	2,474,825
Wyoming	153,635	148,140	10.2	17,934	62,212	2,755,230	.0535	2,181,915	642	388,407	824	44,939	252	254,766	45,241
Micropolitan Statistical Area Totals	30,034,218	29,412,298	10.0	16,228	11,702,873	487,405,540	9.0556	316,905,065	93,225	52,706,414	111,879	11,579,749	64,892	48,966,496	16,130,159
U. S. Totals	274,129,922	261,992,238	13.6	20,038	104,998,830	5,493,122,910	94.7450	3,238,790,398	952,715	452,554,531	960,683	175,155,745	981,614	477,511,871	183,330,633

Source: Devonshire Associates Ltd. and Scan/US, Inc. 2004.

[#] Estimates for Total Retail Sales, General Merchandise, Apparel Store Sales, Food Store Sales, and Health and Drug Store Sales are based on data from the U.S. Census Bureau's 1997 Economic Census and utilize the North American Industry Classification System (NAICS).

[†] State totals are for Metropolitan Core Based Statistical Areas. A U.S. total for Micropolitan Core Based Statistical Areas is also provided.

150 Largest Core Based Statistical Areas (CBSAs): Population/Income/Sales#

The table lists the 150 largest Core Based Statistical Areas (CBSAs) ranked by July 1, 2004 estimated population. The data shown are consistent with the data on the CBSA Table which appears on pages 45-47. A map showing the CBSAs, with a detailed explanation of how they are determined, appears on pages 38-39. An explanation of CBSAs may also be found in the Introduction on pages 5-9.

RANK	CORE BASED STATISTICAL AREA	POPULATION Estimate 7/1/04	POPULATION Census 4/1/00	POPULATION % Change 4/1/90-4/1/00	PER CAPITA INCOME 2003	HOUSE-HOLDS Estimate 7/1/04	DISPOSABLE INCOME 2003 ($1,000)	MARKET ABILITY INDEX 2003	TOTAL RETAIL SALES 2003 Sales ($1,000)	TOTAL RETAIL SALES Ranally Sales Units	GENERAL MERCHANDISE 2003 Sales ($1,000)	GENERAL MERCHANDISE Ranally Sales Units	APPAREL STORE SALES 2003 Sales ($1,000)	APPAREL STORE SALES Ranally Sales Units	FOOD STORE SALES 2003 ($1,000)	HEALTH & DRUG STORE 2003 ($1,000)
1	New York-Northern New Jersey-Long Island, NY-NJ-PA	18,735,483	18,323,002	8.8	22,813	6,824,880	427,405,790	6.7022	196,107,217	57,688	17,839,877	37,868	21,256,522	119,126	32,996,658	16,282,004
2	Los Angeles-Long Beach-Santa Ana, CA	12,971,790	12,365,627	9.7	18,420	4,242,787	238,946,190	4.1072	131,191,725	38,591	14,965,879	31,769	10,877,435	60,961	21,595,780	7,400,000
3	Chicago-Naperville-Joliet, IL-IN-WI	9,405,026	9,098,316	11.2	21,277	3,404,592	200,106,090	3.3284	108,533,325	31,926	12,448,491	26,424	5,997,775	33,613	14,973,121	8,989,067
4	Philadelphia-Camden-Wilmington, PA-NJ-DE-MD	5,799,622	5,687,147	4.6	22,110	2,236,988	128,230,550	2.1466	72,846,541	21,429	6,701,179	14,226	4,338,211	24,312	12,163,100	5,245,024
5	Dallas-Fort Worth-Arlington, TX	5,720,764	5,161,544	29.4	21,519	2,136,210	123,103,990	2.1099	74,314,243	21,860	9,970,829	21,167	3,745,975	20,995	9,998,227	2,946,274
6	Miami-Fort Lauderdale-Miami Beach, FL	5,375,613	5,007,564	23.5	20,322	2,173,822	109,241,680	1.8943	66,142,729	19,456	7,603,750	16,141	5,336,086	29,905	9,219,868	4,758,075
7	Houston-Baytown-Sugar Land, TX	5,187,158	4,715,407	25.2	19,599	1,897,350	101,663,440	1.7618	60,014,131	17,654	9,252,065	19,640	3,382,371	18,955	9,117,678	2,819,147
8	Washington-Arlington-Alexandria, DC-VA-MD-WV	5,179,798	4,796,183	16.3	27,551	1,993,702	142,708,760	2.0960	57,695,266	16,970	7,221,135	15,329	3,808,065	21,343	9,724,167	2,981,653
9	Atlanta-Sandy Springs-Marietta, GA	4,719,358	4,247,981	38.4	22,702	1,809,292	107,137,870	1.8008	62,669,946	18,435	8,088,545	17,171	3,346,251	18,754	9,016,906	2,471,415
10	Detroit-Warren-Livonia, MI	4,492,464	4,452,557	4.8	22,202	1,773,948	99,740,930	1.7090	61,289,437	18,030	9,672,534	20,533	2,789,100	15,630	7,328,480	4,281,485
11	Boston-Cambridge-Quincy, MA-NH	4,452,771	4,391,344	6.2	24,996	1,723,822	111,299,830	1.8013	60,701,542	17,855	5,700,756	12,102	4,396,572	24,640	10,266,378	4,205,252
12	San Francisco-Oakland-Fremont, CA	4,164,518	4,123,740	11.9	27,769	1,599,450	115,645,660	1.7698	55,099,848	16,208	6,134,889	13,023	4,808,658	26,949	10,425,434	3,036,124
13	Riverside-San Bernardino-Ontario, CA	3,763,495	3,254,821	25.7	16,568	1,190,886	62,352,000	1.0820	32,473,181	9,552	4,207,194	8,931	1,932,948	10,833	5,780,775	1,423,456
14	Phoenix-Mesa-Scottsdale, AZ	3,698,598	3,251,876	45.3	19,860	1,390,757	73,453,060	1.2676	43,123,015	12,685	5,754,543	12,215	1,636,357	9,171	5,887,002	2,114,223
15	Seattle-Tacoma-Bellevue, WA	3,171,685	3,043,878	18.9	23,150	1,271,838	73,423,950	1.2254	42,438,914	12,483	6,116,628	12,985	2,512,922	14,083	5,998,962	1,694,877
16	Minneapolis-St. Paul-Bloomington, MN-WI	3,117,850	2,968,806	16.9	23,599	1,239,180	73,576,940	1.2830	49,271,803	14,494	6,752,377	14,336	1,762,104	9,874	6,271,900	2,151,420
17	San Diego-Carlsbad-San Marcos, CA	2,966,135	2,813,833	12.6	20,344	1,059,703	60,342,670	1.0169	33,222,905	9,773	3,825,198	8,120	2,426,068	13,596	5,326,312	1,680,462
18	St. Louis, MO-IL	2,747,415	2,698,687	4.6	20,789	1,108,215	57,115,590	.9597	31,592,542	9,293	4,808,411	10,207	1,105,126	6,193	4,681,186	2,086,819
19	Baltimore-Towson, MD	2,635,941	2,552,994	7.2	22,837	1,025,342	60,196,130	.9507	28,414,112	8,358	3,697,296	7,848	1,633,456	9,155	5,055,123	1,789,340
20	Tampa-St. Petersburg-Clearwater, FL	2,574,498	2,395,997	15.9	21,239	1,157,320	54,679,370	.9513	34,351,447	10,104	4,164,175	8,840	1,446,023	8,104	4,811,738	2,259,763
21	Pittsburgh, PA	2,404,027	2,431,087	-1.5	18,638	1,011,774	44,806,500	.7956	27,697,371	8,147	3,082,330	6,544	1,291,132	7,236	4,492,970	2,114,185
22	Denver-Aurora, CO	2,337,049	2,179,240	30.7	23,285	921,916	54,418,490	.8985	30,460,849	8,960	4,356,686	9,248	1,347,655	7,553	4,236,864	1,085,958
23	Cleveland-Elyria-Mentor, OH	2,136,733	2,148,143	2.2	20,295	877,176	43,365,710	.7537	26,427,730	7,774	2,836,585	6,022	1,297,232	7,270	3,847,381	2,724,980
24	Portland-Vancouver-Beaverton, OR-WA	2,075,083	1,927,881	26.5	20,972	810,015	43,519,560	.7602	27,483,047	8,085	4,981,840	10,575	1,438,297	8,061	3,677,838	843,089
25	Cincinnati-Middletown, OH-KY-IN	2,058,374	2,009,632	8.9	21,001	833,063	43,228,550	.7288	24,347,704	7,162	3,578,925	7,597	1,088,721	6,102	3,474,232	1,334,996
26	Sacramento--Arden-Arcade--Roseville, CA	2,030,311	1,796,857	21.3	20,798	748,723	42,226,880	.6904	21,200,359	6,236	2,531,448	5,374	1,154,590	6,471	3,816,935	889,781
27	Kansas City, MO-KS	1,925,595	1,836,038	12.2	21,378	772,932	41,166,020	.7074	24,965,001	7,342	3,716,868	7,890	953,702	5,346	3,040,182	1,272,430
28	San Antonio, TX	1,854,472	1,711,703	21.6	17,270	676,131	32,027,530	.5891	21,068,159	6,196	2,980,108	6,327	1,116,149	6,257	3,285,955	808,729
29	Orlando, FL	1,851,873	1,644,561	34.3	20,739	737,616	38,405,230	.6825	25,416,119	7,476	3,495,555	7,420	1,661,395	9,310	3,372,844	1,393,435
30	San Jose-Sunnyvale-Santa Clara, CA	1,732,851	1,735,819	13.1	29,594	602,990	51,282,100	.8039	27,476,573	8,082	3,204,551	6,802	2,295,067	12,862	4,468,811	1,364,979
31	Columbus, OH	1,693,064	1,612,694	14.8	21,863	711,298	37,016,120	.6479	24,084,728	7,085	3,114,519	6,612	1,026,104	5,750	2,879,390	943,488
32	Virginia Beach-Norfolk-Newport News, VA-NC	1,656,100	1,576,370	8.8	18,493	631,044	30,626,410	.5304	17,321,808	5,098	2,782,538	5,908	968,399	5,426	2,405,325	788,584
33	Las Vegas-Paradise, NV	1,637,622	1,375,765	85.5	19,574	620,349	32,054,670	.5564	19,011,943	5,593	2,590,700	5,500	1,238,316	6,940	2,927,642	777,477
34	Providence-New Bedford-Fall River, RI-MA	1,635,332	1,582,997	4.8	19,915	645,096	32,567,900	.5469	17,438,480	5,130	2,043,845	4,338	1,093,558	6,128	3,321,275	1,620,497
35	Indianapolis, IN	1,616,900	1,525,104	17.8	21,197	653,495	34,273,110	.6066	22,689,052	6,673	3,846,247	8,165	876,562	4,912	2,181,248	1,455,903
36	Milwaukee-Waukesha-West Allis, WI	1,518,392	1,500,741	4.8	21,091	626,347	32,024,760	.5377	17,828,356	5,244	2,468,920	5,241	607,112	3,403	2,663,965	1,200,135
37	Charlotte-Gastonia-Concord, NC-SC	1,470,003	1,330,448	29.8	22,345	602,683	32,847,930	.5571	19,602,323	5,766	2,646,389	5,617	926,940	5,194	2,486,119	978,597
38	Austin-Round Rock, TX	1,415,292	1,249,763	47.7	22,947	561,961	32,477,300	.6303	28,689,214	8,440	2,281,526	4,844	1,085,483	6,083	3,148,162	1,386,529
39	Nashville-Davidson--Murfreesboro, TN	1,389,376	1,311,789	25.1	21,436	566,503	29,783,080	.5276	19,889,768	5,849	3,310,027	7,027	996,971	5,587	2,462,695	1,078,959
40	New Orleans-Metairie-Kenner, LA	1,318,235	1,316,510	4.1	17,916	535,050	23,617,510	.4235	14,673,543	4,317	2,489,535	5,286	876,417	4,912	2,131,086	1,101,031
41	Memphis, TN-MS-AR	1,249,702	1,205,204	12.9	18,305	480,832	22,875,320	.4105	14,456,493	4,253	2,489,377	5,285	825,463	4,627	1,493,064	919,941
42	Jacksonville, FL	1,228,504	1,122,750	21.4	21,558	497,528	26,483,630	.4471	15,231,569	4,480	1,973,993	4,190	715,024	4,007	2,176,928	768,741
43	Louisville, KY-IN	1,198,515	1,161,975	10.0	20,338	503,792	24,375,560	.4092	13,227,081	3,890	2,142,103	4,548	518,818	2,908	1,495,463	819,693
44	Hartford-West Hartford-East Hartford, CT	1,186,956	1,148,618	2.2	26,395	467,168	31,330,290	.4795	14,476,166	4,258	1,272,994	2,702	1,069,247	5,993	2,502,419	1,079,752
45	Buffalo-Niagara Falls, NY	1,156,288	1,170,111	-1.6	19,600	470,582	22,662,690	.3756	11,435,256	3,364	1,227,487	2,605	661,291	3,706	2,043,522	900,419
46	Richmond, VA	1,150,973	1,096,957	15.6	21,215	469,750	24,417,590	.4073	13,361,603	3,931	2,185,048	4,639	638,822	3,581	1,922,958	786,818
47	Oklahoma City, OK	1,144,287	1,095,421	12.8	18,079	464,505	20,687,690	.3717	13,035,439	3,834	2,207,799	4,686	447,625	2,509	1,473,089	692,412
48	Birmingham-Hoover, AL	1,079,089	1,052,238	10.0	18,944	433,567	20,442,380	.3654	13,037,366	3,835	2,092,263	4,441	676,907	3,793	1,773,260	634,458
49	Rochester, NY	1,042,130	1,037,831	3.5	21,618	414,464	22,528,540	.3645	11,200,585	3,295	1,291,364	2,741	517,944	2,903	2,214,017	566,798
50	Salt Lake City, UT	1,016,207	968,858	26.1	18,190	343,458	18,484,430	.3608	14,942,479	4,395	2,202,106	4,675	702,153	3,935	2,115,978	302,204
51	Honolulu, HI	911,719	876,156	4.8	19,820	301,773	18,070,470	.3029	9,586,291	2,820	1,932,186	4,102	1,213,597	6,801	1,460,075	815,873
52	Raleigh-Cary, NC	911,301	797,071	47.3	24,193	371,773	22,047,240	.3722	13,547,177	3,985	1,817,305	3,858	670,995	3,760	1,750,243	571,253
53	Tucson, AZ	907,511	843,746	26.5	17,888	365,815	16,233,410	.2752	8,272,791	2,434	1,284,384	2,726	326,802	1,831	1,268,524	505,873
54	Bridgeport-Stamford-Norwalk, CT	904,001	882,567	6.6	30,224	334,894	27,322,330	.4561	17,926,178	5,273	934,028	1,983	1,149,371	6,441	2,396,980	817,269
55	Tulsa, OK	886,021	859,532	12.9	18,696	363,016	16,564,680	.2949	10,343,623	3,044	2,059,466	4,371	319,925	1,793	1,142,592	558,925
56	Fresno, CA	866,423	799,407	19.8	13,541	269,842	11,732,460	.2231	7,104,904	2,090	970,831	2,061	301,911	1,692	1,214,541	433,499
57	New Haven-Milford, CT	847,502	824,008	2.5	24,399	331,415	20,678,310	.3304	10,642,435	3,131	1,078,401	2,289	607,778	3,406	1,706,678	797,297
58	Dayton, OH	845,439	848,153	0.5	20,594	357,985	17,411,280	.2977	10,158,179	2,988	1,735,989	3,686	431,765	2,419	1,342,338	491,936
59	Albany-Schenectady-Troy, NY	845,300	825,875	2.0	22,081	345,122	18,665,030	.3014	9,338,794	2,747	1,066,101	2,263	520,678	2,919	1,296,966	616,121
60	Oxnard-Thousand Oaks-Ventura, CA	802,627	753,197	12.6	22,864	258,964	18,351,220	.2961	9,381,128	2,760	941,078	1,998	513,106	2,876	1,505,559	540,323
61	Omaha-Council Bluffs, NE-IA	801,189	767,041	11.8	19,834	317,131	15,890,860	.2901	11,130,228	3,275	1,359,230	2,886	395,984	2,218	1,441,414	616,912
62	Worcester, MA	784,595	750,963	5.8	21,778	300,867	17,087,140	.2811	9,059,973	2,665	882,285	1,873	405,829	2,274	1,627,115	628,138
63	Allentown-Bethlehem-Easton, PA-NJ	776,747	740,395	7.8	20,869	305,639	16,210,200	.2761	9,403,351	2,767	979,519	2,079	367,959	2,063	1,723,108	631,887
64	Albuquerque, NM	775,936	729,649	21.7	18,586	308,223	14,421,760	.2591	9,239,198	2,718	1,680,359	3,567	321,444	1,801	858,890	506,985
65	Grand Rapids-Wyoming, MI	768,430	740,482	14.6	19,201	289,500	14,755,000	.2671	9,880,515	2,906	1,851,881	3,931	352,570	1,976	891,877	446,099
66	Bakersfield, CA	729,553	661,645	21.7	13,779	226,881	10,052,420	.1858	5,580,342	1,642	732,780	1,556	216,564	1,214	895,681	350,750
67	Baton Rouge, LA	727,723	705,973	13.2	17,814	279,668	12,963,740	.2350	8,307,961	2,442	1,491,216	3,166	347,124	1,946	1,093,197	391,446
68	El Paso, TX	713,340	679,622	14.9	12,037	226,278	8,586,800	.1799	6,462,611	1,901	1,356,263	2,879	425,599	2,385	831,659	312,642
69	Akron, OH	703,530	694,960	5.7	20,270	288,070	14,260,790	.2526	9,231,659	2,716	949,148	2,015	365,016	2,046	1,289,167	791,147
70	Springfield, MA	691,167	680,014	1.0	19,479	269,913	13,463,310	.2241	6,876,412	2,023	689,313	1,463	327,408	1,835	1,412,300	508,321
71	Columbia, SC	678,866	647,158	18.0	19,288	271,665	13,094,270	.2312	8,121,937	2,388	1,461,358	3,102	391,616	2,196	1,104,551	415,843
72	Greensboro-High Point, NC	666,943	643,430	19.1	19,789	276,895	13,198,200	.2387	8,968,096	2,638	1,092,366	2,319	404,136	2,265	1,135,820	551,736
73	Poughkeepsie-Newburgh-Middletown, NY	664,094	621,517	9.6	22,088	231,447	14,668,650	.2322	6,806,419	2,002	978,011	2,076	561,093	3,144	1,135,631	396,977
74	Toledo, OH	661,399	659,188	0.8	19,068	271,511	12,611,450	.2286	8,447,768	2,485	1,321,643	2,807	324,354	1,817	1,182,481	472,292
75	McAllen-Edinburg-Pharr, TX	656,072	569,463	48.5	8,644	182,386	5,671,110	.1419	5,457,211	1,605	1,064,900	2,261	420,429	2,356	833,469	231,799
76	Syracuse, NY	655,449	650,154	-1.5	19,766	260,632	12,955,600	.2165	6,781,841	1,995	712,363	1,513	343,366	1,924	1,314,851	467,463
77	Stockton, CA	654,288	563,598	17.3	16,392	210,061	10,725,080	.1822	5,087,457	1,497	677,193	1,438	219,393	1,230	911,463	340,141
78	Sarasota-Bradenton-Venice, FL	647,224	589,959	20.5	22,658	289,616	14,664,530	.2443	8,331,292	2,450	976,820	2,074	496,718	2,784	1,292,386	548,115
79	Knoxville, TN	643,341	616,079	15.2	19,141	273,658	12,314,110	.2435	10,569,943	3,110	1,711,283	3,632	420,316	2,355	1,167,051	538,607
80	Little Rock-North Little Rock, AR	633,708	610,518	14.1	19,291	262,285	12,224,550	.2274	8,899,092	2,617	1,776,498	3,770	318,812	1,786	766,679	282,051
81	Youngstown-Warren-Boardman, OH-PA	590,415	602,964	-1.7	17,455	241,263	10,305,630	.1917	7,069,168	2,079	954,927	2,027	377,795	2,118	939,871	470,637
82	Wichita, KS	586,332	571,166	11.7	18,629	228,064	10,922,760	.1897	6,269,005	1,844	1,192,543	2,531	248,202	1,391	932,851	282,840
83	Greenville, SC	584,065	559,940	18.6	18,610	232,657	10,869,420	.1983	7,315,362	2,152	987,107	2,096	339,854	1,905	952,644	389,823
84	Colorado Springs, CO	582,962	537,484	31.3	19,915	217,598	11,609,510	.2043	7,281,101	2,142	1,150,804	2,443	191,586	1,074	801,447	279,729
85	Charleston-North Charleston, SC	578,716	549,033	8.3	18,762	232,024	10,857,930	.1907	6,506,338	1,913	1,101,200	2,338	413,126	2,315	1,082,356	277,047
86	Scranton--Wilkes-Barre, PA	549,692	560,625	-2.5	17,114	232,147	9,407,410	.1763	6,528,589	1,921	861,310	1,829	306,501	1,718	1,190,018	453,584
87	Madison, WI	534,379	501,774	16.1	21,802	222,637	11,650,780	.2146	8,783,205	2,584	1,026,224	2,178	252,590	1,416	929,642	346,073
88	Boise City-Nampa, ID	524,915	464,840	45.4	17,931	192,987	9,412,420	.1764	6,725,318	1,978	1,140,423	2,421	208,330	1,168	905,562	211,288
89	Harrisburg-Carlisle, PA	520,152	509,074	7.3	20,822	213,483	10,830,400	.1940	7,355,835	2,164	722,807	1,534	278,217	1,559	1,057,504	405,259
90	Lakeland, FL	518,809	483,924	19.4	19,073	217,966	9,895,440	.1713	5,716,090	1,681	873,686	1,855	196,846	1,103	977,731	287,481
91	Augusta-Richmond County, GA-SC	515,207	499,684	14.7	17,290	197,259	8,907,760	.1584	5,243,476	1,542	906,628	1,924	235,924	1,322	754,220	247,507
92	Palm Bay-Melbourne-Titusville, FL	515,004	476,230	19.4	22,229	228,764	11,447,810	.1835	5,603,865	1,648	916,795	1,946	235,423	1,319	919,936	384,085
93	Jackson, MS	513,973	497,197	11.2	17,308	193,505	8,895,610	.1691	6,473,402	1,905	1,301,508	2,763	270,673	1,517	666,464	365,773
94	Portland-South Portland-Biddeford, ME	510,775	487,568	10.5	20,763	210,713	10,605,030	.1948	7,739,008	2,276	666,059	1,414	510,079	2,859	1,535,545	296,960
95	Des Moines, IA	509,323	481,394	15.6	20,607	204,097	10,495,510	.1817	6,384,753	1,877	861,094	1,829	229,830	1,288	846,810	314,243
96	Cape Coral-Fort Myers, FL	508,350	440,888	31.6	21,735	219,630	11,049,150	.1922	7,029,399	2,068	988,622	2,099	443,513	2,486	986,313	442,891
97	Modesto, CA	506,378	446,997	20.6	15,862	162,035	8,032,070	.1459	4,753,556	1,398	669,983	1,422	178,855	1,002	913,403	315,443
98	Chattanooga, TN-GA	488,857	476,531	10.0	18,410	200,415	8,999,930	.1610	5,656,736	1,663	931,010	1,976	299,207	1,677	771,836	342,749
99	Lancaster, PA	486,469	470,658	11.3	19,463	180,573	9,468,350	.1739	6,676,478	1,964	579,937	1,231	367,776	2,061	1,109,981	332,301
100	Ogden-Clearfield, UT	476,951	442,656	25.8	17,543	154,038	8,367,310	.1517	5,317,040	1,564	947,833	2,012	146,125	819	848,133	109,399
101	Deltona-Daytona Beach-Ormond Beach, FL	476,562	443,343	19.6	20,089	215,582	9,573,780	.1631	5,410,480	1,592	719,210	1,527	211,817	1,187	893,089	358,640
102	Santa Rosa-Petaluma, CA	468,851	458,614	18.1	23,674	174,821	11,099,560	.1798	5,877,135	1,729	619,805	1,316	256,127	1,435	1,187,270	345,374
103	Lansing-East Lansing, MI	458,301	447,728	3.5	20,004	182,777	9,167,820	.1606	5,685,892	1,672	1,278,910	2,715	207,150	1,161	673,930	297,591
104	Durham, NC	454,080	426,493	23.8	20,825	189,975	9,456,370	.1584	5,184,875	1,526	512,260	1,088	270,260	1,514	920,987	312,899
105	Flint, MI	444,011	436,141	1.3	19,539	181,093	8,675,620	.1515	5,238,928	1,541	1,038,212	2,204	183,929	1,031	608,615	347,323
106	Winston-Salem, NC	442,297	421,961	16.7	19,940	182,853	8,819,330	.1580	5,846,125	1,719	774,596	1,645	280,777	1,574	717,320	323,855
107	Spokane, WA	435,145	417,939	15.7	17,174	170,747	7,473,250	.1385	5,018,057	1,476	886,324	1,881	231,274	1,296	770,118	205,222
108	Pensacola-Ferry Pass-Brent, FL	434,387	412,153	19.7	19,068	176,993	8,282,890	.1411	4,519,358	1,330	756,204	1,605	179,965	1,008	666,395	295,741
109	Lexington-Fayette, KY	426,494	408,326	17.2	20,850	182,897	8,892,490	.1577	5,875,286	1,728	841,380	1,785	317,551	1,780	630,731	340,223
110	Salinas, CA	418,251	401,762	13.0	17,064	123,111	7,137,110	.1276	4,236,459	1,246	473,268	1,005	285,175	1,598	741,345	267,217
111	Vallejo-Fairfield, CA	417,390	394,542	15.9	21,717	140,762	9,064,370	.1414	3,923,677	1,154	663,323	1,408	193,021	1,082	753,501	156,794
112	Provo-Orem, UT	416,085	376,774	39.9	14,326	117,341	5,961,030	.1174	4,250,508	1,250	810,841	1,721	141,362	792	710,129	74,681
113	Corpus Christi, TX	408,027	403,280	9.7	15,844	149,535	6,464,610	.1214	4,287,745	1,261	695,672	1,477	198,700	1,113	763,556	160,495
114	Canton-Massillon, OH	407,161	406,934	3.3	18,397	162,941	7,490,370	.1367	5,012,905	1,474	691,501	1,468	239,306	1,341	727,029	449,795
115	Santa Barbara-Santa Maria-Goleta, CA	404,260	399,347	8.0	19,379	138,188	7,834,290	.1368	4,700,898	1,383	454,866	966	331,262	1,856	859,109	335,658
116	Fort Wayne, IN	402,608	390,156	10.1	19,308	160,633	7,773,560	.1393	5,065,354	1,490	978,547	2,078	200,064	1,121	533,792	288,823
117	Mobile, AL	399,635	399,843	5.6	15,819	152,735	6,321,850	.1148	3,735,954	1,099	796,502	1,691	159,638	895	512,300	206,288
118	York-Hanover, PA	398,969	381,751	12.4	20,544	157,278	8,196,390	.1339	4,069,282	1,197	563,866	1,197	146,775	823	757,223	207,738
119	Manchester-Nashua, NH	398,775	380,841	13.3	22,726	152,823	9,062,560	.1736	7,717,723	2,270	1,155,385	2,453	304,995	1,709	1,064,120	259,831
120	Visalia-Porterville, CA	398,103	368,021	18.0	12,544	117,213	4,993,740	.0943	2,716,977	799	427,942	908	106,651	598	549,480	145,301
121	Springfield, MO	389,665	368,374	23.3	16,682	160,518	6,500,430	.1280	5,132,095	1,509	778,420	1,652	108,006	606	536,260	223,210
122	Reading, PA	388,909	373,638	11.0	19,644	147,702	7,639,890	.1301	4,256,088	1,252	525,747	1,116	342,408	1,919	683,206	249,524
123	Fayetteville-Springdale-Rogers, AR-MO	387,515	347,045	44.9	16,721	147,765	6,479,530	.1198	4,236,529	1,247	1,303,952	2,767	118,052	661	408,743	125,206
124	Asheville, NC	385,591	369,171	19.9	18,343	164,470	7,072,740	.1350	5,386,669	1,584	728,627	1,546	246,536	1,381	661,500	302,324
125	Reno-Sparks, NV	384,239	342,885	33.3	20,419	148,610	7,845,900	.1375	4,936,356	1,452	767,107	1,628	166,226	932	744,305	194,817
126	Beaumont-Port Arthur, TX	381,930	385,090	6.6	16,834	147,921	6,429,600	.1227	4,650,610	1,368	746,358	1,584	194,534	1,090	630,665	250,353
127	Shreveport-Bossier City, LA	379,073	375,965	4.5	16,335	150,373	6,192,250	.1182	4,392,052	1,292	805,798	1,711	183,191	1,027	541,120	191,964
128	Davenport-Moline-Rock Island, IA-IL	374,674	376,019	2.1	18,885	151,084	7,075,850	.1301	4,913,588	1,445	679,541	1,443	190,384	1,067	610,777	312,800
129	Brownsville-Harlingen, TX	371,857	335,227	28.9	9,563	109,025	3,556,070	.0806	2,774,996	816	641,360	1,361	195,601	1,096	531,733	106,356
130	Salem, OR	367,908	347,214	24.9	16,849	130,863	6,199,000	.1128	3,871,527	1,139	789,346	1,676	136,871	767	556,517	124,085
131	Peoria, IL	365,775	366,899	2.3	19,857	146,334	7,263,210	.1276	4,523,862	1,330	617,644	1,311	118,036	661	677,785	305,743
132	Trenton-Ewing, NJ	365,448	350,761	7.7	25,680	133,605	9,384,820	.1447	4,366,020	1,284	398,348	846	330,116	1,850	753,962	416,720
133	Huntsville, AL	362,704	342,376	16.8	21,319	148,388	7,732,470	.1305	4,408,012	1,296	884,283	1,877	227,112	1,272	579,797	171,413
134	Port St. Lucie-Fort Pierce, FL	357,906	319,426	27.2	21,220	155,543	7,594,610	.1252	3,987,293	1,173	507,921	1,078	135,595	759	652,399	314,490
135	Montgomery, AL	354,386	346,528	13.6	17,853	138,358	6,327,020	.1162	4,233,247	1,246	800,152	1,699	200,979	1,126	523,663	246,613
136	Hickory-Lenoir-Morganton, NC	352,521	341,851	16.9	18,165	142,926	6,403,660	.1160	4,138,266	1,217	589,803	1,251	146,720	822	530,183	248,052
137	Killeen-Temple-Fort Hood, TX	347,063	330,714	23.0	15,926	123,423	5,527,190	.0969	2,888,916	850	420,155	892	82,598	463	411,687	56,125
138	Evansville, IN-KY	346,581	342,815	5.5	18,394	143,502	6,374,920	.1198	4,662,329	1,372	814,297	1,728	208,187	1,166	505,130	238,148
139	Anchorage, AK	345,540	319,605	20.1	21,960	125,280	7,587,970	.1340	5,082,299	1,495	1,142,505	2,426	225,729	1,265	643,803	61,438
140	Ann Arbor, MI	343,273	322,895	14.1	22,856	135,907	7,845,780	.1371	5,202,501	1,530	846,525	1,797	217,383	1,218	569,099	240,364
141	Fayetteville, NC	343,212	336,609	13.2	16,906	131,814	5,802,500	.1052	3,586,986	1,056	702,675	1,492	168,678	945	468,641	155,360
142	Rockford, IL	334,044	320,204	12.9	20,196	129,921	6,746,450	.1163	3,993,279	1,175	607,860	1,290	144,964	813	669,329	238,494
143	Eugene-Springfield, OR	332,896	322,959	14.2	17,777	136,131	5,917,890	.1118	4,302,190	1,266	807,668	1,715	128,392	720	679,603	134,140
144	Tallahassee, FL	330,177	320,304	23.6	19,051	136,318	6,290,160	.1088	3,627,111	1,066	608,524	1,291	168,444	944	601,027	232,307
145	Kalamazoo-Portage, MI	322,014	314,866	7.3	18,958	128,810	6,104,720	.1086	3,844,226	1,131	1,043,323	2,215	128,321	719	354,799	188,470
146	South Bend-Mishawaka, IN-MI	317,967	316,663	6.8	17,891	124,276	5,688,590	.1047	3,837,330	1,129	708,062	1,503	142,891	801	441,894	270,890
147	Savannah, GA	307,995	293,000	13.5	18,342	121,256	5,649,240	.1028	3,741,300	1,100	694,530	1,474	206,990	1,160	521,531	132,810
148	Charleston, WV	305,986	309,635	0.6	17,654	130,915	5,401,750	.1008	3,763,965	1,107	582,070	1,235	144,059	808	470,411	278,964
149	Kingsport-Bristol-Bristol, TN-VA	300,120	298,484	8.3	16,826	130,987	5,049,720	.0947	3,471,046	1,020	662,608	1,406	102,870	577	455,487	193,453
150	Wilmington, NC	299,048	274,532	37.2	20,437	135,026	6,111,590	.1138	4,591,501	1,351	591,267	1,255	185,424	1,040	656,474	236,236

Source: Devonshire Associates Ltd. and Scan/US, Inc. 2004.

Estimates for Total Retail Sales, General Merchandise, Apparel Store Sales, Food Store Sales, and Health and Drug Store Sales are based on data from the U.S. Census Bureau's 1997 Economic Census and utilize the North American Industry Classification System (NAICS).

150 Largest Counties: Population / Income / Sales#

The table lists the 150 largest counties, ranked by July 1, 2004 estimated population. The data shown are consistent with the data in the County Table on pages 52-73.

COUNTY RANK	COUNTY OR COUNTY EQUIVALENT	POPULATION Estimate 7/1/04	POPULATION Census 4/1/00	PER CAPITA INCOME 2003	HOUSEHOLDS Estimate 7/1/04	MEDIAN HOUSEHOLD INCOME 2003	DISPOSABLE INCOME 2003 ($1,000)	MARKET ABILITY INDEX 2003	TOTAL RETAIL SALES Sales 2003 ($1,000)	TOTAL RETAIL SALES Ranally Sales Units	GENERAL MERCHANDISE Sales 2003 ($1,000)	GENERAL MERCHANDISE Ranally Sales Units	APPAREL STORE Sales 2003 ($1,000)	APPAREL STORE Ranally Sales Units	FOOD STORE SALES 2003 ($1,000)	HEALTH & DRUG STORE 2003 ($1,000)	PASSENGER CAR REGIS-TRATIONS 2003	COUNTY OR COUNTY EQUIVALENT
1	Los Angeles, CA	9,980,271	9,519,338	17,007	3,253,579	39,263	169,739,220	2.9601	92,102,910	27,093	10,418,455	22,116	7,736,176	43,356	15,567,979	5,237,037	5,402,514	Los Angeles, CA
2	Cook, IL	5,342,990	5,376,741	19,364	1,958,774	42,017	103,460,480	1.7512	55,847,602	16,428	6,363,904	13,509	3,835,408	21,495	8,716,172	5,532,411	2,689,788	Cook, IL
3	Harris, TX	3,656,415	3,400,578	19,156	1,366,273	39,780	70,043,350	1.2571	45,604,263	13,415	6,510,937	13,821	2,724,895	15,271	6,954,242	2,262,853	2,278,306	Harris, TX
4	Maricopa, AZ	3,486,879	3,072,149	20,135	1,315,734	42,033	70,207,570	1.2176	42,274,027	12,435	5,654,014	12,002	1,598,779	8,960	5,669,314	2,068,177	2,235,443	Maricopa, AZ
5	Orange, CA	2,991,519	2,846,289	23,134	989,208	52,726	69,206,970	1.1471	39,088,814	11,498	4,547,424	9,653	3,141,259	17,605	6,027,801	2,162,963	1,881,977	Orange, CA
6	San Diego, CA	2,966,135	2,813,833	20,344	1,059,703	43,062	60,342,670	1.0169	33,222,905	9,773	3,825,198	8,120	2,426,068	13,596	5,326,312	1,680,462	1,896,665	San Diego, CA
7	Kings, NY	2,474,606	2,465,326	14,547	881,635	30,614	35,997,160	.5722	10,466,614	3,079	767,014	1,628	1,160,613	6,504	2,143,715	1,483,608	515,321	Kings, NY
8	Miami-Dade, FL	2,368,141	2,253,362	16,237	848,751	33,807	38,452,660	.7039	23,817,798	7,006	2,737,682	5,812	2,321,232	13,009	3,289,971	2,034,323	1,315,697	Miami-Dade, FL
9	Dallas, TX	2,303,656	2,218,899	19,854	879,140	40,264	45,736,380	.8476	33,451,662	9,840	4,430,302	9,405	1,869,463	10,477	4,036,338	1,256,109	1,465,267	Dallas, TX
10	Queens, NY	2,223,681	2,229,379	18,150	764,334	39,684	40,359,890	.6009	11,384,793	3,349	859,878	1,825	952,047	5,336	2,389,910	1,551,898	700,819	Queens, NY
11	Wayne, MI	2,018,715	2,061,162	17,902	775,513	37,867	36,139,680	.6319	20,620,588	6,066	3,085,690	6,550	845,136	4,736	3,016,073	1,664,074	1,187,181	Wayne, MI
12	San Bernardino, CA	1,906,582	1,709,434	15,731	577,938	39,247	29,993,250	.5254	15,434,681	4,540	2,058,856	4,371	921,132	5,162	2,897,822	690,175	1,061,255	San Bernardino, CA
13	Riverside, CA	1,856,913	1,545,387	17,426	612,948	40,149	32,358,750	.5566	17,038,501	5,012	2,148,339	4,560	1,011,815	5,671	2,882,953	733,280	1,097,238	Riverside, CA
14	King, WA	1,768,908	1,737,034	25,184	747,678	47,975	44,548,900	.7506	27,758,761	8,165	3,692,856	7,839	1,895,327	10,622	3,777,936	1,119,320	1,298,697	King, WA
15	Broward, FL	1,764,315	1,623,018	21,989	747,072	39,017	38,796,200	.6810	25,541,193	7,513	2,758,291	5,855	1,486,450	8,330	3,491,409	1,626,468	1,136,899	Broward, FL
16	Santa Clara, CA	1,675,734	1,682,585	29,915	586,292	63,995	50,130,310	.7861	27,026,688	7,950	3,149,778	6,686	2,287,248	12,818	4,358,160	1,341,238	1,182,391	Santa Clara, CA
17	Clark, NV	1,637,622	1,375,765	19,574	620,349	41,939	32,054,670	.5564	19,011,943	5,593	2,590,700	5,500	1,238,316	6,940	2,927,642	777,477	1,010,299	Clark, NV
18	Tarrant, TX	1,594,027	1,446,219	20,395	594,919	42,490	32,509,940	.5787	21,425,283	6,302	2,273,907	4,827	991,965	5,559	2,852,327	869,163	1,059,397	Tarrant, TX
19	New York, NY	1,572,971	1,537,195	27,536	755,471	42,974	43,312,660	.7442	29,759,526	8,754	3,335,801	7,081	7,850,059	43,994	3,182,106	3,006,187	244,302	New York, NY
20	Bexar, TX	1,496,237	1,392,931	17,042	546,717	36,239	25,498,880	.4814	18,023,363	5,302	2,641,735	5,608	1,062,045	5,952	2,826,300	720,590	905,649	Bexar, TX
21	Suffolk, NY	1,482,695	1,419,369	25,754	495,648	57,696	38,185,710	.5999	19,116,915	5,623	1,904,296	4,042	1,303,778	7,307	3,087,748	1,312,249	960,491	Suffolk, NY
22	Middlesex, MA	1,472,613	1,465,396	27,568	570,806	54,245	40,596,290	.6440	21,837,015	6,424	1,784,616	3,788	1,474,755	8,265	3,433,808	1,436,414	932,605	Middlesex, MA
23	Philadelphia, PA	1,468,025	1,517,550	15,022	601,909	29,054	22,053,340	.3781	9,909,696	2,915	787,764	1,672	1,123,454	6,296	2,158,817	1,423,825	558,681	Philadelphia, PA
24	Alameda, CA	1,464,561	1,443,741	24,879	543,926	50,332	36,436,510	.5632	16,818,889	4,947	1,539,004	3,267	822,751	4,611	3,380,727	836,556	941,438	Alameda, CA
25	Bronx, NY	1,372,845	1,332,650	12,312	475,273	26,489	16,903,080	.2758	4,095,462	1,205	309,892	658	444,319	2,490	1,041,583	661,888	275,811	Bronx, NY
26	Sacramento, CA	1,364,259	1,223,499	19,771	502,254	40,668	26,972,550	.4497	14,000,552	4,118	1,963,249	4,168	927,762	5,199	2,424,575	546,905	855,031	Sacramento, CA
27	Cuyahoga, OH	1,354,570	1,393,978	19,390	574,816	36,481	26,265,070	.4671	16,746,639	4,926	1,726,440	3,665	1,000,946	5,610	2,530,102	1,914,969	861,511	Cuyahoga, OH
28	Nassau, NY	1,340,495	1,334,544	28,131	449,205	62,549	37,709,860	.6058	21,358,727	6,283	2,023,462	4,295	2,058,858	11,538	2,881,936	1,547,265	810,911	Nassau, NY
29	Allegheny, PA	1,255,103	1,281,666	19,668	544,809	35,911	24,685,840	.4430	16,329,315	4,803	1,644,479	3,491	930,187	5,213	2,650,249	1,228,708	774,262	Allegheny, PA
30	Palm Beach, FL	1,243,157	1,131,184	25,735	577,999	41,513	31,992,820	.5094	16,783,738	4,937	2,107,777	4,474	1,528,403	8,566	2,438,488	1,097,284	887,478	Palm Beach, FL
31	Oakland, MI	1,211,605	1,194,156	28,205	501,036	55,351	34,173,660	.5871	23,701,409	6,972	3,558,982	7,555	1,452,306	8,139	2,343,296	1,542,909	922,079	Oakland, MI
32	Hennepin, MN	1,122,141	1,116,200	24,363	482,887	46,697	27,339,130	.5278	24,368,319	7,168	3,167,395	6,724	1,151,822	6,455	2,601,449	1,097,317	792,808	Hennepin, MN
33	Hillsborough, FL	1,096,848	998,948	20,713	447,410	38,148	22,719,030	.4079	15,488,441	4,556	1,744,239	3,703	734,792	4,118	1,878,578	933,207	725,956	Hillsborough, FL
34	Franklin, OH	1,094,640	1,068,978	21,981	485,707	40,002	24,061,440	.4446	18,354,640	5,399	2,435,257	5,170	882,936	4,948	1,927,076	705,483	813,931	Franklin, OH
35	Contra Costa, CA	1,016,987	948,816	27,259	366,930	56,753	27,721,930	.4057	10,964,225	3,225	1,459,422	3,098	690,609	3,870	2,161,709	539,050	694,666	Contra Costa, CA
36	St. Louis, MO	1,012,010	1,016,315	23,763	419,881	45,642	24,048,260	.4165	15,821,758	4,654	2,258,961	4,795	654,144	3,666	2,241,869	1,093,563	728,515	St. Louis, MO
37	Fairfax, VA	1,008,761	969,749	31,608	379,329	68,938	31,885,260	.4521	12,202,621	3,589	1,701,234	3,611	950,635	5,328	1,927,644	553,025	729,219	Fairfax, VA
38	Orange, FL	985,714	896,344	20,336	389,821	38,271	20,045,770	.3781	15,595,075	4,587	1,894,240	4,021	1,111,012	6,226	1,715,435	748,454	663,159	Orange, FL
39	Westchester, NY	945,092	923,459	27,571	343,503	56,811	26,056,760	.3984	12,325,881	3,626	1,199,362	2,546	1,138,107	6,378	2,060,965	898,751	527,102	Westchester, NY
40	Erie, NY	938,615	950,265	19,617	381,701	36,146	18,412,490	.3082	9,641,934	2,836	1,002,594	2,128	519,748	2,913	1,707,214	737,087	557,927	Erie, NY
41	Montgomery, MD	932,558	873,341	29,947	348,724	62,328	27,926,860	.4048	11,315,031	3,328	1,090,746	2,315	786,479	4,408	1,973,237	534,996	610,330	Montgomery, MD
42	Salt Lake, UT	932,116	898,387	18,076	315,979	43,911	16,848,950	.3344	14,197,599	4,176	2,146,480	4,557	629,720	3,529	1,909,655	284,826	618,154	Salt Lake, UT
43	DuPage, IL	931,347	904,161	28,264	347,373	59,992	26,323,230	.4354	16,357,713	4,812	1,865,219	3,959	930,586	5,215	1,647,963	985,602	646,619	DuPage, IL
44	Milwaukee, WI	931,139	940,164	18,177	396,455	35,739	16,925,060	.2897	9,057,242	2,664	1,299,485	2,759	380,038	2,130	1,354,928	795,995	558,736	Milwaukee, WI
45	Pinellas, FL	927,459	921,482	23,287	461,636	35,033	21,598,100	.3746	14,136,003	4,158	1,510,037	3,206	547,277	3,067	2,046,794	971,804	683,573	Pinellas, FL
46	Honolulu, HI	911,719	876,156	19,820	301,773	46,881	18,070,470	.3029	9,586,291	2,820	1,932,186	4,102	1,213,597	6,801	1,460,075	815,873	491,636	Honolulu, HI
47	Shelby, TN	908,843	897,472	18,512	354,604	37,304	16,824,190	.3088	11,499,693	3,383	1,899,212	4,032	788,357	4,418	1,174,545	760,875	569,371	Shelby, TN
48	Pima, AZ	907,511	843,746	17,888	365,815	34,848	16,233,410	.2752	8,272,791	2,434	1,284,384	2,726	326,802	1,831	1,268,524	505,873	600,419	Pima, AZ
49	Fairfield, CT	904,001	882,567	30,224	334,894	57,713	27,322,330	.4561	17,926,178	5,273	934,028	1,983	1,149,371	6,441	2,396,980	817,269	598,025	Fairfield, CT
50	Bergen, NJ	901,514	884,118	29,771	337,645	57,565	26,839,400	.4186	14,185,109	4,173	1,146,228	2,433	1,080,249	6,054	2,513,556	912,387	567,867	Bergen, NJ
51	Hartford, CT	875,839	857,183	25,542	347,172	45,845	22,370,720	.3556	11,613,745	3,416	1,138,535	2,417	857,713	4,807	1,896,608	820,397	573,213	Hartford, CT
52	Travis, TX	869,648	812,280	23,492	369,393	43,353	20,430,020	.4461	23,826,388	7,009	1,684,916	3,577	731,191	4,098	2,348,135	1,178,319	636,248	Travis, TX
53	Fresno, CA	866,423	799,407	13,541	269,842	32,738	11,732,460	.2231	7,104,904	2,090	970,831	2,061	301,911	1,692	1,214,541	433,499	448,709	Fresno, CA
54	Marion, IN	864,200	860,454	19,809	374,706	37,772	17,118,820	.3328	14,275,351	4,199	2,066,852	4,388	680,543	3,814	1,293,766	1,136,820	610,821	Marion, IN
55	Prince George's, MD	850,384	801,515	23,076	309,453	49,466	19,623,650	.2951	7,654,460	2,252	821,084	1,743	370,328	2,075	1,530,168	396,833	518,153	Prince George's, MD
56	New Haven, CT	847,502	824,008	24,399	331,415	44,342	20,678,310	.3304	10,642,435	3,131	1,078,401	2,289	607,778	3,406	1,706,678	797,297	531,720	New Haven, CT
57	Duval, FL	830,101	778,879	20,810	340,796	37,826	17,274,610	.3088	11,661,697	3,430	1,508,879	3,203	489,864	2,745	1,536,319	590,820	554,170	Duval, FL
58	Macomb, MI	821,634	788,149	23,470	333,076	47,184	19,283,770	.3278	11,914,351	3,505	2,039,828	4,330	339,902	1,905	1,371,719	832,069	608,856	Macomb, MI
59	Fulton, GA	818,745	816,006	23,184	350,031	43,777	18,981,830	.3384	13,432,538	3,951	1,776,324	3,771	1,134,661	6,359	1,914,053	493,971	532,322	Fulton, GA
60	Hamilton, OH	816,699	845,303	20,471	351,774	38,076	16,718,410	.3043	11,803,553	3,472	1,568,275	3,329	769,112	4,310	1,638,199	716,873	557,775	Hamilton, OH
61	Ventura, CA	802,627	753,197	22,864	258,964	53,222	18,351,220	.2961	9,381,128	2,760	941,078	1,998	513,106	2,876	1,505,559	540,323	514,113	Ventura, CA
62	Essex, NJ	797,608	793,633	20,351	286,063	41,124	16,232,360	.2476	5,999,085	1,765	443,360	941	634,867	3,558	1,434,553	556,838	365,477	Essex, NJ
63	Middlesex, NJ	790,283	750,162	26,682	279,135	55,077	21,086,420	.3203	9,535,695	2,805	993,678	2,109	668,688	3,748	1,498,042	545,125	483,989	Middlesex, NJ
64	Worcester, MA	784,595	750,963	21,778	300,867	43,766	17,087,140	.2811	9,059,973	2,665	882,285	1,873	405,829	2,274	1,627,115	628,138	500,744	Worcester, MA
65	Baltimore, MD	784,253	754,292	23,634	318,414	45,692	18,534,880	.3058	10,445,834	3,073	1,386,024	2,942	654,900	3,670	1,754,208	634,897	532,627	Baltimore, MD
66	Montgomery, PA	777,323	750,097	26,422	299,358	54,506	20,538,650	.3398	12,384,781	3,643	1,357,627	2,882	1,085,383	6,083	2,034,819	813,275	529,277	Montgomery, PA
67	Mecklenburg, NC	769,746	695,454	24,604	330,418	45,884	18,938,570	.3225	12,050,279	3,545	1,587,011	3,369	647,070	3,626	1,388,365	545,530	569,655	Mecklenburg, NC
68	Pierce, WA	753,288	700,820	19,217	281,633	41,564	14,476,220	.2441	7,660,414	2,253	1,311,305	2,784	277,368	1,554	1,116,419	309,143	535,609	Pierce, WA
69	San Francisco, CA	743,549	776,733	29,636	332,844	49,555	22,035,600	.3392	11,112,197	3,269	976,344	2,073	2,204,589	12,355	2,006,342	801,356	387,396	San Francisco, CA
70	Essex, MA	741,982	723,419	23,365	284,819	46,702	17,336,360	.2716	8,061,631	2,371	716,046	1,520	552,584	3,097	1,361,166	687,648	458,919	Essex, MA
71	Monroe, NY	737,090	735,343	22,358	300,310	41,277	16,479,510	.2646	8,154,678	2,399	895,104	1,900	405,080	2,270	1,666,922	387,759	476,708	Monroe, NY
72	Kern, CA	729,553	661,645	13,779	226,881	33,407	10,052,420	.1858	5,580,342	1,642	732,780	1,556	216,564	1,214	895,681	350,750	390,843	Kern, CA
73	Wake, NC	716,522	627,846	25,888	297,602	49,553	18,549,530	.3149	11,976,718	3,523	1,643,862	3,490	582,053	3,262	1,495,808	500,884	557,144	Wake, NC
74	El Paso, TX	713,340	679,622	12,037	226,278	29,352	8,586,800	.1799	6,462,611	1,901	1,356,263	2,879	425,599	2,385	831,659	312,642	384,245	El Paso, TX
75	Jefferson, KY	700,741	693,604	20,948	310,484	36,725	14,679,060	.2549	9,096,692	2,676	1,530,818	3,250	445,930	2,499	1,057,025	575,841	490,999	Jefferson, KY
76	Gwinnett, GA	698,970	588,448	24,524	252,225	53,739	17,141,460	.2953	11,272,844	3,316	1,191,909	2,530	541,674	3,036	1,267,631	344,933	503,862	Gwinnett, GA
77	Lake, IL	697,152	644,356	25,051	235,727	59,180	17,464,310	.3153	13,240,975	3,895	902,314	1,915	488,750	2,739	1,167,922	746,979	444,779	Lake, IL
78	San Mateo, CA	693,861	707,161	30,470	255,953	61,761	21,141,720	.3373	12,146,055	3,573	1,793,452	3,807	750,808	4,208	2,113,776	643,255	492,210	San Mateo, CA
79	Multnomah, OR	683,283	660,486	20,230	287,648	38,205	13,822,920	.2610	10,755,184	3,164	1,785,405	3,790	719,360	4,032	1,367,754	296,973	452,776	Multnomah, OR
80	Oklahoma, OK	680,880	660,448	17,709	284,991	32,996	12,057,680	.2343	9,485,296	2,790	1,430,668	3,037	345,116	1,934	1,064,675	499,860	468,898	Oklahoma, OK
81	Suffolk, MA	677,616	689,807	19,586	276,467	36,405	13,271,520	.2203	6,731,224	1,980	349,969	743	1,142,268	6,402	1,510,063	762,737	274,387	Suffolk, MA
82	DeKalb, GA	676,338	665,865	22,651	275,054	44,429	15,319,680	.2420	7,195,702	2,117	809,603	1,719	421,385	2,362	1,115,500	360,276	452,409	DeKalb, GA
83	Cobb, GA	663,776	607,751	25,338	255,316	51,893	16,818,690	.2977	12,131,803	3,569	1,738,439	3,690	617,922	3,463	1,744,223	513,483	493,135	Cobb, GA
84	Jackson, MO	661,091	654,880	19,461	278,123	36,714	12,865,690	.2332	8,722,745	2,566	1,217,102	2,584	287,608	1,612	998,114	489,946	446,304	Jackson, MO
85	Jefferson, AL	656,840	662,047	18,494	268,913	34,844	12,147,880	.2347	9,626,051	2,832	1,451,329	3,081	607,484	3,405	1,247,422	446,142	460,600	Jefferson, AL
86	Hidalgo, TX	656,072	569,463	8,644	182,386	23,710	5,671,110	.1419	5,457,211	1,605	1,064,900	2,261	420,429	2,356	833,469	231,799	292,420	Hidalgo, TX
87	Norfolk, MA	655,356	650,308	28,792	254,854	56,562	18,869,140	.2901	9,325,464	2,743	920,840	1,955	634,516	3,556	1,428,176	652,122	422,582	Norfolk, MA
88	San Joaquin, CA	654,288	563,598	16,392	210,061	38,879	10,725,080	.1822	5,087,457	1,497	677,193	1,438	219,393	1,230	911,463	340,141	375,176	San Joaquin, CA
89	Snohomish, WA	649,489	606,024	22,169	242,527	47,838	14,398,830	.2307	7,019,739	2,065	1,112,466	2,362	340,226	1,907	1,104,607	266,413	481,145	Snohomish, WA
90	Providence, RI	645,010	621,602	17,167	251,477	34,841	11,072,780	.1883	5,511,135	1,621	358,237	760	391,194	2,192	1,226,374	641,525	382,516	Providence, RI
91	Monmouth, NJ	637,323	615,301	29,858	242,133	57,205	19,028,990	.2853	8,763,022	2,578	898,154	1,907	616,738	3,456	1,699,393	544,526	430,244	Monmouth, NJ
92	Collin, TX	629,504	491,675	30,078	235,198	62,074	18,934,140	.2739	7,628,247	2,244	1,165,805	2,475	439,800	2,465	1,149,768	271,602	446,194	Collin, TX
93	Baltimore, MD*	622,161	651,154	14,778	252,858	28,372	9,194,170	.1554	3,805,364	1,119	176,726	375	270,683	1,517	764,403	570,095	239,292	Baltimore, MD
94	Bucks, PA	617,667	597,635	25,011	229,938	53,229	15,448,380	.2654	10,173,907	2,993	862,474	1,831	396,331	2,221	1,660,147	571,612	435,191	Bucks, PA
95	Will, IL	612,859	502,266	23,631	206,961	55,981	14,482,720	.2101	4,883,120	1,436	571,676	1,214	112,172	629	741,107	423,063	410,440	Will, IL
96	Hudson, NJ	606,768	608,975	19,564	230,298	37,691	11,870,940	.1835	4,478,993	1,318	376,234	799	508,737	2,851	872,848	396,886	232,544	Hudson, NJ
97	Kent, MI	595,142	574,335	19,704	226,967	41,981	11,726,700	.2185	8,679,963	2,553	1,669,042	3,543	340,879	1,910	704,075	371,296	403,375	Kent, MI
98	Bernalillo, NM	589,389	556,678	19,178	242,179	36,484	11,303,220	.2103	8,213,325	2,416	1,543,360	3,276	298,070	1,670	669,674	458,941	421,677	Bernalillo, NM
99	Tulsa, OK	572,493	563,299	19,808	245,488	36,079	11,339,830	.2144	8,762,357	2,578	1,667,077	3,539	298,004	1,670	887,933	469,521	413,115	Tulsa, OK
100	Davidson, TN	569,819	569,891	21,077	252,137	36,973	12,010,290	.2437	11,447,682	3,367	1,704,728	3,619	678,403	3,802	1,223,906	710,680	412,800	Davidson, TN
101	El Paso, CO	560,804	516,929	19,819	208,877	42,957	11,114,350	.1975	7,166,545	2,108	1,150,622	2,443	190,170	1,066	768,575	274,941	395,953	El Paso, CO
102	District of Columbia, DC	560,725	572,059	26,337	256,560	37,242	14,767,850	.1959	3,408,245	1,003	145,053	308	469,245	2,630	940,510	481,206	235,770	District of Columbia, DC
103	Denver, CO	558,164	554,636	20,119	243,468	36,894	11,229,470	.2038	7,783,528	2,290	789,445	1,676	388,679	2,178	972,182	306,321	363,719	Denver, CO
104	Ocean, NJ	556,907	510,916	22,970	219,758	42,349	12,792,330	.2037	6,251,600	1,839	571,002	1,212	283,079	1,586	1,327,959	381,234	361,309	Ocean, NJ
105	Delaware, PA	555,177	550,864	21,555	211,118	45,199	11,966,590	.1969	6,300,243	1,853	580,206	1,232	329,248	1,845	1,445,011	569,327	330,274	Delaware, PA
106	Bristol, MA	550,668	534,678	20,512	215,547	40,369	11,295,090	.1942	6,687,807	1,967	1,085,891	2,305	417,656	2,341	1,215,690	477,021	347,693	Bristol, MA
107	Montgomery, OH	550,095	559,062	20,419	240,514	37,391	11,232,240	.1964	7,005,152	2,061	1,206,160	2,560	252,696	1,416	961,401	351,148	400,807	Montgomery, OH
108	Summit, OH	547,831	542,899	20,446	227,872	39,616	11,201,050	.2030	7,805,081	2,296	848,366	1,801	292,381	1,639	1,080,716	703,305	398,640	Summit, OH
109	Denton, TX	534,784	432,976	25,097	198,246	52,161	13,421,650	.1999	5,369,605	1,580	1,025,492	2,177	270,665	1,517	942,760	311,855	385,894	Denton, TX
110	Union, NJ	531,425	522,541	24,155	187,611	49,425	12,836,720	.2064	6,714,919	1,975	322,651	685	315,677	1,769	1,223,960	502,225	302,189	Union, NJ
111	Jefferson, CO[1]	529,255	527,056	25,721	211,565	51,534	13,613,150	.2132	6,739,430	1,982	1,262,709	2,680	259,540	1,455	1,080,297	279,148	421,604	Jefferson, CO
112	Arapahoe, CO	524,236	487,967	23,988	209,391	48,885	12,575,600	.2262	9,263,209	2,725	1,336,753	2,838	352,534	1,976	1,165,486	335,101	388,599	Arapahoe, CO
113	New Castle, DE	519,483	500,265	22,851	201,742	47,492	11,870,500	.2069	7,800,947	2,295	962,699	2,044	351,000	1,967	1,257,968	460,327	344,559	New Castle, DE
114	Polk, FL	518,809	483,924	19,073	217,966	33,882	9,895,440	.1713	5,716,090	1,681	873,686	1,855	196,846	1,103	977,731	287,481	353,833	Polk, FL
115	Camden, NJ	515,644	508,932	22,547	193,883	43,633	11,626,000	.1904	6,208,300	1,826	490,606	1,041	357,773	2,005	1,098,611	472,331	302,389	Camden, NJ
116	Brevard, FL	515,004	476,230	22,229	228,764	37,303	11,447,810	.1835	5,603,865	1,648	916,795	1,946	235,423	1,319	919,936	384,085	382,238	Brevard, FL
117	Anne Arundel, MD	511,686	489,656	26,554	192,675	55,112	13,587,060	.2085	6,366,826	1,873	1,031,207	2,189	374,093	2,097	1,048,749	237,230	371,804	Anne Arundel, MD
118	Lee, FL	508,350	440,888	21,735	219,630	37,791	11,049,150	.1922	7,029,399	2,068	988,622	2,099	443,513	2,486	986,313	442,891	346,632	Lee, FL
119	Stanislaus, CA	506,378	446,997	15,862	162,035	37,383	8,032,070	.1459	4,753,556	1,398	669,983	1,422	178,855	1,002	913,403	315,443	289,267	Stanislaus, CA
120	Ramsey, MN	504,693	511,035	20,942	208,056	41,825	10,569,240	.1887	7,129,858	2,097	1,001,316	2,126	287,208	1,610	1,074,152	392,943	326,880	Ramsey, MN
121	Passaic, NJ	500,842	489,049	20,176	165,703	44,405	10,104,900	.1718	5,698,627	1,676	691,748	1,468	538,403	3,017	952,625	354,527	256,900	Passaic, NJ
122	Johnson, KS	497,146	451,086	26,902	199,850	55,444	13,374,160	.2223	8,245,920	2,426	1,292,625	2,744	541,572	3,035	958,395	395,530	386,163	Johnson, KS
123	Plymouth, MA	491,878	472,822	23,666	178,256	49,953	11,640,650	.1930	6,674,991	1,963	500,163	1,062	260,215	1,458	1,135,648	379,977	321,312	Plymouth, MA
124	Washington, OR	489,844	445,342	22,579	187,584	46,925	11,060,140	.1991	7,944,734	2,337	1,624,383	3,448	429,674	2,408	945,725	171,562	337,164	Washington, OR
125	Lake, IN	488,435	484,564	17,996	186,605	38,958	8,790,030	.1592	5,662,680	1,666	780,761	1,657	220,519	1,236	793,568	428,726	308,377	Lake, IN
126	Morris, NJ	487,077	470,212	33,265	177,679	66,233	16,202,730	.2606	9,892,322	2,910	717,571	1,523	720,280	4,037	1,517,929	581,899	342,536	Morris, NJ
127	Lancaster, PA	486,469	470,658	19,463	180,573	41,641	9,468,350	.1739	6,676,478	1,964	579,937	1,231	367,776	2,061	1,109,981	332,301	314,284	Lancaster, PA
128	Douglas, NE	480,743	463,585	19,874	195,621	40,406	9,554,330	.1828	7,643,874	2,249	893,521	1,897	317,534	1,780	1,014,835	438,791	333,093	Douglas, NE
129	Volusia, FL	476,562	443,343	20,089	215,582	33,201	9,573,780	.1631	5,410,480	1,592	719,210	1,527	211,817	1,187	893,089	358,640	348,665	Volusia, FL
130	Kane, IL	473,610	404,119	21,930	155,884	53,177	10,386,400	.1602	4,319,835	1,271	762,342	1,618	178,346	1,000	700,500	313,932	299,918	Kane, IL
131	Sonoma, CA	468,851	458,614	23,674	174,821	47,810	11,099,560	.1798	5,877,135	1,729	619,805	1,316	256,127	1,435	1,187,270	345,374	332,483	Sonoma, CA
132	Sedgwick, KS	466,006	452,869	18,809	183,088	39,789	8,764,970	.1549	5,372,337	1,580	1,070,450	2,272	228,796	1,282	758,415	256,512	328,115	Sedgwick, KS
133	Chester, PA	464,595	433,501	26,853	171,516	57,890	12,475,900	.2210	9,231,586	2,716	287,925	611	210,579	1,180	841,079	318,928	323,182	Chester, PA
134	Richmond, NY	464,513	443,728	23,528	165,500	49,528	10,929,120	.1517	2,895,764	852	255,426	542	295,732	1,657	695,315	287,014	228,404	Richmond, NY
135	Orleans, LA**	464,268	484,674	14,976	200,992	26,183	6,952,920	.1218	3,405,199	1,002	369,787	785	320,165	1,794	607,673	312,588	227,920	Orleans, LA
136	Hampden, MA	462,756	456,228	18,792	180,216	36,909	8,696,140	.1517	5,101,077	1,501	577,698	1,226	253,956	1,423	956,738	393,607	268,379	Hampden, MA
137	Onondaga, NY	461,207	458,336	20,540	187,155	38,024	9,473,410	.1598	5,272,041	1,551	579,198	1,230	324,363	1,818	984,776	346,688	286,171	Onondaga, NY
138	Dane, WI	456,369	426,526	22,239	191,747	44,581	10,149,360	.1798	6,914,106	2,034	889,619	1,888	241,263	1,352	833,571	318,717	333,858	Dane, WI
139	Lucas, OH	453,978	455,054	18,791	191,320	35,748	8,530,580	.1602	6,292,688	1,851	1,085,178	2,304	285,564	1,600	823,643	370,063	309,782	Lucas, OH
140	Jefferson, LA**	451,699	455,466	19,661	187,132	35,955	8,880,910	.1751	7,657,930	2,253	1,503,975	3,193	440,632	2,469	896,207	499,909	301,304	Jefferson, LA
141	Burlington, NJ	450,960	423,394	26,999	168,471	52,354	12,175,570	.1918	6,326,103	1,861	681,485	1,447	225,239	1,262	975,414	352,366	306,025	Burlington, NJ
142	Genesee, MI	444,011	436,141	19,539	181,093	39,188	8,675,620	.1515	5,238,928	1,541	1,038,212	2,204	183,929	1,031	608,615	347,323	315,266	Genesee, MI
143	Virginia Beach, VA*	443,729	425,257	20,360	168,045	44,057	9,034,270	.1485	4,554,427	1,340	658,328	1,398	284,570	1,595	698,331	198,624	316,083	Virginia Beach, VA
144	Fort Bend, TX	440,039	354,452	23,114	138,170	57,154	10,171,250	.1548	4,184,720	1,231	794,145	1,686	192,539	1,079	534,909	154,139	279,399	Fort Bend, TX
145	Guilford, NC	437,629	421,048	21,145	185,744	39,764	9,253,770	.1714	6,975,821	2,052	810,989	1,722	335,257	1,879	794,262	386,953	327,461	Guilford, NC
146	Spokane, WA	435,145	417,939	17,174	170,747	35,190	7,473,250	.1385	5,018,057	1,476	886,324	1,881	231,274	1,296	770,118	205,222	308,300	Spokane, WA
147	Monterey, CA	418,251	401,762	17,064	123,111	43,679	7,137,110	.1276	4,236,459	1,246	473,268	1,005	285,175	1,598	741,345	267,217	230,362	Monterey, CA
148	Solano, CA	417,390	394,542	21,717	140,762	48,626	9,064,370	.1414	3,923,677	1,154	663,323	1,408	193,021	1,082	753,501	156,794	276,917	Solano, CA
149	East Baton Rouge, LA**	412,326	412,852	18,957	168,774	35,234	7,816,260	.1495	6,096,122	1,793	1,154,525	2,451	274,753	1,540	690,508	288,030	283,614	East Baton Rouge, LA
150	Utah, UT	407,123	368,536	14,363	114,713	41,815	5,847,380	.1153	4,189,283	1,232	806,151	1,711	141,362	792	704,861	73,449	255,562	Utah, UT

*Independent City **Parish Source: Devonshire Associates Ltd. and Scan/US, Inc. 2004.
#Estimates for Total Retail Sales, General Merchandise, Apparel Store Sales, Food Store Sales, and Health and Drug Store Sales are based on data from the U.S. Census Bureau's 1997 Economic Census and utilize the North American Industry Classification System (NAICS).

[1]Census population includes a portion of Broomfield county.

Counties: Population / Income / Sales

This table presents 2000 Census populations, 2004 estimates of population and households, and 2003 estimates of income, purchasing power, retail sales (total and by various store groups) and passenger car registrations. All data except 2000 Census populations are from Devonshire Associates Ltd. and Scan/US, Inc. State and County Codes are from the Federal Information Processing Standards (FIPS) of the National Bureau of Standards. Statistics for Total Retail Sales, General Merchandise, Apparel Store, Food Store Sales, and Health and Drug Store Sales in this edition are estimates based on data from the U.S. Census Bureau, and utilize the 1997 North American Industry Classification System (NAICS).

COUNTY OR COUNTY EQUIVALENT	FIPS CO. CODE	POPULATION Estimate 7/1/04	POPULATION Census 4/1/00	PER CAPITA INCOME 2003	HOUSEHOLDS Estimate 7/1/04	MEDIAN HOUSEHOLD INCOME 2003	DISPOSABLE INCOME 2003 ($1,000)	MARKET ABILITY INDEX 2003	TOTAL RETAIL SALES Sales 2003 ($1,000)	TOTAL RETAIL SALES Ranally Sales Units	GENERAL MERCHANDISE Sales 2003 ($1,000)	GENERAL MERCHANDISE Ranally Sales Units	APPAREL STORE Sales 2003 ($1,000)	APPAREL STORE Ranally Sales Units	FOOD STORE SALES 2003 ($1,000)	HEALTH & DRUG STORE 2003 ($1,000)	PASSENGER CAR REGIS-TRATIONS 2003	COUNTY OR COUNTY EQUIVALENT
ALABAMA (AL; CODE 01; 67 Counties)																		
Autauga*	001	47,354	43,671	19,774	18,350	39,099	936,360	.0162	549,883	**162**	149,726	**318**	9,268	**52**	57,113	62,265	35,544	Autauga
Baldwin**	003	155,304	140,415	19,698	62,614	37,228	3,059,190	.0545	1,980,120	**582**	333,275	**707**	174,971	**981**	257,273	114,101	116,371	Baldwin
Barbour**	005	28,740	29,038	11,646	10,598	24,297	334,700	.0069	226,613	**67**	47,141	**100**	6,040	**34**	43,201	13,043	18,155	Barbour
Bibb*	007	21,630	20,826	14,316	7,975	30,746	309,660	.0052	118,692	**35**	19,514	**41**	....	**....**	28,213	10,046	15,282	Bibb
Blount*	009	55,111	51,024	16,561	20,992	33,133	912,690	.0144	310,041	**91**	75,356	**160**	3,467	**19**	34,460	14,973	43,489	Blount
Bullock	011	11,248	11,714	9,147	3,900	20,241	102,880	.0021	51,867	**15**	10,816	**23**	....	**....**	9,215	4,489	5,890	Bullock
Butler	013	20,485	21,399	12,671	8,321	23,957	259,560	.0054	196,970	**58**	37,818	**80**	4,280	**24**	50,373	8,688	14,121	Butler
Calhoun*	015	112,234	112,249	16,515	47,412	30,063	1,853,520	.0344	1,213,266	**357**	270,566	**574**	36,994	**207**	176,829	51,711	87,861	Calhoun
Chambers**	017	35,478	36,583	14,940	14,465	28,132	530,040	.0094	271,500	**80**	57,569	**122**	2,438	**14**	46,950	14,189	24,901	Chambers
Cherokee	019	24,553	23,988	15,767	10,251	28,977	387,130	.0065	170,157	**50**	26,166	**56**	2,528	**14**	36,664	9,065	21,026	Cherokee
Chilton*	021	41,236	39,593	15,847	16,170	30,924	653,480	.0115	342,170	**101**	85,877	**182**	5,291	**30**	50,430	18,689	31,896	Chilton
Choctaw	023	15,094	15,922	13,041	6,321	23,664	196,840	.0035	84,348	**25**	4,465	**9**	1,719	**10**	20,229	8,309	11,304	Choctaw
Clarke	025	27,370	27,867	13,619	10,777	26,421	372,740	.0076	286,518	**84**	70,804	**150**	8,698	**49**	55,208	17,768	18,449	Clarke
Clay	027	14,155	14,254	14,545	5,909	26,643	205,880	.0033	61,170	**18**	6,945	**15**	....	**....**	13,922	6,759	11,662	Clay
Cleburne	029	14,843	14,123	15,232	6,019	28,751	226,090	.0037	85,120	**25**	7,420	**16**	....	**....**	7,774	2,106	12,428	Cleburne
Coffee**	031	44,984	43,615	16,925	18,431	31,642	761,350	.0143	529,824	**156**	102,336	**217**	15,594	**87**	37,424	19,327	34,237	Coffee
Colbert*	033	54,367	54,984	16,456	22,728	30,348	894,690	.0172	657,153	**193**	119,805	**254**	7,325	**41**	74,519	28,030	43,486	Colbert
Conecuh	035	13,437	14,089	12,551	5,742	22,273	168,650	.0028	51,495	**15**	7,171	**15**	....	**....**	10,410	4,615	9,852	Conecuh
Coosa**	037	11,376	12,202	15,006	4,622	28,244	170,710	.0025	23,622	**7**	1,739	**4**	....	**....**	6,176	2,103	9,021	Coosa
Covington	039	36,748	37,631	14,021	15,616	25,285	515,230	.0101	356,347	**105**	50,573	**107**	12,018	**67**	63,474	23,902	28,081	Covington
Crenshaw	041	13,540	13,665	13,679	5,661	25,004	185,220	.0032	73,499	**22**	6,641	**14**	....	**....**	18,189	5,273	10,114	Crenshaw
Cullman**	043	78,501	77,483	16,272	31,920	30,667	1,277,370	.0236	814,354	**240**	126,777	**269**	19,332	**108**	129,818	38,722	62,765	Cullman
Dale**	045	49,358	49,129	15,583	19,513	30,379	769,140	.0124	267,957	**79**	46,873	**100**	4,009	**22**	51,958	15,858	37,033	Dale
Dallas**	047	44,568	46,365	11,931	18,031	22,401	531,720	.0110	383,922	**113**	82,344	**175**	20,739	**116**	55,539	27,128	28,251	Dallas
DeKalb**	049	67,072	64,452	14,591	26,372	28,207	978,640	.0176	514,179	**151**	124,919	**265**	14,031	**79**	70,957	34,625	51,190	DeKalb
Elmore*	051	72,168	65,874	18,048	26,066	38,269	1,302,490	.0199	420,212	**124**	57,651	**122**	3,256	**18**	86,883	28,390	52,852	Elmore
Escambia	053	38,101	38,440	13,394	14,502	26,920	510,340	.0105	391,710	**115**	60,997	**129**	7,949	**45**	58,627	18,260	25,942	Escambia
Etowah*	055	102,945	103,459	15,783	42,212	29,640	1,624,740	.0296	962,832	**283**	197,166	**419**	41,883	**235**	187,328	55,255	77,749	Etowah
Fayette	057	18,166	18,495	14,751	7,572	27,008	267,960	.0049	152,889	**45**	25,827	**55**	2,889	**16**	23,281	11,045	14,601	Fayette
Franklin	059	30,662	31,223	13,426	12,078	26,076	411,680	.0075	210,887	**62**	28,082	**60**	2,256	**13**	44,277	14,257	22,615	Franklin
Geneva*	061	25,387	25,764	13,690	10,527	25,382	347,540	.0059	129,215	**38**	25,193	**53**	1,162	**7**	33,752	6,882	19,183	Geneva
Greene*	063	9,879	9,974	10,618	4,116	19,469	104,900	.0020	42,296	**12**	9,447	**20**	....	**....**	6,931	1,921	6,458	Greene
Hale*	065	18,295	17,185	11,638	6,609	25,106	212,910	.0037	67,003	**20**	4,477	**10**	....	**....**	24,585	6,405	10,731	Hale
Henry*	067	16,468	16,310	15,123	6,781	28,400	249,050	.0043	116,059	**34**	5,696	**12**	1,849	**10**	17,441	9,417	12,255	Henry
Houston*	069	92,234	88,787	17,586	38,276	32,418	1,622,020	.0350	1,664,605	**490**	332,542	**706**	79,254	**444**	128,117	57,966	66,477	Houston
Jackson**	071	53,727	53,926	16,163	22,137	30,179	868,410	.0152	451,646	**133**	78,800	**167**	16,834	**94**	74,479	23,138	44,311	Jackson
Jefferson*	073	656,840	662,047	18,494	268,913	34,844	12,147,880	.2347	9,626,051	**2,832**	1,451,329	**3,081**	607,484	**3,405**	1,247,422	446,142	460,600	Jefferson
Lamar	075	14,899	15,904	14,584	6,219	26,577	217,290	.0036	82,759	**24**	5,929	**13**	....	**....**	26,536	6,601	11,744	Lamar
Lauderdale*	077	86,633	87,966	17,468	36,668	31,770	1,513,290	.0273	947,014	**279**	258,602	**549**	65,189	**365**	97,357	37,188	70,899	Lauderdale
Lawrence*	079	34,504	34,803	15,641	13,844	30,126	539,690	.0085	168,556	**50**	27,206	**58**	5,251	**29**	27,535	14,832	27,873	Lawrence
Lee*	081	120,927	115,092	15,916	50,646	29,728	1,924,700	.0344	1,074,311	**316**	212,560	**451**	52,646	**295**	208,266	33,042	95,162	Lee
Limestone*	083	69,013	65,676	18,017	27,016	35,191	1,243,440	.0209	613,369	**180**	124,949	**265**	19,174	**107**	76,249	33,726	54,102	Limestone
Lowndes*	085	13,339	13,473	11,360	5,135	22,499	151,530	.0026	46,767	**14**	7,834	**17**	....	**....**	6,999	2,330	8,470	Lowndes
Macon**	087	23,242	24,105	10,649	8,878	20,953	247,500	.0044	78,498	**23**	9,456	**20**	....	**....**	16,973	4,933	13,678	Macon
Madison*	089	293,691	276,700	22,095	121,372	41,214	6,489,030	.1096	3,794,643	**1,116**	759,334	**1,612**	207,939	**1,165**	503,548	137,687	233,045	Madison
Marengo	091	22,269	22,539	13,894	9,022	26,188	309,400	.0058	177,635	**52**	26,060	**55**	5,378	**30**	29,379	8,316	14,712	Marengo
Marion	093	29,862	31,214	14,550	12,435	26,685	434,490	.0077	211,201	**62**	43,660	**93**	2,733	**15**	40,798	9,829	22,959	Marion
Marshall**	095	84,160	82,231	16,249	34,209	30,678	1,367,540	.0292	1,324,374	**390**	198,899	**422**	75,342	**422**	146,143	56,174	64,546	Marshall
Mobile*	097	399,635	399,843	15,819	152,735	31,921	6,321,850	.1148	3,735,954	**1,099**	796,502	**1,691**	159,638	**895**	512,300	206,288	261,879	Mobile
Monroe	099	23,740	24,324	14,436	9,542	27,322	342,700	.0065	215,708	**63**	31,150	**66**	13,169	**74**	41,426	14,069	16,686	Monroe
Montgomery*	101	221,525	223,510	17,771	88,807	34,484	3,936,640	.0775	3,216,384	**946**	584,941	**1,242**	188,455	**1,056**	372,668	153,629	148,872	Montgomery
Morgan*	103	113,078	111,064	18,971	46,246	35,559	2,145,210	.0394	1,487,082	**437**	211,686	**449**	60,588	**340**	140,817	71,192	88,943	Morgan
Perry	105	11,668	11,861	9,902	4,386	20,000	115,540	.0021	38,945	**11**	3,982	**8**	....	**....**	14,822	4,692	6,561	Perry
Pickens	107	20,420	20,949	13,005	8,057	25,682	265,570	.0050	148,571	**44**	7,271	**15**	3,694	**21**	21,164	11,126	14,099	Pickens
Pike**	109	29,126	29,605	13,797	12,474	24,917	401,860	.0082	310,721	**91**	46,085	**98**	8,272	**46**	47,926	17,546	20,957	Pike
Randolph	111	22,223	22,380	13,970	8,738	26,752	310,460	.0053	123,134	**36**	23,794	**51**	1,486	**8**	35,017	5,781	16,833	Randolph
Russell*	113	48,750	49,756	15,183	21,358	26,656	740,160	.0125	316,805	**93**	101,522	**216**	6,301	**35**	90,315	17,898	35,832	Russell
St. Clair*	115	69,841	64,742	17,607	26,685	35,242	1,229,670	.0187	371,977	**109**	56,089	**119**	4,866	**27**	81,250	17,906	53,741	St. Clair
Shelby*	117	164,416	143,293	25,255	63,993	49,366	4,152,380	.0595	1,399,866	**412**	237,333	**504**	20,768	**116**	231,366	74,410	128,859	Shelby
Sumter	119	13,999	14,798	9,661	5,607	18,281	135,240	.0029	83,554	**25**	13,603	**29**	....	**....**	14,589	5,639	8,125	Sumter
Talladega**	121	79,784	80,321	15,346	31,628	29,813	1,224,380	.0215	617,950	**182**	129,614	**275**	18,782	**105**	104,962	36,584	57,896	Talladega
Tallapoosa**	123	40,456	41,475	16,176	17,234	29,501	654,410	.0111	307,250	**90**	70,085	**149**	10,859	**61**	51,260	17,554	31,604	Tallapoosa
Tuscaloosa*	125	166,903	164,875	17,741	69,787	32,908	2,960,990	.0545	1,988,420	**585**	344,218	**731**	96,127	**539**	243,985	106,668	125,950	Tuscaloosa
Walker*	127	70,015	70,713	14,806	28,839	27,509	1,036,620	.0214	868,568	**255**	166,765	**354**	34,079	**191**	100,119	52,291	54,064	Walker
Washington	129	17,804	18,097	14,729	6,822	29,512	262,230	.0040	61,565	**18**	6,595	**14**	....	**....**	13,283	6,131	12,950	Washington
Wilcox	131	13,030	13,183	8,387	5,015	16,362	109,280	.0024	62,189	**18**	5,748	**12**	....	**....**	15,956	4,914	7,606	Wilcox
Winston	133	24,526	24,843	14,511	10,192	26,671	355,890	.0060	139,162	**41**	31,270	**66**	....	**....**	20,805	12,505	19,175	Winston
The State		4,517,136	4,447,100	17,135	1,822,088	32,557	77,402,380	1.3998	47,869,124	**14,080**	8,692,589	**18,451**	2,181,663	**12,224**	6,673,254	2,416,340	3,324,005	The State
ALASKA (AK; CODE 02; 27 Census Divisions)																		
Aleutians East	013	2,646	2,697	10,435	525	42,630	27,610	.0005	9,533	**3**	1,201	**3**	....	**....**	4,361	....	631	Aleutians East
Aleutians West	016	5,176	5,465	17,544	1,342	54,524	90,810	.0014	34,663	**10**	3,489	**7**	....	**....**	14,357	....	2,354	Aleutians West
Anchorage*	020	274,398	260,283	22,488	100,252	49,752	6,170,610	.1105	4,355,756	**1,281**	1,057,357	**2,245**	209,835	**1,176**	511,166	47,012	179,002	Anchorage
Bethel	050	17,133	16,006	10,973	4,508	33,802	188,000	.0036	96,625	**28**	37,577	**80**	....	**....**	34,001	....	3,145	Bethel
Bristol Bay	060	1,058	1,258	23,043	427	46,279	24,380	.0004	13,549	**4**	3,176	**7**	....	**....**	5,240	....	699	Bristol Bay
Denali	068	1,864	1,893	27,082	842	48,026	50,480	.0006	5,034	**1**	....	**....**	....	**....**	1,430	....	1,671	Denali
Dillingham	070	4,934	4,922	15,191	1,550	39,213	74,950	.0013	31,990	**9**	2,664	**6**	....	**....**	18,755	....	1,469	Dillingham
Fairbanks North Star*	090	87,045	82,840	19,956	31,711	44,447	1,737,030	.0312	1,166,641	**343**	299,064	**635**	34,508	**193**	97,107	13,360	58,639	Fairbanks North Star
Haines	100	2,263	2,392	19,956	966	37,709	45,160	.0007	19,422	**6**	1,309	**3**	....	**....**	9,110	....	1,594	Haines
Juneau**	110	31,357	30,711	25,997	11,883	55,454	815,200	.0121	329,922	**97**	120,780	**256**	19,867	**111**	38,860	8,122	20,034	Juneau
Kenai Peninsula	122	51,635	49,691	19,939	19,672	42,247	1,029,570	.0180	627,930	**185**	83,993	**178**	14,751	**83**	137,279	17,456	36,441	Kenai Peninsula
Ketchikan Gateway**	130	13,105	14,070	22,307	5,128	46,536	292,330	.0053	213,308	**63**	9,003	**19**	22,205	**124**	70,139	5,561	7,789	Ketchikan Gateway
Kodiak Island**	150	13,234	13,913	19,219	4,189	48,978	254,350	.0041	117,682	**35**	5,951	**13**	1,559	**9**	49,745	1,916	7,248	Kodiak Island
Lake and Peninsula	164	1,474	1,823	13,928	482	34,145	20,530	.0003	4,030	**1**	2,373	**5**	....	**....**	....	....	430	Lake and Peninsula
Matanuska-Susitna*	170	71,142	59,322	19,923	25,028	45,822	1,417,360	.0235	726,542	**214**	85,149	**181**	15,894	**89**	132,636	14,427	51,068	Matanuska-Susitna
Nome	180	9,158	9,196	14,126	2,711	38,092	129,370	.0023	63,537	**19**	2,111	**4**	....	**....**	38,027	....	1,763	Nome
North Slope	185	7,165	7,385	19,932	2,051	56,412	142,810	.0022	58,217	**17**	23,045	**49**	....	**....**	17,073	....	1,371	North Slope
Northwest Arctic	188	7,425	7,208	12,928	1,853	42,024	95,990	.0017	42,738	**13**	19,896	**42**	....	**....**	17,160	....	742	Northwest Arctic
Prince of Wales-Outer Ketchikan	201	5,703	6,146	17,905	2,169	37,697	102,110	.0015	25,681	**8**	2,315	**5**	....	**....**	11,651	....	3,008	Prince of Wales-Outer Ketchikan
Sitka	220	8,888	8,835	21,931	3,404	46,143	194,920	.0032	97,603	**29**	3,195	**7**	8,828	**49**	35,059	6,560	5,089	Sitka
Skagway-Hoonah-Angoon	232	3,024	3,436	19,884	1,293	37,694	60,130	.0010	28,779	**8**	2,047	**4**	....	**....**	8,603	....	1,578	Skagway-Hoonah-Angoon
Southeast Fairbanks	240	5,727	6,174	15,710	2,002	36,075	89,970	.0014	29,317	**9**	1,191	**3**	....	**....**	5,900	....	3,786	Southeast Fairbanks
Valdez-Cordova	261	9,831	10,195	21,422	3,850	44,398	210,600	.0033	95,781	**28**	3,893	**8**	2,231	**13**	32,227	1,438	6,439	Valdez-Cordova
Wade Hampton	270	7,404	7,028	7,905	1,664	28,404	58,530	.0013	35,597	**10**	10,384	**22**	....	**....**	18,515	....	581	Wade Hampton
Wrangell-Petersburg	280	6,170	6,684	20,749	2,460	42,005	128,020	.0021	60,483	**18**	2,133	**5**	2,006	**11**	25,942	1,195	3,590	Wrangell-Petersburg
Yakutat	282	683	808	17,408	224	42,627	11,890	.0002	5,095	**2**	....	**....**	....	**....**	....	....	313	Yakutat
Yukon-Koyukuk	290	6,257	6,551	12,052	2,247	26,920	75,410	.0012	18,631	**5**	3,999	**8**	....	**....**	5,918	....	1,606	Yukon-Koyukuk
The State		655,899	626,932	20,641	234,433	46,727	13,538,120	.2349	8,314,088	**2,446**	1,788,280	**3,797**	335,023	**1,876**	1,342,127	118,165	402,080	The State
ARIZONA (AZ; CODE 04; 15 Counties)																		
Apache	001	67,789	69,423	8,731	20,403	22,022	591,870	.0114	188,295	**55**	16,659	**35**	4,943	**28**	49,647	6,238	30,689	Apache
Cochise**	003	123,522	117,755	15,016	47,093	30,810	1,854,760	.0322	881,412	**259**	165,558	**351**	26,535	**149**	187,070	22,214	82,354	Cochise
Coconino*	005	122,854	116,320	16,664	44,020	36,077	2,047,190	.0374	1,282,069	**377**	284,754	**604**	31,842	**178**	226,079	29,172	80,390	Coconino
Gila**	007	51,475	51,335	14,790	20,403	29,183	761,340	.0131	341,948	**101**	70,176	**149**	3,595	**20**	81,162	9,208	35,529	Gila
Graham**	009	32,905	33,489	11,018	10,060	28,073	362,560	.0074	231,423	**68**	49,773	**106**	4,936	**28**	45,818	3,305	18,023	Graham
Greenlee**	011	7,202	8,547	17,441	2,671	36,409	125,610	.0018	27,979	**8**	1,436	**3**	1,232	**7**	13,174	....	5,561	Greenlee
La Paz	012	19,470	19,715	14,133	8,597	25,092	275,170	.0062	277,443	**82**	4,177	**9**	....	**....**	28,896	....	14,941	La Paz
Maricopa*	013	3,486,879	3,072,149	20,135	1,315,734	42,033	70,207,570	1.2176	42,274,027	**12,435**	5,654,014	**12,002**	1,598,779	**8,960**	5,669,314	2,068,177	2,235,443	Maricopa
Mohave**	015	176,406	155,032	15,550	71,821	29,905	2,743,200	.0514	1,779,504	**523**	271,732	**577**	32,714	**183**	334,770	77,701	126,330	Mohave
Navajo	017	106,398	97,470	11,271	34,037	27,325	1,199,190	.0245	782,417	**230**	137,447	**292**	11,680	**65**	163,482	11,266	55,231	Navajo
Pima*	019	907,511	843,746	17,888	365,815	34,848	16,233,410	.2752	8,272,791	**2,434**	1,284,384	**2,726**	326,802	**1,831**	1,268,524	505,873	600,419	Pima
Pinal*	021	211,719	179,727	15,329	75,023	33,658	3,245,490	.0500	848,988	**250**	100,529	**213**	37,578	**211**	217,688	46,046	127,720	Pinal
Santa Cruz**	023	40,833	38,381	11,327	12,760	28,427	462,500	.0106	436,479	**128**	104,751	**222**	47,253	**265**	88,596	12,094	22,791	Santa Cruz
Yavapai*	025	189,588	167,517	17,740	79,896	32,607	3,363,380	.0565	1,644,997	**484**	297,003	**630**	44,109	**247**	338,416	63,090	145,395	Yavapai
Yuma*	027	174,609	160,026	13,194	58,992	30,258	2,303,760	.0445	1,439,675	**423**	334,372	**710**	34,477	**193**	209,344	71,584	99,509	Yuma
The State		5,719,160	5,130,632	18,495	2,167,325	38,284	105,777,000	1.8398	60,709,448	**17,857**	8,776,765	**18,629**	2,207,368	**12,370**	8,921,980	2,926,679	3,680,325	The State
ARKANSAS (AR; CODE 05; 75 Counties)																		
Arkansas	001	19,992	20,749	15,310	8,322	28,704	306,080	.0065	284,296	**84**	82,601	**175**	7,336	**41**	29,647	15,472	13,679	Arkansas
Ashley	003	23,384	24,209	15,324	9,280	30,278	358,330	.0062	171,202	**50**	39,881	**85**	6,848	**38**	35,692	9,573	15,574	Ashley
Baxter**	005	39,329	38,386	16,000	17,715	27,541	629,270	.0120	435,398	**128**	107,354	**228**	7,795	**44**	74,355	12,018	30,027	Baxter
Benton*	007	177,727	153,406	18,095	67,027	37,349	3,215,960	.0561	1,834,280	**540**	514,256	**1,092**	27,893	**156**	135,087	55,986	123,026	Benton
Boone**	009	34,966	33,948	15,068	14,513	28,228	526,870	.0113	491,669	**145**	141,845	**301**	12,700	**71**	28,133	14,604	26,368	Boone
Bradley	011	12,352	12,600	11,948	4,806	23,805	147,580	.0028	73,545	**22**	6,450	**14**	2,178	**12**	12,329	3,032	7,793	Bradley
Calhoun**	013	5,591	5,744	14,443	2,329	26,729	80,750	.0012	15,906	**5**	1,529	**3**	....	**....**	2,984	2,821	3,992	Calhoun
Carroll	015	26,672	25,357	13,754	10,692	26,662	366,860	.0072	253,820	**75**	70,783	**150**	6,889	**39**	40,924	9,418	19,721	Carroll
Chicot	017	13,288	14,117	10,772	5,064	21,874	143,140	.0032	115,480	**34**	11,491	**24**	2,878	**16**	19,544	6,349	7,201	Chicot
Clark**	019	23,605	23,546	13,228	8,946	27,049	312,240	.0063	225,853	**66**	43,509	**92**	5,021	**28**	21,717	18,905	14,760	Clark
Clay	021	16,705	17,609	13,225	7,076	24,360	220,930	.0042	131,539	**39**	19,016	**40**	1,124	**6**	17,665	7,439	11,923	Clay
Cleburne	023	24,927	24,046	16,452	10,714	29,901	410,090	.0070	198,526	**58**	49,708	**106**	1,434	**8**	33,327	10,459	19,152	Cleburne
Cleveland*	025	8,761	8,571	15,251	3,395	31,834	133,610	.0019	13,432	**4**	2,475	**5**	....	**....**	1,181	....	6,260	Cleveland
Columbia**	027	24,856	25,603	13,469	9,849	26,514	334,790	.0063	188,963	**56**	52,918	**112**	12,740	**71**	29,193	6,906	16,590	Columbia
Conway	029	20,534	20,336	15,125	8,189	29,680	310,580	.0060	219,284	**65**	67,495	**143**	2,585	**14**	30,727	6,784	14,889	Conway
Craighead*	031	85,334	82,148	15,727	34,061	30,826	1,342,040	.0281	1,210,679	**356**	330,305	**701**	77,711	**436**	91,604	43,446	58,588	Craighead
Crawford*	033	56,398	53,247	14,931	21,112	31,023	842,090	.0145	377,868	**111**	87,963	**187**	1,915	**11**	59,810	13,814	38,327	Crawford
Crittenden*	035	51,207	50,866	13,674	19,076	28,858	700,180	.0150	623,252	**183**	120,650	**256**	11,696	**66**	46,778	31,868	28,336	Crittenden
Cross	037	19,109	19,526	13,867	7,466	27,490	264,980	.0048	139,739	**41**	27,436	**58**	4,386	**25**	20,218	3,426	11,853	Cross
Dallas	039	8,563	9,210	12,665	3,331	25,403	108,450	.0022	80,592	**24**	14,652	**31**	2,130	**12**	10,889	4,521	5,146	Dallas
Desha	041	14,398	15,341	12,021	5,748	23,320	173,080	.0042	192,781	**57**	37,371	**79**	1,976	**11**	20,297	7,817	8,168	Desha

Source: Devonshire Associates Ltd. and Scan/US, Inc. 2004.
* Component of a Metropolitan Core Based Statistical Area.
** Component of a Micropolitan Core Based Statistical Area.

.... Data less than 1,000.

(d) Data not available.

Counties: Population / Income / Sales, *Continued*

COUNTY OR COUNTY EQUIVALENT	FIPS CO. CODE	POPULATION Estimate 7/1/04	POPULATION Census 4/1/00	PER CAPITA INCOME 2003	HOUSEHOLDS Estimate 7/1/04	MEDIAN HOUSEHOLD INCOME 2003	DISPOSABLE INCOME 2003 ($1,000)	MARKET ABILITY INDEX 2003	TOTAL RETAIL SALES Sales 2003 ($1,000)	TOTAL RETAIL SALES Ranally Sales Units	GENERAL MERCHANDISE Sales 2003 ($1,000)	GENERAL MERCHANDISE Ranally Sales Units	APPAREL STORE Sales 2003 ($1,000)	APPAREL STORE Ranally Sales Units	FOOD STORE SALES 2003 ($1,000)	HEALTH & DRUG STORE 2003 ($1,000)	PASSENGER CAR REGIS-TRATIONS 2003	COUNTY OR COUNTY EQUIVALENT
Drew	043	18,389	18,723	14,298	7,458	27,421	262,920	.0054	212,322	**62**	78,295	**166**	5,374	**30**	12,646	4,207	12,918	Drew
Faulkner*	045	93,944	86,014	17,402	35,593	35,783	1,634,820	.0283	875,162	**257**	236,658	**502**	35,049	**196**	51,694	38,647	64,107	Faulkner
Franklin*	047	18,093	17,771	14,611	7,095	29,098	264,360	.0045	109,583	**32**	22,237	**47**	....	**....**	22,146	7,947	13,014	Franklin
Fulton	049	11,621	11,642	13,192	4,865	24,680	153,300	.0024	29,235	**9**	3,077	**7**	....	**....**	7,858	5,162	9,120	Fulton
Garland*	051	92,118	88,068	17,312	41,928	29,899	1,594,770	.0311	1,248,087	**367**	312,850	**664**	38,691	**217**	120,441	58,699	67,663	Garland
Grant*	053	17,074	16,464	17,268	6,573	34,890	294,840	.0045	85,402	**25**	29,793	**63**	....	**....**	15,229	1,884	12,528	Grant
Greene**	055	38,632	37,331	15,266	15,745	29,369	589,760	.0110	365,591	**108**	109,930	**233**	9,745	**55**	38,518	16,686	27,926	Greene
Hempstead**	057	23,381	23,587	13,231	8,852	27,103	309,350	.0058	171,650	**50**	44,663	**95**	6,807	**38**	25,896	5,727	14,858	Hempstead
Hot Spring	059	30,772	30,353	15,184	12,270	29,943	467,230	.0079	195,757	**58**	48,677	**103**	2,903	**16**	29,656	6,055	22,353	Hot Spring
Howard	061	14,526	14,300	13,748	5,651	27,509	199,710	.0038	122,488	**36**	36,376	**77**	1,239	**7**	28,485	6,901	9,826	Howard
Independence**	063	34,469	34,233	15,392	13,796	30,079	530,540	.0105	405,509	**119**	139,967	**297**	19,977	**112**	36,067	16,052	24,786	Independence
Izard	065	13,176	13,249	13,160	5,475	24,788	173,390	.0032	95,499	**28**	4,773	**10**	....	**....**	11,768	6,927	9,643	Izard
Jackson	067	17,148	18,418	12,017	6,576	24,546	206,070	.0044	167,151	**49**	30,377	**64**	3,889	**22**	26,300	6,584	10,516	Jackson
Jefferson*	069	82,445	84,278	13,976	30,359	29,854	1,152,220	.0238	933,401	**275**	187,094	**397**	55,965	**314**	129,323	102,357	48,167	Jefferson
Johnson	071	23,857	22,781	13,048	9,075	26,591	311,280	.0061	199,986	**59**	46,336	**98**	3,375	**19**	25,259	5,892	16,069	Johnson
Lafayette	073	8,234	8,559	12,820	3,415	23,939	105,560	.0017	29,360	**9**	3,587	**8**	....	**....**	8,181	2,933	5,435	Lafayette
Lawrence	075	17,509	17,774	13,345	7,066	25,616	233,660	.0046	153,434	**45**	27,048	**57**	2,375	**13**	14,666	7,120	12,050	Lawrence
Lee	077	11,639	12,580	8,827	3,952	20,584	102,740	.0021	47,938	**14**	6,001	**13**	....	**....**	8,077	3,988	5,756	Lee
Lincoln*	079	14,378	14,492	10,405	4,157	28,024	149,600	.0027	49,050	**14**	4,559	**10**	....	**....**	9,492	5,150	6,851	Lincoln
Little River	081	13,269	13,628	14,929	5,516	27,900	198,090	.0034	93,058	**27**	18,586	**39**	....	**....**	18,054	4,771	9,590	Little River
Logan	083	22,906	22,486	13,603	8,969	26,920	311,580	.0056	157,819	**46**	35,558	**75**	4,994	**28**	23,080	8,947	16,304	Logan
Lonoke*	085	57,901	52,828	17,840	21,416	37,553	1,032,980	.0164	402,217	**118**	112,243	**238**	3,031	**17**	41,225	14,142	40,361	Lonoke
Madison*	087	14,374	14,243	13,177	5,546	26,473	189,400	.0032	70,116	**21**	17,189	**36**	....	**....**	4,026	3,886	11,029	Madison
Marion	089	16,320	16,140	13,954	6,896	25,693	227,730	.0036	62,206	**18**	14,388	**31**	....	**....**	19,447	3,217	12,565	Marion
Miller*	091	42,371	40,443	14,755	16,744	29,294	625,200	.0110	306,783	**90**	70,823	**150**	9,532	**53**	64,670	8,866	27,468	Miller
Mississippi**	093	48,138	51,979	12,701	18,226	26,173	611,410	.0123	417,697	**123**	88,053	**187**	12,828	**72**	53,521	19,860	27,756	Mississippi
Monroe	095	9,457	10,254	11,456	3,848	21,689	108,340	.0026	118,394	**35**	14,574	**31**	1,371	**8**	17,797	7,987	5,601	Monroe
Montgomery	097	9,066	9,245	14,472	3,742	27,433	131,200	.0020	26,812	**8**	1,855	**4**	....	**....**	7,818	2,660	6,994	Montgomery
Nevada**	099	9,545	9,955	13,067	3,803	25,488	124,720	.0021	46,356	**14**	4,317	**9**	....	**....**	7,259	4,259	6,392	Nevada
Newton**	101	8,510	8,608	13,074	3,613	23,923	111,260	.0018	26,165	**8**	1,817	**4**	....	**....**	....	1,808	6,442	Newton
Ouachita**	103	27,369	28,790	14,649	11,273	27,637	400,920	.0074	234,084	**69**	47,842	**102**	12,373	**69**	33,568	9,334	18,226	Ouachita
Perry*	105	10,533	10,209	14,895	4,159	29,623	156,890	.0023	27,437	**8**	3,772	**8**	....	**....**	8,045	2,447	7,876	Perry
Phillips**	107	24,091	26,445	10,429	8,981	21,536	251,240	.0057	216,034	**64**	59,243	**126**	4,686	**26**	30,078	7,956	11,935	Phillips
Pike	109	11,055	11,303	13,688	4,480	26,141	151,320	.0029	90,080	**27**	7,329	**16**	....	**....**	15,750	6,367	8,275	Pike
Poinsett*	111	25,345	25,614	12,982	10,065	25,538	329,030	.0057	133,495	**39**	23,507	**50**	....	**....**	28,073	11,279	16,424	Poinsett
Polk	113	20,206	20,229	12,467	8,069	24,399	251,900	.0050	159,000	**47**	73,550	**156**	3,068	**17**	11,180	6,421	14,368	Polk
Pope**	115	55,417	54,469	14,935	21,242	30,322	827,670	.0173	717,477	**211**	151,329	**321**	18,720	**105**	72,783	24,050	38,866	Pope
Prairie	117	9,289	9,539	14,927	3,896	27,675	138,660	.0023	58,505	**17**	5,578	**12**	....	**....**	8,494	2,389	6,786	Prairie
Pulaski*	119	365,501	361,474	20,056	159,533	35,839	7,330,380	.1437	6,282,433	**1,848**	1,234,221	**2,620**	264,578	**1,483**	587,460	193,618	258,251	Pulaski
Randolph	121	18,169	18,195	13,843	7,347	26,517	251,520	.0045	122,080	**36**	44,546	**95**	....	**....**	17,664	5,706	12,923	Randolph
St. Francis**	123	28,264	29,329	11,102	9,906	24,869	313,780	.0076	340,322	**100**	85,049	**181**	6,775	**38**	50,132	14,792	14,442	St. Francis
Saline*	125	88,755	83,529	19,995	35,011	39,602	1,774,640	.0322	1,226,442	**361**	159,810	**339**	15,917	**89**	63,025	31,312	65,891	Saline
Scott	127	10,947	10,996	12,902	4,317	25,432	141,240	.0024	47,070	**14**	13,436	**29**	....	**....**	6,873	4,680	7,525	Scott
Searcy	129	7,876	8,261	11,822	3,454	20,876	93,110	.0018	47,646	**14**	16,269	**35**	....	**....**	10,058	3,268	6,170	Searcy
Sebastian*	131	117,824	115,071	16,201	46,440	31,983	1,908,920	.0409	1,853,378	**545**	543,960	**1,155**	64,266	**360**	165,102	77,003	78,243	Sebastian
Sevier	133	15,895	15,757	12,930	5,659	28,252	205,520	.0038	109,777	**32**	31,960	**68**	....	**....**	17,050	5,458	10,414	Sevier
Sharp	135	17,554	17,119	13,202	7,454	24,208	231,740	.0045	151,843	**45**	60,618	**129**	....	**....**	15,832	4,098	12,729	Sharp
Stone	137	11,665	11,499	12,065	4,937	21,986	140,740	.0027	81,873	**24**	10,506	**22**	....	**....**	13,685	2,679	9,127	Stone
Union**	139	44,583	45,629	14,544	17,842	28,341	648,400	.0133	532,585	**157**	139,920	**297**	19,892	**111**	58,274	31,305	29,198	Union
Van Buren	141	16,389	16,192	14,355	7,037	25,993	235,260	.0040	96,121	**28**	29,077	**62**	1,208	**7**	9,760	4,138	12,289	Van Buren
Washington*	143	173,341	157,715	16,189	66,984	32,484	2,806,290	.0556	2,208,663	**650**	769,926	**1,634**	89,729	**503**	215,132	61,242	119,861	Washington
White**	145	70,832	67,165	14,916	26,860	30,555	1,056,560	.0203	717,945	**211**	212,988	**452**	33,279	**187**	60,432	33,339	48,257	White
Woodruff	147	8,099	8,741	11,683	3,352	21,701	94,620	.0018	43,774	**13**	5,785	**12**	....	**....**	14,413	5,487	5,142	Woodruff
Yell**	149	21,552	21,139	13,112	7,994	27,538	282,580	.0047	93,475	**28**	19,454	**41**	....	**....**	16,725	7,236	14,623	Yell
The State		2,741,511	2,673,400	15,816	1,093,223	30,798	43,358,860	.8272	30,093,872	**8,855**	7,331,064	**15,559**	960,545	**5,382**	3,171,092	1,230,502	1,873,302	The State

CALIFORNIA (CA; CODE 06; 58 Counties)

COUNTY OR COUNTY EQUIVALENT	FIPS CO. CODE	POPULATION Estimate 7/1/04	POPULATION Census 4/1/00	PER CAPITA INCOME 2003	HOUSEHOLDS Estimate 7/1/04	MEDIAN HOUSEHOLD INCOME 2003	DISPOSABLE INCOME 2003 ($1,000)	MARKET ABILITY INDEX 2003	TOTAL RETAIL SALES Sales 2003 ($1,000)	TOTAL RETAIL SALES Ranally Sales Units	GENERAL MERCHANDISE Sales 2003 ($1,000)	GENERAL MERCHANDISE Ranally Sales Units	APPAREL STORE Sales 2003 ($1,000)	APPAREL STORE Ranally Sales Units	FOOD STORE SALES 2003 ($1,000)	HEALTH & DRUG STORE 2003 ($1,000)	PASSENGER CAR REGIS-TRATIONS 2003	COUNTY OR COUNTY EQUIVALENT
Alameda*	001	1,464,561	1,443,741	24,879	543,926	50,332	36,436,510	.5632	16,818,889	**4,947**	1,539,004	**3,267**	822,751	**4,611**	3,380,727	836,556	941,438	Alameda
Alpine	003	1,210	1,208	20,711	481	39,533	25,060	.0003	4,121	**1**	....	**....**	....	**....**	....	....	923	Alpine
Amador	005	37,967	35,100	19,413	14,032	39,586	737,060	.0151	694,524	**204**	59,982	**127**	7,057	**40**	91,154	15,521	27,479	Amador
Butte*	007	213,422	203,171	15,710	83,496	30,391	3,352,780	.0619	2,084,387	**613**	302,336	**642**	76,186	**427**	422,545	147,515	151,091	Butte
Calaveras	009	45,803	40,554	20,872	18,835	38,117	956,010	.0133	214,602	**63**	2,933	**6**	2,782	**16**	52,736	24,530	38,054	Calaveras
Colusa	011	19,958	18,804	14,018	6,333	33,092	279,770	.0050	137,542	**40**	3,670	**8**	1,818	**10**	19,549	8,640	11,454	Colusa
Contra Costa*	013	1,016,987	948,816	27,259	366,930	56,753	27,721,930	.4057	10,964,225	**3,225**	1,459,422	**3,098**	690,609	**3,870**	2,161,709	539,050	694,666	Contra Costa
Del Norte**	015	28,062	27,507	12,558	9,468	27,895	352,390	.0062	141,014	**41**	32,211	**68**	3,185	**18**	42,505	8,966	15,686	Del Norte
El Dorado*	017	172,703	156,299	23,428	65,465	46,748	4,046,000	.0587	1,354,818	**399**	45,820	**97**	85,407	**479**	370,362	82,579	133,682	El Dorado
Fresno*	019	866,423	799,407	13,541	269,842	32,738	11,732,460	.2231	7,104,904	**2,090**	970,831	**2,061**	301,911	**1,692**	1,214,541	433,499	448,709	Fresno
Glenn	021	27,524	26,453	13,594	9,448	29,917	374,170	.0061	111,590	**33**	22,164	**47**	1,550	**9**	29,346	5,450	17,754	Glenn
Humboldt**	023	128,447	126,518	16,089	52,854	29,492	2,066,640	.0380	1,286,476	**378**	126,205	**268**	45,776	**257**	281,194	104,815	90,026	Humboldt
Imperial*	025	151,466	142,361	10,979	41,707	30,340	1,662,980	.0370	1,392,918	**410**	261,116	**554**	82,208	**461**	254,019	62,708	71,483	Imperial
Inyo**	027	18,460	17,945	18,984	7,986	32,800	350,440	.0061	206,810	**61**	17,014	**36**	8,468	**47**	40,365	14,311	14,467	Inyo
Kern*	029	729,553	661,645	13,779	226,881	33,407	10,052,420	.1858	5,580,342	**1,642**	732,780	**1,556**	216,564	**1,214**	895,681	350,750	390,843	Kern
Kings*	031	141,461	129,461	11,732	37,363	33,191	1,659,660	.0307	763,680	**225**	108,758	**231**	31,613	**177**	181,021	34,944	64,905	Kings
Lake**	033	64,960	58,309	15,357	26,706	28,047	997,580	.0166	407,177	**120**	56,179	**119**	4,482	**25**	117,931	32,441	46,919	Lake
Lassen**	035	33,980	33,828	13,009	9,766	34,227	442,040	.0074	145,131	**43**	17,774	**38**	7,931	**44**	34,436	5,461	19,029	Lassen
Los Angeles*	037	9,980,271	9,519,338	17,007	3,253,579	39,263	169,739,220	2.9601	92,102,910	**27,093**	10,418,455	**22,116**	7,736,176	**43,356**	15,567,979	5,237,037	5,402,514	Los Angeles
Madera*	039	136,739	123,109	13,247	39,936	34,242	1,811,380	.0307	646,914	**190**	57,541	**122**	10,665	**60**	210,767	44,922	73,700	Madera
Marin*	041	245,560	247,289	33,841	99,797	62,101	8,309,900	.1244	4,058,483	**1,194**	366,668	**778**	339,901	**1,905**	762,881	215,907	180,697	Marin
Mariposa	043	18,022	17,130	16,953	7,058	32,400	305,520	.0045	70,089	**21**	14,548	**31**	4,308	**24**	19,655	4,181	13,985	Mariposa
Mendocino**	045	89,009	86,265	17,486	34,594	33,774	1,556,380	.0277	930,565	**274**	88,297	**187**	10,800	**61**	226,768	55,439	60,900	Mendocino
Merced*	047	238,219	210,554	13,234	71,028	33,536	3,152,650	.0571	1,544,511	**454**	256,600	**545**	38,860	**218**	298,155	86,520	125,915	Merced
Modoc	049	9,417	9,449	14,553	3,840	26,641	137,050	.0021	35,731	**11**	....	**....**	....	**....**	9,610	2,555	7,169	Modoc
Mono	051	13,029	12,853	22,153	5,277	41,248	288,630	.0044	119,416	**35**	5,808	**12**	5,853	**33**	43,408	6,956	9,856	Mono
Monterey*	053	418,251	401,762	17,064	123,111	43,679	7,137,110	.1276	4,236,459	**1,246**	473,268	**1,005**	285,175	**1,598**	741,345	267,217	230,362	Monterey
Napa*	055	133,946	124,279	22,584	48,804	46,532	3,024,970	.0481	1,452,122	**427**	87,608	**186**	125,152	**701**	369,317	82,039	92,106	Napa
Nevada**	057	97,292	92,033	22,509	39,292	41,967	2,189,940	.0342	975,608	**287**	36,246	**77**	51,625	**289**	252,253	79,334	78,206	Nevada
Orange*	059	2,991,519	2,846,289	23,134	989,208	52,726	69,206,970	1.1471	39,088,814	**11,498**	4,547,424	**9,653**	3,141,259	**17,605**	6,027,801	2,162,963	1,881,977	Orange
Placer*	061	305,883	248,399	25,937	115,804	51,291	7,933,730	.1283	4,410,614	**1,297**	430,363	**914**	113,290	**635**	683,453	189,460	228,833	Placer
Plumas	063	21,270	20,824	20,064	9,396	34,317	426,760	.0065	158,377	**47**	2,975	**6**	3,798	**21**	50,967	7,669	17,701	Plumas
Riverside*	065	1,856,913	1,545,387	17,426	612,948	40,149	32,358,750	.5566	17,038,501	**5,012**	2,148,339	**4,560**	1,011,815	**5,671**	2,882,953	733,280	1,097,238	Riverside
Sacramento*	067	1,364,259	1,223,499	19,771	502,254	40,668	26,972,550	.4497	14,000,552	**4,118**	1,963,249	**4,168**	927,762	**5,199**	2,424,575	546,905	855,031	Sacramento
San Benito*	069	57,117	53,234	20,165	16,698	51,609	1,151,790	.0178	449,884	**132**	54,773	**116**	7,819	**44**	110,651	23,741	35,632	San Benito
San Bernardino*	071	1,906,582	1,709,434	15,731	577,938	39,247	29,993,250	.5254	15,434,681	**4,540**	2,058,856	**4,371**	921,132	**5,162**	2,897,822	690,175	1,061,255	San Bernardino
San Diego*	073	2,966,135	2,813,833	20,344	1,059,703	43,062	60,342,670	1.0169	33,222,905	**9,773**	3,825,198	**8,120**	2,426,068	**13,596**	5,326,312	1,680,462	1,896,665	San Diego
San Francisco*	075	743,549	776,733	29,636	332,844	49,555	22,035,600	.3392	11,112,197	**3,269**	976,344	**2,073**	2,204,589	**12,355**	2,006,342	801,356	387,396	San Francisco
San Joaquin*	077	654,288	563,598	16,392	210,061	38,879	10,725,080	.1822	5,087,457	**1,497**	677,193	**1,438**	219,393	**1,230**	911,463	340,141	375,176	San Joaquin
San Luis Obispo*	079	254,929	246,681	20,201	98,521	39,519	5,149,890	.0859	2,720,316	**800**	246,788	**524**	150,585	**844**	543,527	192,222	190,418	San Luis Obispo
San Mateo*	081	693,861	707,161	30,470	255,953	61,761	21,141,720	.3373	12,146,055	**3,573**	1,793,452	**3,807**	750,808	**4,208**	2,113,776	643,255	492,210	San Mateo
Santa Barbara*	083	404,260	399,347	19,379	138,188	42,605	7,834,290	.1368	4,700,898	**1,383**	454,866	**966**	331,262	**1,856**	859,109	335,658	258,132	Santa Barbara
Santa Clara*	085	1,675,734	1,682,585	29,915	586,292	63,995	50,130,310	.7861	27,026,688	**7,950**	3,149,778	**6,686**	2,287,248	**12,818**	4,358,160	1,341,238	1,182,391	Santa Clara
Santa Cruz*	087	250,198	255,602	23,542	91,446	48,471	5,890,220	.0942	2,967,816	**873**	302,380	**642**	153,966	**863**	615,612	266,818	176,389	Santa Cruz
Shasta*	089	179,590	163,256	16,828	70,586	32,198	3,022,140	.0528	1,632,661	**480**	274,967	**584**	44,756	**251**	319,925	87,215	127,629	Shasta
Sierra	091	3,477	3,555	19,646	1,523	33,461	68,310	.0009	6,687	**2**	....	**....**	....	**....**	1,027	1,153	2,935	Sierra
Siskiyou	093	44,747	44,301	15,833	19,148	27,808	708,460	.0121	330,270	**97**	34,052	**72**	1,389	**8**	85,044	26,072	34,565	Siskiyou
Solano*	095	417,390	394,542	21,717	140,762	48,626	9,064,370	.1414	3,923,677	**1,154**	663,323	**1,408**	193,021	**1,082**	753,501	156,794	276,917	Solano
Sonoma*	097	468,851	458,614	23,674	174,821	47,810	11,099,560	.1798	5,877,135	**1,729**	619,805	**1,316**	256,127	**1,435**	1,187,270	345,374	332,483	Sonoma
Stanislaus*	099	506,378	446,997	15,862	162,035	37,383	8,032,070	.1459	4,753,556	**1,398**	669,983	**1,422**	178,855	**1,002**	913,403	315,443	289,267	Stanislaus
Sutter*	101	86,547	78,930	16,040	29,165	35,738	1,388,200	.0255	856,231	**252**	200,031	**425**	27,956	**157**	177,822	39,926	53,707	Sutter
Tehama**	103	59,393	56,039	14,714	22,234	29,753	873,930	.0169	597,558	**176**	60,147	**128**	6,236	**35**	119,125	17,908	40,480	Tehama
Trinity	105	13,630	13,022	15,755	6,064	26,603	214,740	.0033	53,639	**16**	1,445	**3**	1,336	**7**	19,366	5,764	11,471	Trinity
Tulare*	107	398,103	368,021	12,544	117,213	32,005	4,993,740	.0943	2,716,977	**799**	427,942	**908**	106,651	**598**	549,480	145,301	204,116	Tulare
Tuolumne**	109	57,450	54,501	18,898	22,603	35,905	1,085,710	.0171	425,315	**125**	62,603	**133**	4,494	**25**	113,995	33,160	43,769	Tuolumne
Ventura*	111	802,627	753,197	22,864	258,964	53,222	18,351,220	.2961	9,381,128	**2,760**	941,078	**1,998**	513,106	**2,876**	1,505,559	540,323	514,113	Ventura
Yolo*	113	187,466	168,660	17,468	65,200	37,916	3,274,600	.0537	1,434,376	**422**	92,016	**195**	28,130	**158**	338,545	70,836	115,311	Yolo
Yuba*	115	64,463	60,219	13,026	21,932	28,817	839,710	.0140	263,867	**78**	18,836	**40**	....	**....**	65,970	35,242	39,171	Yuba
The State		35,979,311	33,871,648	19,878	12,227,339	43,562	715,208,990	11.9649	377,404,791	**111,017**	44,262,037	**93,959**	27,013,524	**151,394**	66,055,029	20,565,700	21,676,396	The State

COLORADO (CO; CODE 08; 64 Counties)

COUNTY OR COUNTY EQUIVALENT	FIPS CO. CODE	POPULATION Estimate 7/1/04	POPULATION Census 4/1/00	PER CAPITA INCOME 2003	HOUSEHOLDS Estimate 7/1/04	MEDIAN HOUSEHOLD INCOME 2003	DISPOSABLE INCOME 2003 ($1,000)	MARKET ABILITY INDEX 2003	TOTAL RETAIL SALES Sales 2003 ($1,000)	TOTAL RETAIL SALES Ranally Sales Units	GENERAL MERCHANDISE Sales 2003 ($1,000)	GENERAL MERCHANDISE Ranally Sales Units	APPAREL STORE Sales 2003 ($1,000)	APPAREL STORE Ranally Sales Units	FOOD STORE SALES 2003 ($1,000)	HEALTH & DRUG STORE 2003 ($1,000)	PASSENGER CAR REGIS-TRATIONS 2003	COUNTY OR COUNTY EQUIVALENT
Adams*[1]	001	389,997	363,857	18,623	137,035	42,572	7,262,850	.1259	4,143,475	**1,219**	515,383	**1,094**	57,856	**324**	620,825	89,463	264,063	Adams
Alamosa	003	15,177	14,966	13,117	5,656	28,246	199,080	.0047	223,384	**66**	62,121	**132**	2,912	**16**	33,520	4,542	10,667	Alamosa
Arapahoe*	005	524,236	487,967	23,988	209,391	48,885	12,575,600	.2262	9,263,209	**2,725**	1,336,753	**2,838**	352,534	**1,976**	1,165,486	335,101	388,599	Arapahoe
Archuleta	007	11,737	9,898	18,640	4,880	35,745	218,780	.0034	83,786	**25**	....	**....**	....	**....**	16,265	3,673	9,786	Archuleta
Baca	009	4,134	4,517	13,972	1,761	26,234	57,760	.0009	18,382	**5**	1,439	**3**	....	**....**	4,892	....	3,668	Baca
Bent	011	5,498	5,998	11,340	1,848	26,914	62,350	.0010	13,975	**4**	....	**....**	....	**....**	5,383	....	3,650	Bent
Boulder*[1]	013	280,533	291,288	24,908	112,423	50,206	6,987,540	.1145	3,962,671	**1,166**	385,734	**819**	126,037	**706**	729,202	128,964	212,581	Boulder
Broomfield*[2]	014	43,078	(d)	27,853	16,723	58,226	1,199,860	.0158	285,950	**84**	46,987	**100**	....	**....**	56,562	10,324	34,298	Broomfield
Chaffee	015	17,021	16,242	16,842	7,080	32,491	286,660	.0053	190,175	**56**	24,955	**53**	1,146	**6**	41,880	6,473	13,936	Chaffee
Cheyenne	017	1,997	2,231	17,356	800	34,902	34,660	.0006	14,797	**4**	....	**....**	....	**....**	1,332	....	1,736	Cheyenne
Clear Creek*	019	9,612	9,322	25,147	4,214	46,379	241,710	.0032	48,326	**14**	....	**....**	1,289	**7**	12,996	3,853	8,834	Clear Creek
Conejos	021	8,400	8,400	10,861	3,058	23,867	91,230	.0016	29,953	**9**	....	**....**	....	**....**	9,101	3,355	6,082	Conejos
Costilla	023	3,528	3,663	10,272	1,505	19,343	36,240	.0006	5,809	**2**	....	**....**	....	**....**	1,567	....	2,473	Costilla
Crowley	025	5,421	5,518	7,619	1,301	25,376	41,300	.0009	19,844	**6**	....	**....**	....	**....**	....	3,323	2,586	Crowley
Custer	027	3,874	3,503	17,987	1,679	33,032	69,680	.0011	23,846	**7**	....	**....**	....	**....**	6,244	1,267	3,693	Custer
Delta	029	29,910	27,834	15,372	11,935	30,962	459,780	.0078	203,957	**60**	7,758	**16**	1,312	**7**	53,271	10,095	24,603	Delta
Denver*	031	558,164	554,636	20,119	243,468	36,894	11,229,470	.2038	7,783,528	**2,290**	789,445	**1,676**	388,679	**2,178**	972,182	306,321	363,719	Denver
Dolores	033	1,817	1,844	16,758	806	30,391	30,450	.0004	5,856	**2**	....	**....**	....	**....**	3,547	....	1,589	Dolores
Douglas*	035	237,826	175,766	30,340	82,611	70,405	7,215,580	.0971	2,095,279	**616**	404,685	**859**	286,583	**1,606**	319,317	59,457	179,705	Douglas
Eagle**	037	47,366	41,659	25,216	16,935	56,358	1,194,360	.0194	663,949	**195**	34,769	**74**	90,608	**508**	158,046	13,783	34,755	Eagle
Elbert*	039	22,964	19,872	23,694	7,728	55,822	544,110	.0068	59,712	**18**	....	**....**	....	**....**	4,221	2,087	19,690	Elbert
El Paso*	041	560,804	516,929	19,819	208,877	42,957	11,114,350	.1975	7,166,545	**2,108**	1,150,622	**2,443**	190,170	**1,066**	768,575	274,941	395,953	El Paso
Fremont**	043	47,971	46,145	13,350	15,962	32,598	640,430	.0112	275,573	**81**	49,144	**104**	....	**....**	55,451	18,788	31,190	Fremont
Garfield	045	48,740	43,791	19,703	17,963	42,811	960,320	.0189	826,982	**243**	100,900	**214**	19,082	**107**	103,554	23,754	35,746	Garfield
Gilpin*	047	4,861	4,757	24,908	2,098	46,254	121,080	.0014	4,368	**1**	....	**....**	....	**....**	1,744	....	4,562	Gilpin
Grand	049	13,403	12,442	22,726	5,592	43,656	304,600	.0047	130,541	**38**	....	**....**	2,387	**13**	33,745	5,338	11,857	Grand
Gunnison	051	14,062	13,956	18,066	5,783	35,628	254,050	.0047	173,961	**51**	9,685	**21**	4,444	**25**	34,173	4,036	11,200	Gunnison
Hinsdale	053	750	790	19,813	339	34,690	14,860	.0002	7,445	**2**	1,086	**2**	....	**....**	1,696	....	684	Hinsdale
Huerfano	055	7,828	7,862	12,422	3,155	25,067	97,240	.0018	48,257	**14**	....	**....**	....	**....**	12,427	2,077	5,586	Huerfano
Jackson	057	1,484	1,577	16,260	638	30,367	24,130	.0004	9,749	**3**	....	**....**	....	**....**	2,177	....	1,333	Jackson
Jefferson*[1]	059	529,255	527,056	25,721	211,565	51,534	13,613,150	.2132	6,739,430	**1,982**	1,262,709	**2,680**	259,540	**1,455**	1,080,297	279,148	421,604	Jefferson
Kiowa	061	1,392	1,622	14,734	579	27,982	20,510	.0003	5,469	**2**	....	**....**	....	**....**	1,017	....	1,254	Kiowa
Kit Carson	063	7,885	8,011	14,711	2,958	31,332	116,000	.0025	111,588	**33**	....	**....**	1,877	**11**	8,036	3,908	6,018	Kit Carson
Lake**	065	7,704	7,812	16,839	2,897	35,844	129,730	.0019	32,456	**10**	....	**....**	....	**....**	14,678	1,302	6,045	Lake
La Plata**	067	46,913	43,941	18,912	18,976	37,520	887,220	.0160	583,783	**172**	42,571	**90**	21,098	**118**	95,493	16,916	38,027	La Plata
Larimer*	069	271,165	251,494	21,864	107,740	44,515	5,928,820	.1012	3,560,752	**1,047**	603,249	**1,281**	139,359	**781**	480,045	104,785	220,754	Larimer
Las Animas	071	15,571	15,207	13,736	6,400	26,731	213,880	.0041	140,390	**41**	17,409	**37**	....	**....**	33,091	3,096	11,672	Las Animas

Source: Devonshire Associates Ltd. and Scan/US, Inc. 2004.
* Component of a Metropolitan Core Based Statistical Area.
** Component of a Micropolitan Core Based Statistical Area.

.... Data less than 1,000. (d) Data not available.
[1]Census population includes a portion of Broomfield county.
[2]Created on November 15, 2001 from parts of Adams, Boulder, Jefferson, and Weld counties.

continued on next page

Counties: Population / Income / Sales, *Continued*

COUNTY OR COUNTY EQUIVALENT	FIPS CO. CODE	POPULATION Estimate 7/1/04	POPULATION Census 4/1/00	PER CAPITA INCOME 2003	HOUSEHOLDS Estimate 7/1/04	MEDIAN HOUSEHOLD INCOME 2003	DISPOSABLE INCOME 2003 ($1,000)	MARKET ABILITY INDEX 2003	TOTAL RETAIL SALES Sales 2003 ($1,000)	TOTAL RETAIL SALES Ranally Sales Units	GENERAL MERCHANDISE Sales 2003 ($1,000)	GENERAL MERCHANDISE Ranally Sales Units	APPAREL STORE Sales 2003 ($1,000)	APPAREL STORE Ranally Sales Units	FOOD STORE SALES 2003 ($1,000)	HEALTH & DRUG STORE 2003 ($1,000)	PASSENGER CAR REGISTRATIONS 2003	COUNTY OR COUNTY EQUIVALENT
Lincoln	073	5,819	6,087	12,817	1,945	30,687	74,580	.0017	77,017	23	....	....	....	....	7,113	3,560	3,998	Lincoln
Logan**	075	21,018	20,504	14,227	7,773	31,152	299,020	.0062	242,804	71	56,172	119	5,824	33	21,164	9,262	14,837	Logan
Mesa*	077	127,075	116,255	16,763	50,551	33,713	2,130,220	.0407	1,540,898	453	347,773	738	31,679	178	205,091	40,014	98,921	Mesa
Mineral	079	895	831	18,804	410	32,636	16,830	.0003	5,391	2	....	....	....	....	1,279	....	815	Mineral
Moffat	081	13,644	13,184	18,347	5,248	38,441	250,320	.0044	145,921	43	10,956	23	....	....	29,080	2,928	10,946	Moffat
Montezuma	083	24,485	23,830	15,185	9,763	30,656	371,810	.0075	295,447	87	41,858	89	1,335	7	51,556	4,032	18,814	Montezuma
Montrose**	085	36,781	33,432	16,305	14,452	33,210	599,700	.0118	469,361	138	73,458	156	6,304	35	80,230	11,770	28,212	Montrose
Morgan**	087	28,145	27,171	13,968	9,655	32,544	393,120	.0071	197,595	58	16,153	34	1,918	11	40,096	10,306	19,266	Morgan
Otero	089	19,590	20,311	13,792	7,760	27,850	270,180	.0053	189,504	56	50,895	108	....	....	27,646	6,912	14,181	Otero
Ouray	091	4,102	3,742	20,863	1,746	39,665	85,580	.0012	15,984	5	....	....	1,490	8	3,880	1,404	3,590	Ouray
Park*	093	17,056	14,523	24,336	7,083	46,336	415,080	.0051	37,571	11	....	....	....	....	3,232	....	15,930	Park
Phillips	095	4,527	4,480	15,271	1,782	31,004	69,130	.0013	39,230	12	....	....	....	....	6,935	4,588	3,410	Phillips
Pitkin	097	15,081	14,872	30,432	6,901	53,081	458,950	.0084	381,685	112	....	....	98,803	554	50,943	29,337	12,651	Pitkin
Prowers	099	14,067	14,483	12,989	5,125	28,499	182,720	.0040	162,523	48	28,471	60	1,287	7	28,033	5,401	9,467	Prowers
Pueblo*	101	151,054	141,472	15,098	58,747	31,495	2,280,620	.0447	1,659,496	488	395,824	840	30,025	168	218,342	61,578	105,762	Pueblo
Rio Blanco	103	5,922	5,986	17,570	2,346	35,529	104,050	.0015	27,443	8	....	....	....	....	9,885	3,458	4,935	Rio Blanco
Rio Grande	105	12,316	12,413	14,402	4,742	30,320	177,380	.0036	138,762	41	1,268	3	1,199	7	28,400	4,906	9,223	Rio Grande
Routt	107	21,109	19,690	24,532	8,675	48,168	517,840	.0082	257,477	76	25,647	54	15,618	88	60,098	5,088	17,464	Routt
Saguache	109	6,946	5,917	12,263	2,790	24,533	85,180	.0015	36,534	11	1,103	2	....	....	4,799	1,602	5,058	Saguache
San Juan	111	577	558	18,596	307	27,699	10,730	.0002	6,867	2	....	....	1,589	9	1,746	....	532	San Juan
San Miguel	113	7,329	6,594	26,294	3,500	44,208	192,710	.0028	68,145	20	....	....	4,875	27	21,505	2,639	6,349	San Miguel
Sedgwick	115	2,661	2,747	14,363	1,132	26,947	38,220	.0007	24,858	7	....	....	....	....	2,776	1,697	2,266	Sedgwick
Summit**	117	25,634	23,548	24,363	9,862	50,960	624,520	.0116	502,350	148	31,457	67	95,896	537	86,358	10,145	20,256	Summit
Teller*	119	22,158	20,555	22,347	8,721	45,745	495,160	.0068	114,555	34	....	....	1,416	8	32,871	4,788	18,873	Teller
Washington	121	4,768	4,926	15,491	1,936	30,603	73,860	.0012	26,503	8	1,238	3	....	....	5,136	2,542	4,476	Washington
Weld*[1]	123	220,667	180,936	16,913	76,443	39,793	3,732,100	.0638	1,875,716	552	261,111	554	24,309	136	242,183	53,013	157,962	Weld
Yuma	125	9,789	9,841	15,114	3,796	31,214	147,950	.0030	120,896	36	....	....	1,605	9	17,856	6,129	7,800	Yuma
The State		4,625,293	4,301,261	21,313	1,797,550	43,810	98,576,980	1.6756	57,617,687	16,951	8,201,622	17,407	2,278,329	12,767	8,231,077	2,010,478	3,410,192	The State

CONNECTICUT (CT; CODE 09; 8 Counties)

COUNTY OR COUNTY EQUIVALENT	FIPS CO. CODE	POPULATION Estimate 7/1/04	POPULATION Census 4/1/00	PER CAPITA INCOME 2003	HOUSEHOLDS Estimate 7/1/04	MEDIAN HOUSEHOLD INCOME 2003	DISPOSABLE INCOME 2003 ($1,000)	MARKET ABILITY INDEX 2003	TOTAL RETAIL SALES Sales 2003 ($1,000)	TOTAL RETAIL SALES Ranally Sales Units	GENERAL MERCHANDISE Sales 2003 ($1,000)	GENERAL MERCHANDISE Ranally Sales Units	APPAREL STORE Sales 2003 ($1,000)	APPAREL STORE Ranally Sales Units	FOOD STORE SALES 2003 ($1,000)	HEALTH & DRUG STORE 2003 ($1,000)	PASSENGER CAR REGISTRATIONS 2003	COUNTY OR COUNTY EQUIVALENT
Fairfield*	001	904,001	882,567	30,224	334,894	57,713	27,322,330	.4561	17,926,178	5,273	934,028	1,983	1,149,371	6,441	2,396,980	817,269	598,025	Fairfield
Hartford*	003	875,839	857,183	25,542	347,172	45,845	22,370,720	.3556	11,613,745	3,416	1,138,535	2,417	857,713	4,807	1,896,608	820,397	573,213	Hartford
Litchfield**	005	189,521	182,193	28,335	75,405	50,340	5,370,040	.0817	2,536,776	746	132,967	282	55,845	313	437,399	162,195	141,764	Litchfield
Middlesex*	007	163,370	155,071	30,042	65,706	52,696	4,907,910	.0700	1,861,027	547	99,621	211	178,567	1,001	392,826	167,362	121,199	Middlesex
New Haven*	009	847,502	824,008	24,399	331,415	44,342	20,678,310	.3304	10,642,435	3,131	1,078,401	2,289	607,778	3,406	1,706,678	797,297	531,720	New Haven
New London*	011	265,499	259,088	25,332	104,602	45,747	6,725,490	.1054	3,310,747	974	430,241	913	173,428	972	509,295	214,890	185,995	New London
Tolland*	013	147,747	136,364	27,423	54,290	52,684	4,051,660	.0539	1,001,394	295	34,838	74	32,967	185	212,985	91,992	105,099	Tolland
Windham**	015	113,767	109,091	22,353	43,649	41,333	2,543,030	.0378	914,690	269	94,432	200	5,747	32	212,130	75,689	78,049	Windham
The State		3,507,246	3,405,565	26,793	1,357,133	48,638	93,969,490	1.4909	49,806,992	14,651	3,943,062	8,369	3,061,415	17,157	7,764,901	3,147,093	2,335,064	The State

DELAWARE (DE; CODE 10; 3 Counties)

COUNTY OR COUNTY EQUIVALENT	FIPS CO. CODE	POPULATION Estimate 7/1/04	POPULATION Census 4/1/00	PER CAPITA INCOME 2003	HOUSEHOLDS Estimate 7/1/04	MEDIAN HOUSEHOLD INCOME 2003	DISPOSABLE INCOME 2003 ($1,000)	MARKET ABILITY INDEX 2003	TOTAL RETAIL SALES Sales 2003 ($1,000)	TOTAL RETAIL SALES Ranally Sales Units	GENERAL MERCHANDISE Sales 2003 ($1,000)	GENERAL MERCHANDISE Ranally Sales Units	APPAREL STORE Sales 2003 ($1,000)	APPAREL STORE Ranally Sales Units	FOOD STORE SALES 2003 ($1,000)	HEALTH & DRUG STORE 2003 ($1,000)	PASSENGER CAR REGISTRATIONS 2003	COUNTY OR COUNTY EQUIVALENT
Kent*	001	136,821	126,697	17,831	51,808	37,755	2,439,640	.0448	1,634,075	481	336,656	715	44,077	247	195,425	69,449	91,956	Kent
New Castle*	003	519,483	500,265	22,851	201,742	47,492	11,870,500	.2069	7,800,947	2,295	962,699	2,044	351,000	1,967	1,257,968	460,327	344,559	New Castle
Sussex**	005	171,552	156,638	18,525	69,809	36,427	3,177,980	.0597	2,325,039	684	240,821	511	219,905	1,232	327,183	127,141	125,281	Sussex
The State		827,856	783,600	21,125	323,359	43,394	17,488,120	.3114	11,760,062	3,460	1,540,177	3,270	614,981	3,446	1,780,576	656,918	561,796	The State

DISTRICT OF COLUMBIA (DC; CODE 11; 1 District)

COUNTY OR COUNTY EQUIVALENT	FIPS CO. CODE	POPULATION Estimate 7/1/04	POPULATION Census 4/1/00	PER CAPITA INCOME 2003	HOUSEHOLDS Estimate 7/1/04	MEDIAN HOUSEHOLD INCOME 2003	DISPOSABLE INCOME 2003 ($1,000)	MARKET ABILITY INDEX 2003	TOTAL RETAIL SALES Sales 2003 ($1,000)	TOTAL RETAIL SALES Ranally Sales Units	GENERAL MERCHANDISE Sales 2003 ($1,000)	GENERAL MERCHANDISE Ranally Sales Units	APPAREL STORE Sales 2003 ($1,000)	APPAREL STORE Ranally Sales Units	FOOD STORE SALES 2003 ($1,000)	HEALTH & DRUG STORE 2003 ($1,000)	PASSENGER CAR REGISTRATIONS 2003	COUNTY OR COUNTY EQUIVALENT
District of Columbia*	001	560,725	572,059	26,337	256,560	37,242	14,767,850	.1959	3,408,245	1,003	145,053	308	469,245	2,630	940,510	481,206	235,770	District of Columbia
The District		560,725	572,059	26,337	256,560	37,242	14,767,850	.1959	3,408,245	1,003	145,053	308	469,245	2,630	940,510	481,206	235,770	The District

FLORIDA (FL; CODE 12; 67 Counties)

COUNTY OR COUNTY EQUIVALENT	FIPS CO. CODE	POPULATION Estimate 7/1/04	POPULATION Census 4/1/00	PER CAPITA INCOME 2003	HOUSEHOLDS Estimate 7/1/04	MEDIAN HOUSEHOLD INCOME 2003	DISPOSABLE INCOME 2003 ($1,000)	MARKET ABILITY INDEX 2003	TOTAL RETAIL SALES Sales 2003 ($1,000)	TOTAL RETAIL SALES Ranally Sales Units	GENERAL MERCHANDISE Sales 2003 ($1,000)	GENERAL MERCHANDISE Ranally Sales Units	APPAREL STORE Sales 2003 ($1,000)	APPAREL STORE Ranally Sales Units	FOOD STORE SALES 2003 ($1,000)	HEALTH & DRUG STORE 2003 ($1,000)	PASSENGER CAR REGISTRATIONS 2003	COUNTY OR COUNTY EQUIVALENT
Alachua*	001	225,339	217,955	16,166	91,355	30,000	3,642,780	.0696	2,576,067	758	374,123	794	132,681	744	467,971	106,898	158,414	Alachua
Baker*	003	23,769	22,259	15,960	7,663	36,751	379,360	.0063	156,131	46	21,852	46	1,267	7	42,341	10,744	14,381	Baker
Bay*	005	157,510	148,217	18,652	64,529	33,795	2,937,810	.0539	2,015,801	593	435,643	925	81,428	456	299,060	98,266	110,021	Bay
Bradford	007	27,211	26,088	13,994	8,991	31,376	380,800	.0068	190,476	56	23,927	51	4,027	23	35,728	7,265	15,724	Bradford
Brevard*	009	515,004	476,230	22,229	228,764	37,303	11,447,810	.1835	5,603,865	1,648	916,795	1,946	235,423	1,319	919,936	384,085	382,238	Brevard
Broward*	011	1,764,315	1,623,018	21,989	747,072	39,017	38,796,200	.6810	25,541,193	7,513	2,758,291	5,855	1,486,450	8,330	3,491,409	1,626,468	1,136,899	Broward
Calhoun	013	12,880	13,017	12,012	4,515	25,666	154,710	.0030	87,739	26	2,175	5	....	....	19,870	2,543	7,442	Calhoun
Charlotte*	015	157,100	141,627	20,982	71,830	34,340	3,296,280	.0530	1,568,354	461	366,846	779	83,926	470	252,565	99,775	112,269	Charlotte
Citrus**	017	129,066	118,085	18,526	60,792	29,482	2,391,070	.0388	1,060,391	312	140,575	298	33,343	187	229,108	61,255	97,410	Citrus
Clay*	019	162,779	140,814	21,699	59,596	44,073	3,532,200	.0559	1,615,809	475	272,051	578	78,284	439	228,365	80,101	117,149	Clay
Collier*	021	297,488	251,377	24,228	122,501	44,121	7,207,470	.1199	4,228,159	1,244	421,375	895	411,527	2,306	713,495	233,244	201,527	Collier
Columbia**	023	61,407	56,513	14,696	23,143	29,238	902,460	.0197	869,207	256	185,272	393	31,719	178	87,338	38,448	39,175	Columbia
DeSoto**	027	34,409	32,209	12,938	11,484	29,062	445,180	.0085	263,408	77	23,970	51	2,019	11	39,543	7,367	17,517	DeSoto
Dixie	029	14,034	13,827	12,966	5,473	24,747	181,960	.0030	52,203	15	2,164	5	....	....	14,947	3,577	9,464	Dixie
Duval*	031	830,101	778,879	20,810	340,796	37,826	17,274,610	.3088	11,661,697	3,430	1,508,879	3,203	489,864	2,745	1,536,319	590,820	554,170	Duval
Escambia*	033	296,422	294,410	18,472	123,038	33,238	5,475,560	.0993	3,595,558	1,058	602,244	1,278	167,034	936	478,726	231,413	201,268	Escambia
Flagler**	035	66,083	49,832	22,412	29,444	37,377	1,481,060	.0205	359,021	106	50,918	108	7,616	43	74,968	27,963	50,091	Flagler
Franklin	037	10,059	11,057	14,803	4,276	26,139	148,900	.0029	101,198	30	2,441	5	1,069	6	24,874	9,981	6,732	Franklin
Gadsden*	039	45,161	45,087	14,286	16,327	29,599	645,190	.0106	225,978	66	17,057	36	3,269	18	52,153	16,301	26,942	Gadsden
Gilchrist*	041	15,996	14,437	13,592	5,662	29,606	217,410	.0034	44,231	13	1,216	3	....	....	11,731	3,663	10,185	Gilchrist
Glades	043	11,351	10,576	14,331	4,172	29,126	162,670	.0025	36,352	11	1,745	4	....	....	14,185	....	6,949	Glades
Gulf	045	15,464	13,332	13,035	5,206	28,998	201,580	.0034	72,771	21	1,838	4	....	....	26,684	5,341	8,866	Gulf
Hamilton	047	14,112	13,327	10,399	4,424	24,929	146,750	.0028	62,572	18	2,322	5	....	....	12,711	3,710	7,069	Hamilton
Hardee**	049	27,908	26,938	11,283	8,240	28,361	314,880	.0060	160,210	47	18,219	39	4,127	23	42,525	5,866	13,554	Hardee
Hendry**	051	37,303	36,210	12,995	11,339	31,471	484,760	.0095	312,039	92	46,463	99	3,192	18	63,594	4,686	18,784	Hendry
Hernando*	053	147,435	130,802	18,359	65,491	31,019	2,706,740	.0467	1,503,695	442	264,966	562	60,492	339	316,438	115,151	104,467	Hernando
Highlands**	055	92,254	87,366	16,351	39,482	28,483	1,508,410	.0264	806,576	237	105,926	225	25,767	144	164,100	44,881	58,744	Highlands
Hillsborough*	057	1,096,848	998,948	20,713	447,410	38,148	22,719,030	.4079	15,488,441	4,556	1,744,239	3,703	734,792	4,118	1,878,578	933,207	725,956	Hillsborough
Holmes	059	19,137	18,564	13,393	7,252	26,190	256,310	.0040	56,798	17	2,183	5	1,359	8	9,439	2,177	12,245	Holmes
Indian River*	061	122,827	112,947	24,627	61,075	36,750	3,024,800	.0496	1,708,268	503	244,642	519	159,902	896	262,262	129,783	96,767	Indian River
Jackson	063	46,424	46,755	13,778	16,879	28,177	639,610	.0128	468,855	138	64,911	138	21,208	119	59,267	22,172	28,649	Jackson
Jefferson*	065	14,410	12,902	15,044	5,239	31,077	216,780	.0034	59,226	17	2,095	4	....	....	16,557	5,177	9,117	Jefferson
Lafayette	067	7,424	7,022	11,981	2,298	28,956	88,950	.0014	18,079	5	5,807	12	....	....	2,133	....	4,140	Lafayette
Lake*	069	256,893	210,528	19,735	109,035	34,754	5,069,690	.0829	2,444,930	719	342,660	727	57,819	324	450,660	170,962	177,856	Lake
Lee*	071	508,350	440,888	21,735	219,630	37,791	11,049,150	.1922	7,029,399	2,068	988,622	2,099	443,513	2,486	986,313	442,891	346,632	Lee
Leon*	073	243,428	239,452	20,356	104,635	35,281	4,955,100	.0881	3,251,618	956	585,892	1,244	163,941	919	500,146	204,438	180,814	Leon
Levy	075	36,821	34,450	14,264	15,062	25,944	525,200	.0099	327,645	96	75,459	160	3,402	19	57,963	18,050	25,412	Levy
Liberty	077	7,424	7,021	12,150	2,425	27,763	90,200	.0014	16,337	5	....	....	....	....	2,804	1,837	4,162	Liberty
Madison	079	18,774	18,733	12,310	6,805	25,363	231,110	.0040	86,673	25	2,274	5	1,124	6	24,897	9,215	11,429	Madison
Manatee*	081	293,837	264,002	20,694	125,359	36,517	6,080,790	.1013	3,258,327	958	455,564	967	210,356	1,179	554,538	213,861	193,897	Manatee
Marion*	083	286,954	258,916	17,412	123,754	30,192	4,996,440	.0912	3,225,186	949	498,732	1,059	83,149	466	433,921	186,643	199,083	Marion
Martin*	085	137,796	126,731	23,598	60,827	39,735	3,251,690	.0559	2,086,389	614	256,781	545	93,757	525	304,359	164,391	96,342	Martin
Miami-Dade*	086	2,368,141	2,253,362	16,237	848,751	33,807	38,452,660	.7039	23,817,798	7,006	2,737,682	5,812	2,321,232	13,009	3,289,971	2,034,323	1,315,697	Miami-Dade
Monroe**	087	78,768	79,589	23,410	34,778	39,615	1,843,930	.0325	1,272,789	374	88,282	187	111,055	622	329,009	111,262	54,166	Monroe
Nassau*	089	62,849	57,663	22,255	24,872	42,099	1,398,730	.0204	459,220	135	49,554	105	16,222	91	113,460	18,578	46,040	Nassau
Okaloosa*	091	180,485	170,498	23,214	81,167	38,459	4,189,840	.0711	2,557,865	752	468,067	994	183,928	1,031	285,709	117,808	147,712	Okaloosa
Okeechobee**	093	38,007	35,910	14,340	14,028	29,004	545,020	.0104	349,704	103	48,465	103	13,343	75	68,932	21,632	22,175	Okeechobee
Orange*	095	985,714	896,344	20,336	389,821	38,271	20,045,770	.3781	15,595,075	4,587	1,894,240	4,021	1,111,012	6,226	1,715,435	748,454	663,159	Orange
Osceola*	097	216,437	172,493	18,243	82,128	35,796	3,948,390	.0665	1,994,231	587	373,120	792	121,023	678	355,513	133,231	143,588	Osceola
Palm Beach*	099	1,243,157	1,131,184	25,735	577,999	41,513	31,992,820	.5094	16,783,738	4,937	2,107,777	4,474	1,528,403	8,566	2,438,488	1,097,284	887,478	Palm Beach
Pasco*	101	402,756	344,765	19,008	182,783	31,481	7,655,500	.1221	3,223,308	948	644,933	1,369	103,462	580	569,928	239,600	284,236	Pasco
Pinellas*	103	927,459	921,482	23,287	461,636	35,033	21,598,100	.3746	14,136,003	4,158	1,510,037	3,206	547,277	3,067	2,046,794	971,804	683,573	Pinellas
Polk*	105	518,809	483,924	19,073	217,966	33,882	9,895,440	.1713	5,716,090	1,681	873,686	1,855	196,846	1,103	977,731	287,481	353,833	Polk
Putnam**	107	72,313	70,423	14,537	28,942	26,959	1,051,230	.0186	524,508	154	78,367	166	16,812	94	94,972	36,175	47,745	Putnam
St. Johns*	109	149,006	123,135	26,165	64,601	45,324	3,898,730	.0557	1,338,712	394	121,658	258	129,388	725	256,443	68,497	115,184	St. Johns
St. Lucie*	111	220,110	192,695	19,731	94,716	34,445	4,342,920	.0693	1,900,905	559	251,140	533	41,838	234	348,040	150,099	152,439	St. Lucie
Santa Rosa*	113	137,965	117,743	20,348	53,955	38,776	2,807,330	.0418	923,801	272	153,961	327	12,931	72	187,669	64,328	102,334	Santa Rosa
Sarasota*	115	353,387	325,957	24,290	164,257	39,145	8,583,740	.1430	5,072,965	1,492	521,256	1,107	286,362	1,605	737,847	334,254	255,084	Sarasota
Seminole*	117	392,829	365,196	23,780	156,632	44,558	9,341,380	.1550	5,381,883	1,583	885,535	1,880	371,542	2,082	851,236	340,788	285,020	Seminole
Sumter**	119	60,637	53,345	15,787	23,810	30,134	957,260	.0144	229,304	67	22,543	48	....	....	55,521	7,858	36,704	Sumter
Suwannee	121	37,248	34,844	14,926	14,586	28,391	555,970	.0099	285,171	84	25,028	53	4,180	23	53,574	15,889	24,848	Suwannee
Taylor	123	19,484	19,256	14,398	7,372	28,325	280,530	.0050	137,994	41	16,017	34	1,617	9	22,510	13,298	12,106	Taylor
Union	125	14,185	13,442	11,212	3,683	31,897	159,040	.0027	35,087	10	1,657	4	....	....	5,930	3,616	6,712	Union
Volusia*	127	476,562	443,343	20,089	215,582	33,201	9,573,780	.1631	5,410,480	1,592	719,210	1,527	211,817	1,187	893,089	358,640	348,665	Volusia
Wakulla*	129	27,178	22,863	17,407	10,117	34,954	473,090	.0067	90,289	27	3,480	7	....	....	32,171	6,391	18,444	Wakulla
Walton	131	48,227	40,601	17,124	20,087	30,945	825,820	.0147	488,339	144	61,379	130	24,493	137	95,926	29,321	34,878	Walton
Washington	133	21,802	20,973	13,684	8,318	26,711	298,340	.0054	153,242	45	48,308	103	1,104	6	20,545	20,220	14,591	Washington
The State		17,342,822	15,982,378	20,434	7,255,877	36,556	354,374,820	6.1173	212,175,371	62,409	27,544,533	58,474	12,679,713	71,057	31,050,963	13,555,446	11,656,363	The State

GEORGIA (GA; CODE 13; 159 Counties)

COUNTY OR COUNTY EQUIVALENT	FIPS CO. CODE	POPULATION Estimate 7/1/04	POPULATION Census 4/1/00	PER CAPITA INCOME 2003	HOUSEHOLDS Estimate 7/1/04	MEDIAN HOUSEHOLD INCOME 2003	DISPOSABLE INCOME 2003 ($1,000)	MARKET ABILITY INDEX 2003	TOTAL RETAIL SALES Sales 2003 ($1,000)	TOTAL RETAIL SALES Ranally Sales Units	GENERAL MERCHANDISE Sales 2003 ($1,000)	GENERAL MERCHANDISE Ranally Sales Units	APPAREL STORE Sales 2003 ($1,000)	APPAREL STORE Ranally Sales Units	FOOD STORE SALES 2003 ($1,000)	HEALTH & DRUG STORE 2003 ($1,000)	PASSENGER CAR REGISTRATIONS 2003	COUNTY OR COUNTY EQUIVALENT
Appling	001	17,922	17,419	13,658	6,861	28,322	244,780	.0045	136,292	40	3,907	8	2,369	13	22,847	8,989	12,551	Appling
Atkinson**	003	7,985	7,609	11,421	2,865	25,435	91,200	.0015	22,993	7	7,072	15	....	....	3,824	2,679	5,037	Atkinson
Bacon	005	10,138	10,103	12,443	3,934	25,596	126,150	.0022	51,790	15	3,439	7	....	....	11,310	6,413	6,699	Bacon
Baker*	007	4,392	4,074	13,440	1,655	28,089	59,030	.0009	5,154	2	....	....	....	....	1,977	....	2,839	Baker
Baldwin**	009	45,020	44,700	14,246	15,394	33,309	641,340	.0129	491,075	144	118,843	252	22,040	124	86,989	21,115	27,206	Baldwin
Banks	011	15,800	14,422	16,992	5,911	35,582	268,470	.0042	85,621	25	3,828	8	25,286	142	4,907	1,895	12,653	Banks
Barrow*	013	55,787	46,144	18,282	19,700	41,112	1,019,910	.0175	558,932	164	80,685	171	8,344	47	98,133	46,537	39,434	Barrow
Bartow*	015	87,405	76,019	18,882	32,735	40,320	1,650,340	.0280	885,621	261	159,207	338	19,518	109	100,682	34,051	64,825	Bartow
Ben Hill**	017	17,149	17,484	12,596	6,650	25,998	216,010	.0046	176,252	52	28,153	60	4,378	25	32,455	8,294	10,457	Ben Hill
Berrien	019	16,552	16,235	14,059	6,515	28,288	232,700	.0039	84,439	25	2,775	6	....	....	15,063	4,458	11,435	Berrien
Bibb*	021	154,445	153,887	16,510	61,996	32,978	2,549,900	.0544	2,476,433	728	462,364	982	131,320	736	326,277	125,199	100,418	Bibb
Bleckley	023	11,891	11,666	15,146	4,549	31,501	180,100	.0030	70,946	21	4,551	10	....	....	14,897	9,877	8,364	Bleckley
Brantley*	025	15,474	14,629	14,000	5,955	29,018	216,630	.0033	42,029	12	1,295	3	....	....	10,999	2,050	11,204	Brantley
Brooks*	027	16,165	16,450	12,370	6,211	26,182	199,960	.0034	63,926	19	3,465	7	1,054	6	11,919	4,837	10,870	Brooks
Bryan*	029	27,274	23,417	19,364	9,615	44,117	528,140	.0074	113,719	33	8,892	19	....	....	14,983	5,921	19,212	Bryan
Bulloch**	031	59,093	55,983	13,380	22,353	28,136	790,650	.0170	699,764	206	161,434	343	31,818	178	94,932	33,365	42,547	Bulloch
Burke*	033	23,167	22,243	11,992	8,419	25,796	277,820	.0054	163,521	48	8,192	17	2,189	12	32,332	10,019	14,466	Burke
Butts*	035	22,885	19,522	15,958	7,852	37,164	365,210	.0060	144,202	42	3,118	7	1,332	7	23,742	11,651	15,850	Butts
Calhoun	037	6,057	6,320	9,505	1,914	23,892	57,570	.0013	42,533	13	3,363	7	....	....	6,550	2,751	2,985	Calhoun
Camden**	039	46,046	43,664	16,085	15,514	38,032	740,650	.0133	429,348	126	78,089	166	5,430	30	50,919	10,044	28,545	Camden
Candler	043	10,170	9,577	10,632	3,543	23,956	108,130	.0024	90,705	27	2,922	6	....	....	14,887	8,130	5,926	Candler
Carroll*	045	102,023	87,268	16,681	37,429	36,023	1,701,820	.0287	800,677	236	145,514	309	29,742	167	140,484	48,010	71,966	Carroll
Catoosa*	047	59,560	53,282	18,138	23,175	36,962	1,080,280	.0178	503,142	148	134,002	284	8,519	48	32,609	28,371	45,869	Catoosa
Charlton	049	10,853	10,282	11,122	3,568	26,510	120,710	.0022	42,306	12	3,719	8	....	....	5,213	5,302	5,987	Charlton
Chatham*	051	236,368	232,048	18,136	95,877	35,583	4,286,760	.0830	3,380,287	994	625,777	1,328	203,592	1,141	469,715	119,229	151,799	Chatham
Chattahoochee*	053	20,780	14,882	7,659	3,603	34,752	159,150	.0028	4,010	1	....	....	....	....	....	....	9,181	Chattahoochee
Chattooga**	055	26,729	25,470	14,059	10,298	29,095	375,780	.0064	156,288	46	29,884	63	2,887	16	35,385	14,076	18,722	Chattooga

Source: Devonshire Associates Ltd. and Scan/US, Inc. 2004.
* Component of a Metropolitan Core Based Statistical Area.
** Component of a Micropolitan Core Based Statistical Area.

.... Data less than 1,000.
[1]Census population includes a portion of Broomfield county.

(d) Data not available.

Counties: Population / Income / Sales, *Continued*

COUNTY OR COUNTY EQUIVALENT	FIPS CO. CODE	POPULATION Estimate 7/1/04	POPULATION Census 4/1/00	PER CAPITA INCOME 2003	HOUSEHOLDS Estimate 7/1/04	MEDIAN HOUSEHOLD INCOME 2003	DISPOSABLE INCOME 2003 ($1,000)	MARKET ABILITY INDEX 2003	TOTAL RETAIL SALES Sales 2003 ($1,000)	TOTAL RETAIL SALES Ranally Sales Units	GENERAL MERCHANDISE Sales 2003 ($1,000)	GENERAL MERCHANDISE Ranally Sales Units	APPAREL STORE Sales 2003 ($1,000)	APPAREL STORE Ranally Sales Units	FOOD STORE SALES 2003 ($1,000)	HEALTH & DRUG STORE 2003 ($1,000)	PASSENGER CAR REGIS-TRATIONS 2003	COUNTY OR COUNTY EQUIVALENT
Cherokee*	057	174,257	141,903	25,199	64,349	53,679	4,391,050	.0656	1,783,841	525	187,029	397	14,085	79	357,004	51,878	134,763	Cherokee
Clarke*	059	104,327	101,489	14,627	44,578	27,074	1,526,040	.0331	1,448,385	426	286,150	607	79,852	448	218,706	58,876	81,613	Clarke
Clay	061	3,359	3,357	11,176	1,410	20,827	37,540	.0007	12,431	4	....	....	....	....	4,887	....	2,192	Clay
Clayton*	063	266,814	236,517	17,343	92,950	39,749	4,627,420	.0894	3,533,228	1,039	650,295	1,380	140,607	788	359,127	122,449	167,474	Clayton
Clinch	065	7,002	6,878	12,115	2,638	25,462	84,830	.0015	27,202	8	3,018	6	....	....	5,769	5,238	4,259	Clinch
Cobb*	067	663,776	607,751	25,338	255,316	51,893	16,818,690	.2977	12,131,803	3,569	1,738,439	3,690	617,922	3,463	1,744,223	513,483	493,135	Cobb
Coffee**	069	39,469	37,413	12,995	14,069	29,025	512,890	.0116	508,738	150	112,546	239	12,204	68	51,783	15,485	23,759	Coffee
Colquitt**	071	43,561	42,053	12,777	16,152	27,465	556,570	.0122	500,321	147	63,411	135	19,512	109	82,112	19,537	26,324	Colquitt
Columbia*	073	100,062	89,288	22,328	35,539	49,458	2,234,190	.0355	1,059,631	312	159,794	339	13,308	75	199,379	32,737	73,157	Columbia
Cook	075	15,989	15,771	12,574	6,041	26,406	201,050	.0041	144,070	42	3,875	8	5,927	33	28,036	5,524	10,658	Cook
Coweta*	077	105,145	89,215	21,257	37,419	47,286	2,235,070	.0345	913,216	269	84,785	180	33,642	189	238,154	49,047	75,070	Coweta
Crawford*	079	12,586	12,495	16,116	4,556	35,418	202,830	.0027	15,122	4	....	....	....	....	10,100	....	8,970	Crawford
Crisp**	081	21,998	21,996	12,248	8,480	25,567	269,440	.0062	266,171	78	48,638	103	14,598	82	39,496	9,167	13,023	Crisp
Dade*	083	16,151	15,154	15,595	6,119	32,520	251,870	.0047	156,185	46	5,272	11	....	....	31,258	8,490	11,995	Dade
Dawson*	085	19,341	15,999	21,245	7,546	43,184	410,900	.0066	190,887	56	....	....	78,963	443	33,678	10,549	16,106	Dawson
Decatur**	087	28,201	28,240	12,863	10,564	27,249	362,750	.0071	228,534	67	19,684	42	8,796	49	36,700	8,239	18,103	Decatur
DeKalb*	089	676,338	665,865	22,651	275,054	44,429	15,319,680	.2420	7,195,702	2,117	809,603	1,719	421,385	2,362	1,115,500	360,276	452,409	DeKalb
Dodge	091	19,451	19,171	12,419	7,267	26,981	241,560	.0047	148,384	44	31,923	68	4,043	23	27,259	12,096	12,652	Dodge
Dooly	093	11,568	11,525	11,465	3,980	26,478	132,630	.0025	66,606	20	2,263	5	....	....	6,250	3,045	6,614	Dooly
Dougherty*	095	95,611	96,065	14,195	36,773	29,460	1,357,180	.0314	1,487,356	438	303,214	644	71,491	401	212,874	55,991	56,317	Dougherty
Douglas*	097	105,116	92,174	21,951	40,872	44,910	2,307,350	.0416	1,639,444	482	126,625	269	25,644	144	236,488	42,967	80,629	Douglas
Early	099	12,184	12,354	12,159	4,749	24,896	148,140	.0027	67,468	20	4,125	9	1,975	11	18,404	6,233	7,559	Early
Echols*	101	4,068	3,754	10,494	1,345	25,334	42,690	.0006	....	....	....	....	....	....	....	....	2,532	Echols
Effingham*	103	44,353	37,535	18,811	15,764	41,824	834,340	.0124	247,295	73	59,862	127	3,398	19	36,832	7,661	31,861	Effingham
Elbert	105	20,680	20,511	13,645	8,197	27,385	282,180	.0053	161,260	47	23,067	49	3,114	17	35,610	11,384	15,195	Elbert
Emanuel	107	21,889	21,837	11,174	8,204	23,417	244,590	.0051	170,127	50	24,401	52	7,294	41	37,234	9,069	13,389	Emanuel
Evans	109	11,628	10,495	11,164	4,222	24,604	129,820	.0028	95,576	28	4,075	9	....	....	11,563	5,515	6,836	Evans
Fannin	111	21,666	19,798	15,668	9,415	28,529	339,460	.0061	190,982	56	20,313	43	4,962	28	35,650	13,981	17,326	Fannin
Fayette*	113	101,180	91,263	28,416	36,632	62,052	2,875,170	.0423	1,190,255	350	143,232	304	74,858	420	210,348	46,729	79,732	Fayette
Floyd*	115	94,225	90,565	15,797	35,418	33,709	1,488,480	.0280	991,673	292	214,757	456	49,258	276	103,109	65,750	63,973	Floyd
Forsyth*	117	131,575	98,407	26,490	45,766	59,979	3,485,450	.0500	1,233,280	363	168,150	357	12,260	69	201,305	32,935	97,290	Forsyth
Franklin	119	21,441	20,285	14,924	8,448	30,305	319,990	.0066	264,148	78	7,890	17	1,885	11	32,993	12,148	16,749	Franklin
Fulton*	121	818,745	816,006	23,184	350,031	43,777	18,981,830	.3384	13,432,538	3,951	1,776,324	3,771	1,134,661	6,359	1,914,053	493,971	532,322	Fulton
Gilmer	123	26,706	23,456	15,937	10,376	32,481	425,620	.0072	191,570	56	45,313	96	1,691	9	34,463	15,530	20,089	Gilmer
Glascock	125	2,663	2,556	14,262	1,073	28,363	37,980	.0005	3,715	1	....	....	....	....	....	....	2,079	Glascock
Glynn*	127	70,354	67,568	20,563	31,879	36,699	1,459,040	.0252	880,046	259	140,049	297	47,934	269	138,807	43,174	54,242	Glynn
Gordon**	129	48,915	44,104	16,741	18,009	35,959	818,910	.0149	506,058	149	94,184	200	48,320	271	57,801	23,386	34,330	Gordon
Grady	131	24,362	23,659	12,813	9,148	27,350	312,160	.0058	167,824	49	22,961	49	3,122	18	29,972	10,197	15,483	Grady
Greene	133	15,532	14,406	15,963	6,153	33,510	247,940	.0040	92,379	27	5,046	11	....	....	30,085	8,038	10,814	Greene
Gwinnett*	135	698,970	588,448	24,524	252,225	53,739	17,141,460	.2953	11,272,844	3,316	1,191,909	2,530	541,674	3,036	1,267,631	344,933	503,862	Gwinnett
Habersham**	137	39,215	35,902	15,885	14,572	33,989	622,920	.0113	370,702	109	78,347	166	6,112	34	70,655	21,823	28,219	Habersham
Hall*	139	161,175	139,277	18,827	58,724	41,073	3,034,450	.0521	1,689,280	497	323,483	687	47,462	266	181,864	83,409	115,498	Hall
Hancock**	141	9,952	10,076	9,172	3,334	22,799	91,280	.0016	20,543	6	2,507	5	....	....	6,381	3,235	5,020	Hancock
Haralson*	143	28,009	25,690	14,571	10,806	30,227	408,120	.0073	208,170	61	23,861	51	....	....	42,102	16,800	20,410	Haralson
Harris*	145	26,586	23,695	20,670	10,000	44,128	549,530	.0070	47,563	14	2,049	4	....	....	3,125	3,616	20,911	Harris
Hart	147	23,561	22,997	15,825	9,544	31,101	372,860	.0061	141,585	42	34,463	73	5,108	29	31,990	10,580	18,288	Hart
Heard*	149	11,168	11,012	14,893	4,133	32,571	166,320	.0024	20,357	6	2,177	5	....	....	2,119	2,115	7,910	Heard
Henry*	151	159,460	119,341	23,583	58,170	51,019	3,760,520	.0545	1,257,715	370	185,918	395	69,303	388	187,266	53,328	122,892	Henry
Houston*	153	123,475	110,765	19,588	47,679	40,812	2,418,660	.0411	1,338,286	394	191,144	406	58,498	328	182,002	37,920	91,218	Houston
Irwin**	155	10,089	9,931	13,280	3,756	28,733	133,980	.0023	46,490	14	3,480	7	....	....	3,400	4,684	6,508	Irwin
Jackson	157	48,692	41,589	17,131	17,760	37,205	834,150	.0153	537,475	158	52,606	112	84,208	472	79,894	26,226	35,406	Jackson
Jasper*	159	12,896	11,426	17,335	4,755	37,348	223,550	.0030	23,772	7	2,859	6	....	....	4,629	3,856	9,384	Jasper
Jeff Davis	161	12,943	12,684	12,676	5,034	26,003	164,070	.0036	152,932	45	22,664	48	3,216	18	18,327	6,769	8,637	Jeff Davis
Jefferson	163	16,920	17,266	11,683	6,339	24,735	197,670	.0039	117,796	35	6,168	13	1,536	9	23,790	10,070	10,371	Jefferson
Jenkins	165	8,820	8,575	11,231	3,369	23,056	99,060	.0019	48,342	14	2,908	6	....	....	5,482	7,171	5,724	Jenkins
Johnson**	167	9,708	8,560	10,196	3,362	23,068	98,980	.0018	34,910	10	4,029	9	....	....	9,189	4,350	5,831	Johnson
Jones*	169	26,065	23,639	18,829	9,724	40,026	490,780	.0066	71,140	21	1,534	3	....	....	26,895	4,787	20,139	Jones
Lamar*	171	16,316	15,912	16,535	6,099	35,305	269,790	.0042	88,081	26	4,390	9	....	....	23,142	5,243	11,312	Lamar
Lanier*	173	7,393	7,241	12,728	2,692	28,079	94,100	.0016	30,504	9	2,864	6	....	....	7,952	2,374	4,782	Lanier
Laurens**	175	46,487	44,874	14,758	18,163	30,388	686,050	.0143	587,280	173	93,716	199	24,406	137	108,215	24,978	31,519	Laurens
Lee*	177	29,584	24,757	18,950	9,997	44,191	560,620	.0077	98,181	29	....	....	....	....	37,702	2,899	20,015	Lee
Liberty*	179	58,129	61,610	13,989	20,363	31,694	813,140	.0145	397,956	117	89,537	190	17,953	101	56,033	10,548	36,332	Liberty
Lincoln	181	8,596	8,348	15,247	3,452	30,591	131,060	.0019	21,661	6	2,569	5	....	....	4,786	3,415	6,367	Lincoln
Long*	183	10,926	10,304	12,386	3,736	28,875	135,330	.0020	10,193	3	....	....	....	....	....	....	6,780	Long
Lowndes*	185	95,395	92,115	14,890	36,636	31,142	1,420,450	.0308	1,361,449	400	195,486	415	87,706	492	163,463	35,948	64,512	Lowndes
Lumpkin	187	23,857	21,016	18,149	9,466	36,293	432,970	.0073	223,219	66	73,310	156	....	....	11,083	10,412	19,402	Lumpkin
McDuffie*	189	21,501	21,231	14,621	8,211	30,362	314,370	.0076	385,509	113	87,623	186	6,778	38	35,699	12,114	14,623	McDuffie
McIntosh*	191	10,878	10,847	14,490	4,390	28,404	157,620	.0033	130,997	39	11,258	24	37,829	212	16,379	6,430	7,424	McIntosh
Macon	193	14,014	14,074	10,440	4,370	23,397	146,310	.0027	59,695	18	4,500	10	....	....	15,857	8,495	8,190	Macon
Madison*	195	27,481	25,730	16,594	10,623	34,162	456,030	.0068	113,505	33	6,886	15	2,205	12	20,131	11,269	20,939	Madison
Marion*	197	7,165	7,144	13,411	2,744	28,016	96,090	.0017	39,715	12	4,085	9	....	....	5,412	3,119	4,971	Marion
Meriwether*	199	22,870	22,534	14,210	8,593	31,029	324,980	.0055	124,851	37	5,983	13	....	....	14,894	11,333	15,220	Meriwether
Miller	201	6,311	6,383	13,114	2,510	25,914	82,760	.0016	47,455	14	5,860	12	....	....	12,970	2,569	4,524	Miller
Mitchell	205	23,786	23,932	11,205	8,294	25,716	266,530	.0052	146,211	43	16,715	35	2,299	13	28,703	11,437	13,607	Mitchell
Monroe*	207	23,707	21,757	18,405	8,540	40,752	436,330	.0062	94,059	28	20,290	43	....	....	17,600	7,812	17,278	Monroe
Montgomery**	209	8,830	8,270	13,089	3,179	28,992	115,580	.0018	16,937	5	1,270	3	....	....	1,478	2,162	5,603	Montgomery
Morgan	211	17,196	15,457	17,328	6,310	37,441	297,980	.0051	157,274	46	55,178	117	1,894	11	20,558	6,431	12,779	Morgan
Murray*	213	40,328	36,506	16,082	14,778	35,000	648,560	.0106	255,025	75	10,862	23	....	....	79,038	12,714	27,376	Murray
Muscogee*	215	185,443	186,291	16,720	74,930	32,824	3,100,680	.0614	2,484,340	731	366,813	779	172,369	966	328,647	148,484	119,306	Muscogee
Newton*	217	80,554	62,001	18,794	29,305	41,207	1,513,930	.0231	513,618	151	74,793	159	24,071	135	120,165	16,868	58,548	Newton
Oconee*	219	28,647	26,225	21,675	10,027	49,162	620,910	.0098	279,787	82	8,505	18	....	....	14,072	8,272	21,516	Oconee
Oglethorpe*	221	13,598	12,635	16,417	5,316	34,420	223,240	.0033	45,498	13	....	....	....	....	3,254	3,822	10,969	Oglethorpe
Paulding*	223	105,749	81,678	21,219	37,994	47,185	2,243,930	.0328	701,362	206	144,979	308	6,612	37	114,069	17,437	79,130	Paulding
Peach**	225	24,491	23,668	14,727	8,921	32,307	360,670	.0068	224,275	66	10,219	22	14,876	83	39,200	8,166	15,520	Peach
Pickens*	227	28,084	22,983	19,120	11,150	38,669	536,980	.0097	361,135	106	16,903	36	1,785	10	33,909	16,623	22,505	Pickens
Pierce**	229	16,532	15,636	13,778	6,451	28,071	227,780	.0041	114,346	34	5,191	11	....	....	14,459	7,432	11,561	Pierce
Pike*	231	15,372	13,688	18,046	5,409	40,809	277,400	.0036	19,541	6	1,638	3	....	....	3,399	1,650	11,847	Pike
Polk**	233	40,315	38,127	14,377	15,014	30,802	579,620	.0100	254,523	75	45,353	96	4,144	23	67,663	20,717	27,035	Polk
Pulaski	235	9,768	9,588	13,637	3,542	30,143	133,210	.0025	74,726	22	2,805	6	....	....	25,107	6,217	6,427	Pulaski
Putnam	237	19,814	18,812	17,556	7,991	35,254	347,860	.0056	145,234	43	4,896	10	....	....	25,756	16,316	15,483	Putnam
Quitman**	239	2,439	2,598	12,821	998	25,314	31,270	.0005	7,762	2	....	....	....	....	4,491	....	1,669	Quitman
Rabun	241	15,978	15,050	17,288	6,824	32,023	276,220	.0049	158,230	47	3,762	8	1,238	7	31,254	15,313	13,075	Rabun
Randolph	243	7,370	7,791	10,327	2,790	21,524	76,110	.0015	36,033	11	2,685	6	....	....	8,760	2,624	4,058	Randolph
Richmond*	245	197,685	199,775	15,426	77,585	31,351	3,049,400	.0608	2,371,484	698	437,488	929	160,053	897	246,108	125,219	120,902	Richmond
Rockdale*	247	76,406	70,111	22,625	28,459	48,525	1,728,690	.0319	1,334,878	393	206,990	439	46,455	260	186,590	66,886	56,753	Rockdale
Schley**	249	3,985	3,766	14,610	1,545	30,112	58,220	.0009	11,488	3	1,406	3	....	....	2,476	....	2,601	Schley
Screven	251	15,420	15,374	13,211	5,835	27,363	203,720	.0037	103,540	30	3,853	8	....	....	18,268	9,702	10,061	Screven
Seminole	253	9,237	9,369	12,871	3,602	25,997	118,890	.0024	82,134	24	3,847	8	....	....	13,419	8,121	6,047	Seminole
Spalding*	255	61,151	58,417	16,221	23,162	34,032	991,940	.0193	745,783	219	114,518	243	37,314	209	147,748	33,978	40,696	Spalding
Stephens**	257	25,191	25,435	14,392	10,288	28,144	362,540	.0068	224,985	66	39,251	83	1,470	8	42,178	10,858	19,166	Stephens
Stewart	259	4,924	5,252	12,049	1,970	23,790	59,330	.0010	21,881	6	4,559	10	....	....	4,787	4,002	2,921	Stewart
Sumter**	261	33,208	33,200	13,417	12,191	29,098	445,540	.0093	364,001	107	67,901	144	11,133	62	44,909	15,038	19,715	Sumter
Talbot	263	6,572	6,498	12,934	2,660	25,450	85,000	.0013	11,519	3	1,551	3	....	....	1,301	1,470	4,223	Talbot
Taliaferro	265	1,919	2,077	12,809	841	22,803	24,580	.0004	3,874	1	....	....	....	....	....	....	1,296	Taliaferro
Tattnall	267	22,408	22,305	10,986	7,180	27,166	246,170	.0048	128,998	38	14,833	31	6,625	37	22,454	12,712	12,077	Tattnall
Taylor	269	8,928	8,815	11,555	3,394	23,990	103,160	.0020	58,172	17	8,378	18	1,346	8	11,609	3,618	5,553	Taylor
Telfair	271	11,431	11,794	11,406	4,146	24,954	130,380	.0025	67,491	20	4,886	10	1,615	9	22,330	7,625	6,787	Telfair
Terrell*	273	10,814	10,970	11,943	4,016	25,741	129,150	.0025	62,736	19	2,962	6	1,618	9	15,645	3,788	6,212	Terrell
Thomas**	275	43,940	42,737	14,386	17,072	29,697	632,120	.0138	601,166	177	110,414	234	24,266	136	73,416	34,580	28,022	Thomas
Tift**	277	39,884	38,407	14,486	14,717	31,008	577,760	.0127	563,753	166	85,424	181	25,473	143	71,250	22,751	24,856	Tift
Toombs**	279	26,586	26,067	12,758	10,245	26,155	339,180	.0077	340,620	100	70,025	149	8,252	46	41,627	18,839	16,494	Toombs
Towns	281	10,078	9,319	16,362	4,400	30,034	164,900	.0027	68,271	20	12,709	27	....	....	12,849	10,791	8,214	Towns
Treutlen	283	6,975	6,854	11,254	2,596	24,251	78,500	.0013	19,510	6	1,466	3	....	....	4,181	4,087	4,480	Treutlen
Troup**	285	60,648	58,779	16,428	23,848	33,337	996,320	.0196	779,390	229	106,604	226	38,680	217	133,792	30,913	40,418	Troup
Turner	287	9,588	9,504	11,362	3,515	24,920	108,940	.0022	71,667	21	3,237	7	....	....	10,675	6,315	5,508	Turner
Twiggs*	289	10,424	10,590	14,060	3,893	30,165	146,560	.0022	24,727	7	....	....	....	....	7,451	....	6,859	Twiggs
Union	291	19,686	17,289	16,188	8,381	30,300	318,670	.0056	173,099	51	9,379	20	1,644	9	37,416	15,177	16,798	Union
Upson**	293	28,094	27,597	14,582	11,054	29,568	409,680	.0069	167,922	49	34,225	73	6,969	39	31,359	8,354	19,218	Upson
Walker*	295	63,070	61,053	15,290	24,741	30,945	964,310	.0158	360,134	106	33,122	70	9,735	55	69,517	24,159	45,346	Walker
Walton*	297	71,966	60,687	18,903	25,381	42,737	1,360,370	.0199	364,212	107	37,864	80	4,239	24	96,319	15,830	52,403	Walton
Ware**	299	35,519	35,483	13,535	14,075	27,016	480,750	.0107	471,933	139	121,740	258	16,073	90	70,760	23,785	22,777	Ware
Warren	301	6,073	6,336	13,336	2,427	26,259	80,990	.0012	13,593	4	1,335	3	....	....	4,873	1,556	4,098	Warren
Washington	303	20,652	21,176	12,699	7,383	28,230	262,250	.0052	170,604	50	23,877	51	4,156	23	25,852	10,737	12,517	Washington
Wayne**	305	27,808	26,565	14,023	10,037	31,067	389,960	.0078	285,169	84	29,299	62	9,018	51	56,995	16,671	17,752	Wayne
Webster	307	2,264	2,390	13,295	892	26,719	30,100	.0005	10,034	3	3,934	8	....	....	1,226	....	1,611	Webster
Wheeler	309	6,732	6,179	9,165	2,107	22,870	61,700	.0012	19,113	6	....	....	....	....	3,691	2,285	3,430	Wheeler
White	311	23,711	19,944	16,667	9,284	33,923	395,190	.0082	357,354	105	4,369	9	7,740	43	38,097	11,719	18,758	White
Whitfield*	313	89,077	83,525	17,686	34,061	36,517	1,575,460	.0329	1,500,158	441	216,133	459	60,753	340	175,600	52,157	63,459	Whitfield
Wilcox	315	8,830	8,577	11,096	2,908	26,566	97,980	.0016	20,730	6	1,979	4	....	....	3,647	1,975	5,217	Wilcox
Wilkes	317	10,645	10,687	14,162	4,415	27,017	150,750	.0027	75,661	22	6,024	13	2,399	13	21,509	8,684	7,524	Wilkes
Wilkinson	319	10,278	10,220	14,977	3,945	31,067	153,930	.0023	25,744	8	1,141	2	....	....	5,409	1,807	7,478	Wilkinson
Worth*	321	21,822	21,967	14,527	8,251	30,553	317,010	.0053	116,810	34	4,885	10	1,501	8	22,191	7,093	14,854	Worth
The State		8,836,255	8,186,453	19,456	3,380,788	40,065	171,919,420	3.0099	104,473,500	30,730	14,825,265	31,467	5,186,391	29,068	15,093,586	4,528,319	6,119,599	The State

HAWAII (HI; CODE 15; 5 Counties)

COUNTY OR COUNTY EQUIVALENT	FIPS CO. CODE	POPULATION Estimate 7/1/04	POPULATION Census 4/1/00	PER CAPITA INCOME 2003	HOUSEHOLDS Estimate 7/1/04	MEDIAN HOUSEHOLD INCOME 2003	DISPOSABLE INCOME 2003 ($1,000)	MARKET ABILITY INDEX 2003	TOTAL RETAIL SALES Sales 2003 ($1,000)	TOTAL RETAIL SALES Ranally Sales Units	GENERAL MERCHANDISE Sales 2003 ($1,000)	GENERAL MERCHANDISE Ranally Sales Units	APPAREL STORE Sales 2003 ($1,000)	APPAREL STORE Ranally Sales Units	FOOD STORE SALES 2003 ($1,000)	HEALTH & DRUG STORE 2003 ($1,000)	PASSENGER CAR REGIS-TRATIONS 2003	COUNTY OR COUNTY EQUIVALENT
Hawaii**	001	161,480	148,677	17,181	58,557	36,816	2,774,430	.0493	1,616,503	476	330,370	701	95,334	534	384,822	103,208	101,893	Hawaii
Honolulu*	003	911,719	876,156	19,820	301,773	46,881	18,070,470	.3029	9,586,291	2,820	1,932,186	4,102	1,213,597	6,801	1,460,075	815,873	491,636	Honolulu
Kalawao	005	124	147	4,516	99	4,999	....	....	....	....	....	....	....	....	....	....	122	Kalawao
Kauai**	007	61,484	58,463	18,874	21,950	41,402	1,160,430	.0210	768,146	226	142,289	302	55,045	308	192,388	54,416	40,058	Kauai
Maui**	009	137,889	128,094	19,535	47,345	44,772	2,693,690	.0492	1,874,641	551	302,956	643	202,723	1,136	403,376	141,222	85,107	Maui
The State		1,272,696	1,211,537	19,407	429,724	45,164	24,699,580	.4224	13,845,580	4,073	2,707,801	5,748	1,566,698	8,779	2,440,661	1,114,719	718,816	The State

IDAHO (ID; CODE 16; 44 Counties)

COUNTY OR COUNTY EQUIVALENT	FIPS CO. CODE	POPULATION Estimate 7/1/04	POPULATION Census 4/1/00	PER CAPITA INCOME 2003	HOUSEHOLDS Estimate 7/1/04	MEDIAN HOUSEHOLD INCOME 2003	DISPOSABLE INCOME 2003 ($1,000)	MARKET ABILITY INDEX 2003	TOTAL RETAIL SALES Sales 2003 ($1,000)	TOTAL RETAIL SALES Ranally Sales Units	GENERAL MERCHANDISE Sales 2003 ($1,000)	GENERAL MERCHANDISE Ranally Sales Units	APPAREL STORE Sales 2003 ($1,000)	APPAREL STORE Ranally Sales Units	FOOD STORE SALES 2003 ($1,000)	HEALTH & DRUG STORE 2003 ($1,000)	PASSENGER CAR REGIS-TRATIONS 2003	COUNTY OR COUNTY EQUIVALENT
Ada*	001	332,530	300,904	20,006	126,574	42,429	6,652,480	.1252	5,109,049	1,503	965,860	2,050	184,468	1,034	655,812	146,161	244,788	Ada
Adams	003	3,531	3,476	14,359	1,486	27,467	50,700	.0009	22,905	7	....	....	....	....	7,149	1,488	3,157	Adams
Bannock*	005	75,644	75,565	15,671	27,584	34,554	1,185,420	.0234	903,112	266	153,687	326	18,959	106	145,567	41,229	55,010	Bannock
Bear Lake	007	6,266	6,411	13,838	2,271	30,613	86,710	.0016	50,751	15	2,356	5	....	....	11,932	2,108	4,841	Bear Lake
Benewah	009	8,975	9,171	14,598	3,565	29,701	131,020	.0023	63,933	19	....	....	....	....	26,533	1,862	7,461	Benewah
Bingham**	011	43,298	41,735	13,803	14,055	34,071	597,660	.0107	297,602	88	29,591	63	....	....	57,160	8,154	30,615	Bingham
Blaine	013	21,346	18,991	23,293	8,813	45,485	497,210	.0086	321,993	95	10,967	23	26,120	146	72,265	16,405	17,471	Blaine
Boise*	015	7,399	6,670	17,858	2,936	36,096	132,130	.0017	9,402	3	....	....	....	....	4,337	....	6,181	Boise
Bonner	017	39,874	36,835	15,677	16,158	31,036	625,090	.0154	824,452	243	61,370	130	14,262	80	79,110	15,418	32,724	Bonner
Bonneville*	019	88,379	82,522	17,161	31,331	39,019	1,516,670	.0305	1,283,022	377	302,766	643	31,419	176	167,142	46,930	62,892	Bonneville
Boundary	021	10,255	9,871	14,180	3,959	29,669	145,420	.0027	80,121	24	....	....	....	....	27,485	....	8,429	Boundary

Source: Devonshire Associates Ltd. and Scan/US, Inc. 2004.
* Component of a Metropolitan Core Based Statistical Area.
** Component of a Micropolitan Core Based Statistical Area.

.... Data less than 1,000. (d) Data not available.

continued on next page

Counties: Population / Income / Sales, *Continued*

COUNTY OR COUNTY EQUIVALENT	FIPS CO. CODE	POPULATION Estimate 7/1/04	POPULATION Census 4/1/00	PER CAPITA INCOME 2003	HOUSEHOLDS Estimate 7/1/04	MEDIAN HOUSEHOLD INCOME 2003	DISPOSABLE INCOME 2003 ($1,000)	MARKET ABILITY INDEX 2003	TOTAL RETAIL SALES Sales 2003 ($1,000)	TOTAL RETAIL SALES Ranally Sales Units	GENERAL MERCHANDISE Sales 2003 ($1,000)	GENERAL MERCHANDISE Ranally Sales Units	APPAREL STORE Sales 2003 ($1,000)	APPAREL STORE Ranally Sales Units	FOOD STORE SALES 2003 ($1,000)	HEALTH & DRUG STORE 2003 ($1,000)	PASSENGER CAR REGIS-TRATIONS 2003	COUNTY OR COUNTY EQUIVALENT
Butte	023	2,864	2,899	14,131	1,114	29,448	40,470	.0006	10,358	**3**	....	**....**	....	**....**	....	....	2,386	Butte
Camas	025	1,072	991	16,894	439	32,884	18,110	.0003	3,892	**1**	....	**....**	....	**....**	....	....	938	Camas
Canyon*	027	157,648	131,441	14,340	53,748	33,766	2,260,690	.0435	1,500,338	**441**	173,281	**368**	23,320	**131**	211,447	61,279	106,745	Canyon
Caribou	029	7,100	7,304	15,900	2,573	35,221	112,890	.0022	80,471	**24**	....	**....**	....	**....**	8,838	4,229	5,404	Caribou
Cassia**	031	21,676	21,416	13,012	7,200	31,463	282,040	.0058	216,592	**64**	36,968	**78**	4,229	**24**	38,998	9,857	14,542	Cassia
Clark	033	866	1,022	12,021	274	30,248	10,410	.0002	4,948	**1**	3,096	**7**	....	**....**	....	....	518	Clark
Clearwater	035	8,244	8,930	14,806	3,213	30,664	122,060	.0022	60,695	**18**	....	**....**	....	**....**	23,787	4,290	6,595	Clearwater
Custer	037	4,010	4,342	16,157	1,693	30,739	64,790	.0010	16,846	**5**	....	**....**	....	**....**	4,491	....	3,568	Custer
Elmore**	039	28,794	29,130	12,822	9,050	32,670	369,210	.0078	303,163	**89**	62,534	**133**	1,005	**6**	32,504	6,374	17,686	Elmore
Franklin*	041	12,043	11,329	13,076	3,705	33,938	157,480	.0028	74,201	**22**	2,284	**5**	....	**....**	18,445	3,524	8,451	Franklin
Fremont**	043	12,211	11,819	13,160	4,104	31,292	160,700	.0028	66,240	**19**	4,307	**9**	....	**....**	13,156	5,237	8,768	Fremont
Gem*	045	15,988	15,181	14,582	5,777	32,324	233,130	.0037	65,483	**19**	....	**....**	....	**....**	21,209	3,259	12,139	Gem
Gooding	047	14,372	14,155	13,073	5,017	30,221	187,890	.0033	75,300	**22**	....	**....**	1,131	**6**	16,033	4,700	10,500	Gooding
Idaho	049	15,394	15,511	13,757	6,115	27,682	211,770	.0037	95,924	**28**	....	**....**	....	**....**	33,490	8,917	12,507	Idaho
Jefferson*	051	20,514	19,155	13,830	6,445	35,254	283,700	.0046	80,822	**24**	3,749	**8**	....	**....**	25,660	....	14,855	Jefferson
Jerome**	053	19,070	18,342	13,674	6,453	32,308	260,770	.0050	162,768	**48**	....	**....**	....	**....**	29,538	1,868	13,422	Jerome
Kootenai*	055	120,129	108,685	16,722	45,406	35,437	2,008,850	.0384	1,461,817	**430**	200,422	**425**	48,677	**273**	245,170	51,863	92,398	Kootenai
Latah**	057	35,151	34,935	14,515	13,273	30,971	510,230	.0096	322,039	**95**	62,654	**133**	11,848	**66**	78,915	16,706	25,849	Latah
Lemhi	059	7,726	7,806	15,124	3,297	28,428	116,850	.0022	69,800	**21**	....	**....**	1,926	**11**	19,592	5,179	7,136	Lemhi
Lewis	061	3,749	3,747	15,447	1,587	29,353	57,910	.0010	26,792	**8**	....	**....**	....	**....**	5,029	....	3,197	Lewis
Lincoln	063	4,408	4,044	13,730	1,573	30,865	60,520	.0010	20,068	**6**	....	**....**	....	**....**	4,713	....	3,319	Lincoln
Madison**	065	30,691	27,467	10,538	8,370	30,871	323,420	.0072	260,180	**77**	39,955	**85**	4,912	**28**	33,240	2,491	18,361	Madison
Minidoka**	067	19,104	20,174	13,047	6,689	30,033	249,250	.0048	150,559	**44**	26,339	**56**	1,374	**8**	20,231	1,933	13,791	Minidoka
Nez Perce*	069	37,804	37,410	17,430	15,526	34,015	658,920	.0128	511,892	**151**	103,032	**219**	9,407	**53**	85,380	14,734	30,659	Nez Perce
Oneida	071	4,133	4,125	14,203	1,458	32,112	58,700	.0009	16,177	**5**	....	**....**	....	**....**	1,045	....	3,225	Oneida
Owyhee*	073	11,350	10,644	11,805	3,952	27,199	133,990	.0023	41,046	**12**	....	**....**	....	**....**	12,757	....	8,280	Owyhee
Payette**	075	21,743	20,578	13,788	7,696	31,266	299,790	.0050	103,190	**30**	....	**....**	....	**....**	25,324	....	15,394	Payette
Power*	077	7,327	7,538	13,074	2,506	30,658	95,790	.0017	44,675	**13**	....	**....**	....	**....**	7,644	1,459	5,219	Power
Shoshone	079	12,751	13,771	14,764	5,581	26,975	188,250	.0055	343,189	**101**	3,240	**7**	....	**....**	71,019	14,871	10,230	Shoshone
Teton**	081	7,373	5,999	17,198	2,615	38,920	126,800	.0020	46,709	**14**	....	**....**	....	**....**	3,178	3,169	5,723	Teton
Twin Falls**	083	67,992	64,284	15,009	25,334	32,284	1,020,480	.0222	994,906	**293**	237,979	**505**	35,559	**199**	102,115	38,889	50,228	Twin Falls
Valley	085	7,777	7,651	18,520	3,349	34,430	144,030	.0026	91,138	**27**	....	**....**	1,571	**9**	27,341	5,221	6,938	Valley
Washington	087	10,002	9,977	13,490	3,759	28,722	134,930	.0024	63,828	**19**	....	**....**	....	**....**	13,965	2,391	7,491	Washington
The State		1,388,573	1,293,953	16,265	507,623	35,643	22,585,330	.4341	16,352,387	**4,814**	2,495,026	**5,297**	429,271	**2,407**	2,489,674	555,695	1,020,031	The State

ILLINOIS (IL; CODE 17; 102 Counties)

COUNTY OR COUNTY EQUIVALENT	FIPS CO. CODE	POPULATION Estimate 7/1/04	POPULATION Census 4/1/00	PER CAPITA INCOME 2003	HOUSEHOLDS Estimate 7/1/04	MEDIAN HOUSEHOLD INCOME 2003	DISPOSABLE INCOME 2003 ($1,000)	MARKET ABILITY INDEX 2003	TOTAL RETAIL SALES Sales 2003 ($1,000)	TOTAL RETAIL SALES Ranally Sales Units	GENERAL MERCHANDISE Sales 2003 ($1,000)	GENERAL MERCHANDISE Ranally Sales Units	APPAREL STORE Sales 2003 ($1,000)	APPAREL STORE Ranally Sales Units	FOOD STORE SALES 2003 ($1,000)	HEALTH & DRUG STORE 2003 ($1,000)	PASSENGER CAR REGIS-TRATIONS 2003	COUNTY OR COUNTY EQUIVALENT
Adams**	001	67,378	68,277	16,250	26,741	32,700	1,094,860	.0219	891,232	**262**	170,328	**362**	26,914	**151**	137,757	50,266	46,983	Adams
Alexander**	003	9,242	9,590	12,623	3,730	25,038	116,660	.0019	33,274	**10**	2,581	**5**	....	**....**	8,372	....	5,451	Alexander
Bond*	005	18,040	17,633	15,896	6,391	35,852	286,770	.0049	131,550	**39**	9,801	**21**	2,131	**12**	26,834	8,351	11,832	Bond
Boone*	007	47,945	41,786	20,449	16,615	46,955	980,420	.0145	314,742	**93**	54,274	**115**	2,254	**13**	58,219	7,740	32,995	Boone
Brown	009	6,854	6,950	12,791	2,102	33,282	87,670	.0014	24,651	**7**	4,106	**9**	....	**....**	4,051	1,171	3,952	Brown
Bureau**	011	35,130	35,503	19,054	14,227	37,334	669,350	.0107	285,935	**84**	29,588	**63**	9,001	**50**	36,830	8,158	26,514	Bureau
Calhoun*	013	5,062	5,084	16,640	2,072	32,246	84,230	.0014	38,917	**11**	....	**....**	....	**....**	5,095	....	4,093	Calhoun
Carroll	015	16,118	16,674	17,961	6,649	34,832	289,500	.0047	119,576	**35**	11,104	**24**	1,260	**7**	23,905	1,764	12,276	Carroll
Cass	017	13,896	13,695	16,182	5,430	32,936	224,870	.0036	78,138	**23**	15,116	**32**	....	**....**	17,795	5,283	9,822	Cass
Champaign*	019	189,076	179,669	17,848	75,340	35,436	3,374,700	.0620	2,245,429	**661**	485,103	**1,030**	92,343	**518**	297,615	167,268	125,379	Champaign
Christian**	021	35,051	35,372	17,114	13,973	34,338	599,870	.0109	374,919	**110**	54,781	**116**	6,247	**35**	58,964	21,012	25,083	Christian
Clark	023	17,000	17,008	17,360	7,024	33,485	295,120	.0048	127,031	**37**	15,672	**33**	1,471	**8**	14,854	8,414	13,223	Clark
Clay	025	14,239	14,560	14,712	5,765	28,922	209,480	.0037	105,218	**31**	15,270	**32**	....	**....**	15,591	3,526	10,396	Clay
Clinton*	027	36,327	35,535	18,970	13,383	40,990	689,120	.0109	274,696	**81**	21,246	**45**	6,051	**34**	42,542	13,467	25,526	Clinton
Coles**	029	51,497	53,196	15,710	21,035	30,560	809,030	.0169	727,955	**214**	200,194	**425**	8,735	**49**	66,096	45,648	36,313	Coles
Cook*	031	5,342,990	5,376,741	19,364	1,958,774	42,017	103,460,480	1.7512	55,847,602	**16,428**	6,363,904	**13,509**	3,835,408	**21,495**	8,716,172	5,532,411	2,689,788	Cook
Crawford	033	19,734	20,452	15,110	7,658	31,010	298,190	.0053	159,217	**47**	13,455	**29**	2,432	**14**	28,350	11,080	13,998	Crawford
Cumberland**	035	10,997	11,253	16,812	4,329	34,043	184,880	.0028	50,127	**15**	1,527	**3**	....	**....**	7,773	1,487	8,599	Cumberland
DeKalb*	037	95,619	88,969	18,757	34,016	41,914	1,793,560	.0300	904,587	**266**	118,105	**251**	25,960	**145**	103,362	45,662	65,624	DeKalb
De Witt	039	16,642	16,798	19,680	6,782	38,606	327,520	.0055	176,008	**52**	13,067	**28**	....	**....**	23,869	7,651	12,950	De Witt
Douglas	041	19,923	19,922	17,800	7,658	36,783	354,620	.0066	248,445	**73**	5,002	**11**	36,969	**207**	26,849	10,696	13,706	Douglas
DuPage*	043	931,347	904,161	28,264	347,373	59,992	26,323,230	.4354	16,357,713	**4,812**	1,865,219	**3,959**	930,586	**5,215**	1,647,963	985,602	646,619	DuPage
Edgar	045	19,310	19,704	16,488	7,774	32,447	318,380	.0054	146,871	**43**	10,964	**23**	....	**....**	21,005	9,481	14,498	Edgar
Edwards	047	6,812	6,971	15,942	2,870	30,015	108,600	.0018	41,752	**12**	1,052	**2**	....	**....**	10,110	1,021	5,395	Edwards
Effingham**	049	34,618	34,264	17,775	13,404	36,267	615,320	.0143	753,819	**222**	87,854	**187**	27,817	**156**	72,990	23,218	24,771	Effingham
Fayette	051	21,453	21,802	14,295	8,114	30,178	306,680	.0059	199,289	**59**	25,299	**54**	1,204	**7**	27,808	6,773	15,202	Fayette
Ford*	053	14,052	14,241	17,824	5,593	35,537	250,460	.0044	148,563	**44**	11,138	**24**	1,741	**10**	22,635	9,992	10,310	Ford
Franklin	055	39,144	39,018	14,483	16,634	27,039	566,920	.0112	412,500	**121**	55,463	**118**	15,286	**86**	60,108	33,173	28,084	Franklin
Fulton**	057	37,466	38,250	15,790	14,693	31,914	591,600	.0103	295,442	**87**	47,907	**102**	7,359	**41**	57,184	23,443	26,649	Fulton
Gallatin	059	6,150	6,445	13,598	2,639	25,222	83,630	.0013	22,171	**7**	....	**....**	....	**....**	2,668	....	4,818	Gallatin
Greene	061	14,695	14,761	14,651	5,773	29,873	215,300	.0037	89,901	**26**	1,107	**2**	....	**....**	16,155	7,693	10,574	Greene
Grundy*	063	40,142	37,535	22,589	15,468	46,709	906,770	.0144	435,104	**128**	44,507	**94**	5,565	**31**	50,300	28,255	29,765	Grundy
Hamilton**	065	8,248	8,621	14,475	3,298	28,738	119,390	.0020	41,092	**12**	3,121	**7**	....	**....**	5,123	....	6,155	Hamilton
Hancock	067	19,166	20,121	17,571	7,743	34,680	336,770	.0053	128,047	**38**	1,744	**4**	1,401	**8**	13,961	9,431	15,101	Hancock
Hardin	069	4,686	4,800	13,950	1,999	26,197	65,370	.0010	10,720	**3**	....	**....**	....	**....**	1,141	1,067	3,475	Hardin
Henderson**	071	8,026	8,213	17,800	3,329	34,097	142,860	.0020	27,090	**8**	....	**....**	....	**....**	9,304	1,995	6,532	Henderson
Henry*	073	50,508	51,020	18,507	20,099	36,967	934,740	.0160	503,278	**148**	78,188	**166**	8,435	**47**	54,688	18,888	38,341	Henry
Iroquois	075	30,473	31,334	17,698	11,982	35,717	539,310	.0085	203,638	**60**	23,488	**50**	....	**....**	33,457	8,839	22,891	Iroquois
Jackson**	077	58,775	59,612	12,818	24,705	24,302	753,380	.0164	669,968	**197**	172,867	**367**	32,906	**184**	85,503	32,707	40,226	Jackson
Jasper	079	9,917	10,117	16,448	3,916	34,029	163,110	.0029	90,890	**27**	4,570	**10**	1,524	**9**	5,108	1,207	8,030	Jasper
Jefferson**	081	40,422	40,045	15,529	15,720	31,986	627,720	.0145	712,597	**210**	129,822	**276**	21,061	**118**	57,058	37,015	27,498	Jefferson
Jersey*	083	22,361	21,668	18,686	8,513	39,142	417,840	.0071	220,860	**65**	62,554	**133**	6,545	**37**	22,972	8,217	17,001	Jersey
Jo Daviess	085	22,606	22,289	20,053	9,663	37,373	453,320	.0074	214,850	**63**	2,301	**5**	7,030	**39**	46,679	9,750	18,313	Jo Daviess
Johnson	087	12,960	12,878	13,379	4,395	31,343	173,390	.0030	66,184	**19**	1,516	**3**	....	**....**	10,195	....	8,284	Johnson
Kane*	089	473,610	404,119	21,930	155,884	53,177	10,386,400	.1602	4,319,835	**1,271**	762,342	**1,618**	178,346	**1,000**	700,500	313,932	299,918	Kane
Kankakee*	091	106,207	103,833	17,954	39,387	38,535	1,906,840	.0346	1,230,032	**362**	251,524	**534**	43,569	**244**	124,754	93,525	67,696	Kankakee
Kendall*	093	70,354	54,544	24,826	24,452	56,949	1,746,580	.0259	683,529	**201**	93,365	**198**	5,133	**29**	113,031	39,191	50,862	Kendall
Knox**	095	54,075	55,836	16,805	21,662	33,281	908,720	.0171	627,035	**184**	129,719	**275**	13,477	**76**	94,904	34,816	37,329	Knox
Lake*	097	697,152	644,356	25,051	235,727	59,180	17,464,310	.3153	13,240,975	**3,895**	902,314	**1,915**	488,750	**2,739**	1,167,922	746,979	444,779	Lake
La Salle**	099	112,214	111,509	18,539	44,088	37,548	2,080,380	.0412	1,766,540	**520**	300,434	**638**	49,577	**278**	248,444	102,319	78,011	La Salle
Lawrence	101	15,247	15,452	14,889	6,303	28,833	227,010	.0037	80,809	**24**	17,638	**37**	....	**....**	14,284	5,700	11,434	Lawrence
Lee**	103	35,365	36,062	17,955	13,298	37,889	634,990	.0105	289,866	**85**	33,204	**70**	2,772	**16**	33,450	23,870	24,849	Lee
Livingston**	105	39,061	39,678	17,684	14,446	37,929	690,740	.0124	427,230	**126**	49,110	**104**	5,326	**30**	64,255	17,202	26,041	Livingston
Logan**	107	30,571	31,183	16,481	10,921	36,706	503,830	.0093	321,966	**95**	42,949	**91**	3,840	**22**	42,195	19,314	19,807	Logan
McDonough**	109	32,846	32,913	14,884	12,851	30,427	488,880	.0094	337,652	**99**	80,012	**170**	11,937	**67**	63,259	26,934	23,429	McDonough
McHenry*	111	294,238	260,077	25,272	103,203	57,465	7,435,880	.1106	2,974,564	**875**	412,195	**875**	78,854	**442**	505,280	212,505	206,090	McHenry
McLean*	113	158,878	150,433	20,577	60,568	43,291	3,269,280	.0581	2,158,777	**635**	294,644	**625**	128,048	**718**	227,004	144,519	109,194	McLean
Macon*	115	110,093	114,706	18,388	45,406	35,505	2,024,380	.0388	1,560,720	**459**	284,280	**603**	50,446	**283**	216,372	109,137	78,073	Macon
Macoupin*	117	49,072	49,019	17,042	19,494	34,249	836,270	.0140	385,541	**113**	29,612	**63**	3,909	**22**	52,991	26,257	37,137	Macoupin
Madison*	119	262,550	258,941	19,635	106,177	38,707	5,155,210	.0871	2,795,199	**822**	419,264	**890**	51,421	**288**	520,780	181,203	186,388	Madison
Marion**	121	40,438	41,691	16,661	16,274	32,862	673,730	.0119	372,945	**110**	73,980	**157**	9,511	**53**	52,989	22,931	28,264	Marion
Marshall*	123	13,003	13,180	19,445	5,232	38,425	252,840	.0037	68,879	**20**	1,344	**3**	....	**....**	10,620	6,218	10,117	Marshall
Mason	125	15,841	16,038	17,145	6,374	33,785	271,590	.0046	133,904	**39**	7,535	**16**	1,241	**7**	17,234	9,268	12,004	Mason
Massac**	127	15,143	15,161	15,585	6,331	29,632	236,010	.0039	91,166	**27**	....	**....**	....	**....**	17,014	9,782	10,872	Massac
Menard*	129	12,619	12,486	21,069	4,997	42,422	265,870	.0040	92,870	**27**	....	**....**	....	**....**	13,146	2,780	9,770	Menard
Mercer*	131	17,018	16,957	18,771	6,722	37,474	319,440	.0049	105,291	**31**	12,157	**26**	1,032	**6**	12,149	3,805	13,630	Mercer
Monroe*	133	30,375	27,619	23,343	11,402	49,228	709,030	.0108	300,223	**88**	29,243	**62**	1,408	**8**	47,153	13,185	23,615	Monroe
Montgomery	135	30,253	30,652	14,982	11,489	31,551	453,250	.0089	327,300	**96**	46,728	**99**	4,196	**24**	46,545	17,186	20,533	Montgomery
Morgan**	137	35,786	36,616	16,979	13,897	35,025	607,600	.0111	385,076	**113**	67,615	**144**	15,565	**87**	57,109	24,791	24,641	Morgan
Moultrie	139	14,512	14,287	17,838	5,538	37,132	258,870	.0037	57,757	**17**	1,136	**2**	1,890	**11**	11,767	8,418	10,136	Moultrie
Ogle**	141	53,421	51,032	19,823	20,298	41,455	1,058,990	.0158	345,463	**102**	31,809	**68**	2,075	**12**	35,498	10,773	39,362	Ogle
Peoria*	143	182,043	183,433	19,103	74,169	37,301	3,477,640	.0633	2,363,944	**695**	411,616	**874**	77,103	**432**	359,380	204,002	123,749	Peoria
Perry	145	22,559	23,094	14,790	8,434	31,340	333,640	.0057	150,101	**44**	19,570	**42**	1,517	**9**	27,559	8,814	14,915	Perry
Piatt*	147	16,444	16,365	20,998	6,596	41,505	345,290	.0052	125,950	**37**	2,322	**5**	1,584	**9**	15,083	5,948	12,573	Piatt
Pike	149	16,790	17,384	14,726	6,685	29,510	247,250	.0045	139,515	**41**	18,725	**40**	....	**....**	19,140	1,346	12,355	Pike
Pope	151	4,208	4,413	14,425	1,695	28,494	60,700	.0009	10,275	**3**	....	**....**	....	**....**	....	....	3,123	Pope
Pulaski	153	6,997	7,348	12,184	2,788	24,363	85,250	.0014	23,678	**7**	1,333	**3**	....	**....**	6,651	1,484	4,517	Pulaski
Putnam**	155	6,129	6,086	20,844	2,466	40,635	127,750	.0017	21,620	**6**	....	**....**	....	**....**	2,817	2,064	4,891	Putnam
Randolph	157	33,025	33,893	16,065	12,086	34,954	530,550	.0096	312,994	**92**	46,831	**99**	1,294	**7**	36,605	14,247	22,459	Randolph
Richland	159	15,957	16,149	15,473	6,684	29,716	246,900	.0053	236,865	**70**	30,130	**64**	3,917	**22**	39,001	10,582	12,039	Richland
Rock Island*	161	147,511	149,374	18,627	60,534	36,020	2,747,640	.0504	1,884,467	**554**	234,180	**497**	78,832	**442**	269,630	165,245	101,934	Rock Island
St. Clair*	163	259,386	256,082	17,888	101,160	36,325	4,639,910	.0829	2,849,884	**838**	611,043	**1,297**	141,160	**791**	401,453	187,192	169,166	St. Clair
Saline**	165	25,999	26,733	14,272	10,751	27,355	371,070	.0078	318,207	**94**	44,487	**94**	3,624	**20**	90,150	25,772	18,048	Saline
Sangamon*	167	192,815	188,951	21,082	81,439	40,027	4,064,860	.0699	2,446,801	**720**	447,894	**951**	79,808	**447**	321,686	157,676	137,162	Sangamon
Schuyler	169	6,967	7,189	17,280	2,921	32,524	120,390	.0020	54,698	**16**	2,370	**5**	1,088	**6**	4,486	3,852	5,619	Schuyler
Scott**	171	5,491	5,537	17,683	2,234	35,225	97,100	.0014	25,762	**8**	1,031	**2**	....	**....**	5,829	1,558	4,426	Scott
Shelby	173	22,269	22,893	17,696	8,923	35,112	394,080	.0061	134,241	**39**	4,698	**10**	2,606	**15**	16,995	8,041	17,235	Shelby
Stark*	175	6,159	6,332	17,282	2,492	34,041	106,440	.0016	33,653	**10**	....	**....**	....	**....**	3,022	2,454	4,609	Stark
Stephenson**	177	47,902	48,979	19,223	19,575	37,358	920,810	.0158	521,699	**153**	87,532	**186**	15,633	**88**	91,926	40,934	34,984	Stephenson
Tazewell*	179	127,916	128,485	20,727	51,017	41,403	2,651,300	.0469	1,733,091	**510**	199,326	**423**	39,132	**219**	268,630	80,821	94,067	Tazewell
Union	181	18,141	18,293	14,750	7,283	29,418	267,580	.0049	155,108	**46**	26,002	**55**	2,180	**12**	40,523	3,331	12,485	Union
Vermilion*	183	82,467	83,919	16,270	33,283	31,937	1,341,740	.0248	858,593	**253**	169,014	**359**	22,640	**127**	137,428	58,020	55,335	Vermilion
Wabash	185	12,608	12,937	16,539	5,147	32,288	208,520	.0035	95,337	**28**	14,570	**31**	....	**....**	10,456	7,386	9,314	Wabash
Warren**	187	18,101	18,735	16,483	6,947	34,171	298,360	.0049	122,905	**36**	24,825	**53**	....	**....**	15,809	6,235	12,591	Warren
Washington	189	15,183	15,148	18,492	5,904	37,684	280,760	.0052	198,902	**59**	6,895	**15**	1,785	**10**	15,297	6,705	11,735	Washington
Wayne	191	16,883	17,151	15,362	7,141	28,872	259,350	.0047	146,506	**43**	26,112	**55**	2,716	**15**	15,919	7,646	13,315	Wayne
White	193	15,029	15,371	15,101	6,469	27,937	226,950	.0041	130,067	**38**	17,084	**36**	1,249	**7**	21,305	5,648	11,606	White
Whiteside**	195	59,633	60,653	18,697	23,645	37,347	1,114,980	.0198	693,865	**204**	137,216	**291**	8,800	**49**	87,410	44,166	42,554	Whiteside
Will*	197	612,859	502,266	23,631	206,961	55,981	14,482,720	.2101	4,883,120	**1,436**	571,676	**1,214**	112,172	**629**	741,107	423,063	410,440	Will
Williamson**	199	62,854	61,296	15,981	26,324	30,575	1,004,470	.0183	602,656	**177**	162,352	**345**	15,156	**85**	54,113	25,879	44,383	Williamson
Winnebago*	201	286,099	278,418	20,154	113,306	40,763	5,766,030	.1018	3,678,536	**1,082**	553,586	**1,175**	142,711	**800**	611,110	230,754	199,043	Winnebago
Woodford*	203	36,654	35,469	21,143	13,424	46,346	774,990	.0121	324,294	**95**	5,358	**11**	1,491	**8**	36,132	12,248	27,483	Woodford
The State		12,725,117	12,419,293	20,409	4,736,295	43,163	259,706,930	4.3979	145,710,068	**42,860**	18,490,509	**39,252**	7,048,659	**39,509**	20,333,294	11,192,197	7,775,171	The State

INDIANA (IN; CODE 18; 92 Counties)

COUNTY OR COUNTY EQUIVALENT	FIPS CO. CODE	POPULATION Estimate 7/1/04	POPULATION Census 4/1/00	PER CAPITA INCOME 2003	HOUSEHOLDS Estimate 7/1/04	MEDIAN HOUSEHOLD INCOME 2003	DISPOSABLE INCOME 2003 ($1,000)	MARKET ABILITY INDEX 2003	TOTAL RETAIL SALES Sales 2003 ($1,000)	TOTAL RETAIL SALES Ranally Sales Units	GENERAL MERCHANDISE Sales 2003 ($1,000)	GENERAL MERCHANDISE Ranally Sales Units	APPAREL STORE Sales 2003 ($1,000)	APPAREL STORE Ranally Sales Units	FOOD STORE SALES 2003 ($1,000)	HEALTH & DRUG STORE 2003 ($1,000)	PASSENGER CAR REGIS-TRATIONS 2003	COUNTY OR COUNTY EQUIVALENT
Adams**	001	33,583	33,625	16,335	12,007	37,534	548,580	.0110	454,284	**134**	49,888	**106**	4,506	**25**	51,824	13,147	22,087	Adams
Allen*	003	342,644	331,849	19,275	137,207	39,929	6,604,320	.1202	4,509,389	**1,326**	924,241	**1,962**	192,471	**1,079**	432,904	253,776	242,659	Allen
Bartholomew*	005	72,553	71,435	19,548	28,769	40,479	1,418,280	.0243	799,523	**235**	148,891	**316**	53,440	**300**	105,411	57,214	55,439	Bartholomew
Benton*	007	9,125	9,421	17,106	3,474	36,896	156,090	.0029	100,292	**30**	....	**....**	....	**....**	10,076	7,274	6,773	Benton
Blackford	009	13,830	14,048	16,481	5,723	32,801	227,930	.0040	118,575	**35**	1,599	**3**	....	**....**	23,545	13,150	10,857	Blackford
Boone*	011	50,364	46,107	20,334	18,851	44,874	1,024,100	.0155	369,381	**109**	33,414	**71**	15,200	**85**	62,023	20,709	38,598	Boone
Brown*	013	15,417	14,957	19,473	6,175	40,195	300,220	.0041	52,660	**15**	....	**....**	3,471	**19**	8,653	2,503	13,551	Brown
Carroll*	015	20,609	20,165	18,701	7,948	40,062	385,410	.0059	133,835	**39**	3,777	**8**	....	**....**	12,280	3,981	15,986	Carroll
Cass**	017	40,228	40,930	17,141	15,489	36,567	689,540	.0124	419,948	**124**	63,608	**135**	16,879	**95**	47,347	26,401	28,443	Cass
Clark*	019	100,377	96,472	19,305	43,051	36,932	1,937,730	.0371	1,526,497	**449**	266,556	**566**	38,387	**215**	148,757	68,135	77,846	Clark
Clay*	021	26,843	26,556	16,189	10,378	34,803	434,560	.0078	247,380	**73**	24,308	**52**	....	**....**	28,111	20,806	20,552	Clay
Clinton**	023	33,939	33,866	17,049	12,607	37,793	578,640	.0095	246,135	**72**	26,815	**57**	2,591	**15**	33,841	19,563	23,869	Clinton
Crawford	025	11,262	10,743	14,833	4,486	30,604	167,050	.0026	46,574	**14**	2,337	**5**	....	**....**	15,240	1,552	9,283	Crawford

Source: Devonshire Associates Ltd. and Scan/US, Inc. 2004.
* Component of a Metropolitan Core Based Statistical Area.
** Component of a Micropolitan Core Based Statistical Area.

.... Data less than 1,000.

(d) Data not available.

Counties: Population / Income / Sales, *Continued*

COUNTY OR COUNTY EQUIVALENT	FIPS CO. CODE	POPULATION Estimate 7/1/04	POPULATION Census 4/1/00	PER CAPITA INCOME 2003	HOUSEHOLDS Estimate 7/1/04	MEDIAN HOUSEHOLD INCOME 2003	DISPOSABLE INCOME 2003 ($1,000)	MARKET ABILITY INDEX 2003	TOTAL RETAIL SALES Sales 2003 ($1,000)	TOTAL RETAIL SALES Ranally Sales Units	GENERAL MERCHANDISE Sales 2003 ($1,000)	GENERAL MERCHANDISE Ranally Sales Units	APPAREL STORE Sales 2003 ($1,000)	APPAREL STORE Ranally Sales Units	FOOD STORE SALES 2003 ($1,000)	HEALTH & DRUG STORE 2003 ($1,000)	PASSENGER CAR REGIS-TRATIONS 2003	COUNTY OR COUNTY EQUIVALENT
Daviess**	027	30,121	29,820	14,307	11,021	32,147	430,940	.0089	349,746	103	18,673	40	4,396	25	34,756	21,109	19,690	Daviess
Dearborn*	029	48,349	46,109	20,600	18,656	43,947	995,990	.0163	496,569	146	54,524	116	7,693	43	53,458	13,727	39,430	Dearborn
Decatur**	031	24,805	24,555	17,843	9,765	37,211	442,590	.0085	336,020	99	45,276	96	4,134	23	39,144	14,958	19,010	Decatur
De Kalb**	033	41,373	40,285	19,069	15,832	40,880	788,940	.0131	390,188	115	37,299	79	5,672	32	66,044	18,598	32,427	De Kalb
Delaware*	035	117,094	118,769	16,012	47,338	32,615	1,874,870	.0364	1,381,187	406	331,237	703	55,373	310	137,963	69,463	86,473	Delaware
Dubois**	037	40,365	39,674	19,269	15,765	40,707	777,810	.0167	822,189	242	96,733	205	25,354	142	62,231	16,000	31,617	Dubois
Elkhart*	039	190,535	182,791	18,034	69,272	40,953	3,436,030	.0660	2,636,787	776	432,046	917	35,241	198	276,343	119,557	125,120	Elkhart
Fayette**	041	24,819	25,588	18,467	10,462	36,043	458,330	.0077	234,214	69	34,533	73	7,010	39	32,924	28,960	19,412	Fayette
Floyd*	043	71,234	70,823	20,059	29,067	40,822	1,428,880	.0212	450,170	132	75,999	161	6,189	35	61,612	51,749	55,196	Floyd
Fountain	045	17,691	17,954	17,093	6,987	35,606	302,400	.0051	150,304	44	2,907	6	1,245	7	28,240	10,368	13,446	Fountain
Franklin*	047	22,956	22,151	20,041	9,414	40,456	460,060	.0064	95,603	28	....	....	....	....	23,050	4,785	20,641	Franklin
Fulton	049	20,491	20,511	17,224	8,104	35,751	352,930	.0062	203,591	60	17,970	38	3,720	21	47,330	12,041	15,231	Fulton
Gibson*	051	33,139	32,500	17,239	13,280	35,223	571,280	.0099	306,758	90	51,445	109	5,226	29	47,167	10,827	25,545	Gibson
Grant**	053	71,013	73,403	16,214	27,908	34,046	1,151,430	.0210	706,960	208	91,804	195	14,792	83	82,411	46,156	50,072	Grant
Greene*	055	33,255	33,157	15,826	13,599	32,075	526,290	.0088	224,202	66	50,939	108	....	....	31,090	18,313	26,677	Greene
Hamilton*	057	227,306	182,740	27,462	82,595	62,094	6,242,200	.0956	2,965,713	872	524,335	1,113	45,409	254	287,798	96,648	165,856	Hamilton
Hancock*	059	60,709	55,391	23,324	23,318	49,843	1,415,960	.0208	504,901	149	49,061	104	5,909	33	60,617	19,946	48,680	Hancock
Harrison*	061	36,107	34,325	18,785	13,944	40,084	678,260	.0115	356,732	105	90,036	191	9,168	51	38,438	28,467	29,997	Harrison
Hendricks*	063	123,336	104,093	22,029	45,098	49,470	2,716,930	.0458	1,571,190	462	469,851	997	27,251	153	168,956	45,129	94,809	Hendricks
Henry**	065	47,446	48,508	17,828	19,352	36,157	845,880	.0148	483,914	142	53,839	114	6,624	37	49,528	30,253	37,866	Henry
Howard*	067	84,849	84,964	20,951	36,408	40,491	1,777,690	.0320	1,230,888	362	322,718	685	34,854	195	116,902	86,737	63,673	Howard
Huntington**	069	38,158	38,075	17,833	14,521	38,496	680,470	.0120	398,031	117	61,897	131	7,063	40	45,975	17,578	28,179	Huntington
Jackson**	071	41,716	41,335	17,697	16,520	36,558	738,260	.0142	569,294	167	108,034	229	43,115	242	56,964	30,487	31,443	Jackson
Jasper*	073	31,372	30,043	17,773	11,386	40,674	557,560	.0103	383,071	113	32,778	70	1,850	10	33,306	32,576	23,058	Jasper
Jay	075	21,708	21,806	15,866	8,418	33,582	344,410	.0057	138,923	41	26,184	56	1,183	7	17,181	9,866	16,176	Jay
Jefferson**	077	32,425	31,705	17,253	12,853	35,838	559,430	.0101	341,168	100	83,080	176	12,059	68	38,072	12,350	23,942	Jefferson
Jennings**	079	28,250	27,554	16,544	10,525	36,383	467,380	.0077	199,768	59	31,371	67	....	....	28,990	11,044	21,664	Jennings
Johnson*	081	125,682	115,209	21,500	47,030	47,308	2,702,160	.0465	1,651,605	486	546,324	1,160	80,951	454	113,138	70,872	94,745	Johnson
Knox**	083	38,600	39,256	14,402	15,507	29,888	555,930	.0114	450,017	132	95,975	204	26,074	146	40,807	27,355	27,035	Knox
Kosciusko**	085	75,657	74,057	18,290	28,202	40,450	1,383,730	.0236	739,220	217	101,038	214	19,336	108	96,223	41,082	53,906	Kosciusko
Lagrange	087	36,387	34,909	15,497	11,803	39,331	563,880	.0099	288,835	85	10,058	21	2,781	16	37,695	20,590	19,284	Lagrange
Lake*	089	488,435	484,564	17,996	186,605	38,958	8,790,030	.1592	5,662,680	1,666	780,761	1,657	220,519	1,236	793,568	428,726	308,377	Lake
La Porte*	091	109,775	110,106	17,742	41,606	38,618	1,947,620	.0356	1,280,452	377	223,881	475	120,176	674	134,138	82,101	74,565	La Porte
Lawrence**	093	46,285	45,922	17,323	19,188	34,598	801,790	.0139	432,022	127	78,924	168	17,490	98	61,653	28,202	36,631	Lawrence
Madison*	095	130,409	133,358	17,867	52,787	36,297	2,330,070	.0408	1,337,055	393	226,170	480	32,209	181	168,264	98,737	94,372	Madison
Marion*	097	864,200	860,454	19,809	374,706	37,772	17,118,820	.3328	14,275,351	4,199	2,066,852	4,388	680,543	3,814	1,293,766	1,136,820	610,821	Marion
Marshall**	099	46,720	45,128	17,947	17,528	39,290	838,500	.0146	477,770	141	66,057	140	12,625	71	62,803	21,064	33,986	Marshall
Martin	101	10,344	10,369	17,194	4,302	33,892	177,850	.0029	70,717	21	1,562	3	....	....	13,435	2,632	8,363	Martin
Miami**	103	36,178	36,082	17,260	14,103	36,574	624,440	.0103	279,048	82	6,575	14	3,758	21	42,645	26,209	27,292	Miami
Monroe*	105	123,639	120,563	16,262	52,250	31,922	2,010,580	.0381	1,394,254	410	291,567	619	59,345	333	194,840	66,862	95,316	Monroe
Montgomery**	107	38,008	37,629	18,094	14,784	38,394	687,720	.0118	371,576	109	63,378	135	4,189	23	51,717	20,691	27,325	Montgomery
Morgan*	109	69,244	66,689	19,621	25,886	43,396	1,358,630	.0215	565,892	166	55,034	117	7,180	40	81,093	27,569	55,206	Morgan
Newton*	111	14,353	14,566	17,138	5,323	38,169	245,980	.0038	79,219	23	....	....	....	....	15,557	9,236	10,594	Newton
Noble**	113	47,239	46,275	17,400	17,165	39,381	821,960	.0133	336,289	99	45,840	97	4,898	27	49,575	14,722	33,454	Noble
Ohio*	115	5,762	5,623	18,691	2,301	38,486	107,700	.0016	25,713	8	....	....	....	....	4,773	1,919	4,884	Ohio
Orange	117	19,714	19,306	14,630	7,962	30,091	288,420	.0054	174,298	51	5,646	12	1,009	6	31,966	13,656	15,005	Orange
Owen*	119	23,137	21,786	16,024	8,922	34,246	370,740	.0057	100,668	30	12,890	27	....	....	20,044	6,239	18,204	Owen
Parke	121	17,360	17,241	15,192	6,508	33,608	263,740	.0040	66,125	19	....	....	....	....	11,043	7,633	12,927	Parke
Perry	123	18,661	18,899	16,413	7,430	34,246	306,280	.0054	168,322	50	23,929	51	4,435	25	26,513	14,674	14,444	Perry
Pike**	125	12,969	12,837	15,828	5,211	32,471	205,270	.0031	54,722	16	....	....	....	....	5,440	5,975	10,619	Pike
Porter*	127	154,300	146,798	22,165	58,906	47,829	3,420,080	.0533	1,496,265	440	299,569	636	20,042	112	184,097	114,389	115,580	Porter
Posey*	129	26,811	27,061	18,933	10,240	41,090	507,620	.0081	213,222	63	8,077	17	....	....	20,235	11,962	20,987	Posey
Pulaski	131	13,863	13,755	15,364	5,265	33,133	212,990	.0035	84,288	25	....	....	1,760	10	11,030	7,430	10,563	Pulaski
Putnam*	133	36,886	36,019	15,392	12,847	36,553	567,750	.0100	292,446	86	52,843	112	3,842	22	51,157	16,028	25,917	Putnam
Randolph	135	26,648	27,401	16,011	10,804	32,510	426,660	.0070	173,420	51	17,406	37	2,148	12	29,247	9,733	20,711	Randolph
Ripley	137	27,539	26,523	17,583	10,393	38,391	484,230	.0084	266,654	78	11,698	25	1,672	9	42,528	19,359	21,124	Ripley
Rush	139	17,949	18,261	16,647	6,928	35,509	298,800	.0050	135,681	40	18,728	40	....	....	20,100	11,057	13,622	Rush
St. Joseph*	141	266,508	265,559	17,775	104,015	37,629	4,737,260	.0911	3,620,979	1,065	700,006	1,486	140,246	786	399,407	257,464	179,859	St. Joseph
Scott**	143	23,725	22,960	16,061	9,646	32,414	381,040	.0068	212,818	63	49,196	104	....	....	22,288	16,434	19,054	Scott
Shelby*	145	43,756	43,445	18,885	16,989	40,231	826,340	.0140	439,912	129	47,990	102	6,805	38	54,047	19,678	33,903	Shelby
Spencer	147	20,321	20,391	17,899	7,632	39,449	363,730	.0058	139,912	41	....	....	....	....	23,958	3,823	15,939	Spencer
Starke	149	23,006	23,556	17,990	9,694	35,113	413,870	.0063	136,141	40	15,458	33	....	....	27,974	7,000	18,375	Starke
Steuben**	151	33,837	33,214	19,179	13,159	40,695	648,950	.0133	615,244	181	93,774	199	53,915	302	83,651	12,270	24,898	Steuben
Sullivan*	153	21,900	21,751	13,728	7,950	31,185	300,650	.0052	125,788	37	16,988	36	1,934	11	16,072	5,316	15,472	Sullivan
Switzerland	155	9,549	9,065	16,244	3,665	35,148	155,110	.0022	23,401	7	....	....	....	....	4,858	2,475	7,378	Switzerland
Tippecanoe*	157	156,683	148,955	16,684	59,605	36,211	2,614,100	.0504	1,936,052	570	482,853	1,025	82,694	463	169,538	98,172	107,748	Tippecanoe
Tipton*	159	16,378	16,577	21,094	6,507	43,890	345,480	.0055	154,334	45	4,458	9	....	....	17,851	11,943	13,085	Tipton
Union	161	7,201	7,349	16,228	2,765	35,024	116,860	.0019	40,235	12	....	....	....	....	9,632	2,291	5,599	Union
Vanderburgh*	163	171,902	171,922	18,310	74,662	34,933	3,147,450	.0683	3,333,628	981	670,569	1,423	186,305	1,044	307,456	148,418	124,350	Vanderburgh
Vermillion*	165	16,504	16,788	16,358	6,705	33,120	269,970	.0047	137,542	40	18,108	38	1,002	6	13,549	5,297	12,894	Vermillion
Vigo*	167	104,149	105,848	15,436	42,378	31,256	1,607,650	.0457	2,794,606	822	452,914	961	104,153	584	158,483	68,793	72,425	Vigo
Wabash**	169	34,129	34,960	17,459	13,154	37,384	595,860	.0105	343,763	101	43,331	92	23,801	133	40,618	22,528	24,893	Wabash
Warren	171	8,788	8,419	18,383	3,416	38,805	161,550	.0023	35,602	10	....	....	....	....	6,744	....	7,167	Warren
Warrick*	173	55,468	52,383	20,353	21,058	44,235	1,128,920	.0159	272,394	80	15,862	34	....	....	63,132	21,158	44,502	Warrick
Washington*	175	27,735	27,223	16,240	10,836	34,360	450,410	.0077	219,810	65	2,574	5	1,719	10	23,634	12,539	21,871	Washington
Wayne**	177	69,968	71,097	16,299	28,483	33,012	1,140,400	.0229	932,393	274	188,648	400	21,466	120	134,752	43,272	50,463	Wayne
Wells*	179	28,011	27,600	18,732	10,717	40,524	524,690	.0085	233,295	69	15,305	33	3,971	22	44,441	17,929	21,545	Wells
White	181	24,725	25,267	17,661	9,539	37,602	436,670	.0081	297,231	87	28,665	61	4,722	26	44,311	11,199	18,123	White
Whitley*	183	31,953	30,707	20,172	12,709	41,815	644,550	.0106	322,670	95	39,000	83	3,621	20	56,447	17,118	25,331	Whitley
The State		6,230,346	6,080,485	18,767	2,465,349	38,967	116,927,130	2.1082	76,264,128	22,432	12,742,454	27,046	2,672,856	14,978	8,378,432	4,554,552	4,512,006	The State

IOWA (IA; CODE 19; 99 Counties)

COUNTY OR COUNTY EQUIVALENT	FIPS CO. CODE	POPULATION Estimate 7/1/04	POPULATION Census 4/1/00	PER CAPITA INCOME 2003	HOUSEHOLDS Estimate 7/1/04	MEDIAN HOUSEHOLD INCOME 2003	DISPOSABLE INCOME 2003 ($1,000)	MARKET ABILITY INDEX 2003	TOTAL RETAIL SALES Sales 2003 ($1,000)	TOTAL RETAIL SALES Ranally Sales Units	GENERAL MERCHANDISE Sales 2003 ($1,000)	GENERAL MERCHANDISE Ranally Sales Units	APPAREL STORE Sales 2003 ($1,000)	APPAREL STORE Ranally Sales Units	FOOD STORE SALES 2003 ($1,000)	HEALTH & DRUG STORE 2003 ($1,000)	PASSENGER CAR REGIS-TRATIONS 2003	COUNTY OR COUNTY EQUIVALENT
Adair	001	7,829	8,243	16,795	3,251	33,095	131,490	.0023	75,893	22	2,057	4	....	....	11,633	4,348	6,488	Adair
Adams	003	4,336	4,482	14,769	1,814	29,115	64,040	.0010	19,855	6	....	....	....	....	2,924	....	3,859	Adams
Allamakee	005	14,503	14,675	15,411	5,724	31,901	223,510	.0041	133,310	39	5,496	12	3,297	18	24,097	6,235	11,228	Allamakee
Appanoose	007	13,552	13,721	14,081	5,784	26,895	190,830	.0035	105,016	31	25,979	55	3,404	19	20,500	4,216	10,965	Appanoose
Audubon	009	6,373	6,830	15,228	2,594	30,704	97,050	.0018	63,288	19	1,754	4	....	....	5,882	1,167	5,102	Audubon
Benton*	011	26,543	25,308	18,451	10,272	39,284	489,740	.0078	203,543	60	8,854	19	2,337	13	20,714	4,938	22,275	Benton
Black Hawk*	013	125,922	128,012	16,904	50,103	35,032	2,128,580	.0428	1,787,507	526	297,139	631	58,515	328	206,762	93,056	93,697	Black Hawk
Boone**	015	26,245	26,224	18,342	10,437	37,761	481,390	.0080	231,328	68	38,782	82	2,885	16	31,994	11,791	21,045	Boone
Bremer*	017	23,391	23,325	17,842	9,004	37,923	417,350	.0068	175,949	52	19,349	41	2,683	15	30,062	8,595	18,632	Bremer
Buchanan	019	20,844	21,093	16,736	7,978	35,720	348,850	.0064	222,932	66	28,707	61	4,264	24	19,356	3,593	15,633	Buchanan
Buena Vista**	021	20,152	20,411	14,628	7,334	32,777	294,780	.0059	220,524	65	31,964	68	7,138	40	29,371	7,685	13,787	Buena Vista
Butler	023	14,852	15,305	16,937	6,125	33,474	251,550	.0039	84,698	25	3,318	7	....	....	9,443	2,886	13,041	Butler
Calhoun	025	10,512	11,115	15,375	4,267	31,125	161,620	.0029	83,788	25	....	....	....	....	7,804	2,398	8,456	Calhoun
Carroll	027	20,993	21,421	17,229	8,539	34,715	361,680	.0072	299,498	88	44,508	94	10,345	58	48,875	11,524	16,086	Carroll
Cass	029	14,192	14,684	16,145	5,982	31,318	229,130	.0043	157,306	46	14,180	30	4,027	23	30,079	9,269	11,320	Cass
Cedar	031	18,279	18,187	18,916	7,258	39,151	345,760	.0053	116,035	34	14,657	31	....	....	15,770	....	15,558	Cedar
Cerro Gordo**	033	44,720	46,447	17,963	19,513	33,803	803,310	.0169	787,014	232	184,524	392	17,132	96	94,978	17,197	35,372	Cerro Gordo
Cherokee	035	12,386	13,035	16,950	5,225	32,815	209,940	.0039	136,130	40	13,143	28	1,918	11	22,400	10,489	10,268	Cherokee
Chickasaw	037	12,580	13,095	17,439	5,083	35,258	219,380	.0036	92,568	27	5,791	12	1,087	6	15,167	5,516	10,508	Chickasaw
Clarke	039	9,258	9,133	15,280	3,597	32,218	141,460	.0025	77,301	23	8,158	17	....	....	20,576	1,298	7,214	Clarke
Clay**	041	16,969	17,372	17,278	7,218	33,177	293,190	.0063	298,800	88	42,515	90	18,950	106	37,528	10,756	13,434	Clay
Clayton	043	18,397	18,678	15,679	7,419	31,758	288,440	.0052	170,330	50	1,497	3	1,253	7	14,500	5,881	14,883	Clayton
Clinton**	045	49,713	50,149	17,472	20,267	35,012	868,600	.0157	542,140	159	66,531	141	9,546	54	87,858	34,549	37,734	Clinton
Crawford	047	16,928	16,942	14,761	6,441	31,649	249,870	.0046	140,977	41	18,949	40	2,383	13	28,858	6,146	12,752	Crawford
Dallas*	049	47,845	40,750	20,472	18,397	44,063	979,490	.0144	307,424	90	9,438	20	1,839	10	36,622	7,313	37,968	Dallas
Davis	051	8,560	8,541	14,325	3,224	30,530	122,620	.0021	55,503	16	5,881	12	....	....	5,442	4,280	6,496	Davis
Decatur	053	8,711	8,689	12,385	3,361	26,251	107,890	.0019	38,409	11	1,551	3	....	....	9,151	3,361	6,397	Decatur
Delaware	055	18,055	18,404	16,125	6,833	35,095	291,130	.0050	146,922	43	21,255	45	1,508	8	21,755	8,269	14,191	Delaware
Des Moines**	057	40,904	42,351	17,535	16,964	34,852	717,240	.0148	662,456	195	139,354	296	20,363	114	119,824	29,913	31,059	Des Moines
Dickinson**	059	16,376	16,424	19,564	7,178	36,509	320,380	.0062	262,966	77	35,707	76	6,728	38	38,253	10,176	13,612	Dickinson
Dubuque*	061	90,309	89,143	17,549	35,087	37,014	1,584,810	.0308	1,245,748	366	204,332	434	31,824	178	148,726	70,539	63,564	Dubuque
Emmet	063	10,742	11,027	15,714	4,417	31,290	168,800	.0031	97,937	29	5,314	11	1,062	6	20,087	6,353	8,579	Emmet
Fayette	065	21,212	22,008	15,134	8,604	30,567	321,020	.0062	221,888	65	19,842	42	3,153	18	28,142	10,796	16,513	Fayette
Floyd	067	16,523	16,900	16,285	6,751	32,487	269,070	.0048	148,091	44	19,735	42	2,739	15	29,689	....	13,305	Floyd
Franklin	069	10,694	10,704	16,816	4,379	33,611	179,830	.0030	79,573	23	3,415	7	....	....	14,081	3,718	8,865	Franklin
Fremont	071	7,816	8,010	17,579	3,145	35,692	137,400	.0020	36,699	11	....	....	....	....	4,627	5,984	6,404	Fremont
Greene	073	9,949	10,366	15,674	4,001	31,973	155,940	.0025	58,732	17	5,752	12	....	....	10,791	4,761	7,734	Greene
Grundy*	075	12,330	12,369	18,328	5,000	36,866	225,980	.0036	91,667	27	....	....	....	....	9,498	5,473	10,061	Grundy
Guthrie*	077	11,550	11,353	17,253	4,762	34,261	199,270	.0032	82,787	24	....	....	....	....	7,417	4,888	9,892	Guthrie
Hamilton	079	16,279	16,438	18,134	6,692	36,023	295,200	.0047	115,272	34	9,825	21	1,424	8	20,774	6,886	12,702	Hamilton
Hancock	081	11,893	12,100	17,446	4,772	35,478	207,490	.0033	75,208	22	3,689	8	....	....	11,749	3,881	10,013	Hancock
Hardin	083	18,123	18,812	16,475	7,373	33,056	298,570	.0055	186,026	55	25,312	54	1,285	7	30,543	7,843	14,238	Hardin
Harrison*	085	15,654	15,666	17,053	6,152	35,555	266,940	.0052	207,145	61	2,237	5	1,065	6	13,961	8,854	12,692	Harrison
Henry	087	19,930	20,336	16,864	7,570	36,269	336,090	.0062	221,153	65	24,382	52	2,254	13	21,674	6,344	14,770	Henry
Howard	089	9,741	9,932	16,226	3,932	32,670	158,060	.0026	69,692	21	3,371	7	....	....	13,665	5,285	7,972	Howard
Humboldt	091	9,998	10,381	18,116	4,180	35,411	181,120	.0031	95,145	28	7,409	16	1,909	11	24,722	1,598	8,309	Humboldt
Ida	093	7,416	7,837	16,814	3,115	32,634	124,690	.0021	57,626	17	5,199	11	1,359	8	9,375	3,507	6,145	Ida
Iowa	095	15,988	15,671	18,217	6,296	37,870	291,260	.0052	176,219	52	....	....	46,261	259	20,358	6,412	12,894	Iowa
Jackson	097	20,191	20,296	16,173	8,231	32,430	326,550	.0059	195,147	57	20,279	43	1,777	10	38,229	7,390	16,297	Jackson
Jasper**	099	37,859	37,213	18,783	15,151	38,361	711,100	.0123	401,408	118	42,455	90	6,171	35	64,808	28,457	29,865	Jasper
Jefferson	101	15,975	16,181	16,032	6,651	31,610	256,110	.0058	287,117	84	72,731	154	2,092	12	54,543	10,394	12,193	Jefferson
Johnson*	103	116,938	111,006	18,537	47,437	37,475	2,167,730	.0404	1,554,147	457	220,859	469	55,000	308	270,763	77,087	86,731	Johnson
Jones*	105	20,326	20,221	16,454	7,743	35,359	334,440	.0057	162,168	48	20,697	44	....	....	19,005	4,586	15,910	Jones
Keokuk	107	11,329	11,400	15,918	4,610	31,958	180,340	.0033	113,600	33	....	....	....	....	4,398	....	9,540	Keokuk
Kossuth	109	16,220	17,163	16,284	6,737	32,136	264,120	.0049	173,680	51	16,480	35	3,138	18	27,591	4,481	13,513	Kossuth
Lee**	111	36,314	38,052	16,786	14,661	34,201	609,580	.0114	416,228	122	54,626	116	11,851	66	67,853	17,385	27,547	Lee
Linn*	113	197,521	191,701	20,875	80,191	42,130	4,123,340	.0744	2,872,078	845	447,566	950	120,082	673	374,981	149,724	150,321	Linn
Louisa**	115	12,209	12,183	16,397	4,518	36,207	200,190	.0030	51,471	15	....	....	....	....	7,035	....	9,496	Louisa
Lucas	117	9,533	9,422	14,209	3,811	29,356	135,450	.0025	74,730	22	8,383	18	....	....	14,187	1,243	7,675	Lucas
Lyon	119	11,745	11,763	16,246	4,514	34,743	190,810	.0031	72,626	21	1,082	2	1,492	8	11,536	4,918	9,737	Lyon
Madison*	121	14,659	14,019	18,065	5,617	38,928	264,820	.0042	106,919	31	6,602	14	....	....	20,105	5,764	12,253	Madison
Mahaska**	123	22,302	22,335	16,864	8,859	34,960	376,090	.0068	235,354	69	32,417	69	7,608	43	40,892	9,074	17,050	Mahaska
Marion**	125	32,527	32,052	18,067	12,258	39,333	587,660	.0104	355,103	104	29,717	63	5,596	31	51,066	14,476	24,727	Marion
Marshall**	127	39,027	39,311	17,095	15,228	35,787	667,180	.0120	403,258	119	74,850	159	22,143	124	67,687	24,331	29,055	Marshall
Mills*	129	15,021	14,547	17,740	5,552	39,731	266,470	.0039	67,679	20	....	....	....	....	14,317	4,032	11,713	Mills
Mitchell	131	10,972	10,874	15,675	4,341	32,392	171,990	.0030	85,426	25	....	....	1,052	6	11,809	4,926	8,770	Mitchell
Monona	133	9,661	10,020	16,146	4,101	31,174	155,990	.0030	116,238	34	8,446	18	....	....	13,279	9,386	7,849	Monona
Monroe	135	7,731	8,016	16,054	3,142	32,426	124,110	.0023	73,817	22	4,932	10	....	....	13,193	3,683	6,617	Monroe
Montgomery	137	11,126	11,771	15,860	4,628	31,199	176,460	.0031	95,119	28	10,751	23	1,215	7	22,394	7,524	8,408	Montgomery
Muscatine**	139	42,192	41,722	18,107	16,213	38,554	763,970	.0137	473,812	139	75,463	160	10,332	58	72,464	23,812	31,059	Muscatine
O'Brien	141	14,482	15,102	16,393	5,822	33,363	237,400	.0047	188,767	56	8,709	18	3,799	21	24,159	9,213	11,184	O'Brien
Osceola	143	6,765	7,003	15,895	2,709	32,329	107,530	.0018	43,263	13	....	....	....	....	5,153	4,693	5,438	Osceola
Page	145	16,156	16,976	16,091	6,443	32,972	259,960	.0048	164,172	48	29,103	62	2,807	16	28,491	7,700	11,887	Page

Source: Devonshire Associates Ltd. and Scan/US, Inc. 2004.
* Component of a Metropolitan Core Based Statistical Area.
** Component of a Micropolitan Core Based Statistical Area.

.... Data less than 1,000.

(d) Data not available.

continued on next page

Counties: Population / Income / Sales, *Continued*

COUNTY OR COUNTY EQUIVALENT	FIPS CO. CODE	POPULATION Estimate 7/1/04	POPULATION Census 4/1/00	PER CAPITA INCOME 2003	HOUSEHOLDS Estimate 7/1/04	MEDIAN HOUSEHOLD INCOME 2003	DISPOSABLE INCOME 2003 ($1,000)	MARKET ABILITY INDEX 2003	TOTAL RETAIL SALES Sales 2003 ($1,000)	TOTAL RETAIL SALES Ranally Sales Units	GENERAL MERCHANDISE Sales 2003 ($1,000)	GENERAL MERCHANDISE Ranally Sales Units	APPAREL STORE Sales 2003 ($1,000)	APPAREL STORE Ranally Sales Units	FOOD STORE SALES 2003 ($1,000)	HEALTH & DRUG STORE 2003 ($1,000)	PASSENGER CAR REGIS-TRATIONS 2003	COUNTY OR COUNTY EQUIVALENT
Palo Alto	147	9,564	10,147	15,622	3,938	30,950	149,410	.0027	87,125	26	4,700	10	....	....	10,835	3,744	7,732	Palo Alto
Plymouth	149	24,669	24,849	18,112	9,443	38,854	446,810	.0077	243,278	72	25,963	55	2,943	17	31,279	7,672	19,333	Plymouth
Pocahontas	151	8,134	8,662	16,288	3,447	31,287	132,490	.0021	42,219	12	....	....	....	....	7,496	....	6,761	Pocahontas
Polk*	153	392,872	374,601	20,852	159,696	42,430	8,192,090	.1460	5,487,233	1,614	812,043	1,724	225,270	1,262	730,371	279,745	285,777	Polk
Pottawattamie*	155	88,639	87,704	17,704	34,567	37,291	1,569,270	.0318	1,379,131	406	140,240	298	39,447	221	152,907	76,203	64,010	Pottawattamie
Poweshiek	157	19,092	18,815	17,548	7,698	35,537	335,030	.0064	255,109	75	24,147	51	1,445	8	34,151	7,907	14,660	Poweshiek
Ringgold	159	5,406	5,469	13,744	2,222	27,230	74,300	.0014	47,265	14	....	....	....	....	6,288	....	4,600	Ringgold
Sac	161	10,678	11,529	15,741	4,465	30,848	168,080	.0031	98,839	29	....	....	....	....	10,946	....	8,755	Sac
Scott*	163	159,637	158,668	19,256	63,729	39,861	3,074,030	.0588	2,420,552	712	355,016	754	102,085	572	274,310	124,863	115,681	Scott
Shelby	165	12,597	13,173	17,183	5,024	35,257	216,460	.0040	141,502	42	7,417	16	1,034	6	22,154	6,546	10,236	Shelby
Sioux	167	32,279	31,589	15,584	11,042	37,222	503,040	.0102	408,949	120	27,815	59	3,701	21	47,944	12,439	22,292	Sioux
Story*	169	83,964	79,981	16,929	30,985	37,751	1,421,410	.0258	880,205	259	164,956	350	36,753	206	145,918	35,233	60,468	Story
Tama	171	17,806	18,103	16,530	6,916	34,922	294,330	.0049	124,517	37	6,374	14	....	....	20,962	6,708	14,154	Tama
Taylor	173	6,729	6,958	14,469	2,743	29,133	97,360	.0016	33,345	10	....	....	....	....	5,366	....	5,863	Taylor
Union	175	11,818	12,309	15,895	5,140	30,264	187,850	.0037	138,417	41	27,555	59	1,724	10	29,636	4,209	9,785	Union
Van Buren	177	7,763	7,809	14,672	3,189	29,421	113,900	.0017	25,178	7	....	....	....	....	2,700	....	6,463	Van Buren
Wapello**	179	35,843	36,051	15,218	14,773	30,464	545,460	.0107	396,910	117	88,650	188	15,260	86	65,275	19,691	27,220	Wapello
Warren*	181	42,397	40,671	20,281	15,625	45,358	859,840	.0139	400,390	118	32,275	69	1,608	9	52,294	16,533	33,012	Warren
Washington*	183	21,511	20,670	17,451	8,463	36,223	375,390	.0065	202,687	60	18,859	40	4,231	24	30,507	6,816	16,601	Washington
Wayne	185	6,648	6,730	14,260	2,800	27,598	94,800	.0016	39,057	11	1,400	3	....	....	5,770	1,474	5,751	Wayne
Webster**	187	39,388	40,235	15,946	15,598	33,037	628,080	.0130	554,657	163	125,210	266	12,017	67	72,883	28,810	29,337	Webster
Winnebago	189	11,343	11,723	17,994	4,693	35,594	204,110	.0035	106,081	31	5,553	12	....	....	20,917	6,543	9,048	Winnebago
Winneshiek	191	21,304	21,310	16,356	7,912	35,979	348,440	.0066	244,065	72	34,823	74	6,400	36	33,901	4,367	15,963	Winneshiek
Woodbury*	193	103,007	103,877	16,599	38,828	36,036	1,709,790	.0346	1,452,174	427	213,902	454	60,237	338	197,997	54,566	69,985	Woodbury
Worth**	195	7,728	7,909	17,330	3,227	33,923	133,930	.0020	35,848	11	....	....	....	....	6,560	....	6,718	Worth
Wright	197	13,581	14,334	17,297	5,644	34,046	234,910	.0035	62,675	18	3,963	8	....	....	11,747	4,593	10,750	Wright
The State		2,949,245	2,926,324	17,971	1,174,389	36,973	53,001,830	.9684	35,056,752	10,310	4,745,603	10,074	1,063,855	5,963	4,879,104	1,640,777	2,239,502	The State

KANSAS (KS; CODE 20; 105 Counties)

COUNTY OR COUNTY EQUIVALENT	FIPS CO. CODE	POPULATION Estimate 7/1/04	POPULATION Census 4/1/00	PER CAPITA INCOME 2003	HOUSEHOLDS Estimate 7/1/04	MEDIAN HOUSEHOLD INCOME 2003	DISPOSABLE INCOME 2003 ($1,000)	MARKET ABILITY INDEX 2003	TOTAL RETAIL SALES Sales 2003 ($1,000)	TOTAL RETAIL SALES Ranally Sales Units	GENERAL MERCHANDISE Sales 2003 ($1,000)	GENERAL MERCHANDISE Ranally Sales Units	APPAREL STORE Sales 2003 ($1,000)	APPAREL STORE Ranally Sales Units	FOOD STORE SALES 2003 ($1,000)	HEALTH & DRUG STORE 2003 ($1,000)	PASSENGER CAR REGIS-TRATIONS 2003	COUNTY OR COUNTY EQUIVALENT
Allen	001	13,753	14,385	14,523	5,580	29,619	199,740	.0041	161,667	48	30,144	64	3,899	22	28,188	12,616	10,872	Allen
Anderson	003	8,244	8,110	15,123	3,286	31,105	124,670	.0023	70,626	21	1,902	4	....	....	7,851	2,987	6,648	Anderson
Atchison**	005	16,734	16,774	14,839	6,319	32,224	248,310	.0045	134,558	40	26,170	56	2,436	14	26,773	10,289	11,895	Atchison
Barber	007	4,951	5,307	16,338	2,117	31,316	80,890	.0015	47,815	14	3,033	6	....	....	7,661	4,356	4,169	Barber
Barton**	009	27,250	28,205	14,913	11,127	30,204	406,390	.0083	335,622	99	58,314	124	8,356	47	53,911	17,066	20,828	Barton
Bourbon	011	14,986	15,379	14,622	6,158	29,456	219,130	.0041	133,561	39	32,353	69	1,679	9	23,296	8,060	11,737	Bourbon
Brown	013	10,353	10,724	14,715	4,209	30,057	152,340	.0029	104,294	31	13,931	30	....	....	17,831	5,430	7,792	Brown
Butler*	015	61,602	59,482	18,365	22,389	41,764	1,131,320	.0183	485,609	143	49,576	105	4,437	25	83,352	12,435	47,421	Butler
Chase**	017	3,132	3,030	15,792	1,310	30,305	49,460	.0007	8,806	3	....	....	....	....	1,673	....	2,688	Chase
Chautauqua	019	4,131	4,359	13,469	1,691	27,116	55,640	.0009	14,268	4	....	....	....	....	3,710	3,495	3,546	Chautauqua
Cherokee	021	21,571	22,605	13,757	8,464	28,839	296,750	.0051	122,477	36	13,867	29	....	....	19,522	8,976	16,565	Cherokee
Cheyenne	023	2,890	3,165	14,997	1,242	28,548	43,340	.0007	16,701	5	....	....	....	....	4,800	....	2,473	Cheyenne
Clark	025	2,316	2,390	15,630	939	31,729	36,200	.0005	8,434	2	....	....	....	....	2,052	....	1,874	Clark
Clay	027	8,488	8,822	15,930	3,509	31,585	135,210	.0026	96,990	29	11,042	23	1,431	8	14,408	5,076	7,080	Clay
Cloud	029	9,740	10,268	14,732	3,968	29,914	143,490	.0027	93,378	27	12,990	28	1,981	11	13,490	5,418	7,807	Cloud
Coffey	031	8,792	8,865	16,953	3,457	35,492	149,050	.0025	66,577	20	....	....	....	....	7,859	4,167	7,577	Coffey
Comanche	033	1,902	1,967	15,521	866	28,215	29,520	.0005	10,861	3	....	....	....	....	2,843	....	1,735	Comanche
Cowley**	035	35,718	36,291	15,420	13,998	32,349	550,770	.0101	326,163	96	42,412	90	8,265	46	63,257	25,972	26,406	Cowley
Crawford**	037	38,454	38,242	13,785	15,555	28,156	530,070	.0106	387,404	114	130,270	277	7,964	45	54,336	10,142	28,931	Crawford
Decatur	039	3,241	3,472	14,955	1,417	28,081	48,470	.0007	11,642	3	....	....	....	....	3,559	1,025	2,866	Decatur
Dickinson	041	19,215	19,344	16,995	7,921	33,957	326,550	.0056	170,046	50	7,871	17	....	....	30,795	8,030	15,978	Dickinson
Doniphan*	043	8,116	8,249	14,576	3,163	30,527	118,300	.0020	51,551	15	....	....	....	....	7,745	....	6,292	Doniphan
Douglas*	045	103,909	99,962	16,965	40,944	35,598	1,762,840	.0319	1,084,623	319	155,726	331	56,394	316	198,476	47,982	76,691	Douglas
Edwards	047	3,225	3,449	14,828	1,359	28,909	47,820	.0007	9,467	3	....	....	....	....	4,737	....	2,600	Edwards
Elk	049	3,148	3,261	13,774	1,362	26,132	43,360	.0006	5,005	1	....	....	....	....	....	....	2,742	Elk
Ellis**	051	27,140	27,507	15,831	11,272	31,424	429,650	.0097	472,673	139	75,697	161	25,686	144	74,164	13,178	21,285	Ellis
Ellsworth	053	6,286	6,525	15,523	2,401	33,458	97,580	.0016	33,455	10	5,445	12	....	....	6,896	1,305	4,910	Ellsworth
Finney**	055	38,704	40,523	14,209	12,567	35,808	549,960	.0120	525,075	154	97,720	207	28,016	157	74,396	10,152	23,006	Finney
Ford**	057	33,156	32,458	14,039	10,730	35,594	465,470	.0103	452,144	133	83,404	177	12,528	70	43,648	9,700	19,791	Ford
Franklin*	059	25,761	24,784	16,961	9,868	36,320	436,940	.0078	256,253	75	93,291	198	2,183	12	25,702	10,648	20,124	Franklin
Geary**	061	25,846	27,947	17,785	12,560	30,316	459,660	.0078	231,775	68	48,258	102	1,734	10	45,428	2,921	21,658	Geary
Gove	063	2,859	3,068	15,883	1,171	31,687	45,410	.0008	28,220	8	....	....	....	....	4,975	1,608	2,653	Gove
Graham	065	2,771	2,946	15,756	1,219	29,571	43,660	.0008	29,255	9	....	....	....	....	5,254	1,780	2,604	Graham
Grant	067	7,698	7,909	16,060	2,708	37,571	123,630	.0023	77,991	23	10,240	22	....	....	15,998	3,698	5,194	Grant
Gray	069	6,110	5,904	15,550	2,103	36,979	95,010	.0016	39,360	12	....	....	....	....	4,320	1,462	4,292	Gray
Greeley	071	1,382	1,534	15,774	554	32,245	21,800	.0004	10,901	3	....	....	....	....	1,354	1,159	1,221	Greeley
Greenwood	073	7,424	7,673	14,659	3,135	28,664	108,830	.0019	46,947	14	4,416	9	....	....	6,881	3,485	6,348	Greenwood
Hamilton	075	2,666	2,670	14,430	1,028	30,634	38,470	.0007	18,279	5	....	....	....	....	3,189	1,121	2,061	Hamilton
Harper	077	6,109	6,536	14,490	2,598	28,038	88,520	.0015	38,292	11	2,529	5	....	....	6,375	3,423	5,119	Harper
Harvey*	079	33,707	32,869	17,803	13,002	38,010	600,070	.0099	271,715	80	52,231	111	13,437	75	64,140	10,746	25,396	Harvey
Haskell	081	4,224	4,307	14,910	1,436	35,862	62,980	.0009	12,522	4	....	....	....	....	1,364	....	2,892	Haskell
Hodgeman	083	2,172	2,085	15,405	830	32,948	33,460	.0006	14,742	4	....	....	....	....	5,031	....	1,884	Hodgeman
Jackson*	085	13,129	12,657	17,008	4,934	37,154	223,300	.0038	108,881	32	18,366	39	....	....	18,675	1,772	11,167	Jackson
Jefferson*	087	18,908	18,426	18,739	7,033	41,388	354,320	.0049	63,518	19	....	....	2,622	15	12,473	2,053	16,139	Jefferson
Jewell	089	3,330	3,791	15,844	1,522	28,345	52,760	.0008	10,281	3	....	....	....	....	2,501	....	3,145	Jewell
Johnson*	091	497,146	451,086	26,902	199,850	55,444	13,374,160	.2223	8,245,920	2,426	1,292,625	2,744	541,572	3,035	958,395	395,530	386,163	Johnson
Kearny	093	4,616	4,531	15,175	1,566	36,660	70,050	.0010	8,439	2	....	....	....	....	4,398	....	3,265	Kearny
Kingman	095	8,285	8,673	16,809	3,237	35,360	139,260	.0022	49,526	15	4,814	10	....	....	13,138	3,523	6,965	Kingman
Kiowa	097	3,118	3,278	15,414	1,311	30,345	48,060	.0008	22,054	6	....	....	2,073	12	3,406	4,308	2,539	Kiowa
Labette**	099	22,096	22,835	14,239	8,965	28,945	314,620	.0059	184,293	54	26,611	57	3,969	22	33,826	16,071	17,132	Labette
Lane	101	1,884	2,155	17,251	803	33,350	32,500	.0005	8,812	3	....	....	....	....	2,347	....	1,718	Lane
Leavenworth*	103	72,419	68,691	18,171	24,893	43,649	1,315,940	.0209	514,628	151	86,624	184	7,670	43	76,294	23,808	50,406	Leavenworth
Lincoln	105	3,473	3,578	15,024	1,495	28,619	52,180	.0008	16,610	5	....	....	....	....	3,756	1,019	3,175	Lincoln
Linn*	107	9,761	9,570	16,372	3,904	33,720	159,810	.0024	42,385	12	....	....	....	....	14,193	2,563	8,434	Linn
Logan	109	2,794	3,046	15,190	1,152	30,528	42,440	.0009	37,094	11	....	....	....	....	3,707	....	2,437	Logan
Lyon**	111	35,750	35,935	14,806	13,923	31,251	529,320	.0103	372,922	110	69,988	149	18,885	106	59,206	14,281	25,523	Lyon
McPherson**	113	29,265	29,554	17,484	11,129	37,605	511,670	.0087	258,577	76	31,322	67	3,795	21	22,742	7,135	22,284	McPherson
Marion	115	13,273	13,361	14,879	5,046	32,599	197,490	.0037	118,512	35	4,214	9	....	....	11,780	6,187	10,321	Marion
Marshall	117	10,474	10,965	15,188	4,276	30,666	159,080	.0031	110,504	33	25,128	53	2,140	12	16,448	2,110	8,575	Marshall
Meade	119	4,670	4,631	15,214	1,707	34,283	71,050	.0011	22,973	7	....	....	....	....	4,913	1,089	3,448	Meade
Miami*	121	29,415	28,351	18,955	10,779	42,930	557,570	.0093	283,710	83	29,277	62	2,613	15	110,394	13,945	23,731	Miami
Mitchell	123	6,638	6,932	16,067	2,771	31,553	106,650	.0023	101,817	30	5,842	12	....	....	11,591	4,056	5,524	Mitchell
Montgomery**	125	34,520	36,252	14,634	14,300	29,187	505,180	.0097	333,168	98	68,489	145	9,750	55	55,474	19,042	25,846	Montgomery
Morris	127	5,956	6,104	15,547	2,493	30,482	92,600	.0016	50,139	15	....	....	1,798	10	8,022	1,446	5,002	Morris
Morton	129	3,263	3,496	15,789	1,220	34,800	51,520	.0008	12,961	4	....	....	....	....	4,574	1,228	2,497	Morton
Nemaha	131	10,436	10,717	14,443	3,856	32,085	150,730	.0028	93,027	27	4,590	10	....	....	18,745	6,688	7,861	Nemaha
Neosho	133	16,459	16,997	14,572	6,520	30,421	239,840	.0052	224,932	66	29,582	63	8,051	45	43,854	8,444	12,986	Neosho
Ness	135	3,069	3,454	17,002	1,381	31,068	52,180	.0008	18,019	5	....	....	....	....	1,907	....	3,081	Ness
Norton	137	5,744	5,953	13,451	2,188	29,061	77,260	.0014	35,183	10	4,086	9	....	....	8,116	2,835	4,109	Norton
Osage*	139	16,789	16,712	16,837	6,553	35,576	282,670	.0043	78,397	23	....	....	....	....	13,878	4,465	14,402	Osage
Osborne	141	4,098	4,452	14,624	1,804	27,131	59,930	.0012	45,705	13	....	....	....	....	9,779	3,700	3,570	Osborne
Ottawa**	143	6,170	6,163	17,060	2,421	35,682	105,260	.0015	18,069	5	....	....	....	....	6,958	1,062	5,379	Ottawa
Pawnee	145	6,660	7,233	15,152	2,513	32,953	100,910	.0018	50,469	15	4,275	9	....	....	12,660	4,452	4,812	Pawnee
Phillips	147	5,547	6,001	16,402	2,315	32,305	90,980	.0015	38,327	11	5,262	11	....	....	8,851	1,417	4,865	Phillips
Pottawatomie**	149	18,856	18,209	16,918	7,031	37,302	319,000	.0054	153,558	45	....	....	2,854	16	64,552	7,441	15,103	Pottawatomie
Pratt	151	9,373	9,647	16,689	3,878	33,275	156,430	.0030	112,749	33	27,130	58	3,848	22	18,688	3,554	7,320	Pratt
Rawlins	153	2,805	2,966	16,018	1,235	30,065	44,930	.0007	13,977	4	....	....	....	....	4,339	....	2,514	Rawlins
Reno**	155	63,546	64,790	16,091	25,173	33,352	1,022,500	.0197	737,385	217	120,567	256	20,622	116	90,943	25,122	46,860	Reno
Republic	157	5,151	5,835	15,352	2,266	28,745	79,080	.0014	40,615	12	1,837	4	....	....	7,025	2,915	4,562	Republic
Rice	159	10,305	10,761	15,142	3,859	33,145	156,040	.0024	44,663	13	3,029	6	....	....	10,710	3,299	7,500	Rice
Riley**	161	62,085	62,843	13,210	22,417	30,253	820,130	.0169	631,787	186	133,015	282	36,036	202	53,293	16,002	44,337	Riley
Rooks	163	5,338	5,685	14,685	2,244	28,685	78,390	.0014	44,468	13	....	....	....	....	7,278	2,311	4,514	Rooks
Rush	165	3,378	3,551	15,577	1,484	29,261	52,620	.0008	15,335	5	....	....	....	....	5,104	....	3,118	Rush
Russell	167	6,765	7,370	14,871	2,960	27,907	100,600	.0017	47,126	14	4,919	10	....	....	8,926	3,413	5,831	Russell
Saline**	169	53,778	53,597	17,333	21,931	35,028	932,110	.0202	952,296	280	223,498	474	45,552	255	105,471	29,876	41,666	Saline
Scott	171	4,712	5,120	18,202	1,914	36,931	85,770	.0016	63,076	19	4,247	9	....	....	8,751	1,376	3,865	Scott
Sedgwick*	173	466,006	452,869	18,809	183,088	39,789	8,764,970	.1549	5,372,337	1,580	1,070,450	2,272	228,796	1,282	758,415	256,512	328,115	Sedgwick
Seward**	175	23,272	22,510	13,527	7,473	34,605	314,790	.0072	325,568	96	64,275	136	24,029	135	48,058	7,689	12,822	Seward
Shawnee*	177	171,175	169,871	19,419	71,974	38,175	3,324,050	.0605	2,278,937	670	477,160	1,013	75,794	425	295,682	164,466	126,814	Shawnee
Sheridan	179	2,617	2,813	15,464	1,062	31,327	40,470	.0007	21,943	6	....	....	....	....	3,668	1,440	2,319	Sheridan
Sherman	181	6,129	6,760	16,180	2,635	30,923	99,170	.0024	130,904	39	24,577	52	3,816	21	12,572	4,639	5,565	Sherman
Smith	183	4,073	4,536	14,081	1,751	27,052	57,350	.0010	29,494	9	1,887	4	....	....	7,789	2,045	3,662	Smith
Stafford	185	4,531	4,789	15,067	1,906	29,562	68,270	.0010	12,535	4	....	....	....	....	4,618	....	3,842	Stafford
Stanton	187	2,404	2,406	16,206	861	36,868	38,960	.0006	16,551	5	1,133	2	....	....	....	....	1,777	Stanton
Stevens	189	5,365	5,463	16,895	1,930	38,631	90,640	.0016	45,561	13	1,144	2	1,393	8	9,341	3,784	3,865	Stevens
Sumner*	191	25,017	25,946	17,044	9,585	36,651	426,400	.0066	139,344	41	20,286	43	1,532	9	26,945	3,147	19,944	Sumner
Thomas	193	7,853	8,180	16,870	3,150	34,558	132,480	.0026	107,460	32	23,201	49	5,860	33	18,699	3,566	6,369	Thomas
Trego	195	3,044	3,319	15,279	1,342	28,399	46,510	.0008	18,719	6	....	....	....	....	4,483	2,344	2,815	Trego
Wabaunsee*	197	6,730	6,885	18,058	2,591	38,514	121,530	.0017	24,477	7	....	....	....	....	1,352	....	6,056	Wabaunsee
Wallace	199	1,584	1,749	15,069	618	31,466	23,870	.0004	8,287	2	....	....	....	....	2,486	....	1,482	Wallace
Washington	201	6,022	6,483	14,132	2,507	27,788	85,100	.0014	23,256	7	....	....	....	....	4,989	....	5,058	Washington
Wichita	203	2,422	2,531	15,334	945	32,056	37,140	.0006	17,449	5	....	....	....	....	1,427	....	1,982	Wichita
Wilson	205	10,005	10,332	14,011	4,071	28,202	140,180	.0021	25,296	7	1,563	3	....	....	5,940	4,570	8,012	Wilson
Woodson	207	3,588	3,788	13,010	1,580	24,206	46,680	.0008	15,488	5	....	....	....	....	4,929	1,024	3,252	Woodson
Wyandotte*	209	156,835	157,882	14,658	59,163	31,935	2,298,960	.0407	1,147,799	338	130,478	277	17,299	97	193,326	71,298	95,845	Wyandotte
The State		2,733,795	2,688,418	18,567	1,074,016	38,314	50,757,140	.8961	30,716,045	9,035	5,120,974	10,869	1,266,790	7,099	4,438,950	1,456,353	2,038,938	The State

KENTUCKY (KY; CODE 21; 120 Counties)

COUNTY OR COUNTY EQUIVALENT	FIPS CO. CODE	POPULATION Estimate 7/1/04	POPULATION Census 4/1/00	PER CAPITA INCOME 2003	HOUSEHOLDS Estimate 7/1/04	MEDIAN HOUSEHOLD INCOME 2003	DISPOSABLE INCOME 2003 ($1,000)	MARKET ABILITY INDEX 2003	TOTAL RETAIL SALES Sales 2003 ($1,000)	TOTAL RETAIL SALES Ranally Sales Units	GENERAL MERCHANDISE Sales 2003 ($1,000)	GENERAL MERCHANDISE Ranally Sales Units	APPAREL STORE Sales 2003 ($1,000)	APPAREL STORE Ranally Sales Units	FOOD STORE SALES 2003 ($1,000)	HEALTH & DRUG STORE 2003 ($1,000)	PASSENGER CAR REGIS-TRATIONS 2003	COUNTY OR COUNTY EQUIVALENT
Adair	001	17,516	17,244	11,980	7,009	23,126	209,840	.0039	95,764	28	18,216	39	....	....	10,918	12,284	12,178	Adair
Allen	003	18,410	17,800	15,359	7,490	29,625	282,760	.0044	80,104	24	5,266	11	....	....	13,407	9,681	13,518	Allen
Anderson**	005	20,021	19,111	21,162	8,004	40,872	423,680	.0059	99,898	29	15,105	32	....	....	11,628	10,207	16,508	Anderson
Ballard**	007	8,155	8,286	16,461	3,369	31,071	134,240	.0022	54,854	16	1,989	4	....	....	9,142	3,625	6,172	Ballard
Barren**	009	39,469	38,033	15,488	16,214	29,677	611,280	.0120	458,181	135	110,350	234	10,016	56	49,439	25,150	29,541	Barren
Bath**	011	11,507	11,085	12,994	4,730	24,567	149,520	.0025	46,026	14	1,512	3	....	....	8,025	4,416	8,437	Bath
Bell**	013	29,925	30,060	10,120	12,460	18,668	302,850	.0077	343,002	101	108,261	230	15,385	86	85,997	21,535	17,990	Bell
Boone*	015	100,516	85,991	24,248	39,486	48,522	2,437,350	.0479	2,266,025	667	496,161	1,053	95,802	537	138,669	80,679	76,732	Boone
Bourbon*	017	19,673	19,360	17,117	7,984	32,425	336,750	.0055	142,816	42	15,455	33	....	....	28,697	12,169	14,189	Bourbon
Boyd*	019	49,520	49,752	16,775	20,832	31,058	830,680	.0177	804,251	237	168,085	357	55,488	311	95,343	47,678	34,797	Boyd
Boyle**	021	27,881	27,697	16,596	10,959	32,817	462,700	.0091	366,457	108	89,604	190	18,935	106	32,543	15,142	18,694	Boyle
Bracken*	023	8,554	8,279	16,492	3,405	32,167	141,070	.0020	24,715	7	1,228	3	....	....	7,065	1,476	6,760	Bracken
Breathitt	025	15,780	16,100	9,714	6,276	18,776	153,290	.0034	108,191	32	23,199	49	2,127	12	15,682	10,274	9,202	Breathitt
Breckinridge	027	19,119	18,648	14,775	7,663	28,496	282,480	.0047	113,251	33	20,136	43	....	....	17,706	10,982	14,452	Breckinridge
Bullitt*	029	65,997	61,236	19,838	24,703	40,981	1,309,280	.0188	334,402	98	8,939	19	....	....	44,113	18,010	50,450	Bullitt
Butler	031	13,257	13,010	14,123	5,254	27,711	187,230	.0029	48,505	14	1,566	3	....	....	12,571	6,674	9,989	Butler
Caldwell	033	12,755	13,060	14,706	5,396	27,012	187,580	.0038	147,926	44	27,075	57	1,725	10	21,281	12,695	10,113	Caldwell
Calloway**	035	34,843	34,177	15,497	14,749	28,471	539,950	.0111	455,288	134	86,107	183	19,063	107	31,205	21,693	26,813	Calloway

Source: Devonshire Associates Ltd. and Scan/US, Inc. 2004. .... Data less than 1,000. (d) Data not available.
* Component of a Metropolitan Core Based Statistical Area.
** Component of a Micropolitan Core Based Statistical Area.

Counties: Population / Income / Sales, *Continued*

COUNTY OR COUNTY EQUIVALENT	FIPS CO. CODE	POPULATION Estimate 7/1/04	POPULATION Census 4/1/00	PER CAPITA INCOME 2003	HOUSEHOLDS Estimate 7/1/04	MEDIAN HOUSEHOLD INCOME 2003	DISPOSABLE INCOME 2003 ($1,000)	MARKET ABILITY INDEX 2003	TOTAL RETAIL SALES Sales 2003 ($1,000)	TOTAL RETAIL SALES Ranally Sales Units	GENERAL MERCHANDISE Sales 2003 ($1,000)	GENERAL MERCHANDISE Ranally Sales Units	APPAREL STORE Sales 2003 ($1,000)	APPAREL STORE Ranally Sales Units	FOOD STORE SALES 2003 ($1,000)	HEALTH & DRUG STORE SALES 2003 ($1,000)	PASSENGER CAR REGIS-TRATIONS 2003	COUNTY OR COUNTY EQUIVALENT
Campbell*	037	87,745	88,616	20,502	36,026	39,096	1,798,960	.0287	815,887	240	99,422	211	24,267	136	184,963	57,249	60,661	Campbell
Carlisle	039	5,397	5,351	15,110	2,262	28,009	81,550	.0013	26,713	8	1,249	3	....	....	8,908	1,752	4,238	Carlisle
Carroll	041	10,248	10,155	17,183	4,040	34,273	176,090	.0036	159,380	47	4,308	9	5,395	30	21,856	9,137	6,915	Carroll
Carter	043	27,234	26,889	13,061	10,836	25,440	355,710	.0071	243,034	71	27,256	58	8,320	47	39,881	17,979	19,108	Carter
Casey	045	16,143	15,447	11,514	6,720	21,285	185,870	.0033	62,360	18	3,218	7	3,422	19	9,829	9,445	11,327	Casey
Christian*	047	69,170	72,265	14,035	25,620	29,715	970,820	.0181	570,961	168	106,314	226	24,148	135	53,598	32,833	42,609	Christian
Clark*	049	34,197	33,144	19,832	14,156	37,515	678,190	.0120	433,377	127	78,891	167	6,507	36	91,587	16,659	25,596	Clark
Clay	051	24,298	24,556	7,640	8,874	15,956	185,630	.0043	120,064	35	30,088	64	3,373	19	22,596	14,305	13,514	Clay
Clinton	053	9,595	9,634	10,944	4,199	19,386	105,010	.0020	54,445	16	2,232	5	....	....	14,171	8,229	7,347	Clinton
Crittenden	055	8,991	9,384	15,007	3,761	27,892	134,930	.0021	33,232	10	3,366	7	....	....	12,528	3,257	6,724	Crittenden
Cumberland	057	7,156	7,147	11,695	3,034	21,376	83,690	.0016	40,420	12	2,477	5	....	....	7,869	5,345	5,248	Cumberland
Daviess*	059	92,851	91,545	17,937	37,583	34,622	1,665,490	.0297	1,020,908	300	225,267	478	38,656	217	109,897	72,292	67,120	Daviess
Edmonson*	061	11,936	11,644	12,974	4,904	24,787	154,860	.0024	24,146	7	1,784	4	....	....	7,365	2,381	9,107	Edmonson
Elliott	063	6,989	6,748	10,816	2,840	20,698	75,590	.0012	13,497	4	....	....	....	....	3,703	2,897	4,843	Elliott
Estill	065	15,153	15,307	12,197	6,271	22,698	184,820	.0033	72,808	21	3,699	8	....	....	17,837	9,235	10,701	Estill
Fayette*	067	268,741	260,512	21,504	121,067	37,210	5,779,130	.1053	4,201,331	1,236	606,834	1,288	282,706	1,584	422,432	267,743	201,879	Fayette
Fleming	069	14,555	13,792	13,663	5,770	26,787	198,870	.0039	140,236	41	4,028	9	....	....	12,131	7,979	10,468	Fleming
Floyd	071	42,233	42,441	11,161	17,655	20,607	471,370	.0096	295,266	87	72,151	153	6,665	37	51,190	35,649	27,505	Floyd
Franklin**	073	48,119	47,687	21,336	21,369	37,424	1,026,670	.0174	593,702	175	114,637	243	20,450	115	62,613	35,311	36,152	Franklin
Fulton**	075	7,326	7,752	12,912	3,109	23,685	94,590	.0020	74,817	22	21,874	46	1,183	7	17,983	9,742	4,619	Fulton
Gallatin*	077	8,041	7,870	16,417	3,002	34,148	132,010	.0019	25,018	7	2,019	4	....	....	4,985	1,186	5,593	Gallatin
Garrard	079	16,173	14,792	16,389	6,308	32,100	265,060	.0038	40,502	12	1,302	3	....	....	10,616	6,075	11,920	Garrard
Grant*	081	24,461	22,384	17,424	9,137	36,338	426,210	.0075	240,794	71	33,972	72	21,041	118	27,692	13,875	17,610	Grant
Graves**	083	37,313	37,028	15,062	15,024	29,318	561,990	.0102	317,557	93	64,849	138	5,236	29	25,851	18,050	26,420	Graves
Grayson	085	24,764	24,053	13,909	10,108	26,355	344,440	.0060	156,232	46	37,478	80	....	....	23,724	13,232	18,794	Grayson
Green	087	11,868	11,518	13,074	4,919	24,671	155,160	.0025	41,082	12	2,384	5	....	....	7,569	6,241	9,035	Green
Greenup*	089	36,989	36,891	15,972	15,056	30,369	590,770	.0087	124,495	37	6,210	13	....	....	25,429	18,868	27,396	Greenup
Hancock*	091	8,436	8,392	17,720	3,334	34,909	149,490	.0022	39,731	12	2,373	5	....	....	11,305	3,087	6,870	Hancock
Hardin*	093	96,607	94,174	17,518	37,065	35,448	1,692,350	.0311	1,118,769	329	249,519	530	58,498	328	86,180	47,317	69,797	Hardin
Harlan	095	31,790	33,202	9,921	13,288	18,154	315,400	.0064	174,973	51	43,343	92	5,224	29	38,953	14,009	19,887	Harlan
Harrison	097	18,294	17,983	17,597	7,336	34,349	321,920	.0052	134,095	39	24,595	52	1,921	11	28,060	13,467	13,821	Harrison
Hart	099	17,992	17,445	12,293	7,033	24,651	221,180	.0039	81,497	24	3,973	8	5,692	32	16,219	10,697	12,542	Hart
Henderson*	101	45,235	44,829	17,837	18,679	33,929	806,860	.0142	468,521	138	67,758	144	14,737	83	53,172	39,757	32,048	Henderson
Henry*	103	15,691	15,060	17,708	6,129	35,353	277,860	.0043	90,440	27	8,268	18	....	....	9,518	7,802	11,602	Henry
Hickman	105	5,138	5,262	16,407	2,187	30,057	84,300	.0012	17,146	5	....	....	....	....	7,130	2,166	3,911	Hickman
Hopkins**	107	46,961	46,519	15,478	19,422	29,123	726,850	.0136	461,681	136	99,767	212	27,544	154	57,417	38,572	33,612	Hopkins
Jackson	109	13,623	13,495	10,347	5,525	19,795	140,960	.0025	42,977	13	5,963	13	....	....	7,734	7,388	9,570	Jackson
Jefferson*	111	700,741	693,604	20,948	310,484	36,725	14,679,060	.2549	9,096,692	2,676	1,530,818	3,250	445,930	2,499	1,057,025	575,841	490,999	Jefferson
Jessamine*	113	42,270	39,041	17,997	15,842	37,030	760,730	.0149	615,940	181	65,103	138	9,449	53	55,232	15,422	29,467	Jessamine
Johnson	115	23,749	23,445	12,317	9,511	23,809	292,520	.0062	234,005	69	59,305	126	8,178	46	35,894	8,297	15,857	Johnson
Kenton*	117	152,501	151,464	21,239	62,260	40,683	3,239,010	.0484	1,133,495	333	114,974	244	29,803	167	262,672	125,760	106,018	Kenton
Knott	119	17,607	17,649	10,388	7,049	20,181	182,900	.0032	51,258	15	1,433	3	....	....	17,519	6,334	11,309	Knott
Knox	121	31,657	31,795	9,433	12,788	17,960	298,630	.0071	269,918	79	47,114	100	22,244	125	45,406	17,379	19,683	Knox
Larue*	123	13,450	13,373	15,881	5,366	31,041	213,600	.0032	52,167	15	1,207	3	....	....	12,904	9,472	10,344	Larue
Laurel*	125	56,343	52,715	13,332	22,466	25,881	751,170	.0155	585,752	172	136,379	290	13,820	77	47,689	19,151	39,156	Laurel
Lawrence	127	15,994	15,569	10,473	6,297	20,664	167,500	.0033	89,007	26	10,980	23	1,742	10	24,940	12,748	10,719	Lawrence
Lee	129	7,891	7,916	9,442	3,095	18,483	74,510	.0014	29,097	9	2,756	6	....	....	6,752	5,393	5,015	Lee
Leslie	131	12,144	12,401	9,727	5,064	17,795	118,120	.0022	42,252	12	3,392	7	....	....	13,688	10,556	8,131	Leslie
Letcher	133	24,714	25,277	11,017	10,309	20,412	272,280	.0051	122,177	36	26,577	56	6,779	38	29,756	19,944	17,069	Letcher
Lewis**	135	13,686	14,092	11,117	5,415	21,640	152,150	.0025	26,621	8	....	....	....	....	7,596	4,929	9,373	Lewis
Lincoln**	137	24,891	23,361	13,139	10,078	25,391	327,040	.0053	89,987	26	12,407	26	....	....	17,804	2,031	18,220	Lincoln
Livingston**	139	9,697	9,804	15,815	4,003	30,037	153,360	.0023	30,440	9	....	....	....	....	9,232	4,921	7,918	Livingston
Logan	141	26,920	26,573	15,886	10,822	30,894	427,660	.0071	176,146	52	29,334	62	1,246	7	27,419	14,099	19,851	Logan
Lyon	143	8,067	8,080	14,091	2,921	30,522	113,670	.0019	45,766	13	....	....	9,800	55	6,315	3,311	5,479	Lyon
McCracken**	145	64,547	65,514	18,508	29,051	32,131	1,194,640	.0260	1,276,363	375	370,374	786	88,815	498	95,930	66,288	48,748	McCracken
McCreary	147	17,234	17,080	9,702	6,843	18,734	167,200	.0033	81,148	24	4,023	9	....	....	16,279	17,166	10,775	McCreary
McLean*	149	9,837	9,938	14,792	4,025	28,094	145,510	.0024	55,887	16	1,898	4	....	....	5,515	4,444	7,443	McLean
Madison**	151	75,994	70,872	15,968	30,537	31,064	1,213,510	.0218	690,716	203	168,477	358	34,766	195	86,030	39,599	55,264	Madison
Magoffin	153	13,337	13,332	9,637	5,249	18,842	128,530	.0025	54,081	16	1,406	3	1,016	6	11,049	11,402	8,368	Magoffin
Marion	155	18,636	18,212	13,775	6,980	28,696	256,710	.0044	101,977	30	24,168	51	1,802	10	26,907	6,602	12,602	Marion
Marshall	157	30,699	30,125	18,164	13,033	33,345	557,620	.0089	224,977	66	32,378	69	....	....	25,363	14,541	24,655	Marshall
Martin	159	12,505	12,578	9,259	4,968	17,872	115,790	.0024	67,423	20	4,102	9	....	....	17,340	14,860	7,944	Martin
Mason**	161	16,821	16,800	15,779	7,333	28,408	265,420	.0063	326,546	96	69,388	147	19,615	110	60,199	10,133	12,463	Mason
Meade*	163	27,972	26,349	16,662	10,444	34,588	466,070	.0072	144,259	42	3,216	7	....	....	16,013	11,669	21,332	Meade
Menifee**	165	6,623	6,556	11,360	2,644	21,932	75,240	.0012	11,500	3	....	....	....	....	3,372	1,379	4,664	Menifee
Mercer	167	21,599	20,817	17,578	8,706	33,246	379,670	.0062	159,630	47	36,956	78	1,764	10	23,003	6,152	16,437	Mercer
Metcalfe**	169	10,052	10,037	12,190	4,094	23,150	122,530	.0022	47,383	14	1,102	2	1,048	6	12,736	6,115	7,713	Metcalfe
Monroe	171	11,741	11,756	11,600	4,775	21,966	136,190	.0029	99,473	29	2,699	6	1,352	8	22,884	11,565	8,202	Monroe
Montgomery**	173	23,827	22,554	15,488	9,649	29,874	369,040	.0080	361,343	106	88,599	188	16,945	95	43,190	20,343	17,102	Montgomery
Morgan	175	14,385	13,948	9,921	5,081	21,663	142,720	.0029	82,073	24	7,928	17	....	....	12,559	12,720	8,912	Morgan
Muhlenberg**	177	31,657	31,839	13,814	12,635	26,677	437,310	.0082	252,231	74	74,753	159	3,366	19	33,010	13,543	23,258	Muhlenberg
Nelson*	179	40,283	37,477	17,848	15,404	36,115	718,980	.0114	279,953	82	40,954	87	6,635	37	35,852	14,328	30,082	Nelson
Nicholas	181	6,986	6,813	15,527	2,995	28,003	108,470	.0016	19,550	6	2,675	6	....	....	6,506	2,126	5,334	Nicholas
Ohio	183	23,242	22,916	14,249	9,214	27,874	331,180	.0057	142,398	42	23,001	49	1,329	7	23,901	20,149	17,387	Ohio
Oldham*	185	51,680	46,178	24,117	17,098	56,225	1,246,360	.0166	261,238	77	53,378	113	1,019	6	16,037	13,510	36,739	Oldham
Owen	187	11,265	10,547	15,598	4,408	31,104	175,710	.0028	60,462	18	1,045	2	....	....	8,378	3,728	8,532	Owen
Owsley	189	4,721	4,858	8,028	1,885	15,398	37,900	.0009	25,974	8	....	....	....	....	19,108	1,550	2,892	Owsley
Pendleton*	191	15,286	14,390	16,611	5,504	35,800	253,920	.0035	34,768	10	....	....	....	....	6,441	2,447	10,908	Pendleton
Perry	193	29,565	29,390	11,361	12,098	21,379	335,890	.0082	368,692	108	80,291	170	18,681	105	49,482	26,567	18,991	Perry
Pike	195	67,152	68,736	12,585	28,282	23,088	845,090	.0190	803,106	236	155,898	331	35,814	201	109,130	73,916	45,957	Pike
Powell	197	13,369	13,237	12,572	5,300	24,656	168,080	.0028	52,696	16	3,229	7	....	....	11,176	9,573	8,990	Powell
Pulaski**	199	58,578	56,217	13,869	24,284	25,955	812,400	.0173	718,036	211	144,158	306	31,091	174	77,860	35,369	42,887	Pulaski
Robertson	201	2,338	2,266	13,901	899	28,106	32,500	.0005	3,150	1	....	....	....	....	....	....	1,701	Robertson
Rockcastle**	203	16,648	16,582	12,043	6,780	22,937	200,500	.0034	57,682	17	5,093	11	....	....	19,665	8,104	12,161	Rockcastle
Rowan	205	22,502	22,094	12,614	8,361	26,207	283,830	.0061	244,778	72	47,827	102	12,725	71	43,363	19,503	14,879	Rowan
Russell	207	16,670	16,315	12,158	7,284	21,386	202,680	.0042	148,172	44	25,417	54	1,716	10	30,094	12,780	12,725	Russell
Scott*	209	37,824	33,061	21,227	14,512	42,910	802,880	.0124	328,679	97	47,285	100	15,825	89	23,705	18,333	27,237	Scott
Shelby*	211	36,679	33,337	19,850	13,646	41,290	728,060	.0125	415,482	122	59,611	127	7,761	44	25,747	10,904	26,654	Shelby
Simpson	213	16,744	16,405	18,122	6,922	34,205	303,430	.0061	260,675	77	20,938	44	....	....	31,740	18,472	12,444	Simpson
Spencer*	215	15,064	11,766	20,086	5,464	42,676	302,570	.0039	31,737	9	1,470	3	....	....	13,531	4,592	11,956	Spencer
Taylor**	217	23,492	22,927	14,349	9,817	26,523	337,090	.0074	325,075	96	78,198	166	10,920	61	33,360	13,256	16,760	Taylor
Todd	219	12,038	11,971	13,894	4,633	27,965	167,250	.0028	64,238	19	2,107	4	....	....	17,503	6,068	8,076	Todd
Trigg*	221	12,954	12,597	16,990	5,452	31,404	220,090	.0034	71,518	21	4,692	10	....	....	15,412	3,715	10,445	Trigg
Trimble*	223	8,955	8,125	16,978	3,522	33,723	152,040	.0021	19,671	6	....	....	....	....	5,187	2,146	6,877	Trimble
Union	225	15,800	15,637	15,755	5,927	32,586	248,930	.0043	116,008	34	20,927	44	....	....	23,187	9,258	11,220	Union
Warren*	227	96,776	92,522	17,988	39,668	34,016	1,740,830	.0330	1,287,810	379	235,115	499	73,389	411	124,554	50,719	70,636	Warren
Washington	229	11,371	10,916	16,185	4,625	31,060	184,040	.0029	64,028	19	1,419	3	....	....	11,332	8,209	8,709	Washington
Wayne	231	20,374	19,923	10,694	8,313	20,007	217,870	.0043	112,422	33	24,893	53	....	....	25,080	13,913	14,368	Wayne
Webster*	233	14,026	14,120	15,171	5,583	29,837	212,790	.0034	67,806	20	....	....	....	....	13,968	6,025	10,599	Webster
Whitley**	235	37,695	35,865	11,110	14,839	21,653	418,800	.0097	394,592	116	102,908	218	6,716	38	26,076	25,802	24,217	Whitley
Wolfe	237	6,886	7,065	9,898	2,825	18,499	68,160	.0014	37,041	11	4,811	10	....	....	11,055	5,321	4,917	Wolfe
Woodford*	239	23,789	23,208	22,481	9,336	44,697	534,810	.0076	153,143	45	27,810	59	2,256	13	9,079	9,895	17,860	Woodford
The State		4,140,891	4,041,769	17,241	1,704,528	32,136	71,393,920	1.2721	42,260,060	12,428	7,415,661	15,743	1,749,071	9,806	5,305,305	2,780,005	2,956,274	The State

LOUISIANA (LA; CODE 22; 64 Parishes)

COUNTY OR COUNTY EQUIVALENT	FIPS CO. CODE	POPULATION Estimate 7/1/04	POPULATION Census 4/1/00	PER CAPITA INCOME 2003	HOUSEHOLDS Estimate 7/1/04	MEDIAN HOUSEHOLD INCOME 2003	DISPOSABLE INCOME 2003 ($1,000)	MARKET ABILITY INDEX 2003	TOTAL RETAIL SALES Sales 2003 ($1,000)	TOTAL RETAIL SALES Ranally Sales Units	GENERAL MERCHANDISE Sales 2003 ($1,000)	GENERAL MERCHANDISE Ranally Sales Units	APPAREL STORE Sales 2003 ($1,000)	APPAREL STORE Ranally Sales Units	FOOD STORE SALES 2003 ($1,000)	HEALTH & DRUG STORE SALES 2003 ($1,000)	PASSENGER CAR REGIS-TRATIONS 2003	COUNTY OR COUNTY EQUIVALENT
Acadia**	001	59,384	58,861	12,319	21,726	25,703	731,580	.0141	423,361	125	79,317	168	9,245	52	77,375	29,499	34,001	Acadia
Allen	003	25,218	25,440	11,435	8,298	26,343	288,380	.0054	136,883	40	24,975	53	1,814	10	28,009	7,854	13,124	Allen
Ascension*	005	86,777	76,627	19,068	30,874	40,948	1,654,690	.0272	796,805	234	126,506	269	62,835	352	118,332	41,517	55,528	Ascension
Assumption**	007	23,229	23,388	14,138	8,472	28,834	328,400	.0053	98,589	29	23,810	51	....	....	20,795	4,473	13,635	Assumption
Avoyelles	009	41,891	41,481	11,096	15,286	22,631	464,820	.0093	270,878	80	55,174	117	2,685	15	54,131	21,831	23,638	Avoyelles
Beauregard**	011	33,660	32,986	15,221	12,678	30,756	512,330	.0092	279,748	82	86,712	184	9,463	53	29,689	6,854	21,868	Beauregard
Bienville	013	15,189	15,752	11,967	6,013	22,674	181,760	.0032	66,835	20	4,268	9	12,552	70	10,820	3,895	9,339	Bienville
Bossier*	015	103,123	98,310	18,362	39,327	36,405	1,893,520	.0341	1,207,650	355	293,349	623	45,929	257	125,073	31,638	86,616	Bossier
Caddo*	017	249,805	252,161	15,777	100,861	29,976	3,941,140	.0779	3,035,118	893	488,126	1,036	134,674	755	396,194	152,668	156,433	Caddo
Calcasieu*	019	184,005	183,577	17,572	74,088	33,191	3,233,420	.0603	2,249,684	662	538,185	1,142	91,221	511	274,045	119,468	122,134	Calcasieu
Caldwell	021	10,609	10,560	13,203	4,081	26,023	140,070	.0025	65,470	19	....	....	....	....	17,702	6,942	6,689	Caldwell
Cameron*	023	9,628	9,991	15,621	3,542	32,207	150,400	.0023	38,884	11	5,628	12	....	....	15,319	....	5,994	Cameron
Catahoula	025	10,518	10,920	11,276	4,067	21,883	118,600	.0026	102,061	30	11,507	24	....	....	27,451	10,060	6,790	Catahoula
Claiborne	027	16,454	16,851	12,113	6,197	24,402	199,310	.0035	77,949	23	14,068	30	1,065	6	19,044	4,342	9,732	Claiborne
Concordia**	029	19,568	20,247	11,403	7,489	22,422	223,140	.0048	170,072	50	20,956	44	....	....	37,275	7,808	11,463	Concordia
De Soto*	031	26,145	25,494	13,677	10,185	26,885	357,590	.0062	149,284	44	24,324	52	2,588	15	19,853	7,659	16,681	De Soto
East Baton Rouge*	033	412,326	412,852	18,957	168,774	35,234	7,816,260	.1495	6,096,122	1,793	1,154,525	2,451	274,753	1,540	690,508	288,030	283,614	East Baton Rouge
East Carroll	035	8,867	9,421	8,743	2,935	20,032	77,520	.0016	42,163	12	7,332	16	....	....	4,716	1,682	3,766	East Carroll
East Feliciana*	037	21,001	21,360	13,021	6,906	31,770	273,450	.0044	66,071	19	1,152	2	....	....	15,228	7,228	11,716	East Feliciana
Evangeline	039	35,063	35,434	9,740	12,859	20,349	341,520	.0070	193,359	57	24,194	51	2,914	16	42,861	25,103	19,281	Evangeline
Franklin	041	20,726	21,263	11,181	7,758	22,403	231,740	.0052	197,613	58	63,443	135	2,761	15	18,874	6,151	12,149	Franklin
Grant*	043	18,945	18,698	14,202	7,340	27,762	269,060	.0041	60,116	18	2,778	6	....	....	3,946	2,428	12,751	Grant
Iberia**	045	74,437	73,266	13,579	26,307	29,359	1,010,790	.0214	864,919	254	112,453	239	37,432	210	126,173	40,574	42,017	Iberia
Iberville*	047	32,647	33,320	11,933	11,645	27,541	389,570	.0077	237,764	70	30,926	66	4,238	24	44,843	16,417	16,790	Iberville
Jackson**	049	15,216	15,397	14,530	6,182	27,341	221,090	.0036	79,342	23	17,623	37	1,041	6	8,720	6,183	10,131	Jackson
Jefferson*	051	451,699	455,466	19,661	187,132	35,955	8,880,910	.1751	7,657,930	2,253	1,503,975	3,193	440,632	2,469	896,207	499,909	301,304	Jefferson
Jefferson Davis**	053	31,015	31,435	12,992	11,571	26,399	402,940	.0084	312,862	92	76,993	163	4,165	23	31,336	16,808	18,813	Jefferson Davis
Lafayette*	055	195,453	190,503	18,099	78,317	34,407	3,537,500	.0742	3,429,683	1,009	689,078	1,463	161,032	902	314,109	220,626	128,399	Lafayette
Lafourche*	057	91,720	89,974	15,747	33,558	32,649	1,444,340	.0261	838,577	247	158,073	336	19,029	107	192,043	37,787	55,344	Lafourche
La Salle	059	14,144	14,282	13,517	5,335	27,000	191,180	.0035	95,305	28	19,055	40	....	....	17,489	8,161	9,082	La Salle
Lincoln**	061	42,384	42,509	12,950	15,976	26,115	548,860	.0117	462,580	136	101,939	216	16,920	95	50,644	13,170	26,251	Lincoln
Livingston*	063	105,200	91,814	17,428	38,244	36,255	1,833,380	.0279	556,613	164	117,178	249	3,677	21	118,790	29,520	70,383	Livingston
Madison**	065	12,874	13,728	8,893	4,284	20,258	114,490	.0028	110,785	33	10,227	22	....	....	16,409	6,507	5,610	Madison
Morehouse**	067	30,568	31,021	12,144	11,575	24,463	371,230	.0077	269,583	79	48,752	104	5,020	28	38,777	14,169	17,709	Morehouse
Natchitoches**	069	38,974	39,080	12,131	14,515	24,781	472,810	.0094	304,713	90	71,511	152	8,195	46	37,610	16,388	22,614	Natchitoches
Orleans*	071	464,268	484,674	14,976	200,992	26,183	6,952,920	.1218	3,405,199	1,002	369,787	785	320,165	1,794	607,673	312,588	227,920	Orleans
Ouachita*	073	148,118	147,250	16,229	56,112	30,577	2,403,800	.0467	1,793,330	528	499,482	1,060	92,642	519	175,892	80,637	95,032	Ouachita
Plaquemines*	075	28,450	26,757	16,179	9,830	35,383	460,290	.0070	117,943	35	5,552	12	....	....	41,545	8,381	16,125	Plaquemines
Pointe Coupee*	077	22,497	22,763	14,512	8,566	29,205	326,470	.0071	306,914	90	31,098	66	....	....	57,266	5,162	14,166	Pointe Coupee
Rapides*	079	127,716	126,337	14,314	48,977	28,332	1,828,070	.0384	1,572,058	462	373,937	794	65,982	370	180,477	98,802	77,034	Rapides
Red River	081	9,498	9,622	10,780	3,389	23,106	102,390	.0022	73,580	22	6,778	14	....	....	6,642	1,723	5,270	Red River
Richland	083	20,516	20,981	11,241	7,534	23,083	230,630	.0055	242,379	71	23,078	49	....	....	24,313	9,197	11,538	Richland
Sabine	085	23,373	23,459	13,497	9,409	25,617	315,460	.0060	191,820	56	40,933	87	3,645	20	39,809	10,824	15,550	Sabine
St. Bernard*	087	65,813	67,229	17,232	25,528	35,171	1,134,110	.0185	471,725	139	135,028	287	15,462	87	116,098	45,205	40,489	St. Bernard
St. Charles*	089	49,737	48,072	18,626	17,083	41,195	926,390	.0134	231,943	68	23,600	50	1,360	8	50,325	16,641	31,434	St. Charles
St. Helena*	091	10,240	10,525	12,013	3,906	23,794	123,010	.0019	18,154	5	4,543	10	....	....	5,462	1,108	6,157	St. Helena
St. James	093	21,092	21,216	15,004	7,166	33,488	316,460	.0051	105,973	31	3,594	8	....	....	39,323	4,857	12,243	St. James
St. John The Baptist*	095	45,373	43,044	16,385	15,381	36,648	743,440	.0123	320,759	94	64,882	138	8,227	46	64,964	27,756	26,334	St. John The Baptist
St. Landry**	097	89,466	87,700	11,199	34,086	22,245	1,001,890	.0210	704,553	207	163,152	346	27,388	154	131,711	54,343	50,255	St. Landry
St. Martin*	099	50,325	48,583	13,863	18,304	29,109	697,640	.0118	270,293	80	32,686	69	....	....	54,863	13,421	29,809	St. Martin

Source: Devonshire Associates Ltd. and Scan/US, Inc. 2004.
* Component of a Metropolitan Core Based Statistical Area.
** Component of a Micropolitan Core Based Statistical Area.

.... Data less than 1,000.

(d) Data not available.

continued on next page

Counties: Population / Income / Sales, *Continued*

COUNTY OR COUNTY EQUIVALENT	FIPS CO. CODE	POPULATION Estimate 7/1/04	POPULATION Census 4/1/00	PER CAPITA INCOME 2003	HOUSEHOLDS Estimate 7/1/04	MEDIAN HOUSEHOLD INCOME 2003	DISPOSABLE INCOME 2003 ($1,000)	MARKET ABILITY INDEX 2003	TOTAL RETAIL SALES Sales 2003 ($1,000)	TOTAL RETAIL SALES Ranally Sales Units	GENERAL MERCHANDISE Sales 2003 ($1,000)	GENERAL MERCHANDISE Ranally Sales Units	APPAREL STORE Sales 2003 ($1,000)	APPAREL STORE Ranally Sales Units	FOOD STORE SALES 2003 ($1,000)	HEALTH & DRUG STORE 2003 ($1,000)	PASSENGER CAR REGISTRATIONS 2003	COUNTY OR COUNTY EQUIVALENT
St. Mary**	101	52,045	53,500	13,245	19,396	26,921	689,350	.0143	543,980	**160**	127,777	**271**	15,277	**86**	101,993	57,279	29,232	St. Mary
St. Tammany*	103	212,895	191,268	21,229	79,104	43,213	4,519,450	.0754	2,468,044	**726**	386,710	**821**	90,081	**505**	354,273	190,551	147,592	St. Tammany
Tangipahoa**	105	104,512	100,588	13,621	38,803	27,964	1,423,600	.0296	1,153,217	**339**	201,638	**428**	33,917	**190**	142,219	56,353	62,757	Tangipahoa
Tensas	107	6,139	6,618	9,788	2,312	19,822	60,090	.0013	37,557	**11**	1,243	**3**	....	....	5,885	....	3,155	Tensas
Terrebonne*	109	106,631	104,503	15,413	37,794	32,996	1,643,510	.0349	1,521,872	**448**	319,850	**679**	57,918	**325**	196,020	68,019	61,614	Terrebonne
Union*	111	23,028	22,803	14,650	9,217	27,656	337,370	.0057	137,654	**40**	20,415	**43**	....	....	36,268	4,991	15,450	Union
Vermilion**	113	54,364	53,807	13,923	20,649	27,986	756,890	.0137	395,458	**116**	55,478	**118**	7,104	**40**	80,350	25,646	33,252	Vermilion
Vernon**	115	50,060	52,531	13,752	17,795	29,430	688,450	.0120	293,605	**86**	43,431	**92**	6,536	**37**	25,512	11,563	31,449	Vernon
Washington**	117	43,960	43,926	12,524	17,811	23,362	550,570	.0104	296,615	**87**	45,150	**96**	8,823	**49**	53,296	21,443	27,861	Washington
Webster**	119	41,293	41,831	14,339	16,620	27,129	592,100	.0114	391,521	**115**	65,762	**140**	11,888	**67**	65,420	15,510	27,613	Webster
West Baton Rouge*	121	21,767	21,601	16,670	7,920	35,000	362,860	.0060	157,084	**46**	22,744	**48**	....	....	25,145	....	13,277	West Baton Rouge
West Carroll	123	12,217	12,314	11,658	4,517	23,857	142,420	.0027	75,329	**22**	34,644	**74**	....	....	11,897	....	7,581	West Carroll
West Feliciana*	125	15,268	15,111	12,055	3,771	37,042	184,050	.0033	72,436	**21**	2,544	**5**	....	....	17,624	1,817	6,762	West Feliciana
Winn	127	16,250	16,894	11,507	5,807	24,571	186,990	.0037	106,843	**31**	25,283	**54**	....	....	15,965	7,031	8,817	Winn
The State		4,505,373	4,468,976	16,103	1,755,361	31,236	72,548,460	1.3623	48,523,208	**14,270**	9,139,874	**19,404**	2,130,023	**11,940**	6,668,639	2,866,560	2,779,013	The State

MAINE (ME; CODE 23; 16 Counties)

COUNTY OR COUNTY EQUIVALENT	FIPS CO. CODE	POPULATION Estimate 7/1/04	POPULATION Census 4/1/00	PER CAPITA INCOME 2003	HOUSEHOLDS Estimate 7/1/04	MEDIAN HOUSEHOLD INCOME 2003	DISPOSABLE INCOME 2003 ($1,000)	MARKET ABILITY INDEX 2003	TOTAL RETAIL SALES Sales 2003 ($1,000)	TOTAL RETAIL SALES Ranally Sales Units	GENERAL MERCHANDISE Sales 2003 ($1,000)	GENERAL MERCHANDISE Ranally Sales Units	APPAREL STORE Sales 2003 ($1,000)	APPAREL STORE Ranally Sales Units	FOOD STORE SALES 2003 ($1,000)	HEALTH & DRUG STORE 2003 ($1,000)	PASSENGER CAR REGISTRATIONS 2003	COUNTY OR COUNTY EQUIVALENT
Androscoggin*	001	106,865	103,793	17,501	44,561	33,858	1,870,230	.0390	1,762,740	**519**	215,665	**458**	23,086	**129**	262,314	67,601	73,393	Androscoggin
Aroostook	003	73,272	73,938	14,719	31,453	27,323	1,078,520	.0204	695,130	**204**	99,864	**212**	13,418	**75**	162,373	41,627	53,034	Aroostook
Cumberland*	005	272,577	265,612	21,003	113,068	40,728	5,724,970	.1170	5,541,891	**1,630**	521,839	**1,108**	379,457	**2,127**	989,094	216,268	190,484	Cumberland
Franklin	007	29,858	29,467	15,324	12,375	29,645	457,540	.0088	316,219	**93**	34,839	**74**	5,385	**30**	100,208	14,435	22,157	Franklin
Hancock	009	53,100	51,791	18,256	23,113	33,530	969,410	.0184	727,090	**214**	63,053	**134**	21,665	**121**	202,157	34,336	40,819	Hancock
Kennebec**	011	120,507	117,114	17,865	50,560	34,251	2,152,840	.0435	1,893,163	**557**	212,524	**451**	40,009	**224**	334,051	73,874	85,445	Kennebec
Knox**	013	40,644	39,618	18,548	17,488	34,601	753,870	.0142	555,250	**163**	47,336	**100**	15,078	**85**	142,378	27,200	29,773	Knox
Lincoln	015	35,071	33,616	19,502	15,221	35,828	683,970	.0123	453,363	**133**	11,880	**25**	7,746	**43**	106,745	19,373	27,835	Lincoln
Oxford	017	56,595	54,755	16,557	23,739	31,603	937,070	.0159	443,547	**130**	43,505	**92**	3,832	**21**	126,645	31,435	42,200	Oxford
Penobscot*	019	147,681	144,919	16,681	61,206	32,190	2,463,420	.0509	2,209,724	**650**	278,391	**591**	50,449	**283**	427,296	83,225	103,569	Penobscot
Piscataquis	021	17,437	17,235	14,712	7,652	26,740	256,530	.0046	138,879	**41**	18,616	**40**	....	....	40,982	9,691	13,553	Piscataquis
Sagadahoc*	023	36,859	35,214	20,074	15,154	39,108	739,920	.0115	288,808	**85**	7,502	**16**	....	....	97,616	14,621	27,437	Sagadahoc
Somerset	025	51,232	50,888	15,118	21,380	28,997	774,550	.0146	504,235	**148**	64,889	**138**	2,942	**16**	107,292	30,406	37,218	Somerset
Waldo	027	38,835	36,280	16,772	16,313	31,880	651,360	.0111	317,999	**94**	24,047	**51**	1,947	**11**	83,160	10,208	29,455	Waldo
Washington	029	33,339	33,941	13,354	14,389	24,794	445,220	.0090	323,943	**95**	32,963	**70**	1,909	**11**	92,452	8,643	24,332	Washington
York*	031	201,339	186,742	20,563	82,491	40,290	4,140,140	.0663	1,908,308	**561**	136,718	**290**	130,437	**731**	448,835	66,071	148,723	York
The State		1,315,211	1,274,923	18,324	550,163	35,140	24,099,560	.4575	18,080,289	**5,317**	1,813,632	**3,850**	697,964	**3,910**	3,723,597	749,012	949,427	The State

MARYLAND (MD; CODE 24; 23 Counties, 1 Independent City)

COUNTY OR COUNTY EQUIVALENT	FIPS CO. CODE	POPULATION Estimate 7/1/04	POPULATION Census 4/1/00	PER CAPITA INCOME 2003	HOUSEHOLDS Estimate 7/1/04	MEDIAN HOUSEHOLD INCOME 2003	DISPOSABLE INCOME 2003 ($1,000)	MARKET ABILITY INDEX 2003	TOTAL RETAIL SALES Sales 2003 ($1,000)	TOTAL RETAIL SALES Ranally Sales Units	GENERAL MERCHANDISE Sales 2003 ($1,000)	GENERAL MERCHANDISE Ranally Sales Units	APPAREL STORE Sales 2003 ($1,000)	APPAREL STORE Ranally Sales Units	FOOD STORE SALES 2003 ($1,000)	HEALTH & DRUG STORE 2003 ($1,000)	PASSENGER CAR REGISTRATIONS 2003	COUNTY OR COUNTY EQUIVALENT
Allegany*	001	73,291	74,930	14,695	29,019	29,067	1,077,040	.0209	748,596	**220**	150,753	**320**	40,011	**224**	119,657	63,896	49,632	Allegany
Anne Arundel*	003	511,686	489,656	26,554	192,675	55,112	13,587,060	.2085	6,366,826	**1,873**	1,031,207	**2,189**	374,093	**2,097**	1,048,749	237,230	371,804	Anne Arundel
Baltimore*	005	784,253	754,292	23,634	318,414	45,692	18,534,880	.3058	10,445,834	**3,073**	1,386,024	**2,942**	654,900	**3,670**	1,754,208	634,897	532,627	Baltimore
Calvert*	009	87,081	74,563	25,721	30,186	57,851	2,239,830	.0303	564,239	**166**	66,384	**141**	13,970	**78**	146,107	27,603	65,624	Calvert
Caroline	011	31,196	29,772	17,358	11,668	36,445	541,490	.0093	277,640	**82**	10,887	**23**	1,787	**10**	38,257	15,899	22,032	Caroline
Carroll*	013	167,068	150,897	23,951	58,627	53,201	4,001,470	.0603	1,609,973	**474**	274,655	**583**	30,968	**174**	373,520	95,391	124,818	Carroll
Cecil*	015	94,837	85,951	21,343	34,976	45,288	2,024,100	.0312	821,602	**242**	100,079	**212**	40,370	**226**	147,577	36,087	67,370	Cecil
Charles*	017	136,969	120,546	25,161	48,546	55,636	3,446,330	.0540	1,680,940	**494**	336,721	**715**	95,742	**537**	254,507	55,900	100,426	Charles
Dorchester**	019	30,616	30,674	17,247	12,881	32,196	528,030	.0101	393,882	**116**	119,290	**253**	12,394	**69**	81,148	25,059	21,265	Dorchester
Frederick*	021	219,345	195,277	24,892	79,679	53,477	5,459,840	.0875	2,870,448	**844**	383,445	**814**	105,802	**593**	494,993	117,849	163,888	Frederick
Garrett	023	30,121	29,846	15,238	11,941	30,257	458,990	.0088	315,913	**93**	9,075	**19**	2,474	**14**	58,553	21,856	21,275	Garrett
Harford*	025	236,397	218,590	24,222	87,585	51,010	5,725,960	.0892	2,676,980	**787**	371,255	**788**	87,917	**493**	487,840	124,197	169,106	Harford
Howard*	027	269,157	247,842	29,772	97,881	63,859	8,013,320	.1145	3,042,851	**895**	424,512	**901**	152,617	**855**	546,425	114,018	191,412	Howard
Kent	029	19,813	19,197	19,214	8,097	36,649	380,680	.0061	169,056	**50**	13,237	**28**	8,404	**47**	49,474	23,314	14,213	Kent
Montgomery*	031	932,558	873,341	29,947	348,724	62,328	27,926,860	.4048	11,315,031	**3,328**	1,090,746	**2,315**	786,479	**4,408**	1,973,237	534,996	610,330	Montgomery
Prince George's*	033	850,384	801,515	23,076	309,453	49,466	19,623,650	.2951	7,654,460	**2,252**	821,084	**1,743**	370,328	**2,075**	1,530,168	396,833	518,153	Prince George's
Queen Anne's*	035	45,219	40,563	25,194	17,302	51,090	1,139,270	.0170	466,284	**137**	32,918	**70**	62,277	**349**	79,980	13,511	35,205	Queen Anne's
St. Mary's**	037	94,832	86,211	22,905	34,535	48,925	2,172,150	.0326	829,104	**244**	138,603	**294**	25,920	**145**	198,182	46,006	68,717	St. Mary's
Somerset*	039	25,685	24,747	12,400	8,771	28,317	318,500	.0053	87,388	**26**	7,001	**15**	1,824	**10**	27,458	10,074	14,528	Somerset
Talbot**	041	34,925	33,812	21,977	14,939	40,378	767,540	.0147	641,645	**189**	59,895	**127**	27,755	**156**	97,588	31,191	26,547	Talbot
Washington*	043	138,354	131,923	18,511	52,912	37,952	2,561,100	.0458	1,617,258	**476**	276,893	**588**	42,981	**241**	256,199	86,461	93,985	Washington
Wicomico*	045	88,204	84,644	17,874	33,806	36,609	1,576,540	.0311	1,297,364	**382**	283,800	**602**	56,128	**315**	153,889	75,224	59,267	Wicomico
Worcester**	047	50,550	46,543	20,815	21,846	37,783	1,052,190	.0192	751,845	**221**	87,276	**185**	98,393	**551**	148,453	45,086	37,770	Worcester
INDEPENDENT CITY																		
Baltimore*	510	622,161	651,154	14,778	252,858	28,372	9,194,170	.1554	3,805,364	**1,119**	176,726	**375**	270,683	**1,517**	764,403	570,095	239,292	Baltimore
The State		5,574,702	5,296,486	23,741	2,117,321	48,136	132,350,990	2.0575	60,450,524	**17,783**	7,652,465	**16,242**	3,364,219	**18,854**	10,830,571	3,402,675	3,619,286	The State

MASSACHUSETTS (MA; CODE 25; 14 Counties)

COUNTY OR COUNTY EQUIVALENT	FIPS CO. CODE	POPULATION Estimate 7/1/04	POPULATION Census 4/1/00	PER CAPITA INCOME 2003	HOUSEHOLDS Estimate 7/1/04	MEDIAN HOUSEHOLD INCOME 2003	DISPOSABLE INCOME 2003 ($1,000)	MARKET ABILITY INDEX 2003	TOTAL RETAIL SALES Sales 2003 ($1,000)	TOTAL RETAIL SALES Ranally Sales Units	GENERAL MERCHANDISE Sales 2003 ($1,000)	GENERAL MERCHANDISE Ranally Sales Units	APPAREL STORE Sales 2003 ($1,000)	APPAREL STORE Ranally Sales Units	FOOD STORE SALES 2003 ($1,000)	HEALTH & DRUG STORE 2003 ($1,000)	PASSENGER CAR REGISTRATIONS 2003	COUNTY OR COUNTY EQUIVALENT
Barnstable*	001	231,645	222,230	23,742	100,221	42,027	5,499,830	.0935	3,415,754	**1,005**	174,648	**371**	229,079	**1,284**	801,769	241,440	170,415	Barnstable
Berkshire*	003	132,813	134,953	20,327	56,564	36,446	2,699,630	.0461	1,559,390	**459**	144,111	**306**	120,070	**673**	319,913	115,743	87,675	Berkshire
Bristol*	005	550,668	534,678	20,512	215,547	40,369	11,295,090	.1942	6,687,807	**1,967**	1,085,891	**2,305**	417,656	**2,341**	1,215,690	477,021	347,693	Bristol
Dukes	007	15,775	14,987	23,355	6,773	41,720	368,430	.0067	273,473	**80**	7,541	**16**	21,544	**121**	85,018	11,781	12,321	Dukes
Essex*	009	741,982	723,419	23,365	284,819	46,702	17,336,360	.2716	8,061,631	**2,371**	716,046	**1,520**	552,584	**3,097**	1,361,166	687,648	458,919	Essex
Franklin*	011	72,431	71,535	20,847	30,397	37,916	1,509,940	.0226	524,992	**154**	43,397	**92**	11,539	**65**	113,750	30,889	50,768	Franklin
Hampden*	013	462,756	456,228	18,792	180,216	36,909	8,696,140	.1517	5,101,077	**1,501**	577,698	**1,226**	253,956	**1,423**	956,738	393,607	268,379	Hampden
Hampshire*	015	155,980	152,251	20,882	59,300	42,028	3,257,230	.0498	1,250,342	**368**	68,218	**145**	61,913	**347**	341,813	83,824	101,684	Hampshire
Middlesex*	017	1,472,613	1,465,396	27,568	570,806	54,245	40,596,290	.6440	21,837,015	**6,424**	1,784,616	**3,788**	1,474,755	**8,265**	3,433,808	1,436,414	932,605	Middlesex
Nantucket	019	11,096	9,520	25,564	4,301	50,938	283,660	.0057	282,168	**83**	....	....	35,370	**198**	65,873	12,591	7,877	Nantucket
Norfolk*	021	655,356	650,308	28,792	254,854	56,562	18,869,140	.2901	9,325,464	**2,743**	920,840	**1,955**	634,516	**3,556**	1,428,176	652,122	422,582	Norfolk
Plymouth*	023	491,878	472,822	23,666	178,256	49,953	11,640,650	.1930	6,674,991	**1,963**	500,163	**1,062**	260,215	**1,458**	1,135,648	379,977	321,312	Plymouth
Suffolk*	025	677,616	689,807	19,586	276,467	36,405	13,271,520	.2203	6,731,224	**1,980**	349,969	**743**	1,142,268	**6,402**	1,510,063	762,737	274,387	Suffolk
Worcester*	027	784,595	750,963	21,778	300,867	43,766	17,087,140	.2811	9,059,973	**2,665**	882,285	**1,873**	405,829	**2,274**	1,627,115	628,138	500,744	Worcester
The State		6,457,204	6,349,097	23,603	2,519,388	45,822	152,411,050	2.4704	80,785,302	**23,763**	7,255,897	**15,403**	5,621,295	**31,504**	14,396,539	5,913,933	3,957,361	The State

MICHIGAN (MI; CODE 26; 83 Counties)

COUNTY OR COUNTY EQUIVALENT	FIPS CO. CODE	POPULATION Estimate 7/1/04	POPULATION Census 4/1/00	PER CAPITA INCOME 2003	HOUSEHOLDS Estimate 7/1/04	MEDIAN HOUSEHOLD INCOME 2003	DISPOSABLE INCOME 2003 ($1,000)	MARKET ABILITY INDEX 2003	TOTAL RETAIL SALES Sales 2003 ($1,000)	TOTAL RETAIL SALES Ranally Sales Units	GENERAL MERCHANDISE Sales 2003 ($1,000)	GENERAL MERCHANDISE Ranally Sales Units	APPAREL STORE Sales 2003 ($1,000)	APPAREL STORE Ranally Sales Units	FOOD STORE SALES 2003 ($1,000)	HEALTH & DRUG STORE 2003 ($1,000)	PASSENGER CAR REGISTRATIONS 2003	COUNTY OR COUNTY EQUIVALENT
Alcona	001	11,528	11,719	16,160	5,150	29,398	186,290	.0029	58,742	**17**	1,943	**4**	1,636	**9**	7,089	1,321	9,407	Alcona
Alger	003	9,743	9,862	16,442	3,853	33,669	160,190	.0025	48,402	**14**	1,528	**3**	....	....	16,794	1,172	6,838	Alger
Allegan**	005	111,737	105,665	18,888	40,974	41,791	2,110,450	.0342	944,747	**278**	85,472	**181**	11,954	**67**	179,334	62,280	81,095	Allegan
Alpena**	007	30,613	31,314	16,769	12,876	32,305	513,340	.0101	408,790	**120**	95,176	**202**	17,826	**100**	33,466	27,238	22,749	Alpena
Antrim	009	24,369	23,110	17,916	9,898	35,664	436,590	.0070	180,059	**53**	4,150	**9**	2,957	**17**	51,758	11,699	18,592	Antrim
Arenac	011	17,312	17,269	15,030	6,896	30,740	260,200	.0048	151,317	**45**	11,111	**24**	1,903	**11**	21,914	12,571	12,742	Arenac
Baraga	013	8,796	8,746	15,142	3,410	31,718	133,190	.0024	72,342	**21**	2,585	**5**	1,388	**8**	14,251	5,118	5,869	Baraga
Barry*	015	59,395	56,755	19,652	22,342	42,386	1,167,210	.0178	412,587	**121**	42,230	**90**	4,907	**28**	68,031	26,457	46,554	Barry
Bay*	017	109,229	110,157	18,379	45,170	36,069	2,007,490	.0384	1,531,992	**451**	331,992	**705**	47,788	**268**	152,433	75,791	81,372	Bay
Benzie**	019	17,400	15,998	17,928	7,204	35,220	311,950	.0051	140,965	**41**	4,120	**9**	1,977	**11**	29,775	8,418	13,590	Benzie
Berrien*	021	162,816	162,453	17,983	66,098	35,934	2,927,880	.0504	1,585,823	**466**	298,008	**633**	29,166	**163**	230,436	105,137	115,292	Berrien
Branch**	023	46,594	45,787	15,942	16,641	36,067	742,800	.0149	599,709	**176**	108,849	**231**	13,644	**76**	97,949	21,461	30,904	Branch
Calhoun*	025	139,106	137,985	18,718	57,969	36,408	2,603,740	.0454	1,519,459	**447**	407,580	**865**	38,743	**217**	160,456	95,039	99,764	Calhoun
Cass*	027	51,459	51,104	18,487	20,261	38,168	951,330	.0136	216,352	**64**	8,057	**17**	2,645	**15**	42,487	13,427	39,293	Cass
Charlevoix	029	26,898	26,090	18,601	10,919	37,177	500,340	.0087	293,449	**86**	26,321	**56**	8,420	**47**	74,927	18,935	20,366	Charlevoix
Cheboygan	031	27,684	26,448	16,243	11,684	31,228	449,680	.0091	375,919	**111**	64,121	**136**	8,265	**46**	63,139	13,854	20,923	Cheboygan
Chippewa**	033	38,907	38,543	14,293	13,973	32,282	556,110	.0103	324,562	**95**	65,180	**138**	14,622	**82**	50,599	13,629	23,368	Chippewa
Clare	035	31,659	31,252	14,031	13,112	27,454	444,220	.0085	281,376	**83**	2,602	**6**	3,948	**22**	43,489	23,284	22,558	Clare
Clinton*	037	68,489	64,753	21,934	25,596	47,658	1,502,250	.0225	554,421	**163**	62,592	**133**	15,989	**90**	76,005	34,648	53,105	Clinton
Crawford	039	14,962	14,273	15,553	6,047	31,084	232,710	.0045	161,273	**47**	14,722	**31**	1,614	**9**	23,140	3,882	10,922	Crawford
Delta**	041	38,234	38,520	17,354	16,188	33,347	663,530	.0114	349,987	**103**	50,183	**107**	13,860	**78**	56,345	17,487	29,050	Delta
Dickinson**	043	27,089	27,472	17,031	11,461	32,604	461,350	.0091	369,924	**109**	71,167	**151**	12,261	**69**	53,071	18,025	19,998	Dickinson
Eaton*	045	106,959	103,655	21,777	42,548	44,539	2,329,290	.0402	1,453,015	**427**	416,784	**885**	32,625	**183**	220,529	53,246	81,402	Eaton
Emmet	047	33,141	31,437	18,910	13,646	37,288	626,680	.0133	636,596	**187**	87,711	**186**	37,076	**208**	73,003	31,301	24,244	Emmet
Genesee*	049	444,011	436,141	19,539	181,093	39,188	8,675,620	.1515	5,238,928	**1,541**	1,038,212	**2,204**	183,929	**1,031**	608,615	347,323	315,266	Genesee
Gladwin	051	27,210	26,023	15,417	11,356	30,183	419,510	.0072	195,029	**57**	18,325	**39**	2,038	**11**	20,525	10,921	20,386	Gladwin
Gogebic	053	17,331	17,370	13,528	7,294	26,136	234,460	.0049	187,083	**55**	29,427	**62**	8,547	**48**	28,950	9,382	11,464	Gogebic
Grand Traverse**	055	83,355	77,654	20,493	34,820	40,021	1,708,200	.0361	1,772,568	**521**	451,225	**958**	94,569	**530**	150,173	66,461	65,186	Grand Traverse
Gratiot**	057	42,563	42,285	15,121	14,864	35,075	643,610	.0116	357,492	**105**	73,953	**157**	3,847	**22**	57,733	16,672	27,517	Gratiot
Hillsdale	059	47,410	46,527	17,453	17,985	37,340	827,440	.0134	344,515	**101**	59,119	**126**	6,609	**37**	45,263	17,232	34,312	Hillsdale
Houghton**	061	36,331	36,016	13,080	14,054	27,457	475,220	.0098	367,791	**108**	72,078	**153**	14,859	**83**	72,612	12,327	23,889	Houghton
Huron	063	34,941	36,079	17,016	14,541	33,125	594,540	.0103	311,338	**92**	58,918	**125**	7,345	**41**	58,253	15,369	26,462	Huron
Ingham*	065	282,853	279,320	18,866	114,633	37,866	5,336,280	.0979	3,678,456	**1,082**	799,534	**1,697**	158,536	**888**	377,396	209,697	197,947	Ingham
Ionia*	067	64,207	61,518	16,627	21,746	39,901	1,067,600	.0176	448,102	**132**	96,799	**205**	2,011	**11**	77,194	24,470	43,644	Ionia
Iosco	069	26,740	27,339	16,204	11,932	29,615	433,290	.0078	254,821	**75**	25,661	**54**	5,302	**30**	52,112	22,224	20,589	Iosco
Iron	071	12,680	13,138	14,846	5,633	27,078	188,250	.0034	106,904	**31**	6,960	**15**	1,212	**7**	23,410	9,690	9,375	Iron
Isabella**	073	65,094	63,351	15,076	24,571	31,977	981,370	.0187	651,096	**192**	247,100	**525**	25,544	**143**	49,850	19,947	47,575	Isabella
Jackson*	075	163,516	158,422	18,372	61,219	40,080	3,004,140	.0530	1,801,553	**530**	486,032	**1,032**	45,211	**253**	190,509	85,531	111,165	Jackson
Kalamazoo*	077	243,185	238,603	19,646	99,529	39,223	4,777,590	.0863	3,220,254	**947**	988,865	**2,099**	125,653	**704**	247,662	147,891	179,847	Kalamazoo
Kalkaska**	079	17,360	16,571	16,616	6,916	33,766	288,460	.0054	193,811	**57**	1,854	**4**	....	....	28,676	9,153	13,159	Kalkaska
Kent*	081	595,142	574,335	19,704	226,967	41,981	11,726,700	.2185	8,679,963	**2,553**	1,669,042	**3,543**	340,879	**1,910**	704,075	371,296	403,375	Kent
Keweenaw**	083	2,200	2,301	15,427	998	27,508	33,940	.0005	4,700	**1**	....	....	....	....	....	....	1,749	Keweenaw
Lake	085	11,929	11,333	13,139	4,988	25,615	156,740	.0026	52,935	**16**	2,144	**5**	....	....	11,112	2,027	8,335	Lake
Lapeer*	087	92,313	87,904	20,576	33,054	46,676	1,899,450	.0314	989,044	**291**	216,084	**459**	16,639	**93**	116,392	59,037	69,828	Lapeer
Leelanau**	089	22,059	21,119	21,535	9,023	42,712	475,030	.0069	151,177	**44**	....	....	11,003	**62**	51,789	11,356	17,572	Leelanau
Lenawee**	091	101,344	98,890	19,258	37,894	41,892	1,951,730	.0346	1,228,128	**361**	242,181	**514**	16,434	**92**	138,341	72,763	73,111	Lenawee
Livingston*	093	177,683	156,951	26,688	64,073	59,675	4,741,980	.0720	2,143,942	**631**	381,446	**810**	53,423	**299**	227,861	88,733	137,877	Livingston
Luce	095	6,889	7,024	13,314	2,500	29,977	91,720	.0021	90,383	**27**	2,268	**5**	1,125	**6**	18,131	6,199	4,258	Luce
Mackinac	097	11,323	11,943	16,845	4,946	31,209	190,740	.0035	121,098	**36**	3,195	**7**	7,223	**40**	26,008	2,828	8,213	Mackinac
Macomb*	099	821,634	788,149	23,470	333,076	47,184	19,283,770	.3278	11,914,351	**3,505**	2,039,828	**4,330**	339,902	**1,905**	1,371,719	832,069	608,856	Macomb
Manistee	101	25,543	24,527	16,184	10,414	32,118	413,390	.0081	312,053	**92**	66,190	**141**	7,844	**44**	44,107	15,864	18,693	Manistee
Marquette**	103	64,616	64,634	17,089	26,794	33,435	1,104,210	.0204	730,812	**215**	155,466	**330**	22,974	**129**	92,574	42,492	48,703	Marquette
Mason	105	28,801	28,274	16,315	11,782	32,443	469,900	.0094	383,524	**113**	86,576	**184**	8,303	**47**	57,220	28,570	21,231	Mason
Mecosta**	107	42,083	40,553	14,824	15,968	31,809	623,840	.0123	457,088	**134**	105,214	**223**	13,544	**76**	80,370	25,521	29,188	Mecosta
Menominee**	109	25,015	25,326	16,310	10,675	31,091	408,000	.0069	192,624	**57**	39,485	**84**	1,823	**10**	38,065	5,521	18,830	Menominee
Midland**	111	84,980	82,874	20,547	33,998	41,441	1,746,070	.0305	1,087,735	**320**	242,444	**515**	40,219	**225**	97,191	79,159	64,532	Midland
Missaukee**	113	15,402	14,478	15,521	5,910	32,680	239,050	.0044	148,268	**44**	6,885	**15**	....	....	18,070	1,854	11,140	Missaukee
Monroe*	115	152,069	145,945	21,641	57,434	46,429	3,290,970	.0534	1,655,186	**487**	319,220	**678**	56,627	**317**	191,344	93,565	114,043	Monroe
Montcalm	117	63,419	61,266	15,731	23,261	34,984	997,640	.0178	546,889	**161**	131,065	**278**	11,669	**65**	77,105	20,665	43,971	Montcalm
Montmorency	119	10,531	10,315	15,417	4,685	28,046	162,360	.0029	90,551	**27**	4,576	**10**	....	....	23,819	7,683	8,538	Montmorency
Muskegon*	121	173,945	170,200	17,223	68,024	35,910	2,995,780	.0552	1,977,190	**582**	527,223	**1,119**	54,416	**305**	204,944	128,039	123,720	Muskegon
Newaygo*	123	49,686	47,874	15,970	18,445	34,963	793,490	.0132	339,863	**100**	43,810	**93**	4,772	**27**	42,578	23,875	35,587	Newaygo
Oakland*	125	1,211,605	1,194,156	28,205	501,036	55,351	34,173,660	.5871	23,701,409	**6,972**	3,558,982	**7,555**	1,452,306	**8,139**	2,343,296	1,542,909	922,079	Oakland
Oceana	127	28,442	26,873	15,059	10,491	33,084	428,300	.0072	179,317	**53**	6,942	**15**	1,708	**10**	42,488	7,111	20,494	Oceana
Ogemaw	129	21,826	21,645	14,727	9,149	28,579	321,440	.0076	379,421	**112**	51,509	**109**	31,968	**179**	53,871	26,787	16,521	Ogemaw
Ontonagon	131	7,496	7,818	15,696	3,422	27,853	117,660	.0022	71,961	**21**	8,181	**17**	1,116	**6**	9,486	1,446	5,963	Ontonagon
Osceola	133	23,598	23,197	15,398	9,210	31,903	363,370	.0064	184,301	**54**	2,143	**5**	1,052	**6**	37,676	20,394	16,710	Osceola

Source: Devonshire Associates Ltd. and Scan/US, Inc. 2004.
* Component of a Metropolitan Core Based Statistical Area.
** Component of a Micropolitan Core Based Statistical Area.

.... Data less than 1,000.

(d) Data not available.

Counties: Population / Income / Sales, *Continued*

COUNTY OR COUNTY EQUIVALENT	FIPS CO. CODE	POPULATION Estimate 7/1/04	POPULATION Census 4/1/00	PER CAPITA INCOME 2003	HOUSEHOLDS Estimate 7/1/04	MEDIAN HOUSEHOLD INCOME 2003	DISPOSABLE INCOME 2003 ($1,000)	MARKET ABILITY INDEX 2003	TOTAL RETAIL SALES Sales 2003 ($1,000)	TOTAL RETAIL SALES Ranally Sales Units	GENERAL MERCHANDISE Sales 2003 ($1,000)	GENERAL MERCHANDISE Ranally Sales Units	APPAREL STORE Sales 2003 ($1,000)	APPAREL STORE Ranally Sales Units	FOOD STORE SALES 2003 ($1,000)	HEALTH & DRUG STORE 2003 ($1,000)	PASSENGER CAR REGIS-TRATIONS 2003	COUNTY OR COUNTY EQUIVALENT
Oscoda	135	9,474	9,418	14,057	3,989	26,959	133,180	.0024	70,621	**21**	2,462	**5**	1,248	**7**	19,886	4,960	7,025	Oscoda
Otsego	137	24,548	23,301	18,443	9,714	37,827	452,740	.0097	470,908	**139**	90,487	**192**	11,936	**67**	49,325	11,334	17,868	Otsego
Ottawa*	139	252,694	238,314	20,891	90,801	47,243	5,278,990	.0893	2,991,989	**880**	749,974	**1,592**	94,721	**531**	278,265	106,669	180,602	Ottawa
Presque Isle	141	14,257	14,411	16,321	6,337	30,039	232,690	.0044	157,480	**46**	4,787	**10**	1,332	**7**	44,421	10,051	11,555	Presque Isle
Roscommon	143	26,464	25,469	15,666	11,849	28,416	414,580	.0089	396,611	**117**	73,716	**156**	2,880	**16**	65,693	8,464	19,365	Roscommon
Saginaw*	145	209,117	210,039	17,419	81,984	36,133	3,642,550	.0737	3,169,109	**932**	578,286	**1,228**	275,821	**1,546**	294,087	145,571	144,001	Saginaw
St. Clair*	147	170,514	164,235	20,540	67,196	42,350	3,502,390	.0588	1,920,103	**565**	390,504	**829**	81,694	**458**	253,138	94,662	127,474	St. Clair
St. Joseph**	149	62,973	62,422	17,662	24,106	37,416	1,112,200	.0190	579,269	**170**	101,768	**216**	12,933	**72**	134,310	26,968	44,377	St. Joseph
Sanilac	151	44,597	44,547	16,295	17,173	34,414	726,690	.0127	380,074	**112**	24,544	**52**	3,385	**19**	58,527	35,196	32,445	Sanilac
Schoolcraft	153	8,725	8,903	14,738	3,611	29,034	128,590	.0026	100,870	**30**	3,455	**7**	2,356	**13**	13,915	7,776	6,211	Schoolcraft
Shiawassee**	155	72,823	71,687	18,540	27,936	39,330	1,350,170	.0244	876,130	**258**	177,143	**376**	8,356	**47**	89,759	56,015	55,396	Shiawassee
Tuscola	157	58,413	58,266	17,413	21,999	37,390	1,017,120	.0181	609,007	**179**	52,523	**112**	6,514	**37**	92,327	28,870	43,166	Tuscola
Van Buren*	159	78,829	76,263	16,836	29,281	36,716	1,327,130	.0223	623,973	**184**	54,458	**116**	2,667	**15**	107,137	40,579	56,890	Van Buren
Washtenaw*	161	343,273	322,895	22,856	135,907	47,286	7,845,780	.1371	5,202,501	**1,530**	846,525	**1,797**	217,383	**1,218**	569,099	240,364	244,973	Washtenaw
Wayne*	163	2,018,715	2,061,162	17,902	775,513	37,867	36,139,680	.6319	20,620,588	**6,066**	3,085,690	**6,550**	845,136	**4,736**	3,016,073	1,664,074	1,187,181	Wayne
Wexford**	165	31,487	30,484	15,989	12,387	32,860	503,460	.0116	580,632	**171**	110,070	**234**	13,994	**78**	79,584	29,732	22,373	Wexford
The State		10,121,382	9,938,444	20,249	3,984,102	41,324	204,943,260	3.5938	128,365,324	**37,760**	22,978,581	**48,782**	5,093,061	**28,541**	15,214,693	7,748,758	7,091,799	The State

MINNESOTA (MN; CODE 27; 87 Counties)

COUNTY OR COUNTY EQUIVALENT	FIPS CO. CODE	POPULATION Estimate 7/1/04	POPULATION Census 4/1/00	PER CAPITA INCOME 2003	HOUSEHOLDS Estimate 7/1/04	MEDIAN HOUSEHOLD INCOME 2003	DISPOSABLE INCOME 2003 ($1,000)	MARKET ABILITY INDEX 2003	TOTAL RETAIL SALES Sales 2003 ($1,000)	TOTAL RETAIL SALES Ranally Sales Units	GENERAL MERCHANDISE Sales 2003 ($1,000)	GENERAL MERCHANDISE Ranally Sales Units	APPAREL STORE Sales 2003 ($1,000)	APPAREL STORE Ranally Sales Units	FOOD STORE SALES 2003 ($1,000)	HEALTH & DRUG STORE 2003 ($1,000)	PASSENGER CAR REGIS-TRATIONS 2003	COUNTY OR COUNTY EQUIVALENT
Aitkin	001	15,928	15,301	15,763	7,062	29,292	251,070	.0042	109,381	**32**	9,859	**21**	....	**....**	23,951	4,916	13,018	Aitkin
Anoka*	003	318,838	298,084	23,025	116,565	51,677	7,341,260	.1155	3,440,179	**1,012**	585,897	**1,244**	65,725	**368**	549,456	169,790	233,282	Anoka
Becker	005	31,538	30,000	16,008	12,729	32,540	504,870	.0099	384,770	**113**	54,369	**115**	10,482	**59**	57,112	9,071	24,478	Becker
Beltrami**	007	42,464	39,650	13,956	15,568	31,515	592,630	.0139	668,410	**197**	116,992	**248**	35,775	**201**	104,506	20,345	28,212	Beltrami
Benton*	009	37,738	34,226	18,520	14,781	38,929	698,920	.0105	216,241	**64**	27,671	**59**	....	**....**	34,675	11,332	27,485	Benton
Big Stone	011	5,606	5,820	14,513	2,309	29,029	81,360	.0013	28,515	**8**	1,042	**2**	....	**....**	6,964	5,051	4,208	Big Stone
Blue Earth**	013	57,766	55,941	17,006	22,221	36,228	982,390	.0207	942,346	**277**	221,221	**470**	49,538	**278**	148,870	43,985	42,465	Blue Earth
Brown**	015	26,385	26,911	18,730	10,971	36,851	494,200	.0088	303,860	**89**	31,702	**67**	4,162	**23**	72,754	10,163	20,015	Brown
Carlton*	017	33,484	31,671	17,579	13,008	37,132	588,600	.0098	271,065	**80**	35,442	**75**	....	**....**	45,456	13,758	24,872	Carlton
Carver*	019	81,656	70,205	24,331	28,355	57,691	1,986,780	.0287	680,728	**200**	99,228	**211**	....	**....**	132,996	26,222	57,072	Carver
Cass**	021	28,509	27,150	16,045	11,648	32,258	457,430	.0077	200,015	**59**	2,094	**4**	1,962	**11**	29,213	6,501	22,022	Cass
Chippewa	023	12,721	13,088	16,962	5,290	33,527	215,770	.0038	115,386	**34**	11,949	**25**	....	**....**	13,347	5,384	9,819	Chippewa
Chisago*	025	47,700	41,101	20,690	17,376	47,002	986,890	.0147	327,674	**96**	2,793	**6**	21,795	**122**	42,772	8,005	37,534	Chisago
Clay*	027	52,205	51,229	16,026	19,382	35,464	836,660	.0157	553,024	**163**	105,493	**224**	5,862	**33**	71,305	22,463	36,150	Clay
Clearwater	029	8,438	8,423	14,116	3,431	28,567	119,110	.0020	43,504	**13**	2,788	**6**	....	**....**	7,324	2,278	6,586	Clearwater
Cook	031	5,310	5,168	19,676	2,486	34,652	104,480	.0018	58,495	**17**	7,311	**16**	1,308	**7**	11,266	1,546	4,178	Cook
Cottonwood	033	11,980	12,167	15,008	4,884	30,473	179,800	.0036	139,772	**41**	7,850	**17**	....	**....**	19,203	7,491	8,879	Cottonwood
Crow Wing**	035	59,463	55,099	17,613	24,402	35,479	1,047,330	.0216	961,941	**283**	206,368	**438**	7,502	**42**	112,715	27,068	44,500	Crow Wing
Dakota*	037	378,473	355,904	25,918	145,666	55,276	9,809,150	.1672	6,420,326	**1,889**	935,622	**1,986**	147,458	**826**	873,260	243,768	280,399	Dakota
Dodge*	039	19,288	17,731	19,205	7,072	43,153	370,430	.0054	103,079	**30**	3,169	**7**	....	**....**	23,952	3,897	14,760	Dodge
Douglas**	041	34,520	32,821	17,735	14,301	35,168	612,210	.0120	494,851	**146**	133,771	**284**	12,174	**68**	77,858	17,348	26,956	Douglas
Faribault	043	15,604	16,181	16,420	6,504	32,235	256,210	.0040	86,597	**25**	11,809	**25**	....	**....**	16,504	5,647	12,218	Faribault
Fillmore	045	21,365	21,122	16,507	8,447	34,353	352,670	.0061	184,975	**54**	4,603	**10**	....	**....**	24,949	11,145	16,293	Fillmore
Freeborn**	047	31,766	32,584	17,539	13,224	34,791	557,130	.0106	395,145	**116**	63,974	**136**	3,807	**21**	44,829	11,230	24,279	Freeborn
Goodhue**	049	45,501	44,127	20,194	17,714	42,742	918,860	.0147	419,120	**123**	22,471	**48**	13,720	**77**	86,966	26,228	35,079	Goodhue
Grant	051	6,232	6,289	15,751	2,539	31,698	98,160	.0017	53,649	**16**	....	**....**	....	**....**	4,400	2,279	4,942	Grant
Hennepin*	053	1,122,141	1,116,200	24,363	482,887	46,697	27,339,130	.5278	24,368,319	**7,168**	3,167,395	**6,724**	1,151,822	**6,455**	2,601,449	1,097,317	792,808	Hennepin
Houston*	055	20,056	19,718	18,090	7,921	37,443	362,810	.0055	115,216	**34**	4,700	**10**	....	**....**	20,269	2,279	14,930	Houston
Hubbard	057	18,703	18,376	16,603	7,703	33,194	310,520	.0055	176,761	**52**	12,120	**26**	1,869	**10**	57,239	10,001	14,793	Hubbard
Isanti*	059	36,651	31,287	20,004	13,434	45,120	733,170	.0114	294,559	**87**	52,645	**112**	2,529	**14**	45,214	8,419	29,041	Isanti
Itasca	061	44,345	43,992	17,136	18,449	33,964	759,900	.0135	441,036	**130**	68,451	**145**	7,437	**42**	82,873	19,344	34,020	Itasca
Jackson	063	11,147	11,268	17,121	4,592	34,125	190,850	.0029	57,383	**17**	....	**....**	....	**....**	9,307	1,671	9,043	Jackson
Kanabec	065	16,133	14,996	16,985	6,290	35,735	274,020	.0048	146,431	**43**	13,473	**29**	....	**....**	28,783	3,049	12,909	Kanabec
Kandiyohi**	067	41,142	41,203	17,610	16,187	36,740	724,500	.0136	517,832	**152**	101,970	**216**	13,071	**73**	63,771	18,875	29,993	Kandiyohi
Kittson	069	4,872	5,285	15,640	2,025	30,889	76,200	.0013	33,874	**10**	....	**....**	....	**....**	5,459	1,570	3,704	Kittson
Koochiching	071	13,922	14,355	17,847	6,110	33,573	248,460	.0042	129,598	**38**	14,258	**30**	2,812	**16**	25,913	7,404	10,635	Koochiching
Lac qui Parle	073	7,806	8,067	15,660	3,267	30,685	122,240	.0021	58,745	**17**	2,209	**5**	....	**....**	9,488	3,064	6,498	Lac qui Parle
Lake	075	11,192	11,058	19,368	4,786	37,213	216,770	.0038	134,427	**40**	6,337	**13**	....	**....**	15,791	2,391	8,811	Lake
Lake of the Woods	077	4,343	4,522	16,631	1,890	31,315	72,230	.0012	30,967	**9**	....	**....**	....	**....**	9,293	1,495	3,591	Lake of the Woods
Le Sueur	079	27,185	25,426	19,581	10,468	41,725	532,320	.0083	211,039	**62**	2,835	**6**	1,436	**8**	32,170	16,479	21,114	Le Sueur
Lincoln	081	6,078	6,429	15,140	2,559	29,684	92,020	.0016	44,380	**13**	....	**....**	....	**....**	6,287	1,985	4,938	Lincoln
Lyon**	083	24,617	25,425	17,425	9,657	36,355	428,950	.0082	315,019	**93**	49,889	**106**	5,930	**33**	50,554	7,737	17,867	Lyon
McLeod**	085	36,194	34,898	19,955	14,216	41,744	722,240	.0117	341,151	**100**	79,331	**168**	14,123	**79**	63,672	14,666	27,358	McLeod
Mahnomen	087	5,093	5,190	13,277	1,978	28,077	67,620	.0012	35,285	**10**	....	**....**	....	**....**	4,703	1,103	3,650	Mahnomen
Marshall	089	9,955	10,155	16,396	4,119	32,517	163,220	.0029	92,158	**27**	....	**....**	....	**....**	8,550	4,450	8,128	Marshall
Martin**	091	21,039	21,802	17,016	8,912	32,775	358,010	.0069	270,946	**80**	30,507	**65**	3,531	**20**	36,982	7,860	15,998	Martin
Meeker	093	23,378	22,644	17,848	9,012	37,953	417,260	.0066	156,802	**46**	9,819	**21**	....	**....**	21,214	4,443	17,532	Meeker
Mille Lacs	095	24,937	22,330	16,717	9,870	34,815	416,880	.0067	161,230	**47**	10,867	**23**	....	**....**	42,551	6,927	18,951	Mille Lacs
Morrison	097	32,854	31,712	16,019	12,554	34,276	526,300	.0104	405,529	**119**	36,298	**77**	2,924	**16**	95,482	6,148	24,275	Morrison
Mower**	099	38,863	38,603	16,957	15,736	34,875	658,990	.0112	325,293	**96**	51,477	**109**	10,926	**61**	70,639	14,604	28,152	Mower
Murray	101	8,928	9,165	16,638	3,693	32,881	148,540	.0024	57,187	**17**	....	**....**	....	**....**	13,730	1,947	7,296	Murray
Nicollet**	103	31,006	29,771	18,970	11,502	42,070	588,190	.0086	158,782	**47**	3,587	**8**	....	**....**	28,118	3,774	21,971	Nicollet
Nobles**	105	20,558	20,832	15,502	7,805	33,531	318,700	.0063	247,510	**73**	23,506	**50**	10,965	**61**	45,025	10,420	14,374	Nobles
Norman	107	7,111	7,442	15,266	2,909	30,719	108,560	.0023	97,178	**29**	....	**....**	....	**....**	7,976	2,403	5,536	Norman
Olmsted*	109	133,562	124,277	22,785	54,231	46,373	3,043,170	.0530	1,995,060	**587**	455,521	**967**	66,575	**373**	199,272	72,562	98,407	Olmsted
Otter Tail**	111	59,382	57,159	16,158	23,868	32,951	959,520	.0174	575,507	**169**	79,934	**170**	7,617	**43**	77,539	17,268	45,778	Otter Tail
Pennington	113	13,665	13,584	16,244	5,681	31,982	221,970	.0042	157,129	**46**	19,853	**42**	5,128	**29**	33,675	6,415	10,158	Pennington
Pine	115	28,107	26,530	16,302	10,712	35,141	458,200	.0077	201,087	**59**	20,025	**43**	....	**....**	30,268	3,596	21,029	Pine
Pipestone	117	9,626	9,895	15,366	4,050	30,206	147,910	.0029	105,723	**31**	5,590	**12**	....	**....**	13,413	5,245	7,250	Pipestone
Polk*	119	30,748	31,369	15,696	12,106	32,711	482,620	.0084	237,769	**70**	15,334	**33**	1,455	**8**	45,703	10,848	21,645	Polk
Pope	121	11,255	11,236	16,591	4,613	33,190	186,730	.0030	70,107	**21**	5,904	**13**	....	**....**	10,086	4,705	8,889	Pope
Ramsey*	123	504,693	511,035	20,942	208,056	41,825	10,569,240	.1887	7,129,858	**2,097**	1,001,316	**2,126**	287,208	**1,610**	1,074,152	392,943	326,880	Ramsey
Red Lake	125	4,331	4,299	15,276	1,796	30,099	66,160	.0012	40,878	**12**	1,608	**3**	....	**....**	4,792	1,205	3,461	Red Lake
Redwood	127	16,061	16,815	17,362	6,497	35,280	278,850	.0051	181,755	**53**	22,522	**48**	....	**....**	27,274	7,276	12,081	Redwood
Renville	129	16,757	17,154	17,304	6,699	35,512	289,960	.0049	143,006	**42**	3,392	**7**	....	**....**	19,254	5,595	12,752	Renville
Rice**	131	60,613	56,665	18,540	21,110	43,894	1,123,790	.0188	558,552	**164**	68,335	**145**	13,673	**77**	102,755	18,411	40,515	Rice
Rock	133	9,582	9,721	17,334	3,853	35,486	166,090	.0029	90,421	**27**	6,078	**13**	....	**....**	12,236	2,940	7,274	Rock
Roseau	135	16,322	16,338	17,370	6,316	36,654	283,510	.0047	128,419	**38**	10,119	**21**	2,802	**16**	21,107	6,215	12,451	Roseau
St. Louis*	137	198,256	200,528	17,502	83,613	34,264	3,469,940	.0644	2,372,961	**698**	443,926	**942**	66,200	**371**	303,533	127,047	144,839	St. Louis
Scott*	139	114,403	89,498	24,845	39,851	58,927	2,842,330	.0385	699,790	**206**	45,616	**97**	5,602	**31**	102,448	21,481	83,893	Scott
Sherburne*	141	77,790	64,417	21,633	27,090	51,038	1,682,800	.0277	892,438	**263**	56,434	**120**	3,435	**19**	132,180	22,260	59,408	Sherburne
Sibley	143	15,250	15,356	17,593	5,786	38,440	268,300	.0041	80,051	**24**	3,410	**7**	....	**....**	12,787	5,253	11,718	Sibley
Stearns*	145	138,332	133,166	17,588	50,817	39,486	2,432,970	.0514	2,368,831	**697**	457,867	**972**	60,143	**337**	289,731	66,379	99,292	Stearns
Steele**	147	35,071	33,680	19,643	13,540	41,842	688,890	.0126	478,056	**141**	66,849	**142**	35,328	**198**	82,429	16,376	25,782	Steele
Stevens	149	9,843	10,053	16,051	3,721	34,896	157,990	.0033	142,464	**42**	5,575	**12**	2,430	**14**	18,392	7,442	6,886	Stevens
Swift	151	11,569	11,956	14,441	4,185	33,076	167,070	.0029	74,307	**22**	3,105	**7**	....	**....**	14,275	3,727	7,711	Swift
Todd	153	24,270	24,426	14,506	9,448	30,676	352,070	.0056	105,759	**31**	4,645	**10**	....	**....**	19,752	6,944	17,938	Todd
Traverse	155	3,843	4,134	14,900	1,620	29,253	57,260	.0010	28,466	**8**	....	**....**	....	**....**	5,218	1,044	2,961	Traverse
Wabasha*	157	22,303	21,610	18,568	8,694	39,155	414,130	.0065	156,000	**46**	3,671	**8**	....	**....**	30,401	8,599	17,532	Wabasha
Wadena	159	13,567	13,713	14,063	5,473	28,615	190,790	.0037	128,792	**38**	8,192	**17**	1,123	**6**	23,300	8,580	9,746	Wadena
Waseca	161	19,405	19,526	18,441	7,516	39,152	357,840	.0056	130,670	**38**	20,181	**43**	....	**....**	22,476	3,330	14,973	Waseca
Washington*	163	217,209	201,130	26,103	80,145	58,324	5,669,700	.0891	2,868,108	**844**	475,995	**1,010**	67,643	**379**	437,304	112,823	161,392	Washington
Watonwan	165	11,554	11,876	15,801	4,505	33,178	182,560	.0030	69,035	**20**	4,445	**9**	....	**....**	14,144	4,393	8,213	Watonwan
Wilkin**	167	6,885	7,138	16,908	2,693	35,471	116,410	.0017	30,148	**9**	....	**....**	....	**....**	2,806	2,034	5,180	Wilkin
Winona**	169	49,300	49,985	16,865	18,943	36,153	831,450	.0147	471,573	**139**	75,183	**160**	12,388	**69**	66,147	8,528	34,481	Winona
Wright*	171	106,446	89,986	20,947	37,945	48,343	2,229,720	.0362	1,101,087	**324**	112,913	**240**	2,341	**13**	149,149	28,978	79,695	Wright
Yellow Medicine	173	10,557	11,080	15,896	4,265	32,266	167,810	.0031	107,464	**32**	1,460	**3**	....	**....**	22,915	4,403	8,387	Yellow Medicine
The State		5,101,284	4,919,479	21,167	2,027,904	43,431	107,980,720	1.9068	70,948,964	**20,871**	9,955,951	**21,137**	2,272,044	**12,730**	9,560,017	3,013,581	3,696,214	The State

MISSISSIPPI (MS; CODE 28; 82 Counties)

COUNTY OR COUNTY EQUIVALENT	FIPS CO. CODE	POPULATION Estimate 7/1/04	POPULATION Census 4/1/00	PER CAPITA INCOME 2003	HOUSEHOLDS Estimate 7/1/04	MEDIAN HOUSEHOLD INCOME 2003	DISPOSABLE INCOME 2003 ($1,000)	MARKET ABILITY INDEX 2003	TOTAL RETAIL SALES Sales 2003 ($1,000)	TOTAL RETAIL SALES Ranally Sales Units	GENERAL MERCHANDISE Sales 2003 ($1,000)	GENERAL MERCHANDISE Ranally Sales Units	APPAREL STORE Sales 2003 ($1,000)	APPAREL STORE Ranally Sales Units	FOOD STORE SALES 2003 ($1,000)	HEALTH & DRUG STORE 2003 ($1,000)	PASSENGER CAR REGIS-TRATIONS 2003	COUNTY OR COUNTY EQUIVALENT
Adams**	001	32,903	34,340	13,098	13,613	24,287	430,970	.0096	410,657	**121**	153,361	**326**	19,937	**112**	35,680	18,096	21,892	Adams
Alcorn**	003	35,037	34,558	15,111	14,752	27,665	529,430	.0110	462,038	**136**	148,426	**315**	21,364	**120**	32,703	18,648	26,953	Alcorn
Amite**	005	13,597	13,599	12,721	5,401	24,757	172,970	.0029	56,627	**17**	2,484	**5**	....	**....**	6,726	2,691	9,371	Amite
Attala	007	19,679	19,661	12,188	7,684	24,044	239,840	.0054	224,333	**66**	48,148	**102**	8,737	**49**	34,036	23,237	12,195	Attala
Benton	009	7,692	8,026	11,793	2,956	23,487	90,710	.0015	26,305	**8**	2,438	**5**	....	**....**	5,969	1,691	5,394	Benton
Bolivar**	011	38,827	40,633	10,529	13,672	22,745	408,820	.0096	388,027	**114**	53,851	**114**	10,407	**58**	51,962	16,214	19,907	Bolivar
Calhoun	013	14,753	15,069	13,626	6,026	25,643	201,030	.0035	86,011	**25**	8,452	**18**	3,441	**19**	22,270	7,452	10,373	Calhoun
Carroll**	015	10,359	10,769	13,859	4,040	27,400	143,570	.0021	22,352	**7**	1,678	**4**	....	**....**	....	1,064	7,327	Carroll
Chickasaw	017	19,141	19,440	12,624	7,273	25,684	241,630	.0045	128,728	**38**	32,516	**69**	2,300	**13**	21,612	7,381	12,926	Chickasaw
Choctaw	019	9,630	9,758	13,019	3,750	25,238	125,370	.0023	63,773	**19**	6,762	**14**	....	**....**	12,250	6,294	6,611	Choctaw
Claiborne	021	11,394	11,831	9,189	3,632	21,773	104,700	.0022	55,912	**16**	4,631	**10**	....	**....**	8,962	2,334	5,446	Claiborne
Clarke**	023	17,674	17,955	13,338	7,044	25,706	235,730	.0036	43,233	**13**	7,024	**15**	....	**....**	11,362	5,109	12,519	Clarke
Clay**	025	21,511	21,979	13,220	8,206	26,656	284,370	.0051	132,868	**39**	24,335	**52**	2,656	**15**	20,918	9,114	13,791	Clay
Coahoma**	027	29,213	30,622	10,058	10,211	21,727	293,820	.0071	286,610	**84**	44,452	**94**	12,253	**69**	39,375	17,981	14,026	Coahoma
Copiah*	029	28,982	28,757	11,886	10,397	25,523	344,470	.0062	141,703	**42**	34,010	**72**	1,945	**11**	29,616	12,964	17,600	Copiah
Covington	031	20,417	19,407	12,475	7,695	25,493	254,700	.0049	142,666	**42**	9,991	**21**	....	**....**	20,468	9,332	13,716	Covington
DeSoto*	033	129,632	107,199	21,498	48,949	43,978	2,786,860	.0449	1,359,111	**400**	299,088	**635**	15,092	**85**	154,987	77,597	94,964	DeSoto
Forrest*	035	74,924	72,604	13,182	28,599	26,347	987,670	.0244	1,217,181	**358**	398,963	**847**	16,782	**94**	82,649	78,931	47,148	Forrest
Franklin	037	8,300	8,448	11,927	3,200	23,888	98,990	.0017	30,603	**9**	2,120	**5**	....	**....**	5,022	1,751	5,699	Franklin
George*	039	20,808	19,144	15,306	7,490	32,582	318,490	.0053	122,970	**36**	38,006	**81**	....	**....**	18,932	8,626	14,597	George
Greene	041	13,122	13,299	11,154	4,198	26,531	146,360	.0025	38,697	**11**	5,519	**12**	....	**....**	6,264	3,756	7,817	Greene
Grenada**	043	22,681	23,263	14,367	9,342	26,780	325,850	.0074	340,758	**100**	96,495	**205**	6,862	**38**	35,182	10,421	15,055	Grenada
Hancock*	045	45,765	42,967	17,198	18,373	32,916	787,080	.0127	309,180	**91**	68,516	**145**	2,913	**16**	59,178	8,212	32,973	Hancock
Harrison*	047	189,590	189,601	17,895	77,866	33,507	3,392,700	.0639	2,454,602	**722**	623,556	**1,324**	104,270	**584**	224,504	111,813	136,086	Harrison
Hinds*	049	248,578	250,800	15,785	94,316	31,999	3,923,920	.0828	3,619,186	**1,065**	689,668	**1,464**	165,418	**927**	352,046	216,248	157,222	Hinds
Holmes	051	21,261	21,609	7,782	7,238	17,124	165,450	.0039	113,003	**33**	9,880	**21**	1,402	**8**	19,756	9,631	9,922	Holmes
Humphreys	053	10,590	11,206	9,028	3,617	20,108	95,610	.0022	71,877	**21**	4,838	**10**	1,194	**7**	10,568	3,374	5,038	Humphreys
Issaquena	055	1,941	2,274	8,542	646	20,060	16,580	.0003	3,085	**1**	....	**....**	....	**....**	3,049	....	975	Issaquena
Itawamba**	057	22,999	22,770	14,826	8,977	29,251	340,990	.0056	122,424	**36**	29,342	**62**	1,505	**8**	15,656	10,489	17,117	Itawamba
Jackson*	059	134,605	131,420	18,233	51,693	36,546	2,454,230	.0416	1,271,057	**374**	299,380	**636**	29,205	**164**	171,679	47,181	96,405	Jackson
Jasper**	061	18,332	18,149	11,736	6,961	24,458	215,150	.0040	98,142	**29**	5,815	**12**	....	**....**	8,814	7,265	12,144	Jasper
Jefferson	063	9,472	9,740	8,466	3,365	18,535	80,190	.0015	17,630	**5**	1,933	**4**	....	**....**	3,324	1,208	5,167	Jefferson
Jefferson Davis	065	13,245	13,962	10,788	5,090	21,363	142,890	.0027	59,447	**17**	9,509	**20**	....	**....**	14,084	6,472	8,617	Jefferson Davis
Jones**	067	65,230	64,958	13,634	24,696	27,660	889,330	.0173	587,062	**173**	138,440	**294**	22,746	**127**	69,213	37,702	43,984	Jones
Kemper**	069	10,439	10,453	11,598	3,956	22,892	121,070	.0021	42,267	**12**	4,649	**10**	....	**....**	8,484	2,745	6,850	Kemper
Lafayette**	071	40,657	38,744	13,494	15,519	27,032	548,630	.0109	383,215	**113**	74,722	**159**	29,014	**163**	57,444	33,730	27,408	Lafayette
Lamar*	073	42,827	39,070	17,672	16,409	35,398	756,830	.0127	362,672	**107**	78,602	**167**	47,662	**267**	31,540	27,131	31,605	Lamar
Lauderdale**	075	77,582	78,161	14,651	30,249	29,242	1,136,670	.0243	1,042,761	**307**	237,693	**505**	33,306	**187**	127,606	52,751	49,970	Lauderdale
Lawrence	077	13,595	13,258	13,855	5,277	27,318	188,360	.0030	46,860	**14**	3,925	**8**	....	**....**	5,577	6,188	9,950	Lawrence
Leake	079	22,112	20,940	12,070	7,935	25,869	266,900	.0055	185,817	**55**	46,375	**98**	7,801	**44**	24,135	8,623	13,690	Leake
Lee**	081	78,261	75,755	17,294	30,676	33,811	1,353,430	.0290	1,354,165	**398**	400,396	**850**	91,936	**515**	86,140	51,109	54,422	Lee
Leflore**	083	36,017	37,947	9,674	12,522	21,175	348,440	.0084	329,210	**97**	56,934	**121**	22,444	**126**	47,510	19,593	17,055	Leflore
Lincoln**	085	33,675	33,166	13,611	13,329	26,519	458,360	.0103	459,067	**135**	145,635	**309**	18,648	**105**	31,765	17,490	23,772	Lincoln
Lowndes**	087	60,373	61,586	14,834	22,735	30,477	895,550	.0197	891,538	**262**	198,351	**421**	43,420	**243**	108,492	47,419	39,320	Lowndes
Madison*	089	81,322	74,674	20,878	30,471	43,365	1,697,840	.0298	1,084,900	**319**	315,647	**670**	87,242	**489**	101,772	53,341	56,366	Madison

Source: Devonshire Associates Ltd. and Scan/US, Inc. 2004.
* Component of a Metropolitan Core Based Statistical Area.
** Component of a Micropolitan Core Based Statistical Area.

.... Data less than 1,000.

(d) Data not available.

continued on next page

Counties: Population / Income / Sales, *Continued*

COUNTY OR COUNTY EQUIVALENT	FIPS CO. CODE	POPULATION Estimate 7/1/04	POPULATION Census 4/1/00	PER CAPITA INCOME 2003	HOUSEHOLDS Estimate 7/1/04	MEDIAN HOUSEHOLD INCOME 2003	DISPOSABLE INCOME 2003 ($1,000)	MARKET ABILITY INDEX 2003	TOTAL RETAIL SALES Sales 2003 ($1,000)	TOTAL RETAIL SALES Ranally Sales Units	GENERAL MERCHANDISE Sales 2003 ($1,000)	GENERAL MERCHANDISE Ranally Sales Units	APPAREL STORE Sales 2003 ($1,000)	APPAREL STORE Ranally Sales Units	FOOD STORE SALES 2003 ($1,000)	HEALTH & DRUG STORE 2003 ($1,000)	PASSENGER CAR REGIS-TRATIONS 2003	COUNTY OR COUNTY EQUIVALENT
Marion	091	24,927	25,595	12,161	9,836	23,632	303,130	.0066	257,001	**76**	58,374	**124**	6,620	**37**	37,686	12,480	17,108	Marion
Marshall*	093	35,565	34,993	12,894	12,772	27,642	458,570	.0076	135,151	**40**	32,407	**69**	2,127	**12**	19,592	13,280	22,731	Marshall
Monroe	095	37,786	38,014	14,641	14,843	28,709	553,230	.0098	281,773	**83**	81,108	**172**	5,277	**30**	28,155	21,949	26,528	Monroe
Montgomery	097	11,866	12,189	12,500	4,665	24,333	148,320	.0029	87,153	**26**	24,548	**52**	2,188	**12**	10,935	5,410	7,718	Montgomery
Neshoba	099	29,275	28,684	13,595	11,349	27,013	397,980	.0078	265,810	**78**	68,775	**146**	8,332	**47**	36,448	11,420	20,171	Neshoba
Newton	101	22,101	21,838	13,734	8,475	27,493	303,530	.0054	144,678	**43**	22,055	**47**	1,355	**8**	18,496	15,882	15,117	Newton
Noxubee	103	12,243	12,548	10,673	4,537	21,891	130,670	.0025	60,339	**18**	4,435	**9**	....	**....**	10,546	7,678	6,807	Noxubee
Oktibbeha**	105	42,432	42,902	13,104	17,815	24,283	556,040	.0109	364,229	**107**	88,815	**189**	22,309	**125**	44,051	7,468	31,498	Oktibbeha
Panola	107	35,526	34,274	12,181	12,988	25,755	432,750	.0093	358,865	**106**	55,989	**119**	19,910	**112**	38,966	16,348	21,745	Panola
Pearl River**	109	51,596	48,621	15,086	20,463	29,285	778,370	.0148	517,201	**152**	143,238	**304**	17,018	**95**	46,792	24,166	37,500	Pearl River
Perry*	111	12,322	12,138	12,707	4,570	26,272	156,580	.0025	40,241	**12**	6,547	**14**	....	**....**	8,531	4,353	8,481	Perry
Pike**	113	38,917	38,940	11,976	15,094	23,645	466,060	.0110	491,987	**145**	88,980	**189**	25,553	**143**	56,119	31,954	25,104	Pike
Pontotoc**	115	27,843	26,726	15,211	10,604	30,678	423,520	.0072	186,455	**55**	41,167	**87**	4,918	**28**	28,138	11,471	19,623	Pontotoc
Prentiss	117	25,575	25,556	13,894	10,027	27,198	355,350	.0063	168,380	**50**	31,343	**67**	2,261	**13**	23,543	9,568	18,705	Prentiss
Quitman	119	9,638	10,117	9,424	3,462	19,947	90,830	.0020	60,076	**18**	15,071	**32**	....	**....**	6,774	2,664	4,924	Quitman
Rankin*	121	127,528	115,327	20,150	48,055	41,160	2,569,690	.0433	1,401,276	**412**	212,941	**452**	12,856	**72**	154,569	60,549	91,471	Rankin
Scott	123	28,465	28,423	12,140	10,285	25,840	345,560	.0066	195,142	**57**	32,449	**69**	3,635	**20**	41,355	18,380	17,244	Scott
Sharkey	125	6,121	6,580	9,866	2,112	21,779	60,390	.0012	29,630	**9**	4,305	**9**	....	**....**	8,293	3,775	2,975	Sharkey
Simpson*	127	27,563	27,639	13,050	10,266	26,715	359,690	.0070	226,337	**67**	49,242	**105**	3,212	**18**	28,461	22,672	18,258	Simpson
Smith	129	15,719	16,182	14,374	5,988	29,067	225,950	.0035	58,840	**17**	5,407	**11**	....	**....**	13,427	4,695	11,210	Smith
Stone*	131	14,384	13,622	13,183	5,034	29,108	189,630	.0034	87,295	**26**	6,674	**14**	....	**....**	17,692	9,661	9,536	Stone
Sunflower**	133	33,078	34,369	8,720	9,147	24,417	288,440	.0076	321,933	**95**	42,715	**91**	4,965	**28**	46,435	17,631	13,940	Sunflower
Tallahatchie	135	14,235	14,903	10,464	5,168	21,860	148,960	.0028	60,503	**18**	7,963	**17**	....	**....**	4,127	7,288	8,012	Tallahatchie
Tate*	137	25,907	25,370	15,727	9,313	33,732	407,430	.0077	269,800	**79**	65,909	**140**	3,357	**19**	12,701	10,741	17,120	Tate
Tippah	139	20,938	20,826	14,342	8,369	27,459	300,300	.0051	127,732	**38**	31,959	**68**	....	**....**	16,877	11,098	15,373	Tippah
Tishomingo	141	18,901	19,163	14,754	7,945	26,829	278,870	.0049	133,259	**39**	25,864	**55**	....	**....**	19,330	10,775	15,418	Tishomingo
Tunica*	143	10,146	9,227	10,992	3,806	23,052	111,520	.0024	83,377	**25**	9,322	**20**	....	**....**	6,932	1,462	5,179	Tunica
Union	145	26,285	25,362	15,584	10,318	30,621	409,630	.0073	222,339	**65**	69,087	**147**	8,065	**45**	34,435	11,356	19,584	Union
Walthall	147	15,219	15,156	11,303	5,756	22,819	172,020	.0032	74,229	**22**	8,229	**17**	2,608	**15**	11,886	2,087	10,180	Walthall
Warren**	149	48,799	49,644	17,470	19,905	33,109	852,530	.0159	587,501	**173**	118,290	**251**	31,259	**175**	77,162	23,583	33,701	Warren
Washington**	151	59,560	62,977	11,603	21,478	24,690	691,100	.0159	659,824	**194**	172,908	**367**	37,803	**212**	57,766	28,847	31,245	Washington
Wayne	153	21,132	21,216	12,217	8,018	24,699	258,170	.0051	159,538	**47**	48,435	**103**	2,838	**16**	17,510	10,752	13,849	Wayne
Webster	155	10,114	10,294	15,898	4,555	27,053	160,790	.0026	60,215	**18**	6,541	**14**	....	**....**	11,797	2,101	8,379	Webster
Wilkinson	157	10,223	10,312	8,873	3,678	19,017	90,710	.0018	33,570	**10**	4,138	**9**	....	**....**	9,774	4,619	5,630	Wilkinson
Winston	159	19,829	20,160	13,353	7,639	26,512	264,780	.0048	137,086	**40**	36,741	**78**	3,974	**22**	19,261	7,189	13,383	Winston
Yalobusha	161	13,417	13,051	13,391	5,524	25,164	179,670	.0030	66,025	**19**	9,229	**20**	....	**....**	17,765	5,807	9,205	Yalobusha
Yazoo**	163	28,309	28,149	10,134	9,261	23,849	286,880	.0066	248,086	**73**	31,949	**68**	4,521	**25**	29,785	9,824	14,623	Yazoo
The State		2,892,228	2,844,658	14,954	1,103,166	30,008	43,250,190	.8302	29,353,211	**8,639**	6,629,705	**14,076**	1,080,695	**6,056**	3,312,054	1,601,382	1,920,660	The State

MISSOURI (MO; CODE 29; 114 Counties, 1 Independent City)

COUNTY OR COUNTY EQUIVALENT	FIPS CO. CODE	POPULATION Estimate 7/1/04	POPULATION Census 4/1/00	PER CAPITA INCOME 2003	HOUSEHOLDS Estimate 7/1/04	MEDIAN HOUSEHOLD INCOME 2003	DISPOSABLE INCOME 2003 ($1,000)	MARKET ABILITY INDEX 2003	TOTAL RETAIL SALES Sales 2003 ($1,000)	TOTAL RETAIL SALES Ranally Sales Units	GENERAL MERCHANDISE Sales 2003 ($1,000)	GENERAL MERCHANDISE Ranally Sales Units	APPAREL STORE Sales 2003 ($1,000)	APPAREL STORE Ranally Sales Units	FOOD STORE SALES 2003 ($1,000)	HEALTH & DRUG STORE 2003 ($1,000)	PASSENGER CAR REGIS-TRATIONS 2003	COUNTY OR COUNTY EQUIVALENT
Adair**	001	24,737	24,977	12,602	9,659	25,741	311,730	.0067	266,719	**78**	48,829	**104**	10,459	**59**	38,648	16,547	17,381	Adair
Andrew*	003	16,904	16,492	18,276	6,489	37,765	308,930	.0047	100,381	**30**	22,751	**48**	....	**....**	8,127	4,729	13,082	Andrew
Atchison	005	6,246	6,430	15,876	2,688	29,327	99,160	.0019	66,070	**19**	1,909	**4**	1,066	**6**	6,796	2,926	4,960	Atchison
Audrain**	007	25,688	25,853	14,815	9,768	31,165	380,560	.0069	210,336	**62**	28,386	**60**	4,904	**27**	33,142	15,550	16,835	Audrain
Barry	009	34,820	34,010	13,684	13,704	27,396	476,490	.0095	345,157	**102**	44,948	**95**	5,170	**29**	62,251	10,446	24,970	Barry
Barton	011	13,148	12,541	13,597	5,080	27,830	178,770	.0034	110,028	**32**	14,128	**30**	....	**....**	14,344	3,438	9,778	Barton
Bates*	013	17,008	16,653	14,231	6,623	28,936	242,040	.0040	89,127	**26**	10,525	**22**	....	**....**	17,705	3,020	12,801	Bates
Benton	015	18,350	17,180	14,192	8,058	25,753	260,430	.0048	144,085	**42**	22,464	**48**	....	**....**	14,203	9,945	14,816	Benton
Bollinger**	017	12,402	12,029	13,849	4,763	28,013	171,750	.0028	57,386	**17**	2,379	**5**	....	**....**	9,177	1,642	9,255	Bollinger
Boone*	019	142,884	135,454	18,274	58,480	35,461	2,611,020	.0487	1,863,303	**548**	297,344	**631**	54,706	**307**	214,028	75,677	103,821	Boone
Buchanan*	021	84,529	85,998	17,305	35,650	32,575	1,462,760	.0281	1,098,105	**323**	265,246	**563**	21,813	**122**	142,194	40,624	59,473	Buchanan
Butler**	023	40,866	40,867	13,787	17,141	26,176	563,420	.0121	508,477	**150**	113,749	**241**	16,241	**91**	44,261	32,457	27,873	Butler
Caldwell*	025	9,214	8,969	14,589	3,638	29,567	134,420	.0020	28,786	**8**	....	**....**	....	**....**	6,660	1,569	6,985	Caldwell
Callaway*	027	42,657	40,766	16,440	15,370	36,160	701,260	.0113	259,007	**76**	33,635	**71**	1,477	**8**	26,956	6,544	29,579	Callaway
Camden	029	38,659	37,051	18,400	16,764	33,565	711,310	.0141	603,155	**177**	123,319	**262**	72,085	**404**	58,954	11,617	31,035	Camden
Cape Girardeau**	031	70,244	68,693	17,186	27,964	34,462	1,207,210	.0263	1,256,476	**370**	296,075	**629**	32,316	**181**	108,789	59,740	49,256	Cape Girardeau
Carroll	033	10,107	10,285	15,230	4,225	28,901	153,930	.0024	44,835	**13**	6,649	**14**	1,164	**7**	8,602	3,309	7,958	Carroll
Carter	035	5,983	5,941	11,655	2,436	22,440	69,730	.0012	22,608	**7**	....	**....**	....	**....**	7,535	....	4,379	Carter
Cass*	037	90,899	82,092	20,863	33,770	44,764	1,896,390	.0288	698,960	**206**	149,782	**318**	1,407	**8**	100,271	27,076	67,186	Cass
Cedar	039	13,874	13,733	13,553	5,756	26,126	188,040	.0034	91,539	**27**	5,396	**11**	....	**....**	21,905	4,087	10,157	Cedar
Chariton	041	8,195	8,438	15,844	3,424	30,056	129,840	.0024	76,565	**23**	1,358	**3**	....	**....**	8,629	6,394	6,748	Chariton
Christian*	043	63,776	54,285	17,343	24,329	36,016	1,106,070	.0176	415,803	**122**	32,090	**68**	1,786	**10**	47,907	22,793	46,920	Christian
Clark**	045	7,430	7,416	14,661	3,045	28,182	108,930	.0019	50,888	**15**	2,583	**5**	....	**....**	6,044	3,806	6,000	Clark
Clay*	047	197,398	184,006	22,322	79,821	44,280	4,406,280	.0808	3,315,806	**975**	575,156	**1,221**	64,864	**364**	330,937	160,756	146,262	Clay
Clinton*	049	20,502	18,979	18,542	7,821	38,840	380,140	.0066	218,374	**64**	48,353	**103**	....	**....**	11,879	8,162	15,642	Clinton
Cole*	051	72,781	71,397	20,318	29,499	40,079	1,478,730	.0290	1,275,055	**375**	271,105	**576**	23,630	**132**	165,456	61,103	53,899	Cole
Cooper	053	17,106	16,670	15,177	6,212	33,061	259,620	.0044	115,492	**34**	15,749	**33**	....	**....**	22,325	1,474	12,034	Cooper
Crawford	055	23,729	22,804	14,377	9,312	29,099	341,150	.0074	321,570	**95**	18,387	**39**	....	**....**	26,780	7,878	17,261	Crawford
Dade	057	7,822	7,923	14,059	3,157	27,505	109,970	.0017	26,740	**8**	....	**....**	....	**....**	5,084	....	6,277	Dade
Dallas*	059	16,253	15,661	12,894	6,239	26,447	209,560	.0036	82,091	**24**	9,091	**19**	....	**....**	18,433	2,146	11,659	Dallas
Daviess	061	8,004	8,016	14,689	3,238	28,836	117,570	.0019	33,908	**10**	1,098	**2**	....	**....**	8,072	3,136	6,055	Daviess
DeKalb*	063	13,050	11,597	10,076	3,509	29,957	131,490	.0026	68,394	**20**	1,386	**3**	....	**....**	10,892	2,337	6,547	DeKalb
Dent	065	14,915	14,927	13,445	6,063	26,127	200,530	.0039	133,068	**39**	24,529	**52**	....	**....**	32,831	5,642	10,793	Dent
Douglas	067	13,450	13,084	12,528	5,413	24,495	168,500	.0028	51,702	**15**	11,455	**24**	....	**....**	15,634	2,583	10,209	Douglas
Dunklin**	069	32,505	33,155	12,293	13,276	23,755	399,590	.0084	304,616	**90**	64,539	**137**	5,218	**29**	57,379	20,776	20,528	Dunklin
Franklin*	071	97,849	93,807	19,171	37,096	40,304	1,875,910	.0319	1,016,996	**299**	211,215	**448**	17,684	**99**	86,056	48,500	71,975	Franklin
Gasconade	073	15,593	15,342	16,825	6,319	32,752	262,360	.0044	125,129	**37**	19,182	**41**	....	**....**	17,132	4,465	11,988	Gasconade
Gentry	075	6,471	6,861	14,121	2,668	27,009	91,380	.0017	52,785	**16**	....	**....**	....	**....**	9,513	5,369	4,824	Gentry
Greene*	077	247,471	240,391	17,582	107,232	32,279	4,350,940	.0913	4,170,871	**1,227**	668,184	**1,418**	102,893	**577**	381,809	179,316	185,720	Greene
Grundy	079	10,279	10,432	14,352	4,456	26,093	147,520	.0027	85,215	**25**	15,022	**32**	2,104	**12**	21,199	5,046	7,594	Grundy
Harrison	081	8,816	8,850	14,114	3,617	27,164	124,430	.0028	132,248	**39**	22,209	**47**	....	**....**	17,689	1,302	6,869	Harrison
Henry	083	22,527	21,997	15,732	9,658	29,128	354,400	.0067	243,253	**72**	24,749	**53**	5,547	**31**	36,896	17,319	17,324	Henry
Hickory	085	9,025	8,940	13,315	3,956	23,879	120,170	.0019	24,397	**7**	....	**....**	....	**....**	5,397	1,723	7,471	Hickory
Holt	087	5,085	5,351	14,887	2,151	27,763	75,700	.0014	43,394	**13**	....	**....**	....	**....**	4,348	1,385	3,970	Holt
Howard*	089	9,949	10,212	14,250	3,774	30,046	141,770	.0022	32,062	**9**	1,017	**2**	....	**....**	10,316	1,842	7,044	Howard
Howell**	091	37,587	37,238	13,537	16,432	24,765	508,830	.0110	460,536	**135**	130,970	**278**	14,932	**84**	40,712	24,526	29,531	Howell
Iron	093	10,199	10,697	12,581	4,077	25,159	128,310	.0023	58,340	**17**	2,539	**5**	....	**....**	16,433	4,199	7,120	Iron
Jackson*	095	661,091	654,880	19,461	278,123	36,714	12,865,690	.2332	8,722,745	**2,566**	1,217,102	**2,584**	287,608	**1,612**	998,114	489,946	446,304	Jackson
Jasper*	097	109,158	104,686	14,656	43,068	29,747	1,599,850	.0339	1,426,792	**420**	317,364	**674**	43,117	**242**	112,760	57,219	75,101	Jasper
Jefferson*	099	209,444	198,099	19,752	77,416	42,383	4,136,960	.0635	1,522,664	**448**	293,562	**623**	12,490	**70**	296,149	62,470	153,118	Jefferson
Johnson**	101	50,858	48,258	15,158	18,435	33,231	770,910	.0130	324,967	**96**	89,837	**191**	4,695	**26**	32,014	9,026	35,643	Johnson
Knox	103	4,295	4,361	13,306	1,768	25,422	57,150	.0011	30,781	**9**	1,805	**4**	....	**....**	9,764	2,087	3,391	Knox
Laclede**	105	33,569	32,513	14,194	13,413	28,167	476,470	.0101	413,223	**122**	68,302	**145**	15,599	**87**	52,935	8,745	23,961	Laclede
Lafayette*	107	32,925	32,960	17,413	12,614	36,182	573,320	.0096	271,007	**80**	19,917	**42**	20,499	**115**	38,833	17,354	24,414	Lafayette
Lawrence	109	36,792	35,204	14,375	14,257	29,673	528,890	.0105	384,630	**113**	25,008	**53**	1,352	**8**	47,307	12,176	26,177	Lawrence
Lewis**	111	10,130	10,494	13,603	3,825	28,568	137,800	.0024	57,810	**17**	4,837	**10**	....	**....**	7,043	2,228	7,290	Lewis
Lincoln*	113	45,856	38,944	17,684	16,337	39,206	810,920	.0133	362,830	**107**	72,448	**154**	1,124	**6**	40,778	18,309	33,295	Lincoln
Linn	115	13,372	13,754	14,565	5,708	26,992	194,760	.0034	94,707	**28**	17,886	**38**	1,222	**7**	13,085	4,108	10,321	Linn
Livingston	117	14,350	14,558	15,216	5,720	30,328	218,350	.0044	168,301	**50**	29,144	**62**	6,644	**37**	32,585	3,268	10,087	Livingston
McDonald*	119	22,073	21,681	12,136	8,208	25,847	267,880	.0049	123,471	**36**	2,581	**5**	....	**....**	54,498	4,092	14,579	McDonald
Macon	121	15,518	15,762	15,677	6,795	28,338	243,270	.0040	98,255	**29**	18,654	**40**	....	**....**	14,273	6,787	12,455	Macon
Madison	123	11,803	11,800	12,664	4,828	25,140	149,470	.0028	82,339	**24**	7,228	**15**	....	**....**	18,961	2,306	8,680	Madison
Maries	125	8,818	8,903	15,081	3,540	29,896	132,980	.0021	35,841	**11**	2,234	**5**	....	**....**	6,035	1,285	7,117	Maries
Marion**	127	28,290	28,289	15,381	11,464	30,537	435,140	.0090	374,525	**110**	67,470	**143**	3,718	**21**	65,786	21,913	19,642	Marion
Mercer	129	3,541	3,757	15,016	1,508	27,769	53,170	.0008	16,745	**5**	....	**....**	....	**....**	1,028	1,006	2,921	Mercer
Miller	131	24,464	23,564	14,646	9,757	29,136	358,290	.0071	260,122	**77**	14,045	**30**	2,263	**13**	45,907	7,743	18,204	Miller
Mississippi	133	14,728	13,427	10,781	5,551	22,422	158,780	.0034	111,303	**33**	7,997	**17**	....	**....**	16,677	6,191	8,152	Mississippi
Moniteau*	135	15,005	14,827	15,663	5,381	35,147	235,020	.0043	136,543	**40**	4,863	**10**	....	**....**	15,961	2,349	10,257	Moniteau
Monroe	137	9,418	9,311	14,541	3,741	29,020	136,950	.0023	50,720	**15**	3,516	**7**	....	**....**	1,948	2,638	7,290	Monroe
Montgomery	139	12,048	12,136	15,505	4,796	30,840	186,810	.0033	98,749	**29**	4,255	**9**	....	**....**	22,523	3,004	9,435	Montgomery
Morgan	141	20,207	19,309	14,748	8,242	28,780	298,010	.0056	181,351	**53**	11,949	**25**	1,473	**8**	45,881	6,595	15,074	Morgan
New Madrid	143	19,028	19,760	13,214	7,737	25,792	251,430	.0054	218,457	**64**	8,209	**17**	1,852	**10**	20,077	9,824	12,014	New Madrid
Newton*	145	54,463	52,636	15,906	20,938	32,602	866,290	.0145	377,919	**111**	102,589	**218**	2,930	**16**	50,395	22,064	39,470	Newton
Nodaway**	147	21,702	21,912	14,432	8,272	30,080	313,200	.0058	183,713	**54**	22,484	**48**	5,275	**30**	54,295	1,755	15,250	Nodaway
Oregon	149	10,295	10,344	11,475	4,264	21,736	118,130	.0023	70,098	**21**	14,016	**30**	....	**....**	17,975	2,297	7,431	Oregon
Osage*	151	13,151	13,062	17,904	5,088	36,592	235,450	.0040	122,694	**36**	1,100	**2**	1,150	**6**	11,448	2,651	10,935	Osage
Ozark	153	9,486	9,542	13,004	3,954	24,708	123,360	.0022	52,888	**16**	....	**....**	....	**....**	13,433	....	7,722	Ozark
Pemiscot	155	19,630	20,047	10,843	7,827	21,506	212,850	.0046	159,530	**47**	15,946	**34**	....	**....**	32,321	14,347	11,462	Pemiscot
Perry	157	18,249	18,132	16,620	7,057	34,106	303,290	.0059	230,889	**68**	40,899	**87**	....	**....**	9,444	....	13,614	Perry
Pettis**	159	39,309	39,403	15,533	16,049	30,335	610,600	.0121	467,542	**138**	104,241	**221**	16,098	**90**	50,526	22,671	28,074	Pettis
Phelps**	161	42,250	39,825	14,179	16,922	28,022	599,070	.0119	440,081	**129**	95,307	**202**	11,523	**65**	49,384	12,629	29,259	Phelps
Pike	163	18,583	18,351	13,703	6,606	30,560	254,650	.0045	120,410	**35**	13,871	**29**	....	**....**	19,970	14,764	12,202	Pike
Platte*	165	81,115	73,781	25,600	32,925	50,056	2,076,550	.0322	989,260	**291**	50,609	**107**	6,383	**36**	134,485	39,421	63,206	Platte
Polk*	167	28,417	26,992	12,950	10,450	28,166	367,990	.0074	258,141	**76**	48,837	**104**	2,497	**14**	56,030	13,506	19,796	Polk
Pulaski**	169	46,394	41,165	12,892	14,788	32,559	598,090	.0106	257,254	**76**	35,119	**75**	2,090	**12**	17,694	7,115	27,479	Pulaski
Putnam	171	5,117	5,223	13,533	2,177	25,239	69,250	.0011	22,340	**7**	....	**....**	....	**....**	10,066	1,514	4,021	Putnam
Ralls**	173	9,650	9,626	17,210	3,778	35,106	166,080	.0024	35,590	**10**	....	**....**	....	**....**	9,096	....	7,731	Ralls
Randolph**	175	25,172	24,663	14,163	9,526	30,087	356,500	.0075	309,533	**91**	74,879	**159**	6,067	**34**	35,250	16,569	16,563	Randolph
Ray*	177	24,106	23,354	18,577	9,140	38,857	447,810	.0068	140,242	**41**	11,976	**25**	....	**....**	22,994	7,335	18,486	Ray
Reynolds	179	6,529	6,689	13,147	2,736	24,957	85,840	.0014	25,445	**7**	1,515	**3**	....	**....**	9,356	2,506	5,015	Reynolds
Ripley	181	13,875	13,509	11,502	5,637	22,299	159,590	.0031	90,878	**27**	7,193	**15**	....	**....**	23,506	1,478	9,843	Ripley
St. Charles*	183	319,977	283,883	23,984	118,558	51,227	7,674,380	.1140	2,933,745	**863**	485,076	**1,030**	101,740	**570**	426,460	153,329	237,731	St. Charles
St. Clair	185	9,677	9,652	12,917	4,064	24,469	125,000	.0022	52,962	**16**	1,845	**4**	....	**....**	13,181	1,122	7,616	St. Clair
Ste. Genevieve	186	18,153	17,842	17,304	6,821	36,432	314,120	.0049	103,909	**31**	9,305	**20**	....	**....**	13,006	6,082	13,501	Ste. Genevieve
St. Francois**	187	58,648	55,641	14,198	22,390	29,639	832,710	.0163	576,238	**170**	156,268	**332**	18,833	**106**	79,456	47,788	39,152	St. Francois
St. Louis*	189	1,012,010	1,016,315	23,763	419,881	45,642	24,048,260	.4165	15,821,758	**4,654**	2,258,961	**4,795**	654,144	**3,666**	2,241,869	1,093,563	728,515	St. Louis
Saline**	195	22,609	23,756	15,228	8,764	31,105	344,280	.0059	159,186	**47**	21,778	**46**	2,730	**15**	36,558	13,793	15,112	Saline
Schuyler**	197	4,220	4,170	13,983	1,754	26,607	59,010	.0010	26,641	**8**	....	**....**	....	**....**	4,008	....	3,367	Schuyler
Scotland	199	4,882	4,983	12,403	1,815	26,324	60,550	.0011	24,478	**7**	....	**....**	....	**....**	4,653	1,263	3,572	Scotland
Scott**	201	40,908	40,422	14,552	16,037	29,617	595,310	.0115	401,222	**118**	56,889	**121**	16,108	**90**	57,953	27,968	26,983	Scott
Shannon	203	8,283	8,324	10,474	3,352	20,410	86,760	.0016	27,473	**8**	5,802	**12**	....	**....**	7,025	2,627	6,134	Shannon
Shelby	205	6,675	6,799	14,124	2,698	27,520	94,280	.0016	35,513	**10**	....	**....**	....	**....**	4,384	1,810	5,109	Shelby
Stoddard	207	29,601	29,705	13,438	12,197	25,859	397,790	.0083	319,840	**94**	27,685	**59**	1,953	**11**	46,181	23,888	21,288	Stoddard
Stone**	209	30,341	28,658	16,011	12,508	30,689	485,790	.0078	173,746	**51**	50,594	**107**	....	**....**	33,178	6,938	23,399	Stone
Sullivan	211	7,034	7,219	12,920	2,885	25,293	90,880	.0017	53,309	**16**	1,222	**3**	....	**....**	6,706	4,333	5,294	Sullivan
Taney**	213	41,899	39,703	14,986	17,074	29,231	627,880	.0134	567,403	**167**	86,088	**183**	82,216	**461**	66,456	24,592	29,792	Taney
Texas	215	24,520	23,003	11,813	9,717	23,487	289,650	.0056	158,377	**47**	14,100	**30**	2,930	**16**	24,490	7,935	17,890	Texas
Vernon	217	20,237	20,454	13,958	7,910	28,247	282,470	.0053	166,932	**49**	28,926	**61**	2,407	**14**	22,559	28,744	14,770	Vernon
Warren*	219	27,570	24,525	18,240	10,486	38,404	502,890	.0086	271,022	**80**	36,959	**78**	23,318	**131**	28,823	15,634	21,260	Warren
Washington*	221	24,034	23,344	12,036	8,902	25,789	289,280	.0053	135,333	**40**	18,151	**39**	....	**....**	28,896	1,149	16,248	Washington
Wayne	223	13,033	13,259	12,498	5,556	22,852	162,880	.0030	74,147	**22**	7,813	**17**	....	**....**	16,507	5,917	9,668	Wayne
Webster*	225	33,748	31,045	13,804	12,268	30,276	465,870	.0081	205,189	**60**	20,219	**43**	....	**....**	32,080	5,449	23,587	Webster
Worth	227	2,235	2,382	13,861	940	26,146	30,980	.0005	6,926	**2**	....	**....**	....	**....**	....	....	1,887	Worth
Wright	229	18,258	17,955	11,945	7,248	23,848	218,090	.0045	157,894	**46**	41,525	**88**	....	**....**	16,994	8,298	13,153	Wright

Source: Devonshire Associates Ltd. and Scan/US, Inc. 2004.
* Component of a Metropolitan Core Based Statistical Area.
** Component of a Micropolitan Core Based Statistical Area.

.... Data less than 1,000.

(d) Data not available.

Counties: Population / Income / Sales, *Continued*

COUNTY OR COUNTY EQUIVALENT	FIPS CO. CODE	POPULATION Estimate 7/1/04	POPULATION Census 4/1/00	PER CAPITA INCOME 2003	HOUSEHOLDS Estimate 7/1/04	MEDIAN HOUSEHOLD INCOME 2003	DISPOSABLE INCOME 2003 ($1,000)	MARKET ABILITY INDEX 2003	TOTAL RETAIL SALES Sales 2003 ($1,000)	TOTAL RETAIL SALES Ranally Sales Units	GENERAL MERCHANDISE Sales 2003 ($1,000)	GENERAL MERCHANDISE Ranally Sales Units	APPAREL STORE Sales 2003 ($1,000)	APPAREL STORE Ranally Sales Units	FOOD STORE SALES 2003 ($1,000)	HEALTH & DRUG STORE 2003 ($1,000)	PASSENGER CAR REGIS-TRATIONS 2003	COUNTY OR COUNTY EQUIVALENT
INDEPENDENT CITY																		
St. Louis*	510	327,502	348,189	15,141	150,947	25,961	4,958,610	.0875	2,531,321	**745**	248,810	**528**	81,582	**457**	412,334	255,453	173,755	St. Louis
The State		5,737,314	5,595,211	18,500	2,318,958	35,927	106,139,620	1.8883	65,707,730	**19,332**	10,192,466	**21,631**	1,925,945	**10,793**	8,623,093	3,620,047	4,061,108	The State
MONTANA (MT; CODE 30; 56 Counties)																		
Beaverhead	001	8,827	9,202	14,390	3,616	27,680	127,020	.0025	91,904	**27**	....	....	3,156	**18**	19,463	2,719	7,196	Beaverhead
Big Horn	003	12,967	12,671	10,275	4,058	26,069	133,240	.0026	68,313	**20**	....	....	....	....	17,262	....	7,235	Big Horn
Blaine	005	6,645	7,009	10,969	2,364	24,525	72,890	.0014	35,745	**11**	....	....	....	....	8,146	1,709	4,525	Blaine
Broadwater	007	4,449	4,385	15,678	1,806	31,306	69,750	.0010	14,557	**4**	....	....	....	....	4,479	....	4,015	Broadwater
Carbon*	009	9,840	9,552	16,816	4,278	30,720	165,470	.0025	45,458	**13**	....	....	....	....	7,606	1,828	8,846	Carbon
Carter	011	1,327	1,360	12,931	533	25,395	17,160	.0003	2,521	**1**	....	....	....	....	....	....	1,330	Carter
Cascade*	013	79,349	80,357	16,141	32,601	31,047	1,280,800	.0252	989,385	**291**	223,772	**475**	22,782	**128**	109,989	41,908	60,061	Cascade
Chouteau	015	5,447	5,970	13,081	2,016	28,459	71,250	.0013	34,103	**10**	....	....	....	....	4,938	1,452	4,469	Chouteau
Custer	017	11,271	11,696	14,812	4,648	28,524	166,950	.0035	151,695	**45**	27,222	**58**	6,235	**35**	28,566	3,710	9,114	Custer
Daniels	019	1,916	2,017	15,230	878	26,334	29,180	.0006	27,366	**8**	....	....	....	....	7,365	2,410	1,844	Daniels
Dawson	021	8,688	9,059	15,229	3,572	29,298	132,310	.0025	89,123	**26**	7,297	**16**	1,262	**7**	6,578	9,264	7,249	Dawson
Deer Lodge	023	8,812	9,417	14,441	3,941	25,970	127,250	.0023	63,005	**19**	....	....	....	....	18,733	6,795	7,134	Deer Lodge
Fallon	025	2,733	2,837	14,885	1,133	28,259	40,680	.0008	33,035	**10**	1,169	**2**	....	....	8,830	3,944	2,460	Fallon
Fergus	027	11,628	11,893	15,097	4,877	28,464	175,550	.0033	110,302	**32**	6,873	**15**	3,617	**20**	21,691	3,626	10,113	Fergus
Flathead**	029	81,063	74,471	16,408	32,674	32,152	1,330,090	.0258	998,648	**294**	208,225	**442**	19,172	**107**	142,619	23,731	65,277	Flathead
Gallatin**	031	74,887	67,831	17,735	29,421	35,726	1,328,150	.0263	1,096,297	**322**	123,460	**262**	34,160	**191**	175,338	27,195	60,863	Gallatin
Garfield	033	1,222	1,279	13,732	538	24,795	16,780	.0003	5,843	**2**	....	....	....	....	3,204	1,154	1,293	Garfield
Glacier	035	13,264	13,247	10,786	4,308	26,297	143,070	.0029	84,292	**25**	2,133	**5**	4,095	**23**	25,412	....	7,433	Glacier
Golden Valley	037	1,055	1,042	11,374	372	25,459	12,000	.0002	1,545	**0**	....	....	....	....	1,161	....	792	Golden Valley
Granite	039	2,912	2,830	14,811	1,251	27,068	43,130	.0007	16,283	**5**	....	....	....	....	4,407	....	2,577	Granite
Hill**	041	16,257	16,673	14,454	6,408	29,237	234,980	.0046	162,898	**48**	24,381	**52**	6,964	**39**	33,234	3,026	12,273	Hill
Jefferson**	043	10,637	10,049	18,372	4,005	37,055	195,420	.0026	25,094	**7**	....	....	....	....	9,174	1,312	9,251	Jefferson
Judith Basin	045	2,146	2,329	13,984	874	27,298	30,010	.0005	5,039	**1**	....	....	....	....	2,120	....	2,108	Judith Basin
Lake	047	27,385	26,507	13,517	10,678	27,522	370,150	.0071	232,025	**68**	28,072	**60**	1,330	**7**	49,024	7,853	21,804	Lake
Lewis and Clark**	049	57,554	55,716	18,475	23,990	35,161	1,063,310	.0198	753,024	**222**	128,558	**273**	11,123	**62**	126,141	20,534	46,533	Lewis and Clark
Liberty	051	2,025	2,158	14,262	788	28,971	28,880	.0005	11,840	**3**	....	....	....	....	5,907	1,194	1,673	Liberty
Lincoln	053	18,832	18,837	13,859	8,030	25,645	261,000	.0045	112,378	**33**	7,860	**17**	1,293	**7**	28,722	5,041	15,300	Lincoln
McCone	055	1,771	1,977	15,195	751	28,563	26,910	.0004	8,758	**3**	....	....	....	....	2,058	....	1,809	McCone
Madison	057	6,998	6,851	15,976	3,094	28,733	111,800	.0018	35,065	**10**	....	....	....	....	10,634	3,318	6,426	Madison
Meagher	059	1,978	1,932	14,191	825	26,718	28,070	.0005	8,863	**3**	....	....	....	....	1,095	1,267	1,606	Meagher
Mineral	061	3,884	3,884	13,973	1,620	26,218	54,270	.0010	28,371	**8**	....	....	....	....	8,146	....	3,183	Mineral
Missoula*	063	99,453	95,802	16,676	40,452	32,609	1,658,450	.0346	1,528,262	**450**	329,816	**700**	38,925	**218**	173,741	41,515	77,751	Missoula
Musselshell	065	4,453	4,497	13,187	1,884	25,113	58,720	.0010	15,829	**5**	....	....	....	....	7,041	1,076	4,033	Musselshell
Park	067	15,876	15,694	16,937	7,148	30,274	268,890	.0047	142,105	**42**	6,159	**13**	2,976	**17**	16,953	6,054	13,473	Park
Petroleum	069	491	493	13,075	215	22,829	6,420	.0001	....	....	....	....	....	....	....	....	471	Petroleum
Phillips	071	4,180	4,601	14,232	1,717	27,302	59,490	.0011	36,611	**11**	....	....	....	....	7,117	1,036	3,604	Phillips
Pondera	073	6,096	6,424	13,401	2,286	28,211	81,690	.0017	61,269	**18**	1,092	**2**	....	....	9,029	3,654	4,776	Pondera
Powder River	075	1,826	1,858	13,894	733	27,378	25,370	.0004	11,932	**4**	....	....	....	....	6,275	....	1,858	Powder River
Powell	077	6,948	7,180	12,311	2,348	28,895	85,540	.0014	20,602	**6**	....	....	....	....	9,747	....	4,697	Powell
Prairie	079	1,143	1,199	14,488	532	24,472	16,560	.0003	5,985	**2**	....	....	....	....	1,068	....	1,227	Prairie
Ravalli	081	39,433	36,070	15,404	15,776	30,672	607,440	.0105	285,375	**84**	33,173	**70**	5,035	**28**	81,250	9,805	32,647	Ravalli
Richland	083	9,002	9,667	15,708	3,737	30,106	141,400	.0027	92,895	**27**	4,631	**10**	4,540	**25**	17,981	5,621	7,469	Richland
Roosevelt	085	10,393	10,620	10,250	3,525	23,811	106,530	.0022	68,759	**20**	....	....	1,771	**10**	14,522	2,086	6,418	Roosevelt
Rosebud	087	9,275	9,383	15,286	3,351	33,432	141,780	.0023	55,235	**16**	....	....	....	....	11,204	....	6,848	Rosebud
Sanders	089	10,521	10,227	13,892	4,539	25,590	146,160	.0024	48,228	**14**	....	....	....	....	17,395	1,516	9,307	Sanders
Sheridan	091	3,540	4,105	15,274	1,534	27,798	54,070	.0010	31,992	**9**	....	....	....	....	7,765	1,958	3,216	Sheridan
Silver Bow**	093	32,777	34,606	16,349	14,828	28,916	535,880	.0110	471,473	**139**	73,057	**155**	28,009	**157**	72,264	17,984	26,979	Silver Bow
Stillwater	095	8,536	8,195	18,254	3,414	36,018	155,820	.0024	55,693	**16**	....	....	....	....	6,909	1,491	7,638	Stillwater
Sweet Grass	097	3,593	3,609	16,165	1,473	31,179	58,080	.0011	44,082	**13**	....	....	....	....	4,902	1,207	3,007	Sweet Grass
Teton	099	6,345	6,445	14,249	2,509	28,628	90,410	.0017	59,039	**17**	....	....	....	....	5,515	2,106	5,475	Teton
Toole	101	5,364	5,267	13,041	1,934	28,634	69,950	.0013	33,776	**10**	8,016	**17**	....	....	7,866	1,362	3,805	Toole
Treasure	103	699	861	14,592	298	26,828	10,200	.0002	2,711	**1**	....	....	....	....	....	....	642	Treasure
Valley	105	7,254	7,675	15,471	3,030	29,316	112,230	.0020	65,129	**19**	2,629	**6**	2,085	**12**	14,168	3,683	6,390	Valley
Wheatland	107	2,060	2,259	11,451	777	24,028	23,590	.0005	12,498	**4**	....	....	....	....	3,805	....	1,609	Wheatland
Wibaux	109	947	1,068	13,464	377	27,071	12,750	.0002	1,028	**0**	....	....	....	....	....	....	832	Wibaux
Yellowstone*	111	134,394	129,352	17,704	54,783	34,508	2,379,280	.0484	2,120,345	**624**	389,726	**827**	70,846	**397**	212,932	63,204	102,211	Yellowstone
The State		922,368	902,195	16,039	373,148	31,423	14,794,220	.2845	10,614,488	**3,122**	1,640,523	**3,483**	279,805	**1,566**	1,604,676	344,921	732,175	The State
NEBRASKA (NE; CODE 31; 93 Counties)																		
Adams**	001	30,797	31,151	16,470	12,011	34,485	507,240	.0097	361,195	**106**	60,107	**128**	7,507	**42**	75,517	22,384	22,858	Adams
Antelope	003	7,135	7,452	13,929	2,872	28,329	99,380	.0018	55,087	**16**	....	....	....	....	7,033	....	5,984	Antelope
Arthur	005	384	444	13,490	161	26,180	5,180	.0001	....	....	....	....	....	....	....	....	372	Arthur
Banner**	007	758	819	14,525	295	30,444	11,010	.0001	....	....	....	....	....	....	....	....	742	Banner
Blaine	009	518	583	12,413	213	24,558	6,430	.0001	....	....	....	....	....	....	....	....	495	Blaine
Boone	011	5,828	6,259	14,242	2,302	29,739	83,000	.0018	74,113	**22**	1,772	**4**	....	....	3,601	2,181	4,874	Boone
Box Butte	013	11,523	12,158	18,092	4,636	36,441	208,470	.0036	112,547	**33**	13,029	**28**	2,014	**11**	21,785	4,789	9,363	Box Butte
Boyd	015	2,299	2,438	12,923	964	25,000	29,710	.0005	10,913	**3**	....	....	....	....	2,472	....	2,058	Boyd
Brown	017	3,480	3,525	14,641	1,547	26,825	50,950	.0010	32,023	**9**	....	....	....	....	3,099	1,091	3,015	Brown
Buffalo**	019	43,282	42,259	16,139	16,495	34,807	698,510	.0146	639,416	**188**	140,859	**299**	25,358	**142**	63,638	27,591	34,138	Buffalo
Burt	021	7,486	7,791	15,854	3,035	31,839	118,680	.0021	58,700	**17**	....	....	....	....	3,910	3,977	6,119	Burt
Butler	023	8,909	8,767	16,610	3,534	34,128	147,980	.0023	42,224	**12**	....	....	....	....	10,136	1,818	7,818	Butler
Cass*	025	25,522	24,334	19,751	9,717	42,326	504,090	.0076	174,172	**51**	10,728	**23**	....	....	18,042	5,991	21,140	Cass
Cedar	027	9,130	9,615	14,652	3,497	31,242	133,770	.0025	81,914	**24**	....	....	....	....	6,001	2,291	7,246	Cedar
Chase	029	4,039	4,068	15,699	1,687	30,617	63,410	.0013	57,249	**17**	....	....	....	....	7,314	....	3,442	Chase
Cherry	031	6,023	6,148	14,400	2,515	28,016	86,730	.0019	86,265	**25**	8,313	**18**	2,555	**14**	16,185	1,318	5,302	Cherry
Cheyenne	033	9,975	9,830	15,996	4,169	31,261	159,560	.0110	1,012,734	**298**	30,463	**65**	3,993	**22**	31,807	21,871	7,854	Cheyenne
Clay**	035	6,851	7,039	15,531	2,692	32,176	106,400	.0019	58,214	**17**	....	....	....	....	11,452	....	5,726	Clay
Colfax	037	10,513	10,441	13,874	3,554	33,456	145,860	.0028	98,632	**29**	1,087	**2**	....	....	15,472	3,097	7,178	Colfax
Cuming	039	9,760	10,203	14,980	3,792	31,425	146,200	.0030	120,370	**35**	3,942	**8**	1,177	**7**	18,160	6,127	7,640	Cuming
Custer	041	11,457	11,793	14,593	4,712	29,000	167,190	.0032	110,075	**32**	6,544	**14**	....	....	20,735	11,357	9,957	Custer
Dakota*	043	20,562	20,253	15,254	7,114	35,638	313,650	.0052	128,596	**38**	19,521	**41**	....	....	37,571	8,238	13,290	Dakota
Dawes	045	8,970	9,060	13,540	3,536	27,682	121,450	.0029	137,012	**40**	27,104	**58**	1,885	**11**	22,762	7,613	7,260	Dawes
Dawson**	047	24,659	24,365	14,540	8,662	33,675	358,530	.0070	249,062	**73**	31,743	**67**	3,724	**21**	41,754	14,836	17,246	Dawson
Deuel	049	2,035	2,098	16,948	900	31,279	34,490	.0006	21,619	**6**	1,012	**2**	....	....	3,738	1,169	1,922	Deuel
Dixon*	051	6,057	6,339	15,059	2,302	32,248	91,210	.0014	23,754	**7**	....	....	....	....	5,056	1,256	4,872	Dixon
Dodge**	053	35,869	36,160	17,043	14,452	34,636	611,320	.0141	724,006	**213**	112,137	**238**	15,239	**85**	69,590	45,176	26,840	Dodge
Douglas*	055	480,743	463,585	19,874	195,621	40,406	9,554,330	.1828	7,643,874	**2,249**	893,521	**1,897**	317,534	**1,780**	1,014,835	438,791	333,093	Douglas
Dundy	057	2,202	2,292	13,483	926	26,247	29,690	.0005	15,116	**4**	....	....	....	....	2,246	....	1,937	Dundy
Fillmore	059	6,362	6,634	16,323	2,599	32,841	103,850	.0018	49,277	**14**	1,317	**3**	....	....	4,461	2,806	5,301	Fillmore
Franklin	061	3,407	3,574	14,071	1,409	27,684	47,940	.0008	15,910	**5**	....	....	....	....	5,368	....	3,147	Franklin
Frontier	063	2,845	3,099	14,467	1,098	30,703	41,160	.0006	8,092	**2**	....	....	....	....	1,347	....	2,501	Frontier
Furnas	065	5,161	5,324	14,962	2,208	28,418	77,220	.0015	52,488	**15**	....	....	....	....	5,385	....	4,419	Furnas
Gage**	067	23,489	22,993	16,395	9,606	32,722	385,100	.0069	221,319	**65**	25,785	**55**	6,921	**39**	34,819	13,124	19,011	Gage
Garden	069	2,165	2,292	14,088	983	25,435	30,500	.0005	12,073	**4**	....	....	....	....	3,517	....	2,098	Garden
Garfield	071	1,823	1,902	13,758	796	25,722	25,080	.0006	34,908	**10**	....	....	....	....	....	....	1,659	Garfield
Gosper**	073	2,072	2,143	17,042	837	34,447	35,310	.0005	2,849	**1**	....	....	....	....	....	....	1,886	Gosper
Grant	075	678	747	15,413	264	32,097	10,450	.0002	3,377	**1**	....	....	....	....	....	....	612	Grant
Greeley	077	2,570	2,714	13,440	1,039	27,020	34,540	.0008	41,016	**12**	....	....	....	....	2,483	....	2,260	Greeley
Hall**	079	54,556	53,534	16,108	20,712	34,901	878,810	.0193	902,645	**266**	245,907	**522**	36,199	**203**	56,139	26,966	39,188	Hall
Hamilton	081	9,507	9,403	17,033	3,559	37,100	161,930	.0024	42,040	**12**	....	....	....	....	3,184	3,379	7,808	Hamilton
Harlan	083	3,627	3,786	14,852	1,537	28,627	53,870	.0009	22,616	**7**	....	....	....	....	3,423	1,056	3,290	Harlan
Hayes	085	1,114	1,068	12,630	453	25,247	14,070	.0002	1,300	**0**	....	....	....	....	1,119	....	1,083	Hayes
Hitchcock	087	3,008	3,111	13,949	1,268	26,252	41,960	.0007	17,101	**5**	....	....	....	....	2,263	....	2,803	Hitchcock
Holt	089	10,942	11,551	14,492	4,476	29,000	158,570	.0033	129,523	**38**	13,358	**28**	2,067	**12**	13,626	15,955	9,235	Holt
Hooker	091	723	783	14,219	310	26,704	10,280	.0002	3,280	**1**	....	....	....	....	....	....	713	Hooker
Howard**	093	6,658	6,567	15,074	2,592	31,592	100,360	.0016	35,794	**11**	....	....	....	....	2,841	....	5,694	Howard
Jefferson	095	7,999	8,333	15,733	3,419	30,229	125,850	.0023	79,651	**23**	13,610	**29**	....	....	13,072	....	6,941	Jefferson
Johnson	097	4,410	4,488	15,902	1,859	30,700	70,130	.0012	38,503	**11**	....	....	....	....	5,769	....	3,857	Johnson
Kearney**	099	6,855	6,882	17,275	2,646	36,300	118,420	.0018	31,694	**9**	....	....	....	....	6,555	1,033	5,872	Kearney
Keith	101	8,347	8,875	16,056	3,550	30,848	134,020	.0029	136,043	**40**	12,529	**27**	1,719	**10**	15,898	7,098	7,291	Keith
Keya Paha	103	945	983	12,201	396	23,577	11,530	.0002	2,637	**1**	....	....	....	....	....	....	966	Keya Paha
Kimball	105	3,786	4,089	15,161	1,629	28,708	57,400	.0010	28,409	**8**	....	....	....	....	4,005	1,015	3,380	Kimball
Knox	107	8,959	9,374	13,075	3,663	26,087	117,140	.0025	93,833	**28**	1,281	**3**	....	....	15,294	3,198	7,186	Knox
Lancaster*	109	264,249	250,291	19,213	107,177	39,122	5,076,970	.0902	3,206,420	**943**	559,295	**1,187**	111,717	**626**	493,547	221,103	193,074	Lancaster
Lincoln**	111	34,850	34,632	17,399	14,443	34,055	606,350	.0111	393,809	**116**	91,544	**194**	8,759	**49**	50,742	22,329	29,298	Lincoln
Logan**	113	691	774	16,093	296	30,588	11,120	.0002	1,313	**0**	....	....	....	....	....	....	761	Logan
Loup	115	754	712	12,294	306	24,696	9,270	.0002	2,197	**1**	....	....	....	....	....	....	730	Loup
McPherson**	117	546	533	11,355	204	24,776	6,200	.0001	1,276	**0**	....	....	....	....	....	....	510	McPherson
Madison**	119	35,979	35,226	15,771	13,831	33,506	567,430	.0130	638,121	**188**	137,773	**292**	23,297	**131**	82,246	26,295	25,603	Madison
Merrick**	121	8,122	8,204	15,669	3,204	32,422	127,260	.0020	40,029	**12**	....	....	....	....	4,139	....	6,757	Merrick
Morrill	123	5,232	5,440	13,807	2,073	28,431	72,240	.0013	31,358	**9**	2,776	**6**	....	....	8,213	....	4,471	Morrill
Nance	125	3,646	4,038	14,361	1,441	29,979	52,360	.0008	16,451	**5**	....	....	....	....	4,028	....	3,104	Nance
Nemaha	127	6,998	7,576	15,332	2,857	31,033	107,290	.0021	74,421	**22**	4,811	**10**	....	....	15,782	8,922	5,707	Nemaha
Nuckolls	129	4,781	5,057	14,991	2,151	27,102	71,670	.0014	55,639	**16**	5,041	**11**	....	....	10,086	1,264	4,390	Nuckolls
Otoe	131	15,529	15,396	16,920	6,091	35,251	262,750	.0044	125,661	**37**	1,610	**3**	11,386	**64**	19,275	10,662	12,251	Otoe
Pawnee	133	2,865	3,087	14,754	1,251	27,518	42,270	.0007	12,327	**4**	....	....	....	....	....	2,001	2,564	Pawnee
Perkins	135	3,018	3,200	15,987	1,224	32,202	48,250	.0008	14,970	**4**	....	....	....	....	....	....	2,684	Perkins
Phelps	137	9,593	9,747	17,079	3,808	35,116	163,840	.0030	106,424	**31**	3,056	**6**	....	....	17,644	10,318	8,141	Phelps
Pierce**	139	7,667	7,857	14,133	2,920	30,489	108,360	.0020	65,102	**19**	....	....	....	....	7,798	....	6,273	Pierce
Platte**	141	31,085	31,662	17,240	12,023	36,373	535,900	.0099	357,800	**105**	54,815	**116**	10,675	**60**	59,638	22,221	23,638	Platte
Polk	143	5,433	5,639	17,425	2,194	35,083	94,670	.0015	30,621	**9**	....	....	....	....	6,736	2,060	4,664	Polk
Red Willow	145	11,185	11,448	15,643	4,650	30,889	174,970	.0044	239,972	**71**	55,012	**117**	6,137	**34**	28,056	14,557	9,376	Red Willow
Richardson	147	8,845	9,531	14,346	3,709	27,878	126,890	.0024	75,097	**22**	3,943	**8**	....	....	12,426	6,079	7,265	Richardson
Rock	149	1,567	1,756	13,555	710	24,157	21,240	.0004	6,777	**2**	....	....	....	....	....	....	1,490	Rock
Saline	151	14,298	13,843	15,338	5,323	33,558	219,300	.0038	105,011	**31**	4,211	**9**	....	....	17,279	6,897	11,437	Saline
Sarpy*	153	135,564	122,595	21,890	50,439	48,759	2,967,530	.0447	1,116,828	**329**	286,952	**609**	24,881	**139**	152,897	51,018	103,463	Sarpy
Saunders*	155	20,059	19,830	18,106	7,634	38,882	363,190	.0056	125,553	**37**	4,399	**9**	1,235	**7**	27,699	3,977	16,535	Saunders
Scotts Bluff**	157	36,941	36,951	15,034	15,085	30,227	555,380	.0115	473,877	**139**	104,077	**221**	13,486	**76**	66,354	12,506	28,209	Scotts Bluff
Seward*	159	16,717	16,496	17,706	6,144	39,447	295,990	.0047	110,445	**32**	17,866	**38**	....	....	5,179	6,161	13,154	Seward
Sheridan	161	5,689	6,198	14,284	2,393	27,729	81,260	.0017	67,482	**20**	5,220	**11**	....	....	16,461	1,108	4,880	Sheridan
Sherman	163	3,073	3,318	14,390	1,337	26,873	44,220	.0008	24,021	**7**	....	....	....	....	6,319	1,339	2,715	Sherman
Sioux	165	1,497	1,475	14,349	623	28,184	21,480	.0003	2,684	**1**	....	....	....	....	....	....	1,424	Sioux
Stanton**	167	6,634	6,455	15,303	2,394	34,881	101,520	.0014	11,715	**3**	....	....	....	....	1,667	....	5,366	Stanton
Thayer	169	5,540	6,055	15,094	2,354	29,074	83,620	.0016	61,801	**18**	....	....	....	....	9,702	....	4,795	Thayer
Thomas	171	649	729	15,886	312	26,816	10,310	.0002	5,725	**2**	....	....	....	....	....	....	711	Thomas
Thurston	173	7,129	7,171	10,130	2,196	26,604	72,220	.0016	55,629	**16**	....	....	....	....	8,132	1,893	4,098	Thurston
Valley	175	4,547	4,647	13,857	1,938	26,713	63,010	.0011	29,701	**9**	3,184	**7**	....	....	4,504	....	3,870	Valley

Source: Devonshire Associates Ltd. and Scan/US, Inc. 2004.
* Component of a Metropolitan Core Based Statistical Area.
** Component of a Micropolitan Core Based Statistical Area.

.... Data less than 1,000.

(d) Data not available.

continued on next page

Counties: Population / Income / Sales, *Continued*

COUNTY OR COUNTY EQUIVALENT	FIPS CO. CODE	POPULATION Estimate 7/1/04	POPULATION Census 4/1/00	PER CAPITA INCOME 2003	HOUSEHOLDS Estimate 7/1/04	MEDIAN HOUSEHOLD INCOME 2003	DISPOSABLE INCOME 2003 ($1,000)	MARKET ABILITY INDEX 2003	TOTAL RETAIL SALES Sales 2003 ($1,000)	TOTAL RETAIL SALES Ranally Sales Units	GENERAL MERCHANDISE Sales 2003 ($1,000)	GENERAL MERCHANDISE Ranally Sales Units	APPAREL STORE Sales 2003 ($1,000)	APPAREL STORE Ranally Sales Units	FOOD STORE SALES 2003 ($1,000)	HEALTH & DRUG STORE 2003 ($1,000)	PASSENGER CAR REGIS-TRATIONS 2003	COUNTY OR COUNTY EQUIVALENT
Washington*	177	19,987	18,780	19,965	7,449	44,033	399,040	.0085	415,845	**122**	20,291	**43**	10,422	**58**	46,755	28,045	15,998	Washington
Wayne	179	9,367	9,851	12,884	3,262	30,350	120,680	.0022	64,423	**19**	4,222	**9**	1,222	**7**	12,715	6,125	6,914	Wayne
Webster	181	3,807	4,061	14,652	1,615	28,152	55,780	.0010	27,836	**8**	....	**....**	....	**....**	4,455	....	3,403	Webster
Wheeler	183	801	886	13,221	328	26,191	10,590	.0002	2,157	**1**	....	**....**	....	**....**	....	....	731	Wheeler
York	185	14,292	14,598	16,830	5,658	34,828	240,530	.0051	236,993	**70**	32,484	**69**	4,333	**24**	31,896	10,559	11,112	York
The State		1,748,000	1,711,263	17,982	693,868	37,045	31,432,860	.5900	22,569,932	**6,633**	3,089,792	**6,560**	674,009	**3,779**	2,972,244	1,198,067	1,319,548	The State
NEVADA (NV; CODE 32; 16 Counties, 1 Independent City)																		
Churchill**	001	25,027	23,982	17,881	9,289	38,243	447,510	.0075	217,654	**64**	19,331	**41**	....	**....**	44,862	7,606	18,752	Churchill
Clark*	003	1,637,622	1,375,765	19,574	620,349	41,939	32,054,670	.5564	19,011,943	**5,593**	2,590,700	**5,500**	1,238,316	**6,940**	2,927,642	777,477	1,010,299	Clark
Douglas**	005	44,993	41,259	23,820	18,169	46,965	1,071,730	.0148	277,567	**82**	....	**....**	1,883	**11**	92,066	17,596	38,306	Douglas
Elko**	007	43,706	45,291	18,883	14,965	44,135	825,290	.0138	421,441	**124**	45,268	**96**	11,004	**62**	93,308	26,021	29,347	Elko
Esmeralda	009	823	971	19,113	397	31,639	15,730	.0002	....	**....**	....	**....**	....	**....**	....	....	726	Esmeralda
Eureka**	011	1,473	1,651	19,280	596	37,788	28,400	.0004	3,145	**1**	....	**....**	....	**....**	....	....	1,188	Eureka
Humboldt	013	14,324	16,106	19,273	5,083	43,218	276,070	.0050	185,401	**55**	4,259	**9**	1,081	**6**	14,774	7,904	10,345	Humboldt
Lander	015	4,845	5,794	19,174	1,769	41,722	92,900	.0014	26,845	**8**	....	**....**	....	**....**	6,790	4,231	3,544	Lander
Lincoln	017	4,293	4,165	14,757	1,633	30,948	63,350	.0010	15,619	**5**	....	**....**	....	**....**	2,428	4,336	2,870	Lincoln
Lyon	019	41,870	34,501	17,796	15,747	37,513	745,100	.0115	246,227	**72**	1,808	**4**	....	**....**	64,876	12,114	32,672	Lyon
Mineral	021	4,720	5,071	17,356	2,133	30,417	81,920	.0013	25,164	**7**	....	**....**	....	**....**	3,869	....	3,968	Mineral
Nye**	023	36,650	32,485	17,695	15,220	33,699	648,510	.0100	218,402	**64**	1,081	**2**	....	**....**	44,883	39,702	29,767	Nye
Pershing	027	6,371	6,693	13,557	1,831	37,114	86,370	.0015	31,032	**9**	....	**....**	....	**....**	1,991	....	3,552	Pershing
Storey*	029	3,551	3,399	23,644	1,559	42,868	83,960	.0010	8,895	**3**	....	**....**	....	**....**	....	....	3,155	Storey
Washoe*	031	380,688	339,486	20,389	147,051	42,063	7,761,940	.1365	4,927,460	**1,449**	767,107	**1,628**	165,864	**930**	743,396	194,817	266,228	Washoe
White Pine	033	8,315	9,181	16,120	3,010	35,294	134,040	.0021	42,651	**13**	....	**....**	2,043	**11**	10,205	6,209	5,763	White Pine
INDEPENDENT CITY																		
Carson City*	510	56,233	52,457	18,970	21,701	38,794	1,066,760	.0212	927,961	**273**	53,850	**114**	1,745	**10**	156,266	105,836	39,250	Carson City
The State		2,315,504	1,998,257	19,643	880,502	41,908	45,484,250	.7856	26,588,237	**7,822**	3,484,703	**7,396**	1,425,802	**7,992**	4,208,328	1,204,678	1,499,732	The State
NEW HAMPSHIRE (NH; CODE 33; 10 Counties)																		
Belknap**	001	61,617	56,325	20,172	25,132	40,283	1,242,950	.0242	1,052,485	**310**	155,884	**331**	62,392	**350**	186,108	33,393	45,555	Belknap
Carroll	003	46,872	43,666	19,671	20,090	37,060	922,010	.0171	674,578	**198**	29,856	**63**	71,228	**399**	147,168	22,507	37,381	Carroll
Cheshire**	005	76,625	73,825	18,949	29,903	39,390	1,452,000	.0307	1,460,285	**430**	155,972	**331**	29,843	**167**	230,684	51,633	55,507	Cheshire
Coos**	007	32,972	33,111	16,887	14,290	31,583	556,810	.0118	540,180	**159**	13,272	**28**	5,042	**28**	85,706	27,709	23,720	Coos
Grafton**	009	84,766	81,743	18,922	33,469	38,837	1,603,970	.0331	1,525,253	**449**	155,045	**329**	43,193	**242**	361,211	59,291	58,750	Grafton
Hillsborough*	011	398,775	380,841	22,726	152,823	48,238	9,062,560	.1736	7,717,723	**2,270**	1,155,385	**2,453**	304,995	**1,709**	1,064,120	259,831	279,600	Hillsborough
Merrimack**	013	145,924	136,225	20,996	56,552	44,028	3,063,870	.0570	2,326,480	**684**	249,001	**529**	55,269	**310**	401,747	95,346	104,060	Merrimack
Rockingham*	015	293,899	277,359	24,646	112,432	52,040	7,243,540	.1402	6,516,590	**1,917**	1,281,686	**2,721**	303,054	**1,698**	1,053,560	207,457	220,506	Rockingham
Strafford*	017	119,427	112,233	19,613	46,188	41,151	2,342,330	.0421	1,554,626	**457**	147,435	**313**	29,181	**164**	343,958	78,897	84,613	Strafford
Sullivan**	019	42,548	40,458	19,716	17,846	38,069	838,890	.0148	524,863	**154**	75,488	**160**	7,748	**43**	114,518	25,863	32,233	Sullivan
The State		1,303,425	1,235,786	21,734	508,725	44,904	28,328,930	.5446	23,893,063	**7,028**	3,419,023	**7,258**	911,944	**5,110**	3,988,780	861,928	941,925	The State
NEW JERSEY (NJ; CODE 34; 21 Counties)																		
Atlantic*	001	266,864	252,552	20,882	100,111	40,608	5,572,680	.0947	3,215,273	**946**	412,580	**876**	217,853	**1,221**	682,910	190,310	148,128	Atlantic
Bergen*	003	901,514	884,118	29,771	337,645	57,565	26,839,400	.4186	14,185,109	**4,173**	1,146,228	**2,433**	1,080,249	**6,054**	2,513,556	912,387	567,867	Bergen
Burlington*	005	450,960	423,394	26,999	168,471	52,354	12,175,570	.1918	6,326,103	**1,861**	681,485	**1,447**	225,239	**1,262**	975,414	352,366	306,025	Burlington
Camden*	007	515,644	508,932	22,547	193,883	43,633	11,626,000	.1904	6,208,300	**1,826**	490,606	**1,041**	357,773	**2,005**	1,098,611	472,331	302,389	Camden
Cape May*	009	101,693	102,326	22,111	42,450	38,602	2,248,490	.0378	1,300,707	**383**	56,977	**121**	99,381	**557**	373,396	94,871	65,228	Cape May
Cumberland*	011	150,283	146,438	17,007	50,856	36,573	2,555,870	.0455	1,488,762	**438**	144,840	**307**	48,684	**273**	322,667	121,082	78,584	Cumberland
Essex*	013	797,608	793,633	20,351	286,063	41,124	16,232,360	.2476	5,999,085	**1,765**	443,360	**941**	634,867	**3,558**	1,434,553	556,838	365,477	Essex
Gloucester*	015	270,847	254,673	24,441	99,146	48,616	6,619,780	.1039	3,193,520	**939**	548,593	**1,165**	201,614	**1,130**	441,088	186,780	180,471	Gloucester
Hudson*	017	606,768	608,975	19,564	230,298	37,691	11,870,940	.1835	4,478,993	**1,318**	376,234	**799**	508,737	**2,851**	872,848	396,886	232,544	Hudson
Hunterdon*	019	130,155	121,989	33,935	47,162	68,391	4,416,860	.0680	2,372,636	**698**	76,807	**163**	105,426	**591**	499,832	107,564	97,541	Hunterdon
Mercer*	021	365,448	350,761	25,680	133,605	50,948	9,384,820	.1447	4,366,020	**1,284**	398,348	**846**	330,116	**1,850**	753,962	416,720	218,377	Mercer
Middlesex*	023	790,283	750,162	26,682	279,135	55,077	21,086,420	.3203	9,535,695	**2,805**	993,678	**2,109**	668,688	**3,748**	1,498,042	545,125	483,989	Middlesex
Monmouth*	025	637,323	615,301	29,858	242,133	57,205	19,028,990	.2853	8,763,022	**2,578**	898,154	**1,907**	616,738	**3,456**	1,699,393	544,526	430,244	Monmouth
Morris*	027	487,077	470,212	33,265	177,679	66,233	16,202,730	.2606	9,892,322	**2,910**	717,571	**1,523**	720,280	**4,037**	1,517,929	581,899	342,536	Morris
Ocean*	029	556,907	510,916	22,970	219,758	42,349	12,792,330	.2037	6,251,600	**1,839**	571,002	**1,212**	283,079	**1,586**	1,327,959	381,234	361,309	Ocean
Passaic*	031	500,842	489,049	20,176	165,703	44,405	10,104,900	.1718	5,698,627	**1,676**	691,748	**1,468**	538,403	**3,017**	952,625	354,527	256,900	Passaic
Salem*	033	65,064	64,285	22,005	24,931	41,888	1,431,740	.0212	495,855	**146**	41,722	**89**	17,221	**97**	102,570	40,166	42,388	Salem
Somerset*	035	315,847	297,490	33,150	115,435	66,254	10,470,420	.1604	5,480,476	**1,612**	473,104	**1,004**	318,208	**1,783**	889,602	260,093	215,721	Somerset
Sussex*	037	153,303	144,166	28,423	54,931	57,704	4,357,290	.0603	1,376,403	**405**	49,545	**105**	23,665	**133**	360,718	69,672	109,146	Sussex
Union*	039	531,425	522,541	24,155	187,611	49,425	12,836,720	.2064	6,714,919	**1,975**	322,651	**685**	315,677	**1,769**	1,223,960	502,225	302,189	Union
Warren*	041	111,301	102,437	26,438	42,375	50,717	2,942,560	.0449	1,341,189	**395**	127,867	**271**	44,375	**249**	287,500	70,195	76,435	Warren
The State		8,707,156	8,414,350	25,358	3,199,381	49,568	220,796,870	3.4614	108,684,617	**31,972**	9,663,099	**20,512**	7,356,272	**41,227**	19,829,135	7,157,799	5,183,488	The State
NEW MEXICO (NM; CODE 35; 33 Counties)																		
Bernalillo*	001	589,389	556,678	19,178	242,179	36,484	11,303,220	.2103	8,213,325	**2,416**	1,543,360	**3,276**	298,070	**1,670**	669,674	458,941	421,677	Bernalillo
Catron	003	3,368	3,543	14,213	1,591	23,222	47,870	.0007	3,706	**1**	1,200	**3**	....	**....**	....	....	3,111	Catron
Chaves**	005	60,348	61,382	13,029	22,431	27,150	786,300	.0152	488,056	**144**	114,371	**243**	20,092	**113**	68,064	32,387	39,003	Chaves
Cibola**	006	26,715	25,595	11,559	8,978	26,471	308,800	.0064	217,822	**64**	12,276	**26**	2,623	**15**	37,952	2,685	16,447	Cibola
Colfax	007	13,995	14,189	15,824	5,904	29,334	221,460	.0041	138,392	**41**	13,481	**29**	3,185	**18**	17,649	6,435	11,076	Colfax
Curry**	009	45,601	45,044	13,774	17,652	27,504	628,110	.0123	431,019	**127**	111,877	**238**	23,920	**134**	52,977	23,063	31,347	Curry
De Baca	011	2,051	2,240	12,969	850	24,570	26,600	.0005	12,461	**4**	....	**....**	....	**....**	3,352	....	1,565	De Baca
Dona Ana*	013	184,554	174,682	12,499	63,683	28,278	2,306,790	.0444	1,344,907	**396**	259,830	**552**	39,961	**224**	154,238	70,219	117,993	Dona Ana
Eddy**	015	51,476	51,658	14,681	19,673	30,124	755,700	.0137	409,266	**120**	76,011	**161**	13,585	**76**	73,217	23,461	35,248	Eddy
Grant**	017	29,459	31,002	14,521	12,045	27,667	427,770	.0078	237,316	**70**	55,606	**118**	6,694	**38**	48,800	7,020	22,192	Grant
Guadalupe	019	4,538	4,680	11,018	1,653	23,034	50,000	.0010	33,052	**10**	....	**....**	....	**....**	2,471	....	2,847	Guadalupe
Harding	021	730	810	15,534	353	24,921	11,340	.0002	7,730	**2**	3,338	**7**	....	**....**	....	....	725	Harding
Hidalgo	023	5,067	5,932	11,441	1,889	23,716	57,970	.0014	68,304	**20**	....	**....**	....	**....**	9,052	1,545	3,358	Hidalgo
Lea**	025	55,610	55,511	13,200	20,136	28,344	734,040	.0144	481,606	**142**	87,874	**187**	16,851	**94**	63,323	23,656	35,788	Lea
Lincoln	027	20,582	19,411	17,755	8,918	31,920	365,430	.0065	224,490	**66**	52,423	**111**	8,846	**50**	38,759	9,095	16,841	Lincoln
Los Alamos**	028	18,970	18,343	36,571	8,079	66,676	693,750	.0081	86,257	**25**	2,333	**5**	2,644	**15**	43,309	2,589	17,196	Los Alamos
Luna**	029	25,978	25,016	9,902	9,758	20,489	257,230	.0061	236,185	**69**	30,874	**66**	2,707	**15**	40,599	2,028	16,435	Luna
McKinley**	031	71,782	74,798	9,083	21,029	23,899	651,980	.0168	708,827	**209**	135,858	**288**	46,949	**263**	102,369	16,868	32,842	McKinley
Mora	033	5,220	5,180	12,209	2,116	22,969	63,730	.0010	10,613	**3**	....	**....**	....	**....**	2,518	....	4,050	Mora
Otero**	035	62,396	62,298	14,103	23,444	29,253	879,990	.0152	375,570	**110**	67,093	**142**	17,309	**97**	54,779	13,480	43,071	Otero
Quay	037	9,452	10,155	13,025	4,011	23,932	123,110	.0027	118,000	**35**	11,994	**25**	1,156	**6**	13,956	8,633	7,087	Quay
Rio Arriba**	039	40,558	41,190	13,681	15,395	27,962	554,880	.0103	309,439	**91**	10,357	**22**	2,321	**13**	62,838	31,798	30,365	Rio Arriba
Roosevelt**	041	18,142	18,018	12,108	6,668	25,560	219,670	.0042	120,937	**36**	9,138	**19**	1,868	**10**	16,384	4,184	12,001	Roosevelt
Sandoval*	043	101,506	89,908	18,961	36,449	41,022	1,924,690	.0268	363,916	**107**	13,213	**28**	14,821	**83**	77,098	15,092	70,130	Sandoval
San Juan*	045	124,961	113,801	13,937	42,462	31,642	1,741,540	.0356	1,362,112	**401**	346,139	**735**	41,368	**232**	147,324	41,633	80,305	San Juan
San Miguel**	047	29,529	30,126	12,494	11,304	25,496	368,930	.0070	199,164	**59**	35,255	**75**	3,521	**20**	41,938	14,441	19,864	San Miguel
Santa Fe*	049	138,622	129,292	20,935	57,574	39,173	2,902,080	.0510	1,871,483	**551**	391,438	**831**	142,197	**797**	198,157	110,379	107,286	Santa Fe
Sierra	051	13,082	13,270	13,872	6,065	23,143	181,470	.0032	81,107	**24**	6,496	**14**	1,413	**8**	24,500	2,465	10,263	Sierra
Socorro	053	18,212	18,078	11,292	6,860	23,063	205,650	.0036	71,137	**21**	2,646	**6**	1,324	**7**	18,615	2,051	11,785	Socorro
Taos**	055	31,667	29,979	14,772	14,093	25,901	467,770	.0085	256,917	**76**	34,734	**74**	17,669	**99**	55,328	10,376	25,512	Taos
Torrance*	057	16,743	16,911	13,348	6,034	29,168	223,490	.0040	102,393	**30**	....	**....**	....	**....**	14,725	3,843	11,581	Torrance
Union	059	3,703	4,174	14,737	1,568	27,085	54,570	.0009	18,592	**5**	1,225	**3**	....	**....**	4,845	....	2,995	Union
Valencia*	061	68,298	66,152	14,208	23,561	31,795	970,360	.0180	559,563	**165**	123,363	**262**	8,216	**46**	97,393	29,109	47,858	Valencia
The State		1,892,304	1,819,046	16,127	724,405	32,551	30,516,290	.5619	19,163,663	**5,640**	3,554,349	**7,547**	741,490	**4,155**	2,256,342	969,660	1,309,844	The State
NEW YORK (NY; CODE 36; 62 Counties)																		
Albany*	001	298,933	294,565	22,046	124,061	40,048	6,590,240	.1152	4,289,265	**1,262**	512,457	**1,088**	331,096	**1,856**	446,094	274,938	183,954	Albany
Allegany	003	50,780	49,927	14,712	18,571	30,266	747,060	.0120	231,119	**68**	17,405	**37**	3,712	**21**	55,964	25,932	30,594	Allegany
Bronx*	005	1,372,845	1,332,650	12,312	475,273	26,489	16,903,080	.2758	4,095,462	**1,205**	309,892	**658**	444,319	**2,490**	1,041,583	661,888	275,811	Bronx
Broome*	007	199,049	200,536	18,215	81,700	33,279	3,625,760	.0642	2,188,690	**644**	350,715	**745**	93,876	**526**	390,801	173,687	125,688	Broome
Cattaraugus**	009	83,168	83,955	16,297	32,394	31,331	1,355,430	.0243	787,989	**232**	125,366	**266**	27,410	**154**	132,840	64,554	52,400	Cattaraugus
Cayuga**	011	81,655	81,963	18,147	31,370	35,369	1,481,790	.0239	629,252	**185**	86,964	**185**	17,404	**98**	113,339	60,237	51,561	Cayuga
Chautauqua**	013	137,003	139,750	16,599	54,280	31,416	2,274,060	.0391	1,147,289	**337**	182,331	**387**	28,227	**158**	227,354	80,263	84,594	Chautauqua
Chemung*	015	90,205	91,070	17,997	35,627	34,145	1,623,380	.0298	1,092,065	**321**	190,558	**405**	53,956	**302**	157,479	68,541	55,785	Chemung
Chenango	017	51,743	51,401	16,744	20,534	31,612	866,370	.0140	341,684	**101**	39,802	**85**	....	**....**	40,274	33,153	34,990	Chenango
Clinton**	019	81,842	79,894	17,614	31,227	34,689	1,441,560	.0255	851,287	**250**	133,135	**283**	47,224	**265**	128,223	52,061	53,122	Clinton
Columbia**	021	63,516	63,094	20,797	25,565	38,871	1,320,970	.0207	563,573	**166**	59,097	**125**	1,117	**6**	125,026	26,548	43,705	Columbia
Cortland**	023	48,729	48,599	16,631	18,762	32,341	810,410	.0152	550,358	**162**	57,678	**122**	7,572	**42**	133,501	30,411	30,856	Cortland
Delaware	025	46,981	48,055	16,977	19,382	30,889	797,590	.0133	367,058	**108**	24,195	**51**	3,412	**19**	56,936	22,905	32,061	Delaware
Dutchess*	027	294,234	280,150	23,067	105,960	48,176	6,787,060	.1043	2,893,122	**851**	352,228	**748**	190,468	**1,067**	564,313	160,219	191,793	Dutchess
Erie*	029	938,615	950,265	19,617	381,701	36,146	18,412,490	.3082	9,641,934	**2,836**	1,002,594	**2,128**	519,748	**2,913**	1,707,214	737,087	557,927	Erie
Essex	031	39,028	38,851	17,321	15,483	32,626	676,020	.0123	431,923	**127**	22,377	**48**	10,640	**60**	96,548	21,488	25,613	Essex
Franklin**	033	51,036	51,134	14,289	18,466	29,835	729,260	.0129	351,437	**103**	23,827	**51**	....	**....**	65,797	33,202	29,422	Franklin
Fulton**	035	55,272	55,073	17,076	22,422	31,555	943,830	.0158	436,457	**128**	44,076	**94**	....	**....**	103,285	36,043	36,129	Fulton
Genesee**	037	59,919	60,370	19,356	23,086	37,593	1,159,820	.0181	450,996	**133**	63,967	**136**	17,053	**96**	70,876	20,080	40,469	Genesee
Greene	039	49,072	48,195	17,716	18,968	34,440	869,360	.0141	370,934	**109**	25,245	**54**	3,594	**20**	86,343	30,292	31,920	Greene
Hamilton	041	5,242	5,379	18,216	2,374	30,343	95,490	.0014	29,107	**9**	3,704	**8**	3,124	**18**	5,678	....	4,176	Hamilton
Herkimer*	043	63,477	64,427	16,936	25,912	31,226	1,075,060	.0170	385,901	**114**	29,543	**63**	7,157	**40**	72,998	44,317	41,010	Herkimer
Jefferson**	045	115,704	111,738	15,568	42,207	31,966	1,801,310	.0349	1,294,072	**381**	148,470	**315**	56,647	**317**	176,042	90,277	66,528	Jefferson
Kings*	047	2,474,606	2,465,326	14,547	881,635	30,614	35,997,160	.5722	10,466,614	**3,079**	767,014	**1,628**	1,160,613	**6,504**	2,143,715	1,483,608	515,321	Kings
Lewis	049	26,520	26,944	16,517	10,193	32,200	438,040	.0072	176,479	**52**	6,341	**13**	2,007	**11**	29,753	16,932	18,538	Lewis
Livingston*	051	64,750	64,328	18,052	22,518	39,012	1,168,860	.0192	531,185	**156**	42,624	**90**	3,520	**20**	117,853	34,166	41,688	Livingston
Madison*	053	70,428	69,441	18,785	26,420	37,296	1,322,980	.0218	625,741	**184**	56,351	**120**	5,366	**30**	133,295	58,008	45,726	Madison
Monroe*	055	737,090	735,343	22,358	300,310	41,277	16,479,510	.2646	8,154,678	**2,399**	895,104	**1,900**	405,080	**2,270**	1,666,922	387,759	476,708	Monroe
Montgomery**	057	49,269	49,708	16,690	20,210	30,611	822,280	.0143	437,677	**129**	46,149	**98**	14,621	**82**	75,309	31,344	31,033	Montgomery
Nassau*	059	1,340,495	1,334,544	28,131	449,205	62,549	37,709,860	.6058	21,358,727	**6,283**	2,023,462	**4,295**	2,058,858	**11,538**	2,881,936	1,547,265	810,911	Nassau
New York*	061	1,572,971	1,537,195	27,536	755,471	42,974	43,312,660	.7442	29,759,526	**8,754**	3,335,801	**7,081**	7,850,059	**43,994**	3,182,106	3,006,187	244,302	New York
Niagara*	063	217,673	219,846	19,526	88,881	35,855	4,250,200	.0674	1,793,323	**528**	224,893	**477**	141,543	**793**	336,308	163,331	141,585	Niagara
Oneida*	065	234,094	235,469	17,674	91,874	33,808	4,137,270	.0721	2,309,743	**679**	356,183	**756**	94,579	**530**	371,073	208,739	142,219	Oneida
Onondaga*	067	461,207	458,336	20,540	187,155	38,024	9,473,410	.1598	5,272,041	**1,551**	579,198	**1,230**	324,363	**1,818**	984,776	346,688	286,171	Onondaga
Ontario*	069	103,127	100,224	21,379	40,339	41,122	2,204,730	.0397	1,541,995	**454**	281,104	**597**	106,720	**598**	235,657	81,966	71,474	Ontario
Orange*	071	369,860	341,367	21,310	125,487	47,145	7,881,590	.1279	3,913,297	**1,151**	625,784	**1,328**	370,625	**2,077**	571,319	236,758	218,626	Orange
Orleans*	073	43,448	44,171	16,901	15,454	35,500	734,330	.0114	240,818	**71**	20,532	**44**	1,452	**8**	64,591	17,503	27,266	Orleans
Oswego*	075	123,814	122,377	17,439	47,057	34,479	2,159,210	.0349	884,059	**260**	76,815	**163**	13,636	**76**	196,779	62,768	78,885	Oswego
Otsego**	077	62,377	61,676	16,249	24,037	31,611	1,013,590	.0187	647,345	**190**	85,765	**182**	14,667	**82**	90,937	32,366	40,374	Otsego
Putnam*	079	100,694	95,745	29,233	34,869	63,102	2,943,570	.0378	619,617	**182**	28,677	**61**	3,062	**17**	171,073	56,526	71,810	Putnam
Queens*	081	2,223,681	2,229,379	18,150	764,334	39,684	40,359,890	.6009	11,384,793	**3,349**	859,878	**1,825**	952,047	**5,336**	2,389,910	1,551,898	700,819	Queens
Rensselaer*	083	154,473	152,538	21,256	61,950	39,997	3,283,540	.0495	1,194,639	**351**	122,093	**259**	10,444	**59**	263,755	110,466	99,540	Rensselaer
Richmond*	085	464,513	443,728	23,528	165,500	49,528	10,929,120	.1517	2,895,764	**852**	255,426	**542**	295,732	**1,657**	695,315	287,014	228,404	Richmond

Source: Devonshire Associates Ltd. and Scan/US, Inc. 2004.
.... Data less than 1,000.
(d) Data not available.
* Component of a Metropolitan Core Based Statistical Area.
** Component of a Micropolitan Core Based Statistical Area.

Counties: Population / Income / Sales, *Continued*

COUNTY OR COUNTY EQUIVALENT	FIPS CO. CODE	POPULATION Estimate 7/1/04	POPULATION Census 4/1/00	PER CAPITA INCOME 2003	HOUSEHOLDS Estimate 7/1/04	MEDIAN HOUSEHOLD INCOME 2003	DISPOSABLE INCOME 2003 ($1,000)	MARKET ABILITY INDEX 2003	TOTAL RETAIL SALES Sales 2003 ($1,000)	TOTAL RETAIL SALES Ranally Sales Units	GENERAL MERCHANDISE Sales 2003 ($1,000)	GENERAL MERCHANDISE Ranally Sales Units	APPAREL STORE Sales 2003 ($1,000)	APPAREL STORE Ranally Sales Units	FOOD STORE SALES 2003 ($1,000)	HEALTH & DRUG STORE 2003 ($1,000)	PASSENGER CAR REGIS-TRATIONS 2003	COUNTY OR COUNTY EQUIVALENT
Rockland*	087	294,839	286,753	26,183	95,567	60,181	7,719,900	.1141	3,089,876	909	337,199	716	230,555	1,292	509,710	254,241	170,839	Rockland
St. Lawrence**	089	111,586	111,931	15,145	41,561	30,509	1,689,950	.0304	928,708	273	126,582	269	27,227	153	175,558	88,512	66,203	St. Lawrence
Saratoga*	091	212,606	200,635	23,751	85,083	44,632	5,049,680	.0764	2,072,197	610	224,741	477	107,584	603	282,209	112,465	150,450	Saratoga
Schenectady*	093	147,572	146,555	21,511	61,672	38,694	3,174,380	.0506	1,489,432	438	172,285	366	56,271	315	257,305	104,098	94,332	Schenectady
Schoharie*	095	31,716	31,582	17,883	12,356	34,649	567,190	.0097	293,261	86	34,525	73	15,283	86	47,604	14,153	22,070	Schoharie
Schuyler	097	19,517	19,224	17,618	7,672	33,512	343,860	.0056	146,847	43	1,752	4	9,154	51	56,130	....	13,769	Schuyler
Seneca**	099	35,787	33,342	17,275	13,326	34,798	618,230	.0111	371,817	109	28,843	61	80,924	454	42,187	19,393	22,708	Seneca
Steuben**	101	99,084	98,726	17,902	39,966	33,189	1,773,850	.0294	830,099	244	90,777	193	15,128	85	183,318	55,714	65,685	Steuben
Suffolk*	103	1,482,695	1,419,369	25,754	495,648	57,696	38,185,710	.5999	19,116,915	5,623	1,904,296	4,042	1,303,778	7,307	3,087,748	1,312,249	960,491	Suffolk
Sullivan	105	75,246	73,966	17,621	28,707	34,690	1,325,890	.0218	590,767	174	29,468	63	7,195	40	122,931	46,779	46,053	Sullivan
Tioga*	107	51,744	51,784	19,513	20,211	37,223	1,009,660	.0148	287,167	84	5,925	13	2,005	11	44,965	23,096	36,377	Tioga
Tompkins*	109	102,983	96,501	18,179	39,852	35,127	1,872,090	.0299	758,836	223	72,786	155	32,607	183	186,312	57,099	62,802	Tompkins
Ulster*	111	182,183	177,749	20,318	70,543	39,394	3,701,600	.0588	1,627,487	479	152,573	324	65,662	368	322,318	116,080	121,282	Ulster
Warren*	113	65,172	63,303	20,384	27,264	36,555	1,328,490	.0248	1,010,937	297	101,762	216	98,221	550	163,891	44,841	44,649	Warren
Washington*	115	62,162	61,042	18,049	23,632	35,561	1,121,980	.0168	321,512	95	18,814	40	1,771	10	49,655	37,481	40,599	Washington
Wayne*	117	93,715	93,765	20,713	35,843	40,527	1,941,110	.0296	731,909	215	52,000	110	1,173	7	128,994	45,404	65,229	Wayne
Westchester*	119	945,092	923,459	27,571	343,503	56,811	26,056,760	.3984	12,325,881	3,626	1,199,362	2,546	1,138,107	6,378	2,060,965	898,751	527,102	Westchester
Wyoming	121	42,780	43,424	17,427	15,099	36,830	745,530	.0119	289,642	85	23,022	49	1,182	7	68,793	15,964	27,105	Wyoming
Yates	123	24,755	24,621	16,158	9,150	32,678	399,990	.0065	155,399	46	9,290	20	1,155	6	39,692	11,543	15,474	Yates
The State		19,254,372	18,976,457	20,652	7,204,879	40,353	397,635,050	6.3736	184,067,719	54,145	19,080,822	40,508	18,893,160	105,882	30,431,174	15,727,930	8,924,727	The State

NORTH CAROLINA (NC; CODE 37; 100 Counties)

COUNTY OR COUNTY EQUIVALENT	FIPS CO. CODE	POPULATION Estimate 7/1/04	POPULATION Census 4/1/00	PER CAPITA INCOME 2003	HOUSEHOLDS Estimate 7/1/04	MEDIAN HOUSEHOLD INCOME 2003	DISPOSABLE INCOME 2003 ($1,000)	MARKET ABILITY INDEX 2003	TOTAL RETAIL SALES Sales 2003 ($1,000)	TOTAL RETAIL SALES Ranally Sales Units	GENERAL MERCHANDISE Sales 2003 ($1,000)	GENERAL MERCHANDISE Ranally Sales Units	APPAREL STORE Sales 2003 ($1,000)	APPAREL STORE Ranally Sales Units	FOOD STORE SALES 2003 ($1,000)	HEALTH & DRUG STORE 2003 ($1,000)	PASSENGER CAR REGIS-TRATIONS 2003	COUNTY OR COUNTY EQUIVALENT
Alamance*	001	138,548	130,800	18,658	56,281	36,368	2,585,040	.0472	1,747,387	514	210,583	447	106,370	596	236,792	102,793	105,187	Alamance
Alexander*	003	35,156	33,603	18,129	13,969	35,627	637,350	.0099	223,070	66	28,464	60	2,045	11	46,692	6,133	28,834	Alexander
Alleghany	005	10,932	10,677	15,495	4,813	27,766	169,390	.0030	89,915	26	3,625	8	....	....	20,640	7,039	9,100	Alleghany
Anson*	007	25,140	25,275	13,259	9,332	28,461	333,320	.0059	145,996	43	19,956	42	4,512	25	37,364	15,969	16,297	Anson
Ashe	009	25,276	24,384	15,179	11,124	27,429	383,670	.0071	231,223	68	33,762	72	3,308	19	39,636	14,083	20,792	Ashe
Avery	011	17,869	17,167	14,048	6,926	28,646	251,030	.0051	197,214	58	37,136	79	6,315	35	49,530	11,879	13,284	Avery
Beaufort**	013	45,548	44,958	15,378	19,076	29,375	700,450	.0144	590,290	174	77,891	165	16,798	94	111,127	38,945	33,662	Beaufort
Bertie	015	19,484	19,773	12,312	7,903	23,951	239,890	.0042	94,954	28	3,251	7	....	....	16,758	8,593	13,113	Bertie
Bladen	017	32,882	32,278	13,443	13,506	26,071	442,040	.0078	200,763	59	25,841	55	7,554	42	43,705	21,816	23,668	Bladen
Brunswick*	019	84,206	73,143	18,113	35,920	33,716	1,525,240	.0257	766,555	225	99,980	212	16,389	92	180,217	58,362	64,404	Brunswick
Buncombe*	021	214,572	206,330	18,420	91,128	34,591	3,952,400	.0765	3,137,657	923	492,704	1,046	174,236	976	362,568	179,131	161,197	Buncombe
Burke*	023	89,791	89,148	16,443	35,013	33,303	1,476,430	.0255	747,888	220	79,267	168	22,276	125	121,949	57,755	65,730	Burke
Cabarrus*	025	146,248	131,063	21,080	58,122	42,073	3,082,970	.0559	2,189,227	644	350,602	744	84,948	476	267,129	119,867	112,092	Cabarrus
Caldwell*	027	79,103	77,415	17,039	31,943	33,565	1,347,870	.0233	704,603	207	91,838	195	11,712	66	113,292	41,315	63,620	Caldwell
Camden**	029	8,174	6,885	18,400	3,217	36,855	150,400	.0021	25,493	8	2,666	6	....	....	4,840	....	6,832	Camden
Carteret**	031	61,352	59,383	19,643	26,568	35,952	1,205,150	.0221	852,892	251	176,070	374	26,558	149	136,013	39,407	47,350	Carteret
Caswell	033	23,659	23,501	15,713	8,889	33,112	371,750	.0055	70,906	21	4,315	9	....	....	20,984	3,889	17,769	Caswell
Catawba*	035	148,471	141,685	19,815	62,001	37,650	2,942,010	.0573	2,462,705	724	390,234	828	110,686	620	248,249	142,850	119,531	Catawba
Chatham*	037	57,081	49,329	20,208	23,021	39,970	1,153,490	.0168	332,583	98	40,143	85	10,250	57	72,377	9,462	44,858	Chatham
Cherokee	039	25,269	24,298	14,800	11,096	26,673	373,970	.0080	342,931	101	87,491	186	10,055	56	59,769	12,009	20,305	Cherokee
Chowan	041	14,537	14,526	14,753	5,844	29,469	214,470	.0042	151,575	45	7,090	15	4,369	24	31,899	8,836	9,437	Chowan
Clay	043	9,446	8,775	16,829	4,294	29,533	158,970	.0031	125,339	37	4,150	9	2,159	12	21,977	6,179	7,995	Clay
Cleveland**	045	98,808	96,287	16,297	38,414	33,271	1,610,280	.0282	861,036	253	121,533	258	29,840	167	143,077	58,308	71,217	Cleveland
Columbus	047	54,440	54,749	12,907	21,703	25,710	702,680	.0144	519,820	153	70,836	150	15,114	85	85,873	41,665	37,245	Columbus
Craven**	049	91,802	91,436	17,558	37,871	33,674	1,611,870	.0295	1,055,851	311	136,137	289	41,052	230	145,350	40,952	65,444	Craven
Cumberland*	051	304,324	302,963	17,357	118,570	35,270	5,282,290	.0972	3,493,381	1,028	695,105	1,476	168,128	942	434,080	148,723	205,861	Cumberland
Currituck*	053	21,665	18,190	18,280	8,318	37,856	396,030	.0065	182,714	54	6,237	13	4,187	23	42,765	1,429	16,317	Currituck
Dare**	055	34,090	29,967	21,448	14,626	39,853	731,150	.0153	753,048	222	123,876	263	57,883	324	170,648	32,663	26,530	Dare
Davidson**	057	153,692	147,246	18,245	61,350	36,250	2,804,120	.0449	1,153,850	339	131,198	279	32,350	181	209,293	89,221	119,855	Davidson
Davie*	059	37,846	34,835	19,023	15,073	37,695	719,930	.0114	289,939	85	40,792	87	2,990	17	40,345	17,847	30,515	Davie
Duplin	061	51,843	49,063	13,196	19,315	27,986	684,120	.0126	357,151	105	45,826	97	6,970	39	69,401	26,315	35,309	Duplin
Durham*	063	240,859	223,314	20,943	99,786	40,667	5,044,380	.0876	3,127,432	920	357,799	760	216,625	1,214	483,561	212,368	166,635	Durham
Edgecombe*	065	54,761	55,606	13,620	20,273	29,365	745,840	.0126	276,688	81	25,191	53	12,906	72	49,949	34,343	32,519	Edgecombe
Forsyth*	067	321,453	306,067	20,601	134,569	39,193	6,622,140	.1242	5,103,704	1,501	714,448	1,517	271,729	1,523	592,663	259,635	236,537	Forsyth
Franklin*	069	53,474	47,260	17,486	20,412	36,435	935,070	.0141	272,781	80	33,562	71	5,947	33	57,675	16,364	39,566	Franklin
Gaston*	071	193,911	190,365	18,664	78,093	36,677	3,619,220	.0633	2,128,937	626	309,405	657	87,621	491	314,524	148,908	141,123	Gaston
Gates	073	10,835	10,516	15,720	4,076	33,047	170,330	.0026	43,410	13	1,574	3	....	....	8,492	....	7,919	Gates
Graham	075	7,994	7,993	13,918	3,490	25,417	111,260	.0020	59,384	17	2,664	6	....	....	9,484	5,506	6,207	Graham
Granville	077	52,887	48,498	16,374	18,662	36,780	865,970	.0139	316,201	93	33,152	70	6,723	38	66,272	26,503	36,226	Granville
Greene*	079	20,302	18,974	13,377	7,245	29,699	271,570	.0043	61,514	18	2,683	6	....	....	17,036	2,441	13,272	Greene
Guilford*	081	437,629	421,048	21,145	185,744	39,764	9,253,770	.1714	6,975,821	2,052	810,989	1,722	335,257	1,879	794,262	386,953	327,461	Guilford
Halifax**	083	56,226	57,370	12,597	22,176	25,392	708,300	.0151	578,814	170	87,639	186	28,925	162	99,749	41,446	35,671	Halifax
Harnett**	085	102,013	91,025	15,345	37,852	32,893	1,565,370	.0264	668,943	197	106,947	227	10,892	61	120,950	44,597	69,687	Harnett
Haywood*	087	55,887	54,033	17,835	24,708	32,000	996,770	.0192	769,010	226	98,536	209	19,333	108	93,948	38,724	45,799	Haywood
Henderson*	089	95,222	89,173	19,094	40,296	35,765	1,818,160	.0346	1,405,008	413	133,057	282	51,572	289	182,833	71,865	73,835	Henderson
Hertford	091	22,102	22,601	12,783	8,840	25,557	282,540	.0064	279,678	82	36,729	78	11,511	65	61,336	28,710	14,855	Hertford
Hoke*	093	38,888	33,646	13,377	13,244	31,938	520,210	.0080	93,605	28	7,569	16	....	....	34,562	6,637	24,083	Hoke
Hyde	095	5,495	5,826	13,305	2,119	27,249	73,110	.0014	40,432	12	10,100	21	....	....	6,207	....	3,461	Hyde
Iredell**	097	136,650	122,660	19,318	53,965	39,219	2,639,860	.0463	1,605,691	472	225,790	479	63,581	356	211,236	93,119	105,212	Iredell
Jackson	099	34,647	33,121	15,909	14,194	30,812	551,200	.0104	368,655	108	103,632	220	6,137	34	61,687	16,346	25,708	Jackson
Johnston*	101	141,305	121,965	18,136	53,759	38,150	2,562,640	.0432	1,297,678	382	139,881	297	82,994	465	196,760	54,005	101,490	Johnston
Jones**	103	10,131	10,381	14,578	4,074	29,309	147,690	.0024	53,352	16	1,354	3	....	....	6,224	....	7,356	Jones
Lee**	105	49,042	49,040	18,883	20,160	36,340	926,070	.0187	828,698	244	90,453	192	24,202	136	140,918	36,620	37,376	Lee
Lenoir**	107	58,240	59,648	16,005	25,017	29,757	932,110	.0185	735,617	216	99,498	211	34,125	191	114,897	40,705	41,921	Lenoir
Lincoln**	109	68,354	63,780	18,410	25,949	38,474	1,258,420	.0211	625,189	184	92,331	196	7,364	41	110,499	66,247	53,671	Lincoln
McDowell	111	43,082	42,151	15,454	17,289	30,658	665,780	.0122	395,673	116	54,654	116	7,640	43	74,446	15,140	32,006	McDowell
Macon	113	31,576	29,811	16,536	13,736	30,260	522,150	.0111	504,346	148	83,309	177	25,292	142	69,800	13,468	24,500	Macon
Madison*	115	19,910	19,635	15,340	8,338	29,046	305,410	.0047	74,994	22	4,330	9	1,394	8	22,150	12,605	15,566	Madison
Martin	117	24,924	25,593	13,816	9,978	27,332	344,340	.0067	232,738	68	33,182	70	7,789	44	36,497	13,745	16,490	Martin
Mecklenburg*	119	769,746	695,454	24,604	330,418	45,884	18,938,570	.3225	12,050,279	3,545	1,587,011	3,369	647,070	3,626	1,388,365	545,530	569,655	Mecklenburg
Mitchell	121	15,867	15,687	15,406	6,752	28,688	244,440	.0047	169,522	50	5,334	11	4,061	23	32,028	18,108	12,309	Mitchell
Montgomery	123	27,429	26,822	14,528	10,195	31,139	398,500	.0074	231,963	68	7,553	16	7,876	44	45,247	18,109	18,742	Montgomery
Moore**	125	80,638	74,769	20,044	33,482	38,286	1,616,310	.0275	907,095	267	138,270	294	51,668	290	119,796	80,633	61,947	Moore
Nash*	127	90,391	87,420	17,155	35,197	35,213	1,550,670	.0294	1,113,283	327	140,808	299	67,830	380	118,179	51,806	64,460	Nash
New Hanover*	129	170,562	160,307	22,524	81,552	37,352	3,841,670	.0765	3,585,290	1,055	483,847	1,027	162,109	909	409,604	164,737	138,092	New Hanover
Northampton**	131	21,682	22,086	13,072	8,818	25,496	283,430	.0049	105,541	31	9,784	21	....	....	15,216	3,966	14,791	Northampton
Onslow*	133	146,634	150,355	14,600	53,106	31,872	2,140,860	.0420	1,534,013	451	261,489	555	47,943	269	197,933	55,794	95,880	Onslow
Orange*	135	118,905	118,227	21,848	52,169	40,035	2,597,810	.0426	1,369,526	403	67,921	144	32,910	184	287,940	71,157	96,622	Orange
Pamlico**	137	12,730	12,934	16,617	5,165	32,350	211,530	.0033	66,750	20	3,366	7	....	....	21,255	7,324	8,957	Pamlico
Pasquotank**	139	36,468	34,897	14,353	14,404	28,924	523,430	.0122	591,580	174	95,264	202	21,621	121	74,240	28,798	23,711	Pasquotank
Pender*	141	44,280	41,082	16,818	17,554	33,375	744,680	.0116	239,656	71	7,440	16	6,925	39	66,653	13,137	32,598	Pender
Perquimans**	143	11,722	11,368	14,809	4,924	27,984	173,590	.0026	38,942	11	2,915	6	....	....	15,089	4,110	8,594	Perquimans
Person*	145	37,235	35,623	17,744	14,999	35,267	660,690	.0114	355,334	105	46,397	99	10,476	59	77,109	19,912	30,813	Person
Pitt*	147	140,223	133,798	16,079	56,933	31,558	2,254,600	.0463	1,950,066	574	211,126	448	117,144	657	258,694	92,355	96,072	Pitt
Polk	149	18,963	18,324	18,805	8,252	34,252	356,590	.0052	92,903	27	2,000	4	....	....	29,565	10,122	15,436	Polk
Randolph*	151	136,509	130,454	17,610	53,187	35,752	2,403,890	.0406	1,196,104	352	178,995	380	47,096	264	190,871	103,534	104,492	Randolph
Richmond**	153	46,666	46,564	13,395	18,129	27,305	625,090	.0126	458,959	135	51,076	108	16,218	91	69,858	27,255	30,242	Richmond
Robeson**	155	126,549	123,339	12,168	45,509	26,876	1,539,800	.0327	1,218,173	358	141,075	299	52,508	294	168,047	57,983	79,080	Robeson
Rockingham*	157	92,805	91,928	16,600	37,964	32,281	1,540,540	.0267	796,170	234	102,382	217	21,783	122	150,687	61,248	72,114	Rockingham
Rowan**	159	135,024	130,340	17,058	51,761	35,338	2,303,210	.0402	1,253,559	369	129,952	276	51,196	287	220,101	79,451	97,203	Rowan
Rutherford**	161	63,726	62,899	15,064	25,950	29,550	959,970	.0177	575,141	169	98,879	210	15,807	89	92,860	37,324	47,367	Rutherford
Sampson	163	62,617	60,161	14,137	23,305	30,338	885,220	.0165	518,637	153	52,680	112	6,927	39	85,474	38,521	43,151	Sampson
Scotland**	165	35,671	35,998	14,372	13,885	29,627	512,650	.0095	302,279	89	68,116	145	15,261	86	57,747	17,813	23,549	Scotland
Stanly**	167	59,068	58,100	16,737	22,661	34,782	988,630	.0187	690,220	203	80,441	171	17,873	100	111,762	39,954	45,621	Stanly
Stokes*	169	45,273	44,711	18,189	18,105	35,805	823,490	.0120	208,845	61	12,421	26	2,115	12	38,161	27,180	38,454	Stokes
Surry**	171	72,629	71,219	15,867	29,232	31,262	1,152,410	.0241	1,044,682	307	193,017	410	40,972	230	144,007	63,130	56,744	Surry
Swain	173	13,163	12,968	13,947	5,329	27,327	183,580	.0034	109,267	32	5,090	11	2,319	13	25,710	12,909	9,412	Swain
Transylvania**	175	29,416	29,334	19,677	12,728	36,070	578,820	.0091	236,069	69	55,564	118	8,437	47	51,366	9,278	23,445	Transylvania
Tyrrell	177	4,159	4,149	11,546	1,546	24,887	48,020	.0009	21,790	6	2,418	5	....	....	4,498	....	2,436	Tyrrell
Union*	179	152,765	123,677	20,141	53,761	45,569	3,076,800	.0476	1,196,668	352	140,841	299	37,158	208	156,509	51,833	110,349	Union
Vance**	181	43,932	42,954	14,195	16,935	29,559	623,600	.0138	612,000	180	90,076	191	24,450	137	85,820	32,696	28,848	Vance
Wake*	183	716,522	627,846	25,888	297,602	49,553	18,549,530	.3149	11,976,718	3,523	1,643,862	3,490	582,053	3,262	1,495,808	500,884	557,144	Wake
Warren	185	19,772	19,972	13,603	7,869	27,830	268,960	.0043	66,179	19	5,311	11	....	....	24,566	3,698	14,433	Warren
Washington	187	13,297	13,723	13,929	5,373	27,496	185,220	.0034	95,980	28	5,608	12	3,816	21	23,583	3,753	8,628	Washington
Watauga**	189	42,829	42,695	15,404	16,948	31,050	659,730	.0152	749,898	221	97,714	207	54,891	308	82,227	36,052	32,470	Watauga
Wayne*	191	113,028	113,329	15,911	44,258	32,198	1,798,380	.0346	1,286,204	378	226,878	482	56,081	314	170,727	62,907	78,730	Wayne
Wilkes**	193	67,472	65,632	16,814	27,998	32,047	1,134,480	.0221	874,308	257	143,274	304	29,969	168	102,636	48,155	55,451	Wilkes
Wilson**	195	75,810	73,814	16,728	31,913	31,748	1,268,130	.0251	1,012,919	298	121,300	258	43,925	246	128,967	56,379	55,066	Wilson
Yadkin*	197	37,725	36,348	17,330	15,106	34,342	653,770	.0104	243,636	72	6,936	15	3,942	22	46,151	19,192	31,291	Yadkin
Yancey	199	18,155	17,774	15,219	7,806	27,969	276,300	.0050	157,497	46	18,899	40	1,543	9	28,025	10,021	14,492	Yancey
The State		8,517,110	8,049,313	19,053	3,462,050	37,022	162,277,040	2.9042	104,325,590	30,685	14,082,382	29,893	4,617,950	25,880	14,536,034	5,639,210	6,298,393	The State

NORTH DAKOTA (ND; CODE 38; 53 Counties)

COUNTY OR COUNTY EQUIVALENT	FIPS CO. CODE	POPULATION Estimate 7/1/04	POPULATION Census 4/1/00	PER CAPITA INCOME 2003	HOUSEHOLDS Estimate 7/1/04	MEDIAN HOUSEHOLD INCOME 2003	DISPOSABLE INCOME 2003 ($1,000)	MARKET ABILITY INDEX 2003	TOTAL RETAIL SALES Sales 2003 ($1,000)	TOTAL RETAIL SALES Ranally Sales Units	GENERAL MERCHANDISE Sales 2003 ($1,000)	GENERAL MERCHANDISE Ranally Sales Units	APPAREL STORE Sales 2003 ($1,000)	APPAREL STORE Ranally Sales Units	FOOD STORE SALES 2003 ($1,000)	HEALTH & DRUG STORE 2003 ($1,000)	PASSENGER CAR REGIS-TRATIONS 2003	COUNTY OR COUNTY EQUIVALENT
Adams	001	2,481	2,593	14,909	1,109	27,048	36,990	.0009	45,219	13	....	....	....	....	7,445	3,360	2,337	Adams
Barnes	003	10,877	11,775	15,410	4,611	29,590	167,620	.0031	99,562	29	3,718	8	....	....	15,159	7,250	9,226	Barnes
Benson	005	6,854	6,964	10,636	2,290	25,853	72,900	.0013	18,849	6	....	....	....	....	1,404	1,393	4,336	Benson
Billings**	007	842	888	16,342	372	30,000	13,760	.0002	2,100	1	....	....	....	....	....	....	996	Billings
Bottineau	009	6,722	7,149	14,795	2,856	28,216	99,450	.0019	63,392	19	4,182	9	....	....	7,895	2,310	5,929	Bottineau
Bowman	011	2,986	3,242	15,988	1,284	30,240	47,740	.0011	57,581	17	....	....	....	....	6,031	1,335	2,775	Bowman
Burke	013	2,055	2,242	14,024	958	24,223	28,820	.0005	14,399	4	....	....	....	....	6,551	....	2,254	Burke
Burleigh*	015	72,410	69,416	19,627	30,153	38,298	1,421,170	.0277	1,182,985	348	244,172	518	31,430	176	132,630	75,881	57,931	Burleigh
Cass*	017	128,372	123,138	19,129	55,524	36,028	2,455,660	.0523	2,524,829	743	346,425	735	86,129	483	199,738	123,846	102,764	Cass
Cavalier	019	4,380	4,831	15,749	1,881	29,956	68,980	.0013	51,033	15	2,992	6	....	....	5,820	2,071	3,952	Cavalier
Dickey	021	5,407	5,757	13,553	2,163	27,447	73,280	.0016	62,799	18	1,145	2	....	....	5,754	1,670	4,335	Dickey
Divide	023	2,241	2,283	15,520	1,015	27,835	34,780	.0005	10,497	3	....	....	....	....	1,025	1,012	2,364	Divide
Dunn	025	3,518	3,600	13,570	1,387	27,939	47,740	.0010	39,703	12	....	....	....	....	8,915	1,348	3,024	Dunn
Eddy	027	2,553	2,757	14,156	1,094	26,899	36,140	.0006	14,329	4	....	....	....	....	5,777	....	2,209	Eddy
Emmons	029	3,909	4,331	13,019	1,664	24,931	50,890	.0012	54,869	16	....	....	....	....	5,548	....	3,383	Emmons
Foster	031	3,415	3,759	15,839	1,428	30,700	54,090	.0012	52,945	16	5,208	11	....	....	6,916	4,457	2,797	Foster
Golden Valley	033	1,799	1,924	13,897	723	27,822	25,000	.0005	20,728	6	....	....	....	....	2,371	....	1,566	Golden Valley
Grand Forks*	035	64,352	66,109	16,151	25,113	33,825	1,039,380	.0249	1,307,693	385	279,043	592	44,650	250	104,858	46,792	45,696	Grand Forks
Grant	037	2,610	2,841	12,345	1,143	22,580	32,220	.0006	15,750	5	....	....	....	....	2,251	....	2,505	Grant
Griggs	039	2,529	2,754	15,437	1,123	27,931	39,040	.0008	27,243	8	....	....	....	....	5,300	2,144	2,480	Griggs
Hettinger	041	2,502	2,715	14,820	1,102	27,191	37,080	.0007	20,398	6	....	....	....	....	3,466	3,363	2,342	Hettinger
Kidder	043	2,526	2,753	13,211	1,116	24,207	33,370	.0006	19,083	6	....	....	....	....	1,797	1,502	2,499	Kidder
LaMoure	045	4,457	4,701	14,689	1,893	27,934	65,470	.0011	22,615	7	....	....	....	....	3,568	1,007	4,177	LaMoure
Logan	047	2,113	2,308	14,056	911	26,347	29,700	.0005	16,459	5	....	....	....	....	1,074	1,151	1,935	Logan
McHenry**	049	5,647	5,987	14,250	2,463	26,436	80,470	.0012	13,478	4	....	....	....	....	2,757	....	5,316	McHenry
McIntosh	051	3,113	3,390	13,521	1,368	25,027	42,090	.0009	38,271	11	....	....	....	....	6,252	2,115	2,757	McIntosh
McKenzie	053	5,581	5,737	13,026	2,129	27,573	72,700	.0013	29,555	9	....	....	....	....	4,511	2,292	4,488	McKenzie
McLean	055	8,827	9,311	16,105	3,744	30,485	142,160	.0023	56,346	17	....	....	....	....	9,486	3,701	8,413	McLean
Mercer	057	8,397	8,644	19,284	3,342	39,504	161,930	.0026	66,033	19	2,977	6	....	....	13,086	7,330	7,896	Mercer
Morton*	059	25,068	25,303	17,167	10,077	34,817	430,340	.0077	255,697	75	1,843	4	....	....	15,620	7,816	20,846	Morton

Source: Devonshire Associates Ltd. and Scan/US, Inc. 2004.
* Component of a Metropolitan Core Based Statistical Area.
** Component of a Micropolitan Core Based Statistical Area.

.... Data less than 1,000.

(d) Data not available.

continued on next page

Counties: Population / Income / Sales, *Continued*

COUNTY OR COUNTY EQUIVALENT	FIPS CO. CODE	POPULATION Estimate 7/1/04	POPULATION Census 4/1/00	PER CAPITA INCOME 2003	HOUSEHOLDS Estimate 7/1/04	MEDIAN HOUSEHOLD INCOME 2003	DISPOSABLE INCOME 2003 ($1,000)	MARKET ABILITY INDEX 2003	TOTAL RETAIL SALES Sales 2003 ($1,000)	TOTAL RETAIL SALES Ranally Sales Units	GENERAL MERCHANDISE Sales 2003 ($1,000)	GENERAL MERCHANDISE Ranally Sales Units	APPAREL STORE Sales 2003 ($1,000)	APPAREL STORE Ranally Sales Units	FOOD STORE SALES 2003 ($1,000)	HEALTH & DRUG STORE 2003 ($1,000)	PASSENGER CAR REGIS-TRATIONS 2003	COUNTY OR COUNTY EQUIVALENT
Mountrail	061	6,439	6,631	12,379	2,532	25,599	79,710	.0017	60,048	**18**	....	**....**	....	**....**	13,057	3,852	5,131	Mountrail
Nelson	063	3,375	3,715	15,188	1,508	27,379	51,260	.0008	15,879	**5**	....	**....**	....	**....**	2,603	1,152	2,901	Nelson
Oliver	065	1,857	2,065	17,221	748	34,562	31,980	.0004	4,101	**1**	....	**....**	....	**....**	1,273	....	1,933	Oliver
Pembina	067	8,085	8,585	17,960	3,422	34,495	145,210	.0029	125,744	**37**	2,431	**5**	2,126	**12**	16,876	4,078	6,796	Pembina
Pierce	069	4,420	4,675	13,514	1,899	25,632	59,730	.0013	55,353	**16**	4,927	**10**	1,203	**7**	6,555	3,235	3,702	Pierce
Ramsey	071	11,481	12,066	16,966	4,783	33,247	194,790	.0039	164,260	**48**	30,378	**64**	3,426	**19**	19,620	7,685	8,653	Ramsey
Ransom	073	5,819	5,890	17,570	2,353	35,127	102,240	.0018	53,714	**16**	3,196	**7**	....	**....**	8,263	3,075	4,891	Ransom
Renville**	075	2,434	2,610	15,308	1,047	28,681	37,260	.0007	27,141	**8**	....	**....**	....	**....**	....	....	2,327	Renville
Richland**	077	17,478	17,998	16,349	6,818	34,005	285,740	.0051	163,596	**48**	4,876	**10**	3,083	**17**	30,076	8,183	13,441	Richland
Rolette	079	13,746	13,674	10,283	4,628	24,971	141,350	.0030	97,445	**29**	4,099	**9**	....	**....**	21,390	1,992	8,279	Rolette
Sargent	081	4,181	4,366	17,917	1,745	34,873	74,910	.0012	33,546	**10**	....	**....**	....	**....**	3,691	....	3,828	Sargent
Sheridan	083	1,491	1,710	12,964	654	24,507	19,330	.0003	7,207	**2**	....	**....**	....	**....**	1,603	....	1,476	Sheridan
Sioux	085	4,072	4,044	7,434	1,108	21,990	30,270	.0007	15,519	**5**	....	**....**	....	**....**	1,943	....	1,953	Sioux
Slope	087	742	767	12,588	316	23,767	9,340	.0001	....	**....**	....	**....**	....	**....**	....	....	877	Slope
Stark**	089	21,990	22,636	15,302	8,909	30,554	336,480	.0074	335,777	**99**	51,589	**110**	10,156	**57**	35,100	18,531	16,906	Stark
Steele	091	2,031	2,258	16,859	829	33,341	34,240	.0006	20,230	**6**	....	**....**	....	**....**	1,766	....	1,806	Steele
Stutsman**	093	21,057	21,908	16,204	8,776	31,651	341,210	.0068	278,743	**82**	43,063	**91**	14,057	**79**	33,053	20,593	16,650	Stutsman
Towner	095	2,606	2,876	16,435	1,133	30,498	42,830	.0006	9,757	**3**	....	**....**	....	**....**	1,177	....	2,316	Towner
Traill	097	8,215	8,477	17,372	3,281	35,211	142,710	.0023	58,650	**17**	3,080	**7**	....	**....**	4,656	6,423	6,624	Traill
Walsh	099	11,513	12,389	16,384	4,804	31,816	188,630	.0036	133,837	**39**	6,913	**15**	....	**....**	23,525	6,877	9,288	Walsh
Ward**	101	56,085	58,795	15,708	22,444	31,771	880,990	.0199	964,538	**284**	140,890	**299**	24,540	**138**	93,714	44,111	44,412	Ward
Wells	103	4,581	5,102	16,400	2,034	29,964	75,130	.0014	53,893	**16**	....	**....**	....	**....**	6,853	4,095	4,127	Wells
Williams**	105	19,199	19,761	15,329	8,130	29,499	294,310	.0063	275,034	**81**	51,078	**108**	7,407	**42**	36,813	14,423	15,420	Williams
The State		631,440	642,200	16,693	259,937	32,825	10,540,610	.2149	9,158,577	**2,697**	1,243,759	**2,638**	235,762	**1,322**	958,312	457,880	507,265	The State

OHIO (OH; CODE 39; 88 Counties)

COUNTY OR COUNTY EQUIVALENT	FIPS CO. CODE	POPULATION Estimate 7/1/04	POPULATION Census 4/1/00	PER CAPITA INCOME 2003	HOUSEHOLDS Estimate 7/1/04	MEDIAN HOUSEHOLD INCOME 2003	DISPOSABLE INCOME 2003 ($1,000)	MARKET ABILITY INDEX 2003	TOTAL RETAIL SALES Sales 2003 ($1,000)	TOTAL RETAIL SALES Ranally Sales Units	GENERAL MERCHANDISE Sales 2003 ($1,000)	GENERAL MERCHANDISE Ranally Sales Units	APPAREL STORE Sales 2003 ($1,000)	APPAREL STORE Ranally Sales Units	FOOD STORE SALES 2003 ($1,000)	HEALTH & DRUG STORE 2003 ($1,000)	PASSENGER CAR REGIS-TRATIONS 2003	COUNTY OR COUNTY EQUIVALENT
Adams	001	28,256	27,330	13,667	11,125	27,640	386,180	.0070	193,302	**57**	31,117	**66**	1,119	**6**	26,392	16,022	21,217	Adams
Allen*	003	108,137	108,473	17,241	42,785	35,036	1,864,400	.0376	1,597,704	**470**	367,555	**780**	46,191	**259**	132,113	97,404	76,902	Allen
Ashland**	005	54,141	52,523	17,187	20,397	36,363	930,530	.0155	429,704	**126**	48,279	**102**	9,024	**51**	72,787	29,980	39,748	Ashland
Ashtabula**	007	103,234	102,728	16,316	40,105	33,736	1,684,410	.0290	837,567	**246**	121,774	**259**	24,400	**137**	142,532	71,498	73,630	Ashtabula
Athens**	009	65,043	62,223	12,069	23,980	26,142	785,010	.0151	437,925	**129**	47,674	**101**	20,926	**117**	110,885	29,926	44,510	Athens
Auglaize**	011	46,780	46,611	19,045	17,822	40,014	890,940	.0146	421,927	**124**	46,713	**99**	17,466	**98**	57,546	23,114	35,318	Auglaize
Belmont*	013	69,474	70,226	14,374	28,495	28,061	998,610	.0224	1,027,807	**302**	229,576	**487**	58,851	**330**	160,340	80,119	49,729	Belmont
Brown*	015	44,217	42,285	16,698	16,526	35,774	738,330	.0113	202,833	**60**	15,599	**33**	2,496	**14**	50,957	18,552	35,165	Brown
Butler*	017	346,371	332,807	21,345	135,917	43,599	7,393,210	.1154	3,165,589	**931**	461,306	**979**	61,907	**347**	531,475	168,698	256,714	Butler
Carroll*	019	29,838	28,836	16,462	11,774	33,369	491,190	.0080	198,524	**58**	3,809	**8**	1,789	**10**	43,537	26,116	23,931	Carroll
Champaign**	021	39,745	38,890	19,530	15,571	40,206	776,230	.0119	275,834	**81**	28,426	**60**	2,243	**13**	58,869	15,221	29,840	Champaign
Clark*	023	142,925	144,742	18,956	57,971	37,452	2,709,270	.0460	1,449,668	**426**	256,832	**545**	30,877	**173**	231,995	132,395	104,744	Clark
Clermont*	025	188,179	177,977	21,062	71,471	44,527	3,963,500	.0663	2,181,259	**642**	478,064	**1,015**	51,779	**290**	197,500	62,204	143,397	Clermont
Clinton**	027	42,113	40,543	18,780	16,811	37,706	790,870	.0149	585,698	**172**	66,039	**140**	6,215	**35**	88,006	17,979	31,912	Clinton
Columbiana**	029	111,328	112,075	15,685	43,451	32,142	1,746,210	.0314	992,742	**292**	98,533	**209**	20,824	**117**	173,190	73,404	80,842	Columbiana
Coshocton**	031	37,273	36,655	16,664	15,211	32,615	621,110	.0102	254,135	**75**	36,220	**77**	9,028	**51**	55,990	15,435	28,944	Coshocton
Crawford**	033	45,825	46,966	17,538	18,899	34,005	803,660	.0129	323,318	**95**	17,274	**37**	5,435	**30**	58,237	48,259	34,967	Crawford
Cuyahoga*	035	1,354,570	1,393,978	19,390	574,816	36,481	26,265,070	.4671	16,746,639	**4,926**	1,726,440	**3,665**	1,000,946	**5,610**	2,530,102	1,914,969	861,511	Cuyahoga
Darke**	037	52,842	53,309	17,984	20,707	36,711	950,290	.0165	532,154	**157**	75,676	**161**	15,579	**87**	84,120	17,797	40,985	Darke
Defiance**	039	38,923	39,500	20,233	15,327	41,123	787,530	.0143	553,784	**163**	82,492	**175**	11,312	**63**	84,847	20,290	30,123	Defiance
Delaware*	041	139,819	109,989	28,480	53,450	59,695	3,982,080	.0578	1,563,825	**460**	138,629	**294**	18,296	**103**	310,134	45,176	110,256	Delaware
Erie*	043	78,417	79,551	20,237	32,184	39,816	1,586,900	.0274	941,112	**277**	206,509	**438**	50,006	**280**	117,156	69,561	58,268	Erie
Fairfield*	045	135,586	122,759	20,486	51,127	43,609	2,777,630	.0436	1,176,899	**346**	166,125	**353**	61,849	**347**	209,733	57,712	103,408	Fairfield
Fayette**	047	28,066	28,433	17,230	11,198	34,518	483,570	.0105	502,596	**148**	41,272	**88**	131,816	**739**	70,016	18,345	20,617	Fayette
Franklin*	049	1,094,640	1,068,978	21,981	485,707	40,002	24,061,440	.4446	18,354,640	**5,399**	2,435,257	**5,170**	882,936	**4,948**	1,927,076	705,483	813,931	Franklin
Fulton*	051	42,546	42,084	19,041	15,972	40,672	810,100	.0132	374,110	**110**	37,041	**79**	2,860	**16**	61,825	23,367	32,829	Fulton
Gallia**	053	31,500	31,069	14,089	12,519	28,382	443,800	.0094	384,469	**113**	45,774	**97**	7,215	**40**	62,516	19,484	23,721	Gallia
Geauga*	055	94,840	90,895	23,871	33,718	53,280	2,263,930	.0330	790,968	**233**	24,358	**52**	11,859	**66**	191,537	75,822	69,089	Geauga
Greene*	057	152,266	147,886	22,010	61,010	44,303	3,351,340	.0556	1,843,877	**542**	348,904	**741**	137,107	**768**	205,089	65,899	119,376	Greene
Guernsey**	059	41,552	40,792	14,163	16,570	28,420	588,500	.0116	419,053	**123**	60,406	**128**	6,984	**39**	79,107	17,744	30,728	Guernsey
Hamilton*	061	816,699	845,303	20,471	351,774	38,076	16,718,410	.3043	11,803,553	**3,472**	1,568,275	**3,329**	769,112	**4,310**	1,638,199	716,873	557,775	Hamilton
Hancock**	063	73,736	71,295	20,094	29,417	40,318	1,481,620	.0277	1,123,567	**331**	249,280	**529**	28,414	**159**	100,481	41,382	55,073	Hancock
Hardin	065	31,498	31,945	15,392	11,934	32,331	484,820	.0082	216,615	**64**	25,355	**54**	3,207	**18**	47,097	13,470	22,345	Hardin
Harrison	067	16,001	15,856	14,798	6,625	28,576	236,780	.0038	72,472	**21**	3,430	**7**	....	**....**	16,227	7,221	12,925	Harrison
Henry	069	29,352	29,210	18,877	11,259	39,328	554,080	.0090	248,980	**73**	19,759	**42**	3,028	**17**	34,665	20,416	22,849	Henry
Highland	071	42,277	40,875	15,928	16,316	32,931	673,380	.0116	323,605	**95**	56,910	**121**	3,925	**22**	48,976	25,383	31,788	Highland
Hocking	073	28,778	28,241	15,837	11,284	32,348	455,750	.0078	212,316	**62**	18,392	**39**	2,337	**13**	44,726	16,304	21,760	Hocking
Holmes	075	41,223	38,943	12,741	12,119	34,698	525,240	.0106	365,592	**108**	31,100	**66**	1,748	**10**	43,063	16,330	18,240	Holmes
Huron**	077	60,438	59,487	17,975	23,074	37,527	1,086,370	.0184	557,047	**164**	52,417	**111**	8,494	**48**	99,678	40,069	43,371	Huron
Jackson	079	33,219	32,641	14,373	13,271	28,766	477,450	.0091	301,789	**89**	53,311	**113**	2,209	**12**	55,933	23,058	24,604	Jackson
Jefferson*	081	71,299	73,894	15,394	30,104	29,333	1,097,590	.0201	656,154	**193**	103,038	**219**	18,658	**105**	122,657	75,354	51,671	Jefferson
Knox**	083	57,690	54,500	16,764	21,293	36,380	967,130	.0160	424,097	**125**	68,391	**145**	12,624	**71**	80,791	28,978	40,993	Knox
Lake*	085	229,287	227,511	22,354	93,173	44,099	5,125,450	.0939	3,849,466	**1,132**	499,865	**1,061**	137,493	**771**	460,199	289,205	173,198	Lake
Lawrence*	087	62,637	62,319	14,095	25,588	27,650	882,840	.0156	419,554	**123**	135,638	**288**	4,114	**23**	68,204	34,803	45,243	Lawrence
Licking*	089	152,155	145,491	19,687	59,092	40,749	2,995,490	.0509	1,663,248	**489**	235,651	**500**	49,313	**276**	208,301	64,752	115,432	Licking
Logan**	091	46,542	46,005	18,963	18,439	38,399	882,560	.0144	403,836	**119**	54,114	**115**	12,174	**68**	79,347	25,525	35,247	Logan
Lorain*	093	293,138	284,664	20,150	114,489	41,469	5,906,600	.0988	3,141,482	**924**	401,414	**852**	94,102	**527**	424,393	289,887	211,564	Lorain
Lucas*	095	453,978	455,054	18,791	191,320	35,748	8,530,580	.1602	6,292,688	**1,851**	1,085,178	**2,304**	285,564	**1,600**	823,643	370,063	309,782	Lucas
Madison*	097	40,757	40,213	17,946	14,405	40,597	731,430	.0122	352,075	**104**	23,123	**49**	1,673	**9**	51,415	14,117	28,429	Madison
Mahoning*	099	249,884	257,555	17,292	104,311	33,206	4,321,080	.0800	2,904,872	**854**	385,938	**819**	127,060	**712**	351,917	190,352	177,212	Mahoning
Marion**	101	66,481	66,217	16,976	25,090	35,941	1,128,570	.0205	706,766	**208**	178,272	**378**	20,323	**114**	90,631	38,621	44,293	Marion
Medina*	103	164,898	151,095	23,073	60,980	49,911	3,804,660	.0609	1,899,175	**559**	184,510	**392**	52,832	**296**	241,150	155,098	125,661	Medina
Meigs	105	23,310	23,072	13,278	9,568	26,001	309,520	.0055	135,626	**40**	10,311	**22**	1,547	**9**	32,391	12,808	18,335	Meigs
Mercer**	107	40,938	40,924	18,350	15,137	39,829	751,220	.0133	451,089	**133**	28,837	**61**	7,970	**45**	64,934	25,642	30,612	Mercer
Miami*	109	100,642	98,868	20,138	40,030	40,584	2,026,720	.0333	1,014,106	**298**	163,716	**348**	38,046	**213**	127,738	57,034	77,437	Miami
Monroe	111	14,845	15,180	14,684	6,051	28,873	217,990	.0034	55,735	**16**	....	**....**	....	**....**	15,545	6,227	12,001	Monroe
Montgomery*	113	550,095	559,062	20,419	240,514	37,391	11,232,240	.1964	7,005,152	**2,061**	1,206,160	**2,560**	252,696	**1,416**	961,401	351,148	400,807	Montgomery
Morgan	115	14,829	14,897	14,033	6,057	27,407	208,100	.0033	55,891	**16**	4,440	**9**	....	**....**	14,882	3,104	11,970	Morgan
Morrow*	117	34,155	31,628	17,582	12,677	37,767	600,500	.0090	172,175	**51**	9,774	**21**	1,788	**10**	41,213	9,789	27,172	Morrow
Muskingum**	119	85,650	84,585	16,108	33,357	33,161	1,379,610	.0279	1,150,335	**338**	150,214	**319**	78,026	**437**	154,137	75,149	62,092	Muskingum
Noble	121	14,039	14,058	13,443	4,840	31,185	188,730	.0032	73,734	**22**	1,298	**3**	....	**....**	17,997	6,914	9,867	Noble
Ottawa*	123	41,255	40,985	20,960	17,016	40,717	864,690	.0147	498,248	**147**	29,495	**63**	5,431	**30**	77,782	24,742	32,864	Ottawa
Paulding	125	19,480	20,293	18,401	7,712	37,077	358,450	.0056	136,799	**40**	5,204	**11**	....	**....**	22,684	7,991	15,926	Paulding
Perry	127	35,390	34,078	15,067	13,130	32,512	533,220	.0082	138,430	**41**	10,258	**22**	1,085	**6**	43,465	13,429	25,935	Perry
Pickaway*	129	51,354	52,727	17,478	18,169	39,681	897,550	.0146	375,830	**111**	58,431	**124**	5,536	**31**	60,430	27,564	36,554	Pickaway
Pike	131	28,341	27,695	15,019	11,492	29,679	425,650	.0076	223,401	**66**	43,224	**92**	2,948	**17**	49,264	21,800	21,743	Pike
Portage*	133	155,699	152,061	19,652	60,198	40,815	3,059,740	.0496	1,426,579	**420**	100,782	**214**	72,635	**407**	208,451	87,842	118,812	Portage
Preble*	135	42,436	42,337	18,875	16,431	39,083	800,980	.0124	295,045	**87**	17,209	**37**	3,916	**22**	48,110	17,855	34,184	Preble
Putnam	137	34,751	34,726	19,101	12,584	42,104	663,790	.0102	239,953	**71**	23,394	**50**	5,092	**29**	38,455	36,631	26,445	Putnam
Richland*	139	128,091	128,852	17,420	50,750	35,159	2,231,330	.0429	1,684,909	**496**	397,813	**844**	53,078	**297**	174,139	81,338	92,516	Richland
Ross**	141	74,752	73,345	16,497	28,363	34,993	1,233,170	.0221	716,221	**211**	175,494	**373**	19,952	**112**	122,565	38,284	53,912	Ross
Sandusky**	143	61,733	61,792	18,864	24,605	37,704	1,164,550	.0197	610,258	**180**	101,794	**216**	12,701	**71**	98,209	33,192	46,956	Sandusky
Scioto**	145	76,918	79,195	13,301	30,571	26,747	1,023,120	.0198	653,311	**192**	111,138	**236**	24,073	**135**	111,974	47,980	53,908	Scioto
Seneca**	147	57,438	58,683	17,294	22,377	35,438	993,340	.0170	505,939	**149**	43,313	**92**	15,932	**89**	79,288	29,897	42,329	Seneca
Shelby**	149	48,760	47,910	19,254	18,366	40,951	938,810	.0154	446,509	**131**	49,177	**104**	8,848	**50**	71,366	28,307	35,432	Shelby
Stark*	151	377,323	378,098	18,550	151,167	37,011	6,999,180	.1287	4,814,381	**1,416**	687,692	**1,460**	237,517	**1,331**	683,492	423,679	275,318	Stark
Summit*	153	547,831	542,899	20,446	227,872	39,616	11,201,050	.2030	7,805,081	**2,296**	848,366	**1,801**	292,381	**1,639**	1,080,716	703,305	398,640	Summit
Trumbull*	155	220,736	225,116	18,298	89,774	35,981	4,038,930	.0712	2,404,298	**707**	323,048	**686**	86,988	**488**	359,830	172,926	160,762	Trumbull
Tuscarawas**	157	91,928	90,914	16,554	36,539	33,231	1,521,810	.0277	935,184	**275**	137,056	**291**	37,510	**210**	174,825	68,586	67,671	Tuscarawas
Union*	159	44,598	40,909	21,750	16,671	46,745	970,000	.0152	426,035	**125**	47,528	**101**	4,711	**26**	71,088	18,895	34,907	Union
Van Wert**	161	29,158	29,659	18,335	11,663	36,533	534,610	.0090	276,615	**81**	40,990	**87**	5,300	**30**	44,403	15,165	22,603	Van Wert
Vinton	163	13,371	12,806	13,398	5,202	27,428	179,150	.0028	38,071	**11**	1,980	**4**	....	**....**	14,400	3,189	9,934	Vinton
Warren*	165	188,737	158,383	23,434	68,184	51,876	4,422,820	.0673	1,835,882	**540**	250,673	**532**	23,349	**131**	342,332	65,566	139,622	Warren
Washington*	167	62,279	63,251	16,435	25,266	32,359	1,023,530	.0191	676,315	**199**	85,353	**181**	10,002	**56**	117,910	30,893	47,489	Washington
Wayne**	169	113,591	111,564	17,605	41,720	38,316	1,999,720	.0344	1,067,460	**314**	101,249	**215**	30,458	**171**	192,702	54,760	79,152	Wayne
Williams	171	38,669	39,188	18,564	15,211	37,619	717,870	.0115	299,389	**88**	48,052	**102**	6,043	**34**	51,368	21,955	28,876	Williams
Wood*	173	123,620	121,065	19,464	47,203	40,896	2,406,080	.0405	1,282,722	**377**	169,929	**361**	30,499	**171**	219,230	54,120	91,386	Wood
Wyandot	175	22,797	22,908	17,926	9,044	36,047	408,660	.0064	148,364	**44**	6,941	**15**	1,289	**7**	24,463	17,508	18,099	Wyandot
The State		11,459,952	11,353,140	19,504	4,663,484	38,353	223,520,150	3.9200	136,773,683	**40,233**	18,668,355	**39,630**	5,729,403	**32,109**	19,270,480	9,170,449	8,258,075	The State

OKLAHOMA (OK; CODE 40; 77 Counties)

COUNTY OR COUNTY EQUIVALENT	FIPS CO. CODE	POPULATION Estimate 7/1/04	POPULATION Census 4/1/00	PER CAPITA INCOME 2003	HOUSEHOLDS Estimate 7/1/04	MEDIAN HOUSEHOLD INCOME 2003	DISPOSABLE INCOME 2003 ($1,000)	MARKET ABILITY INDEX 2003	TOTAL RETAIL SALES Sales 2003 ($1,000)	TOTAL RETAIL SALES Ranally Sales Units	GENERAL MERCHANDISE Sales 2003 ($1,000)	GENERAL MERCHANDISE Ranally Sales Units	APPAREL STORE Sales 2003 ($1,000)	APPAREL STORE Ranally Sales Units	FOOD STORE SALES 2003 ($1,000)	HEALTH & DRUG STORE 2003 ($1,000)	PASSENGER CAR REGIS-TRATIONS 2003	COUNTY OR COUNTY EQUIVALENT
Adair	001	21,794	21,038	11,104	7,849	23,689	242,000	.0043	86,167	**25**	18,565	**39**	....	**....**	12,872	3,208	13,664	Adair
Alfalfa	003	5,851	6,105	13,092	2,102	28,279	76,600	.0013	22,404	**7**	3,000	**6**	....	**....**	3,787	1,874	4,231	Alfalfa
Atoka	005	14,241	13,879	11,134	5,213	23,459	158,560	.0032	95,969	**28**	27,401	**58**	1,107	**6**	13,126	4,119	9,179	Atoka
Beaver	007	5,514	5,857	16,890	2,109	34,253	93,130	.0013	16,069	**5**	2,316	**5**	....	**....**	2,932	....	4,606	Beaver
Beckham**	009	19,942	19,799	12,806	7,511	26,417	255,380	.0061	289,992	**85**	60,998	**129**	7,472	**42**	34,681	9,874	13,483	Beckham
Blaine	011	11,583	11,976	12,375	4,089	27,134	143,340	.0024	47,279	**14**	6,503	**14**	....	**....**	11,224	2,489	8,041	Blaine
Bryan**	013	37,533	36,534	13,622	14,874	26,685	511,260	.0093	257,971	**76**	47,166	**100**	4,015	**23**	39,289	11,589	26,121	Bryan
Caddo	015	30,055	30,150	12,352	10,950	26,170	371,240	.0069	184,289	**54**	38,920	**83**	2,983	**17**	31,899	13,166	19,633	Caddo
Canadian*	017	94,470	87,697	19,790	35,011	41,605	1,869,590	.0295	780,921	**230**	206,421	**438**	6,046	**34**	49,736	33,369	68,540	Canadian
Carter**	019	46,663	45,621	14,264	18,570	27,896	665,590	.0140	579,792	**171**	134,900	**286**	25,796	**145**	53,922	38,101	32,052	Carter
Cherokee**	021	44,157	42,521	12,535	16,890	25,641	553,520	.0107	323,787	**95**	72,670	**154**	9,512	**53**	72,068	10,852	29,559	Cherokee
Choctaw	023	15,461	15,342	11,739	6,375	21,994	181,500	.0034	86,180	**25**	22,623	**48**	1,979	**11**	14,633	4,986	10,611	Choctaw
Cimarron	025	2,901	3,148	14,736	1,165	28,391	42,750	.0009	33,927	**10**	....	**....**	....	**....**	5,423	1,640	2,258	Cimarron
Cleveland*	027	223,830	208,016	20,005	89,574	39,142	4,477,710	.0703	1,857,076	**546**	443,400	**941**	70,153	**393**	237,622	121,731	170,479	Cleveland
Coal	029	5,926	6,031	11,591	2,329	22,927	68,690	.0012	20,034	**6**	2,780	**6**	....	**....**	5,414	1,275	4,069	Coal
Comanche*	031	113,664	114,996	14,565	40,239	32,093	1,655,550	.0289	779,898	**229**	245,081	**520**	21,843	**122**	72,711	30,150	70,163	Comanche
Cotton	033	6,559	6,614	13,688	2,610	26,758	89,780	.0015	26,103	**8**	4,521	**10**	....	**....**	6,558	2,801	4,963	Cotton
Craig	035	14,856	14,950	13,998	5,578	29,360	207,960	.0039	122,900	**36**	23,347	**50**	....	**....**	16,963	6,359	10,409	Craig
Creek*	037	69,207	67,367	15,312	26,174	31,353	1,059,710	.0174	400,252	**118**	89,532	**190**	4,861	**27**	70,467	31,387	49,214	Creek
Custer	039	24,607	26,142	13,931	9,690	27,573	342,810	.0073	306,723	**90**	64,814	**138**	10,930	**61**	44,203	17,768	17,456	Custer
Delaware	041	39,213	37,077	14,054	15,841	26,998	551,080	.0092	184,168	**54**	67,866	**144**	1,835	**10**	14,800	6,599	29,064	Delaware
Dewey	043	4,495	4,743	14,489	1,892	26,635	65,130	.0010	19,347	**6**	1,574	**3**	....	**....**	1,712	1,142	3,996	Dewey
Ellis	045	3,978	4,075	15,475	1,776	26,797	61,560	.0010	21,455	**6**	1,921	**4**	....	**....**	5,125	1,517	3,558	Ellis
Garfield**	047	56,916	57,813	16,295	23,194	31,078	927,440	.0174	620,785	**183**	145,515	**309**	17,180	**96**	98,379	26,289	41,392	Garfield
Garvin	049	27,197	27,210	13,920	10,900	26,964	378,570	.0073	250,791	**74**	39,664	**84**	4,329	**24**	40,701	11,648	19,398	Garvin
Grady*	051	48,055	45,516	15,337	18,500	31,407	737,000	.0126	338,100	**99**	41,524	**88**	9,399	**53**	54,365	16,360	35,182	Grady
Grant	053	4,922	5,144	14,411	1,991	27,733	70,930	.0011	12,470	**4**	2,073	**4**	....	**....**	2,807	....	4,127	Grant
Greer	055	5,843	6,061	11,169	2,083	24,295	65,260	.0011	17,137	**5**	1,718	**4**	....	**....**	6,234	1,517	3,786	Greer
Harmon	057	2,980	3,283	10,896	1,138	21,850	32,470	.0006	17,180	**5**	2,306	**5**	....	**....**	3,732	1,081	1,948	Harmon
Harper	059	3,350	3,562	17,693	1,440	31,766	59,270	.0009	14,224	**4**	1,595	**3**	....	**....**	3,968	1,557	3,084	Harper
Haskell	061	12,118	11,792	11,959	4,744	23,325	144,920	.0027	70,774	**21**	19,000	**40**	1,076	**6**	12,593	1,823	8,327	Haskell
Hughes	063	13,820	14,154	10,894	5,180	22,430	150,560	.0028	64,442	**19**	16,226	**34**	....	**....**	9,337	2,716	8,906	Hughes
Jackson**	065	27,034	28,439	14,063	10,121	29,538	380,190	.0077	290,780	**86**	88,633	**188**	10,564	**59**	36,051	9,911	17,222	Jackson
Jefferson	067	6,454	6,818	11,780	2,569	22,857	76,030	.0014	36,125	**11**	5,883	**13**	....	**....**	6,005	4,247	4,622	Jefferson
Johnston	069	10,526	10,513	11,783	4,074	23,557	124,030	.0021	35,317	**10**	2,261	**5**	....	**....**	9,448	4,922	7,204	Johnston
Kay**	071	47,032	48,080	15,683	19,785	29,068	737,600	.0140	498,805	**147**	136,583	**290**	12,712	**71**	50,706	30,538	34,386	Kay
Kingfisher	073	14,130	13,926	16,946	5,355	34,942	239,450	.0041	122,826	**36**	17,382	**37**	....	**....**	12,724	8,726	10,720	Kingfisher
Kiowa	075	9,902	10,227	13,375	4,126	25,115	132,440	.0023	51,169	**15**	11,489	**24**	....	**....**	12,100	6,479	7,224	Kiowa

Source: Devonshire Associates Ltd. and Scan/US, Inc. 2004.
* Component of a Metropolitan Core Based Statistical Area.
** Component of a Micropolitan Core Based Statistical Area.

.... Data less than 1,000.

(d) Data not available.

Counties: Population / Income / Sales, *Continued*

COUNTY OR COUNTY EQUIVALENT	FIPS CO. CODE	POPULATION Estimate 7/1/04	POPULATION Census 4/1/00	PER CAPITA INCOME 2003	HOUSEHOLDS Estimate 7/1/04	MEDIAN HOUSEHOLD INCOME 2003	DISPOSABLE INCOME 2003 ($1,000)	MARKET ABILITY INDEX 2003	TOTAL RETAIL SALES Sales 2003 ($1,000)	TOTAL RETAIL SALES Ranally Sales Units	GENERAL MERCHANDISE Sales 2003 ($1,000)	GENERAL MERCHANDISE Ranally Sales Units	APPAREL STORE Sales 2003 ($1,000)	APPAREL STORE Ranally Sales Units	FOOD STORE SALES 2003 ($1,000)	HEALTH & DRUG STORE 2003 ($1,000)	PASSENGER CAR REGIS-TRATIONS 2003	COUNTY OR COUNTY EQUIVALENT
Latimer	077	10,541	10,692	11,255	3,956	23,238	118,640	.0020	29,411	**9**	9,476	**20**	....	**....**	6,444	2,388	6,976	Latimer
Le Flore*	079	49,143	48,109	12,618	18,370	26,190	620,100	.0119	362,414	**107**	110,972	**236**	3,222	**18**	63,469	10,277	33,473	Le Flore
Lincoln*	081	32,301	32,080	14,500	12,415	29,476	468,370	.0075	138,256	**41**	17,497	**37**	15,073	**84**	18,250	5,082	23,961	Lincoln
Logan*	083	35,908	33,924	16,355	13,190	35,152	587,280	.0092	193,586	**57**	29,941	**64**	....	**....**	23,306	5,760	26,335	Logan
Love**	085	8,931	8,831	15,501	3,502	30,801	138,440	.0024	71,601	**21**	5,309	**11**	....	**....**	21,422	3,264	6,856	Love
McClain*	087	28,843	27,740	16,991	10,824	35,352	490,060	.0083	242,205	**71**	38,350	**81**	1,011	**6**	25,134	10,250	22,144	McClain
McCurtain	089	33,875	34,402	11,853	13,281	23,426	401,520	.0077	221,829	**65**	56,067	**119**	6,299	**35**	37,215	10,117	22,311	McCurtain
McIntosh	091	19,821	19,456	13,426	8,326	25,027	266,110	.0055	207,938	**61**	63,359	**135**	2,872	**16**	41,932	6,555	14,858	McIntosh
Major	093	7,384	7,545	15,512	3,033	29,529	114,540	.0022	75,559	**22**	5,522	**12**	....	**....**	8,090	4,154	6,184	Major
Marshall	095	13,811	13,184	13,302	5,640	25,389	183,720	.0032	77,306	**23**	22,050	**47**	....	**....**	19,073	6,129	9,993	Marshall
Mayes	097	39,014	38,369	14,666	15,217	29,359	572,170	.0098	247,849	**73**	49,420	**105**	3,082	**17**	52,936	13,500	29,097	Mayes
Murray	099	12,753	12,623	14,607	5,092	28,567	186,280	.0036	130,999	**39**	24,207	**51**	....	**....**	15,831	4,950	9,293	Murray
Muskogee**	101	70,522	69,451	13,443	27,250	27,023	948,050	.0189	667,831	**196**	148,008	**314**	17,507	**98**	91,227	43,464	45,582	Muskogee
Noble	103	11,210	11,411	16,383	4,478	31,997	183,650	.0032	92,085	**27**	9,883	**21**	....	**....**	8,197	4,849	9,018	Noble
Nowata	105	10,918	10,569	14,031	4,251	27,717	153,190	.0023	24,456	**7**	4,111	**9**	....	**....**	4,903	1,859	7,913	Nowata
Okfuskee	107	11,638	11,814	11,014	4,248	23,042	128,180	.0023	44,787	**13**	5,641	**12**	....	**....**	5,949	6,193	7,519	Okfuskee
Oklahoma*	109	680,880	660,448	17,709	284,991	32,996	12,057,680	.2343	9,485,296	**2,790**	1,430,668	**3,037**	345,116	**1,934**	1,064,675	499,860	468,898	Oklahoma
Okmulgee*	111	39,692	39,685	13,190	15,327	26,837	523,540	.0096	270,773	**80**	81,059	**172**	4,916	**28**	39,062	8,312	26,190	Okmulgee
Osage*	113	45,482	44,437	15,710	17,150	32,625	714,540	.0103	118,262	**35**	11,843	**25**	....	**....**	35,787	9,654	32,528	Osage
Ottawa**	115	32,597	33,194	13,447	12,989	26,196	438,340	.0081	233,507	**69**	40,123	**85**	3,199	**18**	35,163	12,643	23,154	Ottawa
Pawnee*	117	16,820	16,612	14,721	6,460	30,031	247,610	.0042	98,288	**29**	24,054	**51**	1,462	**8**	24,340	7,948	12,628	Pawnee
Payne**	119	71,992	68,190	14,003	28,525	27,589	1,008,100	.0194	660,551	**194**	188,651	**400**	26,125	**146**	70,061	33,908	51,940	Payne
Pittsburg**	121	44,235	43,953	13,647	17,381	26,929	603,660	.0122	451,913	**133**	131,857	**280**	13,966	**78**	31,676	16,132	29,553	Pittsburg
Pontotoc**	123	35,183	35,143	13,448	14,008	26,411	473,150	.0096	349,237	**103**	103,362	**219**	13,520	**76**	39,160	18,743	24,766	Pontotoc
Pottawatomie**	125	67,896	65,521	14,487	25,696	29,894	983,640	.0177	517,432	**152**	136,748	**290**	25,468	**143**	63,056	42,768	46,571	Pottawatomie
Pushmataha	127	11,781	11,667	11,591	4,832	21,632	136,550	.0025	55,726	**16**	4,988	**11**	....	**....**	11,610	6,345	8,349	Pushmataha
Roger Mills	129	3,131	3,436	15,679	1,348	28,300	49,090	.0009	25,524	**8**	3,896	**8**	....	**....**	1,171	2,291	3,002	Roger Mills
Rogers*	131	79,136	70,641	19,209	29,010	40,916	1,520,150	.0227	475,432	**140**	120,820	**256**	8,244	**46**	47,588	20,508	58,827	Rogers
Seminole	133	24,356	24,894	12,150	9,407	24,531	295,920	.0056	152,206	**45**	31,833	**68**	3,322	**19**	27,601	11,250	16,300	Seminole
Sequoyah*	135	40,284	38,972	13,021	15,505	26,281	524,530	.0098	283,761	**83**	35,594	**76**	1,723	**10**	63,719	14,299	27,377	Sequoyah
Stephens**	137	42,275	43,182	15,361	17,507	28,910	649,370	.0127	471,251	**139**	93,228	**198**	11,435	**64**	66,237	27,878	31,950	Stephens
Texas**	139	19,853	20,107	14,863	6,872	33,260	295,070	.0052	145,936	**43**	32,730	**69**	2,873	**16**	20,850	6,644	12,959	Texas
Tillman	141	8,700	9,287	12,191	3,410	24,074	106,060	.0018	34,790	**10**	4,280	**9**	2,813	**16**	9,859	2,641	5,959	Tillman
Tulsa*	143	572,493	563,299	19,808	245,488	36,079	11,339,830	.2144	8,762,357	**2,578**	1,667,077	**3,539**	298,004	**1,670**	887,933	469,521	413,115	Tulsa
Wagoner*	145	63,191	57,491	18,346	23,407	38,487	1,159,300	.0163	218,259	**64**	65,082	**138**	1,629	**9**	37,414	11,595	46,804	Wagoner
Washington**	147	49,164	48,996	18,003	20,493	33,748	885,110	.0145	401,693	**118**	135,138	**287**	13,880	**78**	34,488	20,620	36,732	Washington
Washita	149	11,160	11,508	14,212	4,389	28,125	158,610	.0027	58,990	**17**	3,240	**7**	....	**....**	9,799	3,534	8,375	Washita
Woods	151	8,549	9,089	14,788	3,610	27,183	126,420	.0024	84,814	**25**	30,163	**64**	1,251	**7**	11,138	4,078	6,602	Woods
Woodward**	153	18,469	18,486	15,967	7,226	31,571	294,900	.0062	266,362	**78**	82,279	**175**	7,454	**42**	29,546	12,210	13,746	Woodward
The State		3,530,711	3,450,654	16,470	1,411,715	31,990	58,152,070	1.0562	35,434,102	**10,424**	7,177,620	**15,234**	1,071,686	**6,003**	4,285,633	1,887,068	2,500,715	The State

OREGON (OR; CODE 41; 36 Counties)

COUNTY OR COUNTY EQUIVALENT	FIPS CO. CODE	POPULATION Estimate 7/1/04	POPULATION Census 4/1/00	PER CAPITA INCOME 2003	HOUSEHOLDS Estimate 7/1/04	MEDIAN HOUSEHOLD INCOME 2003	DISPOSABLE INCOME 2003 ($1,000)	MARKET ABILITY INDEX 2003	TOTAL RETAIL SALES Sales 2003 ($1,000)	TOTAL RETAIL SALES Ranally Sales Units	GENERAL MERCHANDISE Sales 2003 ($1,000)	GENERAL MERCHANDISE Ranally Sales Units	APPAREL STORE Sales 2003 ($1,000)	APPAREL STORE Ranally Sales Units	FOOD STORE SALES 2003 ($1,000)	HEALTH & DRUG STORE 2003 ($1,000)	PASSENGER CAR REGIS-TRATIONS 2003	COUNTY OR COUNTY EQUIVALENT
Baker	001	16,259	16,741	14,846	6,777	28,517	241,380	.0046	164,930	**49**	4,925	**10**	1,500	**8**	36,679	11,207	12,811	Baker
Benton*	003	79,726	78,153	19,582	32,175	38,800	1,561,160	.0243	609,433	**179**	82,549	**175**	24,628	**138**	136,155	28,413	60,491	Benton
Clackamas*	005	363,386	338,391	22,481	138,857	46,833	8,169,240	.1336	4,329,290	**1,273**	746,301	**1,584**	164,662	**923**	596,731	110,937	274,204	Clackamas
Clatsop**	007	35,896	35,630	17,914	15,031	34,226	643,040	.0119	441,022	**130**	115,333	**245**	25,380	**142**	75,248	21,154	25,629	Clatsop
Columbia*	009	47,125	43,560	19,766	17,832	41,769	931,490	.0138	289,136	**85**	26,168	**56**	3,510	**20**	76,771	30,086	37,058	Columbia
Coos**	011	63,130	62,779	15,870	26,884	29,840	1,001,860	.0184	616,301	**181**	128,661	**273**	13,259	**74**	116,110	24,983	48,055	Coos
Crook**	013	21,020	19,182	16,103	8,053	33,439	338,490	.0055	130,927	**39**	....	**....**	1,497	**8**	29,211	15,619	16,357	Crook
Curry**	015	22,045	21,137	16,456	10,184	28,445	362,780	.0064	199,746	**59**	52,960	**112**	3,206	**18**	30,962	14,634	17,767	Curry
Deschutes*	017	133,790	115,367	19,248	53,268	38,594	2,575,130	.0496	2,062,744	**607**	494,038	**1,049**	64,588	**362**	296,027	49,603	107,804	Deschutes
Douglas**	019	102,953	100,399	15,988	41,645	31,451	1,646,060	.0291	891,484	**262**	180,243	**383**	23,823	**134**	176,421	47,329	80,480	Douglas
Gilliam	021	1,736	1,915	17,408	762	31,921	30,220	.0005	12,031	**4**	....	**....**	....	**....**	2,135	1,239	1,504	Gilliam
Grant	023	7,312	7,935	16,026	3,045	30,663	117,180	.0021	62,896	**19**	1,658	**4**	....	**....**	24,012	6,705	5,969	Grant
Harney	025	7,047	7,609	14,825	2,847	29,331	104,470	.0021	78,659	**23**	....	**....**	1,215	**7**	24,068	3,159	5,605	Harney
Hood River**	027	20,854	20,411	16,047	7,409	35,721	334,640	.0066	261,229	**77**	44,727	**95**	7,208	**40**	74,516	12,335	14,581	Hood River
Jackson*	029	192,822	181,269	17,054	76,466	34,326	3,288,420	.0707	3,296,101	**970**	569,323	**1,209**	84,470	**473**	347,160	87,002	144,677	Jackson
Jefferson	031	19,853	19,009	14,953	7,071	33,570	296,860	.0052	148,613	**44**	2,834	**6**	3,258	**18**	38,897	3,660	14,499	Jefferson
Josephine**	033	80,080	75,726	15,171	33,085	29,346	1,214,910	.0228	775,560	**228**	167,118	**355**	14,814	**83**	120,977	29,963	62,577	Josephine
Klamath**	035	65,050	63,775	14,776	25,933	29,756	961,180	.0189	698,968	**206**	148,089	**314**	12,784	**72**	126,641	21,084	48,739	Klamath
Lake	037	7,450	7,422	14,989	3,191	27,748	111,670	.0020	56,797	**17**	1,045	**2**	....	**....**	18,620	4,479	6,069	Lake
Lane*	039	332,896	322,959	17,777	136,131	34,734	5,917,890	.1118	4,302,190	**1,266**	807,668	**1,715**	128,392	**720**	679,603	134,140	246,882	Lane
Lincoln	041	44,777	44,479	17,044	19,667	30,871	763,160	.0143	525,343	**155**	99,620	**211**	55,518	**311**	113,849	25,000	32,366	Lincoln
Linn**	043	107,154	103,069	17,141	41,277	35,471	1,836,740	.0328	1,087,080	**320**	287,763	**611**	31,844	**178**	168,781	36,564	80,031	Linn
Malheur**	045	31,140	31,615	11,445	9,963	28,398	356,410	.0087	394,873	**116**	104,203	**221**	13,327	**75**	66,706	12,449	18,936	Malheur
Marion*	047	300,798	284,834	16,523	105,914	37,360	4,970,010	.0951	3,584,881	**1,055**	755,154	**1,603**	135,010	**757**	472,284	109,297	191,331	Marion
Morrow**	049	11,815	10,995	14,649	3,947	34,840	173,080	.0029	62,332	**18**	....	**....**	....	**....**	8,341	4,627	8,371	Morrow
Multnomah*	051	683,283	660,486	20,230	287,648	38,205	13,822,920	.2610	10,755,184	**3,164**	1,785,405	**3,790**	719,360	**4,032**	1,367,754	296,973	452,776	Multnomah
Polk*	053	67,110	62,380	18,313	24,949	39,355	1,228,990	.0177	286,645	**84**	34,192	**73**	1,861	**10**	84,233	14,787	48,647	Polk
Sherman	055	1,701	1,934	16,802	703	32,668	28,580	.0005	19,790	**6**	2,150	**5**	....	**....**	8,116	....	1,420	Sherman
Tillamook	057	24,700	24,262	17,207	10,489	32,270	425,020	.0071	194,191	**57**	31,948	**68**	3,361	**19**	43,933	9,469	18,342	Tillamook
Umatilla**	059	72,450	70,548	15,094	25,626	34,093	1,093,560	.0235	1,033,843	**304**	145,893	**310**	30,825	**173**	184,481	32,820	50,945	Umatilla
Union**	061	24,564	24,530	16,128	9,916	31,695	396,180	.0080	325,651	**96**	56,586	**120**	12,413	**70**	64,084	11,381	19,344	Union
Wallowa	063	7,037	7,226	16,091	3,000	30,138	113,230	.0022	78,608	**23**	1,522	**3**	....	**....**	17,969	2,548	5,919	Wallowa
Wasco**	065	23,514	23,791	16,770	9,303	33,814	394,320	.0077	302,490	**89**	67,031	**142**	9,167	**51**	34,428	13,223	17,979	Wasco
Washington*	067	489,844	445,342	22,579	187,584	46,925	11,060,140	.1991	7,944,734	**2,337**	1,624,383	**3,448**	429,674	**2,408**	945,725	171,562	337,164	Washington
Wheeler	069	1,492	1,547	14,926	635	28,073	22,270	.0004	11,506	**3**	....	**....**	....	**....**	2,729	....	1,321	Wheeler
Yamhill*	071	90,750	84,992	17,194	30,754	40,513	1,560,370	.0266	787,105	**232**	148,044	**314**	19,696	**110**	94,481	27,598	61,788	Yamhill
The State		3,602,559	3,421,399	18,901	1,418,021	38,140	68,093,050	1.2475	46,822,313	**13,777**	8,720,416	**18,513**	2,042,078	**11,444**	6,704,837	1,426,266	2,578,438	The State

PENNSYLVANIA (PA; CODE 42; 67 Counties)

COUNTY OR COUNTY EQUIVALENT	FIPS CO. CODE	POPULATION Estimate 7/1/04	POPULATION Census 4/1/00	PER CAPITA INCOME 2003	HOUSEHOLDS Estimate 7/1/04	MEDIAN HOUSEHOLD INCOME 2003	DISPOSABLE INCOME 2003 ($1,000)	MARKET ABILITY INDEX 2003	TOTAL RETAIL SALES Sales 2003 ($1,000)	TOTAL RETAIL SALES Ranally Sales Units	GENERAL MERCHANDISE Sales 2003 ($1,000)	GENERAL MERCHANDISE Ranally Sales Units	APPAREL STORE Sales 2003 ($1,000)	APPAREL STORE Ranally Sales Units	FOOD STORE SALES 2003 ($1,000)	HEALTH & DRUG STORE 2003 ($1,000)	PASSENGER CAR REGIS-TRATIONS 2003	COUNTY OR COUNTY EQUIVALENT
Adams**	001	98,071	91,292	18,638	36,632	39,658	1,827,830	.0275	573,984	**169**	54,779	**116**	11,060	**62**	131,219	21,655	71,386	Adams
Allegheny*	003	1,255,103	1,281,666	19,668	544,809	35,911	24,685,840	.4430	16,329,315	**4,803**	1,644,479	**3,491**	930,187	**5,213**	2,650,249	1,228,708	774,262	Allegheny
Armstrong*	005	71,442	72,392	15,265	29,175	29,858	1,090,590	.0196	598,907	**176**	58,831	**125**	8,487	**48**	105,289	88,216	50,488	Armstrong
Beaver*	007	177,885	181,412	17,911	72,783	34,953	3,186,150	.0520	1,398,278	**411**	237,773	**505**	54,754	**307**	281,915	134,703	121,903	Beaver
Bedford	009	49,909	49,984	15,655	20,179	30,754	781,310	.0163	694,303	**204**	52,333	**111**	3,660	**21**	74,609	26,216	38,946	Bedford
Berks*	011	388,909	373,638	19,644	147,702	41,188	7,639,890	.1301	4,256,088	**1,252**	525,747	**1,116**	342,408	**1,919**	683,206	249,524	256,404	Berks
Blair*	013	126,555	129,144	16,075	52,018	31,133	2,034,420	.0417	1,752,849	**516**	316,759	**672**	58,130	**326**	267,824	121,301	86,217	Blair
Bradford**	015	62,593	62,761	16,480	24,981	32,658	1,031,520	.0188	632,459	**186**	79,629	**169**	13,905	**78**	84,624	34,821	44,012	Bradford
Bucks*	017	617,667	597,635	25,011	229,938	53,229	15,448,380	.2654	10,173,907	**2,993**	862,474	**1,831**	396,331	**2,221**	1,660,147	571,612	435,191	Bucks
Butler*	019	181,858	174,083	19,063	70,122	39,341	3,466,830	.0605	2,051,759	**604**	270,149	**573**	51,283	**287**	333,292	133,119	129,693	Butler
Cambria*	021	148,535	152,598	14,525	60,133	28,351	2,157,510	.0416	1,455,184	**428**	194,854	**414**	35,359	**198**	276,792	104,805	96,672	Cambria
Cameron	023	5,723	5,974	16,044	2,383	30,498	91,820	.0015	34,208	**10**	1,342	**3**	....	**....**	8,042	2,747	3,761	Cameron
Carbon*	025	60,563	58,802	17,095	24,884	32,910	1,035,300	.0173	478,381	**141**	43,705	**93**	....	**....**	131,806	38,245	44,239	Carbon
Centre*	027	143,518	135,758	15,772	52,665	34,149	2,263,590	.0432	1,572,637	**463**	206,017	**437**	90,830	**509**	222,749	82,855	92,657	Centre
Chester*	029	464,595	433,501	26,853	171,516	57,890	12,475,900	.2210	9,231,586	**2,716**	287,925	**611**	210,579	**1,180**	841,079	318,928	323,182	Chester
Clarion	031	41,032	41,765	14,347	16,148	28,937	588,690	.0119	449,405	**132**	43,390	**92**	14,831	**83**	87,321	25,268	28,109	Clarion
Clearfield**	033	82,705	83,382	14,888	33,108	29,700	1,231,350	.0248	961,684	**283**	153,334	**326**	35,001	**196**	135,340	45,868	57,613	Clearfield
Clinton**	035	37,273	37,914	14,571	14,786	29,298	543,090	.0107	397,165	**117**	34,432	**73**	16,825	**94**	62,841	18,648	24,837	Clinton
Columbia**	037	64,770	64,151	15,929	25,498	32,116	1,031,730	.0189	628,655	**185**	77,005	**163**	20,466	**115**	95,625	43,497	46,085	Columbia
Crawford**	039	89,668	90,366	15,527	34,875	31,627	1,392,310	.0252	799,528	**235**	81,499	**173**	20,749	**116**	133,921	49,372	58,613	Crawford
Cumberland*	041	221,861	213,674	21,436	88,599	42,601	4,755,730	.0904	3,870,146	**1,138**	373,604	**793**	111,360	**624**	476,863	168,420	159,948	Cumberland
Dauphin*	043	253,912	251,798	20,579	107,481	38,592	5,225,190	.0906	3,190,528	**939**	346,399	**735**	166,335	**932**	514,031	219,529	172,799	Dauphin
Delaware*	045	555,177	550,864	21,555	211,118	45,199	11,966,590	.1969	6,300,243	**1,853**	580,206	**1,232**	329,248	**1,845**	1,445,011	569,327	330,274	Delaware
Elk**	047	34,071	35,112	18,532	14,108	35,434	631,390	.0101	257,569	**76**	33,836	**72**	3,898	**22**	56,486	25,972	23,877	Elk
Erie*	049	279,718	280,843	17,187	111,157	34,537	4,807,540	.0901	3,333,544	**981**	445,349	**945**	129,279	**725**	546,498	194,903	176,959	Erie
Fayette*	051	145,333	148,644	13,750	59,925	26,429	1,998,260	.0386	1,297,894	**382**	244,733	**520**	45,366	**254**	229,076	103,649	99,006	Fayette
Forest	053	5,006	4,946	13,338	2,029	26,194	66,770	.0013	41,651	**12**	....	**....**	....	**....**	4,789	....	3,465	Forest
Franklin**	055	134,355	129,313	18,931	53,575	37,587	2,543,470	.0443	1,488,277	**438**	171,018	**363**	32,387	**182**	252,298	81,124	101,580	Franklin
Fulton	057	14,624	14,261	16,951	5,975	32,753	247,890	.0040	97,055	**29**	3,398	**7**	....	**....**	14,664	1,188	12,115	Fulton
Greene	059	40,302	40,672	13,690	15,232	28,646	551,720	.0104	323,560	**95**	10,309	**22**	....	**....**	48,752	31,817	26,125	Greene
Huntingdon**	061	45,954	45,586	14,907	17,264	31,775	685,020	.0121	341,278	**100**	17,186	**36**	4,288	**24**	71,454	23,910	31,930	Huntingdon
Indiana**	063	88,892	89,605	14,140	34,895	28,525	1,256,920	.0250	918,658	**270**	153,968	**327**	25,096	**141**	145,092	47,127	60,915	Indiana
Jefferson	065	45,946	45,932	15,367	18,771	30,065	706,030	.0120	319,104	**94**	8,059	**17**	2,329	**13**	67,324	25,170	32,012	Jefferson
Juniata	067	23,134	22,821	15,679	8,793	32,390	362,720	.0061	159,401	**47**	3,576	**8**	....	**....**	20,606	5,162	17,081	Juniata
Lackawanna*	069	209,643	213,295	17,104	87,869	32,376	3,585,670	.0677	2,544,865	**749**	319,242	**678**	142,068	**796**	524,904	185,619	136,327	Lackawanna
Lancaster*	071	486,469	470,658	19,463	180,573	41,641	9,468,350	.1739	6,676,478	**1,964**	579,937	**1,231**	367,776	**2,061**	1,109,981	332,301	314,284	Lancaster
Lawrence**	073	93,007	94,643	15,756	37,010	31,528	1,465,450	.0267	873,282	**257**	103,569	**220**	12,674	**71**	145,503	57,560	62,926	Lawrence
Lebanon*	075	123,395	120,327	18,733	48,483	37,889	2,311,520	.0423	1,571,295	**462**	187,305	**398**	28,005	**157**	226,517	70,127	86,140	Lebanon
Lehigh*	077	323,155	312,090	20,290	129,486	40,440	6,556,780	.1236	5,085,421	**1,496**	602,266	**1,278**	264,918	**1,485**	758,492	341,943	217,971	Lehigh
Luzerne*	079	311,854	319,250	17,134	133,173	31,877	5,343,430	.1001	3,705,084	**1,090**	501,993	**1,066**	161,778	**907**	612,257	255,136	211,768	Luzerne
Lycoming*	081	117,940	120,044	16,296	47,574	32,061	1,921,940	.0378	1,491,653	**439**	223,336	**474**	62,585	**351**	255,638	108,531	78,734	Lycoming
McKean**	083	45,049	45,936	15,672	17,896	31,169	706,020	.0125	379,470	**112**	17,701	**38**	4,410	**25**	84,864	38,535	28,358	McKean
Mercer*	085	119,795	120,293	16,241	47,178	32,701	1,945,620	.0405	1,759,998	**518**	245,942	**522**	163,746	**918**	228,125	107,358	79,080	Mercer
Mifflin**	087	46,282	46,486	15,518	18,621	30,714	718,190	.0132	437,259	**129**	67,389	**143**	18,606	**104**	76,163	23,445	31,675	Mifflin
Monroe**	089	159,381	138,687	18,883	56,652	42,234	3,009,580	.0523	1,746,834	**514**	263,869	**560**	167,624	**939**	350,528	113,936	109,779	Monroe
Montgomery*	091	777,323	750,097	26,422	299,358	54,506	20,538,650	.3398	12,384,781	**3,643**	1,357,627	**2,882**	1,085,383	**6,083**	2,034,819	813,275	529,277	Montgomery
Montour**	093	18,027	18,236	18,275	7,281	35,917	329,440	.0056	170,634	**50**	4,329	**9**	2,106	**12**	39,936	3,286	12,448	Montour
Northampton*	095	281,728	267,066	20,146	108,894	41,418	5,675,560	.0903	2,498,359	**735**	205,681	**437**	57,956	**325**	545,310	181,503	194,894	Northampton
Northumberland**	097	92,940	94,556	15,544	38,885	29,838	1,444,660	.0255	753,732	**222**	38,767	**82**	6,722	**38**	109,562	65,160	62,706	Northumberland
Perry*	099	44,379	43,602	19,141	17,403	38,747	849,480	.0130	295,161	**87**	2,804	**6**	....	**....**	66,610	17,310	33,678	Perry
Philadelphia*	101	1,468,025	1,517,550	15,022	601,909	29,054	22,053,340	.3781	9,909,696	**2,915**	787,764	**1,672**	1,123,454	**6,296**	2,158,817	1,423,825	558,681	Philadelphia
Pike*	103	54,000	46,302	19,421	20,322	41,076	1,048,720	.0149	245,156	**72**	58,787	**125**	5,376	**30**	41,581	9,401	38,360	Pike
Potter	105	18,138	18,080	15,287	7,138	30,783	277,270	.0047	125,902	**37**	4,866	**10**	....	**....**	32,059	9,698	12,265	Potter
Schuylkill**	107	147,221	150,336	15,903	60,111	30,966	2,341,200	.0435	1,496,557	**440**	131,524	**279**	31,556	**177**	277,785	213,434	99,248	Schuylkill
Snyder**	109	38,171	37,546	15,835	14,185	33,665	604,440	.0128	567,806	**167**	139,900	**297**	22,788	**128**	82,981	21,977	26,294	Snyder
Somerset**	111	79,144	80,023	14,586	31,492	29,148	1,154,400	.0211	654,128	**192**	41,968	**89**	23,075	**129**	69,255	47,346	55,126	Somerset
Sullivan	113	6,383	6,556	14,999	2,647	28,748	95,740	.0015	30,202	**9**	2,088	**4**	....	**....**	6,140	2,460	4,801	Sullivan
Susquehanna	115	41,666	42,238	16,079	16,726	31,669	669,940	.0113	299,614	**88**	7,135	**15**	....	**....**	56,478	18,865	30,374	Susquehanna
Tioga	117	41,622	41,373	14,912	16,402	30,169	620,670	.0111	329,931	**97**	45,969	**98**	4,808	**27**	57,403	15,485	29,358	Tioga
Union**	119	42,848	41,624	15,151	13,813	37,355	649,180	.0111	293,853	**86**	30,320	**64**	3,200	**18**	60,884	10,439	24,824	Union
Venango**	121	56,311	57,565	15,658	22,724	30,743	881,710	.0166	584,845	**172**	78,648	**167**	16,790	**94**	108,473	41,052	37,867	Venango
Warren**	123	42,501	43,863	17,543	17,519	33,824	745,590	.0170	863,208	**254**	77,277	**164**	23,209	**130**	72,040	22,109	29,540	Warren
Washington*	125	204,705	202,897	18,173	83,244	35,549	3,720,170	.0626	1,863,723	**548**	153,837	**327**	55,829	**313**	354,299	129,940	141,997	Washington
Wayne	127	49,483	47,722	16,044	19,611	31,971	793,890	.0151	555,473	**163**	53,266	**113**	8,591	**48**	122,334	39,913	35,242	Wayne
Westmoreland*	129	367,701	369,993	18,109	151,716	35,029	6,658,660	.1193	4,157,496	**1,223**	472,527	**1,003**	145,227	**814**	538,851	295,851	260,105	Westmoreland
Wyoming*	131	28,195	28,080	16,964	11,105	34,127	478,310	.0085	278,641	**82**	40,074	**85**	2,655	**15**	52,857	12,829	20,944	Wyoming
York*	133	398,969	381,751	20,544	157,278	41,447	8,196,390	.1339	4,069,282	**1,197**	563,866	**1,197**	146,775	**823**	757,223	207,738	293,087	York
The State		12,392,109	12,281,054	19,098	4,937,535	37,549	236,669,250	4.1708	145,109,009	**42,687**	15,030,581	**31,906**	7,327,780	**41,069**	24,179,500	10,075,015	7,920,514	The State

Source: Devonshire Associates Ltd. and Scan/US, Inc. 2004.
* Component of a Metropolitan Core Based Statistical Area.
** Component of a Micropolitan Core Based Statistical Area.

.... Data less than 1,000.

(d) Data not available.

continued on next page

Counties: Population / Income / Sales, *Continued*

COUNTY OR COUNTY EQUIVALENT	FIPS CO. CODE	POPULATION Estimate 7/1/04	POPULATION Census 4/1/00	PER CAPITA INCOME 2003	HOUSEHOLDS Estimate 7/1/04	MEDIAN HOUSEHOLD INCOME 2003	DISPOSABLE INCOME 2003 ($1,000)	MARKET ABILITY INDEX 2003	TOTAL RETAIL SALES Sales 2003 ($1,000)	TOTAL RETAIL SALES Ranally Sales Units	GENERAL MERCHANDISE Sales 2003 ($1,000)	GENERAL MERCHANDISE Ranally Sales Units	APPAREL STORE Sales 2003 ($1,000)	APPAREL STORE Ranally Sales Units	FOOD STORE SALES 2003 ($1,000)	HEALTH & DRUG STORE 2003 ($1,000)	PASSENGER CAR REGIS-TRATIONS 2003	COUNTY OR COUNTY EQUIVALENT
RHODE ISLAND (RI; CODE 44; 5 Counties)																		
Bristol*	001	51,073	50,648	22,127	19,616	45,673	1,130,100	.0159	297,840	**88**	16,489	**35**	18,572	**104**	70,640	40,003	34,937	Bristol
Kent*	003	172,563	167,090	22,481	70,867	43,210	3,879,400	.0672	2,478,932	**729**	428,202	**909**	140,083	**785**	284,030	234,581	124,237	Kent
Newport*	005	86,020	85,433	24,787	37,163	45,411	2,132,190	.0325	931,057	**274**	28,207	**60**	63,222	**354**	167,062	95,060	62,851	Newport
Providence*	007	645,010	621,602	17,167	251,477	34,841	11,072,780	.1883	5,511,135	**1,621**	358,237	**760**	391,194	**2,192**	1,226,374	641,525	382,516	Providence
Washington*	009	129,998	123,546	23,526	50,426	48,067	3,058,340	.0488	1,531,710	**451**	126,819	**269**	62,830	**352**	357,479	132,308	96,640	Washington
The State		1,084,664	1,048,319	19,612	429,549	39,260	21,272,810	.3527	10,750,673	**3,163**	957,954	**2,033**	675,902	**3,787**	2,105,585	1,143,477	701,181	The State
SOUTH CAROLINA (SC; CODE 45; 46 Counties)																		
Abbeville	001	26,434	26,167	15,449	10,423	30,880	408,370	.0062	99,809	**29**	4,102	**9**	....	**....**	35,776	9,677	19,616	Abbeville
Aiken*	003	148,054	142,552	18,068	59,002	35,528	2,674,970	.0434	1,152,915	**339**	212,036	**450**	52,505	**294**	223,060	59,589	106,672	Aiken
Allendale	005	10,852	11,211	9,335	3,894	20,460	101,300	.0022	68,640	**20**	1,314	**3**	....	**....**	12,059	3,946	5,374	Allendale
Anderson*	007	173,238	165,740	17,671	69,852	34,509	3,061,330	.0557	1,976,565	**581**	309,476	**657**	87,099	**488**	315,932	122,398	129,115	Anderson
Bamberg	009	15,851	16,658	11,449	6,085	23,312	181,480	.0038	125,696	**37**	7,552	**16**	2,734	**15**	32,281	17,653	9,217	Bamberg
Barnwell	011	23,337	23,478	13,907	9,319	27,275	324,540	.0056	138,615	**41**	34,302	**73**	4,398	**25**	32,667	13,105	15,610	Barnwell
Beaufort**	013	136,525	120,937	20,736	51,643	43,453	2,830,970	.0518	2,039,780	**600**	280,532	**596**	193,449	**1,084**	313,404	69,332	88,407	Beaufort
Berkeley*	015	147,602	142,651	17,228	53,791	37,191	2,542,860	.0405	959,508	**282**	87,045	**185**	19,321	**108**	240,098	42,248	97,250	Berkeley
Calhoun*	017	15,410	15,185	16,105	6,277	31,084	248,180	.0036	41,871	**12**	1,166	**2**	1,083	**6**	9,267	6,823	11,750	Calhoun
Charleston*	019	324,460	309,969	19,185	137,273	35,737	6,224,920	.1186	4,838,715	**1,423**	862,994	**1,832**	385,849	**2,162**	696,085	191,478	214,738	Charleston
Cherokee**	021	53,850	52,537	16,269	21,541	31,887	876,070	.0161	553,212	**163**	69,001	**146**	75,472	**423**	83,850	31,964	37,390	Cherokee
Chester**	023	33,833	34,068	15,233	13,155	30,917	515,370	.0090	257,677	**76**	26,856	**57**	5,610	**31**	53,761	15,647	22,972	Chester
Chesterfield	025	43,366	42,768	14,145	17,276	27,988	613,420	.0120	420,390	**124**	46,378	**98**	11,227	**63**	92,684	32,189	29,410	Chesterfield
Clarendon	027	32,979	32,502	12,848	12,556	26,577	423,700	.0080	232,254	**68**	28,455	**60**	6,664	**37**	57,080	13,588	19,913	Clarendon
Colleton**	029	39,448	38,264	14,071	15,419	28,136	555,070	.0103	323,321	**95**	46,486	**99**	10,817	**61**	71,764	16,985	25,028	Colleton
Darlington*	031	68,115	67,394	14,813	26,913	29,522	1,009,000	.0179	517,417	**152**	58,355	**124**	21,249	**119**	109,527	36,572	44,465	Darlington
Dillon**	033	31,133	30,722	12,300	11,716	25,730	382,940	.0078	266,697	**78**	38,052	**81**	8,170	**46**	50,810	20,018	18,551	Dillon
Dorchester*	035	106,654	96,413	19,597	40,960	40,298	2,090,150	.0316	708,115	**208**	151,161	**321**	7,955	**45**	146,174	43,321	74,076	Dorchester
Edgefield*	037	24,738	24,595	14,432	8,503	33,051	357,010	.0057	110,417	**32**	1,495	**3**	1,093	**6**	17,642	7,829	16,280	Edgefield
Fairfield*	039	23,939	23,454	14,330	9,383	28,992	343,040	.0054	87,773	**26**	12,395	**26**	....	**....**	23,095	11,103	16,415	Fairfield
Florence*	041	129,181	125,761	16,191	49,954	32,707	2,091,520	.0429	1,820,488	**536**	303,217	**644**	86,872	**487**	225,269	102,383	84,627	Florence
Georgetown**	043	59,865	55,797	17,274	24,319	33,819	1,034,090	.0189	666,531	**196**	134,871	**286**	55,347	**310**	108,176	51,420	40,907	Georgetown
Greenville*	045	400,132	379,616	19,605	161,236	38,512	7,844,780	.1473	5,917,931	**1,741**	797,823	**1,694**	310,906	**1,742**	674,001	288,117	282,933	Greenville
Greenwood**	047	67,894	66,271	16,500	27,084	32,417	1,120,220	.0208	741,033	**218**	144,697	**307**	39,898	**224**	115,513	39,480	45,767	Greenwood
Hampton	049	21,400	21,386	12,526	7,736	27,087	268,050	.0050	144,285	**42**	7,526	**16**	4,375	**25**	37,294	9,319	12,233	Hampton
Horry*	051	214,999	196,629	18,682	91,843	34,451	4,016,570	.0819	3,690,442	**1,086**	611,740	**1,299**	391,423	**2,194**	536,626	149,542	154,459	Horry
Jasper**	053	21,087	20,678	12,964	7,340	29,431	273,370	.0049	123,082	**36**	2,794	**6**	....	**....**	22,938	6,622	11,951	Jasper
Kershaw*	055	55,026	52,647	18,076	21,620	35,979	994,630	.0162	436,820	**128**	74,517	**158**	11,361	**64**	81,975	24,709	39,893	Kershaw
Lancaster**	057	62,895	61,351	16,217	24,419	32,826	1,019,980	.0171	456,426	**134**	81,844	**174**	12,448	**70**	93,482	28,238	44,740	Lancaster
Laurens*	059	70,472	69,567	15,660	27,241	31,934	1,103,610	.0179	406,968	**120**	63,455	**135**	7,951	**45**	78,576	28,375	49,043	Laurens
Lee	061	20,396	20,119	11,861	7,345	26,357	241,910	.0043	93,242	**27**	3,051	**6**	2,421	**14**	19,938	6,560	11,411	Lee
Lexington*	063	229,751	216,014	21,041	92,730	40,914	4,834,200	.0813	2,708,543	**797**	324,358	**689**	75,070	**421**	455,734	136,243	174,294	Lexington
McCormick	065	10,314	9,958	14,297	3,919	30,241	147,460	.0022	26,812	**8**	1,041	**2**	....	**....**	9,948	3,964	6,874	McCormick
Marion	067	34,996	35,466	12,548	13,571	25,543	439,120	.0083	243,889	**72**	30,908	**66**	9,940	**56**	48,171	21,551	20,517	Marion
Marlboro**	069	28,280	28,818	12,138	10,587	25,469	343,250	.0063	157,411	**46**	8,869	**19**	3,459	**19**	42,179	13,005	15,755	Marlboro
Newberry**	071	37,076	36,108	15,723	14,728	31,218	582,960	.0100	270,971	**80**	49,305	**105**	7,917	**44**	48,168	14,244	26,291	Newberry
Oconee**	073	69,222	66,215	18,429	29,269	34,283	1,275,690	.0209	588,003	**173**	104,331	**221**	15,340	**86**	101,548	38,382	54,926	Oconee
Orangeburg**	075	90,870	91,582	13,742	35,038	27,870	1,248,750	.0250	907,616	**267**	121,855	**259**	37,974	**213**	153,155	54,906	58,098	Orangeburg
Pickens*	077	113,461	110,757	16,931	44,180	34,249	1,921,030	.0331	990,463	**291**	125,830	**267**	20,998	**118**	200,067	73,331	84,477	Pickens
Richland*	079	335,685	320,677	18,968	134,464	37,010	6,367,140	.1198	4,743,325	**1,395**	1,044,218	**2,217**	301,643	**1,691**	513,885	228,162	226,638	Richland
Saluda*	081	19,055	19,181	16,115	7,191	33,452	307,080	.0049	103,604	**30**	4,704	**10**	1,631	**9**	20,595	8,804	13,604	Saluda
Spartanburg*	083	263,575	253,791	17,658	103,158	35,503	4,654,080	.0862	3,173,259	**933**	462,662	**982**	129,536	**726**	417,776	215,655	185,920	Spartanburg
Sumter*	085	106,361	104,646	15,246	40,297	31,423	1,621,630	.0297	959,454	**282**	136,905	**291**	50,276	**282**	128,249	45,197	69,485	Sumter
Union**	087	28,853	29,881	15,848	12,067	30,018	457,270	.0078	214,455	**63**	36,634	**78**	9,143	**51**	50,294	15,660	20,455	Union
Williamsburg	089	35,636	37,217	11,555	13,804	23,235	411,790	.0076	181,372	**53**	13,540	**29**	5,290	**30**	36,819	17,430	21,953	Williamsburg
York*	091	182,193	164,614	20,841	72,957	40,897	3,797,050	.0619	1,891,217	**556**	238,574	**506**	65,630	**368**	322,228	96,489	137,155	York
The State		4,188,493	4,012,012	17,711	1,663,078	35,157	74,181,920	1.3374	46,577,029	**13,696**	7,208,418	**15,304**	2,553,727	**14,315**	7,159,615	2,483,253	2,896,655	The State
SOUTH DAKOTA (SD; CODE 46; 66 Counties)																		
Aurora	003	2,881	3,058	13,572	1,108	28,522	39,100	.0009	37,914	**11**	....	**....**	....	**....**	....	....	2,506	Aurora
Beadle**	005	16,037	17,023	15,434	6,938	28,836	247,520	.0055	260,650	**77**	12,595	**27**	9,901	**55**	11,795	14,268	12,875	Beadle
Bennett	007	3,515	3,574	9,263	1,092	23,638	32,560	.0008	29,596	**9**	....	**....**	....	**....**	....	....	1,837	Bennett
Bon Homme	009	7,055	7,260	12,883	2,548	28,580	90,890	.0018	57,989	**17**	1,559	**3**	....	**....**	1,599	3,056	5,242	Bon Homme
Brookings**	011	28,258	28,220	15,809	10,749	33,312	446,730	.0085	308,020	**91**	55,995	**119**	15,354	**86**	15,133	4,987	21,851	Brookings
Brown**	013	34,430	35,460	17,329	14,591	32,972	596,630	.0158	935,127	**275**	63,942	**136**	9,431	**53**	53,658	5,216	26,623	Brown
Brule	015	5,157	5,364	14,377	1,942	30,645	74,140	.0017	83,167	**24**	4,596	**10**	....	**....**	10,057	....	3,944	Brule
Buffalo	017	1,991	2,032	3,827	517	11,548	7,620	.0002	3,152	**1**	....	**....**	....	**....**	1,458	....	795	Buffalo
Butte	019	9,244	9,094	13,291	3,584	27,602	122,860	.0027	113,692	**33**	3,250	**7**	....	**....**	13,228	1,810	7,848	Butte
Campbell	021	1,646	1,782	13,967	680	26,948	22,990	.0004	12,235	**4**	....	**....**	....	**....**	....	....	1,576	Campbell
Charles Mix	023	9,122	9,350	11,015	3,263	25,098	100,480	.0024	103,453	**30**	4,896	**10**	....	**....**	19,284	....	6,142	Charles Mix
Clark	025	3,847	4,143	13,556	1,487	28,261	52,150	.0010	30,496	**9**	....	**....**	....	**....**	1,048	....	3,168	Clark
Clay**	027	13,092	13,537	12,062	4,881	26,193	157,910	.0034	131,467	**39**	6,793	**14**	....	**....**	19,214	3,139	9,441	Clay
Codington**	029	25,934	25,897	17,374	10,709	34,101	450,590	.0109	589,803	**173**	54,819	**116**	25,136	**141**	62,901	7,843	20,548	Codington
Corson	031	4,312	4,181	7,537	1,299	20,108	32,500	.0007	12,483	**4**	....	**....**	....	**....**	....	....	2,508	Corson
Custer	033	7,679	7,275	17,730	3,221	34,013	136,150	.0022	58,693	**17**	....	**....**	....	**....**	2,989	4,028	6,778	Custer
Davison**	035	18,751	18,741	15,846	7,658	31,249	297,130	.0081	473,811	**139**	75,629	**161**	11,290	**63**	31,102	10,320	14,356	Davison
Day	037	5,776	6,267	14,929	2,436	28,632	86,230	.0018	72,395	**21**	1,919	**4**	....	**....**	4,940	....	4,863	Day
Deuel	039	4,318	4,498	15,343	1,804	29,733	66,250	.0012	35,702	**11**	2,374	**5**	....	**....**	....	....	3,799	Deuel
Dewey	041	6,181	5,972	9,089	1,945	23,294	56,180	.0012	31,502	**9**	1,663	**4**	....	**....**	1,299	....	3,543	Dewey
Douglas	043	3,268	3,458	13,274	1,277	27,216	43,380	.0010	45,975	**14**	....	**....**	....	**....**	1,410	3,628	2,744	Douglas
Edmunds**	045	4,178	4,367	14,296	1,608	30,219	59,730	.0013	52,445	**15**	....	**....**	....	**....**	2,184	....	3,455	Edmunds
Fall River	047	7,270	7,453	14,828	3,110	27,903	107,800	.0020	68,439	**20**	3,953	**8**	....	**....**	6,789	....	5,963	Fall River
Faulk	049	2,418	2,640	13,354	925	28,012	32,290	.0007	25,646	**8**	....	**....**	....	**....**	....	....	1,858	Faulk
Grant	051	7,558	7,847	15,525	3,077	31,269	117,340	.0026	118,454	**35**	5,124	**11**	....	**....**	14,720	3,365	6,140	Grant
Gregory	053	4,415	4,792	12,097	1,909	22,309	53,410	.0011	42,475	**12**	2,035	**4**	....	**....**	5,943	....	4,019	Gregory
Haakon	055	1,954	2,196	14,887	813	28,846	29,090	.0006	26,919	**8**	1,746	**4**	....	**....**	1,283	1,064	1,782	Haakon
Hamlin**	057	5,636	5,540	14,679	2,075	31,979	82,730	.0015	44,816	**13**	....	**....**	....	**....**	....	....	4,527	Hamlin
Hand	059	3,458	3,741	16,038	1,465	30,317	55,460	.0011	40,782	**12**	....	**....**	....	**....**	....	1,178	2,985	Hand
Hanson**	061	3,629	3,139	13,794	1,284	31,418	50,060	.0008	9,698	**3**	....	**....**	....	**....**	....	....	2,887	Hanson
Harding	063	1,270	1,353	11,945	512	23,827	15,170	.0003	7,615	**2**	....	**....**	....	**....**	....	....	1,298	Harding
Hughes**	065	16,744	16,481	19,298	6,722	39,015	323,130	.0069	340,017	**100**	55,623	**118**	13,555	**76**	8,447	3,034	12,625	Hughes
Hutchinson	067	7,619	8,075	13,999	3,023	28,300	106,660	.0024	105,239	**31**	3,993	**8**	1,231	**7**	4,485	3,872	6,150	Hutchinson
Hyde	069	1,543	1,671	14,913	628	29,623	23,010	.0004	14,129	**4**	....	**....**	....	**....**	....	1,242	1,374	Hyde
Jackson	071	2,826	2,930	9,200	913	22,356	26,000	.0007	29,163	**9**	1,382	**3**	....	**....**	....	....	1,816	Jackson
Jerauld	073	2,147	2,295	15,589	952	28,467	33,470	.0010	63,614	**19**	2,656	**6**	....	**....**	2,441	....	1,900	Jerauld
Jones	075	1,057	1,193	15,582	467	28,216	16,470	.0004	19,573	**6**	....	**....**	....	**....**	....	....	1,075	Jones
Kingsbury	077	5,472	5,815	15,367	2,297	29,851	84,090	.0015	40,608	**12**	....	**....**	....	**....**	9,177	1,028	4,918	Kingsbury
Lake	079	10,970	11,276	15,757	4,338	32,136	172,850	.0041	205,427	**60**	11,618	**25**	1,856	**10**	16,494	7,608	9,029	Lake
Lawrence**	081	21,917	21,802	15,559	9,194	30,248	341,000	.0080	400,133	**118**	60,426	**128**	5,266	**30**	14,846	5,781	18,265	Lawrence
Lincoln*	083	30,883	24,131	19,909	11,352	45,038	614,850	.0110	401,646	**118**	1,991	**4**	....	**....**	18,116	3,715	24,876	Lincoln
Lyman	085	3,918	3,895	12,307	1,428	27,101	48,220	.0012	60,268	**18**	1,760	**4**	....	**....**	4,275	1,070	2,878	Lyman
McCook*	087	5,868	5,832	15,639	2,215	33,248	91,770	.0018	74,375	**22**	....	**....**	....	**....**	1,223	2,393	4,791	McCook
McPherson	089	2,668	2,904	11,897	1,138	22,287	31,740	.0006	20,934	**6**	....	**....**	....	**....**	6,032	....	2,218	McPherson
Marshall	091	4,175	4,576	14,446	1,695	28,878	60,310	.0012	43,169	**13**	....	**....**	....	**....**	3,702	....	3,475	Marshall
Meade*	093	24,873	24,253	16,027	9,363	34,636	398,650	.0069	198,332	**58**	6,839	**15**	2,016	**11**	13,434	2,978	20,116	Meade
Mellette	095	2,129	2,083	9,338	722	22,029	19,880	.0004	9,883	**3**	....	**....**	....	**....**	6,242	....	1,437	Mellette
Miner	097	2,663	2,884	14,976	1,149	28,135	39,880	.0007	24,438	**7**	....	**....**	....	**....**	2,904	....	2,508	Miner
Minnehaha*	099	156,477	148,281	19,916	63,806	39,501	3,116,350	.0726	3,966,491	**1,167**	641,968	**1,363**	65,539	**367**	333,660	178,588	121,564	Minnehaha
Moody	101	6,486	6,595	16,093	2,523	33,299	104,380	.0017	40,139	**12**	2,026	**4**	....	**....**	....	....	5,350	Moody
Pennington*	103	92,908	88,565	17,302	37,133	35,022	1,607,490	.0379	2,003,457	**589**	417,197	**886**	84,303	**472**	173,874	75,403	73,093	Pennington
Perkins	105	3,138	3,363	14,222	1,362	26,202	44,630	.0008	25,253	**7**	2,516	**5**	....	**....**	1,067	....	3,038	Perkins
Potter	107	2,453	2,693	15,532	1,079	28,377	38,100	.0009	48,827	**14**	2,118	**5**	....	**....**	....	2,200	2,157	Potter
Roberts	109	10,168	10,016	12,347	3,749	26,869	125,540	.0024	74,997	**22**	5,302	**11**	....	**....**	1,252	2,274	7,669	Roberts
Sanborn	111	2,592	2,675	15,340	1,026	31,010	39,760	.0007	15,011	**4**	....	**....**	....	**....**	....	....	2,415	Sanborn
Shannon	113	13,431	12,466	5,926	3,029	20,814	79,590	.0020	43,805	**13**	1,730	**4**	....	**....**	9,986	4,163	4,670	Shannon
Spink	115	6,825	7,454	14,126	2,618	29,844	96,410	.0020	79,466	**23**	7,328	**16**	....	**....**	1,665	....	5,227	Spink
Stanley**	117	2,742	2,772	19,748	1,131	38,536	54,150	.0010	34,068	**10**	1,798	**4**	....	**....**	5,800	....	2,472	Stanley
Sully	119	1,425	1,556	15,832	585	30,971	22,560	.0006	32,117	**9**	....	**....**	....	**....**	....	....	1,275	Sully
Todd	121	9,594	9,050	6,713	2,647	19,408	64,400	.0015	29,627	**9**	1,136	**2**	....	**....**	10,479	....	4,245	Todd
Tripp	123	6,108	6,430	13,551	2,487	26,663	82,770	.0019	86,406	**25**	7,366	**16**	....	**....**	10,357	1,779	5,188	Tripp
Turner*	125	8,506	8,849	16,699	3,398	33,689	142,040	.0023	52,344	**15**	....	**....**	....	**....**	1,751	2,524	7,553	Turner
Union*	127	13,166	12,584	20,119	5,225	41,267	264,890	.0535	5,696,987	**1,676**	....	**....**	....	**....**	24,282	2,433	10,778	Union
Walworth	129	5,442	5,974	14,061	2,318	26,519	76,520	.0018	92,421	**27**	11,135	**24**	....	**....**	....	2,516	4,100	Walworth
Yankton**	135	21,398	21,652	15,719	8,206	33,316	336,360	.0079	399,013	**117**	71,826	**152**	22,443	**126**	12,392	9,701	15,561	Yankton
Ziebach	137	2,573	2,519	6,825	768	18,043	17,560	.0004	7,312	**2**	....	**....**	....	**....**	2,284	....	1,340	Ziebach
The State		767,184	754,844	16,304	301,193	33,574	12,508,550	.3253	18,643,300	**5,481**	1,622,620	**3,446**	276,406	**1,548**	989,470	385,056	595,047	The State
TENNESSEE (TN; CODE 47; 95 Counties)																		
Anderson*	001	72,110	71,330	18,137	30,658	33,071	1,307,870	.0240	886,529	**261**	166,264	**353**	26,282	**147**	137,959	55,450	56,609	Anderson
Bedford**	003	41,066	37,586	16,463	15,247	34,662	676,080	.0117	346,949	**102**	66,779	**142**	5,273	**30**	63,428	11,746	29,769	Bedford
Benton	005	16,490	16,537	14,883	7,009	27,089	245,420	.0042	112,580	**33**	22,210	**47**	1,627	**9**	21,645	5,172	12,658	Benton
Bledsoe	007	12,604	12,367	12,990	4,619	27,397	163,720	.0026	35,773	**11**	5,949	**13**	....	**....**	7,186	3,496	9,086	Bledsoe
Blount*	009	113,265	105,823	18,937	47,058	35,344	2,144,950	.0398	1,531,706	**451**	240,857	**511**	22,142	**124**	151,253	69,979	90,742	Blount
Bradley*	011	90,961	87,965	17,148	36,804	32,909	1,559,830	.0282	965,747	**284**	186,905	**397**	33,782	**189**	108,900	62,902	70,231	Bradley
Campbell**	013	40,188	39,854	13,009	16,826	24,125	522,800	.0097	279,021	**82**	47,718	**101**	5,192	**29**	62,926	24,593	28,400	Campbell
Cannon*	015	13,300	12,826	16,005	5,317	31,069	212,860	.0032	56,316	**17**	4,351	**9**	....	**....**	10,899	3,859	10,684	Cannon
Carroll	017	29,303	29,475	14,867	11,815	28,776	435,650	.0070	142,902	**42**	22,461	**48**	2,597	**15**	29,025	10,109	22,045	Carroll
Carter*	019	58,913	56,742	13,984	24,311	26,222	823,830	.0141	332,588	**98**	66,438	**141**	2,234	**13**	71,807	15,617	46,333	Carter
Cheatham*	021	37,783	35,912	19,692	13,869	41,845	744,030	.0107	197,111	**58**	24,853	**53**	1,355	**8**	44,135	11,253	28,929	Cheatham
Chester*	023	15,941	15,540	16,832	6,414	32,412	268,320	.0046	138,634	**41**	7,126	**15**	2,172	**12**	14,307	9,103	12,120	Chester
Claiborne	025	30,581	29,862	12,951	12,446	24,675	396,060	.0070	166,404	**49**	51,023	**108**	1,918	**11**	39,787	13,765	23,362	Claiborne
Clay	027	7,935	7,976	13,112	3,465	22,969	104,040	.0017	30,403	**9**	1,141	**2**	....	**....**	11,778	4,559	6,654	Clay
Cocke**	029	34,566	33,565	13,242	14,580	24,353	457,710	.0083	225,466	**66**	68,770	**146**	7,664	**43**	42,696	13,496	27,241	Cocke
Coffee**	031	50,135	48,014	17,017	20,234	32,754	853,150	.0171	716,678	**211**	153,367	**326**	25,349	**142**	96,599	34,735	38,595	Coffee
Crockett	033	14,472	14,532	14,086	5,608	28,203	203,850	.0035	84,241	**25**	9,046	**19**	....	**....**	13,284	11,309	9,624	Crockett
Cumberland**	035	50,183	46,802	16,258	21,893	28,953	815,890	.0155	569,653	**168**	143,603	**305**	44,402	**249**	68,797	18,692	40,454	Cumberland
Davidson*	037	569,819	569,891	21,077	252,137	36,973	12,010,290	.2437	11,447,682	**3,367**	1,704,728	**3,619**	678,403	**3,802**	1,223,906	710,680	412,800	Davidson
Decatur	039	11,578	11,731	14,914	4,935	27,090	172,670	.0029	65,135	**19**	8,734	**19**	....	**....**	7,994	4,491	9,058	Decatur
DeKalb	041	18,230	17,423	14,901	7,376	28,706	271,650	.0045	98,990	**29**	6,675	**14**	1,664	**9**	20,203	12,721	13,661	DeKalb
Dickson*	043	45,469	43,156	18,353	17,711	36,661	834,470	.0149	516,999	**152**	140,371	**298**	15,629	**88**	55,859	15,738	33,974	Dickson
Dyer**	045	37,305	37,279	16,180	15,162	31,149	603,580	.0121	491,453	**145**	116,678	**248**	30,851	**173**	58,438	23,293	25,764	Dyer

Source: Devonshire Associates Ltd. and Scan/US, Inc. 2004. .... Data less than 1,000. (d) Data not available.
* Component of a Metropolitan Core Based Statistical Area.
** Component of a Micropolitan Core Based Statistical Area.

Counties: Population / Income / Sales, *Continued*

COUNTY OR COUNTY EQUIVALENT	FIPS CO. CODE	POPULATION Estimate 7/1/04	POPULATION Census 4/1/00	PER CAPITA INCOME 2003	HOUSEHOLDS Estimate 7/1/04	MEDIAN HOUSEHOLD INCOME 2003	DISPOSABLE INCOME 2003 ($1,000)	MARKET ABILITY INDEX 2003	TOTAL RETAIL SALES Sales 2003 ($1,000)	TOTAL RETAIL SALES Ranally Sales Units	GENERAL MERCHANDISE Sales 2003 ($1,000)	GENERAL MERCHANDISE Ranally Sales Units	APPAREL STORE Sales 2003 ($1,000)	APPAREL STORE Ranally Sales Units	FOOD STORE SALES 2003 ($1,000)	HEALTH & DRUG STORE 2003 ($1,000)	PASSENGER CAR REGIS-TRATIONS 2003	COUNTY OR COUNTY EQUIVALENT
Fayette*	047	33,345	28,806	18,028	12,612	37,314	601,160	.0087	134,001	**39**	20,312	**43**	....	**....**	14,199	10,307	24,491	Fayette
Fentress	049	17,032	16,625	12,065	7,067	22,803	205,490	.0038	101,648	**30**	21,863	**46**	1,206	**7**	30,222	5,981	12,586	Fentress
Franklin**	051	40,901	39,270	16,860	15,891	33,726	689,610	.0113	293,028	**86**	67,641	**144**	4,491	**25**	48,589	16,548	30,869	Franklin
Gibson**	053	47,841	48,152	15,462	19,624	29,518	739,710	.0125	326,634	**96**	56,963	**121**	5,363	**30**	44,393	15,452	33,848	Gibson
Giles	055	29,365	29,447	17,035	11,904	32,692	500,230	.0089	286,634	**84**	39,141	**83**	5,882	**33**	47,461	9,913	23,105	Giles
Grainger*	057	21,687	20,659	14,109	8,931	26,442	305,990	.0047	70,692	**21**	1,776	**4**	....	**....**	18,741	6,457	17,940	Grainger
Greene**	059	64,308	62,909	16,058	27,903	28,858	1,032,690	.0201	769,167	**226**	128,769	**273**	24,766	**139**	145,961	60,734	53,681	Greene
Grundy	061	14,409	14,332	11,568	5,784	22,038	166,690	.0029	53,522	**16**	4,586	**10**	....	**....**	10,209	6,138	10,756	Grundy
Hamblen*	063	59,059	58,128	16,334	24,456	30,690	964,690	.0213	1,008,713	**297**	176,185	**374**	39,960	**224**	111,529	51,834	45,544	Hamblen
Hamilton*	065	310,020	307,896	19,631	130,066	36,401	6,086,050	.1112	4,249,816	**1,250**	682,996	**1,450**	273,791	**1,534**	572,264	260,120	232,869	Hamilton
Hancock	067	6,678	6,786	10,524	2,842	19,060	70,280	.0012	18,252	**5**	1,408	**3**	....	**....**	5,227	1,639	4,884	Hancock
Hardeman	069	28,188	28,105	12,161	9,719	27,305	342,800	.0060	130,593	**38**	26,635	**57**	1,043	**6**	16,479	11,024	16,695	Hardeman
Hardin	071	26,043	25,578	14,316	10,899	26,450	372,820	.0071	239,149	**70**	46,859	**99**	2,320	**13**	33,600	11,137	19,825	Hardin
Hawkins*	073	55,484	53,563	15,944	23,341	29,540	884,650	.0140	296,741	**87**	33,623	**71**	6,458	**36**	67,903	25,312	44,999	Hawkins
Haywood**	075	19,561	19,797	13,257	7,656	26,248	259,320	.0053	194,010	**57**	21,937	**47**	1,999	**11**	26,066	6,014	12,058	Haywood
Henderson	077	25,999	25,522	15,999	10,671	30,485	415,960	.0073	221,602	**65**	34,302	**73**	4,411	**25**	32,413	17,854	20,044	Henderson
Henry**	079	31,198	31,115	16,015	13,585	28,655	499,640	.0096	356,528	**105**	95,268	**202**	9,014	**51**	51,671	12,788	24,333	Henry
Hickman*	081	23,657	22,295	14,104	8,898	29,260	333,670	.0051	71,738	**21**	2,885	**6**	....	**....**	23,620	4,359	16,716	Hickman
Houston	083	8,106	8,088	14,587	3,275	27,995	118,240	.0019	34,952	**10**	1,928	**4**	....	**....**	14,143	2,047	6,247	Houston
Humphreys	085	18,188	17,929	17,802	7,495	33,557	323,790	.0051	125,203	**37**	18,494	**39**	....	**....**	19,214	13,393	14,314	Humphreys
Jackson**	087	11,269	10,984	13,464	4,655	25,447	151,730	.0024	33,043	**10**	5,510	**12**	....	**....**	13,638	....	9,130	Jackson
Jefferson*	089	47,699	44,294	15,745	18,745	31,194	751,000	.0125	316,196	**93**	86,381	**183**	1,088	**6**	41,782	17,075	36,915	Jefferson
Johnson	091	18,093	17,499	11,607	7,193	22,452	210,000	.0040	111,017	**33**	7,681	**16**	1,155	**6**	25,193	10,222	13,134	Johnson
Knox*	093	396,391	382,032	19,553	170,567	35,506	7,750,740	.1622	7,731,279	**2,274**	1,263,307	**2,682**	370,834	**2,078**	818,073	382,810	304,396	Knox
Lake	095	7,785	7,954	8,380	2,324	21,661	65,240	.0014	31,818	**9**	5,506	**12**	....	**....**	8,837	3,416	3,501	Lake
Lauderdale	097	27,086	27,101	12,904	9,718	28,094	349,510	.0064	168,547	**50**	37,159	**79**	5,652	**32**	29,686	13,947	15,794	Lauderdale
Lawrence**	099	40,953	39,926	14,544	16,121	28,859	595,620	.0116	415,384	**122**	100,438	**213**	7,385	**41**	60,112	22,509	30,148	Lawrence
Lewis	101	11,459	11,367	14,280	4,442	28,795	163,640	.0030	86,419	**25**	15,531	**33**	....	**....**	14,852	4,279	8,548	Lewis
Lincoln	103	31,894	31,340	17,119	13,449	31,675	545,980	.0094	288,620	**85**	69,215	**147**	7,994	**45**	40,599	13,201	26,396	Lincoln
Loudon*	105	42,424	39,086	20,292	17,969	37,323	860,860	.0136	373,888	**110**	34,983	**74**	....	**....**	51,929	25,402	35,249	Loudon
McMinn**	107	51,117	49,015	15,716	20,931	30,200	803,330	.0145	465,627	**137**	83,448	**177**	9,545	**54**	70,636	26,395	39,662	McMinn
McNairy	109	25,011	24,653	14,914	10,290	27,908	373,010	.0065	182,673	**54**	22,766	**48**	1,201	**7**	24,388	11,038	19,474	McNairy
Macon*	111	21,213	20,386	14,443	8,364	28,518	306,380	.0053	138,254	**41**	36,983	**79**	2,161	**12**	25,704	9,844	16,284	Macon
Madison*	113	94,495	91,837	17,905	37,801	34,831	1,691,900	.0350	1,584,048	**466**	374,910	**796**	108,075	**606**	136,991	81,287	66,075	Madison
Marion*	115	27,916	27,776	15,548	11,427	29,651	434,050	.0084	307,643	**90**	65,952	**140**	6,372	**36**	58,144	17,184	21,943	Marion
Marshall**	117	27,758	26,767	17,924	10,755	36,091	497,530	.0082	229,022	**67**	27,462	**58**	6,931	**39**	45,473	13,917	20,907	Marshall
Maury**	119	74,356	69,498	19,403	29,143	38,797	1,442,720	.0236	687,944	**202**	117,800	**250**	30,000	**168**	114,288	32,026	56,047	Maury
Meigs	121	11,530	11,086	14,088	4,548	27,667	162,440	.0025	33,706	**10**	1,707	**4**	....	**....**	11,802	1,178	8,932	Meigs
Monroe	123	41,674	38,961	14,698	16,743	28,416	612,540	.0112	347,409	**102**	60,867	**129**	5,073	**28**	80,395	24,182	32,428	Monroe
Montgomery*	125	142,942	134,768	17,292	52,983	36,276	2,471,710	.0450	1,575,410	**463**	419,227	**890**	70,386	**394**	119,866	37,714	98,968	Montgomery
Moore**	127	5,959	5,740	17,394	2,362	34,035	103,650	.0014	10,011	**3**	1,258	**3**	....	**....**	3,962	1,056	4,923	Moore
Morgan	129	20,180	19,757	12,539	7,351	26,556	253,040	.0039	37,147	**11**	6,824	**14**	....	**....**	10,097	2,512	14,629	Morgan
Obion**	131	32,351	32,450	16,490	13,386	31,064	533,460	.0101	374,485	**110**	104,778	**222**	25,093	**141**	20,731	10,934	24,030	Obion
Overton**	133	20,137	20,118	13,780	8,297	25,859	277,480	.0045	86,803	**26**	8,182	**17**	1,246	**7**	22,497	7,170	15,687	Overton
Perry	135	7,621	7,631	14,003	3,067	26,990	106,720	.0017	29,641	**9**	10,526	**22**	....	**....**	7,972	....	5,985	Perry
Pickett	137	5,030	4,945	13,551	2,197	24,385	68,160	.0012	33,770	**10**	5,868	**12**	....	**....**	1,363	3,110	4,233	Pickett
Polk*	139	16,195	16,050	15,166	6,726	28,464	245,610	.0039	71,894	**21**	2,616	**6**	....	**....**	13,396	6,537	13,153	Polk
Putnam**	141	65,804	62,315	15,420	27,002	29,217	1,014,710	.0208	859,073	**253**	171,322	**364**	47,770	**268**	107,669	33,446	51,536	Putnam
Rhea	143	29,560	28,400	14,656	11,832	28,418	433,230	.0073	172,395	**51**	33,329	**71**	3,829	**21**	39,991	13,514	22,502	Rhea
Roane**	145	52,584	51,910	17,180	22,238	31,528	903,400	.0149	400,325	**118**	65,661	**139**	2,705	**15**	74,851	27,508	43,061	Roane
Robertson*	147	59,290	54,433	19,201	22,365	39,880	1,138,450	.0184	506,583	**149**	76,607	**163**	6,293	**35**	99,005	27,933	44,437	Robertson
Rutherford*	149	208,605	182,023	20,983	80,795	42,041	4,377,230	.0719	2,245,244	**660**	483,467	**1,026**	67,271	**377**	264,298	81,079	161,822	Rutherford
Scott	151	21,840	21,127	12,042	8,802	22,951	263,000	.0050	140,323	**41**	33,963	**72**	....	**....**	32,943	18,333	16,418	Scott
Sequatchie*	153	12,140	11,370	15,105	4,887	29,244	183,370	.0031	79,816	**23**	9,666	**21**	....	**....**	8,043	4,425	9,937	Sequatchie
Sevier**	155	76,768	71,170	17,091	31,268	32,452	1,312,010	.0277	1,257,325	**370**	143,073	**304**	247,681	**1,388**	159,641	36,319	60,118	Sevier
Shelby*	157	908,843	897,472	18,512	354,604	37,304	16,824,190	.3088	11,499,693	**3,383**	1,899,212	**4,032**	788,357	**4,418**	1,174,545	760,875	569,371	Shelby
Smith*	159	18,361	17,712	16,807	7,201	33,480	308,590	.0052	140,572	**41**	30,177	**64**	4,777	**27**	21,578	9,263	14,202	Smith
Stewart*	161	12,979	12,370	16,594	5,345	31,222	215,380	.0033	59,549	**18**	8,099	**17**	....	**....**	10,148	2,104	10,577	Stewart
Sullivan*	163	153,090	153,048	17,981	67,650	31,646	2,752,750	.0511	1,914,169	**563**	410,047	**870**	59,021	**331**	211,093	100,881	126,650	Sullivan
Sumner*	165	141,292	130,449	20,791	54,594	41,779	2,937,590	.0444	1,067,617	**314**	212,488	**451**	20,419	**114**	190,307	71,944	105,678	Sumner
Tipton*	167	55,057	51,271	17,898	19,700	39,282	985,410	.0154	352,108	**104**	42,477	**90**	3,820	**21**	63,329	13,810	37,288	Tipton
Trousdale*	169	7,488	7,259	15,199	2,874	30,883	113,810	.0018	38,973	**11**	2,064	**4**	....	**....**	10,974	5,508	5,495	Trousdale
Unicoi*	171	17,729	17,667	15,837	7,750	28,106	280,780	.0042	62,939	**19**	3,810	**8**	....	**....**	14,187	9,239	15,091	Unicoi
Union*	173	19,151	17,808	13,038	7,406	26,111	249,690	.0039	46,540	**14**	5,872	**12**	....	**....**	7,836	4,966	14,489	Union
Van Buren	175	5,465	5,508	14,269	2,234	26,947	77,980	.0012	13,111	**4**	....	**....**	....	**....**	2,604	....	4,292	Van Buren
Warren**	177	39,370	38,276	15,179	15,880	29,742	597,610	.0111	363,309	**107**	132,229	**281**	15,234	**85**	59,388	22,967	29,384	Warren
Washington*	179	110,949	107,198	17,561	48,621	31,047	1,948,340	.0390	1,659,147	**488**	315,664	**670**	123,209	**691**	159,103	96,195	88,709	Washington
Wayne	181	16,984	16,842	11,717	6,098	25,400	199,000	.0034	63,170	**19**	7,071	**15**	....	**....**	17,315	11,724	11,598	Wayne
Weakley**	183	34,120	34,895	14,758	13,648	28,883	503,560	.0086	216,251	**64**	39,052	**83**	5,346	**30**	32,227	12,398	24,567	Weakley
White	185	23,735	23,102	14,932	9,905	27,720	354,400	.0070	262,540	**77**	27,367	**58**	1,743	**10**	33,633	14,713	18,605	White
Williamson*	187	145,703	126,638	29,545	55,065	60,420	4,304,760	.0703	2,621,948	**771**	430,040	**913**	170,459	**955**	337,296	97,593	115,452	Williamson
Wilson*	189	97,396	88,809	22,187	37,313	45,079	2,160,950	.0327	840,732	**247**	161,011	**342**	28,634	**160**	155,112	29,906	76,303	Wilson
The State		5,888,107	5,689,283	18,174	2,394,744	34,491	107,010,440	1.9529	71,056,732	**20,902**	12,470,271	**26,471**	3,556,934	**19,936**	8,856,237	3,983,306	4,348,750	The State

TEXAS (TX; CODE 48; 254 Counties)

COUNTY OR COUNTY EQUIVALENT	FIPS CO. CODE	POPULATION Estimate 7/1/04	POPULATION Census 4/1/00	PER CAPITA INCOME 2003	HOUSEHOLDS Estimate 7/1/04	MEDIAN HOUSEHOLD INCOME 2003	DISPOSABLE INCOME 2003 ($1,000)	MARKET ABILITY INDEX 2003	TOTAL RETAIL SALES Sales 2003 ($1,000)	TOTAL RETAIL SALES Ranally Sales Units	GENERAL MERCHANDISE Sales 2003 ($1,000)	GENERAL MERCHANDISE Ranally Sales Units	APPAREL STORE Sales 2003 ($1,000)	APPAREL STORE Ranally Sales Units	FOOD STORE SALES 2003 ($1,000)	HEALTH & DRUG STORE 2003 ($1,000)	PASSENGER CAR REGIS-TRATIONS 2003	COUNTY OR COUNTY EQUIVALENT
Anderson**	001	54,691	55,109	11,400	16,195	29,982	623,490	.0124	374,727	**110**	88,859	**189**	15,149	**85**	53,595	17,561	27,624	Anderson
Andrews**	003	12,845	13,004	15,155	4,669	31,982	194,660	.0032	76,768	**23**	3,771	**8**	1,037	**6**	5,252	4,850	8,202	Andrews
Angelina**	005	81,163	80,130	15,234	29,926	31,889	1,236,450	.0243	914,392	**269**	188,236	**400**	30,903	**173**	157,084	31,770	51,146	Angelina
Aransas*	007	23,921	22,497	15,596	9,899	29,281	373,080	.0062	156,300	**46**	27,571	**59**	5,025	**28**	48,527	1,515	16,297	Aransas
Archer*	009	9,261	8,854	17,727	3,521	35,867	164,170	.0024	36,448	**11**	....	**....**	....	**....**	2,602	1,053	7,102	Archer
Armstrong*	011	2,020	2,148	17,218	747	35,762	34,780	.0005	3,208	**1**	....	**....**	....	**....**	....	....	1,628	Armstrong
Atascosa*	013	42,850	38,628	13,481	14,312	31,182	577,680	.0106	300,101	**88**	36,913	**78**	3,544	**20**	84,617	7,369	25,572	Atascosa
Austin*	015	25,488	23,590	17,360	9,383	36,315	442,470	.0079	270,325	**80**	23,532	**50**	17,573	**98**	32,427	10,415	17,670	Austin
Bailey	017	6,683	6,594	12,451	2,409	26,531	83,210	.0015	41,102	**12**	3,375	**7**	....	**....**	6,969	....	4,301	Bailey
Bandera*	019	19,851	17,645	18,782	7,850	36,526	372,840	.0053	85,567	**25**	....	**....**	1,341	**8**	21,190	7,948	14,823	Bandera
Bastrop*	021	69,998	57,733	18,370	24,484	40,608	1,285,850	.0214	624,966	**184**	81,841	**174**	3,945	**22**	99,039	6,780	46,425	Bastrop
Baylor	023	3,854	4,093	13,552	1,686	24,051	52,230	.0009	21,215	**6**	3,793	**8**	....	**....**	2,886	....	2,870	Baylor
Bee**	025	32,486	32,359	10,159	9,277	27,173	330,020	.0067	187,620	**55**	22,439	**48**	7,581	**42**	40,072	8,879	14,997	Bee
Bell*	027	251,967	237,974	16,984	95,105	35,049	4,279,440	.0748	2,343,021	**689**	315,312	**669**	75,969	**426**	319,109	39,740	166,616	Bell
Bexar*	029	1,496,237	1,392,931	17,042	546,717	36,239	25,498,880	.4814	18,023,363	**5,302**	2,641,735	**5,608**	1,062,045	**5,952**	2,826,300	720,590	905,649	Bexar
Blanco	031	8,924	8,418	18,424	3,481	37,161	164,420	.0025	49,965	**15**	....	**....**	....	**....**	2,918	....	6,655	Blanco
Borden	033	671	729	15,022	278	27,700	10,080	.0002	3,832	**1**	....	**....**	....	**....**	3,832	....	577	Borden
Bosque	035	17,847	17,204	16,209	6,974	32,243	289,290	.0046	100,096	**29**	2,690	**6**	....	**....**	24,163	6,321	12,974	Bosque
Bowie*	037	89,837	89,306	15,207	33,787	31,488	1,366,140	.0292	1,277,286	**376**	235,492	**500**	69,871	**392**	106,148	32,525	56,901	Bowie
Brazoria*	039	269,789	241,767	19,523	92,394	44,643	5,267,100	.0842	2,299,176	**676**	524,335	**1,113**	58,745	**329**	344,993	82,707	173,787	Brazoria
Brazos*	041	162,171	152,415	13,684	61,901	27,396	2,219,150	.0464	1,835,194	**540**	347,968	**739**	92,157	**516**	241,085	42,860	110,706	Brazos
Brewster	043	9,372	8,866	14,121	3,936	26,095	132,340	.0025	81,430	**24**	7,686	**16**	....	**....**	24,227	6,177	6,330	Brewster
Briscoe	045	1,626	1,790	14,705	659	27,790	23,910	.0004	7,059	**2**	....	**....**	....	**....**	1,586	....	1,223	Briscoe
Brooks	047	7,644	7,976	8,306	2,642	18,561	63,490	.0015	49,650	**15**	6,520	**14**	....	**....**	7,914	1,294	3,635	Brooks
Brown**	049	38,231	37,674	14,432	14,600	29,271	551,760	.0110	415,088	**122**	90,134	**191**	17,601	**99**	39,310	24,586	25,474	Brown
Burleson*	051	17,071	16,470	15,540	6,607	30,927	265,280	.0045	121,881	**36**	16,436	**35**	....	**....**	29,249	....	11,831	Burleson
Burnet	053	40,228	34,147	17,479	15,373	35,538	703,150	.0130	474,656	**140**	98,945	**210**	9,745	**55**	85,066	14,141	28,047	Burnet
Caldwell*	055	36,601	32,194	15,141	12,387	35,018	554,160	.0090	196,208	**58**	13,427	**29**	....	**....**	45,916	7,207	22,212	Caldwell
Calhoun*	057	20,387	20,647	15,510	7,378	32,789	316,210	.0055	151,415	**45**	19,413	**41**	4,794	**27**	44,830	1,306	12,603	Calhoun
Callahan*	059	13,173	12,905	15,628	5,196	30,495	205,870	.0034	79,153	**23**	1,017	**2**	....	**....**	7,064	1,372	9,578	Callahan
Cameron*	061	371,857	335,227	9,563	109,025	25,289	3,556,070	.0806	2,774,996	**816**	641,360	**1,361**	195,601	**1,096**	531,733	106,356	168,989	Cameron
Camp	063	11,809	11,549	14,448	4,554	28,926	170,620	.0037	159,085	**47**	3,144	**7**	4,909	**28**	29,352	13,982	7,893	Camp
Carson*	065	6,507	6,516	18,603	2,506	37,194	121,050	.0018	31,076	**9**	....	**....**	....	**....**	1,109	....	5,200	Carson
Cass	067	29,854	30,438	14,512	12,279	27,155	433,250	.0074	182,724	**54**	34,236	**73**	3,412	**19**	26,457	14,056	21,093	Cass
Castro	069	7,794	8,285	12,737	2,652	28,959	99,270	.0019	62,309	**18**	8,344	**18**	....	**....**	14,182	2,857	4,923	Castro
Chambers*	071	28,050	26,031	19,904	9,938	43,673	558,320	.0079	132,895	**39**	4,482	**10**	1,247	**7**	16,171	5,234	18,722	Chambers
Cherokee**	073	47,864	46,659	12,958	17,119	28,103	620,240	.0119	369,200	**109**	74,757	**159**	7,731	**43**	66,858	12,757	29,422	Cherokee
Childress	075	7,523	7,688	11,361	2,408	27,126	85,470	.0017	53,687	**16**	17,084	**36**	....	**....**	5,754	1,681	3,916	Childress
Clay*	077	11,240	11,006	17,316	4,474	33,615	194,630	.0031	79,172	**23**	1,368	**3**	....	**....**	7,318	1,155	8,975	Clay
Cochran	079	3,414	3,730	12,460	1,228	26,648	42,540	.0007	16,323	**5**	....	**....**	....	**....**	1,559	....	2,228	Cochran
Coke	081	3,683	3,864	14,415	1,494	27,144	53,090	.0010	31,986	**9**	....	**....**	....	**....**	3,690	1,056	2,723	Coke
Coleman	083	8,644	9,235	13,446	3,653	24,640	116,230	.0021	61,780	**18**	2,149	**5**	....	**....**	9,763	3,986	6,346	Coleman
Collin*	085	629,504	491,675	30,078	235,198	62,074	18,934,140	.2739	7,628,247	**2,244**	1,165,805	**2,475**	439,800	**2,465**	1,149,768	271,602	446,194	Collin
Collingsworth	087	2,967	3,206	12,757	1,188	24,560	37,850	.0007	20,686	**6**	....	**....**	....	**....**	4,998	....	2,228	Collingsworth
Colorado	089	20,739	20,390	14,876	7,778	30,723	308,510	.0062	243,967	**72**	21,854	**46**	1,762	**10**	43,324	10,160	13,484	Colorado
Comal*	091	90,783	78,021	20,911	34,779	42,248	1,898,380	.0299	822,187	**242**	124,605	**265**	23,504	**132**	96,634	30,751	66,772	Comal
Comanche	093	13,391	14,026	13,627	5,254	26,944	182,480	.0034	98,624	**29**	2,494	**5**	....	**....**	18,723	3,855	9,449	Comanche
Concho	095	3,716	3,966	9,952	968	29,243	36,980	.0007	14,868	**4**	....	**....**	....	**....**	4,314	....	1,855	Concho
Cooke**	097	38,507	36,363	17,265	14,468	35,783	664,820	.0130	519,070	**153**	59,962	**127**	43,959	**246**	64,701	19,706	26,897	Cooke
Coryell*	099	75,191	74,978	12,319	20,977	34,561	926,260	.0166	394,049	**116**	95,527	**203**	5,235	**29**	74,415	8,510	39,810	Coryell
Cottle	101	1,710	1,904	13,965	754	24,607	23,880	.0005	14,436	**4**	....	**....**	1,687	**9**	1,523	....	1,242	Cottle
Crane	103	3,862	3,996	13,814	1,325	30,888	53,350	.0009	21,377	**6**	....	**....**	....	**....**	4,234	....	2,314	Crane
Crockett	105	3,902	4,099	13,770	1,474	27,856	53,730	.0010	30,447	**9**	....	**....**	....	**....**	6,873	....	2,410	Crockett
Crosby*	107	6,640	7,072	11,447	2,386	24,597	76,010	.0016	57,735	**17**	....	**....**	....	**....**	19,430	2,223	4,107	Crosby
Culberson	109	2,701	2,975	11,751	1,000	24,336	31,740	.0009	54,486	**16**	....	**....**	....	**....**	1,985	....	1,709	Culberson
Dallam	111	6,059	6,222	12,854	2,215	26,921	77,880	.0018	84,657	**25**	7,224	**15**	....	**....**	5,556	....	3,800	Dallam
Dallas*	113	2,303,656	2,218,899	19,854	879,140	40,264	45,736,380	.8476	33,451,662	**9,840**	4,430,302	**9,405**	1,869,463	**10,477**	4,036,338	1,256,109	1,465,267	Dallas
Dawson**	115	14,232	14,985	11,056	4,523	26,671	157,350	.0033	106,328	**31**	9,040	**19**	2,245	**13**	19,631	5,471	7,288	Dawson
Deaf Smith**	117	18,382	18,561	12,297	6,200	27,969	226,050	.0043	125,094	**37**	5,109	**11**	2,582	**14**	21,924	2,483	10,720	Deaf Smith
Delta*	119	5,487	5,327	14,467	2,151	28,614	79,380	.0012	17,450	**5**	....	**....**	....	**....**	3,089	1,001	3,599	Delta
Denton*	121	534,784	432,976	25,097	198,246	52,161	13,421,650	.1999	5,369,605	**1,580**	1,025,492	**2,177**	270,665	**1,517**	942,760	311,855	385,894	Denton
DeWitt	123	20,137	20,013	12,855	7,279	27,161	258,860	.0046	115,868	**34**	11,367	**24**	2,302	**13**	25,300	10,946	12,102	DeWitt
Dickens	125	2,697	2,762	11,342	961	24,562	30,590	.0005	8,795	**3**	....	**....**	....	**....**	1,804	....	1,764	Dickens
Dimmit	127	10,383	10,248	9,328	3,496	21,162	96,850	.0022	70,332	**21**	17,614	**37**	....	**....**	6,062	....	5,382	Dimmit
Donley	129	3,891	3,828	14,865	1,615	27,402	57,840	.0010	30,415	**9**	1,101	**2**	....	**....**	5,904	1,113	2,993	Donley
Duval	131	12,474	13,120	9,775	4,250	21,937	121,930	.0023	41,099	**12**	1,004	**2**	....	**....**	6,799	1,052	6,428	Duval
Eastland	133	18,296	18,297	13,385	7,301	25,853	244,900	.0049	175,341	**52**	22,041	**47**	....	**....**	26,002	9,963	12,830	Eastland
Ector*	135	123,354	121,123	14,193	45,834	29,410	1,750,810	.0368	1,501,339	**442**	332,254	**705**	45,562	**255**	201,630	64,347	76,428	Ector
Edwards	137	1,992	2,162	11,878	757	24,197	23,660	.0004	6,378	**2**	....	**....**	....	**....**	1,718	....	1,412	Edwards
Ellis*	139	128,389	111,360	19,479	42,646	45,414	2,500,890	.0385	926,190	**272**	141,264	**300**	17,260	**97**	189,406	55,206	84,857	Ellis
El Paso*	141	713,340	679,622	12,037	226,278	29,352	8,586,800	.1799	6,462,611	**1,901**	1,356,263	**2,879**	425,599	**2,385**	831,659	312,642	384,245	El Paso
Erath**	143	33,483	33,001	14,417	12,815	29,446	482,740	.0097	370,957	**109**	77,218	**164**	16,570	**93**	46,005	17,783	22,740	Erath
Falls	145	17,642	18,576	11,596	6,188	26,567	204,580	.0038	94,036	**28**	16,723	**36**	....	**....**	30,671	3,185	10,169	Falls
Fannin	147	32,575	31,242	14,860	11,522	32,766	484,050	.0091	307,011	**90**	50,280	**107**	1,758	**10**	27,627	11,973	21,091	Fannin
Fayette	149	22,554	21,804	16,822	9,032	32,215	379,400	.0071	255,484	**75**	24,997	**53**	6,113	**34**	39,584	5,501	16,632	Fayette
Fisher	151	4,080	4,344	14,684	1,714	26,737	59,910	.0009	12,804	**4**	....	**....**	....	**....**	4,713	....	3,108	Fisher
Floyd	153	7,349	7,771	12,021	2,586	26,163	88,340	.0017	49,467	**15**	....	**....**	....	**....**	4,919	1,429	4,660	Floyd
Foard	155	1,519	1,622	13,173	625	25,179	20,010	.0003	5,217	**2**	....	**....**	....	**....**	....	....	1,151	Foard
Fort Bend*	157	440,039	354,452	23,114	138,170	57,154	10,171,250	.1548	4,184,720	**1,231**	794,145	**1,686**	192,539	**1,079**	534,909	154,139	279,399	Fort Bend
Franklin	159	10,049	9,458	15,668	4,037	30,391	157,450	.0025	56,787	**17**	3,014	**6**	....	**....**	4,046	2,331	7,414	Franklin

Source: Devonshire Associates Ltd. and Scan/US, Inc. 2004.
* Component of a Metropolitan Core Based Statistical Area.
** Component of a Micropolitan Core Based Statistical Area.

.... Data less than 1,000.

(d) Data not available.

continued on next page

Counties: Population / Income / Sales, *Continued*

COUNTY OR COUNTY EQUIVALENT	FIPS CO. CODE	POPULATION Estimate 7/1/04	POPULATION Census 4/1/00	PER CAPITA INCOME 2003	HOUSEHOLDS Estimate 7/1/04	MEDIAN HOUSEHOLD INCOME 2003	DISPOSABLE INCOME 2003 ($1,000)	MARKET ABILITY INDEX 2003	TOTAL RETAIL SALES Sales 2003 ($1,000)	TOTAL RETAIL SALES Ranally Sales Units	GENERAL MERCHANDISE Sales 2003 ($1,000)	GENERAL MERCHANDISE Ranally Sales Units	APPAREL STORE Sales 2003 ($1,000)	APPAREL STORE Ranally Sales Units	FOOD STORE SALES 2003 ($1,000)	HEALTH & DRUG STORE 2003 ($1,000)	PASSENGER CAR REGIS-TRATIONS 2003	COUNTY OR COUNTY EQUIVALENT
Freestone	161	18,834	17,867	14,425	7,031	30,229	271,680	.0053	185,869	55	7,605	16	2,415	14	32,345	10,626	12,794	Freestone
Frio	163	16,390	16,252	9,214	4,941	23,696	151,020	.0034	116,171	34	16,352	35	1,528	9	21,899	2,096	7,625	Frio
Gaines	165	14,431	14,467	12,071	4,708	28,518	174,200	.0036	127,159	37	20,184	43	1,499	8	35,865	4,603	8,341	Gaines
Galveston*	167	272,122	250,158	20,011	106,277	39,871	5,445,530	.0870	2,419,704	712	413,687	878	149,310	837	487,505	149,368	179,765	Galveston
Garza	169	5,060	4,872	11,789	1,755	26,061	59,650	.0010	20,381	6	....	....	....	....	4,228	1,269	2,891	Garza
Gillespie	171	22,660	20,814	19,264	9,425	35,567	436,520	.0075	244,024	72	23,663	50	9,469	53	62,204	4,664	17,509	Gillespie
Glasscock	173	1,339	1,406	15,833	476	34,586	21,200	.0003	6,131	2	....	....	....	....	....	....	1,017	Glasscock
Goliad*	175	7,163	6,928	16,112	2,784	31,958	115,410	.0017	26,262	8	1,216	3	....	....	7,801	1,223	5,115	Goliad
Gonzales	177	19,193	18,628	12,912	7,034	27,039	247,820	.0046	133,074	39	21,677	46	1,898	11	31,771	4,370	11,597	Gonzales
Gray**	179	21,145	22,744	15,185	8,301	29,831	321,080	.0060	205,180	60	29,557	63	6,549	37	33,414	8,456	14,912	Gray
Grayson*	181	116,532	110,595	17,785	45,226	35,555	2,072,480	.0389	1,481,541	436	372,920	792	32,470	182	172,110	55,084	81,589	Grayson
Gregg*	183	114,824	111,379	16,919	45,346	32,933	1,942,760	.0424	2,017,742	594	372,882	792	70,029	392	253,971	80,891	76,731	Gregg
Grimes	185	25,411	23,552	13,429	8,523	30,741	341,250	.0061	159,456	47	11,376	24	....	....	42,631	....	14,706	Grimes
Guadalupe*	187	99,505	89,023	18,802	35,676	40,562	1,870,890	.0301	807,046	237	101,980	216	20,822	117	88,728	26,309	68,159	Guadalupe
Hale**	189	35,642	36,602	12,573	11,719	29,619	448,110	.0090	301,700	89	59,099	125	14,615	82	42,633	11,081	20,157	Hale
Hall	191	3,855	3,782	11,209	1,549	21,223	43,210	.0010	45,910	14	1,578	3	....	....	1,846	1,740	2,391	Hall
Hamilton	193	8,081	8,229	15,461	3,275	29,815	124,940	.0022	62,513	18	....	....	....	....	14,977	5,075	6,046	Hamilton
Hansford	195	5,162	5,369	16,246	1,955	33,073	83,860	.0015	51,164	15	....	....	3,544	20	6,783	....	3,813	Hansford
Hardeman	197	4,352	4,724	14,476	1,804	26,877	63,000	.0010	18,554	5	1,220	3	....	....	5,562	1,211	3,231	Hardeman
Hardin*	199	50,132	48,073	17,049	18,908	34,985	854,680	.0149	465,684	137	69,709	148	2,928	16	70,922	10,783	33,946	Hardin
Harris*	201	3,656,415	3,400,578	19,156	1,366,273	39,780	70,043,350	1.2571	45,604,263	13,415	6,510,937	13,821	2,724,895	15,271	6,954,242	2,262,853	2,278,306	Harris
Harrison**	203	62,916	62,110	15,426	23,562	31,808	970,570	.0174	538,676	158	78,763	167	19,827	111	68,989	23,168	42,114	Harrison
Hartley	205	5,121	5,537	17,045	1,590	42,365	87,290	.0012	15,032	4	....	....	1,257	7	8,798	....	3,038	Hartley
Haskell	207	5,640	6,093	12,949	2,415	23,058	73,030	.0016	61,531	18	....	....	....	....	7,641	....	4,149	Haskell
Hays*	209	119,256	97,589	19,066	42,644	41,196	2,273,780	.0382	1,185,258	349	93,809	199	261,908	1,468	153,154	42,761	83,356	Hays
Hemphill	211	3,336	3,351	16,805	1,320	32,775	56,060	.0009	22,133	7	4,261	9	....	....	1,539	1,348	2,601	Hemphill
Henderson**	213	78,507	73,277	15,820	30,896	30,915	1,241,960	.0209	543,715	160	120,059	255	13,253	74	122,394	32,786	54,667	Henderson
Hidalgo*	215	656,072	569,463	8,644	182,386	23,710	5,671,110	.1419	5,457,211	1,605	1,064,900	2,261	420,429	2,356	833,469	231,799	292,420	Hidalgo
Hill	217	35,058	32,321	14,530	13,217	30,056	509,380	.0111	485,994	143	31,751	67	84,316	473	76,956	12,266	23,391	Hill
Hockley**	219	22,854	22,716	13,760	8,275	29,386	314,470	.0061	201,632	59	26,943	57	4,316	24	30,162	7,037	14,514	Hockley
Hood**	221	46,225	41,100	20,747	18,415	40,363	959,020	.0161	531,523	156	76,598	163	6,664	37	75,607	17,680	34,766	Hood
Hopkins**	223	32,901	31,960	15,371	12,711	30,783	505,730	.0103	418,379	123	38,866	83	26,772	150	31,827	22,696	22,556	Hopkins
Houston	225	23,084	23,185	12,498	8,326	26,703	288,500	.0056	175,336	52	18,374	39	2,839	16	36,022	12,625	13,553	Houston
Howard**	227	32,647	33,627	12,743	11,162	28,829	416,030	.0084	297,481	88	51,763	110	8,420	47	37,086	13,259	17,867	Howard
Hudspeth	229	3,142	3,344	8,670	1,016	20,541	27,240	.0005	8,873	3	....	....	....	....	2,433	....	1,800	Hudspeth
Hunt*	231	82,370	76,596	16,694	30,671	35,426	1,375,070	.0242	757,672	223	156,310	332	27,410	154	139,848	37,141	55,818	Hunt
Hutchinson**	233	22,692	23,857	17,459	8,947	34,165	396,190	.0065	176,261	52	25,933	55	7,481	42	37,114	8,469	16,841	Hutchinson
Irion*	235	1,731	1,771	18,030	695	34,422	31,210	.0004	1,362	0	....	....	....	....	....	....	1,326	Irion
Jack	237	9,010	8,763	13,799	3,141	30,297	124,330	.0019	28,605	8	1,111	2	....	....	7,471	3,696	5,586	Jack
Jackson	239	14,183	14,391	16,021	5,270	33,172	227,230	.0037	87,410	26	6,577	14	....	....	17,232	....	9,190	Jackson
Jasper	241	35,471	35,604	14,421	13,654	28,894	511,530	.0099	341,640	100	72,252	153	7,054	40	52,744	18,253	23,045	Jasper
Jeff Davis	243	2,237	2,207	16,294	915	30,573	36,450	.0005	4,578	1	....	....	....	....	3,589	....	1,663	Jeff Davis
Jefferson*	245	247,599	252,051	16,518	96,577	32,639	4,089,940	.0831	3,495,542	1,028	562,045	1,193	171,960	964	442,121	195,079	151,797	Jefferson
Jim Hogg	247	4,944	5,281	11,169	1,738	24,503	55,220	.0011	36,625	11	1,654	4	....	....	7,016	....	2,523	Jim Hogg
Jim Wells**	249	40,830	39,326	11,817	13,677	26,964	482,480	.0099	330,740	97	47,311	100	13,124	74	64,285	16,383	22,186	Jim Wells
Johnson*	251	142,744	126,811	18,278	49,203	40,941	2,609,090	.0415	1,050,188	309	213,689	454	30,443	171	150,990	35,095	96,244	Johnson
Jones*	253	19,809	20,785	10,666	5,815	27,980	211,290	.0049	196,574	58	15,637	33	....	....	9,770	3,302	10,344	Jones
Karnes	255	15,220	15,446	9,715	4,482	25,418	147,860	.0031	89,974	26	12,386	26	....	....	19,480	1,212	7,347	Karnes
Kaufman*	257	85,224	71,313	18,241	29,194	41,013	1,554,610	.0276	941,176	277	67,456	143	46,882	263	153,616	32,053	57,120	Kaufman
Kendall*	259	26,915	23,743	22,130	10,345	44,391	595,640	.0117	537,686	158	36,095	77	2,618	15	87,291	1,104	21,056	Kendall
Kenedy**	261	406	414	10,714	137	24,086	4,350	.0001	....	....	....	....	....	....	....	....	213	Kenedy
Kent	263	745	859	15,678	313	28,856	11,680	.0002	6,047	2	....	....	....	....	....	....	615	Kent
Kerr**	265	45,804	43,653	17,135	18,813	32,079	784,860	.0160	689,337	203	112,563	239	37,302	209	221,124	37,263	31,593	Kerr
Kimble	267	4,548	4,468	15,523	1,945	27,877	70,600	.0013	41,862	12	....	....	....	....	12,001	....	3,489	Kimble
King	269	306	356	12,549	91	32,280	3,840	.0001	....	....	....	....	....	....	....	....	175	King
Kinney	271	3,288	3,379	13,707	1,286	26,874	45,070	.0007	6,022	2	....	....	....	....	3,731	....	2,028	Kinney
Kleberg**	273	31,238	31,549	12,574	10,996	27,545	392,800	.0082	299,066	88	67,426	143	13,157	74	46,219	11,561	16,775	Kleberg
Knox	275	3,827	4,253	12,642	1,539	24,601	48,380	.0009	25,583	8	....	....	....	....	5,763	....	2,519	Knox
Lamar**	277	49,741	48,499	15,332	19,769	30,073	762,610	.0157	650,929	191	128,903	274	31,115	174	71,467	32,389	33,473	Lamar
Lamb	279	14,628	14,709	12,709	5,350	26,662	185,900	.0034	85,090	25	4,852	10	1,423	8	21,813	1,963	9,465	Lamb
Lampasas*	281	19,905	17,762	16,151	7,341	34,097	321,490	.0055	151,846	45	9,316	20	1,395	8	18,163	7,874	13,632	Lampasas
La Salle	283	5,801	5,866	8,771	1,849	20,984	50,880	.0011	30,208	9	2,760	6	....	....	4,036	1,392	2,602	La Salle
Lavaca	285	19,019	19,210	14,611	7,672	27,925	277,880	.0051	157,802	46	16,732	36	1,884	11	35,554	6,556	13,565	Lavaca
Lee	287	16,797	15,657	15,748	6,057	33,750	264,520	.0044	114,344	34	19,783	42	1,820	10	15,779	2,299	11,143	Lee
Leon	289	16,208	15,335	15,310	6,596	28,947	248,140	.0043	114,929	34	....	....	....	....	35,400	3,278	11,465	Leon
Liberty*	291	75,275	70,154	15,530	25,085	36,252	1,169,040	.0205	595,347	175	127,282	270	18,690	105	108,553	29,571	43,069	Liberty
Limestone	293	22,808	22,051	13,032	8,194	28,064	297,240	.0059	196,649	58	22,540	48	2,603	15	47,873	9,383	14,369	Limestone
Lipscomb	295	3,108	3,057	15,441	1,233	30,021	47,990	.0007	12,386	4	....	....	....	....	1,950	....	2,377	Lipscomb
Live Oak	297	11,777	12,309	13,670	4,108	30,455	160,990	.0030	94,865	28	1,901	4	....	....	12,121	2,528	7,055	Live Oak
Llano	299	18,341	17,044	19,939	8,523	32,963	365,710	.0053	102,447	30	....	....	1,429	8	25,599	5,966	15,056	Llano
Loving	301	61	67	25,574	30	40,000	1,560	....	....	....	....	....	....	....	....	....	68	Loving
Lubbock*	303	252,962	242,628	15,382	98,160	30,626	3,891,160	.0818	3,504,726	1,031	536,684	1,139	164,044	919	496,093	106,005	166,391	Lubbock
Lynn	305	6,077	6,550	12,088	2,201	25,877	73,460	.0013	27,202	8	....	....	....	....	....	1,103	3,978	Lynn
McCulloch	307	7,805	8,205	12,926	3,150	24,959	100,890	.0024	111,195	33	27,893	59	1,782	10	8,495	1,581	5,102	McCulloch
McLennan*	309	221,739	213,517	15,426	83,405	31,836	3,420,440	.0655	2,358,225	694	434,782	923	83,366	467	383,400	91,734	143,027	McLennan
McMullen	311	873	851	17,239	373	30,931	15,050	.0002	2,282	1	....	....	....	....	....	....	677	McMullen
Madison	313	12,768	12,940	11,201	3,927	28,052	143,010	.0044	255,166	75	42,597	90	....	....	31,675	11,461	6,637	Madison
Marion	315	11,054	10,941	13,624	4,734	24,607	150,600	.0026	62,522	18	....	....	....	....	9,992	....	7,728	Marion
Martin	317	4,560	4,746	13,436	1,584	29,961	61,270	.0012	44,150	13	....	....	....	....	4,715	2,137	2,818	Martin
Mason	319	3,788	3,738	16,312	1,637	29,290	61,790	.0009	14,936	4	....	....	....	....	5,034	1,013	3,089	Mason
Matagorda**	321	38,404	37,957	14,797	14,269	30,931	568,250	.0102	306,282	90	36,687	78	11,875	67	82,843	11,788	23,597	Matagorda
Maverick**	323	51,111	47,297	7,610	14,309	21,005	388,980	.0101	370,947	109	74,862	159	55,161	309	111,851	10,772	21,624	Maverick
Medina*	325	42,244	39,304	14,422	13,937	33,592	609,260	.0110	327,620	96	21,078	45	1,719	10	53,290	4,972	26,284	Medina
Menard	327	2,353	2,360	13,158	992	24,347	30,960	.0006	14,426	4	....	....	....	....	....	....	1,679	Menard
Midland*	329	119,655	116,009	18,305	46,067	36,657	2,190,260	.0412	1,600,790	471	285,960	607	75,888	425	182,330	53,538	80,446	Midland
Milam	331	25,378	24,238	15,431	9,664	31,179	391,610	.0064	143,500	42	24,062	51	1,623	9	33,613	7,699	17,037	Milam
Mills	333	5,005	5,151	14,254	1,930	28,416	71,340	.0015	58,036	17	....	....	1,129	6	5,205	....	3,578	Mills
Mitchell	335	9,210	9,698	9,268	2,674	24,632	85,360	.0017	41,104	12	....	....	1,622	9	10,507	3,030	4,464	Mitchell
Montague	337	19,511	19,117	15,636	8,012	29,545	305,070	.0050	121,426	36	16,359	35	1,850	10	25,456	8,091	14,866	Montague
Montgomery*	339	360,419	293,768	21,236	128,798	45,764	7,653,950	.1244	3,821,596	1,124	792,232	1,682	212,774	1,192	563,094	114,105	243,085	Montgomery
Moore**	341	20,275	20,121	14,240	6,788	32,601	288,710	.0052	153,535	45	27,154	58	5,490	31	30,756	5,819	13,033	Moore
Morris	343	13,206	13,048	14,730	5,398	27,736	194,520	.0031	55,999	16	2,574	5	....	....	13,634	4,898	9,341	Morris
Motley	345	1,262	1,426	14,707	537	26,622	18,560	.0003	8,009	2	....	....	....	....	....	....	1,003	Motley
Nacogdoches**	347	59,703	59,203	13,173	22,505	27,179	786,480	.0170	692,782	204	113,899	242	40,820	229	102,472	24,304	38,684	Nacogdoches
Navarro**	349	48,002	45,124	13,859	17,375	30,016	665,250	.0129	441,431	130	69,619	148	22,169	124	68,576	15,012	29,395	Navarro
Newton	351	14,808	15,072	13,282	5,616	26,771	196,680	.0030	31,393	9	....	....	....	....	16,338	....	9,362	Newton
Nolan**	353	14,899	15,802	13,085	5,918	25,486	194,960	.0040	142,739	42	16,358	35	5,184	29	19,952	8,367	9,592	Nolan
Nueces*	355	315,797	313,645	16,165	116,490	33,978	5,104,820	.0975	3,614,459	1,063	617,544	1,311	185,248	1,038	572,149	132,270	189,835	Nueces
Ochiltree	357	8,983	9,006	16,745	3,248	35,538	150,420	.0026	77,186	23	7,154	15	2,896	16	9,422	4,781	5,951	Ochiltree
Oldham	359	2,148	2,185	14,274	738	32,210	30,660	.0005	10,890	3	....	....	....	....	....	....	1,345	Oldham
Orange*	361	84,199	84,966	17,637	32,436	35,414	1,484,980	.0247	689,384	203	114,604	243	19,645	110	117,622	44,491	57,039	Orange
Palo Pinto**	363	27,404	27,026	15,045	10,837	29,561	412,290	.0074	226,027	66	30,320	64	16,859	94	43,151	10,609	18,658	Palo Pinto
Panola	365	22,558	22,756	15,328	8,907	30,003	345,760	.0059	154,001	45	17,878	38	4,350	24	37,721	15,804	15,197	Panola
Parker*	367	100,215	88,495	19,122	35,473	41,543	1,916,360	.0325	1,029,472	303	123,069	261	24,260	136	175,390	34,615	70,558	Parker
Parmer	369	9,860	10,016	12,505	3,291	28,856	123,300	.0022	54,777	16	....	....	....	....	6,077	1,368	6,174	Parmer
Pecos	371	15,821	16,809	11,183	4,949	27,389	176,930	.0035	101,897	30	19,399	41	1,805	10	16,323	1,498	8,909	Pecos
Polk	373	46,570	41,133	14,049	17,525	28,919	654,240	.0123	394,143	116	98,804	210	11,496	64	60,933	12,125	28,949	Polk
Potter*	375	118,540	113,546	12,979	42,419	27,966	1,538,540	.0389	1,989,561	585	253,708	539	101,411	568	147,980	101,017	68,757	Potter
Presidio	377	7,671	7,304	8,824	2,682	19,137	67,690	.0014	32,889	10	11,949	25	....	....	6,240	....	4,117	Presidio
Rains	379	11,404	9,139	16,350	4,540	31,595	186,460	.0027	38,094	11	....	....	....	....	18,623	1,135	8,410	Rains
Randall*	381	108,220	104,312	20,587	43,301	39,889	2,227,920	.0357	1,021,898	301	165,449	351	22,814	128	103,566	28,315	80,458	Randall
Reagan	383	2,978	3,326	14,066	1,041	30,977	41,890	.0007	20,182	6	1,181	3	....	....	4,022	....	1,915	Reagan
Real	385	3,006	3,047	13,466	1,289	24,548	40,480	.0006	8,452	2	....	....	....	....	2,641	....	2,282	Real
Red River	387	13,660	14,314	13,979	5,601	26,331	190,950	.0032	70,529	21	12,204	26	....	....	10,214	6,038	9,928	Red River
Reeves**	389	11,975	13,137	9,298	3,801	22,327	111,340	.0025	79,588	23	18,239	39	2,478	14	2,417	8,841	5,887	Reeves
Refugio	391	7,559	7,828	14,194	2,930	28,200	107,290	.0021	71,176	21	1,286	3	....	....	14,194	2,034	4,697	Refugio
Roberts**	393	800	887	22,038	336	40,368	17,630	.0002	2,277	1	....	....	....	....	....	....	691	Roberts
Robertson*	395	15,769	16,000	14,075	6,181	27,587	221,950	.0037	75,526	22	4,211	9	....	....	20,339	5,345	10,167	Robertson
Rockwall*	397	58,223	43,080	25,194	19,566	57,432	1,466,860	.0219	592,754	174	104,945	223	15,870	89	161,607	33,377	41,028	Rockwall
Runnels	399	10,727	11,495	13,357	4,152	26,360	143,280	.0026	76,152	22	3,995	8	1,001	6	10,197	1,504	7,545	Runnels
Rusk*	401	47,219	47,372	14,860	17,515	30,780	701,670	.0117	276,531	81	49,613	105	7,011	39	55,376	16,095	31,124	Rusk
Sabine	403	10,357	10,469	14,472	4,497	25,683	149,890	.0024	50,112	15	1,661	4	....	....	13,789	4,351	7,508	Sabine
San Augustine	405	8,901	8,946	13,527	3,589	25,773	120,400	.0021	53,035	16	1,649	4	....	....	13,484	3,449	5,996	San Augustine
San Jacinto*	407	24,408	22,246	15,453	9,590	30,166	377,170	.0053	46,099	14	1,043	2	....	....	21,456	1,196	16,465	San Jacinto
San Patricio*	409	68,309	67,138	14,445	23,146	32,932	986,710	.0177	516,985	152	50,557	107	8,427	47	142,880	26,711	38,912	San Patricio
San Saba	411	6,006	6,186	13,533	2,217	28,193	81,280	.0018	76,921	23	7,287	15	....	....	8,849	4,137	3,966	San Saba
Schleicher	413	2,781	2,935	14,613	1,091	28,882	40,640	.0006	7,644	2	....	....	....	....	....	....	1,979	Schleicher
Scurry**	415	16,025	16,361	14,046	5,807	30,062	225,080	.0046	178,930	53	25,229	54	2,881	16	20,876	8,880	9,810	Scurry
Shackelford	417	3,308	3,302	14,670	1,290	28,957	48,530	.0008	18,035	5	....	....	....	....	1,891	....	2,360	Shackelford
Shelby	419	26,086	25,224	13,486	9,878	27,350	351,790	.0068	209,322	62	20,679	44	3,660	21	56,138	16,684	16,346	Shelby
Sherman	421	3,147	3,186	14,398	1,095	31,736	45,310	.0007	8,644	3	1,349	3	....	....	....	....	2,045	Sherman
Smith*	423	186,882	174,706	17,504	72,108	35,103	3,271,110	.0660	2,829,077	832	474,715	1,008	187,114	1,049	337,370	129,863	126,800	Smith
Somervell**	425	7,494	6,809	17,176	2,695	36,856	128,720	.0020	45,179	13	10,719	23	....	....	6,240	6,432	5,175	Somervell
Starr**	427	58,958	53,597	5,876	16,241	16,109	346,420	.0097	302,490	89	54,881	117	12,673	71	84,655	6,893	24,073	Starr
Stephens	429	9,385	9,674	13,999	3,568	28,449	131,380	.0024	65,790	19	8,928	19	1,557	9	12,857	3,868	5,999	Stephens
Sterling	431	1,331	1,393	16,258	505	32,742	21,640	.0003	6,570	2	....	....	....	....	....	....	950	Sterling
Stonewall	433	1,379	1,693	14,917	593	26,706	20,570	.0003	7,535	2	....	....	....	....	....	....	1,019	Stonewall
Sutton	435	4,134	4,077	15,989	1,564	32,060	66,100	.0014	62,804	18	....	....	....	....	6,201	....	2,707	Sutton
Swisher	437	7,901	8,378	12,991	2,764	28,668	102,640	.0018	41,376	12	2,943	6	....	....	4,323	....	4,834	Swisher
Tarrant*	439	1,594,027	1,446,219	20,395	594,919	42,490	32,509,940	.5787	21,425,283	6,302	2,273,907	4,827	991,965	5,559	2,852,327	869,163	1,059,397	Tarrant
Taylor*	441	124,966	126,555	16,319	48,929	31,963	2,039,260	.0409	1,676,253	493	364,443	774	57,487	322	193,312	67,243	85,049	Taylor
Terrell	443	1,026	1,081	12,934	438	22,971	13,270	.0002	2,144	1	....	....	....	....	....	....	774	Terrell
Terry	445	12,367	12,761	12,077	4,245	26,903	149,360	.0029	87,757	26	12,087	26	1,939	11	15,259	4,054	7,476	Terry
Throckmorton	447	1,654	1,850	14,359	676	26,957	23,750	.0004	5,317	2	....	....	....	....	....	....	1,266	Throckmorton
Titus**	449	28,765	28,118	13,375	9,620	30,891	384,730	.0085	362,934	107	79,071	168	14,820	83	38,892	18,204	16,719	Titus
Tom Green*	451	103,389	104,010	16,149	41,302	31,241	1,669,670	.0320	1,193,948	351	241,597	513	46,860	263	165,713	36,321	69,173	Tom Green
Travis*	453	869,648	812,280	23,492	369,393	43,353	20,430,020	.4461	23,826,388	7,009	1,684,916	3,577	731,191	4,098	2,348,135	1,178,319	636,248	Travis
Trinity	455	14,259	13,779	13,995	5,978	25,683	199,560	.0032	58,960	17	....	....	....	....	25,354	....	9,633	Trinity
Tyler	457	20,581	20,871	13,741	7,741	28,205	282,800	.0046	90,712	27	13,165	28	....	....	19,932	3,428	13,084	Tyler
Upshur*	459	37,485	35,291	15,590	14,281	31,453	584,390	.0093	195,091	57	42,124	89	1,918	11	37,894	8,930	26,352	Upshur
Upton	461	3,080	3,404	14,101	1,190	28,233	43,430	.0007	15,042	4	....	....	....	....	2,830	....	2,152	Upton
Uvalde**	463	27,070	25,926	11,381	9,040	26,099	308,090	.0066	241,322	71	30,798	65	6,310	35	59,180	6,492	14,643	Uvalde
Val Verde**	465	47,089	44,856	11,281	15,191	27,026	531,200	.0115	421,297	124	82,419	175	24,902	140	88,639	6,705	26,075	Val Verde
Van Zandt	467	51,430	48,140	16,111	19,478	32,740	828,590	.0138	351,715	103	70,403	149	3,766	21	42,655	22,853	36,421	Van Zandt
Victoria*	469	85,853	84,088	16,969	30,982	36,332	1,456,800	.0287	1,163,146	342	236,603	502	51,763	290	156,770	50,391	53,651	Victoria
Walker**	471	62,155	61,758	11,659	18,713	29,837	724,660	.0154	555,154	163	110,029	234	24,793	139	58,183	25,711	31,001	Walker
Waller*	473	35,153	32,663	15,227	11,442	36,043	535,260	.0127	640,006	188	60,390	128	5,785	32	54,330	9,559	20,220	Waller
Ward	475	10,123	10,909	13,509	3,790	27,591	136,750	.0024	63,149	19	7,338	16	1,380	8	11,931	1,184	6,285	Ward

Source: Devonshire Associates Ltd. and Scan/US, Inc. 2004.
* Component of a Metropolitan Core Based Statistical Area.
** Component of a Micropolitan Core Based Statistical Area.

.... Data less than 1,000.

(d) Data not available.

Counties: Population / Income / Sales, *Continued*

COUNTY OR COUNTY EQUIVALENT	FIPS CO. CODE	POPULATION Estimate 7/1/04	POPULATION Census 4/1/00	PER CAPITA INCOME 2003	HOUSEHOLDS Estimate 7/1/04	MEDIAN HOUSEHOLD INCOME 2003	DISPOSABLE INCOME 2003 ($1,000)	MARKET ABILITY INDEX 2003	TOTAL RETAIL SALES Sales 2003 ($1,000)	TOTAL RETAIL SALES Ranally Sales Units	GENERAL MERCHANDISE Sales 2003 ($1,000)	GENERAL MERCHANDISE Ranally Sales Units	APPAREL STORE Sales 2003 ($1,000)	APPAREL STORE Ranally Sales Units	FOOD STORE SALES 2003 ($1,000)	HEALTH & DRUG STORE 2003 ($1,000)	PASSENGER CAR REGIS-TRATIONS 2003	COUNTY OR COUNTY EQUIVALENT
Washington**	477	31,123	30,373	16,944	11,895	34,316	527,340	.0101	385,639	**113**	66,797	**142**	16,638	**93**	63,127	14,269	20,789	Washington
Webb*	479	219,931	193,117	9,311	58,756	26,721	2,047,880	.0538	2,387,548	**702**	472,368	**1,003**	296,511	**1,662**	370,036	96,388	95,585	Webb
Wharton**	481	41,117	41,188	14,045	14,850	30,115	577,470	.0114	410,434	**121**	32,850	**70**	9,024	**51**	91,226	13,634	24,723	Wharton
Wheeler	483	4,672	5,284	15,381	1,921	28,787	71,860	.0013	35,757	**11**	....	**....**	....	**....**	7,295	2,320	3,518	Wheeler
Wichita*	485	128,562	131,664	16,068	49,711	31,962	2,065,790	.0400	1,522,128	**448**	308,562	**655**	45,504	**255**	228,335	73,350	84,729	Wichita
Wilbarger**	487	13,610	14,676	14,490	5,401	28,130	197,210	.0039	148,659	**44**	11,318	**24**	3,584	**20**	29,155	13,683	9,247	Wilbarger
Willacy**	489	20,101	20,082	7,939	5,639	21,525	159,590	.0034	76,060	**22**	7,721	**16**	....	**....**	8,696	8,876	8,542	Willacy
Williamson*	491	319,789	249,967	24,809	113,053	54,080	7,933,490	.1156	2,856,394	**840**	407,533	**865**	87,519	**490**	501,917	151,463	222,264	Williamson
Wilson*	493	36,087	32,408	16,736	12,515	37,356	603,960	.0091	164,590	**48**	17,255	**37**	....	**....**	27,904	9,686	25,272	Wilson
Winkler	495	6,679	7,173	13,788	2,467	28,585	92,090	.0017	50,792	**15**	3,445	**7**	....	**....**	5,383	....	4,216	Winkler
Wise*	497	56,141	48,793	17,806	19,803	39,684	999,620	.0224	1,124,543	**331**	268,590	**570**	11,958	**67**	43,088	9,057	39,417	Wise
Wood	499	40,087	36,752	16,155	16,152	31,002	647,600	.0110	303,241	**89**	78,547	**167**	3,066	**17**	39,469	11,832	28,857	Wood
Yoakum	501	7,237	7,322	13,392	2,487	30,231	96,920	.0017	37,998	**11**	....	**....**	1,246	**7**	8,571	1,639	4,571	Yoakum
Young	503	17,894	17,943	15,183	7,224	29,192	271,690	.0048	140,344	**41**	27,533	**58**	2,342	**13**	31,246	8,390	12,692	Young
Zapata	505	13,132	12,182	10,047	4,303	23,486	131,940	.0024	38,519	**11**	....	**....**	....	**....**	14,656	....	6,619	Zapata
Zavala	507	11,590	11,600	6,765	3,539	16,811	78,410	.0017	30,543	**9**	1,354	**3**	....	**....**	13,301	....	4,959	Zavala
The State		22,508,240	20,851,820	17,983	8,216,915	37,699	404,761,890	7.3813	266,234,582	**78,314**	38,630,480	**82,010**	13,168,126	**73,800**	37,916,175	11,288,000	14,256,695	The State

UTAH (UT; CODE 49; 29 Counties)

COUNTY OR COUNTY EQUIVALENT	FIPS CO. CODE	POPULATION Estimate 7/1/04	POPULATION Census 4/1/00	PER CAPITA INCOME 2003	HOUSEHOLDS Estimate 7/1/04	MEDIAN HOUSEHOLD INCOME 2003	DISPOSABLE INCOME 2003 ($1,000)	MARKET ABILITY INDEX 2003	TOTAL RETAIL SALES Sales 2003 ($1,000)	TOTAL RETAIL SALES Ranally Sales Units	GENERAL MERCHANDISE Sales 2003 ($1,000)	GENERAL MERCHANDISE Ranally Sales Units	APPAREL STORE Sales 2003 ($1,000)	APPAREL STORE Ranally Sales Units	FOOD STORE SALES 2003 ($1,000)	HEALTH & DRUG STORE 2003 ($1,000)	PASSENGER CAR REGIS-TRATIONS 2003	COUNTY OR COUNTY EQUIVALENT
Beaver	001	6,133	6,005	13,134	2,033	32,406	80,550	.0015	43,651	**13**	....	**....**	....	**....**	9,231	4,172	4,214	Beaver
Box Elder**	003	45,045	42,745	15,588	14,019	41,296	702,170	.0126	387,746	**114**	40,311	**86**	8,987	**50**	72,888	5,912	30,781	Box Elder
Cache*	005	96,982	91,391	13,518	29,271	36,955	1,311,050	.0265	973,767	**286**	189,427	**402**	30,031	**168**	147,656	25,012	64,239	Cache
Carbon**	007	19,565	20,422	14,633	7,344	32,044	286,290	.0060	252,843	**74**	75,238	**160**	8,840	**50**	34,664	3,161	15,658	Carbon
Daggett	009	876	921	13,961	335	29,918	12,230	.0002	2,564	**1**	....	**....**	....	**....**	....	....	660	Daggett
Davis*	011	260,687	238,994	18,200	80,958	47,843	4,744,380	.0829	2,736,370	**805**	392,739	**834**	70,460	**395**	431,717	58,089	179,177	Davis
Duchesne	013	15,003	14,371	11,888	4,946	29,781	178,360	.0037	131,542	**39**	4,737	**10**	....	**....**	27,249	2,595	10,187	Duchesne
Emery	015	10,585	10,860	14,858	3,524	36,454	157,270	.0027	67,180	**20**	....	**....**	....	**....**	5,584	4,807	8,189	Emery
Garfield	017	4,475	4,735	13,415	1,503	32,695	60,030	.0010	22,172	**7**	....	**....**	....	**....**	3,090	1,337	3,276	Garfield
Grand	019	8,841	8,485	15,624	3,697	30,604	138,130	.0027	100,415	**30**	3,237	**7**	1,784	**10**	29,531	5,318	6,618	Grand
Iron**	021	36,332	33,779	12,346	11,579	32,007	448,540	.0100	413,772	**122**	76,573	**163**	7,690	**43**	67,258	5,014	24,320	Iron
Juab*	023	8,962	8,238	12,681	2,628	35,421	113,650	.0021	61,225	**18**	4,690	**10**	....	**....**	5,268	1,232	5,967	Juab
Kane	025	6,026	6,046	15,139	2,335	32,036	91,230	.0015	33,735	**10**	....	**....**	....	**....**	11,821	1,696	4,518	Kane
Millard	027	12,469	12,405	13,061	3,944	34,050	162,860	.0032	111,069	**33**	....	**....**	1,266	**7**	25,374	4,014	8,396	Millard
Morgan*	029	7,637	7,129	15,971	2,209	45,689	121,970	.0019	40,780	**12**	....	**....**	....	**....**	7,111	1,830	5,633	Morgan
Piute	031	1,361	1,435	12,153	486	27,804	16,540	.0003	3,794	**1**	....	**....**	....	**....**	1,324	....	1,088	Piute
Rich	033	2,036	1,961	15,437	693	37,360	31,430	.0005	6,760	**2**	....	**....**	....	**....**	....	....	1,572	Rich
Salt Lake*	035	932,116	898,387	18,076	315,979	43,911	16,848,950	.3344	14,197,599	**4,176**	2,146,480	**4,557**	629,720	**3,529**	1,909,655	284,826	618,154	Salt Lake
San Juan	037	13,747	14,413	9,560	4,008	26,783	131,420	.0025	49,389	**15**	....	**....**	....	**....**	13,739	2,183	6,890	San Juan
Sanpete	039	23,981	22,763	10,914	6,900	31,128	261,720	.0052	148,470	**44**	....	**....**	....	**....**	46,480	4,981	14,969	Sanpete
Sevier	041	19,177	18,842	13,468	6,273	33,881	258,270	.0058	255,581	**75**	30,026	**64**	8,213	**46**	44,837	6,285	13,356	Sevier
Summit*	043	34,029	29,736	24,670	11,897	57,984	839,500	.0134	432,968	**127**	33,266	**71**	71,027	**398**	108,300	11,487	25,434	Summit
Tooele*	045	50,062	40,735	15,900	15,582	42,552	795,980	.0130	311,912	**92**	22,359	**47**	1,406	**8**	98,023	5,892	33,318	Tooele
Uintah**	047	26,639	25,224	13,431	8,959	32,772	357,780	.0073	273,772	**81**	60,402	**128**	5,850	**33**	48,963	....	18,402	Uintah
Utah*	049	407,123	368,536	14,363	114,713	41,815	5,847,380	.1153	4,189,283	**1,232**	806,151	**1,711**	141,362	**792**	704,861	73,449	255,562	Utah
Wasatch**	051	18,201	15,215	17,141	5,738	45,046	311,980	.0050	122,654	**36**	9,215	**20**	1,017	**6**	26,744	1,894	12,272	Wasatch
Washington*	053	108,436	90,354	14,542	36,802	35,121	1,576,890	.0343	1,509,158	**444**	206,294	**438**	52,171	**292**	198,002	27,281	70,800	Washington
Wayne	055	2,427	2,509	13,766	893	30,758	33,410	.0006	17,449	**5**	1,587	**3**	....	**....**	5,715	....	1,916	Wayne
Weber*	057	208,627	196,533	16,781	70,871	40,788	3,500,960	.0669	2,539,890	**747**	555,094	**1,178**	75,665	**424**	409,306	49,479	139,319	Weber
The State		2,387,580	2,233,169	16,511	770,119	42,165	39,420,920	.7630	29,437,510	**8,661**	4,659,955	**9,894**	1,117,682	**6,263**	4,494,871	592,029	1,584,885	The State

VERMONT (VT; CODE 50; 14 Counties)

COUNTY OR COUNTY EQUIVALENT	FIPS CO. CODE	POPULATION Estimate 7/1/04	POPULATION Census 4/1/00	PER CAPITA INCOME 2003	HOUSEHOLDS Estimate 7/1/04	MEDIAN HOUSEHOLD INCOME 2003	DISPOSABLE INCOME 2003 ($1,000)	MARKET ABILITY INDEX 2003	TOTAL RETAIL SALES Sales 2003 ($1,000)	TOTAL RETAIL SALES Ranally Sales Units	GENERAL MERCHANDISE Sales 2003 ($1,000)	GENERAL MERCHANDISE Ranally Sales Units	APPAREL STORE Sales 2003 ($1,000)	APPAREL STORE Ranally Sales Units	FOOD STORE SALES 2003 ($1,000)	HEALTH & DRUG STORE 2003 ($1,000)	PASSENGER CAR REGIS-TRATIONS 2003	COUNTY OR COUNTY EQUIVALENT
Addison	001	37,097	35,974	18,309	13,778	39,871	679,200	.0126	479,669	**141**	16,365	**35**	7,092	**40**	80,323	21,559	25,813	Addison
Bennington**	003	37,239	36,994	18,760	15,294	36,799	698,610	.0151	742,588	**218**	48,977	**104**	86,996	**488**	117,991	33,245	26,398	Bennington
Caledonia	005	30,001	29,702	16,188	12,051	32,582	485,660	.0087	281,052	**83**	19,859	**42**	12,405	**70**	50,231	20,371	21,011	Caledonia
Chittenden*	007	149,664	146,571	21,554	59,949	43,716	3,225,860	.0625	2,762,434	**813**	288,774	**613**	140,758	**789**	461,576	139,109	106,698	Chittenden
Essex**	009	6,606	6,459	14,581	2,721	28,578	96,320	.0014	9,341	**3**	....	**....**	....	**....**	5,313	....	4,751	Essex
Franklin*	011	47,499	45,417	17,815	17,772	38,537	846,210	.0149	498,092	**147**	20,989	**45**	14,856	**83**	94,870	39,916	32,691	Franklin
Grand Isle*	013	7,675	6,901	20,227	3,140	40,089	155,240	.0021	21,738	**6**	....	**....**	....	**....**	6,916	....	6,064	Grand Isle
Lamoille	015	24,594	23,233	18,452	9,954	36,748	453,800	.0075	212,887	**63**	11,991	**25**	7,434	**42**	62,807	16,024	17,905	Lamoille
Orange**	017	29,339	28,226	18,307	11,688	36,893	537,100	.0084	199,364	**59**	5,352	**11**	....	**....**	36,549	10,971	21,911	Orange
Orleans	019	27,357	26,277	14,967	11,284	29,451	409,440	.0081	306,137	**90**	25,813	**55**	3,487	**20**	52,907	22,418	19,399	Orleans
Rutland**	021	63,534	63,400	17,698	26,331	34,582	1,124,410	.0218	875,662	**258**	74,609	**158**	41,764	**234**	160,944	56,822	44,533	Rutland
Washington**	023	59,089	58,039	19,665	24,693	37,976	1,162,000	.0207	755,051	**222**	32,438	**69**	25,119	**141**	160,241	53,335	41,468	Washington
Windham	025	44,445	44,216	18,971	18,949	35,840	843,150	.0151	542,100	**159**	12,733	**27**	16,185	**91**	102,251	31,968	32,922	Windham
Windsor**	027	58,026	57,418	20,078	24,972	37,611	1,165,040	.0187	532,160	**157**	18,929	**40**	12,514	**70**	87,536	17,701	44,241	Windsor
The State		622,165	608,827	19,098	252,576	38,040	11,882,040	.2176	8,218,275	**2,419**	577,615	**1,226**	369,536	**2,074**	1,480,456	463,438	445,805	The State

VIRGINIA (VA; CODE 51; 95 Counties, 39 Independent Cities)

COUNTY OR COUNTY EQUIVALENT	FIPS CO. CODE	POPULATION Estimate 7/1/04	POPULATION Census 4/1/00	PER CAPITA INCOME 2003	HOUSEHOLDS Estimate 7/1/04	MEDIAN HOUSEHOLD INCOME 2003	DISPOSABLE INCOME 2003 ($1,000)	MARKET ABILITY INDEX 2003	TOTAL RETAIL SALES Sales 2003 ($1,000)	TOTAL RETAIL SALES Ranally Sales Units	GENERAL MERCHANDISE Sales 2003 ($1,000)	GENERAL MERCHANDISE Ranally Sales Units	APPAREL STORE Sales 2003 ($1,000)	APPAREL STORE Ranally Sales Units	FOOD STORE SALES 2003 ($1,000)	HEALTH & DRUG STORE 2003 ($1,000)	PASSENGER CAR REGIS-TRATIONS 2003	COUNTY OR COUNTY EQUIVALENT
Accomack	001	39,235	38,305	13,872	15,705	28,173	544,270	.0092	206,047	**61**	18,954	**40**	8,984	**50**	41,753	12,678	25,973	Accomack
Albemarle*	003	88,692	79,236	21,677	34,352	45,907	1,922,580	.0322	1,076,739	**317**	223,078	**474**	46,168	**259**	139,418	64,636	65,493	Albemarle
Alleghany[3]	005	16,699	12,926	16,802	6,930	33,220	280,580	.0046	115,301	**34**	11,927	**25**	1,454	**8**	19,590	11,282	13,288	Alleghany
Amelia*	007	11,831	11,400	18,144	4,701	37,152	214,660	.0030	36,750	**11**	....	**....**	....	**....**	8,493	1,227	10,080	Amelia
Amherst*	009	31,890	31,894	16,619	12,312	35,235	529,970	.0089	246,131	**72**	50,919	**108**	2,388	**13**	51,131	16,601	24,529	Amherst
Appomattox*	011	13,712	13,705	16,540	5,439	33,815	226,800	.0038	102,306	**30**	4,143	**9**	1,642	**9**	28,541	8,970	10,901	Appomattox
Arlington*	013	187,390	189,453	35,379	95,852	56,477	6,629,700	.0909	2,363,900	**695**	385,462	**818**	288,147	**1,615**	311,525	143,568	138,554	Arlington
Augusta**	015	67,974	65,615	18,853	26,295	40,048	1,281,540	.0204	531,201	**156**	19,334	**41**	16,940	**95**	87,087	36,386	57,579	Augusta
Bath	017	5,005	5,048	17,173	2,095	33,334	85,950	.0012	12,337	**4**	....	**....**	....	**....**	2,348	....	4,646	Bath
Bedford*	019	63,337	60,371	19,970	25,745	40,080	1,264,830	.0162	108,596	**32**	....	**....**	....	**....**	8,540	7,525	55,955	Bedford
Bland	021	7,000	6,871	13,653	2,704	28,928	95,570	.0015	17,770	**5**	....	**....**	....	**....**	....	....	5,557	Bland
Botetourt*	023	31,742	30,496	20,793	12,361	43,949	660,020	.0096	194,591	**57**	....	**....**	1,526	**9**	36,977	12,361	27,619	Botetourt
Brunswick	025	18,123	18,419	12,553	6,313	29,571	227,500	.0038	71,821	**21**	1,568	**3**	3,350	**19**	16,652	6,018	11,308	Brunswick
Buchanan	027	25,204	26,978	11,037	10,257	21,923	278,170	.0051	111,967	**33**	1,133	**2**	1,695	**10**	30,818	23,625	18,609	Buchanan
Buckingham	029	15,908	15,623	12,203	5,583	28,429	194,130	.0032	52,585	**15**	5,429	**12**	1,050	**6**	6,077	1,011	10,632	Buckingham
Campbell*	031	51,384	51,078	17,922	21,413	35,123	920,910	.0149	385,791	**113**	23,406	**50**	12,292	**69**	75,963	11,678	42,107	Campbell
Caroline*	033	23,543	22,121	17,019	8,778	37,257	400,680	.0064	150,316	**44**	2,453	**5**	1,730	**10**	18,468	6,175	18,073	Caroline
Carroll	035	29,351	29,245	14,983	12,552	28,567	439,760	.0076	205,218	**60**	6,845	**15**	8,893	**50**	32,385	11,120	23,780	Carroll
Charles City*	036	7,181	6,926	19,166	2,905	39,014	137,630	.0017	5,864	**2**	....	**....**	....	**....**	3,450	....	6,270	Charles City
Charlotte	037	12,450	12,472	13,735	5,096	27,700	171,000	.0029	60,437	**18**	....	**....**	....	**....**	14,496	3,446	9,190	Charlotte
Chesterfield*	041	282,130	259,903	24,250	106,846	52,082	6,841,560	.1080	3,358,713	**988**	701,322	**1,489**	144,690	**811**	459,317	158,839	221,203	Chesterfield
Clarke*	043	13,582	12,652	23,238	5,554	46,651	315,620	.0042	67,334	**20**	....	**....**	....	**....**	12,265	1,024	11,788	Clarke
Craig*	045	5,179	5,091	17,304	2,147	34,138	89,620	.0012	7,477	**2**	....	**....**	....	**....**	3,639	....	4,522	Craig
Culpeper	047	39,908	34,262	18,444	14,498	41,474	736,050	.0130	439,267	**129**	54,679	**116**	8,978	**50**	44,978	19,489	29,394	Culpeper
Cumberland*	049	9,250	9,017	14,877	3,749	30,340	137,610	.0022	47,998	**14**	....	**....**	....	**....**	8,268	1,989	7,301	Cumberland
Dickenson	051	16,043	16,395	11,930	6,915	22,396	191,400	.0034	79,313	**23**	2,354	**5**	....	**....**	19,670	5,293	11,704	Dickenson
Dinwiddie*	053	24,932	24,533	18,436	9,670	38,929	459,640	.0063	75,521	**22**	3,042	**6**	1,000	**6**	26,091	8,189	19,729	Dinwiddie
Essex	057	10,349	9,989	17,733	4,253	35,157	183,520	.0038	168,512	**50**	59,665	**127**	4,529	**25**	15,260	7,193	8,317	Essex
Fairfax*	059	1,008,761	969,749	31,608	379,329	68,938	31,885,260	.4521	12,202,621	**3,589**	1,701,234	**3,611**	950,635	**5,328**	1,927,644	553,025	729,219	Fairfax
Fauquier*	061	62,992	55,139	25,028	23,174	55,370	1,576,570	.0228	551,215	**162**	47,843	**102**	13,826	**77**	113,824	37,094	52,056	Fauquier
Floyd	063	14,483	13,874	15,545	6,173	30,036	225,140	.0035	66,974	**20**	1,828	**4**	1,246	**7**	7,242	4,189	12,793	Floyd
Fluvanna*	065	24,026	20,047	19,373	9,022	42,272	465,460	.0060	40,107	**12**	....	**....**	....	**....**	12,593	1,550	18,776	Fluvanna
Franklin*	067	49,641	47,286	17,969	20,433	35,740	892,000	.0148	414,479	**122**	50,975	**108**	8,477	**48**	57,516	9,967	42,578	Franklin
Frederick*	069	66,224	59,209	19,896	25,206	42,636	1,317,620	.0211	592,531	**174**	84,018	**178**	17,695	**99**	47,716	47,820	53,299	Frederick
Giles*	071	17,040	16,657	17,142	7,340	32,465	292,100	.0049	139,308	**41**	9,226	**20**	1,096	**6**	37,225	7,596	13,635	Giles
Gloucester*	073	37,303	34,780	19,441	14,297	41,436	725,200	.0117	327,368	**96**	53,688	**114**	8,601	**48**	65,760	28,818	29,260	Gloucester
Goochland*	075	18,538	16,863	23,122	6,965	49,773	428,630	.0059	102,893	**30**	....	**....**	....	**....**	12,501	....	15,077	Goochland
Grayson	077	16,449	17,917	14,843	7,292	27,179	244,160	.0036	43,568	**13**	....	**....**	....	**....**	11,496	....	13,691	Grayson
Greene*	079	17,251	15,244	18,740	6,351	41,337	323,280	.0044	53,259	**16**	....	**....**	1,099	**6**	9,180	1,993	13,664	Greene
Greensville	081	11,590	11,560	13,454	4,223	30,357	155,930	.0024	32,159	**9**	1,025	**2**	....	**....**	....	....	8,163	Greensville
Halifax	083	36,406	37,355	14,441	15,106	28,469	525,730	.0101	343,121	**101**	64,145	**136**	8,269	**46**	71,286	24,006	28,462	Halifax
Hanover*	085	96,438	86,320	23,468	34,998	52,657	2,263,180	.0357	1,083,695	**319**	112,226	**238**	12,280	**69**	223,707	51,870	75,727	Hanover
Henrico*	087	273,683	262,300	23,940	121,010	44,556	6,551,970	.1142	4,411,902	**1,298**	859,506	**1,825**	257,623	**1,444**	538,539	291,254	219,772	Henrico
Henry**	089	56,818	57,930	15,605	24,167	30,202	886,660	.0151	403,405	**119**	51,239	**109**	11,847	**66**	74,079	30,470	45,348	Henry
Highland	091	2,494	2,536	16,047	1,151	28,449	40,020	.0006	5,295	**2**	....	**....**	....	**....**	....	....	2,345	Highland
Isle of Wight*	093	32,606	29,728	19,865	12,699	42,004	647,730	.0096	200,486	**59**	5,050	**11**	3,840	**22**	51,488	11,871	26,405	Isle of Wight
James City*	095	55,145	48,102	24,993	22,402	50,205	1,378,240	.0190	382,122	**112**	27,801	**59**	80,722	**452**	82,080	16,030	42,878	James City
King and Queen*	097	6,578	6,630	17,071	2,743	33,344	112,290	.0015	7,619	**2**	....	**....**	....	**....**	....	....	5,834	King and Queen
King George	099	18,655	16,803	20,112	6,867	43,907	375,190	.0052	80,268	**24**	1,316	**3**	1,278	**7**	19,775	2,414	15,131	King George
King William*	101	14,440	13,146	20,530	5,436	44,578	296,460	.0046	119,684	**35**	....	**....**	1,170	**7**	20,323	6,802	11,612	King William
Lancaster	103	12,236	11,567	16,367	5,201	31,434	200,270	.0037	133,926	**39**	4,101	**9**	4,165	**23**	36,100	7,414	9,151	Lancaster
Lee	105	23,798	23,589	11,738	10,168	22,246	279,340	.0051	115,123	**34**	2,900	**6**	....	**....**	32,980	17,682	17,010	Lee
Loudoun*	107	237,678	169,599	29,560	83,870	69,014	7,025,710	.0987	2,465,074	**725**	495,113	**1,051**	81,469	**457**	441,736	95,507	171,566	Loudoun
Louisa*	109	28,789	25,627	17,881	11,451	36,590	514,780	.0073	105,578	**31**	4,250	**9**	....	**....**	28,887	3,692	23,854	Louisa
Lunenburg	111	13,191	13,146	12,591	5,162	26,099	166,090	.0028	57,627	**17**	2,322	**5**	....	**....**	9,610	5,722	9,080	Lunenburg
Madison	113	13,195	12,520	17,739	5,183	36,816	234,060	.0042	139,644	**41**	....	**....**	....	**....**	15,514	1,910	10,985	Madison
Mathews*	115	9,220	9,207	20,767	3,953	39,598	191,470	.0026	39,962	**12**	....	**....**	....	**....**	9,973	1,004	7,789	Mathews
Mecklenburg	117	32,613	32,380	14,810	13,351	29,767	482,990	.0094	344,992	**101**	46,827	**99**	11,326	**63**	59,778	20,469	24,184	Mecklenburg
Middlesex	119	10,292	9,932	18,840	4,515	35,006	193,900	.0030	70,116	**21**	....	**....**	....	**....**	9,575	2,584	8,473	Middlesex
Montgomery*	121	86,230	83,629	14,232	32,580	30,617	1,227,260	.0257	1,046,561	**308**	244,175	**518**	36,105	**202**	85,841	40,176	65,540	Montgomery
Nelson*	125	15,097	14,445	17,929	6,376	34,349	270,680	.0038	51,668	**15**	....	**....**	....	**....**	18,110	2,403	13,003	Nelson
New Kent*	127	15,279	13,462	22,196	5,710	48,682	339,130	.0047	76,946	**23**	....	**....**	1,835	**10**	24,643	6,122	12,855	New Kent
Northampton	131	13,358	13,093	13,616	5,532	26,768	181,880	.0033	95,687	**28**	19,251	**41**	1,466	**8**	32,999	5,740	8,682	Northampton
Northumberland	133	12,895	12,259	19,955	5,863	35,812	257,320	.0036	56,488	**17**	....	**....**	1,004	**6**	16,054	4,537	10,934	Northumberland
Nottoway	135	15,558	15,725	12,976	5,714	28,922	201,880	.0039	128,985	**38**	4,091	**9**	3,908	**22**	26,701	12,800	9,864	Nottoway
Orange	137	28,683	25,881	19,414	11,545	39,395	556,850	.0085	198,319	**58**	6,409	**14**	1,109	**6**	47,029	28,492	22,530	Orange
Page	139	23,717	23,177	16,035	9,849	31,441	380,300	.0062	143,068	**42**	9,640	**20**	7,176	**40**	31,294	15,435	19,246	Page
Patrick	141	19,103	19,407	14,543	8,219	27,445	277,820	.0044	79,251	**23**	2,634	**6**	....	**....**	20,309	9,740	16,697	Patrick
Pittsylvania*	143	61,594	61,745	16,570	25,429	32,777	1,020,620	.0167	413,976	**122**	65,144	**138**	12,582	**71**	100,786	12,995	51,380	Pittsylvania
Powhatan*	145	25,328	22,377	19,963	8,536	48,373	505,630	.0073	137,831	**41**	....	**....**	....	**....**	16,353	2,096	19,744	Powhatan
Prince Edward	147	20,342	19,720	12,282	6,913	29,603	249,840	.0062	303,315	**89**	87,362	**185**	7,254	**41**	29,701	7,326	11,786	Prince Edward
Prince George*	149	34,661	33,047	18,495	11,737	44,636	641,070	.0089	113,800	**33**	....	**....**	2,070	**12**	17,957	13,298	24,760	Prince George
Prince William*	153	339,149	280,813	24,334	115,978	58,620	8,252,760	.1251	3,461,208	**1,018**	464,094	**985**	316,989	**1,777**	419,711	94,355	237,650	Prince William
Pulaski*	155	34,995	35,127	16,858	15,013	32,247	589,940	.0103	323,397	**95**	44,185	**94**	3,903	**22**	75,053	25,700	27,220	Pulaski
Rappahannock	157	7,157	6,983	21,080	2,926	42,152	150,870	.0024	68,596	**20**	....	**....**	....	**....**	1,210	1,406	6,503	Rappahannock
Richmond	159	9,076	8,809	13,230	3,119	31,409	120,080	.0024	85,776	**25**	11,657	**25**	1,186	**7**	21,817	8,315	5,842	Richmond
Roanoke*	161	87,854	85,778	22,789	37,835	43,257	2,002,110	.0276	485,309	**143**	24,006	**51**	19,352	**108**	107,639	15,243	75,519	Roanoke
Rockbridge	163	21,015	20,808	17,254	8,717	33,999	362,600	.0066	230,542	**68**	18,792	**40**	....	**....**	39,450	....	18,273	Rockbridge
Rockingham*	165	69,878	67,725	17,516	26,508	37,658	1,223,980	.0203	564,056	**166**	4,251	**9**	1,376	**8**	85,152	49,895	55,018	Rockingham
Russell	167	28,721	30,308	13,198	11,988	25,922	379,070	.0070	199,170	**59**	7,935	**17**	....	**....**	31,235	12,215	22,043	Russell
Scott*	169	22,883	23,403	13,738	9,930	25,942	314,360	.0059	181,325	**53**	5,682	**12**	1,298	**7**	47,282	12,101	17,307	Scott
Shenandoah	171	37,852	35,075	18,532	15,659	36,420	701,490	.0123	410,381	**121**	8,730	**19**	2,846	**16**	65,445	20,999	31,545	Shenandoah
Smyth	173	32,575	33,081	14,502	13,684	28,108	472,390	.0089	290,616	**85**	43,270	**92**	4,633	**26**	63,767	22,964	24,396	Smyth
Southampton	175	17,443	17,482	14,463	6,387	32,211	252,270	.0038	51,329	**15**	3,006	**6**	....	**....**	8,520	10,868	11,812	Southampton

Source: Devonshire Associates Ltd. and Scan/US, Inc. 2004.
* Component of a Metropolitan Core Based Statistical Area.
** Component of a Micropolitan Core Based Statistical Area.

.... Data less than 1,000. (d) Data not available.
[3]Clifton Forge independent city merged with Alleghany county on July 1, 2001.

continued on next page

Counties: Population / Income / Sales, *Continued*

COUNTY OR COUNTY EQUIVALENT	FIPS CO. CODE	POPULATION Estimate 7/1/04	POPULATION Census 4/1/00	PER CAPITA INCOME 2003	HOUSEHOLDS Estimate 7/1/04	MEDIAN HOUSEHOLD INCOME 2003	DISPOSABLE INCOME 2003 ($1,000)	MARKET ABILITY INDEX 2003	TOTAL RETAIL SALES Sales 2003 ($1,000)	TOTAL RETAIL SALES Ranally Sales Units	GENERAL MERCHANDISE Sales 2003 ($1,000)	GENERAL MERCHANDISE Ranally Sales Units	APPAREL STORE Sales 2003 ($1,000)	APPAREL STORE Ranally Sales Units	FOOD STORE SALES 2003 ($1,000)	HEALTH & DRUG STORE 2003 ($1,000)	PASSENGER CAR REGIS-TRATIONS 2003	COUNTY OR COUNTY EQUIVALENT
Spotsylvania*	177	113,260	90,395	22,217	40,088	51,023	2,516,320	.0411	1,318,328	**388**	392,646	**834**	25,576	**143**	165,447	51,428	86,667	Spotsylvania
Stafford*	179	116,821	92,446	23,553	38,420	58,474	2,751,450	.0370	593,801	**175**	80,818	**172**	6,996	**39**	106,195	35,476	84,413	Stafford
Surry*	181	7,065	6,829	16,379	2,743	34,574	115,720	.0016	12,277	**4**	....	**....**	....	**....**	1,147	....	5,457	Surry
Sussex*	183	11,784	12,504	12,366	4,050	29,517	145,720	.0029	96,163	**28**	1,894	**4**	1,512	**8**	9,355	6,912	6,990	Sussex
Tazewell**	185	44,332	44,598	13,744	18,841	26,485	609,320	.0140	644,956	**190**	158,165	**336**	10,601	**59**	105,767	44,784	32,932	Tazewell
Warren*	187	34,587	31,584	18,509	13,315	39,545	640,170	.0113	381,324	**112**	39,441	**84**	12,333	**69**	80,668	16,489	26,422	Warren
Washington*	191	51,487	51,103	16,244	21,926	31,163	836,350	.0169	700,301	**206**	78,125	**166**	24,915	**140**	88,073	29,043	41,211	Washington
Westmoreland	193	17,033	16,718	17,068	7,123	33,382	290,720	.0047	112,376	**33**	....	**....**	2,344	**13**	31,312	5,907	12,991	Westmoreland
Wise	195	41,678	40,123	12,143	16,466	25,222	506,100	.0104	359,803	**106**	46,908	**100**	9,531	**53**	63,943	30,962	28,355	Wise
Wythe	197	28,044	27,599	15,955	12,090	30,475	447,430	.0100	482,382	**142**	31,912	**68**	27,645	**155**	44,153	22,889	22,249	Wythe
York*	199	62,379	56,297	24,642	24,274	51,178	1,537,150	.0213	423,781	**125**	102,263	**217**	44,442	**249**	63,872	30,802	51,051	York
INDEPENDENT CITIES																		
Alexandria*	510	128,847	128,283	32,583	67,671	51,397	4,198,170	.0646	2,209,715	**650**	303,923	**645**	97,294	**545**	255,880	138,676	96,115	Alexandria
Bedford*	515	6,352	6,299	13,295	2,572	26,792	84,450	.0027	172,764	**51**	27,643	**59**	3,585	**20**	34,301	17,016	4,058	Bedford
Bristol*	520	17,176	17,367	15,231	8,140	26,274	261,610	.0068	378,509	**111**	135,129	**287**	11,179	**63**	41,136	26,116	12,255	Bristol
Buena Vista	530	6,307	6,349	15,648	2,610	31,040	98,690	.0017	42,261	**12**	....	**....**	....	**....**	13,939	1,223	4,249	Buena Vista
Charlottesville*	540	38,847	45,049	16,614	18,021	29,335	645,400	.0174	1,044,121	**307**	85,431	**181**	78,648	**441**	210,240	48,830	30,097	Charlottesville
Chesapeake*	550	214,295	199,184	19,823	76,328	45,725	4,247,960	.0793	3,175,219	**934**	769,152	**1,633**	155,482	**871**	348,243	131,796	144,398	Chesapeake
Clifton Forge[3]	560	(d)	4,289	(d)	(d)	(d)	(d)	(d)	(d)	**(d)**	(d)	**(d)**	(d)	**(d)**	(d)	(d)	(d)	Clifton Forge
Colonial Heights*	570	17,408	16,897	21,278	7,602	39,837	370,400	.0110	754,700	**222**	345,892	**734**	56,820	**318**	41,957	26,050	13,706	Colonial Heights
Covington	580	6,278	6,303	16,860	3,024	28,645	105,850	.0026	145,156	**43**	6,772	**14**	7,170	**40**	38,696	5,629	4,602	Covington
Danville*	590	46,575	48,411	14,075	20,713	25,876	655,530	.0149	683,485	**201**	133,549	**284**	20,909	**117**	91,603	43,717	30,439	Danville
Emporia	595	5,653	5,665	13,904	2,245	28,565	78,600	.0022	128,187	**38**	....	**....**	5,774	**32**	30,026	12,817	3,155	Emporia
Fairfax*	600	22,181	21,498	27,678	8,297	60,438	613,920	.0233	1,866,855	**549**	121,768	**258**	86,807	**487**	194,511	61,550	15,935	Fairfax
Falls Church*	610	10,500	10,377	36,247	4,827	64,378	380,590	.0081	464,863	**137**	10,330	**22**	9,207	**52**	48,467	25,387	7,514	Falls Church
Franklin	620	8,244	8,346	15,391	3,511	29,946	126,880	.0029	139,366	**41**	4,598	**10**	6,134	**34**	28,034	7,718	5,525	Franklin
Fredericksburg*	630	20,481	19,279	17,445	8,893	32,339	357,290	.0120	846,352	**249**	113,743	**241**	47,921	**269**	66,001	41,982	13,983	Fredericksburg
Galax	640	6,592	6,837	14,935	2,974	26,845	98,450	.0032	213,401	**63**	60,247	**128**	4,951	**28**	31,368	14,514	4,426	Galax
Hampton*	650	147,010	146,437	17,330	56,725	36,600	2,547,690	.0501	2,048,799	**603**	410,417	**871**	91,269	**512**	176,772	77,081	97,371	Hampton
Harrisonburg*	660	41,444	40,468	11,769	14,013	28,360	487,740	.0152	924,894	**272**	220,645	**468**	38,917	**218**	117,807	24,439	28,142	Harrisonburg
Hopewell*	670	22,421	22,354	16,593	9,771	31,076	372,040	.0057	111,491	**33**	3,629	**8**	4,767	**27**	25,710	9,139	15,776	Hopewell
Lexington	678	7,155	6,867	11,672	2,510	27,184	83,510	.0025	151,110	**44**	23,508	**50**	4,798	**27**	19,390	15,750	3,714	Lexington
Lynchburg*	680	65,067	65,269	15,392	26,744	30,800	1,001,510	.0257	1,431,477	**421**	242,617	**515**	51,281	**287**	134,326	117,670	41,364	Lynchburg
Manassas*	683	37,756	35,135	22,060	12,584	54,129	832,900	.0187	1,016,742	**299**	199,045	**423**	24,343	**136**	163,271	29,592	24,081	Manassas
Manassas Park*	685	11,209	10,290	23,735	3,998	56,245	266,050	.0036	58,181	**17**	....	**....**	....	**....**	14,442	1,887	8,153	Manassas Park
Martinsville**	690	15,036	15,416	13,784	6,423	26,140	207,250	.0058	340,624	**100**	118,085	**251**	21,824	**122**	36,413	15,372	9,471	Martinsville
Newport News*	700	182,162	180,150	17,471	75,375	34,449	3,182,560	.0581	2,059,355	**606**	272,220	**578**	88,222	**494**	255,528	66,152	121,983	Newport News
Norfolk*	710	244,163	234,403	13,604	90,292	30,190	3,321,570	.0650	2,221,985	**654**	352,759	**749**	114,908	**644**	275,793	85,136	127,654	Norfolk
Norton	720	3,917	3,904	12,706	1,822	22,077	49,770	.0022	166,776	**49**	67,992	**144**	11,771	**66**	18,763	6,110	2,621	Norton
Petersburg*	730	32,931	33,740	15,266	14,812	27,700	502,720	.0098	359,200	**106**	3,170	**7**	5,696	**32**	47,644	23,740	20,239	Petersburg
Poquoson*	735	11,929	11,566	24,585	4,391	54,530	293,270	.0038	53,351	**16**	....	**....**	....	**....**	19,779	3,308	9,741	Poquoson
Portsmouth*	740	99,349	100,565	15,424	39,297	32,019	1,532,310	.0249	553,459	**163**	21,042	**45**	10,708	**60**	145,199	94,689	59,709	Portsmouth
Radford*	750	14,744	15,859	11,935	5,994	24,085	175,970	.0033	88,619	**26**	....	**....**	1,898	**11**	15,564	7,031	11,137	Radford
Richmond*	760	193,828	197,790	16,416	88,280	29,642	3,181,790	.0602	2,204,942	**649**	144,939	**308**	145,084	**813**	390,643	168,439	114,140	Richmond
Roanoke*	770	92,245	94,911	16,670	43,436	28,971	1,537,720	.0414	2,472,562	**727**	500,035	**1,061**	128,264	**719**	222,410	122,114	66,406	Roanoke
Salem*	775	24,544	24,747	18,733	10,408	36,033	459,790	.0106	559,985	**165**	51,732	**110**	8,178	**46**	85,715	18,275	18,768	Salem
Staunton**	790	23,850	23,853	16,119	10,084	31,124	384,450	.0093	489,094	**144**	145,165	**308**	13,141	**74**	71,133	25,536	17,006	Staunton
Suffolk*	800	76,604	63,677	17,281	28,431	38,227	1,323,800	.0218	576,665	**170**	96,924	**206**	4,524	**25**	88,432	20,950	51,241	Suffolk
Virginia Beach*	810	443,729	425,257	20,360	168,045	44,057	9,034,270	.1485	4,554,427	**1,340**	658,328	**1,398**	284,570	**1,595**	698,331	198,624	316,083	Virginia Beach
Waynesboro**	820	20,650	19,520	16,533	8,959	30,845	341,410	.0067	262,079	**77**	32,087	**68**	9,722	**54**	61,387	18,759	14,920	Waynesboro
Williamsburg*	830	11,476	11,998	13,196	3,474	35,976	151,440	.0066	509,838	**150**	6,617	**14**	75,856	**425**	80,163	20,369	5,439	Williamsburg
Winchester*	840	24,691	23,585	17,369	10,778	32,630	428,850	.0136	931,597	**274**	268,523	**570**	38,993	**219**	116,988	48,236	17,503	Winchester
The State		7,480,156	7,078,515	21,619	2,955,415	43,389	161,711,520	2.6676	86,111,217	**25,331**	13,177,237	**27,978**	4,411,228	**24,723**	12,503,309	4,398,343	5,463,924	The State

WASHINGTON (WA; CODE 53; 39 Counties)

COUNTY OR COUNTY EQUIVALENT	FIPS CO. CODE	POPULATION Estimate 7/1/04	POPULATION Census 4/1/00	PER CAPITA INCOME 2003	HOUSEHOLDS Estimate 7/1/04	MEDIAN HOUSEHOLD INCOME 2003	DISPOSABLE INCOME 2003 ($1,000)	MARKET ABILITY INDEX 2003	TOTAL RETAIL SALES Sales 2003 ($1,000)	TOTAL RETAIL SALES Ranally Sales Units	GENERAL MERCHANDISE Sales 2003 ($1,000)	GENERAL MERCHANDISE Ranally Sales Units	APPAREL STORE Sales 2003 ($1,000)	APPAREL STORE Ranally Sales Units	FOOD STORE SALES 2003 ($1,000)	HEALTH & DRUG STORE 2003 ($1,000)	PASSENGER CAR REGIS-TRATIONS 2003	COUNTY OR COUNTY EQUIVALENT
Adams	001	16,650	16,428	12,429	5,190	32,124	206,940	.0041	129,712	**38**	20,766	**44**	1,661	**9**	12,955	7,965	10,295	Adams
Asotin*	003	20,647	20,551	16,184	8,486	31,617	334,160	.0060	196,766	**58**	81,242	**172**	1,393	**8**	38,178	12,558	16,271	Asotin
Benton*	005	157,183	142,475	19,658	58,099	43,063	3,089,940	.0534	1,808,952	**532**	444,288	**943**	62,500	**350**	394,780	77,024	118,235	Benton
Chelan*	007	68,388	66,616	16,054	25,155	34,977	1,097,890	.0224	935,231	**275**	152,676	**324**	17,484	**98**	140,702	34,065	47,654	Chelan
Clallam**	009	67,749	64,525	18,353	29,204	34,308	1,243,390	.0208	611,022	**180**	129,403	**275**	18,779	**105**	149,764	30,757	52,627	Clallam
Clark*	011	390,272	345,238	19,962	143,323	44,003	7,790,750	.1236	3,357,522	**988**	651,539	**1,383**	101,395	**568**	589,111	205,201	276,565	Clark
Columbia	013	4,099	4,064	16,646	1,724	31,650	68,230	.0011	28,260	**8**	10,370	**22**	....	**....**	3,240	....	3,454	Columbia
Cowlitz*	015	95,850	92,948	17,792	37,022	36,998	1,705,340	.0301	1,001,310	**295**	212,859	**452**	17,384	**97**	191,898	39,276	72,020	Cowlitz
Douglas*	017	34,114	32,603	16,010	12,128	35,927	546,170	.0096	284,507	**84**	81,015	**172**	10,041	**56**	88,673	8,383	24,308	Douglas
Ferry	019	7,459	7,260	14,200	3,001	28,285	105,920	.0018	42,851	**13**	....	**....**	....	**....**	10,547	....	6,071	Ferry
Franklin*	021	58,316	49,347	13,179	17,046	36,282	768,520	.0164	649,960	**191**	57,937	**123**	3,591	**20**	36,927	22,330	34,446	Franklin
Garfield	023	2,364	2,397	15,876	973	31,505	37,530	.0006	14,090	**4**	....	**....**	....	**....**	4,488	....	1,889	Garfield
Grant**	025	79,916	74,698	13,454	26,303	32,705	1,075,160	.0211	722,524	**213**	94,878	**201**	12,689	**71**	134,450	29,934	51,326	Grant
Grays Harbor**	027	70,145	67,194	15,420	27,219	31,906	1,081,660	.0191	567,126	**167**	99,486	**211**	7,834	**44**	146,082	42,723	48,852	Grays Harbor
Island**	029	77,898	71,558	20,433	30,833	41,523	1,591,720	.0229	433,824	**128**	38,804	**82**	6,640	**37**	108,596	25,212	61,593	Island
Jefferson	031	28,140	25,953	19,959	12,706	35,586	561,660	.0085	196,309	**58**	25,244	**54**	4,419	**25**	61,021	5,495	23,907	Jefferson
King*	033	1,768,908	1,737,034	25,184	747,678	47,975	44,548,900	.7506	27,758,761	**8,165**	3,692,856	**7,839**	1,895,327	**10,622**	3,777,936	1,119,320	1,298,697	King
Kitsap*	035	243,450	231,969	19,816	90,966	42,766	4,824,290	.0783	2,263,687	**666**	520,165	**1,104**	67,059	**376**	338,124	110,073	177,217	Kitsap
Kittitas**	037	35,779	33,362	15,227	14,207	31,119	544,800	.0099	311,447	**92**	26,779	**57**	3,365	**19**	71,452	7,256	27,889	Kittitas
Klickitat	039	19,649	19,161	15,886	7,798	32,148	312,150	.0047	71,427	**21**	6,355	**14**	....	**....**	22,019	3,123	15,789	Klickitat
Lewis**	041	70,994	68,600	16,004	27,374	33,330	1,136,190	.0220	833,926	**245**	165,919	**352**	36,029	**202**	155,153	38,436	55,680	Lewis
Lincoln	043	10,207	10,184	16,801	4,165	32,894	171,490	.0028	65,876	**19**	....	**....**	....	**....**	7,403	3,561	8,814	Lincoln
Mason**	045	52,980	49,405	17,658	20,488	36,615	935,540	.0146	328,062	**97**	55,121	**117**	4,376	**25**	86,737	12,553	41,440	Mason
Okanogan	047	38,991	39,564	13,237	14,832	28,074	516,140	.0092	233,732	**69**	37,001	**79**	....	**....**	64,384	13,036	28,709	Okanogan
Pacific	049	21,156	20,984	16,002	9,305	29,214	338,530	.0053	110,842	**33**	13,132	**28**	1,790	**10**	28,390	13,149	16,433	Pacific
Pend Oreille	051	12,424	11,732	14,911	4,993	30,120	185,260	.0028	41,528	**12**	2,524	**5**	....	**....**	23,120	....	10,127	Pend Oreille
Pierce*	053	753,288	700,820	19,217	281,633	41,564	14,476,220	.2441	7,660,414	**2,253**	1,311,305	**2,784**	277,368	**1,554**	1,116,419	309,143	535,609	Pierce
San Juan	055	14,961	14,077	23,232	6,996	39,767	347,580	.0051	125,789	**37**	4,402	**9**	....	**....**	55,547	9,248	13,209	San Juan
Skagit*	057	111,156	102,979	18,370	41,628	39,462	2,041,940	.0384	1,490,007	**438**	281,875	**598**	60,566	**339**	212,366	60,042	83,052	Skagit
Skamania*	059	10,423	9,872	17,716	4,017	36,790	184,650	.0025	20,075	**6**	....	**....**	....	**....**	7,266	....	8,720	Skamania
Snohomish*	061	649,489	606,024	22,169	242,527	47,838	14,398,830	.2307	7,019,739	**2,065**	1,112,466	**2,362**	340,226	**1,907**	1,104,607	266,413	481,145	Snohomish
Spokane*	063	435,145	417,939	17,174	170,747	35,190	7,473,250	.1385	5,018,057	**1,476**	886,324	**1,881**	231,274	**1,296**	770,118	205,222	308,300	Spokane
Stevens	065	40,954	40,066	15,408	15,568	32,474	631,030	.0104	245,192	**72**	49,935	**106**	5,765	**32**	71,923	8,121	32,329	Stevens
Thurston*	067	226,479	207,355	21,081	90,097	42,493	4,774,330	.0817	2,831,219	**833**	658,091	**1,397**	78,248	**439**	496,829	97,280	173,484	Thurston
Wahkiakum	069	3,719	3,824	18,623	1,523	36,536	69,260	.0009	9,068	**3**	2,409	**5**	....	**....**	....	....	3,181	Wahkiakum
Walla Walla**	071	57,240	55,180	14,848	20,327	33,675	849,910	.0152	453,591	**133**	78,175	**166**	15,474	**87**	98,416	17,914	37,409	Walla Walla
Whatcom*	073	179,561	166,814	18,388	71,394	37,115	3,301,690	.0602	2,206,779	**649**	395,974	**841**	93,233	**523**	482,145	104,046	135,400	Whatcom
Whitman**	075	40,703	40,740	13,067	15,706	27,323	531,850	.0098	274,645	**81**	57,582	**122**	3,289	**18**	20,662	10,040	28,828	Whitman
Yakima*	077	228,066	222,581	13,316	74,206	32,868	3,037,030	.0593	1,979,472	**582**	431,605	**916**	60,404	**339**	329,183	54,696	141,938	Yakima
The State		6,204,912	5,894,121	20,457	2,416,587	42,189	126,935,840	2.1585	72,333,303	**21,279**	11,890,507	**25,240**	3,443,847	**19,300**	11,452,141	3,006,491	4,512,912	The State

WEST VIRGINIA (WV; CODE 54; 55 Counties)

COUNTY OR COUNTY EQUIVALENT	FIPS CO. CODE	POPULATION Estimate 7/1/04	POPULATION Census 4/1/00	PER CAPITA INCOME 2003	HOUSEHOLDS Estimate 7/1/04	MEDIAN HOUSEHOLD INCOME 2003	DISPOSABLE INCOME 2003 ($1,000)	MARKET ABILITY INDEX 2003	TOTAL RETAIL SALES Sales 2003 ($1,000)	TOTAL RETAIL SALES Ranally Sales Units	GENERAL MERCHANDISE Sales 2003 ($1,000)	GENERAL MERCHANDISE Ranally Sales Units	APPAREL STORE Sales 2003 ($1,000)	APPAREL STORE Ranally Sales Units	FOOD STORE SALES 2003 ($1,000)	HEALTH & DRUG STORE 2003 ($1,000)	PASSENGER CAR REGIS-TRATIONS 2003	COUNTY OR COUNTY EQUIVALENT
Barbour	001	15,688	15,557	12,571	6,322	23,338	197,210	.0034	71,260	**21**	5,391	**11**	....	**....**	13,695	7,003	10,749	Barbour
Berkeley*	003	88,214	75,905	18,887	34,879	36,332	1,666,130	.0266	702,696	**207**	115,550	**245**	61,401	**344**	101,655	43,829	62,727	Berkeley
Boone*	005	25,875	25,535	13,497	10,787	24,665	349,240	.0062	163,203	**48**	8,027	**17**	....	**....**	34,393	22,465	16,792	Boone
Braxton	007	14,789	14,702	12,490	5,957	23,287	184,710	.0038	139,227	**41**	3,998	**8**	5,509	**31**	23,799	8,360	9,635	Braxton
Brooke*	009	24,796	25,447	17,356	10,475	31,143	430,370	.0064	108,246	**32**	8,081	**17**	1,454	**8**	24,399	15,911	17,514	Brooke
Cabell*	011	94,503	96,784	16,189	42,685	27,311	1,529,870	.0312	1,309,696	**385**	220,188	**467**	84,843	**475**	125,470	181,596	63,457	Cabell
Calhoun	013	7,201	7,582	11,560	3,007	20,771	83,240	.0014	25,436	**7**	3,228	**7**	....	**....**	7,609	4,027	4,840	Calhoun
Clay*	015	10,355	10,330	11,599	4,161	21,604	120,110	.0022	52,255	**15**	3,312	**7**	....	**....**	15,431	1,485	6,734	Clay
Doddridge**	017	7,516	7,403	13,210	2,937	25,588	99,290	.0015	13,001	**4**	3,273	**7**	....	**....**	....	....	5,089	Doddridge
Fayette**	019	47,185	47,579	12,797	19,194	23,813	603,840	.0118	386,114	**114**	82,734	**176**	10,312	**58**	58,773	27,221	29,585	Fayette
Gilmer	021	6,995	7,160	11,618	2,783	22,018	81,270	.0014	23,811	**7**	2,128	**5**	....	**....**	7,970	1,700	4,634	Gilmer
Grant	023	11,483	11,299	14,919	4,815	26,956	171,320	.0028	59,099	**17**	1,896	**4**	....	**....**	7,993	6,511	8,520	Grant
Greenbrier	025	34,733	34,453	14,612	15,055	25,670	507,520	.0101	384,729	**113**	89,360	**190**	9,508	**53**	38,444	15,864	25,718	Greenbrier
Hampshire*	027	21,556	20,203	15,901	8,702	30,017	342,770	.0052	81,553	**24**	2,648	**6**	....	**....**	14,559	8,603	16,567	Hampshire
Hancock*	029	31,452	32,667	18,150	13,568	31,772	570,850	.0092	245,943	**72**	64,628	**137**	12,381	**69**	56,831	16,417	22,804	Hancock
Hardy	031	13,089	12,669	16,591	5,497	30,217	217,160	.0036	89,352	**26**	14,058	**30**	1,394	**8**	25,607	....	10,122	Hardy
Harrison**	033	67,845	68,652	15,676	28,122	28,792	1,063,570	.0228	1,019,075	**300**	191,959	**407**	47,354	**265**	110,985	67,034	45,199	Harrison
Jackson	035	28,360	28,000	16,363	11,497	30,922	464,050	.0094	392,858	**116**	68,190	**145**	2,347	**13**	40,207	16,555	20,266	Jackson
Jefferson*	037	47,542	42,190	21,074	18,704	40,895	1,001,920	.0149	334,391	**98**	21,331	**45**	4,080	**23**	63,057	40,225	36,485	Jefferson
Kanawha*	039	194,003	200,073	18,452	85,611	31,732	3,579,820	.0703	2,957,136	**870**	509,400	**1,081**	139,510	**782**	321,503	227,301	129,656	Kanawha
Lewis	041	17,238	16,919	14,300	7,247	25,905	246,510	.0048	164,003	**48**	50,288	**107**	2,550	**14**	15,621	7,462	12,166	Lewis
Lincoln*	043	22,291	22,108	11,942	9,081	22,033	266,190	.0044	66,970	**20**	7,633	**16**	....	**....**	29,430	2,115	13,907	Lincoln
Logan	045	36,468	37,710	12,892	15,041	23,708	470,150	.0106	464,256	**137**	67,777	**144**	13,229	**74**	73,592	50,827	22,638	Logan
McDowell	047	24,768	27,329	9,496	10,624	16,508	235,190	.0047	106,470	**31**	30,943	**66**	....	**....**	19,569	17,100	14,449	McDowell
Marion**	049	56,470	56,598	15,391	24,156	27,410	869,130	.0158	505,817	**149**	111,506	**237**	8,265	**46**	80,110	34,573	39,369	Marion
Marshall*	051	34,730	35,519	15,806	14,217	29,572	548,950	.0091	225,128	**66**	52,440	**111**	4,658	**26**	41,978	9,011	24,118	Marshall
Mason**	053	26,116	25,957	14,397	10,961	26,475	375,980	.0060	111,031	**33**	4,068	**9**	....	**....**	20,786	19,444	18,680	Mason
Mercer**	055	61,835	62,980	14,595	26,911	25,542	902,490	.0190	796,107	**234**	157,193	**334**	28,314	**159**	86,514	69,580	42,462	Mercer
Mineral*	057	27,182	27,078	15,649	11,113	29,252	425,360	.0076	234,045	**69**	82,162	**174**	2,676	**15**	34,207	18,455	20,068	Mineral
Mingo	059	27,436	28,253	11,660	11,606	20,775	319,900	.0062	173,351	**51**	7,551	**16**	1,722	**10**	31,922	13,923	16,727	Mingo
Monongalia*	061	85,180	81,866	14,952	35,310	27,462	1,273,600	.0248	905,500	**266**	193,589	**411**	62,458	**350**	106,055	61,465	57,316	Monongalia
Monroe	063	13,597	14,583	15,011	5,776	26,824	204,110	.0030	36,216	**11**	3,515	**7**	....	**....**	7,839	1,696	10,709	Monroe
Morgan*	065	15,680	14,943	18,078	6,585	32,642	283,460	.0043	83,145	**24**	4,221	**9**	....	**....**	14,698	9,135	12,344	Morgan
Nicholas	067	26,139	26,562	14,116	10,924	25,764	368,980	.0074	279,467	**82**	53,217	**113**	7,667	**43**	28,003	19,982	18,373	Nicholas
Ohio*	069	45,334	47,427	17,931	21,294	29,276	812,880	.0140	438,568	**129**	18,711	**40**	6,707	**38**	62,620	28,546	30,981	Ohio
Pendleton	071	7,807	8,196	15,758	3,291	28,416	123,020	.0019	37,630	**11**	2,064	**4**	....	**....**	5,881	6,635	6,381	Pendleton
Pleasants*	073	7,526	7,514	15,640	2,915	30,613	117,710	.0020	56,725	**17**	6,989	**15**	....	**....**	7,464	1,449	4,931	Pleasants
Pocahontas	075	8,890	9,131	14,205	3,818	25,252	126,280	.0022	59,306	**17**	....	**....**	2,248	**13**	6,291	5,979	6,615	Pocahontas
Preston*	077	29,837	29,334	14,225	12,129	26,484	424,440	.0074	193,515	**57**	21,672	**46**	....	**....**	19,759	13,428	21,878	Preston
Putnam*	079	53,462	51,589	20,321	21,275	39,017	1,086,390	.0177	524,400	**154**	53,698	**114**	3,845	**22**	69,654	25,598	38,704	Putnam
Raleigh**	081	79,307	79,220	14,667	32,899	26,767	1,163,210	.0245	1,019,072	**300**	218,487	**464**	19,135	**107**	94,976	69,454	52,269	Raleigh
Randolph	083	28,266	28,262	13,831	11,290	26,273	390,960	.0077	272,851	**80**	73,056	**155**	6,852	**38**	38,637	15,486	18,116	Randolph
Ritchie	085	10,575	10,343	14,514	4,366	26,548	153,490	.0024	45,627	**13**	3,180	**7**	....	**....**	9,880	5,494	7,623	Ritchie
Roane	087	15,325	15,446	12,779	6,293	23,571	195,840	.0036	103,413	**30**	3,018	**6**	....	**....**	26,924	11,159	10,306	Roane
Summers	089	13,783	12,999	10,774	5,444	20,739	148,500	.0026	47,690	**14**	7,160	**15**	....	**....**	13,823	6,705	8,957	Summers
Taylor**	091	16,134	16,089	13,625	6,431	25,789	219,820	.0036	67,487	**20**	5,934	**13**	....	**....**	11,105	2,155	10,743	Taylor
Tucker	093	7,118	7,321	14,199	3,048	25,245	101,070	.0018	54,897	**16**	....	**....**	....	**....**	12,357	5,148	5,118	Tucker
Tyler	095	9,388	9,592	15,031	3,848	27,821	141,110	.0021	29,492	**9**	4,421	**9**	....	**....**	9,689	3,272	6,574	Tyler
Upshur	097	23,754	23,404	13,461	9,359	26,105	319,760	.0064	229,673	**68**	21,154	**45**	2,528	**14**	41,778	10,209	16,123	Upshur
Wayne*	099	42,253	42,903	14,271	17,484	26,124	602,990	.0101	230,948	**68**	51,316	**109**	2,597	**15**	26,717	14,619	27,872	Wayne
Webster	101	9,820	9,719	11,627	4,232	20,325	114,180	.0020	40,372	**12**	7,080	**15**	....	**....**	13,447	1,404	6,793	Webster
Wetzel	103	16,990	17,693	15,860	7,072	28,897	269,460	.0052	189,260	**56**	31,701	**67**	2,968	**17**	35,054	17,927	11,686	Wetzel
Wirt*	105	5,760	5,873	14,981	2,279	28,632	86,290	.0013	13,574	**4**	1,884	**4**	....	**....**	4,840	....	4,141	Wirt
Wood*	107	87,147	87,986	17,711	37,439	31,353	1,543,420	.0312	1,348,847	**397**	344,134	**731**	52,640	**295**	103,807	78,780	61,618	Wood
Wyoming	109	24,577	25,708	13,021	10,516	22,933	320,020	.0056	129,959	**38**	17,724	**38**	....	**....**	27,831	26,330	16,187	Wyoming
The State		1,811,363	1,808,344	15,742	761,032	28,351	28,515,100	.5272	17,843,892	**5,248**	3,140,755	**6,667**	619,656	**3,471**	2,325,919	1,398,368	1,244,035	The State

Source: Devonshire Associates Ltd. and Scan/US, Inc. 2004.
* Component of a Metropolitan Core Based Statistical Area.
** Component of a Micropolitan Core Based Statistical Area.

.... Data less than 1,000. (d) Data not available.
[3]Clifton Forge independent city merged with Alleghany county on July 1, 2001.

Counties: Population / Income / Sales, *Continued*

COUNTY OR COUNTY EQUIVALENT	FIPS CO. CODE	POPULATION Estimate 7/1/04	POPULATION Census 4/1/00	PER CAPITA INCOME 2003	HOUSEHOLDS Estimate 7/1/04	MEDIAN HOUSEHOLD INCOME 2003	DISPOSABLE INCOME 2003 ($1,000)	MARKET ABILITY INDEX 2003	TOTAL RETAIL SALES Sales 2003 ($1,000)	TOTAL RETAIL SALES Ranally Sales Units	GENERAL MERCHANDISE Sales 2003 ($1,000)	GENERAL MERCHANDISE Ranally Sales Units	APPAREL STORE Sales 2003 ($1,000)	APPAREL STORE Ranally Sales Units	FOOD STORE SALES 2003 ($1,000)	HEALTH & DRUG STORE 2003 ($1,000)	PASSENGER CAR REGIS-TRATIONS 2003	COUNTY OR COUNTY EQUIVALENT
WISCONSIN (WI; CODE 55; 72 Counties)																		
Adams	001	20,751	18,643	15,366	8,438	31,569	318,860	.0050	97,059	29	15,294	32	1,234	7	18,039	....	16,303	Adams
Ashland	003	16,586	16,866	14,417	6,727	30,004	239,120	.0051	218,590	64	44,244	94	5,045	28	24,081	8,632	11,136	Ashland
Barron	005	45,670	44,963	16,841	18,487	35,013	769,150	.0155	647,155	190	153,215	325	14,809	83	91,959	15,351	34,931	Barron
Bayfield	007	15,139	15,013	15,799	6,391	31,263	239,180	.0037	64,696	19	5,413	12	....	....	15,753	2,296	12,450	Bayfield
Brown*	009	236,097	226,778	20,278	94,899	42,531	4,787,460	.0877	3,417,482	1,005	818,139	1,737	88,904	498	354,646	101,190	169,637	Brown
Buffalo	011	13,812	13,804	17,048	5,648	34,975	235,470	.0036	71,956	21	11,488	24	....	....	12,991	....	11,345	Buffalo
Burnett	013	16,415	15,674	16,663	7,076	32,128	273,530	.0043	97,709	29	5,893	13	1,169	7	18,870	3,578	13,801	Burnett
Calumet*	015	44,268	40,631	21,241	16,730	47,214	940,310	.0142	347,115	102	33,584	71	4,686	26	96,551	....	33,120	Calumet
Chippewa*	017	57,253	55,195	17,415	22,712	36,641	997,060	.0191	746,907	220	110,848	235	5,369	30	72,225	20,578	44,228	Chippewa
Clark	019	34,080	33,557	13,992	12,305	32,348	476,860	.0088	264,056	78	22,852	49	1,040	6	39,103	6,407	23,799	Clark
Columbia*	021	54,563	52,468	19,541	21,666	41,267	1,066,230	.0179	558,211	164	70,335	149	8,920	50	79,980	24,274	42,053	Columbia
Crawford	023	16,852	17,243	15,282	6,702	32,070	257,530	.0056	246,930	73	68,246	145	7,838	44	34,811	5,751	12,277	Crawford
Dane*	025	456,369	426,526	22,239	191,747	44,581	10,149,360	.1798	6,914,106	2,034	889,619	1,888	241,263	1,352	833,571	318,717	333,858	Dane
Dodge**	027	87,482	85,897	18,495	32,794	41,399	1,617,990	.0267	769,244	226	148,088	314	15,889	89	79,983	14,606	62,214	Dodge
Door	029	28,527	27,961	19,061	12,472	36,492	543,740	.0100	380,228	112	53,988	115	17,329	97	68,676	11,785	23,931	Door
Douglas*	031	44,322	43,287	16,593	18,594	33,163	735,430	.0133	446,232	131	74,501	158	5,972	33	76,071	13,874	33,630	Douglas
Dunn**	033	41,499	39,858	15,874	15,244	36,192	658,740	.0127	478,940	141	82,978	176	4,674	26	54,573	50,555	31,745	Dunn
Eau Claire*	035	94,488	93,142	17,903	38,534	36,710	1,691,640	.0377	1,887,616	555	434,918	923	95,344	534	215,166	74,265	72,766	Eau Claire
Florence**	037	5,075	5,088	16,883	2,207	32,296	85,680	.0012	17,760	5	....	....	....	....	7,035	....	4,157	Florence
Fond du Lac*	039	97,983	97,296	19,536	38,650	41,382	1,914,180	.0329	1,099,443	323	211,554	449	23,267	130	159,938	50,532	71,829	Fond du Lac
Forest	041	9,904	10,024	15,037	4,129	30,453	148,930	.0025	63,181	19	6,924	15	....	....	9,248	....	7,313	Forest
Grant**	043	49,313	49,597	15,444	18,817	33,838	761,600	.0141	470,338	138	74,413	158	8,029	45	68,047	13,519	36,041	Grant
Green**	045	34,466	33,647	18,924	13,734	39,813	652,240	.0144	721,733	212	63,916	136	6,671	37	51,976	11,815	26,350	Green
Green Lake	047	19,240	19,105	18,099	7,922	36,709	348,230	.0065	241,431	71	23,440	50	3,751	21	63,480	6,147	14,922	Green Lake
Iowa*	049	23,447	22,780	18,561	9,224	39,255	435,190	.0169	1,310,888	386	66,270	141	2,408	14	16,092	3,082	18,535	Iowa
Iron	051	6,684	6,861	15,477	3,076	28,141	103,450	.0018	55,336	16	2,292	5	....	....	16,846	....	5,231	Iron
Jackson	053	19,672	19,100	15,607	7,414	34,660	307,030	.0054	161,797	48	30,874	66	....	....	23,311	5,060	14,246	Jackson
Jefferson**	055	77,915	74,021	19,919	30,491	42,584	1,552,020	.0253	748,720	220	116,976	248	10,227	57	119,518	20,116	58,244	Jefferson
Juneau	057	25,251	24,316	16,030	10,258	32,981	404,780	.0072	229,504	68	19,071	40	1,734	10	34,224	16,986	19,390	Juneau
Kenosha*	059	158,255	149,577	19,541	60,514	43,059	3,092,510	.0487	1,265,061	372	201,089	427	94,119	527	200,957	76,540	106,754	Kenosha
Kewaunee*	061	20,539	20,187	18,662	7,989	40,295	383,300	.0060	143,193	42	6,564	14	....	....	24,617	2,154	16,137	Kewaunee
La Crosse*	063	109,063	107,120	17,641	43,894	36,724	1,923,960	.0384	1,624,271	478	323,643	687	35,592	199	207,311	45,123	79,059	La Crosse
Lafayette	065	16,410	16,137	16,423	6,463	35,028	269,500	.0044	104,769	31	....	....	....	....	11,056	4,121	12,838	Lafayette
Langlade	067	20,805	20,740	15,637	8,646	31,483	325,320	.0071	323,503	95	53,317	113	3,908	22	52,884	1,349	15,724	Langlade
Lincoln**	069	30,196	29,641	17,554	12,232	36,237	530,060	.0092	295,677	87	42,939	91	4,386	25	38,202	13,281	23,040	Lincoln
Manitowoc**	071	81,775	82,887	19,213	33,021	39,959	1,571,170	.0255	714,591	210	146,084	310	11,334	64	125,916	17,862	60,246	Manitowoc
Marathon*	073	127,589	125,834	19,297	50,040	41,174	2,462,120	.0466	1,887,978	555	362,120	769	42,550	238	218,595	38,765	95,110	Marathon
Marinette**	075	43,167	43,384	16,408	18,001	32,832	708,270	.0125	386,653	114	90,116	191	13,183	74	59,319	22,197	33,081	Marinette
Marquette	077	14,933	15,832	16,719	6,265	33,261	249,670	.0039	79,488	23	1,080	2	....	....	13,295	....	12,168	Marquette
Menominee	078	4,636	4,562	10,255	1,404	28,679	47,540	.0009	23,802	7	....	....	....	....	6,211	....	2,362	Menominee
Milwaukee*	079	931,139	940,164	18,177	396,455	35,739	16,925,060	.2897	9,057,242	2,664	1,299,485	2,759	380,038	2,130	1,354,928	795,995	558,736	Milwaukee
Monroe	081	42,054	40,899	15,928	16,114	35,021	669,840	.0124	425,026	125	64,674	137	3,936	22	58,185	13,006	29,925	Monroe
Oconto*	083	37,278	35,634	18,190	14,950	38,003	678,090	.0106	249,718	73	8,575	18	....	....	48,331	8,794	29,868	Oconto
Oneida	085	37,312	36,776	17,790	15,844	35,095	663,770	.0146	715,645	211	129,726	275	23,486	132	75,166	11,728	28,915	Oneida
Outagamie*	087	169,283	160,971	20,992	66,824	44,812	3,553,570	.0660	2,692,886	792	420,225	892	121,623	682	278,178	84,039	124,525	Outagamie
Ozaukee*	089	85,508	82,317	26,438	33,756	55,847	2,260,640	.0365	1,257,320	370	103,314	219	24,737	139	160,191	47,875	66,345	Ozaukee
Pepin	091	7,447	7,213	16,282	2,889	35,063	121,250	.0026	117,665	35	10,605	23	1,325	7	5,854	2,018	5,745	Pepin
Pierce*	093	38,196	36,804	19,227	13,819	44,645	734,410	.0105	174,068	51	3,266	7	....	....	41,340	7,222	29,843	Pierce
Polk	095	43,871	41,319	18,270	17,618	38,068	801,510	.0128	329,590	97	49,410	105	1,252	7	48,276	12,568	35,274	Polk
Portage**	097	67,436	67,182	18,752	26,401	40,245	1,264,580	.0219	724,094	213	162,397	345	20,535	115	91,059	5,235	50,498	Portage
Price	099	15,263	15,822	16,778	6,521	32,948	256,080	.0046	149,725	44	14,255	30	1,627	9	35,015	5,382	11,977	Price
Racine*	101	193,383	188,831	20,192	75,070	43,775	3,904,770	.0646	2,000,747	589	328,944	698	47,858	268	321,126	122,733	132,220	Racine
Richland	103	18,250	17,924	15,572	7,427	32,052	284,180	.0055	205,272	60	43,423	92	6,435	36	19,512	9,938	13,975	Richland
Rock*	105	155,545	152,307	19,859	62,205	41,742	3,088,910	.0555	2,063,534	607	359,494	763	32,652	183	282,095	98,760	113,939	Rock
Rusk	107	15,240	15,347	14,359	6,202	29,713	218,830	.0038	99,957	29	13,368	28	....	....	19,062	4,669	11,593	Rusk
St. Croix*	109	73,654	63,155	22,434	27,991	49,135	1,652,360	.0270	874,667	257	213,257	453	4,757	27	90,180	12,191	58,673	St. Croix
Sauk**	111	56,794	55,225	19,037	23,294	38,850	1,081,210	.0211	897,173	264	135,768	288	18,398	103	122,025	31,461	43,159	Sauk
Sawyer	113	16,870	16,196	15,076	7,033	30,384	254,330	.0050	191,383	56	17,771	38	4,506	25	35,384	3,486	12,966	Sawyer
Shawano	115	41,138	40,664	16,868	16,341	35,471	693,900	.0117	326,390	96	63,659	135	7,540	42	47,033	9,490	31,271	Shawano
Sheboygan*	117	113,582	112,646	20,355	45,994	42,122	2,311,980	.0379	1,149,763	338	226,999	482	16,678	93	182,279	51,099	81,145	Sheboygan
Taylor	119	19,478	19,680	17,038	7,704	36,015	331,870	.0061	215,252	63	41,246	88	1,775	10	23,500	1,191	15,152	Taylor
Trempealeau	121	27,383	27,010	17,275	11,150	35,506	473,030	.0078	206,860	61	5,052	11	2,276	13	23,741	5,603	21,711	Trempealeau
Vernon	123	28,638	28,056	14,572	11,136	31,285	417,320	.0076	228,739	67	21,591	46	3,372	19	29,682	13,095	20,607	Vernon
Vilas	125	22,345	21,033	16,686	9,819	31,817	372,850	.0063	180,018	53	13,486	29	....	....	30,403	10,139	18,089	Vilas
Walworth**	127	98,278	93,759	19,033	37,142	42,285	1,870,510	.0305	870,290	256	142,645	303	16,471	92	140,787	42,587	71,745	Walworth
Washburn	129	16,588	16,036	15,936	6,951	31,726	264,340	.0053	209,042	61	26,529	56	1,964	11	32,169	3,235	13,122	Washburn
Washington*	131	123,666	117,493	23,399	47,670	50,539	2,893,620	.0481	1,655,762	487	154,121	327	19,028	107	201,490	54,607	94,152	Washington
Waukesha*	133	378,079	360,767	26,305	148,466	56,005	9,945,440	.1634	5,858,033	1,723	911,999	1,936	183,308	1,027	947,357	301,658	291,182	Waukesha
Waupaca	135	52,763	51,731	17,818	20,757	37,819	940,150	.0167	568,133	167	83,940	178	4,944	28	92,962	24,470	39,671	Waupaca
Waushara	137	23,793	23,154	16,946	9,764	34,558	403,190	.0068	197,141	58	10,886	23	....	....	30,566	....	19,183	Waushara
Winnebago*	139	158,990	156,763	20,432	66,789	40,875	3,248,480	.0566	2,005,674	590	247,543	525	70,315	394	217,440	119,790	121,078	Winnebago
Wood**	141	75,348	75,555	19,157	31,305	38,707	1,443,470	.0283	1,212,078	357	243,709	517	17,042	96	121,683	15,639	57,378	Wood
The State		5,505,083	5,363,675	19,672	2,222,958	40,624	108,297,950	1.8999	66,732,238	19,627	10,457,690	22,198	1,825,386	10,228	8,922,128	2,954,461	3,969,663	The State
WYOMING (WY; CODE 56; 23 Counties)																		
Albany**	001	31,898	32,014	14,713	13,904	27,193	469,300	.0103	458,492	135	116,848	248	6,836	38	51,741	4,936	27,386	Albany
Big Horn	003	11,125	11,461	14,413	4,214	30,320	160,340	.0027	63,938	19	2,697	6	....	....	13,155	1,955	8,909	Big Horn
Campbell**	005	36,992	33,698	20,527	13,784	44,510	759,330	.0124	376,709	111	81,813	174	7,529	42	54,088	4,106	31,220	Campbell
Carbon	007	15,206	15,639	17,214	6,274	33,794	261,750	.0049	186,956	55	13,023	28	1,261	7	29,598	4,518	12,808	Carbon
Converse	009	12,405	12,052	18,490	4,977	37,368	229,370	.0036	91,196	27	8,275	18	....	....	19,145	4,791	10,547	Converse
Crook	011	5,939	5,887	17,114	2,427	33,580	101,640	.0016	34,537	10	....	....	....	....	5,756	....	5,755	Crook
Fremont**	013	35,937	35,804	14,745	13,953	30,726	529,880	.0108	428,106	126	71,459	152	5,410	30	56,495	6,630	27,791	Fremont
Goshen	015	12,110	12,538	15,486	5,015	30,210	187,530	.0032	85,727	25	10,119	21	....	....	18,381	7,564	10,068	Goshen
Hot Springs	017	4,600	4,882	15,696	2,033	28,746	72,200	.0012	29,233	9	4,726	10	....	....	8,560	1,694	3,981	Hot Springs
Johnson	019	7,688	7,075	17,146	3,300	32,079	131,820	.0021	55,135	16	1,141	2	....	....	7,367	3,579	6,666	Johnson
Laramie*	021	84,872	81,607	18,223	33,925	36,764	1,546,640	.0303	1,264,795	372	198,396	421	22,697	127	146,267	25,711	66,070	Laramie
Lincoln	023	15,398	14,573	17,735	5,813	37,845	273,080	.0046	132,565	39	5,200	11	1,061	6	26,817	4,557	12,330	Lincoln
Natrona*	025	68,763	66,533	17,576	28,287	34,625	1,208,590	.0232	917,121	270	190,011	403	22,242	125	108,499	19,530	54,497	Natrona
Niobrara	027	2,188	2,407	14,511	937	27,346	31,750	.0006	16,334	5	1,161	2	....	....	4,390	....	2,147	Niobrara
Park	029	26,440	25,786	17,084	10,897	33,585	451,710	.0087	339,865	100	60,139	128	7,237	41	49,571	7,285	22,333	Park
Platte	031	8,585	8,807	16,904	3,615	32,183	145,120	.0028	104,380	31	9,123	19	....	....	16,017	1,361	7,765	Platte
Sheridan**	033	27,278	26,560	17,277	11,728	32,377	471,290	.0090	352,369	104	61,877	131	6,911	39	41,165	4,298	22,214	Sheridan
Sublette	035	6,507	5,920	18,373	2,666	36,101	119,550	.0019	44,463	13	5,224	11	....	....	9,257	1,664	5,677	Sublette
Sweetwater**	037	36,862	37,613	20,301	14,268	42,391	748,330	.0138	541,644	159	86,239	183	13,088	73	77,637	7,441	30,680	Sweetwater
Teton**	039	18,715	18,251	25,633	7,982	48,717	479,730	.0093	439,483	129	55,531	118	37,186	208	74,059	6,259	16,412	Teton
Uinta**	041	19,697	19,742	18,166	7,086	40,701	357,810	.0067	255,052	75	38,103	81	1,837	10	43,895	3,576	15,061	Uinta
Washakie	043	7,760	8,289	16,424	3,136	32,733	127,450	.0024	88,931	26	14,615	31	1,137	6	10,518	2,587	6,177	Washakie
Weston	045	6,665	6,644	15,499	2,736	30,551	103,300	.0017	40,475	12	6,141	13	....	....	9,522	1,593	6,298	Weston
The State		503,630	493,782	17,806	202,957	35,757	8,967,510	.1678	6,347,503	1,868	1,042,029	2,211	138,786	777	881,902	126,808	412,792	The State
The United States		293,687,162	281,421,906	19,691	112,708,735	39,328	5,782,884,870	100.0000	3,399,544,000	1,000,000	471,078,000	1,000,000	178,435,000	1,000,000	505,933,000	192,191,000	193,017,681	The United States

Source: Devonshire Associates Ltd. and Scan/US, Inc. 2004.
* Component of a Metropolitan Core Based Statistical Area.
** Component of a Micropolitan Core Based Statistical Area.

.... Data less than 1,000.

(d) Data not available.

Principal Business Centers and Other Places with 27,500 or More: Population / Income / Sales

This table presents, for Principal Business Centers and other selected places over 27,500 in population, July 1, 2004 estimates of population and households; and 2003 estimates of per capita income; median household income; disposable income and market ability index; total retail sales; and general merchandise, apparel, food, and drug store sales. Ranally Sales Units are shown for total retail sales, general merchandise store sales and apparel store sales. Also shown are 1997 manufacturers value added and Ranally Manufacturing Units. Source for population, income, and sales estimates: Devonshire Associates Ltd. and Scan/US, Inc. 2004. Place Codes are from the Federal Information Processing Standards (FIPS) of the National Bureau of Standards. Each place carries a number unique in its relationship to the state in which it is located. Central cities of Ranally Metro Areas (RMAs) and suburbs located within them are identified by the abbreviation of the Metro Area name. An alphabetical list of RMAs appears on pages 126-127. The Ranally City Rating classifies Principal Business Centers according to their relative business and economic importance; for a complete explanation, see the Introduction on pages 5-9. A list of cities and other places of 35,000 or more, ranked according to 2000 Census population, appears on pages 129-131. Statistics for Total Retail Trade, General Merchandise, Apparel Store, Food Store Sales, and Health and Drug Store Sales in this edition are estimates based on data from the U.S. Census Bureau, and utilize the 1997 North American Industry Classification System (NAICS).

PLACE NAME	RANALLY METRO AREA	FIPS PLACE CODE	RANALLY CITY RATING	POPULATION Estimate 7/1/04	POPULATION Census 4/1/00	PER CAPITA INCOME 2003	HOUSE-HOLDS Estimate 7/1/04	MEDIAN HOUSEHOLD INCOME 2003	DISPOSABLE INCOME 2003 ($1,000)	MARKET ABILITY INDEX 2003	TOTAL RETAIL TRADE Sales 2003 ($1,000)	TOTAL RETAIL TRADE Ranally Sales Units	GENERAL MERCHANDISE Sales 2003 ($1,000)	GENERAL MERCHANDISE Ranally Sales Units	APPAREL STORES Sales 2003 ($1,000)	APPAREL STORES Ranally Sales Units	FOOD STORE SALES 2003 ($1,000)	HEALTH & DRUG STORE SALES 2003 ($1,000)	MANUFACTURERS VALUE ADDED 1997* ($1,000)	MANUFACTURERS Ranally Mfg Units	PLACE TYPE
Alabama																					
Anniston	ANNI	01852	3-A	23,925	24,276	18,191	10,755	28,689	435,229	.0092	431,741	127	59,944	127	14,000	78	71,148	21,934	355,623	195	Incorporated Place
Auburn	AU-OP	03076	3-B	43,695	42,987	14,765	19,783	20,496	645,175	.0126	463,047	136	124,640	265	31,437	176	91,555	15,266	149,929	82	Incorporated Place
Bessemer	BIR	05980	4-S	28,442	29,672	12,466	11,391	25,162	354,551	.0088	435,058	128	124,877	265	13,039	73	58,247	15,602	162,160	89	Incorporated Place
Birmingham	BIR	07000	2-AA	232,203	242,820	14,925	97,167	27,128	3,465,676	.0790	3,768,231	1,108	310,066	658	230,028	1,289	385,097	158,341	1,239,064	678	Incorporated Place
Cullman		18976	4-C	13,572	13,995	18,015	6,025	29,426	244,493	.0066	408,495	120	87,546	186	12,314	69	62,006	22,715	281,334	154	Incorporated Place
Decatur	DEC	20104	3-A	53,078	53,929	19,860	22,383	34,903	1,054,139	.0218	1,027,338	302	134,751	286	48,209	270	88,451	54,179	1,218,480	667	Incorporated Place
Dothan	DOTH	21184	3-A	59,605	57,737	18,446	25,142	32,877	1,099,480	.0245	1,237,776	364	270,477	574	63,436	356	89,162	42,359	622,171	341	Incorporated Place
Enterprise		24184	4-B	21,256	21,178	17,454	8,769	34,511	370,995	.0076	336,111	99	79,759	169	11,637	65	26,400	12,536	102,743	56	Incorporated Place
Florence	FLO	26896	3-AA	32,088	36,264	17,055	14,428	25,869	547,253	.0137	764,278	225	247,914	526	62,407	350	68,045	30,551	345,750	189	Incorporated Place
Gadsden	GAD	28696	3-A	37,114	38,978	15,837	15,945	27,035	587,757	.0119	491,335	145	107,419	228	30,970	174	94,067	25,451	568,276	311	Incorporated Place
Homewood	BIR	35800	4-Sm	25,227	25,043	21,287	11,100	37,499	536,999	.0139	852,183	251	230,156	489	73,335	411	72,316	32,324	103,797	57	Incorporated Place
Hoover	BIR	35896	◇	64,086	62,742	28,168	26,493	54,724	1,805,144	.0277	871,083	256	135,321	287	31,482	176	97,089	50,422	(d)	....	Incorporated Place
Huntsville	HNTS	37000	3-AA	163,931	158,216	23,119	71,887	39,985	3,789,992	.0691	2,854,321	840	557,428	1,183	173,810	974	326,574	101,039	2,668,556	1,461	Incorporated Place
Jasper		38416	4-C	13,566	14,052	16,600	5,667	29,168	225,202	.0067	430,905	127	108,047	229	22,286	125	42,035	16,237	57,480	31	Incorporated Place
Madison	HNTS	45784	◇	34,207	29,329	24,868	13,512	54,493	850,656	.0127	337,444	99	85,545	182	2,232	13	86,706	18,948	....	....	Incorporated Place
Mobile	MOB	50000	2-A	195,711	198,915	16,576	78,651	30,371	3,244,081	.0626	2,401,000	706	399,318	848	129,196	724	289,576	139,842	968,844	530	Incorporated Place
Montgomery	MTGY	51000	2-A	201,565	201,568	17,643	81,686	35,127	3,556,312	.0707	2,975,724	875	564,409	1,198	176,536	989	356,428	144,658	901,160	493	Incorporated Place
Opelika	AU-OP	57048	3-A	23,110	23,498	16,511	9,557	30,981	381,559	.0086	423,612	125	73,622	156	15,678	88	97,427	10,846	502,652	275	Incorporated Place
Phenix City	COL	59472	◇	28,970	28,265	16,675	13,018	28,655	483,069	.0085	265,679	78	97,994	208	5,293	30	69,508	13,551	477,147	261	Incorporated Place
Selma		69120	4-A	18,837	20,512	12,520	7,912	23,571	235,841	.0050	187,314	55	43,322	92	11,005	62	28,508	12,756	405,078	222	Incorporated Place
Talladega		74592	4-C	14,436	15,143	15,293	5,775	28,530	220,764	.0039	118,736	35	25,968	55	5,233	29	28,609	8,211	91,562	50	Incorporated Place
Tuscaloosa	TUSC	77256	3-AA	75,559	77,906	17,384	32,480	29,129	1,313,530	.0264	1,122,423	330	186,925	397	59,600	334	93,152	67,291	415,687	228	Incorporated Place
Alaska																					
Anchorage	ANCH	03000	2-A	274,398	260,283	22,488	100,252	49,752	6,170,610	.1105	4,355,756	1,281	1,057,357	2,245	209,835	1,176	511,166	47,012	157,819	86	Incorporated Place
Fairbanks	FRBK	24230	3-A	31,089	30,224	18,385	11,546	38,253	571,579	.0143	817,277	240	175,592	373	31,642	177	68,924	7,415	(d)	....	Incorporated Place
Juneau		36400	4-A	31,357	30,711	25,997	11,883	55,454	815,200	.0121	329,922	97	120,780	256	19,867	111	38,860	8,122	(d)	....	Incorporated Place
Ketchikan		38970	4-B	7,537	7,922	23,279	3,106	46,380	175,451	.0038	204,671	60	8,515	18	21,449	120	67,750	5,372	....	....	Incorporated Place
Arizona																					
Apache Junction	PHOE	02830	◇	43,863	31,814	17,928	19,732	33,340	786,367	.0112	162,711	48	34,372	73	2,391	13	53,826	9,995	(d)	....	Incorporated Place
Avondale	PHOE	04720	◇	48,710	35,883	14,510	14,781	43,735	706,777	.0119	278,212	82	87,199	185	1,036	6	61,890	12,769	(d)	....	Incorporated Place
Bullhead City		08220	◇	38,701	33,769	15,662	15,991	28,184	606,139	.0107	323,988	95	85,671	182	12,585	71	40,322	28,655	(d)	....	Incorporated Place
Casa Grande		10530	◇	27,748	25,224	16,291	10,172	32,360	452,053	.0084	297,668	88	42,136	89	30,012	168	58,884	14,189	141,970	78	Incorporated Place
Casas Adobes	TUC	10670	◇	58,091	54,011	20,967	24,239	43,715	1,217,986	.0199	617,352	182	132,226	281	37,197	208	140,125	45,837	(d)	....	Census Designated Place
Catalina Foothills	TUC	11230	◇	57,859	53,794	37,626	26,404	56,309	2,176,990	.0244	186,198	55	12,202	26	13,566	76	61,586	17,703	(d)	....	Census Designated Place
Chandler	PHOE	12000	◇	210,586	176,581	20,359	76,057	51,328	4,287,321	.0662	1,673,155	492	289,594	615	20,073	112	257,884	91,487	3,984,780	2,182	Incorporated Place
Douglas		20050	4-B	14,693	14,312	9,716	4,760	20,445	142,762	.0033	118,744	35	28,203	60	6,875	39	42,243	4,081	(d)	....	Incorporated Place
Flagstaff		23620	3-A	54,664	52,894	18,561	20,570	37,682	1,014,621	.0182	642,098	189	182,694	388	13,989	78	75,803	15,206	307,423	168	Incorporated Place
Gilbert	PHOE	27400	◇	143,984	109,697	20,465	47,488	59,587	2,946,669	.0426	827,603	243	58,704	125	10,202	57	168,680	48,017	150,797	83	Incorporated Place
Glendale	PHOE	27820	3-S	250,386	218,812	17,162	88,561	42,244	4,297,248	.0757	2,436,744	717	350,263	744	61,916	347	381,095	102,108	649,555	356	Incorporated Place
Lake Havasu City		39370	◇	47,888	41,938	17,787	20,548	33,248	851,785	.0160	604,269	178	91,421	194	11,191	63	124,048	21,152	139,072	76	Incorporated Place
Mesa	PHOE	46000	2-S	448,697	396,375	17,448	169,831	39,400	7,828,781	.1554	6,475,474	1,905	1,147,745	2,436	229,932	1,289	855,866	297,361	2,404,733	1,317	Incorporated Place
Nogales	NOGLS	49640	4-A	20,425	20,878	9,702	5,942	23,178	198,167	.0061	334,626	98	95,524	203	42,170	236	63,424	10,679	25,820	14	Incorporated Place
Oro Valley	TUC	51600	◇	35,021	29,700	25,180	14,793	53,324	881,830	.0110	113,443	33	32,707	69	1,215	7	44,312	1,301	(d)	....	Incorporated Place
Peoria	PHOE	54050	◇	145,610	108,364	19,461	53,919	47,203	2,833,722	.0435	1,034,366	304	112,180	238	18,951	106	156,120	39,665	30,265	17	Incorporated Place
Phoenix	PHOE	55000	1-A	1,473,643	1,321,045	18,427	532,238	39,867	27,154,359	.4883	17,355,613	5,105	2,345,800	4,980	664,537	3,724	2,304,720	871,234	10,283,805	5,630	Incorporated Place
Prescott		57380	4-A	35,351	33,938	21,359	15,855	34,674	755,074	.0147	650,991	191	154,531	328	20,470	115	103,910	29,299	106,421	58	Incorporated Place
Prescott Valley		57450	◇	30,343	23,535	13,855	11,635	31,684	420,414	.0069	136,583	40	33,241	71	1,235	7	23,141	3,428	(d)	....	Incorporated Place
Scottsdale	PHOE	65000	3-SS	221,385	202,705	34,517	101,376	56,055	7,641,488	.1225	4,683,538	1,378	621,704	1,320	325,729	1,825	522,532	224,528	756,260	414	Incorporated Place
Sierra Vista		66820	4-A	39,762	37,775	16,867	15,263	35,597	670,662	.0119	382,559	113	105,222	223	12,913	72	67,539	11,727	(d)	....	Incorporated Place
Sun City	PHOE	70320	◇	43,480	38,309	25,545	27,362	31,555	1,110,696	.0149	264,206	78	....	....	11,917	67	98,472	44,834	(d)	....	Census Designated Place
Sun City West	PHOE	70355	◇	29,902	26,344	29,731	17,426	40,117	889,008	.0105	90,526	27	7,243	15	4,388	25	33,616	18,660	(d)	....	Census Designated Place
Surprise	PHOE	71510	◇	41,875	30,848	18,832	17,319	40,837	788,572	.0106	104,762	31	20,338	43	1,993	11	9,268	4,093	(d)	....	Incorporated Place
Tempe	PHOE	73000	3-S	160,992	158,625	20,378	66,053	40,733	3,280,729	.0744	3,972,545	1,169	345,746	734	149,268	837	354,904	174,970	3,345,256	1,831	Incorporated Place
Tucson	TUC	77000	2-AA	517,271	486,699	15,326	209,836	30,561	7,927,934	.1566	5,991,710	1,763	870,423	1,848	228,864	1,283	821,990	366,775	1,767,480	968	Incorporated Place
Yuma	YUMA	85540	3-A	83,663	77,515	14,150	28,921	31,239	1,183,838	.0241	922,285	271	246,015	522	21,865	123	89,801	55,626	136,486	75	Incorporated Place
Arkansas																					
Batesville		04030	4-C	9,251	9,445	16,257	3,761	30,115	150,396	.0032	145,341	43	53,657	114	7,335	41	9,013	6,105	454,299	249	Incorporated Place
Benton	L.R.	05290	4-S	22,565	21,906	21,140	9,302	38,651	477,023	.0105	546,361	161	86,125	183	8,135	46	15,876	13,730	54,892	30	Incorporated Place
Blytheville		07330	4-A	15,768	18,272	13,921	6,136	27,587	219,501	.0047	191,154	56	45,910	97	6,594	37	21,656	6,613	503,204	275	Incorporated Place
Camden		10720	4-B	11,970	13,154	14,816	5,040	27,771	177,353	.0036	141,030	41	34,225	73	6,689	37	19,489	6,248	159,485	87	Incorporated Place
Conway		15190	4-C	48,251	43,167	17,672	18,325	35,700	852,711	.0142	399,316	117	125,463	266	18,538	104	20,829	14,998	570,840	313	Incorporated Place
El Dorado		21070	4-A	20,829	21,530	15,213	8,522	28,894	316,869	.0066	274,924	81	82,725	176	11,798	66	25,342	17,622	739,456	405	Incorporated Place
Fayetteville	FAY-	23290	3-A	63,491	58,047	17,539	26,335	30,836	1,113,583	.0244	1,187,266	349	502,770	1,067	59,858	335	95,629	33,276	449,049	246	Incorporated Place
Fort Smith	FTSM	24550	3-AA	80,943	80,268	16,823	32,661	31,208	1,361,706	.0322	1,692,786	498	539,531	1,145	63,990	359	124,356	72,186	1,786,206	978	Incorporated Place
Harrison		30460	4-A	12,469	12,152	16,169	5,491	28,497	201,612	.0048	251,728	74	74,652	158	6,878	39	15,432	7,014	210,623	115	Incorporated Place
Hot Springs	HTSPR	33400	3-A	36,907	35,750	17,839	17,584	27,596	658,366	.0139	644,499	190	146,041	310	21,498	120	68,671	28,192	180,271	99	Incorporated Place
Jacksonville	L.R.	34750	4-S	30,157	29,916	14,540	11,719	32,920	438,484	.0082	265,300	78	62,980	134	3,772	21	27,819	2,977	127,726	70	Incorporated Place
Jonesboro	JONES	35710	3-A	58,273	55,515	16,325	23,675	31,263	951,333	.0203	922,869	271	288,217	612	66,727	374	71,121	36,539	469,336	257	Incorporated Place
Little Rock	L.R.	41000	2-AA	187,008	183,133	21,781	84,065	37,251	4,073,174	.0789	3,504,180	1,031	705,702	1,498	183,420	1,028	339,453	117,737	977,106	535	Incorporated Place
Magnolia		43460	4-B	10,487	10,858	13,719	4,124	26,830	143,869	.0029	110,630	33	34,242	73	8,122	46	15,484	3,103	248,206	136	Incorporated Place
North Little Rock	L.R.	50450	3-S	59,640	60,433	18,402	26,924	33,610	1,097,514	.0273	1,552,790	457	344,303	731	66,572	373	119,415	49,544	582,299	319	Incorporated Place
Paragould		53390	4-B	22,980	22,017	15,789	9,613	29,878	362,825	.0069	243,418	72	78,118	166	5,942	33	25,761	10,489	390,803	214	Incorporated Place
Pine Bluff	PNBLF	55310	3-A	54,594	55,085	13,848	20,056	29,434	756,010	.0164	693,656	204	163,216	346	47,836	268	86,774	73,264	....	....	Incorporated Place
Rogers		60410	4-B	43,710	38,829	17,862	15,694	37,566	780,748	.0142	507,840	149	139,625	296	12,176	68	25,899	19,090	533,180	292	Incorporated Place
Russellville		61670	4-A	22,720	23,682	15,437	8,957	29,765	350,739	.0092	520,726	153	145,605	309	17,827	100	56,421	20,030	457,849	251	Incorporated Place
Searcy		63020	4-C	20,288	18,928	15,433	7,415	31,445	313,105	.0074	373,898	110	133,081	283	20,244	113	20,528	16,176	260,338	143	Incorporated Place
Springdale	FAY-	66080	4-B	51,860	45,798	15,483	18,546	35,127	802,935	.0158	603,350	177	164,485	349	12,423	70	62,308	15,586	....	....	Incorporated Place
Texarkana	TEXR-	68810	4-B	28,242	26,448	15,268	11,344	28,822	431,203	.0079	249,778	73	59,588	126	8,042	45	53,141	7,481	261,331	143	Incorporated Place
West Memphis	MEM	74540	4-S	27,869	27,666	13,547	10,398	26,711	377,534	.0090	436,337	128	109,849	233	11,348	64	39,976	30,214	....	....	Incorporated Place
California																					
Alameda	SF-O-	00562	3-S	70,844	72,259	29,364	30,385	51,540	2,080,255	.0280	585,973	172	62,855	133	25,248	141	138,390	52,477	578,741	317	Incorporated Place
Alhambra	L.A.	00884	3-S	89,110	85,804	14,266	29,902	36,786	1,271,214	.0269	1,117,960	329	118,953	253	33,545	188	143,325	42,336	175,929	96	Incorporated Place
Aliso Viejo	L.A.	00947	◇	42,193	40,166	29,141	17,061	62,852	1,229,536	.0181	516,976	152	86,753	184	31,525	177	94,214	28,965	(d)	....	Incorporated Place
Altadena	L.A.	01290	◇	44,672	42,610	21,620	15,353	53,508	965,807	.0123	100,324	30	4,466	9	1,389	8	34,184	23,786	(d)	....	Census Designated Place
Anaheim	L.A.	02000	2-S	347,733	328,014	16,652	103,390	45,227	5,790,420	.1075	3,830,225	1,127	324,598	689	111,884	627	675,933	208,275	3,402,548	1,863	Incorporated Place
Antioch	SF-O-	02252	3-S	106,725	90,532	19,439	34,357	51,718	2,074,582	.0332	910,621	268	191,029	406	40,421	227	193,679	36,069	61,317	34	Incorporated Place
Apple Valley	HESP-	02364	◇	56,890	54,239	16,901	19,077	37,010	961,474	.0145	259,651	76	51,968	110	1,867	10	88,945	21,739	(d)	....	Incorporated Place
Arcadia	L.A.	02462	3-Sm	57,497	53,054	23,075	20,543	48,854	1,326,759	.0213	674,186	198	127,865	271	186,941	1,048	116,021	55,982	151,017	83	Incorporated Place
Atascadero		03064	◇	27,592	26,411	19,079	10,251	43,492	526,424	.0094	341,303	100	16,148	34	22,592	127	66,959	28,158	(d)	....	Incorporated Place
Auburn	SAC	03204	4-C	12,476	12,462	26,210	5,340	43,383	326,995	.0072	399,472	118	34,099	72	12,200	68	60,914	27,290	70,443	39	Incorporated Place
Azusa	L.A.	03386	◇	48,348	44,712	11,929	13,452	39,507	576,720	.0110	310,522	91	65,340	139	4,247	24	29,023	9,927	488,689	268	Incorporated Place
Bakersfield	BAK	03526	2-A	298,683	247,057	15,328	99,482	36,366	4,578,105	.0865	3,016,876	887	457,708	972	147,395	826	396,617	208,492	217,840	119	Incorporated Place
Baldwin Park	L.A.	03666	◇	81,493	75,837	9,338	18,068	38,725	760,988	.0155	381,395	112	38,693	82	6,751	38	52,989	22,349	146,985	80	Incorporated Place
Barstow		04030	4-C	21,874	21,119	15,500	7,758	34,906	339,051	.0074	341,016	100	27,260	58	81,017	454	36,636	7,728	(d)	....	Incorporated Place
Bell	L.A.	04870	◇	38,858	36,664	7,878	9,368	28,235	306,122	.0067	164,889	49	14,861	32	10,163	57	36,757	11,461	68,969	38	Incorporated Place
Bellflower	L.A.	04982	4-S	79,556	72,878	13,029	25,246	36,561	1,036,568	.0192	551,119	162	33,391	71	13,687	77	81,243	33,942	(d)	....	Incorporated Place
Bell Gardens	L.A.	04996	◇	45,045	44,054	6,933	9,580	28,194	312,287	.0075	193,426	57	15,998	34	14,247	80	39,882	12,571	81,355	45	Incorporated Place
Berkeley	SF-O-	06000	3-S	100,922	102,743	29,574	45,168	43,851	2,984,682	.0448	1,376,645	405	5,807	12	80,518	451	343,080	59,192	656,470	359	Incorporated Place
Beverly Hills	L.A.	06308	3-SS	35,911	33,784	52,865	15,852	67,346	1,898,452	.0286	1,105,312	325	90,579	192	307,209	1,722	257,264	59,931	21,698	12	Incorporated Place
Brea	L.A.	08100	3-Sm	37,009	35,410	23,559	13,754	51,543	871,912	.0196	1,084,185	319	247,303	525	197,569	1,107	104,311	50,692	603,175	330	Incorporated Place
Brentwood	SF-O-	08142	◇	28,738	23,302	21,545	9,191	59,322	619,153	.0093	231,019	68	....	....	....	....	82,578	5,098	(d)	....	Incorporated Place
Buena Park	L.A.	08786	3-S	83,460	78,282	15,959	25,036	44,445	1,331,955	.0282	1,249,738	368	174,516	370	70,899	397	199,220	63,527	675,959	370	Incorporated Place
Burbank	L.A.	08954	3-S	104,409	100,316	21,061	42,853	43,093	2,198,924	.0475	2,426,661	714	311,778	662	208,905	1,171	460,846	289,235	725,796	397	Incorporated Place
Burlingame	SF-O-	09066	4-Sr	27,563	28,158	56,297	12,578	69,514	1,551,713	.0219	743,895	219	....	....	45,490	255	94,717	59,072	237,210	130	Incorporated Place
Calexico	CLEX	09710	4-B	29,923	27,109	8,851	7,490	27,200	264,859	.0081	423,909	125	69,082	147	64,744	363	115,262	16,936	(d)	....	Incorporated Place
Camarillo	OXN-	10046	4-Sr	57,849	57,077	29,036	21,748	57,855	1,679,699	.0250	744,056	219	34,014	72	93,007	521	109,482	45,984	875,556	479	Incorporated Place
Campbell	SF-O-	10345	4-S	36,596	38,138	32,248	15,864	60,683	1,180,138	.0193	747,425	220	48,454	103	42,571	239	135,984	33,302	351,993	193	Incorporated Place
Carlsbad	SDGO	11194	4-S	86,753	78,247	29,884	35,256	58,439	2,592,506	.0420	1,551,963	457	208,742	443	145,262	814	183,061	70,006	1,482,216	811	Incorporated Place
Carmichael	SAC	11390	◇	55,465	49,742	24,964	22,808	42,610	1,384,654	.0191	384,962	113	12,623	27	12,166	68	111,158	28,240	(d)	....	Census Designated Place
Carson	L.A.	11530	3-S	93,698	89,730	13,642	25,497	46,204	1,278,257	.0254	905,690	266	181,318	385	29,704	166	115,828	29,071	2,235,168	1,224	Incorporated Place
Castro Valley	SF-O-	11964	◇	58,119	57,292	26,368	22,491	55,505	1,532,460	.0206	385,346	113	10,873	23	20,784	116	161,041	34,641	(d)	....	Census Designated Place
Cathedral City	PSPR-	12048	◇	54,224	42,647	16,135	17,986	36,969	874,908	.0180	767,257	226	97,323	207	10,225	57	95,112	16,697	(d)	....	Incorporated Place
Ceres	MOD	12524	◇	38,841	34,609	12,690	11,540	33,546	492,881	.0094	286,958	84	59,242	126	2,626	15	56,400	28,960	67,702	37	Incorporated Place
Cerritos	L.A.	12552	3-Sm	52,401	51,488	20,135	15,491	62,586	1,055,112	.0264	1,555,125	457	226,537	481	115,371	647	5,327	29,524	347,984	191	Incorporated Place
Chico	CHICO	13014	3-A	66,935	59,954	16,039	26,223	30,512	1,073,572	.0227	1,004,449	295	185,985	395	41,471	232	140,823	52,379	195,298	107	Incorporated Place
Chino	L.A.	13210	4-Sr	72,729	67,168	15,084	18,386	48,405	1,097,056	.0205	686,339	202	87,485	186	52,894	296	137,769	25,042	621,175	340	Incorporated Place
Chino Hills	L.A.	13214	◇	86,201	66,787	23,065	25,369	67,091	1,988,232	.0262	360,388	106	44,902	95	8,707	49	122,160	18,775	(d)	....	Incorporated Place
Chula Vista	SDGO	13392	3-S	197,617	173,556	16,896	66,436	42,770	3,338,891	.0589	1,882,373	554	467,154	992	139,852	784	267,857	126,008	390,041	214	Incorporated Place
Citrus Heights	SAC	13588	◇	93,036	85,071	19,957	36,308	40,395	1,856,710	.0326	1,158,229	341	340,207	722	119,400	669	161,002	43,003	(d)	....	Incorporated Place
Claremont	L.A.	13756	◇	34,773	33,998	22,678	11,437	56,808	788,573	.0117	283,314	83	1,460	3	6,718	38	53,788	17,436	100,936	55	Incorporated Place
Clovis	FRES	14218	4-Sr	76,482	68,468	16,681	26,806	40,888	1,275,792	.0249	980,887	289	197,653	420	49,712	279	141,542	46,486	117,467	64	Incorporated Place
Coachella	IND-	14260	◇	27,851	22,724	6,926	5,932	26,678	192,884	.0052	190,759	56	....	....	3,080	17	49,773	6,906	(d)	....	Incorporated Place
Colton	RIV-	14890	◇	55,342	47,662	13,543	16,534	34,007	749,508	.0136	374,781	110	46,465	99	5,112	29	70,953	22,759	139,694	76	Incorporated Place
Commerce	L.A.	14974	4-S	13,122	12,568	9,231	3,394	31,320	121,132	.0050	343,391	101	3,479	7	69,424	389	9,190	5,853	1,853,748	1,015	Incorporated Place
Compton	L.A.	15044	4-Sr	96,653	93,493	8,751	22,857	30,587	845,848	.0167	317,556	93	40,651	86	11,940	67	86,308	13,322	562,951	308	Incorporated Place
Concord	SF-O-	16000	3-SS	129,042	121,780	22,500	46,322	51,060	2,903,391	.0543	2,309,672	679	308,804	656	161,427	905	246,137	76,055	167,754	92	Incorporated Place
Corona	RIV-	16350	4-S	162,414	124,966	18,900	49,490	52,580	3,069,563	.0489	1,279,158	376	146,465	311	37,202	208	215,733	38,934	859,544	471	Incorporated Place
Costa Mesa	L.A.	16532	2-S	114,504	108,724	21,103	41,488	46,295	2,416,337	.0580	3,325,854	978	461,786	980	690,609	3,870	276,483	109,733	985,993	540	Incorporated Place
Covina	L.A.	16742	3-S	50,175	46,837	16,612	16,952	44,014	833,522	.0158	581,397	171	84,060	178	13,823	77	94,236	29,201	236,567	130	Incorporated Place
Culver City	L.A.	17568	3-S	39,545	38,816	22,777	16,785	43,772	900,734	.0180	850,581	250	120,564	256	79,663	446	82,936	29,812	160,294	88	Incorporated Place
Cupertino	SF-O-	17610	3-Sm	55,239	50,546	41,581	20,684	80,442	2,296,872	.0325	1,003,295	295	240,215	510	117,936	661	184,228	38,466	188,380	103	Incorporated Place
Cypress	L.A.	17750	◇	47,716	46,229	23,299	16,241	55,093	1,111,757	.0159	346,986	102	71,314	151	20,411	114	37,931	29,411	132,698	73	Incorporated Place
Daly City	SF-O-	17918	3-Sm	105,556	103,621	18,263	32,208	54,941	1,927,788	.0390	1,716,489	505	369,812	785	144,525	810	213,711	76,597	(d)	....	Incorporated Place
Dana Point	L.A.	17946	◇	36,318	35,110	35,231	15,047	56,679	1,279,533	.0160	284,238	84	....	....	18,116	102	88,141	17,144	(d)	....	Incorporated Place
Danville	SF-O-	17988	◇	44,349	41,715	47,908	15,694	95,708	2,124,693	.0252	432,214	127	79,732	169	21,249	119	71,102	26,612	(d)	....	Incorporated Place
Davis	DAV	18100	◇	67,346	60,308	20,726	25,358	38,951	1,395,835	.0205	431,292	127	2,698	6	6,827	38	97,499	26,848	(d)	....	Incorporated Place
Delano		18394	◇	46,539	38,824	7,604	9,943	26,107	353,874	.0084	251,293	74	30,403	65	15,618	88	66,949	15,558	(d)	....	Incorporated Place
Diamond Bar	L.A.	19192	◇	59,694	56,287	20,992	18,529	61,158	1,253,115	.0172	264,809	78	24,347	52	7,201	40	64,956	19,146	(d)	....	Incorporated Place
Downey	L.A.	19766	3-S	117,264	107,323	15,381	36,743	42,190	1,803,681	.0353	1,325,071	390	244,172	518	81,215	455	137,522	78,746	841,582	461	Incorporated Place
Dublin	SF-O-	20018	◇	31,937	29,973	24,729	10,177	66,042	789,758	.0192	1,156,318	340	91,749	195	57,389	322	61,731	18,147	50,125	27	Incorporated Place

.... Data less than 1,000.
(d) Data not available.
◇ Not classified as a Principal Business Center.

* Data from 1997 Census of Manufactures.

Principal Business Centers and Other Places with 27,500 or More: Population / Income / Sales, *Continued*

PLACE NAME	RANALLY METRO AREA	FIPS PLACE CODE	RANALLY CITY RATING	POPULATION Estimate 7/1/04	POPULATION Census 4/1/00	PER CAPITA INCOME 2003	HOUSE-HOLDS Estimate 7/1/04	MEDIAN HOUSEHOLD INCOME 2003	DISPOSABLE INCOME 2003 ($1,000)	MARKET ABILITY INDEX 2003	TOTAL RETAIL TRADE Sales 2003 ($1,000)	TOTAL RETAIL TRADE Ranally Sales Units	GENERAL MERCHANDISE Sales 2003 ($1,000)	GENERAL MERCHANDISE Ranally Sales Units	APPAREL STORES Sales 2003 ($1,000)	APPAREL STORES Ranally Sales Units	FOOD STORE SALES 2003 ($1,000)	HEALTH & DRUG STORE SALES 2003 ($1,000)	MANUFACTURERS VALUE ADDED 1997* ($1,000)	MANUFACTURERS Ranally Mfg Units	PLACE TYPE
East Los Angeles	**L.A.**	20802	◇	130,301	124,283	8,006	30,962	26,813	1,043,130	.0230	580,209	**171**	114,363	**243**	48,382	**271**	114,458	33,535	(d)	....	Census Designated Place
East Palo Alto	**SF-O-**	20956	◇	31,179	29,506	20,852	7,566	58,094	650,159	.0082	53,957	**16**	....	....	....	....	8,263	....	117,577	**64**	Incorporated Place
El Cajon	**SDGO**	21712	**3-SS**	97,891	94,869	17,838	35,632	37,742	1,746,162	.0360	1,616,635	**476**	252,148	**535**	106,336	**596**	169,234	69,668	390,270	**214**	Incorporated Place
El Centro		21782	**3-A**	38,777	37,835	12,928	11,669	32,451	501,323	.0111	469,637	**138**	137,073	**291**	10,974	**62**	49,327	20,957	(d)	....	Incorporated Place
Elk Grove	**SAC**	22020	◇	65,492	59,984	18,772	20,117	51,082	1,229,416	.0194	485,068	**143**	42,512	**90**	15,690	**88**	153,703	12,614	(d)	....	Incorporated Place
El Monte	**L.A.**	22230	**4-S**	123,373	115,965	8,649	28,497	31,231	1,067,026	.0303	1,441,103	**424**	90,262	**192**	26,347	**148**	171,691	27,862	484,262	**265**	Incorporated Place
El Segundo	**L.A.**	22412	**4-Sr**	16,349	16,033	26,359	7,123	54,813	430,936	.0067	206,449	**61**	....	....	12,072	**68**	24,312	16,050	5,336,252	**2,921**	Incorporated Place
El Toro	**L.A.**	39496	◇	60,468	58,707	24,627	20,721	58,360	1,489,132	.0224	618,123	**182**	3,793	**8**	37,042	**208**	129,770	58,991	161,562	**88**	Incorporated Place
Encinitas	**SDGO**	22678	◇	60,016	58,014	30,839	23,910	56,855	1,850,843	.0272	806,291	**237**	31,179	**66**	45,476	**255**	152,029	45,093	(d)	....	Incorporated Place
Escondido	**SDGO**	22804	**3-S**	146,927	133,559	18,102	48,747	42,012	2,659,633	.0523	2,182,561	**642**	296,784	**630**	178,635	**1,001**	320,915	90,841	296,410	**162**	Incorporated Place
Eureka	**EUR-**	23042	**3-A**	26,262	26,128	15,981	11,205	27,376	419,684	.0099	505,120	**149**	82,636	**175**	32,511	**182**	68,293	53,669	61,779	**34**	Incorporated Place
Fairfield	**FRFL-**	23182	**3-C**	103,862	96,178	20,447	33,979	47,573	2,123,718	.0361	1,208,045	**355**	315,473	**670**	74,011	**415**	207,407	33,710	561,814	**308**	Incorporated Place
Fair Oaks	**SAC**	23294	◇	31,231	28,008	28,079	12,383	52,823	876,949	.0114	189,752	**56**	2,174	**5**	11,448	**64**	84,392	4,783	(d)	....	Census Designated Place
Fallbrook	**SDGO**	23462	◇	30,674	29,100	18,804	9,981	43,895	576,806	.0085	164,323	**48**	....	....	2,909	**16**	62,755	17,183	(d)	....	Census Designated Place
Florin	**SAC**	24498	◇	30,834	27,653	16,171	10,161	39,992	498,622	.0083	209,167	**62**	27,879	**59**	6,595	**37**	54,109	12,987	(d)	....	Census Designated Place
Folsom	**SAC**	24638	◇	63,536	51,884	25,389	20,937	63,194	1,613,085	.0281	1,111,735	**327**	156,383	**332**	86,076	**482**	132,906	41,719	44,599	**24**	Incorporated Place
Fontana	**RIV-**	24680	**4-Sr**	166,588	128,929	13,353	43,108	42,229	2,224,419	.0371	743,051	**219**	84,822	**180**	24,453	**137**	160,579	39,294	460,803	**252**	Incorporated Place
Fountain Valley	**L.A.**	25380	**3-S**	56,673	54,978	23,429	18,846	60,647	1,327,782	.0243	1,019,879	**300**	166,540	**354**	30,564	**171**	146,850	62,367	737,093	**404**	Incorporated Place
Fremont	**SF-O-**	26000	**3-SS**	207,628	203,413	29,332	71,241	67,303	6,090,077	.0854	2,105,417	**619**	74,666	**159**	39,924	**224**	418,473	117,975	4,280,594	**2,343**	Incorporated Place
Fresno	**FRES**	27000	**2-A**	473,574	427,652	13,902	152,466	33,814	6,583,700	.1270	4,282,632	**1,260**	598,991	**1,272**	210,185	**1,178**	704,244	294,304	1,298,165	**711**	Incorporated Place
Fullerton	**L.A.**	28000	**3-SS**	130,138	126,003	21,733	45,365	45,908	2,828,321	.0466	1,503,491	**442**	208,473	**443**	75,337	**422**	278,186	82,589	1,202,024	**658**	Incorporated Place
Gardena	**L.A.**	28168	**3-S**	62,010	57,746	14,317	21,611	35,945	887,805	.0176	642,144	**189**	57,937	**123**	8,089	**45**	98,416	24,882	469,309	**257**	Incorporated Place
Garden Grove	**L.A.**	29000	**3-S**	174,139	165,196	14,309	48,629	43,328	2,491,825	.0459	1,416,824	**417**	157,524	**334**	38,469	**216**	253,729	85,301	1,158,058	**634**	Incorporated Place
Gilroy	**SF-O-**	29504	◇	45,214	41,464	20,617	13,456	56,241	932,185	.0191	896,944	**264**	76,441	**162**	154,222	**864**	114,237	31,281	145,886	**80**	Incorporated Place
Glendale	**L.A.**	30000	**3-SS**	208,259	194,973	18,433	76,050	40,034	3,838,760	.0655	2,057,304	**605**	217,632	**462**	72,556	**407**	297,795	132,782	511,036	**280**	Incorporated Place
Glendora	**L.A.**	30014	**4-S**	50,315	49,415	20,244	16,941	52,935	1,018,599	.0164	472,090	**139**	68,077	**145**	4,519	**25**	81,950	24,071	131,403	**72**	Incorporated Place
Goleta	**S.BAR**	30378	◇	56,017	55,204	21,686	20,268	47,114	1,214,767	.0178	389,231	**114**	29,202	**62**	7,063	**40**	99,034	28,566	(d)	....	Incorporated Place
Hacienda Heights	**L.A.**	31596	◇	55,694	53,122	18,332	16,612	52,234	1,020,985	.0156	335,277	**99**	33,625	**71**	9,327	**52**	106,644	45,038	(d)	....	Census Designated Place
Hanford		31960	**4-B**	46,659	41,686	15,493	15,503	34,653	722,889	.0132	430,142	**127**	68,629	**146**	23,659	**133**	109,576	21,646	113,947	**62**	Incorporated Place
Hawthorne	**L.A.**	32548	**3-S**	91,813	84,112	13,211	30,808	31,598	1,212,976	.0220	591,540	**174**	68,916	**146**	38,045	**213**	100,475	30,260	793,906	**435**	Incorporated Place
Hayward	**SF-O-**	33000	**3-SS**	142,347	140,030	18,788	46,665	47,128	2,674,356	.0492	1,856,656	**546**	160,786	**341**	74,323	**417**	274,696	86,614	1,036,271	**567**	Incorporated Place
Hemet	**HEM**	33182	**3-C**	68,271	58,812	16,300	29,516	27,070	1,112,795	.0226	949,361	**279**	184,804	**392**	14,891	**83**	133,248	71,115	69,079	**38**	Incorporated Place
Hesperia	**HESP-**	33434	◇	67,835	62,582	15,254	21,232	38,308	1,034,740	.0166	340,564	**100**	11,296	**24**	6,727	**38**	99,286	19,572	68,444	**37**	Incorporated Place
Highland	**RIV-**	33588	◇	51,589	44,605	14,938	15,273	38,776	770,613	.0121	221,598	**65**	59,294	**126**	8,169	**46**	59,984	9,523	(d)	....	Incorporated Place
Hollister		34120	◇	39,900	34,413	19,024	11,027	52,075	759,075	.0119	298,124	**88**	41,333	**88**	....	....	55,936	17,450	105,640	**58**	Incorporated Place
Huntington Beach	**L.A.**	36000	**3-SS**	198,280	189,594	28,222	77,392	57,253	5,595,834	.0862	2,754,841	**810**	179,133	**380**	187,441	**1,050**	345,844	199,766	906,253	**496**	Incorporated Place
Huntington Park	**L.A.**	36056	**4-S**	65,665	61,348	8,110	15,754	28,456	532,556	.0120	329,095	**97**	20,871	**44**	62,441	**350**	84,403	28,394	301,720	**165**	Incorporated Place
Indio	**IND-**	36448	**3-C**	60,321	49,116	13,281	17,190	34,613	801,101	.0153	488,306	**144**	76,393	**162**	12,320	**69**	59,338	22,594	(d)	....	Incorporated Place
Industry	**L.A.**	13630	**3-Sm**	786	777	7,939	122	45,325	6,240	.0117	1,314,333	**387**	157,792	**335**	35,281	**198**	254,606	86,656	2,335,206	**1,278**	Incorporated Place
Inglewood	**L.A.**	36546	**3-S**	114,651	112,580	12,387	37,093	32,348	1,420,145	.0250	557,861	**164**	81,475	**173**	19,478	**109**	136,534	43,231	204,869	**112**	Incorporated Place
Irvine	**L.A.**	36770	**4-Sr**	155,581	143,072	28,798	55,971	62,620	4,480,348	.0736	2,753,804	**810**	210,752	**447**	105,266	**590**	243,548	143,062	4,143,406	**2,268**	Incorporated Place
Laguna	**SAC**	39173	◇	38,256	34,309	22,852	12,523	59,713	874,211	.0123	239,236	**70**	74,286	**158**	4,136	**23**	53,396	1,559	(d)	....	Census Designated Place
Laguna Hills	**L.A.**	39220	◇	32,111	31,178	24,285	11,311	44,396	779,810	.0141	583,318	**172**	125,160	**266**	66,581	**373**	73,802	45,323	59,032	**32**	Incorporated Place
Laguna Niguel	**L.A.**	39248	◇	66,384	61,891	34,693	25,041	67,383	2,303,067	.0303	664,612	**196**	108,632	**231**	31,733	**178**	102,398	34,279	(d)	....	Incorporated Place
La Habra	**L.A.**	39290	**4-S**	62,147	58,974	19,445	20,072	46,170	1,208,455	.0220	828,795	**244**	116,588	**247**	19,867	**111**	356,103	32,473	95,388	**52**	Incorporated Place
Lake Elsinore		39486	◇	35,206	28,928	14,939	10,825	38,626	525,960	.0102	373,784	**110**	52,131	**111**	49,249	**276**	93,723	18,989	36,935	**20**	Incorporated Place
Lakewood	**L.A.**	39892	**3-S**	83,924	79,345	17,716	28,161	50,774	1,486,828	.0260	840,385	**247**	183,459	**389**	108,580	**609**	203,581	40,765	(d)	....	Incorporated Place
La Mesa	**SDGO**	40004	**3-S**	54,729	54,749	22,794	24,397	40,399	1,247,513	.0234	1,012,206	**298**	149,152	**317**	64,449	**361**	167,234	43,494	(d)	....	Incorporated Place
La Mirada	**L.A.**	40032	**4-S**	50,213	46,783	17,242	15,489	53,781	865,778	.0157	539,346	**159**	15,590	**33**	12,334	**69**	77,253	22,170	360,387	**197**	Incorporated Place
Lancaster	**L.A.**	40130	**3-C**	123,118	118,718	13,672	39,194	37,579	1,683,277	.0347	1,333,068	**392**	153,134	**325**	49,014	**275**	168,359	101,738	56,845	**31**	Incorporated Place
La Presa	**SDGO**	40326	◇	34,491	32,721	15,362	10,673	42,290	529,862	.0080	117,783	**35**	15,814	**34**	1,496	**8**	17,595	9,033	(d)	....	Census Designated Place
La Puente	**L.A.**	40340	◇	44,288	41,063	10,362	10,112	42,055	458,921	.0092	255,820	**75**	36,714	**78**	5,323	**30**	40,250	10,789	(d)	....	Incorporated Place
La Quinta	**PSPR-**	40354	◇	33,096	23,694	25,663	11,874	48,149	849,336	.0125	326,506	**96**	80,500	**171**	4,468	**25**	54,937	1,795	(d)	....	Incorporated Place
La Verne	**L.A.**	40830	◇	32,583	31,638	20,569	11,277	54,500	670,203	.0106	297,062	**87**	51,232	**109**	13,806	**77**	51,021	8,001	105,763	**58**	Incorporated Place
Lawndale	**L.A.**	40886	◇	34,908	31,711	12,181	10,412	37,670	425,206	.0083	249,316	**73**	42,326	**90**	5,186	**29**	33,846	5,421	(d)	....	Incorporated Place
Livermore	**SF-O-**	41992	**4-S**	76,452	73,345	28,849	27,907	64,140	2,205,526	.0312	786,554	**231**	129,550	**275**	12,656	**71**	160,451	32,257	210,999	**116**	Incorporated Place
Lodi	**STOC**	42202	**4-C**	63,682	56,999	18,981	23,029	37,196	1,208,749	.0211	711,945	**209**	85,352	**181**	15,325	**86**	99,755	71,503	220,170	**121**	Incorporated Place
Lompoc	**LOMP**	42524	**4-C**	40,254	41,103	14,469	12,767	38,902	582,431	.0105	309,195	**91**	73,172	**155**	8,452	**47**	73,136	23,514	(d)	....	Incorporated Place
Long Beach	**L.A.**	43000	**2-S**	502,320	461,522	15,975	175,680	36,806	8,024,341	.1353	3,592,006	**1,057**	401,992	**853**	148,678	**833**	655,103	200,561	2,238,957	**1,226**	Incorporated Place
Los Angeles	**L.A.**	44000	**1-AAA**	3,863,201	3,694,820	17,023	1,318,606	36,989	65,762,793	1.1100	31,538,878	**9,277**	3,058,053	**6,492**	3,030,102	**16,982**	5,850,926	1,965,505	14,314,915	**7,837**	Incorporated Place
Los Banos		44028	◇	34,834	25,869	13,991	10,228	40,077	487,349	.0085	218,204	**64**	44,329	**94**	10,249	**57**	47,187	7,709	....	....	Incorporated Place
Los Gatos	**SF-O-**	44112	**4-Sr**	27,245	28,592	55,761	11,859	83,566	1,519,204	.0204	610,155	**179**	2,091	**4**	17,661	**99**	144,711	43,176	80,486	**44**	Incorporated Place
Lynwood	**L.A.**	44574	**4-S**	76,396	69,845	7,345	15,581	33,307	561,166	.0117	188,385	**55**	4,035	**9**	7,140	**40**	80,493	13,235	119,863	**66**	Incorporated Place
Madera	**FRES**	45022	◇	51,263	43,207	12,251	14,115	34,145	628,001	.0114	284,731	**84**	36,143	**77**	6,033	**34**	83,145	22,382	90,532	**50**	Incorporated Place
Manhattan Beach	**L.A.**	45400	**4-S**	35,333	33,852	49,632	14,934	83,357	1,753,638	.0227	576,685	**170**	67,935	**144**	53,996	**303**	102,022	32,684	(d)	....	Incorporated Place
Manteca		45484	◇	56,315	49,258	17,557	18,674	42,487	988,697	.0165	471,160	**139**	76,244	**162**	6,364	**36**	111,795	25,744	92,914	**51**	Incorporated Place
Martinez	**SF-O-**	46114	◇	36,311	35,866	25,813	14,379	53,655	937,313	.0136	341,890	**101**	32,071	**68**	2,432	**14**	72,311	20,972	....	....	Incorporated Place
Marysville	**YUCY**	46170	**3-B**	13,525	12,268	14,801	5,156	27,770	200,178	.0036	110,958	**33**	10,335	**22**	....	....	21,690	15,755	41,157	**23**	Incorporated Place
Maywood	**L.A.**	46492	◇	28,557	28,083	7,817	6,521	28,357	223,241	.0050	122,445	**36**	7,192	**15**	....	....	58,794	7,553	19,870	**11**	Incorporated Place
Menlo Park	**SF-O-**	46870	**4-Sr**	30,414	30,785	45,342	12,547	72,927	1,379,041	.0198	656,242	**193**	....	....	20,863	**117**	156,557	38,505	950,119	**520**	Incorporated Place
Merced	**MRCD**	46898	**3-A**	72,262	63,893	13,836	22,705	31,043	999,817	.0199	712,551	**210**	147,357	**313**	18,712	**105**	121,873	41,956	208,550	**114**	Incorporated Place
Milpitas	**SF-O-**	47766	◇	63,749	62,698	25,087	18,146	70,880	1,599,271	.0320	1,562,529	**460**	168,520	**358**	300,998	**1,687**	236,048	59,524	4,486,657	**2,456**	Incorporated Place
Mission Viejo	**L.A.**	48256	◇	96,923	93,102	28,500	34,022	66,765	2,762,260	.0411	1,199,412	**353**	185,160	**393**	69,876	**392**	201,040	70,536	151,272	**83**	Incorporated Place
Modesto	**MOD**	48354	**2-A**	206,490	188,856	17,000	69,968	37,257	3,510,234	.0667	2,521,877	**742**	415,247	**881**	125,552	**704**	331,146	172,518	946,491	**518**	Incorporated Place
Monrovia	**L.A.**	48648	**4-S**	37,846	36,929	17,297	13,719	41,972	654,633	.0136	605,962	**178**	29,100	**62**	14,562	**82**	78,282	7,924	395,645	**217**	Incorporated Place
Montclair	**L.A.**	48788	**3-Sm**	37,902	33,049	12,412	9,886	36,895	470,425	.0158	1,040,414	**306**	224,766	**477**	180,289	**1,010**	68,390	29,382	40,858	**22**	Incorporated Place
Montebello	**L.A.**	48816	**4-S**	65,025	62,150	13,053	19,512	35,841	848,743	.0192	843,198	**248**	211,602	**449**	109,438	**613**	120,973	43,433	367,836	**201**	Incorporated Place
Monterey	**MTRY-**	48872	**3-BB**	29,475	29,674	24,807	12,204	44,869	731,192	.0128	506,525	**149**	68,098	**145**	38,256	**214**	134,821	47,161	80,163	**44**	Incorporated Place
Monterey Park	**L.A.**	48914	**4-S**	61,779	60,051	14,397	19,923	37,854	889,447	.0159	453,982	**134**	....	....	32,001	**179**	153,504	64,722	106,065	**58**	Incorporated Place
Moorpark	**L.A.**	49138	◇	33,944	31,415	22,716	9,698	65,403	771,056	.0104	164,864	**48**	22,523	**48**	1,523	**9**	54,329	16,204	221,189	**121**	Incorporated Place
Moreno Valley	**RIV-**	49270	◇	154,564	142,381	14,716	42,958	43,534	2,274,552	.0396	1,066,879	**314**	198,066	**420**	57,304	**321**	204,335	65,195	58,033	**32**	Incorporated Place
Morgan Hill	**SF-O-**	49278	◇	35,707	33,556	30,043	11,994	69,712	1,072,729	.0150	374,514	**110**	88,994	**189**	11,190	**63**	58,668	15,112	220,090	**120**	Incorporated Place
Mountain View	**SF-O-**	49670	**3-SS**	68,398	70,708	36,204	31,478	61,038	2,476,301	.0377	1,312,712	**386**	243,401	**517**	39,333	**220**	255,791	108,900	6,251,610	**3,423**	Incorporated Place
Murrieta		50076	◇	75,052	44,282	20,365	24,493	51,469	1,528,401	.0229	519,667	**153**	7,466	**16**	9,296	**52**	165,079	12,629	71,974	**39**	Incorporated Place
Napa	**NAPA**	50258	**3-S**	80,170	72,585	22,700	29,701	46,708	1,819,863	.0289	869,905	**256**	73,456	**156**	59,103	**331**	173,260	49,609	400,475	**219**	Incorporated Place
National City	**SDGO**	50398	**3-S**	54,481	54,260	10,142	15,229	28,678	552,566	.0222	1,553,068	**457**	169,693	**360**	116,603	**653**	125,860	45,513	133,607	**73**	Incorporated Place
Newark	**SF-O-**	50916	◇	42,917	42,471	21,952	13,469	60,266	942,118	.0188	875,746	**258**	230,393	**489**	90,207	**506**	141,258	24,192	337,105	**185**	Incorporated Place
Newport Beach	**L.A.**	51182	**3-SS**	73,864	70,032	54,399	35,056	71,714	4,018,111	.0536	1,563,739	**460**	216,618	**460**	168,464	**944**	271,372	92,115	1,295,162	**709**	Incorporated Place
North Highlands	**SAC**	51924	◇	49,268	44,187	14,351	17,024	31,630	707,027	.0156	693,904	**204**	51,562	**109**	4,439	**25**	90,072	10,422	(d)	....	Census Designated Place
Norwalk	**L.A.**	52526	**4-S**	111,303	103,298	11,448	28,715	41,436	1,274,214	.0254	768,703	**226**	119,058	**253**	15,306	**86**	163,988	25,007	73,073	**40**	Incorporated Place
Novato	**SF-O-**	52582	◇	46,469	47,630	25,300	18,061	58,415	1,175,650	.0181	544,874	**160**	89,083	**189**	31,344	**176**	93,577	21,210	122,525	**67**	Incorporated Place
Oakland	**SF-O-**	53000	**2-BB**	393,854	399,484	21,677	152,412	39,417	8,537,548	.1293	3,248,340	**956**	147,609	**313**	87,847	**492**	781,322	224,355	1,196,774	**655**	Incorporated Place
Oceanside	**SDGO**	53322	**3-C**	175,419	161,029	17,854	62,284	41,774	3,131,885	.0490	1,126,373	**331**	207,606	**441**	30,903	**173**	215,941	64,628	256,252	**140**	Incorporated Place
Oildale	**BAK**	53448	◇	30,748	27,885	16,879	11,928	31,406	518,981	.0097	349,382	**103**	22,393	**48**	1,388	**8**	50,865	13,576	(d)	....	Census Designated Place
Ontario	**L.A.**	53896	**3-S**	180,009	158,007	13,608	48,623	39,524	2,449,481	.0520	2,105,749	**619**	191,382	**406**	215,164	**1,206**	276,174	55,442	1,692,554	**927**	Incorporated Place
Orange	**L.A.**	53980	**3-SS**	134,689	128,821	21,424	43,088	52,841	2,885,615	.0498	1,771,435	**521**	186,029	**395**	181,304	**1,016**	135,431	116,199	767,521	**420**	Incorporated Place
Orangevale	**SAC**	54092	◇	29,779	26,705	22,806	10,895	49,520	679,129	.0089	113,734	**33**	1,049	**2**	9,795	**55**	22,609	1,648	(d)	....	Census Designated Place
Orcutt	**S.MAR**	54120	◇	29,183	28,830	19,651	10,520	47,236	573,470	.0088	212,135	**62**	54,458	**116**	....	....	43,421	7,157	(d)	....	Census Designated Place
Oroville		54386	**4-B**	13,471	13,004	12,853	5,060	26,654	173,146	.0040	177,133	**52**	24,998	**53**	2,748	**15**	38,332	18,514	79,370	**43**	Incorporated Place
Oxnard	**OXN-**	54652	**3-CC**	193,860	170,358	14,358	49,582	43,650	2,783,390	.0524	1,718,640	**506**	191,917	**407**	87,720	**492**	210,696	59,619	749,006	**410**	Incorporated Place
Pacifica	**SF-O-**	54806	◇	35,539	38,390	24,780	13,280	61,953	880,648	.0117	191,847	**56**	4,291	**9**	5,589	**31**	102,633	15,304	(d)	....	Incorporated Place
Palmdale	**L.A.**	55156	◇	128,228	116,670	13,584	37,349	43,302	1,741,895	.0328	1,022,060	**301**	205,105	**435**	66,203	**371**	206,914	35,400	....	....	Incorporated Place
Palm Desert	**PSPR-**	55184	◇	53,694	41,155	30,370	25,266	42,553	1,630,708	.0266	997,191	**293**	182,452	**387**	184,060	**1,032**	203,212	49,554	40,973	**22**	Incorporated Place
Palm Springs	**PSPR-**	55254	**3-C**	45,925	42,807	25,537	22,230	33,511	1,172,776	.0184	581,620	**171**	17,872	**38**	72,548	**407**	151,134	37,764	73,771	**40**	Incorporated Place
Palo Alto	**SF-O-**	55282	**3-SS**	56,508	58,598	47,759	25,337	70,197	2,698,780	.0433	1,824,720	**537**	347,959	**739**	365,009	**2,046**	202,630	67,186	1,825,277	**999**	Incorporated Place
Paramount	**L.A.**	55618	◇	60,437	55,266	9,679	15,120	34,264	584,962	.0119	306,648	**90**	82,599	**175**	7,965	**45**	75,556	12,544	450,626	**247**	Incorporated Place
Pasadena	**L.A.**	56000	**2-S**	136,618	133,936	22,709	52,393	42,981	3,102,482	.0529	1,895,004	**557**	186,345	**396**	152,033	**852**	324,823	84,222	207,570	**114**	Incorporated Place
Perris	**RIV-**	56700	◇	44,003	36,189	11,768	11,839	35,114	517,845	.0136	698,723	**206**	76,098	**162**	3,018	**17**	38,757	7,669	170,290	**93**	Incorporated Place
Petaluma	**SF-O-**	56784	**4-S**	56,472	54,548	25,328	20,473	55,883	1,430,317	.0228	741,851	**218**	68,563	**146**	47,274	**265**	103,017	67,071	665,302	**364**	Incorporated Place
Pico Rivera	**L.A.**	56924	**4-S**	68,032	63,428	10,992	17,507	38,623	747,832	.0140	328,906	**97**	76,137	**162**	8,936	**50**	62,618	22,064	259,350	**142**	Incorporated Place
Pittsburg	**SF-O-**	57456	**4-S**	63,439	56,769	16,400	19,722	43,979	1,040,399	.0168	393,410	**116**	84,186	**179**	26,373	**148**	95,087	12,286	616,901	**338**	Incorporated Place
Placentia	**L.A.**	57526	◇	49,781	46,488	21,323	16,182	54,894	1,061,456	.0165	442,054	**130**	6,751	**14**	9,603	**54**	69,029	43,707	288,940	**158**	Incorporated Place
Pleasant Hill	**SF-O-**	57764	**4-Sm**	32,880	32,837	30,191	13,672	60,100	992,668	.0161	602,235	**177**	159,278	**338**	26,728	**150**	94,447	30,132	(d)	....	Incorporated Place
Pleasanton	**SF-O-**	57792	**4-S**	66,165	63,654	37,198	24,857	75,534	2,461,216	.0375	1,322,003	**389**	243,467	**517**	153,565	**861**	226,663	69,252	188,177	**103**	Incorporated Place
Pomona	**L.A.**	58072	**3-SS**	163,957	149,473	10,948	41,124	37,853	1,795,024	.0363	1,086,736	**320**	76,362	**162**	10,476	**59**	203,413	54,864	742,598	**407**	Incorporated Place
Porterville	**PORT**	58240	**4-B**	45,153	39,615	11,132	13,297	29,322	502,636	.0103	331,805	**98**	63,815	**135**	12,068	**68**	60,095	24,577	96,988	**53**	Incorporated Place
Poway	**SDGO**	58520	◇	48,919	48,044	25,678	15,917	61,938	1,256,140	.0209	759,815	**224**	124,897	**265**	9,759	**55**	92,896	19,099	104,298	**57**	Incorporated Place
Rancho Cordova	**SAC**	59444	◇	61,394	55,060	20,073	22,628	40,431	1,232,375	.0214	742,142	**218**	126,488	**269**	28,719	**161**	117,321	20,043	(d)	....	Census Designated Place
Rancho Cucamonga	**L.A.**	59451	◇	148,419	127,743	20,394	46,602	54,601	3,026,846	.0440	880,075	**259**	161,106	**342**	27,113	**152**	224,911	45,632	977,336	**535**	Incorporated Place
Rancho Palos Verdes	**L.A.**	59514	◇	42,191	41,145	39,894	15,464	78,720	1,683,161	.0182	88,265	**26**	....	....	5,338	**30**	8,910	8,827	(d)	....	Incorporated Place
Rancho Santa Margarita	**L.A.**	59587	◇	49,824	47,214	29,928	17,250	70,403	1,491,121	.0188	281,927	**83**	31,132	**66**	16,816	**94**	59,137	13,558	(d)	....	Incorporated Place
Redding	**REDD**	59920	**3-A**	90,557	80,865	17,942	36,407	33,171	1,624,775	.0293	1,028,019	**302**	213,744	**454**	21,446	**120**	177,975	55,423	77,257	**42**	Incorporated Place
Redlands	**RIV-**	59962	**3-S**	64,564	63,591	22,458	23,489	43,010	1,449,949	.0238	778,834	**229**	121,539	**258**	21,710	**122**	145,361	48,042	99,920	**55**	Incorporated Place
Redondo Beach	**L.A.**	60018	**3-S**	65,456	63,261	30,377	29,286	60,154	1,988,382	.0304	995,782	**293**	155,102	**329**	251,652	**1,410**	155,807	65,107	....	....	Incorporated Place
Redwood City	**SF-O-**	60102	**3-S**	75,967	75,402	30,622	29,017	63,434	2,326,229	.0352	1,126,444	**331**	163,038	**346**	36,700	**206**	214,795	40,015	632,348	**346**	Incorporated Place
Rialto	**RIV-**	60466	◇	105,594	91,873	12,957	27,761	37,679	1,368,132	.0222	363,835	**107**	51,187	**109**	9,349	**52**	134,547	25,115	140,246	**77**	Incorporated Place
Richmond	**SF-O-**	60620	**3-S**	107,138	99,216	17,430	37,253	39,576	1,867,405	.0289	619,124	**182**	99,227	**211**	30,291	**170**	119,643	33,624	985,497	**540**	Incorporated Place
Riverside	**RIV-**	62000	**2-C**	279,527	255,166	17,672	90,638	40,560	4,939,769	.0895	3,145,411	**925**	507,847	**1,078**	193,496	**1,084**	382,369	173,469	789,082	**432**	Incorporated Place
Rocklin	**SAC**	62364	◇	49,494	36,330	25,141	18,170	57,076	1,244,327	.0184	480,702	**141**	121,762	**258**	1,630	**9**	106,017	16,645	85,041	**47**	Incorporated Place
Rohnert Park	**S.ROS**	62546	◇	42,475	42,236	20,978	15,456	46,835	891,061	.0157	579,496	**170**	108,686	**231**	16,529	**93**	137,123	23,920	80,853	**44**	Incorporated Place
Rosemead	**L.A.**	62896	**4-S**	54,805	53,505	10,383	14,103	35,854	569,031	.0112	283,323	**83**	35,200	**75**	17,499	**98**	67,217	17,695	86,277	**47**	Incorporated Place
Roseville	**SAC**	62938	**4-Sr**	103,014	79,921	25,106	40,007	50,625	2,586,219	.0493	2,254,933	**663**	177,240	**376**	73,626	**413**	214,054	87,692	....	....	Incorporated Place
Rowland Heights	**L.A.**	63218	◇	50,903	48,553	16,565	14,698	48,166	843,207	.0230	1,385,530	**408**	205,594	**436**	86,958	**487**	121,211	27,342	(d)	....	Census Designated Place
Rubidoux	**RIV-**	63260	◇	35,064	29,180	14,216	9,666	41,674	498,461	.0082	167,308	**49**	8,502	**18**	2,733	**15**	42,027	3,348	(d)	....	Census Designated Place
Sacramento	**SAC**	64000	**2-AA**	429,197	407,018	17,820	161,790	35,301	7,648,462	.1359	4,592,542	**1,351**	664,727	**1,411**	462,848	**2,594**	757,151	189,499	1,965,437	**1,076**	Incorporated Place
Salinas	**SLNS**	64224	**3-AA**	163,460	151,060	12,169	40,404	40,756	1,989,130	.0436	1,730,009	**509**	215,410	**457**	101,042	**566**	233,851	113,303	345,127	**189**	Incorporated Place
San Bernardino	**RIV-**	65000	**2-C**	193,228	185,401	12,568	57,555	29,851	2,428,430	.0526	2,095,606	**616**	334,384	**710**	86,760	**486**	237,966	62,955	269,114	**147**	Incorporated Place
San Bruno	**SF-O-**	65028	**4-Sm**	38,885	40,165	22,326	14,583	54,797	868,155	.0184	935,783	**275**	330,511	**702**	36,250	**203**	130,411	35,920	(d)	....	Incorporated Place
San Clemente	**L.A.**	65084	◇	53,344	49,936	30,516	20,821	58,190	1,627,834	.0205	311,678	**92**	25,721	**55**	11,294	**63**	94,493	32,673	100,164	**55**	Incorporated Place
San Diego	**SDGO**	66000	**1-A**	1,282,597	1,223,400	21,080	477,165	43,745	27,037,777	.4502	14,625,414	**4,302**	1,342,016	**2,849**	1,350,296	**7,567**	2,446,816	759,655	6,680,426	**3,657**	Incorporated Place
San Dimas	**L.A.**	66070	◇	35,787	34,980	22,188	12,342	55,944	794,052	.0119	296,144	**87**	37,097	**79**	23,788	**133**	82,905	22,221	183,111	**100**	Incorporated Place
San Francisco	**SF-O-**	67000	**1-AA**	743,549	776,733	29,636	332,844	49,555	22,035,600	.3392	11,112,197	**3,269**	976,344	**2,073**	2,204,589	**12,355**	2,006,342	801,356	1,998,438	**1,094**	Incorporated Place
San Gabriel	**L.A.**	67042	**4-S**	43,173	39,804	13,250	13,528	38,584	572,055	.0112	378,766	**111**	35,087	**74**	15,421	**86**	90,736	12,217	22,580	**12**	Incorporated Place
San Jose	**SF-O-**	68000	**2-BB**	913,340	894,943	24,240	293,585	61,164	22,139,043	.3532	11,284,438	**3,319**	1,233,893	**2,619**	574,498	**3,220**	1,979,127	597,618	14,933,197	**8,175**	Incorporated Place
San Juan Capistrano	**L.A.**	68028	◇	36,802	33,826	26,250	11,963	55,753	966,042	.0172	723,417	**213**	82,041	**174**	25,575	**143**	84,668	36,440	125,726	**69**	Incorporated Place
San Leandro	**SF-O-**	68084	**3-SS**	80,466	79,452	22,861	31,735	46,064	1,839,566	.0344	1,470,725	**433**	274,488	**583**	130,344	**730**	196,808	47,408	1,027,711	**563**	Incorporated Place
San Luis Obispo	**S.LUIS**	68154	**3-A**	44,199	44,174	21,756	19,205	32,919	961,584	.0186	821,148	**242**	62,401	**132**	51,678	**290**	123,288	59,983	124,966	**68**	Incorporated Place
San Marcos	**SDGO**	68196	◇	62,260	54,977	17,519	20,725	43,377	1,090,706	.0187	568,801	**167**	32,164	**68**	15,783	**88**	86,449	20,855	500,039	**274**	Incorporated Place
San Mateo	**SF-O-**	68252	**3-SS**	91,614	92,482	30,596	37,946	58,360	2,803,038	.0519	2,425,437	**713**	495,023	**1,051**	350,492	**1,964**	305,843	162,318	39,341	**22**	Incorporated Place
San Pablo	**SF-O-**	68294	**4-S**	34,712	30,215	14,784	10,340	40,519	513,197	.0102	384,345	**113**	69,899	**148**	32,221	**181**	60,739	12,351	(d)	....	Incorporated Place
San Rafael	**SF-O-**	68364	**3-S**	56,513	56,063	27,201	22,491	55,410	1,537,219	.0269	1,101,458	**324**	104,590	**222**	35,342	**198**	120,984	32,683	129,558	**71**	Incorporated Place
San Ramon	**SF-O-**	68378	◇	46,251	44,722	37,445	17,417	80,333	1,731,891	.0233	582,237	**171**	40,608	**86**	14,755	**83**	180,562	39,780	(d)	....	Incorporated Place
Santa Ana	**L.A.**	69000	**2-S**	355,526	337,977	11,266	77,291	41,672	4,005,339	.0849	2,954,225	**869**	307,657	**653**	281,365	**1,577**	526,471	131,719	2,343,812	**1,283**	Incorporated Place
Santa Barbara	**S.BAR**	69070	**3-AA**	95,212	92,325	23,410	36,700	45,156	2,228,903	.0402	1,633,391	**480**	65,785	**140**	199,658	**1,119**	250,846	114,450	146,777	**80**	Incorporated Place
Santa Clara	**SF-O-**	69084	**3-S**	102,724	102,361	28,021	40,193	60,291	2,878,403	.0600	3,182,490	**936**	359,659	**763**	431,628	**2,419**	303,023	152,160	7,469,243	**4,089**	Incorporated Place
Santa Clarita	**L.A.**	69088	◇	168,950	151,088	22,081	56,312	58,318	3,730,646	.0560	1,382,713	**407**	218,651	**464**	78,319	**439**	201,813	71,805	101,915	**56**	Incorporated Place
Santa Cruz	**S.CRZ**	69112	**3-C**	53,084	54,593	23,792	20,339	46,830	1,262,986	.0195	565,120	**166**	41,066	**87**	32,987	**185**	95,038	75,785	498,363	**273**	Incorporated Place
Santa Fe Springs	**L.A.**	69154	**4-S**	19,295	17,438	11,858	5,294	41,799	228,800	.0090	641,908	**189**	36,387	**77**	8,178	**46**	25,221	14,282	1,504,180	**823**	Incorporated Place
Santa Maria	**S.MAR**	69196	**3-B**	81,050	77,423	12,269	23,141	34,971	994,388	.0231	1,019,569	**300**	164,237	**349**	52,244	**293**	129,006	64,378	283,543	**155**	Incorporated Place
Santa Monica	**L.A.**	70000	**3-SS**	87,456	84,084	36,009	45,719	48,574	3,149,245	.0544	2,404,290	**707**	150,049	**319**	318,024	**1,782**	250,372	139,596	330,028	**181**	Incorporated Place
Santa Paula	**OXN-**	70042	◇	31,087	28,598	15,556	8,832	39,399	483,596	.0078	173,827	**51**	16,053	**34**	2,612	**15**	50,274	12,394	(d)	....	Incorporated Place
Santa Rosa	**S.ROS**	70098	**3-CC**	156,149	147,595	23,366	58,754	46,785	3,648,607	.0636	2,427,546	**714**	283,662	**602**	165,125	**925**	395,779	171,395	1,199,566	**657**	Incorporated Place
Santee	**SDGO**	70224	◇	53,077	52,975	18,662	18,714	48,280	990,546	.0166	506,317	**149**	120,094	**255**	9,977	**56**	42,398	25,217	132,407	**72**	Incorporated Place
Saratoga	**SF-O-**	70280	◇	28,904	29,843	60,939	10,521	111,298	1,761,371	.0183	126,312	**37**	....	....	4,760	**27**	38,447	15,701	(d)	....	Incorporated Place

. . . . Data less than 1,000.
(d) Data not available.
◇ Not classified as a Principal Business Center.

* Data from 1997 Census of Manufactures.

continued on next page

Principal Business Centers and Other Places with 27,500 or More: Population / Income / Sales, *Continued*

PLACE NAME	RANALLY METRO AREA	FIPS PLACE CODE	RANALLY CITY RATING	POPULATION Estimate 7/1/04	POPULATION Census 4/1/00	PER CAPITA INCOME 2003	HOUSE-HOLDS Estimate 7/1/04	MEDIAN HOUSEHOLD INCOME 2003	DISPOSABLE INCOME 2003 ($1,000)	MARKET ABILITY INDEX 2003	TOTAL RETAIL TRADE Sales 2003 ($1,000)	TOTAL RETAIL TRADE Ranally Sales Units	GENERAL MERCHANDISE Sales 2003 ($1,000)	GENERAL MERCHANDISE Ranally Sales Units	APPAREL STORES Sales 2003 ($1,000)	APPAREL STORES Ranally Sales Units	FOOD STORE SALES 2003 ($1,000)	HEALTH & DRUG STORE SALES 2003 ($1,000)	MANUFACTURERS VALUE ADDED 1997* ($1,000)	Ranally Mfg Units	PLACE TYPE
Seaside	MTRY-	70742	◇	33,379	31,696	13,500	10,109	38,129	450,602	.0111	561,979	165	68,972	146	12,411	70	25,251	16,566	(d)	....	Incorporated Place
Simi Valley	L.A.	72016	3-S	117,157	111,351	24,756	38,287	61,658	2,900,287	.0444	1,289,710	379	123,372	262	50,029	280	227,465	66,768	646,633	354	Incorporated Place
South Gate	L.A.	73080	4-Sr	105,303	96,375	8,810	25,142	33,435	927,690	.0198	518,805	153	75,469	160	11,887	67	110,476	25,736	591,688	324	Incorporated Place
South Lake Tahoe		73108	4-C	25,677	23,609	20,693	10,273	37,042	531,342	.0081	203,408	60	14,533	31	33,075	185	48,110	10,830	(d)	....	Incorporated Place
South San Francisco	SF-O-	73262	4-S	61,359	60,552	19,576	20,480	54,164	1,201,162	.0228	938,679	276	91,409	194	7,284	41	188,264	56,896	1,477,988	809	Incorporated Place
South Whittier	L.A.	73430	◇	57,866	55,193	13,348	15,245	44,676	772,411	.0132	288,249	85	....	....	8,214	46	57,889	6,057	(d)	....	Census Designated Place
Spring Valley	SDGO	73696	◇	28,106	26,663	17,647	9,741	42,550	495,973	.0075	148,233	44	12,123	26	1,297	7	15,932	19,634	(d)	....	Census Designated Place
Stanton	L.A.	73962	◇	39,431	37,403	13,452	11,421	38,632	530,407	.0101	315,447	93	43,929	93	10,752	60	83,298	12,189	66,689	37	Incorporated Place
Stockton	STOC	75000	2-A	272,349	243,771	15,216	87,405	34,895	4,144,165	.0712	1,911,681	562	267,921	569	116,152	651	393,228	138,030	774,595	424	Incorporated Place
Sunnyvale	SF-O-	77000	3-S	132,258	131,760	32,919	54,829	64,759	4,353,849	.0673	2,339,078	688	224,982	478	106,674	598	331,790	97,671	7,469,489	4,089	Incorporated Place
Temecula		78120	◇	89,807	57,716	19,887	28,660	54,360	1,786,016	.0300	951,260	280	130,147	276	30,935	173	126,557	26,131	843,028	462	Incorporated Place
Temple City	L.A.	78148	◇	35,571	33,377	16,752	11,977	43,645	595,882	.0095	214,197	63	37,018	79	21,431	120	56,517	17,227	(d)	....	Incorporated Place
Thousand Oaks	OXN-	78582	3-S	123,506	117,005	32,323	44,110	66,367	3,992,122	.0615	2,099,200	617	218,225	463	134,111	752	359,005	126,142	342,749	188	Incorporated Place
Torrance	L.A.	80000	2-S	141,062	137,946	22,364	55,161	49,585	3,154,720	.0659	3,289,088	968	387,099	822	321,415	1,801	271,375	148,894	1,849,269	1,012	Incorporated Place
Tracy		80238	◇	75,538	56,929	18,860	23,269	55,825	1,424,682	.0243	775,214	228	143,696	305	61,244	343	117,372	43,095	264,366	145	Incorporated Place
Tulare	VISL	80644	◇	49,818	43,994	12,240	15,076	31,734	609,756	.0114	312,198	92	65,057	138	23,298	131	41,638	12,183	206,316	113	Incorporated Place
Turlock	MOD	80812	4-C	65,787	55,810	15,594	21,412	36,169	1,025,911	.0189	631,763	186	86,720	184	23,935	134	159,204	33,468	409,913	224	Incorporated Place
Tustin	L.A.	80854	4-S	72,613	67,504	23,313	25,757	52,416	1,692,837	.0329	1,512,286	445	113,314	241	106,543	597	184,137	72,854	833,818	456	Incorporated Place
Ukiah		81134	4-C	15,985	15,497	17,963	6,232	34,049	287,131	.0060	273,744	81	41,173	87	2,312	13	60,567	12,898	39,321	22	Incorporated Place
Union City	SF-O-	81204	◇	69,162	66,869	20,489	19,776	62,353	1,417,090	.0216	528,272	155	72,487	154	7,825	44	174,573	26,878	360,615	197	Incorporated Place
Upland	L.A.	81344	3-S	73,026	68,393	21,793	25,713	44,657	1,591,428	.0248	689,268	203	75,297	160	15,825	89	149,486	44,261	99,138	54	Incorporated Place
Vacaville	FRFL-	81554	◇	95,239	88,625	21,421	30,861	51,624	2,040,094	.0332	1,025,073	302	155,874	331	83,880	470	213,437	42,748	217,827	119	Incorporated Place
Vallejo	SF-O-	81666	3-S	121,499	116,760	20,579	42,039	45,336	2,500,304	.0391	1,042,932	307	191,112	406	25,311	142	144,482	58,765	84,067	46	Incorporated Place
Ventura	OXN-	65042	3-CC	105,271	100,916	23,313	40,181	47,045	2,454,197	.0440	1,767,110	520	125,146	266	54,352	305	241,784	100,363	225,031	123	Incorporated Place
Victorville	HESP-	82590	4-C	67,020	64,029	14,867	21,452	35,573	996,358	.0213	922,470	271	164,767	350	51,597	289	131,252	39,643	128,099	70	Incorporated Place
Visalia	VISL	82954	3-AA	101,106	91,565	16,255	33,472	38,518	1,643,522	.0301	1,023,556	301	183,098	389	52,232	293	194,525	50,526	373,411	204	Incorporated Place
Vista	SDGO	82996	◇	98,379	89,857	16,831	31,907	41,800	1,655,851	.0278	769,268	226	102,603	218	25,046	140	141,035	41,298	390,261	214	Incorporated Place
Walnut	L.A.	83332	◇	30,638	30,004	18,873	8,360	62,965	578,218	.0085	163,329	48	....	....	4,829	27	33,687	5,322	77,308	42	Incorporated Place
Walnut Creek	SF-O-	83346	3-SS	65,352	64,296	37,704	30,619	58,928	2,464,004	.0378	1,363,819	401	118,259	251	183,325	1,027	181,264	87,675	239,193	131	Incorporated Place
Watsonville	WATS	83668	4-C	46,814	44,265	14,022	12,326	41,192	656,437	.0116	315,468	93	39,477	84	9,491	53	72,113	11,419	268,444	147	Incorporated Place
West Covina	L.A.	84200	3-S	113,640	105,080	15,817	33,594	47,792	1,797,411	.0348	1,302,683	383	277,990	590	163,860	918	149,800	49,109	(d)	....	Incorporated Place
West Hollywood	L.A.	84410	◇	35,562	35,716	41,195	22,789	40,994	1,464,961	.0198	537,017	158	20,568	44	88,925	498	116,448	48,101	(d)	....	Incorporated Place
Westminster	L.A.	84550	3-S	92,055	88,207	16,028	27,696	44,095	1,475,423	.0346	1,770,348	521	316,462	672	140,826	789	285,275	75,222	96,068	53	Incorporated Place
Westmont	L.A.	84592	◇	33,153	31,623	9,162	9,601	25,708	303,739	.0055	69,509	20	14,490	31	3,096	17	26,001	4,161	(d)	....	Census Designated Place
West Sacramento	SAC	84816	◇	33,505	31,615	14,487	11,935	31,057	485,386	.0093	315,880	93	4,566	10	8,901	50	83,795	6,901	342,378	187	Incorporated Place
Whittier	L.A.	85292	3-S	89,226	83,680	17,832	29,840	44,673	1,591,051	.0258	674,543	198	99,793	212	43,145	242	123,961	43,089	158,062	87	Incorporated Place
Willowbrook	L.A.	85614	◇	35,791	34,138	8,060	8,800	25,399	288,478	.0056	80,976	24	3,122	7	1,449	8	24,753	5,031	(d)	....	Census Designated Place
Woodland		86328	4-C	54,828	49,151	16,473	18,468	40,674	903,203	.0161	513,146	151	78,275	166	10,755	60	110,431	32,132	205,393	112	Incorporated Place
Yorba Linda	L.A.	86832	◇	62,331	58,918	31,153	20,525	73,986	1,941,820	.0261	572,446	168	85,287	181	11,713	66	137,892	30,850	116,866	64	Incorporated Place
Yuba City	YUCY	86972	3-A	42,701	36,758	15,669	15,175	33,485	669,077	.0129	479,279	141	114,222	242	20,532	115	81,477	23,780	116,044	64	Incorporated Place
Yucaipa	RIV-	87042	◇	49,883	41,207	19,158	18,014	36,716	955,656	.0131	165,651	49	5,178	11	2,229	12	64,617	15,575	(d)	....	Incorporated Place
Colorado																					
Arvada	DEN	03455	4-S	102,446	102,153	22,673	40,011	49,983	2,322,751	.0335	725,630	213	108,178	230	16,753	94	192,712	37,227	251,554	138	Incorporated Place
Aurora	DEN	04000	3-SS	305,447	276,393	18,609	119,114	43,735	5,684,104	.1061	4,098,897	1,206	749,132	1,590	156,359	876	573,456	155,902	172,675	95	Incorporated Place
Boulder	BOUL-	07850	3-CC	93,562	94,673	25,050	39,845	45,390	2,343,715	.0390	1,399,646	412	92,990	197	79,247	444	304,189	42,708	1,002,806	549	Incorporated Place
Broomfield	DEN	09280	◇	43,078	....	27,853	16,723	58,226	1,199,860	.0158	285,950	84	46,987	100	....	....	56,562	10,324	919,582	503	Incorporated Place
Castle Rock	DEN	12415	◇	29,812	20,224	28,314	10,668	61,785	844,104	.0119	290,542	85	20,827	44	59,995	336	39,762	7,842	(d)	....	Incorporated Place
Colorado Springs	CSPG	16000	2-A	382,538	360,890	20,474	150,072	42,208	7,832,053	.1491	6,268,180	1,844	1,032,355	2,191	179,629	1,007	645,884	246,756	2,600,880	1,424	Incorporated Place
Denver	DEN	20000	1-A	558,164	554,636	20,119	243,468	36,894	11,229,470	.2038	7,783,528	2,290	789,445	1,676	388,679	2,178	972,182	306,321	2,525,048	1,382	Incorporated Place
Durango		22035	4-B	14,725	13,922	19,029	5,956	35,689	280,209	.0061	301,117	89	25,254	54	12,516	70	48,527	9,240	(d)	....	Incorporated Place
Englewood	DEN	24785	3-S	32,221	31,727	27,506	14,895	38,727	886,258	.0185	984,075	289	52,423	111	19,972	112	116,200	36,710	351,086	192	Incorporated Place
Fort Collins	FTCL-	27425	3-A	126,771	118,652	21,547	50,436	43,242	2,731,473	.0486	1,852,647	545	360,258	765	65,297	366	244,340	57,991	1,099,468	602	Incorporated Place
Grand Junction	GDJC	31660	3-A	43,228	41,986	18,637	18,528	32,449	805,624	.0189	1,016,143	299	250,491	532	23,625	132	87,652	28,387	241,154	132	Incorporated Place
Greeley	GRLY	32155	3-A	83,659	76,930	16,955	29,785	36,112	1,418,432	.0281	1,149,618	338	223,549	475	19,820	111	115,077	38,239	376,315	206	Incorporated Place
Highlands Ranch	DEN	36410	◇	95,975	70,931	29,191	33,276	72,138	2,801,624	.0354	531,398	156	158,569	337	47,747	268	95,384	22,364	(d)	....	Census Designated Place
Ken Caryl	DEN	40377	◇	31,622	30,887	26,680	11,431	61,552	843,687	.0119	272,352	80	64,979	138	11,575	65	48,334	18,668	(d)	....	Census Designated Place
Lakewood	DEN	43000	3-SS	146,344	144,126	23,785	62,944	44,248	3,480,728	.0579	2,023,815	595	461,007	979	93,085	522	291,994	75,503	278,422	152	Incorporated Place
Littleton	DEN	45255	4-S	41,004	40,340	24,845	17,980	47,446	1,018,759	.0210	1,060,165	312	184,271	391	45,935	257	136,154	65,699	165,055	90	Incorporated Place
Longmont	BOUL-	45970	4-C	81,708	71,093	19,514	31,147	47,898	1,594,433	.0304	1,248,919	367	230,246	489	21,910	123	191,215	50,327	305,367	167	Incorporated Place
Loveland	FTCL-	46465	4-B	54,223	50,608	21,616	21,742	45,353	1,172,108	.0202	717,698	211	134,760	286	36,567	205	103,283	15,798	734,884	402	Incorporated Place
Northglenn	DEN	54330	4-Sm	36,344	31,575	19,618	13,319	46,872	713,004	.0112	288,379	85	27,688	59	1,094	6	36,062	10,146	47,252	26	Incorporated Place
Parker	DEN	57630	◇	41,153	23,558	26,711	13,884	68,506	1,099,235	.0137	153,823	45	26,647	57	1,973	11	60,018	2,981	(d)	....	Incorporated Place
Pueblo	PUEB	62000	3-AA	99,388	102,121	14,706	39,530	28,717	1,461,611	.0319	1,410,407	415	364,836	774	23,984	134	179,883	46,409	264,716	145	Incorporated Place
Southglenn	DEN	72505	◇	46,753	43,520	30,656	18,025	62,525	1,433,268	.0295	1,578,103	464	261,243	555	92,836	520	232,469	33,187	(d)	....	Census Designated Place
Sterling		73935	4-C	10,966	11,360	15,880	4,471	30,707	174,136	.0036	156,958	46	38,543	82	3,996	22	13,971	6,355	(d)	....	Incorporated Place
Thornton	DEN	77290	4-S	98,305	82,384	18,610	34,386	46,812	1,829,414	.0278	603,720	178	81,629	173	1,631	9	105,689	11,679	122,070	67	Incorporated Place
Westminster	DEN	83835	4-S	109,336	100,940	23,039	41,432	50,362	2,519,011	.0398	1,198,085	352	194,940	414	53,359	299	190,685	38,303	203,426	111	Incorporated Place
Wheat Ridge	DEN	84440	4-Sr	33,989	32,913	20,485	15,398	36,487	696,265	.0156	820,560	241	111,785	237	11,969	67	139,499	17,904	145,842	80	Incorporated Place
Connecticut																					
Ansonia	N.Y.	01150	4-S	19,147	18,554	20,116	7,838	39,745	385,164	.0067	237,240	70	....	....	2,905	16	79,704	18,795	74,334	41	Incorporated Place
Branford	N.HAV	07310	◇	29,992	28,683	31,746	13,247	50,884	952,140	.0149	526,569	155	37,633	80	17,477	98	79,636	35,906	269,377	147	Minor Civil Division-Town
Bridgeport	N.Y.	08000	2-C	139,187	139,529	13,420	50,672	32,727	1,867,834	.0364	1,218,018	358	19,802	42	37,472	210	161,156	100,840	757,957	415	Incorporated Place
Bristol	H-NB	08420	3-S	60,120	60,062	23,138	25,310	42,780	1,391,041	.0222	692,325	204	35,513	75	30,513	171	186,215	50,446	361,069	198	Incorporated Place
Cheshire	N.HAV	14160	◇	30,379	28,543	31,590	10,063	66,466	959,666	.0160	633,846	186		....	11,157	63	54,393	32,972	187,434	103	Minor Civil Division-Town
Danbury	N.Y.	18430	3-SS	78,727	74,848	19,521	28,869	49,031	1,536,823	.0390	2,306,216	678	264,233	561	233,147	1,307	299,937	114,332	731,675	401	Incorporated Place
Derby	N.Y.	19480	4-S	12,718	12,391	22,968	5,450	41,804	292,111	.0054	229,760	68	38,585	82	14,337	80	3,740	28,237	(d)	....	Incorporated Place
East Hartford	H-NB	22630	4-S	51,290	49,575	21,487	21,239	38,577	1,102,045	.0201	797,619	235	30,355	64	32,365	181	127,096	62,675	867,842	475	Minor Civil Division-Town
East Haven	N.HAV	22910	◇	29,484	28,189	20,665	11,830	39,011	609,274	.0097	275,411	81	14,829	31	15,040	84	66,705	26,187	46,498	25	Minor Civil Division-Town
Enfield	H-NB	25990	4-S	46,647	45,212	21,908	17,200	47,098	1,021,922	.0181	689,823	203	120,666	256	54,149	303	141,320	45,913	269,800	148	Minor Civil Division-Town
Fairfield	N.Y.	26620	4-S	59,245	57,340	33,273	21,262	72,184	1,971,243	.0333	1,384,109	407	67,108	142	83,276	467	165,346	67,545	103,514	57	Minor Civil Division-Town
Glastonbury	H-NB	31240	◇	33,714	31,876	36,265	13,152	67,862	1,222,649	.0162	375,465	110	....	....	28,069	157	94,324	24,218	93,391	51	Minor Civil Division-Town
Greenwich	N.Y.	33620	3-S	62,622	61,101	54,455	24,012	83,356	3,410,073	.0463	1,427,504	420	12,896	27	122,764	688	147,784	62,413	169,150	93	Minor Civil Division-Town
Groton	N.LON-	34250	◇	40,208	39,907	23,908	15,910	42,897	961,288	.0185	843,036	248	110,233	234	37,907	212	127,144	45,983	59,542	33	Minor Civil Division-Town
Hamden	N.HAV	35650	4-S	60,396	56,913	26,377	24,040	47,162	1,593,039	.0236	645,300	190	37,631	80	80,614	452	135,359	52,037	114,958	63	Minor Civil Division-Town
Hartford	H-NB	37000	2-AA	121,199	121,578	14,442	45,523	23,948	1,750,316	.0326	1,040,929	306	18,659	40	55,821	313	126,646	98,744	130,684	72	Incorporated Place
Manchester	H-NB	44700	3-S	56,312	54,740	25,795	24,211	44,555	1,452,577	.0314	1,701,176	500	371,801	789	142,807	800	195,754	64,101	456,245	250	Minor Civil Division-Town
Meriden	N.HAV	46450	3-B	58,956	58,244	20,734	23,467	40,154	1,222,397	.0210	732,223	215	117,388	249	97,905	549	101,787	55,982	378,759	207	Incorporated Place
Middletown	H-NB	47290	3-S	43,468	43,167	27,678	18,970	43,343	1,203,090	.0181	540,592	159	30,583	65	20,920	117	71,858	60,288	705,669	386	Incorporated Place
Milford	N.Y.	47515	3-S	53,159	50,594	27,644	21,328	53,809	1,469,552	.0271	1,223,004	360	157,487	334	103,852	582	89,793	62,570	720,445	394	Incorporated Place
Naugatuck	WATB	49880	◇	31,453	30,989	22,899	12,136	45,407	720,250	.0109	284,700	84	38,814	82	3,666	21	111,451	16,839	378,644	207	Incorporated Place
New Britain	H-NB	50370	3-C	71,765	71,538	18,698	29,004	32,534	1,341,882	.0210	516,498	152	41,204	87	10,892	61	68,520	42,963	497,710	272	Incorporated Place
New Haven	N.HAV	52000	2-AA	123,832	123,626	17,726	47,598	29,189	2,195,029	.0365	1,032,779	304	58,194	124	74,466	417	160,833	129,987	413,807	227	Incorporated Place
Newington	H-NB	52140	◇	29,868	29,306	26,603	12,419	51,132	794,578	.0151	698,917	206	59,152	126	19,817	111	103,804	46,885	216,162	118	Minor Civil Division-Town
New London	N.LON-	52280	3-AA	25,711	25,671	19,339	10,416	31,744	497,212	.0100	443,729	131	....	....	20,466	115	21,571	26,211	(d)	....	Incorporated Place
New Milford	N.Y.	52630	◇	30,017	27,121	29,202	11,224	58,593	876,542	.0134	423,013	124	40,358	86	5,406	30	87,681	16,348	612,707	335	Minor Civil Division-Town
Norwalk	N.Y.	55990	3-SS	85,226	82,951	26,256	33,837	54,294	2,237,698	.0468	2,452,437	721	81,443	173	90,661	508	283,846	65,360	889,946	487	Incorporated Place
Norwich	N.LON-	56200	4-B	36,250	36,117	22,203	15,489	36,485	804,864	.0141	528,633	156	93,082	198	18,161	102	104,335	40,768	138,999	76	Incorporated Place
Orange	N.HAV	57600	4-Sm	13,850	13,233	35,217	5,017	66,570	487,760	.0115	723,554	213	121,485	258	21,139	118	113,877	33,324	60,288	33	Minor Civil Division-Town
Shelton	N.Y.	68100	◇	39,023	38,101	23,015	14,629	58,782	898,107	.0150	515,971	152	39,519	84	11,569	65	124,144	4,625	441,241	242	Incorporated Place
Southington	H-NB	70550	4-S	40,324	39,728	25,223	15,550	53,261	1,017,090	.0168	594,581	175	43,773	93	18,873	106	119,331	53,116	181,417	99	Minor Civil Division-Town
Stamford	N.Y.	73000	2-S	120,350	117,083	27,301	47,041	54,780	3,285,673	.0555	2,143,830	631	166,274	353	169,647	951	224,302	87,008	1,644,778	900	Incorporated Place
Stratford	N.Y.	74190	4-S	49,955	49,976	20,855	20,070	48,062	1,041,790	.0255	1,484,194	437	24,064	51	46,962	263	167,676	55,832	1,119,345	613	Minor Civil Division-Town
Torrington	TORR	76500	4-C	36,769	35,202	22,727	15,596	39,049	835,643	.0160	708,436	208	68,923	146	25,894	145	131,649	38,661	240,502	132	Incorporated Place
Trumbull	N.Y.	77200	4-Sm	34,738	34,243	26,477	12,163	66,698	919,773	.0191	995,590	293	202,896	431	137,570	771	93,405	29,465	41,104	23	Minor Civil Division-Town
Vernon	H-NB	78250	4-S	27,946	28,063	28,322	12,403	42,903	791,488	.0126	436,047	128	25,584	54	26,798	150	92,687	52,525	44,272	24	Minor Civil Division-Town
Wallingford	N.HAV	78740	4-S	45,013	43,026	26,075	17,638	51,384	1,173,692	.0196	726,811	214	98,645	209	11,684	65	105,193	28,905	596,755	327	Minor Civil Division-Town
Waterbury	WATB	80000	3-BB	107,891	107,271	18,263	43,287	32,736	1,970,407	.0359	1,302,283	383	239,519	508	81,784	458	207,258	102,195	531,402	291	Incorporated Place
West Hartford	H-NB	82590	3-S	66,640	63,589	32,695	26,097	54,638	2,178,768	.0299	736,508	217	92,613	197	98,322	551	96,211	77,168	319,242	175	Minor Civil Division-Town
West Haven	N.HAV	82800	4-S	52,588	52,360	21,295	21,354	39,363	1,119,885	.0164	354,130	104	15,232	32	8,730	49	54,657	47,535	1,116,307	611	Incorporated Place
Westport	N.Y.	83500	4-S	26,556	25,749	64,864	9,956	100,052	1,722,540	.0238	807,708	238	2,701	6	116,735	654	96,233	44,026	(d)	....	Minor Civil Division-Town
Wethersfield	H-NB	84900	4-S	26,973	26,271	28,350	11,696	48,191	764,695	.0107	250,996	74	5,776	12	25,187	141	71,889	38,338	(d)	....	Minor Civil Division-Town
Windsor	H-NB	87000	◇	28,608	28,237	27,880	10,867	55,557	797,599	.0110	248,114	73	34,839	74	3,936	22	47,993	19,015	364,719	200	Minor Civil Division-Town
Delaware																					
Dover	DOVR	21200	3-A	33,931	32,135	19,027	13,252	38,046	645,600	.0130	577,106	170	151,020	321	19,485	109	68,836	26,122	845,914	463	Incorporated Place
Newark	PHIL-	50670	4-S	29,148	28,547	20,338	9,429	53,054	592,826	.0116	504,470	148	26,291	56	14,228	80	91,268	29,700	....	....	Incorporated Place
Wilmington	PHIL-	77580	2-BB	72,942	72,664	18,757	29,564	33,898	1,368,200	.0246	887,818	261	51,951	110	34,070	191	139,868	61,449	....	....	Incorporated Place
District of Columbia																					
Washington	WASH	50000	1-AA	560,725	572,059	26,337	256,560	37,242	14,767,850	.1959	3,408,245	1,003	145,053	308	469,245	2,630	940,510	481,206	170,849	94	Incorporated Place
Florida																					
Altamonte Springs	ORL	00950	3-Sm	43,175	41,200	24,610	20,619	39,322	1,062,542	.0201	905,228	266	235,683	500	115,457	647	83,855	53,956	(d)	....	Incorporated Place
Apopka	ORL	01700	◇	32,928	26,642	19,049	12,453	40,417	627,255	.0095	208,104	61	24,839	53	3,733	21	51,117	12,456	72,884	40	Incorporated Place
Aventura	MIA-	02681	◇	28,229	25,267	33,873	16,268	41,072	956,197	.0162	678,339	200	252,700	536	153,307	859	43,859	43,386	(d)	....	Incorporated Place
Bal Harbour	MIA-	03275	4-Sm	3,347	3,305	38,942	2,007	41,106	130,338	.0023	108,895	32	22,465	48	60,858	341	3,969	8,151	(d)	....	Incorporated Place
Boca Raton	MIA-	07300	3-B	77,835	74,764	37,565	36,759	51,238	2,923,839	.0453	1,665,528	490	268,585	570	357,128	2,001	249,619	143,220	300,389	164	Incorporated Place
Bonita Springs	NAP	07525	◇	35,618	32,797	30,622	16,244	44,614	1,090,679	.0157	437,616	129	31,628	67	9,025	51	62,438	33,545	(d)	....	Incorporated Place
Boynton Beach	MIA-	07875	◇	69,460	60,389	21,834	33,371	37,192	1,516,603	.0275	1,091,593	321	255,206	542	120,414	675	160,667	89,290	....	....	Incorporated Place
Bradenton	SAR-B	07950	3-B	51,385	49,504	19,630	22,272	33,423	1,008,674	.0197	843,695	248	138,560	294	80,170	449	108,857	68,314	....	....	Incorporated Place
Brandon	TAM	08150	◇	85,529	77,895	21,443	32,969	46,405	1,833,959	.0327	1,243,798	366	309,184	656	105,677	592	151,426	96,110	(d)	....	Census Designated Place
Cape Coral	FTMY-	10275	◇	118,762	102,286	19,224	47,880	40,246	2,283,111	.0368	1,013,027	298	206,968	439	41,545	233	188,432	78,844	24,819	14	Incorporated Place
Carol City	MIA-	10650	◇	62,472	59,443	11,253	17,902	36,152	703,015	.0118	166,586	49	2,193	5	3,029	17	28,478	14,512	(d)	....	Census Designated Place
Clearwater	ST.PET	12875	2-B	111,048	108,787	23,907	54,742	35,050	2,654,871	.0559	2,876,270	846	425,199	903	158,936	891	282,991	135,688	198,000	108	Incorporated Place
Cocoa	MELB-	13150	3-S	15,981	16,412	17,610	7,201	26,218	281,430	.0059	271,558	80	5,114	11	2,759	15	37,483	9,099	(d)	....	Incorporated Place
Coconut Creek	MIA-	13275	◇	53,145	43,566	24,805	25,700	41,451	1,318,245	.0222	814,460	240	8,448	18	20,547	115	56,160	28,327	(d)	....	Incorporated Place
Cooper City	MIA-	14125	◇	28,887	27,939	22,623	9,919	56,101	653,516	.0101	279,965	82	101,238	215	31,312	175	30,146	15,879	(d)	....	Incorporated Place
Coral Gables	MIA-	14250	3-S	42,227	42,249	33,358	17,479	52,736	1,408,615	.0233	933,761	275	72,415	154	83,637	469	110,260	52,571	(d)	....	Incorporated Place
Coral Springs	MIA-	14400	◇	127,789	117,549	24,157	45,056	54,892	3,087,005	.0476	1,387,856	408	272,481	578	118,566	664	281,464	108,759	70,588	39	Incorporated Place
Country Club	MIA-	14895	◇	38,158	36,310	17,199	14,114	39,808	656,273	.0115	360,559	106	58,509	124	6,707	38	69,665	46,802	(d)	....	Census Designated Place
Davie	MIA-	16475	◇	87,866	75,720	22,477	34,955	46,151	1,974,941	.0317	982,390	289	95,291	202	49,107	275	190,837	68,738	85,217	47	Incorporated Place
Daytona Beach	D.BCH	16525	2-A	62,550	64,112	18,208	30,287	25,492	1,138,929	.0313	1,945,722	572	281,981	599	125,775	705	128,654	104,352	102,946	56	Incorporated Place
Deerfield Beach	MIA-	16725	◇	72,126	64,583	23,355	36,733	32,754	1,684,519	.0312	1,329,476	391	114,016	242	42,659	239	196,844	104,355	174,195	95	Incorporated Place
De Land	DL	16875	4-C	23,778	20,904	19,217	10,357	31,832	456,933	.0085	336,283	99	34,503	73	12,632	71	72,370	29,336	92,053	50	Incorporated Place
Delray Beach	MIA-	17100	4-S	67,820	60,020	26,477	33,602	40,202	1,795,685	.0352	1,707,119	502	86,951	185	72,508	406	101,236	44,117	44,625	24	Incorporated Place
Deltona	ORL	17200	◇	84,436	69,543	17,083	32,824	37,197	1,442,417	.0199	190,369	56	1,696	4	1,014	6	122,385	18,930	(d)	....	Incorporated Place
Dunedin	ST.PET	18575	◇	35,150	35,691	24,031	18,750	33,331	844,700	.0127	338,316	100	5,466	12	7,382	41	136,093	34,926	(d)	....	Incorporated Place
East Lake	ST.PET	19206	◇	29,583	29,394	31,674	13,171	58,390	937,013	.0123	244,521	72	29,479	63	2,181	12	55,657	25,147	(d)	....	Census Designated Place
Egypt Lake-Leto	TAM	20108	◇	35,996	32,782	17,067	15,417	31,266	614,333	.0142	727,437	214	4,141	9	16,042	90	32,187	25,438	(d)	....	Census Designated Place
Fort Lauderdale	MIA-	24000	2-BB	155,792	152,397	26,543	73,650	36,679	4,135,231	.0786	3,647,393	1,073	208,898	443	222,177	1,245	423,108	231,663	543,417	298	Incorporated Place
Fort Myers	FTMY-	24125	2-A	51,292	48,208	16,010	20,514	28,421	821,205	.0248	1,606,806	473	288,140	612	110,926	622	74,723	75,375	179,260	98	Incorporated Place
Fort Pierce	FTPI	24300	3-A	38,826	37,516	16,469	16,048	26,343	639,438	.0133	577,340	170	76,953	163	13,640	76	66,080	40,721	(d)	....	Incorporated Place
Fort Walton Beach	FTWL	24475	3-A	19,940	19,973	23,403	9,770	35,817	466,660	.0114	677,093	199	30,057	64	11,217	63	49,850	19,147	113,486	62	Incorporated Place
Fountainbleau	MIA-	24562	◇	62,583	59,549	13,062	22,825	31,274	817,436	.0187	830,200	244	209,889	446	81,179	455	46,030	48,294	(d)	....	Census Designated Place
Gainesville	GAIN	25175	3-AA	91,090	95,447	15,144	35,947	29,634	1,379,481	.0309	1,442,272	424	233,931	497	96,475	541	210,301	63,562	162,917	89	Incorporated Place
Golden Glades	MIA-	26375	◇	34,285	32,623	11,636	10,740	30,043	398,942	.0090	362,643	107	24,388	52	17,788	100	42,176	23,888	(d)	....	Census Designated Place
Greenacres City	MIA-	27322	◇	31,881	27,569	20,675	15,451	37,833	659,151	.0106	313,475	92	74,298	158	14,216	80	38,381	27,145	(d)	....	Incorporated Place
Hallandale Beach	MIA-	28450	4-S	37,933	34,282	21,317	20,937	26,286	808,629	.0140	501,247	147	35,602	76	19,820	111	112,360	35,413	43,814	24	Incorporated Place
Hialeah	MIA-	30000	2-S	238,229	226,419	11,935	77,412	29,340	2,843,378	.0606	2,239,087	659	238,712	507	187,084	1,048	410,175	224,545	939,116	514	Incorporated Place
Hollywood	MIA-	32000	2-S	147,594	139,357	21,664	66,495	35,803	3,197,407	.0578	2,279,392	670	102,720	218	100,878	565	282,804	130,134	461,892	253	Incorporated Place
Homestead	MIA-	32275	4-S	32,357	31,909	11,407	10,648	28,160	369,086	.0080	296,212	87	14,089	30	6,211	35	82,139	19,996	(d)	....	Incorporated Place

.... Data less than 1,000.
(d) Data not available.
◇ Not classified as a Principal Business Center.

* Data from 1997 Census of Manufactures.

Principal Business Centers and Other Places with 27,500 or More: Population / Income / Sales, *Continued*

Place Name	Ranally Metro Area	FIPS Place Code	Ranally City Rating	Population Estimate 7/1/04	Population Census 4/1/00	Per Capita Income 2003	House-holds Estimate 7/1/04	Median Household Income 2003	Disposable Income 2003 ($1,000)	Market Ability Index 2003	Total Retail Trade Sales 2003 ($1,000)	Total Retail Trade Ranally Sales Units	General Merchandise Sales 2003 ($1,000)	General Merchandise Ranally Sales Units	Apparel Stores Sales 2003 ($1,000)	Apparel Stores Ranally Sales Units	Food Store Sales 2003 ($1,000)	Health & Drug Store Sales 2003 ($1,000)	Manufacturers Value Added 1997* ($1,000)	Ranally Mfg Units	Place Type
Jacksonville	JAX	35000	2-AA	792,345	735,617	20,380	322,819	37,813	16,148,368	.2922	11,172,138	3,286	1,440,952	3,059	466,447	2,614	1,413,776	563,866	3,878,378	2,123	Incorporated Place
Jupiter	MIA-	35875	◇	47,397	39,328	32,220	22,674	51,185	1,527,122	.0211	532,237	157	64,864	138	22,079	124	138,490	40,182	(d)	....	Incorporated Place
Kendale Lakes	MIA-	36062	◇	59,799	56,901	15,691	19,739	41,659	938,319	.0152	337,729	99	51,901	110	61,529	345	61,356	31,378	(d)	....	Census Designated Place
Kendall	MIA-	36100	◇	79,059	75,226	27,541	31,119	50,072	2,177,357	.0369	1,435,865	422	243,799	518	246,283	1,380	151,050	110,765	(d)	....	Census Designated Place
Key West		36550	4-C	25,894	25,478	21,901	11,220	39,749	567,116	.0103	415,828	122	42,663	91	59,801	335	97,485	30,744	(d)	....	Incorporated Place
Kissimmee	KISS	36950	4-C	60,761	47,814	17,100	23,348	32,539	1,038,986	.0190	662,687	195	89,454	190	36,139	203	99,047	37,317	37,813	21	Incorporated Place
Lake City		37775	4-C	10,416	9,980	16,145	4,288	28,161	168,170	.0043	245,417	72	55,874	119	7,522	42	26,098	11,414	41,231	23	Incorporated Place
Lakeland	LKLD	38250	3-AA	82,940	78,452	20,651	38,446	33,104	1,712,762	.0322	1,331,987	392	198,866	422	52,483	294	227,280	68,941	349,513	191	Incorporated Place
Lake Magdalene	TAM	38350	◇	31,573	28,755	22,556	13,806	35,611	712,150	.0150	757,822	223	149,616	318	42,721	239	83,529	49,196	(d)	....	Census Designated Place
Lake Park	MIA-	38600	4-S	9,811	8,721	16,190	4,172	32,079	158,843	.0073	594,889	175	52,264	111	9,852	55	11,315	4,923	(d)	....	Incorporated Place
Lakeside	JAX	38813	◇	35,751	30,927	20,761	12,743	43,811	742,236	.0129	459,271	135	65,555	139	23,218	130	60,646	25,416	(d)	....	Census Designated Place
Lake Worth	MIA-	39075	4-S	39,396	35,133	14,654	17,213	28,902	577,329	.0094	200,899	59	2,568	5	9,752	55	33,231	32,687	22,295	12	Incorporated Place
Largo	ST.PET	39425	4-S	68,890	69,371	22,936	37,289	32,100	1,580,061	.0276	1,045,748	308	92,171	196	33,315	187	190,086	85,185	135,963	74	Incorporated Place
Lauderdale Lakes	MIA-	39525	4-S	34,299	31,705	15,940	13,748	30,713	546,710	.0096	285,499	84	6,976	15	14,543	82	32,375	29,669	(d)	....	Incorporated Place
Lauderhill	MIA-	39550	4-S	63,604	57,585	16,678	26,502	30,586	1,060,815	.0177	470,625	138	52,506	111	26,149	147	66,030	51,079	(d)	....	Incorporated Place
Leesburg		39875	4-C	15,494	15,956	18,833	6,657	31,036	291,801	.0065	334,175	98	60,880	129	11,119	62	37,675	27,581	39,462	22	Incorporated Place
Lehigh Acres	FTMY-	39925	◇	38,547	33,430	15,615	14,772	36,144	601,898	.0099	234,347	69	98,350	209	7,944	45	62,842	11,269	(d)	....	Census Designated Place
Margate	MIA-	43125	◇	55,939	53,909	19,366	24,778	36,393	1,083,320	.0199	762,691	224	53,393	113	12,284	69	153,309	67,811	(d)	....	Incorporated Place
Melbourne	MELB-	43975	2-A	76,627	71,382	20,624	35,278	33,118	1,580,333	.0327	1,561,557	459	169,592	360	66,821	374	161,258	96,102	737,586	404	Incorporated Place
Merritt Island	MELB-	44275	◇	39,028	36,090	25,080	17,294	42,400	978,805	.0176	730,600	215	186,740	396	31,497	177	67,989	37,535	(d)	....	Census Designated Place
Miami	MIA-	45000	1-AA	365,059	362,470	14,018	140,511	26,033	5,117,496	.1014	3,660,398	1,077	240,468	510	449,996	2,522	439,332	380,844	546,582	299	Incorporated Place
Miami Beach	MIA-	45025	3-S	90,226	87,933	25,063	49,273	28,824	2,261,374	.0314	644,699	190	18,768	40	109,244	612	177,773	124,466	(d)	....	Incorporated Place
Miramar	MIA-	45975	◇	88,982	72,739	15,711	29,592	40,419	1,398,027	.0246	730,458	215	94,466	201	8,260	46	95,131	29,967	73,431	40	Incorporated Place
Naples	NAP	47625	3-A	20,354	20,976	43,842	10,534	53,083	892,357	.0191	1,137,291	335	164,345	349	171,827	963	137,484	78,657	48,299	26	Incorporated Place
New Port Richey	ST.PET	48500	4-S	17,618	16,117	18,836	8,390	27,796	331,855	.0055	163,382	48	34,380	73	4,313	24	26,639	17,820	(d)	....	Incorporated Place
North Fort Myers	FTMY-	49350	◇	46,369	40,214	19,707	22,909	31,733	913,792	.0142	351,984	104	93,916	199	8,343	47	79,347	21,606	(d)	....	Census Designated Place
North Lauderdale	MIA-	49425	◇	35,287	32,264	15,039	12,401	36,818	530,687	.0086	182,365	54	46,797	99	3,606	20	35,217	4,511	(d)	....	Incorporated Place
North Miami	MIA-	49450	4-Sr	62,366	59,880	13,774	22,278	28,871	859,050	.0179	704,994	207	62,361	132	7,818	44	78,951	41,288	24,279	13	Incorporated Place
North Miami Beach	MIA-	49475	3-S	42,514	40,786	14,269	15,135	30,923	606,643	.0122	463,360	136	45,021	96	47,012	263	54,965	35,011	42,539	23	Incorporated Place
North Port	PUN-	49675	◇	29,107	22,797	14,813	11,736	34,514	431,159	.0063	63,552	19	3,067	7	1,209	7	27,279	5,743	(d)	....	Incorporated Place
Oakland Park	MIA-	50575	4-S	34,029	30,966	19,777	15,597	34,790	673,002	.0123	476,529	140	36,509	78	23,447	131	60,142	39,928	99,232	54	Incorporated Place
Ocala	OCA	50750	3-AA	47,120	45,943	18,382	20,041	30,811	866,163	.0232	1,420,875	418	290,702	617	44,609	250	111,878	81,308	510,922	280	Incorporated Place
Ocoee	ORL	51075	◇	28,390	24,391	20,056	9,920	46,326	569,382	.0105	412,844	121	145,364	309	61,957	347	64,102	13,665	(d)	....	Incorporated Place
Orlando	ORL	53000	2-AA	195,010	185,951	21,690	89,465	34,719	4,229,829	.0820	3,642,790	1,072	336,133	714	194,840	1,092	436,822	179,327	1,553,663	851	Incorporated Place
Ormond Beach	D.BCH	53150	◇	38,138	36,301	24,724	17,829	37,675	942,906	.0135	312,490	92	64,748	137	8,131	46	73,814	26,461	56,129	31	Incorporated Place
Oviedo	ORL	53575	◇	31,443	26,316	21,859	10,663	54,767	687,312	.0104	257,391	76	52,831	112	29,545	166	70,149	19,787	(d)	....	Incorporated Place
Palatka		53875	4-C	10,314	10,033	14,383	4,035	27,454	148,343	.0032	140,647	41	30,757	65	6,872	39	15,901	9,612	277,085	152	Incorporated Place
Palm Bay	MELB-	54000	◇	86,531	79,413	17,798	35,258	34,471	1,540,118	.0232	453,208	133	53,466	113	11,218	63	109,530	39,814	544,829	298	Incorporated Place
Palm Beach	MIA-	54025	4-S	11,071	10,468	82,609	6,789	73,461	914,569	.0106	225,148	66	3,388	7	123,382	691	27,671	9,255	(d)	....	Incorporated Place
Palm Beach Gardens	MIA-	54075	◇	38,128	35,058	34,268	18,806	53,689	1,306,585	.0208	780,899	230	167,485	356	169,396	949	119,169	43,577	(d)	....	Incorporated Place
Palm Coast		54200	◇	41,981	32,732	22,503	18,190	38,278	944,703	.0125	161,719	48	43,813	93	5,691	32	39,610	19,329	(d)	....	Incorporated Place
Palm Harbor	ST.PET	54350	◇	59,633	59,248	25,076	28,382	41,171	1,495,384	.0222	591,187	174	59,580	126	17,084	96	164,522	49,458	(d)	....	Census Designated Place
Panama City	PNCY	54700	3-A	38,423	36,417	17,187	15,905	30,045	660,379	.0159	860,412	253	166,854	354	32,424	182	81,551	42,710	247,806	136	Incorporated Place
Pembroke Pines	MIA-	55775	◇	168,116	137,427	21,923	66,880	48,966	3,685,678	.0568	1,527,310	449	376,445	799	120,335	674	222,496	99,658	54,183	30	Incorporated Place
Pensacola	PENS	55925	2-A	52,302	56,255	21,888	25,099	31,453	1,144,776	.0236	1,149,310	338	263,582	560	110,930	622	139,563	88,514	226,643	124	Incorporated Place
Pine Hills	ORL	56825	◇	45,928	41,764	14,070	15,483	32,029	646,202	.0163	863,783	254	77,702	165	17,989	101	60,252	29,314	(d)	....	Census Designated Place
Pinellas Park	ST.PET	56975	4-S	44,717	45,658	19,113	21,012	33,423	854,697	.0191	976,562	287	237,413	504	24,743	139	76,922	140,608	630,218	345	Incorporated Place
Plantation	MIA-	57425	3-Sm	85,012	82,934	23,052	35,848	41,319	1,959,697	.0377	1,701,033	500	176,925	376	143,004	801	215,226	77,377	....	....	Incorporated Place
Plant City	TAM	57550	◇	32,967	29,915	16,922	12,432	34,110	557,872	.0110	442,872	130	77,463	164	10,275	58	76,111	19,507	461,663	253	Incorporated Place
Pompano Beach	MIA-	58050	3-S	79,726	78,191	23,372	37,690	34,714	1,863,387	.0366	1,710,820	503	80,243	170	39,274	220	158,830	66,198	436,553	239	Incorporated Place
Port Charlotte	PUN-	58350	◇	51,527	46,451	18,266	23,052	31,424	941,173	.0186	792,693	233	279,346	593	51,741	290	86,648	50,159	(d)	....	Census Designated Place
Port Orange	D.BCH	58575	◇	48,653	45,823	21,629	22,551	36,606	1,052,314	.0145	237,240	70	70,515	150	2,521	14	40,450	28,295	(d)	....	Incorporated Place
Port Saint Lucie	FTPI	58715	◇	109,127	88,769	19,428	44,932	37,345	2,120,125	.0304	524,721	154	92,906	197	14,578	82	153,746	68,748	(d)	....	Incorporated Place
Richmond West	MIA-	60230	◇	29,513	28,082	14,064	8,551	46,381	415,060	.0063	78,140	23	5,816	12	....	....	28,035	4,905	(d)	....	Census Designated Place
Riviera Beach	MIA-	60975	◇	31,180	29,884	18,303	13,158	31,513	570,701	.0107	409,563	120	24,444	52	19,046	107	25,865	30,531	127,279	70	Incorporated Place
Saint Augustine		62500	4-C	11,209	11,592	21,901	5,174	33,622	245,488	.0045	178,754	53	6,878	15	15,708	88	31,269	10,877	38,415	21	Incorporated Place
Saint Petersburg	ST.PET	63000	2-BB	250,359	248,232	21,119	122,323	32,643	5,287,379	.0945	3,596,736	1,058	360,934	766	149,250	836	511,558	243,277	650,404	356	Incorporated Place
Sanford	ORL	63650	4-S	41,011	38,291	17,861	15,931	33,872	732,517	.0152	688,608	203	130,078	276	61,678	346	68,952	43,343	124,812	68	Incorporated Place
Sarasota	SAR-B	64175	2-A	53,293	52,715	20,186	23,982	33,058	1,075,753	.0232	1,167,393	343	38,887	83	125,863	705	97,619	82,398	85,588	47	Incorporated Place
South Miami Heights	MIA-	67575	◇	35,229	33,522	14,728	10,840	42,227	518,852	.0092	265,416	78	33,304	71	5,605	31	43,097	14,703	(d)	....	Census Designated Place
Spring Hill	SPR.H	68350	◇	77,862	69,078	17,733	33,379	32,164	1,380,761	.0221	550,627	162	67,763	144	13,576	76	182,364	44,721	(d)	....	Census Designated Place
Stuart	STU	68875	3-B	15,939	14,633	24,141	7,962	33,637	384,787	.0080	406,320	120	25,442	54	18,196	102	58,151	26,439	194,673	107	Incorporated Place
Sunrise	MIA-	69700	◇	90,692	85,779	20,182	36,915	39,932	1,830,302	.0362	1,606,384	473	253,905	539	283,822	1,591	155,057	123,421	104,360	57	Incorporated Place
Tallahassee	TALL	70600	3-AA	156,172	150,624	19,002	69,932	32,927	2,967,636	.0598	2,659,877	782	423,983	900	136,892	767	415,277	168,757	....	....	Incorporated Place
Tamarac	MIA-	70675	◇	59,039	55,588	21,863	30,660	32,408	1,290,782	.0197	510,651	150	41,164	87	22,624	127	203,592	61,377	(d)	....	Incorporated Place
Tamiami	MIA-	70700	◇	57,578	54,788	15,435	17,768	44,504	888,710	.0134	197,927	58	21,661	46	9,036	51	67,541	31,875	(d)	....	Census Designated Place
Tampa	TAM	71000	2-AA	320,694	303,447	21,253	137,353	34,848	6,815,651	.1304	5,621,160	1,654	566,454	1,202	352,484	1,975	656,166	370,666	1,125,623	616	Incorporated Place
The Hammocks	MIA-	71569	◇	49,792	47,379	17,000	16,594	47,397	846,486	.0131	276,355	81	63,656	135	12,397	69	58,139	28,093	(d)	....	Census Designated Place
Titusville	TITUS	71900	4-B	40,681	40,670	21,733	18,333	35,767	884,108	.0146	473,299	139	138,840	295	10,887	61	84,552	36,642	29,319	16	Incorporated Place
Town 'n' Country	TAM	72145	◇	79,631	72,523	20,625	33,019	39,470	1,642,371	.0294	1,107,466	326	114,896	244	16,714	94	98,183	67,118	(d)	....	Census Designated Place
University Park	MIA-	73287	◇	27,890	26,538	14,653	9,445	37,035	408,669	.0071	188,399	55	10,181	22	8,986	50	65,939	24,995	(d)	....	Census Designated Place
Venice	VEN	73900	4-C	17,499	17,764	25,164	9,639	35,500	440,337	.0068	205,919	61	4,893	10	11,279	63	37,835	11,273	(d)	....	Incorporated Place
Vero Beach	VERO	74150	3-B	17,443	17,705	33,766	9,595	44,189	588,980	.0099	406,630	120	16,087	34	23,731	133	80,452	36,844	39,036	21	Incorporated Place
Wellington	MIA-	75812	◇	45,791	38,216	25,156	17,168	61,029	1,151,905	.0151	225,598	66	73,476	156	3,905	22	44,710	24,570	(d)	....	Incorporated Place
Westchester	MIA-	76075	◇	31,813	30,271	14,751	10,669	38,023	469,283	.0094	361,376	106	21,004	45	24,360	137	75,213	42,127	(d)	....	Census Designated Place
West Little River	MIA-	76487	◇	34,152	32,498	8,889	10,386	21,483	303,589	.0063	158,062	46	2,487	5	6,121	34	22,390	16,336	(d)	....	Census Designated Place
Weston	MIA-	76582	◇	57,541	49,286	30,836	20,356	67,455	1,774,337	.0209	190,047	56	....	....	10,200	57	80,962	29,780	(d)	....	Incorporated Place
West Palm Beach	MIA-	76600	2-AA	88,873	82,103	20,351	41,795	33,609	1,808,675	.0414	2,230,399	656	260,394	553	128,970	723	242,070	104,469	1,886,388	1,033	Incorporated Place
Winter Haven	WNHV	78275	3-B	27,124	26,487	21,089	13,135	30,857	572,015	.0102	384,462	113	52,333	111	14,995	84	63,099	24,161	74,698	41	Incorporated Place
Winter Park	ORL	78300	3-S	24,096	24,090	34,230	11,300	41,289	824,799	.0151	711,567	209	54,408	115	34,779	195	60,397	48,554	(d)	....	Incorporated Place
Winter Springs	ORL	78325	◇	35,728	31,666	24,840	13,879	47,854	887,487	.0109	91,536	27	14,701	31	1,090	6	23,371	20,451	(d)	....	Incorporated Place

Georgia

Place Name	Ranally Metro Area	FIPS Place Code	Ranally City Rating	Population Estimate 7/1/04	Population Census 4/1/00	Per Capita Income 2003	House-holds Estimate 7/1/04	Median Household Income 2003	Disposable Income 2003 ($1,000)	Market Ability Index 2003	Total Retail Trade Sales 2003 ($1,000)	Total Retail Trade Ranally Sales Units	General Merchandise Sales 2003 ($1,000)	General Merchandise Ranally Sales Units	Apparel Stores Sales 2003 ($1,000)	Apparel Stores Ranally Sales Units	Food Store Sales 2003 ($1,000)	Health & Drug Store Sales 2003 ($1,000)	Manufacturers Value Added 1997* ($1,000)	Ranally Mfg Units	Place Type
Albany	ALB	01052	3-AA	76,068	76,939	14,431	29,409	30,457	1,097,706	.0249	1,158,970	341	245,971	522	56,010	314	168,750	47,431	....	....	Incorporated Place
Alpharetta	ATL	01696	◇	40,054	34,854	30,748	17,385	69,579	1,231,563	.0193	675,525	199	90,501	192	34,069	191	111,889	19,097	330,203	181	Incorporated Place
Athens	ATH	03440	3-A	104,409	100,266	14,887	44,556	27,636	1,554,360	.0331	1,417,177	417	268,615	570	72,113	404	224,139	59,331	577,408	316	Incorporated Place
Atlanta	ATL	04000	1-AA	395,142	416,474	19,800	173,596	36,819	7,824,000	.1399	5,138,733	1,512	662,809	1,407	675,594	3,786	671,845	232,910	3,093,862	1,694	Incorporated Place
Augusta	AUG	04204	2-A	193,417	195,182	15,649	76,036	31,417	3,026,773	.0614	2,504,806	737	462,200	981	160,465	899	270,336	129,032	....	....	Incorporated Place
Brunswick	BRUNS	11560	3-A	15,887	15,600	14,361	6,911	23,959	228,157	.0066	405,251	119	12,800	27	8,217	46	78,555	20,810	370,515	203	Incorporated Place
Carrollton		13492	4-C	23,595	19,843	16,763	8,586	32,591	395,531	.0077	307,289	90	75,840	161	15,768	88	45,088	15,679	462,998	253	Incorporated Place
Cartersville		13688	4-C	18,607	15,925	19,891	7,191	40,560	370,105	.0073	326,436	96	61,889	131	5,237	29	44,145	14,551	1,157,973	634	Incorporated Place
Chamblee	ATL	15172	4-Sr	10,176	9,552	17,339	3,091	45,695	176,443	.0044	246,732	73	....	....	2,231	13	18,675	4,551	190,956	105	Incorporated Place
Columbus	COL	19007	3-AA	185,692	185,781	16,718	75,006	33,035	3,104,314	.0610	2,432,983	716	366,939	779	168,305	943	319,472	138,414	....	....	Incorporated Place
Dalton		21380	3-A	31,639	27,912	19,014	11,924	36,472	601,582	.0136	712,578	210	121,877	259	35,287	198	86,620	25,127	1,986,334	1,087	Incorporated Place
Decatur	ATL	22052	4-Sr	17,177	18,147	24,459	8,267	42,178	420,127	.0056	91,361	27	....	....	4,367	24	6,254	6,079	(d)	....	Incorporated Place
Doraville	ATL	23536	4-S	10,686	9,862	16,681	3,533	39,554	178,252	.0037	160,120	47	10,938	23	3,168	18	10,055	5,288	....	....	Incorporated Place
Dublin		24376	4-C	16,296	15,857	15,593	6,473	30,484	254,098	.0060	303,310	89	55,008	117	13,343	75	55,093	12,993	367,801	201	Incorporated Place
Duluth	ATL	24600	◇	28,701	22,122	29,864	11,887	54,989	857,124	.0185	1,033,458	304	197,017	418	103,225	579	66,520	26,618	(d)	....	Incorporated Place
Dunwoody	ATL	24768	◇	33,323	32,808	39,469	15,165	64,297	1,315,241	.0213	865,660	255	174,614	371	150,731	845	71,615	39,304	(d)	....	Census Designated Place
East Point	ATL	25720	4-Sr	40,645	39,595	13,302	16,215	30,451	540,653	.0114	446,593	131	36,621	78	10,084	57	142,047	35,154	122,681	67	Incorporated Place
Gainesville		31908	3-A	31,965	25,578	17,779	11,433	34,840	568,292	.0131	681,269	200	156,303	332	28,834	162	67,241	38,351	598,564	328	Incorporated Place
Griffin		35324	4-C	25,243	23,451	17,255	9,832	35,090	435,565	.0079	278,950	82	39,611	84	13,290	74	56,664	13,537	381,753	209	Incorporated Place
Hinesville		38964	◇	33,823	30,392	15,098	13,026	32,479	510,650	.0095	312,706	92	77,137	164	15,957	89	47,982	8,008	(d)	....	Incorporated Place
Kennesaw	ATL	43192	◇	28,693	21,675	24,275	11,014	55,451	696,514	.0171	1,028,308	302	208,322	442	102,224	573	60,703	30,891	(d)	....	Incorporated Place
Lagrange		44340	4-A	27,164	25,998	17,295	11,026	34,163	469,806	.0095	406,111	119	57,066	121	21,514	121	66,699	14,751	651,225	357	Incorporated Place
Lawrenceville	ATL	45488	4-Sr	25,986	22,397	20,792	9,113	48,829	540,289	.0127	712,269	210	66,515	141	7,616	43	71,630	17,115	305,851	167	Incorporated Place
Mableton	ATL	48288	◇	32,475	29,733	19,614	12,238	43,188	636,980	.0109	356,911	105	58,644	124	6,113	34	96,325	21,424	(d)	....	Census Designated Place
Macon	MAC	49000	3-AA	95,665	97,255	14,635	39,136	28,446	1,400,031	.0343	1,781,800	524	361,430	767	82,282	461	236,859	95,350	3,709,119	2,031	Incorporated Place
Marietta	ATL	49756	3-S	66,713	58,748	27,011	27,899	49,243	1,801,953	.0291	1,014,959	299	86,793	184	24,083	135	159,025	33,020	462,440	253	Incorporated Place
Martinez	AUG	50036	◇	31,097	27,749	23,078	11,273	49,483	717,642	.0126	479,245	141	86,546	184	7,459	42	77,531	14,467	(d)	....	Census Designated Place
Milledgeville		51492	4-C	18,503	18,757	10,986	4,857	33,479	203,281	.0053	259,252	76	62,958	134	11,676	65	46,083	11,186	....	....	Incorporated Place
Morrow	ATL	53004	4-Sm	5,209	4,882	17,334	1,848	37,899	90,294	.0035	268,114	79	79,044	168	19,276	108	12,731	7,113	(d)	....	Incorporated Place
Moultrie		53060	4-C	13,906	14,387	13,565	5,516	26,418	188,639	.0045	222,887	66	33,918	72	9,397	53	39,465	8,022	99,754	55	Incorporated Place
North Atlanta	ATL	56000	◇	39,185	38,579	29,972	17,539	49,805	1,174,453	.0154	289,989	85	15,965	34	12,664	71	82,061	25,601	(d)	....	Census Designated Place
Peachtree City	ATL	59724	◇	33,495	31,580	29,946	12,078	64,625	1,003,045	.0138	320,272	94	29,609	63	20,536	115	88,431	10,942	597,925	327	Incorporated Place
Redan	ATL	63952	◇	34,373	33,841	19,734	12,981	45,681	678,331	.0091	105,257	31	2,364	5	1,499	8	43,960	5,518	(d)	....	Census Designated Place
Rome	ROME	66668	3-A	36,727	34,980	15,853	14,015	32,419	582,230	.0122	531,380	156	122,132	259	27,871	156	47,347	36,672	425,547	233	Incorporated Place
Roswell	ATL	67284	4-S	86,004	79,334	28,710	35,621	66,453	2,469,147	.0428	1,772,497	521	118,239	251	84,195	472	256,465	36,665	85,639	47	Incorporated Place
Sandy Springs	ATL	68516	◇	86,069	85,781	36,368	42,842	55,968	3,130,150	.0453	1,402,722	413	136,134	289	77,095	432	174,680	38,828	(d)	....	Census Designated Place
Savannah	SAV	69000	2-A	128,045	131,510	15,985	52,362	29,930	2,046,767	.0416	1,721,394	506	320,124	680	111,842	627	253,047	63,224	450,528	247	Incorporated Place
Smyrna	ATL	71492	3-S	46,153	40,999	25,524	21,292	43,072	1,178,026	.0215	922,743	271	109,372	232	24,831	139	103,513	44,743	75,948	42	Incorporated Place
Statesboro		73256	4-C	23,182	22,698	12,549	8,913	24,042	290,916	.0075	380,988	112	107,589	228	21,103	118	58,474	21,387	169,079	93	Incorporated Place
Thomasville		76224	4-C	18,390	18,162	15,129	7,245	30,072	278,215	.0073	409,213	120	84,347	179	17,478	98	54,203	26,759	374,101	205	Incorporated Place
Tifton		76476	4-B	15,584	15,060	14,588	5,830	29,655	227,342	.0056	288,297	85	52,056	111	12,066	68	41,531	13,410	162,820	89	Incorporated Place
Union City	ATL	78324	4-Sm	12,087	11,621	16,129	5,629	35,520	194,957	.0096	800,253	235	130,545	277	40,446	227	33,586	19,378	(d)	....	Incorporated Place
Valdosta	VALD	78800	3-A	43,340	43,724	16,028	17,956	30,588	694,674	.0162	819,963	241	118,768	252	54,284	304	97,632	20,896	366,069	200	Incorporated Place
Warner Robins	MAC	80508	4-B	53,922	48,804	20,220	22,576	39,117	1,090,302	.0185	616,085	181	92,727	197	7,887	44	87,161	17,421	....	....	Incorporated Place
Waycross		80956	3-A	15,076	15,333	14,482	6,256	26,605	218,328	.0052	264,043	78	87,132	185	7,724	43	40,446	16,764	89,718	49	Incorporated Place

Hawaii

Place Name	Ranally Metro Area	FIPS Place Code	Ranally City Rating	Population Estimate 7/1/04	Population Census 4/1/00	Per Capita Income 2003	House-holds Estimate 7/1/04	Median Household Income 2003	Disposable Income 2003 ($1,000)	Market Ability Index 2003	Total Retail Trade Sales 2003 ($1,000)	Total Retail Trade Ranally Sales Units	General Merchandise Sales 2003 ($1,000)	General Merchandise Ranally Sales Units	Apparel Stores Sales 2003 ($1,000)	Apparel Stores Ranally Sales Units	Food Store Sales 2003 ($1,000)	Health & Drug Store Sales 2003 ($1,000)	Manufacturers Value Added 1997* ($1,000)	Ranally Mfg Units	Place Type
Aiea	HON	00550	4-Sm	9,385	9,019	20,190	2,905	52,842	189,484	.0047	273,717	81	60,102	128	32,025	179	17,418	19,802	105,365	58	Census Designated Place
Hilo	HILO	14650	3-A	44,269	40,759	17,022	16,138	36,375	753,549	.0164	774,120	228	129,788	276	37,541	210	179,342	56,186	34,467	19	Census Designated Place
Honolulu	HON	17000	2-AA	391,884	371,657	22,496	149,840	42,632	8,815,719	.1558	5,996,774	1,764	1,159,722	2,462	935,838	5,245	810,594	514,218	446,893	245	Census Designated Place
Kahului		22700	4-A	21,687	20,146	16,551	6,393	43,137	358,933	.0131	965,925	284	263,159	559	59,191	332	100,227	61,982	41,776	23	Census Designated Place
Kailua	HON	23150	4-S	37,996	36,513	24,274	12,870	58,000	922,307	.0128	255,875	75	37,425	79	4,643	26	58,701	15,559	(d)	....	Census Designated Place
Kaneohe	HON	28250	4-S	36,391	34,970	21,704	11,551	60,104	789,824	.0122	327,010	96	38,083	81	33,704	189	63,078	33,799	(d)	....	Census Designated Place
Lahaina		42950	4-B	9,816	9,118	17,852	2,829	48,378	175,237	.0042	226,618	67	9,517	20	65,159	365	62,048	15,943	(d)	....	Census Designated Place
Lihue		45200	4-A	5,966	5,674	21,176	2,372	43,783	126,335	.0033	199,870	59	57,390	122	4,340	24	25,738	12,519	(d)	....	Census Designated Place
Mililani Town	HON	51050	◇	29,770	28,608	20,697	9,480	60,548	616,150	.0091	202,253	59	96,971	206	2,887	16	27,848	32,088	(d)	....	Census Designated Place
Pearl City	HON	62600	◇	32,232	30,976	18,839	9,403	54,487	607,205	.0094	221,485	65	100,762	214	23,039	129	19,513	19,021	(d)	....	Census Designated Place
Wailuku		77450	4-B	13,235	12,296	20,474	4,942	45,131	270,971	.0041	101,085	30	6,767	14	2,597	15	35,305	5,143	(d)	....	Census Designated Place
Waimalu	HON	77750	◇	30,563	29,371	23,636	11,098	53,234	722,385	.0116	374,645	110	90,534	192	43,378	243	24,701	27,580	(d)	....	Census Designated Place
Waipahu	HON	79700	◇	34,450	33,108	14,218	7,976	53,118	489,813	.0103	421,433	124	100,733	214	36,043	202	65,340	26,758	(d)	....	Census Designated Place

Idaho

Place Name	Ranally Metro Area	FIPS Place Code	Ranally City Rating	Population Estimate 7/1/04	Population Census 4/1/00	Per Capita Income 2003	House-holds Estimate 7/1/04	Median Household Income 2003	Disposable Income 2003 ($1,000)	Market Ability Index 2003	Total Retail Trade Sales 2003 ($1,000)	Total Retail Trade Ranally Sales Units	General Merchandise Sales 2003 ($1,000)	General Merchandise Ranally Sales Units	Apparel Stores Sales 2003 ($1,000)	Apparel Stores Ranally Sales Units	Food Store Sales 2003 ($1,000)	Health & Drug Store Sales 2003 ($1,000)	Manufacturers Value Added 1997* ($1,000)	Ranally Mfg Units	Place Type
Boise	BOIS	08830	3-AA	201,901	185,787	21,129	81,807	39,996	4,265,945	.0811	3,453,262	1,016	599,179	1,272	163,389	916	491,911	122,842	1,990,826	1,090	Incorporated Place
Caldwell		12250	◇	31,732	25,967	14,055	10,903	29,720	446,008	.0100	454,505	134	17,179	36	1,057	6	73,784	19,641	75,740	41	Incorporated Place
Coeur d'Alene		16750	4-C	37,779	34,514	17,694	15,220	33,500	668,473	.0149	740,505	218	145,420	309	22,527	126	94,450	23,832	81,665	45	Incorporated Place
Idaho Falls	IDFL	39700	3-A	54,737	50,730	18,745	20,616	39,888	1,026,020	.0184	658,793	194	185,016	393	21,032	118	77,596	34,504	110,555	61	Incorporated Place
Lewiston	LEW	46540	3-A	31,770	30,904	17,764	13,232	34,377	564,352	.0113	483,622	142	99,341	211	9,070	51	75,917	14,206	....	....	Incorporated Place
Meridian	BOIS	52120	◇	45,038	34,919	18,371	15,403	48,137	827,375	.0137	397,927	117	84,615	180	1,693	9	50,589	6,442	56,374	31	Incorporated Place
Moscow		54550	4-B	21,487	21,291	13,384	7,886	28,418	287,584	.0061	245,695	72	53,408	113	9,934	56	58,649	12,715	(d)	....	Incorporated Place
Nampa	BOIS	56260	3-B	70,541	51,867	14,387	24,493	34,555	1,014,900	.0200	729,503	215	142,634	303	20,664	116	90,985	26,198	936,799	513	Incorporated Place
Pocatello	POC	64090	3-A	50,038	51,466	16,304	19,069	33,456	815,821	.0163	662,414	195	73,737	157	10,985	62	124,002	37,178	208,058	114	Incorporated Place
Twin Falls		82810	3-A	37,218	34,469	15,939	14,414	32,293	593,235	.0142	743,196	219	200,950	427	30,037	168	65,668	25,396	177,258	97	Incorporated Place

Illinois

Place Name	Ranally Metro Area	FIPS Place Code	Ranally City Rating	Population Estimate 7/1/04	Population Census 4/1/00	Per Capita Income 2003	House-holds Estimate 7/1/04	Median Household Income 2003	Disposable Income 2003 ($1,000)	Market Ability Index 2003	Total Retail Trade Sales 2003 ($1,000)	Total Retail Trade Ranally Sales Units	General Merchandise Sales 2003 ($1,000)	General Merchandise Ranally Sales Units	Apparel Stores Sales 2003 ($1,000)	Apparel Stores Ranally Sales Units	Food Store Sales 2003 ($1,000)	Health & Drug Store Sales 2003 ($1,000)	Manufacturers Value Added 1997* ($1,000)	Ranally Mfg Units	Place Type
Addison	CHI	00243	4-S	36,993	35,914	19,819	12,419	47,814	733,175	.0146	649,862	191	57,421	122	11,399	64	77,471	16,436	820,700	449	Incorporated Place
Algonquin	CHI	00685	◇	28,611	23,276	27,217	9,666	65,450	778,716	.0110	261,043	77	....	....	....	....	95,403	48,352	(d)	....	Incorporated Place
Alton	ST.L	01114	3-S	30,155	30,496	17,577	12,732	32,773	530,045	.0112	520,442	153	105,926	225	12,333	69	71,455	34,732	76,615	42	Incorporated Place
Arlington Heights	CHI	02154	3-S	73,693	76,031	26,264	29,789	56,501	1,935,467	.0319	1,148,471	338	94,555	201	59,082	331	234,350	107,872	902,885	494	Incorporated Place
Aurora	CHI	03012	3-SS	182,473	142,990	20,303	58,943	50,583	3,704,774	.0570	1,420,434	418	307,058	652	119,673	671	197,565	130,014	1,415,118	775	Incorporated Place
Bartlett	CHI	04013	◇	38,726	36,706	25,207	13,304	67,167	976,173	.0124	149,208	44	....	....	2,625	15	33,243	23,274	147,760	81	Incorporated Place
Belleville	ST.L	04845	3-S	42,745	41,410	20,793	18,743	37,663	888,783	.0146	459,444	135	46,446	99	7,735	43	59,371	49,190	159,016	87	Incorporated Place

continued on next page

.... Data less than 1,000.
(d) Data not available.
◇ Not classified as a Principal Business Center.

* Data from 1997 Census of Manufactures.

Principal Business Centers and Other Places with 27,500 or More: Population / Income / Sales, *Continued*

PLACE NAME	RANALLY METRO AREA	FIPS PLACE CODE	RANALLY CITY RATING	POPULATION Estimate 7/1/04	POPULATION Census 4/1/00	PER CAPITA INCOME 2003	HOUSEHOLDS Estimate 7/1/04	MEDIAN HOUSEHOLD INCOME 2003	DISPOSABLE INCOME 2003 ($1,000)	MARKET ABILITY INDEX 2003	TOTAL RETAIL TRADE Sales 2003 ($1,000)	TOTAL RETAIL TRADE Ranally Sales Units	GENERAL MERCHANDISE Sales 2003 ($1,000)	GENERAL MERCHANDISE Ranally Sales Units	APPAREL STORES Sales 2003 ($1,000)	APPAREL STORES Ranally Sales Units	FOOD STORE SALES 2003 ($1,000)	HEALTH & DRUG STORE SALES 2003 ($1,000)	MANUFACTURERS VALUE ADDED 1997* ($1,000)	MANUFACTURERS Ranally Mfg Units	PLACE TYPE
Berwyn	CHI	05573	4-S	55,216	54,016	16,537	20,121	40,226	913,135	.0158	466,299	137	12,634	27	20,497	115	90,288	62,102	47,120	26	Incorporated Place
Bloomingdale	CHI	06587	4-Sm	22,417	21,675	29,392	8,813	60,295	658,877	.0146	836,001	246	275,556	585	103,906	582	29,341	57,116	37,434	20	Incorporated Place
Bloomington	BLOOM-	06613	3-AA	71,163	64,808	22,922	29,591	44,975	1,631,233	.0297	1,214,571	357	139,767	297	81,373	456	132,537	96,568	. . . .	. . . .	Incorporated Place
Bolingbrook	CHI	07133	◇	61,713	56,321	23,149	19,304	59,425	1,428,618	.0228	705,053	207	147,198	312	10,243	57	87,922	54,355	530,148	290	Incorporated Place
Buffalo Grove	CHI	09447	◇	43,587	42,909	29,190	16,087	68,749	1,272,311	.0201	689,369	203	1,875	4	6,427	36	55,682	72,556	337,885	185	Incorporated Place
Calumet City	CHI	10487	3-Sm	40,268	39,071	15,521	15,584	36,365	625,008	.0163	926,086	272	268,120	569	107,104	600	50,979	59,829	77,996	43	Incorporated Place
Canton		11007	4-C	15,514	15,288	15,174	5,799	30,994	235,413	.0046	167,040	49	34,341	73	5,172	29	25,287	16,479	(d)	. . . .	Incorporated Place
Carbondale	CARB-	11163	3-A	19,222	20,681	12,730	9,604	17,419	244,704	.0070	400,087	118	117,496	249	21,318	119	38,791	24,239	(d)	. . . .	Incorporated Place
Carol Stream	CHI	11332	◇	41,365	40,438	23,122	14,699	58,343	956,449	.0150	445,407	131	14,026	30	1,936	11	38,694	16,480	503,514	276	Incorporated Place
Carpentersville	CHI	11358	◇	40,243	30,586	16,521	11,605	49,242	664,861	.0091	71,195	21	7,444	16	2,753	15	19,147	6,388	137,041	75	Incorporated Place
Centralia		12164	4-B	13,782	14,136	18,132	5,685	32,024	249,901	.0047	184,019	54	43,637	93	7,513	42	29,446	8,851	103,956	57	Incorporated Place
Champaign	CH-U	12385	3-AA	70,220	67,518	17,143	28,567	31,966	1,203,794	.0260	1,221,875	359	391,357	831	79,455	445	110,865	86,832	219,205	120	Incorporated Place
Chicago	CHI	14000	1-AAA	2,897,405	2,896,016	16,792	1,059,656	37,072	48,651,845	.7932	19,857,932	5,841	1,887,367	4,006	1,715,149	9,612	3,897,051	2,785,914	13,497,813	7,390	Incorporated Place
Chicago Heights	CHI	14026	4-S	32,591	32,776	13,761	10,633	38,295	448,477	.0090	326,670	96	2,814	6	1,087	6	64,780	28,320	419,292	230	Incorporated Place
Cicero	CHI	14351	4-Sr	90,010	85,616	10,455	24,289	35,498	941,017	.0178	398,455	117	79,772	169	16,484	92	66,042	35,775	499,866	274	Incorporated Place
Crystal Lake	CHI	17887	4-S	44,806	38,000	26,586	15,708	61,100	1,191,194	.0213	898,340	264	172,942	367	22,295	125	87,518	45,794	449,038	246	Incorporated Place
Danville	DANV	18563	3-A	33,715	33,904	15,749	13,455	29,801	530,971	.0113	502,307	148	124,461	264	18,197	102	75,317	38,036	507,484	278	Incorporated Place
Decatur	DEC	18823	3-AA	78,988	81,860	17,937	33,409	33,009	1,416,779	.0277	1,141,624	336	208,233	442	36,122	202	157,579	89,959	. . . .	. . . .	Incorporated Place
DeKalb	DKLB	19161	4-C	41,272	39,018	15,183	13,812	33,222	626,630	.0123	456,807	134	76,594	163	15,884	89	62,896	29,698	271,271	149	Incorporated Place
Des Plaines	CHI	19642	3-S	58,739	58,720	19,027	22,299	44,761	1,117,627	.0192	627,550	185	49,986	106	8,725	49	115,564	68,315	988,977	541	Incorporated Place
Downers Grove	CHI	20591	4-S	49,159	48,724	28,735	19,856	57,300	1,412,592	.0304	1,684,302	495	51,014	108	32,742	183	124,074	64,105	426,765	234	Incorporated Place
East St. Louis	ST.L	22255	4-S	30,981	31,542	11,142	11,313	21,058	345,186	.0062	119,961	35	2,997	6	. . . .	. . . .	44,211	12,298	63,825	35	Incorporated Place
Effingham		22736	4-B	12,290	12,384	20,596	5,399	36,287	253,123	.0068	432,618	127	56,305	120	16,719	94	37,248	13,877	288,900	158	Incorporated Place
Elgin	CHI	23074	3-S	108,824	94,487	19,906	36,090	49,071	2,166,231	.0349	987,935	291	82,380	175	5,396	30	161,993	55,558	909,017	498	Incorporated Place
Elk Grove Village	CHI	23256	4-Sr	33,511	34,727	22,487	12,771	54,170	753,564	.0156	767,098	226	109,718	233	2,289	13	95,172	19,950	2,109,266	1,155	Incorporated Place
Elmhurst	CHI	23620	4-Sr	43,457	42,762	28,956	16,460	61,299	1,258,356	.0239	1,134,707	334	. . . .	. . . .	14,212	80	128,337	90,301	226,566	124	Incorporated Place
Evanston	CHI	24582	3-S	73,860	74,239	27,023	29,498	50,131	1,995,937	.0312	1,014,513	298	84,212	179	40,336	226	202,638	149,292	167,457	92	Incorporated Place
Evergreen Park	CHI	24634	3-Sm	20,443	20,821	18,972	7,315	48,125	387,845	.0073	292,845	86	94,890	201	59,013	331	20,214	10,385	(d)	. . . .	Incorporated Place
Fairview Heights	ST.L	25141	3-Sm	15,806	15,034	21,355	6,539	41,638	337,534	.0114	837,023	246	295,443	627	110,912	622	49,582	47,931	(d)	. . . .	Incorporated Place
Franklin Park	CHI	27702	4-S	20,077	19,434	14,650	6,682	42,045	294,124	.0062	262,027	77	28,936	61	2,711	15	39,355	10,858	1,963,752	1,075	Incorporated Place
Freeport		27884	4-C	26,075	26,443	19,701	11,185	35,712	513,693	.0093	351,424	103	68,938	146	12,089	68	65,489	30,832	595,642	326	Incorporated Place
Galesburg	GLSB	28326	3-A	33,299	33,706	16,271	13,238	31,053	541,816	.0114	506,836	149	115,955	246	11,856	66	74,125	31,370	. . . .	. . . .	Incorporated Place
Glendale Heights	CHI	29730	◇	32,573	31,765	20,353	11,456	51,438	662,944	.0104	279,807	82	33,869	72	. . . .	. . . .	41,154	20,002	190,122	104	Incorporated Place
Glen Ellyn	CHI	29756	◇	27,821	26,999	32,726	10,897	61,540	910,473	.0123	282,425	83	20,396	43	7,214	40	53,756	17,204	(d)	. . . .	Incorporated Place
Glenview	CHI	29938	4-Sr	41,832	41,847	34,376	15,412	64,994	1,438,002	.0211	658,001	194	45,615	97	23,212	130	78,205	55,335	102,240	56	Incorporated Place
Granite City	ST.L	30926	4-S	31,617	31,301	18,425	13,240	35,140	582,543	.0098	300,066	88	44,429	94	5,698	32	77,274	22,478	813,853	446	Incorporated Place
Gurnee	CHI	32018	◇	34,805	28,834	23,317	12,940	63,712	811,539	.0160	753,239	222	176,487	375	148,827	834	69,808	46,931	278,780	153	Incorporated Place
Hanover Park	CHI	32746	◇	39,364	38,278	17,252	11,392	55,092	679,116	.0097	134,194	39	8,766	19	2,200	12	23,297	14,256	(d)	. . . .	Incorporated Place
Harvey	CHI	33383	4-Sr	29,498	30,000	11,017	8,817	32,294	324,990	.0069	231,546	68	2,853	6	6,776	38	34,160	22,255	315,510	173	Incorporated Place
Highland Park	CHI	34722	4-S	31,779	31,365	45,337	11,771	82,867	1,440,766	.0222	857,933	252	34,382	73	62,234	349	131,978	51,674	. . . .	. . . .	Incorporated Place
Hinsdale	CHI	35307	4-S	18,175	17,349	54,702	6,481	86,182	994,207	.0125	306,018	90	55,305	117	64,440	361	9,270	15,810	(d)	. . . .	Incorporated Place
Hoffman Estates	CHI	35411	◇	48,850	49,495	22,232	16,761	58,485	1,086,025	.0178	575,555	169	22,578	48	28,066	157	72,085	30,601	104,649	57	Incorporated Place
Homewood	CHI	35879	4-S	19,316	19,543	22,349	7,447	50,961	431,697	.0094	491,635	145	61,434	130	13,280	74	78,486	34,921	(d)	. . . .	Incorporated Place
Jacksonville		38115	3-A	18,821	18,940	17,202	7,389	34,005	323,760	.0064	263,418	77	50,293	107	11,435	64	36,830	17,526	. . . .	. . . .	Incorporated Place
Joliet	CHI	38570	3-SS	134,127	106,221	19,738	46,251	44,699	2,647,457	.0461	1,594,184	469	249,054	529	61,639	345	182,509	161,428	1,304,353	714	Incorporated Place
Kankakee	KANK	38934	3-A	27,724	27,491	16,544	10,208	33,660	458,667	.0087	327,592	96	12,149	26	1,767	10	59,398	44,297	288,232	158	Incorporated Place
Lake in the Hills	CHI	41183	◇	29,554	23,152	25,300	9,951	63,502	747,705	.0088	32,323	10	. . . .	. . . .	3,629	20	7,571	3,662	(d)	. . . .	Incorporated Place
La Salle		42184	3-A	9,812	9,796	19,118	4,205	32,460	187,586	.0036	144,405	42	3,799	8	2,413	14	15,303	5,542	77,519	42	Incorporated Place
Libertyville	CHI	43250	4-Sr	21,151	20,742	34,877	7,503	77,207	737,675	.0162	953,822	281	. . . .	. . . .	7,023	39	71,008	11,923	1,937,093	1,060	Incorporated Place
Lombard	CHI	44407	3-Sm	42,198	42,322	25,502	17,044	53,339	1,076,137	.0203	922,721	271	162,614	345	108,480	608	53,452	30,566	146,397	80	Incorporated Place
Macomb		45889	4-C	19,282	18,558	13,471	7,121	27,835	259,741	.0057	240,606	71	67,088	142	8,826	49	44,846	22,045	59,507	33	Incorporated Place
Marion	CARB-	46916	4-B	16,219	16,035	18,729	7,077	31,468	303,769	.0075	432,406	127	136,424	290	13,316	75	36,736	9,991	. . . .	. . . .	Incorporated Place
Matteson	CHI	47540	4-Sm	12,631	12,928	19,761	4,456	49,705	249,607	.0083	603,983	178	202,264	429	78,118	438	32,174	14,236	(d)	. . . .	Incorporated Place
Mattoon		47553	4-A	17,591	18,291	17,891	8,063	32,375	314,716	.0074	393,831	116	129,420	275	4,489	25	16,793	19,625	497,769	273	Incorporated Place
Melrose Park	CHI	48242	3-S	23,934	23,171	14,310	7,861	37,715	342,493	.0095	558,385	164	70,772	150	23,268	130	69,288	27,521	1,093,761	599	Incorporated Place
Moline	D-RI-M	49867	3-B	43,808	43,768	20,115	18,685	36,270	881,187	.0195	1,007,592	296	202,686	430	69,351	389	90,472	104,127	237,831	130	Incorporated Place
Morton Grove	CHI	50647	4-S	22,126	22,451	22,320	8,062	56,221	493,853	.0099	472,665	139	3,907	8	28,263	158	34,787	39,908	717,167	393	Incorporated Place
Mount Prospect	CHI	51089	3-S	57,053	56,265	22,325	21,826	50,957	1,273,735	.0222	824,271	242	208,164	442	52,189	292	114,413	76,118	270,726	148	Incorporated Place
Mount Vernon		51180	3-A	16,348	16,269	17,325	7,113	29,836	283,226	.0076	457,507	135	86,129	183	13,972	78	35,793	24,557	368,582	202	Incorporated Place
Mundelein	CHI	51349	◇	33,976	30,935	21,340	10,903	60,746	725,051	.0112	291,350	86	24,120	51	9,309	52	49,025	32,997	305,034	167	Incorporated Place
Naperville	CHI	51622	4-S	138,753	128,358	31,556	48,967	73,996	4,378,506	.0644	1,932,398	568	185,824	394	68,769	385	194,008	117,043	193,251	106	Incorporated Place
Niles	CHI	53000	3-S	29,662	30,068	19,743	11,799	44,244	585,617	.0191	1,362,152	401	223,654	475	46,479	260	225,416	80,701	588,352	322	Incorporated Place
Normal	BLOOM-	53234	4-S	47,810	45,386	16,371	16,144	38,006	782,715	.0156	626,729	184	155,023	329	46,374	260	68,932	40,827	. . . .	. . . .	Incorporated Place
Norridge	CHI	53377	4-Sm	14,428	14,582	19,461	5,649	42,148	280,780	.0060	291,218	86	. . . .	. . . .	34,936	196	95,098	25,849	48,441	27	Incorporated Place
Northbrook	CHI	53481	3-Sm	32,708	33,435	39,661	11,919	73,629	1,297,233	.0201	750,230	221	117,686	250	109,855	616	62,159	38,430	474,909	260	Incorporated Place
North Chicago	CHI	53559	◇	36,386	35,918	9,046	7,817	36,148	329,162	.0069	182,325	54	. . . .	. . . .	. . . .	. . . .	28,519	3,607	130,015	71	Incorporated Place
North Riverside	CHI	54144	4-Sm	6,903	6,688	26,043	3,023	49,039	179,773	.0050	337,305	99	86,308	183	70,532	395	38,543	15,251	(d)	. . . .	Incorporated Place
Oak Brook	CHI	54534	3-S	8,723	8,702	52,268	3,245	84,267	455,935	.0095	563,876	166	229,121	486	81,583	457	2,742	7,656	220,093	120	Incorporated Place
Oak Lawn	CHI	54820	3-S	52,069	55,245	20,610	20,879	42,981	1,073,144	.0259	1,476,313	434	112,566	239	42,561	239	215,032	100,228	30,654	17	Incorporated Place
Oak Park	CHI	54885	4-S	48,895	52,524	29,800	21,412	52,336	1,457,054	.0194	395,036	116	. . . .	. . . .	27,390	154	108,974	57,376	49,041	27	Incorporated Place
Olney		55912	4-C	8,234	8,631	16,645	3,634	29,561	137,054	.0033	171,599	50	22,954	49	2,875	16	27,863	8,062	(d)	. . . .	Incorporated Place
Orland Park	CHI	56640	3-Sm	49,821	51,077	24,625	18,154	60,405	1,226,856	.0269	1,457,999	429	301,482	640	152,296	854	105,863	116,862	359,992	197	Incorporated Place
Ottawa		56926	4-B	18,246	18,307	19,858	7,562	36,191	362,329	.0076	364,299	107	81,198	172	7,368	41	54,068	21,377	54,605	30	Incorporated Place
Palatine	CHI	57225	◇	69,254	65,479	26,978	26,905	57,637	1,868,331	.0263	619,637	182	38,883	83	14,242	80	111,637	45,965	258,005	141	Incorporated Place
Park Ridge	CHI	57875	4-S	37,072	37,775	29,427	13,915	62,925	1,090,927	.0152	364,445	107	. . . .	. . . .	14,940	84	67,406	39,903	(d)	. . . .	Incorporated Place
Pekin	PEOR	58447	3-S	33,916	33,857	18,769	13,634	36,987	636,568	.0127	556,641	164	57,958	123	16,207	91	71,317	25,475	. . . .	. . . .	Incorporated Place
Peoria	PEOR	59000	2-AA	112,542	112,936	18,675	46,284	35,351	2,101,671	.0412	1,739,905	512	280,641	596	32,834	184	253,793	146,820	541,527	296	Incorporated Place
Peru		59234	3-B	9,702	9,835	20,443	4,122	36,086	198,334	.0069	516,530	152	155,261	330	24,940	140	60,144	26,029	133,136	73	Incorporated Place
Quincy	QUIN	62367	3-A	39,145	40,366	16,351	16,204	30,396	640,060	.0152	798,538	235	161,728	343	25,039	140	125,668	44,038	405,817	222	Incorporated Place
Rockford	RKFD	65000	2-A	153,198	150,115	19,990	61,712	38,357	3,062,359	.0541	1,944,778	572	274,012	582	46,584	261	372,335	133,910	2,524,850	1,382	Incorporated Place
Rock Island	D-RI-M	65078	3-C	40,078	39,684	17,640	16,466	32,774	706,957	.0112	270,586	80	18,084	38	4,435	25	45,492	24,977	137,352	75	Incorporated Place
Round Lake Beach	CHI	66040	◇	30,040	25,859	13,872	8,598	50,764	416,728	.0082	293,107	86	71,279	151	9,427	53	48,424	12,562	(d)	. . . .	Incorporated Place
St. Charles	CHI	66703	4-S	33,145	27,896	31,146	12,213	61,531	1,032,321	.0175	716,930	211	119,230	253	31,534	177	157,466	47,158	764,899	419	Incorporated Place
Schaumburg	CHI	68003	3-SSm	73,056	75,386	25,499	30,777	54,472	1,862,843	.0419	2,363,265	695	331,021	703	286,602	1,606	96,400	105,122	920,387	504	Incorporated Place
Skokie	CHI	70122	3-SSm	66,007	63,348	22,673	24,141	52,044	1,496,596	.0296	1,379,862	406	208,976	444	248,484	1,393	109,532	123,833	1,176,843	644	Incorporated Place
Springfield	SPRG	72000	2-A	113,810	111,454	20,998	50,408	37,062	2,389,771	.0449	1,869,211	550	384,504	816	69,393	389	250,100	128,591	211,854	116	Incorporated Place
Sterling		72546	3-B	15,319	15,451	20,575	6,269	37,540	315,196	.0060	249,040	73	76,601	163	5,153	29	21,973	13,789	226,595	124	Incorporated Place
Streamwood	CHI	73157	◇	36,391	36,407	19,551	12,070	56,935	711,491	.0102	173,341	51	56,545	120	8,982	50	36,028	. . . .	84,209	46	Incorporated Place
Streator		73170	4-B	13,832	14,190	16,909	5,662	33,315	233,890	.0043	147,533	43	12,698	27	5,761	32	24,504	14,205	101,438	56	Incorporated Place
Tinley Park	CHI	75484	◇	48,115	48,401	19,936	17,343	54,546	959,197	.0180	724,166	213	119,562	254	23,848	134	75,177	45,615	104,667	57	Incorporated Place
Urbana	CH-U	77005	4-B	37,991	36,395	14,904	15,151	26,767	566,235	.0109	388,131	114	42,308	90	6,455	36	104,646	53,309	. . . .	. . . .	Incorporated Place
Vernon Hills	CHI	77694	4-Sm	22,905	20,120	24,870	8,675	62,478	569,650	.0229	1,857,268	546	241,821	513	121,342	680	25,208	41,671	179,070	98	Incorporated Place
Villa Park	CHI	77993	4-S	22,146	22,075	22,160	8,120	49,144	490,752	.0105	541,243	159	134,333	285	15,499	87	39,645	39,705	79,212	43	Incorporated Place
Waukegan	CHI	79293	3-SS	99,460	87,901	13,842	31,712	40,542	1,376,722	.0303	1,318,904	388	137,366	292	29,209	164	185,452	142,872	453,546	248	Incorporated Place
Wheaton	CHI	81048	◇	55,126	55,416	31,996	19,931	65,292	1,763,818	.0246	629,159	185	66,462	141	56,769	318	135,007	56,128	37,664	21	Incorporated Place
Wheeling	CHI	81087	◇	36,479	34,496	21,438	14,008	49,734	782,047	.0131	433,051	127	66,906	142	5,401	30	83,692	41,561	1,234,260	676	Incorporated Place
Wilmette	CHI	82075	◇	28,257	27,651	44,225	10,259	87,222	1,249,664	.0155	316,766	93	50,043	106	17,729	99	43,657	41,570	(d)	. . . .	Incorporated Place
Woodridge	CHI	83245	◇	32,049	30,934	24,657	12,228	55,557	790,246	.0113	257,450	76	106,945	227	15,809	89	27,590	10,013	92,332	51	Incorporated Place

Indiana

PLACE NAME	RANALLY METRO AREA	FIPS PLACE CODE	RANALLY CITY RATING	POPULATION Estimate 7/1/04	POPULATION Census 4/1/00	PER CAPITA INCOME 2003	HOUSEHOLDS Estimate 7/1/04	MEDIAN HOUSEHOLD INCOME 2003	DISPOSABLE INCOME 2003 ($1,000)	MARKET ABILITY INDEX 2003	TOTAL RETAIL TRADE Sales 2003 ($1,000)	TOTAL RETAIL TRADE Ranally Sales Units	GENERAL MERCHANDISE Sales 2003 ($1,000)	GENERAL MERCHANDISE Ranally Sales Units	APPAREL STORES Sales 2003 ($1,000)	APPAREL STORES Ranally Sales Units	FOOD STORE SALES 2003 ($1,000)	HEALTH & DRUG STORE SALES 2003 ($1,000)	MANUFACTURERS VALUE ADDED 1997* ($1,000)	MANUFACTURERS Ranally Mfg Units	PLACE TYPE
Anderson	AND	01468	3-A	58,855	59,734	18,041	25,348	33,872	1,061,805	.0199	757,813	223	180,121	382	22,917	128	75,484	60,048	717,721	393	Incorporated Place
Bedford		04114	4-B	13,407	13,768	19,017	6,049	34,335	254,963	.0048	190,142	56	45,496	97	10,374	58	21,626	12,473	311,883	171	Incorporated Place
Bloomington	BLMNG	05860	3-A	71,037	69,291	15,903	29,468	31,270	1,129,694	.0219	830,877	244	170,363	362	38,603	216	139,459	39,756	641,806	351	Incorporated Place
Carmel	IND	10342	◇	37,926	37,733	36,277	13,770	77,687	1,375,842	.0187	483,423	142	139,105	295	16,886	95	48,969	24,794	77,728	43	Incorporated Place
Clarksville	LOU	12934	4-Sm	21,796	21,400	19,985	9,755	32,321	435,593	.0109	638,301	188	88,577	188	22,856	128	40,103	31,885	149,981	82	Incorporated Place
Columbus	COL	14734	3-A	40,648	39,059	20,770	16,835	40,726	844,249	.0140	448,397	132	83,111	176	28,194	158	61,224	36,242	1,055,077	578	Incorporated Place
Crawfordsville		15742	4-C	15,280	15,243	18,924	6,146	37,744	289,164	.0052	184,899	54	36,299	77	2,399	13	28,737	11,737	. . . .	. . . .	Incorporated Place
East Chicago	CHI	19486	4-S	32,466	32,414	13,384	11,968	25,431	434,527	.0073	151,543	45	. . . .	. . . .	5,907	33	45,319	20,589	2,405,111	1,317	Incorporated Place
Elkhart	ELK	20728	3-A	53,493	51,874	18,783	20,753	38,590	1,004,736	.0187	721,822	212	81,188	172	11,997	67	95,633	40,360	1,481,111	811	Incorporated Place
Evansville	EV	22000	2-A	117,446	121,582	17,903	53,326	32,539	2,102,578	.0482	2,492,611	733	517,404	1,098	150,083	841	227,942	116,190	2,148,005	1,176	Incorporated Place
Fishers	IND	23278	◇	60,990	37,835	26,176	22,803	63,616	1,596,500	.0251	810,537	238	115,377	245	6,086	34	89,489	24,866	50,937	28	Incorporated Place
Fort Wayne	FTWA	25000	2-A	211,007	205,727	17,779	88,213	36,047	3,751,507	.0736	3,034,718	893	613,784	1,303	167,621	939	276,906	200,442	2,043,352	1,119	Incorporated Place
Gary	CHI	27000	3-S	103,129	102,746	13,676	39,155	26,926	1,410,413	.0240	547,460	161	26,605	56	17,058	96	95,778	66,788	1,802,488	987	Incorporated Place
Goshen	ELK	28386	4-S	31,715	29,383	17,805	11,589	41,073	564,680	.0121	573,020	169	178,849	380	6,386	36	35,175	18,164	449,604	246	Incorporated Place
Granger	S.B.	28800	◇	28,384	28,284	25,330	9,490	63,395	718,957	.0096	167,597	49	1,494	3	3,483	20	42,600	19,802	(d)	. . . .	Census Designated Place
Greenwood	IND	29898	4-Sm	39,661	36,037	25,838	16,726	49,812	1,024,777	.0180	728,335	214	289,500	615	48,416	271	39,084	32,426	78,753	43	Incorporated Place
Hammond	CHI	31000	3-S	83,180	83,048	15,459	32,683	33,130	1,285,846	.0238	800,288	235	49,096	104	19,634	110	124,067	66,375	556,299	305	Incorporated Place
Highland	CHI	33466	4-Sr	23,783	23,546	22,301	9,922	45,956	530,384	.0118	630,001	185	100,821	214	15,039	84	83,235	33,327	(d)	. . . .	Incorporated Place
Indianapolis	IND	36003	1-A	783,029	781,870	19,621	338,932	38,103	15,363,865	.3055	13,525,845	3,979	2,050,225	4,352	641,412	3,595	1,165,665	1,053,983	11,048,165	6,049	Incorporated Place
Jasper		37782	4-C	12,574	12,100	22,947	5,296	42,133	288,539	.0067	379,604	112	59,873	127	14,354	80	25,779	5,979	474,014	260	Incorporated Place
Jeffersonville	LOU	38358	4-S	28,481	27,362	20,080	12,967	37,636	571,898	.0108	442,633	130	124,339	264	10,358	58	39,784	17,191	252,575	138	Incorporated Place
Kokomo	KOK	40392	3-A	45,958	46,113	22,014	21,175	38,707	1,011,729	.0181	709,400	209	198,818	422	20,744	116	73,366	54,136	. . . .	. . . .	Incorporated Place
Lafayette	LAF-	40788	3-AA	63,099	56,397	18,467	27,643	36,638	1,165,267	.0235	1,035,043	304	257,755	547	47,572	267	62,118	53,896	. . . .	. . . .	Incorporated Place
La Porte	MICH	42246	4-B	21,590	21,621	20,084	9,062	40,345	433,618	.0071	218,220	64	28,493	60	5,546	31	32,839	13,739	308,059	169	Incorporated Place
Lawrence	IND	42426	◇	41,530	38,915	22,944	16,805	48,174	952,852	.0134	264,832	78	15,854	34	3,425	19	34,828	36,926	30,313	17	Incorporated Place
Logansport		44658	4-B	19,428	19,684	16,645	7,513	34,779	323,379	.0063	245,928	72	40,887	87	10,850	61	28,511	16,970	202,466	111	Incorporated Place
Madison		45990	4-C	11,855	12,004	19,280	5,214	35,546	228,570	.0044	186,934	55	47,876	102	6,983	39	20,013	6,153	230,263	126	Incorporated Place
Marion	MRN	46908	3-A	30,821	31,320	16,606	12,482	32,764	511,818	.0103	433,069	127	57,578	122	10,138	57	41,260	28,795	642,317	352	Incorporated Place
Merrillville	CHI	48528	3-S	30,736	30,560	20,159	11,985	43,684	619,615	.0202	1,446,852	426	423,148	898	114,808	643	88,224	56,292	44,774	25	Incorporated Place
Michigan City	MICH	48798	3-A	32,420	32,900	17,979	12,565	36,085	582,885	.0117	504,717	148	117,913	250	76,191	427	38,069	36,688	516,876	283	Incorporated Place
Mishawaka	S.B.	49932	3-B	46,763	46,557	18,189	20,961	34,620	850,594	.0226	1,365,524	402	356,990	758	78,807	442	87,603	64,864	360,347	197	Incorporated Place
Muncie	MUN	51876	3-AA	65,062	67,430	15,395	26,810	30,502	1,001,655	.0206	849,800	250	212,815	452	29,262	164	87,904	45,636	614,293	336	Incorporated Place
New Albany	LOU	52326	4-S	36,879	37,603	19,427	16,415	36,353	716,449	.0113	293,397	86	59,083	125	4,137	23	41,944	34,211	634,275	347	Incorporated Place
New Castle		52740	4-C	17,513	17,780	18,064	7,468	34,593	316,354	.0059	224,898	66	31,907	68	3,783	21	23,807	14,059	212,960	117	Incorporated Place
Noblesville	IND	54180	◇	33,367	28,590	23,966	12,428	54,719	799,676	.0136	496,869	146	78,122	166	4,029	23	41,687	8,631	201,491	110	Incorporated Place
Portage	CHI	61092	◇	35,790	33,496	19,728	13,974	43,096	706,073	.0107	242,399	71	118,080	251	1,107	6	30,636	29,323	359,426	197	Incorporated Place
Richmond	RICH	64260	3-A	39,620	39,124	16,669	16,770	31,449	660,419	.0140	633,934	186	143,715	305	15,628	88	88,336	27,739	660,737	362	Incorporated Place
Shelbyville		69318	4-S	18,512	17,951	19,232	7,689	37,985	356,019	.0061	200,385	59	29,233	62	. . . .	. . . .	28,293	8,501	383,386	210	Incorporated Place
South Bend	S.B.	71000	2-A	110,206	107,789	16,646	45,067	33,283	1,834,525	.0325	1,034,857	304	178,706	379	20,643	116	135,783	80,513	956,514	524	Incorporated Place
Terre Haute	T.H.	75428	3-AA	61,788	59,614	14,579	24,880	29,536	900,799	.0301	2,053,224	604	223,708	475	48,048	269	110,045	47,919	788,416	432	Incorporated Place
Valparaiso	CHI	78326	4-S	29,435	27,428	23,608	11,951	47,024	694,899	.0118	429,884	126	81,470	173	9,262	52	60,351	40,533	276,909	152	Incorporated Place
Vincennes		79208	3-A	18,743	18,701	14,657	7,724	29,387	274,719	.0062	286,520	84	67,259	143	18,320	103	26,181	16,704	92,644	51	Incorporated Place
Warsaw		80306	4-C	12,821	12,415	18,962	5,012	38,819	243,110	.0051	236,169	69	48,581	103	8,550	48	31,596	13,454	966,257	529	Incorporated Place
Washington		80504	4-B	11,097	11,380	15,393	4,552	30,232	170,820	.0036	158,404	47	12,535	27	3,050	17	20,238	11,585	95,059	52	Incorporated Place
West Lafayette	LAF-	82862	◇	28,286	28,778	15,937	10,538	30,516	450,801	.0070	132,190	39	42,790	91	4,233	24	20,235	10,713	. . . .	. . . .	Incorporated Place

Iowa

PLACE NAME	RANALLY METRO AREA	FIPS PLACE CODE	RANALLY CITY RATING	POPULATION Estimate 7/1/04	POPULATION Census 4/1/00	PER CAPITA INCOME 2003	HOUSEHOLDS Estimate 7/1/04	MEDIAN HOUSEHOLD INCOME 2003	DISPOSABLE INCOME 2003 ($1,000)	MARKET ABILITY INDEX 2003	TOTAL RETAIL TRADE Sales 2003 ($1,000)	TOTAL RETAIL TRADE Ranally Sales Units	GENERAL MERCHANDISE Sales 2003 ($1,000)	GENERAL MERCHANDISE Ranally Sales Units	APPAREL STORES Sales 2003 ($1,000)	APPAREL STORES Ranally Sales Units	FOOD STORE SALES 2003 ($1,000)	HEALTH & DRUG STORE SALES 2003 ($1,000)	MANUFACTURERS VALUE ADDED 1997* ($1,000)	MANUFACTURERS Ranally Mfg Units	PLACE TYPE
Ames	AMES	01855	3-C	54,087	50,731	16,415	19,399	35,910	887,820	.0176	704,016	207	156,477	332	27,969	157	126,049	32,123	568,081	311	Incorporated Place
Ankeny	DES	02305	◇	29,644	27,117	22,229	11,544	51,344	658,961	.0111	380,634	112	32,989	70	3,709	21	56,327	13,884	487,377	267	Incorporated Place
Bettendorf	D-RI-M	06355	4-S	31,032	31,275	24,766	12,561	48,504	768,552	.0119	353,986	104	34,642	74	14,159	79	61,929	17,844	72,831	40	Incorporated Place
Burlington	BUR	09550	3-A	26,103	26,839	17,511	10,971	32,910	457,083	.0086	324,965	96	51,239	109	5,105	29	91,536	21,207	295,043	162	Incorporated Place
Cedar Falls	WATL	11755	4-B	35,798	36,145	16,561	13,022	38,215	592,850	.0117	464,017	136	42,317	90	24,774	139	58,637	16,382	162,403	89	Incorporated Place
Cedar Rapids	CEDR	12000	3-AA	124,124	120,758	20,961	52,025	40,627	2,601,804	.0507	2,237,840	658	437,789	929	110,907	622	264,756	119,579	3,517,315	1,926	Incorporated Place
Clinton	CLNT	14430	3-A	27,014	27,772	17,273	11,302	32,303	466,617	.0092	371,554	109	58,176	123	7,351	41	52,241	25,268	909,683	498	Incorporated Place
Council Bluffs	OMA	16860	3-S	59,413	58,268	17,443	23,572	36,093	1,036,330	.0231	1,144,906	337	113,249	240	35,821	201	125,880	62,383	. . . .	. . . .	Incorporated Place
Davenport	D-RI-M	19000	2-A	99,603	98,359	17,379	40,318	35,654	1,731,015	.0379	1,832,478	539	322,272	684	85,031	477	187,007	96,657	1,363,190	746	Incorporated Place
Des Moines	DES	21000	2-AA	201,934	198,682	17,867	83,406	36,599	3,607,999	.0704	2,888,336	850	551,844	1,171	124,524	698	410,260	165,403	1,027,848	563	Incorporated Place
Dubuque	DUB	22395	3-A	58,365	57,686	17,506	23,446	35,359	1,021,757	.0204	863,398	254	150,917	320	24,897	140	119,036	55,304	. . . .	. . . .	Incorporated Place
Fort Dodge		28515	3-A	23,516	25,136	16,483	9,845	32,202	387,605	.0087	421,721	124	103,851	220	9,967	56	57,421	23,895	634,072	347	Incorporated Place
Iowa City	IACY	38595	3-A	62,057	62,220	18,533	25,655	35,157	1,150,088	.0209	764,497	225	75,613	161	19,356	108	166,017	47,245	1,769,541	969	Incorporated Place
Marion	CEDR	49485	◇	28,331	26,294	22,185	11,447	44,949	628,534	.0096	248,590	73	2,311	5	3,708	21	62,140	17,141	44,341	24	Incorporated Place
Marshalltown		49755	4-A	25,845	26,009	17,095	10,100	34,997	441,829	.0083	313,752	92	61,767	131	18,273	102	52,905	20,079	. . . .	. . . .	Incorporated Place
Mason City		50160	3-A	28,296	29,172	18,349	12,562	32,992	519,198	.0115	580,439	171	168,672	358	14,227	80	71,696	12,077	252,177	138	Incorporated Place

. . . . Data less than 1,000.
(d) Data not available.
◇ Not classified as a Principal Business Center.

* Data from 1997 Census of Manufactures.

Principal Business Centers and Other Places with 27,500 or More: Population / Income / Sales, *Continued*

Place Name	Ranally Metro Area	FIPS Place Code	Ranally City Rating	Population Estimate 7/1/04	Population Census 4/1/00	Per Capita Income 2003	Households Estimate 7/1/04	Median Household Income 2003	Disposable Income 2003 ($1,000)	Market Ability Index 2003	Total Retail Trade Sales 2003 ($1,000)	Total Retail Trade Ranally Sales Units	General Merchandise Sales 2003 ($1,000)	General Merchandise Ranally Sales Units	Apparel Stores Sales 2003 ($1,000)	Apparel Stores Ranally Sales Units	Food Store Sales 2003 ($1,000)	Health & Drug Store Sales 2003 ($1,000)	Manufacturers Value Added 1997* ($1,000)	Manufacturers Ranally Mfg Units	Place Type
Muscatine		55110	4-C	22,612	22,697	19,168	8,981	38,236	433,421	.0080	308,231	91	54,986	117	7,534	42	49,957	16,950	564,392	309	Incorporated Place
Ottumwa		60465	4-A	25,282	24,998	15,335	10,570	30,107	387,694	.0078	308,415	91	70,798	150	12,118	68	51,917	15,726	....	....	Incorporated Place
Sioux City	SXCY	73335	3-AA	84,235	85,013	16,790	31,784	36,033	1,414,344	.0287	1,211,724	356	207,388	440	52,273	293	179,841	49,826	476,963	261	Incorporated Place
Urbandale	DES	79950	◇	30,908	29,072	24,990	12,463	54,158	772,403	.0134	523,146	154	36,294	77	5,614	31	75,923	29,670	126,660	69	Incorporated Place
Waterloo	WATL	82425	3-AA	69,727	68,747	17,020	29,329	33,255	1,186,755	.0244	1,065,764	314	248,306	527	29,653	166	125,241	70,710	2,082,662	1,140	Incorporated Place
West Des Moines	DES	83910	4-Sm	50,726	46,403	27,881	22,116	48,726	1,414,303	.0210	597,535	176	83,830	178	65,978	370	86,819	38,551	113,983	62	Incorporated Place
Kansas																					
Coffeyville		14600	4-A	9,831	11,021	14,512	4,224	27,501	142,669	.0028	103,045	30	24,866	53	4,621	26	19,577	7,607	53,112	29	Incorporated Place
Dodge City		18250	4-A	25,962	25,176	13,948	8,392	35,268	362,127	.0081	363,414	107	71,967	153	10,810	61	35,287	8,082	....	....	Incorporated Place
Emporia		21275	4-A	27,092	26,760	14,723	10,609	30,194	398,862	.0081	323,345	95	62,115	132	16,761	94	51,098	12,674	....	....	Incorporated Place
Garden City		25325	4-A	28,944	28,451	14,469	9,666	35,548	418,792	.0088	363,052	107	74,484	158	21,333	120	51,272	6,139	(d)	....	Incorporated Place
Great Bend		28300	3-A	14,866	15,345	15,444	6,241	30,638	229,597	.0051	239,776	71	44,572	95	4,988	28	36,006	11,075	44,919	25	Incorporated Place
Hays		31100	4-A	19,878	20,013	16,427	8,335	31,763	326,528	.0076	385,631	113	65,656	139	22,279	125	51,074	11,430	43,301	24	Incorporated Place
Hutchinson	HUCH	33625	3-A	40,525	40,787	16,469	16,347	33,531	667,412	.0130	511,583	150	92,053	195	16,424	92	64,031	18,587	232,041	127	Incorporated Place
Junction City		35750	4-B	17,495	18,886	18,662	9,012	29,406	326,499	.0057	196,608	58	41,131	87	1,478	8	38,719	2,490	(d)	....	Incorporated Place
Kansas City	K.C.	36000	3-SS	145,423	146,866	14,542	54,794	31,917	2,114,813	.0377	1,074,730	316	129,771	275	17,118	96	182,270	69,732	2,826,709	1,548	Incorporated Place
Lawrence	LAWR	38900	3-A	83,562	80,098	16,955	33,536	35,136	1,416,762	.0265	965,921	284	145,085	308	53,340	299	172,272	41,270	325,174	178	Incorporated Place
Leavenworth	LEAV	39000	4-C	33,933	35,420	17,549	11,793	39,413	595,495	.0096	244,770	72	54,634	116	4,885	27	32,123	15,191	(d)	....	Incorporated Place
Leawood	K.C.	39075	◇	30,400	27,656	37,831	11,225	78,262	1,150,055	.0150	342,661	101	....	....	68,585	384	60,725	31,436	(d)	....	Incorporated Place
Lenexa	K.C.	39350	4-Sr	44,257	40,238	26,600	17,800	58,829	1,177,244	.0203	810,140	238	120,713	256	21,116	118	83,205	48,898	658,743	361	Incorporated Place
Liberal		39825	4-A	20,486	19,666	13,441	6,588	34,426	275,349	.0064	299,046	88	61,577	131	21,684	122	46,041	7,098	....	....	Incorporated Place
Manhattan	MANH	44250	3-A	49,436	44,831	14,182	19,130	30,358	701,109	.0141	526,380	155	114,873	244	30,632	172	44,986	13,529	(d)	....	Incorporated Place
Olathe	K.C.	52575	4-S	109,785	92,962	21,541	39,691	54,604	2,364,904	.0433	1,744,512	513	213,964	454	56,395	316	169,763	53,615	523,679	287	Incorporated Place
Overland Park	K.C.	53775	3-SSm	169,244	149,080	27,936	70,525	58,185	4,727,953	.0819	3,336,853	982	739,441	1,570	280,597	1,573	267,975	161,115	115,593	63	Incorporated Place
Parsons		54675	4-B	11,268	11,514	15,394	4,681	28,880	173,457	.0034	130,357	38	22,282	47	3,364	19	22,551	8,638	101,120	55	Incorporated Place
Pittsburg		56025	4-A	19,310	19,243	13,990	7,998	26,786	270,152	.0059	259,754	76	101,864	216	6,323	35	35,998	6,999	187,244	103	Incorporated Place
Salina	SLN	62700	3-A	45,939	45,679	17,392	19,031	34,660	798,993	.0173	819,389	241	207,354	440	41,015	230	97,364	27,718	329,695	180	Incorporated Place
Shawnee	K.C.	64500	◇	54,628	47,996	24,782	21,885	54,785	1,353,785	.0225	800,577	235	105,835	225	69,392	389	132,951	39,013	....	....	Incorporated Place
Topeka	TOP	71000	3-AA	122,261	122,377	19,187	53,977	35,427	2,345,850	.0461	1,985,384	584	444,329	943	68,594	384	256,482	141,565	....	....	Incorporated Place
Wichita	WICH	79000	2-AA	357,893	344,284	18,895	146,053	38,501	6,762,227	.1231	4,563,292	1,342	906,382	1,924	219,543	1,230	587,065	230,822	4,011,147	2,196	Incorporated Place
Kentucky																					
Ashland	HNTG	02368	3-B	21,441	21,981	18,385	9,866	29,756	394,191	.0092	489,633	144	84,397	179	31,410	176	61,692	36,501	....	....	Incorporated Place
Bowling Green	BOWLG	08902	3-A	53,197	49,296	18,250	22,291	33,428	970,872	.0193	827,883	244	162,533	345	49,678	278	83,970	34,484	....	....	Incorporated Place
Corbin		17362	4-A	7,580	7,742	13,771	3,311	23,826	104,387	.0033	218,350	64	50,364	107	4,854	27	14,228	13,815	51,297	28	Incorporated Place
Covington	CIN	17848	4-S	44,039	43,370	19,519	19,289	33,843	859,607	.0133	330,109	97	23,994	51	8,177	46	76,315	38,893	148,337	81	Incorporated Place
Danville		19882	4-C	14,967	15,477	17,748	6,202	32,699	265,634	.0056	263,877	78	69,478	147	14,646	82	25,352	11,864	313,948	172	Incorporated Place
Elizabethtown		24274	4-C	23,953	22,542	21,357	10,378	36,479	511,571	.0105	503,768	148	135,788	288	34,485	193	31,407	29,576	693,186	379	Incorporated Place
Florence	CIN	27982	3-S	27,556	23,551	24,586	12,213	43,137	677,489	.0173	1,084,145	319	256,200	544	51,212	287	45,629	28,977	476,098	261	Incorporated Place
Frankfort		28900	4-C	27,923	27,741	22,778	13,172	37,524	636,039	.0102	321,899	95	63,804	135	11,633	65	35,618	17,755	266,113	146	Incorporated Place
Glasgow		31114	4-B	13,340	13,019	16,756	5,853	30,347	223,519	.0049	236,192	69	62,721	133	5,971	33	26,134	13,490	298,275	163	Incorporated Place
Harlan		34732	4-B	1,873	2,081	11,915	869	20,358	22,316	.0011	91,790	27	29,818	63	3,549	20	15,786	6,631	(d)	....	Incorporated Place
Henderson	EV	35866	4-S	27,978	27,373	18,718	12,206	32,570	523,699	.0099	389,086	114	57,772	123	12,565	70	44,772	33,898	784,611	430	Incorporated Place
Hopkinsville	HPKNV	37918	4-B	27,559	30,089	16,893	12,017	30,326	465,568	.0091	360,885	106	80,367	171	17,297	97	35,395	23,491	329,419	180	Incorporated Place
Lexington	LEX	46027	2-AA	272,540	260,512	21,394	122,985	37,928	5,830,726	.1062	4,220,467	1,241	615,292	1,306	286,312	1,605	425,898	272,346	2,147,695	1,176	Incorporated Place
Louisville	LOU	48000	2-AA	249,085	256,231	17,751	115,876	28,452	4,421,418	.0768	2,451,273	721	194,202	412	95,852	537	354,803	190,215	9,819,972	5,376	Incorporated Place
Madisonville		49368	4-A	19,057	19,307	16,839	8,134	30,368	320,892	.0066	291,337	86	67,858	144	15,834	89	33,654	23,800	....	....	Incorporated Place
Mayfield		50898	4-B	9,718	10,349	15,446	4,113	27,367	150,104	.0032	138,813	41	29,721	63	2,400	13	10,689	8,273	105,930	58	Incorporated Place
Maysville		51024	4-C	8,864	8,993	16,483	4,063	28,094	146,102	.0036	198,266	58	43,996	93	12,437	70	36,224	6,425	....	....	Incorporated Place
Middlesboro		51924	4-A	10,281	10,384	11,325	4,586	19,587	116,432	.0035	207,160	61	79,712	169	10,634	60	46,073	7,358	....	....	Incorporated Place
Murray		54642	4-B	14,638	14,950	15,229	6,125	28,181	222,922	.0052	258,663	76	50,719	108	11,108	62	18,184	12,778	....	....	Incorporated Place
Newport	CIN	55884	4-S	16,957	17,048	17,469	7,253	30,605	296,230	.0059	247,629	73	22,292	47	7,652	43	51,006	18,503	187,672	103	Incorporated Place
Owensboro	OWNS	58620	3-A	54,373	54,067	18,658	23,467	33,260	1,014,496	.0189	730,220	215	166,208	353	27,380	153	84,776	52,669	....	....	Incorporated Place
Paducah	PAD	58836	3-A	25,807	26,307	20,467	12,351	32,909	528,196	.0127	723,197	213	225,031	478	44,915	252	56,417	35,197	152,607	84	Incorporated Place
Pikeville		60852	4-B	6,417	6,295	14,769	2,885	24,083	94,774	.0031	205,646	60	44,974	95	12,330	69	21,106	11,208	(d)	....	Incorporated Place
Richmond		65226	4-C	29,318	27,152	16,908	12,210	30,823	495,712	.0095	362,402	107	67,334	143	23,044	129	53,200	18,192	314,947	172	Incorporated Place
St. Matthews	LOU	67944	4-Sm	15,682	15,852	36,752	8,438	48,054	576,346	.0112	584,263	172	103,816	220	64,915	364	37,767	37,331	(d)	....	Incorporated Place
Somerset		71688	4-A	11,968	11,352	14,265	5,236	25,713	170,720	.0047	268,711	79	46,418	99	15,070	84	35,339	17,083	138,120	76	Incorporated Place
Louisiana																					
Alexandria	ALEX	00975	3-AA	46,525	46,342	14,388	18,398	25,366	669,409	.0179	1,009,470	297	279,130	593	57,339	321	81,674	52,746	....	....	Incorporated Place
Baton Rouge	B.R.	05000	2-AA	230,715	227,818	17,842	97,291	30,682	4,116,314	.0858	3,910,057	1,150	712,971	1,513	184,044	1,031	429,520	169,595	547,351	300	Incorporated Place
Bossier City	SHRE	08920	3-S	58,559	56,461	17,976	22,515	35,221	1,052,679	.0219	1,001,350	295	258,928	550	41,533	233	83,428	24,271	87,128	48	Incorporated Place
Chalmette	N.O.	14135	◇	31,394	32,069	17,795	12,517	34,416	558,647	.0090	232,988	69	77,590	165	11,631	65	43,506	30,149	(d)	....	Census Designated Place
Gretna	N.O.	31915	4-S	17,904	17,423	15,270	7,657	26,308	273,399	.0087	582,610	171	171,850	365	62,349	349	36,746	19,512	45,832	25	Incorporated Place
Hammond		32755	3-A	18,060	17,639	13,308	6,531	27,138	240,342	.0076	486,055	143	131,697	280	18,993	106	44,001	29,618	63,528	35	Incorporated Place
Houma	HOMA-	36255	3-A	32,642	32,393	17,311	12,051	34,963	565,059	.0143	811,689	239	196,647	417	26,084	146	89,710	33,572	157,888	86	Incorporated Place
Kenner	N.O.	39475	4-S	67,986	70,517	19,426	26,520	37,779	1,320,730	.0251	1,023,223	301	258,973	550	104,115	583	108,267	64,090	88,945	49	Incorporated Place
Lafayette	LAF	40735	2-A	105,908	110,257	19,158	44,140	34,423	2,029,002	.0475	2,575,219	758	578,148	1,227	148,723	833	214,473	182,532	258,729	142	Incorporated Place
Lake Charles	LKCH	41155	3-AA	69,998	71,757	17,785	29,398	30,302	1,244,919	.0262	1,213,952	357	308,897	656	67,535	378	154,123	84,641	....	....	Incorporated Place
La Place	N.O.	42030	◇	29,182	27,684	17,752	9,881	40,616	518,025	.0086	245,270	72	60,127	128	7,624	43	43,041	21,744	(d)	....	Census Designated Place
Marrero	N.O.	48785	◇	35,867	36,165	15,622	13,217	35,409	560,329	.0092	222,331	65	23,442	50	11,755	66	61,293	27,575	(d)	....	Census Designated Place
Metairie	N.O.	50115	◇	144,927	146,136	24,251	67,689	38,032	3,514,564	.0682	3,164,993	931	655,772	1,392	202,427	1,134	357,100	234,854	(d)	....	Census Designated Place
Monroe	MONR	51410	3-AA	53,551	53,107	16,437	21,214	28,963	880,235	.0201	1,002,004	295	257,032	546	48,273	271	100,956	36,097	182,363	100	Incorporated Place
Morgan City		52040	4-C	11,891	12,703	15,502	4,863	28,408	184,331	.0033	100,169	29	16,840	36	....	....	17,341	8,338	102,469	56	Incorporated Place
New Iberia	LAF	54035	3-B	32,508	32,623	14,047	11,949	29,589	456,655	.0097	395,342	116	48,784	104	23,258	130	54,439	22,389	100,458	55	Incorporated Place
New Orleans	N.O.	55000	1-A	464,268	484,674	14,976	200,992	26,183	6,952,920	.1218	3,405,199	1,002	369,787	785	320,165	1,794	607,673	312,588	1,064,555	583	Incorporated Place
Opelousas		58045	4-C	23,361	22,860	11,287	9,172	20,807	263,674	.0060	246,480	73	75,512	160	12,839	72	40,628	20,539	38,738	21	Incorporated Place
Ruston		66655	4-C	20,336	20,546	13,595	7,926	24,505	276,477	.0061	268,597	79	68,457	145	10,774	60	32,469	8,199	103,768	57	Incorporated Place
Shreveport	SHRE	70000	2-AA	203,427	200,145	16,047	83,141	30,402	3,264,430	.0648	2,578,527	758	452,765	961	129,551	726	323,574	132,318	....	....	Incorporated Place
Slidell	N.O.	70805	3-S	26,505	25,695	20,295	10,035	41,434	537,911	.0110	512,603	151	82,167	174	19,137	107	49,379	35,480	27,179	15	Incorporated Place
Thibodaux	HOMA-	75425	4-B	14,615	14,431	17,094	5,731	31,847	249,834	.0043	134,516	40	20,992	45	3,465	19	33,416	8,628	38,585	21	Incorporated Place
West Monroe	MONR	80955	4-S	12,768	13,250	19,724	5,982	35,388	251,842	.0048	199,844	59	66,434	141	5,735	32	29,837	12,742	61,912	34	Incorporated Place
Maine																					
Auburn	LEW-	02060	4-B	23,853	23,203	18,917	10,324	33,335	451,234	.0114	666,874	196	131,215	279	17,615	99	89,947	23,036	441,155	242	Incorporated Place
Augusta	AUG	02100	3-B	18,463	18,560	18,961	8,778	30,948	350,075	.0094	579,210	170	104,473	222	8,161	46	80,972	14,262	76,394	42	Incorporated Place
Bangor	BANG	02795	3-AA	31,249	31,473	19,170	14,102	30,647	599,053	.0157	950,320	280	152,521	324	34,966	196	142,660	40,482	....	....	Incorporated Place
Biddeford		04860	4-S	20,428	20,942	17,842	8,641	33,574	364,486	.0067	242,396	71	31,007	66	5,672	32	75,403	5,842	153,791	84	Incorporated Place
Brunswick	BR-BA	08430	4-B	21,444	21,172	17,648	8,434	37,570	378,436	.0094	527,658	155	109,040	231	19,949	112	86,219	12,663	72,496	40	Minor Civil Division-Town
Lewiston	LEW-	38740	3-A	35,709	35,690	16,619	15,722	27,741	593,443	.0145	790,151	232	66,461	141	4,708	26	113,816	30,760	....	....	Incorporated Place
Portland	POR	60545	2-A	65,335	64,249	19,730	30,839	34,056	1,289,059	.0305	1,693,726	498	48,096	102	33,208	186	290,785	71,652	319,168	175	Incorporated Place
Presque Isle		60825	4-A	9,424	9,511	15,950	4,105	27,745	150,310	.0038	206,939	61	51,985	110	9,740	55	44,536	9,895	(d)	....	Incorporated Place
South Portland	POR	71990	4-Sm	23,293	23,324	19,746	10,233	39,741	459,942	.0147	1,038,076	305	175,837	373	121,332	680	126,024	41,926	....	....	Incorporated Place
Waterville	WATRVL	80740	3-A	15,575	15,605	16,456	6,394	30,354	256,303	.0058	289,962	85	34,552	73	13,999	78	83,554	9,808	103,350	57	Incorporated Place
Maryland																					
Annapolis	ANPLS	01600	3-C	38,072	35,838	33,461	16,780	55,179	1,273,919	.0195	664,488	195	79,410	169	71,852	403	82,656	24,663	(d)	....	Incorporated Place
Aspen Hill	WASH	02825	◇	53,634	50,228	24,660	19,555	57,308	1,322,617	.0167	178,755	53	18,750	40	3,051	17	58,927	16,923	(d)	....	Census Designated Place
Baltimore	BAL	04000	1-A	622,161	651,154	14,778	252,858	28,372	9,194,170	.1554	3,805,364	1,119	176,726	375	270,683	1,517	764,403	570,095	4,452,897	2,438	Independent City
Bel Air	BAL	05550	4-Sm	10,975	10,080	30,479	4,689	55,184	334,512	.0064	308,424	91	46,840	99	14,639	82	33,964	12,372	(d)	....	Incorporated Place
Bethesda	WASH	07125	◇	59,024	55,277	50,340	25,381	83,257	2,971,264	.0417	1,354,001	398	105,740	224	212,249	1,190	129,764	59,300	(d)	....	Census Designated Place
Bowie	WASH	08775	◇	57,292	50,269	29,779	21,092	65,508	1,706,103	.0229	480,407	141	103,804	220	9,373	53	104,846	15,043	(d)	....	Incorporated Place
Carney	BAL	13325	◇	29,386	28,264	21,547	12,833	42,661	633,184	.0115	455,586	134	66,503	141	21,353	120	77,757	24,476	(d)	....	Census Designated Place
Catonsville	BAL	14125	◇	41,400	39,820	22,445	16,457	48,262	929,219	.0168	676,675	199	68,458	145	25,859	145	74,053	32,895	(d)	....	Census Designated Place
Chillum	WASH	16875	◇	36,341	34,252	19,560	13,048	40,520	710,845	.0108	251,692	74	37,543	80	35,549	199	102,198	24,211	(d)	....	Census Designated Place
Clinton	WASH	17900	◇	27,652	26,064	24,365	9,304	61,404	673,747	.0102	277,781	82	35,382	75	4,159	23	85,346	13,248	(d)	....	Census Designated Place
Columbia	BAL	19125	◇	94,697	88,254	31,398	36,720	62,158	2,973,276	.0431	1,235,541	363	260,271	553	120,754	677	197,593	55,979	(d)	....	Census Designated Place
Cumberland	CUMB	21325	3-A	19,859	21,518	16,995	8,896	29,272	337,510	.0069	294,072	87	67,099	142	17,545	98	40,022	25,719	35,080	19	Incorporated Place
Dundalk	BAL	23975	◇	64,781	62,306	16,616	26,264	35,720	1,076,415	.0192	618,828	182	32,070	68	12,016	67	128,238	77,395	(d)	....	Census Designated Place
Easton		24475	4-C	12,621	11,708	21,348	5,483	37,978	269,435	.0062	343,915	101	35,245	75	14,762	83	46,564	17,592	368,001	201	Incorporated Place
Eldersburg	BAL	25575	◇	30,349	27,741	25,916	10,079	61,993	786,527	.0107	210,997	62	28,947	61	5,121	29	91,274	10,945	(d)	....	Census Designated Place
Ellicott City	BAL	26000	◇	61,248	56,397	31,228	22,041	68,715	1,912,654	.0271	727,032	214	124,904	265	14,330	80	159,114	27,228	(d)	....	Census Designated Place
Essex	BAL	26600	◇	40,629	39,078	16,619	16,945	33,826	675,201	.0108	247,900	73	21,253	45	6,063	34	65,307	12,071	(d)	....	Census Designated Place
Frederick	WASH	30325	3-C	62,236	52,767	26,028	24,934	48,371	1,619,858	.0289	1,208,742	356	244,072	518	64,523	362	185,304	47,432	221,392	121	Incorporated Place
Gaithersburg	WASH	31175	3-S	61,876	52,613	25,889	23,234	60,603	1,601,919	.0271	1,018,340	300	188,940	401	66,852	375	114,795	25,391	205,980	113	Incorporated Place
Germantown	WASH	32025	◇	59,176	55,419	24,022	22,471	57,999	1,421,516	.0196	375,564	110	68,454	145	7,289	41	133,323	16,636	(d)	....	Census Designated Place
Glen Burnie	BAL	32650	◇	40,672	38,922	20,989	16,379	42,188	853,654	.0170	775,047	228	188,404	400	29,228	164	94,804	20,687	(d)	....	Census Designated Place
Hagerstown	HAG	36075	3-A	38,730	36,687	19,637	16,946	34,341	760,530	.0142	568,140	167	133,993	284	20,338	114	76,897	34,051	347,549	190	Incorporated Place
Laurel	WASH	45900	3-Sm	21,479	19,960	29,343	9,787	48,384	630,266	.0123	615,656	181	84,533	179	42,600	239	62,572	25,809	(d)	....	Incorporated Place
Milford Mill	BAL	52562	◇	27,580	26,527	20,682	11,093	42,473	570,404	.0095	299,413	88	81,375	173	14,698	82	21,384	26,810	(d)	....	Census Designated Place
Montgomery Village	WASH	53325	◇	40,630	38,051	24,231	15,199	57,507	984,489	.0134	243,474	72	21,327	45	2,268	13	35,279	10,414	(d)	....	Census Designated Place
North Bethesda	WASH	56337	◇	41,229	38,610	37,274	18,604	60,860	1,536,785	.0281	1,364,136	401	28,352	60	114,856	644	177,272	72,801	(d)	....	Census Designated Place
Olney	WASH	58900	◇	33,569	31,438	27,972	11,039	75,703	938,993	.0117	146,265	43	....	....	2,623	15	78,561	11,333	(d)	....	Census Designated Place
Oxon Hill-Glassmanor	WASH	59505	◇	37,510	35,355	24,470	14,773	47,976	917,877	.0127	252,339	74	23,810	51	18,119	102	75,922	13,300	(d)	....	Census Designated Place
Parkville	BAL	60275	◇	32,354	31,118	20,372	13,834	41,276	659,100	.0117	435,092	128	21,751	46	11,029	62	79,479	25,489	(d)	....	Census Designated Place
Perry Hall	BAL	60975	◇	29,846	28,705	21,659	12,052	45,979	646,440	.0132	628,074	185	189,324	402	50,310	282	95,932	28,803	(d)	....	Census Designated Place
Pikesville	BAL	61400	◇	30,279	29,123	30,724	13,514	47,366	930,281	.0120	209,463	62	1,025	2	15,932	89	71,873	19,351	(d)	....	Census Designated Place
Potomac	WASH	63300	◇	47,861	44,822	54,322	16,839	108,680	2,599,924	.0291	377,657	111	38,499	82	79,498	446	73,151	19,476	(d)	....	Census Designated Place
Randallstown	BAL	64950	◇	32,098	30,870	22,161	12,097	50,568	711,322	.0110	307,486	90	19,763	42	7,027	39	67,558	15,980	(d)	....	Census Designated Place
Rockville	WASH	67675	3-SS	50,180	47,388	30,133	18,362	65,144	1,512,061	.0225	684,570	201	....	....	33,469	188	152,187	36,728	102,631	56	Incorporated Place
St. Charles	WASH	69350	◇	37,926	33,379	23,749	13,467	52,496	900,701	.0139	405,287	119	142,635	303	39,927	224	46,606	15,439	(d)	....	Census Designated Place
Salisbury	SLSB	69925	3-A	25,584	23,743	17,767	9,849	35,919	454,555	.0109	589,374	173	139,215	296	27,027	151	70,385	36,584	419,783	230	Incorporated Place
Severn	BAL	71150	◇	36,656	35,076	22,946	12,936	56,622	841,098	.0108	122,077	36	2,639	6	3,482	20	30,749	16,929	(d)	....	Census Designated Place
Severna Park	BAL	71200	◇	29,791	28,507	32,524	10,477	68,858	968,925	.0126	247,446	73	26,151	56	6,438	36	70,569	12,759	(d)	....	Census Designated Place
Silver Spring	WASH	72450	◇	81,732	76,540	23,342	32,637	48,509	1,907,801	.0273	589,029	173	40,461	86	48,732	273	180,474	45,986	(d)	....	Census Designated Place
South Gate	BAL	73550	◇	29,961	28,672	23,420	12,161	46,051	701,691	.0150	780,000	229	173,274	368	45,282	254	89,130	25,072	(d)	....	Census Designated Place
Towson	BAL	78425	◇	53,852	51,793	28,724	22,368	46,476	1,546,842	.0267	1,097,551	323	133,979	284	207,091	1,161	145,231	82,124	(d)	....	Census Designated Place
Woodlawn	BAL	86475	◇	37,512	36,079	19,336	14,796	42,507	725,346	.0128	448,282	132	70,896	150	22,906	128	60,825	26,025	(d)	....	Census Designated Place
Massachusetts																					
Agawam	SPRG	00765	◇	28,810	28,144	21,746	11,684	44,382	626,496	.0101	304,292	90	12,503	27	1,733	10	49,974	23,122	177,802	97	Incorporated Place
Amherst	SPRG	01325	◇	35,804	34,874	16,028	9,741	38,868	573,872	.0088	153,865	45	....	....	3,695	21	60,460	11,513	(d)	....	Minor Civil Division-Town
Andover	BOS	01465	◇	31,587	31,247	36,395	11,513	72,852	1,149,605	.0138	189,735	56	....	....	24,150	135	59,238	21,382	1,585,271	868	Minor Civil Division-Town
Arlington	BOS	01605	◇	40,530	42,389	30,214	18,409	56,173	1,224,554	.0167	378,351	111	....	....	3,694	21	67,254	62,877	(d)	....	Minor Civil Division-Town
Attleboro	PROV-	02690	3-S	44,870	42,068	21,524	17,432	45,302	965,761	.0188	840,246	247	82,490	175	24,061	135	109,120	43,113	704,774	386	Incorporated Place
Barnstable	BARN	03600	◇	48,997	47,821	23,650	20,370	42,459	1,158,757	.0242	1,225,394	360	125,164	266	84,748	475	168,256	79,329	....	....	Incorporated Place
Beverly	BOS	05595	4-S	40,172	39,862	24,646	16,035	48,703	990,074	.0163	564,577	166	13,289	28	12,104	68	116,547	57,211	469,110	257	Incorporated Place
Billerica	BOS	05805	◇	38,278	38,981	21,714	12,823	59,271	831,187	.0136	431,128	127	17,381	37	29,737	167	94,300	35,125	1,045,186	572	Minor Civil Division-Town
Boston	BOS	07000	1-AA	583,303	589,141	19,855	239,820	37,522	11,581,744	.1942	6,159,059	1,812	287,887	611	1,095,286	6,138	1,360,262	677,532	2,424,545	1,327	Incorporated Place
Braintree	BOS	07665	3-Sm	33,796	33,828	24,970	12,859	54,992	843,890	.0193	1,103,128	324	296,405	629	150,615	844	70,960	64,049	333,808	183	Minor Civil Division-Town
Brockton	BOS	09000	3-SS	96,964	94,304	17,372	35,220	36,714	1,684,475	.0340	1,454,912	428	132,003	280	46,406	260	198,306	103,485	217,622	119	Incorporated Place
Brookline	BOS	09175	4-Sr	56,687	57,107	39,408	25,844	58,395	2,233,908	.0274	478,722	141	50,175	107	67,874	380	112,959	75,460	(d)	....	Minor Civil Division-Town
Burlington	BOS	09840	3-SSm	22,322	22,876	27,361	8,184	63,522	610,745	.0161	1,048,947	309	299,769	636	166,986	936	44,361	40,248	219,369	120	Minor Civil Division-Town
Cambridge	BOS	11000	3-SS	103,297	101,355	26,633	43,950	44,322	2,751,151	.0502	2,196,568	646	140,182	298	338,617	1,898	412,179	147,086	356,954	195	Incorporated Place
Chelmsford	BOS	13135	4-S	33,491	33,858	26,618	12,841	60,366	891,466	.0144	505,390	149	53,421	113	22,627	127	89,492	24,073	483,546	265	Minor Civil Division-Town
Chelsea	BOS	13205	4-S	37,055	35,080	12,679	12,696	28,662	469,803	.0087	235,102	69	11,540	24	8,756	49	100,645	23,571	163,069	89	Incorporated Place
Chicopee	SPRG	13660	4-S	55,318	54,653	18,487	23,669	33,619	1,022,657	.0161	395,814	116	68,223	145	12,691	71	73,246	46,329	560,843	307	Incorporated Place
Danvers	BOS	16250	3-S	25,666	25,212	23,749	9,817	51,484	609,536	.0157	988,464	291	145,544	309	70,624	396	90,290	33,206	364,443	200	Minor Civil Division-Town
Dartmouth	N.BED	16425	◇	31,950	30,666	21,614	11,210	45,009	690,558	.0129	541,760	159	154,170	327	49,092	275	40,215	30,389	17,896	10	Minor Civil Division-Town
Dedham	BOS	16495	3-Sm	23,307	23,464	25,059	8,737	54,278	584,057	.0105	432,502	127	79,655	169	37,194	208	28,170	28,573	(d)	....	Minor Civil Division-Town

.... Data less than 1,000.
(d) Data not available.
◇ Not classified as a Principal Business Center.

* Data from 1997 Census of Manufactures.

continued on next page

Principal Business Centers and Other Places with 27,500 or More: Population / Income / Sales, *Continued*

PLACE NAME	RANALLY METRO AREA	FIPS PLACE CODE	RANALLY CITY RATING	POPULATION Estimate 7/1/04	POPULATION Census 4/1/00	PER CAPITA INCOME 2003	HOUSE-HOLDS Estimate 7/1/04	MEDIAN HOUSEHOLD INCOME 2003	DISPOSABLE INCOME 2003 ($1,000)	MARKET ABILITY INDEX 2003	TOTAL RETAIL TRADE Sales 2003 ($1,000)	TOTAL RETAIL TRADE Ranally Sales Units	GENERAL MERCHANDISE Sales 2003 ($1,000)	GENERAL MERCHANDISE Ranally Sales Units	APPAREL STORES Sales 2003 ($1,000)	APPAREL STORES Ranally Sales Units	FOOD STORE SALES 2003 ($1,000)	HEALTH & DRUG STORE SALES 2003 ($1,000)	MANUFACTURERS VALUE ADDED 1997* ($1,000)	MANUFACTURERS Ranally Mfg Units	PLACE TYPE
Dracut	**BOS**	17475	◇	28,582	28,562	21,298	10,596	51,158	608,735	.0081	101,694	**30**	....	**....**	2,296	**13**	34,581	7,098	101,081	**55**	Minor Civil Division-Town
Everett	**BOS**	21990	◇	38,698	38,037	17,826	15,863	37,279	689,813	.0108	247,293	**73**	3,476	**7**	3,918	**22**	19,613	37,675	172,010	**94**	Incorporated Place
Fall River	**F.R.**	23000	**3-BB**	92,160	91,938	16,581	39,597	27,802	1,528,094	.0255	681,337	**200**	55,530	**118**	52,881	**296**	156,837	48,898	720,215	**394**	Incorporated Place
Falmouth		23105	◇	33,266	32,660	25,187	14,300	43,540	837,872	.0137	472,376	**139**	13,945	**30**	30,235	**169**	107,596	47,414	(d)	**....**	Minor Civil Division-Town
Fitchburg	**BOS**	23875	**3-B**	38,373	39,102	16,994	14,862	34,760	652,105	.0126	496,419	**146**	36,532	**78**	17,224	**97**	102,054	31,949	349,671	**191**	Incorporated Place
Framingham	**BOS**	24925	**3-SS**	67,431	66,910	24,829	26,664	49,482	1,674,241	.0328	1,558,292	**458**	111,916	**238**	98,162	**550**	152,359	80,260	348,488	**191**	Minor Civil Division-Town
Franklin	**BOS**	25100	◇	30,254	29,560	24,849	10,558	62,105	751,770	.0125	448,633	**132**	16,792	**36**	19,226	**108**	74,539	17,852	333,457	**183**	Incorporated Place
Gloucester	**BOS**	26150	**4-Sr**	30,551	30,273	22,165	12,805	43,027	677,171	.0102	260,497	**77**	13,283	**28**	7,179	**40**	57,348	37,728	419,058	**229**	Incorporated Place
Greenfield		27025	**4-C**	18,170	18,168	19,562	8,074	31,712	355,446	.0072	326,901	**96**	24,823	**53**	10,523	**59**	69,901	19,637	52,231	**29**	Minor Civil Division-Town
Haverhill	**BOS**	29405	**4-S**	62,126	58,969	20,416	24,412	44,552	1,268,344	.0197	508,274	**150**	17,930	**38**	16,561	**93**	103,667	61,894	260,228	**142**	Incorporated Place
Holyoke	**SPRG**	30840	**3-B**	40,231	39,838	14,941	15,330	28,971	601,083	.0136	645,273	**190**	90,000	**191**	111,840	**627**	63,920	51,621	410,882	**225**	Incorporated Place
Lawrence	**BOS**	34550	**3-SS**	74,467	72,043	12,564	25,480	27,403	935,584	.0173	473,441	**139**	2,255	**5**	10,601	**59**	45,446	41,522	607,999	**333**	Incorporated Place
Leominster	**BOS**	35075	**3-B**	42,819	41,303	20,995	17,314	41,318	898,965	.0178	800,500	**235**	75,711	**161**	67,631	**379**	126,141	46,270	547,996	**300**	Incorporated Place
Lexington	**BOS**	35215	◇	30,551	30,355	41,961	11,326	79,904	1,281,938	.0153	236,996	**70**	....	**....**	13,324	**75**	29,473	29,371	180,585	**99**	Minor Civil Division-Town
Lowell	**BOS**	37000	**3-SS**	106,626	105,167	15,894	38,816	36,171	1,694,675	.0292	828,208	**244**	27,934	**59**	8,282	**46**	141,933	70,614	454,856	**249**	Incorporated Place
Lynn	**BOS**	37490	**3-S**	91,859	89,050	16,121	34,869	35,509	1,480,818	.0263	816,970	**240**	52,833	**112**	14,322	**80**	110,502	61,919	788,084	**431**	Incorporated Place
Malden	**BOS**	37875	**4-S**	57,555	56,340	20,215	23,785	41,547	1,163,454	.0184	497,978	**146**	36,273	**77**	14,335	**80**	136,081	32,251	162,999	**89**	Incorporated Place
Marlborough	**BOS**	38715	**4-S**	37,592	36,255	24,792	15,224	51,002	931,972	.0174	773,207	**227**	138,355	**294**	116,589	**653**	86,507	77,735	1,102,649	**604**	Incorporated Place
Medford	**BOS**	39835	**3-S**	53,909	55,765	22,378	21,571	46,517	1,206,391	.0218	872,274	**257**	72,727	**154**	51,861	**291**	184,808	56,502	66,273	**36**	Incorporated Place
Methuen	**BOS**	40710	**3-Sm**	45,417	43,789	19,973	17,305	44,446	907,107	.0135	294,210	**87**	14,836	**31**	5,305	**30**	61,105	38,592	88,104	**48**	Incorporated Place
Milford	**BOS**	41165	**4-S**	28,487	26,799	22,373	11,249	45,786	637,342	.0108	378,083	**111**	30,413	**65**	18,900	**106**	86,571	47,765	467,394	**256**	Minor Civil Division-Town
Natick	**BOS**	43895	**3-S**	32,236	32,170	31,702	13,268	60,646	1,021,931	.0264	1,741,230	**512**	362,299	**769**	173,219	**971**	83,251	59,461	387,534	**212**	Minor Civil Division-Town
Needham	**BOS**	44105	**4-S**	29,066	28,911	39,278	10,855	74,724	1,141,656	.0150	351,742	**103**	....	**....**	6,452	**36**	63,144	37,829	618,775	**339**	Minor Civil Division-Town
New Bedford	**N.BED**	45000	**3-BB**	92,152	93,768	16,128	38,296	27,242	1,486,212	.0249	651,424	**192**	46,843	**99**	15,303	**86**	198,916	71,253	650,558	**356**	Incorporated Place
Newton	**BOS**	45560	**3-SS**	85,756	83,829	40,799	32,266	73,903	3,498,725	.0463	1,159,591	**341**	81,456	**173**	116,189	**651**	212,110	76,543	282,327	**155**	Incorporated Place
North Adams		46225	**4-C**	14,012	14,681	15,699	6,175	27,551	219,974	.0044	171,418	**50**	28,804	**61**	3,166	**18**	43,422	13,791	45,824	**25**	Incorporated Place
Northampton	**SPRG**	46330	**4-C**	29,554	28,978	21,889	12,527	39,029	646,919	.0114	426,150	**125**	17,487	**37**	25,715	**144**	90,551	28,426	133,498	**73**	Incorporated Place
North Andover	**BOS**	46365	◇	27,609	27,202	29,166	9,955	62,631	805,254	.0111	256,801	**76**	16,005	**34**	21,346	**120**	129,467	21,958	1,669,908	**914**	Minor Civil Division-Town
North Attleborough	**PROV-**	46575	◇	28,755	27,143	25,173	11,214	52,534	723,848	.0151	776,439	**228**	245,945	**522**	96,734	**542**	80,380	111,838	133,917	**73**	Minor Civil Division-Town
Norwood	**BOS**	50250	**4-S**	28,684	28,587	24,998	11,850	51,585	717,043	.0194	1,277,256	**376**	13,627	**29**	27,626	**155**	95,689	34,423	300,302	**164**	Minor Civil Division-Town
Peabody	**BOS**	52490	**3-Sm**	48,552	48,129	21,931	18,931	48,759	1,064,818	.0217	1,043,905	**307**	194,255	**412**	140,333	**786**	73,001	84,711	370,468	**203**	Incorporated Place
Pittsfield	**PTSF**	53960	**3-A**	44,586	45,793	19,740	19,652	34,330	880,117	.0151	509,302	**150**	32,879	**70**	12,668	**71**	147,643	28,171	....	**....**	Incorporated Place
Plymouth	**BOS**	54310	◇	55,501	51,701	22,285	20,160	49,246	1,236,853	.0177	369,674	**109**	40,630	**86**	9,006	**50**	122,926	18,732	133,330	**73**	Minor Civil Division-Town
Quincy	**BOS**	55745	**3-S**	88,726	88,025	23,515	39,911	42,915	2,086,366	.0327	975,632	**287**	45,132	**96**	22,176	**124**	265,869	93,612	54,217	**30**	Incorporated Place
Randolph	**BOS**	55955	◇	30,990	30,963	20,801	11,488	49,996	644,623	.0095	209,907	**62**	1,144	**2**	18,186	**102**	47,171	30,295	134,611	**74**	Minor Civil Division-Town
Revere	**BOS**	56585	◇	49,940	47,283	17,805	20,787	34,924	889,172	.0139	320,325	**94**	13,170	**28**	37,985	**213**	66,892	62,403	(d)	**....**	Incorporated Place
Salem	**BOS**	59105	**3-S**	41,960	40,407	21,632	18,352	40,535	907,662	.0149	478,615	**141**	50,806	**108**	9,564	**54**	70,351	58,469	120,791	**66**	Incorporated Place
Saugus	**BOS**	60015	**4-Sm**	26,295	26,078	23,009	10,135	50,231	605,030	.0138	768,252	**226**	179,824	**382**	118,989	**667**	100,238	33,051	51,042	**28**	Minor Civil Division-Town
Shrewsbury	**WORC**	61800	**4-S**	35,740	31,640	28,588	14,168	55,938	1,021,734	.0169	642,466	**189**	60,902	**129**	17,356	**97**	101,672	29,097	110,480	**60**	Minor Civil Division-Town
Somerville	**BOS**	62535	**4-S**	78,578	77,478	20,546	32,342	42,464	1,614,428	.0257	729,710	**215**	54,985	**117**	12,539	**70**	198,092	63,343	244,804	**134**	Incorporated Place
Springfield	**SPRG**	67000	**2-AA**	153,856	152,082	15,158	58,624	29,266	2,332,167	.0440	1,518,560	**447**	170,699	**362**	55,318	**310**	260,583	152,919	665,713	**364**	Incorporated Place
Swansea	**F.R.**	68750	**4-Sm**	16,075	15,901	21,987	6,059	47,249	353,436	.0069	306,097	**90**	89,348	**190**	49,515	**277**	23,791	17,601	(d)	**....**	Minor Civil Division-Town
Taunton	**BOS**	69170	**4-C**	59,115	55,976	19,695	23,692	39,755	1,164,264	.0199	656,109	**193**	109,849	**233**	83,092	**466**	108,127	49,464	396,091	**217**	Incorporated Place
Tewksbury	**BOS**	69415	◇	28,479	28,851	22,648	9,971	60,272	644,979	.0117	477,890	**141**	100,349	**213**	12,781	**72**	93,381	37,010	218,291	**120**	Minor Civil Division-Town
Waltham	**BOS**	72600	**3-S**	59,055	59,226	22,861	23,444	48,054	1,350,069	.0238	912,889	**269**	59,174	**126**	38,184	**214**	106,618	63,116	622,299	**341**	Incorporated Place
Watertown	**BOS**	73440	◇	32,678	32,986	30,159	14,645	52,604	985,534	.0170	708,312	**208**	47,262	**100**	69,347	**389**	103,164	29,002	436,208	**239**	Incorporated Place
Wellesley	**BOS**	74175	**4-S**	26,523	26,613	46,066	8,717	92,956	1,221,817	.0161	424,907	**125**	....	**....**	42,410	**238**	74,335	27,072	(d)	**....**	Minor Civil Division-Town
Westfield	**SPRG**	76030	**4-S**	41,020	40,072	19,241	15,340	41,665	789,283	.0134	432,922	**127**	47,485	**101**	12,187	**68**	85,622	32,074	321,101	**176**	Incorporated Place
West Springfield	**SPRG**	77885	**4-S**	28,299	27,899	20,506	12,159	37,177	580,301	.0137	770,561	**227**	42,641	**91**	31,280	**175**	109,592	29,782	(d)	**....**	Incorporated Place
Weymouth	**BOS**	78865	**4-S**	54,431	53,988	22,824	22,577	46,677	1,242,322	.0200	629,644	**185**	80,422	**171**	10,181	**57**	114,113	67,823	106,560	**58**	Minor Civil Division-Town
Woburn	**BOS**	81035	**3-S**	36,723	37,258	23,380	14,932	49,718	858,570	.0198	1,116,729	**328**	72,524	**154**	25,090	**141**	97,085	53,989	526,184	**288**	Incorporated Place
Worcester	**WORC**	82000	**2-A**	178,801	172,648	18,177	70,328	33,639	3,250,061	.0603	2,273,517	**669**	136,560	**290**	161,030	**902**	402,802	253,353	1,210,485	**663**	Incorporated Place
Michigan																					
Adrian		00440	**3-A**	21,158	21,574	18,607	7,979	38,753	393,680	.0085	412,332	**121**	122,008	**259**	7,574	**42**	26,737	21,000	353,205	**193**	Incorporated Place
Allen Park	**DET**	01380	◇	27,764	29,376	21,892	11,662	46,655	607,801	.0086	166,605	**49**	....	**....**	....	**....**	50,664	16,024	....	**....**	Incorporated Place
Alpena		01740	**4-A**	10,786	11,304	17,882	4,782	32,414	192,880	.0039	175,380	**52**	43,575	**93**	8,178	**46**	15,036	12,496	234,813	**129**	Incorporated Place
Ann Arbor	**DET**	03000	**2-C**	117,943	114,024	25,183	48,274	46,186	2,970,190	.0521	2,083,782	**613**	293,325	**623**	136,147	**763**	251,880	100,046	347,274	**190**	Incorporated Place
Battle Creek	**BTLCK**	05920	**3-A**	54,240	53,364	19,242	23,077	35,863	1,043,665	.0191	725,379	**213**	230,450	**489**	23,690	**133**	66,011	45,761	1,726,943	**945**	Incorporated Place
Bay City	**SAG-**	06020	**3-B**	36,731	36,817	17,888	15,755	32,914	657,062	.0127	517,105	**152**	94,866	**201**	19,299	**108**	40,069	26,078	317,934	**174**	Incorporated Place
Bedford	**TOL**	06740	◇	31,044	28,606	23,130	11,500	51,753	718,050	.0106	263,463	**77**	....	**....**	2,182	**12**	50,893	13,847	79,050	**43**	Minor Civil Division-Township
Benton Harbor	**BNTH-**	07520	**3-A**	10,980	11,182	11,561	3,841	25,240	126,936	.0036	200,714	**59**	72,298	**153**	5,937	**33**	10,041	5,567	159,131	**87**	Incorporated Place
Birmingham	**DET**	08640	**4-S**	18,630	19,291	52,121	9,256	68,174	971,023	.0135	429,904	**126**	1,259	**3**	90,797	**509**	43,962	29,942	34,681	**19**	Incorporated Place
Bloomfield	**DET**	09110	◇	42,722	43,023	57,867	17,482	87,157	2,472,194	.0318	848,467	**250**	37,250	**79**	25,880	**145**	83,157	38,681	(d)	**....**	Minor Civil Division-Township
Burton	**FLN**	12060	**4-Sm**	32,088	30,308	19,071	12,965	40,240	611,956	.0138	719,031	**212**	229,768	**488**	49,706	**279**	59,488	55,348	....	**....**	Incorporated Place
Cadillac		12320	**4-C**	10,059	10,000	18,004	4,200	33,899	181,101	.0046	267,573	**79**	54,614	**116**	6,944	**39**	33,362	11,685	336,875	**184**	Incorporated Place
Canton	**DET**	13120	◇	76,945	76,366	23,845	28,586	62,850	1,834,742	.0279	772,357	**227**	235,420	**500**	10,554	**59**	79,187	46,803	201,543	**110**	Minor Civil Division-Charter Township
Chesterfield	**DET**	15340	◇	42,059	37,405	22,675	15,525	54,174	953,683	.0138	307,597	**90**	40,597	**86**	1,339	**8**	40,656	31,358	629,160	**344**	Minor Civil Division-Charter Township
Clinton	**DET**	16520	◇	95,841	95,648	25,219	41,676	44,762	2,417,056	.0383	1,234,775	**363**	75,414	**160**	8,801	**49**	105,724	52,621	489,177	**268**	Minor Civil Division-Charter Township
Commerce	**DET**	17640	◇	36,518	34,764	25,225	13,608	58,656	921,162	.0164	670,749	**197**	231,888	**492**	3,851	**22**	93,876	33,493	139,482	**76**	Minor Civil Division-Charter Township
Dearborn	**DET**	21000	**2-S**	98,208	97,775	19,504	37,994	40,763	1,915,411	.0520	3,256,093	**958**	533,980	**1,134**	176,152	**987**	321,768	194,787	2,440,365	**1,336**	Incorporated Place
Dearborn Heights	**DET**	21020	**4-Sr**	58,359	58,264	20,456	24,022	42,843	1,193,790	.0184	468,309	**138**	25,753	**55**	6,116	**34**	106,573	78,881	(d)	**....**	Incorporated Place
Delta	**LANS**	21520	◇	30,821	29,682	24,621	13,379	43,899	758,840	.0151	728,942	**214**	298,500	**634**	24,869	**139**	86,423	25,040	(d)	**....**	Minor Civil Division-Charter Township
Detroit	**DET**	22000	**1-AA**	937,359	951,270	13,420	342,066	28,493	12,579,324	.2084	4,055,955	**1,193**	279,346	**593**	140,921	**790**	1,016,876	406,477	6,445,938	**3,529**	Incorporated Place
East Lansing	**LANS**	24120	**4-S**	47,860	46,525	15,659	15,445	31,760	749,437	.0126	327,815	**96**	105,268	**223**	7,600	**43**	53,381	8,533	(d)	**....**	Incorporated Place
Eastpointe	**DET**	24290	**4-Sr**	34,434	34,077	20,975	14,192	42,212	722,257	.0136	564,285	**166**	31,180	**66**	7,704	**43**	54,946	84,317	(d)	**....**	Incorporated Place
Escanaba		26360	**4-A**	13,029	13,140	18,035	5,915	30,495	234,984	.0056	304,379	**90**	49,922	**106**	13,773	**77**	45,384	14,408	331,046	**181**	Incorporated Place
Farmington Hills	**DET**	27440	**4-S**	84,032	82,111	31,928	35,936	59,468	2,683,000	.0421	1,489,464	**438**	140,936	**299**	91,707	**514**	157,876	138,172	476,776	**261**	Incorporated Place
Flint	**FLN**	29000	**2-A**	123,330	124,943	15,984	50,418	28,698	1,971,335	.0411	1,776,663	**523**	397,252	**843**	67,712	**379**	167,267	115,223	....	**....**	Incorporated Place
Garden City	**DET**	31420	◇	28,357	30,047	19,615	11,181	45,650	556,231	.0099	363,026	**107**	25,829	**55**	9,795	**55**	37,212	23,353	(d)	**....**	Incorporated Place
Georgetown	**GDR**	31880	◇	43,692	41,658	21,065	15,524	50,663	920,353	.0171	698,451	**205**	271,532	**576**	6,152	**34**	75,641	11,460	38,852	**21**	Minor Civil Division-Charter Township
Grand Blanc	**FLN**	33300	◇	31,730	29,827	25,124	13,126	51,269	797,176	.0130	449,346	**132**	72,145	**153**	15,743	**88**	42,139	28,747	138,255	**76**	Minor Civil Division-Charter Township
Grand Haven		33340	**4-C**	10,885	11,168	26,473	5,099	45,614	288,155	.0054	249,484	**73**	87,306	**185**	5,514	**31**	15,034	11,563	518,674	**284**	Incorporated Place
Grand Rapids	**GDR**	34000	**2-AA**	198,445	197,800	17,864	75,450	37,061	3,544,947	.0670	2,587,186	**761**	493,688	**1,048**	90,416	**507**	322,611	146,882	3,123,985	**1,710**	Incorporated Place
Greenville	**GDR**	35100	**4-C**	8,105	7,935	19,562	3,438	35,345	158,550	.0031	135,596	**40**	59,588	**126**	5,369	**30**	9,060	2,597	383,569	**210**	Incorporated Place
Grosse Pointe	**DET**	35480	**4-S**	5,640	5,670	42,513	2,449	68,366	239,773	.0031	70,950	**21**	....	**....**	16,043	**90**	17,040	11,027	(d)	**....**	Incorporated Place
Harper Woods	**DET**	36700	**4-Sm**	13,606	14,254	21,859	6,196	42,614	297,410	.0067	366,832	**108**	145,746	**309**	49,814	**279**	49,659	34,920	(d)	**....**	Incorporated Place
Highland Park	**DET**	38180	**4-S**	15,589	16,746	11,885	5,941	21,228	185,271	.0035	91,776	**27**	....	**....**	3,881	**22**	18,896	5,445	(d)	**....**	Incorporated Place
Holland	**HLND**	38640	**3-C**	35,347	35,048	20,007	12,646	41,624	707,194	.0116	350,317	**103**	43,608	**93**	5,141	**29**	49,984	29,176	1,757,132	**962**	Incorporated Place
Houghton		39360	**4-A**	6,822	7,010	10,075	2,076	24,786	68,729	.0017	69,789	**21**	18,061	**38**	8,708	**49**	2,214	....	(d)	**....**	Incorporated Place
Independence	**DET**	40400	◇	33,977	32,581	26,717	12,844	62,913	907,750	.0131	327,979	**96**	....	**....**	4,652	**26**	44,222	31,134	(d)	**....**	Minor Civil Division-Charter Township
Inkster	**DET**	40680	◇	29,393	30,115	14,898	11,245	33,761	437,895	.0067	105,449	**31**	2,614	**6**	1,477	**8**	21,945	26,402	(d)	**....**	Incorporated Place
Iron Mountain		40960	**4-A**	7,648	8,154	18,137	3,317	33,219	138,711	.0033	177,860	**52**	48,389	**103**	5,232	**29**	26,016	10,361	(d)	**....**	Incorporated Place
Ironwood		41060	**4-A**	6,172	6,293	13,854	2,745	24,933	85,505	.0020	91,088	**27**	21,185	**45**	4,775	**27**	15,716	4,784	(d)	**....**	Incorporated Place
Jackson	**JAC**	41420	**3-AA**	36,834	36,316	18,116	14,679	35,866	667,282	.0143	687,788	**202**	226,102	**480**	21,044	**118**	59,231	28,835	425,876	**233**	Incorporated Place
Kalamazoo	**KZOO**	42160	**2-A**	75,811	77,145	16,322	30,186	32,218	1,237,353	.0268	1,236,447	**364**	404,863	**859**	38,556	**216**	112,637	53,825	699,046	**383**	Incorporated Place
Kentwood	**GDR**	42820	**4-Sm**	47,699	45,255	20,951	20,068	41,370	999,331	.0311	2,175,272	**640**	494,149	**1,049**	125,510	**703**	51,460	69,710	859,766	**471**	Incorporated Place
Lansing	**LANS**	46000	**2-A**	118,010	119,128	17,160	51,152	33,920	2,025,090	.0429	1,961,671	**577**	341,651	**725**	34,090	**191**	181,808	137,339	....	**....**	Incorporated Place
Lincoln Park	**DET**	47800	**4-S**	38,165	40,008	18,204	15,901	39,589	694,767	.0125	437,480	**129**	107,038	**227**	17,303	**97**	87,841	46,357	(d)	**....**	Incorporated Place
Livonia	**DET**	49000	**3-SS**	100,837	100,545	24,005	39,308	55,933	2,420,594	.0458	2,043,059	**601**	351,760	**747**	167,244	**937**	259,465	143,184	1,810,408	**991**	Incorporated Place
Macomb	**DET**	50480	◇	56,757	50,478	23,867	19,678	63,172	1,354,625	.0180	275,756	**81**	....	**....**	6,912	**39**	80,043	24,222	68,537	**38**	Minor Civil Division-Township
Madison Heights	**DET**	50560	**4-S**	30,011	31,101	20,557	13,440	39,729	616,925	.0155	915,135	**269**	176,042	**374**	27,125	**152**	86,961	45,669	586,821	**321**	Incorporated Place
Marquette		51900	**4-A**	19,087	19,661	18,785	8,139	33,505	358,550	.0072	319,114	**94**	87,301	**185**	12,597	**71**	26,265	14,633	(d)	**....**	Incorporated Place
Menominee		53020	**4-B**	9,122	9,131	17,890	4,169	31,366	163,189	.0029	97,720	**29**	17,956	**38**	1,301	**7**	20,665	3,770	196,657	**108**	Incorporated Place
Meridian	**LANS**	53140	◇	40,242	39,116	26,827	17,591	47,150	1,079,581	.0200	900,213	**265**	316,118	**671**	100,468	**563**	56,784	28,685	(d)	**....**	Minor Civil Division-Charter Township
Midland	**SAG-**	53780	**3-C**	42,582	41,685	22,980	17,836	43,421	978,536	.0170	637,151	**187**	154,182	**327**	25,790	**145**	52,690	45,321	760,472	**416**	Incorporated Place
Monroe	**MONR**	55020	**3-C**	22,478	22,076	21,663	8,981	41,833	486,938	.0094	411,718	**121**	122,975	**261**	20,434	**115**	31,139	25,654	756,010	**414**	Incorporated Place
Mount Clemens	**DET**	55820	**3-S**	17,110	17,312	20,596	7,226	35,240	352,404	.0082	456,792	**134**	35,670	**76**	11,939	**67**	70,962	44,367	531,194	**291**	Incorporated Place
Mount Pleasant		56020	**4-A**	26,857	25,946	13,638	9,338	29,138	366,270	.0081	352,213	**104**	143,352	**304**	14,787	**83**	20,722	9,886	....	**....**	Incorporated Place
Muskegon	**MUS**	56320	**3-AA**	39,834	40,105	15,638	15,229	31,908	622,924	.0127	519,304	**153**	112,738	**239**	23,422	**131**	45,315	46,745	630,574	**345**	Incorporated Place
Muskegon Heights	**MUS**	56360	**4-Sm**	11,925	12,049	15,958	4,696	31,121	190,299	.0042	198,180	**58**	54,175	**115**	7,342	**41**	17,628	3,303	130,874	**72**	Incorporated Place
Novi	**DET**	59440	**3-Sm**	49,973	47,386	29,473	20,692	63,044	1,472,877	.0293	1,487,236	**437**	393,274	**835**	102,283	**573**	77,384	72,655	204,136	**112**	Incorporated Place
Oak Park	**DET**	59920	◇	29,830	29,793	18,316	11,657	40,944	546,356	.0115	532,364	**157**	50,285	**107**	35,674	**200**	99,919	41,942	122,025	**67**	Incorporated Place
Orion	**DET**	61100	◇	35,192	33,463	25,095	13,500	60,892	883,128	.0125	283,638	**83**	41,006	**87**	3,288	**18**	39,598	13,755	....	**....**	Minor Civil Division-Charter Township
Owosso		61940	**4-C**	16,063	15,713	18,592	6,636	35,545	298,643	.0061	269,040	**79**	39,793	**84**	3,684	**21**	26,066	20,789	135,157	**74**	Incorporated Place
Petoskey		63820	**4-A**	6,253	6,080	22,211	2,856	37,840	138,884	.0035	207,092	**61**	32,407	**69**	10,599	**59**	25,033	11,448	30,212	**17**	Incorporated Place
Pittsfield	**DET**	64560	◇	33,548	30,167	21,208	13,407	45,668	711,494	.0146	703,796	**207**	203,544	**432**	50,011	**280**	44,814	26,268	96,264	**53**	Minor Civil Division-Charter Township
Plainfield	**GDR**	64660	◇	31,272	30,195	22,185	11,759	48,138	693,767	.0118	415,493	**122**	124,308	**264**	2,313	**13**	11,108	3,337	145,495	**80**	Minor Civil Division-Charter Township
Pontiac	**DET**	65440	**3-SS**	63,930	66,337	14,544	24,524	29,890	929,808	.0206	926,150	**272**	40,698	**86**	20,262	**114**	104,876	65,935	1,526,591	**836**	Incorporated Place
Portage	**KZOO**	65560	**3-Sm**	45,604	44,897	22,503	19,266	44,955	1,026,223	.0205	967,365	**285**	333,069	**707**	56,160	**315**	30,913	39,401	400,741	**219**	Incorporated Place
Port Huron	**PTHU**	65820	**3-C**	32,165	32,338	17,734	13,463	31,897	570,408	.0112	461,018	**136**	73,327	**156**	14,739	**83**	59,074	23,819	519,145	**284**	Incorporated Place
Redford	**DET**	67625	◇	48,638	51,622	19,854	19,629	43,848	965,655	.0169	590,000	**174**	25,870	**55**	19,203	**108**	53,069	31,881	222,469	**122**	Minor Civil Division-Charter Township
Rochester Hills	**DET**	69035	◇	70,254	68,825	31,942	28,195	65,339	2,244,039	.0323	915,610	**269**	66,205	**141**	44,873	**251**	79,592	114,229	638,058	**349**	Incorporated Place
Roseville	**DET**	69800	**3-S**	46,705	48,129	20,023	20,054	38,238	935,185	.0224	1,266,948	**373**	331,538	**704**	49,715	**279**	84,720	36,470	551,795	**302**	Incorporated Place
Royal Oak	**DET**	70040	**3-S**	57,609	60,062	27,627	29,040	47,332	1,591,563	.0318	1,597,160	**470**	267,365	**568**	27,108	**152**	141,938	149,314	274,330	**150**	Incorporated Place
Saginaw	**SAG-**	70520	**2-A**	60,574	61,799	13,897	23,265	27,929	841,774	.0158	500,380	**147**	31,078	**66**	29,273	**164**	70,393	62,175	738,336	**404**	Incorporated Place
St. Clair Shores	**DET**	70760	**4-S**	61,104	63,096	24,835	27,502	43,880	1,517,488	.0236	719,629	**212**	25,972	**55**	27,819	**156**	149,903	70,702	158,426	**87**	Incorporated Place
St. Joseph	**BNTH-**	70960	**4-C**	8,598	8,789	27,476	4,186	44,517	236,241	.0031	58,767	**17**	....	**....**	1,429	**8**	19,245	10,944	172,813	**95**	Incorporated Place
Sault Ste. Marie	**SOO**	71740	**4-A**	17,341	16,542	14,255	6,180	31,250	247,187	.0051	200,564	**59**	49,391	**105**	10,131	**57**	27,122	9,969	17,447	**10**	Incorporated Place
Shelby	**DET**	72820	◇	69,913	65,159	27,205	27,176	57,039	1,901,953	.0277	740,040	**218**	181,113	**384**	14,136	**79**	52,740	49,917	517,779	**283**	Minor Civil Division-Charter Township
Southfield	**DET**	74900	**2-S**	79,844	78,296	25,947	36,381	47,570	2,071,695	.0469	2,667,257	**785**	405,477	**861**	202,420	**1,134**	160,658	145,245	326,834	**179**	Incorporated Place
Southgate	**DET**	74960	**4-S**	28,799	30,136	20,591	12,665	42,457	592,988	.0158	986,949	**290**	220,771	**469**	18,824	**105**	56,099	38,906	(d)	**....**	Incorporated Place
Sterling Heights	**DET**	76460	**3-SSm**	129,301	124,471	23,744	49,698	53,129	3,070,118	.0542	2,139,489	**629**	705,770	**1,498**	118,229	**663**	166,917	110,517	2,423,167	**1,327**	Incorporated Place
Taylor	**DET**	79000	**3-Sm**	62,371	65,868	17,325	24,130	39,623	1,080,601	.0249	1,281,779	**377**	299,399	**636**	65,333	**366**	104,215	84,498	225,464	**123**	Incorporated Place
Traverse City		80340	**3-A**	13,771	14,532	24,562	6,528	40,272	338,250	.0070	357,248	**105**	92,044	**195**	19,430	**109**	28,585	12,849	254,006	**139**	Incorporated Place
Troy	**DET**	80700	**2-Sm**	82,432	80,959	29,885	32,094	69,100	2,463,462	.0548	3,157,160	**929**	673,444	**1,430**	480,532	**2,693**	197,384	149,703	898,252	**492**	Incorporated Place
Walker	**GDR**	82960	**4-Sm**	23,490	21,842	20,682	9,723	43,452	485,831	.0093	401,142	**118**	76,437	**162**	5,464	**31**	8,773	7,190	574,342	**314**	Incorporated Place
Warren	**DET**	84000	**3-SS**	136,405	138,247	21,366	56,673	40,959	2,914,496	.0528	2,077,294	**611**	199,934	**424**	35,971	**202**	307,197	158,131	2,210,392	**1,210**	Incorporated Place
Waterford	**DET**	84240	◇	73,485	73,150	22,897	30,918	48,413	1,682,554	.0351	1,757,158	**517**	491,652	**1,044**	68,334	**383**	124,184	94,042	77,419	**42**	Minor Civil Division-Charter Township
West Bloomfield	**DET**	85480	◇	67,726	64,860	38,176	25,604	76,732	2,585,533	.0316	522,292	**154**	4,193	**9**	37,841	**212**	120,511	51,297	(d)	**....**	Minor Civil Division-Charter Township
Westland	**DET**	86000	**3-S**	86,995	86,602	20,349	37,774	42,032	1,770,243	.0324	1,270,694	**374**	370,994	**788**	53,319	**299**	164,429	104,173	199,408	**109**	Incorporated Place
White Lake	**DET**	86860	◇	29,287	28,219	23,720	10,992	58,264	694,702	.0101	242,241	**71**	37,179	**79**	1,342	**8**	52,959	14,056	(d)	**....**	Minor Civil Division-Charter Township
Wyandotte	**DET**	88900	**4-Sr**	26,477	28,006	20,863	11,496	41,125	552,378	.0083	197,642	**58**	....	**....**	4,704	**26**	35,240	42,199	175,763	**96**	Incorporated Place
Wyoming	**GDR**	88940	**3-S**	71,504	69,368	17,638	28,124	39,413	1,261,153	.0259	1,143,569	**336**	271,876	**577**	57,901	**324**	88,960	48,598	965,374	**529**	Incorporated Place
Ypsilanti	**DET**	89140	**4-S**	22,926	22,362	18,520	8,951	40,243	424,595	.0088	405,945	**119**	111,376	**236**	3,851	**22**	43,603	17,971	....	**....**	Incorporated Place
Minnesota																					
Albert Lea		00694	**4-B**	17,968	18,356	17,810	7,729	32,883	320,012	.0065	285,502	**84**	53,352	**113**	3,276	**18**	33,246	9,664	186,785	**102**	Incorporated Place
Andover	**MPLS-**	01486	◇	31,615	26,588	24,474	9,876	63,001	773,760	.0097	99,340	**29**	....	**....**	2,359	**13**	16,381	5,287	(d)	**....**	Incorporated Place
Apple Valley	**MPLS-**	01900	◇	49,253	45,527	28,146	18,448	60,128	1,386,295	.0226	819,566	**241**	172,108	**365**	8,148	**46**	137,195	28,811	(d)	**....**	Incorporated Place

.... Data less than 1,000.
(d) Data not available.
◇ Not classified as a Principal Business Center.

* Data from 1997 Census of Manufactures.

Principal Business Centers and Other Places with 27,500 or More: Population / Income / Sales, *Continued*

PLACE NAME	RANALLY METRO AREA	FIPS PLACE CODE	RANALLY CITY RATING	POPULATION Estimate 7/1/04	POPULATION Census 4/1/00	PER CAPITA INCOME 2003	HOUSE-HOLDS Estimate 7/1/04	MEDIAN HOUSEHOLD INCOME 2003	DISPOSABLE INCOME 2003 ($1,000)	MARKET ABILITY INDEX 2003	TOTAL RETAIL TRADE Sales 2003 ($1,000)	TOTAL RETAIL TRADE Ranally Sales Units	GENERAL MERCHANDISE Sales 2003 ($1,000)	GENERAL MERCHANDISE Ranally Sales Units	APPAREL STORES Sales 2003 ($1,000)	APPAREL STORES Ranally Sales Units	FOOD STORE SALES 2003 ($1,000)	HEALTH & DRUG STORE SALES 2003 ($1,000)	MANUFACTURERS VALUE ADDED 1997* ($1,000)	Ranally Mfg Units	PLACE TYPE
Austin		02908	4-B	23,636	23,314	17,774	10,081	32,740	420,115	.0073	237,949	70	44,992	96	9,399	53	52,460	12,428	....	....	Incorporated Place
Bemidji		05068	4-A	12,475	11,917	15,853	4,956	33,568	197,763	.0047	246,456	72	47,126	100	14,394	81	38,820	8,263	34,085	19	Incorporated Place
Blaine	MPLS-	06382	4-Sm	48,248	44,942	22,394	17,485	52,766	1,080,480	.0182	627,183	184	119,401	253	29,925	168	137,672	38,274	240,778	132	Incorporated Place
Bloomington	MPLS-	06616	3-SS	80,976	85,172	25,894	36,398	49,851	2,096,803	.0513	3,138,893	923	473,500	1,005	384,375	2,154	220,110	119,629	783,566	429	Incorporated Place
Brainerd		07300	4-A	13,531	13,178	18,347	5,879	34,014	248,248	.0056	285,861	84	52,554	112	2,790	16	23,407	9,181	158,562	87	Incorporated Place
Brooklyn Center	MPLS-	07948	3-S	28,996	29,172	17,146	11,960	38,978	497,159	.0131	778,140	229	198,111	421	17,769	100	21,205	12,764	147,969	81	Incorporated Place
Brooklyn Park	MPLS-	07966	◇	69,861	67,388	20,374	26,721	51,352	1,423,351	.0280	1,236,667	364	132,185	281	20,764	116	117,328	41,373	416,075	228	Incorporated Place
Burnsville	MPLS-	08794	3-Sm	61,929	60,220	26,897	25,489	51,197	1,665,709	.0350	1,851,721	545	388,711	825	96,566	541	199,410	70,223	384,578	211	Incorporated Place
Coon Rapids	MPLS-	13114	4-S	61,749	61,607	23,057	23,203	49,581	1,423,754	.0228	716,676	211	186,139	395	7,098	40	70,049	25,518	220,496	121	Incorporated Place
Cottage Grove	MPLS-	13456	◇	30,908	30,582	21,777	10,408	57,422	673,095	.0108	323,924	95	59,679	127	1,410	8	71,024	24,353	....	....	Incorporated Place
Duluth	DUL	17000	3-AA	87,850	86,918	17,484	36,800	33,134	1,535,973	.0298	1,192,304	351	219,447	466	36,624	205	131,136	77,987	286,310	157	Incorporated Place
Eagan	MPLS-	17288	◇	67,051	63,557	28,244	26,150	58,442	1,893,790	.0316	1,212,217	357	213,945	454	17,957	101	188,340	60,019	1,114,607	610	Incorporated Place
Eden Prairie	MPLS-	18116	◇	58,262	54,901	31,351	22,866	67,988	1,826,578	.0293	1,077,688	317	258,705	549	9,342	52	168,293	27,020	917,355	502	Incorporated Place
Edina	MPLS-	18188	3-SSm	46,817	47,425	37,515	21,788	58,171	1,756,321	.0398	2,432,096	715	591,559	1,256	164,119	920	171,351	100,534	289,215	158	Incorporated Place
Fairmont		20330	4-B	10,615	10,889	18,493	4,675	33,194	196,298	.0039	170,534	50	24,942	53	2,887	16	26,053	6,223	151,114	83	Incorporated Place
Fergus Falls		20906	4-A	14,037	13,471	18,359	5,957	33,198	257,703	.0051	221,937	65	50,973	108	3,370	19	21,890	3,663	101,735	56	Incorporated Place
Fridley	MPLS-	22814	3-Sm	27,261	27,449	23,465	11,519	43,012	639,678	.0115	461,627	136	88,063	187	6,156	35	50,518	20,901	866,141	474	Incorporated Place
Golden Valley	MPLS-	24308	4-Sr	19,264	20,281	23,641	8,443	47,279	455,428	.0123	797,088	234	50,521	107	10,898	61	177,574	79,767	734,806	402	Incorporated Place
Hibbing		28790	4-C	16,297	17,071	18,297	7,276	32,407	298,183	.0052	175,808	52	35,232	75	4,476	25	26,996	10,099	93,067	51	Incorporated Place
Inver Grove Heights	MPLS-	31076	◇	32,573	29,751	24,662	12,897	52,713	803,318	.0142	567,642	167	35,956	76	....	....	54,849	1,850	(d)	....	Incorporated Place
Lakeville	MPLS-	35180	◇	49,218	43,128	24,124	16,218	62,998	1,187,354	.0179	481,882	142	13,052	28	2,797	16	53,762	13,770	285,133	156	Incorporated Place
Mankato	MNKT	39878	3-A	33,745	32,427	17,064	13,127	34,592	575,814	.0135	703,189	207	188,422	400	41,467	232	106,671	33,068	340,281	186	Incorporated Place
Maple Grove	MPLS-	40166	◇	50,907	50,365	24,541	18,656	65,497	1,249,292	.0193	571,049	168	134,116	285	23,901	134	82,023	31,172	616,158	337	Incorporated Place
Maplewood	MPLS-	40382	4-S	33,954	34,947	19,828	13,980	43,011	673,229	.0151	785,845	231	147,907	314	38,763	217	91,572	26,199	46,245	25	Incorporated Place
Marshall		40688	4-B	12,468	12,735	18,362	4,943	37,042	228,936	.0049	233,333	69	44,046	94	4,755	27	33,981	6,108	100,289	55	Incorporated Place
Minneapolis	MPLS-	43000	1-AA	390,465	382,618	19,405	174,764	36,330	7,576,851	.1317	4,489,768	1,321	527,492	1,120	217,185	1,217	635,533	329,518	2,106,593	1,153	Incorporated Place
Minnetonka	MPLS-	43252	3-Sm	49,123	51,301	33,130	21,528	58,066	1,627,424	.0345	1,941,228	571	401,060	851	97,369	546	156,521	83,486	971,589	532	Incorporated Place
Moorhead	FAR-	43864	◇	31,883	32,177	16,184	11,790	34,133	515,987	.0101	392,489	115	66,323	141	5,332	30	57,006	17,806	44,584	24	Incorporated Place
New Ulm		46042	4-C	13,151	13,594	19,498	5,615	38,123	256,415	.0049	197,775	58	26,421	56	2,470	14	47,997	5,855	734,237	402	Incorporated Place
Oakdale	MPLS-	47680	◇	27,650	26,653	22,840	11,035	49,397	631,524	.0114	458,649	135	75,707	161	....	....	66,312	16,463	(d)	....	Incorporated Place
Owatonna		49300	4-C	23,495	22,434	20,238	9,223	41,904	475,496	.0087	337,656	99	54,806	116	4,481	25	60,472	11,815	505,543	277	Incorporated Place
Plymouth	MPLS-	51730	◇	68,442	65,894	29,528	27,165	65,031	2,020,987	.0405	2,082,623	613	83,363	177	13,540	76	175,771	26,292	1,138,178	623	Incorporated Place
Richfield	MPLS-	54214	4-S	33,280	34,439	20,841	15,353	41,318	693,604	.0164	926,386	273	23,322	50	23,930	134	97,864	39,353	(d)	....	Incorporated Place
Rochester	ROCH	54880	3-AA	95,448	85,806	23,955	40,024	46,644	2,286,467	.0410	1,665,705	490	406,415	863	56,174	315	171,029	63,301	....	....	Incorporated Place
Roseville	MPLS-	55852	3-Sm	31,520	33,690	24,700	14,269	46,430	778,539	.0223	1,526,493	449	305,581	649	112,729	632	160,203	89,888	248,830	136	Incorporated Place
St. Cloud	ST.CLD	56896	3-A	60,375	59,107	19,063	23,782	36,910	1,150,957	.0246	1,192,617	351	310,769	660	41,731	234	103,752	34,235	499,285	273	Incorporated Place
St. Louis Park	MPLS-	57220	4-S	43,529	44,126	27,481	21,596	46,167	1,196,200	.0257	1,402,569	413	176,208	374	30,553	171	103,446	58,164	388,369	213	Incorporated Place
St. Paul	MPLS-	58000	2-BB	292,505	287,151	18,463	119,488	37,257	5,400,534	.0888	2,512,359	739	229,272	487	89,969	504	523,457	175,492	2,873,925	1,573	Incorporated Place
Savage	MPLS-	58738	◇	29,034	21,115	25,411	9,495	64,600	737,793	.0092	90,766	27	....	....	1,011	6	7,130	....	73,359	40	Incorporated Place
Shakopee	MPLS-	59350	◇	30,540	20,568	24,007	11,382	53,000	733,170	.0109	277,430	82	40,015	85	3,239	18	18,014	9,213	(d)	....	Incorporated Place
Virginia		67288	4-C	9,091	9,157	17,319	4,406	29,478	157,445	.0040	229,748	68	60,634	129	7,961	45	21,968	8,909	(d)	....	Incorporated Place
West St. Paul	MPLS-	69700	4-Sm	19,392	19,405	30,478	9,015	44,354	591,027	.0092	317,194	93	53,093	113	9,280	52	87,288	21,218	67,097	37	Incorporated Place
Willmar		70420	3-A	17,659	18,351	17,716	7,152	34,578	312,848	.0072	369,163	109	82,807	176	10,516	59	45,579	13,295	142,260	78	Incorporated Place
Winona		71032	4-B	27,370	27,069	16,761	10,672	34,235	458,751	.0083	281,055	83	57,704	122	9,425	53	39,118	4,759	425,999	233	Incorporated Place
Woodbury	MPLS-	71428	◇	55,676	46,463	29,850	20,778	65,002	1,661,931	.0253	811,181	239	183,402	389	59,429	333	124,114	40,086	96,502	53	Incorporated Place
Worthington		71734	4-A	11,740	11,283	16,058	4,468	34,186	188,522	.0042	196,157	58	21,536	46	10,046	56	27,963	8,656	233,396	128	Incorporated Place

Mississippi

PLACE NAME	RANALLY METRO AREA	FIPS PLACE CODE	RANALLY CITY RATING	POPULATION Estimate 7/1/04	POPULATION Census 4/1/00	PER CAPITA INCOME 2003	HOUSE-HOLDS Estimate 7/1/04	MEDIAN HOUSEHOLD INCOME 2003	DISPOSABLE INCOME 2003 ($1,000)	MARKET ABILITY INDEX 2003	TOTAL RETAIL TRADE Sales 2003 ($1,000)	TOTAL RETAIL TRADE Ranally Sales Units	GENERAL MERCHANDISE Sales 2003 ($1,000)	GENERAL MERCHANDISE Ranally Sales Units	APPAREL STORES Sales 2003 ($1,000)	APPAREL STORES Ranally Sales Units	FOOD STORE SALES 2003 ($1,000)	HEALTH & DRUG STORE SALES 2003 ($1,000)	MANUFACTURERS VALUE ADDED 1997* ($1,000)	Ranally Mfg Units	PLACE TYPE
Biloxi	BIL-	06220	3-AA	51,377	50,644	17,178	21,655	31,974	882,573	.0179	765,333	225	289,339	614	51,003	286	47,472	33,826	....	....	Incorporated Place
Brookhaven		08820	4-B	9,656	9,861	13,983	3,902	25,759	135,017	.0034	175,396	52	59,990	127	7,836	44	13,348	7,350	119,874	66	Incorporated Place
Clarksdale		13820	4-C	20,069	20,645	10,344	7,135	22,045	207,592	.0051	219,046	64	34,653	74	9,640	54	29,827	14,147	60,412	33	Incorporated Place
Columbus	COL	15380	3-A	25,264	25,944	14,777	9,934	27,462	373,322	.0098	544,528	160	143,903	305	30,939	173	71,570	28,824	....	....	Incorporated Place
Corinth		15700	4-B	13,849	14,054	16,327	6,259	27,520	226,108	.0050	234,073	69	78,625	167	11,013	62	16,809	9,913	....	....	Incorporated Place
Greenville	GRNV	29180	3-A	40,236	41,633	11,889	14,618	25,031	478,372	.0111	481,291	142	146,955	312	32,376	181	43,446	17,985	416,767	228	Incorporated Place
Greenwood		29340	4-B	16,717	18,425	10,854	6,391	21,356	181,440	.0047	221,669	65	42,690	91	16,663	93	30,476	14,346	....	....	Incorporated Place
Gulfport	BIL-	29700	3-B	73,212	71,127	17,044	30,155	32,085	1,247,806	.0260	1,154,067	339	211,521	449	40,895	229	100,433	52,396	115,299	63	Incorporated Place
Hattiesburg	HATT	31020	3-A	46,591	44,779	13,673	18,342	26,298	637,055	.0162	857,052	252	288,846	613	26,388	148	61,832	62,406	387,501	212	Incorporated Place
Jackson	JAC	36000	2-AA	181,683	184,256	15,700	69,897	30,382	2,852,417	.0656	3,233,186	951	616,730	1,309	157,925	885	282,873	189,412	828,738	454	Incorporated Place
Laurel	LAUR	39640	3-A	17,321	18,393	14,443	6,597	25,376	250,168	.0069	399,706	118	114,028	242	18,138	102	50,360	27,800	412,886	226	Incorporated Place
McComb		43280	4-A	13,035	13,337	12,302	5,252	22,733	160,359	.0043	234,076	69	54,336	115	14,718	82	27,671	17,964	19,427	11	Incorporated Place
Meridian	MRID	46640	3-A	37,473	39,968	14,817	15,220	28,071	555,254	.0134	688,212	202	172,457	366	21,059	118	84,326	35,792	....	....	Incorporated Place
Natchez	NCHZ	50440	3-A	17,581	18,464	13,401	7,518	24,178	235,605	.0056	262,470	77	110,698	235	14,379	81	25,517	13,180	89,625	49	Incorporated Place
Olive Branch	MEM	54040	◇	32,260	21,054	23,085	12,055	50,489	744,713	.0107	231,159	68	8,202	17	....	....	28,450	2,390	(d)	....	Incorporated Place
Pascagoula	PSCG	55360	3-B	25,895	26,200	17,827	10,337	30,355	461,641	.0122	734,233	216	147,846	314	14,006	78	105,730	19,880	....	....	Incorporated Place
Southaven	MEM	69280	◇	36,005	28,977	21,987	14,276	42,765	791,629	.0158	740,351	218	287,400	610	10,832	61	61,944	43,137	(d)	....	Incorporated Place
Starkville		70240	4-B	21,741	21,869	15,220	10,633	24,154	330,903	.0061	195,085	57	51,775	110	12,115	68	24,246	3,939	....	....	Incorporated Place
Tupelo		74840	3-A	35,530	34,211	18,345	14,163	34,563	651,795	.0156	849,635	250	276,376	587	62,562	351	50,250	33,506	664,511	364	Incorporated Place
Vicksburg	VICK	76720	3-A	25,497	26,407	18,003	10,786	33,473	459,029	.0084	299,922	88	19,065	40	19,216	108	46,995	14,066	236,691	130	Incorporated Place

Missouri

PLACE NAME	RANALLY METRO AREA	FIPS PLACE CODE	RANALLY CITY RATING	POPULATION Estimate 7/1/04	POPULATION Census 4/1/00	PER CAPITA INCOME 2003	HOUSE-HOLDS Estimate 7/1/04	MEDIAN HOUSEHOLD INCOME 2003	DISPOSABLE INCOME 2003 ($1,000)	MARKET ABILITY INDEX 2003	TOTAL RETAIL TRADE Sales 2003 ($1,000)	TOTAL RETAIL TRADE Ranally Sales Units	GENERAL MERCHANDISE Sales 2003 ($1,000)	GENERAL MERCHANDISE Ranally Sales Units	APPAREL STORES Sales 2003 ($1,000)	APPAREL STORES Ranally Sales Units	FOOD STORE SALES 2003 ($1,000)	HEALTH & DRUG STORE SALES 2003 ($1,000)	MANUFACTURERS VALUE ADDED 1997* ($1,000)	Ranally Mfg Units	PLACE TYPE
Ballwin	ST.L	03160	◇	31,376	31,283	27,118	12,335	61,449	850,840	.0152	645,916	190	55,862	119	11,937	67	78,397	33,006	(d)	....	Incorporated Place
Blue Springs	K.C.	06652	4-S	48,367	48,080	21,164	18,023	49,093	1,023,617	.0175	608,193	179	68,634	146	2,226	12	114,790	20,922	74,315	41	Incorporated Place
Bridgeton	ST.L	08398	3-S	15,190	15,550	19,994	6,357	43,628	303,714	.0095	662,517	195	98,212	208	13,135	74	37,325	39,349	481,935	264	Incorporated Place
Cape Girardeau	CPGIR	11242	3-A	35,130	35,349	17,680	14,479	32,314	621,091	.0152	847,720	249	201,023	427	23,047	129	44,731	51,552	721,404	395	Incorporated Place
Chesterfield	ST.L	13600	◇	47,662	46,802	39,472	19,173	74,520	1,881,330	.0246	573,386	169	158,473	336	63,395	355	94,662	52,897	108,081	59	Incorporated Place
Clayton	ST.L	14572	3-S	12,637	12,825	42,197	5,510	56,979	533,245	.0093	432,313	127	....	....	9,745	55	15,146	8,800	(d)	....	Incorporated Place
Columbia	COL	15670	3-A	90,750	84,531	18,712	37,779	34,814	1,698,132	.0326	1,329,102	391	241,140	512	44,102	247	132,844	57,250	739,533	405	Incorporated Place
Crestwood	ST.L	17218	4-Sm	11,691	11,863	22,923	5,252	47,142	267,992	.0065	379,391	112	119,082	253	31,699	178	29,330	30,734	81,873	45	Incorporated Place
Creve Coeur	ST.L	17272	4-S	16,446	16,500	48,382	7,263	66,981	795,684	.0123	486,548	143	....	....	15,514	87	136,867	39,835	305,915	167	Incorporated Place
Des Peres	ST.L	19270	4-Sm	8,752	8,592	42,761	3,187	83,395	374,240	.0058	224,637	66	83,430	177	36,133	202	16,850	9,950	(d)	....	Incorporated Place
Florissant	ST.L	24778	4-S	49,167	50,497	19,781	20,743	43,549	972,596	.0165	534,172	157	59,832	127	9,889	55	115,097	62,742	(d)	....	Incorporated Place
Frontenac	ST.L	26110	4-Sm	3,537	3,483	49,151	1,374	88,676	173,847	.0026	98,969	29	38,740	82	16,930	95	6,932	4,191	(d)	....	Incorporated Place
Hannibal		30214	4-B	17,410	17,757	15,897	7,137	29,902	276,764	.0058	249,612	73	52,087	111	2,705	15	47,357	15,732	....	....	Incorporated Place
Independence	K.C.	35000	3-S	114,206	113,288	18,467	49,528	36,262	2,109,020	.0402	1,603,797	472	340,345	722	66,628	373	145,096	114,508	521,830	286	Incorporated Place
Jefferson City	JFCY	37000	3-A	40,776	39,636	21,221	17,362	39,500	865,299	.0169	755,953	222	160,910	342	14,466	81	105,771	40,394	610,123	334	Incorporated Place
Jennings	ST.L	37178	4-Sm	15,407	15,469	14,957	6,422	29,646	230,447	.0046	177,621	52	40,412	86	4,345	24	37,474	10,973	(d)	....	Incorporated Place
Joplin	JOP	37592	3-A	46,659	45,504	16,699	19,563	30,586	779,147	.0170	803,689	236	184,573	392	26,600	149	57,600	39,478	390,960	214	Incorporated Place
Kansas City	K.C.	38000	1-A	452,805	441,545	19,885	195,547	35,866	9,004,147	.1658	6,466,825	1,902	997,434	2,117	235,370	1,319	641,816	403,292	4,235,403	2,319	Incorporated Place
Kirksville		39026	4-A	16,418	16,988	12,552	6,421	24,988	206,077	.0048	214,960	63	40,322	86	8,637	48	30,912	13,664	221,671	121	Incorporated Place
Kirkwood	ST.L	39044	4-S	26,849	27,324	30,977	12,063	53,100	831,699	.0127	417,856	123	42,125	89	8,785	49	55,116	27,291	74,903	41	Incorporated Place
Lees Summit	K.C.	41348	◇	72,894	70,700	24,108	28,178	54,742	1,757,328	.0254	598,939	176	71,194	151	10,570	59	144,218	28,974	296,146	162	Incorporated Place
Liberty	K.C.	42032	◇	27,738	26,232	21,574	10,316	47,315	598,427	.0097	295,691	87	15,219	32	6,239	35	64,837	18,258	....	....	Incorporated Place
Mehlville	ST.L	47180	◇	28,699	28,822	21,165	13,007	44,048	607,415	.0110	435,105	128	103,870	220	17,486	98	45,774	19,815	(d)	....	Census Designated Place
Mexico		47648	4-C	10,173	11,320	16,937	4,307	31,281	172,295	.0033	123,797	36	16,851	36	3,545	20	22,100	9,978	150,391	82	Incorporated Place
Moberly		49034	4-C	12,038	11,945	15,744	5,114	28,755	189,526	.0047	253,696	75	62,621	133	5,074	28	29,479	13,856	78,951	43	Incorporated Place
North Kansas City	K.C.	53102	4-S	5,073	4,714	28,347	2,805	34,245	143,804	.0027	129,736	38	....	....	....	....	2,201	4,895	441,655	242	Incorporated Place
Oakville	ST.L	53876	◇	35,161	35,309	20,416	13,033	53,660	717,836	.0117	345,928	102	131,550	279	30,009	168	47,635	33,526	(d)	....	Census Designated Place
O'Fallon	ST.L	54074	◇	65,585	46,169	21,492	22,627	51,722	1,409,580	.0204	423,427	125	88,788	188	8,614	48	58,114	24,530	....	....	Incorporated Place
Poplar Bluff		59096	3-A	15,595	16,651	14,619	6,803	26,383	227,987	.0061	348,944	103	84,816	180	11,429	64	28,079	23,808	249,438	137	Incorporated Place
Raytown	K.C.	60788	◇	30,283	30,388	20,380	13,243	39,570	617,165	.0120	523,057	154	154,126	327	15,002	84	47,228	27,306	32,176	18	Incorporated Place
Rolla		62912	4-A	17,710	16,367	14,499	7,174	29,124	256,785	.0056	243,180	72	63,857	136	7,144	40	24,813	7,341	83,013	45	Incorporated Place
Saint Ann	ST.L	63956	4-Sm	13,286	13,607	17,088	6,296	31,916	227,036	.0076	534,893	157	216,480	460	50,327	282	40,404	32,498	(d)	....	Incorporated Place
Saint Charles	ST.L	64082	3-S	63,539	60,321	24,774	26,429	43,677	1,574,101	.0237	655,880	193	82,730	176	15,105	85	97,497	43,068	187,380	103	Incorporated Place
Saint Joseph	ST.JO	64550	3-AA	73,900	73,990	17,407	31,354	32,718	1,286,385	.0250	1,004,051	295	256,313	544	20,905	117	126,451	38,731	....	....	Incorporated Place
St. Louis	ST.L	65000	1-AA	327,502	348,189	15,141	150,947	25,961	4,958,610	.0875	2,531,321	745	248,810	528	81,582	457	412,334	255,453	5,088,636	2,786	Independent City
Saint Peters	ST.L	65126	◇	54,233	51,381	24,783	20,124	53,531	1,344,031	.0229	855,135	252	122,231	259	51,570	289	95,563	37,647	1,227,392	672	Incorporated Place
Sedalia		66440	4-A	19,132	20,339	16,636	8,372	30,134	318,275	.0065	282,255	83	66,436	141	9,950	56	31,973	14,449	269,557	148	Incorporated Place
Sikeston		67790	4-B	17,015	16,992	14,834	6,876	28,374	252,407	.0055	248,348	73	39,290	83	11,789	66	32,780	19,998	145,424	80	Incorporated Place
Springfield	SPRG	70000	2-A	154,363	151,580	17,243	70,178	30,329	2,661,679	.0600	3,000,955	883	550,360	1,168	96,864	543	273,611	144,655	1,670,752	915	Incorporated Place
University City	ST.L	75220	◇	36,907	37,428	26,408	16,949	41,173	974,651	.0150	458,458	135	22,940	49	9,933	56	140,644	35,264	(d)	....	Incorporated Place
West Plains		78928	4-A	10,092	10,866	14,552	4,627	25,710	146,861	.0038	203,767	60	59,499	126	7,262	41	12,001	10,830	168,465	92	Incorporated Place
Wildwood	ST.L	79820	◇	33,738	32,884	28,413	11,594	72,202	958,594	.0108	18,828	6	1,432	3	....	....	2,987	1,064	(d)	....	Incorporated Place

Montana

PLACE NAME	RANALLY METRO AREA	FIPS PLACE CODE	RANALLY CITY RATING	POPULATION Estimate 7/1/04	POPULATION Census 4/1/00	PER CAPITA INCOME 2003	HOUSE-HOLDS Estimate 7/1/04	MEDIAN HOUSEHOLD INCOME 2003	DISPOSABLE INCOME 2003 ($1,000)	MARKET ABILITY INDEX 2003	TOTAL RETAIL TRADE Sales 2003 ($1,000)	TOTAL RETAIL TRADE Ranally Sales Units	GENERAL MERCHANDISE Sales 2003 ($1,000)	GENERAL MERCHANDISE Ranally Sales Units	APPAREL STORES Sales 2003 ($1,000)	APPAREL STORES Ranally Sales Units	FOOD STORE SALES 2003 ($1,000)	HEALTH & DRUG STORE SALES 2003 ($1,000)	MANUFACTURERS VALUE ADDED 1997* ($1,000)	Ranally Mfg Units	PLACE TYPE
Billings	BIL	06550	3-AA	93,254	89,847	18,023	39,382	34,536	1,680,677	.0357	1,684,015	495	387,242	822	65,447	367	169,965	53,573	....	....	Incorporated Place
Bozeman		08950	3-A	31,409	27,509	18,031	12,582	34,296	566,348	.0115	509,079	150	47,519	101	19,927	112	60,164	15,017	41,788	23	Incorporated Place
Butte	BUT	11397	3-A	32,255	33,892	16,264	14,589	28,874	524,601	.0104	412,944	121	71,390	152	27,036	152	70,386	17,632	(d)	....	Incorporated Place
Great Falls	GTFA	32800	3-A	55,291	56,690	16,382	23,556	30,894	905,785	.0181	734,304	216	168,823	358	16,897	95	83,917	33,649	54,936	30	Incorporated Place
Havre		35050	4-C	8,851	9,621	15,818	3,766	29,117	140,008	.0028	114,466	34	18,030	38	5,150	29	24,366	2,238	(d)	....	Incorporated Place
Helena		35600	3-A	25,689	25,780	20,044	11,715	33,556	514,908	.0112	561,161	165	117,948	250	9,750	55	102,624	18,821	(d)	....	Incorporated Place
Kalispell		40075	4-A	15,623	14,223	17,391	6,840	31,285	271,692	.0057	256,219	75	71,475	152	4,377	25	32,438	6,062	(d)	....	Incorporated Place
Missoula	MSLA	50200	3-A	55,922	57,053	16,443	23,939	30,014	919,522	.0214	1,097,115	323	302,590	642	36,389	204	144,808	34,068	65,422	36	Incorporated Place

Nebraska

PLACE NAME	RANALLY METRO AREA	FIPS PLACE CODE	RANALLY CITY RATING	POPULATION Estimate 7/1/04	POPULATION Census 4/1/00	PER CAPITA INCOME 2003	HOUSE-HOLDS Estimate 7/1/04	MEDIAN HOUSEHOLD INCOME 2003	DISPOSABLE INCOME 2003 ($1,000)	MARKET ABILITY INDEX 2003	TOTAL RETAIL TRADE Sales 2003 ($1,000)	TOTAL RETAIL TRADE Ranally Sales Units	GENERAL MERCHANDISE Sales 2003 ($1,000)	GENERAL MERCHANDISE Ranally Sales Units	APPAREL STORES Sales 2003 ($1,000)	APPAREL STORES Ranally Sales Units	FOOD STORE SALES 2003 ($1,000)	HEALTH & DRUG STORE SALES 2003 ($1,000)	MANUFACTURERS VALUE ADDED 1997* ($1,000)	Ranally Mfg Units	PLACE TYPE
Beatrice		03390	4-C	12,912	12,496	17,413	5,629	32,419	224,842	.0043	166,930	49	21,715	46	5,880	33	26,224	10,844	42,581	23	Incorporated Place
Bellevue	OMA	03950	4-Sm	47,338	44,382	21,682	19,003	42,885	1,026,362	.0166	511,769	151	131,105	278	6,054	34	82,236	26,876	86,962	48	Incorporated Place
Columbus		10110	4-C	20,124	20,971	18,027	8,064	36,798	362,777	.0068	254,502	75	43,625	93	6,281	35	45,193	17,777	197,603	108	Incorporated Place
Fremont		17670	4-C	25,003	25,174	17,792	10,190	35,401	444,854	.0100	506,275	149	95,373	202	12,884	72	54,668	36,231	107,041	59	Incorporated Place
Grand Island	GDIS	19595	3-A	44,082	42,940	16,072	16,869	34,548	708,490	.0154	715,862	211	222,696	473	31,070	174	46,339	22,528	414,467	227	Incorporated Place
Hastings		21415	3-A	25,120	24,064	16,703	10,020	33,987	419,574	.0080	301,389	89	54,805	116	6,714	38	67,474	20,410	196,653	108	Incorporated Place
Kearney		25055	4-B	27,311	27,431	16,623	10,628	34,607	453,988	.0100	481,189	142	127,589	271	15,696	88	50,926	24,305	129,585	71	Incorporated Place
Lincoln	LINC	28000	3-AA	239,834	225,581	19,001	98,321	38,797	4,557,085	.0830	3,087,309	908	529,819	1,125	111,397	624	484,733	221,591	....	....	Incorporated Place
McCook		29925	4-A	7,779	7,994	16,410	3,320	30,991	127,650	.0033	190,942	56	47,116	100	5,256	29	24,030	12,467	(d)	....	Incorporated Place
Norfolk		34615	3-A	23,968	23,516	16,650	9,600	34,048	399,063	.0092	461,946	136	108,855	231	18,273	102	53,574	20,020	56,492	31	Incorporated Place
North Platte		35000	3-A	23,875	23,878	17,827	10,133	33,497	425,618	.0080	300,747	88	78,360	166	7,232	41	40,625	19,113	(d)	....	Incorporated Place
Omaha	OMA	37000	2-AA	397,239	390,007	19,126	165,464	39,031	7,597,438	.1528	6,801,543	2,001	824,942	1,751	311,482	1,746	903,508	411,815	2,939,121	1,609	Incorporated Place
Scottsbluff		44245	3-A	14,597	14,732	15,374	6,116	29,307	224,421	.0059	335,496	99	83,320	177	10,888	61	51,264	8,848	45,664	25	Incorporated Place

Nevada

PLACE NAME	RANALLY METRO AREA	FIPS PLACE CODE	RANALLY CITY RATING	POPULATION Estimate 7/1/04	POPULATION Census 4/1/00	PER CAPITA INCOME 2003	HOUSE-HOLDS Estimate 7/1/04	MEDIAN HOUSEHOLD INCOME 2003	DISPOSABLE INCOME 2003 ($1,000)	MARKET ABILITY INDEX 2003	TOTAL RETAIL TRADE Sales 2003 ($1,000)	TOTAL RETAIL TRADE Ranally Sales Units	GENERAL MERCHANDISE Sales 2003 ($1,000)	GENERAL MERCHANDISE Ranally Sales Units	APPAREL STORES Sales 2003 ($1,000)	APPAREL STORES Ranally Sales Units	FOOD STORE SALES 2003 ($1,000)	HEALTH & DRUG STORE SALES 2003 ($1,000)	MANUFACTURERS VALUE ADDED 1997* ($1,000)	Ranally Mfg Units	PLACE TYPE
Carson City		09700	4-C	56,233	52,457	18,970	21,701	38,794	1,066,760	.0212	927,961	273	53,850	114	1,745	10	156,266	105,836	297,324	163	Independent City
Henderson	LASV	31900	◇	215,979	175,381	22,641	83,089	50,926	4,890,073	.0778	2,357,442	693	353,860	751	84,191	472	319,373	72,653	544,072	298	Incorporated Place
Las Vegas	LASV	40000	2-AA	552,823	478,434	20,670	207,967	43,024	11,426,595	.1921	6,312,302	1,857	836,955	1,777	193,616	1,085	1,012,969	294,212	272,972	149	Incorporated Place
North Las Vegas	LASV	51800	◇	150,501	115,488	13,784	45,127	42,550	2,074,477	.0359	872,918	257	133,362	283	9,471	53	197,114	50,824	195,723	107	Incorporated Place
Paradise	LASV	54600	◇	221,486	186,070	19,422	93,693	37,438	4,301,761	.0869	3,921,112	1,153	727,607	1,545	546,403	3,062	615,967	165,702	(d)	....	Census Designated Place
Reno	RENO	60600	2-A	204,639	180,480	20,748	83,192	40,026	4,245,937	.0790	3,216,961	946	598,957	1,271	137,893	773	454,858	119,164	446,658	245	Incorporated Place
Sparks	RENO	68400	4-S	74,337	66,346	17,432	27,321	42,649	1,295,854	.0249	982,053	289	133,760	284	8,719	49	162,572	51,234	390,132	214	Incorporated Place
Spring Valley	LASV	68585	◇	139,733	117,390	23,231	58,145	44,181	3,246,134	.0549	1,965,766	578	122,853	261	35,562	199	162,647	53,112	(d)	....	Census Designated Place
Sunrise Manor	LASV	71400	◇	185,833	156,120	14,982	65,103	36,989	2,784,218	.0489	1,384,641	407	140,733	299	26,424	148	210,996	58,844	(d)	....	Census Designated Place
Winchester	LASV	84600	◇	32,090	26,958	18,454	14,540	31,124	592,193	.0177	1,175,924	346	285,701	606	248,898	1,395	186,484	55,130	(d)	....	Census Designated Place

New Hampshire

PLACE NAME	RANALLY METRO AREA	FIPS PLACE CODE	RANALLY CITY RATING	POPULATION Estimate 7/1/04	POPULATION Census 4/1/00	PER CAPITA INCOME 2003	HOUSE-HOLDS Estimate 7/1/04	MEDIAN HOUSEHOLD INCOME 2003	DISPOSABLE INCOME 2003 ($1,000)	MARKET ABILITY INDEX 2003	TOTAL RETAIL TRADE Sales 2003 ($1,000)	TOTAL RETAIL TRADE Ranally Sales Units	GENERAL MERCHANDISE Sales 2003 ($1,000)	GENERAL MERCHANDISE Ranally Sales Units	APPAREL STORES Sales 2003 ($1,000)	APPAREL STORES Ranally Sales Units	FOOD STORE SALES 2003 ($1,000)	HEALTH & DRUG STORE SALES 2003 ($1,000)	MANUFACTURERS VALUE ADDED 1997* ($1,000)	Ranally Mfg Units	PLACE TYPE
Claremont		12900	4-B	12,909	13,151	18,836	5,723	32,938	243,158	.0056	293,572	86	60,992	129	4,456	25	67,252	18,758	223,256	122	Incorporated Place
Concord	CONC	14200	3-B	42,069	40,687	20,810	17,131	39,044	875,440	.0211	1,203,100	354	165,849	352	35,133	197	212,758	46,467	216,070	118	Incorporated Place
Derry	BOS	17940	◇	36,788	34,021	21,206	13,527	49,575	780,131	.0124	351,325	103	57,477	122	3,441	19	51,998	13,771	163,961	90	Minor Civil Division-Town
Dover	PTSM-	18820	4-C	28,157	26,884	22,045	12,370	41,251	620,715	.0112	439,829	129	34,525	73	11,044	62	115,232	25,574	291,829	160	Incorporated Place
Keene		39300	4-A	23,194	22,563	19,259	9,361	35,913	446,693	.0118	719,258	212	70,185	149	22,627	127	78,720	37,856	257,672	141	Incorporated Place
Laconia		40180	4-C	15,700	16,411	17,778	6,574	35,446	279,114	.0082	537,479	158	93,240	198	41,255	231	84,978	14,626	191,406	105	Incorporated Place
Lebanon		41300	3-A	12,934	12,568	21,835	5,783	39,243	282,410	.0077	491,355	145	100,161	213	16,388	92	87,623	21,297	172,031	94	Incorporated Place
Manchester	MNCH	45140	3-AA	110,296	107,006	19,977	46,114	38,355	2,203,373	.0460	2,205,150	649	355,804	755	104,242	584	239,569	93,481	705,764	386	Incorporated Place
Nashua	BOS	50260	3-B	89,600	86,605	22,908	36,112	47,109	2,052,550	.0490	2,851,565	839	485,942	1,032	166,027	930	323,612	93,558	1,255,871	688	Incorporated Place
Portsmouth	PTSM-	62900	3-C	20,097	20,784	26,054	9,677	42,017	523,610	.0194	1,525,037	449	296,147	629	76,947	431	204,882	41,348	159,643	87	Incorporated Place
Rochester	PTSM-	65140	4-C	29,742	28,461	19,024	12,170	37,804	565,803	.0109	451,538	133	43,458	92	9,647	54	86,079	25,054	808,492	443	Incorporated Place
Salem	BOS	66660	4-S	29,098	28,112	25,291	10,938	51,852	735,920	.0227	1,631,832	480	566,264	1,202	135,785	761	174,046	48,192	....	....	Minor Civil Division-Town

.... Data less than 1,000.
(d) Data not available.
◇ Not classified as a Principal Business Center.

* Data from 1997 Census of Manufactures.

continued on next page

Principal Business Centers and Other Places with 27,500 or More: Population / Income / Sales, *Continued*

PLACE NAME	RANALLY METRO AREA	FIPS PLACE CODE	RANALLY CITY RATING	POPULATION Estimate 7/1/04	POPULATION Census 4/1/00	PER CAPITA INCOME 2003	HOUSE-HOLDS Estimate 7/1/04	MEDIAN HOUSEHOLD INCOME 2003	DISPOSABLE INCOME 2003 ($1,000)	MARKET ABILITY INDEX 2003	TOTAL RETAIL TRADE Sales 2003 ($1,000)	TOTAL RETAIL TRADE Ranally Sales Units	GENERAL MERCHANDISE Sales 2003 ($1,000)	GENERAL MERCHANDISE Ranally Sales Units	APPAREL STORES Sales 2003 ($1,000)	APPAREL STORES Ranally Sales Units	FOOD STORE SALES 2003 ($1,000)	HEALTH & DRUG STORE SALES 2003 ($1,000)	MANUFACTURERS VALUE ADDED 1997* ($1,000)	Ranally Mfg Units	PLACE TYPE
New Jersey																					
Asbury Park	**N.Y.**	01960	**4-S**	16,986	16,930	24,228	7,069	37,442	411,539	.0064	194,787	**57**	42,748	**91**	4,846	**27**	23,722	24,074	(d)	....	Incorporated Place
Atlantic City	**ATCY**	02080	**3-AA**	42,300	40,517	16,279	16,486	25,870	688,604	.0140	587,955	**173**	63,303	**134**	80,866	**453**	138,267	52,812	(d)	....	Incorporated Place
Bayonne	**N.Y.**	03580	**4-S**	57,481	61,842	20,384	23,793	38,525	1,171,706	.0172	357,629	**105**	5,895	**13**	21,205	**119**	97,742	41,049	243,949	**134**	Incorporated Place
Belleville	**N.Y.**	04695	**4-Sr**	36,304	35,928	18,053	13,894	43,347	655,400	.0108	301,712	**89**	23,445	**50**	10,531	**59**	101,627	10,844	219,662	**120**	Minor Civil Division-Township
Berkeley	**N.Y.**	05305	◇	39,232	39,991	23,959	19,607	34,466	939,942	.0117	102,443	**30**	1,408	**3**	1,356	**8**	42,457	9,200	(d)	....	Minor Civil Division-Township
Bloomfield	**N.Y.**	06260	**4-S**	48,182	47,683	20,884	19,249	48,309	1,006,227	.0159	442,287	**130**	1,488	**3**	24,789	**139**	144,755	41,412	163,327	**89**	Minor Civil Division-Township
Brick	**N.Y.**	07420	**4-S**	78,909	76,119	24,593	30,724	47,043	1,940,587	.0299	881,266	**259**	151,309	**321**	57,333	**321**	223,800	41,665	(d)	....	Minor Civil Division-Township
Bridgewater	**N.Y.**	07720	**4-S**	46,511	42,940	34,715	16,818	72,575	1,614,625	.0295	1,397,924	**411**	385,788	**819**	217,862	**1,221**	67,314	42,732	609,867	**334**	Minor Civil Division-Township
Burlington	**PHIL-**	08920	**4-S**	10,219	9,736	25,363	4,197	48,942	259,184	.0053	266,003	**78**	62,237	**132**	14,738	**83**	26,696	12,746	181,828	**100**	Incorporated Place
Camden	**PHIL-**	10000	**3-S**	80,723	79,904	10,238	25,187	23,170	826,482	.0149	261,243	**77**	5,206	**11**	8,710	**49**	69,221	37,163	340,536	**186**	Incorporated Place
Cherry Hill	**PHIL-**	12280	**3-SS**	71,287	69,965	32,065	27,512	60,117	2,285,853	.0388	1,602,265	**471**	137,801	**293**	201,828	**1,131**	211,363	93,704	468,629	**257**	Minor Civil Division-Township
City of Orange	**N.Y.**	13045	**4-S**	33,464	32,868	14,028	12,158	34,892	469,427	.0083	219,445	**65**	7,250	**15**	18,592	**104**	29,933	26,593	35,818	**20**	Minor Civil Division-Township
Clifton	**N.Y.**	13690	**4-S**	80,849	78,672	22,894	30,670	46,037	1,850,951	.0297	932,267	**274**	95,602	**203**	53,048	**297**	156,508	58,605	932,625	**511**	Incorporated Place
Deptford	**PHIL-**	17710	◇	30,117	26,763	24,176	11,580	45,595	728,120	.0150	755,877	**222**	179,523	**381**	79,892	**448**	46,120	31,033	43,727	**24**	Minor Civil Division-Township
Dover	**N.Y.**	18070	**4-S**	18,997	18,188	17,502	5,732	51,709	332,479	.0073	354,151	**104**	35,788	**76**	9,611	**54**	93,526	4,364	61,647	**34**	Incorporated Place
Dover	**N.Y.**	18130	**3-S**	95,750	89,706	24,640	36,025	48,508	2,359,256	.0417	1,670,903	**492**	294,173	**624**	107,691	**604**	291,568	112,983	53,097	**29**	Minor Civil Division-Township
East Brunswick	**N.Y.**	19000	**3-S**	50,231	46,756	32,206	17,521	64,816	1,617,751	.0263	1,010,166	**297**	180,555	**383**	105,911	**594**	125,358	55,074	70,733	**39**	Minor Civil Division-Township
East Orange	**N.Y.**	19390	**4-Sr**	68,895	69,824	13,857	25,777	30,798	954,665	.0145	180,155	**53**	3,990	**8**	20,975	**118**	60,313	22,471	(d)	....	Incorporated Place
Eatontown	**N.Y.**	19840	**4-Sm**	14,251	14,008	28,082	6,127	51,737	400,199	.0090	512,753	**151**	95,703	**203**	86,659	**486**	45,460	16,406	154,367	**85**	Incorporated Place
Edison	**N.Y.**	20230	**3-S**	102,187	97,687	29,740	36,671	60,271	3,039,076	.0502	1,918,937	**564**	190,095	**404**	219,675	**1,231**	207,267	121,416	1,317,847	**721**	Minor Civil Division-Township
Egg Harbor	**ATCY**	20290	◇	34,349	30,726	21,586	12,463	46,935	741,467	.0122	394,980	**116**	29,089	**62**	23,642	**132**	18,379	21,154	(d)	....	Minor Civil Division-Township
Elizabeth	**N.Y.**	21000	**3-S**	125,595	120,568	13,939	41,736	33,043	1,750,637	.0309	819,897	**241**	27,742	**59**	57,859	**324**	204,916	71,345	544,705	**298**	Incorporated Place
Englewood	**N.Y.**	21480	**4-S**	26,749	26,203	30,091	9,492	52,450	804,897	.0139	584,285	**172**	....	....	25,894	**145**	82,482	13,945	181,081	**99**	Incorporated Place
Evesham	**PHIL-**	22110	◇	48,424	42,275	28,595	18,471	58,918	1,384,687	.0227	843,280	**248**	113,830	**242**	48,647	**273**	166,021	45,304	(d)	....	Minor Civil Division-Township
Ewing	**PHIL-**	22185	◇	36,717	35,707	19,916	13,155	43,109	731,247	.0115	298,279	**88**	3,278	**7**	22,059	**124**	74,967	29,096	161,663	**89**	Minor Civil Division-Township
Fair Lawn	**N.Y.**	22470	◇	32,053	31,637	28,373	11,968	62,181	909,434	.0129	321,265	**95**	....	....	4,803	**27**	53,282	30,185	346,422	**190**	Incorporated Place
Flemington	**N.Y.**	23700	**4-S**	4,412	4,200	41,795	1,919	68,105	184,400	.0034	173,723	**51**	4,870	**10**	14,461	**81**	30,046	6,346	297,403	**163**	Incorporated Place
Fort Lee	**N.Y.**	24420	◇	37,143	35,461	35,407	17,368	51,597	1,315,113	.0167	316,425	**93**	1,290	**3**	19,260	**108**	131,825	52,595	(d)	....	Incorporated Place
Franklin	**N.Y.**	24900	◇	52,836	50,903	27,158	20,050	59,779	1,434,934	.0221	689,184	**203**	43,872	**93**	23,648	**133**	167,392	56,123	368,354	**202**	Minor Civil Division-Township
Freehold	**N.Y.**	25230	◇	32,663	31,537	26,847	11,678	58,317	876,905	.0187	1,003,290	**295**	109,309	**232**	133,091	**746**	102,893	40,296	143,750	**79**	Minor Civil Division-Township
Galloway	**ATCY**	25560	◇	34,634	31,209	20,414	11,916	45,532	707,013	.0090	60,322	**18**	1,694	**4**	....	....	13,514	2,324	....	....	Minor Civil Division-Township
Garfield	**N.Y.**	25770	◇	30,569	29,786	17,321	11,543	40,127	529,491	.0085	211,933	**62**	1,357	**3**	....	....	44,420	16,626	293,514	**161**	Incorporated Place
Gloucester	**PHIL-**	26760	◇	65,671	64,350	21,658	24,337	46,504	1,422,272	.0209	465,598	**137**	56,796	**121**	11,069	**62**	97,281	28,347	95,649	**52**	Minor Civil Division-Township
Hackensack	**N.Y.**	28680	**3-SS**	43,789	42,677	23,618	18,567	44,264	1,034,223	.0225	1,197,514	**352**	231,492	**491**	93,275	**523**	163,218	127,057	191,180	**105**	Incorporated Place
Hamilton	**PHIL-**	29310	◇	89,423	87,109	23,300	35,132	50,077	2,083,586	.0317	863,614	**254**	46,750	**99**	28,648	**161**	205,883	111,828	338,838	**186**	Minor Civil Division-Township
Hillsborough	**N.Y.**	31890	◇	38,625	36,634	28,381	13,292	70,585	1,096,207	.0134	141,095	**42**	1,153	**2**	1,758	**10**	95,048	....	363,691	**199**	Minor Civil Division-Township
Hoboken	**N.Y.**	32250	**4-S**	41,282	38,577	36,475	20,884	56,667	1,505,754	.0173	166,147	**49**	2,149	**5**	8,190	**46**	66,398	34,638	120,572	**66**	Incorporated Place
Howell	**N.Y.**	33300	◇	52,545	48,903	24,318	17,983	60,358	1,277,791	.0180	386,198	**114**	66,903	**142**	24,769	**139**	79,351	15,289	73,223	**40**	Minor Civil Division-Township
Irvington	**N.Y.**	34450	**4-S**	61,136	60,695	13,958	22,292	34,512	853,339	.0134	215,882	**64**	25,572	**54**	19,876	**111**	47,059	24,819	94,478	**52**	Minor Civil Division-Township
Jackson	**N.Y.**	34680	◇	48,436	42,816	22,830	16,111	57,130	1,105,796	.0150	243,151	**72**	1,054	**2**	49,527	**278**	64,679	18,193	(d)	....	Minor Civil Division-Township
Jersey City	**N.Y.**	36000	**3-SS**	228,062	240,055	18,093	84,296	36,248	4,126,240	.0657	1,639,019	**482**	256,025	**543**	175,966	**986**	245,951	140,089	534,551	**293**	Incorporated Place
Kearny	**N.Y.**	36510	**4-S**	42,023	40,513	18,730	14,079	43,444	787,080	.0130	373,813	**110**	37,420	**79**	22,381	**125**	144,064	28,939	180,388	**99**	Incorporated Place
Lakewood	**N.Y.**	38550	**4-Sr**	77,272	60,352	16,837	25,618	33,665	1,301,027	.0306	1,591,801	**468**	11,011	**23**	5,955	**33**	116,794	55,538	364,429	**200**	Minor Civil Division-Township
Lawrence	**PHIL-**	39510	◇	30,529	29,159	29,185	11,505	59,230	890,998	.0200	1,156,308	**340**	209,565	**445**	122,052	**684**	85,589	68,910	37,003	**20**	Minor Civil Division-Township
Linden	**N.Y.**	40350	**4-S**	41,106	39,394	18,783	15,589	41,911	772,106	.0152	648,550	**191**	74,475	**158**	35,561	**199**	92,374	39,725	1,951,317	**1,068**	Incorporated Place
Livingston	**N.Y.**	40890	**3-Sm**	27,357	27,391	37,062	9,330	81,499	1,013,918	.0166	674,830	**199**	153,956	**327**	103,507	**580**	97,714	66,981	43,463	**24**	Minor Civil Division-Township
Long Branch	**N.Y.**	41310	**4-Sr**	32,422	31,340	21,622	13,602	36,724	701,044	.0099	189,159	**56**	2,138	**5**	1,422	**8**	104,142	18,574	31,106	**17**	Incorporated Place
Manalapan	**N.Y.**	42990	◇	34,951	33,423	30,097	11,768	70,924	1,051,905	.0143	315,353	**93**	38,574	**82**	17,576	**98**	93,522	17,522	(d)	....	Minor Civil Division-Township
Manchester	**N.Y.**	43140	◇	41,263	38,928	22,764	22,048	26,805	939,306	.0117	91,366	**27**	....	....	....	....	46,127	23,833	(d)	....	Minor Civil Division-Township
Marlboro	**N.Y.**	44070	◇	38,293	36,398	36,282	12,609	82,158	1,389,358	.0158	129,330	**38**	12,218	**26**	2,963	**17**	43,736	13,774	76,189	**42**	Minor Civil Division-Township
Middletown	**N.Y.**	45990	◇	66,503	66,327	31,051	24,277	61,770	2,064,974	.0299	848,746	**250**	107,406	**228**	37,012	**207**	230,426	70,051	(d)	....	Minor Civil Division-Township
Millburn	**N.Y.**	46380	**4-Sm**	20,008	19,765	61,989	7,114	117,216	1,240,281	.0174	605,392	**178**	114,754	**244**	224,346	**1,257**	83,907	40,379	(d)	....	Minor Civil Division-Township
Millville	**VINL**	46680	**4-S**	27,346	26,847	19,106	10,298	37,513	522,476	.0082	208,795	**61**	27,915	**59**	3,773	**21**	69,912	15,905	344,652	**189**	Incorporated Place
Monroe	**PHIL-**	47250	◇	30,083	28,967	22,011	11,229	44,494	662,165	.0098	234,432	**69**	....	....	5,999	**34**	70,352	13,569	54,788	**30**	Minor Civil Division-Township
Monroe	**N.Y.**	47280	◇	30,485	27,999	33,012	13,576	50,294	1,006,357	.0114	66,919	**20**	....	....	....	....	18,809	6,546	80,316	**44**	Minor Civil Division-Township
Montclair	**N.Y.**	47500	**4-S**	39,617	38,977	36,249	15,338	64,896	1,436,079	.0179	312,524	**92**	....	....	18,516	**104**	113,263	30,301	(d)	....	Minor Civil Division-Township
Moorestown	**PHIL-**	47880	**3-Sm**	22,351	19,017	44,921	8,400	67,838	1,004,021	.0154	592,760	**174**	109,965	**233**	76,918	**431**	16,808	49,040	742,519	**407**	Minor Civil Division-Township
Morristown	**N.Y.**	48300	**3-S**	19,610	18,544	42,237	7,751	68,687	828,260	.0123	427,909	**126**	15,000	**32**	27,558	**154**	35,449	17,544	182,698	**100**	Incorporated Place
Mount Laurel	**PHIL-**	49020	◇	45,352	40,221	33,982	19,167	56,570	1,541,149	.0222	661,265	**195**	....	....	9,318	**52**	100,720	26,309	162,553	**89**	Minor Civil Division-Township
Neptune	**N.Y.**	49890	◇	27,710	27,690	22,274	11,395	41,184	617,215	.0095	259,753	**76**	12,531	**27**	....	....	97,556	29,646	(d)	....	Minor Civil Division-Township
Newark	**N.Y.**	51000	**2-CC**	273,968	273,546	11,104	91,879	26,147	3,042,245	.0573	1,394,096	**410**	53,012	**113**	112,685	**632**	343,894	144,900	1,817,277	**995**	Incorporated Place
New Brunswick	**N.Y.**	51210	**3-S**	50,455	48,573	14,400	13,530	34,338	726,539	.0120	254,338	**75**	61,489	**131**	18,712	**105**	34,325	22,989	497,120	**272**	Incorporated Place
Newton	**N.Y.**	51930	**4-S**	8,857	8,244	29,001	3,557	52,693	256,859	.0044	175,569	**52**	6,075	**13**	1,829	**10**	37,096	7,530	(d)	....	Incorporated Place
North Bergen	**N.Y.**	52470	**4-Sr**	60,664	58,092	18,299	22,259	37,884	1,110,091	.0169	362,638	**107**	35,546	**75**	9,124	**51**	144,922	23,897	358,769	**196**	Minor Civil Division-Township
North Brunswick	**N.Y.**	52560	◇	38,084	36,287	29,396	14,284	54,234	1,119,517	.0179	632,837	**186**	81,778	**174**	26,412	**148**	74,607	21,020	256,716	**141**	Minor Civil Division-Township
Nutley	**N.Y.**	53680	◇	27,544	27,362	22,093	11,004	52,510	608,538	.0092	234,063	**69**	....	....	13,125	**74**	90,039	35,966	....	....	Minor Civil Division-Township
Ocean Township	**N.Y.**	54270	**4-Sm**	27,480	26,959	25,110	10,912	43,815	690,025	.0112	380,917	**112**	47,139	**100**	8,380	**47**	53,927	42,951	(d)	....	Minor Civil Division-Township
Old Bridge	**N.Y.**	54705	◇	63,700	60,456	26,312	22,535	56,921	1,676,048	.0240	583,955	**172**	24,803	**53**	12,928	**72**	144,033	30,457	159,870	**88**	Minor Civil Division-Township
Orange	**N.Y.**	55020	◇	33,032	32,868	14,042	12,000	34,878	463,824	.0082	218,723	**64**	7,226	**15**	18,531	**104**	29,835	26,506	(d)	....	Census Designated Place
Paramus	**N.Y.**	55950	**2-Sm**	25,781	25,737	25,126	8,113	65,363	647,781	.0340	3,021,164	**889**	634,071	**1,346**	591,396	**3,314**	121,075	91,768	124,562	**68**	Incorporated Place
Parsippany-Troy Hills	**N.Y.**	56460	**4-S**	52,618	50,649	28,179	20,635	59,724	1,482,712	.0291	1,440,342	**424**	79,230	**168**	56,107	**314**	205,409	70,391	693,569	**380**	Minor Civil Division-Township
Passaic	**N.Y.**	56550	**4-S**	69,756	67,861	12,735	19,733	31,771	888,354	.0159	390,423	**115**	13,406	**28**	38,428	**215**	133,686	31,931	237,872	**130**	Incorporated Place
Paterson	**N.Y.**	57000	**3-S**	151,031	149,222	13,068	44,638	31,667	1,973,628	.0324	567,593	**167**	20,815	**44**	34,823	**195**	159,358	53,437	929,443	**509**	Incorporated Place
Pemberton	**PHIL-**	57510	◇	28,139	28,691	20,198	10,091	43,480	568,363	.0077	95,261	**28**	....	....	....	....	44,118	9,203	(d)	....	Minor Civil Division-Township
Pennsauken	**PHIL-**	57660	**4-S**	36,204	35,737	19,639	12,950	42,530	711,005	.0124	426,969	**126**	6,981	**15**	13,373	**75**	47,100	28,601	601,437	**329**	Minor Civil Division-Township
Perth Amboy	**N.Y.**	58200	**4-S**	49,919	47,303	15,771	15,324	35,965	787,271	.0128	292,296	**86**	2,439	**5**	15,962	**89**	75,132	23,960	220,395	**121**	Incorporated Place
Piscataway	**N.Y.**	59010	◇	53,301	50,482	25,670	17,377	59,830	1,368,210	.0173	204,275	**60**	32,186	**68**	1,289	**7**	51,453	9,209	879,274	**481**	Minor Civil Division-Township
Plainfield	**N.Y.**	59190	**4-S**	48,355	47,829	17,925	15,157	45,097	866,780	.0162	617,958	**182**	68,052	**144**	24,359	**137**	104,051	47,275	64,566	**35**	Incorporated Place
Pleasantville	**ATCY**	59640	**4-S**	20,129	19,012	15,804	6,762	36,194	318,112	.0090	558,348	**164**	57,779	**123**	21,516	**121**	94,623	28,879	(d)	....	Incorporated Place
Princeton		60900	**4-C**	14,826	14,203	25,627	3,542	71,311	379,949	.0072	331,416	**97**	20,501	**44**	47,458	**266**	40,535	22,978	(d)	....	Incorporated Place
Red Bank	**N.Y.**	62430	**4-S**	12,311	11,844	32,318	5,643	52,808	397,869	.0070	312,710	**92**	3,129	**7**	36,011	**202**	45,772	18,700	(d)	....	Incorporated Place
Ridgewood	**N.Y.**	63000	**4-S**	24,960	24,936	47,242	8,612	85,595	1,179,154	.0156	415,063	**122**	....	....	40,704	**228**	63,337	22,619	(d)	....	Incorporated Place
Sayreville	**N.Y.**	65790	◇	42,705	40,377	25,570	15,779	51,619	1,091,982	.0142	212,582	**63**	1,384	**3**	12,533	**70**	65,905	10,518	540,416	**296**	Incorporated Place
Secaucus	**N.Y.**	66570	**4-S**	16,577	15,931	27,376	6,486	53,387	453,805	.0128	876,534	**258**	32,550	**69**	188,317	**1,055**	45,372	19,710	280,395	**154**	Incorporated Place
Somerville	**N.Y.**	68460	**4-S**	12,834	12,423	28,199	4,889	58,768	361,902	.0084	494,511	**145**	10,347	**22**	8,857	**50**	43,590	18,821	400,495	**219**	Incorporated Place
South Brunswick	**N.Y.**	68790	◇	41,098	37,734	31,819	14,591	66,802	1,307,710	.0183	474,855	**140**	8,963	**19**	9,038	**51**	54,012	17,612	435,944	**239**	Minor Civil Division-Township
South Plainfield	**N.Y.**	69390	**4-S**	23,311	21,810	24,705	7,624	58,822	575,887	.0115	557,600	**164**	87,010	**185**	18,931	**106**	88,796	25,468	391,340	**214**	Incorporated Place
Stafford	**N.Y.**	70320	◇	28,853	22,532	23,042	10,979	46,642	664,817	.0116	436,465	**128**	88,242	**187**	10,913	**61**	109,005	11,277	(d)	....	Minor Civil Division-Township
Summit	**N.Y.**	71430	**4-S**	21,947	21,131	55,193	8,137	79,040	1,211,327	.0151	360,430	**106**	....	....	15,323	**86**	18,740	18,079	244,006	**134**	Incorporated Place
Teaneck	**N.Y.**	72360	**4-Sr**	39,240	39,260	28,400	13,401	63,247	1,114,435	.0145	246,082	**72**	....	....	3,796	**21**	76,050	46,403	(d)	....	Minor Civil Division-Township
Toms River	**N.Y.**	73110	◇	94,099	86,327	24,403	34,753	49,529	2,296,275	.0410	1,669,949	**491**	297,423	**631**	107,828	**604**	286,865	112,699	(d)	....	Census Designated Place
Trenton	**PHIL-**	74000	**2-B**	85,884	85,403	15,651	30,134	33,990	1,344,135	.0214	441,229	**130**	7,114	**15**	30,406	**170**	97,658	77,164	185,692	**102**	Incorporated Place
Union	**N.Y.**	74480	**4-S**	56,898	54,405	21,885	20,263	51,898	1,245,198	.0250	1,173,578	**345**	43,793	**93**	61,537	**345**	184,274	91,823	433,782	**237**	Minor Civil Division-Township
Union City	**N.Y.**	74630	**3-S**	69,842	67,088	13,456	23,877	28,836	939,801	.0164	399,933	**118**	5,664	**12**	43,499	**244**	77,246	69,197	61,780	**34**	Incorporated Place
Vernon	**N.Y.**	75740	◇	27,805	24,686	25,451	9,571	55,487	707,667	.0093	151,539	**45**	8,828	**19**	2,140	**12**	41,722	9,705	(d)	....	Minor Civil Division-Township
Vineland	**VINL**	76070	**3-C**	57,046	56,271	18,662	20,341	37,883	1,064,617	.0196	734,317	**216**	89,348	**190**	38,265	**214**	89,672	57,952	494,402	**271**	Incorporated Place
Voorhees	**PHIL-**	76220	◇	28,703	28,126	32,939	11,036	60,056	945,453	.0140	433,316	**127**	93,343	**198**	72,709	**407**	55,272	58,529	(d)	....	Minor Civil Division-Township
Washington	**PHIL-**	77180	◇	51,323	47,114	25,570	17,497	55,179	1,312,336	.0194	516,187	**152**	71,791	**152**	15,304	**86**	119,661	37,746	(d)	....	Minor Civil Division-Township
Watchung	**N.Y.**	77600	**4-Sm**	5,738	5,613	58,060	2,137	83,460	333,146	.0042	103,288	**30**	....	....	4,785	**27**	3,398	37,503	(d)	....	Incorporated Place
Wayne	**N.Y.**	77840	**3-SSm**	55,841	54,069	32,378	19,132	69,903	1,808,008	.0360	1,881,173	**553**	503,200	**1,068**	318,173	**1,783**	157,107	97,842	419,140	**229**	Minor Civil Division-Township
Westfield	**N.Y.**	79040	◇	29,755	29,644	40,498	10,559	80,327	1,205,024	.0147	257,573	**76**	35,726	**76**	26,798	**150**	48,490	30,898	(d)	....	Incorporated Place
West New York	**N.Y.**	79610	**4-S**	49,079	45,768	17,426	17,943	33,065	855,260	.0123	179,995	**53**	5,382	**11**	27,148	**152**	37,593	28,411	73,110	**40**	Incorporated Place
West Orange	**N.Y.**	79800	**4-S**	45,910	44,943	27,406	16,863	60,978	1,258,194	.0162	253,429	**75**	53,602	**114**	15,868	**89**	71,532	27,586	302,909	**166**	Minor Civil Division-Township
Willingboro	**PHIL-**	81440	**4-S**	32,271	33,008	23,879	10,741	53,341	770,606	.0104	170,298	**50**	14,061	**30**	2,223	**12**	82,108	17,025	(d)	....	Minor Civil Division-Township
Winslow	**PHIL-**	81740	◇	35,287	34,611	21,192	12,238	50,850	747,799	.0109	234,664	**69**	9,577	**20**	3,018	**17**	64,517	13,784	(d)	....	Minor Civil Division-Township
Woodbridge Township	**N.Y.**	82000	**3-SSm**	101,123	97,203	25,426	35,901	53,849	2,571,160	.0466	1,985,411	**584**	272,218	**578**	214,486	**1,202**	177,776	80,923	753,472	**413**	Minor Civil Division-Township
Woodbury	**PHIL-**	82120	**4-S**	10,335	10,307	24,889	4,177	44,524	257,226	.0070	462,823	**136**	121,835	**259**	55,181	**309**	20,030	20,504	(d)	....	Incorporated Place
New Mexico																					
Alamogordo		01780	**4-C**	39,473	35,582	14,960	15,453	29,991	590,527	.0105	301,020	**89**	57,063	**121**	14,154	**79**	42,740	11,464	45,990	**25**	Incorporated Place
Albuquerque	**ALBU**	02000	**2-AA**	483,489	448,607	19,378	204,455	36,563	9,369,192	.1774	7,186,364	**2,114**	1,329,928	**2,823**	266,811	**1,495**	613,139	425,442	....	....	Incorporated Place
Carlsbad		12150	**4-A**	25,714	25,625	15,711	10,183	30,777	403,986	.0071	207,949	**61**	44,428	**94**	9,168	**51**	32,266	14,300	(d)	....	Incorporated Place
Clovis	**CLOV**	16420	**4-A**	33,148	32,667	14,184	13,147	27,688	470,176	.0091	319,029	**94**	86,592	**184**	18,106	**101**	40,309	17,154	(d)	....	Incorporated Place
Farmington	**FARM**	25800	**3-A**	41,123	37,844	16,921	15,590	33,378	695,825	.0165	872,520	**257**	289,578	**615**	31,036	**174**	58,440	23,890	46,426	**25**	Incorporated Place
Gallup		28460	**3-A**	17,275	20,209	12,169	5,947	27,215	210,217	.0061	353,200	**104**	74,606	**158**	31,390	**176**	28,334	9,598	(d)	....	Incorporated Place
Hobbs		32520	**4-A**	29,215	28,657	13,160	10,437	27,498	384,471	.0084	351,978	**104**	67,872	**144**	12,494	**70**	40,107	18,813	(d)	....	Incorporated Place
Las Cruces	**LSCR**	39380	**3-A**	75,934	74,267	14,679	30,171	29,870	1,114,663	.0225	871,498	**256**	218,391	**464**	29,110	**163**	96,970	54,249	106,241	**58**	Incorporated Place
Rio Rancho	**ALBU**	63460	◇	61,235	51,765	19,378	23,104	42,725	1,186,596	.0173	322,450	**95**	15,507	**33**	6,501	**36**	78,097	15,425	....	....	Incorporated Place
Roswell	**RSWL**	64930	**3-A**	43,443	45,293	13,324	16,528	27,479	578,853	.0110	340,344	**100**	92,186	**196**	16,194	**91**	41,493	18,583	....	....	Incorporated Place
Santa Fe	**S.FE**	70500	**3-A**	62,768	62,203	23,338	28,404	38,407	1,464,863	.0316	1,661,373	**489**	370,270	**786**	136,577	**765**	179,991	105,412	55,489	**30**	Incorporated Place
South Valley	**ALBU**	74520	◇	41,356	39,060	12,317	14,037	29,920	509,399	.0094	244,373	**72**	39,512	**84**	3,588	**20**	34,770	13,791	(d)	....	Census Designated Place
New York																					
Albany	**A-S-T**	01000	**2-AA**	98,009	95,658	18,721	42,289	31,319	1,834,843	.0320	1,070,600	**315**	93,662	**199**	121,246	**679**	106,294	109,406	157,323	**86**	Incorporated Place
Amherst	**BUF**	02000	◇	118,343	116,510	26,278	46,508	49,145	3,109,855	.0553	2,306,149	**678**	249,909	**531**	175,995	**986**	397,858	118,404	247,985	**136**	Minor Civil Division-Town
Amsterdam	**A-S-T**	02066	**4-S**	17,637	18,355	18,300	7,797	30,367	322,755	.0057	192,339	**57**	23,891	**51**	8,412	**47**	33,645	14,671	128,831	**71**	Incorporated Place
Auburn	**SYR**	03078	**3-C**	27,920	28,574	19,230	11,469	33,482	536,890	.0096	347,305	**102**	59,216	**126**	4,607	**26**	56,572	36,871	275,943	**151**	Incorporated Place
Babylon	**N.Y.**	04000	◇	216,425	211,792	22,400	71,273	52,868	4,847,826	.0760	2,186,816	**643**	168,345	**357**	103,853	**582**	406,093	176,843	1,166,916	**639**	Minor Civil Division-Town
Batavia		04715	**4-C**	16,594	16,256	19,097	6,738	32,641	316,902	.0058	220,714	**65**	43,912	**93**	11,307	**63**	25,475	9,847	155,700	**85**	Incorporated Place
Bethlehem	**A-S-T**	06354	◇	32,239	31,304	28,894	12,665	54,704	931,515	.0120	195,524	**58**	22,984	**49**	13,746	**77**	51,802	19,163	377,096	**206**	Minor Civil Division-Town
Binghamton	**BING**	06607	**3-AA**	46,475	47,380	18,348	21,113	30,042	852,737	.0139	385,437	**113**	22,042	**47**	6,749	**38**	92,225	43,973	718,099	**393**	Incorporated Place
Brentwood	**N.Y.**	08026	◇	56,323	53,917	15,365	13,292	51,929	865,418	.0138	282,566	**83**	14,354	**30**	13,198	**74**	77,142	23,615	(d)	....	Census Designated Place
Brighton	**ROCH**	08246	◇	36,095	35,588	32,645	16,792	46,472	1,178,326	.0183	646,282	**190**	64,143	**136**	73,605	**413**	74,280	44,060	64,018	**35**	Minor Civil Division-Town
Brookhaven	**N.Y.**	10000	◇	478,805	448,248	23,153	158,717	55,846	11,085,541	.1754	5,321,869	**1,565**	773,674	**1,642**	426,331	**2,389**	937,875	340,471	279,526	**153**	Minor Civil Division-Town
Buffalo	**BUF**	11000	**2-AA**	279,681	292,648	15,358	119,187	24,732	4,295,391	.0707	1,641,888	**483**	89,604	**190**	70,185	**393**	386,908	208,518	2,491,343	**1,364**	Incorporated Place
Carmel	**N.Y.**	12529	◇	35,438	33,006	28,338	11,814	65,133	1,004,246	.0132	232,898	**69**	20,711	**44**	....	....	59,883	25,929	67,685	**37**	Minor Civil Division-Town
Centereach	**N.Y.**	13376	◇	28,501	27,285	21,284	8,625	59,336	606,611	.0102	341,616	**100**	80,512	**171**	20,741	**116**	40,471	17,371	(d)	....	Census Designated Place
Central Islip	**N.Y.**	13552	◇	33,374	31,950	17,667	9,290	51,170	589,617	.0094	234,176	**69**	1,809	**4**	20,627	**116**	68,887	18,909	(d)	....	Census Designated Place
Cheektowaga	**BUF**	15011	◇	90,796	94,019	18,666	39,190	34,228	1,694,768	.0339	1,478,281	**435**	238,793	**507**	160,530	**900**	270,308	97,028	433,728	**237**	Minor Civil Division-Town
Cicero	**SYR**	15704	◇	28,499	27,982	20,394	11,033	46,017	581,216	.0105	405,794	**119**	3,323	**7**	13,536	**76**	100,098	21,633	57,243	**31**	Minor Civil Division-Town
Clarkstown	**N.Y.**	15968	◇	84,379	82,082	30,232	28,558	68,520	2,550,942	.0418	1,584,014	**466**	290,954	**618**	170,582	**956**	165,312	132,050	377,465	**207**	Minor Civil Division-Town
Clay	**SYR**	16067	◇	59,290	58,805	20,985	23,040	44,465	1,244,225	.0223	847,023	**249**	140,210	**298**	53,759	**301**	172,380	59,389	113,254	**62**	Minor Civil Division-Town
Clifton Park	**A-S-T**	16353	◇	34,192	32,995	27,841	13,417	52,621	951,935	.0140	393,734	**116**	54,525	**116**	28,821	**162**	63,911	19,858	40,758	**22**	Minor Civil Division-Town
Colonie	**A-S-T**	17343	◇	79,883	79,258	22,226	31,630	44,338	1,775,460	.0421	2,416,655	**711**	350,339	**744**	143,084	**802**	157,175	91,459	198,300	**109**	Minor Civil Division-Town
Commack	**N.Y.**	17530	◇	37,989	36,367	27,984	12,349	68,899	1,063,088	.0195	870,830	**256**	142,225	**302**	62,851	**352**	139,650	51,493	(d)	....	Census Designated Place
Coram	**N.Y.**	18157	◇	36,482	34,923	24,132	13,224	54,281	880,377	.0122	241,802	**71**	4,025	**9**	8,188	**46**	86,712	12,688	(d)	....	Census Designated Place
Corning		18256	**4-B**	10,617	10,842	23,447	4,982	35,107	248,933	.0038	99,878	**29**	....	....	1,791	**10**	41,054	11,654	131,021	**72**	Incorporated Place
Cortland		18388	**4-C**	18,959	18,740	15,439	7,190	29,306	292,705	.0067	325,970	**96**	37,782	**80**	4,473	**25**	75,165	19,730	287,213	**157**	Incorporated Place
Cortlandt	**N.Y.**	18410	◇	39,328	38,467	24,290	13,749	64,525	955,265	.0125	172,207	**51**	3,215	**7**	1,015	**6**	50,708	12,489	(d)	....	Minor Civil Division-Town
Deer Park	**N.Y.**	19972	◇	29,578	28,316	23,471	10,036	53,194	694,233	.0102	249,550	**73**	....	....	3,817	**21**	64,853	34,251	(d)	....	Census Designated Place
Dunkirk		21105	**4-B**	12,912	13,131	17,346	5,461	27,671	223,974	.0039	128,217	**38**	22,786	**48**	6,304	**35**	43,636	13,344	138,438	**76**	Incorporated Place
Eastchester	**N.Y.**	21820	◇	32,169	31,318	39,160	12,924	68,489	1,259,732	.0160	330,594	**97**	24,517	**52**	29,656	**166**	102,613	27,333	(d)	....	Minor Civil Division-Town
East Meadow	**N.Y.**	22502	◇	37,628	37,461	23,052	12,250	58,412	867,382	.0146	516,464	**152**	8,810	**19**	28,890	**162**	118,990	56,734	(d)	....	Census Designated Place
Elmira	**ELM**	24229	**3-AA**	30,363	30,940	15,211	11,559	29,079	461,857	.0083	259,031	**76**	2,881	**6**	8,907	**50**	61,242	18,108	221,899	**121**	Incorporated Place
Elmont	**N.Y.**	24273	◇	32,802	32,657	18,403	9,934	55,621	603,640	.0101	297,355	**87**	3,085	**7**	8,413	**47**	71,740	24,450	(d)	....	Census Designated Place
Endicott	**BING**	24515	**4-S**	12,883	13,038	21,878	6,042	35,862	281,859	.0042	102,637	**30**	11,567	**25**	2,379	**13**	26,983	9,982	....	....	Incorporated Place
Franklin Square	**N.Y.**	27309	◇	29,472	29,342	21,995	10,227	55,228	648,235	.0101	282,162	**83**	....	....	6,944	**39**	78,783	14,819	(d)	....	Census Designated Place
Freeport	**N.Y.**	27485	**4-Sr**	44,786	43,783	18,166	13,814	50,268	813,598	.0156	630,007	**185**	32,528	**69**	14,975	**84**	57,266	36,426	175,742	**96**	Incorporated Place
Garden City	**N.Y.**	28178	**3-Sm**	21,322	21,672	41,749	7,272	79,900	890,162	.0209	1,334,113	**392**	375,247	**797**	296,664	**1,663**	41,483	102,932	76,856	**42**	Incorporated Place
Gates	**ROCH**	28442	◇	29,083	29,275	20,488	12,170	40,550	595,858	.0092	229,832	**68**	11,566	**25**	1,557	**9**	93,704	8,032	612,841	**336**	Minor Civil Division-Town
Geneva		28640	**3-C**	13,641	13,617	16,927	5,136	33,784	230,895	.0048	217,507	**64**	35,567	**76**	4,867	**27**	55,601	10,719	76,547	**42**	Incorporated Place
Glen Cove	**N.Y.**	29113	**4-Sr**	27,585	26,622	23,908	9,810	50,469	659,502	.0111	394,553	**116**	....	....	8,146	**46**	94,197	44,950	245,265	**134**	Incorporated Place
Glens Falls	**GLFLS**	29333	**3-A**	14,193	14,354	19,082	6,387	28,959	270,832	.0062	325,246	**96**	14,652	**31**	26,288	**147**	112,901	10,487	350,068	**192**	Incorporated Place

.... Data less than 1,000.
(d) Data not available.
◇ Not classified as a Principal Business Center.

* Data from 1997 Census of Manufactures.

Principal Business Centers and Other Places with 27,500 or More: Population / Income / Sales, *Continued*

PLACE NAME	RANALLY METRO AREA	FIPS PLACE CODE	RANALLY CITY RATING	POPULATION Estimate 7/1/04	POPULATION Census 4/1/00	PER CAPITA INCOME 2003	HOUSE-HOLDS Estimate 7/1/04	MEDIAN HOUSEHOLD INCOME 2003	DISPOSABLE INCOME 2003 ($1,000)	MARKET ABILITY INDEX 2003	TOTAL RETAIL TRADE Sales 2003 ($1,000)	TOTAL RETAIL TRADE Ranally Sales Units	GENERAL MERCHANDISE Sales 2003 ($1,000)	GENERAL MERCHANDISE Ranally Sales Units	APPAREL STORES Sales 2003 ($1,000)	APPAREL STORES Ranally Sales Units	FOOD STORE SALES 2003 ($1,000)	HEALTH & DRUG STORE SALES 2003 ($1,000)	MANUFACTURERS VALUE ADDED 1997* ($1,000)	MANUFACTURERS Ranally Mfg Units	PLACE TYPE
Glenville	A-S-T	29366	◇	28,354	28,183	23,058	11,504	46,578	653,777	.0108	360,474	106	27,376	58	7,681	43	71,098	16,910	73,507	40	Minor Civil Division-Town
Gloversville		29443	4-C	15,337	15,413	18,046	6,598	29,271	276,767	.0046	130,708	38	26,400	56	....	....	37,635	10,357	121,622	67	Incorporated Place
Greece	ROCH	30290	◇	94,379	94,141	21,877	38,719	42,325	2,064,762	.0366	1,390,669	409	244,001	518	90,006	504	231,864	61,931	65,108	36	Minor Civil Division-Town
Greenburgh	N.Y.	30367	◇	89,133	86,764	32,024	33,769	68,880	2,854,400	.0423	1,310,514	385	123,212	262	118,643	665	224,960	97,739	124,255	68	Minor Civil Division-Town
Guilderland	A-S-T	31104	◇	33,665	32,688	23,946	14,045	44,562	806,129	.0118	288,537	85	34,668	74	41,228	231	71,942	26,484	(d)	....	Minor Civil Division-Town
Hamburg	BUF	31654	◇	57,190	56,259	20,760	22,651	42,914	1,187,236	.0224	932,461	274	169,060	359	51,157	287	99,994	43,300	415,458	227	Minor Civil Division-Town
Haverstraw	N.Y.	32765	◇	34,498	33,811	21,774	11,520	49,878	751,168	.0094	58,694	17	....	....	....	....	16,326	2,366	(d)	....	Minor Civil Division-Town
Hempstead	N.Y.	33139	3-S	58,379	56,554	14,620	15,684	41,885	853,509	.0172	666,866	196	4,985	11	11,753	66	41,253	43,438	44,926	25	Incorporated Place
Henrietta	ROCH	34099	◇	40,087	39,028	19,267	13,787	46,481	772,351	.0213	1,350,718	397	229,138	486	101,155	567	117,745	42,916	361,255	198	Minor Civil Division-Town
Hicksville	N.Y.	34374	◇	41,443	41,260	23,680	13,760	60,466	981,380	.0244	1,486,451	437	150,048	319	119,417	669	85,637	95,867	(d)	....	Census Designated Place
Holbrook	N.Y.	35056	◇	28,740	27,512	25,024	9,527	62,471	719,201	.0106	274,329	81	31,864	68	10,315	58	69,880	8,832	(d)	....	Census Designated Place
Hornell		35672	4-B	8,831	9,019	15,522	3,594	28,970	137,071	.0029	121,932	36	21,247	45	2,598	15	27,645	7,086	....	....	Incorporated Place
Huntington	N.Y.	37000	◇	196,779	195,289	36,877	67,220	70,547	7,256,611	.0995	2,650,725	780	267,977	569	251,925	1,412	388,514	188,428	1,680,966	920	Minor Civil Division-Town
Huntington Station	N.Y.	37044	◇	31,244	29,910	32,361	10,289	66,300	1,011,096	.0149	458,421	135	47,145	100	60,977	342	45,988	28,517	(d)	....	Census Designated Place
Irondequoit	ROCH	37726	◇	52,264	52,354	22,723	23,175	40,044	1,187,571	.0179	460,910	136	98,745	210	47,941	269	100,185	36,359	(d)	....	Minor Civil Division-Town
Islip	N.Y.	38000	◇	337,059	322,612	22,844	104,511	57,400	7,699,835	.1240	3,908,447	1,150	350,051	743	175,575	984	701,980	291,415	2,893,322	1,584	Minor Civil Division-Town
Ithaca	ITH	38077	3-A	31,575	29,287	17,155	11,356	31,797	541,670	.0098	340,576	100	37,614	80	16,688	94	80,948	27,492	246,969	135	Incorporated Place
Jamestown	JMST	38264	3-A	29,940	31,730	17,143	12,988	27,663	513,270	.0097	366,632	108	47,771	101	2,874	16	67,479	23,583	405,316	222	Incorporated Place
Johnson City	BING	38748	3-Sm	15,325	15,535	17,434	7,025	28,508	267,173	.0063	339,223	100	78,539	167	42,825	240	82,473	27,544	22,369	12	Incorporated Place
Kingston	KNGST	39727	3-B	23,429	23,456	20,908	10,066	33,418	489,849	.0103	510,711	150	90,007	191	32,385	181	91,319	31,098	60,921	33	Incorporated Place
Lancaster	BUF	41146	◇	39,388	39,019	20,243	15,419	44,431	797,323	.0113	197,448	58	11,651	25	4,254	24	43,657	13,090	61,943	34	Minor Civil Division-Town
Levittown	N.Y.	42081	◇	53,304	53,067	22,306	17,295	60,792	1,189,011	.0196	639,602	188	112,524	239	43,470	244	95,673	54,116	(d)	....	Census Designated Place
Lindenhurst	N.Y.	42554	◇	29,118	27,819	22,320	9,589	53,963	649,913	.0097	235,733	69	1,734	4	4,744	27	45,066	21,834	49,093	27	Incorporated Place
Lockport	LOCK	43082	3-C	21,616	22,279	22,070	9,391	37,959	477,074	.0081	287,947	85	38,919	83	6,858	38	46,497	24,277	1,104,815	605	Incorporated Place
Long Beach	N.Y.	43335	◇	36,162	35,462	28,287	15,186	52,195	1,022,929	.0123	115,082	34	....	....	4,550	26	40,815	20,157	(d)	....	Incorporated Place
Mamaroneck	N.Y.	44842	◇	29,530	28,967	43,694	11,103	82,506	1,290,290	.0173	463,050	136	1,296	3	22,495	126	77,689	35,060	(d)	....	Minor Civil Division-Town
Manlius	SYR	45029	◇	32,344	31,872	29,866	13,066	51,363	965,994	.0126	233,677	69	19,520	41	5,767	32	71,196	11,074	(d)	....	Minor Civil Division-Town
Middletown	MIDD	47042	3-C	27,253	25,388	21,518	10,240	40,601	586,417	.0124	623,172	183	190,794	405	45,111	253	63,557	30,859	110,409	60	Incorporated Place
Mineola	N.Y.	47636	4-Sr	19,231	19,234	25,030	7,478	54,333	481,351	.0092	422,467	124	....	....	16,934	95	52,401	56,245	85,962	47	Incorporated Place
Monroe	N.Y.	47999	◇	38,583	31,407	16,576	10,196	49,400	639,549	.0102	234,159	69	14,392	31	8,869	50	58,776	19,973	(d)	....	Minor Civil Division-Town
Mount Kisco	N.Y.	48890	4-S	10,360	9,983	43,003	4,130	64,576	445,510	.0076	344,816	101	....	....	38,557	216	20,160	18,817	49,380	27	Incorporated Place
Mount Pleasant	N.Y.	49011	◇	44,289	43,221	26,952	14,009	71,139	1,193,683	.0192	665,668	196	3,514	7	9,569	54	103,762	34,909	(d)	....	Minor Civil Division-Town
Mount Vernon	N.Y.	49121	4-Sr	69,325	68,381	15,989	25,968	38,696	1,108,468	.0181	435,357	128	4,337	9	26,669	149	132,394	48,398	287,052	157	Incorporated Place
Newburgh	NWBG	50034	3-C	31,085	28,259	18,444	10,163	39,673	573,341	.0107	415,956	122	81,424	173	18,157	102	59,503	26,223	59,176	32	Incorporated Place
New City	N.Y.	50100	◇	34,999	34,038	32,625	11,384	75,495	1,141,851	.0150	312,445	92	39,169	83	28,661	161	83,793	45,074	(d)	....	Census Designated Place
New Rochelle	N.Y.	50617	3-S	73,379	72,182	25,518	26,491	55,524	1,872,478	.0274	702,654	207	83,175	177	30,307	170	92,197	45,624	84,171	46	Incorporated Place
New York	N.Y.	51000	1-AAAA	8,108,616	8,008,278	18,191	3,042,213	36,347	147,501,910	2.3448	58,602,159	17,238	5,528,011	11,735	10,702,770	59,981	9,452,629	6,990,595	13,875,950	7,597	Incorporated Place
Niagara Falls	BUF	51055	3-BB	53,613	55,593	17,045	23,698	27,025	913,859	.0161	519,533	153	72,541	154	76,959	431	105,865	49,892	683,992	374	Incorporated Place
North Hempstead	N.Y.	53000	◇	228,094	222,611	36,878	78,605	72,106	8,411,711	.1357	5,371,629	1,580	330,308	701	636,389	3,567	584,553	292,348	539,300	295	Minor Civil Division-Town
North Tonawanda	BUF	53682	4-S	33,122	33,262	20,735	13,915	39,337	686,795	.0094	141,359	42	12,386	26	2,693	15	28,014	16,060	300,857	165	Incorporated Place
Oceanside	N.Y.	54441	◇	32,879	32,733	25,503	11,253	64,093	838,504	.0153	660,856	194	64,547	137	61,071	342	99,353	88,431	(d)	....	Census Designated Place
Olean		54716	3-A	14,731	15,347	18,258	6,307	30,162	268,960	.0060	299,734	88	51,212	109	17,462	98	44,943	20,311	394,390	216	Incorporated Place
Oneonta		54881	4-A	13,557	13,292	13,069	4,421	27,964	177,174	.0047	248,878	73	49,098	104	7,125	40	33,787	9,749	86,341	47	Incorporated Place
Orangetown	N.Y.	55211	◇	48,863	47,711	31,667	17,801	61,355	1,547,325	.0202	391,049	115	11,612	25	17,567	98	98,104	43,643	711,652	390	Minor Civil Division-Town
Orchard Park	BUF	55277	◇	28,084	27,637	25,115	10,583	51,163	705,330	.0112	360,469	106	25,710	55	4,091	23	38,251	16,621	157,685	86	Minor Civil Division-Town
Ossining	N.Y.	55541	◇	37,735	36,534	26,823	12,703	64,183	1,012,184	.0133	225,832	66	....	....	2,971	17	58,274	24,884	(d)	....	Minor Civil Division-Town
Oswego		55574	4-C	18,140	17,954	19,119	7,574	32,510	346,818	.0053	119,803	35	16,223	34	4,780	27	29,556	11,458	....	....	Incorporated Place
Oyster Bay	N.Y.	56000	◇	291,998	293,925	31,060	98,588	68,813	9,069,453	.1463	5,442,967	1,601	496,674	1,054	421,069	2,360	773,397	375,427	2,026,739	1,110	Minor Civil Division-Town
Patchogue	N.Y.	56660	4-S	12,566	11,919	24,032	4,946	49,403	301,980	.0058	258,797	76	23,303	49	17,607	99	36,053	12,050	(d)	....	Incorporated Place
Peekskill	N.Y.	56979	3-S	23,352	22,441	17,192	9,018	42,536	401,474	.0083	371,192	109	37,763	80	2,523	14	87,587	25,387	(d)	....	Incorporated Place
Penfield	ROCH	57144	◇	35,827	34,645	27,404	14,195	54,808	981,807	.0141	354,323	104	17,700	38	5,075	28	93,652	11,286	99,688	55	Minor Civil Division-Town
Perinton	ROCH	57221	◇	45,381	46,090	29,980	18,119	61,266	1,360,509	.0171	252,862	74	12,135	26	3,645	20	128,970	6,624	121,601	67	Minor Civil Division-Town
Pittsford	ROCH	58365	◇	27,604	27,219	34,461	10,023	66,792	951,252	.0118	196,067	58	....	....	18,854	106	74,688	13,145	111,523	61	Minor Civil Division-Town
Plattsburgh	PLATT	58574	3-A	19,156	18,816	19,048	8,027	31,469	364,881	.0080	401,811	118	75,264	160	26,765	150	59,603	24,189	220,743	121	Incorporated Place
Port Chester	N.Y.	59223	4-S	28,300	27,867	20,251	9,625	48,252	573,115	.0097	320,197	94	27,312	58	17,108	96	102,354	28,558	70,946	39	Incorporated Place
Port Washington North	N.Y.	59531	4-Sm	2,658	2,700	44,486	1,045	72,583	118,244	.0019	75,511	22	....	....	....	....	4,070	1,809	(d)	....	Incorporated Place
Poughkeepsie	POK	59641	3-AA	31,568	29,871	21,137	12,861	36,511	667,258	.0128	553,905	163	108,956	231	86,670	486	74,415	27,482	....	....	Incorporated Place
Ramapo	N.Y.	60510	◇	112,488	108,905	21,960	32,664	53,581	2,470,226	.0358	763,182	224	32,273	69	42,523	238	144,817	52,225	(d)	....	Minor Civil Division-Town
Riverhead		61984	◇	30,932	27,680	23,636	12,129	42,428	731,095	.0138	606,802	178	67,968	144	116,056	650	57,777	18,410	57,507	31	Minor Civil Division-Town
Rochester	ROCH	63000	2-AA	216,733	219,773	17,010	91,808	28,222	3,686,612	.0591	1,410,422	415	40,781	87	45,922	257	253,461	108,206	7,098,433	3,886	Incorporated Place
Rockville Centre	N.Y.	63264	4-S	24,133	24,568	35,817	9,032	67,565	864,380	.0126	398,836	117	....	....	12,405	70	64,803	34,592	(d)	....	Incorporated Place
Rome	UT-R	63418	3-B	34,272	34,950	17,617	13,648	34,312	603,761	.0102	297,209	87	67,407	143	9,620	54	41,936	24,679	148,075	81	Incorporated Place
Rotterdam	A-S-T	63935	◇	28,486	28,316	21,001	11,936	39,100	598,239	.0099	319,276	94	83,600	177	22,668	127	35,679	29,551	(d)	....	Minor Civil Division-Town
Rye	N.Y.	64320	◇	44,819	43,880	22,255	15,670	49,889	997,447	.0163	527,596	155	35,798	76	24,726	139	161,512	44,650	(d)	....	Minor Civil Division-Town
Salina	SYR	64815	◇	33,563	33,290	21,301	14,914	37,788	714,919	.0122	417,640	123	38,722	82	4,563	26	57,684	57,259	112,281	61	Minor Civil Division-Town
Saratoga Springs	A-S-T	65255	4-S	27,814	26,186	25,984	11,774	42,910	722,721	.0134	592,330	174	96,767	205	42,020	235	73,829	29,375	174,855	96	Incorporated Place
Schenectady	A-S-T	65508	3-BB	61,890	61,821	19,652	27,040	32,825	1,216,280	.0204	641,664	189	60,866	129	19,655	110	74,519	52,562	568,643	311	Incorporated Place
Smithtown	N.Y.	68000	◇	116,991	115,715	29,869	39,298	67,363	3,494,349	.0556	1,971,411	580	163,454	347	79,788	447	291,243	127,223	701,960	384	Minor Civil Division-Town
Southampton		68473	◇	60,444	54,712	28,927	23,981	49,073	1,748,456	.0283	1,025,206	302	57,598	122	76,444	428	122,177	58,140	(d)	....	Minor Civil Division-Town
Syracuse	SYR	73000	2-AA	146,810	147,306	15,362	60,747	25,559	2,255,255	.0417	1,387,206	408	105,781	225	71,078	398	180,272	89,192	1,111,876	609	Incorporated Place
Tonawanda	BUF	75000	◇	75,220	78,155	20,010	32,467	37,761	1,505,170	.0240	661,154	194	45,047	96	10,608	59	98,645	93,564	907,013	497	Minor Civil Division-Town
Troy	A-S-T	75484	3-C	49,164	49,170	19,638	20,460	33,284	965,504	.0153	406,661	120	42,683	91	3,551	20	83,207	42,489	77,144	42	Incorporated Place
Union	BING	76056	◇	55,792	56,298	19,454	24,788	33,393	1,085,372	.0178	523,404	154	93,027	197	41,787	234	131,997	46,240	171,412	94	Minor Civil Division-Town
Utica	UT-R	76540	3-AA	60,183	60,651	16,025	25,464	25,327	964,438	.0160	398,801	117	72,988	155	3,318	19	88,303	42,114	251,483	138	Incorporated Place
Valley Stream	N.Y.	76705	4-S	37,058	36,368	23,655	12,727	58,047	876,591	.0166	731,290	215	162,386	345	83,077	466	64,294	47,681	(d)	....	Incorporated Place
Warwick	N.Y.	78366	◇	33,982	30,764	25,097	12,091	54,422	852,837	.0114	191,988	56	....	....	2,210	12	62,745	14,593	(d)	....	Minor Civil Division-Town
Watertown	WATN	78608	3-A	26,534	26,705	17,891	11,168	29,910	474,708	.0116	640,894	189	103,540	220	38,472	216	73,043	55,378	138,761	76	Incorporated Place
Webster	ROCH	78971	◇	39,221	37,926	25,551	15,964	51,791	1,002,154	.0147	380,170	112	68,761	146	4,074	23	131,070	12,707	76,243	42	Minor Civil Division-Town
West Babylon	N.Y.	79246	◇	45,390	43,452	21,714	15,046	53,266	985,599	.0161	505,868	149	68,700	146	31,977	179	106,663	25,002	(d)	....	Census Designated Place
West Islip	N.Y.	80302	◇	30,195	28,907	27,921	9,391	64,384	843,081	.0141	541,351	159	11,865	25	3,597	20	82,332	51,687	(d)	....	Census Designated Place
West Seneca	BUF	80918	◇	44,415	45,920	19,632	18,015	40,737	871,958	.0153	539,437	159	25,684	55	14,352	80	126,066	40,408	222,121	122	Minor Civil Division-Town
White Plains	N.Y.	81677	2-S	54,425	53,077	24,557	21,350	54,388	1,336,526	.0289	1,540,655	453	244,766	520	393,258	2,204	75,380	91,012	(d)	....	Incorporated Place
Yonkers	N.Y.	84000	3-SS	200,454	196,086	18,164	75,657	42,159	3,641,087	.0626	1,978,321	582	210,854	448	180,027	1,009	375,750	200,840	274,591	150	Incorporated Place
Yorktown	N.Y.	84077	◇	37,364	36,318	23,666	12,882	68,348	884,266	.0197	1,075,383	316	245,100	520	119,232	668	126,512	58,128	(d)	....	Minor Civil Division-Town

North Carolina

PLACE NAME	RANALLY METRO AREA	FIPS PLACE CODE	RANALLY CITY RATING	POPULATION Estimate 7/1/04	POPULATION Census 4/1/00	PER CAPITA INCOME 2003	HOUSE-HOLDS Estimate 7/1/04	MEDIAN HOUSEHOLD INCOME 2003	DISPOSABLE INCOME 2003 ($1,000)	MARKET ABILITY INDEX 2003	TOTAL RETAIL TRADE Sales 2003 ($1,000)	TOTAL RETAIL TRADE Ranally Sales Units	GENERAL MERCHANDISE Sales 2003 ($1,000)	GENERAL MERCHANDISE Ranally Sales Units	APPAREL STORES Sales 2003 ($1,000)	APPAREL STORES Ranally Sales Units	FOOD STORE SALES 2003 ($1,000)	HEALTH & DRUG STORE SALES 2003 ($1,000)	MANUFACTURERS VALUE ADDED 1997* ($1,000)	MANUFACTURERS Ranally Mfg Units	PLACE TYPE
Asheboro		02080	3-C	23,217	21,672	16,454	9,422	30,833	382,015	.0104	624,600	184	91,761	195	30,008	168	75,888	50,143	978,623	536	Incorporated Place
Asheville	ASHE	02140	3-AA	69,433	68,889	19,542	31,551	32,597	1,356,853	.0308	1,624,744	478	304,832	647	101,972	571	153,096	87,157	628,646	344	Incorporated Place
Burlington	BUR	09060	3-A	46,101	44,917	19,286	19,365	35,745	889,119	.0184	858,598	253	155,264	330	75,617	424	95,022	48,738	600,468	329	Incorporated Place
Cary	RAL	10740	◇	108,276	94,536	29,588	43,067	62,477	3,203,631	.0530	2,032,962	598	450,475	956	144,897	812	289,452	118,430	217,430	119	Incorporated Place
Chapel Hill	DUR	11800	3-C	50,168	48,715	23,639	20,752	41,066	1,185,923	.0190	606,605	178	43,050	91	25,928	145	186,337	46,543	(d)	....	Incorporated Place
Charlotte	CHRLT	12000	2-AA	575,926	540,828	24,705	250,263	45,928	14,228,287	.2415	8,978,482	2,641	1,088,224	2,310	485,723	2,722	1,069,838	416,368	3,235,192	1,771	Incorporated Place
Clinton		13240	4-C	8,322	8,600	15,326	3,250	30,000	127,540	.0027	116,947	34	15,033	32	1,863	10	16,704	6,733	63,816	35	Incorporated Place
Concord	CHRLT	14100	4-C	65,638	55,977	21,839	25,855	42,511	1,433,467	.0244	850,738	250	166,521	353	40,848	229	92,755	48,117	5,678,518	3,109	Incorporated Place
Dunn		18320	4-C	9,876	9,196	17,072	4,075	29,905	168,604	.0034	142,222	42	18,976	40	2,747	15	23,396	12,496	84,152	46	Incorporated Place
Durham	DUR	19000	3-BB	208,104	187,035	20,629	86,782	39,576	4,293,073	.0755	2,741,799	807	340,071	722	214,321	1,201	420,150	193,779	....	....	Incorporated Place
Eden	MRTNV	20080	4-C	16,069	15,908	15,253	6,833	28,296	245,102	.0048	177,207	52	28,325	60	5,559	31	37,926	15,493	501,895	275	Incorporated Place
Elizabeth City		20580	4-C	18,514	17,188	14,728	7,563	28,924	272,681	.0062	287,977	85	47,529	101	10,130	57	37,173	14,420	....	....	Incorporated Place
Fayetteville	FAY	22920	2-A	128,304	121,015	20,243	56,341	34,498	2,597,245	.0489	2,010,375	591	496,645	1,054	117,905	661	194,005	73,712	1,107,190	606	Incorporated Place
Forest City		24080	4-C	7,470	7,549	16,231	3,259	27,762	121,245	.0030	165,044	49	34,345	73	4,489	25	13,818	8,465	167,023	91	Incorporated Place
Fort Bragg	FAY	24260	◇	29,314	29,183	5,857	4,763	28,730	171,698	.0036	8,754	3	....	....	1,286	7	2,407	....	(d)	....	Census Designated Place
Gastonia	CHRLT	25580	3-BB	68,187	66,277	18,480	27,699	34,837	1,260,102	.0250	1,072,363	315	245,995	522	60,338	338	96,910	68,196	1,193,568	653	Incorporated Place
Goldsboro	GLDS	26880	3-A	34,818	39,043	16,169	13,571	32,567	562,961	.0127	614,930	181	116,070	246	32,434	182	88,144	34,712	305,196	167	Incorporated Place
Greensboro	GRNS-	28000	2-A	236,075	223,891	22,064	103,192	39,590	5,208,675	.0957	3,918,566	1,153	552,112	1,172	219,126	1,228	416,197	258,540	3,497,301	1,915	Incorporated Place
Greenville	GRNV	28080	3-A	64,786	60,476	17,272	27,885	31,662	1,119,011	.0229	995,330	293	122,755	261	77,933	437	110,121	41,835	1,330,242	728	Incorporated Place
Henderson		30660	4-C	15,618	16,095	14,060	6,285	23,759	219,591	.0073	491,793	145	74,877	159	20,324	114	71,340	27,179	....	....	Incorporated Place
Hendersonville		30720	3-B	10,987	10,420	20,020	4,870	34,963	219,962	.0063	418,305	123	52,287	111	14,981	84	56,698	24,106	146,708	80	Incorporated Place
Hickory	HICK	31060	3-A	42,375	37,222	22,150	18,625	37,800	938,605	.0198	996,942	293	150,728	320	52,905	296	123,778	59,832	965,332	528	Incorporated Place
High Point	GRNS-	31400	3-B	91,251	85,839	19,245	37,706	37,705	1,756,128	.0343	1,462,379	430	155,499	330	68,032	381	187,117	70,322	972,213	532	Incorporated Place
Huntersville	CHRLT	33120	◇	30,338	24,960	23,854	12,166	60,490	723,691	.0108	277,378	82	60,253	128	8,750	49	32,973	11,067	(d)	....	Incorporated Place
Jacksonville	JAX	34200	3-A	61,114	66,715	11,566	17,804	32,239	706,833	.0160	644,281	190	130,347	277	19,342	108	59,790	21,216	(d)	....	Incorporated Place
Kannapolis	CHRLT	35200	3-C	38,576	36,910	18,451	16,295	34,465	711,761	.0138	564,096	166	113,467	241	14,708	82	66,075	27,278	....	....	Incorporated Place
Kinston		35920	3-B	21,629	23,688	15,733	9,625	27,250	340,283	.0078	384,487	113	70,789	150	18,697	105	67,008	28,790	345,211	189	Incorporated Place
Lenoir		37760	4-B	16,671	16,793	17,022	6,970	31,440	283,772	.0058	250,786	74	45,249	96	4,238	24	37,634	13,226	528,077	289	Incorporated Place
Lexington		38060	4-C	20,373	19,953	17,615	8,181	33,745	358,865	.0076	353,223	104	59,185	126	10,273	58	51,102	21,899	446,189	244	Incorporated Place
Lumberton		39700	4-B	20,398	20,795	13,122	7,783	27,964	267,662	.0077	450,936	133	58,927	125	24,668	138	46,486	15,966	344,256	188	Incorporated Place
Monroe		43920	3-S	33,353	26,228	18,858	11,528	41,749	628,957	.0110	376,911	111	57,269	122	15,126	85	50,372	11,718	964,429	528	Incorporated Place
Morganton		44400	4-B	17,650	17,310	17,068	7,009	33,305	301,253	.0058	227,046	67	29,145	62	8,362	47	39,395	13,326	496,535	272	Incorporated Place
Mount Airy		44800	4-C	8,642	8,484	17,023	3,766	30,093	147,110	.0043	272,533	80	48,750	103	11,411	64	30,162	16,122	442,323	242	Incorporated Place
New Bern		46340	3-A	23,856	23,128	21,484	11,237	35,614	512,528	.0099	439,011	129	83,258	177	19,538	109	54,124	15,624	144,518	79	Incorporated Place
Raleigh	RAL	55000	2-AA	302,564	276,093	26,438	133,116	46,111	7,999,321	.1456	6,324,150	1,860	809,134	1,718	350,228	1,963	716,183	261,995	1,057,542	579	Incorporated Place
Roanoke Rapids		56900	4-A	17,088	16,957	14,148	7,115	27,226	241,762	.0056	271,456	80	49,053	104	16,277	91	42,045	16,651	95,705	52	Incorporated Place
Rockingham		57260	4-C	9,501	9,672	14,790	3,942	27,200	140,517	.0038	220,807	65	33,550	71	10,308	58	33,866	10,884	253,762	139	Incorporated Place
Rocky Mount	RKYMT	57500	3-A	57,089	55,893	16,740	22,149	33,135	955,657	.0193	814,911	240	124,842	265	60,706	340	84,391	44,269	767,332	420	Incorporated Place
Salisbury	SLSB	58860	3-C	27,168	26,462	17,550	10,569	32,144	476,807	.0101	462,368	136	92,392	196	28,656	161	65,026	35,404	456,869	250	Incorporated Place
Sanford		59280	4-C	24,100	23,220	18,140	9,675	36,064	437,174	.0096	477,043	140	54,247	115	14,394	81	80,507	21,962	1,091,937	598	Incorporated Place
Shelby		61200	4-C	19,722	19,477	17,632	8,111	32,477	347,746	.0066	259,731	76	52,551	112	12,265	69	47,363	17,491	605,864	332	Incorporated Place
Statesville		64740	4-C	25,549	23,320	18,144	10,479	33,744	463,554	.0094	410,303	121	64,873	138	23,403	131	50,827	28,269	878,716	481	Incorporated Place
Thomasville	GRNS-	67420	4-S	20,966	19,788	17,698	8,555	33,692	371,049	.0060	155,912	46	16,733	36	2,681	15	34,527	13,755	352,217	193	Incorporated Place
Washington		71220	4-B	9,653	9,583	15,367	4,104	29,325	148,341	.0034	164,082	48	27,141	58	6,129	34	23,003	11,638	119,903	66	Incorporated Place
Wilmington	WILM	74440	3-AA	85,551	75,838	21,094	43,648	31,508	1,804,617	.0447	2,633,442	775	431,754	917	137,377	770	320,485	125,929	700,865	384	Incorporated Place
Wilson		74540	3-B	46,260	44,405	17,175	19,573	31,749	794,506	.0160	680,298	200	96,663	205	34,128	191	82,832	40,704	833,769	456	Incorporated Place
Winston Salem	WNS	75000	2-B	195,346	185,776	20,689	83,099	37,102	4,041,574	.0791	3,490,742	1,027	577,648	1,226	225,613	1,264	350,371	181,638	2,444,535	1,338	Incorporated Place

North Dakota

PLACE NAME	RANALLY METRO AREA	FIPS PLACE CODE	RANALLY CITY RATING	POPULATION Estimate 7/1/04	POPULATION Census 4/1/00	PER CAPITA INCOME 2003	HOUSE-HOLDS Estimate 7/1/04	MEDIAN HOUSEHOLD INCOME 2003	DISPOSABLE INCOME 2003 ($1,000)	MARKET ABILITY INDEX 2003	TOTAL RETAIL TRADE Sales 2003 ($1,000)	TOTAL RETAIL TRADE Ranally Sales Units	GENERAL MERCHANDISE Sales 2003 ($1,000)	GENERAL MERCHANDISE Ranally Sales Units	APPAREL STORES Sales 2003 ($1,000)	APPAREL STORES Ranally Sales Units	FOOD STORE SALES 2003 ($1,000)	HEALTH & DRUG STORE SALES 2003 ($1,000)	MANUFACTURERS VALUE ADDED 1997* ($1,000)	MANUFACTURERS Ranally Mfg Units	PLACE TYPE
Bismarck	BIS	07200	3-A	57,238	55,532	20,415	24,958	38,031	1,168,528	.0228	999,307	294	213,258	453	27,041	152	115,056	62,840	....	....	Incorporated Place
Dickinson		19620	4-A	15,296	16,010	15,977	6,380	30,844	244,389	.0054	252,876	74	43,540	92	8,086	45	28,421	14,462	(d)	....	Incorporated Place
Fargo	FAR-	25700	3-AA	93,980	90,599	19,610	42,346	34,799	1,842,906	.0415	2,172,812	639	352,595	748	77,168	432	132,264	109,780	493,433	270	Incorporated Place
Grand Forks	GDFK	32060	3-A	50,750	49,321	16,779	20,542	33,040	851,534	.0207	1,124,690	331	273,094	580	43,703	245	97,000	42,303	131,601	72	Incorporated Place
Jamestown		40580	4-C	15,012	15,527	16,244	6,408	31,193	243,852	.0049	197,104	58	37,104	79	10,475	59	27,767	17,743	....	....	Incorporated Place
Minot		53380	3-A	36,042	36,567	17,365	15,634	31,932	625,885	.0137	664,860	196	116,934	248	20,270	114	73,026	34,477	....	....	Incorporated Place
Williston		86220	4-A	12,318	12,512	15,788	5,344	29,722	194,479	.0042	190,362	56	40,168	85	5,728	32	26,918	10,472	(d)	....	Incorporated Place

Ohio

PLACE NAME	RANALLY METRO AREA	FIPS PLACE CODE	RANALLY CITY RATING	POPULATION Estimate 7/1/04	POPULATION Census 4/1/00	PER CAPITA INCOME 2003	HOUSE-HOLDS Estimate 7/1/04	MEDIAN HOUSEHOLD INCOME 2003	DISPOSABLE INCOME 2003 ($1,000)	MARKET ABILITY INDEX 2003	TOTAL RETAIL TRADE Sales 2003 ($1,000)	TOTAL RETAIL TRADE Ranally Sales Units	GENERAL MERCHANDISE Sales 2003 ($1,000)	GENERAL MERCHANDISE Ranally Sales Units	APPAREL STORES Sales 2003 ($1,000)	APPAREL STORES Ranally Sales Units	FOOD STORE SALES 2003 ($1,000)	HEALTH & DRUG STORE SALES 2003 ($1,000)	MANUFACTURERS VALUE ADDED 1997* ($1,000)	MANUFACTURERS Ranally Mfg Units	PLACE TYPE
Akron	AKR	01000	2-BB	216,462	217,074	16,544	93,145	31,043	3,581,140	.0694	2,680,199	788	350,590	744	120,910	678	256,011	263,198	1,129,973	619	Incorporated Place
Alliance	ALLI	01420	4-C	23,422	23,253	15,821	9,162	32,005	370,557	.0081	368,667	108	64,012	136	13,254	74	44,929	27,281	208,454	114	Incorporated Place
Ashland		02568	4-C	21,469	21,249	18,042	8,531	35,691	387,338	.0068	226,661	67	30,393	65	4,864	27	38,059	18,273	378,066	207	Incorporated Place
Ashtabula	ASHT	02638	3-A	20,858	20,962	16,011	8,515	30,516	333,954	.0065	245,916	72	62,612	133	12,600	71	34,965	20,577	166,562	91	Incorporated Place
Athens		02736	4-A	21,691	21,342	9,934	6,499	24,993	215,470	.0055	239,765	71	29,464	63	14,967	84	52,877	16,188	59,591	33	Incorporated Place
Barberton	AKR	03828	4-S	28,337	27,899	17,605	12,143	34,695	498,866	.0088	288,023	85	20,907	44	5,290	30	62,279	24,600	233,165	128	Incorporated Place
Beachwood	CLEV	04500	4-Sm	12,284	12,186	35,565	5,299	52,942	436,883	.0080	382,058	112	32,493	69	110,577	620	28,998	39,660	(d)	....	Incorporated Place
Beavercreek	DAY	04720	◇	39,361	37,984	24,087	15,618	51,225	948,105	.0156	534,884	157	86,806	184	61,551	345	72,550	22,574	76,333	42	Incorporated Place
Bedford	CLEV	04878	4-Sr	14,300	14,214	19,338	6,923	36,011	276,535	.0082	550,189	162	45,687	97	4,738	27	32,815	9,999	122,475	67	Incorporated Place
Bellefontaine		05130	4-C	13,403	13,069	20,070	5,531	37,659	268,995	.0050	202,796	60	34,793	74	7,778	44	37,762	13,735	....	....	Incorporated Place
Bowling Green		07972	4-C	30,221	29,636	15,016	10,707	32,491	453,792	.0092	360,919	106	53,270	113	11,207	63	64,427	10,090	255,711	140	Incorporated Place
Brooklyn	CLEV	09246	4-Sm	11,587	11,586	18,345	5,531	34,474	212,558	.0054	310,965	91	52,631	112	17,109	96	75,639	75,134	220,033	120	Incorporated Place
Brunswick	CLEV	09680	◇	35,423	33,388	21,985	12,936	50,464	778,790	.0126	391,599	115	18,077	38	17,122	96	35,781	23,914	48,428	27	Incorporated Place
Cambridge		10996	4-B	11,644	11,520	15,679	5,037	27,704	182,571	.0038	167,254	49	31,312	66	3,161	18	30,381	7,651	125,188	69	Incorporated Place
Canton	CAN	12000	2-A	80,992	80,806	16,219	33,215	30,859	1,313,612	.0250	915,246	269	103,064	219	34,499	193	158,982	104,333	1,745,086	955	Incorporated Place
Celina		12868	4-C	10,176	10,303	20,007	4,247	37,133	203,594	.0037	139,228	41	14,706	31	3,807	21	17,157	5,923	255,222	140	Incorporated Place
Chillicothe		14184	3-A	22,097	21,796	19,615	9,841	34,850	433,437	.0078	285,038	84	75,235	160	8,554	48	46,114	16,215	....	....	Incorporated Place
Cincinnati	CIN	15000	1-A	317,273	331,285	18,210	149,198	30,143	5,777,565	.1012	3,358,849	988	275,515	585	219,817	1,232	588,383	271,661	3,778,697	2,069	Incorporated Place
Cleveland	CLEV	16000	1-AA	443,046	478,403	13,553	182,728	26,031	6,004,786	.1161	3,852,861	1,133	206,398	438	202,950	1,137	772,665	463,584	4,128,581	2,260	Incorporated Place
Cleveland Heights	CLEV	16014	4-S	46,015	49,958	21,268	19,935	39,691	978,648	.0155	446,676	131	42,755	91	10,906	61	115,047	101,232	(d)	....	Incorporated Place

.... Data less than 1,000.
(d) Data not available.
◇ Not classified as a Principal Business Center.

* Data from 1997 Census of Manufactures.

continued on next page

Principal Business Centers and Other Places with 27,500 or More: Population / Income / Sales, *Continued*

Place Name	Ranally Metro Area	FIPS Place Code	Ranally City Rating	Population Estimate 7/1/04	Population Census 4/1/00	Per Capita Income 2003	House-holds Estimate 7/1/04	Median Household Income 2003	Disposable Income 2003 ($1,000)	Market Ability Index 2003	Total Retail Trade Sales 2003 ($1,000)	Total Retail Trade Ranally Sales Units	General Merchandise Sales 2003 ($1,000)	General Merchandise Ranally Sales Units	Apparel Stores Sales 2003 ($1,000)	Apparel Stores Ranally Sales Units	Food Store Sales 2003 ($1,000)	Health & Drug Store Sales 2003 ($1,000)	Manufacturers Value Added 1997* ($1,000)	Ranally Mfg Units	Place Type
Columbus	**COL**	18000	**1-A**	736,256	711,470	21,271	337,305	37,747	15,660,729	.2978	12,724,694	**3,743**	1,546,931	**3,284**	640,418	**3,589**	1,340,019	505,442	4,498,713	**2,463**	Incorporated Place
Coshocton		18868	**4-C**	11,748	11,682	18,667	5,280	30,928	219,300	.0039	131,462	**39**	20,209	**43**	4,166	**23**	29,609	8,689	407,354	**223**	Incorporated Place
Cuyahoga Falls	**AKR**	19778	**4-S**	49,286	49,374	20,983	22,422	40,163	1,034,147	.0205	930,676	**274**	60,757	**129**	21,943	**123**	113,098	95,819	315,078	**172**	Incorporated Place
Dayton	**DAY**	21000	**2-AA**	163,241	166,179	15,685	70,634	27,903	2,560,383	.0464	1,489,629	**438**	141,580	**301**	37,590	**211**	267,865	110,407	1,599,319	**876**	Incorporated Place
Defiance		21308	**4-C**	16,486	16,465	21,249	6,749	41,474	350,318	.0066	273,890	**81**	45,883	**97**	6,257	**35**	44,142	10,955	493,455	**270**	Incorporated Place
Delaware		21434	**4-C**	26,623	25,243	23,326	10,655	45,641	621,015	.0117	512,080	**151**	15,234	**32**	6,344	**36**	71,922	16,620	497,673	**272**	Incorporated Place
Dover		22456	**3-C**	11,952	12,210	18,842	4,947	36,630	225,198	.0041	151,845	**45**	5,305	**11**	1,661	**9**	37,200	10,201	256,287	**140**	Incorporated Place
Dublin	**COL**	22694	◇	33,935	31,392	32,206	13,096	64,367	1,092,899	.0201	939,852	**276**	192,201	**408**	81,905	**459**	67,887	34,174	100,764	**55**	Incorporated Place
East Liverpool	**E.LIV**	23730	**4-A**	13,096	13,089	14,497	5,347	26,501	189,857	.0040	165,869	**49**	39,072	**83**	6,305	**35**	27,503	11,111	46,553	**25**	Incorporated Place
Elyria	**CLEV**	25256	**3-S**	55,956	55,953	19,467	23,546	36,763	1,089,313	.0223	1,029,775	**303**	218,372	**464**	55,228	**310**	82,633	61,808	858,688	**470**	Incorporated Place
Euclid	**CLEV**	25704	**3-S**	53,065	52,717	18,317	25,332	32,937	972,011	.0165	504,523	**148**	113,467	**241**	23,633	**132**	47,487	67,061	725,724	**397**	Incorporated Place
Fairborn	**DAY**	25914	◇	33,210	32,052	19,816	15,092	34,722	658,089	.0116	419,068	**123**	84,722	**180**	7,718	**43**	33,966	10,860	83,286	**46**	Incorporated Place
Fairfield	**CIN**	25970	**4-S**	43,057	42,097	23,931	18,436	45,003	1,030,390	.0200	925,850	**272**	48,846	**104**	29,621	**166**	126,809	29,362	245,037	**134**	Incorporated Place
Fairlawn	**AKR**	26166	**4-Sm**	7,463	7,307	37,949	3,159	64,474	283,214	.0055	292,627	**86**	36,895	**78**	37,401	**210**	42,348	28,013	(d)	. . . .	Incorporated Place
Findlay	**FIND**	27048	**3-A**	38,637	38,967	21,284	16,059	40,147	822,357	.0164	751,608	**221**	181,894	**386**	20,733	**116**	62,935	28,130	696,898	**382**	Incorporated Place
Fremont		28826	**4-C**	17,424	17,375	19,334	7,131	35,634	336,871	.0062	241,712	**71**	53,266	**113**	6,502	**36**	35,448	8,663	573,001	**314**	Incorporated Place
Gahanna	**COL**	29106	◇	34,204	32,636	24,548	13,588	54,030	839,643	.0130	382,809	**113**	96,391	**205**	7,283	**41**	65,652	12,034	36,513	**20**	Incorporated Place
Garfield Heights	**CLEV**	29428	◇	30,955	30,734	16,660	12,974	36,307	515,696	.0094	326,150	**96**	17,335	**37**	3,614	**20**	36,869	49,421	102,517	**56**	Incorporated Place
Greenville		32340	**4-C**	13,374	13,294	19,598	5,809	34,740	262,104	.0048	186,703	**55**	29,442	**62**	8,616	**48**	25,923	8,143	398,008	**218**	Incorporated Place
Hamilton	**CIN**	33012	**3-C**	60,852	60,690	21,224	25,743	40,321	1,291,508	.0192	436,366	**128**	96,955	**206**	5,159	**29**	86,709	30,304	363,002	**199**	Incorporated Place
Huber Heights	**DAY**	36610	◇	36,716	38,212	20,342	14,743	44,665	746,893	.0128	430,008	**126**	189,596	**402**	10,380	**58**	58,740	24,353	. . . .	. . . .	Incorporated Place
Kent	**AKR**	39872	**4-S**	27,870	27,906	16,151	10,149	32,343	450,135	.0087	329,099	**97**	19,463	**41**	6,907	**39**	33,284	12,781	155,054	**85**	Incorporated Place
Kettering	**DAY**	40040	**3-S**	57,408	57,502	25,639	27,291	42,356	1,471,871	.0221	623,960	**184**	95,464	**203**	29,877	**167**	81,360	46,152	457,138	**250**	Incorporated Place
Lakewood	**CLEV**	41664	**4-Sr**	56,413	56,646	21,155	27,567	37,326	1,193,418	.0179	423,759	**125**	. . . .	. . . .	18,969	**106**	81,540	83,473	103,812	**57**	Incorporated Place
Lancaster	**LANC**	41720	**3-C**	37,176	35,335	19,576	15,921	35,695	727,752	.0133	504,651	**148**	104,979	**223**	37,045	**208**	63,787	27,156	366,487	**201**	Incorporated Place
Lima	**LIMA**	43554	**3-AA**	39,605	40,081	16,232	16,104	30,927	642,887	.0142	671,049	**197**	196,134	**416**	22,957	**129**	53,499	41,961	623,253	**341**	Incorporated Place
Lorain	**CLEV**	44856	**3-S**	69,449	68,652	16,791	28,091	32,277	1,166,105	.0196	541,931	**159**	72,970	**155**	16,560	**93**	78,951	75,523	3,215,673	**1,760**	Incorporated Place
Mansfield	**MANS**	47138	**3-AA**	47,528	49,346	17,932	20,058	32,733	852,266	.0170	726,304	**214**	202,489	**430**	31,124	**174**	89,923	40,643	643,978	**353**	Incorporated Place
Marietta	**PRKB**	47628	**4-B**	13,751	14,515	17,269	5,719	31,791	237,472	.0055	283,599	**83**	45,693	**97**	5,325	**30**	39,500	8,530	151,178	**83**	Incorporated Place
Marion	**MRN**	47754	**3-A**	34,827	35,318	17,129	13,595	34,540	596,548	.0113	431,775	**127**	115,768	**246**	13,198	**74**	54,271	23,871	300,441	**164**	Incorporated Place
Mason	**CIN**	48188	◇	28,599	22,016	26,195	10,327	61,254	749,145	.0115	344,988	**101**	1,056	**2**	. . . .	. . . .	75,123	10,364	(d)	. . . .	Incorporated Place
Massillon	**CAN**	48244	**4-C**	31,421	31,325	18,487	12,991	37,175	580,873	.0096	276,239	**81**	30,774	**65**	4,800	**27**	46,520	29,707	273,150	**150**	Incorporated Place
Maumee	**TOL**	48342	**4-S**	14,870	15,237	25,611	6,487	45,949	380,832	.0080	416,735	**123**	101,603	**216**	2,752	**15**	11,590	16,228	283,703	**155**	Incorporated Place
Mayfield Heights	**CLEV**	48482	**4-S**	19,536	19,386	30,126	10,278	42,309	588,534	.0096	359,971	**106**	1,201	**3**	27,596	**155**	42,252	40,275	. . . .	. . . .	Incorporated Place
Medina	**CLEV**	48790	**4-S**	29,369	25,139	25,319	11,335	51,879	743,608	.0118	384,678	**113**	67,327	**143**	11,169	**63**	45,187	23,143	348,114	**191**	Incorporated Place
Mentor	**CLEV**	49056	**3-Sm**	50,673	50,278	23,476	19,505	49,801	1,189,609	.0263	1,425,378	**419**	275,807	**585**	86,708	**486**	122,481	101,267	870,739	**477**	Incorporated Place
Middleburg Heights	**CLEV**	49644	**3-S**	16,005	15,542	19,120	7,144	39,335	306,008	.0079	468,985	**138**	88,148	**187**	13,019	**73**	23,184	38,612	39,752	**22**	Incorporated Place
Middletown	**MIDD**	49840	**3-C**	51,852	51,605	21,645	22,850	38,233	1,122,341	.0164	362,803	**107**	57,300	**122**	4,942	**28**	59,994	25,394	2,807,989	**1,537**	Incorporated Place
Mount Vernon		53102	**4-C**	14,559	14,375	19,068	6,308	32,961	277,610	.0050	179,872	**53**	36,234	**77**	6,517	**37**	29,012	13,033	285,930	**157**	Incorporated Place
Newark	**NWRK**	54040	**3-C**	48,380	46,279	18,088	20,489	34,235	875,081	.0142	381,503	**112**	57,085	**121**	1,713	**10**	67,218	20,237	441,871	**242**	Incorporated Place
New Philadelphia		55216	**3-B**	16,769	17,056	18,432	7,299	32,426	309,086	.0063	279,669	**82**	83,237	**177**	23,025	**129**	22,703	24,246	239,302	**131**	Incorporated Place
Niles	**YNGS-**	55916	**3-Sm**	20,649	20,932	18,278	8,978	32,714	377,429	.0087	451,504	**133**	87,750	**186**	53,482	**300**	58,601	38,541	294,789	**161**	Incorporated Place
North Olmsted	**CLEV**	56882	**4-Sm**	34,227	34,113	21,353	14,060	47,223	730,855	.0184	1,109,135	**326**	209,125	**444**	85,019	**476**	101,309	85,320	(d)	. . . .	Incorporated Place
North Royalton	**CLEV**	57008	◇	29,821	28,648	21,385	12,105	50,460	637,714	.0088	137,308	**40**	. . . .	. . . .	2,021	**11**	32,932	11,204	80,988	**44**	Incorporated Place
Ontario	**MANS**	58520	**4-Sm**	5,431	5,303	18,557	2,311	33,892	100,785	.0046	381,786	**112**	166,025	**352**	17,028	**95**	12,459	13,301	222,232	**122**	Incorporated Place
Painesville	**CLEV**	59416	**4-S**	17,433	17,503	20,827	6,711	42,566	363,083	.0056	149,037	**44**	. . . .	. . . .	. . . .	. . . .	30,015	16,530	431,320	**236**	Incorporated Place
Parma	**CLEV**	61000	**3-S**	86,340	85,655	18,274	36,635	39,843	1,577,809	.0322	1,439,540	**423**	261,831	**556**	83,740	**469**	181,928	174,522	388,141	**212**	Incorporated Place
Piqua		62848	**4-C**	20,954	20,738	18,577	8,557	35,484	389,260	.0074	297,621	**88**	22,726	**48**	24,240	**136**	43,993	14,978	313,018	**171**	Incorporated Place
Portsmouth	**PTSM**	64304	**3-A**	19,254	20,909	14,309	8,558	23,754	275,499	.0066	332,438	**98**	69,639	**148**	16,017	**90**	57,901	23,436	46,428	**25**	Incorporated Place
Ravenna	**AKR**	65592	**4-Sr**	11,685	11,771	19,823	5,142	38,110	231,628	.0037	106,290	**31**	14,024	**30**	. . . .	. . . .	14,859	6,152	213,918	**117**	Incorporated Place
Reynoldsburg	**COL**	66390	◇	33,979	32,069	21,799	14,692	44,919	740,707	.0111	268,462	**79**	40,264	**85**	12,945	**73**	32,431	8,564	95,827	**52**	Incorporated Place
Richmond Heights	**CLEV**	66894	**4-Sm**	11,075	10,944	26,710	5,098	48,226	295,810	.0051	198,021	**58**	34,467	**73**	9,145	**51**	40,051	11,906	(d)	. . . .	Incorporated Place
St. Clairsville	**WHL**	69526	**4-Sm**	5,165	5,057	18,931	2,354	34,348	97,780	.0028	184,811	**54**	66,441	**141**	18,351	**103**	18,008	14,468	(d)	. . . .	Incorporated Place
Salem		69834	**4-B**	12,360	12,197	19,082	5,304	34,188	235,856	.0039	115,821	**34**	5,579	**12**	2,773	**16**	21,470	13,323	297,446	**163**	Incorporated Place
Sandusky	**SNDSK**	70380	**3-A**	26,533	27,844	19,552	11,630	34,152	518,782	.0103	452,433	**133**	125,970	**267**	28,697	**161**	42,290	31,656	303,519	**166**	Incorporated Place
Shaker Heights	**CLEV**	71682	◇	29,216	29,405	27,596	12,551	40,913	806,248	.0119	335,523	**99**	24,855	**53**	79,429	**445**	39,002	41,303	(d)	. . . .	Incorporated Place
Springdale	**CIN**	74104	**3-Sm**	10,604	10,563	21,129	4,651	41,846	224,056	.0100	836,824	**246**	188,432	**400**	102,433	**574**	15,947	47,148	823,722	**451**	Incorporated Place
Springfield	**SPR**	74118	**3-BB**	64,431	65,358	18,044	26,776	33,741	1,162,571	.0203	669,176	**197**	74,887	**159**	17,555	**98**	123,397	65,569	. . . .	. . . .	Incorporated Place
Steubenville	**STU-**	74608	**3-A**	18,085	19,015	16,233	8,147	26,493	293,578	.0074	409,149	**120**	83,491	**177**	14,569	**82**	67,319	46,589	. . . .	. . . .	Incorporated Place
Stow	**AKR**	74944	◇	32,502	32,139	23,130	12,909	50,692	751,761	.0125	431,536	**127**	78,801	**167**	8,850	**50**	102,662	57,627	179,497	**98**	Incorporated Place
Strongsville	**CLEV**	75098	◇	45,423	43,858	23,873	17,346	59,924	1,084,386	.0190	743,355	**219**	171,122	**363**	88,662	**497**	96,066	60,195	340,221	**186**	Incorporated Place
Tiffin		76778	**4-B**	17,993	18,135	18,871	7,448	35,581	339,538	.0056	160,693	**47**	19,629	**42**	7,501	**42**	21,162	9,471	271,920	**149**	Incorporated Place
Toledo	**TOL**	77000	**2-AA**	310,336	313,619	16,977	133,711	31,820	5,268,504	.0993	3,696,947	**1,087**	562,153	**1,193**	220,057	**1,233**	553,815	244,286	2,764,850	**1,514**	Incorporated Place
Trotwood	**DAY**	77504	**4-Sm**	26,706	27,420	17,191	11,555	32,794	459,115	.0106	542,065	**159**	115,905	**246**	28,864	**162**	59,816	15,972	43,093	**24**	Incorporated Place
Troy		77588	**4-C**	22,321	21,999	21,182	9,265	40,781	472,810	.0085	327,644	**96**	94,262	**200**	5,144	**29**	26,610	9,362	718,818	**394**	Incorporated Place
Upper Arlington	**COL**	79002	**4-S**	34,779	33,686	31,022	15,602	51,298	1,078,899	.0150	374,884	**110**	42,193	**90**	35,161	**197**	59,015	31,740	(d)	. . . .	Incorporated Place
Warren	**YNGS-**	80892	**3-B**	44,596	46,832	17,761	18,906	32,056	792,049	.0152	597,348	**176**	100,733	**214**	5,791	**32**	97,059	41,915	1,097,861	**601**	Incorporated Place
Westerville	**COL**	83342	◇	35,764	35,318	25,645	13,851	56,936	917,153	.0134	342,066	**101**	39,028	**83**	2,931	**16**	69,928	11,084	99,567	**55**	Incorporated Place
Westlake	**CLEV**	83622	◇	32,485	31,719	30,894	13,616	56,448	1,003,603	.0163	615,919	**181**	25,408	**54**	11,429	**64**	49,536	70,727	145,672	**80**	Incorporated Place
Whitehall	**COL**	84742	**4-S**	18,399	19,201	20,226	8,650	33,102	372,132	.0094	561,109	**165**	55,858	**119**	17,544	**98**	102,527	18,272	. . . .	. . . .	Incorporated Place
Willoughby	**CLEV**	85484	**4-Sr**	22,625	22,621	26,560	10,577	42,666	600,930	.0109	470,584	**138**	28,376	**60**	6,712	**38**	67,462	42,755	583,386	**319**	Incorporated Place
Wooster		86548	**3-C**	25,520	24,811	20,547	10,471	37,935	524,355	.0096	373,695	**110**	57,222	**121**	6,875	**39**	61,764	19,275	856,510	**469**	Incorporated Place
Xenia	**DAY**	86772	**4-S**	24,504	24,164	19,404	10,180	38,762	475,475	.0077	220,884	**65**	21,544	**46**	6,373	**36**	31,498	7,731	45,847	**25**	Incorporated Place
Youngstown	**YNGS-**	88000	**2-AA**	76,559	82,026	13,943	31,509	25,466	1,067,428	.0198	605,604	**178**	55,593	**118**	18,094	**101**	96,980	63,354	413,577	**226**	Incorporated Place
Zanesville	**ZAN**	88084	**3-A**	25,500	25,586	17,206	10,677	31,237	438,761	.0095	451,524	**133**	68,166	**145**	34,467	**193**	60,300	29,079	356,455	**195**	Incorporated Place

Oklahoma

Place Name	Ranally Metro Area	FIPS Place Code	Ranally City Rating	Population Estimate 7/1/04	Population Census 4/1/00	Per Capita Income 2003	House-holds Estimate 7/1/04	Median Household Income 2003	Disposable Income 2003 ($1,000)	Market Ability Index 2003	Total Retail Trade Sales 2003 ($1,000)	Total Retail Trade Ranally Sales Units	General Merchandise Sales 2003 ($1,000)	General Merchandise Ranally Sales Units	Apparel Stores Sales 2003 ($1,000)	Apparel Stores Ranally Sales Units	Food Store Sales 2003 ($1,000)	Health & Drug Store Sales 2003 ($1,000)	Manufacturers Value Added 1997* ($1,000)	Ranally Mfg Units	Place Type
Ada		00200	**4-A**	15,881	15,691	14,516	6,784	26,231	230,523	.0049	205,528	**60**	64,324	**137**	8,345	**47**	22,368	10,343	44,306	**24**	Incorporated Place
Altus		01700	**4-C**	20,929	21,447	14,099	7,751	29,301	295,081	.0061	241,701	**71**	83,761	**178**	9,983	**56**	33,657	9,050	. . . .	. . . .	Incorporated Place
Ardmore		02600	**3-A**	24,269	23,711	15,390	9,972	28,739	373,511	.0082	372,670	**110**	96,544	**205**	17,590	**99**	32,823	23,009	. . . .	. . . .	Incorporated Place
Bartlesville	**BART**	04450	**3-A**	34,900	34,748	19,145	14,792	34,578	668,143	.0115	384,256	**113**	131,267	**279**	13,571	**76**	35,770	22,270	86,510	**47**	Incorporated Place
Broken Arrow	**TUL**	09050	**4-S**	76,146	74,859	19,256	28,335	47,810	1,466,234	.0255	870,718	**256**	161,932	**344**	10,479	**59**	116,569	37,562	340,699	**187**	Incorporated Place
Chickasha		13950	**4-C**	16,093	15,850	16,128	6,591	27,037	259,543	.0051	198,433	**58**	33,422	**71**	7,565	**42**	37,139	10,382	347,937	**190**	Incorporated Place
Duncan		21900	**4-B**	22,569	22,505	16,731	9,646	30,050	377,605	.0073	286,724	**84**	51,805	**110**	7,554	**42**	35,535	18,035	279,551	**153**	Incorporated Place
Edmond	**O.C.**	23200	**4-S**	71,328	68,315	23,005	27,298	48,627	1,640,893	.0234	489,204	**144**	67,945	**144**	16,159	**91**	97,801	36,180	56,473	**31**	Incorporated Place
Elk City		23500	**4-C**	10,414	10,510	14,469	4,176	28,090	150,678	.0037	194,651	**57**	49,237	**105**	6,216	**35**	23,562	7,564	(d)	. . . .	Incorporated Place
Enid	**ENID**	23950	**3-A**	47,481	47,045	16,559	19,434	31,445	786,231	.0145	504,461	**148**	138,097	**293**	10,612	**59**	65,815	23,936	. . . .	. . . .	Incorporated Place
Lawton	**LAWT**	41850	**3-AA**	99,162	92,757	14,321	34,697	31,468	1,420,112	.0253	715,424	**210**	236,458	**502**	19,892	**111**	64,051	27,170	. . . .	. . . .	Incorporated Place
McAlester		44800	**4-A**	17,810	17,783	13,632	6,649	28,016	242,787	.0053	228,508	**67**	81,679	**173**	8,780	**49**	13,912	8,280	79,959	**44**	Incorporated Place
Miami		48000	**4-B**	12,923	13,704	14,752	5,366	26,062	190,641	.0037	128,446	**38**	31,113	**66**	2,313	**13**	20,687	9,864	76,290	**42**	Incorporated Place
Midwest City	**O.C.**	48350	**3-S**	53,304	54,088	15,910	22,666	32,856	848,043	.0184	847,221	**249**	262,245	**557**	20,143	**113**	57,811	36,715	. . . .	. . . .	Incorporated Place
Moore	**O.C.**	49200	◇	43,694	41,138	18,314	16,572	41,000	800,219	.0130	355,565	**105**	172,551	**366**	6,840	**38**	44,833	24,204	(d)	. . . .	Incorporated Place
Muskogee	**MSKOG**	50050	**3-A**	39,098	38,310	14,833	16,054	27,091	579,941	.0115	427,895	**126**	112,015	**238**	12,163	**68**	29,417	32,960	475,830	**261**	Incorporated Place
Norman	**O.C.**	52500	**3-S**	102,233	95,694	20,645	43,679	35,574	2,110,588	.0368	1,313,964	**387**	246,921	**524**	62,601	**351**	152,634	72,427	331,946	**182**	Incorporated Place
Oklahoma City	**O.C.**	55000	**1-A**	538,368	506,132	17,457	225,221	33,885	9,398,357	.1830	7,369,044	**2,168**	1,099,682	**2,334**	283,457	**1,589**	723,296	369,285	4,451,920	**2,437**	Incorporated Place
Ponca City		59850	**4-A**	24,860	25,919	16,557	10,750	30,706	411,619	.0082	339,321	**100**	107,917	**229**	8,865	**50**	28,231	21,769	. . . .	. . . .	Incorporated Place
Shawnee		66800	**3-C**	29,285	28,692	15,541	11,665	29,634	455,111	.0089	339,962	**100**	96,137	**204**	18,287	**102**	37,371	29,635	272,407	**149**	Incorporated Place
Stillwater		70300	**4-A**	41,067	39,065	14,378	16,582	27,505	590,455	.0115	412,290	**121**	136,436	**290**	19,361	**109**	41,134	15,613	438,949	**240**	Incorporated Place
Tulsa	**TUL**	75000	**2-AA**	397,055	393,049	20,483	178,301	34,783	8,132,848	.1583	6,908,813	**2,032**	1,386,280	**2,943**	273,402	**1,532**	641,741	395,312	2,656,935	**1,455**	Incorporated Place
Woodward		82150	**4-C**	11,590	11,853	16,523	4,732	31,068	191,496	.0043	205,396	**60**	70,446	**150**	6,279	**35**	21,422	10,454	(d)	. . . .	Incorporated Place

Oregon

Place Name	Ranally Metro Area	FIPS Place Code	Ranally City Rating	Population Estimate 7/1/04	Population Census 4/1/00	Per Capita Income 2003	House-holds Estimate 7/1/04	Median Household Income 2003	Disposable Income 2003 ($1,000)	Market Ability Index 2003	Total Retail Trade Sales 2003 ($1,000)	Total Retail Trade Ranally Sales Units	General Merchandise Sales 2003 ($1,000)	General Merchandise Ranally Sales Units	Apparel Stores Sales 2003 ($1,000)	Apparel Stores Ranally Sales Units	Food Store Sales 2003 ($1,000)	Health & Drug Store Sales 2003 ($1,000)	Manufacturers Value Added 1997* ($1,000)	Ranally Mfg Units	Place Type
Albany	**CORV-**	01000	**3-B**	43,547	40,852	18,508	17,268	37,937	805,988	.0155	635,510	**187**	206,740	**439**	22,656	**127**	63,059	15,563	345,138	**189**	Incorporated Place
Aloha	**POR**	01650	◇	45,301	41,741	20,464	15,542	47,437	927,059	.0135	276,646	**81**	75,367	**160**	17,085	**96**	55,179	8,778	(d)	. . . .	Census Designated Place
Beaverton	**POR**	05350	**3-S**	85,458	76,129	22,484	34,898	43,529	1,921,396	.0405	2,044,575	**601**	279,278	**593**	134,945	**756**	182,832	28,162	1,336,393	**732**	Incorporated Place
Bend		05800	**3-A**	71,934	52,029	20,015	29,300	40,146	1,439,757	.0268	1,070,445	**315**	301,564	**640**	41,807	**234**	99,368	23,053	225,835	**124**	Incorporated Place
Coos Bay		15250	**4-A**	15,372	15,374	15,578	6,636	29,646	239,466	.0052	231,581	**68**	62,636	**133**	. . . .	. . . .	24,197	4,706	16,077	**9**	Incorporated Place
Corvallis	**CORV-**	15800	**3-B**	50,113	49,322	19,096	20,835	36,063	956,934	.0159	478,318	**141**	68,468	**145**	20,624	**116**	107,065	22,252	553,900	**303**	Incorporated Place
Eugene	**EUG**	23850	**2-A**	150,343	137,893	19,106	64,025	33,806	2,872,475	.0585	2,653,464	**781**	456,453	**969**	93,688	**525**	378,484	98,206	614,945	**337**	Incorporated Place
Grants Pass		30550	**3-B**	24,564	23,003	15,740	10,097	30,301	386,642	.0085	389,387	**115**	96,534	**205**	9,099	**51**	52,198	14,582	125,680	**69**	Incorporated Place
Gresham	**POR**	31250	**4-S**	95,542	90,205	18,071	36,039	40,773	1,726,551	.0327	1,272,137	**374**	209,402	**445**	25,688	**144**	201,781	40,474	476,797	**261**	Incorporated Place
Hillsboro	**POR**	34100	**4-S**	82,099	70,186	20,126	29,574	46,946	1,652,360	.0298	1,127,885	**332**	170,700	**362**	15,911	**89**	152,205	32,662	788,238	**432**	Incorporated Place
Keizer	**SAL**	38500	◇	36,490	32,203	15,647	13,525	36,174	570,964	.0095	232,022	**68**	25,739	**55**	1,120	**6**	39,747	9,760	(d)	. . . .	Incorporated Place
Klamath Falls		39700	**3-A**	19,728	19,462	15,174	8,105	28,288	299,349	.0063	270,487	**80**	17,350	**37**	6,593	**37**	65,034	5,453	123,925	**68**	Incorporated Place
Lake Oswego	**POR**	40550	◇	37,262	35,278	35,880	15,762	60,985	1,336,957	.0170	332,596	**98**	. . . .	. . . .	13,153	**74**	115,961	24,967	70,004	**38**	Incorporated Place
McMinnville		45000	◇	28,476	26,499	17,006	10,075	37,649	484,263	.0096	394,536	**116**	46,357	**98**	12,865	**72**	54,036	13,711	193,283	**106**	Incorporated Place
Medford	**MEDF**	47000	**3-AA**	69,370	63,154	18,260	27,751	35,973	1,266,699	.0338	2,049,612	**603**	394,129	**837**	51,533	**289**	150,849	37,485	132,508	**73**	Incorporated Place
Milwaukie	**POR**	48650	**4-S**	21,891	20,490	18,792	9,221	37,956	411,385	.0072	241,519	**71**	86,597	**184**	5,094	**29**	18,796	9,349	365,995	**200**	Incorporated Place
North Bend		53000	**4-B**	9,348	9,544	17,150	3,968	32,465	160,316	.0029	102,124	**30**	22,879	**49**	7,045	**39**	26,958	6,315	(d)	. . . .	Incorporated Place
Ontario		54900	**4-C**	10,001	10,985	14,075	3,683	28,673	140,763	.0037	201,990	**59**	60,204	**128**	7,700	**43**	28,575	5,166	. . . .	. . . .	Incorporated Place
Oregon City	**POR**	55200	**4-S**	30,300	25,754	19,434	11,256	45,267	588,838	.0098	301,578	**89**	94,552	**201**	13,365	**75**	42,437	7,984	90,863	**50**	Incorporated Place
Pendleton		57150	**4-B**	16,017	16,354	15,365	5,781	35,723	246,097	.0050	207,337	**61**	21,073	**45**	12,296	**69**	49,723	3,612	69,300	**38**	Incorporated Place
Portland	**POR**	59000	**1-A**	551,390	529,121	20,350	237,821	37,909	11,221,029	.2121	8,783,713	**2,584**	1,489,257	**3,161**	624,779	**3,501**	1,079,098	245,232	3,465,307	**1,897**	Incorporated Place
Roseburg		63650	**3-A**	20,610	20,017	17,954	8,641	33,637	370,036	.0079	374,738	**110**	99,924	**212**	10,482	**59**	54,293	19,276	54,371	**30**	Incorporated Place
Salem	**SAL**	64900	**2-A**	147,771	136,924	18,393	53,962	39,313	2,717,957	.0493	1,788,589	**526**	438,810	**932**	70,159	**393**	239,454	62,506	644,920	**353**	Incorporated Place
Springfield	**EUG**	69600	**3-B**	55,955	52,864	15,597	21,975	33,573	872,740	.0163	561,204	**165**	163,659	**347**	20,854	**117**	105,156	10,589	373,038	**204**	Incorporated Place
The Dalles		13425	**4-C**	11,988	12,156	17,173	4,838	34,144	205,871	.0046	228,289	**67**	51,190	**109**	7,024	**39**	24,361	10,131	(d)	. . . .	Incorporated Place
Tigard	**POR**	73650	◇	44,168	41,223	23,163	17,820	45,350	1,023,085	.0229	1,249,614	**368**	404,179	**858**	112,543	**631**	104,675	30,593	290,001	**159**	Incorporated Place
Tualatin	**POR**	74950	**4-Sm**	24,723	22,791	25,322	9,446	50,295	626,043	.0096	288,159	**85**	120,970	**257**	4,847	**27**	37,564	2,486	364,262	**199**	Incorporated Place

Pennsylvania

Place Name	Ranally Metro Area	FIPS Place Code	Ranally City Rating	Population Estimate 7/1/04	Population Census 4/1/00	Per Capita Income 2003	House-holds Estimate 7/1/04	Median Household Income 2003	Disposable Income 2003 ($1,000)	Market Ability Index 2003	Total Retail Trade Sales 2003 ($1,000)	Total Retail Trade Ranally Sales Units	General Merchandise Sales 2003 ($1,000)	General Merchandise Ranally Sales Units	Apparel Stores Sales 2003 ($1,000)	Apparel Stores Ranally Sales Units	Food Store Sales 2003 ($1,000)	Health & Drug Store Sales 2003 ($1,000)	Manufacturers Value Added 1997* ($1,000)	Ranally Mfg Units	Place Type
Abington Township	**PHIL-**	00156	**3-S**	55,503	56,103	27,305	21,672	53,190	1,515,509	.0265	1,095,028	**322**	43,458	**92**	76,094	**426**	141,326	102,219	(d)	. . . .	Minor Civil Division-Township
Allentown	**ALL-**	02000	**2-AA**	108,583	106,632	17,335	43,937	32,815	1,882,322	.0360	1,400,801	**412**	105,833	**225**	42,459	**238**	266,898	104,221	3,362,309	**1,841**	Incorporated Place
Altoona	**ALT**	02184	**3-AA**	48,603	49,523	15,142	20,245	28,711	735,948	.0175	889,457	**262**	225,308	**478**	40,224	**225**	126,442	61,869	253,069	**139**	Incorporated Place
Beaver	**PGH**	04688	**4-S**	4,684	4,775	24,323	2,117	40,277	113,927	.0018	58,847	**17**	. . . .	. . . .	. . . .	. . . .	7,506	7,621	. . . .	. . . .	Incorporated Place
Bensalem Township	**PHIL-**	05616	**3-Sm**	59,063	58,434	21,082	23,270	44,825	1,245,154	.0272	1,403,604	**413**	184,840	**392**	51,044	**286**	191,063	82,228	292,518	**160**	Minor Civil Division-Township
Bethel Park	**PGH**	06064	◇	33,079	33,556	23,093	13,635	48,337	763,901	.0125	418,247	**123**	38,551	**82**	18,504	**104**	141,196	31,508	28,725	**16**	Incorporated Place
Bethlehem	**ALL-**	06088	**3-B**	73,793	71,329	19,987	29,517	37,521	1,474,898	.0250	823,414	**242**	59,572	**126**	17,832	**100**	175,571	64,077	527,214	**289**	Incorporated Place
Bloomsburg		07128	**4-C**	12,350	12,375	14,227	4,122	33,247	175,698	.0041	199,992	**59**	31,786	**67**	7,960	**45**	21,044	11,360	128,049	**70**	Incorporated Place
Bradford		08040	**4-B**	8,835	9,175	17,527	3,818	30,245	154,848	.0029	112,471	**33**	7,977	**17**	1,961	**11**	19,455	7,890	240,008	**131**	Incorporated Place
Bristol	**PHIL-**	08768	◇	54,771	55,521	18,193	19,806	42,467	996,470	.0181	655,182	**193**	39,025	**83**	17,186	**96**	129,532	43,430	478,417	**262**	Minor Civil Division-Township
Butler	**BUTL**	10464	**3-C**	15,184	15,121	19,553	6,905	33,217	296,891	.0063	308,389	**91**	62,830	**133**	11,525	**65**	40,849	25,144	76,227	**42**	Incorporated Place
Camp Hill	**HRBG**	11000	**3-Sm**	7,793	7,636	26,070	3,556	44,547	203,164	.0040	192,805	**57**	47,649	**101**	16,418	**92**	17,081	17,523	. . . .	. . . .	Incorporated Place
Carlisle	**CARL**	11272	**3-C**	18,356	17,970	21,429	7,787	40,300	393,359	.0065	211,949	**62**	22,331	**47**	5,060	**28**	29,298	5,918	569,478	**312**	Incorporated Place
Chambersburg		12536	**3-B**	18,387	17,862	21,266	8,103	36,867	391,020	.0077	344,621	**101**	55,988	**119**	10,476	**59**	54,476	17,848	196,945	**108**	Incorporated Place
Charleroi	**PGH**	12704	**4-S**	5,072	4,871	16,654	2,387	29,027	84,470	.0014	40,756	**12**	6,754	**14**	1,823	**10**	7,874	3,845	84,346	**46**	Incorporated Place
Cheltenham Township	**PHIL-**	12968	**4-S**	38,265	36,875	28,193	15,058	53,466	1,078,795	.0139	223,253	**66**	33,761	**72**	8,732	**49**	52,769	28,055	136,174	**75**	Minor Civil Division-Township
Chester	**PHIL-**	13208	**4-Sr**	36,987	36,854	11,050	13,043	24,691	408,719	.0075	169,426	**50**	6,567	**14**	3,725	**21**	28,830	17,147	534,383	**293**	Incorporated Place
Clearfield		14064	**4-B**	6,492	6,631	17,088	3,053	27,451	110,935	.0026	136,629	**40**	29,248	**62**	4,943	**28**	15,173	6,622	92,597	**51**	Incorporated Place
Connellsville		15776	**4-C**	9,235	9,146	15,282	4,095	26,308	141,133	.0026	86,168	**25**	6,131	**13**	. . . .	. . . .	5,678	7,723	(d)	. . . .	Incorporated Place
Doylestown	**PHIL-**	19784	**4-S**	8,100	8,227	40,404	3,963	63,806	327,275	.0051	199,626	**59**	8,353	**18**	5,729	**32**	25,294	11,500	(d)	. . . .	Incorporated Place
Drexel Hill	**PHIL-**	19920	◇	29,594	29,364	22,168	12,175	44,857	656,030	.0091	164,138	**48**	4,016	**9**	7,242	**41**	41,335	34,077	(d)	. . . .	Census Designated Place
Du Bois		20136	**4-A**	7,870	8,123	19,923	3,569	33,234	156,795	.0036	199,228	**59**	37,169	**79**	10,209	**57**	31,668	10,655	92,425	**51**	Incorporated Place
Easton	**ALL-**	21648	**3-B**	27,197	26,263	15,835	10,045	34,177	430,669	.0077	236,726	**70**	13,529	**29**	9,732	**55**	49,257	30,373	430,301	**236**	Incorporated Place
Erie	**ERIE**	24000	**2-A**	103,853	103,717	15,049	42,957	29,085	1,562,859	.0289	941,544	**277**	98,270	**209**	22,811	**128**	183,198	87,042	937,786	**513**	Incorporated Place
Falls	**PHIL-**	25112	**4-S**	35,668	34,865	24,570	13,681	51,417	876,358	.0155	621,326	**183**	56,443	**120**	25,570	**143**	111,622	42,144	187,571	**103**	Minor Civil Division-Township
Franklin	**OILC-F**	27456	**4-B**	7,156	7,212	17,731	3,064	31,139	126,884	.0024	97,278	**29**	10,762	**23**	. . . .	. . . .	20,602	7,931	195,969	**107**	Incorporated Place
Greensburg	**PGH**	31200	**3-SS**	15,909	15,889	21,611	7,294	36,290	343,811	.0089	552,667	**163**	94,272	**200**	43,496	**244**	52,603	34,932	73,940	**40**	Incorporated Place
Hanover	**HANV**	32448	**3-B**	14,657	14,535	23,142	6,770	40,371	339,195	.0066	302,605	**89**	50,702	**108**	9,593	**54**	46,991	9,853	588,939	**322**	Incorporated Place
Harrisburg	**HRBG**	32800	**2-AA**	47,483	48,950	17,318	20,730	28,520	822,329	.0141	431,059	**127**	7,094	**15**	12,164	**68**	64,923	35,161	223,366	**122**	Incorporated Place
Hatboro	**PHIL-**	33088	**4-S**	7,266	7,393	21,753	3,012	46,132	158,057	.0024	56,332	**17**	8,781	**19**	3,975	**22**	4,779	3,466	36,287	**20**	Incorporated Place
Haverford Township	**PHIL-**	33144	◇	48,627	48,498	26,888	18,363	56,764	1,307,466	.0181	392,542	**115**	32,378	**69**	29,773	**167**	78,559	48,626	(d)	. . . .	Minor Civil Division-Township
Hazleton	**HAZ**	33408	**3-B**	22,420	23,329	17,789	10,327	27,070	398,822	.0100	571,608	**168**	116,280	**247**	28,282	**159**	93,135	34,897	625,358	**342**	Incorporated Place
Hempfield	**PGH**	33792	◇	39,986	40,721	18,349	16,013	36,086	733,712	.0099	97,289	**29**	13,970	**30**	6,500	**36**	10,052	6,279	45,275	**25**	Minor Civil Division-Township
Hermitage	**SHAR**	34064	**4-Sm**	16,208	16,157	20,983	6,931	36,437	340,096	.0083	486,243	**143**	153,269	**325**	10,507	**59**	72,840	21,287	67,573	**37**	Incorporated Place

. . . . Data less than 1,000.
(d) Data not available.
◇ Not classified as a Principal Business Center.

* Data from 1997 Census of Manufactures.

Principal Business Centers and Other Places with 27,500 or More: Population / Income / Sales, *Continued*

PLACE NAME	RANALLY METRO AREA	FIPS PLACE CODE	RANALLY CITY RATING	POPULATION Estimate 7/1/04	POPULATION Census 4/1/00	PER CAPITA INCOME 2003	HOUSE-HOLDS Estimate 7/1/04	MEDIAN HOUSEHOLD INCOME 2003	DISPOSABLE INCOME 2003 ($1,000)	MARKET ABILITY INDEX 2003	TOTAL RETAIL TRADE Sales 2003 ($1,000)	TOTAL RETAIL TRADE Ranally Sales Units	GENERAL MERCHANDISE Sales 2003 ($1,000)	GENERAL MERCHANDISE Ranally Sales Units	APPAREL STORES Sales 2003 ($1,000)	APPAREL STORES Ranally Sales Units	FOOD STORE SALES 2003 ($1,000)	HEALTH & DRUG STORE SALES 2003 ($1,000)	MANUFACTURERS VALUE ADDED 1997* ($1,000)	Ranally Mfg Units	PLACE TYPE
Indiana		36816	3-A	14,701	14,895	13,152	4,895	27,466	193,353	.0050	259,658	76	58,161	123	9,473	53	34,645	13,006	34,285	19	Incorporated Place
Jenkintown	PHIL-	38000	4-S	4,538	4,478	39,803	2,077	54,189	180,628	.0031	140,615	41	....	....	7,593	43	10,336	10,061	(d)	....	Incorporated Place
Johnstown	JNST	38288	3-AA	22,166	23,906	13,986	10,546	22,606	310,006	.0057	167,214	49	6,000	13	1,992	11	20,992	18,387	348,876	191	Incorporated Place
Lancaster	LANC	41216	2-A	56,473	56,348	17,527	21,262	34,910	989,787	.0188	725,823	214	66,981	142	104,902	588	103,776	52,873	1,148,243	629	Incorporated Place
Lansdale	PHIL-	41432	4-S	15,964	16,071	26,499	6,645	55,268	423,036	.0066	205,574	60	11,868	25	13,091	73	41,538	18,748	305,402	167	Incorporated Place
Latrobe	LTROB	41680	4-C	8,789	8,994	18,594	3,958	33,364	163,421	.0029	97,122	29	8,185	17	1,584	9	9,230	7,770	272,124	149	Incorporated Place
Lebanon	LEB	42168	3-C	24,605	24,461	19,159	10,495	34,925	471,419	.0087	333,862	98	51,046	108	6,514	37	40,182	14,362	307,861	169	Incorporated Place
Levittown	PHIL-	42928	4-Sr	55,775	53,966	18,727	19,541	45,424	1,044,503	.0149	238,700	70	3,897	8	7,702	43	82,128	36,376	(d)	....	Census Designated Place
Lewistown		43000	4-C	8,877	8,998	16,593	4,024	28,193	147,295	.0027	97,568	29	19,703	42	3,995	22	7,690	4,123	165,264	90	Incorporated Place
Lock Haven	WMSPT	44128	4-C	8,897	9,149	13,266	3,275	27,326	118,027	.0024	82,730	24	1,057	2	1,702	10	16,225	4,082	(d)	....	Incorporated Place
Lower Makefield	PHIL-	44968	◇	33,421	32,681	31,175	12,173	61,653	1,041,901	.0123	118,349	35	7,293	15	2,194	12	42,267	20,156	(d)	....	Minor Civil Division-Township
Lower Merion Township	PHIL-	44976	3-S	61,885	59,850	43,642	23,887	72,447	2,700,805	.0354	885,925	261	41,920	89	109,947	616	208,969	66,158	48,584	27	Minor Civil Division-Township
Lower Paxton	HRBG	45056	◇	45,811	44,424	23,159	19,916	43,755	1,060,938	.0197	840,625	247	137,423	292	47,663	267	126,082	30,463	(d)	....	Minor Civil Division-Township
Manheim	LANC	46896	◇	35,150	33,697	24,764	13,694	47,752	870,454	.0190	1,025,781	302	169,743	360	69,105	387	80,461	53,686	265,430	145	Minor Civil Division-Township
Marple Township	PHIL-	47616	4-Sm	23,974	23,737	23,805	8,855	52,635	570,691	.0106	459,304	135	51,813	110	20,954	117	107,034	29,608	(d)	....	Minor Civil Division-Township
McCandless	PGH	45900	◇	28,026	29,022	25,709	11,150	53,499	720,508	.0123	467,402	137	72,908	155	38,401	215	56,325	30,827	(d)	....	Minor Civil Division-Town
McKeesport	PGH	46256	4-S	23,744	24,040	11,620	9,866	23,647	275,905	.0056	179,011	53	11,608	25	3,847	22	38,844	7,540	67,127	37	Incorporated Place
Meadville		48360	3-A	13,065	13,685	16,986	5,250	31,112	221,917	.0050	251,195	74	36,603	78	9,038	51	36,068	20,752	345,762	189	Incorporated Place
Mechanicsburg	HRBG	48376	4-Sr	9,014	9,042	26,402	4,115	45,541	237,985	.0065	439,173	129	18,262	39	4,782	27	37,338	10,010	116,324	64	Incorporated Place
Middletown	PHIL-	49120	◇	44,056	44,141	21,766	15,542	53,335	958,909	.0246	1,504,821	443	168,256	357	121,379	680	91,527	80,038	119,874	66	Minor Civil Division-Township
Middletown	PHIL-	49136	4-Sm	16,241	16,064	25,421	5,668	54,584	412,856	.0083	406,258	120	56,041	119	29,696	166	41,393	20,954	82,097	45	Minor Civil Division-Township
Millcreek	ERIE	49548	4-Sm	51,741	52,129	23,236	22,104	40,352	1,202,252	.0245	1,193,480	351	259,212	550	92,678	519	152,199	61,640	413,260	226	Minor Civil Division-Township
Monessen	PGH	50344	4-S	8,470	8,669	14,890	3,901	25,803	126,118	.0021	48,111	14	....	....	....	....	3,110	6,635	(d)	....	Incorporated Place
Monroeville	PGH	52330	3-Sm	29,219	29,349	20,831	12,759	40,653	608,671	.0194	1,371,173	403	220,080	467	128,804	722	89,185	56,640	42,987	24	Incorporated Place
Mount Lebanon	PGH	51696	◇	32,685	33,017	26,100	13,975	48,061	853,072	.0117	240,523	71	....	....	28,223	158	52,781	19,245	(d)	....	Minor Civil Division-Township
Natrona Heights	PGH	32868	4-S	10,708	10,934	15,987	4,861	31,925	171,184	.0037	170,620	50	25,690	55	2,678	15	38,786	11,338	(d)	....	Census Designated Place
New Castle	NWCS	53368	3-A	26,037	26,309	16,308	10,781	30,607	424,617	.0079	277,739	82	46,264	98	4,391	25	47,854	18,769	201,272	110	Incorporated Place
New Kensington	PGH	53736	4-S	14,611	14,701	18,315	6,609	32,828	267,596	.0046	141,634	42	22,111	47	3,324	19	20,271	14,952	41,339	23	Incorporated Place
Norristown	PHIL-	54656	3-S	32,285	31,282	17,575	12,557	36,617	567,411	.0096	287,468	85	24,934	53	16,993	95	80,640	31,623	113,434	62	Incorporated Place
Northampton	PHIL-	54688	◇	40,408	39,384	26,264	13,593	62,317	1,061,277	.0153	381,525	112	14,032	30	8,414	47	103,923	28,270	133,943	73	Minor Civil Division-Township
North Huntingdon	PGH	55128	◇	29,055	29,123	18,648	11,411	40,130	541,814	.0095	317,756	93	8,361	18	5,917	33	42,670	19,217	51,315	28	Minor Civil Division-Township
North Wales	PHIL-	55512	4-Sm	3,308	3,342	28,917	1,297	61,146	95,659	.0017	76,059	22	20,882	44	13,967	78	7,601	6,685	(d)	....	Incorporated Place
Oil City	OILC-F	56456	4-A	11,362	11,504	15,520	4,804	28,568	176,342	.0028	60,665	18	1,761	4	....	....	21,242	7,280	(d)	....	Incorporated Place
Penn Hills	PGH	59032	◇	44,927	46,809	18,675	19,371	37,486	839,000	.0147	492,754	145	23,348	50	2,773	16	46,345	13,948	40,186	22	Minor Civil Division-Township
Philadelphia	PHIL-	60000	1-AA	1,468,025	1,517,550	15,022	601,909	29,054	22,053,340	.3781	9,909,696	2,915	787,764	1,672	1,123,454	6,296	2,158,817	1,423,825	3,997,488	2,188	Incorporated Place
Pittsburgh	PGH	61000	1-AA	316,832	334,563	17,069	140,727	28,402	5,408,101	.0973	3,281,979	965	178,925	380	253,073	1,418	594,683	361,761	1,183,746	648	Incorporated Place
Plymouth Township	PHIL-	61664	4-Sm	15,925	16,045	24,829	6,521	50,308	395,404	.0088	483,789	142	46,910	100	46,832	262	38,866	35,190	41,577	23	Minor Civil Division-Township
Pottstown	PTSTN	62416	3-C	21,924	21,859	19,278	9,279	40,397	422,655	.0083	354,303	104	83,052	176	20,020	112	51,761	26,245	476,162	261	Incorporated Place
Pottsville	PTSVL	62432	3-A	14,964	15,549	17,159	6,237	31,640	256,766	.0057	275,231	81	23,927	51	4,659	26	33,230	79,903	123,763	68	Incorporated Place
Radnor	PHIL-	63264	4-Sm	31,181	30,878	37,809	10,624	71,801	1,178,922	.0155	365,183	107	13,813	29	25,028	140	111,743	30,331	144,564	79	Minor Civil Division-Township
Reading	READ	63624	2-A	83,331	81,207	13,882	31,024	27,164	1,156,795	.0204	536,325	158	24,886	53	106,915	599	84,755	56,066	1,893,280	1,037	Incorporated Place
Ridley Township	PHIL-	64800	◇	31,093	30,791	19,841	12,437	43,403	616,925	.0116	466,891	137	37,507	80	10,544	59	187,172	42,586	(d)	....	Minor Civil Division-Township
Ross	PGH	66264	4-S	31,929	32,551	22,671	14,122	43,307	723,862	.0141	638,311	188	132,892	282	65,888	369	105,358	36,390	(d)	....	Minor Civil Division-Township
Scranton	SCR-	69000	2-A	74,727	76,415	15,160	31,690	27,658	1,132,849	.0244	1,077,353	317	184,077	391	103,887	582	195,545	85,913	340,419	186	Incorporated Place
Shaler	PGH	69584	◇	29,202	29,757	20,321	12,134	42,140	593,415	.0089	202,811	60	6,400	14	1,139	6	50,945	11,710	69,616	38	Minor Civil Division-Township
Shamokin		69600	4-B	7,541	8,009	12,477	3,584	20,857	94,087	.0022	99,915	29	3,488	7	1,811	10	17,123	17,048	(d)	....	Incorporated Place
Sharon	SHAR	69720	3-A	16,361	16,328	15,364	6,908	26,102	251,366	.0056	265,115	78	38,601	82	37,546	210	28,040	30,416	132,316	72	Incorporated Place
Springfield	PHIL-	73032	3-Sm	23,909	23,677	24,340	8,831	56,493	581,937	.0145	885,821	261	150,928	320	93,724	525	95,332	41,408	(d)	....	Minor Civil Division-Township
State College	STCOL	73808	3-A	38,649	38,420	12,709	12,207	27,971	491,196	.0122	601,400	177	108,359	230	58,391	327	71,744	35,543	172,952	95	Incorporated Place
Stroudsburg		74888	3-A	6,097	5,756	22,741	2,553	41,310	138,653	.0030	161,133	47	33,789	72	8,833	50	21,534	8,321	(d)	....	Incorporated Place
Sunbury		75304	4-A	10,421	10,610	15,487	4,548	30,014	161,390	.0036	171,915	51	6,419	14	1,596	9	27,346	12,009	125,470	69	Incorporated Place
Swatara Township	HRBG	75672	4-S	23,682	22,611	19,266	9,462	40,600	456,265	.0096	461,035	136	98,335	209	32,369	181	19,316	20,674	84,204	46	Minor Civil Division-Township
Tredyffrin	PHIL-	77344	◇	29,263	29,062	41,016	12,468	68,397	1,200,265	.0199	851,425	250	14,419	31	26,956	151	103,339	31,426	(d)	....	Minor Civil Division-Township
Uniontown	UNTN	78528	3-C	12,628	12,422	15,202	5,624	25,186	191,972	.0050	276,610	81	88,073	187	14,841	83	28,267	19,879	125,513	69	Incorporated Place
Upper Darby	PHIL-	79000	3-S	82,625	81,821	18,609	33,314	39,230	1,537,587	.0261	811,242	239	70,889	150	34,462	193	197,718	79,538	(d)	....	Minor Civil Division-Township
Upper Merion Township	PHIL-	79136	3-Sm	27,049	26,863	27,820	11,745	55,469	752,493	.0236	1,727,200	508	461,023	979	399,418	2,238	105,555	71,514	743,921	407	Minor Civil Division-Township
Upper St. Clair	PGH	79274	4-Sm	20,017	20,053	33,328	7,212	69,139	667,133	.0108	410,651	121	99,983	212	72,900	409	23,012	21,536	(d)	....	Minor Civil Division-Township
Warminster	PHIL-	80952	4-Sr	31,258	31,383	22,551	11,509	51,275	704,888	.0138	635,822	187	67,858	144	23,274	130	103,100	22,213	281,222	154	Minor Civil Division-Township
Warren		81000	4-B	9,818	10,259	20,036	4,471	33,649	196,710	.0076	587,750	173	62,131	132	17,948	101	33,754	9,987	267,826	147	Incorporated Place
Washington	WASH	81328	3-C	15,898	15,268	17,473	6,619	33,044	277,786	.0052	195,833	58	24,662	52	12,213	68	35,159	9,830	384,068	210	Incorporated Place
Waynesboro	HAG	81824	4-C	9,740	9,614	20,969	4,369	36,269	204,238	.0031	76,073	22	6,842	15	....	....	14,647	7,292	130,961	72	Incorporated Place
West Chester	PHIL-	82704	4-S	17,874	17,861	27,879	6,355	61,543	498,316	.0149	1,063,644	313	7,650	16	3,445	19	46,739	16,528	221,308	121	Incorporated Place
West Mifflin	PGH	83512	3-Sm	21,911	22,464	16,585	9,608	34,627	363,398	.0112	740,128	218	235,148	499	36,578	205	141,109	22,923	327,381	179	Incorporated Place
Wilkes Barre	SCR-	85152	3-BB	41,570	43,123	15,540	18,027	27,748	645,982	.0174	1,017,120	299	218,079	463	68,787	385	142,362	55,062	241,438	132	Incorporated Place
Williamsport	WMSPT	85312	3-A	30,207	30,706	16,166	12,372	28,281	488,330	.0107	496,558	146	34,177	73	14,569	82	107,113	41,861	587,735	322	Incorporated Place
Wyomissing	READ	86880	4-Sm	8,853	8,587	34,536	3,477	54,858	305,744	.0064	353,994	104	74,233	158	98,943	555	32,693	18,986	206,410	113	Incorporated Place
York	YORK	87048	3-AA	41,587	40,862	19,552	16,693	34,532	813,094	.0138	444,084	131	46,823	99	16,779	94	70,181	32,951	1,257,244	688	Incorporated Place
Rhode Island																					
Coventry	PROV-	18640	◇	34,706	33,668	20,616	13,226	46,212	715,490	.0103	199,840	59	30,228	64	....	....	49,705	22,280	....	....	Minor Civil Division-Town
Cranston	PROV-	19180	4-S	80,837	79,269	18,867	31,930	39,698	1,525,133	.0262	849,537	250	31,065	66	120,240	674	103,017	80,520	523,274	286	Incorporated Place
Cumberland	PROV-	20080	◇	32,842	31,840	21,427	12,723	48,285	703,695	.0110	303,186	89	87,463	186	18,462	103	96,725	19,172	92,384	51	Minor Civil Division-Town
East Providence	PROV-	22960	4-S	49,215	48,688	17,996	21,005	36,263	885,656	.0166	633,642	186	22,171	47	47,954	269	109,728	41,283	328,540	180	Incorporated Place
Johnston	PROV-	37720	◇	29,032	28,195	18,330	11,649	40,217	532,169	.0107	472,407	139	57,669	122	13,066	73	109,819	47,507	112,825	62	Minor Civil Division-Town
Newport	NWPT	49960	3-C	26,974	26,475	23,617	12,338	38,297	637,043	.0115	472,863	139	18,728	40	63,174	354	119,552	71,986	(d)	....	Incorporated Place
North Providence	PROV-	51760	◇	32,933	32,411	19,015	14,743	33,608	626,224	.0110	378,333	111	15,384	33	12,531	70	82,385	38,194	62,544	34	Minor Civil Division-Town
Pawtucket	PROV-	54640	3-BB	74,902	72,958	15,960	31,174	30,131	1,195,428	.0204	557,009	164	51,776	110	13,747	77	132,448	66,861	682,512	374	Incorporated Place
Providence	PROV-	59000	2-AA	185,951	173,618	14,993	67,615	28,064	2,787,943	.0470	1,161,174	342	26,520	56	88,747	497	296,946	140,780	739,896	405	Incorporated Place
South Kingstown	PROV-	67460	◇	29,814	27,921	21,179	10,096	50,682	631,439	.0104	326,594	96	5,292	11	9,518	53	59,875	46,600	224,186	123	Minor Civil Division-Town
Warwick	PROV-	74300	3-CC	87,021	85,808	22,597	36,756	42,585	1,966,385	.0371	1,603,993	472	322,178	684	127,982	717	180,205	138,233	611,016	335	Incorporated Place
Westerly	N.LON-	77000	4-S	23,401	22,966	23,441	9,783	40,862	548,547	.0104	463,148	136	58,247	124	11,548	65	108,665	31,439	71,213	39	Minor Civil Division-Town
West Warwick	PROV-	78440	◇	29,860	29,581	19,806	12,881	36,795	591,406	.0107	399,967	118	1,335	3	8,061	45	25,286	43,621	95,186	52	Minor Civil Division-Town
Woonsocket	PROV-	80780	3-S	43,454	43,224	14,706	18,011	29,030	639,015	.0129	502,874	148	45,008	96	23,753	133	140,720	109,454	169,199	93	Incorporated Place
South Carolina																					
Aiken	AUG	00550	4-C	26,993	25,337	20,475	11,201	38,687	552,695	.0094	318,503	94	66,628	141	14,711	82	55,207	22,268	652,632	357	Incorporated Place
Anderson	AND	01360	3-A	24,528	25,514	19,592	10,400	34,829	480,548	.0104	519,871	153	105,705	224	32,904	184	63,348	28,247	962,649	527	Incorporated Place
Charleston	CHAS	13330	2-A	104,143	96,650	20,052	46,731	33,661	2,088,227	.0398	1,662,434	489	258,960	550	214,487	1,202	280,062	87,169	362,268	198	Incorporated Place
Columbia	COL	16000	2-AA	118,658	116,278	17,219	46,029	32,376	2,043,167	.0425	1,899,984	559	364,516	774	140,717	789	211,437	102,383	763,766	418	Incorporated Place
Florence	FLO	25810	3-A	30,232	30,248	18,870	12,276	35,618	570,487	.0120	563,919	166	110,215	234	28,815	161	64,472	33,161	343,276	188	Incorporated Place
Goose Creek	CHAS	29815	◇	31,070	29,208	15,736	9,914	40,354	488,920	.0072	93,977	28	1,678	4	1,368	8	40,965	8,154	388,649	213	Incorporated Place
Greenville	GRNV	30850	2-A	54,575	56,002	21,098	24,292	33,421	1,151,425	.0312	1,987,479	585	318,446	676	159,437	894	131,023	87,471	1,955,952	1,071	Incorporated Place
Greenwood	GREEN	30895	3-A	21,979	22,071	16,261	8,693	31,687	357,398	.0076	345,966	102	73,259	156	18,041	101	69,486	20,808	581,116	318	Incorporated Place
Hilton Head Island		34045	◇	38,709	33,862	31,028	16,545	54,703	1,201,071	.0195	737,438	217	125,268	266	105,270	590	146,462	33,211	(d)	....	Incorporated Place
Mount Pleasant	CHAS	48535	◇	51,778	47,609	25,330	22,016	52,496	1,311,539	.0192	490,664	144	89,812	191	34,793	195	121,190	28,653	(d)	....	Incorporated Place
Myrtle Beach	MYR.B	49075	3-A	22,804	22,759	23,382	10,733	34,485	533,201	.0167	1,188,449	350	267,510	568	178,980	1,003	112,159	46,227	....	....	Incorporated Place
North Charleston	CHAS	50875	3-S	80,886	79,641	13,875	32,186	29,262	1,122,303	.0269	1,325,201	390	259,607	551	72,559	407	104,374	37,081	573,669	314	Incorporated Place
Orangeburg		53080	3-A	11,802	12,765	13,116	4,321	27,983	154,789	.0041	221,645	65	40,890	87	10,798	61	34,677	14,558	293,434	161	Incorporated Place
Rock Hill	CHRLT	61405	3-C	54,679	49,765	20,391	22,276	38,699	1,114,951	.0197	713,846	210	98,281	209	30,071	169	118,412	33,129	420,258	230	Incorporated Place
Spartanburg	SPRT	68290	3-BB	38,229	39,673	18,740	15,664	32,089	716,413	.0148	679,606	200	134,860	286	31,694	178	69,901	51,065	754,617	413	Incorporated Place
Summerville	CHAS	70270	◇	32,484	27,752	20,925	12,952	41,643	679,730	.0110	335,038	99	80,465	171	3,547	20	71,152	17,738	114,427	63	Incorporated Place
Sumter	SUMT	70405	3-A	38,415	39,643	15,467	14,816	30,224	594,155	.0134	636,214	187	103,680	220	36,652	205	83,623	33,306	810,636	444	Incorporated Place
South Dakota																					
Aberdeen		00100	3-A	23,836	24,658	17,920	10,481	32,720	427,141	.0117	727,140	214	55,254	117	7,574	42	43,744	4,440	....	....	Incorporated Place
Huron		31060	4-A	11,112	11,893	16,131	5,014	28,133	179,247	.0042	219,810	65	10,723	23	8,429	47	9,964	12,148	....	....	Incorporated Place
Mitchell		43100	4-A	14,239	14,558	16,534	6,046	30,904	235,432	.0062	356,969	105	65,211	138	9,735	55	26,600	8,898	192,540	105	Incorporated Place
Rapid City	RAP	52980	3-A	62,951	59,607	17,867	25,905	33,884	1,124,774	.0280	1,588,790	467	395,968	841	75,101	421	154,631	53,873	268,013	147	Incorporated Place
Sioux Falls	SXFL	59020	3-AA	132,443	123,975	20,613	55,345	39,433	2,729,986	.0648	3,651,530	1,074	598,528	1,271	64,718	363	290,703	169,739	579,979	318	Incorporated Place
Watertown		69300	4-A	20,048	20,237	17,854	8,559	33,680	357,940	.0089	504,982	149	47,439	101	21,752	122	54,434	6,787	....	....	Incorporated Place
Yankton		73060	4-C	12,683	13,528	16,642	5,106	33,286	211,069	.0053	296,381	87	54,108	115	16,907	95	8,510	7,308	116,134	64	Incorporated Place
Tennessee																					
Alcoa	KNOX	00540	4-S	8,018	7,734	19,683	3,725	30,341	157,816	.0100	913,959	269	125,418	266	4,452	25	55,236	31,144	....	....	Incorporated Place
Athens		02320	4-C	13,666	13,220	16,175	5,842	30,326	221,047	.0052	267,145	79	59,153	126	6,428	36	40,683	11,937	303,516	166	Incorporated Place
Bartlett	MEM	03440	◇	43,405	40,543	18,476	15,244	49,966	801,961	.0136	422,266	124	100,843	214	37,268	209	36,082	25,762	59,149	32	Incorporated Place
Bristol	JNSC-	08540	3-B	24,507	24,821	17,796	11,172	29,502	436,116	.0083	321,097	94	48,362	103	2,261	13	35,429	14,354	89,082	49	Incorporated Place
Chattanooga	CHTN	14000	2-A	156,183	155,554	18,458	68,124	31,837	2,882,899	.0594	2,698,914	794	390,118	828	193,732	1,086	307,530	168,261	1,844,947	1,010	Incorporated Place
Clarksville	CLRKV	15160	3-A	111,864	103,455	16,744	41,364	35,565	1,873,061	.0349	1,261,169	371	353,181	750	56,241	315	79,147	30,485	688,667	377	Incorporated Place
Cleveland	CLEV	15400	3-A	38,103	37,192	17,446	16,005	31,396	664,737	.0136	592,586	174	112,739	239	19,783	111	64,968	43,190	1,440,780	789	Incorporated Place
Collierville	MEM	16420	◇	34,279	31,872	24,914	11,529	67,150	854,040	.0126	323,339	95	66,251	141	5,211	29	30,576	13,219	188,553	103	Incorporated Place
Columbia		16540	4-C	35,468	33,055	20,301	14,411	38,428	720,039	.0128	467,528	138	91,192	194	23,532	132	60,614	22,335	....	....	Incorporated Place
Cookeville		16920	3-A	25,070	23,923	15,634	10,711	27,777	391,946	.0096	506,463	149	115,267	245	27,390	154	64,393	19,278	605,190	331	Incorporated Place
Dyersburg		22200	4-A	17,685	17,452	16,599	7,312	30,592	293,560	.0061	266,808	78	68,873	146	18,478	104	30,955	11,998	338,169	185	Incorporated Place
Elizabethton	JNSC-	23500	4-S	13,407	13,372	13,739	5,444	26,268	184,203	.0041	184,536	54	41,599	88	3,827	21	34,618	8,937	118,140	65	Incorporated Place
Franklin	NASH	27740	◇	59,861	41,842	29,606	24,681	59,515	1,772,264	.0312	1,335,841	393	280,061	595	91,543	513	124,748	47,250	299,224	164	Incorporated Place
Germantown	MEM	28960	◇	37,178	37,348	35,407	13,612	77,960	1,316,346	.0179	452,154	133	93,026	197	67,077	376	78,045	41,796	(d)	....	Incorporated Place
Goodlettsville	NASH	29920	4-Sm	13,659	13,780	20,442	5,902	41,868	279,224	.0060	304,999	90	99,776	212	41,109	230	27,786	11,690	(d)	....	Incorporated Place
Greeneville		30980	4-C	14,949	15,198	17,626	6,934	28,027	263,494	.0058	279,858	82	55,202	117	9,692	54	54,087	23,600	343,548	188	Incorporated Place
Hendersonville	NASH	33280	◇	43,557	40,620	24,738	17,506	46,245	1,077,527	.0150	309,517	91	23,662	50	7,556	42	72,996	35,790	78,734	43	Incorporated Place
Jackson	JAC	37640	3-A	63,554	59,643	17,825	25,877	33,752	1,132,838	.0240	1,121,973	330	271,462	576	76,388	428	103,075	61,941	....	....	Incorporated Place
Johnson City	JNSC-	38320	3-B	57,872	55,469	17,409	26,251	28,787	1,007,470	.0220	1,053,978	310	230,714	490	90,451	507	86,541	63,200	444,653	243	Incorporated Place
Kingsport	JNSC-	39560	3-AA	46,091	44,905	18,381	21,473	30,551	847,189	.0178	836,470	246	227,914	484	31,923	179	83,229	48,024	....	....	Incorporated Place
Knoxville	KNOX	40000	2-AA	181,112	173,890	17,388	83,100	29,135	3,149,142	.0745	3,960,068	1,165	557,982	1,184	195,973	1,098	441,820	205,238	1,060,551	581	Incorporated Place
Lebanon		41520	4-C	21,713	20,235	20,695	8,900	37,612	449,343	.0087	376,640	111	96,559	205	8,771	49	59,207	8,768	318,155	174	Incorporated Place
Maryville	KNOX	46380	4-C	24,482	23,120	18,689	9,858	36,462	457,544	.0079	263,320	77	42,663	91	6,116	34	44,614	20,344	523,202	286	Incorporated Place
Memphis	MEM	48000	2-AA	667,392	650,100	16,490	266,045	32,110	11,005,478	.2169	8,648,626	2,544	1,159,475	2,461	548,260	3,073	895,361	610,578	3,593,510	1,967	Incorporated Place
Morristown	MORR	50280	3-C	25,253	24,965	16,718	10,778	29,823	422,181	.0099	517,619	152	83,889	178	21,176	119	59,580	28,057	896,655	491	Incorporated Place
Murfreesboro	MUR	51560	3-C	85,260	68,816	21,083	34,843	37,222	1,797,569	.0302	1,000,085	294	195,454	415	34,996	196	138,493	37,703	661,302	362	Incorporated Place
Nashville	NASH	52006	2-AA	549,295	545,524	20,905	243,295	37,730	11,483,281	.2306	10,635,716	3,129	1,519,019	3,225	565,286	3,168	1,153,206	674,715	....	....	Incorporated Place
Oak Ridge	KNOX	55120	3-C	27,502	27,387	23,337	12,331	38,651	641,805	.0126	586,306	172	83,110	176	24,676	138	82,278	42,976	774,483	424	Incorporated Place
Paris		56720	4-C	9,134	9,763	17,677	4,287	28,355	161,461	.0036	178,250	52	49,248	105	4,624	26	25,713	6,683	142,382	78	Incorporated Place
Smyrna	NASH	69420	◇	27,897	25,569	21,781	11,141	42,848	607,636	.0098	302,957	89	102,179	217	1,734	10	50,795	9,138	....	....	Incorporated Place
Union City		75940	4-B	11,026	10,876	18,146	4,714	32,177	200,074	.0043	208,697	61	70,857	150	16,420	92	9,857	5,883	595,958	326	Incorporated Place
Texas																					
Abilene	ABIL	01000	3-AA	118,221	115,930	15,626	44,434	31,724	1,847,380	.0384	1,625,044	478	356,601	757	54,781	307	183,620	66,768	519,341	284	Incorporated Place
Addison	D-FW	01240	4-Sr	14,730	14,166	32,453	8,291	45,093	478,035	.0079	316,830	93	42,852	91	8,537	48	48,178	8,880	48,687	27	Incorporated Place
Allen	D-FW	01924	◇	55,572	43,554	25,503	18,308	69,380	1,417,264	.0193	367,114	108	49,707	106	8,427	47	116,909	5,284	57,494	31	Incorporated Place
Amarillo	AMA	03000	2-A	177,534	173,627	16,429	68,950	33,695	2,916,784	.0593	2,497,317	735	358,540	761	123,579	693	242,613	129,165	....	....	Incorporated Place
Arlington	D-FW	04000	2-S	372,209	332,969	20,467	141,131	44,511	7,617,862	.1397	5,499,317	1,618	620,752	1,318	301,971	1,692	689,667	214,728	1,374,814	753	Incorporated Place
Atascocita	HOU	04462	◇	38,446	35,757	20,654	12,461	59,187	794,075	.0112	191,260	56	39,342	84	6,229	35	64,623	6,505	(d)	....	Census Designated Place
Austin	AUS	05000	2-AA	692,237	656,562	22,489	300,808	42,658	15,567,749	.3638	20,631,763	6,069	1,456,318	3,091	632,844	3,547	1,975,595	1,024,858	10,541,882	5,771	Incorporated Place
Bay City		05984	4-C	18,206	18,667	14,832	6,841	30,446	270,035	.0053	195,251	57	26,187	56	9,500	53	48,575	8,111	(d)	....	Incorporated Place
Baytown	HOU	06128	3-S	69,547	66,430	17,034	25,875	39,309	1,184,645	.0197	532,655	157	112,481	239	35,680	200	75,475	25,139	....	....	Incorporated Place
Beaumont	B-PA	07000	2-A	110,795	113,866	18,217	45,718	33,453	2,018,298	.0420	1,924,405	566	338,184	718	117,250	657	213,533	122,463	1,210,461	663	Incorporated Place
Bedford	D-FW	07132	◇	48,308	47,152	26,309	20,990	49,226	1,270,914	.0191	550,179	162	66,865	142	8,160	46	98,229	32,602	....	....	Incorporated Place
Big Spring		08236	3-A	25,873	25,233	12,077	8,449	28,541	312,471	.0065	232,532	68	42,187	90	6,767	38	29,097	10,806	....	....	Incorporated Place
Borger		09556	4-C	13,550	14,302	17,802	5,361	33,610	241,215	.0042	131,637	39	24,343	52	6,862	38	27,045	6,923	(d)	....	Incorporated Place
Brownsville	BRNS	10768	3-AA	151,514	139,722	8,340	41,851	23,342	1,263,565	.0313	1,143,523	336	296,244	629	96,854	543	245,538	38,015	443,267	243	Incorporated Place
Brownwood		10780	4-A	18,459	18,813	13,904	7,019	27,843	256,658	.0058	268,602	79	65,907	140	6,926	39	23,559	14,827	476,667	261	Incorporated Place

continued on next page

.... Data less than 1,000.
(d) Data not available.
◇ Not classified as a Principal Business Center.

* Data from 1997 Census of Manufactures.

Principal Business Centers and Other Places with 27,500 or More: Population / Income / Sales, *Continued*

PLACE NAME / RANALLY METRO AREA	FIPS PLACE CODE	RANALLY CITY RATING	POPULATION Estimate 7/1/04	POPULATION Census 4/1/00	PER CAPITA INCOME 2003	HOUSE-HOLDS Estimate 7/1/04	MEDIAN HOUSEHOLD INCOME 2003	DISPOSABLE INCOME 2003 ($1,000)	MARKET ABILITY INDEX 2003	TOTAL RETAIL TRADE Sales 2003 ($1,000)	TOTAL RETAIL TRADE Ranally Sales Units	GENERAL MERCHANDISE Sales 2003 ($1,000)	GENERAL MERCHANDISE Ranally Sales Units	APPAREL STORES Sales 2003 ($1,000)	APPAREL STORES Ranally Sales Units	FOOD STORE SALES 2003 ($1,000)	HEALTH & DRUG STORE SALES 2003 ($1,000)	MANUFACTURERS VALUE ADDED 1997* ($1,000)	MANUFACTURERS Ranally Mfg Units	PLACE TYPE
Bryan **BRY-**	10912	**3-A**	69,782	65,660	13,159	26,600	31,271	918,276	.0208	920,959	**271**	127,492	**271**	14,176	**79**	115,060	16,631	134,588	**74**	Incorporated Place
Carrollton **D-FW**	13024	**4-S**	117,598	109,576	26,223	42,463	55,464	3,083,825	.0472	1,420,050	**418**	167,984	**357**	42,511	**238**	237,690	92,376	1,362,395	**746**	Incorporated Place
Cedar Hill **D-FW**	13492	◇	35,296	32,093	19,344	12,383	52,229	682,776	.0099	183,101	**54**	27,987	**59**	1,654	**9**	48,380	5,655	(d)	....	Incorporated Place
Cedar Park **AUS**	13552	◇	35,676	26,049	24,834	12,025	60,256	885,981	.0138	425,480	**125**	148,894	**316**	48,200	**270**	28,025	46,399	....	....	Incorporated Place
Channelview **HOU**	14236	◇	31,920	29,685	14,271	10,410	39,161	455,527	.0074	145,558	**43**	9,447	**20**	3,839	**22**	26,170	17,139	(d)	....	Census Designated Place
Cleburne **D-FW**	15364	**4-S**	27,346	26,005	18,463	9,849	36,580	504,882	.0095	371,932	**109**	79,050	**168**	10,759	**60**	37,404	12,648	288,797	**158**	Incorporated Place
College Station **BRY-**	15976	**3-B**	73,716	67,890	12,601	28,306	24,128	928,900	.0204	832,677	**245**	228,990	**486**	78,198	**438**	114,998	25,421	(d)	....	Incorporated Place
Conroe	16432	**3-S**	37,855	36,811	16,129	13,734	33,300	610,546	.0197	1,342,505	**395**	250,606	**532**	41,796	**234**	127,195	26,019	321,502	**176**	Incorporated Place
Coppell **D-FW**	16612	◇	39,583	35,958	30,306	14,075	78,819	1,199,602	.0155	280,903	**83**	....	....	3,073	**17**	90,642	16,538	(d)	....	Incorporated Place
Copperas Cove **KILL-**	16624	◇	28,234	29,592	16,860	10,293	37,075	476,030	.0071	116,411	**34**	11,431	**24**	1,740	**10**	2,387	4,120	(d)	....	Incorporated Place
Corpus Christi **CRPX**	17000	**2-A**	277,665	277,454	16,544	103,603	34,894	4,593,674	.0888	3,417,897	**1,005**	617,972	**1,312**	177,332	**994**	526,089	130,180	....	....	Incorporated Place
Corsicana	17060	**4-C**	25,049	24,485	13,808	8,875	28,061	345,875	.0077	337,567	**99**	57,701	**122**	18,622	**104**	50,529	11,597	....	....	Incorporated Place
Dallas **D-FW**	19000	**1-AA**	1,247,153	1,188,580	20,192	497,226	37,014	25,182,046	.4474	16,401,442	**4,825**	1,912,334	**4,059**	1,127,790	**6,320**	1,984,255	539,068	9,756,190	**5,341**	Incorporated Place
Deer Park **HOU**	19624	◇	29,533	28,520	20,328	10,506	54,823	600,359	.0085	146,933	**43**	2,084	**4**	7,286	**41**	47,704	14,474	4,599,765	**2,518**	Incorporated Place
Del Rio	19792	**4-B**	34,464	33,867	11,388	11,221	27,112	392,483	.0086	321,213	**94**	64,921	**138**	19,432	**109**	69,092	5,281	(d)	....	Incorporated Place
Denison **SHRM-**	19900	**4-B**	21,937	22,773	18,411	8,857	32,955	403,891	.0080	336,527	**99**	71,951	**153**	5,406	**30**	35,309	11,004	463,961	**254**	Incorporated Place
Denton **DENT**	19972	**3-S**	89,116	80,537	18,923	34,521	35,270	1,686,372	.0321	1,297,152	**382**	291,398	**619**	46,301	**259**	241,746	75,282	519,941	**285**	Incorporated Place
Desoto **D-FW**	20092	◇	38,612	37,646	21,553	14,724	51,059	832,223	.0132	378,523	**111**	21,099	**45**	26,596	**149**	155,548	21,307	(d)	....	Incorporated Place
Duncanville **D-FW**	21628	**4-Sr**	35,810	36,081	20,473	13,414	47,038	733,130	.0131	485,112	**143**	106,182	**225**	9,884	**55**	68,460	16,785	146,646	**80**	Incorporated Place
Eagle Pass	21892	**4-A**	24,794	22,413	8,452	7,747	21,127	209,559	.0051	179,264	**53**	38,267	**81**	26,603	**149**	55,252	5,506	....	....	Incorporated Place
Edinburg **MCAL**	22660	**4-C**	57,107	48,465	9,142	16,873	25,263	522,086	.0108	277,255	**82**	49,088	**104**	10,799	**61**	58,933	9,294	236,144	**129**	Incorporated Place
El Paso **ELP**	24000	**2-AA**	592,983	563,662	12,983	196,469	31,596	7,698,795	.1613	6,153,496	**1,810**	1,368,374	**2,905**	428,272	**2,400**	718,776	309,262	3,115,892	**1,706**	Incorporated Place
Euless **D-FW**	24768	◇	49,063	46,005	21,547	20,696	43,350	1,057,139	.0166	469,458	**138**	2,272	**5**	21,348	**120**	121,636	18,357	68,365	**37**	Incorporated Place
Farmers Branch **D-FW**	25452	◇	27,874	27,508	21,220	10,367	46,298	591,492	.0138	774,589	**228**	48,567	**103**	36,337	**204**	61,144	18,412	795,433	**435**	Incorporated Place
Flower Mound **D-FW**	26232	◇	65,586	50,702	28,955	21,118	77,869	1,899,060	.0230	238,959	**70**	....	....	3,617	**20**	154,204	30,542	(d)	....	Incorporated Place
Fort Hood **KILL-**	26736	◇	35,694	33,711	6,473	6,475	30,912	231,052	.0045	3,006	**1**	....	....	....	....	....	....	(d)	....	Census Designated Place
Fort Worth **D-FW**	27000	**2-BB**	604,370	534,694	17,319	223,305	35,405	10,467,044	.2026	8,040,589	**2,365**	779,938	**1,656**	348,323	**1,952**	986,027	340,635	5,885,255	**3,222**	Incorporated Place
Friendswood **HOU**	27648	**4-Sm**	32,000	29,037	24,879	11,472	60,857	796,119	.0122	354,124	**104**	100,846	**214**	48,947	**274**	70,131	35,446	(d)	....	Incorporated Place
Frisco **D-FW**	27684	◇	49,463	33,714	27,753	17,872	64,493	1,372,736	.0176	262,718	**77**	3,210	**7**	3,109	**17**	71,387	20,413	84,976	**47**	Incorporated Place
Galveston **GLV-**	28068	**3-C**	56,741	57,247	18,261	24,325	29,210	1,036,147	.0170	473,812	**139**	64,719	**137**	35,519	**199**	116,360	34,265	24,149	**13**	Incorporated Place
Garland **D-FW**	29000	**3-S**	224,313	215,768	17,475	79,762	44,458	3,919,760	.0671	2,033,574	**598**	376,431	**799**	47,201	**265**	303,429	94,463	1,467,003	**803**	Incorporated Place
Georgetown **AUS**	29336	◇	29,915	28,339	26,465	11,194	52,349	791,704	.0123	381,889	**112**	19,638	**42**	3,293	**18**	102,385	13,087	....	....	Incorporated Place
Grand Prairie **D-FW**	30464	**4-S**	137,246	127,427	17,212	49,472	43,279	2,362,292	.0439	1,600,972	**471**	163,224	**346**	12,769	**72**	178,441	70,842	1,121,505	**614**	Incorporated Place
Grapevine **D-FW**	30644	◇	45,252	42,059	27,615	17,093	61,611	1,249,631	.0247	1,219,789	**359**	78,075	**166**	153,152	**858**	160,876	22,803	139,495	**76**	Incorporated Place
Greenville	30920	**4-C**	25,219	23,960	17,563	9,546	35,411	442,926	.0087	360,987	**106**	91,296	**194**	19,879	**111**	49,908	18,938	146,685	**80**	Incorporated Place
Haltom City **D-FW**	31928	◇	42,208	39,018	17,581	16,309	39,160	742,071	.0140	532,880	**157**	31,328	**67**	3,702	**21**	80,892	19,912	183,132	**100**	Incorporated Place
Harlingen **BRNS**	32372	**3-B**	62,216	57,564	12,081	20,770	28,163	751,663	.0175	766,674	**226**	131,164	**278**	46,572	**261**	132,084	29,579	229,228	**125**	Incorporated Place
Houston **HOU**	35000	**1-AA**	2,117,667	1,953,631	18,628	819,631	36,928	39,447,563	.7202	26,619,396	**7,830**	3,311,886	**7,030**	1,825,401	**10,230**	4,048,440	1,411,408	13,318,807	**7,292**	Incorporated Place
Humble **HOU**	35348	**4-S**	15,575	14,579	17,121	6,142	40,206	266,652	.0094	683,692	**201**	220,473	**468**	50,936	**285**	29,023	15,112	57,767	**32**	Incorporated Place
Huntsville	35528	**4-C**	34,572	35,078	11,444	10,280	29,396	395,638	.0093	401,047	**118**	85,838	**182**	19,152	**107**	38,616	19,575	(d)	....	Incorporated Place
Hurst **D-FW**	35576	**3-Sm**	36,723	36,273	22,367	14,411	48,672	821,379	.0190	1,060,845	**312**	220,418	**468**	75,364	**422**	140,718	39,144	48,617	**27**	Incorporated Place
Irving **D-FW**	37000	**3-S**	198,195	191,615	21,175	82,781	42,409	4,196,697	.0840	3,876,463	**1,140**	385,098	**817**	144,181	**808**	296,363	141,244	1,256,787	**688**	Incorporated Place
Jacksonville	37216	**4-C**	13,942	13,868	12,979	4,922	26,994	180,953	.0038	145,421	**43**	47,057	**100**	4,693	**26**	14,923	4,508	141,924	**78**	Incorporated Place
Keller **D-FW**	38632	◇	33,501	27,345	25,369	10,940	67,180	849,896	.0107	123,581	**36**	1,858	**4**	....	....	54,510	4,875	(d)	....	Incorporated Place
Kerrville	39040	**4-C**	20,834	20,425	18,097	8,792	31,746	377,034	.0081	387,658	**114**	64,261	**136**	21,817	**122**	128,741	22,588	33,970	**19**	Incorporated Place
Killeen **KILL-**	39148	**3-B**	95,364	86,911	15,540	37,451	33,659	1,481,931	.0275	930,092	**274**	132,852	**282**	35,801	**201**	113,508	12,273	(d)	....	Incorporated Place
Lake Jackson **L.JAC-**	40588	**3-C**	27,472	26,386	25,519	10,069	53,330	701,061	.0121	474,412	**140**	217,704	**462**	22,714	**127**	19,417	23,803	(d)	....	Incorporated Place
La Porte **HOU**	41440	◇	34,132	31,880	18,825	12,351	50,897	642,546	.0105	293,475	**86**	4,741	**10**	5,096	**29**	65,189	20,404	785,420	**430**	Incorporated Place
Laredo **LAR**	41464	**3-AA**	196,572	176,576	9,457	53,055	28,135	1,858,956	.0494	2,261,250	**665**	478,607	**1,016**	251,809	**1,411**	348,985	97,255	....	....	Incorporated Place
League City **HOU**	41980	◇	52,329	45,444	23,393	19,230	56,573	1,224,124	.0174	372,393	**110**	3,628	**8**	3,636	**20**	106,895	18,534	(d)	....	Incorporated Place
Lewisville **D-FW**	42508	◇	91,756	77,737	25,153	35,818	51,143	2,307,963	.0460	2,247,319	**661**	478,944	**1,017**	186,532	**1,045**	143,860	121,186	617,939	**338**	Incorporated Place
Longview **LNGV**	43888	**3-AA**	74,905	73,344	17,533	29,877	33,645	1,313,334	.0297	1,497,340	**440**	278,169	**590**	61,587	**345**	184,932	51,323	1,249,706	**684**	Incorporated Place
Lubbock **LUB**	45000	**2-A**	206,965	199,564	15,542	81,921	31,343	3,216,732	.0682	2,978,692	**876**	501,812	**1,065**	158,716	**889**	396,988	96,509	828,864	**454**	Incorporated Place
Lufkin **LUFK**	45072	**3-A**	31,829	32,709	16,257	12,257	32,280	517,435	.0114	539,789	**159**	128,074	**272**	20,824	**117**	84,883	18,289	283,175	**155**	Incorporated Place
Mansfield **D-FW**	46452	◇	35,493	28,031	20,959	11,371	56,912	743,883	.0106	197,992	**58**	51,612	**110**	1,467	**8**	57,057	7,269	180,286	**99**	Incorporated Place
Marshall **MAR**	46776	**4-B**	22,880	23,935	14,003	8,411	28,807	320,389	.0067	269,592	**79**	58,266	**124**	14,459	**81**	37,103	10,617	105,716	**58**	Incorporated Place
McAllen **MCAL**	45384	**2-A**	117,684	106,414	12,783	37,054	32,036	1,504,412	.0435	2,550,151	**750**	671,219	**1,425**	311,658	**1,747**	262,467	129,938	260,836	**143**	Incorporated Place
McKinney **D-FW**	45744	◇	92,154	54,369	23,772	31,069	59,220	2,190,707	.0347	1,076,721	**317**	138,377	**294**	20,478	**115**	163,693	34,673	720,084	**394**	Incorporated Place
Mesquite **D-FW**	47892	**3-Sm**	130,765	124,523	17,612	48,293	44,982	2,302,992	.0532	2,759,380	**812**	697,437	**1,481**	223,631	**1,253**	221,033	143,041	739,695	**405**	Incorporated Place
Midland **MIDL-**	48072	**3-AA**	97,195	94,996	18,503	38,112	37,468	1,798,381	.0348	1,433,279	**422**	239,961	**509**	67,043	**376**	175,792	51,869	77,473	**42**	Incorporated Place
Mission **MCAL**	48768	◇	51,927	45,408	8,963	15,903	23,261	465,432	.0097	247,010	**73**	48,870	**104**	6,514	**37**	47,777	7,798	88,371	**48**	Incorporated Place
Mission Bend **HOU**	48772	◇	38,275	30,831	17,076	11,190	48,687	653,578	.0111	321,832	**95**	73,581	**156**	4,565	**26**	67,657	14,009	(d)	....	Census Designated Place
Missouri City **HOU**	48804	◇	56,875	52,913	24,174	18,397	60,962	1,374,879	.0189	357,712	**105**	91,948	**195**	6,102	**34**	107,519	28,092	75,115	**41**	Incorporated Place
Mount Pleasant	49800	**4-C**	13,674	13,935	13,014	4,404	29,958	177,960	.0046	242,934	**71**	58,887	**125**	10,021	**56**	24,458	13,590	178,062	**97**	Incorporated Place
Nacogdoches	50256	**4-B**	27,575	29,914	13,539	10,502	27,603	373,333	.0080	331,220	**97**	61,020	**130**	21,766	**122**	52,396	12,607	232,756	**127**	Incorporated Place
New Braunfels	50820	◇	39,260	36,494	18,328	15,003	38,195	719,563	.0127	429,545	**126**	58,562	**124**	10,300	**58**	41,765	11,152	274,768	**150**	Incorporated Place
North Richland Hills **D-FW**	52356	**4-S**	60,033	55,635	22,053	22,678	49,977	1,323,918	.0258	1,160,977	**342**	107,795	**229**	31,289	**175**	88,420	52,725	233,129	**128**	Incorporated Place
Odessa **MIDL-**	53388	**3-AA**	92,520	90,943	14,970	35,205	30,018	1,384,983	.0288	1,195,958	**352**	309,890	**658**	38,150	**214**	160,470	34,594	201,812	**110**	Incorporated Place
Orange **B-PA**	54132	**3-C**	17,353	18,643	18,129	7,037	34,046	314,589	.0055	181,941	**54**	29,884	**63**	6,701	**38**	24,284	13,463	377,681	**207**	Incorporated Place
Palestine	54708	**4-C**	17,365	17,598	15,270	6,834	29,463	265,157	.0052	199,579	**59**	58,724	**125**	9,720	**54**	13,793	10,373	48,160	**26**	Incorporated Place
Pampa	54912	**4-C**	17,026	17,887	16,125	7,149	30,018	274,542	.0050	163,467	**48**	25,706	**55**	5,748	**32**	28,049	7,105	(d)	....	Incorporated Place
Paris	55080	**3-A**	25,918	25,898	15,619	10,695	27,678	404,806	.0099	523,227	**154**	120,157	**255**	24,863	**139**	55,406	29,125	1,329,043	**728**	Incorporated Place
Pasadena **HOU**	56000	**3-S**	151,155	141,674	15,054	52,885	37,890	2,275,432	.0433	1,512,913	**445**	335,278	**712**	65,232	**366**	212,168	77,748	1,434,970	**786**	Incorporated Place
Pearland **HOU**	56348	◇	45,756	37,640	23,706	16,182	55,388	1,084,687	.0162	422,010	**124**	109,064	**232**	17,237	**97**	83,397	21,025	39,435	**22**	Incorporated Place
Pharr **MCAL**	57200	**4-S**	52,603	46,660	8,187	14,560	23,600	430,685	.0116	483,840	**142**	43,558	**92**	17,394	**97**	78,332	9,738	(d)	....	Incorporated Place
Plainview	57980	**4-C**	21,008	22,336	13,049	7,218	29,785	274,139	.0055	191,091	**56**	35,789	**76**	11,227	**63**	28,410	7,882	....	....	Incorporated Place
Plano **D-FW**	58016	**3-S**	232,864	222,030	34,657	85,673	68,935	8,070,385	.1320	5,248,987	**1,544**	910,102	**1,932**	370,270	**2,075**	707,154	195,525	1,478,608	**809**	Incorporated Place
Port Arthur **B-PA**	58820	**3-B**	55,413	57,755	13,879	22,172	25,421	769,053	.0156	591,176	**174**	76,394	**162**	47,784	**268**	105,290	34,918	1,454,445	**796**	Incorporated Place
Richardson **D-FW**	61796	**3-S**	97,132	91,802	25,953	39,022	55,982	2,520,865	.0456	1,947,769	**573**	204,762	**435**	90,889	**509**	254,497	74,002	1,883,412	**1,031**	Incorporated Place
Rosenberg **HOU**	63284	**4-S**	25,813	24,043	15,281	8,542	35,143	394,455	.0110	665,121	**196**	96,326	**204**	15,595	**87**	53,905	23,453	154,345	**84**	Incorporated Place
Round Rock **AUS**	63500	◇	68,525	61,136	25,453	24,051	55,270	1,744,137	.0276	889,859	**262**	92,162	**196**	15,850	**89**	202,619	36,806	....	....	Incorporated Place
Rowlett **D-FW**	63572	◇	48,992	44,503	21,171	16,475	61,251	1,037,233	.0141	207,197	**61**	8,395	**18**	2,152	**12**	77,567	11,936	33,283	**18**	Incorporated Place
San Angelo **SANG**	64472	**3-AA**	87,328	88,439	16,185	35,301	31,285	1,413,368	.0274	1,050,217	**309**	215,623	**458**	39,726	**223**	147,764	33,125	353,578	**194**	Incorporated Place
San Antonio **SANT**	65000	**1-A**	1,223,175	1,144,646	16,624	450,546	36,338	20,334,345	.4017	16,155,862	**4,752**	2,479,280	**5,263**	1,003,308	**5,623**	2,538,530	674,047	2,552,048	**1,397**	Incorporated Place
San Juan **MCAL**	65516	◇	31,755	26,229	6,969	8,080	21,719	221,295	.0048	79,257	**23**	1,522	**3**	1,947	**11**	26,144	3,028	(d)	....	Incorporated Place
San Marcos	65600	◇	34,438	34,733	16,126	13,093	30,217	555,337	.0128	639,164	**188**	59,834	**127**	174,143	**976**	82,679	25,305	122,874	**67**	Incorporated Place
Sherman **SHRM-**	67496	**3-A**	35,696	35,082	18,368	14,017	34,344	655,681	.0143	707,888	**208**	229,538	**487**	19,715	**110**	65,332	31,450	1,681,085	**920**	Incorporated Place
Socorro **ELP**	68636	◇	29,694	27,152	6,882	7,581	23,900	204,350	.0043	58,207	**17**	....	....	....	....	17,121	....	(d)	....	Incorporated Place
Spring **HOU**	69596	◇	39,122	36,385	18,428	13,966	50,484	720,930	.0119	343,816	**101**	41,716	**89**	8,937	**50**	139,802	32,626	(d)	....	Census Designated Place
Sugar Land **HOU**	70808	◇	70,327	63,328	29,488	22,897	68,936	2,073,815	.0305	884,297	**260**	182,339	**387**	65,775	**369**	124,155	49,203	414,019	**227**	Incorporated Place
Temple **KILL-**	72176	**3-A**	55,909	54,514	19,585	23,171	34,049	1,094,984	.0205	820,936	**241**	128,404	**273**	25,783	**144**	88,722	15,566	596,066	**326**	Incorporated Place
Texarkana **TEXR-**	72368	**3-AA**	34,994	34,782	18,184	13,879	34,943	636,343	.0139	685,707	**202**	123,446	**262**	51,773	**290**	54,577	16,715	289,887	**159**	Incorporated Place
Texas City **GLV-**	72392	**3-C**	42,482	41,521	16,217	16,309	33,767	688,926	.0137	551,536	**162**	196,040	**416**	28,207	**158**	58,372	29,568	1,632,210	**894**	Incorporated Place
The Colony **D-FW**	72530	◇	30,211	26,531	21,114	9,727	55,958	637,861	.0090	160,756	**47**	61,971	**132**	5,736	**32**	50,323	8,328	(d)	....	Incorporated Place
The Woodlands **HOU**	72656	◇	68,273	55,649	32,043	24,769	71,008	2,187,649	.0305	790,992	**233**	251,295	**533**	80,625	**452**	170,787	47,706	(d)	....	Census Designated Place
Tyler **TYL**	74144	**3-AA**	86,303	83,650	18,583	34,417	33,531	1,603,752	.0372	1,980,562	**583**	329,403	**699**	139,255	**780**	206,470	102,758	996,129	**545**	Incorporated Place
Victoria **VICT**	75428	**3-A**	61,562	60,603	17,255	22,700	36,185	1,062,225	.0223	1,012,210	**298**	208,122	**442**	45,414	**255**	151,584	48,149	569,184	**312**	Incorporated Place
Waco **WACO**	76000	**3-AA**	119,030	113,726	14,126	45,055	27,679	1,681,445	.0379	1,727,781	**508**	346,517	**736**	77,380	**434**	252,883	68,274	1,987,836	**1,088**	Incorporated Place
Weslaco **MCAL**	77272	◇	29,729	26,935	9,124	9,244	23,246	271,252	.0071	304,844	**90**	70,007	**149**	23,656	**133**	47,804	11,032	12,374	**7**	Incorporated Place
Wichita Falls **WIFL**	79000	**3-AA**	105,010	104,197	15,937	40,291	31,553	1,673,531	.0333	1,319,049	**388**	268,174	**569**	42,119	**236**	176,473	63,833	570,299	**312**	Incorporated Place

Utah

PLACE NAME / RANALLY METRO AREA	FIPS PLACE CODE	RANALLY CITY RATING	POPULATION Estimate 7/1/04	POPULATION Census 4/1/00	PER CAPITA INCOME 2003	HOUSE-HOLDS Estimate 7/1/04	MEDIAN HOUSEHOLD INCOME 2003	DISPOSABLE INCOME 2003 ($1,000)	MARKET ABILITY INDEX 2003	TOTAL RETAIL TRADE Sales 2003 ($1,000)	TOTAL RETAIL TRADE Ranally Sales Units	GENERAL MERCHANDISE Sales 2003 ($1,000)	GENERAL MERCHANDISE Ranally Sales Units	APPAREL STORES Sales 2003 ($1,000)	APPAREL STORES Ranally Sales Units	FOOD STORE SALES 2003 ($1,000)	HEALTH & DRUG STORE SALES 2003 ($1,000)	MANUFACTURERS VALUE ADDED 1997* ($1,000)	MANUFACTURERS Ranally Mfg Units	PLACE TYPE
Bountiful **S.L.C.**	07690	**4-S**	41,767	41,301	22,881	14,076	48,536	955,673	.0167	632,696	**186**	54,383	**115**	5,999	**34**	96,841	25,972	26,982	**15**	Incorporated Place
Clearfield **OGD**	13850	◇	29,410	25,974	14,931	9,336	41,541	439,106	.0070	131,008	**39**	2,738	**6**	....	....	42,117	2,429	297,448	**163**	Incorporated Place
Cottonwood Heights **S.L.C.**	16270	◇	28,604	27,569	25,844	10,110	56,055	739,232	.0106	255,377	**75**	56,717	**120**	6,493	**36**	61,287	3,395	(d)	....	Census Designated Place
Draper **S.L.C.**	20120	◇	28,687	25,220	17,461	7,402	62,302	500,912	.0098	400,363	**118**	42,097	**89**	18,435	**103**	57,663	30,396	134,257	**74**	Incorporated Place
Kearns **S.L.C.**	40470	◇	34,923	33,659	14,186	9,849	44,273	495,425	.0085	206,073	**61**	24,385	**52**	1,360	**8**	85,899	3,998	(d)	....	Census Designated Place
Layton **OGD**	43660	**4-S**	66,125	58,474	17,874	21,517	47,587	1,181,943	.0242	1,071,158	**315**	246,008	**522**	52,363	**293**	126,012	21,241	(d)	....	Incorporated Place
Logan **LOGN**	45860	**4-A**	45,603	42,670	13,398	14,894	31,810	610,979	.0141	648,061	**191**	162,052	**344**	23,346	**131**	88,261	14,682	283,940	**155**	Incorporated Place
Midvale **S.L.C.**	49710	◇	28,128	27,029	17,221	10,833	37,179	484,400	.0114	598,563	**176**	136,163	**289**	24,023	**135**	65,806	22,189	(d)	....	Incorporated Place
Millcreek **S.L.C.**	50150	◇	31,517	30,377	22,211	13,442	40,861	700,024	.0150	772,424	**227**	118,697	**252**	54,554	**306**	76,278	17,628	(d)	....	Census Designated Place
Murray **S.L.C.**	53230	**3-S**	34,651	34,024	17,588	13,295	37,860	609,426	.0194	1,338,807	**394**	206,132	**438**	79,965	**448**	77,844	18,819	136,911	**75**	Incorporated Place
Ogden **OGD**	55980	**3-BB**	81,190	77,226	16,404	29,261	35,851	1,331,880	.0273	1,157,112	**340**	238,909	**507**	26,177	**147**	183,859	28,069	1,546,457	**847**	Incorporated Place
Orem **PRVO-**	57300	**3-B**	92,357	84,324	15,329	26,611	43,391	1,415,732	.0342	1,776,455	**523**	357,415	**759**	72,701	**407**	215,536	20,152	142,014	**78**	Incorporated Place
Provo **PRVO-**	62470	**3-AA**	113,860	105,166	12,462	32,806	32,394	1,418,875	.0290	1,018,098	**299**	234,738	**498**	56,012	**314**	189,767	29,984	191,371	**105**	Incorporated Place
Riverton **S.L.C.**	64340	◇	28,449	25,011	14,864	7,452	55,871	422,862	.0068	138,512	**41**	1,391	**3**	....	....	62,833	1,707	(d)	....	Incorporated Place
Roy **OGD**	65110	◇	36,076	32,885	16,616	11,905	44,565	599,427	.0094	205,096	**60**	....	....	3,982	**22**	73,473	3,867	....	....	Incorporated Place
St. George	65330	**4-A**	58,915	49,663	15,762	21,085	34,536	928,640	.0233	1,280,481	**377**	191,883	**407**	51,611	**289**	126,526	25,648	107,637	**59**	Incorporated Place
Salt Lake City **S.L.C.**	67000	**2-AA**	181,399	181,743	19,330	73,711	35,636	3,506,471	.0713	3,248,614	**956**	281,097	**597**	151,505	**849**	470,614	54,086	2,306,155	**1,263**	Incorporated Place
Sandy **S.L.C.**	67440	◇	88,735	88,418	20,491	26,623	57,444	1,818,228	.0363	1,644,628	**484**	394,867	**838**	74,001	**415**	167,746	24,848	187,820	**103**	Incorporated Place
South Jordan **S.L.C.**	70850	◇	31,943	29,437	17,174	8,411	62,002	548,584	.0076	74,237	**22**	2,126	**5**	....	....	3,616	....	....	....	Incorporated Place
Taylorsville **S.L.C.**	75360	◇	56,148	57,439	15,973	18,695	42,075	896,850	.0164	551,831	**162**	114,740	**244**	7,888	**44**	103,211	7,760	....	....	Incorporated Place
Tooele	76680	◇	30,541	22,502	17,360	10,113	43,064	530,205	.0085	208,211	**61**	18,005	**38**	1,006	**6**	65,463	3,451	....	....	Incorporated Place
West Jordan **S.L.C.**	82950	◇	74,019	68,336	15,006	21,104	49,531	1,110,725	.0188	474,583	**140**	129,899	**276**	4,992	**28**	110,498	4,766	155,966	**85**	Incorporated Place
West Valley **S.L.C.**	83470	**3-S**	117,699	108,896	13,765	35,941	40,939	1,620,121	.0388	1,904,747	**560**	319,908	**679**	39,938	**224**	179,827	26,752	637,803	**349**	Incorporated Place

Vermont

PLACE NAME / RANALLY METRO AREA	FIPS PLACE CODE	RANALLY CITY RATING	POPULATION Estimate 7/1/04	POPULATION Census 4/1/00	PER CAPITA INCOME 2003	HOUSE-HOLDS Estimate 7/1/04	MEDIAN HOUSEHOLD INCOME 2003	DISPOSABLE INCOME 2003 ($1,000)	MARKET ABILITY INDEX 2003	TOTAL RETAIL TRADE Sales 2003 ($1,000)	TOTAL RETAIL TRADE Ranally Sales Units	GENERAL MERCHANDISE Sales 2003 ($1,000)	GENERAL MERCHANDISE Ranally Sales Units	APPAREL STORES Sales 2003 ($1,000)	APPAREL STORES Ranally Sales Units	FOOD STORE SALES 2003 ($1,000)	HEALTH & DRUG STORE SALES 2003 ($1,000)	MANUFACTURERS VALUE ADDED 1997* ($1,000)	MANUFACTURERS Ranally Mfg Units	PLACE TYPE
Barre	03175	**4-C**	9,206	9,291	20,005	4,281	33,545	184,165	.0035	143,970	**42**	4,789	**10**	4,957	**28**	28,573	13,933	63,395	**35**	Incorporated Place
Bennington	04825	**4-B**	15,708	15,737	15,773	6,288	32,132	247,766	.0063	355,342	**105**	43,351	**92**	15,505	**87**	68,808	15,956	156,465	**86**	Minor Civil Division-Town
Burlington **BUR**	10675	**3-AA**	38,677	38,889	17,768	16,404	31,444	687,208	.0146	677,408	**199**	61,530	**131**	51,574	**289**	123,563	36,340	....	....	Incorporated Place
Rutland	61225	**3-A**	17,643	17,292	18,531	7,765	31,504	326,935	.0081	456,532	**134**	54,342	**115**	30,610	**172**	67,620	32,543	189,099	**104**	Incorporated Place
South Burlington **BUR**	66175	**4-S**	16,462	15,814	23,808	6,842	46,612	391,923	.0104	663,577	**195**	104,875	**223**	21,745	**122**	28,665	35,065	(d)	....	Incorporated Place

Virginia

PLACE NAME / RANALLY METRO AREA	FIPS PLACE CODE	RANALLY CITY RATING	POPULATION Estimate 7/1/04	POPULATION Census 4/1/00	PER CAPITA INCOME 2003	HOUSE-HOLDS Estimate 7/1/04	MEDIAN HOUSEHOLD INCOME 2003	DISPOSABLE INCOME 2003 ($1,000)	MARKET ABILITY INDEX 2003	TOTAL RETAIL TRADE Sales 2003 ($1,000)	TOTAL RETAIL TRADE Ranally Sales Units	GENERAL MERCHANDISE Sales 2003 ($1,000)	GENERAL MERCHANDISE Ranally Sales Units	APPAREL STORES Sales 2003 ($1,000)	APPAREL STORES Ranally Sales Units	FOOD STORE SALES 2003 ($1,000)	HEALTH & DRUG STORE SALES 2003 ($1,000)	MANUFACTURERS VALUE ADDED 1997* ($1,000)	MANUFACTURERS Ranally Mfg Units	PLACE TYPE
Alexandria **WASH**	01000	**3-SS**	128,847	128,283	32,583	67,671	51,397	4,198,170	.0646	2,209,715	**650**	303,923	**645**	97,294	**545**	255,880	138,676	194,752	**107**	Independent City
Annandale **WASH**	01912	◇	57,140	54,994	28,206	21,510	63,133	1,611,702	.0219	466,154	**137**	39,843	**85**	6,596	**37**	131,249	39,072	(d)	....	Census Designated Place
Arlington **WASH**	03000	**3-SS**	187,390	189,453	35,379	95,852	56,477	6,629,700	.0909	2,363,900	**695**	385,462	**818**	288,147	**1,615**	311,525	143,568	(d)	....	Census Designated Place
Blacksburg	07784	◇	43,091	39,573	12,294	14,616	24,903	529,741	.0095	224,299	**66**	....	....	6,302	**35**	42,856	14,580	149,272	**82**	Incorporated Place
Bristol **JNSC-**	09816	**3-B**	17,176	17,367	15,231	8,140	26,274	261,610	.0068	378,509	**111**	135,129	**287**	11,179	**63**	41,136	26,116	474,903	**260**	Independent City
Burke **WASH**	11464	◇	60,058	57,737	28,844	20,800	75,225	1,732,326	.0218	314,607	**93**	27,689	**59**	8,311	**47**	120,590	17,484	(d)	....	Census Designated Place
Centreville **WASH**	14440	◇	50,619	48,661	28,086	19,265	67,672	1,421,675	.0176	206,513	**61**	....	....	1,291	**7**	117,443	8,460	(d)	....	Census Designated Place
Chantilly **WASH**	14744	◇	42,692	41,041	29,798	16,072	69,813	1,272,118	.0251	1,270,889	**374**	391,938	**832**	132,717	**744**	108,257	28,162	(d)	....	Census Designated Place
Charlottesville **CHRLTV**	14968	**3-AA**	38,847	45,049	16,614	18,021	29,335	645,400	.0174	1,044,121	**307**	85,431	**181**	78,648	**441**	210,240	48,830	....	....	Independent City
Chesapeake **NORF-**	16000	**3-S**	214,295	199,184	19,823	76,328	45,725	4,247,960	.0793	3,175,219	**934**	769,152	**1,633**	155,482	**871**	348,243	131,796	336,679	**184**	Independent City
Dale City **WASH**	21088	◇	67,598	55,971	22,189	21,588	59,107	1,499,912	.0194	205,955	**61**	33,733	**72**	5,581	**31**	53,909	5,318	(d)	....	Census Designated Place
Danville **DANV**	21344	**3-A**	46,575	48,411	14,075	20,713	25,876	655,530	.0149	683,485	**201**	133,549	**283**	20,909	**117**	91,603	43,717	....	....	Independent City
Fairfax **WASH**	26496	**3-SS**	22,181	21,498	27,678	8,297	60,438	613,920	.0233	1,866,855	**549**	121,768	**258**	86,807	**486**	194,511	61,550	(d)	....	Independent City
Falls Church **WASH**	27200	**3-S**	10,500	10,377	36,247	4,827	64,378	380,590	.0081	464,863	**137**	10,330	**22**	9,207	**52**	48,467	25,387	(d)	....	Independent City
Franconia **WASH**	29552	◇	33,190	31,907	32,111	14,368	67,675	1,065,780	.0131	182,359	**54**	93,146	**198**	4,678	**26**	41,788	5,359	(d)	....	Census Designated Place
Fredericksburg **FRED**	29744	**3-A**	20,481	19,279	17,445	8,893	32,339	357,290	.0120	846,352	**249**	113,743	**241**	47,921	**269**	66,001	41,982	88,499	**48**	Independent City
Hampton **NN-H**	35000	**3-BB**	147,010	146,437	17,330	56,725	36,600	2,547,690	.0501	2,048,799	**603**	410,417	**871**	91,269	**511**	176,772	77,081	422,730	**231**	Independent City
Harrisonburg	35624	**3-A**	41,444	40,468	11,769	14,013	28,360	487,740	.0152	924,894	**272**	220,645	**468**	38,917	**218**	117,807	24,439	254,261	**139**	Independent City
Hopewell **RICH**	38424	**4-S**	22,421	22,354	16,593	9,771	31,076	372,040	.0057	111,491	**33**	3,629	**8**	4,767	**27**	25,710	9,139	743,916	**407**	Independent City
Jefferson **WASH**	40584	◇	28,526	27,422	25,124	10,817	58,018	716,683	.0112	350,196	**103**	3,387	**7**	11,924	**67**	47,061	35,066	(d)	....	Census Designated Place
Lake Ridge **WASH**	43432	◇	36,719	30,404	28,467	13,468	62,115	1,045,277	.0170	623,768	**183**	95,821	**203**	136,118	**763**	62,188	27,617	(d)	....	Census Designated Place
Leesburg **WASH**	44984	◇	33,572	28,311	30,586	12,242	63,181	1,026,821	.0162	574,974	**169**	83,414	**177**	25,513	**143**	113,678	28,611	(d)	....	Incorporated Place
Lynchburg **LYNCH**	47672	**3-AA**	65,067	65,269	15,392	26,744	30,800	1,001,510	.0257	1,431,477	**421**	242,617	**515**	51,281	**287**	134,326	117,670	1,602,612	**877**	Independent City
Manassas **WASH**	48952	**4-S**	37,756	35,135	22,060	12,584	54,129	832,900	.0187	1,016,742	**299**	199,045	**423**	24,343	**136**	163,271	29,592	594,660	**326**	Independent City
Martinsville **MRTNV**	49784	**3-A**	15,036	15,416	13,784	6,423	26,140	207,250	.0058	340,624	**100**	118,085	**251**	21,824	**122**	36,413	15,372	345,425	**189**	Independent City
McLean **WASH**	48376	◇	40,497	38,929	48,368	15,526	91,161	1,958,754	.0258	692,251	**204**	185,703	**394**	114,886	**644**	154,847	35,580	(d)	....	Census Designated Place
Mechanicsville **RICH**	50856	◇	34,035	30,464	24,321	13,057	52,234	827,778	.0128	377,925	**111**	71,844	**153**	3,066	**17**	98,856	25,733	(d)	....	Census Designated Place
Mount Vernon **WASH**	54144	◇	29,732	28,582	25,227	11,441	53,309	750,040	.0096	119,564	**35**	....	....	....	....	44,136	8,720	(d)	....	Census Designated Place
Newport News **NN-H**	56000	**2-B**	182,162	180,150	17,471	75,375	34,449	3,182,560	.0581	2,059,355	**606**	272,220	**578**	88,222	**494**	255,528	66,152	1,653,589	**905**	Independent City
Norfolk **NORF-**	57000	**2-AA**	244,163	234,403	13,604	90,292	30,190	3,321,570	.0650	2,221,985	**654**	352,759	**749**	114,908	**644**	275,793	85,136	2,789,712	**1,527**	Independent City

.... Data less than 1,000.
(d) Data not available.
◇ Not classified as a Principal Business Center.

* Data from 1997 Census of Manufactures.

Principal Business Centers and Other Places with 27,500 or More: Population / Income / Sales, *Continued*

PLACE NAME	RANALLY METRO AREA	FIPS PLACE CODE	RANALLY CITY RATING	POPULATION Estimate 7/1/04	POPULATION Census 4/1/00	PER CAPITA INCOME 2003	HOUSE-HOLDS Estimate 7/1/04	MEDIAN HOUSEHOLD INCOME 2003	DISPOSABLE INCOME 2003 ($1,000)	MARKET ABILITY INDEX 2003	TOTAL RETAIL TRADE Sales 2003 ($1,000)	TOTAL RETAIL TRADE Ranally Sales Units	GENERAL MERCHANDISE Sales 2003 ($1,000)	GENERAL MERCHANDISE Ranally Sales Units	APPAREL STORES Sales 2003 ($1,000)	APPAREL STORES Ranally Sales Units	FOOD STORE SALES 2003 ($1,000)	HEALTH & DRUG STORE SALES 2003 ($1,000)	MANUFACTURERS VALUE ADDED 1997* ($1,000)	MANUFACTURERS Ranally Mfg Units	PLACE TYPE
Oakton	**WASH**	58472	◇	30,529	29,348	42,198	12,015	85,817	1,288,269	.0158	292,000	**86**	8,206	**17**	16,648	**93**	26,940	14,617	(d)	....	Census Designated Place
Petersburg	**RICH**	61832	**3-B**	32,931	33,740	15,266	14,812	27,700	502,720	.0098	359,200	**106**	3,170	**7**	5,696	**32**	47,644	23,740	145,376	**80**	Independent City
Portsmouth	**NORF-**	64000	**3-C**	99,349	100,565	15,424	39,297	32,019	1,532,310	.0249	553,459	**163**	21,042	**45**	10,708	**60**	145,199	94,689	143,648	**79**	Independent City
Reston	**WASH**	66672	◇	58,676	56,407	36,109	25,192	69,018	2,118,720	.0277	607,041	**179**	36,264	**77**	48,926	**274**	154,793	38,158	(d)	....	Census Designated Place
Richmond	**RICH**	67000	**2-AA**	193,828	197,790	16,416	88,280	29,642	3,181,790	.0602	2,204,942	**649**	144,939	**308**	145,084	**813**	390,643	168,439	8,229,631	**4,505**	Independent City
Roanoke	**ROAN**	68000	**2-A**	92,245	94,911	16,670	43,436	28,971	1,537,720	.0414	2,472,562	**727**	500,035	**1,061**	128,264	**719**	222,410	122,114	1,213,436	**664**	Independent City
Salem	**ROAN**	70000	**4-S**	24,544	24,747	18,733	10,408	36,033	459,790	.0106	559,985	**165**	51,732	**110**	8,178	**46**	85,715	18,275	555,145	**304**	Independent City
Springfield	**WASH**	74592	◇	31,641	30,417	24,085	11,336	60,165	762,086	.0184	1,094,810	**322**	131,706	**280**	132,806	**744**	59,312	65,519	(d)	....	Census Designated Place
Staunton		75216	**3-A**	23,850	23,853	16,119	10,084	31,124	384,450	.0093	489,094	**144**	145,165	**308**	13,141	**74**	71,133	25,536	(d)	....	Independent City
Suffolk	**NORF-**	76432	**4-S**	76,604	63,677	17,281	28,431	38,227	1,323,800	.0218	576,665	**170**	96,924	**206**	4,524	**25**	88,432	20,950	539,571	**295**	Independent City
Tuckahoe	**RICH**	79560	◇	45,118	43,242	33,359	20,311	52,567	1,505,091	.0222	690,777	**203**	214,360	**455**	119,506	**670**	108,641	58,225	(d)	....	Census Designated Place
Virginia Beach	**NORF-**	82000	**2-B**	443,729	425,257	20,360	168,045	44,057	9,034,270	.1485	4,554,427	**1,340**	658,328	**1,397**	284,570	**1,595**	698,331	198,624	380,394	**208**	Independent City
Waynesboro		83680	**4-B**	20,650	19,520	16,533	8,959	30,845	341,410	.0067	262,079	**77**	32,087	**68**	9,722	**54**	61,387	18,759	452,490	**248**	Independent City
West Springfield	**WASH**	84976	◇	29,521	28,378	29,044	11,114	68,276	857,415	.0107	141,510	**42**	3,592	**8**	2,893	**16**	59,560	8,256	(d)	....	Census Designated Place
Williamsburg	**NN-H**	86160	**4-S**	11,476	11,998	13,196	3,474	35,976	151,440	.0066	509,838	**150**	6,617	**14**	75,856	**425**	80,163	20,369	....	....	Independent City
Winchester		86720	**3-A**	24,691	23,585	17,369	10,778	32,630	428,850	.0136	931,597	**274**	268,523	**570**	38,993	**219**	116,988	48,236	791,080	**433**	Independent City
Woodbridge	**WASH**	87312	◇	38,575	31,941	19,540	13,104	45,472	753,761	.0155	717,873	**211**	20,917	**44**	12,101	**68**	69,621	6,166	(d)	....	Census Designated Place

Washington

PLACE NAME	RANALLY METRO AREA	FIPS PLACE CODE	RANALLY CITY RATING	POPULATION Estimate 7/1/04	POPULATION Census 4/1/00	PER CAPITA INCOME 2003	HOUSE-HOLDS Estimate 7/1/04	MEDIAN HOUSEHOLD INCOME 2003	DISPOSABLE INCOME 2003 ($1,000)	MARKET ABILITY INDEX 2003	TOTAL RETAIL TRADE Sales 2003 ($1,000)	TOTAL RETAIL TRADE Ranally Sales Units	GENERAL MERCHANDISE Sales 2003 ($1,000)	GENERAL MERCHANDISE Ranally Sales Units	APPAREL STORES Sales 2003 ($1,000)	APPAREL STORES Ranally Sales Units	FOOD STORE SALES 2003 ($1,000)	HEALTH & DRUG STORE SALES 2003 ($1,000)	MANUFACTURERS VALUE ADDED 1997* ($1,000)	MANUFACTURERS Ranally Mfg Units	PLACE TYPE
Aberdeen		00100	**4-A**	16,938	16,461	15,827	6,513	31,158	268,075	.0060	286,673	**84**	72,644	**154**	4,808	**27**	71,750	18,063	(d)	....	Incorporated Place
Auburn	**SEAT**	03180	**4-S**	42,485	40,314	18,134	17,541	38,535	770,419	.0183	991,166	**292**	127,518	**271**	28,749	**161**	186,778	16,036	1,205,661	**660**	Incorporated Place
Bellevue	**SEAT**	05210	**3-SS**	111,917	109,569	32,389	48,335	56,661	3,624,880	.0618	2,588,523	**761**	344,942	**732**	318,503	**1,785**	226,368	103,343	281,164	**154**	Incorporated Place
Bellingham	**BELNG**	05280	**3-A**	74,157	67,171	18,490	31,752	33,199	1,371,127	.0270	1,139,769	**335**	240,320	**510**	45,229	**253**	219,068	53,602	235,158	**129**	Incorporated Place
Bothell	**SEAT**	07380	◇	30,133	30,150	24,106	12,294	54,848	726,378	.0125	471,206	**139**	....	....	18,477	**104**	147,313	31,222	383,068	**210**	Incorporated Place
Bremerton	**BREM**	07695	**3-A**	36,373	37,259	17,020	14,796	33,719	619,086	.0113	395,969	**116**	73,304	**156**	2,488	**14**	36,128	24,178	(d)	....	Incorporated Place
Burien	**SEAT**	08850	◇	33,796	31,881	22,331	14,657	41,010	754,708	.0119	342,677	**101**	23,274	**49**	8,670	**49**	73,189	24,375	(d)	....	Incorporated Place
Centralia		11160	**3-B**	15,405	14,742	17,285	6,238	30,860	266,282	.0049	172,799	**51**	....	....	17,134	**96**	32,639	17,004	(d)	....	Incorporated Place
Des Moines	**SEAT**	17635	◇	29,950	29,267	20,480	11,982	41,692	613,365	.0090	188,466	**55**	13,312	**28**	3,031	**17**	32,423	6,361	(d)	....	Incorporated Place
Edmonds	**SEAT**	20750	◇	38,817	39,515	30,193	16,676	50,679	1,171,985	.0151	263,476	**78**	11,443	**24**	15,499	**87**	77,420	11,994	(d)	....	Incorporated Place
Everett	**SEAT**	22640	**3-CC**	98,677	91,488	20,880	39,365	40,511	2,060,357	.0405	1,809,714	**532**	225,531	**479**	32,005	**179**	214,278	44,551	....	....	Incorporated Place
Federal Way	**SEAT**	23515	◇	86,831	83,259	20,628	33,822	45,781	1,791,151	.0306	1,045,546	**308**	323,331	**686**	56,577	**317**	161,057	26,543	46,205	**25**	Incorporated Place
Kennewick	**RICH-**	35275	**3-A**	63,501	54,693	18,231	24,077	38,277	1,157,697	.0244	1,140,607	**336**	333,745	**708**	53,105	**298**	209,608	43,496	....	....	Incorporated Place
Kent	**SEAT**	35415	**4-S**	83,088	79,524	19,869	33,633	43,378	1,650,905	.0309	1,248,460	**367**	280,777	**596**	21,308	**119**	149,459	63,344	2,503,653	**1,371**	Incorporated Place
Kirkland	**SEAT**	35940	**4-S**	43,596	45,054	33,972	20,737	58,210	1,481,039	.0239	918,316	**270**	128,883	**274**	24,428	**137**	171,532	32,560	194,142	**106**	Incorporated Place
Lacey	**OLYM**	36745	◇	34,293	31,226	20,711	13,830	42,542	710,234	.0125	454,671	**134**	174,568	**371**	4,758	**27**	82,834	16,199	(d)	....	Incorporated Place
Lakewood	**SEAT**	38038	◇	60,497	58,211	19,511	24,880	34,825	1,180,345	.0212	773,872	**228**	169,636	**360**	33,747	**189**	143,241	43,263	33,679	**18**	Incorporated Place
Longview	**LNGV**	40245	**3-A**	35,452	34,660	18,844	14,428	35,683	668,063	.0127	508,873	**150**	110,284	**234**	2,654	**15**	92,551	15,508	336,920	**184**	Incorporated Place
Lynnwood	**SEAT**	40840	**3-Sm**	34,159	33,847	21,232	13,520	44,397	725,274	.0163	877,950	**258**	224,547	**477**	114,079	**639**	82,966	31,472	75,004	**41**	Incorporated Place
Marysville	**SEAT**	43955	◇	29,420	25,315	20,269	10,995	46,076	596,319	.0091	214,600	**63**	76,091	**162**	11,080	**62**	33,427	10,031	91,262	**50**	Incorporated Place
Mount Vernon		47560	**4-C**	29,106	26,232	17,559	10,225	39,052	511,075	.0097	377,349	**111**	52,295	**111**	3,530	**20**	65,499	16,863	32,585	**18**	Incorporated Place
North Creek	**SEAT**	49665	◇	27,589	25,742	25,555	9,905	57,429	705,029	.0091	128,762	**38**	5,610	**12**	2,984	**17**	36,280	11,277	(d)	....	Census Designated Place
Olympia	**OLYM**	51300	**3-A**	47,693	42,514	23,986	21,185	41,506	1,143,979	.0208	873,733	**257**	171,112	**363**	36,372	**204**	127,388	24,006	155,664	**85**	Incorporated Place
Pasco	**RICH-**	53545	**3-B**	42,631	32,066	13,187	12,415	37,210	562,154	.0116	436,108	**128**	44,052	**94**	2,730	**15**	26,544	15,044	....	....	Incorporated Place
Port Angeles		55365	**4-A**	18,261	18,397	19,036	8,200	34,229	347,616	.0062	215,414	**63**	56,293	**119**	6,079	**34**	36,000	8,665	108,889	**60**	Incorporated Place
Puyallup	**SEAT**	56695	**4-S**	37,482	33,011	20,990	14,692	44,328	786,731	.0158	731,231	**215**	131,717	**280**	12,893	**72**	62,392	9,531	223,122	**122**	Incorporated Place
Redmond	**SEAT**	57535	**4-S**	44,835	45,256	30,475	19,527	60,784	1,366,363	.0230	916,628	**270**	142,719	**303**	80,260	**450**	129,872	64,170	1,297,879	**711**	Incorporated Place
Renton	**SEAT**	57745	**3-S**	53,069	50,052	24,081	23,816	46,339	1,277,931	.0285	1,568,261	**461**	287,278	**610**	15,249	**85**	148,853	37,641	....	....	Incorporated Place
Richland	**RICH-**	58235	**3-B**	43,091	38,708	23,699	17,257	48,312	1,021,200	.0158	453,373	**133**	89,581	**190**	5,322	**30**	130,870	29,596	138,617	**76**	Incorporated Place
Sammamish	**SEAT**	61115	◇	34,759	34,104	35,717	11,725	82,964	1,241,482	.0131	2,221	**1**	....	....	....	....	1,079	....	(d)	....	Incorporated Place
Seattle	**SEAT**	63000	**1-A**	570,290	563,374	25,367	270,027	41,950	14,466,518	.2469	9,398,646	**2,765**	569,844	**1,210**	723,813	**4,056**	1,329,356	429,387	2,722,952	**1,491**	Incorporated Place
Shoreline	**SEAT**	63960	◇	53,762	53,025	21,836	21,677	45,804	1,173,930	.0194	629,791	**185**	145,995	**310**	12,515	**70**	118,796	26,456	(d)	....	Incorporated Place
South Hill	**SEAT**	65922	◇	33,990	31,623	19,893	11,802	50,180	676,155	.0110	319,206	**94**	103,059	**219**	17,690	**99**	46,150	11,272	(d)	....	Census Designated Place
Spokane	**SPOK**	67000	**2-AA**	203,039	195,629	17,043	84,727	32,431	3,460,459	.0663	2,556,401	**752**	483,886	**1,027**	163,731	**918**	389,638	127,500	447,426	**245**	Incorporated Place
Tacoma	**SEAT**	70000	**2-B**	215,039	193,556	18,017	84,956	35,999	3,874,260	.0739	2,919,458	**859**	574,706	**1,220**	151,733	**850**	369,636	110,864	1,037,083	**568**	Incorporated Place
Tukwila	**SEAT**	72625	**4-Sm**	17,548	17,181	19,247	7,578	38,256	337,745	.0113	809,231	**238**	215,100	**457**	100,125	**561**	60,629	16,623	200,283	**110**	Incorporated Place
University Place	**SEAT**	73465	◇	34,287	29,933	23,462	13,987	44,158	804,442	.0106	149,209	**44**	17,490	**37**	3,080	**17**	24,094	21,463	(d)	....	Incorporated Place
Vancouver	**POR**	74060	**3-SS**	179,932	143,560	20,004	70,652	40,130	3,599,323	.0560	1,428,853	**420**	342,996	**728**	36,298	**203**	277,215	116,875	1,316,796	**721**	Incorporated Place
Walla Walla	**WALL**	75775	**3-A**	31,150	29,686	15,125	11,103	33,369	471,157	.0091	330,393	**97**	61,912	**131**	12,168	**68**	66,153	14,215	95,598	**52**	Incorporated Place
Wenatchee		77105	**3-A**	29,763	27,856	16,925	11,222	34,563	503,730	.0114	567,930	**167**	116,637	**248**	9,586	**54**	74,197	20,329	42,191	**23**	Incorporated Place
Yakima	**YAK**	80010	**3-AA**	72,812	71,845	14,322	26,249	30,783	1,042,846	.0225	970,929	**286**	228,043	**484**	31,409	**176**	121,641	31,197	320,084	**175**	Incorporated Place

West Virginia

PLACE NAME	RANALLY METRO AREA	FIPS PLACE CODE	RANALLY CITY RATING	POPULATION Estimate 7/1/04	POPULATION Census 4/1/00	PER CAPITA INCOME 2003	HOUSE-HOLDS Estimate 7/1/04	MEDIAN HOUSEHOLD INCOME 2003	DISPOSABLE INCOME 2003 ($1,000)	MARKET ABILITY INDEX 2003	TOTAL RETAIL TRADE Sales 2003 ($1,000)	TOTAL RETAIL TRADE Ranally Sales Units	GENERAL MERCHANDISE Sales 2003 ($1,000)	GENERAL MERCHANDISE Ranally Sales Units	APPAREL STORES Sales 2003 ($1,000)	APPAREL STORES Ranally Sales Units	FOOD STORE SALES 2003 ($1,000)	HEALTH & DRUG STORE SALES 2003 ($1,000)	MANUFACTURERS VALUE ADDED 1997* ($1,000)	MANUFACTURERS Ranally Mfg Units	PLACE TYPE
Barboursville	**HNTG**	04276	**4-Sm**	2,867	3,183	18,933	1,304	34,355	54,280	.0030	262,054	**77**	59,835	**127**	33,320	**187**	15,845	50,366	(d)	....	Incorporated Place
Beckley	**BECK**	05332	**3-A**	16,386	17,254	16,489	7,523	27,190	270,196	.0066	358,706	**106**	102,143	**217**	8,854	**50**	23,147	22,292	(d)	....	Incorporated Place
Bluefield		08524	**3-A**	10,595	11,451	15,437	4,825	25,442	163,553	.0040	216,373	**64**	68,255	**145**	13,617	**76**	20,275	19,670	(d)	....	Incorporated Place
Charleston	**CHAS**	14600	**2-A**	50,321	53,421	22,969	23,682	34,018	1,155,805	.0206	812,493	**239**	161,169	**342**	27,139	**152**	91,146	80,157	113,803	**62**	Incorporated Place
Clarksburg	**CLRKB**	15628	**3-A**	16,448	16,743	15,923	7,457	25,711	261,907	.0061	311,248	**92**	72,891	**155**	3,752	**21**	52,465	21,149	(d)	....	Incorporated Place
Elkins		24580	**4-B**	6,903	7,032	16,080	2,988	27,148	111,001	.0026	127,996	**38**	37,144	**79**	3,502	**20**	17,711	7,628	(d)	....	Incorporated Place
Fairmont	**FAIRM**	26452	**3-A**	18,641	19,097	16,787	8,423	28,097	312,927	.0058	203,570	**60**	50,083	**106**	3,514	**20**	28,981	11,361	129,865	**71**	Incorporated Place
Huntington	**HNTG**	39460	**2-A**	47,926	51,475	16,403	22,674	24,846	786,143	.0155	613,399	**180**	85,191	**181**	18,108	**101**	68,337	59,590	569,709	**312**	Incorporated Place
Logan		48148	**4-A**	1,469	1,630	15,387	708	23,473	22,603	.0006	32,056	**9**	8,562	**18**	1,026	**6**	1,535	1,718	(d)	....	Incorporated Place
Martinsburg		52060	**4-B**	14,695	14,972	21,748	6,666	34,481	319,586	.0057	220,366	**65**	42,013	**89**	22,540	**126**	32,065	15,634	212,791	**116**	Incorporated Place
Morgantown	**MORG**	55756	**3-A**	26,737	26,809	13,333	10,910	22,226	356,496	.0088	440,462	**130**	105,726	**224**	33,390	**187**	55,224	35,416	....	....	Incorporated Place
Parkersburg	**PRKB**	62140	**3-AA**	32,818	33,099	16,752	14,969	27,462	549,754	.0126	632,711	**186**	108,151	**230**	26,627	**149**	65,194	41,067	67,949	**37**	Incorporated Place
Vienna	**PRKB**	83500	**4-Sm**	10,364	10,861	22,191	4,706	36,049	229,990	.0057	344,662	**101**	191,597	**407**	16,710	**94**	11,591	13,029	(d)	....	Incorporated Place
Weirton	**STU-**	85156	**4-B**	19,653	20,411	19,521	8,879	32,996	383,645	.0065	204,785	**60**	61,168	**130**	11,718	**66**	42,870	12,293	760,589	**416**	Incorporated Place
Wheeling	**WHL**	86452	**3-AA**	28,920	31,419	19,102	14,258	29,278	552,422	.0095	317,137	**93**	14,805	**31**	5,226	**29**	48,240	22,588	....	....	Incorporated Place
Williamson		87508	**4-A**	3,202	3,414	14,543	1,555	21,727	46,567	.0012	69,880	**21**	1,066	**2**	1,491	**8**	16,120	6,093	(d)	....	Incorporated Place

Wisconsin

PLACE NAME	RANALLY METRO AREA	FIPS PLACE CODE	RANALLY CITY RATING	POPULATION Estimate 7/1/04	POPULATION Census 4/1/00	PER CAPITA INCOME 2003	HOUSE-HOLDS Estimate 7/1/04	MEDIAN HOUSEHOLD INCOME 2003	DISPOSABLE INCOME 2003 ($1,000)	MARKET ABILITY INDEX 2003	TOTAL RETAIL TRADE Sales 2003 ($1,000)	TOTAL RETAIL TRADE Ranally Sales Units	GENERAL MERCHANDISE Sales 2003 ($1,000)	GENERAL MERCHANDISE Ranally Sales Units	APPAREL STORES Sales 2003 ($1,000)	APPAREL STORES Ranally Sales Units	FOOD STORE SALES 2003 ($1,000)	HEALTH & DRUG STORE SALES 2003 ($1,000)	MANUFACTURERS VALUE ADDED 1997* ($1,000)	MANUFACTURERS Ranally Mfg Units	PLACE TYPE
Antigo		02250	**4-C**	8,336	8,560	16,747	3,613	31,605	139,602	.0034	182,466	**54**	31,336	**67**	2,386	**13**	30,769	....	73,861	**40**	Incorporated Place
Appleton	**APP**	02375	**3-AA**	73,388	70,087	21,796	29,483	43,564	1,599,536	.0309	1,371,730	**404**	215,199	**457**	71,824	**403**	135,195	52,340	949,942	**520**	Incorporated Place
Beaver Dam		05900	**4-C**	15,334	15,169	20,623	6,586	38,598	316,231	.0066	320,294	**94**	100,062	**212**	9,807	**55**	22,259	5,743	108,005	**59**	Incorporated Place
Beloit	**RKFD**	06500	**3-B**	35,609	35,775	17,632	13,811	36,849	627,871	.0111	369,643	**109**	78,060	**166**	2,429	**14**	42,797	19,112	666,913	**365**	Incorporated Place
Brookfield	**MILW**	10025	**3-Sm**	39,798	38,649	33,481	14,990	64,411	1,332,470	.0261	1,345,644	**396**	228,918	**486**	126,640	**710**	222,624	55,228	244,100	**134**	Incorporated Place
Eau Claire	**EAUC**	22300	**3-AA**	61,963	61,704	18,054	25,621	36,678	1,118,689	.0261	1,386,930	**408**	334,893	**711**	73,639	**413**	129,245	58,353	369,935	**203**	Incorporated Place
Fond du Lac	**FDLC**	26275	**3-A**	42,352	42,203	19,989	17,346	39,884	846,574	.0144	478,076	**141**	144,044	**306**	16,823	**94**	88,793	21,441	888,756	**487**	Incorporated Place
Franklin	**MILW**	27300	◇	30,131	29,494	22,307	11,485	57,075	672,132	.0103	278,932	**82**	77,916	**165**	....	....	51,590	5,499	179,206	**98**	Incorporated Place
Glendale	**MILW**	29400	**4-S**	12,799	13,367	26,178	5,850	42,311	335,048	.0069	355,620	**105**	50,208	**107**	17,721	**99**	66,112	43,186	302,716	**166**	Incorporated Place
Green Bay	**GRBY**	31000	**2-A**	102,880	102,313	19,098	43,630	38,073	1,964,802	.0423	2,074,578	**610**	492,851	**1,046**	52,182	**292**	227,698	63,409	1,768,420	**968**	Incorporated Place
Greendale	**MILW**	31125	**4-Sm**	13,776	14,405	24,844	6,086	48,688	342,248	.0069	340,383	**100**	183,505	**390**	50,288	**282**	15,051	24,921	40,895	**22**	Incorporated Place
Greenfield	**MILW**	31175	**4-S**	34,753	35,476	20,795	16,308	40,923	722,699	.0143	649,697	**191**	79,597	**169**	12,183	**68**	68,188	45,999	(d)	....	Incorporated Place
Janesville	**JNSV**	37825	**3-A**	60,903	59,498	21,690	25,431	42,958	1,321,000	.0249	1,057,492	**311**	196,961	**418**	23,986	**134**	130,576	54,807	3,016,117	**1,651**	Incorporated Place
Kenosha	**KEN**	39225	**3-S**	92,833	90,352	18,814	36,035	39,716	1,746,583	.0296	924,151	**272**	151,820	**322**	70,418	**395**	133,823	62,006	533,449	**292**	Incorporated Place
La Crosse	**LACRO**	40775	**3-AA**	51,544	51,818	17,934	21,793	32,155	924,399	.0190	852,720	**251**	141,136	**300**	25,439	**143**	81,905	26,444	367,439	**201**	Incorporated Place
Madison	**MAD**	48000	**2-AA**	220,718	208,054	21,552	97,403	39,203	4,756,904	.0907	3,913,723	**1,151**	706,548	**1,500**	208,417	**1,168**	527,923	206,699	1,344,489	**736**	Incorporated Place
Manitowoc	**MNTW**	48500	**3-A**	34,210	34,053	19,797	14,614	37,237	677,239	.0116	390,850	**115**	113,938	**242**	6,886	**39**	55,560	13,747	819,379	**449**	Incorporated Place
Marinette		49300	**3-A**	11,235	11,749	18,638	5,009	33,520	209,402	.0042	182,570	**54**	65,699	**139**	9,507	**53**	24,139	7,441	332,748	**182**	Incorporated Place
Marshfield		49675	**3-B**	17,968	18,800	22,715	8,213	37,997	408,136	.0093	519,234	**153**	105,851	**225**	4,098	**23**	30,414	6,086	199,746	**109**	Incorporated Place
Menomonee Falls	**MILW**	51000	**4-S**	34,655	32,647	24,523	14,297	50,950	849,842	.0164	754,861	**222**	170,093	**361**	11,466	**64**	80,477	59,557	745,816	**408**	Incorporated Place
Milwaukee	**MILW**	53000	**1-A**	595,260	596,974	15,457	245,501	31,423	9,201,031	.1575	4,241,760	**1,248**	421,073	**894**	157,649	**884**	708,425	438,582	4,168,514	**2,282**	Incorporated Place
Neenah	**APP**	55750	**4-S**	23,814	24,507	24,743	10,293	45,258	589,234	.0095	311,111	**92**	37,341	**79**	4,153	**23**	39,253	24,479	966,968	**529**	Incorporated Place
New Berlin	**MILW**	56375	◇	40,457	38,220	27,160	16,053	59,130	1,098,801	.0153	349,315	**103**	33,438	**71**	3,830	**21**	66,435	8,779	732,623	**401**	Incorporated Place
Oak Creek	**MILW**	58800	◇	27,947	28,456	20,658	11,709	48,016	577,339	.0097	321,326	**95**	48,800	**104**	3,435	**19**	69,416	10,298	1,105,457	**605**	Incorporated Place
Oshkosh	**OSH**	60500	**3-B**	64,307	62,916	18,037	26,513	37,035	1,159,898	.0252	1,218,166	**358**	163,932	**348**	48,381	**271**	129,740	67,994	718,814	**394**	Incorporated Place
Racine	**MILW**	66000	**3-CC**	81,139	81,855	19,546	32,266	39,300	1,585,970	.0246	608,088	**179**	99,914	**212**	18,638	**104**	108,289	48,346	1,118,610	**612**	Incorporated Place
Rhinelander		67200	**4-B**	7,432	7,735	17,007	3,152	34,119	126,397	.0032	180,746	**53**	29,699	**63**	6,886	**39**	16,465	2,649	151,695	**83**	Incorporated Place
Sheboygan	**SHEB**	72975	**3-A**	50,156	50,792	20,006	21,502	38,650	1,003,440	.0180	671,097	**197**	175,513	**373**	11,903	**67**	94,060	38,311	664,045	**364**	Incorporated Place
Stevens Point		77200	**3-A**	24,800	24,551	18,196	9,868	37,200	451,272	.0087	351,086	**103**	94,861	**201**	12,578	**70**	42,540	3,204	192,516	**105**	Incorporated Place
Superior	**DUL**	78650	**4-C**	27,642	27,368	16,770	11,932	31,320	463,548	.0091	362,731	**107**	64,595	**137**	5,332	**30**	62,919	12,386	....	....	Incorporated Place
Watertown		83975	**4-C**	23,220	21,598	18,252	8,855	40,810	423,800	.0073	233,367	**69**	66,800	**142**	3,361	**19**	40,665	7,355	240,119	**131**	Incorporated Place
Waukesha	**MILW**	84250	**3-S**	68,185	64,825	23,250	28,240	48,095	1,585,316	.0286	1,166,965	**343**	222,172	**472**	17,606	**99**	129,933	48,803	1,361,225	**745**	Incorporated Place
Wausau	**WAUS**	84475	**3-A**	38,504	38,426	21,071	16,227	39,037	811,335	.0165	775,633	**228**	190,313	**404**	22,705	**127**	63,306	21,785	564,657	**309**	Incorporated Place
Wauwatosa	**MILW**	84675	**3-S**	46,995	47,271	23,892	21,480	45,815	1,122,782	.0206	867,135	**255**	161,276	**342**	67,520	**378**	65,593	74,807	877,711	**481**	Incorporated Place
West Allis	**MILW**	85300	**3-S**	60,462	61,254	19,016	28,885	36,555	1,149,749	.0222	920,008	**271**	96,670	**205**	12,612	**71**	81,795	50,805	422,228	**231**	Incorporated Place
West Bend		85350	**4-C**	28,910	28,152	24,659	12,052	47,270	712,887	.0129	539,333	**159**	77,691	**165**	6,605	**37**	57,320	18,108	327,249	**179**	Incorporated Place
Wisconsin Rapids		88200	**3-B**	18,087	18,435	20,366	8,160	38,607	368,353	.0064	219,485	**65**	45,635	**97**	5,858	**33**	37,744	3,324	395,393	**216**	Incorporated Place

Wyoming

PLACE NAME	RANALLY METRO AREA	FIPS PLACE CODE	RANALLY CITY RATING	POPULATION Estimate 7/1/04	POPULATION Census 4/1/00	PER CAPITA INCOME 2003	HOUSE-HOLDS Estimate 7/1/04	MEDIAN HOUSEHOLD INCOME 2003	DISPOSABLE INCOME 2003 ($1,000)	MARKET ABILITY INDEX 2003	TOTAL RETAIL TRADE Sales 2003 ($1,000)	TOTAL RETAIL TRADE Ranally Sales Units	GENERAL MERCHANDISE Sales 2003 ($1,000)	GENERAL MERCHANDISE Ranally Sales Units	APPAREL STORES Sales 2003 ($1,000)	APPAREL STORES Ranally Sales Units	FOOD STORE SALES 2003 ($1,000)	HEALTH & DRUG STORE SALES 2003 ($1,000)	MANUFACTURERS VALUE ADDED 1997* ($1,000)	MANUFACTURERS Ranally Mfg Units	PLACE TYPE
Casper	**CASP**	13150	**3-A**	50,641	49,644	17,959	21,159	34,771	909,444	.0176	716,255	**211**	188,408	**400**	20,841	**117**	85,720	15,614	(d)	....	Incorporated Place
Cheyenne	**CHEY**	13900	**3-A**	54,416	53,011	19,495	23,451	37,304	1,060,865	.0196	758,714	**223**	136,263	**289**	16,104	**90**	106,426	20,047	....	....	Incorporated Place
Gillette		31855	**4-B**	20,713	19,646	20,890	8,019	43,253	432,696	.0072	233,402	**69**	49,653	**105**	5,156	**29**	33,133	2,219	(d)	....	Incorporated Place
Laramie		45050	**4-C**	26,994	27,204	14,528	11,853	27,296	392,174	.0085	370,566	**109**	93,094	**198**	5,533	**31**	41,429	4,017	(d)	....	Incorporated Place
Riverton		66220	**4-A**	9,503	9,310	15,364	4,003	30,268	146,001	.0032	141,017	**41**	30,977	**66**	1,879	**11**	18,765	2,483	(d)	....	Incorporated Place
Rock Springs		67235	**4-A**	18,739	18,708	20,190	7,606	40,577	378,335	.0074	321,828	**95**	61,657	**131**	9,819	**55**	41,680	3,702	(d)	....	Incorporated Place
Sheridan		69845	**4-C**	16,195	15,804	18,387	7,354	32,241	297,784	.0058	238,916	**70**	44,074	**94**	4,832	**27**	28,026	3,061	(d)	....	Incorporated Place

.... Data less than 1,000.
(d) Data not available.
◇ Not classified as a Principal Business Center.

* Data from 1997 Census of Manufactures.

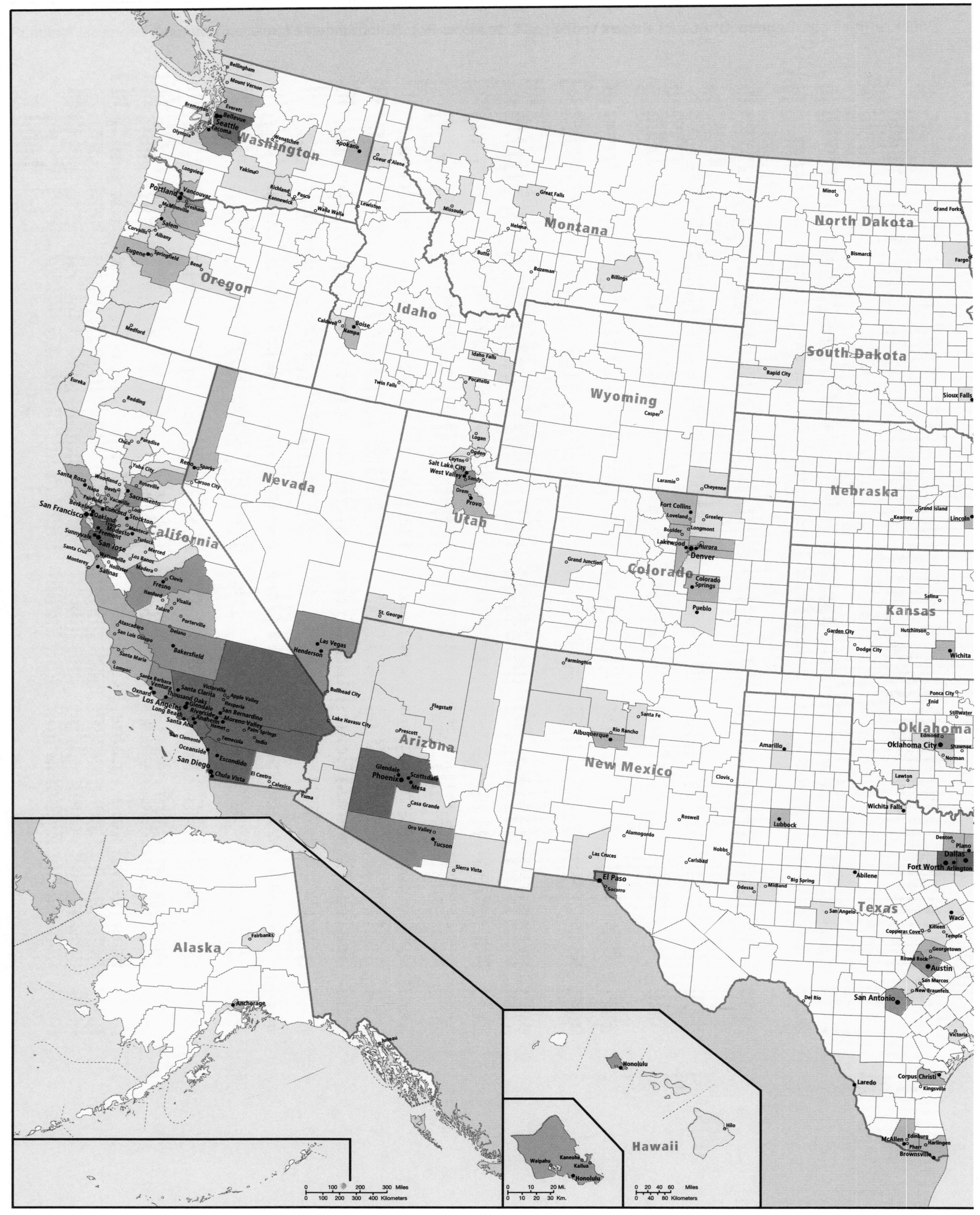

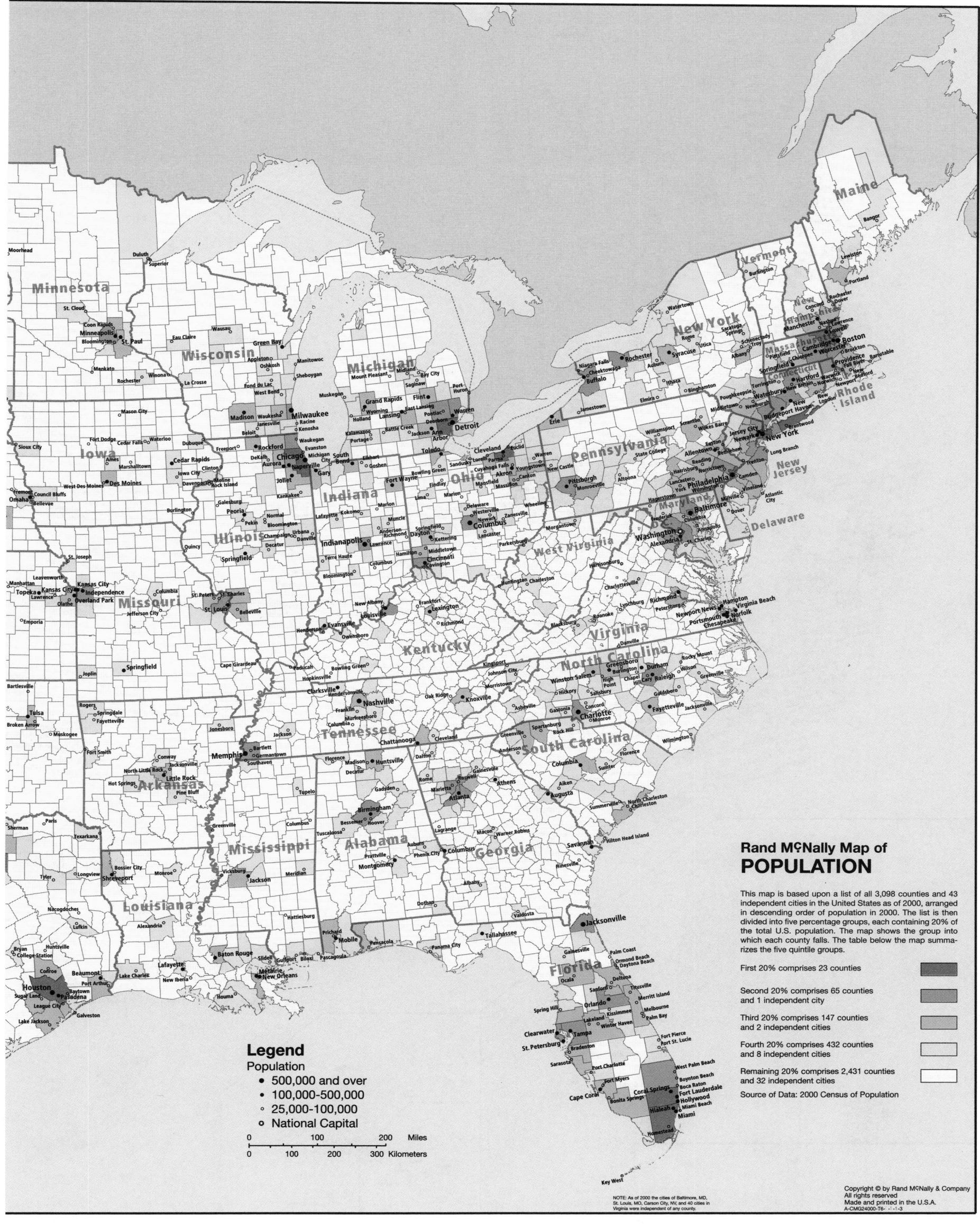

Rand McNally Map of
POPULATION

This map is based upon a list of all 3,098 counties and 43 independent cities in the United States as of 2000, arranged in descending order of population in 2000. The list is then divided into five percentage groups, each containing 20% of the total U.S. population. The map shows the group into which each county falls. The table below the map summarizes the five quintile groups.

First 20% comprises 23 counties

Second 20% comprises 65 counties and 1 independent city

Third 20% comprises 147 counties and 2 independent cities

Fourth 20% comprises 432 counties and 8 independent cities

Remaining 20% comprises 2,431 counties and 32 independent cities

Source of Data: 2000 Census of Population

Legend
Population
- 500,000 and over
- 100,000-500,000
- ○ 25,000-100,000
- ◉ National Capital

```
0        100        200   Miles
0    100    200    300 Kilometers
```

NOTE: As of 2000 the cities of Baltimore, MD, St. Louis, MO, Carson City, NV, and 40 cities in Virginia were independent of any county.

QUINTILE GROUPING OF COUNTIES AND INDEPENDENT CITIES ACCORDING TO TOTAL POPULATION, 2000

Group	Range in population of counties and independent cities in each group — Largest	Smallest	Total population of each group	Population of each group plus all preceding groups	% of total U.S. population contained in each group	% of total U.S. population contained in each group plus all preceding groups	Number of counties & indep. cities in each group	% of the total number of counties & indep. cities in each group	Numbers of counties & indep. cities in each group plus all preceding groups	% of the total number of counties & indep. cities in each group plus all preceding groups
1	9,519,338 to	1,393,978	56,777,962	56,777,962	20.1	20.1	23	0.7	23	0.7
2	1,392,931 to	607,751	56,207,218	112,985,180	20.0	40.1	66	2.1	89	2.8
3	606,024 to	241,767	55,968,411	168,953,591	19.9	60.0	149	4.8	238	7.6
4	240,391 to	73,825	56,234,029	225,187,620	20.0	80.0	440	14.0	678	21.6
5	73,814 to	67	56,234,286	281,421,906	20.0	100.0	2,463	78.4	3,141	100.0

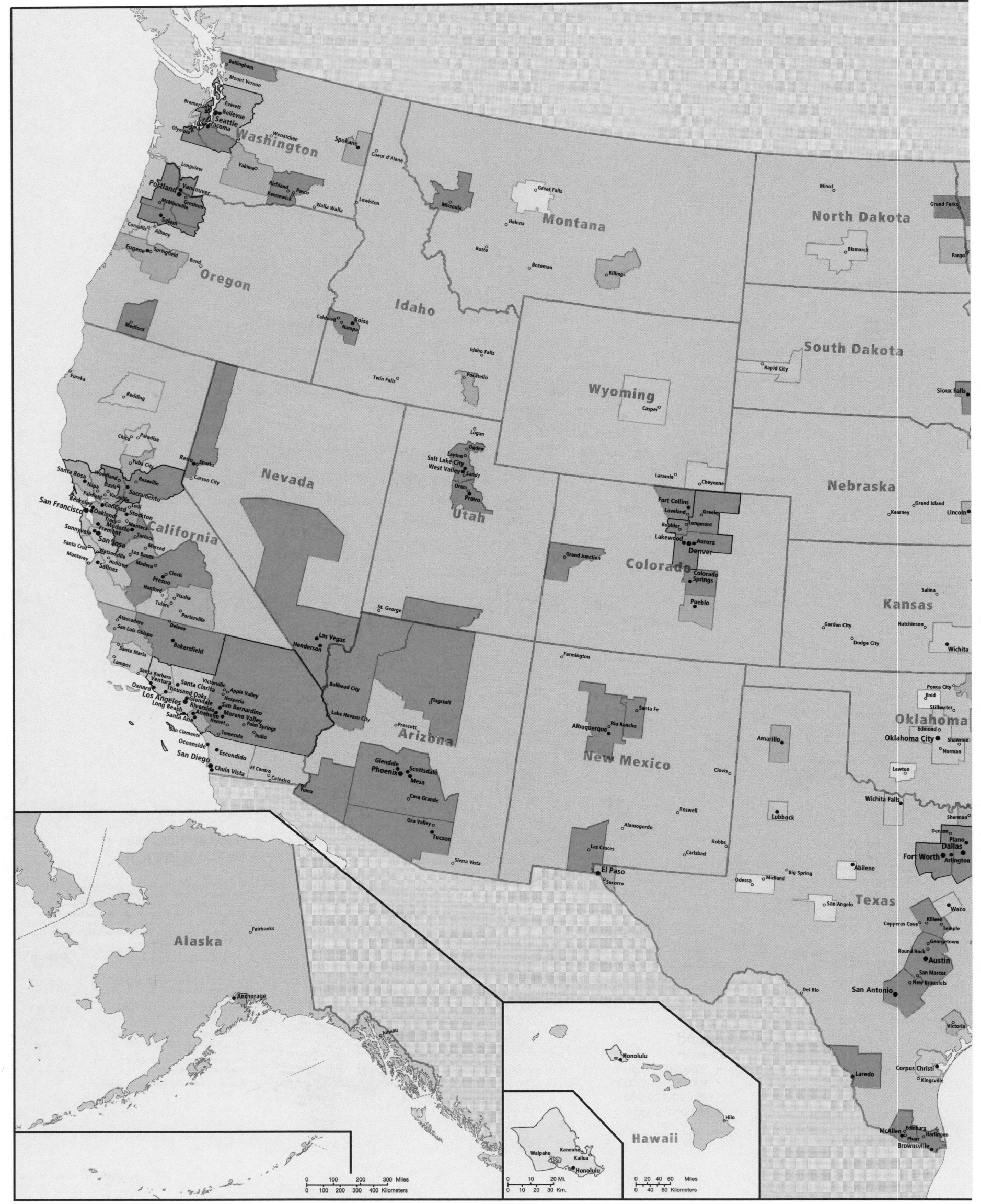

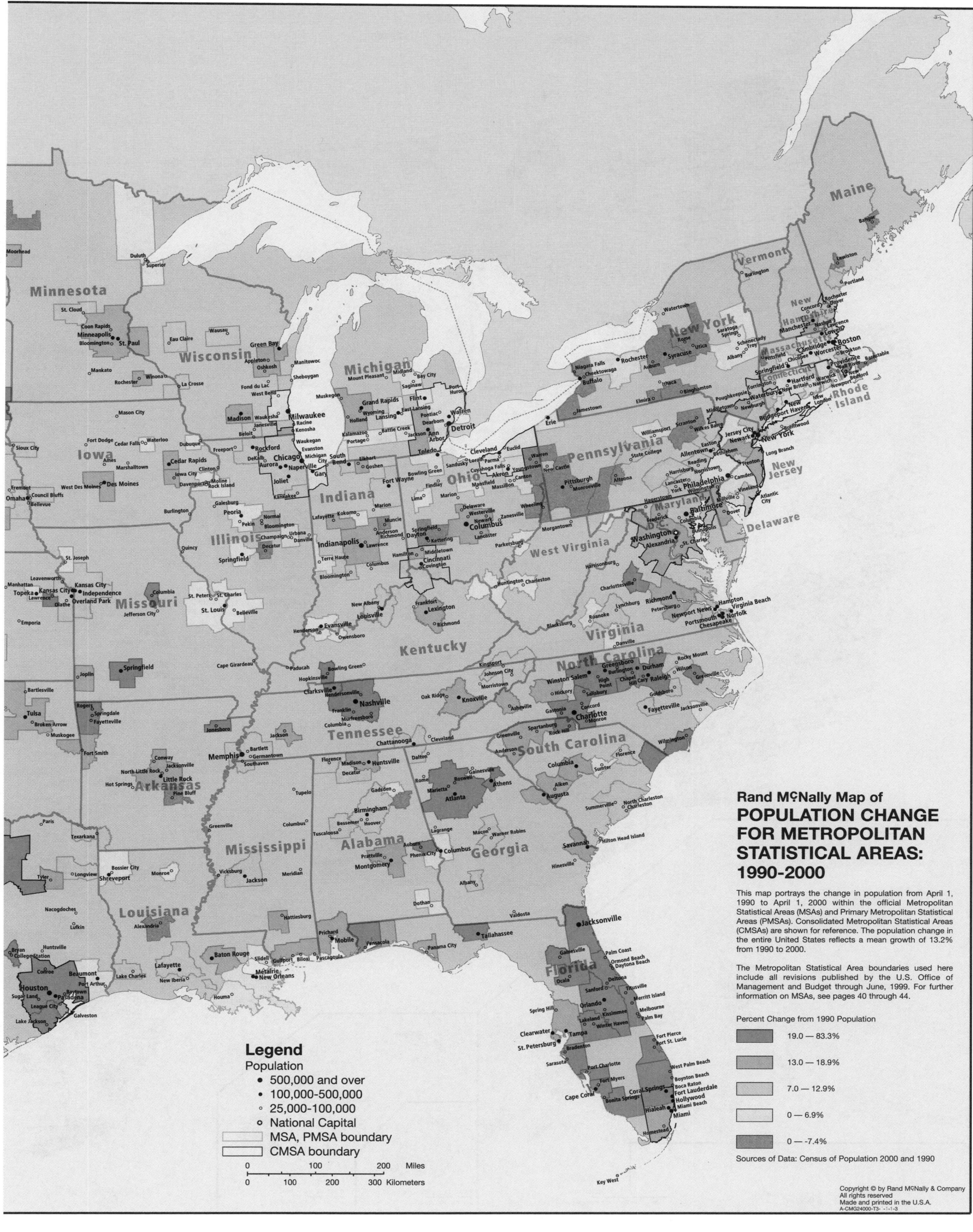

Rand McNally Map of
POPULATION CHANGE FOR METROPOLITAN STATISTICAL AREAS: 1990-2000

This map portrays the change in population from April 1, 1990 to April 1, 2000 within the official Metropolitan Statistical Areas (MSAs) and Primary Metropolitan Statistical Areas (PMSAs). Consolidated Metropolitan Statistical Areas (CMSAs) are shown for reference. The population change in the entire United States reflects a mean growth of 13.2% from 1990 to 2000.

The Metropolitan Statistical Area boundaries used here include all revisions published by the U.S. Office of Management and Budget through June, 1999. For further information on MSAs, see pages 40 through 44.

Percent Change from 1990 Population

19.0 — 83.3%

13.0 — 18.9%

7.0 — 12.9%

0 — 6.9%

0 — -7.4%

Sources of Data: Census of Population 2000 and 1990

Legend
Population
- 500,000 and over
- 100,000-500,000
- 25,000-100,000
- National Capital
- MSA, PMSA boundary
- CMSA boundary

0   100   200 Miles
0   100   200   300 Kilometers

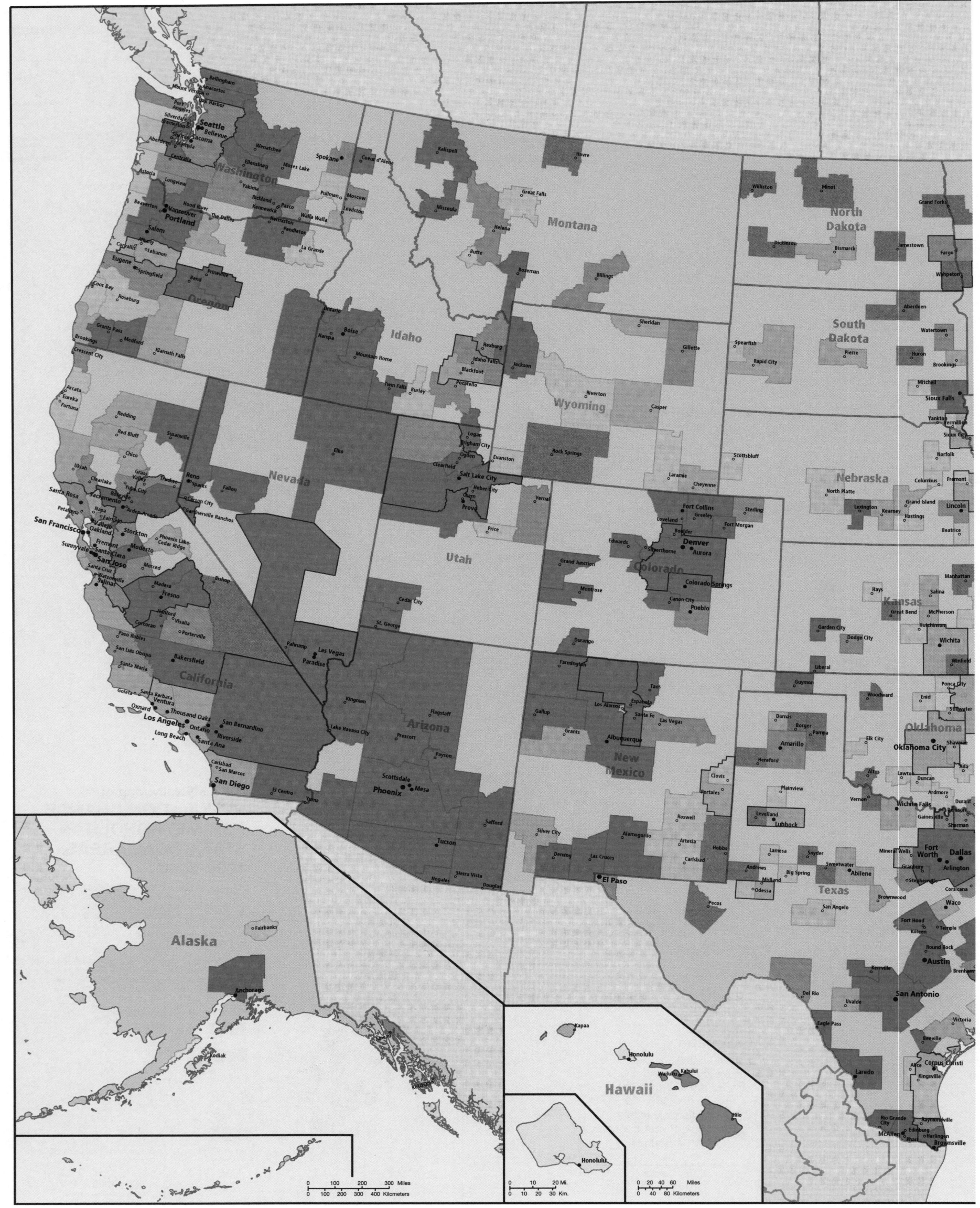

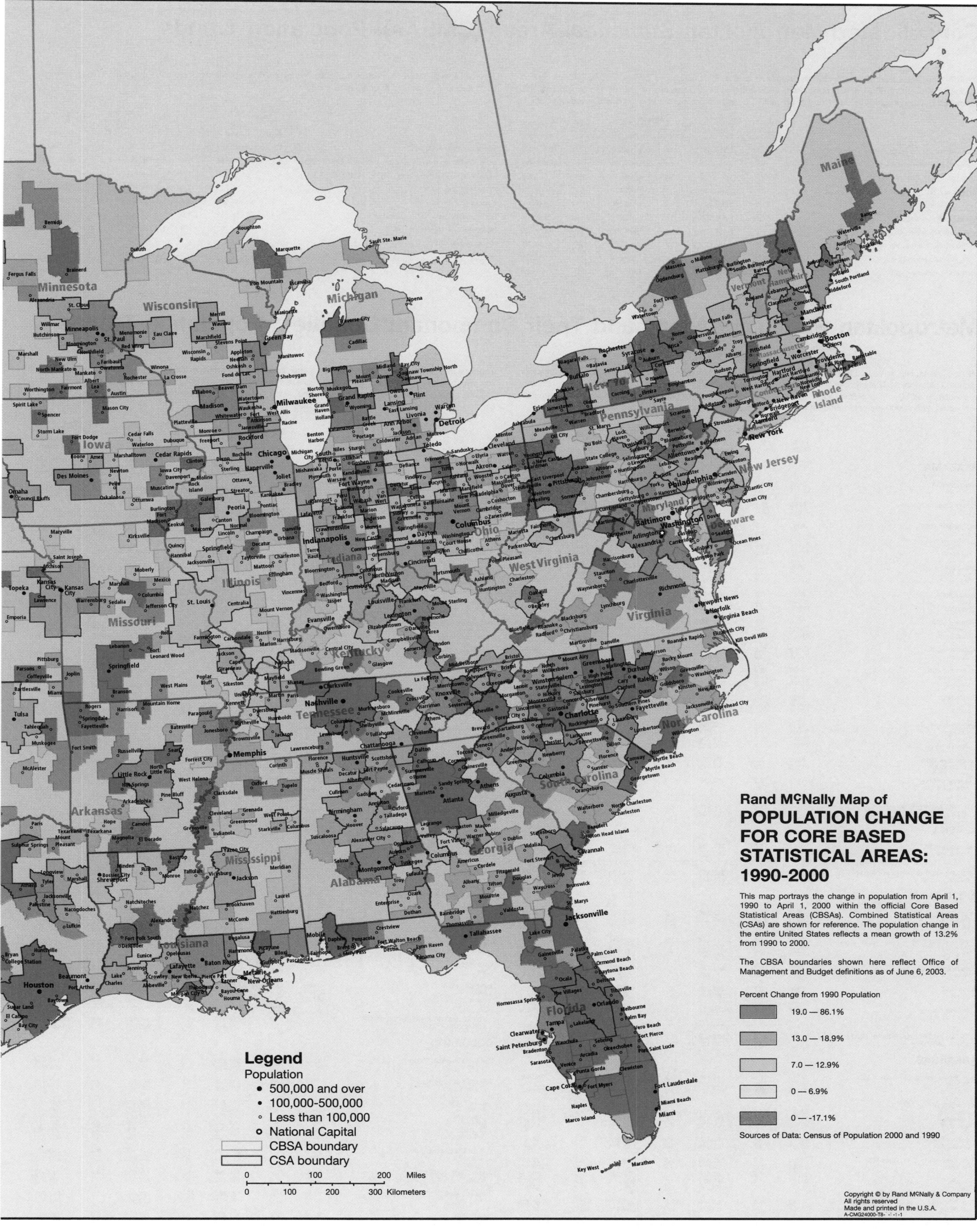

Rand McNally Map of
**POPULATION CHANGE
FOR CORE BASED
STATISTICAL AREAS:
1990-2000**

This map portrays the change in population from April 1, 1990 to April 1, 2000 within the official Core Based Statistical Areas (CBSAs). Combined Statistical Areas (CSAs) are shown for reference. The population change in the entire United States reflects a mean growth of 13.2% from 1990 to 2000.

The CBSA boundaries shown here reflect Office of Management and Budget definitions as of June 6, 2003.

Percent Change from 1990 Population

19.0 — 86.1%

13.0 — 18.9%

7.0 — 12.9%

0 — 6.9%

0 — -17.1%

Sources of Data: Census of Population 2000 and 1990

Legend
Population
- ● 500,000 and over
- ● 100,000-500,000
- ○ Less than 100,000
- ◉ National Capital
- CBSA boundary
- CSA boundary

0   100   200   Miles

0   100   200   300 Kilometers

Consolidated Metropolitan Statistical Areas (CMSAs): Population Trends

The following data are presented for Consolidated Metropolitan Statistical Areas (CMSAs): 1990-2000 percent of change in population; 2000 **actual** population; 2000-2004 estimated percent of change in population; 2004 **estimated** population; 2004-2009 projected percent of change in population; and 2009 **projected** population.

The data reflect CMSAs as defined and published by the Office of Management and Budget (OMB) on December 31, 1992, and as revised through June 30, 1999.

	PAST		PRESENT		FUTURE	
	1990-2000 % Change	2000 Census	2000-2004 % Change	7/1/04 Estimate	2004-2009 % Change	2009 Projection
Boston-Worcester-Lawrence, MA-NH-ME-CT	6.7	5,819,100	2.4	5,958,412	1.9	6,070,300
Chicago-Gary-Kenosha, IL-IN-WI	11.1	9,157,540	3.4	9,465,508	3.8	9,824,261
Cincinnati-Hamilton, OH-KY-IN	8.9	1,979,202	2.4	2,026,864	2.7	2,081,274
Cleveland-Akron, OH	3.0	2,945,831	-0.1	2,943,497	-0.1	2,939,931
Dallas-Fort Worth, TX	29.3	5,221,801	10.8	5,783,868	11.4	6,442,376
Denver-Boulder-Greeley, CO	30.4	2,581,506	6.2	2,740,678	8.3	2,967,224
Detroit-Ann Arbor-Flint, MI	5.2	5,456,428	1.4	5,533,161	1.5	5,618,602
Houston-Galveston-Brazoria, TX	25.2	4,669,571	10.0	5,137,262	10.7	5,689,389
Los Angeles-Riverside-Orange County, CA	12.7	16,373,645	7.1	17,537,912	7.8	18,912,925
Miami-Fort Lauderdale, FL	21.4	3,876,380	6.6	4,132,456	7.3	4,432,174
Milwaukee-Racine, WI	5.1	1,689,572	1.3	1,711,775	1.5	1,737,692
New York-Northern NJ-Long Island, NY-NJ-CT-PA	8.4	21,199,865	2.5	21,728,432	2.7	22,325,597
Philadelphia-Wilmington-Atlantic City, PA-NJ-DE-MD	5.0	6,188,463	2.1	6,318,462	2.5	6,473,706
Portland-Salem, OR-WA	26.3	2,265,223	7.4	2,432,568	8.1	2,630,541
Sacramento-Yolo, CA	21.3	1,796,857	13.0	2,030,311	13.7	2,307,706
San Francisco-Oakland-San Jose, CA	12.6	7,039,362	1.0	7,110,637	0.9	7,175,037
Seattle-Tacoma-Bremerton, WA	19.7	3,554,760	4.6	3,719,512	5.2	3,912,921
Washington-Baltimore, DC-MD-VA-WV	13.1	7,608,070	6.5	8,100,870	7.1	8,677,739
TOTAL: CMSA PORTION OF COUNTRY	**12.5**	**109,423,176**	**4.6**	**114,412,185**	**5.1**	**120,219,395**

Metropolitan Statistical Areas and Their Component Counties: Population Trends

MSAs, PMSAs, NECMAs, and their component counties are listed by state. The following data are presented for each: the Metropolitan Statistical Area FIPS Code and State-County FIPS Code(s); 1990-2000 percent of change in population; 2000 **actual** population; 2000-2004 estimated percent of change in population; 2004 **estimated** population; 2004-2009 projected percent of change in population; and 2009 **projected** population.

The total metropolitan population within the state (**Total: Metro Portion of State**) and the total state population are also given. Data shown in **bold face** represent in-state metropolitan area totals. The data reflect MSAs, PMSAs, and NECMAs as defined and published by the Office of Management and Budget (OMB) on December 31, 1992, and as revised through June 30, 1999.

		PAST		PRESENT		FUTURE	
	FIPS CODE	1990-2000 % Change	2000 Census	2000-2004 % Change	7/1/04 Estimate	2004-2009 % Change	2009 Projection
ALABAMA							
Anniston MSA	**0450**	**-3.3**	**112,249**	**-0.0**	**112,234**	**1.0**	**113,328**
Calhoun	01015	-3.3	112,249	-0.0	112,234	1.0	113,328
Auburn-Opelika MSA	**0580**	**32.1**	**115,092**	**5.1**	**120,927**	**5.6**	**127,735**
Lee	01081	32.1	115,092	5.1	120,927	5.6	127,735
Birmingham MSA	**1000**	**9.6**	**921,106**	**2.7**	**946,208**	**3.1**	**975,243**
Blount	01009	30.0	51,024	8.0	55,111	8.8	59,975
Jefferson	01073	1.6	662,047	-0.8	656,840	-1.0	650,292
St. Clair	01115	29.5	64,742	7.9	69,841	8.4	75,736
Shelby	01117	44.2	143,293	14.7	164,416	15.1	189,240
Decatur MSA	**2030**	**10.9**	**145,867**	**1.2**	**147,582**	**1.3**	**149,459**
Lawrence	01079	10.4	34,803	-0.9	34,504	-1.3	34,058
Morgan	01103	11.0	111,064	1.8	113,078	2.1	115,401
Dothan MSA	**2180**	**5.3**	**137,916**	**2.7**	**141,592**	**3.1**	**145,995**
Dale	01045	-1.0	49,129	0.5	49,358	0.6	49,650
Houston	01069	9.2	88,787	3.9	92,234	4.5	96,345
Florence MSA	**2650**	**8.9**	**142,950**	**-1.4**	**141,000**	**-1.8**	**138,513**
Colbert	01033	6.4	54,984	-1.1	54,367	-1.5	53,547
Lauderdale	01077	10.4	87,966	-1.5	86,633	-1.9	84,966
Gadsden MSA	**2880**	**3.6**	**103,459**	**-0.5**	**102,945**	**-0.4**	**102,482**
Etowah	01055	3.6	103,459	-0.5	102,945	-0.4	102,482
Huntsville MSA	**3440**	**16.8**	**342,376**	**5.9**	**362,704**	**6.6**	**386,635**
Limestone	01083	21.3	65,676	5.1	69,013	5.5	72,841
Madison	01089	15.8	276,700	6.1	293,691	6.8	313,794
Mobile MSA	**5160**	**13.3**	**540,258**	**2.7**	**554,939**	**3.0**	**571,665**
Baldwin	01003	42.9	140,415	10.6	155,304	11.2	172,642
Mobile	01097	5.6	399,843	-0.1	399,635	-0.2	399,023
Montgomery MSA	**5240**	**13.9**	**333,055**	**2.4**	**341,047**	**2.8**	**350,440**
Autauga	01001	27.6	43,671	8.4	47,354	9.1	51,660
Elmore	01051	33.9	65,874	9.6	72,168	10.2	79,543
Montgomery	01101	6.9	223,510	-0.9	221,525	-1.0	219,237
Tuscaloosa MSA	**8600**	**9.5**	**164,875**	**1.2**	**166,903**	**1.4**	**169,166**
Tuscaloosa	01125	9.5	164,875	1.2	166,903	1.4	169,166
* **Russell County** (See Columbus, GA-AL MSA.)	**01113**	**6.2**	**49,756**	**-2.0**	**48,750**	**-2.4**	**47,582**
TOTAL: METRO PORTION OF STATE		**11.2**	**3,108,959**	**2.5**	**3,186,831**	**2.9**	**3,278,243**
TOTAL: ALABAMA		10.1	4,447,100	1.6	4,517,136	1.8	4,599,054
ALASKA							
Anchorage MSA	**0380**	**15.0**	**260,283**	**5.4**	**274,398**	**6.2**	**291,471**
Anchorage	02020	15.0	260,283	5.4	274,398	6.2	291,471
TOTAL: METRO PORTION OF STATE		**15.0**	**260,283**	**5.4**	**274,398**	**6.2**	**291,471**
TOTAL: ALASKA		14.0	626,932	4.6	655,899	5.4	691,302
ARIZONA							
Flagstaff, AZ-UT MSA	2620	20.2	122,366	5.3	128,880	6.0	136,576
Coconino	**04005**	**20.4**	**116,320**	**5.6**	**122,854**	**6.3**	**130,614**
Kane, UT	49025	17.0	6,046	-0.3	6,026	-1.1	5,962
Phoenix-Mesa MSA	**6200**	**45.3**	**3,251,876**	**13.7**	**3,698,598**	**14.2**	**4,224,395**
Maricopa	04013	44.8	3,072,149	13.5	3,486,879	14.0	3,974,832
Pinal	04021	54.4	179,727	17.8	211,719	17.9	249,563
Tucson MSA	**8520**	**26.5**	**843,746**	**7.6**	**907,511**	**8.1**	**981,041**
Pima	04019	26.5	843,746	7.6	907,511	8.1	981,041
Yuma MSA	**9360**	**49.7**	**160,026**	**9.1**	**174,609**	**9.9**	**191,975**
Yuma	04027	49.7	160,026	9.1	174,609	9.9	191,975
* **Mohave County** (See Las Vegas, NV-AZ MSA.)	**04015**	**65.8**	**155,032**	**13.8**	**176,406**	**14.3**	**201,594**
TOTAL: METRO PORTION OF STATE		**41.4**	**4,527,000**	**12.2**	**5,079,978**	**12.8**	**5,729,619**
TOTAL: ARIZONA		40.0	5,130,632	11.5	5,719,160	12.1	6,410,903
ARKANSAS							
Fayetteville-Springdale-Rogers MSA	**2580**	**47.5**	**311,121**	**12.8**	**351,068**	**13.3**	**397,810**
Benton	05007	57.3	153,406	15.9	177,727	16.1	206,263
Washington	05143	39.1	157,715	9.9	173,341	10.5	191,547
Fort Smith, AR-OK MSA	2720	17.8	207,290	3.5	214,506	3.8	222,569
Crawford	**05033**	**25.3**	**53,247**	**5.9**	**56,398**	**6.6**	**60,126**
Sebastian	**05131**	**15.5**	**115,071**	**2.4**	**117,824**	**2.4**	**120,635**
Sequoyah, OK	40135	15.2	38,972	3.4	40,284	3.8	41,808
Jonesboro MSA	**3700**	**19.1**	**82,148**	**3.9**	**85,334**	**4.1**	**88,843**
Craighead	05031	19.1	82,148	3.9	85,334	4.1	88,843
Little Rock-North Little Rock MSA	**4400**	**13.8**	**583,845**	**3.8**	**606,101**	**4.3**	**631,866**
Faulkner	05045	43.3	86,014	9.2	93,944	10.0	103,323
Lonoke	05085	34.5	52,828	9.6	57,901	10.2	63,789
Pulaski	05119	3.4	361,474	1.1	365,501	1.2	370,029
Saline	05125	30.1	83,529	6.3	88,755	6.7	94,725
Pine Bluff MSA	**6240**	**-1.4**	**84,278**	**-2.2**	**82,445**	**-2.7**	**80,235**
Jefferson	05069	-1.4	84,278	-2.2	82,445	-2.7	80,235
* **Crittenden County** (See Memphis, TN-AR-MS MSA.)	**05035**	**1.9**	**50,866**	**0.7**	**51,207**	**0.5**	**51,447**
* **Miller County** (See Texarkana, TX-AR MSA.)	**05091**	**5.1**	**40,443**	**4.8**	**42,371**	**5.6**	**44,746**
TOTAL: METRO PORTION OF STATE		**19.1**	**1,321,019**	**5.4**	**1,392,748**	**6.0**	**1,475,708**
TOTAL: ARKANSAS		13.7	2,673,400	2.5	2,741,511	2.9	2,820,498
CALIFORNIA							
Bakersfield MSA	**0680**	**21.7**	**661,645**	**10.3**	**729,553**	**11.3**	**811,845**
Kern	06029	21.7	661,645	10.3	729,553	11.3	811,845
Chico-Paradise MSA	**1620**	**11.6**	**203,171**	**5.0**	**213,422**	**5.6**	**225,471**
Butte	06007	11.6	203,171	5.0	213,422	5.6	225,471
Fresno MSA	**2840**	**22.1**	**922,516**	**8.7**	**1,003,162**	**9.7**	**1,099,980**
Fresno	06019	19.8	799,407	8.4	866,423	9.3	946,868
Madera	06039	39.8	123,109	11.1	136,739	12.0	153,112
Los Angeles-Long Beach PMSA	**4480**	**7.4**	**9,519,338**	**4.8**	**9,980,271**	**5.4**	**10,523,607**
Los Angeles	06037	7.4	9,519,338	4.8	9,980,271	5.4	10,523,607
Merced MSA	**4940**	**18.0**	**210,554**	**13.1**	**238,219**	**13.9**	**271,433**
Merced	06047	18.0	210,554	13.1	238,219	13.9	271,433
Modesto MSA	**5170**	**20.6**	**446,997**	**13.3**	**506,378**	**14.0**	**577,071**
Stanislaus	06099	20.6	446,997	13.3	506,378	14.0	577,071
Oakland PMSA	**5775**	**14.9**	**2,392,557**	**3.7**	**2,481,548**	**3.9**	**2,578,342**
Alameda	06001	12.9	1,443,741	1.4	1,464,561	1.2	1,482,152
Contra Costa	06013	18.1	948,816	7.2	1,016,987	7.8	1,096,190
Orange County PMSA	**5945**	**18.1**	**2,846,289**	**5.1**	**2,991,519**	**5.6**	**3,160,141**
Orange	06059	18.1	2,846,289	5.1	2,991,519	5.6	3,160,141
Redding MSA	**6690**	**11.0**	**163,256**	**10.0**	**179,590**	**11.0**	**199,281**
Shasta	06089	11.0	163,256	10.0	179,590	11.0	199,281
Riverside-San Bernardino PMSA	**6780**	**25.7**	**3,254,821**	**15.6**	**3,763,495**	**16.1**	**4,369,109**
Riverside	06065	32.0	1,545,387	20.2	1,856,913	20.0	2,228,111
San Bernardino	06071	20.5	1,709,434	11.5	1,906,582	12.3	2,140,998
Sacramento PMSA	**6920**	**21.5**	**1,628,197**	**13.2**	**1,842,845**	**13.9**	**2,098,130**
El Dorado	06017	24.1	156,299	10.5	172,703	11.2	192,098
Placer	06061	43.8	248,399	23.1	305,883	22.3	374,106
Sacramento	06067	17.5	1,223,499	11.5	1,364,259	12.3	1,531,926
Salinas MSA	**7120**	**13.0**	**401,762**	**4.1**	**418,251**	**4.5**	**437,244**
Monterey	06053	13.0	401,762	4.1	418,251	4.5	437,244
San Diego MSA	**7320**	**12.6**	**2,813,833**	**5.4**	**2,966,135**	**5.9**	**3,142,238**
San Diego	06073	12.6	2,813,833	5.4	2,966,135	5.9	3,142,238
San Francisco PMSA	**7360**	**8.0**	**1,731,183**	**-2.8**	**1,682,970**	**-3.5**	**1,623,296**
Marin	06041	7.5	247,289	-0.7	245,560	-1.0	243,006
San Francisco	06075	7.3	776,733	-4.3	743,549	-5.3	704,156
San Mateo	06081	8.9	707,161	-1.9	693,861	-2.6	676,134
San Jose PMSA	**7400**	**12.4**	**1,682,585**	**-0.4**	**1,675,734**	**-0.8**	**1,662,290**
Santa Clara	06085	12.4	1,682,585	-0.4	1,675,734	-0.8	1,662,290
San Luis Obispo-Atascadero-Paso Robles MSA	**7460**	**13.6**	**246,681**	**3.3**	**254,929**	**3.5**	**263,976**
San Luis Obispo	06079	13.6	246,681	3.3	254,929	3.5	263,976
Santa Barbara-Santa Maria-Lompoc MSA	**7480**	**8.0**	**399,347**	**1.2**	**404,260**	**1.4**	**409,876**
Santa Barbara	06083	8.0	399,347	1.2	404,260	1.4	409,876
Santa Cruz-Watsonville PMSA	**7485**	**11.3**	**255,602**	**-2.1**	**250,198**	**-2.7**	**243,374**
Santa Cruz	06087	11.3	255,602	-2.1	250,198	-2.7	243,374
Santa Rosa PMSA	**7500**	**18.1**	**458,614**	**2.2**	**468,851**	**2.3**	**479,459**
Sonoma	06097	18.1	458,614	2.2	468,851	2.3	479,459
Stockton-Lodi MSA	**8120**	**17.3**	**563,598**	**16.1**	**654,288**	**16.4**	**761,890**
San Joaquin	06077	17.3	563,598	16.1	654,288	16.4	761,890
Vallejo-Fairfield-Napa PMSA	**8720**	**15.0**	**518,821**	**6.3**	**551,336**	**6.7**	**588,276**
Napa	06055	12.2	124,279	7.8	133,946	8.7	145,637
Solano	06095	15.9	394,542	5.8	417,390	6.0	442,639
Ventura PMSA	**8735**	**12.6**	**753,197**	**6.6**	**802,627**	**7.2**	**860,068**
Ventura	06111	12.6	753,197	6.6	802,627	7.2	860,068
Visalia-Tulare-Porterville MSA	**8780**	**18.0**	**368,021**	**8.2**	**398,103**	**9.2**	**434,646**
Tulare	06107	18.0	368,021	8.2	398,103	9.2	434,646
Yolo PMSA	**9270**	**19.5**	**168,660**	**11.2**	**187,466**	**11.8**	**209,576**
Yolo	06113	19.5	168,660	11.2	187,466	11.8	209,576
Yuba City MSA	**9340**	**13.5**	**139,149**	**8.5**	**151,010**	**9.5**	**165,375**
Sutter	06101	22.5	78,930	9.7	86,547	10.7	95,765
Yuba	06115	3.4	60,219	7.0	64,463	8.0	69,610
TOTAL: METRO PORTION OF STATE		**13.7**	**32,750,394**	**6.2**	**34,796,160**	**6.9**	**37,195,994**
TOTAL: CALIFORNIA		13.8	33,871,648	6.2	35,979,311	6.9	38,453,601
COLORADO							
Boulder-Longmont PMSA	**1125**	**29.3**	**291,288**	**-3.7**	**280,533**	**4.1**	**292,034**
Boulder	08013	29.3	291,288[1]	-3.7	280,533	4.1	292,034
Colorado Springs MSA	**1720**	**30.2**	**516,929**	**8.5**	**560,804**	**9.2**	**612,412**
El Paso	08041	30.2	516,929	8.5	560,804	9.2	612,412
Denver PMSA	**2080**	**30.0**	**2,109,282**	**6.2**	**2,239,478**	**7.5**	**2,407,561**
Adams	08001	37.3	363,857[1]	7.2	389,997	12.5	438,602
Arapahoe	08005	24.6	487,967	7.4	524,236	7.8	565,097
Denver	08031	18.6	554,636	0.6	558,164	0.6	561,577
Douglas	08035	191.0	175,766	35.3	237,826	30.2	309,585
Jefferson	08059	20.2	527,056[1]	0.4	529,255	0.7	532,700
Fort Collins-Loveland MSA	**2670**	**35.1**	**251,494**	**7.8**	**271,165**	**8.4**	**293,935**
Larimer	08069	35.1	251,494	7.8	271,165	8.4	293,935
Grand Junction MSA	**2995**	**24.8**	**116,255**	**9.3**	**127,075**	**9.4**	**139,069**
Mesa	08077	24.8	116,255	9.3	127,075	9.4	139,069
Greeley PMSA	**3060**	**37.3**	**180,936**	**22.0**	**220,667**	**21.3**	**267,629**
Weld	08123	37.3	180,936[1]	22.0	220,667	21.3	267,629
Pueblo MSA	**6560**	**15.0**	**141,472**	**6.8**	**151,054**	**7.6**	**162,566**
Pueblo	08101	15.0	141,472	6.8	151,054	7.6	162,566
TOTAL: METRO PORTION OF STATE		**29.8**	**3,607,656**	**6.7**	**3,850,776**	**8.4**	**4,175,206**
TOTAL: COLORADO		30.6	4,301,261	7.5	4,625,293	8.1	4,998,320
CONNECTICUT							
Hartford NECMA	**3283**	**2.2**	**1,148,618**	**3.3**	**1,186,956**	**3.8**	**1,232,061**
Hartford	09003	0.6	857,183	2.2	875,839	2.5	897,751
Middlesex	09007	8.3	155,071	5.4	163,370	5.9	173,023
Tolland	09013	6.0	136,364	8.3	147,747	9.2	161,287
New Haven-Bridgeport-Stamford-Danbury-Waterbury NECMA	**5483**	**4.6**	**1,706,575**	**2.6**	**1,751,503**	**3.0**	**1,803,893**
Fairfield	09001	6.6	882,567	2.4	904,001	2.7	928,248
New Haven	09009	2.5	824,008	2.9	847,502	3.3	875,645

* Indicates county is included from metro in different state.
Source: Devonshire Associates Ltd. and Scan/US, Inc. 2004.

[1] Includes a portion of Broomfield county.

Metropolitan Statistical Areas and Their Component Counties: Population Trends, *Continued*

	FIPS CODE	PAST 1990-2000 % Change	PAST 2000 Census	PRESENT 2000-2004 % Change	PRESENT 7/1/04 Estimate	FUTURE 2004-2009 % Change	FUTURE 2009 Projection
New London-Norwich NECMA	**5523**	**1.6**	**259,088**	**2.5**	**265,499**	**2.8**	**273,047**
New London	09011	1.6	259,088	2.5	265,499	2.8	273,047
TOTAL: METRO PORTION OF STATE		**3.4**	**3,114,281**	**2.9**	**3,203,958**	**3.3**	**3,309,001**
TOTAL: CONNECTICUT		3.6	3,405,565	3.0	3,507,246	3.4	3,626,616

DELAWARE

	FIPS CODE	PAST 1990-2000 % Change	PAST 2000 Census	PRESENT 2000-2004 % Change	PRESENT 7/1/04 Estimate	FUTURE 2004-2009 % Change	FUTURE 2009 Projection
Dover MSA	**2190**	**14.1**	**126,697**	**8.0**	**136,821**	**8.9**	**148,978**
Kent	10001	14.1	126,697	8.0	136,821	8.9	148,978
Wilmington-Newark, DE-MD PMSA	9160	14.2	586,216	4.8	614,320	5.3	646,791
New Castle	**10003**	**13.2**	**500,265**	**3.8**	**519,483**	**4.2**	**541,522**
Cecil, MD	24015	20.5	85,951	10.3	94,837	11.0	105,269
TOTAL: METRO PORTION OF STATE		**13.4**	**626,962**	**4.7**	**656,304**	**5.2**	**690,500**
TOTAL: DELAWARE		17.6	783,600	5.6	827,856	6.3	879,679

DISTRICT OF COLUMBIA

	FIPS CODE	PAST 1990-2000 % Change	PAST 2000 Census	PRESENT 2000-2004 % Change	PRESENT 7/1/04 Estimate	FUTURE 2004-2009 % Change	FUTURE 2009 Projection
Washington, DC-MD-VA-WV PMSA	8840	16.6	4,923,153	8.2	5,326,575	8.8	5,796,584
District of Columbia	**11001**	**-5.7**	**572,059**	**-2.0**	**560,725**	**-2.3**	**547,617**
Calvert, MD	24009	45.1	74,563	16.8	87,081	17.0	101,916
Charles, MD	24017	19.2	120,546	13.6	136,969	14.3	156,536
Frederick, MD	24021	30.0	195,277	12.3	219,345	12.9	247,718
Montgomery, MD	24031	15.4	873,341	6.8	932,558	7.3	1,000,765
Prince George's, MD	24033	9.9	801,515	6.1	850,384	6.8	908,563
Alexandria, VA (Ind. City)	51510	15.4	128,283	0.4	128,847	-0.3	128,458
Arlington, VA	51013	10.8	189,453	-1.1	187,390	-1.3	184,980
Clarke, VA	51043	4.6	12,652	7.4	13,582	8.0	14,672
Culpeper, VA	51047	23.3	34,262	16.5	39,908	17.0	46,675
Fairfax, VA	51059	18.5	969,749	4.0	1,008,761	4.1	1,050,462
Fairfax, VA (Ind. City)	51600	9.6	21,498	3.2	22,181	3.4	22,928
Falls Church, VA (Ind. City)	51610	8.3	10,377	1.2	10,500	0.7	10,576
Fauquier, VA	51061	13.1	55,139	14.2	62,992	14.7	72,263
Fredericksburg, VA (Ind. City)	51630	1.3	19,279	6.2	20,481	7.1	21,938
King George, VA	51099	24.2	16,803	11.0	18,655	11.8	20,862
Loudoun, VA	51107	96.9	169,599	40.1	237,678	33.5	317,314
Manassas, VA (Ind. City)	51683	25.7	35,135	7.5	37,756	7.8	40,708
Manassas Park, VA (Ind. City)	51685	52.8	10,290	8.9	11,209	9.8	12,302
Prince William, VA	51153	30.2	280,813	20.8	339,149	20.4	408,242
Spotsylvania, VA	51177	57.5	90,395	25.3	113,260	23.9	140,355
Stafford, VA	51179	51.0	92,446	26.4	116,821	24.8	145,805
Warren, VA	51187	20.8	31,584	9.5	34,587	10.4	38,170
Berkeley, WV	54003	28.1	75,905	16.2	88,214	16.6	102,878
Jefferson, WV	54037	17.4	42,190	12.7	47,542	13.3	53,881
TOTAL: METRO PORTION OF DISTRICT		**-5.7**	**572,059**	**-2.0**	**560,725**	**-2.3**	**547,617**
TOTAL: DISTRICT OF COLUMBIA		-5.7	572,059	-2.0	560,725	-2.3	547,617

FLORIDA

	FIPS CODE	PAST 1990-2000 % Change	PAST 2000 Census	PRESENT 2000-2004 % Change	PRESENT 7/1/04 Estimate	FUTURE 2004-2009 % Change	FUTURE 2009 Projection
Daytona Beach MSA	**2020**	**23.5**	**493,175**	**10.0**	**542,645**	**10.9**	**601,522**
Flagler	12035	73.6	49,832	32.6	66,083	29.3	85,466
Volusia	12127	19.6	443,343	7.5	476,562	8.3	516,056
Fort Lauderdale PMSA	**2680**	**29.3**	**1,623,018**	**8.7**	**1,764,315**	**9.3**	**1,929,159**
Broward	12011	29.3	1,623,018	8.7	1,764,315	9.3	1,929,159
Fort Myers-Cape Coral MSA	**2700**	**31.6**	**440,888**	**15.3**	**508,350**	**15.9**	**589,051**
Lee	12071	31.6	440,888	15.3	508,350	15.9	589,051
Fort Pierce-Port St. Lucie MSA	**2710**	**27.2**	**319,426**	**12.0**	**357,906**	**13.0**	**404,587**
Martin	12085	25.6	126,731	8.7	137,796	9.7	151,164
St. Lucie	12111	28.3	192,695	14.2	220,110	15.1	253,423
Fort Walton Beach MSA	**2750**	**18.6**	**170,498**	**5.9**	**180,485**	**6.6**	**192,392**
Okaloosa	12091	18.6	170,498	5.9	180,485	6.6	192,392
Gainesville MSA	**2900**	**20.0**	**217,955**	**3.4**	**225,339**	**3.9**	**234,144**
Alachua	12001	20.0	217,955	3.4	225,339	3.9	234,144
Jacksonville MSA	**3600**	**21.4**	**1,100,491**	**9.5**	**1,204,735**	**10.5**	**1,331,027**
Clay	12019	32.9	140,814	15.6	162,779	16.2	189,164
Duval	12031	15.7	778,879	6.6	830,101	7.6	893,203
Nassau	12089	31.2	57,663	9.0	62,849	9.7	68,969
St. Johns	12109	46.9	123,135	21.0	149,006	20.6	179,691
Lakeland-Winter Haven MSA	**3980**	**19.4**	**483,924**	**7.2**	**518,809**	**8.0**	**560,565**
Polk	12105	19.4	483,924	7.2	518,809	8.0	560,565
Melbourne-Titusville-Palm Bay MSA	**4900**	**19.4**	**476,230**	**8.1**	**515,004**	**9.0**	**561,468**
Brevard	12009	19.4	476,230	8.1	515,004	9.0	561,468
Miami PMSA	**5000**	**16.3**	**2,253,362**	**5.1**	**2,368,141**	**5.7**	**2,503,015**
Miami-Dade	12086	16.3	2,253,362	5.1	2,368,141	5.7	2,503,015
Naples MSA	**5345**	**65.3**	**251,377**	**18.3**	**297,488**	**18.2**	**351,759**
Collier	12021	65.3	251,377	18.3	297,488	18.2	351,759
Ocala MSA	**5790**	**32.9**	**258,916**	**10.8**	**286,954**	**11.6**	**320,284**
Marion	12083	32.9	258,916	10.8	286,954	11.6	320,284
Orlando MSA	**5960**	**34.3**	**1,644,561**	**12.6**	**1,851,873**	**13.2**	**2,096,306**
Lake	12069	38.4	210,528	22.0	256,893	21.4	311,975
Orange	12095	32.3	896,344	10.0	985,714	10.6	1,089,958
Osceola	12097	60.1	172,493	25.5	216,437	24.4	269,272
Seminole	12117	27.0	365,196	7.6	392,829	8.2	425,101
Panama City MSA	**6015**	**16.7**	**148,217**	**6.3**	**157,510**	**7.4**	**169,093**
Bay	12005	16.7	148,217	6.3	157,510	7.4	169,093
Pensacola MSA	**6080**	**19.7**	**412,153**	**5.4**	**434,387**	**6.2**	**461,432**
Escambia	12033	12.0	294,410	0.7	296,422	0.9	299,104
Santa Rosa	12113	44.3	117,743	17.2	137,965	17.7	162,328
Punta Gorda MSA	**6580**	**27.6**	**141,627**	**10.9**	**157,100**	**11.8**	**175,640**
Charlotte	12015	27.6	141,627	10.9	157,100	11.8	175,640
Sarasota-Bradenton MSA	**7510**	**20.5**	**589,959**	**9.7**	**647,224**	**10.5**	**715,358**
Manatee	12081	24.7	264,002	11.3	293,837	12.0	329,004
Sarasota	12115	17.3	325,957	8.4	353,387	9.3	386,354
Tallahassee MSA	**8240**	**21.8**	**284,539**	**1.4**	**288,589**	**1.5**	**292,977**
Gadsden	12039	9.7	45,087	0.2	45,161	0.3	45,296
Leon	12073	24.4	239,452	1.7	243,428	1.7	247,681
Tampa-St. Petersburg-Clearwater MSA	**8280**	**15.9**	**2,395,997**	**7.4**	**2,574,498**	**8.3**	**2,787,447**
Hernando	12053	29.4	130,802	12.7	147,435	13.5	167,363
Hillsborough	12057	19.8	998,948	9.8	1,096,848	10.7	1,214,056
Pasco	12101	22.6	344,765	16.8	402,756	17.2	472,007
Pinellas	12103	8.2	921,482	0.6	927,459	0.7	934,021
West Palm Beach-Boca Raton MSA	**8960**	**31.0**	**1,131,184**	**9.9**	**1,243,157**	**10.8**	**1,377,535**
Palm Beach	12099	31.0	1,131,184	9.9	1,243,157	10.8	1,377,535
TOTAL: METRO PORTION OF STATE		**23.4**	**14,837,497**	**8.7**	**16,124,509**	**9.5**	**17,654,761**
TOTAL: FLORIDA		23.5	15,982,378	8.5	17,342,822	9.3	18,961,590

GEORGIA

	FIPS CODE	PAST 1990-2000 % Change	PAST 2000 Census	PRESENT 2000-2004 % Change	PRESENT 7/1/04 Estimate	FUTURE 2004-2009 % Change	FUTURE 2009 Projection
Albany MSA	**0120**	**7.3**	**120,822**	**3.6**	**125,195**	**4.4**	**130,699**
Dougherty	13095	-0.3	96,065	-0.5	95,611	-0.4	95,249
Lee	13177	52.4	24,757	19.5	29,584	19.8	35,450
Athens MSA	**0500**	**21.5**	**153,444**	**4.6**	**160,455**	**5.0**	**168,461**
Clarke	13059	15.9	101,489	2.8	104,327	3.0	107,507
Madison	13195	22.2	25,730	6.8	27,481	7.4	29,507
Oconee	13219	48.9	26,225	9.2	28,647	9.8	31,447
Atlanta MSA	**0520**	**38.9**	**4,112,198**	**11.1**	**4,570,501**	**11.6**	**5,101,872**
Barrow	13013	55.3	46,144	20.9	55,787	20.7	67,325
Bartow	13015	36.0	76,019	15.0	87,405	15.3	100,778
Carroll	13045	22.2	87,268	16.9	102,023	17.1	119,514
Cherokee	13057	57.3	141,903	22.8	174,257	21.9	212,338
Clayton	13063	29.9	236,517	12.8	266,814	13.3	302,190
Cobb	13067	35.7	607,751	9.2	663,776	9.6	727,493
Coweta	13077	65.7	89,215	17.9	105,145	17.8	123,894
DeKalb	13089	22.0	665,865	1.6	676,338	1.5	686,337
Douglas	13097	29.6	92,174	14.0	105,116	14.8	120,622
Fayette	13113	46.2	91,263	10.9	101,180	11.2	112,509
Forsyth	13117	123.2	98,407	33.7	131,575	29.5	170,391
Fulton	13121	25.7	816,006	0.3	818,745	0.3	820,832
Gwinnett	13135	66.7	588,448	18.8	698,970	18.3	827,071
Henry	13151	103.2	119,341	33.6	159,460	29.7	206,741
Newton	13217	48.3	62,001	29.9	80,554	27.4	102,604
Paulding	13223	96.3	81,678	29.5	105,749	26.8	134,135
Pickens	13227	59.3	22,983	22.2	28,084	21.0	33,979
Rockdale	13247	29.6	70,111	9.0	76,406	9.6	83,732
Spalding	13255	7.3	58,417	4.7	61,151	5.5	64,495
Walton	13297	57.3	60,687	18.6	71,966	18.0	84,892
Augusta-Aiken, GA-SC MSA	0600	15.0	477,441	3.1	492,040	3.6	509,549
Columbia	**13073**	**35.2**	**89,288**	**12.1**	**100,062**	**12.8**	**112,848**
McDuffie	**13189**	**5.5**	**21,231**	**1.3**	**21,501**	**1.3**	**21,780**
Richmond	**13245**	**5.3**	**199,775**	**-1.0**	**197,685**	**-1.2**	**195,374**
Aiken, SC	45003	17.9	142,552	3.9	148,054	4.4	154,638
Edgefield, SC	45037	33.9	24,595	0.6	24,738	0.7	24,909
Columbus, GA-AL MSA	1800	5.3	274,624	2.5	281,559	2.9	289,799
Russell, AL	01113	6.2	49,756	-2.0	48,750	-2.4	47,582
Chattahoochee	**13053**	**-12.1**	**14,882**	**39.6**	**20,780**	**34.8**	**28,013**
Harris	**13145**	**33.2**	**23,695**	**12.2**	**26,586**	**13.1**	**30,057**
Muscogee	**13215**	**3.9**	**186,291**	**-0.5**	**185,443**	**-0.7**	**184,147**
Macon MSA	**4680**	**10.9**	**322,549**	**5.1**	**338,900**	**5.8**	**358,497**
Bibb	13021	2.6	153,887	0.4	154,445	0.5	155,230
Houston	13153	24.2	110,765	11.5	123,475	12.3	138,676
Jones	13169	14.0	23,639	10.3	26,065	11.4	29,028
Peach	13225	11.7	23,668	3.5	24,491	3.5	25,346
Twiggs	13289	8.0	10,590	-1.6	10,424	-2.0	10,217
Savannah MSA	**7520**	**13.5**	**293,000**	**5.1**	**307,995**	**6.0**	**326,328**
Bryan	13029	51.7	23,417	16.5	27,274	17.1	31,942
Chatham	13051	7.0	232,048	1.9	236,368	2.3	241,848
Effingham	13103	46.1	37,535	18.2	44,353	18.5	52,538
*** Catoosa County**	**13047**	**25.5**	**53,282**	**11.8**	**59,560**	**12.4**	**66,931**
*** Dade County**	**13083**	**15.3**	**15,154**	**6.6**	**16,151**	**7.4**	**17,353**
*** Walker County**	**13295**	**4.7**	**61,053**	**3.3**	**63,070**	**3.9**	**65,504**
(See Chattanooga, TN-GA MSA.)							
TOTAL: METRO PORTION OF STATE		**30.2**	**5,666,664**	**9.3**	**6,193,884**	**9.9**	**6,807,864**
TOTAL: GEORGIA		26.4	8,186,453	7.9	8,836,255	8.6	9,593,957

HAWAII

	FIPS CODE	PAST 1990-2000 % Change	PAST 2000 Census	PRESENT 2000-2004 % Change	PRESENT 7/1/04 Estimate	FUTURE 2004-2009 % Change	FUTURE 2009 Projection
Honolulu MSA	**3320**	**4.8**	**876,156**	**4.1**	**911,719**	**4.9**	**956,800**
Honolulu	15003	4.8	876,156	4.1	911,719	4.9	956,800
TOTAL: METRO PORTION OF STATE		**4.8**	**876,156**	**4.1**	**911,719**	**4.9**	**956,800**
TOTAL: HAWAII		9.3	1,211,537	5.0	1,272,696	5.9	1,348,138

IDAHO

	FIPS CODE	PAST 1990-2000 % Change	PAST 2000 Census	PRESENT 2000-2004 % Change	PRESENT 7/1/04 Estimate	FUTURE 2004-2009 % Change	FUTURE 2009 Projection
Boise City MSA	**1080**	**46.1**	**432,345**	**13.4**	**490,178**	**13.8**	**557,690**
Ada	16001	46.2	300,904	10.5	332,530	11.1	369,368
Canyon	16027	45.9	131,441	19.9	157,648	19.5	188,322
Pocatello MSA	**6340**	**14.4**	**75,565**	**0.1**	**75,644**	**0.1**	**75,705**
Bannock	16005	14.4	75,565	0.1	75,644	0.1	75,705
TOTAL: METRO PORTION OF STATE		**40.4**	**507,910**	**11.4**	**565,822**	**11.9**	**633,395**
TOTAL: IDAHO		28.5	1,293,953	7.3	1,388,573	8.0	1,499,776

ILLINOIS

	FIPS CODE	PAST 1990-2000 % Change	PAST 2000 Census	PRESENT 2000-2004 % Change	PRESENT 7/1/04 Estimate	FUTURE 2004-2009 % Change	FUTURE 2009 Projection
Bloomington-Normal MSA	**1040**	**16.5**	**150,433**	**5.6**	**158,878**	**6.3**	**168,862**
McLean	17113	16.5	150,433	5.6	158,878	6.3	168,862
Champaign-Urbana MSA	**1400**	**3.8**	**179,669**	**5.2**	**189,076**	**6.0**	**200,443**
Champaign	17019	3.8	179,669	5.2	189,076	6.0	200,443
Chicago PMSA	**1600**	**11.6**	**8,272,768**	**3.5**	**8,558,311**	**3.9**	**8,890,349**
Cook	17031	5.3	5,376,741	-0.6	5,342,990	-0.8	5,299,999
DeKalb	17037	14.2	88,969	7.5	95,619	8.2	103,501
DuPage	17043	15.7	904,161	3.0	931,347	3.3	962,070
Grundy	17063	16.1	37,535	6.9	40,142	7.6	43,212
Kane	17089	27.3	404,119	17.2	473,610	17.4	556,007
Kendall	17093	38.4	54,544	29.0	70,354	26.9	89,295
Lake	17097	24.8	644,356	8.2	697,152	8.7	757,754
McHenry	17111	41.9	260,077	13.1	294,238	13.8	334,948
Will	17197	40.6	502,266	22.0	612,859	21.3	743,563
Decatur MSA	**2040**	**-2.1**	**114,706**	**-4.0**	**110,093**	**-4.8**	**104,829**
Macon	17115	-2.1	114,706	-4.0	110,093	-4.8	104,829
Kankakee PMSA	**3740**	**7.9**	**103,833**	**2.3**	**106,207**	**2.7**	**109,106**
Kankakee	17091	7.9	103,833	2.3	106,207	2.7	109,106
Peoria-Pekin MSA	**6120**	**2.4**	**347,387**	**-0.2**	**346,613**	**-0.2**	**345,872**
Peoria	17143	0.3	183,433	-0.8	182,043	-0.8	180,577
Tazewell	17179	3.9	128,485	-0.4	127,916	-0.6	127,205
Woodford	17203	8.6	35,469	3.3	36,654	3.9	38,090
Rockford MSA	**6880**	**12.6**	**371,236**	**4.4**	**387,465**	**4.9**	**406,531**
Boone	17007	35.6	41,786	14.7	47,945	15.3	55,286
Ogle	17141	11.0	51,032	4.7	53,421	5.3	56,236
Winnebago	17201	10.1	278,418	2.8	286,099	3.1	295,009
Springfield MSA	**7880**	**6.3**	**201,437**	**2.0**	**205,434**	**2.3**	**210,247**
Menard	17129	11.8	12,486	1.1	12,619	1.0	12,749
Sangamon	17167	5.9	188,951	2.0	192,815	2.4	197,498
*** Henry County**	**17073**	**-0.3**	**51,020**	**-1.0**	**50,508**	**-1.3**	**49,831**
*** Rock Island County**	**17161**	**0.4**	**149,374**	**-1.2**	**147,511**	**-1.4**	**145,513**
(See Davenport-Moline-Rock Island, IA-IL MSA.)							
*** Clinton County**	**17027**	**4.7**	**35,535**	**2.2**	**36,327**	**2.6**	**37,288**
*** Jersey County**	**17083**	**5.5**	**21,668**	**3.2**	**22,361**	**3.9**	**23,223**
*** Madison County**	**17119**	**3.9**	**258,941**	**1.4**	**262,550**	**1.6**	**266,835**
*** Monroe County**	**17133**	**23.2**	**27,619**	**10.0**	**30,375**	**10.7**	**33,630**
*** St. Clair County**	**17163**	**-2.6**	**256,082**	**1.3**	**259,386**	**1.5**	**263,266**
(See St. Louis, MO-IL MSA.)							
TOTAL: METRO PORTION OF STATE		**10.1**	**10,541,708**	**3.1**	**10,871,095**	**3.5**	**11,255,825**
TOTAL: ILLINOIS		8.6	12,419,293	2.5	12,725,117	2.8	13,082,984

INDIANA

	FIPS CODE	PAST 1990-2000 % Change	PAST 2000 Census	PRESENT 2000-2004 % Change	PRESENT 7/1/04 Estimate	FUTURE 2004-2009 % Change	FUTURE 2009 Projection
Bloomington MSA	**1020**	**10.6**	**120,563**	**2.6**	**123,639**	**3.0**	**127,311**
Monroe	18105	10.6	120,563	2.6	123,639	3.0	127,311
Elkhart-Goshen MSA	**2330**	**17.0**	**182,791**	**4.2**	**190,535**	**4.6**	**199,304**
Elkhart	18039	17.0	182,791	4.2	190,535	4.6	199,304
Evansville-Henderson, IN-KY MSA	2440	6.2	296,195	1.1	299,416	1.3	303,292
Posey	**18129**	**4.2**	**27,061**	**-0.9**	**26,811**	**-1.2**	**26,484**
Vanderburgh	**18163**	**4.2**	**171,922**	**-0.0**	**171,902**	**0.0**	**171,959**
Warrick	**18173**	**16.6**	**52,383**	**5.9**	**55,468**	**6.5**	**59,086**
Henderson, KY	21101	4.1	44,829	0.9	45,235	1.2	45,763
Fort Wayne MSA	**2760**	**10.1**	**502,141**	**2.7**	**515,722**	**3.0**	**531,394**
Adams	18001	8.1	33,625	-0.1	33,583	-0.1	33,537
Allen	18003	10.3	331,849	3.3	342,644	3.6	355,080
De Kalb	18033	14.0	40,285	2.7	41,373	2.9	42,587
Huntington	18069	7.5	38,075	0.2	38,158	0.2	38,229
Wells	18179	6.4	27,600	1.5	28,011	1.7	28,501
Whitley	18183	11.1	30,707	4.1	31,953	4.7	33,460
Gary PMSA	**2960**	**4.4**	**631,362**	**1.8**	**642,735**	**2.1**	**656,324**
Lake	18089	1.9	484,564	0.8	488,435	1.0	493,200
Porter	18127	13.9	146,798	5.1	154,300	5.7	163,124
Indianapolis MSA	**3480**	**16.4**	**1,607,486**	**5.4**	**1,695,006**	**6.1**	**1,797,554**
Boone	18011	20.9	46,107	9.2	50,364	9.9	55,335
Hamilton	18057	67.7	182,740	24.4	227,306	23.0	279,692
Hancock	18059	21.7	55,391	9.6	60,709	10.4	67,026
Hendricks	18063	37.5	104,093	18.5	123,336	18.2	145,760
Johnson	18081	30.8	115,209	9.1	125,682	9.6	137,807
Madison	18095	2.1	133,358	-2.2	130,409	-2.7	126,901
Marion	18097	7.9	860,454	0.4	864,200	0.5	868,901
Morgan	18109	19.3	66,689	3.8	69,244	4.2	72,185
Shelby	18145	7.8	43,445	0.7	43,756	0.4	43,947
Kokomo MSA	**3850**	**4.7**	**101,541**	**-0.3**	**101,227**	**-0.4**	**100,848**
Howard	18067	5.1	84,964	-0.1	84,849	-0.2	84,692
Tipton	18159	2.8	16,577	-1.2	16,378	-1.4	16,156
Lafayette MSA	**3920**	**13.2**	**182,821**	**4.3**	**190,622**	**4.8**	**199,744**
Clinton	18023	9.3	33,866	0.2	33,939	-0.1	33,898
Tippecanoe	18157	14.1	148,955	5.2	156,683	5.8	165,846
Muncie MSA	**5280**	**-0.7**	**118,769**	**-1.4**	**117,094**	**-1.7**	**115,140**
Delaware	18035	-0.7	118,769	-1.4	117,094	-1.7	115,140
South Bend MSA	**7800**	**7.5**	**265,559**	**0.4**	**266,508**	**0.3**	**267,297**
St. Joseph	18141	7.5	265,559	0.4	266,508	0.3	267,297
Terre Haute MSA	**8320**	**1.1**	**149,192**	**-1.1**	**147,496**	**-1.3**	**145,577**
Clay	18021	7.5	26,556	1.1	26,843	1.3	27,197
Vermillion	18165	0.1	16,788	-1.7	16,504	-2.0	16,167
Vigo	18167	-0.2	105,848	-1.6	104,149	-1.9	102,213
*** Clark County**	**18019**	**9.9**	**96,472**	**4.0**	**100,377**	**4.5**	**104,846**
*** Floyd County**	**18043**	**10.0**	**70,823**	**0.6**	**71,234**	**0.6**	**71,661**
*** Harrison County**	**18061**	**14.8**	**34,325**	**5.2**	**36,107**	**5.5**	**38,110**
*** Scott County**	**18143**	**9.4**	**22,960**	**3.3**	**23,725**	**3.6**	**24,568**
(See Louisville, KY-IN MSA.)							
*** Dearborn County**	**18029**	**18.7**	**46,109**	**4.9**	**48,349**	**5.2**	**50,848**
*** Ohio County**	**18115**	**5.8**	**5,623**	**2.5**	**5,762**	**2.6**	**5,911**
(See Cincinnati, OH-KY-IN PMSA.)							
TOTAL: METRO PORTION OF STATE		**10.8**	**4,389,903**	**3.2**	**4,530,319**	**3.6**	**4,693,966**
TOTAL: INDIANA		9.7	6,080,485	2.5	6,230,346	2.8	6,403,859

IOWA

	FIPS CODE	PAST 1990-2000 % Change	PAST 2000 Census	PRESENT 2000-2004 % Change	PRESENT 7/1/04 Estimate	FUTURE 2004-2009 % Change	FUTURE 2009 Projection
Cedar Rapids MSA	**1360**	**13.6**	**191,701**	**3.0**	**197,521**	**3.3**	**204,051**
Linn	19113	13.6	191,701	3.0	197,521	3.3	204,051
Davenport-Moline-Rock Island, IA-IL MSA	1960	2.3	359,062	-0.4	357,656	-0.5	356,045
Henry, IL	17073	-0.3	51,020	-1.0	50,508	-1.3	49,831
Rock Island, IL	17161	0.4	149,374	-1.2	147,511	-1.4	145,513
Scott	**19163**	**5.1**	**158,668**	**0.6**	**159,637**	**0.7**	**160,701**

* Indicates county is included from metro in different state.
Source: Devonshire Associates Ltd. and Scan/US, Inc. 2004.

continued on next page

Metropolitan Statistical Areas and Their Component Counties: Population Trends, *Continued*

	FIPS CODE	PAST 1990-2000 % Change	PAST 2000 Census	PRESENT 2000-2004 % Change	PRESENT 7/1/04 Estimate	FUTURE 2004-2009 % Change	FUTURE 2009 Projection
Des Moines MSA	2120	16.1	456,022	5.9	483,114	6.6	514,766
Dallas	19049	37.0	40,750	17.4	47,845	17.7	56,309
Polk	19153	14.5	374,601	4.9	392,872	5.4	414,072
Warren	19181	12.9	40,671	4.2	42,397	4.7	44,385
Dubuque MSA	2200	3.2	89,143	1.3	90,309	1.4	91,581
Dubuque	19061	3.2	89,143	1.3	90,309	1.4	91,581
Iowa City MSA	3500	15.5	111,006	5.3	116,938	5.9	123,853
Johnson	19103	15.5	111,006	5.3	116,938	5.9	123,853
Sioux City, IA-NE MSA	7720	7.9	124,130	-0.5	123,569	-0.6	122,823
Woodbury	19193	5.7	103,877	-0.8	103,007	-1.1	101,918
Dakota, NE	31043	21.0	20,253	1.5	20,562	1.7	20,905
Waterloo-Cedar Falls MSA	8920	3.4	128,012	-1.6	125,922	-2.0	123,434
Black Hawk	19013	3.4	128,012	-1.6	125,922	-2.0	123,434
*** Pottawattamie County** (See Omaha, NE-IA MSA.)	19155	6.1	87,704	1.1	88,639	0.9	89,425
TOTAL: METRO PORTION OF STATE		10.5	1,326,133	2.9	1,365,087	3.3	1,409,729
TOTAL: IOWA		5.4	2,926,324	0.8	2,949,245	0.9	2,975,158

KANSAS

	FIPS CODE	PAST 1990-2000 % Change	PAST 2000 Census	PRESENT 2000-2004 % Change	PRESENT 7/1/04 Estimate	FUTURE 2004-2009 % Change	FUTURE 2009 Projection
Lawrence MSA	4150	22.2	99,962	3.9	103,909	4.4	108,485
Douglas	20045	22.2	99,962	3.9	103,909	4.4	108,485
Topeka MSA	8440	5.5	169,871	0.8	171,175	0.7	172,453
Shawnee	20177	5.5	169,871	0.8	171,175	0.7	172,453
Wichita MSA[2]	9040	12.8	512,351	3.0	527,608	3.3	545,261
Butler	20015	17.6	59,482	3.6	61,602	3.8	63,942
Sedgwick	20173	12.2	452,869	2.9	466,006	3.3	481,319
*** Johnson County**	20091	27.0	451,086	10.2	497,146	10.6	550,011
*** Leavenworth County**	20103	6.7	68,691	5.4	72,419	6.0	76,745
*** Miami County**	20121	20.8	28,351	3.8	29,415	3.8	30,539
*** Wyandotte County** (See Kansas City, MO-KS MSA.)	20209	-2.5	157,882	-0.7	156,835	-0.9	155,484
TOTAL: METRO PORTION OF STATE		14.3	1,488,194	4.7	1,558,507	5.2	1,638,978
TOTAL: KANSAS		8.5	2,688,418	1.7	2,733,795	1.9	2,785,235

KENTUCKY

	FIPS CODE	PAST 1990-2000 % Change	PAST 2000 Census	PRESENT 2000-2004 % Change	PRESENT 7/1/04 Estimate	FUTURE 2004-2009 % Change	FUTURE 2009 Projection
Lexington MSA	4280	18.0	479,198	4.9	502,488	5.4	529,590
Bourbon	21017	0.6	19,360	1.6	19,673	1.9	20,047
Clark	21049	12.4	33,144	3.2	34,197	3.5	35,385
Fayette	21067	15.6	260,512	3.2	268,741	3.6	278,436
Jessamine	21113	28.0	39,041	8.3	42,270	9.0	46,080
Madison	21151	23.2	70,872	7.2	75,994	7.8	81,890
Scott	21209	38.5	33,061	14.4	37,824	14.5	43,314
Woodford	21239	16.3	23,208	2.5	23,789	2.7	24,438
Louisville, KY-IN MSA	4520	8.1	1,025,598	2.4	1,049,861	2.6	1,077,421
Clark, IN	18019	9.9	96,472	4.0	100,377	4.5	104,846
Floyd, IN	18043	10.0	70,823	0.6	71,234	0.6	71,661
Harrison, IN	18061	14.8	34,325	5.2	36,107	5.5	38,110
Scott, IN	18143	9.4	22,960	3.3	23,725	3.6	24,568
Bullitt	21029	28.7	61,236	7.8	65,997	8.2	71,436
Jefferson	21111	4.3	693,604	1.0	700,741	1.2	709,304
Oldham	21185	38.8	46,178	11.9	51,680	11.3	57,496
Owensboro MSA	5990	5.0	91,545	1.4	92,851	1.7	94,400
Daviess	21059	5.0	91,545	1.4	92,851	1.7	94,400
*** Henderson County** (See Evansville-Henderson, IN-KY MSA.)	21101	4.1	44,829	0.9	45,235	1.2	45,763
*** Boone County**	21015	49.3	85,991	16.9	100,516	16.8	117,390
*** Campbell County**	21037	5.7	88,616	-1.0	87,745	-1.3	86,626
*** Gallatin County**	21077	45.9	7,870	2.2	8,041	2.8	8,268
*** Grant County**	21081	42.2	22,384	9.3	24,461	9.8	26,848
*** Kenton County**	21117	6.6	151,464	0.7	152,501	0.7	153,565
*** Pendleton County** (See Cincinnati, OH-KY-IN PMSA.)	21191	19.6	14,390	6.2	15,286	6.4	16,262
*** Christian County** (See Clarksville-Hopkinsville, TN-KY MSA.)	21047	4.8	72,265	-4.3	69,170	-5.2	65,576
*** Boyd County**	21019	-2.7	49,752	-0.5	49,520	-0.3	49,349
*** Carter County**	21043	10.5	26,889	1.3	27,234	1.6	27,682
*** Greenup County** (See Huntington-Ashland, WV-KY-OH MSA.)	21089	0.4	36,891	0.3	36,989	0.5	37,173
TOTAL: METRO PORTION OF STATE		10.9	1,973,102	2.9	2,030,455	3.3	2,096,728
TOTAL: KENTUCKY		9.7	4,041,769	2.5	4,140,891	2.8	4,256,211

LOUISIANA (Parishes)

	FIPS CODE	PAST 1990-2000 % Change	PAST 2000 Census	PRESENT 2000-2004 % Change	PRESENT 7/1/04 Estimate	FUTURE 2004-2009 % Change	FUTURE 2009 Projection
Alexandria MSA	0220	-4.0	126,337	1.1	127,716	1.2	129,296
Rapides	22079	-4.0	126,337	1.1	127,716	1.2	129,296
Baton Rouge MSA	0760	14.1	602,894	3.8	626,070	4.3	653,081
Ascension	22005	31.6	76,627	13.2	86,777	13.5	98,512
East Baton Rouge	22033	8.6	412,852	-0.1	412,326	-0.2	411,618
Livingston	22063	30.2	91,814	14.6	105,200	15.0	120,940
West Baton Rouge	22121	11.2	21,601	0.8	21,767	1.1	22,011
Houma MSA	3350	6.4	194,477	2.0	198,351	2.4	203,111
Lafourche	22057	4.8	89,974	1.9	91,720	2.4	93,889
Terrebonne	22109	7.8	104,503	2.0	106,631	2.4	109,222
Lafayette MSA	3880	11.8	385,647	2.3	394,628	2.7	405,476
Acadia	22001	5.3	58,861	0.9	59,384	1.1	60,056
Lafayette	22055	15.6	190,503	2.6	195,453	3.1	201,469
St. Landry	22097	9.2	87,700	2.0	89,466	2.3	91,566
St. Martin	22099	10.5	48,583	3.6	50,325	4.1	52,385
Lake Charles MSA	3960	9.2	183,577	0.2	184,005	0.3	184,541
Calcasieu	22019	9.2	183,577	0.2	184,005	0.3	184,541
Monroe MSA	5200	3.6	147,250	0.6	148,118	0.7	149,179
Ouachita	22073	3.6	147,250	0.6	148,118	0.7	149,179
New Orleans MSA	5560	4.1	1,337,726	0.1	1,339,327	0.3	1,343,083
Jefferson	22051	1.6	455,466	-0.8	451,699	-0.9	447,807
Orleans	22071	-2.5	484,674	-4.2	464,268	-5.0	441,054
Plaquemines	22075	4.6	26,757	6.3	28,450	7.4	30,569
St. Bernard	22087	0.9	67,229	-2.1	65,813	-2.3	64,315
St. Charles	22089	13.3	48,072	3.5	49,737	3.8	51,643
St. James	22093	1.6	21,216	-0.6	21,092	-0.6	20,957
St. John The Baptist	22095	7.6	43,044	5.4	45,373	6.1	48,148
St. Tammany	22103	32.4	191,268	11.3	212,895	12.1	238,590
Shreveport-Bossier City MSA	7680	4.2	392,302	0.5	394,221	0.6	396,524
Bossier	22015	14.2	98,310	4.9	103,123	5.4	108,716
Caddo	22017	1.6	252,161	-0.9	249,805	-1.1	247,077
Webster	22119	-0.4	41,831	-1.3	41,293	-1.4	40,731
TOTAL: METRO PORTION OF STATE		6.7	3,370,210	1.3	3,412,436	1.5	3,464,291
TOTAL: LOUISIANA		5.9	4,468,976	0.8	4,505,373	1.0	4,550,570

MAINE

	FIPS CODE	PAST 1990-2000 % Change	PAST 2000 Census	PRESENT 2000-2004 % Change	PRESENT 7/1/04 Estimate	FUTURE 2004-2009 % Change	FUTURE 2009 Projection
Bangor NECMA	0733	-1.1	144,919	1.9	147,681	2.4	151,173
Penobscot	23019	-1.1	144,919	1.9	147,681	2.4	151,173
Lewiston-Auburn NECMA	4243	-1.4	103,793	3.0	106,865	3.5	110,613
Androscoggin	23001	-1.4	103,793	3.0	106,865	3.5	110,613
Portland NECMA	6403	9.2	265,612	2.6	272,577	3.0	280,846
Cumberland	23005	9.2	265,612	2.6	272,577	3.0	280,846
TOTAL: METRO PORTION OF STATE		3.9	514,324	2.5	527,123	2.9	542,632
TOTAL: MAINE		3.8	1,274,923	3.2	1,315,211	3.6	1,362,624

MARYLAND

	FIPS CODE	PAST 1990-2000 % Change	PAST 2000 Census	PRESENT 2000-2004 % Change	PRESENT 7/1/04 Estimate	FUTURE 2004-2009 % Change	FUTURE 2009 Projection
Baltimore PMSA	0720	7.2	2,552,994	3.2	2,635,941	3.8	2,735,037
Anne Arundel	24003	14.6	489,656	4.5	511,686	4.9	536,925
Baltimore	24005	9.0	754,292	4.0	784,253	4.5	819,459
Baltimore (Ind. City)	24510	-11.5	651,154	-4.5	622,161	-5.1	590,521
Carroll	24013	22.3	150,897	10.7	167,068	11.5	186,338
Harford	24025	20.0	218,590	8.1	236,397	8.9	257,462
Howard	24027	32.3	247,842	8.6	269,157	9.1	293,568
Queen Anne's	24035	19.5	40,563	11.5	45,219	12.3	50,764
Cumberland, MD-WV MSA	1900	0.4	102,008	-1.5	100,473	-1.7	98,767
Allegany	24001	-0.0	74,930	-2.2	73,291	-2.6	71,421
Mineral, WV	54057	1.4	27,078	0.4	27,182	0.6	27,346
Hagerstown PMSA	3180	8.7	131,923	4.9	138,354	5.6	146,118
Washington	24043	8.7	131,923	4.9	138,354	5.6	146,118
*** Cecil County** (See Wilmington-Newark, DE-MD PMSA.)	24015	20.5	85,951	10.3	94,837	11.0	105,269
*** Calvert County**	24009	45.1	74,563	16.8	87,081	17.0	101,916
*** Charles County**	24017	19.2	120,546	13.6	136,969	14.3	156,536
*** Frederick County**	24021	30.0	195,277	12.3	219,345	12.9	247,718
*** Montgomery County**	24031	15.4	873,341	6.8	932,558	7.3	1,000,765
*** Prince George's County** (See Washington, DC-MD-VA-WV PMSA.)	24033	9.9	801,515	6.1	850,384	6.8	908,563
TOTAL: METRO PORTION OF STATE		10.6	4,911,040	5.2	5,168,760	5.9	5,473,343
TOTAL: MARYLAND		10.8	5,296,486	5.3	5,574,702	5.9	5,903,665

MASSACHUSETTS

	FIPS CODE	PAST 1990-2000 % Change	PAST 2000 Census	PRESENT 2000-2004 % Change	PRESENT 7/1/04 Estimate	FUTURE 2004-2009 % Change	FUTURE 2009 Projection
Barnstable-Yarmouth NECMA	0743	19.1	222,230	4.2	231,645	4.5	242,135
Barnstable	25001	19.1	222,230	4.2	231,645	4.5	242,135
Boston-Worcester-Lawrence-Lowell-Brockton, MA-NH NECMA	1123	6.5	6,057,826	2.1	6,186,809	2.3	6,329,608
Bristol	25005	5.6	534,678	3.0	550,668	3.3	568,949
Essex	25009	8.0	723,419	2.6	741,982	2.8	762,628
Middlesex	25017	4.8	1,465,396	0.5	1,472,613	0.3	1,477,006
Norfolk	25021	5.6	650,308	0.8	655,356	0.8	660,454
Plymouth	25023	8.6	472,822	4.0	491,878	4.4	513,646
Suffolk	25025	3.9	689,807	-1.8	677,616	-2.3	662,356
Worcester	25027	5.8	750,963	4.5	784,595	5.1	824,492
Hillsborough, NH	33011	13.3	380,841	4.7	398,775	5.2	419,332
Rockingham, NH	33015	12.8	277,359	6.0	293,899	6.5	312,885
Strafford, NH	33017	7.7	112,233	6.4	119,427	7.1	127,860
Pittsfield NECMA	6323	-3.2	134,953	-1.6	132,813	-1.9	130,354
Berkshire	25003	-3.2	134,953	-1.6	132,813	-1.9	130,354
Springfield NECMA	8003	0.9	608,479	1.7	618,736	2.0	630,934
Hampden	25013	-0.0	456,228	1.4	462,756	1.7	470,565
Hampshire	25015	3.9	152,251	2.4	155,980	2.8	160,369
TOTAL: METRO PORTION OF STATE		5.5	6,253,055	1.7	6,357,902	1.8	6,472,954
TOTAL: MASSACHUSETTS		5.5	6,349,097	1.7	6,457,204	1.8	6,576,114

MICHIGAN

	FIPS CODE	PAST 1990-2000 % Change	PAST 2000 Census	PRESENT 2000-2004 % Change	PRESENT 7/1/04 Estimate	FUTURE 2004-2009 % Change	FUTURE 2009 Projection
Ann Arbor PMSA	0440	18.1	578,736	7.5	622,300	8.1	672,589
Lenawee	26091	8.1	98,890	2.5	101,344	2.7	104,124
Livingston	26093	35.7	156,951	13.2	177,683	13.5	201,672
Washtenaw	26161	14.1	322,895	6.3	343,273	6.9	366,793
Benton Harbor MSA	0870	0.7	162,453	0.2	162,816	0.1	163,051
Berrien	26021	0.7	162,453	0.2	162,816	0.1	163,051
Detroit PMSA	2160	4.1	4,441,551	0.6	4,466,850	0.6	4,493,239
Lapeer	26087	17.6	87,904	5.0	92,313	5.4	97,299
Macomb	26099	9.9	788,149	4.2	821,634	4.7	859,988
Monroe	26115	9.2	145,945	4.2	152,069	4.6	159,036
Oakland	26125	10.2	1,194,156	1.5	1,211,605	1.5	1,230,186
St. Clair	26147	12.8	164,235	3.8	170,514	4.2	177,753
Wayne	26163	-2.4	2,061,162	-2.1	2,018,715	-2.5	1,968,977
Flint PMSA	2640	1.3	436,141	1.8	444,011	2.0	452,774
Genesee	26049	1.3	436,141	1.8	444,011	2.0	452,774
Grand Rapids-Muskegon-Holland MSA	3000	16.1	1,088,514	4.1	1,133,518	4.5	1,184,859
Allegan	26005	16.7	105,665	5.7	111,737	6.3	118,757
Kent	26081	14.7	574,335	3.6	595,142	4.0	618,715
Muskegon	26121	7.1	170,200	2.2	173,945	2.4	178,202
Ottawa	26139	26.9	238,314	6.0	252,694	6.5	269,185
Jackson MSA	3520	5.8	158,422	3.2	163,516	3.6	169,477
Jackson	26075	5.8	158,422	3.2	163,516	3.6	169,477
Kalamazoo-Battle Creek MSA	3720	5.4	452,851	1.8	461,120	2.1	470,810
Calhoun	26025	1.5	137,985	0.8	139,106	0.9	140,354
Kalamazoo	26077	6.8	238,603	1.9	243,185	2.2	248,537
Van Buren	26159	8.9	76,263	3.4	78,829	3.9	81,919
Lansing-East Lansing MSA	4040	3.5	447,728	2.4	458,301	2.7	470,587
Clinton	26037	11.9	64,753	5.8	68,489	6.4	72,882
Eaton	26045	11.6	103,655	3.2	106,959	3.6	110,760
Ingham	26065	-0.9	279,320	1.3	282,853	1.4	286,945
Saginaw-Bay City-Midland MSA	6960	0.9	403,070	0.1	403,326	0.1	403,578
Bay	26017	-1.4	110,157	-0.8	109,229	-1.0	108,107
Midland	26111	9.5	82,874	2.5	84,980	2.9	87,412
Saginaw	26145	-0.9	210,039	-0.4	209,117	-0.5	208,059
TOTAL: METRO PORTION OF STATE		6.1	8,169,466	1.8	8,315,758	2.0	8,480,964
TOTAL: MICHIGAN		6.9	9,938,444	1.8	10,121,382	2.0	10,328,365

MINNESOTA

	FIPS CODE	PAST 1990-2000 % Change	PAST 2000 Census	PRESENT 2000-2004 % Change	PRESENT 7/1/04 Estimate	FUTURE 2004-2009 % Change	FUTURE 2009 Projection
Duluth-Superior, MN-WI MSA	2240	1.6	243,815	-0.5	242,578	-0.6	241,009
St. Louis	27137	1.2	200,528	-1.1	198,256	-1.4	195,546
Douglas, WI	55031	3.7	43,287	2.4	44,322	2.6	45,463
Minneapolis-St. Paul, MN-WI MSA	5120	16.9	2,968,806	5.0	3,117,850	5.5	3,288,729
Anoka	27003	22.3	298,084	7.0	318,838	7.5	342,630
Carver	27019	46.5	70,205	16.3	81,656	16.5	95,126
Chisago	27025	34.7	41,101	16.1	47,700	16.1	55,373
Dakota	27037	29.3	355,904	6.3	378,473	6.8	404,250
Hennepin	27053	8.1	1,116,200	0.5	1,122,141	0.5	1,127,580
Isanti	27059	20.7	31,287	17.1	36,651	17.4	43,044
Ramsey	27123	5.2	511,035	-1.2	504,693	-1.6	496,428
Scott	27139	54.7	89,498	27.8	114,403	25.4	143,515
Sherburne	27141	53.6	64,417	20.8	77,790	20.1	93,397
Washington	27163	37.9	201,130	8.0	217,209	8.4	235,409
Wright	27171	31.0	89,986	18.3	106,446	18.4	126,017
Pierce, WI	55093	12.3	36,804	3.8	38,196	4.2	39,816
St. Croix, WI	55109	25.7	63,155	16.6	73,654	17.0	86,144
Rochester MSA	6820	16.7	124,277	7.5	133,562	8.1	144,443
Olmsted	27109	16.7	124,277	7.5	133,562	8.1	144,443
St. Cloud MSA	6980	12.4	167,392	5.2	176,070	5.7	186,043
Benton	27009	13.4	34,226	10.3	37,738	10.8	41,805
Stearns	27145	12.1	133,166	3.9	138,332	4.3	144,238
*** Clay County** (See Fargo-Moorhead, ND-MN MSA.)	27027	1.6	51,229	1.9	52,205	2.1	53,311
*** Polk County** (See Grand Forks, ND-MN MSA.)	27119	-3.5	31,369	-2.0	30,748	-2.5	29,972
*** Houston County** (See La Crosse, WI-MN MSA.)	27055	6.6	19,718	1.7	20,056	1.9	20,435
TOTAL: METRO PORTION OF STATE		15.0	3,463,360	4.4	3,616,897	4.9	3,792,519
TOTAL: MINNESOTA		12.4	4,919,479	3.7	5,101,284	4.1	5,310,829

MISSISSIPPI

	FIPS CODE	PAST 1990-2000 % Change	PAST 2000 Census	PRESENT 2000-2004 % Change	PRESENT 7/1/04 Estimate	FUTURE 2004-2009 % Change	FUTURE 2009 Projection
Biloxi-Gulfport-Pascagoula MSA	0920	16.5	363,988	1.6	369,960	1.7	376,230
Hancock	28045	35.3	42,967	6.5	45,765	6.7	48,851
Harrison	28047	14.7	189,601	-0.0	189,590	-0.1	189,423
Jackson	28059	14.0	131,420	2.4	134,605	2.5	137,956
Hattiesburg MSA	3285	13.1	111,674	5.4	117,751	6.0	124,760
Forrest	28035	6.3	72,604	3.2	74,924	3.6	77,594
Lamar	28073	28.4	39,070	9.6	42,827	10.1	47,166
Jackson MSA	3560	11.5	440,801	3.8	457,428	4.2	476,750
Hinds	28049	-1.4	250,800	-0.9	248,578	-1.0	245,985
Madison	28089	38.8	74,674	8.9	81,322	9.6	89,114
Rankin	28121	32.3	115,327	10.6	127,528	11.1	141,651
*** DeSoto County** (See Memphis, TN-AR-MS MSA.)	28033	57.9	107,199	20.9	129,632	20.2	155,853
TOTAL: METRO PORTION OF STATE		17.1	1,023,662	5.0	1,074,771	5.5	1,133,593
TOTAL: MISSISSIPPI		10.5	2,844,658	1.7	2,892,228	1.9	2,946,963

MISSOURI

	FIPS CODE	PAST 1990-2000 % Change	PAST 2000 Census	PRESENT 2000-2004 % Change	PRESENT 7/1/04 Estimate	FUTURE 2004-2009 % Change	FUTURE 2009 Projection
Columbia MSA	1740	20.5	135,454	5.5	142,884	6.1	151,657
Boone	29019	20.5	135,454	5.5	142,884	6.1	151,657
Joplin MSA	3710	16.6	157,322	4.0	163,621	4.5	170,964
Jasper	29097	15.7	104,686	4.3	109,158	4.8	114,363
Newton	29145	18.4	52,636	3.5	54,463	3.9	56,601
Kansas City, MO-KS MSA	3760	12.2	1,776,062	4.9	1,863,851	5.4	1,964,702
Johnson, KS	20091	27.0	451,086	10.2	497,146	10.6	550,011
Leavenworth, KS	20103	6.7	68,691	5.4	72,419	6.0	76,745
Miami, KS	20121	20.8	28,351	3.8	29,415	3.8	30,539
Wyandotte, KS	20209	-2.5	157,882	-0.7	156,835	-0.9	155,484
Cass	29037	28.7	82,092	10.7	90,899	11.3	101,203
Clay	29047	19.9	184,006	7.3	197,398	8.0	213,104
Clinton	29049	14.4	18,979	8.0	20,502	8.8	22,311
Jackson	29095	3.4	654,880	0.9	661,091	1.0	667,791
Lafayette	29107	6.0	32,960	-0.1	32,925	-0.4	32,789
Platte	29165	27.5	73,781	9.9	81,115	10.6	89,721
Ray	29177	6.3	23,354	3.2	24,106	3.7	25,004
St. Joseph MSA	7000	4.9	102,490	-1.0	101,433	-1.4	99,998
Andrew	29003	12.7	16,492	2.5	16,904	2.7	17,360
Buchanan	29021	3.5	85,998	-1.7	84,529	-2.2	82,638

* Indicates county is included from metro in different state.
Source: Devonshire Associates Ltd. and Scan/US, Inc. 2004.

[2] Data exclude Harvey County, Kansas (2000 Census population 32,869; 2004 estimated population 33,707; and 2009 projected population 34,714), which fails to meet published standards for MSA inclusion, but has been included with the Wichita MSA as the result of Congressional action.

Metropolitan Statistical Areas and Their Component Counties: Population Trends, *Continued*

	FIPS CODE	PAST 1990-2000 % Change	PAST 2000 Census	PRESENT 2000-2004 % Change	PRESENT 7/1/04 Estimate	FUTURE 2004-2009 % Change	FUTURE 2009 Projection
St. Louis, MO-IL MSA	7040	4.5	2,603,607	1.8	2,651,207	2.1	2,707,853
Clinton, IL	17027	4.7	35,535	2.2	36,327	2.6	37,288
Jersey, IL	17083	5.5	21,668	3.2	22,361	3.9	23,223
Madison, IL	17119	3.9	258,941	1.4	262,550	1.6	266,835
Monroe, IL	17133	23.2	27,619	10.0	30,375	10.7	33,630
St. Clair, IL	17163	-2.6	256,082	1.3	259,386	1.5	263,266
Franklin	29071	16.4	93,807	4.3	97,849	4.8	102,549
Jefferson	29099	15.6	198,099	5.7	209,444	6.3	222,683
Lincoln	29113	34.8	38,944	17.7	45,856	17.9	54,086
St. Charles	29183	33.3	283,883	12.7	319,977	13.2	362,124
St. Louis	29189	2.3	1,016,315	-0.4	1,012,010	-0.6	1,006,248
St. Louis (Ind. City)	29510	-12.2	348,189	-5.9	327,502	-6.9	304,819
Warren	29219	25.6	24,525	12.4	27,570	12.8	31,102
Springfield MSA	7920	23.2	325,721	5.9	344,995	6.5	367,587
Christian	29043	66.3	54,285	17.5	63,776	17.3	74,782
Greene	29077	15.6	240,391	2.9	247,471	3.4	255,945
Webster	29225	30.7	31,045	8.7	33,748	9.2	36,860
TOTAL: METRO PORTION OF STATE		8.7	3,794,801	2.8	3,901,177	3.2	4,025,740
TOTAL: MISSOURI		9.3	5,595,211	2.5	5,737,314	2.9	5,901,462

MONTANA

	FIPS CODE	1990-2000 % Change	2000 Census	2000-2004 % Change	7/1/04 Estimate	2004-2009 % Change	2009 Projection
Billings MSA	0880	14.0	129,352	3.9	134,394	4.4	140,329
Yellowstone	30111	14.0	129,352	3.9	134,394	4.4	140,329
Great Falls MSA	3040	3.4	80,357	-1.3	79,349	-1.4	78,254
Cascade	30013	3.4	80,357	-1.3	79,349	-1.4	78,254
Missoula MSA	5140	21.8	95,802	3.8	99,453	4.2	103,582
Missoula	30063	21.8	95,802	3.8	99,453	4.2	103,582
TOTAL: METRO PORTION OF STATE		13.2	305,511	2.5	313,196	2.9	322,165
TOTAL: MONTANA		12.9	902,195	2.2	922,368	2.6	946,103

NEBRASKA

	FIPS CODE	1990-2000 % Change	2000 Census	2000-2004 % Change	7/1/04 Estimate	2004-2009 % Change	2009 Projection
Lincoln MSA	4360	17.2	250,291	5.6	264,249	6.1	280,408
Lancaster	31109	17.2	250,291	5.6	264,249	6.1	280,408
Omaha, NE-IA MSA	5920	12.1	716,998	4.7	750,455	5.2	789,482
Pottawattamie, IA	19155	6.1	87,704	1.1	88,639	0.9	89,425
Cass	31025	14.1	24,334	4.9	25,522	5.4	26,911
Douglas	31055	11.3	463,585	3.7	480,743	4.2	500,745
Sarpy	31153	19.5	122,595	10.6	135,564	11.3	150,940
Washington	31177	13.1	18,780	6.4	19,987	7.4	21,461
* **Dakota County** (See Sioux City, IA-NE MSA.)	31043	21.0	20,253	1.5	20,562	1.7	20,905
TOTAL: METRO PORTION OF STATE		14.3	899,838	5.2	946,627	5.8	1,001,370
TOTAL: NEBRASKA		8.4	1,711,263	2.1	1,748,000	2.5	1,791,543

NEVADA

	FIPS CODE	1990-2000 % Change	2000 Census	2000-2004 % Change	7/1/04 Estimate	2004-2009 % Change	2009 Projection
Las Vegas, NV-AZ MSA	4120	83.3	1,563,282	18.4	1,850,678	18.1	2,185,608
Mohave, AZ	04015	65.8	155,032	13.8	176,406	14.3	201,594
Clark	32003	85.5	1,375,765	19.0	1,637,622	18.6	1,942,707
Nye	32023	82.7	32,485	12.8	36,650	12.7	41,307
Reno MSA	6720	33.3	339,486	12.1	380,688	12.9	429,797
Washoe	32031	33.3	339,486	12.1	380,688	12.9	429,797
TOTAL: METRO PORTION OF STATE		72.4	1,747,736	17.6	2,054,960	17.5	2,413,811
TOTAL: NEVADA		66.3	1,998,257	15.9	2,315,504	16.1	2,687,254

NEW HAMPSHIRE

	FIPS CODE	1990-2000 % Change	2000 Census	2000-2004 % Change	7/1/04 Estimate	2004-2009 % Change	2009 Projection
* **Hillsborough County**	33011	13.3	380,841	4.7	398,775	5.2	419,332
* **Rockingham County**	33015	12.8	277,359	6.0	293,899	6.5	312,885
* **Strafford County** (See Boston-Worcester-Lawrence-Lowell-Brockton, MA-NH NECMA.)	33017	7.7	112,233	6.4	119,427	7.1	127,860
TOTAL: METRO PORTION OF STATE		12.3	770,433	5.4	812,101	5.9	860,077
TOTAL: NEW HAMPSHIRE		11.4	1,235,786	5.5	1,303,425	6.0	1,382,117

NEW JERSEY

	FIPS CODE	1990-2000 % Change	2000 Census	2000-2004 % Change	7/1/04 Estimate	2004-2009 % Change	2009 Projection
Atlantic-Cape May PMSA	0560	11.1	354,878	3.9	368,557	4.5	385,070
Atlantic	34001	12.6	252,552	5.7	266,864	6.5	284,131
Cape May	34009	7.6	102,326	-0.6	101,693	-0.7	100,939
Bergen-Passaic PMSA	0875	7.4	1,373,167	2.1	1,402,356	2.3	1,434,510
Bergen	34003	7.1	884,118	2.0	901,514	2.2	921,244
Passaic	34031	7.9	489,049	2.4	500,842	2.5	513,266
Jersey City PMSA	3640	10.1	608,975	-0.4	606,768	-0.5	603,520
Hudson	34017	10.1	608,975	-0.4	606,768	-0.5	603,520
Middlesex-Somerset-Hunterdon PMSA	5015	14.7	1,169,641	5.7	1,236,285	6.2	1,313,407
Hunterdon	34019	13.2	121,989	6.7	130,155	7.3	139,607
Middlesex	34023	11.7	750,162	5.3	790,283	5.9	836,721
Somerset	34035	23.8	297,490	6.2	315,847	6.7	337,079
Monmouth-Ocean PMSA	5190	14.2	1,126,217	6.0	1,194,230	6.6	1,273,605
Monmouth	34025	11.2	615,301	3.6	637,323	4.0	662,568
Ocean	34029	17.9	510,916	9.0	556,907	9.7	611,037
Newark PMSA	5640	6.1	2,032,989	2.3	2,080,714	2.8	2,138,338
Essex	34013	2.0	793,633	0.5	797,608	0.8	804,081
Morris	34027	11.6	470,212	3.6	487,077	4.0	506,709
Sussex	34037	10.1	144,166	6.3	153,303	7.0	164,089
Union	34039	5.8	522,541	1.7	531,425	1.9	541,750
Warren	34041	11.8	102,437	8.7	111,301	9.4	121,709
Trenton PMSA	8480	7.7	350,761	4.2	365,448	4.7	382,782
Mercer	34021	7.7	350,761	4.2	365,448	4.7	382,782
Vineland-Millville-Bridgeton PMSA	8760	6.1	146,438	2.6	150,283	3.3	155,170
Cumberland	34011	6.1	146,438	2.6	150,283	3.3	155,170
* **Burlington County**	34005	7.2	423,394	6.5	450,960	7.3	483,852
* **Camden County**	34007	1.2	508,932	1.3	515,644	1.7	524,315
* **Gloucester County**	34015	10.7	254,673	6.4	270,847	7.2	290,271
* **Salem County** (See Philadelphia, PA-NJ PMSA.)	34033	-1.5	64,285	1.2	65,064	1.6	66,116
TOTAL: METRO PORTION OF STATE		8.9	8,414,350	3.5	8,707,156	3.9	9,050,956
TOTAL: NEW JERSEY		8.9	8,414,350	3.5	8,707,156	3.9	9,050,956

NEW MEXICO

	FIPS CODE	1990-2000 % Change	2000 Census	2000-2004 % Change	7/1/04 Estimate	2004-2009 % Change	2009 Projection
Albuquerque MSA	0200	21.0	712,738	6.5	759,193	7.3	814,647
Bernalillo	35001	15.8	556,678	5.9	589,389	6.7	628,991
Sandoval	35043	42.0	89,908	12.9	101,506	13.4	115,077
Valencia	35061	46.2	66,152	3.2	68,298	3.3	70,579
Las Cruces MSA	4100	28.9	174,682	5.7	184,554	6.5	196,459
Dona Ana	35013	28.9	174,682	5.7	184,554	6.5	196,459
Santa Fe MSA	7490	26.1	147,635	6.7	157,592	7.5	169,389
Los Alamos	35028	1.3	18,343	3.4	18,970	4.4	19,808
Santa Fe	35049	30.7	129,292	7.2	138,622	7.9	149,581
TOTAL: METRO PORTION OF STATE		23.0	1,035,055	6.4	1,101,339	7.2	1,180,495
TOTAL: NEW MEXICO		20.1	1,819,046	4.0	1,892,304	4.7	1,980,754

NEW YORK

	FIPS CODE	1990-2000 % Change	2000 Census	2000-2004 % Change	7/1/04 Estimate	2004-2009 % Change	2009 Projection
Albany-Schenectady-Troy MSA	0160	1.6	875,583	2.2	894,569	2.5	917,335
Albany	36001	0.7	294,565	1.5	298,933	1.8	304,373
Montgomery	36057	-4.4	49,708	-0.9	49,269	-1.0	48,764
Rensselaer	36083	-1.2	152,538	1.3	154,473	1.5	156,803
Saratoga	36091	10.7	200,635	6.0	212,606	6.6	226,546
Schenectady	36093	-1.8	146,555	0.7	147,572	1.0	148,981
Schoharie	36095	-0.9	31,582	0.4	31,716	0.5	31,868
Binghamton MSA	0960	-4.6	252,320	-0.6	250,793	-0.6	249,233
Broome	36007	-5.5	200,536	-0.7	199,049	-0.8	197,500
Tioga	36107	-1.1	51,784	-0.1	51,744	-0.0	51,733
Buffalo-Niagara Falls MSA	1280	-1.6	1,170,111	-1.2	1,156,288	-1.4	1,140,627
Erie	36029	-1.9	950,265	-1.2	938,615	-1.4	925,325
Niagara	36063	-0.4	219,846	-1.0	217,673	-1.1	215,302
Dutchess County PMSA	2281	8.0	280,150	5.0	294,234	5.7	310,975
Dutchess	36027	8.0	280,150	5.0	294,234	5.7	310,975
Elmira MSA	2335	-4.3	91,070	-0.9	90,205	-1.1	89,168
Chemung	36015	-4.3	91,070	-0.9	90,205	-1.1	89,168
Glens Falls MSA	2975	4.9	124,345	2.4	127,334	2.9	131,063
Warren	36113	6.9	63,303	3.0	65,172	3.5	67,455
Washington	36115	2.9	61,042	1.8	62,162	2.3	63,608
Jamestown MSA	3610	-1.5	139,750	-2.0	137,003	-2.3	133,834
Chautauqua	36013	-1.5	139,750	-2.0	137,003	-2.3	133,834
Nassau-Suffolk PMSA	5380	5.5	2,753,913	2.5	2,823,190	2.8	2,901,600
Nassau	36059	3.7	1,334,544	0.4	1,340,495	0.4	1,345,637
Suffolk	36103	7.4	1,419,369	4.5	1,482,695	4.6	1,555,963
Newburgh, NY-PA PMSA	5660	15.5	387,669	9.3	423,860	10.1	466,560
Orange	36071	11.0	341,367	8.3	369,860	9.1	403,392
Pike, PA	42103	65.6	46,302	16.6	54,000	17.0	63,168
New York PMSA	5600	9.0	9,314,235	1.4	9,449,241	1.6	9,602,418
Bronx	36005	10.7	1,332,650	3.0	1,372,845	3.5	1,421,060
Kings	36047	7.2	2,465,326	0.4	2,474,606	0.4	2,484,985
New York	36061	3.3	1,537,195	2.3	1,572,971	2.6	1,613,813
Putnam	36079	14.1	95,745	5.2	100,694	5.7	106,411
Queens	36081	14.2	2,229,379	-0.3	2,223,681	-0.4	2,214,646
Richmond	36085	17.1	443,728	4.7	464,513	5.1	488,386
Rockland	36087	8.0	286,753	2.8	294,839	3.1	304,089
Westchester	36119	5.6	923,459	2.3	945,092	2.5	969,028
Rochester MSA	6840	3.4	1,098,201	0.4	1,102,049	0.4	1,106,192
Genesee	36037	0.5	60,370	-0.7	59,919	-0.8	59,415
Livingston	36051	3.1	64,328	0.7	64,750	0.7	65,206
Monroe	36055	3.0	735,343	0.2	737,090	0.2	738,840
Ontario	36069	5.4	100,224	2.9	103,127	3.3	106,536
Orleans	36073	5.6	44,171	-1.6	43,448	-2.1	42,550
Wayne	36117	5.2	93,765	-0.1	93,715	-0.1	93,645
Syracuse MSA	8160	-1.4	732,117	0.7	737,104	0.8	743,017
Cayuga	36011	-0.4	81,963	-0.4	81,655	-0.4	81,302
Madison	36053	0.5	69,441	1.4	70,428	1.7	71,656
Onondaga	36067	-2.3	458,336	0.6	461,207	0.7	464,651
Oswego	36075	0.5	122,377	1.2	123,814	1.3	125,408
Utica-Rome MSA	8680	-5.3	299,896	-0.8	297,571	-0.8	295,056
Herkimer	36043	-2.1	64,427	-1.5	63,477	-1.8	62,350
Oneida	36065	-6.1	235,469	-0.6	234,094	-0.6	232,706
TOTAL: METRO PORTION OF STATE		5.8	17,473,058	1.5	17,729,441	1.7	18,023,910
TOTAL: NEW YORK		5.5	18,976,457	1.5	19,254,372	1.7	19,575,657

NORTH CAROLINA

	FIPS CODE	1990-2000 % Change	2000 Census	2000-2004 % Change	7/1/04 Estimate	2004-2009 % Change	2009 Projection
Asheville MSA	0480	17.8	225,965	3.8	234,482	4.2	244,239
Buncombe	37021	18.0	206,330	4.0	214,572	4.4	224,068
Madison	37115	15.8	19,635	1.4	19,910	1.3	20,171
Charlotte-Gastonia-Rock Hill, NC-SC MSA	1520	29.0	1,499,293	9.9	1,648,241	10.5	1,822,085
Cabarrus	37025	32.5	131,063	11.6	146,248	12.0	163,785
Gaston	37071	8.7	190,365	1.9	193,911	2.1	197,978
Lincoln	37109	26.8	63,780	7.2	68,354	7.9	73,744
Mecklenburg	37119	36.0	695,454	10.7	769,746	11.3	856,626
Rowan	37159	17.8	130,340	3.6	135,024	4.0	140,481
Union	37179	46.9	123,677	23.5	152,765	22.2	186,658
York, SC	45091	25.2	164,614	10.7	182,193	11.3	202,803
Fayetteville MSA	2560	10.3	302,963	0.4	304,324	0.6	306,169
Cumberland	37051	10.3	302,963	0.4	304,324	0.6	306,169
Goldsboro MSA	2980	8.3	113,329	-0.3	113,028	-0.3	112,648
Wayne	37191	8.3	113,329	-0.3	113,028	-0.3	112,648
Greensboro--Winston-Salem--High Point MSA	3120	19.2	1,251,509	4.6	1,308,675	5.1	1,374,822
Alamance	37001	20.9	130,800	5.9	138,548	6.4	147,422
Davidson	37057	16.2	147,246	4.4	153,692	4.9	161,263
Davie	37059	25.0	34,835	8.6	37,846	9.2	41,321
Forsyth	37067	15.1	306,067	5.0	321,453	5.7	339,659
Guilford	37081	21.2	421,048	3.9	437,629	4.4	456,823
Randolph	37151	22.4	130,454	4.6	136,509	5.0	143,297
Stokes	37169	20.1	44,711	1.3	45,273	1.2	45,796
Yadkin	37197	19.2	36,348	3.8	37,725	4.0	39,241
Greenville MSA	3150	24.0	133,798	4.8	140,223	5.5	147,885
Pitt	37147	24.0	133,798	4.8	140,223	5.5	147,885
Hickory-Morganton-Lenoir MSA	3290	16.9	341,851	3.1	352,521	3.4	364,417
Alexander	37003	22.0	33,603	4.6	35,156	5.3	37,012
Burke	37023	17.7	89,148	0.7	89,791	0.7	90,457
Caldwell	37027	9.5	77,415	2.2	79,103	2.4	80,976
Catawba	37035	19.7	141,685	4.8	148,471	5.1	155,972
Jacksonville MSA	3605	0.3	150,355	-2.5	146,634	-3.0	142,265
Onslow	37133	0.3	150,355	-2.5	146,634	-3.0	142,265
Raleigh-Durham-Chapel Hill MSA	6640	38.9	1,187,941	11.8	1,328,146	12.6	1,495,394
Chatham	37037	27.3	49,329	15.7	57,081	16.1	66,293
Durham	37063	22.8	223,314	7.9	240,859	8.5	261,245
Franklin	37069	29.8	47,260	13.1	53,474	13.7	60,811
Johnston	37101	50.0	121,965	15.9	141,305	15.9	163,817
Orange	37135	26.0	118,227	0.6	118,905	3.0	122,518
Wake	37183	48.3	627,846	14.1	716,522	14.5	820,710
Rocky Mount MSA	6895	7.3	143,026	1.5	145,152	1.8	147,778
Edgecombe	37065	-1.7	55,606	-1.5	54,761	-1.2	54,096
Nash	37127	14.0	87,420	3.4	90,391	3.6	93,682
Wilmington MSA	9200	36.3	233,450	9.1	254,768	10.0	280,202
Brunswick	37019	43.5	73,143	15.1	84,206	15.5	97,272
New Hanover	37129	33.3	160,307	6.4	170,562	7.3	182,930
* **Currituck County** (See Norfolk-Virginia Beach-Newport News, VA-NC MSA.)	37053	32.4	18,190	19.1	21,665	19.2	25,821
TOTAL: METRO PORTION OF STATE		24.3	5,437,056	7.0	5,815,666	7.7	6,260,922
TOTAL: NORTH CAROLINA		21.4	8,049,313	5.8	8,517,110	6.4	9,066,420

NORTH DAKOTA

	FIPS CODE	1990-2000 % Change	2000 Census	2000-2004 % Change	7/1/04 Estimate	2004-2009 % Change	2009 Projection
Bismarck MSA	1010	13.0	94,719	2.9	97,478	3.2	100,607
Burleigh	38015	15.4	69,416	4.3	72,410	4.8	75,902
Morton	38059	6.8	25,303	-0.9	25,068	-1.4	24,705
Fargo-Moorhead, ND-MN MSA	2520	13.7	174,367	3.6	180,577	3.9	187,692
Clay, MN	27027	1.6	51,229	1.9	52,205	2.1	53,311
Cass	38017	19.7	123,138	4.3	128,372	4.7	134,381
Grand Forks, ND-MN MSA	2985	-5.5	97,478	-2.4	95,100	-2.9	92,367
Polk, MN	27119	-3.5	31,369	-2.0	30,748	-2.5	29,972
Grand Forks	38035	-6.5	66,109	-2.7	64,352	-3.0	62,395
TOTAL: METRO PORTION OF STATE		10.3	283,966	2.2	290,202	2.5	297,383
TOTAL: NORTH DAKOTA		0.5	642,200	-1.7	631,440	-1.9	619,592

OHIO

	FIPS CODE	1990-2000 % Change	2000 Census	2000-2004 % Change	7/1/04 Estimate	2004-2009 % Change	2009 Projection
Akron PMSA	0080	5.7	694,960	1.2	703,530	1.3	712,812
Portage	39133	6.6	152,061	2.4	155,699	2.6	159,812
Summit	39153	5.4	542,899	0.9	547,831	0.9	553,000
Canton-Massillon MSA	1320	3.3	406,934	0.1	407,161	0.0	407,290
Carroll	39019	8.7	28,836	3.5	29,838	4.0	31,027
Stark	39151	2.9	378,098	-0.2	377,323	-0.3	376,263
Cincinnati, OH-KY-IN PMSA	1640	7.9	1,646,395	2.1	1,680,493	2.3	1,719,163
Dearborn, IN	18029	18.7	46,109	4.9	48,349	5.2	50,848
Ohio, IN	18115	5.8	5,623	2.5	5,762	2.6	5,911
Boone, KY	21015	49.3	85,991	16.9	100,516	16.8	117,390
Campbell, KY	21037	5.7	88,616	-1.0	87,745	-1.3	86,626
Gallatin, KY	21077	45.9	7,870	2.2	8,041	2.8	8,268
Grant, KY	21081	42.2	22,384	9.3	24,461	9.8	26,848
Kenton, KY	21117	6.6	151,464	0.7	152,501	0.7	153,565
Pendleton, KY	21191	19.6	14,390	6.2	15,286	6.4	16,262
Brown	39015	20.9	42,285	4.6	44,217	4.6	46,255
Clermont	39025	18.5	177,977	5.7	188,179	6.3	200,037
Hamilton	39061	-2.4	845,303	-3.4	816,699	-4.1	783,497
Warren	39165	39.0	158,383	19.2	188,737	18.5	223,656
Cleveland-Lorain-Elyria PMSA	1680	2.2	2,250,871	-0.5	2,239,967	-0.6	2,227,119
Ashtabula	39007	2.9	102,728	0.5	103,234	0.5	103,780
Cuyahoga	39035	-1.3	1,393,978	-2.8	1,354,570	-3.4	1,308,652
Geauga	39055	12.0	90,895	4.3	94,840	4.7	99,314
Lake	39085	5.6	227,511	0.8	229,287	0.9	231,284
Lorain	39093	5.0	284,664	3.0	293,138	3.3	302,944
Medina	39103	23.5	151,095	9.1	164,898	9.9	181,145
Columbus MSA	1840	14.5	1,540,157	4.8	1,614,311	5.3	1,699,176
Delaware	39041	64.3	109,989	27.1	139,819	25.1	174,883
Fairfield	39045	18.7	122,759	10.4	135,586	11.2	150,735
Franklin	39049	11.2	1,068,978	2.4	1,094,640	2.6	1,122,878
Licking	39089	13.4	145,491	4.6	152,155	5.0	159,728
Madison	39097	8.5	40,213	1.4	40,757	1.6	41,412
Pickaway	39129	9.3	52,727	-2.6	51,354	-3.5	49,540
Dayton-Springfield MSA	2000	-0.1	950,558	-0.5	945,928	-0.6	940,380
Clark	39023	-1.9	144,742	-1.3	142,925	-1.5	140,785
Greene	39057	8.2	147,886	3.0	152,266	3.3	157,280
Miami	39109	6.1	98,868	1.8	100,642	2.0	102,678
Montgomery	39113	-2.6	559,062	-1.6	550,095	-1.9	539,637
Hamilton-Middletown PMSA	3200	14.2	332,807	4.1	346,371	4.5	362,111
Butler	39017	14.2	332,807	4.1	346,371	4.5	362,111
Lima MSA	4320	0.5	155,084	-0.1	154,917	-0.2	154,564
Allen	39003	-1.2	108,473	-0.3	108,137	-0.5	107,596
Auglaize	39011	4.5	46,611	0.4	46,780	0.4	46,968

* Indicates county is included from metro in different state.
Source: Devonshire Associates Ltd. and Scan/US, Inc. 2004.

continued on next page

Metropolitan Statistical Areas and Their Component Counties: Population Trends, *Continued*

	FIPS CODE	PAST 1990-2000 % Change	PAST 2000 Census	PRESENT 2000-2004 % Change	PRESENT 7/1/04 Estimate	FUTURE 2004-2009 % Change	FUTURE 2009 Projection
Mansfield MSA	4800	1.0	175,818	-1.1	173,916	-1.3	171,695
Crawford	39033	-1.9	46,966	-2.4	45,825	-2.9	44,507
Richland	39139	2.2	128,852	-0.6	128,091	-0.7	127,188
Steubenville-Weirton, OH-WV MSA	8080	-7.4	132,008	-3.4	127,547	-3.9	122,519
Jefferson	39081	-8.0	73,894	-3.5	71,299	-4.1	68,410
Brooke, WV	54009	-5.7	25,447	-2.6	24,796	-2.9	24,079
Hancock, WV	54029	-7.3	32,667	-3.7	31,452	-4.5	30,030
Toledo MSA	8400	0.7	618,203	0.3	620,144	0.4	622,319
Fulton	39051	9.3	42,084	1.1	42,546	1.1	43,035
Lucas	39095	-1.6	455,054	-0.2	453,978	-0.3	452,689
Wood	39173	6.9	121,065	2.1	123,620	2.4	126,595
Youngstown-Warren MSA	9320	-1.0	594,746	-2.2	581,948	-2.6	566,986
Columbiana	39029	3.5	112,075	-0.7	111,328	-0.9	110,331
Mahoning	39099	-2.7	257,555	-3.0	249,884	-3.5	241,134
Trumbull	39155	-1.2	225,116	-1.9	220,736	-2.4	215,521
*** Lawrence County** (See Huntington-Ashland, WV-KY-OH MSA.)	39087	0.8	62,319	0.5	62,637	0.7	63,060
*** Washington County** (See Parkersburg-Marietta, WV-OH MSA.)	39167	1.6	63,251	-1.5	62,279	-1.8	61,151
*** Belmont County** (See Wheeling, WV-OH MSA.)	39013	-1.2	70,226	-1.1	69,474	-1.2	68,653
TOTAL: METRO PORTION OF STATE		4.4	9,213,776	0.8	9,291,714	0.9	9,379,171
TOTAL: OHIO		4.7	11,353,140	0.9	11,459,952	1.1	11,580,720

OKLAHOMA

	FIPS CODE	PAST 1990-2000 % Change	PAST 2000 Census	PRESENT 2000-2004 % Change	PRESENT 7/1/04 Estimate	FUTURE 2004-2009 % Change	FUTURE 2009 Projection
Enid MSA	2340	1.9	57,813	-1.6	56,916	-1.7	55,975
Garfield	40047	1.9	57,813	-1.6	56,916	-1.7	55,975
Lawton MSA	4200	3.1	114,996	-1.2	113,664	-1.0	112,529
Comanche	40031	3.1	114,996	-1.2	113,664	-1.0	112,529
Oklahoma City MSA	5880	13.0	1,083,346	4.5	1,131,827	5.1	1,189,331
Canadian	40017	17.9	87,697	7.7	94,470	8.3	102,289
Cleveland	40027	19.4	208,016	7.6	223,830	8.6	243,120
Logan	40083	16.9	33,924	5.8	35,908	6.8	38,347
McClain	40087	21.7	27,740	4.0	28,843	4.3	30,084
Oklahoma	40109	10.1	660,448	3.1	680,880	3.5	704,863
Pottawatomie	40125	11.5	65,521	3.6	67,896	4.0	70,628
Tulsa MSA	8560	13.3	803,235	3.3	829,509	3.7	860,064
Creek	40037	10.6	67,367	2.7	69,207	3.0	71,260
Osage	40113	6.7	44,437	2.4	45,482	2.6	46,643
Rogers	40131	28.0	70,641	12.0	79,136	12.3	88,837
Tulsa	40143	11.9	563,299	1.6	572,493	1.9	583,325
Wagoner	40145	20.1	57,491	9.9	63,191	10.8	69,999
*** Sequoyah County** (See Fort Smith, AR-OK MSA.)	40135	15.2	38,972	3.4	40,284	3.8	41,808
TOTAL: METRO PORTION OF STATE		12.2	2,098,362	3.5	2,172,200	4.0	2,259,707
TOTAL: OKLAHOMA		9.7	3,450,654	2.3	3,530,711	2.7	3,626,604

OREGON

	FIPS CODE	PAST 1990-2000 % Change	PAST 2000 Census	PRESENT 2000-2004 % Change	PRESENT 7/1/04 Estimate	FUTURE 2004-2009 % Change	FUTURE 2009 Projection
Corvallis MSA	1890	10.4	78,153	2.0	79,726	2.5	81,681
Benton	41003	10.4	78,153	2.0	79,726	2.5	81,681
Eugene-Springfield MSA	2400	14.2	322,959	3.1	332,896	3.6	344,731
Lane	41039	14.2	322,959	3.1	332,896	3.6	344,731
Medford-Ashland MSA	4890	23.8	181,269	6.4	192,822	7.1	206,537
Jackson	41029	23.8	181,269	6.4	192,822	7.1	206,537
Portland-Vancouver, OR-WA PMSA	6440	26.6	1,918,009	7.6	2,064,660	8.4	2,238,058
Clackamas	41005	21.4	338,391	7.4	363,386	8.2	393,126
Columbia	41009	16.0	43,560	8.2	47,125	9.2	51,439
Multnomah	41051	13.1	660,486	3.5	683,283	4.0	710,606
Washington	41067	42.9	445,342	10.0	489,844	10.6	541,567
Yamhill	41071	29.7	84,992	6.8	90,750	7.5	97,577
Clark, WA	53011	45.0	345,238	13.0	390,272	13.7	443,743
Salem PMSA	7080	24.9	347,214	6.0	367,908	6.7	392,483
Marion	41047	24.7	284,834	5.6	300,798	6.3	319,801
Polk	41053	25.9	62,380	7.6	67,110	8.3	72,682
TOTAL: METRO PORTION OF STATE		21.7	2,502,366	5.8	2,647,740	6.5	2,819,747
TOTAL: OREGON		20.4	3,421,399	5.3	3,602,559	6.0	3,817,376

PENNSYLVANIA

	FIPS CODE	PAST 1990-2000 % Change	PAST 2000 Census	PRESENT 2000-2004 % Change	PRESENT 7/1/04 Estimate	FUTURE 2004-2009 % Change	FUTURE 2009 Projection
Allentown-Bethlehem-Easton MSA	0240	7.2	637,958	4.3	665,446	5.0	698,456
Carbon	42025	3.4	58,802	3.0	60,563	3.5	62,711
Lehigh	42077	7.2	312,090	3.5	323,155	4.1	336,281
Northampton	42095	8.1	267,066	5.5	281,728	6.3	299,464
Altoona MSA	0280	-1.1	129,144	-2.0	126,555	-2.4	123,474
Blair	42013	-1.1	129,144	-2.0	126,555	-2.4	123,474
Erie MSA	2360	1.9	280,843	-0.4	279,718	-0.5	278,430
Erie	42049	1.9	280,843	-0.4	279,718	-0.5	278,430
Harrisburg-Lebanon-Carlisle MSA	3240	7.0	629,401	2.2	643,547	2.6	660,546
Cumberland	42041	9.4	213,674	3.8	221,861	4.4	231,657
Dauphin	42043	5.9	251,798	0.8	253,912	1.0	256,480
Lebanon	42075	5.8	120,327	2.5	123,395	3.0	127,083
Perry	42099	5.9	43,602	1.8	44,379	2.1	45,326
Johnstown MSA	3680	-3.6	232,621	-2.1	227,679	-2.5	222,031
Cambria	42021	-6.4	152,598	-2.7	148,535	-3.1	143,998
Somerset	42111	2.3	80,023	-1.1	79,144	-1.4	78,033
Lancaster MSA	4000	11.3	470,658	3.4	486,469	3.8	504,836
Lancaster	42071	11.3	470,658	3.4	486,469	3.8	504,836
Philadelphia, PA-NJ PMSA	6160	3.6	5,100,931	1.7	5,185,302	2.0	5,286,675
Burlington, NJ	34005	7.2	423,394	6.5	450,960	7.3	483,852
Camden, NJ	34007	1.2	508,932	1.3	515,644	1.7	524,315
Gloucester, NJ	34015	10.7	254,673	6.4	270,847	7.2	290,271
Salem, NJ	34033	-1.5	64,285	1.2	65,064	1.6	66,116
Bucks	42017	10.4	597,635	3.4	617,667	3.7	640,325
Chester	42029	15.2	433,501	7.2	464,595	7.7	500,504
Delaware	42045	0.6	550,864	0.8	555,177	0.7	558,790
Montgomery	42091	10.6	750,097	3.6	777,323	4.2	810,039
Philadelphia	42101	-4.3	1,517,550	-3.3	1,468,025	-3.8	1,412,463
Pittsburgh MSA	6280	-1.5	2,358,695	-1.1	2,332,585	-1.3	2,302,295
Allegheny	42003	-4.1	1,281,666	-2.1	1,255,103	-2.5	1,224,321
Beaver	42007	-2.5	181,412	-1.9	177,885	-2.3	173,845
Butler	42019	14.5	174,083	4.5	181,858	5.0	190,912
Fayette	42051	2.3	148,644	-2.2	145,333	-2.7	141,431
Washington	42125	-0.8	202,897	0.9	204,705	1.0	206,762
Westmoreland	42129	-0.1	369,993	-0.6	367,701	-0.7	365,024
Reading MSA	6680	11.0	373,638	4.1	388,909	4.6	406,841
Berks	42011	11.0	373,638	4.1	388,909	4.6	406,841
Scranton--Wilkes-Barre--Hazleton MSA	7560	-2.1	624,776	-1.7	614,462	-1.8	603,115
Columbia	42037	1.5	64,151	1.0	64,770	1.3	65,582
Lackawanna	42069	-2.6	213,295	-1.7	209,643	-1.9	205,576
Luzerne	42079	-2.7	319,250	-2.3	311,854	-2.7	303,556
Wyoming	42131	0.0	28,080	0.4	28,195	0.7	28,401
Sharon MSA	7610	-0.6	120,293	-0.4	119,795	-0.4	119,272
Mercer	42085	-0.6	120,293	-0.4	119,795	-0.4	119,272
State College MSA	8050	9.7	135,758	5.7	143,518	6.5	152,895
Centre	42027	9.7	135,758	5.7	143,518	6.5	152,895
Williamsport MSA	9140	1.1	120,044	-1.8	117,940	-2.1	115,459
Lycoming	42081	1.1	120,044	-1.8	117,940	-2.1	115,459
York MSA	9280	12.4	381,751	4.5	398,969	5.1	419,155
York	42133	12.4	381,751	4.5	398,969	5.1	419,155
*** Pike County** (See Newburgh, NY-PA PMSA.)	42103	65.6	46,302	16.6	54,000	17.0	63,168
TOTAL: METRO PORTION OF STATE		3.1	10,391,529	0.9	10,482,379	1.0	10,592,094
TOTAL: PENNSYLVANIA		3.4	12,281,054	0.9	12,392,109	1.1	12,525,381

RHODE ISLAND

	FIPS CODE	PAST 1990-2000 % Change	PAST 2000 Census	PRESENT 2000-2004 % Change	PRESENT 7/1/04 Estimate	FUTURE 2004-2009 % Change	FUTURE 2009 Projection
Providence-Warwick-Pawtucket NECMA	6483	5.1	962,886	3.7	998,644	4.2	1,040,712
Bristol	44001	3.7	50,648	0.8	51,073	0.8	51,493
Kent	44003	3.7	167,090	3.3	172,563	3.7	178,891
Providence	44007	4.2	621,602	3.8	645,010	4.3	672,848
Washington	44009	12.3	123,546	5.2	129,998	5.8	137,480
TOTAL: METRO PORTION OF STATE		5.1	962,886	3.7	998,644	4.2	1,040,712
TOTAL: RHODE ISLAND		4.5	1,048,319	3.5	1,084,664	3.9	1,127,164

* Indicates county is included from metro in different state.
Source: Devonshire Associates Ltd. and Scan/US, Inc. 2004.

SOUTH CAROLINA

	FIPS CODE	PAST 1990-2000 % Change	PAST 2000 Census	PRESENT 2000-2004 % Change	PRESENT 7/1/04 Estimate	FUTURE 2004-2009 % Change	FUTURE 2009 Projection
Charleston-North Charleston MSA	1440	8.3	549,033	5.4	578,716	6.1	614,123
Berkeley	45015	10.8	142,651	3.5	147,602	3.9	153,361
Charleston	45019	5.1	309,969	4.7	324,460	5.3	341,682
Dorchester	45035	16.1	96,413	10.6	106,654	11.7	119,080
Columbia MSA	1760	18.4	536,691	5.4	565,436	6.0	599,434
Lexington	45063	28.9	216,014	6.4	229,751	7.0	245,856
Richland	45079	12.2	320,677	4.7	335,685	5.3	353,578
Florence MSA	2655	10.0	125,761	2.7	129,181	3.3	133,411
Florence	45041	10.0	125,761	2.7	129,181	3.3	133,411
Greenville-Spartanburg-Anderson MSA	3160	15.9	962,441	4.3	1,004,256	4.8	1,052,690
Anderson	45007	14.1	165,740	4.5	173,238	5.0	181,872
Cherokee	45021	18.0	52,537	2.5	53,850	2.7	55,322
Greenville	45045	18.6	379,616	5.4	400,132	6.0	423,990
Pickens	45077	18.0	110,757	2.4	113,461	2.7	116,470
Spartanburg	45083	11.9	253,791	3.9	263,575	4.3	275,036
Myrtle Beach MSA	5330	36.5	196,629	9.3	214,999	9.9	236,202
Horry	45051	36.5	196,629	9.3	214,999	9.9	236,202
Sumter MSA	8140	2.0	104,646	1.6	106,361	1.9	108,382
Sumter	45085	2.0	104,646	1.6	106,361	1.9	108,382
*** Aiken County**	45003	17.9	142,552	3.9	148,054	4.4	154,638
*** Edgefield County** (See Augusta-Aiken, GA-SC MSA.)	45037	33.9	24,595	0.6	24,738	0.7	24,909
*** York County** (See Charlotte-Gastonia-Rock Hill, NC-SC MSA.)	45091	25.2	164,614	10.7	182,193	11.3	202,803
TOTAL: METRO PORTION OF STATE		15.9	2,806,962	5.2	2,953,934	5.8	3,126,592
TOTAL: SOUTH CAROLINA		15.1	4,012,012	4.4	4,188,493	4.9	4,395,198

SOUTH DAKOTA

	FIPS CODE	PAST 1990-2000 % Change	PAST 2000 Census	PRESENT 2000-2004 % Change	PRESENT 7/1/04 Estimate	FUTURE 2004-2009 % Change	FUTURE 2009 Projection
Rapid City MSA	6660	8.9	88,565	4.9	92,908	5.4	97,969
Pennington	46103	8.9	88,565	4.9	92,908	5.4	97,969
Sioux Falls MSA	7760	23.8	172,412	8.7	187,360	9.1	204,406
Lincoln	46083	56.4	24,131	28.0	30,883	25.5	38,756
Minnehaha	46099	19.8	148,281	5.5	156,477	5.9	165,650
TOTAL: METRO PORTION OF STATE		18.3	260,977	7.4	280,268	7.9	302,375
TOTAL: SOUTH DAKOTA		8.5	754,844	1.6	767,184	1.9	781,561

TENNESSEE

	FIPS CODE	PAST 1990-2000 % Change	PAST 2000 Census	PRESENT 2000-2004 % Change	PRESENT 7/1/04 Estimate	FUTURE 2004-2009 % Change	FUTURE 2009 Projection
Chattanooga, TN-GA MSA	1560	9.6	465,161	2.5	476,717	2.9	490,453
Catoosa, GA	13047	25.5	53,282	11.8	59,560	12.4	66,931
Dade, GA	13083	15.3	15,154	6.6	16,151	7.4	17,353
Walker, GA	13295	4.7	61,053	3.3	63,070	3.9	65,504
Hamilton	47065	7.8	307,896	0.7	310,020	0.8	312,567
Marion	47115	11.7	27,776	0.5	27,916	0.7	28,098
Clarksville-Hopkinsville, TN-KY MSA	1660	22.2	207,033	2.5	212,112	2.7	217,907
Christian, KY	21047	4.8	72,265	-4.3	69,170	-5.2	65,576
Montgomery	47125	34.1	134,768	6.1	142,942	6.6	152,331
Jackson MSA	3580	18.3	107,377	2.8	110,436	3.3	114,042
Chester	47023	21.2	15,540	2.6	15,941	3.1	16,436
Madison	47113	17.8	91,837	2.9	94,495	3.3	97,606
Johnson City-Kingsport-Bristol, TN-VA MSA	3660	10.1	480,091	1.6	487,711	1.9	496,840
Carter	47019	10.2	56,742	3.8	58,913	4.4	61,505
Hawkins	47073	20.2	53,563	3.6	55,484	4.0	57,720
Sullivan	47163	6.6	153,048	0.0	153,090	0.1	153,289
Unicoi	47171	6.8	17,667	0.4	17,729	0.6	17,827
Washington	47179	16.1	107,198	3.5	110,949	3.9	115,303
Bristol, VA (Ind. City)	51520	-5.7	17,367	-1.1	17,176	-0.9	17,023
Scott, VA	51169	0.9	23,403	-2.2	22,883	-2.6	22,279
Washington, VA	51191	11.4	51,103	0.8	51,487	0.8	51,894
Knoxville MSA	3840	17.3	687,249	4.8	720,109	5.4	758,822
Anderson	47001	4.5	71,330	1.1	72,110	1.4	73,141
Blount	47009	23.1	105,823	7.0	113,265	7.7	122,041
Knox	47093	13.8	382,032	3.8	396,391	4.3	413,365
Loudon	47105	25.1	39,086	8.5	42,424	9.4	46,425
Sevier	47155	39.4	71,170	7.9	76,768	8.2	83,094
Union	47173	30.0	17,808	7.5	19,151	8.4	20,756
Memphis, TN-AR-MS MSA	4920	12.7	1,135,614	3.7	1,178,084	4.2	1,227,496
Crittenden, AR	05035	1.9	50,866	0.7	51,207	0.5	51,447
DeSoto, MS	28033	57.9	107,199	20.9	129,632	20.2	155,853
Fayette	47047	12.7	28,806	15.8	33,345	15.8	38,625
Shelby	47157	8.6	897,472	1.3	908,843	1.5	922,152
Tipton	47167	36.5	51,271	7.4	55,057	7.9	59,419
Nashville MSA	5360	25.0	1,231,311	6.0	1,305,357	6.6	1,391,875
Cheatham	47021	32.3	35,912	5.2	37,783	5.5	39,876
Davidson	47037	11.6	569,891	-0.0	569,819	-0.0	569,701
Dickson	47043	23.1	43,156	5.4	45,469	5.9	48,138
Robertson	47147	31.2	54,433	8.9	59,290	9.4	64,834
Rutherford	47149	53.5	182,023	14.6	208,605	15.1	240,080
Sumner	47165	26.3	130,449	8.3	141,292	9.0	153,992
Williamson	47187	56.3	126,638	15.1	145,703	15.1	167,711
Wilson	47189	31.2	88,809	9.7	97,396	10.4	107,543
TOTAL: METRO PORTION OF STATE		16.7	3,862,144	3.8	4,010,190	4.3	4,183,575
TOTAL: TENNESSEE		16.7	5,689,283	3.5	5,888,107	3.9	6,119,904

TEXAS

	FIPS CODE	PAST 1990-2000 % Change	PAST 2000 Census	PRESENT 2000-2004 % Change	PRESENT 7/1/04 Estimate	FUTURE 2004-2009 % Change	FUTURE 2009 Projection
Abilene MSA	0040	5.8	126,555	-1.3	124,966	-1.5	123,107
Taylor	48441	5.8	126,555	-1.3	124,966	-1.5	123,107
Amarillo MSA	0320	16.2	217,858	4.1	226,760	4.6	237,204
Potter	48375	16.0	113,546	4.4	118,540	5.1	124,557
Randall	48381	16.3	104,312	3.7	108,220	4.1	112,647
Austin-San Marcos MSA	0640	47.7	1,249,763	13.2	1,415,292	13.3	1,603,483
Bastrop	48021	50.9	57,733	21.2	69,998	20.9	84,598
Caldwell	48055	22.0	32,194	13.7	36,601	14.1	41,747
Hays	48209	48.7	97,589	22.2	119,256	21.2	144,559
Travis	48453	40.9	812,280	7.1	869,648	7.1	931,805
Williamson	48491	79.1	249,967	27.9	319,789	25.3	400,774
Beaumont-Port Arthur MSA	0840	6.6	385,090	-0.8	381,930	-0.9	378,485
Hardin	48199	16.3	48,073	4.3	50,132	5.0	52,623
Jefferson	48245	5.3	252,051	-1.8	247,599	-2.0	242,615
Orange	48361	5.5	84,966	-0.9	84,199	-1.1	83,247
Brazoria PMSA	1145	26.1	241,767	11.6	269,789	12.3	302,968
Brazoria	48039	26.1	241,767	11.6	269,789	12.3	302,968
Brownsville-Harlingen-San Benito MSA	1240	28.9	335,227	10.9	371,857	11.8	415,655
Cameron	48061	28.9	335,227	10.9	371,857	11.8	415,655
Bryan-College Station MSA	1260	25.1	152,415	6.4	162,171	7.2	173,866
Brazos	48041	25.1	152,415	6.4	162,171	7.2	173,866
Corpus Christi MSA	1880	8.8	380,783	0.9	384,106	1.1	388,338
Nueces	48355	7.7	313,645	0.7	315,797	0.9	318,737
San Patricio	48409	14.3	67,138	1.7	68,309	1.9	69,601
Dallas PMSA	1920	31.5	3,519,176	10.8	3,900,657	11.4	4,346,969
Collin	48085	86.2	491,675	28.0	629,504	25.7	791,230
Dallas	48113	19.8	2,218,899	3.8	2,303,656	4.2	2,401,298
Denton	48121	58.3	432,976	23.5	534,784	22.4	654,680
Ellis	48139	30.8	111,360	15.3	128,389	15.5	148,272
Henderson	48213	25.2	73,277	7.1	78,507	7.8	84,652
Hunt	48231	19.0	76,596	7.5	82,370	8.2	89,093
Kaufman	48257	36.6	71,313	19.5	85,224	19.2	101,560
Rockwall	48397	68.3	43,080	35.2	58,223	30.8	76,184
El Paso MSA	2320	14.9	679,622	5.0	713,340	5.5	752,812
El Paso	48141	14.9	679,622	5.0	713,340	5.5	752,812
Fort Worth-Arlington PMSA	2800	25.1	1,702,625	10.6	1,883,211	11.3	2,095,407
Hood	48221	41.8	41,100	12.5	46,225	12.7	52,117
Johnson	48251	30.5	126,811	12.6	142,744	12.9	161,115
Parker	48367	36.6	88,495	13.2	100,215	13.6	113,879
Tarrant	48439	23.6	1,446,219	10.2	1,594,027	10.9	1,768,296
Galveston-Texas City PMSA	2920	15.1	250,158	8.8	272,122	9.8	298,837
Galveston	48167	15.1	250,158	8.8	272,122	9.8	298,837
Houston PMSA	3360	25.8	4,177,646	10.0	4,595,351	10.7	5,087,584
Chambers	48071	29.6	26,031	7.8	28,050	8.3	30,391
Fort Bend	48157	57.2	354,452	24.1	440,039	23.0	541,335
Harris	48201	20.7	3,400,578	7.5	3,656,415	8.2	3,957,791
Liberty	48291	33.1	70,154	7.3	75,275	7.7	81,059
Montgomery	48339	61.2	293,768	22.7	360,419	21.8	438,982
Waller	48473	39.6	32,663	7.6	35,153	8.2	38,026
Killeen-Temple MSA	3810	22.6	312,952	4.5	327,158	4.9	343,318
Bell	48027	24.5	237,974	5.9	251,967	6.4	268,153
Coryell	48099	16.8	74,978	0.3	75,191	-0.0	75,165
Laredo MSA	4080	44.9	193,117	13.9	219,931	14.3	251,491
Webb	48479	44.9	193,117	13.9	219,931	14.3	251,491

Metropolitan Statistical Areas and Their Component Counties: Population Trends, *Continued*

	FIPS CODE	PAST 1990-2000 % Change	PAST 2000 Census	PRESENT 2000-2004 % Change	PRESENT 7/1/04 Estimate	FUTURE 2004-2009 % Change	FUTURE 2009 Projection
Longview-Marshall MSA	4420	7.7	208,780	3.1	215,225	3.8	223,302
Gregg	48183	6.1	111,379	3.1	114,824	3.8	119,232
Harrison	48203	8.0	62,110	1.3	62,916	1.7	63,956
Upshur	48459	12.5	35,291	6.2	37,485	7.0	40,114
Lubbock MSA	4600	9.0	242,628	4.3	252,962	5.0	265,524
Lubbock	48303	9.0	242,628	4.3	252,962	5.0	265,524
McAllen-Edinburg-Mission MSA	4880	48.5	569,463	15.2	656,072	15.6	758,677
Hidalgo	48215	48.5	569,463	15.2	656,072	15.6	758,677
Odessa-Midland MSA	5800	5.1	237,132	2.5	243,009	3.5	251,452
Ector	48135	1.8	121,123	1.8	123,354	2.7	126,654
Midland	48329	8.8	116,009	3.1	119,655	4.3	124,798
San Angelo MSA	7200	5.6	104,010	-0.6	103,389	-0.7	102,692
Tom Green	48451	5.6	104,010	-0.6	103,389	-0.7	102,692
San Antonio MSA	7240	20.2	1,592,383	8.2	1,722,612	8.9	1,876,678
Bexar	48029	17.5	1,392,931	7.4	1,496,237	8.2	1,619,092
Comal	48091	50.5	78,021	16.4	90,783	16.5	105,766
Guadalupe	48187	37.2	89,023	11.8	99,505	12.1	111,519
Wilson	48493	43.1	32,408	11.4	36,087	11.7	40,301
Sherman-Denison MSA	7640	16.4	110,595	5.4	116,532	5.9	123,419
Grayson	48181	16.4	110,595	5.4	116,532	5.9	123,419
Texarkana, TX-AR MSA	8360	8.0	129,749	1.9	132,208	2.3	135,265
Miller, AR	05091	5.1	40,443	4.8	42,371	5.6	44,746
Bowie	48037	9.4	89,306	0.6	89,837	0.8	90,519
Tyler MSA	8640	15.5	174,706	7.0	186,882	7.7	201,203
Smith	48423	15.5	174,706	7.0	186,882	7.7	201,203
Victoria MSA	8750	13.1	84,088	2.1	85,853	2.7	88,140
Victoria	48469	13.1	84,088	2.1	85,853	2.7	88,140
Waco MSA	8800	12.9	213,517	3.9	221,739	4.4	231,389
McLennan	48309	12.9	213,517	3.9	221,739	4.4	231,389
Wichita Falls MSA	9080	7.8	140,518	-1.9	137,823	-2.2	134,757
Archer	48009	11.0	8,854	4.6	9,261	3.9	9,618
Wichita	48485	7.6	131,664	-2.4	128,562	-2.7	125,139
TOTAL: METRO PORTION OF STATE		24.9	17,691,880	9.0	19,280,576	9.7	21,147,276
TOTAL: TEXAS		22.8	20,851,820	7.9	22,508,240	8.7	24,456,895

UTAH

	FIPS CODE	PAST 1990-2000 % Change	PAST 2000 Census	PRESENT 2000-2004 % Change	PRESENT 7/1/04 Estimate	FUTURE 2004-2009 % Change	FUTURE 2009 Projection
Provo-Orem MSA	6520	39.8	368,536	10.5	407,123	11.1	452,429
Utah	49049	39.8	368,536	10.5	407,123	11.1	452,429
Salt Lake City-Ogden MSA	7160	24.4	1,333,914	5.1	1,401,430	5.6	1,480,173
Davis	49011	27.2	238,994	9.1	260,687	9.8	286,123
Salt Lake	49035	23.8	898,387	3.8	932,116	4.2	971,433
Weber	49057	24.1	196,533	6.2	208,627	6.7	222,617
* **Kane County**	49025	17.0	6,046	-0.3	6,026	-1.1	5,962
(See Flagstaff, AZ-UT MSA.)							
TOTAL: METRO PORTION OF STATE		27.4	1,708,496	6.2	1,814,579	6.8	1,938,564
TOTAL: UTAH		29.6	2,233,169	6.9	2,387,580	7.6	2,568,143

VERMONT

	FIPS CODE	PAST 1990-2000 % Change	PAST 2000 Census	PRESENT 2000-2004 % Change	PRESENT 7/1/04 Estimate	FUTURE 2004-2009 % Change	FUTURE 2009 Projection
Burlington NECMA	1303	12.3	198,889	3.0	204,838	3.3	211,517
Chittenden	50007	11.2	146,571	2.1	149,664	2.3	153,038
Franklin	50011	13.6	45,417	4.6	47,499	5.0	49,879
Grand Isle	50013	29.8	6,901	11.2	7,675	12.1	8,600
TOTAL: METRO PORTION OF STATE		12.3	198,889	3.0	204,838	3.3	211,517
TOTAL: VERMONT		8.2	608,827	2.2	622,165	2.5	637,457

VIRGINIA

	FIPS CODE	PAST 1990-2000 % Change	PAST 2000 Census	PRESENT 2000-2004 % Change	PRESENT 7/1/04 Estimate	FUTURE 2004-2009 % Change	FUTURE 2009 Projection
Charlottesville MSA	1540	21.7	159,576	5.8	168,816	6.3	179,480
Albemarle	51003	16.5	79,236	11.9	88,692	5.8	93,797
Charlottesville (Ind. City)	51540	11.7	45,049	-13.8	38,847	-4.0	37,309
Fluvanna	51065	61.3	20,047	19.8	24,026	19.7	28,764
Greene	51079	48.0	15,244	13.2	17,251	13.7	19,610
Danville MSA	1950	1.3	110,156	-1.8	108,169	-2.1	105,930
Danville (Ind. City)	51590	-8.8	48,411	-3.8	46,575	-4.3	44,565
Pittsylvania	51143	10.9	61,745	-0.2	61,594	-0.4	61,365
Lynchburg MSA	4640	10.8	214,911	1.5	218,030	1.6	221,539
Amherst	51009	11.6	31,894	-0.0	31,890	-0.0	31,881
Bedford	51019	32.2	60,371	4.9	63,337	5.3	66,712
Bedford (Ind. City)	51515	3.7	6,299	0.8	6,352	1.0	6,414
Campbell	51031	7.4	51,078	0.6	51,384	0.6	51,695
Lynchburg (Ind. City)	51680	-1.2	65,269	-0.3	65,067	-0.4	64,837
Norfolk-Virginia Beach-Newport News, VA-NC MSA	5720	8.8	1,569,541	5.1	1,649,035	5.7	1,742,898
Currituck, NC	37053	32.4	18,190	19.1	21,665	19.2	25,821
Chesapeake (Ind. City)	51550	31.1	199,184	7.6	214,295	8.1	231,578
Gloucester	51073	15.4	34,780	7.3	37,303	8.1	40,326
Hampton (Ind. City)	51650	9.5	146,437	0.4	147,010	0.4	147,660
Isle of Wight	51093	18.7	29,728	9.7	32,606	10.4	36,004
James City	51095	38.0	48,102	14.6	55,145	15.0	63,432
Mathews	51115	10.3	9,207	0.1	9,220	0.2	9,237
Newport News (Ind. City)	51700	5.9	180,150	1.1	182,162	1.4	184,721
Norfolk (Ind. City)	51710	-10.3	234,403	4.2	244,163	5.0	256,324
Poquoson (Ind. City)	51735	5.1	11,566	3.1	11,929	3.5	12,352
Portsmouth (Ind. City)	51740	-3.2	100,565	-1.2	99,349	-1.3	98,010
Suffolk (Ind. City)	51800	22.1	63,677	20.3	76,604	20.2	92,042
Virginia Beach (Ind. City)	51810	8.2	425,257	4.3	443,729	4.8	465,007
Williamsburg (Ind. City)	51830	4.1	11,998	-4.4	11,476	-5.4	10,852
York	51199	32.7	56,297	10.8	62,379	11.5	69,532
Richmond-Petersburg MSA	6760	15.1	996,512	4.8	1,044,758	5.4	1,101,510
Charles City	51036	10.3	6,926	3.7	7,181	4.4	7,495
Chesterfield	51041	24.2	259,903	8.6	282,130	9.4	308,557
Colonial Heights (Ind. City)	51570	5.2	16,897	3.0	17,408	3.5	18,018
Dinwiddie	51053	17.0	24,533	1.6	24,932	1.6	25,325
Goochland	51075	19.1	16,863	9.9	18,538	10.8	20,537
Hanover	51085	36.4	86,320	11.7	96,438	12.2	108,214
Henrico	51087	20.4	262,300	4.3	273,683	4.7	286,663
Hopewell (Ind. City)	51670	-3.2	22,354	0.3	22,421	0.7	22,568
New Kent	51127	28.9	13,462	13.5	15,279	14.2	17,455
Petersburg (Ind. City)	51730	-12.1	33,740	-2.4	32,931	-2.4	32,140
Powhatan	51145	46.0	22,377	13.2	25,328	13.4	28,721
Prince George	51149	20.6	33,047	4.9	34,661	5.1	36,444
Richmond (Ind. City)	51760	-2.6	197,790	-2.0	193,828	-2.3	189,373
Roanoke MSA	6800	5.1	235,932	0.2	236,385	0.3	237,135
Botetourt	51023	22.0	30,496	4.1	31,742	4.6	33,207
Roanoke	51161	8.1	85,778	2.4	87,854	3.0	90,472
Roanoke (Ind. City)	51770	-1.5	94,911	-2.8	92,245	-3.3	89,208
Salem (Ind. City)	51775	4.2	24,747	-0.8	24,544	-1.2	24,248
* **Alexandria City**	51510	15.4	128,283	0.4	128,847	-0.3	128,458
* **Arlington County**	51013	10.8	189,453	-1.1	187,390	-1.3	184,980
* **Clarke County**	51043	4.6	12,652	7.4	13,582	8.0	14,672
* **Culpeper County**	51047	23.3	34,262	16.5	39,908	17.0	46,675
* **Fairfax County**	51059	18.5	969,749	4.0	1,008,761	4.1	1,050,462
* **Fairfax City**	51600	9.6	21,498	3.2	22,181	3.4	22,928
* **Falls Church City**	51610	8.3	10,377	1.2	10,500	0.7	10,576
* **Fauquier County**	51061	13.1	55,139	14.2	62,992	14.7	72,263
* **Fredericksburg City**	51630	1.3	19,279	6.2	20,481	7.1	21,938
* **King George County**	51099	24.2	16,803	11.0	18,655	11.8	20,862
* **Loudoun County**	51107	96.9	169,599	40.1	237,678	33.5	317,314
* **Manassas City**	51683	25.7	35,135	7.5	37,756	7.8	40,708
* **Manassas Park City**	51685	52.8	10,290	8.9	11,209	9.8	12,302
* **Prince William County**	51153	30.2	280,813	20.8	339,149	20.4	408,242
* **Spotsylvania County**	51177	57.5	90,395	25.3	113,260	23.9	140,355
* **Stafford County**	51179	51.0	92,446	26.4	116,821	24.8	145,805
* **Warren County**	51187	20.8	31,584	9.5	34,587	10.4	38,170
(See Washington, DC-MD-VA-WV PMSA.)							
* **Bristol City**	51520	-5.7	17,367	-1.1	17,176	-0.9	17,023
* **Scott County**	51169	0.9	23,403	-2.2	22,883	-2.6	22,279
* **Washington County**	51191	11.4	51,103	0.8	51,487	0.8	51,894
(See Johnson City-Kingsport-Bristol, TN-VA MSA.)							
TOTAL: METRO PORTION OF STATE		15.8	5,528,068	6.7	5,898,831	7.3	6,330,577
TOTAL: VIRGINIA		14.4	7,078,515	5.7	7,480,156	6.3	7,949,286

WASHINGTON

	FIPS CODE	PAST 1990-2000 % Change	PAST 2000 Census	PRESENT 2000-2004 % Change	PRESENT 7/1/04 Estimate	FUTURE 2004-2009 % Change	FUTURE 2009 Projection
Bellingham MSA	0860	30.5	166,814	7.6	179,561	8.3	194,508
Whatcom	53073	30.5	166,814	7.6	179,561	8.3	194,508
Bremerton PMSA	1150	22.3	231,969	4.9	243,450	5.6	257,104
Kitsap	53035	22.3	231,969	4.9	243,450	5.6	257,104
Olympia PMSA	5910	28.6	207,355	9.2	226,479	10.0	249,121
Thurston	53067	28.6	207,355	9.2	226,479	10.0	249,121
Richland-Kennewick-Pasco MSA	6740	27.9	191,822	12.3	215,499	13.3	244,065
Benton	53005	26.6	142,475	10.3	157,183	11.2	174,797
Franklin	53021	31.7	49,347	18.2	58,316	18.8	69,268
Seattle-Bellevue-Everett PMSA	7600	18.8	2,414,616	3.4	2,496,295	3.8	2,591,750
Island	53029	18.9	71,558	8.9	77,898	9.7	85,466
King	53033	15.2	1,737,034	1.8	1,768,908	2.1	1,806,395
Snohomish	53061	30.1	606,024	7.2	649,489	7.8	699,889
Spokane MSA	7840	15.7	417,939	4.1	435,145	4.7	455,733
Spokane	53063	15.7	417,939	4.1	435,145	4.7	455,733
Tacoma PMSA	8200	19.6	700,820	7.5	753,288	8.2	814,946
Pierce	53053	19.6	700,820	7.5	753,288	8.2	814,946
Yakima MSA	9260	17.9	222,581	2.5	228,066	2.9	234,762
Yakima	53077	17.9	222,581	2.5	228,066	2.9	234,762
* **Clark County**	53011	45.0	345,238	13.0	390,272	13.7	443,743
(See Portland-Vancouver, OR-WA PMSA.)							
TOTAL: METRO PORTION OF STATE		21.4	4,899,154	5.5	5,168,055	6.1	5,485,732
TOTAL: WASHINGTON		21.1	5,894,121	5.3	6,204,912	5.9	6,572,249

WEST VIRGINIA

	FIPS CODE	PAST 1990-2000 % Change	PAST 2000 Census	PRESENT 2000-2004 % Change	PRESENT 7/1/04 Estimate	FUTURE 2004-2009 % Change	FUTURE 2009 Projection
Charleston MSA	1480	0.5	251,662	-1.7	247,465	-2.0	242,600
Kanawha	54039	-3.6	200,073	-3.0	194,003	-3.6	187,025
Putnam	54079	20.4	51,589	3.6	53,462	4.0	55,575
Huntington-Ashland, WV-KY-OH MSA	3400	1.0	315,538	-0.8	313,136	-0.8	310,489
Boyd, KY	21019	-2.7	49,752	-0.5	49,520	-0.3	49,349
Carter, KY	21043	10.5	26,889	1.3	27,234	1.6	27,682
Greenup, KY	21089	0.4	36,891	0.3	36,989	0.5	37,173
Lawrence, OH	39087	0.8	62,319	0.5	62,637	0.7	63,060
Cabell	54011	-0.0	96,784	-2.4	94,503	-2.9	91,807
Wayne	54099	3.0	42,903	-1.5	42,253	-2.0	41,418
Parkersburg-Marietta, WV-OH MSA	6020	1.4	151,237	-1.2	149,426	-1.4	147,322
Washington, OH	39167	1.6	63,251	-1.5	62,279	-1.8	61,151
Wood	54107	1.2	87,986	-1.0	87,147	-1.1	86,171
Wheeling, WV-OH MSA	9000	-3.8	153,172	-2.4	149,538	-2.7	145,471
Belmont, OH	39013	-1.2	70,226	-1.1	69,474	-1.2	68,653
Marshall	54051	-4.9	35,519	-2.2	34,730	-2.4	33,892
Ohio	54069	-6.8	47,427	-4.4	45,334	-5.3	42,926
* **Berkeley County**	54003	28.1	75,905	16.2	88,214	16.6	102,878
* **Jefferson County**	54037	17.4	42,190	12.7	47,542	13.3	53,881
(See Washington, DC-MD-VA-WV PMSA.)							
* **Mineral County**	54057	1.4	27,078	0.4	27,182	0.6	27,346
(See Cumberland, MD-WV MSA.)							
* **Brooke County**	54009	-5.7	25,447	-2.6	24,796	-2.9	24,079
* **Hancock County**	54029	-7.3	32,667	-3.7	31,452	-4.5	30,030
(See Steubenville-Weirton, OH-WV MSA.)							
TOTAL: METRO PORTION OF STATE		2.3	765,568	0.7	770,618	0.8	777,028
TOTAL: WEST VIRGINIA		0.8	1,808,344	0.2	1,811,363	0.3	1,816,410

WISCONSIN

	FIPS CODE	PAST 1990-2000 % Change	PAST 2000 Census	PRESENT 2000-2004 % Change	PRESENT 7/1/04 Estimate	FUTURE 2004-2009 % Change	FUTURE 2009 Projection
Appleton-Oshkosh-Neenah MSA	0460	13.7	358,365	4.0	372,541	4.4	388,774
Calumet	55015	18.5	40,631	9.0	44,268	10.0	48,693
Outagamie	55087	14.6	160,971	5.2	169,283	5.5	178,644
Winnebago	55139	11.7	156,763	1.4	158,990	1.5	161,437
Eau Claire MSA	2290	7.8	148,337	2.3	151,741	2.6	155,653
Chippewa	55017	5.4	55,195	3.7	57,253	4.2	59,651
Eau Claire	55035	9.3	93,142	1.4	94,488	1.6	96,002
Green Bay MSA	3080	16.5	226,778	4.1	236,097	4.7	247,140
Brown	55009	16.5	226,778	4.1	236,097	4.7	247,140
Janesville-Beloit MSA	3620	9.2	152,307	2.1	155,545	2.4	159,300
Rock	55105	9.2	152,307	2.1	155,545	2.4	159,300
Kenosha PMSA	3800	16.7	149,577	5.8	158,255	6.5	168,482
Kenosha	55059	16.7	149,577	5.8	158,255	6.5	168,482
La Crosse, WI-MN MSA	3870	9.0	126,838	1.8	129,119	2.0	131,755
Houston, MN	27055	6.6	19,718	1.7	20,056	1.9	20,435
La Crosse	55063	9.4	107,120	1.8	109,063	2.1	111,320
Madison MSA	4720	16.2	426,526	7.0	456,369	7.7	491,316
Dane	55025	16.2	426,526	7.0	456,369	7.7	491,316
Milwaukee-Waukesha PMSA	5080	4.8	1,500,741	1.2	1,518,392	1.3	1,538,818
Milwaukee	55079	-2.0	940,164	-1.0	931,139	-1.1	920,777
Ozaukee	55089	13.0	82,317	3.9	85,508	4.3	89,182
Washington	55131	23.3	117,493	5.3	123,666	5.8	130,790
Waukesha	55133	18.4	360,767	4.8	378,079	5.3	398,069
Racine PMSA	6600	7.9	188,831	2.4	193,383	2.8	198,874
Racine	55101	7.9	188,831	2.4	193,383	2.8	198,874
Sheboygan MSA	7620	8.4	112,646	0.8	113,582	0.9	114,615
Sheboygan	55117	8.4	112,646	0.8	113,582	0.9	114,615
Wausau MSA	8940	9.0	125,834	1.4	127,589	1.7	129,695
Marathon	55073	9.0	125,834	1.4	127,589	1.7	129,695
* **Douglas County**	55031	3.7	43,287	2.4	44,322	2.6	45,463
(See Duluth-Superior, MN-WI MSA.)							
* **Pierce County**	55093	12.3	36,804	3.8	38,196	4.2	39,816
* **St. Croix County**	55109	25.7	63,155	16.6	73,654	17.0	86,144
(See Minneapolis-St. Paul, MN-WI MSA.)							
TOTAL: METRO PORTION OF STATE		9.3	3,640,308	3.0	3,748,729	3.4	3,875,410
TOTAL: WISCONSIN		9.6	5,363,675	2.6	5,505,083	3.0	5,669,003

WYOMING

	FIPS CODE	PAST 1990-2000 % Change	PAST 2000 Census	PRESENT 2000-2004 % Change	PRESENT 7/1/04 Estimate	FUTURE 2004-2009 % Change	FUTURE 2009 Projection
Casper MSA	1350	8.7	66,533	3.4	68,763	4.0	71,508
Natrona	56025	8.7	66,533	3.4	68,763	4.0	71,508
Cheyenne MSA	1580	11.6	81,607	4.0	84,872	4.6	88,799
Laramie	56021	11.6	81,607	4.0	84,872	4.6	88,799
TOTAL: METRO PORTION OF STATE		10.2	148,140	3.7	153,635	4.3	160,307
TOTAL: WYOMING		8.9	493,782	2.0	503,630	2.4	515,570
TOTAL: METRO PORTION OF UNITED STATES		13.9	226,042,306	4.9	237,175,717	5.5	250,268,914
TOTAL: UNITED STATES		13.2	281,421,906	4.4	293,687,162	4.9	308,074,407

* Indicates county is included from metro in different state.
Source: Devonshire Associates Ltd. and Scan/US, Inc. 2004.

150 Largest Metropolitan Statistical Areas: Population Trends

The following data are presented for the 150 largest MSAs, PMSAs, and NECMAs (based on 2009 population projections): the Metropolitan Statistical Area FIPS Code, 1990-2000 percent of change in population; 2000 **actual** population; 2000-2004 estimated percent of change in population; 2004 **estimated** population; 2004-2009 projected percent of change in population; and 2009 **projected** population. MSAs, PMSAs, and NECMAs are ranked and listed in descending order according to their 2009 projected population figures. (A ranking of MSAs and PMSAs according to their 2004 estimated population figures can be found on page 44.) The data reflect MSAs, PMSAs, and NECMAs as defined and published by the Office of Management and Budget (OMB) on December 31, 1992, and as revised through June 30, 1999.

		PAST		PRESENT		FUTURE		
	FIPS CODE	1990-2000 % Change	2000 Census	2000-2004 % Change	7/1/04 Estimate	2004-2009 % Change	2009 Projection	2009 Rank
Los Angeles-Long Beach, CA PMSA	4480	7.4	9,519,338	4.8	9,980,271	5.4	10,523,607	1
New York, NY PMSA	5600	9.0	9,314,235	1.4	9,449,241	1.6	9,602,418	2
Chicago, IL PMSA	1600	11.6	8,272,768	3.5	8,558,311	3.9	8,890,349	3
Boston-Worcester-Lawrence-Lowell-Brockton, MA-NH NECMA	1123	6.5	6,057,826	2.1	6,186,809	2.3	6,329,608	4
Washington, DC-MD-VA-WV PMSA	8840	16.6	4,923,153	8.2	5,326,575	8.8	5,796,584	5
Philadelphia, PA-NJ PMSA	6160	3.6	5,100,931	1.7	5,185,302	2.0	5,286,675	6
Atlanta, GA MSA	0520	38.9	4,112,198	11.1	4,570,501	11.6	5,101,872	7
Houston, TX PMSA	3360	25.8	4,177,646	10.0	4,595,351	10.7	5,087,584	8
Detroit, MI PMSA	2160	4.1	4,441,551	0.6	4,466,850	0.6	4,493,239	9
Riverside-San Bernardino, CA PMSA	6780	25.7	3,254,821	15.6	3,763,495	16.1	4,369,109	10
Dallas, TX PMSA	1920	31.5	3,519,176	10.8	3,900,657	11.4	4,346,969	11
Phoenix-Mesa, AZ MSA	6200	45.3	3,251,876	13.7	3,698,598	14.2	4,224,395	12
Minneapolis-St. Paul, MN-WI MSA	5120	16.9	2,968,806	5.0	3,117,850	5.5	3,288,729	13
Orange County, CA PMSA	5945	18.1	2,846,289	5.1	2,991,519	5.6	3,160,141	14
San Diego, CA MSA	7320	12.6	2,813,833	5.4	2,966,135	5.9	3,142,238	15
Nassau-Suffolk, NY PMSA	5380	5.5	2,753,913	2.5	2,823,190	2.8	2,901,600	16
Tampa-St. Petersburg-Clearwater, FL MSA	8280	15.9	2,395,997	7.4	2,574,498	8.3	2,787,447	17
Baltimore, MD PMSA	0720	7.2	2,552,994	3.2	2,635,941	3.8	2,735,037	18
St. Louis, MO-IL MSA	7040	4.5	2,603,607	1.8	2,651,207	2.1	2,707,853	19
Seattle-Bellevue-Everett, WA PMSA	7600	18.8	2,414,616	3.4	2,496,295	3.8	2,591,750	20
Oakland, CA PMSA	5775	14.9	2,392,557	3.7	2,481,548	3.9	2,578,342	21
Miami, FL PMSA	5000	16.3	2,253,362	5.1	2,368,141	5.7	2,503,015	22
Denver, CO PMSA[1]	2080	30.0	2,109,282	6.2	2,239,478	7.5	2,407,561	23
Pittsburgh, PA MSA	6280	-1.5	2,358,695	-1.1	2,332,585	-1.3	2,302,295	24
Portland-Vancouver, OR-WA PMSA	6440	26.6	1,918,009	7.6	2,064,660	8.4	2,238,058	25
Cleveland-Lorain-Elyria, OH PMSA	1680	2.2	2,250,871	-0.5	2,239,967	-0.6	2,227,119	26
Las Vegas, NV-AZ MSA	4120	83.3	1,563,282	18.4	1,850,678	18.1	2,185,608	27
Newark, NJ PMSA	5640	6.1	2,032,989	2.3	2,080,714	2.8	2,138,338	28
Sacramento, CA PMSA	6920	21.5	1,628,197	13.2	1,842,845	13.9	2,098,130	29
Orlando, FL MSA	5960	34.3	1,644,561	12.6	1,851,873	13.2	2,096,306	30
Fort Worth-Arlington, TX PMSA	2800	25.1	1,702,625	10.6	1,883,211	11.3	2,095,407	31
Kansas City, MO-KS MSA	3760	12.2	1,776,062	4.9	1,863,851	5.4	1,964,702	32
Fort Lauderdale, FL PMSA	2680	29.3	1,623,018	8.7	1,764,315	9.3	1,929,159	33
San Antonio, TX MSA	7240	20.2	1,592,383	8.2	1,722,612	8.9	1,876,678	34
Charlotte-Gastonia-Rock Hill, NC-SC MSA	1520	29.0	1,499,293	9.9	1,648,241	10.5	1,822,085	35
New Haven-Bridgeport-Stamford-Danbury-Waterbury, CT NECMA	5483	4.6	1,706,575	2.6	1,751,503	3.0	1,803,893	36
Indianapolis, IN MSA	3480	16.4	1,607,486	5.4	1,695,006	6.1	1,797,554	37
Norfolk-Virginia Beach-Newport News, VA-NC MSA	5720	8.8	1,569,541	5.1	1,649,035	5.7	1,742,898	38
Cincinnati, OH-KY-IN PMSA	1640	7.9	1,646,395	2.1	1,680,493	2.3	1,719,163	39
Columbus, OH MSA	1840	14.5	1,540,157	4.8	1,614,311	5.3	1,699,176	40
San Jose, CA PMSA	7400	12.4	1,682,585	-0.4	1,675,734	-0.8	1,662,290	41
San Francisco, CA PMSA	7360	8.0	1,731,183	-2.8	1,682,970	-3.5	1,623,296	42
Austin-San Marcos, TX MSA	0640	47.7	1,249,763	13.2	1,415,292	13.3	1,603,483	43
Milwaukee-Waukesha, WI PMSA	5080	4.8	1,500,741	1.2	1,518,392	1.3	1,538,818	44
Raleigh-Durham-Chapel Hill, NC MSA	6640	38.9	1,187,941	11.8	1,328,146	12.6	1,495,394	45
Salt Lake City-Ogden, UT MSA	7160	24.4	1,333,914	5.1	1,401,430	5.6	1,480,173	46
Bergen-Passaic, NJ PMSA	0875	7.4	1,373,167	2.1	1,402,356	2.3	1,434,510	47
Nashville, TN MSA	5360	25.0	1,231,311	6.0	1,305,357	6.6	1,391,875	48
West Palm Beach-Boca Raton, FL MSA	8960	31.0	1,131,184	9.9	1,243,157	10.8	1,377,535	49
Greensboro--Winston-Salem--High Point, NC MSA	3120	19.2	1,251,509	4.6	1,308,675	5.1	1,374,822	50
New Orleans, LA MSA	5560	4.1	1,337,726	0.1	1,339,327	0.3	1,343,083	51
Jacksonville, FL MSA	3600	21.4	1,100,491	9.5	1,204,735	10.5	1,331,027	52
Middlesex-Somerset-Hunterdon, NJ PMSA	5015	14.7	1,169,641	5.7	1,236,285	6.2	1,313,407	53
Monmouth-Ocean, NJ PMSA	5190	14.2	1,126,217	6.0	1,194,230	6.6	1,273,605	54
Hartford, CT NECMA	3283	2.2	1,148,618	3.3	1,186,956	3.8	1,232,061	55
Memphis, TN-AR-MS MSA	4920	12.7	1,135,614	3.7	1,178,084	4.2	1,227,496	56
Oklahoma City, OK MSA	5880	13.0	1,083,346	4.5	1,131,827	5.1	1,189,331	57
Grand Rapids-Muskegon-Holland, MI MSA	3000	16.1	1,088,514	4.1	1,133,518	4.5	1,184,859	58
Buffalo-Niagara Falls, NY MSA	1280	-1.6	1,170,111	-1.2	1,156,288	-1.4	1,140,627	59
Rochester, NY MSA	6840	3.4	1,098,201	0.4	1,102,049	0.4	1,106,192	60
Richmond-Petersburg, VA MSA	6760	15.1	996,512	4.8	1,044,758	5.4	1,101,510	61
Fresno, CA MSA	2840	22.1	922,516	8.7	1,003,162	9.7	1,099,980	62
Louisville, KY-IN MSA	4520	8.1	1,025,598	2.4	1,049,861	2.6	1,077,421	63
Greenville-Spartanburg-Anderson, SC MSA	3160	15.9	962,441	4.3	1,004,256	4.8	1,052,690	64
Providence-Warwick-Pawtucket, RI NECMA	6483	5.1	962,886	3.7	998,644	4.2	1,040,712	65
Tucson, AZ MSA	8520	26.5	843,746	7.6	907,511	8.1	981,041	66
Birmingham, AL MSA	1000	9.6	921,106	2.7	946,208	3.1	975,243	67
Honolulu, HI MSA	3320	4.8	876,156	4.1	911,719	4.9	956,800	68
Dayton-Springfield, OH MSA	2000	-0.1	950,558	-0.5	945,928	-0.6	940,380	69
Albany-Schenectady-Troy, NY MSA	0160	1.6	875,583	2.2	894,569	2.5	917,335	70
Ventura, CA PMSA	8735	12.6	753,197	6.6	802,627	7.2	860,068	71
Tulsa, OK MSA	8560	13.3	803,235	3.3	829,509	3.7	860,064	72
Tacoma, WA PMSA	8200	19.6	700,820	7.5	753,288	8.2	814,946	73
Albuquerque, NM MSA	0200	21.0	712,738	6.5	759,193	7.3	814,647	74
Bakersfield, CA MSA	0680	21.7	661,645	10.3	729,553	11.3	811,845	75
Omaha, NE-IA MSA	5920	12.1	716,998	4.7	750,455	5.2	789,482	76
Stockton-Lodi, CA MSA	8120	17.3	563,598	16.1	654,288	16.4	761,890	77
Knoxville, TN MSA	3840	17.3	687,249	4.8	720,109	5.4	758,822	78
McAllen-Edinburg-Mission, TX MSA	4880	48.5	569,463	15.2	656,072	15.6	758,677	79
El Paso, TX MSA	2320	14.9	679,622	5.0	713,340	5.5	752,812	80
Syracuse, NY MSA	8160	-1.4	732,117	0.7	737,104	0.8	743,017	81
Sarasota-Bradenton, FL MSA	7510	20.5	589,959	9.7	647,224	10.5	715,358	82
Akron, OH PMSA	0080	5.7	694,960	1.2	703,530	1.3	712,812	83
Allentown-Bethlehem-Easton, PA MSA	0240	7.2	637,958	4.3	665,446	5.0	698,456	84
Ann Arbor, MI PMSA	0440	18.1	578,736	7.5	622,300	8.1	672,589	85
Harrisburg-Lebanon-Carlisle, PA MSA	3240	7.0	629,401	2.2	643,547	2.6	660,546	86
Gary, IN PMSA	2960	4.4	631,362	1.8	642,735	2.1	656,324	87
Baton Rouge, LA MSA	0760	14.1	602,894	3.8	626,070	4.3	653,081	88
Wilmington-Newark, DE-MD PMSA	9160	14.2	586,216	4.8	614,320	5.3	646,791	89
Little Rock-North Little Rock, AR MSA	4400	13.8	583,845	3.8	606,101	4.3	631,866	90
Springfield, MA NECMA	8003	0.9	608,479	1.7	618,736	2.0	630,934	91
Toledo, OH MSA	8400	0.7	618,203	0.3	620,144	0.4	622,319	92
Charleston-North Charleston, SC MSA	1440	8.3	549,033	5.4	578,716	6.1	614,123	93
Colorado Springs, CO MSA	1720	30.2	516,929	8.5	560,804	9.2	612,412	94
Jersey City, NJ PMSA	3640	10.1	608,975	-0.4	606,768	-0.5	603,520	95
Scranton--Wilkes-Barre--Hazleton, PA MSA	7560	-2.1	624,776	-1.7	614,462	-1.8	603,115	96
Daytona Beach, FL MSA	2020	23.5	493,175	10.0	542,645	10.9	601,522	97
Columbia, SC MSA	1760	18.4	536,691	5.4	565,436	6.0	599,434	98
Fort Myers-Cape Coral, FL MSA	2700	31.6	440,888	15.3	508,350	15.9	589,051	99
Vallejo-Fairfield-Napa, CA PMSA	8720	15.0	518,821	6.3	551,336	6.7	588,276	100
Modesto, CA MSA	5170	20.6	446,997	13.3	506,378	14.0	577,071	101
Mobile, AL MSA	5160	13.3	540,258	2.7	554,939	3.0	571,665	102
Youngstown-Warren, OH MSA	9320	-1.0	594,746	-2.2	581,948	-2.6	566,986	103
Melbourne-Titusville-Palm Bay, FL MSA	4900	19.4	476,230	8.1	515,004	9.0	561,468	104
Lakeland-Winter Haven, FL MSA	3980	19.4	483,924	7.2	518,809	8.0	560,565	105
Boise City, ID MSA	1080	46.1	432,345	13.4	490,178	13.8	557,690	106
Wichita, KS MSA[2]	9040	12.8	512,351	3.0	527,608	3.3	545,261	107
Fort Wayne, IN MSA	2760	10.1	502,141	2.7	515,722	3.0	531,394	108
Lexington, KY MSA	4280	18.0	479,198	4.9	502,488	5.4	529,590	109
Des Moines, IA MSA	2120	16.1	456,022	5.9	483,114	6.6	514,766	110
Augusta-Aiken, GA-SC MSA	0600	15.0	477,441	3.1	492,040	3.6	509,549	111
Lancaster, PA MSA	4000	11.3	470,658	3.4	486,469	3.8	504,836	112
Johnson City-Kingsport-Bristol, TN-VA MSA	3660	10.1	480,091	1.6	487,711	1.9	496,840	113
Madison, WI MSA	4720	16.2	426,526	7.0	456,369	7.7	491,316	114
Chattanooga, TN-GA MSA	1560	9.6	465,161	2.5	476,717	2.9	490,453	115
Santa Rosa, CA PMSA	7500	18.1	458,614	2.2	468,851	2.3	479,459	116
Jackson, MS MSA	3560	11.5	440,801	3.8	457,428	4.2	476,750	117
Kalamazoo-Battle Creek, MI MSA	3720	5.4	452,851	1.8	461,120	2.1	470,810	118
Lansing-East Lansing, MI MSA	4040	3.5	447,728	2.4	458,301	2.7	470,587	119
Newburgh, NY-PA PMSA	5660	15.5	387,669	9.3	423,860	10.1	466,560	120
Pensacola, FL MSA	6080	19.7	412,153	5.4	434,387	6.2	461,432	121
Spokane, WA MSA	7840	15.7	417,939	4.1	435,145	4.7	455,733	122
Flint, MI PMSA	2640	1.3	436,141	1.8	444,011	2.0	452,774	123
Provo-Orem, UT MSA	6520	39.8	368,536	10.5	407,123	11.1	452,429	124
Salinas, CA MSA	7120	13.0	401,762	4.1	418,251	4.5	437,244	125
Visalia-Tulare-Porterville, CA MSA	8780	18.0	368,021	8.2	398,103	9.2	434,646	126
Reno, NV MSA	6720	33.3	339,486	12.1	380,688	12.9	429,797	127
York, PA MSA	9280	12.4	381,751	4.5	398,969	5.1	419,155	128
Brownsville-Harlingen-San Benito, TX MSA	1240	28.9	335,227	10.9	371,857	11.8	415,655	129
Santa Barbara-Santa Maria-Lompoc, CA MSA	7480	8.0	399,347	1.2	404,260	1.4	409,876	130
Canton-Massillon, OH MSA	1320	3.3	406,934	0.1	407,161	0.0	407,290	131
Reading, PA MSA	6680	11.0	373,638	4.1	388,909	4.6	406,841	132
Rockford, IL MSA	6880	12.6	371,236	4.4	387,465	4.9	406,531	133
Lafayette, LA MSA	3880	11.8	385,647	2.3	394,628	2.7	405,476	134
Fort Pierce-Port St. Lucie, FL MSA	2710	27.2	319,426	12.0	357,906	13.0	404,587	135
Saginaw-Bay City-Midland, MI MSA	6960	0.9	403,070	0.1	403,326	0.1	403,578	136
Fayetteville-Springdale-Rogers, AR MSA	2580	47.5	311,121	12.8	351,068	13.3	397,810	137
Shreveport-Bossier City, LA MSA	7680	4.2	392,302	0.5	394,221	0.6	396,524	138
Salem, OR PMSA	7080	24.9	347,214	6.0	367,908	6.7	392,483	139
Appleton-Oshkosh-Neenah, WI MSA	0460	13.7	358,365	4.0	372,541	4.4	388,774	140
Corpus Christi, TX MSA	1880	8.8	380,783	0.9	384,106	1.1	388,338	141
Huntsville, AL MSA	3440	16.8	342,376	5.9	362,704	6.6	386,635	142
Atlantic-Cape May, NJ PMSA	0560	11.1	354,878	3.9	368,557	4.5	385,070	143
Trenton, NJ PMSA	8480	7.7	350,761	4.2	365,448	4.7	382,782	144
Beaumont-Port Arthur, TX MSA	0840	6.6	385,090	-0.8	381,930	-0.9	378,485	145
Biloxi-Gulfport-Pascagoula, MS MSA	0920	16.5	363,988	1.6	369,960	1.7	376,230	146
Springfield, MO MSA	7920	23.2	325,721	5.9	344,995	6.5	367,587	147
Hickory-Morganton-Lenoir, NC MSA	3290	16.9	341,851	3.1	352,521	3.4	364,417	148
Hamilton-Middletown, OH PMSA	3200	14.2	332,807	4.1	346,371	4.5	362,111	149
Macon, GA MSA	4680	10.9	322,549	5.1	338,900	5.8	358,497	150

Source: Devonshire Associates Ltd. and Scan/US, Inc. 2004.

[1] Census population includes a portion of Broomfield county.
[2] Data exclude Harvey County, Kansas (2000 Census population 32,869; 2004 estimated population 33,707; and 2009 projected population 34,714), which fails to meet published standards for MSA inclusion, but has been included with the Wichita MSA as the result of Congressional action.

Combined Statistical Areas (CSAs): Population Trends

The following data are presented for Combined Statistical Areas (CSAs): 1990-2000 percent of change in population; 2000 **actual** population; 2000-2004 estimated percent of change in population; 2004 **estimated** population; 2004-2009 projected percent of change in population; and 2009 **projected** population.

	PAST		PRESENT		FUTURE	
	1990-2000 % Change	2000 Census	2000-2004 % Change	7/1/04 Estimate	2004-2009 % Change	2009 Projection
Albany-Corvallis-Lebanon, OR	11.8	181,222	3.1	186,880	3.8	193,998
Albany-Schenectady-Amsterdam, NY	1.9	1,118,095	2.0	1,140,691	2.4	1,168,063
Ames-Boone, IA	6.8	106,205	3.8	110,209	4.2	114,874
Appleton-Oshkosh-Neenah, WI	13.7	358,365	4.0	372,541	4.4	388,774
Asheville-Brevard, NC	19.5	398,505	4.1	415,007	4.6	434,057
Atlanta-Sandy Springs-Gainesville, GA-AL	37.1	4,548,344	10.9	5,045,068	11.4	5,620,886
Baton Rouge-Pierre Part, LA	12.8	729,361	3.0	750,952	3.3	775,970
Beckley-Oak Hill, WV	1.6	126,799	-0.2	126,492	-0.2	126,283
Bend-Prineville, OR	51.1	134,549	15.1	154,810	15.2	178,397
Birmingham-Hoover-Cullman, AL	10.3	1,129,721	2.5	1,157,590	2.9	1,190,835
Boston-Worcester-Manchester, MA-NH	6.9	5,715,698	2.2	5,843,682	2.4	5,986,013
Brownsville-Harlingen-Raymondville, TX	27.9	355,309	10.3	391,958	11.2	435,788
Buffalo-Niagara-Cattaraugus, NY	-1.5	1,254,066	-1.2	1,239,456	-1.3	1,222,868
Cape Girardeau-Sikeston-Jackson, MO-IL	6.9	130,734	1.6	132,796	1.9	135,255
Charlotte-Gastonia-Salisbury, NC-SC	26.3	1,897,034	8.8	2,064,635	9.5	2,260,054
Chattanooga-Cleveland-Athens, TN-GA	11.8	629,561	2.8	647,130	3.2	667,804
Chicago-Naperville-Michigan City, IL-IN-WI	11.1	9,312,255	3.3	9,621,008	3.7	9,980,464
Cincinnati-Middletown-Wilmington, OH-KY-IN	9.0	2,050,175	2.5	2,100,487	2.7	2,157,914
Claremont-Lebanon, NH-VT	7.3	207,845	3.3	214,679	3.8	222,766
Cleveland-Akron-Elyria, OH	3.0	2,945,831	-0.1	2,943,497	-0.1	2,939,931
Clovis-Portales, NM	7.0	63,062	1.1	63,743	1.5	64,716
Columbia-Newberry, SC	17.5	683,266	4.8	715,942	5.4	754,384
Columbus-Auburn-Opelika, GA-AL	11.2	420,965	2.8	432,893	3.2	446,907
Columbus-Marion-Chillicothe, OH	13.7	1,835,189	4.6	1,920,053	5.1	2,017,430
Columbus-West Point, MS	3.9	83,565	-2.0	81,884	-2.4	79,894
Corbin-London, KY	15.4	88,580	6.2	94,038	6.9	100,484
Corpus Christi-Kingsville, TX	9.2	435,243	1.0	439,671	1.3	445,273
Dallas-Fort Worth, TX	29.2	5,346,119	10.7	5,918,901	11.3	6,589,725
Dayton-Springfield-Greenville, OH	0.4	1,085,094	-0.4	1,080,951	-0.5	1,075,888
Deltona-Daytona Beach-Palm Coast, FL	23.5	493,175	10.0	542,645	10.9	601,522
Denver-Aurora-Boulder, CO	30.6	2,449,054	6.9	2,617,582	7.3	2,808,663
Des Moines-Newton-Pella, IA	14.4	550,659	5.3	579,709	5.8	613,598
Detroit-Warren-Flint, MI	5.1	5,357,538	1.4	5,431,817	1.5	5,514,478
Dothan-Enterprise-Ozark, AL	6.4	223,605	2.2	228,431	2.6	234,266
Eau Claire-Menomonie, WI	8.5	188,195	2.7	193,240	3.0	199,077
Fairmont-Clarksburg, WV	-0.0	148,742	-0.5	147,965	-0.6	147,069
Fargo-Wahpeton, ND-MN	11.5	199,503	2.7	204,940	3.0	211,158
Findlay-Tiffin, OH	3.8	129,978	0.9	131,174	1.2	132,705
Fond du Lac-Beaver Dam, WI	9.9	183,193	1.2	185,465	1.4	188,044
Fort Polk South-De Ridder, LA	-7.1	85,517	-2.1	83,720	-2.7	81,490
Fort Wayne-Huntington-Auburn, IN	11.0	548,416	2.7	562,961	3.0	579,637
Fresno-Madera, CA	22.1	922,516	8.7	1,003,162	9.7	1,099,980
Grand Rapids-Muskegon-Holland, MI	15.8	1,254,661	4.2	1,306,806	4.6	1,366,491
Greensboro--Winston-Salem--High Point, NC	18.1	1,414,656	4.2	1,474,109	4.7	1,543,079
Greenville-Spartanburg-Anderson, SC	15.5	1,128,104	4.0	1,172,803	4.4	1,224,524
Gulfport-Biloxi-Pascagoula, MS	16.8	396,754	2.1	405,152	2.3	414,312
Harrisburg-Carlisle-Lebanon, PA	7.0	629,401	2.2	643,547	2.6	660,546
Hartford-West Hartford-Willimantic, CT	2.6	1,257,709	3.4	1,300,723	3.9	1,351,553
Houston-Baytown-Huntsville, TX	24.9	4,815,122	9.8	5,287,717	10.6	5,845,599
Huntsville-Decatur, AL	15.0	488,243	4.5	510,286	5.1	536,094
Idaho Falls-Blackfoot, ID	13.5	143,412	6.1	152,191	6.8	162,493
Indianapolis-Anderson-Columbus, IN	15.6	1,843,588	4.9	1,933,566	5.4	2,038,592
Ithaca-Cortland, NY	1.4	145,100	4.6	151,712	5.3	159,762
Jackson-Humboldt, TN	13.4	155,529	1.8	158,277	2.0	161,479
Jackson-Yazoo City, MS	11.2	525,346	3.2	542,282	3.6	561,890
Johnson City-Kingsport-Bristol (Tri-Cities), TN-VA	10.1	480,091	1.6	487,711	1.9	496,840
Kansas City-Overland Park-Kansas City, MO-KS	12.1	1,901,070	4.8	1,993,187	5.3	2,098,874
Knoxville-Sevierville-La Follette, TN	16.6	779,013	4.3	812,881	4.9	852,710
Kokomo-Peru, IN	2.8	137,623	-0.2	137,405	-0.3	137,030
Lafayette-Acadiana, LA	10.7	512,720	2.1	523,429	2.5	536,409
Lafayette-Frankfort, IN	11.9	212,407	3.7	220,356	4.2	229,711
Lake Charles-Jennings, LA	8.1	225,003	-0.2	224,648	-0.2	224,292
Lansing-East Lansing-Owosso, MI	3.4	519,415	2.3	531,124	2.6	544,802
Las Vegas-Paradise-Pahrump, NV	85.5	1,408,250	18.9	1,674,272	18.5	1,984,014
Lexington-Fayette--Frankfort--Richmond, KY	17.4	602,773	4.4	629,233	4.8	659,690
Lima-Van Wert-Wapakoneta, OH	-0.0	184,743	-0.4	184,075	-0.5	183,131
Little Rock-North Little Rock-Pine Bluff, AR	12.7	785,024	3.2	810,124	3.6	839,091
Longview-Marshall, TX	7.8	256,152	2.5	262,444	3.0	270,342
Los Angeles-Long Beach-Riverside, CA	12.7	16,373,645	7.1	17,537,912	7.8	18,912,925
Louisville-Elizabethtown-Scottsburg, KY-IN	9.7	1,292,482	3.1	1,332,297	3.4	1,377,691
Lubbock-Levelland, TX	7.2	272,416	3.7	282,456	4.4	294,764
Lumberton-Laurinburg, NC	14.7	159,337	1.8	162,220	2.2	165,757
Macon-Warner Robins-Fort Valley, GA	12.6	356,801	5.2	375,193	5.9	397,263
Madison-Baraboo, WI	16.2	556,999	6.1	591,173	6.8	631,153
Mansfield-Bucyrus, OH	1.0	175,818	-1.1	173,916	-1.3	171,695
Midland-Odessa, TX	5.1	237,132	2.5	243,009	3.5	251,452
Milwaukee-Racine-Waukesha, WI	5.1	1,689,572	1.3	1,711,775	1.5	1,737,692
Minneapolis-St. Paul-St. Cloud, MN-WI	16.4	3,271,888	5.0	3,436,228	5.5	3,625,127
Mobile-Daphne-Fairhope, AL	13.3	540,258	2.7	554,939	3.0	571,665
Monroe-Bastrop, LA	3.2	201,074	0.3	201,714	0.4	202,558
Montgomery-Alexander City, AL	12.7	400,205	1.5	406,218	1.7	413,316
Morristown-Newport, TN	20.7	156,646	4.1	163,011	4.5	170,344
Myrtle Beach-Conway-Georgetown, SC	32.6	252,426	8.9	274,864	9.4	300,766
Nashville-Davidson--Murfreesboro--Columbia, TN	25.2	1,381,287	6.0	1,463,732	6.6	1,559,887
New Orleans-Metairie-Bogalusa, LA	4.0	1,360,436	0.1	1,362,195	0.3	1,366,143
New York-Newark-Bridgeport, NY-NJ-CT-PA	8.4	21,361,797	2.5	21,888,232	2.8	22,495,568
Oklahoma City-Shawnee, OK	12.7	1,160,942	4.4	1,212,183	5.0	1,272,956
Omaha-Council Bluffs-Fremont, NE-IA	11.5	803,201	4.2	837,058	4.7	876,356
Orlando-The Villages, FL	35.1	1,697,906	12.6	1,912,510	13.2	2,165,753
Paducah-Mayfield, KY-IL	6.0	135,793	-0.7	134,855	-0.8	133,759
Peoria-Canton, IL	2.1	405,149	-0.5	403,241	-0.5	401,183
Philadelphia-Camden-Vineland, PA-NJ-DE-MD	4.7	5,833,585	2.0	5,949,905	2.3	6,088,636
Pittsburgh-New Castle, PA	-1.5	2,525,730	-1.1	2,497,034	-1.3	2,463,663
Portland-Lewiston-South Portland, ME	8.2	591,361	4.4	617,640	5.0	648,241
Raleigh-Durham-Cary, NC	37.9	1,314,589	11.6	1,467,394	12.4	1,649,526
Rochester-Batavia-Seneca Falls, NY	3.2	1,131,543	0.6	1,137,836	0.6	1,144,996
Rockford-Freeport-Rochelle, IL	11.2	420,215	3.6	435,367	4.1	453,208
Sacramento--Arden-Arcade--Truckee, CA-NV	21.6	1,930,149	12.6	2,172,596	13.2	2,460,363
Saginaw-Bay City-Saginaw Township North, MI	-1.1	320,196	-0.6	318,346	-0.7	316,166
St. Louis-St. Charles-Farmington, MO-IL	4.7	2,754,328	1.9	2,806,063	2.2	2,867,577
Salisbury-Ocean Pines, MD	17.4	155,934	5.5	164,439	6.1	174,473
Salt Lake City-Ogden-Clearfield, UT	26.0	1,469,474	5.9	1,556,404	6.5	1,657,423
San Jose-San Francisco-Oakland, CA	12.8	7,092,596	1.1	7,167,754	1.0	7,236,234
Santa Fe-Espanola, NM	27.9	170,482	5.1	179,180	5.6	189,279
Savannah-Hinesville-Fort Stewart, GA	15.1	364,914	3.3	377,050	4.0	392,287
Seattle-Tacoma-Olympia, WA	19.8	3,604,165	4.7	3,772,492	5.2	3,970,156
Shreveport-Bossier City-Minden, LA	4.0	417,796	0.6	420,366	0.7	423,439
Sioux City-Vermillion, IA-NE-SD	8.3	156,590	-0.5	155,884	-0.6	155,026
Sunbury-Lewisburg-Selinsgrove, PA	2.4	173,726	0.1	173,959	0.2	174,291
Syracuse-Auburn, NY	-1.4	732,117	0.7	737,104	0.8	743,017
Toledo-Fremont, OH	0.7	720,980	0.3	723,132	0.3	725,500
Tulsa-Bartlesville, OK	12.3	908,528	2.9	935,185	3.3	966,149
Tyler-Jacksonville, TX	15.1	221,365	6.0	234,746	6.7	250,545
Union City-Martin, TN-KY	4.4	75,097	-1.7	73,797	-2.1	72,220
Washington-Baltimore-Northern Virginia, DC-MD-VA-WV	13.1	7,538,385	6.4	8,023,042	7.1	8,589,988
Wausau-Merrill, WI	9.2	155,475	1.5	157,785	1.7	160,488
Wichita-Winfield, KS	10.8	607,457	2.4	622,050	2.7	638,821
Williamsport-Lock Haven, PA	1.3	157,958	-1.7	155,213	-2.1	151,928
York-Hanover-Gettysburg, PA	13.2	473,043	5.1	497,040	5.7	525,283
Youngstown-Warren-East Liverpool, OH-PA	-1.0	715,039	-1.9	701,743	-2.2	686,258
TOTAL: CMSA PORTION OF COUNTRY	12.7	174,028,784	4.4	181,741,992	5.0	190,741,686

Core Based Statistical Areas and Their Component Counties: Population Trends

Metropolitan CBSAs and their component counties are listed by state. The following data are presented for each: the CBSA FIPS Code and State-County FIPS Code(s); 1990-2000 percent of change in population; 2000 **actual** population; 2000-2004 estimated percent of change in population; 2004 **estimated** population; 2004-2009 projected percent of change in population; and 2009 **projected** population.

The total Metropolitan CBSA population within the state (**Total: Metro Portion of State**), the total Micropolitan CBSA population within the state (**Total: Micro Portion of State**), and the total state population are also given. Data shown in **bold face** represent in-state metropolitan area totals. A U.S. total for Micropolitan CBSAs is also provided.

ALABAMA

	FIPS CODE	PAST 1990-2000 % Change	PAST 2000 Census	PRESENT 2000-2004 % Change	PRESENT 7/1/04 Estimate	FUTURE 2004-2009 % Change	FUTURE 2009 Projection
Anniston-Oxford AL	**11500**	**-3.3**	**112,249**	**-0.0**	**112,234**	**1.0**	**113,328**
Calhoun	01015	-3.3	112,249	-0.0	112,234	1.0	113,328
Auburn-Opelika AL	**12220**	**32.1**	**115,092**	**5.1**	**120,927**	**5.6**	**127,735**
Lee	01081	32.1	115,092	5.1	120,927	5.6	127,735
Birmingham-Hoover AL	**13820**	**10.0**	**1,052,238**	**2.6**	**1,079,089**	**3.0**	**1,111,187**
Bibb	01007	25.6	20,826	3.9	21,630	9.8	23,744
Blount	01009	30.0	51,024	8.0	55,111	8.8	59,975
Chilton	01021	22.0	39,593	4.1	41,236	4.3	43,021
Jefferson	01073	1.6	662,047	-0.8	656,840	-1.0	650,292
Shelby	01117	44.2	143,293	14.7	164,416	15.1	189,240
St. Clair	01115	29.5	64,742	7.9	69,841	8.4	75,736
Walker	01127	4.5	70,713	-1.0	70,015	-1.2	69,179
Decatur AL	**19460**	**10.9**	**145,867**	**1.2**	**147,582**	**1.3**	**149,459**
Lawrence	01079	10.4	34,803	-0.9	34,504	-1.3	34,058
Morgan	01103	11.0	111,064	1.8	113,078	2.1	115,401
Dothan AL	**20020**	**8.7**	**130,861**	**2.5**	**134,089**	**2.8**	**137,845**
Geneva	01061	9.0	25,764	-1.5	25,387	-2.0	24,879
Henry	01067	6.1	16,310	1.0	16,468	0.9	16,621
Houston	01069	9.2	88,787	3.9	92,234	4.5	96,345
Florence-Muscle Shoals AL	**22520**	**8.9**	**142,950**	**-1.4**	**141,000**	**-1.8**	**138,513**
Colbert	01033	6.4	54,984	-1.1	54,367	-1.5	53,547
Lauderdale	01077	10.4	87,966	-1.5	86,633	-1.9	84,966
Gadsden AL	**23460**	**3.6**	**103,459**	**-0.5**	**102,945**	**-0.4**	**102,482**
Etowah	01055	3.6	103,459	-0.5	102,945	-0.4	102,482
Huntsville AL	**26620**	**16.8**	**342,376**	**5.9**	**362,704**	**6.6**	**386,635**
Limestone	01083	21.3	65,676	5.1	69,013	5.5	72,841
Madison	01089	15.8	276,700	6.1	293,691	6.8	313,794
Mobile AL	**33660**	**5.6**	**399,843**	**-0.1**	**399,635**	**-0.2**	**399,023**
Mobile	01097	5.6	399,843	-0.1	399,635	-0.2	399,023
Montgomery AL	**33860**	**13.6**	**346,528**	**2.3**	**354,386**	**2.6**	**363,600**
Autauga	01001	27.6	43,671	8.4	47,354	9.1	51,660
Elmore	01051	33.9	65,874	9.6	72,168	10.2	79,543
Lowndes	01085	6.4	13,473	-1.0	13,339	-1.3	13,160
Montgomery	01101	6.9	223,510	-0.9	221,525	-1.0	219,237
Tuscaloosa AL	**46220**	**9.0**	**192,034**	**1.6**	**195,077**	**1.1**	**197,209**
Greene	01063	-1.8	9,974	-1.0	9,879	-1.1	9,775
Hale	01065	10.9	17,185	6.5	18,295	-0.1	18,268
Tuscaloosa	01125	9.5	164,875	1.2	166,903	1.4	169,166
* **Russell** (See Columbus, GA-AL.)	**01113**	**6.2**	**49,756**	**-2.0**	**48,750**	**-2.4**	**47,582**
TOTAL: METRO PORTION OF STATE		**10.2**	**3,133,253**	**2.1**	**3,198,418**	**2.4**	**3,274,598**
TOTAL: MICRO PORTION OF STATE		**13.3**	**810,945**	**1.8**	**825,876**	**2.1**	**843,072**
TOTAL: ALABAMA		10.1	4,447,100	1.6	4,517,136	1.8	4,599,054

ALASKA

	FIPS CODE	PAST 1990-2000 % Change	PAST 2000 Census	PRESENT 2000-2004 % Change	PRESENT 7/1/04 Estimate	FUTURE 2004-2009 % Change	FUTURE 2009 Projection
Anchorage AK	**11260**	**20.1**	**319,605**	**8.1**	**345,540**	**9.0**	**376,599**
Anchorage	02020	15.0	260,283	5.4	274,398	6.2	291,471
Matanuska-Susitna	02170	49.5	59,322	19.9	71,142	19.7	85,128
Fairbanks AK	**21820**	**6.6**	**82,840**	**5.1**	**87,045**	**6.1**	**92,333**
Fairbanks North Star	02090	6.6	82,840	5.1	87,045	6.1	92,333
TOTAL: METRO PORTION OF STATE		**17.1**	**402,445**	**7.5**	**432,585**	**8.4**	**468,932**
TOTAL: MICRO PORTION OF STATE		**8.9**	**58,694**	**-1.7**	**57,696**	**-1.9**	**56,603**
TOTAL: ALASKA		14.0	626,932	4.6	655,899	5.4	691,302

ARIZONA

	FIPS CODE	PAST 1990-2000 % Change	PAST 2000 Census	PRESENT 2000-2004 % Change	PRESENT 7/1/04 Estimate	FUTURE 2004-2009 % Change	FUTURE 2009 Projection
Flagstaff AZ	**22380**	**20.4**	**116,320**	**5.6**	**122,854**	**6.3**	**130,614**
Coconino	04005	20.4	116,320	5.6	122,854	6.3	130,614
Phoenix-Mesa-Scottsdale AZ	**38060**	**45.3**	**3,251,876**	**13.7**	**3,698,598**	**14.2**	**4,224,395**
Maricopa	04013	44.8	3,072,149	13.5	3,486,879	14.0	3,974,832
Pinal	04021	54.4	179,727	17.8	211,719	17.9	249,563
Prescott AZ	**39140**	**55.5**	**167,517**	**13.2**	**189,588**	**13.6**	**215,355**
Yavapai	04025	55.5	167,517	13.2	189,588	13.6	215,355
Tucson AZ	**46060**	**26.5**	**843,746**	**7.6**	**907,511**	**8.1**	**981,041**
Pima	04019	26.5	843,746	7.6	907,511	8.1	981,041
Yuma AZ	**49740**	**49.7**	**160,026**	**9.1**	**174,609**	**9.9**	**191,975**
Yuma	04027	49.7	160,026	9.1	174,609	9.9	191,975
TOTAL: METRO PORTION OF STATE		**41.1**	**4,539,485**	**12.2**	**5,093,160**	**12.8**	**5,743,380**
TOTAL: MICRO PORTION OF STATE		**36.9**	**404,539**	**6.9**	**432,343**	**7.6**	**465,185**
TOTAL: ARIZONA		40.0	5,130,632	11.5	5,719,160	12.1	6,410,903

ARKANSAS

	FIPS CODE	PAST 1990-2000 % Change	PAST 2000 Census	PRESENT 2000-2004 % Change	PRESENT 7/1/04 Estimate	FUTURE 2004-2009 % Change	FUTURE 2009 Projection
Fayetteville-Springdale-Rogers, AR-MO	22220	44.9	347,045	11.7	387,515	12.2	434,846
Benton	**05007**	**57.3**	**153,406**	**15.9**	**177,727**	**16.1**	**206,263**
Madison	**05087**	**22.6**	**14,243**	**0.9**	**14,374**	**0.7**	**14,468**
Washington	**05143**	**39.1**	**157,715**	**9.9**	**173,341**	**10.5**	**191,547**
McDonald, MO	29119	28.0	21,681	1.8	22,073	2.2	22,568
Fort Smith, AR-OK	22900	16.7	273,170	3.1	281,742	3.5	291,476
Crawford	**05033**	**25.3**	**53,247**	**5.9**	**56,398**	**6.6**	**60,126**
Franklin	**05047**	**19.3**	**17,771**	**1.8**	**18,093**	**2.4**	**18,534**
Sebastian	**05131**	**15.5**	**115,071**	**2.4**	**117,824**	**2.4**	**120,635**
Le Flore, OK	40079	11.2	48,109	2.1	49,143	2.5	50,373
Sequoyah, OK	40135	15.2	38,972	3.4	40,284	3.8	41,808
Hot Springs AR	**26300**	**20.0**	**88,068**	**4.6**	**92,118**	**5.0**	**96,731**
Garland	05051	20.0	88,068	4.6	92,118	5.0	96,731
Jonesboro AR	**27860**	**15.1**	**107,762**	**2.7**	**110,679**	**2.8**	**113,827**
Craighead	05031	19.1	82,148	3.9	85,334	4.1	88,843
Poinsett	05111	3.9	25,614	-1.1	25,345	-1.4	24,984
Little Rock-North Little Rock AR	**30780**	**14.1**	**610,518**	**3.8**	**633,708**	**4.2**	**660,529**
Faulkner	05045	43.3	86,014	9.2	93,944	10.0	103,323
Grant	05053	18.0	16,464	3.7	17,074	4.1	17,774
Lonoke	05085	34.5	52,828	9.6	57,901	10.2	63,789
Perry	05105	28.1	10,209	3.2	10,533	3.4	10,889
Pulaski	05119	3.4	361,474	1.1	365,501	1.2	370,029
Saline	05125	30.1	83,529	6.3	88,755	6.7	94,725
Pine Bluff AR	**38220**	**0.4**	**107,341**	**-1.6**	**105,584**	**-2.0**	**103,504**
Cleveland	05025	10.2	8,571	2.2	8,761	2.9	9,017
Jefferson	05069	-1.4	84,278	-2.2	82,445	-2.7	80,235
Lincoln	05079	5.9	14,492	-0.8	14,378	-0.9	14,252
* **Crittenden** (See Memphis, TN-MS-AR.)	**05035**	**1.9**	**50,866**	**0.7**	**51,207**	**0.5**	**51,447**
* **Miller** (See Texarkana, TX-Texarkana, AR.)	**05091**	**5.1**	**40,443**	**4.8**	**42,371**	**5.6**	**44,746**
TOTAL: METRO PORTION OF STATE		**18.8**	**1,516,451**	**5.1**	**1,593,424**	**5.6**	**1,682,357**
TOTAL: MICRO PORTION OF STATE		**7.7**	**565,886**	**-0.5**	**563,130**	**-0.5**	**560,049**
TOTAL: ARKANSAS		13.7	2,673,400	2.5	2,741,511	2.9	2,820,498

CALIFORNIA

	FIPS CODE	PAST 1990-2000 % Change	PAST 2000 Census	PRESENT 2000-2004 % Change	PRESENT 7/1/04 Estimate	FUTURE 2004-2009 % Change	FUTURE 2009 Projection
Bakersfield CA	**12540**	**21.7**	**661,645**	**10.3**	**729,553**	**11.3**	**811,845**
Kern	06029	21.7	661,645	10.3	729,553	11.3	811,845
Chico CA	**17020**	**11.6**	**203,171**	**5.0**	**213,422**	**5.6**	**225,471**
Butte	06007	11.6	203,171	5.0	213,422	5.6	225,471
El Centro CA	**20940**	**30.2**	**142,361**	**6.4**	**151,466**	**7.4**	**162,630**
Imperial	06025	30.2	142,361	6.4	151,466	7.4	162,630
Fresno CA	**23420**	**19.8**	**799,407**	**8.4**	**866,423**	**9.3**	**946,868**
Fresno	06019	19.8	799,407	8.4	866,423	9.3	946,868
Hanford-Corcoran CA	**25260**	**27.6**	**129,461**	**9.3**	**141,461**	**10.2**	**155,937**
Kings	06031	27.6	129,461	9.3	141,461	10.2	155,937
Los Angeles-Long Beach-Santa Ana CA	**31100**	**9.7**	**12,365,627**	**4.9**	**12,971,790**	**5.5**	**13,683,748**
Los Angeles	06037	7.4	9,519,338	4.8	9,980,271	5.4	10,523,607
Orange	06059	18.1	2,846,289	5.1	2,991,519	5.6	3,160,141
Madera CA	**31460**	**39.8**	**123,109**	**11.1**	**136,739**	**12.0**	**153,112**
Madera	06039	39.8	123,109	11.1	136,739	12.0	153,112
Merced CA	**32900**	**18.0**	**210,554**	**13.1**	**238,219**	**13.9**	**271,433**
Merced	06047	18.0	210,554	13.1	238,219	13.9	271,433
Modesto CA	**33700**	**20.6**	**446,997**	**13.3**	**506,378**	**14.0**	**577,071**
Stanislaus	06099	20.6	446,997	13.3	506,378	14.0	577,071
Napa CA	**34900**	**12.2**	**124,279**	**7.8**	**133,946**	**8.7**	**145,637**
Napa	06055	12.2	124,279	7.8	133,946	8.7	145,637
Oxnard-Thousand Oaks-Ventura CA	**37100**	**12.6**	**753,197**	**6.6**	**802,627**	**7.2**	**860,068**
Ventura	06111	12.6	753,197	6.6	802,627	7.2	860,068
Redding CA	**39820**	**11.0**	**163,256**	**10.0**	**179,590**	**11.0**	**199,281**
Shasta	06089	11.0	163,256	10.0	179,590	11.0	199,281
Riverside-San Bernardino-Ontario CA	**40140**	**25.7**	**3,254,821**	**15.6**	**3,763,495**	**16.1**	**4,369,109**
Riverside	06065	32.0	1,545,387	20.2	1,856,913	20.0	2,228,111
San Bernardino	06071	20.5	1,709,434	11.5	1,906,582	12.3	2,140,998
Sacramento--Arden-Arcade--Roseville CA	**40900**	**21.3**	**1,796,857**	**13.0**	**2,030,311**	**13.7**	**2,307,706**
El Dorado	06017	24.1	156,299	10.5	172,703	11.2	192,098
Placer	06061	43.8	248,399	23.1	305,883	22.3	374,106
Sacramento	06067	17.5	1,223,499	11.5	1,364,259	12.3	1,531,926
Yolo	06113	19.5	168,660	11.2	187,466	11.8	209,576
Salinas CA	**41500**	**13.0**	**401,762**	**4.1**	**418,251**	**4.5**	**437,244**
Monterey	06053	13.0	401,762	4.1	418,251	4.5	437,244
San Diego-Carlsbad-San Marcos CA	**41740**	**12.6**	**2,813,833**	**5.4**	**2,966,135**	**5.9**	**3,142,238**
San Diego	06073	12.6	2,813,833	5.4	2,966,135	5.9	3,142,238
San Francisco-Oakland-Fremont CA	**41860**	**11.9**	**4,123,740**	**1.0**	**4,164,518**	**0.9**	**4,201,638**
Alameda	06001	12.9	1,443,741	1.4	1,464,561	1.2	1,482,152
Contra Costa	06013	18.1	948,816	7.2	1,016,987	7.8	1,096,190
Marin	06041	7.5	247,289	-0.7	245,560	-1.0	243,006
San Francisco	06075	7.3	776,733	-4.3	743,549	-5.3	704,156
San Mateo	06081	8.9	707,161	-1.9	693,861	-2.6	676,134
San Jose-Sunnyvale-Santa Clara CA	**41940**	**13.1**	**1,735,819**	**-0.2**	**1,732,851**	**-0.5**	**1,723,487**
San Benito	06069	45.1	53,234	7.3	57,117	7.1	61,197
Santa Clara	06085	12.4	1,682,585	-0.4	1,675,734	-0.8	1,662,290
San Luis Obispo-Paso Robles CA	**42020**	**13.6**	**246,681**	**3.3**	**254,929**	**3.5**	**263,976**
San Luis Obispo	06079	13.6	246,681	3.3	254,929	3.5	263,976
Santa Barbara-Santa Maria-Goleta CA	**42060**	**8.0**	**399,347**	**1.2**	**404,260**	**1.4**	**409,876**
Santa Barbara	06083	8.0	399,347	1.2	404,260	1.4	409,876
Santa Cruz-Watsonville CA	**42100**	**11.3**	**255,602**	**-2.1**	**250,198**	**-2.7**	**243,374**
Santa Cruz	06087	11.3	255,602	-2.1	250,198	-2.7	243,374
Santa Rosa-Petaluma CA	**42220**	**18.1**	**458,614**	**2.2**	**468,851**	**2.3**	**479,459**
Sonoma	06097	18.1	458,614	2.2	468,851	2.3	479,459
Stockton CA	**44700**	**17.3**	**563,598**	**16.1**	**654,288**	**16.4**	**761,890**
San Joaquin	06077	17.3	563,598	16.1	654,288	16.4	761,890
Vallejo-Fairfield CA	**46700**	**15.9**	**394,542**	**5.8**	**417,390**	**6.0**	**442,639**
Solano	06095	15.9	394,542	5.8	417,390	6.0	442,639
Visalia-Porterville CA	**47300**	**18.0**	**368,021**	**8.2**	**398,103**	**9.2**	**434,646**
Tulare	06107	18.0	368,021	8.2	398,103	9.2	434,646
Yuba City CA	**49700**	**13.5**	**139,149**	**8.5**	**151,010**	**9.5**	**165,375**
Sutter	06101	22.5	78,930	9.7	86,547	10.7	95,765
Yuba	06115	3.4	60,219	7.0	64,463	8.0	69,610
TOTAL: METRO PORTION OF STATE		**13.9**	**33,075,450**	**6.3**	**35,146,204**	**6.9**	**37,575,758**
TOTAL: MICRO PORTION OF STATE		**11.5**	**552,945**	**4.4**	**577,053**	**5.0**	**606,072**
TOTAL: CALIFORNIA		13.8	33,871,648	6.2	35,979,311	6.9	38,453,601

COLORADO

	FIPS CODE	PAST 1990-2000 % Change	PAST 2000 Census	PRESENT 2000-2004 % Change	PRESENT 7/1/04 Estimate	FUTURE 2004-2009 % Change	FUTURE 2009 Projection
Boulder CO	**14500**	**29.1**	**269,814**	**4.0**	**280,533**	**4.1**	**292,034**
Boulder	08013	29.1	269,814	4.0	280,533	4.1	292,034
Colorado Springs CO	**17820**	**31.3**	**537,484**	**8.5**	**582,962**	**9.2**	**636,428**
El Paso	08041	30.2	516,929	8.5	560,804	9.2	612,412
Teller	08119	64.9	20,555	7.8	22,158	8.4	24,016
Denver-Aurora CO	**19740**	**30.7**	**2,179,240**	**7.2**	**2,337,049**	**7.7**	**2,516,629**
Adams	08001	35.0	348,618	11.9	389,997	12.5	438,602
Arapahoe	08005	24.6	487,967	7.4	524,236	7.8	565,097
Broomfield	08014	55.3	38,272	12.6	43,078	10.5	47,622
Clear Creek	08019	22.4	9,322	3.1	9,612	3.8	9,981
Denver	08031	18.6	554,636	0.6	558,164	0.6	561,577
Douglas	08035	191.0	175,766	35.3	237,826	30.2	309,585
Elbert	08039	106.0	19,872	15.6	22,964	15.5	26,514
Gilpin	08047	55.0	4,757	2.2	4,861	1.6	4,939
Jefferson	08059	20.3	525,507	0.7	529,255	0.7	532,700
Park	08093	102.4	14,523	17.4	17,056	17.3	20,012
Fort Collins-Loveland CO	**22660**	**35.1**	**251,494**	**7.8**	**271,165**	**8.4**	**293,935**
Larimer	08069	35.1	251,494	7.8	271,165	8.4	293,935
Grand Junction CO	**24300**	**24.8**	**116,255**	**9.3**	**127,075**	**9.4**	**139,069**
Mesa	08077	24.8	116,255	9.3	127,075	9.4	139,069
Greeley CO	**24540**	**37.3**	**180,926**	**22.0**	**220,667**	**21.3**	**267,629**
Weld	08123	37.3	180,926	22.0	220,667	21.3	267,629
Pueblo CO	**39380**	**15.0**	**141,472**	**6.8**	**151,054**	**7.6**	**162,566**
Pueblo	08101	15.0	141,472	6.8	151,054	7.6	162,566
TOTAL: METRO PORTION OF STATE		**30.4**	**3,676,685**	**8.0**	**3,970,505**	**8.5**	**4,308,290**
TOTAL: MICRO PORTION OF STATE		**44.2**	**244,212**	**7.1**	**261,532**	**7.7**	**281,614**
TOTAL: COLORADO		30.6	4,301,261	7.5	4,625,293	8.1	4,998,320

CONNECTICUT

	FIPS CODE	PAST 1990-2000 % Change	PAST 2000 Census	PRESENT 2000-2004 % Change	PRESENT 7/1/04 Estimate	FUTURE 2004-2009 % Change	FUTURE 2009 Projection
Bridgeport-Stamford-Norwalk CT	**14860**	**6.6**	**882,567**	**2.4**	**904,001**	**2.7**	**928,248**
Fairfield	09001	6.6	882,567	2.4	904,001	2.7	928,248
Hartford-West Hartford-East Hartford CT	**25540**	**2.2**	**1,148,618**	**3.3**	**1,186,956**	**3.8**	**1,232,061**
Hartford	09003	0.6	857,183	2.2	875,839	2.5	897,751
Middlesex	09007	8.3	155,071	5.4	163,370	5.9	173,023
Tolland	09013	6.0	136,364	8.3	147,747	9.2	161,287
New Haven-Milford CT	**35300**	**2.5**	**824,008**	**2.9**	**847,502**	**3.3**	**875,645**
New Haven	09009	2.5	824,008	2.9	847,502	3.3	875,645
Norwich-New London CT	**35980**	**1.6**	**259,088**	**2.5**	**265,499**	**2.8**	**273,047**
New London	09011	1.6	259,088	2.5	265,499	2.8	273,047
TOTAL: METRO PORTION OF STATE		**3.4**	**3,114,281**	**2.9**	**3,203,958**	**3.3**	**3,309,001**
TOTAL: MICRO PORTION OF STATE		**5.3**	**291,284**	**4.1**	**303,288**	**4.7**	**317,615**
TOTAL: CONNECTICUT		3.6	3,405,565	3.0	3,507,246	3.4	3,626,616

DELAWARE

	FIPS CODE	PAST 1990-2000 % Change	PAST 2000 Census	PRESENT 2000-2004 % Change	PRESENT 7/1/04 Estimate	FUTURE 2004-2009 % Change	FUTURE 2009 Projection
Dover DE	**20100**	**14.1**	**126,697**	**8.0**	**136,821**	**8.9**	**148,978**
Kent	10001	14.1	126,697	8.0	136,821	8.9	148,978
* **New Castle** (See Philadelphia-Camden-Wilmington, PA-NJ-DE-MD.)	**10003**	**13.2**	**500,265**	**3.8**	**519,483**	**4.2**	**541,522**
TOTAL: METRO PORTION OF STATE		**13.4**	**626,962**	**4.7**	**656,304**	**5.2**	**690,500**
TOTAL: MICRO PORTION OF STATE		**38.3**	**156,638**	**9.5**	**171,552**	**10.3**	**189,179**
TOTAL: DELAWARE		17.6	783,600	5.6	827,856	6.3	879,679

* Indicates county is included from metro in different state.
Source: Devonshire Associates Ltd. and Scan/US, Inc. 2004.

Core Based Statistical Areas and Their Component Counties: Population Trends, *Continued*

DISTRICT OF COLUMBIA

	FIPS CODE	PAST 1990-2000 % Change	PAST 2000 Census	PRESENT 2000-2004 % Change	PRESENT 7/1/04 Estimate	FUTURE 2004-2009 % Change	FUTURE 2009 Projection
Washington-Arlington-Alexandria, DC-VA-MD-WV	47900	16.3	4,796,183	8.0	5,179,798	8.6	5,626,169
District of Columbia	**11001**	**-5.7**	**572,059**	**-2.0**	**560,725**	**-2.3**	**547,617**
Calvert, MD	24009	45.1	74,563	16.8	87,081	17.0	101,916
Charles, MD	24017	19.2	120,546	13.6	136,969	14.3	156,536
Frederick, MD	24021	30.0	195,277	12.3	219,345	12.9	247,718
Montgomery, MD	24031	15.4	873,341	6.8	932,558	7.3	1,000,765
Prince George's, MD	24033	9.9	801,515	6.1	850,384	6.8	908,563
Alexandria, VA	51510	15.4	128,283	0.4	128,847	-0.3	128,458
Arlington, VA	51013	10.8	189,453	-1.1	187,390	-1.3	184,980
Clarke, VA	51043	4.6	12,652	7.4	13,582	8.0	14,672
Fairfax, VA	51059	18.5	969,749	4.0	1,008,761	4.1	1,050,462
Fairfax, VA	51600	9.6	21,498	3.2	22,181	3.4	22,928
Falls Church, VA	51610	8.3	10,377	1.2	10,500	0.7	10,576
Fauquier, VA	51061	13.1	55,139	14.2	62,992	14.7	72,263
Fredericksburg, VA	51630	1.3	19,279	6.2	20,481	7.1	21,938
Loudoun, VA	51107	96.9	169,599	40.1	237,678	33.5	317,314
Manassas, VA	51683	25.7	35,135	7.5	37,756	7.8	40,708
Manassas Park, VA	51685	52.8	10,290	8.9	11,209	9.8	12,302
Prince William, VA	51153	30.2	280,813	20.8	339,149	20.4	408,242
Spotsylvania, VA	51177	57.5	90,395	25.3	113,260	23.9	140,355
Stafford, VA	51179	51.0	92,446	26.4	116,821	24.8	145,805
Warren, VA	51187	20.8	31,584	9.5	34,587	10.4	38,170
Jefferson, WV	54037	17.4	42,190	12.7	47,542	13.3	53,881
TOTAL: METRO PORTION OF DISTRICT		**-5.7**	**572,059**	**-2.0**	**560,725**	**-2.3**	**547,617**
TOTAL: DISTRICT OF COLUMBIA		-5.7	572,059	-2.0	560,725	-2.3	547,617

FLORIDA

	FIPS CODE	PAST 1990-2000 % Change	PAST 2000 Census	PRESENT 2000-2004 % Change	PRESENT 7/1/04 Estimate	FUTURE 2004-2009 % Change	FUTURE 2009 Projection
Cape Coral-Fort Myers FL	**15980**	**31.6**	**440,888**	**15.3**	**508,350**	**15.9**	**589,051**
Lee	12071	31.6	440,888	15.3	508,350	15.9	589,051
Deltona-Daytona Beach-Ormond Beach FL	**19660**	**19.6**	**443,343**	**7.5**	**476,562**	**8.3**	**516,056**
Volusia	12127	19.6	443,343	7.5	476,562	8.3	516,056
Fort Walton Beach-Crestview-Destin FL	**23020**	**18.6**	**170,498**	**5.9**	**180,485**	**6.6**	**192,392**
Okaloosa	12091	18.6	170,498	5.9	180,485	6.6	192,392
Gainesville FL	**23540**	**21.5**	**232,392**	**3.8**	**241,335**	**4.4**	**251,953**
Alachua	12001	20.0	217,955	3.4	225,339	3.9	234,144
Gilchrist	12041	49.3	14,437	10.8	15,996	11.3	17,809
Jacksonville FL	**27260**	**21.4**	**1,122,750**	**9.4**	**1,228,504**	**10.4**	**1,356,521**
Baker	12003	20.4	22,259	6.8	23,769	7.3	25,494
Clay	12019	32.9	140,814	15.6	162,779	16.2	189,164
Duval	12031	15.7	778,879	6.6	830,101	7.6	893,203
Nassau	12089	31.2	57,663	9.0	62,849	9.7	68,969
St. Johns	12109	46.9	123,135	21.0	149,006	20.6	179,691
Lakeland FL	**29460**	**19.4**	**483,924**	**7.2**	**518,809**	**8.0**	**560,565**
Polk	12105	19.4	483,924	7.2	518,809	8.0	560,565
Miami-Fort Lauderdale-Miami Beach FL	**33100**	**23.5**	**5,007,564**	**7.3**	**5,375,613**	**8.1**	**5,809,709**
Broward	12011	29.3	1,623,018	8.7	1,764,315	9.3	1,929,159
Miami-Dade	12086	16.3	2,253,362	5.1	2,368,141	5.7	2,503,015
Palm Beach	12099	31.0	1,131,184	9.9	1,243,157	10.8	1,377,535
Naples-Marco Island FL	**34940**	**65.3**	**251,377**	**18.3**	**297,488**	**18.2**	**351,759**
Collier	12021	65.3	251,377	18.3	297,488	18.2	351,759
Ocala FL	**36100**	**32.9**	**258,916**	**10.8**	**286,954**	**11.6**	**320,284**
Marion	12083	32.9	258,916	10.8	286,954	11.6	320,284
Orlando FL	**36740**	**34.3**	**1,644,561**	**12.6**	**1,851,873**	**13.2**	**2,096,306**
Lake	12069	38.4	210,528	22.0	256,893	21.4	311,975
Orange	12095	32.3	896,344	10.0	985,714	10.6	1,089,958
Osceola	12097	60.1	172,493	25.5	216,437	24.4	269,272
Seminole	12117	27.0	365,196	7.6	392,829	8.2	425,101
Palm Bay-Melbourne-Titusville FL	**37340**	**19.4**	**476,230**	**8.1**	**515,004**	**9.0**	**561,468**
Brevard	12009	19.4	476,230	8.1	515,004	9.0	561,468
Panama City-Lynn Haven FL	**37460**	**16.7**	**148,217**	**6.3**	**157,510**	**7.4**	**169,093**
Bay	12005	16.7	148,217	6.3	157,510	7.4	169,093
Pensacola-Ferry Pass-Brent FL	**37860**	**19.7**	**412,153**	**5.4**	**434,387**	**6.2**	**461,432**
Escambia	12033	12.0	294,410	0.7	296,422	0.9	299,104
Santa Rosa	12113	44.3	117,743	17.2	137,965	17.7	162,328
Port St. Lucie-Fort Pierce FL	**38940**	**27.2**	**319,426**	**12.0**	**357,906**	**13.0**	**404,587**
Martin	12085	25.6	126,731	8.7	137,796	9.7	151,164
St. Lucie	12111	28.3	192,695	14.2	220,110	15.1	253,423
Punta Gorda FL	**39460**	**27.6**	**141,627**	**10.9**	**157,100**	**11.8**	**175,640**
Charlotte	12015	27.6	141,627	10.9	157,100	11.8	175,640
Sarasota-Bradenton-Venice FL	**42260**	**20.5**	**589,959**	**9.7**	**647,224**	**10.5**	**715,358**
Manatee	12081	24.7	264,002	11.3	293,837	12.0	329,004
Sarasota	12115	17.3	325,957	8.4	353,387	9.3	386,354
Tallahassee FL	**45220**	**23.6**	**320,304**	**3.1**	**330,177**	**3.5**	**341,665**
Gadsden	12039	9.7	45,087	0.2	45,161	0.3	45,296
Jefferson	12065	14.2	12,902	11.7	14,410	12.9	16,275
Leon	12073	24.4	239,452	1.7	243,428	1.7	247,681
Wakulla	12129	61.0	22,863	18.9	27,178	19.3	32,413
Tampa-St. Petersburg-Clearwater FL	**45300**	**15.9**	**2,395,997**	**7.4**	**2,574,498**	**8.3**	**2,787,447**
Hernando	12053	29.4	130,802	12.7	147,435	13.5	167,363
Hillsborough	12057	19.8	998,948	9.8	1,096,848	10.7	1,214,056
Pasco	12101	22.6	344,765	16.8	402,756	17.2	472,007
Pinellas	12103	8.2	921,482	0.6	927,459	0.7	934,021
Vero Beach FL	**46940**	**25.2**	**112,947**	**8.7**	**122,827**	**9.6**	**134,647**
Indian River	12061	25.2	112,947	8.7	122,827	9.6	134,647
TOTAL: METRO PORTION OF STATE		**23.4**	**14,973,073**	**8.6**	**16,262,606**	**9.4**	**17,795,933**
TOTAL: MICRO PORTION OF STATE		**27.6**	**646,420**	**8.0**	**698,155**	**8.9**	**760,440**
TOTAL: FLORIDA		23.5	15,982,378	8.5	17,342,822	9.3	18,961,590

GEORGIA

	FIPS CODE	PAST 1990-2000 % Change	PAST 2000 Census	PRESENT 2000-2004 % Change	PRESENT 7/1/04 Estimate	FUTURE 2004-2009 % Change	FUTURE 2009 Projection
Albany GA	**10500**	**7.7**	**157,833**	**2.8**	**162,223**	**3.5**	**167,822**
Baker	13007	12.7	4,074	7.8	4,392	9.7	4,817
Dougherty	13095	-0.3	96,065	-0.5	95,611	-0.4	95,249
Lee	13177	52.4	24,757	19.5	29,584	19.8	35,450
Terrell	13273	3.0	10,970	-1.4	10,814	-1.8	10,617
Worth	13321	11.3	21,967	-0.7	21,822	-0.6	21,689
Athens-Clarke County GA	**12020**	**22.1**	**166,079**	**4.8**	**174,053**	**5.2**	**183,151**
Clarke	13059	15.9	101,489	2.8	104,327	3.0	107,507
Madison	13195	22.2	25,730	6.8	27,481	7.4	29,507
Oconee	13219	48.9	26,225	9.2	28,647	9.8	31,447
Oglethorpe	13221	29.4	12,635	7.6	13,598	8.0	14,690
Atlanta-Sandy Springs-Marietta GA	**12060**	**38.4**	**4,247,981**	**11.1**	**4,719,358**	**11.6**	**5,265,848**
Barrow	13013	55.3	46,144	20.9	55,787	20.7	67,325
Bartow	13015	36.0	76,019	15.0	87,405	15.3	100,778
Butts	13035	27.4	19,522	17.2	22,885	17.2	26,815
Carroll	13045	22.2	87,268	16.9	102,023	17.1	119,514
Cherokee	13057	57.3	141,903	22.8	174,257	21.9	212,338
Clayton	13063	29.9	236,517	12.8	266,814	13.3	302,190
Cobb	13067	35.7	607,751	9.2	663,776	9.6	727,493
Coweta	13077	65.7	89,215	17.9	105,145	17.8	123,894
Dawson	13085	69.7	15,999	20.9	19,341	19.8	23,172
DeKalb	13089	22.0	665,865	1.6	676,338	1.5	686,337
Douglas	13097	29.6	92,174	14.0	105,116	14.8	120,622
Fayette	13113	46.2	91,263	10.9	101,180	11.2	112,509
Forsyth	13117	123.2	98,407	33.7	131,575	29.5	170,391
Fulton	13121	25.7	816,006	0.3	818,745	0.3	820,832
Gwinnett	13135	66.7	588,448	18.8	698,970	18.3	827,071
Haralson	13143	17.0	25,690	9.0	28,009	9.8	30,750
Heard	13149	27.6	11,012	1.4	11,168	0.7	11,249
Henry	13151	103.2	119,341	33.6	159,460	29.7	206,741
Jasper	13159	35.2	11,426	12.9	12,896	13.5	14,642
Lamar	13171	22.0	15,912	2.5	16,316	2.5	16,723
Meriwether	13199	0.5	22,534	1.5	22,870	1.8	23,289
Newton	13217	48.3	62,001	29.9	80,554	27.4	102,604
Paulding	13223	96.3	81,678	29.5	105,749	26.8	134,135
Pickens	13227	59.3	22,983	22.2	28,084	21.0	33,979
Pike	13231	33.9	13,688	12.3	15,372	12.8	17,336
Rockdale	13247	29.6	70,111	9.0	76,406	9.6	83,732
Spalding	13255	7.3	58,417	4.7	61,151	5.5	64,495
Walton	13297	57.3	60,687	18.6	71,966	18.0	84,892
Augusta-Richmond County, GA-SC	12260	14.7	499,684	3.1	515,207	3.6	533,805
Burke	**13033**	**8.1**	**22,243**	**4.2**	**23,167**	**4.7**	**24,256**
Columbia	**13073**	**35.2**	**89,288**	**12.1**	**100,062**	**12.8**	**112,848**
McDuffie	**13189**	**5.5**	**21,231**	**1.3**	**21,501**	**1.3**	**21,780**
Richmond	**13245**	**5.3**	**199,775**	**-1.0**	**197,685**	**-1.2**	**195,374**
Aiken, SC	45003	17.9	142,552	3.9	148,054	4.4	154,638
Edgefield, SC	45037	33.9	24,595	0.6	24,738	0.7	24,909
Brunswick GA	**15260**	**13.2**	**93,044**	**4.6**	**97,306**	**5.2**	**102,361**
Brantley	13025	32.1	14,629	5.8	15,474	6.3	16,450
Glynn	13127	8.1	67,568	5.0	70,954	5.8	75,069
McIntosh	13191	25.6	10,847	0.3	10,878	-0.3	10,842
Columbus, GA-AL	17980	5.7	281,768	2.5	288,724	2.8	296,937
Russell, AL	01113	6.2	49,756	-2.0	48,750	-2.4	47,582
Chattahoochee	**13053**	**-12.1**	**14,882**	**39.6**	**20,780**	**34.8**	**28,013**
Harris	**13145**	**33.2**	**23,695**	**12.2**	**26,586**	**13.1**	**30,057**
Marion	**13197**	**27.8**	**7,144**	**0.3**	**7,165**	**-0.4**	**7,138**
Muscogee	**13215**	**3.9**	**186,291**	**-0.5**	**185,443**	**-0.7**	**184,147**
Dalton GA	**19140**	**21.7**	**120,031**	**7.8**	**129,405**	**8.2**	**140,030**
Murray	13213	39.6	36,506	10.5	40,328	10.9	44,735
Whitfield	13313	15.3	83,525	6.6	89,077	7.0	95,295
Gainesville GA	**23580**	**45.9**	**139,277**	**15.7**	**161,175**	**15.7**	**186,542**
Hall	13139	45.9	139,277	15.7	161,175	15.7	186,542
Hinesville-Fort Stewart GA	**25980**	**22.0**	**71,914**	**-4.0**	**69,055**	**-4.5**	**65,959**
Liberty	13179	16.8	61,610	-5.7	58,129	-6.6	54,306
Long	13183	66.1	10,304	6.0	10,926	6.7	11,653
Macon GA	**31420**	**7.6**	**222,368**	**2.2**	**227,227**	**2.6**	**233,241**
Bibb	13021	2.6	153,887	0.4	154,445	0.5	155,230
Crawford	13079	39.0	12,495	0.7	12,586	1.3	12,748
Jones	13169	14.0	23,639	10.3	26,065	11.4	29,028
Monroe	13207	27.1	21,757	9.0	23,707	9.7	26,018
Twiggs	13289	8.0	10,590	-1.6	10,424	-2.0	10,217
Rome GA	**40660**	**11.5**	**90,565**	**4.0**	**94,225**	**4.5**	**98,508**
Floyd	13115	11.5	90,565	4.0	94,225	4.5	98,508
Savannah GA	**42340**	**13.5**	**293,000**	**5.1**	**307,995**	**6.0**	**326,328**
Bryan	13029	51.7	23,417	16.5	27,274	17.1	31,942
Chatham	13051	7.0	232,048	1.9	236,368	2.3	241,848
Effingham	13103	46.1	37,535	18.2	44,353	18.5	52,538
Valdosta GA	**46660**	**20.5**	**119,560**	**2.9**	**123,021**	**3.4**	**127,228**
Brooks	13027	6.8	16,450	-1.7	16,165	-2.4	15,783
Echols	13101	60.8	3,754	8.4	4,068	8.5	4,413
Lanier	13173	30.9	7,241	2.1	7,393	2.2	7,555
Lowndes	13185	21.2	92,115	3.6	95,395	4.3	99,477
Warner Robins GA	**47580**	**24.2**	**110,765**	**11.5**	**123,475**	**12.3**	**138,676**
Houston	13153	24.2	110,765	11.5	123,475	12.3	138,676
* **Catoosa**	**13047**	**25.5**	**53,282**	**11.8**	**59,560**	**12.4**	**66,931**
* **Dade**	**13083**	**15.3**	**15,154**	**6.6**	**16,151**	**7.4**	**17,353**
* **Walker**	**13295**	**4.7**	**61,053**	**3.3**	**63,070**	**3.9**	**65,504**
(See Chattanooga, TN-GA.)							
TOTAL: METRO PORTION OF STATE		**29.2**	**6,526,455**	**8.9**	**7,109,688**	**9.6**	**7,789,095**
TOTAL: MICRO PORTION OF STATE		**14.8**	**884,394**	**3.7**	**917,087**	**4.2**	**955,366**
TOTAL: GEORGIA		26.4	8,186,453	7.9	8,836,255	8.6	9,593,957

HAWAII

	FIPS CODE	PAST 1990-2000 % Change	PAST 2000 Census	PRESENT 2000-2004 % Change	PRESENT 7/1/04 Estimate	FUTURE 2004-2009 % Change	FUTURE 2009 Projection
Honolulu HI	**26180**	**4.8**	**876,156**	**4.1**	**911,719**	**4.9**	**956,800**
Honolulu	15003	4.8	876,156	4.1	911,719	4.9	956,800
TOTAL: METRO PORTION OF STATE		**4.8**	**876,156**	**4.1**	**911,719**	**4.9**	**956,800**
TOTAL: MICRO PORTION OF STATE		**23.3**	**335,234**	**7.6**	**360,853**	**8.4**	**391,237**
TOTAL: HAWAII		9.3	1,211,537	5.0	1,272,696	5.9	1,348,138

IDAHO

	FIPS CODE	PAST 1990-2000 % Change	PAST 2000 Census	PRESENT 2000-2004 % Change	PRESENT 7/1/04 Estimate	FUTURE 2004-2009 % Change	FUTURE 2009 Projection
Boise City-Nampa ID	**14260**	**45.4**	**464,840**	**12.9**	**524,915**	**13.4**	**595,013**
Ada	16001	46.2	300,904	10.5	332,530	11.1	369,368
Boise	16015	90.1	6,670	10.9	7,399	11.0	8,212
Canyon	16027	45.9	131,441	19.9	157,648	19.5	188,322
Gem	16045	28.2	15,181	5.3	15,988	6.0	16,946
Owyhee	16073	26.8	10,644	6.6	11,350	7.2	12,165
Coeur d'Alene ID	**17660**	**55.7**	**108,685**	**10.5**	**120,129**	**11.0**	**133,350**
Kootenai	16055	55.7	108,685	10.5	120,129	11.0	133,350
Idaho Falls ID	**26820**	**14.6**	**101,677**	**7.1**	**108,893**	**7.8**	**117,341**
Bonneville	16019	14.3	82,522	7.1	88,379	7.7	95,227
Jefferson	16051	15.8	19,155	7.1	20,514	7.8	22,114
Lewiston, ID-WA	30300	12.9	57,961	0.8	58,451	1.1	59,079
Nez Perce	**16069**	**10.8**	**37,410**	**1.1**	**37,804**	**1.4**	**38,324**
Asotin, WA	53003	16.7	20,551	0.5	20,647	0.5	20,755
Pocatello ID	**38540**	**13.7**	**83,103**	**-0.2**	**82,971**	**-0.2**	**82,806**
Bannock	16005	14.4	75,565	0.1	75,644	0.1	75,705
Power	16077	6.4	7,538	-2.8	7,327	-3.1	7,101
* **Franklin**	**16041**	**22.7**	**11,329**	**6.3**	**12,043**	**7.0**	**12,884**
(See Logan, UT-ID.)							
TOTAL: METRO PORTION OF STATE		**35.8**	**807,044**	**9.9**	**886,755**	**10.5**	**979,718**
TOTAL: MICRO PORTION OF STATE		**17.6**	**295,879**	**3.8**	**307,103**	**4.5**	**320,895**
TOTAL: IDAHO		28.5	1,293,953	7.3	1,388,573	8.0	1,499,776

ILLINOIS

	FIPS CODE	PAST 1990-2000 % Change	PAST 2000 Census	PRESENT 2000-2004 % Change	PRESENT 7/1/04 Estimate	FUTURE 2004-2009 % Change	FUTURE 2009 Projection
Bloomington-Normal IL	**14060**	**16.5**	**150,433**	**5.6**	**158,878**	**6.3**	**168,862**
McLean	17113	16.5	150,433	5.6	158,878	6.3	168,862
Champaign-Urbana IL	**16580**	**3.7**	**210,275**	**4.4**	**219,572**	**5.1**	**230,816**
Champaign	17019	3.8	179,669	5.2	189,076	6.0	200,443
Ford	17053	-0.2	14,241	-1.3	14,052	-1.5	13,839
Piatt	17147	5.3	16,365	0.5	16,444	0.5	16,534
Chicago-Naperville-Joliet, IL-IN-WI	16980	11.2	9,098,316	3.4	9,405,026	3.8	9,762,099
Cook	**17031**	**5.3**	**5,376,741**	**-0.6**	**5,342,990**	**-0.8**	**5,299,999**
DeKalb	**17037**	**14.2**	**88,969**	**7.5**	**95,619**	**8.2**	**103,501**
DuPage	**17043**	**15.7**	**904,161**	**3.0**	**931,347**	**3.3**	**962,070**
Grundy	**17063**	**16.1**	**37,535**	**6.9**	**40,142**	**7.6**	**43,212**
Kane	**17089**	**27.3**	**404,119**	**17.2**	**473,610**	**17.4**	**556,007**
Kendall	**17093**	**38.4**	**54,544**	**29.0**	**70,354**	**26.9**	**89,295**
Lake	**17097**	**24.8**	**644,356**	**8.2**	**697,152**	**8.7**	**757,754**
McHenry	**17111**	**41.9**	**260,077**	**13.1**	**294,238**	**13.8**	**334,948**
Will	**17197**	**40.6**	**502,266**	**22.0**	**612,859**	**21.3**	**743,563**
Jasper, IN	18073	20.4	30,043	4.4	31,372	4.7	32,839
Lake, IN	18089	1.9	484,564	0.8	488,435	1.0	493,200
Newton, IN	18111	7.5	14,566	-1.5	14,353	-1.7	14,105
Porter, IN	18127	13.9	146,798	5.1	154,300	5.7	163,124
Kenosha, WI	55059	16.7	149,577	5.8	158,255	6.5	168,482
Danville IL	**19180**	**-4.9**	**83,919**	**-1.7**	**82,467**	**-2.0**	**80,800**
Vermilion	17183	-4.9	83,919	-1.7	82,467	-2.0	80,800
Decatur IL	**19500**	**-2.1**	**114,706**	**-4.0**	**110,093**	**-4.8**	**104,829**
Macon	17115	-2.1	114,706	-4.0	110,093	-4.8	104,829
Kankakee-Bradley IL	**28100**	**7.9**	**103,833**	**2.3**	**106,207**	**2.7**	**109,106**
Kankakee	17091	7.9	103,833	2.3	106,207	2.7	109,106
Peoria IL	**37900**	**2.3**	**366,899**	**-0.3**	**365,775**	**-0.3**	**364,660**
Marshall	17123	2.6	13,180	-1.3	13,003	-1.4	12,822
Peoria	17143	0.3	183,433	-0.8	182,043	-0.8	180,577
Stark	17175	-3.1	6,332	-2.7	6,159	-3.1	5,966
Tazewell	17179	3.9	128,485	-0.4	127,916	-0.6	127,205
Woodford	17203	8.6	35,469	3.3	36,654	3.9	38,090
Rockford IL	**40420**	**12.9**	**320,204**	**4.3**	**334,044**	**4.9**	**350,295**
Boone	17007	35.6	41,786	14.7	47,945	15.3	55,286
Winnebago	17201	10.1	278,418	2.8	286,099	3.1	295,009
Springfield IL	**44100**	**6.3**	**201,437**	**2.0**	**205,434**	**2.3**	**210,247**
Menard	17129	11.8	12,486	1.1	12,619	1.0	12,749
Sangamon	17167	5.9	188,951	2.0	192,815	2.4	197,498
* **Henry**	**17073**	**-0.3**	**51,020**	**-1.0**	**50,508**	**-1.3**	**49,831**
* **Mercer**	**17131**	**-1.9**	**16,957**	**0.4**	**17,018**	**0.4**	**17,089**
* **Rock Island**	**17161**	**0.4**	**149,374**	**-1.2**	**147,511**	**-1.4**	**145,513**
(See Davenport-Moline-Rock Island, IA-IL.)							
* **Bond**	**17005**	**17.6**	**17,633**	**2.3**	**18,040**	**2.7**	**18,533**
* **Calhoun**	**17013**	**-4.5**	**5,084**	**-0.4**	**5,062**	**-0.8**	**5,024**
* **Clinton**	**17027**	**4.7**	**35,535**	**2.2**	**36,327**	**2.6**	**37,288**
* **Jersey**	**17083**	**5.5**	**21,668**	**3.2**	**22,361**	**3.9**	**23,223**
* **Macoupin**	**17117**	**2.8**	**49,019**	**0.1**	**49,072**	**0.2**	**49,154**
* **Madison**	**17119**	**3.9**	**258,941**	**1.4**	**262,550**	**1.6**	**266,835**
* **Monroe**	**17133**	**23.2**	**27,619**	**10.0**	**30,375**	**10.7**	**33,630**
* **St. Clair**	**17163**	**-2.6**	**256,082**	**1.3**	**259,386**	**1.5**	**263,266**
(See St. Louis, MO-IL.)							
TOTAL: METRO PORTION OF STATE		**9.9**	**10,713,406**	**3.0**	**11,038,991**	**3.4**	**11,419,350**
TOTAL: MICRO PORTION OF STATE		**2.2**	**1,081,896**	**-0.9**	**1,071,879**	**-1.1**	**1,060,565**
TOTAL: ILLINOIS		8.6	12,419,293	2.5	12,725,117	2.8	13,082,984

INDIANA

	FIPS CODE	PAST 1990-2000 % Change	PAST 2000 Census	PRESENT 2000-2004 % Change	PRESENT 7/1/04 Estimate	FUTURE 2004-2009 % Change	FUTURE 2009 Projection
Anderson IN	**11300**	**2.1**	**133,358**	**-2.2**	**130,409**	**-2.7**	**126,901**
Madison	18095	2.1	133,358	-2.2	130,409	-2.7	126,901
Bloomington IN	**14020**	**12.0**	**175,506**	**2.6**	**180,031**	**2.9**	**185,301**
Greene	18055	9.0	33,157	0.3	33,255	0.2	33,305
Monroe	18105	10.6	120,563	2.6	123,639	3.0	127,311
Owen	18119	26.1	21,786	6.2	23,137	6.7	24,685
Columbus IN	**18020**	**12.2**	**71,435**	**1.6**	**72,553**	**1.5**	**73,612**
Bartholomew	18005	12.2	71,435	1.6	72,553	1.5	73,612
Elkhart-Goshen IN	**21140**	**17.0**	**182,791**	**4.2**	**190,535**	**4.6**	**199,304**
Elkhart	18039	17.0	182,791	4.2	190,535	4.6	199,304
Evansville, IN-KY	21780	5.5	342,815	1.1	346,581	1.3	351,066
Gibson	**18051**	**1.8**	**32,500**	**2.0**	**33,139**	**2.2**	**33,876**
Posey	**18129**	**4.2**	**27,061**	**-0.9**	**26,811**	**-1.2**	**26,484**
Vanderburgh	**18163**	**4.2**	**171,922**	**-0.0**	**171,902**	**0.0**	**171,959**
Warrick	**18173**	**16.6**	**52,383**	**5.9**	**55,468**	**6.5**	**59,086**
Henderson, KY	21101	4.1	44,829	0.9	45,235	1.2	45,763
Webster, KY	21233	1.2	14,120	-0.7	14,026	-0.9	13,898

* Indicates county is included from metro in different state.
Source: Devonshire Associates Ltd. and Scan/US, Inc. 2004.

continued on next page

Core Based Statistical Areas and Their Component Counties: Population Trends, *Continued*

	FIPS CODE	PAST 1990-2000 % Change	PAST 2000 Census	PRESENT 2000-2004 % Change	PRESENT 7/1/04 Estimate	FUTURE 2004-2009 % Change	FUTURE 2009 Projection
Fort Wayne IN	**23060**	**10.1**	**390,156**	**3.2**	**402,608**	**3.6**	**417,041**
Allen	18003	10.3	331,849	3.3	342,644	3.6	355,080
Wells	18179	6.4	27,600	1.5	28,011	1.7	28,501
Whitley	18183	11.1	30,707	4.1	31,953	4.7	33,460
Indianapolis IN	**26900**	**17.8**	**1,525,104**	**6.0**	**1,616,900**	**6.7**	**1,724,443**
Boone	18011	20.9	46,107	9.2	50,364	9.9	55,335
Brown	18013	6.2	14,957	3.1	15,417	3.4	15,936
Hamilton	18057	67.7	182,740	24.4	227,306	23.0	279,692
Hancock	18059	21.7	55,391	9.6	60,709	10.4	67,026
Hendricks	18063	37.5	104,093	18.5	123,336	18.2	145,760
Johnson	18081	30.8	115,209	9.1	125,682	9.6	137,807
Marion	18097	7.9	860,454	0.4	864,200	0.5	868,901
Morgan	18109	19.3	66,689	3.8	69,244	4.2	72,185
Putnam	18133	18.8	36,019	2.4	36,886	2.6	37,854
Shelby	18145	7.8	43,445	0.7	43,756	0.4	43,947
Kokomo IN	**29020**	**4.7**	**101,541**	**-0.3**	**101,227**	**-0.4**	**100,848**
Howard	18067	5.1	84,964	-0.1	84,849	-0.2	84,692
Tipton	18159	2.8	16,577	-1.2	16,378	-1.4	16,156
Lafayette IN	**29140**	**12.4**	**178,541**	**4.4**	**186,417**	**5.0**	**195,813**
Benton	18007	-0.2	9,421	-3.1	9,125	-3.5	8,810
Carroll	18015	7.2	20,165	2.2	20,609	2.7	21,157
Tippecanoe	18157	14.1	148,955	5.2	156,683	5.8	165,846
Michigan City-La Porte IN	**33140**	**2.8**	**110,106**	**-0.3**	**109,775**	**-0.5**	**109,259**
La Porte	18091	2.8	110,106	-0.3	109,775	-0.5	109,259
Muncie IN	**34620**	**-0.7**	**118,769**	**-1.4**	**117,094**	**-1.7**	**115,140**
Delaware	18035	-0.7	118,769	-1.4	117,094	-1.7	115,140
South Bend-Mishawaka, IN-MI	43780	6.8	316,663	0.4	317,967	0.4	319,124
St. Joseph	**18141**	**7.5**	**265,559**	**0.4**	**266,508**	**0.3**	**267,297**
Cass, MI	26027	3.3	51,104	0.7	51,459	0.7	51,827
Terre Haute IN	**45460**	**2.6**	**170,943**	**-0.9**	**169,396**	**-1.0**	**167,668**
Clay	18021	7.5	26,556	1.1	26,843	1.3	27,197
Sullivan	18153	14.5	21,751	0.7	21,900	0.9	22,091
Vermillion	18165	0.1	16,788	-1.7	16,504	-2.0	16,167
Vigo	18167	-0.2	105,848	-1.6	104,149	-1.9	102,213
* **Jasper**	**18073**	**20.4**	**30,043**	**4.4**	**31,372**	**4.7**	**32,839**
* **Lake**	**18089**	**1.9**	**484,564**	**0.8**	**488,435**	**1.0**	**493,200**
* **Newton**	**18111**	**7.5**	**14,566**	**-1.5**	**14,353**	**-1.7**	**14,105**
* **Porter**	**18127**	**13.9**	**146,798**	**5.1**	**154,300**	**5.7**	**163,124**
(See Chicago-Naperville-Joliet, IL-IN-WI.)							
* **Clark**	**18019**	**9.9**	**96,472**	**4.0**	**100,377**	**4.5**	**104,846**
* **Floyd**	**18043**	**10.0**	**70,823**	**0.6**	**71,234**	**0.6**	**71,661**
* **Harrison**	**18061**	**14.8**	**34,325**	**5.2**	**36,107**	**5.5**	**38,110**
* **Washington**	**18175**	**14.8**	**27,223**	**1.9**	**27,735**	**2.1**	**28,317**
(See Louisville, KY-IN.)							
* **Dearborn**	**18029**	**18.7**	**46,109**	**4.9**	**48,349**	**5.2**	**50,848**
* **Franklin**	**18047**	**13.1**	**22,151**	**3.6**	**22,956**	**4.0**	**23,867**
* **Ohio**	**18115**	**5.8**	**5,623**	**2.5**	**5,762**	**2.6**	**5,911**
(See Cincinnati-Middletown, OH-KY-IN.)							
TOTAL: METRO PORTION OF STATE		**10.7**	**4,686,372**	**3.1**	**4,831,753**	**3.5**	**5,000,860**
TOTAL: MICRO PORTION OF STATE		**6.5**	**1,028,340**	**0.3**	**1,031,556**	**0.3**	**1,034,544**
TOTAL: INDIANA		9.7	6,080,485	2.5	6,230,346	2.8	6,403,859

IOWA

	FIPS CODE	PAST 1990-2000 % Change	PAST 2000 Census	PRESENT 2000-2004 % Change	PRESENT 7/1/04 Estimate	FUTURE 2004-2009 % Change	FUTURE 2009 Projection
Ames IA	**11180**	**7.7**	**79,981**	**5.0**	**83,964**	**5.6**	**88,649**
Story	19169	7.7	79,981	5.0	83,964	5.6	88,649
Cedar Rapids IA	**16300**	**12.6**	**237,230**	**3.0**	**244,390**	**3.3**	**252,543**
Benton	19011	12.8	25,308	4.9	26,543	5.6	28,034
Jones	19105	4.0	20,221	0.5	20,326	0.6	20,458
Linn	19113	13.6	191,701	3.0	197,521	3.3	204,051
Davenport-Moline-Rock Island, IA-IL	19340	2.1	376,019	-0.4	374,674	-0.4	373,134
Henry, IL	17073	-0.3	51,020	-1.0	50,508	-1.3	49,831
Mercer, IL	17131	-1.9	16,957	0.4	17,018	0.4	17,089
Rock Island, IL	17161	0.4	149,374	-1.2	147,511	-1.4	145,513
Scott	**19163**	**5.1**	**158,668**	**0.6**	**159,637**	**0.7**	**160,701**
Des Moines IA	**19780**	**15.6**	**481,394**	**5.8**	**509,323**	**6.4**	**541,966**
Dallas	19049	37.0	40,750	17.4	47,845	17.7	56,309
Guthrie	19077	3.8	11,353	1.7	11,550	2.1	11,796
Madison	19121	12.3	14,019	4.6	14,659	5.1	15,404
Polk	19153	14.5	374,601	4.9	392,872	5.4	414,072
Warren	19181	12.9	40,671	4.2	42,397	4.7	44,385
Dubuque IA	**20220**	**3.2**	**89,143**	**1.3**	**90,309**	**1.4**	**91,581**
Dubuque	19061	3.2	89,143	1.3	90,309	1.4	91,581
Iowa City IA	**26980**	**13.8**	**131,676**	**5.1**	**138,449**	**5.7**	**146,341**
Johnson	19103	15.5	111,006	5.3	116,938	5.9	123,853
Washington	19183	5.4	20,670	4.1	21,511	4.5	22,488
Sioux City, IA-NE-SD	43580	8.9	143,053	-0.2	142,792	-0.3	142,427
Woodbury	**19193**	**5.7**	**103,877**	**-0.8**	**103,007**	**-1.1**	**101,918**
Dakota, NE	31043	21.0	20,253	1.5	20,562	1.7	20,905
Dixon, NE	31051	3.2	6,339	-4.4	6,057	-5.2	5,741
Union, SD	46127	23.5	12,584	4.6	13,166	5.3	13,863
Waterloo-Cedar Falls IA	**47940**	**3.2**	**163,706**	**-1.3**	**161,643**	**-1.5**	**159,197**
Black Hawk	19013	3.4	128,012	-1.6	125,922	-2.0	123,434
Bremer	19017	2.2	23,325	0.3	23,391	0.5	23,497
Grundy	19075	2.8	12,369	-0.3	12,330	-0.5	12,266
* **Harrison**	**19085**	**6.4**	**15,666**	**-0.1**	**15,654**	**-0.4**	**15,587**
* **Mills**	**19129**	**10.2**	**14,547**	**3.3**	**15,021**	**3.7**	**15,581**
* **Pottawattamie**	**19155**	**6.1**	**87,704**	**1.1**	**88,639**	**0.9**	**89,425**
(See Omaha-Council Bluffs, NE-IA.)							
TOTAL: METRO PORTION OF STATE		**10.0**	**1,563,592**	**3.0**	**1,610,036**	**3.3**	**1,663,489**
TOTAL: MICRO PORTION OF STATE		**1.9**	**526,441**	**-1.1**	**520,468**	**-1.4**	**513,415**
TOTAL: IOWA		5.4	2,926,324	0.8	2,949,245	0.9	2,975,158

KANSAS

	FIPS CODE	PAST 1990-2000 % Change	PAST 2000 Census	PRESENT 2000-2004 % Change	PRESENT 7/1/04 Estimate	FUTURE 2004-2009 % Change	FUTURE 2009 Projection
Lawrence KS	**29940**	**22.2**	**99,962**	**3.9**	**103,909**	**4.4**	**108,485**
Douglas	20045	22.2	99,962	3.9	103,909	4.4	108,485
Topeka KS	**45820**	**6.8**	**224,551**	**1.0**	**226,731**	**1.0**	**228,930**
Jackson	20085	9.8	12,657	3.7	13,129	4.2	13,680
Jefferson	20087	15.9	18,426	2.6	18,908	2.8	19,446
Osage	20139	9.6	16,712	0.5	16,789	0.1	16,803
Shawnee	20177	5.5	169,871	0.8	171,175	0.7	172,453
Wabaunsee	20197	4.3	6,885	-2.3	6,730	-2.7	6,548
Wichita KS	**48620**	**11.7**	**571,166**	**2.7**	**586,332**	**3.0**	**603,817**
Butler	20015	17.6	59,482	3.6	61,602	3.8	63,942
Harvey	20079	5.9	32,869	2.5	33,707	3.0	34,714
Sedgwick	20173	12.2	452,869	2.9	466,006	3.3	481,319
Sumner	20191	0.4	25,946	-3.6	25,017	-4.7	23,842
* **Franklin**	**20059**	**12.7**	**24,784**	**3.9**	**25,761**	**4.2**	**26,851**
* **Johnson**	**20091**	**27.0**	**451,086**	**10.2**	**497,146**	**10.6**	**550,011**
* **Leavenworth**	**20103**	**6.7**	**68,691**	**5.4**	**72,419**	**6.0**	**76,745**
* **Linn**	**20107**	**15.9**	**9,570**	**2.0**	**9,761**	**2.0**	**9,953**
* **Miami**	**20121**	**20.8**	**28,351**	**3.8**	**29,415**	**3.8**	**30,539**
* **Wyandotte**	**20209**	**-2.5**	**157,882**	**-0.7**	**156,835**	**-0.9**	**155,484**
(See Kansas City, MO-KS.)							
* **Doniphan**	**20043**	**1.4**	**8,249**	**-1.6**	**8,116**	**-2.1**	**7,949**
(See St. Joseph, MO-KS.)							
TOTAL: METRO PORTION OF STATE		**13.7**	**1,644,292**	**4.4**	**1,716,425**	**4.8**	**1,798,764**
TOTAL: MICRO PORTION OF STATE		**3.6**	**603,665**	**-1.4**	**595,472**	**-1.7**	**585,573**
TOTAL: KANSAS		8.5	2,688,418	1.7	2,733,795	1.9	2,785,235

KENTUCKY

	FIPS CODE	PAST 1990-2000 % Change	PAST 2000 Census	PRESENT 2000-2004 % Change	PRESENT 7/1/04 Estimate	FUTURE 2004-2009 % Change	FUTURE 2009 Projection
Bowling Green KY	**14540**	**19.7**	**104,166**	**4.4**	**108,712**	**4.9**	**114,026**
Edmonson	21061	12.4	11,644	2.5	11,936	2.8	12,267
Warren	21227	20.7	92,522	4.6	96,776	5.1	101,759
Elizabethtown KY	**21060**	**6.6**	**107,547**	**2.3**	**110,057**	**2.6**	**112,888**
Hardin	21093	5.5	94,174	2.6	96,607	2.9	99,375
Larue	21123	14.5	13,373	0.6	13,450	0.5	13,513
Lexington-Fayette KY	**30460**	**17.2**	**408,326**	**4.4**	**426,494**	**5.0**	**447,700**
Bourbon	21017	0.6	19,360	1.6	19,673	1.9	20,047
Clark	21049	12.4	33,144	3.2	34,197	3.5	35,385
Fayette	21067	15.6	260,512	3.2	268,741	3.6	278,436
Jessamine	21113	28.0	39,041	8.3	42,270	9.0	46,080
Scott	21209	38.5	33,061	14.4	37,824	14.5	43,314
Woodford	21239	16.3	23,208	2.5	23,789	2.7	24,438
Louisville, KY-IN	31140	10.0	1,161,975	3.1	1,198,515	3.5	1,240,235
Clark, IN	18019	9.9	96,472	4.0	100,377	4.5	104,846
Floyd, IN	18043	10.0	70,823	0.6	71,234	0.6	71,661
Harrison, IN	18061	14.8	34,325	5.2	36,107	5.5	38,110
Washington, IN	18175	14.8	27,223	1.9	27,735	2.1	28,317
Bullitt	**21029**	**28.7**	**61,236**	**7.8**	**65,997**	**8.2**	**71,436**
Henry	**21103**	**17.4**	**15,060**	**4.2**	**15,691**	**4.7**	**16,427**
Jefferson	**21111**	**4.3**	**693,604**	**1.0**	**700,741**	**1.2**	**709,304**
Meade	**21163**	**9.0**	**26,349**	**6.2**	**27,972**	**6.3**	**29,733**
Nelson	**21179**	**26.1**	**37,477**	**7.5**	**40,283**	**8.0**	**43,523**
Oldham	**21185**	**38.8**	**46,178**	**11.9**	**51,680**	**11.3**	**57,496**
Shelby	**21211**	**34.3**	**33,337**	**10.0**	**36,679**	**10.6**	**40,571**
Spencer	**21215**	**73.0**	**11,766**	**28.0**	**15,064**	**25.3**	**18,879**
Trimble	**21223**	**33.4**	**8,125**	**10.2**	**8,955**	**10.9**	**9,932**
Owensboro KY	**36980**	**5.0**	**109,875**	**1.1**	**111,124**	**1.2**	**112,512**
Daviess	21059	5.0	91,545	1.4	92,851	1.7	94,400
Hancock	21091	6.7	8,392	0.5	8,436	0.2	8,452
McLean	21149	3.2	9,938	-1.0	9,837	-1.8	9,660
* **Henderson**	**21101**	**4.1**	**44,829**	**0.9**	**45,235**	**1.2**	**45,763**
* **Webster**	**21233**	**1.2**	**14,120**	**-0.7**	**14,026**	**-0.9**	**13,898**
(See Evansville, IN-KY.)							
* **Boone**	**21015**	**49.3**	**85,991**	**16.9**	**100,516**	**16.8**	**117,390**
* **Bracken**	**21023**	**6.6**	**8,279**	**3.3**	**8,554**	**3.9**	**8,888**
* **Campbell**	**21037**	**5.7**	**88,616**	**-1.0**	**87,745**	**-1.3**	**86,626**
* **Gallatin**	**21077**	**45.9**	**7,870**	**2.2**	**8,041**	**2.8**	**8,268**
* **Grant**	**21081**	**42.2**	**22,384**	**9.3**	**24,461**	**9.8**	**26,848**
* **Kenton**	**21117**	**6.6**	**151,464**	**0.7**	**152,501**	**0.7**	**153,565**
* **Pendleton**	**21191**	**19.6**	**14,390**	**6.2**	**15,286**	**6.4**	**16,262**
(See Cincinnati-Middletown, OH-KY-IN.)							
* **Christian**	**21047**	**4.8**	**72,265**	**-4.3**	**69,170**	**-5.2**	**65,576**
* **Trigg**	**21221**	**21.6**	**12,597**	**2.8**	**12,954**	**3.0**	**13,339**
(See Clarksville, TN-KY.)							
* **Boyd**	**21019**	**-2.7**	**49,752**	**-0.5**	**49,520**	**-0.3**	**49,349**
* **Greenup**	**21089**	**0.4**	**36,891**	**0.3**	**36,989**	**0.5**	**37,173**
(See Huntington-Ashland, WV-KY-OH.)							
TOTAL: METRO PORTION OF STATE		**11.4**	**2,272,494**	**3.2**	**2,344,447**	**3.5**	**2,427,372**
TOTAL: MICRO PORTION OF STATE		**10.3**	**763,170**	**2.5**	**782,071**	**2.8**	**804,104**
TOTAL: KENTUCKY		9.7	4,041,769	2.5	4,140,891	2.8	4,256,211

* Indicates county is included from metro in different state.
Source: Devonshire Associates Ltd. and Scan/US, Inc. 2004.

LOUISIANA (Parishes)

	FIPS CODE	PAST 1990-2000 % Change	PAST 2000 Census	PRESENT 2000-2004 % Change	PRESENT 7/1/04 Estimate	FUTURE 2004-2009 % Change	FUTURE 2009 Projection
Alexandria LA	**10780**	**-2.7**	**145,035**	**1.1**	**146,661**	**1.3**	**148,528**
Grant	22043	6.7	18,698	1.3	18,945	1.5	19,232
Rapides	22079	-4.0	126,337	1.1	127,716	1.2	129,296
Baton Rouge LA	**12940**	**13.2**	**705,973**	**3.1**	**727,723**	**3.5**	**752,944**
Ascension	22005	31.6	76,627	13.2	86,777	13.5	98,512
East Baton Rouge	22033	8.6	412,852	-0.1	412,326	-0.2	411,618
East Feliciana	22037	11.2	21,360	-1.7	21,001	-2.2	20,536
Iberville	22047	7.3	33,320	-2.0	32,647	-2.5	31,828
Livingston	22063	30.2	91,814	14.6	105,200	15.0	120,940
Pointe Coupee	22077	1.0	22,763	-1.2	22,497	-1.5	22,161
St. Helena	22091	6.6	10,525	-2.7	10,240	-3.3	9,904
West Baton Rouge	22121	11.2	21,601	0.8	21,767	1.1	22,011
West Feliciana	22125	17.0	15,111	1.0	15,268	1.1	15,434
Houma-Bayou Cane-Thibodaux LA	**26380**	**6.4**	**194,477**	**2.0**	**198,351**	**2.4**	**203,111**
Lafourche	22057	4.8	89,974	1.9	91,720	2.4	93,889
Terrebonne	22109	7.8	104,503	2.0	106,631	2.4	109,222
Lafayette LA	**29180**	**14.5**	**239,086**	**2.8**	**245,778**	**3.3**	**253,854**
Lafayette	22055	15.6	190,503	2.6	195,453	3.1	201,469
St. Martin	22099	10.5	48,583	3.6	50,325	4.1	52,385
Lake Charles LA	**29340**	**9.1**	**193,568**	**0.0**	**193,633**	**0.1**	**193,773**
Calcasieu	22019	9.2	183,577	0.2	184,005	0.3	184,541
Cameron	22023	7.9	9,991	-3.6	9,628	-4.1	9,232
Monroe LA	**33740**	**4.4**	**170,053**	**0.6**	**171,146**	**0.8**	**172,510**
Ouachita	22073	3.6	147,250	0.6	148,118	0.7	149,179
Union	22111	10.2	22,803	1.0	23,028	1.3	23,331
New Orleans-Metairie-Kenner LA	**35380**	**4.1**	**1,316,510**	**0.1**	**1,318,235**	**0.3**	**1,322,126**
Jefferson	22051	1.6	455,466	-0.8	451,699	-0.9	447,807
Orleans	22071	-2.5	484,674	-4.2	464,268	-5.0	441,054
Plaquemines	22075	4.6	26,757	6.3	28,450	7.4	30,569
St. Bernard	22087	0.9	67,229	-2.1	65,813	-2.3	64,315
St. Charles	22089	13.3	48,072	3.5	49,737	3.8	51,643
St. John The Baptist	22095	7.6	43,044	5.4	45,373	6.1	48,148
St. Tammany	22103	32.4	191,268	11.3	212,895	12.1	238,590
Shreveport-Bossier City LA	**43340**	**4.5**	**375,965**	**0.8**	**379,073**	**1.0**	**382,708**
Bossier	22015	14.2	98,310	4.9	103,123	5.4	108,716
Caddo	22017	1.6	252,161	-0.9	249,805	-1.1	247,077
De Soto	22031	0.6	25,494	2.6	26,145	2.9	26,915
TOTAL: METRO PORTION OF STATE		**6.8**	**3,340,667**	**1.2**	**3,380,600**	**1.4**	**3,429,554**
TOTAL: MICRO PORTION OF STATE		**3.5**	**815,801**	**0.1**	**817,009**	**0.2**	**818,686**
TOTAL: LOUISIANA		5.9	4,468,976	0.8	4,505,373	1.0	4,550,570

MAINE

	FIPS CODE	PAST 1990-2000 % Change	PAST 2000 Census	PRESENT 2000-2004 % Change	PRESENT 7/1/04 Estimate	FUTURE 2004-2009 % Change	FUTURE 2009 Projection
Bangor ME	**12620**	**-1.1**	**144,919**	**1.9**	**147,681**	**2.4**	**151,173**
Penobscot	23019	-1.1	144,919	1.9	147,681	2.4	151,173
Lewiston-Auburn ME	**30340**	**-1.4**	**103,793**	**3.0**	**106,865**	**3.5**	**110,613**
Androscoggin	23001	-1.4	103,793	3.0	106,865	3.5	110,613
Portland-South Portland-Biddeford ME	**38860**	**10.5**	**487,568**	**4.8**	**510,775**	**5.3**	**537,628**
Cumberland	23005	9.2	265,612	2.6	272,577	3.0	280,846
Sagadahoc	23023	5.0	35,214	4.7	36,859	5.5	38,878
York	23031	13.5	186,742	7.8	201,339	8.2	217,904
TOTAL: METRO PORTION OF STATE		**6.2**	**736,280**	**3.9**	**765,321**	**4.5**	**799,414**
TOTAL: MICRO PORTION OF STATE		**3.0**	**156,732**	**2.8**	**161,151**	**3.3**	**166,462**
TOTAL: MAINE		3.8	1,274,923	3.2	1,315,211	3.6	1,362,624

MARYLAND

	FIPS CODE	PAST 1990-2000 % Change	PAST 2000 Census	PRESENT 2000-2004 % Change	PRESENT 7/1/04 Estimate	FUTURE 2004-2009 % Change	FUTURE 2009 Projection
Baltimore-Towson MD	**12580**	**7.2**	**2,552,994**	**3.2**	**2,635,941**	**3.8**	**2,735,037**
Anne Arundel	24003	14.6	489,656	4.5	511,686	4.9	536,925
Baltimore	24005	9.0	754,292	4.0	784,253	4.5	819,459
Baltimore (Ind. City)	24510	-11.5	651,154	-4.5	622,161	-5.1	590,521
Carroll	24013	22.3	150,897	10.7	167,068	11.5	186,338
Harford	24025	20.0	218,590	8.1	236,397	8.9	257,462
Howard	24027	32.3	247,842	8.6	269,157	9.1	293,568
Queen Anne's	24035	19.5	40,563	11.5	45,219	12.3	50,764
Cumberland, MD-WV	19060	0.4	102,008	-1.5	100,473	-1.7	98,767
Allegany	**24001**	**-0.0**	**74,930**	**-2.2**	**73,291**	**-2.6**	**71,421**
Mineral, WV	54057	1.4	27,078	0.4	27,182	0.6	27,346
Hagerstown-Martinsburg, MD-WV	25180	15.6	222,771	8.7	242,248	9.6	265,500
Washington	**24043**	**8.7**	**131,923**	**4.9**	**138,354**	**5.6**	**146,118**
Berkeley, WV	54003	28.1	75,905	16.2	88,214	16.6	102,878
Morgan, WV	54065	23.2	14,943	4.9	15,680	5.3	16,504
Salisbury MD	**41540**	**11.9**	**109,391**	**4.1**	**113,889**	**4.7**	**119,202**
Somerset	24039	5.6	24,747	3.8	25,685	4.6	26,872
Wicomico	24045	13.9	84,644	4.2	88,204	4.7	92,330
* **Calvert**	**24009**	**45.1**	**74,563**	**16.8**	**87,081**	**17.0**	**101,916**
* **Charles**	**24017**	**19.2**	**120,546**	**13.6**	**136,969**	**14.3**	**156,536**
* **Frederick**	**24021**	**30.0**	**195,277**	**12.3**	**219,345**	**12.9**	**247,718**
* **Montgomery**	**24031**	**15.4**	**873,341**	**6.8**	**932,558**	**7.3**	**1,000,765**
* **Prince George's**	**24033**	**9.9**	**801,515**	**6.1**	**850,384**	**6.8**	**908,563**
(See Washington-Arlington-Alexandria, DC-VA-MD-WV.)							
* **Cecil**	**24015**	**20.5**	**85,951**	**10.3**	**94,837**	**11.0**	**105,269**
(See Philadelphia-Camden-Wilmington, PA-NJ-DE-MD.)							
TOTAL: METRO PORTION OF STATE		**10.7**	**5,020,431**	**5.2**	**5,282,649**	**5.9**	**5,592,545**
TOTAL: MICRO PORTION OF STATE		**14.8**	**197,240**	**6.9**	**210,923**	**7.8**	**227,301**
TOTAL: MARYLAND		10.8	5,296,486	5.3	5,574,702	5.9	5,903,665

MASSACHUSETTS

	FIPS CODE	PAST 1990-2000 % Change	PAST 2000 Census	PRESENT 2000-2004 % Change	PRESENT 7/1/04 Estimate	FUTURE 2004-2009 % Change	FUTURE 2009 Projection
Barnstable Town MA	**12700**	**19.1**	**222,230**	**4.2**	**231,645**	**4.5**	**242,135**
Barnstable	25001	19.1	222,230	4.2	231,645	4.5	242,135
Boston-Cambridge-Quincy, MA-NH	14460	6.2	4,391,344	1.4	4,452,771	1.4	4,516,835
Essex	**25009**	**8.0**	**723,419**	**2.6**	**741,982**	**2.8**	**762,628**
Middlesex	**25017**	**4.8**	**1,465,396**	**0.5**	**1,472,613**	**0.3**	**1,477,006**
Norfolk	**25021**	**5.6**	**650,308**	**0.8**	**655,356**	**0.8**	**660,454**
Plymouth	**25023**	**8.6**	**472,822**	**4.0**	**491,878**	**4.4**	**513,646**
Suffolk	**25025**	**3.9**	**689,807**	**-1.8**	**677,616**	**-2.3**	**662,356**
Rockingham, NH	33015	12.8	277,359	6.0	293,899	6.5	312,885
Strafford, NH	33017	7.7	112,233	6.4	119,427	7.1	127,860
Pittsfield MA	**38340**	**-3.2**	**134,953**	**-1.6**	**132,813**	**-1.9**	**130,354**
Berkshire	25003	-3.2	134,953	-1.6	132,813	-1.9	130,354
Springfield MA	**44140**	**1.0**	**680,014**	**1.6**	**691,167**	**1.9**	**704,493**
Franklin	25011	2.1	71,535	1.3	72,431	1.6	73,559
Hampden	25013	-0.0	456,228	1.4	462,756	1.7	470,565
Hampshire	25015	3.9	152,251	2.4	155,980	2.8	160,369
Worcester MA	**49340**	**5.8**	**750,963**	**4.5**	**784,595**	**5.1**	**824,492**
Worcester	25027	5.8	750,963	4.5	784,595	5.1	824,492
* **Bristol**	**25005**	**5.6**	**534,678**	**3.0**	**550,668**	**3.3**	**568,949**
(See Providence-New Bedford-Fall River, RI-MA.)							
TOTAL: METRO PORTION OF STATE		**5.4**	**6,324,590**	**1.7**	**6,430,333**	**1.8**	**6,546,513**
TOTAL: MASSACHUSETTS		5.5	6,349,097	1.7	6,457,204	1.8	6,576,114

Core Based Statistical Areas and Their Component Counties: Population Trends, *Continued*

	FIPS CODE	PAST 1990-2000 % Change	PAST 2000 Census	PRESENT 2000-2004 % Change	PRESENT 7/1/04 Estimate	FUTURE 2004-2009 % Change	FUTURE 2009 Projection
MICHIGAN							
Ann Arbor MI	11460	14.1	322,895	6.3	343,273	6.9	366,793
Washtenaw	26161	14.1	322,895	6.3	343,273	6.9	366,793
Battle Creek MI	12980	1.5	137,985	0.8	139,106	0.9	140,354
Calhoun	26025	1.5	137,985	0.8	139,106	0.9	140,354
Bay City MI	13020	-1.4	110,157	-0.8	109,229	-1.0	108,107
Bay	26017	-1.4	110,157	-0.8	109,229	-1.0	108,107
Detroit-Warren-Livonia MI	19820	4.8	4,452,557	0.9	4,492,464	1.0	4,535,875
Lapeer	26087	17.6	87,904	5.0	92,313	5.4	97,299
Livingston	26093	35.7	156,951	13.2	177,683	13.5	201,672
Macomb	26099	9.9	788,149	4.2	821,634	4.7	859,988
Oakland	26125	10.2	1,194,156	1.5	1,211,605	1.5	1,230,186
St. Clair	26147	12.8	164,235	3.8	170,514	4.2	177,753
Wayne	26163	-2.4	2,061,162	-2.1	2,018,715	-2.5	1,968,977
Flint MI	22420	1.3	436,141	1.8	444,011	2.0	452,774
Genesee	26049	1.3	436,141	1.8	444,011	2.0	452,774
Grand Rapids-Wyoming MI	24340	14.6	740,482	3.8	768,430	4.2	800,347
Barry	26015	13.4	56,755	4.7	59,395	5.2	62,496
Ionia	26067	7.9	61,518	4.4	64,207	4.9	67,375
Kent	26081	14.7	574,335	3.6	595,142	4.0	618,715
Newaygo	26123	25.3	47,874	3.8	49,686	4.2	51,761
Holland-Grand Haven MI	26100	26.9	238,314	6.0	252,694	6.5	269,185
Ottawa	26139	26.9	238,314	6.0	252,694	6.5	269,185
Jackson MI	27100	5.8	158,422	3.2	163,516	3.6	169,477
Jackson	26075	5.8	158,422	3.2	163,516	3.6	169,477
Kalamazoo-Portage MI	28020	7.3	314,866	2.3	322,014	2.6	330,456
Kalamazoo	26077	6.8	238,603	1.9	243,185	2.2	248,537
Van Buren	26159	8.9	76,263	3.4	78,829	3.9	81,919
Lansing-East Lansing MI	29620	3.5	447,728	2.4	458,301	2.7	470,587
Clinton	26037	11.9	64,753	5.8	68,489	6.4	72,882
Eaton	26045	11.6	103,655	3.2	106,959	3.6	110,760
Ingham	26065	-0.9	279,320	1.3	282,853	1.4	286,945
Monroe MI	33780	9.2	145,945	4.2	152,069	4.6	159,036
Monroe	26115	9.2	145,945	4.2	152,069	4.6	159,036
Muskegon-Norton Shores MI	34740	7.1	170,200	2.2	173,945	2.4	178,202
Muskegon	26121	7.1	170,200	2.2	173,945	2.4	178,202
Niles-Benton Harbor MI	35660	0.7	162,453	0.2	162,816	0.1	163,051
Berrien	26021	0.7	162,453	0.2	162,816	0.1	163,051
Saginaw-Saginaw Township North MI	40980	-0.9	210,039	-0.4	209,117	-0.5	208,059
Saginaw	26145	-0.9	210,039	-0.4	209,117	-0.5	208,059
* **Cass** (See South Bend-Mishawaka, IN-MI.)	26027	3.3	51,104	0.7	51,459	0.7	51,827
TOTAL: METRO PORTION OF STATE		6.1	8,099,288	1.8	8,242,444	2.0	8,404,130
TOTAL: MICRO PORTION OF STATE		9.0	1,053,944	2.5	1,080,259	2.8	1,110,635
TOTAL: MICHIGAN		6.9	9,938,444	1.8	10,121,382	2.0	10,328,365
MINNESOTA							
Duluth, MN-WI	20260	2.3	275,486	0.2	276,062	0.2	276,690
Carlton	27017	8.2	31,671	5.7	33,484	6.6	35,681
St. Louis	27137	1.2	200,528	-1.1	198,256	-1.4	195,546
Douglas, WI	55031	3.7	43,287	2.4	44,322	2.6	45,463
Minneapolis-St. Paul-Bloomington, MN-WI	33460	16.9	2,968,806	5.0	3,117,850	5.5	3,288,729
Anoka	27003	22.3	298,084	7.0	318,838	7.5	342,630
Carver	27019	46.5	70,205	16.3	81,656	16.5	95,126
Chisago	27025	34.7	41,101	16.1	47,700	16.0	55,373
Dakota	27037	29.3	355,904	6.3	378,473	6.8	404,250
Hennepin	27053	8.1	1,116,200	0.5	1,122,141	0.5	1,127,580
Isanti	27059	20.7	31,287	17.1	36,651	17.4	43,044
Ramsey	27123	5.2	511,035	-1.2	504,693	-1.6	496,428
Scott	27139	54.7	89,498	27.8	114,403	25.4	143,515
Sherburne	27141	53.6	64,417	20.8	77,790	20.1	93,397
Washington	27163	37.9	201,130	8.0	217,209	8.4	235,409
Wright	27171	31.0	89,986	18.3	106,446	18.4	126,017
Pierce, WI	55093	12.3	36,804	3.8	38,196	4.2	39,816
St. Croix, WI	55109	25.7	63,155	16.6	73,654	17.0	86,144
Rochester MN	40340	15.3	163,618	7.0	175,153	7.7	188,610
Dodge	27039	12.7	17,731	8.8	19,288	9.2	21,070
Olmsted	27109	16.7	124,277	7.5	133,562	8.1	144,443
Wabasha	27157	9.5	21,610	3.2	22,303	3.6	23,097
St. Cloud MN	41060	12.4	167,392	5.2	176,070	5.7	186,043
Benton	27009	13.4	34,226	10.3	37,738	10.8	41,805
Stearns	27145	12.1	133,166	3.9	138,332	4.3	144,238
* **Clay** (See Fargo, ND-MN.)	27027	1.6	51,229	1.9	52,205	2.1	53,311
* **Polk** (See Grand Forks, ND-MN.)	27119	-3.5	31,369	-2.0	30,748	-2.5	29,972
* **Houston** (See La Crosse, WI-MN.)	27055	6.6	19,718	1.7	20,056	1.9	20,435
TOTAL: METRO PORTION OF STATE		14.9	3,534,372	4.5	3,691,972	4.9	3,872,367
TOTAL: MICRO PORTION OF STATE		8.5	731,444	2.7	751,044	3.1	774,262
TOTAL: MINNESOTA		12.4	4,919,479	3.7	5,101,284	4.1	5,310,829
MISSISSIPPI							
Gulfport-Biloxi MS	25060	18.4	246,190	1.4	249,739	1.5	253,546
Hancock	28045	35.3	42,967	6.5	45,765	6.7	48,851
Harrison	28047	14.7	189,601	-0.0	189,590	-0.1	189,423
Stone	28131	26.7	13,622	5.6	14,384	6.2	15,272
Hattiesburg MS	25620	13.0	123,812	5.1	130,073	5.5	137,254
Forrest	28035	6.3	72,604	3.2	74,924	3.6	77,594
Lamar	28073	28.4	39,070	9.6	42,827	10.1	47,166
Perry	28111	11.7	12,138	1.5	12,322	1.4	12,494
Jackson MS	27140	11.2	497,197	3.4	513,973	3.8	533,404
Copiah	28029	4.2	28,757	0.8	28,982	0.9	29,242
Hinds	28049	-1.4	250,800	-0.9	248,578	-1.1	245,985
Madison	28089	38.8	74,674	8.9	81,322	9.6	89,114
Rankin	28121	32.3	115,327	10.6	127,528	11.1	141,651
Simpson	28127	15.4	27,639	-0.3	27,563	-0.5	27,412
Pascagoula MS	37700	14.1	150,564	3.2	155,413	3.4	160,766
George	28039	14.8	19,144	8.7	20,808	9.6	22,810
Jackson	28059	14.0	131,420	2.4	134,605	2.5	137,956
* **DeSoto**	28033	57.9	107,199	20.9	129,632	20.2	155,853
* **Marshall**	28093	15.3	34,993	1.6	35,565	1.7	36,168
* **Tate**	28137	18.4	25,370	2.1	25,907	2.2	26,465
* **Tunica** (See Memphis, TN-MS-AR.)	28143	13.0	9,227	10.0	10,146	11.2	11,283
TOTAL: METRO PORTION OF STATE		16.6	1,194,552	4.7	1,250,448	5.1	1,314,739
TOTAL: MICRO PORTION OF STATE		6.2	1,001,735	-0.6	995,901	-0.7	989,398
TOTAL: MISSISSIPPI		10.5	2,844,658	1.7	2,892,228	1.9	2,946,963
MISSOURI							
Columbia MO	17860	19.4	145,666	4.9	152,833	5.6	161,317
Boone	29019	20.5	135,454	5.5	142,884	6.1	151,657
Howard	29089	6.0	10,212	-2.6	9,949	-2.9	9,660
Jefferson City MO	27620	16.0	140,052	2.5	143,594	2.8	147,649
Callaway	29027	24.3	40,766	4.6	42,657	5.0	44,808
Cole	29051	12.3	71,397	1.9	72,781	2.2	74,401
Moniteau	29135	20.6	14,827	1.2	15,005	1.3	15,207
Osage	29151	8.7	13,062	0.7	13,151	0.6	13,233
Joplin MO	27900	16.6	157,322	4.0	163,621	4.5	170,964
Jasper	29097	15.7	104,686	4.3	109,158	4.8	114,363
Newton	29145	18.4	52,636	3.5	54,463	3.9	56,601
Kansas City, MO-KS	28140	12.2	1,836,038	4.9	1,925,595	5.3	2,028,351
Franklin, KS	20059	12.7	24,784	3.9	25,761	4.2	26,851
Johnson, KS	20091	27.0	451,086	10.2	497,146	10.6	550,011
Leavenworth, KS	20103	6.7	68,691	5.4	72,419	6.0	76,745
Linn, KS	20107	15.9	9,570	2.0	9,761	2.0	9,953
Miami, KS	20121	20.8	28,351	3.8	29,415	3.8	30,539
Wyandotte, KS	20209	-2.5	157,882	-0.7	156,835	-0.9	155,484
Bates	29013	10.8	16,653	2.1	17,008	2.1	17,362
Caldwell	29025	7.0	8,969	2.7	9,214	2.9	9,483
Cass	29037	28.7	82,092	10.7	90,899	11.3	101,203
Clay	29047	19.9	184,006	7.3	197,398	8.0	213,104
Clinton	29049	14.4	18,979	8.0	20,502	8.8	22,311
Jackson	29095	3.4	654,880	0.9	661,091	1.0	667,791
Lafayette	29107	6.0	32,960	-0.1	32,925	-0.4	32,789
Platte	29165	27.5	73,781	9.9	81,115	10.6	89,721
Ray	29177	6.3	23,354	3.2	24,106	3.7	25,004
Springfield MO	44180	23.3	368,374	5.8	389,665	6.4	414,630
Christian	29043	66.3	54,285	17.5	63,776	17.3	74,782
Dallas	29059	23.8	15,661	3.8	16,253	4.3	16,954
Greene	29077	15.6	240,391	2.9	247,471	3.4	255,945
Polk	29167	23.7	26,992	5.3	28,417	5.9	30,089
Webster	29225	30.7	31,045	8.7	33,748	9.2	36,860
St. Joseph, MO-KS	41140	5.6	122,336	0.2	122,599	-1.4	120,925
Doniphan, KS	20043	1.4	8,249	-1.6	8,116	-2.1	7,949
Andrew	29003	12.7	16,492	2.5	16,904	2.7	17,360
Buchanan	29021	3.5	85,998	-1.7	84,529	-2.2	82,638
DeKalb	29063	16.4	11,597	12.5	13,050	-0.6	12,978
St. Louis, MO-IL	41180	4.6	2,698,687	1.8	2,747,415	2.1	2,805,346
Bond, IL	17005	17.6	17,633	2.3	18,040	2.7	18,533
Calhoun, IL	17013	-4.5	5,084	-0.4	5,062	-0.8	5,024
Clinton, IL	17027	4.7	35,535	2.2	36,327	2.6	37,288
Jersey, IL	17083	5.5	21,668	3.2	22,361	3.9	23,223
Macoupin, IL	17117	2.8	49,019	0.1	49,072	0.2	49,154
Madison, IL	17119	3.9	258,941	1.4	262,550	1.6	266,835
Monroe, IL	17133	23.2	27,619	10.0	30,375	10.7	33,630
St. Clair, IL	17163	-2.6	256,082	1.3	259,386	1.5	263,266
Franklin	29071	16.4	93,807	4.3	97,849	4.8	102,549
Jefferson	29099	15.6	198,099	5.7	209,444	6.3	222,683
Lincoln	29113	34.8	38,944	17.7	45,856	17.9	54,086
St. Charles	29183	33.3	283,883	12.7	319,977	13.2	362,124
St. Louis	29189	2.3	1,016,315	-0.4	1,012,010	-0.6	1,006,248
St. Louis (Ind. City)	29510	-12.2	348,189	-5.9	327,502	-6.9	304,819
Warren	29219	25.6	24,525	12.4	27,570	12.8	31,102
Washington	29221	14.5	23,344	3.0	24,034	3.1	24,782
* **McDonald** (See Fayetteville-Springdale-Rogers, AR-MO.)	29119	28.0	21,681	1.8	22,073	2.2	22,568
TOTAL: METRO PORTION OF STATE		9.2	4,069,962	2.8	4,184,769	3.2	4,317,265
TOTAL: MICRO PORTION OF STATE		10.9	738,726	2.5	757,408	2.8	778,925
TOTAL: MISSOURI		9.3	5,595,211	2.5	5,737,314	2.9	5,901,462
MONTANA							
Billings MT	13740	14.3	138,904	3.8	144,234	4.4	150,517
Carbon	30009	18.2	9,552	3.0	9,840	3.5	10,188
Yellowstone	30111	14.0	129,352	3.9	134,394	4.4	140,329
Great Falls MT	24500	3.4	80,357	-1.3	79,349	-1.4	78,254
Cascade	30013	3.4	80,357	-1.3	79,349	-1.4	78,254
Missoula MT	33540	21.8	95,802	3.8	99,453	4.2	103,582
Missoula	30063	21.8	95,802	3.8	99,453	4.2	103,582
TOTAL: METRO PORTION OF STATE		13.4	315,063	2.5	323,036	2.9	332,353
TOTAL: MICRO PORTION OF STATE		19.7	259,346	5.3	273,175	5.9	289,369
TOTAL: MONTANA		12.9	902,195	2.2	922,368	2.6	946,103
NEBRASKA							
Lincoln NE	30700	16.5	266,787	5.3	280,966	5.8	297,349
Lancaster	31109	17.2	250,291	5.6	264,249	6.1	280,408
Seward	31159	6.8	16,496	1.3	16,717	1.3	16,941
Omaha-Council Bluffs, NE-IA	36540	11.8	767,041	4.5	801,189	5.0	840,954
Harrison, IA	19085	6.4	15,666	-0.1	15,654	-0.4	15,587
Mills, IA	19129	10.2	14,547	3.3	15,021	3.7	15,581
Pottawattamie, IA	19155	6.1	87,704	1.1	88,639	0.9	89,425
Cass	31025	14.1	24,334	4.9	25,522	5.4	26,911
Douglas	31055	11.3	463,585	3.7	480,743	4.2	500,745
Sarpy	31153	19.5	122,595	10.6	135,564	11.3	150,940
Saunders	31155	8.4	19,830	1.2	20,059	1.2	20,304
Washington	31177	13.1	18,780	6.4	19,987	7.4	21,461
* **Dakota**	31043	21.0	20,253	1.5	20,562	1.7	20,905
* **Dixon** (See Sioux City, IA-NE-SD.)	31051	3.2	6,339	-4.4	6,057	-5.2	5,741
TOTAL: METRO PORTION OF STATE		13.9	942,503	5.0	989,460	5.5	1,044,356
TOTAL: MICRO PORTION OF STATE		7.0	396,206	0.5	398,361	0.7	400,977
TOTAL: NEBRASKA		8.4	1,711,263	2.1	1,748,000	2.5	1,791,543
NEVADA							
Carson City NV	16180	29.7	52,457	7.2	56,233	8.2	60,837
Carson City (Ind. City)	32510	29.7	52,457	7.2	56,233	8.2	60,837
Las Vegas-Paradise NV	29820	85.5	1,375,765	19.0	1,637,622	18.6	1,942,707
Clark	32003	85.5	1,375,765	19.0	1,637,622	18.6	1,942,707
Reno-Sparks NV	39900	33.3	342,885	12.1	384,239	12.8	433,545
Storey	32029	34.6	3,399	4.5	3,551	5.5	3,748
Washoe	32031	33.3	339,486	12.1	380,688	12.9	429,797
TOTAL: METRO PORTION OF STATE		70.4	1,771,107	17.3	2,078,094	17.3	2,437,089
TOTAL: MICRO PORTION OF STATE		47.0	144,668	5.0	151,849	5.4	160,098
TOTAL: NEVADA		66.3	1,998,257	15.9	2,315,504	16.1	2,687,254
NEW HAMPSHIRE							
Manchester-Nashua NH	31700	13.3	380,841	4.7	398,775	5.2	419,332
Hillsborough	33011	13.3	380,841	4.7	398,775	5.2	419,332
* **Rockingham**	33015	12.8	277,359	6.0	293,899	6.5	312,885
* **Strafford** (See Boston-Cambridge-Quincy, MA-NH.)	33017	7.7	112,233	6.4	119,427	7.1	127,860
TOTAL: METRO PORTION OF STATE		12.3	770,433	5.4	812,101	5.9	860,077
TOTAL: MICRO PORTION OF STATE		8.8	421,687	5.4	444,452	6.1	471,476
TOTAL: NEW HAMPSHIRE		11.4	1,235,786	5.5	1,303,425	6.0	1,382,117
NEW JERSEY							
Atlantic City NJ	12100	12.6	252,552	5.7	266,864	6.5	284,131
Atlantic	34001	12.6	252,552	5.7	266,864	6.5	284,131
Ocean City NJ	36140	7.6	102,326	-0.6	101,693	-0.7	100,939
Cape May	34009	7.6	102,326	-0.6	101,693	-0.7	100,939
Trenton-Ewing NJ	45940	7.7	350,761	4.2	365,448	4.7	382,782
Mercer	34021	7.7	350,761	4.2	365,448	4.7	382,782
Vineland-Millville-Bridgeton NJ	47220	6.1	146,438	2.6	150,283	3.3	155,170
Cumberland	34011	6.1	146,438	2.6	150,283	3.3	155,170
* **Bergen**	34003	7.1	884,118	2.0	901,514	2.2	921,244
* **Essex**	34013	2.0	793,633	0.5	797,608	0.8	804,081
* **Hudson**	34017	10.1	608,975	-0.4	606,768	-0.5	603,520
* **Hunterdon**	34019	13.2	121,989	6.7	130,155	7.3	139,607
* **Middlesex**	34023	11.7	750,162	5.3	790,283	5.9	836,721
* **Monmouth**	34025	11.2	615,301	3.6	637,323	4.0	662,568
* **Morris**	34027	11.6	470,212	3.6	487,077	4.0	506,709
* **Ocean**	34029	17.9	510,916	9.0	556,907	9.7	611,037
* **Passaic**	34031	7.9	489,049	2.4	500,842	2.5	513,266
* **Somerset**	34035	23.8	297,490	6.2	315,847	6.7	337,079
* **Sussex**	34037	10.1	144,166	6.3	153,303	7.0	164,089
* **Union** (See New York-Northern New Jersey-Long Island, NY-NJ-PA.)	34039	5.8	522,541	1.7	531,425	1.9	541,750
* **Warren** (See Allentown-Bethlehem-Easton, PA-NJ.)	34041	11.8	102,437	8.7	111,301	9.4	121,709
* **Burlington**	34005	7.2	423,394	6.5	450,960	7.3	483,852
* **Camden**	34007	1.2	508,932	1.3	515,644	1.7	524,315
* **Gloucester**	34015	10.7	254,673	6.4	270,847	7.2	290,271
* **Salem** (See Philadelphia-Camden-Wilmington, PA-NJ-DE-MD.)	34033	-1.5	64,285	1.2	65,064	1.6	66,116
TOTAL: METRO PORTION OF STATE		8.9	8,414,350	3.5	8,707,156	3.9	9,050,956
TOTAL: NEW JERSEY		8.9	8,414,350	3.5	8,707,156	3.9	9,050,956
NEW MEXICO							
Albuquerque NM	10740	21.7	729,649	6.3	775,936	7.1	831,100
Bernalillo	35001	15.8	556,678	5.9	589,389	6.7	628,991
Sandoval	35043	42.0	89,908	12.9	101,506	13.4	115,077
Torrance	35057	64.4	16,911	-1.0	16,743	-1.7	16,453
Valencia	35061	46.2	66,152	3.2	68,298	3.3	70,579
Farmington NM	22140	24.2	113,801	9.8	124,961	10.7	138,374
San Juan	35045	24.2	113,801	9.8	124,961	10.7	138,374
Las Cruces NM	29740	28.9	174,682	5.7	184,554	6.5	196,459
Dona Ana	35013	28.9	174,682	5.7	184,554	6.5	196,459
Santa Fe NM	42140	30.7	129,292	7.2	138,622	7.9	149,581
Santa Fe	35049	30.7	129,292	7.2	138,622	7.9	149,581
TOTAL: METRO PORTION OF STATE		24.0	1,147,424	6.7	1,224,073	7.5	1,315,514
TOTAL: MICRO PORTION OF STATE		12.9	569,960	-0.3	568,231	-0.2	566,931
TOTAL: NEW MEXICO		20.1	1,819,046	4.0	1,892,304	4.7	1,980,754

* Indicates county is included from metro in different state.
Source: Devonshire Associates Ltd. and Scan/US, Inc. 2004.

continued on next page

Core Based Statistical Areas and Their Component Counties: Population Trends, *Continued*

NEW YORK

	FIPS CODE	PAST 1990-2000 % Change	PAST 2000 Census	PRESENT 2000-2004 % Change	PRESENT 7/1/04 Estimate	FUTURE 2004-2009 % Change	FUTURE 2009 Projection
Albany-Schenectady-Troy NY	10580	2.0	825,875	2.4	845,300	2.8	868,571
Albany	36001	0.7	294,565	1.5	298,933	1.8	304,373
Rensselaer	36083	-1.2	152,538	1.3	154,473	1.5	156,803
Saratoga	36091	10.7	200,635	6.0	212,606	6.6	226,546
Schenectady	36093	-1.8	146,555	0.7	147,572	1.0	148,981
Schoharie	36095	-0.9	31,582	0.4	31,716	0.5	31,868
Binghamton NY	13780	-4.6	252,320	-0.6	250,793	-0.6	249,233
Broome	36007	-5.5	200,536	-0.7	199,049	-0.8	197,500
Tioga	36107	-1.1	51,784	-0.1	51,744	-0.0	51,733
Buffalo-Niagara Falls NY	15380	-1.6	1,170,111	-1.2	1,156,288	-1.4	1,140,627
Erie	36029	-1.9	950,265	-1.2	938,615	-1.4	925,325
Niagara	36063	-0.4	219,846	-1.0	217,673	-1.1	215,302
Elmira NY	21300	-4.3	91,070	-0.9	90,205	-1.1	89,168
Chemung	36015	-4.3	91,070	-0.9	90,205	-1.1	89,168
Glens Falls NY	24020	4.9	124,345	2.4	127,334	2.9	131,063
Warren	36113	6.9	63,303	3.0	65,172	3.5	67,455
Washington	36115	2.9	61,042	1.8	62,162	2.3	63,608
Ithaca NY	27060	2.6	96,501	6.7	102,983	7.6	110,842
Tompkins	36109	2.6	96,501	6.7	102,983	7.6	110,842
Kingston NY	28740	7.5	177,749	2.5	182,183	2.9	187,546
Ulster	36111	7.5	177,749	2.5	182,183	2.9	187,546
New York-Northern New Jersey-Long Island, NY-NJ-PA	35620	8.8	18,323,002	2.3	18,735,483	2.5	19,208,857
Bergen, NJ	34003	7.1	884,118	2.0	901,514	2.2	921,244
Essex, NJ	34013	2.0	793,633	0.5	797,608	0.8	804,081
Hudson, NJ	34017	10.1	608,975	-0.4	606,768	-0.5	603,520
Hunterdon, NJ	34019	13.2	121,989	6.7	130,155	7.3	139,607
Middlesex, NJ	34023	11.7	750,162	5.3	790,283	5.9	836,721
Monmouth, NJ	34025	11.2	615,301	3.6	637,323	4.0	662,568
Morris, NJ	34027	11.6	470,212	3.6	487,077	4.0	506,709
Ocean, NJ	34029	17.9	510,916	9.0	556,907	9.7	611,037
Passaic, NJ	34031	7.9	489,049	2.4	500,842	2.5	513,266
Somerset, NJ	34035	23.8	297,490	6.2	315,847	6.7	337,079
Sussex, NJ	34037	10.1	144,166	6.3	153,303	7.0	164,089
Union, NJ	34039	5.8	522,541	1.7	531,425	1.9	541,750
Bronx	36005	10.7	1,332,650	3.0	1,372,845	3.5	1,421,060
Kings	36047	7.2	2,465,326	0.4	2,474,606	0.4	2,484,985
Nassau	36059	3.7	1,334,544	0.4	1,340,495	0.4	1,345,637
New York	36061	3.3	1,537,195	2.3	1,572,971	2.6	1,613,813
Putnam	36079	14.1	95,745	5.2	100,694	5.7	106,411
Queens	36081	14.2	2,229,379	-0.3	2,223,681	-0.4	2,214,646
Richmond	36085	17.1	443,728	4.7	464,513	5.1	488,386
Rockland	36087	8.0	286,753	2.8	294,839	3.1	304,089
Suffolk	36103	7.4	1,419,369	4.5	1,482,695	4.9	1,555,963
Westchester	36119	5.6	923,459	2.3	945,092	2.5	969,028
Pike, PA	42103	65.6	46,302	16.6	54,000	17.0	63,168
Poughkeepsie-Newburgh-Middletown NY	39100	9.6	621,517	6.9	664,094	7.6	714,367
Dutchess	36027	8.0	280,150	5.0	294,234	5.7	310,975
Orange	36071	11.0	341,367	8.3	369,860	9.1	403,392
Rochester NY	40380	3.5	1,037,831	0.4	1,042,130	0.4	1,046,777
Livingston	36051	3.1	64,328	0.7	64,750	0.7	65,206
Monroe	36055	3.0	735,343	0.2	737,090	0.2	738,840
Ontario	36069	5.4	100,224	2.9	103,127	3.3	106,536
Orleans	36073	5.6	44,171	-1.6	43,448	-2.1	42,550
Wayne	36117	5.2	93,765	-0.1	93,715	-0.1	93,645
Syracuse NY	45060	-1.5	650,154	0.8	655,449	1.0	661,715
Madison	36053	0.5	69,441	1.4	70,428	1.7	71,656
Onondaga	36067	-2.3	458,336	0.6	461,207	0.7	464,651
Oswego	36075	0.5	122,377	1.2	123,814	1.3	125,408
Utica-Rome NY	46540	-5.3	299,896	-0.8	297,571	-0.8	295,056
Herkimer	36043	-2.1	64,427	-1.5	63,477	-1.8	62,350
Oneida	36065	-6.1	235,469	-0.6	234,094	-0.6	232,706
TOTAL: METRO PORTION OF STATE		5.9	17,415,517	1.6	17,686,761	1.8	17,998,983
TOTAL: MICRO PORTION OF STATE		-0.4	1,130,953	0.4	1,135,947	0.6	1,143,028
TOTAL: NEW YORK		5.5	18,976,457	1.5	19,254,372	1.7	19,575,657

NORTH CAROLINA

	FIPS CODE	PAST 1990-2000 % Change	PAST 2000 Census	PRESENT 2000-2004 % Change	PRESENT 7/1/04 Estimate	FUTURE 2004-2009 % Change	FUTURE 2009 Projection
Asheville NC	11700	19.9	369,171	4.4	385,591	4.9	404,590
Buncombe	37021	18.0	206,330	4.0	214,572	4.4	224,068
Haywood	37087	15.1	54,033	3.4	55,887	4.0	58,111
Henderson	37089	28.7	89,173	6.8	95,222	7.4	102,240
Madison	37115	15.8	19,635	1.4	19,910	1.3	20,171
Burlington NC	15500	20.9	130,800	5.9	138,548	6.4	147,422
Alamance	37001	20.9	130,800	5.9	138,548	6.4	147,422
Charlotte-Gastonia-Concord, NC-SC	16740	29.8	1,330,448	10.5	1,470,003	11.1	1,632,848
Anson	37007	7.7	25,275	-0.5	25,140	-0.6	24,998
Cabarrus	37025	32.5	131,063	11.6	146,248	12.0	163,785
Gaston	37071	8.7	190,365	1.9	193,911	2.1	197,978
Mecklenburg	37119	36.0	695,454	10.7	769,746	11.3	856,626
Union	37179	46.9	123,677	23.5	152,765	22.2	186,658
York, SC	45091	25.2	164,614	10.7	182,193	11.3	202,803
Durham NC	20500	23.8	426,493	6.5	454,080	7.7	489,144
Chatham	37037	27.3	49,329	15.7	57,081	16.1	66,293
Durham	37063	22.8	223,314	7.9	240,859	8.5	261,245
Orange	37135	26.0	118,227	0.6	118,905	3.0	122,518
Person	37145	18.0	35,623	4.5	37,235	5.0	39,088
Fayetteville NC	22180	13.2	336,609	2.0	343,212	2.4	351,282
Cumberland	37051	10.3	302,963	0.4	304,324	0.6	306,169
Hoke	37093	47.2	33,646	15.6	38,888	16.0	45,113
Goldsboro NC	24140	8.3	113,329	-0.3	113,028	-0.3	112,648
Wayne	37191	8.3	113,329	-0.3	113,028	-0.3	112,648
Greensboro-High Point NC	24660	19.1	643,430	3.7	666,943	4.1	693,996
Guilford	37081	21.2	421,048	3.9	437,629	4.4	456,823
Randolph	37151	22.4	130,454	4.6	136,509	5.0	143,297
Rockingham	37157	6.8	91,928	1.0	92,805	1.2	93,876
Greenville NC	24780	23.9	152,772	5.1	160,525	5.7	169,748
Greene	37079	23.3	18,974	7.0	20,302	7.7	21,863
Pitt	37147	24.0	133,798	4.8	140,223	5.5	147,885
Hickory-Lenoir-Morganton NC	25860	16.9	341,851	3.1	352,521	3.4	364,417
Alexander	37003	22.0	33,603	4.6	35,156	5.3	37,012
Burke	37023	17.7	89,148	0.7	89,791	0.7	90,457
Caldwell	37027	9.5	77,415	2.2	79,103	2.4	80,976
Catawba	37035	19.7	141,685	4.8	148,471	5.1	155,972
Jacksonville NC	27340	0.3	150,355	-2.5	146,634	-3.0	142,265
Onslow	37133	0.3	150,355	-2.5	146,634	-3.0	142,265
Raleigh-Cary NC	39580	47.3	797,071	14.3	911,301	14.7	1,045,338
Franklin	37069	29.8	47,260	13.1	53,474	13.7	60,811
Johnston	37101	50.0	121,965	15.9	141,305	15.9	163,817
Wake	37183	48.3	627,846	14.1	716,522	14.5	820,710
Rocky Mount NC	40580	7.3	143,026	1.5	145,152	1.8	147,778
Edgecombe	37065	-1.7	55,606	-1.5	54,761	-1.2	54,096
Nash	37127	14.0	87,420	3.4	90,391	3.6	93,682
Wilmington NC	48900	37.2	274,532	8.9	299,048	9.8	328,247
Brunswick	37019	43.5	73,143	15.1	84,206	15.5	97,272
New Hanover	37129	33.3	160,307	6.4	170,562	7.3	182,930
Pender	37141	42.4	41,082	7.8	44,280	8.5	48,045
Winston-Salem NC	49180	16.7	421,961	4.8	442,297	5.4	466,017
Davie	37059	25.0	34,835	8.6	37,846	9.2	41,321
Forsyth	37067	15.1	306,067	5.0	321,453	5.7	339,659
Stokes	37169	20.1	44,711	1.3	45,273	1.2	45,796
Yadkin	37197	19.2	36,348	3.8	37,725	4.0	39,241
* **Currituck** (See Virginia Beach-Norfolk-Newport News, VA-NC.)	37053	32.4	18,190	19.1	21,665	19.2	25,821
TOTAL: METRO PORTION OF STATE		24.3	5,485,424	7.0	5,868,355	7.7	6,318,758
TOTAL: MICRO PORTION OF STATE		15.7	1,869,008	3.6	1,936,154	4.0	2,014,345
TOTAL: NORTH CAROLINA		21.4	8,049,313	5.8	8,517,110	6.4	9,066,420

NORTH DAKOTA

	FIPS CODE	PAST 1990-2000 % Change	PAST 2000 Census	PRESENT 2000-2004 % Change	PRESENT 7/1/04 Estimate	FUTURE 2004-2009 % Change	FUTURE 2009 Projection
Bismarck ND	13900	13.0	94,719	2.9	97,478	3.2	100,607
Burleigh	38015	15.4	69,416	4.3	72,410	4.8	75,902
Morton	38059	6.8	25,303	-0.9	25,068	-1.4	24,705
Fargo, ND-MN	22020	13.7	174,367	3.6	180,577	3.9	187,692
Clay, MN	27027	1.6	51,229	1.9	52,205	2.1	53,311
Cass	38017	19.7	123,138	4.3	128,372	4.7	134,381
Grand Forks, ND-MN	24220	-5.5	97,478	-2.4	95,100	-2.9	92,367
Polk, MN	27119	-3.5	31,369	-2.0	30,748	-2.5	29,972
Grand Forks	38035	-6.5	66,109	-2.7	64,352	-3.0	62,395
TOTAL: METRO PORTION OF STATE		10.3	283,966	2.2	290,202	2.5	297,383
TOTAL: MICRO PORTION OF STATE		-1.6	150,583	-3.9	144,732	-4.6	138,098
TOTAL: NORTH DAKOTA		0.5	642,200	-1.7	631,440	-1.9	619,592

* Indicates county is included from metro in different state.
Source: Devonshire Associates Ltd. and Scan/US, Inc. 2004.

OHIO

	FIPS CODE	PAST 1990-2000 % Change	PAST 2000 Census	PRESENT 2000-2004 % Change	PRESENT 7/1/04 Estimate	FUTURE 2004-2009 % Change	FUTURE 2009 Projection
Akron OH	10420	5.7	694,960	1.2	703,530	1.3	712,812
Portage	39133	6.6	152,061	2.4	155,699	2.6	159,812
Summit	39153	5.4	542,899	0.9	547,831	0.9	553,000
Canton-Massillon OH	15940	3.3	406,934	0.1	407,161	0.0	407,290
Carroll	39019	8.7	28,836	3.5	29,838	4.0	31,027
Stark	39151	2.9	378,098	-0.2	377,323	-0.3	376,263
Cincinnati-Middletown, OH-KY-IN	17140	8.9	2,009,632	2.4	2,058,374	2.7	2,114,029
Dearborn, IN	18029	18.7	46,109	4.9	48,349	5.2	50,848
Franklin, IN	18047	13.1	22,151	3.6	22,956	4.0	23,867
Ohio, IN	18115	5.8	5,623	2.5	5,762	2.6	5,911
Boone, KY	21015	49.3	85,991	16.9	100,516	16.8	117,390
Bracken, KY	21023	6.6	8,279	3.3	8,554	3.9	8,888
Campbell, KY	21037	5.7	88,616	-1.0	87,745	-1.3	86,626
Gallatin, KY	21077	45.9	7,870	2.2	8,041	2.8	8,268
Grant, KY	21081	42.2	22,384	9.3	24,461	9.8	26,848
Kenton, KY	21117	6.6	151,464	0.7	152,501	0.7	153,565
Pendleton, KY	21191	19.6	14,390	6.2	15,286	6.4	16,262
Brown	39015	20.9	42,285	4.6	44,217	4.6	46,255
Butler	39017	14.2	332,807	4.1	346,371	4.5	362,111
Clermont	39025	18.5	177,977	5.7	188,179	6.3	200,037
Hamilton	39061	-2.4	845,303	-3.4	816,699	-4.1	783,497
Warren	39165	39.0	158,383	19.2	188,737	18.5	223,656
Cleveland-Elyria-Mentor OH	17460	2.2	2,148,143	-0.5	2,136,733	-0.6	2,123,339
Cuyahoga	39035	-1.3	1,393,978	-2.8	1,354,570	-3.4	1,308,652
Geauga	39055	12.0	90,895	4.3	94,840	4.7	99,314
Lake	39085	5.6	227,511	0.8	229,287	0.9	231,284
Lorain	39093	5.0	284,664	3.0	293,138	3.3	302,944
Medina	39103	23.5	151,095	9.1	164,898	9.9	181,145
Columbus OH	18140	14.8	1,612,694	5.0	1,693,064	5.4	1,785,083
Delaware	39041	64.3	109,989	27.1	139,819	25.1	174,883
Fairfield	39045	18.7	122,759	10.4	135,586	11.2	150,735
Franklin	39049	11.2	1,068,978	2.4	1,094,640	2.6	1,122,878
Licking	39089	13.4	145,491	4.6	152,155	5.0	159,728
Madison	39097	8.5	40,213	1.4	40,757	1.6	41,412
Morrow	39117	14.0	31,628	8.0	34,155	8.6	37,080
Pickaway	39129	9.3	52,727	-2.6	51,354	-3.5	49,540
Union	39159	28.0	40,909	9.0	44,598	9.5	48,827
Dayton OH	19380	0.5	848,153	-0.3	845,439	-0.4	842,116
Greene	39057	8.2	147,886	3.0	152,266	3.3	157,280
Miami	39109	6.1	98,868	1.8	100,642	2.0	102,678
Montgomery	39113	-2.6	559,062	-1.6	550,095	-1.9	539,637
Preble	39135	5.5	42,337	0.2	42,436	0.2	42,521
Lima OH	30620	-1.2	108,473	-0.3	108,137	-0.5	107,596
Allen	39003	-1.2	108,473	-0.3	108,137	-0.5	107,596
Mansfield OH	31900	2.2	128,852	-0.6	128,091	-0.7	127,188
Richland	39139	2.2	128,852	-0.6	128,091	-0.7	127,188
Sandusky OH	41780	3.6	79,551	-1.4	78,417	-1.9	76,958
Erie	39043	3.6	79,551	-1.4	78,417	-1.9	76,958
Springfield OH	44220	-1.9	144,742	-1.3	142,925	-1.5	140,785
Clark	39023	-1.9	144,742	-1.3	142,925	-1.5	140,785
Toledo OH	45780	0.8	659,188	0.3	661,399	0.4	663,881
Fulton	39051	9.3	42,084	1.1	42,546	1.1	43,035
Lucas	39095	-1.6	455,054	-0.2	453,978	-0.3	452,689
Ottawa	39123	2.4	40,985	0.7	41,255	0.7	41,562
Wood	39173	6.9	121,065	2.1	123,620	2.4	126,595
Youngstown-Warren-Boardman, OH-PA	49660	-1.7	602,964	-2.1	590,415	-2.5	575,927
Mahoning	39099	-2.7	257,555	-3.0	249,884	-3.5	241,134
Trumbull	39155	-1.2	225,116	-1.9	220,736	-2.4	215,521
Mercer, PA	42085	-0.6	120,293	-0.4	119,795	-0.4	119,272
* **Lawrence** (See Huntington-Ashland, WV-KY-OH.)	39087	0.8	62,319	0.5	62,637	0.7	63,060
* **Washington** (See Parkersburg-Marietta, WV-OH.)	39167	1.6	63,251	-1.5	62,279	-1.8	61,151
* **Jefferson** (See Weirton-Steubenville, WV-OH.)	39081	-8.0	73,894	-3.5	71,299	-4.1	68,410
* **Belmont** (See Wheeling, WV-OH.)	39013	-1.2	70,226	-1.1	69,474	-1.2	68,653
TOTAL: METRO PORTION OF STATE		4.6	9,140,806	0.9	9,225,408	1.0	9,320,533
TOTAL: MICRO PORTION OF STATE		4.5	1,708,392	0.9	1,724,118	1.0	1,742,158
TOTAL: OHIO		4.7	11,353,140	0.9	11,459,952	1.1	11,580,720

OKLAHOMA

	FIPS CODE	PAST 1990-2000 % Change	PAST 2000 Census	PRESENT 2000-2004 % Change	PRESENT 7/1/04 Estimate	FUTURE 2004-2009 % Change	FUTURE 2009 Projection
Lawton OK	30020	3.1	114,996	-1.2	113,664	-1.0	112,529
Comanche	40031	3.1	114,996	-1.2	113,664	-1.0	112,529
Oklahoma City OK	36420	12.8	1,095,421	4.5	1,144,287	5.1	1,202,328
Canadian	40017	17.9	87,697	7.7	94,470	8.3	102,289
Cleveland	40027	19.4	208,016	7.6	223,830	8.6	243,120
Grady	40051	9.0	45,516	5.6	48,055	6.4	51,130
Lincoln	40081	9.8	32,080	0.7	32,301	0.6	32,495
Logan	40083	16.9	33,924	5.8	35,908	6.8	38,347
McClain	40087	21.7	27,740	4.0	28,843	4.3	30,084
Oklahoma	40109	10.1	660,448	3.1	680,880	3.5	704,863
Tulsa OK	46140	12.9	859,532	3.1	886,021	3.5	916,777
Creek	40037	10.6	67,367	2.7	69,207	3.0	71,260
Okmulgee	40111	8.8	39,685	0.0	39,692	0.1	39,744
Osage	40113	6.7	44,437	2.4	45,482	2.6	46,643
Pawnee	40117	6.7	16,612	1.3	16,820	0.9	16,969
Rogers	40131	28.0	70,641	12.0	79,136	12.3	88,837
Tulsa	40143	11.9	563,299	1.6	572,493	1.9	583,325
Wagoner	40145	20.1	57,491	9.9	63,191	10.8	69,999
* **Le Flore**	40079	11.2	48,109	2.1	49,143	2.5	50,373
* **Sequoyah** (See Fort Smith, AR-OK.)	40135	15.2	38,972	3.4	40,284	3.8	41,808
TOTAL: METRO PORTION OF STATE		12.3	2,157,030	3.5	2,233,399	4.0	2,323,815
TOTAL: MICRO PORTION OF STATE		6.5	733,861	0.9	740,394	1.1	748,678
TOTAL: OKLAHOMA		9.7	3,450,654	2.3	3,530,711	2.7	3,626,604

OREGON

	FIPS CODE	PAST 1990-2000 % Change	PAST 2000 Census	PRESENT 2000-2004 % Change	PRESENT 7/1/04 Estimate	FUTURE 2004-2009 % Change	FUTURE 2009 Projection
Bend OR	13460	53.9	115,367	16.0	133,790	16.1	155,277
Deschutes	41017	53.9	115,367	16.0	133,790	16.1	155,277
Corvallis OR	18700	10.4	78,153	2.0	79,726	2.5	81,681
Benton	41003	10.4	78,153	2.0	79,726	2.5	81,681
Eugene-Springfield OR	21660	14.2	322,959	3.1	332,896	3.6	344,731
Lane	41039	14.2	322,959	3.1	332,896	3.6	344,731
Medford OR	32780	23.8	181,269	6.4	192,822	7.1	206,537
Jackson	41029	23.8	181,269	6.4	192,822	7.1	206,537
Portland-Vancouver-Beaverton, OR-WA	38900	26.5	1,927,881	7.6	2,075,083	8.4	2,249,134
Clackamas	41005	21.4	338,391	7.4	363,386	8.2	393,126
Columbia	41009	16.0	43,560	8.2	47,125	9.2	51,439
Multnomah	41051	13.1	660,486	3.5	683,283	4.0	710,606
Washington	41067	42.9	445,342	10.0	489,844	10.6	541,567
Yamhill	41071	29.7	84,992	6.8	90,750	7.5	97,577
Clark, WA	53011	45.0	345,238	13.0	390,272	13.7	443,743
Skamania, WA	53059	19.1	9,872	5.6	10,423	6.3	11,076
Salem OR	41420	24.9	347,214	6.0	367,908	6.7	392,483
Marion	41047	24.7	284,834	5.6	300,798	6.3	319,801
Polk	41053	25.9	62,380	7.6	67,110	8.3	72,682
TOTAL: METRO PORTION OF STATE		22.9	2,617,733	6.3	2,781,530	7.0	2,975,024
TOTAL: MICRO PORTION OF STATE		12.8	663,587	2.7	681,665	3.2	703,528
TOTAL: OREGON		20.4	3,421,399	5.3	3,602,559	6.0	3,817,376

PENNSYLVANIA

	FIPS CODE	PAST 1990-2000 % Change	PAST 2000 Census	PRESENT 2000-2004 % Change	PRESENT 7/1/04 Estimate	FUTURE 2004-2009 % Change	FUTURE 2009 Projection
Allentown-Bethlehem-Easton, PA-NJ	10900	7.8	740,395	4.9	776,747	5.6	820,165
Warren, NJ	34041	11.8	102,437	8.7	111,301	9.4	121,709
Carbon	42025	3.4	58,802	3.0	60,563	3.5	62,711
Lehigh	42077	7.2	312,090	3.5	323,155	4.1	336,281
Northampton	42095	8.1	267,066	5.5	281,728	6.3	299,464
Altoona PA	11020	-1.1	129,144	-2.0	126,555	-2.4	123,474
Blair	42013	-1.1	129,144	-2.0	126,555	-2.4	123,474
Erie PA	21500	1.9	280,843	-0.4	279,718	-0.5	278,430
Erie	42049	1.9	280,843	-0.4	279,718	-0.5	278,430
Harrisburg-Carlisle PA	25420	7.3	509,074	2.2	520,152	2.6	533,463
Cumberland	42041	9.4	213,674	3.8	221,861	4.4	231,657
Dauphin	42043	5.9	251,798	0.8	253,912	1.0	256,480
Perry	42099	5.9	43,602	1.8	44,379	2.1	45,326
Johnstown PA	27780	-6.4	152,598	-2.7	148,535	-3.1	143,998
Cambria	42021	-6.4	152,598	-2.7	148,535	-3.1	143,998
Lancaster PA	29540	11.3	470,658	3.4	486,469	3.8	504,836
Lancaster	42071	11.3	470,658	3.4	486,469	3.8	504,836

Core Based Statistical Areas and Their Component Counties: Population Trends, *Continued*

	FIPS CODE	PAST 1990-2000 % Change	PAST 2000 Census	PRESENT 2000-2004 % Change	PRESENT 7/1/04 Estimate	FUTURE 2004-2009 % Change	FUTURE 2009 Projection
Lebanon PA	**30140**	**5.8**	**120,327**	**2.5**	**123,395**	**3.0**	**127,083**
Lebanon	42075	5.8	120,327	2.5	123,395	3.0	127,083
Philadelphia-Camden-Wilmington, PA-NJ-DE-MD	37980	4.6	5,687,147	2.0	5,799,622	2.3	5,933,466
New Castle, DE	10003	13.2	500,265	3.8	519,483	4.2	541,522
Cecil, MD	24015	20.5	85,951	10.3	94,837	11.0	105,269
Burlington, NJ	34005	7.2	423,394	6.5	450,960	7.3	483,852
Camden, NJ	34007	1.2	508,932	1.3	515,644	1.7	524,315
Gloucester, NJ	34015	10.7	254,673	6.4	270,847	7.2	290,271
Salem, NJ	34033	-1.5	64,285	1.2	65,064	1.6	66,116
Bucks	**42017**	**10.4**	**597,635**	**3.4**	**617,667**	**3.7**	**640,325**
Chester	**42029**	**15.2**	**433,501**	**7.2**	**464,595**	**7.7**	**500,504**
Delaware	**42045**	**0.6**	**550,864**	**0.8**	**555,177**	**0.7**	**558,790**
Montgomery	**42091**	**10.6**	**750,097**	**3.6**	**777,323**	**4.2**	**810,039**
Philadelphia	**42101**	**-4.3**	**1,517,550**	**-3.3**	**1,468,025**	**-3.8**	**1,412,463**
Pittsburgh PA	**38300**	**-1.5**	**2,431,087**	**-1.1**	**2,404,027**	**-1.3**	**2,372,650**
Allegheny	42003	-4.1	1,281,666	-2.1	1,255,103	-2.5	1,224,321
Armstrong	42005	-1.5	72,392	-1.3	71,442	-1.5	70,355
Beaver	42007	-2.5	181,412	-1.9	177,885	-2.3	173,845
Butler	42019	14.5	174,083	4.5	181,858	5.0	190,912
Fayette	42051	2.3	148,644	-2.2	145,333	-2.7	141,431
Washington	42125	-0.8	202,897	0.9	204,705	1.0	206,762
Westmoreland	42129	-0.1	369,993	-0.6	367,701	-0.7	365,024
Reading PA	**39740**	**11.0**	**373,638**	**4.1**	**388,909**	**4.6**	**406,841**
Berks	42011	11.0	373,638	4.1	388,909	4.6	406,841
Scranton--Wilkes-Barre PA	**42540**	**-2.5**	**560,625**	**-2.0**	**549,692**	**-2.2**	**537,533**
Lackawanna	42069	-2.6	213,295	-1.7	209,643	-1.9	205,576
Luzerne	42079	-2.7	319,250	-2.3	311,854	-2.7	303,556
Wyoming	42131	0.0	28,080	0.4	28,195	0.7	28,401
State College PA	**44300**	**9.7**	**135,758**	**5.7**	**143,518**	**6.5**	**152,895**
Centre	42027	9.7	135,758	5.7	143,518	6.5	152,895
Williamsport PA	**48700**	**1.1**	**120,044**	**-1.8**	**117,940**	**-2.1**	**115,459**
Lycoming	42081	1.1	120,044	-1.8	117,940	-2.1	115,459
York-Hanover PA	**49620**	**12.4**	**381,751**	**4.5**	**398,969**	**5.1**	**419,155**
York	42133	12.4	381,751	4.5	398,969	5.1	419,155
*** Pike** (See New York-Northern New Jersey-Long Island, NY-NJ-PA.)	**42103**	**65.6**	**46,302**	**16.6**	**54,000**	**17.0**	**63,168**
*** Mercer** (See Youngstown-Warren-Boardman, OH-PA.)	**42085**	**-0.6**	**120,293**	**-0.4**	**119,795**	**-0.4**	**119,272**
TOTAL: METRO PORTION OF STATE		**3.0**	**10,319,747**	**0.9**	**10,409,907**	**1.0**	**10,518,834**
TOTAL: MICRO PORTION OF STATE		**5.1**	**1,578,983**	**1.3**	**1,599,234**	**1.5**	**1,623,217**
TOTAL: PENNSYLVANIA		3.4	12,281,054	0.9	12,392,109	1.1	12,525,381

RHODE ISLAND

	FIPS CODE	1990-2000 % Change	2000 Census	2000-2004 % Change	7/1/04 Estimate	2004-2009 % Change	2009 Projection
Providence-New Bedford-Fall River, RI-MA	39300	4.8	1,582,997	3.3	1,635,332	3.7	1,696,113
Bristol, MA	25005	5.6	534,678	3.0	550,668	3.3	568,949
Bristol	**44001**	**3.7**	**50,648**	**0.8**	**51,073**	**0.8**	**51,493**
Kent	**44003**	**3.7**	**167,090**	**3.3**	**172,563**	**3.7**	**178,891**
Newport	**44005**	**-2.0**	**85,433**	**0.7**	**86,020**	**0.5**	**86,452**
Providence	**44007**	**4.2**	**621,602**	**3.8**	**645,010**	**4.3**	**672,848**
Washington	**44009**	**12.3**	**123,546**	**5.2**	**129,998**	**5.8**	**137,480**
TOTAL: METRO PORTION OF STATE		**4.5**	**1,048,319**	**3.5**	**1,084,664**	**3.9**	**1,127,164**
TOTAL: RHODE ISLAND		4.5	1,048,319	3.5	1,084,664	3.9	1,127,164

SOUTH CAROLINA

	FIPS CODE	1990-2000 % Change	2000 Census	2000-2004 % Change	7/1/04 Estimate	2004-2009 % Change	2009 Projection
Anderson SC	**11340**	**14.1**	**165,740**	**4.5**	**173,238**	**5.0**	**181,872**
Anderson	45007	14.1	165,740	4.5	173,238	5.0	181,872
Charleston-North Charleston SC	**16700**	**8.3**	**549,033**	**5.4**	**578,716**	**6.1**	**614,123**
Berkeley	45015	10.8	142,651	3.5	147,602	3.9	153,361
Charleston	45019	5.1	309,969	4.7	324,460	5.3	341,682
Dorchester	45035	16.1	96,413	10.6	106,654	11.7	119,080
Columbia SC	**17900**	**18.0**	**647,158**	**4.9**	**678,866**	**5.5**	**716,130**
Calhoun	45017	19.1	15,185	1.5	15,410	1.4	15,624
Fairfield	45039	5.2	23,454	2.1	23,939	2.1	24,432
Kershaw	45055	20.8	52,647	4.5	55,026	4.9	57,745
Lexington	45063	28.9	216,014	6.4	229,751	7.0	245,856
Richland	45079	12.2	320,677	4.7	335,685	5.3	353,578
Saluda	45081	17.3	19,181	-0.7	19,055	-0.8	18,895
Florence SC	**22500**	**9.6**	**193,155**	**2.1**	**197,296**	**2.5**	**202,319**
Darlington	45031	9.0	67,394	1.1	68,115	1.2	68,908
Florence	45041	10.0	125,761	2.7	129,181	3.3	133,411
Greenville SC	**24860**	**18.6**	**559,940**	**4.3**	**584,065**	**4.8**	**611,950**
Greenville	45045	18.6	379,616	5.4	400,132	6.0	423,990
Laurens	45059	19.8	69,567	1.3	70,472	1.4	71,490
Pickens	45077	18.0	110,757	2.4	113,461	2.7	116,470
Myrtle Beach-Conway-North Myrtle Beach SC	**34820**	**36.5**	**196,629**	**9.3**	**214,999**	**9.9**	**236,202**
Horry	45051	36.5	196,629	9.3	214,999	9.9	236,202
Spartanburg SC	**43900**	**11.9**	**253,791**	**3.9**	**263,575**	**4.3**	**275,036**
Spartanburg	45083	11.9	253,791	3.9	263,575	4.3	275,036
Sumter SC	**44940**	**2.0**	**104,646**	**1.6**	**106,361**	**1.9**	**108,382**
Sumter	45085	2.0	104,646	1.6	106,361	1.9	108,382
*** Aiken**	**45003**	**17.9**	**142,552**	**3.9**	**148,054**	**4.4**	**154,638**
*** Edgefield** (See Augusta-Richmond County, GA-SC.)	**45037**	**33.9**	**24,595**	**0.6**	**24,738**	**0.7**	**24,909**
*** York** (See Charlotte-Gastonia-Concord, NC-SC.)	**45091**	**25.2**	**164,614**	**10.7**	**182,193**	**11.3**	**202,803**
TOTAL: METRO PORTION OF STATE		**15.8**	**3,001,853**	**5.0**	**3,152,101**	**5.6**	**3,328,364**
TOTAL: MICRO PORTION OF STATE		**15.0**	**733,229**	**3.8**	**760,831**	**4.2**	**792,994**
TOTAL: SOUTH CAROLINA		15.1	4,012,012	4.4	4,188,493	4.9	4,395,198

SOUTH DAKOTA

	FIPS CODE	1990-2000 % Change	2000 Census	2000-2004 % Change	7/1/04 Estimate	2004-2009 % Change	2009 Projection
Rapid City SD	**39660**	**9.3**	**112,818**	**4.4**	**117,781**	**5.0**	**123,618**
Meade	46093	10.9	24,253	2.6	24,873	3.1	25,649
Pennington	46103	8.9	88,565	4.9	92,908	5.4	97,969
Sioux Falls SD	**43620**	**21.9**	**187,093**	**7.8**	**201,734**	**8.2**	**218,369**
Lincoln	46083	56.4	24,131	28.0	30,883	25.5	38,756
McCook	46087	2.5	5,832	0.6	5,868	0.3	5,888
Minnehaha	46099	19.8	148,281	5.5	156,477	5.9	165,650
Turner	46125	3.2	8,849	-3.9	8,506	-5.1	8,075
*** Union** (See Sioux City, IA-NE-SD.)	**46127**	**23.5**	**12,584**	**4.6**	**13,166**	**5.3**	**13,863**
TOTAL: METRO PORTION OF STATE		**17.1**	**312,495**	**6.5**	**332,681**	**7.0**	**355,850**
TOTAL: MICRO PORTION OF STATE		**6.3**	**214,631**	**-0.9**	**212,746**	**-1.0**	**210,525**
TOTAL: SOUTH DAKOTA		8.5	754,844	1.6	767,184	1.9	781,561

TENNESSEE

	FIPS CODE	1990-2000 % Change	2000 Census	2000-2004 % Change	7/1/04 Estimate	2004-2009 % Change	2009 Projection
Chattanooga, TN-GA	16860	10.0	476,531	2.6	488,857	3.0	503,503
Catoosa, GA	13047	25.5	53,282	11.8	59,560	12.4	66,931
Dade, GA	13083	15.3	15,154	6.6	16,151	7.4	17,353
Walker, GA	13295	4.7	61,053	3.3	63,070	3.9	65,504
Hamilton	**47065**	**7.8**	**307,896**	**0.7**	**310,020**	**0.8**	**312,567**
Marion	**47115**	**11.7**	**27,776**	**0.5**	**27,916**	**0.7**	**28,098**
Sequatchie	**47153**	**28.3**	**11,370**	**6.8**	**12,140**	**7.5**	**13,050**
Clarksville, TN-KY	17300	22.6	232,000	2.6	238,045	2.9	244,887
Christian, KY	21047	4.8	72,265	-4.3	69,170	-5.2	65,576
Trigg, KY	21221	21.6	12,597	2.8	12,954	3.0	13,339
Montgomery	**47125**	**34.1**	**134,768**	**6.1**	**142,942**	**6.6**	**152,331**
Stewart	**47161**	**30.5**	**12,370**	**4.9**	**12,979**	**5.1**	**13,641**
Cleveland TN	**17420**	**19.1**	**104,015**	**3.0**	**107,156**	**3.4**	**110,762**
Bradley	47011	19.3	87,965	3.4	90,961	3.8	94,447
Polk	47139	17.6	16,050	0.9	16,195	0.7	16,315
Jackson TN	**27180**	**18.3**	**107,377**	**2.8**	**110,436**	**3.3**	**114,042**
Chester	47023	21.2	15,540	2.6	15,941	3.1	16,436
Madison	47113	17.8	91,837	2.9	94,495	3.3	97,606
Johnson City TN	**27740**	**13.2**	**181,607**	**3.3**	**187,591**	**3.8**	**194,635**
Carter	47019	10.2	56,742	3.8	58,913	4.4	61,505
Unicoi	47171	6.8	17,667	0.4	17,729	0.6	17,827
Washington	47179	16.1	107,198	3.5	110,949	3.9	115,303
Kingsport-Bristol-Bristol, TN-VA	28700	8.3	298,484	0.5	300,120	0.7	302,205
Hawkins	**47073**	**20.2**	**53,563**	**3.6**	**55,484**	**4.0**	**57,720**
Sullivan	**47163**	**6.6**	**153,048**	**0.0**	**153,090**	**0.1**	**153,289**
Bristol, VA	51520	-5.7	17,367	-1.1	17,176	-0.9	17,023
Scott, VA	51169	0.9	23,403	-2.2	22,883	-2.6	22,279
Washington, VA	51191	11.4	51,103	0.8	51,487	0.8	51,894
Knoxville TN	**28940**	**15.2**	**616,079**	**4.4**	**643,341**	**5.0**	**675,728**
Anderson	47001	4.5	71,330	1.1	72,110	1.4	73,141
Blount	47009	23.1	105,823	7.0	113,265	7.7	122,041
Knox	47093	13.8	382,032	3.8	396,391	4.3	413,365
Loudon	47105	25.1	39,086	8.5	42,424	9.4	46,425
Union	47173	30.0	17,808	7.5	19,151	8.4	20,756
Memphis, TN-MS-AR	32820	12.9	1,205,204	3.7	1,249,702	4.1	1,301,412
Crittenden, AR	05035	1.9	50,866	0.7	51,207	0.5	51,447
DeSoto, MS	28033	57.9	107,199	20.9	129,632	20.2	155,853
Marshall, MS	28093	15.3	34,993	1.6	35,565	1.7	36,168
Tate, MS	28137	18.4	25,370	2.1	25,907	2.2	26,465
Tunica, MS	28143	13.0	9,227	10.0	10,146	11.2	11,283
Fayette	**47047**	**12.7**	**28,806**	**15.8**	**33,345**	**15.8**	**38,625**
Shelby	**47157**	**8.6**	**897,472**	**1.3**	**908,843**	**1.5**	**922,152**
Tipton	**47167**	**36.5**	**51,271**	**7.4**	**55,057**	**7.9**	**59,419**
Morristown TN	**34100**	**22.4**	**123,081**	**4.4**	**128,445**	**4.8**	**134,591**
Grainger	47057	20.8	20,659	5.0	21,687	5.6	22,897
Hamblen	47063	15.2	58,128	1.6	59,059	1.8	60,098
Jefferson	47089	34.2	44,294	7.7	47,699	8.2	51,596
Nashville-Davidson--Murfreesboro TN	**34980**	**25.1**	**1,311,789**	**5.9**	**1,389,376**	**6.5**	**1,479,740**
Cannon	47015	22.5	12,826	3.7	13,300	3.6	13,782
Cheatham	47021	32.3	35,912	5.2	37,783	5.5	39,876
Davidson	47037	11.6	569,891	-0.0	569,819	-0.0	569,701
Dickson	47043	23.1	43,156	5.4	45,469	5.9	48,138
Hickman	47081	33.1	22,295	6.1	23,657	6.4	25,180
Macon	47111	28.2	20,386	4.1	21,213	4.5	22,165
Robertson	47147	31.2	54,433	8.9	59,290	9.4	64,834
Rutherford	47149	53.5	182,023	14.6	208,605	15.1	240,080
Smith	47159	25.2	17,712	3.7	18,361	3.7	19,043
Sumner	47165	26.3	130,449	8.3	141,292	9.0	153,992
Trousdale	47169	22.6	7,259	3.2	7,488	2.8	7,695
Williamson	47187	56.3	126,638	15.1	145,703	15.1	167,711
Wilson	47189	31.2	88,809	9.7	97,396	10.4	107,543
TOTAL: METRO PORTION OF STATE		**16.8**	**4,122,288**	**3.8**	**4,278,161**	**4.3**	**4,460,390**
TOTAL: MICRO PORTION OF STATE		**16.6**	**957,407**	**3.4**	**989,798**	**3.8**	**1,027,026**
TOTAL: TENNESSEE		16.7	5,689,283	3.5	5,888,107	3.9	6,119,904

TEXAS

	FIPS CODE	1990-2000 % Change	2000 Census	2000-2004 % Change	7/1/04 Estimate	2004-2009 % Change	2009 Projection
Abilene TX	**10180**	**8.3**	**160,245**	**-1.4**	**157,948**	**-1.7**	**155,289**
Callahan	48059	8.8	12,905	2.1	13,173	2.4	13,484
Jones	48253	26.0	20,785	-4.7	19,809	-5.6	18,698
Taylor	48441	5.8	126,555	-1.3	124,966	-1.5	123,107
Amarillo TX	**11100**	**15.5**	**226,522**	**3.9**	**235,287**	**4.4**	**245,559**
Armstrong	48011	6.3	2,148	-6.0	2,020	-8.5	1,849
Carson	48065	-0.9	6,516	-0.1	6,507	-0.0	6,506
Potter	48375	16.0	113,546	4.4	118,546	5.1	124,557
Randall	48381	16.3	104,312	3.7	108,220	4.1	112,647
Austin-Round Rock TX	**12420**	**47.7**	**1,249,763**	**13.2**	**1,415,292**	**13.3**	**1,603,483**
Bastrop	48021	50.9	57,733	21.2	69,998	20.9	84,598
Caldwell	48055	22.0	32,194	13.7	36,601	14.1	41,747
Hays	48209	48.7	97,589	22.2	119,256	21.2	144,559
Travis	48453	40.9	812,280	7.0	869,648	7.1	931,805
Williamson	48491	79.1	249,967	27.9	319,789	25.3	400,774
Beaumont-Port Arthur TX	**13140**	**6.6**	**385,090**	**-0.8**	**381,930**	**-0.9**	**378,485**
Hardin	48199	16.3	48,073	4.3	50,132	5.0	52,623
Jefferson	48245	5.3	252,051	-1.8	247,599	-2.0	242,615
Orange	48361	5.5	84,966	-0.9	84,199	-1.1	83,247
Brownsville-Harlingen TX	**15180**	**28.9**	**335,227**	**10.9**	**371,857**	**11.8**	**415,655**
Cameron	48061	28.9	335,227	10.9	371,857	11.8	415,655
College Station-Bryan TX	**17780**	**22.4**	**184,885**	**5.5**	**195,011**	**6.2**	**207,038**
Brazos	48041	25.1	152,415	6.4	162,171	7.2	173,866
Burleson	48051	20.9	16,470	3.6	17,071	3.8	17,719
Robertson	48395	3.2	16,000	-1.4	15,769	-2.0	15,453
Corpus Christi TX	**18580**	**9.7**	**403,280**	**1.2**	**408,027**	**1.5**	**413,993**
Aransas	48007	25.7	22,497	6.3	23,921	7.2	25,655
Nueces	48355	7.7	313,645	0.7	315,797	0.9	318,737
San Patricio	48409	14.3	67,138	1.7	68,309	1.9	69,601
Dallas-Fort Worth-Arlington TX	**19100**	**29.4**	**5,161,544**	**10.8**	**5,720,764**	**11.4**	**6,375,790**
Collin	48085	86.2	491,675	28.0	629,504	25.7	791,230
Dallas	48113	19.8	2,218,899	3.8	2,303,656	4.2	2,401,298
Delta	48119	9.7	5,327	3.0	5,487	3.3	5,666
Denton	48121	58.3	432,976	23.5	534,784	22.4	654,680
Ellis	48139	30.8	111,360	15.3	128,389	15.5	148,272
Hunt	48231	19.0	76,596	7.5	82,370	8.2	89,093
Johnson	48251	30.5	126,811	12.6	142,744	12.9	161,115
Kaufman	48257	36.6	71,313	19.5	85,224	19.2	101,560
Parker	48367	36.6	88,495	13.2	100,215	13.6	113,879
Rockwall	48397	68.3	43,080	35.2	58,223	30.8	76,184
Tarrant	48439	23.6	1,446,219	10.2	1,594,027	10.9	1,768,296
Wise	48497	40.7	48,793	15.1	56,141	14.9	64,517
El Paso TX	**21340**	**14.9**	**679,622**	**5.0**	**713,340**	**5.5**	**752,812**
El Paso	48141	14.9	679,622	5.0	713,340	5.5	752,812
Houston-Baytown-Sugar Land TX	**26420**	**25.2**	**4,715,407**	**10.0**	**5,187,158**	**10.7**	**5,743,884**
Austin	48015	18.9	23,590	8.0	25,488	8.4	27,637
Brazoria	48039	26.1	241,767	11.6	269,789	12.3	302,968
Chambers	48071	29.6	26,031	7.8	28,050	8.3	30,391
Fort Bend	48157	57.2	354,452	24.1	440,039	23.0	541,335
Galveston	48167	15.1	250,158	8.8	272,122	9.8	298,837
Harris	48201	20.7	3,400,578	7.5	3,656,415	8.2	3,957,791
Liberty	48291	33.1	70,154	7.3	75,275	7.7	81,059
Montgomery	48339	61.2	293,768	22.7	360,419	21.8	438,982
San Jacinto	48407	35.9	22,246	9.7	24,408	10.0	26,858
Waller	48473	39.6	32,663	7.6	35,153	8.2	38,026
Killeen-Temple-Fort Hood TX	**28660**	**23.0**	**330,714**	**4.9**	**347,063**	**5.4**	**365,712**
Bell	48027	24.5	237,974	5.9	251,967	6.4	268,153
Coryell	48099	16.8	74,978	0.3	75,191	-0.0	75,165
Lampasas	48281	31.4	17,762	12.1	19,905	12.5	22,394
Laredo TX	**29700**	**44.9**	**193,117**	**13.9**	**219,931**	**14.3**	**251,491**
Webb	48479	44.9	193,117	13.9	219,931	14.3	251,491
Longview TX	**30980**	**7.8**	**194,042**	**2.8**	**199,528**	**3.4**	**206,386**
Gregg	48183	6.1	111,379	3.1	114,824	3.8	119,232
Rusk	48401	8.3	47,372	-0.3	47,219	-0.4	47,040
Upshur	48459	12.5	35,291	6.2	37,485	7.0	40,114
Lubbock TX	**31180**	**8.6**	**249,700**	**4.0**	**259,602**	**4.7**	**271,678**
Crosby	48107	-3.2	7,072	-6.1	6,640	-7.3	6,154
Lubbock	48303	9.0	242,628	4.3	252,962	5.0	265,524
McAllen-Edinburg-Pharr TX	**32580**	**48.5**	**569,463**	**15.2**	**656,072**	**15.6**	**758,677**
Hidalgo	48215	48.5	569,463	15.2	656,072	15.6	758,677
Midland TX	**33260**	**8.8**	**116,009**	**3.1**	**119,655**	**4.3**	**124,798**
Midland	48329	8.8	116,009	3.1	119,655	4.3	124,798
Odessa TX	**36220**	**1.8**	**121,123**	**1.8**	**123,354**	**2.7**	**126,654**
Ector	48135	1.8	121,123	1.8	123,354	2.7	126,654
San Angelo TX	**41660**	**5.7**	**105,781**	**-0.6**	**105,120**	**-0.7**	**104,370**
Irion	48235	8.7	1,771	-2.3	1,731	-3.1	1,678
Tom Green	48451	5.6	104,010	-0.6	103,389	-0.7	102,692
San Antonio TX	**41700**	**21.6**	**1,711,703**	**8.3**	**1,854,472**	**9.1**	**2,023,104**
Atascosa	48013	26.5	38,628	10.9	42,850	11.5	47,765
Bandera	48019	67.1	17,645	12.5	19,851	12.7	22,366
Bexar	48029	17.5	1,392,931	7.4	1,496,237	8.2	1,619,092
Comal	48091	50.5	78,021	16.4	90,783	16.5	105,766
Guadalupe	48187	37.2	89,023	11.8	99,505	12.1	111,519
Kendall	48259	62.7	23,743	13.4	26,915	13.7	30,598
Medina	48325	43.9	39,304	7.5	42,244	8.2	45,697
Wilson	48493	43.1	32,408	11.4	36,087	11.7	40,301
Sherman-Denison TX	**43300**	**16.4**	**110,595**	**5.4**	**116,532**	**5.9**	**123,419**
Grayson	48181	16.4	110,595	5.4	116,532	5.9	123,419
Texarkana, TX-Texarkana, AR	45500	8.0	129,749	1.9	132,208	2.3	135,265
Miller, AR	05091	5.1	40,443	4.8	42,371	5.6	44,746
Bowie	**48037**	**9.4**	**89,306**	**0.6**	**89,837**	**0.8**	**90,519**
Tyler TX	**46340**	**15.5**	**174,706**	**7.0**	**186,882**	**7.7**	**201,203**
Smith	48423	15.5	174,706	7.0	186,882	7.7	201,203
Victoria TX	**47020**	**12.3**	**111,663**	**1.6**	**113,403**	**1.9**	**115,590**
Calhoun	48057	8.4	20,647	-1.3	20,387	-1.6	20,051
Goliad	48175	15.9	6,928	3.4	7,163	3.3	7,399
Victoria	48469	13.1	84,088	2.1	85,853	2.7	88,140
Waco TX	**47380**	**12.9**	**213,517**	**3.9**	**221,739**	**4.4**	**231,389**
McLennan	48309	12.9	213,517	3.9	221,739	4.4	231,389
Wichita Falls TX	**48660**	**7.9**	**151,524**	**-1.6**	**149,063**	**-1.9**	**146,159**
Archer	48009	11.0	8,854	4.6	9,261	3.9	9,618
Clay	48077	9.8	11,006	2.1	11,240	1.4	11,402
Wichita	48485	7.6	131,664	-2.4	128,562	-2.7	125,139
TOTAL: METRO PORTION OF STATE		**24.9**	**17,944,548**	**8.9**	**19,548,867**	**9.6**	**21,433,137**
TOTAL: MICRO PORTION OF STATE		**11.7**	**1,489,577**	**2.1**	**1,521,512**	**2.6**	**1,560,464**
TOTAL: TEXAS		22.8	20,851,820	7.9	22,508,240	8.7	24,456,895

UTAH

	FIPS CODE	1990-2000 % Change	2000 Census	2000-2004 % Change	7/1/04 Estimate	2004-2009 % Change	2009 Projection
Logan, UT-ID	30860	29.3	102,720	6.1	109,025	6.8	116,458
Franklin, ID	16041	22.7	11,329	6.3	12,043	7.0	12,884
Cache	**49005**	**30.2**	**91,391**	**6.1**	**96,982**	**6.8**	**103,574**
Ogden-Clearfield UT	**36260**	**25.8**	**442,656**	**7.7**	**476,951**	**8.4**	**516,972**
Davis	49011	27.2	238,994	9.1	260,687	9.8	286,123
Morgan	49029	29.0	7,129	7.1	7,637	7.8	8,232
Weber	49057	24.1	196,533	6.2	208,627	6.7	222,617

* Indicates county is included from metro in different state.
Source: Devonshire Associates Ltd. and Scan/US, Inc. 2004.

continued on next page

Core Based Statistical Areas and Their Component Counties: Population Trends, *Continued*

	FIPS CODE	PAST 1990-2000 % Change	PAST 2000 Census	PRESENT 2000-2004 % Change	PRESENT 7/1/04 Estimate	FUTURE 2004-2009 % Change	FUTURE 2009 Projection
Provo-Orem UT	39340	39.9	376,774	10.4	416,085	11.1	462,240
Juab	49023	41.6	8,238	8.8	8,962	9.5	9,811
Utah	49049	39.8	368,536	10.5	407,123	11.1	452,429
Salt Lake City UT	41620	26.1	968,858	4.9	1,016,207	5.4	1,071,048
Salt Lake	49035	23.8	898,387	3.8	932,116	4.2	971,433
Summit	49043	91.6	29,736	14.4	34,029	14.8	39,074
Tooele	49045	53.1	40,735	22.9	50,062	20.9	60,541
St. George UT	41100	86.1	90,354	20.0	108,436	19.8	129,952
Washington	49053	86.1	90,354	20.0	108,436	19.8	129,952
TOTAL: METRO PORTION OF STATE		30.6	1,970,033	7.3	2,114,661	8.0	2,283,786
TOTAL: MICRO PORTION OF STATE		25.1	137,385	6.1	145,782	6.8	155,641
TOTAL: UTAH		29.6	2,233,169	6.9	2,387,580	7.6	2,568,143

VERMONT

	FIPS CODE	PAST 1990-2000 % Change	PAST 2000 Census	PRESENT 2000-2004 % Change	PRESENT 7/1/04 Estimate	FUTURE 2004-2009 % Change	FUTURE 2009 Projection
Burlington-South Burlington VT	15540	12.3	198,889	3.0	204,838	3.3	211,517
Chittenden	50007	11.2	146,571	2.1	149,664	2.3	153,038
Franklin	50011	13.6	45,417	4.6	47,499	5.0	49,879
Grand Isle	50013	29.8	6,901	11.2	7,675	12.1	8,600
TOTAL: METRO PORTION OF STATE		12.3	198,889	3.0	204,838	3.3	211,517
TOTAL: MICRO PORTION OF STATE		4.6	250,536	1.3	253,833	1.5	257,683
TOTAL: VERMONT		8.2	608,827	2.2	622,165	2.5	637,457

VIRGINIA

	FIPS CODE	PAST 1990-2000 % Change	PAST 2000 Census	PRESENT 2000-2004 % Change	PRESENT 7/1/04 Estimate	FUTURE 2004-2009 % Change	FUTURE 2009 Projection
Blacksburg-Christiansburg-Radford VA	13980	7.5	151,272	1.1	153,009	1.4	155,084
Giles	51071	1.8	16,657	2.3	17,040	2.5	17,458
Montgomery	51121	13.1	83,629	3.1	86,230	3.6	89,306
Pulaski	51155	1.8	35,127	-0.4	34,995	-0.5	34,822
Radford (Ind. City)	51750	-0.5	15,859	-7.0	14,744	-8.5	13,498
Charlottesville VA	16820	20.9	174,021	5.7	183,913	6.2	195,350
Albemarle	51003	16.5	79,236	11.9	88,692	5.8	93,797
Charlottesville (Ind. City)	51540	11.7	45,049	-13.8	38,847	-4.0	37,309
Fluvanna	51065	61.3	20,047	19.8	24,026	19.7	28,764
Greene	51079	48.0	15,244	13.2	17,251	13.7	19,610
Nelson	51125	13.0	14,445	4.5	15,097	5.1	15,870
Danville VA	19260	1.3	110,156	-1.8	108,169	-2.1	105,930
Danville (Ind. City)	51590	-8.8	48,411	-3.8	46,575	-4.3	44,565
Pittsylvania	51143	10.9	61,745	-0.2	61,594	-0.4	61,365
Harrisonburg VA	25500	22.7	108,193	2.9	111,322	3.5	115,255
Harrisonburg (Ind. City)	51660	31.8	40,468	2.4	41,444	3.3	42,816
Rockingham	51165	17.8	67,725	3.2	69,878	3.7	72,439
Lynchburg VA	31340	10.9	228,616	1.4	231,742	1.5	235,259
Amherst	51009	11.6	31,894	-0.0	31,890	-0.0	31,881
Appomattox	51011	11.4	13,705	0.1	13,712	0.1	13,720
Bedford	51019	32.2	60,371	4.9	63,337	5.3	66,712
Bedford (Ind. City)	51515	3.7	6,299	0.8	6,352	1.0	6,414
Campbell	51031	7.4	51,078	0.6	51,384	0.6	51,695
Lynchburg (Ind. City)	51680	-1.2	65,269	-0.3	65,067	-0.4	64,837
Richmond VA	40060	15.6	1,096,957	4.9	1,150,973	5.5	1,214,683
Amelia	51007	29.7	11,400	3.8	11,831	3.7	12,274
Caroline	51033	15.1	22,121	6.4	23,543	7.5	25,302
Charles City	51036	10.3	6,926	3.7	7,181	4.4	7,495
Chesterfield	51041	24.2	259,903	8.6	282,130	9.4	308,557
Colonial Heights (Ind. City)	51570	5.2	16,897	3.0	17,408	3.5	18,018
Cumberland	51049	15.2	9,017	2.6	9,250	3.3	9,554
Dinwiddie	51053	17.0	24,533	1.6	24,932	1.6	25,325
Goochland	51075	19.1	16,863	9.9	18,538	10.8	20,537
Hanover	51085	36.4	86,320	11.7	96,438	12.2	108,214
Henrico	51087	20.4	262,300	4.3	273,683	4.7	286,663
Hopewell (Ind. City)	51670	-3.2	22,354	0.3	22,421	0.7	22,568
King William	51101	20.5	13,146	9.8	14,440	10.7	15,985
King and Queen	51097	5.4	6,630	-0.8	6,578	-0.8	6,525
Louisa	51109	26.1	25,627	12.3	28,789	13.2	32,576
New Kent	51127	28.9	13,462	13.5	15,279	14.2	17,455
Petersburg (Ind. City)	51730	-12.1	33,740	-2.4	32,931	-2.4	32,140
Powhatan	51145	46.0	22,377	13.2	25,328	13.4	28,721
Prince George	51149	20.6	33,047	4.9	34,661	5.1	36,444
Richmond (Ind. City)	51760	-2.6	197,790	-2.0	193,828	-2.3	189,373
Sussex	51183	22.0	12,504	-5.8	11,784	-7.0	10,957
Roanoke VA	40220	7.4	288,309	1.0	291,205	1.2	294,783
Botetourt	51023	22.0	30,496	4.1	31,742	4.6	33,207
Craig	51045	16.4	5,091	1.7	5,179	2.0	5,280
Franklin	51067	19.6	47,286	5.0	49,641	5.5	52,368
Roanoke	51161	8.1	85,778	2.4	87,854	3.0	90,472
Roanoke (Ind. City)	51770	-1.5	94,911	-2.8	92,245	-3.3	89,208
Salem (Ind. City)	51775	4.2	24,747	-0.8	24,544	-1.2	24,248
Virginia Beach-Norfolk-Newport News, VA-NC	47260	8.8	1,576,370	5.1	1,656,100	5.7	1,750,240
Currituck, NC	37053	32.4	18,190	19.1	21,665	19.2	25,821
Chesapeake (Ind. City)	51550	31.1	199,184	7.6	214,295	8.1	231,578
Gloucester	51073	15.4	34,780	7.3	37,303	8.1	40,326
Hampton (Ind. City)	51650	9.5	146,437	0.4	147,010	0.4	147,660
Isle of Wight	51093	18.7	29,728	9.7	32,606	10.4	36,004
James City	51095	38.0	48,102	14.6	55,145	15.0	63,432
Mathews	51115	10.3	9,207	0.1	9,220	0.2	9,237
Newport News (Ind. City)	51700	5.9	180,150	1.1	182,162	1.4	184,721
Norfolk (Ind. City)	51710	-10.3	234,403	4.2	244,163	5.0	256,324
Poquoson (Ind. City)	51735	5.1	11,566	3.1	11,929	3.5	12,352
Portsmouth (Ind. City)	51740	-3.2	100,565	-1.2	99,349	-1.3	98,010
Suffolk (Ind. City)	51800	22.1	63,677	20.3	76,604	20.2	92,042
Surry	51181	11.1	6,829	3.5	7,065	3.9	7,342
Virginia Beach (Ind. City)	51810	8.2	425,257	4.3	443,729	4.8	465,007
Williamsburg (Ind. City)	51830	4.1	11,998	-4.4	11,476	-5.4	10,852
York	51199	32.7	56,297	10.8	62,379	11.5	69,532
Winchester, VA-WV	49020	22.4	102,997	9.2	112,471	9.9	123,579
Frederick	51069	29.5	59,209	11.8	66,224	12.5	74,515
Winchester (Ind. City)	51840	7.5	23,585	4.7	24,691	5.2	25,974
Hampshire, WV	54027	22.5	20,203	6.7	21,556	7.1	23,090
* **Alexandria City**	51510	15.4	128,283	0.4	128,847	-0.3	128,458
* **Arlington County**	51013	10.8	189,453	-1.1	187,390	-1.3	184,980
* **Clarke County**	51043	4.6	12,652	7.4	13,582	8.0	14,672
* **Fairfax County**	51059	18.5	969,749	4.0	1,008,761	4.1	1,050,462
* **Fairfax City**	51600	9.6	21,498	3.2	22,181	3.4	22,928
* **Falls Church City**	51610	8.3	10,377	1.2	10,500	0.7	10,576
* **Fauquier County**	51061	13.1	55,139	14.2	62,992	14.7	72,263
* **Fredericksburg City**	51630	1.3	19,279	6.2	20,481	7.1	21,938
* **Loudoun County**	51107	96.9	169,599	40.1	237,678	33.5	317,314
* **Manassas City**	51683	25.7	35,135	7.5	37,756	7.8	40,708
* **Manassas Park City**	51685	52.8	10,290	8.9	11,209	9.8	12,302
* **Prince William County**	51153	30.2	280,813	20.8	339,149	20.4	408,242
* **Spotsylvania County**	51177	57.5	90,395	25.3	113,260	23.9	140,355
* **Stafford County**	51179	51.0	92,446	26.4	116,821	24.8	145,805
* **Warren County**	51187	20.8	31,584	9.5	34,587	10.4	38,170
(See Washington-Arlington-Alexandria, DC-VA-MD-WV.)							
* **Bristol City**	51520	-5.7	17,367	-1.1	17,176	-0.9	17,023
* **Scott County**	51169	0.9	23,403	-2.2	22,883	-2.6	22,279
* **Washington County**	51191	11.4	51,103	0.8	51,487	0.8	51,894
(See Kingsport-Bristol-Bristol, TN-VA.)							
TOTAL: METRO PORTION OF STATE		15.8	6,007,063	6.4	6,392,423	7.0	6,841,621
TOTAL: MICRO PORTION OF STATE		4.7	226,932	0.8	228,660	0.9	230,797
TOTAL: VIRGINIA		14.4	7,078,515	5.7	7,480,156	6.3	7,949,286

WASHINGTON

	FIPS CODE	PAST 1990-2000 % Change	PAST 2000 Census	PRESENT 2000-2004 % Change	PRESENT 7/1/04 Estimate	FUTURE 2004-2009 % Change	FUTURE 2009 Projection
Bellingham WA	13380	30.5	166,814	7.6	179,561	8.3	194,508
Whatcom	53073	30.5	166,814	7.6	179,561	8.3	194,508
Bremerton-Silverdale WA	14740	22.3	231,969	4.9	243,450	5.6	257,104
Kitsap	53035	22.3	231,969	4.9	243,450	5.6	257,104
Kennewick-Richland-Pasco WA	28420	27.9	191,822	12.3	215,499	13.3	244,065
Benton	53005	26.6	142,475	10.3	157,183	11.2	174,797
Franklin	53021	31.7	49,347	18.2	58,316	18.8	69,268
Longview WA	31020	13.2	92,948	3.1	95,850	3.7	99,372
Cowlitz	53015	13.2	92,948	3.1	95,850	3.7	99,372
Mount Vernon-Anacortes WA	34580	29.4	102,979	7.9	111,156	8.6	120,767
Skagit	53057	29.4	102,979	7.9	111,156	8.6	120,767
Olympia WA	36500	28.6	207,355	9.2	226,479	10.0	249,121
Thurston	53067	28.6	207,355	9.2	226,479	10.0	249,121
Seattle-Tacoma-Bellevue WA	42660	18.9	3,043,878	4.2	3,171,685	4.7	3,321,230
King	53033	15.2	1,737,034	1.8	1,768,908	2.1	1,806,395
Pierce	53053	19.6	700,820	7.5	753,288	8.2	814,946
Snohomish	53061	30.1	606,024	7.2	649,489	7.8	699,889
Spokane WA	44060	15.7	417,939	4.1	435,145	4.7	455,733
Spokane	53063	15.7	417,939	4.1	435,145	4.7	455,733
Wenatchee WA	48300	26.5	99,219	3.3	102,502	3.8	106,382
Chelan	53007	27.5	66,616	2.7	68,388	3.0	70,465
Douglas	53017	24.4	32,603	4.6	34,114	5.3	35,917
Yakima WA	49420	17.9	222,581	2.5	228,066	2.9	234,762
Yakima	53077	17.9	222,581	2.5	228,066	2.9	234,762
* **Asotin**	53003	16.7	20,551	0.5	20,647	0.5	20,755
(See Lewiston, ID-WA.)							
* **Clark**	53011	45.0	345,238	13.0	390,272	13.7	443,743
* **Skamania**	53059	19.1	9,872	5.6	10,423	6.3	11,076
(See Portland-Vancouver-Beaverton, OR-WA.)							
TOTAL: METRO PORTION OF STATE		21.5	5,153,165	5.4	5,430,735	6.0	5,758,618
TOTAL: MICRO PORTION OF STATE		17.4	525,262	5.4	553,404	6.2	587,597
TOTAL: WASHINGTON		21.1	5,894,121	5.3	6,204,912	5.9	6,572,249

WEST VIRGINIA

	FIPS CODE	PAST 1990-2000 % Change	PAST 2000 Census	PRESENT 2000-2004 % Change	PRESENT 7/1/04 Estimate	FUTURE 2004-2009 % Change	FUTURE 2009 Projection
Charleston WV	16620	0.6	309,635	-1.2	305,986	-1.4	301,761
Boone	54005	-1.3	25,535	1.3	25,875	1.7	26,313
Clay	54015	3.5	10,330	0.2	10,355	0.1	10,370
Kanawha	54039	-3.6	200,073	-3.0	194,003	-3.6	187,025
Lincoln	54043	3.4	22,108	0.8	22,291	0.8	22,478
Putnam	54079	20.4	51,589	3.6	53,462	4.0	55,575
Huntington-Ashland, WV-KY-OH	26580	0.2	288,649	-1.0	285,902	-1.1	282,807
Boyd, KY	21019	-2.7	49,752	-0.5	49,520	-0.3	49,349
Greenup, KY	21089	0.4	36,891	0.3	36,989	0.5	37,173
Lawrence, OH	39087	0.8	62,319	0.5	62,637	0.7	63,060
Cabell	54011	-0.0	96,784	-2.4	94,503	-2.9	91,807
Wayne	54099	3.0	42,903	-1.5	42,253	-2.0	41,418
Morgantown WV	34060	6.4	111,200	3.4	115,017	4.1	119,677
Monongalia	54061	8.4	81,866	4.0	85,180	4.7	89,191
Preston	54077	1.0	29,334	1.7	29,837	2.2	30,486
Parkersburg-Marietta, WV-OH	37620	1.7	164,624	-1.2	162,712	-1.4	160,479
Washington, OH	39167	1.6	63,251	-1.5	62,279	-1.8	61,151
Pleasants	54073	-0.4	7,514	0.2	7,526	0.3	7,547
Wirt	54105	13.1	5,873	-1.9	5,760	-2.6	5,610
Wood	54107	1.2	87,986	-1.0	87,147	-1.1	86,171
Weirton-Steubenville, WV-OH	48260	-7.4	132,008	-3.4	127,547	-3.9	122,519
Jefferson, OH	39081	-8.0	73,894	-3.5	71,299	-4.1	68,410
Brooke	54009	-5.7	25,447	-2.6	24,796	-2.9	24,079
Hancock	54029	-7.3	32,667	-3.7	31,452	-4.5	30,030
Wheeling, WV-OH	48540	-3.8	153,172	-2.4	149,538	-2.7	145,471
Belmont, OH	39013	-1.2	70,226	-1.1	69,474	-1.2	68,653
Marshall	54051	-4.9	35,519	-2.2	34,730	-2.4	33,892
Ohio	54069	-6.8	47,427	-4.4	45,334	-5.3	42,926
* **Jefferson**	54037	17.4	42,190	12.7	47,542	13.3	53,881
(See Washington-Arlington-Alexandria, DC-VA-MD-WV.)							
* **Mineral**	54057	1.4	27,078	0.4	27,182	0.6	27,346
(See Cumberland, MD-WV.)							
* **Berkeley**	54003	28.1	75,905	16.2	88,214	16.6	102,878
* **Morgan**	54065	23.2	14,943	4.9	15,680	5.3	16,504
(See Hagerstown-Martinsburg, MD-WV.)							
* **Hampshire**	54027	22.5	20,203	6.7	21,556	7.1	23,090
(See Winchester, VA-WV.)							
TOTAL: METRO PORTION OF STATE		3.4	983,274	1.2	994,678	1.4	1,008,617
TOTAL: MICRO PORTION OF STATE		0.2	364,478	-0.6	362,408	-0.6	360,081
TOTAL: WEST VIRGINIA		0.8	1,808,344	0.2	1,811,363	0.3	1,816,410

WISCONSIN

	FIPS CODE	PAST 1990-2000 % Change	PAST 2000 Census	PRESENT 2000-2004 % Change	PRESENT 7/1/04 Estimate	FUTURE 2004-2009 % Change	FUTURE 2009 Projection
Appleton WI	11540	15.3	201,602	5.9	213,551	6.5	227,337
Calumet	55015	18.5	40,631	9.0	44,268	10.0	48,693
Outagamie	55087	14.6	160,971	5.2	169,283	5.5	178,644
Eau Claire WI	20740	7.8	148,337	2.3	151,741	2.6	155,653
Chippewa	55017	5.4	55,195	3.7	57,253	4.2	59,651
Eau Claire	55035	9.3	93,142	1.4	94,488	1.6	96,002
Fond du Lac WI	22540	8.0	97,296	0.7	97,983	0.8	98,733
Fond du Lac	55039	8.0	97,296	0.7	97,983	0.8	98,733
Green Bay WI	24580	16.0	282,599	4.0	293,914	4.5	307,242
Brown	55009	16.5	226,778	4.1	236,097	4.7	247,140
Kewaunee	55061	6.9	20,187	1.7	20,539	2.0	20,956
Oconto	55083	17.9	35,634	4.6	37,278	5.0	39,146
Janesville WI	27500	9.2	152,307	2.1	155,545	2.4	159,300
Rock	55105	9.2	152,307	2.1	155,545	2.4	159,300
La Crosse, WI-MN	29100	9.0	126,838	1.8	129,119	2.0	131,755
Houston, MN	27055	6.6	19,718	1.7	20,056	1.9	20,435
La Crosse	55063	9.4	107,120	1.8	109,063	2.1	111,320
Madison WI	31540	16.1	501,774	6.5	534,379	7.1	572,553
Columbia	55021	16.4	52,468	4.0	54,563	4.5	56,996
Dane	55025	16.2	426,526	7.0	456,369	7.7	491,316
Iowa	55049	13.1	22,780	2.9	23,447	3.4	24,241
Milwaukee-Waukesha-West Allis WI	33340	4.8	1,500,741	1.2	1,518,392	1.3	1,538,818
Milwaukee	55079	-2.0	940,164	-1.0	931,139	-1.1	920,777
Ozaukee	55089	13.0	82,317	3.9	85,508	4.3	89,182
Washington	55131	23.3	117,493	5.3	123,666	5.8	130,790
Waukesha	55133	18.4	360,767	4.8	378,079	5.3	398,069
Oshkosh-Neenah WI	36780	11.7	156,763	1.4	158,990	1.5	161,437
Winnebago	55139	11.7	156,763	1.4	158,990	1.5	161,437
Racine WI	39540	7.9	188,831	2.4	193,383	2.8	198,874
Racine	55101	7.9	188,831	2.4	193,383	2.8	198,874
Sheboygan WI	43100	8.4	112,646	0.8	113,582	0.9	114,615
Sheboygan	55117	8.4	112,646	0.8	113,582	0.9	114,615
Wausau WI	48140	9.0	125,834	1.4	127,589	1.7	129,695
Marathon	55073	9.0	125,834	1.4	127,589	1.7	129,695
* **Kenosha**	55059	16.7	149,577	5.8	158,255	6.5	168,482
(See Chicago-Naperville-Joliet, IL-IN-WI.)							
* **Douglas**	55031	3.7	43,287	2.4	44,322	2.6	45,463
(See Duluth, MN-WI.)							
* **Pierce**	55093	12.3	36,804	3.8	38,196	4.2	39,816
* **St. Croix**	55109	25.7	63,155	16.6	73,654	17.0	86,144
(See Minneapolis-St. Paul-Bloomington, MN-WI.)							
TOTAL: METRO PORTION OF STATE		9.4	3,868,673	2.9	3,982,539	3.3	4,115,482
TOTAL: MICRO PORTION OF STATE		9.9	735,741	1.8	748,744	2.0	763,515
TOTAL: WISCONSIN		9.6	5,363,675	2.6	5,505,083	3.0	5,669,003

WYOMING

	FIPS CODE	PAST 1990-2000 % Change	PAST 2000 Census	PRESENT 2000-2004 % Change	PRESENT 7/1/04 Estimate	FUTURE 2004-2009 % Change	FUTURE 2009 Projection
Casper WY	16220	8.7	66,533	3.4	68,763	4.0	71,508
Natrona	56025	8.7	66,533	3.4	68,763	4.0	71,508
Cheyenne WY	16940	11.6	81,607	4.0	84,872	4.6	88,799
Laramie	56021	11.6	81,607	4.0	84,872	4.6	88,799
TOTAL: METRO PORTION OF STATE		10.2	148,140	3.7	153,635	4.3	160,307
TOTAL: MICRO PORTION OF STATE		9.5	203,682	1.8	207,379	2.1	211,782
TOTAL: WYOMING		8.9	493,782	2.0	503,630	2.4	515,570
TOTAL: METRO PORTION OF UNITED STATES		14.0	232,579,940	5.0	244,095,704	5.5	257,586,869
TOTAL: MICRO PORTION OF UNITED STATES		10.0	29,412,298	2.1	30,034,218	2.5	30,771,205
TOTAL: UNITED STATES		13.2	281,421,906	4.4	293,687,162	4.9	308,074,407

* Indicates county is included from metro in different state.
Source: Devonshire Associates Ltd. and Scan/US, Inc. 2004.

Metropolitan Core Based Statistical Areas: Population Trends

The following data are presented for metroplitan CBSAs (based on 2009 population projections): the CBSA FIPS Code, 1990-2000 percent of change in population; 2000 **actual** population; 2000-2004 estimated percent of change in population; 2004 **estimated** population; 2004-2009 projected percent of change in population; and 2009 **projected** population. CBSAs are ranked and listed in descending order according to their 2009 projected population figures. (A ranking of CBSAs according to their 2004 estimated population figures can be found on page 50.)

		PAST		PRESENT		FUTURE		
	FIPS CODE	1990-2000 % Change	2000 Census	2000-2004 % Change	7/1/04 Estimate	2004-2009 % Change	2009 Projection	2009 Rank
New York-Northern New Jersey-Long Island, NY-NJ-PA	35620	8.8	18,323,002	2.3	18,735,483	2.5	19,208,857	1
Los Angeles-Long Beach-Santa Ana, CA	31100	9.7	12,365,627	4.9	12,971,790	5.5	13,683,748	2
Chicago-Naperville-Joliet, IL-IN-WI	16980	11.2	9,098,316	3.4	9,405,026	3.8	9,762,099	3
Dallas-Fort Worth-Arlington, TX	19100	29.4	5,161,544	10.8	5,720,764	11.4	6,375,790	4
Philadelphia-Camden-Wilmington, PA-NJ-DE-MD	37980	4.6	5,687,147	2.0	5,799,622	2.3	5,933,466	5
Miami-Fort Lauderdale-Miami Beach, FL	33100	23.5	5,007,564	7.3	5,375,613	8.1	5,809,709	6
Houston-Baytown-Sugar Land, TX	26420	25.2	4,715,407	10.0	5,187,158	10.7	5,743,884	7
Washington-Arlington-Alexandria, DC-VA-MD-WV	47900	16.3	4,796,183	8.0	5,179,798	8.6	5,626,169	8
Atlanta-Sandy Springs-Marietta, GA	12060	38.4	4,247,981	11.1	4,719,358	11.6	5,265,848	9
Detroit-Warren-Livonia, MI	19820	4.8	4,452,557	0.9	4,492,464	1.0	4,535,875	10
Boston-Cambridge-Quincy, MA-NH	14460	6.2	4,391,344	1.4	4,452,771	1.4	4,516,835	11
Riverside-San Bernardino-Ontario, CA	40140	25.7	3,254,821	15.6	3,763,495	16.1	4,369,109	12
Phoenix-Mesa-Scottsdale, AZ	38060	45.3	3,251,876	13.7	3,698,598	14.2	4,224,395	13
San Francisco-Oakland-Fremont, CA	41860	11.9	4,123,740	1.0	4,164,518	0.9	4,201,638	14
Seattle-Tacoma-Bellevue, WA	42660	18.9	3,043,878	4.2	3,171,685	4.7	3,321,230	15
Minneapolis-St. Paul-Bloomington, MN-WI	33460	16.9	2,968,806	5.0	3,117,850	5.5	3,288,729	16
San Diego-Carlsbad-San Marcos, CA	41740	12.6	2,813,833	5.4	2,966,135	5.9	3,142,238	17
St. Louis, MO-IL	41180	4.6	2,698,687	1.8	2,747,415	2.1	2,805,346	18
Tampa-St. Petersburg-Clearwater, FL	45300	15.9	2,395,997	7.4	2,574,498	8.3	2,787,447	19
Baltimore-Towson, MD	12580	7.2	2,552,994	3.2	2,635,941	3.8	2,735,037	20
Denver-Aurora, CO	19740	30.7	2,157,756	8.3	2,337,049	7.7	2,516,629	21
Pittsburgh, PA	38300	-1.5	2,431,087	-1.1	2,404,027	-1.3	2,372,650	22
Sacramento--Arden-Arcade--Roseville, CA	40900	21.3	1,796,857	13.0	2,030,311	13.7	2,307,706	23
Portland-Vancouver-Beaverton, OR-WA	38900	26.5	1,927,881	7.6	2,075,083	8.4	2,249,134	24
Cleveland-Elyria-Mentor, OH	17460	2.2	2,148,143	-0.5	2,136,733	-0.6	2,123,339	25
Cincinnati-Middletown, OH-KY-IN	17140	8.9	2,009,632	2.4	2,058,374	2.7	2,114,029	26
Orlando, FL	36740	34.3	1,644,561	12.6	1,851,873	13.2	2,096,306	27
Kansas City, MO-KS	28140	12.2	1,836,038	4.9	1,925,595	5.3	2,028,351	28
San Antonio, TX	41700	21.6	1,711,703	8.3	1,854,472	9.1	2,023,104	29
Las Vegas-Paradise, NV	29820	85.5	1,375,765	19.0	1,637,622	18.6	1,942,707	30
Columbus, OH	18140	14.8	1,612,694	5.0	1,693,064	5.4	1,785,083	31
Virginia Beach-Norfolk-Newport News, VA-NC	47260	8.8	1,576,370	5.1	1,656,100	5.7	1,750,240	32
Indianapolis, IN	26900	17.8	1,525,104	6.0	1,616,900	6.7	1,724,443	33
San Jose-Sunnyvale-Santa Clara, CA	41940	13.1	1,735,819	-0.2	1,732,851	-0.5	1,723,487	34
Providence-New Bedford-Fall River, RI-MA	39300	4.8	1,582,997	3.3	1,635,332	3.7	1,696,113	35
Charlotte-Gastonia-Concord, NC-SC	16740	29.8	1,330,448	10.5	1,470,003	11.1	1,632,848	36
Austin-Round Rock, TX	12420	47.7	1,249,763	13.2	1,415,292	13.3	1,603,483	37
Milwaukee-Waukesha-West Allis, WI	33340	4.8	1,500,741	1.2	1,518,392	1.3	1,538,818	38
Nashville-Davidson--Murfreesboro, TN	34980	25.1	1,311,789	5.9	1,389,376	6.5	1,479,740	39
Jacksonville, FL	27260	21.4	1,122,750	9.4	1,228,504	10.4	1,356,521	40
New Orleans-Metairie-Kenner, LA	35380	4.1	1,316,510	0.1	1,318,235	0.3	1,322,126	41
Memphis, TN-MS-AR	32820	12.9	1,205,204	3.7	1,249,702	4.1	1,301,412	42
Louisville, KY-IN	31140	10.0	1,161,975	3.1	1,198,515	3.5	1,240,235	43
Hartford-West Hartford-East Hartford, CT	25540	2.2	1,148,618	3.3	1,186,956	3.8	1,232,061	44
Richmond, VA	40060	15.6	1,096,957	4.9	1,150,973	5.5	1,214,683	45
Oklahoma City, OK	36420	12.8	1,095,421	4.5	1,144,287	5.1	1,202,328	46
Buffalo-Niagara Falls, NY	15380	-1.6	1,170,111	-1.2	1,156,288	-1.4	1,140,627	47
Birmingham-Hoover, AL	13820	10.0	1,052,238	2.6	1,079,089	3.0	1,111,187	48
Salt Lake City, UT	41620	26.1	968,858	4.9	1,016,207	5.4	1,071,048	49
Rochester, NY	40380	3.5	1,037,831	0.4	1,042,130	0.4	1,046,777	50
Raleigh-Cary, NC	39580	47.3	797,071	14.3	911,301	14.7	1,045,338	51
Tucson, AZ	46060	26.5	843,746	7.6	907,511	8.1	981,041	52
Honolulu, HI	26180	4.8	876,156	4.1	911,719	4.9	956,800	53
Fresno, CA	23420	19.8	799,407	8.4	866,423	9.3	946,868	54
Bridgeport-Stamford-Norwalk, CT	14860	6.6	882,567	2.4	904,001	2.7	928,248	55
Tulsa, OK	46140	12.9	859,532	3.1	886,021	3.5	916,777	56
New Haven-Milford, CT	35300	2.5	824,008	2.9	847,502	3.3	875,645	57
Albany-Schenectady-Troy, NY	10580	2.0	825,875	2.4	845,300	2.8	868,571	58
Oxnard-Thousand Oaks-Ventura, CA	37100	12.6	753,197	6.6	802,627	7.2	860,068	59
Dayton, OH	19380	0.5	848,153	-0.3	845,439	-0.4	842,116	60
Omaha-Council Bluffs, NE-IA	36540	11.8	767,041	4.5	801,189	5.0	840,954	61
Albuquerque, NM	10740	21.7	729,649	6.3	775,936	7.1	831,100	62
Worcester, MA	49340	5.8	750,963	4.5	784,595	5.1	824,492	63
Allentown-Bethlehem-Easton, PA-NJ	10900	7.8	740,395	4.9	776,747	5.6	820,165	64
Bakersfield, CA	12540	21.7	661,645	10.3	729,553	11.3	811,845	65
Grand Rapids-Wyoming, MI	24340	14.6	740,482	3.8	768,430	4.2	800,347	66
Stockton, CA	44700	17.3	563,598	16.1	654,288	16.4	761,890	67
McAllen-Edinburg-Pharr, TX	32580	48.5	569,463	15.2	656,072	15.6	758,677	68
Baton Rouge, LA	12940	13.2	705,973	3.1	727,723	3.5	752,944	69
El Paso, TX	21340	14.9	679,622	5.0	713,340	5.5	752,812	70
Columbia, SC	17900	18.0	647,158	4.9	678,866	5.5	716,130	71
Sarasota-Bradenton-Venice, FL	42260	20.5	589,959	9.7	647,224	10.5	715,358	72
Poughkeepsie-Newburgh-Middletown, NY	39100	9.6	621,517	6.9	664,094	7.6	714,367	73
Akron, OH	10420	5.7	694,960	1.2	703,530	1.3	712,812	74
Springfield, MA	44140	1.0	680,014	1.6	691,167	1.9	704,493	75
Greensboro-High Point, NC	24660	19.1	643,430	3.7	666,943	4.1	693,996	76
Knoxville, TN	28940	15.2	616,079	4.4	643,341	5.0	675,728	77
Toledo, OH	45780	0.8	659,188	0.3	661,399	0.4	663,881	78
Syracuse, NY	45060	-1.5	650,154	0.8	655,449	1.0	661,715	79
Little Rock-North Little Rock, AR	30780	14.1	610,518	3.8	633,708	4.2	660,529	80
Colorado Springs, CO	17820	31.3	537,484	8.5	582,962	9.2	636,428	81
Charleston-North Charleston, SC	16700	8.3	549,033	5.4	578,716	6.1	614,123	82
Greenville, SC	24860	18.6	559,940	4.3	584,065	4.8	611,950	83
Wichita, KS	48620	11.7	571,166	2.7	586,332	3.0	603,817	84
Boise City-Nampa, ID	14260	45.4	464,840	12.9	524,915	13.4	595,013	85
Cape Coral-Fort Myers, FL	15980	31.6	440,888	15.3	508,350	15.9	589,051	86
Modesto, CA	33700	20.6	446,997	13.3	506,378	14.0	577,071	87
Youngstown-Warren-Boardman, OH-PA	49660	-1.7	602,964	-2.1	590,415	-2.5	575,927	88
Madison, WI	31540	16.1	501,774	6.5	534,379	7.1	572,553	89
Palm Bay-Melbourne-Titusville, FL	37340	19.4	476,230	8.1	515,004	9.0	561,468	90
Lakeland, FL	29460	19.4	483,924	7.2	518,809	8.0	560,565	91
Des Moines, IA	19780	15.6	481,394	5.8	509,323	6.4	541,966	92
Portland-South Portland-Biddeford, ME	38860	10.5	487,568	4.8	510,775	5.3	537,628	93
Scranton--Wilkes-Barre, PA	42540	-2.5	560,625	-2.0	549,692	-2.2	537,533	94
Augusta-Richmond County, GA-SC	12260	14.7	499,684	3.1	515,207	3.6	533,805	95
Harrisburg-Carlisle, PA	25420	7.3	509,074	2.2	520,152	2.6	533,463	96
Jackson, MS	27140	11.2	497,197	3.4	513,973	3.8	533,404	97
Ogden-Clearfield, UT	36260	25.8	442,656	7.7	476,951	8.4	516,972	98
Deltona-Daytona Beach-Ormond Beach, FL	19660	19.6	443,343	7.5	476,562	8.3	516,056	99
Lancaster, PA	29540	11.3	470,658	3.4	486,469	3.8	504,836	100
Chattanooga, TN-GA	16860	10.0	476,531	2.6	488,857	3.0	503,503	101
Durham, NC	20500	23.8	426,493	6.5	454,080	7.7	489,144	102
Santa Rosa-Petaluma, CA	42220	18.1	458,614	2.2	468,851	2.3	479,459	103
Lansing-East Lansing, MI	29620	3.5	447,728	2.4	458,301	2.7	470,587	104
Winston-Salem, NC	49180	16.7	421,961	4.8	442,297	5.4	466,017	105
Provo-Orem, UT	39340	39.9	376,774	10.4	416,085	11.1	462,240	106
Pensacola-Ferry Pass-Brent, FL	37860	19.7	412,153	5.4	434,387	6.2	461,432	107
Spokane, WA	44060	15.7	417,939	4.1	435,145	4.7	455,733	108
Flint, MI	22420	1.3	436,141	1.8	444,011	2.0	452,774	109
Lexington-Fayette, KY	30460	17.2	408,326	4.4	426,494	5.0	447,700	110
Vallejo-Fairfield, CA	46700	15.9	394,542	5.8	417,390	6.0	442,639	111
Salinas, CA	41500	13.0	401,762	4.1	418,251	4.5	437,244	112
Fayetteville-Springdale-Rogers, AR-MO	22220	44.9	347,045	11.7	387,515	12.2	434,846	113
Visalia-Porterville, CA	47300	18.0	368,021	8.2	398,103	9.2	434,646	114
Reno-Sparks, NV	39900	33.3	342,885	12.1	384,239	12.8	433,545	115
Manchester-Nashua, NH	31700	13.3	380,841	4.7	398,775	5.2	419,332	116
York-Hanover, PA	49620	12.4	381,751	4.5	398,969	5.1	419,155	117
Fort Wayne, IN	23060	10.1	390,156	3.2	402,608	3.6	417,041	118
Brownsville-Harlingen, TX	15180	28.9	335,227	10.9	371,857	11.8	415,655	119
Springfield, MO	44180	23.3	368,374	5.8	389,665	6.4	414,630	120
Corpus Christi, TX	18580	9.7	403,280	1.2	408,027	1.5	413,993	121
Santa Barbara-Santa Maria-Goleta, CA	42060	8.0	399,347	1.2	404,260	1.4	409,876	122
Canton-Massillon, OH	15940	3.3	406,934	0.1	407,161	0.0	407,290	123
Reading, PA	39740	11.0	373,638	4.1	388,909	4.6	406,841	124
Asheville, NC	11700	19.9	369,171	4.4	385,591	4.9	404,590	125
Port St. Lucie-Fort Pierce, FL	38940	27.2	319,426	12.0	357,906	13.0	404,587	126
Mobile, AL	33660	5.6	399,843	-0.1	399,635	-0.2	399,023	127
Salem, OR	41420	24.9	347,214	6.0	367,908	6.7	392,483	128
Huntsville, AL	26620	16.8	342,376	5.9	362,704	6.6	386,635	129
Trenton-Ewing, NJ	45940	7.7	350,761	4.2	365,448	4.7	382,782	130
Shreveport-Bossier City, LA	43340	4.5	375,965	0.8	379,073	1.0	382,708	131
Beaumont-Port Arthur, TX	13140	6.6	385,090	-0.8	381,930	-0.9	378,485	132
Anchorage, AK	11260	20.1	319,605	8.1	345,540	9.0	376,599	133
Davenport-Moline-Rock Island, IA-IL	19340	2.1	376,019	-0.4	374,674	-0.4	373,134	134
Ann Arbor, MI	11460	14.1	322,895	6.3	343,273	6.9	366,793	135
Killeen-Temple-Fort Hood, TX	28660	23.0	330,714	4.9	347,063	5.4	365,712	136
Peoria, IL	37900	2.3	366,899	-0.3	365,775	-0.3	364,660	137
Hickory-Lenoir-Morganton, NC	25860	16.9	341,851	3.1	352,521	3.4	364,417	138
Montgomery, AL	33860	13.6	346,528	2.3	354,386	2.6	363,600	139
Naples-Marco Island, FL	34940	65.3	251,377	18.3	297,488	18.2	351,759	140
Fayetteville, NC	22180	13.2	336,609	2.0	343,212	2.4	351,282	141
Evansville, IN-KY	21780	5.5	342,815	1.1	346,581	1.3	351,066	142
Rockford, IL	40420	12.9	320,204	4.3	334,044	4.9	350,295	143
Eugene-Springfield, OR	21660	14.2	322,959	3.1	332,896	3.6	344,731	144
Tallahassee, FL	45220	23.6	320,304	3.1	330,177	3.5	341,665	145
Kalamazoo-Portage, MI	28020	7.3	314,866	2.3	322,014	2.6	330,456	146
Wilmington, NC	48900	37.2	274,532	8.9	299,048	9.8	328,247	147
Savannah, GA	42340	13.5	293,000	5.1	307,995	6.0	326,328	148
Ocala, FL	36100	32.9	258,916	10.8	286,954	11.6	320,284	149
South Bend-Mishawaka, IN-MI	43780	6.8	316,663	0.4	317,967	0.4	319,124	150
Green Bay, WI	24580	16.0	282,599	4.0	293,914	4.5	307,242	151
Kingsport-Bristol-Bristol, TN-VA	28700	8.3	298,484	0.5	300,120	0.7	302,205	152
Charleston, WV	16620	0.6	309,635	-1.2	305,986	-1.4	301,761	153
Lincoln, NE	30700	16.5	266,787	5.3	280,966	5.8	297,349	154
Columbus, GA-AL	17980	5.7	281,768	2.5	288,724	2.8	296,937	155
Utica-Rome, NY	46540	-5.3	299,896	-0.8	297,571	-0.8	295,056	156
Roanoke, VA	40220	7.4	288,309	1.0	291,205	1.2	294,783	157
Fort Collins-Loveland, CO	22660	35.1	251,494	7.8	271,165	8.4	293,935	158
Boulder, CO	14500	29.3	291,288	-3.7	280,533	4.1	292,034	159
Fort Smith, AR-OK	22900	16.7	273,170	3.1	281,742	3.5	291,476	160
Atlantic City, NJ	12100	12.6	252,552	5.7	266,864	6.5	284,131	161
Huntington-Ashland, WV-KY-OH	26580	0.2	288,649	-1.0	285,902	-1.1	282,807	162
Erie, PA	21500	1.9	280,843	-0.4	279,718	-0.5	278,430	163
Duluth, MN-WI	20260	2.3	275,486	0.2	276,062	0.2	276,690	164
Spartanburg, SC	43900	11.9	253,791	3.9	263,575	4.3	275,036	165
Norwich-New London, CT	35980	1.6	259,088	2.5	265,499	2.8	273,047	166
Lubbock, TX	31180	8.6	249,700	4.0	259,602	4.7	271,678	167
Merced, CA	32900	18.0	210,554	13.1	238,219	13.9	271,433	168
Holland-Grand Haven, MI	26100	26.9	238,314	6.0	252,694	6.5	269,185	169
Greeley, CO	24540	37.3	180,936	22.0	220,667	21.3	267,629	170
Hagerstown-Martinsburg, MD-WV	25180	15.6	222,771	8.7	242,248	9.6	265,500	171
San Luis Obispo-Paso Robles, CA	42020	13.6	246,681	3.3	254,929	3.5	263,976	172
Bremerton-Silverdale, WA	14740	22.3	231,969	4.9	243,450	5.6	257,104	173
Lafayette, LA	29180	14.5	239,086	2.8	245,778	3.3	253,854	174
Gulfport-Biloxi, MS	25060	18.4	246,190	1.4	249,739	1.5	253,546	175
Cedar Rapids, IA	16300	12.6	237,230	3.0	244,390	3.3	252,543	176
Gainesville, FL	23540	21.5	232,392	3.8	241,335	4.4	251,953	177
Laredo, TX	29700	44.9	193,117	13.9	219,931	14.3	251,491	178
Binghamton, NY	13780	-4.6	252,320	-0.6	250,793	-0.6	249,233	179
Olympia, WA	36500	28.6	207,355	9.2	226,479	10.0	249,121	180
Amarillo, TX	11100	15.5	226,522	3.9	235,287	4.4	245,559	181
Clarksville, TN-KY	17300	22.6	232,000	2.6	238,045	2.9	244,887	182
Kennewick-Richland-Pasco, WA	28420	27.9	191,822	12.3	215,499	13.3	244,065	183
Santa Cruz-Watsonville, CA	42100	11.3	255,602	-2.1	250,198	-2.7	243,374	184
Barnstable Town, MA	12700	19.1	222,230	4.2	231,645	4.5	242,135	185
Myrtle Beach-Conway-North Myrtle Beach, SC	34820	36.5	196,629	9.3	214,999	9.9	236,202	186
Lynchburg, VA	31340	10.9	228,616	1.4	231,742	1.5	235,259	187
Yakima, WA	49420	17.9	222,581	2.5	228,066	2.9	234,762	188
Macon, GA	31420	7.6	222,368	2.2	227,227	2.6	233,241	189
Waco, TX	47380	12.9	213,517	3.9	221,739	4.4	231,389	190
Champaign-Urbana, IL	16580	3.7	210,275	4.4	219,572	5.1	230,816	191
Topeka, KS	45820	6.8	224,551	1.0	226,731	1.0	228,930	192
Appleton, WI	11540	15.3	201,602	5.9	213,551	6.5	227,337	193
Chico, CA	17020	11.6	203,171	5.0	213,422	5.6	225,471	194
Sioux Falls, SD	43620	21.9	187,093	7.8	201,734	8.2	218,369	195
Prescott, AZ	39140	55.5	167,517	13.2	189,588	13.6	215,355	196
Burlington-South Burlington, VT	15540	12.3	198,889	3.0	204,838	3.3	211,517	197
Springfield, IL	44100	6.3	201,437	2.0	205,434	2.3	210,247	198
Saginaw-Saginaw Township North, MI	40980	-0.9	210,039	-0.4	209,117	-0.5	208,059	199
College Station-Bryan, TX	17780	22.4	184,885	5.5	195,011	6.2	207,038	200
Medford, OR	32780	23.8	181,269	6.4	192,822	7.1	206,537	201
Longview, TX	30980	7.8	194,042	2.8	199,528	3.4	206,386	202
Houma-Bayou Cane-Thibodaux, LA	26380	6.4	194,477	2.0	198,351	2.4	203,111	203
Florence, SC	22500	9.6	193,155	2.1	197,296	2.5	202,319	204
Tyler, TX	46340	15.5	174,706	7.0	186,882	7.7	201,203	205
Elkhart-Goshen, IN	21140	17.0	182,791	4.2	190,535	4.6	199,304	206
Redding, CA	39820	11.0	163,256	10.0	179,590	11.0	199,281	207
Racine, WI	39540	7.9	188,831	2.4	193,383	2.8	198,874	208
Tuscaloosa, AL	46220	9.0	192,034	1.6	195,077	1.1	197,209	209
Las Cruces, NM	29740	28.9	174,682	5.7	184,554	6.5	196,459	210
Lafayette, IN	29140	12.4	178,541	4.4	186,417	5.0	195,813	211
Charlottesville, VA	16820	20.9	174,021	5.7	183,913	6.2	195,350	212
Johnson City, TN	27740	13.2	181,607	3.3	187,591	3.8	194,635	213
Bellingham, WA	13380	30.5	166,814	7.6	179,561	8.3	194,508	214
Lake Charles, LA	29340	9.1	193,568	0.0	193,633	0.1	193,773	215
Fort Walton Beach-Crestview-Destin, FL	23020	18.6	170,498	5.9	180,485	6.6	192,392	216
Yuma, AZ	49740	49.7	160,026	9.1	174,609	9.9	191,975	217
Rochester, MN	40340	15.3	163,618	7.0	175,153	7.7	188,610	218
Fargo, ND-MN	22020	13.7	174,367	3.6	180,577	3.9	187,692	219
Kingston, NY	28740	7.5	177,749	2.5	182,183	2.9	187,546	220
Gainesville, GA	23580	45.9	139,277	15.7	161,175	15.7	186,542	221
St. Cloud, MN	41060	12.4	167,392	5.2	176,070	5.7	186,043	222
Bloomington, IN	14020	12.0	175,506	2.6	180,031	2.9	185,301	223
Athens-Clarke County, GA	12020	22.1	166,079	4.8	174,053	5.2	183,151	224
Anderson, SC	11340	14.1	165,740	4.5	173,238	5.0	181,872	225
Muskegon-Norton Shores, MI	34740	7.1	170,200	2.2	173,945	2.4	178,202	226
Punta Gorda, FL	39460	27.6	141,627	10.9	157,100	11.8	175,640	227
Monroe, LA	33740	4.4	170,053	0.6	171,146	0.8	172,510	228
Joplin, MO	27900	16.6	157,322	4.0	163,621	4.5	170,964	229
Greenville, NC	24780	23.9	152,772	5.1	160,525	5.7	169,748	230
Jackson, MI	27100	5.8	158,422	3.2	163,516	3.6	169,477	231
Panama City-Lynn Haven, FL	37460	16.7	148,217	6.3	157,510	7.4	169,093	232
Bloomington-Normal, IL	14060	16.5	150,433	5.6	158,878	6.3	168,862	233
Albany, GA	10500	7.7	157,833	2.8	162,223	3.5	167,822	234
Terre Haute, IN	45460	2.6	170,943	-0.9	169,396	-1.0	167,668	235
Yuba City, CA	49700	13.5	139,149	8.5	151,010	9.5	165,375	236
Niles-Benton Harbor, MI	35660	0.7	162,453	0.2	162,816	0.1	163,051	237
El Centro, CA	20940	30.2	142,361	6.4	151,466	7.4	162,630	238
Pueblo, CO	39380	15.0	141,472	6.8	151,054	7.6	162,566	239
Oshkosh-Neenah, WI	36780	11.7	156,763	1.4	158,990	1.5	161,437	240
Columbia, MO	17860	19.4	145,666	4.9	152,833	5.6	161,317	241
Pascagoula, MS	37700	14.1	150,564	3.2	155,413	3.4	160,766	242
Parkersburg-Marietta, WV-OH	37620	1.7	164,624	-1.2	162,712	-1.4	160,479	243
Janesville, WI	27500	9.2	152,307	2.1	155,545	2.4	159,300	244
Waterloo-Cedar Falls, IA	47940	3.2	163,706	-1.3	161,643	-1.5	159,197	245
Monroe, MI	33780	9.2	145,945	4.2	152,069	4.6	159,036	246
Hanford-Corcoran, CA	25260	27.6	129,461	9.3	141,461	10.2	155,937	247
Eau Claire, WI	20740	7.8	148,337	2.3	151,741	2.6	155,653	248
Abilene, TX	10180	8.3	160,245	-1.4	157,948	-1.7	155,289	249
Bend, OR	13460	53.9	115,367	16.0	133,790	16.1	155,277	250
Vineland-Millville-Bridgeton, NJ	47220	6.1	146,438	2.6	150,283	3.3	155,170	251
Blacksburg-Christiansburg-Radford, VA	13980	7.5	151,272	1.1	153,009	1.4	155,084	252
Madera, CA	31460	39.8	123,109	11.1	136,739	12.0	153,112	253
State College, PA	44300	9.7	135,758	5.7	143,518	6.5	152,895	254
Bangor, ME	12620	-1.1	144,919	1.9	147,681	2.4	151,173	255
Billings, MT	13740	14.3	138,904	3.8	144,234	4.4	150,517	256
Santa Fe, NM	42140	30.7	129,292	7.2	138,622	7.9	149,581	257
Decatur, AL	19460	10.9	145,867	1.2	147,582	1.3	149,459	258
Dover, DE	20100	14.1	126,697	8.0	136,821	8.9	148,978	259
Alexandria, LA	10780	-2.7	145,035	1.1	146,661	1.3	148,528	260
Rocky Mount, NC	40580	7.3	143,026	1.5	145,152	1.8	147,778	261
Jefferson City, MO	27620	16.0	140,052	2.5	143,594	2.8	147,649	262
Burlington, NC	15500	20.9	130,800	5.9	138,548	6.4	147,422	263
Iowa City, IA	26980	13.8	131,676	5.1	138,449	5.7	146,341	264
Wichita Falls, TX	48660	7.9	151,524	-1.6	149,063	-1.9	146,159	265
Napa, CA	34900	12.2	124,279	7.8	133,946	8.7	145,637	266
Wheeling, WV-OH	48540	-3.8	153,172	-2.4	149,538	-2.7	145,471	267
Johnstown, PA	27780	-6.4	152,598	-2.7	148,535	-3.1	143,998	268
Sioux City, IA-NE-SD	43580	8.9	143,053	-0.2	142,792	-0.3	142,427	269
Jacksonville, NC	27340	0.3	150,355	-2.5	146,634	-3.0	142,265	270
Springfield, OH	44220	-1.9	144,742	-1.3	142,925	-1.5	140,785	271
Battle Creek, MI	12980	1.5	137,985	0.8	139,106	0.9	140,354	272
Dalton, GA	19140	21.7	120,031	7.8	129,405	8.2	140,030	273
Grand Junction, CO	24300	24.8	116,255	9.3	127,075	9.4	139,069	274
Warner Robins, GA	47580	24.2	110,765	11.5	123,475	12.3	138,676	275
Florence-Muscle Shoals, AL	22520	8.9	142,950	-1.4	141,000	-1.8	138,513	276
Farmington, NM	22140	24.2	113,801	9.8	124,961	10.7	138,374	277
Dothan, AL	20020	8.7	130,861	2.5	134,089	2.8	137,845	278
Hattiesburg, MS	25620	13.0	123,812	5.1	130,073	5.5	137,254	279
Texarkana, TX-Texarkana, AR	45500	8.0	129,749	1.9	132,208	2.3	135,265	280
Vero Beach, FL	46940	25.2	112,947	8.7	122,827	9.6	134,647	281
Morristown, TN	34100	22.4	123,081	4.4	128,445	4.8	134,591	282
Coeur d'Alene, ID	17660	55.7	108,685	10.5	120,129	11.0	133,350	283
La Crosse, WI-MN	29100	9.0	126,838	1.8	129,119	2.0	131,755	284
Glens Falls, NY	24020	4.9	124,345	2.4	127,334	2.9	131,063	285
Flagstaff, AZ	22380	20.4	116,320	5.6	122,854	6.3	130,614	286
Pittsfield, MA	38340	-3.2	134,953	-1.6	132,813	-1.9	130,354	287
St. George, UT	41100	86.1	90,354	20.0	108,436	19.8	129,952	288
Wausau, WI	48140	9.0	125,834	1.4	127,589	1.7	129,695	289
Auburn-Opelika, AL	12220	32.1	115,092	5.1	120,927	5.6	127,735	290
Valdosta, GA	46660	20.5	119,560	2.9	123,021	3.4	127,228	291
Mansfield, OH	31900	2.2	128,852	-0.6	128,091	-0.7	127,188	292
Lebanon, PA	30140	5.8	120,327	2.5	123,395	3.0	127,083	293
Anderson, IN	11300	2.1	133,358	-2.2	130,409	-2.7	126,901	294
Odessa, TX	36220	1.8	121,123	1.8	123,354	2.7	126,654	295
Midland, TX	33260	8.8	116,009	3.1	119,655	4.3	124,798	296
Rapid City, SD	39660	9.3	112,818	4.4	117,781	5.0	123,618	297
Winchester, VA-WV	49020	22.4	102,997	9.2	112,471	9.9	123,579	298
Altoona, PA	11020	-1.1	129,144	-2.0	126,555	-2.4	123,474	299
Sherman-Denison, TX	43300	16.4	110,595	5.4	116,532	5.9	123,419	300
Weirton-Steubenville, WV-OH	48260	-7.4	132,008	-3.4	127,547	-3.9	122,519	301
St. Joseph, MO-KS	41140	5.6	122,336	0.2	122,599	-1.4	120,925	302
Mount Vernon-Anacortes, WA	34580	29.4	102,979	7.9	111,156	8.6	120,767	303
Morgantown, WV	34060	6.4	111,200	3.4	115,017	4.1	119,677	304

* Indicates county is included from metro in different state.
Source: Devonshire Associates Ltd. and Scan/US, Inc. 2004.

continued on next page

Metropolitan Core Based Statistical Areas: Population Trends, *Continued*

	FIPS CODE	PAST		PRESENT		FUTURE		2009 Rank
		1990-2000 % Change	2000 Census	2000-2004 % Change	7/1/04 Estimate	2004-2009 % Change	2009 Projection	
Salisbury, MD	41540	11.9	109,391	4.1	113,889	4.7	119,202	305
Idaho Falls, ID	26820	14.6	101,677	7.1	108,893	7.8	117,341	306
Logan, UT-ID	30860	29.3	102,720	6.1	109,025	6.8	116,458	307
Victoria, TX	47020	12.3	111,663	1.6	113,403	1.9	115,590	308
Williamsport, PA	48700	1.1	120,044	-1.8	117,940	-2.1	115,459	309
Harrisonburg, VA	25500	22.7	108,193	2.9	111,322	3.5	115,255	310
Muncie, IN	34620	-0.7	118,769	-1.4	117,094	-1.7	115,140	311
Sheboygan, WI	43100	8.4	112,646	0.8	113,582	0.9	114,615	312
Jackson, TN	27180	18.3	107,377	2.8	110,436	3.3	114,042	313
Bowling Green, KY	14540	19.7	104,166	4.4	108,712	4.9	114,026	314
Jonesboro, AR	27860	15.1	107,762	2.7	110,679	2.8	113,827	315
Anniston-Oxford, AL	11500	-3.3	112,249	-0.0	112,234	1.0	113,328	316
Elizabethtown, KY	21060	6.6	107,547	2.3	110,057	2.6	112,888	317
Goldsboro, NC	24140	8.3	113,329	-0.3	113,028	-0.3	112,648	318
Lawton, OK	30020	3.1	114,996	-1.2	113,664	-1.0	112,529	319
Owensboro, KY	36980	5.0	109,875	1.1	111,124	1.2	112,512	320
Ithaca, NY	27060	2.6	96,501	6.7	102,983	7.6	110,842	321
Cleveland, TN	17420	19.1	104,015	3.0	107,156	3.4	110,762	322
Lewiston-Auburn, ME	30340	-1.4	103,793	3.0	106,865	3.5	110,613	323
Michigan City-La Porte, IN	33140	2.8	110,106	-0.3	109,775	-0.5	109,259	324
Kankakee-Bradley, IL	28100	7.9	103,833	2.3	106,207	2.7	109,106	325
Lawrence, KS	29940	22.2	99,962	3.9	103,909	4.4	108,485	326
Sumter, SC	44940	2.0	104,646	1.6	106,361	1.9	108,382	327
Bay City, MI	13020	-1.4	110,157	-0.8	109,229	-1.0	108,107	328
Lima, OH	30620	-1.2	108,473	-0.3	108,137	-0.5	107,596	329
Wenatchee, WA	48300	26.5	99,219	3.3	102,502	3.8	106,382	330
Danville, VA	19260	1.3	110,156	-1.8	108,169	-2.1	105,930	331
Decatur, IL	19500	-2.1	114,706	-4.0	110,093	-4.8	104,829	332
San Angelo, TX	41660	5.7	105,781	-0.6	105,120	-0.7	104,370	333
Missoula, MT	33540	21.8	95,802	3.8	99,453	4.2	103,582	334
Pine Bluff, AR	38220	0.4	107,341	-1.6	105,584	-2.0	103,504	335
Gadsden, AL	23460	3.6	103,459	-0.5	102,945	-0.4	102,482	336
Brunswick, GA	15260	13.2	93,044	4.6	97,306	5.2	102,361	337
Ocean City, NJ	36140	7.6	102,326	-0.6	101,693	-0.7	100,939	338
Kokomo, IN	29020	4.7	101,541	-0.3	101,227	-0.4	100,848	339
Bismarck, ND	13900	13.0	94,719	2.9	97,478	3.2	100,607	340
Longview, WA	31020	13.2	92,948	3.1	95,850	3.7	99,372	341
Cumberland, MD-WV	19060	0.4	102,008	-1.5	100,473	-1.7	98,767	342
Fond du Lac, WI	22540	8.0	97,296	0.7	97,983	0.8	98,733	343
Rome, GA	40660	11.5	90,565	4.0	94,225	4.5	98,508	344
Hot Springs, AR	26300	20.0	88,068	4.6	92,118	5.0	96,731	345
Grand Forks, ND-MN	24220	-5.5	97,478	-2.4	95,100	-2.9	92,367	346
Fairbanks, AK	21820	6.6	82,840	5.1	87,045	6.1	92,333	347
Dubuque, IA	20220	3.2	89,143	1.3	90,309	1.4	91,581	348
Elmira, NY	21300	-4.3	91,070	-0.9	90,205	-1.1	89,168	349
Cheyenne, WY	16940	11.6	81,607	4.0	84,872	4.6	88,799	350
Ames, IA	11180	7.7	79,981	5.0	83,964	5.6	88,649	351
Pocatello, ID	38540	13.7	83,103	-0.2	82,971	-0.2	82,806	352
Corvallis, OR	18700	10.4	78,153	2.0	79,726	2.5	81,681	353
Danville, IL	19180	-4.9	83,919	-1.7	82,467	-2.0	80,800	354
Great Falls, MT	24500	3.4	80,357	-1.3	79,349	-1.4	78,254	355
Sandusky, OH	41780	3.6	79,551	-1.4	78,417	-1.9	76,958	356
Columbus, IN	18020	12.2	71,435	1.6	72,553	1.5	73,612	357
Casper, WY	16220	8.7	66,533	3.4	68,763	4.0	71,508	358
Hinesville-Fort Stewart, GA	25980	22.0	71,914	-4.0	69,055	-4.5	65,959	359
Carson City, NV	16180	29.7	52,457	7.2	56,233	8.2	60,837	360
Lewiston, ID-WA	30300	12.9	57,961	0.8	58,451	1.1	59,079	361

Source: Devonshire Associates Ltd. and Scan/US, Inc. 2004.

Counties: Population Trends

Counties are arranged by state. The following data are provided for each county: the State-County FIPS Code, 2000-2004 estimated percent of change in population; 2004 estimated population; 2004-2009 projected percent of change in population; and 2009 projected population. Included are Ranally Population Units (RPUs) indicating how each county's population relates to the total population of the United States (due to the rounding of county RPUs, slight differences may occur between the state RPU totals shown and actual totals).

	FIPS CODE	PRESENT 2000-2004 % Change	PRESENT 7/1/04 Estimate	7/1/04 Ranally Population Units	FUTURE 2004-2009 % Change	FUTURE 2009 Projection	2009 Ranally Population Units
ALABAMA							
Autauga*	01001	8.4	47,354	**161**	9.1	51,660	**168**
Baldwin**	01003	10.6	155,304	**529**	11.2	172,642	**560**
Barbour**	01005	-1.0	28,740	**98**	-1.3	28,360	**92**
Bibb*	01007	3.9	21,630	**74**	9.8	23,744	**77**
Blount*	01009	8.0	55,111	**188**	8.8	59,975	**195**
Bullock	01011	-4.0	11,248	**38**	-3.9	10,804	**35**
Butler	01013	-4.3	20,485	**70**	-5.0	19,469	**63**
Calhoun*	01015	-0.0	112,234	**382**	1.0	113,328	**368**
Chambers**	01017	-3.0	35,478	**121**	-3.8	34,141	**111**
Cherokee	01019	2.4	24,553	**84**	2.5	25,173	**82**
Chilton*	01021	4.1	41,236	**140**	4.3	43,021	**140**
Choctaw	01023	-5.2	15,094	**51**	-6.1	14,176	**46**
Clarke	01025	-1.8	27,370	**93**	-2.1	26,789	**87**
Clay	01027	-0.7	14,155	**48**	-1.0	14,020	**46**
Cleburne	01029	5.1	14,843	**51**	5.6	15,679	**51**
Coffee**	01031	3.1	44,984	**153**	4.0	46,771	**152**
Colbert*	01033	-1.1	54,367	**185**	-1.5	53,547	**174**
Conecuh	01035	-4.6	13,437	**46**	-5.5	12,702	**41**
Coosa**	01037	-6.8	11,376	**39**	-5.3	10,771	**35**
Covington	01039	-2.3	36,748	**125**	-2.6	35,798	**116**
Crenshaw	01041	-0.9	13,540	**46**	-1.4	13,346	**43**
Cullman**	01043	1.3	78,501	**267**	1.5	79,648	**259**
Dale**	01045	0.5	49,358	**168**	0.6	49,650	**161**
Dallas**	01047	-3.9	44,568	**152**	-4.5	42,576	**138**
DeKalb**	01049	4.1	67,072	**228**	4.5	70,076	**227**
Elmore*	01051	9.6	72,168	**246**	10.2	79,543	**258**
Escambia	01053	-0.9	38,101	**130**	-1.0	37,708	**122**
Etowah*	01055	-0.5	102,945	**351**	-0.4	102,482	**333**
Fayette	01057	-1.8	18,166	**62**	-2.1	17,789	**58**
Franklin	01059	-1.8	30,662	**104**	-2.3	29,972	**97**
Geneva*	01061	-1.5	25,387	**86**	-2.0	24,879	**81**
Greene*	01063	-1.0	9,879	**34**	-1.1	9,775	**32**
Hale*	01065	6.5	18,295	**62**	-0.1	18,268	**59**
Henry*	01067	1.0	16,468	**56**	0.9	16,621	**54**
Houston*	01069	3.9	92,234	**314**	4.5	96,345	**313**
Jackson**	01071	-0.4	53,727	**183**	-0.7	53,349	**173**
Jefferson*	01073	-0.8	656,840	**2,237**	-1.0	650,292	**2,111**
Lamar	01075	-6.3	14,899	**51**	-7.9	13,722	**45**
Lauderdale*	01077	-1.5	86,633	**295**	-1.9	84,966	**276**
Lawrence*	01079	-0.9	34,504	**117**	-1.3	34,058	**111**
Lee*	01081	5.1	120,927	**412**	5.6	127,735	**415**
Limestone*	01083	5.1	69,013	**235**	5.5	72,841	**236**
Lowndes*	01085	-1.0	13,339	**45**	-1.3	13,160	**43**
Macon**	01087	-3.6	23,242	**79**	-4.3	22,235	**72**
Madison*	01089	6.1	293,691	**1,000**	6.8	313,794	**1,019**
Marengo	01091	-1.2	22,269	**76**	-1.6	21,914	**71**
Marion	01093	-4.3	29,862	**102**	-5.2	28,310	**92**
Marshall**	01095	2.3	84,160	**287**	2.7	86,461	**281**
Mobile*	01097	-0.1	399,635	**1,361**	-0.2	399,023	**1,295**
Monroe	01099	-2.4	23,740	**81**	-2.7	23,094	**75**
Montgomery*	01101	-0.9	221,525	**754**	-1.0	219,237	**712**
Morgan*	01103	1.8	113,078	**385**	2.1	115,401	**375**
Perry	01105	-1.6	11,668	**40**	-1.6	11,483	**37**
Pickens	01107	-2.5	20,420	**70**	-3.0	19,803	**64**
Pike**	01109	-1.6	29,126	**99**	-2.5	28,386	**92**
Randolph	01111	-0.7	22,223	**76**	-1.1	21,975	**71**
Russell*	01113	-2.0	48,750	**166**	-2.4	47,582	**154**
St. Clair*	01115	7.9	69,841	**238**	8.4	75,736	**246**
Shelby*	01117	14.7	164,416	**560**	15.1	189,240	**614**
Sumter	01119	-5.4	13,999	**48**	-6.3	13,113	**43**
Talladega**	01121	-0.7	79,784	**272**	-0.9	79,061	**257**
Tallapoosa**	01123	-2.5	40,456	**138**	-3.7	38,945	**126**
Tuscaloosa*	01125	1.2	166,903	**568**	1.4	169,166	**549**
Walker*	01127	-1.0	70,015	**238**	-1.2	69,179	**225**
Washington	01129	-1.6	17,804	**61**	-2.1	17,425	**57**
Wilcox	01131	-1.2	13,030	**44**	0.2	13,059	**42**
Winston	01133	-1.3	24,526	**84**	-1.9	24,061	**78**
TOTAL: ALABAMA		**1.6**	**4,517,136**	**15,384**	**1.8**	**4,599,054**	**14,931**
ALASKA (Boroughs and Census Areas)							
Aleutians East	02013	-1.9	2,646	**9**	-1.9	2,595	**8**
Aleutians West	02016	-5.3	5,176	**18**	-6.2	4,856	**16**
Anchorage*	02020	5.4	274,398	**934**	6.2	291,471	**946**
Bethel	02050	7.0	17,133	**58**	7.5	18,423	**60**
Bristol Bay	02060	-15.9	1,058	**4**	-17.4	874	**3**
Denali	02068	-1.5	1,864	**6**	-2.2	1,823	**6**
Dillingham	02070	0.2	4,934	**17**	0.0	4,934	**16**
Fairbanks North Star*	02090	5.1	87,045	**296**	6.1	92,333	**300**
Haines	02100	-5.4	2,263	**8**	-7.1	2,103	**7**
Juneau**	02110	2.1	31,357	**107**	2.6	32,185	**104**
Kenai Peninsula	02122	3.9	51,635	**176**	4.7	54,051	**175**
Ketchikan Gateway**	02130	-6.9	13,105	**45**	-7.8	12,077	**39**
Kodiak Island**	02150	-4.9	13,234	**45**	-6.7	12,341	**40**
Lake and Peninsula	02164	-19.1	1,474	**5**	-22.5	1,143	**4**
Matanuska-Susitna*	02170	19.9	71,142	**242**	19.7	85,128	**276**
Nome	02180	-0.4	9,158	**31**	-0.2	9,137	**30**
North Slope	02185	-3.0	7,165	**24**	-3.7	6,903	**22**
Northwest Arctic	02188	3.0	7,425	**25**	3.5	7,686	**25**
Prince of Wales-Outer Ketchikan	02201	-7.2	5,703	**19**	-8.9	5,196	**17**
Sitka	02220	0.6	8,888	**30**	0.7	8,947	**29**
Skagway-Hoonah-Angoon	02232	-12.0	3,024	**10**	-14.7	2,579	**8**
Southeast Fairbanks	02240	-7.2	5,727	**20**	-9.0	5,210	**17**
Valdez-Cordova	02261	-3.6	9,831	**33**	-5.0	9,336	**30**
Wade Hampton	02270	5.4	7,404	**25**	6.1	7,854	**25**
Wrangell-Petersburg	02280	-7.7	6,170	**21**	-9.6	5,575	**18**
Yakutat	02282	-15.5	683	**2**	-17.9	561	**2**
Yukon-Koyukuk	02290	-4.5	6,257	**21**	-4.4	5,981	**19**
TOTAL: ALASKA		**4.6**	**655,899**	**2,231**	**5.4**	**691,302**	**2,242**
ARIZONA							
Apache	04001	-2.4	67,789	**231**	-2.5	66,115	**215**
Cochise**	04003	4.9	123,522	**421**	5.5	130,326	**423**
Coconino*	04005	5.6	122,854	**418**	6.3	130,614	**424**
Gila**	04007	0.3	51,475	**175**	0.3	51,605	**168**
Graham**	04009	-1.7	32,905	**112**	-2.2	32,184	**104**
Greenlee**	04011	-15.7	7,202	**25**	-19.3	5,814	**19**
La Paz	04012	-1.2	19,470	**66**	-1.2	19,237	**62**
Maricopa*	04013	13.5	3,486,879	**11,873**	14.0	3,974,832	**12,902**
Mohave**	04015	13.8	176,406	**601**	14.3	201,594	**654**
Navajo	04017	9.2	106,398	**362**	10.0	116,986	**380**
Pima*	04019	7.6	907,511	**3,090**	8.1	981,041	**3,184**
Pinal*	04021	17.8	211,719	**721**	17.9	249,563	**810**
Santa Cruz**	04023	6.4	40,833	**139**	6.9	43,662	**142**
Yavapai*	04025	13.2	189,588	**646**	13.6	215,355	**699**
Yuma*	04027	9.1	174,609	**595**	9.9	191,975	**623**
TOTAL: ARIZONA		**11.5**	**5,719,160**	**19,475**	**12.1**	**6,410,903**	**20,809**
ARKANSAS							
Arkansas	05001	-3.6	19,992	**68**	-4.1	19,174	**62**
Ashley	05003	-3.4	23,384	**80**	-4.2	22,402	**73**
Baxter**	05005	2.5	39,329	**134**	2.7	40,392	**131**
Benton*	05007	15.9	177,727	**605**	16.1	206,263	**670**
Boone**	05009	3.0	34,966	**119**	3.2	36,080	**117**
Bradley	05011	-2.0	12,352	**42**	-2.5	12,041	**39**
Calhoun**	05013	-2.7	5,591	**19**	-3.1	5,418	**18**
Carroll	05015	5.2	26,672	**91**	5.8	28,223	**92**
Chicot	05017	-5.9	13,288	**45**	-7.1	12,345	**40**
Clark**	05019	0.3	23,605	**80**	0.5	23,712	**77**
Clay	05021	-5.1	16,705	**57**	-6.0	15,704	**51**
Cleburne	05023	3.7	24,927	**85**	4.0	25,935	**84**
Cleveland*	05025	2.2	8,761	**30**	2.9	9,017	**29**
Columbia**	05027	-2.9	24,856	**85**	-3.5	23,975	**78**
Conway	05029	1.0	20,534	**70**	1.1	20,768	**67**
Craighead*	05031	3.9	85,334	**291**	4.1	88,843	**288**
Crawford*	05033	5.9	56,398	**192**	6.6	60,126	**195**
Crittenden*	05035	0.7	51,207	**174**	0.5	51,447	**167**
Cross	05037	-2.1	19,109	**65**	-2.5	18,636	**60**
Dallas	05039	-7.0	8,563	**29**	-8.1	7,869	**26**
Desha	05041	-6.1	14,398	**49**	-7.5	13,322	**43**
Drew	05043	-1.8	18,389	**63**	-2.1	17,994	**58**
Faulkner*	05045	9.2	93,944	**320**	10.0	103,323	**335**
Franklin*	05047	1.8	18,093	**62**	2.4	18,534	**60**
Fulton	05049	-0.2	11,621	**40**	-0.5	11,564	**38**
Garland*	05051	4.6	92,118	**314**	5.0	96,731	**314**
Grant*	05053	3.7	17,074	**58**	4.1	17,774	**58**
Greene**	05055	3.5	38,632	**132**	3.6	40,011	**130**
Hempstead**	05057	-0.9	23,381	**80**	-1.1	23,134	**75**
Hot Spring	05059	1.4	30,772	**105**	1.6	31,252	**101**
Howard	05061	1.6	14,526	**49**	2.2	14,845	**48**
Independence**	05063	0.7	34,469	**117**	0.6	34,669	**113**
Izard	05065	-0.6	13,176	**45**	-1.0	13,046	**42**
Jackson	05067	-6.9	17,148	**58**	-8.2	15,743	**51**
Jefferson*	05069	-2.2	82,445	**281**	-2.7	80,235	**260**
Johnson	05071	4.7	23,857	**81**	5.5	25,172	**82**
Lafayette	05073	-3.8	8,234	**28**	-4.6	7,857	**26**
Lawrence	05075	-1.5	17,509	**60**	-1.3	17,286	**56**
Lee	05077	-7.5	11,639	**40**	-8.8	10,609	**34**
Lincoln*	05079	-0.8	14,378	**49**	-0.9	14,252	**46**
Little River	05081	-2.6	13,269	**45**	-3.3	12,832	**42**
Logan	05083	1.9	22,906	**78**	2.1	23,387	**76**
Lonoke*	05085	9.6	57,901	**197**	10.2	63,789	**207**
Madison*	05087	0.9	14,374	**49**	0.7	14,468	**47**
Marion	05089	1.1	16,320	**56**	1.1	16,497	**54**
Miller*	05091	4.8	42,371	**144**	5.6	44,746	**145**
Mississippi**	05093	-7.4	48,138	**164**	-8.9	43,854	**142**
Monroe	05095	-7.8	9,457	**32**	-8.8	8,621	**28**
Montgomery	05097	-1.9	9,066	**31**	-3.0	8,793	**29**
Nevada**	05099	-4.1	9,545	**33**	-4.8	9,085	**29**
Newton**	05101	-1.1	8,510	**29**	-1.9	8,347	**27**
Ouachita**	05103	-4.9	27,369	**93**	-5.8	25,777	**84**
Perry*	05105	3.2	10,533	**36**	3.4	10,889	**35**
Phillips**	05107	-8.9	24,091	**82**	-10.3	21,599	**70**
Pike	05109	-2.2	11,055	**38**	-3.0	10,722	**35**
Poinsett*	05111	-1.1	25,345	**86**	-1.4	24,984	**81**
Polk	05113	-0.1	20,206	**69**	-0.5	20,106	**65**
Pope**	05115	1.7	55,417	**189**	2.1	56,557	**184**
Prairie	05117	-2.6	9,289	**32**	-2.9	9,020	**29**
Pulaski*	05119	1.1	365,501	**1,245**	1.2	370,029	**1,201**
Randolph	05121	-0.1	18,169	**62**	-0.1	18,152	**59**
St. Francis**	05123	-3.6	28,264	**96**	-4.4	27,022	**88**
Saline*	05125	6.3	88,755	**302**	6.7	94,725	**307**
Scott	05127	-0.4	10,947	**37**	-0.8	10,864	**35**
Searcy	05129	-4.7	7,876	**27**	-6.0	7,402	**24**
Sebastian*	05131	2.4	117,824	**401**	2.4	120,635	**392**
Sevier	05133	0.9	15,895	**54**	1.1	16,075	**52**
Sharp	05135	2.5	17,554	**60**	2.6	18,012	**58**
Stone	05137	1.4	11,665	**40**	1.4	11,826	**38**
Union**	05139	-2.3	44,583	**152**	-2.8	43,352	**141**
Van Buren	05141	1.2	16,389	**56**	1.2	16,590	**54**
Washington*	05143	9.9	173,341	**590**	10.5	191,547	**622**
White**	05145	5.5	70,832	**241**	6.0	75,058	**244**
Woodruff	05147	-7.3	8,099	**28**	-8.6	7,406	**24**
Yell**	05149	2.0	21,552	**73**	2.1	22,007	**71**
TOTAL: ARKANSAS		**2.5**	**2,741,511**	**9,339**	**2.9**	**2,820,498**	**9,153**
CALIFORNIA							
Alameda*	06001	1.4	1,464,561	**4,987**	1.2	1,482,152	**4,811**
Alpine	06003	0.2	1,210	**4**	0.2	1,213	**4**
Amador	06005	8.2	37,967	**129**	9.1	41,435	**134**
Butte*	06007	5.0	213,422	**727**	5.6	225,471	**732**
Calaveras	06009	12.9	45,803	**156**	13.9	52,149	**169**
Colusa	06011	6.1	19,958	**68**	7.0	21,358	**69**
Contra Costa*	06013	7.2	1,016,987	**3,463**	7.8	1,096,190	**3,558**
Del Norte**	06015	2.0	28,062	**96**	2.6	28,803	**93**
El Dorado*	06017	10.5	172,703	**588**	11.2	192,098	**624**
Fresno*	06019	8.4	866,423	**2,950**	9.3	946,868	**3,074**
Glenn	06021	4.0	27,524	**94**	4.9	28,860	**94**
Humboldt**	06023	1.5	128,447	**437**	2.1	131,102	**426**
Imperial*	06025	6.4	151,466	**516**	7.4	162,630	**528**
Inyo**	06027	2.9	18,460	**63**	3.6	19,126	**62**
Kern*	06029	10.3	729,553	**2,484**	11.3	811,845	**2,635**
Kings*	06031	9.3	141,461	**482**	10.2	155,937	**506**
Lake**	06033	11.4	64,960	**221**	12.2	72,913	**237**
Lassen**	06035	0.4	33,980	**116**	0.8	34,249	**111**
Los Angeles*	06037	4.8	9,980,271	**33,983**	5.4	10,523,607	**34,159**
Madera*	06039	11.1	136,739	**466**	12.0	153,112	**497**
Marin*	06041	-0.7	245,560	**836**	-1.0	243,006	**789**
Mariposa	06043	5.2	18,022	**61**	6.1	19,117	**62**
Mendocino**	06045	3.2	89,009	**303**	3.7	92,264	**299**
Merced*	06047	13.1	238,219	**811**	13.9	271,433	**881**
Modoc	06049	-0.3	9,417	**32**	-0.0	9,416	**31**
Mono	06051	1.4	13,029	**44**	1.6	13,235	**43**
Monterey*	06053	4.1	418,251	**1,424**	4.5	437,244	**1,419**
Napa*	06055	7.8	133,946	**456**	8.7	145,637	**473**
Nevada**	06057	5.7	97,292	**331**	6.1	103,256	**335**
Orange*	06059	5.1	2,991,519	**10,186**	5.6	3,160,141	**10,258**
Placer*	06061	23.1	305,883	**1,042**	22.3	374,106	**1,214**
Plumas	06063	2.1	21,270	**72**	2.9	21,880	**71**
Riverside*	06065	20.2	1,856,913	**6,323**	20.0	2,228,111	**7,232**
Sacramento*	06067	11.5	1,364,259	**4,645**	12.3	1,531,926	**4,973**
San Benito*	06069	7.3	57,117	**194**	7.1	61,197	**199**
San Bernardino*	06071	11.5	1,906,582	**6,492**	12.3	2,140,998	**6,950**
San Diego*	06073	5.4	2,966,135	**10,100**	5.9	3,142,238	**10,200**
San Francisco*	06075	-4.3	743,549	**2,532**	-5.3	704,156	**2,286**
San Joaquin*	06077	16.1	654,288	**2,228**	16.4	761,890	**2,473**
San Luis Obispo*	06079	3.3	254,929	**868**	3.5	263,976	**857**
San Mateo*	06081	-1.9	693,861	**2,363**	-2.6	676,134	**2,195**
Santa Barbara*	06083	1.2	404,260	**1,376**	1.4	409,876	**1,330**
Santa Clara*	06085	-0.4	1,675,734	**5,706**	-0.8	1,662,290	**5,396**
Santa Cruz*	06087	-2.1	250,198	**852**	-2.7	243,374	**790**
Shasta*	06089	10.0	179,590	**612**	11.0	199,281	**647**
Sierra	06091	-2.2	3,477	**12**	-3.5	3,357	**11**
Siskiyou	06093	1.0	44,747	**152**	1.3	45,350	**147**
Solano*	06095	5.8	417,390	**1,421**	6.0	442,639	**1,437**
Sonoma*	06097	2.2	468,851	**1,596**	2.3	479,459	**1,556**
Stanislaus*	06099	13.3	506,378	**1,724**	14.0	577,071	**1,873**
Sutter*	06101	9.7	86,547	**295**	10.7	95,765	**311**
Tehama**	06103	6.0	59,393	**202**	6.8	63,441	**206**
Trinity	06105	4.7	13,630	**46**	5.7	14,401	**47**
Tulare*	06107	8.2	398,103	**1,356**	9.2	434,646	**1,411**
Tuolumne**	06109	5.4	57,450	**196**	6.0	60,918	**198**
Ventura*	06111	6.6	802,627	**2,733**	7.2	860,068	**2,792**
Yolo*	06113	11.2	187,466	**638**	11.8	209,576	**680**
Yuba*	06115	7.0	64,463	**219**	8.0	69,610	**226**
TOTAL: CALIFORNIA		**6.2**	**35,979,311**	**122,509**	**6.9**	**38,453,601**	**124,821**
COLORADO							
Adams*[1]	08001	7.2	389,997	**1,328**	12.5	438,602	**1,424**
Alamosa	08003	1.4	15,177	**52**	1.7	15,429	**50**
Arapahoe*	08005	7.4	524,236	**1,785**	7.8	565,097	**1,834**
Archuleta	08007	18.6	11,737	**40**	18.1	13,858	**45**
Baca	08009	-8.5	4,134	**14**	-10.1	3,717	**12**
Bent	08011	-8.3	5,498	**19**	-9.8	4,957	**16**
Boulder*[1]	08013	-3.7	280,533	**955**	4.1	292,034	**948**
Broomfield*[2]	08014	(d)	43,078	**147**	10.5	47,622	**155**
Chaffee	08015	4.8	17,021	**58**	5.3	17,922	**58**
Cheyenne	08017	-10.5	1,997	**7**	-12.6	1,745	**6**
Clear Creek*	08019	3.1	9,612	**33**	3.8	9,981	**32**

Source: Devonshire Associates Ltd. and Scan/US, Inc. 2004.
* Component of a Metropolitan Core Based Statistical Area.
** Component of a Micropolitan Core Based Statistical Area.

[1]Census population includes a portion of Broomfield county.
[2]Created on November 15, 2001 from parts of Adams, Boulder, Jefferson, and Weld counties.

(d) Data not available.

continued on next page

Counties: Population Trends, *Continued*

County	FIPS CODE	PRESENT 2000-2004 % Change	PRESENT 7/1/04 Estimate	7/1/04 Ranally Population Units	FUTURE 2004-2009 % Change	FUTURE 2009 Projection	2009 Ranally Population Units
Conejos	08021	0.0	8,400	**29**	-0.2	8,386	**27**
Costilla	08023	-3.7	3,528	**12**	-4.8	3,358	**11**
Crowley	08025	-1.8	5,421	**18**	-2.6	5,281	**17**
Custer	08027	10.6	3,874	**13**	11.6	4,322	**14**
Delta	08029	7.5	29,910	**102**	8.4	32,415	**105**
Denver*	08031	0.6	558,164	**1,901**	0.6	561,577	**1,823**
Dolores	08033	-1.5	1,817	**6**	-2.1	1,778	**6**
Douglas*	08035	35.3	237,826	**810**	30.2	309,585	**1,005**
Eagle**	08037	13.7	47,366	**161**	14.2	54,094	**176**
Elbert*	08039	15.6	22,964	**78**	15.5	26,514	**86**
El Paso*	08041	8.5	560,804	**1,910**	9.2	612,412	**1,988**
Fremont**	08043	4.0	47,971	**163**	4.3	50,051	**162**
Garfield	08045	11.3	48,740	**166**	11.6	54,385	**177**
Gilpin*	08047	2.2	4,861	**17**	1.6	4,939	**16**
Grand	08049	7.7	13,403	**46**	8.6	14,550	**47**
Gunnison	08051	0.8	14,062	**48**	0.6	14,143	**46**
Hinsdale	08053	-5.1	750	**3**	-5.9	706	**2**
Huerfano	08055	-0.4	7,828	**27**	0.0	7,830	**25**
Jackson	08057	-5.9	1,484	**5**	-7.4	1,374	**4**
Jefferson*[1]	08059	0.4	529,255	**1,802**	0.7	532,700	**1,729**
Kiowa	08061	-14.2	1,392	**5**	-16.7	1,160	**4**
Kit Carson	08063	-1.6	7,885	**27**	-1.7	7,752	**25**
Lake**	08065	-1.4	7,704	**26**	-1.8	7,568	**25**
La Plata**	08067	6.8	46,913	**160**	7.3	50,332	**163**
Larimer*	08069	7.8	271,165	**923**	8.4	293,935	**954**
Las Animas	08071	2.4	15,571	**53**	2.3	15,928	**52**
Lincoln	08073	-4.4	5,819	**20**	-5.2	5,519	**18**
Logan**	08075	2.5	21,018	**72**	2.1	21,465	**70**
Mesa*	08077	9.3	127,075	**433**	9.4	139,069	**451**
Mineral	08079	7.7	895	**3**	8.0	967	**3**
Moffat	08081	3.5	13,644	**46**	4.3	14,228	**46**
Montezuma	08083	2.7	24,485	**83**	3.1	25,235	**82**
Montrose**	08085	10.0	36,781	**125**	10.8	40,761	**132**
Morgan**	08087	3.6	28,145	**96**	4.0	29,258	**95**
Otero	08089	-3.5	19,590	**67**	-4.1	18,788	**61**
Ouray	08091	9.6	4,102	**14**	9.9	4,507	**15**
Park*	08093	17.4	17,056	**58**	17.3	20,012	**65**
Phillips	08095	1.0	4,527	**15**	1.8	4,607	**15**
Pitkin	08097	1.4	15,081	**51**	2.6	15,475	**50**
Prowers	08099	-2.9	14,067	**48**	-3.4	13,589	**44**
Pueblo*	08101	6.8	151,054	**514**	7.6	162,566	**528**
Rio Blanco	08103	-1.1	5,922	**20**	-1.4	5,841	**19**
Rio Grande	08105	-0.8	12,316	**42**	-1.2	12,169	**40**
Routt	08107	7.2	21,109	**72**	7.6	22,711	**74**
Saguache	08109	17.4	6,946	**24**	17.1	8,137	**26**
San Juan	08111	3.4	577	**2**	4.3	602	**2**
San Miguel	08113	11.1	7,329	**25**	12.0	8,205	**27**
Sedgwick	08115	-3.1	2,661	**9**	-3.9	2,556	**8**
Summit**	08117	8.9	25,634	**87**	9.6	28,085	**91**
Teller*	08119	7.8	22,158	**75**	8.4	24,016	**78**
Washington	08121	-3.2	4,768	**16**	-4.6	4,548	**15**
Weld*[1]	08123	22.0	220,667	**751**	21.3	267,629	**869**
Yuma	08125	-0.5	9,789	**33**	-0.5	9,736	**32**
TOTAL: COLORADO		**7.5**	**4,625,293**	**15,750**	**8.1**	**4,998,320**	**16,225**

CONNECTICUT

County	FIPS CODE	2000-2004 % Change	7/1/04 Estimate	7/1/04 Ranally Population Units	2004-2009 % Change	2009 Projection	2009 Ranally Population Units
Fairfield*	09001	2.4	904,001	**3,078**	2.7	928,248	**3,013**
Hartford*	09003	2.2	875,839	**2,982**	2.5	897,751	**2,914**
Litchfield**	09005	4.0	189,521	**645**	4.5	198,123	**643**
Middlesex*	09007	5.4	163,370	**556**	5.9	173,023	**562**
New Haven*	09009	2.9	847,502	**2,886**	3.3	875,645	**2,842**
New London*	09011	2.5	265,499	**904**	2.8	273,047	**886**
Tolland*	09013	8.3	147,747	**503**	9.2	161,287	**524**
Windham**	09015	4.3	113,767	**387**	5.0	119,492	**388**
TOTAL: CONNECTICUT		**3.0**	**3,507,246**	**11,941**	**3.4**	**3,626,616**	**11,772**

DELAWARE

County	FIPS CODE	2000-2004 % Change	7/1/04 Estimate	7/1/04 Ranally Population Units	2004-2009 % Change	2009 Projection	2009 Ranally Population Units
Kent*	10001	8.0	136,821	**466**	8.9	148,978	**484**
New Castle*	10003	3.8	519,483	**1,769**	4.2	541,522	**1,758**
Sussex**	10005	9.5	171,552	**584**	10.3	189,179	**614**
TOTAL: DELAWARE		**5.6**	**827,856**	**2,819**	**6.3**	**879,679**	**2,856**

DISTRICT OF COLUMBIA (District)

County	FIPS CODE	2000-2004 % Change	7/1/04 Estimate	7/1/04 Ranally Population Units	2004-2009 % Change	2009 Projection	2009 Ranally Population Units
District of Columbia*	11001	-2.0	560,725	**1,909**	-2.3	547,617	**1,778**
TOTAL: DISTRICT OF COLUMBIA		**-2.0**	**560,725**	**1,909**	**-2.3**	**547,617**	**1,778**

FLORIDA

County	FIPS CODE	2000-2004 % Change	7/1/04 Estimate	7/1/04 Ranally Population Units	2004-2009 % Change	2009 Projection	2009 Ranally Population Units
Alachua*	12001	3.4	225,339	**767**	3.9	234,144	**760**
Baker*	12003	6.8	23,769	**81**	7.3	25,494	**83**
Bay*	12005	6.3	157,510	**536**	7.4	169,093	**549**
Bradford	12007	4.3	27,211	**93**	5.2	28,628	**93**
Brevard*	12009	8.1	515,004	**1,754**	9.0	561,468	**1,823**
Broward*	12011	8.7	1,764,315	**6,007**	9.3	1,929,159	**6,262**
Calhoun	12013	-1.1	12,880	**44**	-1.6	12,678	**41**
Charlotte*	12015	10.9	157,100	**535**	11.8	175,640	**570**
Citrus**	12017	9.3	129,066	**439**	10.1	142,106	**461**
Clay*	12019	15.6	162,779	**554**	16.2	189,164	**614**
Collier*	12021	18.3	297,488	**1,013**	18.2	351,759	**1,142**
Columbia**	12023	8.7	61,407	**209**	9.5	67,220	**218**
DeSoto**	12027	6.8	34,409	**117**	7.7	37,057	**120**
Dixie	12029	1.5	14,034	**48**	1.9	14,294	**46**
Duval*	12031	6.6	830,101	**2,826**	7.6	893,203	**2,899**
Escambia*	12033	0.7	296,422	**1,009**	0.9	299,104	**971**
Flagler**	12035	32.6	66,083	**225**	29.3	85,466	**277**
Franklin	12037	-9.0	10,059	**34**	2.8	10,337	**34**
Gadsden*	12039	0.2	45,161	**154**	0.3	45,296	**147**
Gilchrist*	12041	10.8	15,996	**54**	11.3	17,809	**58**
Glades	12043	7.3	11,351	**39**	8.2	12,283	**40**
Gulf	12045	16.0	15,464	**53**	7.0	16,549	**54**
Hamilton	12047	5.9	14,112	**48**	6.9	15,087	**49**
Hardee**	12049	3.6	27,908	**95**	4.5	29,151	**95**
Hendry**	12051	3.0	37,303	**127**	3.2	38,496	**125**
Hernando*	12053	12.7	147,435	**502**	13.5	167,363	**543**
Highlands**	12055	5.6	92,254	**314**	6.5	98,271	**319**
Hillsborough*	12057	9.8	1,096,848	**3,735**	10.7	1,214,056	**3,941**
Holmes	12059	3.1	19,137	**65**	4.0	19,894	**65**
Indian River*	12061	8.7	122,827	**418**	9.6	134,647	**437**
Jackson	12063	-0.7	46,424	**158**	-0.9	46,004	**149**
Jefferson*	12065	11.7	14,410	**49**	12.9	16,275	**53**
Lafayette	12067	5.7	7,424	**25**	6.2	7,881	**26**
Lake*	12069	22.0	256,893	**875**	21.4	311,975	**1,013**
Lee*	12071	15.3	508,350	**1,731**	15.9	589,051	**1,912**
Leon*	12073	1.7	243,428	**829**	1.7	247,681	**804**
Levy	12075	6.9	36,821	**125**	7.5	39,576	**128**
Liberty	12077	5.7	7,424	**25**	7.3	7,967	**26**
Madison	12079	0.2	18,774	**64**	0.2	18,812	**61**
Manatee*	12081	11.3	293,837	**1,001**	12.0	329,004	**1,068**
Marion*	12083	10.8	286,954	**977**	11.6	320,284	**1,040**
Martin*	12085	8.7	137,796	**469**	9.7	151,164	**491**
Miami-Dade*	12086	5.1	2,368,141	**8,063**	5.7	2,503,015	**8,125**
Monroe**	12087	-1.0	78,768	**268**	-1.1	77,916	**253**
Nassau*	12089	9.0	62,849	**214**	9.7	68,969	**224**
Okaloosa*	12091	5.9	180,485	**615**	6.6	192,392	**625**
Okeechobee**	12093	5.8	38,007	**129**	6.9	40,635	**132**
Orange*	12095	10.0	985,714	**3,356**	10.6	1,089,958	**3,538**
Osceola*	12097	25.5	216,437	**737**	24.4	269,272	**874**
Palm Beach*	12099	9.9	1,243,157	**4,233**	10.8	1,377,535	**4,471**
Pasco*	12101	16.8	402,756	**1,371**	17.2	472,007	**1,532**
Pinellas*	12103	0.6	927,459	**3,158**	0.7	934,021	**3,032**
Polk*	12105	7.2	518,809	**1,767**	8.0	560,565	**1,820**
Putnam**	12107	2.7	72,313	**246**	3.3	74,675	**242**
St. Johns*	12109	21.0	149,006	**507**	20.6	179,691	**583**
St. Lucie*	12111	14.2	220,110	**749**	15.1	253,423	**823**
Santa Rosa*	12113	17.2	137,965	**470**	17.7	162,328	**527**
Sarasota*	12115	8.4	353,387	**1,203**	9.3	386,354	**1,254**
Seminole*	12117	7.6	392,829	**1,338**	8.2	425,101	**1,380**
Sumter**	12119	13.7	60,637	**206**	14.5	69,447	**225**
Suwannee	12121	6.9	37,248	**127**	7.4	40,011	**130**
Taylor	12123	1.2	19,484	**66**	1.8	19,831	**64**
Union	12125	5.5	14,185	**48**	6.4	15,098	**49**
Volusia*	12127	7.5	476,562	**1,623**	8.3	516,056	**1,675**
Wakulla*	12129	18.9	27,178	**93**	19.3	32,413	**105**
Walton	12131	18.8	48,227	**164**	19.2	57,497	**187**
Washington	12133	4.0	21,802	**74**	4.5	22,790	**74**
TOTAL: FLORIDA		**8.5**	**17,342,822**	**59,048**	**9.3**	**18,961,590**	**61,551**

GEORGIA

County	FIPS CODE	2000-2004 % Change	7/1/04 Estimate	7/1/04 Ranally Population Units	2004-2009 % Change	2009 Projection	2009 Ranally Population Units
Appling	13001	2.9	17,922	**61**	3.5	18,548	**60**
Atkinson**	13003	4.9	7,985	**27**	5.9	8,453	**27**
Bacon	13005	0.3	10,138	**35**	0.1	10,152	**33**
Baker*	13007	7.8	4,392	**15**	9.7	4,817	**16**
Baldwin**	13009	0.7	45,020	**153**	0.7	45,354	**147**
Banks	13011	9.6	15,800	**54**	10.1	17,391	**56**
Barrow*	13013	20.9	55,787	**190**	20.7	67,325	**219**
Bartow*	13015	15.0	87,405	**298**	15.3	100,778	**327**
Ben Hill**	13017	-1.9	17,149	**58**	-2.5	16,724	**54**
Berrien	13019	2.0	16,552	**56**	2.1	16,893	**55**
Bibb*	13021	0.4	154,445	**526**	0.5	155,230	**504**
Bleckley	13023	1.9	11,891	**40**	2.1	12,137	**39**
Brantley*	13025	5.8	15,474	**53**	6.3	16,450	**53**
Brooks*	13027	-1.7	16,165	**55**	-2.4	15,783	**51**
Bryan*	13029	16.5	27,274	**93**	17.1	31,942	**104**
Bulloch**	13031	5.6	59,093	**201**	6.2	62,756	**204**
Burke*	13033	4.2	23,167	**79**	4.7	24,256	**79**
Butts*	13035	17.2	22,885	**78**	17.2	26,815	**87**
Calhoun	13037	-4.2	6,057	**21**	-5.2	5,741	**19**
Camden**	13039	5.5	46,046	**157**	6.3	48,925	**159**
Candler	13043	6.2	10,170	**35**	7.2	10,902	**35**
Carroll*	13045	16.9	102,023	**347**	17.1	119,514	**388**
Catoosa*	13047	11.8	59,560	**203**	12.4	66,931	**217**
Charlton	13049	5.6	10,853	**37**	6.7	11,584	**38**
Chatham*	13051	1.9	236,368	**805**	2.3	241,848	**785**
Chattahoochee*	13053	39.6	20,780	**71**	34.8	28,013	**91**
Chattooga**	13055	4.9	26,729	**91**	5.7	28,262	**92**
Cherokee*	13057	22.8	174,257	**593**	21.9	212,338	**689**
Clarke*	13059	2.8	104,327	**355**	3.0	107,507	**349**
Clay	13061	0.1	3,359	**11**	0.1	3,362	**11**
Clayton*	13063	12.8	266,814	**908**	13.3	302,190	**981**
Clinch	13065	1.8	7,002	**24**	2.5	7,175	**23**
Cobb*	13067	9.2	663,776	**2,260**	9.6	727,493	**2,361**
Coffee**	13069	5.5	39,469	**134**	6.0	41,842	**136**
Colquitt**	13071	3.6	43,561	**148**	4.1	45,350	**147**
Columbia*	13073	12.1	100,062	**341**	12.8	112,848	**366**
Cook	13075	1.4	15,989	**54**	1.2	16,180	**53**
Coweta*	13077	17.9	105,145	**358**	17.8	123,894	**402**
Crawford*	13079	0.7	12,586	**43**	1.3	12,748	**41**
Crisp**	13081	0.0	21,998	**75**	0.1	22,019	**71**
Dade*	13083	6.6	16,151	**55**	7.4	17,353	**56**
Dawson*	13085	20.9	19,341	**66**	19.8	23,172	**75**
Decatur**	13087	-0.1	28,201	**96**	-0.2	28,142	**91**
DeKalb*	13089	1.6	676,338	**2,303**	1.5	686,337	**2,228**
Dodge	13091	1.5	19,451	**66**	2.0	19,835	**64**
Dooly	13093	0.4	11,568	**39**	0.7	11,647	**38**
Dougherty*	13095	-0.5	95,611	**326**	-0.4	95,249	**309**
Douglas*	13097	14.0	105,116	**358**	14.8	120,622	**392**
Early	13099	-1.4	12,184	**41**	-1.6	11,986	**39**
Echols*	13101	8.4	4,068	**14**	8.5	4,413	**14**
Effingham*	13103	18.2	44,353	**151**	18.5	52,538	**171**
Elbert	13105	0.8	20,680	**70**	1.0	20,897	**68**
Emanuel	13107	0.2	21,889	**75**	0.1	21,906	**71**
Evans	13109	10.8	11,628	**40**	11.3	12,944	**42**
Fannin	13111	9.4	21,666	**74**	10.0	23,823	**77**
Fayette*	13113	10.9	101,180	**345**	11.2	112,509	**365**
Floyd*	13115	4.0	94,225	**321**	4.5	98,508	**320**
Forsyth*	13117	33.7	131,575	**448**	29.5	170,391	**553**
Franklin	13119	5.7	21,441	**73**	6.5	22,827	**74**
Fulton*	13121	0.3	818,745	**2,788**	0.3	820,832	**2,664**
Gilmer	13123	13.9	26,706	**91**	13.7	30,367	**99**
Glascock	13125	4.2	2,663	**9**	5.0	2,796	**9**
Glynn*	13127	5.0	70,954	**242**	5.8	75,069	**244**
Gordon**	13129	10.9	48,915	**167**	11.6	54,600	**177**
Grady	13131	3.0	24,362	**83**	3.6	25,244	**82**
Greene	13133	7.8	15,532	**53**	8.6	16,874	**55**
Gwinnett*	13135	18.8	698,970	**2,380**	18.3	827,071	**2,685**
Habersham**	13137	9.2	39,215	**134**	9.8	43,059	**140**
Hall*	13139	15.7	161,175	**549**	15.7	186,542	**606**
Hancock**	13141	-1.2	9,952	**34**	-1.2	9,830	**32**
Haralson*	13143	9.0	28,009	**95**	9.8	30,750	**100**
Harris*	13145	12.2	26,586	**91**	13.1	30,057	**98**
Hart	13147	2.5	23,561	**80**	2.7	24,203	**79**
Heard*	13149	1.4	11,168	**38**	0.7	11,249	**37**
Henry*	13151	33.6	159,460	**543**	29.7	206,741	**671**
Houston*	13153	11.5	123,475	**420**	12.3	138,676	**450**
Irwin**	13155	1.6	10,089	**34**	1.4	10,233	**33**
Jackson	13157	17.1	48,692	**166**	17.4	57,161	**186**
Jasper*	13159	12.9	12,896	**44**	13.5	14,642	**48**
Jeff Davis	13161	2.0	12,943	**44**	2.1	13,217	**43**
Jefferson	13163	-2.0	16,920	**58**	-2.4	16,520	**54**
Jenkins	13165	2.9	8,820	**30**	3.1	9,096	**30**
Johnson**	13167	13.4	9,708	**33**	14.8	11,142	**36**
Jones*	13169	10.3	26,065	**89**	11.4	29,028	**94**
Lamar*	13171	2.5	16,316	**56**	2.5	16,723	**54**
Lanier*	13173	2.1	7,393	**25**	2.2	7,555	**25**
Laurens**	13175	3.6	46,487	**158**	4.1	48,377	**157**
Lee*	13177	19.5	29,584	**101**	19.8	35,450	**115**
Liberty*	13179	-5.7	58,129	**198**	-6.6	54,306	**176**
Lincoln	13181	3.0	8,596	**29**	3.5	8,893	**29**
Long*	13183	6.0	10,926	**37**	6.7	11,653	**38**
Lowndes*	13185	3.6	95,395	**325**	4.3	99,477	**323**
Lumpkin	13187	13.5	23,857	**81**	14.1	27,215	**88**
McDuffie*	13189	1.3	21,501	**73**	1.3	21,780	**71**
McIntosh*	13191	0.3	10,878	**37**	-0.3	10,842	**35**
Macon	13193	-0.4	14,014	**48**	-0.4	13,958	**45**
Madison*	13195	6.8	27,481	**94**	7.4	29,507	**96**
Marion*	13197	0.3	7,165	**24**	-0.4	7,138	**23**
Meriwether*	13199	1.5	22,870	**78**	1.8	23,289	**76**
Miller	13201	-1.1	6,311	**21**	-1.4	6,225	**20**
Mitchell	13205	-0.6	23,786	**81**	-1.0	23,557	**76**
Monroe*	13207	9.0	23,707	**81**	9.7	26,018	**84**
Montgomery**	13209	6.8	8,830	**30**	7.8	9,522	**31**
Morgan	13211	11.3	17,196	**59**	12.2	19,302	**63**
Murray*	13213	10.5	40,328	**137**	10.9	44,735	**145**
Muscogee*	13215	-0.5	185,443	**631**	-0.7	184,147	**598**
Newton*	13217	29.9	80,554	**274**	27.4	102,604	**333**
Oconee*	13219	9.2	28,647	**98**	9.8	31,447	**102**
Oglethorpe*	13221	7.6	13,598	**46**	8.0	14,690	**48**
Paulding*	13223	29.5	105,749	**360**	26.8	134,135	**435**
Peach**	13225	3.5	24,491	**83**	3.5	25,346	**82**
Pickens*	13227	22.2	28,084	**96**	21.0	33,979	**110**
Pierce**	13229	5.7	16,532	**56**	6.2	17,556	**57**
Pike*	13231	12.3	15,372	**52**	12.8	17,336	**56**
Polk**	13233	5.7	40,315	**137**	6.4	42,889	**139**
Pulaski	13235	1.9	9,768	**33**	2.3	9,989	**32**
Putnam	13237	5.3	19,814	**67**	6.0	21,008	**68**
Quitman**	13239	-6.1	2,439	**8**	-8.0	2,244	**7**
Rabun	13241	6.2	15,978	**54**	6.9	17,082	**55**
Randolph	13243	-5.4	7,370	**25**	-6.2	6,914	**22**
Richmond*	13245	-1.0	197,685	**673**	-1.2	195,374	**634**
Rockdale*	13247	9.0	76,406	**260**	9.6	83,732	**272**
Schley**	13249	5.8	3,985	**14**	6.3	4,235	**14**
Screven	13251	0.3	15,420	**53**	0.4	15,484	**50**
Seminole	13253	-1.4	9,237	**31**	-1.8	9,072	**29**
Spalding*	13255	4.7	61,151	**208**	5.5	64,495	**209**
Stephens**	13257	-1.0	25,191	**86**	-1.4	24,827	**81**
Stewart	13259	-6.2	4,924	**17**	-7.4	4,559	**15**
Sumter**	13261	0.0	33,208	**113**	-0.1	33,161	**108**
Talbot	13263	1.1	6,572	**22**	0.8	6,624	**22**
Taliaferro	13265	-7.6	1,919	**7**	-9.4	1,739	**6**
Tattnall	13267	0.5	22,408	**76**	0.5	22,522	**73**
Taylor	13269	1.3	8,928	**30**	1.5	9,062	**29**
Telfair	13271	-3.1	11,431	**39**	-3.9	10,982	**36**
Terrell*	13273	-1.4	10,814	**37**	-1.8	10,617	**34**
Thomas**	13275	2.8	43,940	**150**	3.1	45,300	**147**
Tift**	13277	3.8	39,884	**136**	4.5	41,685	**135**
Toombs**	13279	2.0	26,586	**91**	2.2	27,171	**88**

Source: Devonshire Associates Ltd. and Scan/US, Inc. 2004.
* Component of a Metropolitan Core Based Statistical Area.
** Component of a Micropolitan Core Based Statistical Area.

[1]Census population includes a portion of Broomfield county.

Counties: Population Trends, *Continued*

	FIPS CODE	PRESENT 2000-2004 % Change	PRESENT 7/1/04 Estimate	7/1/04 Ranally Population Units	FUTURE 2004-2009 % Change	FUTURE 2009 Projection	2009 Ranally Population Units
Towns	13281	8.1	10,078	**34**	8.8	10,960	**36**
Treutlen	13283	1.8	6,975	**24**	1.6	7,088	**23**
Troup**	13285	3.2	60,648	**207**	3.5	62,794	**204**
Turner	13287	0.9	9,588	**33**	0.9	9,677	**31**
Twiggs*	13289	-1.6	10,424	**35**	-2.0	10,217	**33**
Union	13291	13.9	19,686	**67**	14.4	22,522	**73**
Upson**	13293	1.8	28,094	**96**	2.1	28,672	**93**
Walker*	13295	3.3	63,070	**215**	3.9	65,504	**213**
Walton*	13297	18.6	71,966	**245**	18.0	84,892	**276**
Ware**	13299	0.1	35,519	**121**	0.2	35,597	**116**
Warren	13301	-4.2	6,073	**21**	-4.5	5,799	**19**
Washington	13303	-2.5	20,652	**70**	-3.1	20,020	**65**
Wayne**	13305	4.7	27,808	**95**	5.4	29,299	**95**
Webster	13307	-5.3	2,264	**8**	-6.5	2,116	**7**
Wheeler	13309	8.9	6,732	**23**	10.4	7,429	**24**
White	13311	18.9	23,711	**81**	18.9	28,191	**92**
Whitfield*	13313	6.6	89,077	**303**	7.0	95,295	**309**
Wilcox	13315	2.9	8,830	**30**	3.7	9,159	**30**
Wilkes	13317	-0.4	10,645	**36**	-0.4	10,606	**34**
Wilkinson	13319	0.6	10,278	**35**	0.5	10,334	**34**
Worth*	13321	-0.7	21,822	**74**	-0.6	21,689	**70**
TOTAL: GEORGIA		**7.9**	**8,836,255**	**30,088**	**8.6**	**9,593,957**	**31,141**

HAWAII

	FIPS CODE	PRESENT 2000-2004 % Change	PRESENT 7/1/04 Estimate	7/1/04 Ranally Population Units	FUTURE 2004-2009 % Change	FUTURE 2009 Projection	2009 Ranally Population Units
Hawaii**	15001	8.6	161,480	**550**	9.5	176,764	**574**
Honolulu*	15003	4.1	911,719	**3,104**	4.9	956,800	**3,106**
Kalawao	15005	-15.6	124	**0**	-18.5	101	**0**
Kauai**	15007	5.2	61,484	**209**	6.0	65,167	**212**
Maui**	15009	7.6	137,889	**470**	8.3	149,306	**485**
TOTAL: HAWAII		**5.0**	**1,272,696**	**4,333**	**5.9**	**1,348,138**	**4,377**

IDAHO

	FIPS CODE	PRESENT 2000-2004 % Change	PRESENT 7/1/04 Estimate	7/1/04 Ranally Population Units	FUTURE 2004-2009 % Change	FUTURE 2009 Projection	2009 Ranally Population Units
Ada*	16001	10.5	332,530	**1,132**	11.1	369,368	**1,199**
Adams	16003	1.6	3,531	**12**	2.2	3,610	**12**
Bannock*	16005	0.1	75,644	**258**	0.1	75,705	**246**
Bear Lake	16007	-2.3	6,266	**21**	-3.1	6,069	**20**
Benewah	16009	-2.1	8,975	**31**	-3.0	8,708	**28**
Bingham**	16011	3.7	43,298	**147**	4.3	45,152	**147**
Blaine	16013	12.4	21,346	**73**	13.0	24,118	**78**
Boise*	16015	10.9	7,399	**25**	11.0	8,212	**27**
Bonner	16017	8.3	39,874	**136**	8.9	43,428	**141**
Bonneville*	16019	7.1	88,379	**301**	7.7	95,227	**309**
Boundary	16021	3.9	10,255	**35**	4.0	10,662	**35**
Butte	16023	-1.2	2,864	**10**	-1.6	2,819	**9**
Camas	16025	8.2	1,072	**4**	10.5	1,185	**4**
Canyon*	16027	19.9	157,648	**537**	19.5	188,322	**611**
Caribou	16029	-2.8	7,100	**24**	-3.6	6,844	**22**
Cassia**	16031	1.2	21,676	**74**	1.5	22,004	**71**
Clark	16033	-15.3	866	**3**	-19.6	696	**2**
Clearwater	16035	-7.7	8,244	**28**	-9.0	7,499	**24**
Custer	16037	-7.6	4,010	**14**	-9.5	3,631	**12**
Elmore**	16039	-1.2	28,794	**98**	-1.3	28,407	**92**
Franklin*	16041	6.3	12,043	**41**	7.0	12,884	**42**
Fremont**	16043	3.3	12,211	**42**	4.3	12,730	**41**
Gem*	16045	5.3	15,988	**54**	6.0	16,946	**55**
Gooding	16047	1.5	14,372	**49**	1.5	14,581	**47**
Idaho	16049	-0.8	15,394	**52**	-0.6	15,296	**50**
Jefferson*	16051	7.1	20,514	**70**	7.8	22,114	**72**
Jerome**	16053	4.0	19,070	**65**	4.1	19,850	**64**
Kootenai*	16055	10.5	120,129	**409**	11.0	133,350	**433**
Latah**	16057	0.6	35,151	**120**	0.9	35,467	**115**
Lemhi	16059	-1.0	7,726	**26**	-0.3	7,701	**25**
Lewis	16061	0.1	3,749	**13**	0.1	3,751	**12**
Lincoln	16063	9.0	4,408	**15**	9.8	4,842	**16**
Madison**	16065	11.7	30,691	**105**	13.2	34,754	**113**
Minidoka**	16067	-5.3	19,104	**65**	-6.2	17,927	**58**
Nez Perce*	16069	1.1	37,804	**129**	1.4	38,324	**124**
Oneida	16071	0.2	4,133	**14**	0.1	4,139	**13**
Owyhee*	16073	6.6	11,350	**39**	7.2	12,165	**39**
Payette**	16075	5.7	21,743	**74**	6.4	23,126	**75**
Power*	16077	-2.8	7,327	**25**	-3.1	7,101	**23**
Shoshone	16079	-7.4	12,751	**43**	-9.0	11,605	**38**
Teton**	16081	22.9	7,373	**25**	21.3	8,946	**29**
Twin Falls**	16083	5.8	67,992	**232**	6.7	72,532	**235**
Valley	16085	1.6	7,777	**26**	2.1	7,943	**26**
Washington	16087	0.3	10,002	**34**	0.3	10,036	**33**
TOTAL: IDAHO		**7.3**	**1,388,573**	**4,730**	**8.0**	**1,499,776**	**4,867**

ILLINOIS

	FIPS CODE	PRESENT 2000-2004 % Change	PRESENT 7/1/04 Estimate	7/1/04 Ranally Population Units	FUTURE 2004-2009 % Change	FUTURE 2009 Projection	2009 Ranally Population Units
Adams**	17001	-1.3	67,378	**229**	-1.5	66,365	**215**
Alexander**	17003	-3.6	9,242	**31**	-4.5	8,829	**29**
Bond*	17005	2.3	18,040	**61**	2.7	18,533	**60**
Boone*	17007	14.7	47,945	**163**	15.3	55,286	**179**
Brown	17009	-1.4	6,854	**23**	-1.9	6,727	**22**
Bureau**	17011	-1.1	35,130	**120**	-1.3	34,672	**113**
Calhoun*	17013	-0.4	5,062	**17**	-0.8	5,024	**16**
Carroll	17015	-3.3	16,118	**55**	-3.8	15,508	**50**
Cass	17017	1.5	13,896	**47**	2.0	14,167	**46**
Champaign*	17019	5.2	189,076	**644**	6.0	200,443	**651**
Christian**	17021	-0.9	35,051	**119**	-1.1	34,668	**113**
Clark	17023	-0.0	17,000	**58**	0.0	17,008	**55**
Clay	17025	-2.2	14,239	**48**	-2.7	13,855	**45**
Clinton*	17027	2.2	36,327	**124**	2.6	37,288	**121**
Coles**	17029	-3.2	51,497	**175**	-3.6	49,625	**161**
Cook*	17031	-0.6	5,342,990	**18,193**	-0.8	5,299,999	**17,204**
Crawford	17033	-3.5	19,734	**67**	-4.1	18,925	**61**
Cumberland**	17035	-2.3	10,997	**37**	-2.9	10,674	**35**
DeKalb*	17037	7.5	95,619	**326**	8.2	103,501	**336**
De Witt	17039	-0.9	16,642	**57**	-1.1	16,455	**53**
Douglas	17041	0.0	19,923	**68**	-0.0	19,922	**65**
DuPage*	17043	3.0	931,347	**3,171**	3.3	962,070	**3,123**
Edgar	17045	-2.0	19,310	**66**	-2.2	18,881	**61**
Edwards	17047	-2.3	6,812	**23**	-2.7	6,627	**22**
Effingham**	17049	1.0	34,618	**118**	1.3	35,058	**114**
Fayette	17051	-1.6	21,453	**73**	-2.0	21,025	**68**
Ford*	17053	-1.3	14,052	**48**	-1.5	13,839	**45**
Franklin	17055	0.3	39,144	**133**	0.3	39,280	**128**
Fulton**	17057	-2.0	37,466	**128**	-2.5	36,523	**119**
Gallatin	17059	-4.6	6,150	**21**	-5.5	5,812	**19**
Greene	17061	-0.4	14,695	**50**	-0.5	14,626	**47**
Grundy*	17063	6.9	40,142	**137**	7.6	43,212	**140**
Hamilton**	17065	-4.3	8,248	**28**	-5.1	7,829	**25**
Hancock	17067	-4.7	19,166	**65**	-5.7	18,069	**59**
Hardin	17069	-2.4	4,686	**16**	-2.7	4,560	**15**
Henderson**	17071	-2.3	8,026	**27**	-2.9	7,793	**25**
Henry*	17073	-1.0	50,508	**172**	-1.3	49,831	**162**
Iroquois	17075	-2.7	30,473	**104**	-3.4	29,437	**96**
Jackson**	17077	-1.4	58,775	**200**	-1.7	57,780	**188**
Jasper	17079	-2.0	9,917	**34**	-1.9	9,730	**32**
Jefferson**	17081	0.9	40,422	**138**	1.1	40,860	**133**
Jersey*	17083	3.2	22,361	**76**	3.9	23,223	**75**
Jo Daviess	17085	1.4	22,606	**77**	1.8	23,005	**75**
Johnson	17087	0.6	12,960	**44**	0.3	13,005	**42**
Kane*	17089	17.2	473,610	**1,613**	17.4	556,007	**1,805**
Kankakee*	17091	2.3	106,207	**362**	2.7	109,106	**354**
Kendall*	17093	29.0	70,354	**240**	26.9	89,295	**290**
Knox**	17095	-3.2	54,075	**184**	-3.8	52,041	**169**
Lake*	17097	8.2	697,152	**2,374**	8.7	757,754	**2,460**
La Salle**	17099	0.6	112,214	**382**	0.8	113,088	**367**
Lawrence	17101	-1.3	15,247	**52**	-1.3	15,046	**49**
Lee**	17103	-1.9	35,365	**120**	-2.4	34,514	**112**
Livingston**	17105	-1.6	39,061	**133**	-1.9	38,336	**124**
Logan**	17107	-2.0	30,571	**104**	-2.3	29,854	**97**
McDonough**	17109	-0.2	32,846	**112**	-0.1	32,812	**107**
McHenry*	17111	13.1	294,238	**1,002**	13.8	334,948	**1,087**
McLean*	17113	5.6	158,878	**541**	6.3	168,862	**548**
Macon*	17115	-4.0	110,093	**375**	-4.8	104,829	**340**
Macoupin*	17117	0.1	49,072	**167**	0.2	49,154	**160**
Madison*	17119	1.4	262,550	**894**	1.6	266,835	**866**
Marion**	17121	-3.0	40,438	**138**	-3.8	38,912	**126**
Marshall*	17123	-1.3	13,003	**44**	-1.4	12,822	**42**
Mason	17125	-1.2	15,841	**54**	-1.4	15,623	**51**
Massac**	17127	-0.1	15,143	**52**	0.2	15,168	**49**
Menard*	17129	1.1	12,619	**43**	1.0	12,749	**41**
Mercer*	17131	0.4	17,018	**58**	0.4	17,089	**55**
Monroe*	17133	10.0	30,375	**103**	10.7	33,630	**109**
Montgomery	17135	-1.3	30,253	**103**	-1.6	29,761	**97**
Morgan**	17137	-2.3	35,786	**122**	-2.8	34,780	**113**
Moultrie	17139	1.6	14,512	**49**	1.5	14,727	**48**
Ogle**	17141	4.7	53,421	**182**	5.3	56,236	**183**
Peoria*	17143	-0.8	182,043	**620**	-0.8	180,577	**586**
Perry	17145	-2.3	22,559	**77**	-2.7	21,942	**71**
Piatt*	17147	0.5	16,444	**56**	0.5	16,534	**54**
Pike	17149	-3.4	16,790	**57**	-4.0	16,119	**52**
Pope	17151	-4.6	4,208	**14**	-6.1	3,952	**13**
Pulaski	17153	-4.8	6,997	**24**	-5.5	6,610	**21**
Putnam**	17155	0.7	6,129	**21**	0.8	6,180	**20**
Randolph	17157	-2.6	33,025	**112**	-3.3	31,945	**104**
Richland	17159	-1.2	15,957	**54**	-1.2	15,758	**51**
Rock Island*	17161	-1.2	147,511	**502**	-1.4	145,513	**472**
St. Clair*	17163	1.3	259,386	**883**	1.5	263,266	**855**
Saline**	17165	-2.7	25,999	**89**	-3.0	25,215	**82**
Sangamon*	17167	2.0	192,815	**657**	2.4	197,498	**641**
Schuyler	17169	-3.1	6,967	**24**	-3.8	6,701	**22**
Scott**	17171	-0.8	5,491	**19**	-1.3	5,421	**18**
Shelby	17173	-2.7	22,269	**76**	-3.1	21,589	**70**
Stark*	17175	-2.7	6,159	**21**	-3.1	5,966	**19**
Stephenson**	17177	-2.2	47,902	**163**	-2.6	46,677	**152**
Tazewell*	17179	-0.4	127,916	**436**	-0.6	127,205	**413**
Union	17181	-0.8	18,141	**62**	-0.8	17,995	**58**
Vermilion*	17183	-1.7	82,467	**281**	-2.0	80,800	**262**
Wabash	17185	-2.5	12,608	**43**	-2.8	12,253	**40**
Warren**	17187	-3.4	18,101	**62**	-3.9	17,391	**56**
Washington	17189	0.2	15,183	**52**	0.1	15,199	**49**
Wayne	17191	-1.6	16,883	**57**	-1.8	16,578	**54**
White	17193	-2.2	15,029	**51**	-2.5	14,647	**48**
Whiteside**	17195	-1.7	59,633	**203**	-2.1	58,385	**190**
Will*	17197	22.0	612,859	**2,087**	21.3	743,563	**2,414**
Williamson**	17199	2.5	62,854	**214**	3.2	64,879	**211**
Winnebago*	17201	2.8	286,099	**974**	3.1	295,009	**958**
Woodford*	17203	3.3	36,654	**125**	3.9	38,090	**124**
TOTAL: ILLINOIS		**2.5**	**12,725,117**	**43,330**	**2.8**	**13,082,984**	**42,472**

INDIANA

	FIPS CODE	PRESENT 2000-2004 % Change	PRESENT 7/1/04 Estimate	7/1/04 Ranally Population Units	FUTURE 2004-2009 % Change	FUTURE 2009 Projection	2009 Ranally Population Units
Adams**	18001	-0.1	33,583	**114**	-0.1	33,537	**109**
Allen*	18003	3.3	342,644	**1,167**	3.6	355,080	**1,153**
Bartholomew*	18005	1.6	72,553	**247**	1.5	73,612	**239**
Benton*	18007	-3.1	9,125	**31**	-3.5	8,810	**29**
Blackford	18009	-1.6	13,830	**47**	-1.6	13,603	**44**
Boone*	18011	9.2	50,364	**171**	9.9	55,335	**180**
Brown*	18013	3.1	15,417	**52**	3.4	15,936	**52**
Carroll*	18015	2.2	20,609	**70**	2.7	21,157	**69**
Cass**	18017	-1.7	40,228	**137**	-2.3	39,304	**128**
Clark*	18019	4.0	100,377	**342**	4.5	104,846	**340**
Clay*	18021	1.1	26,843	**91**	1.3	27,197	**88**
Clinton**	18023	0.2	33,939	**116**	-0.1	33,898	**110**
Crawford	18025	4.8	11,262	**38**	5.1	11,839	**38**
Daviess**	18027	1.0	30,121	**103**	1.2	30,490	**99**
Dearborn*	18029	4.9	48,349	**165**	5.2	50,848	**165**
Decatur**	18031	1.0	24,805	**84**	1.2	25,095	**81**
De Kalb**	18033	2.7	41,373	**141**	2.9	42,587	**138**
Delaware*	18035	-1.4	117,094	**399**	-1.7	115,140	**374**
Dubois**	18037	1.7	40,365	**137**	2.0	41,188	**134**
Elkhart*	18039	4.2	190,535	**649**	4.6	199,304	**647**
Fayette**	18041	-3.0	24,819	**85**	-3.6	23,934	**78**
Floyd*	18043	0.6	71,234	**243**	0.6	71,661	**233**
Fountain	18045	-1.5	17,691	**60**	-1.7	17,397	**56**
Franklin*	18047	3.6	22,956	**78**	4.0	23,867	**77**
Fulton	18049	-0.1	20,491	**70**	-0.4	20,404	**66**
Gibson*	18051	2.0	33,139	**113**	2.2	33,876	**110**
Grant**	18053	-3.3	71,013	**242**	-3.8	68,285	**222**
Greene*	18055	0.3	33,255	**113**	0.2	33,305	**108**
Hamilton*	18057	24.4	227,306	**774**	23.0	279,692	**908**
Hancock*	18059	9.6	60,709	**207**	10.4	67,026	**218**
Harrison*	18061	5.2	36,107	**123**	5.5	38,110	**124**
Hendricks*	18063	18.5	123,336	**420**	18.2	145,760	**473**
Henry**	18065	-2.2	47,446	**162**	-2.6	46,205	**150**
Howard*	18067	-0.1	84,849	**289**	-0.2	84,692	**275**
Huntington**	18069	0.2	38,158	**130**	0.2	38,229	**124**
Jackson**	18071	0.9	41,716	**142**	0.9	42,095	**137**
Jasper*	18073	4.4	31,372	**107**	4.7	32,839	**107**
Jay	18075	-0.4	21,708	**74**	-0.6	21,585	**70**
Jefferson**	18077	2.3	32,425	**110**	2.7	33,297	**108**
Jennings**	18079	2.5	28,250	**96**	2.4	28,942	**94**
Johnson*	18081	9.1	125,682	**428**	9.6	137,807	**447**
Knox**	18083	-1.7	38,600	**131**	-1.9	37,880	**123**
Kosciusko**	18085	2.2	75,657	**258**	2.4	77,436	**251**
Lagrange	18087	4.2	36,387	**124**	4.9	38,188	**124**
Lake*	18089	0.8	488,435	**1,663**	1.0	493,200	**1,601**
La Porte*	18091	-0.3	109,775	**374**	-0.5	109,259	**355**
Lawrence**	18093	0.8	46,285	**157**	0.9	46,709	**152**
Madison*	18095	-2.2	130,409	**444**	-2.7	126,901	**412**
Marion*	18097	0.4	864,200	**2,943**	0.5	868,901	**2,820**
Marshall**	18099	3.5	46,720	**159**	3.9	48,561	**158**
Martin	18101	-0.2	10,344	**35**	-0.2	10,328	**34**
Miami**	18103	0.3	36,178	**123**	0.0	36,182	**117**
Monroe*	18105	2.6	123,639	**421**	3.0	127,311	**413**
Montgomery**	18107	1.0	38,008	**129**	1.3	38,489	**125**
Morgan*	18109	3.8	69,244	**236**	4.2	72,185	**234**
Newton*	18111	-1.5	14,353	**49**	-1.7	14,105	**46**
Noble**	18113	2.1	47,239	**161**	2.1	48,243	**157**
Ohio*	18115	2.5	5,762	**20**	2.6	5,911	**19**
Orange	18117	2.1	19,714	**67**	2.5	20,202	**66**
Owen*	18119	6.2	23,137	**79**	6.7	24,685	**80**
Parke	18121	0.7	17,360	**59**	0.9	17,511	**57**
Perry	18123	-1.3	18,661	**64**	-1.5	18,383	**60**
Pike**	18125	1.0	12,969	**44**	1.5	13,160	**43**
Porter*	18127	5.1	154,300	**525**	5.7	163,124	**529**
Posey*	18129	-0.9	26,811	**91**	-1.2	26,484	**86**
Pulaski	18131	0.8	13,863	**47**	1.0	14,004	**45**
Putnam*	18133	2.4	36,886	**126**	2.6	37,854	**123**
Randolph	18135	-2.7	26,648	**91**	-3.4	25,739	**84**
Ripley	18137	3.8	27,539	**94**	4.0	28,651	**93**
Rush	18139	-1.7	17,949	**61**	-1.9	17,615	**57**
St. Joseph*	18141	0.4	266,508	**907**	0.3	267,297	**868**
Scott**	18143	3.3	23,725	**81**	3.6	24,568	**80**
Shelby*	18145	0.7	43,756	**149**	0.4	43,947	**143**
Spencer	18147	-0.3	20,321	**69**	-0.5	20,210	**66**
Starke	18149	-2.3	23,006	**78**	-2.9	22,350	**73**
Steuben**	18151	1.9	33,837	**115**	1.9	34,489	**112**
Sullivan*	18153	0.7	21,900	**75**	0.9	22,091	**72**
Switzerland	18155	5.3	9,549	**33**	6.0	10,118	**33**
Tippecanoe*	18157	5.2	156,683	**534**	5.8	165,846	**538**
Tipton*	18159	-1.2	16,378	**56**	-1.4	16,156	**52**
Union	18161	-2.0	7,201	**25**	-2.5	7,018	**23**
Vanderburgh*	18163	-0.0	171,902	**585**	0.0	171,959	**558**
Vermillion*	18165	-1.7	16,504	**56**	-2.0	16,167	**52**
Vigo*	18167	-1.6	104,149	**355**	-1.9	102,213	**332**
Wabash**	18169	-2.4	34,129	**116**	-3.0	33,095	**107**
Warren	18171	4.4	8,788	**30**	4.8	9,214	**30**
Warrick*	18173	5.9	55,468	**189**	6.5	59,086	**192**
Washington*	18175	1.9	27,735	**94**	2.1	28,317	**92**
Wayne**	18177	-1.6	69,968	**238**	-1.9	68,646	**223**
Wells*	18179	1.5	28,011	**95**	1.7	28,501	**93**
White	18181	-2.1	24,725	**84**	-2.5	24,096	**78**
Whitley*	18183	4.1	31,953	**109**	4.7	33,460	**109**
TOTAL: INDIANA		**2.5**	**6,230,346**	**21,215**	**2.8**	**6,403,859**	**20,792**

IOWA

	FIPS CODE	PRESENT 2000-2004 % Change	PRESENT 7/1/04 Estimate	7/1/04 Ranally Population Units	FUTURE 2004-2009 % Change	FUTURE 2009 Projection	2009 Ranally Population Units
Adair	19001	-5.0	7,829	**27**	-5.8	7,374	**24**
Adams	19003	-3.3	4,336	**15**	-4.0	4,163	**14**
Allamakee	19005	-1.2	14,503	**49**	-1.6	14,265	**46**
Appanoose	19007	-1.2	13,552	**46**	-1.4	13,360	**43**

Source: Devonshire Associates Ltd. and Scan/US, Inc. 2004.
* Component of a Metropolitan Core Based Statistical Area.
** Component of a Micropolitan Core Based Statistical Area.

continued on next page

Counties: Population Trends, *Continued*

	FIPS CODE	PRESENT 2000-2004 % Change	PRESENT 7/1/04 Estimate	7/1/04 Ranally Population Units	FUTURE 2004-2009 % Change	FUTURE 2009 Projection	2009 Ranally Population Units
Audubon	19009	-6.7	6,373	**22**	-7.9	5,867	**19**
Benton*	19011	4.9	26,543	**90**	5.6	28,034	**91**
Black Hawk*	19013	-1.6	125,922	**429**	-2.0	123,434	**401**
Boone**	19015	0.1	26,245	**89**	-0.1	26,225	**85**
Bremer*	19017	0.3	23,391	**80**	0.5	23,497	**76**
Buchanan	19019	-1.2	20,844	**71**	-1.4	20,548	**67**
Buena Vista**	19021	-1.3	20,152	**69**	-1.3	19,886	**65**
Butler	19023	-3.0	14,852	**51**	-3.8	14,286	**46**
Calhoun	19025	-5.4	10,512	**36**	-6.5	9,832	**32**
Carroll	19027	-2.0	20,993	**71**	-2.2	20,530	**67**
Cass	19029	-3.4	14,192	**48**	-4.2	13,597	**44**
Cedar	19031	0.5	18,279	**62**	0.4	18,348	**60**
Cerro Gordo**	19033	-3.7	44,720	**152**	-4.4	42,769	**139**
Cherokee	19035	-5.0	12,386	**42**	-6.0	11,638	**38**
Chickasaw	19037	-3.9	12,580	**43**	-4.7	11,988	**39**
Clarke	19039	1.4	9,258	**32**	0.8	9,335	**30**
Clay**	19041	-2.3	16,969	**58**	-3.0	16,457	**53**
Clayton	19043	-1.5	18,397	**63**	-1.6	18,111	**59**
Clinton**	19045	-0.9	49,713	**169**	-0.9	49,247	**160**
Crawford	19047	-0.1	16,928	**58**	-0.1	16,913	**55**
Dallas*	19049	17.4	47,845	**163**	17.7	56,309	**183**
Davis	19051	0.2	8,560	**29**	0.1	8,570	**28**
Decatur	19053	0.3	8,711	**30**	0.2	8,731	**28**
Delaware	19055	-1.9	18,055	**61**	-2.3	17,634	**57**
Des Moines**	19057	-3.4	40,904	**139**	-4.1	39,222	**127**
Dickinson**	19059	-0.3	16,376	**56**	-0.7	16,257	**53**
Dubuque*	19061	1.3	90,309	**308**	1.4	91,581	**297**
Emmet	19063	-2.6	10,742	**37**	-2.9	10,429	**34**
Fayette	19065	-3.6	21,212	**72**	-4.5	20,253	**66**
Floyd	19067	-2.2	16,523	**56**	-2.6	16,101	**52**
Franklin	19069	-0.1	10,694	**36**	0.0	10,695	**35**
Fremont	19071	-2.4	7,816	**27**	-2.9	7,587	**25**
Greene	19073	-4.0	9,949	**34**	-4.8	9,470	**31**
Grundy*	19075	-0.3	12,330	**42**	-0.5	12,266	**40**
Guthrie*	19077	1.7	11,550	**39**	2.1	11,796	**38**
Hamilton	19079	-1.0	16,279	**55**	-1.1	16,093	**52**
Hancock	19081	-1.7	11,893	**40**	-2.2	11,629	**38**
Hardin	19083	-3.7	18,123	**62**	-4.7	17,276	**56**
Harrison*	19085	-0.1	15,654	**53**	-0.4	15,587	**51**
Henry	19087	-2.0	19,930	**68**	-2.3	19,467	**63**
Howard	19089	-1.9	9,741	**33**	-2.2	9,524	**31**
Humboldt	19091	-3.7	9,998	**34**	-4.5	9,547	**31**
Ida	19093	-5.4	7,416	**25**	-6.3	6,951	**23**
Iowa	19095	2.0	15,988	**54**	2.1	16,325	**53**
Jackson	19097	-0.5	20,191	**69**	-0.8	20,035	**65**
Jasper**	19099	1.7	37,859	**129**	2.0	38,605	**125**
Jefferson	19101	-1.3	15,975	**54**	-1.5	15,737	**51**
Johnson*	19103	5.3	116,938	**398**	5.9	123,853	**402**
Jones*	19105	0.5	20,326	**69**	0.6	20,458	**66**
Keokuk	19107	-0.6	11,329	**39**	-1.1	11,207	**36**
Kossuth	19109	-5.5	16,220	**55**	-6.6	15,148	**49**
Lee**	19111	-4.6	36,314	**124**	-5.4	34,364	**112**
Linn*	19113	3.0	197,521	**673**	3.3	204,051	**662**
Louisa**	19115	0.2	12,209	**42**	0.3	12,244	**40**
Lucas	19117	1.2	9,533	**32**	1.6	9,686	**31**
Lyon	19119	-0.2	11,745	**40**	-0.1	11,736	**38**
Madison*	19121	4.6	14,659	**50**	5.1	15,404	**50**
Mahaska**	19123	-0.1	22,302	**76**	-0.0	22,291	**72**
Marion**	19125	1.5	32,527	**111**	1.5	33,027	**107**
Marshall**	19127	-0.7	39,027	**133**	-1.0	38,642	**125**
Mills*	19129	3.3	15,021	**51**	3.7	15,581	**51**
Mitchell	19131	0.9	10,972	**37**	1.1	11,094	**36**
Monona	19133	-3.6	9,661	**33**	-4.3	9,245	**30**
Monroe	19135	-3.6	7,731	**26**	-4.1	7,411	**24**
Montgomery	19137	-5.5	11,126	**38**	-7.1	10,340	**34**
Muscatine**	19139	1.1	42,192	**144**	1.1	42,676	**139**
O'Brien	19141	-4.1	14,482	**49**	-4.9	13,776	**45**
Osceola	19143	-3.4	6,765	**23**	-3.9	6,498	**21**
Page	19145	-4.8	16,156	**55**	-5.7	15,235	**49**
Palo Alto	19147	-5.7	9,564	**33**	-7.1	8,883	**29**
Plymouth	19149	-0.7	24,669	**84**	-1.0	24,415	**79**
Pocahontas	19151	-6.1	8,134	**28**	-6.9	7,570	**25**
Polk*	19153	4.9	392,872	**1,338**	5.4	414,072	**1,344**
Pottawattamie*	19155	1.1	88,639	**302**	0.9	89,425	**290**
Poweshiek	19157	1.5	19,092	**65**	1.5	19,384	**63**
Ringgold	19159	-1.2	5,406	**18**	-1.4	5,331	**17**
Sac	19161	-7.4	10,678	**36**	-8.7	9,753	**32**
Scott*	19163	0.6	159,637	**544**	0.7	160,701	**522**
Shelby	19165	-4.4	12,597	**43**	-4.6	12,012	**39**
Sioux	19167	2.2	32,279	**110**	2.7	33,144	**108**
Story*	19169	5.0	83,964	**286**	5.6	88,649	**288**
Tama	19171	-1.6	17,806	**61**	-2.0	17,456	**57**
Taylor	19173	-3.3	6,729	**23**	-4.7	6,416	**21**
Union	19175	-4.0	11,818	**40**	-4.8	11,256	**37**
Van Buren	19177	-0.6	7,763	**26**	-0.9	7,690	**25**
Wapello**	19179	-0.6	35,843	**122**	-0.6	35,619	**116**
Warren*	19181	4.2	42,397	**144**	4.7	44,385	**144**
Washington*	19183	4.1	21,511	**73**	4.5	22,488	**73**
Wayne	19185	-1.2	6,648	**23**	-1.6	6,539	**21**
Webster**	19187	-2.1	39,388	**134**	-2.5	38,384	**125**
Winnebago	19189	-3.2	11,343	**39**	-4.5	10,838	**35**
Winneshiek	19191	-0.0	21,304	**73**	-0.1	21,285	**69**
Woodbury*	19193	-0.8	103,007	**351**	-1.1	101,918	**331**
Worth**	19195	-2.3	7,728	**26**	-3.0	7,500	**24**
Wright	19197	-5.3	13,581	**46**	-6.5	12,697	**41**
TOTAL: IOWA		**0.8**	**2,949,245**	**10,043**	**0.9**	**2,975,158**	**9,660**

KANSAS

	FIPS CODE	PRESENT 2000-2004 % Change	PRESENT 7/1/04 Estimate	7/1/04 Ranally Population Units	FUTURE 2004-2009 % Change	FUTURE 2009 Projection	2009 Ranally Population Units
Allen	20001	-4.4	13,753	**47**	-5.5	13,001	**42**
Anderson	20003	1.7	8,244	**28**	2.1	8,420	**27**
Atchison**	20005	-0.2	16,734	**57**	-0.3	16,692	**54**
Barber	20007	-6.7	4,951	**17**	-8.0	4,553	**15**
Barton**	20009	-3.4	27,250	**93**	-3.9	26,177	**85**
Bourbon	20011	-2.6	14,986	**51**	-3.3	14,487	**47**
Brown	20013	-3.5	10,353	**35**	-4.2	9,915	**32**
Butler*	20015	3.6	61,602	**210**	3.8	63,942	**208**
Chase**	20017	3.4	3,132	**11**	3.9	3,254	**11**
Chautauqua	20019	-5.2	4,131	**14**	-6.3	3,870	**13**
Cherokee	20021	-4.6	21,571	**73**	-5.5	20,386	**66**
Cheyenne	20023	-8.7	2,890	**10**	-10.6	2,584	**8**
Clark	20025	-3.1	2,316	**8**	-3.8	2,229	**7**
Clay	20027	-3.8	8,488	**29**	-4.9	8,072	**26**
Cloud	20029	-5.1	9,740	**33**	-5.9	9,165	**30**
Coffey	20031	-0.8	8,792	**30**	-1.3	8,678	**28**
Comanche	20033	-3.3	1,902	**6**	-3.6	1,834	**6**
Cowley**	20035	-1.6	35,718	**122**	-2.0	35,004	**114**
Crawford**	20037	0.6	38,454	**131**	0.7	38,714	**126**
Decatur	20039	-6.7	3,241	**11**	-7.9	2,984	**10**
Dickinson	20041	-0.7	19,215	**65**	-1.1	19,006	**62**
Doniphan*	20043	-1.6	8,116	**28**	-2.1	7,949	**26**
Douglas*	20045	3.9	103,909	**354**	4.4	108,485	**352**
Edwards	20047	-6.5	3,225	**11**	-7.5	2,983	**10**
Elk	20049	-3.5	3,148	**11**	-3.1	3,049	**10**
Ellis**	20051	-1.3	27,140	**92**	-1.4	26,772	**87**
Ellsworth	20053	-3.7	6,286	**21**	-4.7	5,993	**19**
Finney**	20055	-4.5	38,704	**132**	-5.9	36,413	**118**
Ford**	20057	2.2	33,156	**113**	2.1	33,859	**110**
Franklin*	20059	3.9	25,761	**88**	4.2	26,851	**87**
Geary**	20061	-7.5	25,846	**88**	-8.6	23,619	**77**
Gove	20063	-6.8	2,859	**10**	-8.4	2,618	**8**
Graham	20065	-5.9	2,771	**9**	-6.5	2,591	**8**
Grant	20067	-2.7	7,698	**26**	-3.0	7,465	**24**
Gray	20069	3.5	6,110	**21**	3.7	6,339	**21**
Greeley	20071	-9.9	1,382	**5**	-13.0	1,203	**4**
Greenwood	20073	-3.2	7,424	**25**	-4.0	7,125	**23**
Hamilton	20075	-0.1	2,666	**9**	0.0	2,666	**9**
Harper	20077	-6.5	6,109	**21**	-7.6	5,647	**18**
Harvey*	20079	2.5	33,707	**115**	3.0	34,714	**113**
Haskell	20081	-1.9	4,224	**14**	-2.7	4,111	**13**
Hodgeman	20083	4.2	2,172	**7**	4.8	2,277	**7**
Jackson*	20085	3.7	13,129	**45**	4.2	13,680	**44**
Jefferson*	20087	2.6	18,908	**64**	2.8	19,446	**63**
Jewell	20089	-12.2	3,330	**11**	-14.3	2,854	**9**
Johnson*	20091	10.2	497,146	**1,693**	10.6	550,011	**1,785**
Kearny	20093	1.9	4,616	**16**	2.7	4,739	**15**
Kingman	20095	-4.5	8,285	**28**	-5.7	7,815	**25**
Kiowa	20097	-4.9	3,118	**11**	-5.3	2,953	**10**
Labette**	20099	-3.2	22,096	**75**	-3.7	21,289	**69**
Lane	20101	-12.6	1,884	**6**	-15.0	1,602	**5**
Leavenworth*	20103	5.4	72,419	**247**	6.0	76,745	**249**
Lincoln	20105	-2.9	3,473	**12**	-3.6	3,348	**11**
Linn*	20107	2.0	9,761	**33**	2.0	9,953	**32**
Logan	20109	-8.3	2,794	**10**	-10.3	2,505	**8**
Lyon**	20111	-0.5	35,750	**122**	-0.8	35,460	**115**
McPherson**	20113	-1.0	29,265	**100**	-1.4	28,847	**94**
Marion	20115	-0.7	13,273	**45**	-1.0	13,136	**43**
Marshall	20117	-4.5	10,474	**36**	-5.3	9,917	**32**
Meade	20119	0.8	4,670	**16**	0.8	4,706	**15**
Miami*	20121	3.8	29,415	**100**	3.8	30,539	**99**
Mitchell	20123	-4.2	6,638	**23**	-5.0	6,305	**20**
Montgomery**	20125	-4.8	34,520	**118**	-5.8	32,510	**106**
Morris	20127	-2.4	5,956	**20**	-3.3	5,761	**19**
Morton	20129	-6.7	3,263	**11**	-8.0	3,002	**10**
Nemaha	20131	-2.6	10,436	**36**	-3.1	10,117	**33**
Neosho	20133	-3.2	16,459	**56**	-3.7	15,857	**51**
Ness	20135	-11.1	3,069	**10**	-13.5	2,656	**9**
Norton	20137	-3.5	5,744	**20**	-4.5	5,487	**18**
Osage*	20139	0.5	16,789	**57**	0.1	16,803	**55**
Osborne	20141	-8.0	4,098	**14**	-9.4	3,711	**12**
Ottawa**	20143	0.1	6,170	**21**	-0.6	6,135	**20**
Pawnee	20145	-7.9	6,660	**23**	-9.7	6,017	**20**
Phillips	20147	-7.6	5,547	**19**	-9.4	5,024	**16**
Pottawatomie**	20149	3.6	18,856	**64**	3.7	19,554	**63**
Pratt	20151	-2.8	9,373	**32**	-3.4	9,055	**29**
Rawlins	20153	-5.4	2,805	**10**	-6.6	2,621	**9**
Reno**	20155	-1.9	63,546	**216**	-2.3	62,110	**202**
Republic	20157	-11.7	5,151	**18**	-13.9	4,433	**14**
Rice	20159	-4.2	10,305	**35**	-5.1	9,780	**32**
Riley**	20161	-1.2	62,085	**211**	-1.7	61,040	**198**
Rooks	20163	-6.1	5,338	**18**	-7.2	4,953	**16**
Rush	20165	-4.9	3,378	**12**	-5.8	3,182	**10**
Russell	20167	-8.2	6,765	**23**	-9.9	6,095	**20**
Saline**	20169	0.3	53,778	**183**	0.3	53,955	**175**
Scott	20171	-8.0	4,712	**16**	-9.5	4,266	**14**
Sedgwick*	20173	2.9	466,006	**1,587**	3.3	481,319	**1,562**
Seward**	20175	3.4	23,272	**79**	3.9	24,169	**78**
Shawnee*	20177	0.8	171,175	**583**	0.7	172,453	**560**
Sheridan	20179	-7.0	2,617	**9**	-8.3	2,401	**8**
Sherman	20181	-9.3	6,129	**21**	-11.2	5,442	**18**
Smith	20183	-10.2	4,073	**14**	-12.3	3,571	**12**
Stafford	20185	-5.4	4,531	**15**	-6.3	4,247	**14**
Stanton	20187	-0.1	2,404	**8**	-0.2	2,400	**8**
Stevens	20189	-1.8	5,365	**18**	-2.3	5,239	**17**
Sumner*	20191	-3.6	25,017	**85**	-4.7	23,842	**77**
Thomas	20193	-4.0	7,853	**27**	-5.0	7,463	**24**
Trego	20195	-8.3	3,044	**10**	-9.2	2,764	**9**
Wabaunsee*	20197	-2.3	6,730	**23**	-2.7	6,548	**21**
Wallace	20199	-9.4	1,584	**5**	-10.9	1,411	**5**
Washington	20201	-7.1	6,022	**21**	-8.6	5,502	**18**
Wichita	20203	-4.3	2,422	**8**	-5.0	2,300	**7**
Wilson	20205	-3.2	10,005	**34**	-3.7	9,634	**31**
Woodson	20207	-5.3	3,588	**12**	-5.9	3,376	**11**
Wyandotte*	20209	-0.7	156,835	**534**	-0.9	155,484	**505**
TOTAL: KANSAS		**1.7**	**2,733,795**	**9,310**	**1.9**	**2,785,235**	**9,040**

KENTUCKY

	FIPS CODE	PRESENT 2000-2004 % Change	PRESENT 7/1/04 Estimate	7/1/04 Ranally Population Units	FUTURE 2004-2009 % Change	FUTURE 2009 Projection	2009 Ranally Population Units
Adair	21001	1.6	17,516	**60**	1.6	17,804	**58**
Allen	21003	3.4	18,410	**63**	4.0	19,146	**62**
Anderson**	21005	4.8	20,021	**68**	5.2	21,061	**68**
Ballard**	21007	-1.6	8,155	**28**	-2.3	7,969	**26**
Barren**	21009	3.8	39,469	**134**	4.3	41,148	**134**
Bath**	21011	3.8	11,507	**39**	4.1	11,975	**39**
Bell**	21013	-0.4	29,925	**102**	-0.5	29,784	**97**
Boone*	21015	16.9	100,516	**342**	16.8	117,390	**381**
Bourbon*	21017	1.6	19,673	**67**	1.9	20,047	**65**
Boyd*	21019	-0.5	49,520	**169**	-0.3	49,349	**160**
Boyle**	21021	0.7	27,881	**95**	0.8	28,097	**91**
Bracken*	21023	3.3	8,554	**29**	3.9	8,888	**29**
Breathitt	21025	-2.0	15,780	**54**	-2.2	15,434	**50**
Breckinridge	21027	2.5	19,119	**65**	2.8	19,659	**64**
Bullitt*	21029	7.8	65,997	**225**	8.2	71,436	**232**
Butler	21031	1.9	13,257	**45**	2.2	13,543	**44**
Caldwell	21033	-2.3	12,755	**43**	-2.7	12,414	**40**
Calloway**	21035	1.9	34,843	**119**	2.4	35,696	**116**
Campbell*	21037	-1.0	87,745	**299**	-1.3	86,626	**281**
Carlisle	21039	0.9	5,397	**18**	1.2	5,463	**18**
Carroll	21041	0.9	10,248	**35**	0.9	10,339	**34**
Carter	21043	1.3	27,234	**93**	1.6	27,682	**90**
Casey	21045	4.5	16,143	**55**	5.1	16,969	**55**
Christian*	21047	-4.3	69,170	**236**	-5.2	65,576	**213**
Clark*	21049	3.2	34,197	**116**	3.5	35,385	**115**
Clay	21051	-1.1	24,298	**83**	-1.0	24,058	**78**
Clinton	21053	-0.4	9,595	**33**	-0.5	9,546	**31**
Crittenden	21055	-4.2	8,991	**31**	-5.4	8,503	**28**
Cumberland	21057	0.1	7,156	**24**	-0.2	7,142	**23**
Daviess*	21059	1.4	92,851	**316**	1.7	94,400	**306**
Edmonson*	21061	2.5	11,936	**41**	2.8	12,267	**40**
Elliott	21063	3.6	6,989	**24**	3.8	7,256	**24**
Estill	21065	-1.0	15,153	**52**	-1.3	14,959	**49**
Fayette*	21067	3.2	268,741	**915**	3.6	278,436	**904**
Fleming	21069	5.5	14,555	**50**	6.0	15,433	**50**
Floyd	21071	-0.5	42,233	**144**	-0.5	42,038	**136**
Franklin**	21073	0.9	48,119	**164**	0.7	48,461	**157**
Fulton**	21075	-5.5	7,326	**25**	-6.1	6,879	**22**
Gallatin*	21077	2.2	8,041	**27**	2.8	8,268	**27**
Garrard	21079	9.3	16,173	**55**	10.0	17,784	**58**
Grant*	21081	9.3	24,461	**83**	9.8	26,848	**87**
Graves**	21083	0.8	37,313	**127**	0.8	37,617	**122**
Grayson	21085	3.0	24,764	**84**	3.3	25,579	**83**
Green	21087	3.0	11,868	**40**	3.4	12,273	**40**
Greenup*	21089	0.3	36,989	**126**	0.5	37,173	**121**
Hancock*	21091	0.5	8,436	**29**	0.2	8,452	**27**
Hardin*	21093	2.6	96,607	**329**	2.9	99,375	**323**
Harlan	21095	-4.3	31,790	**108**	-4.7	30,305	**98**
Harrison	21097	1.7	18,294	**62**	1.8	18,627	**60**
Hart	21099	3.1	17,992	**61**	3.1	18,553	**60**
Henderson*	21101	0.9	45,235	**154**	1.2	45,763	**149**
Henry*	21103	4.2	15,691	**53**	4.7	16,427	**53**
Hickman	21105	-2.4	5,138	**17**	-2.6	5,006	**16**
Hopkins**	21107	1.0	46,961	**160**	1.3	47,571	**154**
Jackson	21109	0.9	13,623	**46**	1.0	13,763	**45**
Jefferson*	21111	1.0	700,741	**2,386**	1.2	709,304	**2,302**
Jessamine*	21113	8.3	42,270	**144**	9.0	46,080	**150**
Johnson	21115	1.3	23,749	**81**	2.1	24,254	**79**
Kenton*	21117	0.7	152,501	**519**	0.7	153,565	**498**
Knott	21119	-0.2	17,607	**60**	-0.2	17,572	**57**
Knox	21121	-0.4	31,657	**108**	-0.8	31,400	**102**
Larue*	21123	0.6	13,450	**46**	0.5	13,513	**44**
Laurel**	21125	6.9	56,343	**192**	7.6	60,618	**197**
Lawrence	21127	2.7	15,994	**54**	3.1	16,487	**54**
Lee	21129	-0.3	7,891	**27**	-0.6	7,847	**25**
Leslie	21131	-2.1	12,144	**41**	-2.4	11,852	**38**
Letcher	21133	-2.2	24,714	**84**	-2.6	24,076	**78**
Lewis**	21135	-2.9	13,686	**47**	-3.9	13,149	**43**
Lincoln**	21137	6.5	24,891	**85**	7.1	26,670	**87**
Livingston**	21139	-1.1	9,697	**33**	-1.5	9,551	**31**
Logan	21141	1.3	26,920	**92**	1.5	27,314	**89**
Lyon	21143	-0.2	8,067	**27**	-0.7	8,011	**26**
McCracken**	21145	-1.5	64,547	**220**	-1.7	63,454	**206**
McCreary	21147	0.9	17,234	**59**	1.3	17,450	**57**
McLean*	21149	-1.0	9,837	**33**	-1.8	9,660	**31**
Madison**	21151	7.2	75,994	**259**	7.8	81,890	**266**
Magoffin	21153	0.0	13,337	**45**	0.1	13,348	**43**
Marion	21155	2.3	18,636	**63**	2.8	19,149	**62**
Marshall	21157	1.9	30,699	**105**	2.3	31,395	**102**
Martin	21159	-0.6	12,505	**43**	-0.6	12,424	**40**
Mason**	21161	0.1	16,821	**57**	0.2	16,847	**55**

Source: Devonshire Associates Ltd. and Scan/US, Inc. 2004.
* Component of a Metropolitan Core Based Statistical Area.
** Component of a Micropolitan Core Based Statistical Area.

Counties: Population Trends, *Continued*

	FIPS CODE	PRESENT 2000-2004 % Change	PRESENT 7/1/04 Estimate	7/1/04 Ranally Population Units	FUTURE 2004-2009 % Change	FUTURE 2009 Projection	2009 Ranally Population Units
Meade*	21163	6.2	27,972	**95**	6.3	29,733	**97**
Menifee**	21165	1.0	6,623	**23**	0.4	6,649	**22**
Mercer	21167	3.8	21,599	**74**	4.4	22,541	**73**
Metcalfe**	21169	0.1	10,052	**34**	0.5	10,099	**33**
Monroe	21171	-0.1	11,741	**40**	0.0	11,743	**38**
Montgomery**	21173	5.6	23,827	**81**	6.1	25,286	**82**
Morgan	21175	3.1	14,385	**49**	3.7	14,920	**48**
Muhlenberg**	21177	-0.6	31,657	**108**	-0.6	31,482	**102**
Nelson*	21179	7.5	40,283	**137**	8.0	43,523	**141**
Nicholas	21181	2.5	6,986	**24**	3.5	7,230	**23**
Ohio	21183	1.4	23,242	**79**	1.6	23,624	**77**
Oldham*	21185	11.9	51,680	**176**	11.3	57,496	**187**
Owen	21187	6.8	11,265	**38**	7.6	12,126	**39**
Owsley	21189	-2.8	4,721	**16**	-3.5	4,556	**15**
Pendleton*	21191	6.2	15,286	**52**	6.4	16,262	**53**
Perry	21193	0.6	29,565	**101**	1.2	29,924	**97**
Pike	21195	-2.3	67,152	**229**	-2.5	65,462	**212**
Powell	21197	1.0	13,369	**46**	0.8	13,479	**44**
Pulaski**	21199	4.2	58,578	**199**	4.8	61,403	**199**
Robertson	21201	3.2	2,338	**8**	3.9	2,430	**8**
Rockcastle**	21203	0.4	16,648	**57**	0.1	16,668	**54**
Rowan	21205	1.8	22,502	**77**	2.3	23,024	**75**
Russell	21207	2.2	16,670	**57**	2.5	17,088	**55**
Scott*	21209	14.4	37,824	**129**	14.5	43,314	**141**
Shelby*	21211	10.0	36,679	**125**	10.6	40,571	**132**
Simpson	21213	2.1	16,744	**57**	2.4	17,144	**56**
Spencer*	21215	28.0	15,064	**51**	25.3	18,879	**61**
Taylor**	21217	2.5	23,492	**80**	3.1	24,214	**79**
Todd	21219	0.6	12,038	**41**	0.8	12,131	**39**
Trigg*	21221	2.8	12,954	**44**	3.0	13,339	**43**
Trimble*	21223	10.2	8,955	**30**	10.9	9,932	**32**
Union	21225	1.0	15,800	**54**	1.5	16,043	**52**
Warren*	21227	4.6	96,776	**330**	5.1	101,759	**330**
Washington	21229	4.2	11,371	**39**	4.9	11,926	**39**
Wayne	21231	2.3	20,374	**69**	2.4	20,858	**68**
Webster*	21233	-0.7	14,026	**48**	-0.9	13,898	**45**
Whitley**	21235	5.1	37,695	**128**	5.8	39,866	**129**
Wolfe	21237	-2.5	6,886	**23**	-3.7	6,629	**22**
Woodford*	21239	2.5	23,789	**81**	2.7	24,438	**79**
TOTAL: KENTUCKY		**2.5**	**4,140,891**	**14,101**	**2.8**	**4,256,211**	**13,816**

LOUISIANA (Parishes)

	FIPS CODE	PRESENT 2000-2004 % Change	PRESENT 7/1/04 Estimate	7/1/04 Ranally Population Units	FUTURE 2004-2009 % Change	FUTURE 2009 Projection	2009 Ranally Population Units
Acadia**	22001	0.9	59,384	**202**	1.1	60,056	**195**
Allen	22003	-0.9	25,218	**86**	-1.0	24,963	**81**
Ascension*	22005	13.2	86,777	**295**	13.5	98,512	**320**
Assumption**	22007	-0.7	23,229	**79**	-0.9	23,026	**75**
Avoyelles	22009	1.0	41,891	**143**	1.2	42,379	**138**
Beauregard**	22011	2.0	33,660	**115**	2.1	34,380	**112**
Bienville	22013	-3.6	15,189	**52**	-4.2	14,545	**47**
Bossier*	22015	4.9	103,123	**351**	5.4	108,716	**353**
Caddo*	22017	-0.9	249,805	**851**	-1.1	247,077	**802**
Calcasieu*	22019	0.2	184,005	**627**	0.3	184,541	**599**
Caldwell	22021	0.5	10,609	**36**	0.4	10,656	**35**
Cameron*	22023	-3.6	9,628	**33**	-4.1	9,232	**30**
Catahoula	22025	-3.7	10,518	**36**	-4.5	10,042	**33**
Claiborne	22027	-2.4	16,454	**56**	-2.4	16,057	**52**
Concordia**	22029	-3.4	19,568	**67**	-4.1	18,774	**61**
De Soto*	22031	2.6	26,145	**89**	2.9	26,915	**87**
East Baton Rouge*	22033	-0.1	412,326	**1,404**	-0.2	411,618	**1,336**
East Carroll	22035	-5.9	8,867	**30**	-7.0	8,243	**27**
East Feliciana*	22037	-1.7	21,001	**72**	-2.2	20,536	**67**
Evangeline	22039	-1.0	35,063	**119**	-1.2	34,627	**112**
Franklin	22041	-2.5	20,726	**71**	-3.2	20,066	**65**
Grant*	22043	1.3	18,945	**65**	1.5	19,232	**62**
Iberia**	22045	1.6	74,437	**253**	1.9	75,875	**246**
Iberville*	22047	-2.0	32,647	**111**	-2.5	31,828	**103**
Jackson**	22049	-1.2	15,216	**52**	-1.4	14,997	**49**
Jefferson*	22051	-0.8	451,699	**1,538**	-0.9	447,807	**1,454**
Jefferson Davis**	22053	-1.3	31,015	**106**	-1.6	30,519	**99**
Lafayette*	22055	2.6	195,453	**666**	3.1	201,469	**654**
Lafourche*	22057	1.9	91,720	**312**	2.4	93,889	**305**
La Salle	22059	-1.0	14,144	**48**	-1.3	13,965	**45**
Lincoln**	22061	-0.3	42,384	**144**	-0.4	42,224	**137**
Livingston*	22063	14.6	105,200	**358**	15.0	120,940	**393**
Madison**	22065	-6.2	12,874	**44**	-7.6	11,890	**39**
Morehouse**	22067	-1.5	30,568	**104**	-1.7	30,048	**98**
Natchitoches**	22069	-0.3	38,974	**133**	-0.4	38,823	**126**
Orleans*	22071	-4.2	464,268	**1,581**	-5.0	441,054	**1,432**
Ouachita*	22073	0.6	148,118	**504**	0.7	149,179	**484**
Plaquemines*	22075	6.3	28,450	**97**	7.4	30,569	**99**
Pointe Coupee*	22077	-1.2	22,497	**77**	-1.5	22,161	**72**
Rapides*	22079	1.1	127,716	**435**	1.2	129,296	**420**
Red River	22081	-1.3	9,498	**32**	-1.4	9,364	**30**
Richland	22083	-2.2	20,516	**70**	-2.6	19,987	**65**
Sabine	22085	-0.4	23,373	**80**	-0.7	23,206	**75**
St. Bernard*	22087	-2.1	65,813	**224**	-2.3	64,315	**209**
St. Charles*	22089	3.5	49,737	**169**	3.8	51,643	**168**
St. Helena*	22091	-2.7	10,240	**35**	-3.3	9,904	**32**
St. James	22093	-0.6	21,092	**72**	-0.6	20,957	**68**
St. John The Baptist*	22095	5.4	45,373	**154**	6.1	48,148	**156**
St. Landry**	22097	2.0	89,466	**305**	2.3	91,566	**297**
St. Martin*	22099	3.6	50,325	**171**	4.1	52,385	**170**
St. Mary**	22101	-2.7	52,045	**177**	-3.0	50,502	**164**
St. Tammany*	22103	11.3	212,895	**725**	12.1	238,590	**774**
Tangipahoa**	22105	3.9	104,512	**356**	4.4	109,090	**354**
Tensas	22107	-7.2	6,139	**21**	-8.4	5,623	**18**
Terrebonne*	22109	2.0	106,631	**363**	2.4	109,222	**355**
Union*	22111	1.0	23,028	**78**	1.3	23,331	**76**
Vermilion**	22113	1.0	54,364	**185**	1.3	55,058	**179**
Vernon**	22115	-4.7	50,060	**170**	-5.9	47,110	**153**
Washington**	22117	0.1	43,960	**150**	0.1	44,017	**143**
Webster**	22119	-1.3	41,293	**141**	-1.4	40,731	**132**
West Baton Rouge*	22121	0.8	21,767	**74**	1.1	22,011	**71**
West Carroll	22123	-0.8	12,217	**42**	-0.8	12,117	**39**
West Feliciana*	22125	1.0	15,268	**52**	1.1	15,434	**50**
Winn	22127	-3.8	16,250	**55**	-4.4	15,533	**50**
TOTAL: LOUISIANA		**0.8**	**4,505,373**	**15,343**	**1.0**	**4,550,570**	**14,772**

MAINE

	FIPS CODE	PRESENT 2000-2004 % Change	PRESENT 7/1/04 Estimate	7/1/04 Ranally Population Units	FUTURE 2004-2009 % Change	FUTURE 2009 Projection	2009 Ranally Population Units
Androscoggin*	23001	3.0	106,865	**364**	3.5	110,613	**359**
Aroostook	23003	-0.9	73,272	**249**	-1.1	72,496	**235**
Cumberland*	23005	2.6	272,577	**928**	3.0	280,846	**912**
Franklin	23007	1.3	29,858	**102**	1.6	30,331	**98**
Hancock	23009	2.5	53,100	**181**	2.9	54,641	**177**
Kennebec**	23011	2.9	120,507	**410**	3.4	124,627	**405**
Knox**	23013	2.6	40,644	**138**	2.9	41,835	**136**
Lincoln	23015	4.3	35,071	**119**	4.9	36,782	**119**
Oxford	23017	3.4	56,595	**193**	3.9	58,812	**191**
Penobscot*	23019	1.9	147,681	**503**	2.4	151,173	**491**
Piscataquis	23021	1.2	17,437	**59**	1.2	17,652	**57**
Sagadahoc*	23023	4.7	36,859	**126**	5.5	38,878	**126**
Somerset	23025	0.7	51,232	**174**	0.8	51,621	**168**
Waldo	23027	7.0	38,835	**132**	7.6	41,769	**136**
Washington	23029	-1.8	33,339	**114**	-2.1	32,644	**106**
York*	23031	7.8	201,339	**686**	8.2	217,904	**707**
TOTAL: MAINE		**3.2**	**1,315,211**	**4,478**	**3.6**	**1,362,624**	**4,423**

MARYLAND

	FIPS CODE	PRESENT 2000-2004 % Change	PRESENT 7/1/04 Estimate	7/1/04 Ranally Population Units	FUTURE 2004-2009 % Change	FUTURE 2009 Projection	2009 Ranally Population Units
Allegany*	24001	-2.2	73,291	**250**	-2.6	71,421	**232**
Anne Arundel*	24003	4.5	511,686	**1,742**	4.9	536,925	**1,743**
Baltimore*	24005	4.0	784,253	**2,670**	4.5	819,459	**2,660**
Calvert*	24009	16.8	87,081	**297**	17.0	101,916	**331**
Caroline	24011	4.8	31,196	**106**	5.4	32,867	**107**
Carroll*	24013	10.7	167,068	**569**	11.5	186,338	**605**
Cecil*	24015	10.3	94,837	**323**	11.0	105,269	**342**
Charles*	24017	13.6	136,969	**466**	14.3	156,536	**508**
Dorchester**	24019	-0.2	30,616	**104**	0.1	30,632	**99**
Frederick*	24021	12.3	219,345	**747**	12.9	247,718	**804**
Garrett	24023	0.9	30,121	**103**	1.2	30,475	**99**
Harford*	24025	8.1	236,397	**805**	8.9	257,462	**836**
Howard*	24027	8.6	269,157	**916**	9.1	293,568	**953**
Kent	24029	3.2	19,813	**67**	3.4	20,477	**66**
Montgomery*	24031	6.8	932,558	**3,175**	7.3	1,000,765	**3,248**
Prince George's*	24033	6.1	850,384	**2,896**	6.8	908,563	**2,949**
Queen Anne's*	24035	11.5	45,219	**154**	12.3	50,764	**165**
St. Mary's**	24037	10.0	94,832	**323**	10.9	105,203	**341**
Somerset*	24039	3.8	25,685	**87**	4.6	26,872	**87**
Talbot**	24041	3.3	34,925	**119**	3.6	36,195	**117**
Washington*	24043	4.9	138,354	**471**	5.6	146,118	**474**
Wicomico*	24045	4.2	88,204	**300**	4.7	92,330	**300**
Worcester**	24047	8.6	50,550	**172**	9.3	55,271	**179**
INDEPENDENT CITY							
Baltimore*	24510	-4.5	622,161	**2,118**	-5.1	590,521	**1,917**
TOTAL: MARYLAND		**5.3**	**5,574,702**	**18,980**	**5.9**	**5,903,665**	**19,162**

MASSACHUSETTS

	FIPS CODE	PRESENT 2000-2004 % Change	PRESENT 7/1/04 Estimate	7/1/04 Ranally Population Units	FUTURE 2004-2009 % Change	FUTURE 2009 Projection	2009 Ranally Population Units
Barnstable*	25001	4.2	231,645	**789**	4.5	242,135	**786**
Berkshire*	25003	-1.6	132,813	**452**	-1.9	130,354	**423**
Bristol*	25005	3.0	550,668	**1,875**	3.3	568,949	**1,847**
Dukes	25007	5.3	15,775	**54**	5.5	16,646	**54**
Essex*	25009	2.6	741,982	**2,526**	2.8	762,628	**2,475**
Franklin*	25011	1.3	72,431	**247**	1.6	73,559	**239**
Hampden*	25013	1.4	462,756	**1,576**	1.7	470,565	**1,527**
Hampshire*	25015	2.4	155,980	**531**	2.8	160,369	**521**
Middlesex*	25017	0.5	1,472,613	**5,014**	0.3	1,477,006	**4,794**
Nantucket	25019	16.6	11,096	**38**	16.8	12,955	**42**
Norfolk*	25021	0.8	655,356	**2,231**	0.8	660,454	**2,144**
Plymouth*	25023	4.0	491,878	**1,675**	4.4	513,646	**1,667**
Suffolk*	25025	-1.8	677,616	**2,307**	-2.3	662,356	**2,150**
Worcester*	25027	4.5	784,595	**2,672**	5.1	824,492	**2,676**
TOTAL: MASSACHUSETTS		**1.7**	**6,457,204**	**21,987**	**1.8**	**6,576,114**	**21,345**

MICHIGAN

	FIPS CODE	PRESENT 2000-2004 % Change	PRESENT 7/1/04 Estimate	7/1/04 Ranally Population Units	FUTURE 2004-2009 % Change	FUTURE 2009 Projection	2009 Ranally Population Units
Alcona	26001	-1.6	11,528	**39**	-1.9	11,307	**37**
Alger	26003	-1.2	9,743	**33**	-1.3	9,621	**31**
Allegan**	26005	5.7	111,737	**380**	6.3	118,757	**385**
Alpena**	26007	-2.2	30,613	**104**	-2.7	29,779	**97**
Antrim	26009	5.4	24,369	**83**	5.6	25,742	**84**
Arenac	26011	0.2	17,312	**59**	0.1	17,326	**56**
Baraga	26013	0.6	8,796	**30**	0.8	8,863	**29**
Barry*	26015	4.7	59,395	**202**	5.2	62,496	**203**
Bay*	26017	-0.8	109,229	**372**	-1.0	108,107	**351**
Benzie**	26019	8.8	17,400	**59**	9.2	19,007	**62**
Berrien*	26021	0.2	162,816	**554**	0.1	163,051	**529**
Branch**	26023	1.8	46,594	**159**	1.9	47,495	**154**
Calhoun*	26025	0.8	139,106	**474**	0.9	140,354	**456**
Cass*	26027	0.7	51,459	**175**	0.7	51,827	**168**
Charlevoix	26029	3.1	26,898	**92**	3.4	27,822	**90**
Cheboygan	26031	4.7	27,684	**94**	5.0	29,076	**94**
Chippewa**	26033	0.9	38,907	**132**	1.1	39,330	**128**
Clare	26035	1.3	31,659	**108**	1.1	32,008	**104**
Clinton*	26037	5.8	68,489	**233**	6.4	72,882	**237**
Crawford	26039	4.8	14,962	**51**	5.1	15,732	**51**
Delta**	26041	-0.7	38,234	**130**	-1.1	37,824	**123**
Dickinson**	26043	-1.4	27,089	**92**	-1.8	26,603	**86**
Eaton*	26045	3.2	106,959	**364**	3.6	110,760	**360**
Emmet	26047	5.4	33,141	**113**	6.0	35,142	**114**
Genesee*	26049	1.8	444,011	**1,512**	2.0	452,774	**1,470**
Gladwin	26051	4.6	27,210	**93**	5.0	28,561	**93**
Gogebic	26053	-0.2	17,331	**59**	0.0	17,338	**56**
Grand Traverse**	26055	7.3	83,355	**284**	8.0	90,065	**292**
Gratiot**	26057	0.7	42,563	**145**	0.7	42,872	**139**
Hillsdale	26059	1.9	47,410	**161**	1.9	48,306	**157**
Houghton**	26061	0.9	36,331	**124**	1.1	36,741	**119**
Huron	26063	-3.2	34,941	**119**	-3.8	33,597	**109**
Ingham*	26065	1.3	282,853	**963**	1.4	286,945	**931**
Ionia*	26067	4.4	64,207	**219**	4.9	67,375	**219**
Iosco	26069	-2.2	26,740	**91**	-2.7	26,010	**84**
Iron	26071	-3.5	12,680	**43**	-4.1	12,159	**39**
Isabella**	26073	2.8	65,094	**222**	3.3	67,243	**218**
Jackson*	26075	3.2	163,516	**557**	3.6	169,477	**550**
Kalamazoo*	26077	1.9	243,185	**828**	2.2	248,537	**807**
Kalkaska**	26079	4.8	17,360	**59**	5.3	18,274	**59**
Kent*	26081	3.6	595,142	**2,026**	4.0	618,715	**2,008**
Keweenaw**	26083	-4.4	2,200	**7**	-5.8	2,072	**7**
Lake	26085	5.3	11,929	**41**	5.6	12,599	**41**
Lapeer*	26087	5.0	92,313	**314**	5.4	97,299	**316**
Leelanau**	26089	4.5	22,059	**75**	4.5	23,048	**75**
Lenawee**	26091	2.5	101,344	**345**	2.7	104,124	**338**
Livingston*	26093	13.2	177,683	**605**	13.5	201,672	**655**
Luce	26095	-1.9	6,889	**23**	-2.1	6,741	**22**
Mackinac	26097	-5.2	11,323	**39**	-6.3	10,615	**34**
Macomb*	26099	4.2	821,634	**2,798**	4.7	859,988	**2,791**
Manistee	26101	4.1	25,543	**87**	4.4	26,671	**87**
Marquette**	26103	-0.0	64,616	**220**	-0.0	64,610	**210**
Mason	26105	1.9	28,801	**98**	2.0	29,376	**95**
Mecosta**	26107	3.8	42,083	**143**	4.2	43,859	**142**
Menominee**	26109	-1.2	25,015	**85**	-1.4	24,669	**80**
Midland**	26111	2.5	84,980	**289**	2.9	87,412	**284**
Missaukee**	26113	6.4	15,402	**52**	6.9	16,462	**53**
Monroe*	26115	4.2	152,069	**518**	4.6	159,036	**516**
Montcalm	26117	3.5	63,419	**216**	3.9	65,882	**214**
Montmorency	26119	2.1	10,531	**36**	1.8	10,722	**35**
Muskegon*	26121	2.2	173,945	**592**	2.4	178,202	**578**
Newaygo*	26123	3.8	49,686	**169**	4.2	51,761	**168**
Oakland*	26125	1.5	1,211,605	**4,125**	1.5	1,230,186	**3,993**
Oceana	26127	5.8	28,442	**97**	6.5	30,277	**98**
Ogemaw	26129	0.8	21,826	**74**	0.8	21,993	**71**
Ontonagon	26131	-4.1	7,496	**26**	-4.9	7,128	**23**
Osceola	26133	1.7	23,598	**80**	1.9	24,037	**78**
Oscoda	26135	0.6	9,474	**32**	0.7	9,540	**31**
Otsego	26137	5.4	24,548	**84**	5.7	25,946	**84**
Ottawa*	26139	6.0	252,694	**860**	6.5	269,185	**874**
Presque Isle	26141	-1.1	14,257	**49**	-1.0	14,110	**46**
Roscommon	26143	3.9	26,464	**90**	4.4	27,630	**90**
Saginaw*	26145	-0.4	209,117	**712**	-0.5	208,059	**675**
St. Clair*	26147	3.8	170,514	**581**	4.2	177,753	**577**
St. Joseph**	26149	0.9	62,973	**214**	0.9	63,514	**206**
Sanilac	26151	0.1	44,597	**152**	0.2	44,666	**145**
Schoolcraft	26153	-2.0	8,725	**30**	-2.6	8,494	**28**
Shiawassee**	26155	1.6	72,823	**248**	1.9	74,215	**241**
Tuscola	26157	0.3	58,413	**199**	0.3	58,563	**190**
Van Buren*	26159	3.4	78,829	**268**	3.9	81,919	**266**
Washtenaw*	26161	6.3	343,273	**1,169**	6.9	366,793	**1,191**
Wayne*	26163	-2.1	2,018,715	**6,874**	-2.5	1,968,977	**6,391**
Wexford**	26165	3.3	31,487	**107**	3.7	32,660	**106**
TOTAL: MICHIGAN		**1.8**	**10,121,382**	**34,460**	**2.0**	**10,328,365**	**33,524**

MINNESOTA

	FIPS CODE	PRESENT 2000-2004 % Change	PRESENT 7/1/04 Estimate	7/1/04 Ranally Population Units	FUTURE 2004-2009 % Change	FUTURE 2009 Projection	2009 Ranally Population Units
Aitkin	27001	4.1	15,928	**54**	4.6	16,654	**54**
Anoka*	27003	7.0	318,838	**1,086**	7.5	342,630	**1,112**
Becker	27005	5.1	31,538	**107**	5.8	33,355	**108**
Beltrami**	27007	7.1	42,464	**145**	7.8	45,796	**149**
Benton*	27009	10.3	37,738	**128**	10.8	41,805	**136**
Big Stone	27011	-3.7	5,606	**19**	-4.1	5,378	**17**
Blue Earth**	27013	3.3	57,766	**197**	4.0	60,065	**195**
Brown**	27015	-2.0	26,385	**90**	-2.3	25,790	**84**
Carlton*	27017	5.7	33,484	**114**	6.6	35,681	**116**
Carver*	27019	16.3	81,656	**278**	16.5	95,126	**309**
Cass**	27021	5.0	28,509	**97**	5.3	30,025	**97**
Chippewa	27023	-2.8	12,721	**43**	-3.4	12,294	**40**
Chisago*	27025	16.1	47,700	**162**	16.1	55,373	**180**
Clay*	27027	1.9	52,205	**178**	2.1	53,311	**173**
Clearwater	27029	0.2	8,438	**29**	0.8	8,509	**28**
Cook	27031	2.7	5,310	**18**	2.6	5,449	**18**
Cottonwood	27033	-1.5	11,980	**41**	-1.6	11,784	**38**
Crow Wing**	27035	7.9	59,463	**202**	8.7	64,625	**210**
Dakota*	27037	6.3	378,473	**1,289**	6.8	404,250	**1,312**
Dodge*	27039	8.8	19,288	**66**	9.2	21,070	**68**
Douglas**	27041	5.2	34,520	**118**	5.8	36,534	**119**
Faribault	27043	-3.6	15,604	**53**	-4.2	14,953	**49**
Fillmore	27045	1.2	21,365	**73**	1.2	21,619	**70**

Source: Devonshire Associates Ltd. and Scan/US, Inc. 2004.
* Component of a Metropolitan Core Based Statistical Area.
** Component of a Micropolitan Core Based Statistical Area.

continued on next page

Counties: Population Trends, *Continued*

	FIPS CODE	PRESENT 2000-2004 % Change	PRESENT 7/1/04 Estimate	7/1/04 Ranally Population Units	FUTURE 2004-2009 % Change	FUTURE 2009 Projection	2009 Ranally Population Units
Freeborn**	27047	-2.5	31,766	**108**	-3.0	30,802	**100**
Goodhue**	27049	3.1	45,501	**155**	3.7	47,172	**153**
Grant	27051	-0.9	6,232	**21**	-0.9	6,178	**20**
Hennepin*	27053	0.5	1,122,141	**3,821**	0.5	1,127,580	**3,660**
Houston*	27055	1.7	20,056	**68**	1.9	20,435	**66**
Hubbard	27057	1.8	18,703	**64**	1.8	19,042	**62**
Isanti*	27059	17.1	36,651	**125**	17.4	43,044	**140**
Itasca	27061	0.8	44,345	**151**	0.9	44,746	**145**
Jackson	27063	-1.1	11,147	**38**	-1.1	11,029	**36**
Kanabec	27065	7.6	16,133	**55**	8.2	17,462	**57**
Kandiyohi**	27067	-0.1	41,142	**140**	-0.1	41,112	**133**
Kittson	27069	-7.8	4,872	**17**	-9.3	4,417	**14**
Koochiching	27071	-3.0	13,922	**47**	-3.4	13,452	**44**
Lac qui Parle	27073	-3.2	7,806	**27**	-3.8	7,509	**24**
Lake	27075	1.2	11,192	**38**	1.4	11,350	**37**
Lake of the Woods	27077	-4.0	4,343	**15**	-4.6	4,145	**13**
Le Sueur	27079	6.9	27,185	**93**	7.7	29,289	**95**
Lincoln	27081	-5.5	6,078	**21**	-6.4	5,690	**18**
Lyon**	27083	-3.2	24,617	**84**	-4.0	23,627	**77**
McLeod**	27085	3.7	36,194	**123**	4.6	37,842	**123**
Mahnomen	27087	-1.9	5,093	**17**	-2.0	4,992	**16**
Marshall	27089	-2.0	9,955	**34**	-2.1	9,747	**32**
Martin**	27091	-3.5	21,039	**72**	-4.2	20,148	**65**
Meeker	27093	3.2	23,378	**80**	3.7	24,239	**79**
Mille Lacs	27095	11.7	24,937	**85**	12.4	28,033	**91**
Morrison	27097	3.6	32,854	**112**	4.0	34,176	**111**
Mower**	27099	0.7	38,863	**132**	0.5	39,061	**127**
Murray	27101	-2.6	8,928	**30**	-2.9	8,665	**28**
Nicollet**	27103	4.1	31,006	**106**	4.4	32,366	**105**
Nobles**	27105	-1.3	20,558	**70**	-1.5	20,243	**66**
Norman	27107	-4.4	7,111	**24**	-5.4	6,724	**22**
Olmsted*	27109	7.5	133,562	**455**	8.1	144,443	**469**
Otter Tail**	27111	3.9	59,382	**202**	4.5	62,056	**201**
Pennington	27113	0.6	13,665	**47**	1.1	13,810	**45**
Pine	27115	5.9	28,107	**96**	6.4	29,910	**97**
Pipestone	27117	-2.7	9,626	**33**	-2.8	9,354	**30**
Polk*	27119	-2.0	30,748	**105**	-2.5	29,972	**97**
Pope	27121	0.2	11,255	**38**	0.1	11,266	**37**
Ramsey*	27123	-1.2	504,693	**1,718**	-1.6	496,428	**1,611**
Red Lake	27125	0.7	4,331	**15**	1.4	4,392	**14**
Redwood	27127	-4.5	16,061	**55**	-5.1	15,235	**49**
Renville	27129	-2.3	16,757	**57**	-2.8	16,291	**53**
Rice**	27131	7.0	60,613	**206**	7.8	65,341	**212**
Rock	27133	-1.4	9,582	**33**	-1.7	9,420	**31**
Roseau	27135	-0.1	16,322	**56**	0.1	16,338	**53**
St. Louis*	27137	-1.1	198,256	**675**	-1.4	195,546	**635**
Scott*	27139	27.8	114,403	**390**	25.4	143,515	**466**
Sherburne*	27141	20.8	77,790	**265**	20.1	93,397	**303**
Sibley	27143	-0.7	15,250	**52**	-0.9	15,116	**49**
Stearns*	27145	3.9	138,332	**471**	4.3	144,238	**468**
Steele**	27147	4.1	35,071	**119**	4.5	36,662	**119**
Stevens	27149	-2.1	9,843	**34**	-2.3	9,621	**31**
Swift	27151	-3.2	11,569	**39**	-3.7	11,140	**36**
Todd	27153	-0.6	24,270	**83**	-0.8	24,073	**78**
Traverse	27155	-7.0	3,843	**13**	-8.4	3,520	**11**
Wabasha*	27157	3.2	22,303	**76**	3.6	23,097	**75**
Wadena	27159	-1.1	13,567	**46**	-1.3	13,384	**43**
Waseca	27161	-0.6	19,405	**66**	-0.8	19,251	**62**
Washington*	27163	8.0	217,209	**740**	8.4	235,409	**764**
Watonwan	27165	-2.7	11,554	**39**	-2.9	11,223	**36**
Wilkin**	27167	-3.5	6,885	**23**	-4.2	6,594	**21**
Winona**	27169	-1.4	49,300	**168**	-1.8	48,401	**157**
Wright*	27171	18.3	106,446	**362**	18.4	126,017	**409**
Yellow Medicine	27173	-4.7	10,557	**36**	-5.5	9,976	**32**
TOTAL: MINNESOTA		**3.7**	**5,101,284**	**17,373**	**4.1**	**5,310,829**	**17,235**

MISSISSIPPI

	FIPS CODE	PRESENT 2000-2004 % Change	PRESENT 7/1/04 Estimate	7/1/04 Ranally Population Units	FUTURE 2004-2009 % Change	FUTURE 2009 Projection	2009 Ranally Population Units
Adams**	28001	-4.2	32,903	**112**	-4.9	31,290	**102**
Alcorn**	28003	1.4	35,037	**119**	1.5	35,558	**115**
Amite**	28005	-0.0	13,597	**46**	0.1	13,609	**44**
Attala	28007	0.1	19,679	**67**	0.1	19,703	**64**
Benton	28009	-4.2	7,692	**26**	-5.2	7,293	**24**
Bolivar**	28011	-4.4	38,827	**132**	-5.1	36,841	**120**
Calhoun	28013	-2.1	14,753	**50**	-2.5	14,386	**47**
Carroll**	28015	-3.8	10,359	**35**	-4.9	9,853	**32**
Chickasaw	28017	-1.5	19,141	**65**	-1.7	18,824	**61**
Choctaw	28019	-1.3	9,630	**33**	-1.6	9,473	**31**
Claiborne	28021	-3.7	11,394	**39**	-4.7	10,864	**35**
Clarke**	28023	-1.6	17,674	**60**	-2.0	17,313	**56**
Clay**	28025	-2.1	21,511	**73**	-2.6	20,943	**68**
Coahoma**	28027	-4.6	29,213	**99**	-5.5	27,595	**90**
Copiah*	28029	0.8	28,982	**99**	0.9	29,242	**95**
Covington	28031	5.2	20,417	**70**	5.9	21,612	**70**
DeSoto*	28033	20.9	129,632	**441**	20.2	155,853	**506**
Forrest*	28035	3.2	74,924	**255**	3.6	77,594	**252**
Franklin	28037	-1.8	8,300	**28**	-2.4	8,101	**26**
George*	28039	8.7	20,808	**71**	9.6	22,810	**74**
Greene	28041	-1.3	13,122	**45**	-1.8	12,887	**42**
Grenada**	28043	-2.5	22,681	**77**	-2.8	22,045	**72**
Hancock*	28045	6.5	45,765	**156**	6.7	48,851	**159**
Harrison*	28047	-0.0	189,590	**646**	-0.1	189,423	**615**
Hinds*	28049	-0.9	248,578	**846**	-1.0	245,985	**798**
Holmes	28051	-1.6	21,261	**72**	-2.0	20,834	**68**
Humphreys	28053	-5.5	10,590	**36**	-6.1	9,947	**32**
Issaquena	28055	-14.6	1,941	**7**	-17.3	1,605	**5**
Itawamba**	28057	1.0	22,999	**78**	0.7	23,171	**75**
Jackson*	28059	2.4	134,605	**458**	2.5	137,956	**448**
Jasper**	28061	1.0	18,332	**62**	1.4	18,587	**60**
Jefferson	28063	-2.8	9,472	**32**	-3.2	9,167	**30**
Jefferson Davis	28065	-5.1	13,245	**45**	-5.6	12,498	**41**
Jones**	28067	0.4	65,230	**222**	0.5	65,528	**213**
Kemper**	28069	-0.1	10,439	**36**	0.1	10,454	**34**
Lafayette**	28071	4.9	40,657	**138**	5.8	42,995	**140**
Lamar*	28073	9.6	42,827	**146**	10.1	47,166	**153**
Lauderdale**	28075	-0.7	77,582	**264**	-0.8	76,943	**250**
Lawrence	28077	2.5	13,595	**46**	2.7	13,967	**45**
Leake	28079	5.6	22,112	**75**	6.6	23,568	**77**
Lee**	28081	3.3	78,261	**266**	3.6	81,094	**263**
Leflore**	28083	-5.1	36,017	**123**	-6.1	33,822	**110**
Lincoln**	28085	1.5	33,675	**115**	1.8	34,292	**111**
Lowndes**	28087	-2.0	60,373	**206**	-2.4	58,951	**191**
Madison*	28089	8.9	81,322	**277**	9.6	89,114	**289**
Marion	28091	-2.6	24,927	**85**	-3.2	24,120	**78**
Marshall*	28093	1.6	35,565	**121**	1.7	36,168	**117**
Monroe	28095	-0.6	37,786	**129**	-0.8	37,502	**122**
Montgomery	28097	-2.6	11,866	**40**	-2.9	11,526	**37**
Neshoba	28099	2.1	29,275	**100**	2.4	29,969	**97**
Newton	28101	1.2	22,101	**75**	1.3	22,383	**73**
Noxubee	28103	-2.4	12,243	**42**	-3.0	11,876	**39**
Oktibbeha**	28105	-1.1	42,432	**144**	-1.7	41,722	**135**
Panola	28107	3.7	35,526	**121**	4.0	36,931	**120**
Pearl River**	28109	6.1	51,596	**176**	6.8	55,091	**179**
Perry*	28111	1.5	12,322	**42**	1.4	12,494	**41**
Pike**	28113	-0.1	38,917	**133**	-0.2	38,820	**126**
Pontotoc**	28115	4.2	27,843	**95**	4.8	29,173	**95**
Prentiss	28117	0.1	25,575	**87**	-0.1	25,540	**83**
Quitman	28119	-4.7	9,638	**33**	-5.2	9,137	**30**
Rankin*	28121	10.6	127,528	**434**	11.1	141,651	**460**
Scott	28123	0.1	28,465	**97**	0.2	28,534	**93**
Sharkey	28125	-7.0	6,121	**21**	-8.1	5,625	**18**
Simpson*	28127	-0.3	27,563	**94**	-0.5	27,412	**89**
Smith	28129	-2.9	15,719	**54**	-3.6	15,153	**49**
Stone*	28131	5.6	14,384	**49**	6.2	15,272	**50**
Sunflower**	28133	-3.8	33,078	**113**	-4.4	31,625	**103**
Tallahatchie	28135	-4.5	14,235	**48**	-5.4	13,462	**44**
Tate*	28137	2.1	25,907	**88**	2.2	26,465	**86**
Tippah	28139	0.5	20,938	**71**	0.4	21,022	**68**
Tishomingo	28141	-1.4	18,901	**64**	-1.7	18,575	**60**
Tunica*	28143	10.0	10,146	**35**	11.2	11,283	**37**
Union	28145	3.6	26,285	**89**	3.2	27,138	**88**
Walthall	28147	0.4	15,219	**52**	0.9	15,359	**50**
Warren**	28149	-1.7	48,799	**166**	-2.0	47,825	**155**
Washington**	28151	-5.4	59,560	**203**	-6.4	55,772	**181**
Wayne	28153	-0.4	21,132	**72**	-0.4	21,043	**68**
Webster	28155	-1.7	10,114	**34**	-2.3	9,885	**32**
Wilkinson	28157	-0.9	10,223	**35**	-0.9	10,131	**33**
Winston	28159	-1.6	19,829	**68**	-2.1	19,418	**63**
Yalobusha	28161	2.8	13,417	**46**	2.6	13,768	**45**
Yazoo**	28163	0.6	28,309	**96**	0.6	28,486	**92**
TOTAL: MISSISSIPPI		**1.7**	**2,892,228**	**9,846**	**1.9**	**2,946,963**	**9,569**

MISSOURI

	FIPS CODE	PRESENT 2000-2004 % Change	PRESENT 7/1/04 Estimate	7/1/04 Ranally Population Units	FUTURE 2004-2009 % Change	FUTURE 2009 Projection	2009 Ranally Population Units
Adair**	29001	-1.0	24,737	**84**	-1.1	24,469	**79**
Andrew*	29003	2.5	16,904	**58**	2.7	17,360	**56**
Atchison	29005	-2.9	6,246	**21**	-3.2	6,045	**20**
Audrain**	29007	-0.6	25,688	**87**	-0.6	25,543	**83**
Barry	29009	2.4	34,820	**119**	2.7	35,765	**116**
Barton	29011	4.8	13,148	**45**	5.6	13,890	**45**
Bates*	29013	2.1	17,008	**58**	2.1	17,362	**56**
Benton	29015	6.8	18,350	**62**	7.5	19,720	**64**
Bollinger**	29017	3.1	12,402	**42**	3.3	12,815	**42**
Boone*	29019	5.5	142,884	**487**	6.1	151,657	**492**
Buchanan*	29021	-1.7	84,529	**288**	-2.2	82,638	**268**
Butler**	29023	-0.0	40,866	**139**	0.1	40,914	**133**
Caldwell*	29025	2.7	9,214	**31**	2.9	9,483	**31**
Callaway*	29027	4.6	42,657	**145**	5.0	44,808	**145**
Camden	29029	4.3	38,659	**132**	4.6	40,432	**131**
Cape Girardeau**	29031	2.3	70,244	**239**	2.6	72,066	**234**
Carroll	29033	-1.7	10,107	**34**	-2.1	9,894	**32**
Carter	29035	0.7	5,983	**20**	0.8	6,028	**20**
Cass*	29037	10.7	90,899	**310**	11.3	101,203	**329**
Cedar	29039	1.0	13,874	**47**	1.3	14,049	**46**
Chariton	29041	-2.9	8,195	**28**	-3.4	7,920	**26**
Christian*	29043	17.5	63,776	**217**	17.3	74,782	**243**
Clark**	29045	0.2	7,430	**25**	0.6	7,475	**24**
Clay*	29047	7.3	197,398	**672**	8.0	213,104	**692**
Clinton*	29049	8.0	20,502	**70**	8.8	22,311	**72**
Cole*	29051	1.9	72,781	**248**	2.2	74,401	**242**
Cooper	29053	2.6	17,106	**58**	2.8	17,588	**57**
Crawford	29055	4.1	23,729	**81**	4.5	24,805	**81**
Dade	29057	-1.3	7,822	**27**	-1.5	7,704	**25**
Dallas*	29059	3.8	16,253	**55**	4.3	16,954	**55**
Daviess	29061	-0.1	8,004	**27**	-0.0	8,003	**26**
DeKalb*	29063	12.5	13,050	**44**	-0.6	12,978	**42**
Dent	29065	-0.1	14,915	**51**	-0.2	14,887	**48**
Douglas	29067	2.8	13,450	**46**	3.2	13,882	**45**
Dunklin**	29069	-2.0	32,505	**111**	-2.3	31,766	**103**
Franklin*	29071	4.3	97,849	**333**	4.8	102,549	**333**
Gasconade	29073	1.6	15,593	**53**	1.6	15,850	**51**
Gentry	29075	-5.7	6,471	**22**	-7.0	6,017	**20**
Greene*	29077	2.9	247,471	**843**	3.4	255,945	**831**
Grundy	29079	-1.5	10,279	**35**	-1.6	10,118	**33**
Harrison	29081	-0.4	8,816	**30**	-0.7	8,755	**28**
Henry	29083	2.4	22,527	**77**	2.4	23,062	**75**
Hickory	29085	1.0	9,025	**31**	1.1	9,123	**30**
Holt	29087	-5.0	5,085	**17**	-5.7	4,796	**16**
Howard*	29089	-2.6	9,949	**34**	-2.9	9,660	**31**
Howell**	29091	0.9	37,587	**128**	1.2	38,020	**123**
Iron	29093	-4.7	10,199	**35**	-5.1	9,678	**31**
Jackson*	29095	0.9	661,091	**2,251**	1.0	667,791	**2,168**
Jasper*	29097	4.3	109,158	**372**	4.8	114,363	**371**
Jefferson*	29099	5.7	209,444	**713**	6.3	222,683	**723**
Johnson**	29101	5.4	50,858	**173**	5.8	53,831	**175**
Knox	29103	-1.5	4,295	**15**	-1.9	4,213	**14**
Laclede**	29105	3.2	33,569	**114**	3.6	34,774	**113**
Lafayette*	29107	-0.1	32,925	**112**	-0.4	32,789	**106**
Lawrence	29109	4.5	36,792	**125**	4.9	38,613	**125**
Lewis**	29111	-3.5	10,130	**34**	-4.6	9,662	**31**
Lincoln*	29113	17.7	45,856	**156**	17.9	54,086	**176**
Linn	29115	-2.8	13,372	**46**	-3.3	12,935	**42**
Livingston	29117	-1.4	14,350	**49**	-1.3	14,159	**46**
McDonald*	29119	1.8	22,073	**75**	2.2	22,568	**73**
Macon	29121	-1.5	15,518	**53**	-1.9	15,227	**49**
Madison	29123	0.0	11,803	**40**	-0.1	11,791	**38**
Maries	29125	-1.0	8,818	**30**	-1.3	8,704	**28**
Marion**	29127	0.0	28,290	**96**	-0.0	28,288	**92**
Mercer	29129	-5.7	3,541	**12**	-7.5	3,276	**11**
Miller	29131	3.8	24,464	**83**	4.3	25,507	**83**
Mississippi	29133	9.7	14,728	**50**	11.6	16,436	**53**
Moniteau*	29135	1.2	15,005	**51**	1.3	15,207	**49**
Monroe	29137	1.1	9,418	**32**	1.1	9,522	**31**
Montgomery	29139	-0.7	12,048	**41**	-0.8	11,946	**39**
Morgan	29141	4.7	20,207	**69**	5.1	21,242	**69**
New Madrid	29143	-3.7	19,028	**65**	-4.1	18,251	**59**
Newton*	29145	3.5	54,463	**185**	3.9	56,601	**184**
Nodaway**	29147	-1.0	21,702	**74**	-0.9	21,497	**70**
Oregon	29149	-0.5	10,295	**35**	-0.3	10,261	**33**
Osage*	29151	0.7	13,151	**45**	0.6	13,233	**43**
Ozark	29153	-0.6	9,486	**32**	-0.7	9,422	**31**
Pemiscot	29155	-2.1	19,630	**67**	-2.5	19,143	**62**
Perry	29157	0.6	18,249	**62**	0.7	18,368	**60**
Pettis**	29159	-0.2	39,309	**134**	-0.5	39,128	**127**
Phelps**	29161	6.1	42,250	**144**	6.9	45,148	**147**
Pike	29163	1.3	18,583	**63**	1.7	18,904	**61**
Platte*	29165	9.9	81,115	**276**	10.6	89,721	**291**
Polk*	29167	5.3	28,417	**97**	5.9	30,089	**98**
Pulaski**	29169	12.7	46,394	**158**	12.3	52,078	**169**
Putnam	29171	-2.0	5,117	**17**	-3.0	4,963	**16**
Ralls**	29173	0.2	9,650	**33**	-0.2	9,633	**31**
Randolph**	29175	2.1	25,172	**86**	2.5	25,801	**84**
Ray*	29177	3.2	24,106	**82**	3.7	25,004	**81**
Reynolds	29179	-2.4	6,529	**22**	-3.9	6,272	**20**
Ripley	29181	2.7	13,875	**47**	3.4	14,341	**47**
St. Charles*	29183	12.7	319,977	**1,090**	13.2	362,124	**1,175**
St. Clair	29185	0.3	9,677	**33**	-0.2	9,661	**31**
Ste. Genevieve	29186	1.7	18,153	**62**	1.6	18,449	**60**
St. Francois**	29187	5.4	58,648	**200**	6.1	62,231	**202**
St. Louis*	29189	-0.4	1,012,010	**3,446**	-0.6	1,006,248	**3,266**
Saline**	29195	-4.8	22,609	**77**	-5.9	21,264	**69**
Schuyler**	29197	1.2	4,220	**14**	1.3	4,275	**14**
Scotland	29199	-2.0	4,882	**17**	-2.4	4,764	**15**
Scott**	29201	1.2	40,908	**139**	1.6	41,545	**135**
Shannon	29203	-0.5	8,283	**28**	-0.6	8,230	**27**
Shelby	29205	-1.8	6,675	**23**	-2.1	6,536	**21**
Stoddard	29207	-0.4	29,601	**101**	-0.4	29,472	**96**
Stone**	29209	5.9	30,341	**103**	6.6	32,332	**105**
Sullivan	29211	-2.6	7,034	**24**	-3.2	6,807	**22**
Taney**	29213	5.5	41,899	**143**	5.9	44,370	**144**
Texas	29215	6.6	24,520	**83**	7.7	26,404	**86**
Vernon	29217	-1.1	20,237	**69**	-1.1	20,006	**65**
Warren*	29219	12.4	27,570	**94**	12.8	31,102	**101**
Washington*	29221	3.0	24,034	**82**	3.1	24,782	**80**
Wayne	29223	-1.7	13,033	**44**	-2.2	12,750	**41**
Webster*	29225	8.7	33,748	**115**	9.2	36,860	**120**
Worth	29227	-6.2	2,235	**8**	-7.4	2,069	**7**
Wright	29229	1.7	18,258	**62**	2.0	18,617	**60**
INDEPENDENT CITY							
St. Louis*	29510	-5.9	327,502	**1,115**	-6.9	304,819	**989**
TOTAL: MISSOURI		**2.5**	**5,737,314**	**19,534**	**2.9**	**5,901,462**	**19,155**

MONTANA

	FIPS CODE	PRESENT 2000-2004 % Change	PRESENT 7/1/04 Estimate	7/1/04 Ranally Population Units	FUTURE 2004-2009 % Change	FUTURE 2009 Projection	2009 Ranally Population Units
Beaverhead	30001	-4.1	8,827	**30**	-5.1	8,376	**27**
Big Horn	30003	2.3	12,967	**44**	2.7	13,323	**43**
Blaine	30005	-5.2	6,645	**23**	-6.1	6,239	**20**
Broadwater	30007	1.5	4,449	**15**	2.0	4,538	**15**
Carbon*	30009	3.0	9,840	**34**	3.5	10,188	**33**
Carter	30011	-2.4	1,327	**5**	-2.1	1,299	**4**
Cascade*	30013	-1.3	79,349	**270**	-1.4	78,254	**254**
Chouteau	30015	-8.8	5,447	**19**	-11.1	4,841	**16**
Custer	30017	-3.6	11,271	**38**	-4.3	10,790	**35**
Daniels	30019	-5.0	1,916	**7**	-6.1	1,800	**6**
Dawson	30021	-4.1	8,688	**30**	-5.0	8,257	**27**
Deer Lodge	30023	-6.4	8,812	**30**	-7.6	8,138	**26**
Fallon	30025	-3.7	2,733	**9**	-3.6	2,635	**9**
Fergus	30027	-2.2	11,628	**40**	-2.9	11,296	**37**

Source: Devonshire Associates Ltd. and Scan/US, Inc. 2004.
* Component of a Metropolitan Core Based Statistical Area.
** Component of a Micropolitan Core Based Statistical Area.

Counties: Population Trends, *Continued*

	FIPS CODE	PRESENT 2000-2004 % Change	PRESENT 7/1/04 Estimate	7/1/04 Ranally Population Units	FUTURE 2004-2009 % Change	FUTURE 2009 Projection	2009 Ranally Population Units
Flathead**	30029	8.9	81,063	**276**	9.7	88,903	**289**
Gallatin**	30031	10.4	74,887	**255**	10.9	83,063	**270**
Garfield	30033	-4.5	1,222	**4**	-4.5	1,167	**4**
Glacier	30035	0.1	13,264	**45**	0.5	13,329	**43**
Golden Valley	30037	1.2	1,055	**4**	3.5	1,092	**4**
Granite	30039	2.9	2,912	**10**	2.9	2,997	**10**
Hill**	30041	-2.5	16,257	**55**	-2.9	15,788	**51**
Jefferson**	30043	5.9	10,637	**36**	6.4	11,320	**37**
Judith Basin	30045	-7.9	2,146	**7**	-10.3	1,926	**6**
Lake	30047	3.3	27,385	**93**	3.4	28,307	**92**
Lewis and Clark**	30049	3.3	57,554	**196**	3.6	59,604	**193**
Liberty	30051	-6.2	2,025	**7**	-7.3	1,877	**6**
Lincoln	30053	-0.0	18,832	**64**	-0.1	18,806	**61**
McCone	30055	-10.4	1,771	**6**	-12.2	1,555	**5**
Madison	30057	2.1	6,998	**24**	2.2	7,154	**23**
Meagher	30059	2.4	1,978	**7**	2.8	2,033	**7**
Mineral	30061	0.0	3,884	**13**	-0.1	3,880	**13**
Missoula*	30063	3.8	99,453	**339**	4.2	103,582	**336**
Musselshell	30065	-1.0	4,453	**15**	-1.3	4,393	**14**
Park	30067	1.2	15,876	**54**	1.1	16,046	**52**
Petroleum	30069	-0.4	491	**2**	-0.4	489	**2**
Phillips	30071	-9.2	4,180	**14**	-10.3	3,749	**12**
Pondera	30073	-5.1	6,096	**21**	-5.5	5,759	**19**
Powder River	30075	-1.7	1,826	**6**	-2.1	1,787	**6**
Powell	30077	-3.2	6,948	**24**	-4.1	6,662	**22**
Prairie	30079	-4.7	1,143	**4**	-4.8	1,088	**4**
Ravalli	30081	9.3	39,433	**134**	9.7	43,265	**140**
Richland	30083	-6.9	9,002	**31**	-8.1	8,273	**27**
Roosevelt	30085	-2.1	10,393	**35**	-2.8	10,103	**33**
Rosebud	30087	-1.2	9,275	**32**	-1.5	9,136	**30**
Sanders	30089	2.9	10,521	**36**	3.1	10,848	**35**
Sheridan	30091	-13.8	3,540	**12**	-16.4	2,960	**10**
Silver Bow**	30093	-5.3	32,777	**112**	-6.4	30,691	**100**
Stillwater	30095	4.2	8,536	**29**	4.5	8,918	**29**
Sweet Grass	30097	-0.4	3,593	**12**	-1.5	3,538	**11**
Teton	30099	-1.6	6,345	**22**	-1.9	6,227	**20**
Toole	30101	1.8	5,364	**18**	2.4	5,492	**18**
Treasure	30103	-18.8	699	**2**	-22.3	543	**2**
Valley	30105	-5.5	7,254	**25**	-6.3	6,798	**22**
Wheatland	30107	-8.8	2,060	**7**	-10.5	1,843	**6**
Wibaux	30109	-11.3	947	**3**	-14.6	809	**3**
Yellowstone*	30111	3.9	134,394	**458**	4.4	140,329	**456**
TOTAL: MONTANA		**2.2**	**922,368**	**3,143**	**2.6**	**946,103**	**3,075**

NEBRASKA

	FIPS CODE	PRESENT 2000-2004 % Change	PRESENT 7/1/04 Estimate	7/1/04 Ranally Population Units	FUTURE 2004-2009 % Change	FUTURE 2009 Projection	2009 Ranally Population Units
Adams**	31001	-1.1	30,797	**105**	-1.5	30,324	**98**
Antelope	31003	-4.3	7,135	**24**	-5.2	6,762	**22**
Arthur	31005	-13.5	384	**1**	-15.9	323	**1**
Banner**	31007	-7.4	758	**3**	-10.0	682	**2**
Blaine	31009	-11.1	518	**2**	-13.3	449	**1**
Boone	31011	-6.9	5,828	**20**	-7.8	5,374	**17**
Box Butte	31013	-5.2	11,523	**39**	-6.1	10,819	**35**
Boyd	31015	-5.7	2,299	**8**	-6.7	2,145	**7**
Brown	31017	-1.3	3,480	**12**	-1.5	3,427	**11**
Buffalo**	31019	2.4	43,282	**147**	2.7	44,458	**144**
Burt	31021	-3.9	7,486	**25**	-5.0	7,114	**23**
Butler	31023	1.6	8,909	**30**	0.6	8,961	**29**
Cass*	31025	4.9	25,522	**87**	5.4	26,911	**87**
Cedar	31027	-5.0	9,130	**31**	-5.9	8,588	**28**
Chase	31029	-0.7	4,039	**14**	-0.4	4,024	**13**
Cherry	31031	-2.0	6,023	**21**	-2.5	5,873	**19**
Cheyenne	31033	1.5	9,975	**34**	1.8	10,151	**33**
Clay**	31035	-2.7	6,851	**23**	-3.3	6,627	**22**
Colfax	31037	0.7	10,513	**36**	0.7	10,590	**34**
Cuming	31039	-4.3	9,760	**33**	-5.1	9,262	**30**
Custer	31041	-2.8	11,457	**39**	-3.6	11,040	**36**
Dakota*	31043	1.5	20,562	**70**	1.7	20,905	**68**
Dawes	31045	-1.0	8,970	**31**	-0.8	8,896	**29**
Dawson**	31047	1.2	24,659	**84**	1.2	24,952	**81**
Deuel	31049	-3.0	2,035	**7**	-4.4	1,946	**6**
Dixon*	31051	-4.4	6,057	**21**	-5.2	5,741	**19**
Dodge**	31053	-0.8	35,869	**122**	-1.3	35,402	**115**
Douglas*	31055	3.7	480,743	**1,637**	4.2	500,745	**1,625**
Dundy	31057	-3.9	2,202	**7**	-5.0	2,092	**7**
Fillmore	31059	-4.1	6,362	**22**	-4.9	6,050	**20**
Franklin	31061	-4.7	3,407	**12**	-5.0	3,237	**11**
Frontier	31063	-8.2	2,845	**10**	-9.8	2,566	**8**
Furnas	31065	-3.1	5,161	**18**	-3.4	4,986	**16**
Gage**	31067	2.2	23,489	**80**	2.6	24,106	**78**
Garden	31069	-5.5	2,165	**7**	-6.3	2,028	**7**
Garfield	31071	-4.2	1,823	**6**	-4.7	1,737	**6**
Gosper**	31073	-3.3	2,072	**7**	-4.2	1,986	**6**
Grant	31075	-9.2	678	**2**	-11.2	602	**2**
Greeley	31077	-5.3	2,570	**9**	-6.3	2,408	**8**
Hall**	31079	1.9	54,556	**186**	2.4	55,848	**181**
Hamilton	31081	1.1	9,507	**32**	1.5	9,649	**31**
Harlan	31083	-4.2	3,627	**12**	-5.0	3,446	**11**
Hayes	31085	4.3	1,114	**4**	4.6	1,165	**4**
Hitchcock	31087	-3.3	3,008	**10**	-3.9	2,892	**9**
Holt	31089	-5.3	10,942	**37**	-6.0	10,287	**33**
Hooker	31091	-7.7	723	**2**	-9.3	656	**2**
Howard**	31093	1.4	6,658	**23**	1.9	6,783	**22**
Jefferson	31095	-4.0	7,999	**27**	-5.0	7,597	**25**
Johnson	31097	-1.7	4,410	**15**	-2.2	4,312	**14**
Kearney**	31099	-0.4	6,855	**23**	-0.6	6,815	**22**
Keith	31101	-5.9	8,347	**28**	-7.1	7,752	**25**
Keya Paha	31103	-3.9	945	**3**	-4.3	904	**3**
Kimball	31105	-7.4	3,786	**13**	-8.5	3,465	**11**
Knox	31107	-4.4	8,959	**31**	-5.2	8,497	**28**
Lancaster*	31109	5.6	264,249	**900**	6.1	280,408	**910**
Lincoln**	31111	0.6	34,850	**119**	0.7	35,077	**114**
Logan**	31113	-10.7	691	**2**	-12.9	602	**2**
Loup	31115	5.9	754	**3**	6.8	805	**3**
McPherson**	31117	2.4	546	**2**	3.3	564	**2**
Madison**	31119	2.1	35,979	**123**	2.8	36,973	**120**
Merrick**	31121	-1.0	8,122	**28**	-0.7	8,062	**26**
Morrill	31123	-3.8	5,232	**18**	-4.9	4,974	**16**
Nance	31125	-9.7	3,646	**12**	-12.1	3,204	**10**
Nemaha	31127	-7.6	6,998	**24**	-9.4	6,342	**21**
Nuckolls	31129	-5.5	4,781	**16**	-6.1	4,490	**15**
Otoe	31131	0.9	15,529	**53**	0.8	15,651	**51**
Pawnee	31133	-7.2	2,865	**10**	-8.8	2,612	**8**
Perkins	31135	-5.7	3,018	**10**	-6.2	2,830	**9**
Phelps	31137	-1.6	9,593	**33**	-1.9	9,407	**31**
Pierce**	31139	-2.4	7,667	**26**	-2.9	7,443	**24**
Platte**	31141	-1.8	31,085	**106**	-1.8	30,522	**99**
Polk	31143	-3.7	5,433	**18**	-4.1	5,210	**17**
Red Willow	31145	-2.3	11,185	**38**	-2.9	10,856	**35**
Richardson	31147	-7.2	8,845	**30**	-8.7	8,074	**26**
Rock	31149	-10.8	1,567	**5**	-13.4	1,357	**4**
Saline	31151	3.3	14,298	**49**	3.8	14,839	**48**
Sarpy*	31153	10.6	135,564	**462**	11.3	150,940	**490**
Saunders*	31155	1.2	20,059	**68**	1.2	20,304	**66**
Scotts Bluff**	31157	-0.0	36,941	**126**	-0.2	36,862	**120**
Seward*	31159	1.3	16,717	**57**	1.3	16,941	**55**
Sheridan	31161	-8.2	5,689	**19**	-9.9	5,127	**17**
Sherman	31163	-7.4	3,073	**10**	-8.4	2,816	**9**
Sioux	31165	1.5	1,497	**5**	2.1	1,528	**5**
Stanton**	31167	2.8	6,634	**23**	3.8	6,889	**22**
Thayer	31169	-8.5	5,540	**19**	-10.4	4,965	**16**
Thomas	31171	-11.0	649	**2**	-14.3	556	**2**
Thurston	31173	-0.6	7,129	**24**	-0.9	7,062	**23**
Valley	31175	-2.2	4,547	**15**	-2.7	4,423	**14**
Washington*	31177	6.4	19,987	**68**	7.4	21,461	**70**
Wayne	31179	-4.9	9,367	**32**	-5.5	8,848	**29**
Webster	31181	-6.3	3,807	**13**	-7.6	3,516	**11**
Wheeler	31183	-9.6	801	**3**	-11.9	706	**2**
York	31185	-2.1	14,292	**49**	-2.5	13,940	**45**
TOTAL: NEBRASKA		**2.1**	**1,748,000**	**5,952**	**2.5**	**1,791,543**	**5,812**

Source: Devonshire Associates Ltd. and Scan/US, Inc. 2004.
* Component of a Metropolitan Core Based Statistical Area.
** Component of a Micropolitan Core Based Statistical Area.

NEVADA

	FIPS CODE	PRESENT 2000-2004 % Change	PRESENT 7/1/04 Estimate	7/1/04 Ranally Population Units	FUTURE 2004-2009 % Change	FUTURE 2009 Projection	2009 Ranally Population Units
Churchill**	32001	4.4	25,027	**85**	5.1	26,293	**85**
Clark*	32003	19.0	1,637,622	**5,576**	18.6	1,942,707	**6,306**
Douglas**	32005	9.1	44,993	**153**	9.8	49,401	**160**
Elko**	32007	-3.5	43,706	**149**	-4.3	41,807	**136**
Esmeralda	32009	-15.2	823	**3**	-18.6	670	**2**
Eureka**	32011	-10.8	1,473	**5**	-12.4	1,290	**4**
Humboldt	32013	-11.1	14,324	**49**	-12.4	12,548	**41**
Lander	32015	-16.4	4,845	**16**	-18.7	3,940	**13**
Lincoln	32017	3.1	4,293	**15**	3.3	4,435	**14**
Lyon	32019	21.4	41,870	**143**	20.8	50,581	**164**
Mineral	32021	-6.9	4,720	**16**	-7.2	4,382	**14**
Nye**	32023	12.8	36,650	**125**	12.7	41,307	**134**
Pershing	32027	-4.8	6,371	**22**	-5.5	6,018	**20**
Storey*	32029	4.5	3,551	**12**	5.5	3,748	**12**
Washoe*	32031	12.1	380,688	**1,296**	12.9	429,797	**1,395**
White Pine	32033	-9.4	8,315	**28**	-9.9	7,493	**24**
INDEPENDENT CITY							
Carson City*	32510	7.2	56,233	**191**	8.2	60,837	**197**
TOTAL: NEVADA		**15.9**	**2,315,504**	**7,884**	**16.1**	**2,687,254**	**8,721**

NEW HAMPSHIRE

	FIPS CODE	PRESENT 2000-2004 % Change	PRESENT 7/1/04 Estimate	7/1/04 Ranally Population Units	FUTURE 2004-2009 % Change	FUTURE 2009 Projection	2009 Ranally Population Units
Belknap**	33001	9.4	61,617	**210**	10.2	67,920	**220**
Carroll	33003	7.3	46,872	**160**	7.9	50,564	**164**
Cheshire**	33005	3.8	76,625	**261**	4.3	79,925	**259**
Coos**	33007	-0.4	32,972	**112**	-0.7	32,741	**106**
Grafton**	33009	3.7	84,766	**289**	4.3	88,408	**287**
Hillsborough*	33011	4.7	398,775	**1,358**	5.2	419,332	**1,361**
Merrimack**	33013	7.1	145,924	**497**	7.9	157,434	**511**
Rockingham*	33015	6.0	293,899	**1,001**	6.5	312,885	**1,016**
Strafford*	33017	6.4	119,427	**407**	7.1	127,860	**415**
Sullivan**	33019	5.2	42,548	**145**	5.9	45,048	**146**
TOTAL: NEW HAMPSHIRE		**5.5**	**1,303,425**	**4,440**	**6.0**	**1,382,117**	**4,485**

NEW JERSEY

	FIPS CODE	PRESENT 2000-2004 % Change	PRESENT 7/1/04 Estimate	7/1/04 Ranally Population Units	FUTURE 2004-2009 % Change	FUTURE 2009 Projection	2009 Ranally Population Units
Atlantic*	34001	5.7	266,864	**909**	6.5	284,131	**922**
Bergen*	34003	2.0	901,514	**3,070**	2.2	921,244	**2,990**
Burlington*	34005	6.5	450,960	**1,536**	7.3	483,852	**1,571**
Camden*	34007	1.3	515,644	**1,756**	1.7	524,315	**1,702**
Cape May*	34009	-0.6	101,693	**346**	-0.7	100,939	**328**
Cumberland*	34011	2.6	150,283	**512**	3.3	155,170	**504**
Essex*	34013	0.5	797,608	**2,716**	0.8	804,081	**2,610**
Gloucester*	34015	6.4	270,847	**922**	7.2	290,271	**942**
Hudson*	34017	-0.4	606,768	**2,066**	-0.5	603,520	**1,959**
Hunterdon*	34019	6.7	130,155	**443**	7.3	139,607	**453**
Mercer*	34021	4.2	365,448	**1,244**	4.7	382,782	**1,243**
Middlesex*	34023	5.3	790,283	**2,691**	5.9	836,721	**2,716**
Monmouth*	34025	3.6	637,323	**2,170**	4.0	662,568	**2,151**
Morris*	34027	3.6	487,077	**1,658**	4.0	506,709	**1,645**
Ocean*	34029	9.0	556,907	**1,896**	9.7	611,037	**1,983**
Passaic*	34031	2.4	500,842	**1,705**	2.5	513,266	**1,666**
Salem*	34033	1.2	65,064	**222**	1.6	66,116	**215**
Somerset*	34035	6.2	315,847	**1,075**	6.7	337,079	**1,094**
Sussex*	34037	6.3	153,303	**522**	7.0	164,089	**533**
Union*	34039	1.7	531,425	**1,809**	1.9	541,750	**1,759**
Warren*	34041	8.7	111,301	**379**	9.4	121,709	**395**
TOTAL: NEW JERSEY		**3.5**	**8,707,156**	**29,647**	**3.9**	**9,050,956**	**29,381**

NEW MEXICO

	FIPS CODE	PRESENT 2000-2004 % Change	PRESENT 7/1/04 Estimate	7/1/04 Ranally Population Units	FUTURE 2004-2009 % Change	FUTURE 2009 Projection	2009 Ranally Population Units
Bernalillo*	35001	5.9	589,389	**2,007**	6.7	628,991	**2,042**
Catron	35003	-4.9	3,368	**11**	-6.8	3,140	**10**
Chaves**	35005	-1.7	60,348	**205**	-2.0	59,136	**192**
Cibola**	35006	4.4	26,715	**91**	4.9	28,022	**91**
Colfax	35007	-1.4	13,995	**48**	-2.0	13,712	**45**
Curry**	35009	1.2	45,601	**155**	1.8	46,400	**151**
De Baca	35011	-8.4	2,051	**7**	-9.3	1,861	**6**
Dona Ana*	35013	5.7	184,554	**628**	6.5	196,459	**638**
Eddy**	35015	-0.4	51,476	**175**	0.0	51,496	**167**
Grant**	35017	-5.0	29,459	**100**	-5.9	27,721	**90**
Guadalupe	35019	-3.0	4,538	**15**	-3.9	4,360	**14**
Harding	35021	-9.9	730	**2**	-11.0	650	**2**
Hidalgo	35023	-14.6	5,067	**17**	-15.0	4,308	**14**
Lea**	35025	0.2	55,610	**189**	0.9	56,128	**182**
Lincoln	35027	6.0	20,582	**70**	6.3	21,879	**71**
Los Alamos**	35028	3.4	18,970	**65**	4.4	19,808	**64**
Luna**	35029	3.8	25,978	**88**	4.7	27,203	**88**
McKinley**	35031	-4.0	71,782	**244**	-5.2	68,021	**221**
Mora	35033	0.8	5,220	**18**	0.4	5,240	**17**
Otero**	35035	0.2	62,396	**212**	0.2	62,507	**203**
Quay	35037	-6.9	9,452	**32**	-7.8	8,718	**28**
Rio Arriba**	35039	-1.5	40,558	**138**	-2.1	39,698	**129**
Roosevelt**	35041	0.7	18,142	**62**	1.0	18,316	**59**
Sandoval*	35043	12.9	101,506	**346**	13.4	115,077	**374**
San Juan*	35045	9.8	124,961	**425**	10.7	138,374	**449**
San Miguel**	35047	-2.0	29,529	**101**	-2.4	28,827	**94**
Santa Fe*	35049	7.2	138,622	**472**	7.9	149,581	**486**
Sierra	35051	-1.4	13,082	**45**	-1.7	12,862	**42**
Socorro	35053	0.7	18,212	**62**	0.9	18,383	**60**
Taos**	35055	5.6	31,667	**108**	6.3	33,648	**109**
Torrance*	35057	-1.0	16,743	**57**	-1.7	16,453	**53**
Union	35059	-11.3	3,703	**13**	-13.7	3,196	**10**
Valencia*	35061	3.2	68,298	**233**	3.3	70,579	**229**
TOTAL: NEW MEXICO		**4.0**	**1,892,304**	**6,441**	**4.7**	**1,980,754**	**6,430**

NEW YORK

	FIPS CODE	PRESENT 2000-2004 % Change	PRESENT 7/1/04 Estimate	7/1/04 Ranally Population Units	FUTURE 2004-2009 % Change	FUTURE 2009 Projection	2009 Ranally Population Units
Albany*	36001	1.5	298,933	**1,018**	1.8	304,373	**988**
Allegany	36003	1.7	50,780	**173**	2.1	51,867	**168**
Bronx*	36005	3.0	1,372,845	**4,675**	3.5	1,421,060	**4,613**
Broome*	36007	-0.7	199,049	**678**	-0.8	197,500	**641**
Cattaraugus**	36009	-0.9	83,168	**283**	-1.1	82,241	**267**
Cayuga**	36011	-0.4	81,655	**278**	-0.4	81,302	**264**
Chautauqua**	36013	-2.0	137,003	**466**	-2.3	133,834	**434**
Chemung*	36015	-0.9	90,205	**307**	-1.1	89,168	**289**
Chenango	36017	0.7	51,743	**176**	0.8	52,160	**169**
Clinton**	36019	2.4	81,842	**279**	2.9	84,222	**273**
Columbia**	36021	0.7	63,516	**216**	0.9	64,067	**208**
Cortland**	36023	0.3	48,729	**166**	0.4	48,920	**159**
Delaware	36025	-2.2	46,981	**160**	-2.6	45,773	**149**
Dutchess*	36027	5.0	294,234	**1,002**	5.7	310,975	**1,009**
Erie*	36029	-1.2	938,615	**3,196**	-1.4	925,325	**3,004**
Essex	36031	0.5	39,028	**133**	0.5	39,205	**127**
Franklin**	36033	-0.2	51,036	**174**	-0.2	50,933	**165**
Fulton**	36035	0.4	55,272	**188**	0.6	55,598	**180**
Genesee**	36037	-0.7	59,919	**204**	-0.8	59,415	**193**
Greene	36039	1.8	49,072	**167**	2.1	50,108	**163**
Hamilton	36041	-2.5	5,242	**18**	-3.3	5,068	**16**
Herkimer*	36043	-1.5	63,477	**216**	-1.8	62,350	**202**
Jefferson**	36045	3.5	115,704	**394**	4.5	120,968	**393**
Kings*	36047	0.4	2,474,606	**8,426**	0.4	2,484,985	**8,066**
Lewis	36049	-1.6	26,520	**90**	-2.2	25,947	**84**
Livingston*	36051	0.7	64,750	**220**	0.7	65,206	**212**
Madison*	36053	1.4	70,428	**240**	1.7	71,656	**233**
Monroe*	36055	0.2	737,090	**2,510**	0.2	738,840	**2,398**
Montgomery**	36057	-0.9	49,269	**168**	-1.0	48,764	**158**
Nassau*	36059	0.4	1,340,495	**4,564**	0.4	1,345,637	**4,368**
New York*	36061	2.3	1,572,971	**5,356**	2.6	1,613,813	**5,238**
Niagara*	36063	-1.0	217,673	**741**	-1.1	215,302	**699**
Oneida*	36065	-0.6	234,094	**797**	-0.6	232,706	**755**
Onondaga*	36067	0.6	461,207	**1,570**	0.7	464,651	**1,508**
Ontario*	36069	2.9	103,127	**351**	3.3	106,536	**346**
Orange*	36071	8.3	369,860	**1,259**	9.1	403,392	**1,309**
Orleans*	36073	-1.6	43,448	**148**	-2.1	42,550	**138**
Oswego*	36075	1.2	123,814	**422**	1.3	125,408	**407**
Otsego**	36077	1.1	62,377	**212**	1.4	63,278	**205**
Putnam*	36079	5.2	100,694	**343**	5.7	106,411	**345**
Queens*	36081	-0.3	2,223,681	**7,572**	-0.4	2,214,646	**7,189**
Rensselaer*	36083	1.3	154,473	**526**	1.5	156,803	**509**
Richmond*	36085	4.7	464,513	**1,582**	5.1	488,386	**1,585**
Rockland*	36087	2.8	294,839	**1,004**	3.1	304,089	**987**

continued on next page

Counties: Population Trends, *Continued*

	FIPS CODE	PRESENT 2000-2004 % Change	PRESENT 7/1/04 Estimate	7/1/04 Ranally Population Units	FUTURE 2004-2009 % Change	FUTURE 2009 Projection	2009 Ranally Population Units
St. Lawrence**	36089	-0.3	111,586	380	-0.3	111,239	361
Saratoga*	36091	6.0	212,606	724	6.6	226,546	735
Schenectady*	36093	0.7	147,572	502	1.0	148,981	484
Schoharie*	36095	0.4	31,716	108	0.5	31,868	103
Schuyler	36097	1.5	19,517	66	1.6	19,828	64
Seneca**	36099	7.3	35,787	122	8.4	38,804	126
Steuben**	36101	0.4	99,084	337	0.4	99,443	323
Suffolk*	36103	4.5	1,482,695	5,049	4.9	1,555,963	5,051
Sullivan	36105	1.7	75,246	256	2.0	76,732	249
Tioga*	36107	-0.1	51,744	176	-0.0	51,733	168
Tompkins*	36109	6.7	102,983	351	7.6	110,842	360
Ulster*	36111	2.5	182,183	620	2.9	187,546	609
Warren*	36113	3.0	65,172	222	3.5	67,455	219
Washington*	36115	1.8	62,162	212	2.3	63,608	206
Wayne*	36117	-0.1	93,715	319	-0.1	93,645	304
Westchester*	36119	2.3	945,092	3,218	2.5	969,028	3,145
Wyoming	36121	-1.5	42,780	146	-1.8	42,029	136
Yates	36123	0.5	24,755	84	0.7	24,929	81
TOTAL: NEW YORK		**1.5**	**19,254,372**	**65,560**	**1.7**	**19,575,657**	**63,537**

NORTH CAROLINA

	FIPS CODE	PRESENT 2000-2004 % Change	PRESENT 7/1/04 Estimate	7/1/04 Ranally Population Units	FUTURE 2004-2009 % Change	FUTURE 2009 Projection	2009 Ranally Population Units
Alamance*	37001	5.9	138,548	472	6.4	147,422	479
Alexander*	37003	4.6	35,156	120	5.3	37,012	120
Alleghany	37005	2.4	10,932	37	2.6	11,220	36
Anson*	37007	-0.5	25,140	86	-0.6	24,998	81
Ashe	37009	3.7	25,276	86	4.0	26,298	85
Avery	37011	4.1	17,869	61	4.7	18,713	61
Beaufort**	37013	1.3	45,548	155	1.5	46,249	150
Bertie	37015	-1.5	19,484	66	-1.5	19,184	62
Bladen	37017	1.9	32,882	112	2.4	33,675	109
Brunswick*	37019	15.1	84,206	287	15.5	97,272	316
Buncombe*	37021	4.0	214,572	731	4.4	224,068	727
Burke*	37023	0.7	89,791	306	0.7	90,457	294
Cabarrus*	37025	11.6	146,248	498	12.0	163,785	532
Caldwell*	37027	2.2	79,103	269	2.4	80,976	263
Camden**	37029	18.7	8,174	28	19.0	9,731	32
Carteret**	37031	3.3	61,352	209	4.0	63,782	207
Caswell	37033	0.7	23,659	81	0.6	23,795	77
Catawba*	37035	4.8	148,471	506	5.1	155,972	506
Chatham*	37037	15.7	57,081	194	16.1	66,293	215
Cherokee	37039	4.0	25,269	86	4.4	26,373	86
Chowan	37041	0.1	14,537	49	3.6	15,058	49
Clay	37043	7.6	9,446	32	8.3	10,234	33
Cleveland**	37045	2.6	98,808	336	2.8	101,598	330
Columbus	37047	-0.6	54,440	185	-0.7	54,051	175
Craven**	37049	0.4	91,802	313	0.3	92,038	299
Cumberland*	37051	0.4	304,324	1,036	0.6	306,169	994
Currituck*	37053	19.1	21,665	74	19.2	25,821	84
Dare**	37055	13.8	34,090	116	14.3	38,960	126
Davidson**	37057	4.4	153,692	523	4.9	161,263	523
Davie*	37059	8.6	37,846	129	9.2	41,321	134
Duplin	37061	5.7	51,843	177	6.4	55,153	179
Durham*	37063	7.9	240,859	820	8.5	261,245	848
Edgecombe*	37065	-1.5	54,761	186	-1.2	54,096	176
Forsyth*	37067	5.0	321,453	1,095	5.7	339,659	1,103
Franklin*	37069	13.1	53,474	182	13.7	60,811	197
Gaston*	37071	1.9	193,911	660	2.1	197,978	643
Gates	37073	3.0	10,835	37	3.7	11,241	36
Graham	37075	0.0	7,994	27	0.0	7,994	26
Granville	37077	9.0	52,887	180	9.8	58,057	188
Greene*	37079	7.0	20,302	69	7.7	21,863	71
Guilford*	37081	3.9	437,629	1,490	4.4	456,823	1,483
Halifax**	37083	-2.0	56,226	191	-2.3	54,920	178
Harnett**	37085	12.1	102,013	347	12.8	115,044	373
Haywood*	37087	3.4	55,887	190	4.0	58,111	189
Henderson*	37089	6.8	95,222	324	7.4	102,240	332
Hertford	37091	-2.2	22,102	75	-4.6	21,088	68
Hoke*	37093	15.6	38,888	132	16.0	45,113	146
Hyde	37095	-5.7	5,495	19	-6.3	5,148	17
Iredell**	37097	11.4	136,650	465	11.9	152,964	497
Jackson	37099	4.6	34,647	118	4.9	36,362	118
Johnston*	37101	15.9	141,305	481	15.9	163,817	532
Jones**	37103	-2.4	10,131	34	-3.2	9,805	32
Lee**	37105	0.0	49,042	167	-1.0	48,565	158
Lenoir**	37107	-2.4	58,240	198	-2.6	56,718	184
Lincoln**	37109	7.2	68,354	233	7.9	73,744	239
McDowell	37111	2.2	43,082	147	2.5	44,153	143
Macon	37113	5.9	31,576	108	6.3	33,579	109
Madison*	37115	1.4	19,910	68	1.3	20,171	65
Martin	37117	-2.6	24,924	85	-2.9	24,204	79
Mecklenburg*	37119	10.7	769,746	2,621	11.3	856,626	2,781
Mitchell	37121	1.1	15,867	54	1.1	16,046	52
Montgomery	37123	2.3	27,429	93	2.2	28,043	91
Moore**	37125	7.8	80,638	275	8.5	87,487	284
Nash*	37127	3.4	90,391	308	3.6	93,682	304
New Hanover*	37129	6.4	170,562	581	7.3	182,930	594
Northampton**	37131	-1.8	21,682	74	-2.3	21,185	69
Onslow*	37133	-2.5	146,634	499	-3.0	142,265	462
Orange*	37135	0.6	118,905	405	3.0	122,518	398
Pamlico**	37137	-1.6	12,730	43	-2.1	12,466	40
Pasquotank**	37139	4.5	36,468	124	5.4	38,449	125
Pender*	37141	7.8	44,280	151	8.5	48,045	156
Perquimans**	37143	3.1	11,722	40	3.3	12,113	39
Person*	37145	4.5	37,235	127	5.0	39,088	127
Pitt*	37147	4.8	140,223	477	5.5	147,885	480
Polk	37149	3.5	18,963	65	3.7	19,657	64
Randolph*	37151	4.6	136,509	465	5.0	143,297	465
Richmond**	37153	0.2	46,666	159	0.2	46,777	152
Robeson**	37155	2.6	126,549	431	3.1	130,512	424
Rockingham*	37157	1.0	92,805	316	1.2	93,876	305
Rowan**	37159	3.6	135,024	460	4.0	140,491	456
Rutherford**	37161	1.3	63,726	217	1.5	64,655	210
Sampson	37163	4.1	62,617	213	4.6	65,516	213
Scotland**	37165	-0.9	35,671	121	-1.2	35,245	114
Stanly**	37167	1.7	59,068	201	1.9	60,175	195
Stokes*	37169	1.3	45,273	154	1.2	45,796	149
Surry**	37171	2.0	72,629	247	2.4	74,381	241
Swain	37173	1.5	13,163	45	1.4	13,349	43
Transylvania**	37175	0.3	29,416	100	0.2	29,467	96
Tyrrell	37177	0.2	4,159	14	0.4	4,174	14
Union*	37179	23.5	152,765	520	22.2	186,658	606
Vance**	37181	2.3	43,932	150	2.2	44,910	146
Wake*	37183	14.1	716,522	2,440	14.5	820,710	2,664
Warren	37185	-1.0	19,772	67	-1.0	19,573	64
Washington	37187	-3.1	13,297	45	-3.8	12,797	42
Watauga**	37189	0.3	42,829	146	0.2	42,930	139
Wayne*	37191	-0.3	113,028	385	-0.3	112,648	366
Wilkes**	37193	2.8	67,472	230	3.1	69,552	226
Wilson**	37195	2.7	75,810	258	3.1	78,169	254
Yadkin*	37197	3.8	37,725	128	4.0	39,241	127
Yancey	37199	2.1	18,155	62	2.4	18,582	60
TOTAL: NORTH CAROLINA		**5.8**	**8,517,110**	**28,999**	**6.4**	**9,066,420**	**29,431**

NORTH DAKOTA

	FIPS CODE	PRESENT 2000-2004 % Change	PRESENT 7/1/04 Estimate	7/1/04 Ranally Population Units	FUTURE 2004-2009 % Change	FUTURE 2009 Projection	2009 Ranally Population Units
Adams	38001	-4.3	2,481	8	-4.9	2,360	8
Barnes	38003	-7.6	10,877	37	-9.0	9,895	32
Benson	38005	-1.6	6,854	23	-2.1	6,711	22
Billings**	38007	-5.2	842	3	-4.8	802	3
Bottineau	38009	-6.0	6,722	23	-7.1	6,247	20
Bowman	38011	-7.9	2,986	10	-9.4	2,705	9
Burke	38013	-8.3	2,055	7	-10.1	1,848	6
Burleigh*	38015	4.3	72,410	247	4.8	75,902	246
Cass*	38017	4.3	128,372	437	4.7	134,381	436
Cavalier	38019	-9.3	4,380	15	-11.2	3,890	13
Dickey	38021	-6.1	5,407	18	-7.6	4,996	16
Divide	38023	-1.8	2,241	8	-1.6	2,206	7
Dunn	38025	-2.3	3,518	12	-3.0	3,413	11
Eddy	38027	-7.4	2,553	9	-8.7	2,332	8
Emmons	38029	-9.7	3,909	13	-11.5	3,461	11
Foster	38031	-9.2	3,415	12	-10.9	3,042	10
Golden Valley	38033	-6.5	1,799	6	-7.9	1,656	5
Grand Forks*	38035	-2.7	64,352	219	-3.0	62,395	203
Grant	38037	-8.1	2,610	9	-10.0	2,350	8
Griggs	38039	-8.2	2,529	9	-9.4	2,292	7
Hettinger	38041	-7.8	2,502	9	-8.9	2,279	7
Kidder	38043	-8.2	2,526	9	-9.6	2,283	7
LaMoure	38045	-5.2	4,457	15	-6.0	4,188	14
Logan	38047	-8.4	2,113	7	-10.1	1,900	6
McHenry**	38049	-5.7	5,647	19	-6.5	5,281	17
McIntosh	38051	-8.2	3,113	10	-9.8	2,807	9
McKenzie	38053	-2.7	5,581	19	-3.1	5,408	18
McLean	38055	-5.2	8,827	30	-6.0	8,297	27
Mercer	38057	-2.9	8,397	29	-3.2	8,129	26
Morton*	38059	-0.9	25,068	85	-1.4	24,705	80
Mountrail	38061	-2.9	6,439	22	-3.3	6,228	20
Nelson	38063	-9.2	3,375	11	-10.9	3,006	10
Oliver	38065	-10.1	1,857	6	-12.1	1,633	5
Pembina	38067	-5.8	8,085	28	-7.0	7,517	24
Pierce	38069	-5.5	4,420	15	-6.6	4,128	13
Ramsey	38071	-4.8	11,481	39	-5.8	10,816	35
Ransom	38073	-1.2	5,819	20	-1.7	5,718	19
Renville**	38075	-6.7	2,434	8	-7.8	2,244	7
Richland**	38077	-2.9	17,478	60	-3.5	16,872	55
Rolette	38079	0.5	13,746	47	0.4	13,800	45
Sargent	38081	-4.2	4,181	14	-5.2	3,964	13
Sheridan	38083	-12.8	1,491	5	-15.2	1,265	4
Sioux	38085	0.7	4,072	14	0.2	4,081	13
Slope	38087	-3.3	742	3	-3.1	719	2
Stark**	38089	-2.9	21,990	75	-3.3	21,274	69
Steele	38091	-10.1	2,031	7	-11.8	1,792	6
Stutsman**	38093	-3.9	21,057	72	-4.7	20,072	65
Towner	38095	-9.4	2,606	9	-11.0	2,319	8
Traill	38097	-3.1	8,215	28	-3.9	7,894	26
Walsh	38099	-7.1	11,513	39	-8.6	10,518	34
Ward**	38101	-4.6	56,085	191	-5.6	52,949	172
Wells	38103	-10.2	4,581	16	-12.3	4,018	13
Williams**	38105	-2.8	19,199	65	-3.1	18,604	60
TOTAL: NORTH DAKOTA		**-1.7**	**631,440**	**2,151**	**-1.9**	**619,592**	**2,010**

OHIO

	FIPS CODE	PRESENT 2000-2004 % Change	PRESENT 7/1/04 Estimate	7/1/04 Ranally Population Units	FUTURE 2004-2009 % Change	FUTURE 2009 Projection	2009 Ranally Population Units
Adams	39001	3.4	28,256	96	4.0	29,399	95
Allen*	39003	-0.3	108,137	368	-0.5	107,596	349
Ashland**	39005	3.1	54,141	184	3.6	56,091	182
Ashtabula**	39007	0.5	103,234	352	0.5	103,780	337
Athens**	39009	4.5	65,043	221	5.1	68,345	222
Auglaize**	39011	0.4	46,780	159	0.4	46,968	152
Belmont*	39013	-1.1	69,474	237	-1.2	68,653	223
Brown*	39015	4.6	44,217	151	4.6	46,255	150
Butler*	39017	4.1	346,371	1,179	4.5	362,111	1,175
Carroll*	39019	3.5	29,838	102	4.0	31,027	101
Champaign**	39021	2.2	39,745	135	2.5	40,738	132
Clark*	39023	-1.3	142,925	487	-1.5	140,785	457
Clermont*	39025	5.7	188,179	641	6.3	200,037	649
Clinton**	39027	3.9	42,113	143	4.2	43,885	142
Columbiana**	39029	-0.7	111,328	379	-0.9	110,331	358
Coshocton**	39031	1.7	37,273	127	1.9	37,971	123
Crawford**	39033	-2.4	45,825	156	-2.9	44,507	144
Cuyahoga*	39035	-2.8	1,354,570	4,612	-3.4	1,308,652	4,248
Darke**	39037	-0.9	52,842	180	-1.1	52,249	170
Defiance**	39039	-1.5	38,923	133	-1.7	38,263	124
Delaware*	39041	27.1	139,819	476	25.1	174,883	568
Erie*	39043	-1.4	78,417	267	-1.9	76,958	250
Fairfield*	39045	10.4	135,586	462	11.2	150,735	489
Fayette**	39047	-1.3	28,066	96	-1.6	27,603	90
Franklin*	39049	2.4	1,094,640	3,727	2.6	1,122,878	3,645
Fulton*	39051	1.1	42,546	145	1.1	43,035	140
Gallia**	39053	1.4	31,500	107	1.6	32,002	104
Geauga*	39055	4.3	94,840	323	4.7	99,314	322
Greene*	39057	3.0	152,266	518	3.3	157,280	511
Guernsey**	39059	1.9	41,552	141	2.3	42,490	138
Hamilton*	39061	-3.4	816,699	2,781	-4.1	783,497	2,543
Hancock**	39063	3.4	73,736	251	4.1	76,733	249
Hardin	39065	-1.4	31,498	107	-1.8	30,946	100
Harrison	39067	0.9	16,001	54	1.1	16,173	52
Henry	39069	0.5	29,352	100	0.6	29,517	96
Highland	39071	3.4	42,277	144	3.7	43,838	142
Hocking	39073	1.9	28,778	98	2.3	29,441	96
Holmes	39075	5.9	41,223	140	6.5	43,920	143
Huron**	39077	1.6	60,438	206	1.7	61,459	199
Jackson	39079	1.8	33,219	113	2.2	33,937	110
Jefferson*	39081	-3.5	71,299	243	-4.1	68,410	222
Knox**	39083	5.9	57,690	196	6.6	61,480	200
Lake*	39085	0.8	229,287	781	0.9	231,284	751
Lawrence*	39087	0.5	62,637	213	0.7	63,060	205
Licking*	39089	4.6	152,155	518	5.0	159,728	518
Logan**	39091	1.2	46,542	158	1.4	47,187	153
Lorain*	39093	3.0	293,138	998	3.3	302,944	983
Lucas*	39095	-0.2	453,978	1,546	-0.3	452,689	1,469
Madison*	39097	1.4	40,757	139	1.6	41,412	134
Mahoning*	39099	-3.0	249,884	851	-3.5	241,134	783
Marion**	39101	0.4	66,481	226	0.6	66,892	217
Medina*	39103	9.1	164,898	561	9.9	181,145	588
Meigs	39105	1.0	23,310	79	1.4	23,647	77
Mercer**	39107	0.0	40,938	139	0.0	40,953	133
Miami*	39109	1.8	100,642	343	2.0	102,678	333
Monroe	39111	-2.2	14,845	51	-2.7	14,437	47
Montgomery*	39113	-1.6	550,095	1,873	-1.9	539,637	1,752
Morgan	39115	-0.5	14,829	50	-0.5	14,753	48
Morrow*	39117	8.0	34,155	116	8.6	37,080	120
Muskingum**	39119	1.3	85,650	292	1.3	86,769	282
Noble	39121	-0.1	14,039	48	-0.6	13,961	45
Ottawa*	39123	0.7	41,255	140	0.7	41,562	135
Paulding	39125	-4.0	19,480	66	-4.6	18,579	60
Perry	39127	3.8	35,390	121	4.4	36,962	120
Pickaway*	39129	-2.6	51,354	175	-3.5	49,540	161
Pike	39131	2.3	28,341	97	2.6	29,069	94
Portage*	39133	2.4	155,699	530	2.6	159,812	519
Preble*	39135	0.2	42,436	144	0.2	42,521	138
Putnam	39137	0.1	34,751	118	-0.1	34,731	113
Richland*	39139	-0.6	128,091	436	-0.7	127,188	413
Ross**	39141	1.9	74,752	255	2.2	76,372	248
Sandusky**	39143	-0.1	61,733	210	-0.2	61,619	200
Scioto**	39145	-2.9	76,918	262	-3.4	74,281	241
Seneca**	39147	-2.1	57,438	196	-2.6	55,972	182
Shelby**	39149	1.8	48,760	166	2.0	49,715	161
Stark*	39151	-0.2	377,323	1,285	-0.3	376,263	1,221
Summit*	39153	0.9	547,831	1,865	0.9	553,000	1,795
Trumbull*	39155	-1.9	220,736	752	-2.4	215,521	700
Tuscarawas**	39157	1.1	91,928	313	1.2	93,022	302
Union*	39159	9.0	44,598	152	9.5	48,827	158
Van Wert**	39161	-1.7	29,158	99	-2.0	28,567	93
Vinton	39163	4.4	13,371	46	5.2	14,068	46
Warren*	39165	19.2	188,737	643	18.5	223,656	726
Washington*	39167	-1.5	62,279	212	-1.8	61,151	198
Wayne**	39169	1.8	113,591	387	2.0	115,914	376
Williams	39171	-1.3	38,669	132	-1.7	38,001	123
Wood*	39173	2.1	123,620	421	2.4	126,595	411
Wyandot	39175	-0.5	22,797	78	-0.6	22,650	74
TOTAL: OHIO		**0.9**	**11,459,952**	**39,020**	**1.1**	**11,580,720**	**37,588**

OKLAHOMA

	FIPS CODE	PRESENT 2000-2004 % Change	PRESENT 7/1/04 Estimate	7/1/04 Ranally Population Units	FUTURE 2004-2009 % Change	FUTURE 2009 Projection	2009 Ranally Population Units
Adair	40001	3.6	21,794	74	4.1	22,691	74
Alfalfa	40003	-4.2	5,851	20	-4.9	5,563	18
Atoka	40005	2.6	14,241	48	3.4	14,731	48
Beaver	40007	-5.9	5,514	19	-6.0	5,185	17
Beckham**	40009	0.7	19,942	68	1.2	20,175	65
Blaine	40011	-3.3	11,583	39	-4.0	11,117	36
Bryan**	40013	2.7	37,533	128	3.0	38,667	126
Caddo	40015	-0.3	30,055	102	-0.2	29,981	97
Canadian*	40017	7.7	94,470	322	8.3	102,289	332
Carter**	40019	2.3	46,663	159	2.9	47,995	156
Cherokee**	40021	3.8	44,157	150	4.2	46,021	149
Choctaw	40023	0.8	15,461	53	0.9	15,605	51
Cimarron	40025	-7.8	2,901	10	-9.9	2,615	8
Cleveland*	40027	7.6	223,830	762	8.6	243,120	789

Source: Devonshire Associates Ltd. and Scan/US, Inc. 2004.
* Component of a Metropolitan Core Based Statistical Area.
** Component of a Micropolitan Core Based Statistical Area.

Counties: Population Trends, *Continued*

	FIPS CODE	PRESENT 2000-2004 % Change	PRESENT 7/1/04 Estimate	7/1/04 Ranally Population Units	FUTURE 2004-2009 % Change	FUTURE 2009 Projection	2009 Ranally Population Units
Coal	40029	-1.7	5,926	**20**	-1.7	5,825	**19**
Comanche*	40031	-1.2	113,664	**387**	-1.0	112,529	**365**
Cotton	40033	-0.8	6,559	**22**	-1.7	6,445	**21**
Craig	40035	-0.6	14,856	**51**	-0.8	14,736	**48**
Creek*	40037	2.7	69,207	**236**	3.0	71,260	**231**
Custer	40039	-5.9	24,607	**84**	-6.9	22,907	**74**
Delaware	40041	5.8	39,213	**134**	6.4	41,732	**135**
Dewey	40043	-5.2	4,495	**15**	-5.8	4,233	**14**
Ellis	40045	-2.4	3,978	**14**	-2.3	3,885	**13**
Garfield**	40047	-1.6	56,916	**194**	-1.7	55,975	**182**
Garvin	40049	-0.0	27,197	**93**	-0.4	27,092	**88**
Grady*	40051	5.6	48,055	**164**	6.4	51,130	**166**
Grant	40053	-4.3	4,922	**17**	-5.1	4,672	**15**
Greer	40055	-3.6	5,843	**20**	-3.8	5,620	**18**
Harmon	40057	-9.2	2,980	**10**	-11.4	2,641	**9**
Harper	40059	-6.0	3,350	**11**	-6.8	3,121	**10**
Haskell	40061	2.8	12,118	**41**	3.0	12,483	**41**
Hughes	40063	-2.4	13,820	**47**	-2.8	13,433	**44**
Jackson**	40065	-4.9	27,034	**92**	-5.4	25,565	**83**
Jefferson	40067	-5.3	6,454	**22**	-6.0	6,065	**20**
Johnston	40069	0.1	10,526	**36**	0.2	10,542	**34**
Kay**	40071	-2.2	47,032	**160**	-2.4	45,905	**149**
Kingfisher	40073	1.5	14,130	**48**	2.0	14,417	**47**
Kiowa	40075	-3.2	9,902	**34**	-3.7	9,532	**31**
Latimer	40077	-1.4	10,541	**36**	-1.6	10,372	**34**
Le Flore*	40079	2.1	49,143	**167**	2.5	50,373	**164**
Lincoln*	40081	0.7	32,301	**110**	0.6	32,495	**105**
Logan*	40083	5.8	35,908	**122**	6.8	38,347	**124**
Love**	40085	1.1	8,931	**30**	1.4	9,059	**29**
McClain*	40087	4.0	28,843	**98**	4.3	30,084	**98**
McCurtain	40089	-1.5	33,875	**115**	-1.9	33,224	**108**
McIntosh	40091	1.9	19,821	**67**	2.1	20,244	**66**
Major	40093	-2.1	7,384	**25**	-2.6	7,193	**23**
Marshall	40095	4.8	13,811	**47**	5.7	14,603	**47**
Mayes	40097	1.7	39,014	**133**	1.8	39,729	**129**
Murray	40099	1.0	12,753	**43**	1.4	12,927	**42**
Muskogee**	40101	1.5	70,522	**240**	1.9	71,847	**233**
Noble	40103	-1.8	11,210	**38**	-1.8	11,003	**36**
Nowata	40105	3.3	10,918	**37**	3.7	11,325	**37**
Okfuskee	40107	-1.5	11,638	**40**	-1.8	11,434	**37**
Oklahoma*	40109	3.1	680,880	**2,318**	3.5	704,863	**2,288**
Okmulgee*	40111	0.0	39,692	**135**	0.1	39,744	**129**
Osage*	40113	2.4	45,482	**155**	2.6	46,643	**151**
Ottawa**	40115	-1.8	32,597	**111**	-2.5	31,790	**103**
Pawnee*	40117	1.3	16,820	**57**	0.9	16,969	**55**
Payne**	40119	5.6	71,992	**245**	6.5	76,648	**249**
Pittsburg**	40121	0.6	44,235	**151**	0.7	44,566	**145**
Pontotoc**	40123	0.1	35,183	**120**	0.1	35,226	**114**
Pottawatomie**	40125	3.6	67,896	**231**	4.0	70,628	**229**
Pushmataha	40127	1.0	11,781	**40**	1.3	11,935	**39**
Roger Mills	40129	-8.9	3,131	**11**	-10.6	2,800	**9**
Rogers*	40131	12.0	79,136	**269**	12.3	88,837	**288**
Seminole	40133	-2.2	24,356	**83**	-2.7	23,699	**77**
Sequoyah*	40135	3.4	40,284	**137**	3.8	41,808	**136**
Stephens**	40137	-2.1	42,275	**144**	-2.3	41,288	**134**
Texas**	40139	-1.3	19,853	**67**	-2.1	19,444	**63**
Tillman	40141	-6.3	8,700	**30**	-7.4	8,053	**26**
Tulsa*	40143	1.6	572,493	**1,949**	1.9	583,325	**1,893**
Wagoner*	40145	9.9	63,191	**215**	10.8	69,999	**227**
Washington**	40147	0.3	49,164	**167**	0.4	49,372	**160**
Washita	40149	-3.0	11,160	**38**	-3.8	10,735	**35**
Woods	40151	-5.9	8,549	**29**	-6.8	7,966	**26**
Woodward**	40153	-0.1	18,469	**63**	0.2	18,507	**60**
TOTAL: OKLAHOMA		**2.3**	**3,530,711**	**12,019**	**2.7**	**3,626,604**	**11,771**

OREGON

	FIPS CODE	2000-2004 % Change	7/1/04 Estimate	7/1/04 Ranally Population Units	2004-2009 % Change	2009 Projection	2009 Ranally Population Units
Baker	41001	-2.9	16,259	**55**	-3.5	15,692	**51**
Benton*	41003	2.0	79,726	**271**	2.5	81,681	**265**
Clackamas*	41005	7.4	363,386	**1,237**	8.2	393,126	**1,276**
Clatsop**	41007	0.7	35,896	**122**	1.1	36,274	**118**
Columbia*	41009	8.2	47,125	**160**	9.2	51,439	**167**
Coos**	41011	0.6	63,130	**215**	0.9	63,681	**207**
Crook**	41013	9.6	21,020	**72**	10.0	23,120	**75**
Curry**	41015	4.3	22,045	**75**	5.3	23,203	**75**
Deschutes*	41017	16.0	133,790	**456**	16.1	155,277	**504**
Douglas**	41019	2.5	102,953	**351**	3.0	106,059	**344**
Gilliam	41021	-9.3	1,736	**6**	-11.3	1,539	**5**
Grant	41023	-7.9	7,312	**25**	-9.2	6,639	**22**
Harney	41025	-7.4	7,047	**24**	-9.2	6,399	**21**
Hood River**	41027	2.2	20,854	**71**	2.3	21,325	**69**
Jackson*	41029	6.4	192,822	**657**	7.1	206,537	**670**
Jefferson	41031	4.4	19,853	**67**	4.7	20,782	**67**
Josephine**	41033	5.7	80,080	**273**	6.6	85,332	**277**
Klamath**	41035	2.0	65,050	**221**	2.1	66,448	**216**
Lake	41037	0.4	7,450	**25**	0.6	7,497	**24**
Lane*	41039	3.1	332,896	**1,134**	3.6	344,731	**1,119**
Lincoln	41041	0.7	44,777	**152**	1.2	45,324	**147**
Linn**	41043	4.0	107,154	**365**	4.8	112,317	**365**
Malheur**	41045	-1.5	31,140	**106**	-1.6	30,647	**99**
Marion*	41047	5.6	300,798	**1,024**	6.3	319,801	**1,038**
Morrow**	41049	7.5	11,815	**40**	8.0	12,756	**41**
Multnomah*	41051	3.5	683,283	**2,327**	4.0	710,606	**2,307**
Polk*	41053	7.6	67,110	**229**	8.3	72,682	**236**
Sherman	41055	-12.0	1,701	**6**	-14.3	1,458	**5**
Tillamook	41057	1.8	24,700	**84**	2.2	25,250	**82**
Umatilla**	41059	2.7	72,450	**247**	3.0	74,655	**242**
Union**	41061	0.1	24,564	**84**	0.1	24,577	**80**
Wallowa	41063	-2.6	7,037	**24**	-3.1	6,816	**22**
Wasco**	41065	-1.2	23,514	**80**	-1.6	23,134	**75**
Washington*	41067	10.0	489,844	**1,668**	10.6	541,567	**1,758**
Wheeler	41069	-3.6	1,492	**5**	-4.3	1,428	**5**
Yamhill*	41071	6.8	90,750	**309**	7.5	97,577	**317**
TOTAL: OREGON		**5.3**	**3,602,559**	**12,267**	**6.0**	**3,817,376**	**12,391**

PENNSYLVANIA

	FIPS CODE	2000-2004 % Change	7/1/04 Estimate	7/1/04 Ranally Population Units	2004-2009 % Change	2009 Projection	2009 Ranally Population Units
Adams**	42001	7.4	98,071	**334**	8.2	106,128	**344**
Allegheny*	42003	-2.1	1,255,103	**4,274**	-2.5	1,224,321	**3,974**
Armstrong*	42005	-1.3	71,442	**243**	-1.5	70,355	**228**
Beaver*	42007	-1.9	177,885	**606**	-2.3	173,845	**564**
Bedford	42009	-0.2	49,909	**170**	-0.3	49,736	**161**
Berks*	42011	4.1	388,909	**1,324**	4.6	406,841	**1,321**
Blair*	42013	-2.0	126,555	**431**	-2.4	123,474	**401**
Bradford**	42015	-0.3	62,593	**213**	-0.4	62,332	**202**
Bucks*	42017	3.4	617,667	**2,103**	3.7	640,325	**2,078**
Butler*	42019	4.5	181,858	**619**	5.0	190,912	**620**
Cambria*	42021	-2.7	148,535	**506**	-3.1	143,998	**467**
Cameron	42023	-4.2	5,723	**19**	-4.6	5,459	**18**
Carbon*	42025	3.0	60,563	**206**	3.5	62,711	**204**
Centre*	42027	5.7	143,518	**489**	6.5	152,895	**496**
Chester*	42029	7.2	464,595	**1,582**	7.7	500,504	**1,625**
Clarion	42031	-1.8	41,032	**140**	-2.1	40,152	**130**
Clearfield**	42033	-0.8	82,705	**282**	-1.0	81,846	**266**
Clinton**	42035	-1.7	37,273	**127**	-2.2	36,469	**118**
Columbia**	42037	1.0	64,770	**221**	1.3	65,582	**213**
Crawford**	42039	-0.8	89,668	**305**	-1.0	88,761	**288**
Cumberland*	42041	3.8	221,861	**755**	4.4	231,657	**752**
Dauphin*	42043	0.8	253,912	**865**	1.0	256,480	**833**
Delaware*	42045	0.8	555,177	**1,890**	0.7	558,790	**1,814**
Elk**	42047	-3.0	34,071	**116**	-3.5	32,893	**107**
Erie*	42049	-0.4	279,718	**952**	-0.5	278,430	**904**
Fayette*	42051	-2.2	145,333	**495**	-2.7	141,431	**459**
Forest	42053	1.2	5,006	**17**	1.6	5,087	**17**
Franklin**	42055	3.9	134,355	**457**	4.4	140,331	**456**
Fulton	42057	2.5	14,624	**50**	3.0	15,067	**49**
Greene	42059	-0.9	40,302	**137**	-1.2	39,818	**129**
Huntingdon**	42061	0.8	45,954	**156**	0.9	46,386	**151**
Indiana**	42063	-0.8	88,892	**303**	-0.9	88,064	**286**
Jefferson	42065	0.0	45,946	**156**	-0.0	45,943	**149**
Juniata	42067	1.4	23,134	**79**	1.5	23,477	**76**
Lackawanna*	42069	-1.7	209,643	**714**	-1.9	205,576	**667**
Lancaster*	42071	3.4	486,469	**1,656**	3.8	504,836	**1,639**
Lawrence**	42073	-1.7	93,007	**317**	-2.1	91,013	**295**
Lebanon*	42075	2.5	123,395	**420**	3.0	127,083	**413**
Lehigh*	42077	3.5	323,155	**1,100**	4.1	336,281	**1,092**
Luzerne*	42079	-2.3	311,854	**1,062**	-2.7	303,556	**985**
Lycoming*	42081	-1.8	117,940	**402**	-2.1	115,459	**375**
McKean**	42083	-1.9	45,049	**153**	-2.1	44,117	**143**
Mercer*	42085	-0.4	119,795	**408**	-0.4	119,272	**387**
Mifflin**	42087	-0.4	46,282	**158**	-0.6	46,009	**149**
Monroe**	42089	14.9	159,381	**543**	15.3	183,769	**597**
Montgomery*	42091	3.6	777,323	**2,647**	4.2	810,039	**2,629**
Montour**	42093	-1.1	18,027	**61**	-1.5	17,748	**58**
Northampton*	42095	5.5	281,728	**959**	6.3	299,464	**972**
Northumberland**	42097	-1.7	92,940	**316**	-2.1	91,034	**295**
Perry*	42099	1.8	44,379	**151**	2.1	45,326	**147**
Philadelphia*	42101	-3.3	1,468,025	**4,999**	-3.8	1,412,463	**4,585**
Pike*	42103	16.6	54,000	**184**	17.0	63,168	**205**
Potter	42105	0.3	18,138	**62**	-0.1	18,125	**59**
Schuylkill**	42107	-2.1	147,221	**501**	-2.4	143,633	**466**
Snyder**	42109	1.7	38,171	**130**	2.0	38,941	**126**
Somerset**	42111	-1.1	79,144	**269**	-1.4	78,033	**253**
Sullivan	42113	-2.6	6,383	**22**	-3.4	6,165	**20**
Susquehanna	42115	-1.4	41,666	**142**	-1.7	40,937	**133**
Tioga	42117	0.6	41,622	**142**	0.8	41,940	**136**
Union**	42119	2.9	42,848	**146**	3.4	44,316	**144**
Venango**	42121	-2.2	56,311	**192**	-2.5	54,879	**178**
Warren**	42123	-3.1	42,501	**145**	-3.7	40,933	**133**
Washington*	42125	0.9	204,705	**697**	1.0	206,762	**671**
Wayne	42127	3.7	49,483	**168**	3.9	51,424	**167**
Westmoreland*	42129	-0.6	367,701	**1,252**	-0.7	365,024	**1,185**
Wyoming*	42131	0.4	28,195	**96**	0.7	28,401	**92**
York*	42133	4.5	398,969	**1,358**	5.1	419,155	**1,361**
TOTAL: PENNSYLVANIA		**0.9**	**12,392,109**	**42,194**	**1.1**	**12,525,381**	**40,657**

RHODE ISLAND

	FIPS CODE	2000-2004 % Change	7/1/04 Estimate	7/1/04 Ranally Population Units	2004-2009 % Change	2009 Projection	2009 Ranally Population Units
Bristol*	44001	0.8	51,073	**174**	0.8	51,493	**167**
Kent*	44003	3.3	172,563	**588**	3.7	178,891	**581**
Newport*	44005	0.7	86,020	**293**	0.5	86,452	**281**
Providence*	44007	3.8	645,010	**2,196**	4.3	672,848	**2,184**
Washington*	44009	5.2	129,998	**443**	5.8	137,480	**446**
TOTAL: RHODE ISLAND		**3.5**	**1,084,664**	**3,694**	**3.9**	**1,127,164**	**3,659**

SOUTH CAROLINA

	FIPS CODE	2000-2004 % Change	7/1/04 Estimate	7/1/04 Ranally Population Units	2004-2009 % Change	2009 Projection	2009 Ranally Population Units
Abbeville	45001	1.0	26,434	**90**	1.0	26,699	**87**
Aiken*	45003	3.9	148,054	**504**	4.4	154,638	**502**
Allendale	45005	-3.2	10,852	**37**	-3.7	10,448	**34**
Anderson*	45007	4.5	173,238	**590**	5.0	181,872	**590**
Bamberg	45009	-4.8	15,851	**54**	-5.8	14,935	**48**
Barnwell	45011	-0.6	23,337	**79**	-0.7	23,175	**75**
Beaufort**	45013	12.9	136,525	**465**	13.3	154,703	**502**
Berkeley*	45015	3.5	147,602	**503**	3.9	153,361	**498**
Calhoun*	45017	1.5	15,410	**52**	1.4	15,624	**51**
Charleston*	45019	4.7	324,460	**1,105**	5.3	341,682	**1,109**
Cherokee**	45021	2.5	53,850	**183**	2.7	55,322	**180**
Chester**	45023	-0.7	33,833	**115**	-1.1	33,466	**109**
Chesterfield	45025	1.4	43,366	**148**	1.3	43,936	**143**
Clarendon	45027	1.5	32,979	**112**	1.6	33,515	**109**
Colleton**	45029	3.1	39,448	**134**	3.5	40,822	**133**
Darlington*	45031	1.1	68,115	**232**	1.2	68,908	**224**
Dillon**	45033	1.3	31,133	**106**	1.7	31,661	**103**
Dorchester*	45035	10.6	106,654	**363**	11.7	119,080	**387**
Edgefield*	45037	0.6	24,738	**84**	0.7	24,909	**81**
Fairfield*	45039	2.1	23,939	**82**	2.1	24,432	**79**
Florence*	45041	2.7	129,181	**440**	3.3	133,411	**433**
Georgetown**	45043	7.3	59,865	**204**	7.8	64,564	**210**
Greenville*	45045	5.4	400,132	**1,362**	6.0	423,990	**1,376**
Greenwood**	45047	2.4	67,894	**231**	2.9	69,847	**227**
Hampton	45049	0.1	21,400	**73**	0.2	21,446	**70**
Horry*	45051	9.3	214,999	**732**	9.9	236,202	**767**
Jasper**	45053	2.0	21,087	**72**	2.1	21,531	**70**
Kershaw*	45055	4.5	55,026	**187**	4.9	57,745	**187**
Lancaster**	45057	2.5	62,895	**214**	3.0	64,768	**210**
Laurens*	45059	1.3	70,472	**240**	1.4	71,490	**232**
Lee	45061	1.4	20,396	**69**	1.6	20,722	**67**
Lexington*	45063	6.4	229,751	**782**	7.0	245,856	**798**
McCormick	45065	3.6	10,314	**35**	3.9	10,718	**35**
Marion	45067	-1.3	34,996	**119**	-1.7	34,414	**112**
Marlboro**	45069	-1.9	28,280	**96**	-2.3	27,629	**90**
Newberry**	45071	2.7	37,076	**126**	3.2	38,254	**124**
Oconee**	45073	4.5	69,222	**236**	5.1	72,718	**236**
Orangeburg**	45075	-0.8	90,870	**309**	-0.9	90,083	**292**
Pickens*	45077	2.4	113,461	**386**	2.7	116,470	**378**
Richland*	45079	4.7	335,685	**1,143**	5.3	353,578	**1,148**
Saluda*	45081	-0.7	19,055	**65**	-0.8	18,895	**61**
Spartanburg*	45083	3.9	263,575	**897**	4.3	275,036	**893**
Sumter*	45085	1.6	106,361	**362**	1.9	108,382	**352**
Union**	45087	-3.4	28,853	**98**	-4.3	27,626	**90**
Williamsburg	45089	-4.2	35,636	**121**	-5.1	33,832	**110**
York*	45091	10.7	182,193	**620**	11.3	202,803	**658**
TOTAL: SOUTH CAROLINA		**4.4**	**4,188,493**	**14,257**	**4.9**	**4,395,198**	**14,270**

SOUTH DAKOTA

	FIPS CODE	2000-2004 % Change	7/1/04 Estimate	7/1/04 Ranally Population Units	2004-2009 % Change	2009 Projection	2009 Ranally Population Units
Aurora	46003	-5.8	2,881	**10**	-7.5	2,664	**9**
Beadle**	46005	-5.8	16,037	**55**	-7.0	14,919	**48**
Bennett	46007	-1.7	3,515	**12**	-2.2	3,439	**11**
Bon Homme	46009	-2.8	7,055	**24**	-3.5	6,810	**22**
Brookings**	46011	0.1	28,258	**96**	-0.2	28,201	**92**
Brown**	46013	-2.9	34,430	**117**	-3.4	33,253	**108**
Brule	46015	-3.9	5,157	**18**	-4.6	4,922	**16**
Buffalo	46017	-2.0	1,991	**7**	-0.9	1,973	**6**
Butte	46019	1.6	9,244	**31**	1.7	9,399	**31**
Campbell	46021	-7.6	1,646	**6**	-9.5	1,490	**5**
Charles Mix	46023	-2.4	9,122	**31**	-3.1	8,843	**29**
Clark	46025	-7.1	3,847	**13**	-8.4	3,522	**11**
Clay**	46027	-3.3	13,092	**45**	-3.8	12,599	**41**
Codington**	46029	0.1	25,934	**88**	0.0	25,944	**84**
Corson	46031	3.1	4,312	**15**	2.8	4,432	**14**
Custer	46033	5.6	7,679	**26**	6.1	8,146	**26**
Davison**	46035	0.1	18,751	**64**	0.1	18,771	**61**
Day	46037	-7.8	5,776	**20**	-9.4	5,232	**17**
Deuel	46039	-4.0	4,318	**15**	-5.2	4,094	**13**
Dewey	46041	3.5	6,181	**21**	3.9	6,420	**21**
Douglas	46043	-5.5	3,268	**11**	-6.3	3,062	**10**
Edmunds**	46045	-4.3	4,178	**14**	-5.1	3,966	**13**
Fall River	46047	-2.5	7,270	**25**	-2.4	7,092	**23**
Faulk	46049	-8.4	2,418	**8**	-10.1	2,173	**7**
Grant	46051	-3.7	7,558	**26**	-4.4	7,225	**23**
Gregory	46053	-7.9	4,415	**15**	-9.1	4,015	**13**
Haakon	46055	-11.0	1,954	**7**	-12.6	1,708	**6**
Hamlin**	46057	1.7	5,636	**19**	1.8	5,737	**19**
Hand	46059	-7.6	3,458	**12**	-8.6	3,160	**10**
Hanson**	46061	15.6	3,629	**12**	16.2	4,216	**14**
Harding	46063	-6.1	1,270	**4**	-7.0	1,181	**4**
Hughes**	46065	1.6	16,744	**57**	1.7	17,033	**55**
Hutchinson	46067	-5.6	7,619	**26**	-7.1	7,077	**23**
Hyde	46069	-7.7	1,543	**5**	-9.3	1,399	**5**
Jackson	46071	-3.5	2,826	**10**	-4.8	2,690	**9**
Jerauld	46073	-6.4	2,147	**7**	-7.4	1,988	**6**
Jones	46075	-11.4	1,057	**3**	-13.2	918	**3**
Kingsbury	46077	-5.9	5,472	**19**	-7.3	5,071	**16**
Lake	46079	-2.7	10,970	**37**	-3.2	10,620	**34**
Lawrence**	46081	0.5	21,917	**75**	0.8	22,082	**72**
Lincoln*	46083	28.0	30,883	**105**	25.5	38,756	**126**
Lyman	46085	0.6	3,918	**13**	0.2	3,925	**13**
McCook*	46087	0.6	5,868	**20**	0.3	5,888	**19**
McPherson	46089	-8.1	2,668	**9**	-9.7	2,408	**8**
Marshall	46091	-8.8	4,175	**14**	-11.0	3,717	**12**
Meade*	46093	2.6	24,873	**85**	3.1	25,649	**83**
Mellette	46095	2.2	2,129	**7**	2.3	2,179	**7**
Miner	46097	-7.7	2,663	**9**	-9.8	2,403	**8**
Minnehaha*	46099	5.5	156,477	**533**	5.9	165,650	**538**
Moody	46101	-1.7	6,486	**22**	-1.9	6,361	**21**
Pennington*	46103	4.9	92,908	**316**	5.4	97,969	**318**
Perkins	46105	-6.7	3,138	**11**	-7.6	2,899	**9**

Source: Devonshire Associates Ltd. and Scan/US, Inc. 2004.
* Component of a Metropolitan Core Based Statistical Area.
** Component of a Micropolitan Core Based Statistical Area.

continued on next page

Counties: Population Trends, *Continued*

	FIPS CODE	PRESENT 2000-2004 % Change	PRESENT 7/1/04 Estimate	7/1/04 Ranally Population Units	FUTURE 2004-2009 % Change	FUTURE 2009 Projection	2009 Ranally Population Units
Potter	46107	-8.9	2,453	**8**	-10.6	2,193	**7**
Roberts	46109	1.5	10,168	**35**	1.9	10,362	**34**
Sanborn	46111	-3.1	2,592	**9**	-3.8	2,493	**8**
Shannon	46113	7.7	13,431	**46**	8.2	14,528	**47**
Spink	46115	-8.4	6,825	**23**	-10.2	6,131	**20**
Stanley**	46117	-1.1	2,742	**9**	-1.9	2,691	**9**
Sully	46119	-8.4	1,425	**5**	-10.2	1,279	**4**
Todd	46121	6.0	9,594	**33**	6.5	10,214	**33**
Tripp	46123	-5.0	6,108	**21**	-5.5	5,771	**19**
Turner*	46125	-3.9	8,506	**29**	-5.1	8,075	**26**
Union*	46127	4.6	13,166	**45**	5.3	13,863	**45**
Walworth	46129	-8.9	5,442	**19**	-10.4	4,877	**16**
Yankton**	46135	-1.2	21,398	**73**	-1.3	21,113	**69**
Ziebach	46137	2.1	2,573	**9**	4.2	2,681	**9**
TOTAL: SOUTH DAKOTA		**1.6**	**767,184**	**2,614**	**1.9**	**781,561**	**2,538**
TENNESSEE							
Anderson*	47001	1.1	72,110	**246**	1.4	73,141	**237**
Bedford**	47003	9.3	41,066	**140**	9.9	45,128	**146**
Benton	47005	-0.3	16,490	**56**	-0.3	16,440	**53**
Bledsoe	47007	1.9	12,604	**43**	1.9	12,842	**42**
Blount*	47009	7.0	113,265	**386**	7.7	122,041	**396**
Bradley*	47011	3.4	90,961	**310**	3.8	94,447	**307**
Campbell**	47013	0.8	40,188	**137**	0.8	40,505	**131**
Cannon*	47015	3.7	13,300	**45**	3.6	13,782	**45**
Carroll	47017	-0.6	29,303	**100**	-0.7	29,107	**94**
Carter*	47019	3.8	58,913	**201**	4.4	61,505	**200**
Cheatham*	47021	5.2	37,783	**129**	5.5	39,876	**129**
Chester*	47023	2.6	15,941	**54**	3.1	16,436	**53**
Claiborne	47025	2.4	30,581	**104**	2.7	31,409	**102**
Clay	47027	-0.5	7,935	**27**	-0.8	7,874	**26**
Cocke**	47029	3.0	34,566	**118**	3.4	35,753	**116**
Coffee**	47031	4.4	50,135	**171**	4.9	52,594	**171**
Crockett	47033	-0.4	14,472	**49**	-0.6	14,378	**47**
Cumberland**	47035	7.2	50,183	**171**	7.9	54,142	**176**
Davidson*	47037	-0.0	569,819	**1,940**	-0.0	569,701	**1,849**
Decatur	47039	-1.3	11,578	**39**	-1.4	11,420	**37**
DeKalb	47041	4.6	18,230	**62**	5.3	19,195	**62**
Dickson*	47043	5.4	45,469	**155**	5.9	48,138	**156**
Dyer**	47045	0.1	37,305	**127**	-0.0	37,288	**121**
Fayette*	47047	15.8	33,345	**114**	15.8	38,625	**125**
Fentress	47049	2.4	17,032	**58**	2.9	17,519	**57**
Franklin**	47051	4.2	40,901	**139**	4.7	42,843	**139**
Gibson**	47053	-0.6	47,841	**163**	-0.8	47,437	**154**
Giles	47055	-0.3	29,365	**100**	-0.4	29,243	**95**
Grainger*	47057	5.0	21,687	**74**	5.6	22,897	**74**
Greene**	47059	2.2	64,308	**219**	2.5	65,892	**214**
Grundy	47061	0.5	14,409	**49**	0.7	14,511	**47**
Hamblen*	47063	1.6	59,059	**201**	1.8	60,098	**195**
Hamilton*	47065	0.7	310,020	**1,056**	0.8	312,567	**1,015**
Hancock	47067	-1.6	6,678	**23**	-1.8	6,556	**21**
Hardeman	47069	0.3	28,188	**96**	0.3	28,260	**92**
Hardin	47071	1.8	26,043	**89**	2.2	26,621	**86**
Hawkins*	47073	3.6	55,484	**189**	4.0	57,720	**187**
Haywood**	47075	-1.2	19,561	**67**	-1.6	19,240	**62**
Henderson	47077	1.9	25,999	**89**	1.9	26,494	**86**
Henry**	47079	0.3	31,198	**106**	0.2	31,263	**101**
Hickman*	47081	6.1	23,657	**81**	6.4	25,180	**82**
Houston	47083	0.2	8,106	**28**	1.3	8,213	**27**
Humphreys	47085	1.4	18,188	**62**	1.8	18,515	**60**
Jackson**	47087	2.6	11,269	**38**	2.7	11,572	**38**
Jefferson*	47089	7.7	47,699	**162**	8.2	51,596	**167**
Johnson	47091	3.4	18,093	**62**	4.0	18,818	**61**
Knox*	47093	3.8	396,391	**1,350**	4.3	413,365	**1,342**
Lake	47095	-2.1	7,785	**27**	-2.4	7,595	**25**
Lauderdale	47097	-0.1	27,086	**92**	0.2	27,133	**88**
Lawrence**	47099	2.6	40,953	**139**	3.0	42,199	**137**
Lewis	47101	0.8	11,459	**39**	0.9	11,566	**38**
Lincoln	47103	1.8	31,894	**109**	1.9	32,497	**105**
Loudon*	47105	8.5	42,424	**144**	9.4	46,425	**151**
McMinn**	47107	4.3	51,117	**174**	4.7	53,539	**174**
McNairy	47109	1.5	25,011	**85**	1.5	25,374	**82**
Macon*	47111	4.1	21,213	**72**	4.5	22,165	**72**
Madison*	47113	2.9	94,495	**322**	3.3	97,606	**317**
Marion*	47115	0.5	27,916	**95**	0.7	28,098	**91**
Marshall**	47117	3.7	27,758	**95**	4.0	28,861	**94**
Maury**	47119	7.0	74,356	**253**	7.8	80,147	**260**
Meigs	47121	4.0	11,530	**39**	4.4	12,032	**39**
Monroe	47123	7.0	41,674	**142**	7.5	44,790	**145**
Montgomery*	47125	6.1	142,942	**487**	6.6	152,331	**494**
Moore**	47127	3.8	5,959	**20**	4.0	6,199	**20**
Morgan	47129	2.1	20,180	**69**	2.5	20,682	**67**
Obion**	47131	-0.3	32,351	**110**	-0.5	32,175	**104**
Overton**	47133	0.1	20,137	**69**	-0.3	20,069	**65**
Perry	47135	-0.1	7,621	**26**	-0.4	7,593	**25**
Pickett	47137	1.7	5,030	**17**	2.3	5,148	**17**
Polk*	47139	0.9	16,195	**55**	0.7	16,315	**53**
Putnam**	47141	5.6	65,804	**224**	6.3	69,960	**227**
Rhea	47143	4.1	29,560	**101**	4.6	30,932	**100**
Roane**	47145	1.3	52,584	**179**	1.5	53,383	**173**
Robertson*	47147	8.9	59,290	**202**	9.4	64,834	**210**
Rutherford*	47149	14.6	208,605	**710**	15.1	240,080	**779**
Scott	47151	3.4	21,840	**74**	3.8	22,667	**74**
Sequatchie*	47153	6.8	12,140	**41**	7.5	13,050	**42**
Sevier**	47155	7.9	76,768	**261**	8.2	83,094	**270**
Shelby*	47157	1.3	908,843	**3,095**	1.5	922,152	**2,993**
Smith*	47159	3.7	18,361	**63**	3.7	19,043	**62**
Stewart*	47161	4.9	12,979	**44**	5.1	13,641	**44**
Sullivan*	47163	0.0	153,090	**521**	0.1	153,289	**498**
Sumner*	47165	8.3	141,292	**481**	9.0	153,992	**500**
Tipton*	47167	7.4	55,057	**187**	7.9	59,419	**193**
Trousdale*	47169	3.2	7,488	**25**	2.8	7,695	**25**
Unicoi*	47171	0.4	17,729	**60**	0.6	17,827	**58**
Union*	47173	7.5	19,151	**65**	8.4	20,756	**67**
Van Buren	47175	-0.8	5,465	**19**	-1.1	5,403	**18**
Warren**	47177	2.9	39,370	**134**	3.1	40,577	**132**
Washington*	47179	3.5	110,949	**378**	3.9	115,303	**374**
Wayne	47181	0.8	16,984	**58**	1.1	17,171	**56**
Weakley**	47183	-2.2	34,120	**116**	-2.8	33,166	**108**
White	47185	2.7	23,735	**81**	3.2	24,490	**79**
Williamson*	47187	15.1	145,703	**496**	15.1	167,711	**544**
Wilson*	47189	9.7	97,396	**332**	10.4	107,543	**349**
TOTAL: TENNESSEE		**3.5**	**5,888,107**	**20,052**	**3.9**	**6,119,904**	**19,861**
TEXAS							
Anderson**	48001	-0.8	54,691	**186**	-0.9	54,198	**176**
Andrews**	48003	-1.2	12,845	**44**	-0.9	12,731	**41**
Angelina**	48005	1.3	81,163	**276**	1.4	82,298	**267**
Aransas*	48007	6.3	23,921	**81**	7.2	25,655	**83**
Archer*	48009	4.6	9,261	**32**	3.9	9,618	**31**
Armstrong*	48011	-6.0	2,020	**7**	-8.5	1,849	**6**
Atascosa*	48013	10.9	42,850	**146**	11.5	47,765	**155**
Austin*	48015	8.0	25,488	**87**	8.4	27,637	**90**
Bailey	48017	1.3	6,683	**23**	1.7	6,795	**22**
Bandera*	48019	12.5	19,851	**68**	12.7	22,366	**73**
Bastrop*	48021	21.2	69,998	**238**	20.9	84,598	**275**
Baylor	48023	-5.8	3,854	**13**	-6.9	3,590	**12**
Bee**	48025	0.4	32,486	**111**	0.8	32,759	**106**
Bell*	48027	5.9	251,967	**858**	6.4	268,153	**870**
Bexar*	48029	7.4	1,496,237	**5,095**	8.2	1,619,092	**5,256**
Blanco	48031	6.0	8,924	**30**	6.4	9,496	**31**
Borden	48033	-8.0	671	**2**	-7.7	619	**2**
Bosque	48035	3.7	17,847	**61**	4.2	18,600	**60**
Bowie*	48037	0.6	89,837	**306**	0.8	90,519	**294**
Brazoria*	48039	11.6	269,789	**919**	12.3	302,968	**983**
Brazos*	48041	6.4	162,171	**552**	7.2	173,866	**564**
Brewster	48043	5.7	9,372	**32**	6.7	9,996	**32**
Briscoe	48045	-9.2	1,626	**6**	-10.7	1,452	**5**
Brooks	48047	-4.2	7,644	**26**	-4.8	7,275	**24**
Brown**	48049	1.5	38,231	**130**	1.7	38,870	**126**
Burleson*	48051	3.6	17,071	**58**	3.8	17,719	**58**
Burnet	48053	17.8	40,228	**137**	17.6	47,323	**154**
Caldwell*	48055	13.7	36,601	**125**	14.1	41,747	**136**
Calhoun*	48057	-1.3	20,387	**69**	-1.6	20,051	**65**
Callahan*	48059	2.1	13,173	**45**	2.4	13,484	**44**
Cameron*	48061	10.9	371,857	**1,266**	11.8	415,655	**1,349**
Camp	48063	2.3	11,809	**40**	2.2	12,070	**39**
Carson*	48065	-0.1	6,507	**22**	-0.0	6,506	**21**
Cass	48067	-1.9	29,854	**102**	-2.3	29,155	**95**
Castro	48069	-5.9	7,794	**27**	-6.6	7,283	**24**
Chambers*	48071	7.8	28,050	**96**	8.3	30,391	**99**
Cherokee**	48073	2.6	47,864	**163**	3.1	49,342	**160**
Childress	48075	-2.1	7,523	**26**	-2.6	7,326	**24**
Clay*	48077	2.1	11,240	**38**	1.4	11,402	**37**
Cochran	48079	-8.5	3,414	**12**	-9.8	3,078	**10**
Coke	48081	-4.7	3,683	**13**	-5.5	3,482	**11**
Coleman	48083	-6.4	8,644	**29**	-7.4	8,007	**26**
Collin*	48085	28.0	629,504	**2,143**	25.7	791,230	**2,568**
Collingsworth	48087	-7.5	2,967	**10**	-8.8	2,705	**9**
Colorado	48089	1.7	20,739	**71**	2.3	21,214	**69**
Comal*	48091	16.4	90,783	**309**	16.5	105,766	**343**
Comanche	48093	-4.5	13,391	**46**	-5.4	12,662	**41**
Concho	48095	-6.3	3,716	**13**	-7.5	3,436	**11**
Cooke**	48097	5.9	38,507	**131**	6.6	41,063	**133**
Coryell*	48099	0.3	75,191	**256**	-0.0	75,165	**244**
Cottle	48101	-10.2	1,710	**6**	-11.5	1,513	**5**
Crane	48103	-3.4	3,862	**13**	-2.9	3,749	**12**
Crockett	48105	-4.8	3,902	**13**	-4.0	3,745	**12**
Crosby*	48107	-6.1	6,640	**23**	-7.3	6,154	**20**
Culberson	48109	-9.2	2,701	**9**	-10.2	2,426	**8**
Dallam	48111	-2.6	6,059	**21**	-3.4	5,856	**19**
Dallas*	48113	3.8	2,303,656	**7,844**	4.2	2,401,298	**7,795**
Dawson**	48115	-5.0	14,232	**48**	-6.1	13,367	**43**
Deaf Smith**	48117	-1.0	18,382	**63**	-0.9	18,217	**59**
Delta*	48119	3.0	5,487	**19**	3.3	5,666	**18**
Denton*	48121	23.5	534,784	**1,821**	22.4	654,680	**2,125**
DeWitt	48123	0.6	20,137	**69**	0.9	20,317	**66**
Dickens	48125	-2.4	2,697	**9**	-1.5	2,656	**9**
Dimmit	48127	1.3	10,383	**35**	2.0	10,590	**34**
Donley	48129	1.6	3,891	**13**	1.8	3,962	**13**
Duval	48131	-4.9	12,474	**42**	-5.5	11,783	**38**
Eastland	48133	-0.0	18,296	**62**	-0.1	18,272	**59**
Ector*	48135	1.8	123,354	**420**	2.7	126,654	**411**
Edwards	48137	-7.9	1,992	**7**	-9.3	1,807	**6**
Ellis*	48139	15.3	128,389	**437**	15.5	148,272	**481**
El Paso*	48141	5.0	713,340	**2,429**	5.5	752,812	**2,444**
Erath**	48143	1.5	33,483	**114**	1.7	34,042	**111**
Falls	48145	-5.0	17,642	**60**	-6.0	16,592	**54**
Fannin	48147	4.3	32,575	**111**	4.6	34,066	**111**
Fayette	48149	3.4	22,554	**77**	4.1	23,471	**76**
Fisher	48151	-6.1	4,080	**14**	-7.3	3,781	**12**
Floyd	48153	-5.4	7,349	**25**	-6.3	6,883	**22**
Foard	48155	-6.4	1,519	**5**	-6.9	1,414	**5**
Fort Bend*	48157	24.1	440,039	**1,498**	23.0	541,335	**1,757**
Franklin	48159	6.2	10,049	**34**	7.1	10,761	**35**
Freestone	48161	5.4	18,834	**64**	6.1	19,978	**65**
Frio	48163	0.8	16,390	**56**	1.4	16,613	**54**
Gaines	48165	-0.2	14,431	**49**	-0.3	14,394	**47**
Galveston*	48167	8.8	272,122	**927**	9.8	298,837	**970**
Garza	48169	3.9	5,060	**17**	4.8	5,304	**17**
Gillespie	48171	8.9	22,660	**77**	9.6	24,825	**81**
Glasscock	48173	-4.8	1,339	**5**	-5.8	1,262	**4**
Goliad*	48175	3.4	7,163	**24**	3.3	7,399	**24**
Gonzales	48177	3.0	19,193	**65**	3.5	19,870	**64**
Gray**	48179	-7.0	21,145	**72**	-7.9	19,474	**63**
Grayson*	48181	5.4	116,532	**397**	5.9	123,419	**401**
Gregg*	48183	3.1	114,824	**391**	3.8	119,232	**387**
Grimes	48185	7.9	25,411	**87**	8.8	27,645	**90**
Guadalupe*	48187	11.8	99,505	**339**	12.1	111,519	**362**
Hale**	48189	-2.6	35,642	**121**	-3.2	34,508	**112**
Hall	48191	1.9	3,855	**13**	2.8	3,964	**13**
Hamilton	48193	-1.8	8,081	**28**	-2.3	7,896	**26**
Hansford	48195	-3.9	5,162	**18**	-4.6	4,925	**16**
Hardeman	48197	-7.9	4,352	**15**	-9.6	3,935	**13**
Hardin*	48199	4.3	50,132	**171**	5.0	52,623	**171**
Harris*	48201	7.5	3,656,415	**12,450**	8.2	3,957,791	**12,847**
Harrison**	48203	1.3	62,916	**214**	1.7	63,956	**208**
Hartley	48205	-7.5	5,121	**17**	-9.4	4,638	**15**
Haskell	48207	-7.4	5,640	**19**	-8.4	5,168	**17**
Hays*	48209	22.2	119,256	**406**	21.2	144,559	**469**
Hemphill	48211	-0.4	3,336	**11**	0.4	3,351	**11**
Henderson**	48213	7.1	78,507	**267**	7.8	84,652	**275**
Hidalgo*	48215	15.2	656,072	**2,234**	15.6	758,677	**2,463**
Hill	48217	8.5	35,058	**119**	8.8	38,127	**124**
Hockley**	48219	0.6	22,854	**78**	1.0	23,086	**75**
Hood**	48221	12.5	46,225	**157**	12.7	52,117	**169**
Hopkins**	48223	2.9	32,901	**112**	3.3	33,995	**110**
Houston	48225	-0.4	23,084	**79**	-0.5	22,959	**75**
Howard**	48227	-2.9	32,647	**111**	-3.1	31,649	**103**
Hudspeth	48229	-6.0	3,142	**11**	-7.7	2,901	**9**
Hunt*	48231	7.5	82,370	**280**	8.2	89,093	**289**
Hutchinson**	48233	-4.9	22,692	**77**	-5.7	21,400	**69**
Irion*	48235	-2.3	1,731	**6**	-3.1	1,678	**5**
Jack	48237	2.8	9,010	**31**	3.4	9,314	**30**
Jackson	48239	-1.4	14,183	**48**	-2.3	13,863	**45**
Jasper	48241	-0.4	35,471	**121**	-0.5	35,283	**115**
Jeff Davis	48243	1.4	2,237	**8**	0.3	2,244	**7**
Jefferson*	48245	-1.8	247,599	**843**	-2.0	242,615	**788**
Jim Hogg	48247	-6.4	4,944	**17**	-7.7	4,561	**15**
Jim Wells**	48249	3.8	40,830	**139**	4.4	42,636	**138**
Johnson*	48251	12.6	142,744	**486**	12.9	161,115	**523**
Jones*	48253	-4.7	19,809	**67**	-5.6	18,698	**61**
Karnes	48255	-1.5	15,220	**52**	-1.8	14,940	**48**
Kaufman*	48257	19.5	85,224	**290**	19.2	101,560	**330**
Kendall*	48259	13.4	26,915	**92**	13.7	30,598	**99**
Kenedy**	48261	-1.9	406	**1**	-3.0	394	**1**
Kent	48263	-13.3	745	**3**	-15.0	633	**2**
Kerr**	48265	4.9	45,804	**156**	5.4	48,271	**157**
Kimble	48267	1.8	4,548	**15**	1.5	4,614	**15**
King	48269	-14.0	306	**1**	-18.3	250	**1**
Kinney	48271	-2.7	3,288	**11**	-3.4	3,177	**10**
Kleberg**	48273	-1.0	31,238	**106**	-1.1	30,886	**100**
Knox	48275	-10.0	3,827	**13**	-12.2	3,360	**11**
Lamar**	48277	2.6	49,741	**169**	2.8	51,125	**166**
Lamb	48279	-0.6	14,628	**50**	-0.3	14,581	**47**
Lampasas*	48281	12.1	19,905	**68**	12.5	22,394	**73**
La Salle	48283	-1.1	5,801	**20**	-1.8	5,699	**19**
Lavaca	48285	-1.0	19,019	**65**	-1.2	18,796	**61**
Lee	48287	7.3	16,797	**57**	7.9	18,132	**59**
Leon	48289	5.7	16,208	**55**	5.9	17,163	**56**
Liberty*	48291	7.3	75,275	**256**	7.7	81,059	**263**
Limestone	48293	3.4	22,808	**78**	4.1	23,742	**77**
Lipscomb	48295	1.7	3,108	**11**	2.5	3,186	**10**
Live Oak	48297	-4.3	11,777	**40**	-5.2	11,169	**36**
Llano	48299	7.6	18,341	**62**	8.4	19,873	**65**
Loving	48301	-9.0	61	**0**	-8.2	56	**0**
Lubbock*	48303	4.3	252,962	**861**	5.0	265,524	**862**
Lynn	48305	-7.2	6,077	**21**	-8.2	5,579	**18**
McCulloch	48307	-4.9	7,805	**27**	-5.6	7,367	**24**
McLennan*	48309	3.9	221,739	**755**	4.4	231,389	**751**
McMullen	48311	2.6	873	**3**	2.6	896	**3**
Madison	48313	-1.3	12,768	**43**	-2.1	12,503	**41**
Marion	48315	1.0	11,054	**38**	1.1	11,181	**36**
Martin	48317	-3.9	4,560	**16**	-4.3	4,363	**14**
Mason	48319	1.3	3,788	**13**	1.4	3,841	**12**
Matagorda**	48321	1.2	38,404	**131**	1.5	38,975	**127**
Maverick**	48323	8.1	51,111	**174**	9.1	55,773	**181**
Medina*	48325	7.5	42,244	**144**	8.2	45,697	**148**
Menard	48327	-0.3	2,353	**8**	-0.1	2,350	**8**
Midland*	48329	3.1	119,655	**407**	4.3	124,798	**405**
Milam	48331	4.7	25,378	**86**	5.4	26,750	**87**
Mills	48333	-2.8	5,005	**17**	-3.2	4,843	**16**
Mitchell	48335	-5.0	9,210	**31**	-5.5	8,699	**28**
Montague	48337	2.1	19,511	**66**	2.4	19,985	**65**
Montgomery*	48339	22.7	360,419	**1,227**	21.8	438,982	**1,425**
Moore**	48341	0.8	20,275	**69**	1.0	20,479	**66**

Source: Devonshire Associates Ltd. and Scan/US, Inc. 2004.
* Component of a Metropolitan Core Based Statistical Area.
** Component of a Micropolitan Core Based Statistical Area.

Counties: Population Trends, *Continued*

	FIPS CODE	PRESENT 2000-2004 % Change	7/1/04 Estimate	7/1/04 Ranally Population Units	FUTURE 2004-2009 % Change	2009 Projection	2009 Ranally Population Units
Morris	48343	1.2	13,206	45	1.4	13,397	43
Motley	48345	-11.5	1,262	4	-15.1	1,071	3
Nacogdoches**	48347	0.8	59,703	203	1.0	60,294	196
Navarro**	48349	6.4	48,002	163	7.0	51,354	167
Newton	48351	-1.8	14,808	50	-2.0	14,506	47
Nolan**	48353	-5.7	14,899	51	-6.8	13,884	45
Nueces*	48355	0.7	315,797	1,075	0.9	318,737	1,035
Ochiltree	48357	-0.3	8,983	31	-0.2	8,967	29
Oldham	48359	-1.7	2,148	7	-2.6	2,093	7
Orange*	48361	-0.9	84,199	287	-1.1	83,247	270
Palo Pinto**	48363	1.4	27,404	93	1.4	27,797	90
Panola	48365	-0.9	22,558	77	-1.1	22,318	72
Parker*	48367	13.2	100,215	341	13.6	113,879	370
Parmer	48369	-1.6	9,860	34	-1.8	9,682	31
Pecos	48371	-5.9	15,821	54	-6.6	14,773	48
Polk	48373	13.2	46,570	159	13.4	52,802	171
Potter*	48375	4.4	118,540	404	5.1	124,557	404
Presidio	48377	5.0	7,671	26	5.2	8,070	26
Rains	48379	24.8	11,404	39	23.9	14,135	46
Randall*	48381	3.7	108,220	368	4.1	112,647	366
Reagan	48383	-10.5	2,978	10	-11.8	2,627	9
Real	48385	-1.3	3,006	10	-2.3	2,936	10
Red River	48387	-4.6	13,660	47	-5.4	12,925	42
Reeves**	48389	-8.8	11,975	41	-10.3	10,742	35
Refugio	48391	-3.4	7,559	26	-4.3	7,236	23
Roberts**	48393	-9.8	800	3	-11.4	709	2
Robertson*	48395	-1.4	15,769	54	-2.0	15,453	50
Rockwall*	48397	35.2	58,223	198	30.8	76,184	247
Runnels	48399	-6.7	10,727	37	-8.2	9,852	32
Rusk*	48401	-0.3	47,219	161	-0.4	47,040	153
Sabine	48403	-1.1	10,357	35	-1.1	10,247	33
San Augustine	48405	-0.5	8,901	30	-0.7	8,840	29
San Jacinto*	48407	9.7	24,408	83	10.0	26,858	87
San Patricio*	48409	1.7	68,309	233	1.9	69,601	226
San Saba	48411	-2.9	6,006	20	-3.9	5,774	19
Schleicher	48413	-5.2	2,781	9	-6.0	2,614	8
Scurry**	48415	-2.1	16,025	55	-1.7	15,746	51
Shackelford	48417	0.2	3,308	11	0.5	3,323	11
Shelby	48419	3.4	26,086	89	3.9	27,103	88
Sherman	48421	-1.2	3,147	11	-1.8	3,091	10
Smith*	48423	7.0	186,882	636	7.7	201,203	653
Somervell**	48425	10.1	7,494	26	10.8	8,306	27
Starr**	48427	10.0	58,958	201	10.8	65,354	212
Stephens	48429	-3.0	9,385	32	-3.4	9,070	29
Sterling	48431	-4.5	1,331	5	-4.1	1,276	4
Stonewall	48433	-18.5	1,379	5	-21.8	1,078	4
Sutton	48435	1.4	4,134	14	2.9	4,253	14
Swisher	48437	-5.7	7,901	27	-6.9	7,354	24
Tarrant*	48439	10.2	1,594,027	5,428	10.9	1,768,296	5,740
Taylor*	48441	-1.3	124,966	426	-1.5	123,107	400
Terrell	48443	-5.1	1,026	3	-3.9	986	3
Terry	48445	-3.1	12,367	42	-3.4	11,945	39
Throckmorton	48447	-10.6	1,654	6	-12.2	1,453	5
Titus**	48449	2.3	28,765	98	2.8	29,571	96
Tom Green*	48451	-0.6	103,389	352	-0.7	102,692	333
Travis*	48453	7.1	869,648	2,961	7.1	931,805	3,025
Trinity	48455	3.5	14,259	49	3.8	14,797	48
Tyler	48457	-1.4	20,581	70	-1.7	20,232	66
Upshur*	48459	6.2	37,485	128	7.0	40,114	130
Upton	48461	-9.5	3,080	10	-11.0	2,742	9
Uvalde**	48463	4.4	27,070	92	5.2	28,483	92
Val Verde**	48465	5.0	47,089	160	5.5	49,689	161
Van Zandt	48467	6.8	51,430	175	7.4	55,257	179
Victoria*	48469	2.1	85,853	292	2.7	88,140	286
Walker**	48471	0.6	62,155	212	0.9	62,740	204
Waller*	48473	7.6	35,153	120	8.2	38,026	123
Ward	48475	-7.2	10,123	34	-8.0	9,315	30
Washington**	48477	2.5	31,123	106	2.8	31,984	104
Webb*	48479	13.9	219,931	749	14.3	251,491	816
Wharton**	48481	-0.2	41,117	140	-0.3	40,985	133
Wheeler	48483	-11.6	4,672	16	-13.5	4,042	13
Wichita*	48485	-2.4	128,562	438	-2.7	125,139	406
Wilbarger**	48487	-7.3	13,610	46	-8.7	12,430	40
Willacy**	48489	0.1	20,101	68	0.2	20,133	65
Williamson*	48491	27.9	319,789	1,089	25.3	400,774	1,301
Wilson*	48493	11.4	36,087	123	11.7	40,301	131
Winkler	48495	-6.9	6,679	23	-7.2	6,197	20
Wise*	48497	15.1	56,141	191	14.9	64,517	209
Wood	48499	9.1	40,087	136	10.0	44,092	143
Yoakum	48501	-1.2	7,237	25	-0.9	7,175	23
Young	48503	-0.3	17,894	61	-0.2	17,855	58
Zapata	48505	7.8	13,132	45	8.6	14,263	46
Zavala	48507	-0.1	11,590	39	-0.1	11,574	38
TOTAL: TEXAS		**7.9**	**22,508,240**	**76,642**	**8.7**	**24,456,895**	**79,385**

UTAH

	FIPS CODE	2000-2004 % Change	7/1/04 Estimate	7/1/04 Ranally Population Units	2004-2009 % Change	2009 Projection	2009 Ranally Population Units
Beaver	49001	2.1	6,133	21	2.3	6,275	20
Box Elder**	49003	5.4	45,045	153	6.0	47,745	155
Cache*	49005	6.1	96,982	330	6.8	103,574	336
Carbon**	49007	-4.2	19,565	67	-4.9	18,599	60
Daggett	49009	-4.9	876	3	-7.1	814	3
Davis*	49011	9.1	260,687	888	9.8	286,123	929
Duchesne	49013	4.4	15,003	51	5.2	15,789	51
Emery	49015	-2.5	10,585	36	-3.1	10,261	33
Garfield	49017	-5.5	4,475	15	-7.1	4,156	13
Grand	49019	4.2	8,841	30	4.6	9,250	30
Iron**	49021	7.6	36,332	124	8.1	39,285	128
Juab*	49023	8.8	8,962	31	9.5	9,811	32
Kane	49025	-0.3	6,026	21	-1.1	5,962	19
Millard	49027	0.5	12,469	42	0.5	12,536	41
Morgan*	49029	7.1	7,637	26	7.8	8,232	27
Piute	49031	-5.2	1,361	5	-6.6	1,271	4
Rich	49033	3.8	2,036	7	4.2	2,121	7
Salt Lake*	49035	3.8	932,116	3,174	4.2	971,433	3,153
San Juan	49037	-4.6	13,747	47	-5.4	13,000	42
Sanpete	49039	5.4	23,981	82	6.1	25,437	83
Sevier	49041	1.8	19,177	65	1.9	19,546	63
Summit*	49043	14.4	34,029	116	14.8	39,074	127
Tooele*	49045	22.9	50,062	170	20.9	60,541	197
Uintah**	49047	5.6	26,639	91	6.4	28,354	92
Utah*	49049	10.5	407,123	1,386	11.1	452,429	1,469
Wasatch**	49051	19.6	18,201	62	19.0	21,658	70
Washington*	49053	20.0	108,436	369	19.8	129,952	422
Wayne	49055	-3.3	2,427	8	-5.3	2,298	7
Weber*	49057	6.2	208,627	710	6.7	222,617	723
TOTAL: UTAH		**6.9**	**2,387,580**	**8,130**	**7.6**	**2,568,143**	**8,336**

VERMONT

	FIPS CODE	2000-2004 % Change	7/1/04 Estimate	7/1/04 Ranally Population Units	2004-2009 % Change	2009 Projection	2009 Ranally Population Units
Addison	50001	3.1	37,097	126	3.5	38,407	125
Bennington**	50003	0.7	37,239	127	0.8	37,542	122
Caledonia	50005	1.0	30,001	102	1.0	30,306	98
Chittenden*	50007	2.1	149,664	510	2.3	153,038	497
Essex**	50009	2.3	6,606	22	2.8	6,791	22
Franklin*	50011	4.6	47,499	162	5.0	49,879	162
Grand Isle*	50013	11.2	7,675	26	12.1	8,600	28
Lamoille	50015	5.9	24,594	84	6.3	26,142	85
Orange**	50017	3.9	29,339	100	4.4	30,627	99
Orleans	50019	4.1	27,357	93	4.6	28,629	93
Rutland**	50021	0.2	63,534	216	0.2	63,684	207
Washington**	50023	1.8	59,089	201	2.1	60,356	196
Windham	50025	0.5	44,445	151	0.7	44,773	145
Windsor**	50027	1.1	58,026	198	1.1	58,683	190
TOTAL: VERMONT		**2.2**	**622,165**	**2,118**	**2.5**	**637,457**	**2,069**

VIRGINIA

	FIPS CODE	2000-2004 % Change	7/1/04 Estimate	7/1/04 Ranally Population Units	2004-2009 % Change	2009 Projection	2009 Ranally Population Units
Accomack	51001	2.4	39,235	134	2.7	40,287	131
Albemarle*	51003	11.9	88,692	302	5.8	93,797	304
Alleghany[3]	51005	9.2	16,699	57	-3.5	16,122	52
Amelia*	51007	3.8	11,831	40	3.7	12,274	40
Amherst*	51009	-0.0	31,890	109	-0.0	31,881	103
Appomattox*	51011	0.1	13,712	47	0.1	13,720	45
Arlington*	51013	-1.1	187,390	638	-1.3	184,980	600
Augusta**	51015	3.6	67,974	231	4.0	70,705	230
Bath	51017	-0.9	5,005	17	-0.8	4,964	16
Bedford*	51019	4.9	63,337	216	5.3	66,712	217
Bland	51021	1.9	7,000	24	2.5	7,176	23
Botetourt*	51023	4.1	31,742	108	4.6	33,207	108
Brunswick	51025	-1.6	18,123	62	-2.1	17,744	58
Buchanan	51027	-6.6	25,204	86	-7.5	23,319	76
Buckingham	51029	1.8	15,908	54	2.2	16,251	53
Campbell*	51031	0.6	51,384	175	0.6	51,695	168
Caroline*	51033	6.4	23,543	80	7.5	25,302	82
Carroll	51035	0.4	29,351	100	0.2	29,420	95
Charles City*	51036	3.7	7,181	24	4.4	7,495	24
Charlotte	51037	-0.2	12,450	42	-0.1	12,440	40
Chesterfield*	51041	8.6	282,130	961	9.4	308,557	1,002
Clarke*	51043	7.4	13,582	46	8.0	14,672	48
Craig*	51045	1.7	5,179	18	2.0	5,280	17
Culpeper	51047	16.5	39,908	136	17.0	46,675	152
Cumberland*	51049	2.6	9,250	31	3.3	9,554	31
Dickenson	51051	-2.1	16,043	55	-2.4	15,665	51
Dinwiddie*	51053	1.6	24,932	85	1.6	25,325	82
Essex	51057	3.6	10,349	35	4.3	10,790	35
Fairfax*	51059	4.0	1,008,761	3,435	4.1	1,050,462	3,410
Fauquier*	51061	14.2	62,992	214	14.7	72,263	235
Floyd	51063	4.4	14,483	49	4.6	15,144	49
Fluvanna*	51065	19.8	24,026	82	19.7	28,764	93
Franklin*	51067	5.0	49,641	169	5.5	52,368	170
Frederick*	51069	11.8	66,224	225	12.5	74,515	242
Giles*	51071	2.3	17,040	58	2.5	17,458	57
Gloucester*	51073	7.3	37,303	127	8.1	40,326	131
Goochland*	51075	9.9	18,538	63	10.8	20,537	67
Grayson	51077	-8.2	16,449	56	-3.2	15,920	52
Greene*	51079	13.2	17,251	59	13.7	19,610	64
Greensville	51081	0.3	11,590	39	0.4	11,631	38
Halifax	51083	-2.5	36,406	124	-3.0	35,296	115
Hanover*	51085	11.7	96,438	328	12.2	108,214	351
Henrico*	51087	4.3	273,683	932	4.7	286,663	931
Henry**	51089	-1.9	56,818	193	-2.4	55,477	180
Highland	51091	-1.7	2,494	8	-2.0	2,445	8
Isle of Wight*	51093	9.7	32,606	111	10.4	36,004	117
James City*	51095	14.6	55,145	188	15.0	63,432	206
King and Queen*	51097	-0.8	6,578	22	-0.8	6,525	21
King George	51099	11.0	18,655	64	11.8	20,862	68
King William*	51101	9.8	14,440	49	10.7	15,985	52
Lancaster	51103	5.8	12,236	42	6.6	13,042	42
Lee	51105	0.9	23,798	81	1.3	24,115	78
Loudoun*	51107	40.1	237,678	809	33.5	317,314	1,030
Louisa*	51109	12.3	28,789	98	13.2	32,576	106
Lunenburg	51111	0.3	13,191	45	0.9	13,309	43
Madison	51113	5.4	13,195	45	6.0	13,988	45
Mathews*	51115	0.1	9,220	31	0.2	9,237	30
Mecklenburg	51117	0.7	32,613	111	0.9	32,920	107
Middlesex	51119	3.6	10,292	35	3.9	10,698	35
Montgomery*	51121	3.1	86,230	294	3.6	89,306	290
Nelson*	51125	4.5	15,097	51	5.1	15,870	52
New Kent*	51127	13.5	15,279	52	14.2	17,455	57
Northampton	51131	2.0	13,358	45	2.7	13,723	45
Northumberland	51133	5.2	12,895	44	5.9	13,658	44
Nottoway	51135	-1.1	15,558	53	-1.5	15,331	50
Orange	51137	10.8	28,683	98	11.6	32,006	104
Page	51139	2.3	23,717	81	2.7	24,354	79
Patrick	51141	-1.6	19,103	65	-2.0	18,712	61
Pittsylvania*	51143	-0.2	61,594	210	-0.4	61,365	199
Powhatan*	51145	13.2	25,328	86	13.4	28,721	93
Prince Edward	51147	3.2	20,342	69	4.0	21,149	69
Prince George*	51149	4.9	34,661	118	5.1	36,444	118
Prince William*	51153	20.8	339,149	1,155	20.4	408,242	1,325
Pulaski*	51155	-0.4	34,995	119	-0.5	34,822	113
Rappahannock	51157	2.5	7,157	24	3.3	7,393	24
Richmond	51159	3.0	9,076	31	3.9	9,427	31
Roanoke*	51161	2.4	87,854	299	3.0	90,472	294
Rockbridge	51163	1.0	21,015	72	1.0	21,220	69
Rockingham*	51165	3.2	69,878	238	3.7	72,439	235
Russell	51167	-5.2	28,721	98	-2.4	28,027	91
Scott*	51169	-2.2	22,883	78	-2.6	22,279	72
Shenandoah	51171	7.9	37,852	129	8.6	41,117	133
Smyth	51173	-1.5	32,575	111	-1.9	31,951	104
Southampton	51175	-0.2	17,443	59	-0.3	17,393	56
Spotsylvania*	51177	25.3	113,260	386	23.9	140,355	456
Stafford*	51179	26.4	116,821	398	24.8	145,805	473
Surry*	51181	3.5	7,065	24	3.9	7,342	24
Sussex*	51183	-5.8	11,784	40	-7.0	10,957	36
Tazewell**	51185	-0.6	44,332	151	-0.3	44,183	143
Warren*	51187	9.5	34,587	118	10.4	38,170	124
Washington*	51191	0.8	51,487	175	0.8	51,894	168
Westmoreland	51193	1.9	17,033	58	2.5	17,466	57
Wise	51195	3.9	41,678	142	-1.5	41,057	133
Wythe	51197	1.6	28,044	95	1.8	28,557	93
York*	51199	10.8	62,379	212	11.5	69,532	226
INDEPENDENT CITIES							
Alexandria*	51510	0.4	128,847	439	-0.3	128,458	417
Bedford*	51515	0.8	6,352	22	1.0	6,414	21
Bristol*	51520	-1.1	17,176	58	-0.9	17,023	55
Buena Vista	51530	-0.7	6,307	21	-1.1	6,240	20
Charlottesville*	51540	-13.8	38,847	132	-4.0	37,309	121
Chesapeake*	51550	7.6	214,295	730	8.1	231,578	752
Clifton Forge[3]	51560	(d)	(d)	(d)	(d)	(d)	(d)
Colonial Heights*	51570	3.0	17,408	59	3.5	18,018	58
Covington	51580	-0.4	6,278	21	-0.5	6,245	20
Danville*	51590	-3.8	46,575	159	-4.3	44,565	145
Emporia	51595	-0.2	5,653	19	-0.3	5,635	18
Fairfax*	51600	3.2	22,181	76	3.4	22,928	74
Falls Church*	51610	1.2	10,500	36	0.7	10,576	34
Franklin	51620	-1.2	8,244	28	-0.6	8,191	27
Fredericksburg*	51630	6.2	20,481	70	7.1	21,938	71
Galax	51640	-3.6	6,592	22	-4.6	6,286	20
Hampton*	51650	0.4	147,010	501	0.4	147,660	479
Harrisonburg*	51660	2.4	41,444	141	3.3	42,816	139
Hopewell*	51670	0.3	22,421	76	0.7	22,568	73
Lexington	51678	4.2	7,155	24	5.5	7,549	25
Lynchburg*	51680	-0.3	65,067	222	-0.4	64,837	210
Manassas*	51683	7.5	37,756	129	7.8	40,708	132
Manassas Park*	51685	8.9	11,209	38	9.8	12,302	40
Martinsville**	51690	-2.5	15,036	51	-2.8	14,614	47
Newport News*	51700	1.1	182,162	620	1.4	184,721	600
Norfolk*	51710	4.2	244,163	831	5.0	256,324	832
Norton	51720	0.3	3,917	13	1.0	3,958	13
Petersburg*	51730	-2.4	32,931	112	-2.4	32,140	104
Poquoson*	51735	3.1	11,929	41	3.5	12,352	40
Portsmouth*	51740	-1.2	99,349	338	-1.3	98,010	318
Radford*	51750	-7.0	14,744	50	-8.5	13,498	44
Richmond*	51760	-2.0	193,828	660	-2.3	189,373	615
Roanoke*	51770	-2.8	92,245	314	-3.3	89,208	290
Salem*	51775	-0.8	24,544	84	-1.2	24,248	79
Staunton**	51790	-0.0	23,850	81	0.0	23,859	77
Suffolk*	51800	20.3	76,604	261	20.2	92,042	299
Virginia Beach*	51810	4.3	443,729	1,511	4.8	465,007	1,509
Waynesboro**	51820	5.8	20,650	70	6.3	21,959	71
Williamsburg*	51830	-4.4	11,476	39	-5.4	10,852	35
Winchester*	51840	4.7	24,691	84	5.2	25,974	84
TOTAL: VIRGINIA		**5.7**	**7,480,156**	**25,466**	**6.3**	**7,949,286**	**25,805**

WASHINGTON

	FIPS CODE	2000-2004 % Change	7/1/04 Estimate	7/1/04 Ranally Population Units	2004-2009 % Change	2009 Projection	2009 Ranally Population Units
Adams	53001	1.4	16,650	57	1.4	16,888	55
Asotin*	53003	0.5	20,647	70	0.5	20,755	67
Benton*	53005	10.3	157,183	535	11.2	174,797	567
Chelan*	53007	2.7	68,388	233	3.0	70,465	229
Clallam**	53009	5.0	67,749	231	6.3	72,032	234
Clark*	53011	13.0	390,272	1,329	13.7	443,743	1,440
Columbia	53013	0.9	4,099	14	0.8	4,131	13
Cowlitz*	53015	3.1	95,850	326	3.7	99,372	323
Douglas*	53017	4.6	34,114	116	5.3	35,917	117
Ferry	53019	2.7	7,459	25	2.8	7,667	25
Franklin*	53021	18.2	58,316	199	18.8	69,268	225

Source: Devonshire Associates Ltd. and Scan/US, Inc. 2004.
* Component of a Metropolitan Core Based Statistical Area.
** Component of a Micropolitan Core Based Statistical Area.

[3]Clifton Forge independent city merged with Alleghany county on July 1, 2001.

(d) Data not available.

continued on next page

Counties: Population Trends, *Continued*

	FIPS CODE	PRESENT 2000-2004 % Change	PRESENT 7/1/04 Estimate	7/1/04 Ranally Population Units	FUTURE 2004-2009 % Change	FUTURE 2009 Projection	2009 Ranally Population Units
Garfield	53023	-1.4	2,364	8	-1.4	2,330	8
Grant**	53025	7.0	79,916	272	7.7	86,041	279
Grays Harbor**	53027	4.4	70,145	239	5.3	73,842	240
Island**	53029	8.9	77,898	265	9.7	85,466	277
Jefferson	53031	8.4	28,140	96	7.5	30,260	98
King*	53033	1.8	1,768,908	6,023	2.1	1,806,395	5,864
Kitsap*	53035	4.9	243,450	829	5.6	257,104	835
Kittitas**	53037	7.2	35,779	122	8.0	38,644	125
Klickitat	53039	2.5	19,649	67	2.6	20,159	65
Lewis**	53041	3.5	70,994	242	4.2	73,946	240
Lincoln	53043	0.2	10,207	35	0.3	10,237	33
Mason**	53045	7.2	52,980	180	8.0	57,235	186
Okanogan	53047	-1.4	38,991	133	-1.8	38,284	124
Pacific	53049	0.8	21,156	72	1.3	21,421	70
Pend Oreille	53051	5.9	12,424	42	6.8	13,272	43
Pierce*	53053	7.5	753,288	2,565	8.2	814,946	2,645
San Juan	53055	6.3	14,961	51	6.7	15,963	52
Skagit*	53057	7.9	111,156	378	8.6	120,767	392
Skamania*	53059	5.6	10,423	35	6.3	11,076	36
Snohomish*	53061	7.2	649,489	2,211	7.8	699,889	2,272
Spokane*	53063	4.1	435,145	1,482	4.7	455,733	1,479
Stevens	53065	2.2	40,954	139	2.2	41,842	136
Thurston*	53067	9.2	226,479	771	10.0	249,121	809
Wahkiakum	53069	-2.7	3,719	13	-3.7	3,580	12
Walla Walla**	53071	3.7	57,240	195	4.3	59,685	194
Whatcom*	53073	7.6	179,561	611	8.3	194,508	631
Whitman**	53075	-0.1	40,703	139	0.0	40,706	132
Yakima*	53077	2.5	228,066	777	2.9	234,762	762
TOTAL: WASHINGTON		**5.3**	**6,204,912**	**21,127**	**5.9**	**6,572,249**	**21,334**

WEST VIRGINIA

	FIPS CODE	PRESENT 2000-2004 % Change	PRESENT 7/1/04 Estimate	7/1/04 Ranally Population Units	FUTURE 2004-2009 % Change	FUTURE 2009 Projection	2009 Ranally Population Units
Barbour	54001	0.8	15,688	53	1.1	15,857	51
Berkeley*	54003	16.2	88,214	300	16.6	102,878	334
Boone*	54005	1.3	25,875	88	1.7	26,313	85
Braxton	54007	0.6	14,789	50	0.6	14,876	48
Brooke*	54009	-2.6	24,796	84	-2.9	24,079	78
Cabell*	54011	-2.4	94,503	322	-2.9	91,807	298
Calhoun	54013	-5.0	7,201	25	-6.3	6,747	22
Clay*	54015	0.2	10,355	35	0.1	10,370	34
Doddridge**	54017	1.5	7,516	26	1.6	7,637	25
Fayette**	54019	-0.8	47,185	161	-0.9	46,743	152
Gilmer	54021	-2.3	6,995	24	-3.0	6,787	22
Grant	54023	1.6	11,483	39	2.1	11,723	38
Greenbrier	54025	0.8	34,733	118	1.1	35,103	114
Hampshire*	54027	6.7	21,556	73	7.1	23,090	75
Hancock*	54029	-3.7	31,452	107	-4.5	30,030	97
Hardy	54031	3.3	13,089	45	3.7	13,578	44
Harrison**	54033	-1.2	67,845	231	-1.4	66,892	217
Jackson	54035	1.3	28,360	97	1.3	28,725	93
Jefferson*	54037	12.7	47,542	162	13.3	53,881	175
Kanawha*	54039	-3.0	194,003	661	-3.6	187,025	607
Lewis	54041	1.9	17,238	59	2.6	17,679	57
Lincoln*	54043	0.8	22,291	76	0.8	22,478	73
Logan	54045	-3.3	36,468	124	-3.7	35,101	114
McDowell	54047	-9.4	24,768	84	-11.0	22,052	72
Marion**	54049	-0.2	56,470	192	-0.2	56,375	183
Marshall*	54051	-2.2	34,730	118	-2.4	33,892	110
Mason**	54053	0.6	26,116	89	0.7	26,289	85
Mercer**	54055	-1.8	61,835	211	-2.3	60,440	196
Mineral*	54057	0.4	27,182	93	0.6	27,346	89
Mingo	54059	-2.9	27,436	93	-2.7	26,696	87
Monongalia*	54061	4.0	85,180	290	4.7	89,191	290
Monroe	54063	-6.8	13,597	46	3.4	14,062	46
Morgan*	54065	4.9	15,680	53	5.3	16,504	54
Nicholas	54067	-1.6	26,139	89	-2.0	25,615	83
Ohio*	54069	-4.4	45,334	154	-5.3	42,926	139
Pendleton	54071	-4.7	7,807	27	-5.6	7,369	24
Pleasants*	54073	0.2	7,526	26	0.3	7,547	24
Pocahontas	54075	-2.6	8,890	30	-3.0	8,621	28
Preston*	54077	1.7	29,837	102	2.2	30,486	99
Putnam*	54079	3.6	53,462	182	4.0	55,575	180
Raleigh**	54081	0.1	79,307	270	0.3	79,540	258
Randolph	54083	0.0	28,266	96	0.2	28,317	92
Ritchie	54085	2.2	10,575	36	2.8	10,871	35
Roane	54087	-0.8	15,325	52	-1.2	15,139	49
Summers	54089	6.0	13,783	47	-4.7	13,129	43
Taylor**	54091	0.3	16,134	55	0.2	16,165	52
Tucker	54093	-2.8	7,118	24	-3.1	6,894	22
Tyler	54095	-2.1	9,388	32	-2.7	9,137	30
Upshur	54097	1.5	23,754	81	1.8	24,170	78
Wayne*	54099	-1.5	42,253	144	-2.0	41,418	134
Webster	54101	1.0	9,820	33	1.5	9,966	32
Wetzel	54103	-4.0	16,990	58	-4.9	16,161	52
Wirt*	54105	-1.9	5,760	20	-2.6	5,610	18
Wood*	54107	-1.0	87,147	297	-1.1	86,171	280
Wyoming	54109	-4.4	24,577	84	-5.0	23,337	76
TOTAL: WEST VIRGINIA		**0.2**	**1,811,363**	**6,168**	**0.3**	**1,816,410**	**5,893**

WISCONSIN

	FIPS CODE	PRESENT 2000-2004 % Change	PRESENT 7/1/04 Estimate	7/1/04 Ranally Population Units	FUTURE 2004-2009 % Change	FUTURE 2009 Projection	2009 Ranally Population Units
Adams	55001	11.3	20,751	71	4.4	21,670	70
Ashland	55003	-1.7	16,586	56	-2.0	16,261	53
Barron	55005	1.6	45,670	156	1.7	46,446	151
Bayfield	55007	0.8	15,139	52	0.8	15,263	50
Brown*	55009	4.1	236,097	804	4.7	247,140	802
Buffalo	55011	0.1	13,812	47	-0.1	13,799	45
Burnett	55013	4.7	16,415	56	5.3	17,277	56
Calumet*	55015	9.0	44,268	151	10.0	48,693	158
Chippewa*	55017	3.7	57,253	195	4.2	59,651	194
Clark	55019	1.6	34,080	116	1.6	34,634	112
Columbia*	55021	4.0	54,563	186	4.5	56,996	185
Crawford	55023	-2.3	16,852	57	-2.8	16,377	53
Dane*	55025	7.0	456,369	1,554	7.7	491,316	1,595
Dodge**	55027	1.8	87,482	298	2.1	89,311	290
Door	55029	2.0	28,527	97	2.2	29,151	95
Douglas*	55031	2.4	44,322	151	2.6	45,463	148
Dunn**	55033	4.1	41,499	141	4.6	43,424	141
Eau Claire*	55035	1.4	94,488	322	1.6	96,002	312
Florence**	55037	-0.3	5,075	17	-0.6	5,045	16
Fond du Lac*	55039	0.7	97,983	334	0.8	98,733	320
Forest	55041	-1.2	9,904	34	-1.7	9,735	32
Grant**	55043	-0.6	49,313	168	-0.6	49,040	159
Green**	55045	2.4	34,466	117	2.7	35,397	115
Green Lake	55047	0.7	19,240	66	0.9	19,417	63
Iowa*	55049	2.9	23,447	80	3.4	24,241	79
Iron	55051	-2.6	6,684	23	-3.2	6,471	21
Jackson	55053	3.0	19,672	67	3.4	20,341	66
Jefferson**	55055	5.3	77,915	265	3.2	80,382	261
Juneau	55057	3.8	25,251	86	4.4	26,362	86
Kenosha*	55059	5.8	158,255	539	6.5	168,482	547
Kewaunee*	55061	1.7	20,539	70	2.0	20,956	68
La Crosse*	55063	1.8	109,063	371	2.1	111,320	361
Lafayette	55065	1.7	16,410	56	2.1	16,756	54
Langlade	55067	0.3	20,805	71	0.4	20,889	68
Lincoln**	55069	1.9	30,196	103	2.0	30,793	100
Manitowoc**	55071	-1.3	81,775	278	-1.8	80,338	261
Marathon*	55073	1.4	127,589	434	1.7	129,695	421
Marinette**	55075	-0.5	43,167	147	-0.8	42,816	139
Marquette	55077	-5.7	14,933	51	2.7	15,332	50
Menominee	55078	1.6	4,636	16	1.4	4,701	15
Milwaukee*	55079	-1.0	931,139	3,171	-1.1	920,777	2,989
Monroe	55081	2.8	42,054	143	3.1	43,344	141
Oconto*	55083	4.6	37,278	127	5.0	39,146	127
Oneida	55085	1.5	37,312	127	1.7	37,938	123
Outagamie*	55087	5.2	169,283	576	5.5	178,644	580
Ozaukee*	55089	3.9	85,508	291	4.3	89,182	289
Pepin	55091	3.2	7,447	25	4.3	7,767	25
Pierce*	55093	3.8	38,196	130	4.2	39,816	129
Polk	55095	6.2	43,871	149	6.8	46,874	152
Portage**	55097	0.4	67,436	230	0.4	67,681	220
Price	55099	-3.5	15,263	52	-4.4	14,591	47
Racine*	55101	2.4	193,383	658	2.8	198,874	646
Richland	55103	1.8	18,250	62	1.6	18,534	60
Rock*	55105	2.1	155,545	530	2.4	159,300	517
Rusk	55107	-0.7	15,240	52	-0.9	15,098	49
St. Croix*	55109	16.6	73,654	251	17.0	86,144	280
Sauk**	55111	2.8	56,794	193	3.2	58,600	190
Sawyer	55113	4.2	16,870	57	4.6	17,652	57
Shawano	55115	1.2	41,138	140	1.1	41,576	135
Sheboygan*	55117	0.8	113,582	387	0.9	114,615	372
Taylor	55119	-1.0	19,478	66	-1.5	19,177	62
Trempealeau	55121	1.4	27,383	93	1.4	27,769	90
Vernon	55123	2.1	28,638	98	2.5	29,349	95
Vilas	55125	6.2	22,345	76	6.8	23,862	77
Walworth**	55127	4.8	98,278	335	7.5	105,612	343
Washburn	55129	3.4	16,588	56	3.7	17,197	56
Washington*	55131	5.3	123,666	421	5.8	130,790	425
Waukesha*	55133	4.8	378,079	1,287	5.3	398,069	1,292
Waupaca	55135	2.0	52,763	180	1.9	53,756	174
Waushara	55137	2.8	23,793	81	3.6	24,640	80
Winnebago*	55139	1.4	158,990	541	1.5	161,437	524
Wood**	55141	-0.3	75,348	257	-0.4	75,076	244
TOTAL: WISCONSIN		**2.6**	**5,505,083**	**18,745**	**3.0**	**5,669,003**	**18,402**

WYOMING

	FIPS CODE	PRESENT 2000-2004 % Change	PRESENT 7/1/04 Estimate	7/1/04 Ranally Population Units	FUTURE 2004-2009 % Change	FUTURE 2009 Projection	2009 Ranally Population Units
Albany**	56001	-0.4	31,898	109	0.2	31,948	104
Big Horn	56003	-2.9	11,125	38	-3.3	10,758	35
Campbell**	56005	9.8	36,992	126	10.1	40,744	132
Carbon	56007	-2.8	15,206	52	-3.1	14,729	48
Converse	56009	2.9	12,405	42	3.0	12,777	41
Crook	56011	0.9	5,939	20	0.9	5,992	19
Fremont**	56013	0.4	35,937	122	0.3	36,047	117
Goshen	56015	-3.4	12,110	41	-4.4	11,575	38
Hot Springs	56017	-5.8	4,600	16	-6.8	4,288	14
Johnson	56019	8.7	7,688	26	9.4	8,410	27
Laramie*	56021	4.0	84,872	289	4.6	88,799	288
Lincoln	56023	5.7	15,398	52	6.1	16,344	53
Natrona*	56025	3.4	68,763	234	4.0	71,508	232
Niobrara	56027	-9.1	2,188	7	-10.5	1,959	6
Park	56029	2.5	26,440	90	2.9	27,216	88
Platte	56031	-2.5	8,585	29	-2.5	8,373	27
Sheridan**	56033	2.7	27,278	93	3.1	28,111	91
Sublette	56035	9.9	6,507	22	10.6	7,197	23
Sweetwater**	56037	-2.0	36,862	126	-2.1	36,085	117
Teton**	56039	2.5	18,715	64	2.4	19,164	62
Uinta**	56041	-0.2	19,697	67	-0.1	19,683	64
Washakie	56043	-6.4	7,760	26	-7.6	7,172	23
Weston	56045	0.3	6,665	23	0.4	6,691	22
TOTAL: WYOMING		**2.0**	**503,630**	**1,714**	**2.4**	**515,570**	**1,671**
TOTAL: UNITED STATES		**4.4**	**293,687,162**	**1,000,000**	**4.9**	**308,074,407**	**1,000,000**

Source: Devonshire Associates Ltd. and Scan/US, Inc. 2004.
* Component of a Metropolitan Core Based Statistical Area.
** Component of a Micropolitan Core Based Statistical Area.

150 Largest Counties: Population Trends

The following data are provided for the 150 largest counties (or county equivalents): the State-County FIPS Code, 2000-2004 estimated percent of change in population; 2004 estimated population; 2004-2009 projected percent of change in population; and 2009 projected population. Counties are ranked by population according to their 2004 estimated and their 2009 projected figures. Counties are listed in descending order by their 2009 projected population figures.

	FIPS Code	PRESENT			FUTURE		
		2000-2004 % Change	7/1/04 Estimate	2004 Rank	2004-2009 %	2009 Projection	2009 Rank
Los Angeles, CA	06037	4.8	9,980,271	1	5.4	10,523,607	1
Cook, IL	17031	-0.6	5,342,990	2	-0.8	5,299,999	2
Maricopa, AZ	04013	13.5	3,486,879	4	14.0	3,974,832	3
Harris, TX	48201	7.5	3,656,415	3	8.2	3,957,791	4
Orange, CA	06059	5.1	2,991,519	5	5.6	3,160,141	5
San Diego, CA	06073	5.4	2,966,135	6	5.9	3,142,238	6
Miami-Dade, FL	12086	5.1	2,368,141	8	5.7	2,503,015	7
Kings, NY	36047	0.4	2,474,606	7	0.4	2,484,985	8
Dallas, TX	48113	3.8	2,303,656	9	4.2	2,401,298	9
Riverside, CA	06065	20.2	1,856,913	13	20.0	2,228,111	10
Queens, NY	36081	-0.3	2,223,681	10	-0.4	2,214,646	11
San Bernardino, CA	06071	11.5	1,906,582	12	12.3	2,140,998	12
Wayne, MI	26163	-2.1	2,018,715	11	-2.5	1,968,977	13
Clark, NV	32003	19.0	1,637,622	17	18.6	1,942,707	14
Broward, FL	12011	8.7	1,764,315	15	9.3	1,929,159	15
King, WA	53033	1.8	1,768,908	14	2.1	1,806,395	16
Tarrant, TX	48439	10.2	1,594,027	18	10.9	1,768,296	17
Santa Clara, CA	06085	-0.4	1,675,734	16	-0.8	1,662,290	18
Bexar, TX	48029	7.4	1,496,237	20	8.2	1,619,092	19
New York, NY	36061	2.3	1,572,971	19	2.6	1,613,813	20
Suffolk, NY	36103	4.5	1,482,695	21	4.9	1,555,963	21
Sacramento, CA	06067	11.5	1,364,259	26	12.3	1,531,926	22
Alameda, CA	06001	1.4	1,464,561	24	1.2	1,482,152	23
Middlesex, MA	25017	0.5	1,472,613	22	0.3	1,477,006	24
Bronx, NY	36005	3.0	1,372,845	25	3.5	1,421,060	25
Philadelphia, PA	42101	-3.3	1,468,025	23	-3.8	1,412,463	26
Palm Beach, FL	12099	9.9	1,243,157	30	10.8	1,377,535	27
Nassau, NY	36059	0.4	1,340,495	28	0.4	1,345,637	28
Cuyahoga, OH	39035	-2.8	1,354,570	27	-3.4	1,308,652	29
Oakland, MI	26125	1.5	1,211,605	31	1.5	1,230,186	30
Allegheny, PA	42003	-2.1	1,255,103	29	-2.5	1,224,321	31
Hillsborough, FL	12057	9.8	1,096,848	33	10.7	1,214,056	32
Hennepin, MN	27053	0.5	1,122,141	32	0.5	1,127,580	33
Franklin, OH	39049	2.4	1,094,640	34	2.6	1,122,878	34
Contra Costa, CA	06013	7.2	1,016,987	35	7.8	1,096,190	35
Orange, FL	12095	10.0	985,714	38	10.6	1,089,958	36
Fairfax, VA (County)	51059	4.0	1,008,761	37	4.1	1,050,462	37
St. Louis, MO (County)	29189	-0.4	1,012,010	36	-0.6	1,006,248	38
Montgomery, MD	24031	6.8	932,558	41	7.3	1,000,765	39
Pima, AZ	04019	7.6	907,511	48	8.1	981,041	40
Salt Lake, UT	49035	3.8	932,116	42	4.2	971,433	41
Westchester, NY	36119	2.3	945,092	39	2.5	969,028	42
DuPage, IL	17043	3.0	931,347	43	3.3	962,070	43
Honolulu, HI	15003	4.1	911,719	46	4.9	956,800	44
Fresno, CA	06019	8.4	866,423	53	9.3	946,868	45
Pinellas, FL	12103	0.6	927,459	45	0.7	934,021	46
Travis, TX	48453	7.1	869,648	52	7.1	931,805	47
Fairfield, CT	09001	2.4	904,001	49	2.7	928,248	48
Erie, NY	36029	-1.2	938,615	40	-1.4	925,325	49
Shelby, TN	47157	1.3	908,843	47	1.5	922,152	50
Bergen, NJ	34003	2.0	901,514	50	2.2	921,244	51
Milwaukee, WI	55079	-1.0	931,139	44	-1.1	920,777	52
Prince George's, MD	24033	6.1	850,384	55	6.8	908,563	53
Hartford, CT	09003	2.2	875,839	51	2.5	897,751	54
Duval, FL	12031	6.6	830,101	57	7.6	893,203	55
New Haven, CT	09009	2.9	847,502	56	3.3	875,645	56
Marion, IN	18097	0.4	864,200	54	0.5	868,901	57
Ventura, CA	06111	6.6	802,627	61	7.2	860,068	58
Macomb, MI	26099	4.2	821,634	58	4.7	859,988	59
Mecklenburg, NC	37119	10.7	769,746	67	11.3	856,626	60
Middlesex, NJ	34023	5.3	790,283	63	5.9	836,721	61
Gwinnett, GA	13135	18.8	698,970	76	18.3	827,071	62
Worcester, MA	25027	4.5	784,595	64	5.1	824,492	63
Fulton, GA	13121	0.3	818,745	59	0.3	820,832	64
Wake, NC	37183	14.1	716,522	73	14.5	820,710	65
Baltimore, MD (County)	24005	4.0	784,253	65	4.5	819,459	66
Pierce, WA	53053	7.5	753,288	68	8.2	814,946	67
Kern, CA	06029	10.3	729,553	72	11.3	811,845	68
Montgomery, PA	42091	3.6	777,323	66	4.2	810,039	69
Essex, NJ	34013	0.5	797,608	62	0.8	804,081	70
Collin, TX	48085	28.0	629,504	92	25.7	791,230	71
Hamilton, OH	39061	-3.4	816,699	60	-4.1	783,497	72
Essex, MA	25009	2.6	741,982	70	2.8	762,628	73
San Joaquin, CA	06077	16.1	654,288	88	16.4	761,890	74
Hidalgo, TX	48215	15.2	656,072	86	15.6	758,677	75

	FIPS Code	PRESENT			FUTURE		
		2000-2004 % Change	7/1/04 Estimate	2004 Rank	2004-2009 %	2009 Projection	2009 Rank
Lake, IL	17097	8.2	697,152	77	8.7	757,754	76
El Paso, TX	48141	5.0	713,340	74	5.5	752,812	77
Will, IL	17197	22.0	612,859	95	21.3	743,563	78
Monroe, NY	36055	0.2	737,090	71	0.2	738,840	79
Cobb, GA	13067	9.2	663,776	83	9.6	727,493	80
Multnomah, OR	41051	3.5	683,283	79	4.0	710,606	81
Jefferson, KY	21111	1.0	700,741	75	1.2	709,304	82
Oklahoma, OK	40109	3.1	680,880	80	3.5	704,863	83
San Francisco, CA	06075	-4.3	743,549	69	-5.3	704,156	84
Snohomish, WA	53061	7.2	649,489	89	7.8	699,889	85
DeKalb, GA	13089	1.6	676,338	82	1.5	686,337	86
San Mateo, CA	06081	-1.9	693,861	78	-2.6	676,134	87
Providence, RI	44007	3.8	645,010	90	4.3	672,848	88
Jackson, MO	29095	0.9	661,091	84	1.0	667,791	89
Monmouth, NJ	34025	3.6	637,323	91	4.0	662,568	90
Suffolk, MA	25025	-1.8	677,616	81	-2.3	662,356	91
Norfolk, MA	25021	0.8	655,356	87	0.8	660,454	92
Denton, TX	48121	23.5	534,784	109	22.4	654,680	93
Jefferson, AL	01073	-0.8	656,840	85	-1.0	650,292	94
Bucks, PA	42017	3.4	617,667	94	3.7	640,325	95
Bernalillo, NM	35001	5.9	589,389	98	6.7	628,991	96
Kent, MI	26081	3.6	595,142	97	4.0	618,715	97
El Paso, CO	08041	8.5	560,804	101	9.2	612,412	98
Ocean, NJ	34029	9.0	556,907	104	9.7	611,037	99
Hudson, NJ	34017	-0.4	606,768	96	-0.5	603,520	100
Baltimore, MD (Ind. City)	24510	-4.5	622,161	93	-5.1	590,521	101
Lee, FL	12071	15.3	508,350	118	15.9	589,051	102
Tulsa, OK	40143	1.6	572,493	99	1.9	583,325	103
Stanislaus, CA	06099	13.3	506,378	119	14.0	577,071	104
Davidson, TN	47037	-0.0	569,819	100	-0.0	569,701	105
Bristol, MA	25005	3.0	550,668	106	3.3	568,949	106
Arapahoe, CO	08005	7.4	524,236	112	7.8	565,097	107
Denver, CO	08031	0.6	558,164	103	0.6	561,577	108
Brevard, FL	12009	8.1	515,004	116	9.0	561,468	109
Polk, FL	12105	7.2	518,809	114	8.0	560,565	110
Delaware, PA	42045	0.8	555,177	105	0.7	558,790	111
Kane, IL	17089	17.2	473,610	130	17.4	556,007	112
Summit, OH	39153	0.9	547,831	108	0.9	553,000	113
Johnson, KS	20091	10.2	497,146	122	10.6	550,011	114
District of Columbia, DC	11001	-2.0	560,725	102	-2.3	547,617	115
Union, NJ	34039	1.7	531,425	110	1.9	541,750	116
Washington, OR	41067	10.0	489,844	124	10.6	541,567	117
New Castle, DE	10003	3.8	519,483	113	4.2	541,522	118
Fort Bend, TX	48157	24.1	440,039	144	23.0	541,335	119
Montgomery, OH	39113	-1.6	550,095	107	-1.9	539,637	120
Anne Arundel, MD	24003	4.5	511,686	117	4.9	536,925	121
Jefferson, CO[1]	08059	0.4	529,255	111	0.7	532,700	122
Camden, NJ	34007	1.3	515,644	115	1.7	524,315	123
Volusia, FL	12127	7.5	476,562	129	8.3	516,056	124
Plymouth, MA	25023	4.0	491,878	123	4.4	513,646	125
Passaic, NJ	34031	2.4	500,842	121	2.5	513,266	126
Morris, NJ	34027	3.6	487,077	126	4.0	506,709	127
Lancaster, PA	42071	3.4	486,469	127	3.8	504,836	128
Douglas, NE	31055	3.7	480,743	128	4.2	500,745	129
Chester, PA	42029	7.2	464,595	133	7.7	500,504	130
Ramsey, MN	27123	-1.2	504,693	120	-1.6	496,428	131
Lake, IN	18089	0.8	488,435	125	1.0	493,200	132
Dane, WI	55025	7.0	456,369	138	7.7	491,316	133
Richmond, NY	36085	4.7	464,513	134	5.1	488,386	134
Burlington, NJ	34005	6.5	450,960	141	7.3	483,852	135
Sedgwick, KS	20173	2.9	466,006	132	3.3	481,319	136
Sonoma, CA	06097	2.2	468,851	131	2.3	479,459	137
Pasco, FL	12101	16.8	402,756	152	17.2	472,007	138
Hampden, MA	25013	1.4	462,756	136	1.7	470,565	139
Virginia Beach, VA (Ind. City)	51810	4.3	443,729	143	4.8	465,007	140
Onondaga, NY	36067	0.6	461,207	137	0.7	464,651	141
Guilford, NC	37081	3.9	437,629	145	4.4	456,823	142
Spokane, WA	53063	4.1	435,145	146	4.7	455,733	143
Genesee, MI	26049	1.8	444,011	142	2.0	452,774	144
Lucas, OH	39095	-0.2	453,978	139	-0.3	452,689	145
Utah, UT	49049	10.5	407,123	150	11.1	452,429	146
Jefferson, LA*	22051	-0.8	451,699	140	-0.9	447,807	147
Clark, WA	53011	13.0	390,272	161	13.7	443,743	148
Solano, CA	06095	5.8	417,390	148	6.0	442,639	149
Orleans, LA*	22071	-4.2	464,268	135	-5.0	441,054	150

* Parish
Source: Devonshire Associates Ltd. and Scan/US, Inc. 2004.   [1] Census population includes a portion of Broomfield county.

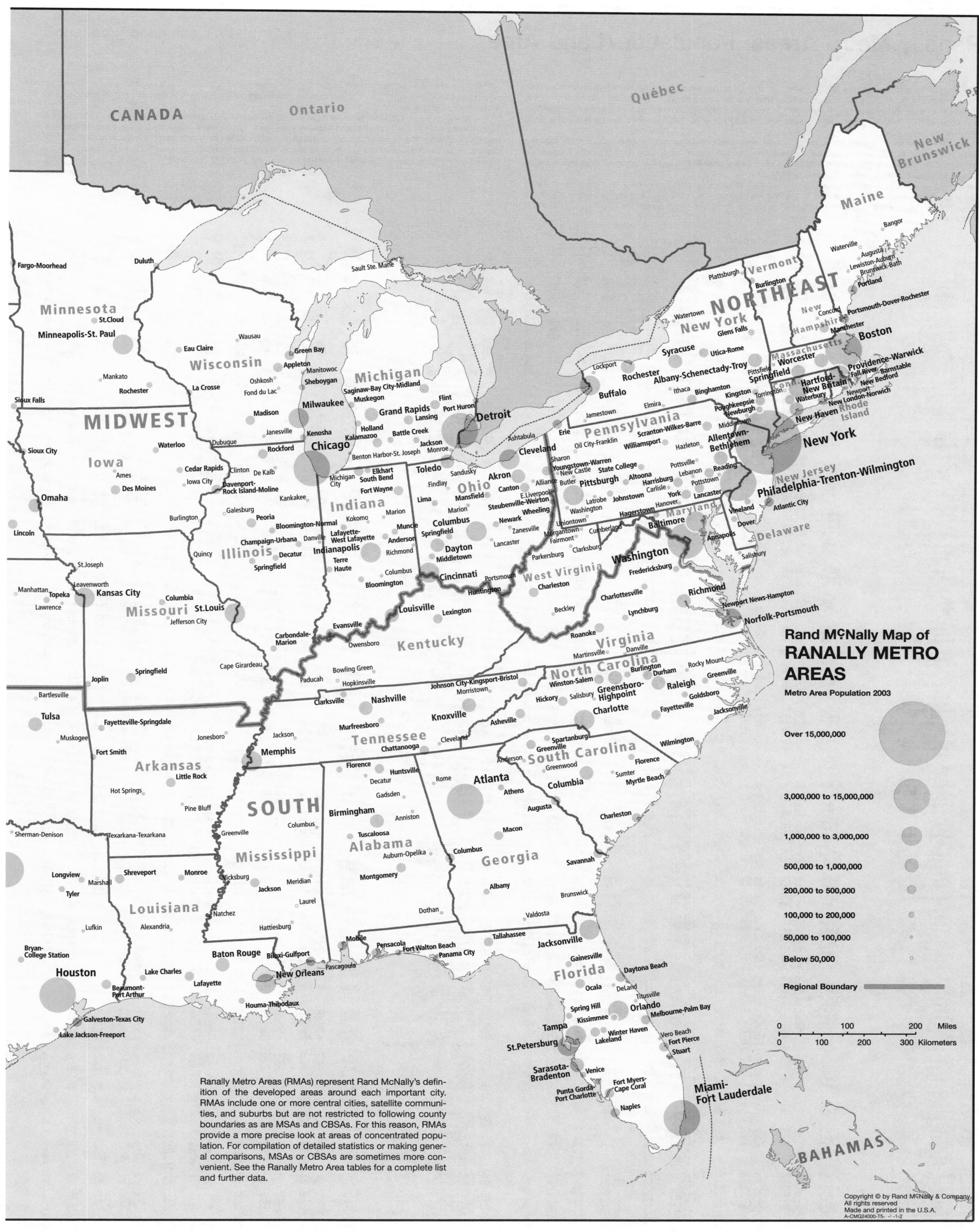

Rand McNally Map of
RANALLY METRO AREAS

Metro Area Population 2003

Over 15,000,000

3,000,000 to 15,000,000

1,000,000 to 3,000,000

500,000 to 1,000,000

200,000 to 500,000

100,000 to 200,000

50,000 to 100,000

Below 50,000

Regional Boundary

Ranally Metro Areas (RMAs) represent Rand McNally's definition of the developed areas around each important city. RMAs include one or more central cities, satellite communities, and suburbs but are not restricted to following county boundaries as are MSAs and CBSAs. For this reason, RMAs provide a more precise look at areas of concentrated population. For compilation of detailed statistics or making general comparisons, MSAs or CBSAs are sometimes more convenient. See the Ranally Metro Area tables for a complete list and further data.

Ranally Metro Areas: Population/Land Area

The Ranally Metropolitan Areas (RMAs) listed in this table represent Rand McNally's definitions of the metropolitan areas of the nation's major cities. They are designed to provide accurate information on the population change and areal extent of each metropolitan area. The RMAs are defined on a sub-county basis; this is in contrast with the U.S. government's Metropolitan Statistical Areas (MSAs), which are generally defined in terms of whole counties.

The RMAs have been defined for all areas with an estimated population of at least 50,000 and for selected areas of less than 50,000. A more detailed description of the criteria used for defining RMAs is in the Introduction on pages 5-9. The map on pages 124–125 shows the location of all RMAs and the individual state maps, pages 142–254, depict the areal extent of individual RMAs.

The table contains 2004 estimated populations for each RMA, its central city (or cities), and suburbs. All RMAs with a population over 50,000 are ranked. In addition the table presents the 2000 Census population for RMAs; a 2000–2004 percent of population change for RMAs, central cities, and suburbs; and the land area of RMAs and central cities.

Following this table are summaries of the RMA population by region and by state, and a list of RMAs by population size in descending order. Two tables on page 135 list the RMAs that are most rapidly growing, and most rapidly losing in population.

The tables on page 128 indicate several population trends that are currently underway in the nation. Since 2000, most RMAs in the Northeast and Midwest have experienced lower rates of population growth than the country as a whole. The highest rates of population growth for RMAs have occurred in the South and West. In all regions, RMA Central Cities have grown more slowly since 2000 than the suburban parts of RMAs.

Source for city estimates: Devonshire Associates Ltd. and Scan/US, Inc. 2004.

Rank 2004		RMA Abbrev.	Ranally Metro Area: Population Estimate 7/1/04	Ranally Metro Area: Population Census 4/1/00	Ranally Metro Area: Percent Change 2000-2004	Central City: Population Estimate 7/1/04	Central City: Percent Change 2000-2004	Suburbs: Population Estimate 7/1/04	Suburbs: Percent Change 2000-2004	Land Area (Sq. Miles): Metro Area	Land Area (Sq. Miles): City 2000
258	Abilene, TX	ABIL	118,421	117,689	.6	118,221	2.0	200	-88.7	211	103
59	Akron, OH	AKR	718,210	708,043	1.4	216,462	-.3	501,748	2.2	825	62
271	Albany, GA	ALB	109,171	107,244	1.8	76,068	-1.1	33,103	9.2	277	56
54	Albany-, NY	A-S-T	810,303	793,886	2.1	209,063	1.8	601,240	2.1	1,675	42
	Albany, NY					98,009	3.9				21
	Schenectady, NY					61,890	.1				11
	Troy, NY					49,164	.0				10
62	Albuquerque, NM	ALBU	710,693	668,334	6.3	483,489	7.8	227,204	3.4	778	132
297	Alexandria, LA	ALEX	97,760	96,705	1.1	46,525	.4	51,235	1.7	394	25
65	Allentown-, PA-NJ	ALL-	639,160	608,943	5.0	182,376	2.5	456,784	6.0	790	37
	Allentown, PA					108,583	1.8				18
	Bethlehem, PA					73,793	3.5				19
414	Alliance, OH	ALLI	51,346	51,753	-.8	23,422	.7	27,924	-2.0	167	8
245	Altoona, PA	ALT	123,008	125,517	-2.0	48,603	-1.9	74,405	-2.1	408	9
174	Amarillo, TX	AMA	195,917	188,149	4.1	177,534	2.3	18,383	26.6	153	88
375	Ames, IA	AMES	65,925	62,798	5.0	54,087	6.6	11,838	-1.9	146	20
118	Anchorage, AK†	ANCH	313,971	293,276	7.1	274,398	5.4	39,573	19.9	1,754	1,698
232	Anderson, IN	AND	134,698	137,711	-2.2	58,855	-1.5	75,843	-2.7	440	38
290	Anderson, SC	AND	99,269	94,972	4.5	24,528	-3.9	74,741	7.6	294	12
204	Annapolis, MD	ANPLS	152,909	144,778	5.6	38,072	6.2	114,837	5.4	146	6
296	Anniston, AL	ANNI	98,512	98,571	-.1	23,925	-1.4	74,587	.4	382	20
163	Appleton, WI	APP	220,077	210,894	4.4	73,388	4.7	146,689	4.2	299	17
139	Asheville, NC	ASHE	261,378	251,012	4.1	69,433	.8	191,945	5.4	727	35
	Ashtabula, OH	ASHT	42,298	42,091	.5	20,858	-.5	21,440	1.5	96	8
199	Athens, GA	ATH	160,915	151,357	6.3	104,409	4.1	56,506	10.6	452	17
12	Atlanta, GA	ATL	3,992,259	3,623,062	10.2	395,142	-5.1	3,597,117	12.2	3,132	132
125	Atlantic City, NJ	ATCY	296,782	281,933	5.3	42,300	4.4	254,482	5.4	565	11
325	Auburn-, AL	AU-OP	84,923	80,826	5.1	66,805	.5	18,118	26.3	137	78
	Auburn, AL					43,695	1.6				33
	Opelika, AL					23,110	-1.7				45
94	Augusta, GA-SC	AUG	415,417	402,891	3.1	193,417	-.9	222,000	6.9	783	20
372	Augusta, ME	AUG	66,518	64,589	3.0	18,463	-.5	48,055	4.4	365	55
37	Austin, TX	AUS	1,122,107	1,009,196	11.2	692,237	5.4	429,870	21.9	1,071	218
86	Bakersfield, CA	BAK	450,236	408,328	10.3	298,683	21.0	151,553	-6.1	492	92
18	Baltimore, MD-PA	BAL	2,302,482	2,241,860	2.7	622,161	-4.5	1,680,321	5.6	1,780	81
311	Bangor, ME	BANG	92,916	91,001	2.1	31,249	-.7	61,667	3.6	398	35
194	Barnstable, MA	BARN	167,584	160,772	4.2	48,997	2.5	118,587	5.0	260	60
	Bartlesville, OK	BART	40,914	40,774	.3	34,900	.4	6,014	-.2	40	21
71	Baton Rouge, LA	B.R.	558,224	542,403	2.9	230,715	1.3	327,509	4.1	821	74
276	Battle Creek, MI	BTLCK	106,455	105,471	.9	54,240	1.6	52,215	.2	251	43
108	Beaumont-, TX	B-PA	355,597	359,418	-1.1	166,208	-3.2	189,389	.8	722	157
	Beaumont, TX					110,795	-2.7				80
	Port Arthur, TX					55,413	-4.1				77
328	Beckley, WV	BECK	84,490	84,587	-.1	16,386	-5.0	68,104	1.1	441	9
210	Bellingham, WA	BELNG	149,799	139,165	7.6	74,157	10.4	75,642	5.1	338	22
293	Benton Harbor-, MI	BNTH-	98,918	98,418	.5	19,578	-2.0	79,340	1.1	278	7
	Benton Harbor, MI					10,980	-1.8				4
	St. Joseph, MI					8,598	-2.2				3
255	Billings, MT	BIL	117,847	113,426	3.9	93,254	3.8	24,593	4.3	107	33
141	Biloxi-, MS	BIL-	255,906	252,892	1.2	124,589	2.3	131,317	.1	309	43
	Biloxi, MS					51,377	1.4				20
	Gulfport, MS					73,212	2.9				23
161	Binghamton, NY-PA	BING	222,109	223,650	-.7	46,475	-1.9	175,634	-.4	705	10
53	Birmingham, AL	BIR	812,325	800,495	1.5	232,203	-4.4	580,122	4.0	1,622	149
332	Bismarck, ND	BIS	83,308	80,754	3.2	57,238	3.3	26,070	2.8	159	24
254	Bloomington-, IL	BLOOM-	119,173	112,143	6.3	118,973	8.0	200	-89.7	76	29
	Bloomington, IL					71,163	9.8				17
	Normal, IL					47,810	5.3				12
257	Bloomington, IN	BLMNG	117,598	114,767	2.5	71,037	2.5	46,561	2.4	210	15
97	Boise, ID	BOIS	392,581	349,941	12.2	201,901	8.7	190,680	16.2	306	46
9	Boston, MA-NH	BOS	4,748,174	4,679,465	1.5	583,303	-1.0	4,164,871	1.8	3,609	48
146	Boulder-, CO	BOUL-	247,385	256,431	-3.5	175,270	5.7	72,115	-20.5	248	36
	Boulder, CO					93,562	-1.2				23
	Longmont, CO					81,708	14.9				13
415	Bowling Green, KY	BOWLG	53,397	48,992	9.0	53,197	8.0	200	.0	188	29
178	Bremerton, WA	BREM	194,364	185,060	5.0	36,373	-2.4	157,991	6.9	257	20
111	Brownsville, TX-MEX.	BRNS	340,948	307,363	10.9	151,514	8.4	189,434	13.0	393	28
	incl. Matamoros, MEX.		*790,948*	*587,363*	*34.7*					*418*	
374	Brunswick, GA	BRUNS	65,963	62,815	5.0	15,887	1.8	50,076	6.1	131	17
395	Brunswick-, ME††	BR-BA	59,450	57,361	3.6	24,380	1.2	35,070	5.4	211	22
	Brunswick, ME					15,172	2.4				13
	Bath, ME					9,208	-.6				9
212	Bryan-, TX	BRY-	149,047	140,080	6.4	143,498	7.4	5,549	-15.0	95	63
	Bryan, TX					69,782	6.3				33
	College Station, TX					73,716	8.6				30
41	Buffalo, NY-CAN.	BUF	1,075,752	1,088,729	-1.2	279,681	-4.4	796,071	.0	1,128	41
	incl. St. Catharines-Niagara Falls, CAN.		*1,467,652*	*1,451,929*	*1.1*					*1,668*	
	Burlington, IA	BUR	34,172	35,380	-3.4	26,103	-2.7	8,069	-5.5	83	13
229	Burlington, NC	BUR	135,592	128,179	5.8	46,101	2.6	89,491	7.5	317	20
187	Burlington, VT	BUR	174,136	169,535	2.7	38,677	-2.9	135,459	4.4	562	11
367	Butler, PA	BUTL	67,951	65,046	4.5	15,184	.4	52,767	5.7	170	3
	Butte, MT†	BUT	32,737	34,564	-5.3	32,255	-4.8	482	-28.3	718	716
	Calexico, CA-MEX.	CLEX	30,123	24,616	22.4	29,923	10.4	200	.0	8	4
	incl. Mexicali, MEX.		*650,123*	*474,616*	*37.0*					*48*	
109	Canton, OH	CAN	343,578	343,794	-.1	80,992	.2	262,586	-.2	585	20
373	Cape Girardeau, MO	CPGIR	66,379	65,017	2.1	35,130	-.6	31,249	5.3	163	23
244	Carbondale-, IL	CARB-	123,153	122,444	.6	35,441	-14.9	87,712	8.5	504	21
	Carbondale, IL					19,222	-24.9				10
	Marion, IL					16,219	1.1				11
376	Carlisle, PA	CARL	65,902	63,470	3.8	18,356	2.1	47,546	4.5	197	5
382	Casper, WY	CASP	64,241	62,158	3.4	50,641	2.0	13,600	8.7	98	21
185	Cedar Rapids, IA	CEDR	177,315	172,024	3.1	124,124	2.8	53,191	3.8	259	54
226	Champaign-, IL	CH-U	136,269	129,489	5.2	108,211	2.7	28,058	16.1	145	21
	Champaign, IL					70,220	3.3				13
	Urbana, IL					37,991	1.7				8
78	Charleston, SC	CHAS	500,855	475,333	5.4	104,143	7.8	396,712	4.8	635	43
158	Charleston, WV	CHAS	230,496	234,573	-1.7	50,321	-5.8	180,175	-.5	826	30
32	Charlotte, NC-SC	CHRLT	1,427,035	1,301,901	9.6	575,926	6.6	851,109	11.7	2,106	174
250	Charlottesville, VA	CHRLTV	119,767	116,978	2.4	38,847	-3.1	80,920	5.3	373	10
91	Chattanooga, TN-GA	CHTN	423,203	412,643	2.6	156,183	.4	267,020	3.9	863	118
349	Cheyenne, WY	CHEY	75,772	72,857	4.0	54,416	2.7	21,356	7.6	56	19
3	Chicago, IL-IN-WI	CHI	9,026,690	8,748,587	3.2	2,897,405	.0	6,129,285	4.7	4,068	227
302	Chico, CA	CHICO	95,626	91,033	5.0	66,935	10.6	28,691	-6.0	135	22
25	Cincinnati, OH-KY-IN	CIN	1,713,279	1,691,894	1.3	317,273	-4.2	1,396,006	2.6	2,139	77
406	Clarksburg, WV	CLRKB	53,888	54,529	-1.2	16,448	-1.8	37,440	-.9	195	8
205	Clarksville, TN-KY	CLRKV	152,058	145,582	4.4	111,864	8.1	40,194	-4.6	299	73
20	Cleveland, OH	CLEV	2,166,582	2,182,254	-.7	443,046	-7.2	1,723,536	1.1	1,985	77
313	Cleveland, TN	CLEV	90,946	87,951	3.4	38,103	2.4	52,843	4.1	329	20
	Clinton, IA-IL	CLNT	37,281	37,644	-1.0	27,014	-2.7	10,267	4.0	73	36
	Clovis, NM	CLOV	39,543	39,060	1.2	33,148	1.5	6,395	.0	32	14
72	Colorado Springs, CO	CSPG	549,350	506,440	8.5	382,538	6.0	166,812	14.6	510	183
273	Columbia, MO	COL	107,183	101,609	5.5	90,750	7.4	16,433	-3.8	104	44
73	Columbia, SC	COL	539,290	512,179	5.3	118,658	2.4	420,632	6.1	1,070	117
144	Columbus, GA-AL	COL	252,711	248,565	1.7	185,692	-.3	67,019	7.6	315	216
365	Columbus, IN	COL	68,420	66,969	2.2	40,648	4.1	27,772	-.5	262	20
407	Columbus, MS	COL	53,035	54,101	-2.0	25,264	-2.6	27,771	-1.4	150	12
33	Columbus, OH	COL	1,270,575	1,225,821	3.7	736,256	3.5	534,319	3.9	1,211	191
314	Concord, NH	CONC	90,591	84,570	7.1	42,069	3.4	48,522	10.6	329	64
116	Corpus Christi, TX	CRPX	320,081	317,717	.7	277,665	.1	42,416	5.3	334	135
262	Corvallis-, OR	CORV-	112,928	109,900	2.8	93,660	3.9	19,268	-2.3	194	25
	Corvallis, OR					50,113	1.6				13
	Albany, OR					43,547	6.6				12
346	Cumberland, MD-WV	CUMB	77,658	79,128	-1.9	19,859	-7.7	57,799	.3	289	8
7	Dallas-, TX	D-FW	5,154,855	4,681,646	10.1	1,851,523	7.4	3,303,332	11.7	3,360	623
	Dallas, TX					1,247,153	4.9				342
	Fort Worth, TX					604,370	13.0				281
381	Danville, IL	DANV	64,286	65,418	-1.7	33,715	-.6	30,571	-3.0	238	15
353	Danville, VA-NC	DANV	72,110	73,986	-2.5	46,575	-3.8	25,535	-.2	265	43
122	Davenport-, IA-IL	D-RI-M	301,101	302,080	-.3	183,489	.9	117,612	-2.2	446	91
	Davenport, IA					99,603	1.3				61
	Moline, IL					43,808	.1				15
	Rock Island, IL					40,078	1.0				15
368	Davis, CA	DAV	67,763	60,966	11.1	67,346	11.7	417	-36.6	38	8
56	Dayton, OH	DAY	785,527	785,027	.1	163,241	-1.8	622,286	.6	1,100	55
119	Daytona Beach, FL	D.BCH	310,526	286,852	8.3	62,550	-2.4	247,976	11.3	281	32
299	Decatur, AL	DEC	96,559	95,099	1.5	53,078	-1.6	43,481	5.6	248	47
289	Decatur, IL	DEC	99,661	103,836	-4.0	78,988	-3.5	20,673	-5.9	238	37
364	De Kalb, IL	DKLB	69,200	64,388	7.5	41,272	5.8	27,928	10.1	141	8
396	DeLand, FL	DL	57,207	53,219	7.5	23,778	13.7	33,429	3.4	114	10
200	Denton, TX	DENT	158,173	128,061	23.5	89,116	10.7	69,057	45.3	145	53
19	Denver, CO	DEN	2,210,500	2,088,925	5.8	558,164	.8	1,652,336	7.6	1,267	153
95	Des Moines, IA	DES	407,604	388,217	5.0	201,934	1.6	205,670	8.5	475	75
10	Detroit, MI-CAN.	DET	4,694,293	4,641,127	1.1	937,359	-1.5	3,756,934	1.8	3,656	139
	incl. Windsor, CAN.		*4,998,793*	*4,899,827*	*2.0*					*3,989*	
317	Dothan, AL	DOTH	89,756	86,801	3.4	59,605	3.2	30,151	3.7	387	80
225	Dover, DE	DOVR	136,367	126,206	8.1	33,931	5.9	102,436	8.8	428	21
350	Dubuque, IA-WI-IL	DUB	74,494	73,570	1.3	58,365	1.2	16,129	1.5	117	23
207	Duluth, MN-WI	DUL	151,105	150,470	.4	87,850	1.8	63,255	-1.4	292	68
103	Durham, NC	DUR	376,581	355,621	5.9	208,104	11.3	168,477	-.1	680	69
	East Liverpool, OH	E.LIV	38,463	38,759	-.8	13,096	.1	25,367	-1.2	156	4
277	Eau Claire, WI	EAUC	105,987	103,894	2.0	61,963	.4	44,024	4.3	197	28
175	Elkhart, IN-MI	ELK	194,724	187,083	4.1	53,493	3.1	141,231	4.5	519	17
339	Elmira, NY	ELM	81,208	81,987	-1.0	30,363	-1.9	50,845	-.4	209	7
57	El Paso, TX-NM-MEX.	ELP	729,987	695,311	5.0	592,983	5.2	137,004	4.1	469	245
	incl. Ciudad Juarez, MEX.		*2,004,987*	*1,490,311*	*34.5*					*529*	
	Enid, OK	ENID	49,156	49,931	-1.6	47,481	.9	1,675	-42.0	168	72
140	Erie, PA	ERIE	258,313	259,365	-.4	103,853	.1	154,460	-.8	537	22
129	Eugene, OR	EUG	284,985	276,455	3.1	150,343	9.0	134,642	-2.8	505	38
292	Eureka-, CA	EUR-	99,097	97,609	1.5	42,619	-.4	56,478	3.0	211	18
	Eureka, CA					26,262	.5				10
	Arcata, CA					16,357	-1.8				8
152	Evansville, IN-KY	EV	243,880	241,874	.8	117,446	-3.4	126,434	5.1	403	41
371	Fairbanks, AK	FRBK	66,639	63,420	5.1	31,089	2.9	35,550	7.1	95	31
154	Fairfield-, CA	FRFL-	237,374	224,380	5.8	199,101	7.7	38,273	-3.3	222	59
	Fairfield, CA					103,862	8.0				36
	Vacaville, CA					95,239	7.5				23
399	Fairmont, WV	FAIRM	56,571	56,699	-.2	18,641	-2.4	37,930	.9	236	8
193	Fall River, MA-RI	F.R.	169,287	164,759	2.7	92,160	.2	77,127	5.9	162	31
213	Fargo-, ND-MN	FAR-	148,975	143,735	3.6	125,863	2.5	23,112	10.3	129	40
	Fargo, ND					93,980	3.7				30
	Moorhead, MN					31,883	-.9				10
360	Farmington, NM	FARM	70,525	64,227	9.8	41,123	8.7	29,402	11.4	134	24
215	Fayetteville-, AR	FAY-	146,395	132,499	10.5	115,351	11.1	31,044	8.3	340	70
	Fayetteville, AR					63,491	9.4				40
	Springdale, AR					51,860	13.2				30
110	Fayetteville, NC	FAY	342,807	336,917	1.7	128,304	6.0	214,503	-.6	724	41
416	Findlay, OH	FIND	50,405	48,737	3.4	38,637	-.8	11,768	20.5	95	14
79	Flint, MI	FLN	497,437	488,625	1.8	123,330	-1.3	374,107	2.9	1,032	34
264	Florence, AL	FLO	112,012	113,578	-1.4	32,088	-11.5	79,924	3.4	455	24
285	Florence, SC	FLO	103,013	100,577	2.4	30,232	-.1	72,781	3.5	298	15
398	Fond du Lac, WI	FDLC	56,996	56,596	.7	42,352	.4	14,644	1.7	115	13
143	Fort Collins-, CO	FTCL-	253,631	235,232	7.8	180,994	6.9	72,637	10.1	356	62
	Fort Collins, CO					126,771	6.8				41
	Loveland, CO					54,223	7.1				21
84	Fort Myers-, FL	FTMY-	455,543	395,089	15.3	170,054	13.0	285,489	16.7	438	127
	Fort Myers, FL					51,292	6.4				22
	Cape Coral, FL					118,762	16.1				105
168	Fort Pierce, FL	FTPI	209,600	183,494	14.2	38,826	3.5	170,774	17.0	205	12
188	Fort Smith, AR-OK	FTSM	173,700	168,369	3.2	80,943	.8	92,757	5.3	441	47
214	Fort Walton Beach, FL	FTWL	148,410	139,781	6.2	19,940	-.2	128,470	7.2	98	7
114	Fort Wayne, IN	FTWA	326,773	316,478	3.3	211,007	2.6	115,766	4.5	424	63
	Frederick, MD, *now part of Washington, DC-MD-VA*										
211	Fredericksburg, VA	FRED	149,190	121,747	22.5	20,481	6.2	128,709	25.6	242	11
55	Fresno, CA	FRES	792,323	729,375	8.6	473,574	10.7	318,749	5.6	7,516	99
318	Gadsden, AL	GAD	89,392	89,619	-.3	37,114	-4.8	52,278	3.2	332	36
184	Gainesville, FL	GAIN	180,300	174,392	3.4	91,090	-4.6	89,210	13.0	166	35
	Galesburg, IL	GLSB	43,246	44,654	-3.2	33,299	-1.2	9,947	-9.1	126	17
172	Galveston-, TX	GLV-	206,407	189,747	8.8	99,223	.5	107,184	17.8	278	108
	Galveston, TX					56,741	-.9				46
	Texas City, TX					42,482	2.3				62
	Gastonia, NC, *now part of Charlotte, NC-SC*										
265	Glens Falls, NY	GLFLS	111,264	107,250	3.7	14,193	-1.1	97,071	4.5	384	4
281	Goldsboro, NC	GLDS	104,440	104,826	-.4	34,818	-11.1	69,622	6.0	371	21
405	Grand Forks, ND-MN	GDFK	54,223	55,642	-2.6	50,750	2.8	3,473	-44.7	61	14
	Grand Island, NE	GDIS	47,057	46,175	1.9	44,082	2.7	2,975	-8.0	61	21
261	Grand Junction, CO	GDJC	114,326	104,591	9.3	43,228	1.3	71,098	14.8	124	15
61	Grand Rapids, MI	GDR	714,237	686,981	4.0	198,445	.3	515,792	5.4	1,357	44
361	Great Falls, MT	GTFA	70,268	71,161	-1.3	55,291	-2.5	14,977	3.5	101	15
240	Greeley, CO	GRLY	125,048	102,533	22.0	83,659	8.7	41,389	61.7	101	28
166	Green Bay, WI	GRBY	217,104	208,515	4.1	102,880	.1	114,224	8.0	267	44
69	Greensboro-, NC	GRNS-	567,581	546,450	3.9	327,326	5.7	240,255	1.5	1,132	123
	Greensboro, NC					236,075	5.4				80
	High Point, NC					91,251	6.3				43
	Greenville, MS	GRNV	42,521	44,961	-5.4	40,236	-3.4	2,285	-31.3	70	26
252	Greenville, NC	GRNV	119,404	113,933	4.8	64,786	5.8	54,618	3.6	357	18
80	Greenville, SC	GRNV	491,651	468,255	5.0	54,575	-2.5	437,076	6.0	914	25
380	Greenwood, SC	GREEN	64,598	63,176	2.3	21,979	-1.1	42,619	4.1	223	13
189	Hagerstown, MD-PA-WV	HAG	173,269	164,726	5.2	38,730	5.6	134,539	5.1	452	10
358	Hanover, PA	HANV	70,697	66,826	5.8	14,657	.8	56,040	7.2	151	4
	Harlingen, TX, *now part of Brownsville, TX-MEX.*										
92	Harrisburg, PA	HRBG	418,648	410,150	2.1	47,483	-3.0	371,165	2.8	700	8
35	Hartford-, CT	H-NB	1,221,331	1,182,480	3.3	192,964	-1.4	1,028,367	4.2	1,677	30
	Hartford, CT					121,199	-2.4				17
	New Britain, CT					71,765	.3				13
336	Hattiesburg, MS	HATT	82,290	78,776	4.5	46,591	4.0	35,699	5.0	171	25
369	Hazleton, PA	HAZ	67,463	68,670	-1.8	22,420	-3.9	45,043	-.7	267	6
206	Hemet, CA	HEM	151,357	125,964	20.2	68,271	16.1	83,086	23.7	135	18
167	Hesperia-, CA	HESP-	215,615	193,320	11.5	191,745	6.0	23,870	91.4	209	157
	Hesperia, CA					67,835	8.4				48
	Victorville, CA					67,020	4.7				42
	Apple Valley, CA					56,890	4.9				67
155	Hickory, NC	HICK	235,269	224,463	4.8	42,375	13.8	192,894	3.0	791	20
384	Hilo, HI††	HILO	63,885	58,820	8.6	44,269	8.6	19,616	8.6	68	54
251	Holland, MI	HLND	119,507	112,747	6.0	35,347	.9	84,160	8.3	246	14
49	Honolulu, HI††	HON	911,683	876,121	4.1	391,884	5.4	519,799	3.0	600	83
	Hopkinsville, KY	HPKNV	33,009	34,486	-4.3	27,559	-8.3	5,450	23.2	88	20
357	Hot Springs, AR	HTSPR	70,912	67,794	4.6	36,907	3.2	34,005	6.1	165	29
239	Houma-, LA	HOMA-	126,642	124,143	2.0	47,257	.9	79,385	2.7	457	18
	Houma, LA					32,642	.8				14
	Thibodaux, LA					14,615	1.3				4
11	Houston, TX	HOU	4,472,646	4,080,199	9.6	2,117,667	8.4	2,354,979	10.7	2,576	540
149	Huntington, WV-KY-OH	HNTG	245,309	247,651	-.9	47,926	-6.9	197,383	.6	756	15
126	Huntsville, AL	HNTS	291,804	274,980	6.1	163,931	3.3	127,873	9.9	639	164
	Hutchinson, KS	HUCH	47,668	48,601	-1.9	40,525	-.6	7,143	-8.6	90	21
308	Idaho Falls, ID	IDFL	93,888	87,666	7.1	54,737	7.9	39,151	6.0	205	15
31	Indianapolis, IN	IND	1,454,456	1,371,830	6.0	783,029	.1	671,427	13.8	1,737	362
272	Indio-, CA	IND-	109,001	90,714	20.2	88,172	22.7	20,829	10.4	92	37
	Indio, CA					60,321	22.8				17
	Coachella, CA					27,851	22.6				20
295	Iowa City, IA	IACY	98,545	93,546	5.3	62,057	-.5	36,488	17.1	113	22
294	Ithaca, NY	ITH	98,866	92,631	6.7	31,575	9.7	67,291	5.4	399	6
201	Jackson, MI	JAC	156,915	152,085	3.2	36,834	1.4	120,081	3.7	544	11
104	Jackson, MS	JAC	371,988	361,423	2.9	181,683	-1.4	190,305	7.4	590	109
340	Jackson, TN	JAC	80,703	78,432	2.9	63,554	6.6	17,149	-8.7	201	40
44	Jacksonville, FL	JAX	1,034,766	955,200	8.3	792,345	7.7	242,421	10.4	1,212	759
236	Jacksonville, NC	JAX	129,935	133,062	-2.4	61,114	-8.4	68,821	3.7	273	13
390	Jamestown, NY	JMST	61,987	63,230	-2.0	29,940	-6.4	32,047	2.6	224	9
331	Janesville, WI	JNSV	83,397	81,661	2.1	60,903	1.2	22,494	4.8	182	24
355	Jefferson City, MO	JFCY	71,250	69,692	2.2	40,776	7.2	30,474	-3.7	190	27
106	Johnson City-, TN-VA	JNSC-	364,016	358,147	1.6	128,470	2.6	235,546	1.1	992	84
	Johnson City, TN					57,872	4.3				31
	Kingsport, TN					46,091	2.6				32
	Bristol, TN					24,507	-1.3				21
249	Johnstown, PA	JNST	120,473	123,321	-2.3	22,166	-7.3	98,307	-1.1	403	6
392	Jonesboro, AR	JONES	61,010	58,732	3.9	58,273	5.0	2,737	-14.9	150	73
253	Joplin, MO-KS	JOP	119,189	114,889	3.7	46,659	2.5	72,530	4.5	371	30
124	Kalamazoo, MI	KZOO	297,200	290,529	2.3	75,811	-1.7	221,389	3.8	839	25
319	Kankakee, IL	KANK	88,980	87,116	2.1	27,724	.8	61,256	2.7	301	10
	Kannapolis, NC, *now part of Charlotte, NC-SC*										
26	Kansas City, MO-KS	K.C.	1,639,476	1,563,527	4.9	452,805	2.6	1,186,671	5.8	1,929	312
243	Kenosha, WI	KEN	123,710	116,926	5.8	92,833	2.7	30,877	16.2	86	22
130	Killeen-, TX	KILL-	283,156	270,163	4.8	151,273	7.0	131,883	2.4	361	71
	Killeen, TX					95,364	9.7				28
	Temple, TX					55,909	2.6				43
279	Kingston, NY	KNGST	105,409	102,928	2.4	23,429	-.1	81,980	3.2	314	8
176	Kissimmee, FL	KISS	194,686	155,541	25.2	60,761	27.1	133,925	24.3	300	12
58	Knoxville, TN	KNOX	722,963	693,948	4.2	181,112	4.2	541,851	4.2	1,802	77
322	Kokomo, IN	KOK	86,622	86,817	-.2	45,958	-.3	40,664	-.1	267	14
280	La Crosse, WI-MN	LACRO	104,821	102,982	1.8	51,544	-.5	53,277	4.1	196	18
218	Lafayette-, IN	LAF-	143,968	136,867	5.2	91,385	7.0	52,583	2.2	223	18
	Lafayette, IN					63,099	11.4				13
	West Lafayette, IN					28,286	-1.7				5
134	Lafayette, LA	LAF	274,755	268,116	2.5	105,908	-3.9	168,847	7.0	882	41
202	Lake Charles, LA	LKCH	154,419	154,060	.2	69,998	-2.5	84,421	2.6	287	32
216	Lake Jackson-, TX	L.JAC-	145,656	130,528	11.6	41,359	5.8	104,297	14.1	508	26
	Lake Jackson, TX					27,472	4.1				14
	Freeport, TX					13,887	9.3				12
147	Lakeland, FL	LKLD	247,259	230,633	7.2	82,940	5.7	164,319	8.0	324	38
359	Lancaster, OH	LANC	70,636	63,954	10.4	37,176	5.2	33,460	16.9	166	16
121	Lancaster, PA	LANC	302,589	292,754	3.4	56,473	.2	246,116	4.1	503	7
101	Lansing, MI	LANS	383,953	376,205	2.1	118,010	-1.1	265,943	3.5	737	34
173	Laredo, TX-MEX.	LAR	205,836	180,740	13.9	196,572	11.3	9,264	122.5	59	33
	incl. Nuevo Laredo, MEX.		*655,836*	*399,740*	*64.1*					*79*	
256	Las Cruces, NM	LSCR	117,670	111,375	5.7	75,934	3.3	41,736	10.3	226	38
28	Las Vegas, NV	LASV	1,600,612	1,344,673	19.0	552,823	15.4	1,047,789	21.1	565	83
403	Latrobe, PA	LTROB	54,972	55,327	-.6	8,789	-2.3	46,183	-.3	190	2
	Laurel, MS	LAUR	49,739	49,532	.4	17,321	-5.8	32,418	4.1	231	15
321	Lawrence, KS	LAWR	86,635	83,344	3.9	83,562	4.3	3,073	-5.3	89	23
305	Lawton, OK	LAWT	99,362	96,238	3.2	99,162	6.9	200	-94.3	101	51
	Leavenworth, KS	LEAV	44,551	42,257	5.4	33,933	-4.2	10,618	55.3	47	23
307	Lebanon, PA	LEB	94,057	91,718	2.6	24,605	.6	69,452	3.3	216	5
411	Lewiston, ID-WA	LEW	51,815	51,385	.8	31,770	2.8	20,045	-2.1	36	16
304	Lewiston-, ME	LEW-	95,130	92,395	3.0	59,562	1.1	35,568	6.2	305	94
	Lewiston, ME					35,709	.1				34
	Auburn, ME					23,853	2.8				60
102	Lexington, KY	LEX	377,581	361,983	4.3	272,540	4.6	105,041	3.5	566	285
278	Lima, OH	LIMA	105,543	105,770	-.2	39,605	-4.8	65,938	2.7	286	13
150	Lincoln, NE	LINC	244,531	231,614	5.6	239,834	6.3	4,697	-22.1	158	63
87	Little Rock, AR	L.R.	441,259	431,800	2.2	187,008	2.1	254,251	2.2	605	103
401	Lockport, NY	LOCK	55,809	56,366	-1.0	21,616	-3.0	34,193	.3	195	9

† To avoid dividing incorporated cities, the Anchorage and Butte RMAs each include some sparsely settled territory that would otherwise be omitted from the RMA.

†† Brunswick, Hilo, and Honolulu are not incorporated cities. Central city data refer to the census designated place.

Ranally Metro Areas: Population / Land Area, *Continued*

Rank 2004		RMA Abbrev.	RANALLY METRO AREA Population Estimate 7/1/04	RANALLY METRO AREA Population Census 4/1/00	RANALLY METRO AREA Percent Change 2000-2004	CENTRAL CITY Population Estimate 7/1/04	CENTRAL CITY Percent Change 2000-2004	SUBURBS Population Estimate 7/1/04	SUBURBS Percent Change 2000-2004	LAND AREA (Sq. Miles) Metro Area	LAND AREA (Sq. Miles) City 2000
330	Logan, UT	LOGN	84,016	79,173	6.1	45,603	6.9	38,413	5.2	120	14
383	Lompoc, CA	LOMP	64,095	63,316	1.2	40,254	-2.1	23,841	7.3	44	11
230	Longview, TX	LNGV	135,260	131,492	2.9	74,905	2.1	60,355	3.8	456	52
344	Longview, WA-OR	LNGV	78,695	76,068	3.5	35,452	2.3	43,243	4.4	120	12
2	Los Angeles, CA	L.A.	13,671,048	12,996,023	5.2	3,863,201	4.6	9,807,847	5.4	3,224	469
46	Louisville, KY-IN	LOU	992,170	970,458	2.2	249,085	-2.8	743,085	4.0	1,171	62
159	Lubbock, TX	LUB	229,287	219,920	4.3	206,965	3.7	22,322	9.7	245	104
387	Lufkin, TX	LUFK	63,180	62,376	1.3	31,829	-2.7	31,351	5.7	143	24
234	Lynchburg, VA	LYNCH	133,146	132,504	.5	65,067	-.3	68,079	1.3	388	49
132	Macon, GA	MAC	277,707	265,193	4.7	95,665	-1.6	182,042	8.4	464	48
93	Madison, WI	MAD	417,349	390,058	7.0	220,718	6.1	196,631	8.0	584	58
171	Manchester, NH	MNCH	206,745	196,727	5.1	110,296	3.1	96,449	7.5	317	33
	Manhattan, KS	MANH	49,636	44,482	11.6	49,436	9.8	200	.0	51	11
404	Manitowoc, WI	MNTW	54,807	55,553	-1.3	34,210	.5	20,597	-4.2	118	14
409	Mankato, MN	MNKT	52,095	50,357	3.5	33,745	4.1	18,350	2.3	81	12
247	Mansfield, OH	MANS	120,906	121,311	-.3	47,528	-7.9	73,378	5.3	420	28
379	Marion, IN	MRN	65,202	67,396	-3.3	30,821	-1.6	34,381	-4.7	250	13
402	Marion, OH	MRN	55,751	55,530	.4	34,827	-6.7	20,924	15.0	150	8
	Marshall, TX	MAR	30,646	30,254	1.3	22,880	-4.4	7,766	22.9	80	24
337	Martinsville, VA-NC	MRTNV	82,042	83,170	-1.4	15,036	-2.5	67,006	-1.1	288	11
75	McAllen, TX-MEX.	MCAL	517,096	448,834	15.2	117,684	10.6	399,412	16.6	615	32
	incl. Reynosa, MEX.		*907,096*	*716,834*	*26.5*					*635*	
203	Medford, OR	MEDF	154,375	145,126	6.4	69,370	8.9	85,005	4.4	240	18
88	Melbourne-, FL	MELB-	438,717	405,677	8.1	163,158	8.2	275,559	8.1	339	93
	Melbourne, FL					76,627	7.3				29
	Palm Bay, FL					86,531	9.0				64
38	Memphis, TN-AR-MS	MEM	1,099,342	1,066,097	3.1	667,392	2.7	431,950	3.8	1,272	256
222	Merced, CA	MRCD	140,070	123,804	13.1	72,262	13.1	67,808	13.2	134	16
389	Meridian, MS	MRID	62,225	62,690	-.7	37,473	-6.2	24,752	8.9	195	36
6	Miami-, FL	MIA-	5,307,359	4,944,670	7.3	520,851	1.2	4,786,508	8.1	1,660	67
	Miami, FL					365,059	.7				36
	Fort Lauderdale, FL					155,792	2.2				31
309	Michigan City, IN	MICH	93,507	93,789	-.3	32,420	-1.5	61,087	.3	242	20
324	Middletown, NY	MIDD	85,290	79,163	7.7	27,253	7.3	58,037	7.9	211	5
223	Middletown, OH	MIDD	139,685	128,847	8.4	51,852	.5	87,833	13.7	164	20
160	Midland-, TX	MIDL-	222,169	216,880	2.4	189,715	2.0	32,454	4.9	234	101
	Midland, TX					97,195	2.3				66
	Odessa, TX					92,520	1.7				35
27	Milwaukee, WI	MILW	1,629,177	1,610,669	1.1	595,260	-.3	1,033,917	2.0	1,494	96
16	Minneapolis-, MN-WI	MPLS-	2,785,442	2,682,362	3.8	682,970	2.0	2,102,472	4.5	2,425	108
	Minneapolis, MN					390,465	2.0				55
	St. Paul, MN					292,505	2.0				53
329	Missoula, MT	MSLA	84,050	80,964	3.8	55,922	-2.0	28,128	17.6	122	17
90	Mobile, AL	MOB	430,472	425,684	1.1	195,711	-1.7	234,761	3.7	849	118
85	Modesto, CA	MOD	452,746	399,512	13.3	206,490	9.3	246,256	16.9	213	30
227	Monroe, LA	MONR	135,940	135,143	.6	53,551	.8	82,389	.4	357	26
388	Monroe, MI	MONR	62,490	59,973	4.2	22,478	1.8	40,012	5.6	116	9
186	Monterey-, CA	MTRY-	174,988	168,089	4.1	89,317	9.3	85,671	-.8	195	26
	Monterey, CA					29,475	-.7				8
	Seaside, CA					33,379	.9				9
	Marina, CA					26,463	39.8				9
133	Montgomery, AL	MTGY	276,733	273,001	1.4	201,565	.0	75,168	5.2	453	135
315	Morgantown, WV-PA	MORG	90,521	87,377	3.6	26,737	-.3	63,784	5.3	360	8
291	Morristown, TN	MORR	99,104	96,411	2.8	25,253	1.2	73,851	3.4	401	16
242	Muncie, IN	MUN	124,158	126,023	-1.5	65,062	-3.5	59,096	.9	375	23
267	Murfreesboro, TN	MUR	111,015	96,869	14.6	85,260	23.9	25,755	-8.2	126	30
195	Muskegon, MI	MUS	167,042	163,319	2.3	39,834	-.7	127,208	3.2	367	14
412	Muskogee, OK	MSKOG	51,778	50,853	1.8	39,098	2.1	12,680	1.1	122	35
190	Myrtle Beach, SC-NC	MYR.B	171,707	156,337	9.8	22,804	.2	148,903	11.5	423	16
323	Napa, CA	NAPA	85,496	79,326	7.8	80,170	10.4	5,326	-21.0	50	17
142	Naples, FL	NAP	255,531	216,383	18.1	20,354	-3.0	235,177	20.4	250	11
47	Nashville, TN	NASH	945,957	907,017	4.3	549,295	.7	396,662	9.7	1,464	398
	Natchez, MS-LA	NCHZ	40,785	42,455	-3.9	17,581	-4.8	23,204	-3.3	333	13
284	Newark, OH	NWRK	103,058	98,544	4.6	48,380	4.5	54,678	4.6	250	18
179	New Bedford, MA	N.BED	191,694	185,971	3.1	92,152	-1.7	99,542	8.0	214	20
260	Newburgh, NY	NWBG	115,726	107,327	7.8	31,085	10.0	84,641	7.0	154	4
397	New Castle, PA	NWCS	57,111	58,116	-1.7	26,037	-1.0	31,074	-2.3	102	9
70	New Haven, CT	N.HAV	560,269	544,274	2.9	123,832	.0	436,437	3.8	431	19
	New Iberia, LA, *now part of Lafayette, LA*										
120	New London-, CT-RI	N.LON-	309,064	300,098	3.0	61,961	-.5	247,103	3.9	662	34
	New London, CT					25,711	-1.8				6
	Norwich, CT					36,250	.4				28
34	New Orleans, LA	N.O.	1,238,026	1,242,139	-.3	464,268	-4.2	773,758	2.2	1,039	181
386	Newport, RI	NWPT	63,632	63,197	.7	26,974	1.9	36,658	-.2	44	8
77	Newport News-, VA	NN-H	506,176	487,244	3.9	329,172	.6	177,004	10.6	686	120
	Newport News, VA					182,162	.8				68
	Hampton, VA					147,010	.4				52
1	New York, NY-NJ-CT	N.Y.	19,799,374	19,360,664	2.3	8,382,584	1.2	11,416,790	3.0	6,905	333
	New York, NY					8,108,616	1.2				309
	Newark, NJ					273,968	.5				24
	Nogales, AZ-MEX.	NOGLS	26,831	25,220	6.4	20,425	-2.2	6,406	47.5	22	21
	incl. Nogales, MEX.		*191,831*	*131,220*	*46.2*					*34*	
40	Norfolk-, VA‡	NORF-	1,078,045	1,023,003	5.4	902,187	5.0	175,858	7.1	1,076	643
	Norfolk, VA					244,163	4.2				54
	Virginia Beach, VA					443,729	4.3				248
	Chesapeake, VA					214,295	7.6				341
157	Ocala, FL	OCA	234,327	211,431	10.8	47,120	2.6	187,207	13.1	588	29
	Odessa, TX, *now part of Midland-, TX*										
115	Ogden, UT	OGD	322,819	300,985	7.3	81,190	5.1	241,629	8.0	220	26
	Oil City-, PA	OILC-F	37,553	38,389	-2.2	18,518	-1.1	19,035	-3.2	176	10
	Oil City, PA					11,362	-1.2				5
	Franklin, PA					7,156	-.8				5
45	Oklahoma City, OK	O.C.	1,017,163	973,684	4.5	538,368	6.4	478,795	2.4	1,606	608
164	Olympia, WA	OLYM	218,244	200,141	9.0	47,693	12.2	170,551	8.2	340	16
63	Omaha, NE-IA	OMA	680,772	650,384	4.7	397,239	1.9	283,533	8.9	513	101
30	Orlando, FL	ORL	1,468,206	1,342,878	9.3	195,010	4.9	1,273,196	10.0	978	67
333	Oshkosh, WI	OSH	83,279	82,112	1.4	64,307	2.2	18,972	-1.2	117	18
352	Owensboro, KY	OWNS	72,522	71,502	1.4	54,373	.6	18,149	4.1	142	15
64	Oxnard-, CA	OXN-	658,793	618,831	6.5	422,637	8.8	236,156	2.4	529	95
	Oxnard, CA					193,860	13.8				24
	Thousand Oaks, CA					123,506	5.6				50
	Ventura, CA					105,271	4.3				21
362	Paducah, KY-IL	PAD	69,900	70,799	-1.3	25,807	-1.9	44,093	-.9	167	18
151	Palm Springs-, CA	PSPR-	244,481	203,466	20.2	153,843	21.5	90,638	17.9	312	115
	Palm Springs, CA					45,925	7.3				77
	Cathedral City, CA					54,224	27.1				19
	Palm Desert, CA					53,694	30.5				19
217	Panama City, FL	PNCY	145,487	136,904	6.3	38,423	5.5	107,064	6.5	161	16
288	Parkersburg, WV-OH	PRKB	99,930	100,987	-1.0	32,818	-.8	67,112	-1.1	363	11
326	Pascagoula, MS	PSCG	84,564	82,563	2.4	25,895	-1.2	58,669	4.1	157	15
99	Pensacola, FL	PENS	388,549	371,095	4.7	52,302	-7.0	336,247	6.8	494	23
123	Peoria, IL	PEOR	297,481	298,602	-.4	112,542	-.3	184,939	-.4	587	41
5	Philadelphia-, PA-NJ-DE-MD	PHIL-	5,931,045	5,814,079	2.0	1,626,851	-2.9	4,304,194	4.0	3,912	154
	Philadelphia, PA					1,468,025	-3.3				135
	Trenton, NJ					85,884	.6				8
	Wilmington, DE					72,942	.4				11
13	Phoenix, AZ	PHOE	3,495,656	3,078,489	13.6	1,473,643	11.6	2,022,013	15.1	2,071	420
378	Pine Bluff, AR	PNBLF	65,677	67,137	-2.2	54,594	-1.0	11,083	-7.7	125	42
21	Pittsburgh, PA	PGH	1,981,722	2,010,337	-1.4	316,832	-5.3	1,664,890	-.6	2,608	56
327	Pittsfield, MA	PTSF	84,538	85,900	-1.6	44,586	-2.6	39,952	-.4	252	41
410	Plattsburgh, NY	PLATT	51,979	50,741	2.4	19,156	1.8	32,823	2.8	228	5
377	Pocatello, ID	POC	65,761	65,692	.1	50,038	-2.8	15,723	10.5	99	28
348	Porterville, CA	PORT	75,811	70,082	8.2	45,153	14.0	30,658	.6	164	11
287	Port Huron, MI-CAN.	PTHU	101,364	97,755	3.7	32,165	-.5	69,199	5.8	185	8
	incl. Sarnia, CAN.		*186,764*	*185,855*	*.5*					*378*	
145	Portland, ME	POR	249,988	242,412	3.1	65,335	1.7	184,653	3.6	626	23
22	Portland, OR-WA	POR	1,898,833	1,764,702	7.6	551,390	4.2	1,347,443	9.1	1,533	125
137	Portsmouth-, NH-ME	PTSM-	263,084	247,111	6.5	77,996	2.5	185,088	8.2	628	88
	Portsmouth, NH					20,097	-3.3				16
	Rochester, NH					29,742	4.5				45
	Dover, NH					28,157	4.7				27
391	Portsmouth, OH-KY	PTSM	61,390	63,075	-2.7	19,254	-7.9	42,136	-.1	210	11
363	Pottstown, PA	PTSTN	69,494	66,225	4.9	21,924	.3	47,570	7.2	66	5
343	Pottsville, PA	PTSVL	78,731	80,397	-2.1	14,964	-3.8	63,767	-1.7	257	4
153	Poughkeepsie, NY	POK	238,746	227,751	4.8	31,568	5.7	207,178	4.7	355	5
42	Providence-, RI-MA	PROV-	1,061,458	1,024,698	3.6	272,972	5.2	788,486	3.0	979	55
	Providence, RI					185,951	7.1				19
	Warwick, RI					87,021	1.4				36
96	Provo-, UT	PRVO-	398,488	360,719	10.5	206,217	8.8	192,271	12.3	286	57
	Provo, UT					113,860	8.0				39
	Orem, UT					92,357	9.8				18
220	Pueblo, CO	PUEB	141,048	132,101	6.8	99,388	-2.7	41,660	39.0	163	36
221	Punta Gorda-, FL	PUN-	140,103	126,731	10.6	68,814	13.2	71,289	8.1	227	36
	Punta Gorda, FL					17,287	20.5				14
	Port Charlotte, FL					51,527	10.9				22
413	Quincy, IL	QUIN	51,586	52,274	-1.3	39,145	-3.0	12,441	4.5	113	13
	Racine, WI, *now part of Milwaukee, WI*										
51	Raleigh, NC	RAL	838,377	733,981	14.2	302,564	9.6	535,813	17.0	1,330	88
316	Rapid City, SD	RAP	90,313	86,248	4.7	62,951	5.7	27,362	2.6	147	35
127	Reading, PA	READ	291,577	280,128	4.1	83,331	2.6	208,246	4.7	410	10
208	Redding, CA	REDD	151,087	137,346	10.0	90,557	12.0	60,530	7.2	322	51
105	Reno, NV	RENO	371,468	331,264	12.1	204,639	13.4	166,829	10.6	473	58
182	Richland-, WA	RICH-	181,955	162,425	12.0	149,223	18.9	32,732	-11.4	213	75
	Richland, WA					43,091	11.3				32
	Kennewick, WA					63,501	16.1				20
	Pasco, WA					42,631	32.9				23
394	Richmond, IN-OH	RICH	60,260	61,141	-1.4	39,620	1.3	20,640	-6.3	203	18
48	Richmond, VA	RICH	936,988	897,287	4.4	193,828	-2.0	743,160	6.2	1,060	60
23	Riverside-, CA	RIV-	1,841,272	1,587,954	16.0	472,755	7.3	1,368,517	19.3	938	133
	Riverside, CA					279,527	9.5				78
	San Bernardino, CA					193,228	4.2				55
148	Roanoke, VA	ROAN	245,562	244,825	.3	92,245	-2.8	153,317	2.3	555	43
237	Rochester, MN	ROCH	128,997	119,927	7.6	95,448	11.2	33,549	-1.7	264	30
50	Rochester, NY	ROCH	875,878	873,504	.3	216,733	-1.4	659,145	.8	1,585	36
113	Rockford, IL-WI	RKFD	329,934	318,096	3.7	153,198	2.1	176,736	5.2	424	45
	Rock Hill, SC, *now part of Charlotte, NC-SC*										
301	Rocky Mount, NC	RKYMT	95,737	93,768	2.1	57,089	2.0	38,648	2.3	351	25
320	Rome, GA	ROME	86,859	83,486	4.0	36,727	5.0	50,132	3.4	269	24
408	Roswell, NM	RSWL	52,786	53,690	-1.7	43,443	-4.1	9,343	11.3	81	29
24	Sacramento, CA	SAC	1,717,079	1,518,806	13.1	429,197	5.4	1,287,882	15.8	1,035	96
107	Saginaw-, MI	SAG-	359,562	359,538	.0	139,887	-.3	219,675	.2	1,028	55
	Saginaw, MI					60,574	-2.0				17
	Midland, MI					42,582	2.2				28
	Bay City, MI					36,731	-.2				10
263	St. Cloud, MN	ST.CLD	112,727	105,361	7.0	60,375	2.1	52,352	13.2	203	15
312	St. Joseph, MO-KS	ST.JO	92,082	93,230	-1.2	73,900	-.1	18,182	-5.5	238	43
17	St. Louis, MO-IL	ST.L	2,364,197	2,337,245	1.2	327,502	-5.9	2,036,695	2.4	2,437	62
36	St. Petersburg, FL	ST.PET	1,197,652	1,152,771	3.9	250,359	.9	947,293	4.7	514	59
128	Salem, OR	SAL	290,929	274,523	6.0	147,771	7.9	143,158	4.0	439	42
	Salina, KS	SLN	47,232	47,073	.3	45,939	.6	1,293	-7.2	42	21
192	Salinas, CA	SLNS	169,931	163,232	4.1	163,460	14.6	6,471	-68.5	234	19
338	Salisbury, MD-DE	SLSB	81,410	77,891	4.5	25,584	7.8	55,826	3.1	210	10
298	Salisbury, NC	SLSB	97,319	93,662	3.9	27,168	2.7	70,151	4.4	333	16
43	Salt Lake City, UT	S.L.C.	1,038,598	994,767	4.4	181,399	-.2	857,199	5.4	461	109
306	San Angelo, TX	SANG	94,508	95,076	-.6	87,328	-1.3	7,180	8.2	103	48
29	San Antonio, TX	SANT	1,511,381	1,405,646	7.5	1,223,175	6.9	288,206	10.4	1,032	333
15	San Diego, CA-MEX.	SDGO	2,884,537	2,736,424	5.4	1,282,597	4.8	1,601,940	5.9	1,373	324
	incl. Tijuana, MEX.		*4,384,537*	*3,471,424*	*26.3*					*1,453*	
335	Sandusky, OH	SNDSK	82,595	83,125	-.6	26,533	-4.7	56,062	1.4	172	10
4	San Francisco-, CA	SF-O-	6,034,656	5,990,557	.7	2,050,743	-1.0	3,983,913	1.6	2,041	274
	San Francisco, CA					743,549	-4.3				47
	San Jose, CA					913,340	2.1				171
	Oakland, CA					393,854	-1.4				56
393	San Luis Obispo, CA	S.LUIS	60,691	58,727	3.3	44,199	.1	16,492	13.3	33	9
169	Santa Barbara, CA	S.BAR	208,032	205,504	1.2	95,212	6.3	112,820	-2.7	153	19
183	Santa Cruz, CA	S.CRZ	181,113	185,025	-2.1	53,084	-2.8	128,029	-1.8	223	13
286	Santa Fe, NM	S.FE	102,291	95,406	7.2	62,768	.9	39,523	19.0	172	37
266	Santa Maria, CA	S.MAR	111,172	109,581	1.5	81,050	4.7	30,122	-6.3	57	17
112	Santa Rosa, CA	S.ROS	335,496	328,170	2.2	156,149	5.8	179,347	-.7	457	34
76	Sarasota-, FL	SAR-B	513,280	466,778	10.0	104,678	2.4	408,602	12.1	242	26
	Sarasota, FL					53,293	1.1				15
	Bradenton, FL					51,385	3.8				11
	Sault Ste. Marie, MI-CAN.	SOO	18,777	18,601	.9	17,341	21.1	1,436	-66.4	40	15
	incl. Sault Ste. Marie, CAN.		*101,277*	*105,001*	*-3.5*					*315*	
135	Savannah, GA	SAV	266,899	257,930	3.5	128,045	-3.7	138,854	11.1	550	63
82	Scranton-, PA	SCR-	460,323	469,087	-1.9	116,297	-2.7	344,026	-1.6	925	32
	Scranton, PA					74,727	-2.2				25
	Wilkes Barre, PA					41,570	-3.6				7
14	Seattle, WA	SEAT	3,165,807	3,036,889	4.2	570,290	1.2	2,595,517	4.9	2,604	84
354	Sharon, PA-OH	SHAR	71,419	71,902	-.7	16,361	.2	55,058	-.9	158	4
282	Sheboygan, WI	SHEB	104,094	103,237	.8	50,156	-1.3	53,938	2.8	314	13
341	Sherman-, TX	SHRM-	80,450	76,351	5.4	57,633	-.4	22,817	23.4	194	59
	Sherman, TX					35,696	1.8				37
	Denison, TX					21,937	-3.7				22
117	Shreveport, LA-TX	SHRE	316,289	314,390	.6	203,427	1.6	112,862	-1.2	599	99
275	Sioux City, IA-NE-SD	SXCY	106,512	106,902	-.4	84,235	-.9	22,277	1.8	130	54
235	Sioux Falls, SD	SXFL	132,981	125,549	5.9	132,443	6.7	538	-61.3	60	45
131	South Bend, IN-MI	S.B.	281,963	280,926	.4	110,206	2.2	171,757	-.8	364	36
180	Spartanburg, SC	SPRT	189,197	182,174	3.9	38,229	-3.6	150,968	5.9	399	18
100	Spokane, WA-ID	SPOK	388,221	371,509	4.5	203,039	3.8	185,182	5.3	315	56
191	Springfield, IL	SPRG	170,456	167,040	2.0	113,810	2.2	56,646	1.7	330	43
66	Springfield, MA	SPRG	603,239	593,284	1.7	153,856	1.2	449,383	1.9	745	32
136	Springfield, MO	SPRG	266,685	254,590	4.8	154,363	1.8	112,322	9.0	437	68
246	Springfield, OH	SPR	121,762	123,310	-1.3	64,431	-2.0	57,331	-.4	293	20
270	Spring Hill, FL	SPR.H	110,215	97,754	12.7	77,862	12.7	32,353	12.8	117	23
274	State College, PA	STCOL	107,013	101,227	5.7	38,649	.6	68,364	8.8	234	5
283	Steubenville-, OH-WV	STU-	103,866	107,478	-3.4	37,738	-6.5	66,128	-1.5	348	26
	Steubenville, OH					18,085	-9.3				8
	Weirton, WV					19,653	-3.7				18
83	Stockton, CA	STOC	460,128	396,350	16.1	272,349	11.7	187,779	23.1	252	53
248	Stuart, FL	STU	120,842	110,885	9.0	15,939	8.9	104,903	9.0	107	4
310	Sumter, SC	SUMT	92,954	91,455	1.6	38,415	-3.1	54,539	5.3	293	23
68	Syracuse, NY	SYR	575,197	571,783	.6	146,810	.3	428,387	.7	1,303	25
165	Tallahassee, FL	TALL	217,259	213,711	1.7	156,172	3.7	61,087	-3.2	241	63
39	Tampa, FL	TAM	1,083,183	984,692	10.0	320,694	5.7	762,489	11.9	870	109
	Temple, TX, *now part of Killeen-, TX*										
269	Terre Haute, IN	T.H.	110,573	112,034	-1.3	61,788	3.6	48,785	-6.9	322	28
303	Texarkana-, TX-AR	TEXR-	95,306	93,525	1.9	63,236	3.3	32,070	-.7	175	38
	Texarkana, TX					34,994	.6				21
	Texarkana, AR					28,242	6.8				17
351	Titusville, FL	TITUS	72,930	67,439	8.1	40,681	.0	32,249	20.5	73	20
67	Toledo, OH-MI	TOL	593,139	590,723	.4	310,336	-1.1	282,803	2.1	879	81
197	Topeka, KS	TOP	162,269	161,033	.8	122,261	-.1	40,008	3.5	256	55
	Torrington, CT	TORR	48,008	46,151	4.0	36,769	4.5	11,239	2.6	113	40
52	Tucson, AZ	TUC	827,659	769,505	7.6	517,271	6.3	310,388	9.8	778	156
60	Tulsa, OK	TUL	717,583	698,105	2.8	397,055	1.0	320,528	5.1	1,169	184
224	Tuscaloosa, AL	TUSC	136,719	135,057	1.2	75,559	-2.9	61,160	6.9	249	47
209	Tyler, TX	TYL	150,553	140,749	7.0	86,303	3.2	64,250	12.5	359	40
345	Uniontown, PA	UNTN	77,691	79,461	-2.2	12,628	1.7	65,063	-2.9	248	2
162	Utica-, NY	UT-R	220,128	221,518	-.6	94,455	-1.1	125,673	-.3	717	91
	Utica, NY					60,183	-.6				16
	Rome, NY					34,272	-1.9				75
342	Valdosta, GA	VALD	80,353	77,590	3.6	43,340	-2.1	37,013	11.1	150	27
238	Venice, FL	VEN	128,440	117,800	9.0	17,499	-2.0	110,941	11.0	144	7
300	Vero Beach, FL	VERO	95,857	88,146	8.7	17,443	-1.5	78,414	11.3	108	11
	Vicksburg, MS-LA	VICK	40,673	41,403	-1.8	25,497	-3.4	15,176	1.2	258	13
366	Victoria, TX	VICT	68,002	66,604	2.1	61,562	1.6	6,440	7.3	63	30
196	Vineland, NJ	VINL	162,869	158,101	3.0	57,046	2.2	105,823	3.5	356	69
170	Visalia, CA	VISL	207,527	191,846	8.2	101,106	10.0	106,421	6.5	3,371	24
181	Waco, TX	WACO	183,724	176,912	3.9	119,030	4.7	64,694	2.4	287	76
400	Walla Walla, WA-OR	WALL	56,288	54,342	3.6	31,150	4.9	25,138	2.0	95	10
8	Washington, DC-MD-VA	WASH	4,904,263	4,581,114	7.1	560,725	-2.0	4,343,538	8.3	3,479	61
385	Washington, PA	WASH	63,637	63,075	.9	15,898	4.1	47,739	-.1	217	3
156	Waterbury, CT	WATB	234,870	227,899	3.1	107,891	.6	126,979	5.3	234	29
259	Waterloo, IA	WATL	116,057	117,984	-1.6	69,727	1.4	46,330	-5.9	233	61
370	Watertown, NY	WATN	67,372	65,063	3.5	26,534	-.6	40,838	6.5	226	9
417	Waterville, ME	WATRVL	50,267	49,192	2.2	15,575	-.2	34,692	3.3	218	14
347	Watsonville, CA	WATS	77,505	78,222	-.9	46,814	5.8	30,691	-9.6	129	6
334	Wausau, WI	WAUS	82,812	81,673	1.4	38,504	.2	44,308	2.5	244	14
	West Palm Beach, FL, *now part of Miami-, FL*										
231	Wheeling, WV-OH	WHL	134,866	138,490	-2.6	28,920	-8.0	105,946	-1.1	487	14
81	Wichita, KS	WICH	473,657	460,520	2.9	357,893	3.2	115,764	1.8	615	115
241	Wichita Falls, TX	WIFL	124,964	127,789	-2.2	105,010	.8	19,954	-15.4	225	54
233	Williamsport, PA	WMSPT	133,933	136,302	-1.7	30,207	-1.6	103,726	-1.8	471	9
177	Wilmington, NC	WILM	194,510	181,109	7.4	85,551	12.8	108,959	3.5	377	30
98	Winston-Salem, NC	WNS	391,062	373,267	4.8	195,346	5.2	195,716	4.4	754	71
219	Winter Haven, FL	WNHV	143,082	133,461	7.2	27,124	2.4	115,958	8.4	173	12
74	Worcester, MA-CT	WORC	528,712	506,130	4.5	178,801	3.6	349,911	4.9	860	38
228	Yakima, WA	YAK	135,761	132,496	2.5	72,812	1.3	62,949	3.8	240	15
138	York, PA	YORK	261,887	250,585	4.5	41,587	1.8	220,300	5.0	416	5
89	Youngstown-, OH-PA	YNGS-	437,406	448,405	-2.5	121,155	-7.0	316,251	-.6	809	50
	Youngstown, OH					76,559	-6.7				34
	Warren, OH					44,596	-7.5				16
268	Yuba City, CA	YUCY	110,977	102,089	8.7	42,701	16.2	68,276	4.5	81	7
198	Yuma, AZ-CA	YUMA	162,088	148,651	9.0	83,663	7.9	78,425	10.2	239	22
356	Zanesville, OH	ZAN	71,164	70,135	1.5	25,500	-.3	45,664	2.5	257	10

‡ To avoid dividing the independent cities of Chesapeake, Suffolk, and Virginia Beach, the Norfolk-Virginia Beach-Chesapeake RMA includes some sparsely settled territory that would otherwise be omitted from the RMA.

Ranally Metro Areas: Summary Tables

GROUPED WITHIN REGIONS/SIZE CLASSES

Northeast (incl. DE, MD, DC and WV)

	RANALLY METRO AREA			CENTRAL CITY		SUBURBS		LAND AREA (Sq. miles)	
	Population Estimate 7/1/04	Population Census 4/1/00	Percent Change 2000-2004	Population Estimate 7/1/04	Percent Change 2000-2004	Population Estimate 7/1/04	Percent Change 2000-2004	Metro Area	City 2000
New York, NY-NJ-CT	**19,799,374**	19,360,664	2.3	8,382,584	1.2	11,416,790	3.1	6,905	333
Philadelphia-, PA-NJ-DE-MD	**5,931,045**	5,814,079	2.0	1,626,851	-2.9	4,304,194	4.0	3,912	154
Boston, MA-NH	**4,748,174**	4,679,465	1.5	583,303	-1.0	4,164,871	1.8	3,609	48
2,500,000 - 4,999,999	**2,874,740**	2,723,237	5.6	560,725	-2.0	2,314,015	7.6	2,392	61
1,000,000 - 2,499,999	**7,642,745**	7,548,104	1.3	1,684,610	-2.7	5,958,135	2.4	8,172	263
500,000 - 999,999	**4,592,758**	4,491,804	2.2	1,211,471	1.0	3,381,287	2.7	7,389	229
300,000 - 499,999	**1,490,624**	1,472,089	1.3	282,214	-1.5	1,208,410	1.9	2,790	81
200,000 - 299,999	**2,974,725**	2,893,652	2.8	855,408	1.0	2,119,317	3.6	6,336	357
100,000 - 199,999	**2,254,669**	2,190,890	2.9	696,023	.4	1,558,646	4.1	5,237	288
70,000 - 99,999	**1,444,550**	1,419,411	1.8	483,815	.1	960,735	2.6	4,800	327
50,000 - 69,999	**1,093,602**	1,080,743	1.2	362,696	-.7	730,906	2.2	3,479	184
LESS THAN 50,000	**143,768**	144,475	-.5	74,940	.8	68,828	-1.9	515	68
Total in RMAs	**54,990,774**	53,818,613	2.2	16,804,640	.0	38,186,134	3.2	55,536	2,393
Not in RMAs	**8,427,424**	8,236,254	2.3					142,587	
TOTAL, NORTHEAST	**63,418,198**	62,054,867	2.2					198,123	

Midwest (North Central)

	RANALLY METRO AREA			CENTRAL CITY		SUBURBS		LAND AREA (Sq. miles)	
	Population Estimate 7/1/04	Population Census 4/1/00	Percent Change 2000-2004	Population Estimate 7/1/04	Percent Change 2000-2004	Population Estimate 7/1/04	Percent Change 2000-2004	Metro Area	City 2000
Chicago, IL-IN-WI	**9,026,690**	8,748,587	3.2	2,897,405	.0	6,129,285	4.7	4,068	227
Detroit, MI-CAN.	**4,694,293**	4,641,127	1.1	937,359	-1.5	3,756,934	1.8	3,656	139
Minneapolis-, MN-WI	**2,785,442**	2,682,362	3.8	682,970	2.0	2,102,472	4.5	2,425	108
1,000,000 - 2,499,999	**11,901,620**	11,660,846	2.1	3,655,171	-.9	8,246,449	3.5	12,429	1,177
500,000 - 999,999	**3,491,885**	3,421,158	2.1	1,285,723	.1	2,206,162	3.3	4,674	343
300,000 - 499,999	**4,266,564**	4,180,019	2.1	1,911,613	1.5	2,354,951	2.5	7,058	640
200,000 - 299,999	**2,038,550**	1,987,445	2.6	986,470	1.8	1,052,080	3.3	3,309	335
100,000 - 199,999	**4,695,899**	4,573,472	2.7	2,524,502	2.4	2,171,397	3.0	9,663	1,019
70,000 - 99,999	**1,538,198**	1,513,020	1.7	896,440	1.1	641,758	2.5	3,517	377
50,000 - 69,999	**1,180,657**	1,175,256	.5	632,198	.9	548,459	-.1	3,297	241
LESS THAN 50,000	**488,067**	483,897	.9	351,626	.9	136,441	.8	1,016	190
Total in RMAs	**46,107,865**	45,067,189	2.3	16,761,477	.5	29,346,388	3.3	55,112	4,796
Not in RMAs	**19,602,277**	19,325,587	1.4					696,328	
TOTAL, MIDWEST	**65,710,142**	64,392,776	2.0					751,440	

South (excl. DE, MD, DC and WV)

	RANALLY METRO AREA			CENTRAL CITY		SUBURBS		LAND AREA (Sq. miles)	
	Population Estimate 7/1/04	Population Census 4/1/00	Percent Change 2000-2004	Population Estimate 7/1/04	Percent Change 2000-2004	Population Estimate 7/1/04	Percent Change 2000-2004	Metro Area	City 2000
Miami-, FL	**5,307,359**	4,944,670	7.3	520,851	1.2	4,786,508	8.1	1,660	67
Dallas-, TX	**5,154,855**	4,681,646	10.1	1,851,523	7.4	3,303,332	11.7	3,360	623
Houston, TX	**4,472,646**	4,080,199	9.6	2,117,667	8.4	2,354,979	10.7	2,576	540
Atlanta, GA	**3,992,259**	3,623,062	10.2	395,142	-5.1	3,597,117	12.2	3,132	132
1,000,000 - 2,499,999	**15,306,429**	14,315,084	6.9	6,621,961	4.9	8,684,468	8.6	13,863	3,407
500,000 - 999,999	**10,194,371**	9,677,593	5.3	4,030,501	2.4	6,163,870	7.3	14,813	1,798
300,000 - 499,999	**7,688,409**	7,368,626	4.3	3,148,219	2.8	4,540,190	5.5	12,423	1,737
200,000 - 299,999	**4,949,555**	4,694,079	5.4	2,398,608	2.4	2,550,947	8.5	8,470	1,378
100,000 - 199,999	**5,742,167**	5,410,025	6.1	2,732,806	3.7	3,009,361	8.4	11,490	1,368
70,000 - 99,999	**2,460,239**	2,397,224	2.6	1,232,089	1.1	1,228,150	4.2	6,683	854
50,000 - 69,999	**789,236**	773,749	2.0	448,741	1.5	340,495	2.7	1,881	339
LESS THAN 50,000	**361,942**	368,012	-1.6	233,455	-3.0	128,487	.9	1,333	204
Total in RMAs	**66,419,467**	62,333,969	6.6	25,731,563	3.8	40,687,904	8.4	81,684	12,447
Not in RMAs	**30,669,566**	29,442,362	4.2					753,269	
TOTAL, SOUTH	**97,089,033**	91,776,331	5.8					834,953	

West

	RANALLY METRO AREA			CENTRAL CITY		SUBURBS		LAND AREA (Sq. miles)	
	Population Estimate 7/1/04	Population Census 4/1/00	Percent Change 2000-2004	Population Estimate 7/1/04	Percent Change 2000-2004	Population Estimate 7/1/04	Percent Change 2000-2004	Metro Area	City 2000
Los Angeles, CA	**13,671,048**	12,996,023	5.2	3,863,201	4.6	9,807,847	5.4	3,224	469
San Francisco-, CA	**6,034,656**	5,990,557	.7	2,050,743	-1.0	3,983,913	1.6	2,041	274
Phoenix, AZ	**3,495,656**	3,078,489	13.6	1,473,643	11.6	2,022,013	15.1	2,071	420
Seattle, WA	**3,165,807**	3,036,889	4.2	570,290	1.2	2,595,517	4.9	2,604	84
San Diego, CA-MEX.	**2,884,537**	2,736,424	5.4	1,282,597	4.8	1,601,940	5.9	1,373	324
1,000,000 - 2,499,999	**10,306,894**	9,299,827	10.8	2,745,728	6.0	7,561,166	12.7	5,799	699
500,000 - 999,999	**4,450,501**	4,168,606	6.8	2,671,393	7.6	1,779,108	5.6	10,711	748
300,000 - 499,999	**3,886,154**	3,540,054	9.8	2,105,055	9.9	1,781,099	9.7	4,768	2,150
200,000 - 299,999	**2,408,203**	2,261,298	6.5	1,443,078	8.6	965,125	3.5	6,155	568
100,000 - 199,999	**3,109,196**	2,888,099	7.7	1,786,363	7.5	1,322,833	7.9	4,087	588
70,000 - 99,999	**990,749**	948,388	4.5	624,235	5.5	366,514	2.8	1,547	190
50,000 - 69,999	**613,964**	592,516	3.6	434,199	2.5	179,765	6.4	687	217
LESS THAN 50,000	**156,745**	149,500	4.8	115,751	1.1	40,994	17.3	836	755
Total in RMAs	**55,174,110**	51,686,670	6.7	21,166,276	5.9	34,007,834	7.3	45,903	7,486
Not in RMAs	**12,295,679**	11,511,262	6.8					1,707,045	
TOTAL, WEST	**67,469,789**	63,197,932	6.8					1,752,948	

United States

	RANALLY METRO AREA			CENTRAL CITY		SUBURBS		LAND AREA (Sq. miles)	
	Population Estimate 7/1/04	Population Census 4/1/00	Percent Change 2000-2004	Population Estimate 7/1/04	Percent Change 2000-2004	Population Estimate 7/1/04	Percent Change 2000-2004	Metro Area	City 2000
10,000,000 AND OVER	**33,470,422**	32,356,687	3.4	12,245,785	2.2	21,224,637	4.1	10,129	802
5,000,000 - 9,999,999	**31,454,605**	30,179,539	4.2	8,947,373	.7	22,507,232	5.7	15,041	1,345
2,500,000 - 4,999,999	**33,113,554**	31,281,254	5.9	8,603,696	4.2	24,509,858	6.5	23,838	1,856
1,000,000 - 2,499,999	**45,157,688**	42,823,861	5.4	14,707,470	2.7	30,450,218	6.9	40,263	5,546
500,000 - 999,999	**22,729,515**	21,759,161	4.5	9,199,088	3.3	13,530,427	5.2	37,587	3,118
300,000 - 499,999	**17,331,751**	16,560,788	4.7	7,447,101	4.2	9,884,650	5.0	27,039	4,608
200,000 - 299,999	**12,371,033**	11,836,474	4.5	5,683,564	3.6	6,687,469	5.3	24,270	2,638
100,000 - 199,999	**15,801,931**	15,062,486	4.9	7,739,694	3.8	8,062,237	6.0	30,477	3,263
70,000 - 99,999	**6,433,736**	6,278,043	2.5	3,236,579	1.8	3,197,157	3.2	16,547	1,748
50,000 - 69,999	**3,677,459**	3,622,264	1.5	1,877,834	1.1	1,799,625	2.0	9,344	981
LESS THAN 50,000	**1,150,522**	1,145,884	.4	775,772	-.3	374,750	1.9	3,700	1,217
Total in RMAs	**222,692,216**	212,906,441	4.6	80,463,956	2.8	142,228,260	5.6	238,235	27,122
Not in RMAs	**70,994,946**	68,515,465	3.6					3,299,229	
TOTAL, UNITED STATES	**293,687,162**	281,421,906	4.4					3,537,464	

POPULATION BY STATE

	RANALLY METRO AREA			CENTRAL CITY		SUBURBS		LAND AREA (Sq. miles)	
	Population Estimate 7/1/04	Population Census 4/1/00	Percent Change 2000-2004	Population Estimate 7/1/04	Percent Change 2000-2004	Population Estimate 7/1/04	Percent Change 2000-2004	Metro Area	City 2000
Alabama	**2,568,559**	2,523,154	1.8	1,141,584	-1.4	1,426,975	4.5	5,843	898
Alaska	**380,610**	356,696	6.7	305,487	5.2	75,123	13.5	1,849	1,729
Arizona	**4,507,938**	4,017,828	12.2	2,095,002	9.9	2,412,936	14.3	3,068	619
Arkansas	**1,007,264**	973,549	3.5	561,318	3.9	445,946	2.9	1,833	381
California	**32,371,542**	30,562,624	5.9	11,881,669	5.6	20,489,873	6.1	24,664	2,383
Colorado	**3,641,288**	3,426,253	6.3	1,523,241	3.5	2,118,047	8.3	2,769	513
Connecticut	**3,395,462**	3,298,426	2.9	523,417	-.2	2,872,045	3.5	3,886	152
Delaware	**645,867**	616,607	4.7	106,873	2.1	538,994	5.3	769	32
District of Columbia	**560,725**	572,059	-2.0	560,725	-2.0	0		61	61
Florida	**14,899,316**	13,763,407	8.3	3,476,767	4.9	11,422,549	9.3	10,424	1,708
Georgia	**5,648,669**	5,216,665	8.3	1,274,392	-2.0	4,374,277	11.7	6,459	620
Hawaii	**975,568**	934,941	4.3	436,153	5.8	539,415	3.2	668	137
Idaho	**609,486**	557,885	9.2	338,446	6.1	271,040	13.4	694	105
Illinois	**10,600,902**	10,302,563	2.9	3,877,609	.3	6,723,293	4.5	7,792	557
Indiana	**4,286,681**	4,164,390	2.9	1,812,775	.8	2,473,906	4.6	7,299	726
Iowa	**1,309,025**	1,277,865	2.4	807,249	1.3	501,776	4.3	1,830	419
Kansas	**1,569,328**	1,500,851	4.6	733,549	2.4	835,779	6.5	1,800	269
Kentucky	**1,881,182**	1,832,624	2.6	682,561	.9	1,198,621	3.7	2,690	429
Louisiana	**2,969,154**	2,943,970	.9	1,221,649	-1.6	1,747,505	2.6	5,041	496
Maine	**658,797**	638,250	3.2	214,564	.8	444,233	4.4	2,285	243
Maryland	**5,082,543**	4,837,731	5.1	744,406	-3.2	4,338,137	6.6	5,010	115
Massachusetts	**6,203,871**	6,102,337	1.7	1,193,855	.1	5,010,016	2.1	5,499	270
Michigan	**7,862,735**	7,733,798	1.7	1,850,659	-.7	6,012,076	2.4	11,033	452
Minnesota	**3,226,647**	3,108,729	3.8	992,271	2.8	2,234,376	4.2	3,212	243
Mississippi	**1,191,353**	1,158,765	2.8	542,130	-1.0	649,223	6.3	2,681	307
Missouri	**3,545,446**	3,470,723	2.2	1,221,885	.3	2,323,561	3.2	4,164	609
Montana	**304,902**	300,115	1.6	236,722	-.3	68,180	8.9	1,048	781
Nebraska	**916,940**	873,272	5.0	681,155	3.4	235,785	9.8	656	185
Nevada	**1,972,080**	1,675,937	17.7	757,462	14.8	1,214,618	19.5	1,038	141
New Hampshire	**870,684**	824,315	5.6	230,361	2.9	640,323	6.6	1,729	185
New Jersey	**8,501,621**	8,214,209	3.5	459,198	1.1	8,042,423	3.6	6,062	112
New Mexico	**1,121,019**	1,058,132	5.9	739,905	5.7	381,114	6.5	1,479	274
New York	**17,175,672**	16,918,374	1.5	9,388,545	1.0	7,787,127	2.2	12,422	625
North Carolina	**5,206,882**	4,873,505	6.8	2,226,005	6.2	2,980,877	7.3	10,378	764
North Dakota	**240,105**	234,263	2.5	201,968	3.4	38,137	-2.0	291	68
Ohio	**8,909,362**	8,857,600	.6	2,897,945	-1.7	6,011,417	1.7	12,292	809
Oklahoma	**1,995,599**	1,928,674	3.5	1,156,064	4.0	839,535	2.8	3,333	971
Oregon	**2,376,750**	2,248,265	5.7	1,012,534	5.7	1,364,216	5.7	2,553	248
Pennsylvania	**9,789,833**	9,723,499	.7	2,786,223	-2.4	7,003,610	2.0	13,127	403
Rhode Island	**1,083,681**	1,047,383	3.5	299,946	4.9	783,735	2.9	1,035	63
South Carolina	**2,510,230**	2,385,797	5.2	453,563	1.1	2,056,667	6.2	5,216	282
South Dakota	**226,395**	214,761	5.4	195,394	6.3	31,001	-.1	224	80
Tennessee	**3,761,851**	3,642,045	3.3	2,006,486	3.2	1,755,365	3.4	6,871	1,112
Texas	**17,412,370**	16,038,228	8.6	9,285,606	6.1	8,126,764	11.6	14,831	3,489
Utah	**1,843,921**	1,735,644	6.2	514,409	4.7	1,329,512	6.8	1,087	206
Vermont	**174,136**	169,535	2.7	38,677	-2.9	135,459	4.4	562	11
Virginia	**5,367,038**	5,053,586	6.2	1,703,438	2.2	3,663,600	8.2	6,084	990
Washington	**4,928,993**	4,677,335	5.4	1,220,189	4.5	3,708,804	5.7	4,832	310
West Virginia	**847,882**	855,888	-.9	257,850	-4.4	590,032	.7	3,089	121
Wisconsin	**3,414,299**	3,328,374	2.6	1,489,018	1.3	1,925,281	3.6	4,519	379
Wyoming	**140,013**	135,015	3.7	105,057	2.3	34,956	8.0	154	40

RANKED BY POPULATION

Rank 2000	RMA	Census 4/1/00
1	New York, NY-NJ-CT	19,360,664
2	Los Angeles, CA	12,996,023
3	Chicago, IL-IN-WI	8,748,587
4	San Francisco-, CA	5,990,557
5	Philadelphia-, PA-NJ-DE-MD	5,814,079
6	Miami-, FL	4,944,670
7	Dallas-, TX	4,681,646
8	Boston, MA-NH	4,679,465
9	Detroit, MI-CAN.	4,641,127
10	Washington, DC-MD-VA	4,581,114
11	Houston, TX	4,080,199
12	Atlanta, GA	3,623,062
13	Phoenix, AZ	3,078,489
14	Seattle, WA	3,036,889
15	San Diego, CA-MEX.	2,736,424
16	Minneapolis-, MN-WI	2,682,362
17	St. Louis, MO-IL	2,337,245
18	Baltimore, MD-PA	2,241,860
19	Cleveland, OH	2,182,254
20	Denver, CO	2,088,925
21	Pittsburgh, PA	2,010,337
22	Portland, OR-WA	1,764,702
23	Cincinnati, OH-KY-IN	1,691,894
24	Milwaukee, WI	1,610,669
25	Riverside-, CA	1,587,954
26	Kansas City, MO-KS	1,563,527
27	Sacramento, CA	1,518,806
28	San Antonio, TX	1,405,646
29	Indianapolis, IN	1,371,830
30	Las Vegas, NV	1,344,673
31	Orlando, FL	1,342,878
32	Charlotte, NC-SC	1,301,901
33	New Orleans, LA	1,242,139
34	Columbus, OH	1,225,821
35	Hartford-, CT	1,182,480
36	St. Petersburg, FL	1,152,771
37	Buffalo, NY-CAN.	1,088,729
38	Memphis, TN-AR-MS	1,066,097
39	Providence-, RI-MA	1,024,698
40	Norfolk-, VA	1,023,003
41	Austin, TX	1,009,196
42	Salt Lake City, UT	994,767
43	Tampa, FL	984,692
44	Oklahoma City, OK	973,684
45	Louisville, KY-IN	970,458
46	Jacksonville, FL	955,200
47	Nashville, TN	907,017
48	Richmond, VA	897,287
49	Honolulu, HI	876,121
50	Rochester, NY	873,504
51	Birmingham, AL	800,495
52	Albany-, NY	793,886
53	Dayton, OH	785,027
54	Tucson, AZ	769,505
55	Raleigh, NC	733,981
56	Fresno, CA	729,375
57	Akron, OH	708,043
58	Tulsa, OK	698,105
59	El Paso, TX-NM-MEX.	695,311
60	Knoxville, TN	693,948
61	Grand Rapids, MI	686,981
62	Albuquerque, NM	668,334
63	Omaha, NE-IA	650,384
64	Oxnard-, CA	618,831
65	Allentown-, PA-NJ	608,943
66	Springfield, MA	593,284
67	Toledo, OH-MI	590,723
68	Syracuse, NY	571,783
69	Greensboro-, NC	546,450
70	New Haven, CT	544,274
71	Baton Rouge, LA	542,403
72	Columbia, SC	512,179
73	Colorado Springs, CO	506,440
74	Worcester, MA-CT	506,130
75	Flint, MI	488,625
76	Newport News-, VA	487,244
77	Charleston, SC	475,333
78	Scranton-, PA	469,087
79	Greenville, SC	468,255
80	Sarasota-, FL	466,778
81	Wichita, KS	460,520
82	McAllen, TX-MEX.	448,834
83	Youngstown-, OH-PA	448,405
84	Little Rock, AR	431,800
85	Mobile, AL	425,684
86	Chattanooga, TN-GA	412,643
87	Harrisburg, PA	410,150
88	Bakersfield, CA	408,328
89	Melbourne-, FL	405,677
90	Augusta, GA-SC	402,891
91	Modesto, CA	399,512
92	Stockton, CA	396,350
93	Fort Myers-, FL	395,089
94	Madison, WI	390,058
95	Des Moines, IA	388,217
96	Lansing, MI	376,205
97	Winston-Salem, NC	373,267
98	Spokane, WA-ID	371,509
99	Pensacola, FL	371,095
100	Lexington, KY	361,983
101	Jackson, MS	361,423
102	Provo-, UT	360,719
103	Saginaw-, MI	359,538
104	Beaumont-, TX	359,418
105	Johnson City-, TN-VA	358,147
106	Durham, NC	355,621
107	Boise, ID	349,941
108	Canton, OH	343,794
109	Fayetteville, NC	336,917
110	Reno, NV	331,264
111	Santa Rosa, CA	328,170
112	Rockford, IL-WI	318,096
113	Corpus Christi, TX	317,717
114	Fort Wayne, IN	316,478
115	Shreveport, LA-TX	314,390
116	Brownsville, TX-MEX.	307,363
117	Davenport-, IA-IL	302,080
118	Ogden, UT	300,985
119	New London-, CT-RI	300,098
120	Peoria, IL	298,602
121	Anchorage, AK	293,276
122	Lancaster, PA	292,754
123	Kalamazoo, MI	290,529
124	Daytona Beach, FL	286,852
125	Atlantic City, NJ	281,933
126	South Bend, IN-MI	280,926
127	Reading, PA	280,128
128	Eugene, OR	276,455
129	Huntsville, AL	274,980
130	Salem, OR	274,523
131	Montgomery, AL	273,001
132	Killeen-, TX	270,163
133	Lafayette, LA	268,116
134	Macon, GA	265,193
135	Erie, PA	259,365
136	Savannah, GA	257,930
137	Boulder-, CO	256,431
138	Springfield, MO	254,590
139	Biloxi-, MS	252,892
140	Asheville, NC	251,012
141	York, PA	250,585
142	Columbus, GA-AL	248,565
143	Huntington, WV-KY-OH	247,651
144	Portsmouth-, NH-ME	247,111
145	Roanoke, VA	244,825
146	Portland, ME	242,412
147	Evansville, IN-KY	241,874
148	Fort Collins-, CO	235,232
149	Charleston, WV	234,573
150	Lincoln, NE	231,614
151	Lakeland, FL	230,633
152	Waterbury, CT	227,899
153	Poughkeepsie, NY	227,751
154	Hickory, NC	224,463
155	Fairfield-, CA	224,380
156	Binghamton, NY-PA	223,650
157	Utica-, NY	221,518
158	Lubbock, TX	219,920
159	Midland-, TX	216,880
160	Naples, FL	216,383
161	Tallahassee, FL	213,711
162	Ocala, FL	211,431
163	Appleton, WI	210,894
164	Green Bay, WI	208,515
165	Santa Barbara, CA	205,504
166	Palm Springs-, CA	203,466
167	Olympia, WA	200,141
168	Manchester, NH	196,727
169	Hesperia-, CA	193,320
170	Visalia, CA	191,846
171	Galveston-, TX	189,747
172	Amarillo, TX	188,149
173	Elkhart, IN-MI	187,083
174	New Bedford, MA	185,971
175	Bremerton, WA	185,060
176	Santa Cruz, CA	185,025
177	Fort Pierce, FL	183,494
178	Spartanburg, SC	182,174
179	Wilmington, NC	181,109
180	Laredo, TX-MEX.	180,740
181	Waco, TX	176,912
182	Gainesville, FL	174,392
183	Cedar Rapids, IA	172,024
184	Burlington, VT	169,535
185	Fort Smith, AR-OK	168,369
186	Monterey-, CA	168,089
187	Springfield, IL	167,040
188	Fall River, MA-RI	164,759
189	Hagerstown, MD-PA-WV	164,726
190	Muskegon, MI	163,319
191	Salinas, CA	163,232
192	Richland-, WA	162,425
193	Topeka, KS	161,033
194	Barnstable, MA	160,772
195	Vineland, NJ	158,101
196	Myrtle Beach, SC-NC	156,337
197	Kissimmee, FL	155,541
198	Lake Charles, LA	154,060
199	Jackson, MI	152,085
200	Athens, GA	151,357
201	Duluth, MN-WI	150,470
202	Yuma, AZ-CA	148,651
203	Clarksville, TN-KY	145,582
204	Medford, OR	145,126
205	Annapolis, MD	144,778
206	Fargo-, ND-MN	143,735
207	Tyler, TX	140,749
208	Bryan-, TX	140,080
209	Fort Walton Beach, FL	139,781
210	Bellingham, WA	139,165
211	Wheeling, WV-OH	138,490
212	Anderson, IN	137,711
213	Redding, CA	137,346
214	Panama City, FL	136,904
215	Lafayette-, IN	136,867
216	Williamsport, PA	136,302
217	Monroe, LA	135,143
218	Tuscaloosa, AL	135,057
219	Winter Haven, FL	133,461
220	Jacksonville, NC	133,062
221	Lynchburg, VA	132,504
222	Fayetteville-, AR	132,499
223	Yakima, WA	132,496
224	Pueblo, CO	132,101
225	Longview, TX	131,492
226	Lake Jackson-, TX	130,528
227	Champaign-, IL	129,489
228	Middletown, OH	128,847
229	Burlington, NC	128,179
230	Denton, TX	128,061
231	Wichita Falls, TX	127,789
232	Punta Gorda-, FL	126,731
233	Dover, DE	126,206
234	Muncie, IN	126,023
235	Hemet, CA	125,964
236	Sioux Falls, SD	125,549
237	Altoona, PA	125,517
238	Houma-, LA	124,143
239	Merced, CA	123,804
240	Johnstown, PA	123,321
241	Springfield, OH	123,310
242	Carbondale-, IL	122,444
243	Fredericksburg, VA	121,747
244	Mansfield, OH	121,311
245	Rochester, MN	119,927
246	Waterloo, IA	117,984
247	Venice, FL	117,800
248	Abilene, TX	117,689
249	Charlottesville, VA	116,978
250	Kenosha, WI	116,926
251	Joplin, MO-KS	114,889
252	Bloomington, IN	114,767
253	Greenville, NC	113,933
254	Florence, AL	113,578
255	Billings, MT	113,426
256	Holland, MI	112,747
257	Bloomington-, IL	112,143
258	Terre Haute, IN	112,034
259	Las Cruces, NM	111,375
260	Stuart, FL	110,885
261	Corvallis-, OR	109,900
262	Santa Maria, CA	109,581
263	Steubenville-, OH-WV	107,478
264	Newburgh, NY	107,327
265	Glens Falls, NY	107,250
266	Albany, GA	107,244
267	Sioux City, IA-NE-SD	106,902
268	Lima, OH	105,770
269	Battle Creek, MI	105,471
270	St. Cloud, MN	105,361
271	Goldsboro, NC	104,826
272	Grand Junction, CO	104,591
273	Eau Claire, WI	103,894
274	Decatur, IL	103,836
275	Sheboygan, WI	103,237
276	La Crosse, WI-MN	102,982
277	Kingston, NY	102,928
278	Greeley, CO	102,533
279	Yuba City, CA	102,089
280	Columbia, MO	101,609
281	State College, PA	101,227
282	Parkersburg, WV-OH	100,987
283	Florence, SC	100,577
284	Anniston, AL	98,571
285	Newark, OH	98,544
286	Benton Harbor-, MI	98,418
287	Port Huron, MI-CAN.	97,755
288	Spring Hill, FL	97,754
289	Eureka-, CA	97,609
290	Murfreesboro, TN	96,869
291	Alexandria, LA	96,705
292	Morristown, TN	96,411
293	Lawton, OK	96,238
294	Santa Fe, NM	95,406
295	Decatur, AL	95,099
296	San Angelo, TX	95,076
297	Anderson, SC	94,972
298	Michigan City, IN	93,789
299	Rocky Mount, NC	93,768
300	Salisbury, NC	93,662
301	Iowa City, IA	93,546
302	Texarkana-, TX-AR	93,525
303	St. Joseph, MO-KS	93,230
304	Ithaca, NY	92,631
305	Lewiston-, ME	92,395
306	Lebanon, PA	91,718
307	Sumter, SC	91,455
308	Chico, CA	91,033
309	Bangor, ME	91,001
310	Indio-, CA	90,714
311	Gadsden, AL	89,619
312	Vero Beach, FL	88,146
313	Cleveland, TN	87,951
314	Idaho Falls, ID	87,666
315	Morgantown, WV-PA	87,377
316	Kankakee, IL	87,116
317	Kokomo, IN	86,817
318	Dothan, AL	86,801
319	Rapid City, SD	86,248
320	Pittsfield, MA	85,900
321	Beckley, WV	84,587
322	Concord, NH	84,570
323	Rome, GA	83,486
324	Lawrence, KS	83,344
325	Martinsville, VA-NC	83,170
326	Sandusky, OH	83,125
327	Pascagoula, MS	82,563
328	Oshkosh, WI	82,112
329	Elmira, NY	81,987
330	Wausau, WI	81,673
331	Janesville, WI	81,661
332	Missoula, MT	80,964
333	Auburn-, AL	80,826
334	Bismarck, ND	80,754
335	Pottsville, PA	80,397
336	Uniontown, PA	79,461
337	Napa, CA	79,326
338	Logan, UT	79,173
339	Middletown, NY	79,163
340	Cumberland, MD-WV	79,128
341	Hattiesburg, MS	78,776
342	Jackson, TN	78,432
343	Watsonville, CA	78,222
344	Salisbury, MD-DE	77,891
345	Valdosta, GA	77,590
346	Sherman-, TX	76,351
347	Longview, WA-OR	76,068
348	Danville, VA-NC	73,986
349	Dubuque, IA-WI-IL	73,570
350	Cheyenne, WY	72,857
351	Sharon, PA-OH	71,902
352	Owensboro, KY	71,502
353	Great Falls, MT	71,161
354	Paducah, KY-IL	70,799
355	Zanesville, OH	70,135
356	Porterville, CA	70,082
357	Jefferson City, MO	69,692
358	Hazleton, PA	68,670
359	Hot Springs, AR	67,794
360	Titusville, FL	67,439
361	Marion, IN	67,396
362	Pine Bluff, AR	67,137
363	Columbus, IN	66,969
364	Hanover, PA	66,826
365	Victoria, TX	66,604
366	Pottstown, PA	66,225
367	Pocatello, ID	65,692
368	Danville, IL	65,418
369	Watertown, NY	65,063
370	Butler, PA	65,046
371	Cape Girardeau, MO	65,017
372	Augusta, ME	64,589
373	De Kalb, IL	64,388
374	Farmington, NM	64,227
375	Lancaster, OH	63,954
376	Carlisle, PA	63,470
377	Fairbanks, AK	63,420
378	Lompoc, CA	63,316
379	Jamestown, NY	63,230
380	Newport, RI	63,197
381	Greenwood, SC	63,176
382	Portsmouth, OH-KY	63,075
383	Washington, PA	63,075
384	Brunswick, GA	62,815
385	Ames, IA	62,798
386	Meridian, MS	62,690
387	Lufkin, TX	62,376
388	Casper, WY	62,158
389	Richmond, IN-OH	61,141
390	Davis, CA	60,966
391	Monroe, MI	59,973
392	Hilo, HI	58,820
393	Jonesboro, AR	58,732
394	San Luis Obispo, CA	58,727
395	New Castle, PA	58,116
396	Brunswick-, ME	57,361
397	Fairmont, WV	56,699
398	Fond du Lac, WI	56,596
399	Lockport, NY	56,366
400	Grand Forks, ND-MN	55,642
401	Manitowoc, WI	55,553
402	Marion, OH	55,530
403	Latrobe, PA	55,327
404	Clarksburg, WV	54,529
405	Walla Walla, WA-OR	54,342
406	Columbus, MS	54,101
407	Roswell, NM	53,690
408	DeLand, FL	53,219
409	Quincy, IL	52,274
410	Alliance, OH	51,753
411	Lewiston, ID-WA	51,385
412	Muskogee, OK	50,853
413	Plattsburgh, NY	50,741
414	Mankato, MN	50,357
	Enid, OK	49,931
	Laurel, MS	49,532
	Waterville, ME	49,192
	Bowling Green, KY	48,992
	Findlay, OH	48,737
	Hutchinson, KS	48,601
	Salina, KS	47,073
	Grand Island, NE	46,175
	Torrington, CT	46,151
	Greenville, MS	44,961
	Galesburg, IL	44,654
	Manhattan, KS	44,482
	Natchez, MS-LA	42,455
	Leavenworth, KS	42,257
	Ashtabula, OH	42,091
	Vicksburg, MS-LA	41,403
	Bartlesville, OK	40,774
	Clovis, NM	39,060
	East Liverpool, OH	38,759
	Oil City-, PA	38,389
	Clinton, IA-IL	37,644
	Burlington, IA	35,380
	Butte, MT	34,564
	Hopkinsville, KY	34,486
	Marshall, TX	30,254
	Nogales, AZ-MEX.	25,220
	Calexico, CA-MEX.	24,616
	Sault Ste. Marie, MI-CAN.	18,601

Cities and Other Places of 35,000 or More

This table lists cities and other places of 35,000 or more, ranked according to 2000 Census population. In addition, the table presents the 1990 Census population and the 1990-2000 percent of population change. The Ranally City Rating classifies Principal Business Centers according to their relative business and economic importance; for a complete explanation, see the Introduction on pages 5-9. A list of all Principal Business Centers and other places with 27,500 or more, arranged in alphabetical order by state, appears on pages 74-87.

CITY RANK 2000	CITY, WITH PLACE TYPE	RANALLY CITY RATING	Population Census 4/1/00	Population Census 4/1/90	PER-CENT CHNG
1	New York, NY (Incorporated Place)	1-AAAA	8,008,278	7,322,564	9.4
2	Los Angeles, CA (Incorporated Place)	1-AAA	3,694,820	3,485,398	6.0
3	Chicago, IL (Incorporated Place)	1-AAA	2,896,016	2,783,726	4.0
4	Houston, TX (Incorporated Place)	1-AA	1,953,631	1,630,864	19.8
5	Philadelphia, PA (Incorporated Place)	1-AA	1,517,550	1,585,577	-4.3
6	Phoenix, AZ (Incorporated Place)	1-A	1,321,045	983,392	34.3
7	San Diego, CA (Incorporated Place)	1-A	1,223,400	1,110,549	10.2
8	Dallas, TX (Incorporated Place)	1-AA	1,188,580	1,006,877	18.0
9	San Antonio, TX (Incorporated Place)	1-A	1,144,646	935,393	22.4
10	Detroit, MI (Incorporated Place)	1-AA	951,270	1,027,974	-7.5
11	San Jose, CA (Incorporated Place)	2-BB	894,943	782,248	14.4
12	Indianapolis, IN (Incorporated Place)	1-A	781,870	731,327	6.9
13	San Francisco, CA (Incorporated Place)	1-AA	776,733	723,959	7.3
14	Hempstead, NY (Minor Civil Division-Town)	◇	755,924	725,639	4.2
15	Jacksonville, FL (Incorporated Place)	2-AA	735,617	635,230	15.8
16	Columbus, OH (Incorporated Place)	1-A	711,470	632,910	12.4
17	Austin, TX (Incorporated Place)	2-AA	656,562	465,648	41.0
18	Baltimore, MD (Independent City)	1-A	651,154	736,014	-11.5
19	Memphis, TN (Incorporated Place)	2-AA	650,100	610,337	6.5
20	Milwaukee, WI (Incorporated Place)	1-A	596,974	628,088	-5.0
21	Boston, MA (Incorporated Place)	1-AA	589,141	574,283	2.6
22	Washington, DC (Incorporated Place)	1-AA	572,059	606,900	-5.7
23	El Paso, TX (Incorporated Place)	2-AA	563,662	515,342	9.4
24	Seattle, WA (Incorporated Place)	1-A	563,374	516,259	9.1
25	Denver, CO (Incorporated Place)	1-A	554,636	467,610	18.6
26	Nashville, TN (Incorporated Place)	2-AA	545,524	488,374	11.7
27	Charlotte, NC (Incorporated Place)	2-AA	540,828	395,934	36.6
28	Fort Worth, TX (Incorporated Place)	2-BB	534,694	447,619	19.5
29	Portland, OR (Incorporated Place)	1-A	529,121	437,319	21.0
30	Oklahoma City, OK (Incorporated Place)	1-A	506,132	444,719	13.8
31	Tucson, AZ (Incorporated Place)	2-AA	486,699	405,371	20.1
32	New Orleans, LA (Incorporated Place)	1-A	484,674	496,938	-2.5
33	Las Vegas, NV (Incorporated Place)	2-AA	478,434	258,295	85.2
34	Cleveland, OH (Incorporated Place)	1-AA	478,403	505,616	-5.4
35	Long Beach, CA (Incorporated Place)	2-S	461,522	429,433	7.5
36	Albuquerque, NM (Incorporated Place)	2-AA	448,607	384,619	16.6
37	Brookhaven, NY (Minor Civil Division-Town)	◇	448,248	407,779	9.9
38	Kansas City, MO (Incorporated Place)	1-A	441,545	435,146	1.5
39	Fresno, CA (Incorporated Place)	2-A	427,652	354,202	20.7
40	Virginia Beach, VA (Independent City)	2-B	425,257	393,069	8.2
41	Atlanta, GA (Incorporated Place)	1-AA	416,474	394,017	5.7
42	Sacramento, CA (Incorporated Place)	2-AA	407,018	369,365	10.2
43	Oakland, CA (Incorporated Place)	2-BB	399,484	372,242	7.3
44	Mesa, AZ (Incorporated Place)	2-S	396,375	288,104	37.6
45	Tulsa, OK (Incorporated Place)	2-AA	393,049	367,302	7.0
46	Omaha, NE (Incorporated Place)	2-AA	390,007	335,719	16.2
47	Minneapolis, MN (Incorporated Place)	1-AA	382,618	368,383	3.9
48	Honolulu, HI (Census Designated Place)	2-AA	371,657	365,272	1.7
49	Miami, FL (Incorporated Place)	1-AA	362,470	358,548	1.1
50	Colorado Springs, CO (Incorporated Place)	2-A	360,890	281,140	28.4
51	St. Louis, MO (Independent City)	1-AA	348,189	396,685	-12.2
52	Wichita, KS (Incorporated Place)	2-AA	344,284	304,011	13.2
53	Santa Ana, CA (Incorporated Place)	2-S	337,977	293,742	15.1
54	Pittsburgh, PA (Incorporated Place)	1-AA	334,563	369,879	-9.5
55	Arlington, TX (Incorporated Place)	2-S	332,969	261,721	27.2
56	Cincinnati, OH (Incorporated Place)	1-A	331,285	364,040	-9.0
57	Anaheim, CA (Incorporated Place)	2-S	328,014	266,406	23.1
58	Islip, NY (Minor Civil Division-Town)	◇	322,612	299,587	7.7
59	Toledo, OH (Incorporated Place)	2-AA	313,619	332,943	-5.8
60	Tampa, FL (Incorporated Place)	2-AA	303,447	280,015	8.4
61	Oyster Bay, NY (Minor Civil Division-Town)	◇	293,925	292,657	0.4
62	Buffalo, NY (Incorporated Place)	2-AA	292,648	328,123	-10.8
63	St. Paul, MN (Incorporated Place)	2-BB	287,151	272,235	5.5
64	Corpus Christi, TX (Incorporated Place)	2-A	277,454	257,453	7.8
65	Aurora, CO (Incorporated Place)	3-SS	276,393	222,103	24.4
66	Raleigh, NC (Incorporated Place)	2-AA	276,093	207,951	32.8
67	Newark, NJ (Incorporated Place)	2-CC	273,546	275,221	-0.6
68	Lexington, KY (Incorporated Place)	2-AA	260,512	225,366	15.6
69	Anchorage, AK (Incorporated Place)	2-A	260,283	226,338	15.0
70	Louisville, KY (Incorporated Place)	2-AA	256,231	269,063	-4.8
71	Riverside, CA (Incorporated Place)	2-C	255,166	226,505	12.7
72	Saint Petersburg, FL (Incorporated Place)	2-BB	248,232	238,629	4.0
73	Bakersfield, CA (Incorporated Place)	2-A	247,057	174,978	41.2
74	Stockton, CA (Incorporated Place)	2-A	243,771	210,943	15.6
75	Birmingham, AL (Incorporated Place)	2-AA	242,820	265,968	-8.7
76	Jersey City, NJ (Incorporated Place)	3-SS	240,055	228,537	5.0
77	Norfolk, VA (Independent City)	2-AA	234,403	261,229	-10.3
78	Baton Rouge, LA (Incorporated Place)	2-AA	227,818	219,531	3.8
79	Hialeah, FL (Incorporated Place)	2-S	226,419	188,004	20.4
80	Lincoln, NE (Incorporated Place)	3-AA	225,581	191,972	17.5
81	Greensboro, NC (Incorporated Place)	2-A	223,891	183,521	22.0
82	North Hempstead, NY (Minor Civil Division-Town)	◇	222,611	211,393	5.3
83	Plano, TX (Incorporated Place)	3-S	222,030	128,713	72.5
84	Rochester, NY (Incorporated Place)	2-AA	219,773	231,636	-5.1
85	Glendale, AZ (Incorporated Place)	3-S	218,812	147,864	48.0
86	Akron, OH (Incorporated Place)	2-BB	217,074	223,019	-2.7
87	Garland, TX (Incorporated Place)	3-S	215,768	180,650	19.4
88	Babylon, NY (Minor Civil Division-Town)	◇	211,792	202,889	4.4
89	Madison, WI (Incorporated Place)	2-AA	208,054	191,262	8.8
90	Fort Wayne, IN (Incorporated Place)	2-A	205,727	172,971	18.9
91	Fremont, CA (Incorporated Place)	3-SS	203,413	173,339	17.3
92	Scottsdale, AZ (Incorporated Place)	3-SS	202,705	130,075	55.8
93	Montgomery, AL (Incorporated Place)	2-A	201,568	187,543	7.5
94	Shreveport, LA (Incorporated Place)	2-AA	200,145	198,525	0.8
95	Lubbock, TX (Incorporated Place)	2-A	199,564	186,206	7.2
96	Chesapeake, VA (Independent City)	3-S	199,184	151,976	31.1
97	Mobile, AL (Incorporated Place)	2-A	198,915	196,263	1.4
98	Des Moines, IA (Incorporated Place)	2-AA	198,682	193,187	2.8
99	Grand Rapids, MI (Incorporated Place)	2-AA	197,800	189,126	4.6
100	Richmond, VA (Independent City)	2-AA	197,790	203,056	-2.6
101	Yonkers, NY (Incorporated Place)	3-SS	196,086	188,082	4.3
102	Spokane, WA (Incorporated Place)	2-AA	195,629	177,196	10.4
103	Huntington, NY (Minor Civil Division-Town)	◇	195,289	191,474	2.0
104	Augusta, GA (Incorporated Place)	2-A	195,182	44,639	337.2
105	Glendale, CA (Incorporated Place)	3-SS	194,973	180,038	8.3
106	Tacoma, WA (Incorporated Place)	2-B	193,556	176,664	9.6
107	Irving, TX (Incorporated Place)	3-S	191,615	155,037	23.6
108	Huntington Beach, CA (Incorporated Place)	3-SS	189,594	181,519	4.4
109	Arlington, VA (Census Designated Place)	3-SS	189,453	170,936	10.8
110	Modesto, CA (Incorporated Place)	2-A	188,856	164,730	14.6
111	Durham, NC (Incorporated Place)	3-BB	187,035	136,612	36.9
112	Paradise, NV (Census Designated Place)	◇	186,070	124,682	49.2
113	Orlando, FL (Incorporated Place)	2-AA	185,951	164,693	12.9
114	Boise, ID (Incorporated Place)	3-AA	185,787	125,551	48.0
115	Columbus, GA (Incorporated Place)	3-AA	185,781	178,681	4.0
116	Winston Salem, NC (Incorporated Place)	2-B	185,776	143,485	29.5
117	San Bernardino, CA (Incorporated Place)	2-C	185,401	164,676	12.6
118	Jackson, MS (Incorporated Place)	2-AA	184,256	196,637	-6.3
119	Little Rock, AR (Incorporated Place)	2-AA	183,133	175,795	4.2
120	Salt Lake City, UT (Incorporated Place)	2-AA	181,743	159,936	13.6
121	Thornton, IL (Minor Civil Division-Township)	◇	180,802	175,896	2.8
122	Reno, NV (Incorporated Place)	2-A	180,480	133,850	34.8
123	Newport News, VA (Independent City)	2-B	180,150	170,045	5.9
124	Rockford, IL (Minor Civil Division-Township)	◇	178,853	173,645	3.0
125	Chandler, AZ (Incorporated Place)	◇	176,581	90,533	95.0
126	Laredo, TX (Incorporated Place)	3-AA	176,576	122,899	43.7
127	Henderson, NV (Incorporated Place)	◇	175,381	64,942	170.1
128	Knoxville, TN (Incorporated Place)	2-AA	173,890	165,039	5.4
129	Amarillo, TX (Incorporated Place)	2-A	173,627	157,615	10.2
130	Providence, RI (Incorporated Place)	2-AA	173,618	160,728	8.0
131	Chula Vista, CA (Incorporated Place)	3-S	173,556	135,163	28.4
132	Worcester, MA (Incorporated Place)	2-A	172,648	169,759	1.7
133	Oxnard, CA (Incorporated Place)	3-CC	170,358	142,216	19.8
134	Center, IN (Minor Civil Division-Township)	◇	167,055	182,140	-8.3
135	Dayton, OH (Incorporated Place)	2-AA	166,179	182,044	-8.7
136	North, IN (Minor Civil Division-Township)	◇	165,656	166,928	-0.8
137	Garden Grove, CA (Incorporated Place)	3-S	165,196	143,050	15.5
138	Oceanside, CA (Incorporated Place)	3-C	161,029	128,398	25.4
139	Tempe, AZ (Incorporated Place)	3-S	158,625	141,865	11.8
140	Huntsville, AL (Incorporated Place)	3-AA	158,216	159,789	-1.0
141	Ontario, CA (Incorporated Place)	3-S	158,007	133,179	18.6
142	Sunrise Manor, NV (Census Designated Place)	◇	156,120	95,362	63.7
143	Wheeling, IL (Minor Civil Division-Township)	◇	155,834	148,641	4.8
144	Proviso, IL (Minor Civil Division-Township)	◇	155,831	152,443	2.2
145	Chattanooga, TN (Incorporated Place)	2-A	155,554	152,466	2.0
146	Fort Lauderdale, FL (Incorporated Place)	2-BB	152,397	149,377	2.0
147	Worth, IL (Minor Civil Division-Township)	◇	152,239	151,144	0.7
148	Springfield, MA (Incorporated Place)	2-AA	152,082	156,983	-3.1
149	Springfield, MO (Incorporated Place)	2-A	151,580	140,494	7.9
150	Santa Clarita, CA (Incorporated Place)	◇	151,088	110,690	36.5
151	Salinas, CA (Incorporated Place)	3-AA	151,060	108,777	38.9
152	Tallahassee, FL (Incorporated Place)	3-AA	150,624	124,773	20.7
153	Rockford, IL (Incorporated Place)	2-A	150,115	140,003	7.2
154	Pomona, CA (Incorporated Place)	3-SS	149,473	131,723	13.5
155	Paterson, NJ (Incorporated Place)	3-S	149,222	140,891	5.9
156	Overland Park, KS (Incorporated Place)	3-SSm	149,080	111,790	33.4
157	Downers Grove, IL (Minor Civil Division-Township)	◇	148,110	137,862	7.4
158	Santa Rosa, CA (Incorporated Place)	3-CC	147,595	113,261	30.3
159	Syracuse, NY (Incorporated Place)	2-AA	147,306	163,860	-10.1
160	Kansas City, KS (Incorporated Place)	3-SS	146,866	149,800	-2.0
161	Hampton, VA (Independent City)	3-BB	146,437	133,793	9.5
162	Metairie, LA (Census Designated Place)	◇	146,136	149,428	-2.2
163	Lakewood, CO (Incorporated Place)	3-SS	144,126	126,481	14.0
164	Vancouver, WA (Incorporated Place)	3-SS	143,560	46,380	209.5
165	Irvine, CA (Incorporated Place)	4-Sr	143,072	110,330	29.7
166	Aurora, IL (Incorporated Place)	3-SS	142,990	99,556	43.6
167	Moreno Valley, CA (Incorporated Place)	◇	142,381	118,779	19.9
168	Pasadena, TX (Incorporated Place)	3-S	141,674	119,363	18.7
169	Hayward, CA (Incorporated Place)	3-SS	140,030	111,343	25.8
170	Brownsville, TX (Incorporated Place)	3-AA	139,722	98,962	41.2
171	Bridgeport, CT (Incorporated Place)	2-C	139,529	141,686	-1.5
172	Bridgeport, CT (Minor Civil Division-Town)	◇	139,529	141,686	-1.5
173	Hollywood, FL (Incorporated Place)	2-S	139,357	121,697	14.5
174	Warren, MI (Incorporated Place)	3-SS	138,247	144,864	-4.6
175	Torrance, CA (Incorporated Place)	2-S	137,946	133,107	3.6
176	Eugene, OR (Incorporated Place)	2-A	137,893	112,669	22.4
177	Pembroke Pines, FL (Incorporated Place)	◇	137,427	65,452	110.0
178	Salem, OR (Incorporated Place)	2-A	136,924	107,786	27.0
179	Maine, IL (Minor Civil Division-Township)	◇	135,623	128,837	5.3
180	Schaumburg, IL (Minor Civil Division-Township)	◇	134,114	127,625	5.1
181	Pasadena, CA (Incorporated Place)	2-S	133,936	131,591	1.8
182	Escondido, CA (Incorporated Place)	3-S	133,559	108,635	22.9
183	Wayne, IN (Minor Civil Division-Township)	◇	133,461	125,699	6.2
184	Washington, IN (Minor Civil Division-Township)	◇	132,927	133,969	-0.8
185	Sunnyvale, CA (Incorporated Place)	3-S	131,760	117,229	12.4
186	Savannah, GA (Incorporated Place)	2-A	131,510	137,560	-4.4
187	Fontana, CA (Incorporated Place)	4-Sr	128,929	87,535	47.3
188	Orange, CA (Incorporated Place)	3-SS	128,821	110,658	16.4
189	Naperville, IL (Incorporated Place)	4-S	128,358	85,351	50.4
190	Alexandria, VA (Independent City)	3-SS	128,283	111,183	15.4
191	Calumet, IN (Minor Civil Division-Township)	◇	127,800	141,875	-9.9
192	Rancho Cucamonga, CA (Incorporated Place)	◇	127,743	101,409	26.0
193	Grand Prairie, TX (Incorporated Place)	4-S	127,427	99,616	27.9
194	Fullerton, CA (Incorporated Place)	3-SS	126,003	114,144	10.4
195	Corona, CA (Incorporated Place)	4-S	124,966	76,095	64.2
196	Flint, MI (Incorporated Place)	2-A	124,943	140,761	-11.2
197	York, IL (Minor Civil Division-Township)	◇	124,553	120,546	3.3
198	Mesquite, TX (Incorporated Place)	3-Sm	124,523	101,484	22.7
199	Sterling Heights, MI (Incorporated Place)	3-SSm	124,471	117,810	5.7
200	East Los Angeles, CA (Census Designated Place)	◇	124,283	126,379	-1.7
201	Sioux Falls, SD (Incorporated Place)	3-AA	123,975	100,814	23.0
202	New Haven, CT (Incorporated Place)	2-AA	123,626	130,474	-5.2
203	New Haven, CT (Minor Civil Division-Town)	◇	123,626	130,474	-5.2
204	Topeka, KS (Incorporated Place)	3-AA	122,377	119,883	2.1
205	Concord, CA (Incorporated Place)	3-SS	121,780	111,348	9.4
206	Evansville, IN (Incorporated Place)	2-A	121,582	126,272	-3.7
207	Hartford, CT (Incorporated Place)	2-AA	121,578	139,739	-13.0
208	Hartford, CT (Minor Civil Division-Town)	◇	121,578	139,739	-13.0
209	Fayetteville, NC (Incorporated Place)	2-A	121,015	75,695	59.9
210	Cedar Rapids, IA (Incorporated Place)	3-AA	120,758	108,751	11.0
211	Elizabeth, NJ (Incorporated Place)	3-S	120,568	110,002	9.6
212	Lansing, MI (Incorporated Place)	2-A	119,128	127,321	-6.4
213	Lancaster, CA (Incorporated Place)	3-C	118,718	97,291	22.0
214	Fort Collins, CO (Incorporated Place)	3-A	118,652	87,758	35.2
215	Milton, IL (Minor Civil Division-Township)	◇	118,616	108,148	9.7
216	Lisle, IL (Minor Civil Division-Township)	◇	117,604	108,452	8.4
217	Coral Springs, FL (Incorporated Place)	◇	117,549	79,443	48.0
218	Spring Valley, NV (Census Designated Place)	◇	117,390	51,726	126.9
219	Stamford, CT (Incorporated Place)	2-S	117,083	108,056	8.4
220	Stamford, CT (Minor Civil Division-Town)	◇	117,083	108,056	8.4
221	Thousand Oaks, CA (Incorporated Place)	3-S	117,005	104,352	12.1
222	Vallejo, CA (Incorporated Place)	3-S	116,760	109,199	6.9
223	Palmdale, CA (Incorporated Place)	◇	116,670	68,946	69.2
224	Amherst, NY (Minor Civil Division-Town)	◇	116,510	111,711	4.3
225	Columbia, SC (Incorporated Place)	2-AA	116,278	103,477	12.4
226	El Monte, CA (Incorporated Place)	4-S	115,965	106,209	9.2
227	Abilene, TX (Incorporated Place)	3-AA	115,930	106,654	8.7
228	Smithtown, NY (Minor Civil Division-Town)	◇	115,715	113,406	2.0
229	Aurora, IL (Minor Civil Division-Township)	◇	115,553	101,769	13.5
230	North Las Vegas, NV (Incorporated Place)	◇	115,488	47,707	142.1
231	Ann Arbor, MI (Incorporated Place)	2-C	114,024	109,592	4.0
232	Beaumont, TX (Incorporated Place)	2-A	113,866	114,323	-0.4
233	Waco, TX (Incorporated Place)	3-AA	113,726	103,590	9.8
234	Independence, MO (Incorporated Place)	3-S	113,288	112,301	0.9
235	Peoria, IL (Incorporated Place)	2-AA	112,936	113,504	-0.5
236	Peoria City, IL (Minor Civil Division-Township)	◇	112,936	113,504	-0.5
237	Palatine, IL (Minor Civil Division-Township)	◇	112,740	103,273	9.2
238	Inglewood, CA (Incorporated Place)	3-S	112,580	109,602	2.7
239	Lawrence, IN (Minor Civil Division-Township)	◇	111,961	94,548	18.4
240	Bloomingdale, IL (Minor Civil Division-Township)	◇	111,709	96,050	16.3
241	Capital, IL (Minor Civil Division-Township)	◇	111,471	104,126	7.1
242	Springfield, IL (Incorporated Place)	2-A	111,454	105,417	5.7
243	Simi Valley, CA (Incorporated Place)	3-S	111,351	100,217	11.1
244	Wayne, IN (Minor Civil Division-Township)	◇	111,117	116,005	-4.2
245	Lafayette, LA (Incorporated Place)	2-A	110,257	94,421	16.8
246	Gilbert, AZ (Incorporated Place)	◇	109,697	29,122	276.7
247	Carrollton, TX (Incorporated Place)	4-S	109,576	82,169	33.4
248	Bremen, IL (Minor Civil Division-Township)	◇	109,575	107,803	1.6
249	Bellevue, WA (Incorporated Place)	3-SS	109,569	86,874	26.1
250	Lyons, IL (Minor Civil Division-Township)	◇	109,264	105,004	4.1
251	Ramapo, NY (Minor Civil Division-Town)	◇	108,905	93,861	16.0
252	West Valley, UT (Incorporated Place)	3-S	108,896	86,976	25.2
253	Clearwater, FL (Incorporated Place)	2-B	108,787	98,784	10.1
254	Costa Mesa, CA (Incorporated Place)	2-S	108,724	96,357	12.8
255	Peoria, AZ (Incorporated Place)	◇	108,364	50,675	113.8
256	South Bend, IN (Incorporated Place)	2-A	107,789	105,511	2.2
257	Downey, CA (Incorporated Place)	3-S	107,323	91,444	17.4
258	Waterbury, CT (Incorporated Place)	3-BB	107,271	108,961	-1.6
259	Waterbury, CT (Minor Civil Division-Town)	◇	107,271	108,961	-1.6
260	Manchester, NH (Incorporated Place)	3-AA	107,006	99,567	7.5
261	Allentown, PA (Incorporated Place)	2-AA	106,632	105,090	1.5
262	McAllen, TX (Incorporated Place)	2-A	106,414	84,021	26.7
263	Joliet, IL (Incorporated Place)	3-SS	106,221	76,836	38.2
264	Lowell, MA (Incorporated Place)	3-SS	105,167	103,439	1.7
265	Provo, UT (Incorporated Place)	3-AA	105,166	86,835	21.1
266	West Covina, CA (Incorporated Place)	3-S	105,080	96,086	9.4
267	Wichita Falls, TX (Incorporated Place)	3-AA	104,197	96,259	8.2
268	Erie, PA (Incorporated Place)	2-A	103,717	108,718	-4.6
269	Daly City, CA (Incorporated Place)	3-Sm	103,621	92,311	12.3
270	Clarksville, TN (Incorporated Place)	3-A	103,455	75,494	37.0
271	Norwalk, CA (Incorporated Place)	4-S	103,298	94,279	9.6
272	Gary, IN (Incorporated Place)	3-S	102,746	116,646	-11.9
273	Berkeley, CA (Incorporated Place)	3-S	102,743	102,724	0.0
274	Niles, IL (Minor Civil Division-Township)	◇	102,638	96,412	6.5
275	Santa Clara, CA (Incorporated Place)	3-S	102,361	93,613	9.3
276	Green Bay, WI (Incorporated Place)	2-A	102,313	96,466	6.1
277	Cape Coral, FL (Incorporated Place)	◇	102,286	74,991	36.4
278	Arvada, CO (Incorporated Place)	4-S	102,153	89,218	14.5
279	Pueblo, CO (Incorporated Place)	3-AA	102,121	98,640	3.5
280	Cambridge, MA (Incorporated Place)	3-SS	101,355	95,802	5.8
281	Westminster, CO (Incorporated Place)	4-S	100,940	74,625	35.3
282	Ventura, CA (Incorporated Place)	3-CC	100,916	92,575	9.0
283	Portsmouth, VA (Independent City)	3-C	100,565	103,907	-3.2
284	Livonia, MI (Incorporated Place)	3-SS	100,545	100,850	-0.3
285	Burbank, CA (Incorporated Place)	3-S	100,316	93,643	7.1
286	Athens, GA (Incorporated Place)	3-A	100,266	45,734	119.2
287	Richmond, CA (Incorporated Place)	3-S	99,216	87,425	13.5
288	Davenport, IA (Incorporated Place)	2-A	98,359	95,333	3.2
289	Dearborn, MI (Incorporated Place)	2-S	97,775	89,286	9.5
290	Edison, NJ (Census Designated Place)	◇	97,687	88,680	10.2
291	Edison, NJ (Minor Civil Division-Township)	3-S	97,687	88,680	10.2
292	Macon, GA (Incorporated Place)	3-AA	97,255	106,612	-8.8
293	Woodbridge, NJ (Minor Civil Division-Township)	3-SSm	97,203	93,086	4.4
294	Charleston, SC (Incorporated Place)	2-A	96,650	80,414	20.2
295	South Gate, CA (Incorporated Place)	4-Sr	96,375	86,284	11.7
296	Fairfield, CA (Incorporated Place)	3-C	96,178	77,211	24.6
297	Arden-Arcade, CA (Census Designated Place-Census Area Only)	◇	96,025	92,040	4.3
298	Norman, OK (Incorporated Place)	3-S	95,694	80,071	19.5
299	Albany, NY (Incorporated Place)	2-AA	95,658	101,082	-5.4
300	Clinton, MI (Minor Civil Division-Charter Township)	◇	95,648	10,838	782.5
301	Clinton Township, MI (Census Designated Place)	◇	95,648	85,866	11.4
302	Gainesville, FL (Incorporated Place)	3-AA	95,447	84,770	12.6
303	Midland, TX (Incorporated Place)	3-AA	94,996	89,443	6.2
304	Elk Grove, IL (Minor Civil Division-Township)	◇	94,969	87,857	8.1
305	Portage, IN (Minor Civil Division-Township)	◇	94,916	101,791	-6.8
306	Roanoke, VA (Independent City)	2-A	94,911	96,397	-1.5
307	El Cajon, CA (Incorporated Place)	3-SS	94,869	88,693	7.0
308	Leyden, IL (Minor Civil Division-Township)	◇	94,685	89,142	6.2
309	Boulder, CO (Incorporated Place)	3-CC	94,673	83,295	13.7
310	Cary, NC (Incorporated Place)	◇	94,536	43,858	115.6
311	Elgin, IL (Incorporated Place)	3-S	94,487	77,010	22.7
312	Brockton, MA (Incorporated Place)	3-SS	94,304	92,788	1.6
313	Greece, NY (Minor Civil Division-Town)	◇	94,141	90,106	4.5
314	Cheektowaga, NY (Minor Civil Division-Town)	◇	94,019	99,314	-5.3
315	Warren, IN (Minor Civil Division-Township)	◇	93,941	87,989	6.8
316	Bloom, IL (Minor Civil Division-Township)	◇	93,901	95,029	-1.2
317	New Bedford, MA (Incorporated Place)	3-BB	93,768	99,922	-6.2
318	Compton, CA (Incorporated Place)	4-Sr	93,493	90,454	3.4
319	Mission Viejo, CA (Incorporated Place)	◇	93,102	72,820	27.9
320	Olathe, KS (Incorporated Place)	4-S	92,962	63,352	46.7
321	Perry, IN (Minor Civil Division-Township)	◇	92,838	85,060	9.1
322	Waukegan, IL (Minor Civil Division-Township)	◇	92,805	78,185	18.7
323	Lawton, OK (Incorporated Place)	3-AA	92,757	80,561	15.1
324	San Mateo, CA (Incorporated Place)	3-SS	92,482	85,486	8.2
325	Santa Barbara, CA (Incorporated Place)	3-AA	92,325	85,571	7.9
326	Fall River, MA (Incorporated Place)	3-BB	91,938	92,703	-0.8
327	Rialto, CA (Incorporated Place)	◇	91,873	72,388	26.9
328	Richardson, TX (Incorporated Place)	3-S	91,802	74,840	22.7
329	Visalia, CA (Incorporated Place)	3-AA	91,565	75,636	21.1
330	Everett, WA (Incorporated Place)	3-CC	91,488	69,974	30.7
331	Orland, IL (Minor Civil Division-Township)	◇	91,418	69,542	31.5
332	Odessa, TX (Incorporated Place)	3-AA	90,943	89,699	1.4
333	Fargo, ND (Incorporated Place)	3-AA	90,599	74,111	22.2
334	Antioch, CA (Incorporated Place)	3-S	90,532	62,195	45.6
335	Elgin, IL (Minor Civil Division-Township)	◇	90,384	72,355	24.9
336	Kenosha, WI (Incorporated Place)	3-S	90,352	80,352	12.4
337	Gresham, OR (Incorporated Place)	4-S	90,205	68,235	32.2
338	Vista, CA (Incorporated Place)	◇	89,857	71,872	25.0
339	Billings, MT (Incorporated Place)	3-AA	89,847	81,151	10.7
340	Carson, CA (Incorporated Place)	3-S	89,730	83,995	6.8
341	Dover, NJ (Minor Civil Division-Township)	3-S	89,706	76,371	17.5
342	Lynn, MA (Incorporated Place)	3-S	89,050	81,245	9.6
343	Addison, IL (Minor Civil Division-Township)	◇	88,900	82,727	7.5
344	Port Saint Lucie, FL (Incorporated Place)	◇	88,769	55,866	58.9
345	Vacaville, CA (Incorporated Place)	◇	88,625	71,479	24.0
346	San Angelo, TX (Incorporated Place)	3-AA	88,439	84,474	4.7
347	Sandy, UT (Incorporated Place)	◇	88,418	75,058	17.8
348	Columbia, MD (Census Designated Place)	◇	88,254	75,883	16.3
349	Westminster, CA (Incorporated Place)	3-S	88,207	78,118	12.9
350	Quincy, MA (Incorporated Place)	3-S	88,025	84,985	3.6
351	Miami Beach, FL (Incorporated Place)	3-S	87,933	92,639	-5.1
352	Waukegan, IL (Incorporated Place)	3-SS	87,901	69,392	26.7
353	Hamilton, NJ (Minor Civil Division-Township)	◇	87,109	86,553	0.6
354	Duluth, MN (Incorporated Place)	3-AA	86,918	85,493	1.7
355	Killeen, TX (Incorporated Place)	3-B	86,911	63,535	36.8
356	Greenburgh, NY (Minor Civil Division-Town)	◇	86,764	83,816	3.5
357	Nashua, NH (Incorporated Place)	3-B	86,605	79,662	8.7
358	Westland, MI (Incorporated Place)	3-S	86,602	84,724	2.2
359	Joliet, IL (Minor Civil Division-Township)	◇	86,468	84,243	2.6
360	Toms River, NJ (Census Designated Place)	◇	86,327	7,524	1,047.4
361	Algonquin, IL (Minor Civil Division-Township)	◇	86,219	57,746	49.3
362	High Point, NC (Incorporated Place)	3-B	85,839	69,496	23.5
363	Warwick, RI (Incorporated Place)	3-CC	85,808	85,427	0.4
364	Rochester, MN (Incorporated Place)	3-AA	85,806	70,745	21.3
365	Alhambra, CA (Incorporated Place)	3-S	85,804	82,106	4.5
366	Sandy Springs, GA (Census Designated Place)	◇	85,781	67,842	26.4
367	Sunrise, FL (Incorporated Place)	◇	85,779	64,407	33.2
368	Naperville, IL (Minor Civil Division-Township)	◇	85,736	49,533	73.1
369	Parma, OH (Incorporated Place)	3-S	85,655	87,876	-2.5
370	Cicero, IL (Incorporated Place)	4-Sr	85,616	67,436	27.0
371	Trenton, NJ (Incorporated Place)	2-B	85,403	88,675	-3.7
372	Bloomington, MN (Incorporated Place)	3-SS	85,172	86,335	-1.3
373	Citrus Heights, CA (Incorporated Place)	◇	85,071	82,045	3.7
374	Sioux City, IA (Incorporated Place)	3-AA	85,013	80,505	5.6
375	Columbia, MO (Incorporated Place)	3-A	84,531	69,101	22.3
376	Orem, UT (Incorporated Place)	3-B	84,324	67,561	24.8
377	Hawthorne, CA (Incorporated Place)	3-S	84,112	71,349	17.9
378	Santa Monica, CA (Incorporated Place)	3-SS	84,084	86,905	-3.2
379	Newton, MA (Incorporated Place)	3-SS	83,829	82,585	1.5
380	Whittier, CA (Incorporated Place)	3-S	83,680	77,671	7.7
381	Tyler, TX (Incorporated Place)	3-AA	83,650	75,450	10.9
382	Hanover, IL (Minor Civil Division-Township)	◇	83,471	62,308	34.0
383	Federal Way, WA (Incorporated Place)	◇	83,259	(d)	(d)
384	Hammond, IN (Incorporated Place)	3-S	83,048	84,236	-1.4
385	Norwalk, CT (Incorporated Place)	3-SS	82,951	78,331	5.9
386	Norwalk, CT (Minor Civil Division-Town)	◇	82,951	(d)	(d)
387	Plantation, FL (Incorporated Place)	3-Sm	82,934	66,692	24.4
388	Northfield, IL (Minor Civil Division-Township)	◇	82,880	78,186	6.0
389	Thornton, CO (Incorporated Place)	4-S	82,384	55,031	49.7
390	Farmington Hills, MI (Incorporated Place)	4-S	82,111	74,652	10.0
391	West Palm Beach, FL (Incorporated Place)	2-AA	82,103	67,643	21.4
392	Clarkstown, NY (Minor Civil Division-Town)	◇	82,082	79,346	3.4
393	Youngstown, OH (Incorporated Place)	2-AA	82,026	95,732	-14.3
394	Decatur, IL (Incorporated Place)	3-AA	81,860	83,885	-2.4
395	Racine, WI (Incorporated Place)	3-CC	81,855	84,298	-2.9
396	Upper Darby, PA (Minor Civil Division-Township)	3-S	81,821	81,177	0.8
397	Reading, PA (Incorporated Place)	2-A	81,207	78,380	3.6
398	Troy, MI (Incorporated Place)	2-Sm	80,959	72,884	11.1
399	Redding, CA (Incorporated Place)	3-A	80,865	66,462	21.7
400	Canton, OH (Incorporated Place)	2-A	80,806	84,161	-4.0
401	Denton, TX (Incorporated Place)	3-S	80,537	66,270	21.5
402	Fort Smith, AR (Incorporated Place)	3-AA	80,268	72,798	10.3
403	Lawrence, KS (Incorporated Place)	3-A	80,098	65,608	22.1
404	Cheektowaga, NY (Census Designated Place)	◇	79,988	84,387	-5.2
405	Roseville, CA (Incorporated Place)	4-Sr	79,921	44,685	78.9
406	Camden, NJ (Incorporated Place)	3-S	79,904	87,492	-8.7
407	North Charleston, SC (Incorporated Place)	3-S	79,641	70,218	13.4
408	Kent, WA (Incorporated Place)	4-S	79,524	37,960	109.5
409	San Leandro, CA (Incorporated Place)	3-SS	79,452	68,223	16.5
410	Palm Bay, FL (Incorporated Place)	◇	79,413	62,632	26.8
411	Lakewood, CA (Incorporated Place)	3-S	79,345	73,557	7.9
412	Roswell, GA (Incorporated Place)	4-S	79,334	47,923	65.5
413	Cranston, RI (Incorporated Place)	4-S	79,269	76,060	4.2
414	Colonie, NY (Minor Civil Division-Town)	◇	79,258	76,494	3.6
415	Clifton, NJ (Incorporated Place)	4-S	78,672	71,742	9.7
416	Lakeland, FL (Incorporated Place)	3-AA	78,452	70,576	11.2
417	Southfield, MI (Incorporated Place)	2-S	78,296	75,728	3.4
418	Buena Park, CA (Incorporated Place)	3-S	78,282	68,784	13.8
419	Carlsbad, CA (Incorporated Place)	4-S	78,247	63,126	24.0
420	Pompano Beach, FL (Incorporated Place)	3-S	78,191	72,411	8.0
421	Tonawanda, NY (Minor Civil Division-Town)	◇	78,155	82,464	-5.2
422	Tuscaloosa, AL (Incorporated Place)	3-AA	77,906	77,759	0.2
423	Brandon, FL (Census Designated Place)	◇	77,895	57,985	34.3
424	Lewisville, TX (Incorporated Place)	◇	77,737	46,521	67.1
425	Yuma, AZ (Incorporated Place)	3-A	77,515	56,966	36.1
426	Somerville, MA (Incorporated Place)	4-S	77,478	76,210	1.7
427	Santa Maria, CA (Incorporated Place)	3-B	77,423	61,284	26.3
428	Ogden, UT (Incorporated Place)	3-BB	77,226	63,909	20.8
429	Kalamazoo, MI (Incorporated Place)	2-A	77,145	80,277	-3.9
430	Albany, GA (Incorporated Place)	3-AA	76,939	78,122	-1.5
431	Greeley, CO (Incorporated Place)	3-A	76,930	60,536	27.1
432	Silver Spring, MD (Census Designated Place)	◇	76,540	76,046	0.6
433	Scranton, PA (Incorporated Place)	2-A	76,415	81,805	-6.6
434	Canton, MI (Census Designated Place)	◇	76,366	57,047	33.9
435	Canton, MI (Minor Civil Division-Charter Township)	◇	76,366	57,040	33.9
436	Beaverton, OR (Incorporated Place)	3-S	76,129	53,310	42.8
437	Brick, NJ (Minor Civil Division-Township)	4-S	76,119	66,473	14.5
438	Arlington Heights, IL (Incorporated Place)	3-S	76,031	75,460	0.8
439	Wilmington, NC (Incorporated Place)	3-AA	75,838	55,530	36.6
440	Baldwin Park, CA (Incorporated Place)	◇	75,837	69,330	9.4
441	Davie, FL (Incorporated Place)	◇	75,720	47,217	60.4
442	Redwood City, CA (Incorporated Place)	3-S	75,402	66,072	14.1
443	Schaumburg, IL (Incorporated Place)	3-SSm	75,386	68,586	9.9
444	Kendall, FL (Census Designated Place)	◇	75,226	87,271	-13.8
445	Broken Arrow, OK (Incorporated Place)	4-S	74,859	58,043	29.0
446	Danbury, CT (Incorporated Place)	3-SS	74,848	65,585	14.1
447	Danbury, CT (Minor Civil Division-Town)	◇	74,848	65,585	14.1
448	Boca Raton, FL (Incorporated Place)	3-B	74,764	61,492	21.6
449	Las Cruces, NM (Incorporated Place)	3-A	74,267	62,126	19.5
450	Evanston, IL (Incorporated Place)	3-S	74,239	73,233	1.4
451	Evanston, IL (Minor Civil Division-Township)	◇	74,239	73,233	1.4
452	Saint Joseph, MO (Incorporated Place)	3-AA	73,990	71,852	3.0
453	Livermore, CA (Incorporated Place)	4-S	73,345	56,741	29.3
454	Longview, TX (Incorporated Place)	3-AA	73,344	70,311	4.3
455	Waterford, MI (Census Designated Place)	◇	73,150	66,692	9.7
456	Waterford, MI (Minor Civil Division-Charter Township)	◇	73,150	66,692	9.7
457	Pawtucket, RI (Incorporated Place)	3-BB	72,958	72,644	0.4
458	Bellflower, CA (Incorporated Place)	4-S	72,878	61,815	17.9
459	Miramar, FL (Incorporated Place)	◇	72,739	40,663	78.9
460	Wilmington, DE (Incorporated Place)	2-BB	72,664	71,529	1.6
461	Napa, CA (Incorporated Place)	3-S	72,585	61,842	17.4
462	Town 'n' Country, FL (Census Designated Place)	◇	72,523	60,946	19.0
463	Alameda, CA (Incorporated Place)	3-S	72,259	76,459	-5.5
464	New Rochelle, NY (Incorporated Place)	3-S	72,182	67,265	7.3
465	Lawrence, MA (Incorporated Place)	3-SS	72,043	70,207	2.6
466	Yakima, WA (Incorporated Place)	3-AA	71,845	54,843	31.0
467	Lake Charles, LA (Incorporated Place)	3-AA	71,757	70,580	1.7
468	Du Page, IL (Minor Civil Division-Township)	◇	71,745	55,444	29.4
469	New Britain, CT (Incorporated Place)	3-C	71,538	75,491	-5.2
470	New Britain, CT (Minor Civil Division-Town)	◇	71,538	75,491	-5.2
471	Pike, IN (Minor Civil Division-Township)	◇	71,465	45,204	58.1
472	Melbourne, FL (Incorporated Place)	2-A	71,382	59,646	19.7
473	Bethlehem, PA (Incorporated Place)	3-B	71,329	71,428	-0.1
474	Gulfport, MS (Incorporated Place)	3-B	71,127	40,775	74.4
475	Center, IN (Minor Civil Division-Township)	◇	71,120	74,656	-4.7
476	Longmont, CO (Incorporated Place)	4-C	71,093	51,529	38.0
477	Highlands Ranch, CO (Census Designated Place)	◇	70,931	10,181	596.7
478	Mountain View, CA (Incorporated Place)	3-SS	70,708	67,460	4.8
479	Lees Summit, MO (Incorporated Place)	◇	70,700	46,418	52.3
480	Kenner, LA (Incorporated Place)	4-S	70,517	72,033	-2.1
481	Hillsboro, OR (Incorporated Place)	4-S	70,186	37,520	87.1
482	Appleton, WI (Incorporated Place)	3-AA	70,087	65,695	6.7
483	Newport Beach, CA (Incorporated Place)	3-SS	70,032	66,643	5.1
484	Cherry Hill, NJ (Minor Civil Division-Township)	3-SS	69,965	69,319	0.9
485	Lynwood, CA (Incorporated Place)	4-S	69,845	61,945	12.8
486	East Orange, NJ (Incorporated Place)	4-Sr	69,824	73,552	-5.1
487	Deltona, FL (Incorporated Place)	◇	69,543	50,828	36.8
488	Largo, FL (Incorporated Place)	4-S	69,371	65,674	5.6
489	Wyoming, MI (Incorporated Place)	3-S	69,368	63,891	8.6
490	Bloomington, IN (Incorporated Place)	3-A	69,291	60,633	14.3
491	Spring Hill, FL (Census Designated Place)	◇	69,078	31,117	122.0
492	Asheville, NC (Incorporated Place)	3-AA	68,889	61,855	11.4
493	Rochester Hills, MI (Incorporated Place)	◇	68,825	61,766	11.4
494	Murfreesboro, TN (Incorporated Place)	3-C	68,816	44,922	53.2
495	Waterloo, IA (Incorporated Place)	3-AA	68,747	66,467	3.4
496	Lorain, OH (Incorporated Place)	3-S	68,652	71,245	-3.6
497	Clovis, CA (Incorporated Place)	4-Sr	68,468	50,323	36.1
498	Upland, CA (Incorporated Place)	3-S	68,393	63,374	7.9
499	Mount Vernon, NY (Incorporated Place)	4-Sr	68,381	67,153	1.8

◇ Not classified as a Principal Business Center.

(d) Data not available.

continued on next page

Cities and Other Places of 35,000 or More, *Continued*

CITY RANK 2000	CITY, WITH PLACE TYPE	RANALLY CITY RATING	Population Census 4/1/00	Population Census 4/1/90	PER-CENT CHNG
500	West Jordan, UT (Incorporated Place)	◇	68,336	42,892	59.3
501	Edmond, OK (Incorporated Place)	4-S	68,315	52,315	30.6
502	St. Joseph, IN (Minor Civil Division-Township)	◇	68,276	61,167	11.6
503	College Station, TX (Incorporated Place)	3-B	67,890	52,456	29.4
504	Passaic, NJ (Incorporated Place)	4-S	67,861	58,041	16.9
505	Rich, IL (Minor Civil Division-Township)	◇	67,623	61,458	10.0
506	Champaign, IL (Incorporated Place)	3-AA	67,518	63,502	6.3
507	Champaign City, IL (Minor Civil Division-Township)	◇	67,518	63,502	6.3
508	Tustin, CA (Incorporated Place)	4-S	67,504	50,689	33.2
509	Knight, IN (Minor Civil Division-Township)	◇	67,491	65,522	3.0
510	Muncie, IN (Incorporated Place)	3-AA	67,430	71,035	-5.1
511	Brooklyn Park, MN (Incorporated Place)	◇	67,388	56,381	19.5
512	Bellingham, WA (Incorporated Place)	3-A	67,171	52,179	28.7
513	Chino, CA (Incorporated Place)	4-Sr	67,168	59,682	12.5
514	Union City, NJ (Incorporated Place)	3-S	67,088	58,012	15.6
515	Framingham, MA (Census Designated Place)	◇	66,910	64,989	3.0
516	Framingham, MA (Minor Civil Division-Town)	3-SS	66,910	64,989	3.0
517	Union City, CA (Incorporated Place)	◇	66,869	53,762	24.4
518	Chino Hills, CA (Incorporated Place)	◇	66,787	37,868	76.4
519	Jacksonville, NC (Incorporated Place)	3-A	66,715	30,398	119.5
520	Baytown, TX (Incorporated Place)	3-S	66,430	63,850	4.0
521	Sparks, NV (Incorporated Place)	4-S	66,346	53,367	24.3
522	Pontiac, MI (Incorporated Place)	3-SS	66,337	71,166	-6.8
523	Middletown, NJ (Minor Civil Division-Township)	◇	66,327	68,183	-2.7
524	Gastonia, NC (Incorporated Place)	3-BB	66,277	54,732	21.1
525	Plymouth, MN (Incorporated Place)	◇	65,894	50,889	29.5
526	Taylor, MI (Incorporated Place)	3-Sm	65,868	70,811	-7.0
527	Bryan, TX (Incorporated Place)	3-A	65,660	55,002	19.4
528	Palatine, IL (Incorporated Place)	◇	65,479	38,894	68.4
529	Springfield, OH (Incorporated Place)	3-BB	65,358	70,487	-7.3
530	Vernon, IL (Minor Civil Division-Township)	◇	65,355	51,141	27.8
531	Lynchburg, VA (Independent City)	3-AA	65,269	66,049	-1.2
532	Shelby, MI (Minor Civil Division-Charter Township)	◇	65,159	48,655	33.9
533	Shelby Township, MI (Census Designated Place)	◇	65,159	48,655	33.9
534	West Bloomfield Township, MI (Census Designated Place)	◇	64,862	54,843	18.3
535	West Bloomfield, MI (Minor Civil Division-Charter Township)	◇	64,860	54,843	18.3
536	Waukesha, WI (Incorporated Place)	3-S	64,825	56,958	13.8
537	Bloomington, IL (Incorporated Place)	3-AA	64,808	51,889	24.9
538	Bloomington City, IL (Minor Civil Division-Township)	◇	64,808	51,889	24.9
539	Clay, IN (Minor Civil Division-Township)	◇	64,709	43,007	50.5
540	Deerfield Beach, FL (Incorporated Place)	◇	64,583	46,325	39.4
541	Gloucester, NJ (Minor Civil Division-Township)	◇	64,350	53,797	19.6
542	Penn, IN (Minor Civil Division-Township)	◇	64,322	59,879	7.4
543	Walnut Creek, CA (Incorporated Place)	3-SS	64,296	60,569	6.2
544	Portland, ME (Incorporated Place)	2-A	64,249	64,358	-0.2
545	Daytona Beach, FL (Incorporated Place)	2-A	64,112	61,921	3.5
546	Victorville, CA (Incorporated Place)	4-C	64,029	40,674	57.4
547	Merced, CA (Incorporated Place)	3-A	63,893	56,216	13.7
548	Wayne, IL (Minor Civil Division-Township)	◇	63,776	40,379	57.9
549	Suffolk, VA (Independent City)	4-S	63,677	52,141	22.1
550	Pleasanton, CA (Incorporated Place)	4-S	63,654	50,553	25.9
551	Redlands, CA (Incorporated Place)	3-S	63,591	60,394	5.3
552	West Hartford, CT (Census Designated Place)	◇	63,589	60,110	5.8
553	West Hartford, CT (Minor Civil Division-Town)	3-S	63,589	60,110	5.8
554	Eagan, MN (Incorporated Place)	◇	63,557	47,409	34.1
555	Pico Rivera, CA (Incorporated Place)	4-S	63,428	59,177	7.2
556	Skokie, IL (Incorporated Place)	3-SSm	63,348	59,432	6.6
557	Sugar Land, TX (Incorporated Place)	◇	63,328	24,549	158.0
558	Redondo Beach, CA (Incorporated Place)	3-S	63,261	60,167	5.1
559	Medford, OR (Incorporated Place)	3-AA	63,154	46,951	34.5
560	St. Clair Shores, MI (Incorporated Place)	4-S	63,096	68,107	-7.4
561	Oshkosh, WI (Incorporated Place)	3-B	62,916	55,006	14.4
562	Hoover, AL (Incorporated Place)	◇	62,742	39,788	57.7
563	Milpitas, CA (Incorporated Place)	◇	62,698	50,686	23.7
564	Hesperia, CA (Incorporated Place)	◇	62,582	50,418	24.1
565	Dundalk, MD (Census Designated Place)	◇	62,306	65,800	-5.3
566	Iowa City, IA (Incorporated Place)	3-A	62,220	59,738	4.2
567	Santa Fe, NM (Incorporated Place)	3-A	62,203	55,859	11.4
568	Montebello, CA (Incorporated Place)	4-S	62,150	59,564	4.3
569	Laguna Niguel, CA (Incorporated Place)	◇	61,891	44,400	39.4
570	Bayonne, NJ (Incorporated Place)	4-S	61,842	61,444	0.6
571	Schenectady, NY (Incorporated Place)	3-BB	61,821	65,566	-5.7
572	Saginaw, MI (Incorporated Place)	2-A	61,799	69,512	-11.1
573	Tonawanda, NY (Census Designated Place)	◇	61,729	65,284	-5.4
574	Eau Claire, WI (Incorporated Place)	3-AA	61,704	56,856	8.5
575	Coon Rapids, MN (Incorporated Place)	4-S	61,607	52,978	16.3
576	Huntington Park, CA (Incorporated Place)	4-S	61,348	56,065	9.4
577	West Allis, WI (Incorporated Place)	3-S	61,254	63,221	-3.1
578	Round Rock, TX (Incorporated Place)	◇	61,136	30,923	97.7
579	Greenwich, CT (Minor Civil Division-Town)	3-S	61,101	58,441	4.6
580	Irvington, NJ (Census Designated Place)	◇	60,695	59,774	1.5
581	Irvington, NJ (Minor Civil Division-Township)	4-S	60,695	61,018	-0.5
582	Hamilton, OH (Incorporated Place)	3-C	60,690	61,368	-1.1
583	Utica, NY (Incorporated Place)	3-AA	60,651	68,637	-11.6
584	Victoria, TX (Incorporated Place)	3-A	60,603	55,076	10.0
585	South San Francisco, CA (Incorporated Place)	4-S	60,552	54,312	11.5
586	Greenville, NC (Incorporated Place)	3-A	60,476	44,972	34.5
587	Old Bridge, NJ (Minor Civil Division-Township)	◇	60,456	56,475	7.0
588	North Little Rock, AR (Incorporated Place)	3-S	60,433	61,741	-2.1
589	Boynton Beach, FL (Incorporated Place)	◇	60,389	46,194	30.7
590	Lakewood, NJ (Minor Civil Division-Township)	4-Sr	60,352	45,048	34.0
591	Saint Charles, MO (Incorporated Place)	3-S	60,321	54,555	10.6
592	Davis, CA (Incorporated Place)	◇	60,308	46,209	30.5
593	Burnsville, MN (Incorporated Place)	3-Sm	60,220	51,288	17.4
594	Florence-Graham, CA (Census Designated Place-Census Area Only)	◇	60,197	57,147	5.3
595	Colerain, OH (Minor Civil Division-Township)	◇	60,144	56,781	5.9
596	Bristol, CT (Incorporated Place)	3-S	60,062	60,640	-1.0
597	Bristol, CT (Minor Civil Division-Town)	◇	60,062	60,640	-1.0
598	Royal Oak, MI (Incorporated Place)	3-S	60,062	65,410	-8.2
599	Monterey Park, CA (Incorporated Place)	4-S	60,051	60,738	-1.1
600	Anderson, IN (Minor Civil Division-Township)	◇	60,026	59,892	0.2
601	Delray Beach, FL (Incorporated Place)	4-S	60,020	47,181	27.2
602	Elk Grove, CA (Incorporated Place)	◇	59,984	17,483	243.1
603	Chico, CA (Incorporated Place)	3-A	59,954	40,079	49.6
604	North Miami, FL (Incorporated Place)	4-Sr	59,880	49,998	19.8
605	Lower Merion, PA (Minor Civil Division-Township)	3-S	59,850	58,003	3.2
606	Anderson, IN (Incorporated Place)	3-A	59,734	59,459	0.5
607	Jackson, TN (Incorporated Place)	3-A	59,643	48,949	21.8
608	Terre Haute, IN (Incorporated Place)	3-AA	59,614	55,439	7.5
609	Rapid City, SD (Incorporated Place)	3-A	59,607	54,523	9.3
610	Fountainbleau, FL (Census Designated Place)	◇	59,549	(d)	(d)
611	Janesville, WI (Incorporated Place)	3-A	59,498	52,133	14.1
612	Carol City, FL (Census Designated Place)	◇	59,443	53,331	11.5
613	Warren, IL (Minor Civil Division-Township)	◇	59,424	34,785	70.8
614	Palm Harbor, FL (Census Designated Place)	◇	59,248	50,256	17.9
615	Waltham, MA (Incorporated Place)	3-S	59,226	57,878	2.3
616	St. Cloud, MN (Incorporated Place)	3-A	59,107	48,812	21.1
617	La Habra, CA (Incorporated Place)	4-S	58,974	51,266	15.0
618	Haverhill, MA (Incorporated Place)	4-S	58,969	51,418	14.7
619	Yorba Linda, CA (Incorporated Place)	◇	58,918	52,422	12.4
620	Hemet, CA (Incorporated Place)	3-C	58,812	36,094	62.9
621	Clay, NY (Minor Civil Division-Town)	◇	58,805	59,749	-1.6
622	Marietta, GA (Incorporated Place)	3-S	58,748	44,129	33.1
623	Des Plaines, IL (Incorporated Place)	3-S	58,720	53,223	10.3
624	El Toro, CA (Incorporated Place)	◇	58,707	56,065	4.7
625	Palo Alto, CA (Incorporated Place)	3-SS	58,598	55,900	4.8
626	Layton, UT (Incorporated Place)	4-S	58,474	41,784	39.9
627	Bensalem, PA (Minor Civil Division-Township)	3-Sm	58,434	56,788	2.9
628	Decatur, IL (Minor Civil Division-Township)	◇	58,355	61,907	-5.7
629	Council Bluffs, IA (Incorporated Place)	3-S	58,268	54,315	7.3
630	Dearborn Heights, MI (Incorporated Place)	4-Sr	58,264	60,838	-4.2
631	Meriden, CT (Incorporated Place)	3-B	58,244	59,479	-2.1
632	Meriden, CT (Minor Civil Division-Town)	◇	58,244	59,479	-2.1
633	Lakewood, WA (Incorporated Place)	◇	58,211	55,937	4.1
634	North Bergen, NJ (Minor Civil Division-Township)	4-Sr	58,092	48,414	20.0
635	Fayetteville, AR (Incorporated Place)	3-A	58,047	42,099	37.9
636	Encinitas, CA (Incorporated Place)	◇	58,014	55,386	4.7
637	Port Arthur, TX (Incorporated Place)	3-B	57,755	58,724	-1.7
638	Gardena, CA (Incorporated Place)	3-S	57,746	49,841	15.9
639	Burke, VA (Census Designated Place)	◇	57,737	57,734	0.0
640	Dothan, AL (Incorporated Place)	3-A	57,737	53,721	7.5
641	Temecula, CA (Incorporated Place)	◇	57,716	27,099	113.0
642	Wheaton-Glenmont, MD (Census Designated Place-Census Area Only)	◇	57,694	53,720	7.4
643	Dubuque, IA (Incorporated Place)	3-A	57,686	57,546	0.2
644	Lauderhill, FL (Incorporated Place)	4-S	57,585	49,708	15.8
645	Harlingen, TX (Incorporated Place)	3-B	57,564	48,735	18.1
646	Kettering, OH (Incorporated Place)	3-S	57,502	60,569	-5.1
647	Taylorsville, UT (Incorporated Place)	◇	57,439	51,500	11.5
648	Fairfield, CT (Minor Civil Division-Town)	4-S	57,340	53,418	7.3
649	Castro Valley, CA (Census Designated Place)	◇	57,292	48,619	17.8
650	Galveston, TX (Incorporated Place)	3-C	57,247	59,070	-3.1
651	Brookline, MA (Census Designated Place)	◇	57,107	54,718	4.4
652	Brookline, MA (Minor Civil Division-Town)	4-Sr	57,107	54,718	4.4
653	Camarillo, CA (Incorporated Place)	4-Sr	57,077	52,303	9.1
654	Missoula, MT (Incorporated Place)	3-A	57,053	42,918	32.9
655	Lodi, CA (Incorporated Place)	4-C	56,999	51,874	9.9
656	Tracy, CA (Incorporated Place)	◇	56,929	33,558	69.6
657	Hamden, CT (Minor Civil Division-Town)	4-S	56,913	52,434	8.5
658	Kendale Lakes, FL (Census Designated Place)	◇	56,901	48,524	17.3
659	Pittsburg, CA (Incorporated Place)	4-S	56,769	47,564	19.4
660	New Trier, IL (Minor Civil Division-Township)	◇	56,716	54,705	3.7
661	Jeffersonville, IN (Minor Civil Division-Township)	◇	56,695	53,449	6.1
662	Great Falls, MT (Incorporated Place)	3-A	56,690	55,097	2.9
663	Lakewood, OH (Incorporated Place)	4-Sr	56,646	59,718	-5.1
664	Hempstead, NY (Incorporated Place)	3-S	56,554	49,453	14.4
665	Bossier City, LA (Incorporated Place)	3-S	56,461	52,721	7.1
666	Reston, VA (Census Designated Place)	◇	56,407	48,556	16.2
667	Ellicott City, MD (Census Designated Place)	◇	56,397	41,396	36.2
668	Lafayette, IN (Incorporated Place)	3-AA	56,397	43,758	28.9
669	Lancaster, PA (Incorporated Place)	2-A	56,348	55,551	1.4
670	Malden, MA (Incorporated Place)	4-S	56,340	53,884	4.6
671	Bolingbrook, IL (Incorporated Place)	◇	56,321	40,843	37.9
672	Union, NY (Minor Civil Division-Town)	◇	56,298	59,786	-5.8
673	Diamond Bar, CA (Incorporated Place)	◇	56,287	53,672	4.9
674	Vineland, NJ (Incorporated Place)	3-C	56,271	54,780	2.7
675	Mount Prospect, IL (Incorporated Place)	3-S	56,265	53,170	5.8
676	Hamburg, NY (Minor Civil Division-Town)	◇	56,259	53,735	4.7
677	Pensacola, FL (Incorporated Place)	2-A	56,255	58,165	-3.3
678	Abington, PA (Minor Civil Division-Township)	3-S	56,103	56,322	-0.4
679	San Rafael, CA (Incorporated Place)	3-S	56,063	48,404	15.8
680	Greenville, SC (Incorporated Place)	2-A	56,002	58,282	-3.9
681	Concord, NC (Incorporated Place)	4-C	55,977	27,347	104.7
682	Taunton, MA (Incorporated Place)	4-C	55,976	49,832	12.3
683	Dale City, VA (Census Designated Place)	◇	55,971	47,170	18.7
684	Elyria, OH (Incorporated Place)	3-S	55,953	56,746	-1.4
685	Rocky Mount, NC (Incorporated Place)	3-A	55,893	48,997	14.1
686	Turlock, CA (Incorporated Place)	4-C	55,810	42,198	32.3
687	Medford, MA (Incorporated Place)	3-S	55,765	57,407	-2.9
688	Green, OH (Minor Civil Division-Township)	◇	55,660	52,687	5.6
689	The Woodlands, TX (Census Designated Place)	◇	55,649	29,205	90.5
690	North Richland Hills, TX (Incorporated Place)	4-S	55,635	45,895	21.2
691	Niagara Falls, NY (Incorporated Place)	3-BB	55,593	61,840	-10.1
692	Tamarac, FL (Incorporated Place)	◇	55,588	44,822	24.0
693	Bismarck, ND (Incorporated Place)	3-A	55,532	49,256	12.7
694	Bristol, PA (Minor Civil Division-Township)	◇	55,521	57,129	-2.8
695	Jonesboro, AR (Incorporated Place)	3-A	55,515	46,535	19.3
696	Johnson City, TN (Incorporated Place)	3-B	55,469	49,479	12.1
697	Germantown, MD (Census Designated Place)	◇	55,419	41,145	34.7
698	Wheaton, IL (Incorporated Place)	◇	55,416	51,464	7.7
699	Concord, IN (Minor Civil Division-Township)	◇	55,377	49,126	12.7
700	Bethesda, MD (Census Designated Place)	◇	55,277	62,936	-12.2
701	Paramount, CA (Incorporated Place)	◇	55,266	47,669	15.9
702	Oak Lawn, IL (Incorporated Place)	3-S	55,245	56,182	-1.7
703	Goleta, CA (Incorporated Place)	◇	55,204	(d)	(d)
704	South Whittier, CA (Census Designated Place)	◇	55,193	49,524	11.4
705	Pine Bluff, AR (Incorporated Place)	3-A	55,085	57,140	-3.6
706	Rancho Cordova, CA (Census Designated Place)	◇	55,060	48,731	13.0
707	Annandale, VA (Census Designated Place)	◇	54,994	50,975	7.9
708	Fountain Valley, CA (Incorporated Place)	3-S	54,978	53,691	2.4
709	San Marcos, CA (Incorporated Place)	◇	54,977	38,974	41.1
710	Avon, IL (Minor Civil Division-Township)	◇	54,957	35,989	52.7
711	Eden Prairie, MN (Incorporated Place)	◇	54,901	39,311	39.7
712	Union, OH (Minor Civil Division-Township)	◇	54,895	39,703	38.3
713	Tamiami, FL (Census Designated Place)	◇	54,788	33,845	61.9
714	La Mesa, CA (Incorporated Place)	3-S	54,749	52,931	3.4
715	Manchester, CT (Minor Civil Division-Town)	3-S	54,740	51,618	6.0
716	Southampton, NY (Minor Civil Division-Town)	◇	54,712	44,976	21.6
717	Kennewick, WA (Incorporated Place)	3-A	54,693	42,155	29.7
718	Chicopee, MA (Incorporated Place)	4-S	54,653	56,632	-3.5
719	Santa Cruz, CA (Incorporated Place)	3-C	54,593	49,040	11.3
720	Petaluma, CA (Incorporated Place)	4-S	54,548	43,184	26.3
721	Temple, TX (Incorporated Place)	3-A	54,514	46,109	18.2
722	Union, NJ (Census Designated Place)	◇	54,405	50,024	8.8
723	Union, NJ (Minor Civil Division-Township)	4-S	54,405	50,024	8.8
724	McKinney, TX (Incorporated Place)	◇	54,369	21,283	155.5
725	National City, CA (Incorporated Place)	3-S	54,260	54,249	0.0
726	Apple Valley, CA (Incorporated Place)	◇	54,239	46,079	17.7
727	Midwest City, OK (Incorporated Place)	3-S	54,088	52,267	3.5
728	Wayne, NJ (Census Designated Place)	◇	54,069	47,025	15.0
729	Wayne, NJ (Minor Civil Division-Township)	3-SSm	54,069	47,025	15.0
730	Owensboro, KY (Incorporated Place)	3-A	54,067	53,549	1.0
731	Berwyn, IL (Incorporated Place)	4-S	54,016	45,426	18.9
732	Berwyn, IL (Minor Civil Division-Township)	◇	54,016	45,426	18.9
733	Casas Adobes, AZ (Census Designated Place)	◇	54,011	(d)	(d)
734	Weymouth, MA (Census Designated Place)	◇	53,988	54,063	-0.1
735	Weymouth, MA (Minor Civil Division-Town)	4-S	53,988	54,063	-0.1
736	Levittown, PA (Census Designated Place)	4-Sr	53,966	55,362	-2.5
737	Decatur, AL (Incorporated Place)	3-A	53,929	48,778	10.6
738	Brentwood, NY (Census Designated Place)	◇	53,917	45,218	19.2
739	Margate, FL (Incorporated Place)	◇	53,909	42,985	25.4
740	Catalina Foothills, AZ (Census Designated Place)	◇	53,794	(d)	(d)
741	St. John, IN (Minor Civil Division-Township)	◇	53,701	41,782	28.5
742	Rosemead, CA (Incorporated Place)	4-S	53,505	51,638	3.6
743	Charleston, WV (Incorporated Place)	2-A	53,421	57,287	-6.7
744	Palos, IL (Minor Civil Division-Township)	◇	53,419	50,916	4.9
745	Battle Creek, MI (Incorporated Place)	3-A	53,364	53,540	-0.3
746	Dundee, IL (Minor Civil Division-Township)	◇	53,207	39,070	36.2
747	Hacienda Heights, CA (Census Designated Place)	◇	53,122	52,354	1.5
748	Monroe, LA (Incorporated Place)	3-AA	53,107	54,909	-3.3
749	White Plains, NY (Incorporated Place)	2-S	53,077	48,718	8.9
750	Levittown, NY (Census Designated Place)	◇	53,067	53,286	-0.4
751	Arcadia, CA (Incorporated Place)	3-Sm	53,054	48,290	9.9
752	Shoreline, WA (Incorporated Place)	◇	53,025	46,979	12.9
753	Cheyenne, WY (Incorporated Place)	3-A	53,011	50,008	6.0
754	Washington, OH (Minor Civil Division-Township)	◇	52,991	46,609	13.7
755	Santee, CA (Incorporated Place)	◇	52,975	52,902	0.1
756	Missouri City, TX (Incorporated Place)	◇	52,913	36,176	46.3
757	Flagstaff, AZ (Incorporated Place)	3-A	52,894	45,857	15.3
758	Springfield, OR (Incorporated Place)	3-B	52,864	44,683	18.3
759	Frederick, MD (Incorporated Place)	3-C	52,767	40,148	31.4
760	Euclid, OH (Incorporated Place)	3-S	52,717	54,875	-3.9
761	Sarasota, FL (Incorporated Place)	2-A	52,715	50,961	3.4
762	Gaithersburg, MD (Incorporated Place)	3-S	52,613	39,542	33.1
763	Oak Park, IL (Incorporated Place)	4-S	52,524	53,648	-2.1
764	Oak Park, IL (Minor Civil Division-Township)	◇	52,524	53,648	-2.1
765	Carson City, NV (Independent City)	4-C	52,457	40,443	29.7
766	West Haven, CT (Incorporated Place)	4-S	52,360	54,021	-3.1
767	West Haven, CT (Minor Civil Division-Town)	◇	52,360	54,021	-3.1
768	Irondequoit, NY (Census Designated Place)	◇	52,354	52,322	0.1
769	Irondequoit, NY (Minor Civil Division-Town)	◇	52,354	52,322	0.1
770	Milford, CT (Minor Civil Division-Town)	◇	52,305	49,938	4.7
771	Millcreek, PA (Minor Civil Division-Township)	4-Sm	52,129	46,820	11.3
772	Bend, OR (Incorporated Place)	3-A	52,029	20,447	154.5
773	Plain, OH (Minor Civil Division-Township)	◇	51,997	49,181	5.7
774	Harrison, IN (Minor Civil Division-Township)	◇	51,898	53,810	-3.6
775	Folsom, CA (Incorporated Place)	◇	51,884	29,802	74.1
776	Elkhart, IN (Incorporated Place)	3-A	51,874	43,627	18.9
777	Nampa, ID (Incorporated Place)	3-B	51,867	28,365	82.9
778	La Crosse, WI (Incorporated Place)	3-AA	51,818	51,003	1.6
779	Towson, MD (Census Designated Place)	◇	51,793	49,445	4.7
780	Rio Rancho, NM (Incorporated Place)	◇	51,765	32,505	59.3
781	Plymouth, MA (Minor Civil Division-Town)	◇	51,701	45,608	13.4
782	Redford, MI (Census Designated Place)	◇	51,622	(d)	(d)
783	Redford, MI (Minor Civil Division-Charter Township)	◇	51,622	54,387	-5.1
784	Middletown, OH (Incorporated Place)	3-C	51,605	46,022	12.1
785	Cerritos, CA (Incorporated Place)	3-Sm	51,488	53,240	-3.3
786	Huntington, WV (Incorporated Place)	2-A	51,475	54,844	-6.1
787	Pocatello, ID (Incorporated Place)	3-A	51,466	46,080	11.7
788	Saint Peters, MO (Incorporated Place)	◇	51,381	45,779	12.2
789	Minnetonka, MN (Incorporated Place)	3-Sm	51,301	48,370	6.1
790	Wabash, IN (Minor Civil Division-Township)	◇	51,261	49,348	3.9
791	Orland Park, IL (Incorporated Place)	3-Sm	51,077	35,720	43.0
792	Franklin, NJ (Minor Civil Division-Township)	◇	50,903	42,780	19.0
793	Sheboygan, WI (Incorporated Place)	3-A	50,792	49,676	2.2
794	Ames, IA (Incorporated Place)	3-C	50,731	47,198	7.5
795	Idaho Falls, ID (Incorporated Place)	3-A	50,730	43,929	15.5
796	Flower Mound, TX (Incorporated Place)	◇	50,702	15,527	226.5
797	Parsippany-Troy Hills, NJ (Minor Civil Division-Township)	4-S	50,649	48,478	4.5
798	Biloxi, MS (Incorporated Place)	3-AA	50,644	46,319	9.3
799	Loveland, CO (Incorporated Place)	4-B	50,608	37,352	35.5
800	Milford, CT (Incorporated Place)	3-S	50,594	48,168	5.0
801	Cupertino, CA (Incorporated Place)	3-Sm	50,546	40,263	25.5
802	Florissant, MO (Incorporated Place)	4-S	50,497	51,206	-1.4
803	Piscataway, NJ (Minor Civil Division-Township)	◇	50,482	(d)	(d)
804	Macomb, MI (Minor Civil Division-Township)	◇	50,478	22,714	122.2
805	Maple Grove, MN (Incorporated Place)	◇	50,365	38,736	30.0
806	Mentor, OH (Incorporated Place)	3-Sm	50,278	47,358	6.2
807	Bowie, MD (Incorporated Place)	◇	50,269	37,589	33.7
808	Aspen Hill, MD (Census Designated Place)	◇	50,228	45,494	10.4
809	Renton, WA (Incorporated Place)	3-S	50,052	41,688	20.1
810	Stratford, CT (Census Designated Place)	◇	49,976	49,389	1.2
811	Stratford, CT (Minor Civil Division-Town)	4-S	49,976	49,389	1.2
812	Fairfield, IN (Minor Civil Division-Township)	◇	49,970	46,166	8.2
813	Cleveland Heights, OH (Incorporated Place)	4-S	49,958	54,052	-7.6
814	San Clemente, CA (Incorporated Place)	◇	49,936	41,100	21.5
815	Rock Hill, SC (Incorporated Place)	3-C	49,765	41,610	19.6
816	Carmichael, CA (Census Designated Place)	◇	49,742	48,702	2.1
817	St. George, UT (Incorporated Place)	4-A	49,663	28,502	74.2
818	Casper, WY (Incorporated Place)	3-A	49,644	46,742	6.2
819	East Hartford, CT (Census Designated Place)	◇	49,575	50,452	-1.7
820	East Hartford, CT (Minor Civil Division-Town)	4-S	49,575	50,452	-1.7
821	Altoona, PA (Incorporated Place)	3-AA	49,523	51,881	-4.5
822	Bradenton, FL (Incorporated Place)	3-B	49,504	43,779	13.1
823	Hoffman Estates, IL (Incorporated Place)	◇	49,495	46,561	6.3
824	Glendora, CA (Incorporated Place)	4-S	49,415	47,828	3.3
825	Cuyahoga Falls, OH (Incorporated Place)	4-S	49,374	48,950	0.9
826	Mansfield, OH (Incorporated Place)	3-AA	49,346	50,627	-2.5
827	Corvallis, OR (Incorporated Place)	3-B	49,322	44,757	10.2
828	Grand Forks, ND (Incorporated Place)	3-A	49,321	49,425	-0.2
829	Bowling Green, KY (Incorporated Place)	3-A	49,296	40,641	21.3
830	Weston, FL (Incorporated Place)	◇	49,286	(d)	(d)
831	Manteca, CA (Incorporated Place)	◇	49,258	40,773	20.8
832	Ypsilanti, MI (Minor Civil Division-Charter Township)	◇	49,182	45,307	8.6
833	Troy, NY (Incorporated Place)	3-C	49,170	54,269	-9.4
834	Woodland, CA (Incorporated Place)	4-C	49,151	39,802	23.5
835	Indio, CA (Incorporated Place)	3-C	49,116	36,793	33.5
836	Harrisburg, PA (Incorporated Place)	2-AA	48,950	52,376	-6.5
837	Libertyville, IL (Minor Civil Division-Township)	◇	48,904	42,436	15.2
838	Howell, NJ (Minor Civil Division-Township)	◇	48,903	38,987	25.4
839	Warner Robins, GA (Incorporated Place)	4-B	48,804	43,726	11.6
840	Downers Grove, IL (Incorporated Place)	4-S	48,724	46,858	4.0
841	Chapel Hill, NC (Incorporated Place)	3-C	48,715	38,719	25.8
842	East Providence, RI (Incorporated Place)	4-S	48,688	50,380	-3.4
843	Centreville, VA (Census Designated Place)	◇	48,661	26,585	83.0
844	New Brunswick, NJ (Incorporated Place)	3-S	48,573	41,711	16.5
845	Rowland Heights, CA (Census Designated Place)	◇	48,553	42,647	13.8
846	Haverford, PA (Minor Civil Division-Township)	◇	48,498	49,848	-2.7
847	New Albany, IN (Minor Civil Division-Township)	◇	48,476	44,958	7.8
848	Edinburg, TX (Incorporated Place)	4-C	48,465	29,885	62.2
849	Danville, VA (Independent City)	3-A	48,411	53,056	-8.8
850	Tinley Park, IL (Incorporated Place)	◇	48,401	37,121	30.4
851	Fort Myers, FL (Incorporated Place)	2-A	48,208	45,206	6.6
852	Peabody, MA (Incorporated Place)	3-Sm	48,129	47,039	2.3
853	Roseville, MI (Incorporated Place)	3-S	48,129	51,412	-6.4
854	Blue Springs, MO (Incorporated Place)	4-S	48,080	40,153	19.7
855	Poway, CA (Incorporated Place)	◇	48,044	43,516	10.4
856	Shawnee, KS (Incorporated Place)	◇	47,996	37,993	26.3
857	Plainfield, NJ (Incorporated Place)	4-S	47,829	46,567	2.7
858	Barnstable, MA (Incorporated Place)	◇	47,821	40,949	16.8
859	Kissimmee, FL (Incorporated Place)	4-C	47,814	30,050	59.1
860	Orangetown, NY (Minor Civil Division-Town)	◇	47,711	46,742	2.1
861	Bloomfield, NJ (Census Designated Place)	◇	47,683	45,061	5.8
862	Bloomfield, NJ (Minor Civil Division-Township)	4-S	47,683	45,061	5.8
863	Colton, CA (Incorporated Place)	◇	47,662	40,213	18.5
864	Novato, CA (Incorporated Place)	◇	47,630	47,585	0.1
865	Center, IN (Minor Civil Division-Township)	◇	47,619	47,354	0.6
866	Mount Pleasant, SC (Incorporated Place)	◇	47,609	30,108	58.1
867	Edina, MN (Incorporated Place)	3-SSm	47,425	46,070	2.9
868	Rockville, MD (Incorporated Place)	3-SS	47,388	44,835	5.7
869	Novi, MI (Incorporated Place)	3-Sm	47,386	32,998	43.6
870	Binghamton, NY (Incorporated Place)	3-AA	47,380	53,008	-10.6
871	The Hammocks, FL (Census Designated Place)	◇	47,379	(d)	(d)
872	Perth Amboy, NJ (Incorporated Place)	4-S	47,303	41,967	12.7
873	Revere, MA (Incorporated Place)	◇	47,283	42,786	10.5
874	Wauwatosa, WI (Incorporated Place)	3-S	47,271	49,366	-4.2
875	Rancho Santa Margarita, CA (Incorporated Place)	◇	47,214	11,390	314.5
876	Bedford, TX (Incorporated Place)	◇	47,152	43,762	7.7
877	Washington, NJ (Minor Civil Division-Township)	◇	47,114	41,960	12.3
878	Enid, OK (Incorporated Place)	3-A	47,045	45,309	3.8
879	Covina, CA (Incorporated Place)	3-S	46,837	43,207	8.4
880	Warren, OH (Incorporated Place)	3-B	46,832	50,793	-7.8
881	Penn Hills, PA (Census Designated Place)	◇	46,809	51,430	-9.0
882	Penn Hills, PA (Minor Civil Division-Township)	◇	46,809	51,430	-9.0
883	Chesterfield, MO (Incorporated Place)	◇	46,802	38,630	21.2
884	La Mirada, CA (Incorporated Place)	4-S	46,783	40,452	15.7
885	East Brunswick, NJ (Census Designated Place)	◇	46,756	43,548	7.4
886	East Brunswick, NJ (Minor Civil Division-Township)	3-S	46,756	43,548	7.4
887	Pharr, TX (Incorporated Place)	4-S	46,660	32,921	41.7
888	Mishawaka, IN (Incorporated Place)	3-B	46,557	42,608	9.3
889	East Lansing, MI (Incorporated Place)	4-S	46,525	50,677	-8.2
890	Placentia, CA (Incorporated Place)	◇	46,488	41,259	12.7
891	Woodbury, MN (Incorporated Place)	◇	46,463	20,075	131.4
892	Port Charlotte, FL (Census Designated Place)	◇	46,451	41,535	11.8
893	West Des Moines, IA (Incorporated Place)	4-Sm	46,403	31,702	46.4
894	Alexandria, LA (Incorporated Place)	3-AA	46,342	49,188	-5.8
895	Newark, OH (Incorporated Place)	3-C	46,279	44,389	4.3
896	Cypress, CA (Incorporated Place)	◇	46,229	42,655	8.4
897	O'Fallon, MO (Incorporated Place)	◇	46,169	18,698	146.9
898	Kokomo, IN (Incorporated Place)	3-A	46,113	44,962	2.6
899	Perinton, NY (Minor Civil Division-Town)	◇	46,090	43,015	7.1
900	Euless, TX (Incorporated Place)	◇	46,005	38,149	20.6
901	Ocala, FL (Incorporated Place)	3-AA	45,943	42,045	9.3
902	West Seneca, NY (Census Designated Place)	◇	45,943	47,866	-4.0
903	West Seneca, NY (Minor Civil Division-Town)	◇	45,920	47,866	-4.1
904	Port Orange, FL (Incorporated Place)	◇	45,823	35,317	29.7
905	Springdale, AR (Incorporated Place)	4-B	45,798	29,941	53.0
906	Pittsfield, MA (Incorporated Place)	3-A	45,793	48,622	-5.8
907	West New York, NJ (Incorporated Place)	4-S	45,768	38,125	20.0
908	Plainfield, IL (Minor Civil Division-Township)	◇	45,691	15,392	196.8
909	Salina, KS (Incorporated Place)	3-A	45,679	42,303	8.0
910	Pinellas Park, FL (Incorporated Place)	4-S	45,658	43,426	5.1
911	Normal, IL (Minor Civil Division-Township)	◇	45,637	40,449	12.8
912	Miami, OH (Minor Civil Division-Township)	◇	45,593	40,700	12.0
913	Apple Valley, MN (Incorporated Place)	◇	45,527	34,598	31.6
914	Joplin, MO (Incorporated Place)	3-A	45,504	40,961	11.1
915	League City, TX (Incorporated Place)	◇	45,444	30,159	50.7
916	Mission, TX (Incorporated Place)	◇	45,408	28,653	58.5
917	Normal, IL (Incorporated Place)	4-S	45,386	40,023	13.4
918	Roswell, NM (Incorporated Place)	3-A	45,293	44,654	1.4
919	Redmond, WA (Incorporated Place)	4-S	45,256	35,800	26.4
920	Kentwood, MI (Incorporated Place)	4-Sm	45,255	37,826	19.6
921	Enfield, CT (Minor Civil Division-Town)	4-S	45,212	45,532	-0.7
922	Winfield, IL (Minor Civil Division-Township)	◇	45,155	37,969	18.9
923	Kirkland, WA (Incorporated Place)	4-S	45,054	40,052	12.5
924	Charlottesville, VA (Independent City)	3-AA	45,049	40,341	11.7
925	West Orange, NJ (Census Designated Place)	◇	44,943	39,103	14.9
926	West Orange, NJ (Minor Civil Division-Township)	4-S	44,943	39,103	14.9
927	Blaine, MN (Incorporated Place)	4-Sm	44,942	38,975	15.3
928	Burlington, NC (Incorporated Place)	3-A	44,917	39,498	13.7
929	Marion, OH (Minor Civil Division-Township)	◇	44,908	43,564	3.1
930	Kingsport, TN (Incorporated Place)	3-AA	44,905	36,353	23.5
931	Portage, MI (Incorporated Place)	3-Sm	44,897	41,042	9.4
932	Manhattan, KS (Incorporated Place)	3-A	44,831	37,737	18.8
933	Potomac, MD (Census Designated Place)	◇	44,822	45,634	-1.8
934	Hattiesburg, MS (Incorporated Place)	3-A	44,779	41,882	6.9
935	San Ramon, CA (Incorporated Place)	◇	44,722	35,303	26.7
936	Azusa, CA (Incorporated Place)	◇	44,712	41,333	8.2
937	Highland, CA (Incorporated Place)	◇	44,605	34,439	29.5
938	Rowlett, TX (Incorporated Place)	◇	44,503	23,260	91.3
939	Lower Paxton, PA (Minor Civil Division-Township)	◇	44,424	39,162	13.4
940	Wilson, NC (Incorporated Place)	3-B	44,405	36,930	20.2
941	Bellevue, NE (Incorporated Place)	4-Sm	44,382	30,928	43.5
942	Wheatland, IL (Minor Civil Division-Township)	◇	44,349	10,746	312.7
943	Murrieta, CA (Incorporated Place)	◇	44,282	18,557	138.6
944	Watsonville, CA (Incorporated Place)	4-C	44,265	31,099	42.3
945	Sylvania, OH (Minor Civil Division-Township)	◇	44,253	39,983	10.7
946	North Highlands, CA (Census Designated Place)	◇	44,187	42,105	4.9
947	San Luis Obispo, CA (Incorporated Place)	3-A	44,174	41,958	5.3
948	Middletown, PA (Minor Civil Division-Township)	◇	44,141	43,063	2.5
949	St. Louis Park, MN (Incorporated Place)	4-S	44,126	43,787	0.8
950	Bell Gardens, CA (Incorporated Place)	◇	44,054	42,355	4.0
951	Tulare, CA (Incorporated Place)	◇	43,994	33,249	32.3
952	Portage, IN (Minor Civil Division-Township)	◇	43,956	40,929	7.4
953	Rye, NY (Minor Civil Division-Town)	◇	43,880	39,524	11.0
954	Strongsville, OH (Incorporated Place)	◇	43,858	35,308	24.2
955	Anderson, OH (Minor Civil Division-Township)	◇	43,857	39,939	9.8
956	Methuen, MA (Incorporated Place)	3-Sm	43,789	39,990	9.5
957	Freeport, NY (Incorporated Place)	4-Sr	43,783	39,894	9.7
958	Moline, IL (Incorporated Place)	3-B	43,768	43,202	1.3
959	Wayne, IN (Minor Civil Division-Township)	◇	43,742	44,743	-2.2
960	Valdosta, GA (Incorporated Place)	3-A	43,724	39,806	9.8
961	Coconut Creek, FL (Incorporated Place)	◇	43,566	27,485	58.5
962	Allen, TX (Incorporated Place)	◇	43,554	18,309	137.9
963	Southglenn, CO (Census Designated Place)	◇	43,520	43,087	1.0
964	West Babylon, NY (Census Designated Place)	◇	43,452	42,410	2.5
965	Shields, IL (Minor Civil Division-Township)	◇	43,382	43,414	-0.1
966	Covington, KY (Incorporated Place)	4-S	43,370	43,264	0.2
967	Tuckahoe, VA (Census Designated Place)	◇	43,242	42,629	1.4
968	Woonsocket, RI (Incorporated Place)	3-S	43,224	43,877	-1.5
969	Mount Pleasant, NY (Minor Civil Division-Town)	◇	43,221	40,590	6.5
970	Madera, CA (Incorporated Place)	◇	43,207	29,281	47.6
971	Conway, AR (Incorporated Place)	4-C	43,167	26,481	63.0
972	Middletown, CT (Incorporated Place)	3-S	43,167	42,762	0.9
973	Middletown, CT (Minor Civil Division-Town)	◇	43,167	42,762	0.9
974	Lakeville, MN (Incorporated Place)	◇	43,128	24,854	73.5
975	Wilkes Barre, PA (Incorporated Place)	3-BB	43,123	47,523	-9.3
976	Wallingford, CT (Minor Civil Division-Town)	4-S	43,026	40,822	5.4
977	Bloomfield, MI (Minor Civil Division-Township)	◇	43,023	42,137	2.1
978	Bloomfield Township, MI (Census Designated Place)	◇	43,021	42,137	2.1
979	Auburn, AL (Incorporated Place)	3-B	42,987	33,830	27.1
980	Bridgewater, NJ (Minor Civil Division-Township)	4-S	42,940	32,509	32.1
981	Grand Island, NE (Incorporated Place)	3-A	42,940	39,386	9.0
982	Buffalo Grove, IL (Incorporated Place)	◇	42,909	36,427	17.8
983	Jackson, NJ (Minor Civil Division-Township)	◇	42,816	33,233	28.8
984	Palm Springs, CA (Incorporated Place)	3-C	42,807	40,181	6.5
985	Poughkeepsie, NY (Minor Civil Division-Town)	◇	42,777	40,143	6.6
986	Elmhurst, IL (Incorporated Place)	4-Sr	42,762	42,029	1.7
987	Hackensack, NJ (Incorporated Place)	3-SS	42,677	37,049	15.2
988	Logan, UT (Incorporated Place)	4-A	42,670	32,762	30.2
989	Cathedral City, CA (Incorporated Place)	◇	42,647	30,085	41.8
990	Altadena, CA (Census Designated Place)	◇	42,610	42,658	-0.1
991	Boardman, OH (Minor Civil Division-Township)	◇	42,518	41,796	1.7
992	Olympia, WA (Incorporated Place)	3-A	42,514	33,840	25.6
993	Newark, CA (Incorporated Place)	◇	42,471	37,861	12.2
994	Arlington, MA (Census Designated Place)	◇	42,389	44,630	-5.0
995	Arlington, MA (Minor Civil Division-Town)	◇	42,389	44,630	-5.0
996	Union, OH (Minor Civil Division-Township)	◇	42,332	33,368	26.9
997	Lombard, IL (Incorporated Place)	3-Sm	42,322	39,408	7.4
998	Evesham, NJ (Minor Civil Division-Township)	◇	42,275	35,309	19.7
999	Coral Gables, FL (Incorporated Place)	3-S	42,249	40,091	5.4
1000	Rohnert Park, CA (Incorporated Place)	◇	42,236	36,326	16.3
1001	Fond du Lac, WI (Incorporated Place)	3-A	42,203	37,757	11.8
1002	DeKalb, IL (Minor Civil Division-Township)	◇	42,189	38,710	9.0
1003	Fairfield, OH (Incorporated Place)	4-S	42,097	39,729	6.0
1004	Attleboro, MA (Incorporated Place)	3-S	42,068	38,383	9.6
1005	Grapevine, TX (Incorporated Place)	◇	42,059	29,202	44.0
1006	St. Charles, IL (Minor Civil Division-Township)	◇	42,051	33,112	27.0
1007	Lockport, IL (Minor Civil Division-Township)	◇	42,048	32,336	30.0
1008	Grand Junction, CO (Incorporated Place)	3-A	41,986	29,255	43.5
1009	Lake Havasu City, AZ (Incorporated Place)	◇	41,938	24,363	72.1
1010	Glenview, IL (Incorporated Place)	4-Sr	41,847	37,052	12.9
1011	Franklin, TN (Incorporated Place)	◇	41,842	20,098	108.2
1012	Pine Hills, FL (Census Designated Place)	◇	41,764	35,322	18.2
1013	Beavercreek, OH (Minor Civil Division-Township)	◇	41,745	35,536	17.5
1014	Aloha, OR (Census Designated Place)	◇	41,741	34,284	21.8
1015	McHenry, IL (Minor Civil Division-Township)	◇	41,740	37,034	12.7
1016	Danville, CA (Incorporated Place)	◇	41,715	31,306	33.2
1017	Hanford, CA (Incorporated Place)	4-B	41,686	30,897	34.9
1018	Midland, MI (Incorporated Place)	3-C	41,685	38,053	9.5
1019	Georgetown, MI (Minor Civil Division-Charter Township)	◇	41,658	32,672	27.5

◇ Not classified as a Principal Business Center.

(d) Data not available.

Cities and Other Places of 35,000 or More, *Continued*

CITY RANK 2000	CITY, WITH PLACE TYPE	RANALLY CITY RATING	Population Census 4/1/00	Population Census 4/1/90	PER-CENT CHNG
1020	Greenville, MS (Incorporated Place)	3-A	41,633	45,226	-7.9
1021	Texas City, TX (Incorporated Place)	3-C	41,521	40,822	1.7
1022	Gilroy, CA (Incorporated Place)	◇	41,464	31,487	31.7
1023	Belleville, IL (Incorporated Place)	3-S	41,410	42,785	-3.2
1024	Belleville, IL (Minor Civil Division-Township)	◇	41,410	42,785	-3.2
1025	Leominster, MA (Incorporated Place)	3-B	41,303	38,145	8.3
1026	Bountiful, UT (Incorporated Place)	4-S	41,301	36,147	14.3
1027	Frankfort, IL (Minor Civil Division-Township)	◇	41,292	25,755	60.3
1028	Hicksville, NY (Census Designated Place)	◇	41,260	40,174	2.7
1029	Tigard, OR (Incorporated Place)	◇	41,223	29,344	40.5
1030	Yucaipa, CA (Incorporated Place)	◇	41,207	32,824	25.5
1031	Altamonte Springs, FL (Incorporated Place)	3-Sm	41,200	34,879	18.1
1032	Columbus, IN (Minor Civil Division-Township)	◇	41,194	37,466	10.0
1033	Palm Desert, CA (Incorporated Place)	◇	41,155	23,252	77.0
1034	Rancho Palos Verdes, CA (Incorporated Place)	◇	41,145	41,659	-1.2
1035	Moore, OK (Incorporated Place)	◇	41,138	40,318	2.0
1036	Lompoc, CA (Incorporated Place)	4-C	41,103	37,649	9.2
1037	La Puente, CA (Incorporated Place)	◇	41,063	36,955	11.1
1038	Chantilly, VA (Census Designated Place)	◇	41,041	29,337	39.9
1039	Bloomington, IN (Minor Civil Division-Township)	◇	41,032	42,156	-2.7
1040	Smyrna, GA (Incorporated Place)	3-S	40,999	30,981	32.3
1041	York, PA (Incorporated Place)	3-AA	40,862	42,192	-3.2
1042	Albany, OR (Incorporated Place)	3-B	40,852	29,540	38.3
1043	Hutchinson, KS (Incorporated Place)	3-A	40,787	39,308	3.8
1044	North Miami Beach, FL (Incorporated Place)	3-S	40,786	35,359	15.3
1045	Hilo, HI (Census Designated Place)	3-A	40,759	37,808	7.8
1046	Hempfield, PA (Minor Civil Division-Township)	◇	40,721	42,609	-4.4
1047	Concord, NH (Incorporated Place)	3-B	40,687	36,006	13.0
1048	Titusville, FL (Incorporated Place)	4-B	40,670	39,394	3.2
1049	Hendersonville, TN (Incorporated Place)	◇	40,620	32,188	26.2
1050	Bartlett, TN (Incorporated Place)	◇	40,543	26,989	50.2
1051	Atlantic City, NJ (Incorporated Place)	3-AA	40,517	37,986	6.7
1052	Kearny, NJ (Incorporated Place)	4-S	40,513	34,874	16.2
1053	Perry, IN (Minor Civil Division-Township)	◇	40,508	31,985	26.6
1054	Harrisonburg, VA (Independent City)	3-A	40,468	30,707	31.8
1055	Carol Stream, IL (Incorporated Place)	◇	40,438	31,759	27.3
1056	Salem, MA (Incorporated Place)	3-S	40,407	38,091	6.1
1057	Sayreville, NJ (Incorporated Place)	◇	40,377	34,986	15.4
1058	Quincy, IL (Incorporated Place)	3-A	40,366	39,682	1.7
1059	Quincy, IL (Minor Civil Division-Township)	◇	40,366	39,682	1.7
1060	Littleton, CO (Incorporated Place)	4-S	40,340	33,685	19.8
1061	Auburn, WA (Incorporated Place)	4-S	40,314	33,102	21.8
1062	Lenexa, KS (Incorporated Place)	4-Sr	40,238	34,034	18.2
1063	Bath, OH (Minor Civil Division-Township)	◇	40,231	38,277	5.1
1064	Mount Laurel, NJ (Minor Civil Division-Township)	◇	40,221	30,270	32.9
1065	North Fort Myers, FL (Census Designated Place)	◇	40,214	30,027	33.9
1066	Aliso Viejo, CA (Incorporated Place)	◇	40,166	7,612	427.7
1067	San Bruno, CA (Incorporated Place)	4-Sm	40,165	38,961	3.1
1068	Muskegon, MI (Incorporated Place)	3-AA	40,105	40,283	-0.4
1069	Lima, OH (Incorporated Place)	3-AA	40,081	45,549	-12.0
1070	Westfield, MA (Incorporated Place)	4-S	40,072	38,372	4.4
1071	Lincoln Park, MI (Incorporated Place)	4-S	40,008	41,832	-4.4
1072	Berkeley, NJ (Minor Civil Division-Township)	◇	39,991	37,319	7.2
1073	Meridian, MS (Incorporated Place)	3-A	39,968	41,036	-2.6
1074	Groton, CT (Minor Civil Division-Town)	◇	39,907	45,144	-11.6
1075	Pleasant, IN (Minor Civil Division-Township)	◇	39,901	28,094	42.0
1076	Beverly, MA (Incorporated Place)	4-S	39,862	38,195	4.4
1077	Holyoke, MA (Incorporated Place)	3-B	39,838	43,704	-8.8
1078	Catonsville, MD (Census Designated Place)	◇	39,820	35,233	13.0
1079	San Gabriel, CA (Incorporated Place)	4-S	39,804	37,120	7.2
1080	Southington, CT (Minor Civil Division-Town)	4-S	39,728	38,518	3.1
1081	Bel Air South, MD (Census Designated Place-Census Area Only)	◇	39,711	26,421	50.3
1082	Ela, IL (Minor Civil Division-Township)	◇	39,688	32,433	22.4
1083	Rock Island, IL (Incorporated Place)	3-C	39,684	40,552	-2.1
1084	Spartanburg, SC (Incorporated Place)	3-BB	39,673	43,467	-8.7
1085	Saginaw, MI (Minor Civil Division-Charter Township)	◇	39,657	37,684	5.2
1086	Sumter, SC (Incorporated Place)	3-A	39,643	40,977	-3.3
1087	Hobart, IN (Minor Civil Division-Township)	◇	39,636	38,942	1.8
1088	Jefferson City, MO (Incorporated Place)	3-A	39,636	35,481	11.7
1089	Porterville, CA (Incorporated Place)	4-B	39,615	29,563	34.0
1090	East Point, GA (Incorporated Place)	4-Sr	39,595	34,402	15.1
1091	Blacksburg, VA (Incorporated Place)	◇	39,573	34,590	14.4
1092	Edmonds, WA (Incorporated Place)	◇	39,515	30,744	28.5
1093	Linden, NJ (Incorporated Place)	4-S	39,394	36,701	7.3
1094	Northampton, PA (Minor Civil Division-Township)	◇	39,384	35,406	11.2
1095	Jupiter, FL (Incorporated Place)	◇	39,328	24,907	57.9
1096	Teaneck, NJ (Census Designated Place)	◇	39,260	37,825	3.8
1097	Teaneck, NJ (Minor Civil Division-Township)	4-Sr	39,260	6,233	529.9
1098	Clay, IN (Minor Civil Division-Township)	◇	39,145	31,033	26.1
1099	Richmond, IN (Incorporated Place)	3-A	39,124	38,705	1.1
1100	Meridian, MI (Minor Civil Division-Charter Township)	◇	39,116	35,644	9.7
1101	Fitchburg, MA (Incorporated Place)	3-B	39,102	41,194	-5.1
1102	Essex, MD (Census Designated Place)	◇	39,078	40,872	-4.4
1103	Calumet City, IL (Incorporated Place)	3-Sm	39,071	37,840	3.3
1104	Stillwater, OK (Incorporated Place)	4-A	39,065	36,676	6.5
1105	South Valley, NM (Census Designated Place)	◇	39,060	35,701	9.4
1106	Columbus, IN (Incorporated Place)	3-A	39,059	31,802	22.8
1107	Goldsboro, NC (Incorporated Place)	3-A	39,043	40,709	-4.1
1108	Henrietta, NY (Minor Civil Division-Town)	◇	39,028	36,376	7.3
1109	Lancaster, NY (Minor Civil Division-Town)	◇	39,019	32,181	21.2
1110	DeKalb, IL (Incorporated Place)	4-C	39,018	34,925	11.7
1111	Haltom City, TX (Incorporated Place)	◇	39,018	32,856	18.8
1112	Billerica, MA (Minor Civil Division-Town)	◇	38,981	37,609	3.6
1113	Gadsden, AL (Incorporated Place)	3-A	38,978	42,523	-8.3
1114	Montclair, NJ (Census Designated Place)	◇	38,977	37,729	3.3
1115	Montclair, NJ (Minor Civil Division-Township)	4-S	38,977	37,729	3.3
1116	Findlay, OH (Incorporated Place)	3-A	38,967	35,703	9.1
1117	McLean, VA (Census Designated Place)	◇	38,929	38,163	2.0
1118	Manchester, NJ (Minor Civil Division-Township)	◇	38,928	35,976	8.2
1119	Glen Burnie, MD (Census Designated Place)	◇	38,922	37,305	4.3
1120	Lawrence, IN (Incorporated Place)	◇	38,915	26,849	44.9
1121	Burlington, VT (Incorporated Place)	3-AA	38,889	39,127	-0.6
1122	Rogers, AR (Incorporated Place)	4-B	38,829	24,692	57.3
1123	Delano, CA (Incorporated Place)	◇	38,824	22,762	70.6
1124	Culver City, CA (Incorporated Place)	3-S	38,816	38,793	0.1
1125	Richland, WA (Incorporated Place)	3-B	38,708	32,315	19.8
1126	Ross, IN (Minor Civil Division-Township)	◇	38,685	34,683	11.5
1127	Stickney, IL (Minor Civil Division-Township)	◇	38,673	37,297	3.7
1128	Brookfield, WI (Incorporated Place)	3-Sm	38,649	35,184	9.8
1129	North Bethesda, MD (Census Designated Place)	◇	38,610	29,656	30.2
1130	North Atlanta, GA (Census Designated Place)	◇	38,579	27,812	38.7
1131	Hoboken, NJ (Incorporated Place)	4-S	38,577	33,397	15.5
1132	Cortlandt, NY (Minor Civil Division-Town)	◇	38,467	37,357	3.0
1133	Wausau, WI (Incorporated Place)	3-A	38,426	37,060	3.7
1134	State College, PA (Incorporated Place)	3-A	38,420	38,923	-1.3
1135	Pacifica, CA (Incorporated Place)	◇	38,390	37,670	1.9
1136	Muskogee, OK (Incorporated Place)	3-A	38,310	37,708	1.6
1137	Sun City, AZ (Census Designated Place)	◇	38,309	38,126	0.5
1138	Sanford, FL (Incorporated Place)	4-S	38,291	32,387	18.2
1139	Hanover Park, IL (Incorporated Place)	◇	38,278	32,918	16.3
1140	New Berlin, WI (Incorporated Place)	◇	38,220	33,592	13.8
1141	Wellington, FL (Incorporated Place)	◇	38,216	20,670	84.9
1142	Huber Heights, OH (Incorporated Place)	◇	38,212	38,696	-1.3
1143	Center, IN (Minor Civil Division-Township)	◇	38,186	32,603	17.1
1144	Campbell, CA (Incorporated Place)	4-S	38,138	36,048	5.8
1145	Shelton, CT (Incorporated Place)	◇	38,101	35,418	7.6
1146	Shelton, CT (Minor Civil Division-Town)	◇	38,101	35,418	7.6
1147	Montgomery Village, MD (Census Designated Place)	◇	38,051	32,315	17.8
1148	Everett, MA (Incorporated Place)	◇	38,037	35,701	6.5
1149	Kendall West, FL (Census Designated Place-Census Area Only)	◇	38,034	(d)	(d)
1150	Austintown, OH (Minor Civil Division-Township)	◇	38,001	36,740	3.4
1151	Crystal Lake, IL (Incorporated Place)	4-S	38,000	24,512	55.0
1152	Beavercreek, OH (Incorporated Place)	◇	37,984	33,626	13.0
1153	Webster, NY (Minor Civil Division-Town)	◇	37,926	31,639	19.9
1154	Farmington, NM (Incorporated Place)	3-A	37,844	33,997	11.3
1155	El Centro, CA (Incorporated Place)	3-A	37,835	31,384	20.6
1156	Fishers, IN (Incorporated Place)	◇	37,835	7,508	403.9
1157	Park Ridge, IL (Incorporated Place)	4-S	37,775	36,175	4.4
1158	Sierra Vista, AZ (Incorporated Place)	4-A	37,775	32,983	14.5
1159	Jackson, OH (Minor Civil Division-Township)	◇	37,744	32,071	17.7
1160	South Brunswick, NJ (Minor Civil Division-Township)	◇	37,734	25,792	46.3
1161	Carmel, IN (Incorporated Place)	◇	37,733	25,380	48.7
1162	Desoto, TX (Incorporated Place)	◇	37,646	30,544	23.3
1163	Pearland, TX (Incorporated Place)	◇	37,640	18,927	98.9
1164	New Albany, IN (Incorporated Place)	4-S	37,603	36,322	3.5
1165	Springfield, OH (Minor Civil Division-Township)	◇	37,587	38,509	-2.4
1166	Fort Pierce, FL (Incorporated Place)	3-A	37,516	36,830	1.9
1167	East Meadow, NY (Census Designated Place)	◇	37,461	36,909	1.5
1168	University City, MO (Incorporated Place)	◇	37,428	40,087	-6.6
1169	Chesterfield, MI (Minor Civil Division-Charter Township)	◇	37,405	25,905	44.4
1170	Stanton, CA (Incorporated Place)	◇	37,403	30,491	22.7
1171	Germantown, TN (Incorporated Place)	◇	37,348	32,893	13.5
1172	Bremerton, WA (Incorporated Place)	3-A	37,259	38,142	-2.3
1173	Woburn, MA (Incorporated Place)	3-S	37,258	35,943	3.7
1174	Hickory, NC (Incorporated Place)	3-A	37,222	28,301	31.5
1175	Boardman, OH (Census Designated Place)	◇	37,215	38,596	-3.6
1176	Cleveland, TN (Incorporated Place)	3-A	37,192	30,354	22.5
1177	Monrovia, CA (Incorporated Place)	4-S	36,929	35,761	3.3
1178	Kannapolis, NC (Incorporated Place)	3-C	36,910	29,709	24.2
1179	Cheltenham, PA (Minor Civil Division-Township)	4-S	36,875	34,923	5.6
1180	Chester, PA (Incorporated Place)	4-Sr	36,854	41,856	-12.0
1181	Bay City, MI (Incorporated Place)	3-B	36,817	38,936	-5.4
1182	Conroe, TX (Incorporated Place)	3-S	36,811	27,610	33.3
1183	Yuba City, CA (Incorporated Place)	3-A	36,758	27,437	34.0
1184	Bartlett, IL (Incorporated Place)	◇	36,706	19,373	89.5
1185	Hagerstown, MD (Incorporated Place)	3-A	36,687	35,445	3.5
1186	Bell, CA (Incorporated Place)	◇	36,664	34,365	6.7
1187	Hillsborough, NJ (Minor Civil Division-Township)	◇	36,634	28,808	27.2
1188	Miami, OH (Minor Civil Division-Township)	◇	36,632	28,199	29.9
1189	South Moline, IL (Minor Civil Division-Township)	◇	36,586	36,781	-0.5
1190	Minot, ND (Incorporated Place)	3-A	36,567	34,544	5.9
1191	Ossining, NY (Minor Civil Division-Town)	◇	36,534	34,124	7.1
1192	Kailua, HI (Census Designated Place)	4-S	36,513	36,818	-0.8
1193	New Braunfels, TX (Incorporated Place)	◇	36,494	27,334	33.5
1194	Parkway-South Sacramento, CA (Census Designated Place-Census Area Only)	◇	36,468	31,903	14.3
1195	Panama City, FL (Incorporated Place)	3-A	36,417	34,378	5.9
1196	Streamwood, IL (Incorporated Place)	◇	36,407	30,987	17.5
1197	Marlboro, NJ (Minor Civil Division-Township)	◇	36,398	27,974	30.1
1198	Cunningham, IL (Minor Civil Division-Township)	◇	36,395	36,344	0.1
1199	Urbana, IL (Incorporated Place)	4-B	36,395	36,344	0.1
1200	Spring, TX (Census Designated Place)	◇	36,385	33,111	9.9
1201	Valley Stream, NY (Incorporated Place)	4-S	36,368	33,946	7.1
1202	Commack, NY (Census Designated Place)	◇	36,367	36,124	0.7
1203	Rocklin, CA (Incorporated Place)	◇	36,330	19,033	90.9
1204	Yorktown, NY (Minor Civil Division-Town)	◇	36,318	33,467	8.5
1205	Jackson, MI (Incorporated Place)	3-AA	36,316	37,446	-3.0
1206	Country Club, FL (Census Designated Place)	◇	36,310	(d)	(d)
1207	Ormond Beach, FL (Incorporated Place)	◇	36,301	29,721	22.1
1208	North Brunswick, NJ (Census Designated Place)	◇	36,287	31,287	16.0
1209	North Brunswick, NJ (Minor Civil Division-Township)	◇	36,287	31,287	16.0
1210	Hurst, TX (Incorporated Place)	3-Sm	36,273	33,574	8.0
1211	Florence, AL (Incorporated Place)	3-AA	36,264	36,426	-0.4
1212	Marlborough, MA (Incorporated Place)	4-S	36,255	31,813	14.0
1213	Perris, CA (Incorporated Place)	◇	36,189	21,460	68.6
1214	Harlem, IL (Minor Civil Division-Township)	◇	36,171	28,453	27.1
1215	Marrero, LA (Census Designated Place)	◇	36,165	36,671	-1.4
1216	Cedar Falls, IA (Incorporated Place)	4-B	36,145	34,298	5.4
1217	Norwich, CT (Incorporated Place)	4-B	36,117	37,391	-3.4
1218	Norwich, CT (Minor Civil Division-Town)	◇	36,117	37,391	-3.4
1219	Merritt Island, FL (Census Designated Place)	◇	36,090	32,886	9.7
1220	Duncanville, TX (Incorporated Place)	4-Sr	36,081	35,748	0.9
1221	Woodlawn, MD (Census Designated Place)	◇	36,079	32,907	9.6
1222	Lakewood, NJ (Census Designated Place)	◇	36,065	26,095	38.2
1223	Greenwood, IN (Incorporated Place)	4-Sm	36,037	26,265	37.2
1224	Coppell, TX (Incorporated Place)	◇	35,958	16,881	113.0
1225	Belleville, NJ (Census Designated Place)	◇	35,928	34,213	5.0
1226	Belleville, NJ (Minor Civil Division-Township)	4-Sr	35,928	34,213	5.0
1227	North Chicago, IL (Incorporated Place)	◇	35,918	34,978	2.7
1228	Addison, IL (Incorporated Place)	4-S	35,914	32,058	12.0
1229	Avondale, AZ (Incorporated Place)	◇	35,883	16,169	121.9
1230	Martinez, CA (Incorporated Place)	◇	35,866	31,808	12.8
1231	Annapolis, MD (Incorporated Place)	3-C	35,838	33,187	8.0
1232	Mifflin, OH (Minor Civil Division-Township)	◇	35,787	28,449	25.8
1233	Beloit, WI (Incorporated Place)	3-B	35,775	35,573	0.6
1234	Atascocita, TX (Census Designated Place)	◇	35,757	(d)	(d)
1235	Hot Springs, AR (Incorporated Place)	3-A	35,750	32,462	10.1
1236	Pennsauken, NJ (Census Designated Place)	◇	35,737	34,738	2.9
1237	Pennsauken, NJ (Minor Civil Division-Township)	4-S	35,737	34,738	2.9
1238	West Hollywood, CA (Incorporated Place)	◇	35,716	36,118	-1.1
1239	Ewing, NJ (Minor Civil Division-Township)	◇	35,707	34,185	4.5
1240	Ewing, NJ (Census Designated Place)	◇	35,707	34,185	4.5
1241	Dunedin, FL (Incorporated Place)	◇	35,691	34,012	4.9
1242	Lewiston, ME (Incorporated Place)	3-A	35,690	39,757	-10.2
1243	Brighton, NY (Minor Civil Division-Town)	◇	35,588	34,455	3.3
1244	Brighton, NY (Census Designated Place)	◇	35,584	34,455	3.3
1245	Alamogordo, NM (Incorporated Place)	4-C	35,582	27,596	28.9
1246	White River, IN (Minor Civil Division-Township)	◇	35,539	28,232	25.9
1247	Greenfield, WI (Incorporated Place)	4-S	35,476	33,403	6.2
1248	Long Beach, NY (Incorporated Place)	◇	35,462	33,510	5.8
1249	Fort Lee, NJ (Incorporated Place)	◇	35,461	31,997	10.8
1250	Leavenworth, KS (Incorporated Place)	4-C	35,420	38,495	-8.0
1251	Brea, CA (Incorporated Place)	3-Sm	35,410	32,873	7.7
1252	Oxon Hill-Glassmanor, MD (Census Designated Place)	◇	35,355	35,794	-1.2
1253	Cape Girardeau, MO (Incorporated Place)	3-A	35,349	34,438	2.6
1254	Lancaster, OH (Incorporated Place)	3-C	35,335	34,507	2.4
1255	Marion, OH (Incorporated Place)	3-A	35,318	34,075	3.6
1256	Westerville, OH (Incorporated Place)	◇	35,318	30,269	16.7
1257	Seattle Hill-Silver Firs, WA (Census Designated Place-Census Area Only)	◇	35,311	(d)	(d)
1258	Oakville, MO (Census Designated Place)	◇	35,309	31,750	11.2
1259	Lake Oswego, OR (Incorporated Place)	◇	35,278	30,576	15.4
1260	Torrington, CT (Minor Civil Division-Town)	◇	35,202	33,687	4.5
1261	Torrington, CT (Incorporated Place)	4-C	35,202	33,687	4.5
1262	Manassas, VA (Independent City)	4-S	35,135	27,957	25.7
1263	Lake Worth, FL (Incorporated Place)	4-S	35,133	28,564	23.0
1264	Dana Point, CA (Incorporated Place)	◇	35,110	31,896	10.1
1265	Nunda, IL (Minor Civil Division-Township)	◇	35,104	24,759	41.8
1266	Sherman, TX (Incorporated Place)	3-A	35,082	31,601	11.0
1267	Chelsea, MA (Incorporated Place)	4-S	35,080	28,710	22.2
1268	Huntsville, TX (Incorporated Place)	4-C	35,078	27,925	25.6
1269	Severn, MD (Census Designated Place)	◇	35,076	24,499	43.2
1270	Palm Beach Gardens, FL (Incorporated Place)	◇	35,058	22,990	52.5
1271	Holland, MI (Incorporated Place)	3-C	35,048	30,745	14.0

◇ Not classified as a Principal Business Center.

(d) Data not available.

U.S. Colleges and Universities: Enrollment

NOTE: This list includes accredited four year colleges and universities with 300 or more students. The colleges and universitites are arranged in alphabetical order, by state. The city or town in which the college or university is located, or is associated with, appears in italic type. The student enrollment for each school is the last item in each entry. These figures are based primarily on Fall,1997 enrollment.

Alabama

Alabama Agricultural and Mechanical University, *Normal* ... 5,100
Alabama State University, *Montgomery* ... 5,300
Andrew Jackson University, *Birmingham* ... 300
Athens State College, *Athens* ... 2,700
Auburn University, *Auburn* ... 21,500
Auburn University at Montgomery, *Montgomery* ... 5,500
Birmingham Southern College, *Birmingham* ... 1,500
Concordia College, *Selma* ... 500
Faulkner University, *Montgomery* ... 2,400
Huntingdon College, *Montgomery* ... 700
Jacksonville State University, *Jacksonville* ... 7,600
Judson College, *Marion* ... 400
Miles College, *Fairfield* ... 1,300
Oakwood College, *Huntsville* ... 1,700
Samford University, *Homewood* ... 4,500
Southeast College of Technology, *Mobile* ... 600
Southern Christian University, *Montgomery* ... 350
Spring Hill College, *Mobile* ... 1,400
Stillman College, *Tuscaloosa* ... 1,000
Talladega College, *Talladega* ... 650
Troy State University - Main Campus, *Troy* ... 6,200
Troy State University at Dothan, *Dothan* ... 2,100
Troy State University at Montgomery, *Montgomery* ... 3,300
Tuskegee University, *Tuskegee* ... 3,000
University of Alabama, *Tuscaloosa* ... 18,300
University of Alabama at Birmingham, *Birmingham* ... 14,900
University of Alabama in Huntsville, *Huntsville* ... 6,500
University of Mobile, *Mobile* ... 2,100
University of Montevallo, *Montevallo* ... 3,100
University of North Alabama, *Florence* ... 5,600
University of South Alabama, *Mobile* ... 1,200
University of West Alabama, *Livingston* ... 1,900
Virginia College, *Birmingham* ... 750

Alaska

Alaska Pacific University, *Anchorage* ... 600
University of Alaska Anchorage, *Anchorage* ... 16,300
University of Alaska Fairbanks, *Fairbanks* ... 9,000
University of Alaska Southeast, *Juneau* ... 4,600

Arizona

Al Collins Graphic Design School, Ltd, *Tempe* ... 1,100
Arizona State University - Main Campus, *Tempe* ... 44,300
Arizona State University - West, *Phoenix* ... 4,800
Arizona State University - East, *Mesa* ... 1,100
Chaparral Career College, *Tucson* ... 400
Devry Institute of Technology, *Phoenix* ... 3,300
Grand Canyon University, *Phoenix* ... 2,200
IIT Technical Institute, *Phoenix* ... 400
Northern Arizona University, *Flagstaff* ... 19,600
Prescott College, *Prescott* ... 900
Thunderbird, The American Graduate School of International Management, *Glendale* ... 1,500
University of Arizona, *Tucson* ... 33,700
University of Phoenix, *Phoenix* ... 42,100
Western International University, *Phoenix* ... 1,200

Arkansas

Arkansas State University, *Jonesboro* ... 10,000
Arkansas Tech University, *Russellville* ... 4,200
Central Baptist College, *Conway* ... 350
Harding University, *Searcy* ... 4,100
Henderson State University, *Arkadelphia* ... 3,600
Hendrix College, *Conway* ... 1,000
John Brown University, *Siloam Springs* ... 1,400
Lyon College, *Batesville* ... 500
Ouachita Baptist University, *Arkadelphia* ... 1,600
Philander Smith College, *Little Rock* ... 900
Southern Arkansas University, *Magnolia* ... 2,700
University of Arkansas at Fayetteville, *Fayetteville* ... 14,300
University of Arkansas at Little Rock, *Little Rock* ... 11,000
University of Arkansas at Monticello, *Monticello* ... 2,200
University of Arkansas at Pine Bluff, *Pine Bluff* ... 3,000
University of Arkansas for Medical Sciences, *Little Rock* ... 1,900
University of Central Arkansas, *Conway* ... 9,000
University of the Ozarks, *Clarksville* ... 550
Williams Baptist College, *Walnut Ridge* ... 700

California

Academy of Art College, *San Francisco* ... 5,000
American Intercontinental University, *Los Angeles* ... 600
Armstrong University, *Oakland* ... 1,000
Art Center College of Design, *Pasadena* ... 1,300
Azusa Pacific University, *Azusa* ... 5,100
Bethany College, *Scotts Valley* ... 600
Biola University, *La Mirada* ... 3,400
Brook Institute, *Santa Barbara* ... 350
California Baptist University, *Riverside* ... 2,000
California College for Health Sciences, *National City* ... 9,000
California College of Arts and Crafts, *Oakland* ... 1,100
California College of Podiatric Medicine, *San Francisco* ... 350
California Institute of Integral Studies, *San Francisco* ... 1,000
California Institute of Technology, *Pasadena* ... 1,900
California Institute of the Arts, *Santa Clarita* ... 1,100
California Lutheran University, *Thousand Oaks* ... 2,600
California Maritime Academy, *Vallejo* ... 400
California Polytechnic State University-San Luis Obispo, *San Luis Obispo* ... 16,700
California School of Professional Psychology-Berkeley/Alameda, *Alameda* ... 750
California School of Professional Psychology-Fresno, *Fresno* ... 400
California School of Professional Psychology-Los Angeles, *Los Angeles* ... 700
California School of Professional Psychology-San Diego, *San Diego* ... 650
California State Polytechnic University-Pomona, *Pomona* ... 17,200
California State University-Dominguez Hills, *Carson* ... 12,500
California State University-Bakersfield, *Bakersfield* ... 5,600
California State University-Chico, *Chico* ... 15,200
California State University-Fresno, *Fresno* ... 18,100
California State University-Fullerton, *Fullerton* ... 24,900
California State University-Hayward, *Hayward* ... 12,900
California State University-Long Beach, *Long Beach* ... 27,800
California State University-Los Angeles, *Los Angeles* ... 19,200
California State University-Monterey Bay, *Seaside* ... 1,500
California State University-Northridge, *Los Angeles* ... 27,700
California State University-Sacramento, *Sacramento* ... 23,500
California State University-San Bernardino, *San Bernardino* ... 13,200
California State University-San Marcos, *San Marcos* ... 4,700
California State University-Stanislaus, *Turlock* ... 6,200
California Western School of Law, *San Diego* ... 700
Chapman University, *Orange* ... 3,900
Charles R. Drew University of Medicine and Science, *Los Angeles* ... 600
Christian Heritage College, *El Cajon* ... 650
Claremont Graduate School, *Claremont* ... 2,100
Claremont McKenna College, *Claremont* ... 1,000
Cleveland Chiropractic College of Los Angeles, *Los Angeles* ... 500
Cogswell Polytechnical College, *Sunnyvale* ... 600
Coleman College, *La Mesa* ... 800
College of Notre Dame, *Belmont* ... 1,800
Concordia University, *Irvine* ... 1,100
Devry Institute of Technology, *Long Beach* ... 1,800
Devry Institute of Technology-Pomona, *Pomona* ... 3,300
Dominican College of San Rafael, *San Rafael* ... 1,500
Emperor's College of Traditional Oriental Medicine, *Santa Monica* ... 400
Fresno Pacific University, *Fresno* ... 1,600
Fuller Theological Seminary, *Pasadena* ... 2,400
Golden Gate Baptist Theological Seminary, *Mill Valley* ... 1,000
Golden Gate University-San Francisco, *San Francisco* ... 7,000
Harvey Mudd Colege, *Claremont* ... 650
Holy Names College, *Oakland* ... 900
Hope International University, *Fullerton* ... 1,000
Humboldt State University, *Arcata* ... 7,500
Humphreys College, *Stockton* ... 700
ITT Technical Institute, *Anaheim* ... 700
ITT Technical Institute, *Rancho Cordova* ... 400
ITT Technical Institute, *San Bernardino* ... 600
ITT Technical Institute, *San Diego* ... 800
ITT Technical Institute, *Sylmar* ... 500
ITT Technical Institute of West Covina, *West Covina* ... 700
Institute of Transpersonal Psychology, *Palo Alto* ... 350
Interior Designers Institute, *Newport Beach* ... 500
John F. Kennedy University, *Orinda* ... 1,800
L.I.F.E Bible College, *San Dimas* ... 400
La Sierra University, *Riverside* ... 1,600
Life Chiropractic College-West, *San Lorenzo* ... 800
Lincoln University, *San Francisco* ... 300
Loma Linda University, *Loma Linda* ... 3,400
Los Angeles College of Chiropractic, *Whittier* ... 800
Loyola Marymount University, *Los Angeles* ... 6,900
Masters Institute, *San Jose* ... 1,000
Menlo College, *Menlo Park* ... 500
Mills College, *Oakland* ... 1,100
Monterey Institute of International Studies, *Monterey* ... 850
Mount Saint Mary's College, *Los Angeles* ... 2,000
National University, *San Diego* ... 13,300
Naval Postgraduate School, *Monterey* ... 1,400
New College of California, *San Francisco* ... 1,700
Northwestern Polytechnic University, *Fremont* ... 400
Occidental College, *Los Angeles* ... 1,600
Otis College of Art and Design, *Los Angeles* ... 750
Pacific College of Oriental Medicine, *San Diego* ... 350
Pacific Graduate School of Psychology, *Palo Alto* ... 300
Pacific Oaks College, *Pasadena* ... 700
Pacific Union College, *Angwin* ... 1,600
Pacifica Graduate Institute, *Carpinteria* ... 40
Palmer College of Chiropractic-West, *San Jose* ... 700
Patten College, *Oakland* ... 800
Pepperdine University, *Malibu* ... 7,800
Pitzer College, *Claremont* ... 900
Point Loma Nazarine College, *San Diego* ... 1,600
Pomona College, *Claremont* ... 1,600
Saint Mary's College of California, *Moraga* ... 4,200
Samra University of Oriental Medicine, *Los Angeles* ... 400
Samuel Merritt College, *Oakland* ... 700
San Diego Mesa College, *San Diego* ... 2,400
San Diego State University, *San Diego* ... 30,600
San Francisco Art Institute, *San Francisco* ... 700
San Francisco State University, *San Francisco* ... 27,000
San Francisco Theological Seminary, *San Anselmo* ... 800
San Jose Christian College, *San Jose* ... 350
San Jose State University, *San Jose* ... 26,500
Santa Clara University, *Santa Clara* ... 7,900
Saybrook Graduate School, *San Francisco* ... 350
School of Theology at Claremont, *Claremont* ... 400
Scripps College, *Claremont* ... 700
Simpson College, *Redding* ... 1,300
Sonoma State University, *Rohnert Park* ... 7,000
South Baylo University, *Anaheim* ... 650
Southern California College, *Costa Mesa* ... 1,300
Southern California College of Optometry, *Fullerton* ... 400
Southern California Institute of Architecture, *Santa Monica* ... 450
Southern California Institute of Technology, *Brea* ... 650
Southwestern University School of Law, *Los Angeles* ... 1,000
Stanford University, *Stanford* ... 16,500
The Advertising Arts College, *San Diego* ... 300
The Fielding Institute, *Santa Barbara* ... 1,100
The Master's College and Seminary, *Santa Clarita* ... 1,200
The National Hispanic University, *San Jose* ... 300
Thomas Jefferson School of Law, *San Diego* ... 600
United States International University, *San Diego* ... 1,300
University of California Hastings College of Law, *San Francisco* ... 1,200
University of California-Berkeley, *Berkeley* ... 30,300
University of California-Davis, *Davis* ... 24,300
University of California-Irvine, *Irvine* ... 17,300
University of California-Los Angeles, *Los Angeles* ... 34,800
University of California-Riverside, *Riverside* ... 10,000
University of California-San Diego, *San Diego* ... 15,100
University of California-San Francisco, *San Francisco* ... 3,500
University of California-Santa Barbara, *Santa Barbara* ... 18,900
University of California-Santa Cruz, *Santa Cruz* ... 10,600
University of La Verne, *La Verne* ... 6,000
University of Redlands, *Redlands* ... 3,500
University of San Diego, *San Diego* ... 6,700
University of San Francisco, *San Francisco* ... 7,800
University of Southern California, *Los Angeles* ... 28,300
University of West Los Angeles, *Los Angeles* ... 600
University of the Pacific, *Stockton* ... 5,600
Western State University College of Law - Fullerton, *Fullerton* ... 900
Western University of Health Sciences, *Pomona* ... 1,200
Westmont College, *Santa Barbara* ... 1,300
Whittier College, *Whittier* ... 2,100
Woodbury University, *Los Angeles* ... 1,000

Colorado

Adams State College, *Alamosa* ... 2,300
College for Financial Planning, *Denver* ... 4,600
Colorado Christian University, *Lakewood* ... 1,900
Colorado College, *Colorado Springs* ... 2,000
Colorado Institute of Art, *Denver* ... 1,700
Colorado School of Mines, *Golden* ... 3,200
Colorado State University, *Fort Collins* ... 22,300
Colorado Technical University, *Greenwood Village* ... 300
Colorado Technical University, *Colorado Springs* ... 1,700
Commonwealth International University, *Denver* ... 550
Denver Seminary, *Englewood* ... 500
Denver Technical College, *Denver* ... 1,600
Fort Lewis College, *Durango* ... 4,400
ITT Technical Institute, *Aurora* ... 350
Iliff School of Theology, *Denver* ... 300
Mesa State College, *Grand Junction* ... 4,700
Metropolitan State College, *Denver* ... 12,600
National Technological University, *Fort Collins* ... 1,500
Nazarene Bible College, *Colorado Springs* ... 950
Regis University, *Denver* ... 7,800
The Naropa Institute, *Boulder* ... 700
United States Air Force Academy, *United States Air Force Academy* ... 4,000
University of Colorado Health Sciences Center, *Denver* ... 2,400
University of Colorado at Boulder, *Boulder* ... 25,100
University of Colorado at Colorado Springs, *Colorado Springs* ... 6,500
University of Colorado at Denver, *Denver* ... 10,900
University of Denver, *Denver* ... 8,700
University of Northern Colorado, *Greeley* ... 11,900
University of Southern Colorado, *Pueblo* ... 5,000
Western State College, *Gunnison* ... 2,500
Westwood College of Technology, *Denver* ... 800

Connecticut

Albertus Magnus College, *New Haven* ... 1,500
Central Connecticut State University, *New Britain* ... 11,700
Charter Oak State College, *Hartford* ... 1,200
Connecticut College, *New London* ... 1,900
Eastern Connecticut State University, *Willimantic* ... 4,600
Fairfield University, *Fairfield* ... 5,200
Quinnipiac College, *Hamden* ... 5,500
Rensselaer at Hartford, *Hartford* ... 1,900
Sacred Heart University, *Bridgeport* ... 5,500
Saint Joseph College, *West Hartford* ... 1,900
Southern Connecticut State University, *New Haven* ... 11,400
Teikyo Post University, *Waterbury* ... 1,300
Trinity College, *Hartford* ... 2,000
United States Coast Guard Academy, *New London* ... 850
University of Bridgeport, *Bridgeport* ... 2,400
University of Connecticut, *Storrs* ... 21,200
University of Connecticut Health Center, *Farmington* ... 350
University of Hartford, *West Hartford* ... 7,100
University of New Haven, *West Haven* ... 5,000
Wesleyan University, *Middletown* ... 3,300
Western Connecticut State University, *Danbury* ... 5,400
Yale University, *New Haven* ... 11,100

Delaware

Delaware State University, *Dover* ... 3,300
Goldey Beacom College, *Sherwood Park* ... 1,600
University of Delaware, *Newark* ... 21,200
Wesley College, *Dover* ... 1,300
Widener University School of Law, *Widener University / Delaware Campus* ... 1,600
Wilmington College, *New Castle* ... 4,200

District of Columbia

American University, *Washington* ... 11,100
Catholic University of America, *Washington* ... 5,600
Corcoran School of Art, *Washington* ... 350
Gallaudet University, *Washington* ... 2,100
George Washington University, *Washington* ... 19,400
Georgetown University, *Washington* ... 12,500
Howard University, *Washington* ... 10,400
Joint Military Intelligence College, *Washington* ... 450
National Defense University, *Washington* ... 900
Southeastern University, *Washington* ... 800
Strayer University, *Washington* ... 9,400
Trinity College, *Washington* ... 1,500
University of the District of Columbia, *Washington* ... 4,800
Wesley Theological Seminary, *Washington* ... 700

Florida

Art Institute of Fort Lauderdale, *Fort Lauderdale* ... 2,300
Barry University, *Miami Shores* ... 7,200
Bethune Cookman College, *Daytona Beach* ... 2,500
Caribbean Center for Advanced Studies / Miami Inst Py, *Miami* ... 650
Christian International, *Santa Rosa Beach* ... 500
Clearwater Christian College, *Clearwater* ... 600
Eckerd College, *St. Petersburg* ... 1,500
Education America-Tampa Technical Institute, *Tampa* ... 1,200
Edward Waters College, *Jacksonville* ... 500
Embry-Riddle Aeronautical University, *Bunnell* ... 4,600
Flagler College, *St. Augustine* ... 1,700
Florida Agricultural and Mechanical University, *Tallahassee* ... 11,100
Florida Atlantic University, *Boca Raton* ... 21,000
Florida Baptist Theological College, *Graceville* ... 550
Florida Institute of Technology, *Melbourne* ... 4,100
Florida International University, *Miami* ... 30,000
Florida Memorial College, *Opa Locka* ... 1,700
Florida Metropolitan University Tampa College, Pinellas, *Clearwater* ... 900
Florida Metropoltan University-Fort Lauderdale College, *Fort Lauderdale* ... 600
Florida Southern College, *Lakeland* ... 2,700
Florida State University, *Tallahassee* ... 30,500
ITT Technical Institute, *Maitland* ... 350
ITT Technical Institute, *Tampa* ... 600
International Academy of Merchandising and Design, *Tampa* ... 600
International College, *Naples* ... 600
Jacksonville University, *Jacksonville* ... 2,200
Jones College Jacksonville, *Jacksonville* ... 1,000
Lynn University, *Boca Raton* ... 1,800
Nova Southeastern University, *Davie* ... 15,800
Orlando College, *Orlando* ... 1,900
Palm Beach Atlantic College, *West Palm Beach* ... 1,900
Reformed Theological Seminary, *Maitland* ... 700
Ringling School of Art and Design, *Sarasota* ... 900
Rollins College, *Winter Park* ... 3,400
Saint Leo College, *St. Leo* ... 7,400
Saint Thomas University, *Opa Locka* ... 2,200
Southeastern College of the Assemblies of God, *Lakeland* ... 1,100
Stetson University, *DeLand* ... 2,900
Tampa College, *Tampa* ... 1,000
Trinity International University, South Florida Campus, *Miami* ... 400
University of Central Florida, *Orlando* ... 28,300
University of Florida, *Gainesville* ... 41,700
University of Miami, *Coral Gables* ... 13,700
University of North Florida, *Jacksonville* ... 11,800
University of Sarasota, *Sarasota* ... 1,600
University of South Florida, *Tampa* ... 34,100
University of Tampa, *Tampa* ... 2,900
University of West Florida, *Pensacola* ... 8,100
Warner Southern College, *Lake Wales* ... 650
Webber College, *Babson Park* ... 450

Georgia

Agnes Scott College, *Decatur* ... 800
Albany State University, *Albany* ... 3,200
American Inter Continental University, *Atlanta* ... 1,100
Armstrong Atlantic State University, *Savannah* ... 5,700
Art Institute of Atlanta, *Atlanta* ... 1,600
Atlanta Christian College, *East Point* ... 300
Atlanta College of Art, *Atlanta* ... 400
Augusta College, *Augusta* ... 5,500
Berry College, *Mount Berry* ... 1,900
Beulah Heights Bible College, *Atlanta* ... 500
Brenau University, *Gainesville* ... 2,600
Brewton - Parker College, *Mount Vernon* ... 1,700
Clark Atlanta University, *Atlanta* ... 5,900
Clayton College and State University, *Morrow* ... 4,700
Columbia Theological Seminary, *Decatur* ... 600
Columbus State University, *Columbus* ... 5,400
Covenant College, *Lookout Mountain* ... 950
Devry Institute of Technology, *Alpharetta* ... 500
Devry Institute of Technology, *Atlanta* ... 2,900
Emmanuel College, *Franklin Springs* ... 800
Emory University, *Atlanta* ... 11,100
Fort Valley State College, *Fort Valley* ... 2,800
Georgia Baptist College of Nursing, *Atlanta* ... 350
Georgia College and State University, *Milledgeville* ... 5,500
Georgia Institute of Technology, *Atlanta* ... 13,100
Georgia School of Professional Psychology, *Atlanta* ... 350
Georgia Southern University, *Statesboro* ... 14,000
Georgia Southwestern State University, *Americus* ... 2,500
Georgia State University, *Atlanta* ... 24,300
Herzing College, *Atlanta* ... 400
Interdenominational Theological Center, *Atlanta* ... 400
Kennesaw State University, *Marietta* ... 13,100
La Grange College, *LaGrange* ... 1,000
Life University, *Marietta* ... 4,000
Luther Rice Seminary, *Lithonia* ... 1,500
Macon State College, *Macon* ... 3,600
Medical College of Georgia, *Augusta* ... 2,000
Mercer University, *Macon* ... 6,800
Morehouse College, *Atlanta* ... 3,000
Morris Brown College, *Atlanta* ... 2,200
North Georgia College and State University, *Dahlonega* ... 3,300
Oglethorpe University, *North Atlanta* ... 1,200
Paine College, *Augusta* ... 800
Piedmont College, *Demorest* ... 1,600
Reinhardt College, *Waleska* ... 1,000
Savannah College of Art and Design, *Savannah* ... 3,500
Savannah State University, *Savannah State College* ... 2,700
Shorter College, *Rome* ... 1,700
South College, *Savannah* ... 400
Southern Polytechnic State University, *Marietta* ... 3,900
Spelman College, *Atlanta* ... 1,900
State University of West Georgia, *Carrollton* ... 8,400
Thomas College, *Thomasville* ... 700
Toccoa Falls College, *Toccoa Falls* ... 1,000
University of Georgia, *Athens* ... 29,700
Valdosta State University, *Valdosta* ... 9,800
Wesleyan College, *Macon* ... 500

Hawaii

Brigham Young University-Hawaii Campus, *Laie* ... 2,300
Chaminade University of Honolulu, *Honolulu* ... 2,600
Hawaii Pacific University, *Honolulu* ... 8,400
University of Hawaii at Hilo, *Hilo* ... 2,700
University of Hawaii at Manoa, *Honolulu* ... 17,400
University of Hawaii at West Oahu, *Pearl City* ... 650

Idaho

Albertson College of Idaho, *Caldwell* ... 700
Boise State University, *Boise* ... 15,500
ITT Technical Institute, *Boise* ... 450
Idaho State University, *Pocatello* ... 11,900
Lewis-Clark State College, *Lewiston* ... 3,000
Northwest Nazarene College, *Nampa* ... 1,100
University of Idaho, *Moscow* ... 11,000

Illinois

Adler School of Professional Psychology, *Chicago* ... 400
American Academy of Art, *Chicago* ... 400
American School of Professional Psychology, *Chicago* ... 2,000
Augustana College, *Rock Island* ... 2,200
Aurora University, *Aurora* ... 2,100
Barat College, *Lake Forest* ... 800
Benedictine University, *Lisle* ... 2,600
Blackburn College, *Carlinville* ... 500
Bradley University, *Peoria* ... 5,900
Catholic Theological Union, *Chicago* ... 400
Chicago State University, *Chicago* ... 9,000
Columbia College, *Chicago* ... 8,500
Concordia University, *River Forest* ... 1,900
De Paul University, *Chicago* ... 17,800
Devry Institute of Technology, *Chicago* ... 3,500
Devry Institute of Technology, *Addison* ... 3,700
Dominican University, *River Forest* ... 1,800
Dr. William Scholl College of Podiatric, *Chicago* ... 400
East-West University, *Chicago* ... 600
Eastern Illinois University, *Charleston* ... 11,800
Elmhurst College, *Elmhurst* ... 2,800
Eureka College, *Eureka* ... 500
Finch University of Health Sciences-Chicago Medical School, *Chicago* ... 1,400
Garrett-Evangelical Theological Seminary, *Evanston* ... 500
Governors State University, *University Park* ... 6,100
Greenville College, *Greenville* ... 1,000
Harrington Institute of Interior Design, *Chicago* ... 400
Illinois College, *Jacksonville* ... 950
Illinois College of Optometry, *Chicago* ... 600
Illinois Institute of Art, *Chicago* ... 1,000
Illinois Institute of Technology, *Chicago* ... 6,100
Illinois State University, *Normal* ... 20,300
Illinois Wesleyan University, *Bloomington* ... 2,000
International Academy of Merchandising and Design, *Chicago* ... 800
John Marshall Law School, *Chicago* ... 1,300
Judson College, *Elgin* ... 950
Keller Graduate School of Management, *Chicago* ... 3,900
Kendall College, *Evanston* ... 500
Knox College, *Galesburg* ... 2,000
Lake Forest College, *Lake Forest* ... 1,200
Lake Forest Graduate of Management, *Lake Forest* ... 850
Lewis University, *Romeoville* ... 4,000
Lincoln Christian College and Seminary, *Lincoln* ... 900
Loyola University of Chicago, *Chicago* ... 13,600
Lutheran School of Theology at Chicago, *Chicago* ... 400
MacMurray College, *Jacksonville* ... 650
McCormick Theological Seminary, *Chicago* ... 500
McKendree College, *Lebanon* ... 1,800
Midwestern University, *Downers Grove* ... 1,300
Millikin University, *Decatur* ... 2,000
Monmouth College, *Monmouth* ... 1,000
Moody Bible Institute, *Chicago* ... 1,500
National College of Chiropractic, *Lombard* ... 900
National-Louis University, *Evanston* ... 7,100
North Central College, *Naperville* ... 2,700
North Park University, *Chicago* ... 2,100
Northeastern Illinois University, *Chicago* ... 10,200
Northern Baptist Theological Seminary, *Lombard* ... 350
Northern Illinois University, *DeKalb* ... 22,100
Northwestern Business College, *Chicago* ... 1,200
Northwestern University, *Evanston* ... 15,000
Olivet Nazarene University, *Bourbonnais* ... 2,300
Principia College, *Elsah* ... 550
Quincy University, *Quincy* ... 1,100
Robert Morris College, *Chicago* ... 3,600
Rockford College, *Rockford* ... 1,800
Roosevelt University, *Chicago* ... 6,600
Rush University, *Chicago* ... 1,500
Saint Augustine College, *Chicago* ... 1,100
Saint Xavier University, *Chicago* ... 4,000
School of the Art Institute of Chicago, *Chicago* ... 2,000
Southern Illinois University at Carbondale, *Carbondale* ... 21,900
Southern Illinois University at Edwardsville, *Edwardsville* ... 11,200
Trinity Christian College, *Palos Heights* ... 600
Trinity International University, *Bannockburn* ... 3,600
University of Chicago, *Chicago* ... 11,800
University of Illinois at Chicago, *Chicago* ... 25,500
University of Illinois at Urbana, *Urbana* ... 36,000
University of Saint Francis, *Joliet* ... 4,300
Western Illinois University, *Macomb* ... 12,200
Wheaton College, *Wheaton* ... 2,700

Indiana

Anderson University, *Anderson* ... 2,200
Ball State University, *Muncie* ... 18,500
Bethel College, *Mishawaka* ... 1,500
Butler University, *Indianapolis* ... 4,000
Calumet College of Saint Joseph, *Whiting* ... 1,000
Christian Theological Seminary, *Indianapolis* ... 400
Concordia Theological Seminary, *Fort Wayne* ... 350
De Pauw University, *De Pauw University* ... 2,300
Earlham College, *Richmond* ... 1,000
Franklin College of Indiana, *Franklin* ... 900
Goshen College, *Goshen* ... 1,000
Grace College and Theological Seminary, *Winona Lake* ... 700
Hanover College, *Hanover* ... 1,100
Huntington College, *Huntington* ... 800
ITT Technical Indianapolis, *Indianapolis* ... 900
ITT Technical Institute, *Fort Wayne* ... 650
Indiana Institute of Technology, *Fort Wayne* ... 1,500
Indiana State University, *Terre Haute* ... 10,800
Indiana University Bloomington, *Bloomington* ... 34,900
Indiana University at Kokomo, *Kokomo* ... 3,400
Indiana University at South Bend, *South Bend* ... 7,200
Indiana University-East, *Richmond* ... 2,300
Indiana University-Northwest, *Gary* ... 5,300
Indiana University-Purdue University at Fort Wayne, *Fort Wayne* ... 10,700
Indiana University-Purdue University at Indianapolis, *Indianapolis* ... 27,000
Indiana University-Southeast, *New Albany* ... 5,500
Indiana Wesleyan University, *Marion* ... 6,100
International Business College, *Fort Wayne* ... 800
Manchester College, *North Manchester* ... 1,100
Marian College, *Indianapolis* ... 1,400
Martin University, *Indianapolis* ... 700
Oakland City University, *Oakland City* ... 1,200
Purdue University Calumet, *Hammond* ... 9,300
Purdue University North Central Campus, *Westville* ... 340
Purdue University Main Campus, *West Lafayette* ... 35,700
Rose-Hulman Institute of Technology, *Terre Haute* ... 1,700
Saint Joseph's College, *Rensselaer* ... 950
Saint Mary's College, *St. Marys* ... 1,400
Saint Mary-of-the-Woods College, *St. Mary-of-the-Woods* ... 1,300
Taylor University-Fort Wayne, *Fort Wayne* ... 400
Taylor University-Upland, *Upland* ... 1,900
Tri-State University, *Angola* ... 1,300
University Of Indianapolis, *Indianapolis* ... 3,800
University of Evansville, *Evansville* ... 3,200
University of Notre Dame, *Notre Dame* ... 10,300
University of Saint Francis, *Fort Wayne* ... 1,600
University of Southern Indiana, *Evansville* ... 8,300
Valparaiso University, *Valparaiso* ... 3,600
Wabash College, *Crawfordsville* ... 800

Iowa

Briar Cliff College, *Sioux City* ... 1,000
Buena Vista College, *Storm Lake* ... 1,300
Central College, *Pella* ... 1,200
Clarke College, *Dubuque* ... 1,200
Coe College, *Cedar Rapids* ... 1,300
Cornell College, *Mount Vernon* ... 1,100
Dordt College, *Sioux Center* ... 1,300
Drake University, *Des Moines* ... 5,200
Faith Baptist Bible College and Seminary, *Ankeny* ... 400
Graceland College, *Lamoni* ... 1,300
Grand View College, *Des Moines* ... 1,400
Grinnell College, *Grinnell* ... 1,300
Hamilton Technical College, *Davenport* ... 350
Iowa State University, *Ames* ... 25,400
Iowa Wesleyan College, *Mount Pleasant* ... 800
Loras College, *Dubuque* ... 1,800
Luther College, *Decorah* ... 2,400
Maharishi University of Management, *Fairfield* ... 1,400
Marycrest International University, *Davenport* ... 800
Mercy College of Health Sciences, *Des Moines* ... 400
Morningside College, *Sioux City* ... 1,200
Mount Mercy College, *Cedar Rapids* ... 1,200
Mount Saint Clare College, *Clinton* ... 600
Northwestern College, *Orange City* ... 1,200
Palmer College of Chiropractic, *Davenport* ... 1,800
Saint Ambrose University, *Davenport* ... 2,800
Simpson College, *Indianola* ... 2,000
University of Dubuque, *Dubuque* ... 1,000
University of Iowa, *Iowa City* ... 27,900
University of Northern Iowa, *Cedar Falls* ... 13,100
University of Osteopathic Medicine and Health Sciences, *Des Moines* ... 1,300
Upper Iowa University, *Fayette* ... 4,100
Waldorf College, *Forest City* ... 700
Wartburg College, *Waverly* ... 1,500
William Penn College, *Oskaloosa* ... 900

Kansas

Baker University, *Baldwin City* ... 1,900
Benedictine College, *Atchison* ... 800
Bethany College, *Lindsborg* ... 700
Bethel College, *North Newton* ... 600
Emporia State University, *Emporia* ... 5,300
Fort Hays State University, *Hays* ... 5,600
Friends University, *Wichita* ... 2,700
Haskell Indian Nations University, *Lawrence* ... 800
Kansas State University, *Manhattan* ... 20,300
Kansas State University-Salina, College of Technology, *Salina* ... 700
Kansas Wesleyan University, *Salina* ... 700
McPherson College, *Mc Pherson* ... 500
Mid-America Nazarene College, *Olathe* ... 1,400
Newman University, *Wichita* ... 1,700
Ottawa University, *Ottawa* ... 2,700
Pittsburg State University, *Pittsburg* ... 6,200
Saint Mary College, *Leavenworth* ... 500
Southwestern College, *Winfield* ... 800
Sterling College, *Sterling* ... 500
Tabor College, *Hillsboro* ... 500
United States Army Command and General Staff College, *United States Army Command and General Staff College* ... 1,000
University of Kansas Main Campus, *Lawrence* ... 25,100
University of Kansas Medical Center, *Kansas City* ... 2,500
Washburn University of Topeka, *Topeka* ... 6,300
Wichita State University, *Wichita* ... 14,100

Kentucky

Alice Lloyd College, *Pippa Passes* ... 500
Asbury College, *Wilmore* ... 1,300
Asbury Theological Seminary, *Wilmore* ... 1,200
Bellarmine College, *Louisville* ... 2,200
Berea College, *Berea* ... 1,500
Brescia College, *Owensboro* ... 700
Campbellsville University, *Campbellsville* ... 1,600
Centre College, *Danville* ... 1,000
Cumberland College, *Williamsburg* ... 1,700
Eastern Kentucky University, *Richmond* ... 15,400
Georgetown College, *Georgetown* ... 1,600
Kentucky Christian College, *Grayson* ... 500
Kentucky State University, *Frankfort* ... 2,300
Kentucky Wesleyan College, *Owensboro* ... 800

U.S. Colleges and Universities: Enrollment, *Continued*

Lindsey Wilson College, *Columbia*	1,400
Midway College, *Midway*	700
Morehead State University, *Morehead*	8,200
Murray State University, *Murray*	8,800
Northern Kentucky University, *Highland Heights*	11,800
Pikeville College, *Pikeville*	750
Southern Baptist Theological Seminary, *Louisville*	1,800
Spalding University, *Louisville*	1,600
Sullivan College, *Louisville*	2,500
Thomas More College, *Crestview Hills*	1,400
Transylvania University, *Lexington*	1,000
Union College, *Barbourville*	1,000
University of Kentucky, *Lexington*	23,500
University of Louisville, *Louisville*	20,900
Western Kentucky University, *Bowling Green*	14,500

Louisiana

Centenary College of Louisiana, *Shreveport*	1,000
Dillard University, *New Orleans*	1,500
Grambling State University, *Grambling*	5,900
Grantham College of Engineering, *Slidell*	2,500
Louisiana College, *Pineville*	1,400
Louisiana State University Medical Center, *New Orleans*	2,900
Louisiana State University and Agricultural and Mechanical College, *Baton Rouge*	28,100
Louisiana State University-Shreveport, *Shreveport*	4,300
Louisiana Tech University, *Ruston*	9,500
Loyola University in New Orleans, *New Orleans*	5,300
McNeese State University, *Lake Charles*	8,100
New Orleans Baptist Theological Seminary, *New Orleans*	1,800
Nicholls State University, *Thibodaux*	7,200
Northeast Louisiana University, *Monroe*	10,900
Northwestern State University, *Natchitoches*	8,900
Our Lady of Holy Cross College, *New Orleans*	1,300
Our Lady of the Lake College, *Baton Rouge*	1,000
Southeastern Louisiana University, *Hammond*	15,300
Southern University and Agricultural & Mechanical College, *Baton Rouge*	9,800
Southern University at New Orleans, *New Orleans*	4,100
Tulane University, *New Orleans*	11,000
University of New Orleans, *New Orleans*	15,800
University of Southwestern Louisiana, *Lafayette*	17,000
Xavier University of Louisiana, *New Orleans*	3,500

Maine

Bates College, *Lewiston*	1,600
Bowdoin College, *Brunswick*	1,600
Colby College, *Waterville*	1,800
Husson College, *Bangor*	2,000
Main College of Art, *Portland*	300
Maine Maritime Academy, *Castine*	650
Saint Joseph's College, *Standish*	5,000
Thomas College, *Waterville*	900
Unity College, *Unity*	500
University of Maine, *Orono*	9,200
University of Maine at Augusta, *Augusta*	5,200
University of Maine at Farmington, *Farmington*	2,000
University of Maine at Fort Kent, *Fort Kent*	700
University of Maine at Machias, *Machias*	900
University of Maine at Presque Isle, *Presque Isle*	1,400
University of New England, *Biddeford*	2,500
University of Southern Maine, *Portland*	10,200

Maryland

Bowie State University, *Bowie*	5,200
Capitol College, *Kensington*	650
College of Notre Dame, *Baltimore*	3,100
Columbia Union College, *Takoma Park*	1,200
Coppin State College, *Baltimore*	3,500
Frostburg State University, *Frostburg*	5,200
Goucher College, *Towson*	1,400
Griggs University, *Silver Spring*	400
Hood College, *Frederick*	1,900
Johns Hopkins University, *Baltimore*	12,300
Loyola College in Maryland, *Baltimore*	6,200
Maryland Institute College of Art, *Baltimore*	1,500
Morgan State University, *Baltimore*	5,800
Mount Saint Mary's College, *Emmitsburg*	1,800
Ner Israel Rabbinical College, *Baltimore*	500
Peabody Institute of Johns Hopkins University, *Baltimore*	700
Saint John's College, *Annapolis*	500
Saint Mary's College of Maryland, *St. Marys City*	1,500
Salisbury State University, *Salisbury*	6,000
Sojourner-Douglas College, *Baltimore*	600
Towson State University, *Towson*	15,500
Uniformed Services University of the Health Sciences, *Bethesda*	700
United States Naval Academy, *Annapolis*	4,000
University of Baltimore, *Baltimore*	4,600
University of Maryland Baltimore, *Baltimore*	6,000
University of Maryland Baltimore County Campus, *Catonsville*	9,900
University of Maryland College Park Campus, *College Park*	32,700
University of Maryland University College, *College Park*	13,800
University of Maryland Eastern Shore, *Princess Anne*	3,200
Villa Julie College, *Stevenson*	2,000
Washington Bible College/Capital Bible Seminary, *Lanham*	400
Washington College, *Chestertown*	1,200
Western Maryland College, *Westminster*	2,800

Massachusetts

American International College, *Springfield*	1,900
Amherst College, *Amherst*	1,800
Andover Newton Theological School, *Newton*	500
Anna Maria College, *Paxton*	1,700
Art Institute of Boston, *Boston*	500
Assumption College, *Worcester*	2,600
Atlantic Union College, *South Lancaster*	600
Babson College, *Wellesley*	3,300
Bay Path College, *Longmeadow*	600
Becker College-Worcester, *Worcester*	600
Bentley College, *Waltham*	6,100
Berklee College of Music, *Boston*	2,900
Boston Architectural Center, *Boston*	650
Boston College, *Newton*	14,700
Boston University, *Boston*	29,400
Bradford College, *Haverhill*	600
Brandeis University, *Waltham*	4,300
Bridgewater State College, *Bridgewater*	8,900
Cambridge College, *Cambridge*	1,700
Clark University, *Worcester*	2,700
College of Our Lady of the Elms, *Chicopee*	1,100
College of the Holy Cross, *Worcester*	2,700
Curry College, *Milton*	1,400
Eastern Nazarene College, *Quincy*	1,400
Emerson College, *Boston*	3,000
Emmanuel College, *Boston*	1,600
Endicott College, *Beverly*	1,300
Fitchburg State College, *Fitchburg*	5,800
Framingham State College, *Framingham*	5,300
Gordon College, *Wenham*	1,300
Gordon-Cornwell Theological Seminary, *South Hamilton*	1,900
Hampshire College, *Amherst*	1,100
Harvard University, *Cambridge*	18,600
Hebrew College, *Brookline*	350
Lasell College, *Newton*	650
Lesley College, *Cambridge*	6,900
MGH Institute of Health Professions, *Boston*	550
Massachusetts College of Art, *Boston*	1,500
Massachusetts College of Liberal Arts, *North Adams*	1,700
Massachusetts College of Pharmacy and Allied Health Sciences, *Boston*	1,700
Massachusetts Institute of Technology, *Cambridge*	9,900
Massachusetts Maritime Academy, *Buzzards Bay*	800
Massachusetts School of Law, *Andover*	500
Merrimack College, *North Andover*	2,700
Mount Holyoke College, *South Hadley*	1,900
Mount Ida College, *Newton*	1,800
New England College of Optometry, *Boston*	400
New England Conservatory of Music, *Boston*	800
New England School of Law, *Boston*	950
Newbury College, *Brookline*	4,800
Nichols College, *Dudley Hill*	1,800
Northeastern University, *Boston*	24,300
Pine Manor College, *Brookline*	400
Radcliffe College, *Cambridge*	800
Regis College, *Weston*	1,300
Salem State College, *Salem*	9,200
School of the Museum of Fine Arts-Boston, *Boston*	700
Simmons College, *Boston*	3,600
Simon's Rock College of Bard, *Great Barrington*	350
Smith College, *Northampton*	3,200
Southern New England School of Law, *North Dartmouth*	400
Springfield College, *Springfield*	3,400
Stonehill College, *North Easton*	2,700
Suffolk University, *Boston*	6,400
The Boston Conservatory, *Boston*	550
The National Graduate School of Quality Management, *Falmouth*	1,500
Tufts University, *Medford*	8,400
University of Massachusetts at Amherst, *Amherst*	23,000
University of Massachusetts at Boston, *Boston*	11,800
University of Massachusetts at Dartmouth, *North Dartmouth*	6,400
University of Massachusetts at Lowell, *Lowell*	12,300
University of Massachusetts at Worcester, *Worcester*	700
Wellesley College, *Wellesley*	2,300
Wentworth Institute of Technology, *Boston*	3,100
Western New England College, *Springfield*	4,700
Westfield State College, *Westfield*	4,900
Wheaton College, *Norton*	1,400
Wheelock College, *Boston*	1,300
Williams College, *Williamstown*	2,000
Worcester Polytechnic Institute, *Worcester*	3,800
Worcester State College, *Worcester*	5,500

Michigan

Adrian College, *Adrian*	1,000
Albion College, *Albion*	1,600
Alma College, *Alma*	1,400
Andrews University, *Andrews*	3,200
Aquinas College, *Grand Rapids*	2,500
Baker College of Auburn Hills, *Auburn Hills*	1,100
Baker College of Cadillac, *Cadillac*	800
Baker College of Jackson, *Jackson*	850
Baker College of Mount Clemens, *Clinton*	1,200
Baker College of Muskegon, *Muskegon*	2,000
Baker College of Owosso, *Owosso*	1,900
Baker College of Port Huron, *Port Huron*	950
Baker College of Flint, *Flint*	4,300
Calvin College, *Grand Rapids*	3,800
Center for Creative Studies - College of Art and Design, *Detroit*	1,000
Central Michigan University, *Mount Pleasant*	24,700
Cleary College, *Ypsilanti*	650
Concordia College, *Ann Arbor*	550
Cornerstone College and Grand Rapids Baptist Seminary, *Grand Rapids*	1,700
Davenport College of Business, *Grand Rapids*	3,700
Detroit College of Business-Dearborn, *Dearborn*	6,400
Eastern Michigan University, *Ypsilanti*	22,700
Ferris State University, *Big Rapids*	9,500
Grand Valley State University, *Allendale*	15,700
Hillsdale College, *Hillsdale*	1,200
Hope College, *Holland*	2,900
Kalamazoo College, *Kalamazoo*	1,200
Kendall College of Art and Design, *Grand Rapids*	600
Kettering University, *Flint*	2,500
Lake Superior State University, *Sault Ste. Marie*	3,400
Lawrence Technological University, *Southfield*	4,200
Madonna University, *Livonia*	3,900
Marygrove College, *Detroit*	3,600
Michigan State University, *East Lansing*	42,600
Michigan Technological University, *Houghton*	6,300
Northern Michigan University, *Marquette*	7,800
Northwood University, *Midland*	6,100
Oakland University, *Rochester Hills*	14,400
Olivet College, *Olivet*	800
Rochester College, *Rochester Hills*	450
Saginaw Valley State University, *Bay City*	7,500
Saint Mary's College, *Orchard Lake*	350
Siena Heights College, *Adrian*	2,000
Spring Arbor College, *Spring Arbor*	2,400
Suomi College, *Hancock*	400
Thomas M. Cooley Law School, *Lansing*	1,600
University of Detroit Mercy, *Detroit*	6,900
University of Michigan-Ann Arbor, *Ann Arbor*	37,000
University of Michigan-Dearborn, *Dearborn*	8,300
University of Michigan-Flint, *Flint*	6,500
Walsh College of Accountancy and Business Administration, *Troy*	3,000
Wayne State University, *Detroit*	30,700
Western Michigan University, *Kalamazoo*	26,100
William Tyndale College, *Farmington Hills*	600

Minnesota

Augsburg College, *Minneapolis*	2,900
Bemidji State University, *Bemidji*	4,700
Bethel College, *St. Paul*	2,600
Bethel Theological Seminary, *St. Paul*	700
Carleton College, *Northfield*	1,900
College of Saint Benedict, *St. Joseph*	2,000
College of Saint Catherine, *St. Paul*	2,800
College of Saint Scholastica, *Duluth*	2,000
Concordia College at Moorhead, *Moorhead*	2,900
Concordia University, *St. Paul*	1,200
Crown College, *St. Bonifacius*	700
Gustavus Adolphus College, *St. Peter*	2,400
Hamline University, *St. Paul*	1,500
Luther Seminary, *St. Paul*	800
Macalester College, *St. Paul*	1,700
Mankato State University, *Mankato*	12,500
Martin Luther College, *New Ulm*	800
Metropolitan State University, *St. Paul*	5,500
Minneapolis College of Art Design, *Minneapolis*	600
Moorhead State University, *Moorhead*	6,500
North Central Bible College, *Minneapolis*	1,000
Northwestern College, *Roseville*	1,700
Northwestern College of Chiropractic, *St. Paul*	800
Saint Cloud State University, *St. Cloud*	14,100
Saint John's University, *Collegeville*	1,800
Saint Mary's University of Minnesota, *Winona*	5,100
Saint Olaf College, *Northfield*	2,900
Southwest State University, *Marshall*	3,100
The Graduate School of America, *Minneapolis*	400
University of Minnesota Twin Cities, *Minneapolis*	34,000
University of Minnesota at Duluth, *Duluth*	7,400
University of Minnesota at Morris, *Morris*	1,900
University of Minnesota-Crookston, *Crookston*	2,200
University of Saint Thomas, *St. Paul*	10,400
Walden University, *Minneapolis*	1,200
William Mitchell College of Law, *St. Paul*	1,000
Winona State University, *Winona*	6,700

Mississippi

Alcorn State University, *Lorman*	2,800
Belhaven College, *Jackson*	1,300
Blue Mountain College, *Blue Mountain*	500
Delta State University, *Cleveland*	4,000
Jackson State University, *Jackson*	6,300
Millsaps College, *Jackson*	1,400
Mississippi College, *Clinton*	3,500
Mississippi State University, *Mississippi State*	15,600
Mississippi University for Women, *Columbus*	3,300
Mississippi Valley State University, *Itta Bena*	2,200
Reformed Theological Seminary, *Jackson*	1,900
Rust College, *Holly Springs*	900
Tougaloo College, *Tougaloo*	900
University of Mississippi, *Oxford*	10,500
University of Mississippi Medical Center, *Jackson*	1,900
University of Southern Mississippi, *Hattiesburg*	14,600
William Carey College, *Hattiesburg*	2,100

Missouri

Avila College, *Kansas City*	1,200
Baptist Bible College, *Springfield*	900
Berean College, *Springfield*	1,000
Calvary Bible College, *Kansas City*	300
Central Bible College, *Springfield*	1,100
Central Methodist College, *Fayette*	1,300
Central Missouri State University, *Warrensburg*	10,300
Cleveland Chiropractic College, *Kansas City*	650
College of the Ozarks, *Point Lookout*	1,600
Columbia College, *Columbia*	7,800
Concordia Seminary, *Clayton*	500
Covenant Theological Seminary, *Creve Coeur*	900
Culver-Stockton College, *Canton*	1,000
Deaconess College of Nursing, *St. Louis*	300
Devry Institute of Technology, *Kansas City*	2,400
Drury College, *Springfield*	1,600
Evangel University, *Springfield*	1,600
Fontbonne College, *Clayton*	2,100
Hannibal-La Grange College, *Hannibal*	1,100
Harris-Stowe State College, *St. Louis*	1,700
ITT Technical Institute, *Earth City*	450
Kansas City Art Institute, *Kansas City*	600
Kirksville College of Osteopathic Medicine, *Kirksville*	600
Lincoln University, *Jefferson City*	3,000
Lindenwood University, *St. Charles*	4,800
Logan College of Chiropractic, *Chesterfield*	1,100
Maryville University of St. Louis, *Creve Coeur*	3,100
Midwestern Baptist Theological Seminary, *Kansas City*	700
Missouri Baptist College, *Creve Coeur*	2,400
Missouri Southern State College, *Joplin*	5,500
Missouri Valley College, *Marshall*	1,300
Missouri Western State College, *St. Joseph*	5,200
Northwest Missouri State University, *Maryville*	6,300
Ozark Christian College, *Joplin*	700
Park College, *Parkville*	8,400
Rockhurst College, *Kansas City*	2,800
Saint Louis College of Pharmacy, *St. Louis*	900
Saint Louis University, *St. Louis*	11,000
Saint Paul School of Theology, *Kansas City*	350
Southeast Missouri State University, *Cape Girardeau*	8,200
Southwest Baptist University, *Bolivar*	3,900
Southwest Missouri State University, *Springfield*	16,500
Stephens College, *Columbia*	800
Truman State University, *Kirksville*	6,400
University of Missouri-Columbia, *Columbia*	22,500
University of Missouri-Kansas City, *Kansas City*	10,400
University of Missouri-Rolla, *Rolla*	5,000
University of Missouri-Saint Louis, *Bellerive*	11,900
Washington University, *University City*	11,600
Webster University, *Webster Groves*	14,600
Westminster College, *Fulton*	700
William Jewell College, *Liberty*	1,500
William Woods University, *Fulton*	1,300

Montana

Carroll College, *Helena*	1,200
Montana State University, *Bozeman*	11,700
Montana State University-Billings, *Billings*	4,300
Montana State University-Northern, *Havre*	1,700
Montana Tech of the University of Montana, *Butte*	1,800
Rocky Mountain College, *Billings*	800
Salish Kootenai College, *Pablo*	1,000
The University of Montana, *Missoula*	12,100
University of Great Falls, *Great Falls*	1,200
Western Montana College, *Dillon*	900

Nebraska

Bellevue University, *Bellevue*	2,900
Chadron State College, *Chadron*	3,000
Clarkson College, *Omaha*	600
College of Saint Mary, *Omaha*	1,100
Concordia College, *Seward*	1,200
Creighton University, *Omaha*	6,300
Dana College, *Blair*	600
Doane College, *Crete*	1,800
Grace University, *Omaha*	500
Hastings College, *Hastings*	1,100
Midland Lutheran College, *Fremont*	1,000
Nebraska Methodist College of Nursing and Allied Health, *Omaha*	400
Nebraska Wesleyan University, *Lincoln*	1,700
Peru State College, *Peru*	1,900
Union College, *Lincoln*	650
University of Nebraska Medical Center, *Omaha*	2,600
University of Nebraska at Kearney, *Kearney*	7,100
University of Nebraska at Lincoln, *Lincoln*	22,800
University of Nebraska at Omaha, *Omaha*	13,700
Wayne State College, *Wayne*	3,800
York College, *York*	500

Nevada

Sierra Nevada College, *Incline Village*	600
University of Nevada-Las Vegas, *Paradise*	20,300
University of Nevada-Reno, *Reno*	11,800

New Hampshire

Colby-Sawyer College, *New London*	800
College for Lifelong Learning, *Durham*	2,500
Daniel Webster College, *Nashua*	700
Dartmouth College, *Hanover*	4,300
Franklin Pierce College, *Franklin Pierce College*	3,300
Franklin Pierce Law Center, *Concord*	400
Hesser College, *Manchester*	2,500
Keene State College, *Keene*	4,600
New England College, *Henniker*	700
New Hampshire College, *Manchester*	6,000
Notre Dame College, *Manchester*	1,300
Plymouth State College, *Plymouth*	3,800
Rivier College, *Nashua*	3,000
Saint Anselm College, *Pinardville*	2,000
University of New Hampshire, *Durham*	13,600
University of New Hampshire at Manchester, *Manchester*	750

New Jersey

Beth Medrash Govoha, *Lakewood*	2,200
Bloomfield College, *Bloomfield*	2,000
Caldwell College, *Caldwell*	1,800
Centenary College, *Hackettstown*	1,000
College of Saint Elizabeth, *Convent Station*	1,800
Drew University, *Madison*	2,300
Farleigh Dickinson University, *Teaneck*	8,900
Felician College, *Lodi*	1,100
Georgian Court College, *Lakewood*	2,300
Kean University, *Union*	11,500
Monmouth University, *West Long Branch*	5,300
Montclair State University, *Montclair*	12,800
New Jersey City University, *Jersey City*	8,500
New Jersey Institute of Technology, *Newark*	8,100
Princeton Theological Seminary, *Princeton*	750
Princeton University, *Princeton*	6,300
Ramapo College of New Jersey, *Mahwah*	4,700
Richard Stockton College of New Jersey, The, *Pomona*	6,000
Rider University, *Lawrenceville*	5,100
Rowan University, *Glassboro*	9,400
Rutgers the State University of New Jersey Camden Campus, *Camden*	5,000
Rutgers the State University of New Jersey New Brunswick Campus, *New Brunswick*	34,400
Rutgers the State University of New Jersey Newark Campus, *Newark*	9,300
Saint Peter's College, *Jersey City*	3,700
Seton Hall University, *South Orange*	9,500
Seton Hall University School of Law, *Newark*	1,200
Stevens Institute of Technology, *Hoboken*	3,200
The College of New Jersey, *Ewing Township*	6,800
Thomas Edison State College, *Trenton*	8,600
University of Medicine and Dentistry of New Jersey, *Newark*	3,300
Westminster Choir College of Rider University, *Princeton*	450
William Paterson University of New Jersey, *Wayne*	9,200

New Mexico

College of Santa Fe, *Santa Fe*	1,400
College of the Southwest, *Hobbs*	700
Eastern New Mexico University, *Portales*	3,500
New Mexico Highlands University, *Las Vegas*	2,500
New Mexico Institute of Mining and Technology, *Socorro*	1,400
New Mexico State University, *University Park*	15,100
Saint John's College, *Santa Fe*	400
University of New Mexico, *Albuquerque*	23,800
Western New Mexico University, *Silver City*	2,600

New York

Adelphi University, *Garden City*	5,600
Albany College of Pharmacy of Union University, *Albany*	650
Albany Law School of Union University, *Albany*	750
Albany Medical College, *Albany*	700
Alfred University, *Alfred*	2,300
Audrey Cohen College, *New York*	1,100
Bank Street College of Education, *New York*	900
Bard College, *Annandale-on-Hudson*	1,100
Barnard College, *New York*	2,300
Boricua College, *New York*	1,100
Brooklyn Law School, *New York*	1,500
Canisius College, *Buffalo*	4,600
Cazenovia College, *Cazenovia*	700
Central Yeshiva Tomchei Tmimin Lubavitz, *New York*	350
City University of New York Bernard Baruch College, *New York*	15,100
City University of New York Brooklyn College, *New York*	15,100
City University of New York City College, *New York*	12,100
City University of New York City Technical College, *New York*	11,200
City University of New York College of Staten Island, *New York*	12,000
City University of New York Graduate School and University Center, *New York*	4,000
City University of New York Hunter College, *New York*	19,700
City University of New York John Jay College of Criminal Justice, *New York*	10,900
City University of New York Lehman College, *New York*	9,400
City University of New York Medgar Evers College, *New York*	5,100
City University of New York Queens College, *New York*	16,500
City University of New York York College, *New York*	5,900
Clarkson University, *Potsdam*	2,700
Colgate University, *Hamilton*	2,800
College of Aeronautics, *La Guardia Airport*	1,100
College of Mount Saint Vincent, *New York*	1,600
College of New Rochelle, *New Rochelle*	7,100
College of Saint Rose, *Albany*	4,000
Columbia University in the City of New York, *New York*	21,100
Concordia College, *Bronxville*	600
Cooper Union, *New York*	900
Cornell University, *Ithaca*	18,400
Cornell University Medical Campus, *New York*	650
Culinary Institute of America, *Hyde Park*	2,100
D'youville College, *Buffalo*	1,800
Daemen College, *Amherst*	1,900
DeVry Institute of Technology, *New York*	500
Dominican College of Blauvelt, *Orangeburg*	1,700
Dowling College, *Oakdale*	6,700
Elmira College, *Elmira*	1,100
Fashion Institute of Technology, *New York*	11,700
Five Towns College, *Seaford*	600
Fordham University, *New York*	13,700
Hamilton College, *Clinton*	1,600
Hartwick College, *Oneonta*	1,500
Hilbert College, *Hamburg*	900
Hobart-William Smith Colleges, *Geneva*	1,800
Hofstra University, *Hempstead*	12,600
Houghton College, *Houghton*	1,400
Iona College, *New Rochelle*	4,900
Ithaca College, *Ithaca*	5,900
Jewish Theological Seminary of America, *New York*	650
Keuka College, *Keuka Park*	850
Le Moyne College, *De Witt*	3,100
Long Island University Brooklyn Campus, *New York*	8,000
Long Island University C W Post Campus, *Brookville*	8,200
Long Island University Southampton College, *Southampton*	1,600
Manhattan College, *New York*	3,000
Manhattan School of Music, *New York*	850
Manhattanville College, *Harrison*	1,800
Marist College, *Fairview*	4,600
Marymount College, *Tarrytown*	900
Marymount Manhattan College, *New York*	2,100
Medaille College, *Buffalo*	900
Mercy College, *Dobbs Ferry*	7,800
Mesivta Torah Vodaath Seminary, *New York*	400
Molloy College, *Rockville Centre*	2,300
Monroe College, *New York*	3,500
Mount Saint Mary College, *Newburgh*	2,100
Mount Sinai School Of Medicine, *New York*	500
Nazareth College of Rochester, *Pittsford*	2,800
New School University, *New York*	7,200
New York Chiropractic College, *Seneca Falls*	950
New York College for Wholistic Health Education and Research, *Syosset*	850
New York College of Podiatric Medicine, *New York*	450
New York Institute of Technology Manhattan Campus, *New York*	2,800
New York Institute of Technology-Old Westbury, *Old Westbury*	5,300
New York Law School, *New York*	1,400
New York Medical College, *Valhalla*	1,600
New York School of Interior Design, *New York*	650
New York State College of Ceramics at Alfred University, *Alfred*	800
New York Theological Seminary, *New York*	300
New York University, *New York*	36,600
Niagara University, *Niagara University*	3,100
Nyack College, *South Nyack*	1,400
Pace University-New York, *New York*	7,800
Pace University-Pleasantville Briarcliff Campus, *Pleasantville*	3,500
Pace University-White Plains Campus, *White Plains*	2,100
Paul Smith's College of Arts and Sciences, *Paul Smiths*	750
Polytechnic University, *New York*	3,400
Pratt Institute, *New York*	3,800
Rabbi Isaac Elchanan Seminary, *New York*	300
Rabbinical College Bobover Yeshiva Bnei Zion, *New York*	400
Regents College, University of the State of NY, *Albany*	17,400
Rensselaer Polytechnic Institute, *Troy*	6,400
Roberts Wesleyan College, *North Chili*	1,400
Rochester Institute of Technology, *Rochester*	13,200
Russell Sage College, *Troy*	1,000
Sage Graduate School, *Troy*	1,100
Saint Bonaventure University, *St. Bonaventure*	2,800
Saint Francis College, *New York*	2,100
Saint John's University, *New York*	18,500
Saint Joseph's College, *New York*	1,400
Saint Joseph's College Suffolk Campus, *Brentwood*	2,800
Saint Lawrence University, *Canton*	2,000
Saint Thomas Aquinas College, *Sparkill*	2,200
Sarah Lawrence College, *Yonkers*	1,400
School of Visual Arts, *New York*	5,200
Siena College, *Loudonville*	3,100
Skidmore College, *Saratoga Springs*	2,600
St. John Fisher College, *East Rochester*	2,200
State Purchase College, State University of New York, *Harrison*	3,300
State Univ. of N.Y. Col. of Agriculture & Technology at Cobleskill, *Cobleskill*	2,500
State Univ. of New York College of Environmental Science and Forestry, *Syracuse*	1,700
State University of New York College at Brockport, *Brockport*	8,500
State University of New York College at Buffalo, *Buffalo*	10,800
State University of New York College at Cortland, *Cortland*	6,300
State University of New York College at Fredonia, *Fredonia*	4,600
State University of New York College at Geneseo, *Geneseo*	5,600
State University of New York College at Old Westbury, *Old Westbury*	3,600
State University of New York College at Oneonta, *Oneonta*	5,400
State University of New York College at Oswego, *Oswego*	8,000
State University of New York College at Plattsburgh, *Plattsburgh*	5,900
State University of New York College at Potsdam, *Potsdam*	4,000
State University of New York College of Technology at Alfred, *Alfred*	2,900
State University of New York College of Technology at Farmingdale, *Farmingdale*	5,600
State University of New York Empire State College, *Saratoga Springs*	7,600
State University of New York Health Science Center at Brooklyn, *New York*	1,500
State University of New York Health Science Center at Stony Brook, *Stony Brook*	2,300
State University of New York Health Science Center at Syracuse, *Syracuse*	1,200
State University of New York Institute of Technology at Utica-Rome, *Utica*	2,500
State University of New York Maritime College, *New York*	800
State University of New York at Albany, *Albany*	16,100
State University of New York at Binghamton, *Binghamton*	12,200
State University of New York at Buffalo, *Buffalo*	23,400
State University of New York at New Paltz, *New Paltz*	7,600
State University of New York at Stony Brook, *South Stony Brook*	15,500
Syracuse University, *Syracuse*	18,400
Teachers College at Columbia University, *New York*	5,000
The College of Insurance, *New York*	400
The Juilliard School, *New York*	750
Touro College, *New York*	9,000
Union College, *Schenectady*	2,000
Union Theological Seminary, *New York*	400
United States Merchant Marine Academy, *Kings Point*	900
United States Military Academy, *West Point*	4,100
United Talmudical Academy, *New York*	1,600
University of Rochester, *Rochester*	8,500
Utica College of Syracuse University, *Utica*	2,000
Vassar College, *Arlington*	2,400
Wagner College, *New York*	2,000
Wells College, *Aurora*	300
Yeshiva University, *New York*	5,400
Yeshivath Viznitz, *Monsey*	400

North Carolina

Appalachian State University, *Boone*	12,100
Barber-Scotia College, *Concord*	500
Barton College, *Wilson*	1,300
Belmont Abbey College, *Belmont*	900
Bennett College, *Greensboro*	600
Brevard College, *Brevard*	700
Campbell University Inc., *Buies Creek*	6,000
Catawba College, *Salisbury*	1,300
Chowan College, *Murfreesboro*	800
Davidson College, *Davidson*	1,600
Duke University, *Durham*	11,600
East Carolina University, *Greenville*	17,800
Elizabeth City State University, *Elizabeth City*	1,900
Elon College, *Elon College*	3,700
Fayetteville State University, *Fayetteville*	3,900
Gardner-Webb University, *Boiling Springs*	3,000
Greensboro College, *Greensboro*	1,100
Guilford College, *Greensboro*	1,300
High Point University, *High Point*	2,700
Johnson C. Smith University, *Charlotte*	1,400
Lees-McRae College, *Banner Elk*	500
Lenoir-Rhyne College, *Hickory*	1,600
Livingstone College, *Salisbury*	900
Mars Hill College, *Mars Hill*	1,200
Meredith College, *Raleigh*	2,600
Methodist College, *Fayetteville*	1,700
Montreat College, *Montreat*	1,000
Mount Olive College, *Mount Olive*	1,600
North Carolina Agricultural and Technical State University, *Greensboro*	7,500
North Carolina Central University, *Durham*	5,700
North Carolina School of the Arts, *Winston-Salem*	1,000
North Carolina State University at Raleigh, *Raleigh*	27,500
North Carolina Wesleyan College, *Rocky Mount*	1,800
Peace College, *Raleigh*	500
Pfeiffer College, *Misenheimer*	1,800
Piedmont Baptist College, *Winston-Salem*	300
Queens College, *Charlotte*	1,700
Reformed Theological Seminary, *Charlotte*	400
Saint Andrew's Presbyterian College, *Laurinburg*	600
Saint Augustine's College, *Raleigh*	1,600
Salem College, *Winston-Salem*	1,000

U.S. Colleges and Universities: Enrollment, *Continued*

Shaw University, *Raleigh* 2,300
Southeastern Baptist Theological Seminary, *Wake Forest* 1,500
University of North Carolina at Asheville, *Asheville* 2,600
University of North Carolina at Chapel Hill, *Chapel Hill* 24,200
University of North Carolina at Charlotte, *Charlotte* 16,400
University of North Carolina at Greensboro, *Greensboro* 12,300
University of North Carolina at Pembroke, *Pembroke* 3,000
University of North Carolina at Wilmington, *Wilmington* 9,200
Wake Forest University, *Winston-Salem* 6,100
Warren Wilson College, *Swannanoa* 700
Warren Wilson College, *Swannanoa* 700
Western Carolina University, *Cullowhee* 6,500
Wingate College, *Wingate* 1,300
Winston-Salem State University, *Winston-Salem* 2,900

North Dakota

Dickinson State University, *Dickinson* 1,700
Jamestown College, *Jamestown* 1,100
Mayville State College, *Mayville* 700
Minot State University, *Minot* 2,900
North Dakota State University, *Fargo* 9,500
Trinity Bible College, *Ellendale* 300
University of Mary, *Bismarck* 2,100
University of North Dakota Main Campus, *Grand Forks* 10,400
Valley City State University, *Valley City* 1,100

Ohio

Air Force Institute of Technology, *Air Force Institute of Technology* 600
Antioch University, *Yellow Springs* 3,800
Ashland University, *Ashland* 5,600
Baldwin-Wallace College, *Berea* 4,500
Bluffton College, *Bluffton* 1,100
Bowling Green State University, *Bowling Green* 18,600
Capital University, *Bexley* 4,000
Case Western Reserve University, *Cleveland* 9,900
Cedarville College, *Cedarville* 2,600
Central State University, *Wilberforce* 1,100
Cincinnati Bible College and Seminary, *Cincinnati* 900
Cleveland College of Jewish Studies, *Beachwood* 1,400
Cleveland Institute of Art, *Cleveland* 500
Cleveland Institute of Music, *Cleveland* 350
Cleveland State University, *Cleveland* 15,700
College of Mount Saint Joseph, *Mount St. Joseph* 2,200
College of Wooster, *Wooster* 1,700
Columbus College of Art and Design, *Columbus* 1,100
David N. Myers College, *Cleveland* 1,100
Defiance College, *Defiance* 800
Denison University, *Granville* 2,000
Devry Institute of Technology, *Columbus* 2,900
Franciscan University of Steunbenville, *Steubenville* 2,000
Franklin University, *Columbus* 4,100
Heidelberg College, *Tiffin* 1,600
Hiram College, *Hiram* 1,100
John Carroll University, *University Heights* 4,400
Kent State University, *Kent* 20,700
Kent State University Stark Campus, *Canton* 2,600
Kenyon College, *Gambier* 1,500
Kettering College of Medical Arts, *Kettering* 500
Lake Erie College, *Painesville* 700
Lourdes College, *Sylvania* 1,400
Malone College, *Canton* 2,200
Marietta College, *Marietta* 1,300
Medical College of Ohio, *Toledo* 1,000
Miami University-Hamilton Campus, *Hamilton* 2,700
Miami University-Oxford Campus, *Oxford* 16,300
Mount Carmel College of Nursing, *Columbus* 350
Mount Union College, *Alliance* 1,800
Mount Vernon Nazarene College, *Mount Vernon* 1,900
Muskingum College, *New Concord* 1,300
Northeastern Ohio University College of Medicine, *Rootstown* 400
Notre Dame College of Ohio, *South Euclid* 650
Oberlin College, *Oberlin* 2,900
Ohio College of Podiatric Medicine, *Cleveland* 500
Ohio Dominican College, *Columbus* 1,900
Ohio Northern University, *Ada* 2,900
Ohio State University-Lima Campus, *Lima* 1,400
Ohio State University-Main Campus, *Columbus* 48,300
Ohio State University-Mansfield Campus, *Mansfield* 1,500
Ohio State University-Marion Campus, *Marion* 1,100
Ohio State University-Newark Campus, *Newark* 1,700
Ohio University Eastern Campus, *St. Clairsville* 900
Ohio University Lancaster Branch, *Lancaster* 1,700
Ohio University Main Campus, *Athens* 19,200
Ohio University Zanesville Branch, *Zanesville* 1,200
Ohio Wesleyan University, *Delaware* 1,900
Otterbein College, *Westerville* 2,700
Shawnee State University, *Portsmouth* 3,200
The Union Institute, *Cincinnati* 2,000
The University of Findlay, *Findlay* 3,300
Tiffin University, *Tiffin* 1,300
United Theological Seminary, *Dayton* 500
University of Akron Main Campus, *Akron* 23,500
University of Cincinnati, *Cincinnati* 28,200
University of Dayton, *Dayton* 10,200
University of Rio Grande, *Rio Grande* 2,000
University of Toledo, *Toledo* 20,300
Urbana University, *Urbana* 1,000
Ursuline College, *Cleveland Heights* 1,200
Walsh University, *Canton* 1,500
Wilberforce University, *Wilberforce* 950
Wilmington College, *Wilmington* 1,700
Wittenberg University, *Springfield* 2,000
Wright State University, *Fairborn* 16,000
Xavier University, *Cincinnati* 6,500
Youngstown State University, *Youngstown* 12,300

Oklahoma

American Bible College and Seminary, *Bethany* 350
Bartlesville Wesleyan College, *Bartlesville* 600
Cameron University, *Lawton* 5,300
East Central University, *Ada* 4,200
Langston University, *Langston* 4,000
Mid America Bible College, *Oklahoma City* 600
Northeastern State University, *Tahlequah* 8,500
Northwestern Oklahoma State University, *Alva* 1,900
Oklahoma Baptist University, *Shawnee* 2,200
Oklahoma Christian University of Science and Arts, *Oklahoma City* 1,700
Oklahoma City University, *Oklahoma City* 4,700
Oklahoma Panhandle State University, *Goodwell* 1,300
Oklahoma State University College of Osteopathic Medicine, *Tulsa* 350
Oklahoma State University Main Campus, *Stillwater* 19,300
Oral Roberts University, *Tulsa* 5,000
Phillips University, *Enid* 600
Southeastern Oklahoma State University, *Durant* 3,900
Southern Nazarene University, *Bethany* 1,800
Southwestern Oklahoma State University, *Weatherford* 4,900
University of Central Oklahoma, *Edmond* 14,100
University of Oklahoma Health Sciences Center, *Oklahoma City* 2,800
University of Oklahoma Norman Campus, *Norman* 23,200
University of Science and Arts of Oklahoma, *Chickasha* 1,400
University of Tulsa, *Tulsa* 4,200

Oregon

Concordia College, *Portland* 1,000
Eastern Oregon State College, *La Grande* 1,900
George Fox University, *Newberg* 2,300
ITT Technical Institute, *Portland* 450
Lewis and Clark College, *Portland* 3,000
Linfield College, *McMinnville* 2,100
Marylhurst University, *Marylhurst* 1,500
Multnomah Bible College and Biblical Seminary, *Portland* 750
National College of Naturopathic Medicine, *Portland* 400
Northwest Christian College, *Eugene* 450
Oregon Graduate Institute of Science and Technology, *Beaverton* 600
Oregon Health Sciences University, *Portland* 1,800
Oregon Institute of Technology, *Klamath Falls* 2,500
Oregon State University, *Corvallis* 14,100
Pacific University, *Forest Grove* 1,900
Portland State University, *Portland* 14,900
Reed College, *Portland* 1,300
Southern Oregon College, *Ashland* 5,100
University of Oregon, *Eugene* 17,200
University of Portland, *Portland* 2,300
Warner Pacific College, *Portland* 650
Western Baptist College, *Salem* 700
Western Seminary, *Portland* 700
Western States Chiropractic College, *Portland* 500
Willamette University, *Salem* 2,500

Pennsylvania

Albright College, *Reading* 1,400
Allegheny College, *Meadville* 1,900
Allegheny University of the Health Sciences, *Philadelphia* 3,300
Allentown College of Saint Francis de Sales, *Center Valley* 1,700
Alvernia College, *Reading* 1,200
American College, *Bryn Mawr* 450
Art Institute of Philadelphia, *Philadelphia* 2,200
Baptist Bible College and Seminary, *Clarks Summit* 850
Beaver College, *Glenside* 2,700
Bloomsburg University of Pennsylvania, *Bloomsburg* 7,500
Bryn Mawr College, *Bryn Mawr* 1,800
Bucknell University, *Lewisburg* 3,500
Cabrini College, *Radnor Township* 2,100
California University of Pennsylvania, *California* 5,800
Carlow College, *Pittsburgh* 2,400
Carnegie-Mellon University, *Pittsburgh* 7,900
Cedar Crest College, *Allentown* 1,800
Chatham College, *Pittsburgh* 900
Chestnut Hill College, *Philadelphia* 1,500
Cheyney University of Pennsylvania, *Cheyney* 1,400
Clarion University of Pennsylvania, *Clarion* 5,900
Clarion University of Pennsylvania-Venango Campus, *Oil City* 500
College Misericordia, *Dallas* 1,700
Delaware Valley College, *Doylestown* 1,400
Dickinson College, *Carlisle* 1,900
Dickinson School of Law, *Carlisle* 500
Drexel University, *Philadelphia* 10,500
Duquesne University, *Pittsburgh* 9,500
East Stroudsburg University of Pennsylvania, *East Stroudsburg* 5,700
Eastern Baptist Theological Seminary, *Philadelphia* 400
Eastern College, *St. Davids* 2,500
Edinboro University of Pennsylvania, *Edinboro* 7,100
Elizabethtown College, *Elizabethtown* 1,700
Franklin and Marshall College, *Lancaster* 1,800
Gannon University, *Erie* 3,200
Geneva College, *Beaver Falls* 1,900
Gettysburg College, *Gettysburg* 2,200
Gratz College, *Melrose Park* 300
Grove City College, *Grove City* 2,300
Gwynedd-Mercy College, *Gwynedd Valley* 1,800
Haverford College, *Haverford* 1,100
Holy Family College, *Philadelphia* 2,600
Immaculata College, *Immaculata* 2,500
Indiana University of Pennsylvania, *Indiana* 13,700
Juniata College, *Huntingdon* 1,200
King's College, *Wilkes-Barre* 2,200
Kutztown University of Pennsylvania, *Kutztown* 7,800
La Roche College, *McCandless Township* 1,600
La Salle University, *Philadelphia* 5,500
Lafayette College, *Easton* 2,200
Lake Erie College of Osteopathic Medicine, *Erie* 400
Lancaster Bible College, *Lancaster* 750
Lebanon Valley College, *Annville* 1,900
Lehigh University, *Bethlehem* 6,300
Lincoln University, *Lincoln University* 2,000
Lock Haven University, *Lock Haven* 3,600
Lycoming College, *Williamsport* 1,500
Mansfield University of Pennsylvania, *Mansfield* 2,900
Marywood University, *Scranton* 2,900
Mercyhurst College, *Erie* 1,900
Messiah College, *Grantham* 2,600
Millersville University of Pennsylvania, *Millersville* 7,600
Moore College of Art and Design, *Philadelphia* 450
Moravian College, *Bethlehem* 1,800
Mount Aloysius College, *Cresson* 1,400
Muhlenberg College, *Allentown* 1,800
Neumann College, *Aston* 1,200
Peirce College, *Philadelphia* 2,300
Pennsylvania College of Optometry, *Philadelphia* 600
Pennsylvania College of Technology, *Williamsport* 5,000
Pennsylvania State University-Abington Campus, *Abington* 3,200
Pennsylvania State University-Altoona Campus, *Altoona* 3,700
Pennsylvania State University-Beaver Campus, *Monaca* 800
Pennsylvania State University-Berks Campus, *Reading* 1,800
Pennsylvania State University-Delaware County Campus, *Media* 1,500
Pennsylvania State University-Du Bois Campus, *Du Bois* 1,100
Pennsylvania State University-Erie Campus, *Erie* 3,300
Pennsylvania State University-Fayette Campus, *Uniontown* 900
Pennsylvania State University-Great Valley, *Malvern* 1,500
Pennsylvania State University-Harrisburg Campus, *Middletown* 3,500
Pennsylvania State University-Hazleton Campus, *Hazleton* 1,300
Pennsylvania State University-Lehigh Valley Campus, *Fogelsville* 600
Pennsylvania State University-McKeesport Campus, *McKeesport* 850
Pennsylvania State University-Milton Hershey Medical Center, *Hershey* 600
Pennsylvania State University-Mont Alto Campus, *Mont Alto* 1,100
Pennsylvania State University-New Kensington Campus, *New Kensington* 850
Pennsylvania State University-Schuylkill Campus, *Schuylkill Haven* 1,000
Pennsylvania State University-Shenango Valley Campus, *Sharon* 1,000
Pennsylvania State University-University Park Campus, *State College* 40,500
Pennsylvania State University-Wilkes-Barre Campus, *Lehman* 800
Pennsylvania State University-Worthington-Scranton, *Dunmore* 1,500
Pennsylvania State University-York Campus, *York* 2,000
Philadelphia College of Osteopatic Medicine, *Philadelphia* 1,100
Philadelphia College of Pharmacy and Science, *Philadelphia* 2,200
Philadelphia College of Textiles and Science, *Philadelphia* 3,300
Philadelphia College of the Bible, *Langhorne Manor* 1,300
Pittsburgh Theological Seminary, *Pittsburgh* 300
Point Park College, *Pittsburgh* 2,200
Robert Morris College, *Coraopolis* 5,000
Rosemont College, *Rosemont* 950
Saint Charles Borromeo Seminary, *Philadelphia* 450
Saint Francis College, *Loretto* 1,900
Saint Joseph's University, *Philadelphia* 7,000
Seton Hill College, *Greensburg* 900
Shippensburg University of Pennsylvania, *Shippensburg* 6,700
Slippery Rock University of Pennsylvania, *Slippery Rock* 7,000
St. Vincent College and Seminary, *Latrobe* 1,100
Susquehanna University, *Selinsgrove* 1,700
Swarthmore College, *Swarthmore* 1,400
Temple University, *Philadelphia* 27,600
The University of The Arts, *Philadelphia* 1,600
Thiel College, *Greenville* 1,000
Thomas Jefferson University, *Philadelphia* 800
University of Pennsylvania, *Philadelphia* 21,500
University of Pittsburgh at Bradford, *Bradford* 1,300
University of Pittsburgh-Greensburg Campus, *Greensburg* 1,500
University of Pittsburgh-Johnstown Campus, *Scalp Level* 3,100
University of Pittsburgh-Main Campus, *Pittsburgh* 25,500
University of Scranton, *Scranton* 4,800
Ursinus College, *Collegeville* 1,200
Valley Forge Christian College, *Phoenixville* 500
Villanova University, *Villanova* 10,000
Washington and Jefferson College, *Washington* 1,200
Waynesburg College, *Waynesburg* 1,300
West Chester University of Pennsylvania, *West Chester* 11,400
Westminster College, *New Wilmington* 1,400
Westminster Theological Seminary, *Philadelphia* 650
Widener University-Main Campus, *Chester* 5,500
Wilkes University, *Wilkes-Barre* 2,800
Wilson College, *Chambersburg* 800
York College of Pennsylvania, *York* 5,000

Rhode Island

Brown University, *Providence* 7,400
Bryant College, *Bryant College* 3,300
Johnson and Wales University, *Providence* 8,000
New England Institute of Technology, *Warwick* 2,400
Providence College, *Providence* 5,500
Rhode Island College, *Providence* 8,600
Rhode Island School of Design, *Providence* 2,000
Roger Williams University, *Bristol* 3,400
Salve Regina University, *Newport* 2,100
University of Rhode Island, *Kingston* 13,400

South Carolina

Allen University, *Columbia* 400
Anderson College, *Anderson* 1,000
Benedict College, *Columbia* 2,200
Charleston Southern University, *Goose Creek* 2,500
Citadel Military College of South Carolina, *Charleston* 3,800
Claflin College, *Orangeburg* 1,000
Clemson University, *Clemson* 16,400
Coastal Carolina University, *Conway* 4,400
Coker College, *Hartsville* 1,000
College of Charleston, *Charleston* 11,000
Columbia College, *Columbia* 1,300
Columbia International University, *Columbia* 450
Converse College, *Spartanburg* 1,300
Erskine College and Seminary, *Due West* 550
Francis Marion University, *Florence* 3,600
Furman University, *Greenville* 2,800
Lander University, *Greenwood* 2,500
Limestone College, *Gaffney* 1,600
Medical University of South Carolina, *Charleston* 2,400
Morris College, *Sumter* 1,000
Newberry College, *Newberry* 700
North Greenville College, *Tigerville* 1,000
Presbyterian College, *Clinton* 1,100
Sherman College of Straight Chiropractic, *Spartanburg* 400
South Carolina State University, *Orangeburg* 4,700
Southern Wesleyan University, *Central* 1,300
University of South Carolina at Aiken, *Aiken* 3,000
University of South Carolina at Columbia, *Columbia* 25,400
University of South Carolina at Spartanburg, *Spartanburg* 3,700
Voorhees College, *Denmark* 600
Winthrop University, *Rock Hill* 5,600
Wofford College, *Spartanburg* 1,100

South Dakota

Augustana College, *Sioux Falls* 1,900
Black Hills State University, *Spearfish* 2,800
Dakota State University, *Madison* 1,300
Dakota Wesleyan University, *Mitchell* 700
Huron University, *Huron* 500
Mount Marty College, *Yankton* 1,000
National American University, *Rapid City* 2,500
Northern State University, *Aberdeen* 2,500
Oglala Lakota College, *Kyle* 1,300
Presentation College, *Aberdeen* 500
Sinte Gleska University, *Rosebud* 1,700
South Dakota School of Mines and Technology, *Rapid City* 2,200
South Dakota State University, *Brookings* 8,200
University of Sioux Falls, *Sioux Falls* 1,000
University of South Dakota Main Campus, *Vermillion* 6,500

Tennessee

Aquinas College, *Nashville* 400
Austin Peay State University, *Clarksville* 7,800
Baptist Memorial College of Health Sciences, *Memphis* 350
Belmont University, *Nashville* 3,000
Bethel College, *McKenzie* 600
Bryan College, *Dayton* 500
Carson-Newman College, *Jefferson City* 2,300
Christian Brothers University, *Memphis* 1,900
Crichton College, *Memphis* 700
Cumberland University, *Lebanon* 1,100
David Lipscomb University, *Nashville* 2,500
East Tennessee State University, *Johnson City* 11,300
Fisk University, *Nashville* 800
Free Will Baptist Bible College, *Nashville* 350
Freed-Hardeman University, *Henderson* 1,600
ITT Technical Institute, *Nashville* 600
ITT Technical Institute, *Knoxville* 450
Johnson Bible College, *Knoxville* 500
King College, *Bristol* 550
Lambuth University, *Jackson* 1,000
Lane College, *Jackson* 700
Le Moyne-Owen College, *Memphis* 1,000
Lee University, *Cleveland* 2,900
Lincoln Memorial University, *Harrogate* 1,800
Martin Methodist College, *Pulaski* 550
Maryville College, *Maryville* 1,000
Meharry Medical College, *Nashville* 900
Mid America Baptist Theological Seminary, *Germantown* 500
Middle Tennessee State University, *Murfreesboro* 18,400
Milligan College, *Milligan College* 900
Rhodes College, *Memphis* 1,400
Southern Adventists University, *Collegedale* 1,700
Southern College of Optometry, *Memphis* 500
Tennessee State University, *Nashville* 8,600
Tennessee Technological University, *Cookeville* 8,300
Tennessee Temple University, *Chattanooga* 650
Tennessee Wesleyan College, *Athens* 800
Trevecca Nazarene University, *Nashville* 1,500
Tusculum College, *Tusculum* 1,500
Union University, *Jackson* 2,000
University of Memphis, *Memphis* 19,900
University of Tennessee at Chattanooga, *Chattanooga* 8,500
University of Tennessee at Knoxville, *Knoxville* 25,000
University of Tennessee at Martin, *Martin* 6,000
University of Tennessee-Memphis, *Memphis* 2,100
University of the South, *Sewanee* 1,300
Vanderbilt University, *Nashville* 10,200

Texas

Abilene Christian University, *Abilene* 4,500
Amber University, *Garland* 1,500
Angelo State University, *San Angelo* 6,200
Austin College, *Sherman* 1,200
Austin Presbyterian Theological Seminary, *Austin* 350
Baylor College of Medicine, *Houston* 1,200
Baylor University, *Waco* 12,500
Concordia University at Austin, *Austin* 800
Criswell College, *Dallas* 500
Dallas Baptist University, *Dallas* 3,500
Dallas Theological Seminary, *Dallas* 1,500
Devry Institute of Technology, *Irving* 2,600
East Texas Baptist University, *Marshall* 1,300
Hardin-Simmons University, *Abilene* 2,300
Houston Baptist University, *Houston* 2,300
Howard Payne University, *Brownwood* 1,500
Huston-Tillotson College, *Austin* 700
ICI University, *Irving* 1,400
Jarvis Christian College, *Hawkins* 500
Lamar University, *Beaumont* 8,100
Le Tourneau University, *Longview* 2,200
Lubbock Christian University, *Lubbock* 1,200
McMurry University, *Abilene* 1,400
Midwestern State University, *Wichita Falls* 5,800
Our Lady of the Lake University of San Antonio, *San Antonio* 3,700
Parker College of Chiropractic, *Irving* 1,100
Paul Quinn College, *Dallas* 650
Prairie View A & M University, *Prairie View* 6,000
Rice University, *Houston* 4,300
Saint Edward's University, *Austin* 3,100
Saint Mary's University of San Antonio, *San Antonio* 4,200
Sam Houston State University, *Huntsville* 12,700
Schreiner College, *Kerrville* 700
South Texas College of Law, *Houston* 1,200
Southern Methodist University, *University Park* 9,700
Southwest Texas State University, *San Marcos* 20,700
Southwestern Adventist College, *Keene* 1,100
Southwestern Assemblies of God University, *Waxahachie* 1,500
Southwestern Baptist Theological Seminary, *Fort Worth* 3,300
Southwestern University, *Georgetown* 1,200
Stephen F. Austin State University, *Nacogdoches* 12,000
Sul Ross State University, *Alpine* 3,300
Tarleton State University, *Stephenville* 6,400
Texas A & M International University, *Laredo* 2,800
Texas A & M University, *College Station* 41,500
Texas A & M University at Galveston, *Galveston* 1,100
Texas A & M University at Kingsville, *Kingsville* 6,000
Texas A & M University-Corpus Christi, *Corpus Christi* 6,000
Texas A & M University System-Baylor College of Dentistry, *Dallas* 500
Texas A & M University-Commerce, *Commerce* 7,700
Texas A & M University-Texarkana, *Texarkana* 1,000
Texas Chiropractic College, *Pasadena* 500
Texas Christian University, *Fort Worth* 7,300
Texas College, *Tyler* 300
Texas Lutheran University, *Seguin* 1,400
Texas Southern University, *Houston* 7,300
Texas Tech University, *Lubbock* 25,000
Texas Tech University Health Sciences Center, *Lubbock* 1,500
Texas Wesleyan University, *Fort Worth* 3,200
Texas Woman's University, *Denton* 9,400
The University of Texas at Brownsville, *Brownsville* 8,300
The University of Texas-Pan American at Edinburg, *Edinburg* 12,500
Trinity University, *San Antonio* 2,600
University of Central Texas, *Killeen* 1,100
University of Dallas, *Irving* 2,900
University of Houston, *Houston* 31,600
University of Houston - Clear Lake, *Houston* 6,900
University of Houston - Downtown, *Houston* 8,200
University of Houston - Victoria, *Victoria* 1,500
University of Mary Hardin Baylor, *Belton* 2,300
University of North Texas, *Denton* 25,000
University of North Texas-Health Science Center at Fort Worth, *Fort Worth* 500
University of Saint Thomas, *Houston* 2,500
University of Texas Health Science Center at Houston, *Houston* 3,100
University of Texas Health Science Center at San Antonio, *San Antonio* 2,700
University of Texas Medical Branch at Galveston, *Galveston* 2,100
University of Texas Southwest Medical Center-Dallas, *Dallas* 1,600
University of Texas at Arlington, *Arlington* 19,300
University of Texas at Austin, *Austin* 48,900
University of Texas at Dallas, *Richardson* 9,300
University of Texas at El Paso, *El Paso* 15,200
University of Texas at San Antonio, *San Antonio* 17,500
University of Texas at Tyler, *Tyler* 3,400
University of Texas of the Permian Basin, *Odessa* 2,100
University of the Incarnate Word, *San Antonio* 3,300
Wayland Baptist University, *Plainview* 4,200
West Texas A & M University, *Canyon* 6,500
Wiley College, *Marshall* 650

Utah

Brigham Young University, *Provo* 31,200
ITT Technical Institute, *Salt Lake City* 500
Southern Utah University, *Cedar City* 6,000
University of Utah, *Salt Lake City* 26,200
Utah State University, *Logan* 21,200
Utah Valley State College, *Orem* 16,000
Weber State University, *Ogden* 14,600
Westminster College of Salt Lake City, *Salt Lake City* 21,100

Vermont

Bennington College, *North Bennington* 450
Burlington College, *Burlington* 800
Castleton State College, *Castleton* 1,800
Champlain College, *Burlington* 2,300
College of Saint Joseph, *Rutland* 500
Goddard College, *Plainfield* 600
Green Mountain College, *Poultney* 600
Johnson State College, *Johnson* 1,600
Lyndon State College, *Lyndonville* 1,100
Middlebury College, *Middlebury* 2,200
Norwich University, *Northfield* 2,700
Saint Michael's College, *Winooski* 2,800
School for International Training, *Brattleboro* 500
Southern Vermont College, *Bennington* 750
Trinity College, *Burlington* 1,000
University of Vermont, *Burlington* 9,100
Vermont College of Norwich University, *Montpelier* 1,000
Vermont Law School, *South Royalton* 500
Vermont Technical College, *South Royalton* 1,000

Virginia

American Military University, *Manassas* 700
Averett College, *Danville* 2,400
Bluefield College, *Bluefield* 800
Bridgewater College, *Bridgewater* 1,100
Christopher Newport University, *Newport News* 4,900
Clinch Valley College of the University of Virginia, *Wise* 1,500
College of William and Mary, *Williamsburg* 7,600
Community Hospital of Roanoke Valley College of Health & Sciences, *Roanoke* 600
Eastern Mennonite University, *Parkview* 1,300
Eastern Virginia Medical School, *Norfolk* 600
Emory and Henry College, *Emory* 900
Ferrum College, *Ferrum* 900
George Mason University, *Fairfax* 23,800
Hampden-Sydney College, *Hampden Sydney* 1,000
Hampton University, *Hampton* 5,700
Hollins College, *Hollins* 1,100
James Madison University, *Harrisonburg* 14,100
Liberty University, *Lynchburg* 6,600
Longwood College, *Farmville* 3,400
Lynchburg College, *Lynchburg* 2,000
Mary Baldwin College, *Staunton* 1,600
Mary Washington College, *Fredericksburg* 3,800
Marymount University, *Arlington* 3,500
National Business College, *Salem* 1,300
Norfolk State University, *Norfolk* 7,700
Old Dominion University, *Norfolk* 18,600
Radford University, *Radford* 8,500
Randolph-Macon College, *Ashland* 1,100
Randolph-Macon Woman's College, *Lynchburg* 700
Regent University, *Virginia Beach* 1,700
Roanoke College, *Salem* 1,700
Saint Paul's College, *Lawrenceville* 700
Shenandoah University, *Winchester* 1,900
Sweet Briar College, *Sweet Briar* 650
The Judge Advocate General's School, *Charlottesville* 3,500
Union Theological Seminary & presbyterian School of Christian Education, *Richmond* 350
University of Richmond, *Richmond* 4,400
University of Virginia, *Charlottesville* 18,000
Virginia Commonwealth University, *Richmond* 22,700
Virginia Intermont College, *Bristol* 850
Virginia Military Institute, *Lexington* 1,300
Virginia Polytechnic Institute and State University, *Blacksburg* 27,200
Virginia State University, *Ettrick* 4,200
Virginia Union University, *Richmond* 1,700
Virginia Wesleyan College, *Norfolk* 1,400
Washington and Lee University, *Lexington* 2,100
World College, *Virginia Beach* 500

Washington

Bastyr University, *Seattle* 1,000
Central Washington University, *Ellensburg* 8,400
City University, *Bellevue* 13,200
Cornish College of the Arts, *Seattle* 700
Eastern Washington University, *Cheney* 7,500
Evergreen State College, *Olympia* 4,100
Gonzaga University, *Spokane* 4,400
Heritage College, *Toppenish* 1,200
ITT Technical Institute, *Seattle* 600
Northwest College, *Kirkland* 900
Pacific Lutheran University, *Parkland* 3,600
Saint Martin's College, *Lacey* 1,700
Seattle Pacific University, *Seattle* 3,300
Seattle University, *Seattle* 5,700
University of Puget Sound, *Tacoma* 3,000
University of Washington, *Seattle* 35,400
Walla Walla College, *College Place* 1,600
Washington State University, *Pullman* 20,200
Western Washington University, *Bellingham* 11,500
Whitman College, *Walla Walla* 1,400
Whitworth College, *Country Homes* 1,800

West Virginia

Alderson Broaddus College, *Broaddus* 700
Appalachian Bible College, *Bradley* 300
Bethany College, *Bethany* 800
Bluefield State College, *Bluefield* 2,500
Concord College, *Athens* 2,800
Davis and Elkins College, *Elkins* 700
Fairmont State College, *Fairmont* 6,600
Glenville State College, *Glenville* 2,300
Marshall University, *Huntington* 15,700
Ohio Valley College, *Parkersburg* 450
Salem-Teikyo University, *Salem* 800
Shepherd College, *Shepherdstown* 4,000
The College of West Virginia, *Beckley* 2,100
University of Charleston, *Charleston* 1,400
West Liberty State College, *West Liberty* 2,400
West Virginia State College, *Institute* 4,600
West Virginia University, *Morgantown* 22,200
West Virginia University Institute of Technology, *Montgomery* 2,600
West Virginia University at Parkersburg, *Parkersburg* 3,400
West Virginia Wesleyan College, *Buckhannon* 1,600
Wheeling Jesuit University, *Wheeling* 1,600

Wisconsin

Alverno College, *Milwaukee* 2,200
Beloit College, *Beloit* 1,200
Cardinal Stritch University, *Glendale* 5,300
Carroll College, *Waukesha* 2,500
Carthage College, *Kenosha* 2,200
Columbia College of Nursing, *Milwaukee* 350
Concordia University-Wisconsin, *Mequon* 4,400
Edgewood College, *Madison* 2,000
Herzing College of Technology, *Madison* 500
ITT Technical Institute, *Greenfield* 400
Lakeland College, *Howards Grove* 3,300
Lawrence University, *Appleton* 1,200
Maranatha Baptist Bible College, *Watertown* 700
Marian College of Fond du Lac, *Fond du Lac* 2,300
Marquette University, *Milwaukee* 10,600
Medical College of Wisconsin, *Milwaukee* 1,200
Milwaukee Institute of Art and Design, *Milwaukee* 500
Milwaukee School of Engineering, *Milwaukee* 3,000
Mount Mary College, *Milwaukee* 1,300
Mount Senario College, *Ladysmith* 750
Northland College, *Ashland* 900
Ripon College, *Ripon* 700
Saint Norbert College, *De Pere* 2,000
Silver Lake College, *Manitowoc* 1,000
University of Wisconsin-Eau Claire, *Eau Claire* 10,500
University of Wisconsin-Green Bay, *Green Bay* 5,400
University of Wisconsin-La Crosse, *La Crosse* 9,100
University of Wisconsin-Madison, *Madison* 40,200
University of Wisconsin-Milwaukee, *Milwaukee* 22,300
University of Wisconsin-Oshkosh, *Oshkosh* 10,600
University of Wisconsin-Parkside, *Kenosha* 4,500
University of Wisconsin-Platteville, *Platteville* 5,100
University of Wisconsin-River Falls, *River Falls* 5,400
University of Wisconsin-Stevens Point, *Stevens Point* 8,500
University of Wisconsin-Stout, *Menomonie* 7,500
University of Wisconsin-Superior, *Superior* 2,600
University of Wisconsin-Whitewater, *Whitewater* 10,600
Viterbo College, *La Crosse* 1,600
Wisconsin Lutheran College, *Milwaukee* 450

Wyoming

University of Wyoming, *Laramie* 11,100

U.S. Summary Tables

The tables below rank the most rapidly growing RMAs, PMSAs, MSAs, and CBSAs from 1990 to 2000. Also ranked are the top RMAs, PMSAs, MSAs, and CBSAs losing population between 1990 and 2000. Both the numerical change and the percentage change are shown.

Counties with more than 50,000 population increase (decrease) between 1990 and 2000 are also ranked. Only the numerical increase or decrease is listed. (For metropolitan area definitions and additional information about RMAs and counties, see the Introduction on pages 5-9.)

Most Rapidly Growing RMAs, 1990–2000

No.	RMA	Population: Census 4/1/00	Population: Census 4/1/90	Population Increase 1990–2000: No.	Population Increase 1990–2000: %
1	Las Vegas, NV	1,344,700	724,700	620,000	85.6
2	Naples, FL	216,400	133,700	82,700	61.9
3	Kissimmee, FL	155,500	97,700	57,800	59.2
4	Denton, TX	128,100	80,900	47,200	58.3
5	Murfreesboro, TN	96,900	63,100	33,800	53.6
6	Yuma, AZ-CA	148,600	99,700	48,900	49.0
7	McAllen, TX-MX	448,800	302,300	146,500	48.5
8	Raleigh, NC	734,000	497,200	236,800	47.6
9	Austin, TX	1,009,200	687,200	322,000	46.9
10	Boise, ID	350,000	239,400	110,600	46.2
11	Laredo, TX-MEX.	180,700	124,700	56,000	44.9
12	Phoenix, AZ	3,078,500	2,124,900	953,600	44.9
13	Fredericksburg, VA	121,800	84,900	36,900	43.5
14	Fayetteville-, AR	132,500	94,200	38,300	40.7
15	Provo-, UT	360,700	258,000	102,700	39.8
16	Atlanta, GA	3,623,100	2,621,100	1,002,000	38.2
17	Greeley, CO	102,500	74,700	27,800	37.2
18	Myrtle Beach, SC-NC	156,300	114,400	41,900	36.6
19	Fort Collins-, CO	235,200	174,100	61,100	35.1
20	Wilmington, NC	181,100	134,800	46,300	34.3
21	Reno, NV	331,300	248,500	82,800	33.3
22	Ocala, FL	211,400	159,100	52,300	32.9
23	Hemet, CA	126,000	95,400	30,600	32.1
24	Palm Springs-, CA	203,500	154,100	49,400	32.1
25	Auburn-, AL	80,800	61,200	19,600	32.0

RMAs Most Rapidly Losing Population, 1990–2000

No.	RMA	Population: Census 4/1/00	Population: Census 4/1/90	Population Decrease 1990–2000: No.	Population Decrease 1990–2000: %
1	Carbondale-, IL	122,400	143,000	-20,600	-14.4
2	Lafayette, LA	268,100	294,700	-26,600	-9.0
3	Steubenville-, OH-WV	107,400	116,000	-8,600	-7.4
4	Greenville, MS	45,000	48,500	-3,500	-7.2
5	Plattsburgh, NY	50,700	54,600	-3,900	-7.1
6	Manhattan, KS	44,500	47,400	-2,900	-6.1
7	Utica-, NY	221,500	235,500	-14,000	-5.9
8	Grand Forks, ND-MN	55,700	59,200	-3,500	-5.9
9	Johnstown, PA	123,300	129,600	-6,300	-4.9
10	Danville, IL	65,400	68,800	-3,400	-4.9
11	Binghamton, NY-PA	223,700	234,600	-10,900	-4.6
12	Wheeling, WV-OH	138,500	144,900	-6,400	-4.4
13	Elmira, NY	82,000	85,700	-3,700	-4.3
14	Alexandria, LA	96,700	100,700	-4,000	-4.0
15	Pittsfield, MA	85,900	88,700	-2,800	-3.2
16	Oil City-, PA	38,400	39,600	-1,200	-3.0
17	Natchez, MS-LA	42,400	43,700	-1,300	-3.0
18	Danville, VA-NC	74,000	76,100	-2,100	-2.8
19	Pittsburgh, PA	2,010,400	2,062,000	-51,600	-2.5
20	Anniston, AL	98,600	101,100	-2,500	-2.5
21	Scranton-, PA	469,200	479,700	-10,500	-2.2
22	Decatur, IL	103,800	106,100	-2,300	-2.2
23	Hazleton, PA	68,600	70,100	-1,500	-2.1
24	Newport, RI	63,200	64,500	-1,300	-2.0
25	Youngstown-, OH-PA	448,400	457,200	-8,800	-1.9

Most Rapidly Growing PMSAs and MSAs, 1990–2000

No.	PMSA & MSA	Population: Census 4/1/00	Population: Census 4/1/90	Population Increase 1990–2000: No.	Population Increase 1990–2000: %
1	Las Vegas, NV-AZ MSA	1,563,282	852,737	710,545	83.3
2	Naples, FL MSA	251,377	152,099	99,278	65.3
3	Yuma, AZ MSA	160,026	106,895	53,131	49.7
4	McAllen-Edinburg-Mission, TX MSA	569,463	383,545	185,918	48.5
5	Austin-San Marcos, TX MSA	1,249,763	846,227	403,536	47.7
6	Fayetteville-Springdale-Rogers, AR MSA	311,121	210,908	100,213	47.5
7	Boise City, ID MSA	432,345	295,851	136,494	46.1
8	Phoenix-Mesa, AZ MSA	3,251,876	2,238,480	1,013,396	45.3
9	Laredo, TX MSA	193,117	133,239	59,878	44.9
10	Provo-Orem, UT MSA	368,536	263,590	104,946	39.8
11	Atlanta, GA MSA	4,112,198	2,959,950	1,152,248	38.9
12	Raleigh-Durham-Chapel Hill, NC MSA	1,187,941	855,545	332,396	38.9
13	Greeley, CO PMSA	180,936	131,821	49,115	37.3
14	Myrtle Beach, SC MSA	196,629	144,053	52,576	36.5
15	Wilmington, NC MSA	233,450	171,269	62,181	36.3
16	Fort Collins-Loveland, CO MSA	251,494	186,136	65,358	35.1
17	Orlando, FL MSA	1,644,561	1,224,852	419,709	34.3
18	Reno, NV MSA	339,486	254,667	84,819	33.3
19	Ocala, FL MSA	258,916	194,833	64,083	32.9
20	Auburn-Opelika, AL MSA	115,092	87,146	27,946	32.1
21	Fort Myers-Cape Coral, FL MSA	440,888	335,113	105,775	31.6
22	Dallas, TX PMSA	3,519,176	2,676,248	842,928	31.5
23	West Palm Beach-Boca Raton, FL MSA	1,131,184	863,518	267,666	31.0
24	Bellingham, WA MSA	166,814	127,780	39,034	30.5
25	Colorado Springs, CO MSA	516,929	397,014	119,915	30.2

PMSAs and MSAs Most Rapidly Losing Population 1990–2000

No.	PSMA & MSA	Population: Census 4/1/00	Population: Census 4/1/90	Population Decrease 1990–2000: No.	Population Decrease 1990–2000: %
1	Steubenville-Weirton, OH-WV MSA	132,008	142,523	-10,515	-7.4
2	Grand Forks, ND-MN MSA	97,478	103,181	-5,703	-5.5
3	Utica-Rome, NY MSA	299,896	316,633	-16,737	-5.3
4	Binghamton, NY MSA	252,320	264,497	-12,177	-4.6
5	Pittsfield, MA MSA	84,699	88,695	-3,996	-4.5
6	Elmira, NY MSA	91,070	95,195	-4,125	-4.3
7	Alexandria, LA MSA	126,337	131,556	-5,219	-4.0
8	Wheeling, WV-OH MSA	153,172	159,301	-6,129	-3.8
9	Johnstown, PA MSA	232,621	241,247	-8,626	-3.6
10	Anniston, AL MSA	112,249	116,034	-3,785	-3.3
11	Lewiston-Auburn, ME MSA	90,830	93,679	-2,849	-3.0
12	Scranton--Wilkes-Barre--Hazleton, PA MSA	624,776	638,466	-13,690	-2.1
13	Decatur, IL MSA	114,706	117,206	-2,500	-2.1
14	Buffalo-Niagara Falls, NY MSA	1,170,111	1,189,288	-19,177	-1.6
15	Pittsburgh, PA MSA	2,358,695	2,394,811	-36,116	-1.5
16	Jamestown, NY MSA	139,750	141,895	-2,145	-1.5
17	Syracuse, NY MSA	732,117	742,177	-10,060	-1.4
18	Pine Bluff, AR MSA	84,278	85,487	-1,209	-1.4
19	Altoona, PA MSA	129,144	130,542	-1,398	-1.1
20	Youngstown-Warren, OH MSA	594,746	600,895	-6,149	-1.0
21	Bangor, ME MSA	90,864	91,611	-747	-0.8
22	Muncie, IN MSA	118,769	119,659	-890	-0.7
23	Sharon, PA MSA	120,293	121,003	-710	-0.6
24	New Bedford, MA PMSA	175,198	175,641	-443	-0.3
25	Dayton-Springfield, OH MSA	950,558	951,270	-712	-0.1

Most Rapidly Growing CBSAs, 1990–2000

No.	CBSA	Population: Census 4/1/00	Population: Census 4/1/90	Population Increase 1990–2000: No.	Population Increase 1990–2000: %
1	St. George, UT	90,354	48,560	41,794	86.1
2	Las Vegas-Paradise, NV	1,375,765	741,459	634,306	85.5
3	Naples-Marco Island, FL	251,377	152,099	99,278	65.3
4	Coeur d'Alene, ID	108,685	69,795	38,890	55.7
5	Prescott, AZ	167,517	107,714	59,803	55.5
6	Bend, OR	115,367	74,958	40,409	53.9
7	Yuma, AZ	160,026	106,895	53,131	49.7
8	McAllen-Edinburg-Pharr, TX	569,463	383,545	185,918	48.5
9	Austin-Round Rock, TX	1,249,763	846,227	403,536	47.7
10	Raleigh-Cary, NC	797,071	541,100	255,971	47.3
11	Gainesville, GA	139,277	95,428	43,849	45.9
12	Boise City-Nampa, ID	464,840	319,596	145,244	45.4
13	Phoenix-Mesa-Scottsdale, AZ	3,251,876	2,238,480	1,013,396	45.3
14	Laredo, TX	193,117	133,239	59,878	44.9
15	Fayetteville-Springdale-Rogers, AR-MO	347,045	239,464	107,581	44.9
16	Provo-Orem, UT	376,774	269,407	107,367	39.9
17	Madera, CA	123,109	88,090	35,019	39.8
18	Atlanta-Sandy Springs-Marietta, GA	4,247,981	3,069,425	1,178,556	38.4
19	Greeley, CO*	180,926	131,817	49,109	37.3
20	Wilmington, NC	274,532	200,124	74,408	37.2
21	Myrtle Beach-Conway-North Myrtle Beach, SC	196,629	144,053	52,576	36.5
22	Fort Collins-Loveland, CO	251,494	186,136	65,358	35.1
23	Orlando, FL	1,644,561	1,224,852	419,709	34.3
24	Reno-Sparks, NV	342,885	257,193	85,692	33.3
25	Ocala, FL	258,916	194,833	64,083	32.9

*For the purposes of this table, Broomfield City is treated as if it were a county at the time of the 1990 and 2000 censuses. Broomfield County was formed from parts of Adams, Boulder, Jefferson, and Weld counties in 2001, and is coextensive with Broomfield City.

CBSAs Most Rapidly Losing Population 1990–2000

No.	CBSA	Population: Census 4/1/00	Population: Census 4/1/90	Population Decrease 1990–2000: No.	Population Decrease 1990–2000: %
1	Weirton-Steubenville, WV-OH	132,008	142,523	-10,515	-7.4
2	Johnstown, PA	152,598	163,029	-10,431	-6.4
3	Grand Forks, ND-MN	97,478	103,181	-5,703	-5.5
4	Utica-Rome, NY	299,896	316,633	-16,737	-5.3
5	Danville, IL	83,919	88,257	-4,338	-4.9
6	Binghamton, NY	252,320	264,497	-12,177	-4.6
7	Elmira, NY	91,070	95,195	-4,125	-4.3
8	Wheeling, WV-OH	153,172	159,301	-6,129	-3.8
9	Anniston-Oxford, AL	112,249	116,034	-3,785	-3.3
10	Pittsfield, MA	134,953	139,352	-4,399	-3.2
11	Alexandria, LA	145,035	149,082	-4,047	-2.7
12	Scranton—Wilkes-Barre, PA	560,625	575,264	-14,639	-2.5
13	Decatur, IL	114,706	117,206	-2,500	-2.1
14	Springfield, OH	144,742	147,548	-2,806	-1.9
15	Youngstown-Warren-Boardman, OH-PA	602,964	613,622	-10,658	-1.7
16	Buffalo-Niagara Falls, NY	1,170,111	1,189,288	-19,177	-1.6
17	Pittsburgh, PA	2,431,087	2,468,289	-37,202	-1.5
18	Syracuse, NY	650,154	659,864	-9,710	-1.5
19	Bay City, MI	110,157	111,723	-1,566	-1.4
20	Lewiston-Auburn, ME	103,793	105,259	-1,466	-1.4
21	Lima, OH	108,473	109,755	-1,282	-1.2
22	Bangor, ME	144,919	146,601	-1,682	-1.1
23	Altoona, PA	129,144	130,542	-1,398	-1.1
24	Saginaw-Saginaw Township North, MI	210,039	211,946	-1,907	-0.9
25	Muncie, IN	118,769	119,659	-890	-0.7

Counties With More Than 50,000 Population Increase, 1990–2000

No.	County (Chief Urban Center)	Population: Census 4/1/00	Population: Census 4/1/90	Numerical Increase 1990–2000
1	Maricopa, AZ (Phoenix)	3,072,149	2,122,101	950,048
2	Los Angeles, CA (Los Angeles)	9,519,338	8,863,164	656,174
3	Clark, NV (Las Vegas)	1,375,765	741,459	634,306
4	Harris, TX (Houston)	3,400,578	2,818,199	582,379
5	Orange, CA (Anaheim)	2,846,289	2,410,556	435,733
6	Riverside, CA (Riverside)	1,545,387	1,170,413	374,974
7	Broward, FL (Fort Lauderdale)	1,623,018	1,255,488	367,530
8	Dallas, TX (Dallas)	2,218,899	1,852,810	366,089
9	Dade, FL (Miami)	2,253,362	1,937,094	316,268
10	San Diego, CA (San Diego)	2,813,833	2,498,016	315,817
11	San Bernardino, CA (Riverside)	1,709,434	1,418,380	291,054
12	Queens, NY (New York)	2,229,379	1,951,598	277,781
13	Tarrant, TX (Fort Worth)	1,446,219	1,170,103	276,116
14	Cook, IL (Chicago)	5,376,741	5,105,067	271,674
15	Palm Beach, FL (West Palm Beach)	1,131,184	863,518	267,666
16	Travis, TX (Austin)	812,280	576,407	235,873
17	Gwinnett, GA (Atlanta)	588,448	352,910	235,538
18	King, WA (Seattle)	1,737,034	1,507,319	229,715
19	Collin, TX (Dallas)	491,675	264,036	227,639
20	Orange, FL (Orlando)	896,344	677,491	218,853
21	Bexar, TX (San Antonio)	1,392,931	1,185,394	207,537
22	Wake, NC (Raleigh)	627,846	423,380	204,466
23	Hidalgo, TX (McAllen)	569,463	383,545	185,918
24	Santa Clara, CA (San Jose)	1,682,585	1,497,577	185,008
25	Mecklenburg, NC (Charlotte)	695,454	511,433	184,021
26	Sacramento, CA (Sacramento)	1,223,499	1,041,219	182,280
27	Pima, AZ (Tucson)	843,746	666,880	176,866
28	Salt Lake, UT (Salt Lake City)	898,387	725,956	172,431
29	Fulton, GA (Atlanta)	816,006	648,951	167,055
30	Hillsborough, FL (Tampa)	998,948	834,054	164,894
31	Kings, NY (New York)	2,465,326	2,300,664	164,662
32	Alameda, CA (Oakland)	1,443,741	1,279,182	164,559
33	Cobb, GA (Atlanta)	607,751	447,745	160,006
34	Denton, TX (Dallas)	432,976	273,525	159,451
35	Fairfax, VA (Washington)	969,749	818,584	151,165
36	Contra Costa, CA (Oakland)	948,816	803,732	145,084
37	Will, IL (Chicago)	502,266	357,313	144,953
38	Snohomish, WA (Seattle)	606,024	465,642	140,382
39	Washington, OR (Portland)	445,342	311,554	133,788
40	Fresno, CA (Fresno)	799,407	667,490	131,917
41	Fort Bend, TX (Houston)	354,452	225,421	129,031
42	Bronx, NY (New York)	1,332,650	1,203,789	128,861
43	Lake, IL (Chicago)	644,356	516,418	127,938
44	DuPage, IL (Chicago)	904,161	781,666	122,495
45	DeKalb, GA (Atlanta)	665,865	545,837	120,028
46	El Paso, CO (Colorado Springs)	516,929	397,014	119,915
47	Kern, CA (Bakersfield)	661,645	543,477	118,168
48	Montgomery, MD (Washington)	873,341	757,027	116,314
49	Douglas, CO (Denver)	175,766	60,391	115,375
50	Pierce, WA (Tacoma)	700,820	586,203	114,617
51	Montgomery, TX (Houston)	293,768	182,201	111,567
52	Oakland, MI (Detroit)	1,194,156	1,083,592	110,564
53	Williamson, TX (Austin)	249,967	139,551	110,416
54	Franklin, OH (Columbus)	1,068,978	961,437	107,541
55	Clark, WA (Portland)	345,238	238,053	107,185
56	Duval, FL (Jacksonville)	778,879	672,971	105,908
57	Lee, FL (Fort Myers)	440,888	335,113	105,775
58	Utah, UT (Provo)	368,536	263,590	104,946
59	Collier, FL (Naples)	251,377	152,099	99,278
60	Adams, CO (Denver)	363,857	265,038	98,819
61	Suffolk, NY (Nassau)	1,419,369	1,321,864	97,505
62	Arapahoe, CO (Denver)	487,967	391,511	96,456
63	Johnson, KS (Kansas City)	451,086	355,054	96,032
64	Ada, ID (Boise City)	300,904	205,775	95,129
65	Jefferson, CO (Denver)	527,056	438,430	88,626
66	El Paso, TX (El Paso)	679,622	591,610	88,012
67	Denver, CO (Denver)	554,636	467,610	87,026
68	Kane, IL (Chicago)	404,119	317,471	86,648
69	Washoe, NV (Reno)	339,486	254,667	84,819
70	Ventura, CA (Ventura)	753,197	669,016	84,181
71	Hennepin, MN (Minneapolis)	1,116,200	1,032,431	83,769
72	Loudoun, VA (Washington)	169,599	86,129	83,470
73	San Joaquin, CA (Stockton)	563,598	480,628	82,970
74	Dakota, MN (Minneapolis)	355,904	275,227	80,677
75	Polk, FL (Lakeland)	483,924	405,382	78,542
76	Middlesex, NJ (New Brunswick)	750,162	671,780	78,382
77	Ocean, NJ (Lakewood)	510,916	433,203	77,713
78	Seminole, FL (Orlando)	365,196	287,529	77,667
79	Brevard, FL (Melbourne)	476,230	398,978	77,252
80	McHenry, IL (Chicago)	260,077	183,241	76,836
81	Multnomah, OR (Portland)	660,486	583,887	76,599
82	Stanislaus, CA (Modesto)	446,997	370,522	76,475
83	Bernalillo, NM (Albuquerque)	556,678	480,577	76,101
84	Placer, CA (Sacramento)	248,399	172,796	75,603
85	Cameron, TX (Brownsville)	335,227	260,120	75,107
86	Hamilton, IN (Indianapolis)	182,740	108,936	73,804
87	Kent, MI (Grand Rapids)	574,335	500,631	73,704
88	Guilford, NC (Greensboro)	421,048	347,420	73,628
89	Volusia, FL (Daytona Beach)	443,343	370,712	72,631
90	Prince George's, MD (Washington)	801,515	729,268	72,247
91	Montgomery, PA (Philadelphia)	750,097	678,111	71,986
92	Shelby, TN (Memphis)	897,472	826,330	71,142
93	St. Charles, MO (St. Louis)	283,883	212,907	70,976
94	Macomb, MI (Detroit)	788,149	717,400	70,749
95	Sonoma, CA (Santa Rosa)	458,614	388,222	70,392
96	Pinellas, FL (St. Petersburg)	921,482	851,659	69,823
97	Middlesex, MA (Boston)	1,465,396	1,398,468	66,928
98	Boulder, CO (Boulder)	291,288	225,339	65,949
99	Larimer, CO (Fort Collins)	251,494	186,136	65,358
100	Prince William, VA (Washington)	280,813	215,686	65,127
101	Osceola, FL (Orlando)	172,493	107,728	64,765
102	Richmond, NY (New York)	443,728	378,977	64,751
103	Marion, FL (Ocala)	258,916	194,833	64,083
104	Pasco, FL (Tampa)	344,765	281,131	63,634
105	Rutherford, TN (Nashville)	182,023	118,570	63,453
106	Pinal, AZ (Phoenix)	179,727	116,379	63,348
107	Marion, IN (Indianapolis)	860,454	797,159	63,295
108	Anne Arundel, MD (Baltimore)	489,656	427,239	62,417
109	Monmouth, NJ (Monmouth)	615,301	553,124	62,177
110	Baltimore, MD (Baltimore)	754,292	692,134	62,158
111	Mohave, AZ (Las Vegas)	155,032	93,497	61,535
112	Oklahoma, OK (Oklahoma City)	660,448	599,611	60,837
113	Henry, GA (Atlanta)	119,341	58,741	60,600
114	Howard, MD (Baltimore)	247,842	187,328	60,514
115	Tulsa, OK (Tulsa)	563,299	503,341	59,958
116	Webb, TX (Laredo)	193,117	133,239	59,878
117	Yavapai, AZ (Prescott)	167,517	107,714	59,803
118	Clackamas, OR (Portland)	338,391	278,850	59,541
119	Greenville, SC (Greenville)	379,616	320,167	59,449
120	Dane, WI (Madison)	426,526	367,085	59,441
121	Davidson, TN (Nashville)	569,891	510,784	59,107
122	Bergen, NJ (Bergen)	884,118	825,380	58,738
123	Lake, FL (Orlando)	210,528	152,104	58,424
124	New Castle, DE (Wilmington)	500,265	441,946	58,319
125	San Mateo, CA (San Francisco)	707,161	649,623	57,538
126	Somerset, NJ (Middlesex)	297,490	240,279	57,211
127	Chester, PA (Philadelphia)	433,501	376,396	57,105
128	Spokane, WA (Spokane)	417,939	361,364	56,575
129	Bucks, PA (Philadelphia)	597,635	541,174	56,461
130	Marion, OR (Salem)	284,834	228,483	56,351
131	Tulare, CA (Visalia)	368,021	311,921	56,100
132	Waukesha, WI (Milwaukee)	360,767	304,715	56,052
133	Benton, AR (Fayetteville)	153,406	97,499	55,907
134	Hudson, NJ (Jersey City)	608,975	553,099	55,876
135	Washington, MN (Minneapolis)	201,130	145,896	55,234
136	Fairfield, CT (Bridgeport)	882,567	827,645	54,922
137	Clayton, GA (Atlanta)	236,517	182,052	54,465
138	Anoka, MN (Minneapolis)	298,084	243,641	54,443
139	Forsyth, GA (Atlanta)	98,407	44,083	54,324
140	Solano, CA (Vallejo)	394,542	340,421	54,121
141	Essex, MA (Boston)	723,419	670,080	53,339
142	Yuma, AZ (Yuma)	160,026	106,895	53,131
143	San Francisco, CA (San Francisco)	776,733	723,959	52,774
144	Horry, SC (Myrtle Beach)	196,629	144,053	52,576
145	Manatee, FL (Bradenton)	264,002	211,707	52,295
146	Cherokee, GA (Atlanta)	141,903	90,204	51,699
147	Davis, UT (Salt Lake City)	238,994	187,941	51,053
148	Chesterfield, VA (Richmond)	259,903	209,274	50,629
149	Ottawa, MI (Grand Rapids)	238,314	187,768	50,546
150	Brazoria, TX (Brazoria)	241,767	191,707	50,060

Counties With More Than 50,000 Population Decrease, 1990–2000

No.	County (Chief Urban Center)	Population: Census 4/1/00	Population: Census 4/1/90	Numerical Decrease 1990–2000
1	Philadelphia, PA (Philadelphia)	1,517,550	1,585,577	-68,027
2	Allegheny, PA (Pittsburgh)	1,281,666	1,336,449	-54,783
3	Wayne, MI (Detroit)	2,061,162	2,111,687	-50,525

U.S.: Population and Agriculture

STATE	CAPITAL	CHIEF CITY OTHER THAN CAPITAL	FIPS STATE CODE†	LAND AREA (Sq. Miles) 2000	POPULATION: TOTAL 4/1/2000	POPULATION: TOTAL 4/1/1990	POPULATION: PERCENT CHANGE 1990-2000	POPULATION: TOTAL 4/1/1980	POPULATION: PERCENT CHANGE 1980-1990	AGRICULTURE*: NUMBER OF FARMS 2002	AGRICULTURE*: LAND IN FARMS (1,000 Acres) 2002	AGRICULTURE*: FINAL AGRICULTURAL OUTPUT ($1,000) 2002
Alabama	Montgomery	•Birmingham	01	50,744	4,447,100	4,040,587	10.1	3,894,046	3.8	45,000	8,900	3,343,000
Alaska	Juneau	•Anchorage	02	571,951	626,932	550,043	14.0	401,851	36.9	1,000	900	48,000
Arizona	•Phoenix	Tucson	04	113,635	5,130,632	3,665,228	40.0	2,716,756	34.9	7,000	26,600	2,427,000
Arkansas	•Little Rock	Fort Smith	05	52,068	2,673,400	2,350,725	13.7	2,286,357	2.8	47,000	14,500	5,189,000
California	Sacramento	•Los Angeles	06	155,959	33,871,648	29,760,021	13.8	23,667,372	25.7	80,000	27,600	25,906,000
Colorado	•Denver	Colorado Springs	08	103,718	4,301,261	3,294,394	30.6	2,889,735	14.0	31,000	31,100	4,651,000
Connecticut	•Hartford	Bridgeport	09	4,845	3,405,565	3,287,116	3.6	3,107,576	5.8	4,000	400	474,000
Delaware	Dover	•Wilmington	10	1,954	783,600	666,168	17.6	594,317	12.1	2,000	500	627,000
District of Columbia	•Washington		11	61	572,059	606,900	-5.7	638,432	-4.9	(n.a.)	(n.a.)	(n.a.)
Florida	Tallahassee	•Miami	12	53,927	15,982,378	12,937,926	23.5	9,747,015	32.7	44,000	10,400	6,264,000
Georgia	•Atlanta	Augusta	13	57,906	8,186,453	6,478,216	26.4	5,462,982	18.6	49,000	10,700	5,030,000
Hawaii	•Honolulu	Hilo	15	6,423	1,211,537	1,108,229	9.3	964,691	14.9	5,000	1,300	534,000
Idaho	•Boise	Nampa	16	82,747	1,293,953	1,006,749	28.5	944,127	6.6	25,000	11,800	4,002,000
Illinois	Springfield	•Chicago	17	55,584	12,419,293	11,430,602	8.6	11,427,414	0.0	73,000	27,300	8,089,000
Indiana	•Indianapolis	Fort Wayne	18	35,867	6,080,485	5,544,159	9.7	5,490,212	1.0	60,000	15,100	5,008,000
Iowa	•Des Moines	Cedar Rapids	19	55,869	2,926,324	2,776,755	5.4	2,913,808	-4.7	91,000	31,700	12,813,000
Kansas	Topeka	•Wichita	20	81,815	2,688,418	2,477,574	8.5	2,364,236	4.8	64,000	47,200	9,074,000
Kentucky	Frankfort	•Louisville	21	39,728	4,041,769	3,685,296	9.7	3,660,324	0.7	87,000	13,800	3,174,000
Louisiana	Baton Rouge	•New Orleans	22	43,562	4,468,976	4,219,973	5.9	4,206,098	0.3	27,000	7,800	1,939,000
Maine	Augusta	•Portland	23	30,862	1,274,923	1,227,928	3.8	1,125,043	9.1	7,000	1,400	472,000
Maryland	Annapolis	•Baltimore	24	9,774	5,296,486	4,781,468	10.8	4,216,933	13.4	12,000	2,100	1,326,000
Massachusetts	•Boston	Worcester	25	7,840	6,349,097	6,016,425	5.5	5,737,093	4.9	6,000	500	389,000
Michigan	Lansing	•Detroit	26	56,804	9,938,444	9,295,297	6.9	9,262,044	0.4	53,000	10,100	3,917,000
Minnesota	St. Paul	•Minneapolis	27	79,610	4,919,479	4,375,099	12.4	4,075,970	7.3	81,000	27,500	8,926,000
Mississippi	•Jackson	Gulfport	28	46,907	2,844,658	2,573,216	10.5	2,520,698	2.1	42,000	11,100	3,262,000
Missouri	Jefferson City	•St. Louis	29	68,886	5,595,211	5,117,073	9.3	4,916,759	4.1	107,000	29,900	5,248,000
Montana	Helena	•Billings	30	145,552	902,195	799,065	12.9	786,624	1.6	28,000	59,600	2,093,000
Nebraska	Lincoln	•Omaha	31	76,872	1,711,263	1,578,385	8.4	1,569,825	0.5	49,000	45,900	10,051,000
Nevada	Carson City	•Las Vegas	32	109,826	1,998,257	1,201,833	66.3	800,508	50.1	3,000	6,300	451,000
New Hampshire	Concord	•Manchester	33	8,968	1,235,786	1,109,252	11.4	920,610	20.5	3,000	400	149,000
New Jersey	Trenton	•Newark	34	7,417	8,414,350	7,730,188	8.9	7,365,011	5.0	10,000	800	754,000
New Mexico	Santa Fe	•Albuquerque	35	121,356	1,819,046	1,515,069	20.1	1,303,542	16.2	15,000	44,800	1,750,000
New York	Albany	•New York	36	47,214	18,976,457	17,990,455	5.5	17,558,165	2.5	37,000	7,700	3,228,000
North Carolina	Raleigh	•Charlotte	37	48,711	8,049,313	6,628,637	21.4	5,880,415	12.7	54,000	9,100	7,059,000
North Dakota	Bismarck	•Fargo	38	68,976	642,200	638,800	0.5	652,717	-2.1	31,000	39,300	3,526,000
Ohio	Columbus	•Cleveland	39	40,948	11,353,140	10,847,115	4.7	10,797,603	0.5	78,000	14,600	4,461,000
Oklahoma	•Oklahoma City	Tulsa	40	68,667	3,450,654	3,145,585	9.7	3,025,487	4.0	83,000	33,700	4,606,000
Oregon	Salem	•Portland	41	95,997	3,421,399	2,842,321	20.4	2,633,156	7.9	40,000	17,100	3,248,000
Pennsylvania	Harrisburg	•Philadelphia	42	44,817	12,281,054	11,881,643	3.4	11,864,751	0.1	58,000	7,700	4,343,000
Rhode Island	•Providence	Warwick	44	1,045	1,048,319	1,003,464	4.5	947,154	5.9	1,000	100	56,000
South Carolina	•Columbia	Charleston	45	30,110	4,012,012	3,486,703	15.1	3,120,730	11.7	25,000	4,800	1,528,000
South Dakota	Pierre	•Sioux Falls	46	75,885	754,844	696,004	8.5	690,768	0.8	32,000	43,800	4,050,000
Tennessee	•Nashville	Memphis	47	41,217	5,689,283	4,877,185	16.7	4,591,023	6.2	88,000	11,700	2,259,000
Texas	Austin	•Dallas	48	261,797	20,851,820	16,986,510	22.8	14,225,288	19.4	229,000	129,900	14,664,000
Utah	•Salt Lake City	West Valley	49	82,144	2,233,169	1,722,850	29.6	1,461,037	17.9	15,000	11,700	1,143,000
Vermont	Montpelier	•Burlington	50	9,250	608,827	562,758	8.2	511,456	10.0	7,000	1,200	497,000
Virginia	Richmond	•Virginia Beach	51	39,594	7,078,515	6,187,358	14.4	5,346,797	15.7	48,000	8,600	2,416,000
Washington	Olympia	•Seattle	53	66,544	5,894,121	4,866,692	21.1	4,132,353	17.8	36,000	15,300	5,465,000
West Virginia	•Charleston	Huntington	54	24,078	1,808,344	1,793,477	0.8	1,950,186	-8.0	21,000	3,600	488,000
Wisconsin	Madison	•Milwaukee	55	54,310	5,363,675	4,891,769	9.6	4,705,642	4.0	77,000	15,700	5,871,000
Wyoming	•Cheyenne	Casper	56	97,100	493,782	453,588	8.9	469,557	-3.4	9,000	34,400	902,000
United States	Washington D.C.	•New York		3,537,438	281,421,906	248,709,873	13.2	226,542,294	9.8	2,129,000	938,300	207,192,000

• Largest city (metropolitan population) in the state.
(n.a.) Not applicable.
† Federal Information Processing Standards (FIPS) code for States, as published by the National Bureau of Standards, U.S. Department of Commerce.

* Source: Statistical Abstract of the United States: 2004-2005.

U.S.: Population Characteristics*

STATE	HOUSEHOLDS 2000	POPULATION IN HOUSEHOLDS 2000	PERSONS PER HOUSEHOLD 2000	POPULATION IN GROUP QUARTERS 2000	TOTAL POPULATION 2000	HISPANIC OR LATINO (OF ANY RACE) 2000†	TOTAL NOT HISPANIC OR LATINO 2000	ONE RACE 2000	WHITE 2000	BLACK OR AFRICAN AMERICAN 2000	AMERICAN INDIAN AND ALASKA NATIVE 2000	ASIAN 2000	NATIVE HAWAIIAN AND OTHER PACIFIC ISLANDER 2000	SOME OTHER RACE 2000	TWO OR MORE RACES 2000
Alabama	1,737,080	4,332,380	2.49	114,720	4,447,100	75,830	4,371,270	4,332,184	3,125,819	1,150,076	21,618	30,989	1,059	2,623	39,086
Alaska	221,600	607,583	2.74	19,349	626,932	25,852	601,080	570,626	423,788	21,073	96,505	24,741	3,181	1,338	30,454
Arizona	1,901,327	5,020,782	2.64	109,850	5,130,632	1,295,617	3,835,015	3,758,643	3,274,258	149,941	233,370	89,315	5,639	6,120	76,372
Arkansas	1,042,696	2,599,492	2.49	73,908	2,673,400	86,866	2,586,534	2,556,170	2,100,135	416,615	16,702	19,892	1,494	1,332	30,364
California	11,502,870	33,051,894	2.87	819,754	33,871,648	10,966,556	22,905,092	22,001,977	15,816,790	2,181,926	178,984	3,648,860	103,736	71,681	903,115
Colorado	1,658,238	4,198,306	2.53	102,955	4,301,261	735,601	3,565,660	3,492,939	3,202,880	158,443	28,982	93,277	3,845	5,512	72,721
Connecticut	1,301,670	3,297,626	2.53	107,939	3,405,565	320,323	3,085,242	3,032,346	2,638,845	295,571	7,267	81,564	958	8,141	52,896
Delaware	298,736	759,017	2.54	24,583	783,600	37,277	746,323	736,101	567,973	148,435	2,324	16,110	234	1,025	10,222
District of Columbia	248,338	536,497	2.16	35,562	572,059	44,953	527,106	517,522	159,178	340,088	1,274	15,039	273	1,670	9,584
Florida	6,337,929	15,593,433	2.46	388,945	15,982,378	2,682,715	13,299,663	13,062,709	10,458,509	2,264,268	42,358	261,693	6,887	28,994	236,954
Georgia	3,006,369	7,952,631	2.65	233,822	8,186,453	435,227	7,751,226	7,663,862	5,128,661	2,331,465	17,670	171,513	3,278	11,275	87,364
Hawaii	403,240	1,175,755	2.92	35,782	1,211,537	87,699	1,123,838	905,138	277,091	20,829	2,539	494,149	108,441	2,089	218,700
Idaho	469,645	1,262,457	2.69	31,496	1,293,953	101,690	1,192,263	1,174,002	1,139,291	4,889	15,789	11,641	1,200	1,192	18,261
Illinois	4,591,779	12,097,512	2.63	321,781	12,419,293	1,530,262	10,889,031	10,735,035	8,424,140	1,856,152	18,232	419,916	3,116	13,479	153,996
Indiana	2,336,306	5,902,331	2.53	178,154	6,080,485	214,536	5,865,949	5,804,834	5,219,373	505,462	13,654	58,424	1,573	6,348	61,115
Iowa	1,149,276	2,822,155	2.46	104,169	2,926,324	82,473	2,843,851	2,818,379	2,710,344	60,744	7,955	36,345	888	2,103	25,472
Kansas	1,037,891	2,606,468	2.51	81,950	2,688,418	188,252	2,500,166	2,457,658	2,233,997	151,407	22,322	46,301	1,154	2,477	42,508
Kentucky	1,590,647	3,926,965	2.47	114,804	4,041,769	59,939	3,981,830	3,944,080	3,608,013	293,639	7,939	29,368	1,275	3,846	37,750
Louisiana	1,656,053	4,333,011	2.62	135,965	4,468,976	107,738	4,361,238	4,321,978	2,794,391	1,443,390	24,129	54,256	1,076	4,736	39,260
Maine	518,200	1,240,011	2.39	34,912	1,274,923	9,360	1,265,563	1,253,832	1,230,297	6,440	6,911	9,014	334	836	11,731
Maryland	1,980,859	5,162,430	2.61	134,056	5,296,486	227,916	5,068,570	4,985,624	3,286,547	1,464,735	13,312	209,738	1,913	9,379	82,946
Massachusetts	2,443,580	6,127,881	2.51	221,216	6,349,097	428,729	5,920,368	5,810,030	5,198,359	318,329	11,264	236,786	1,706	43,586	110,338
Michigan	3,785,661	9,688,555	2.56	249,889	9,938,444	323,877	9,614,567	9,451,080	7,806,691	1,402,047	53,421	175,311	2,145	11,465	163,487
Minnesota	1,895,127	4,783,596	2.52	135,883	4,919,479	143,382	4,776,097	4,705,793	4,337,143	168,813	52,009	141,083	1,714	5,031	70,304
Mississippi	1,046,434	2,749,244	2.63	95,414	2,844,658	39,569	2,805,089	2,787,817	1,727,908	1,028,473	11,224	18,349	569	1,294	17,272
Missouri	2,194,594	5,433,153	2.48	162,058	5,595,211	118,592	5,476,619	5,404,714	4,686,474	625,667	23,302	61,041	2,939	5,291	71,905
Montana	358,667	877,433	2.45	24,762	902,195	18,081	884,114	870,346	807,823	2,534	54,426	4,569	425	569	13,768
Nebraska	666,184	1,660,445	2.49	50,818	1,711,263	94,425	1,616,838	1,599,142	1,494,494	67,537	13,460	21,677	647	1,327	17,696
Nevada	751,165	1,964,582	2.62	33,675	1,998,257	393,970	1,604,287	1,555,056	1,303,001	131,509	21,397	88,593	7,769	2,787	49,231
New Hampshire	474,606	1,200,247	2.53	35,539	1,235,786	20,489	1,215,297	1,203,691	1,175,252	8,354	2,698	15,803	330	1,254	11,606
New Jersey	3,064,645	8,219,529	2.68	194,821	8,414,350	1,117,191	7,297,159	7,163,470	5,557,209	1,096,171	11,338	477,012	2,175	19,565	133,689
New Mexico	677,971	1,782,739	2.63	36,307	1,819,046	765,386	1,053,660	1,027,867	813,495	30,654	161,460	18,257	992	3,009	25,793
New York	7,056,860	18,395,996	2.61	580,461	18,976,457	2,867,583	16,108,874	15,742,758	11,760,981	2,812,623	52,499	1,035,926	5,230	75,499	366,116
North Carolina	3,132,013	7,795,432	2.49	253,881	8,049,313	378,963	7,670,350	7,590,385	5,647,155	1,723,301	95,333	112,416	3,165	9,015	79,965
North Dakota	257,152	618,569	2.41	23,631	642,200	7,786	634,414	627,748	589,149	3,761	30,772	3,566	218	282	6,666
Ohio	4,445,773	11,054,019	2.49	299,121	11,353,140	217,123	11,136,017	10,998,247	9,538,111	1,290,662	21,985	131,670	2,336	13,483	137,770
Oklahoma	1,342,293	3,338,279	2.49	112,375	3,450,654	179,304	3,271,350	3,131,101	2,556,368	257,981	266,158	46,172	2,100	2,322	140,249
Oregon	1,333,723	3,343,908	2.51	77,491	3,421,399	275,314	3,146,085	3,063,352	2,857,616	53,325	40,130	100,333	7,398	4,550	82,733
Pennsylvania	4,777,003	11,847,753	2.48	433,301	12,281,054	394,088	11,886,966	11,773,869	10,322,455	1,202,437	14,904	218,296	2,691	13,086	113,097
Rhode Island	408,424	1,009,503	2.47	38,816	1,048,319	90,820	957,499	936,683	858,433	41,922	4,181	23,416	320	8,411	20,816
South Carolina	1,533,854	3,876,975	2.53	135,037	4,012,012	95,076	3,916,936	3,883,646	2,652,291	1,178,486	12,765	35,568	1,270	3,266	33,290
South Dakota	290,245	726,426	2.50	28,418	754,844	10,903	743,941	734,981	664,585	4,563	60,988	4,316	219	310	8,960
Tennessee	2,232,905	5,541,337	2.48	147,946	5,689,283	123,838	5,565,445	5,510,621	4,505,930	928,204	13,820	56,077	1,810	4,780	54,824
Texas	7,393,354	20,290,711	2.74	561,109	20,851,820	6,669,666	14,182,154	13,951,587	10,933,313	2,364,255	68,859	554,445	10,757	19,958	230,567
Utah	701,281	2,192,689	3.13	40,480	2,233,169	201,559	2,031,610	2,000,302	1,904,265	16,137	26,663	36,483	14,806	1,948	31,308
Vermont	240,634	588,067	2.44	20,760	608,827	5,504	603,323	596,514	585,431	2,921	2,325	5,160	120	557	6,809
Virginia	2,699,173	6,847,117	2.54	231,398	7,078,515	329,540	6,748,975	6,634,953	4,965,637	1,376,378	18,596	259,277	3,380	11,685	114,022
Washington	2,271,398	5,757,739	2.53	136,382	5,894,121	441,509	5,452,612	5,276,686	4,652,490	184,631	85,396	319,401	22,779	11,989	175,926
West Virginia	736,481	1,765,197	2.40	43,147	1,808,344	12,279	1,796,065	1,781,082	1,709,966	56,825	3,456	9,356	335	1,144	14,983
Wisconsin	2,084,544	5,207,717	2.50	155,958	5,363,675	192,921	5,170,754	5,118,833	4,681,630	300,245	43,980	87,995	1,346	3,637	51,921
Wyoming	193,608	479,699	2.48	14,083	493,782	31,669	462,113	455,949	438,799	3,504	10,238	2,670	264	474	6,164
TOTAL	105,480,101	273,643,273	2.59	7,778,633	281,421,906	35,305,818	246,116,088	241,513,942	194,552,774	33,947,837	2,068,883	10,123,169	353,509	467,770	4,602,146

* Total U.S. population of 281,421,906 comprises White, Black, American Indian, Alaska Native, Asian, Native Hawaiian, other Pacific Islander, some other race, and two or more races.
Source: 2000 U.S. Census of Population and Housing.

† "Hispanic or Latino" consists of persons classifying themselves as Mexican, Puerto Rican, Cuban, South or Central American, or of other Spanish/Hispanic culture or origin.
Persons of Hispanic or Latino origin may be of any race.

Map Introduction

This section of the *Commercial Atlas & Marketing Guide* presents a series of maps of the United States. The first map in this series is a United States road map, followed by a map that shows both the distance and the approximate driving time between hundreds of cities across North America. Next is a mileage chart that offers more than 5,300 mileages between 90 North American cities and National Parks.

Next are 113 pages of state reference maps that enable the user to see the geographic location of the counties and places appearing in the *Commercial Atlas* tables and index. These maps include populated places, Ranally Metropolitan Areas (RMAs), major transportation features, time zones, selected parks, and important physical features. Inset maps for major cities provide a greater level of detail for these special areas. Places listed in the *Commercial Atlas* state index in Volume 2 are linked to the state reference maps using letters and numbers along the map border. For example, a place in the index with a key of D-9 would be located at the intersection of row D and column 9 on the map. For more information about the state index see the Introduction beginning on page 5 in Volume 2. A detailed legend for the state reference maps appears at the bottom of this page.

Following the state reference maps are county subdivision maps for New England and other selected states. Maps are included for every state for which townships and other selected county subdivisions are included in the *Commercial Atlas* index and tables. For general information about county subdivisions see the Glossary of Terms beginning on page 5. For detailed information about county subdivisions in an individual state, see the Administrative Divisions section that precedes the state index in Volume 2.

Legend for State Reference Maps

Cities and towns

- Ranally Metropolitan Areas (RMA)
- National capital
- State capital
- County seat
- Other city or town

Administrative areas

- State boundaries
- County boundaries
- COOK County names

Roads and related symbols

- Limited access highway
- Limited access highway — under construction
- Other through highway
- Other road
- Unpaved road
- Interstate highway
- U.S. highway
- State highway
- Secondary state or county highway

Points of interest and parks

- Park
- National Forest
- Campsite
- Indian reservation
- Point of interest, historic site or monument
- Golf course

Other symbols

- Area covered by inset map
- Inset map page indicator
- Hospital, medical center
- Building
- Airport; military installation
- Major airport outside map area
- Cemetery
- Dam
- Mountain peak; highest point in state
- Port of entry
- Tourist information center
- Swamp
- Time zone boundary
- Continental divide

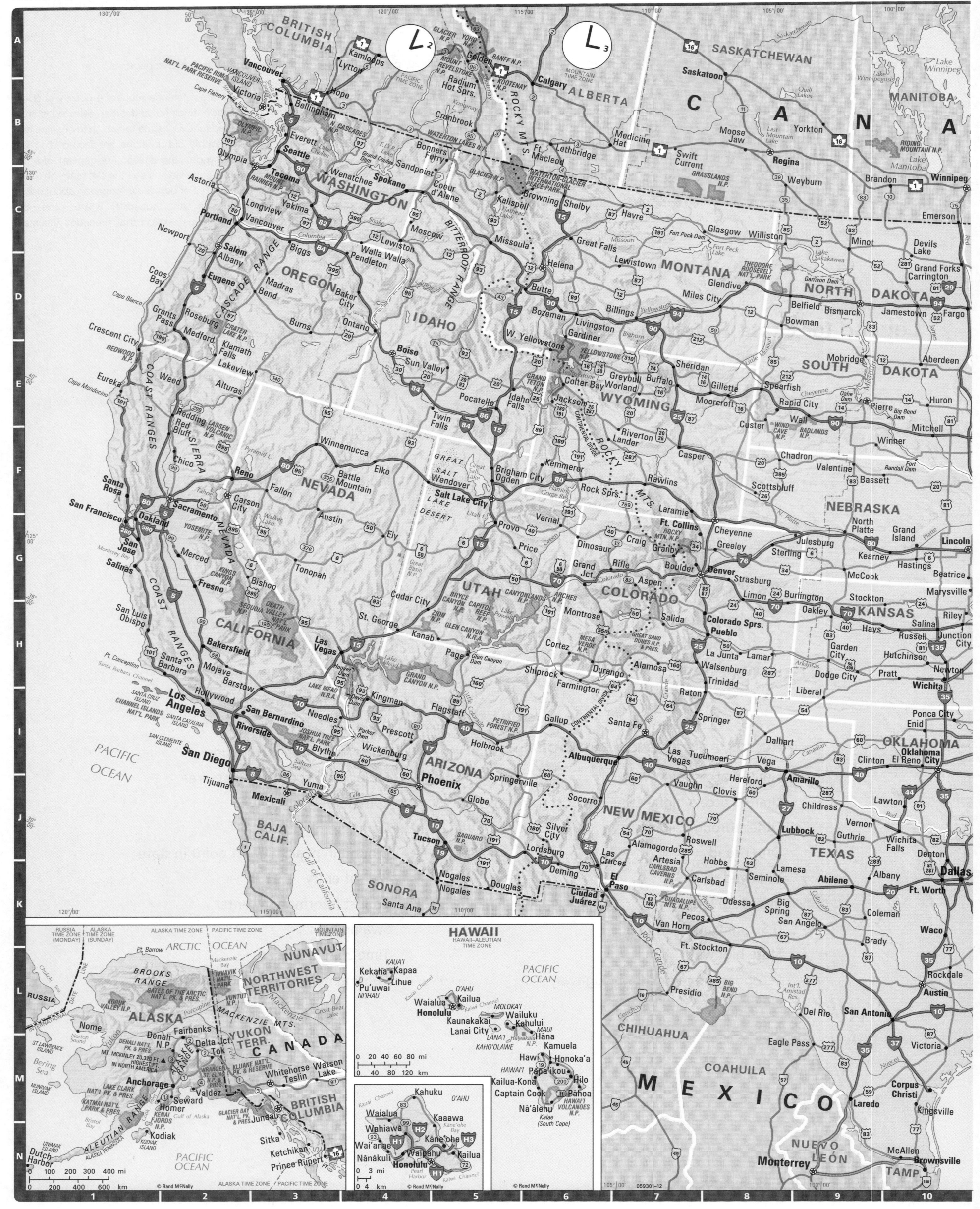

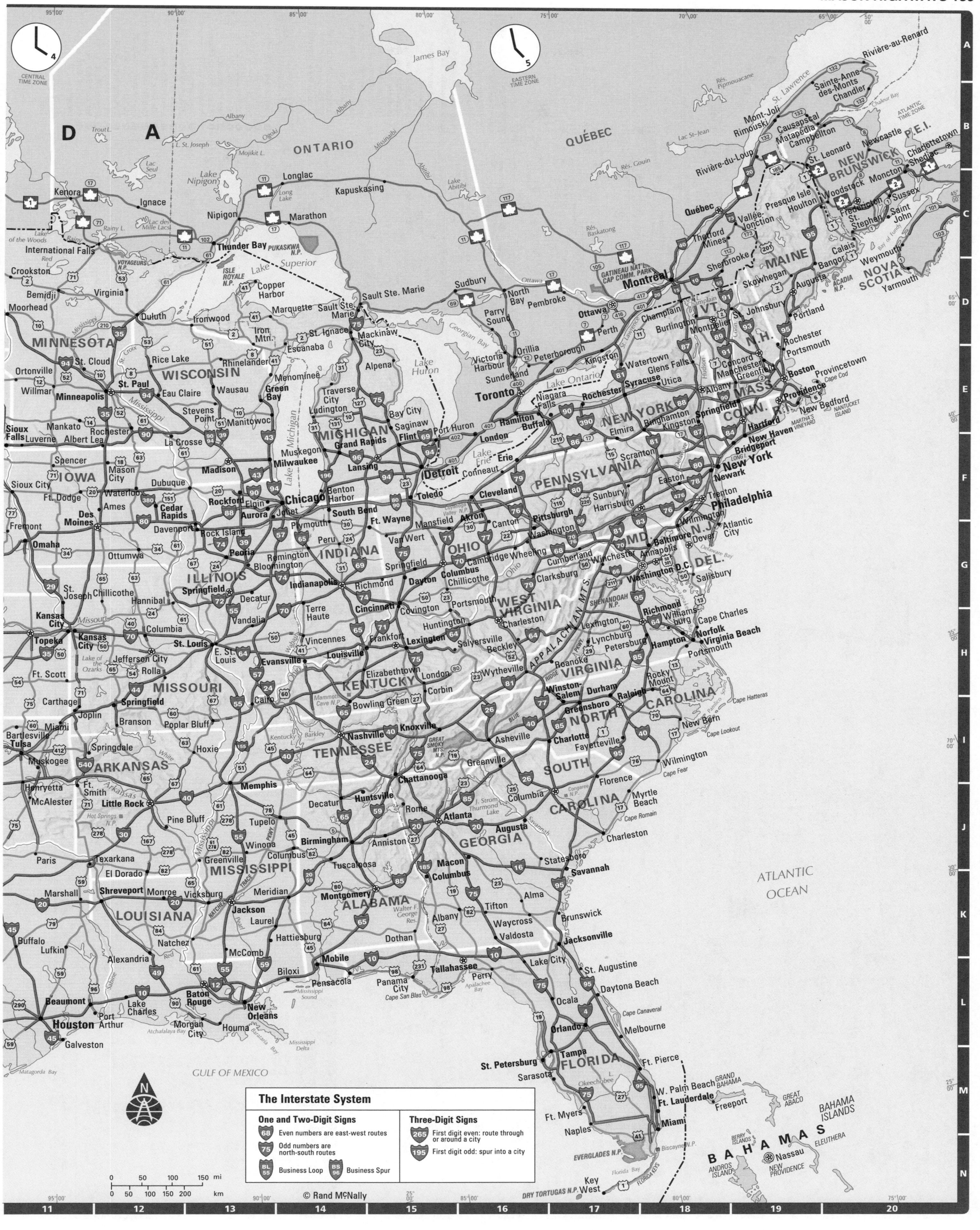

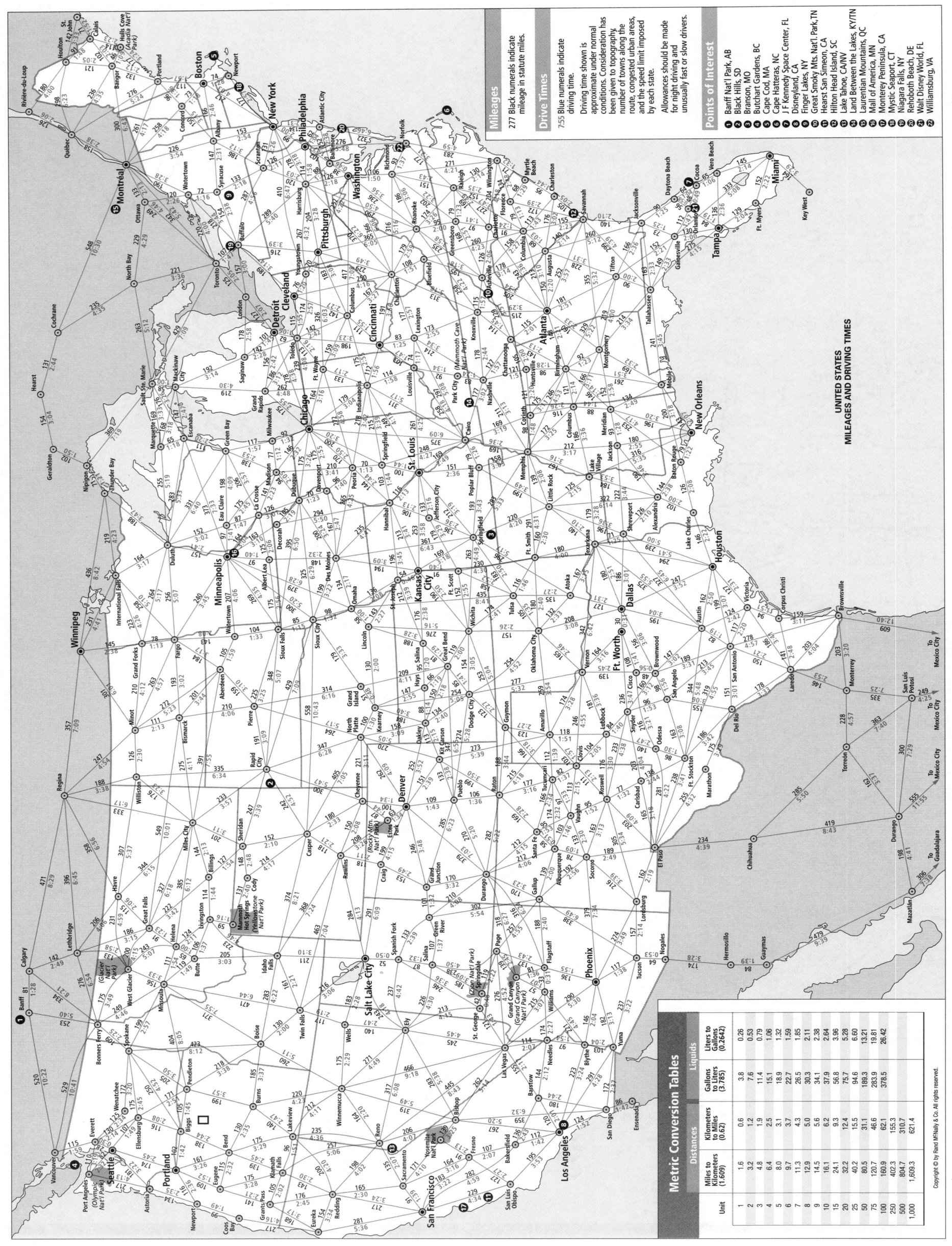

UNITED STATES
MILEAGES AND DRIVING TIMES

Mileages
277 Black numerals indicate mileage in statute miles.

Drive Times
755 Blue numerals indicate driving time.

Driving time shown is approximate under normal conditions. Consideration has been given to topography, the number of towns along the route, congested urban areas, and the speed limit imposed by each state.

Allowances should be made for night driving and unusually fast or slow drivers.

Points of Interest

1. Banff Nat'l Park, AB
2. Black Hills, SD
3. Branson, MO
4. Butchart Gardens, BC
5. Cape Cod, MA
6. Cape Hatteras, NC
7. J F Kennedy Space Center, FL
8. Disneyland, CA
9. Finger Lakes, NY
10. Great Smoky Mts. Nat'l Park, TN
11. Hearst San Simeon, CA
12. Hilton Head Island, SC
13. Lake Between the Lakes, KY/TN
14. Lake Tahoe, CA/NV
15. Laurentian Mountains, QC
16. Mall of America, MN
17. Monterey Peninsula, CA
18. Niagara Falls, NY
19. Mystic Seaport, CT
20. Rehoboth Beach, DE
21. Walt Disney World, FL
22. Williamsburg, VA

Metric Conversion Tables

	Distances		Liquids	
Unit	Miles to Kilometers (1.609)	Kilometers to Miles (0.62)	Gallons to Liters (3.785)	Liters to Gallons (0.2642)
1	1.6	0.6	3.8	0.26
2	3.2	1.2	7.6	0.53
3	4.8	1.9	11.4	0.79
4	6.4	2.5	15.1	1.06
5	8.0	3.1	18.9	1.32
6	9.7	3.7	22.7	1.59
7	11.3	4.3	26.5	1.85
8	12.9	5.0	30.3	2.11
9	14.5	5.6	34.1	2.38
10	16.1	6.2	37.9	2.64
15	24.1	9.3	56.8	3.96
20	32.2	12.4	75.7	5.28
25	40.2	15.5	94.6	6.60
50	80.5	31.1	189.3	13.21
75	120.7	46.6	283.9	19.81
100	160.9	62.1	378.5	26.42
250	402.3	155.3		
500	804.7	310.7		
1,000	1,609.3	621.4		

Mileages in this chart are based upon the routes usually followed by motorists. Highway systems involved include interstate, U.S., and state highways.

Mileages ©Rand McNally

City labels (top, reading down): Wichita KS, Washington DC, Seattle WA, San Francisco CA, San Diego CA, San Antonio TX, Salt Lake City UT, St. Louis MO, Reno NV, Rapid City SD, Portland OR, Portland ME, Pittsburgh PA, Phoenix AZ, Philadelphia PA, Orlando FL, Omaha NE, Oklahoma City OK, Norfolk VA, New York NY, New Orleans LA, Nashville TN, Minneapolis MN, Milwaukee WI, Miami FL, Memphis TN, Louisville KY, Los Angeles CA, Little Rock AR, Las Vegas NV, Kansas City MO, Jacksonville FL, Jackson MS, Indianapolis IN, Houston TX, Hartford CT, Grand Junction CO, Fargo ND, El Paso TX, Detroit MI, Des Moines IA, Denver CO, Dallas TX, Columbus OH, Columbia SC, Cleveland OH, Chicago IL, Cheyenne WY, Charlotte NC, Charleston WV, Charleston SC, Buffalo NY, Boston MA, Boise ID, Birmingham AL, Billings MT, Baltimore MD, Atlanta GA, Albuquerque NM, Albany NY

City labels (left/bottom column): Acadia N.P. ME, Albany NY, Albuquerque NM, Amarillo TX, Atlanta GA, Baltimore MD, Big Bend N.P. TX, Billings MT, Birmingham AL, Boise ID, Boston MA, Brownsville TX, Buffalo NY, Calgary AB, Charleston SC, Charleston WV, Charlotte NC, Cheyenne WY, Chicago IL, Cincinnati OH, Cleveland OH, Columbia SC, Columbus OH, Crater Lake N.P. OR, Dallas TX, Denver CO, Des Moines IA, Detroit MI, El Paso TX, Fargo ND, Grand Canyon N.P. AZ, Grand Junction CO, Great Smoky Mtn N.P., Hartford CT, Houston TX, Indianapolis IN, Jackson MS, Jacksonville FL, Kansas City MO, Las Vegas NV, Little Rock AR, Los Angeles CA, Louisville KY, Memphis TN, Mexico City MX, Miami FL, Milwaukee WI, Minneapolis MN, Mobile AL, Montpelier VT, Montreal QC, Nashville TN, New Orleans LA, New York NY, Norfolk VA, Oklahoma City OK, Omaha NE, Orlando FL, Philadelphia PA, Phoenix AZ, Pittsburgh PA, Portland ME, Portland OR, Quebec QC, Raleigh NC, Rapid City SD, Regina SK, Reno NV, St. Louis MO, Salt Lake City UT, San Antonio TX, San Diego CA, San Francisco CA, Sault Ste. Marie ON, Savannah GA, Seattle WA, Shenandoah N.P. VA, Shreveport LA, Spokane WA, Tampa FL, Thunder Bay ON, Toronto ON, Tucson AZ, Vancouver BC, Washington DC, Wichita KS, Winnipeg MB, Yellowstone N.P. WY, Yosemite N.P. CA

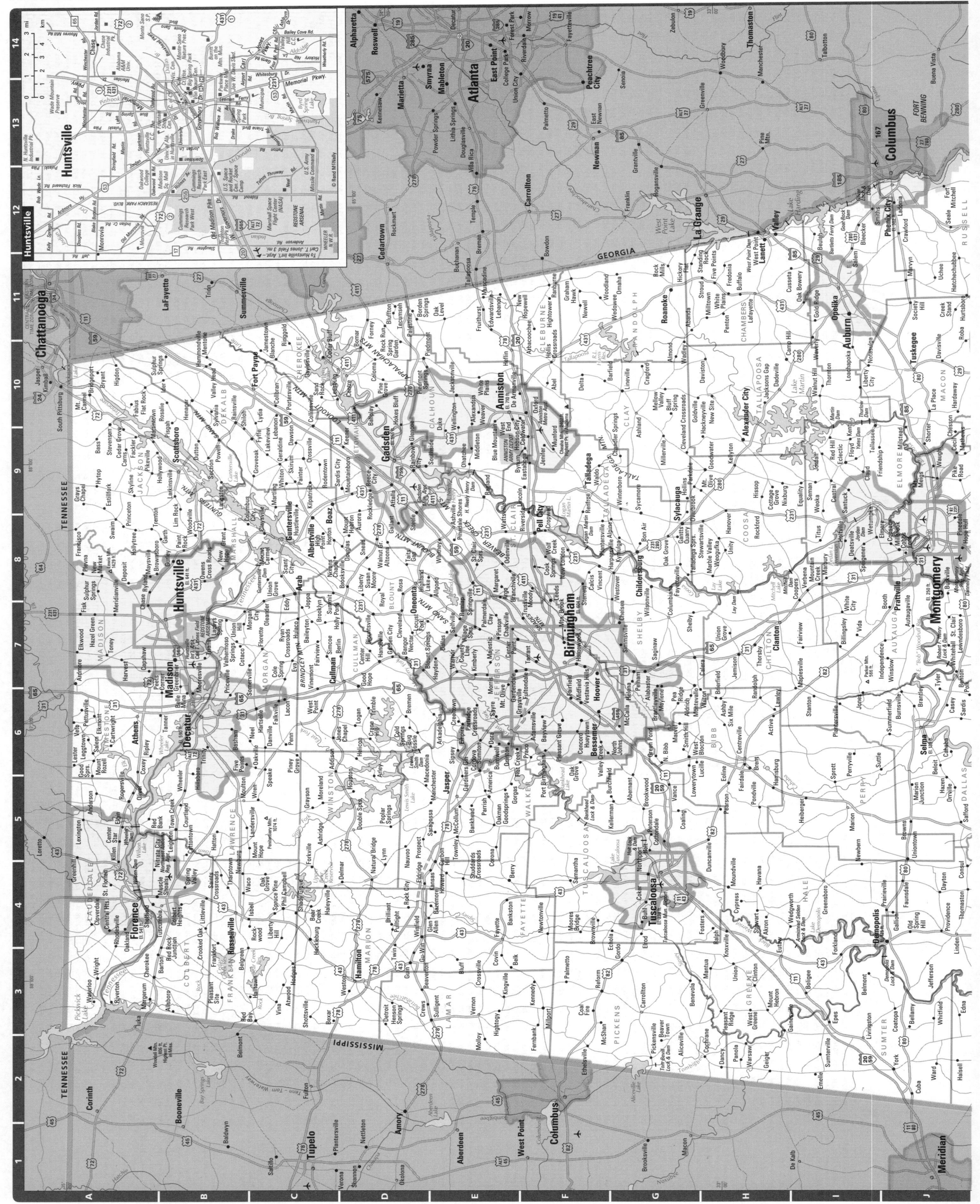

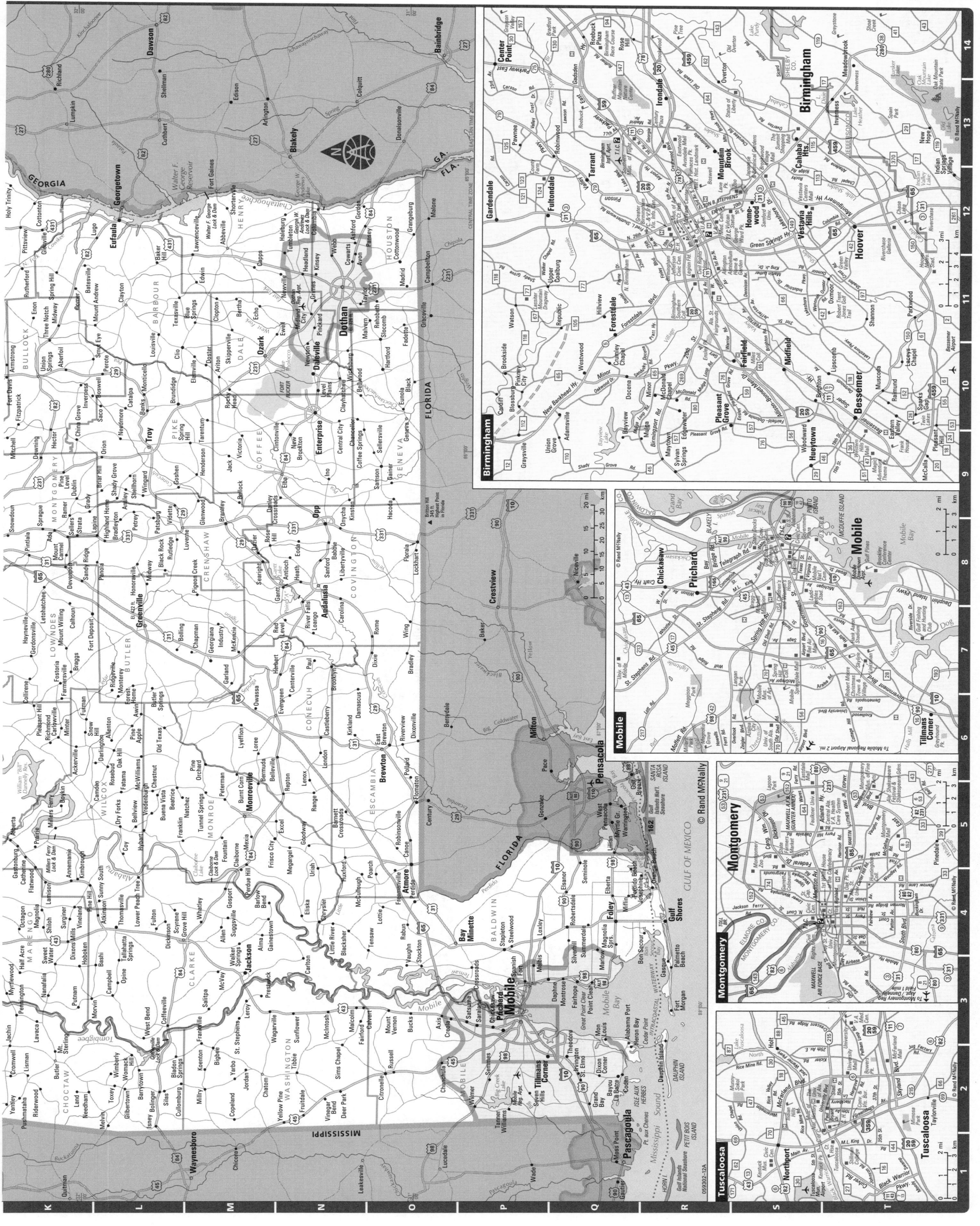

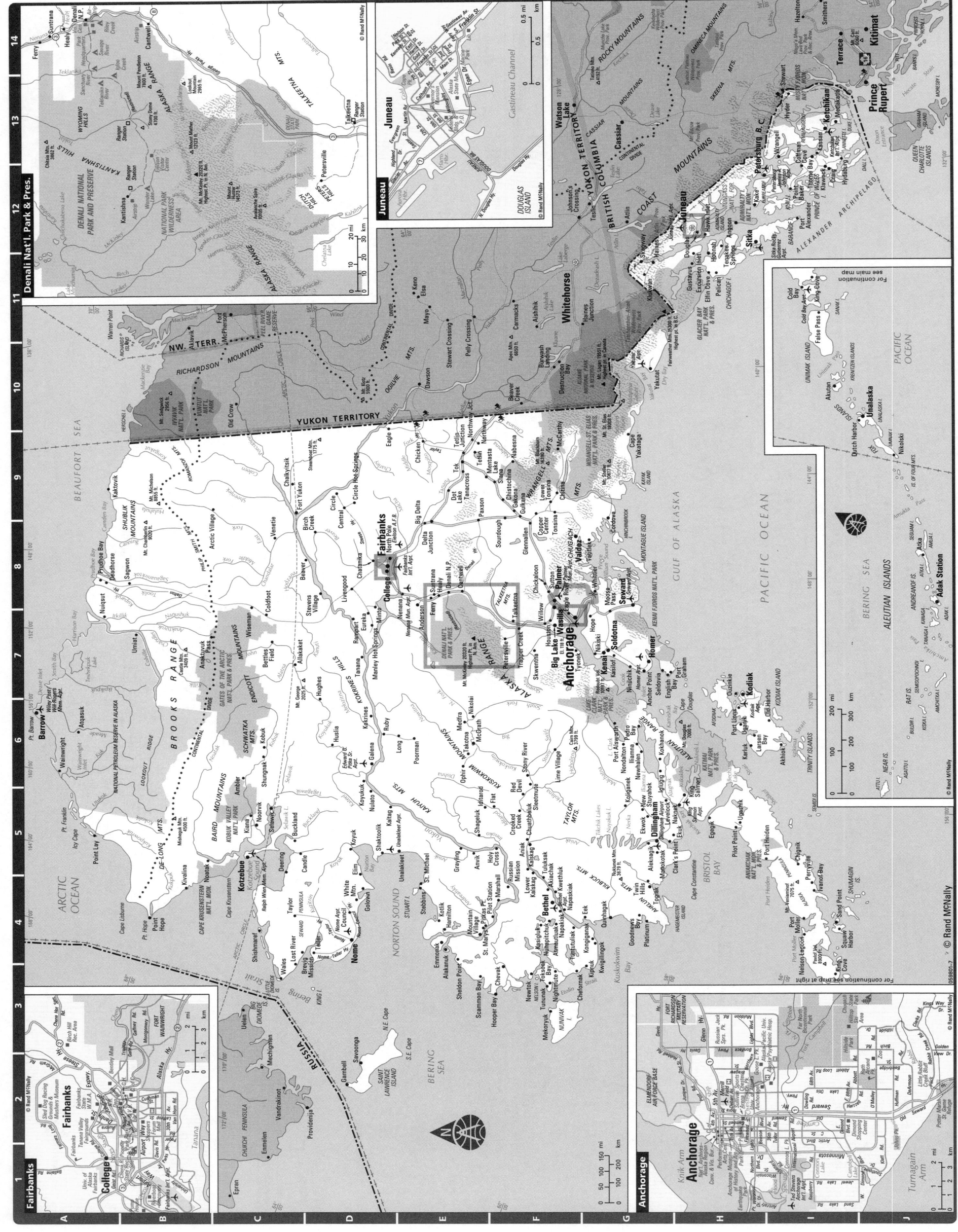

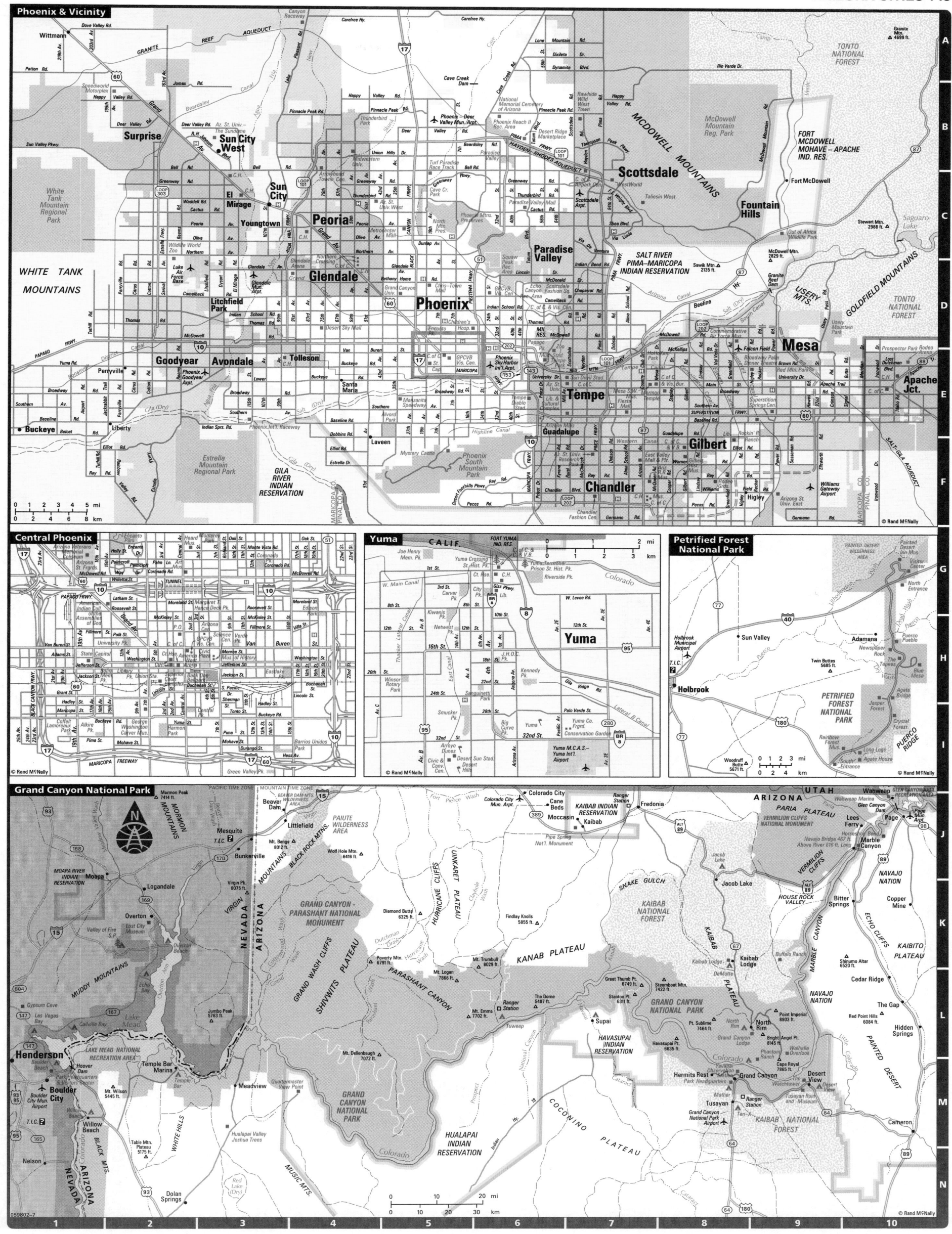

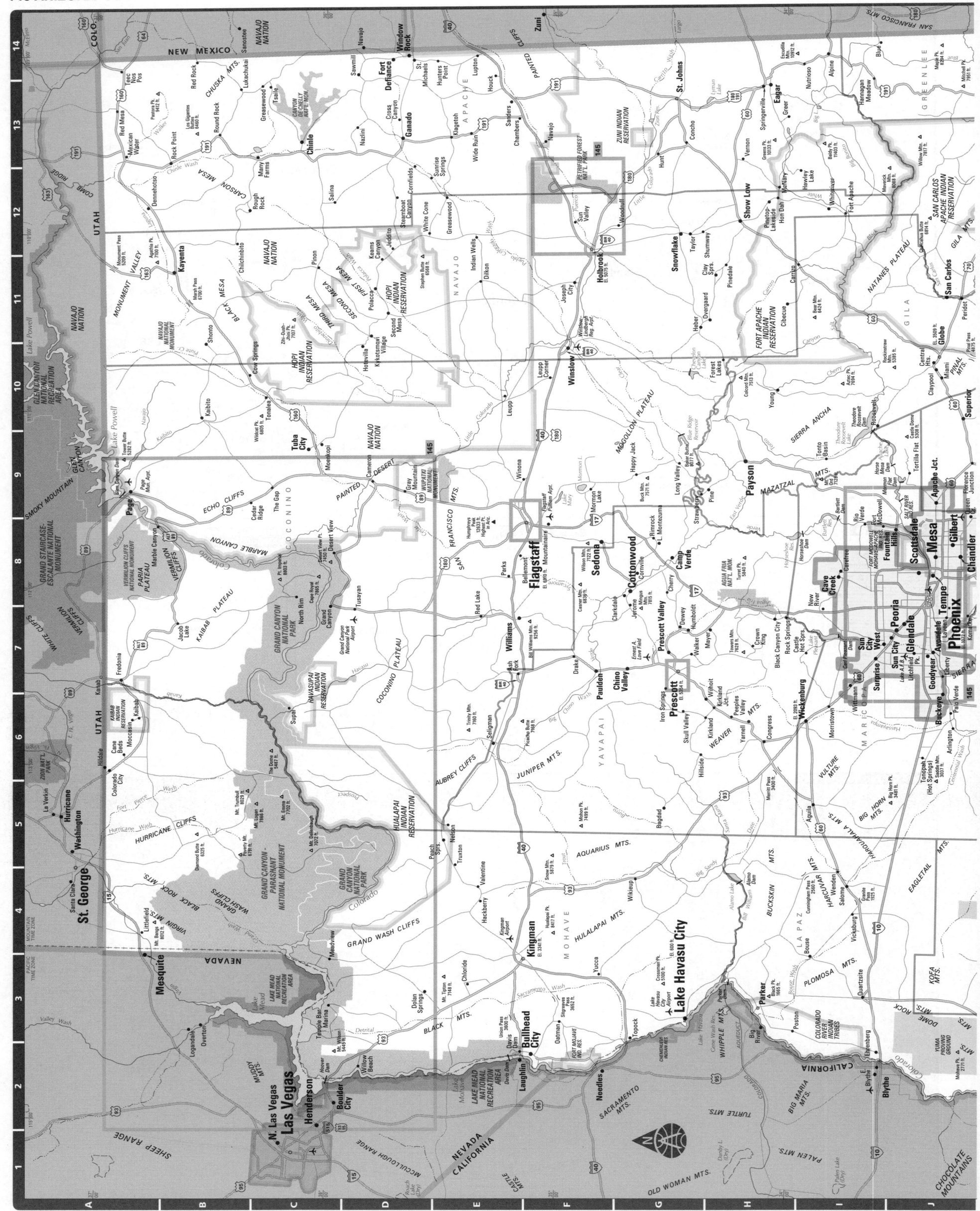

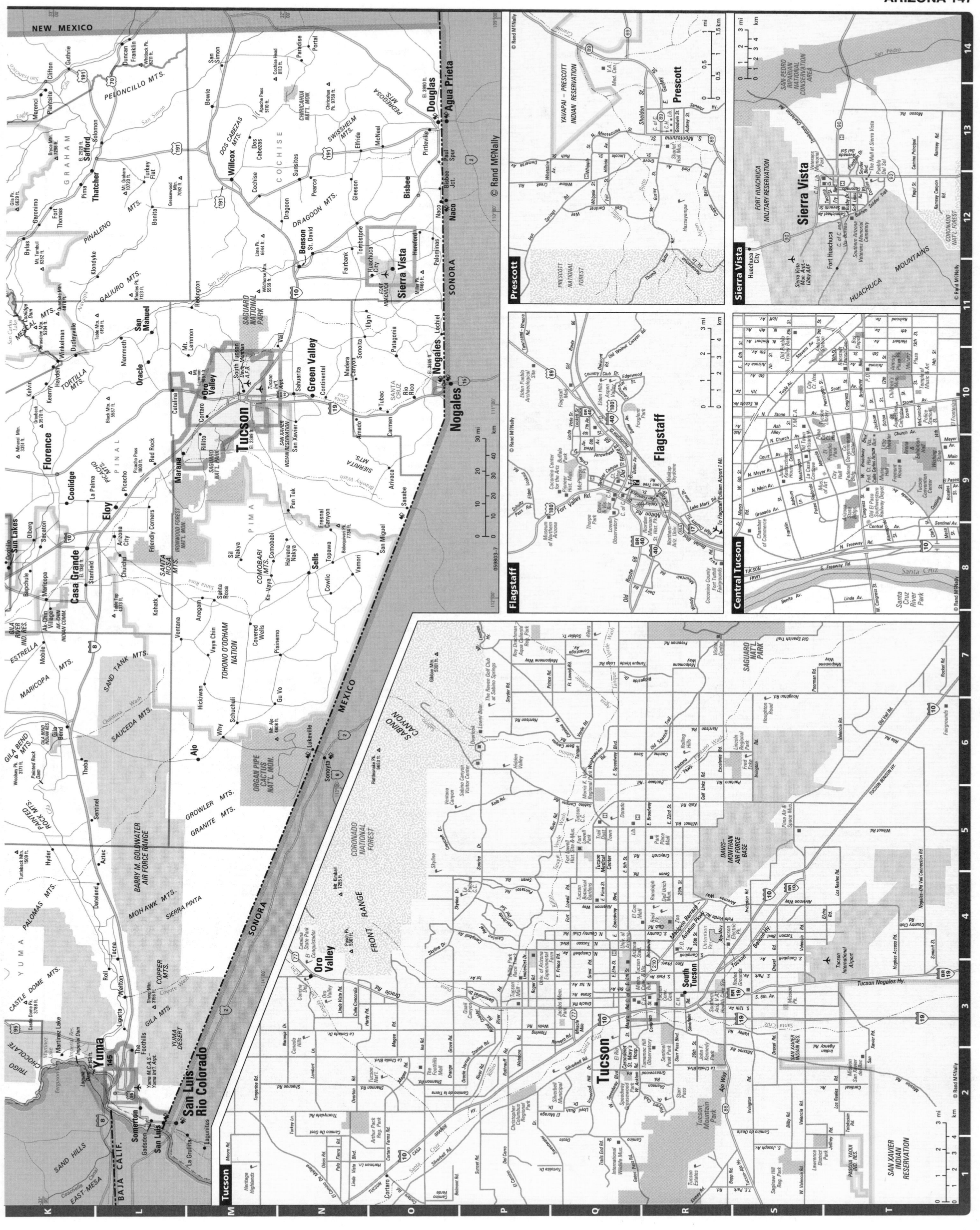

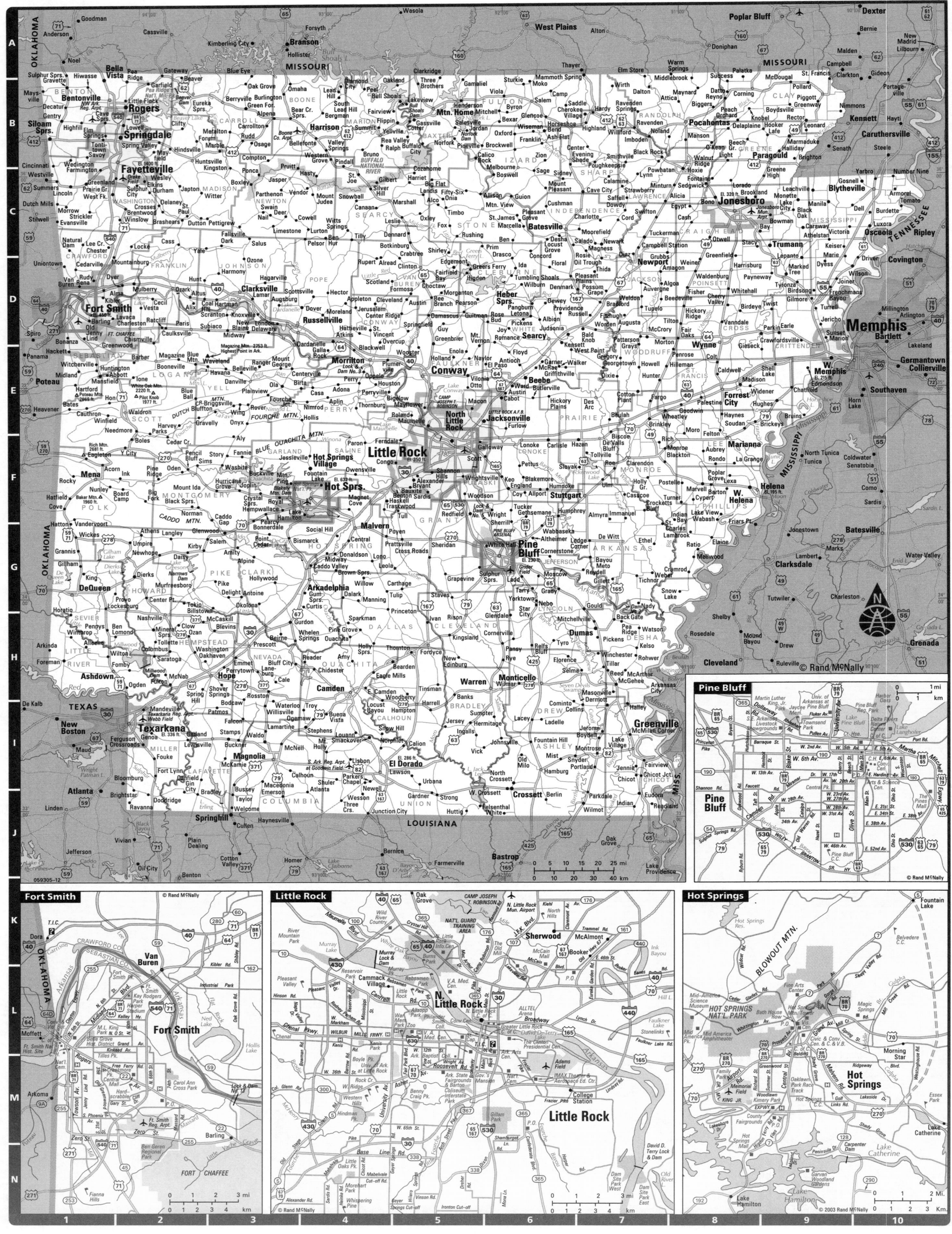

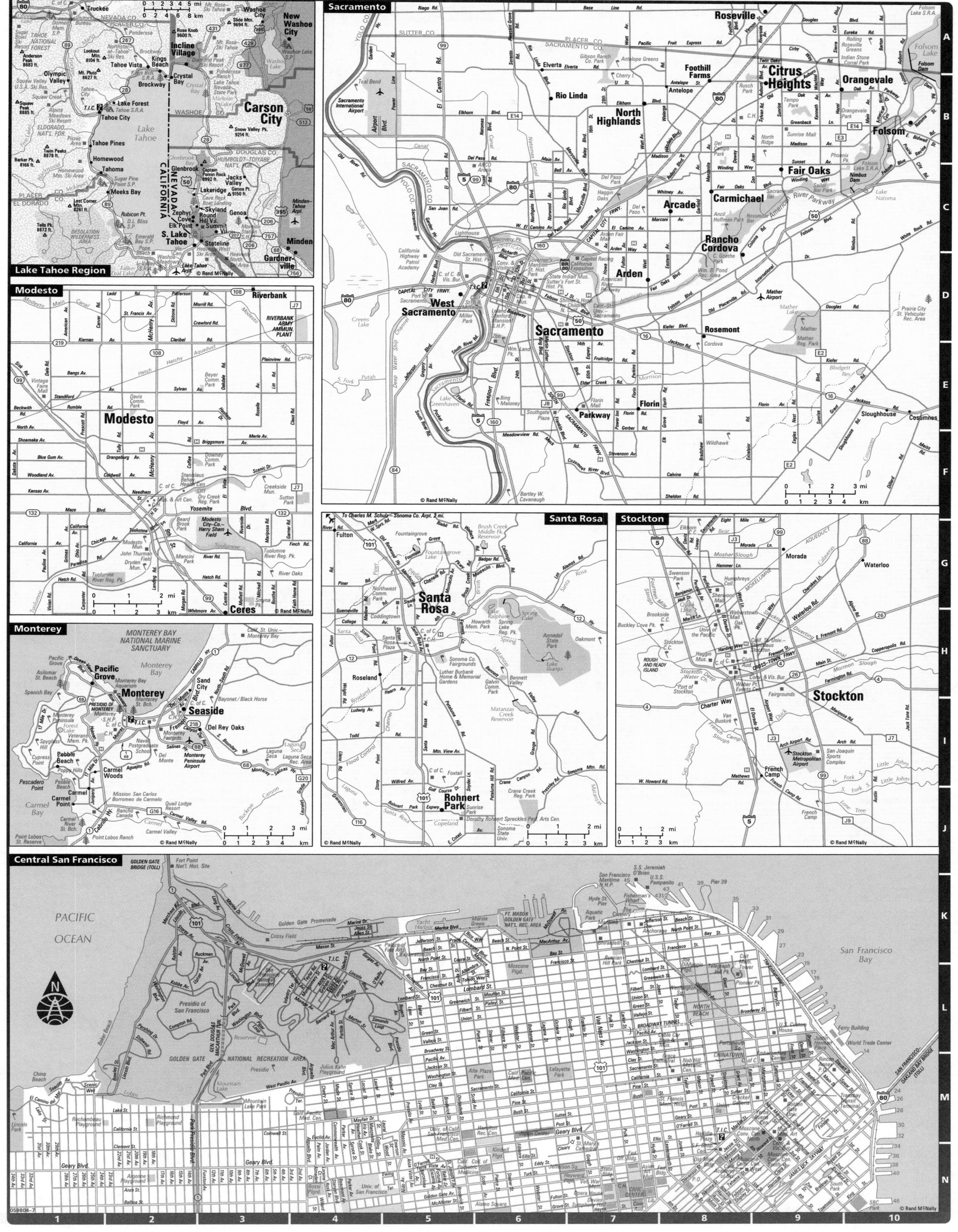

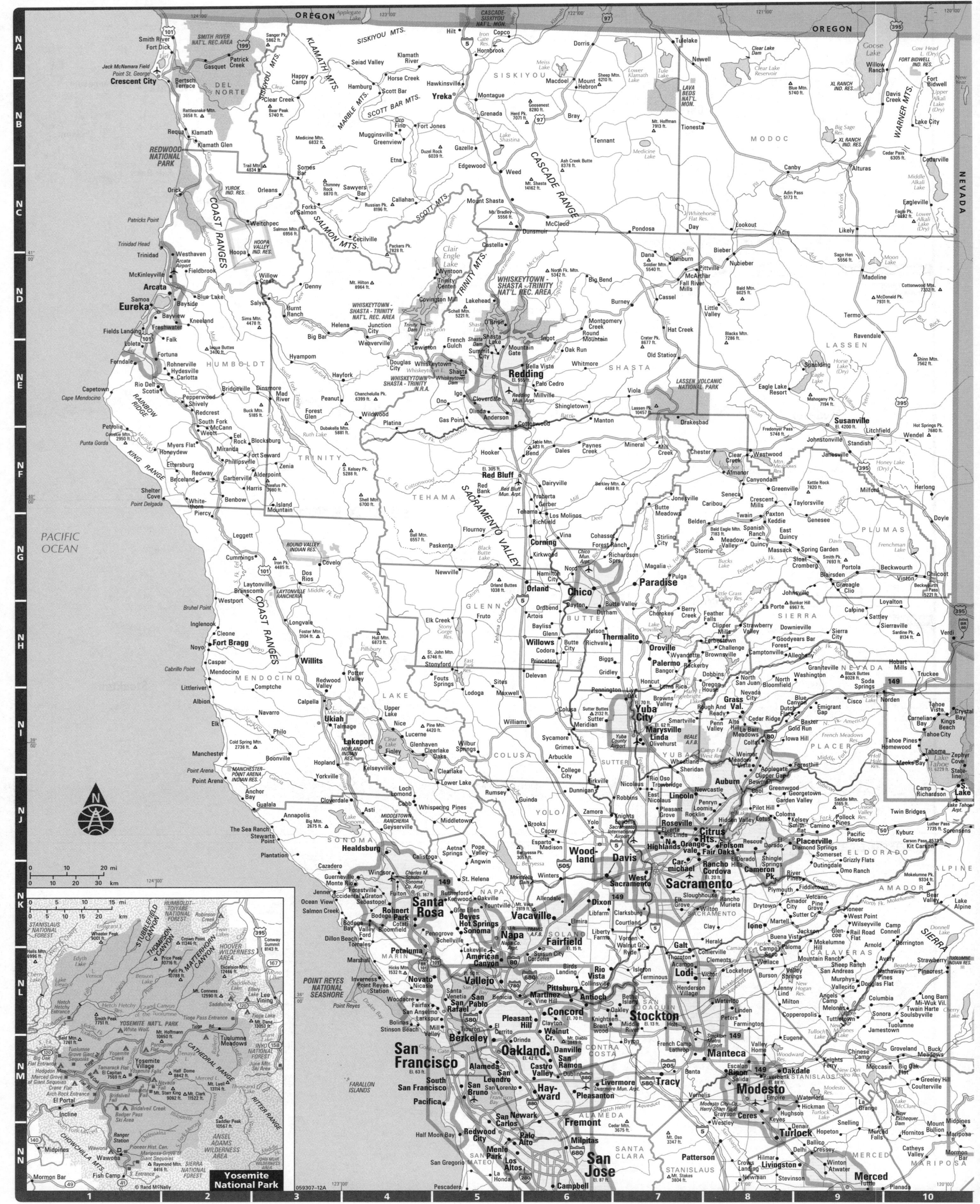

Yosemite National Park

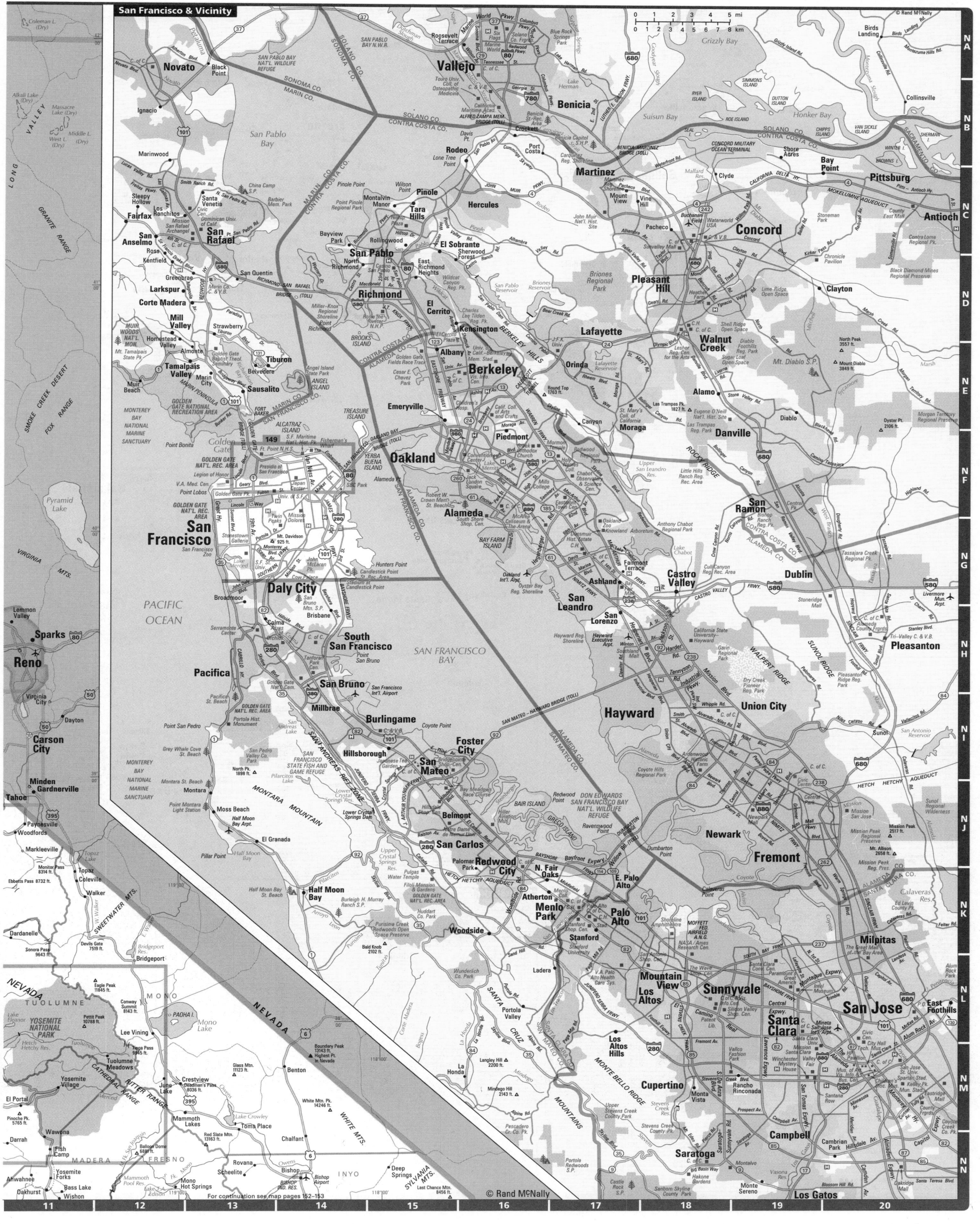

San Francisco & Vicinity

© Rand McNally

For continuation see map pages 152-153

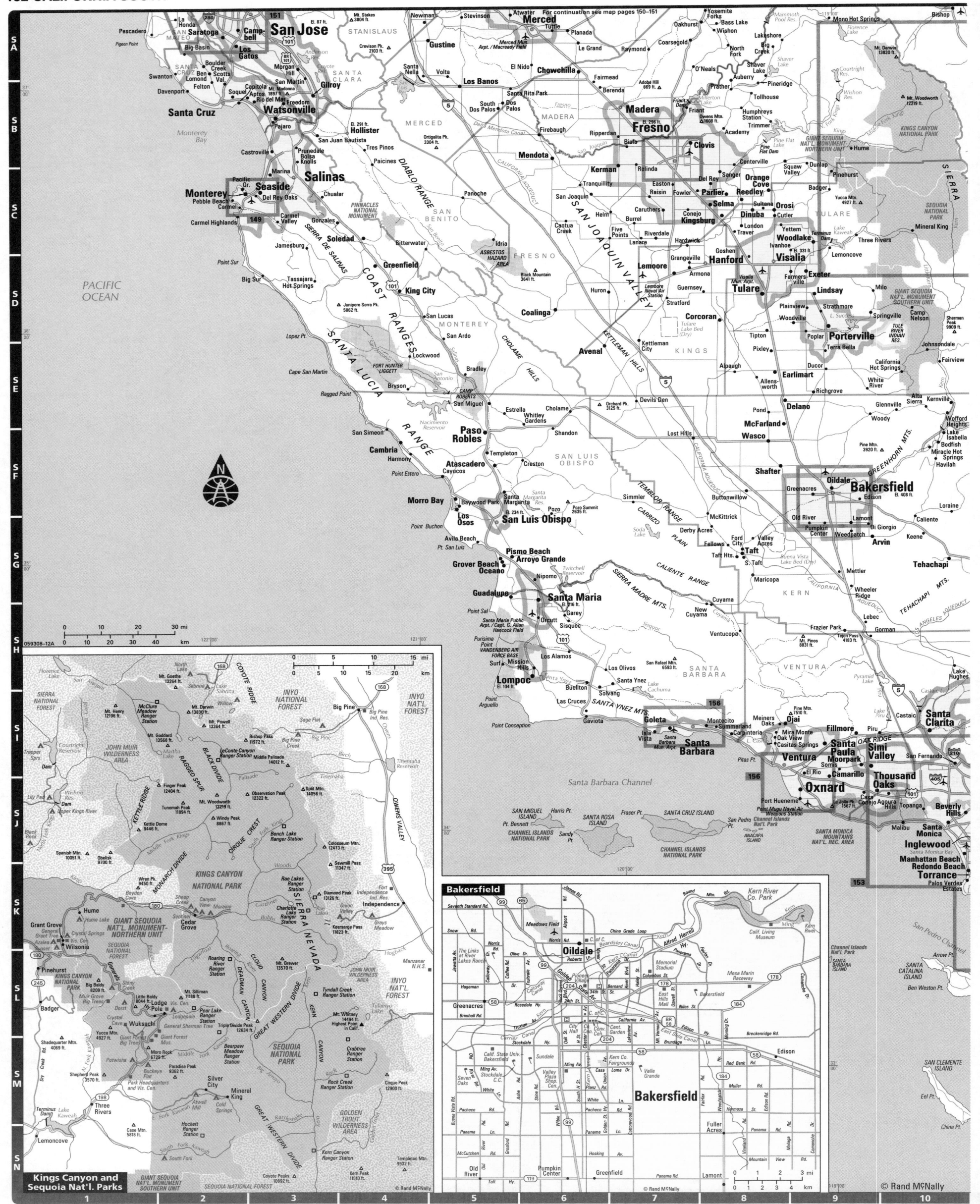

Kings Canyon and
Sequoia Nat'l. Parks

Bakersfield

© Rand McNally

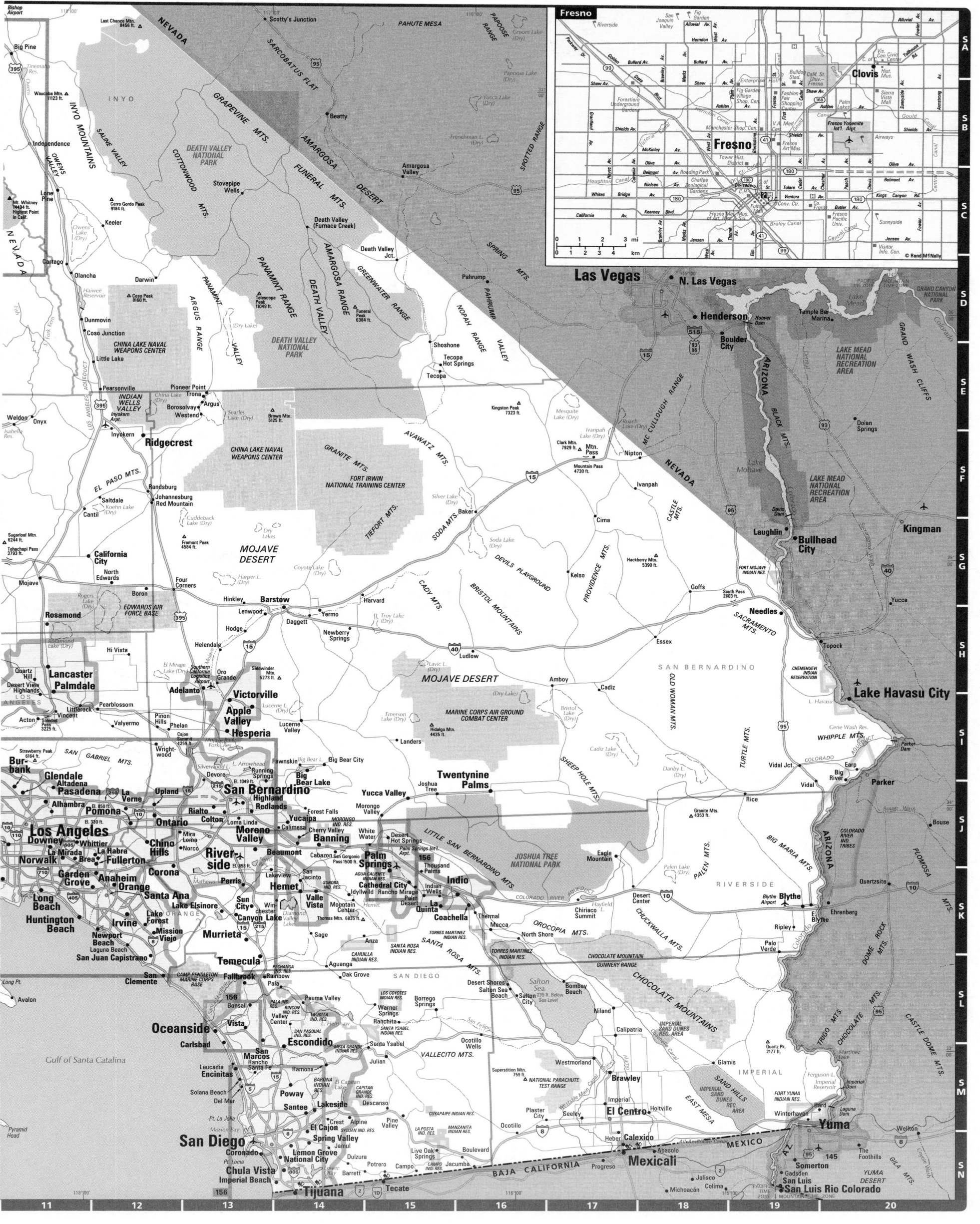

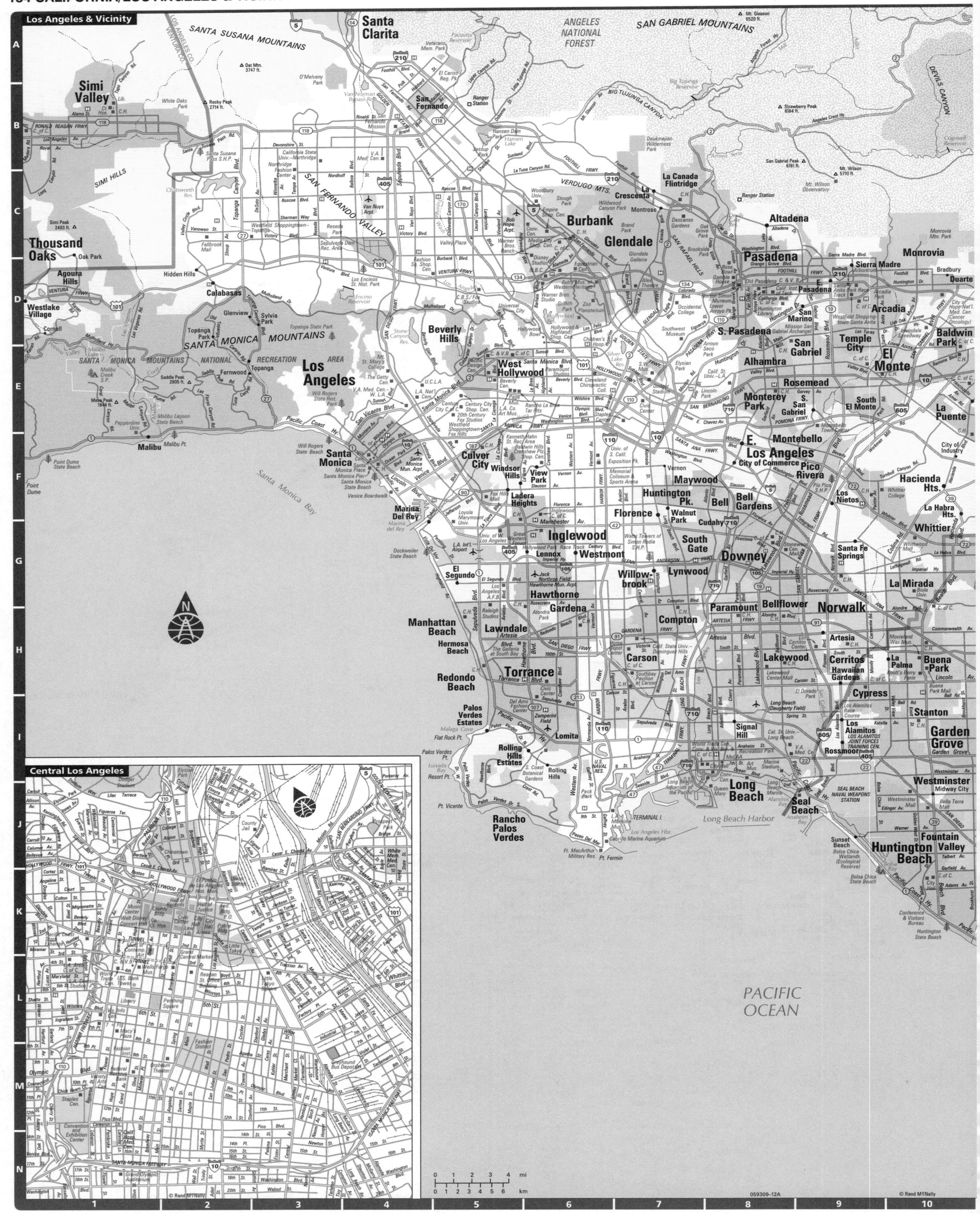

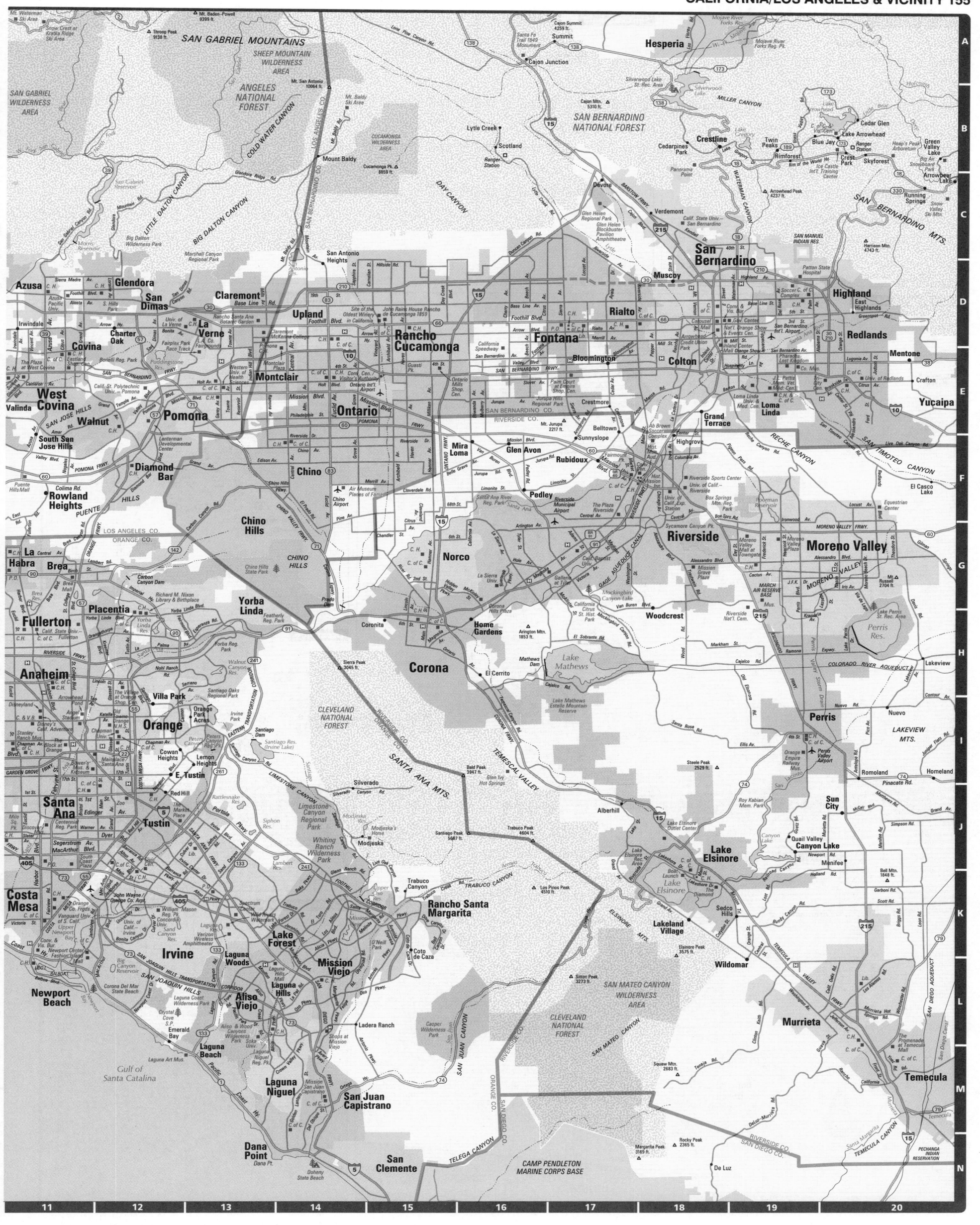

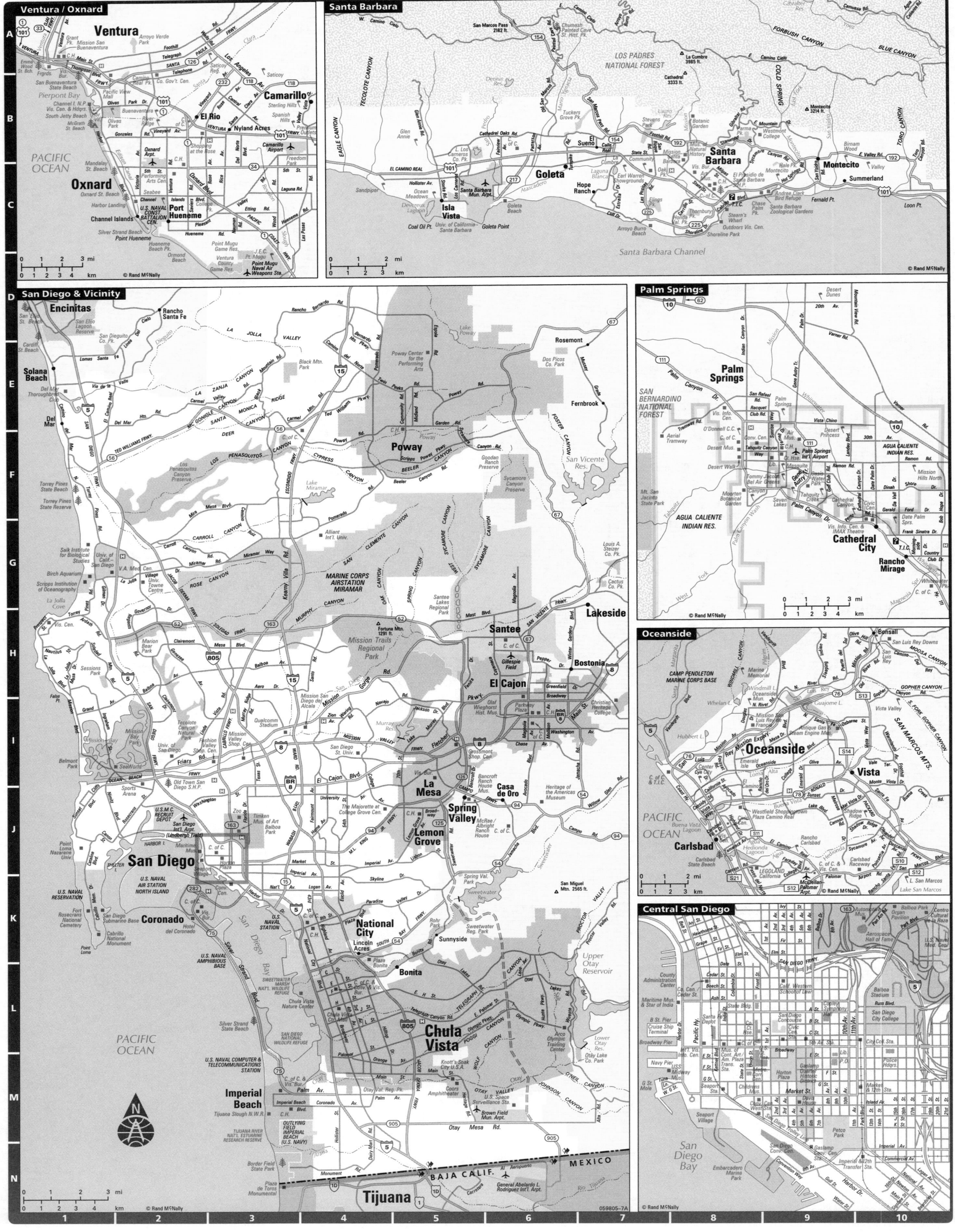

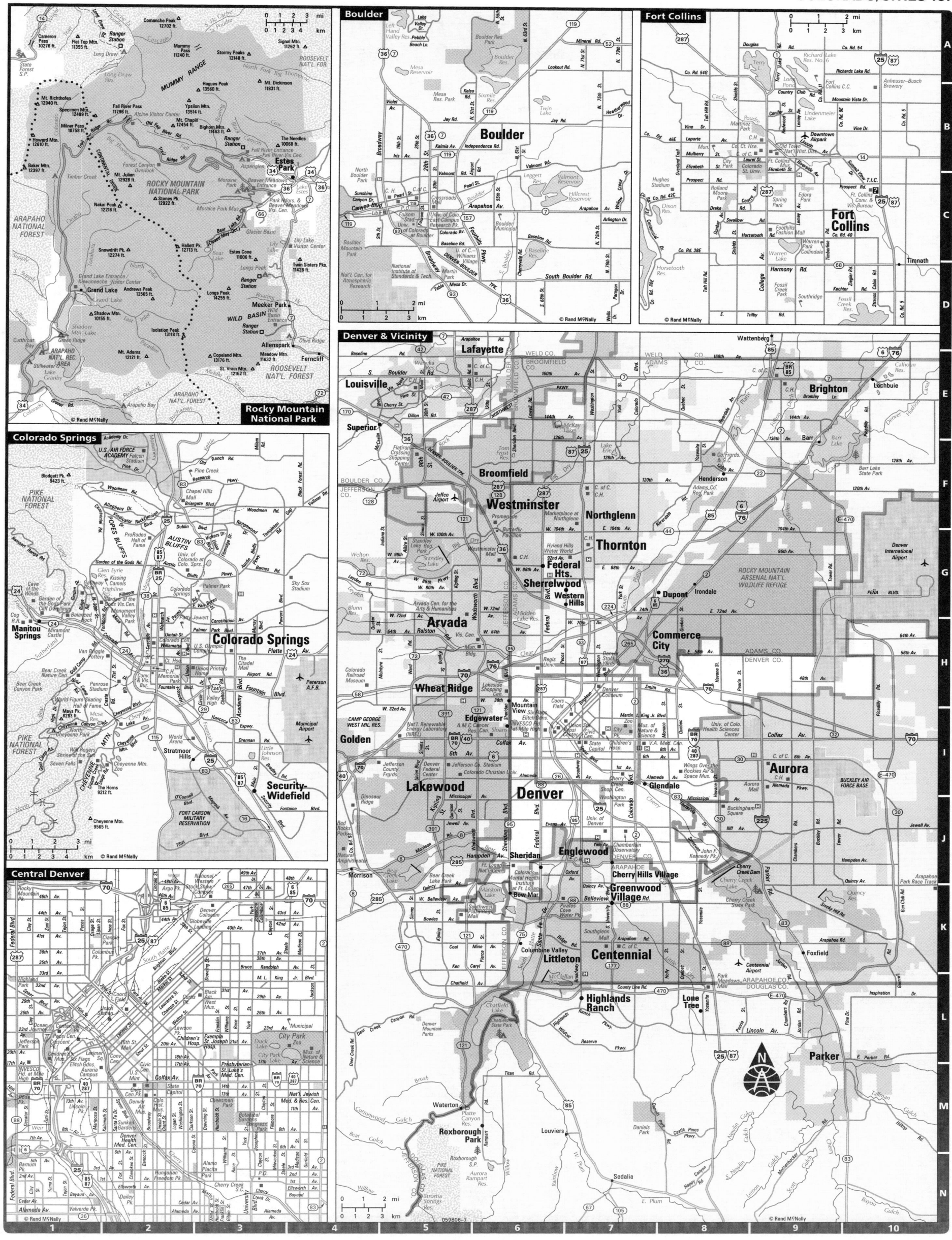

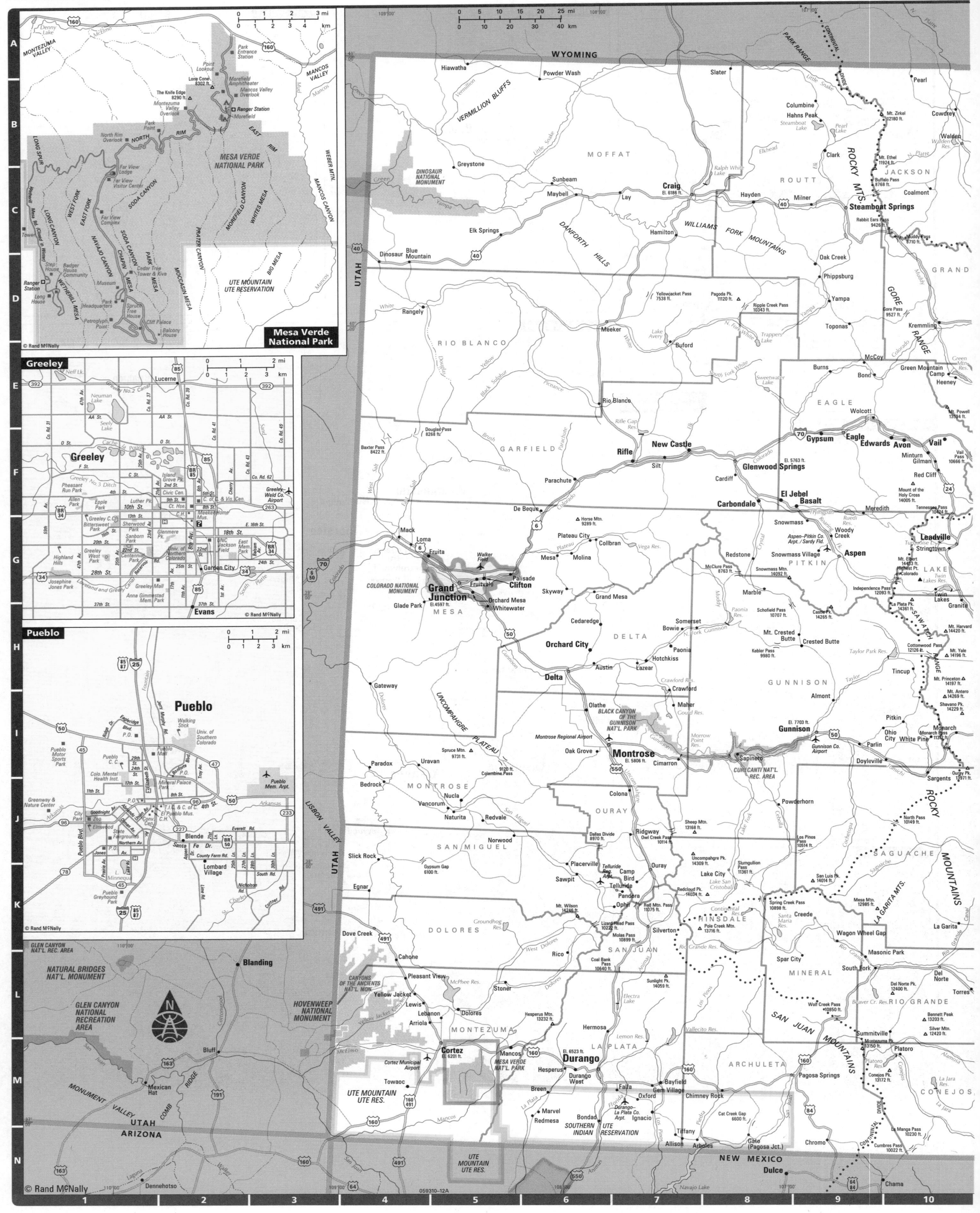

© Rand McNally

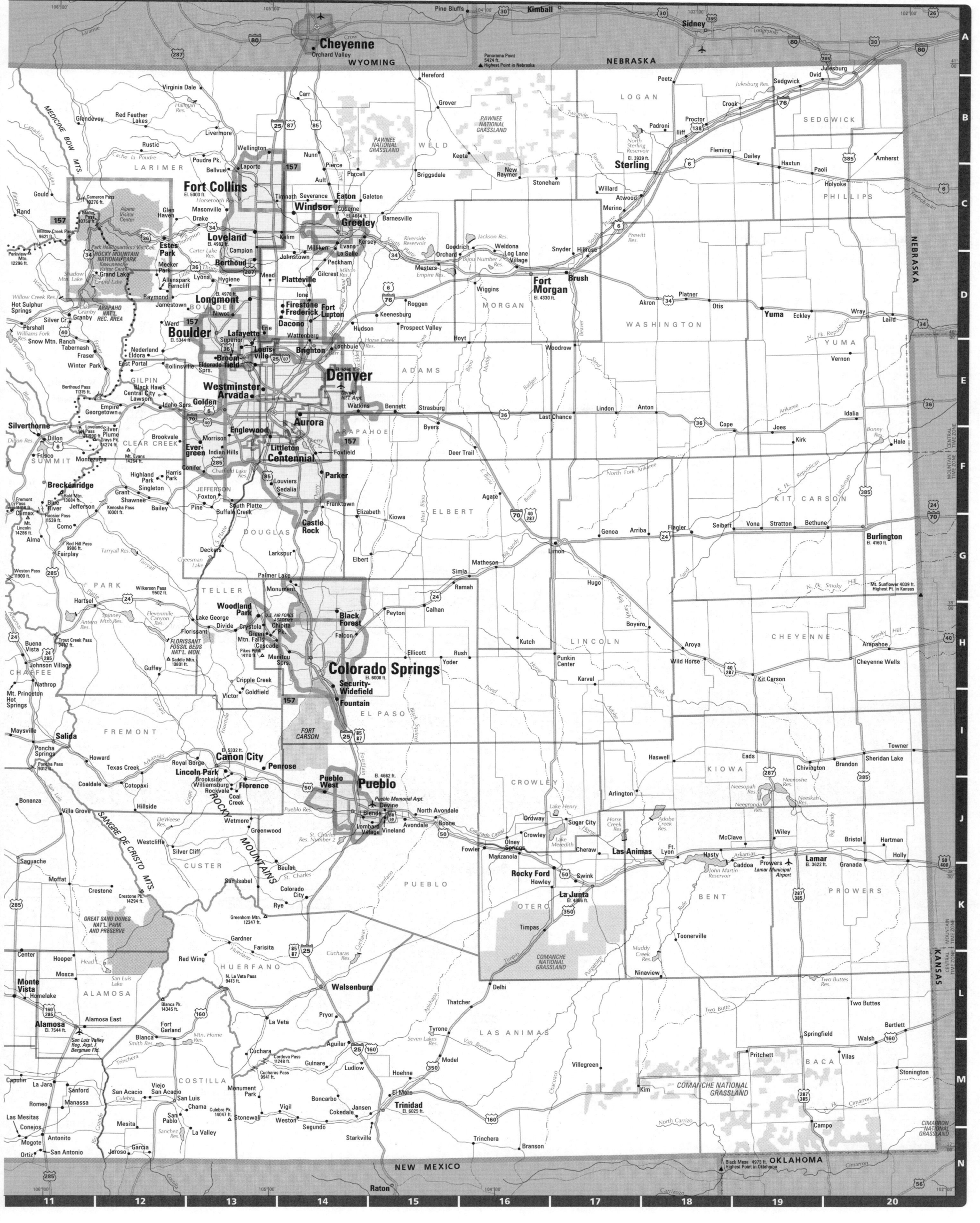

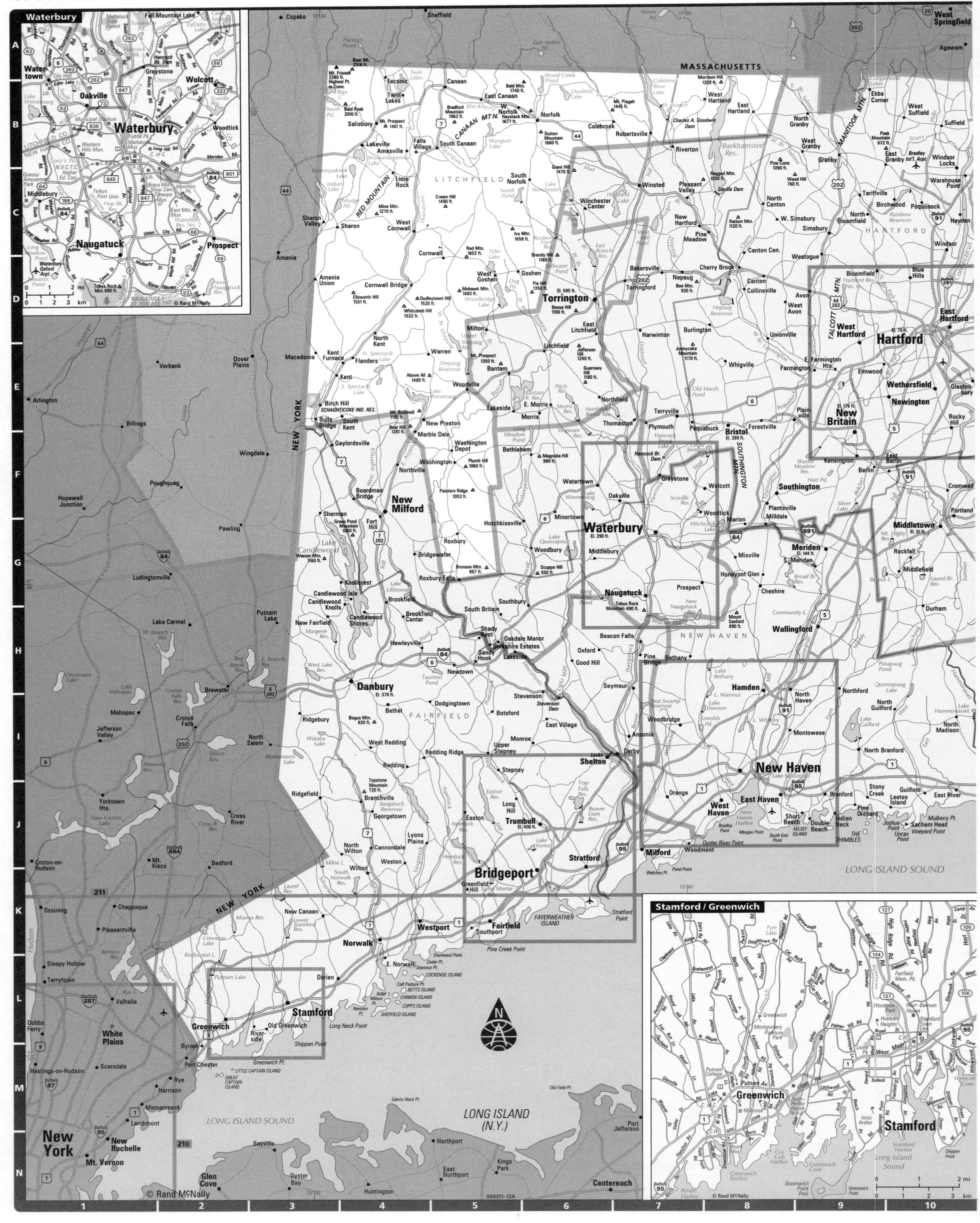

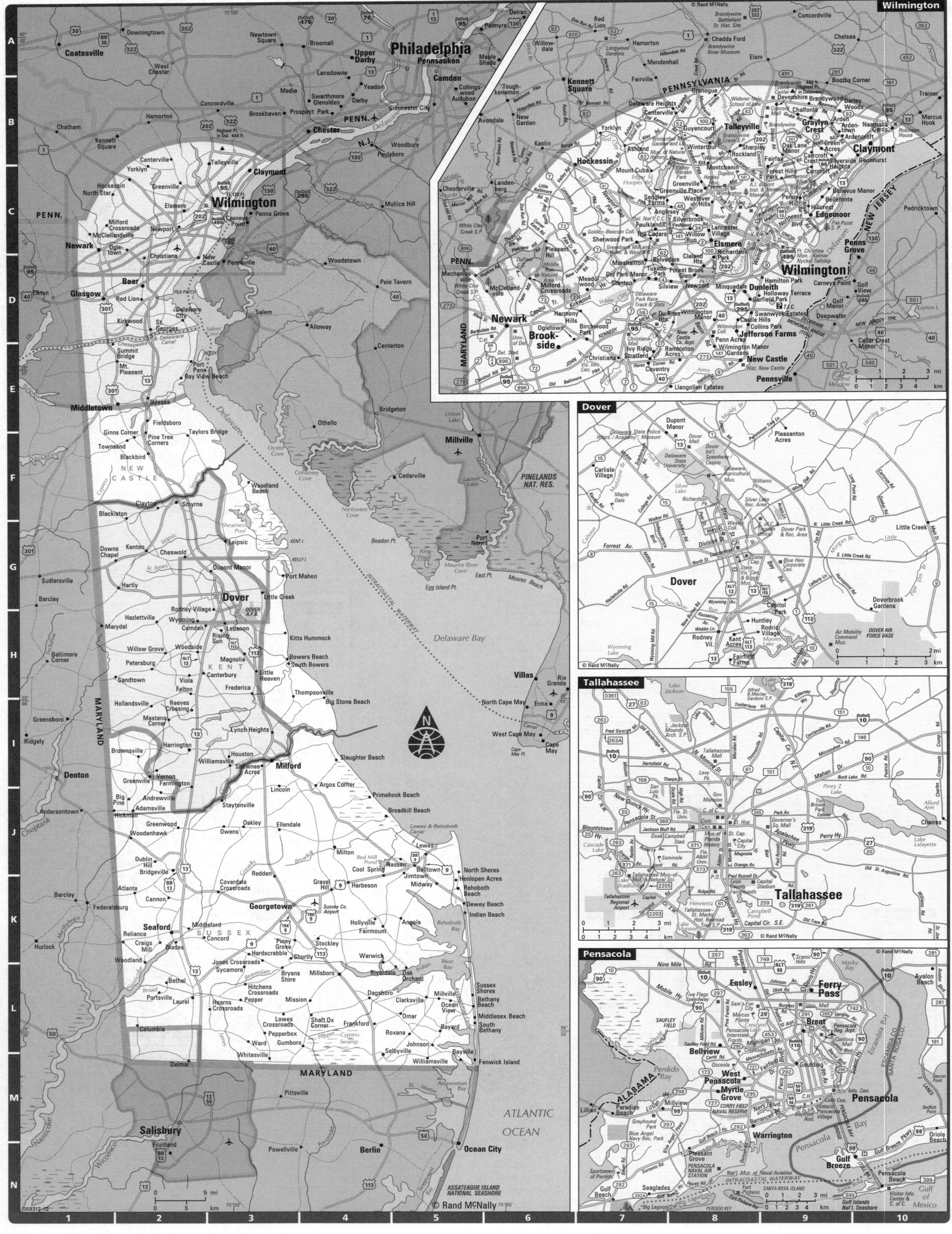

Wilmington

Dover

Tallahassee

Pensacola

© Rand McNally

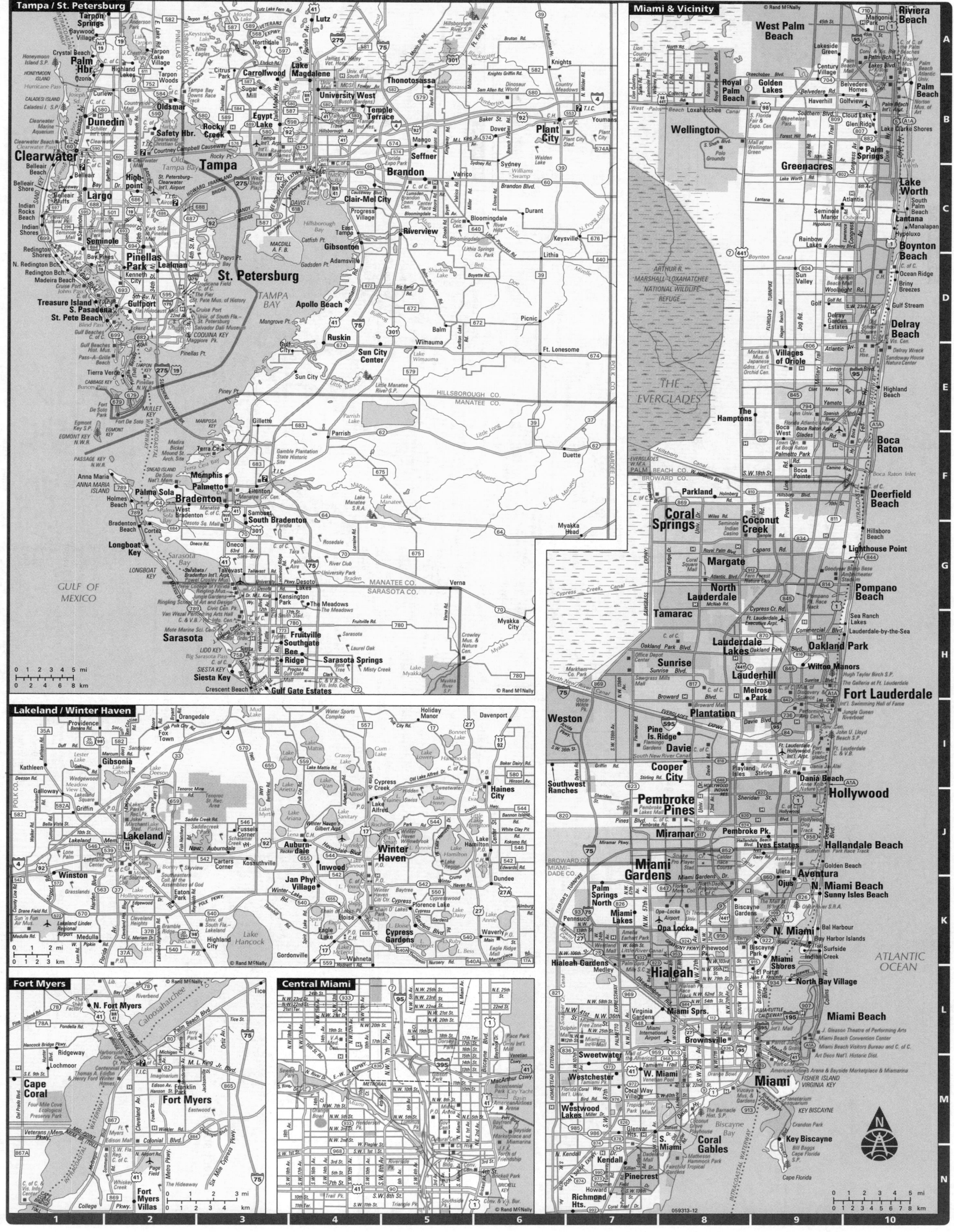

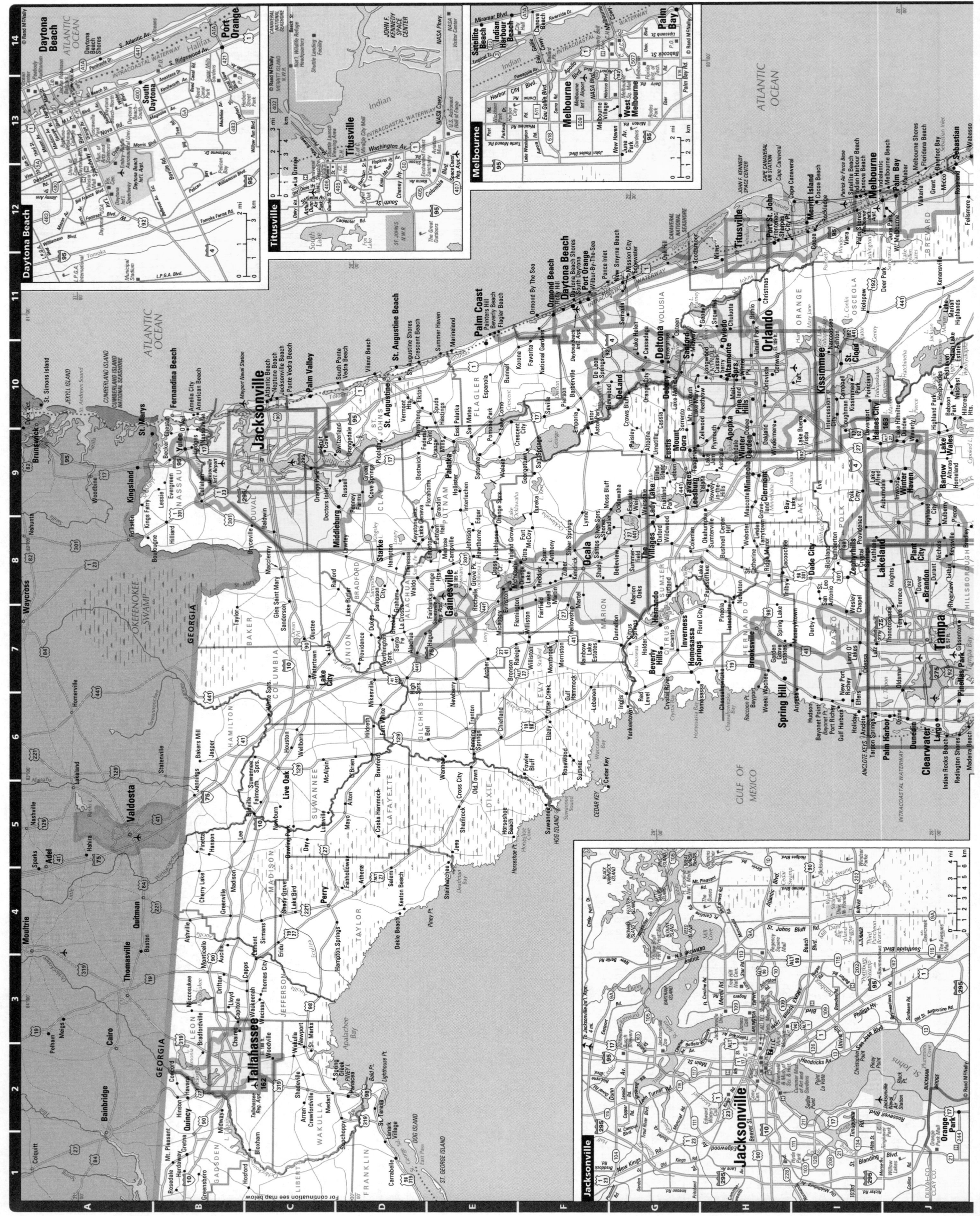

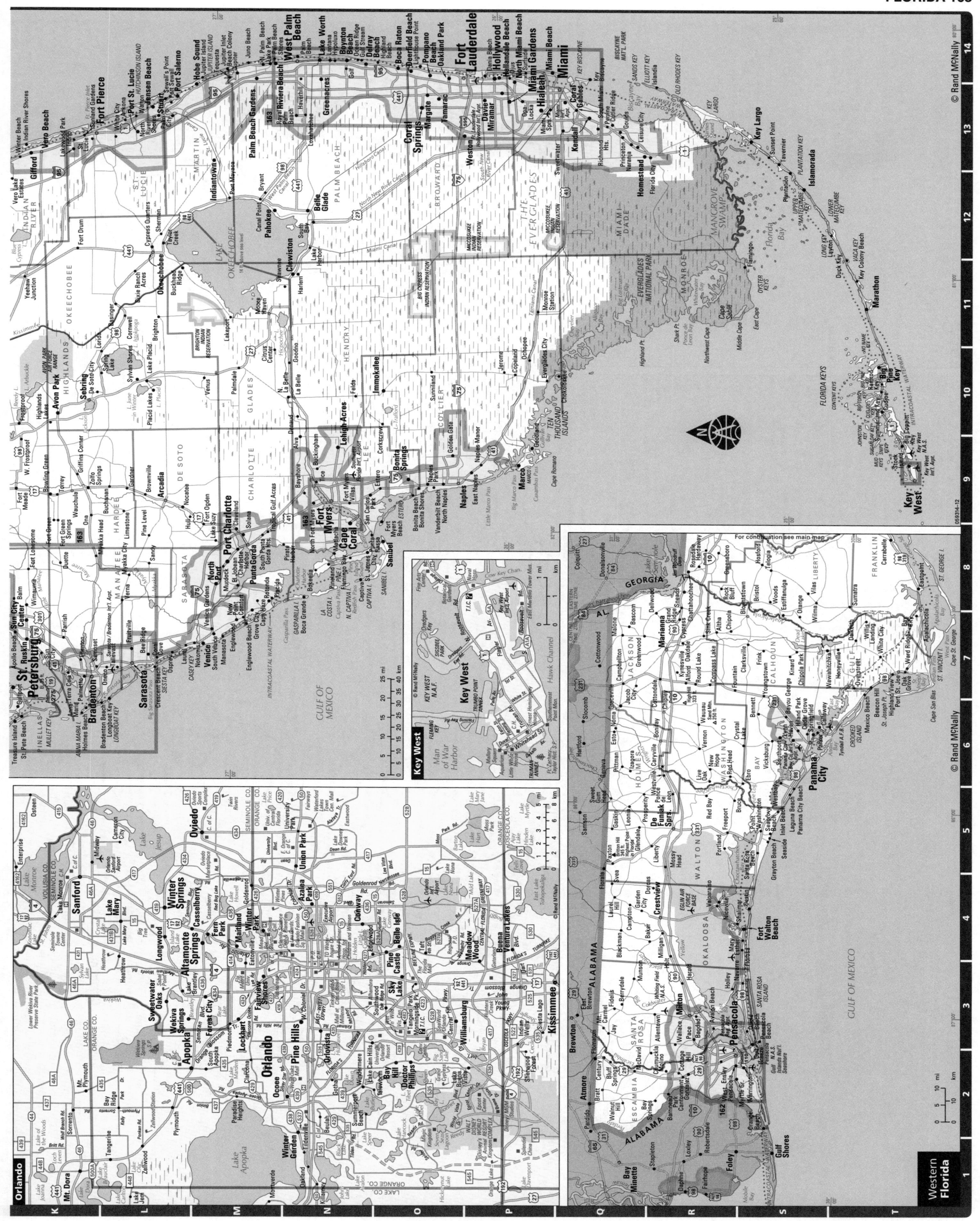

Key West

Orlando

Western Florida

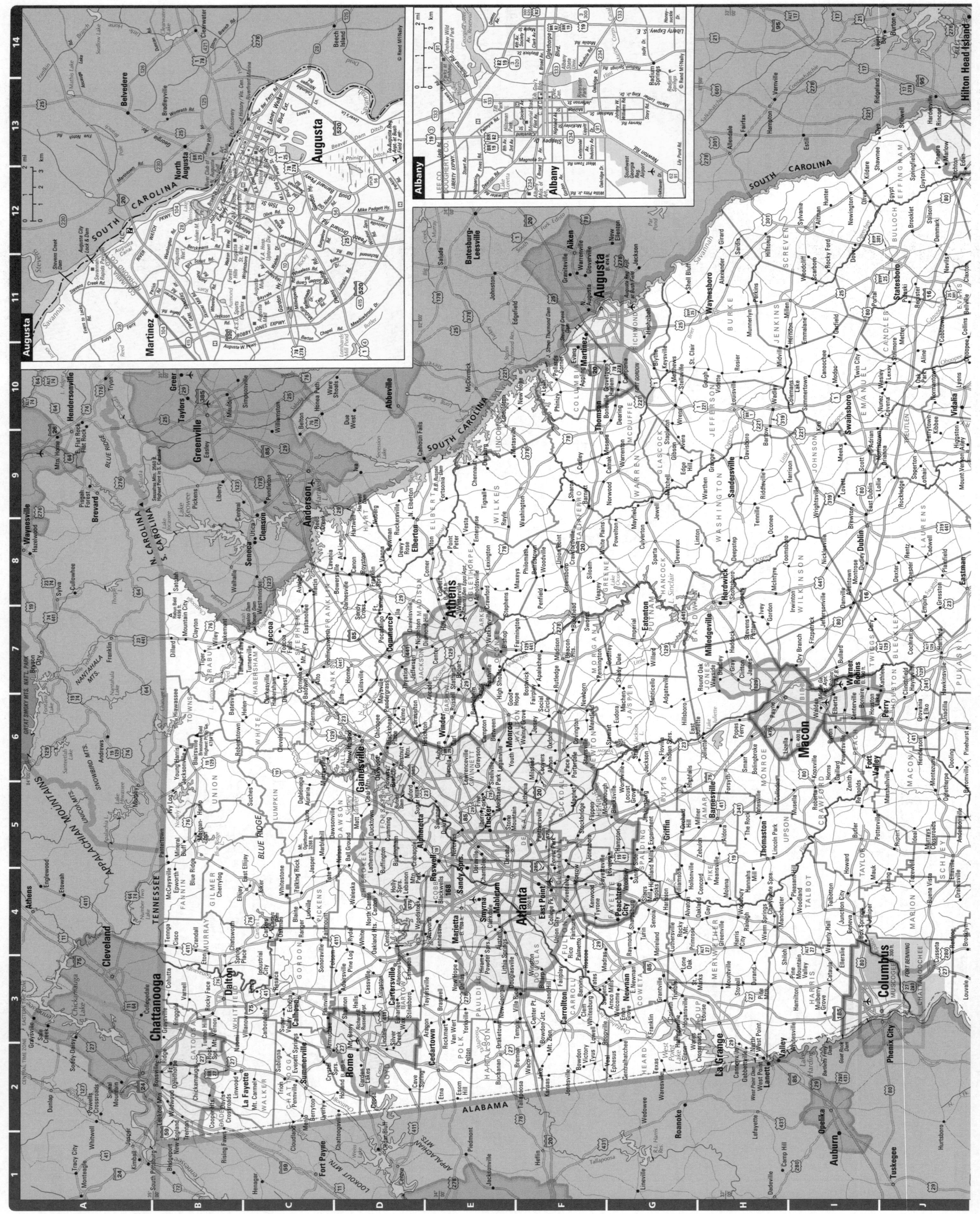

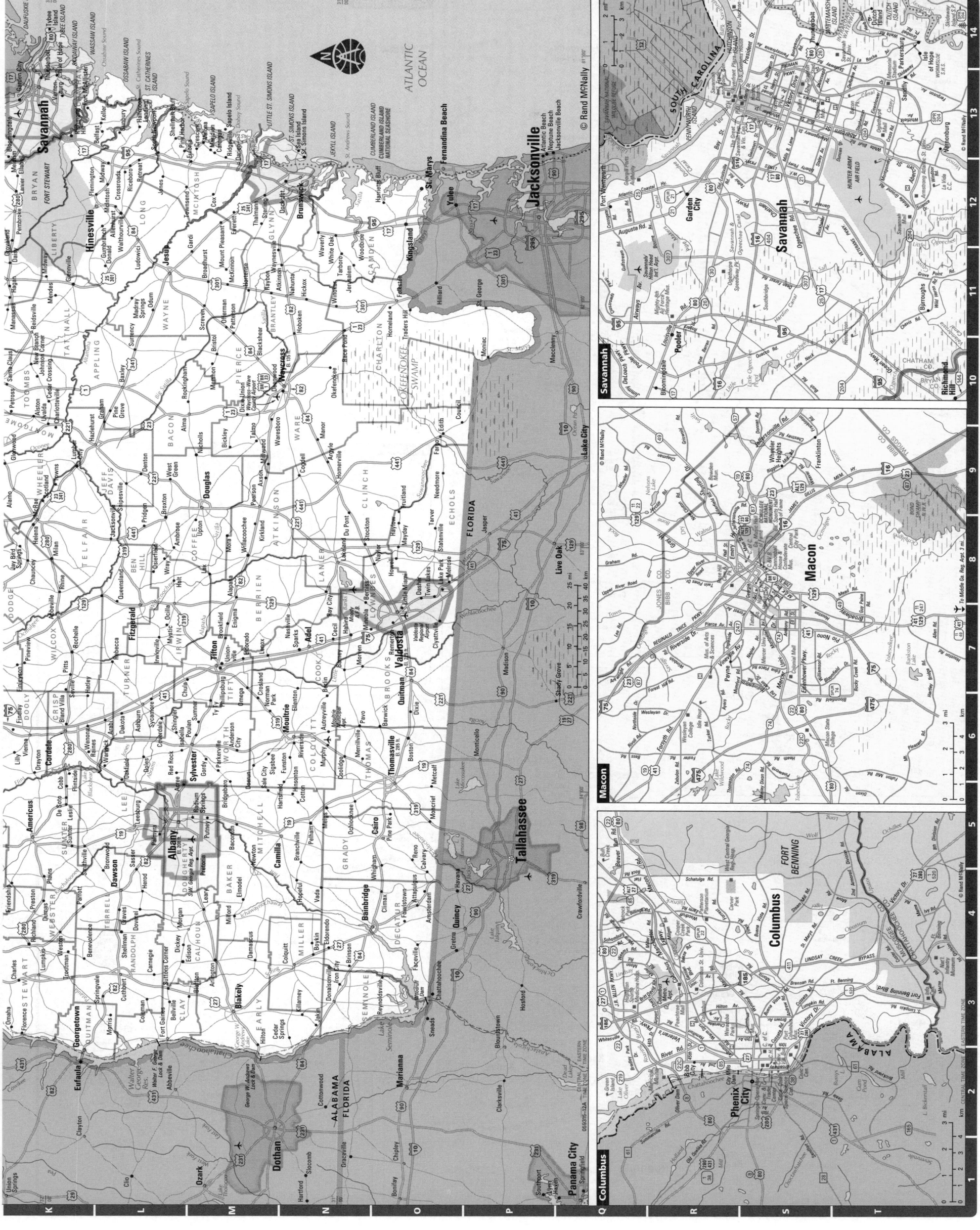

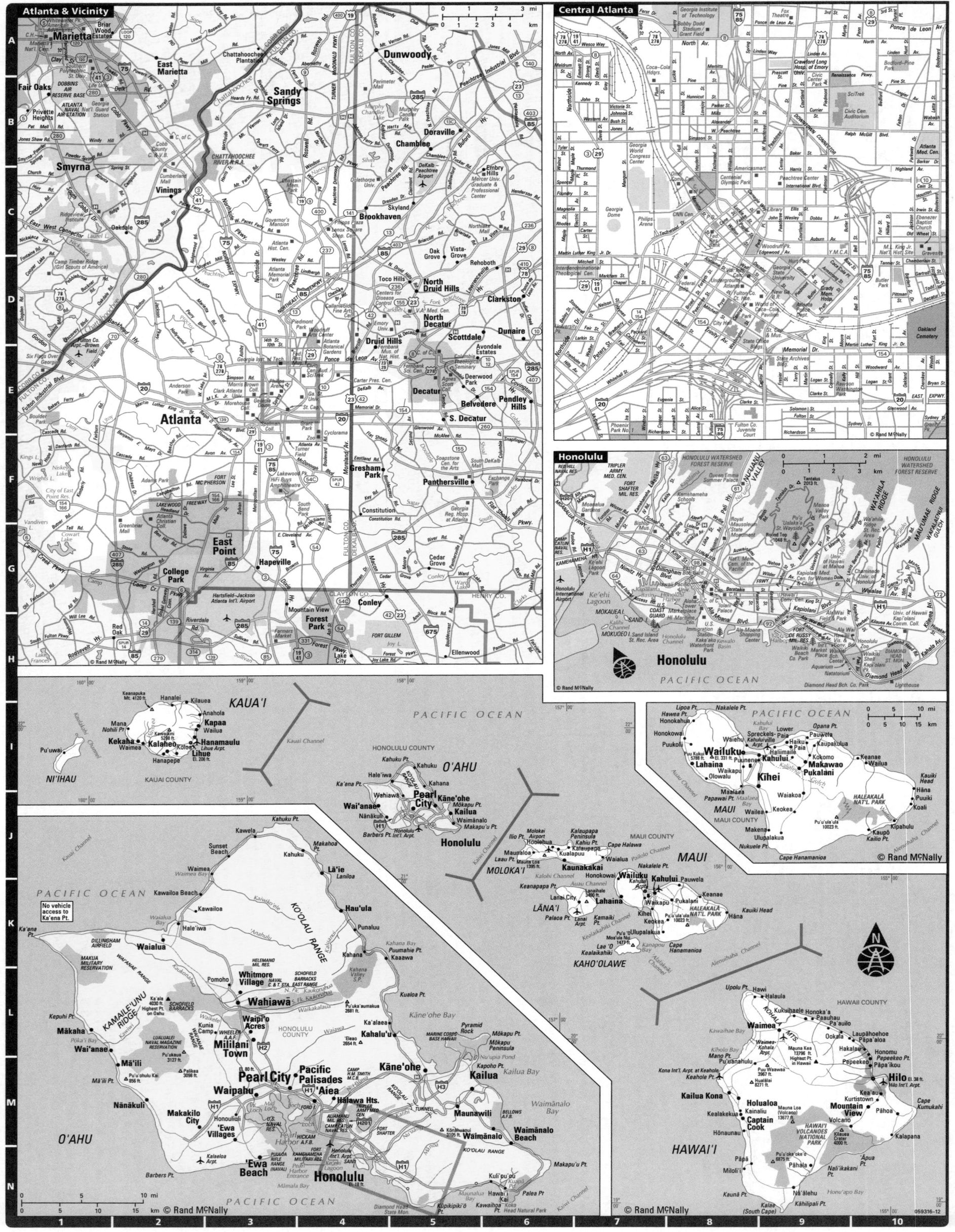

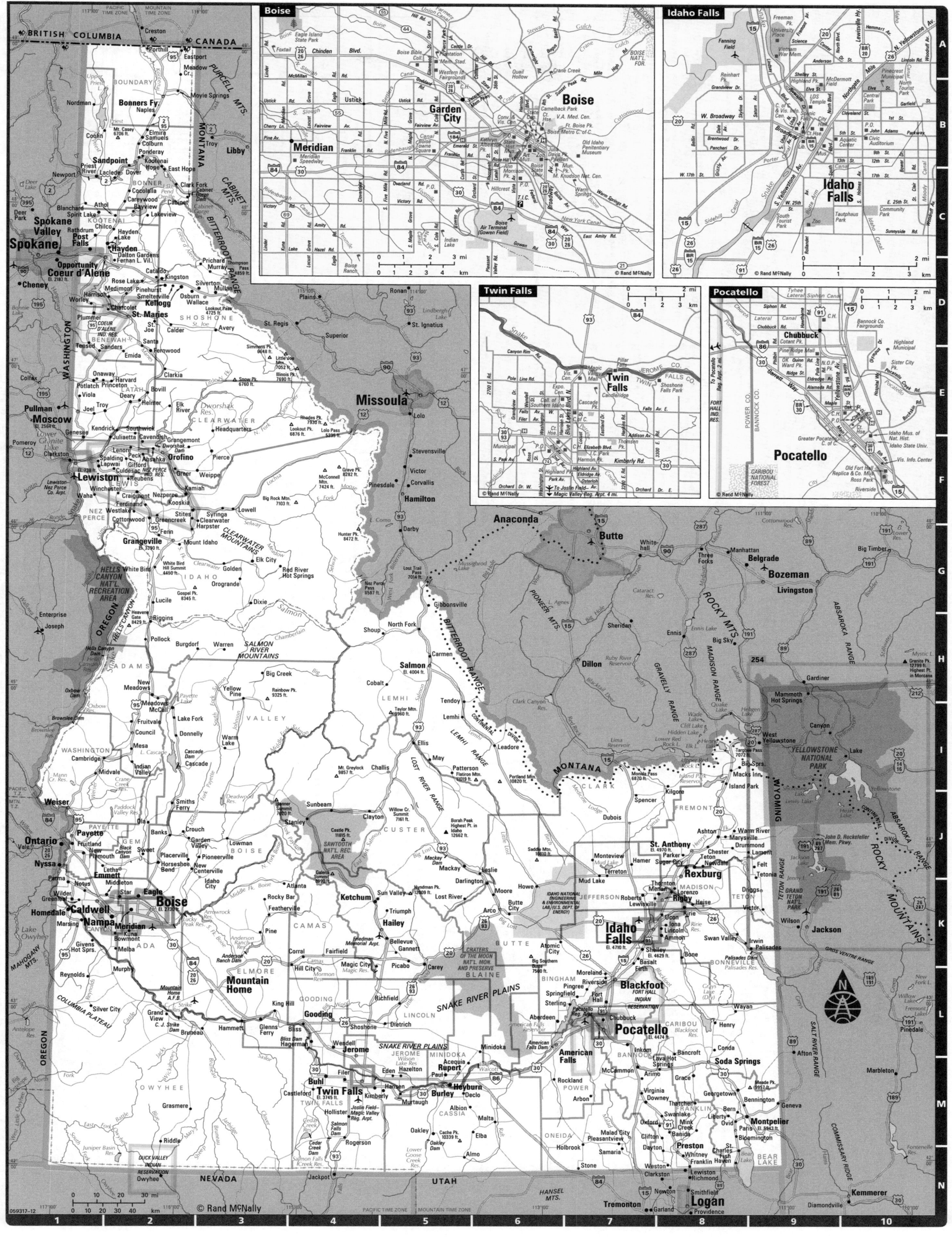

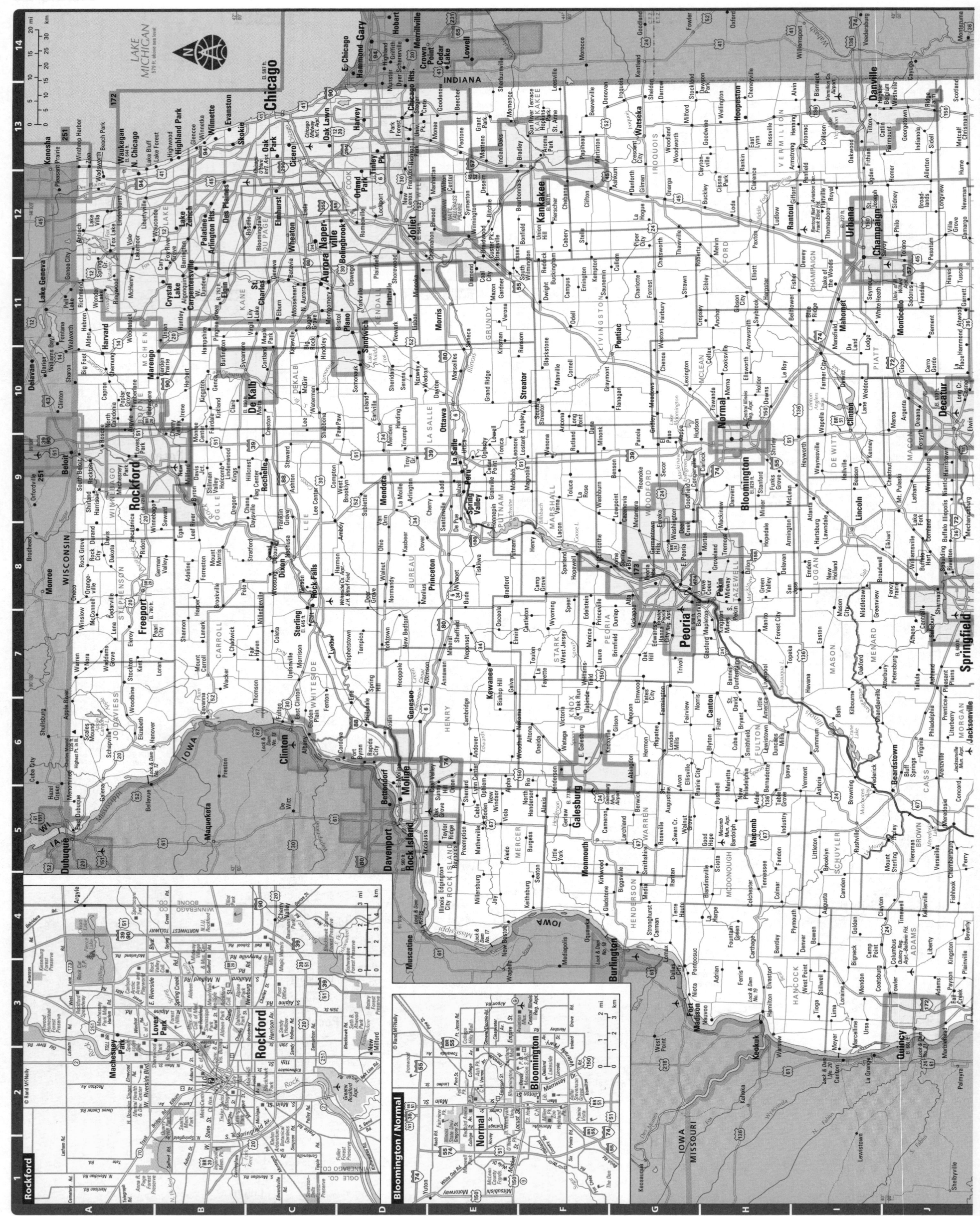

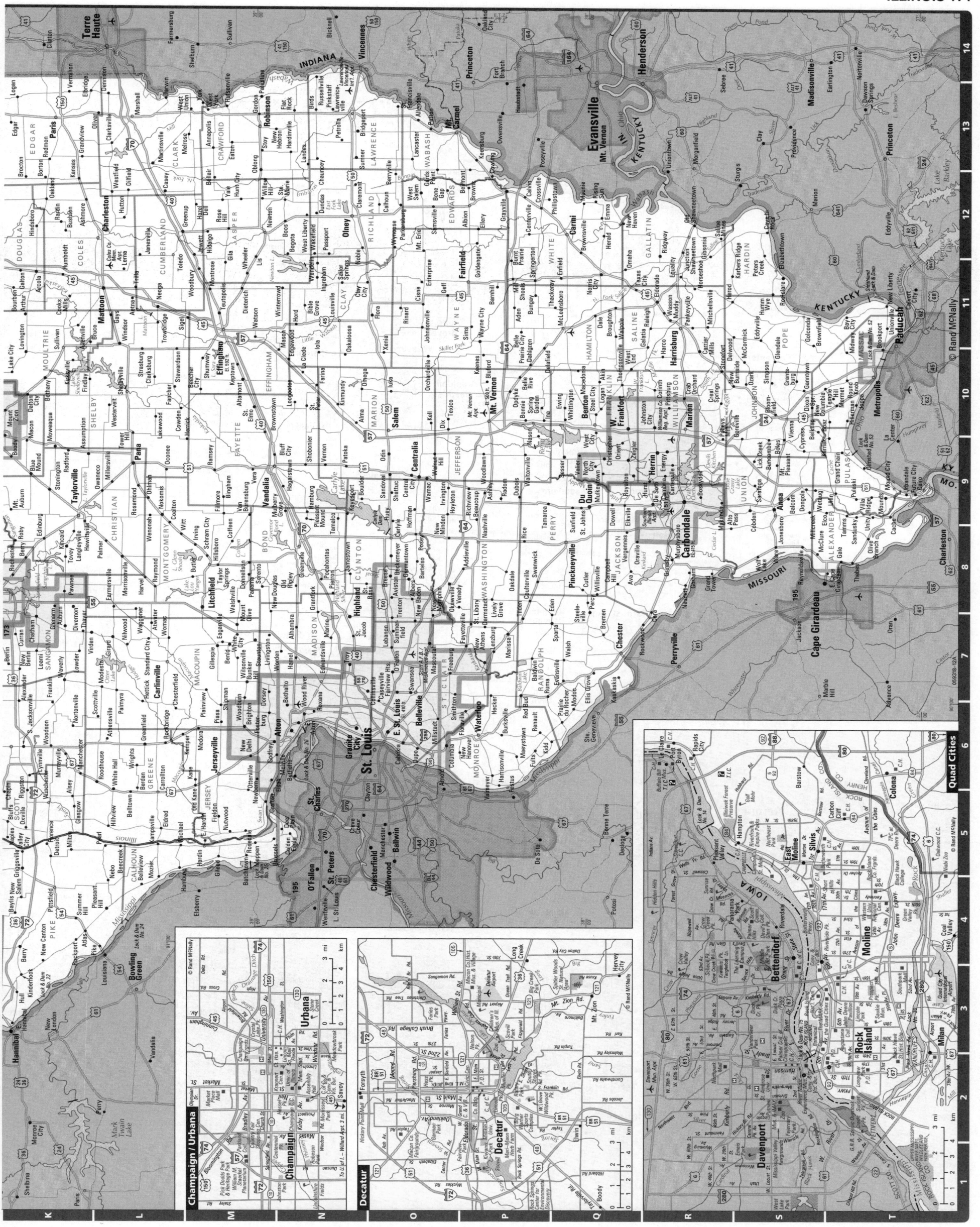

Chicago & Vicinity

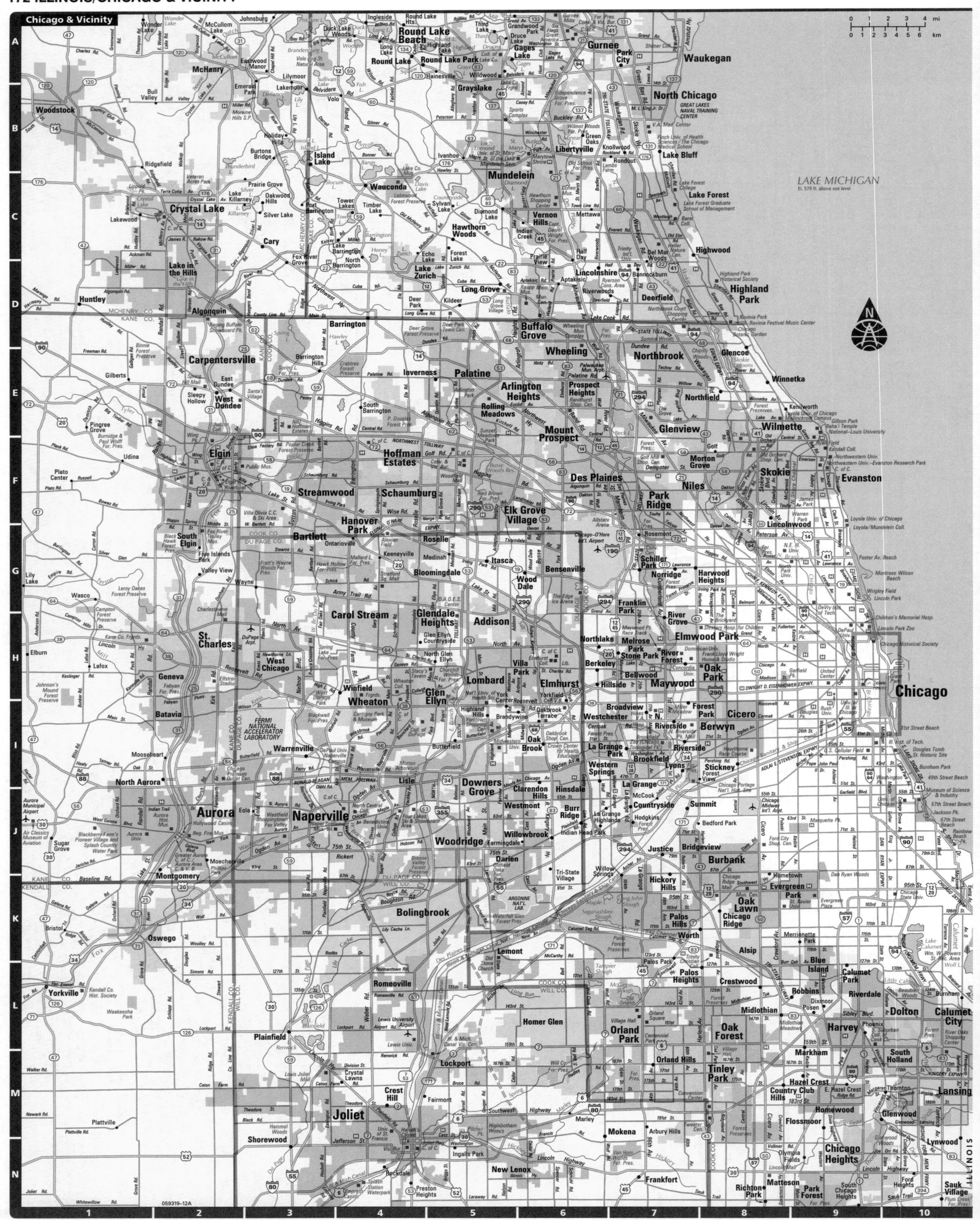

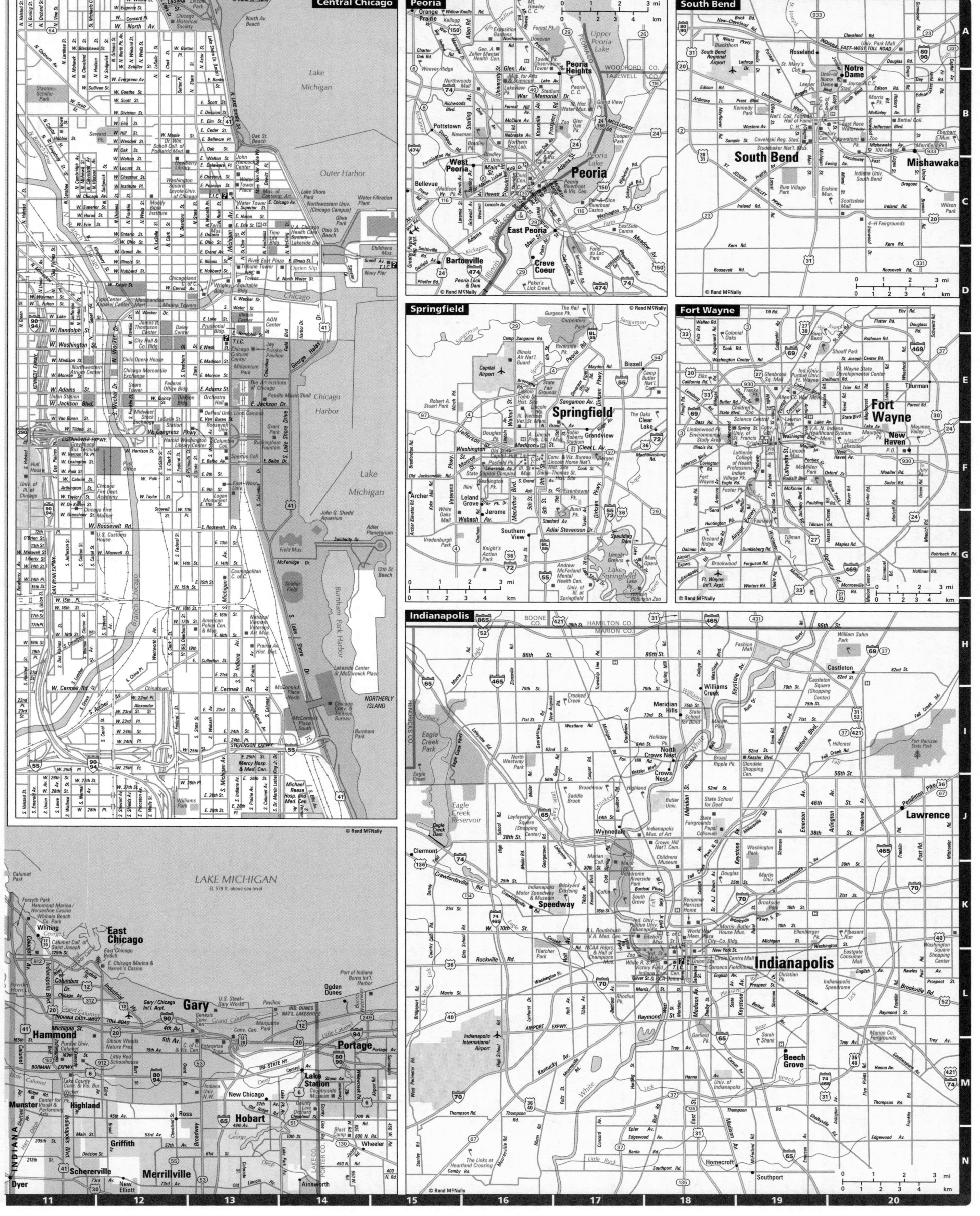

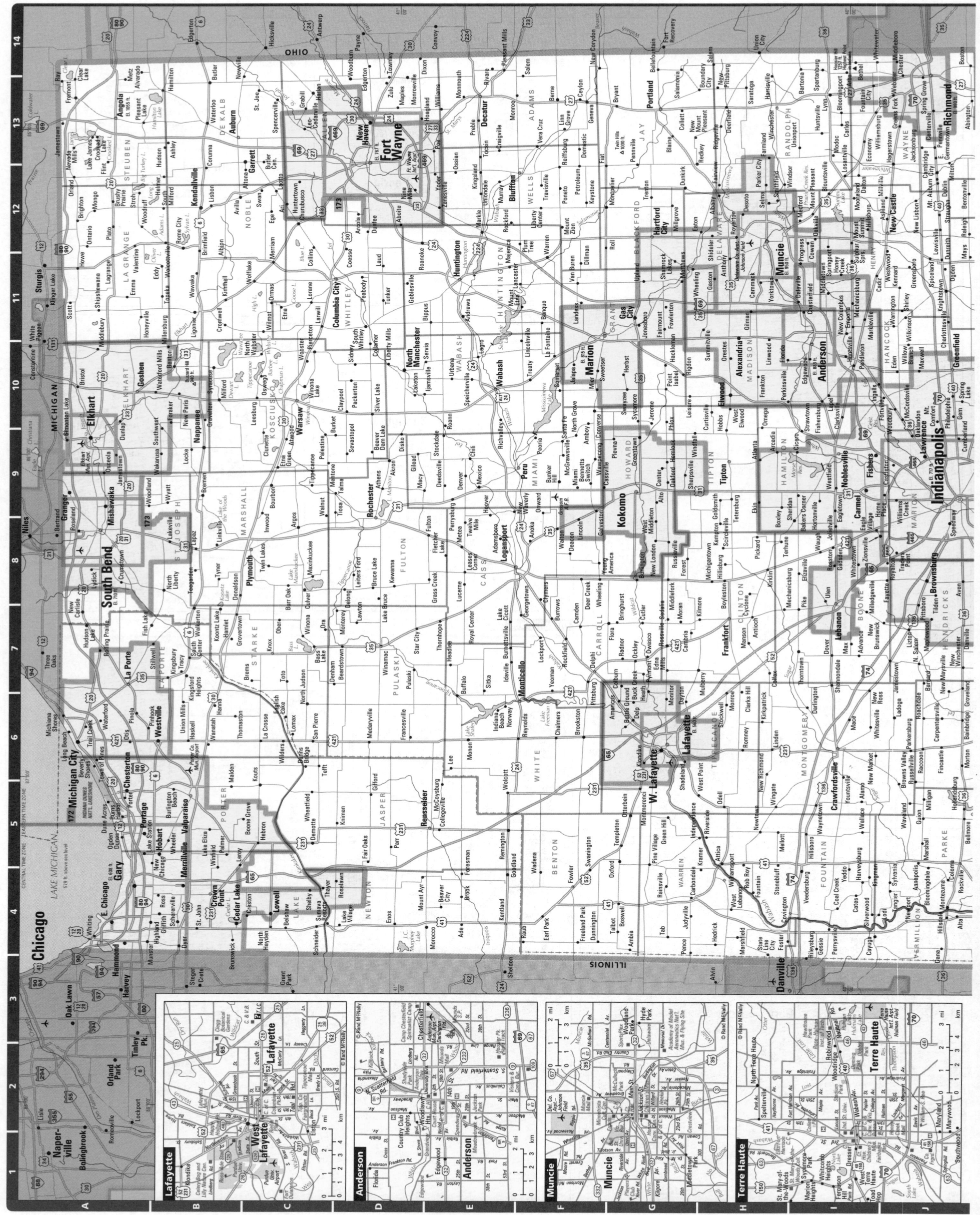

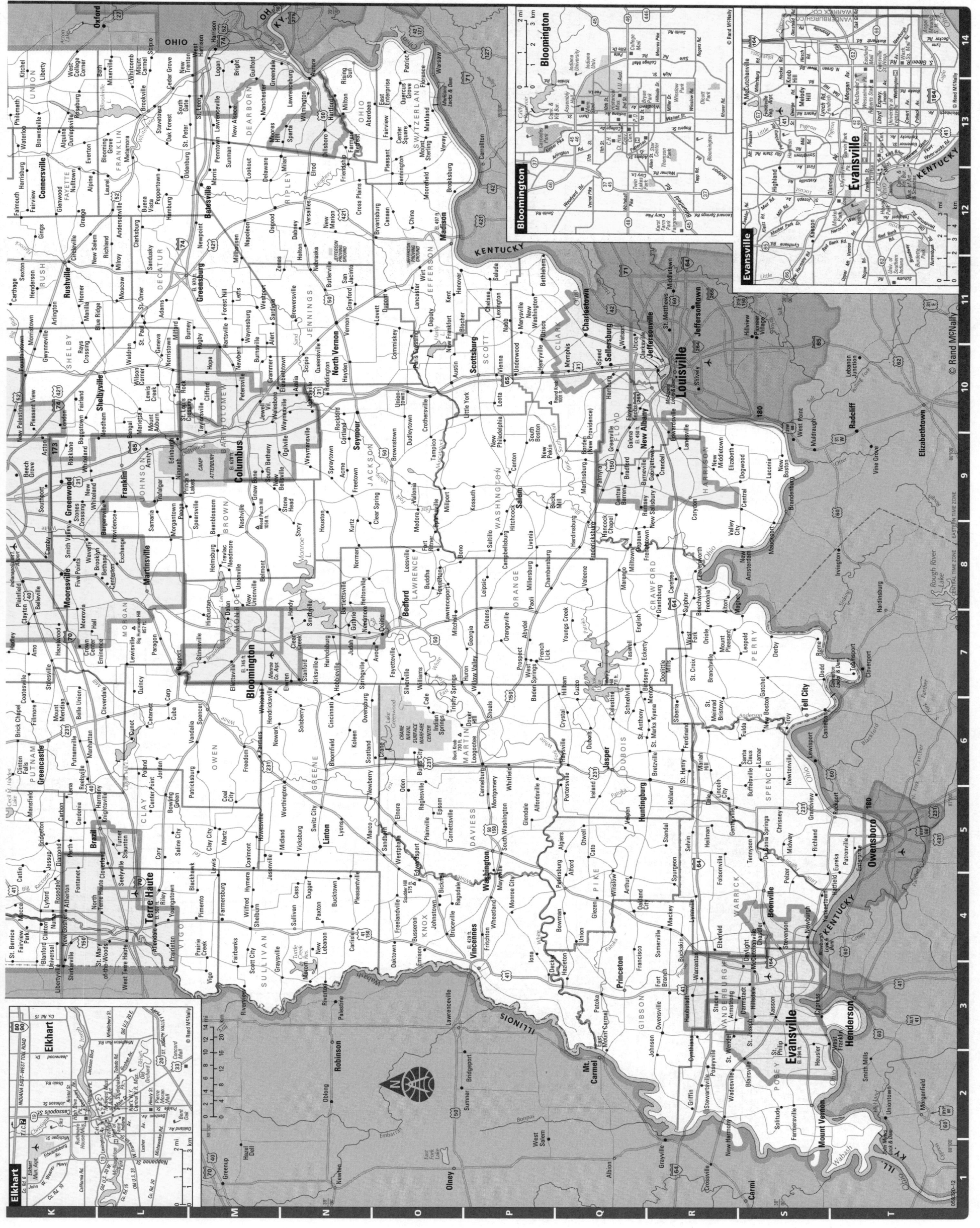

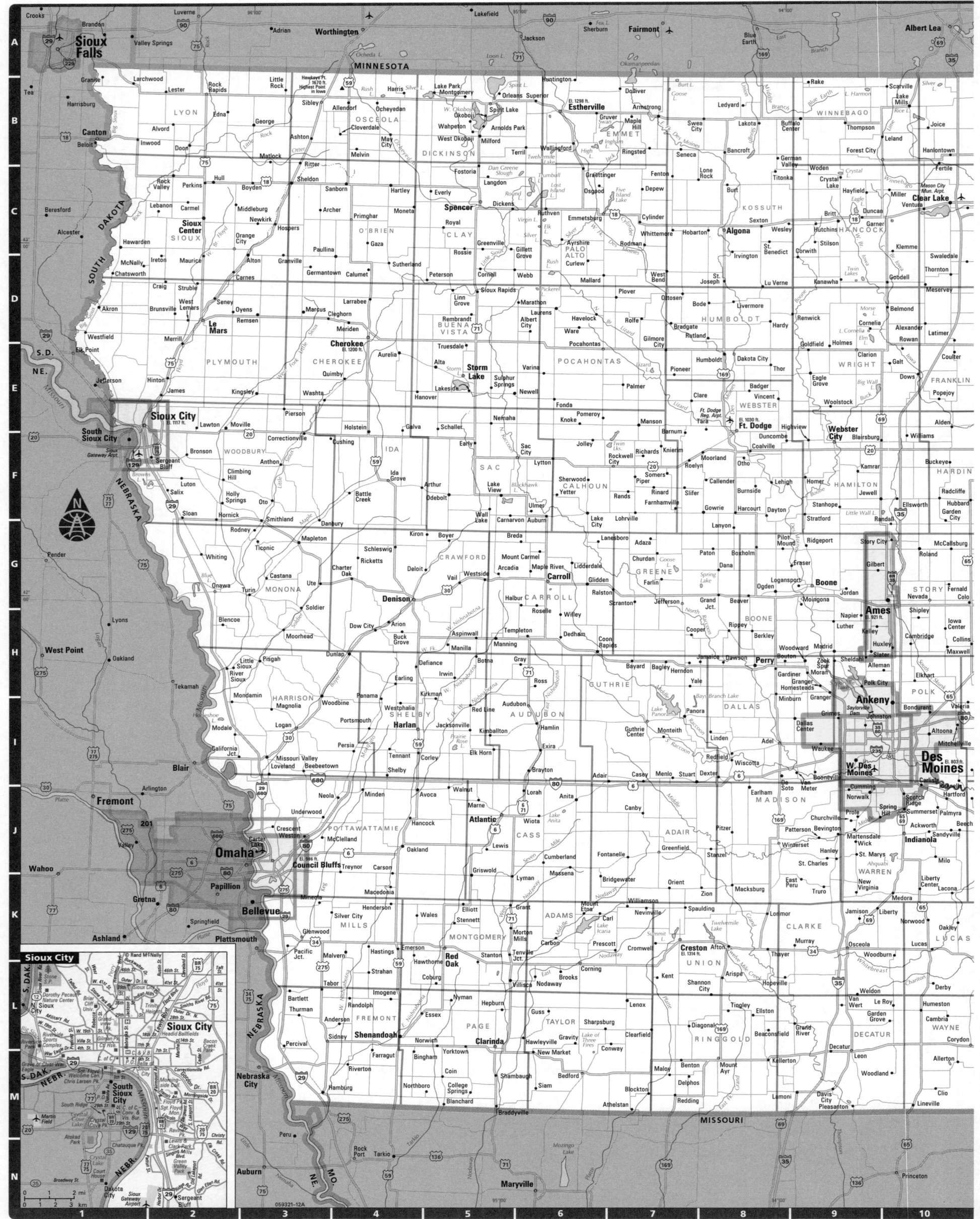

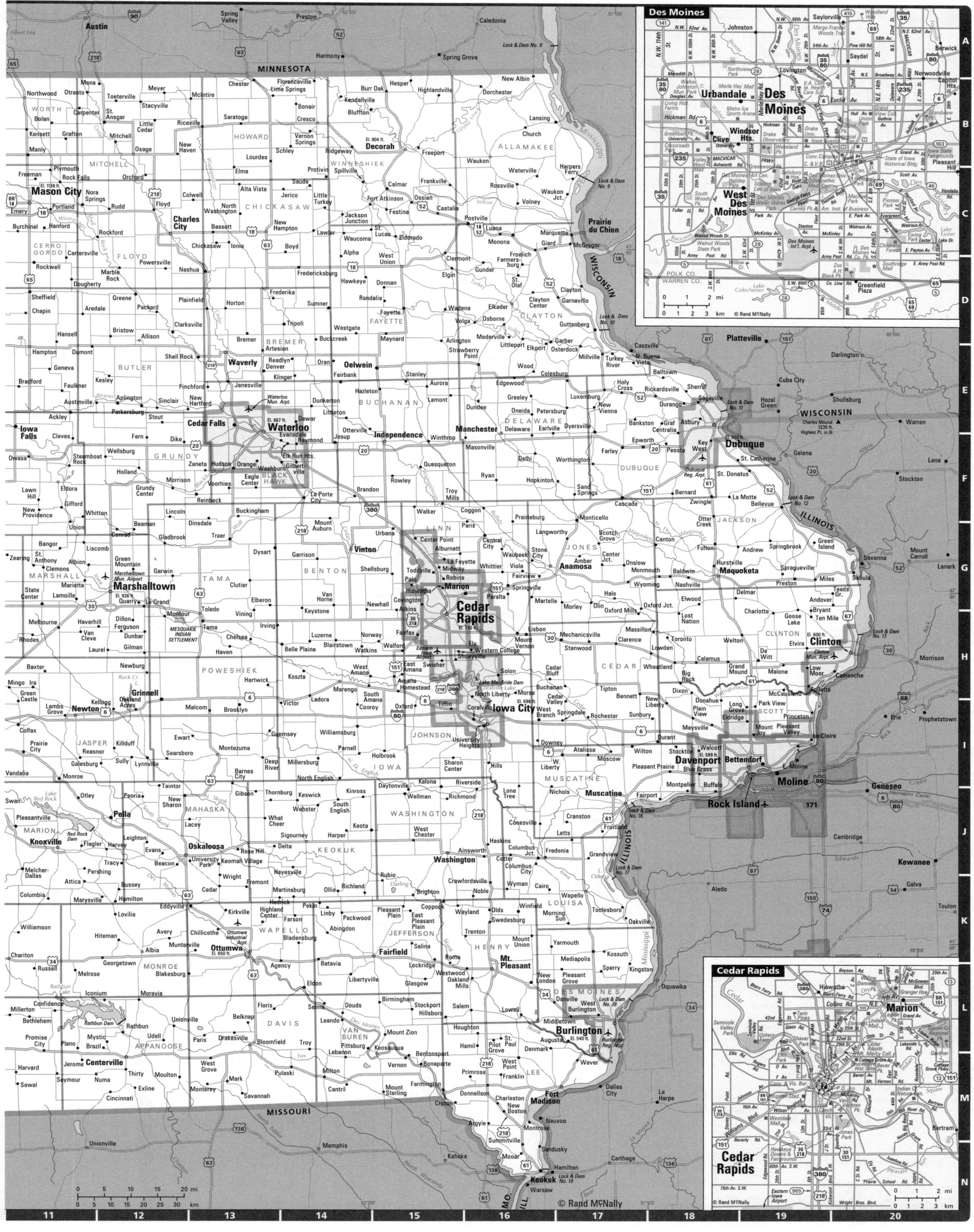

© Rand McNally

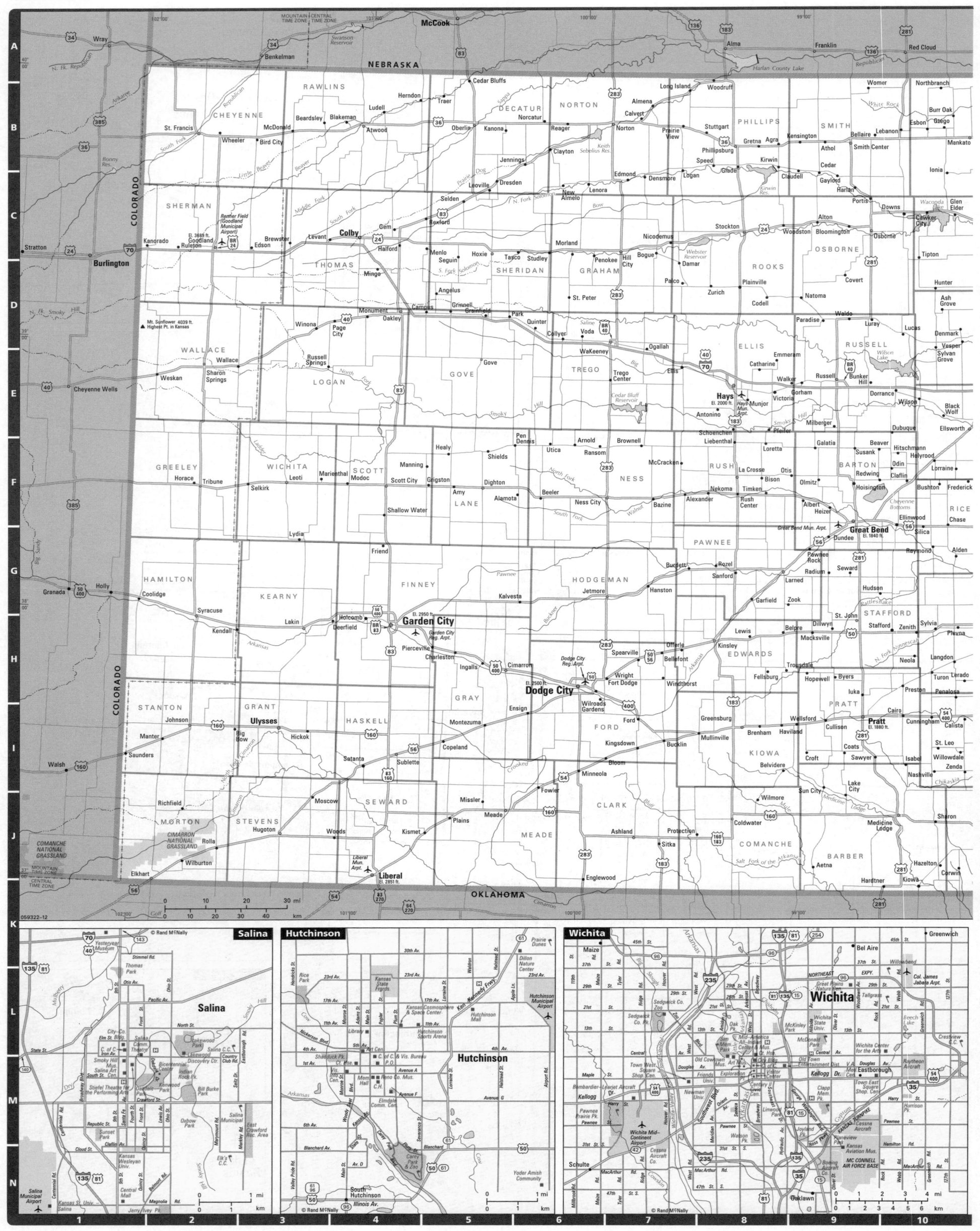

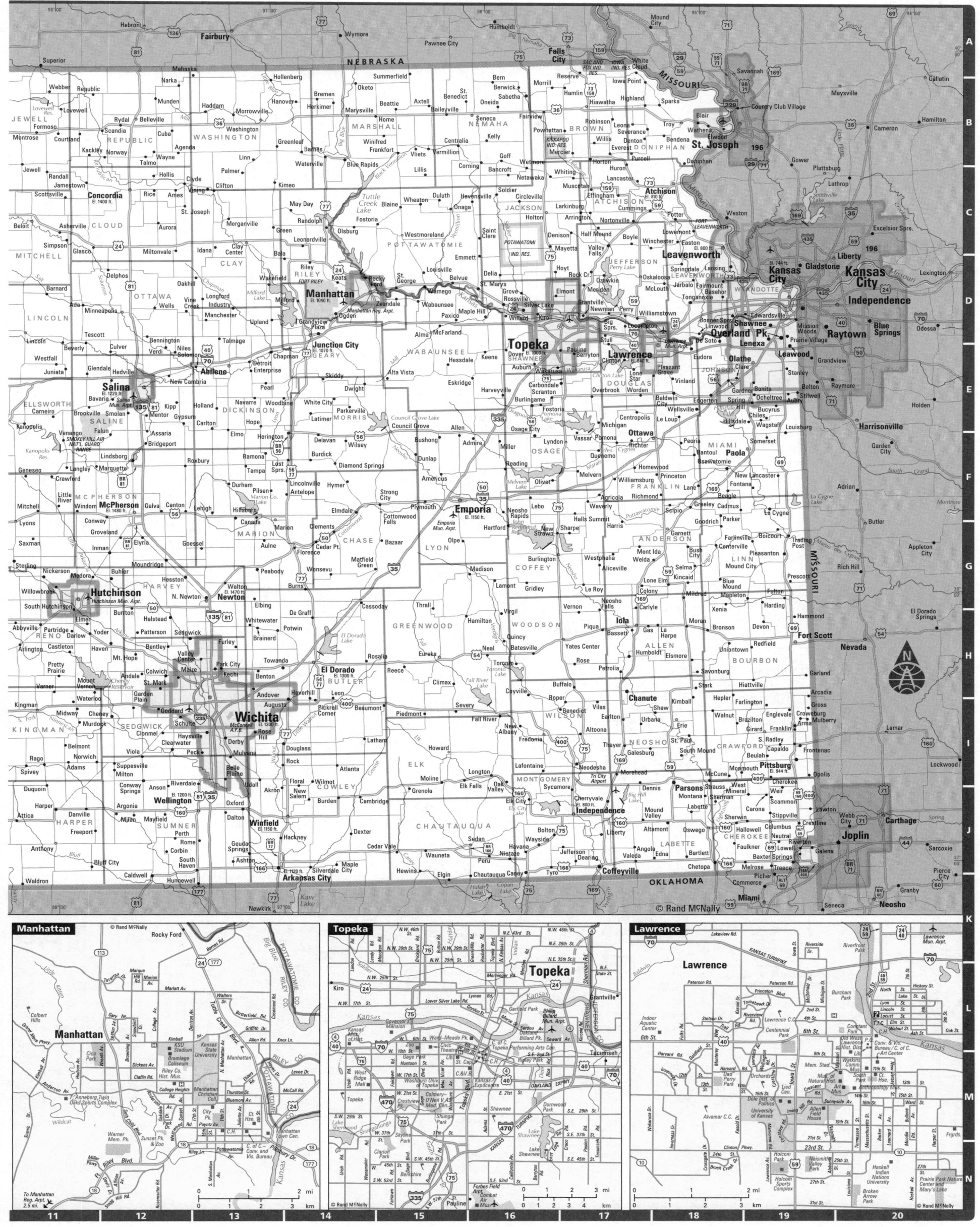

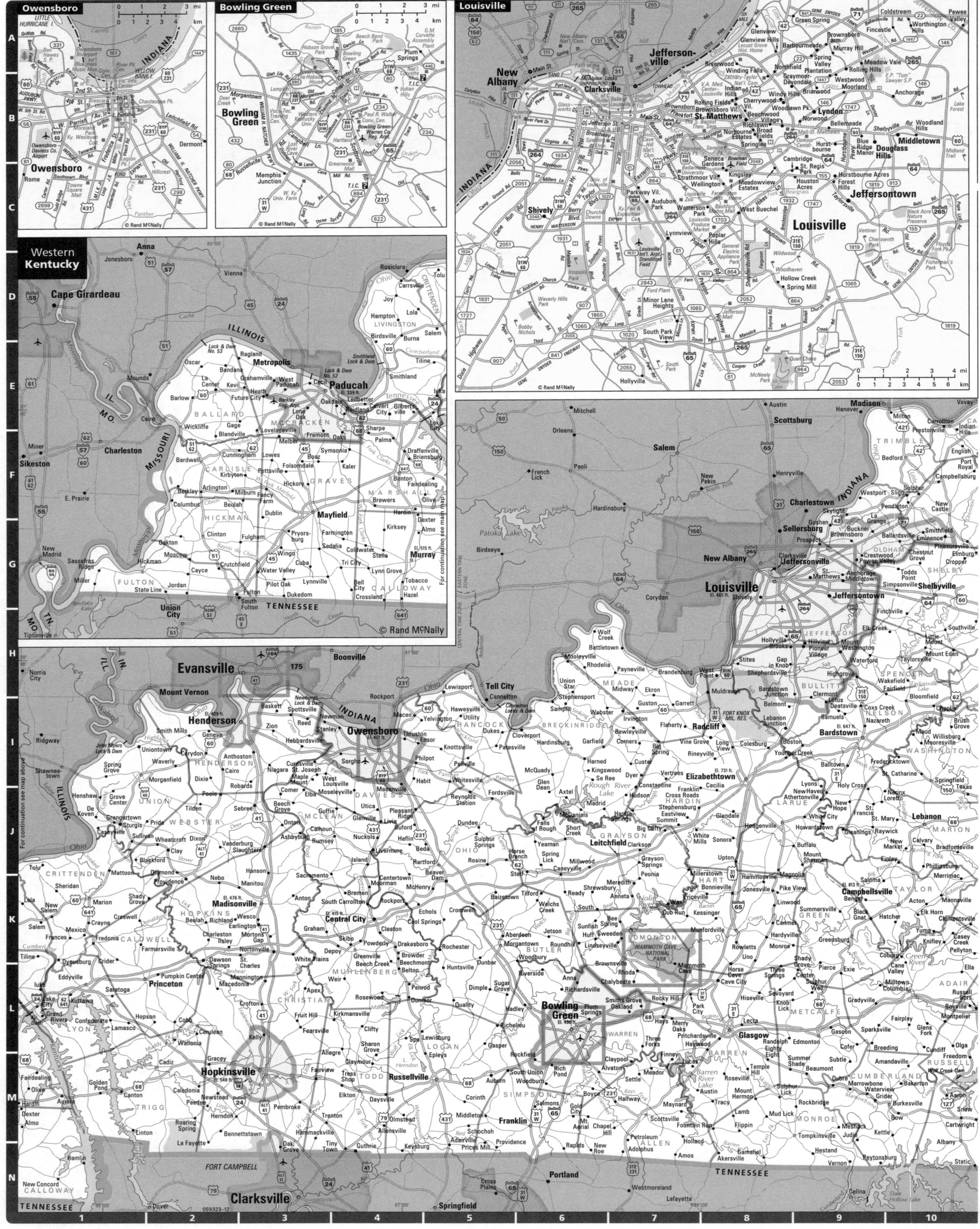

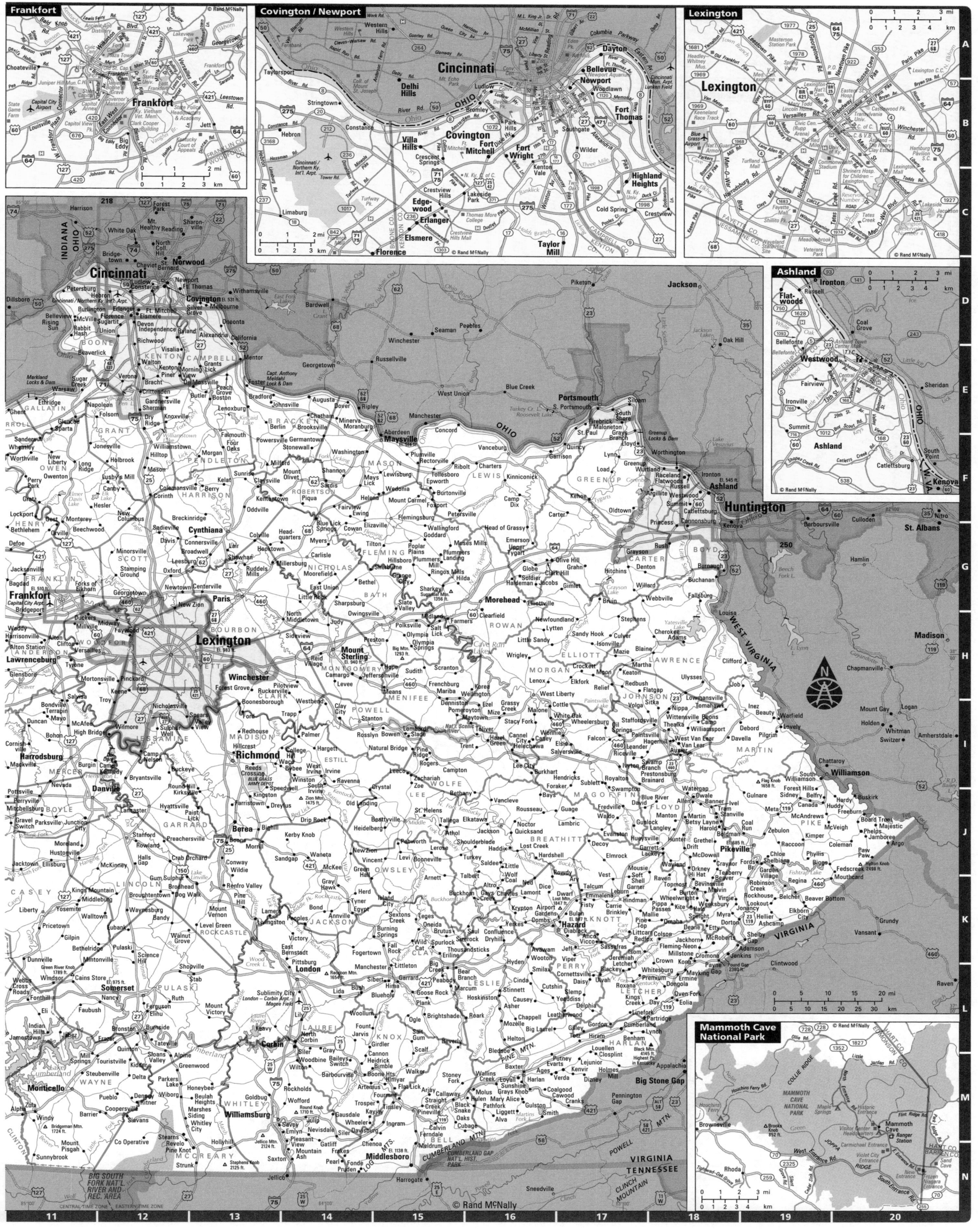

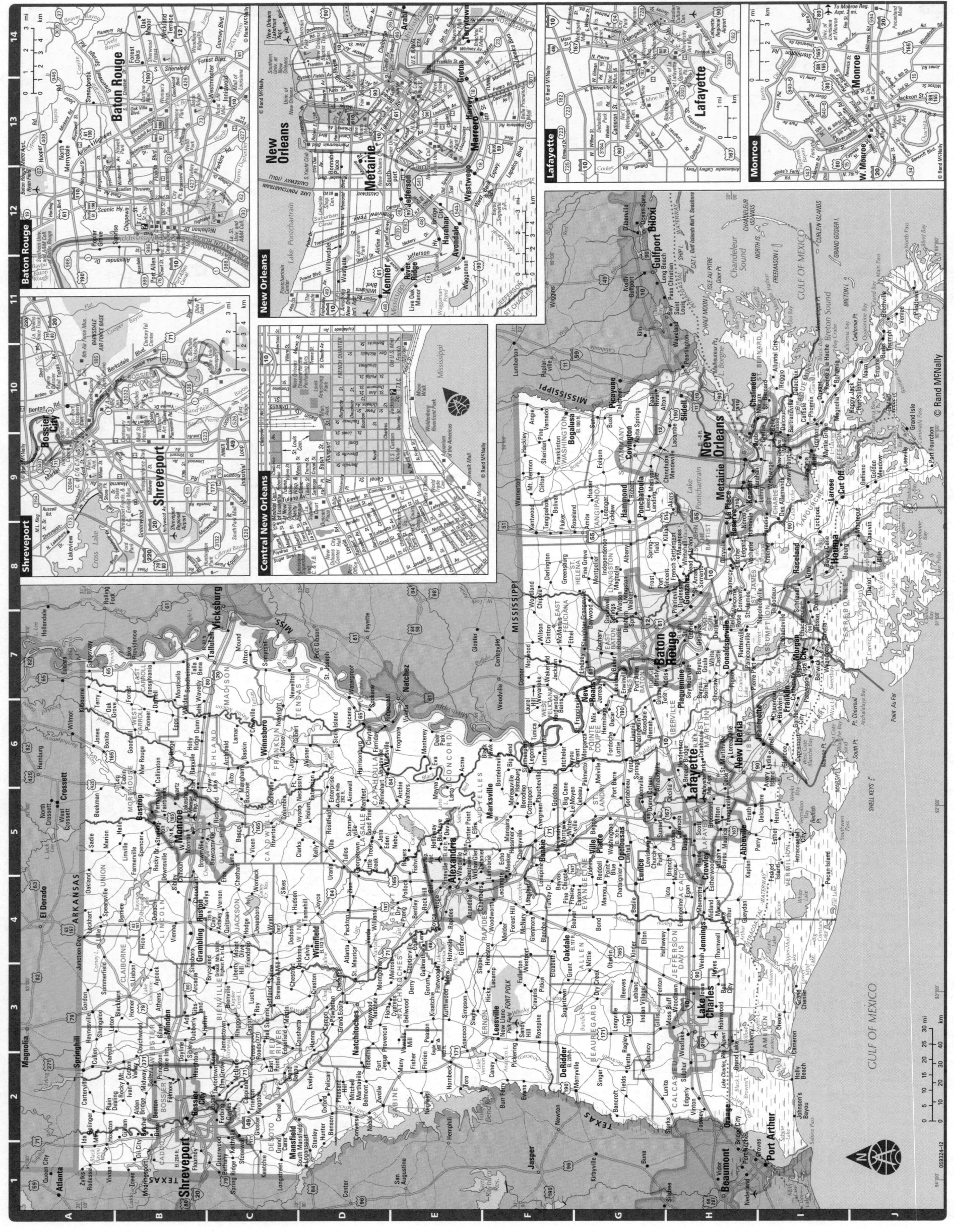

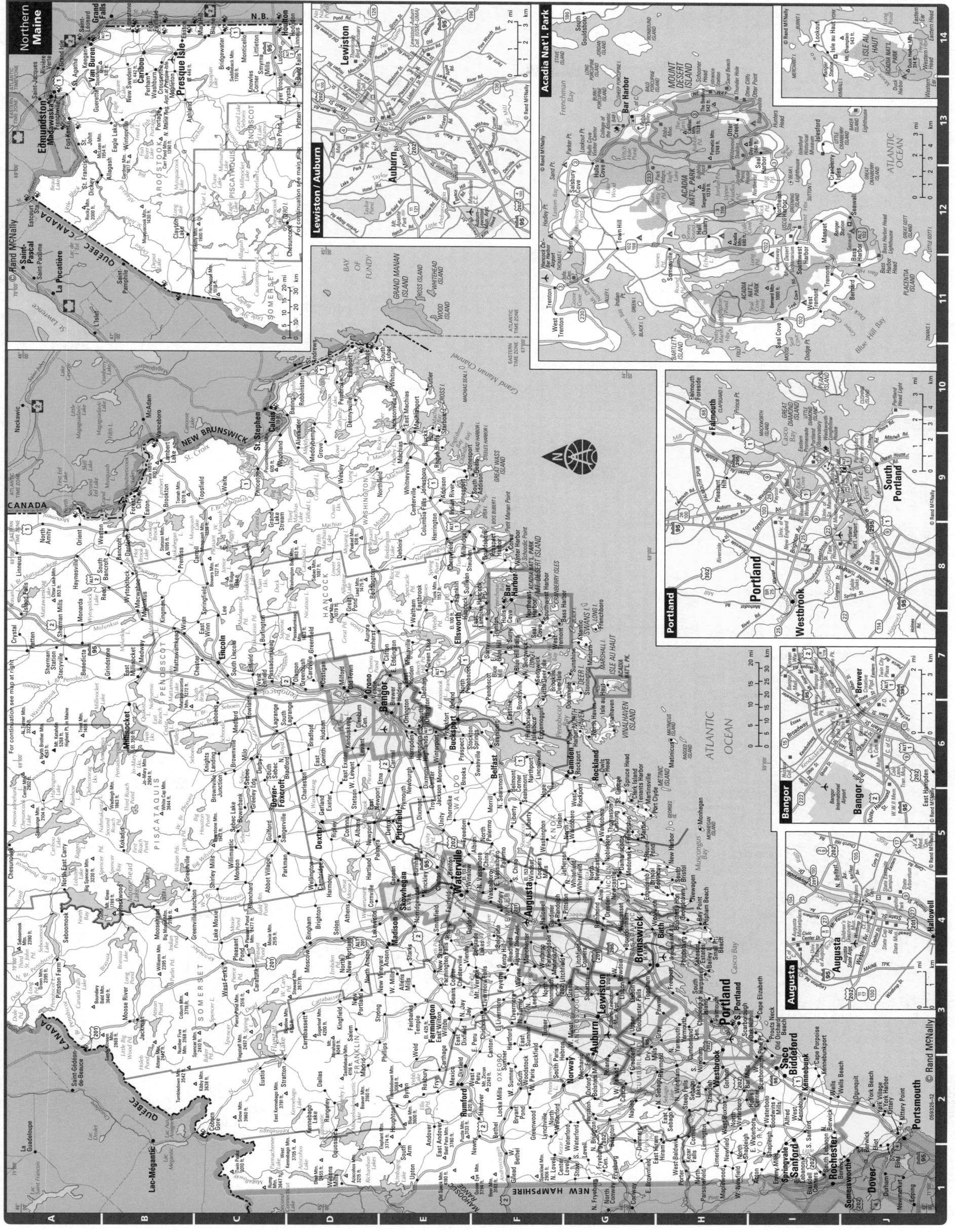

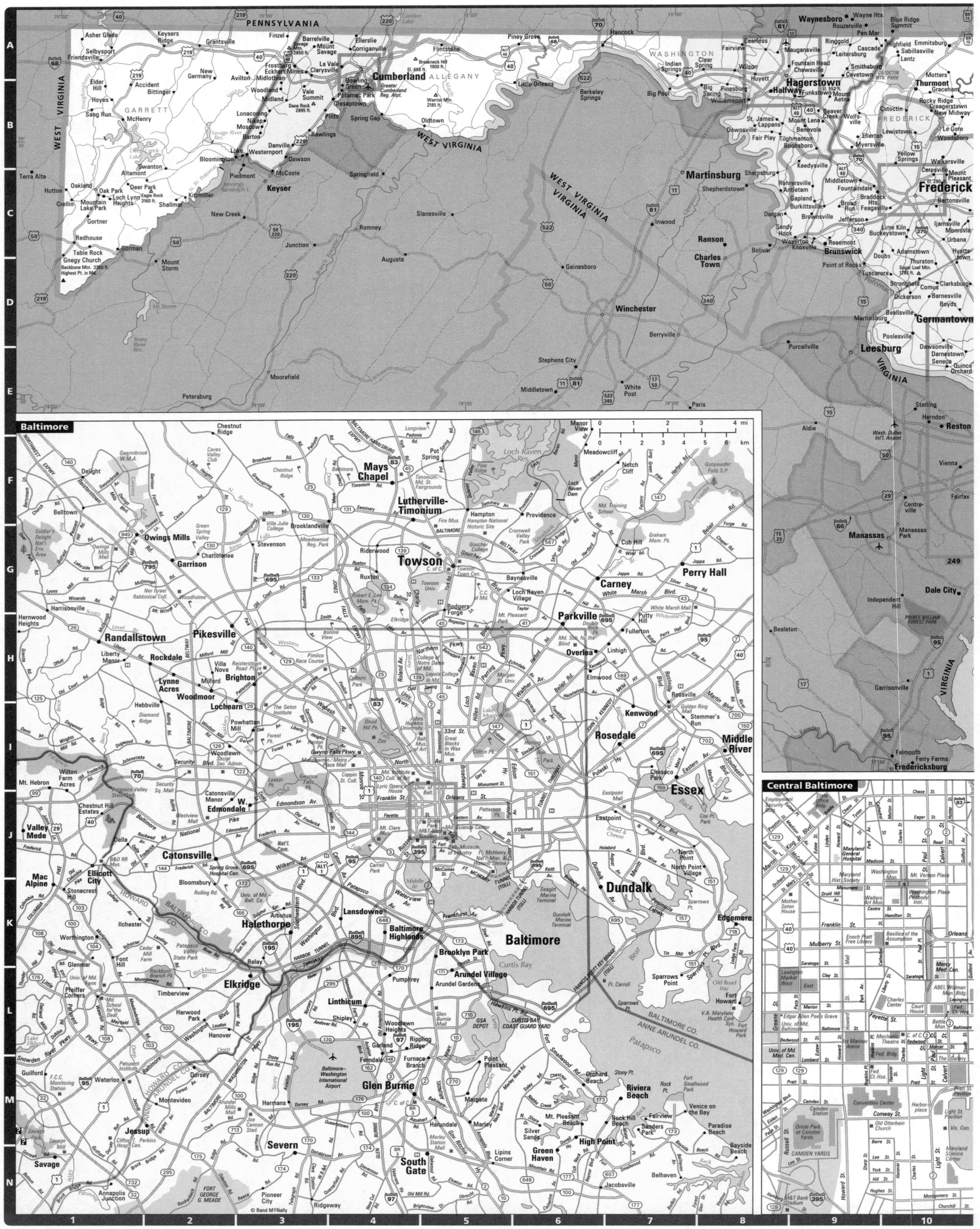

Baltimore

Central Baltimore

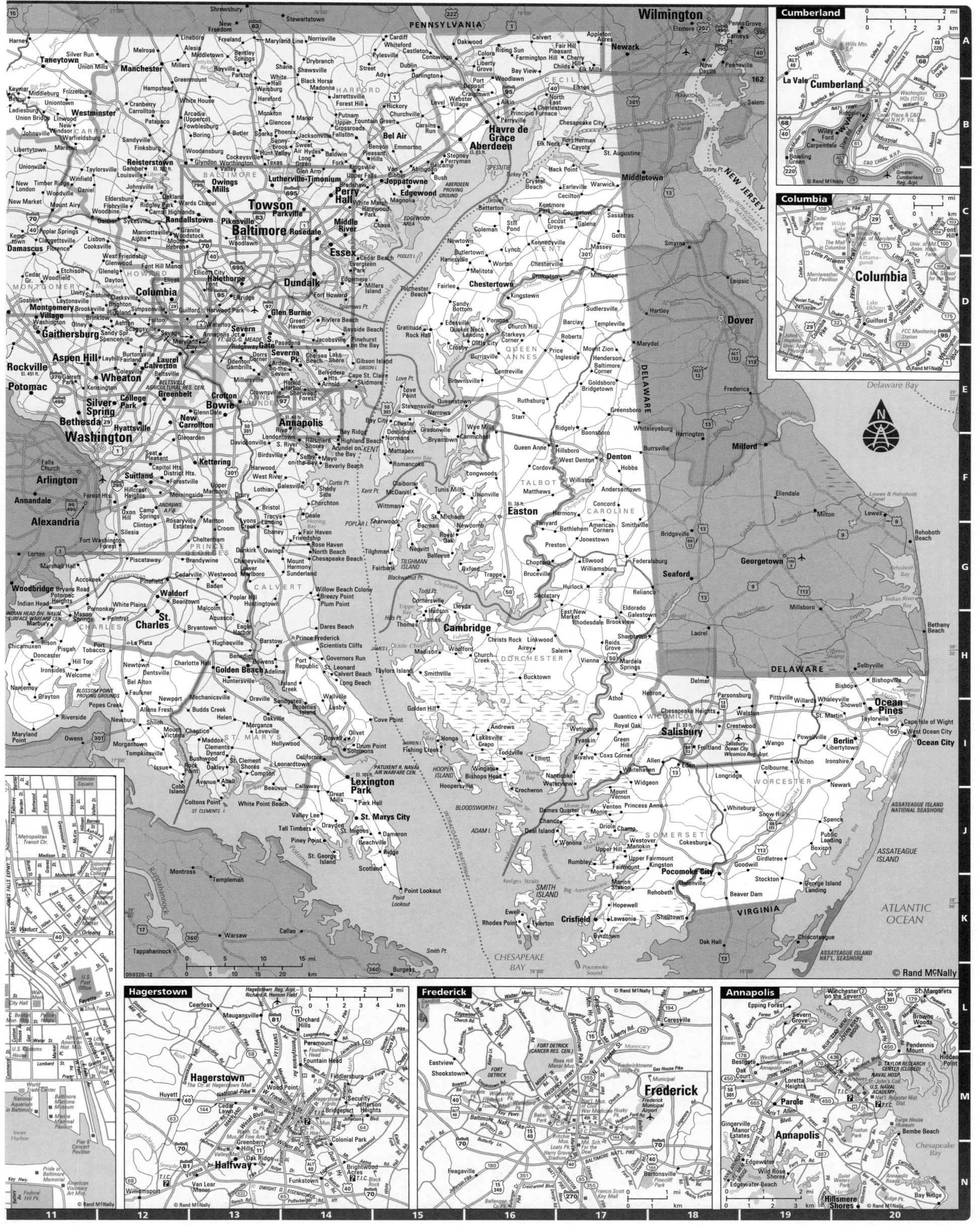

© Rand McNally

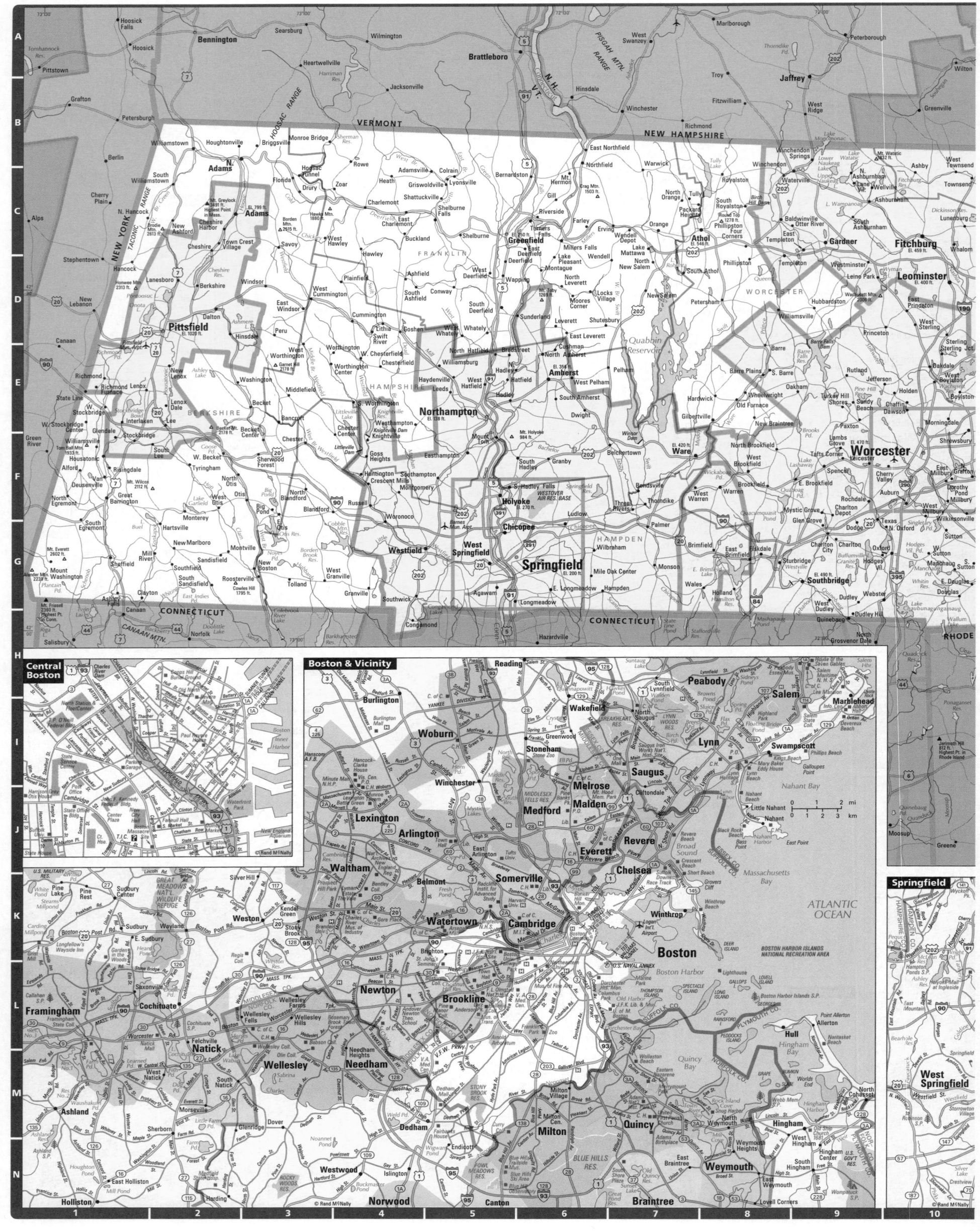

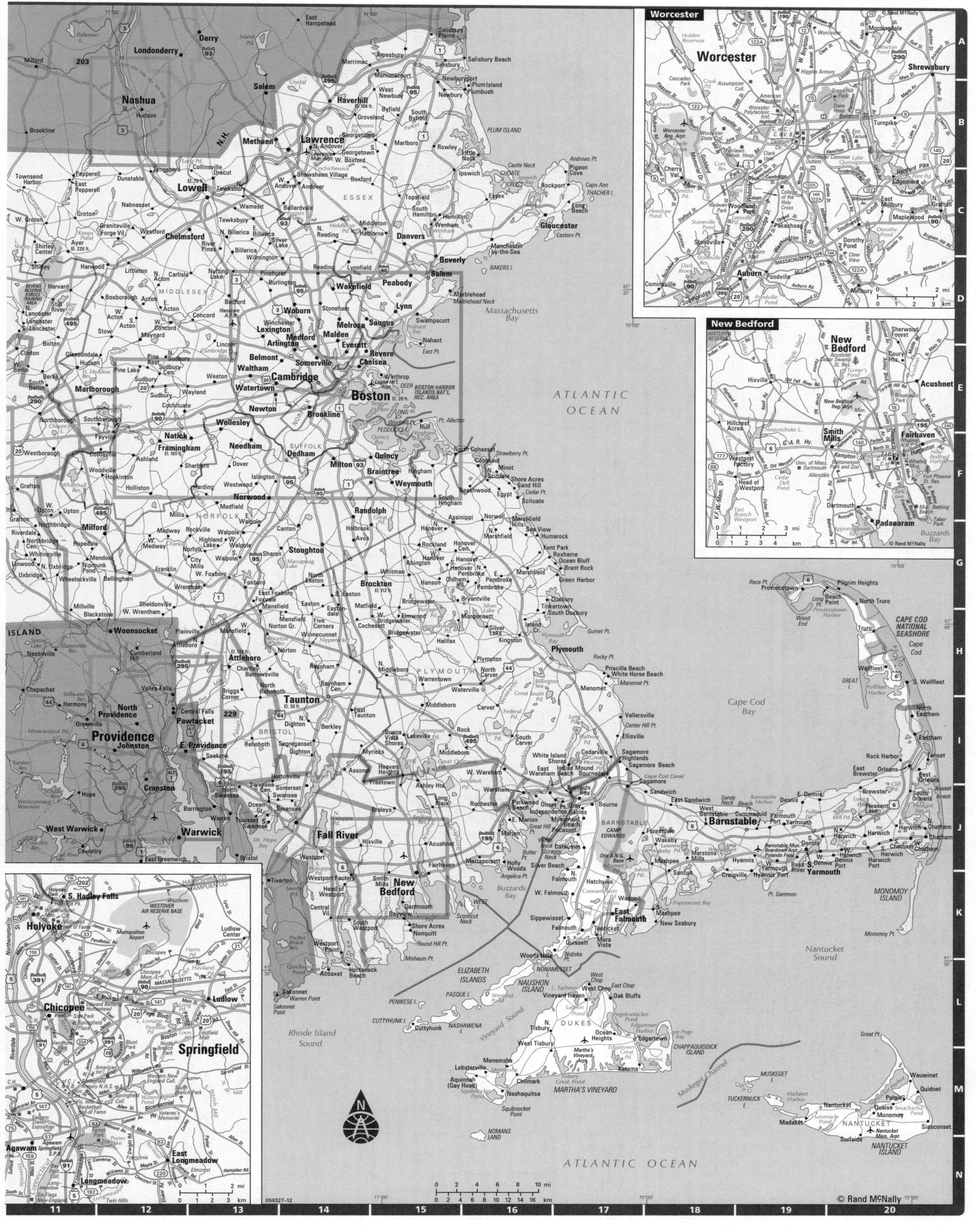

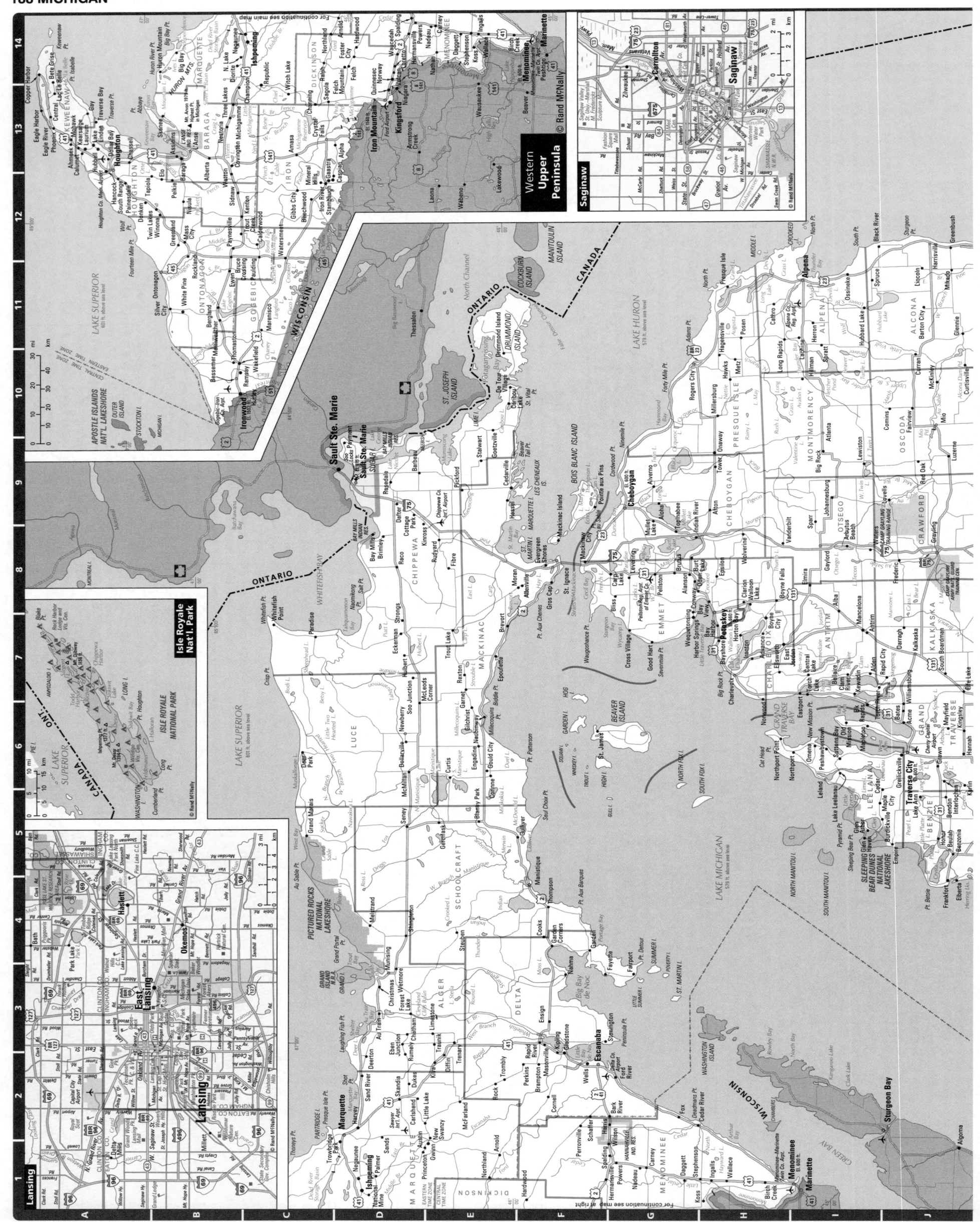

Western Upper Peninsula

Saginaw

Isle Royale Nat'l. Park

Lansing

© Rand McNally

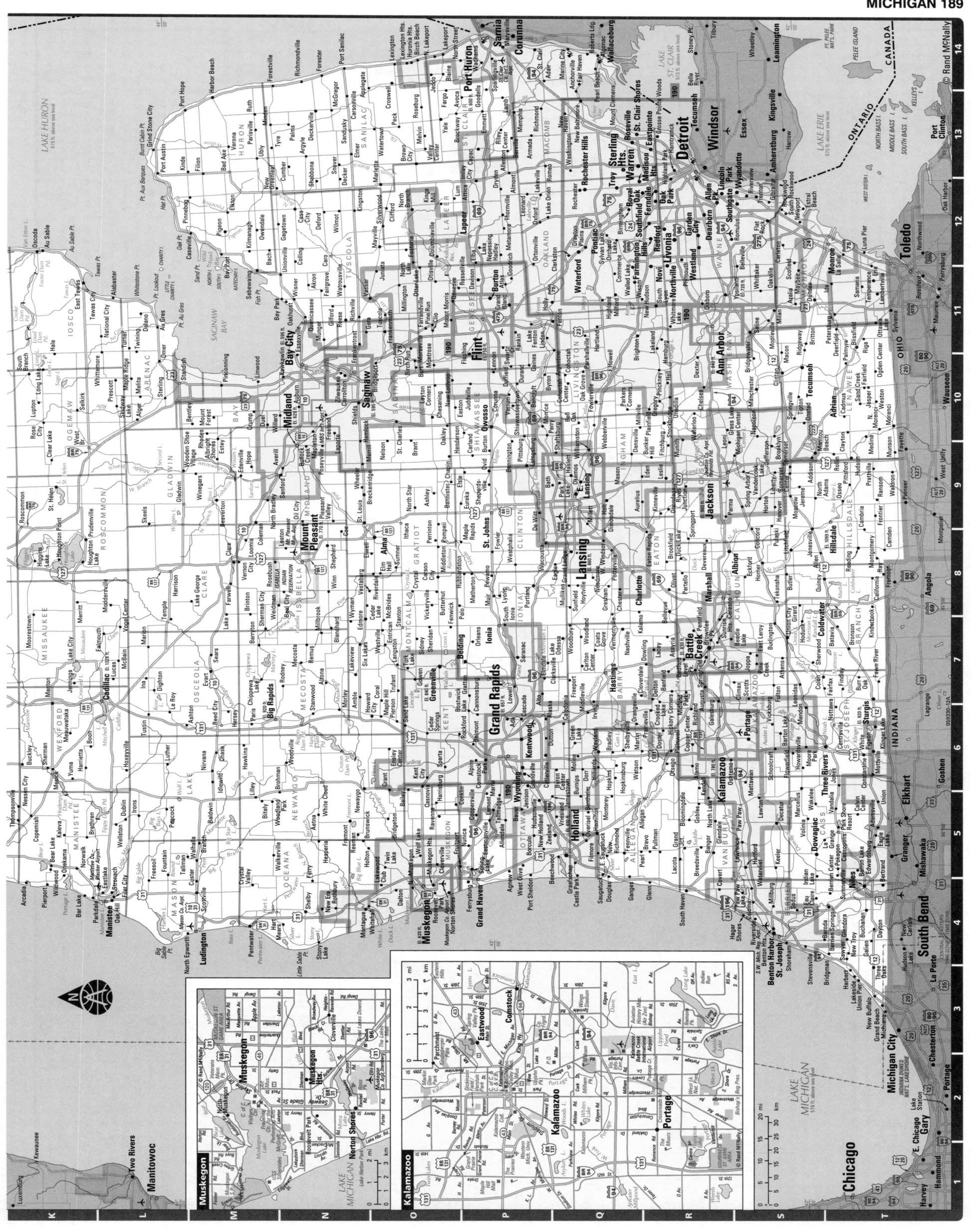

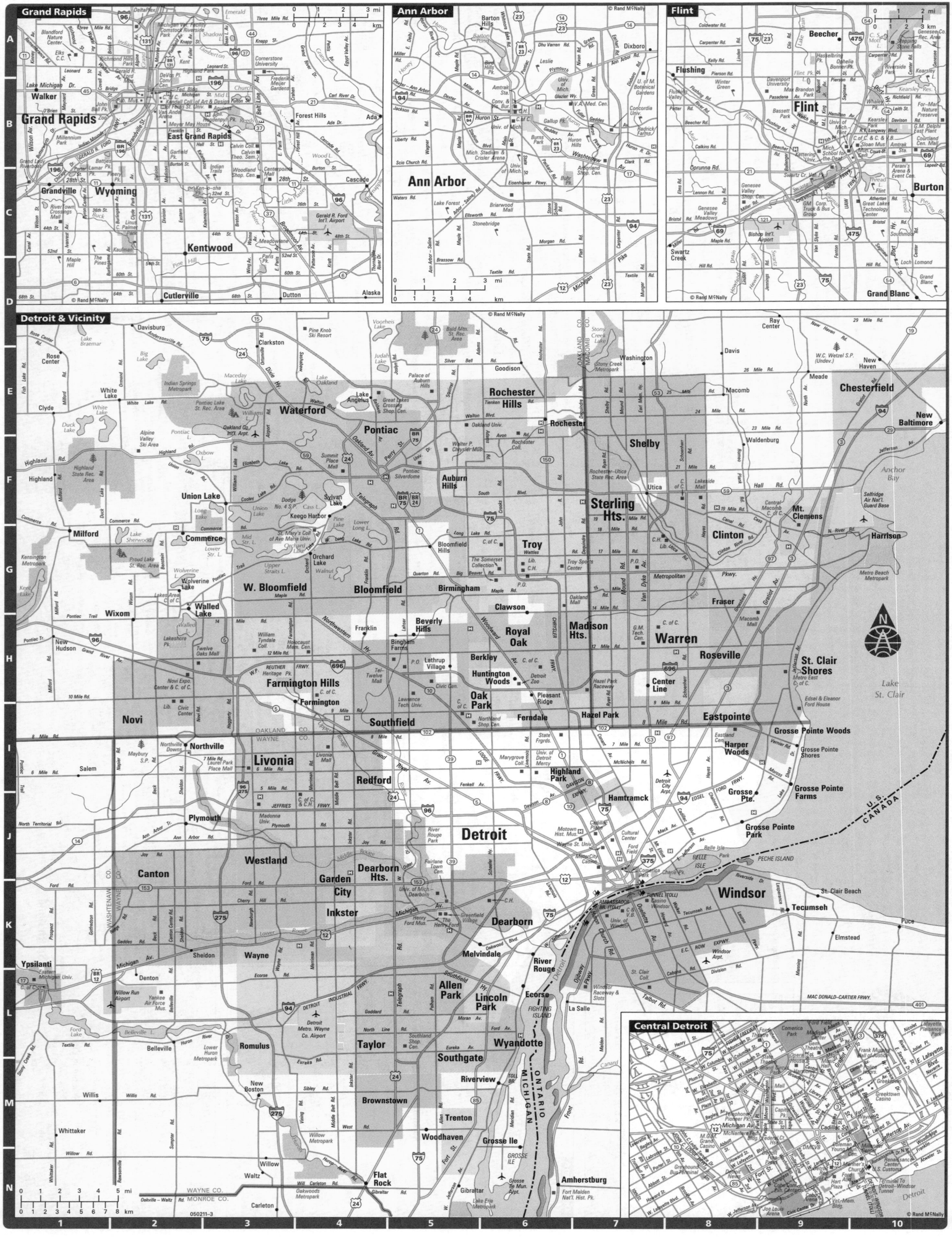

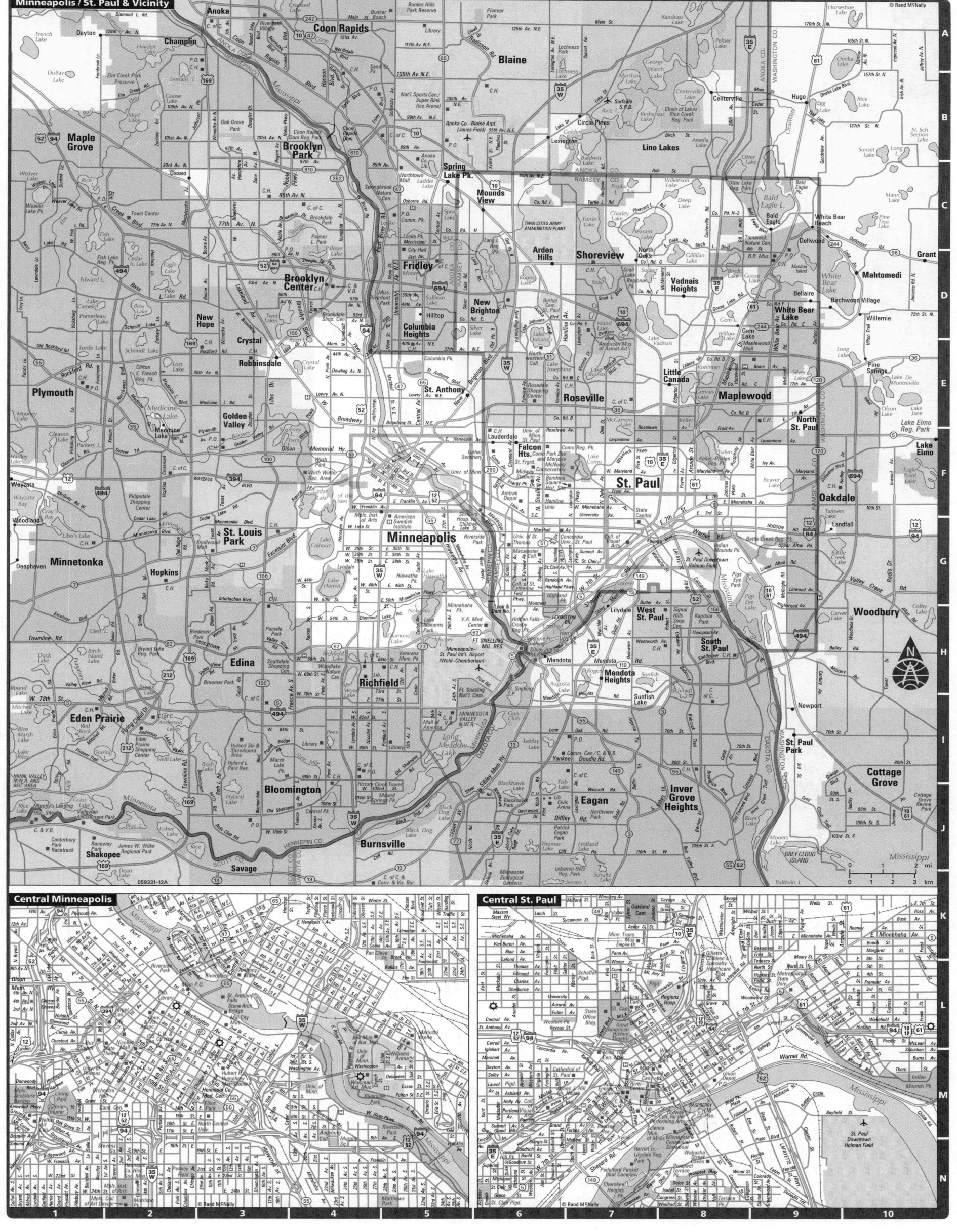

Minneapolis / St. Paul & Vicinity

Central Minneapolis

Central St. Paul

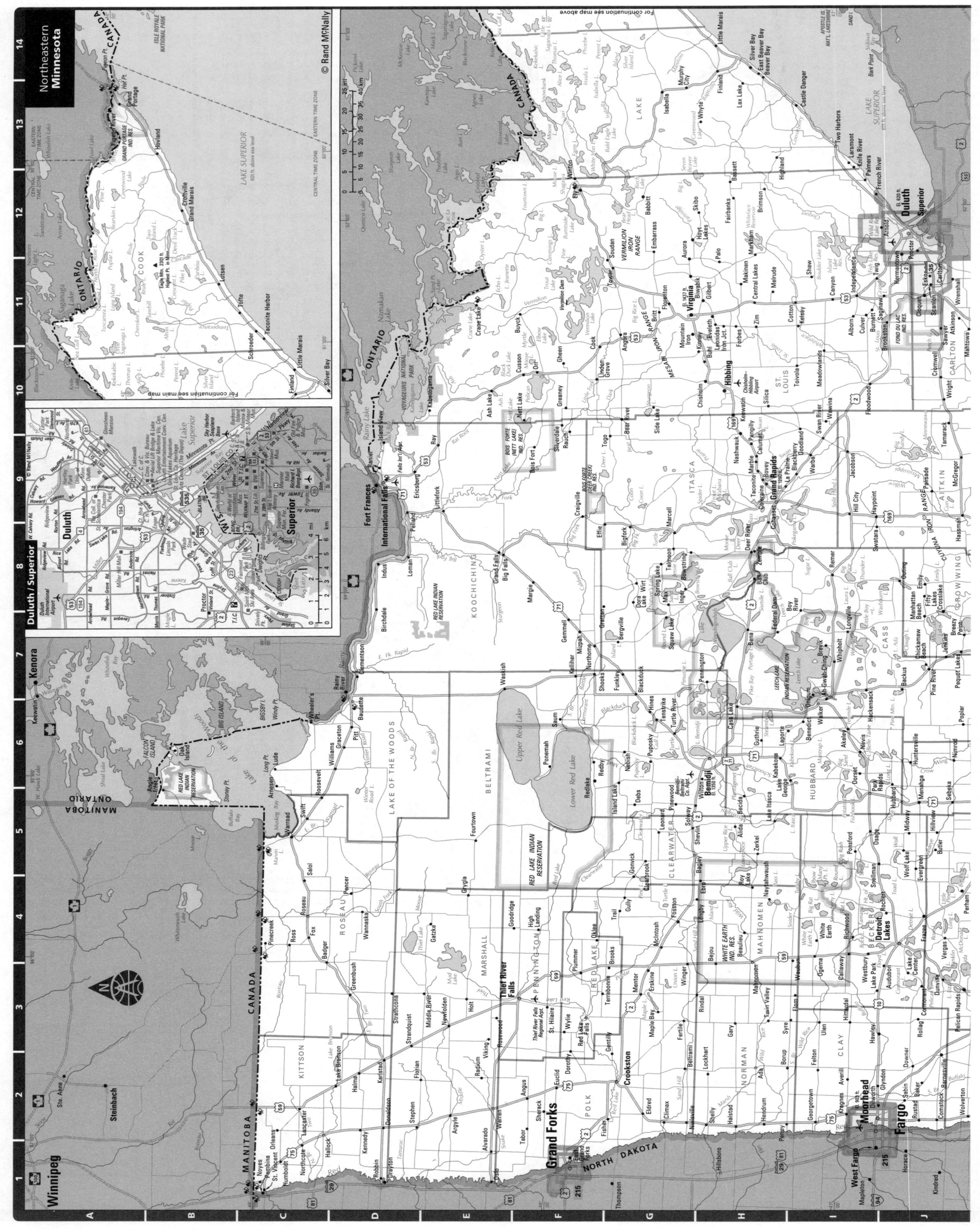

Northeastern
Minnesota

© Rand McNally

Duluth / Superior

Duluth

Superior

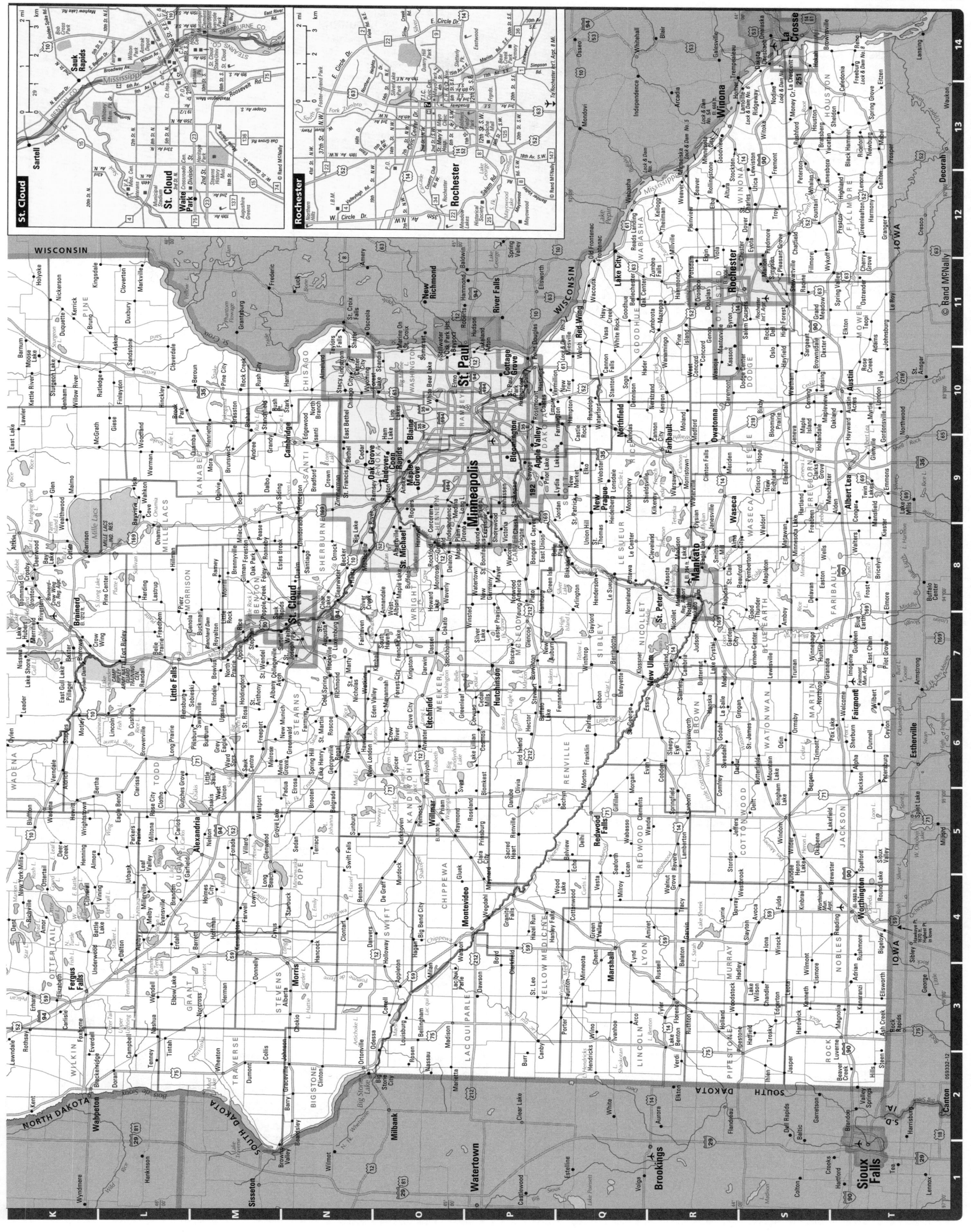

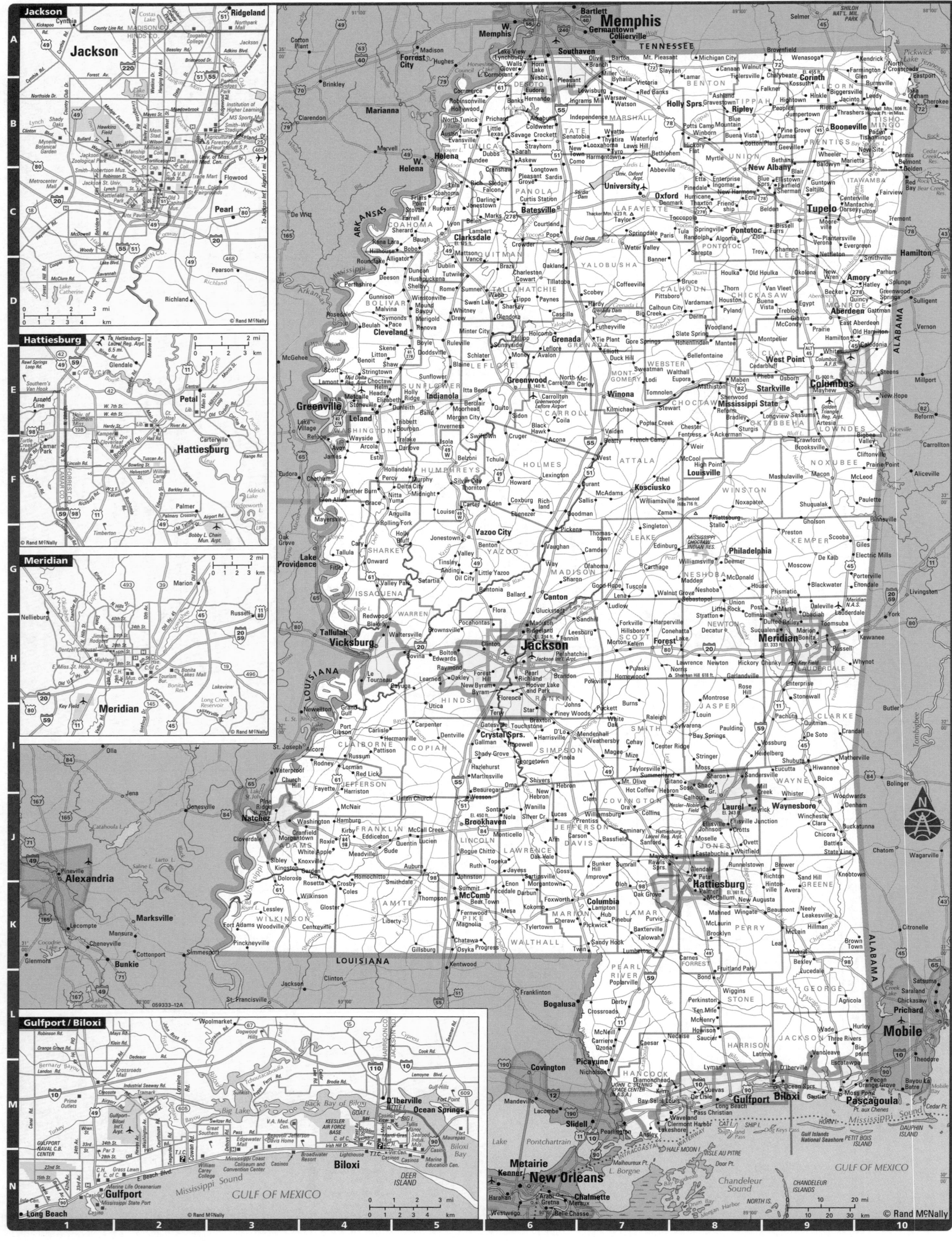

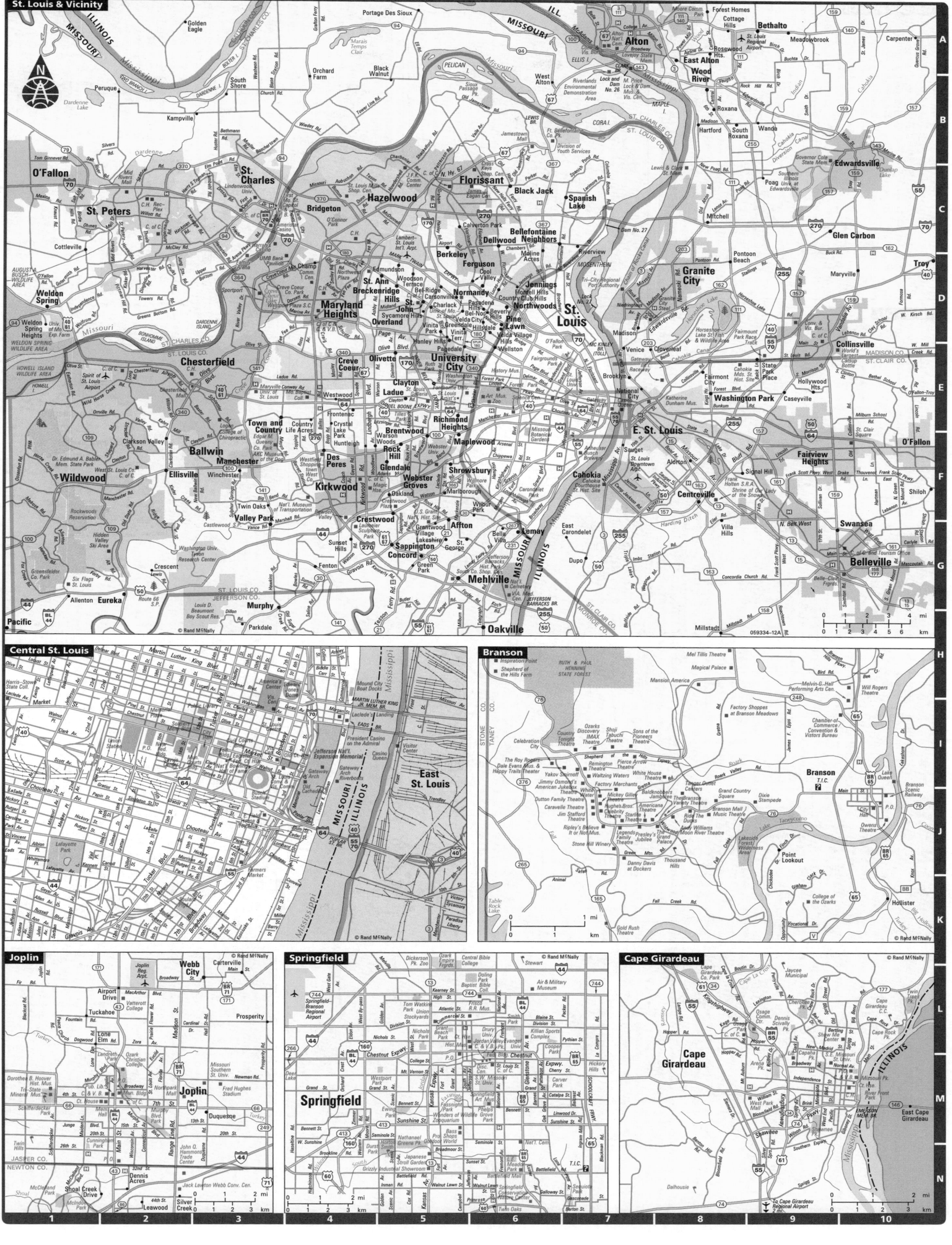

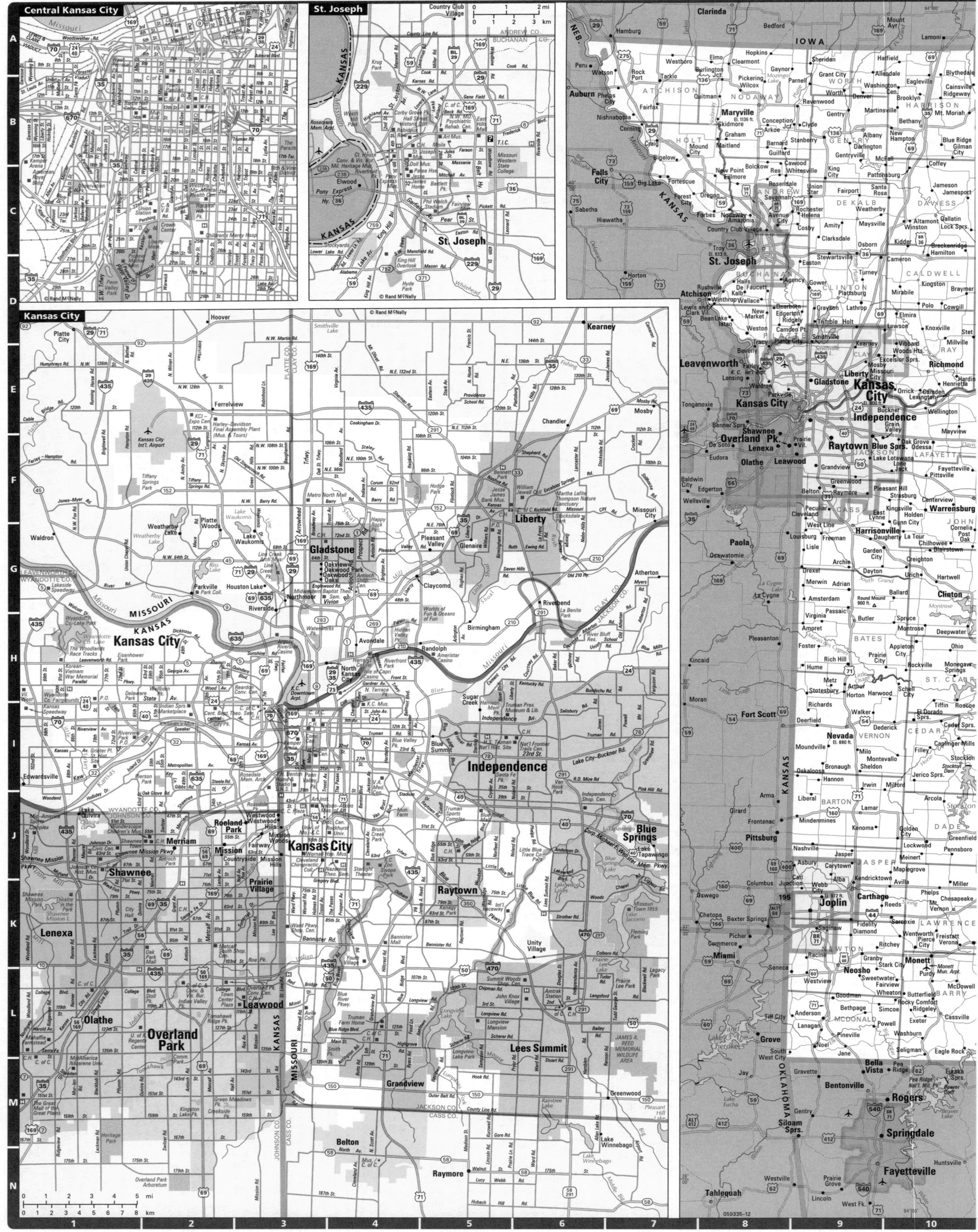

Central Kansas City

St. Joseph

Kansas City

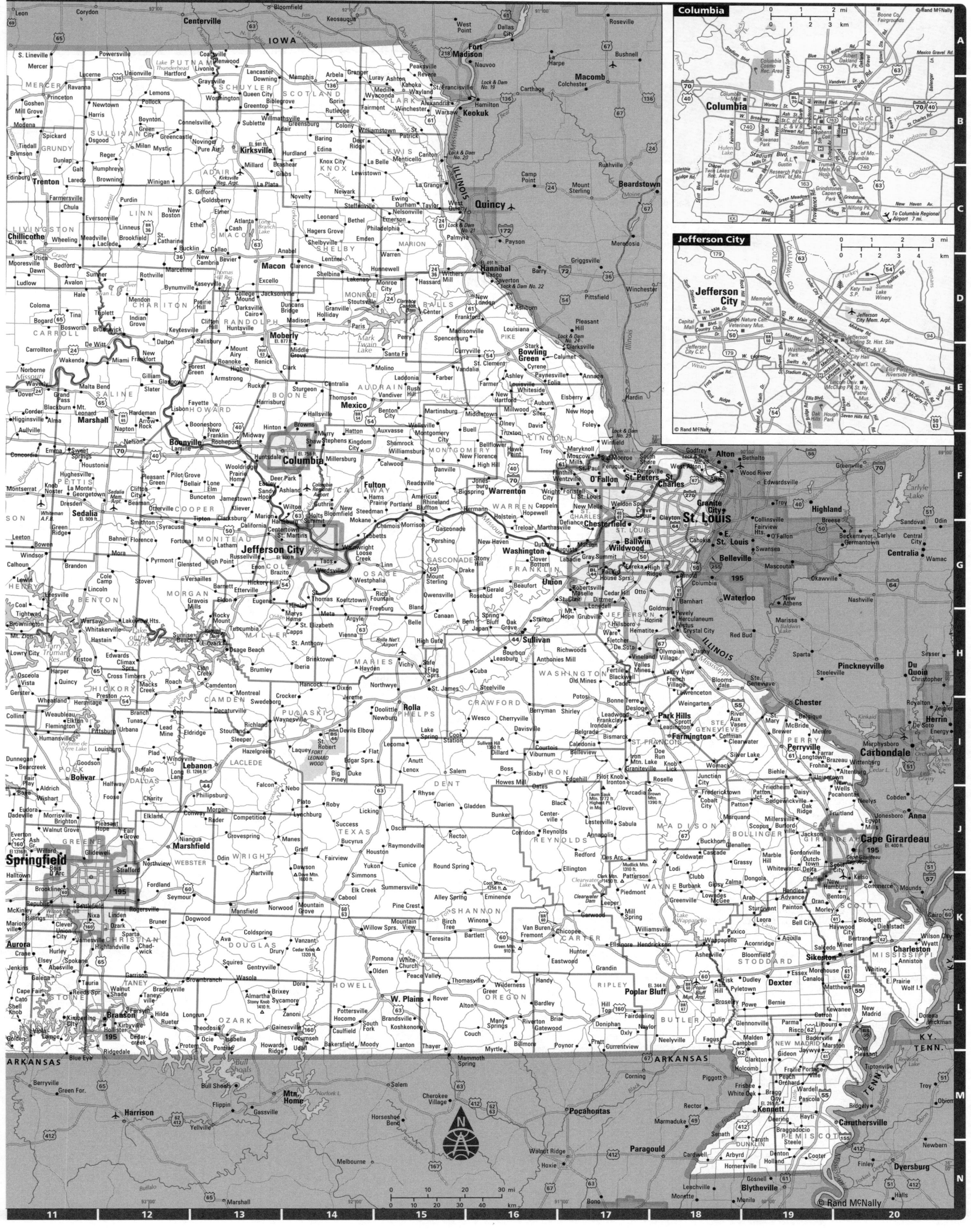

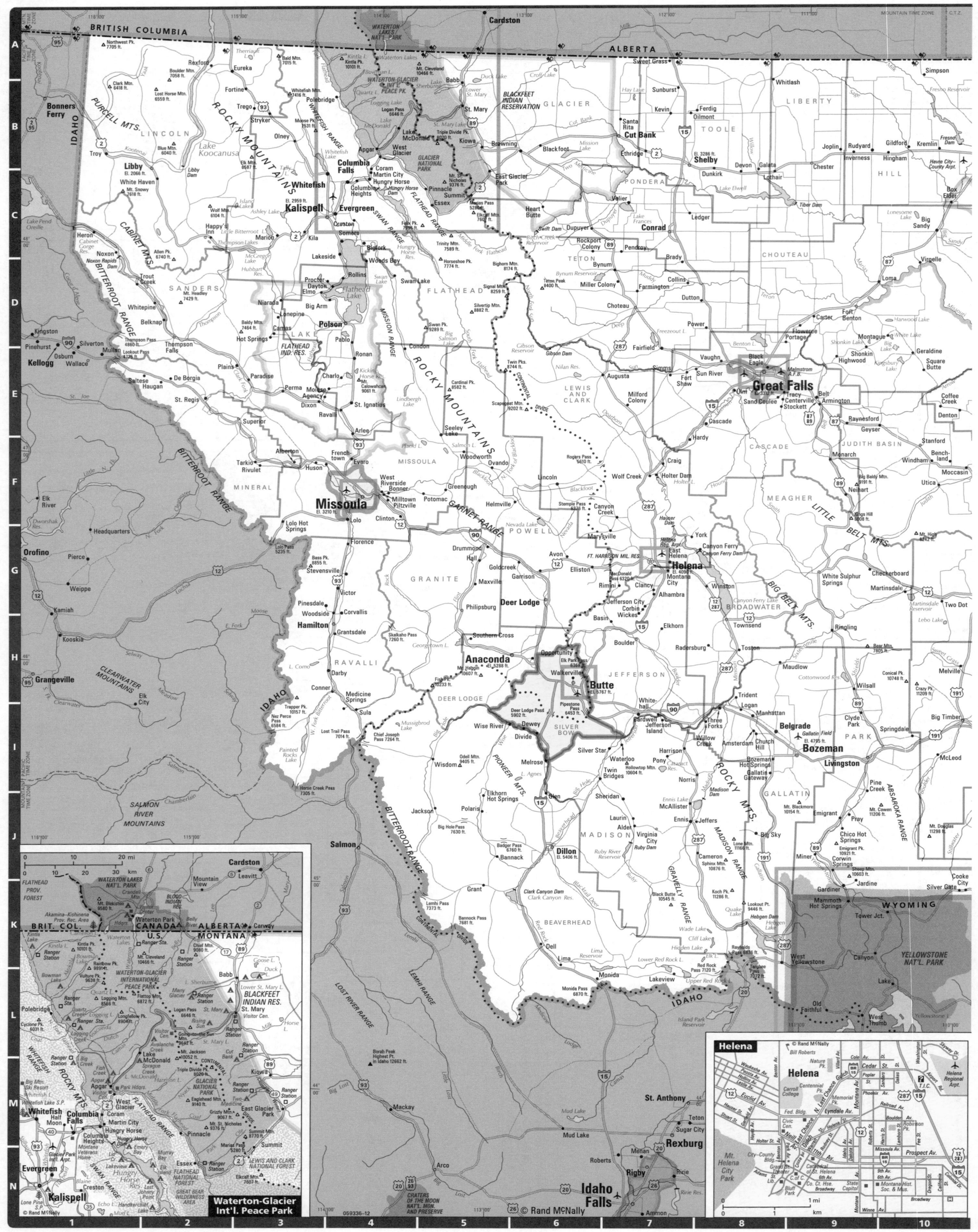

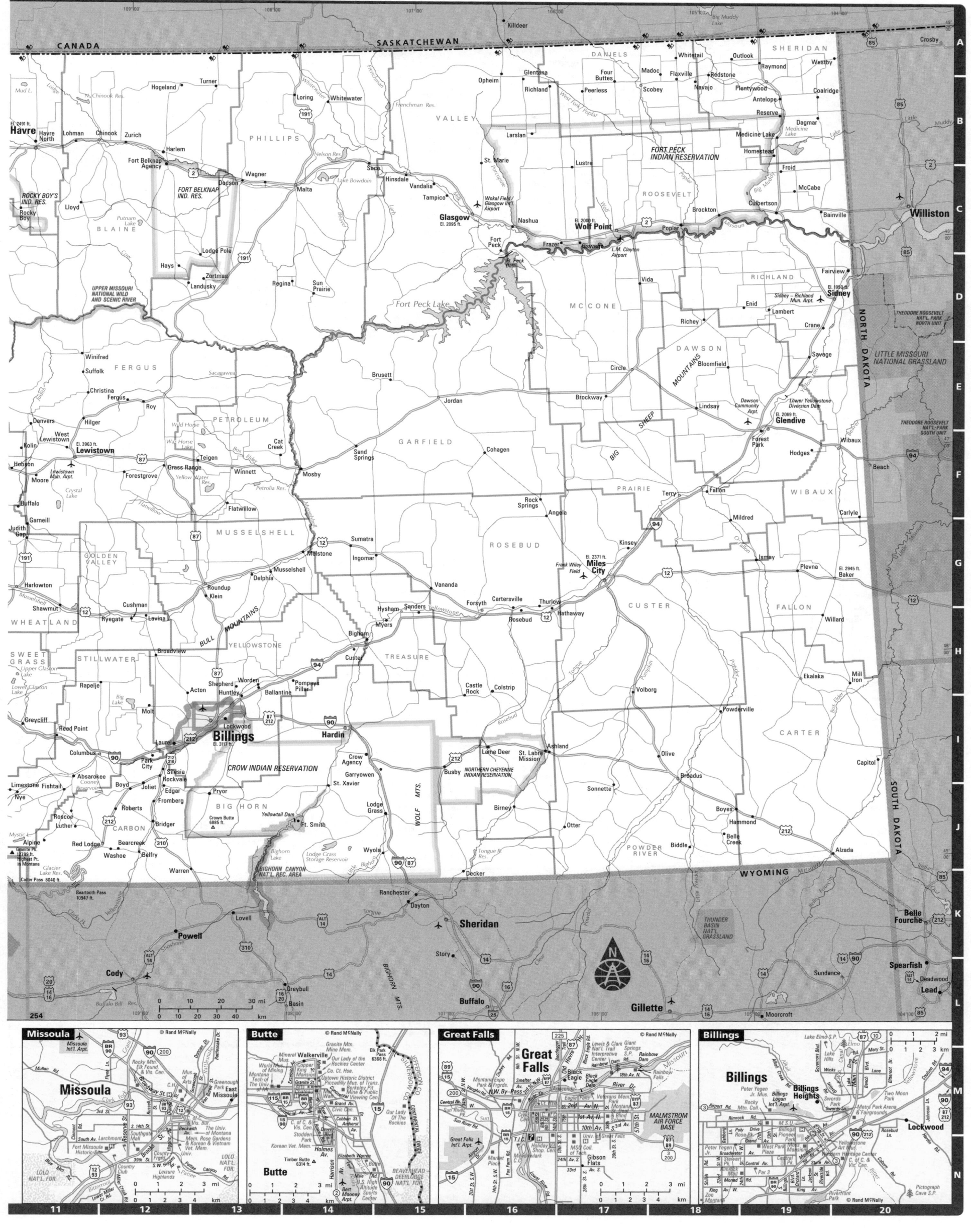

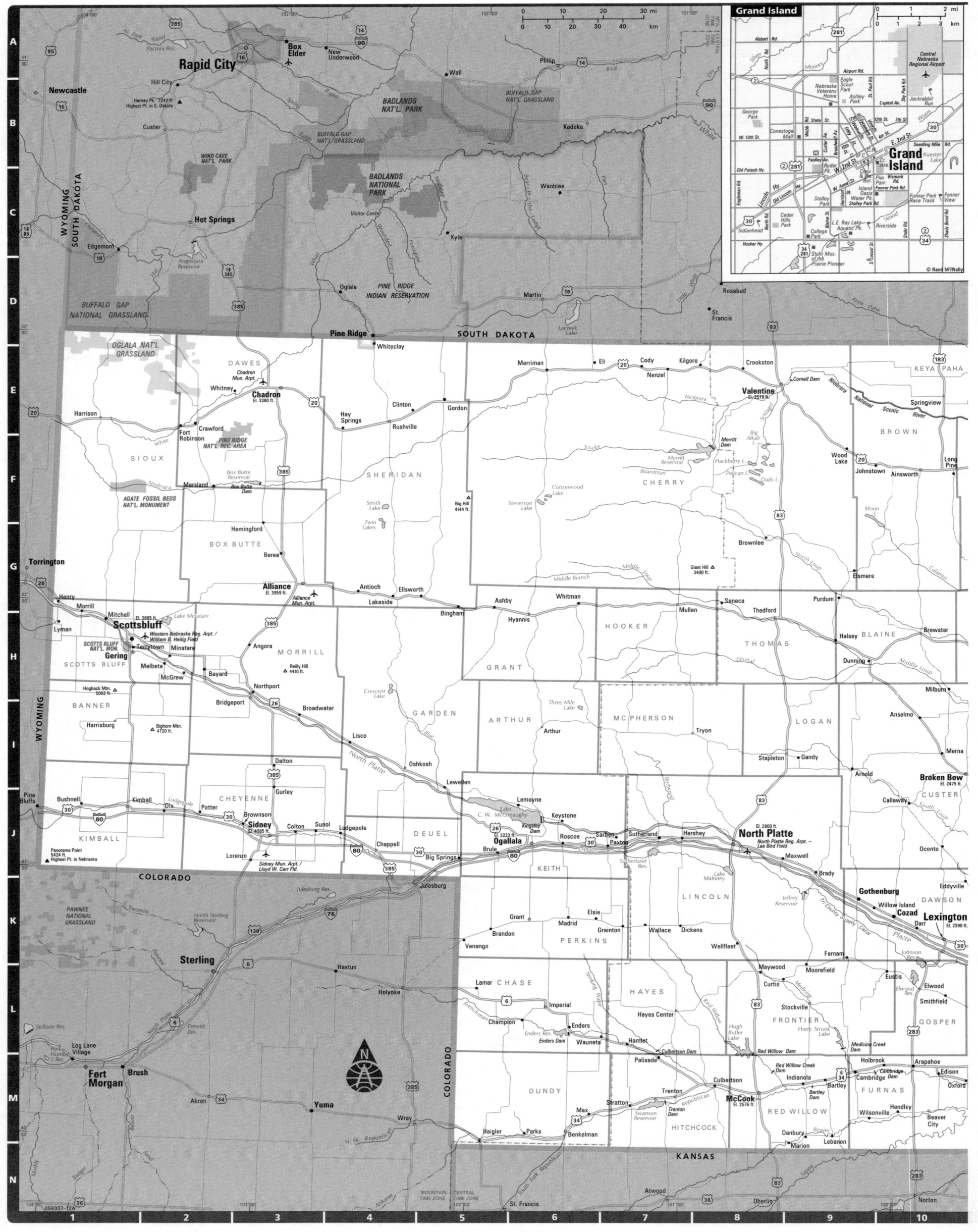

Grand Island

© Rand McNally

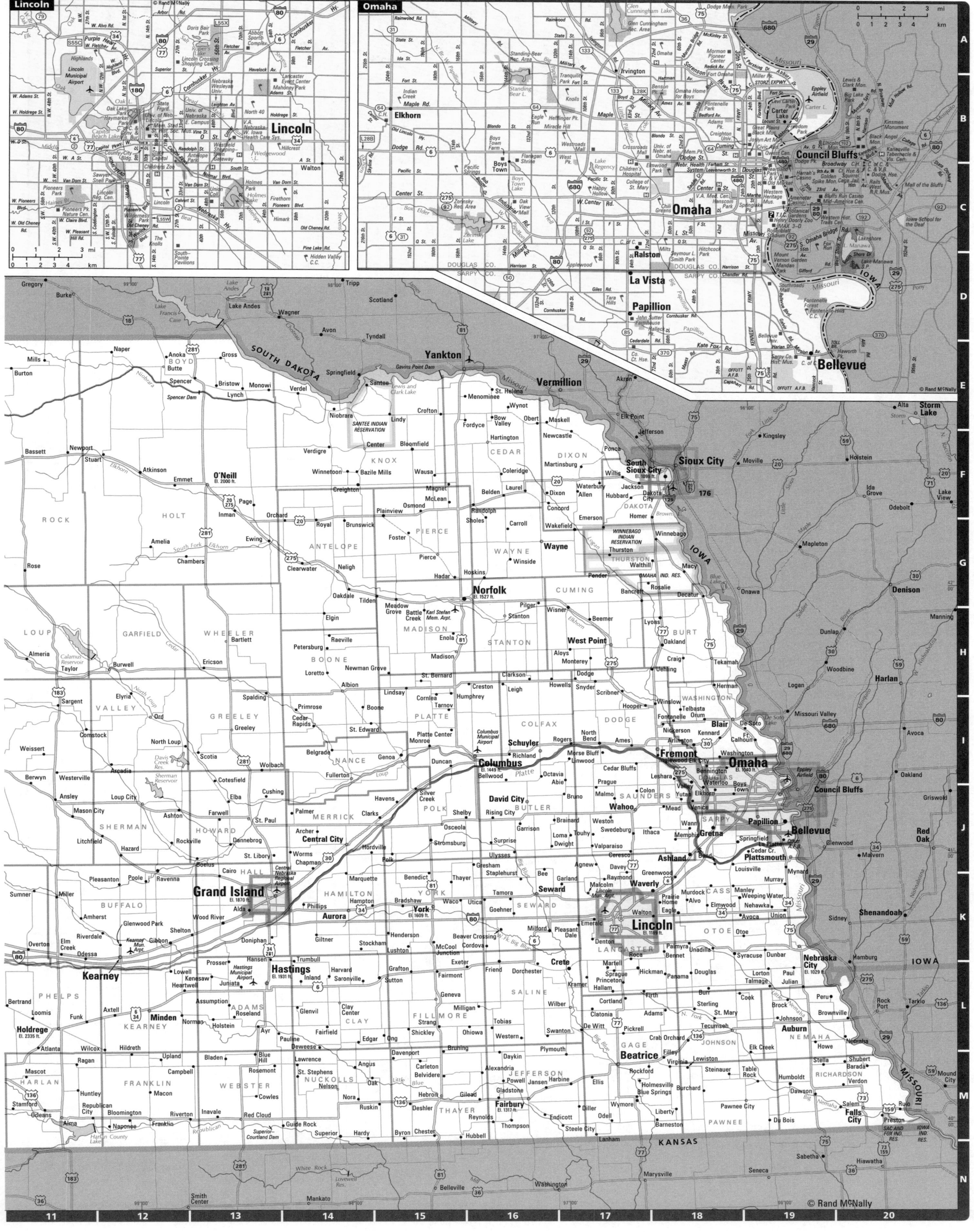

Lincoln

Omaha

© Rand McNally

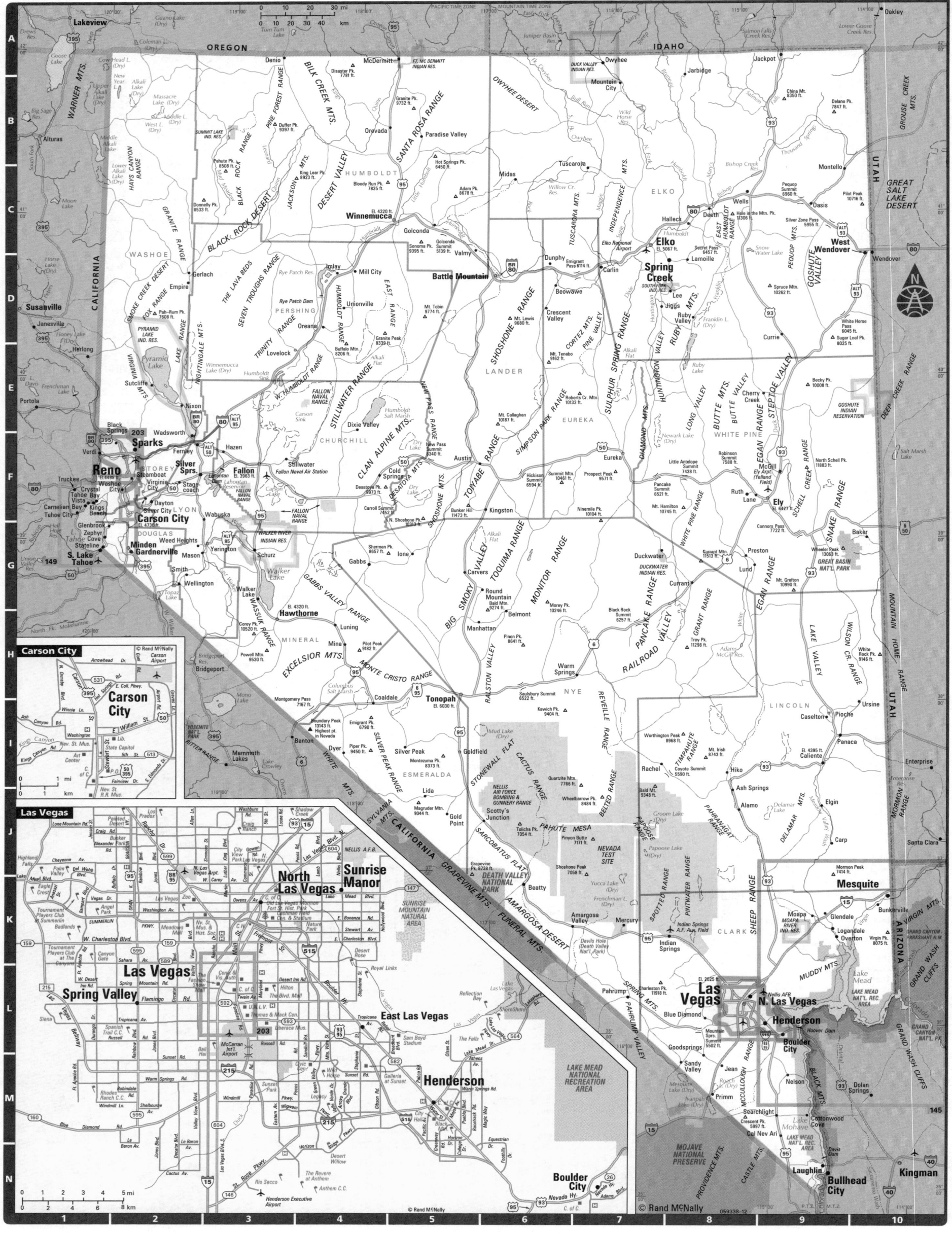

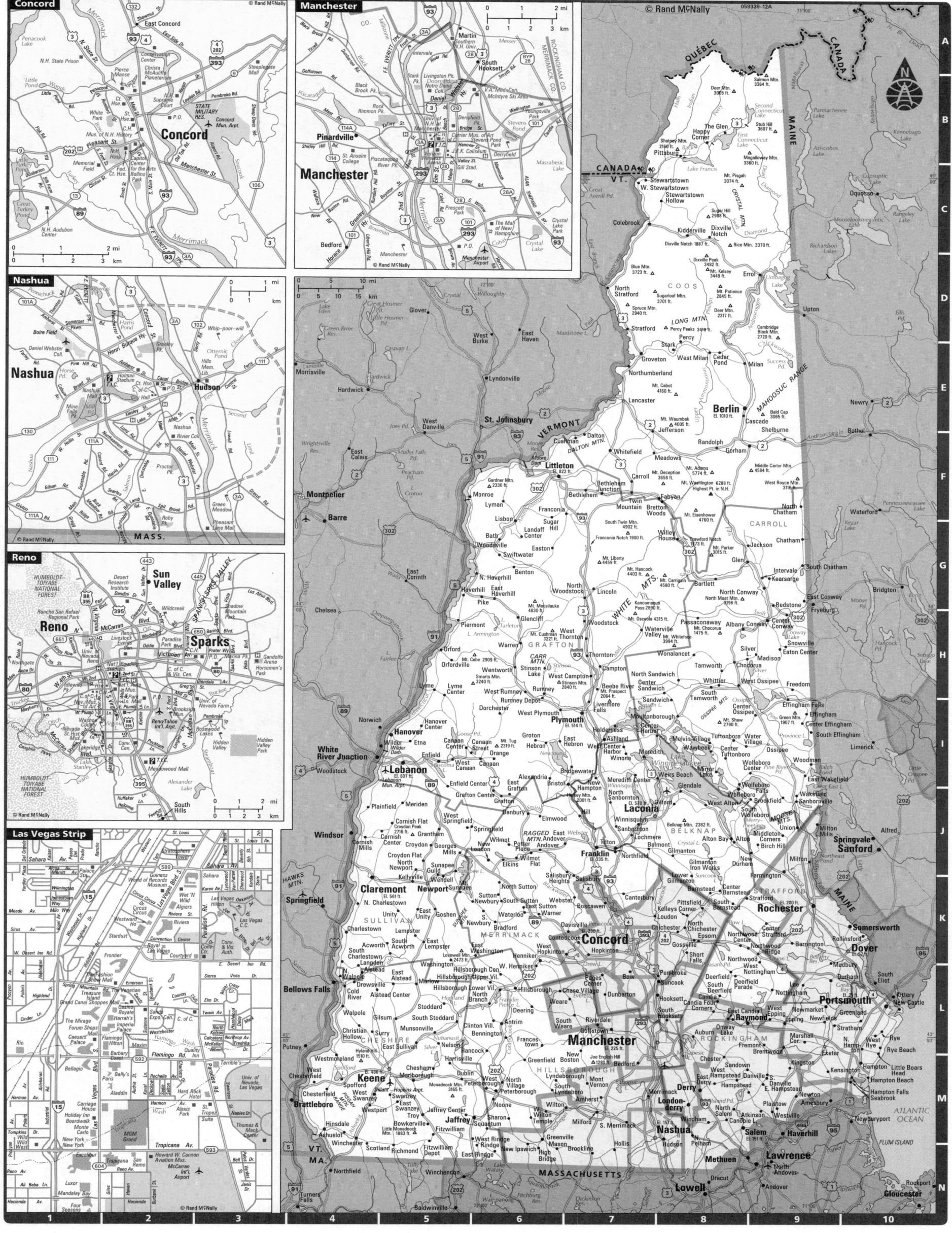

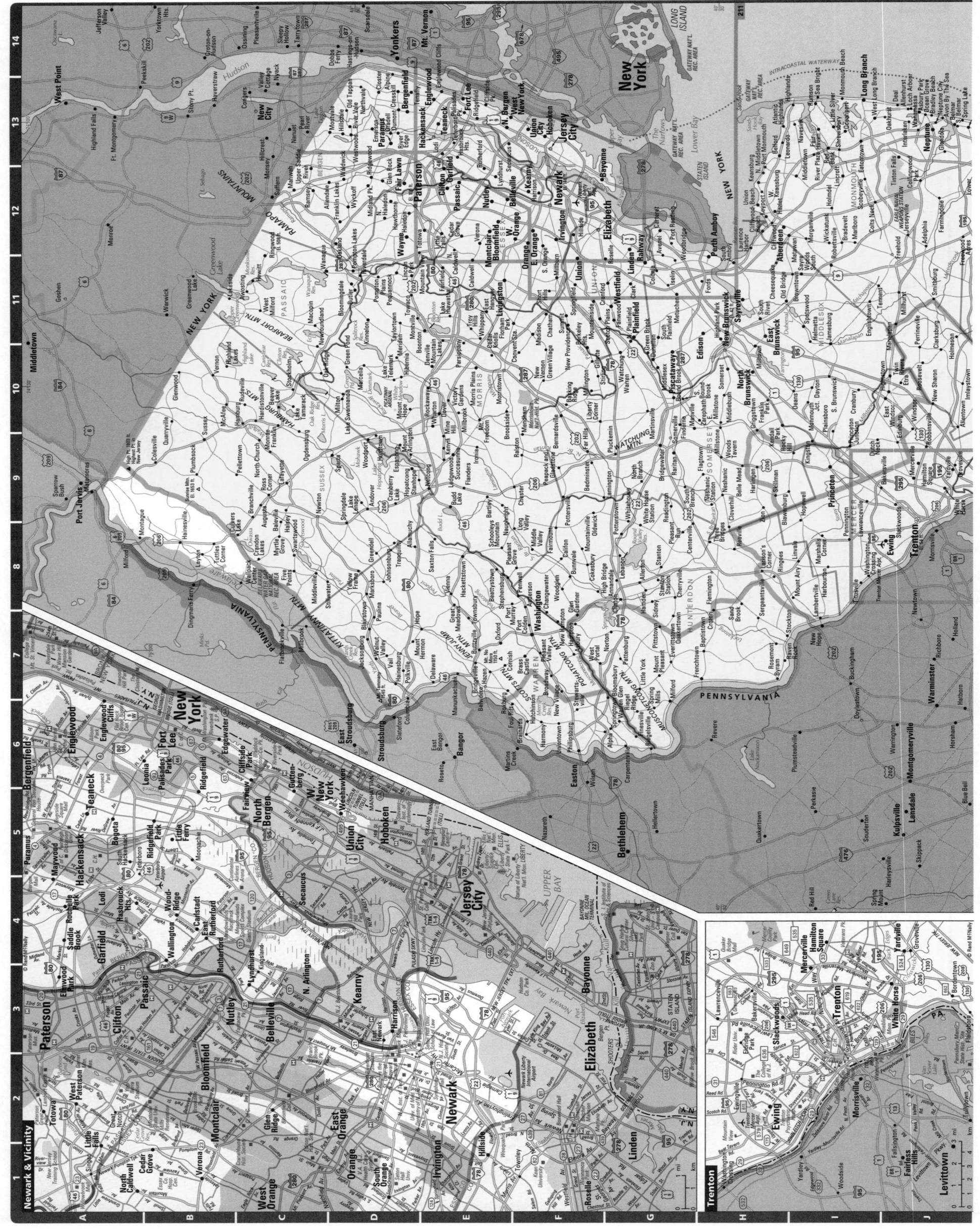

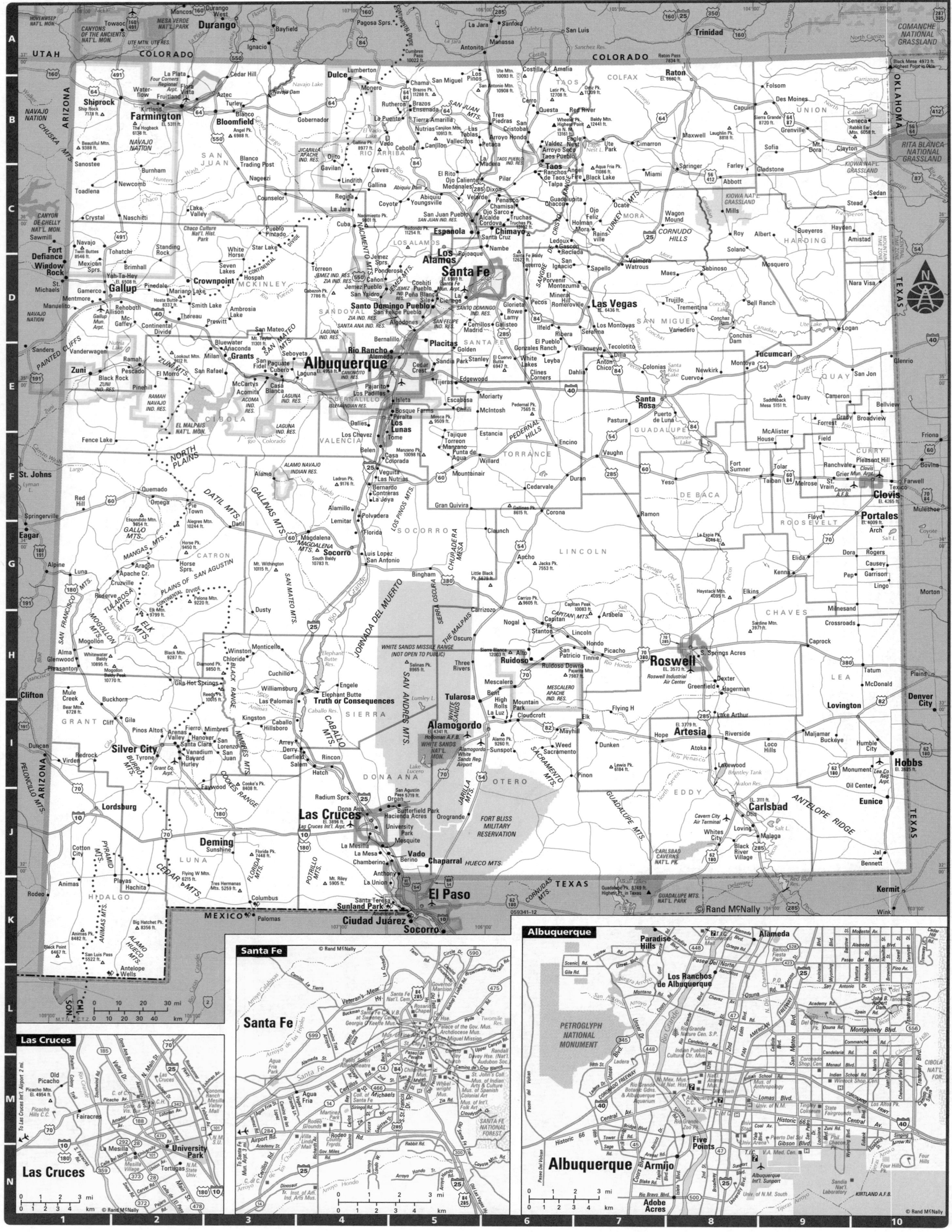

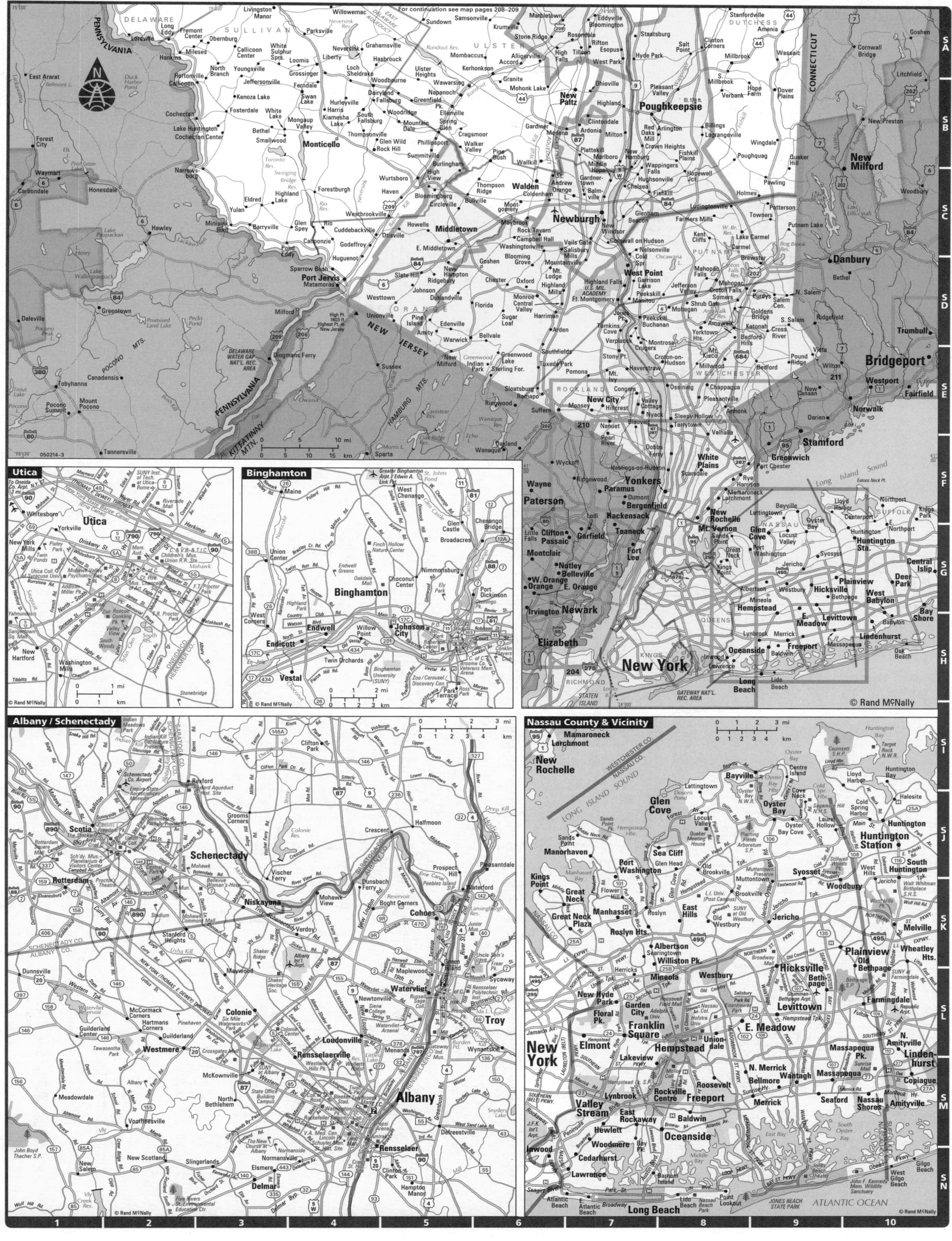

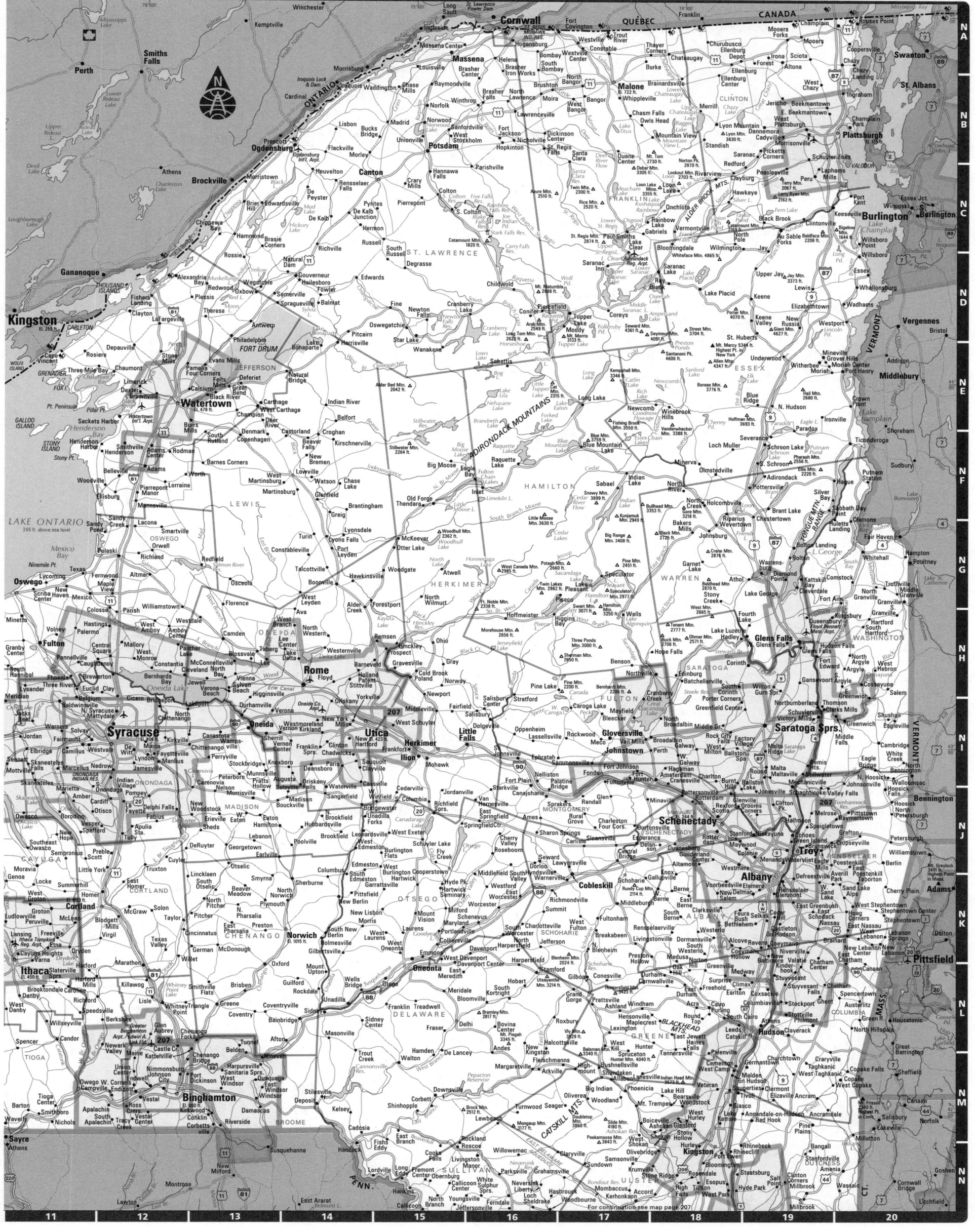

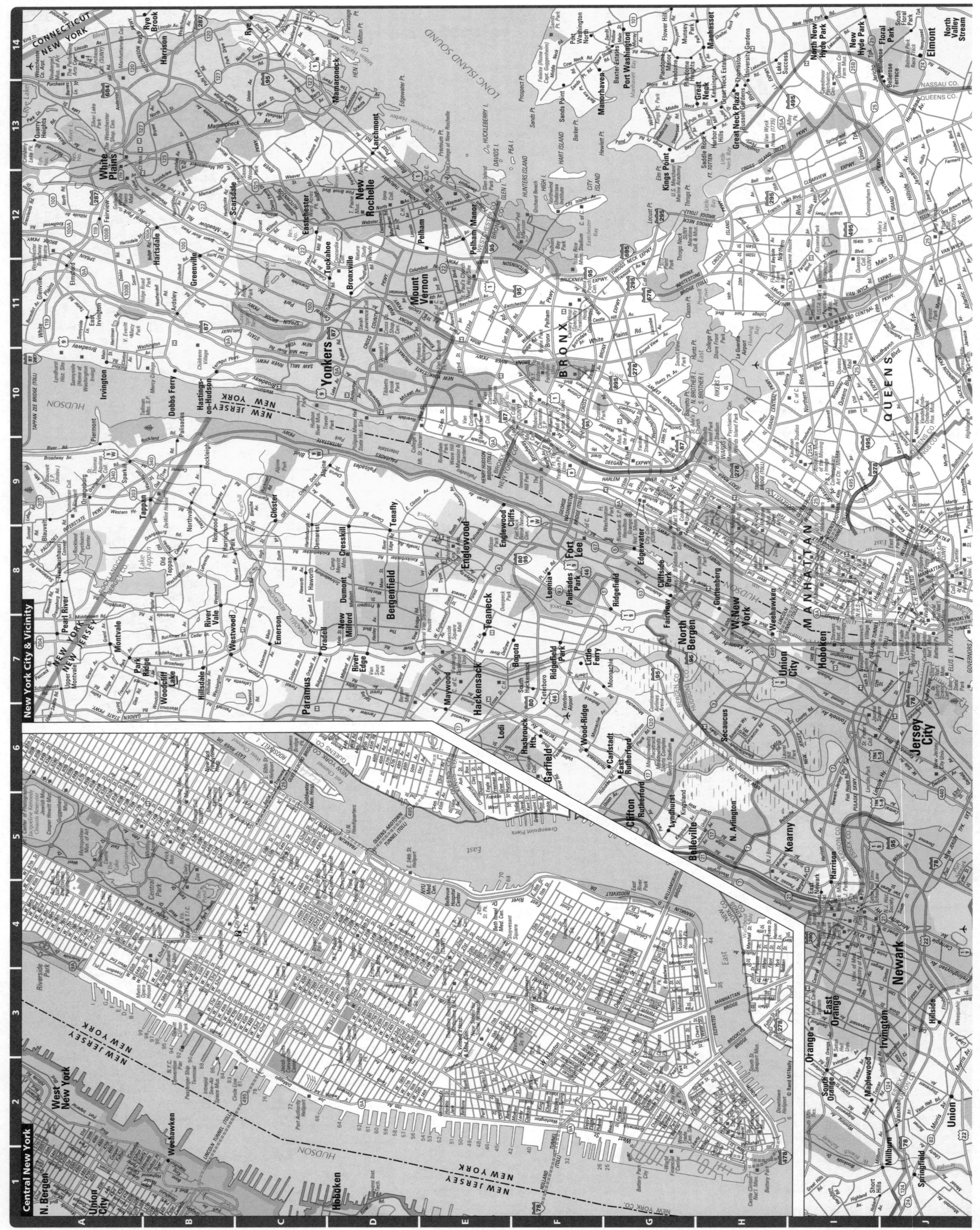

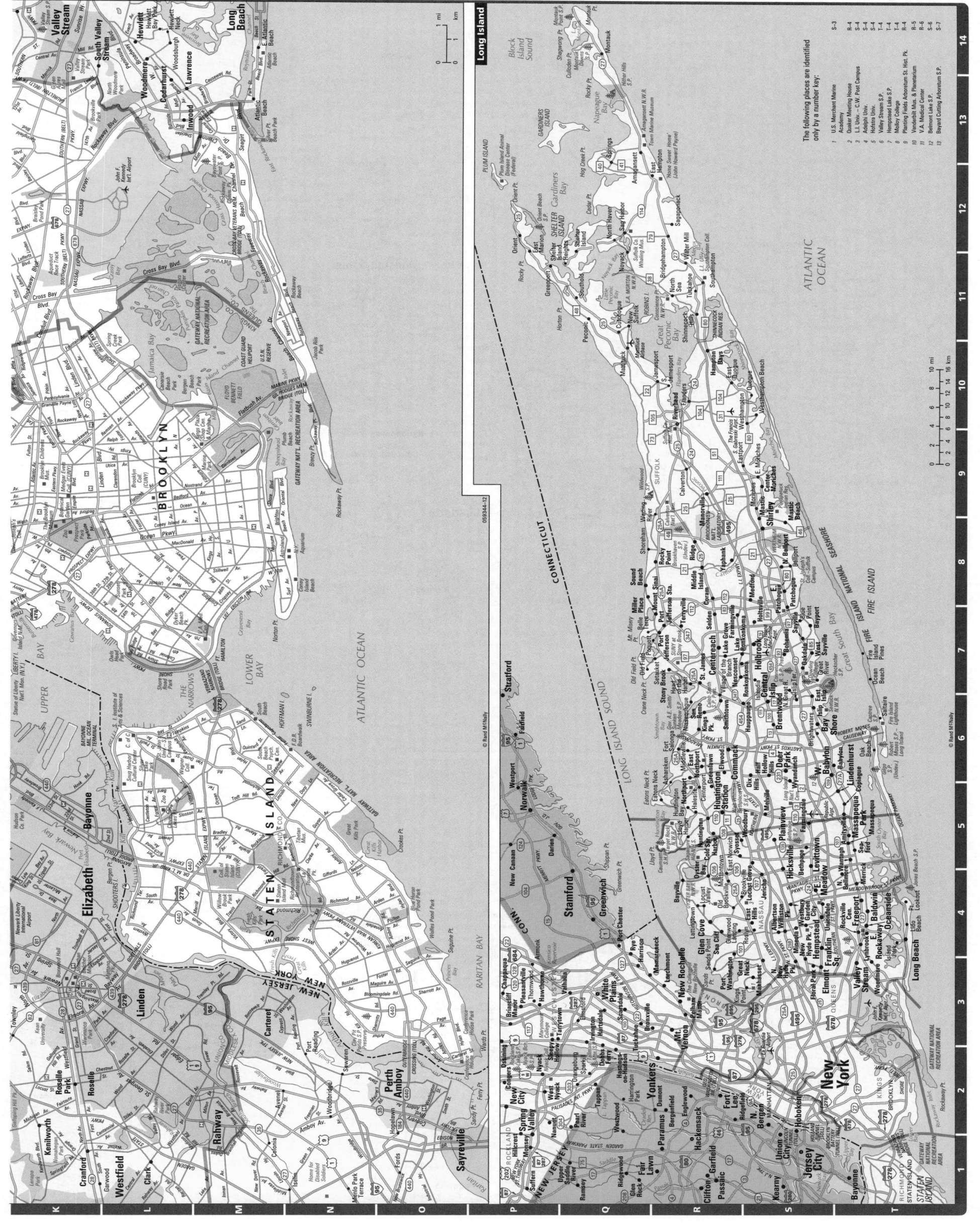

Long Island

The following places are identified only by a number key:

1   U.S. Merchant Marine Academy S-3
2   Quaker Meeting House R-4
3   L.I. Univ. - C.W. Post Campus S-4
4   Adelphi Univ. S-4
5   Hofstra Univ. T-1
6   Valley Stream S.P. T-1
7   Molloy College R-4
8   Planting Fields Arboretum St. Hist. Pk. R-5
9   Hempstead Lake S.P. R-4
10 Vanderbilt Mus. & Planetarium R-5
11 V.A. Medical Center R-6
12 Belmont Lake S.P. S-6
13 Bayard Cutting Arboretum S.P. S-7

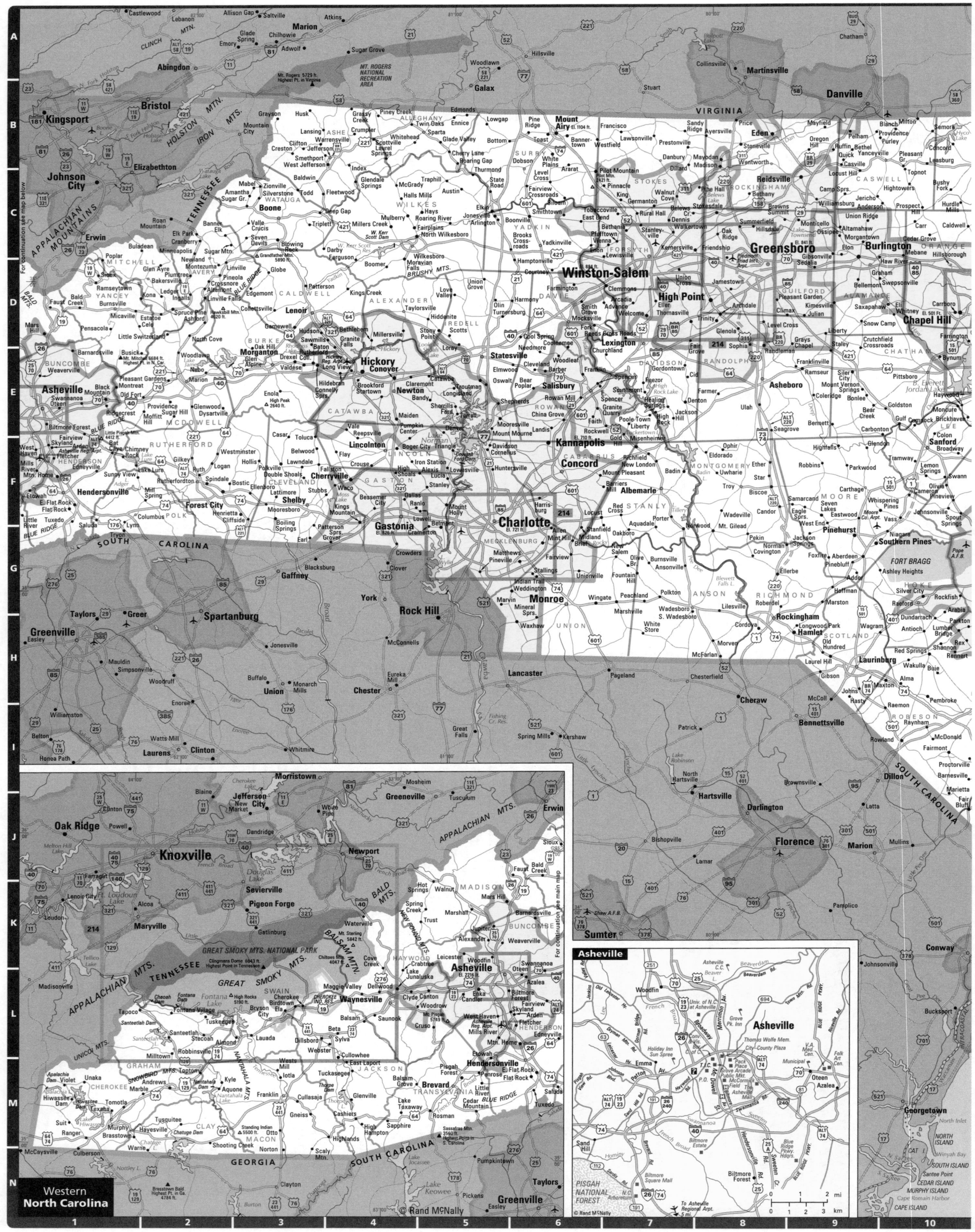

Western
North Carolina

© Rand McNally

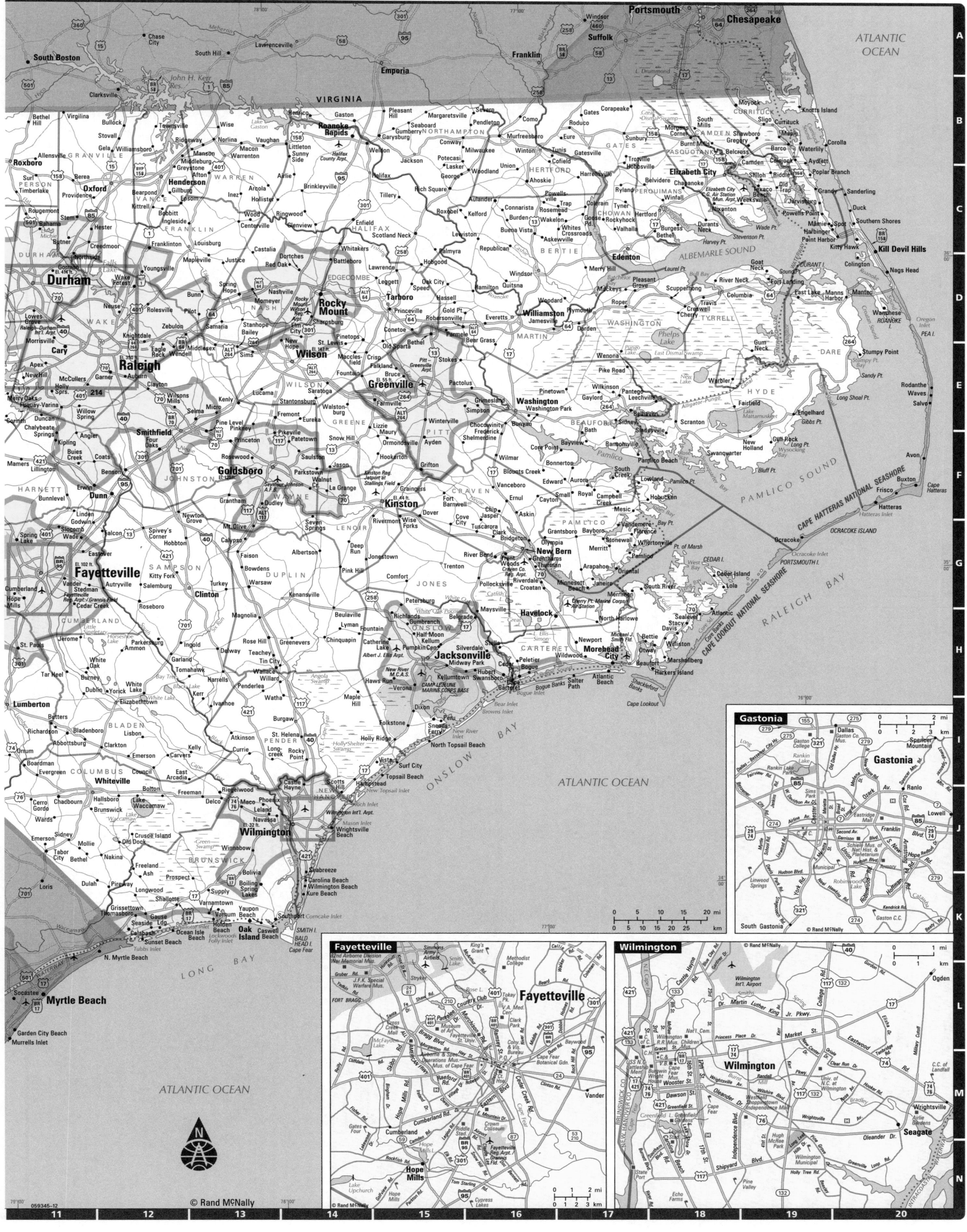

© Rand McNally

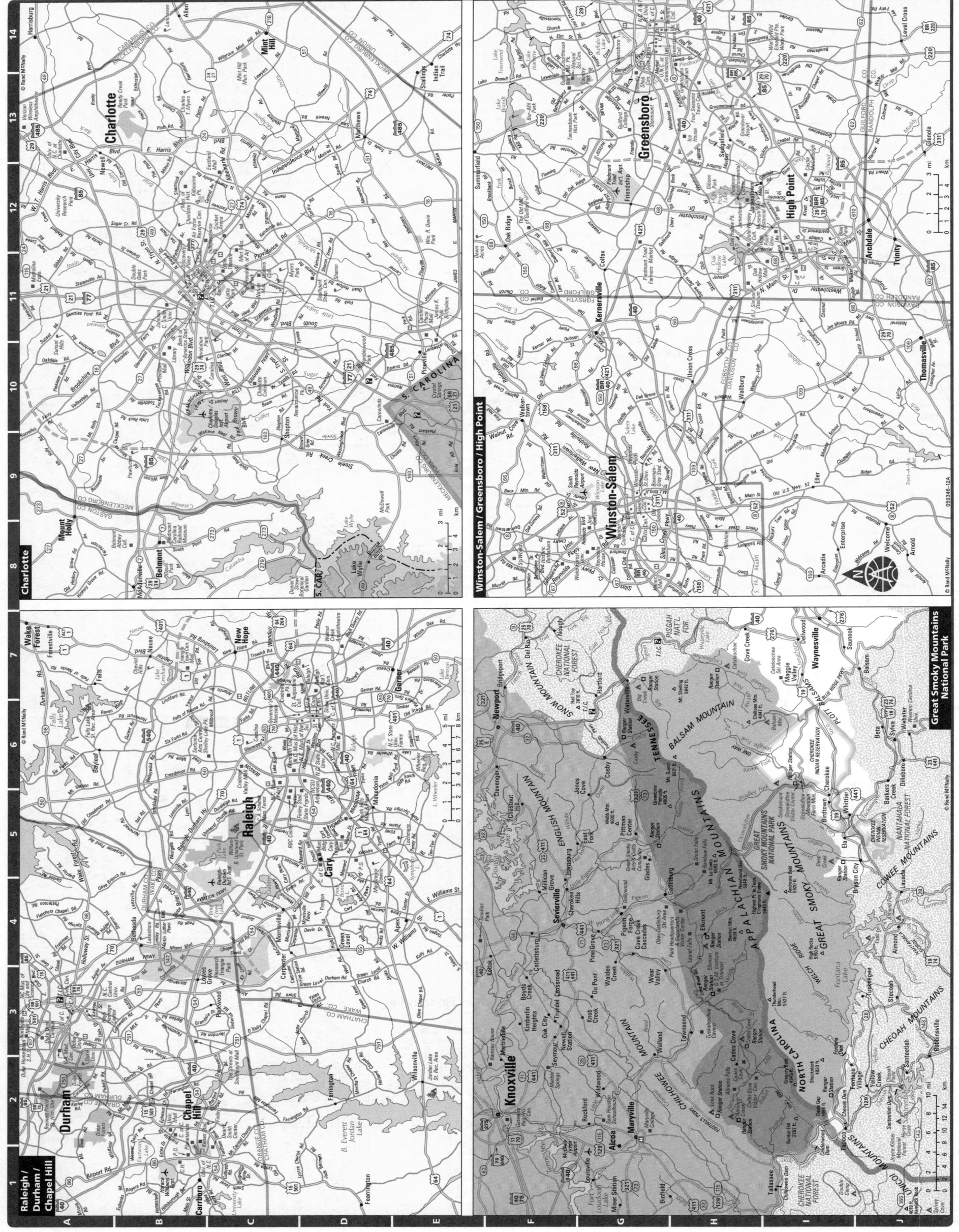

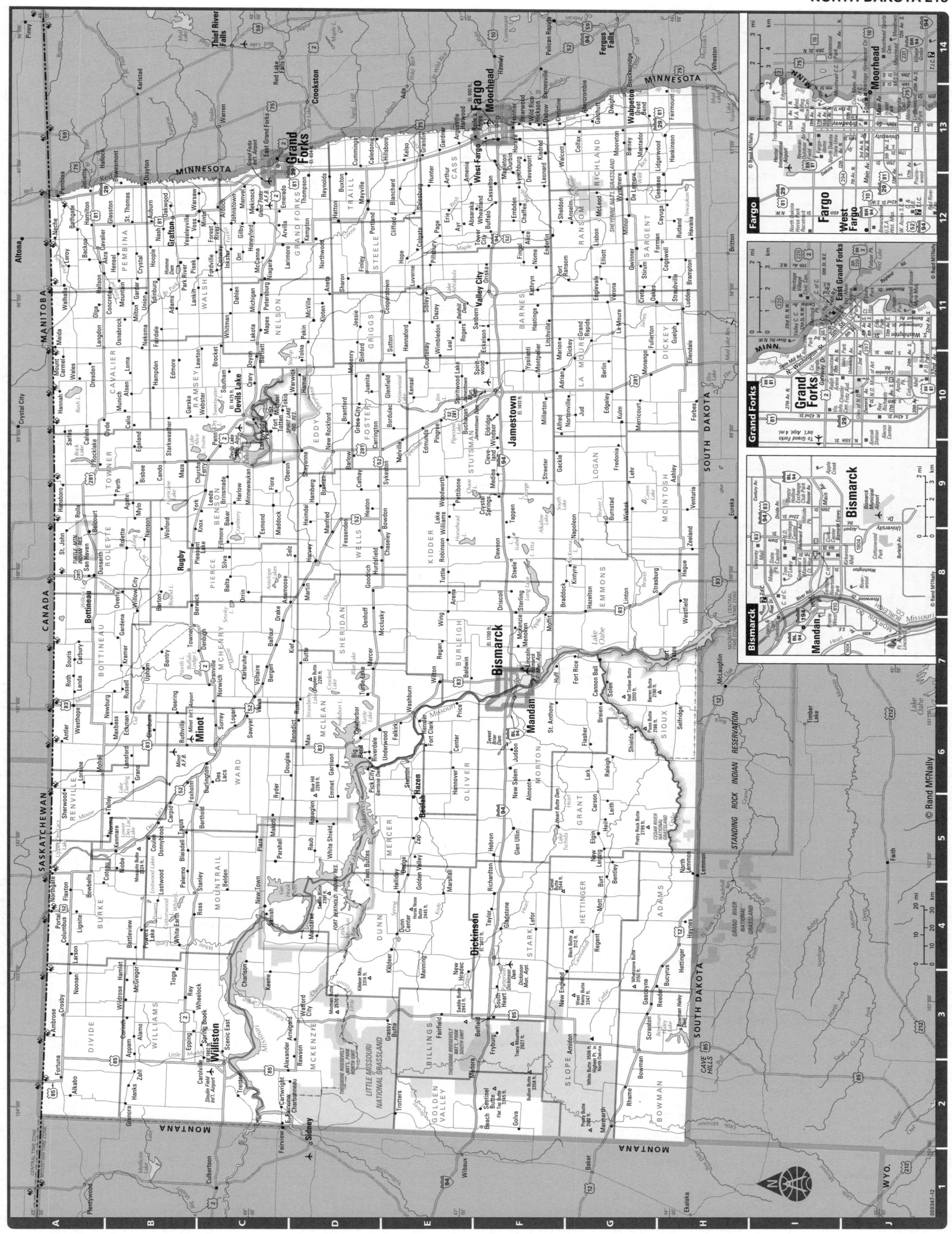

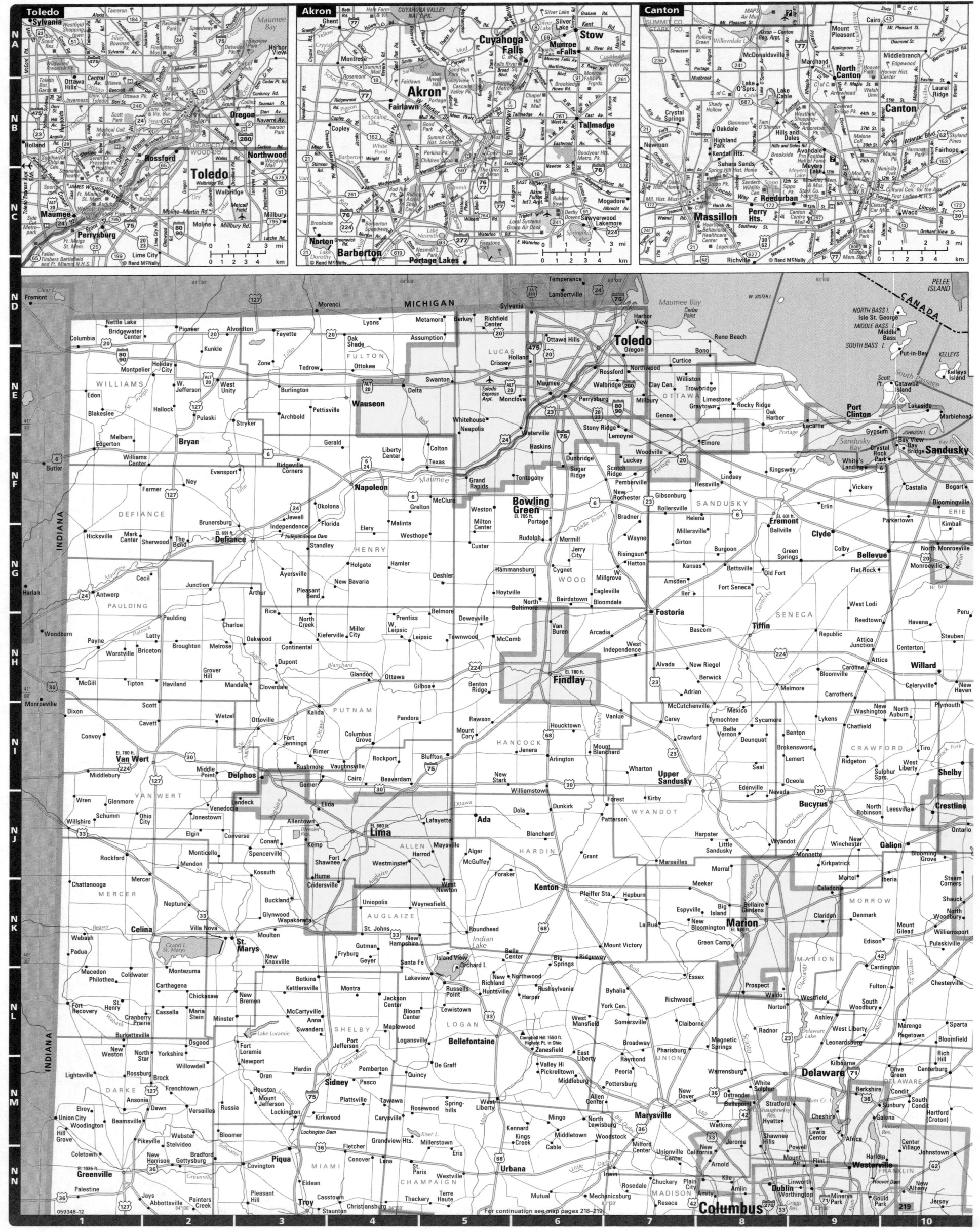

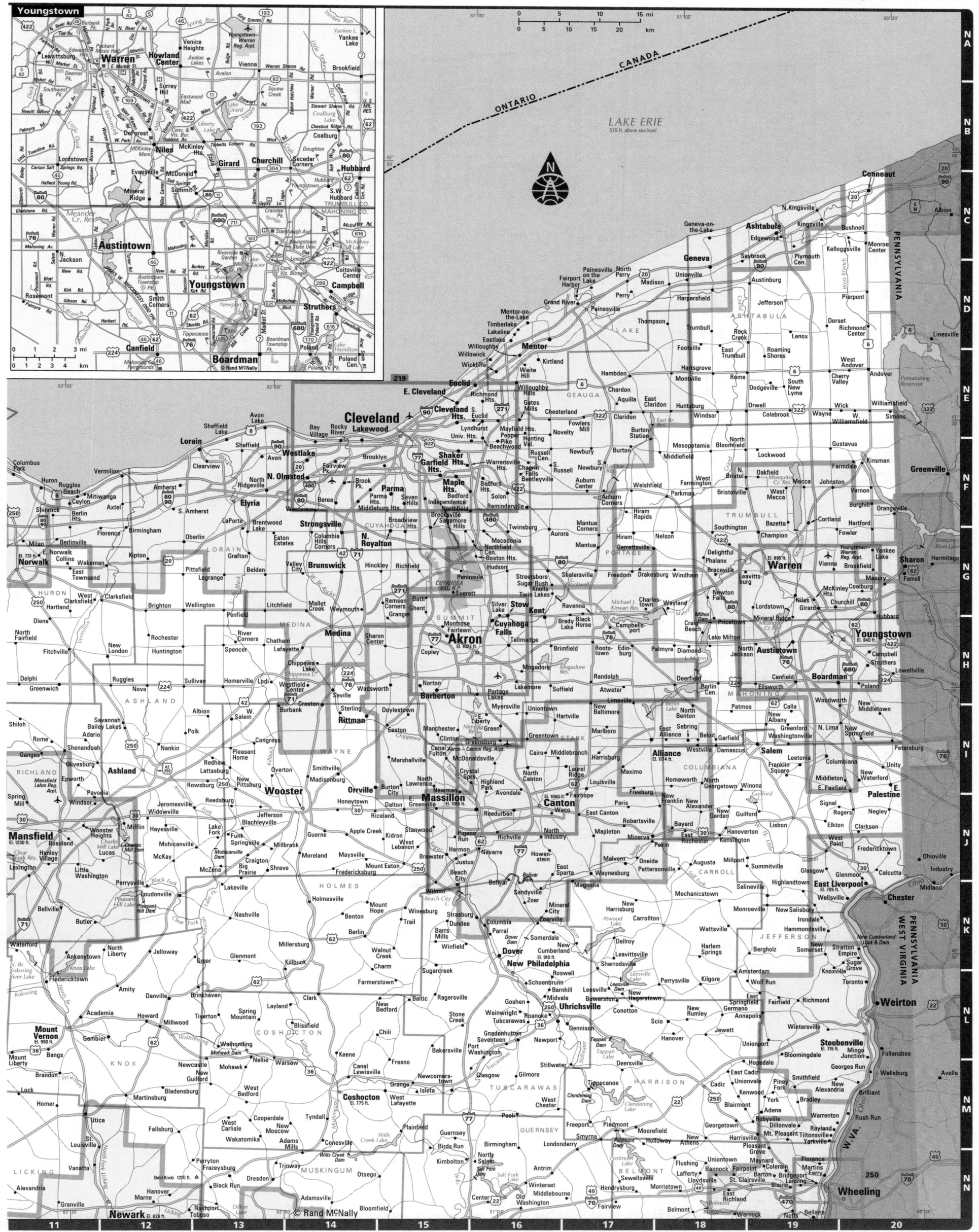

Youngstown

OHIO/NORTHERN 217

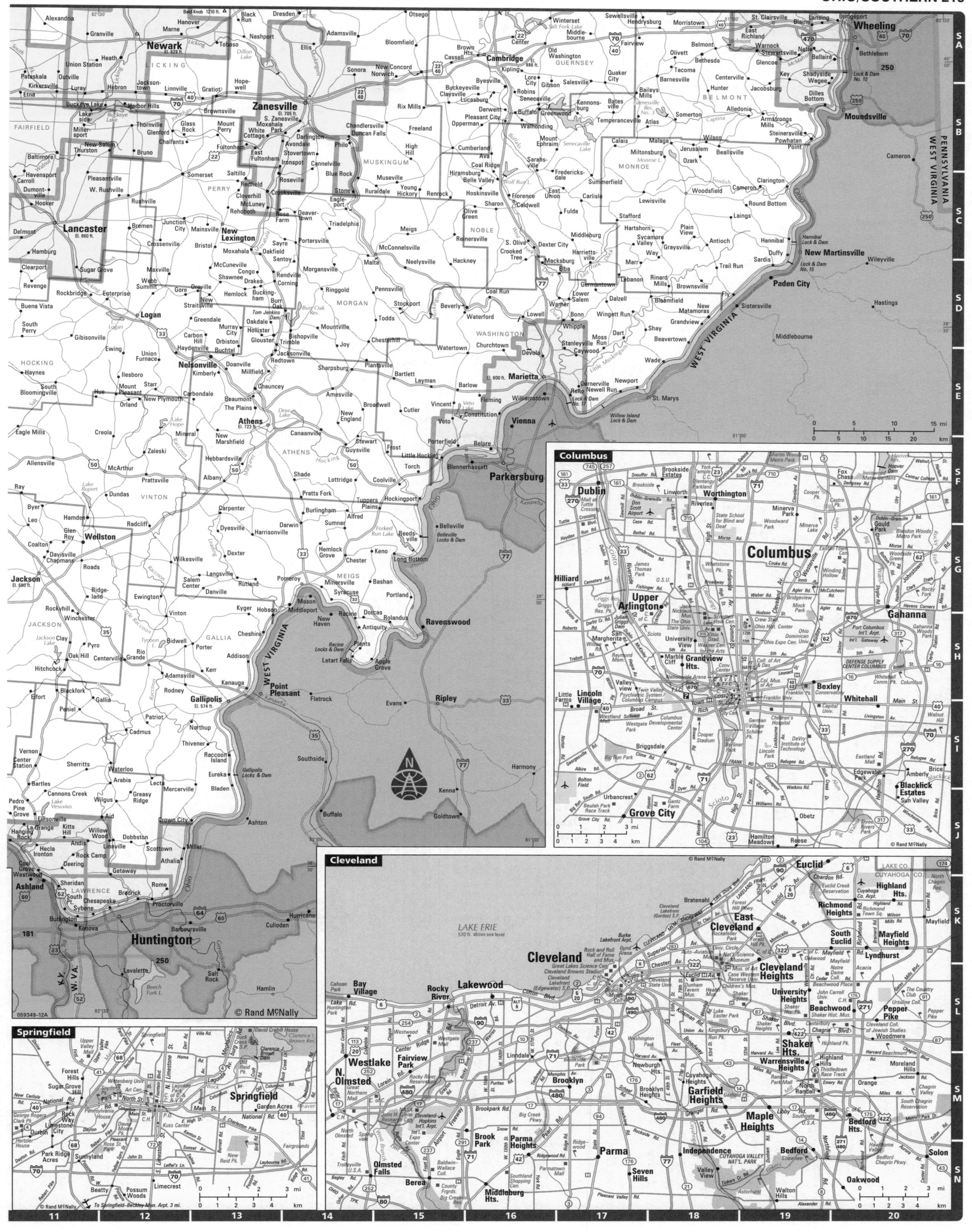

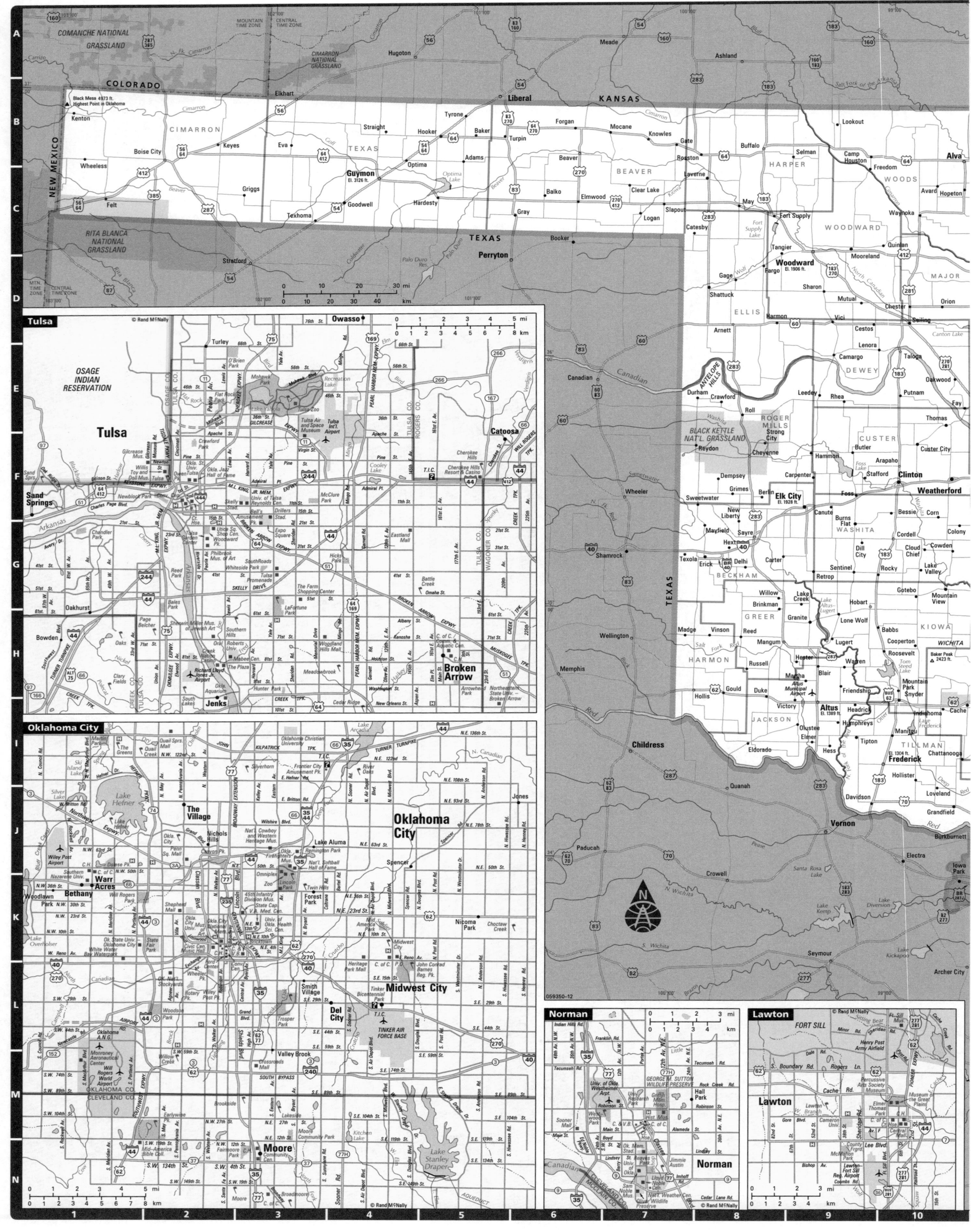

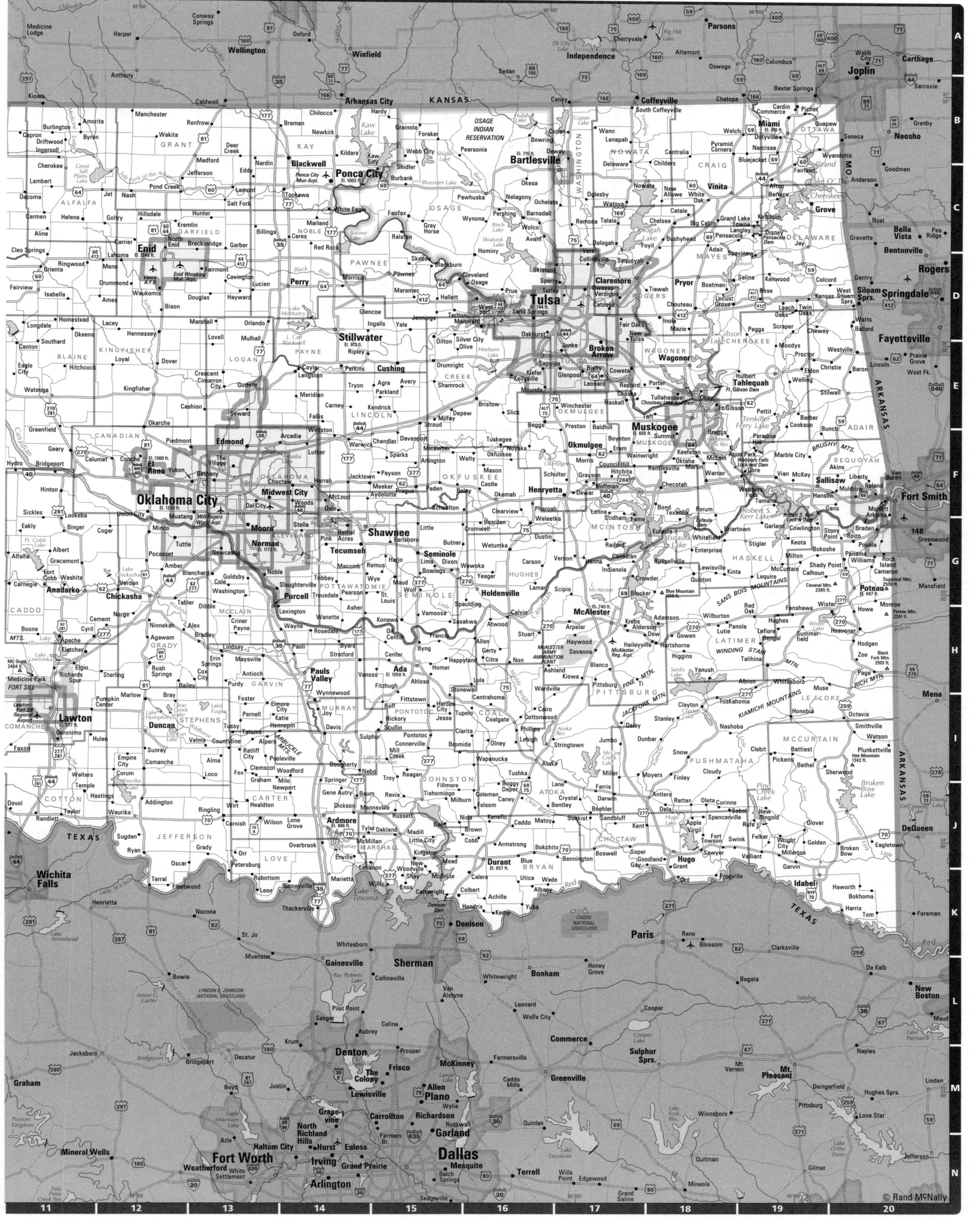

© Rand McNally

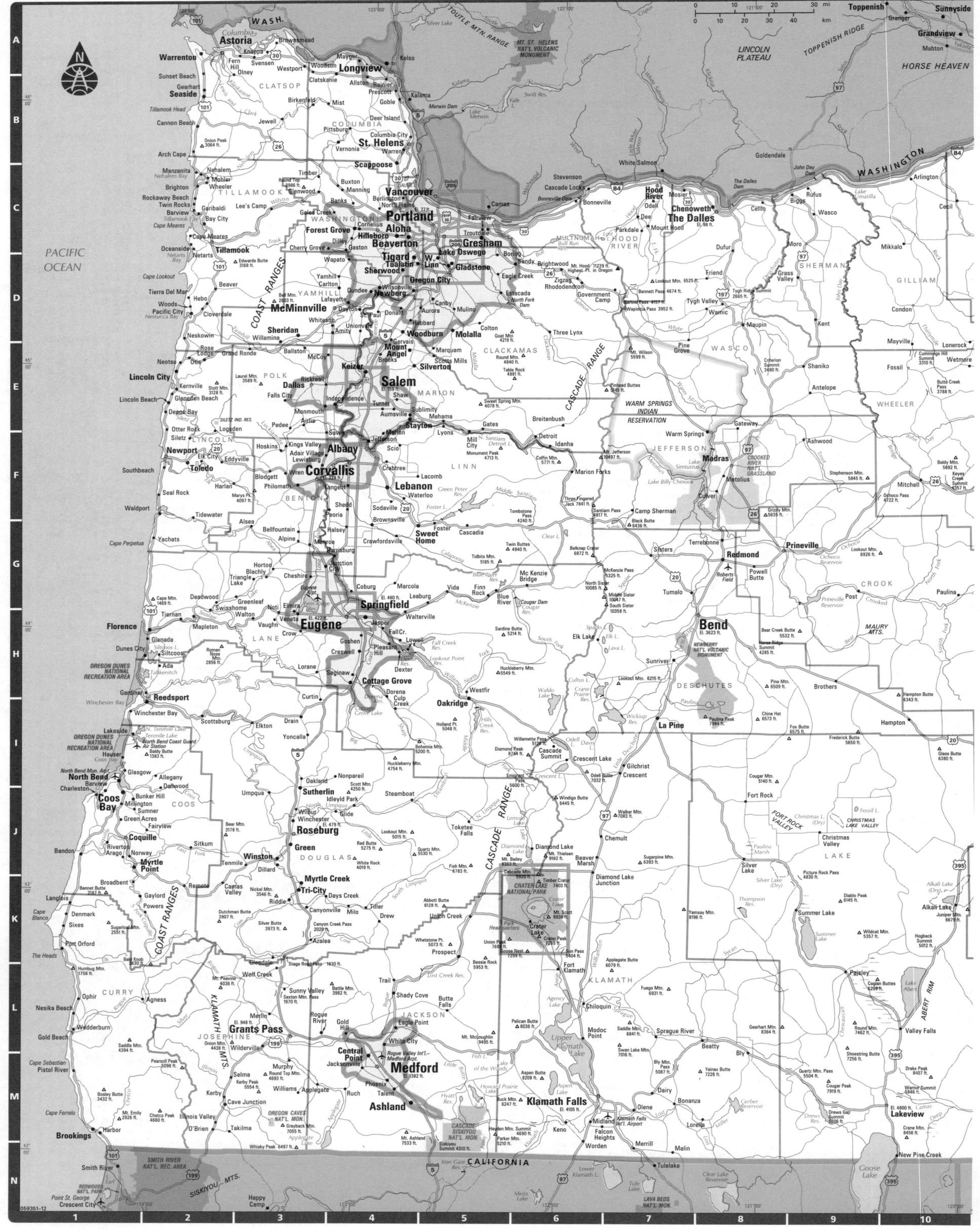

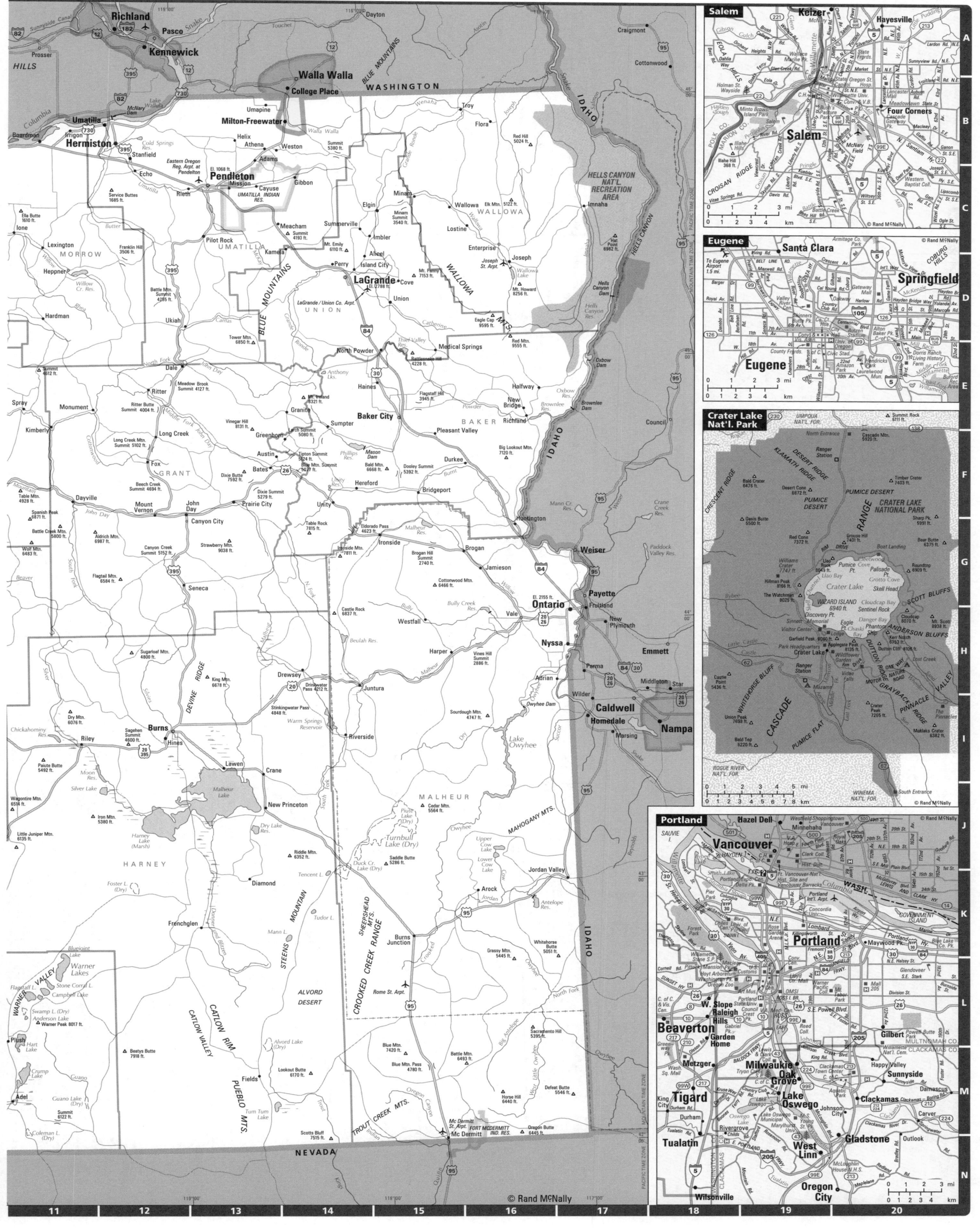

© Rand McNally

For continuation see map pages 226–227

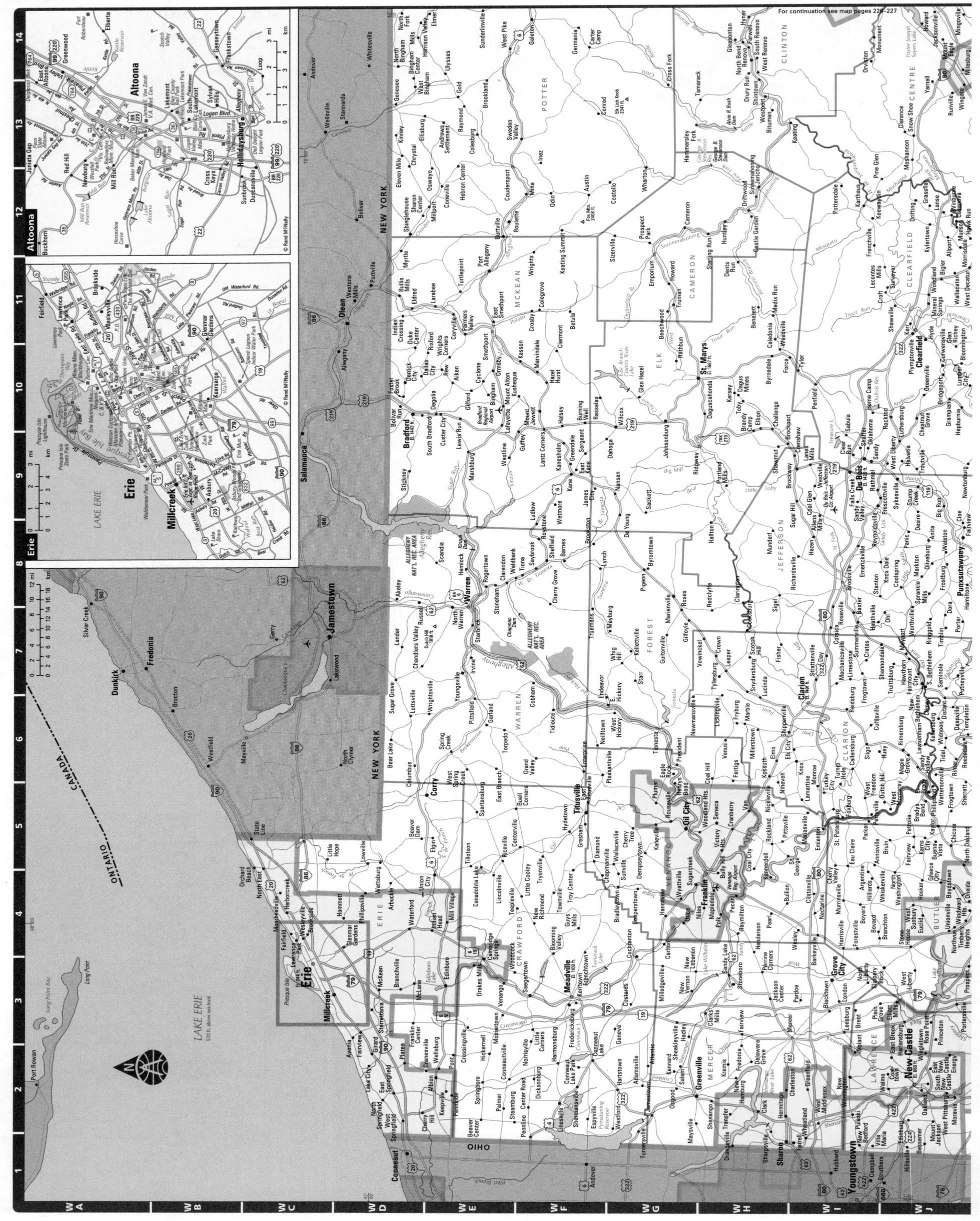

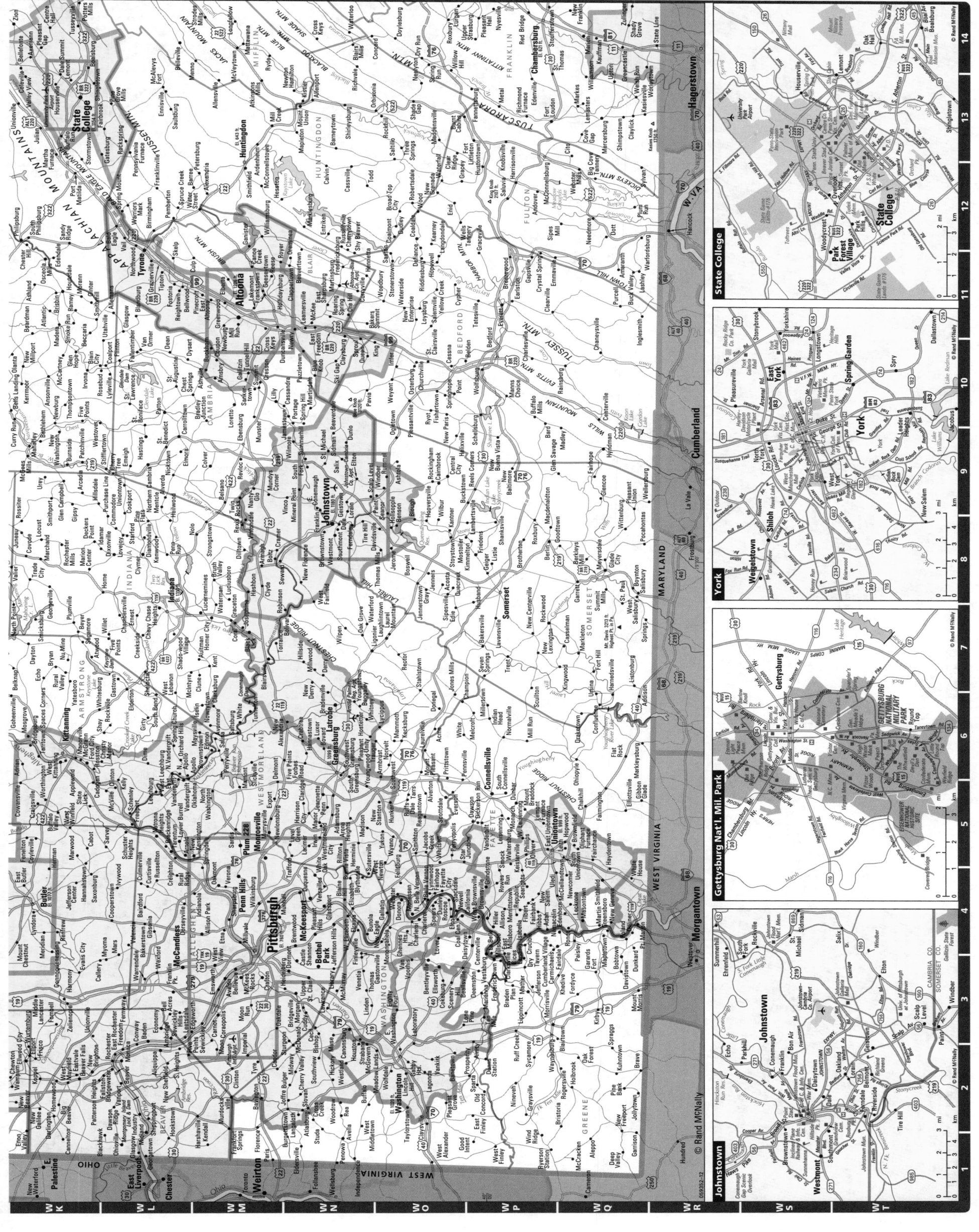

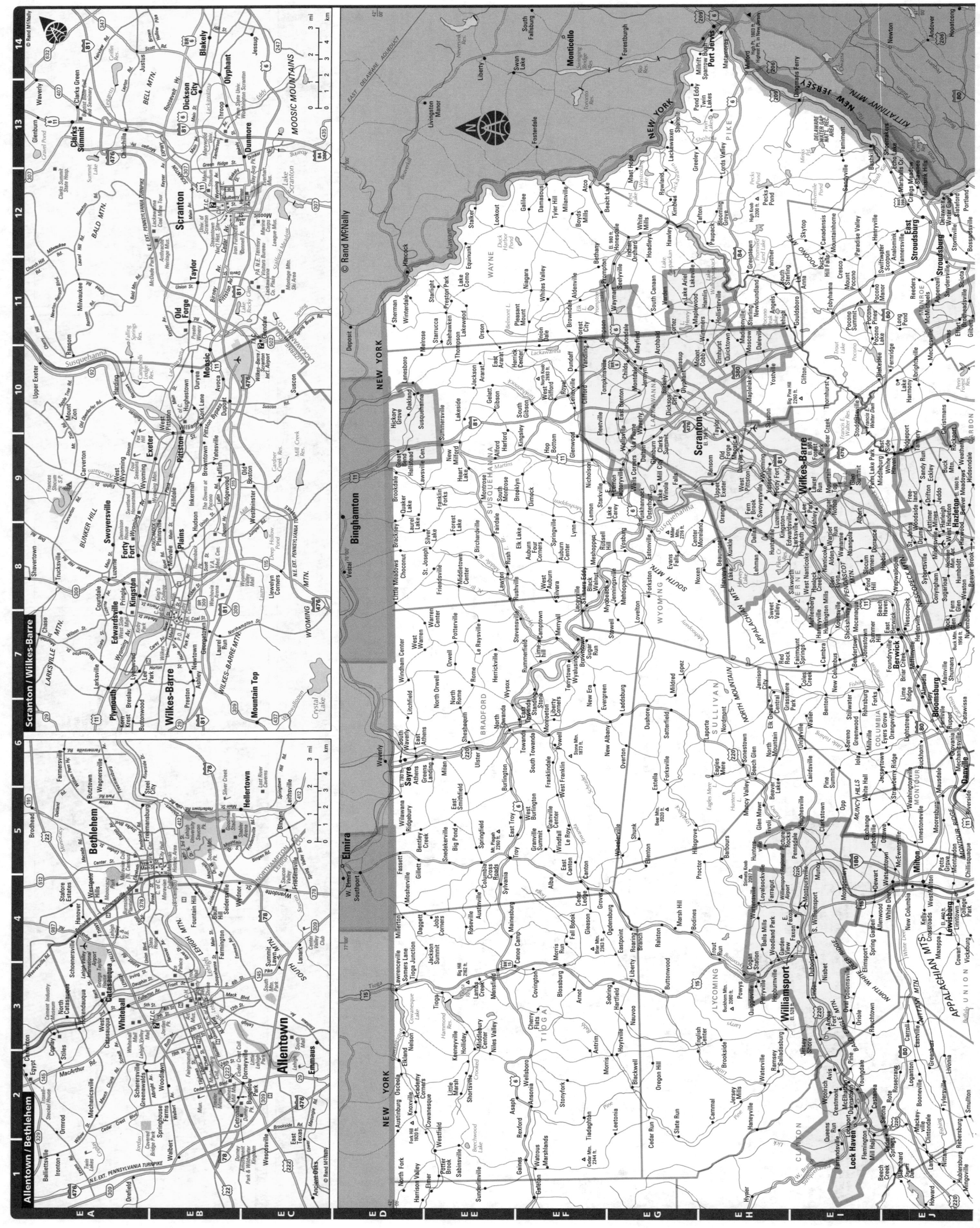

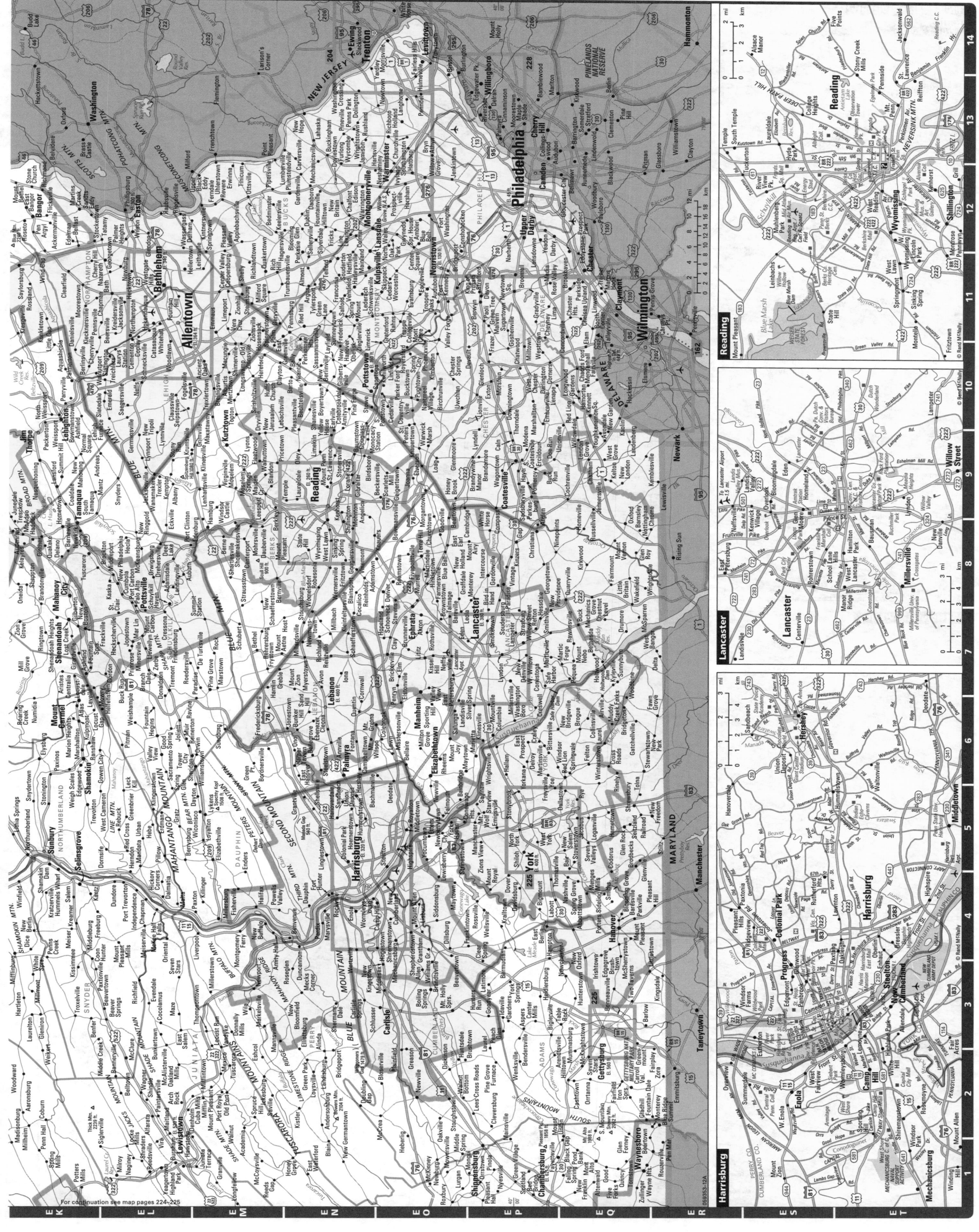

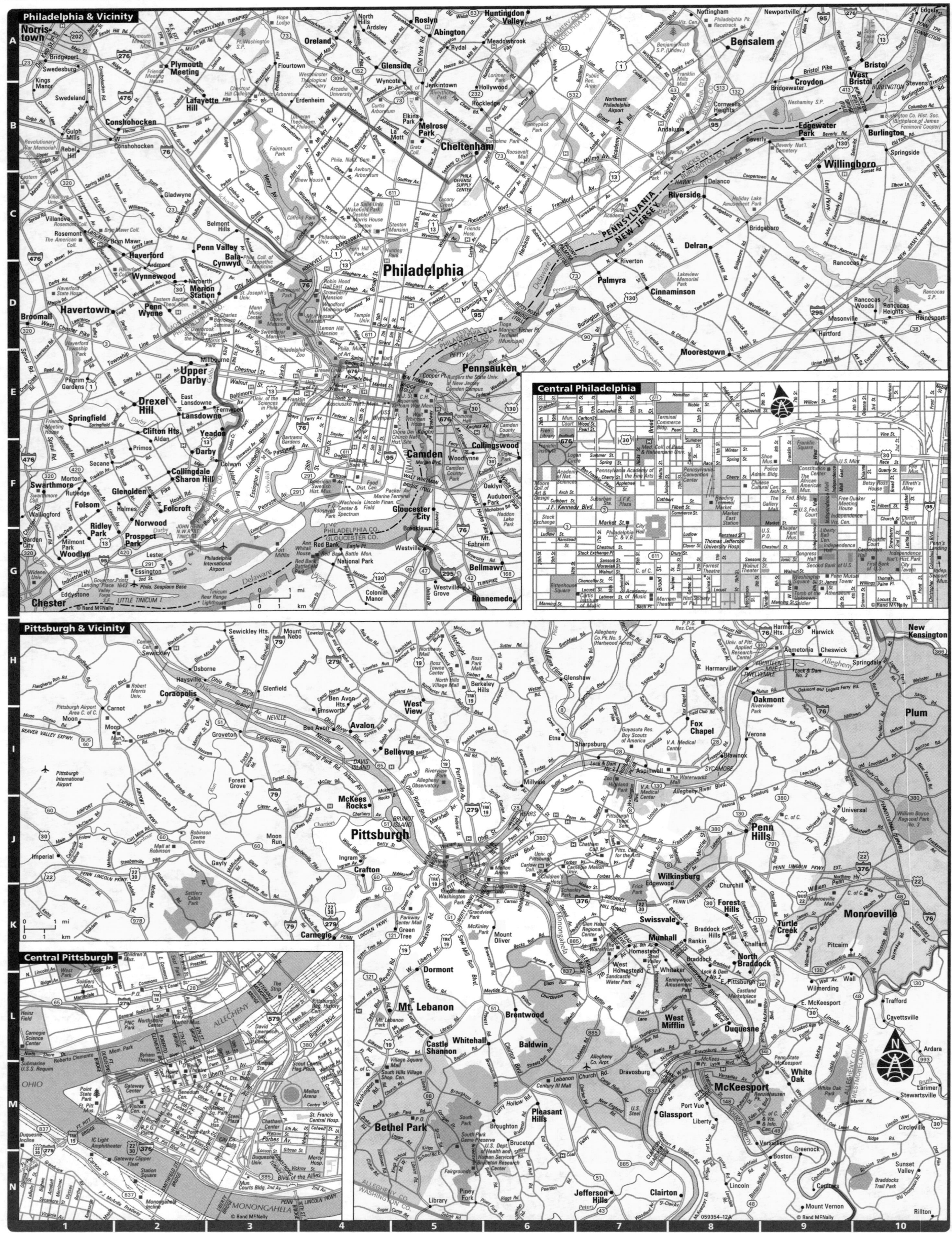

Philadelphia & Vicinity

Central Philadelphia

Pittsburgh & Vicinity

Central Pittsburgh

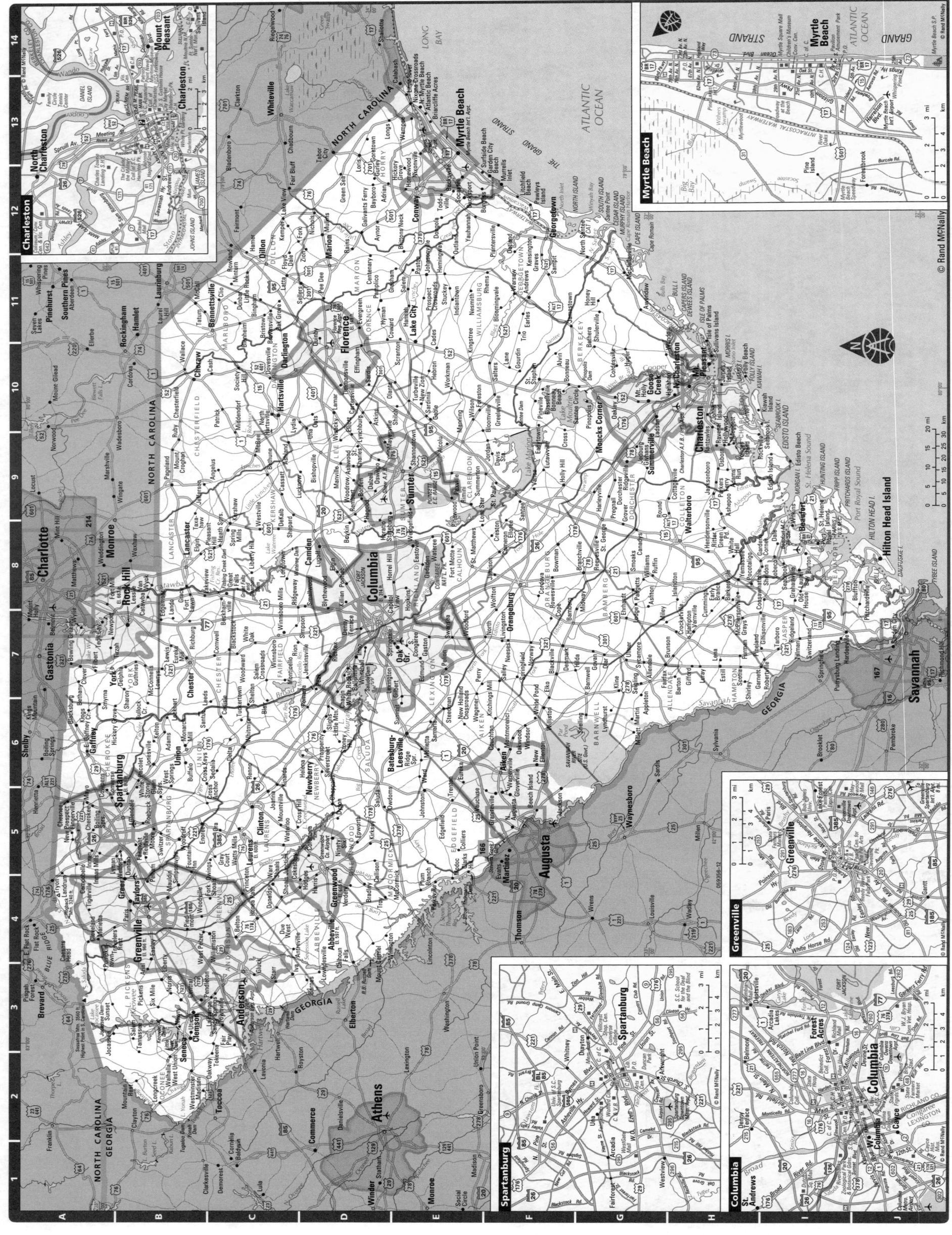

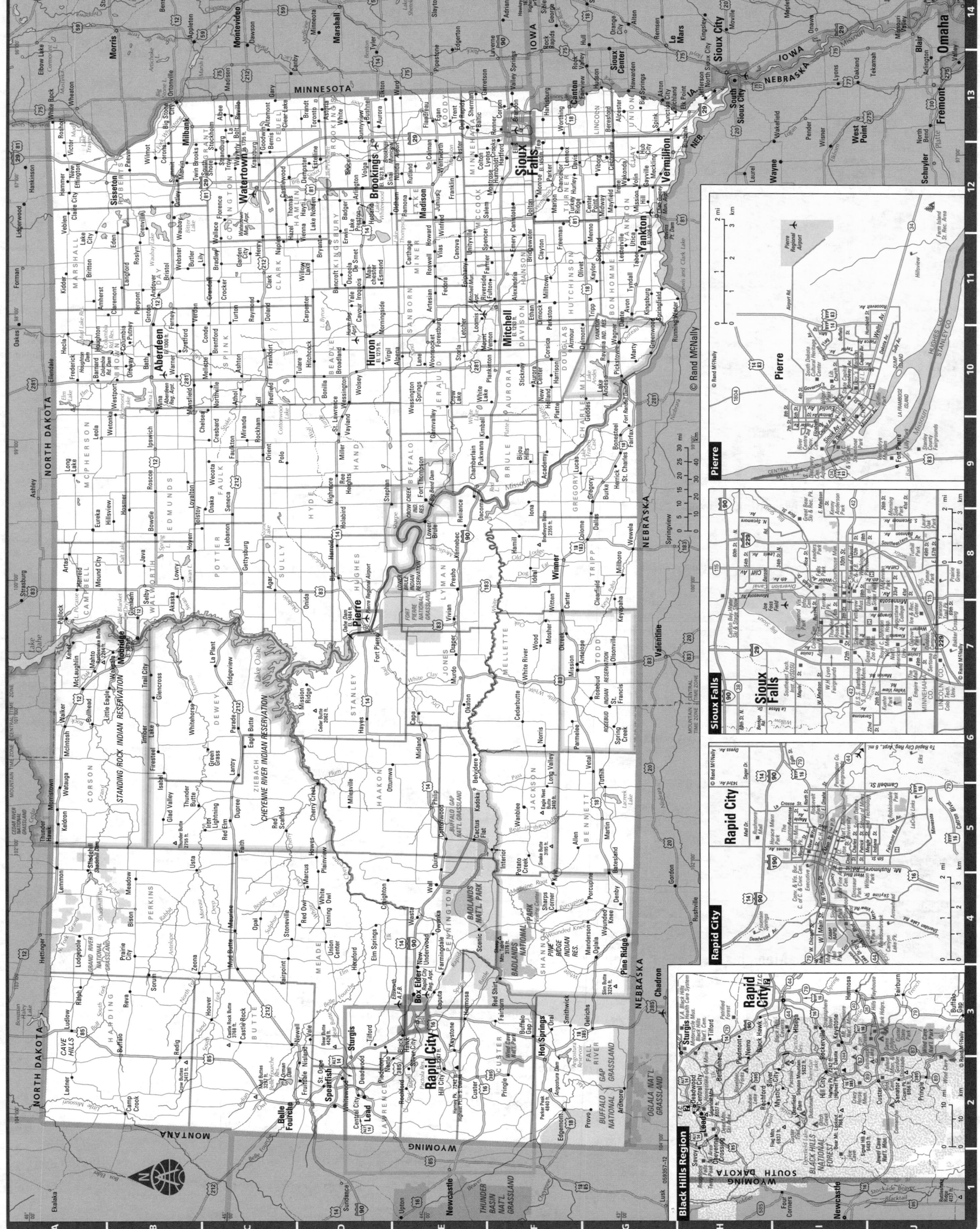

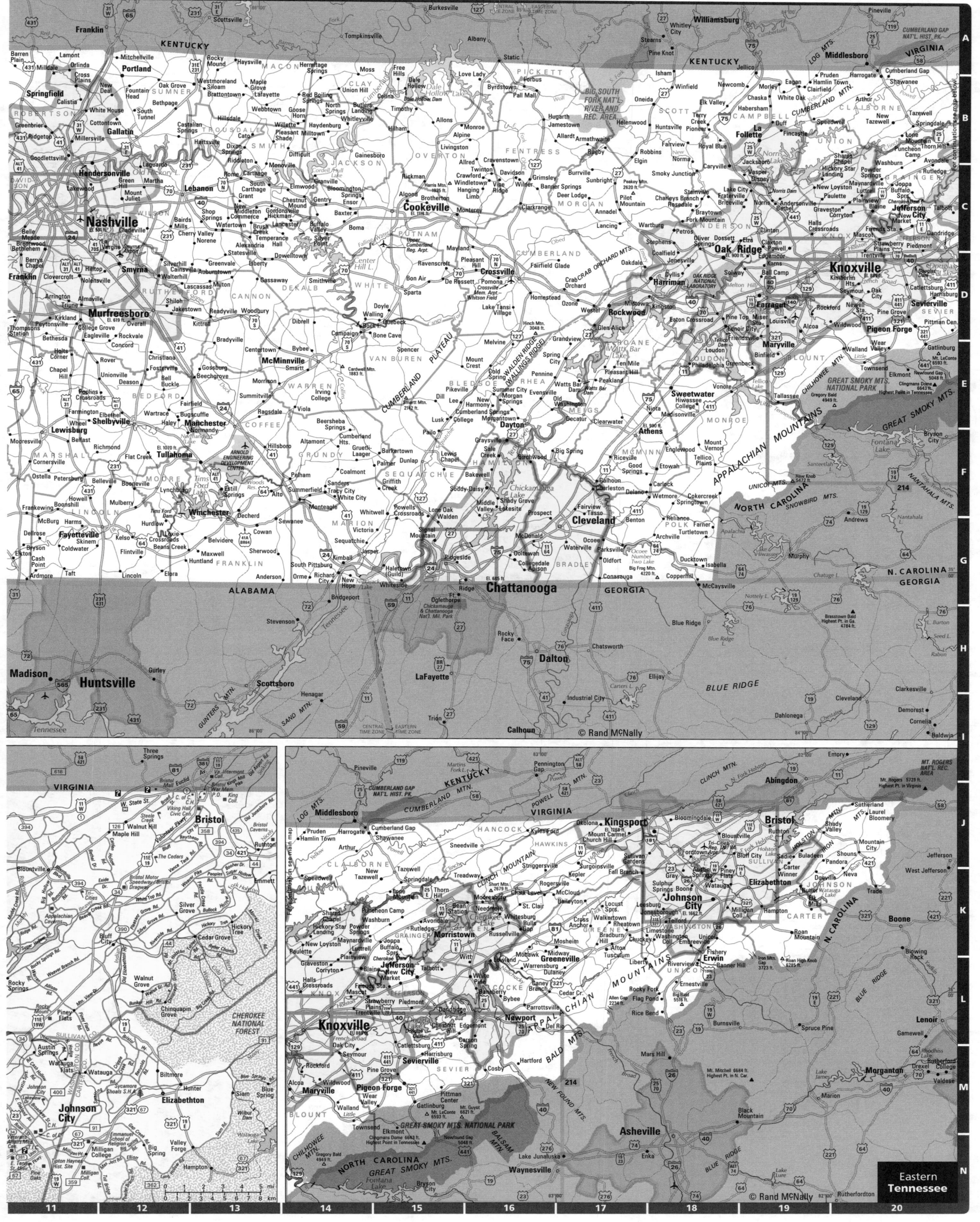

© Rand McNally

Eastern
Tennessee

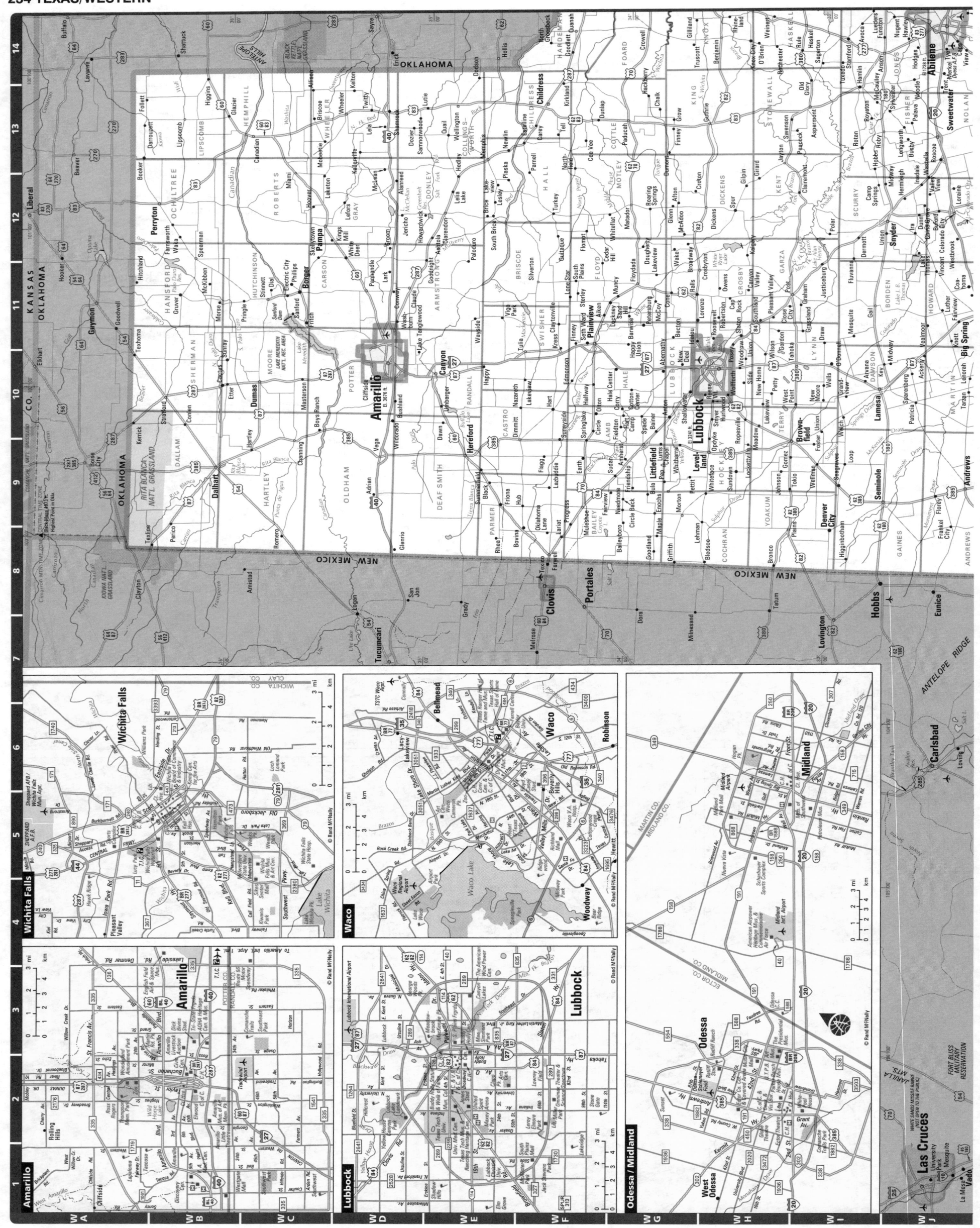

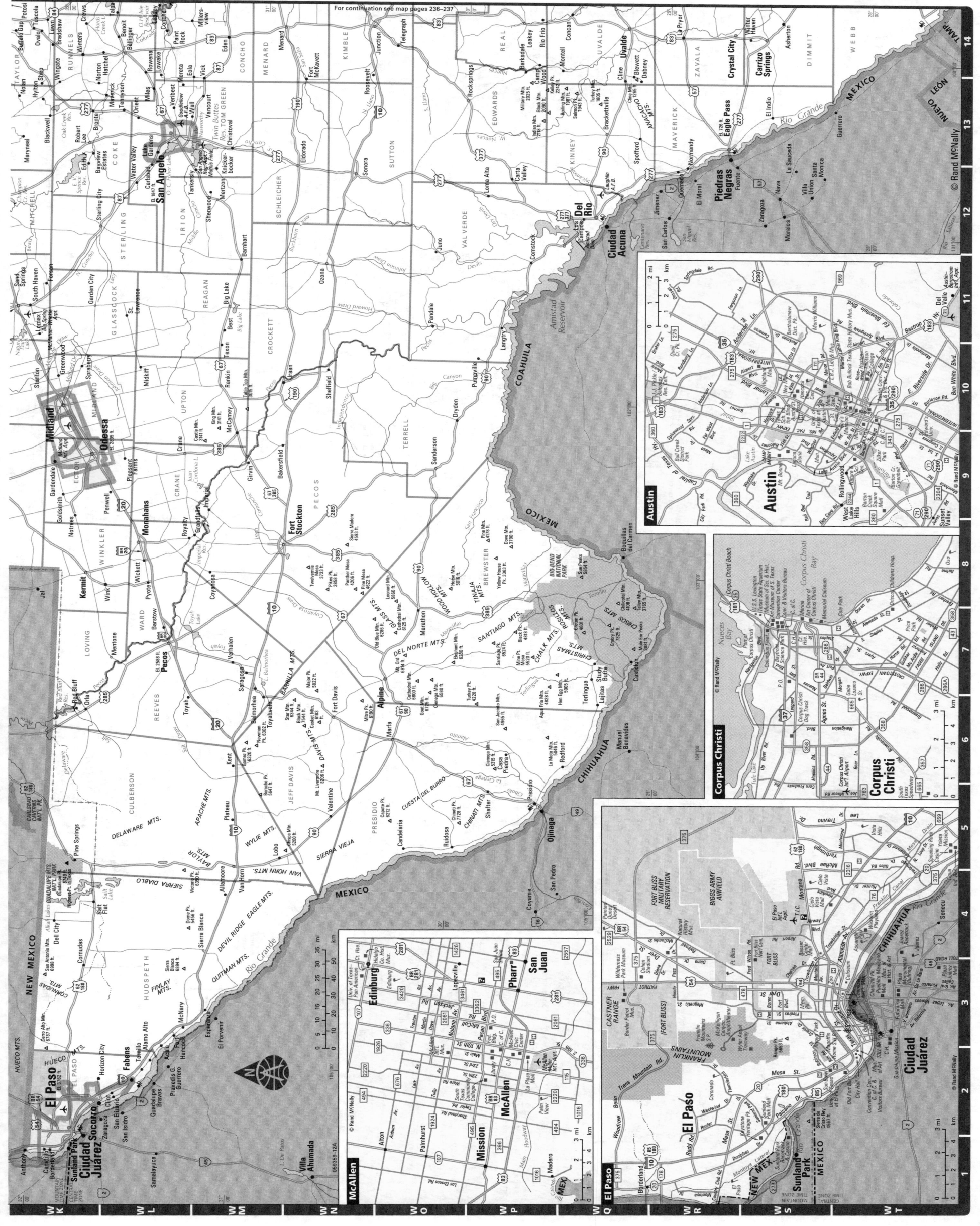

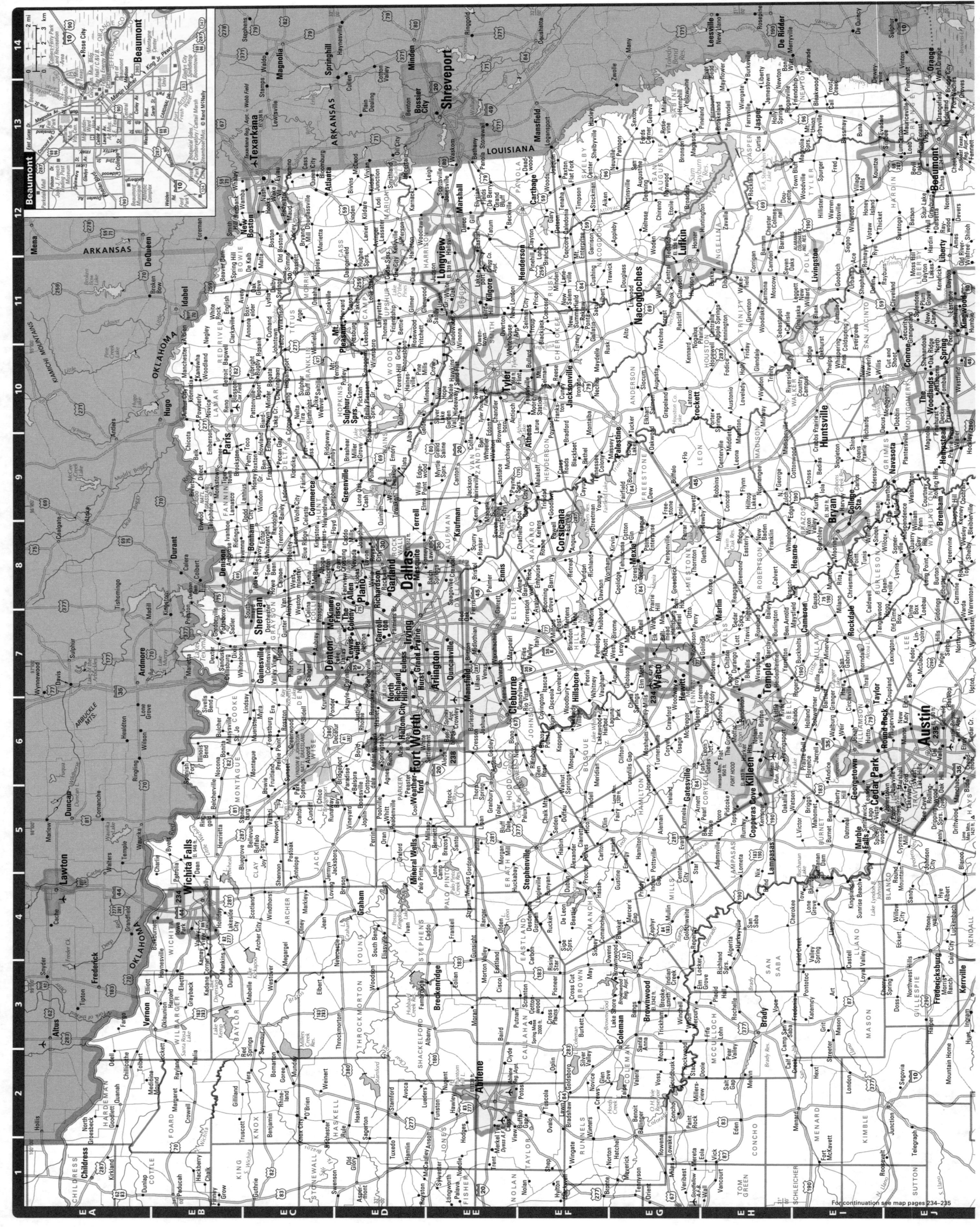

For continuation see map pages 234-235.

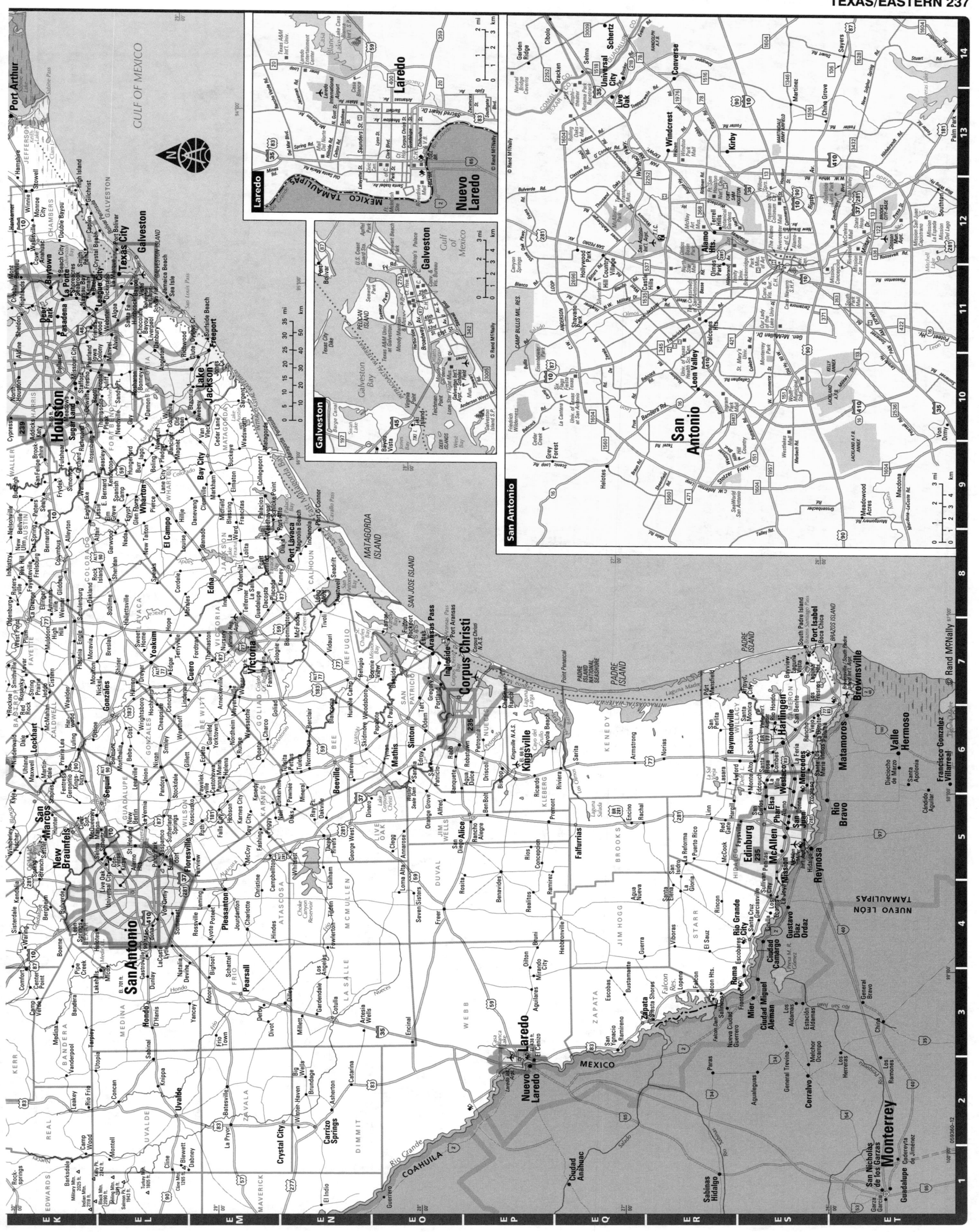

Laredo

Nuevo Laredo

Galveston

San Antonio

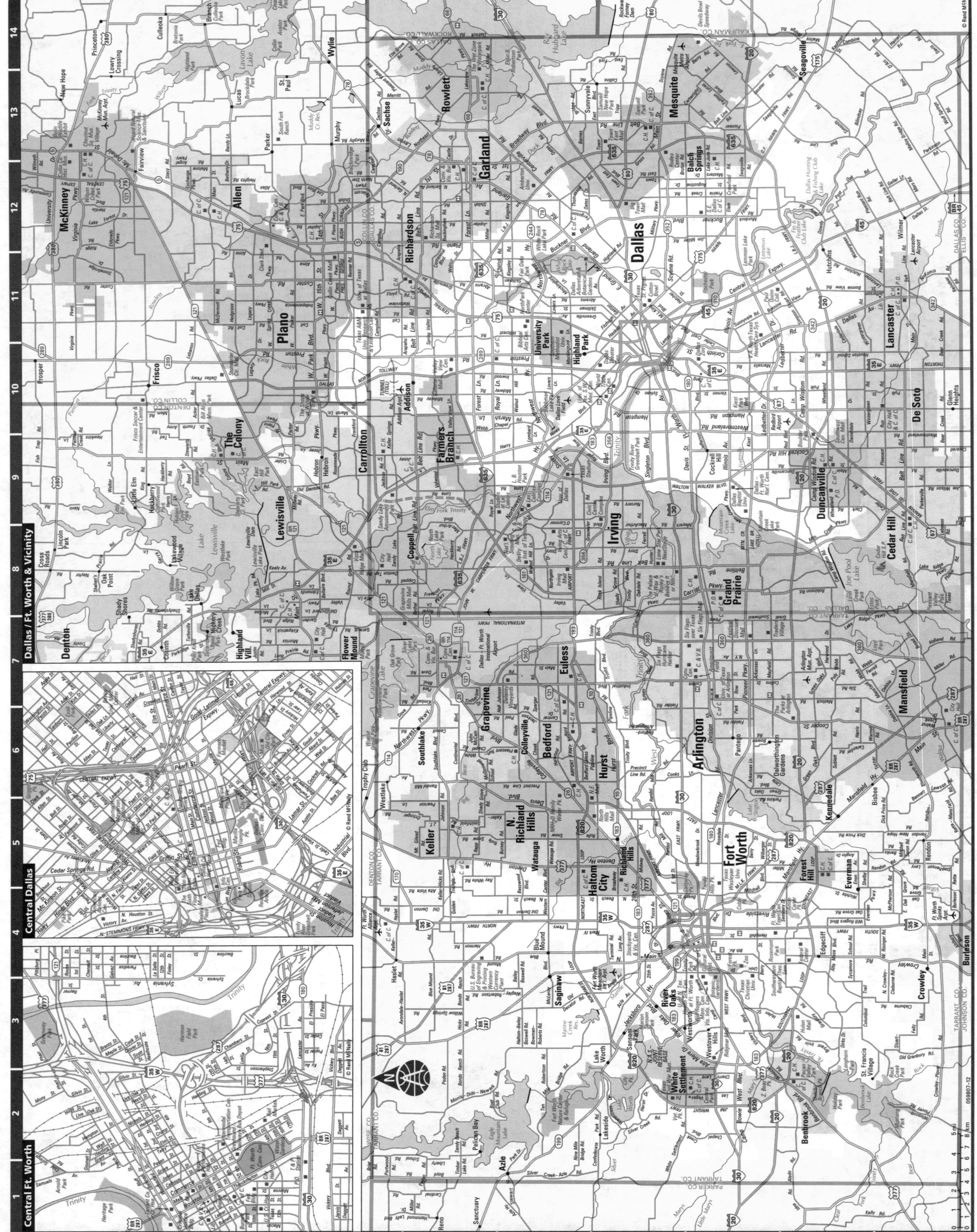

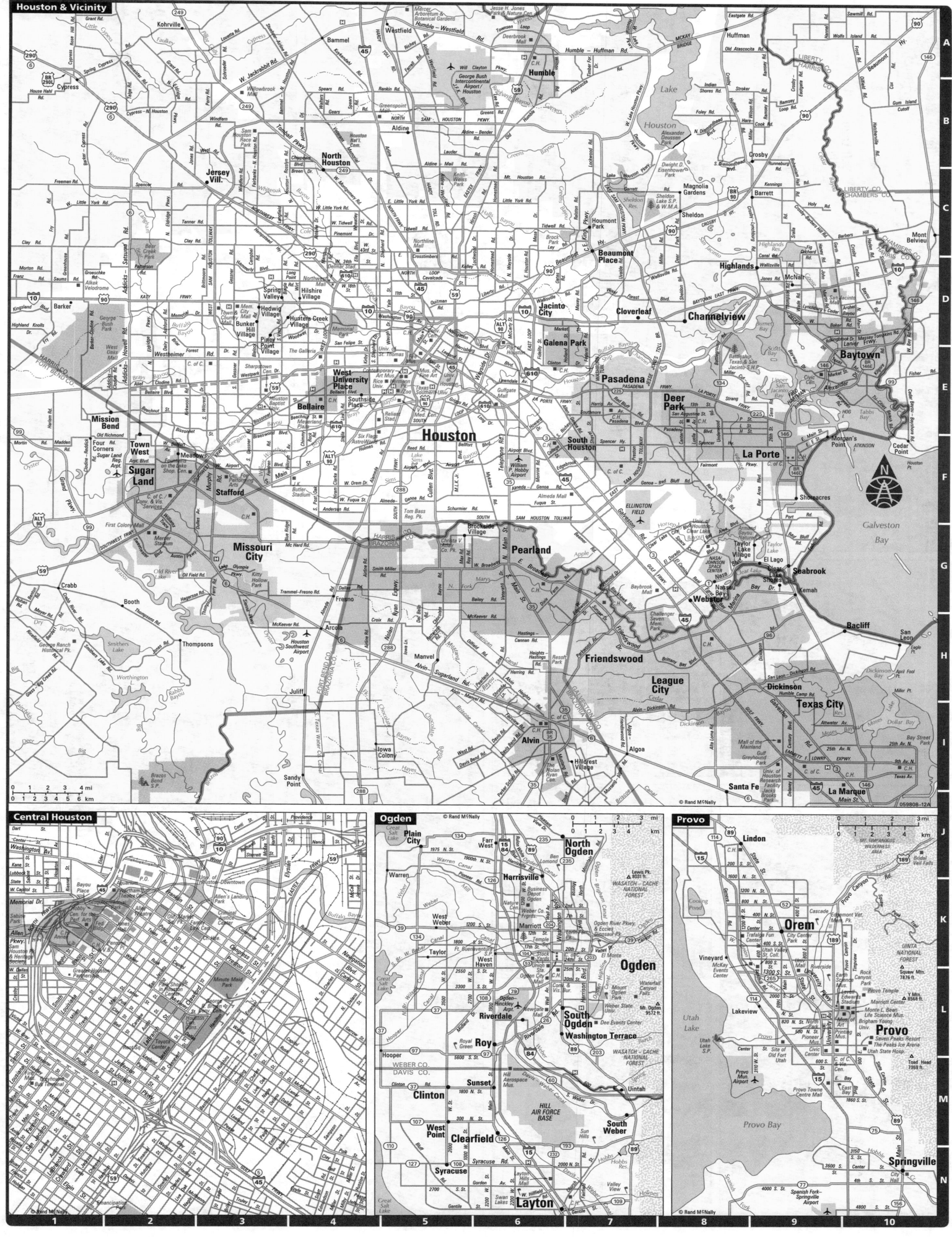

Houston & Vicinity

Central Houston

Ogden

Provo

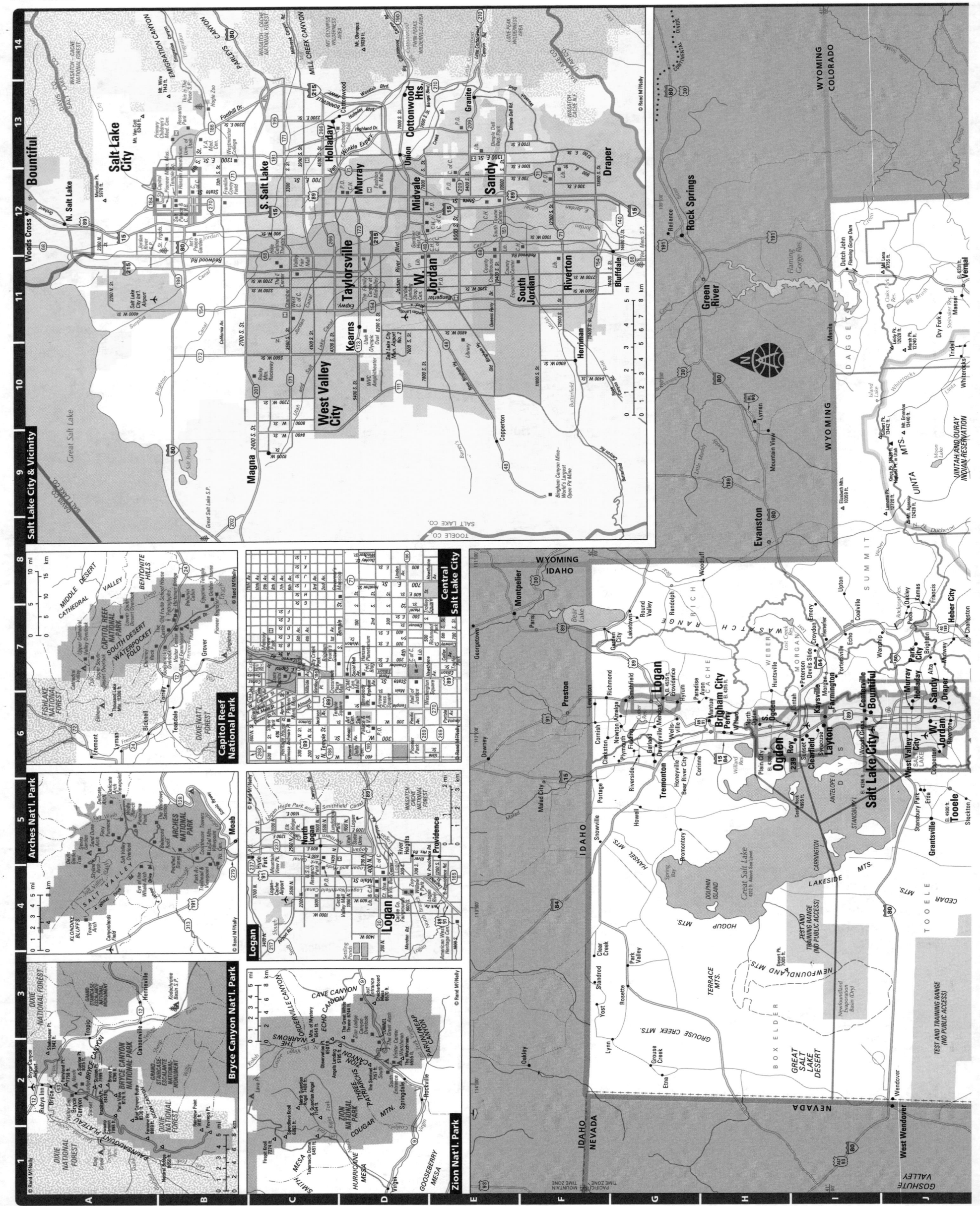

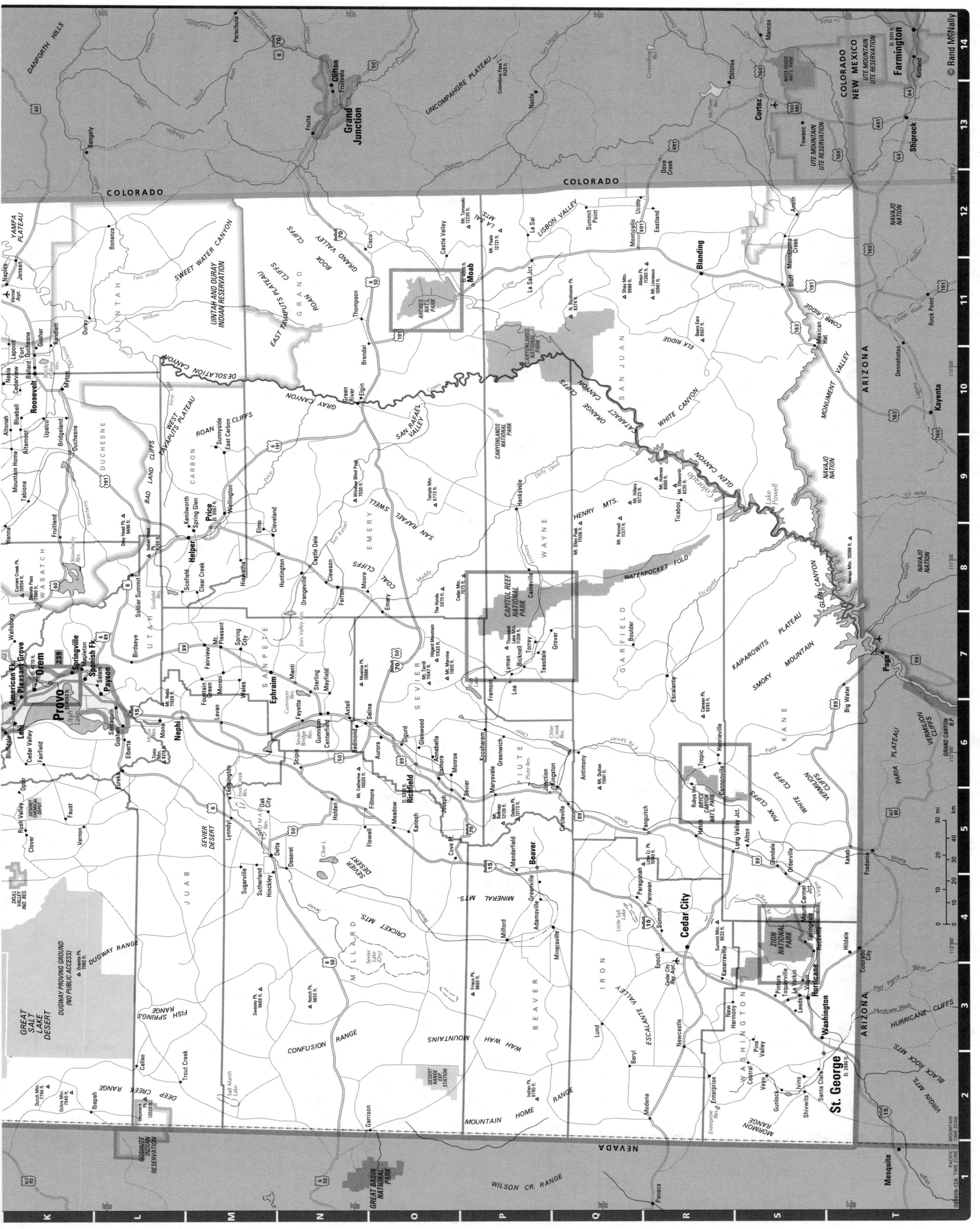

© Rand McNally

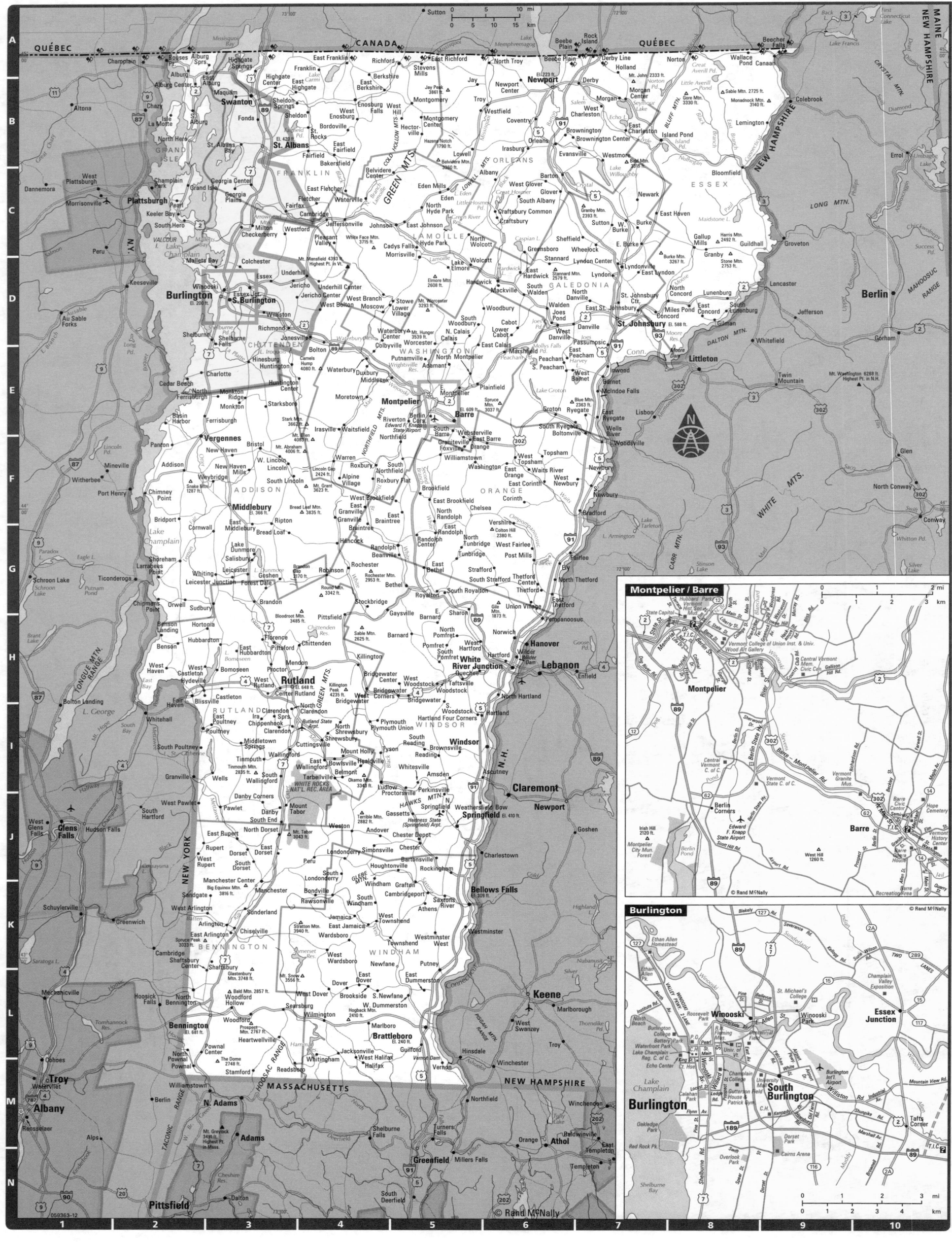

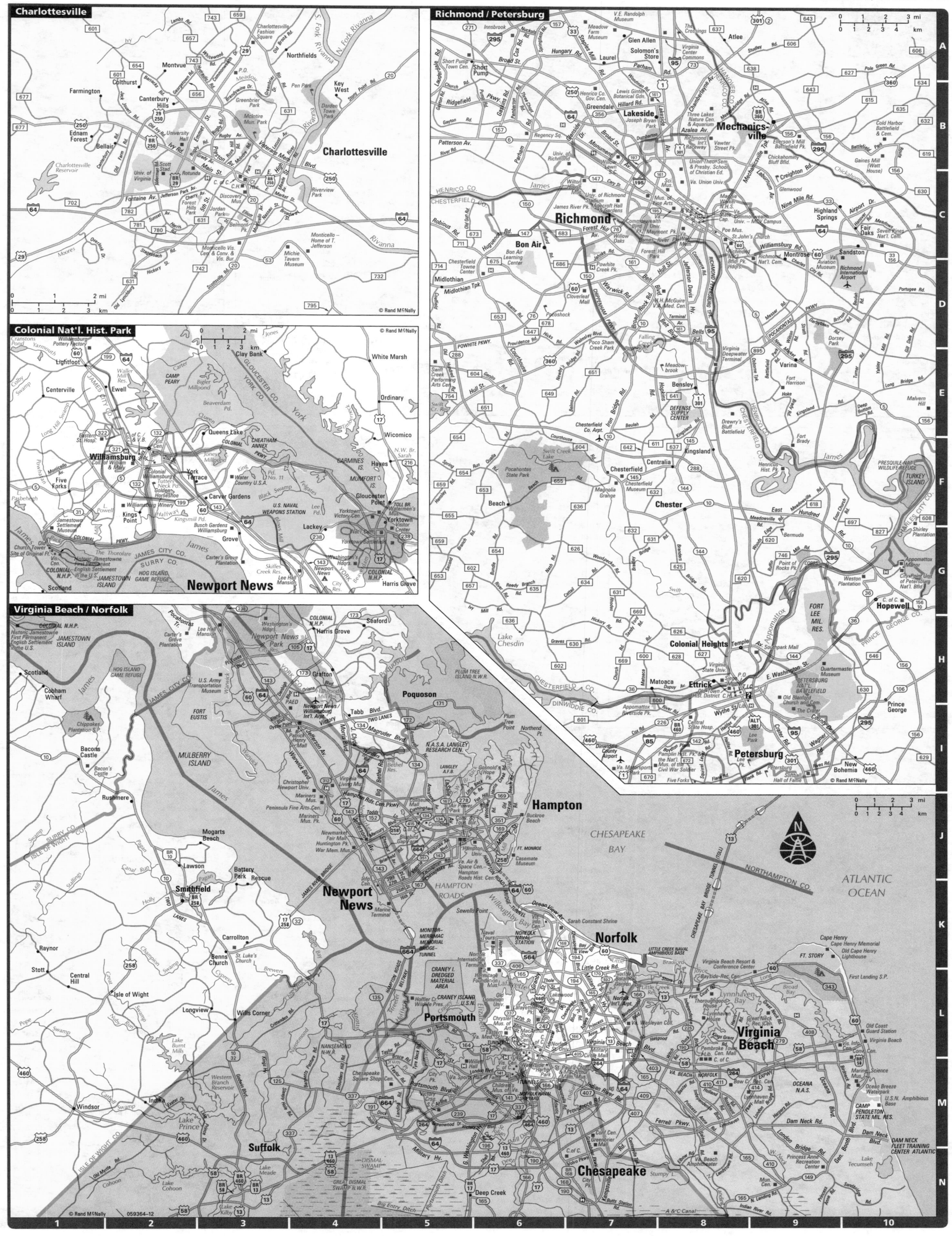

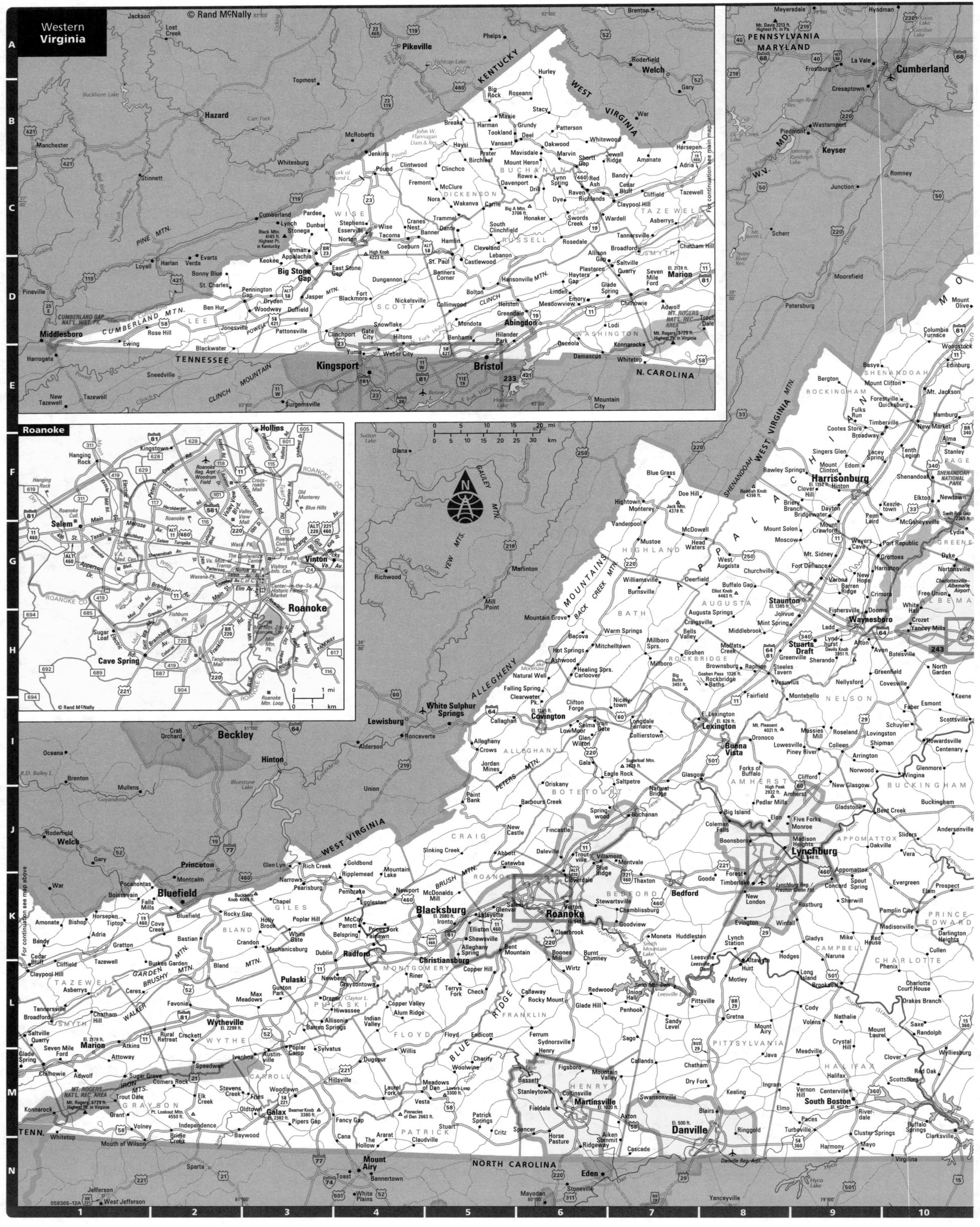

Western Virginia

© RAND McNALLY

Roanoke

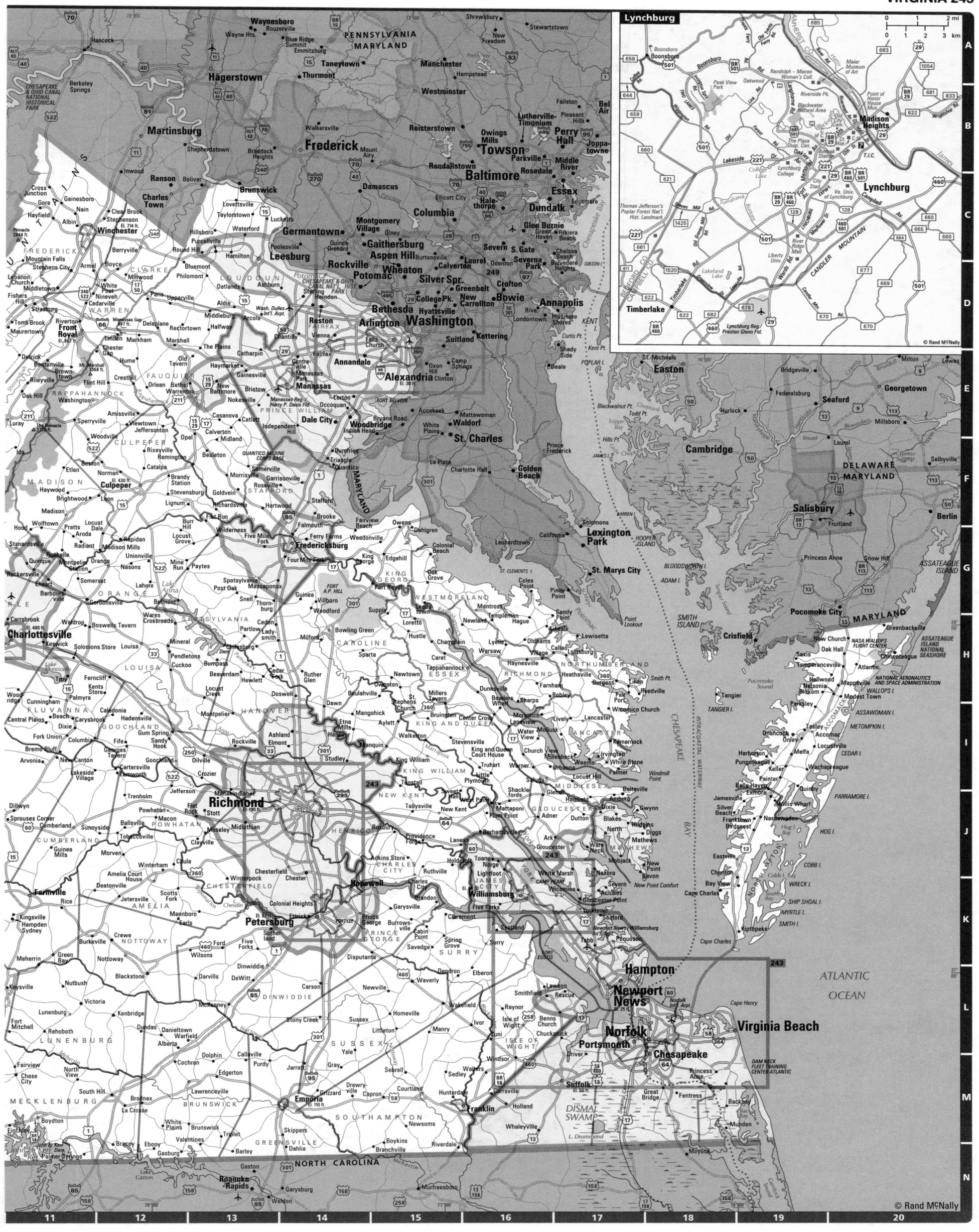

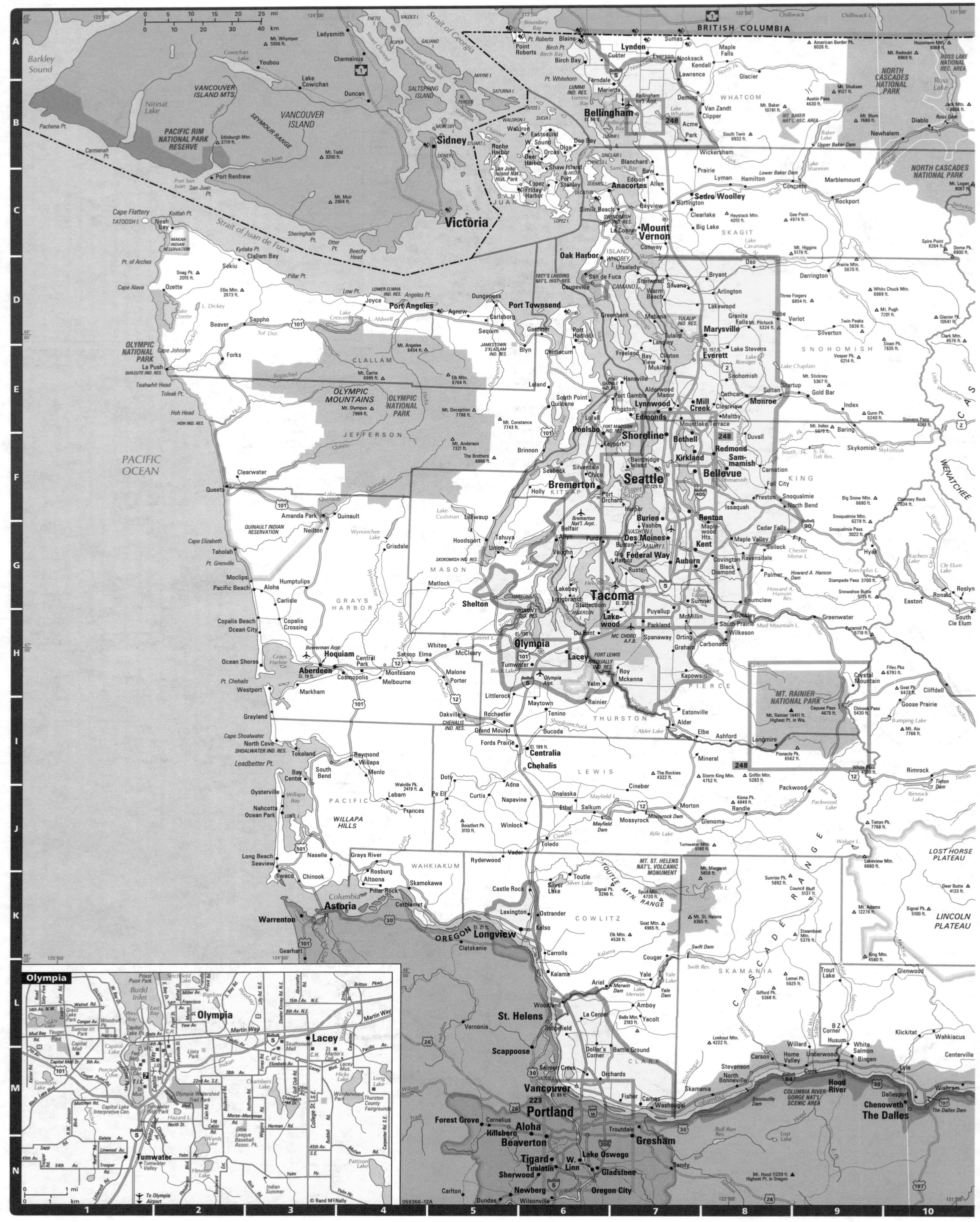

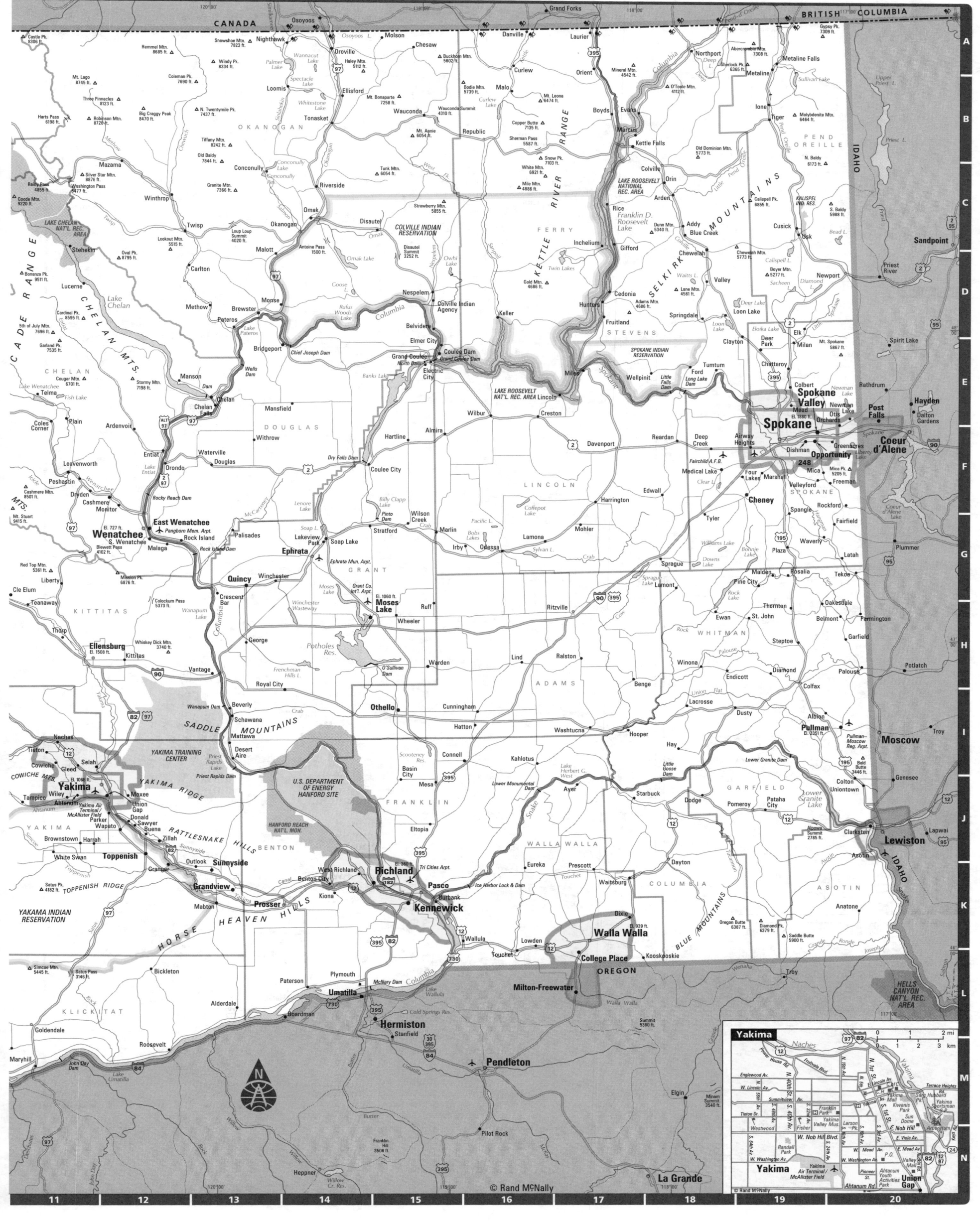

© Rand McNally

Yakima

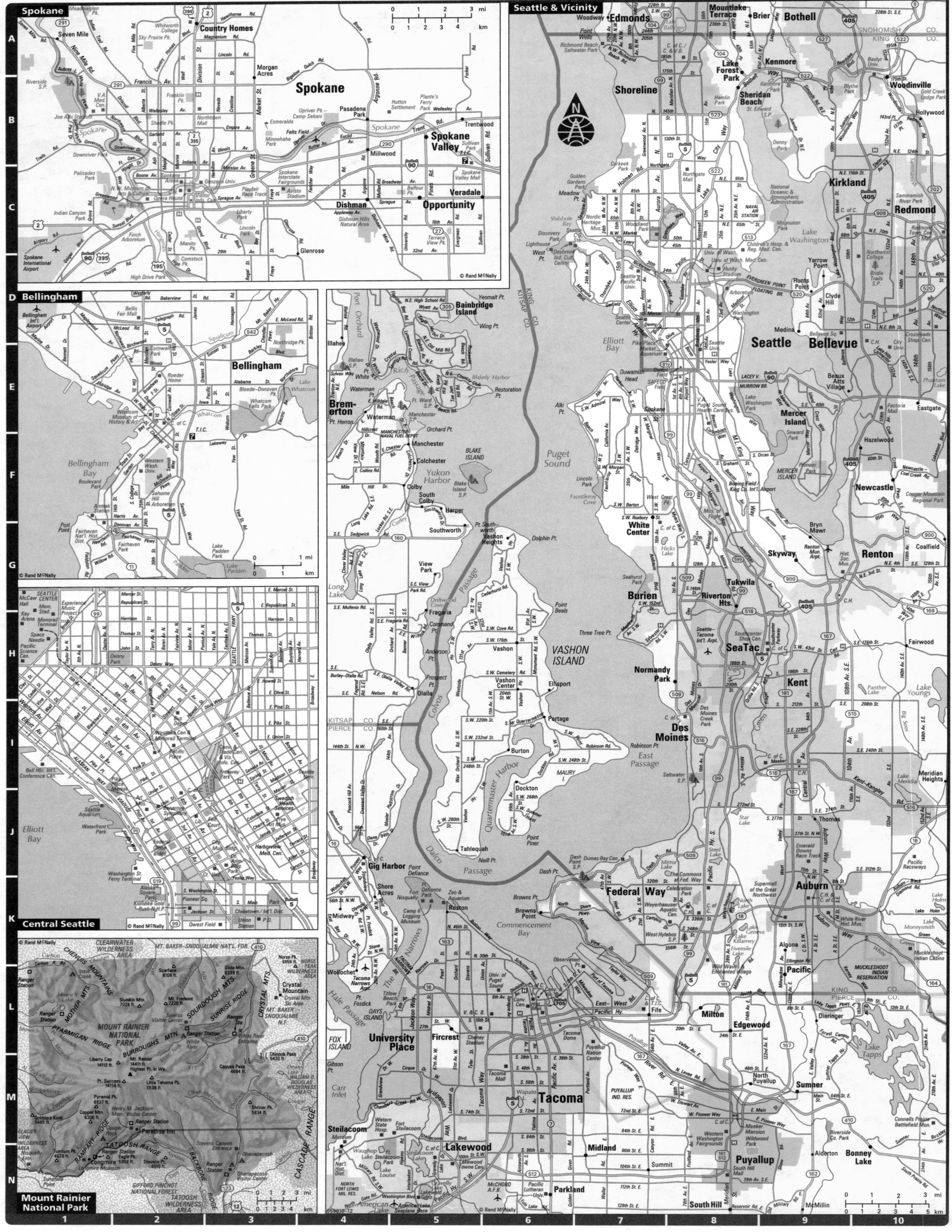

Spokane

Seattle & Vicinity

Bellingham

Central Seattle

Mount Rainier National Park

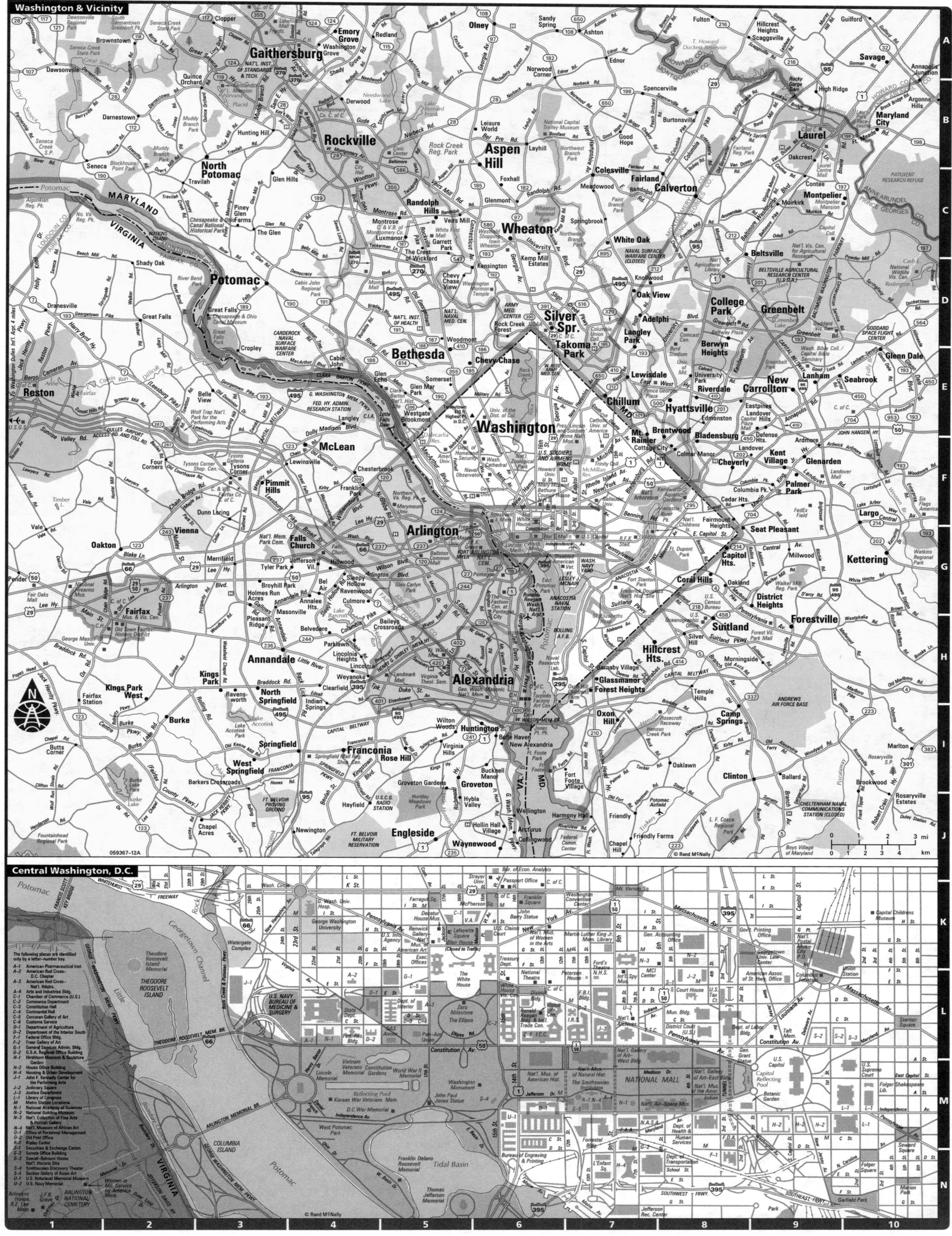

Washington & Vicinity

Central Washington, D.C.

© Rand McNally

059367-12A

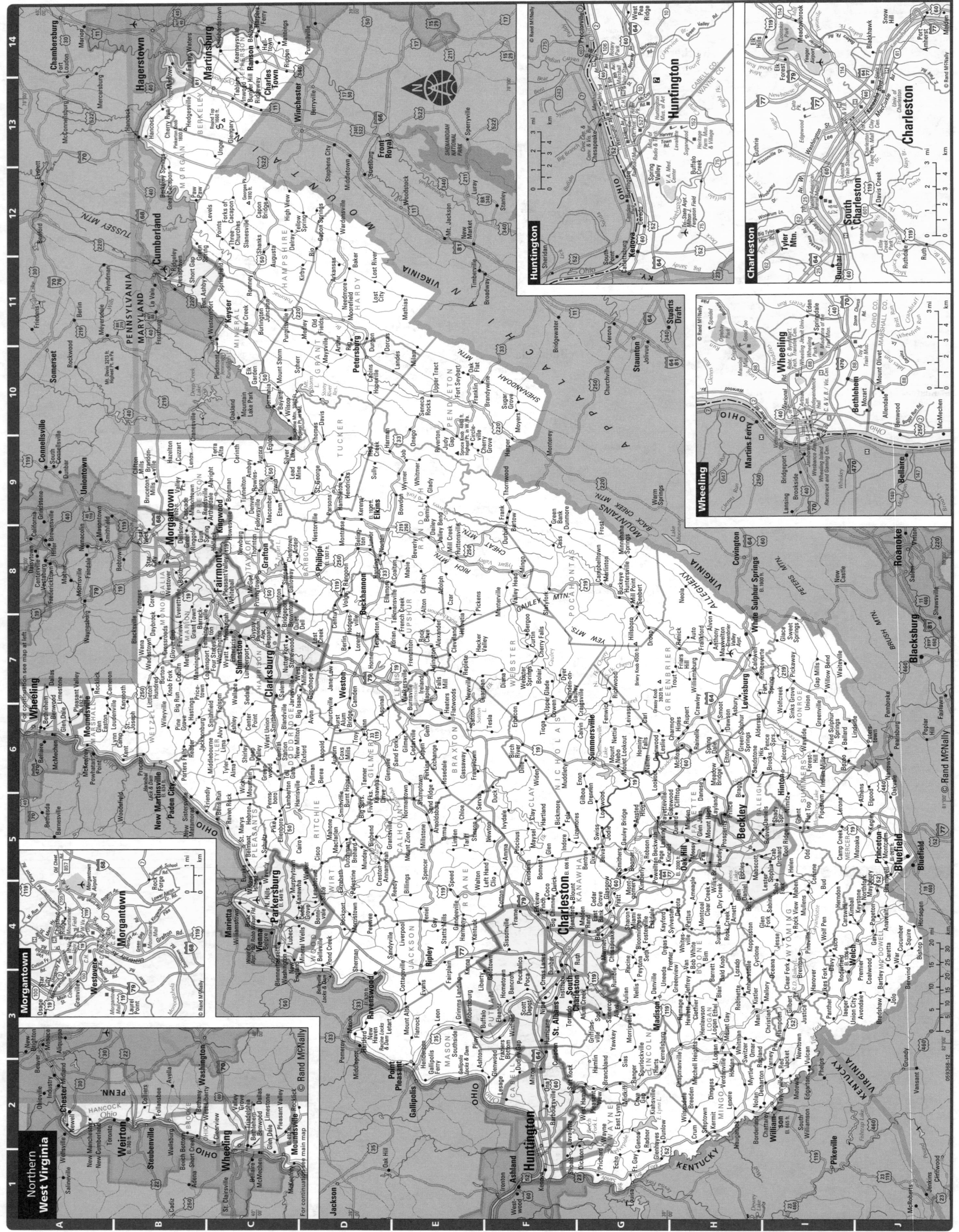

Northern
West Virginia

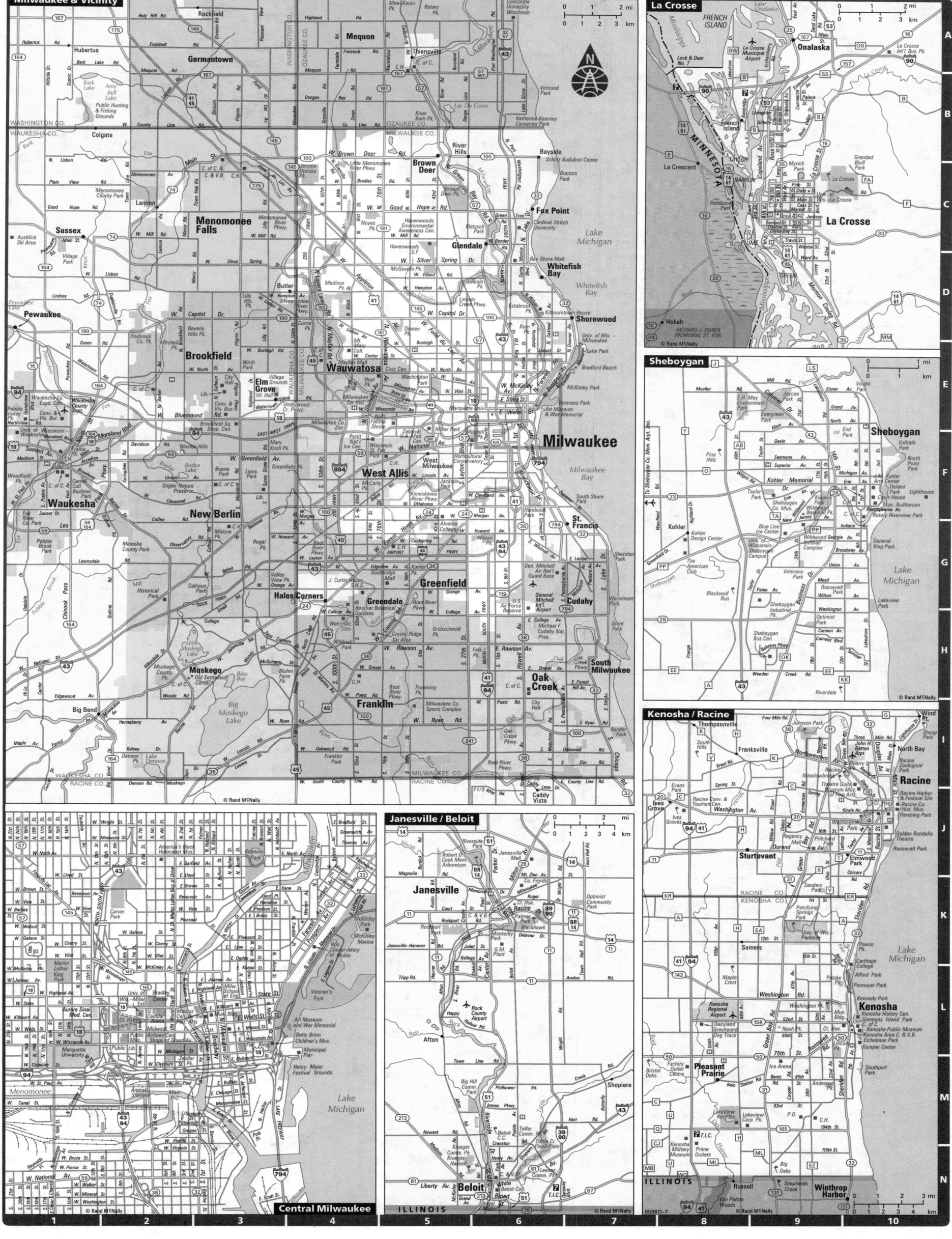

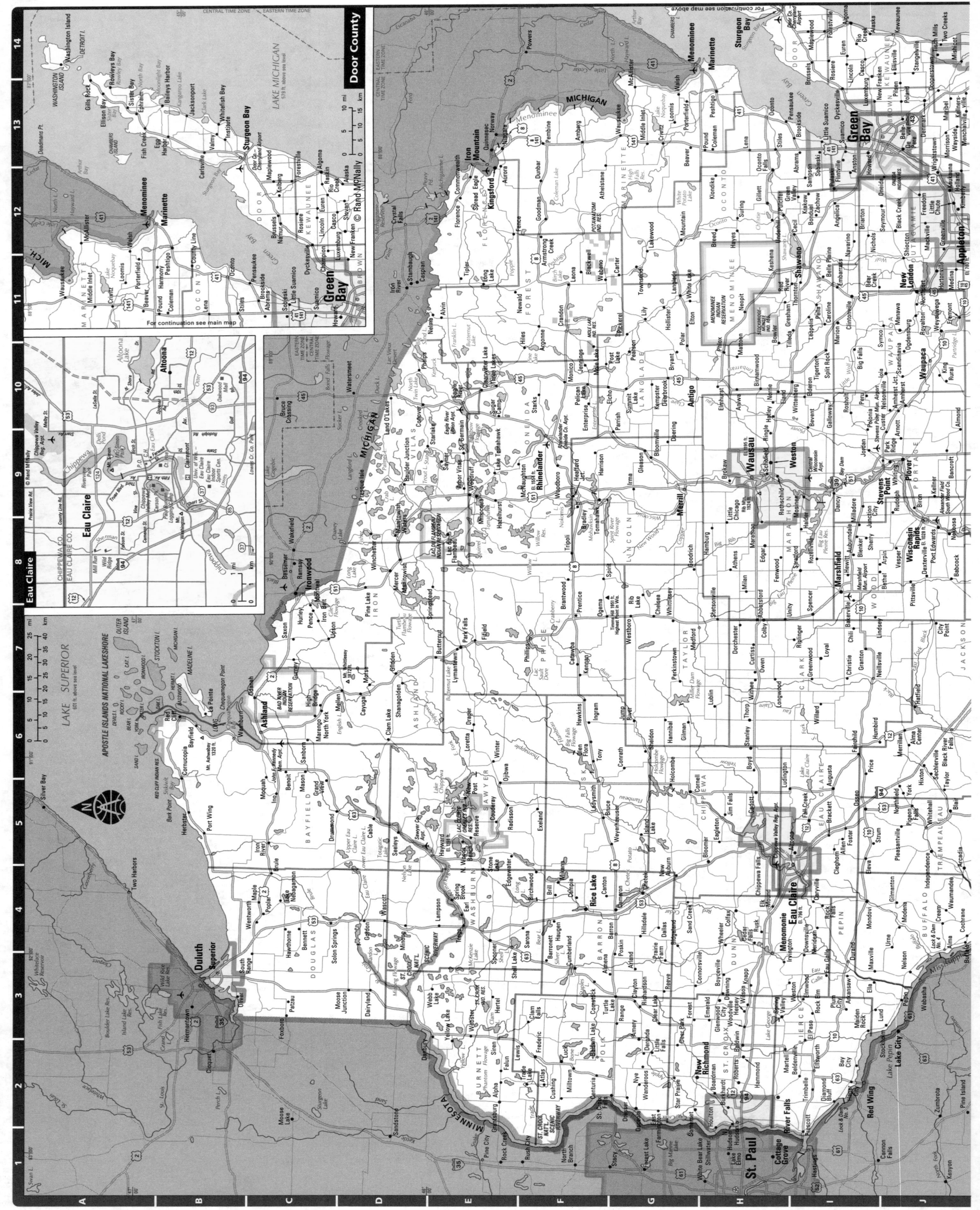

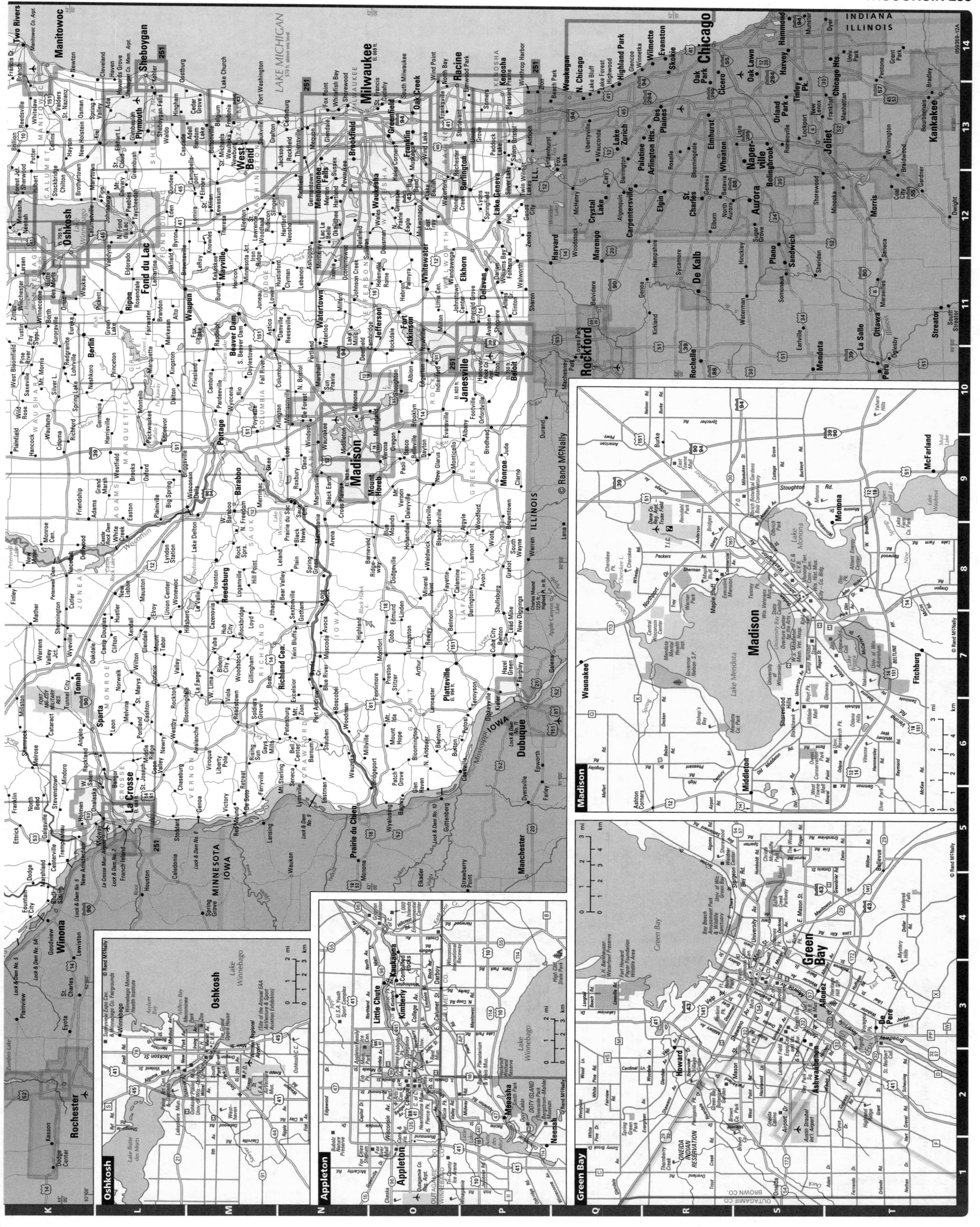

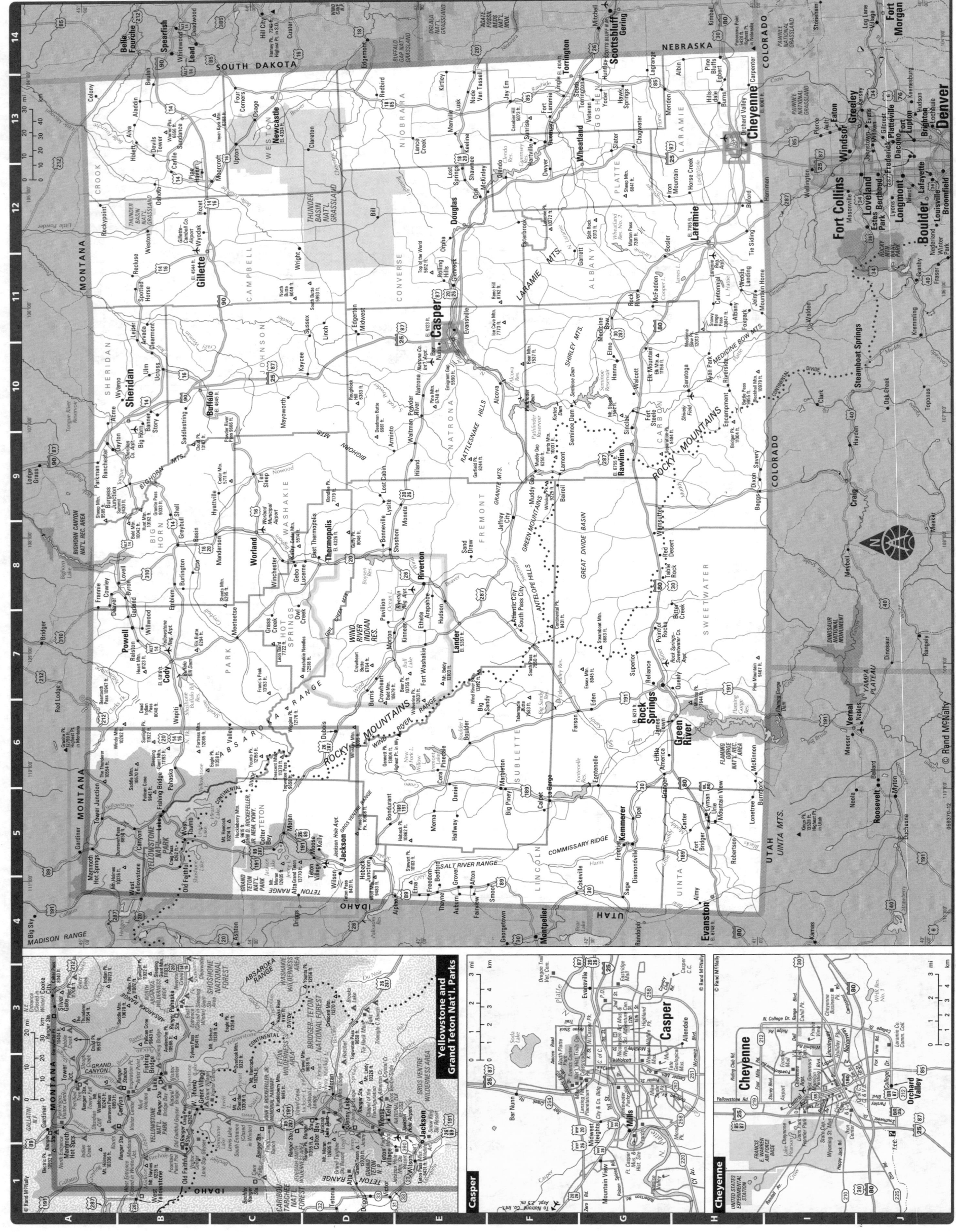

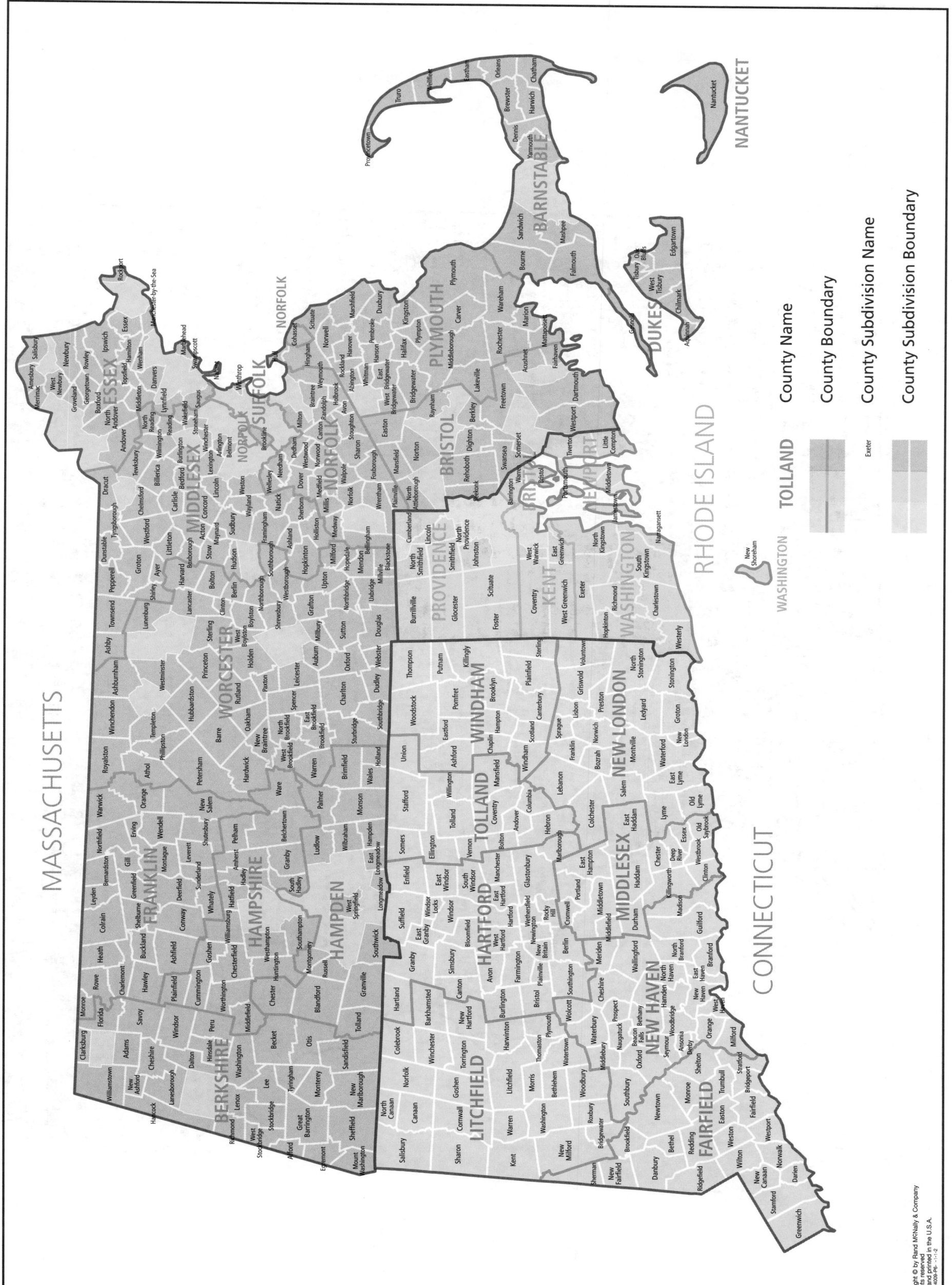

MASSACHUSETTS

CONNECTICUT

RHODE ISLAND

County Name

County Boundary

County Subdivision Name

County Subdivision Boundary

TOLLAND

Exeter

MARION — County Name

County Boundary

Oakdale — County Subdivision Name

County Subdivision Boundary

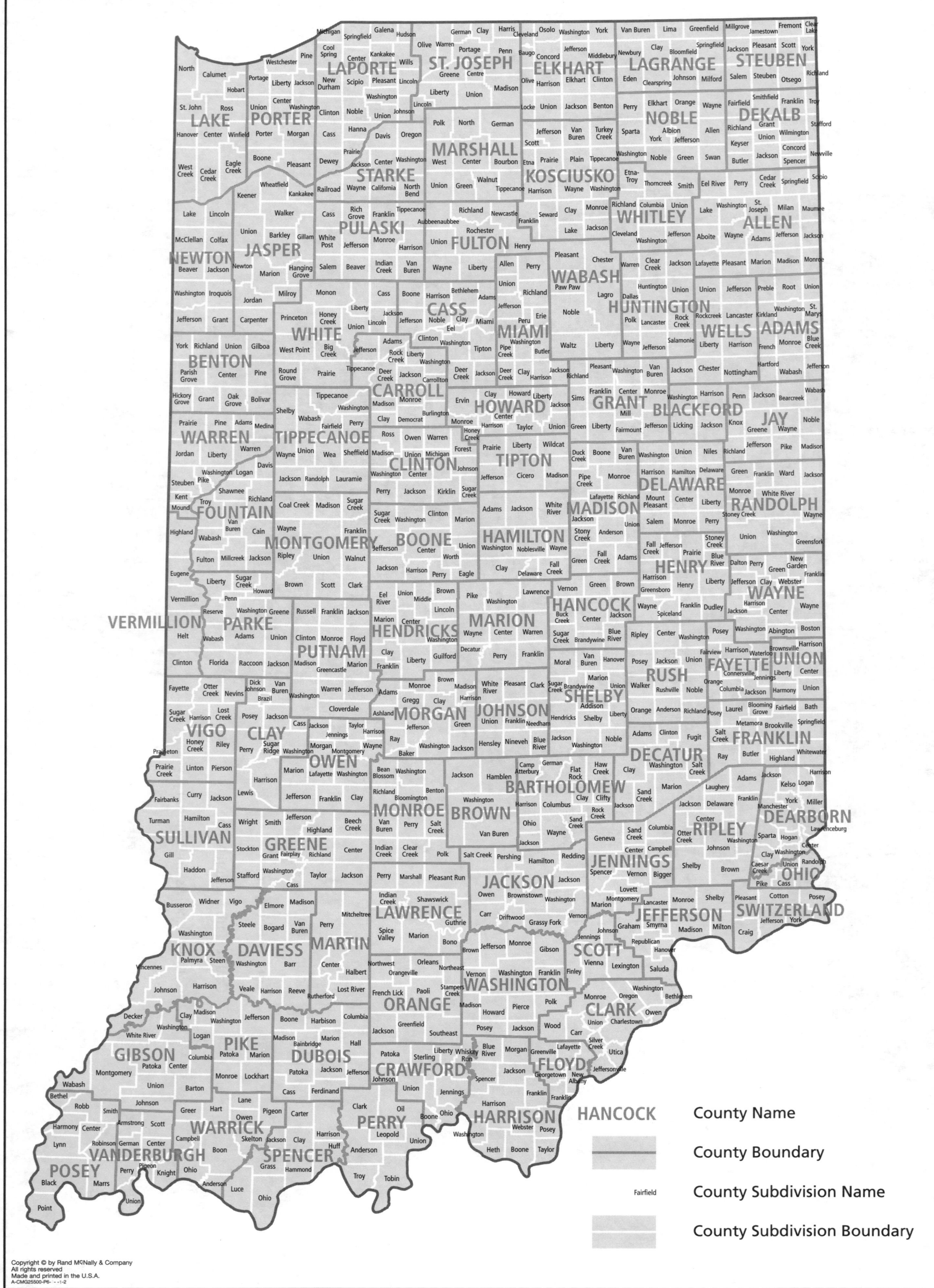

County Name

County Boundary

County Subdivision Name

County Subdivision Boundary

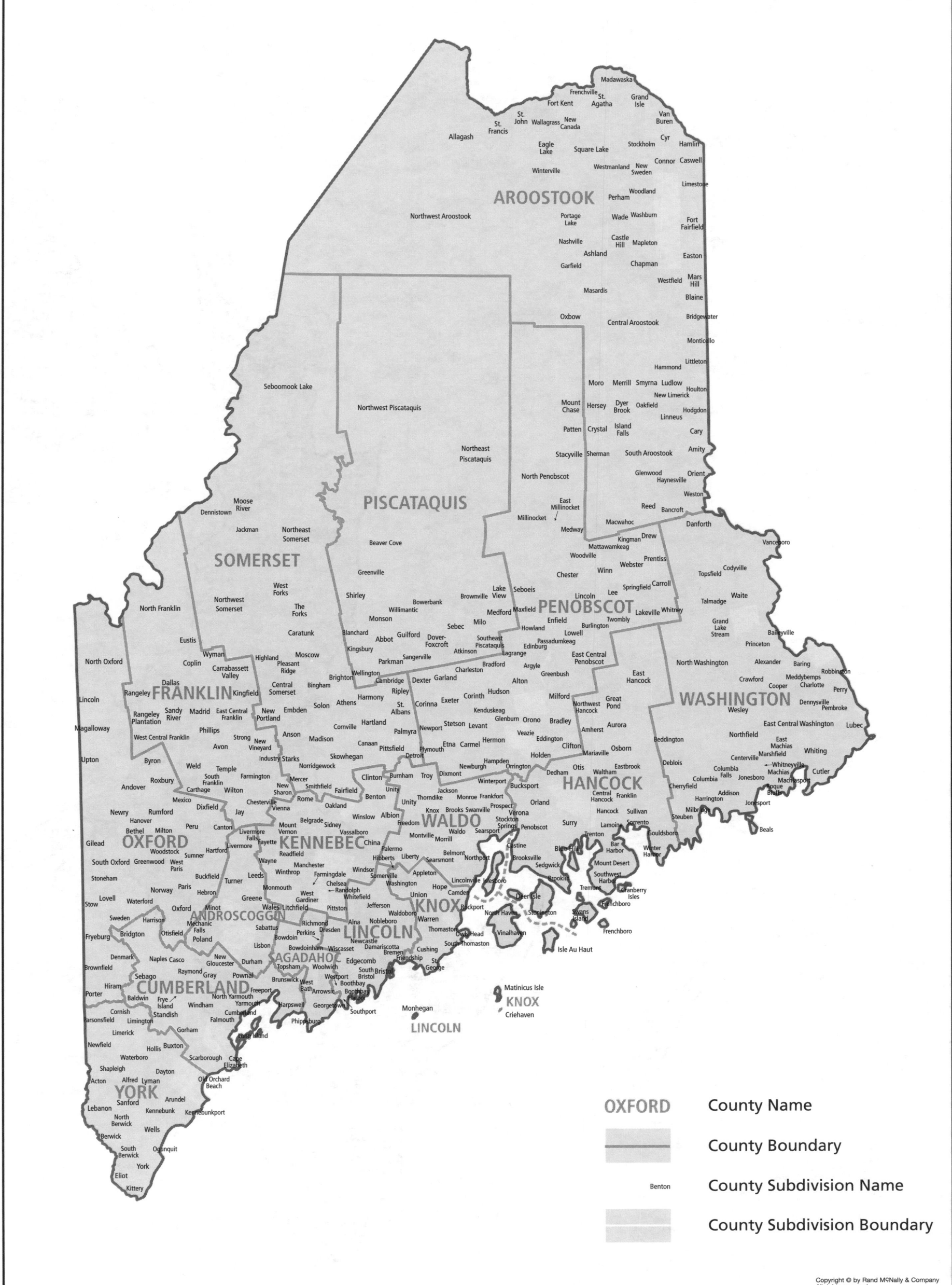

OXFORD — County Name

——— County Boundary

Benton — County Subdivision Name

——— County Subdivision Boundary

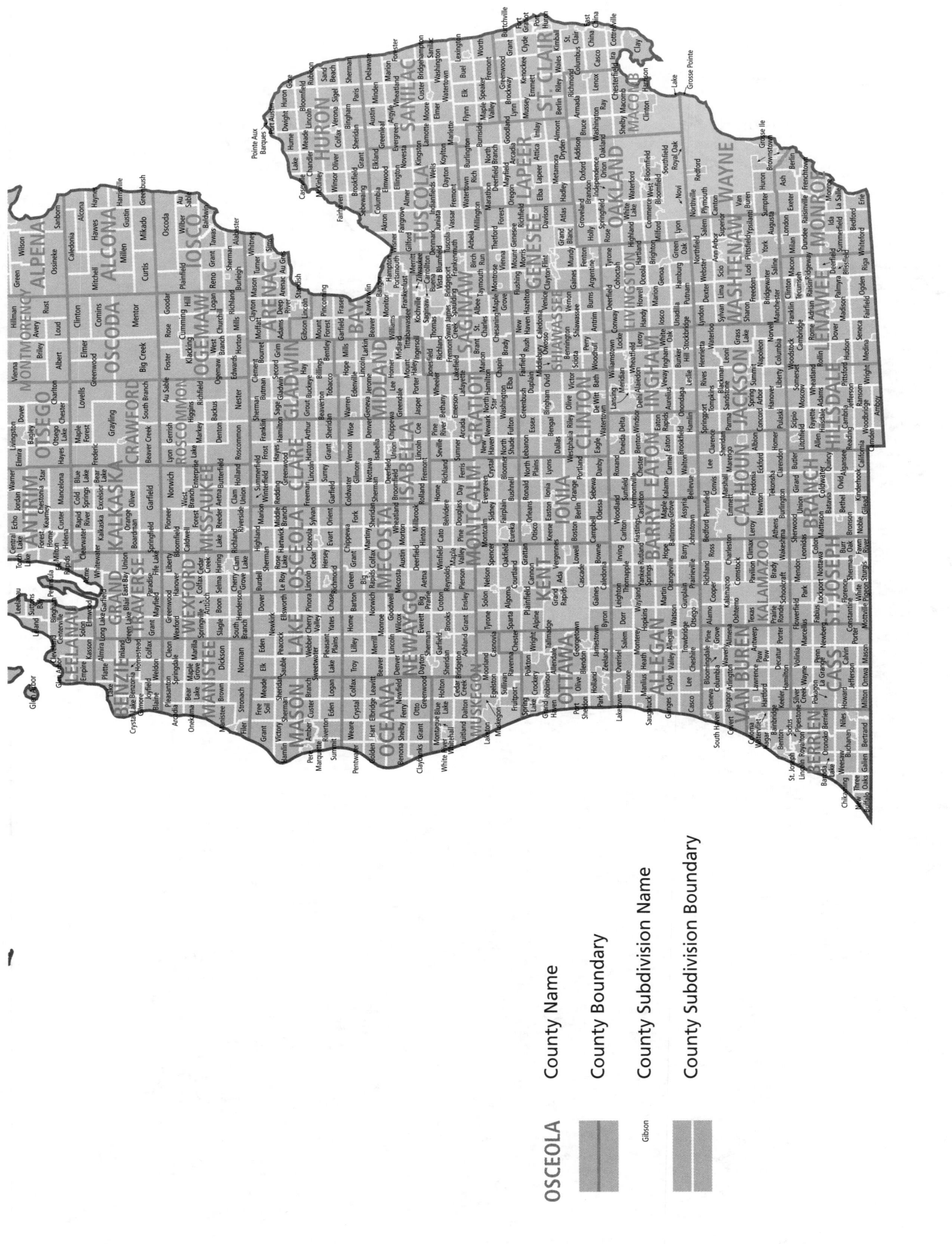

OSCEOLA   County Name

County Boundary

Gibson   County Subdivision Name

County Subdivision Boundary

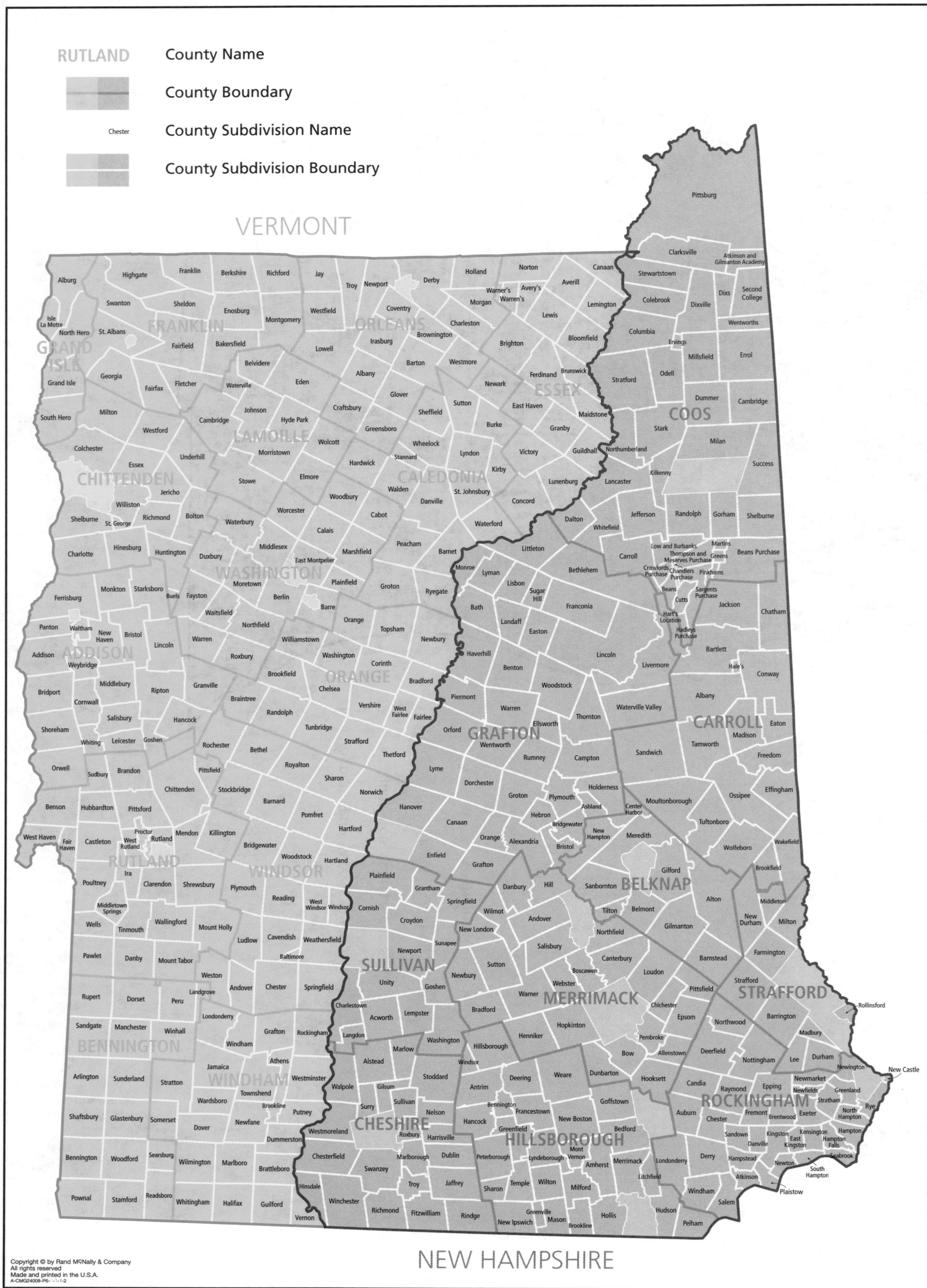

RUTLAND — County Name

County Boundary

Chester — County Subdivision Name

County Subdivision Boundary

VERMONT

NEW HAMPSHIRE

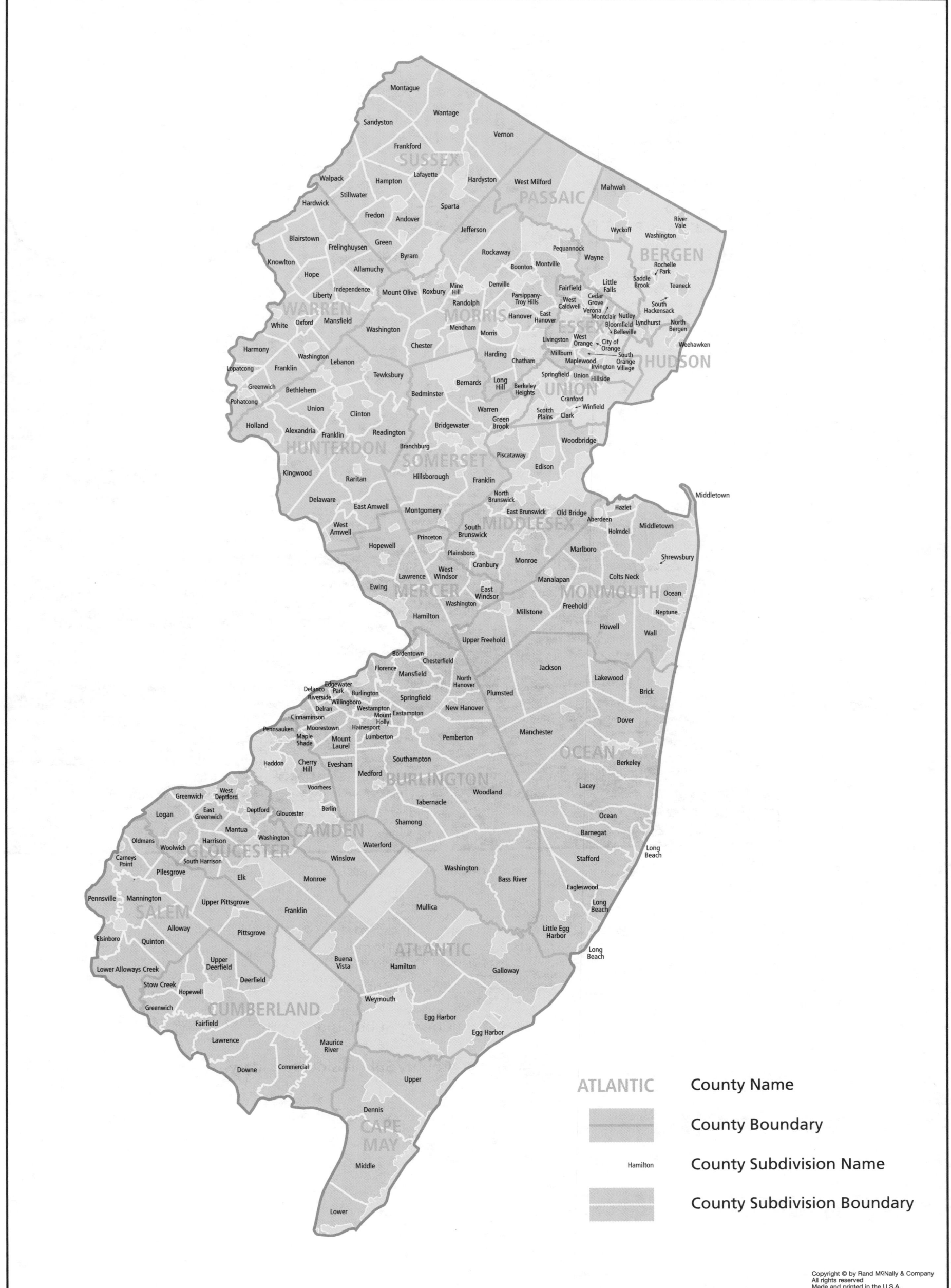

ATLANTIC	County Name
	County Boundary
Hamilton	County Subdivision Name
	County Subdivision Boundary

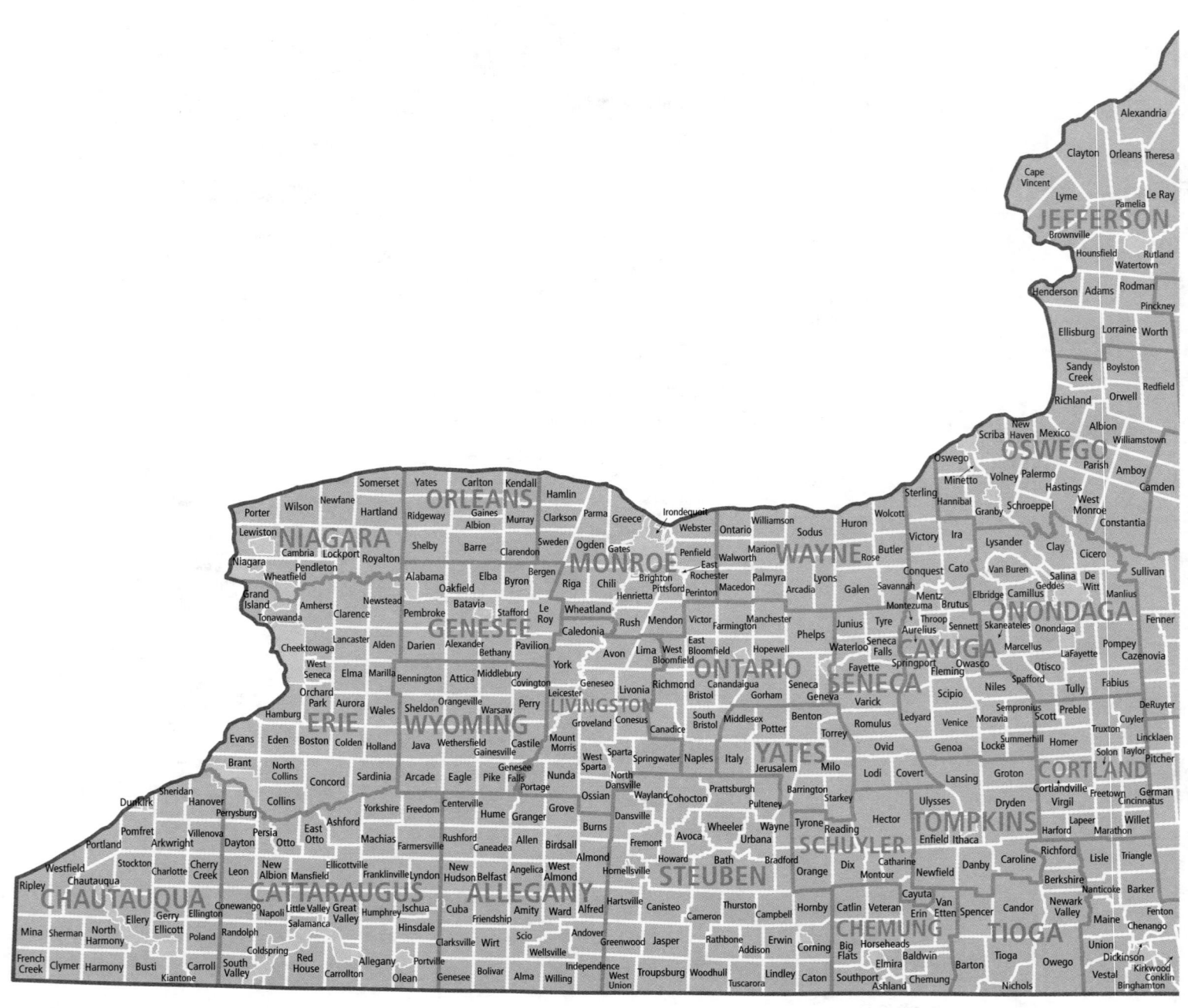

CAYUGA — County Name

County Boundary

Eaton — County Subdivision Name

County Subdivision Boundary

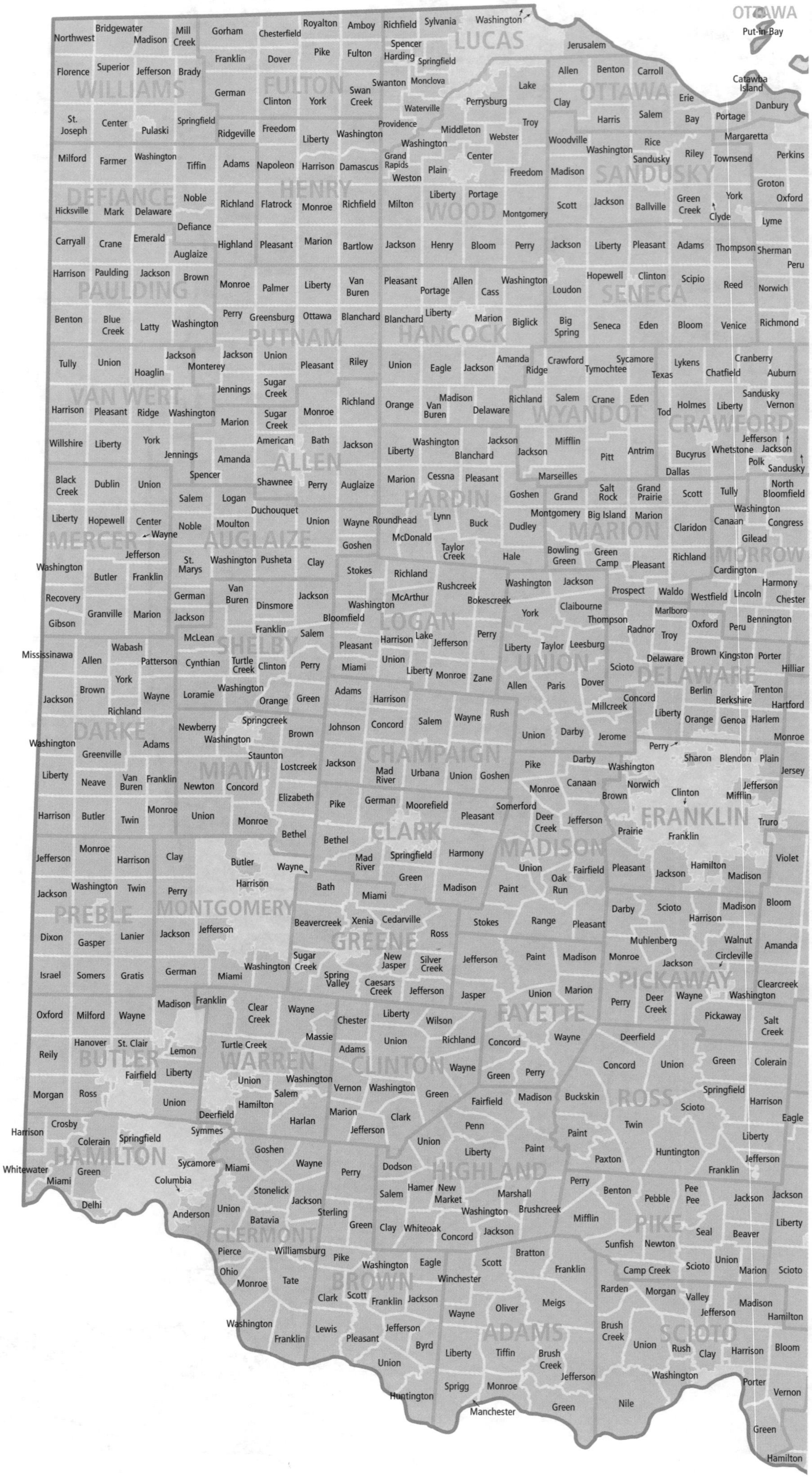

OTTAWA

Put-in-Bay

Northwest Bridgewater Mill Gorham Chesterfield Royalton Amboy Richfield Sylvania Washington
Madison Creek

Franklin Dover Pike Fulton Spencer Harding Springfield Jerusalem

Florence Superior Jefferson Brady LUCAS

Catawba Island

WILLIAMS German Clinton York Swan Creek Swanton Monclova Allen Benton Carroll Erie

FULTON Waterville Perrysburg Lake Clay OTTAWA Bay Portage Danbury

St. Joseph Center Pulaski Springfield Ridgeville Freedom Liberty Washington Providence Middleton Troy Harris Salem Margaretta

Milford Farmer Washington Tiffin Adams Napoleon Harrison Damascus Weston Plain Center Woodville Washington Rice Riley Townsend Perkins

Hicksville Mark Delaware Noble Richland Flatrock Monroe Richfield Milton Liberty Portage Scott Jackson Ballville Green Creek York Clyde Groton Oxford Lyme

DEFIANCE Defiance Montgomery SANDUSKY Thompson Sherman

Carryall Crane Emerald Auglaize Highland Pleasant Marion Bartlow Jackson Henry Bloom Perry Jackson Liberty Pleasant Adams Peru

Harrison Paulding Jackson Brown Monroe Palmer Liberty Van Buren Pleasant Allen Portage Cass Washington Hopewell Clinton Scipio Reed Norwich

PAULDING Loudon SENECA

Benton Blue Creek Latty Washington Perry Greensburg Ottawa Blanchard Blanchard Liberty Marion Biglick Big Spring Seneca Eden Bloom Venice Richmond

PUTNAM HANCOCK

Tully Union Hoaglin Jackson Monterey Jackson Union Pleasant Riley Union Eagle Jackson Amanda Ridge Crawford Tymochtee Sycamore Texas Lykens Chatfield Cranberry Auburn

VAN WERT Jennings Sugar Creek Richland Orange Madison Van Buren Richland Salem Crane Eden Tod Holmes Liberty Sandusky Vernon

Harrison Pleasant Ridge Washington Marion Sugar Creek Monroe WYANDOT CRAWFORD Jefferson Jackson Polk Sandusky

Willshire Liberty York Jennings American Bath Jackson Liberty Washington Jackson Mifflin Pitt Antrim Bucyrus Whetstone Dallas

Black Creek Dublin Union Spencer Amanda Shawnee Perry Auglaize Marion Cessna Pleasant Blanchard Jackson Marseilles Goshen Grand Salt Rock Grand Prairie Scott Tully North Bloomfield

ALLEN HARDIN

Liberty Hopewell Center Noble Salem Logan Moulton Duchouquet Union Wayne Roundhead Lynn Buck Dudley Montgomery Big Island Marion Claridon Canaan Washington Congress

MERCER Wayne AUGLAIZE Goshen McDonald Taylor Creek Hale Bowling Green Green Camp Pleasant Richland Gilead MORROW

Washington Jefferson St. Marys Washington Pusheta Clay Stokes Richland Rushcreek Washington Jackson Prospect Waldo Westfield Lincoln Harmony

Recovery Butler Franklin German Van Buren Jackson Washington McArthur Bokescreek York Claibourne Thompson Radnor Marlboro Oxford Peru Chester

Granville Marion Jackson Dinsmore Bloomfield Franklin Salem LOGAN Harrison Lake Jefferson Perry Liberty Taylor Leesburg Scioto Troy Bennington

Gibson McLean SHELBY Pleasant Miami Union Allen Paris Delaware Brown Kingston Porter

Mississinawa Allen Wabash Patterson Cynthian Turtle Creek Clinton Perry Liberty Monroe Zane UNION Dover Concord Millcreek Liberty Orange Berlin Berkshire Trenton Hartford Hilliar

Jackson Brown York Wayne Loramie Washington Orange Green Adams Harrison Wayne Rush Union Darby Jerome Perry Sharon DELAWARE Genoa Harlem Monroe

Washington Richland Newberry Springcreek Brown Johnson Concord Salem CHAMPAIGN Pike Darby Washington Norwich Clinton Jefferson Mifflin Jersey

DARKE Greenville Adams Staunton Lostcreek Jackson Mad River Urbana Union Goshen Monroe Canaan Brown Clinton FRANKLIN Truro

Liberty Neave Van Buren Franklin Newton Concord Elizabeth Pike German Moorefield Somerford Deer Creek Jefferson Prairie Franklin Hamilton Madison Violet

Harrison Butler Twin Monroe Union Monroe Bethel Bethel CLARK Pleasant MADISON Union Oak Run Fairfield Pleasant Jackson

Jefferson Monroe Harrison Clay Butler Wayne Mad River Springfield Harmony Green Madison Paint Darby Scioto Madison Bloom

PREBLE Jackson Washington Twin Perry Harrison Bath Miami Green MONTGOMERY Muhlenberg Walnut Amanda

Dixon Gasper Lanier Jackson Jefferson Beavercreek Xenia Cedarville Stokes Range Pleasant Monroe Jackson Circleville

Israel Somers Gratis German Miami Washington Creek GREENE Sugar New Jasper Silver Creek Jefferson Paint Madison PICKAWAY Perry Deer Creek Wayne Washington Clearcreek

Oxford Milford Wayne Madison Franklin Clear Creek Spring Valley Caesars Creek Jefferson Jasper Union Marion Perry Pickaway Salt Creek

Reily Hanover St. Clair Lemon Wayne Chester Liberty Wilson FAYETTE Deerfield Concord Union Green Colerain

BUTLER Fairfield Liberty Turtle Creek Massie Adams Union Richland Concord Wayne Green Perry ROSS Springfield Harrison

Morgan Ross Union Salem Vernon Washington Green Fairfield Madison Buckskin Twin Scioto Eagle

Harrison Crosby Deerfield Hamilton Harlan Marion Clark Penn Huntington Liberty Jefferson

Symmes Goshen Jefferson Union Liberty Paint Paxton Franklin

Whitewater Colerain Springfield Sycamore Miami Wayne Perry Dodson HIGHLAND Perry Benton Pebble Pee Pee Jackson Jackson

HAMILTON Green Columbia Stonelick Jackson Salem Hamer New Market Marshall Washington Brushcreek Mifflin PIKE Seal Beaver Liberty

Miami Delhi Anderson Union Batavia Sterling Green Clay Whiteoak Concord Jackson Sunfish Newton Camp Creek Scioto Union Marion Scioto

Pierce CLERMONT Williamsburg Pike Washington Eagle Scott Bratton Franklin Rarden Morgan Valley Madison Hamilton

Ohio Monroe Tate Clark Scott Franklin Winchester Brush Creek Jefferson

Washington Jackson Wayne Oliver Meigs ADAMS SCIOTO Bloom

Franklin Lewis Pleasant Jefferson Byrd Liberty Tiffin Brush Creek Union Rush Clay Harrison

Washington Sprigg Monroe Jefferson Washington Porter Vernon

Huntington Manchester Green Nile Green

Hamilton

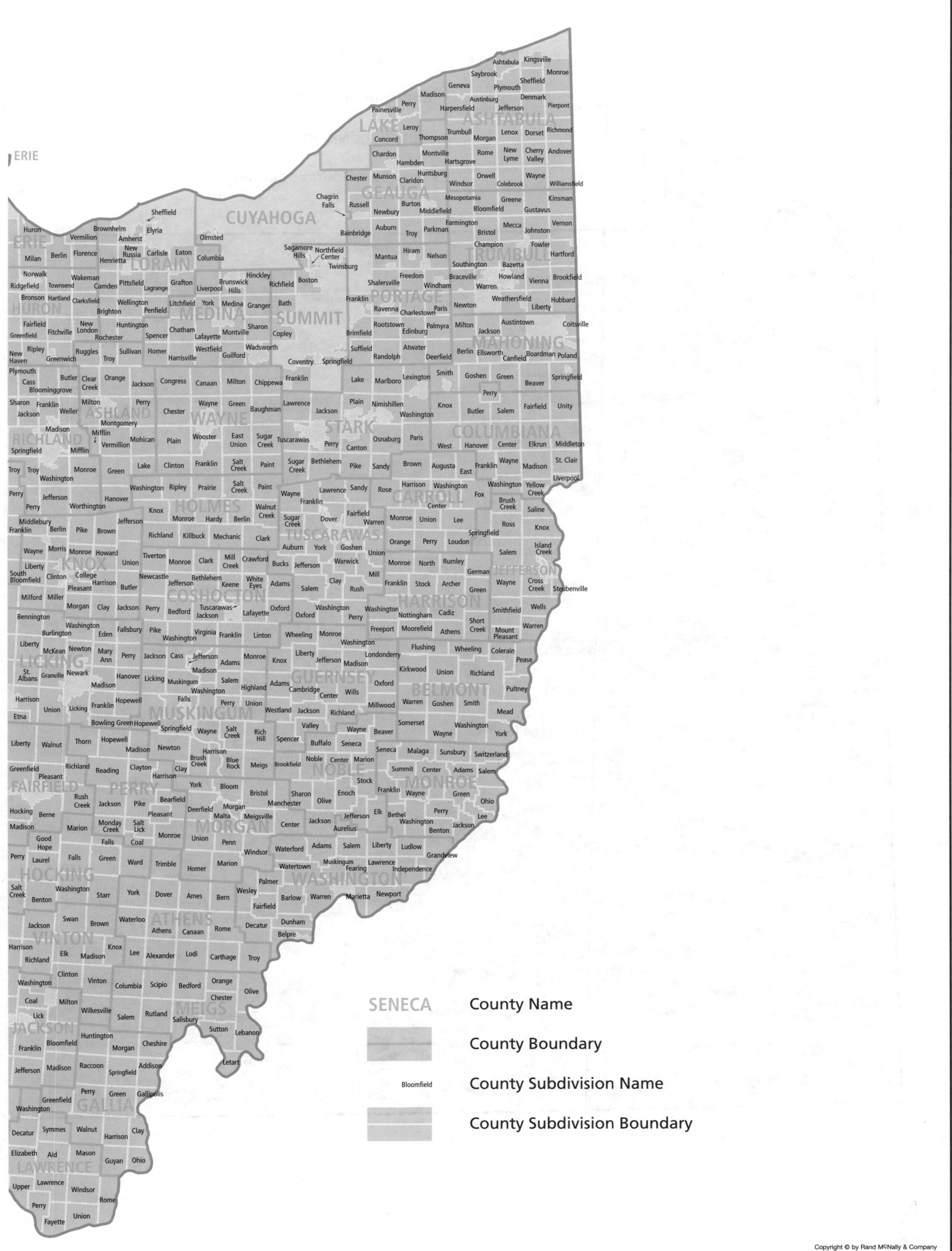

SENECA — County Name

County Boundary

Bloomfield — County Subdivision Name

County Subdivision Boundary

CAMBRIA — County Name

County Boundary

Carroll — County Subdivision Name

County Subdivision Boundary

CHESTER

1 North Coventry	13 Willistown
2 East Coventry	14 Warwick
3 East Vincent	15 East Nantmeal
4 East Pikeland	16 Upper Uwchlan
5 Schuylkill	17 Uwchlan
6 Easttown	18 West Whiteland
7 Easttown	19 West Goshen
8 South Coventry	20 East Goshen
9 West Vincent	21 Westtown
10 West Pikeland	22 Thornbury
11 Charlestown	23 West Nantmeal
12 East Whiteland	24 Wallace

25 East Brandywine	37 East Fallowfield
26 East Caln	38 Newlin
27 East Bradford	39 East Marlborough
28 Birmingham	40 Kennett
29 West Brandywine	41 Sadsbury
30 Caln	42 Highland
31 West Bradford	43 West Marlborough
32 Pocopson	44 London Grove
33 Pennsbury	45 New Garden
34 Honeybrook	46 West Sadsbury
35 West Caln	47 West Fallowfield
36 Valley	48 Londonderry

49 Penn	
50 New London	
51 Franklin	
52 London Britain	
53 Upper Oxford	
54 Lower Oxford	
55 East Nottingham	
56 West Nottingham	
57 Elk	

DELAWARE

1 Radnor	13 Middletown
2 Haverford	14 Aston
3 Upper Darby	15 Chester
4 Newtown	16 Thornbury
5 Marple	17 Concord
6 Springfield	18 Bethel
7 Darby	19 Upper Chichester
8 Upper Providence	20 Lower Chichester
9 Nether Providence	21 Chadds Ford
10 Ridley	
11 Tinicum	
12 Edgmont	

MONTGOMERY

1 Upper Hanover	14 Upper Salford
2 Marlborough	15 Lower Salford
3 Salford	16 Towamencin
4 Franconia	17 Upper Gwynedd
5 Hatfield	18 Lower Gwynedd
6 Montgomery	19 Upper Dublin
7 Horsham	20 Abington
8 Upper Moreland	21 Perkiomen
9 Lower Moreland	22 Skippack
10 Douglass	23 Worcester
11 New Hanover	24 East Norriton
12 Upper Frederick	25 Whitpain
13 Lower Frederick	26 Whitemarsh

27 Springfield	
28 Cheltenham	
29 Upper Pottsgrove	
30 West Pottsgrove	
31 Lower Pottsgrove	
32 Limerick	
33 Upper Providence	
34 Lower Providence	
35 West Norriton	
36 Upper Merion	
37 Plymouth	
38 Lower Merion	

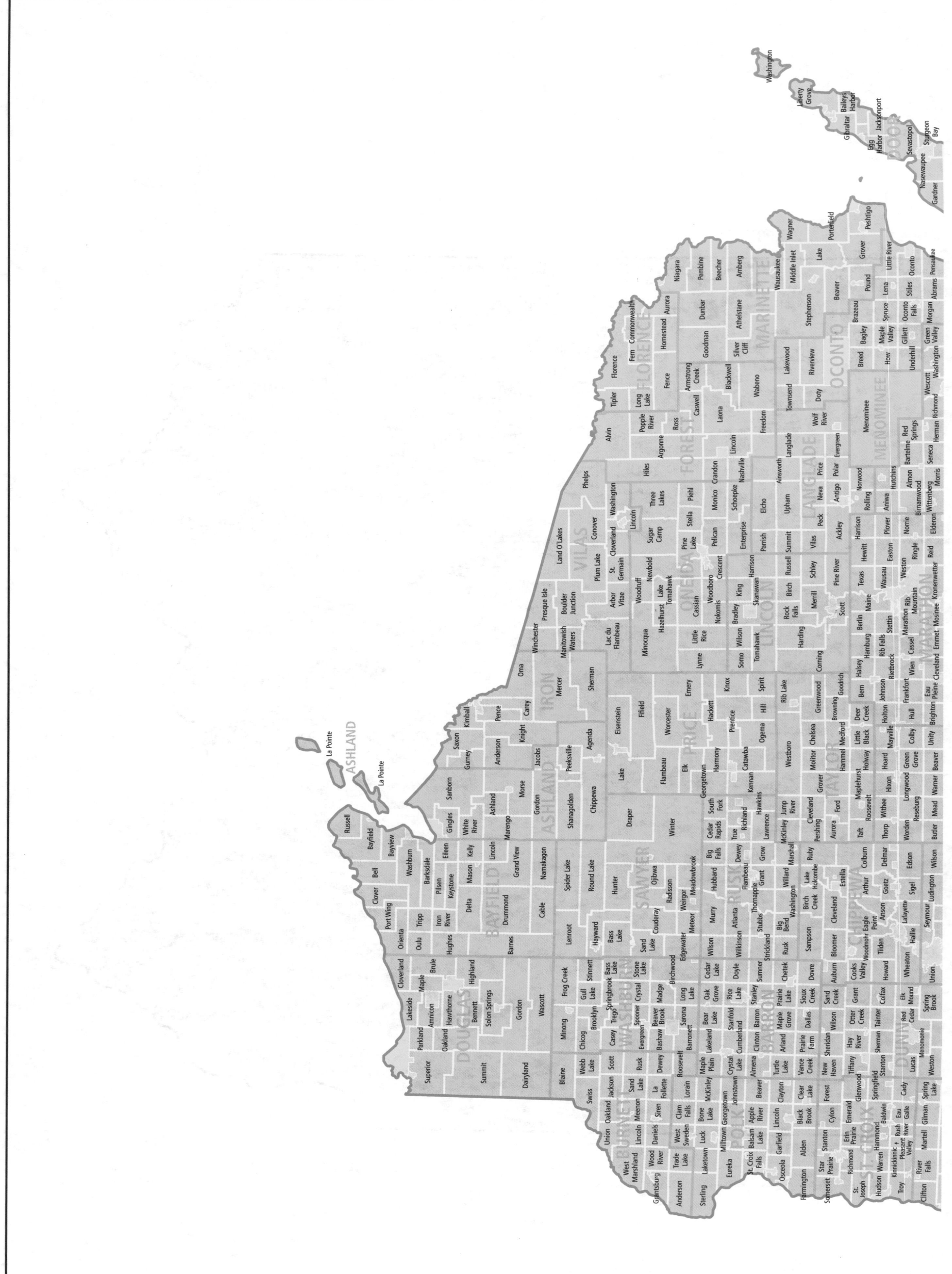

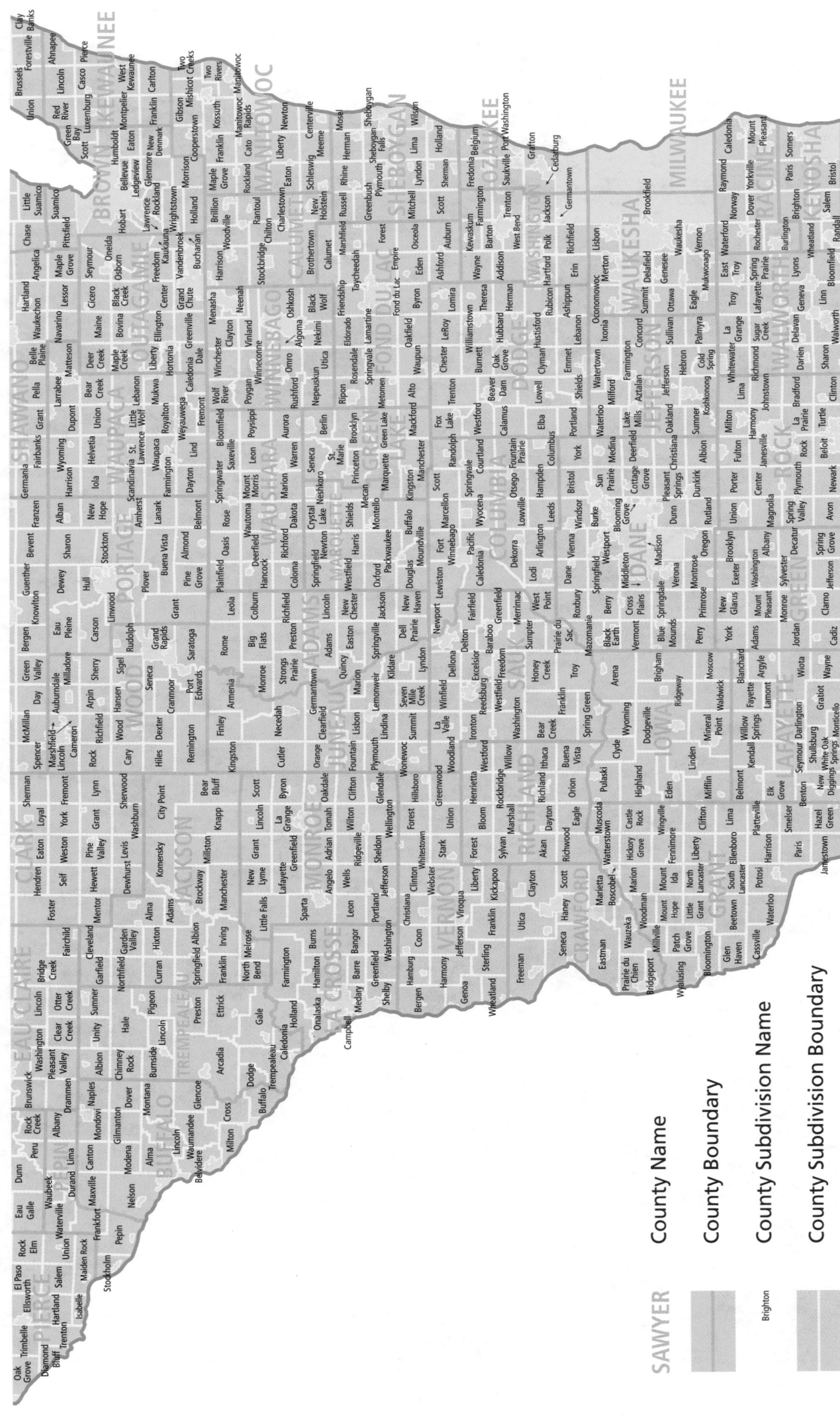

County Name

County Boundary

County Subdivision Name

County Subdivision Boundary

SAWYER

Brighton